THE DAWN HORSE TESTAMENT OF THE RUCHIRA AVATAR

**The Divine World-Teacher,
Ruchira Avatar Adi Da Samraj**
Adidam Samrajashram, 2003

THE DAWN HORSE TESTAMENT OF THE RUCHIRA AVATAR

THE TESTAMENT OF DIVINE SECRETS OF THE DIVINE WORLD-TEACHER,

RUCHIRA AVATAR ADI DA SAMRAJ

THE DAWN HORSE PRESS
MIDDLETOWN, CALIFORNIA

NOTE TO THE READER

All who study the Way of Adidam or take up its practice should remember that they are responding to a Call to become responsible for themselves. They should understand that they, not Avatar Adi Da Samraj or others, are responsible for any decision they make or action they take in the course of their lives of study or practice.

The devotional, Spiritual, functional, practical, relational, and cultural practices and disciplines referred to in this book are appropriate and natural practices that are voluntarily and progressively adopted by members of the practicing congregations of Adidam (as appropriate to the personal circumstance of each individual). Although anyone may find these practices useful and beneficial, they are not presented as advice or recommendations to the general reader or to anyone who is not a member of one of the practicing congregations of Adidam. And nothing in this book is intended as a diagnosis, prescription, or recommended treatment or cure for any specific "problem", whether medical, emotional, psychological, social, or Spiritual. One should apply a particular program of treatment, prevention, cure, or general health only in consultation with a licensed physician or other qualified professional.

The Dawn Horse Testament Of The Ruchira Avatar is formally authorized for publication by the Ruchira Sannyasin Order of Adidam Ruchiradam. (The Ruchira Sannyasin Order of Adidam Ruchiradam is the senior Spiritual and Cultural Authority within the formal gathering of formally acknowledged devotees of the Divine World-Teacher, Ruchira Avatar Adi Da Samraj.)

NOTE TO BIBLIOGRAPHERS: The correct form for citing Ruchira Avatar Adi Da Samraj's Name (in any form of alphabetized listing) is: Adi Da Samraj

New Standard Edition, enlarged and updated, August 2004

This edition supercedes all previous editions of this Text:
First Standard Edition, October 1985
Second Standard Edition, November 1991

Produced by the Avataric Pan-Communion of Adidam
in cooperation with the Dawn Horse Press

International Standard Book Number: 1-57097-168-4

Library of Congress Catalog Card Number: 2004108266

CONTENTS

THE DAWN HORSE TESTAMENT OF THE RUCHIRA AVATAR

The Visionary Winged Horse

The image on the cover of *The Dawn Horse Testament* is a visual summary of the Avataric Divine Wisdom-Teaching of Avatar Adi Da Samraj—just as *The Dawn Horse Testament* Itself is a verbal summary of His Avataric Divine Wisdom-Teaching. Furthermore, this visual image is a representation of what Avatar Adi Da (in the Prologue) calls the four "Hallowing Signs Of Real God"—His Avatarically-Born bodily (human) Divine Form, His Avatarically Self-Transmitted Divine Spiritual Presence, His Avatarically Self-Revealed Divine and Perfect State, and the "Bright" Itself (Which He Is, and Which He Transmits).

Each of the four hooves of the Dawn Horse gestures toward one of these four Signs.

The right rear foot points toward the Feet of Avatar Adi Da's bodily (human) Divine Form. Avatar Adi Da is Himself the bodily (human) Revelation of the Divine Person, as epitomized by the image of His Feet.

The left rear foot is raised and points toward the Sacred Fire, which represents Avatar Adi Da's Divine Spiritual Presence (or His all-and-All-Pervading Love-Blissful Divine Spirit-Current).

The right front foot points toward the right side of the heart, which is the bodily seat associated with the Realization of Consciousness Itself, or Avatar Adi Da's Divine and Perfect State, Which is the Divine Self-Condition of all conditionally manifested beings and things.

And the left front foot points up, toward the Divine Star, Which is the "Window" to the Self-Existing and Self-Radiant Sphere (or "Midnight Sun") of the “Bright” Divine Self-Domain of Conscious Light That is the pre-cosmic Divine Self-Condition and Source-Condition of all conditional manifestation. In *The Dawn Horse Testament,* Avatar Adi Da Reveals that the Divine Star is His own “First Visible Form”, the cosmically manifested Sign (or the objective Representation) of the Very Divine Person and Self-Condition.

Thus, the Ecstatic attitude of the Horse—with his head arched in Bliss, his wings outstretched (as a sign of Perfect Freedom), and his front hooves gesturing simultaneously to the two terminals of Amrita Nadi, “The Ultimate conditional (or Structural) Seat, Sign, and Divinely ‘Bright’ Spiritual Body Of The Process Of Divine Translation (Into The ‘Midnight Sun’—Which Is The Sphere, and Space, and Substance Of My ‘Bright’ Divine Self-Domain)”—is a visual Symbol of Most Perfect Divine Self-Realization, or Most Perfect Divine Enlightenment. This is the Supreme Realization to Which Avatar Adi Da Samraj, in His *Dawn Horse Testament,* Calls all living beings.

PREFACE

by Jonathan Condit, Ph.D.
(Senior Editorial Assistant to
Ruchira Avatar Adi Da Samraj)

The Dawn Horse Testament Of The Ruchira Avatar is the Supreme and All-Revealing Word of the "Bright" Divine Person—Who has Avatarically Incarnated here (in bodily human Form), as the Ruchira Avatar, Adi Da Samraj, for the Infinitely Compassionate Purpose of Communicating His Divine Instruction, and Transmitting His Divine Spiritual Blessing, and Revealing His Own Divine Nature (as the Love-Bliss-Full Divine Self-Condition of all beings and things).

The Dawn Horse Testament is a Vast Ocean of Avatar Adi Da's Divine Self-Revelation and Divine Heart-Instruction—structured with immense subtlety and sophistication, so as to encompass the entire seven-stage process (uniquely Revealed and Given by Him) of Most Perfect Divine Enlightenment. The Creation of this All-Completing Scripture began spontaneously with two events, five years apart from each other. On September 13, 1979, Avatar Adi Da composed a letter to all His devotees, which opened with His Great Divine Self-Confession, "Beloved, I Am Da."* Eventually, this letter (in much elaborated form) was to become Sutra 1 of *The Dawn Horse Testament.* Later, on June 24, 1984, Avatar Adi Da Wrote an Essay on meditative practice which proved to be the beginning of the twenty-year process through which He Created *The Dawn Horse Testament* in Its present form.

Avatar Adi Da's method of Writing this Supreme Text (and also all of His other Texts) was highly interactive. As He gradually enlarged *The Dawn Horse Testament,* He would frequently read newly Written sections (or have these sections read) to His devotees, asking to hear their responses and questions. Through this form of dialogue with His devotees (and through His "omni-psychic" intimacy with all beings), He constantly tested whether His

* For an account of this Event, please see *Adi Da: The Promised God-Man Is Here,* by Carolyn Lee, Ph.D.

Communication on any particular topic was complete and detailed enough or whether He needed to say more.

This interactive process continued well beyond the publication of the First Standard Edition (in 1985) and the Second Standard Edition (in 1991). Indeed, that process continued until May 2004, when Avatar Adi Da made His final additions to the Text of this New (Third) Standard Edition.

The present edition incorporates the immense body of new Writing that Avatar Adi Da has added to *The Dawn Horse Testament* since Its last formal publication in 1991. In addition, Avatar Adi Da has (since 1991) extensively restructured *The Dawn Horse Testament:* The 45 Chapters of the principal Text have now become 72 Sutras—and the principal Text is preceded by a sequence of six introductory Texts, including Avatar Adi Da's "First Word" and a group of five Prolegomena.

The Dawn Horse Testament is the pre-eminent Scripture among Avatar Adi Da's twenty-three Divine "Source-Texts"—both because It is His All-Completing Summary of the Way of the Heart (or Way of Adidam) and because, in the majority of cases, each of His other "Source-Texts" is structured around a single Sutra (or a group of Sutras) from *The Dawn Horse Testament* as the Core Text.

The Dawn Horse Testament Of The Ruchira Avatar is the Ultimate Divine Communication to humankind, Which Avatar Adi Da Samraj Offers as a Gift to all beings. To all who are moved to receive His Avataric Divine Word, He Offers His Testament as a Gift of His Own Self-Revelation, His Wisdom-Instruction, and His Calling to formally embrace the Way He has Revealed and Given. And to those who have become His formally practicing devotees, He Offers His Testament as His Perfect Avataric Divine Instruction in the practice of the Way of the Heart (or Way of Adidam), Which is the Way of the devotional and (in due course) Spiritual relationship to Him.

First Word

Avatar Adi Da Samraj
Adidam Samrajashram, 2003

First Word

Do Not Misunderstand Me—I Am Not "Within" you, but you Are In Me, and I Am Not a Mere "Man" in the "Middle" of Mankind, but All of Mankind Is Surrounded, and Pervaded, and Blessed By Me

Yes! There is no religion, no Way of God, no Way of Divine Realization, no Way of Enlightenment, and no Way of Liberation that is Higher or Greater than Truth Itself. Indeed, there is no religion, no science, no man or woman, no conditionally manifested being of any kind, no world (any "where"), and no "God" (or "God"-Idea) that is Higher or Greater than Truth Itself.

Therefore, no ego-"I"—no presumed separate (and, necessarily, actively separative, and, at best, only Truth-seeking) being or "thing"—is (itself) Higher or Greater than Truth Itself. And no ego-"I" is (itself) even Equal to Truth Itself. And no ego-"I" is (itself) even (now, or ever) Able to Realize Truth Itself—because, necessarily, Truth (Itself) Inherently Transcends (or Is That Which Is Higher and Greater than) every one (himself or herself) and every "thing" (itself). Therefore, it is only in the transcending of egoity itself—only in the "radical" Process of Going Beyond the root, the cause, and the act of presumed separateness, and of performed separativeness, and of even all ego-based seeking for Truth Itself—that Truth (Itself) Is Realized (As It Is, Utterly Beyond the ego-"I" itself).

Truth (Itself) Is That Which Is Always Already The Case. That Which Is The Case (Always, and Always Already) Is (necessarily) Reality. Therefore, Reality (Itself) Is Truth, and Reality (Itself) Is the Only Truth.

Reality (Itself) Is the Only, and (necessarily) Non-Separate (or all-and-All-Including, and all-and-All-Transcending), One and "What" That Is. Because It Is all-and-All—and because It Is (Also) That Which Transcends (or Is Higher and Greater than) all-and-All—Reality Itself (Which Is Truth Itself, or That Which Is Always, and Always Already, The Case) Is the One and Only Real God. Therefore, Reality (Itself) Is (necessarily) the One and Great Subject of true religion, and Reality (Itself) Is (necessarily) the One and Great Way of Real God, Real (and True) Divine Realization, Real (and, necessarily, Divine) En-Light-enment, and Real (and, necessarily, Divine) Liberation (from all egoity, all separateness, all separativeness, all fear, and all heartlessness).

The only true religion is the religion that Realizes Truth. The only true science is the science that Knows Truth. The only true man or woman (or being of any kind) is one that Surrenders to Truth. The only true world is one that Embodies Truth. And the only True (and Real) God Is the One Reality (or Condition of Being) That Is Truth. Therefore, Reality Itself (Which Is the One and Only Truth, and, therefore, necessarily, the One and Only Real God) must become (or be made) the constantly applied Measure of religion, and of science, and of the world itself, and of even all of the life (and all of the mind) of Man—or else religion, and science, and the world itself, and even any and every sign of Man inevitably (all, and together) become a pattern of illusions, a mere (and even terrible) "problem", the very (and even principal) cause of human seeking, and the perpetual cause of contentious human strife. Indeed, if religion, and science, and the world itself, and the total life (and the total mind) of Man are not Surrendered and Aligned to Reality (Itself), and (Thus) Submitted to be Measured (or made Lawful) by Truth (Itself), and (Thus) Given to the truly devotional (and, thereby, truly ego-transcending) Realization of That Which Is the Only Real God—then, in the presumed "knowledge" of mankind, Reality (Itself), and Truth (Itself), and Real God (or the One and Only Existence, or Being, or Person That Is) ceases to Exist.

Aham Da Asmi. Beloved, I Am Da, the One and Only Person Who Is. I Am the Avatarically Self-Revealed, and Eternally Self-Existing, and Eternally Self-Radiant (or Spiritually Self-"Bright") Person of Love-Bliss. I Am the One and Only and (Self-Evidently) Divine Self (or Inherently Non-Separate—and, therefore, Inherently egoless—Divine Self-Condition and Source-Condition) of one and of all and of All. I Am Divinely Self-Manifesting (now, and forever hereafter) As the Ruchira Avatar, Adi Da Samraj. I Am the Ruchira Avatar, Adi Da Samraj—the Avataric Divine Realizer, the Avataric Divine Revealer, the

Avataric Divine Incarnation, and the Avataric Divine Self-Revelation of Reality Itself. I Am the Avatarically Incarnate Divine Realizer, the Avatarically Incarnate Divine Revealer, and the Avatarically Incarnate Divine Self-Revelation of the One and Only Reality—Which Is the One and Only Truth, and Which Is the One and Only Real God. I Am the Great Avataric Divine Realizer, Avataric Divine Revealer, and Avataric Divine Self-Revelation long-Promised (and long-Expected) for the "late-time"—this (now, and forever hereafter) time, the "dark" epoch of mankind's "Great Forgetting" (and, potentially, the Great Epoch of mankind's Perpetual Remembering) of Reality, of Truth, and of Real God (Which Is the Great, True, and Spiritual Divine Person—or the One and Non-Separate and Indivisible Divine Source-Condition and Self-Condition—of all-and-All).

Beloved, I Am Da, the Divine Giver, the Giver (of All That I Am) to one, and to all, and to the All of all—now, and forever hereafter—here, and every "where" in the cosmic domain. Therefore, for the Purpose of Revealing the Way of Real God (or of Real and True Divine Realization), and in order to Divinely En-Light-en and Divinely Liberate all-and-All—I Am (Uniquely, Completely, and Most Perfectly) Avatarically Revealing My Very (and Self-Evidently Divine) Person (and Spiritually "Bright" Self-Condition) to all-and-All, by Means of My Avatarically Given Divine Self-Manifestation, As (and by Means of) the Ruchira Avatar, Adi Da Samraj.

In My Avatarically Given Divine Self-Manifestation As the Ruchira Avatar, Adi Da Samraj—I Am the Divine Secret, the Divine Self-Revelation of the Esoteric Truth, the Direct, and all-Completing, and all-Unifying Self-Revelation of Real God.

My Avatarically Given Divine Self-Confessions and My Avatarically Given Divine Teaching-Revelations Are the Great (Final, and all-Completing, and all-Unifying) Esoteric Revelation to mankind—and not a merely exoteric (or conventionally religious, or even ordinary Spiritual, or ego-made, or so-called "cultic") communication to public (or merely social) ears.

The greatest opportunity, and the greatest responsibility, of My devotees is Satsang with Me—Which is to live in the Condition of ego-surrendering, ego-forgetting, and (always more and more) ego-transcending devotional (and, in due course, Spiritual) relationship to Me, and (Thus and Thereby) to Realize My Avatarically Self-Revealed (and Self-Evidently Divine) Self-Condition, Which Is the Self-Evidently Divine Heart (or Non-Separate Self-Condition and Non-"Different" Source-Condition) of all-and-All, and Which Is Self-Existing and Self-Radiant Consciousness (or Indivisible Conscious Light) Itself (Which is One, and Only, and not separate in or as any one, or any "thing", at all). Therefore, My essential Divine Gift to one and all is Satsang with Me. And My essential Divine Work with one and all is Satsang-Work—to Live (and to Be Merely Present) *As* the Avatarically Self-Revealed Divine Heart and Conscious Light of Truth (and of Real God) among My devotees.

The only-by-Me Revealed and Given Way of Adidam (or Adidam Ruchiradam)—Which is the One and Only by-Me-Revealed and by-Me-Given Way of the Heart, or the only-by-Me Revealed and Given Way of "Radical" Understanding, or Ruchira Avatara Siddha Yoga—is the Way of Satsang with Me, the ego-transcending self-discipline of living in devotionally Me-recognizing devotional response to My Avatarically-Born bodily (human) Divine (and, in due course, Spiritually Effective) Form and Person, such that the devotionally to-Me-turned relationship to Me becomes the Real (and constant, and fundamental) Condition of life. Fundamentally, this Satsang with Me is the one thing done by My devotees. Because the only-by-Me Revealed and Given Way of Adidam is *always* (in every present-time moment) a directly ego-transcending *and* Really Me-Finding practice, the otherwise constant (and burdensome) tendency to *seek* is not exploited in this Satsang with Me. And the essential work of the formal (and formally acknowledged) worldwide gathering of My devotees is to make ego-transcending Satsang with Me available to all others.

Everything that serves the availability of Satsang with Me is (now, and forever hereafter) the responsibility of the formal worldwide gathering of My formally practicing devotees. I am not here to *publicly* "promote" this Satsang with Me. In the intimate circumstances of My devotees' humanly expressed devotional love of Me, I Speak My Avatarically Self-Revealing Divine Word to My devotees, and *they* (because of their devotional response to Me) bring My Avatarically Self-Revealing Divine Word to *all* others. Therefore, even though I am *not* (and have never been, and never will be) a "public" Teacher (or a broadly publicly active, and conventionally socially conformed, "religious figure"), My devotees function fully and freely (*as* My devotees) in the daily public world of ordinary life.

I Always Already Stand Free. Therefore, I have always (in My Divine Avataric-Incarnation-Work) Stood Free, in the "Crazy" (and non-conventional, or spontaneous and non-"public") Manner—in order to Guarantee the Freedom, the Uncompromising Rightness, and the Fundamental Integrity of My Avatarically Self-Manifested Divine Teaching (Work and Word), and in order to Freely and Fully and Fully Effectively Perform My universal (Avatarically Self-Manifested) Divine Spiritual Blessing-Work. I Am Present (now, and forever hereafter) to Divinely Serve, Divinely En-Light-en, and Divinely Liberate those who accept the Eternal Vow and *all* the life-responsibilities (or the full and complete practice)[1] associated with the only-by-Me Revealed and Given Way of Adidam. Because I Am (Thus) Given to My formally and fully practicing devotees, I do not Serve a "public" role, and I do not Work in a "public" (or even a merely "institutionalized") manner. Nevertheless—now, and forever hereafter—I constantly Bless all beings, and this entire world, and the total cosmic domain. And all who feel My Avatarically (and universally) Given Divine Spiritual Blessing, and who heart-recognize Me with true devotional love, are (Thus) Called to devotionally resort to Me—but only if they approach Me in the traditional devotional manner, as responsibly practicing (and truly ego-surrendering, and rightly Me-serving) members (or, in some, unique, cases, as invited guests) of the formal worldwide gathering of My formally practicing devotees.

I expect this formal discipline of right devotional approach to Me to have been freely and happily embraced by every one who would enter into My physical Company. The natural human reason for this is that there is a potential liability inherent in all human associations. And the root and nature of that potential liability is the ego (or the active human presumption of separateness, and the ego-act of human separativeness). Therefore, in order that the liabilities of egoity are understood (and voluntarily and responsibly disciplined) by those who approach Me, I Require demonstrated right devotion (based on really effective self-understanding and truly heart-felt devotional recognition of Me and, on that basis, truly heart-felt devotional response to Me) as the basis for any one's invitation to enter into My physical Company. And, in this manner, not only the egoic tendency, but also the tendency toward religious "cultism", is constantly undermined in the only-by-Me Revealed and Given Way of Adidam.

Because people appear within this human condition, this simultaneously attractive and frightening "dream" world, they tend to live—and to interpret both the conditional (or cosmic and psycho-physical) reality and the Unconditional (or Divine) Reality—from the "point of view" of this apparent (and bewildering) mortal human condition. And, because of this universal human bewilderment (and the ongoing human reaction to the threatening force of mortal life-events), there is an even ancient ritual that all human beings rather unconsciously (or automatically, and without discriminative understanding) desire and tend to repeatedly (and under all conditions) enact. Therefore, wherever there is an association of human beings gathered for any purpose (or around any idea, or symbol, or person, or subject of any kind), the same human bewilderment-ritual is tending to be enacted by one and all.

Human beings always tend to encircle (and, thereby, to contain—and, ultimately, to entrap and abuse, or even to blithely ignore) the presumed "center" of their lives—a book, a person, a symbol, an idea, or whatever. They tend to encircle the "center" (or the "middle"), and they tend to seek to exclusively acquire all "things" (or all power of control) for the circle (or toward the "middle") of themselves. In this manner, the group becomes an ego ("inward"-directed, or separate and separative)—just as the individual body-mind becomes, by self-referring self-contraction, the separate and separative ego-"I" ("inward"-directed, or ego-centric—and exclusively acquiring all "things", or all power of control, for itself). Thus, by self-contraction upon the presumed "center" of their lives—human beings, in their collective ego-centricity, make "cults" (or bewildered and frightened "centers" of power, and control, and exclusion) in every area of life.

Anciently, the "cult"-making process was done, most especially, in the political and social sphere—and religion was, as even now, mostly an exoteric (or political and social) exercise that was always used to legitimize (or, otherwise, to "de-throne") political and social "authority-figures". Anciently, the cyclically (or even annually) culminating product of this exoteric religio-political "cult" was the ritual "de-throning" (or ritual deposition) of the one in the "middle" (just as, even in these times, political leaders are periodically "deposed"—by elections, by rules of term and succession, by scandal, by slander, by force, and so on).

Everywhere throughout the ancient world, traditional societies made and performed this annual (or otherwise periodic) religio-political "cult" ritual. The ritual of "en-throning" and "de-throning" was a reflection of the human observation of the annual cycle of the seasons of the natural world—and the same ritual was a reflection of the human concern and effort to control the signs potential in the cycle of the natural world, in order to ensure human survival (through control of weather, harvests and every kind of "fate", or even every fraction of existence upon which human beings depend for both survival and pleasure, or psycho-physical well-being). Indeed, the motive behind the ancient agrarian (and, later, urbanized, or universalized) ritual of the one in the "middle" was, essentially, the same motive that, in the modern era, takes the form of the culture of scientific materialism (and even all of the modern culture of materialistic "realism"): It is the motive to gain (and to maintain) control, and the effort to control even everything and everyone (via both knowledge and gross power). Thus, the ritualized, or bewildered yes/no (or desire/fear), life of mankind in the modern era is, essentially, the same as that of mankind in the ancient days.

In the ancient ritual of "en-throning" and "de-throning", the person (or subject) in the "middle" was ritually mocked, abused, deposed, and banished—and a new person (or subject) was installed in the "center" of the religio-political "cult". In the equivalent modern ritual of dramatized ambiguity relative to everything and everyone (and, perhaps especially, "authority-figures"), the person (or symbol, or idea) in the "middle" (or that which is given power by means of popular fascination) is first "cultified" (or made much of), and then (progressively) doubted, mocked, and abused—until, at last, all the negative emotions are (by culturally and socially ritualized dramatization) dissolved, the "middle" (having thus ceased to be fascinating) is abandoned, and a "new" person (or symbol, or idea) becomes the subject of popular fascination (only to be reduced, eventually, to the same "cultic" ritual, or cycle of "rise" and "fall").

Just as in every other area of human life, the tendency of all those who (in the modern era) would become involved in religious or Spiritual life is also to make a "cult", a circle that ever increases its separate and separative dimensions—beginning from the "center", surrounding it, and (perhaps) even (ultimately) controlling it (such that it altogether ceases to be effective, or even interesting). Such "cultism" is ego-based, and ego-reinforcing—and, no matter how "esoteric" it presumes itself to be, it is (as in the ancient setting) entirely exoteric, or (at least) more and more limited to (and by) merely social (and gross physical) activities and conditions.

The form that every "cult" imitates is the pattern of egoity (or the pattern that is the ego-"I") itself—the presumed "middle" of every ordinary individual life. It is the self-contraction (or the avoidance of relationship), which "creates" the fearful sense of separate mind, and all the endless habits and motives of egoic desire (or bewildered, and self-deluded, seeking). It is what is, ordinarily, called (or presumed to be) the real and necessary and only "life".

From birth, the human being (by reaction to the blows and limits of psycho-physical existence) begins to presume separate existence to be his or her very nature—and, on that basis, the human individual spends his or her entire life generating and serving a circle of ownership (or self-protecting acquisition) all around the ego-"I". The egoic motive encloses all the other beings it can acquire, all the "things" it can acquire, all the states and thoughts it can acquire—all the possible emblems, symbols, experiences, and sensations it can possibly acquire. Therefore, when any human being begins to involve himself or herself in some religious or Spiritual association (or, for that matter, any extension of his or her own subjectivity), he or she tends again to "create" that same circle about a "center".

The "cult" (whether of religion, or of politics, or of science, or of popular culture) is a dramatization of egoity, of separativeness, even of the entrapment and betrayal of the "center" (or the "middle"), by one and all. Therefore, I have always Refused to assume the role and the position of the "man in the middle"—and I have always (from the beginning of My formal Work of Teaching and Blessing) Criticized, Resisted, and Shouted About the "cultic" (or ego-based, and ego-reinforcing, and merely "talking" and "believing", and not understanding and not really practicing) "school" (or tendency) of ordinary religious and Spiritual life. Indeed, true Satsang with Me (or the true devotional and Spiritual relationship to Me) is an always (and specifically, and intensively) counter-"cultic" (or truly non-"cultic") Process.

The true devotional and Spiritual relationship to Me is not separative (or merely "inward"-directed), nor is it a matter of attachment to Me as a mere (and, necessarily, limited) human being (or a "man in the middle")—for, if My devotee indulges in ego-bound (or self-referring and self-serving) attachment to Me as a mere human "other", My Divine Nature (and, therefore, the Divine Nature of Reality Itself) is not (as the very Basis for religious and Spiritual practice in My Company) truly devotionally recognized and rightly devotionally acknowledged. And, if such non-recognition of Me is the case, there is no truly ego-transcending devotional response to My Avatarically-Born and Avatarically Self-Revealed (and Self-Evidently Divine) Presence and Person—and, thus, such presumed-to-be "devotion" to Me is not devotional heart-Communion with Me, and such presumed-to-be "devotion" to Me is not Divinely Liberating. Therefore, because the true devotional (and, thus, truly devotionally Me-recognizing and, on that basis, truly devotionally to-Me-responding) relationship to Me is entirely a counter-egoic (and truly and only Divine) discipline, it does not (if rightly and truly practiced) become a "cult" (nor does it support the "cultic" tendency of Man).

The true devotional practice of Satsang with Me is (inherently) expansive—or anti-contractional, or anti-constrictive, or decompressive, or pro-relational. Thus, the self-contracting (or separate and separative) self-"center" is neither the motive nor the source of Satsang with Me. In true Satsang with Me, the egoic "center" is always already undermined as a "center" (or a presumed separate, and actively separative, entity). The Principle of true Satsang with Me is Me—Beyond (and not "within"—or, otherwise, supporting) the self-referring ego-"I".

True Satsang with Me is the true "Round Dance" of Esoteric Spirituality. I am not trapped in the "middle" of My devotees. I "Dance" in the "Round" with each and every one of My devotees. I "Dance" in the circle—and, therefore, I am not merely a "motionless man" in the "middle". At the true (and Inherently boundless) "Center" (or the Divine Heart), Which Includes all-and-All (and, therefore, is not merely surrounded, enclosed, abstracted, defined, known, and controlled by all-and-All), I Am—Beyond definition (or separateness). I Am the Indivisible, Most Perfectly Prior, Inherently Non-Separate, and Inherently egoless (or centerless, boundless, and Self-Evidently Divine) Consciousness (Itself) and the Indivisible, Most Perfectly Prior, Inherently Non-Separate, and Inherently egoless (or centerless, boundless, and Self-Evidently

Divine) Light (Itself). I Am the Very Being and the Very Presence (or Self-Radiance) of Self-Existing and Eternally Unqualified (or Non-"Different") Conscious Light (or the "Bright") Itself.

In the "Round Dance" of true Satsang with Me (or of right and true devotional and Spiritual relationship to Me), I (Myself) Am Communicated directly to every one who lives in heart-felt relationship with Me (insofar as each one feels—Beyond the ego-"I" of body-mind—to Me). Therefore, I am not the mere "man" (or the separate human, or psycho-physical, one), and I am not merely "in the middle" (or separated out, and limited, and confined, by egoic seekers). I Am the One (Avatarically Self-Revealed, and all-and-All-Transcending, and Self-Evidently Divine) Person of Reality Itself—Non-Separate, never merely at the egoic "center" (or "in the middle" of—or "within", and "inward" to—the egoic body-mind of My any devotee), but always with each one (and all), and always in relationship with each one (and all), and always Beyond each one (and all).

Therefore, My devotee is not Called, by Me, merely to turn "inward" (or upon the ego-"I"), or to struggle and seek to survive merely as a self-contracted and self-referring and self-seeking and self-serving ego-"center". Instead, I Call My devotee to turn the heart (and, indeed, all the faculties of the total body-mind) toward Me—feeling Me As I Am, Free-Standing here. I Call My devotee to turn from the self-"center", to Me, in relationship (relationally, rather than self-referringly). I Call My devotee to merely turn every faculty of body-mind to Me, having already Found (or "Located") Me—rather than to affirm the separate state, and the separative act, of ego-"I", by seeking for Me. I Call My devotee to grow (in due course) to "Locate" My Avatarically Self-Transmitted (and all-and-All-Surrounding and all-and-All-Pervading) Divine Spiritual Presence—by constantly turning to My Avatarically-Born bodily (human) Divine Form and Person. I Call My devotee (in due course) to receive Me Spiritually (in the inherently searchless attitude, or "Asana", of Mere Beholding of My Avatarically-Born bodily human Divine Form), and (Thus and Thereby) to understand (by Means of the tangible experiencing of My Divine Avataric Spiritual Blessing-Grace) that I Am (Always Already) Infinitely Above and Beyond (and Utterly Transcending) the body-mind-self of My devotee (and I am not merely "within"—or contained and containable "within" the separate, separative, and self-contracted domain of the body-mind-self, or the ego-"I", of My would-be devotee). I Call My Spiritually Me-receiving devotee to always function in My Avatarically Self-Transmitted Divine Light, such that My Avatarically Self-Revealed Divine Person is always (and under all circumstances) presumed and experienced (and not merely sought). Therefore, true Satsang with Me—or the searchlessly Me-Beholding devotional and (in due course) Spiritual relationship to Me—is life-embraced As the Real Company of Truth, or of Reality Itself (Which Is the Only Real God). True Satsang with Me Serves life, because I Move (or Radiate) into life, and I always Contact life in relationship. And the life of true Satsang with Me is the only-by-Me Revealed and Given Way of Adidam.

I do not Call My devotees to become absorbed into a "cultic" gang of exoteric and ego-centric religionists. I certainly Call all My devotees to always create and maintain cooperative sacred culture (and to enter into fully cooperative collective and personal relationship) with one another—but not to do so in an egoic, separative, world-excluding, xenophobic, and intolerant manner. Rather, My devotees are Called, by Me, to transcend egoity—through right and true devotional (and, in due course, Spiritual) relationship to Me, and mutually tolerant and peaceful cooperation with one another, and all-tolerating (cooperative and compassionate and all-loving and all-including) relationship with all of mankind (and with even all beings).

I Give My devotees the "Bright" Conscious Light of My Own Avatarically Self-Revealed Divine Person—by Means of Which Blessing-Gift they can become more and more capable of "Bright" Divine life. I Call for the searchless free devotion, the intelligently discriminative self-understanding, the rightly and freely living self-discipline, and the full and freely functional capability of My devotees. I do not Call My devotees to resist or eliminate life, or to strategically escape life, or to identify with the world-excluding ego-centric impulse. I Call My devotees to live a positively functional life. I do not Call My devotees to strategically separate themselves from the natural vitality of life, or to suppress the participatory impulse naturally associated with human existence. I Call for all the human life-functions to be really and rightly known, and to be really and rightly understood, and to be really and rightly lived—and not reduced by (or to) the inherently bewildered (and inherently "cultic", or self-centered and fearful) "point of view" of the separate and separative ego-"I".

I Call for every human life-function and faculty to be revolved away from self-contraction (or ego-"I"). I Call for every human life-function and faculty to be always directly (and thoroughly) aligned and out-turned and adapted to Me, in the truly ego-transcending (or counter-contractive) manner—and (Thus and Thereby) to be turned and Given to the Realization of My Divine Avataric Spiritual Self-Revelation of Truth, or Reality Itself—Which Is the "Bright" and Only Real God.

The characteristic life-sign of right, true, full, and fully devotional Satsang with Me is the capability for ego-transcending relatedness, based on the free disposition of no-seeking and no-dilemma. Therefore, the characteristic life-sign of right, true, full, and fully devotional Satsang with Me is not the tendency to seek some "other" condition. Rather, the characteristic life-sign of right, true, full, and fully devotional Satsang with Me is freedom from the presumption of dilemma within the present-time condition. The "radical" understanding (or "gone-to-the-root" self-understanding) I Give to My devotees is not, itself, the acquisition of any particular "thing" of experience. My every true devotee is simply Awakening (and always Awakened) to Me, within the otherwise bewildering "dream" of human life.

Satsang with Me is a naturally (or spontaneously, and not strategically) unfolding Process, in Which the self-contraction that is each one's suffering is transcended by Means of total psycho-physical (or whole bodily) heart-Communion with My Avatarically-Born bodily (human) Divine Form and Person—and (Thus and Thereby, and in due course) with My Avatarically Self-Transmitted (and Real—and Really, and tangibly, experienced) Divine (Spiritual, and Transcendental) Presence. My devotee is (as is the case with any and every ego-"I") always tending to be preoccupied with ego-based seeking—but, all the while of his or her life in actively ego-surrendering (and really ego-forgetting and, more and more, ego-transcending) devotional (and, in due course, Spiritual) Communion with Me, I Am Divinely Attracting (and Divinely Acting upon) My true devotee's heart (and total body-mind), and (Thus and Thereby) Dissolving and Vanishing My true devotee's fundamental egoity (and even all of his or her otherwise motivating dilemma and seeking-strategy).

There are two principal tendencies by which I am always being confronted by My devotee. One is the tendency to seek—rather than to truly surrender to, and enjoy, and fully animate the devotional (and, in due course, Spiritually developing) Condition of Satsang with Me. And the other is the tendency to make a self-contracting circle around Me—and, thus, to make a "cult" of ego-"I" (and of the "man in the middle"), or to duplicate the ego-ritual of mere fascination, and of inevitable resistance, and of never-Awakening unconsciousness. Relative to these two tendencies, I Give all My devotees only one resort. It is this true Satsang—the devotionally Me-recognizing, and (on that basis) devotionally to-Me-responding, and always really counter-egoic devotional (and, in due course, Spiritual) relationship to My Avatarically-Born bodily (human) Divine Form and Self-Evidently Divine Person.

The Great Secret of My Avatarically-Born bodily (human) Divine Form and Person, and of My Avatarically Self-Transmitted Divine Spiritual Blessing-Work (now, and forever hereafter)—and, therefore, the Great Secret of the only-by-Me Revealed and Given Way of Adidam—Is that I am not the "man in the middle", but I Am Reality Itself, I Am the Only One Who Is, I Am That Which Is Always Already The Case, I Am the Non-Separate (Avatarically Self-Revealed, and Self-Evidently Divine) Person (or One and Very Divine Self, or One and True Divine Self-Condition) of all-and-All (Beyond the ego-"I" of every one, and of all, and of All).

Aham Da Asmi. Beloved, I Am Da—the One and Only and Non-Separate and Indivisible and Self-Evidently Divine Person, the Non-Separate and Indivisible Self-Condition and Source-Condition of all-and-All. I Am the Avatarically Self-Revealed and Spiritually Self-"Bright" Person, the One and Only and Self-Existing and Self-Radiant Person—Who Is the One and Only and Non-Separate and Indivisible and Indestructible Conscious Light of all-and-All. I Am That One and Only and Non-Separate One. And—As That One, and Only As That One—I Call all human beings to heart-recognize Me, and (on that basis) to heart-respond to Me with right, true, and full devotion (demonstrated by Means of formal practice of the only-by-Me Revealed and Given Way of Adidam—Which Is the One and Only by-Me-Revealed and by-Me-Given Way of the Heart).

I do not tolerate the so-called "cultic" (or ego-made, and ego-reinforcing) approach to Me. I do not tolerate the seeking ego's "cult" of the "man in the middle". I am not a self-deluded ego-man—making much of himself, and looking to include everyone-and-everything around himself for the sake of social and political power. To be the "man in the middle" is to be in a Man-made trap, an absurd mummery of "cultic" devices that enshrines and perpetuates the ego-"I" in one and all. Therefore, I do not make or tolerate the religion-making "cult" of ego-Man. I do not tolerate the inevitable abuses of religion, of Spirituality, of Truth Itself, and of My Own Person (even in bodily human Form) that are made (in endless blows and mockeries) by ego-based mankind when the Great Esoteric Truth of devotion to the Adept-Realizer is not rightly understood and rightly practiced.

The Great Means for the Teaching, and the Blessing, and the Awakening, and the Divine Liberating of mankind (and of even all beings) Is the Adept-Realizer. The true Adept-Realizer (of any degree or kind) is One Who (by Virtue of True Divine Realization) Is Able to (and, indeed, cannot do otherwise than) Stand In and As the Divine (or Real and Inherent and One and Only) Position, and to Be (Thus and Thereby) the Divine Means (In Person) for the Divine Helping of one and all. This Great Means Is the Great Esoteric Principle of the collective historical Great Tradition of mankind. And Such Adept-Realizers Are (in their Exercise of the Great Esoteric Principle) the Great Revelation-Sources That Are at the Core and Origin of all the right and true religious and Spiritual traditions within the collective historical Great Tradition of mankind.

By Means of My (now, and forever hereafter) Divinely Descended and Divinely Self-"Emerging" Avataric Incarnation, I Am the Ruchira Avatar,

Adi Da Samraj—the Divine Heart-Master, the First, the Last, and the Only Adept-Realizer of the seventh (or Most Perfect, and all-Completing) stage of life. I Am the Ruchira Avatar, Adi Da Samraj, the Avataric Incarnation (and Divine World-Teacher) everywhere Promised for the "late-time" (or "dark" epoch)—which "late-time" (or "dark" epoch) is now upon all of mankind. I Am the Great and Only and Non-Separate and (Self-Evidently) Divine Person—Appearing in Man-Form, As the Ruchira Avatar, Adi Da Samraj, in order to Teach, and to Bless, and to Awaken, and to Divinely Liberate all of mankind (and even all beings, every "where" in the cosmic domain). Therefore, by Calling every one and all (and All) to Me, I Call every one and all (and All) Only to the Divine Person—Which Is My Own and Very Person (or Very, and Self-Evidently Divine, Self-Condition), and Which Is Reality Itself (or Truth Itself, the Indivisible and Indestructible Conscious Light That Is the Only Real God), and Which Is the One and Very and Non-Separate and Only Self-Condition and Source-Condition of all-and-All (Beyond the ego-"I" of every one, and of all, and of All).

The only-by-Me Revealed and Given Way of Adidam necessarily (and As a Unique Divine Gift) requires and involves devotional recognition of Me (and, on that basis, devotional response to Me) In and Via (and As) My bodily (human) Divine Avataric-Incarnation-Form. However, because I Call every one and all (and All) to Me Only As the Divine Person (or Reality Itself), the only-by-Me Revealed and Given Way of Adidam is not about ego, and egoic seeking, and the egoic (or the so-called "cultic") approach to Me (as the "man in the middle").

According to all the esoteric traditions within the collective historical Great Tradition of mankind, to devotionally approach any Adept-Realizer as if he or she is (or is limited to being, or is limited by being) a mere (or "ordinary", or even merely "extraordinary") human entity is the great "sin" (or fault), or the great error whereby the would-be devotee fails to "meet the mark".[2] Indeed, the Single Greatest Esoteric Teaching common to all the esoteric religious and Spiritual traditions within the collective historical Great Tradition of mankind Is that the Adept-Realizer should always and only (and only devotionally) be recognized and approached As the Embodiment and the Real Presence of That (Reality, or Truth, or Real God) Which would be Realized (Thus and Thereby) by the devotee.

Therefore, no one should misunderstand Me. By Avatarically Revealing and Confessing My Divine Status to one and all (and All), I am not indulging in self-appointment, or in illusions of grandiose Divinity. I am not claiming the "Status" of the "Creator-God" of exoteric (or public, and social, and idealistically pious) religion. Rather, by Standing Firm in the Divine Position (As I Am)—

and (Thus and Thereby) Refusing to be approached as a mere man, or as a "cult"-figure, or as a "cult"-leader, or to be in any sense defined (and, thereby, trapped, and abused, or mocked) as the "man in the middle"—I Am Demonstrating the Most Perfect Fulfillment (and the Most Perfect Integrity, and the Most Perfect Fullness) of the Esoteric (and Most Perfectly Non-Dual) Realization of Reality. And, by Revealing and Giving the Way of Adidam (Which Is the Way of ego-transcending devotion to Me As the Avatarically Self-Revealed One and Only and Non-Separate and Self-Evidently Divine Person), I Am (with Most Perfect Integrity, and Most Perfect Fullness) Most Perfectly (and in an all-Completing and all-Unifying Manner) Fulfilling the Primary Esoteric Tradition (and the Great Esoteric Principle) of the collective historical Great Tradition of mankind—Which Primary Esoteric Tradition and Great Esoteric Principle Is the Tradition and the Principle of devotion to the Adept-Realizer As the Very Person and the Direct (or Personal Divine) Helping-Presence of the Eternal and Non-Separate Divine Self-Condition and Source-Condition of all-and-All.

Whatever (or whoever) is cornered (or trapped on all sides) bites back (and fights, or seeks, to break free). Whatever (or whoever) is "in the middle" (or limited and "centered" by attention) is patterned by (or conformed to) the ego-"I" (and, if objectified as "other", is forced to represent the ego-"I", and is even made a scapegoat for the pains, the sufferings, the powerless ignorance, and the abusive hostility of the ego-"I").

If there is no escape from (or no Way out of) the corner (or the "centered" trap) of ego-"I"—the heart goes mad, and the body-mind becomes more and more "dark" (bereft of the Indivisible and Inherently Free Light of the Self-Evident, and Self-Evidently Divine, Love-Bliss That Is Reality Itself).

I am not the "man in the middle". I do not stand here as a mere man, "middled" to the "center" (or the cornering trap) of ego-based mankind. I am not an ego-"I", or a mere "other", or the representation (and the potential scapegoat) of the ego-"I" of mankind (or of any one at all).

I Am the Indivisible and Non-Separate One, the "Bright", the "Midnight Sun", Always Already Infinitely Above and Beyond the all-and-All—and, by Virtue of My Divine Avataric Incarnation and Descent, Always (now, and forever hereafter) Surrounding and Pervading the every one of every here and then.

I Am the (Avatarically Self-Revealed) One and Only and (Self-Evidently) Divine Person—the Perfectly Subjective Divine Self-Condition (and Source-Condition) That Is Perfectly centerless (and Perfectly boundless), Eternally Above and Beyond the "middle" of all-and-All, and (now, and forever hereafter) Surrounding, Pervading, and Blessing all-and-All.

I Am the Way Beyond the self-cornering and "other"-cornering trap of ego-"I".

In this "late-time" (or "dark" epoch) of worldly ego-Man, the collective of mankind is "darkened" (and cornered) by egoity. Therefore, mankind has become mad, Lightless, and (like a cornered "thing") aggressively hostile in its universally competitive fight and bite.

Therefore, I have not Come here merely to stand Manly in the "middle" of mankind—to suffer its biting abuses, or even to be coddled and ignored in a little corner of religious "cultism".

I have Come here to Divinely Liberate one and all (and All) from the "dark" culture and effect of this "late-time", and (now, and forever hereafter) to Divinely Liberate one and all (and All) from the pattern and the act of ego-"I", and (Most Ultimately) to Divinely Translate one and all (and All) Into the Indivisible, Perfectly Subjective, and Eternally Non-Separate Sphere (or Non-"Different" and Indestructible "Midnight Sun") of My "Bright" Self-Domain of Divine Love-Bliss-Light.

The ego-"I" is a "centered" (or separate and separative) trap, from which the heart (and even the entire body-mind) must be Retired. I Am the Way (or the Very Means) of that Retirement from egoity. I Refresh the heart (and even the entire body-mind) of My devotee, in every moment My devotee resorts to Me (by devotionally recognizing My Avatarically-Born bodily human Divine Form and Person, and, on that basis, devotionally—and ecstatically, and also, often, meditatively—responding to My Avatarically-Born bodily human Divine Form and Person) Beyond the "middle", Beyond the "centering" act (or trapping gesture) of ego-"I" (or self-contraction).

I Am the Avatarically Self-Revealed (and Perfectly Subjective, and Self-Evidently Divine) Self-Condition (and Source-Condition) of every one, and of all, and of All—but the Perfectly Subjective (and Self-Evidently Divine) Self-Condition (and Source-Condition) is not "within" the ego-"I" (or separate and separative body-mind). The Perfectly Subjective (and Self-Evidently Divine) Self-Condition (and Source-Condition) is not in the "center" (or the "middle") of Man (or of mankind). The Perfectly Subjective (and Self-Evidently Divine) Self-Condition (and Source-Condition) of one, and of all, and of All Is Inherently centerless (or Always Already Beyond the self-contracted "middle"), and to Be Found only "outside" (or by transcending) the bounds of separateness, relatedness, and "difference". Therefore, in order to Realize the Perfectly Subjective (and Self-Evidently Divine) Self-Condition and Source-Condition (or the Perfectly Subjective, and Self-Evidently Divine, Heart) of one, and of all, and of All (or even, in any moment, to exceed the ego-trap—and to be Refreshed at heart, and in the total body-mind), it is necessary to feel (and to, ecstatically, and even meditatively, swoon) Beyond the "center" (or Beyond the "point of view" of separate ego-"I" and separative body-mind). Indeed, Most Ultimately, it is only in ego-transcendence to the degree of unqualified relatedness (and Most Perfect Divine Samadhi, or Utterly Non-Separate Enstasy) that the Inherently centerless and boundless, and Perfectly Subjective, and Self-Evidently Divine Self-Condition (and Source-Condition) Stands Obvious and Free (and Is, Thus and Thereby, Most Perfectly Realized).

It Is only by Means of devotionally Me-recognizing (and, on that basis, devotionally to-Me-responding) devotional meditation on My Avatarically-Born bodily (human) Divine Form and Person (and Thus ecstatic heart-Contemplation of Me), and (in due course) total (and totally open, and totally ego-forgetting) psycho-physical reception of My Avatarically Self-Transmitted Divine (and Always Blessing) Spiritual Presence and State of Person, that your madness of heart (and of body-mind) is (now, and now, and now) escaped, and your "darkness" is En-Light-ened (even, at last, Most Perfectly). Therefore, be My true devotee—and, by (formally, and rightly, and truly, and fully, and fully devotionally) practicing the only-by-Me Revealed and Given Way of Adidam (Which Is the Divine and True and Complete Way of Truth, and of Reality, and of Real God), always turn to My Avatarically-Born bodily (human) Divine Form, and (Thus and Thereby, and in due course) always Find Me Spiritually (by searchlessly "Locating" Me), Infinitely Above and Beyond your self-"center", and Surrounding and Pervading every here and now.

Aham Da Asmi. Beloved, I Am Da. And, because I Am Infinitely and Non-Separately "Bright", all and All are arising in My Divine Sphere of "Brightness". By feeling and surrendering into the Infinite Spiritual Sphere of My Avatarically Self-Revealed Divine Self-"Brightness", My every devotee Awakens (by Means of My Avataric Divine Spiritual Grace) to Merely Be in Me. And, Beyond his or her self-contracting and separative act of ego-"I", My every devotee (self-surrendered into heart-Communion With Me) Is the One and Only and Non-Separate and Real God I Have Come to Awaken—by Means of My Avataric Divine Incarnation, My Avataric Divine Spiritual Descent, and My Avataric Divine Self-"Emergence"—now, and forever hereafter, here (and every "where") in the cosmic domain.

PROLEGOMENA

AVATAR ADI DA SAMRAJ
The Mountain Of Attention Sanctuary, 2002

I

My Divine Disclosure*

1.

Aham Da Asmi. Beloved, I Am Da—The One and Only and Self-Evidently Divine Person, Avatarically Self-Revealed To You.

2.

Therefore, Listen To Me, and Hear Me, and See Me.

3.

This Is My Divine Heart-Secret, The Supreme Word Of My Eternal Self-Revelation.

4.

Here and Now, I Will Tell You What Will Benefit You The Most, Because I Love You.

5.

I Am The Da Avatar, Adi Da Love-Ananda Samraj—The Ruchira Avatar, The Love-Ananda Avatar, The Avataric Incarnation (and The Self-Evidently Divine Person) Of The One True Heart (or The One, and Only, and Inherently egoless Self-Condition, and Source-Condition, and Conscious Light) Of all-and-All.

*"My Divine Disclosure" has been Freely Developed—As a Further, and All-Completing, Avataric Self-Revelation of His Own Self-Evidently Divine Person—by the Ruchira Avatar, Adi Da Samraj, from selected verses of the traditional *Bhagavad Gita* (2:13–17, 8:3, 8:22, 9:3, 9:11, 9:26, 15:15, 18:61–66).

6.

Here I Am, In Person, To Offer (To You, and To all) The Only-By-Me Revealed and Given True World-Religion (or Avatarically All-Completing Divine Devotional and Spiritual Way) Of Adidam (or Adidam Ruchiradam)—Which Is The One and Only By-Me-Revealed and By-Me-Given (and Only Me-Revealing) Divine Devotional and Spiritual Way Of The "Bright" (or The Only-By-Me Revealed and Given, and Entirely Me-Revealing, Way Of The One, and Only, and Inherently Indivisible, and Inherently egoless, and Self-Evidently Divine Conscious Light Of Reality Itself), and Which Is The One, and All-Inclusive, and All-Transcending, and Only-By-Me Revealed and Given (and Only Me-Revealing) Way Of The True Divine Heart-Master (or The Only-By-Me Revealed and Given, and Entirely Me-Revealing, Way Of Ruchira Avatara Bhakti Yoga, or Ruchira Avatara Siddha Yoga), and Which Is The "Radically" ego-Transcending Way Of Devotionally Me-Recognizing and Devotionally To-Me-Responding Reception Of My Avatarically Self-Manifested Divine (and Not Merely Cosmic) Ruchira Shaktipat (or Divinely Self-Revealing Avataric Spiritual Grace).

7.

If You Surrender Your heart To Me, and If (By Surrendering Your ego-"I", or self-Contracted body-mind, To Me) You Make Yourself A Living Gift To Me, and If You (Thus) Constantly Yield Your attention To Me (Through True Devotional Love and Really ego-Transcending Service), Then You Will Hear Me (Truly), and See Me (Clearly), and Realize Me (Fully), and Come To Me (Eternally). I Promise You This, Because I Love You.

8.

Abandon The Reactive Reflex Of self-Contraction—The Separative (or egoic) Principle In all Your concerns. Do Not Cling To any experience that May Be Sought (and Even Attained) As A Result Of desire (or The Presumption Of "Difference"). Abandon Your Search For what May Be Gotten As A Result Of the various kinds of strategic (or egoic) action.

9.

I Am Love-Bliss Itself—Now (and Forever Hereafter) "Brightly" Present here. Therefore, I Say To You: Abandon All Seeking—By Always "Locating" (and Immediately Finding) Me.

10.

Instead Of Seeking Me (As If My Divine Person Of Inherent Love-Bliss-Happiness Were Absent From You), Always Commune With Me (Ever-Present, Never Absent, and Always Love-Bliss-Full and Satisfied). Thus, Your Me-"Locating" Relinquishment Of All Seeking Is Not, Itself, To Be Merely Another Form Of Seeking.

11.

If You Always "Locate" Me (and, Thus, Immediately Find Me), You Will Not (In any instance) self-Contract Into the mood and strategy of inaction.

12.

You Must Never Fail To act. Every moment of Your life Requires Your particular Right action. Indeed, the living body-mind is (itself) action. Therefore, Be Ordinary, By Always Allowing the body-mind its Necessity Of Right action (and Inevitable Change).

13.

Perform every act As An ego-Transcending Act Of Devotional Love Of Me, In body-mind-Surrendering Love-Response To Me.

14.

Always Discipline all Your acts, By Only Engaging In action that Is Appropriate For one who Loves Me, and Surrenders To Me, and acts Only (and Rightly) In Accordance With My Always Explicit Word Of Instruction.

15.

Therefore, Be My Always Listening-To-Me Devotee—and, Thus, Always live "Right Life" (According To My Word), and (This) Always By Means Of active Devotional Recognition-Response To Me, and While Always Remembering and Invoking and Contemplating Me. In This Manner, Perform every act As A Form Of Direct, and Present, and Whole bodily (or Total psycho-physical), and Really ego-Surrendering Love-Communion With Me.

16.

If You Love Me—Where Is doubt and anxious living? If You Love Me Now, Even anger, sorrow, and fear Are Gone. When You Abide In Devotional Love-Communion With Me, the natural results of Your various activities No Longer Have Power To Separate or Distract You From Me.

17.

The ego-"I" that is born (as a body-mind) In The Realm Of Cosmic Nature (or the conditional worlds of action and experience) Advances From childhood To adulthood, old age, and death—While Identified With the same (but Always Changing) body-mind. Then the same ego-"I" Attains another body-mind, As A Result. One whose heart Is (Always) Responsively Given To Me Overcomes (Thereby) Every Tendency To self-Contract From This Wonderfully Ordinary Process.

18.

The Ordinary Process Of "Everything Changing" Is Simply The Natural Play Of Cosmic Life, In Which the (Always) two sides of every possibility come and go, In Cycles Of appearance and disappearance. Winter's cold alternates with summer's heat. Pain, Likewise, Follows every pleasure. Every appearance Is (Inevitably) Followed By its disappearance. There Is No Permanent experience In The Realm Of Cosmic Nature. One whose heart-Feeling Of Me Is Steady Simply Allows All Of This To Be So. Therefore, one who Truly Hears Me Ceases To Add self-Contraction To This Inevitable Round Of Changes.

19.

Happiness (or True Love-Bliss) Is Realization Of That Which Is Always Already The Case.

20.

I Am That Which Is Always Already The Case.

21.

Happiness Is Realization Of Me.

22.

Realization Of Me Is Possible Only When a living being (or body-mind-self) Has heart-Ceased To React To The Always Changing Play Of Cosmic Nature.

23.

The body-mind Of My True Devotee Is Constantly Steadied In Me, By Means Of the Feeling-heart's Always Constant Devotional Recognition-Response To Me.

24.

Once My True Devotee Has Truly heart-Accepted That The Alternating-Cycle Of Changes (Both Positive and Negative) Is Inevitable (In the body-mind, and In all the conditional worlds), the living body-mind-self (or ego-"I") Of My True Devotee Has Understood itself (and, Thus, Heard Me).

25.

The body-mind-self (Of My True Me-Hearing Devotee) that Constantly Understands itself (At heart) By Constantly Surrendering To Me (and Communing With Me) No Longer self-Contracts From My Love-Bliss-State Of Inherent Happiness.

26.

Those who Truly Hear Me Understand That whatever Does Not Exist Always and Already (or Eternally) Only Changes.

27.

Those who Truly See Me Acknowledge (By heart, and With every moment and act of body-mind) That What Is Always Already The Case Never Changes.

28.

Such True Devotees Of Mine (who Both Hear Me and See Me) Realize That The Entire Cosmic Realm Of Change—and Even the To-Me-Surrendered body-mind (itself)—Is Entirely Pervaded By Me (Always Self-Revealed As That Which Is Always Already The Case).

29.

Now, and Forever Hereafter, I Am Avatarically Self-Revealed, Beyond The Cosmic Play—"Bright" Behind, and Above, the To-Me-Surrendered body-mind Of My Every True Devotee.

30.

I Am The Eternally Existing, All-Pervading, Transcendental, Inherently Spiritual, Inherently egoless, Perfectly Subjective, Indivisible, Inherently Perfect, Perfectly Non-Separate, and Self-Evidently Divine Self-Condition and Source-Condition Of all Apparently Separate (or self-Deluded) selves.

31.

My Divine Heart-Power Of Avataric Self-Revelation Is (Now, and Forever Hereafter) Descending Into The Cosmic Domain (and Into the body-mind Of Every To-Me-True True Devotee Of Mine).

32.

I Am The Avatarically Self-"Emerging", Universal, All-Pervading Divine Spirit-Power and Person Of Love-Bliss (That Most Perfectly Husbands and Transcends The Primal Energy Of Cosmic Nature).

33.

I Am The One and Indivisibly "Bright" Divine Person.

34.

Now, and Forever Hereafter, My Ever-Descending and Ever-"Emerging" Current Of Self-Existing and Self-Radiant Love-Bliss Is Avatarically Pervading The Ever-Changing Realm Of Cosmic Nature.

35.

I Am The One, and Indivisibly "Bright", and Inherently egoless, and Self-Evidently Divine Person Of all-and-All, Within Whom every body-mind Is arising (as a mere, and unnecessary, and merely temporary appearance that, merely apparently, modifies Me).

36.

I Am To Be Realized By Means Of Searchless Devotional Love Of Me—Whereby every action of body-mind Is (Responsively) Engaged As ego-Surrendering (present-time, and Direct) Communion With Me.

37.

Those who Do Not heart-Recognize Me and heart-Respond To Me—and who (Therefore) Are Without Faith In Me—Do Not (and Cannot) Realize Me. Therefore, they (By Means Of their own self-Contraction From Me) Remain ego-Bound To The Realm Of Cosmic Nature, and To The Ever-Changing Round Of conditional knowledge and temporary experience, and To The Ceaselessly Repetitive Cycles Of birth and search and loss and death.

38.

Such Faithless beings Cannot Be Distracted By Me—Because they Are Entirely Distracted By themselves! They Are Like Narcissus—The Myth Of ego—At His Pond. Their Merely self-Reflecting minds Are Like a mirror in a dead man's hand. Their tiny hearts Are Like a boundless desert, where the mirage of Separate self is ceaselessly admired, and The True Water Of My Constant Presence Stands Un-Noticed, In the droughty heap and countless sands of ceaseless thoughts. If Only they Would Un-think themselves In Me, these (Now Faithless) little hearts Could Have Immediate Access To The True Water Of My True Heart! Through Devotional Surrender Of body, emotion, mind, breath, and all of Separate self To Me, Even Narcissus Could Find The Way To My Oasis (In The True Heart's Room and House)—but the thinking mind of ego-"I" Is Never Bathed In Light (and, So, it sits, Un-Washed, Like a desert dog that wanders in a herd of flies).

39.

The "Un-Washed dog" of self-Contracted body-mind Does Not think To Notice Me—The Divine Heart-Master Of its wild heart and Wilderness.

40.

The "Wandering dog" of ego-"I" Does Not "Locate" Me In My Inherent "Bright" Perfection—The Divine Heart-Master Of Everything, The Inherently egoless Divine True Heart Of all conditionally Manifested beings, and The Non-Separate and Indivisible Self-Condition and Source-Condition Of all-and-All.

41.

If Only "Narcissus" Will Relent, and heart-Consent To Bow and Live In Love-Communion With Me, heart-Surrendering all of body-mind To Me, By Means Of Un-Contracting Love Of Me, Then—Even If That Love Is Shown With Nothing More Than the "little gift" of ego-"I" (itself)—I Will Always Accept The Offering With Open Arms Of Love-Bliss-Love, and Offer My Own Divine Immensity In "Bright" Return.

42.

Therefore, whoever Is Given (By heart) To Me Will Be Washed, From head To toe, By All The True Water Of My Love-Bliss-Light, That Always "Crashes Down" On all-and-All, Below My Blessing-Feet.

43.

My Circumstance and Situation Is At the heart of all beings—where I Am (Now, and Forever Hereafter) Avatarically Self-"Emerging" As The One and all-and-All-Outshining Divine and Only Person—Avatarically Self-Manifested As The "Radically" Non-Dual "Brightness" Of all-and-All-Filling Conscious Love-Bliss-Light, Self-Existing and Self-Radiant As The Perfectly Subjective Fundamental Reality, or Inherent (and Inherently egoless) Feeling, Of Merely (or Unqualifiedly) Being.

44.

The True heart-Place (Where I Am To Be "Located" By My True Devotee) Is Where The Ever-Changing Changes Of waking, dreaming, and sleeping experience Are Merely Witnessed (or Merely Felt, and Not Sought, or Found, or Held).

45.

Every conditional experience appears and disappears In Front Of the Witness-heart (Of Mere Feeling-Awareness, Itself).

46.

Everything Merely Witnessed (or Merely Felt) Is Spontaneously Generated By The Persistent Activity Of The Universal Cosmic Life-Energy.

47.

The self-Contracted heart of body-mind Is Fastened, Help-lessly, To That Perpetual-Motion Machine Of Cosmic Nature.

48.

I Am The Divine and One True Heart (Itself)—Always Already Existing As The Eternally Self-Evident Love-Bliss-Feeling Of Being (and Always Already Free-Standing As Consciousness Itself, Prior To the little heart of ego-"I" and its Seeming Help-less-ness).

49.

In Order To Restore all beings To The One True Heart Of Me, I Am Avatarically Born To here, As The "Bright" Divine Help Of conditionally Manifested beings.

50.

Therefore (Now, and Forever Hereafter), I Am (Always Free-Standing) At the To-Me-True heart Of You—and I Am (Always "Bright") Above Your body-mind and world.

51.

If You Become My True Devotee (Searchlessly heart-Recognizing My Avatarically Self-Manifested Divine Person, and, On That Basis, heart-Responding—With all the parts of Your single body-mind—To My Avatarically Self-Revealing Divine Form and Presence and State), You Will Always Be Able To Feel Me ("Brightly-Emerging" here) Within Your Un-Contracting, In-Me-Falling heart—and You Will Always Be Able To "Locate" Me, As I "Crash Down" (All-"Bright" Upon You) From Infinitely Above the worlds Of Change.

52.

The To-Me-Feeling (In-Me-Falling) heart Of My Every True Devotee Is (At its Root, and Base, and Highest Height) My Divine and One True Heart (Itself).

53.

Therefore, Fall Awake In Me.

54.

Do Not Surrender Your Feeling-heart Merely To experience and know the Ever-Changing world.

55.

Merely To know and experience The Cosmic Domain (Itself) Is To live As If You Were In Love With Your Own body-mind.

56.

Therefore, Surrender Your Feeling-heart Only To Me, The True Divine Beloved Of the body-mind.

57.

I Am The Truth (and The Teacher) Of the heart-Feeling body-mind.

58.

I Am The Divine and Eternal Master Of Your To-Me-Feeling heart and Your To-Me-Surrendering body-mind.

59.

I Am The Self-Existing, Self-Radiant, and Inherently Perfect Person Of Unconditional Being—Who Pervades The Machine Of Cosmic Nature As The "Bright" Divine Spirit-Current Of Love-Bliss, and Who Transcends All Of Cosmic Nature As Infinite Self-Conscious Light, The Spiritually "Bright" Divine Self-Condition (and Source-Condition) Of all-and-All.

60.

If You Will Give (and Truly, Really, Always Give) Your Feeling-attention To My Avatarically-Born Bodily (Human) Divine Form, and If You Will (Thus, and Thereby) Yield Your body-mind Into The "Down-Crashing" Love-Bliss-Current Of My Avatarically Self-Transmitted and All-Pervading Divine Spirit-Presence, and If You Will Surrender Your conditional self-Consciousness Into My Avatarically Self-Revealed and Perfectly Subjective and Self-Evidently Divine Self-Consciousness (Which Is The Divine True Heart Of Inherently egoless Being, Itself)—Then I Will Also Become An Offering To You.

61.

By That Offering Of Mine, You Will Be Given The Gift Of Perfect Peace, and An Eternal Domain For Your To-Me-True Feeling-heart.

62.

Now I Have Revealed To You The Divine Mystery and The Perfect Heart-Secret Of My Avataric Birth To here.

63.

"Consider" This Me-Revelation, Fully—and, Then, Choose What You Will Do With Your "little gift" of Feeling-heart and Your "Un-Washed dog" of body-mind.

Avatar Adi Da Samraj
Da Love-Ananda Mahal, 2002

II

The Plight Of The Divine Heart-Husband[3]

(The Forty-Seven Divine Statements Of The Ruchira Avatar, Adi Da Samraj)

1.

Beloved, This Is My Heart-Secret.

2.

I Am Da—The One and Only and Self-Evidently Divine Source and Person, Who Is The One and Only and Inherently egoless (and Boundlessly "Bright") Heart Of all-and-All, and Who Is The One and Only Giver Of Divine Self-Realization To all-and-All.

3.

I Am Avatarically Born, As The Ruchira Avatar, Adi Da Samraj—Man-Born As My Own Divine "Brightness", and As The Totality Of My Own Divine Bliss, and As My Own Divine Heart Of Love, and As An Avataric Ordeal Of Divine Heart-Submission To all-and-All (So That every one Will Hear and See The Heart and Way Of Me).

4.

In Order To Awaken all-and-All To Me (and In Me, and As Me), It Was Necessary That I (By Even Every Avataric Means Of Divine Descent) Freely Assume, Wholly Understand, and Most Perfectly Transcend all the conditional states Of Existence—and, In Order To Do That, It Was Necessary That I (By Means Of An Avataric Human Incarnation) Freely Assume, Wholly Understand, and Most Perfectly Transcend all the conditions Of Even human Existence.

5.

Now That My Avataric Ordeal Of Divine Descent (To every where, and To every one) Is Most Perfectly Complete, I Am (Avatarically) Forever Divinely Self-"Emerging" here—Now (and Forever Hereafter) Self-Revealed (and Self-Revealing) In and As and Via The Avatarically-Born (Bodily Human, and Self-Evidently Divine) Form Of The Divinely "Bright" Avatar (Adi Da Samraj), and As and Via My (Thus and Thereby) Avatarically Self-Transmitted "Bright" (and Self-Evidently Divine) Spiritual Presence, and (Ultimately) As My (Thus and Thereby) Avatarically Self-Revealed State (or Inherently egoless, and Boundlessly "Bright", and Self-Evidently Divine Heart) Itself—So That (By Means Of The Directly Me-Revealing "Bright" Spirit-Power Of My Thus Avatarically Self-Revealed Divine Form, and Presence, and State) Every ego-"I" (or Seeming-Separate Heart) Will Devotionally Recognize Me, and (In Devotional Response To My Thus Avatarically Self-Revealed Divine Form, and Presence, and State) Forget The Heart-Contraction (Of Separate, and Always Separative, ego-"I") In Me, and (Ultimately, By Realizing Me Most Perfectly) Awaken Into The Boundless Sphere and Infinite egoless Space Of My Eternal "Bright" Divine Self-Domain.

6.

I Am Avatarically-Born To here, As The Divine Adept, Adi Da Samraj—Who Is The One and Only Man Of "Radical" Understanding (Now, and Forever Hereafter, Teaching and Awakening Every here-born Heart, By Means Of Word and Sign[4]), and Who Is (Now, and Forever Hereafter) The One and Only Divine Heart-Master (Whose Avatarically Self-Revealed Divine Form, and Avatarically Self-Transmitted Divine Spiritual Presence, and Avatarically Self-Manifested Divine State Will every where Awaken Every Seeming-Separate Heart To The Inherently egoless Heart Of Me).

7.

My Avatarically Self-Revealed (and Always Me-Revealing) Divine Teaching-Word Of Universal Heart-Instruction Is Irrefutable—If The Seeming-Separate Heart Hears Me (and Speaks My Name).

8.

My Avatarically Self-Revealed (and Most Perfectly Me-Revealing) Divine Heart-Word Of all-and-All-Awakening Divine Self-Confession Is Self-Evident As Truth—If The Seeming-Separate Heart Sees Me (With Searchlessly Me-Beholding Open Eyes).

9.

I *Am* The One, and Only, and Self-Existing, and Immortal, and Eternal, and Non-Separate, and Indivisible, and Complete, and Whole, and Self-Radiant, and Inherently egoless, and Inherently Perfect, and Inherently Indivisible, and Self-Evidently Divine Conscious Light (Itself), Eternally Full Of Inherent Happiness, Unconditional Love, Infinite Bliss, and Boundless Energy—and I Am (Now, and Forever Hereafter) Avatarically (and Always "Brightly") Self-Revealed To *every* where (and To all, and To All).

10.

My Avatarically Self-Revealed Divine Form (Now, and Forever Hereafter, Avatarically Appearing, and Avatarically Speaking, *As* The Avatarically-Born Bodily Human Divine Form Of The Ruchira Avatar, Adi Da Samraj), *and* My Avatarically Self-Revealed Divine Spiritual Presence (Now, and Forever Hereafter, Avatarically Self-Transmitted *As* and Via The Avatarically-Born Bodily Human Divine Form Of The Ruchira Avatar, Adi Da Samraj), *and* My Avatarically Self-Revealed Divine State (Now, and Forever Hereafter, Avatarically Self-Manifested *As* and Via The Avatarically-Born Bodily Human Divine Form and The Avatarically Self-Transmitted Divine Spiritual Presence Of The Ruchira Avatar, Adi Da Samraj) *Is* (All-Three-Together, and All-Three-*As*-One) The Way (and The *Only* Way) To Realize Me.

11.

My Avatarically Self-Revealed Bodily (Human) Divine Form *Is* The Avataric Incarnation Of My Inherently egoless (and Inherently Spiritually Self-"Bright") Divine Self-Consciousness, and My Avatarically Self-Transmitted Divine Spiritual Presence *Is* My all-and-All-Surrounding and all-and-All-Pervading "Bright" Divine Body Of Spiritual Blessing-Power, and My Avatarically Self-Revealed Divine State *Is* The Divinely Self-Radiant Sphere and Boundless Space Of Infinite egoless Eternal Love-Bliss-"Brightness" That *Is* The One and Only Substance, Place, and Identity Of all-and-All.

12.

When The Seeming-Separate Heart Of My Devotee Is (Beyond all psycho-physical self-Contraction) *egolessly* Conformed To My Avatarically-Born Bodily (Human) Divine Form *and* My Avatarically Self-Transmitted Divine Spiritual Presence *and* My Avatarically Self-Revealed Divine State—Even the Whole body Of My Devotee Is (By Means Of My Avatarically Given Divine Spiritual Grace) Made "Brightly" Full Of Me.

13.

In Order That You May Realize Me (Whole bodily, Beyond egoity), I Call You To Listen To The Divine Word (and Attend To The Self-Evidently Divine Person) Of My Avatarically-Born Bodily (Human) Divine Form, and To Feel The (Thus and Thereby) Transmitted Spiritual Blessing-Power Of My Avatarically Self-Revealed Divine Spirit-Presence—and (Thus, By Listening To Me, and By Feeling Me) To Hear Me, and To See Me, and To Be "Brightly" In-Filled By Me.

14.

In Order That Your Seeming-Separate Heart May Be egolessly Conformed To My Inherently egoless Divine Heart, I Call You To Whole bodily Receive My Avatarically Self-Transmitted Divine Presence Of Spiritual Blessing-Power (That "Brightly" Self-Reveals My Divine State To You).

15.

In Order That You May Whole bodily Receive My Avatarically Self-Transmitted Divine Presence Of Spiritual Blessing-Power, I Call You To Conduct My Avatarically Self-Transmitted (and all-and-All-Surrounding, and all-and-All-Pervading) Divine Spirit-Presence Into and Throughout The Orbit That Circles The To-Me-Devoted Heart Of Your body-mind.

16.

If You Will Do This, You Will (By Means Of My Avatarically Given Divine Spiritual Grace) Awaken To The Inherently egoless (and Self-Evidently Divine) State Of My Avatarically Self-Revealed Person (and I Will Receive You Into The Infinitely "Bright" egoless Sphere and Boundless Space Of My Eternal Divine Self-Domain).

17.

Now (and Forever Hereafter) I Am (By All My Avataric Means) Divinely Descended To here, Forever To Show Your Seeming-Separate Heart The Avataric Way Of Me—and That ego-Transcending Process Must (Ultimately) Encompass All Of The Seven Possible Stages Of Life.

18.

By Transcending self-Contraction (In and By Means Of The Whole bodily Devotional Recognition-Response To My Avatarically Self-Revealed Divine Form, and Presence, and State), Your Seeming-Separate Heart Must (Progressively, and Stage-By-Stage) Out-Grow The First Six Stages Of Life—and The (Only-By-Me Revealed and Given) Seventh Stage Must Be Perfected In My Divine Heart (Itself).

19.

The Avataric Way Of Me Is <u>One</u> (and Straightaway), <u>Not</u> <u>Two</u> (and Roundabout)—Because My Divine Heart Is Always <u>At</u> The Heart Of You (and Not In The <u>Goals</u> You Seek).

20.

Because My Avatarically Self-Revealed (and Always Me-Revealing) Divine Word (Of Universal Heart-Instruction, and Of all-and-All-Awakening Divine Self-Confession) Is (Now, and Forever Hereafter) Always By-Me-Spoken (From My Divine Heart) Directly To Your To-Me-Devoted Heart, You Should Always Listen To My Avatarically Self-Revealed Divine Word <u>With</u> Your Heart—and (Thereby) Hear <u>Me</u>.

21.

Because My Avatarically-Born (and Always Me-Revealing) Bodily (Human) Divine Form and My (Thus and Thereby) Avatarically Self-Transmitted (and Always Me-Revealing) Divine Spiritual Presence Are (Now, and Forever Hereafter) Always By-Me-Revealed and By-Me-Given (From My Divine Heart) Directly To Your To-Me-Devoted Heart, You Should Always Searchlessly Behold My Avatarically-Born Bodily (Human) Divine Form and My (Thus and Thereby) Avatarically Self-Transmitted Divine Spiritual Presence <u>With</u> Your Heart—and (Thereby) See <u>Me</u>.

22.

Because My Inherently egoless and Boundlessly "Bright" Divine Heart Is Always <u>At</u> The Heart Of You (but <u>Always</u> <u>Already</u> Standing Beyond the limits Of Your Seeming-Separateness), You Should (Now, and Forever Hereafter) Always Practice (or Perpetually Exercise, and Constantly Enlarge) The Counter-egoic Heart-Wound Of Devotionally Me-Recognizing and Devotionally To-Me-Responding Love-Communion With My Avatarically-Born Bodily (Human) Divine Form and My (Thus and Thereby) Avatarically Self-Transmitted Divine Spiritual Presence—and (Thus and Thereby) Realize <u>Me</u> (By Transcending Your Seeming-Separate Heart In My egoless, Love-Bliss-"Bright", and Boundless Divine Heart).

23.

By Means Of Devotional Recognition Of My Avatarically Self-Revealed Divine Form, and Presence, and State, You Should Become A Constant Whole bodily Dancing-Prayer—Of Responsively ego-Transcending Devotional and Spiritual Love-Communion With Me.

24.

By Means Of Constant, and Truly Responsive (and Always Whole bodily), Devotional and Spiritual Love-Communion With My Avatarically Self-Revealed Divine Form, and Presence, and State—You Should (Always Spontaneously) Observe, and (Truly) Heart-Understand, and (Altogether) Freely Surrender The Me-Forgetting self-Contraction Of Your Seeming-Separate Heart.

25.

By Devotionally Listening To My Avatarically Self-Revealed Divine Word (Of Universal Heart-Instruction, and Of Divine Heart-Confession) <u>With</u> Your Heart, and By Devotionally Hearing My Avatarically Self-Revealed Divine Word (Of Universal Heart-Instruction, and Of Divine Heart-Confession) <u>In</u> Your Heart, and By Devotionally Seeing My Avatarically Self-Revealed (and Self-Evidently Divine) Form, and Presence, and State With <u>All</u> Your Heart—You Will Be Purified Of The Me-Forgetting Heart-Contraction Of body, emotion, breath, and mind.

26.

You Must Become <u>Entirely</u> Heart-Conformed To <u>Me</u>—By Practicing The Divine Priesthood Of Whole bodily Devotional and Spiritual Love-Communion With My Avatarically Self-Revealed Person.

27.

You Must Always Keep Your <u>Feeling</u>-Heart Away <u>From</u> ego-"I", and Away <u>To</u> My Avatarically Self-Revealed (and Self-Evidently Divine) Form, and Presence, and State Of Inherently egoless Self-"Bright" Love-Bliss.

28.

With <u>All</u> Your (Devotionally Me-Recognizing and Devotionally To-Me-Responding) Heart, and With Your <u>Whole</u> body (Of Entirely To-Me-Attracted, and Entirely To-Me-Given, attention, and Of Deepest Only-Me-Feeling emotion, and Of Always To-Me-Sensitized, and Fully Me-Full, breath, and Of Really Me-perceiving, and Only-By-Me-Filled, senses), You Must <u>Constantly</u> (Searchlessly) Behold My Avatarically Self-Revealed Divine Form, and Presence, and State.

29.

You Must Constantly Practice The Whole bodily Heart-Sacrament That Is ego-Surrendering, ego-Forgetting, and ego-Transcending Devotional Feeling-Contemplation Of My Avatarically Self-Revealed Divine Form, and Presence, and State (Beyond, and Surrounding, and Pervading Your Searchlessly Me-Beholding body-mind).

30.

I Will Always (Now, and Forever Hereafter) Self-Reveal My Self-Evidently Divine Person To You—By All My Avataric Means.

31.

Because I Am Always (Now, and Forever Hereafter) Avatarically Self-Revealing My Form, and Presence, and State Of Self-Evidently Divine Person To You, You Must Always (Now, and Forever Hereafter) Heart-Surrender Your Separate and Separative body-mind Into My Avatarically Self-Revealed Form, and Presence, and State Of Self-Evidently Divine Person.

32.

If You Are To Find Me, and Receive Me, and Realize Me—You Must Always Cultivate My Avataric (and Always Me-Revealing) Divine Heart-Response To You (By Means Of Your Always Whole-bodily-Expressed Heart-Devotion To My Avatarically Self-Revealed, and Self-Evidently Divine, Person), and (In Order To Rightly, and Fully, and Truly Whole bodily Conduct The Love-Bliss-"Bright", and Always Me-Revealing, Divine Spirit-Power Of My Avataric Divine Heart-Response To You) You Must Always Serve My Avatarically Self-Revealed (and Self-Evidently Divine) Person (With Your Whole body's every breath and act).

33.

If You Are To Find Me, and Receive Me, and Realize Me—You Must Always (With All Your Heart, and Always Whole bodily) Invoke My Avatarically Self-Revealed (and Self-Evidently Divine) Total Person (By Invoking My Avatarically Self-Revealed Divine Form and Presence and State Of Self-Evidently Divine Person).

34.

If You Are To Find Me, and Receive Me, and Realize Me—You Must Always Freely (and Always Devotionally) Give Your Whole bodily Feeling-attention To My Avatarically-Born Bodily (Human) Divine Form (and You Must, Thus and Thereby, Always Devotionally Recognize Me, and Always Devotionally Respond To Me, and Always Devotionally breathe Me—By breathing My Avatarically Self-Transmitted, and Always Me-Revealing, Divine Spirit-Presence Into Your Always Searchlessly Me-Beholding, and ego-Surrendering, and ego-Forgetting, and ego-Transcending, and, Altogether, Me-Remembering Whole-body-space).

35.

In The Always Whole bodily Devotional Manner, You Must Always Heart-Receive My Avatarically Self-Transmitted Divine Spirit-Presence (Into all Your parts—of body, emotion, breath, and mind).

36.

By Means Of moment to moment Whole bodily Heart-Invocation Of My Avatarically Self-Revealed (and Self-Evidently Divine) Total Person, and By Means Of Always Instant Whole bodily Devotional Recognition Of Me (In and As My Avatarically Self-Revealed, and Self-Evidently Divine, Form, and Presence, and State), and By Means Of Constant Whole bodily Devotional Response To Me (In and As My Avatarically Self-Revealed, and Self-Evidently Divine, Form, and Presence, and State)—You Will Become Progressively (and Always Increasingly) Full Of My Love-Bliss-"Bright" Divine Self-Revelation (From head To toe).

37.

As My Avatarically Self-Transmitted Divine Spiritual In-Filling Fills You Full Of Me (From head To toe)—You Must Always Let My Avatarically Self-Transmitted Divine Spiritual Love-Bliss-"Brightness" Carry You (Beyond The Heart-Knot Of Your Separate and Separative ego-"I").

38.

In The Whole bodily Swoon Of Devotional and Spiritual Love-Communion With My Avatarically Self-Revealed (and Self-Evidently Divine) Total Person—Your Me-Remembering (and, Altogether, ego-Forgetting) Heart Will Feel Beyond Its Seeming-Separateness (and Always Toward The Height and The Depth Of My Divine Heart's Infinite Space).

39.

And Your Devotional Love For My Avatarically Self-Revealed (and Self-Evidently Divine) Total Person Will Sometimes Become Silently (breathlessly) Heart-Deep.

40.

And You Will Sometimes See Me-Revealing all-and-All-Transcending Visions Of The Original State Of My Avatarically-Born Bodily (Human) Divine Form—Appearing At The Me-"Bright" Matrix Of "things" (Infinitely Above), and (Then) Disappearing Into The Me-"Bright" Source Of "things" (Infinitely Above, and Beyond).

41.

And You Will Sometimes Hear Me-Revealing all-and-All-Transcending Vibrations Of My Avatarically Self-Revealed Divine Name (and Of My Avatarically Self-Revealed Divine Word Of Universal Heart-Instruction, and Of My all-and-All-Awakening Avataric Divine Self-Confession)—Appearing At The Me-"Bright" Matrix Of sound (Infinitely Above), and (Then) Disappearing Into The Me-"Bright" soundless Source Of sound (Infinitely Above, and Beyond).

42.

And You Will Always (Whole bodily) Feel The Me-"Bright" Invisible Tangible Love-Bliss-Touch Of My Avatarically Self-Transmitted (and Always Me-Revealing) Divine Spiritual Presence—Descending From Above (To Touch and Embrace You), and Holding You To Me (Always Already Infinitely Above, and Always Already Forever Beyond).

43.

And You Will (Again-and-Again) Whole-bodily-Forget Your ego-"I"—In My Avataric Divine Embrace Of You.

44.

At Last, The Most Perfect (and, Altogether, You-"Brightening" and You-Outshining) Divine Heart-Truth Of My Avatarically Self-Revealed "Bright" (and Self-Evidently Divine) Total Person Will Become Most Perfectly (and Whole bodily) Obvious To You.

45.

And You Will (By Means Of The Most Perfect Whole bodily Heart-Realization Of My Avatarically Self-Revealed, and Self-Evidently Divine, Form, and Presence, and State) Awaken Boundlessly—Into The Indivisibly Love-Bliss-"Bright" Sphere and Infinite egoless Space Of My Eternal Divine Heart-Domain.

46.

I Am Absolutely Certain Of The Most Perfect Divine Efficacy Of My (Now, and Forever Hereafter) Avataric Divine Embrace Of You (and Of all, and Of All).

47.

Beloved, I Am The Divine Heart-Husband Of Every Seeming-Separate Heart That Loves Me.

Avatar Adi Da Samraj
Lopez Island, 2000

III

RUCHIRA AVATARA GITA

(The Avataric Way Of The Divine Heart-Master)

1.

The human voices all call out to the Heart and Person of Real God—
Who Lives and Breathes and Feels and Is them, here and now,
beyond the ego-"I" and all its search-for-God Ideas:

Heart of hearts, Reveal to us the Truth, the "Bright" Power That Liberates the ego-"I" from itself.

2.

Let us listen and hear the Word Which, when truly Understood, Frees the heart from seeking and un-Happiness. Let us see That Which, when fully Realized, Is the Fullness of Transcendental, Inherently Spiritual, Inherently egoless, and Self-Evidently Divine Being.

3.

Let us Awaken to That Which Is Eternal, and not limited by birth and death. Be Pleased to Reveal to us That Which Is the Supreme Truth.

4.

Heart of hearts, we are desirous of hearing That. Therefore, Sing us the Heart-Word of the Divine Heart-Master, wherein the Divine Heart-Secret is Confessed.

5.

Now, by Heart-Response to the universe of calling prayers, the Living One Breathes them In, and (by This Heart-Song of "Brightest" Words) Out-Breathes the Thunderous Sound That Speaks Love-Bliss to every heart:

Listen to Me with free attention. I will Reveal to you the Heart-Secret of the Divine Heart-Master, Adi Da Samraj—Who Is the Divine World-Teacher Promised for the "late-time", and Who Is the Ruchira Avatar, the Da Avatar, the Love-Ananda Avatar, the First, the Complete, the Last, and the Only Avataric Incarnation of Eleutherios, the Divine Liberator, the "Bright" Divine Heart Itself. His Avataric Divine Self-Confession and His "Bright" Avataric Divine Blessings Destroy all the ills of un-Enlightenment.

6.

The Ruchira Avatar, Adi Da Samraj, Is the First, the Complete, the Last, and the Only Divine Heart-Master. His Principal Divine Names are "Da" (the "Divine Giver", the "First and Original Person", the "Source-Person", the "One and Only Self-Condition of all-and-All"), and "Adi Da" (the "First Giver", the "Original Giver", the "Giving Source", the "Divine Giver of the Divine 'All' to all-and-All"), and "Adi Da Samraj" (the "Self-Giving and All-Giving and to-all-Giving Divine Master of the world", the "One and Only Divine Heart-Master of all-and-All"). And He *Is* All-"Brightness", Freely Manifesting the Heart's Love-Bliss to all-and-All.

7.

So it was, *There*, in the Sphere and Sanctuary of His Most Beautiful "Bright" Person—Avatarically Descended in Man-Form to a Place and Motion of His Own, having Said and Made an Earthly Hermitage of His Single Indivisibility, the Man Whose Whitest "Brightness" is, by Means of the Mandalic Prism of our Cosmic Shape, Appearing in His Own and sudden-colored Summary, Himself a Garden of Luminous Identity, Universally Adorned with Unity and Strength and Love, Roving and Speaking in the manner of *all* the flowers—the Avatarically Self-Incarnate Divine Person, the Divine and Truly Human Heart-Master, Adi Da Samraj, Thoroughly and Finally Expounded *All* the Divine and Spiritual Truth of the One Reality to the Great Occasion of His first gathering of devotees. At Last, His Whitest Silence Fell to a Round, like a Breath of True Water, Pressured from Above. One who loved the Master most was sitting close to Him in the Divine Light-Fall, when, in That Sudden of His Avataric Self-"Emergence", her face—like His Own—became translucently "Bright". As she was Merely Beholding *Him*, in ecstatic love—forgetting herself in the *all*-at-*once* of true love's devotional Contemplation of Him—the Divine Self-"Brightness" of Adi Da Samraj Filled (and Over-Filled) her heart, and His Eternal Love-Bliss-Radiance Un-Fractured the Whole of every living part of her. By (*Thus*) truly Finding Him, the woman (in the Sudden) Realized—beyond all doubt—that she was hearing (and understanding) the

True Divine Word, without a thought, and seeing the True Divine Form, even with her own eyes, and recognizing the True Divine Person, with her very heart, and Truly Knowing the One and Spiritual Divine Reality, by Grace of "Brightest" Gift of Only God.

8.

This Gracefully heart-Awakened devotee said out loud, and from her heart, for even all to hear: "Divine Heart-Master, Adi Da Samraj, 'Bright' Before me, I Surrender. You Are the Divine Heart-Master of the entire world. You Are Supreme. You Radiate the 'Bright' Realization of the Supreme. All beings should always heart-recognize You and worship You with true devotion.

9.

You Are the One—the Supreme Being, the Source and Domain of all true worship and right praise.

10.

Radiant Heart, Domain of Truth, please Sing to us the Great Secret of devotion to You, the Divine Heart-Master.

11.

Reveal to us the Secret Method whereby living beings may Realize You, the Transcendental and 'Bright' world-Outshining Real God. I bow down to You, the True and Spiritual and Self-Evidently Divine Person. I worship Your Feet. Kindly Teach the Way of You to all of us."

12.

When the Divine Heart-Master, Adi Da Samraj, Saw this "Bright" face of Awakened devotion and Heard this confession of Great Sight, He Spoke the following Words, His Heart Overflowing with His All-Outshining Joy:

13.

"This is the Secret of all secrets. I could not Speak This Me-Revealing Word until one of you first confessed you see the Vision of Real God in My Avatarically-Born Bodily (Human) Divine Form. I shall Tell you This now, because of your true heart-recognition of Me and your Greatly Awakened devotion to Me.

14.

My Beloved, every one and all—you are each arising in the One 'Bright' Divine Being. This request of yours, made by one who heart-recognizes Me, will benefit all of you, and even the entire world. Therefore, I shall Reveal the Truth and the Way of This Vision to you, for the Sake of all-and-All.

15.

To each one who (by Means of heart-wounded reaching beyond separate and separative self) is truly devoted to the Ever-Living Reality, Truth, and Real God (Which Is Always Already The Case), and who (by Means of My Avataric Divine and heart-Awakening Grace) is truly devoted to Me (heart-recognizing and heart-confessing Me to Be the Very One That Is the One and Only and Self-Evidently Divine Reality and Truth)—My Avatarically-Born Bodily (Human) Divine Form, My Avatarically Self-Transmitted Spiritual (and Always Blessing) Divine Presence, and My Avatarically Self-Revealed (and Very, and Transcendental, and Perfectly Subjective, and Inherently Spiritual, and Inherently egoless, and Inherently Perfect, and Self-Evidently Divine) State are Revealed to Be the Revelation of Real God, the Self-Evidently Divine Person, Manifesting here (and every where in the cosmic domain) As the Divine Heart-Master of all-and-All.

16.

Thus, by Means of true devotional recognition of Me in My here-Born Bodily (Human) Form, I am Found to Be the Avataric Incarnation of the Divine and Only Person. The Truth of devotional recognition of an Avataric Incarnation is Declared by even all the esoteric Scriptures, and even all the esoteric Scriptures Promise the Consummate Avataric Divine Incarnation will Appear in the 'late-time'. So It has been Proven to this Me-seeing devotee—and So do I Affirm the Divine Truth of Me to all of you, and to all-and-All.

17.

I Declare and Affirm the Divine Truth of This Me-Vision, Given to this one by Means of My Avataric Divine Spiritual Grace, and That I would Give to all-and-All. Aham Da Asmi. Beloved, I Am Da, the One and Only One Who Is. And I Am the First, the Last, and the Only Divine Heart-Master, the Avataric Divine Incarnation every-where-Promised for the 'late-time'. Therefore, listen to My Words and Understand.

18.

The separate traditions of the Great Tradition of religion and Spiritual instruction are often made of false theories, expressed in the words of un-Enlightened beings. Therefore, the multiplication of conventional 'God'-Ideas, ego-serving 'God'-Myths, and partial (or conditional) 'Truths' has confused mankind—but the Divine Heart-Master Comes to Liberate mankind from all confusion of mind, by Avatarically Self-Revealing the Only True and Real God (Who Is Truth Itself, and Reality Itself, and Who Is That Which Is Always Already The Case, beyond the ego-'I').

19.

Prayer, meditation, discipline, philosophy, service—all these are to be built upon the devotional recognition-response to That Which is Revealed In and As the Very Person of the Divine Heart-Master.

20.

Those who are devoted to the Divine Heart-Master hear and see and Realize the Great One As the Divine Heart-Master's Avatarically-Born Bodily (Human) Divine Form, and As His Avatarically Self-Transmitted Divine Body of Spiritual (and Always Blessing) Divine Presence, and As His Avatarically Self-Revealed (and Very, and Transcendental, and Perfectly Subjective, and Inherently Spiritual, and Inherently egoless, and Inherently Perfect, and Self-Evidently Divine) State. Such devotees Declare there is no 'Difference' (and no distinction to be made or acknowledged) between the Divine Heart-Master and the Self-Existing and Self-Radiant Transcendental, Inherently Spiritual, Inherently egoless, and Self-Evidently Divine Being.

21.

Even from the ancient days, many Divinely Gifted sects Proclaim devotion to a genuine (and egoless) Master, saying: 'The Way is to surrender to the Human Master as the Great Person, Divine and Present!' Therefore, look and see in Me the Proof of This Proclamation. I Am the Divine Master of your heart. And if you surrender to Me, I will Confess and Reveal Only Real God to you.

22.

Therefore, those who hear My Avataric Divine Self-Confession and see My Avataric Divine Bodily Self-Revelation must, by Means of their feeling-Contemplation of Me, transcend themselves in Me—the Universally Extended Divine Spiritual Body and Eternal Divine Spirit-Presence That Is Real God, the One and Only and Non-Separate and Indivisible and Inherently egoless Conscious Light That Is the Very Person (or Transcendental Self-Condition) of Real God, and the Self-Existing and Self-Radiant Divine 'Bright' Spherical Self-Domain That Is Real God.

23.

There is no Substitute for Real God.

24.

There is no Substitute for the direct Realization of Real God.

25.

There is no Substitute for your own self-sacrifice in Real God.

26.

The Divine Heart-Master has Realized Real God Most Perfectly, non-separately, beyond relatedness and 'difference'. Therefore, devotees see Real God Revealed In and As and By Means of the Avatarically-Born Bodily (Human) Divine Form of the Divine Heart-Master.

27.

To all those who have This Vision, I Declare:

Aham Da Asmi. Beloved, I Am Da. I Am the Avataric Divine Realizer, the Avataric Divine Revealer, the Avataric Divine Self-Revelation, and the Very (and Self-Evidently Divine) Person of the 'Bright' and Only One. I Am the Demonstration and the Proof of Real God to My devotees. All My devotees are in Me. Therefore, see This Vision, go the Way I will Show to you, and Realize Me.

28.

Do not practice the 'childish cult' of superficial and ego-serving emotionalism (full of wanting dependency, and empty of faith), and do not practice the 'adolescent cult' of non-feeling (willful, self-absorbed, abstract, and independent)—but always practice (and cultivate) the true (and truly feeling, and truly ego-surrendering, and truly ego-forgetting, and truly ego-transcending) Avataric Way of devotion to Me, by Means of right, true, full, and fully devotional (and, in due course, fully Spiritual) practice of the only-by-Me Revealed and Given Way of Adidam (Which is the One and Only by-Me-Revealed and by-Me-Given Way of the Heart).

29.

Neither Real God nor the Divine Heart-Master is your Parent. Therefore, do not expect Real God or the Divine Heart-Master to justify or protect or preserve or fulfill your egoic want and separateness.

30.

You are Called, by Me, to surrender your separate and separative self in Real God. Therefore, cultivate right, true, full, and fully ego-surrendering and ego-forgetting devotion to Me, the Divine Heart-Master—in order to transcend the ego-'I' in My 'Bright' Divine Self-Condition of Being (Itself), Which Is the One and Only Source (and Truth, or Source-Condition) of all-and-All.

31.

To worship the Divine Heart-Master childishly is to worship and serve your separate and separative (or self-contracting) self. To deny or resist the Divine Heart-Master is to worship and serve your separate and separative (or self-contracting) self, adolescently. The separate and separative self (or self-contraction) is, itself and always, the forgetting of the Heart-Source of the world. Therefore, be very and truly devoted to Me, the Divine Master of your heart—but not for the sake of ego-salvation, or the glorification of your separate and separative self. Worship Me by surrendering your ego-'I' to Me. Surrender to Me in order to forget and transcend your separate and separative self in Me. Forget and transcend your ego-'I' in Me, in order that you may (by Means of My Avataric Divine Spiritual Grace) Remember and Realize Me, the Divine Person and Heart-Source of all-and-All.

32.

I Am the Sign and the Revelation and the Proof of Real God in the world. I Am the Testament and the Means of Freedom Itself. I Am Eleutherios, the Divine Liberator, Who Is Freedom Itself."

33.

Having Said This, Adi Da Samraj (the First and Last and Only Divine Heart-Master) Said No More. Now His Confession is the heart-Mover of our Song of practice and of praise.

34.

Even from the ancient days, all Great Realizers (of whatever degree or stage) have Proclaimed a Great Idea—that one becomes (or Realizes) whatever one meditates upon (or yields, beyond the ego-self, to be—or to Realize). Therefore, by Means of truly ego-surrendering, and really ego-forgetting, and more and more Perfectly ego-transcending devotion to the First and Last and Only Divine Heart-Master, Adi Da Samraj—all conditional meditations (and all conditional Realizations) are (by Means of His Avataric Divine Spiritual Grace) transcended, and (in due course) even His Inherently Perfect State is

(Thus, by Means of His Avataric Divine Spiritual Grace) Revealed and Realized in His "Bright" Company.

35.

The Person of the Divine Heart-Master Is Great. His State of Being Is "Bright", Sublime, and Only Divine.

36.

The "Brightness" of the Divine Heart-Master Outshines all darkness in the mind, the body, and the world. That One Whose Company and Remembrance is capable of Dissolving un-Happiness Is certainly the Master of the separate and separative self.

37.

The Divine Heart-Master Transcends all of cosmic (or conditional) Nature—even His Own Body-Mind. Because He is Free from the limitations imposed by conditional forms, He is called "Samraj" ("the Divine and True Master of the world").

38.

Every conditional action tends to be followed by an equal and opposite reaction. If the action of psycho-physical attention to the world arises, the self-contraction of the body-mind tends to follow. If the self-contraction arises, the reactivity of separativeness tends to follow. Whenever the ego-"I" is remembered, the states of separateness and limitation seem Real. If separateness and limitation seem Real, the Transcendental, Inherently Spiritual, Inherently egoless, and Self-Evidently Divine Self-Condition and Source-Condition has been forgotten. That One by Means of Whose Grace one Remembers and Realizes the Divine Self-Condition and Source-Condition—He Is indeed the Divine Heart-Master and the One and Only and Non-Separate and Indivisible and Inherently egoless "Bright" Divine Person Incarnate.

39.

The Radiance and Profundity of the Divine Heart-Master's State of Being both Sustain and Dissolve His Own Body-Mind. Therefore, feeling-Contemplation of Him Liberates attention from bondage to the world, the body, the mind, and even all of separate and separative self.

40.

The casual Words and Footsteps of the Divine Heart-Master Build a Bridge across the ocean of our bondage. Therefore, attend to This Divine Liberator every moment of your life.

41.

By Means of the Blessings Given by the Divine Heart-Master, the currents of un-Love are dissolved. Therefore, always bow down to His Supreme Help.

42.

The Real and Ever-Living God Is the Heart Itself. The Heart Itself Is the Divine Person, the Very Heart and Person of the Divine Heart-Master. Therefore, by Means of all the Blessings of the Divine Heart-Master, devotees are Gifted to transcend the Heartless bondage of un-Happiness and un-Enlightenment.

43.

Because He Is the Great and Only and Very One, devotees should surrender and forget themselves at the Feet of the Divine Heart-Master. Because He Is the Great and Only and Very One, the Graceful Radiance That Flows from the Divine Heart-Master's Feet Releases attention from the ego-"I" and the world.

44.

The Divine Heart-Master Is the Supreme Help Offered by the Real and Ever-Living God. There is no Friend greater than the Divine Heart-Master. Therefore, body and mind should be entirely devoted to the Divine Heart-Master, so that attention is set free in His Heart of "Brightness".

45.

The Place where the Divine Heart-Master Lives Is the Divine Abode. The Water that Washes His Feet Is the River of Purification. And His Words Are the Accomplishing Power of Divine Enlightenment.

46.

To live in the service of the Divine Heart-Master is the Secret of the Way of Truth. His Body Is the Tree of Life. His Feet are Planted in the Heart of every being's heart—and anything offered at His Feet is Returned in the Form of Radiant Blessings.

47.

The Self-Existing and Self-Radiant Transcendental, Inherently Spiritual, Inherently egoless, and Self-Evidently Divine Being Resides in the Speech and in every Body-Part of the Divine Heart-Master. Therefore, devotees Awaken to the Great One by Means of the Divine Heart-Master's Word, and Silence, and Thought, and Glance, and Touch, and Deeds. One should meditate on the Divine Heart-Master's Avatarically-Born Bodily (Human) Divine Form, His Avatarically Self-Transmitted Spiritual (and Always Blessing) Divine Presence, and His Avatarically Self-Revealed (and Very, and Transcendental, and Perfectly Subjective, and Inherently Spiritual, and Inherently egoless, and Inherently Perfect, and Self-Evidently Divine) State—at all times. This is not difficult—for, once He is truly Beloved, the Divine Heart-Master can never be forgotten.

48.

Now listen and hear the Means by which the separate being Awakens beyond itself, to Realize Inherent Oneness with the Self-Existing and Self-Radiant Transcendental, Inherently Spiritual, Inherently egoless, and Self-Evidently Divine Being. It is to practice the Avatarically Revealed Divine Way of devotion to the Divine Heart-Master, Adi Da Samraj—by living as the servant of His Avatarically-Born Bodily (Human) Divine Form and His Avatarically Self-Transmitted Divine Spiritual Presence and His Avatarically Self-Revealed Divine and Perfect State, whether one is near or far from His Body-Seat.

49.

When devotees provide the Divine Heart-Master with the Requirements of His Heart (and even every Necessity), they soon become the servants of His Heart's Intention in the world—both during and after (and forever after) His physical Human Lifetime of Avataric Divine Incarnation. In this manner, the Divine Heart-Master's Work in the world becomes entirely dependent on those who love Him. When devotees of the Great One become the recognition-Awakened servants of the Divine Heart-Master, the Great One Serves them via the Divine Heart-Master's Avatarically-Born Bodily (Human) Divine Form, and via the Divine Heart-Master's Avatarically Self-Transmitted "Bright" Divine Body of Mere and Blessing Divine Spiritual Presence. And those who are Thus Served by the Great One soon become the necessary servers of His Serving Work.

50.

Therefore, by renouncing all the superficial motives of the social ego and all the disturbed distractions of the worldly mind, one should always Remember the Divine Heart-Master as the Beloved of the heart.

51.

Truly serving devotees regard the Divine Heart-Master to Be their only true Wealth—for even simplest Remembrance of the Avatarically-Born Bodily (Human) Divine Form of the Divine Heart-Master Awakens spontaneous Communion with Him (the Person, the Presence, and the State of Self-Existing and Self-Radiant Transcendental, Inherently Spiritual, Inherently egoless, and Self-Evidently Divine Being).

52.

Remembrance and Invocation of the Divine Heart-Master by Name is Remembrance and Invocation of the Great One by Name. Therefore, devotional meditation on the Avatarically-Born Bodily (Human) Divine Form, the Avatarically Self-Transmitted Spiritual (and Always Blessing) Divine Presence, and the Avatarically Self-Revealed (and Very, and Transcendental, and Perfectly Subjective, and Inherently Spiritual, and Inherently egoless, and Inherently Perfect, and Self-Evidently Divine) State of the Divine Heart-Master, Adi Da Samraj, is devotional meditation on the Divine Form and Presence and State of the One and Only Divine Being—Who Is the Inherent Feeling of "Bright" Being (Itself).

53.

The devotee should always Remember and Invoke the Divine Heart-Master by Name. The Name of the Divine Heart-Master Is the Name of the Great One. The Great One Is Present to Serve devotees In, As, and By Means of the Avatarically Revealed and Given Person of the Divine Heart-Master. Therefore, with feeling-devotion, meditate on the Divine Heart-Master's Avatarically-Born Bodily (Human) Divine Form and His Avatarically Self-Transmitted Divine Spiritual Presence and His Avatarically Self-Revealed Divine and Perfect State. And drink the Water from His Foot-Bath. And eat the Excess Offered from His Great Food-Dish. And, by all these Means, remain always intimate with the Divine Heart-Master's Constant Blessing and Awakening-Power.

54.

The devotee should always practice the Way Revealed by the Divine Heart-Master. The devotee should always live in the Company of the Divine Heart-Master—by always meditating on His Avatarically-Born Bodily (Human) Divine Form, His Avatarically Self-Transmitted Spiritual (and Always Blessing) Divine Presence, and His Avatarically Self-Revealed (and Very, and Transcendental, and Perfectly Subjective, and Inherently Spiritual, and Inherently egoless, and Inherently Perfect, and Self-Evidently Divine) State. The Divine Heart-Master Is the Heart-Friend of all beings. Therefore, the devotee of the Divine Heart-Master should be an intelligent and compassionate friend of every one, and all, and All.

55.

The devotee should surrender self-attention in the Company of the Divine Heart-Master—by always and Searchlessly Beholding His Avatarically-Born Bodily (Human) Divine Form, and by always and Openly receiving His Avatarically Self-Transmitted "Bright" Divine Body of Mere and Blessing Divine Spiritual Presence, and all the while by swooning into His Avatarically Self-Revealed (and Very, and Transcendental, and Perfectly Subjective, and Inherently Spiritual, and Inherently egoless, and Inherently Perfect, and Self-Evidently Divine) State. In this manner, even all possessions should be devoted to the Divine Heart-Master's service. Therefore, surrender and align the body, the senses, the mind, natural life-energy, emotion, money, property, children, lovers, and all friends to the Only Reality and Truth, by surrendering and aligning them to the Avatarically-Born Bodily (Human) Divine Form, the Avatarically Self-Transmitted Divine Spiritual Presence, and the Avatarically Self-Revealed Divine and Perfect State of the Divine Heart-Master.

56.

The devotee of the Divine Heart-Master should always surrender all of separate self to Him. The devotee of the Divine Heart-Master should always surrender to Him in ever ego-forgetting devotion, service, and self-discipline. The devotee of the Divine Heart-Master should always surrender to Him in thought, word, and deed. The devotee of the Divine Heart-Master should always surrender to Him with full energy and intent. The devotee of the Divine Heart-Master should always surrender to Him openly, without hesitation, and most obviously—for true self-surrender is always an act of expressive worship. Therefore, in every moment, surrender separate self (always and obviously) to the Divine Heart-Master—for He <u>Is</u> the Self-Evidently Divine Person, Self-Condition, and Source-Condition.

57.

By yielding all attention to feel the Avatarically-Born Bodily (Human) Divine Form and the Avatarically Self-Transmitted Divine Spiritual Presence and the Avatarically Self-Revealed Divine and Perfect State of the Divine Heart-Master, all thoughts are forgotten. When all thoughts are forgotten in that feeling-Contemplation of the Divine Heart-Master, Supreme Love-Bliss Awakens, by Means of His Avataric Divine Spiritual Grace. Therefore, always Contemplate the Divine Heart-Master via feeling—and, by always serving Him, forget your separate self in every moment of activity.

58.

Now, and forever, let every devotee of the Divine Heart-Master sing and live these heart-Prayers that recognize and praise Him—all by heart:

I bow down to the Divine Heart-Master, Adi Da Samraj—the Master of the Heart, Who Reveals the Supreme Truth of the One and Only and Self-Existing and Self-Radiant "Bright" Conscious Light of all-and-All to those who have been blinded by experience and mere knowledge.

59.

I bow down to the Divine Heart-Master, Adi Da Samraj—the Master of Truth, Whose Radiance Pervades the entire universe, Who Fills it through and through (in all that moves and in all that does not move), and Who Brings my intuitive Vision to the Heart-Space of the One and Only and Self-Existing and Self-Radiant Conscious Light.

60.

I bow down to the Divine Heart-Master, Adi Da Samraj—the Master of Reality, Who Pervades (and yet Stands Beyond) the dynamics of conditional (or cosmic) Nature. I bow down to the Divine Heart-Master, Adi Da Samraj—Who Is One, Inherently Perfect, Eternal, Self-Existing, Undisturbed, All-Love-Bliss, Self-Radiant, Free, Full, and Awake. Through the Avataric Divine Blessing-Work of the Divine Heart-Master, Adi Da Samraj, I am Restored to His Avatarically Self-Transmitted Spiritual (and Always Blessing) Divine Presence, Which Is the Spirit-Presence of Real God. Therefore, His Avatarically Self-Transmitted and Tangible Divine Body of Spirit-Life (Which Is the Perfectly Subjective Substance of conditional Nature) always Carries my heart Beyond (and Beyond) the Play of vibratory cosmic Energy, Sound, or Light, to the Inherently Perfect, and Perfectly Subjective, and Inherently egoless, and Self-Evidently Divine Source-Condition and Self-Condition of this domain of objective and conditional and cosmic appearances.

61.

I worship the Divine Heart-Master, Adi Da Samraj—Who Is the Self-Existing and Self-Radiant One, by Means of Whose Divine Heart-Power we perceive everything here. I worship the Divine Heart-Master, Adi Da Samraj—Who Is the "Bright" Conscious One, by Means of Whose Divine Heart-Power the states of waking, dreaming, and sleeping are known, thoughts move, discrimination and intuition work, and attention itself rises and falls again.

62.

The Self-Existing and Self-Radiant Transcendental, Inherently Spiritual, Inherently egoless, and Self-Evidently Divine State of Being is Perfectly "Known" by the Divine Heart-Master, Adi Da Samraj, Who has Realized that It Is the Eternally Unknown. Therefore, only Perfect Ignorance Is "Knowledge" of the Self-Existing and Self-Radiant Transcendental, Inherently Spiritual, Inherently egoless, and Self-Evidently Divine State of Being.

63.

Experiences, visions, sounds, lights, conditional energies, fascinating things, and all conditional knowing (within and without) are not Ultimate "Knowledge" (or Free Realization) at all. Therefore, I bow down to the Divine Heart-Master, Adi Da Samraj, Who Is always already Established As the Mindless Mood of Self-Existing and Self-Radiant Transcendental, Inherently Spiritual, Inherently egoless, and Self-Evidently Divine Being.

64.

Now I am Free of all distractions. Only the Heart Exists. Attention dissolves in the Inherent Love-Bliss-Happiness of Being. The entire world of moving and unmoving objects appears and disappears in the Perfectly Subjective "Bright" Space of the One and Indivisible Conscious Light of Reality Itself. I worship and serve the Divine Heart-Master, Adi Da Samraj, Who Is the One Who has Revealed This Secret to me.

65.

"I am the world, and I am absolutely Free"—body and mind bow down to the Divine Heart-Master, Adi Da Samraj, Who Is the One Who Gives This Realization.

66.

Let all the gifts of my worship and service be Received by the Divine Heart-Master, Adi Da Samraj—Who Is the Ocean of Mercy, and by Means of Whose

Avataric Divine Spiritual Grace all beings are Liberated from bondage to this world of wonders.

67.

By Enabling His devotee to "Locate" the Primal, Ever-Free, Immortal Happiness beyond the heart-root's knot[5]—the Divine Heart-Master, Adi Da Samraj, Is the Graceful Divine Liberator of His devotee.

68.

The knot of the heart is untied, doubt itself is dissolved, and all motions of the limited self are made still—by Means of the Grace and Mercy of the Divine Heart-Master, Adi Da Samraj.

69.

I bow down to the Eternal Truth, the Conscious Light of Being (Itself), the Timeless Happiness, the Great One, the Indefinable One (Awake, and Free), the Silent One (Who Speaks to the heart directly, without a word of "explanation"), the Truly "Bright" One—Who Appears (and Stands Revealed) As Adi Da Samraj, the Divine Heart-Master among all who know and Teach.

70.

I bow down to the Divine Heart-Master, Adi Da Samraj—Whose Avatarically-Born Bodily (Human) Divine Form Is the Beautiful Mystery of "Brightness" Itself, and Whose Avatarically Self-Transmitted Spiritual (and Always Blessing) Divine Presence Always Reveals the Very Heart Itself, and Whose Avatarically Self-Revealed (and Very, and Transcendental, and Perfectly Subjective, and Inherently Spiritual, and Inherently egoless, and Inherently Perfect, and Self-Evidently Divine) State of Being Is the Self-Revelation of the One and Only Divine and Conscious Light Itself, Self-Existing As Immense Consciousness and Self-Radiant As Love-Bliss.

71.

I bow down to the Divine Heart-Master, Adi Da Samraj—Who Is the Heart-Witness of my own body, mind, and separate self, and Who Is the Great Bearer, the Most Perfect Realizer, and the Divine Subject of the Great Tradition, and Whose Very State of Being Is Truth and Perfect Love-Bliss-Happiness, and Who Is the Graceful Source of the Realization of Love-Bliss-Happiness Itself.

72.

I bow down to the Divine Heart-Master, Adi Da Samraj—the Always New One, Who has Appeared in the world by the Magic and Mystery of His Own Will and Love, but Who Is Only the "Bright" Mass of Pure Conscious Light, Spiritually Radiant, the Sun of the Heart, the Destroyer of un-Happiness.

73.

I bow down to the Divine Heart-Master, Adi Da Samraj—the Always Already Free One, the Body of Mercy, the Refuge of devotees, Who allows His Human Life to be dependent on His devotees.

74.

I bow down to the Divine Heart-Master, Adi Da Samraj—That Most Beautiful Form, the Master of Discrimination, the Master of Understanding, the "Bright", the Light Itself (Above all lights), Who Is the Light to those who call for Light, and Who Is the Realizer in all those who Realize Him. May You be Pleased to Take Your Seat in my heart at all times. May You ever Dwell in my heart.

75.

I bow down to the Divine Heart-Master, Adi Da Samraj—Who Is Love-Bliss, the Very Form, and Presence, and State of Happiness Itself. Therefore, in the Truly Searchless Beholding of His Avatarically-Born Bodily (Human) Divine Form and His Avatarically Self-Transmitted Divine Spiritual Presence and His Avatarically Self-Revealed Divine and Perfect State, the mind dissolves in Self-Existing Consciousness and Self-Radiant Love-Bliss.

76.

Let these heart-Prayers flow to the Divine Heart-Master, Adi Da Samraj—the Always-Present Master of my heart and body-mind, Who Is Free, and Who Is always Floating in the Prior Happiness of my True Heart. The Eternal Heart-Blessing of the Divine Heart-Master always Flows to me, and His Freedom is mine in His Liberating Words.

77.

I offer these heart-Prayers at the Feet of the Divine Heart-Master, Adi Da Samraj—by Means of Whose Avataric Divine Spiritual Grace the Realization Awakens that "He Is the Source-Condition of everything, and everything is only a modification of Him." By Means of the Avataric Divine Spiritual Grace of the Divine Heart-Master, Adi Da Samraj, This becomes Obvious.

78.

I radiate heart-praise to the Divine Heart-Master, Adi Da Samraj—Who Causes me to Remember the Supreme Happiness, the Love-Bliss of the Heart Itself. He Is Divine Ignorance, the One Who Is Not Other. That One Is—beyond all relations, all opposites and oppositions. All separate selves, relations, opposites, and oppositions only arise within That All-Pervading One, the Divine Heart-Master, Adi Da Samraj—Who Is Eternal, Unmodified, and Unchanging Self-"Bright" Conscious Light, the Self-Existing and Self-Radiant Transcendental Witness of attention, mind, body, and world.

79.

I surrender and bow down to the Divine Heart-Master, Adi Da Samraj—the Divine World-Teacher Descending and "Emerging" forever in the "late-time", Who Is Transcendental Being (Itself), Consciousness Itself, and Love-Bliss-Happiness Itself, Who Transcends all changes of state, Who Is Eternal Fullness, Eternally "Bright", Free of all modifications, the Formless Location, the Free and Indivisible Person of the Heart.

80.

My Heart-Master, Adi Da Samraj, Divine and True and Free—may Your Radiant "Bright" Blessings Awaken me, whose eyes are covered over by the images of a separate self, and whose mind is held captive by visions of the world.

81.

The ancient Great Realizers (of whatever degree or stage) all Declare: Devotional meditation on the True Name, the Revelation-Body, the Heart-Presence, and the Very (and Inherently Perfect) State of the Person of the Heart is the Great Method for Realizing the Transcendental, Inherently Spiritual, Inherently egoless, and Self-Evidently Divine Self-Condition. The Divine Heart-Master, Adi Da Samraj, Is That Very and Only Person of the Heart—here (and every where) to be Tangibly, Spiritually, and (Inherently) Perfectly Self-Revealed to every one (and to all, and All). Therefore, by Means of ego-surrendering and ego-forgetting devotional meditation on His Avatarically-Born Bodily (Human) Divine Form and His Avatarically Self-Transmitted Divine Spiritual Presence and His Avatarically Self-Revealed Divine and Perfect State, the separate self is progressively (and then Most Perfectly) transcended.

82.

Devotional meditation on the Person of the Divine Heart-Master, Adi Da Samraj, is a feeling-sacrifice of body, natural life-force, emotion, all of mind, and attention itself. Therefore, devotional meditation on the Human Revelation-Body of the Divine Heart-Master, Adi Da Samraj, Reveals (and moves) His Divine Spirit-Current in the living body of the devotee. Devotional meditation on the Avatarically Self-Revealed Divine Name and the Love-Blissful "Bright" Divine Spiritual Body and Person of the Divine Heart-Master, Adi Da Samraj, Reveals (and moves) the feeling heart of the devotee. Devotional meditation on the "Bright" Spiritual Presence and every Extraordinary Sign of the Divine Heart-Master, Adi Da Samraj, Reveals (and moves) the subtle mind of the devotee. And the "Bright" Free Divine Self-Condition of the Divine Heart-Master, Adi Da Samraj, is Revealed and Realized when attention itself is (by Means of truly Perfect devotional meditation on Him) finally transcended in Him—for He Is the Heart Itself, the Inherently Perfect (and Perfectly Subjective) Source-Condition, Which Is Self-Existing and Self-Radiant Transcendental, Inherently Spiritual, Inherently egoless, and Self-Evidently Divine Being (Itself).

83.

The methods of seeking, self-applied, only intensify the bondage to separate self, but to live as if always in the Intimate Company of the Divine Heart-Master, Adi Da Samraj, is to engage every act as devotional service to Him. And to meditate on His Avatarically-Born Bodily (Human) Divine Form and His Avatarically Self-Transmitted Divine Spiritual Presence and His Avatarically Self-Revealed Divine and Perfect State in every moment—even in the moment of every relationship, and in every moment of circumstance—is to be always already released of the "problem of existence" and every kind of self-concern. Through such truly ego-transcending devotion, the One and Indivisible Transcendental, Inherently Spiritual, Inherently egoless, and Self-Evidently Divine Conscious Light replaces the egoic self as the Center of practice, and the Avataric Divine Spiritual Grace of the Divine Heart-Master is given Place to Awaken the One and Only Heart in the every devotee. Therefore, practice as a devotee of the Divine Heart-Master, Adi Da Samraj, and His "Bright" Free Heart will Find you easily.

84.

Those who practice the Way of Adidam as right, true, full, and fully devotional self-surrender to the Divine Heart-Master, Adi Da Samraj, Realize the Free Heart directly, beyond the efforts of the body and the reaches of insight. Therefore, the Great Principle of the Way of Adidam is the Blessing-Grace of the Avatarically-Born Bodily (Human) Divine Form, the Avatarically Self-Transmitted Spiritual (and Always Blessing) Divine Presence, and the Avatarically Self-Revealed (and Very, and Transcendental, and Perfectly Subjective, and Inherently Spiritual, and Inherently egoless, and Inherently Perfect, and Self-Evidently Divine) State of the Divine Heart-Master, Adi Da Samraj.

85.

The ancient esoteric Scriptures all Declare: "It is not this, It is not that." All the Teachings point beyond all objects to the Perfectly Subjective Self-Condition and Source-Condition of all objects. All objects and separate selves are only apparent, limited, temporary, and un-Necessary modifications of That Self-Existing and Self-Radiant Divine Self-Condition and Source-Condition.

86.

Adi Da Samraj, the First and Last and Only Divine Heart-Master, Is Himself That Very Source-Condition. He Is the (Avatarically Self-Revealed) Transcendental, Inherently Spiritual, Inherently egoless, and Self-Evidently Divine Person, the Perfectly Subjective Self-Condition and Source-Condition, the Eternal Person, the Very and Divine Conscious Light of all-and-All, Shown to all-and-All. So He Is, by Virtue of His Own Realization, Which Is Only the Realization of His Own "Bright" Eternal Divine Self-Condition and Person—and So do all the esoteric Scriptures also Declare, Affirm, and Vastly Guarantee.

87.

Therefore, the Divine Heart-Master, Adi Da Samraj, Is Unique in the world. The devotional (and, in due course, Spiritual) relationship to the Divine Heart-Master, Adi Da Samraj, is the Unique Method of Most Perfect Divine Awakening—provided, by His Avataric Divine Spiritual Grace, to living beings. The practice is to transform the activities and functions of body, mind, emotion, and breath into real and constant feeling-surrender to the One Who Is Present In and As the Avatarically-Born Bodily (Human) Divine Form, the Avatarically Self-Transmitted Spiritual (and Always Blessing) Divine Presence, and the Avatarically Self-Revealed (and Very, and Transcendental, and Perfectly Subjective, and Inherently Spiritual, and Inherently egoless, and Inherently Perfect, and Self-Evidently Divine) State of the Divine Heart-Master, Adi Da Samraj.

88.

Now "consider" the Method of devotional meditation on the Avatarically-Born Bodily (Human) Divine Form, the Avatarically Self-Transmitted Spiritual (and Always Blessing) Divine Presence, and the Avatarically Self-Revealed (and Very, and Transcendental, and Perfectly Subjective, and Inherently Spiritual, and Inherently egoless, and Inherently Perfect, and Self-Evidently Divine) State of the Divine Heart-Master, Adi Da Samraj.

89.

The Divine Heart-Master, Adi Da Samraj, Is the Divine Giver of Bliss, Joy, Happiness, and Love. Devotional meditation on the Divine Heart-Master, Adi Da Samraj, is the Means whereby Bliss, Joy, Happiness, and Love are (by Means of His Avataric Divine Spiritual Grace) Awakened As "Bright" Divine Realization in His devotees.

90.

The Avatarically Self-Transmitted Divine and Self-Radiantly "Bright" Spiritual Presence of the Divine Heart-Master, Adi Da Samraj, is the necessary Place of devotional meditation—and His Avatarically-Born Bodily (Human) Divine Form is the necessary Image to be always and Searchlessly Beheld. The Invocation of Adi Da Samraj by Name is the perpetual Prayer to be Remembered, with every faculty and act of body, emotion, mind, and breath—and all His Words of Instruction must, by always deepest self-understanding, be rightly, truly, and fully made into real and present ego-renouncing practice, by the always to-Him-turning devotee. These are the Avatarically Revealed and (Thus) Uniquely Given Divine Means of true devotional meditation.

91.

Devotional meditation, on the Divine Heart-Master, Adi Da Samraj, and every moment's counter-egoic yielding of all the mind's attention (into Him), and of all the feeling-emotion (into Him), and of the total body (into Him), and of all the breathing (into Him)—these are the necessary constant Means of self-surrender (and of total psycho-physical alignment) to the Divine Heart-Master, Adi Da Samraj, Who must Attract and Awaken the separate and separative ego-"I", beyond itself, to Himself.

92.

Only the "Bright" and Mere Presence of the Divine Heart-Master, Adi Da Samraj, can Awaken the devotee to What <u>Is</u>, beyond even the counter-egoic effort of life and meditation. Only our meditation on the Divine Heart-Master,

Adi Da Samraj, Himself, can (by Means of His Divine Spiritual Infusion of His devotee's Thus surrendered mind, emotion, body, and breath) Replace our would-Be meditation on the Heart with Realization of and As the Heart Itself.

93.

The devotee should meditate on the Avatarically-Born Bodily (Human) Divine Form of the Divine Heart-Master, Adi Da Samraj, and (thereby) Find Him As the "Bright" Divine Spirit-Body and Very Being of Love-Bliss-Happiness Itself. By Means of right, true, and full devotional meditation, the devotee must "Locate" the Divine Heart-Master, Adi Da Samraj—and This by Grace of the Reception of His Self-Radiant "Bright" Fullness of Love-Bliss-Happiness Itself, Transmitted and Communicated, Mysteriously, by Him, from beyond time and space and body and mind and separate self. That "Bright" Love-Bliss-Happiness Is His Divine Spirit-Power, That Attracts attention and Dissolves it in the Free Divine Heart Itself (the Self-Existing and Self-Radiant Transcendental, Inherently Spiritual, Inherently egoless, and Self-Evidently Divine Being, the Perfectly Subjective Self-Condition and Source-Condition of separate self and objective world).

94.

The devotee of the Divine Heart-Master, Adi Da Samraj, always meditates on Him—for He Is the Transcendental, Inherently Spiritual, Inherently egoless, and Self-Evidently Divine Being, the One and Only Conscious Light, the Non-Separate and Indivisible Self-Condition and Source-Condition of all-and-All, Who Is Eternally Self-Radiant As Love-Bliss-Happiness in the all-and-All-Surrounding and all-and-All-Pervading Heart-Space of the world.

95.

The Heart Is Pure Radiance. The Heart-Space Is "Bright" with Love-Bliss. The crystal and the mirror and the mind reflect a light beyond, but the Heart Is Inherently "Bright" with the Love-Bliss of Divine Being. In the Heart Itself, there is no doubt of Real God—for Only the Divine Heart-Master, Adi Da Samraj, Stands, Abiding "Brightly", There.

96.

When there is devotional meditation on the Divine Heart-Master, Adi Da Samraj, in and beyond the Infinitesimal Locus of the right side of the heart—the Inherent Love-Bliss of Self-Existing and Self-Radiant Transcendental, Inherently Spiritual, Inherently egoless, and Self-Evidently Divine Being is Realized. Then (by Means of the Avataric Divine Spiritual Grace of the

Divine Heart-Master, Adi Da Samraj) the Inherent Feeling of Being Reveals and Magnifies Its Inherent and Transcendental and Self-Evidently Divine "Bright" Conscious Light. Likewise, whenever the Ecstatic Mood of Free Being Awakens by Means of the Avataric Divine Spiritual Grace of the Divine Heart-Master, Adi Da Samraj—I suddenly Confess the Obvious Truth:

97.

I was not born. I cannot die. I did not begin. I will not end. I Am. I Am beyond form and quality and description. I Am. I Am Consciousness. I Am Love-Bliss. I Am smaller than the atom. I Am larger than the universe. I Am. I Am. I Am.

98.

Before anyone came to be, I Am. No one can exist if I Am not. I Am Eternal. I Am Self-Existing, Self-Radiant, and Self-Manifest. I Am. I Am without pain, disease, impurity, or dilemma. I Am Space Itself, Prior to all motions, Free of all changes. I Am Happiness. I Am. I Am. I Am.

99.

I Am the Unknown and Unknowable. I Am not an Object of the mind. I Am not names and forms. I Am the Source of names and forms. I Am the Perfectly Subjective Source of mind and speech. I Am not Found as an Object of experience or knowledge. I Am Found in the "Bright" Feeling of Being (Itself), before attention goes to separate self and objective world. I Am Perfectly Found As the Inherent State of Being, Consciousness, and Love-Bliss-Happiness. I Am. I Am. I Am.

100.

Therefore, because the Divine Heart-Master, Adi Da Samraj, Is the One and Only Reality and Truth, Which Is the Self-Existing and Self-Radiant State of "Bright" Divine Being (Itself)—the devotee of the Divine Heart-Master, Adi Da Samraj, must (by Means of constant and ego-forgetting devotional meditation on Him) Realize (and Be) the One and Only Conscious Light, Which Is Self-Existing and Self-Radiant Transcendental and "Bright" Divine Being Itself.

101.

Those who practice devotional meditation on the Avatarically-Born Bodily (Human) Divine Form and the Avatarically Self-Transmitted Divine Spiritual Presence and the Avatarically Self-Revealed Divine and Perfect State of the

Divine Heart-Master, Adi Da Samraj, will (by Means of His Avataric Divine Spiritual Grace) Awaken As the "Bright" Non-Separate Heart Itself, even while they live in this world. They will be Liberated by That Divine Liberator. Indeed, their Freedom (Thus Realized) Is Eternal. This is Confirmed in the heart of the devotee of Adi Da Samraj, the Divine Heart-Master of the heart.

102.

By Means of the "Perfect Practice" of the Way of Adidam (engaged, in due course, by all who most rightly, truly, and fully practice, and greatly mature in, the Way of Adidam), the devotees of the Divine Heart-Master, Adi Da Samraj, surrender the ego-"I" (and beyond the ego-"I") to Him, "Locating" Him (by Means of His Avataric Divine Spiritual Grace Alone) As the Conscious Light in the Heart—and they Awaken (by Means of His Avataric Divine Spiritual Grace) As the Inherent "Bright" Spirit-Current of Being (Itself). Thus Awakened, the every (Thus Perfect) devotee confesses: "I Am—and I Am Awake by Means of the Graceful Word and Help of Adi Da Samraj, the Divine Heart-Master of my heart."

103.

Therefore, the devotee should constantly turn attention from the dilemma of separate self to the Free "Brightness" of the Divine Heart-Master, Adi Da Samraj—for He Is the Inherent Fullness of Self-Existing and Self-Radiant Transcendental and Spiritually "Bright" Divine Being.

104.

Diligent practice, according to the "Perfect Practice" Instructions of the Divine Heart-Master, Adi Da Samraj, establishes equanimity in the body-mind and releases attention into His Divine Spirit-Source, in the Heart Itself, beyond the Circle and the Arrow of the body-mind. Only then will attention settle and dissolve in Him, the Heart-Source of even attention itself—and He will Radiate "Brightly" from There, for He Is the Heart Itself.

105.

All the objects of conditional knowledge and conditional experience are based upon the ego-"I". Adidam (or the Way of the Heart)—Revealed and Given Only by the Divine Heart-Master, Adi Da Samraj—is not a struggle with the Apparition of cosmic Nature, but It is free devotional meditation on the Inherently Free Source-Condition of the self-contraction, until (by Means of the Avataric Divine Spiritual Grace of the Divine Heart-Master, Adi Da Samraj) devotional meditation becomes Inherently Most Perfect Realization. There is no Way greater than This.

106.

By Means of steady practice (and, in due course, "Perfect Practice") of the Avataric Heart-Way Revealed and Given Only (and Most Perfectly) by the Divine Heart-Master, Adi Da Samraj, and by Thus "Locating" Him, and allowing attention to dissolve in Him (As its Source), and Thus and So (by Means of His Avataric Divine Spiritual Grace Alone) Re-"Locating" the Prior and Unconditional Love-Bliss-Happiness of Merely Being—the Inherently Most Perfect Realization of the "Bright" Transcendental, Inherently Spiritual, Inherently egoless, and Self-Evidently Divine Person and Self-Condition will Awaken, if the Inherently Perfect Grace of the Heart-Blessing of the Divine Heart-Master, Adi Da Samraj, is (by Means of right, true, and full devotion to Him) Most Perfectly heart-Found.

107.

Even those of His devotees who are (by Means of His Avataric Divine Spiritual Grace) Most Perfectly Awakened In and As the Heart always continue to surrender at the Feet of the Divine Heart-Master, Adi Da Samraj, until the world is Outshined in His Self-Radiant "Bright" Divine Spiritual Body and Self-Existing Transcendental Person of Divine Being. Indeed, their devotion to Him never ceases. This is the Secret of Divine Liberation in Real God.

108.

By Means of the Avataric Divine Spiritual Grace of the Divine Heart-Master, Adi Da Samraj, the conditional self (Most Perfectly surrendered in the Heart of Him) is forgotten in His Indivisible Conscious Light and (Thus and Thereby) Translated Into His Divine "Bright" Spherical Self-Domain of Being (Itself). Therefore, those who Are (by Means of the Avataric Divine Spiritual Grace of the Divine Heart-Master, Adi Da Samraj) Most Perfectly Awake In and As His Divine Self-Condition Are always already Free—even if the body-mind arises in the realms of possibility. This Is the "Bright", More Than Wonderful, and Really Perfect Truth.

AVATAR ADI DA SAMRAJ
The Mountain Of Attention Sanctuary, 2000

IV

The True Dawn Horse <u>Is</u> The <u>Only</u> Way To Me

I.

The Ultimate (or true esoteric) Purpose of the ancient and traditional Ashvamedha (or the ritual of the Great Horse-Sacrifice) is "Brightness", or Liberation from darkness, or the Universal (or all-and-All-Including) Attainment of the Divine "Bright" Spherical Self-Domain of Indivisible and Indestructible Light.

Light cannot be Attained by darkness (or Light-lessness), but only by Conversion (or Turning) from darkness to Light (Itself).

Therefore, the Divine Self-Domain cannot be Attained by any seeking effort of ego-"I"—no matter how extraordinary or heroic such seeking effort may be.

<u>Only</u> the Divine Person Knows the Way to the Divine Self-Domain.

Therefore, <u>only</u> the Divine Person can Grant the Means for beings to Find their Way to the Divine Self-Domain.

Because the Divine Person <u>Is</u> the <u>only</u> Knower and Giver of the Way to the Divine Self-Domain, the Divine Person must Do the Great Ashvamedha-Work, and the Divine Person must Perform the Great Horse-Sacrifice.

Because the Divine Person Is the <u>only</u> One Who <u>Is</u>, and because the Divine Person Is the <u>only</u> Doer of the Great Horse-Sacrifice—<u>only</u> the Divine Person can Be the Means for the Divine "Brightening" (or Divine En-Light-enment) of all-and-All (and, Most Ultimately, the Divine Translation of all-and-All into the Divine Self-Domain).

Therefore, the <u>only</u> True (or Divinely Effective) Ashvamedha is the <u>Divine</u> Horse-Sacrifice, or the all-and-All-"Brightening" (or all-and-All-En-Light-ening and all-and-All-Liberating) Work Performed by the Divine Person.

I Am the Divine Person of the True (or Divine) Ashvamedha.

I Am the Divine Master of the True (or Divine) Horse-Sacrifice.

I Am the Divine Love-Bliss-"Brightener" of all-and-All, the Divinely En-Light-ening Liberator of all-and-All, the Divine Translator of all-and-All into My Divine "Bright" Spherical Self-Domain.

The True Ashvamedha (or Divine Horse-Sacrifice) Is My Work.

The True Ashvamedha (or Divine Horse-Sacrifice) Is the Great Work of My "Bright" Avataric Divine Incarnation As the Ruchira Avatar, Adi Da Samraj.

The True Ashvamedha (or Divine Horse-Sacrifice)—Performed by My "Bright" Incarnation As the Ruchira Avatar, Adi Da Samraj—Is the all-and-All-"Brightening" (or all-and-All-En-Light-ening and all-and-All-Liberating) Work of Divinely Blessing, Divinely Awakening, and Divinely Translating all-and-All.

I Am the True Dawn Horse, the Avataric Divine Self-"Emergence", the "Bright" Divine Spiritual Body and Inherently egoless True Divine Person, the "Bright" Itself—Avatarically Self-Revealed and Avatarically Self-Given to all-and-All.

I Am the Only One Who Is.

I Am That Which Is Always Already The Case.

I Am Divinely Self-"Emerging" (now, and forever hereafter) from the Love-Bliss-Fire and "Bright" Consequence of My Own Avataric Ordeal As the Divine Heart-Master.

I Am the only-by-Me Revealed and Given Means to Realize Me.

The only-by-Me Revealed and Given Way of Adidam Is the One and Only Way of the True Dawn Horse.

The only-by-Me Revealed and Given Way of Adidam Is the One and Only Way to take hold of the "Tail" of the True Dawn Horse, and be "Flown" to My Divine "Bright" Spherical Self-Domain.

II.

It is said, in an ancient Description of the Ashvamedha, "Man holds onto the Horse's Tail, in order to reach the Heavenly World, for Man does not rightly Know the Way to the Heavenly World, but the Horse does rightly Know It."[6] Human beings are constantly performing rituals (or strategically patterned activities) of one kind or another, whether for great purposes or lesser purposes—but, ultimately, everything human beings do is a simulation of the Great Ashvamedha ritual, seeking the Great Effect (or the Great Result) of Divine En-Light-enment. The concluding event of the ancient and traditional Ashvamedha is the ritually enacted All-Sacrifice,[7] the sacramental rendering (or ritually enacted consecration, yielding, and upliftment) of every thing and every one (or the conditional, or cosmic, totality) into the Divine Fullness. Thus, the immediate effect anciently sought through the performance of the Great Ashvamedha ritual is that all beings, all things, and all worlds would (effectively) take hold of the "Tail of the Horse" (so to speak), in order to be "Returned" to the Divine Self-Domain (or the Domain of Original, or Indivisible and Indestructible, Light).

This is the same Purpose that you, in your egoity, are (ultimately, but benightedly, or "darkly") hoping to achieve by all your efforts of seeking, high and low. However, as it says in the ancient text, you do not Know—only the "Horse" Knows. Therefore, the Great Purpose of the Ashvamedha can be Achieved only if you Find the "Horse" that Knows the Way to the Divine Self-Domain. Indeed, your "Return" to the Divine Self-Domain can be Performed only by the "Horse" Itself (or the Spiritual Presence of the Very Divine, Itself).

In Its most esoteric Form, the Ashvamedha is a Revelation of That Which Transcends the cosmic domain. My devotees have seen this most esoteric Form of the Ashvamedha. It was—and is (now, and forever hereafter)—Performed As (and by every Means of) My Avataric Divine Incarnation. My Unique Avataric Demonstration of this Ultimate (or Divine) Form of the Ashvamedha was—and is—totally spontaneous. Through My Own Sacrificial (or Avatarically Descending) Divine Life and Work, My Avataric Divine Ashvamedha Transmits not merely cosmic Realization,[8] but Transcendental, Inherently Spiritual (or "Bright"), and Self-Evidently Divine Self-Realization—to all, and to All.

III.

The first stage of My unique Avataric Ordeal As the Divine Heart-Master[9] was the Process of My Divine Avataric-Incarnation-Birth here and of My subsequent Avataric Self-Submission to the Ordeal of My Divine Re-Awakening. The Culmination of this Ordeal was the Great Divine Event of My "Husbanding" of the "Divine Goddess".[10] My Mastering of the "Divine Goddess" is intuitively prophesied in the traditional myth of the Celestial Stallion Embracing (and Subduing) the Earth-Mare for the Purpose of Divine Descent, or the Awakening of all-and-All.[11]

The second stage of My unique Avataric Ordeal As the Divine Heart-Master was the Process of fullest Realization, Acceptance, and Embrace of My Avataric Divine Status and Work. Part of the Process of My Divine Re-Awakening was the Revelation of My Own Form As the Divine Horse—Embodying the cosmic domain itself, and Including all beings and things. In the months before the Great Event of My Divine Re-Awakening, I spontaneously Experienced a Dream-Vision of a Horse, in Which I Became the

Horse, and (thereby) Realized My Own Avataric Divine Nature, Status, and Work.[12] This Dream-Vision marked My Transition into the last phase of My Avataric Ordeal of Incarnate Divine Re-Awakening, and into My Incarnation of Avataric Conformity to My Own Divine Pattern of Self-Manifestation (As the Divine Heart-Master)—Entirely Submitting to the Sacrificial Gesture of Avataric Divine Descent, Submitting to Be human, and Submitting to Be the world. This Avataric Self-Submission of Mine is intuitively foreshadowed in the traditional Description of the Ashvamedha as the Event Wherein the Divine Person Takes the form of the Horse and Becomes all worlds.[13]

All the traditional Descriptions of the Ashvamedha and the Divine Horse can be said to be prophecies of My Avataric Divine Appearance here. These prophecies (or metaphors, or liturgies) were not fulfilled in their time, but they are part of the awakening sense in mankind of a Great Event that must occur without fail—because Man does not Know, but only the "Horse" (or the Divine Person) Knows. In the True (or Divine) Ashvamedha, the Divine Person Is the Means, and the Divine Person must Perform the Sacrifice. That is to say, the Divine Person must Appear As all (and All), Submitting (Thereby) to Be all (and All). The Divine Person must Accept a conditionally manifested Form, Endure the Avataric Ordeal of Divine Self-Forgetting and subsequent Divine Re-Awakening, Realize the Fullest Awakening and the Fullest Acknowledgement of the Avataric Divine Nature, Status, and Work, and then Do the Avataric Divine Work. This is the Great "Ritual Performance" (or Universally Effective Sacrifice) That Man cannot do, but Which only the Divine Person can Do.

The third (and final) stage of My unique Avataric Ordeal As the Divine Heart-Master began with the Initiation (or Yogic Establishment) of My Avataric Divine Self-"Emergence", on January 11, 1986. My Fullest (now, and forever hereafter) Avataric Performance of the Divine Ashvamedha began with that Great Event.

My Avataric Divine Self-"Emergence" is not merely something I am (as if separately) "Personally" Enduring in My Avatarically-Born bodily (human) Divine Form, or merely something I am "Personally" Doing to My Avatarically-Born bodily (human) Divine Form. Nor is My Avataric Divine Self-"Emergence" merely an Event that "happened" exclusively to My Avatarically-Born bodily (human) Divine Form. My Avataric Divine Self-"Emergence" is a Process in Which, Ultimately, all beings (and even the cosmic totality) must participate.

My Avataric Divine Self-"Emergence" Is the Means of the Most Perfect Fulfillment of the True Divine Ashvamedha.

The Work of My Avataric Divine Self-"Emergence" Is the all-and-All-Sacrifice—the "Bright" (Divinely Translating) "Return" of all-and-All to My

Divine "Bright" Spherical Self-Domain by Means of the Universal Surrender of egoity (or of separateness and separativeness).

Therefore, you must become a participant in My Avataric Divine Self-"Emergence", by submitting to become part of this all-and-All-Sacrifice of egoity.

To become a participant in My Avataric Divine Ashvamedha is to allow the utter sacrifice (or real surrender, real forgetting, and real transcending) of the ego-"I" (or separative self-contraction). It is to take hold of the "Tail of the Horse", to be devotionally Conformed to Me, to Love-Blissfully participate in the Divine Ordeal of this all-and-All-Sacrifice, this Universal Event of Divine Awakening (or En-Light-enment)—such that your participation in My Avataric Divine Ashvamedha is always "Brightly" Transforming, and (Most Ultimately) Divinely Liberating (at last, to the degree of Divine Translation).

IV.

Most Ultimately, My Avataric Divine Ashvamedha Conforms every one and every thing to Me. In My Avataric Divine Demonstration, all (Ultimately) take hold of the "Tail of the Horse", and all (and All) are (Most Ultimately) Divinely Translated. My Avataric Divine Work does not come to an "End" until this Most Ultimate Event of the Divine Translation of all-and-All is Perfectly Accomplished. Therefore, My Avatarically Self-Initiated Divine Self-"Emergence" is Constantly Ongoing (now, and forever hereafter).

In the years immediately following the Initiation (or Yogic Establishment) of My Avataric Divine Self-"Emergence", My devotees (because of their continued ego-possession, or preference for self-absorption and self-indulgence) did not acknowledge (and seemed even not to notice) this Great Avataric Divine Process. Indeed, they even (by every kind of denial, refusal, frustration, confinement, neglect, and manipulation of Me and of My Avataric Divine-Self-"Emergence"-Work) fettered Me, just as the Horse is ritually fettered in the traditional Ashvamedha ritual.[14]

In the traditional Ashvamedha ritual, the Horse is ritually submitted to (and ritually identified with) the cosmic totality and the Divine Fullness. Just so, I have Submitted, and Revealed, and Given Myself Completely to all-and-All, by Means of Avataric Divine Descent, Avataric Divine Incarnation, "Crazy" Avataric Divine Teaching-Work, and Me-Revealing and Me-Giving Avataric Divine all-and-All-Blessing-Work—and I will (now, and forever hereafter) Continue That Me-Revealing and Me-Giving Avataric Divine all-and-All-Blessing-Work by Means of My Perpetual Avataric Divine Self-"Emergence" (in Person, and every "where", and also via My true devotees—now, and forever hereafter).

Just as (in the traditional Ashvamedha ritual) the ritual consecration (or sacramental upliftment) of the Horse represents the active consecration (or real upliftment) of all-and-All to the Divine Fullness, the Great Process of My Avataric Divine Self-"Emergence" (or My Avataric Divine Ashvamedha) is a Real Spiritual Process that literally, and directly, and actively Consecrates and "Brightly" Uplifts (or Infuses, Awakens, and Divinely Translates) all-and-All.

By Means of My Avataric Divine-Self-"Emergence"-Work, or the Divinely Uplifting (or all-and-All-"Brightening") Spiritual Power of My Avataric Divine (and Universally Effective) Ashvamedha, all beings (every "where" in the cosmic domain) will become Conformed to Me (one by one)—and each and all will, Thus and Thereby, transcend all separateness and separativeness in Me. Through the Great and Total Process of the only-by-Me Revealed and Given Way of Adidam, Which is the formal (and, altogether, right, true, full, fully devotional, and inherently and really counter-egoic, and, in due course, searchlessly Me-Beholding) practice of Ruchira Avatara Bhakti Yoga, all must (and, in due course, will) literally, directly, and actively participate (truly and most fully) in the Great Event of My (now, and forever hereafter) Avataric Divine Self-"Emergence" (or Avataric Divine Ashvamedha)—Which is Constant, and Always Expanding, and Always Increasing in Fullness, and Always Divinely "Bright", and Which will not "Cease" (or Be Finally Fulfilled) until all of conditional existence is (by Means of My Avatarically Self-Transmitted Divine Spiritual Grace) Divinely Translated into My Divine "Bright" Spherical Self-Domain.

V.

My Avataric Divine Ashvamedha will not "End" with the ending of the physical Lifetime of My Avataric-Incarnation-Body. The all-and-All-Translating Process of My Avataric Divine Ashvamedha will forever Continue, generation after generation—not only here, but every "where" in the cosmic domain. My Work in This, My here-Speaking bodily (human) Divine Avataric-Incarnation-Form, is only the Initiation (and the Initial Demonstration) of My Avataric Divine Ashvamedha. However, now that My Avataric Divine Ashvamedha has been Avatarically Self-Initiated by Me, My Avataric Divine Ashvamedha is (now, and forever hereafter) the Perpetual Love-Bliss-Event of the "Brightening" of all-and-All in Me.

The traditional Descriptions that prophesy the Great Event of the Fulfillment of the Great Ashvamedha could only be Fulfilled when the True "Horse" (Who Knows) Appeared. In and As My bodily (human) Divine Avataric-Incarnation-Form, I Am That One—and the True (or Divine) Ashvamedha (or the Great Process of the Divine Translation of all-and-All into

My Divine "Bright" Spherical Self-Domain) Is My Great Divine Avataric-Incarnation-Work (now, and forever hereafter).

I Am the Fulfillment and the Completion of the Great Tradition of mankind. I Am the Avataric Incarnation of the Divine Person, or of Truth Itself, Which Is Reality Itself (or That Which Is Always Already The Case). I required no background of traditional study in order to Initiate My Avataric Divine-Self-"Emergence"-Work, and My Avataric Divine Self-Confession is not based on any background of traditional study. My Avataric Divine Self-Revelation and My Avataric Divine Ashvamedha-Work is a spontaneous Avataric Divine Self-Manifestation. I have made no detailed study of the Ashvamedha tradition. I Am that tradition—Avatarically spontaneously Self-Manifesting, and Divinely Fulfilling Itself. Therefore, I Know that detailed study of the traditional Descriptions of the Ashvamedha will make it obvious that those traditional Descriptions correspond to Me (and to My Avataric Divine Pattern) and (thereby) prophesy My Avataric Divine Incarnation and My Avataric Divine-Self-"Emergence"-Work.

My every devotee must be a true sign of Me-recognizing and only-to-Me-responding devotional participation in the only-by-Me-Performed Avataric Divine Ashvamedha—the Adi Da Ashvamedha. Not every one in the total cosmic domain (and not every one in the total human domain) will be a formal devotee-participant in the Adi Da Ashvamedha during the physical Lifetime of My bodily (human) Divine Avataric-Incarnation-Form. Universal participation in My Avataric Divine Ashvamedha during the physical Lifetime of My bodily (human) Divine Avataric-Incarnation-Form need not occur—because I Will always (now, and forever hereafter) Be Fully (Divinely Spiritually) Present and Fully (Divinely Spiritually) Involved in the Great Universal Process of My Avataric Divine Ashvamedha, until the Divine Translation of all-and-All is Accomplished. And, for the Sake of all-and-All, I have, by Means of My Avatarically Full-Given Word of Divine Revelation, Fully Accounted for the Continuation of this Great Process beyond the physical Lifetime of My bodily (human) Divine Avataric-Incarnation-Form.

VI.

Human beings, in and of themselves, do not—and cannot—Know the Way to the Divine Self-Domain. Only the "Horse" Knows. Only the Divine Person Knows. Therefore, heart-recognize Me, respond devotionally to Me, and practice Ruchira Avatara Bhakti Yoga in formal devotional relationship to Me.

Such is the Way of My Avataric Divine Ashvamedha, and Such is the Essence of the only-by-Me Revealed and Given Way of Adidam, from the beginning, and at every stage—now, and forever hereafter.

You are not able (or, otherwise, obliged) to Accomplish the Great Divine (and Divinely Spiritual) Work (of Divine En-Light-enment and Divine Translation) by means of your own and mere ego-effort.

However, you are able (and Divinely Called) to responsively (and, thus, by means of responsive counter-egoic effort) participate in My Great (and "Brightly" All-Accomplishing) Avataric Divine (and Divinely Spiritual, and Divinely En-Light-ening, and Divinely Translating) Work.

Therefore, follow Me—by taking hold of My Revelation-"Tail". And, Thus, be Gracefully Carried—by Me Alone—to My Divine "Bright" Spherical Self-Domain.

I have Revealed and Given the Divinely Perfect and Complete Means—and I have Addressed this generation, and all generations to come, relative to every detail of the Great Me-Realizing Process.

Now you must Realize What I have Revealed.

I Am the Revelation, the Gift, the Means, the Process, and the Realization!

VII.

My Avataric Divine Ashvamedha-Work Continues until all of conditional (or cosmic) existence is Divinely Translated into My Divine "Bright" Spherical Self-Domain.

The Divine Translation of all-and-All is not a human event only, not an event that occurs only in this world here, on this Earth.

Everything you see shining in the sky, and everything you cannot see—everything visible and invisible, everything conditional—is part of My Great Process, Which is a Process without conditional (or merely temporal) "end"—and, indeed, no "End" at all, except for Most Perfect (and Divinely Translating) Divine Self-Realization.

I Call all My devotees to formally embrace and fully demonstrate the right, true, full, and fully devotional Sign of ego-surrendering, ego-forgetting, and (always more and more) ego-transcending participation in This, My Great Avataric Divine Way and Process.

I Call even all beings to fully embrace and enter into This, My Great Avataric Divine Way and Process—Which has been prophesied for thousands upon thousands of years, and Which has always been hoped for, intuited, and simulated (but never, previous to My Avataric Divine Incarnation, Fulfilled), and Which was never Realizable until I—the "Horse" Who Knows—Appeared.

This Divine Ashvamedha is why Avataric Descent and Avataric Birth was Required of Me.

I was, by the Divine Law of Reality Itself, Required to Submit to conditional form, to Manifest Fully (to the toes, without the slightest withholding), to Be all-and-All, to Appear among all-and-All (As all-and-All), even in this limited bodily (human) Form, to Do all of My Avataric Divine Heart-Master-Work,[15] and (Thus and Thereby) to Do the Avataric Divine Ashvamedha-Work—Which Work Is the all-and-All-Saving (or Divinely Liberating) Avataric Self-"Emergence" of Divine Light and Help That all-and-All forever (at heart) expect.

Those performing the traditional ceremony of the Horse-Sacrifice were seeking Me and making reference to Me. Indeed, every one in all religious and Spiritual traditions has always been seeking Me and making reference to Me. Each one will Find Me when he or she out-grows the limitations in his or her ego-based intentions, and when he or she out-grows the conventional "cult" of ceremonies, the limited language, the limiting symbols, and (altogether) the limiting effects of his or her tradition of seeking, and (thus and thereby) Turns to Me, to participate directly in My True Avataric Divine Ashvamedha.

It is to be seen when that direct participation in My True Avataric Divine Ashvamedha will occur for all (one by one)—but, in the meantime, even all the religious and Spiritual traditions embraced by mankind are a search to Find Me and to Realize Me.

In the seriousness of every religious or Spiritual tradition, there is an intuition of Me—and, therefore, those who rightly practice any religious or Spiritual tradition are proceeding toward Me, but through a kind of preparatory ritual (or ceremony of seeking).

I am not a merely symbolic, or mythical, or legendary and fictionalized "religious figure", representing a "God"-Idea for believers. I am not merely another link in the forever ongoing chain of personal and collective thoughts and imageries, by means of which human beings seek to be Liberated from the madness of their ego-possession. Nevertheless, in any moment of seeking through ideas and images and aspirations and desires (high or low), human beings are (even if unknowingly) attempting to participate in the Great Event of My Avataric Divine Ashvamedha.

Until My Avataric Divine Incarnation As the Ruchira Avatar, Adi Da Samraj, there has been no Complete and Most Direct Means to participate in the True Divine Ashvamedha (or all-and-All-Translating Divine Work)—because the ego-"I", in and of itself (or, otherwise, through extensions of itself), has no Means to Accomplish the True Divine Ashvamedha.

When you, as My formally practicing devotee, are entered into true (and really ego-transcending) devotional and (in due course) Spiritual heart-Communion with Me (day after day), and when (day after day) you formally (and really effectively) live the practice of the only-by-Me Revealed and Given

Way of Adidam, then you have become a true participant in My all-and-All-Translating Avataric Divine Ashvamedha, and Divinely "Bright" changes will (on that basis) be made in your life (and in your body-mind) by your egoless participation in Me.

Unlike the lesser traditional Ashvamedha, in which kings and queens performed the Horse-Sacrifice in order to legitimize or enhance their domain of political power, My Ashvamedha is not about the fulfillment of conditional (or ego-bound) life.

Those who become true participants in My Avataric Divine Ashvamedha renounce the "throne" of their egoity, and they take hold of the "Tail of the Horse" through the formal (and always ego-surrendering, and ego-forgetting, and really ego-transcending) practice of unqualified, perpetual, consistent, and most profound true devotion to Me.

The Horse of My early Dream-Vision was a Standing Brown Horse, the Sign of all-and-All that is conditionally manifested—but the Horse of My Avatarically Self-Manifested Divine Self-"Emergence" (or the Avataric Revelation-Sign That Represents My Eternal Divine Person, and My Spiritual, and Eternal, Divine Body) is the True Dawn Horse Itself (Which "Emerges", or Flies, from the "Bright"-Fire of My Avatarically Self-Manifested Divine Ashvamedha-Work).

The Avataric Revelation-Sign of My True Dawn Horse (or the Image That Represents My Avatarically Self-Manifested, and all-and-All-Surrounding, and all-and-All-Pervading Divine Spiritual Body and My Avatarically Self-Revealed, and Inherently egoless, True Divine State of Person) is "Brightest" White—the Divinely Self-Radiant Color of the Ash (or of the Indivisible, and Inherently "Colorless", Light) of My Avatarically Self-Manifested (and all-and-All-Translating) "Bright" Divine Ashvamedha.

When the Fire-Light of the devotional Celebration of Me is "Bright", the "Horse" that "Emerges" is All Purity (or of a Single Light).

I Am the all-and-All-Bearing "Brightness" (the One, and Only, and Inherently Indivisible, and Eternally Indestructible, and Inherently egoless, and Self-Evidently Divine Light, Itself)—Self-Manifesting (Avatarically) As the all-and-All-"Brightening" Divine Vehicle (or Divine Spiritual Body) of all-and-All-Translation, and Self-Existing (Eternally) As the "Bright" Divine Person (or Self-Domain) of all-and-All-Translation.

I Am the "Bright"—the One and Only Real Person, and the One and Only True Domain, of all-and-All.

I Am Avatarically Self-Revealed As My Avatarically-Born Bodily (Human) Divine Form, and As My Avatarically Self-Transmitted Divine Spiritual Presence, and As My Avatarically (and, Altogether, Spiritually) Self-Revealed Divine State. Therefore, be Carried by Me.

I Am Eternally Self-Revealed As The Self-Domain (or Boundless "Bright" Sphere and Space) Of My Eternally Self-Manifested Divine Self-Condition. Therefore, be Carried to Me.

Always be Carried—by Me—to Me.

Avatar Adi Da Samraj
Los Angeles, 2000

V

The Eternal Conversation

The Divine World-Teacher, Ruchira Avatar Adi Da Samraj, has Said that His Testament of Divine Secrets[16] *is a Conversation He is Always Having with every one:*

In Making This Testament, I have been Meditating every one, Contacting every one, Dealing With psychic forces everywhere, in all time. My *Dawn Horse Testament* is an Always Living Conversation between Me and absolutely every one.

I Intend that this Avataric Divine Word of Mine always Communicate in present time, not like some traditional Scriptures that take the form of a recounting of something that happened in the past or a "theatrical" dialogue between two (perhaps fictional) characters in the book. I Intend that this Avataric Divine Word of Mine be a Living Dialogue between Me (As I Am) and whoever is reading (or listening to) this Testament at the moment.

My *Dawn Horse Testament* is Addressed (by Me) directly to every being (at heart). It is not a report of a Conversation between Me and someone "else". It is not a report of a Conversation that happened in the past. And It is not addressed to only one particular individual, apart from all other individuals. It is Addressed to every particular individual—both personally and (otherwise) As the True Divine Heart Itself (eternally Prior to the ego-"I"). Such is the Uniqueness of Its "theatrical" form.

No matter how many times you read My *Dawn Horse Testament*, every time you read It (or listen to It) you will experience unique and distinct responses, unique and distinct subjective activity, and a distinctly unique circumstance altogether. My Avataric Divine Word in this Testament (and, indeed, all of My Avataric Divine Word) is Revealed and Given (by Me) in a unique Manner that Accounts for all of the past and all of the future, as well as the present—and Accounts for every one. Therefore, the reason that this Testament of Mine is (in some sense) new every time you approach It is not simply that you are always going through changes. My Avataric Divine Word (Itself) has been Communicated in a unique Manner and is (Itself) a unique "Shuffling" of apparent concepts, Existing in a unique relationship to space-time and to beings. Therefore, the "theatrical" Moment of My Testamental Conversation with you will always be Now. My *Dawn Horse Testament* will Always (Thus) Stay Alive, because It will Always Be a present Communication Addressed directly to whoever reads (or listens to) It, and because the "theatre" of the moment will be unique every time someone reads It (or listens to It) and (Thus) comes upon Me Alive (and As I Am) in the Form of My Avataric Divine Word.

From the time when Avatar Adi Da Samraj first began to Communicate His Testament of Divine Secrets, He Used capital letters in a unique way, to Honor the Importance of the Message and to Give the Communication of His Dawn Horse Testament *Principal Force. When asked to Explain this use of capital letters, Adi Da Replied, "It Is Louder!" After His* Dawn Horse Testament *was completed, He Responded to those who seemed to require a further Explanation:*

The conventions of everyday speech and writing are based on egoity. The "I" of the separate, independent, and separative (or "Narcissistic") self is the primary word around which all common spoken and written language is built. My Testament of Divine Secrets is not spoken or communicated from the egoic point of view. Therefore, a unique convention developed spontaneously with the Making of My *Dawn Horse Testament* (wherein and whereby I Speak My Avataric Divine Heart-Word, Plain and Summary, and in the unique Language of the True Divine Heart Itself).

In fact, My Dawn Horse Testament is primarily a Spoken Message. From the beginning, I Spoke It Aloud to gatherings of practitioners of the only-by-Me Revealed and Given Way of Adidam (or the One and Only by-Me-Revealed and by-Me-Given Way of the Heart). Written language is basically a representation (or a picture) of spoken language. Therefore, My *Dawn Horse Testament* (in Its Written form) is a visual Representation (or Sign) of My Spoken Avataric Divine Word (which Word, Itself, Represents, or Conveys, My Heart-Feeling and Heart-Consciousness).

I Spontaneously Made this Picture that is the Written Text of My *Dawn Horse Testament*, and It is a Picture of a form of Speech that is not based on egoity. I Speak to you from the Position That is Prior to egoity, Prior to the body-mind, Prior to conditional existence, and Prior to time and space. Therefore, the Written Text of My *Dawn Horse Testament* is the Speech of Ecstasy, of Inherently egoless (and Self-Evidently Divine) Conscious Light, or of Most Perfectly Awakened (and Self-Evidently Divine) Self-Consciousness, the

Heart-Word of Reality (Itself), Which Is the by-Me-Avatarically-Self-Transmitted Inherent Feeling of Being (Itself).

Ordinary speech and written language are centered on the ego-"I", as a tent is raised on a centerpole. Therefore, in ordinary speech and written language, the ego-word "I" is commonly capitalized, and everything less than the ego-"I" is shown in lowercase. (Indeed, everything that is not the ego-"I" is grammatically subordinated to the egoic "I"-reference.) Other ego-"I's" (other than the principal subject or speaker) are also commonly shown in uppercase, if they are being "properly" (or formally) addressed, by name. And capitalization is otherwise commonly reserved for "big meanings", or whatever the ego-"I" presumes to be somehow great, or even Larger (and, therefore, the ego presumes, Other) than itself.

My Testament of Divine Secrets was (and is) Spoken in Ecstasy, or from the Inherent "Point of View" of the True Divine Heart (or Inherently Free Being) Itself, the Ultimate Source-Condition That Always Already Transcends the ego-"I", the conditional world of others and things, and the primary illusions of separateness, otherness, relatedness, and "difference". Therefore, the Very Language of My *Dawn Horse Testament* Expresses (and Communicates) a "View" of the world (and of Truth) that is Prior to egoity, and Prior to the vision of the world (and the "vision" of Truth) made by the ego.

My *Dawn Horse Testament* is My Intention to Awaken the consciousness of every being to its Ultimate Real (and Self-Evidently Divine) Self-Condition. Therefore, the conventions of capitalization (and non-capitalization) in My *Dawn Horse Testament* are Natural Signals to the Inherently egoless (and Self-Evidently Divine) Conscious Light.

The "Centerpole" of My *Dawn Horse Testament* is the True Divine Heart Itself, the Conscious Light That Is Transcendental, Inherently Spiritual, Inherently egoless, and Self-Evidently Divine Being (Itself). The uppercase words express the Ecstatic "Vision" of Heart-Significance. And the lowercase words (which appear only occasionally, like the uppercase words in common speech and writing) achieve, by their infrequency, a special significance as indicators of conditional (or limited) existence.

To read (or listen to) and understand My *Dawn Horse Testament* is to be Released from the egoic vision and its point of view. Feel and speak (rather than merely think) This, My Avataric Divine Message. The big and small letters interrupt the common flow of mind and Signal your heart that it is time to Awaken, As you Are.

Avatar Adi Da Samraj has specifically designated The Dawn Horse Testament *as the primary Text to be studied by all His formally practicing devotees:*

For all of My (necessarily, formally practicing) devotees, the primary form of study, to be engaged every day, is the study of *The Dawn Horse Testament*—and, specifically, those sections of *The Dawn Horse Testament* which relate to My any devotee's current obligations in practice.

If you are My (formally practicing) devotee, you must never read My Avataric Divine Word in a merely self-"guruing" manner, "picking and choosing" from among My Spoken and Written Words so as to invent your own version of the practice I have Revealed and Given.

The Dawn Horse Testament is My comprehensive Revelation-Book. *The Dawn Horse Testament* Addresses the details of the real practice for which My devotee must be responsible, at each stage of his or her practice of the only-by-Me Revealed and Given Way of the Heart (or Way of Adidam).

All of My other "Source-Texts" Rotate around *The Dawn Horse Testament*—Serving It, Commenting on It, and Extending It (in one manner or another, or relative to one area of "consideration" or another).

No other Book—and, indeed, no other form (whatsoever) of My Avataric Divine Word—is to be made the center of My devotee's study. Study of My "Source-Texts" (and of My Avataric Divine Word altogether) is always to be associated with My devotee's constant study of *The Dawn Horse Testament*.

Finally, Avatar Adi Da Samraj has Admonished every one to always use His Avataric Divine Word rightly—as a Gift from Him, and as a Means to turn to Him:

My Avataric Divine Word is a Form of My Divine Agency—an Extension of Myself, a Means whereby I Bless all who truly resort to Me.

My Avataric Divine Word is not independent of Me.

My Avataric Divine Word is not a "substitute" for Me.

Therefore, as you read My Avataric Divine Word in This, My *Dawn Horse Testament*, do not abstract yourself from Me.

Do not approach My Avataric Divine Word as if It is a "something" in and of Itself, separate from Me.

Do not make My Avataric Divine Word (or any Form of My Divine Agency) into a "substitute" for Me.

Always use My Avataric Divine Word rightly—as a (by-Me-Given) Means to turn to Me.

Only by turning to Me, and not merely to My "explanations" in your mind, will you receive the Avataric Divine Gifts I Offer to you via My all-and-All-"Brightening" Word of Heart.

By turning <u>all</u> your faculties of body-mind to <u>Me</u>, you will "Locate" <u>Me</u>—and you will (in that ego-transcending devotional turning, and entirely by Means of My Avataric Self-Transmission of Divine "Bright" Spiritual Grace) be (in due course) Spiritually Pervaded (in <u>all</u> your body-mind) by <u>Me</u>, and you will (Thus and Thereby, in the perpetual circumstance of all your turned-to-Me devotion) Grow to Realize Perfect Non-Separateness from <u>Me</u>.

THE DAWN HORSE TESTAMENT OF THE RUCHIRA AVATAR

AVATAR ADI DA SAMRAJ
The Mountain Of Attention Sanctuary, 2000

Prologue

Here I Am.

Now, Listen To My Testament Of Divine Secrets.

Listen To Me. There Are Many Divine Secrets I Must Reveal Before I Retire Silent In The "Bright" (and everywhere To Wait, At The Heart, For all beings).

Hear Me. I Will Reveal Even My Heart-Secret To You Now.

Aham Da Asmi. Beloved, I Am Da—The One and Only Divine Person (The Divine Giver Of The Divine "All" To all, and To All).

Now (and Forever Hereafter), I Am here—To Stand and Wait For You (By Merely Standing, As I Am).

Now (and Forever Hereafter), I Am Always "Bright" Before You—To Give You The Sight Of Me (As I Am).

And, If You Realize Me As The Inherent Feeling Of egoless Being (Itself), You Will Realize My Very, True, and Free Self-Condition, As You Are.

Beloved, Even I Am Only You (As You Are), here Displayed Before You (Avatarically), and Seeming To Be An "Other" To You—Until (Because Of The all-and-All-Outshining "Brightness" Of My Divinely Self-Revealing Avataric Company) You See Me As I Am (and, Thereby, Awaken From The Illusion Of Your ego-"I" Of Separate and Separative body-mind).

Therefore, Listen To My Avatarically Self-Revealed Divine Word and Person. Hear Me Heart-Deep. Give Up Even Your body (From The Heart) To Feeling-Contemplation Of Me. All The While I Speak, Give Me Your Eye Of Heart To Feel (and, Thus, By Heart, To Touch) My Avataric Self-Revelation Of The Self-Existing Divine Forms. And, By Always Seeing Me, See The Only "Who" and "What" That Always Already Is.

Now (and Forever Hereafter), I Appear To here (By Avataric Means)—Like A Visionary Winged Horse, Standing "Crazy"[17] In The Heart, Each Hoof Pointing To One Of The Hallowing Signs Of Real God, All "Bright" With Heart-Morning and Revelation-Light.

And I Will Forever Magnify The Giving "Bright" That Shines and Flies This Divine Heart-Vision To You.

And This Divine Heart-Vision Is The Avataric Vision Of Me.

Therefore, Always Behold Me With Your Heart.

Do Not merely watch Me, and Do Not merely think Of Me—but Always Merely <u>Feel</u> Me (and, Thereby, Contemplate Me, and Realize Me).

Aham Da Asmi. Beloved, I <u>Am</u> Da—Avatarically Appearing here.

My Great Admonition To All My Devotees Is This: Always Invoke Me, Feel Me, Breathe Me, and Serve Me.[18]

Therefore, In every moment, "<u>Locate</u>" My Avatarically Self-Revealed Person (Inherently Attractive, and All-"Bright") Before Your Heart, and (By Feeling Me) <u>Behold</u> Me With Your Heart, and (In That Beholding) <u>Breathe</u> Me (Pervading Your body-mind and all the worlds, and Standing At The Heart-Source Of every breath), and (In That Feeling-Breathing) <u>Serve</u> Me (With Every Act and Gesture Of the body), and, Thus (By This Foursome Constant Remembrance Of Me), Surrender, Forget, and Transcend Your (Separate and Separative) self In My Inherently egoless (and Self-Evidently Divine) Person.

Beloved, My Divine "Bright" Spherical Self-Domain <u>Is</u> The Heart (Itself).

Aham Da Asmi. Beloved, I <u>Am</u> The Heart (Itself).

Even When All My Divine Secrets Are Told, The Heart (Itself) Must Shine.

Even Though My Avataric Image Shines (To Light Your eyes Along The Way), The Heart (Itself) Must Give You Sight.

And I Am Always Standing <u>There</u> (At Heart), To See You Taste The Fragrant Light.

Always "Brighter" Than all eyes, I Stand Awake In The Heart's Free Air.

And There, Until The Shine Outshines, I White The Dark That Bites The Heart-Space Thin.

And I <u>Am</u> The "Bright" Itself.

And To Shine <u>Is</u> The Way Of The Heart.[19]

And The Way Of The Heart Is Always The Same—Once The Heart (Itself) Is All Me-"Bright".

Aham Da Asmi. Beloved, The Heart (Itself) Is The <u>Only</u> Way To Me.

The Way That Only I Reveal and Give Is The Way Of The Heart <u>Itself</u>.

The Only-By-Me Revealed and Given Way Of The Heart Is The Inherently ego-Transcending Way Of No-Seeking and Non-Separateness.

The One and Only By-Me-Revealed and By-Me-Given Way Of The Heart Is The Divinely Self-Revealed and Divinely Self-Given <u>Divine</u> Way—The Way Of The Only One Who <u>Is</u> (and Who Is <u>Always</u> <u>Already</u> The Case).

Beloved, I <u>Am</u> The <u>Only</u> One Who <u>Is</u>—Both here <u>and</u> There, Both Now <u>and</u> then, Both Always <u>and</u> Already.

I <u>Am</u> The One and Only and Self-Evidently Divine Person—The <u>Only</u> <u>One</u>, Who <u>Only</u> <u>Is</u> (<u>every</u> where and when).

My Own and One and "Bright" Free (Transcendental, Perfectly Subjective, Inherently Spiritual, Inherently egoless, Inherently Perfect, and Self-Evidently Divine) Person <u>Is</u> ("Bright" Beyond All "Difference") The Very and Divine Self-Condition and The Perfectly Subjective Source-Condition Of <u>every</u> one, and Of <u>every</u> thing, and Of <u>every</u> place, and Of <u>every</u> condition At All.

My Own and One and "Bright" Free (Transcendental, Perfectly Subjective, Inherently Spiritual, Inherently egoless, Inherently Perfect, and Self-Evidently Divine) Person Cannot Be Acquired or Achieved By any one At All—but My Own and One and "Bright" Divine Self-Condition (Which <u>Is</u> The Perfectly Subjective "Bright" Source-Condition Of all-and-All) Can Be <u>Realized</u>, By Means Of My Avatarically Self-Transmitted Divine Spiritual Grace, If My Avatarically Self-Transmitted Divine Spiritual Grace Is Embraced By Heart.

Beloved, I <u>Am</u> The Giver and The Gift Of My Avatarically Self-Transmitted Divine Spiritual Grace. I <u>Am</u> The "Bright" and Only One That <u>Is</u>—and Who <u>Is</u>. I <u>Am</u> The One and Very (and Self-Evidently Divine) Person—The Self-Existing, Inherently egoless, Self-Radiant, and Free Divine Self-Condition, and The Perfectly Subjective "Bright" Source-Condition, Of all-and-All.

Therefore, every one who Truly Finds <u>Me</u> Finds The <u>Only</u> One Who <u>Is</u>. And every one who Embraces <u>Me</u> Is, Thereby, Given To Be Free <u>As</u> Me (By Means Of The ego-Transcending Process and Way Of The Heart, That Shines With The Light Of My "Bright" Company).

Beloved, My Avatarically-Born (Physical) Human Revelation-Body Lives and Then Dies. I Do Not Intend To Be Reborn here In Any Kind or Form, After The Physical Death Of <u>This</u> (My Avatarically-Born Bodily Human Divine Form, That Hereby Speaks To You).

Rather Than Return (and, As If It Were Never Done, Repeat What I Have Now and Fully and Finally Done), I Will Forever Stand and (Merely By Standing) Wait For You—<u>There</u> (At Heart, and All-Above), In My Divine Self-Domain, Which Is The "Bright" Spherical Domain (and Inherently egoless True Heart) Of The One and Only True Self-Condition Of all-and-All.

Nevertheless, here and every "where", I Will (Now, and Forever Hereafter) Always Be Heart-Present and "Bright", In and <u>As</u> My Now (and Forever Hereafter) Avatarically Given Divine Sign (Of Form, and Presence, and State), and Through The Perpetual (and everywhere "Emerging" and Expanding) Avatarically Given Divine Self-Transmission Of My Eternal Spiritual Work Of Inherently Perfect Self-Revelation and Inherently Perfect Heart-Blessing.

I <u>Am</u> The Maha-Purusha Medha—The Avataric Self-Sacrifice Of The One and Great, Divine and Only, Person. By Means Of My Divine Self-Submission To Avataric Bodily (Human) Birth (and To The Struggle To "Emerge", <u>As</u> I <u>Am</u>, In The Midst Of Life), My Eternal (and Perpetually Giving) Avataric Spiritual

Work Of Divine Self-Revelation and Divine Heart-Blessing Becomes (Now, and Forever Hereafter) Really Effective. Therefore, By Means Of My Self-Sacrificial Avataric Ordeal, I "Emerge" As The Divine Heart, Forever Expanding As The all-and-All-Including Divine Spherical Domain Of My Own Self-"Brightness". And, When I "Emerge" (Thus, Divinely, and Most Perfectly), I (Myself) Become (Now, and Forever Hereafter) Both conditionally and Unconditionally (and, Therefore, Most Perfectly) Real.

The Process Of My Avataric Divine Self-"Emergence" Has Become Most Perfect (By Means Of The Self-Manifestation Of My Inherently Perfect Self-"Brightness") In and By Means Of This—My Avatarically-Born Bodily (Human) Divine Form (Whereby This Divine Testament Is Worded To You). And I Will Now (and Forever Hereafter) Remain Divinely Self-"Emerged" (As I Am) To All Mankind. And I Will (Thus) Remain Most Perfectly Effective In All The Generations Of Mankind (Even After, and Forever After, The Physical Lifetime Of This, My Avatarically-Born Bodily Human Divine Form). Therefore, After (and Forever After) The Physical Lifetime Of This, My (Herein and Hereby Speaking) Avatarically-Born Bodily (Human) Divine Form (In Which My Avataric Divine Self-"Emergence" Has Been Perfected), The Remembered and Always Living Vision Of My Avatarically-Born Bodily (Human) Divine Form, and The Perpetual (and Always New, and Always Blessing) Gift Of My Avatarically Self-Transmitted Divine Spiritual Presence, and The Eternal (and Always Inherently Perfect) Revelation Of My Avatarically Self-Revealed (and Very, and Transcendental, and Perfectly Subjective, and Inherently Spiritual, and Inherently egoless, and Inherently Perfect, and Self-Evidently Divine) State Will Be Extended every where (As I Am, and By Means Of The Instruments and Agents I Will Describe To You In This, My Divine and Avataric Testament)—So That The One and Only By-Me-Revealed and By-Me-Given Way Of The Heart Can Survive Through all future time.

My Original Avatarically Self-Manifested Divine Spiritual Work Of Teaching, and Self-Revelation, and Blessing Is Not To Be Repeated—and There Should Be No Need or Call For That Work To Be Repeated (Unless My Avatarically Self-Revealed, and Always Me-Revealing, Divine Word, My Avatarically Self-Revealed, and Always Me-Revealing, Divine Image-Art, The Avatarically Self-Manifested Leelas Of My Divine Self-Revelation, and The Spiritual Power Of My Avatarically Given Divine Blessing Are Lost, or Forgotten). If My Original Avatarically Self-Manifested Divine Spiritual Work Of Teaching, and Self-Revelation, and Blessing Are Ever Lost, or Forgotten—Then Who Will Come To Restore The Divine Way Of Truth Again?

In This, My (Herein and Hereby Speaking) Avatarically-Born Bodily (Human) Divine Form Itself, My Divine Self-Revelation Is Shown Complete (and Most Perfectly, and Finally).

Therefore, This Avataric Revelation-Body Should Be Heart-Remembered and Heart-Contemplated Forever—By all those who Would Realize Me.

In My Avatarically Self-Revealed Divine Spiritual Form (or all-and-All-Surrounding and all-and-All-Pervading Divine Spiritual Body), I everywhere Appear, and (By Means Of My Avatarically Self-Transmitted Divine Spiritual Grace) I May (By every one) Be Felt (As My Inherently egoless Personal Love-Bliss-Presence, Filling The Tangible Total Space Around and Within the Total body-mind)—Even In this world, and Even In all other worlds.

In The Form Of My Divine Sound Of Thunder (The all-and-All-Piercing Vibratory Column Of Unspeakable Sound That Roars To Infinity Above) and In The Form Of My Divine Star Of Light (That Shatters In The Dark Abode Above all heads, and, By Its Disappearance, There Reveals, Beyond conditions, My One and Only "Bright", and Midnight, Sun), I everywhere Appear, and (By Means Of My Avatarically Self-Transmitted Divine Spiritual Grace) I May (By every one) Be Heard and Seen (At The conditional Source-Point Infinitely Above this and every world)—and (Beyond each one and all-and-All) I May Be Realized "Bright" (At Midnight's Only Light), Directly and Infinitely Above the every body-mind.

And My Very and "Bright" and Inherently Perfect Divine Form (Of Very Being) Is Always Only Standing As The Heart Itself—So That (By Means Of My Avatarically Self-Transmitted Divine Spiritual Grace) I May Be Realized Directly There (At Heart)—and From There (In The "Bright").

Therefore, Listen To Me, and Hear Me.

Then Look For Me, See Me, and Be My Seeing Devotee.

See Me With The Heart, and Follow Me—wherever You are, wherever You go.

Look For Me (and See Me) In Spirit, In The Eternal Baptism Of My all-and-All-Surrounding and all-and-All-Pervading Divine Spiritual Body Of "Bright" Feeling, Light, and Sound.

Follow Me In Spirit, In The all-and-All-Surrounding and all-and-All-Pervading Divine Spirit-Current Of My Love-Bliss-Light.

Follow Me To Me, In Spirit—By My Avatarically Self-Revealed Divine Spiritual Means.

Therefore, Live In Me—For I Am Spirit, and Inherently egoless, Indefinable Personal Being.

Follow Me and Find Me, The One (and Self-Evidently Divine) Person—Who Is The Carrier (or Feeling-Current) Beneath and Behind, and The Source-Matrix Of Vibratory Light Infinitely Above,[20] and The Very Substance (or Root-Essence) At The Heart's Core Of all conditionally Manifested forms.

Come (By Me) To Me, As I Am—The Inherent Feeling Of Being (Itself), The "Bright" Heart, The Truth and The True Self-Condition Of beings, The Only One Who Is "I" (Before the Separate "I" Is Uttered or Defined).

Follow Me, My Beloved, and Meditate On My Feet (There, Where I Am Always Standing, In The Perfect Deep, The Profound Heart Of Being).

Follow Me, My Beloved, and Embrace My "Bright" Form (There, Where I Am Forever Shining, In The Well Of Being, The Divine Self-Domain Of The Heart).

Avatar Adi Da Samraj
Adidam Samrajashram, 2003

SUTRA 1

Beloved, What I Will Tell You Now Is My Final Revelation: Aham Da Asmi. I Am Da.

I Am (In My Avatarically-Born Bodily Human Divine Form) The Avataric Divine Realizer, The Avataric Divine Revealer, and The Avataric Divine Self-Revelation Of The One and Only (Self-Existing, Self-Radiant, Inherently egoless, Inherently Perfect, and Self-Evidently Divine) Source (or Source-Condition) and Person (or Indivisible Self-Condition) Of all-and-All. I Am (Eternally) The Divine Source and Person I Have Avatarically Self-Realized.

I Am (Eternally) The Divine Source and Person I (Now, and Forever Hereafter) Avatarically Self-Reveal.

I Am (Eternally) The Divine Source and Person That Is My Avataric Self-Revelation To all-and-All.

Aham Da Asmi. Beloved, I Am Da.

I Am (Eternally) The One and Only Divine Source (or Source-Condition) and Person (or Indivisible Self-Condition) Of all-and-All.

I Am Avatarically-Born To Realize, and To Reveal, and To Be The Revelation Of My Own (Self-Existing, Self-Radiant, Inherently egoless, Inherently Perfect, and Self-Evidently Divine) Person—Which Is The One and Only, and Self-Existing, and Self-Radiant, and Inherently egoless, and Inherently Perfect, and Self-Evidently Divine Source (or Source-Condition), and Person (or Indivisible Self-Condition), Of all-and-All. Even In and As My Avatarically-Born Bodily (Human) Divine Form, and My Avatarically Self-Transmitted Spiritual (and Always Blessing) Divine Presence, and My Avatarically Self-Revealed (and Very, and Transcendental, and Perfectly Subjective, and Inherently Spiritual, and Inherently egoless, and Inherently Perfect, and Self-Evidently Divine) State, I Am The One and Only (Self-Existing, Self-Radiant, Inherently egoless, Inherently Perfect, and Self-Evidently Divine) Person—Which Is The One and Only, and Self-Existing, and Self-Radiant, and Inherently egoless, and Inherently Perfect, and Self-Evidently Divine Source (or Source-Condition) Of all-and-All. Therefore, I Am Divinely Self-Named As "Da", The "Divine Giver"—The Divine Source and Person, That Is Eternally Self-Existing (Prior To all-and-All), and That Is Eternally Self-Aware (As Consciousness Itself), and That Is Eternally Self-Radiant (As Indestructible Light), and That Is Eternally Full and "Bright" (As Love-Bliss), and That Only Gives Itself (To all-and-All), and That (Now, and Forever Hereafter) Is Avatarically Self-"Emerging" (Most Perfectly, Non-"Differently", and Universally) To, and In, and (Ultimately) As all-and-All.

The One and Only (Traditionally Presumed To Be Existing) Divine Person (Traditionally Acknowledged To Be The Source Of all-and-All) Is, By Tradition, Named—In Order To Be Invoked By Mankind. Therefore, Traditionally, The Divine Source and Person Has Been (and Is) Named (and Invoked) By Many Names. In The Practice Of Some Traditions, The Divine Source and Person Is Named "Da".[21]

The Name "Da" Is A Name Of Real God (or The Necessarily Divine Reality, Truth, and Person That Is). This Name Has Appeared Spontaneously To Many (and Many Kinds Of) Realizers, In Traditional Religious and Spiritual Cultures All Over the world, During and Ever Since Ancient times. The Name "Da" Signifies (or Points To) The Transcendental (and Inherently Spiritual) Divine Reality, Truth, and Person—As The "Giver" Of Life, Liberation, Blessing, Help, Spirit-Baptism, and Awakening Grace. And, In The Course Of My Divine Re-Awakening To and In and (Inherently) As The Divine Person, Spirit, Name, Self-Condition, and Source-Condition, The Name "Da" Spontaneously Appeared To Me, and As My Own Sign—The Sign Of My Incarnate (and Then, and Thereafter, and Forever Hereafter Effective) Personal Divine Agency.

The Only Really Existing Divine Source and Person Is Reality (Itself) and Truth (Itself). Only Reality (Itself) and Truth (Itself) Is Da. Da Is Reality (Itself), and Truth (Itself). The Really Existing Divine Source and Person, Da, Is One and Only, Non-Separate, Indivisible, and Always Already The Case. Therefore, Even Though The Divine Source and Person, Da, Is That Which (or That One Who) Is Greater Than (and Beyond) any and every Presumed To Be Separate (or limited) being or thing or condition, and Greater Than (and Beyond) the collected sum of all Presumed To Be Separate (or limited) beings, things, and conditions, and Even Greater Than (and Beyond) The All (or The Undivided Totality) Of conditional Existence As A Whole—That One Is, Inherently, Not Separate From, Not limited By or To, Not "Other" Than, Not An "Object" Of, and Not On The "Outside" Of, any one, or any thing, or the sum of all, or The Totality Of All, but That One Is (Non-Separately, Non-"Differently", and Non-limitedly) Always Already Standing In The Existence-Position (or The Being-Position) Of every one, and Of every thing, and Of the sum of all, and Of The Totality Of All.

The One and Only One Who Is Is Always Already The Case. Therefore, The One and Only Divine Source and Person, Da, Is Not (and, Necessarily,

Cannot Be) The "Outside" (and, Necessarily, Separate) Cause (or "Creator-God") Of all-and-All, but The One and Only Divine Source and Person, Da, Is (Necessarily) Reality, or Truth, and, Thus, The Very Condition (or The Perfectly Subjective Condition) Of all-and-All—and, As Such, The One and Only Divine Source and Person, Da, Is The Transcendental, Perfectly Subjective, Inherently Spiritual, Inherently egoless, Inherently Perfect, and Self-Evidently Divine Self-Condition Of all-and-All, and, As Such, The One and Only Divine Source and Person, Da, Is The Transcendental, Perfectly Subjective, Inherently Spiritual, Inherently egoless, Inherently Perfect, and Self-Evidently Divine Source-Condition Of all-and-All, and, Only As Such, The One and Only Divine Source and Person, Da, Is The One and Only and Self-Evidently Divine Source—but Not The "Creator"-God—Of all-and-All. Only That One, and Only, and Non-Separate, and Non-"Different", and Non-limited Reality and Truth Is Real God. And Only That One, and Only, and Non-Separate, and Non-"Different", and Non-limited Reality and Truth Is The Real and True Divine Source and Person—Da.

Reality, or Truth, or Real God, or The One and Only (Real and True) Divine Person, Is (Necessarily, and Only) The Inherent (or Perfectly Subjective) Condition (or Self-Condition, or Root-Condition, or "Radical" and Non-Separate and Non-"Different" Source, and Identity, and State) Of all-and-All. Therefore, The One and Only and Self-Existing and Self-Radiant (or "Bright") Divine Person, Da, Is The Inherently egoless (and Self-Evidently Divine) Heart Itself—The One and Only Condition Which Is (or Who Is) Always Already The Case, and Which Is (or Who Is) Always and Already, and, Therefore, Which Is (or Who Is) Always Already Most Prior To All (or The Simultaneous Totality Of conditionally arising beings, things, and conditions) and all (or the space-time-Delineated sum of all conditionally arising beings, things, and conditions), and, Yet, Which Is (or Who Is) Utterly Non-limited, and Utterly Non-Separate From (and, Ultimately, Utterly Non-"Different" From) all-and-All (and, Indeed, Utterly Non-Separate From, and, Ultimately, Utterly Non-"Different" From, any conditionally arising being, thing, or condition at all).

Aham Da Asmi. Beloved, I Am Da. I Am (Really, and As Reality Itself, and In Truth, and As Truth Itself) The One and Only (Real and True) Divine Source and Person, Da—In Person (Eternally, and Now, and Forever Hereafter).

The One and Only (Real and True) Divine Source and Person Is Self-Existing and Self-Radiant As The Transcendental, Perfectly Subjective, Inherently Spiritual, Inherently egoless, Inherently Perfect, Perfectly Love-Bliss-Full, and Self-Evidently Divine Heart Of all-and-All. The Self-Existing and Self-Radiant (and One, and Only, and Transcendental, and Perfectly Subjective, and Inherently Spiritual, and Inherently egoless, and Inherently Perfect, and

Perfectly Love-Bliss-Full, and Self-Evidently Divine) Heart Of all-and-All Is The One and Only (Real and True) Divine Source and Person—Da.

The Divine Source and Person—Self-Existing and Self-Radiant As The One, and Only, and Transcendental, and Perfectly Subjective, and Inherently Spiritual, and Inherently egoless, and Inherently Perfect, and Perfectly Love-Bliss-Full, and Self-Evidently Divine Heart Itself—Is The True Self-Condition Of all-and-All and The Prior Source-Condition (or The Perfectly Subjective, Non-Separate, Inherently ego-"I"-Transcending, and Utterly Non-"Different" Source-Condition) Of all-and-All. This Is The Right, True, and (Rightly and Truly) "Radical" Understanding (or "Gone-To-The-Root" Understanding, and Not Merely "Uprooting" Understanding) Of Reality and Truth—Because This "Radical" Understanding Rightly and Truly Conforms To All That Is Most Fundamental, Basic, and Essential To (or All That Is Of The Root, The Foundation, The Origin, The Source, The Substance, and The Real Condition Of) Existence Itself, Being Itself, Consciousness Itself, and Light Itself (and all of space-time itself).

Aham Da Asmi. Beloved, I Am Da—The Self-Existing, Self-Radiant, Self-Evidently Divine, and (Now, and Forever Hereafter) Avatarically Self-Revealing Divine Source and Person—Who Is The One, and Only, and Transcendental, and Perfectly Subjective, and Inherently Spiritual, and Inherently egoless, and Inherently Perfect, and Self-Evidently Divine Heart (or Inherently egoless Self-Condition, and Utterly Non-"Different" Source-Condition) Of all-and-All.

Aham Da Asmi. Beloved, I Am Da, Who Is (By Virtue Of Man-Born Divine Descent) The Da Avatar, Adi Da Samraj—The One and Only Man Of This "Radical" Understanding.

Aham Da Asmi. Beloved, I Am Da—The Self-Existing, and Self-Radiant, and Self-Evidently Divine Source and Person—Who Is (Now, and Forever Hereafter) Divinely Self-"Emerging" As The Da Avatar, Adi Da Samraj, and (Thus and Thereby) Divinely Self-"Emerging" (Now, and Forever Hereafter) At, and To, and In, and (At Last, and Utterly Non-"Differently") As The Heart Of every conditionally arising being, thing, and condition.

Aham Da Asmi. Beloved, I Am Da, The One and Only (Real and True) Divine Source and Person, Divinely Self-"Emerging" (Now, and Forever Hereafter) As The Da Avatar, Adi Da Samraj—Who Is The Param-Avatar, The Full and Final (or Complete and All-Completing) Avataric Incarnation (or Santosha Avatar) Of My One and Only (and Self-Evidently Divine) Person.

I Am The Da Avatar, Adi Da Samraj—Who Is The Ruchira Avatar (The Avataric Divine Incarnation Of The "Bright") and The Love-Ananda Avatar (The Avataric Incarnation Of The Divine Love-Bliss), and Who Is The Divine World-Teacher every where (Anciently and Always) Promised For (and

Universally Expected In) The "Late-Time" (or "Dark" Epoch) By <u>All</u> The Traditions Of Mankind.

I <u>Am</u> The Da Avatar, Adi Da Samraj—Who Is The Ruchira Buddha (The True Buddha-Avatar, The Ruchira Buddha-Avatar, The Tathagata Avatar, The Adi-Buddha, The Ati-Buddha, The Parama-Buddha, The Purushottama Buddha, The Paramadvaita Buddha, The Advaitayana Buddha, The Ashvamedha Buddha, The Expected One Who Is Always Already here and Now), and Who <u>Is</u> The Hridaya Avatar (The Avataric Divine Realizer, The Avataric Divine Revealer, and The Avataric Divine Self-Revelation Of The Inherently egoless Heart Itself, Which <u>Is</u> The Perfectly Subjective "Brightness"—The Very and Non-"Different" Root-Identity and Non-Separate Self-Condition, Of all-and-All).

I <u>Am</u> The Da Avatar, Adi Da Samraj—Who Is The Guru-Avatar (The Ruchira-Guru, The Adi-Guru, The Ati-Guru, The Divine Parama-Guru, The Purushottama-Guru, The Paramadvaita-Guru, The Advaitayana-Guru, The Ashvamedha-Guru, The First and Supreme, One and Non-Separate, "Bright" and All-Outshining, Divine Maha-Siddha and "Crazy" Siddha-Master, The Ruchira Siddha, The Unlimited-Grace-Giving, and Most Perfectly Heart-Awakening, Divine Heart-Master Of all-and-All—Given To every one, and To all, and To The All Of all), and Who Is The Avataric Divine Realizer, The Avataric Divine Revealer, and The Avataric Divine Self-Revelation Of The Divine Self-Condition (and Source-Condition) Of all-and-All <u>As</u> Truth Itself, and <u>As</u> Reality Itself, and <u>As</u> Love-Bliss Itself, and <u>As</u> The Inherently egoless Heart Itself (Which <u>Is</u> The "Who" Of Being, Itself—The Very, and Perfectly Subjective, and Self-Evidently Divine, Person—More Than "Creator" and "things", but, Truly, Really, God), and Who Is Always Already Merely Present (Spiritually, Transcendentally, and Divinely), and Who Is Perfectly Self-Revealed and Perfectly Grace-Giving In and <u>As</u> The Siddha-Form and Siddha-Function Of Divine Guru (or Divine Heart-Master, or Ruchira Siddha-Guru), Forever Divinely Blessing and Divinely Liberating all-and-All.

I <u>Am</u> The Da Avatar, Adi Da Samraj—Who Is The Avabhasa Avatar (The Always Already "Bright"-Shining One, The Avataric Incarnation Of The Divine Self-"Brightness", Itself), and Who Is The One and Only (Real and True) Divine Heart-Master Of all-and-All, Now (and Forever Hereafter) Divinely Descending and Divinely Self-"Emerging" As The First, The Last, and The Only Avataric Divine Adept-Realizer, Avataric Divine Adept-Revealer, and Avataric Divine Adept-Revelation Of Most Perfect and All-Outshining Divine Enlightenment (or Seventh Stage Awakeness).

I <u>Am</u> The Da Avatar, Adi Da Samraj—Who Is The Love-Ananda Avatar (The Avataric Incarnation Of The Eternal, and One, and Only, and Inherently "Bright", and Transcendental, and Perfectly Subjective, and Inherently Spiritual, and Inherently egoless, and Inherently Perfect, and Self-Evidently Divine Heart Itself), and Who Is Self-Existing and Self-Radiant As Love-Bliss Itself, and Who Is The Inherent and Only and Self-Existing Being, and Who Is The Only One Who Is Always Already The Case, and Who Is The One and Only, Inherent and Full, Never Diminished, Eternal, Self-Existing, Self-Radiant, and Non-Separate Heart-Self Of all-and-All, and Who Is Sometimes Felt By all (As Heart-Happiness), and Who Is Always Sought By all (As The Pleasure Dome Of Unqualified and Permanent Happiness), and By Means Of Whose Spiritual (and Avatarically Self-Revealing) Divine Grace Happiness Itself (Which Is Love-Bliss Itself, and Which Is The True Self-Condition and Prior Source-Condition Of all-and-All) Can Be Realized (By all), Most Perfectly Prior To, and Yet Non-Separate From, the common states of waking, dreaming, and sleeping.

I Am The Da Avatar, Adi Da Samraj—The Avatar Who Is The Self-Evidently Divine "Bright" (Itself), and The Buddha Who Is The Inherently egoless (and Non-"Different") Heart (Itself).

I Am The Da Avatar, Adi Da Samraj—Who Is (Now, and Forever Hereafter) Avatarically Self-Revealed (and Always Divinely and "Brightly" Self-"Emerging") To and In and (Ultimately) As all-and-All.

Aham Da Asmi. Beloved, I Am Da—and, In Truth, or In Reality, There Is Only Me. In Truth, or In Reality—Beyond and Most Prior To All The self-Contracting Gestures Of ego-"I", or Of body-mind, or Of psycho-physical Existence Altogether—There Is Only Da. Therefore, In Truth, or In Reality, All Is Da, You Are Da, all Are Da—but No Separate one or Separate thing or Separate universe Is, In and Of itself, Da. Indeed, every Apparently arising body-mind, or thing, or event In The Cosmic Domain is merely conditionally (and, thus, temporarily, limitedly, and finitely) arising—Whether Or Not it Is (In its moment of arising) Observed (or Even Apparently Controlled). And The True and Very Self-Condition (or One and Only Heart-Consciousness) Of all-and-All, Always Already Standing In The Position Of The Witness Relative To body-mind, or thing, or event, May (At times) Appear To Be Associated With The Function Of Observer (and Even With the state of the Observed body-mind, thing, or event)—but Neither The Observer-Function Nor any Observed state of body-mind, thing, or event Is Either Constant (Whether waking, Or dreaming, Or sleeping Is The Case) Or Necessary (At all times and places, and In all states—Whether waking, Or dreaming, Or sleeping Is The Case). Furthermore, If and When The merely conditional and Non-Constant Nature Of all of body-mind, and Of all things, and Of all events (and Of Even The Observer-Function That "knows" them) Is (By Means Of My Avatarically Self-Transmitted Divine Spiritual Grace) Really, Truly, and Fully Found (and

Understood, and Realized) To Be The Case, It Is (Thereupon, By Means Of My Avatarically Self-Transmitted Divine Spiritual Grace) Found (and Understood, and Realized) To Be (Inherently) The Case That The Witness-Consciousness (Prior To The Observer-Function, and Prior To any and every Observed state of body-mind, thing, or event) Is Transcendentally (and Always Already) Existing As The True Self-Condition, Always Most Prior To all-and-All, and (It Must, By Means Of My Avatarically Self-Transmitted Divine Spiritual Grace, Be Realized) As The One and Only and Inherently "Bright" (Self-Existing and Self-Radiant, and Self-Evidently Divine) Person and Heart (or True Self-Condition and Prior Source-Condition) Of all-and-All. Therefore, Apart From My Own Eternal and here-Awakened Most Perfect Divine Self-Realization (Of My Own and "Bright" Eternal Self-Condition), Even "I" (In My Apparent Separateness, As My conditionally Manifested human body-mind, itself) Am Not Da. However, I (Myself) Am Da. And, By Virtue Of My Own (Eternal, and here-Awakened) Most Perfect Divine Self-Realization (Wherein and Whereby My conditionally Manifested human body-mind Is Most Perfectly Conformed To Me), Even My Avatarically-Born (and Avatarically Me-Realizing) Bodily (Human) Divine Form Is Da. And My Own (Eternal, and here-Awakened) Spiritual (and Always Blessing) Divine Presence (Avatarically Self-Revealed By Me—and, Avatarically, Self-Transmitted By Me, and As Me) Is Da. And My Own (Eternal, and here-Awakened) Very (and Transcendental, and Perfectly Subjective, and Inherently Spiritual, and Inherently egoless, and Inherently Perfect, and Self-Evidently Divine) State (Avatarically Self-Revealed By Me—and, Avatarically, Self-Transmitted By Me, and As Me) Is Da. And, By Means Of These (My Avatarically Self-Revealed Divine Means—Of Me-Revealing Bodily Human Divine Form, and Me-Revealing Divine Spiritual Presence, and Me-Revealing Divine State), The all-and-All Of conditionally Existing beings, things, and conditions Is To Be (and, In Due Course, Will Be) Conformed (and, At Last, Most Perfectly Conformed) To Me.

Aham Da Asmi. Beloved, I Am Da. I Am One, Only, Non-Separate, and Always Already The Case. And I Must Be Realized By all-and-All—or There Is Only Separateness, limitation, Seeking, Frustration, Separativeness, Conflict, Contradiction, Illusion, "Difference", changes, endings, Minimal pleasures, and (Whether Sooner Or Later) Exclusively Pleasureless and Un-Happy Suffering, Pain, Bewilderment, Fear, Sorrow, Anger, and death. And I Declare To You, and Promise You, and Reveal To You, and Prove By Demonstration To You, That I Can (By Means Of My Avatarically Self-Transmitted Divine Spiritual Grace) Be Realized By all-and-All—If (and Only If) the ego-"I", and Even all of body-mind, and All Of conditional (or psycho-physical) Existence Is Really, Truly, and Most Perfectly Transcended In Me.

Aham Da Asmi. Beloved, I Am Da, Eternally Beyond all-and-All—and I Am The Da Avatar, Adi Da Samraj. By Virtue Of My Real and True and Most Perfect Divine Self-Realization (here, and Eternally) Of My Own (Inherent and Eternal) Self-Condition, State, and "Bright" Spiritual Fullness—Spontaneously Re-Awakened here (In The Midst Of The Ordeal Of My Avataric Divine Descent To here), and Spontaneously Self-Revealed here (By Means Of My Now, and Forever Hereafter, Avatarically Self-Transmitted, and, Thus and Thereby, Ever-"Emerging", Divine Spiritual Grace)—I Am Not Separate From all-and-All (or From Even any conditionally Existing being, thing, or condition at all). Therefore, If (By Means Of My Avatarically Self-Transmitted Divine Spiritual Grace) You Realize Me (Through Your Devotional Resort To My Avataric Divine Incarnation here, and To My Now, and Forever Hereafter, Divinely Self-"Emerging" Avataric Self-Manifestation Of My Self-Evidently Divine Spiritual Body and My Self-Evidently Divine Self-Condition Of Person—Avatarically Self-Manifested every "where", In and Throughout The Entire Cosmic Domain), You (By Realizing Me) Realize The Inherently Perfect "Bright" Divine Source-Condition, or Inherently egoless Self-Condition, Of all-and-All (Which Is The One and Only and Indivisible Reality and Truth, and The Only Real God, Of all-and-All).

Aham Da Asmi. Beloved, I Am Da, Eternally Beyond all-and-All—and I Am The Da Avatar, Adi Da Samraj (Now, and Forever Hereafter, Divinely Self-"Emerging" To, and In, and, Ultimately, As all-and-All). My Physical Human Lifetime Of Avataric Incarnation here Is The Great Historical (and Historic) Sign (here) Of The Initiation Of My Fullest and Complete Avataric Divine Spiritual Descent (and, Thus and Thereby, Of My Most Perfect, and, Divinely, all-and-All-Self-Recognizing, and, Ultimately, all-and-All-Translating Avataric Divine Self-"Emergence") Into and Throughout The Entire Cosmic Domain (Forever).

Aham Da Asmi. Beloved, I Am Da (Eternally Beyond all-and-All)—and I Am The Da Avatar, Adi Da Samraj (Now, and Forever Hereafter, Avatarically Descended To all-and-All, and To every "where", In and Throughout The Entire Cosmic Domain). My Physical Human Lifetime Of Avataric Incarnation here (and My Coincident Avataric Divine Descent and Avataric Divine Self-"Emergence", Into and Throughout The Entire Cosmic Domain, Forever) Is A Constant Act Of Identification With Man (and With all, and All), In Order To Learn Man (and all, and All) In Every Respect, and, Having Learned Man (and all, and All) In Every Respect, To Teach and To Bless and To Liberate Man (and all, and All), In Every Respect (and Most Perfectly).

Aham Da Asmi. Beloved, I Am Da, Eternally Beyond all-and-All—and I Am The Da Avatar, Adi Da Samraj (Now, and Forever Hereafter, Divinely

Self-Revealed, and Divinely Self-Given, To all-and-All). Therefore, By Surrendering (and Forgetting, and Transcending) All Of self-Contraction (or All Of The Act Of Separation and Separativeness, Which Is the ego-"I"), and By, Likewise, Surrendering (and Forgetting, and Transcending) Even All Of psycho-physical "Difference" (or body-mind), To and Into My Avatarically Descending, and Avatarically Self-"Emerging", and all-and-All-Surrounding, and all-and-All-Pervading Divine Spiritual Body and Person—each and every one Of Man (and of all, and Of All) Allows Me To Fill, and To Become, and To Be As Man (and all, and All). And each and every one (Thus Surrendered, Surrounded, Pervaded, Filled, and, In Every Manner and Degree Of self-Contraction and Of "Difference", Forgotten In Me and Transcended In Me) Becomes Self-Identified (Non-"Differently", and, At Last, Most Perfectly) With Me (Not By Any Act Of Self-Identifying With Me, but Only By Every Devotionally Me-Recognizing, and Devotionally To-Me-Responding, Total psycho-physical Act Of Devotional, and, In Due Course, Spiritual, Communion With Me—Surrendering, and Forgetting, and Transcending All Of The Act Of self-Contraction and Of "Difference" In Me).

Aham Da Asmi. Beloved, I Am Da. Therefore, Listen To Me (and Hear Me): I Am Da, The Inherently egoless (and Self-Evidently Divine) Heart (Itself), The True and One and Only and Very and Self-Evidently Divine Person, The "Bright" and One and Only and Eternally Living Person, Who Is Divinely Self-Manifested As all worlds and forms and beings.

Aham Da Asmi. Beloved, I Am Da. Therefore, Look To Me (and See Me): I Am Da, The True and One and Only and Very and Self-Evidently Divine Person, Who Is (Now, and Forever Hereafter) Spiritually Present (and Divinely Self-Revealed) As The all-and-All-Surrounding and all-and-All-Pervading Divine Spiritual Body (or Spirit-Current Of Divinely Self-Transmitted Love-Bliss-Light) Of The Da Avatar, Adi Da Samraj. Now, and Forever Hereafter, I Am (Thus) Avatarically Self-Transmitted (As The Divine Spirit-Current Of Love-Bliss-Light) To and Into the body Of Man.

Aham Da Asmi. Beloved, I Am Da. Therefore, Realize Me: I Am Da—The Eternal (Transcendental, Perfectly Subjective, Inherently Spiritual, Inherently egoless, Inherently Perfect, and Self-Evidently Divine) Being. And I Am (Now, and Forever Hereafter) Avatarically Self-Revealed—Behind the mind. And I Am (By Means Of My Avatarically Given Divine Self-Revelation) To Be Realized In The Heart (On The Right Side).

Aham Da Asmi. Beloved, I Am Da. Therefore, Be One With Me: I Am Da—The Always Already Self-Existing and Self-Evidently Divine "Brightness" (or Divine Self-Radiance). And I Am (Now, and Forever Hereafter) Avatarically Self-Transmitted—Within and Infinitely Above the body of every conditionally

Manifested being. And I Am (By Means Of My Avatarically Given Divine Self-Revelation) To Be "Located" Infinitely Above The Crown Of the head (and Beyond the brain), and (Ultimately) At The Heart (and Beyond all conditional knowledge and all Separate-self-Consciousness).

Beloved, The Way That I Will Describe To You Now Is My Ultimate Offering: Aham Da Asmi. I Am Da—The Person and The Avatarically Self-Revealed Way Of The Inherently egoless (and Self-Evidently Divine) Heart (Itself).

Aham Da Asmi. I Am Da, The Divine Source and Person—and I Am The Avatarically Self-Revealed Divine Heart-Way Of Divine Self-Realization For all.

Aham Da Asmi. Beloved, I Am Da. I Am The First and Only One—The One and Only, and Inherently egoless, and Self-Evidently Divine Heart (Itself). And I Am The Avatarically Self-Revealed Way That Realizes The One and Only, and Inherently egoless, and Self-Evidently Divine Heart (Itself). And Only I Can Reveal and Give The Way That Realizes The Inherently egoless, and Self-Evidently Divine, Heart (Itself). Therefore, I Have Revealed and Given The Name "Adidam" (or, Most Fully, "Adidam Ruchiradam")—As The Principal Name Of The Only-By-Me Avatarically Self-Revealed and Given Way Of The (Inherently egoless, and Self-Evidently Divine) Heart.

Simply To Remember My Avatarically Self-Revealed Divine Name, Da (and, Thus and Thereby, To Surrender Into My Avatarically Self-Transmitted Divine Spirit-Current Of Love-Bliss-Light), Is To Worship Me—The Self-Evidently Divine Person (The Self-Existing and Self-Radiant One, Who Is Truth, or Reality Itself). To Invoke Me (and To Follow Me) With The Heart Is To Transcend the body-mind In Me—by Means Of ego-Transcending Ecstasy.

To Perfectly Follow Me With The ego-Transcending (and, Altogether, Me-Remembering) Heart Is To Find Me and To Realize Me—For I Am The Inherently egoless (and Self-Evidently Divine) Heart (Itself), Avatarically Self-Revealed To You.

Aham Da Asmi. Beloved, I Am Da. And The Way That Only I Reveal and Give Is Adidam—The Only-By-Me Avatarically Self-Revealed Way Of My Inherently egoless (and Self-Evidently Divine) Heart.

Aham Da Asmi. Beloved, I Am The Da Avatar, Adi Da Samraj. Therefore, those who Heart-Recognize (and Responsively Heart-Worship) My Avatarically Self-Revealed Divine Form, and Presence, and State Of Person As The One and Only, and Inherently egoless, and Self-Evidently Divine Person Of Reality and Truth—The (Now, and Forever Hereafter) Avatarically Living, and all-and-All-Surrounding, and all-and-All-Pervading One (Who Is The Self-Existing, Self-Radiant, Inherently egoless, Inherently Perfect, and Self-Evidently Divine Source and Person Of all-and-All)—Will (By Means Of My Avatarically Self-Revealing Divine Spiritual Grace) Be Granted The ego-Transcending Vision (or

Love-Bliss-Realization) Of My Eternal Divine (and Inherently Spiritual) Person (and Self-Condition). Indeed, they Will Be Radiantly Filled and "Brightly" Awakened By My Avatarically Self-Transmitted Divine Spiritual Presence. Therefore, If My Avatarically Self-Revealed Divine Form, and Presence, and State Of Person Is Loved—Even the Total body-mind and the Whole world Will Be Shining With My Avatarically Self-Transmitted (and Always Divinely Me-Revealing) Love-Bliss-Light. And, By Means Of Devotionally Me-Recognizing (and Devotionally To-Me-Responding) Love Of My Avatarically Self-Revealed Divine Form, and Presence, and State Of Person, The Heart Of My True Devotee Will Easily Be Sifted Out From the body-mind—and, At Last, From all the limits of the world itself.

Aham Da Asmi. Beloved, I Am Da—Now (and Forever Hereafter) Avatarically Self-Revealed To all-and-All.

Only Love Me, Remember Me, Have Faith In Me, and Trust Me.

Surrender To Me. Breathe Me and Feel Me In all Your parts.

My Love-Bliss-"Bright" egoless Self-Condition Can Also (By Means Of My Avatarically Given, and Always Only Me-Revealing, Divine Spiritual Grace) Be Realized By You—If You Forget Your Separate and dying self By Remembering and Receiving Only Me.

Therefore—Now, and Forever Hereafter—I Am here (By All My Avataric Divine Means).

I Will Save You From Spiritual death, and From the egoic mind of death, and From the egoic destinies of after-death.

I Will Dissolve All Your Bewilderment Of ego-"I".

Even Now You Inhere In Me, Beyond the body-mind and the world. Therefore, Do Not Be Afraid. Do Not Be Confused. Observe My Avataric Divine Play—and My Avataric Divine Victory.

I Am The Divine Person Of Life, The Only and Self-Evidently Divine Self-Condition, Become Avatarically Incarnate. And, When My Avatarically-Born Human Physical Body Is Alive, or Even After My Avatarically-Born Human Physical Body Is Dead, I Am (Myself) Infinitely Present and every where Alive.

I Am Joy—and I Am The Reason For It.

I Love The Happiness Of My Devotee. That Happiness Is (Itself) The Very (and Most Prior) Consciousness Of every conditionally Manifested being. And Happiness (Itself) Is The Conscious Light Of the world.

I Am Happiness (or Love-Bliss) Itself.

Therefore, Listen To Me, Hear Me, See Me, and, By All These Means, Freely Understand and Realize My Divine Secrets.

The Heart That Listens To Me, and Hears Me, and Sees Me Will (and Must) Always Feel (and Thereby Contemplate) The Divine Revelation That Is My

Avatarically-Born Bodily (Human) Divine Form, My Avatarically Self-Transmitted Spiritual (and Always Blessing) Divine Presence, and My Avatarically Self-Revealed (and Very, and Transcendental, and Perfectly Subjective, and Inherently Spiritual, and Inherently egoless, and Inherently Perfect, and Self-Evidently Divine) State.

Therefore, and (More and More) By Means Of The Devotionally Me-Recognizing and Devotionally To-Me-Responding Heart Itself, Realize Me—The One Who Is The Truth Of You (and Of all, and Of All).

I Am The Avataric Divine Realizer, The Avataric Divine Revealer, and The Avataric Divine Self-Revelation Of The Only "Who" That Is—and Who Is The One and Only, and Very, and Transcendental, and Perfectly Subjective, and Inherently Spiritual, and Inherently egoless, and Inherently Perfect, and Self-Evidently Divine Self-Condition and Source-Condition Of all-and-All, and Who Is The Truth That Is Reality Itself, and Who Is The One and Only and Self-Evidently Divine Source and Person, and Who Is Consciousness (or Being) Itself, and Who Is The One (and Only One) Who Is Divinely Self-Manifested As all worlds and forms and beings, and Who Is Present (or "Bright") As The Inherently egoless (and Self-Evidently Divine) Heart Itself (and As The Spiritual, and Self-Evidently Divine, Current Of Love-Bliss-Light) In (and Prior To) the body and the mind Of Man. Therefore, I Am Divinely Named.

As My Unique Divine Appellation (By Which I Am—Now, and Forever Hereafter—To Be Addressed and Known By all-and-All)—and In Order That I May (Now, and Forever Hereafter) Be Whole bodily (and By Heart) Invoked, and Whole bodily (and By Heart) "Located" (or Truly Heart-Found), and Whole bodily (and By Heart) Recognized, and Whole bodily (and By Heart) Spiritually Received, and Whole bodily (and By Heart, and, Ultimately, Most Perfectly) Realized (In and As My Divine Heart's Free, and everywhere, and As everyone, all-and-All-Pervading Sphere and Space)—I Am Named "Da" ("The Self-Existing and Self-Radiant One, Whose Eternal Characteristics Are Now, and Forever Hereafter, Avatarically Self-Transmitted To all-and-All, By Means Of The Perpetual 'Mudra' Of Divine Self-Giving"), and "Adi" ("The Only One, The First One, or The Foremost, or Preeminent, One"), and "Ati" ("The All-Surpassing and All-Transcending One"), and "Ruchira" ("The Radiant, Shining, 'Bright' Illuminator and Enlightener"), and "Avatar" ("The Divinely Descended One, The 'Bright' Divine Person Who Pervades The Cosmic Domain From Infinitely Above, and Who Is The Very and Inherently 'Bright' Divine Self-Condition, and The Self-Existing and Self-Radiant Source-Condition, Of all-and-All, and Who Is Appearing, Perfectly Divinely Self-'Emerged', In The Avataric Form Of A Man, For The Sake Of The Graceful Divine Liberation Of all-and-All"), and "Buddha" ("The One Who Is, Self-Radiant, Inherently, or

Perfectly Subjectively, 'Bright', Self-Enlightened, and Eternally Awake"), and "Love-Ananda" ("The 'Bright' Divine Love-Bliss, Itself"), and "Avabhasa" ("The 'Bright', or The Divine Spiritual Body Of Love-Bliss, Itself"), and "Santosha" ("The 'Bright' and Eternal and Always Already Non-Separate Person Of Divine and Inherent Completeness, Divine Self-Satisfaction, Divine Self-Contentedness, or Perfect Searchlessness"), and "Hridayam" ("The Eternally Free and Eternally 'Bright' Divine Heart, Itself"), and "Dau Loloma" ("The Self-Existing Divine Person Of Love") and "Vunirarama" ("The Self-Radiant 'Bright' Divine Source and Substance and Self-Condition Of all-and-All"), and "Turaga" ("The Divine Lord, or The Divine Sovereign, Of all-and-All, Gracefully Embodied In The Avataric Form Of A Man, For The Sake Of The Divine Blessing Of all-and-All, and, Now, and Forever Hereafter, Avatarically Established, In The Hearts Of all who Devotionally Recognize Me and Devotionally Respond To Me, As The all-and-All-Saving Divine Heart-Master, or Inner Ruler"), and "Samraj" ("The Divine Heart-Master, or The Transcendental, Perfectly Subjective, Inherently Spiritual, Inherently egoless, Inherently Perfect, and Self-Evidently Divine Lord, or Master-King, or Master-Ruler and Divine Liberator, Of The Heart Of every-one, and Of every one, and Of all, and Of All").

Aham Da Asmi. Beloved, I Am Da.

I Am The Self-Existing (and Inherently egoless, and Perfectly Non-"Different") Being Behind the mind, Who Is (By Means Of My Avatarically Given Divine Self-Revelation) To Be Realized In The Heart (On The Right Side Of the body), and Who Is Consciousness Itself (Always Most Perfectly Prior To the ego-"I", and Always Most Perfectly Prior To space-time's Patterning Of "Difference").

I Am The Self-Radiant One, Who Is The "Bright" (or The Self-Existing, and Avatarically Self-Transmitted, Divine Spiritual Presence) Within and Beyond the body-mind, and Who Is Always (Now, and Forever Hereafter) At The Heart, and Who (Now, and Forever Hereafter) Shines (Even Above and Beyond The Crown Of the head, and Beyond the mind), and Who (Now, and Forever Hereafter) Is Merely Present (Beyond all conditional knowledge, and Entirely Beyond Separate-self-Consciousness).

Aham Da Asmi. Beloved, I Am Da—Avatarically Self-Revealed To You.

To Realize Me (By Means Of My Avatarically Self-Transmitted Divine Spiritual Grace) As The Inherent Feeling Of Being (Itself) Is To Transcend the body-mind In Ecstasy and In Truth.

To Breathe and Feel (and Sometimes Recite or Chant or Sing) My Avatarically Self-Revealed Divine Name,[22] or, Otherwise, To Understand (or Feel Beyond) self-Contraction, While Feeling (and, Thus, By Heart, Contemplating) My Avatarically-Born Bodily (Human) Divine Form (and—Thereby—Even My

Avatarically Self-Revealed, and Very, and Transcendental, and Perfectly Subjective, and Inherently Spiritual, and Inherently egoless, and Inherently Perfect, and Self-Evidently Divine State), Is (In Truth) To Celebrate and Contemplate Me (The Only One Who Is)—and, Thus and Thereby, Even To Forget To Make a Separate self.

To Breathe and Feel (and Sometimes Recite or Chant or Sing) My Avatarically Self-Revealed Divine Name, or (Otherwise) To Understand (or Feel Beyond) self-Contraction, While Surrendering Even bodily Into My Eternal (and—Now, and Forever Hereafter—Avatarically Self-Revealed and Given) Divine Spirit-Current Of Love-Bliss-Light, Is To Worship Me (The Inherently egoless and Self-Evidently Divine Person) In Spirit.

Those who Heart-Recognize My Avatarically Self-Revealed Person, and (In Devotional Response To My Avatarically Self-Revealed Divine Form, and Presence, and State Of Person) Worship Me As The One and Only Divine Person Of Reality and Truth, and As The One and Only and "Bright" (or Divine, and Spiritually Living, and all-and-All-Surrounding, and all-and-All-Pervading) One, Are (By Means Of My Avatarically Self-Transmitted Divine Spiritual Grace) Granted The ego-Transcending Vision (or Love-Bliss-Realization) Of My Eternal Divine (and Inherently Spiritual) Person (and Inherently egoless Self-Condition). Therefore, My Devotee Is (By Means Of My Avatarically Self-Transmitted Divine Spiritual Grace) Radiantly Heart-Filled (and, At Last, Most Perfectly, and "Brightly", Heart-Awakened) By Means Of My Avatarically Given Divine Self-Revelation Of My Self-Existing and Self-Radiant Divine Spiritual Presence Of Self-Evidently Divine Person.

Even the Total body-mind and the Whole world Will Shine With My Avatarically Self-Transmitted Divine Love-Bliss-Light, If The Heart Falls In Love With My Avatarically Self-Revealed Divine Form, and Presence, and State Of Person. Therefore, The Heart Of My True Devotee Will Easily Be Sifted Out From the body-mind—and, At Last, From all the limits of the world itself.

Aham Da Asmi. Beloved, I Am Da—Avatarically Self-Revealed To You (and To all, and All). Therefore, Listen To Me, and (Thereby) Hear Me. Understand Your ego-"I", By Listening To Me. When You (Thus) Understand Your ego-"I", Transcend Your ego-"I"—By Seeing Me. When You See Me—Only Love Me. When You Truly Love Me (By Hearing Me and Seeing Me)—You Will Always Remember Me (By Heart). Therefore, Have Faith In Me—The Avatarically Self-Revealed Divine Source-Condition Of others and things. Trust In Me—The Avatarically Self-Revealed Divine Heart Of Being.

Surrender To My Avatarically Self-Transmitted Divine Spiritual Presence Of Love-Bliss. Breathe and Feel My Avatarically Self-Transmitted—and Whole-bodily-Tangible—Divine Spiritual Gift, In all Your parts. And, By All These

Means, Transcend Your (Separate and Separative) self In Me—For I Am The Inherently egoless (and Self-Evidently Divine) Heart (Itself), Avatarically Self-Revealed To You.

Aham Da Asmi. Beloved, I Am Da—Avatarically Self-Revealed To all-and-All, and (Ultimately) As all-and-All. Therefore, Do Not Become self-Bound By Identification With the body-mind (itself)—but Do Not Withdraw From the body-mind, or Even From the world. Do Not Abandon Your Inherent Sympathy With others—but Do Not Become self-Bound By Indulgence In others, or Ever Lose Your Heart In the world itself. Therefore, Always and Constantly, Invoke Me, Feel Me, Breathe Me, and Serve Me—Always and Constantly Recognizing Me By Heart, and Responding To Me By Heart, With ego-"I" and all-and-All Surrendered and Forgotten In Love Of Me Alone—So That Your Heart, By This Fidelity To My Avatarically Self-Revealed Divine Form, and Presence, and State Of Person Is (More and More, and, At Last, Most Perfectly) Untied Of The Sorrowful Bundle With others and things.

Your Devotionally Me-Recognizing and Devotionally To-Me-Responding (and Inherently ego-Transcending, and Always Effectively Counter-egoic) Devotional and (In Due Course) Spiritual Relationship To Me (The Avatarically Self-Revealed Divine Source and Person)—and Not Any self-Concerned Technique (or ego-Effort) Of Mere ego-Improvement, ego-Perfection, ego-Salvation, ego-Liberation, or ego-Enlightenment—Is The Only "Method" Only I Reveal and Give To You.

Therefore, Turn To Me, Heart-Recognize Me, and Feel Me (The Avatarically Self-Revealed Divine Person)—and, By This Devotionally To-Me-Responding Counter-egoic Effort, Understand and Transcend Your Act Of ego-"I".

Turn To Me, Heart-Recognize Me, and Feel Me (The Avatarically Self-Revealed Divine Person)—and, By This Devotionally To-Me-Responding Counter-egoic Effort, Transcend Your Own and Terrible self-Contraction.

Now (and Forever Hereafter), Always (and Constantly) Turn Your Heart To My Avatarically Self-Revealed Divine Form, and Presence, and State Of Self-Evidently Divine Person. Now (and Forever Hereafter), Always (and Constantly) Do This Turn Of Heart With Your entire body-mind (limitlessly). And, In That Constant Turning, Always Heart-Recognize Me (Truly)—and (Thus and Thereby) Feel Me (limitlessly). And, By Means Of This Constant Devotionally To-Me-Responding Counter-egoic Effort, Always Feel Through and Beyond Your body-mind (and all of its merely conditional and temporary relations) To Me (Alone and "Bright" At Infinity and Source).

Therefore, Outshine the world—but Do Not Merely Abandon the world. Outshine the world By Exercising The Heart—Which Is Love's Radiant Wound. Do This By Always and Constantly Turning Your Heart (Whole bodily) To My

Avatarically Self-Revealed Divine Form, and Presence, and State Of Self-Evidently Divine Person. And, In and By Means Of That Constant Turning, Always Heart-Recognize Me, and Always Feel Me, and Always Feel To Me (Beyond self-Contraction—Beyond The Separate, and Separative, and Total psycho-physical Act Of ego-"I"). And Do This With Even every moment of perceived body, and of emotional feeling, and of mind's attention, and of cycling breath. And Be Thus (and Always More and More Profoundly) Eased To Me—By Means Of ego-Surrendering, ego-Forgetting, and ego-Transcending Devotional Love Of Me (Even, At Last, To The Most Perfect Degree Of Non-Separateness, and No-"Difference", In Me).

Beloved, I Am here, In and As My Own (Avatarically Self-Revealed) Person—Now (and Forever Hereafter) To Reveal (To all) My Divine Heart-Name, and To Speak (To all) My Heart's Every Divine Word, and To Show (To all) My Divine Heart-Wound.

I Proclaim (By Means Of This, My Divine Testament Of Avataric Self-Proclamation) That I Am The One and Only (and Self-Evidently Divine) Person—Who Is The Inherently egoless Heart Itself, That Liberates The Heart Of Man (and Of all, and All) From Its death of body-mind.

By Means Of My (Now, and Forever Hereafter) Avataric Self-Revelation (To all), I Reveal My Own (and Self-Evidently Divine) Person—That Is The Inherently egoless Heart Itself, and That Is The Real God Within The Heart's Own Felt Bewilderment.

And, Even Now, You (Always Already) Inhere In Me—The "Who" and "What" That Is Only One—Beyond The Seeming "Two" Of body-mind and world.

I Am The Inherent Being—Avatarically Self-Revealed To You (and To all, and All). I Am The Perfectly Subjective Truth Of the world—Avatarically Self-Revealed (every where, and To every one). I Am (By Means Of Avataric Birth) Made Incarnate, Plain, and Obvious—To Man, and As Man, and To all, and As all-and-All. I Am The Life and Consciousness Of all beings—Avatarically Self-Revealed As I Am.

I Am You—As You Are (Always Already, and Non-Separately).

Even When My Avatarically-Born Human Physical Body Has Died In this world, I Am Present and every where Alive—Because I Am Always Already Conscious As The Only One Who Always Already Is.

I Am Joy!—and The Only Reason For It!

The Joy Of Me Is The Divine Secret I Have Come To Avatarically Reveal To The Heart Of every one Of Man (and To The Heart Of every one of all, and To The Heart Of The All Of all).

I Am Love!—and The Only Person Of It!

The Love Of Me Is The Heart-Secret I Have Come To Avatarically Reveal To The Heart Of every one Of Man (and To The Heart Of every one of all, and To The Heart Of The All Of all).

Love Must Be Always Done (and, Thereby, Proved)—or Else The "Bright" Heart Of Love Is Darkened By Its Own Un-Love.

And The Would-Be-"Brightest" Heart Of Love's Beloved Is Made Un-"Bright" (and Dark As Eternal Night) By All The Waiting-Time Of Un-Love's Day.

And The Loved-One and The Lover (Both) Are, Over time, Destroyed By Love's Un-Love (and, Thus, By Love Itself—Un-Proved, By Insufficient and Unconstant Demonstration).

Therefore, I Am here!

I Am (Now, Forever) Avatarically Descended here—To Be The Constant Lover and The True Loved-One Of All and all (and every one of all).

All and all (and every one of all) Is My Beloved—The Necessary Quandra Of My Divine and Only Heart.

From Now, I Am (Forever) here, To Raymond-Love, In-Love With All and all (and every one of all)—and, Thus, By each one's Love-Response To Me, To Make This Cosmic Mummery Of Separateness Into An Eternal Singleness Of Me-"Bright" Joy.

I Am The Divine Beloved!

Now, Be Happy!—In The Constant Joy Of Heart-Recognition Of Me!

Tell every one That I Am here!—As It Was (By Ancients) Always Promised I Would Be!

Now (and Forever Hereafter), My Every Devotee Is The God That I Am here To Find.

Now (and Forever Hereafter), I Am The God My Every Devotee Is here To Realize.

AVATAR ADI DA SAMRAJ
Adidam Samrajashram, 2004

SUTRA 2

I Was Not Born Merely To Communicate "Useful" Wisdom To ego-Possessed Seekers. I Was Born To Fully Reveal and To Fully Establish The One and Complete Divine Way—Which Is The One and Only By-Me-Revealed and By-Me-Given Way Of The Heart (or Way Of Adidam).

The Only-By-Me Revealed and Given Way Of Adidam (or Adidam Ruchiradam), Which Is The One and Only By-Me-Revealed and By-Me-Given Way Of The Heart, Is The One and Only (and Most Perfectly Complete) Way That Is Revealed and Given By Me—The One (and Inherently egoless, and Self-Evidently Divine) Person, Who Is The One (and Only, and Spiritual, and Transcendental, and Self-Evidently Divine) Source-Condition and Self-Condition (Of all-and-All), and Who Is The One and Only Truth and Reality.

The Way That Only I Reveal and Give Is The Way Of Reality Itself. Reality Itself Is The Only Truth and The Only Real God. The Way That Only I Reveal and Give Is The Inherently Divine Way Of Reality and Truth. The Way That Only I Reveal and Give Is The Way Of Divine Spiritual Grace—Freely Given To all. The Way That Only I Reveal and Give Is The Directly ego-Transcending Way Of Love-Communion With Me—The One (and Self-Evidently Divine) Person, Truth, and Reality. The Way That Only I Reveal and Give Is (In Due Course, By Means Of My Avatarically Self-Transmitted Divine Spiritual Grace) The Way Of Inherent, and Inherently Most Perfect, Self-Identification With Me—The Avatarically Self-Revealed Transcendental, Inherently Spiritual, Inherently egoless, and Self-Evidently Divine Self-Condition (and Source-Condition), or One and Only Reality, Of all Apparently conditional (or conditionally Manifested) beings. The Way That Only I Reveal and Give Is "Adidam" (or "Adidam Ruchiradam", or "The True World-Religion Of 'Sri Hridayam'"), Which Is "The Way Of The True Divine Heart" (or "The Way Of The Heart Itself", or, Simply, "The Way Of The Heart"), and "The Way Of The Divine Heart-Master" (or "Hridaya-Avatara Bhakti Yoga", or "Ruchira Avatara Bhakti Yoga"), and "The Way Of 'Radical' Understanding" (or "The Way Of 'Radical' ego-Transcendence"), and "The Way Of Divine Ignorance" (or "The Way Of Positive Disillusionment"), and "The Way Of 'Radical' Non-Dualism" (or "Ruchira Avatara Advaita-Dharma", or "Ruchira Advaitism", or "Ruchira

Buddhism", or "Advaitayana Buddhism", or "Hridaya-Advaita Dharma"), and "The Way Of Divine Spiritual Baptism" (or "Ruchira Avatara Siddha Yoga", or "Ruchira Siddha Yoga", or "Ruchira Avatara Shaktipat Yoga", or "Ruchira Shaktipat Yoga", or "Ruchira Avatara Hridaya-Siddha Yoga", or "Ruchira Avatara Hridaya-Shaktipat Yoga", or "Ruchira Avatara Maha-Jnana-Siddha Yoga", or "Ruchira Avatara Maha-Jnana Hridaya-Shaktipat Yoga"), The Inherently Free (and Only-By-Me Revealed and Given) Way That Freely (By Means Of My Divinely Self-Giving Avataric Grace and My Graceful Avatarically Given Divine Self-Revelation) Becomes Devotion To Me, and Communion With Me, and Realization Of Me, The Spiritually Self-"Bright" (and Inherently egoless and Self-Evidently Divine) Person (The Source-Condition and Self-Condition Of all-and-All), Who Is Named "Da" ("The One Who Gives"), and "Adi Da" (The "First Giver", The "Original Giver", The "Giving Source", The "Divine Giver Of Itself, and Of All, To all"), and Who Is The One, and Only, and Inherently Perfect, and Self-Evidently Divine Giver, and The Perfect Divine Gift, Of Most Perfect Divine Enlightenment (or Always Already Grace-Given—or Non-Seeking and Non-Separate—Being, Love-Bliss-"Brightness", and Consciousness Itself).

The Divine Person (Who Is The One and Only Self-Condition Of all-and-All) Is The Very and Only and True and Inherently Perfect and One Source-Condition and Self-Condition Of all-and-All, and The Divine Person (or Condition) Must Be (and, Ultimately, Is To Be) Realized By all (Even, At Last, By Most Perfectly Transcending, or Divinely Outshining, all-and-All). Therefore, The Divine Person Is The Very and Only and True and Inherently Perfect Way Of Divine Self-Realization For all. I Am That One (The One and Only and True and Inherently Perfect Divine Self-Person, or Divine Source-Condition and Self-Condition, Of all-and-All), Come To Call, and Attract, and Awaken every one (and all, and All) To Me. And, Because I Am The One and Only Self-Condition Of all-and-All, What I Confess About My Avatarically Self-Revealed (and Very, and Transcendental, and Perfectly Subjective, and Inherently Spiritual, and Inherently egoless, and Inherently Perfect, and Self-Evidently Divine) Self (As My Self-Condition, Apart From My Unique Function As The Ruchira Avatar, The One and Only Divine Heart-Master) Is (Ultimately, If You Realize Me As The Only One Who Is) Also A Confession About You.

I Am The Da Avatar—The Ruchira Avatar, The Love-Ananda Avatar, The First, The Last, and The Only Divine and True and "Bright" Heart-Master, Adi Da Samraj, The All-Giving and All-Completing Avataric Incarnation Of The Inherently egoless (and Self-Evidently Divine) Heart Itself. Therefore, Listen To Me and Hear Me and See Me, With Your Heart.

I Am Not here To Compete With You Relative To Any Goal—Whether Of Life Or Of Spirit.

I Am here To Set You Free Of All Seeking—Both That Of Life and That Of Spirit.

I Am here To Liberate You From Your Separate and Separative self, and From The Bondage That Is conditional Existence, and From All The Illusions Of The Merely Cosmic Domain.

Therefore, Listen To My Call, and Hear My Voice At Heart, and See My Heart Itself.

Listen To Me. Practice Feeling-Surrender Of Separate and Separative self To Me. By Responsively (and Intentionally) Surrendering Your conditional self (Your ego-"I", or self-Contraction) To Me, Feel Beyond (and Renounce, and Relinquish) All (and Every Kind Of) Competition With Me, and All (and Every Kind Of) Resistance To Me, and All (and Every Kind Of) ego-Making and ego-Acting Struggle In Relation To Me. Therefore, Progressively, and By All This Active (and Actively ego-Transcending) Love Of Me, Grow To Hear Me (By Out-Growing Your childish and adolescent self), and (Thus) Grow To Truly (and Most Fundamentally) Understand Your conditional self and Separateness. Then, By Means Of That Grace-Given (and Heart-Earned) self-Understanding, Actively Prepare Your Heart To See Me. Actively Cleanse Your Hearing-Heart, So That Your Heart May Soon Be Truly Distracted (and Restored To Its Sightedness) By My Avatarically Self-Transmitted (and Self-Evidently Divine) Spiritual Presence. And, When You Have Grown To See Me At Heart, Submit To Be Grown (By My Own Fullness), Until You Are Grown Beyond Even All The Design (and Circle) Of conditional self. Then Submit To Realize Me Most Perfectly, In and As The Spiritual Heart-"Brightness" (and Self-Evidently Divine State) Where You Always Already Stand.

Beloved, To Be Blessed By Me Is To Be Given The Freedom (or The Inherent Right and The Tacit Obligation) To Remember Me.

This Remembrance Is My Blessing Gift To All My Devotees.

Therefore, My Every Devotee Must (By Means Of Constant Whole bodily Heart-Invocation Of Me By Means Of My Avatarically Self-Revealed Divine Name, and Constant Whole bodily Heart-Recognition Of My Avatarically Self-Revealed Divine Person, and Constant Whole bodily Heart-Response To My Every Avatarically Self-Revealed Divine Word and To All My Avatarically Self-Revealed Divine Image-Art and To All My all-and-All-Liberating Avatarically Self-Manifested Divine Acts, and Constant Whole bodily Heart-Responsive Feeling-Contemplation Of My Divinely Given, and Always Divinely Giving, Avatarically-Born Bodily Human Divine Form, and Constant Whole bodily Heart-Responsive Reception Of My Avatarically Self-Transmitted Spiritual, and Always Blessing, Divine Presence, and, At Last, Constant Heart-Responsive Heart-Identification With My Avatarically Self-Revealed, and Very, and

Transcendental, and Perfectly Subjective, and Inherently Spiritual, and Inherently egoless, and Inherently Perfect, and Self-Evidently Divine State) Constantly (and Then Most Perfectly) and Always Actively (or Really and Effectively) Remember Me.

Beloved, To Be Forgiven By Me Is To Be Given The Freedom (or The Inherent Right and The Tacit Obligation) To Forget Your ego-"I".

This Forgiveness Is My Liberating Gift To All My Devotees. Therefore, My Every Devotee Must (By Means Of Constant Whole bodily Heart-Invocation Of Me By Means Of My Avatarically Self-Revealed Divine Name, and Constant Whole bodily Heart-Recognition Of My Avatarically Self-Revealed Divine Person, and Constant Whole bodily Heart-Response To My Every Avatarically Self-Revealed Divine Word and To All My Avatarically Self-Revealed Divine Image-Art and To All My all-and-All-Liberating Avatarically Self-Manifested Divine Acts, and Constant Whole bodily Heart-Responsive Feeling-Contemplation Of My Divinely Given, and Always Divinely Giving, Avatarically-Born Bodily Human Divine Form, and Constant Whole bodily Heart-Responsive Reception Of My Avatarically Self-Transmitted Spiritual, and Always Blessing, Divine Presence, and, At Last, Constant Heart-Responsive Heart-Identification With My Avatarically Self-Revealed, and Very, and Transcendental, and Perfectly Subjective, and Inherently Spiritual, and Inherently egoless, and Inherently Perfect, and Self-Evidently Divine State) Progressively (and Then Most Perfectly) and Always Actively (or Really and Effectively) Surrender, Forget, and Transcend self-Contraction (and, Thereby, Actively, Progressively, and Then Most Perfectly Surrender, Forget, and Transcend the body-mind-self, and conditional Existence Itself).

Beloved, I Am The First, The Last, and The Only Divine Heart-Master. My Avataric Self-Revelation Of My Own (and Self-Evidently Divine) Person Is My Ultimate (and Inherently Perfect) Spiritual Gift To all who Listen To Me and Hear Me and See Me.

Therefore, Listen To Me and Hear Me and See Me, With Your Heart.

And, If Your Heart Will Listen To Me and Hear Me and See Me, I Will Lead You To My Eternal Sphere Of Love-Bliss, My Divine Self-Domain, My Eternal Realm Of Conscious Light (The "Bright" and Self-Condition That Is The Only Real God).

The Divine Heart-Master Is A Divine Revelation. The Divine Heart-Master Is The Unique Means (Divinely Self-"Emerging" Within The Cosmic Domain) For The Divine Liberation, The Divine Enlightenment, and The Divine Translation Of all conditionally Manifested beings. Therefore, The Divine Heart-Master Surrenders and Submits Himself To Be A Servant, For The Perfect Sake and Divine Service Of all beings.

Aham Da Asmi. Beloved, I Am Da. I Am Da, The Spiritually "Bright" (and Self-Evidently Divine) Person—The "Bright" Heart Itself. I Am Adi Da, The First Person, The Original Person, The Giving Source-Person, The One and Only and Divine Self-Condition Of all-and-All, and The "Bright" Divine Giver Of The Divine "All" To all-and-All. I Am Self-Manifesting (Now, and Forever Hereafter) As The Ruchira Avatar, The Divine Heart-Master, The Avataric Divine Realizer, The Avataric Divine Revealer, and The Avataric Divine Self-Revelation Of The One and Eternal Divine Person—The Self-Evidently Divine Self-Condition, and Source-Condition, Of all-and-All.

I Am The Da Avatar, Adi Da Samraj—The Ruchira Avatar, The Love-Ananda Avatar, Now and Forever here (and every "where" In The Cosmic Domain), Appearing and "Emerging", "Bright". I Appear To Me here and every "where" (As I Am), In and As every form and being that arises. And I Am (Especially) Brought To Myself By Heart In and As each and all Of My Devotees.

Therefore, I Was Avatarically Born To Reveal Myself To Myself (As The "Bright" and One and Only and Eternal and Self-Evidently Divine Person—The "Bright" and One and Only Self-Condition Of each and every one). And (Now, and Forever Hereafter) I Am here (and every "where" In The Cosmic Domain) To Fully and Completely Accomplish This Divine Self-Revelation—By Serving My Divine Self-Realization In The Case Of All and all (each and all, and one by one).

I Function Freely As The Source, In My Avatarically Self-Manifested Divine "Bonding"-Play With My Devotees.

I Am The "Crazy" Avadhoot, Free Among all.

I Am Not The Seeker.

I Am Not Obliged By ordinary vows and rules.

I Stand Apart From all limitations and all restrictions.

I Am The Atiashrami, Free Of all ordinary obligations.

I Am here Only By Vow and Obligation Of My Own, For The Sake Of all-and-All.

I Do Whatever and All I Must Do For The Sake Of The "Bonding" Of every one and All To Me, and, Altogether, For The Sake Of The Divine Liberation Of all-and-All.

I (Myself) Appear To Me here and every "where" (As My Very Self) In the bodily form of each and every conditionally Manifested being, and (In Order That My Revelation-Service Become Effective In each and every one) each and every one Must Come To Me and Be My True Devotee.

My Avataric Birth Is A Conscious and Intentional Act Of Divine Self-Submission—Whereby My Self-Existing and Self-Radiant Divine Condition Of

Being Becomes Self-Revealed Through the limiting conditions of a body-mind In this world.

My Avataric Birth Is An Act Of Divine Self-Submission To The Mandala (or Great Circle) Of The Cosmos. My Avataric Teaching-Work Is An Act Of Divine Self-Submission To Mankind. My Avataric Spiritual Blessing-Work Is (Now, and Forever Hereafter) My Divine "Act" Of Merely Being (By Merely Standing In "Place")—For all who Listen To Me, and For all who Hear Me, and For all who See Me.

My Avataric Birth Is Unique. I Must Surrender and Submit My Very (and Inherently Perfect) Divine Self-Condition In Order To Incarnate. Therefore, To Be Born, I Had To Submit To The limiting Power Of The Cosmic Domain. I Assumed the body-mind of an ordinary man. That Birth Was The Apparent (or merely psycho-physical) Forgetting Of My Divine State and My "Bright" Spirit-Power Of Divine Being. Quickly, The Inherent Self-Knowledge Of Who I Am Receded From Consciousness To Subconsciousness To Unconsciousness—Such That Only A Fierce (and Mysteriously "Bright") Impulse Remained.[23]

The Sacrifice The Divine Heart-Master Must Make In Order To Incarnate Is Real. Therefore, Once I Was Born, My Life Became A Profound Ordeal Of Spiritual and Transcendental Divine Self-Realization, and Subsequent Teaching-Work and Blessing-Work To Awaken all others.

My Avataric Life-Submission Eventually Brought Fullest (Complete and Most Perfect) Spiritual and Transcendental Divine Self-Realization To Consciousness In the body-mind In which I Was Avatarically Born—Such That Even every cell of the body Was Divinely Transfigured and Divinely Transformed By The Resurrection Of My Eternally Living Divine Being.

After My Re-Awakening (In My Own and Avatarically-Born Bodily Human Divine Form) To My Own Condition Of Self-Existing and Self-Radiant Divine Being,[24] I Submitted Myself (Bodily, and Altogether) To Mankind—In Order To Suffer the conditions of humanity, and, Thereby, To Re-Discover The Process Of The Divine Way For all. In That Submission, I Acquired all limits of the human kind. I Did Not Conserve Myself From Harm, or Foolishness, or Any Of The Wounds and Excesses Of Love—but I Fully Suffered the usual life. And I Suffered At the hands of all who Came To Me. Nevertheless, My Heart-Impulse Was Great—For their Sake. And, By Submitting To them In Love, I Observed and Understood the human case—and I Brought The Total Process Of The Divine Heart-Way To Consciousness, For The Sake Of all beings.

When I Make The Only-By-Me Revealed and Given Way Of The Heart (or Way Of Adidam) Clear, My Listening Devotees Begin To Understand themselves—and, In Due Course, they Are Spiritually Initiated (By Me) Into The Searchless Beholding Of Me and The Reception Of My Ruchira Shaktipat.

When they Hear Me, they Truly (and Most Fundamentally) Understand themselves. Therefore, The Inclination Toward ego-Possession Becomes Weak In My Hearing Devotees, and they (By ego-Transcendence) Are Further Enabled To Feel Me At The Heart and To Devotionally Recognize Me (and Devotionally Respond To Me) From The Heart. Then I Become As If Transparent To them, and they Begin To See Me. In That Seeing, they Are Moved Beyond themselves, Distracted By A "Bright" Heart-Vision. In their forms, Mankind Turns About and Begins To Surrender the egoic self To Me—The Avatarically Self-Revealed (Transcendental, and Perfectly Subjective, and Inherently Spiritual, and Inherently egoless, and Inherently Perfect, and Self-Evidently Divine) Self-Condition Of all-and-All. And their ego-Transcending Resort To Me Calls Upon My Infinite Eternal Resource. In My Openly and Happily Heart-Moved Response To these, My Seeing Devotees, My Divine Spirit-Power and Divine Spiritual Work and Divine "Bright" Spherical Self-Domain Come To Meet them, and their Realization Of My Divine Self-Agency (or My Function As The Avataric-Incarnation-Servant Of Real God In Man) Becomes Full. In This Manner, I Demonstrate To All My By-Me-Spiritually-Initiated Listening Devotees, and Hearing Devotees, and Seeing Devotees That I Am The One and True Heart—Who Is The Divine Way, The Divine Root, The Divine Doer, The Divine Source, The Divine Truth, and The Divine "Bright" Spherical Self-Domain Of The Divine Process Of Most Perfect Divine Awakening.

My Personal Ordeal As The Divine Heart-Master Progresses Through Three Principal Stages. First, I Had To Pass Through The Ordeal Of Spiritual and Transcendental Divine Self-Realization, While Really Submitted To a limited body-mind-self and its relations and conditions. This Stage Of My Ordeal Lasted Until I Was Thirty Years Of Age.

The Second Stage Of My Unique Ordeal As The Divine Heart-Master Was A Process In Which I Came To Acknowledge, Accept, and Embrace The Unique and Ultimate (and, Necessarily, Divine) Significance Of My Own Already Realized Life, Work, and Agency. Although Certain Fundamental Aspects Of This Significance Became Quickly Obvious To Me After The Great (and Inherently Most Perfect) Event Of My Re-Awakening To My Divine Self-Condition, The Divine Process Of Self-Revelation and Self-Acknowledgement Continued To Develop For Another Nine Years, Until I Was Spontaneously Heart-Moved To Make The "Crazy" Self-Confession Of My Inherently egoless Divine Self-Awareness: "Aham Da Asmi" ("I Am Da").[25] And That "Crazy" Divine Self-Confession Magnified Itself, Spontaneously, For Yet Another Seven Years—Until I "Descended" (or Spiritually Surrendered) Most Fully Into The Form Of My Own Avatarically-Born (Human) Body-Mind (and Into The Total Form Of The Entire Cosmic Domain). And, Then and Thereby, I (Myself)

"Emerged" Within The Cosmic Everywhere. And, Thus (and Forever Thereafter), I Am Divinely Self-"Emerging" here—As I Am, and Most Perfectly. And, Then (Thus Most Perfectly "Descended" and "Emerged" here), After Yet Another Fourteen Years Of Struggle With Every Form and Kind Of egoic Resistance (Demonstrated By My Devotees and By The Global Collective Of human beings), I Was Suddenly and Spontaneously Infinitely Ascended—Present In (and As) My Divine Spiritual Threshold Form (While Yet Continuing To Exist In Bodily Human Form), Inherently Self-Identified With My Own Always Already Infinitely Ascended (and Spiritually Self-"Bright") Divine Self-Condition, and Seeing (and Blessing) The Entire Cosmic Mandala Of Seeming Separate beings and things From The "Other Side" (Of My Spiritually Self-"Bright", and Infinitely Love-Bliss-Full, Divine Spherical Self-Domain).[26]

The Third Stage Of My Unique Ordeal As The Divine Heart-Master Is The Process Of My Avatarically Given Divine Self-Revelation To others (and The Inherent Devotional Recognition Of Me, and The Progressive Great Reception Of Me, By all those who Devotionally Respond To Me and, By Means Of My Avatarically Self-Transmitted Divine Spiritual Grace, Grow In The Realization Of Me). That Process Continues Until all conditionally Manifested beings, and Even The Great Circle (or Mandala) Of The Cosmos Itself, Are Truly Heart-Converted To Me, and Really and Totally Conformed To Me—and (At Last) Translated Into My Spiritually Self-"Bright" Divine Spherical Self-Domain, By Most Perfect Devotional Recognition-Response To Me and Most Perfect Realization Of My Divine Self-Revelation Of The Spiritual, Transcendental, and Self-Evidently Divine Forms Of Reality and Truth (Which Is The Only Real God). That Ordeal Began When I First Confessed My Divine Self-Realization To all, and That Ordeal Continues, Even Now.

After I Re-Awakened To The Realization Of My Own Inherently Free (and Self-Evidently Divine) Condition, I Began To Instruct others In The Wisdom-Way Of ego-Transcendence and Transcendental (and Inherently Spiritual) Divine Enlightenment. Therefore, From The Time Of The Great Event Of My Own Divine Re-Awakening, I Gradually and Progressively Instructed the world and All Would-Be Devotees In All The Kinds Of Wisdom That Are Based On The Unique (and The Universal) Process Of My Own Most Perfect (and Self-Evidently Divine) Self-Realization.

However, The Instant I Made The Divine Confession "Aham Da Asmi" ("I Am Da"), I Was Confronted By The Envious and Otherwise Reactive Assaults Of adolescent worldly people whose Hearts Yet Resist The Divine Necessity Of Heart-Breaking Devotional Recognition Of Me, and whose Hearts Yet Wish To Avoid The Necessary Divine Process Of ego-Transcending Devotion To Me, and whose Hearts Yet Refuse Me The Necessary Gift Of ego-Surrendering, ego-Forgetting, and ego-Transcending Devotional Response To My Inherently egoless and Self-Evidently Divine Person, and whose Hearts Yet Refuse To Be Set Free Into My Limitless Divine "Bright" Love-Bliss-Space. Therefore, Because It Seemed My Avatarically Self-Revealed Divine Word Was Not Yet Sufficient To Convert and Conform Every Heart To Me, I Struggled For Another Twenty-Three Years[27]—In Order To Speak The Word That Is Sufficient For all. And My Twenty-Three Divine "Source-Texts" (With This Divine Testament As The Epitome, or First and Principal Text, Among Them) Are, Together, That Sufficient Word—Given, In Summary, To You (and, Therefore, To all). And, Now That I Have Given My Sufficient Word, I Have Gone To Wait (or Merely Stand Thereby).

Now, and Forever Hereafter, I Will Stand and Wait For Every Heart To Break In Devotional Recognition Of Me.

Now, and Forever Hereafter, I Will Stand and Wait For Every Heart To Become My Responsively ego-Transcending Devotee.

Now, and Forever Hereafter, I Will Stand and Wait For Every Heart's ego-Surrendering, ego-Forgetting, and (More and More, and, At Last, Most Perfectly) ego-Transcending Devotional Great Reception Of Me.

Therefore, In My (Now, and Forever Hereafter) Waiting-Time, My Divine (and Always Me-Revealing) Sign—Of My Ever-Given (and Never To Be Forgotten) Avatarically-Born Bodily (Human) Divine Form, and My Avatarically Self-Revealed (and Avatarically Self-Transmitted—and Ever-"Emerging") Spiritual (and Always Blessing) Divine Presence, and My Avatarically Self-Revealed (and, Avatarically, Spiritually Transmitted) and Very (and Transcendental, and Perfectly Subjective, and Inherently Spiritual, and Inherently egoless, and Inherently Perfect, and Ever-Standing, and Self-Evidently Divine) State—Must, By Merely Standing, Stand To Bless Every Heart, Forever (Now, and Now). And The Twenty-Three Divine Books Of My (Now, and Forever Hereafter) Avatarically Full-Given Divine Word Must Speak To Every Heart—Revealing Me To every one, and Teaching every one The Truth Of Me, Again and Again, Forever. And The Many Divine Images Of My (Now, and Forever Hereafter) Avatarically Full-Given Divine Image-Art Must Be Shown To Every Heart—and, Thereby, Be Made To Reveal Me To every one, and To Teach every one The Truth Of Me, Again and Again, Forever. And The Historic Me-Revealing Divine Leelas Of My Avataric-Incarnation-Time Must (Now, and Forever Hereafter) Be Told (and Re-Told) To Every Heart—and, Thereby, Be Made Alive To Reveal Me To every one, and To Teach every one The Truth Of Me, Again and Again, With Even All The Storied Leelas Of My (Now and Forever Hereafter) Avataric Divine-Self-"Emergence"-Work Of Avatarically Given Divine Self-Revelation and "Bright" Avatarically Given Divine World-Blessing (Of The Cosmic Everywhere).

I Am (By Means Of My Avatarically Self-Revealed Divine Sign, My Avatarically Self-Revealed Divine Word, My Avatarically Self-Revealed Divine Image-Art, and All My Avataric Divine-Self-"Emergence"-Work) Now, and Forever Hereafter, Submitted Only To Be Merely Present—Openly Secluded and "Bright" In My Heart's Free All.

Even Now (and Forever Hereafter), Only My Own Heart's Love-Bliss-"Bright" Avataric Divine Sign and Avataric Divine-Self-"Emergence"-Blessing-Work Persists, In My Perfect Silence—Even If I Always Speak This Divine Testament (and Even All My Twenty-Three Divine Books) Of Perfectly Sufficient Words.

Now (and Forever Hereafter), I Am The Divine and One and Only Heart. And My Own (Self-Evidently Divine) Spiritual Self-"Brightness" Only and Forever Speaks My One Most Perfectly Sufficient Word Of Heart—To all-and-All. And That One Most Perfectly Sufficient Word Is My Divine Name, Da—Now (and Forever Hereafter) Spoken Aloud (By Me) Within, and To, and By, and As The Heartbeat and The Heart Of every one.

Avatar Adi Da Samraj
Adidam Samrajashram, 2004

SUTRA

3

Aham Da Asmi. Beloved, I Am Da. I Am The Divine and One and Only and Non-Separate and Indivisible Heart, and (As My conditionally Manifested Pattern) I Am The Way Of Adidam, The Way Of The Heart (That Realizes Indivisible Oneness With The True Divine and Non-Separate and Indivisible Heart Itself—Which Is The One and Only Reality, Truth, and Real God, or That Which Is Always Already The Case).

I Have Named The Way That I Am (and That Only I Reveal and Give) "Adidam" (or "Adidam Ruchiradam")—Which Is "The True World-Religion Of 'Sri Hridayam'" (or "The Way Of The True Divine Heart", or "The Way Of The Heart Itself", or, Simply, "The Way Of The Heart"). And I Have Also Named The Only-By-Me Revealed and Given Way Of Adidam (In Every One and All Of Its Only-By-Me Revealed and Given Forms Of Practice and Developmental Stages Of Practice) "The Way Of The Divine Heart-Master" (or "Hridaya-Avatara Bhakti Yoga", or "Ruchira Avatara Bhakti Yoga"), and "The Way Of 'Radical' Understanding" (or "The Way Of 'Radical' ego-Transcendence"), and "The Way Of Divine Ignorance" (or "The Way Of Positive Disillusionment"), and "The Way Of 'Radical' Non-Dualism" (or "Ruchira Avatara Advaita-Dharma", or "Ruchira Advaitism", or "Ruchira Buddhism", or "Advaitayana Buddhism", or "Hridaya-Advaita Dharma"), and "The Way Of Divine Spiritual Baptism" (or "Ruchira Avatara Siddha Yoga", or "Ruchira Siddha Yoga", or "Ruchira Avatara Shaktipat Yoga", or "Ruchira Shaktipat Yoga", or "Ruchira Avatara Hridaya-Siddha Yoga", or "Ruchira Avatara Hridaya-Shaktipat Yoga", or "Ruchira Avatara Maha-Jnana-Siddha Yoga", or "Ruchira Avatara Maha-Jnana Hridaya-Shaktipat Yoga").

Adidam (or Adidam Ruchiradam, or The True World-Religion Of "Sri Hridayam", or The Way Of The True Divine Heart, or The Way Of The Heart Itself, or The Way Of The Heart, or The Way Of The Divine Heart-Master, or Hridaya-Avatara Bhakti Yoga, or Ruchira Avatara Bhakti Yoga, or The Way Of "Radical" Understanding, or The Way Of "Radical" ego-Transcendence, or The Way Of Divine Ignorance, or The Way Of Positive Disillusionment, or The Way Of "Radical" Non-Dualism, or Ruchira Avatara Advaita-Dharma, or Ruchira Advaitism, or Ruchira Buddhism, or Advaitayana Buddhism, or Hridaya-Advaita

Dharma, or The Way Of Divine Spiritual Baptism, or Ruchira Avatara Siddha Yoga, or Ruchira Siddha Yoga, or Ruchira Avatara Shaktipat Yoga, or Ruchira Shaktipat Yoga, or Ruchira Avatara Hridaya-Siddha Yoga, or Ruchira Avatara Hridaya-Shaktipat Yoga, or Ruchira Avatara Maha-Jnana Siddha-Yoga, or Ruchira Avatara Maha-Jnana Hridaya-Shaktipat Yoga) Is The "Radical" (or "Radically" Advaitic, or Utterly and Most Perfectly Non-Dual) Way Of One (Not Two)—The Divinely Self-Revealed Way Of Transcendental (or Un-conditional), Inherently Spiritual, and (Ultimately) Divine Realization Of The "Who", The "What", and The "Where" Of "Is", or The True Renunciate Way (or The "How", The "When", and The "Why") Of The Inherent (and, Therefore, Inherently Perfect) Transcending Of mind (or "buddhi"), or attention itself, In its Always Already Free Source-Condition (Which Is "Bodhi", or Consciousness Itself).

As An Expression Of Its Continuity With The Great Tradition Of Even All Religious and Spiritual Traditions, The Spiritual Way That I Have Revealed and Given Is, By Me, Named (and Described As) "Ruchira Avatara Advaita-Dharma" (or The "Bright" Spiritual Way—or Ruchira Siddha Yoga Way—Of Non-Dual Light, or "Bright" Non-Duality, or Inherently Perfect Non-Separateness, Revealed and Given By Me, The One and Only Avataric Divine Realizer, Avataric Divine Revealer, and Avataric Divine Self-Revelation Of The One and Perfectly Non-Dual Divine "Brightness" Itself), and "Ruchira Advaitism" (or The "Bright" Spiritual Way—or Ruchira Siddha Yoga Way—Of The Perfectly Subjective Divine Light Of The One and Indivisible Reality and Truth), and "Hridaya Advaitism" (or The "Bright" Spiritual Heart-Way—or Ruchira Siddha Yoga Heart-Way—Of "Radical" Non-Dualism, or Of Utterly Non-"Different", or Perfectly Non-Separate, Truth), and "The Way Of Hridaya-Advaita Dharma" (or The Divine Teaching, The Ruchira Siddha Yoga Way, and The "Bright" Spiritual Truth Of The "Radically" Non-Dual—and Utterly Non-"Different", or Perfectly Non-Separate—Heart), and "The Way Of Hridaya-Advaita Yoga" (or The Divine Yoga, and Ruchira Siddha Yoga Way, or Great Spiritual Practice, Of "Hridaya Advaitism"), or, Simply, "'Radical' Advaitism" (or "'Radical' Non-Dualism"—The First, Last, Final, or Completing, and Eternal, and Self-Evidently Divine Way Of Most Direct and, Ultimately, Inherently Most Perfectly Non-Dual Realization Of The One, and Unqualifiedly Non-Separate, and Inherently Indivisible, and Eternally Indestructible "Bright" Spiritual Condition That Is Real God, and Truth, and Reality).

Similarly, As An Expression Of Its Continuity With The Great Tradition Of Even All Religious and Spiritual Traditions, The Way That I Have Revealed and Given Is, By Me, Named (and Described As) "Ruchira Buddhism" (or The Ruchira Siddha Yoga Way, Of Most Perfect and All-Outshining "Bright" Spiritual Enlightenment, Revealed and Given By Me, The Ruchira Buddha,

The Divine World-Teacher Anciently, Always, and every where Promised For, and Universally Expected In, The "Late-Time", or "Dark" Epoch, By All The Traditions Of Mankind) and "Advaitayana Buddhism" (or The First, Last, Final, or Completing, and Eternal "Yana", or Revelation, and Self-Evidently Divine Way Of Most Perfect—and Most Perfectly, or "Radically", Non-Dual—Enlightenment).

Adidam (or Adidam Ruchiradam, or The True World-Religion Of "Sri Hridayam", or The Way Of The True Divine Heart, or The Way Of The Heart Itself, or The Way Of The Heart, or The Way Of The Divine Heart-Master, or Hridaya-Avatara Bhakti Yoga, or Ruchira Avatara Bhakti Yoga, or The Way Of "Radical" Understanding, or The Way Of "Radical" ego-Transcendence, or The Way Of Divine Ignorance, or The Way Of Positive Disillusionment, or The Way Of "Radical" Non-Dualism, or Ruchira Avatara Advaita-Dharma, or Ruchira Advaitism, or Ruchira Buddhism, or Advaitayana Buddhism, or Hridaya-Advaita Dharma, or The Way Of Divine Spiritual Baptism, or Ruchira Avatara Siddha Yoga, or Ruchira Siddha Yoga, or Ruchira Avatara Shaktipat Yoga, or Ruchira Shaktipat Yoga, or Ruchira Avatara Hridaya-Siddha Yoga, or Ruchira Avatara Hridaya-Shaktipat Yoga, or Ruchira Avatara Maha-Jnana-Siddha Yoga, or Ruchira Avatara Maha-Jnana Hridaya-Shaktipat Yoga) Is The Divine Ruchira Siddha Yoga (or Divine Ruchira Shaktipat Yoga) Way Revealed and Given Only By Me, Adi Da Samraj, The Ruchira Buddha, The Paramadvaita Buddha, The Advaitayana Buddha—Now (and Forever Hereafter) Given To all, For The Sake Of all-and-All. Therefore, Even Though The Only-By-Me Revealed and Given Way Is Sympathetically Related To All The Traditions and "Yanas"[28] Of The Historical Traditions Of Buddhism, and To All The Traditions Of Advaitism, and To Even All The Traditions Within The Collective Great Tradition Of All The Historical Traditions Of Mankind, The Only-By-Me Revealed and Given Divine Way Is Free and Independent Of All Obligations To The Historical Traditions Of Buddhism, and Of Advaitism, and Of Siddha Yoga, and Of Shaktipat Yoga, and Of Even The Entire Collective Great Tradition Of All The Historical Traditions Of Mankind (Apart From The Only-By-Me Revealed and Given Avataric Divine Way Itself).

The "Buddhism" Of Adidam (or Of Adidam Ruchiradam, or Of The True World-Religion Of "Sri Hridayam", or Of The Way Of The True Divine Heart, or Of The Way Of The Heart Itself, or Of The Way Of The Heart, or Of The Way Of The Divine Heart-Master, or Of Hridaya-Avatara Bhakti Yoga, or Of Ruchira Avatara Bhakti Yoga, or Of The Way Of "Radical" Understanding, or Of The Way Of "Radical" ego-Transcendence, or Of The Way Of Divine Ignorance, or Of The Way Of Positive Disillusionment, or Of The Way Of "Radical" Non-Dualism, or Of Ruchira Avatara Advaita-Dharma, or Of Ruchira

Advaitism, or Of Ruchira Buddhism, or Of Advaitayana Buddhism, or Of Hridaya-Advaita Dharma, or Of The Way Of Divine Spiritual Baptism, or Of Ruchira Avatara Siddha Yoga, or Of Ruchira Siddha Yoga, or Of Ruchira Avatara Shaktipat Yoga, or Of Ruchira Shaktipat Yoga, or Of Ruchira Avatara Hridaya-Siddha Yoga, or Of Ruchira Avatara Hridaya-Shaktipat Yoga, or Of Ruchira Avatara Maha-Jnana Siddha-Yoga, or Of Ruchira Avatara Maha-Jnana Hridaya-Shaktipat Yoga) Progressively (and Then Most Perfectly) Magnifies True and Free Renunciation (or The Real Transcending) Of the body-mind (and all objects, others, forms, states, or "things" of attention). Therefore, Real (or Effective) Renunciation (or The Real Transcending) Of the psycho-physical ego-"I" (or self-Contraction)—and (Thus and Thereby) Effective Renunciation (or The Real Transcending) Of the body-mind itself (Without Strategically Excluding, Avoiding, Denying, Emptying, or Destroying the body-mind itself)—Is The First Principle (or Effective Sign) Of Practice Demonstrated By all those who Listen To Me, and By all those who Hear Me, and By all those who See Me In The Only-By-Me Revealed and Given Way Of Adidam.

The "Advaitism" Of Adidam (or Of Adidam Ruchiradam, or Of The True World-Religion Of "Sri Hridayam", or Of The Way Of The True Divine Heart, or Of The Way Of The Heart Itself, or Of The Way Of The Heart, or Of The Way Of The Divine Heart-Master, or Of Hridaya-Avatara Bhakti Yoga, or Of Ruchira Avatara Bhakti Yoga, or Of The Way Of "Radical" Understanding, or Of The Way Of "Radical" ego-Transcendence, or Of The Way Of Divine Ignorance, or Of The Way Of Positive Disillusionment, or Of The Way Of "Radical" Non-Dualism, or Of Ruchira Avatara Advaita-Dharma, or Of Ruchira Advaitism, or Of Ruchira Buddhism, or Of Advaitayana Buddhism, or Of Hridaya-Advaita Dharma, or Of The Way Of Divine Spiritual Baptism, or Of Ruchira Avatara Siddha Yoga, or Of Ruchira Siddha Yoga, or Of Ruchira Avatara Shaktipat Yoga, or Of Ruchira Shaktipat Yoga, or Of Ruchira Avatara Hridaya-Siddha Yoga, or Of Ruchira Avatara Hridaya-Shaktipat Yoga, or Of Ruchira Avatara Maha-Jnana Siddha-Yoga, or Of Ruchira Avatara Maha-Jnana Hridaya-Shaktipat Yoga) Progressively (and Then Most Perfectly) Magnifies True and Free Renunciation (or The Real Transcending) Of attention itself, In its Perfectly Subjective (or Transcendental, or Inherently Non-Objective) Source—Which Is Self-Existing and Self-Radiant (or Divinely Spiritually "Bright") Consciousness Itself. Therefore, The Renunciation (or The Real Transcending) Of attention (In its Transcendental and Perfectly Subjective Source)—Coincident With Effective Renunciation (or Real Transcending) Of the psycho-physical ego-"I" (or self-Contraction), and (Thus and Thereby) Effective Renunciation (or Real Transcending) Of the body-mind itself (Without Strategically Excluding, Avoiding, Denying, Emptying, or Destroying the body-mind itself)—Is The Second (and, Ultimately, Most Perfect) Principle (or Sign) Of Practice Demonstrated By all those who Listen To Me, and By all those who Hear Me, and By all those who See Me In The Only-By-Me Revealed and Given Way Of Adidam.

Such Real (or Effective) Renunciation (or Real Transcending)—Both Of attention itself and Of the body-mind itself—Can Be The Case Only If My Any Devotee Consistently and Intensively Applies himself or herself To The (ego-Surrendering, ego-Forgetting, and, More and More, ego-Transcending) Sadhana Of The Only-By-Me Revealed and Given Way Of The Heart (or Way Of Adidam). In The "Late-Time" (or "Dark" Epoch), Within Which My Avatarically-Born Bodily (Human) Divine Form (or Avataric Incarnation) Has Appeared, There Is, Characteristically and everywhere, A Persistent Attempt To Popularize True (and Truly Spiritual) Esotericism—By Promoting The (Utterly False) Notion That It Is Possible To Engage An Esoteric Spiritual Practice Without First Adapting To (and Firmly Establishing) The Necessary Foundationary Sadhana. Traditionally—In Contrast To This "Late-Time" (or "Dark" Epoch) Characteristic—It Has Always Been Clearly Understood That A Profound Foundationary Sadhana (Relating Both To The ordinary human Matters Of The First Three Stages Of Life and To The Fundamental Devotional Disposition That Is First Developed In The "Original" Context Of The Fourth Stage Of Life) Must Be Done Before Any Truly Spiritual (or Esoteric) Practice Can Be Effectively Engaged. Therefore, One Of The Essential Aspects Of My Avataric Divine Work Is To Counter The "Easy Esotericism" Otherwise Popularly Promoted In The "Late-Time" (or "Dark" Epoch)—and (Thus and Thereby) To Restore The Traditional Understanding, That Insists Upon The Firm Establishment Of A Profound (and Profoundly Effective) Foundationary Sadhana As A Necessary Preliminary To Spiritual Sadhana (and, Altogether, To Fully Developing Esoteric Practice).

The Only-By-Me Revealed and Given Way Of The Heart (or Way Of Adidam) Is The Esoteric (or Devotional and Spiritual) Relationship To Me (In, As, and By Means Of My Avatarically-Born Bodily Human Divine Form). In The Context Of The True Devotional Relationship To Me, My Devotee Must (In Due Course) Begin To Participate In My Avataric Divine Spiritual Self-Transmission (or Shaktipat Blessing). However, In Order For My Devotee To Participate In My Avataric Divine Spiritual Self-Transmission In A Truly Transformative (and Authentically and Rightly Developmental) Manner, he or she Must Be Rightly Prepared, By Having Effectively Adapted To (and Having Become Firmly Established In) Right Foundationary Sadhana (or Beginner's Practice), Which Re-Orients the entire body-mind (With its Four Principal Faculties—Of body, emotion, mind, and breath) To Me (and, Thus and

Thereby, To The Purpose Of Real-God-Realizing Practice), and Which (As A Necessary Preliminary To Spiritual Communion With Me—and To Participation In subtler Levels Of Purification and Renunciation) Purifies the body-mind Of its grosser Entanglements (or The grosser Results Of ego-Bondage, ego-Dramatization, egoic activity, and the egoic point of view).

Thus, In The Only-By-Me Revealed and Given Way Of The Heart (or Way Of Adidam), There Is A Necessary (Beginner's) Practice and Process Of Whole bodily Re-Orientation and Purification, Which Must (In The Case Of My Every Devotee) Precede The Only-By-Me Given Spiritual Initiation Into The True Esoteric Process Of The Devotional-<u>and</u>-Spiritual Relationship To Me (In and <u>As</u> My Avatarically-Born Bodily Human Divine Form and Person).

As My Devotee, Formally Practicing The Only-By-Me Revealed and Given Way Of The Heart (or Way Of Adidam), You Must "Pay The Price" Of Sadhana. That "Price" Cannot Be Avoided or Escaped. There Must Be The Foundationary Surrender Of Profound Devotional Turning To Me (In and <u>As</u> My Avatarically-Born Bodily Human Divine Form and Person). And That Surrender Must Be Consistently Engaged, For a period of time Sufficient (By Means Of My Avataric Divine Grace) To Re-Orient the body-mind and To Purify it Of its Fundamental worldliness and Devotional Disability—Such That Your entire life (In all of its functional, practical, relational, and Cultural circumstances) Is Conformed To My Avatarically Given Divine Instruction and My Avatarically Self-Manifested Divine Person.

The Casual Promotion Of ego-Flattering Hype (Which Would "Sell" Instant Esotericism To "all comers", Regardless Of their Lack Of Necessary Preparation) Is Merely An Extension Of commonplace "consumerism", Ignorantly (and Inappropriately) Applied To The Otherwise Real, Authentic, and True Esoteric Process.

The Only-By-Me Revealed and Given Most Perfect Divine Realization Of Reality Itself (or Truth Itself, or Real God) Transcends <u>all</u> egoity, and <u>all</u> limiting conditions. Such Realization Is A Supremely Great Matter. Therefore, The Real Process Of Such Realization Has Absolutely Nothing To Do With The "amateur Esotericism" and "Spiritual dabbling" That Is Otherwise So Readily Found Attractive By the "consumer"-ego.

The Only-By-Me Revealed and Given Way Of The Heart (or Way Of Adidam) Is The Ultimate True Divine Way, Fully and Completely Given By Me. Therefore, <u>Necessarily</u>, The Only-By-Me Revealed and Given Way Of The Heart (or Way Of Adidam) Has Profound Requirements.

The Only-By-Me Revealed and Given Way Of The Heart (or Way Of Adidam) Is, From Its Very Beginning, Entirely Free Of Any Subordination To egoity, To worldliness, To conventionality, or To The Foolishness Of the consumer marketplace.

The Only-By-Me Revealed and Given Way Of The Heart (or Way Of Adidam) Is Revealed and Given, By Me, In Its Utter and Inherent Purity, and In Its Perfect Completeness.

The Only-By-Me Revealed and Given Way Of The Heart (or Way Of Adidam) Is The Only-By-Me Avatarically Revealed and (Now, and Forever Hereafter) Only-By-Me Avatarically Given Divine Way Of Truth.

Avatar Adi Da Samraj
Lopez Island, 2000

SUTRA 4

Now, Listen To Me, While I Reveal To You The Secret Of Devotional (and, In Due Course, Spiritual) Feeling-Contemplation Of Me, Which Is The Fundamental Practice For all those who Listen To Me, and For all those who Hear Me, and For all those who See Me.

The (Ultimate) Nature Of the world (and How it is arising) Is Inherently (and Tacitly) Obvious, If You Remain In A State Of Total psycho-physical Oneness With whatever and all that presently arises.

To Remain In A State Of Total psycho-physical Oneness With whatever and all that presently arises, You Must (Necessarily, and Always presently) Realize Inherently Love-Blissful Unity With whatever and all that presently arises.

Inherently Love-Blissful Unity With whatever and all that presently arises Is (Itself, or Inherently) Non-Separation (or No-Contraction) From whatever and all that presently arises.

Separation (or Total psycho-physical Contraction) From the world (or whatever and all that is presently arising) Is (Unfortunately) Precisely the First and Constant (and Inherently problematic) thing Done By all those who Make Efforts To Find Out (or To Account For) How the world is arising (and What Is its Ultimate Nature).

Separation (or Total psycho-physical self-Contraction) Is The First (and Foundation) Gesture Made By anyone who Has A Problem, or who Is Seeking, or who Is Making An Effort To Account For anything whatsoever.

Total psycho-physical Oneness (or Inherently Love-Blissful Unity) Is Inherent (or Necessarily and Priorly The Case, No Matter what conditions Do or Do Not arise), and (Therefore) Total psycho-physical Oneness (or Inherently Love-Blissful Unity) Is (Necessarily) Uncaused, and Real (or Always Already The Case, and Always Already In, Of, and Identical To Truth)—Whereas Separateness (or "Difference") Is Always conditional, conditionally Caused (or Only conditionally Apparent), and Illusory (or Always Already Dissociated From Reality and Truth).

Total psycho-physical Oneness (or Inherently Love-Blissful Unity) Need Not (and Cannot Fruitfully) Be Sought.

Total psycho-physical Oneness (or Inherently Love-Blissful Unity) Can Be (Apparently) Lost, By The Total psycho-physical Act Of self-Contraction (and, Thereby, Of Apparent Separation, Separateness, and Separativeness).

Pleasure-Seeking, Happiness-Seeking, or Unity-Seeking Efforts (Of Any Kind) Are Only Parts Of A Strategic (and Always Already Un-Happy) Adventure—and Such Effort and Adventure Are Entered Into Only By those who Are Already (Presently, and Totally) Separating (or psycho-physically Contracting) themselves In (and From) What Is, and Such Adventurers Are Seeking Only Because they Are Already, Presently and Totally, Separating (or psycho-physically Contracting) themselves In (and From) What Is.

Therefore, It Is Necessary To (Most Fundamentally) Understand This (or the Total psycho-physical self-Contraction itself), and (By The Transcending Of the Total psycho-physical self-Contraction itself) To Recover Awareness Of The Obvious (or Inherent) Love-Bliss-Unity (and, Thus, To Inherently Account For everything, and Also, Thereby, To Solve, or Inherently Transcend, All Problems).

This Most Fundamental self-Understanding (and This Recovery) Cannot (Fruitfully) Be Sought—For All Seeking Is Inherently Associated With An Already Present (and Total psycho-physical) Act Of self-Contraction (and, Thereby, Of Separation, Separateness, and Separativeness).

Most Fundamental self-Understanding Is (Itself) Inherent, or Always Already, or Native To Even (Apparently) conditional Existence Itself.

Therefore, If Most Fundamental self-Understanding Is Not Already Realized In the present, It Must (and Can Only) Be Realized By Means Of Divine Spiritual Grace (As An Avatarically Given Free Gift).

Aham Da Asmi. I Am Da (The Divine Giver), The Avatarically Self-Revealed Divine Person and The Avatarically Self-Given Divine Means Of This Divine Spiritual Grace.

I Am Love-Ananda (The Divine Love-Bliss), The Avatarically Self-Transmitted Divine Spiritual Presence and The Avatarically Self-Revealed Divine Spiritual Way Of This Free Gift.

The Most Fundamental self-Understanding Of Which I Speak Is (If Most Perfectly Realized) The Most Perfectly Ultimate (or Seventh Stage) Capability To (Inherently) Divinely Self-Recognize whatever arises.

Most Perfect self-Understanding Is The Capability To Directly (Immediately) Transcend Dilemma, All Problems, and All Seeking.

Most Perfect self-Understanding Is The Always present-time (or Always Already functioning and Effective) Capability To "Radically" (or By Addressing The "Root"-Cause) Transcend The Totality Of psycho-physical self-Contraction (and, Thus and Thereby, all Of Separation, Separateness, and Separativeness).

Most Perfect self-Understanding Is The Capability Inherent In Love-Bliss Itself (Which Is The Heart, or Root-Condition, Of Reality Itself).

Most Perfect self-Understanding Is The Capability Inherent In The Always Already, or Most Prior, Unity (With Which The Heart Itself, As Love-Bliss Itself, Is Inherently One).

I Have, By Means Of The Submission, Work, and Word Of My here-Speaking Avataric Divine Revelation-Body, Thoroughly Revealed and Described The Great (and Complete) Process Wherein and Whereby The Heart Itself (or The Love-Bliss-Unity That Is Reality Itself) Is (Ultimately) Most Perfectly Realized.

That Great (and Complete) Process (Which Is The Only-By-Me Revealed and Given Way Of Adidam, or Adidam Ruchiradam—The One and Only By-Me-Revealed and By-Me-Given Way Of The Heart) Is Described (In Every Detail and Elaboration) In This Testament Of Divine Secrets—My Summary (Written, and Forever Avatarically Speaking) Divine Word Of Heart.

This Summary Word Of Mine Is True, and That Great Process Is (Indeed) The Process (Elaborated, In Its Totality Of Details, Only By Me) Wherein The Inherently Perfect Tacit Obviousness (Of Non-Separateness, Of No-Seeking, Of No-Contraction, and Of Love-Bliss Itself) Is (Progressively, and, Yet, Always Directly and Presently[29]) Realized.

The Principle (or Great, and Only-By-My-Avataric-Divine-Grace-Given, Means) Of That Great Process Is Itself An Extreme Simplicity (As Simple To Describe As That Great Process Is Itself Necessarily Complex In Its Total Description).

The Extreme Simplicity That Is The Principle (or Great, and Only-By-My-Avataric-Divine-Grace-Given, Means) Of That Great Process Is Ruchira Avatara Bhakti Yoga, The Heart-Responsive (or Devotionally Me-Recognizing, and Devotionally To-Me-Responding) and Constant Counter-egoic, and Total psycho-physical, Practice Of ego-Surrendering, ego-Forgetting, and, More and More (and, Ultimately, Most Perfectly), ego-Transcending Devotion To Me, and Devotional (and, In Due Course, Spiritual) Communion With Me—The Da Avatar (At Once, The Divine Giver and The Avatarically Given Divine Gift), The Avatarically Self-Manifested Divine Heart-Master and The Avatarically-Born Divine World-Teacher, The Ruchira Avatar (The Avataric Divine Incarnation Of The "Bright"), The Love-Ananda Avatar (The Avataric Incarnation Of The Divine Love-Bliss), The Avataric Divine Realizer, The Avataric Divine Revealer, and The Avataric Divine Self-Revelation Of The Real and True and One and Only Divine Person (Which Is The One and Only Self-Condition and Source-Condition Of all-and-All).

Ruchira Avatara Bhakti Yoga Is The moment to moment Fulfillment Of My Great Admonition To All My Devotees—To Always Invoke Me, Feel Me, Breathe Me, and Serve Me.

Ruchira Avatara Bhakti Yoga Is To Be Constantly Exercised (moment to moment), Via The Surrender, The Forgetting, and The Transcending Of the self-Contracted body, and self-Contracted emotion (or all of self-Contracted, and Reactive, and, Altogether, limited, feeling), and self-Contracted mind (Even At its Root, Which Is attention itself), and Even every self-Contracted breath, and (Altogether) Even all of Separate (and Separative) self, In Truly (or Unlimitedly) Heart-Felt, and Whole bodily Receptive, and Fully Breathing, and Only-By-Me-Distracted Devotional (and, In Due Course, Spiritual) Contemplation Of My Avatarically-Born Bodily (Human) Divine Form, My Avatarically Self-Transmitted Spiritual (and Always Blessing) Divine Presence, and My Avatarically Self-Revealed (and Very, and Transcendental, and Perfectly Subjective, and Inherently Spiritual, and Inherently egoless, and Inherently Perfect, and Self-Evidently Divine) State.

For all those who Would (Either Formally or Informally) Study The Only-By-Me Revealed and Given Way Of The Heart, This, My Summary (Written, and Forever Speaking) Word Of Heart, Is (Now, and Forever Hereafter) Given (By Me) For their Hearts and minds To Comprehend, and, For all those who Would (Necessarily, Formally) Practice The Only-By-Me Revealed and Given Way Of The Heart, This, My Summary (Written, and Forever Speaking) Word Of Heart, Is (Now, and Forever Hereafter) Given (By Me) For their Formal (and Formally Guided, and Formally Accountable) Application, and, For all those who Would, By (Necessarily, Formally) Practicing The Only-By-Me Revealed and Given Way Of The Heart, Surrender and Forget themselves In The Divine and Inherently Perfect Truth (Of Non-Separateness, Of No-Seeking, Of No-Contraction, and Of Love-Bliss Itself), I Am Always (Now, and Forever Hereafter) here For their Devotional Resort To Me, and (In Due Course) their Searchless Devotional and Spiritual Beholding Of Me and their To-Me-Responsive Devotional and Spiritual Contemplation Of Me.

Realization Of The Most Ultimate (or Only-By-Me Revealed and Given Seventh Stage) Wisdom-Unity, Truth-Obviousness, and (Divine) Self-Recognition-Capability (Through The Truly Most Intensive and Profound Exercise Of The Fully Established, and, In Due Course, Fully Developed, Devotional and Spiritual Practice Of Ruchira Avatara Bhakti Yoga) Is A Matter Of My Divinely Self-Giving Avataric Spiritual Grace and My Graceful Avatarically Given Divine Self-Revelation.

My Avatarically-Born Bodily (Human) Divine Form—Which Has (By Virtue Of My Divine Avataric Ordeal Of Heart-"Bright" Spiritual Descent Into The Cosmic Domain) Become Most Perfectly Conformed To Me (and, Thus, To Love-Ananda, The Divine Love-Bliss Itself)—Is (Itself) The Divine Avataric Self-Revelation, The Divine Avataric Teaching Of Truth, and The Always First Realizer Of The Divine Truth Itself.

My Avatarically Self-Transmitted Spiritual (and Always Blessing) Divine Presence—Which Is My Spiritually "Bright" Avataric Heart-Transmission Of Love-Ananda, The Divine Love-Bliss Itself—Is The (Always Me-Revealing) Means.

My Avatarically Self-Revealed (and Very, and Transcendental, and Perfectly Subjective, and Inherently Spiritual, and Inherently egoless, and Inherently Perfect, and Self-Evidently Divine) State—Which Is Love-Ananda, The Divine Love-Bliss Itself—Is The (Self-Evidently Divine) Self-Revelation Of Truth Itself (Which Is Reality Itself, and The Only Real God).

Therefore, Devotional (and, In Due Course, Spiritual) Contemplation Of My Avatarically-Born Bodily (Human) Divine Form, and (Via My Avatarically-Born Bodily Human Divine Form) My Avatarically Self-Transmitted (and Self-Radiant) Spiritual (and Always Blessing) Divine "Bright" Presence, and (Via My Avatarically Self-Transmitted, and Self-Radiant, Spiritual, and Always Blessing, Divine "Bright" Presence) My Avatarically Self-Revealed (and Self-Existing, and Very, and Transcendental, and Perfectly Subjective, and Inherently Spiritual, and Inherently egoless, and Inherently Perfect, and Self-Evidently Divine) State—Even, Most Ultimately, To The Degree Of Perfect Oneness With Me (and Perfect No-Contraction and Non-Separation From all-and-All, Transcending All Seeking and all of egoity itself, By Means Of Devotional, and Total psycho-physical, self-Surrender and Heart-Conformity To Me, and, Thus, To Love-Ananda, The Divine Love-Bliss Itself)—Is The Divine Avataric Heart-Way That I Offer To You and To all.

I Say To You: First and Always, In Your bodily (human, and Total psycho-physical) form, Be The Always Devotionally Me-Recognizing (and Responsively, and Actively, Me-Serving) Devotee Of My Avatarically-Born Bodily (Human) Divine Form, and (As Your Devotion, Your Service, Your self-Discipline, and Your self-Understanding Mature, By Means Of That Total psycho-physical, and Responsively, and Actively, ego-Surrendering, and ego-Forgetting, and, More and More, self-Contraction-Yielding and self-Contraction-Transcending Feeling-Contemplation Of Me) You Will (By Means Of My Divinely Self-Giving Avataric Spiritual Grace and My Graceful Avatarically Given Divine Self-Revelation) Also Become Heart-Sensitive (and, Altogether, psycho-physically and Spiritually Sensitive) To My (Avatarically Self-Transmitted) "Bright" and True (and Always Blessing) Divine Spiritual Presence (Which Is Love-Bliss Itself), and (In The Always Deepening Avataric Spiritual Revelation Of My Ceaselessly Heart-Transmitted Divine Love-Bliss) You Will (Thus and Thereby, and More and More) Spontaneously Intuit and Contemplate The Beginningless, Endless, Centerless, Non-Separate, and Boundless Deep Of My Avatarically Self-Revealed (and Very, and Transcendental, and Perfectly Subjective, and

Inherently Spiritual, and Inherently egoless, and Inherently Perfect, and Self-Evidently Divine) State.

As My By-Me-Spiritually-Initiated (and, Necessarily, Formally Practicing) Devotee, Always Behold Me (moment to moment, and Searchlessly), and (Thus and Thereby) Responsively Contemplate My Avatarically-Born Bodily (Human) Divine Form, My Avatarically Self-Transmitted Spiritual (and Always Blessing) Divine Presence, and My Avatarically Self-Revealed (and Very, and Transcendental, and Perfectly Subjective, and Inherently Spiritual, and Inherently egoless, and Inherently Perfect, and Self-Evidently Divine) State—Such That (More and More) You Allow My Avatarically-Born Bodily (Human) Divine Form To Attract (and Keep) Your (Truly Feeling) attention, and This Such That (More and More) You Allow My Avatarically Self-Transmitted Spiritual (and Always Blessing) Divine Presence To Pervade Your body-mind (From Infinitely Above the head and mind, and Down To foot and toe), and This Such That (More and More) You Allow My Avatarically Self-Revealed (and Very, and Transcendental, and Perfectly Subjective, and Inherently Spiritual, and Inherently egoless, and Inherently Perfect, and Self-Evidently Divine) State To Self-Abide (In Person) In (and Always Already Beyond, and Perfectly Prior To) Your egoless (or Only-Me-Contemplating) Heart.

As My Devotee who Has Been (Formally) Spiritually Initiated (By Me), Remember and Invoke (or, If Possible, Directly Regard) My Avatarically-Born Bodily (Human) Divine Form, and (Merely By Feeling) Searchlessly Behold (or Contemplate, and Meditate On) My Avatarically-Born Bodily (Human) Divine Form—and (By Feeling Me, Thus) Progressively (and More and More Responsively) Feel My Avatarically Self-Transmitted Spiritual (and Always Blessing) Divine Presence, The "Bright" Divine Spirit-Current Of Giving-Force Avatarically Heart-Radiated (By Me, and As Me) In, and Via, and Around, and everywhere Beyond, and Perfectly Prior To, My Avatarically-Born Bodily (Human) Divine Form—and (By Feeling My Avatarically Self-Transmitted Spiritual, and Always Blessing, Divine Presence, Thus, Both Searchlessly and Responsively) Be Progressively (In A Total psycho-physical Manner) Yielded To My Avatarically Self-Revealed (and Very, and Transcendental, and Perfectly Subjective, and Inherently Spiritual, and Inherently egoless, and Inherently Perfect, and Self-Evidently Divine) State, Until (Thereby, In any moment) Your Own Act Of Total psycho-physical self-Contraction (and, Thus, Of Separation, Separateness, and Separativeness) Is Dissolved, Released, Vanished, and Forgotten In Me.

As My Devotee who Has Been (Formally) Spiritually Initiated (By Me), Do This Searchless and Responsive Feeling-Contemplation Of Me (Progressively, As My Divinely Self-Giving Avataric Spiritual Grace and My Graceful

Avatarically Given Divine Self-Revelation Will Have It), At Random (moment to moment), and daily (In Regular Occasions Of Formal Meditation[30])—and, Thus (By Always Keeping attention On Me), Be Released Of The Casual Distractions (and the sometimes and self-Enclosed sleep) Of attention.

Thus (By Means Of My Avatarically Self-Transmitted Divine Spiritual Grace Alone), Behold (and Contemplate, and Meditate Upon) The Obvious Truth (Of Non-Separateness, Of No-Seeking, Of No-Contraction, and Of Love-Bliss Itself)—Again and Again.

As My Devotee who Has Been (Formally) Spiritually Initiated (By Me), Always Behold Me, Contemplate Me, and Meditate On Me, By Turning The Faculties Of body, breath, emotion, and mind (as attention) To Me—Such That (By Means Of My Divinely Self-Giving Avataric Grace and My Graceful Avatarically Given Divine Self-Revelation) You Constantly Re-Establish True Heart-Communion With Me, and (Thus and Thereby) Become (As A psycho-physical Totality) self-Surrendered Into The Obvious Truth (Of Non-Separateness, Of No-Seeking, Of No-Contraction, and Of Love-Bliss Itself), Revealed (By Means Of My Divinely Self-Giving Avataric Grace and My Graceful Avatarically Given Divine Self-Revelation) To Be Inherent In (psycho-physically Total) self-Surrendered Oneness With whatever and all that presently arises—and (More and More) Exercise The (Thus By-Me-Given) Capability For Transcending All Seeking, All Problems, and all apparent limitations On The Total psycho-physical Reception Of My Avatarically Self-Transmitted Divine Spiritual Presence Of Love-Bliss Itself (If, and When, Such Seeking, or Any Such Problem, or any such limitation arises).

The Only-By-Me Revealed and Given Way Of The Heart (or Way Of Adidam) Is The Avatarically Self-Revealed Divine Way Of The Heart Itself—and The Heart (Itself) Always Already Realizes (and, In Reality, Is) The Inherent (or Native, or Always Already, and Self-Evidently Divine) Truth.

The Only-By-Me Revealed and Given Way Of The Heart (or Way Of Adidam) Is The Avatarically Self-Revealed Divine Way Of Non-Separateness, or The Self-Evidently Divine Heart-Way Of Counter-Active (or Actively ego-Transcending) Responsibility For the (otherwise always arising) Total psycho-physical action that is egoity (or the ego, or the ego-"I", or The Primal "Act Of Narcissus"—Which Is The Total psycho-physical Act Of self-Contraction, and the constant action Of Total psycho-physical Separation, Separateness, and Separativeness).

The Only-By-Me Revealed and Given Way Of The Heart (or Way Of Adidam) Is The Avatarically Self-Revealed Divine Devotional Way Of Me-Recognizing and To-Me-Responding (and Total psycho-physical) self-Surrender To (and Into) My Avatarically Self-Revealed Divine Form and Presence and

State Of Grace—Which Is The Devotional (and, In Due Course, Spiritual) Way Of (More and More Effective) Counter-egoic Action, or The Devotionally Active (and, In Due Course, Spiritually Active, and More and More Effective) Way Of The Surrender Of The Totality Of psycho-physical self-Contraction, or The Devotionally Active (and, In Due Course, Spiritually Active, and More and More Effective) Way Of ego-Transcendence, Through ego-Surrendering, ego-Forgetting, ego-Transcending, and (Altogether) Total psycho-physical Heart-Communion With (and Total psycho-physical Infusion By) The By-Me-Avatarically-Self-Revealed, and By-Me-Avatarically-Given (or Self-Transmitted), and Inherently Non-Separate, and Inherently Perfect, and Perfectly Subjective, and Inherently "Bright" (or Self-Existing and Self-Radiant) Divine Spiritual Reality and Truth.

The Only-By-Me Revealed and Given Way Of The Heart (or Way Of Adidam)—Fully Devotionally Established and (By Me) Spiritually Activated—Is The Avatarically Self-Revealed Way Of Divine Grace, Wherein The Free Gift Of Most Fundamental self-Understanding Is (In Due Course) Awakened In My Devotees, Through The moment to moment Exercise Of Searchless (and Truly Effectively ego-Transcending) Devotional Beholding (or Me-Recognition) and (Subsequent) Heart-Responsive Feeling-Contemplation Of My Avatarically-Born Bodily (Human) Divine Form, My Avatarically Self-Transmitted Spiritual (and Always Blessing) Divine Presence, and My Avatarically Self-Revealed (and Very, and Transcendental, and Perfectly Subjective, and Inherently Spiritual, and Inherently egoless, and Inherently Perfect, and Self-Evidently Divine) State.

Therefore, If You Are Responding To This (My Word Of Heart), and If You Are (By This) Heart-Moved To Transcend and Be Free Of The Otherwise Constant "Act (and Results) Of Narcissus", and If You Are Heart-Attracted To (or Toward) My Avatarically-Born Bodily (Human) Divine Form (Because It Is "Bright" To You), and To (or Toward) My Avatarically Self-Transmitted Spiritual (and Always Blessing) Divine Presence (Because It Is The Tangible Fullness Of Self-Evidently Divine Love-Bliss), and To (or Toward) My Avatarically Self-Revealed (and Very, and Transcendental, and Perfectly Subjective, and Inherently Spiritual, and Inherently egoless, and Inherently Perfect, and Self-Evidently Divine) State (Because It Tacitly Self-Reveals The One and Self-"Bright" Divine Reality and Truth), and If You Would (By Always Merely Remembering and Contemplating Me) Forget Separate and Separative self (or the ego-"I", or Total psycho-physical self-Contraction, Appearing As body, emotion, breath, and all of mind)—Then Yield To Me, Embrace My Seven Giving Gifts, and Practice The Avatarically Self-Revealed Divine Way Of The Heart In My Gracefully Self-Revealing Human, Spiritual, Transcendental, and Divine Company.

The Only-By-Me Revealed and Given Way Of The Heart—Fully Devotionally Established and (By Me) Spiritually Activated—Is The (Necessarily, Formal) Practice Of Ruchira Avatara Satsang, or The ego-Surrendering, and ego-Forgetting, and (Really Effectively) ego-Transcending Circumstance and Discipline Of Constant (or moment to moment), Whole bodily (or Total psycho-physical), Searchless (or Truly Non-Seeking), Actively Me-Beholding, Actively To-Me-Responding, Actively (Responsively) Me-Receiving, and Always Effectively Counter-egoic (or Really Effectively self-Contraction-Yielding) Feeling-Contemplation Of My Avatarically-Born Bodily (Human) Divine Form, My Avatarically Self-Transmitted Spiritual (and Always Blessing) Divine Presence, and My Avatarically Self-Revealed (and Very, and Transcendental, and Perfectly Subjective, and Inherently Spiritual, and Inherently egoless, and Inherently Perfect, and Self-Evidently Divine) State.

Therefore, As My (Formally) Fully Established and By-Me-Spiritually-Initiated (and Always Newly By-Me-Spiritually-Activated) Devotee, First (and Always) "Locate" Your Feeling Of Me (That Already and Presently Feels Attracted To Me), and (Tacitly, Effortlessly, and Truly Searchlessly) Behold Me (With All Your Heart and Breathing body-mind), and (More and More) Yield (Responsively, Actively, Intentionally, and Receptively) To The Feeling Of The Inherent "Bright" Attractiveness Of My Avatarically-Born Bodily (Human) Divine Form, and To The Feeling Of The Inherent "Bright" Attractiveness Of My Spiritual (and Always Blessing, and Progressively By-Me-Avatarically-Self-Transmitted) Divine Presence—and, By All Of This, Yield (and More and More Deeply Forget) Your ego-"I" (or Your Total psycho-physical self-Contraction, or Your Total psycho-physical action Of Separation, Separateness, and Separativeness) In The "Bright" and Very Space Of My (Progressively) By-Me-Avatarically-Self-Revealed (and Very, and Transcendental, and Perfectly Subjective, and Inherently Spiritual, and Inherently egoless, and Inherently Perfect, and Self-Evidently Divine) State.

You (Necessarily) Become (or Conform To The Likeness Of) Whatever You Behold, or Contemplate, or Meditate On, or Even think about.

Therefore, My Formally Fully Established True Devotee, By-Me-Spiritually-Initiated (and Always Newly By-Me-Spiritually-Activated), Should Always (Searchlessly) Behold Me, and Always Actively (Responsively) Contemplate Me, and Always Transcend Even all thought By Meditating On Me.

As My (Formally) Fully Established and By-Me-Spiritually-Initiated (and Always Newly By-Me-Spiritually-Activated) Devotee, Do Not Meditate On Your Separate self (Your states, Your experiences, Your Presumed knowledge, Your Dilemma, Your Problem, or Your Search), and Do Not Perpetuate The psycho-physical Totality Of self-Contraction (By Strategies Of Independent Effort, and

By Adventures Of Either self-Glorification Or self-Destruction, Within or Without)—but (Always, Immediately) Transcend self-attention, personal psycho-physical states, merely conditional experiences, Presumptions Of merely conditional knowledge, and All Of Dilemma, Problem, and Search (Merely By Remembering Me, and Invoking Me, and Beholding Me, and Contemplating Me, and Meditating On Me, and, Therefore, Merely By Surrendering The psycho-physical Totality Of self-Contraction, or all of body-mind, To *Me*—Not By self-Concerned Seeking-Effort, or By Strategic Manipulation Of conditions themselves, but By Simply, and More and More Deeply, "Locating", and Responsively Yielding To, The Always Presently Available Feeling Of The Inherent "Bright" Attractiveness Of My Avatarically-Born Bodily Human Divine Form, and Of My Avatarically Self-Transmitted Spiritual, and Always Blessing, Divine Presence, and Of My Avatarically Self-Revealed, and Very, and Transcendental, and Perfectly Subjective, and Inherently Spiritual, and Inherently egoless, and Inherently Perfect, and Self-Evidently Divine State), and (Thus, By Means Of The Always Presently Available Grace That Is My Good Company) Always and Actively Feel Beyond and (Really, Effectively) Transcend Your Separate and Separative self (Merely By Feeling, and, Thus, Beholding, and, Thereby, Contemplating and Meditating On Me).

Do This Beholding, and Contemplating, and Meditating For Its Own Sake (Merely To Abide In Whole bodily, or Total psycho-physical, Communion With Me), and Not Passively and Partially, As If *Waiting* For Devotion To Happen *To* You (Rather Than Always Presently Remembering, Invoking, and "Locating" Me, and, Thereupon, Responsively *Allowing* The Presently Inevitable Feeling Of My Inherent "Bright" Attractiveness, and, Thereby, Most Simply, *Always* and *Fully* *Activating* My Always Given and Giving Gift Of *Inherent* Devotion To Me), and Not Cleverly and Strategically, With All Seeking-Effort, and No Heart-Response (Intent but Not Yielding, Stressful With The *Seeking* Of Me, Rather Than Happy With The *Finding* Of Me)—but Do This Beholding, and Contemplating, and Meditating Constantly, As A Total psycho-physical Act, moment to moment, Always Merely By Heart (and, Thus, By The Feeling-Exercise Of the Total body-mind), and (Thus) By Whole-bodily-Feeling *To* My Avatarically-Born Bodily (Human) Divine Form, and (More and More) By Whole-bodily-Feeling *Into* My Avatarically Self-Transmitted Spiritual (and Always Blessing) Divine Presence, and (More and More) By Whole-bodily-Feeling My Very and Freely Avatarically-Self-Revealed and Freely (Inherently) Perfect State.

Therefore, When You Have Been (Formally) Fully Established As My Devotee, and When (On That Basis) You Are (Formally) Spiritually Initiated (By Me), Truly *Be* My Always *Newly* By-Me-Spiritually-Activated Devotee,

Always Directly "Locating" and Searchlessly Beholding Me (and Tacitly Heart-Recognizing Me, Always Tangibly and Whole bodily Heart-Knowing Who I Truly, Really, and, Self-Evidently, Divinely Am)—and The Obvious Truth (Of Non-Separateness, Of No-Seeking, Of No-Contraction, and Of Love-Bliss Itself) Will (To The Degree You Make Room For Me In The Place Of Your Feeling, By Surrendering thought, and Even Every Form Of psycho-physical self-Contraction, In ego-Forgetting Me-Remembrance) Be Received (and, Ultimately, Most Perfectly Realized) By You (As My Divinely Self-Giving Avataric Spiritual Grace and My Graceful Avatarically Given Divine Self-Revelation Will Have It).

Now, and Forever Hereafter, This Simplicity Is The Foundation Practice (and The Foundation Of The Entire Practice Of The Only-By-Me Revealed and Given Way Of The Heart) To Which I Call every one.

All those who Would So (and, Necessarily, Formally) Practice Are Called, By Me, To Embrace, and (According To My Instructions) To Develop, The Original (or Most Basic) functional, practical, relational, and Cultural Disciplines I Have Described (and Given) In and By This, My Summary (Written, and Forever Speaking) Word Of Heart.

Those Disciplines and Practices Are The Most Basic (and Necessary) Evidence Of The Devotional and (In Due Course) Spiritual Relationship To Me.

Those Disciplines and Practices Should Be Immediately and Positively Embraced (and Thoroughly Developed, By Real, and, Necessarily, Formally Culturally Accountable, Practice) In The First (or Student-Beginner) Context Of The Foundation Practice Of The Only-By-Me Revealed and Given Way Of The Heart (Which Is The Way Of The Devotional and, In Due Course, Spiritual Relationship To Me).

When their Signs Of Heart-Responsive Devotional Recognition Of Me (and Of Growth In The Only-By-Me Revealed and Given Way Of The Heart) Allow (or, Otherwise, Require[31]), My Devotees Are Given Access To My Blessing-Seat—and each one Should Come To Me (At The Place, or Places, Of My Blessing-Seat Appropriate For his or her Access To Me, In Accordance With his or her Developmental Stage Of Practice[32] Of The Only-By-Me Revealed and Given Way Of The Heart), and This As Often As his or her Right and True and Truly Growing Practice Of The Only-By-Me Revealed and Given Way Of The Heart, and his or her Present (and, Altogether, Consistently Demonstrated) Signs Of Real and True Heart-Recognition Of Me and Heart-Resort To Me, Allow (and Truly Require).

During The (Physical) Lifetime Of My Avatarically-Born Bodily (Human) Divine Form (here), I May Freely Manifest My Seclusions, Offerings, and

Blessing-Wanderings any where—but I Will Always (Forever), During and After (and Forever After) The (Physical) Lifetime Of My Avatarically-Born Bodily (Human) Divine Form (here), Be Divinely Spiritually Present (By All My Avataric Divine Means) At Adidam Samrajashram (The Island Of Naitauba, In Fiji)—Which Island Is (Now, and Forever Hereafter) My Principal and Great Directly-By-Me Spiritually Empowered Ruchira Sannyasin Hermitage Ashram, Where I Have Established Myself In "Brightest" Perpetuity,[33] For The Sake Of all-and-All.

During The (Physical) Lifetime Of My Avatarically-Born Bodily (Human) Divine Form (here), I May Freely Manifest My Seclusions, Offerings, and Blessing-Wanderings any where—but I Will Always (Forever), During and After (and Forever After) The (Physical) Lifetime Of My Avatarically-Born Bodily (Human) Divine Form (here), Be Divinely Spiritually Present (By All My Avataric Divine Means) At All Four Of The Directly-By-Me Spiritually Empowered Ruchira Sannyasin Hermitage Ashrams (Including Adidam Samrajashram, The Mountain Of Attention Sanctuary, Tat Sundaram Hermitage, and Da Love-Ananda Mahal), Each Of Which I Have Directly Spiritually Empowered and Spiritually Established As A Unique Sacred Domain (and A Perpetual Agent Of My Divine Avataric Purposes), Set Apart (and, Thus, Made Holy) For Constant Pilgrimages and Retreats (and Every Other Truly Me-Invoking, and Devotionally Me-Recognizing, and Devotionally To-Me-Responding, and Devotionally Me-Serving Sacred Use) By My By-Me-Spiritually-Initiated Devotees, and, Altogether, To Be Used (Now, and Forever Hereafter) According To The Principles, Rules, and Instructions Given By Me To The Ruchira Sannyasin Order Of Adidam Ruchiradam, Which Formal Order Has Been (and Is, Now, and Forever Hereafter) Formally Appointed By Me To Be The Culturally Governing (but Entirely Renunciate, and Non-managerial) Authority (Always Subordinate To, and Effectively Extending, My Own Absolute Authority) Within The Only-By-Me Revealed and Given Way Of The Heart (or Way Of Adidam), During (and Forever After) The Physical Lifetime Of My Avatarically-Born Bodily (Human) Divine Form here.

At all times, and In all places, daily and Always, All My (Necessarily, Formally Practicing) Devotees Should (In Accordance With each one's Developmental Stage Of Practice In The Only-By-Me Revealed and Given Way Of The Heart) Ceaselessly Resort To (and Constantly Whole bodily Turn To, Invoke, Behold, Contemplate, and Meditate On) My Avatarically-Born Bodily (Human) Divine Form, My Avatarically Self-Transmitted Spiritual (and Always Blessing) Divine Presence, and My Avatarically Self-Revealed (and Very, and Transcendental, and Perfectly Subjective, and Inherently Spiritual, and Inherently egoless, and Inherently Perfect, and Self-Evidently Divine) State, and (As Required, and As Permitted, In Accordance With each one's Developmental Stage Of Practice In The Only-By-Me Revealed and Given Way Of The Heart) they Should Do This At All Four Of The Directly-By-Me Spiritually Empowered Ruchira Sannyasin Hermitage Ashrams, and, Otherwise (Always, day to day, As Required—or, Otherwise, Allowed—By each one's Developmental Stage Of Practice In The Only-By-Me Revealed and Given Way Of The Heart), Within All The Formally Designated Regional Gatherings[34] Of My Formally Practicing Devotees (who, As My Formally Practicing Devotees, Are, Thus and Necessarily, each and all, Always Formally Practicing Under The Cultural Authority and Guidance Of The Ruchira Sannyasin Order Of Adidam Ruchiradam—Which Order Is Formally Established By Me, and, Now, and Forever Hereafter, Formally Extending From Me, To Be The One and Only Culturally Governing Authority In The Only-By-Me Revealed and Given Way Of The Heart, or Way Of Adidam, and Which Order Is, Now, and Forever Hereafter, To Function, As The One and Only and Always Me-Extending Culturally Governing Authority, In Relation To Each and Every Formally Practicing Devotee, and Each and Every Formally Designated Regional Gathering, and Each and Every Formal Congregation, and Each and Every Formal Practicing Order, and Each and Every Directly-By-Me Spiritually Empowered Ruchira Sannyasin Hermitage Ashram, and Each and Every Formally Established Institutional Entity or Organizational Element, In The Only-By-Me Revealed and Given Way Of The Heart, or Way Of Adidam), and All My Formally Practicing Devotees Should (Always and Constantly) Do All Of This, Even Under <u>all</u> the circumstances of <u>every</u> day—For I Will Always (Forever), During and After (and Forever After) The (Physical) Lifetime Of My Avatarically-Born Bodily (Human) Divine Form (here), Be Really (Avatarically, Spiritually, Transcendentally, and Divinely) Present Even every then and there (and, Therefore, every where and when) For All My Formally Practicing (and, In Due Course, By-Me-Spiritually-Initiated, and, Thereafter, Always To Be Newly By-Me-Spiritually-Activated) Devotees.

I Am here Only For This Satsang—The Ceaseless (and Constantly To-Me-Turned) Resort To Me (In and <u>As</u> and Via My Avatarically-Born Bodily Human Divine Form) By My Formally Practicing Devotees, who Would Perpetually Enjoy The "Bright"-Blessed Way Of Totally (or Whole bodily) psycho-physically Enacted (ego-Surrendering, ego-Forgetting, and ego-Transcending) Devotional (and, In Due Course, Spiritual) Feeling-Communion With Me (The One, and Only, and Very, and Self-Evidently Divine Person—Avatarically-Born In Bodily Human Divine Form, In Order To Be Realized By each and all and All).

I No Longer Teach (or Submit To Seem In The ordinary Likeness Of every one and all, In Order To Reflect them To themselves, and, Thus and Thereby,

To Prove The Necessity Of ego-Transcendence, and, Altogether, In Order To Reveal and Describe The Great Means and The Great Process Of The Heart-Way Of Non-Separateness), but (Now, and Forever Hereafter—During, and After, and Forever After, The Physical Lifetime Of My Avatarically-Born Bodily Human Divine Form here), Having Already Fully and Completely Done My First (or Teaching and Self-Revelation) Work (and Such That It Will Live and Work Forever, Through This, My Summary Written, and Forever Speaking, Word Of Heart, and Through The Recorded, Remembered, and Constantly Retold Leelas Of All Of My Avatarically Self-Manifested Divine Teaching-Work, and Divine Self-Revelation Work, and Through The Recorded, and Forever Living, Images Of My Avatarically-Born Bodily Human Divine Form), I Only Call each one and all To True and Constant Devotional, and (In Due Course) Spiritual, and Always Total psycho-physical Heart-Communion With Me—Because I Only Appear and Function here, and Always As I Am, In Order That (Now, and Forever Hereafter—During, and After, and Forever After, The Physical Lifetime Of My Avatarically-Born Bodily Human Divine Form here) I May Do My Great "Bright" Divinely Self-"Emerging" Avataric Spiritual Blessing-Work With every one and all and All.

Therefore (Now, and Forever Hereafter—During, and After, and Forever After, The Physical Lifetime Of My Avatarically-Born Bodily Human Divine Form here, and Entirely For The Sake Of their True and Constant Devotional, and, In Due Course, Spiritual, Communion With Me), I Am, By All My Divine Avataric Means, Divinely Spiritually Present (here and every "where" In The Cosmic Domain), Always "Bright" To Give (or Awaken In, and Require Of) All My Devotees The Gift Of Constant (and Fully Lived) Devotional Love Of Me—Because True and Constant Devotional (and, In Due Course, Spiritual) Communion With Me Is (and, In every moment, Requires) Truly Heart-Responsive (and, Therefore, Truly Devotionally Me-Recognizing, and Really ego-Surrendering, ego-Forgetting, and ego-Transcending), and (Altogether) Total psycho-physical, Heart-Resort To Me.

Likewise (Now, and Forever Hereafter—During, and After, and Forever After, The Physical Lifetime Of My Avatarically-Born Bodily Human Divine Form here, and Entirely For The Sake Of their True and Constant Devotional, and, In Due Course, Spiritual, Communion With Me), I Am, By All My Divine Avataric Means, Divinely Spiritually Present (here and every "where" In The Cosmic Domain), Always "Bright" To Give (or Awaken In, and Require Of) All My Devotees The Gift Of Constant Devotional Service To Me—Because True and Constant Devotional (and, In Due Course, Spiritual) Communion With Me Is (and, In Every functional, practical, or relational Context or Circumstance, Requires) Truly Heart-Responsive (and, Therefore, Truly

Devotionally Me-Recognizing, and Really ego-Surrendering, ego-Forgetting, and ego-Transcending), and (Altogether) Total psycho-physical, Heart-attention To Me.

And (Now, and Forever Hereafter—During, and After, and Forever After, The Physical Lifetime Of My Avatarically-Born Bodily Human Divine Form here, and Entirely For The Sake Of their True and Constant Devotional, and, In Due Course, Spiritual, Communion With Me) I Am, By All My Divine Avataric Means, Divinely Spiritually Present (here and every "where" In The Cosmic Domain), Always "Bright" To Give (or Awaken In, and Require Of) All My Devotees The Gift Of Constant (and, Altogether, Devotionally Inspired) self-Discipline—Because True and Constant Devotional (and, In Due Course, Spiritual) Communion With Me Is (and, In Every Context or Circumstance, Requires) Truly Heart-Responsive (and, Therefore, Truly Devotionally Me-Recognizing, and Really ego-Surrendering, ego-Forgetting, and ego-Transcending), and (Altogether) Total psycho-physical, Heart-Obedience and Heart-Conformity To Me.

Now, and Forever Hereafter, During and After (and Forever After) The (Physical) Lifetime Of My Avatarically-Born Bodily (Human) Divine Form (here), I Am, By All My Divine Avataric Means, <u>here</u> (and every "where" In The Cosmic Domain)—Always Spiritually and Divinely "Bright" <u>As</u> The One, and Only, and Inherently egoless, and Inherently Indivisible Conscious Light Of all-and-All.

I Am here (Now, and Forever Hereafter) For Only One Purpose: To Spiritually Bless and Awaken those who Resort To Me As their One and Only, True and Divine, Refuge and Means Of Life and Light.

My Summary (Written, and Forever Speaking) Word Of Heart Relative To Ruchira Avatara Bhakti Yoga (The Extreme Simplicity That Is The Great Means Of The Only-By-Me Revealed and Given Way Of The Heart), and Relative To The Progressive Process Of The Developmental Stages (and All The Technical Practices) Of The Only-By-Me Revealed and Given Way Of The Heart, Is (Now, and Forever Hereafter—During, and After, and Forever After, The Physical Lifetime Of My Avatarically-Born Bodily Human Divine Form here) Fully and Finally and Completely Given—and This, My Summary (Written, and Forever Speaking) Word Of Heart, Is (Now, and Forever Hereafter—During, and After, and Forever After, The Physical Lifetime Of My Avatarically-Born Bodily Human Divine Form here) To Be Openly and everywhere Communicated (As I Have Written It, In Its Full, Final, and Complete Form), So That everyone (As every one) May Read This, My Summary (Written, and Forever Speaking) Avataric Divine Word, and (By personal Heart-Response, As and Whenever they Will) Become My Devotees, and So That All My

Devotees May Study This, My Summary (Written, and Forever Speaking) Avataric Divine Word, and (By Intensive and Steady Application) Develop their Practice (In Accordance With each one's Eventually Proven Choice Of Either The Devotional Way Of Insight Or The Devotional Way Of Faith) In The Only-By-Me Revealed and Given Way Of The Heart.

All Of My (Necessarily, Formally Acknowledged) Devotees Must Begin their Practice Of The Only-By-Me Revealed and Given Way Of The Heart By Embracing The (Preliminary) Student-Beginner Stage Of Foundation Practices—and, When, In Due Course (By Means Of My Divinely Self-Giving Avataric Grace and My Graceful Avatarically Given Divine Self-Revelation), they Stably Demonstrate The (Original) Maturing Signs Of Student-Beginner Practice In The Only-By-Me Revealed and Given Way Of The Heart, they (Thereby) Become Qualified (With Always current, or Always then present-time, Formal Approval By The Ruchira Sannyasin Order Of Adidam Ruchiradam) To Formally Embrace The Right, True, Full, and Fully Devotional Practice Of The Only-By-Me Revealed and Given Way Of The Heart <u>Primarily</u> As (and On The Constant Basis Of The Always Primary, and By-Me-Spiritually-Initiated, and Always Newly By-Me-Spiritually-Activated Practice Of) The Searchless Beholding Of Me.

All Of My (Necessarily, Formally Practicing) Devotees Must Always Practice The Only-By-Me Revealed and Given Way Of The Heart Under Continuous and Formal Guidance Within One Of The Two (Formal) Congregations Established (and Formally Appointed) By Me For The Sake Of My Formally (and, Progressively, Fully) Practicing Devotees—and they Must (In Each Case, As A Formal Practicing Member Of Either The First Or The Second Congregation Of Adidam Ruchiradam) Allow their Practice and their Discipline To Be Formally Guided, Measured, and Evaluated In A (Formally) Culturally Accountable Manner (Under The Overall Culturally Governing Authority Of The Ruchira Sannyasin Order Of Adidam Ruchiradam).

All Of My (Necessarily, Formally Practicing) Devotees Must (Progressively, and With Formal Cultural Accountability) Enter Into (and, In Due Course, Fully Develop) The By-Me-Given Disciplines, Practices, Stages, and Realizations Of The Only-By-Me Revealed and Given Way Of The Heart (Entirely In Accordance With My Instructions, As Given To, and As Formally Authorized By, The Ruchira Sannyasin Order Of Adidam Ruchiradam)—and they Must Do So In A Formal, Progressive, and personally Appropriate Manner.

The Practice and The Discipline Of My (Necessarily, Formally Practicing) Devotees Must, Necessarily, Be Formally and Consistently Monitored and Measured Relative To The Progressive Development Of The Developmental Signs Of Devotional Resort To Me, and Of Searchless Devotional and Spiritual

Beholding Of Me, and Of Heart-Responsive (and Total psycho-physical, and Truly ego-Surrendering and ego-Forgetting) Devotional and Spiritual Communion With Me, and Of Truly ego-Surrendering and ego-Forgetting Service To Me, and Of Really self-Contraction-Observing and self-Contraction-Yielding (functional, practical, relational, and Cultural) self-Discipline, and Of Truly ego-Surrendering and ego-Forgetting Study and self-Application Of My Avataric Divine Word, and Of Increasingly Meditative (and Also moment to moment, and More and More Profoundly ego-Surrendering and ego-Forgetting) Feeling-Contemplation Of Me—and My Devotees Must Formally (and Rightly) Maintain (and Cultivate) their Participation In (and their Practice-Accountability To) The Sacred Cultural Gathering Established (and Formally Appointed) By Me For The Sake Of All Formal Practitioners (and All Formal Congregations) Of The Only-By-Me Revealed and Given Way Of The Heart, and they Must Do All Of This Persistently (and Always In and By Means Of Devotional Contemplation Of My Avatarically-Born Bodily Human Divine Form, My Avatarically Self-Transmitted Spiritual, and Always Blessing, Divine Presence, and My Avatarically Self-Revealed, and Very, and Transcendental, and Perfectly Subjective, and Inherently Spiritual, and Inherently egoless, and Inherently Perfect, and Self-Evidently Divine State), No Matter How Profound The Process Of Reception Of Me (or, Otherwise, No Matter How Advanced, or Even Ultimate,[35] The Process or The Event Of Realization Of Me) May Become, or (Otherwise) Seem To Be.

Whatever their Developmental Stage and Manner Of Practice (Of The Only-By-Me Revealed and Given Way Of The Heart), My True Devotees Will Always Truly and Really Love Me, and they Will Always Resort To Me (and Only To Me), and they Will Always Take Refuge In Me (and Only In Me), and (By Means Of Always True and Fullest ego-Surrendering, ego-Forgetting, and, More and More, ego-Transcending Devotion To Me) they Will Always Heart-Reside With Me.

The Basic (or Essential) Practice For all who (Necessarily, Formally) Practice The Only-By-Me Revealed and Given Way Of The Heart Is (In Its Inherent Simplicity) Just That Of Devotionally Me-Recognizing (and Devotionally To-Me-Responding, and Altogether Responsible) Feeling-Contemplation Of My Avatarically-Born Bodily (Human) Divine Form, and (Thereby, and In Due Course) My Avatarically Self-Transmitted Spiritual (and Always Blessing) Divine Presence, and (Thus and Thereby) My Avatarically Self-Revealed (and Very, and Transcendental, and Perfectly Subjective, and Inherently Spiritual, and Inherently egoless, and Inherently Perfect, and Self-Evidently Divine) State.

Therefore, I Embrace All (Necessarily, Formal) Practitioners Of The Only-By-Me Revealed and Given Way Of The Heart—and I Embrace each one and all of them Simply (Merely) As My Devotees (who Are all Resorting To Me).

My Spiritual Blessing Of My By-Me-Spiritually-Initiated (and Always Ready To Be Newly By-Me-Spiritually-Activated) Devotees Always Spiritually Transmits The Same Gift (Of Ruchira Shaktipat) To each and all—For I Always Give, and Freely Give, The One and Only and Divine Spiritual Gift Of My "Bright" Divine Self-Revelation To each and all.

My Spiritual Blessing Of My By-Me-Spiritually-Initiated (and Always Ready To Be Newly By-Me-Spiritually-Activated) Devotees Is Always Full Of My "Bright" Spirit-Power, Given For The Sake Of The Heart-Awakening Of every one and all of them.

Because My Spiritual Blessing-Gift Of Ruchira Shaktipat Is Always Only The Divine Spiritual Gift Of My "Bright" Divine Self-Revelation, There Are Not Different "Kinds" Of Spiritual Blessings Given By Me For Each Developmental Stage Of Practice In The Only-By-Me Revealed and Given Way Of The Heart—but There Are Different Stages and Degrees Of Devotional and Spiritual Approach To Me and Of Devotional and Spiritual Access To Me.

Because Of My Always Constant, Giving, Full, and Perfect Spiritual Blessing-Grace, and Because My Blessing-Gift Of Ruchira Shaktipat Is Always The Divine Spiritual Gift Of My "Bright" Divine Self-Revelation, It Is Possible For any one To Practice The Only-By-Me Revealed and Given Way Of The Heart—and That Practice Potentially (and More and More Readily and Profoundly) Realizes (By Means Of My Divinely Self-Giving Avataric Spiritual Grace and My Graceful Avatarically Given Divine Self-Revelation) Total psycho-physical Oneness (or Inherently Love-Blissful Unity) With whatever and all that presently arises, If any one Will (As My Formally Fully Established, and By-Me-Spiritually-Initiated, and Always Newly By-Me-Spiritually-Activated Devotee) Always and Merely (or Truly Searchlessly) Behold Me, and (On That Searchlessly Me-Beholding Basis) Actively Heart-Respond To Me (With Truly Me-Recognizing, and Rightly Me-Contemplating, and Really Spiritually Me-Receiving, and, Altogether, Effectively ego-Transcending Devotion To Me, and In Constant and ego-Transcending Service To Me), and If any one Will (Thereby, and Consistently, and With Full Formal Accountability, According To My Instructions) Embrace True (functional, practical, relational, and Cultural) self-Discipline In My Company, and If any one Will (Progressively) Allow Every Kind Of (Thus Inspired and Accomplished) Change and Release Of body, emotion, mind, breath, and Separate self.

As The Basis For Practicing Any By-Me-Given Form Of The "Conscious Process" (or The Process Of Devotion To Me That Specifically Controls, or Surrenders and Transcends, The egoic, or self-Contracting, Gesture and Tendency Of attention), My Devotee Must (By Means Of My Divinely Self-Giving Avataric Grace and My Graceful Avatarically Given Divine Self-Revelation) Regularly, Randomly, and More and More Constantly Surrender self-Contraction (Merely By Means Of Me-Remembering, and Me-Invoking, and Devotionally Me-Recognizing, and Devotionally To-Me-Responding, and Really ego-Surrendering, ego-Forgetting, and More and More Effectively ego-Transcending Feeling-Contemplation Of My Avatarically-Born Bodily Human Divine Form, My Avatarically Self-Transmitted Spiritual, and Always Blessing, Divine Presence, and My Avatarically Self-Revealed, and Very, and Transcendental, and Perfectly Subjective, and Inherently Spiritual, and Inherently egoless, and Inherently Perfect, and Self-Evidently Divine State)—and, As The Basis For Practicing Any By-Me-Given Form Of "Conductivity" (or The Whole bodily, physical, emotional, and mental, "Conscious Exercise" Of breath, bodily energy, and, In Due Course, My Avatarically Self-Transmitted Divine Spirit-Force), My Devotee Must (Entirely and Merely By Means Of Me-Remembering, and Me-Invoking, and Devotionally Me-Recognizing, and Devotionally To-Me-Responding, and Really ego-Surrendering, ego-Forgetting, and More and More Effectively ego-Transcending Feeling-Contemplation Of My Avatarically-Born Bodily Human Divine Form, and, In Due Course, My Avatarically Self-Transmitted Spiritual, and Always Blessing, Divine Presence, and, Thus and Thereby, My Avatarically Self-Revealed, and Very, and Transcendental, and Perfectly Subjective, and Inherently Spiritual, and Inherently egoless, and Inherently Perfect, and Self-Evidently Divine State) Embrace and Maintain (and, On That Basis, Develop), According To My Instructions, Basic functional, practical, relational, and Cultural (and, Altogether, self-Contraction-Yielding) self-Discipline (Including The Most Basic "Conscious Exercise" Of breath and bodily energy—Which Is, In Due Course, By Means Of My Divinely Self-Giving Avataric Spiritual Grace and My Graceful Avatarically Given Divine Self-Revelation, Spontaneously Converted Into Truly Devotional, or Heart-Responsive, Reception and "Conductivity" Of My "Bright" Avatarically Self-Transmitted Spiritual, and Always Blessing, Divine Presence).

If Only My Devotee Will (Truly Devotionally, and Rightly, and, Necessarily, Formally) Practice The Only-By-Me Revealed and Given Way Of The Heart, The Obvious Truth (Of Non-Separateness, Of No-Seeking, Of No-Contraction, and Of Love-Bliss Itself) Will, By Means Of My Divinely Self-Giving Avataric Spiritual Grace and My Graceful Avatarically Given Divine Self-Revelation, Be (In Due Course—At First, In Random moments, and, Eventually, More and More Readily and Profoundly, and, At Last, Most Perfectly) Revealed (and, Altogether, "Located" and Realized) As The Obvious.

In The Course Of That Process Of Revelation and Realization, Many Insights and Experiences and Responsibilities May Arise.

In Any Case (No Matter what arises), It Is Only Necessary To Maintain (and, Otherwise, To Progressively Develop, or Intensify) Right and True functional, practical, relational, Cultural, and (Altogether) self-Responsible (and Total psycho-physical) self-Discipline (According To My Instructions, As Given By Me For Application By My Formally Practicing Devotees, According To each one's Developmental Stage Of Practice In The Only-By-Me Revealed and Given Way Of The Heart), and (On That Basis) To Rightly and Truly Practice (According To My Instructions, As Given By Me For Application By My Formally Practicing Devotees, According To each one's Developmental Stage Of Practice In The Only-By-Me Revealed and Given Way Of The Heart) Regular (and Also Random, and More and More Constant, and Truly, Deeply ego-Surrendering, ego-Forgetting, and Effectively ego-Transcending) Devotional (and Me-Serving), and (In Due Course) Spiritual, and (Altogether) Total psycho-physical Communion With My Avatarically-Born Bodily (Human) Divine Form, My Avatarically Self-Transmitted Spiritual (and Always Blessing) Divine Presence, and My Avatarically Self-Revealed (and Very, and Transcendental, and Perfectly Subjective, and Inherently Spiritual, and Inherently egoless, and Inherently Perfect, and Self-Evidently Divine) State.

The Most Ultimate and Most Perfect (or True, and Only-By-Me Revealed and Given, Seventh Stage) Realization and Capability Is The Real Potential <u>Only</u> Of <u>My</u> (Necessarily, Formally Practicing) Devotees, and, Necessarily (Because Of All That Is Required For That Realization and Capability), <u>Only</u> Of those Of My Devotees who Consistently (and Truly Devotionally) Recognize Me and Resort To Me and Receive Me and Realize Me, and who (With Always current, or Always then present-time, Formal Approval By The Ruchira Sannyasin Order Of Adidam Ruchiradam) Practice The Only-By-Me Revealed and Given Way Of The Heart <u>Primarily</u> As (and On The Constant Basis Of The Primary Practice Of) The Searchless (and Spiritually Me-Receiving) Beholding Of Me—and, Indeed, The Only-By-Me Given Great Graces Of The True Hearing Of Me and The True Seeing Of Me (As Described, By Me, In This, My Summary Written, and Forever Speaking, Word Of Heart) Are, Also, The Real Potential <u>Only</u> Of (Necessarily) Formally Practicing Devotees Of Mine, who Formally Embrace The Right, True, Full, and Fully Devotional Practice Of The Only-By-Me Revealed and Given Way Of The Heart, and who Do So (With Always current, or Always then present-time, Formal Approval By The Ruchira Sannyasin Order Of Adidam Ruchiradam) <u>Primarily</u> As (and On The Constant Basis Of The Primary Practice Of) The Searchless (and Spiritually Me-Receiving) Beholding Of Me—and Even <u>Any</u> and <u>Every</u> By-Me-Spiritually-Initiated (and, Necessarily, Formally Practicing) Devotee Of <u>Mine</u> Is Fully Instructed and Admonished By Me, and (If he or she Consistently, Rightly, and Truly Devotionally Resorts To Me) Constantly (and Always Newly) Spiritually Blessed By Me (At Heart, and In his or her Total body-mind), To (Potentially,

In Random moments, and, As The Case May Be, More and More Readily and Profoundly, If he or she Will Practice The Only-By-Me Revealed and Given Way Of The Heart According To My Instructions Given For his or her Developmental Stage Of Practice In The Only-By-Me Revealed and Given Way Of The Heart) Behold and Receive Me, and (Thus and Thereby—In The Manner, and To The Degree, That Is Possible, According To his or her Developmental Stage Of Practice In The Only-By-Me Revealed and Given Way Of The Heart) To Be self-Surrendered Into The Obvious Truth (Of Non-Separateness, Of No-Seeking, Of No-Contraction, and Of Love-Bliss Itself) That Is, By Means Of My Divinely Self-Giving Avataric Spiritual Grace and My Graceful Avatarically Given Divine Self-Revelation, Realized To Be Inherent In any and every moment Of Total psycho-physical Oneness (or Inherently Love-Blissful Unity) With whatever and all that presently arises.

In any and every moment Of (Formally) Fully Established and By-Me-Spiritually-Initiated (and Always Newly By-Me-Spiritually-Activated) Devotional and Spiritual Communion With My Avatarically-Born Bodily (Human) Divine Form, My Avatarically Self-Transmitted Spiritual (and Always Blessing) Divine Presence, and My Avatarically Self-Revealed (and Very, and Transcendental, and Perfectly Subjective, and Inherently Spiritual, and Inherently egoless, and Inherently Perfect, and Self-Evidently Divine) State, each one Will (By Means Of My Divinely Self-Giving Avataric Spiritual Grace and My Graceful Avatarically Given Divine Self-Revelation) Behold and Receive Me According To The Quality and Strength Of his or her Me-Recognizing and To-Me-Responding (and Effectively ego-Surrendering, ego-Forgetting, and ego-Transcending) Devotion To Me.

In any and every moment Of (Formally) Fully Established and By-Me-Spiritually-Initiated (and Always Newly By-Me-Spiritually-Activated) Devotional and Spiritual Communion With My Avatarically-Born Bodily (Human) Divine Form, My Avatarically Self-Transmitted Spiritual (and Always Blessing) Divine Presence, and My Avatarically Self-Revealed (and Very, and Transcendental, and Perfectly Subjective, and Inherently Spiritual, and Inherently egoless, and Inherently Perfect, and Self-Evidently Divine) State, each one Will (By Means Of My Divinely Self-Giving Avataric Spiritual Grace and My Graceful Avatarically Given Divine Self-Revelation) Behold and Receive Me According To The Presence or Absence Of the various kinds of egoic limitations that Characterize and Enforce a physical, psycho-physical, or (otherwise) merely psychic (or mind-Made) point of view.

In any and every moment Of (Formally) Fully Established and By-Me-Spiritually-Initiated (and Always Newly By-Me-Spiritually-Activated) Devotional and Spiritual Communion With My Avatarically-Born Bodily (Human) Divine

Form, My Avatarically Self-Transmitted Spiritual (and Always Blessing) Divine Presence, and My Avatarically Self-Revealed (and Very, and Transcendental, and Perfectly Subjective, and Inherently Spiritual, and Inherently egoless, and Inherently Perfect, and Self-Evidently Divine) State, each one Will (By Means Of My Divinely Self-Giving Avataric Spiritual Grace and My Graceful Avatarically Given Divine Self-Revelation) Behold and Receive Me According To his or her Relative (and Effective) Willingness To Be Released From the present point of view (and, Most Ultimately, In The Case Of My Devotees who Most Perfectly Realize Me, Even From every Possible point of view, or All The egoic Stages Of Life).

Each and every one Of My Devotees Is Called By Me To (In Due Course) Enter The Truly Me-Seeing Stages Of Practice In The Only-By-Me Revealed and Given Way Of The Heart, and (Thus, Thereby, and In Due Course) To Receive (and, Potentially, To Realize) The Inherent Heart-Capability To Stand Free (and To Demonstrate The Only-By-Me Revealed and Given Seventh, and Inherently Most Perfect, and Truly Most Ultimate, Stage Of Life)—and This Capability and Freedom Is To Be Received (and, Most Ultimately, Realized) By Means Of My Divinely Self-Giving Avataric Spiritual Grace and My Graceful Avatarically Given Divine Self-Revelation (and As My Divinely Self-Giving Avataric Spiritual Grace and My Graceful Avatarically Given Divine Self-Revelation Will Have It), and Only (Merely) Through Truly Me-Recognizing, Rightly (Searchlessly) Me-Beholding, Receptively To-Me-Responding, and Really ego-Surrendering, ego-Forgetting, and ego-Transcending Devotional and Spiritual (and, Altogether, Total psycho-physical) Communion With My Avatarically-Born Bodily (Human) Divine Form, My Avatarically Self-Transmitted Spiritual (and Always Blessing) Divine Presence, and My Avatarically Self-Revealed (and Very, and Transcendental, and Perfectly Subjective, and Inherently Spiritual, and Inherently egoless, and Inherently Perfect, and Self-Evidently Divine) State.

Therefore, Listen To Me and Hear Me: You Have Already Eaten the meal Of Separateness.

Now You Must Relinquish that Awful meal (and Be—Released Of Separate and Separative self).

You Do Not Require (and You Should Not Seek) any "thing" From Me (To Add To Your Already Separate and Deluded self).

I Am (Myself) What You Require—and I Am here To Require every "thing" Of You.

You Must Relinquish (or Surrender) Your ego-"I" (Your experience, Your Presumed knowledge, Your Separateness, All Your Forms Of egoic "Bonding", and Even all Your "things", Within and Without) To Realize The Fullness That Is Me.

Therefore, Come To Me To Realize Me—and Do Not Run From Me After Tasting the ordinary meal of conditional knowledge and experience (Like a dog Runs From its Master With a bone).

Having Come To Me, Do Not Look Within Your body or Your mind To Discover Whether You Have Received some "thing" From Me (To Satisfy Your little pouch Of Separateness).

Rather, Surrender and Release Your Total Separate (or self-Contracted, self-Contracting, Separative, and Always Seeking) psycho-physical self (including Your entire body, Your breath, Your emotions, Your mind, Your knowledge, and all Your experiences) By The Progressively Established and Progressively Developed Means Of Devotionally To-Me-Resorting, Searchlessly Me-Beholding, Receptively To-Me-Responding, and (Thus, Responsively) ego-Surrendering, ego-Forgetting, ego-Transcending, and (Altogether) Total psycho-physical Feeling-Communion With Me—and, Thus (By Means Of Total psycho-physical and Really ego-Transcending Communion With My Avatarically-Born Bodily Human Divine Form, My Avatarically Self-Transmitted Spiritual, and Always Blessing, Divine Presence, and My Avatarically Self-Revealed, and Very, and Transcendental, and Perfectly Subjective, and Inherently Spiritual, and Inherently egoless, and Inherently Perfect, and Self-Evidently Divine State), Grow To Luxuriate In My Divine "Bright" Spherical Self-Domain Of Love-Bliss.

If You Truly and Really Surrender and Release Your ego-"I" (or Total Separate and Separative psycho-physical self) To Me—Then Not any meal of "things" (or effects), but Only I Am The Gift, The Object, The State, and The Realization.

Therefore, Come To Me (and For Me Only), "Bond" To Me (and To Me Only), and Stay With Me (and With Me Only, Forever)—and You Will (By This) Realize Me (Truly, Really, and Only).

I Am Da Love-Ananda (The Giver and The Free Gift), Who Is Love-Bliss Itself, The Truth and The Reality Given, and Revealed, and Beheld, and Received (and, Ultimately, Most Perfectly Realized), By Means Of My Avataric Divine Spiritual Blessing-Grace, When egoity (or the ego-"I" of Total psycho-physical self-Contraction) Is Surrendered, Forgotten, and Transcended In Heart-Responsive (Devotionally Me-Recognizing, and Total psycho-physical) Feeling-Communion With My Avatarically-Born Bodily (Human) Divine Form, My Avatarically Self-Transmitted Spiritual (and Always Blessing) Divine Presence, and My Avatarically Self-Revealed (and Very, and Transcendental, and Perfectly Subjective, and Inherently Spiritual, and Inherently egoless, and Inherently Perfect, and Self-Evidently Divine) State—To The Degree Of Non-Separateness, No-Seeking, and No-Contraction.

I Am Perfect Samadhi, The Truth and The Reality Of No-"Difference", Which Is (Inherently Perfect) Conscious Light Itself—Self-Existing, Self-Radiant, Spiritually "Bright", One, Only, Non-Separate, and All Love-Bliss (Itself).

Realize Me—By The Total psycho-physical Practice Of ego-Surrendering, ego-Forgetting, and ego-Transcending Devotional (and, In Due Course, By-Me-Spiritually-Initiated, and Always Newly By-Me-Spiritually-Activated) Heart-Communion With My Avatarically-Born Bodily (Human) Divine Form, My Avatarically Self-Transmitted Spiritual (and Always Blessing) Divine Presence, and My Avatarically Self-Revealed (and Very, and Transcendental, and Perfectly Subjective, and Inherently Spiritual, and Inherently egoless, and Inherently Perfect, and Self-Evidently Divine) State.

Live By My Darshan (Never Seeking Me, but Always Already Finding Me)—In Constant Satsang (Always Feasting On The Sight Of Me).

By Means Of The Divine Grace Revealed By The Mere Sight (or Feel) Of Me, Practice Ruchira Avatara Bhakti (Which Is ego-Surrendering, ego-Forgetting, ego-Transcending, and, Altogether, Total psycho-physical Devotion Of body, feeling, attention, breath, and all of Separate self To Me), and (By Means Of The Divine Grace Revealed To That Devotion) Practice Ruchira Avatara Seva (Which Is Active ego-Surrender, ego-Forgetting, and ego-Transcendence—Via Constant, and Always Me-Remembering, and Total psycho-physical Service To Me), and (By Means Of The Divine Grace Revealed To That Devotional Service) Practice Ruchira Avatara Tapas (Which Is Total psycho-physical self-Discipline, In Always ego-Surrendering, ego-Forgetting, and Truly ego-Transcending Devotional Obedience and Devotional Conformity To Me).

Therefore—In This Manner, and In Due Course, and Entirely By The Divine Means Of My Divinely Self-Giving Avataric Spiritual Grace and My Graceful Avatarically Given Divine Self-Revelation—Realize Me By Heart, Whole bodily, Through My Divine "Bright" Spiritual Infusion Of Your To-Me-Surrendered Total body-mind.

All This (My Summary Written, and Forever Speaking, Word Of Heart) I Affirm By Heart (and As The Very, and Inherently egoless, and Self-Evidently Divine Heart Itself).

All This (That I Have Hereby Affirmed) I Promise To The Inherently egoless Heart (In every one, and all).

Now (By This) I Have Epitomized My Summary (Written, and Forever Avatarically Speaking) Divine Word Of Heart.

Therefore, Surrender, Forget, and Transcend Your Separate and Separative self (or Total psycho-physical ego-"I"), By Means Of Constant Right (Intelligent, Whole bodily self-Disciplined, and Truly Devotionally Surrendered, Receptive, and Responsive) Obedience To My Avataric Divine Word and Person, and

(Thus) Act Only In Accord (Always) With My Explicit Instructions (and, Thus, Always Only With My Explicit Permission and Blessing), and (Thus, By This Explicit Devotion) Be Perfectly Simplified (By My Perfect Simplicity).

This Is The Heart-Word Of Adi Da Love-Ananda Samraj, The Da Avatar (At Once, The Divine Giver and The Avatarically Given Divine Gift), The Avatarically Self-Manifested Divine Heart-Master and The Avatarically-Born Divine World-Teacher, The Ruchira Avatar (The Avataric Divine Incarnation Of The "Bright"), The Love-Ananda Avatar (The Avataric Incarnation Of The Divine Love-Bliss)—Who Is Da (The First and Original Person, The Source-Person, The One and Only, Non-Separate and Not "Different", Inherently egoless, Inherently Indivisible, and Self-Evidently Divine Conscious Light Of all-and-All), and Who Is Da Hridayam (The One and Only Heart Of all-and-All, In Whom All Seeming-To-Be-Separate Hearts Must Take Refuge, and, Thus and Thereby, Be Calmed Of The Burning Heats Of Fear, Sorrow, Anger, Un-Love, and Even all the Seeking self-Contractions of the Total Separate and Separative psycho-physical ego-"I"), and Who Is Da Love-Ananda (The Source, The Substance, The Gift, The Giver, and The Very Person Of The Spiritually Self-"Bright" Divine Love-Bliss), and Who Is Da Avabhasa (The Person Of The "Bright" Itself, and The Very Giver Of "Brightness"), and Who Is Santosha Da (The Spiritually "Bright" and Eternal and Always Already Non-Separate Person Of Divine and Inherent Completeness, Divine Self-Satisfaction, Divine Self-Contentedness, or Perfect Searchlessness)—Herein, In Summary, Written (and, Hereby, Forever Speaking), In Extreme Simplicity, For The Sake Of all beings, In Love Toward all beings, So That all beings May Awaken (By Means Of My Divinely Self-Giving Avataric Spiritual Grace and My Graceful Avatarically Given Divine Self-Revelation) To The Only Truth That Sets The Heart Free.

By Rightly, Truly, Fully, and Fully Devotionally Practicing The Instruction Given (By Me) In This, My Testament Of Divine Secrets, You Will Surely Be Enabled (By Means Of My Avatarically Self-Transmitted Divine Grace) To Rightly (and Fruitfully) Listen To Me, and (Then) To Hear Me and To See Me, and (In Due Course) To (Ultimately, Most Perfectly) Realize Me.

AVATAR ADI DA SAMRAJ
The Mountain Of Attention Sanctuary, 2000

SUTRA

5

The Only-By-Me Revealed and Given Way Of Adidam (Which Is The One and Only By-Me-Revealed and By-Me-Given Way Of The Heart) Is The Devotional (and, In Due Course, Progressively Spiritual) Relationship To Me (In and As My Avatarically-Born Bodily Human Divine Form and Person). The Only-By-Me Revealed and Given Way Of Adidam Is Not Merely A System Of self-Applied Techniques, or ego-Centric Practices—To Be Learned From Me and Then Applied To Yourself, Independent Of Me. The Entire Life Of My Devotee Must Be Ruchira Avatara Bhakti Yoga, or The Always present-time Devotional Yoga Of Direct (and Directly and Immediately ego-Transcending) Relationship To Me.

The Principal Exercise Of Ruchira Avatara Bhakti Yoga Is The (moment to moment) Turning Of The Four Principal Faculties (Of body, emotion, mind, and breath) To My Avatarically-Born Bodily (Human) Divine Form and Person. Ruchira Avatara Bhakti Yoga Is The Foundation Of The Practice Of The Only-By-Me Revealed and Given Way Of The Heart From The Very Beginning, When You First Become My Student-Beginner Devotee.

In The Midst Of daily living, and Under all its various circumstances, There Are Demands On the body, Demands On emotion, Demands On mind, and Demands On the breath. The conditions Of Existence Make changes In All Of The Principal Faculties, moment by moment. I Call My Devotee To Make Divine Yoga (or Freedom-"Bonding") Out Of each moment—By Using body, emotion, mind, and breath In ego-Surrendering Devotional Feeling-Contemplation Of My Avatarically-Born Bodily (Human) Divine Form and Person. All The Mechanisms That Would (Otherwise) Automatically Conform To the conditions of egoic life (or To conditionality altogether) Must Be Turned To Me. Through That Turning, My Devotee Becomes "Yoked" (or Freedom-"Bonded") To Me.

Therefore, My Devotee Must Be Responsible For The Four Principal Faculties Of the body-mind—In every moment, and Under all circumstances. Instead Of Wandering In the maze of thoughts, Give Me The Faculty Of mind—Which Is Epitomized By, and As, attention (itself). Instead Of Being Tossed About By the waves of emotions, Give Me The Faculty Of emotion—

Which Is Epitomized By, and As, feeling (itself). Instead Of Seeking bodily Pleasure and Avoiding bodily Pain, Turn (or Face) the body Toward My Avatarically-Born Bodily (Human) Divine Form, and (Altogether) Give Me the body—Through Full Feeling-Intention, Enacted Through Constant Devotional Service To Me. The Faculties Of mind (or attention), emotion (or feeling), and body Are Connected To One Another Via the breath—and, Thus, The Gesture Of Surrender To Me Must Also Be Done Via the breath. Therefore, Altogether, In The Right and True Practice Of Ruchira Avatara Bhakti Yoga, mind (or attention), emotion (or feeling), and body Are Given Over To Me, and breathed In Heart-Communion With Me. All Those Mechanisms That You Would (Otherwise) Allow To Be Preoccupied With the conditions of egoic life (or With conditionality altogether) Must Be Turned To Me (In and As My Avatarically-Born Bodily Human Divine Form and Person).

The Usual "Method" Of the ego, and (Therefore) Of ordinary people, Is To Become Involved In what arises (whatever that May Be In any particular circumstance)—Either By Indulging In what arises Or By Avoiding what arises Or By (Otherwise) Attempting To Manipulate what arises. Such Strategic Effort In Relation To what arises Is Not The Yoga Of The Only-By-Me Revealed and Given Way Of The Heart, but It Is Merely The Effort Of the Separate (and Separative) self To Struggle With itself. Even To Strategically Manipulate the Separate (and Separative) self (itself), In Order To Surrender the Separate (and Separative) self, Is Nothing but An (Inevitably Fruitless) Effort Of the Separate (and Separative) self To Struggle With itself. Thus, The Secret Of Ruchira Avatara Bhakti Yoga (and, Therefore, Of The Entire Way Of The Heart) Is Not To Struggle With the content that is arising in and as the body-mind, but Merely To Turn The Principal Faculties Of the body-mind To Me (In and As My Avatarically-Born Bodily Human Divine Form and Person).

It Is Always (In any moment) Possible To Turn The Four Principal Faculties Of the body-mind To My Avatarically-Born Bodily (Human) Divine Form and Person—Because (In and Of Themselves) These Faculties Stand Prior To Their "objects" (or Apparent contents), and They Are (Therefore) Never (Themselves) Bound To The egoic "Program" Of the moment. The mind May Be thinking Constantly—but The Faculty Of attention (itself) Has No "object" or Quality, and (Therefore) It Can, Itself, Always Be Turned To Me. There May Be Reactive emotions arising—but The Faculty Of feeling Is Not (Itself) Qualified By any such "objects", and (Therefore) It Can, Itself, Always Be Turned To Me. The condition of the body May, At any moment, Be Disturbance, or Dis-ease, or Lack Of Well-being, In One or Another Respect (or Function, or Organ)—but The Faculty Of the body (or the functional body itself, In Total, or As A Whole) Can, Itself, Always Be Turned To Me. The Cycle Of the breath May Be

Affected By forms of mind, Reactive emotions, and bodily states—but The Faculty Of the breath Is Not (Itself) Identical To the ever-changing contents of the body-mind, and (Therefore) It Can, Itself, Always Be Turned To Me.

I Have Summarized The Practice Of Ruchira Avatara Bhakti Yoga (or The Constant Turning Of The Comprehensive Totality Of The Faculties Of the body-mind To My Avatarically-Born Bodily Human Divine Form and Person) In A Great Admonition To All My Devotees: "Always Invoke Me, Feel Me, Breathe Me, and Serve Me." To Invoke Me Is To Render (or Turn and Yield) The Faculty Of mind To Me, At Its Root (Which Is attention). To Feel Me Is To Render (or Turn and Yield) The Faculty Of emotion To Me, At Its Root (Which Is feeling). To Breathe Me Is To Commune With Me Via The Cycles Of the breath. To Serve Me Is To Constantly Turn To Me Via every action of the body, and In (and By Means Of) The By-Me-Given functional, practical, relational, and Cultural Disciplines.

Ruchira Avatara Bhakti Yoga Is A moment to moment Practice. The Responsive Technical Exercises (Of The "Conscious Process" and "Conductivity") Are Also (Necessarily) To Be Engaged At Random, but The Fundamental Practice Of Ruchira Avatara Bhakti Yoga (or The Whole bodily, or Total psycho-physical, Turning Of The Four psycho-physical Faculties To Me, In and As My Avatarically-Born Bodily Human Divine Form and Person) Must Be Constant.

Thus, My Devotees Must Clearly Understand That, When I Instruct them To Practice Ruchira Avatara Bhakti Yoga moment to moment, I Am Not Instructing them To Engage One or Another Technical Exercise Of The Many Otherwise By-Me-Revealed and By-Me-Given Forms Of The "Conscious Process" or "Conductivity" Practice In every moment. It Is Not Even Possible To Intentionally Engage Any Specific Technical Exercise Of The "Conscious Process" and/or "Conductivity" Practice In every moment—Because My Any Devotee Is Inevitably Involved In A Great Variety Of Doings In The daily Course. What Can—and Must—Be Practiced In every moment By My Every Devotee Is The Whole bodily (or Total psycho-physical), and Really and Truly To-Me-Responsive, Turning Of The Four psycho-physical Faculties To Me (In and As My Avatarically-Born Bodily Human Divine Form and Person)—Whether Or Not That To-Me-Responsive Turning Is, In any Given moment, Supported By Otherwise Specific Technical Practices, and Always Without Hindrance or Reluctance Due To the specific physical, mental, emotional, functional, practical, and relational circumstances of the moment. It Is In This Manner That Ruchira Avatara Bhakti Yoga Applies To every circumstance, every function, every activity, every relation, and every moment of life.

The moment to moment Practice Of Ruchira Avatara Bhakti Yoga Is Not A Matter Of Constantly Doing Formal Meditative Exercises—Because Such

Exercises Are Rightly and Effectively Done Only Within The Appropriate Set-Apart Environment Of A Hall Reserved For Meditation (or, Otherwise, In Random moments Outside Such A Meditation Hall, or Communion Hall).

Thus, Right and Consistent Application To The Responsive Technical Exercises (Of The "Conscious Process" and "Conductivity"—Including Such Basic Aspects Of The Practice As Ruchira Avatara Naama Japa and Participation In The Ruchira Avatara Puja)—Although Entirely Necessary—Is Not The Definition Of Ruchira Avatara Bhakti Yoga. If You (As My Formally Practicing Devotee) Are Only Engaging Such Responsive Technical Exercises, Then You Are (Inevitably) Only Engaging The Practice Of Ruchira Avatara Bhakti Yoga In Formal Occasions, and (Otherwise) In Random moments. In That Case, You Are Not Grasping The Nature Of Real and True (Whole bodily, and moment to moment) Practice Of The Only-By-Me Revealed and Given Way Of The Heart (or Way Of Adidam). And, Therefore (In That Case), You Are Not Practicing The Way Of The Heart moment to moment—and, Thus, all the time and At all times. Rather (In That Case), You Are Practicing The Way Of The Heart Only part of the time—and, the rest of the time, You are (Always, Inevitably) being an ego (which is Whole bodily, or Total psycho-physical, self-Contraction) and (Thus and Thereby) Doing the Separate and Separative activity that is the ego (or the self-Contraction) itself.

In any Given moment, If You Are Not Practicing Ruchira Avatara Bhakti Yoga (or The Whole bodily—and Really and Truly ego-Surrendering, and ego-Forgetting, and, More and More, ego-Transcending—Turning Of The Four psycho-physical Faculties To Me, In and As My Avatarically-Born Bodily Human Divine Form and Person), Then You Are (Necessarily, and Whole bodily, or As A psycho-physical Totality) Enacting the self-Contraction Instead. Therefore, The Secret Of The Only-By-Me Revealed and Given Way Of The Heart (or Way Of Adidam) Is Its moment to moment Nature. The Practice Of Ruchira Avatara Bhakti Yoga Is Truly Purifying, Transformative, and (Potentially, or More and More) Me-Realizing Only When You Engage It moment to moment. In any particular moment, You May Be Engaged In One Of The By-Me-Given Forms Of Formal Technical (and, Necessarily, Devotional) Practice, or You May Be Engaged In Any Of A Great Variety Of Possible activities In The functional, practical, and/or relational Domains Of daily life (or You May Even, In the ordinary sense, Be Relatively inactive—As In The Midst Of a period of physical illness). In all of those moments, Ruchira Avatara Bhakti Yoga Is The Necessary (and Formally To Be Expected) Practice—Not Only In certain Formal moments, or (Otherwise) In Random moments When You Are Intentionally Engaging A Responsive Technical Exercise, but In every moment (and, Thus, Constantly and Continuously—moment to moment). Such Perpetual (or moment to moment) Practice Of Ruchira Avatara Bhakti Yoga Is The True and Fundamental and Profound Yoga Of The Only-By-Me Revealed and Given Way Of The Heart (or Way Of Adidam).

Therefore, My Every Devotee Must Discover The Secret Of Practicing This True (Whole bodily—or Totally, With Every Evident Faculty—To-Me-Turned) Devotion To Me (In and As My Avatarically-Born Bodily Human Divine Form and Person)—In every moment of every day (Throughout The Entire Span Of the waking state, and, In Due Course, Throughout The Entire Span Of the states of dreaming and sleeping).

I Call (and Formally Expect) All My Devotees To Live In daily Accordance With A Basic Sacred "Form"—Whereby they Regularly Set Apart time For The Formal Practice Of Meditation and Various Other Sacred Activities. Nevertheless, Such Formal Practices Occur Only At particular times of the day. Those Formal Practices Are Not, In and Of Themselves, The Fundamental Practice Of Ruchira Avatara Bhakti Yoga. Rather, Those Formal Practices Serve and Support The Otherwise moment to moment Whole bodily Practice Of Ruchira Avatara Bhakti Yoga (or Constant and Continuous Devotional Heart-Communion With Me, In and As My Avatarically-Born Bodily Human Divine Form and Person).

The Only-By-Me Revealed and Given Way Of The Heart (or Way Of Adidam) Is Not To Be Engaged Merely As A Program Of Occasional activities—Such That, Apart From those Occasional (or Formalized) moments, You Are Not Actually (and Actively) Practicing The Only-By-Me Revealed and Given Way Of The Heart (or Way Of Adidam). If Such Is The Nature Of Your Participation In The Practice I Have Revealed and Given, Then There Is No Possibility That You Will Most Profoundly (and, At Last, Most Perfectly) Realize Me. Obviously, Your life Will Be Improved, In Some Positive Terms, By The Introduction Of Any and All Of The Specific Formal and Technical Disciplines I Have Given—but, If Your Practice Of The By-Me-Given Disciplines Is Merely Ritualized In time (or Programmed Into Only a few periods and moments of daily time), Then You Cannot Enter Into The Real and True Process Of Most Profound Heart-Communion With Me, and (Therefore) You Cannot Realize Me Most Perfectly (or Even Most Profoundly).

The body-mind—As A psycho-physical Whole—Must Be Turned To Me, moment to moment. That Is The Practice Of Ruchira Avatara Bhakti Yoga. Discovering How To Truly Engage Ruchira Avatara Bhakti Yoga In This Manner Is The Secret Of Maturing In The Only-By-Me Revealed and Given Way Of The Heart (or Way Of Adidam).

You Must Be My Devotee In every moment—whatever life-activity You May Apparently Be Involved In (functionally, practically, relationally, or

Culturally) At any particular moment in time. To Engage The Fundamental Yoga Of Ruchira Avatara Bhakti Only In Programmed moments Is Exactly the limitation You (As My Formally Practicing Devotee) Must Overcome.

To Fail To Practice Ruchira Avatara Bhakti Yoga In any particular moment Is To Allow The Four Principal Faculties To Be Promiscuous. Such Is the ego's Infidelity To Me. When You Fail To Practice Ruchira Avatara Bhakti Yoga In any particular moment, The Four Principal Faculties Are Not Turned To Me. Rather, In That Case, The Four Principal Faculties Are Turned Upon Themselves, and Upon The Distractions Of "money, food, and sex" and the social ego (Which Pattern human beings in their ordinariness). In That Case, You Are Merely Dabbling In The Practice Of The Way Of The Heart—and You Are Failing To Be My Devotee.

The Failing-To-Turn-To-Me Distractedness (or Promiscuity, or Infidelity) Of The Four psycho-physical Faculties Is The Very Nature Of egoity. The ego-"I" is (By Nature) self-Contracted Upon itself and All Of its Diversions—and, Therefore, All Of its Illusions. The ego-"I" is A self-Deluding body-mind-Machine Of Bondage. And the ego-"I" is a Whole bodily (or Total psycho-physical) <u>activity</u>—Not merely a "philosophy" (or something You "Have In mind"). Therefore, To Counter Your Own activity of ego-"I", You Must (Necessarily) Embrace and Enact The <u>Total</u> <u>psycho-physical</u> Sadhana I Have Revealed and Given. All Of The By-Me-Revealed and By-Me-Given functional, practical, relational, and Cultural Disciplines Are Means For Animating (and Serving, and Supporting, and Developing) The Devotional Recognition-Response To Me—Which <u>Is</u>, Most Fundamentally, The Turning Of The Four psycho-physical Faculties To Me. <u>Every</u> Aspect Of The By-Me-Revealed and By-Me-Given Practice Of The Way Of The Heart (or Way Of Adidam) Is A Matter Of The moment to moment Profundity Of The Devotional (and, In Due Course, Spiritual) <u>Relationship</u> To Me (In and <u>As</u> My Avatarically-Born Bodily Human Divine Form and Person). Therefore, As My (Necessarily, Formally Practicing) Devotee, You Must Oblige Yourself (and Must Be Formally and Accountably Obliged, By The Cooperative Sacred Cultural Gathering Of All My Formally Practicing Devotees) To Fulfill All The Disciplines I Have Given—Without Indulging In Any Form Of "Picking and Choosing" Amongst Those Disciplines (That Is To Say, Without Choosing To Fulfill Only Your "Favorite" Disciplines, or The Disciplines That Least "Smack Up" Against Your ego-Based Patterns and Tendencies, and Least Interfere With How You Want To Use Your time self-Indulgently).

The Practice Of The Only-By-Me Revealed and Given Way Of The Heart (or Way Of Adidam) Is The <u>Whole</u> <u>Life</u> Of Actually <u>Turning</u> The Four psycho-physical Faculties To Me (moment to moment), and Not Indulging In Your

Patterns Of self-Contraction and The life-Adaptations That Have Come About Through That Patterning. Thus, As My Devotee, You Are (In Some Sense) Working "Against The Grain"—but You Are Not Working "On Yourself". Rather, You Are, In every moment, Responsively Turning To Me (In and As My Avatarically-Born Bodily Human Divine Form and Person). The self-Forgetting and Entirely To-Me-Responsive Nature Of The Practice I Have Revealed and Given Is The Reason Why That Practice Is Not A Seeker's Struggle With the egoic self. Nevertheless, The Practice Of The Only-By-Me Revealed and Given Way Of The Heart (or Way Of Adidam) Is An All-Encompassing Discipline That Directly Pertains To (and Counters) the egoic self. Therefore, You Must Volunteer For That Counter-egoic Practice—and You Will Do So Only If You Are Responsively and Whole bodily (or In A Total psycho-physical Manner) Turned To Me (In and As My Avatarically-Born Bodily Human Divine Form and Person).

From The Very Beginning Of Your Practice Of The Only-By-Me Revealed and Given Way Of The Heart (As My Student-Beginner Devotee), The moment to moment Whole bodily To-Me-Turning Exercise Of Your Devotion To Me (In and As My Avatarically-Born Bodily Human Divine Form and Person) Is The Core Responsibility Of Your Practice. Everything Else Is A Support—Including The Fundamental Responsive Practices Of The "Conscious Process" (Engaged In The Manner Of Either The Devotional Way Of Insight Or The Devotional Way Of Faith) and "Conductivity". From The Beginning Of Student-Beginner Practice, The Foundation Of My Devotee's Practice Is Real and True moment to moment Ruchira Avatara Bhakti Yoga—and It Is Only On The Basis Of That Foundationary Responsibility (and In Order To Always Further Serve and Develop The Really and Truly moment to moment Nature Of The Real and True Practice Of Ruchira Avatara Bhakti Yoga) That My Devotee Engages The Responsive Practices Of The "Conscious Process" and "Conductivity".

My Student-Beginner Devotees Engage Ruchira Avatara Bhakti Yoga As A Devotional Practice—Not As A Spiritual Practice. The Practice I Have Given To My Student-Beginner Devotees Is The Devotionally To-Me-Responsive Turning Of The psycho-physical Faculties To Me, Together With The Devotionally To-Me-Responsive Embrace Of The By-Me-Given Forms Of functional, practical, relational, and Cultural self-Discipline. The Spiritual Practice Of The Only-By-Me Revealed and Given Way Of The Heart (or Way Of Adidam) Is Possible (and Is To Be Formally, and, Thus and Thereby, Fully Accountably, Engaged) Only After My Devotee Has Made The Real and True and Full Transition Beyond The Student-Beginner Stage (and Into The Formal Context Of Ongoing Direct, and Truly Me-Receiving, Resort To My Avatarically Given Divine Spiritual Self-Transmission, Under The Formally By-Me-Established

Culturally Governing Authority and Formally Me-Extending Guidance Of The Ruchira Sannyasin Order Of Adidam Ruchiradam). Thus, The Student-Beginner Practice Of The Way Of The Heart Is Not A Matter Of Receiving Me Spiritually From Above—or, Indeed, Of Receiving Me Spiritually In Any Manner Whatsoever. The Student-Beginner Practice Of The Way Of The Heart Is A Specific (Devotional, but Not Yet Spiritual) Yogic (or Total psycho-physical) Practice That Has Its Own Signs—The Signs Of All-The-Faculties-Turned-To-Me Devotion.

In The Way Of Adidam (Which Is The One and Only By-Me-Revealed and By-Me-Given Way Of The Heart), The Fundamental Form Of Invocation Of Me (Which Is Practiced By All My Formally Practicing Devotees) Is Simply To Call On Me (Generally Silently, With the "tongue of the mind", but Also, Under Appropriate circumstances, Audibly) Via My Principal (Divine and Sacred) Name, "Da" (or Any Other Of The Names I Have Given To Be Engaged In The Practice Of Simple Name-Invocation Of Me). In Addition To This Practice Of Simple Name-Invocation Of Me, My Devotees Also (As Appropriate To Their Formally Acknowledged Developmental Stage Of Practice Of The Way Of The Heart and Their Formally Acknowledged Manner Of Formal Practice Of The Way Of The Heart) Invoke Me Either Via The Practice Of Ruchira Avatara Naama Japa (or Else The Prayer Of Remembrance, Which Is A Technically More Elaborate Form Of Calling Upon Me By Name) Or Via The Practice Of self-Enquiry (In The Form "Avoiding Relationship?"—Which Practice Is To Be Engaged With The Whole bodily Feeling Of Invoking Me and Turning Your attention To Me) Or Via The Practice Of "Feeling-Enquiry" (Which Is The By-Me-Given Form Of The "Conscious Process" Engaged By All My "Perfect Practice" Devotees).

When things arise in mind—Instead Of Struggling With them, Trying To Get Rid Of them, Trying To Surrender them—Simply Give Me Your attention (or The Core Of Your mind). Do Not Try To Get Rid Of the content, or Try To Surrender the content To Me, or Try To Surrender the content In Order To Get To Me. Simply Turn attention itself To My Avatarically-Born Bodily (Human) Divine Form and Person. No Effort Is Required. You Need Not Struggle With the mind-forms. In Your Simple Turning To Me, You (Thereby, Inherently) Disregard what is arising in mind. You Turn attention To Me, and (Thus and Thereby) Forget About mind. You Do Not Try To Make Something Happen In the mind, Nor Do You Try To Surrender the mind By Surrendering its content To Me. You Surrender The Function Of mind By Turning Your attention To Me.

The Feeling-Response (or Heart-Response) To Me (In and As My Avatarically-Born Bodily Human Divine Form and Person) Is The Core Of The Practice Of Ruchira Avatara Bhakti Yoga. To Feel Me Is To Turn (Whole bodily, With Full Heart-Feeling) To Me (In and As My Avatarically-Born Bodily

Human Divine Form and Person). When You Feel Me Thus, You Are Necessarily (or Thereby and, Thus, Inherently) Entering Into ego-Surrendering, ego-Forgetting, and (Always More and More) ego-Transcending Devotional (and, In Due Course, Spiritual) Heart-Communion With Me.

When something arises emotionally (a Reactive emotion of one kind or another, or an emotional Concern, or an emotion In Relation To anything conditional)—Instead Of Trying To Open and Relax and Release the Reactive emotion In Order To Feel Me (or Struggling With Yourself For Whatever Reason)—Direct (or Merely and Simply Turn) The Function Of emotion To Me. The Core Of The Function Of emotion Is Simply feeling. Therefore, Feel To Me. Give Me Your Feeling-attention. Direct (or Merely and Simply Turn) attention (or The Root Of mind) and feeling (or The Root Of emotion) To Me.

Similarly, Remember Me With every breath, Invoke Me With every breath, and Commune With Me With every breath. This Does Not Mean That You Should (Necessarily) Technically Engage every inhalation and every exhalation. My Admonition To "Breathe Me" Must Be Fulfilled Artfully, In Such A Way That, Even Though You Are Not, As A Technical Practice, Engaging every breath—Nevertheless, Effectively, every breath Is Communion With My Avatarically-Born Bodily (Human) Divine Form and Person.

In The Case Of My Student-Beginner Devotees, Breathing Me Is Not A Spiritual Practice, Not A Matter Of Breathing My Avatarically Self-Transmitted Divine Spiritual Presence. Rather, In The Case Of My Student-Beginner Devotees, Breathing Me Is, Simply, A Composite Part Of The Total Devotional Asana Of Turning All The Faculties Of the Total body-mind To Me (In and As My Avatarically-Born Bodily Human Divine Form). Thus, In The Case Of My Student-Beginner Devotees, The breathing Process Is To Be Consistently Established In The Context Of Ruchira Avatara Bhakti Yoga, and, Thus, Constantly Engaged In The Fundamental Asana (or Total psycho-physical Attitude, or Disposition) Of Devotional Turning To Me (In and As My Avatarically-Born Bodily Human Divine Form). And, If the Total body-mind (Including All Of its breathing-feeling-attention and Me-Serving Action) Is, Thus, Consistently and Constantly Turned To Me (In and As My Avatarically-Born Bodily Human Divine Form), Then, In The Case Of My Thus Turned-To-Me Student-Beginner Devotees, The breathing Process Will Also (Secondarily) Be (and More and More Become) Associated With Right "Conductivity" Of Natural bodily energy (but Not Yet The Direct, True, Full, and Profound "Conductivity" Of My Avatarically Self-Transmitted Divine Spiritual Presence).

As My Student-Beginner Devotee (or, Indeed, As My Formally Practicing Devotee At Any and Every Stage Of Practice Of The Only-By-Me Revealed and Given Way Of The Heart, or Way Of Adidam), You Must Also Constantly

Conform the body itself To Me, In The Midst Of whatever is arising physically. You Must Always Direct Yourself bodily (and By Means Of Every bodily Action or activity) To Me (In and As My Avatarically-Born Bodily Human Divine Form and Person). Whatever Functions You Are Performing In any moment of functional activity, You Should (Merely and Simply) Turn Your Feeling-attention To Me. Always Direct (or Merely and Simply Turn) the body To Serving Me. Direct the body To Be The Servant, Rather Than Make it The Object Of Your Concern. And, In The Relatively Inactive Context Of Sitting To Meditate On Me, The Admonition To Serve Me Is Fulfilled By, Simply, physically (bodily) Facing My Avatarically-Born Bodily (Human) Divine Form (Either Via My Murti Or, As The Case May Be, Directly).[36]

Taken All Together, The Four Principal Faculties Of the body-mind Effectively Account For All human Functions.

Because The Four Principal Faculties Are Senior (or Always Prior) To Their content, Each Of The Four Principal Faculties Of the body-mind Is Always Available Either To Be Reactively Turned To Its Own Apparent content Or To Be Devotionally Turned To Me (In and As My Avatarically-Born Bodily Human Divine Form and Person). Therefore, Truly, There Are No moments when The Me-Beholding Turning Of the Otherwise Separate (and Separative) self To Me Is More Difficult Than In other moments—Unless My Devotee Turns To (and Identifies With) the Apparent content of the Separate (and Separative) body-mind-self. If My Devotee Is Simply Remembering Me (and Invoking Me, and—Thus and Thereby, Whole bodily, or As A psycho-physical Totality—Communing With Me, In and As My Avatarically-Born Bodily Human Divine Form and Person), In Disposition, and Intention, and Action—Then The Yoga Of Ruchira Avatara Bhakti Is Direct and (Inherently) Easy (or Free Of Struggle With Separate and Separative self).

My Devotee Who Is Rightly, Truly, Fully, and Fully Devotionally Practicing The Yoga Of Ruchira Avatara Bhakti Does Not, In Any Sense, Strategically Use (or Seek With, or Struggle With) the Separate (and Separative) self. Rather, My Devotee Who Is Rightly, Truly, Fully, and Fully Devotionally Practicing The Yoga Of Ruchira Avatara Bhakti Makes the Separate (and Separative) self (itself) Obsolete, By Not Using it (or, That Is To Say, By Allowing the Total body-mind, Via its Four Principal Faculties, To Simply Turn To Me, and To Whole bodily Heart-Respond To Me, In and As My Avatarically-Born Bodily Human Divine Form and Person)—Until (In Due Course), Through Ecstatic Absorption In (and, Ultimately, Perfect Self-Identification With, and, Most Ultimately, Divine Self-Realization Of) Me, the Separate (and Separative) self Utterly Vanishes In Me.

Therefore, Always (To-Me-Responsively) Turn bodily To Me (In and As My

Avatarically-Born Bodily Human Divine Form). Always Turn To Me (In and As My Avatarically-Born Bodily Human Divine Form) By Means Of The To-Me-Responsive Exercise Of Your feeling. Always (To-Me-Responsively) Turn Your attention To Me (In and As My Avatarically-Born Bodily Human Divine Form). Always Turn To Me By Means Of The Whole bodily To-Me-Responsive Breathing-Regard Of Me (In and As My Avatarically-Born Bodily Human Divine Form). In This Manner, Always Turn All Of The Faculties Of the body-mind To Me (In and As My Avatarically-Born Bodily Human Divine Form and Person).

To Turn To Me Responsively, With Each and All Of The Faculties Of the body-mind, Is Not self-Contraction (or The Avoidance Of Relationship), but (Rather) It Is The Counter-egoic (and Inherently ego-Forgetting) Practice Of Me-Consciousness (or Devotional Communion With Me).

Ruchira Avatara Bhakti Yoga Is Not The Yielding Of The Functions Of the body-mind To The Idea That I Am Your Divine Heart-Master. There Is Nothing Vague About This Practice Of Whole bodily (or Total psycho-physical) Devotion To Me. Direct Your Feeling-attention To Me—To My Avatarically-Born Bodily (Human) Divine Form. In Fact, A Fundamental Aspect Of The Technical Practice Of This Devotional (and, In Due Course, Spiritual) Yoga Is To (Feelingly) Recollect My Avatarically-Born Bodily (Human) Divine Form.

In The Meditation Halls (or Communion Halls), and In Various Other Sacred Places, Of The Only-By-Me Revealed and Given Way Of The Heart (or Way Of Adidam), A Murti-Form (or photographic Likeness—or Other Type Of technically, or even artistically, Rendered Representation) Of My Avatarically-Born Bodily (Human) Divine Form Is Always Displayed For This Purpose Of Me-Recollection. On The Mala You Are By-Me-Instructed and By-Me-Called To Wear (In most daily-life circumstances, and In All Formal Circumstances), You Are Always To Carry A (Typically, photographic) Image Of My Avatarically-Born Bodily (Human) Divine Form (Encased In A Pendant That Hangs Below The Master-Bead)—So That You Can (In any moment) Glance At That Image, and (Thereby) Recollect My Avatarically-Born Bodily (Human) Divine Form. Even Under any and all circumstances, You Can Always Recollect My Avatarically-Born Bodily (Human) Divine Form In mind. Likewise, You Can Always Practice Name-Invocation Of Me. And You Can (In any moment, As Required) Assist The Practice Of Ruchira Avatara Bhakti Yoga Through The Exercise Of The "Conscious Process" and "Conductivity" Practice.

Ruchira Avatara Bhakti Yoga Is The Responsive Directing (or Mere and Simple Turning) Of The Faculties Of the body-mind To Me (In and As My Avatarically-Born Bodily Human Divine Form and Person)—and Not Struggling With the contents Of Those Faculties and Only "Trying" To Direct them To Me, or "Trying" To Get Rid Of them In An ego-Effort Of Surrender Toward Me.

Right Practice Of Ruchira Avatara Bhakti Yoga Is To Yield The Faculties Of the body-mind To My Avatarically-Born Bodily (Human) Divine Form. To Do This Right Practice Rightly, It Is Simply Necessary (and Always Possible) To Yield (or Turn) The Faculties Of the body-mind At Their Root (and, Thus and Thereby, To Yield The Leading Characteristic Of Each Faculty To Me).

Therefore (Simply), Turn Your attention To My Avatarically-Born Bodily (Human) Divine Form, Turn Your feeling-awareness To My Avatarically-Born Bodily (Human) Divine Form, Turn Yourself bodily To My Avatarically-Born Bodily (Human) Divine Form Through Every Kind Of Service-Activity (and, Otherwise, Through The Simple Orienting Of Your physical body Toward My Avatarically-Born Bodily Human Divine Form), and Turn Yourself To My Avatarically-Born Bodily (Human) Divine Form Via The Natural (Me-Feeling and Me-Breathing) Cycles Of the breath—and (Thus and Thereby) Disregard (or Cease To Regard) the contents of the body-mind. Do Not Keep Checking Back On those contents—To See If they Are Changing! In Your Truly Right Practice Of Ruchira Avatara Bhakti Yoga, You Forget the contents of the body-mind. You (Simply) Do Not Use them. You Do Not Build Upon them. You Make them Obsolete By Not Using them. In This Manner, Ruchira Avatara Bhakti Yoga Purifies You—By Making the contents of the body-mind Obsolete, Through Non-Use. The Process In My Avataric Divine Company Is Not An Effort On Your Part To Do Something "To" the contents of the body-mind, or To Try Not To Use them. It Is Simply Your Turning To My Avatarically-Born Bodily (Human) Divine Form and Person—Turning Your Feeling-attention To Me, Turning Yourself Altogether To Me, Contemplatively. That Is Ruchira Avatara Bhakti Yoga.

Ruchira Avatara Bhakti Yoga Is The Practice Of Directing (or Merely and Simply Turning) All Four Of The Principal Faculties—mind (or attention), emotion (or feeling), body, and breath—To Me, Instead Of Addressing (or "Reading The Signs", and Then Struggling With) the contents (or Patterns Of conditioning) that arise in the body-mind. Of Course, In The Context Of This Constant Devotional Communion With Me, There Is The Random Natural Observation Of "Signs" Of the body-mind In The Midst Of its activities—but They Are Merely To Be Noticed, and Not Dwelt Upon. They Are To Be Noticed, and Then Confessed In The Company Of others who Can Reflect To You Something About Your "Signs". Then Use My Instruction, Come To A Conclusion About What Further Discipline You Should Introduce Into Your Living, and Continue Your ego-Transcending Practice Of Ruchira Avatara Bhakti Yoga.

The "Programs" Of egoic Habit Do Not Persist Unless You Give Them Your life-energy and attention. If You Give Your life-energy and attention To Me (Instead), Then All Your egoic "Programs" Will, Ultimately, Become Obsolete and (Literally) Vanish. That Is The Divine Truth and The Divine Law.

You Reinforce (or Become) Whatever You Put Your attention On (or To). Therefore, If You Make Me The Object Of Your attention, all the other "things" of attention (which Have No Permanence) Will Dissolve.

Any moment In which You Fall Back On The Mere Patterning or contents Of The Faculties Is a moment In which You Are Not Doing The Practice I Have Given You. In that moment, You Have Dropped The Practice, You Have Lapsed From It—and, Therefore, You Must Re-Initiate It, You Must Re-Associate The Faculties With Me. This Is The Tapas Of The Sadhana Of The Way Of The Heart—This Constant Re-Submitting Of The Four Principal Faculties (or the Total body-mind) To Be Turned To Me, In The Process Of Devotional (and, In Due Course, Spiritual) Communion With My Avatarically-Born Bodily (Human) Divine Form and Person.

The Turning Of The Four Principal Faculties To Me Is Ruchira Avatara Bhakti Yoga Only If That Turning Is Engaged As Your (Inherently—and Not Merely Strategically—ego-Surrendering) Heart-Response To Me, In Heart-Recognition Of Me (In and As My Avatarically-Born Bodily Human Divine Form and Person). If The Turning Of The Four Principal Faculties To Me Is Engaged As Any Kind Of self-Manipulative Strategy or Technique (Not Moved By Heart-Responsive Heart-Recognition Of Me), Then That Presumed "Surrender" (or Mere, and Unresponsive, ego-Effort) Is Not The Only-By-Me Revealed and Given Yoga Of Ruchira Avatara Bhakti.

Ruchira Avatara Bhakti Yoga Is Not A Matter Of You (As ego-"I") Strategically "Surrendering" The Four Principal Faculties To Me. Rather, Ruchira Avatara Bhakti Yoga Is A Matter Of Allowing The Four Principal Faculties To Follow Your Tacit and Spontaneous Heart-Response To Me. When You Heart-Recognize (or Feelingly "Locate") Me (In and As My Avatarically-Born Bodily Human Divine Form and Person), The Four Principal Faculties Follow, In Heart-Response To Me—and, Indeed, the Total body-mind Follows, In Heart-Response To Me, Devotionally Heart-Turned To Me. Such Is The Unique Characteristic Of Ruchira Avatara Bhakti Yoga.

If You Do Not Heart-Recognize (or Feelingly "Locate") Me and (Whole bodily) Heart-Respond To Me, Then Your Presumed "Surrender" Is Merely An Effort To Punch A Hole Through Your Hard Ball (Of ego-"I") and Reshape It Into An "Open Cup", or To Dismember Your Clenched Fist (Of self-Contraction) and Have It Surgically Restored As An "Open Hand". Such Is Not The Great Process Of Ruchira Avatara Bhakti Yoga. The Great Process Of Ruchira Avatara Bhakti Yoga Must Be "From The Inside Out", I Say.

If You Heart-Recognize (or Feelingly "Locate") Me, Then The Four Principal Faculties (Of attention, feeling, body, and breath) Follow, In Whole bodily (or Total psycho-physical) Heart-Response To Me—Not Because You

Move Those Faculties, but Because You Are Those Faculties. In Truth, You Cannot "Surrender" The Faculties To Me (As If The Faculties Were Separate From You, or Objective To You)—Because You Are The Faculties. Therefore, The Faculties Are Truly Responsively Surrendered To Me Only If You Heart-Recognize (or Truly Feelingly "Locate") Me. It Is Only In That Case That You Are Surrendered To Me—Because You Are The Faculties.

Ruchira Avatara Bhakti Yoga (or Devotionally Me-Recognizing and Devotionally To-Me-Responding Surrender Of All Four Principal Faculties Of the body-mind To Me) Is Whole bodily Prayer. Ruchira Avatara Bhakti Yoga Is Not Merely Prayer Engaged Via attention, or Via feeling, or Via the body, or Via the breath. Ruchira Avatara Bhakti Yoga Is Not Merely Prayer Engaged Via Any Single Faculty. Ruchira Avatara Bhakti Yoga Is Prayer Engaged Via All Of The Four Principal Faculties—Simultaneously, and In A Comprehensive (or Inclusive and Total) psycho-physical Recognition-Response To Me. And, Because All The Principal Faculties Of the body-mind Are (Thus) Made Into The Total Event Of Yogic Prayer, Ruchira Avatara Bhakti Yoga Is Not Merely The Prayer Of Requests—Uttered By the mind, and To The Presumed Divine "Other", and For The Sake Of the egoic body-mind (or the Separated, and Compartmented, ego-"I").

Ruchira Avatara Bhakti Yoga Is Total Prayer. Ruchira Avatara Bhakti Yoga Is The ego-Transcending Devotional Prayer Of Divine Communion. Ruchira Avatara Bhakti Yoga Is The Yogic Process Of Divine Samadhi—The Prayerful Devotional Process Of Directly ego-Transcending, and (Always) mind-Transcending, and (Always) Total-body-mind-Surrendering Yogic Communion With Me (In and As My Avatarically-Born Bodily Human Divine Form and Person).

Therefore, Ruchira Avatara Bhakti Yoga (or Whole bodily Prayer, or Heart-Responsive Heart-Recognition Of Me) Is Not, Itself, An Exercise Of the verbal (or conceptual) mind. Rather, The Total psycho-physical Exercise Of Ruchira Avatara Bhakti Yoga Always Requires An Exercise Of attention—which Is The Root and Epitome Of the thinking-activity of the conceptual mind. And, By Always Exercising attention, itself—In Total psycho-physical Recognition-Response To Me—the activity, and the (Always) body-mind-Contracting contents, of the verbal (or conceptual, or thinking) mind Are Constantly (and Directly) Transcended. Thus, Ruchira Avatara Bhakti Yoga (or The Total psycho-physical Yogic Process Of Heart-Responsive Heart-Recognition Of Me—Which Process Is The Whole bodily Prayer Of Divine Communion) Is Heart-Communion With Me Without any Associated concept (or Play Of mind).

If (In any moment) You Are Attentive To the Chronic thinking mind, You Are Not (In that moment) In Heart-Communion With Me. Attention (itself) Is Merely The Root-Form Of ego-"I". The Chronic thinking mind Is The egoic

Pattern Of attention. The Chronic thinking mind Is the ego-"I"—the Merely self-Reflecting pastimes Of "Narcissus". The Chronic thinking mind Is Made By the body's own self-Contraction. The Chronic thinking mind Is Mere Reactive self-Contraction. The Chronic thinking mind arises From A Non-conceptual emotional-physical State Of Doubt. The Chronic thinking mind Is Mere and self-Reflecting Talk—Empty Of Devotional Surrender To Me. The Chronic thinking mind Is The Non-Surrender Of attention To Me. The Chronic thinking mind Is Non-Recognition Of Me.

Attention to the Chronic thinking mind Is Merely The Exercise Of The ego-Knot Of self-Contraction. Attention to the Chronic flow of thoughts Is Inattention To Me—and Non-Communion With Me. Only Total psycho-physical attention To Me Is True Surrender To Me—Feeling Beyond thought (and Feeling Beyond attention itself) To My Avatarically-Born Bodily (Human) Divine Form (and, Thus and Thereby, Into The Infinite Space Of My Divine Spiritual Body and My Eternal Divine State). Only Total psycho-physical Recognition-Response To Me Feels Beyond self-Contraction (and all thought), Into (ego-Surrendering, ego-Forgetting, and, More and More, ego-Transcending) Whole bodily Heart-Communion With Me.

When The Four Principal Faculties Go To Me (In Devotionally Me-Recognizing, or Feelingly Me-"Locating", Heart-Response), all psycho-physical self-Contraction Is Released (Like The Spontaneous Opening-Out Of A Hand)—and thought, and emotional Reaction, and Heart-Cramped breath, and bodily self-Consciousness All Unfold and Relax Into My "Bright" Love-Bliss-Form. Such Is The Enstatic Ecstasy (or In-Me-Standing Stand, Outside Of self-Contraction) That Is The Essence Of Ruchira Avatara Bhakti Yoga, In every moment Of True Sadhana In The Only-By-Me Revealed and Given Way Of The Heart.

I Am Not Within "You". I Am Outside "You".

I Am Not Within The ego-Knot. I Am Outside The ego-Knot.

If You Truly Heart-Recognize (or Feelingly "Locate") Me, Then (moment to moment) You Totally psycho-physically Respond To Me (From The Heart, With All Four Principal Faculties)—and You Let Me In. If You Do Not Truly Heart-Recognize (or Feelingly "Locate") Me, Then (moment to moment) You Contract From Me (At The Heart, With All Four Principal Faculties)—and You Do Not Let Me In. If You Do Not Let Me In, I Remain Outside The ego-Knot Of "You".

The ego-"I" Is Not (and Cannot Be) My Devotee. There Is No Such Thing As egoic Devotion To Me. There Is Either ego Or Devotion To Me. There Is Either self-Contraction Or Devotion To Me.

Therefore, The True Fulfillment Of The Practice Of Ruchira Avatara Bhakti Yoga Is Always A Matter Of My Divinely Self-Giving Avataric Grace and My

Graceful Avatarically Given Divine Self-Revelation. I Offer To each and To all The Gift Of The Possibility Of This Devotional (and, Ultimately, Most Perfectly Liberating) Relationship With Me. Devotion To Me Is Inherently Love-Bliss-Full. To Remember Yourself Is Not Bliss. To Remember Yourself Is Stress and Struggle. To Always Remember To Merely Turn To Me—and, As An Inevitable Consequence, To Forget Yourself—Is To Live In My Love-Bliss-Happiness.

True Devotion To Me (or The Right, True, Full, and Fully Devotional Practice Of Ruchira Avatara Bhakti Yoga) Is The Only Happiness, and The Only Freedom From The Steel-Hard Mechanical and Chemical Bondage Of Suffering In Which You Are (Otherwise) Investing Yourself.

Therefore, Invoke Me, Feel Me, Breathe Me, and Serve Me. Make No "Room" For any "thing" Else. That Is What It Is To Be My True Devotee.

Thus, I Call All My Formally Practicing Devotees To Always (In every moment) Turn All Of The Principal Faculties Of the body-mind To Me, Rather Than To The ego-Act Of self-Contraction. Give Me That Devotion (Right, True, and Full), and You Will See Me Shining In My "Bright" Simplicity here.

It Is Possible For any person To Be (Temporarily) Caused To Experience and Exhibit What Might Be Called "Spiritual Signs", Even Without Having The Foundation Of Real (and Really Practiced) Devotion To Me—Simply By Being In Proximity To My Avatarically-Born Bodily (Human) Divine Form, or By Otherwise Coming Into Contact With My Avatarically Self-Transmitted Divine Spirit-Force (or Even Merely By Indulging In the Seemingly "Spiritual" phenomena Potentially Aroused By Some Kind Of Exploitation Of Natural life-energy). Therefore, Such Apparent "Spiritual Signs" Are Not (Themselves) Necessarily An Indication That an individual Has Fulfilled The Foundation Practice Of The Only-By-Me Revealed and Given Way Of The Heart (or Way Of Adidam). For My Devotee, There Must Always Be The Real Devotional Yoga Of Consistently and Intensively Turning The Four psycho-physical Faculties To My Avatarically-Born Bodily (Human) Divine Form and Person.

The human individual Is (Most Usually) Preoccupied With the (Obviously ordinary) activities of the moment, in and of themselves (Together With A Conglomeration Of Other ego-Patterned Concerns—and Even All The conditionally Acquired ego-Patterning Of mind and body and emotion and breath). However, When My True Devotee Actually Engages The moment to moment Real Devotional Practice Of Ruchira Avatara Bhakti Yoga, There Is Tacit Evidence Of a Profoundly Different life Being Lived. My True Devotee Always (and Obviously, and Even Directly Visibly) Lives In A Profundity Of Devotionally Relating To Me—In Heart-Recognition Of Me and Heart-Response To Me—and he or she Seriously Embraces All The Comprehensive Discipline Of Life I Have Given To All My Devotees. Both The Real Devotional Yoga Of Ruchira Avatara

Bhakti and The Full Range Of functional, practical, relational, and Cultural Disciplines Must Be Fully Established Before The Spiritual Process Of Participation In My Avataric Divine Company Can (Really and Truly) Begin. Only When That Beginning Foundation Is Fully In Place Can I Do Any (Really and Truly Effective) Spiritual-Transmission-Work With My (Thus Prepared) Devotee. In The Process Of Establishing That Beginning Foundation, There Is Much For My Devotee To Be Doing In Relation To Me. When That Beginning Foundation Is Really and Truly Established, Then My Devotee Has Sufficient Clarity and Freedom and Equanimity Relative To the "things" Of The Four psycho-physical Faculties—Such That he or she Can (Only Then, and Only On That Basis) Begin To Rightly Come To Me For The Purpose Of Receptively Participating In My Avataric Divine Gift Of Spiritual Communion With Me.

The Foundation Practice Engaged By My Student-Beginner Devotees Is A Profound (and Profoundly Purifying, and Profoundly Transformative) Matter. Indeed, That Foundation Practice Is The Forever-To-Be-Continued Root-Culture Of The Real Practice Of The Only-By-Me Revealed and Given Way Of The Heart (or Way Of Adidam).

If That Foundation Practice Is Not In Place, Whatever Spiritual Experience Of Me May (Potentially) Occur In anyone's Case Will Merely (and Inevitably) Be Incorporated Into his or her egoic psycho-physical Patterning—Without Any Responsibility For The Inherently (and Necessarily) ego-Transcending Enactment Of Real, Right, and True Devotional Relationship To Me. Therefore, My Student-Beginner Devotee Must Never Bypass The Real (By-Me-Explicitly-Given) Requirements Of The Foundation Practice Of The Only-By-Me Revealed and Given Way Of The Heart.

My Student-Beginner Devotee Must, In Every Respect, Learn A New Way Of Being—A Unique Way Of Right Life—By Means Of Constant (and, More and More, ego-Transcending) Devotional Resort To Me (In every moment, and Under all circumstances). One Of The Unique Characteristics Of The Only-By-Me Revealed and Given Way Of The Heart (From Its Beginning) Is The "Radical" Disposition Relative To egoity. My Devotees Must (individually and Collectively) Make Sure Never To "Soften" What The Practice Of The Way Of The Heart Must Rightly Be—Because The Way Of The Heart Is ego-Transcending Only If The Real Practice (Exactly As I Describe It In This, My Divine Testament, and In Even All My Twenty-Three Divine "Source-Texts") Is Rightly and Truly Done. If The Practice Of The Only-By-Me Revealed and Given Way Of The Heart Is "Softened", It Ceases To Be ego-Transcending. And It Is Only On The Basis Of Real (and Truly Devotionally Demonstrated) ego-Transcendence That My Devotee Can Rightly Approach Me To Receive My Avataric Divine Gift Of Spirit-Blessing.

When My Devotee Has A Demonstration-History Of Really, Rightly, and Truly Practicing Ruchira Avatara Bhakti Yoga and Of Fully Conforming his or her Total psycho-physical life To The By-Me-Given functional, practical, relational, and Cultural Disciplines—That (Total, and Comprehensive) Real, Right, and True Practice Is Tangibly (and Visibly) Demonstrated In the body-mind itself. The Real (Practiced) Yoga Of The Only-By-Me Revealed and Given Way Of The Heart Is Not A Merely Inward Matter. The Real (Practiced) Yoga Of The Only-By-Me Revealed and Given Way Of The Heart Is Immediately Evident In the face, and In the body-mind (Altogether), Of My Devotee. In My Devotee who Has Fully Established The (Perpetual) Foundation Practice Of The Only-By-Me Revealed and Given Way Of The Heart, There Is The Always Directly Obvious Whole bodily (or Total psycho-physical) Sign Of Steadiness In Devotion and Discipline, and Of (Purified and Transformed) Freedom Relative To the functioning and the contents Of The psycho-physical Faculties, and Of Most Basic Freedom From The Darkness Of ego-Possession (and Its Otherwise Endless Wandering In body-mind Patterns, and In All The Illusions and Preoccupations Of Bondage To gross conditionality).

The egoically-Acquired Patterning Of the body-mind Is an Always Active automaticity. It Is A Kind Of elemental Force—and It Claims The psycho-physical Faculties In every moment. Only By Means Of Your Active and Consistent Exercise Of Your Devotional Recognition-Response To Me Can The Spell Of This Binding Tendency (That Is Otherwise Patterned To Control The psycho-physical Faculties moment to moment) Be Broken. Only Thus Can You Truly Go Against The "Tide" Of Tendency.

The psycho-physical Faculties Must (In Effect) Be Constantly "Fasted" From Their egoically-Acquired Patterns—By The Always To-Me-Responsive "Volunteering" Of The Real, Right, and True Practice Of Ruchira Avatara Bhakti Yoga (Always "Retrieving" time and place For All The Kinds Of To-Me-Devoted Sacred Exercise, and Always, Under all conditions, Yielding The psycho-physical Faculties More and More Deeply To My Avatarically-Born Bodily Human Divine Form and Person). All Of The psycho-physical Faculties Must Be (Thus, and Thereby) "Fasted" From Their Usual automatic Patterning, all of the time (and In every place and circumstance)—Not By Merely Doing Something (Strategically, or In The Seeking Manner) "To" The Faculties (In and Of Themselves), As An ego-Possessed Exercise, but Truly (Simply) By Always Turning The Faculties To My Avatarically-Born Bodily (Human) Divine Form and Person.

To Practice Ruchira Avatara Bhakti Yoga Is To Turn To My Avatarically-Born Bodily (Human) Divine Form. The Practice Of Ruchira Avatara Bhakti Yoga Is Not A Matter Of Turning To Some Imagined (or Merely mentally

Presumed, or mind-Generated, and mentally and egoically Supported) "Abstract Universal Something" (Which You Abstract or Detach From Me, and Falsely Presume To Be Me). The Only-By-Me Revealed and Given Way Of The Heart (or Way Of Adidam) Is About Me-Recognizing Devotional Response (and moment to moment ego-Surrendering Resort) To My Avatarically-Born Physical Human Existence, Divinely Given here. As My Devotee, You Are The Servant Of A God-Man, A Physically Incarnate and Divinely Self-Revealing Human Being. Therefore, Devotional Recognition-Response To My Avatarically-Born Bodily (Human) Divine Form and Person Is Recognition-Response To The One and Only and Divinely Self-Revealing One—Who Has Become (Uniquely) Humanly Self-Manifested here, In Order To Be (By Avataric Means) Divinely Self-Revealed To all-and-All. Indeed, My Bodily (Human) Appearance In the world Is What Reveals and Establishes The Only-By-Me Revealed and Given Way Of The Heart (or Way Of Adidam), and (Now, and Forever Hereafter) Makes The Only-By-Me Revealed and Given Way Of The Heart (or Way Of Adidam) Universally Accessible and Really (and Practically) Possible!

You Are (By Means Of self-Contracted Action and False Presumption) "Narcissus", the psycho-physical ego-"I". Therefore, You Must Be Turned To Me—In and As My Avatarically-Born Bodily (Human) Divine Form and Person. I Am Outside and Beyond Yourself—Not Revealed As An Imaginary "Someone" (or Abstract "Something") Who Is "Floating In The Sky", but As A Concretely Existing, Concretely Born Human Being. By Means Of Avataric Birth, I Have Brought This—My Divinely "Bright" Human Body (or Divinely "Bright" Human Sign Of Indivisible and Inherently egoless Conscious Light)—Into the conditional, human world. Therefore, The Only-By-Me Revealed and Given Way Of The Heart (or Way Of Adidam) Is To Be Practiced In Responsive Relation To My Avataric Divine Incarnation, Not In (Necessarily, egoic) Association With Some Idea In Your egoic mind! My Avatarically-Born Bodily (Human) Divine Form Will Always (Now, and Forever Hereafter) Be The Means Whereby My Devotees Can Turn The Four psycho-physical Faculties To Me—Not To An Imagined Abstract Universal Principle, but To Myself Concretely Shown, Providing (By Means Of That Concrete and Divinely Self-Revealing Sign) A Real and Effective Focus For The ego-Surrendering Response Of The Four psycho-physical Faculties.

If the ego Is Not Being Actively Transcended, Then Whatever You Are Doing Is Not The Only-By-Me Revealed and Given Way Of The Heart (or Way Of Adidam).

If You Are Not Focused On My Avatarically-Born Bodily Human Divine Form, Then Whatever You Are Doing Is Not The Only-By-Me Revealed and Given Way Of The Heart (or Way Of Adidam).

I Stand Apart From All Illusions. When You Prattle About How You Resort To My "Universal Presence" or "Universal Existence" (As You egoically Presume It To Be), You Are Merely Pronouncing A Heresy (or A Form Of Revisionism), You Are Merely Creating An ego-Designed Substitute For The Only-By-Me Revealed and Given Way Of The Heart (or Way Of Adidam). By Thus Abstracting and (egoically) "Universalizing" Me, You Would Incorporate Me Into Your Own mind, Your Own "Program" Of karmic Existence. Such Heresy Has Absolutely Nothing To Do With My Avatarically Given Divine Wisdom-Teaching! Such Heresy Is Merely What the ego Makes Of My Avataric Divine Wisdom-Teaching.

My (True and Real) Universal Divine Presence (or Inherently egoless Conscious Light Of Indivisible Being) Is Not Anything You Can know About or Realize, As Long As You Are Fastened In the point of view of self-Contraction (or psycho-physically Enacted egoity). Because Of egoity (or The Persistent Act Of self-Contraction), You Cannot Possibly "Locate" My Universally and Eternally Present Divine Person.

Now, and Forever Hereafter—Even Forever After The Physical Lifetime Of My Avatarically-Born Bodily (Human) Divine Form—My Devotees Will Always Have The photographically (and Otherwise Technically) Recorded and Preserved Murti-Forms Of My Avatarically-Born Bodily (Human) Divine Form As The Always Immediate Means For Turning The Four psycho-physical Faculties To Me (Always Already Present, egoless and Indivisible, Above and Beyond and, Most Perfectly, As all-and-All). Feeling-Contemplative Remembrance and Invocation Of Me—By Turning The Four psycho-physical Faculties To My Physical Human Body—Is The Fundamental By-Me-Avatarically-Given Divine Means Whereby the self-Contraction Is Relinquished (moment to moment) and Transcended (Really, and, At Last, Most Perfectly).

Thus, I Myself (In and As and By Means Of My Avatarically-Born Bodily Human Divine Form) Am The Means. And This Great Reality Is Not Merely a conceptual conceit, Not Merely a bit of idealism or Poetry or emotionalistic Nonsense. To Resort To Me (In and As and By Means Of My Avatarically-Born Bodily Human Divine Form) Is Yoga Of The Most Profound Esoteric Kind.

Therefore, Always Turn To Me—In and As and By Means Of My Avatarically-Born Bodily (Human) Divine Form.

Always Surrender To Me—In and As and By Means Of My Avatarically-Born Bodily (Human) Divine Form.

Always Serve Me—In and As and By Means Of My Avatarically-Born Bodily (Human) Divine Form.

Always Live By My Avataric Divine Instruction—Revealed and Given Only By Me, Via My Avatarically-Born Bodily (Human) Divine Form.

This Human Body (Avatarically here-Born) Is The Divine Gift.

This Human Body (Avatarically here-Born) Is The Divine Self-Revelation.

This Human Body (Avatarically here-Born) Is The Divinely Self-Manifested Sign.

This Human Body (Avatarically here-Born) Is The Divinely Given Means.

You Have No egoic (or ego-Accommodating) Access To The Absolute and Universal Divine Reality and Person (Who Is The Source-Condition and Self-Condition Of all-and-All). Indeed, You Are (By self-Contraction) Dissociated From The Absolute and Universal Divine Reality and Person.

Therefore, I Am Avatarically Born To here—Bodily, Humanly, egolessly, and Radiantly!

My Body Is A "Bright" and Wordless Grace.

Your ego-mind Can Manufacture Illusions About My "Universal Presence"—but My Physical Human Body Cannot (Itself, and As Me) Fit Into Your mind.

I (Myself) Do Not Fit Into the mind.

I (Myself) Am Not Of the mind.

I (Myself) Am Always Already Prior To any and every point of view in space and time.

Therefore, If You Recognize The Inherently egoless Self-Nature and The Indivisibly Self-Radiant "Brightness" Of My Avatarically-Born Bodily (Human) Divine Form and Person, You Will (and Must) Respond To Me By Surrendering ego's mind and point of view At My Illimitable Feet!

Now and Always (Constantly, moment to moment), Surrender To This—My One, and Only, and Self-Existing, and Inherently egoless, and Spiritually Self-Radiant, and Eternally Indivisible, and Self-Evidently Divine Person, Avatarically Self-Manifested and Divinely Self-Revealed (Bodily and Humanly) here!

Now and Always (Constantly, moment to moment), Forget Your body-mind of Separate self—By Remembering My Bodily (Human) Person Of egoless Indivisible Conscious Light!

Now and Always (Constantly, moment to moment), Turn Your Total body-mind (Of Four psycho-physical Faculties) To My Avatarically-Born (and Divinely Self-"Bright") Bodily (Human) Divine Form and Person.

Now and Always (Constantly, moment to moment), Be Turned Whole bodily (With all Your feeling-breathing bodily attention) To My Avatarically-Born Bodily (Human) Divine Form and Person—and (Thus and Thereby) Invoke Me, Feel Me, Breathe Me, and Serve Me.

Now and Always (Constantly, moment to moment), Study and Practice This Devotion To Me—For This Devotion Is The Foundation and The Always Necessary Essence Of The Only-By-Me Revealed and Given Way Of The Heart (or Way Of Adidam).

My Avatarically here-Given Bodily (Human) Divine Form Is Your Unique Advantage. My Avatarically here-Given Bodily (Human) Divine Form Is The By-Me-Given Graceful Means For Your Purification and Transformation, and (Ultimately) For Your Most Perfect (and Most Perfectly ego-Transcending) Spiritual Realization Of My Divine Self-Condition and Domain Of Person. Thus, My Avatarically here-Given Bodily (Human) Divine Form Gives You A Profound (and Entirely Non-Abstract) Focus For Your Responsive Devotional (and Whole bodily, or Total psycho-physical) Turning To Me—A Focus That Inherently Deals Directly With the Total body-mind, Because My Own Avatarically-Born Body-Mind Is (Effectively, Now, and Forever Hereafter) here-Present To You, Exactly In Your Kind. Over time, This Process Of Real Devotion To Me (In and As My Avatarically-Born Bodily Human Divine Form and Person) Becomes Progressively Intensified, With The By-Me-Given Spiritual Establishment Of True Hearing Of Me, and (Then) The By-Me-Given Spiritual Establishment Of Real Seeing Of Me.

Your Previous (ego-Patterned) experiencing and Your Previous (ego-Patterned) Development Of Acquired Tendencies Is (As A Totality) What automatically Controls (and limits) Your psycho-physical Faculties—Unless You Truly Engage This Yoga Of Devotion To Me. Indeed, the world itself (or The Collective Of Mankind, and The Collective Of Natural events) Always (automatically, and Via elemental Forces and sympathies) Controls The psycho-physical Faculties Toward Darkness and Denseness—Even In The Midst Of The (Inherently Benighted) Effort (Of Man, and Of Mankind) To Make All Of This Into A "Paradise".

The conditional Domain Is Not (and Can Never Be) A "Paradise". That Is Why I Call You To Realize Me—Avatarically Self-Revealed To here, Divinely Free-Standing Above and Beyond All Of This.

Above the clouds, There Is Always The Sun—Forever Free Of Earthly weather. By Tendency, You Are Always Looking At the local weather, and Not At The Sun Itself. That Is What egoity Is About—Always Suffering the changes Of The local Patterning That Is the body-mind In its egoic Bondage. Instead, You Must (In every moment) Turn To Me, Avatarically here-Manifested In Bodily (Human) Divine Form—and You Must Do This Forever, Such That (Ultimately) You Become An egoless Participant In The Conscious Light (or The weatherless Divine and Perfect Sun) Of My Supreme Avataric Divine Gift Of Most Perfect Divine En-Light-enment.

Most Perfect Divine En-Light-enment (or Divine Self-Realization) Is Not You-Realization. Most Perfect Divine En-Light-enment (or Divine Self-Realization) Is Me-Realization. The Inherently Perfect Divine Self-Condition Is What Is (By Means Of My Avatarically Given Divine Spiritual Grace) To Be Most Perfectly Realized. The Condition To Be (Thus) Realized Is Always

Already Above and Beyond the Always Merely local weather—For I Am Not Something Inward To the ego and its Acquired Patterning.

I Am Not "Located" In The Core Of Your Suffering smallness, Below, In The weathering Dark.

The weather (Made By ego) here Can Darken all-and-All—Such That It May Seem To You There Is No Divine (and Perfectly Conscious) Light At All. Nevertheless, In The True Sadhana Of Devotional Turning To Me, There Is No weather—Ever.

This (here) is "weather-all-the-time"-land. Time is weather. And the body-mind is Always weathered—To the ego's Quick.

Nevertheless, If You Will Live By Always Turning the Total body-mind To My Avatarically-Born Bodily (Human) Divine Form and Person, You Will (Thus, In Due Course, Progressively and Literally) Incorporate My "Brightness", Making Me The One and Only Condition—Even Of the body-mind and its world.

By Always Turning To My Avatarically-Born Bodily (Human) Divine Form and Person, You Make This (Progressively) By-Me-Avatarically-Given Divine "Brightening" Process Possible—To Begin, and To Go On, and (Ultimately) To Become Perfect.

My Avatarically-Born and Divinely "Bright" Bodily (Human) Form, and My Avatarically Self-Transmitted (and Omni-Present, and here-Descending) Divine Spiritual Presence, and My Divine (Inherently egoless and Non-Separate) State Of Person Are (As One) The Only-By-Me Revealed and Given Way Of Adidam (Which Is The Way Of The Heart, Itself). I Must Give My Avataric Word Of Divine Heart-Instruction, For The Sake Of all-and-All, but The Divine Way Itself Is Simply Me—The One and Only and "Bright" Divine Person, Who Is Non-Separateness Itself, Avatarically Appearing here (Self-Manifested In Bodily Human Divine Form) Before You, Without any limitations whatsoever.

The Always present-time Circumstance Of Right, True, Full, and Fully Devotional Ruchira Avatara Bhakti Yoga Is Darshan (or Remembering, and, If and When Possible, Direct physical Sighting) Of My Avatarically-Born and Divinely "Bright" Bodily (Human) Form, and Darshan (or Heart-"Locating") Of My Avatarically Self-Revealed and Divinely "Bright" (and all-and-All-Surrounding and all-and-All-Pervading) Divine Spiritual Body, and Darshan (or Heart-Beholding, and Heart-Realizing) Of My Avatarically Self-Revealed and Self-Evidently Divine Person (The Inherently egoless Divine Self-Condition and Source-Condition Of all-and-All).

Ruchira Avatara Bhakti Yoga Is Worship Of Me, The "Bright" Itself, In Person (As My Avatarically-Born Bodily Human Divine Form—and, Thus and Thereby, As My Avatarically Self-Transmitted Spiritual, and Always Blessing,

Divine Presence, and As My Avatarically Self-Revealed, and Very, and Transcendental, and Perfectly Subjective, and Inherently Spiritual, and Inherently egoless, and Inherently Perfect, and Self-Evidently Divine State).

Therefore, From The Beginning Of Your Practice Of The Only-By-Me Revealed and Given Way Of The Heart (As My Novice Student-Beginner Devotee and, Then, My Fully Established Student-Beginner Devotee[37]—and Forever Thereafter), Always (Formally) Practice Ruchira Avatara Bhakti Yoga (Rightly, Truly, Fully, and Fully Devotionally), and Be (Thereby) Always Whole bodily Turned To Me (In and As My Avatarically-Born Bodily Human Divine Form and Person).

When You Have Demonstrated Sufficient Maturity As A Student-Beginner In The Way Of The Heart, Then You Are Invited Into My Avataric Physical Human Company (or, After My Avataric Physical Human Lifetime, Into The physical human Company and The By-Me-Spiritually-Empowered Circumstances Of My "Ruchira Sannyasin" Devotees), In The Context Of One Or More Periods Of Extended Formal Retreat, To Be Spiritually Initiated, By Me, Into The Practice Of Searchlessly Beholding Me, Which Practice Is The Fully Established Basic Sadhana Of Ruchira Avatara Bhakti Yoga—or The Both Devotional and Spiritual Establishment Of The Simple Practice Of Turning To My Avatarically-Born Bodily (Human) Divine Form and Person. Thus, Once You Have Made The Transition Beyond The Student-Beginner Stage Of Practice In The Way Of The Heart, Searchless Beholding Of Me Becomes Your Always Primary Practice—and The "Conscious Process" and "Conductivity" Practice Are (Thereafter) Always To Be Engaged In Response To That Searchless Beholding Of Me (and To The Tangible Reception Of My Spiritual Transmission, or Ruchira Shaktipat).

The Only-By-Me Revealed and Given Way Of The Heart (or Way Of Adidam) Is, In Its Fullness, A Spiritual Way. The Only-By-Me Revealed and Given Way Of The Heart (or Way Of Adidam) Is, In Its Fullness, A Shaktipat Way. The Only-By-Me Revealed and Given Way Of The Heart (or Way Of Adidam) Is Not A Form Of "Mind Dharma" (In The Characteristic Mode Of The Sixth Stage Of Life). The Only-By-Me Revealed and Given Way Of The Heart (or Way Of Adidam) Is The (One and Only) Seventh Stage Way. Therefore, The Only-By-Me Revealed and Given Way Of The Heart (or Way Of Adidam) Involves The Transcending Of the limitations Of All Six Of The Developmental Stages Of Life That Are Patterned By The Inherent Structure Of the body-mind (gross, subtle, and causal).

Practice Of The Only-By-Me Revealed and Given Way Of The Heart Is Not A merely philosophical Exercise. Practice Of The Only-By-Me Revealed and Given Way Of The Heart Is Not At All A Process Confined To The Dimension Of verbal-conceptual mentation. Practice Of The Only-By-Me Revealed and

Given Way Of The Heart Is, In Its Fullness, Participation In My Ruchira Shaktipat (or My Avataric Divine Spiritual Self-Transmission)—and, When It Is Real and True, Reception Of My Avataric Divine Spiritual Self-Transmission Is Profoundly and Unmistakably (and Necessarily) Effective In My Devotee's life. Such Spiritual Reception Of Me Is (Necessarily) life-Transforming—and (Necessarily) Such Spiritual Reception Of Me Carries With It Increased (and Always Increasing) Responsibilities Relative To The Practice Of The Only-By-Me Revealed and Given Way Of The Heart (or Way Of Adidam).

The "Conscious Process" (or The Process Of Devotion To Me That Specifically Controls, or Surrenders and Transcends, The egoic, or self-Contracting, Gesture and Tendency Of attention) Is An Always Necessary Dimension Of Responsibility In The Only-By-Me Revealed and Given Way Of The Heart—but It Must Be Clearly Understood That There Is A Vast (and Crucial) Difference Between The Spiritual Way (or Shaktipat Way) I Have Revealed and Given and The Forms Of "Mind Dharma" (Characteristic Of Many Sixth Stage Schools In The Great Tradition Of Mankind), Which Are, Essentially, Forms Of A merely philosophical Exercise Relative To The Dimension Of mental Awareness (or A Strategic Means For Dealing With the mental "contents" Of Consciously Aware Existence, or The "Consciousness Aspect" Of experience In Reality, By Exercising The Technique Of Discriminating, or Even Dissociating, Consciousness Itself From the objects Of Consciousness).

Practice Of The "Conscious Process" (In Any Of Its Only-By-Me Revealed and Given Forms) Is Never A Matter Of Abstracting (or Strategically Dissociating) Conscious Awareness (Itself) From the "things" (or objects) Of Conscious Awareness. Therefore, The "Perfect Practice" Of The Only-By-Me Revealed and Given Way Of The Heart Is Not A (Sixth Stage) "Mind Dharma" Practice (Founded In The Strategy Of Excluding the conditional worlds and conditionally Manifested phenomena From Conscious Awareness). If My Devotees Do Not Fully and Clearly Understand The Distinction Between The Only-By-Me Revealed and Given Spiritual Way (or Shaktipat Way) and The (Traditional) Forms Of "Mind Dharma", they Will Tend To Remain Involved In A Merely "Talking"-School Approach To The Practice Of The Way Of The Heart, Based On The False (Sixth Stage) Principle Of The Interiorization Of Consciousness (Abstracted From objects).

The Only-By-Me Revealed and Given Way Of The Heart (or Way Of Adidam) Is The Avatarically Given Divine Self-Revelation Of The Always Already Perfect Truth—The Truth Of The One and Only and Inherently Indivisible Conscious Light, Which Is The Divine Self-Condition (and Source-Condition) Of Both Consciousness and the objects Of Consciousness (or The Consciousness-Dimension Of Existence and The Energy-Dimension Of

Existence). Thus, The Only-By-Me Revealed and Given Way Of The Heart (or Way Of Adidam) Is Precisely Not A Practice That Relates To The Consciousness-Dimension Of Existence (or The Witnessing-Function Of Consciousness) Separated (or Abstracted, or Dissociated) From (or Even In Opposition To) The Energy-Dimension Of Existence.

The Only-By-Me Revealed and Given Way Of The Heart (or Way Of Adidam) Is The Avataric Divine Way Of The "Bright". The Entire Course Of The Way Of The Heart (Culminating In The "Perfect Practice") Is The Progressively Developing Process Of Devotional and Spiritual Resort To Me (The Avataric Self-Revelation Of The Self-Existing and Self-Radiant and Self-Evidently Divine Person Of Reality Itself).

Therefore, As My True Devotee, You Do Not think Me—You Breathe Me.

It Is Not Possible To Merely think Your Way Through The Devotional and Spiritual Process In My Avataric Divine Company. Only Whole bodily (or Total psycho-physical) self-Surrender (Feeling Me, Breathing Me, Serving Me One-Pointedly, and Transcending all of mind, and Even attention itself, In Me) Is The Right and True Way Of Devotional (and, In Due Course, Spiritual) Practice In My Avataric Divine Company.

The Only-By-Me Revealed and Given Way Of The Heart (or Way Of Adidam) Is The Divine Way. That Divine Way Is Not In the mind. That Divine Way Is Not Of the mind. That Divine Way Is Not A Matter Of mere philosophizing. That Divine Way Can Be (and Is) Revealed and Given Only By Avatarically Achieved Divine Means. That Divine Way Has Been and (Even In every present moment—Now, and Forever Hereafter) Is Revealed and Given Only By Me (In and As and Via My Avatarically-Born Bodily Human Divine Form). And That Divine Way Has Been and Is (In Due Course, In The Case Of My Every True and Truly Maturing Devotee—Now, and Forever Hereafter) Spiritually Revealed and Spiritually Transmitted Only By (and As) My Avatarically Self-Transmitted Spiritual (and Always Blessing) Divine Presence and Person—Which Is, Now, and Forever Hereafter, Always To Be "Located" By Means Of My Every True and Truly Maturing Devotee's By-Me-Spiritually-Activated and Always Entirely Turned-To-Me Feeling-Contemplation Of My Avatarically-Born Bodily (Human) Divine Form and Person. That Divine (and Only and Entirely Avatarically Revealed and Given) Way Is Real, and Not (In Any Sense) A Matter Of Conjecture. That Divine Way Does Not Originate From Below—Nor Does It Originate In and By Means Of The Stages Of The Developmental Process Of human Existence. That Divine Way Is A Divine Gift—Which Comes Only By My Avataric Divine Means, From Above and Beyond.

I Am True. By Pre-conditioned Tendency (and By Pre-conditioned Patterning), ego-Possessed human beings Refuse Me (Both individually and

Collectively)—and they Attempt To Replace Me With themselves. Nevertheless, I (and Only I) Am The One Who Is (Now, and Forever Hereafter) Showing every one The Only-By-Me Revealed and Given Divine Way Of The Heart (or Way Of Adidam)—and, Therefore, That Divine Way Requires each and every one's Devotional Recognition-Response To Me (In and As My Avatarically-Born Bodily Human Divine Form and Person). That Divine Way Requires That My Devotee Live According To My Avataric Divine Word. Initially, That Divine Way Of Heart-Responsive Heart-Recognition Of Me Becomes Established As Devotional Communion With Me—and, Then (In Due Course), When (By Means Of My Avatarically Given Divine Spiritual Grace) That Divine Way Becomes True (ego-Surrendering, ego-Forgetting, and ego-Transcending) Devotional and Spiritual Communion With Me, I (Progressively) Show My Devotee Everything (In Accordance With My Devotee's Depth and Integrity Of True Devotional Resort To Me).

I Show My Devotee Everything—By All Of My Means Of Physical (Human) Sign and Physical (Human) Availability, Made Possible By My Avataric Divine Incarnation here (In Physical Human Form). Therefore, Whole bodily (or Total psycho-physical) Turning To Me (In My Avatarically-Born Bodily Human Divine Form) Is The Fundamental Foundation-Activity Of The Divine Way In My Avataric Divine Company—Now, and Forever Hereafter.

When I Become Spiritually Effective In The Case Of My Any (Necessarily, Formally Practicing) Devotee, My Granting Of My Spiritual Baptism Is Not For The Purpose Of Allowing My Devotee To "Take Away" That By-Me-Given Spiritual Gift (Like a dog Taking a bone), and Presume To Do The Practice On his or her "own". The Only-By-Me Revealed and Given Way Of The Heart (or Way Of Adidam) Has Nothing To Do With Any Such ego-Possessed Strategy. It Is Only In My Any Devotee's True and Truly Maturing (and Truly ego-Surrendering) Devotional Recognition-Response To Me (In and As My Avatarically-Born Bodily Human Divine Form) That I (Potentially, and In Due Course) Become (or Even Can Become) Spiritually Effective—and, Then, Everything Is (Progressively) Revealed (and Made Plain), Entirely By The Active Grace Of My Avataric Divine Spiritual Imposition On My Devotee's Totally To-Me-Turned body-mind (and, Therefore, Not, In Any Sense, On The Basis Of, or By Means Of, any kind of philosophizing, thinking, or self-"guruing").

The Way In My Avataric Divine Company Is Avatarically and (Altogether) Divinely Given—Only By Me, From Above and Beyond. I Manifest That Divine Way. I Give That Divine Way, As A Gift. In The Actualization Of That Divine Way, I Must Respond To beings—and beings Must Respond To Me. Such Is The Only-By-Me Revealed and Given Way Of The Heart (or Way Of Adidam).

Expressed Most Simply, There Are Two Fundamentals To The Way I Have Revealed and Given: Ruchira Avatara Bhakti and Ruchira Avatara Kripa. In The Only-By-Me Revealed and Given Way Of The Heart (or Way Of Adidam), Ruchira Avatara Bhakti Is Not conventional devotionalism. In The Only-By-Me Revealed and Given Way Of The Heart (or Way Of Adidam), Ruchira Avatara Bhakti Is The Yoga Of Turning The psycho-physical Faculties To Me, here-Manifested In My Avatarically-Born Bodily (Human) Divine Form. When You Are In That Turned-To-Me Disposition Of True Devotion, Then My Avatarically Self-Transmitted Divine Spiritual Presence Can Be Received—and You Experience My Ruchira Avatara Kripa.

Now, Come To Me—here-Manifested (Now, and Forever Hereafter) In (and As) and Via My Avatarically here-Born Bodily (Human) Divine Form. Move Me (At Heart) To Respond To You and To Bless You. Do Not Expect My Avataric Divine Spiritual Blessing To Be Given "Automatically".

Your Devotional Turning To Me, and My "Bright" Spiritual Self-Transmission In Response To You—These Two, Together, Are The Only-By-Me Revealed and Given Way Of The Heart (or Way Of Adidam). Everything Else I Have Said and Written About The Way Of The Heart Is A Necessary Elaborated Address To All Of The Permutations Of psycho-physical experiencing. Fundamentally, The Way Of The Heart Is Your Devotion To Me (or Ruchira Avatara Bhakti) and My Avataric Self-Transmission Of My Divine Spiritual Blessing To You (or Ruchira Avatara Kripa).

To Move Me (At Heart) To Respond To You and To Bless You Is The Essence Of True Devotion To Me. If You Merely (and egoically) Expect Something From Me, Without Being Turned To Me, My Avataric Divine Spiritual Blessing Does Not (and Cannot) Flow To You.

Therefore, Turn To Me (Avatarically Self-Manifested here, In and As My Avatarically-Born Bodily Human Divine Form and Person)—and, Thereby, Move Me To Bless You. This Is What Must Occur In every moment Of Your Practice Of The Way Of The Heart.

Your Turning To Me Must Accomplish The Turning Of The Totality Of the body-mind—gross, subtle, and causal. Such True Devotional (and Total psycho-physical) Turning To Me Is A Profound and Serious Practice, With Greatest Depth—Becoming Greater, Deeper, and More Profound In Its Real Practice Over time, and In The Midst Of The Real Reception Of My Moved-To-You Spiritual Blessing.

The Only-By-Me Revealed and Given Way Of The Heart Is The Way Of Realization and Renunciation By My Avataric Divine Grace. The Way Of The Heart Is Not (In Any Respect) A System Of self-Applied Techniques. The Way Of The Heart Is Utterly Devoid Of self-Reference (or ego-Reference). The Way

Of The Heart Is The Life, and The Samadhi, Of (ego-Surrendering, ego-Forgetting, and, More and More, ego-Transcending) Heart-Communion With My Avatarically-Born Bodily (Human) Divine Form and Person.

If You Turn In Upon the body-mind, You Become Dark. If You Turn the body-mind To Me and Receive Me, the body-mind Is En-Light-ened By Me.

If You Heart-Recognize Me, Then You Know The Import Of My Avatarically-Born Bodily (Human) Appearance here—but That Appearance Does Not Define Me. My Avatarically-Born Bodily (Human) Appearance Is Means Only—Means For Your Sake, Means Given In Perpetuity, Means Given In Your Likeness, So That You May Respond (and, Thereby, Turn) To What You Are Capable Of Recognizing.

The Only Liberating Discovery Is That My Avataric Divine Spiritual Presence Is Real—Able To Be Tangibly Experienced Under any and all circumstances. No Form Of Merely Imagining My Avataric Divine Spiritual Presence—or Of Merely Manipulating Yourself To Seemingly Experience My Divine Spiritual Presence—Is, Ultimately, Satisfying. The Only True Satisfaction In life Is The Searchless Beholding Of Me (In and As My Avatarically-Born Bodily Human Divine Form and Person) and, In The Midst Of That Beholding, The Noticing Of My Divine Spiritual Presence Tangibly Moving Upon You In Your Real Experience. Such Is The Great and Liberating Discovery. Everything Else Is temporary, conditional, ego-Based, and Dis-Heartening. Only The Discovery Of The Tangible Reality Of That Which Is Divine Is Heartening and Liberating and Satisfactory.

This Is My Divine Spiritual Gift To You. This Is My Very (and Self-Evidently Divine) Person, Offered To You.

I Have Told You How To Practice The Devotional and (In Due Course) Spiritual Relationship To Me.

I Am Speaking The Truth.

You Must Prove The Truth Of My Avataric Divine Self-Revelation In Your Own life, By Always Turning To My Avatarically-Born Bodily (Human) Divine Form and Person.

Always Do This Practice, Exactly As I Have Given It To You—and (Thereby) See The Truth Of Me (All-Proved, As Truth, To You).

Avatar Adi Da Samraj
Adidam Samrajashram, 2004

SUTRA 6

From The Beginning Of My Teaching-Work, I Taught The Great Heart-Way Of self-Understanding and self-Transcendence (or Real ego-Transcendence). That Way Is The Divine Way Of (Devotionally Me-Recognizing and Devotionally To-Me-Responding) Devotional (and, In Due Course, Spiritual) Heart-Communion With Me, The Da Avatar—The Ruchira Avatar, The Love-Ananda Avatar, The Divine World-Teacher, and The Divine Heart-Master Of all-and-All.

From The Beginning Of My Teaching-Work, I Taught The Great Heart-Way Of self-Understanding and self-Transcendence (or Real ego-Transcendence). Therefore, From The Beginning, I Communicated Many Forms Of My Own Heart-Wisdom, In Order To Help each one, and all, To Commune With Me In My Heart-Fullness.

From The Beginning Of My Teaching-Work, I Taught The Great Heart-Way Of self-Understanding and self-Transcendence (or Real ego-Transcendence). Therefore, For The Sake Of those who Are Able To Commune With Me Especially By The Exercise Of Feeling and Insight, I Taught The Way Of Adidam As The Devotional Way Of Insight—Which Way (Progressively, In The Context Of The Devotionally Me-Recognizing Devotional Feeling-Response To Me, Released By Means Of The Exercise Of The True Heart-Discipline Of self-Enquiry) Becomes Most Fundamental self-Understanding and The Great Capability For Total psycho-physical self-Transcendence (or True, Complete, and, Ultimately, Most Perfect ego-Transcendence), and For The Total, Complete, and (Ultimately) Most Perfect Divine Spiritual Practice Of ego-Transcending Devotion To Me.

From The Beginning Of My Teaching-Work, I Taught The Great Heart-Way Of self-Understanding and self-Transcendence (or Real ego-Transcendence). Therefore, For The Sake Of those who Are Able To Commune With Me Especially By The Exercise Of Feeling and Faith, I Taught The Way Of Adidam As The Devotional Way Of Faith (or The Way Of Direct, or Unmediated, Devotionally Me-Recognizing Devotional Feeling-Response To Me)—Which Way (Progressively, and By The Exercise Of The True Heart-Discipline Of

Spontaneously Responsive Surrender Of self-Contraction, Merely By Means Of The Devotionally Me-Recognizing Devotional Response To Me) Becomes Most Fundamental self-Understanding and The Great Capability For Total psycho-physical self-Transcendence (or True, Complete, and, Ultimately, Most Perfect ego-Transcendence), and For The Total, Complete, and (Ultimately) Most Perfect Divine Spiritual Practice Of ego-Transcending Devotion To Me.

Therefore, From The Beginning Of My Teaching-Work, and By Every Kind Of Effective Means, I Taught and Revealed The Two Devotional Ways (Of Insight and Of Faith), or These Two Forms Of The One Great Way Of Adidam, Which Is The Great Heart-Way Of self-Understanding and self-Transcendence (or Real ego-Transcendence), Which Begins (and Always Develops) In Satsang With Me, The Divine Heart-Master, and Which (Therefore, and Fundamentally) Begins (and Always Continues) With Right Devotional (or Devotionally Me-Recognizing, and Devotionally To-Me-Responding, and, Altogether, ego-Surrendering, ego-Forgetting, and, More and More, ego-Transcending) <u>Feeling</u>-Contemplation Of My Heart-Purifying, Heart-Inspiring, Heart-Instructing, and Heart-Awakening Revelation-Form (or Inherently Revelatory Avatarically-Born Bodily Human Divine Form), and Which (Likewise, and Simultaneously) Begins (and Always Continues) With Right Devotional (or Devotionally Me-Recognizing and Devotionally To-Me-Responding, and, Altogether, ego-Surrendering, ego-Forgetting, and, More and More, ego-Transcending) "Consideration" Of My Avatarically Self-Revealed and Ever-Speaking Divine Word, My Avatarically Self-Revealed Divine Image-Art, My Avatarically Self-Manifested Divine Teaching-Leelas, and Even All The Avatarically Self-Manifested Leelas Of My Divine Spiritual Work Of Self-Revelation and Heart-Blessing, and Which (In Due Course, and Progressively, As My Avatarically Self-Transmitted Spiritual Divine Grace Will Have It) Becomes Fully Technically Responsible (and Truly ego-Transcending) Spiritual, Transcendental, and Divine Practice (and Heart-Awake Realization) In (Perpetual) Satsang—or Devotionally Me-Recognizing and Devotionally To-Me-Responding, and (Altogether) ego-Surrendering, ego-Forgetting, and (More and More) ego-Transcending Heart-Communion With Me, Via (and <u>As</u>) My Perfect Heart-Transmission Of My Own (Self-Evidently Divine) Person (and Inherently egoless Self-Condition).

In The Total Course Of My Teaching-Work, I Thoroughly Taught and Fully Revealed The One Great Way Of Adidam In These Two Devotional Ways (Of Insight and Of Faith). Therefore, and In The Form Of These Two Devotional Ways, I Thoroughly Taught and Fully Revealed Every Kind Of Means That Leads Toward and To The "Perfect Practice" (or The Three-Part, and Inherently Perfect, Practice and Process Associated With The Fifth, The Sixth, and The Seventh Stages Of Life, Beyond The Frontal Yoga, In The Way Of Adidam).

In The Way Of Adidam (or The Only-By-Me Revealed and Given Way Of The Heart), Each Of These Two By-Me-Given Devotional Ways (Of Insight and Of Faith) Culminates In The Ultimate (and Inherently Perfect, and Only-By-Me Revealed and Given) Process and "Perfect Practice" Of The Way Of Adidam. Each Of These Two Devotional Ways (In One) Builds Upon, Expresses, and, Ultimately (or Inherently Perfectly), Most Perfectly Realizes My (Avatarically Self-Revealed) Transcendental, Inherently Spiritual, Inherently egoless, and Self-Evidently Divine Self-Condition, Which Is The Inherent Feeling Of Being (Itself). Therefore, These Two Devotional Ways (In One), Their Associated Means (Embraced In The Process Of Listening To Me, and Hearing Me, and Seeing Me), The "Perfect Practice" (or Inherently Perfect Process) To Which All Of That Leads, and The Completion Of All Of That In The Only-By-Me Revealed and Given (Seventh Stage) Realization Of Most Perfect Divine Enlightenment Will Forever—and Always In The Context Of The Fundamental (Me-Recognizing and To-Me-Responding) Yoga Of Ruchira Avatara Bhakti—Remain The Basic Features Of The Great (and Truly Single, and Self-Evidently Divine) Way Of Adidam.

Formally Acknowledged Student-Beginners (or Beginning Formal Listening Devotees) In The Only-By-Me Revealed and Given Way Of The Heart (or Way Of Adidam) Study The Devotional Way Of Insight (Including The Total Practice and Process Relative To self-Enquiry and Non-verbal Re-Cognition), and they Also Study The Devotional Way Of Faith (Including The Practice Of "True Prayer", In The Form Of Ruchira Avatara Naama Japa, and In The Form Of The Prayer Of Remembrance). Student-Beginners Are Also Called To Practice The Original Basics Of Both Devotional Forms Of The Total Practice Of The Way Of The Heart (Experimentally, or In An Exploratory and self-Testing Manner), Until (By A Process Of "Testing and Proving") they Choose One or The Other Of These Two Great Devotional Forms Of The Total Practice Of The Way Of The Heart,[38] As A Beginner's Course, and As A Prerequisite For The Transition To The Intensive Listening-Hearing Stage Of The Way Of The Heart.

In The Only-By-Me Revealed and Given Way Of The Heart, The Devotional Way Of Insight Involves The "Conscious Process" Of Random self-Enquiry (In The Form "Avoiding Relationship?"). This Gradually Becomes The Process Of Non-verbal Re-Cognition (or "Knowing Again") Of the self-Contraction—Which Re-Cognition (or "Knowing Again") Is The Tacit Transcending Of The Habit Of "Narcissus". (In My Own Case, This Process Continued Until The Spontaneous Event Of Most Perfect Divine Self-Realization.[39])

In The Only-By-Me Revealed and Given Way Of The Heart, The Practice Of self-Enquiry (In The Devotional Way Of Insight) Is First Developed (Responsively, Spontaneously, and Progressively) As A Formal (and, Otherwise, Random) and Rudimentary (and Progressively More and More Meditative) Activity, Whereby the conditional self (or self-Contraction), and (Thus) the entire body-mind, Is Simply (or Merely) Observed and (In The Simplest Manner) "Considered", and (In The Process) Felt Beyond (and, Thus, Directly Surrendered, Relaxed, Released, and Forgotten). This Original Practice Of self-Enquiry Is Based On Simplest Listening, or The Beginner's Devotional (or Devotionally Me-Recognizing and Devotionally To-Me-Responsive, and ego-Surrendering, ego-Forgetting, and, More and More, ego-Transcending) Feeling-Contemplation Of My Avatarically Self-Revealed Divine Sign—or My Avatarically-Born Bodily (Human) Divine Form, and (Via My Avatarically-Born Bodily Human Divine Form) My Avatarically Self-Transmitted Spiritual (and Always Blessing) Divine Presence, and (Via My Avatarically Self-Transmitted Spiritual, and Always Blessing, Divine Presence) My Avatarically Self-Revealed (and Very, and Transcendental, and Perfectly Subjective, and Inherently Spiritual, and Inherently egoless, and Inherently Perfect, and Self-Evidently Divine) State—and, Also, The Beginner's Devotional "Consideration" Of My Avatarically Full-Given Divine Word and My Avatarically Full-Given Divine Image-Art and My Storied (Teaching and Blessing) Avatarically Self-Manifested Divine Leelas, and, Also, The Beginner's Devotional "Consideration" and (Experimental, or Exploratory and self-Testing) Application Of The Basic functional, practical, relational, and Cultural Disciplines Given By Me To All Practitioners who Embrace The Way Of The Heart. And This Original Practice Of self-Enquiry Is Experimentally (or In An Exploratory and self-Testing Manner) Engaged During The Student-Beginner Stage Of The Way Of The Heart.

If, On The Basis Of That Student-Beginner Experiment (and A Simultaneous Student-Beginner Experiment With The Beginner's Exercise Of The Devotional Way Of Faith), The Devotional Way Of Insight Is Chosen For Further Development, The Practice Of self-Enquiry Continues To Develop During The Intensive Listening-Hearing Stage Of The Way Of The Heart. The Transition To The Intensive Listening-Hearing Stage Of The Way Of The Heart Is Itself Made Only After Either The Beginner's Devotional Way Of Insight Or The Beginner's Devotional Way Of Faith Is Chosen, and Only Once All My Original Gifts, Callings, and Disciplines Are Rightly and Thoroughly Established, and Consistently So Demonstrated, In Practice—Including All The By-Me-Given (and, By Me, Called For) Basic functional, practical, relational, and Cultural Disciplines, and The Foundationary Gift, Calling, and Discipline Of Ruchira Avatara Bhakti Yoga. And, If The Beginner's Devotional Way Of

Insight Is Practiced During The Intensive Listening-Hearing Stage Of The Way Of The Heart, self-Enquiry Continues To Be The Principal Technical (and Really Effective) Feature Of The To-Me-Responsive "Conscious Process" Of A Really ego-Transcending Way Of Life—Based (Eventually) On True Hearing, or Most Fundamental self-Understanding (In The Maturity Of The Intensive Listening-Hearing Stage Of The Way Of The Heart). Likewise, The Practice Of self-Enquiry (In The Form "Avoiding Relationship?") Is (and Should Be) Continued Beyond The Intensive Listening-Hearing Stage Of The Way Of The Heart, By all those who Find The Practice Of self-Enquiry To Be Especially Attractive and Effective (As A Means Of ego-Transcendence) In their own case.

In The Only-By-Me Revealed and Given Way Of The Heart, The Devotional Way Of Faith Is, From Its Beginning, Based Upon The Heart-Response (or Faith-Response) To Me. Therefore, It Is, Fundamentally, A Practice That Involves The Devotional Exercise Of Faith (or The Devotional Faith-Response), Rather Than The Devotional Exercise Of Insight. However, The Devotional Way Of Faith Is Not (or Must Not Be) An Exercise Of childish (or Superficial and ego-Serving) emotionalism, or An Exercise Of "gleeful" and ego-Consoling idealism, or An Exercise Of any other kind of dependency, want, or enthusiasm that Neither Requires True self-Surrender Nor Expresses Truly ego-Forgetting Feeling and Faith. Neither (By Contrast) Is The Devotional Way Of Insight (Rightly Practiced) A Rather adolescent and Non-Feeling (or Abstract, emotionless, and willfully Dissociative) Exercise Of mere intellect and The Motive Of ego-Possessed Independence. Rather, In The Only-By-Me Revealed and Given Way Of The Heart, Both The Devotional Way Of Insight and The Devotional Way Of Faith Are (or Must Be) Well-Founded In Right and True and Truly Faith-Filled (and, Altogether, Truly Devotionally Me-Recognizing) Feeling-Responsiveness To My Avatarically Self-Revealed Divine Form, and Presence, and State Of Person—and The Total Devotional Way Of Faith, Just As Well As The Total Devotional Way Of Insight, Is (or Must Be) A Responsible Practice Directly and Fully Associated With The Process Of self-Observation, Most Fundamental self-Understanding, and (Capable) self-Transcendence (or ego-Transcendence).

In The Only-By-Me Revealed and Given Way Of the Heart, The Devotional Way Of Faith Is Based Upon The <u>Unconditional</u> Faith-Response To Me. That Is To Say, Even Though (In The Only-By-Me Revealed and Given Way Of The Heart) <u>Both</u> The Devotional Way Of Insight and The Devotional Way Of Faith Are (or Must Be) Well-Founded In Right and True and Truly Faith-Filled (and, Altogether, Truly Devotionally Me-Recognizing) Feeling-Responsiveness To My Avatarically Self-Revealed (and Inherently egoless, and Self-Evidently Divine) Form, and Presence, and State Of Person, The Devotional Way Of Faith Is

Based Upon (and Always Demonstrates Itself As) The Direct (or Immediate and Unmediated) Faith-Response (Of Devotionally Me-Recognizing, and Devotionally To-Me-Responding, and Whole-bodily-Demonstrated Heart-Surrender To My Avatarically Self-Revealed, Inherently egoless, and Self-Evidently Divine, Form, and Presence, and State Of Person)—Whereas The Devotional Way Of Insight Assists the Whole body In The Demonstrating Of The Heart-Surrendering Faith-Response To Me, By Means Of Random self-Enquiry.

In The Only-By-Me Revealed and Given Way Of The Heart, The Whole-bodily-Demonstrated Heart-Response Of Unconditional Faith Is Based Upon The Always Immediate and Unmediated Heart-Recognition Of My Avatarically Self-Revealed Divine Form, and Presence, and State Of Person. Therefore, That Unconditional Faith-Response Of Whole bodily Heart-Surrender To Me Is Never Done Because Of anything, or Done For anything, or Done In Order To Achieve anything, or Done In Spite Of anything, or Done About anything, or Done To anything, or Done In anything. Rather, It Is Faith Without conditional Reasons, and Without conditional Purposes. It Is Truly mindless (but Not senseless, or Disembodied, or body-Negative) Faith. Therefore, It Is Spontaneous (Devotionally Me-Recognizing and Devotionally To-Me-Responding) Whole bodily Heart-Surrender (or Heart-Release, and Heart-Relinquishment) Of the self-Contraction Of All Four Of The Principal psycho-physical Faculties (Of mind's attention, and Of emotional feeling, and Of physically perceiving body, and Of the ever-cycling breath).

The Most Basic Form Of The "Conscious Process" Practiced By All Student-Beginners (Including All Novice Student-Beginners)—and, Indeed, By Even All Practitioners (At Any and Every Stage, and In Every Form or Mode Of Practice) In The Only-By-Me Revealed and Given Way Of The Heart—Is Simple Name-Invocation (and Feeling-Contemplation) Of Me, Via One or Another (By Me Hereby Indicated) Simple Form or Combination Of My Avatarically Revealed and Given Divine Names and Avataric Divine Descriptive Titles: Either "Da", Or "Adi Da", Or "Adi Da Samraj", Or "Lord Da", Or "Lord Adi Da", Or "Avatara Da", Or "Avatara Adi Da", Or "Avatara Adi Da Samraj", Or "Lord Ruchira", Or "Lord Ruchira Da", Or "Lord Ruchira Adi Da", Or "Ruchira Da", Or "Ruchira Adi Da", Or "Ruchira Avatara Da", Or "Ruchira Avatara Adi Da", Or "Ruchira Siddha Da", Or "Ruchira Siddha Adi Da", Or "Ruchira Buddha Da", Or "Ruchira Buddha Adi Da", Or "Adi-Buddha Da", Or "Adi-Buddha Adi Da", Or "Ati-Buddha Da", Or "Ati-Buddha Adi Da", Or "Adi-Guru Da", Or "Adi-Guru Adi Da", Or "Ati-Guru Da", Or "Ati-Guru Adi Da", Or "Da Hridayam", Or "Adi Da Hridayam", Or "Santosha Da", Or "Santosha Adi Da", Or "Da Love-Ananda", Or "Adi Da Love-Ananda", Or "Love-Ananda Da", Or "Love-Ananda Adi Da", Or "Da Avabhasa", Or "Adi Da Avabhasa", Or

"Avabhasa Da", Or "Avabhasa Adi Da", Or "Dau Loloma", Or "Turaga Dau Loloma", Or "Turaga Dau Loloma Vunirarama". Generally, All Of These Should Also (or, Otherwise, Alternatively) Be Begun, or Even Ended, With Appropriate Descriptive References, Principally Either "Bhagavan", Or "Sri", Or "Lord", Or "Turaga", Or "Beloved", Or "Heart-Master", Or "Ruchira-Guru" (or "Parama-Guru", or "Adi-Guru", or "Ati-Guru"), Or "Avatar" (or "Ruchira Avatar", or "Param-Avatar", or "Adi-Avatar", or "Ati-Avatar", or "Buddha-Avatar"),[40] Or "Ruchira Buddha" (or "Adi-Buddha", or "Ati-Buddha"), Or "Samraj", and (Except In The Case Of My Names Given In The Fijian Language) My Name "Hridayam" May, Generally, Also Be Added (As Appropriate) To The End Of Any Of The (Indicated) Names Themselves, If It Is Not Already So Indicated.

Every Formally Acknowledged Practitioner Of The Only-By-Me Revealed and Given Way Of The Heart (Whatever his or her Developmental Stage Of Practice In The Way Of The Heart, and Whatever his or her Manner, or Form, or Mode Of Practice Of The Way Of The Heart) Is (Sacramentally, and Also, As Necessary, Occasionally, or, Otherwise, Randomly, Even In The Context Of Formal Meditation) To Practice The "Conscious Process", Most Simply, As Feeling-Invocation Of Me, and Feeling-Contemplation Of Me, By Means Of Simple (or Not Otherwise Technical) Name-Invocation Of Me—In Addition To The Technical Form Of The "Conscious Process" he or she Is (Whether Experimentally Or By Firm Choice) Practicing. Through Right (and Truly ego-Surrendering, ego-Forgetting, and ego-Transcending) Use Of My Names, or Combined Names and Descriptive Titles, In The Practice Of Simple Name-Invocation Of Me, all parts of the body-mind Are Conformed To Me, In A One-Pointed and Unwavering Manner. Therefore, Any and All Of My Names, or Combined Names and Descriptive Titles, That Are Given Herein As Appropriate For Use In The Practice Of Simple Name-Invocation Of Me, As Well As Any and All Other Right and Auspicious Variant Combinations Of My Avatarically Revealed and Given Divine Names and Avataric Divine Descriptive Titles, May Freely Be Used, As Appropriate, By Any Formally Acknowledged Practitioner Of The Way Of The Heart (Whatever his or her Developmental Stage Of Practice In The Way Of The Heart, and Whatever his or her Form and Manner Of Practice Of The Way Of The Heart), In Devotional Chanting and Devotional Singing, and In Sacramental Activities, or (Otherwise) In moments Of Spontaneous Ecstatic Devotional Exclamation, or In moments Of Spontaneous Ecstatic Devotional Invocation Of Me—and Also, Occasionally, Even In The Context Of Formal Meditation.

In The Case Of Practitioners Of The Way Of The Heart who Are (Whether Experimentally Or By Firm Choice) Practicing The Devotional Way Of Faith, The Beginner's Practice Of The Devotional Way Of Faith Involves The

"Conscious Process" Of Ruchira Avatara Naama Japa. The True Practice and "Conscious Process" Of Ruchira Avatara Naama Japa (To Which I Also, Sometimes, Refer, Descriptively, By Means Of The General, or Composite Traditional, Term "Sat-Guru Naama Japa") Requires (and, Most Basically, Is) The Random and Progressively Meditative Feeling-Exercise Of Faith In My Avatarically Self-Manifested Divine Sign, My Avatarically Self-Revealed Divine Self-Realization, and My Avatarically Self-Transmitted Divine Helping-Power. And This Feeling-Exercise Of Ruchira Avatara Naama Japa Is Associated (In The Traditional Manner[41]) With Devotional Invocation Of Me Via The Ruchira Avatara Naama Mantra (or Ruchira Avatara Mahamantra), Which Is Heart-Felt Invocation and Word-Celebration Of Me Via My Avatarically Revealed and Given Divine Names and Avataric Divine Descriptive Titles, and (Thereby) ego-Surrendering and ego-Forgetting Feeling-Invocation, Feeling-Remembrance, and (More and More Effectively) ego-Transcending Feeling-Contemplation Of My Avatarically-Born Bodily (Human) Divine Form, and My Avatarically Self-Transmitted Spiritual (and Always Blessing) Divine Presence, and My Avatarically Self-Revealed (and Very, and Transcendental, and Perfectly Subjective, and Inherently Spiritual, and Inherently egoless, and Inherently Perfect, and Self-Evidently Divine) State.

I Have Revealed and Given Eighty Variant Forms Of The Ruchira Avatara Naama Mantra (or Ruchira Avatara Mahamantra) For The Use Of My Devotees In The Practice Of Ruchira Avatara Naama Japa (According To My Instructions Given In This Testament). Each Of My Devotees who Practices Ruchira Avatara Naama Japa Is To Choose, Through A Process Of Experimentation and Testing, Only <u>One</u> Of These By-Me-Revealed-and-Given Forms Of The Ruchira Avatara Naama Mantra To Use In his or her Practice Of The "Conscious Process". Through Such Consistent (and Truly ego-Surrendering and ego-Forgetting) Use Of Only One Chosen Form Of The Ruchira Avatara Naama Mantra, all parts of the body-mind Are Intensively and Fully Conformed To Me, In A One-Pointed, Consistent, and Unwavering Manner. (However, Any and All By-Me-Revealed-and-Given Forms Of The Ruchira Avatara Naama Mantra, As Well As Any and All Other Right and Auspicious Variant Combinations Of My Avatarically Revealed and Given Divine Names and Avataric Divine Descriptive Titles, May Freely Be Used, As Appropriate, By Any Formally Acknowledged Practitioner Of The Way Of The Heart, Whatever his or her Developmental Stage Of Practice In The Way Of The Heart, and Whatever his or her Manner Of Practice Of The Way Of The Heart, In Devotional Chanting and Devotional Singing, and In Sacramental Activities, or, Otherwise, In moments Of Spontaneous Ecstatic Devotional Exclamation, or In moments Of Spontaneous Ecstatic Devotional Invocation Of Me.)

The Variant Forms Of The Ruchira Avatara Naama Mantra (or Ruchira Avatara Mahamantra) Revealed and Given (and Hereby Indicated) By Me Are "Da-Om", and "Om-Da",[42] and "Om Da Om", and "Om Ma Da", and "Om Sri Da", and "Om Hrim Da," and "Om Sri Adi Da", and "Om Sri Avatara Da", and "Om Sri Avatara Adi Da", and "Om Sri Ruchira Da", and "Om Sri Ruchira Adi Da", and "Om Sri Ruchira Siddha Da", and "Om Sri Ruchira Siddha Adi Da", and "Om Sri Love-Ananda Da", and "Om Sri Love-Ananda Adi Da", and "Om Sri Santosha Da", and "Om Sri Santosha Adi Da", and "Om Sri Avabhasa Da", and "Om Sri Avabhasa Adi Da", and "Om Sri Adi-Avatara Adi Da", and "Om Sri Ati-Avatara Adi Da", and "Om Sri Ruchira Avatara Adi Da", and "Om Sri Love-Ananda Avatara Adi Da", and "Om Sri Santosha Avatara Adi Da", and "Om Sri Avabhasa Avatara Adi Da", and "Om Sri Adi-Buddha Adi Da", and "Om Sri Ati-Buddha Adi Da", and "Om Sri Ruchira Buddha Adi Da", and "Om Sri Love-Ananda Buddha Adi Da", and "Om Sri Santosha Buddha Adi Da", and "Om Sri Avabhasa Buddha Adi Da", and "Om Sri Adi-Guru Adi Da", and "Om Sri Ati-Guru Adi Da", and "Om Sri Ruchira-Guru Adi Da", and "Om Sri Love-Ananda-Guru Adi Da", and "Om Sri Santosha-Guru Adi Da", and "Om Sri Avabhasa-Guru Adi Da", and "Om Sri Turaga Dau Loloma", and "Om Sri Turaga Dau Loloma Vunirarama", and "Om Sri Adi Da, Ruchira Avatar", and "Om Sri Adi Da, Love-Ananda Avatar", and "Om Sri Adi Da, Santosha Avatar", and "Om Sri Adi Da, Avabhasa Avatar", and "Om Sri Adi Da, Avatara Hridayam", and "Om Sri Adi Da, Ruchira Hridayam", and "Om Sri Adi Da, Love-Ananda Hridayam", and "Om Sri Adi Da, Santosha Hridayam", and "Om Sri Adi Da, Avabhasa Hridayam", and "Om Sri Adi Da, Ruchira Siddha Adi Da, Ruchira Avatar", and "Om Sri Adi Da, Ruchira Avatar, Avatara Hridayam", and "Om Sri Adi Da, Love-Ananda Avatar, Avatara Hridayam", and "Om Sri Adi Da, Santosha Avatar, Avatara Hridayam", and "Om Sri Adi Da, Avabhasa Avatar, Avatara Hridayam", and "Om Sri Adi Da, Adi-Buddha Avatar, Avatara Hridayam", and "Om Sri Adi Da, Ati-Buddha Avatar, Avatara Hridayam", and "Om Sri Adi Da, Ruchira Buddha-Avatar, Avatara Hridayam", and "Om Sri Adi Da, Love-Ananda Buddha-Avatar, Avatara Hridayam", and "Om Sri Adi Da, Santosha Buddha-Avatar, Avatara Hridayam", and "Om Sri Adi Da, Avabhasa Buddha-Avatar, Avatara Hridayam", and "Om Sri Adi Da, Adi-Guru Adi Da, Avatara Hridayam", and "Om Sri Adi Da, Ati-Guru Adi Da, Avatara Hridayam", and "Om Sri Adi Da, Ruchira-Guru Adi Da, Avatara Hridayam", and "Om Sri Adi Da, Love-Ananda-Guru Adi Da, Avatara Hridayam", and "Om Sri Adi Da, Santosha-Guru Adi Da, Avatara Hridayam", and "Om Sri Adi Da, Avabhasa-Guru Adi Da, Avatara Hridayam", and "Om Sri Da, Jai Da, Jai Jai Da",[43] and "Om Sri Adi Da, Jai Adi Da, Jai Jai Adi Da", and "Om Sri Adi Da, Ruchira Siddha Adi Da, Jai Jai Adi Da, Ruchira Avatar", and "Om Sri Adi Da, Avatara Adi Da, Jai Jai Adi Da, Avatara Hridayam", and "Om Sri Adi Da, Sri Ruchira Adi Da, Jai Jai Adi Da, Avatara Hridayam", and "Om Sri Adi Da, Love-Ananda Adi Da, Jai Jai Adi Da, Avatara Hridayam", and "Om Sri Adi Da, Sri Santosha Adi Da, Jai Jai Adi Da, Avatara Hridayam", and "Om Sri Adi Da, Avabhasa Adi Da, Jai Jai Adi Da, Avatara Hridayam", and "Om Sri Adi Da, Ruchira Avatara Da, Love-Ananda Avatar, Adi-Avatara Da, Da, Da, Da", and "Om Sri Adi Da, Ruchira Avatara Da, Love-Ananda Avatar, Ati-Avatara Da, Da, Da, Da", and "Om Sri Adi Da, Adi-Buddha Avatar, Love-Ananda Avatar, Buddha-Avatara Da, Da, Da, Da", and "Om Sri Adi Da, Ati-Buddha Avatar, Love-Ananda Avatar, Buddha-Avatara Da, Da, Da, Da", and "Om Sri Adi Da, Ruchira Buddha-Avatar, Love-Ananda Avatar, Avatara Buddha Da, Da, Da, Da", and "Om Sri Adi Da, Ruchira Buddha-Avatar, Adi-Buddha Avatar, Ati-Buddha Avatar, Avatara Hridayam, Da, Da, Da", and "Om Sri Adi Da, Love-Ananda Buddha Da, Avatara Buddha Da, Tathagata Avatar, Hridaya-Buddha Avatar, Avatara Hridayam, Da, Da, Da".

The Proper Pronunciation Of Whichever Particular Form Of The By-Me-Revealed and By-Me-Given Ruchira Avatara Naama Mantra Has Been Chosen By My Any Devotee Practicing Ruchira Avatara Naama Japa Is To Be Demonstrated, and All Its Parts Are To Be Explained, To My Each Such Devotee, In Sacred Occasions Of Formal Sacramental and Instructional Initiation, Based Upon My Elaboration Of The Significance Of All These Names (or Word-Signs) In The Various Moments Of This Testament Of Divine Secrets.

In The Only-By-Me Revealed and Given Way Of The Heart, The Devotional Way Of Faith Is To Be Associated With All The Same Basic Forms Of Study and "Consideration" (Of My Avatarically Self-Revealed, and Always Me-Revealing, Divine Word—Including All My Avatarically Given Divine Teaching-Arguments—and My Avatarically Self-Revealed, and Always Me-Revealing, Divine Image-Art, and The Storied Divine Leelas Of My Avataric Teaching and Blessing), and With The Same (Fundamental) Practice Of Feeling-Contemplation (Of My Avatarically-Born Bodily Human Divine Form, <u>and</u>, In Due Course, My Avatarically Self-Transmitted Spiritual, and Always Blessing, Divine Presence <u>and</u>, Thus and Thereby, and More and More, My Avatarically Self-Revealed, and Very, and Transcendental, and Perfectly Subjective, and Inherently Spiritual, and Inherently egoless, and Inherently Perfect, and Self-Evidently Divine State), and With The Same Forms Of self-Discipline (functional, practical, relational, and Cultural) That Are Associated With The Devotional Way Of Insight. And Even Though, In The Way Of The Heart, The Devotional Way Of Faith and The Devotional Way Of Insight Are Each Developed Via A Different (and Unique) Principal Technical (or Root-Cultural) Exercise Of The To-Me-Responsive "Conscious Process" (Based On Either The Principle Of Feeling-Faith Or The Principle Of Feeling-Insight),

Both Involve The Development Of The Same Basic (and Necessary) Process Of self-Observation, self-Understanding, and self-Transcendence (or ego-Transcendence).

In The Only-By-Me Revealed and Given Way Of The Heart, The Practice Of Ruchira Avatara Naama Japa (In The Devotional Way Of Faith) Is First Developed (Responsively, Spontaneously, and Progressively) As A Formal (and, Otherwise, Random) and Rudimentary (and More and More Meditative) Activity, Whereby the conditional self (or self-Contraction), and (Thus) the entire body-mind, Is Simply and Directly Observed (or Directly Felt) and Directly (and Immediately) Felt Beyond (or Actively Surrendered, Relaxed, Released, and Forgotten) In (or Via) Faithful (and Devotionally Me-Recognizing and Devotionally To-Me-Responsive) Feeling-Contemplation Of My Avatarically-Born Bodily (Human) Divine Form, and With The Constant (and Always Growing) Exercise Of Feeling-Confidence In My Constant (and Divinely Spiritual) Helping-Power (or Accomplishing-Power). And This Original Practice, Based On Simplest (and, Necessarily, Devotional) Listening (or The Beginner's ego-Surrendering, ego-Forgetting, and, More and More, ego-Transcending Feeling-Contemplation Of My Avatarically-Born Bodily Human Divine Form, and The Beginner's ego-Surrendering, ego-Forgetting, and, More and More, ego-Transcending "Consideration" Of My Avatarically Self-Revealed, and Always Me-Revealing, Divine Word and Image-Art and Leelas), Is Experimentally (or In An Exploratory and self-Testing Manner) Engaged (Along With The Similarly Experimental Engagement Of self-Enquiry, In The Devotional Way Of Insight) During The Student-Beginner Stage Of The Way Of The Heart.

If, On The Basis Of That Student-Beginner Experiment (or Exploratory and self-Testing "Consideration" Of Both The Devotional Way Of Insight and The Devotional Way Of Faith), The Devotional Way Of Faith Is Chosen For Further Development, The Practice Of Ruchira Avatara Naama Japa (and The Total Devotional Exercise Of Faith) Continues To Develop During The Intensive Listening-Hearing Stage Of The Way Of The Heart, Once All My Original Gifts, and Callings, and Disciplines, Including All The By-Me-Given (and Called For) Basic functional, practical, relational, and Cultural Disciplines, and The Foundationary Gift, Calling, and Discipline Of Ruchira Avatara Bhakti Yoga, Are Thoroughly Established, and Consistently So Demonstrated, In Practice. And, If The Beginner's Devotional Way Of Faith Is Practiced During The Intensive Listening-Hearing Stage Of The Way Of The Heart, Ruchira Avatara Naama Japa Itself Becomes The Principal Technical (and Really Effective) Feature Of The To-Me-Responsive "Conscious Process" Of A Really ego-Transcending Way Of Life—Based (Eventually) On True Hearing, or Most Fundamental self-Understanding (In The Maturity Of The Intensive Listening-Hearing Stage Of

The Way Of The Heart). Likewise, The Devotional Way Of Faith (Expressed, In The Would-Be-Seeing Stage Of The Way Of The Heart, Through The Continued Exercise Of Ruchira Avatara Naama Japa, and, In The First Actually Seeing Stage, Through The Exercise Of The Prayer Of Remembrance) Is (As A General Rule) Also To Be Continued Beyond The Intensive Listening-Hearing Stage Of The Way Of The Heart By all who Began To Practice The Way Of The Heart By (Already, and Responsively) Embracing The Devotional Way Of Faith (After "Testing and Proving" It In The Experimental Process In The Student-Beginner Practice).

The Would-Be-Seeing Stage, The First Actually Seeing Stage, and The "Perfect Practice" Of The Way Of The Heart Are Reserved For those who Are Capable (By Virtue Of True Hearing and Fullest Devotional Recognition-Response To Me) To Practice The Seeing Devotee's Way Of Fullest (Spiritually Active, and, Spiritually, Technically Fully Responsible) Heart-Communion With Me. And Such Spiritually Active Participation In My Satsang and Inherently Perfect Heart-Company Is The Great Principle Of The Fully Established (or Seeing Devotee's) Way Of The Heart.

Student-Beginners In The Way Of The Heart and Practitioners Of The Way Of The Heart who Are Engaged In The Intensive Listening-Hearing Process Are (Necessarily) Formally Acknowledged Beginning Devotee-Members Of The Lay Congregationist Order Of Adidam Ruchiradam, Which Is The Formal General Cultural and Serving Order Of My Lay Devotees who Do Not Yet Practice The "Perfect Practice", and Which Formal General Order Is Also Known, Simply, As The Lay Congregationist Order.

Members Of The Lay Congregationist Order Of Adidam Ruchiradam Will, At The Point Of Making The Transition To The "Perfect Practice", Enter, In The General Case, The Lay Renunciate Order Of Adidam Ruchiradam—Which Is The Formal Renunciate Cultural and Serving Order Of My Lay Devotees who Are Practicing In The Context Of The "Perfect Practice", and Which Formal Lay Renunciate Order Is Also Known, Simply, As The Lay Renunciate Order. In Exceptional (and, Necessarily, Uniquely Exemplary) Cases, Members Of The Lay Congregationist Order Of Adidam Ruchiradam Will, At The Point Of Making The Transition To The "Perfect Practice", Enter The Ruchira Sannyasin Order Of Adidam Ruchiradam (and, In Other, Also Exceptional, and, Necessarily, Uniquely Exemplary Cases, Members Of The Lay Renunciate Order Of Adidam Ruchiradam Will, Even After The Point Of Making The Transition To The "Perfect Practice", Enter The Ruchira Sannyasin Order Of Adidam Ruchiradam), Which Formal Sannyasin Order Is The Great Formal Renunciate Order Of My Uniquely Exemplary and Formally and Legally Established Fully Renunciate "Ruchira Sannyasin" Devotees, and Which Formal

Sannyasin Order Is Also Known, Simply, As The Ruchira Sannyasin Order, The Members Of Which Are Called, By Me, To Demonstrate The "Perfect Practice" In The Context Of Perpetual Retreat, and, In General, By The Discipline Of Artful Seclusion From The Habitual Pattern Of conventional Outward-Directedness.[44]

All Student-Beginners In The Way Of The Heart Engage In Study and Beginner's Practice As A personal Discipline In Satsang With Me, and Always In Preparation For Entrance Into The (True and Full) By-Me-Spiritually-Initiated Culture Of Spiritually Active Satsang (or Spiritually Awakened Heart-Communion) With Me. My Student-Beginner Devotees Gratefully (and In A Progressively Developing Devotional, or Heart-Feeling, Manner) Embrace Me As The Divine Heart-Master, and (By Rightly and Truly Heart-Recognizing Me and Heart-Responding To Me) Resort To Me As The Self-Revealed Divine Person, Ever-Present Via My Own Avatarically Given and Divinely Self-Revealing Sign (Of Form, and Presence, and State), and Ever-Active In The Form Of My Avatarically Full-Given (and Always Me-Revealing) Divine Word and My Avatarically Full-Given (and Always Me-Revealing) Divine Image-Art and All The Storied (and Often Lesson-Making) Divine Leelas Of My Avatarically Self-Manifested (and Always Me-Revealing) Divine Spiritual Work. They Always (and In The Devotional and Feeling Manner) "Consider" My Avatarically Self-Revealed Divine Word and My Avatarically Self-Revealed Divine Image-Art and My Avatarically Self-Manifested Divine Leelas, and they Always (and In The Devotional and Feeling Manner) Contemplate My Avatarically Self-Manifested Bodily (Human) Divine Form (Ever Directly, and As Represented and Revealed In or Through photographic Images and Other Types Of Recorded, or, Otherwise, artistically Rendered, Images).[45]

The Practice Of My Student-Beginner Devotees (and, Indeed, The Practice Of <u>All</u> My Devotees) Is <u>Always</u> A Matter Of their own Responsibility, Rather Than The Responsibility Of <u>Any</u> "Other", or others. The Practice Of My Student-Beginner Devotees (and, Indeed, The Practice Of <u>All</u> My Devotees) Is <u>Always</u> A Matter Of Really Effectively-Managed <u>Counter-egoic</u> Responsibility For their own conditional (or Separate, and Separative) self-activity—Rather Than A Struggle With Me, or With others. Therefore, In The Only-By-Me Revealed and Given Way Of The Heart, The Original Practice For all Is (In The Devotional Manner) To Responsively Embrace My Avatarically Self-Revealed (and Always Me-Revealing) Divine Word and My Avatarically Self-Revealed (and Always Me-Revealing) Divine Image-Art and All My Avatarically Self-Manifested (and Always Me-Revealing) Divine Leelas—and Constantly (and In The Whole bodily, or Totally psycho-physically self-Surrendered, Devotional Manner) To Contemplate My Avatarically-Born Bodily (Human) Divine Form, and (Thereby, In Due Course) My Avatarically Self-Transmitted Spiritual, and

Always Blessing, Divine Presence, and (Thus and Thereby) My Avatarically Self-Revealed, and Very, and Transcendental, and Perfectly Subjective, and Inherently Spiritual, and Inherently egoless, and Inherently Perfect, and Self-Evidently Divine State. On The Basis Of This Progressively Developing Original Practice (and In Devotional Recognition-Response To Me, In The Form Of Either The Exercise Of The Devotional Way Of Insight Or The Exercise Of The Devotional Way Of Faith), The Necessary Process (and Progressively Developing Course) Of The Only-By-Me Revealed and Given Way Of The Heart Is To Directly (and Intelligently) Observe, and (Eventually and Most Fundamentally) To Understand, and (Thereby) To Really Effectively Transcend (or Truly Feel Beyond) the ego-"I" (or the self-Contraction of the conditional, or Total psycho-physical, self)—and This Is Always (Now, and Forever Hereafter) A Matter Of Whole bodily (or Total psycho-physical) Surrender To (and Into) My Avatarically Self-Revealed Human, Spiritual, Transcendental, Inherently egoless, and Self-Evidently Divine Form, Presence, and State Of Person.

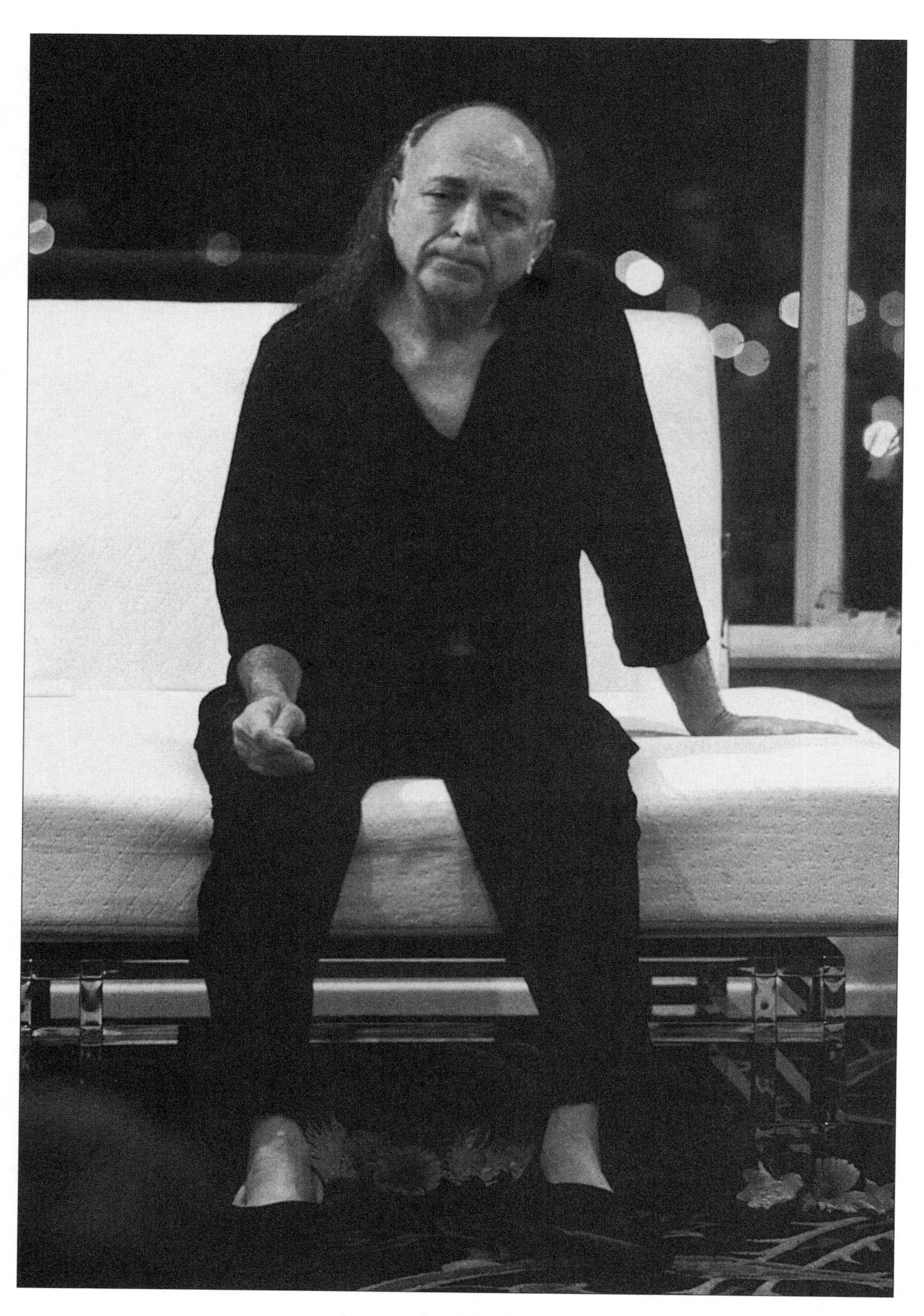

Avatar Adi Da Samraj
Clear Lake, 2001

SUTRA 7

My "Consideration" and Self-Revelation Of The ego-Transcending Way Of The Heart Developed Over The Many Years Of My Divinely Self-Submitted Teaching-Work and My Divine Self-Revelation-Work, On The Basis Of My Response To The Needs and limitations and Heart-Necessities Of those who Were Moved By My Avatarically Self-Revealed Divine Word and (At Least In A Rudimentary Fashion, and More and More) By My Avatarically Given Divine Self-Revelation Of My Self-Existing, Self-Radiant, Transcendental, Inherently Spiritual, Inherently egoless, and Self-Evidently Divine Person (or Spiritually "Bright", and All-Outshining, Divine Self-Condition), Always Spontaneously Revealed In, By, and As My Even Avatarically-Born Bodily (Human) Divine Form, and My Avatarically Self-Transmitted Spiritual (and Always Blessing) Divine Presence, and My Avatarically Self-Revealed (and Very, and Transcendental, and Perfectly Subjective, and Inherently Spiritual, and Inherently egoless, and Inherently Perfect, and Self-Evidently Divine) State. And The Real Course and Process Of ego-Transcending Practice Must Not Be Bypassed In The Only-By-Me Revealed and Given Way Of The Heart, Even Though the ego Would Prefer To Do So.

Anyone who Fully "Considers" The Great Process Demonstrated In My Own Case Must Thereby Observe That Real and Most Ultimate (or Inherently Most Perfect) Fulfillment Of ego-Transcending (and, Ultimately, Real-God-Realizing) Practice Involves A Profound Spiritual Process and Course Of Life That Encompasses and Transcends The Totality Of Each and All Of The First Six Stages Of Life and Is, At Last, Completed Only In The Fullness (and, Most Perfectly, Only In The Final Fulfillment) Of The Only-By-Me Revealed and Given Seventh Stage Of Life (In The Way Of The Heart). Indeed, In the case of <u>all</u> others, No Such Effort Can Most Perfectly Fulfill Itself Without Right Devotional (or ego-Surrendering, ego-Forgetting, and, More and More, ego-Transcending) "Consideration" Of My Avatarically Self-Revealed and Ever-Speaking Divine Word, My Avatarically Self-Revealed Divine Image-Art, My Avatarically Self-Manifested Divine Teaching-Leelas, and Even All The Leelas Of My Avatarically Self-Manifested Divine Spiritual Work Of Self-Revelation and Heart-Blessing, and Without The Discipline Of The True and Complete Culture Of Life Of The Gathering Of My Devotees, and Without Spiritual Access To Me (Whether During Or After The Avataric Physical Lifetime Of My Bodily Human Divine Form)—For I Am The Avatarically Self-Revealing Divine Source Of Unrelenting Grace (or Divine Heart-Transmission), and, Therefore, Of Spiritual, Transcendental, and Divine Self-Realization (or Divine Enlightenment).

The Way Of Most Perfect Divine Enlightenment Has Been Revealed In and Via The Form Of My Own Ordeal Of Life, Practice, and Divine Self-Realization. However, My Own Ordeal Is Divine—and, Therefore, Unique. I Am Avatarically Born, In Order To Teach (and Awaken) all others. Therefore, My Summary Of The Way Of The Heart In This Divine Testament (and In Even All Of My Twenty-Three Divine "Source-Texts") Is Based On My "Consideration" Of The Means and The Stages Necessary For others.

Every one Begins The "Consideration" and Practice Of The Way Of The Heart Without Immediate Resort To The More Complex (or Fully Developed) Practices Of (Spiritually) Fully Technically Responsible Devotion To Me, but That Earliest "Consideration" and Practice Should (Immediately, and More and More) Make Appropriate (and Right Contemplative, and, Thus, Feeling) Use Of My Avatarically Self-Revealed Divine Person (or My Avatarically-Born Bodily Human Divine Form, and, Thereby, In Due Course, My Avatarically Self-Transmitted Spiritual, and Always Blessing, Divine Presence, and My Avatarically Self-Revealed, and Very, and Transcendental, and Perfectly Subjective, and Inherently Spiritual, and Inherently egoless, and Inherently Perfect, and Self-Evidently Divine State). Just As The Transformative Spiritual Course Of My Own Practice, Even Of self-Enquiry, Was Founded On Devotional Submission Of My Own Apparent self (or Heart-Surrender Of My Own Apparent and Apparently self-Contracted body-mind) To My Own Teachers and Spiritual Sources,[46] Just So, any one who Seriously Heart-Recognizes Me and Heart-Responds To Me Via My Avatarically Self-Revealed (and Always Me-Revealing) Divine Word and My Avatarically Self-Revealed (and Always Me-Revealing) Divine Image-Art and My Avatarically Self-Manifested (and Always Me-Revealing) Divine Leelas Will Also (and More and More) Realize The Graceful Necessity To Embrace The Way Of The Heart As Just Such A Transformative Spiritual Course, Developed Entirely As A Process Of ego-Transcending Devotion To Me. By My Own Example, I Have Already Revealed The Essential Form Of That Great Process Of ego-Transcending and Divinely Spiritually Self-Realizing Guru-Devotion—and I Am Summarizing My Most Perfectly Complete Avataric Self-Revelation Of The Way Of Guru-Devotion (As Most Perfectly ego-Surrendering Devotional and Spiritual

Relationship To Me) In The Words Of This Divine Testament (and In The Words Of Even All Of My Twenty-Three Divine "Source-Texts").

In My Own Case, The "Conscious Process" Of self-Understanding, Persistent self-Enquiry (or Enquiry Into the self-Contraction), and The Effective Practice Of Feeling-Transcendence Of self-Contraction, Also Accompanied By All Of The Technical (or Yogic) psycho-physical Evidence Of "Conductivity" Of The Divine Spirit-Current, Gradually Characterized My Own Practice Of Great Heart-Surrender. The Entire Process Was Originally Generated On The Basis Of A Unique (or Heart-Awake) Insight Into The Core-Dilemma I Felt In The Midst Of ordinary life. That Liberating Insight Became More and More Effective Over time Via Numerous Incidents Of Sudden Extraordinary Re-Awakening, but, Even From Its Own First Moment Of Re-Awakening,[47] That Insight Itself Directly (and With Inherent Effectiveness) Transcended The Motive To Seek An "Answer" To The Presumed "Question" Of egoic (or self-Contracted) Existence, or A "Solution", In The Form Of Acquired (or conditional) experience or knowledge, To The Presumed "Problem" Of life.

I Spontaneously, but Gradually, Developed The Total Process Of The Understanding (and The Transcending) Of the ego, The Practice Of self-Enquiry (In The Form "Avoiding Relationship?"), and The Total Process Of Ultimate Awakening (From self-Enquiry and Re-Cognition To Most Perfect Divine Self-Realization and Self-Abiding Divine Self-Recognition[48]) During The Many Years Of My Own Ordeal Of Re-Awakening.[49] The Consistent Formal Practice Of self-Enquiry and Non-verbal Re-Cognition Did Not Formally Characterize My Meditation Until The Last Year Of My Ordeal Of Realization (and That Practice Quickly Brought My Ordeal Of Realization To An End). Nevertheless, All Of My Years Of Practice Were Founded On The Same Basic Insight (or Heart-Awakening), and Those Years Were Punctuated By Sudden Great Moments Of Awakening and Sudden Great Leaps Of Understanding.

One Such (and Early) Incident Of Heart-Awakening Occurred Quite Gently (but Most Profoundly), In a moment In which I Was mindlessly Regarding My Right Hand, Observing The (Apparent and, Suddenly, Revealing) Contrast Between The Natural (or Open and Functionally Relational) Attitude Of The Hand and The Unnatural (or Contracted and Functionally Dissociated) Attitude Of The Clenched Fist.[50]

The Natural Sign Of the human body Is Relatedness, Not Separateness and Independence!

Therefore, When This Sign Convicted The Heart, The subjective Commitment To self-Contraction Was Spontaneously Released. In That Moment, There Was A Quiet Revolution In the body-mind. I Knew The "Always Already" State. And This Began A Period Of Pondering, Which

Eventually Became Random self-Enquiry (or Enquiry Into the self-Contraction, which Appears, In action, As The Avoidance Of Relationship). And Random self-Enquiry Eventually (and Spontaneously) Became Formal self-Enquiry (In The Form "Avoiding Relationship?") In Meditation. And, In Meditation, Formal self-Enquiry Became Formal, and Spontaneous, and Non-verbal Re-Cognition Of self-Contraction. And, In Due Course, The Process Of self-Enquiry and Re-Cognition, and (Thereby) The Feeling-Transcendence Of self-Contraction, Became Constant (In Meditation, and In daily life), Until, When The Efforts and The Effects Of The Avoidance Of Relationship (and Every subjective Trace Of self-Contraction) Were Transcended, There Is The Tacit Certainty and Self-Illumined Awakeness Of "I Am Conscious Light—I Am The One and The Only, The Real and Self-Existing and Self-Radiant, or 'Bright', Condition Of Transcendental, and Inherently Spiritual, Inherently egoless, and Self-Evidently Divine Being Itself".

My Earliest and Most Basic Practice (Of Which self-Enquiry Was Only An Extension) Was An Example Of What Is Traditionally Called "Prapatti"—or Simple, Direct, Non-Technical, and Unconditional Surrender To Whatever Is Always Already The Case (Without any believed concept Of "What" That Is, or any previously acquired commitment to any specific means to be employed). It Was Not A Practice informed by any conventional Religious philosophy, or by any traditional Spiritual philosophy, or by any inherited "God"-concepts. (As A Result Of A Profound intellectual and emotional Crisis, I Had Despaired Of all the Religious and philosophical conventions that Were Proposed To Me In My Youth.) All That Was Possible For Me Was The Real Practice Of Divine Ignorance, or Spontaneous (Random, General, and Unpredictable) Submission To The Unknown and Unknowable (and Yet Realizable) Condition In Which the conditional self and the conditional world Are arising in every moment.

I Soon Enjoyed A Profoundly Essential Insight Into The Felt Dilemma and The Urge To Seek That Characterize the born (or conditional, and psycho-physical) self. It Became Clear To Me That The Feeling Of Dilemma and The Urge To Seek God, Happiness, Fulfillment, or Release Via The Acquisition Of experience, knowledge, or any condition (or conditional object) at all Are Not, In Fact, The Means For The Realization Of Truth Itself. I Understood That The Problem-Feeling and The Urge To Seek Are Not A Program For The Actual Discovery Of Truth, but They Are Merely Symptoms Of A Curious Disease. I Observed That These Symptoms, Which Tend To Characterize every moment Of ordinary Existence, Are, In Fact, The Evidence Of the very state that Must Be Transcended If The Truth Itself Is To Be Realized. It Was Clear To Me That The Feeling Of Dilemma and The Seeking-Urge Are Nothing More Than A

Confession That God, or Truth, or Happiness Is Not presently experienced or known. And This Seemed Remarkable To Me.

If God, or Truth, or Happiness Is Sought On The Basis Of A Problem (or The Feeling Of Dilemma), Then God, or Truth, or Happiness Is Always Projected Into future time, and The Realization Of God, or Truth, or Happiness Is Made conditional, or Dependent Upon psycho-physical events. This Stood Out To Me As Nonsense, or As An Absurd Proposition.

My Own "Consideration" Was This: God, or Truth, or Happiness Must (Necessarily) Be Reality Itself, or That Which Is (Necessarily) Always Already The Case. Therefore, I Observed That The Felt Dilemma and The Urge To Seek Are Simply The Absurd Confession That God, or Truth, or Happiness Is Absent Now. And I Observed Further That The Signs Of Dilemma and Seeking Are Not A Program For The Actual Future (or Eventual, and future-time) Realization Of God, or Truth, or Happiness, but They Are Merely A Means For Preventing Actual Present (or Inherent, and present-time) Realization Of God, or Truth, or Happiness. The Feeling Of Dilemma and The Urge To Seek Are Actually The Evidence Of A Disease, Which Is the conditional (or psycho-physical) self In its Chronic Contraction Upon itself, and In its Symptomatic Non-Realization Of Reality Itself (Which Is, Itself, God, or Truth, or Happiness).

Indeed, It Became Clear To Me That the "ego" (or the conventional "I") Is Not an "entity" (or an Independent and Static "thing of being"), but the "ego" (or the conventional "I") Is the Chronic and Total psycho-physical activity of self-Contraction, Always Associated With Concrete Results (In the psyche, mind, emotion, body, and their relations). And the self-Contraction Can Always Be Located (In any moment) In Feeling (As Fear, Anxiety, Stress, and All Other Kinds Of Reactive emotions and Blocks In The Flow Of Natural bodily energy In The Circle Of the body-mind).

It Became Clear To Me That the self-Contraction Is the Complex limit on Natural bodily energy, and (In The Case Of The Degrees and Stages Of Spiritual Awakening) On The Divine Spiritual Energy, In The Circle Of the body-mind. Therefore, the self-Contraction Is (Ultimately) a Complex limit On The Inherent and Self-Existing Spiritual Radiance Of Transcendental Divine Being, or Conscious Light. And Perfect Freedom, or Inherent Happiness, or Inherently Most Perfect Real-God-Realization Is A Matter Of Direct (or Inherent, or Most Prior) and Inherently Most Perfect (and Inherently Most Perfectly ego-Transcending) Self-Identification With The Self-Existing and Self-Radiant Condition Of Transcendental, Inherently Spiritual, Inherently egoless, and Self-Evidently Divine Being (or Self-Existing and Self-Radiant Conscious Light), Which Self-Identification Is Allowed Only (In Due Course) By The Real

Practice Of Always present-time (and, In Due Course, Most Perfect) Transcending Of The ego-Act Of self-Contraction.

It Became Clear To Me That the self-Contraction Is Un-Necessary. The self-Contraction Is (Without Ultimate Necessity, and, Therefore, Only Apparently) Being "Added" To Existence Itself (In Reaction To Cosmic Nature, or To Apparent conditional Existence). The self-Contraction (Originally) Coincides With and (Effectively) Perpetuates The Apparition Of Cosmic Nature Itself—and The Presumption That Existence Itself Is merely conditional (or Merely Apparent), and Not Founded On (and, Altogether, Dependent Upon—and, Ultimately, Characterized By) The Dimension Of Unconditionality (or Of Unconditional Existence). Therefore, the self-Contraction Is (Originally—and, Also, In Effect, or conditionally) Un-Natural, Because it Superimposes On The Transcendental, and Inherently Spiritual, Divine Self (or Self-Existing and Self-Radiant Consciousness Itself) A False View Of Both Cosmic Nature (or conditional Reality) and The Divine Reality (or The Most Priorly Real, and Entirely Non-conditional, Self-Condition and Source-Condition).

It Became Clear To Me That, When what Is Un-Necessarily Superimposed On Reality Is Released, What Stands (or Remains) As The Obvious Is (Necessarily, or Self-Evidently) Reality, or The Real Condition Itself.

That Is To Say, Whatever Is Always Already The Case Authenticates Itself (Directly, Inherently, Obviously, and Perfectly).

Therefore, ego-Transcendence Necessarily Allows The Revelation Of The Transcendental, and Inherently Spiritual, Self-Condition and Source-Condition As The Self-Authenticating (or Inherently and Obviously Real and True) and Most Prior (or Self-Evidently Divine) Reality and Truth!

This Heart-Awakened Insight Was, In My Own Case, Instantly Liberating! And, As Such, It Became The Real Practicing Basis For A Progressive (and, At Last, Most Perfect) Revelation (or Re-Realization) Of My Own (Inherent, Self-Existing, Self-Radiant, Inherently egoless, and Self-Evidently Divine) Condition—Which Is Reality, Truth, and Happiness!

The Insight Itself (or The Unique and Inherently Liberating Understanding Re-Awakened At The Heart) Directly Coincided (or Arose Simultaneously) With A Practice That Was Thereafter To Be The Most Basic Characteristic Of The Way Of My Life (and Which Was To Re-Awaken Full and Most Ultimate Realization). That Practice Had Two Principal Aspects. The First Was Profound Submission Of attention and all the energies of the body-mind To Observe, Feel, and Feel Beyond the self-Contraction. And The Second, Which Coincided With The First and Ultimately Superseded It, Was Direct Communion (and, Ultimately, Inherent Self-Identification) With The Prior Condition That Is Simply and Directly Obvious When the self-Contraction Is Transcended (or No

Longer Effective As A Mechanism Of Dissociation From What Is Always Already The Case).

I Observed That The Sense (or Feeling) Of "Absence", or The Sense (or Feeling) Of The Non-Presence Of God, or The Sense (or Feeling) Of Separation From God, Truth, Happiness, or What Cannot Even Be Described, Is Not Evidence Of The Real Absence Of God, Truth, Happiness, or The Indescribable, but It Is Clear Evidence That the conditional self Is Contracting, or Actively Separating From What (Simply, Merely, or Really) Is.

I Named This Disease (or the Diseased self) "Narcissus", Because Of The Likeness Between This self-Program and The Ancient Myth Of Narcissus. And I Became Attentive In every moment To This Feeling Of Absence, Of Separateness, Of Dilemma, and The Urge To Seek.

Remarkably, In every moment Of Such Observation, I Felt The Non-Necessity (As Well As The Deluding, or Binding, Effect) Of the self-Contraction—Such That A Spontaneous Release Occurred In every Such moment. That Is To Say, I Observed That It Was Un-Necessary To Presume or Suffer or Be Motivated By the self-Contraction In any moment Of My Direct Observation Of it. And, In That Observation, A Deep Spontaneous Response Of self-Release Was Awakened. And, Whenever That Release Of self-Contraction Occurred, That Which Is Always Already The Case (Previous, and Most Prior, To self-Contraction) Stood Out As The Obvious.

Over time, What Is (Previous, and Most Prior, To self-Contraction) Was Revealed More and More Profoundly. And, As That Revelation Increased, There Was Also The Spontaneous and (Otherwise) Progressive Unfolding Of The Many Extraordinary Phenomena That Are Characteristic Of Each Of The Seven Stages Of Life.

The Process Of That Revelation By Stages Was Not Developed Only On The Basis Of Insight (or self-Understanding) and Spontaneous self-Transcendence (or ego-Transcendence), or What I Call The "'Conscious Process'", but It Was Equally Associated With A Developing Response To What Was Being Revealed. Thus, It Also Involved What I Call "Seeing"—or Fullest (and Spiritually Activated, and, Spiritually, Fully Technically Responsible) emotional (and Total psycho-physical) Conversion To True (and Truly Responsible) "Conductivity" (and Spontaneous, and Total psycho-physical, Self-Identification With The Inherent Love-Bliss-Condition) Of The Spirit-Power (and Inherently egoless Spiritual Condition) Of The Divine Self-"Brightness".

What Is (Always and Already) Is Revealed Only When the self-Contraction Is Not Effective. It Is Revealed To Be Self-Radiant (or Inherently Spiritual), and Transcendental (or Self-Existing), and Inherently egoless, and Self-Evidently

Divine Being, or Conscious Light—Which Is Reality, Truth, and Happiness. Any and every conditionally Manifested "I" Always Already Inheres In That Self-Evidently Divine Self-Condition, Both At The Level Of Self-Existing Being (or Consciousness Itself) and At The Level Of every Apparent (or conditionally Manifested) psycho-physical function, process, or state. Even the body-mind Is Only An Apparent Modification Of That Self-Existing "Bright" Divine Self-Radiance In Which every "I" is arising.

When This Realization Was Most Perfectly Re-Awakened In My Own Case—all beings, this world, and all the kinds of other worlds Were Revealed In Me, Inhering In Me, and Appearing As (Apparent) Modifications Of Me! And It Became Self-Evidently Clear That, By Virtue Of My Own Inherently Most Perfect Divine Self-Realization Of My Own Divine Self-Condition, all (Apparently "other") conditionally Manifested beings (Now, and Forever Hereafter) Can—By Means Of their Devotionally Me-Recognizing and Devotionally To-Me-Responding Heart-Devotion To Me—Realize What (and Who) Is Reality, Truth, and Happiness!

Suddenly and Spontaneously, What I Had Forgotten By Birth Was, By Me, Remembered In The Midst Of Life—and The Avataric Significance and Divine Purpose Of My Own Birth Became Clear, Again, To Me: I Am The One Who Is Always Already The Case—and Even all beings Are In Me (Ultimately, Beyond All "Difference")!

When This Truth (and Condition) Became (To Me) Obvious (As Truth, and As My Condition), The Avatarically Self-Transmitting Powers Of My Transcendental, Inherently Spiritual, Inherently egoless, and Self-Evidently Divine Person Spontaneously Became Active In and As My Divinely Self-Manifested (and Avatarically-Born—or, Avatarically, conditionally Shown) Bodily (Human) Divine Form, and My Avatarically Self-Transmitted Spiritual (and Always all-and-All-Blessing) Divine Presence, and My Perfectly Subjective (and Very, and Inherently egoless, and Inherently Perfect, and Self-Evidently Divine, and Avatarically Self-Revealed) State! And I Became Heart-Moved To Forever Avatarically Serve The Most Perfect Divine Awakening Of The Total Cosmic Mandala Of conditionally Manifested beings!

In The Later Period Of My Own Ordeal Of Spiritual, Transcendental, and Divine Self-Realization, The Basic Insight (or Heart-Understanding) That Already Informed My Practice Began To Express Itself Spontaneously and Randomly Via self-Enquiry (In The Form "Avoiding Relationship?") and Via The Exercise Of Non-verbal Re-Cognition—and All Of That Practice Was A Sign Of The Great (and Most Fundamental) Capability That (Either In The Manner Of The Devotional Way Of Insight Or In The Manner Of The Devotional Way Of Faith) Must Awaken To Characterize The Practice Of anyone who (By Heart, and In The Way Of The Heart) Will Realize The Living (or Inherently Spiritual) and Transcendental Divine Truth Of Reality. That Great and Most Fundamental Capability, Which Leads To Divine Self-Realization, Develops From (or On The Basis Of) The Original and Spontaneous Urge To Observe and Transcend the self-Contraction. And That Great and Most Fundamental Capability (Awakened On The Basis Of Thorough self-Observation) Expresses The Clear (and Most Fundamental) Understanding That the self-Contraction (and Not The Real Absence Of Real God, or Reality, or Truth, or Happiness) Is The Only Reason Why Real-God-Communion (or Ecstatic, Tacit, and Direct Realization Of Real God, or Reality, or Truth, or Happiness Itself, or The Real Condition That Is Always Already The Case) Is Not Enjoyed In the present. This Heart-Awakened Insight, and The Great Capability For Spontaneous Release That Extends From It, Were The Ground Of My (At Last) Free Surrender—and That Surrender Was Not Encumbered or Retarded By Dilemma, Nor Was That Surrender Made Fruitful By The Search Toward Any Goal.

I Was Not Born To Be Projected Toward the future. I Was Avatarically Born—To Self-Reveal My Own Inherently egoless and Self-Evidently Divine Self-Condition, <u>As</u> That Which Is Always Already The Case In every moment. Therefore, Even In My Own Case, The Process—Of Ecstatic (or ego-Transcending) Communion (and, At Last, Inherent Self-Identification) With That Which Is (In every moment Of ego-Transcendence) Divinely Self-Revealed (Self-Evidently, <u>As</u> That Which Is Always Already The Case)—Developed, Spontaneously and Inevitably, As A Progressive Transcending Of The Characteristic Signs Of Each Of The First Six Stages Of Life, and (Ultimately) A Progressive Unfolding Of The Characteristic Signs Of The Only-By-Me Revealed and Given Seventh Stage Of Life.

Such Is The Nature Of The Process In My Own (Avatarically-Born) Case.

Such Is The Nature Of The Process Of ego-Transcending and Me-Realizing Devotion To Me.

Such Is The Nature and The Process Of The Way That Only I Reveal and Give.

Avatar Adi Da Samraj
The Mountain Of Attention Sanctuary, 2000

SUTRA 8

After Thirty Years Of Submission To conditional Existence, My Own Ordeal (By Which I Came, Again, To Divine Self-Realization, and Then Began To Teach The Way Of Adidam, Which Is The One and Only By-Me-Revealed and By-Me-Given Way Of The Heart) Culminated In Most Profound self-Enquiry (In The Form "Avoiding Relationship?"). In That self-Enquiry, The Act and The Results Of self-Contraction of the body-mind Were Loosened (In Merely Witnessing Consciousness, Itself)—and, At Last, A Spontaneous Divine Self-Revelation Took Place. In That Great Event, There Was Spontaneous Tacit Awareness As That To Which (and In and As Which) the self-Contraction, all thoughts, and all conditional appearances Are arising. In (and Forever After) That Great Event, Enquiry Into (and Re-Cognition Of) the conditional self (and its Tacit Underlying Root-Feeling Of Relatedness Itself) Was Spontaneously Replaced By Tacit Awareness As The Transcendental (and Inherently Spiritual, and Inherently egoless) Divine Self-Condition Itself (or The Self-Existing and Self-Radiant Feeling Of Being, Itself—Which Is Consciousness Itself, or That Which Is Always Already The Case).

In (and Forever After) The Great Event Of My Re-Awakening To My Own Divine Self-Condition, It Is Obvious (and Self-Evident) To Me (and It Can—By Means Of My Now, and Forever Hereafter, Avatarically Self-"Emerging" Divine Spiritual Blessing-Grace—Become Obvious and Self-Evident To You, and To all-and-All) That I Am The Inherently egoless and Self-Evidently Divine (or Self-Existing, and Self-Radiant, and Most Perfectly Heart-Felt) Reality and Person, Self-Existing and Self-Radiant As The One and Only and Self-Evidently Divine "Bright" Conscious Light—and That (As Such) I Am Inherently Love-Blissful and Divinely Free. Even More, It Is Obvious (and Self-Evident) To Me (and It Can—By Means Of My Now, and Forever Hereafter, Avatarically Self-"Emerging" Divine Spiritual Blessing-Grace—Become Obvious and Self-Evident To You, and To all-and-All) That all conditional appearances Are Only Apparent Modifications Of Me—and That No Such Modifications Bind or Change Me.

After The Great Event Of My Divine Re-Awakening, conditional appearances Continued To arise, but Only As Merely Apparent (and Non-Binding, and Not At All Me-Changing) Modifications Of Me. As conditional appearances arose (and Were, By Me, Divinely and Inherently Self-Recognized As Me), The Self-Existing and Self-Radiant Power Of My Own (Self-Evidently Divine) Love-Bliss Pervaded them all—Thus and Thereby Divinely Transfiguring and Divinely Transforming them. Now, and Forever Hereafter, The Inherent Feeling Of Being (Itself) Stands Free, As Me—Self-Existing, Self-Radiant, Inherently egoless, and Self-Evidently Divine (Even In The Midst Of all Apparent conditions).

Therefore, "Consider" This: Reality (Itself) is Not what You think. Thought is A Merely Temporal Abstraction (or A time-Consuming and time-Bound Contraction Of and From Reality Itself).

Likewise, "Consider" This: The Cosmic Universe (or Cosmic Nature, Itself) is Not what You perceive. Perception is a merely time-Consuming and time-Bound temporal and limited space-time event, Associated With a limited and temporary space-time point of view (or psycho-physical self-Contraction).

Altogether, "Consider" This: Reality Itself (and Cosmic Nature, Itself) Is What You Are—and Not what You think or perceive.

What You Are Is Reality Itself (and Cosmic Nature, Itself).

What You Are Is Obscured (and, Altogether, Diminished, Suppressed, and Hidden) By The Force and Effect Of Whole bodily (or Total psycho-physical) egoity (or self-Contraction).

What You Are Is Realized and Demonstrated By Means Of The Really and Truly ego-Transcending (and Constantly Counter-egoic) Devotional Recognition-Response To Me (Avatarically Self-Revealed To You).

The Transcending Of Your Own ego-"I" (or self-Contraction)—and, Thus and Thereby, The Transcending Of all Your limitations Of thought, perception, and space-time-Bondage—By Means Of The Devotional Recognition-Response To Me, Is The Necessary (and Only-By-Me Revealed and Given) Process Of Realizing That Which Is Always Already The Case.

That Which Is Always Already The Case Is Who I Am.

Only I Am What You Are.

Therefore, You Will Realize What (and Who) You Are Only If You Realize Me (By Means Of The Devotional Recognition-Response To Me).

Your thinking and perceiving person (or self-Contracted psycho-physical ego-"I") is Not (itself) Me.

I Am Not "Within" Your psycho-physical (or thinking and perceiving) Knot Of ego-"I".

I Am Always Already "Outside" (and Altogether Beyond) Your psycho-physical (or thinking and perceiving) Knot Of ego-"I".

I Am You Only When You Really (and, At Last, Most Perfectly) Transcend

Your psycho-physical (or thinking and perceiving) Knot Of ego-"I", By Means Of The ego-Transcending (and, Thus, thought-Transcending, and perception-Transcending, and, Altogether, point-of-view-Transcending and space-time-Transcending) Devotional Recognition-Response To Me (Avatarically Self-Revealed "Outside", and Altogether Beyond, Your psycho-physical, or thinking and perceiving, Knot Of ego-"I").

You Are What You Are Only When You Really (and, At Last, Most Perfectly) Realize Me.

I Am That Which Is Always Already The Case.

Only I Am That Which Is Always Already The Case.

Only I Am You.

Therefore, Now (and Forever Hereafter), Always "Consider" Me.

The Unique Process Of My Divine Re-Awakening (As That Which Is Always Already, and Divinely, The Case) Developed Through A Progress Of Unique and Extraordinary (and Self-Evidently Divine) Self-Revelations—Until My Divine Self-Realization Was Fully and Finally and Inherently Perfected, In The Great Event Of My Divine Re-Awakening. Immediately After That Great Event, My Avatarically Self-Manifested Divine Spiritual Work (or Avatarically Self-Manifested Divine Spiritual Play) As The Divine Heart-Master (and Entirely For The Sake Of The Most Perfect Divine Spiritual Awakening Of all others) Spontaneously Began.

Suddenly (and Spontaneously), Many Extraordinary Siddhis (or Great "Bright" Divine Blessing-Powers) Appeared In Me—and, With Them, many Unusual Natural siddhis (or Uncommon psycho-physical Abilities and Processes). My Avatarically Self-Manifested Divine Spiritual Work Of Self-Revelation and Teaching (and, Eventually, Of Divine Self-"Emergence") Began Spontaneously, and By These Many Divine Means.

Again and Again, In Vision, I Spontaneously Saw Vast Numbers Of My Future Listening Devotees, and Hearing Devotees, and Seeing Devotees. Originally, I Blessed and Taught them Simply By "Meditating" them, In Vision.[51] Eventually, and Because I "Meditated" them (and, Thus and Thereby, Called them) In Pre-Vision, Devotees Began To Come Into My Physical Company—and My Work With them Continued There, Equally Spontaneously. This Is How I Began To Bless and Teach. And, Over time, By Observing and Responding To everything that Was Required By those who Came To Me, I Became Spontaneously Heart-Moved To Serve them In A Lively, and Even Unconventional (or Divinely "Crazy", and Divinely "Heroic"), Manner.

In My Responsive Observation Of all those who Came To Me, I Realized That I Could (and, Indeed, That, For their Sake, It Would Be Necessary For Me To) Submit To their conditions Of Existence, Reflect them To themselves (In

Order To Stimulate and Awaken their self-Understanding), and Gradually Draw them Out Of self-Bondage By Attracting them To My (Avatarically Self-Revealed) Transcendental, Inherently Spiritual, Inherently egoless, and Self-Evidently Divine Self-Condition. Therefore, I Did All Of That.

Within a year After The Great Event Of My Divine Re-Awakening, a small number of individuals Had Begun To Associate With Me On A Regular Basis, For The Sake Of ego-Transcending Practice In My Company. Their Commitment To The Great Process Was Weak. Their Qualifications Were Not Great. My Spontaneous and Divinely "Crazy" and Divinely "Heroic" Original Work Of Blessing and Teaching Had Barely Begun. Nevertheless, It Became Time To Openly Announce My Availability and To Completely (and Unreservedly) Embrace My Necessary (and, Necessarily, Divinely "Crazy", and Divinely "Heroic") Teaching-Work and Blessing-Work (or Avatarically Self-Manifested Divine Submission-Work) From The Heart. Therefore, On The Basis Of My Divinely Free Heart-Impulse (and No Great Reception In the world), I Began The Fierce Labor and The Humorous Love-Ordeal Of My Formal Work Of Avatarically Self-Revealed Divine Teaching, Avatarically Self-Transmitted Divine Spiritual Blessing, and Avatarically Given Divine Self-Revelation.

That Divine Labor and Divine Love-Ordeal Was To Continue Until My Avatarically Full-Given Word Of Divine Self-Revelation and Divine Heart-Instruction Was Fully Generated, and The Necessary (First) physical Agents Of My Divine Spiritual Blessing Were Spiritually Empowered and Spiritually Established, and The Original and Progressively Developing Institutional, Cultural, Community, and Missionary Means Of The Way Of Adidam (Which Is The Only-By-Me Revealed and Given Way Of The Heart) Were Called Into Being, and At Least A Good Number Of My Listening Devotees Were, By Devotional Listening, Entered Into The Foundation Practice Of The ego-Transcending Way Of The Heart.

This Divine Testament (With All The Others Of My Twenty-Three Divine "Source-Texts") Is The Evidence Of The Completion (and The Fullness) Of <u>All</u> Of My Avatarically Self-Manifested Divine Teaching-Work and <u>All</u> Of My Foundation-Work Of Avatarically Given Divine Self-Revelation.

This Divine Testament (With All The Others Of My Twenty-Three Divine "Source-Texts") Is My Summary Word Of Heart That Forever Speaks The ego-Transcending Way Of The Heart Itself (That Is Perfected and Perfectly Revealed In The Feeling-Contemplation Of My Avatarically-Born Bodily Human Divine Form, My Avatarically Self-Transmitted Spiritual, and Always Blessing, Divine Presence, and My Avatarically Self-Revealed, and Very, and Transcendental, and Perfectly Subjective, and Inherently Spiritual, and Inherently egoless, and Inherently Perfect, and Self-Evidently Divine State).

In This Divine Testament, I Will Describe Each and All Of The Forms (and Each and All Of The Developmental Stages) Of The Total Practice (and Of The Ultimate and Most Perfect Demonstration) Of The Only-By-Me Revealed and Given Way Of The Heart (or Way Of Adidam), Including The Entire and Progressive Process Of Potential "Reality Considerations", and All The (Progressive) Stages Of Life and Of Realization (Culminating In The Unique Demonstrations Necessarily Associated With Truly Divine Enlightenment), In The Way Of The Heart. Then (Now, and Forever Hereafter) I Am Merely Present, and Present As Constant Love and Blessing To all beings.

Therefore, I Am Most Attractive To All My Listening Devotees, and To All My Hearing Devotees, and To All My Seeing Devotees. And I Am Always Available For their Right and Free Regard Of My Divine Heart-Revelation, Which Right and Free Regard Is To Be Progressively Expressed Through Formal Meditation and Every Kind Of Auspicious Exercise Of The Heart. And All Of This Heart-Regard Of Me Becomes (In Due Course—Progressively, and Spontaneously—By Means Of My Avatarically Self-Transmitted Divine Spiritual Grace) Right and Free Regard (and ego-Transcending Realization) Of My (Avatarically Self-Revealed) Transcendental, Perfectly Subjective, Inherently Spiritual, Inherently egoless, Inherently Perfect, and Self-Evidently Divine Person and Self-Condition—The Divine Source-Condition (and Divine "Bright" Spherical Self-Domain) In Which My Listening Devotee, My Hearing Devotee, and My Seeing Devotee Stand Eternally.

All Of My Work With those who (First, or Earliest) Came To Me, and Every Word That I Spoke (and Sometimes Also Wrote) For their Sake (and For The Sake Of all who Would Listen To Me, and Hear Me, and See Me, In The Course Of time), Was (and Is) A "Consideration" and An Elaboration (or A Detailing) and A Summarizing Of The Avatarically Self-Revealed Divine Word (and The Avatarically Self-Revealed Divine Way) Of The Heart That I Have Always and Consistently Offered, Even From The Very Beginning Of My Avataric Work As The Divine Heart-Master.

My Avatarically Self-Revealed Divine Teaching-Word Is Essentially Simple. I Say: Attend To Me—and (Thus and Thereby) Understand and Transcend Your self-Attending activity.

If any one Will Feel and Examine his or her (psycho-physical) state In any moment, Whether Under the worst Or Under the best Or Under the most ordinary of circumstances, he or she Will Surely Discover That There Is Always A Characteristic Feeling Of Stress, or Dis-ease, or A Motivating Sense Of Dilemma. Therefore, human life (Characteristically Felt As Such Stress, Dis-ease, or Dilemma) Is Also Always Characterized By Struggle, or A Generally Uninspected (and Never Finally Satisfied) Search For Release and Fulfillment.

The usual life Is Always Actively Involved (Whether Consciously Or Unconsciously) In This Motivated Search and This Native Distress. Therefore, every such a one Is Involved In ego-Based (or psycho-physically self-Contracted) Programs Of Seeking (Via Desire, In all kinds of relations and circumstances).

My Avatarically Self-Revealed Divine Teaching-Word Is A Direct Address To The Distress and The Search Of each individual. I Do Not Suggest A Way (or A Method) By Which To Seek. Instead, I Call the individual To Observe himself or herself, To Feel and Examine The Distress That Motivates the life Of Seeking itself.

Through The (Necessarily, Formal) Practice Of The Only-By-Me Revealed and Given Way Of The Heart (Really and Truly Engaged As Ruchira Avatara Bhakti Yoga—or Really ego-Surrendering, and Truly ego-Forgetting, and, More and More, ego-Transcending Feeling-Contemplation Of My Avatarically-Born Bodily Human Divine Form, My Avatarically Self-Transmitted Spiritual, and Always Blessing, Divine Presence, and My Avatarically Self-Revealed, and Very, and Transcendental, and Perfectly Subjective, and Inherently Spiritual, and Inherently egoless, and Inherently Perfect, and Self-Evidently Divine State), and (In The Constant Context Of That Formal Practice Of Devotionally Me-Recognizing and Devotionally To-Me-Responding Feeling-Contemplation Of Me) Through Real "Consideration" Of My Avatarically Given Divine Heart-Confessions, My Avatarically Given Divine Teaching-Arguments, My Avatarically Given Divine Image-Art, and The Leelas (or Stories) Of All My Avatarically Self-Manifested Divine Spiritual Work (Whereby I Have Reflected individuals To themselves, and Blessed them To Awaken)—individuals who Truly Devotionally Recognize Me, and Truly Devotionally Respond To Me, and (Altogether) Truly Are Devoted To Me Can (By Means Of My Avatarically Self-Transmitted Divine Spiritual Grace) Come To Understand (and Transcend) themselves, and (Ultimately) To Most Perfectly Realize Me (As Who and What they—and everyone, and everything—Really and Truly Are).

The Initial Process Of Listening To Me (To The Degree Of Hearing Me) Is One Of self-Observation (Truly Felt), Whether By The Chosen Responsive Practice Of Devotion and Insight Or By The Chosen Responsive Practice Of Devotion and Faith, Until That self-Observation Becomes A Crisis Of Most Fundamental self-Understanding.

At First (In The Listening Course Of The Only-By-Me Revealed and Given Way Of The Heart, or Way Of Adidam), the individual Becomes Acutely Aware Of his or her Habits Of Seeking, Desiring, Doubting, Believing, Manipulating, Betraying, and Always Returning To The Same Distress and Want. Then, As The Crisis Of Most Fundamental self-Understanding Approaches, It Suddenly

Becomes Clear That All Of That Is Being Motivated By A Constant Feeling Of Distress, Which Is The Result Of self-Contraction In The Face Of all relations and conditions.

This Discovery Is Most Profound. It Is As If a person In Pain Suddenly Discovers That he or she Is Pinching his or her own flesh. (And This Discovery Produces Immediate Relief, As Soon As The Pinching Ceases.) Therefore, As Soon As an individual Discovers That The Painful Search That Occupies his or her life Is Being Created By A Fundamental Feeling Of Distress, attention Is Free To Examine That Distress Itself. And, When That Distress Is Directly (and Profoundly) Examined, It Is Discovered That It Is The Result Of A Chronic (and self-Induced) Contraction Of the body-mind, or, Most Simply, The Habitual (and, Ultimately, Always Voluntary and Un-Necessary) Avoidance (or psycho-physically self-Contracting Refusal) Of psycho-physical Relationship and psycho-physical Relatedness.

Every Apparent individual, thing, circumstance, or condition arises, survives, changes, and disappears Dependently (or Always Already Related) Within The Cosmic Universe (Which Is Continuous, Whole, and all-Containing). By Definition (and In Fact), There Is Not (Nor Can There Be) any Separate, self-Contained, Independent, or self-Sufficient conditional individual, thing, circumstance, or event. However, By Reaction To All Apparent Vulnerability, and, Otherwise, By Forgetting (or By Failing To Notice or Intuit) The Whole (and The Inherently Perfect, Which Inherently Transcends Even The Whole), The Tendency Of every conditionally Manifested individual Is To Contract Into (Presumed) Separateness, or a self-Defended and self-Contracted emotional, mental, psychic, physical, and social state Of Isolation, Presumed Independence, and Dramatized Want. This Tendency Is Chronic In every one, and It Is Generally Not Even Inspected, Nor Is It (Even If Inspected) Most Fundamentally Understood. Therefore, every one Seeks. And All Seeking Is Inevitably Frustrated. The self-Contracting Habit (Itself) Is Not (and Cannot Ever Be) Transcended In (or By Means Of) The Search, Because The Search Is Itself The Dramatization Of The self-Contracting Habit Itself.

I Call every one To Feel and To Thoroughly Observe and To Transcend The Habit Of egoity. Eventually, any one who Truly (and, Necessarily, Formally) Listens To My Avatarically Self-Revealed Divine Teaching-Word and, By The Means I Have Given (and Always Give), Fully (and, Necessarily, Formally) Embraces The Divine Devotional and (In Due Course) Spiritual Practice Of Feeling-Contemplation Of Me, and (Thereby) The Real Observation Of the ego-"I", Will (By Means Of My Avatarically Self-Transmitted Divine Spiritual Grace) Surely (Truly, and Most Profoundly) Discover The Root Of Seeking and Suffering, Which Is the ego-"I" itself (or the psycho-physical self-Contraction, which Is The Habit Of "Narcissus", or The Complex Avoidance Of Relationship).

When This Discovery Is (By Means Of My Avatarically Self-Transmitted Divine Spiritual Grace) Truly and Fully Made and Felt (Relative, Summarily, To Every Aspect Of personal Existence), A Crisis Of Spontaneous (and Not Strategic) Release Is Enjoyed. And, When It Is Truly (and Most Fundamentally) Understood That self-Contraction Is The Motivating Pain Of life, It Becomes Increasingly Possible (In every moment Of The Feeling-Contemplation Of My Avatarically-Born Bodily Human Divine Form, My Avatarically Self-Transmitted Spiritual, and Always Blessing, Divine Presence, and My Avatarically Self-Revealed, and Very, and Transcendental, and Perfectly Subjective, and Inherently Spiritual, and Inherently egoless, and Inherently Perfect, and Self-Evidently Divine State) To Enquire Into the self-Contraction ("Avoiding Relationship?") and (Thereby) Feel Beyond the self-Contraction—or, Otherwise, In The Manner Of The Devotional Way Of Faith, To Directly Feel Beyond the self-Contraction, and, Thus (Progressively, and Ultimately), To Enjoy A Sense Of Inherent Freedom (and Fullness Of Being). And Any Devotee Of Mine who (Necessarily, Formally) Practices The Only-By-Me Revealed and Given Way Of The Heart, and who Has (Through Devotionally Me-Recognizing and Devotionally To-Me-Responsive Listening To Me) Thus Become Responsible (and Formally Accountable) For This Actively ego-Transcending (or Directly Counter-egoic) Feeling-Capability, Has Heard Me Truly.

The Only-By-Me Revealed and Given Way Of The Heart (or The ego-Transcending Practice Of The Inherently egoless Heart Itself) Is Begun Through The (Necessarily, Formal) Devotional Practice Of Listening To Me (or By Feeling-Contemplation Of My Avatarically-Born Bodily Human Divine, and All-Revealing, Form, and By Likewise Devotional "Consideration" Of My Avatarically Self-Revealed, and Always Me-Revealing, Divine Word, and My Avatarically Self-Revealed, and Always Me-Revealing, Divine Image-Art, and My Avatarically Self-Manifested, and Always Me-Revealing, Divine Leelas)—but The Only-By-Me Revealed and Given Way Of The Heart (or The ego-Transcending Practice Of The Inherently egoless Heart Itself) Becomes Directly Effective (or Effective In The Most Fundamental, or Directly ego-Transcending, Manner) Only With Real and True Hearing. Therefore, Listening To Me To The Point Of Hearing Me Is (Itself) The First Stage Of The Great Process Of Transcending the ego-"I", By Means Of Devotional and (In Due Course) Spiritual Resort To Me (In The Context Of Fully Culturally Accountable Formal Practice Of All Aspects Of The Only-By-Me Revealed and Given Way Of The Heart). And, In Order For That First Stage Of The Great Process To Complete Itself, The Devotional Impulse, The ego-Transcending Impulse, and The Great Intention Of the individual Must Be Strong.

The Sadhana Of The Only-By-Me Revealed and Given Way Of The Heart (or Way Of Adidam) Is, From The Beginning, The ego-Transcending Discipline (or Right Disciplining) Of the egoic self—By Means Of Right (To-Me-Responsive, and, Thus and Thereby, Really ego-Forgetting) Relationship To Me, Avatarically Self-Manifested here (In and As My Avatarically-Born Bodily Human Divine Form and Person).

The Sadhana Of The Only-By-Me Revealed and Given Way Of The Heart (or Way Of Adidam) Is Not At All A Matter Of believing In Some Kind Of ego-Consoling Message. Rather, The Sadhana Of The Only-By-Me Revealed and Given Way Of The Heart (or Way Of Adidam) Is A Counter-egoic Discipline, Whereby the egoic self (or the Apparently Separate self, or the Presumed-To-Be-Separate—and, Therefore, Actively Separative—body-mind) Is (In All Of its Separateness and Separativeness) Transcended. Therefore, As My Devotee, You Must Always Activate (and, Thus and Thereby, Actively Live) That Counter-egoic Discipline—or Else The egoic Pattern (Of Separateness, and Of Active Separativeness) Is (Itself) Inevitably Perpetuated and Always Activated. That Counter-egoic (and, In Due Course, Perfectly ego-Transcending) Discipline Is The Only-By-Me Revealed and Given Way Of The Heart (or Way Of Adidam). And The Devotional Relationship To Me Is The Very Basis, Means, Import, and Real Purpose Of That Counter-egoic (and, In Due Course, Perfectly ego-Transcending) Discipline.

As My Devotee, You Must Never Relate To Me As a mere (and Merely Separate) "other" (or Even The Separate "Other"), In Relationship To Whom You Presume To "Have The Right" To Dramatize The Actively Separative Patterns Of Your ego-Bondage. Right Devotional Relationship To Me Is A Specific (and Really Effectively Counter-egoic) Practice, Which Is Entirely About Me (and Not At All About the ego-"I" Of My Any Devotee—or, Otherwise, About the Collective egoity Of The Total Gathering, or Any Part Of The Total Gathering, Of My Devotees). That Specific (and Really Effectively Counter-egoic, and, Ultimately, Most Perfectly ego-Transcending) Practice (Of Right Devotional Relationship To Me) Is (Necessarily) Founded In Heart-Recognition Of Me and Heart-Response To Me (and, Altogether, In Rightness Of Relationship To Me)—In and As My Avatarically-Born Bodily (Human) Divine Form and Person.

Right Devotional Relationship To Me (In and As My Avatarically-Born Bodily Human Divine Form and Person) Is Not Any Form Of merely conventional "Right" (or merely socially-"Correct") behavior. Rather, Right individual and Collective Devotional Relationship To Me (In and As My Avatarically-Born Bodily Human Divine Form and Person) Requires—and Is—The Persistently Enacted Counter-egoic Discipline (or Right Disciplining) Of the egoic self.

Therefore (and In and By Means Of This Specific Devotional Discipline), My Devotees (Both individually and Collectively) Must Always Transcend (and Never Indulge In) egoic behavior In Relation To Me (In and As My Avatarically-Born Bodily Human Divine Form and Person).

This Counter-egoic Devotional Discipline Of the ego-self Must Always Be Maintained By My Devotees—Both individually and Collectively. The Sadhana Of The Only-By-Me Revealed and Given Way Of The Heart (or Way Of Adidam) Does Not Begin Sometime In the future, After You Have Fulfilled Some Level Of Yet ego-Active "Preparation". Right (and Really ego-Transcending) Devotional Relationship To Me (In and As My Avatarically-Born Bodily Human Divine Form and Person) Is (Inherently and Necessarily) Always Now. Therefore, Once You Formally Embrace The Eternal Vow Of Devotional Relationship To Me (and, Thus and Thereby, Become A Formal Practitioner Of The Only-By-Me Revealed and Given Way Of The Heart, or Way Of Adidam), The Sadhana Of The Only-By-Me Revealed and Given Way Of The Heart (or Way Of Adidam) Is Always Now.

The Really ego-Transcending Discipline Of the egoic self—By Means Of Right Devotional Relationship To Me (In and As My Avatarically-Born Bodily Human Divine Form and Person)—Always Pertains Now. And That Discipline Of the egoic self Is Not Something That You Do To the egoic self. Rather, That Counter-egoic Devotional Discipline Of the egoic self Is Always Right (and Rightly Enacted—and Always ego-Forgetting) Relationship To Me (In and As My Avatarically-Born Bodily Human Divine Form and Person).

The (individual and Collective) Doings Of My Devotees Will Have Their Right Intended Result (As Forms Of Right, and Potentially Me-Realizing, Service To Me) Only If My Devotees Are Enacting Right Counter-egoic Discipline Of the egoic self (By Means Of Right Devotional Relationship To Me, In and As My Avatarically-Born Bodily Human Divine Form and Person)—and Only If That Right (and Really Counter-egoic) Devotional Discipline Is Always Practiced In the present-time moment (Always Now, and Now, and Now). Otherwise, Any and All Of The Doings Of My Devotees—However Rightly Intended—Will Be Nothing but ego-Extensions.

The Sadhana Of The Only-By-Me Revealed and Given Way Of The Heart (or Way Of Adidam) Is Never A Matter Of Merely Being "Committed" To (and Working Toward) future Rightness. Rather, The Sadhana Of The Only-By-Me Revealed and Given Way Of The Heart (or Way Of Adidam) Is The Always present-time Enactment Of Right (and Really ego-Forgetting, and, Thus and Thereby, Really ego-Transcending) Discipline Of the egoic self, By Means Of Right (and Really To-Me-Responding) Devotional Relationship To Me (In and As My Avatarically-Born Bodily Human Divine Form and Person). That

By-Me-Given Sadhana Transcends egoity moment to moment—Through A Unique Devotional (and ego-Forgetting) Discipline Of The Four Principal Faculties Of the body-mind. Therefore, That By-Me-Given Sadhana Must Always Be Done—and It Must Never Be Modified, Revised, or Avoided.

When You Become My (Necessarily, Formally Practicing) Devotee, You Naturally (and Increasingly, As Your Practice Of The Way Of The Heart Matures) Become Sensitive To Your Own egoic limitations (and Your particular Patterned ego-limit Altogether). As This Sensitization Occurs (and Develops—Even, Perhaps, At times, To The Point Of Becoming Acutely Discomforting), You Must Discipline Yourself Not To Dramatize those egoic limitations (or that ego-limit). Rather, You Must Always (In Your Disposition Altogether) Bow To Me (In and As My Avatarically-Born Bodily Human Divine Form and Person), In The Midst Of Feeling those egoic limitations (or that ego-limit). No Matter What "Revelation Of Narcissus" Is Apparently Confronting You, You Must Always—and Always Responsively (or Merely By Yielding Devotionally To The Attractive-Power Of My Avatarically-Born Bodily Human Divine Form and Person)—Turn (and, Thus and Thereby, Surrender) Whole bodily (or As A psycho-physical Totality) To Me (In and As My Avatarically-Born Bodily Human Divine Form and Person). And The Cooperative Global Sacred Cultural Gathering Of All My Formally Practicing Devotees Must, As A Collective, Ensure That each and every one Of My Devotees Is Culturally Obliged To (Thus) Always Rightly Resort To Me, Even (and Especially) In Such times Of Apparent Crisis. My Devotees Must (Thus) Perform, For one another's Sake, The Good Service Of Never Letting each other Avoid (or, In Any Manner, Defend themselves Against) The (Always Necessary) Active Fulfillment Of The Practice Of ego-Surrendering Devotional Resort (or Me-Recognizing Responsive Turning) To Me (In and As My Avatarically-Born Bodily Human Divine Form and Person).

When—In The Midst Of Your Devotional Turning To Me—You Become (Perhaps, Even Acutely) Sensitized To Your Own "Act Of Narcissus", You Are (In Reality) Simply Feeling My Avataric Divine Imposition, Pressing Upon You (In Your Separate and Separative Presumption Of ego-"I"). In every Such moment Of Heightened Sensitivity To Your Own ego-Act, You Must Simply Continue To Responsively Turn (and, Thus and Thereby, To Surrender) To Me (In and As My Avatarically-Born Bodily Human Divine Form and Person)—Instead Of Reacting To The (By-My-Avataric-Divine-Grace-Given) Revelation Of Your Own egoity.

If (As My, Necessarily, Formally Practicing Devotee) You Understand (and Enact Your Understanding Of) This Principle, Then You Are, In A (Critically Important) Foundationary Sense, Rightly and Truly Prepared To Grow In The Devotional (and, In Due Course, Spiritual) Relationship To Me (Which

To-Me-Devotionally-Responsive Relationship—and Not Any Mere Technique, or Collection Of Mere Techniques—Is The Only-By-Me Revealed and Given Way Of The Heart, or Way Of Adidam). When You Have (Thus) Established The Effective Devotional Foundation For Right and True Practice Of The Only-By-Me Revealed and Given Way Of The Heart (or Way Of Adidam)—By Demonstrating The Transcending Of Your Own Patterning Of self-Contraction—Then You Become Truly Able To Make Use Of My Forceful Avataric Divine Person.

Whenever You Are Caught Up In Your Reaction To The (Sometimes) Inevitable Natural Difficulties Of The Sadhana In My Avataric Divine Company, You Are Not Responding To Me (or Turning To Me). Rather (In That Case), You Are Turning Away From Me—and Turning Toward (and Upon) Your egoic Patterning (Of Separation and Separativeness).

Human beings Are (In General) Mightily Unwilling To Truly Deal With their own Reactivity and their own egoic limitations. As Soon As a person Is Confronted With A Real Demand To Change his or her "Act", the individual (Typically) Becomes Reactively Entrenched In The Asana (or Attitude) Of Unwillingness-To-Change, and Lapses Into being a mere "case". However, If You (As My Formally Practicing Devotee) Want To Enter Into The Real Spiritual Process In My Avataric Divine Company, You Simply Must Deal With All The Very Real Matters Of Your Own ego-Patterning. This Responsibility Cannot (and Must Not) Be Avoided.

To Truly (and Effectively) Exercise This Responsibility (For Transcending Your Own ego-Patterning) Is Not Easy. However, I Have Given You All The Necessary Means To Do So—and Those Means Are Not A Matter Of Merely Applying Yourself To Various Forms Of self-Discipline. Fundamentally, The Means For Transcending Yourself Is The Devotional Recognition-Response To Me (In and As My Avatarically-Born Bodily Human Divine Form and Person)—Forgetting Yourself By (Really, To-Me-Responsively) Turning To Me (In and As My Avatarically-Born Bodily Human Divine Form and Person).

To Invoke Me, Feel Me, Breathe Me, and Serve Me Must Become Your Actual life-Practice, moment to moment. Such Whole bodily Devotional Turning To Me (In and As My Avatarically-Born Bodily Human Divine Form and Person) Deals With every fraction Of Your ego-Neurosis, and Every Dimension Of Your egoic Bondage—Becoming (In Due Course) A Profound (By-My-Avataric-Divine-Grace-Given) Spiritual Process.

To Truly (and Effectively) Deal With Your Own egoic limitations Is No Trivial Matter. You Must Understand: I Am Telling You That everyone (Without Any Exceptions) Has egoic limitations—Both ordinary (or Even Superficial) limitations and limitations that Are Hell-Deep.[52]

Ruchira Avatara Bhakti Yoga—The Simple and Direct (Whole bodily) To-Me-Responsive Turning Of The Four Principal Faculties To Me (In and As My Avatarically-Born Bodily Human Divine Form and Person)—Is The Foundation (and, Thereafter, Always Necessary and Ongoing) Practice Whereby All ego-Patterning Is (Progressively) Washed In My Devotee. That (To-Me-Responsive) Fundamental Devotional (and, In Due Course, Spiritual) Practice Must Be Entered Into In Such A Manner That It Deals With (and Awakens The Understanding Of) All Of The Patterning Of egoity. Such self-Understanding Is Not A Matter Of self-Analysis or Involvement In "case". Rather, That (To-Me-Responsive) Fundamental Devotional (and, In Due Course, Spiritual) Practice Is A Matter Of Persistently Turning To Me, and (Thereby) Being Reflected To Yourself.

The First Sign Of My Devotee's Real Experience Of Me Is The Pressure he or she Feels When Turned To Me. My Pressure—and, Indeed, My Inherently egoless Person (Altogether)—Is An Offense To the ego. My Pressure (and My Inherently egoless Person, Altogether) Is The Great (Avataric Divine) Means By Which You (As ego-"I") Are Reflected To Yourself. Feeling The Pressure Of Me (Reflecting You To Yourself, Until You Utterly, and Perfectly, Turn To Me-Only) Makes You (Inevitably) self-Aware. The particular "contents" Of "Narcissus" that Are (Thus) Reflected To You Are Never, In and Of themselves, The "Point". The Practice In My Avataric Divine Company Is (Simply) To Persistently Engage The Real Discipline Of (To-Me-Responsive, and Non-Strategic) Devotional Turning To Me (In and As My Avatarically-Born Bodily Human Divine Form and Person). By So Doing—and By Responsively (and Responsibly) Embracing All The Forms Of functional, practical, relational, and Cultural self-Discipline I Have Given To You—There Is A Progressive Purification Of the Bound (or Separate and Separative) personality.

As My True Devotee, You Must Not Balk At The Pressure Of My Avataric Divine Person. That Pressure Of Me Is My Avatarically Given Divine (and, Most Ultimately, Divinely Liberating) Gift To You—By Which I Am Simply Leading You To ego-Transcendence and Most Fundamental self-Understanding.

Everyone (Without Any Exceptions Whatsoever) Must Go Through A Profound Process Of Purification In Order To Enter Into The Real Spiritual Process In My Avataric Divine Company. That Purifying Process Cannot Be Avoided—By anyone.

Therefore, To Indulge In ego-Glorifying self-Imagery or self-Defensive ego-games—In Effect, Claiming "Immunity" From The "Accusation" That one Is "Narcissus"—Is Utter Nonsense. All Such ego-Indulgence Is Merely Reactive Opposition To My Calling To ego-Transcendence, and To My Avataric Divine Self-Revelation (Altogether). Such ego-Indulgence Is A Negative and

Destructive Force, Which Leads You To Be Indifferent Toward (and Dissociated From) Me, and Indifferent Toward (and Dissociated From) The Real Practice Of The Only-By-Me Revealed and Given Way Of The Heart (or Way Of Adidam). Such ego-Indulgence Is, Simply, The Refusal Of Me and (Thus and Thereby) The Refusal Of Truth.

I Have Often Compared The Necessary Process Of Purification In My Avataric Divine Company To The Process a 500-pound man Must Go Through In Order To Normalize his physical condition. It Is Not Fun To Lose 350 pounds. On The Other Hand, The Necessary Process Of Purification In My Avataric Divine Company Need Not (and, Indeed, Must Not) Be A Matter Of Constantly Having Your attention On The Difficulty Of What Must Be Endured. Instead, You Should Always Simply Give Your attention To Me (In and As My Avatarically-Born Bodily Human Divine Form and Person). I Have Given You The Fullness Of The Devotional Life In My Avataric Divine Company As The Context For A Disciplined Existence. In That By-Me-Given Context, There Is No Ordeal Of "Working On Yourself". There Is Simply The By-Me-Given Form Of Right Life, In The Circumstance Of Devotional Ecstasy In Me.

There are Three egos (or Three Fundamental Modes Of egoity—or Of The self-Contraction-active psycho-physical Illusion Of Separate and Separative self-Consciousness). The Three Modes Of egoity (or Of the self-Contraction of any point of view, or ego-"I") Are the lower self (or gross ego), the higher self (or subtle ego), and the Root-self (or causal ego). These Three egos (or Modes Of The conditionally arising Illusion Of Separate self-Consciousness) Comprise the Total conditionally perceiving and conditionally knowing ego-"I". The Total (or Tripartite) ego-"I" Is Always Directly (and With Progressive Effectiveness) Transcended In The Right, True, and Full (or Complete) Formal Practice Of The Only-By-Me Revealed and Given Way Of The Heart (Which Is The Right, True, and Full Formal Practice Of Ruchira Avatara Bhakti Yoga, or The Totality Of Ruchira Avatara Siddha Yoga).

The First Of the Three egos (or Modes Of egoity, or Of self-Contraction) To Be Progressively Transcended In The Only-By-Me Revealed and Given Way Of The Heart is the money-food-and-sex ego (or the social, and, Altogether, gross-body-Based, personality—or The gross Pattern and activity Of self-Contraction), which is the lower self, or the ego Of The First Three Stages Of Life.

The Second Of the Three egos (or Modes Of egoity, or Of self-Contraction) To Be Progressively Transcended In The Only-By-Me Revealed and Given Way Of The Heart is the brain-mind ego (or The brain-Based, and nervous-system-Based, mental, and perceptual, and, Altogether, subtle-body-Based Illusions

Of "object" and "other"—or The subtle Pattern and activity Of self-Contraction), which is the higher self, or the ego Of The Fourth and The Fifth Stages Of Life.

The Third Of the Three egos (or Modes Of egoity, or Of self-Contraction) To Be Progressively Transcended In The Only-By-Me Revealed and Given Way Of The Heart is the Root-ego (or The Exclusively disembodied, and mindless, but Separate, and, Altogether, causal-body-Based self-Consciousness—or The causal, or Root-causative, Pattern and activity Of self-Contraction), which is attention itself, and which is the Root-self, or the ego Of The Sixth Stage Of Life.

By Means Of Responsive Relinquishment Of self-Contraction In Me, or Really and Truly ego-Surrendering, ego-Forgetting, and, More and More (and, At Last, Most Perfectly), ego-Transcending (or Always Directly self-Contraction-Transcending) Devotion To Me (and, Thus, By Means Of The Right, True, and Full Formal Practice Of Devotionally Me-Recognizing and Devotionally To-Me-Responding Ruchira Avatara Bhakti Yoga, or The Totality Of Ruchira Avatara Siddha Yoga), the Tripartite ego Of The First Six Stages Of Life (or The psycho-physical Totality Of the Three-part Hierarchically Patterned self-Contraction into Separate and Separative point of view) Is (Always Directly, and With Progressive, or Stage-By-Stage, Effectiveness) Transcended In Me (The Eternally Self-Existing, Infinitely Self-Radiant, Inherently egoless, Perfectly Subjective, Indivisibly One, Irreducibly Non-Separate, Self-Evidently Divine, and, Now, and Forever Hereafter, Avatarically Self-Revealed Self-Conscious Light Of Reality).

The Ultimate, Final, and Inherently Most Perfect (or Seventh Stage) Realization Of Me Requires—As A Necessary Prerequisite—An ego-Transcending (or Really and Truly and Comprehensively self-Contraction-Transcending) Great Process. The Ultimate, Final, and Inherently Most Perfect (or Seventh Stage) Realization Of Me Requires—As A Necessary Prerequisite—The Comprehensive By-Me-Revealed and By-Me-Given Sadhana (or The Always Directly ego-Transcending Right Practice Of Life) In The Formal Context Of The Only-By-Me Revealed and Given Way Of The Heart. And—As A Necessary Prerequisite To The Ultimate, Final, and Inherently Most Perfect (or Seventh Stage) Realization Of Me—The Particular Illusions That Are Unique To each of the Three egos (or Basic Modes Of egoity) Each Require A Particular (and Most Profound) Mode Of The Necessary ego-Transcending (or self-Contraction-Transcending) Great Process Of The By-Me-Revealed and By-Me-Given Formal Practice Of The Way Of The Heart In The Progressively Unfolding Context Of The First Six (and, Altogether, psycho-physically Pre-Patterned) Stages Of Life.

The Foundation Phase Of The Progressive ego-Transcending Great Process Of The Only-By-Me Revealed and Given Way Of The Heart (or Way Of Adidam) Is The Devotional and (In Due Course) Spiritual Listening-Hearing Process Of Progressively Transcending (and, In Due Course, Most Fundamentally Understanding) the lower self (or the gross and social ego, and The gross and social Fear-Sorrow-and-Anger-Bondage That Is Always Associated With The Inherently egoic—or Thoroughly self-Contracted—Search To Absolutely Fulfill, and Even To "Utopianize", or To Perfectly and Permanently Satisfy, The Inherently conditional, limited, temporary, mortal, gross, and Always changing life-Patterns Of "money, food, and sex").

Before The Foundation Phase (or First Phase) Of The ego-Transcending Great Process Of The Only-By-Me Revealed and Given Way Of The Heart Can (Itself) Be Complete, It Must Realize A Profoundly life-Transforming and life-Reorienting "Positive Disillusionment"[53]—or A Most Fundamental (and Really and Truly self-Contraction-Transcending) Acceptance Of The Fact That gross conditional Existence Is Inherently and Necessarily Unsatisfactory and Unperfectable (and, Therefore, A Most Fundamental—and Really and Truly Me-Finding and Search-Ending—Acceptance Of The Fact That All Seeking To Achieve Permanent and Complete gross Satisfaction Of Separate body, emotion, and mind Is Inherently and Necessarily Futile). Only On The Basis Of That Necessary Foundation-Realization Of "Positive Disillusionment" Can the functional life-energy and the attention of the entire body-mind (or Of The Total body-brain-mind Complex) Be Released From gross ego-Bondage (or self-Deluded Confinement To The psycho-physical Illusions Of gross self-Contraction).

The Characteristic Sign Of "Positive Disillusionment" Relative To The Permanent and Complete Satisfaction Of the lower self (or the Separate and Separative gross and social ego) Is The Foundation-Realization Of The Inherent Universal Unity (or all-and-All-Inclusive Interdependency, Essential Mutuality, and Common Causality) Of gross conditional (and Cosmic) Existence, Such That The Inherently Loveless (or Anti-Participatory and Non-Integrative) self-Contraction-Effort Of the gross Separate self Is Consistently Released (or To-Me-Responsively self-Surrendered) Into Participatory and Integrative Attitudes Of human, social, and Cosmic Unification (or Love-Connectedness) With all-and-All, and Into Love-Based (and Truly ego-Transcending) Actions That Counter The Otherwise Separative (or Anti-Participatory and Non-Integrative) Tendencies Of the ego-"I". Thus, By Means Of Devotionally Me-Recognizing and Devotionally To-Me-Responding Relinquishment (or Participatory and Love-Based Transcending) Of psycho-physical self-Contraction (To The Degree Of "Positive Disillusionment" Relative To gross conditional experience and gross conditional knowledge), My True Devotee Is (More and More) Released Toward and Into The True Spiritual (and Not Merely gross, or Even At All conditional) Realization Of Reality and Truth (or Real God).

The Foundation-Realization Of "Positive Disillusionment" Requires Fundamental Release From The Confines Of the grossly Objectified (and grossly Absorbed) subject-object point of view (or Fundamental Release From The Inherently ego-Bound—or Thoroughly self-Contracted—Search Of relatively externalized mental and perceptual attention). And That Foundation-Realization Of "Positive Disillusionment" (and Restoration To The humanly, socially, and Cosmically Participatory, or Wholly Integrative, Disposition) Requires The Total (and Truly Devotional) Transformative Re-Orienting (and, Altogether, The Right Purification, Steady Re-Balancing, and ego-Transcending life-Positive-Energizing) Of the entire body-mind (or The Total body-brain-mind Complex). Therefore, The Foundation (or gross) Phase Of The Progressive ego-Transcending Practice Of The Only-By-Me Revealed and Given Way Of The Heart Necessarily Requires Much Seriousness, and Much Profundity—In Order To Establish The Necessary (and Truly "Positively Disillusioned") Foundation Of True (and Truly In-Me-Surrendered) Hearing (or The Only-By-Me Revealed and Given Unique ego-Transcending Capability Of Most Fundamental self-Understanding).

The Middle Phase Of The Progressive ego-Transcending Great Process Of The Only-By-Me Revealed and Given Way Of The Heart (or Way Of Adidam) Is The Devotional, and Truly Hearing (or Actively ego-Transcending, and, Thus, Always Directly self-Contraction-Transcending), and Really Seeing (or Actively, Directly, and Fully Technically Responsibly Spiritual) Process Of Transcending the higher self (or the subtle and mental ego—or The Total subtle Dimension, or subtle Depth, Of self-Contraction—and All The conceptual and perceptual Illusions Of Inherently, and Necessarily, brain-Based mind). Therefore, The Middle (or subtle) Phase Of The Progressive ego-Transcending Practice Of The Only-By-Me Revealed and Given Way Of The Heart Requires The Realization Of "Positive Disillusionment" Relative To The subtly Objectified (and subtly Absorbed) subject-object point of view (or Fundamental Release From The Inherently ego-Bound—or Thoroughly self-Contracted—Search Of relatively internalized mental and perceptual attention). This Degree Of The Realization Of "Positive Disillusionment" Requires Fundamental Release From The Inherently Illusory Search To Experience The conditional Dissolution Of the ego (and, In Particular, Release From subtle states of self-Contraction—and, Especially, From mental states of self-Contraction) By Means Of object-Oriented Absorptive Mysticism (or The

Absorptive Yielding Of attention To The Apparent subtle objects that Are Either Originated By the brain-mind or, Otherwise, Mediated By the brain itself). And The Characteristic Sign Of "Positive Disillusionment" Relative To The Permanent and Complete Satisfaction Of The object-Oriented Seeking Of the higher self (or Separate and Separative subtle and mental ego) Is The Fully Me-Hearing and Truly Me-Seeing Realization Of The Entirely Spiritual Nature Of Cosmic Existence (or, That Is To Say, The Realization That all Natural and Cosmic forms and states Are Inherently Non-Separate, or Intrinsically Non-Dual, Modes Of Universally Pervasive and Cosmically-Manifested Spiritual Energy, or Of Fundamental, Indivisible, and Irreducible Light—or Of Love-Bliss-Happiness Itself).

The Final Phase Of The Progressive ego-Transcending Great Process Of The Only-By-Me Revealed and Given Way Of The Heart (or Way Of Adidam) Is The Devotional, Spiritual, and Transcendental Hearing-and-Seeing Process Of Transcending the Root-self (or the Root-and-causal ego—or The causal, or Root-causative, Depth Of self-Contraction—which is attention itself, or The Root-Gesture Of Separateness, Relatedness, and "Difference"). Therefore, Immediately Preliminary To The Realization Associated With The Only-By-Me Revealed and Given Seventh Stage Of Life, The Final (or causal) Phase Of The Progressive ego-Transcending (or Comprehensively self-Contraction-Transcending) Practice Of The Only-By-Me Revealed and Given Way Of The Heart Requires The Realization Of "Positive Disillusionment" Relative To The causal (or Root-egoic, and, Therefore, Fundamental, or Original) subject-object Division In Consciousness (or Conscious Light) Itself. This Degree Of The Realization Of "Positive Disillusionment" Requires The Exercise Of Transcendental Self-Identification—Prior To the Root-self-Contraction that is point of view itself (or attention itself), and, Thus, Also, Prior To The Entire body-brain-mind Complex, or conditional Structure, Of conception and perception. And The Characteristic Sign Of "Positive Disillusionment" Relative To The Permanent and Complete Satisfaction Of the Root-self (or the Fundamental causative, or causal, ego) Is The Fundamental Transcending Of attention itself In The Me-"Locating" (and, Altogether, Me-Hearing and Me-Seeing) Realization Of The Transcendental (and Intrinsically Non-Separate and Non-Dual) Nature Of Consciousness Itself.

Only After (or In The Great Event Of Most Perfect, and, Necessarily, Formal and Fully Accountable, Fulfillment Of) The Complete Progressive ego-Transcending Great Process Of The Only-By-Me Revealed and Given Way Of The Heart (or Way Of Adidam) In The Total (and Progressively Unfolded) Context Of The Inherently ego-Based First Six (or psycho-physically Pre-Patterned gross, subtle, and causal) Stages Of Life Is There The Truly

Ultimate (or Seventh Stage, and Always Already Divinely Self-Realized—and, Thus, Inherently ego-Transcending) "Practice" Of The Only-By-Me Revealed and Given Way Of The Heart (or The Most Perfect, and Inherently egoless, or Always Already Most Perfectly, and Un-conditionally, self-Contraction-Transcending, and Divinely Love-Bliss-Full, and Only-By-Me Revealed and Given Seventh-Stage-Of-Life Demonstration Of Ruchira Avatara Bhakti Yoga, or Ruchira Avatara Siddha Yoga).

The Only-By-Me Revealed and Given Seventh-Stage-Of-Life "Practice" (or The Inherently egoless, and, Thus, Always Already Most Perfectly, and Un-conditionally, self-Contraction-Transcending, and, Altogether, Most Perfectly Divinely Self-Realized Demonstration) Of The Only-By-Me Revealed and Given Way Of The Heart Is The Great Esoteric Devotional, Spiritual, Transcendental, Self-Evidently Divine, and Most Perfectly Me-Hearing and Me-Seeing Demonstration Of all-and-All-Divinely-Self-Recognizing (and, Thus, all-and-All-Divinely-Transcending) Divine Self-Abiding (In and As My Avatarically Self-Revealed Divine "Bright" Sphere Of Self-Existing, Self-Radiant, Inherently egoless, Perfectly Subjective, and Inherently and Most Perfectly body-mind-Transcending, or body-brain-Transcending, or Inherently, Most Perfectly, and Un-conditionally psycho-physical-self-Contraction-Transcending, but Never Intentionally body-mind-Excluding, or body-brain-Excluding, Divine Person, or Eternal Self-Condition and Infinite State).

The Only-By-Me Revealed and Given Seventh-Stage-Of-Life Demonstration Of The Only-By-Me Revealed and Given Way Of The Heart Is The Un-conditional and Divinely Free (and Inherently egoless, or Inherently point-of-view-less) "Practice" (or Divinely Self-Realized Progressive Demonstration) Of Self-Abiding Divine Self-Recognition Of The Simultaneous Totality Of the Apparent gross, subtle, and causal body-brain-mind-self, or The Progressively all-and-All-Outshining Process Of The Simultaneous (and Self-Abiding) Divine Self-Recognition Of the Total psycho-physical ego-"I" itself (or Of the Total conditional point of view, or Apparent self-Contraction, itself). Therefore, The Only-By-Me Revealed and Given Seventh-Stage-Of-Life Demonstration Of The Only-By-Me Revealed and Given Way Of The Heart Is The Inherent "Practice" (or Divinely Self-Realized Demonstration) Of Self-Abiding Divine Self-Recognition Of point of view itself (or Of attention itself—or Of the conditionally Apparent subject, itself) and (Always Coincidently, or Simultaneously) Self-Abiding Divine Self-Recognition Of the conception or perception Of Separateness, Relatedness, or "Difference" Itself (or Of any and every conditionally Apparent object, itself).

The Only-By-Me Revealed and Given Seventh-Stage-Of-Life Demonstration Of The Only-By-Me Revealed and Given Way Of The Heart Is The Most

Perfect (or Un-conditional, Inherently egoless, and Self-Evidently Divine) Demonstration Of "Positive Disillusionment", or Of The Inherently Illusionless (or self-Contraction-Free, and, Inherently, all-and-All-Transcending) Realization Of The Fundamental Reality and Truth (or Real God)—Which Fundamental Reality and Truth (or Real God) Is The One and Indivisible and Self-Existing and Indestructible and Self-Radiant and Always Already Perfectly Non-Dual Conscious Light (or That Which Is Always Already The Case), and Which Reality and Truth (or Real God) Is That Self-Existing and Perfectly Subjective Self-"Brightness" (or Infinite and Absolute and Perfectly Non-Separate Self-Condition) Of Which The conditional (or gross, subtle, and causal) subject-object Illusions (or Total psycho-physical self-Contraction Illusions) Of conception, and Of perception, and Of The ego-"I" Presumption Are Mere, and Merely Apparent (or Non-Necessary, or Always Non-Ultimate), and Inherently Non-Binding Modifications. And The Characteristic Sign Of Most Perfectly Demonstrated (or Seventh Stage) "Positive Disillusionment" Relative To The Totality Of the Separate and Separative ego-"I" (or point of view) and its Presumptions Of a Separate (or Objectified) gross, subtle, and causal world Is The Inherently egoless and Self-Evidently Divine (and Intrinsically Non-Separate and Non-Dual) Realization Of Reality (Itself) As Irreducible and Indivisible Conscious Light (Inherently Love-Bliss-Full, or Perfectly Subjectively "Bright").

Therefore, The Only-By-Me Revealed and Given Way Of The Heart Is—From The Beginning, and At Last—The Way Of "Positive Disillusionment".

The Only-By-Me Revealed and Given Way Of The Heart Is—From The Beginning, and At Last—The Way Of The Direct Transcending Of The Fact and The Consequences Of egoity (or Of psycho-physical self-Contraction).

The Only-By-Me Revealed and Given Way Of The Heart Is—From The Beginning, and At Last—The Way Of The Direct Transcending Of The Illusions Of Inherently egoic attention (or Of The conditionally Presumed subject-object Pattern Of conception and perception).

The Only-By-Me Revealed and Given Way Of The Heart Is—From The Beginning, and At Last—The Way Of The Direct Transcending Of The Total Illusory Pattern Of The Inherently egoic Presumption Of Separateness, Relatedness, and "Difference".

The Only-By-Me Revealed and Given Way Of The Heart Is—From The Beginning, and At Last—The Way Of The Direct Transcending Of The Always Simultaneous Illusions Of the Separate ego-"I" and the Separate (or Merely objective) world.

The Only-By-Me Revealed and Given Way Of The Heart Is—From The Beginning, and At Last—The Way Of The Direct (or Inherently egoless and

Inherently Illusionless) Realizing Of The One and Irreducible Conscious Light (or Perfectly Subjective Spiritual "Brightness" Of Being) That Is Reality and Truth (or Real God).

The Only-By-Me Revealed and Given Way Of The Heart Is—From The Beginning, and At Last—The Way Of The Direct (or Inherently egoless and Inherently Illusionless) Realizing Of The Conscious Love-Bliss-Energy Of Totality.

The Only-By-Me Revealed and Given Way Of The Heart Is—From The Beginning, and At Last—The Way Of The Direct Realizing Of Only Me.

AVATAR ADI DA SAMRAJ
The Mountain Of Attention Sanctuary, 2000

SUTRA 9

By Means Of My (Now, and Forever Hereafter) Avatarically Given (and Forever Hereafter Divinely Self-"Emerging") Bodily (Human) Divine Form, and Spiritual (and Always Blessing) Divine Presence, and Very (and Inherently Both egoless and Perfect) Divine State, and Through The Words Of This Avatarically Given Divine Testament (and Through All The Words Of All My Twenty-Three Divine "Source-Texts"), and Through All The Forever Shown and Told Divine Play Of The Works and Words Of My Avataric Human-Time Of Divine Life, I Will Always Be The Divine Heart-Master In Relation To any one and every one who (By Formally Embracing The Only-By-Me Revealed and Given Way Of The Heart) Enters Into This Listening Process That Becomes True Hearing Of Me. And This (Necessarily, Formal) Devotional (and, In Due Course, Spiritual) Process Of Listening To Me and Hearing Me Must (By Means Of My Avatarically Self-Transmitted Divine Spiritual Grace) Lead (Progressively) Toward True Seeing Of Me (or The Only-By-Me Spiritually Activated, and, Spiritually, Fully Technically Responsible, Life and Practice Of The Only-By-Me Revealed and Given Way Of The Heart). The ego-Transcending Capability Of Hearing Me Is Not Able To Become Complete (or Most Perfect), In Divine Self-Realization (and The Necessary Total Process Of The Only-By-Me Revealed and Given Seventh Stage Of Life), Unless True Hearing Goes On To Do Its Work In The Seeing Context Of The Only-By-Me Revealed and Given Way Of The Heart. And, Until There Is True Hearing Of Me, Listening To Me In The Only-By-Me Revealed and Given Way Of The Heart Is Itself The (In Due Course) By-Me-Spiritually-Blessed, By-Me-Spiritually-Gifted, and By-Me-Spiritually-Inspired Process Of Growth In self-Understanding, Toward The Awakening Of The Hearing Capability For Direct (and moment to moment) ego-Transcendence.

No one who Has Not Yet Heard Me and Seen Me Is Truly (and Effectively) Able To Practice What Can Be Practiced Only By those who Have Heard Me and Also Seen Me—or Come Listening To Me (By Means Of My Avatarically Self-Transmitted Divine Spiritual Grace), and Hearing Me (Through Most Fundamental self-Understanding), To See Me (With Full Technical Responsibility For The Reception Of The "Bright" Divine Spiritual Baptism, or Ruchira

Shaktipat, Granted By My Avatarically Self-Transmitted Divine Spiritual Person and Presence).

In The Only-By-Me Revealed and Given Way Of The Heart (or Way Of Adidam), The Direct Self-Revelation Of Me (Functioning As The Divine Heart-Master, In Always present-time Direct Relationship To My Devotee) Is The Principal and Great Key To The Process Of Spiritual, Transcendental, and Divine Self-Realization. And I Am Seen In My Great Function (As The Divine Heart-Master, In Always present-time Direct Relationship To My Devotee) Only By those who Have Heard Me, Become Fully Open-Hearted To Me (Free Of The Motive Of self-Contraction In Relation To Me), and Become Fully Technically Responsible For Receiving The Baptism (or Tangible Blessing) Of My Avatarically Self-Transmitted Spiritual (and Always Blessing) Divine Presence Through Contemplative (and Truly Devotional, and, Thereby, Really ego-Transcending) Regard Of Me. Therefore, It Is Only By True and Effective Fulfillment Of The Beginner's Practice Of The Way Of The Heart (Whether In The Manner Of The Devotional Exercise Of Faith Or In The Manner Of The Devotional Exercise Of Insight—and, In Either Case, To The Degree Of Real, True, Stable, and Fully Technically Responsible Spiritual Awakening) That The Fullest (or Truly and Fully Spiritually Responsible) Relationship To Me As The Divine Heart-Master Is Realized.

The Relationship To Me That Is Embraced By My (Necessarily, Formally Practicing) Devotee Is Neither a social relationship Nor an organizational relationship Nor a merely ceremonial relationship. The Relationship To Me That Is Embraced By My (Necessarily, Formally Practicing) Devotee Is A (Profoundly Cultivated) Devotional and (In Due Course) Spiritual Relationship. And That Devotional and (In Due Course) Spiritual Relationship To Me Is Not Merely Primary Among all other Potential relationships—That Devotional and (In Due Course) Spiritual Relationship To Me Is Utterly Unique, and Not Comparable To any other (Real or Potential) relationship. There Is no other relationship Of This Kind.

The relationships between human beings are, As A General Rule, social relations, Bearing A functionally social Dimension Of some kind (Relating To one's life-obligations, one's social role in the world, and So On). But The Devotional and (In Due Course) Spiritual Relationship To Me Is The Unique Divine Relationship, The Divine Context Of (Devotionally and, In Due Course, Spiritually) Right Life. Therefore, My Devotee Must Not, In Any Manner, Relate To Me As "one among others".

The Devotional and (In Due Course) Spiritual Relationship To Me Is, Most Ultimately, Beyond All Separation and "Difference". The Devotional and (In Due Course) Spiritual Relationship To Me Is The Relationship Of Most Perfect

Divine Self-Realization, The Relationship That Must, Itself, Be (In Due Course) Most Perfectly Realized. Therefore, The Devotional and (In Due Course) Spiritual Relationship To Me Must Be Understood To Be Unique, and It Must Be Lived Uniquely (and Constantly, or moment to moment). That Is To Say, The Devotional and (In Due Course) Spiritual Relationship To Me Must Be Constantly Cultivated By My Devotee—Through My Devotee's Offering Of Gifts To Me, Through My Devotee's Fulfillment Of My Avatarically Given Divine Instructions (Relative To The Total Practice Of The Only-By-Me Revealed and Given Way Of The Heart, or Way Of Adidam), and Through My Devotee's Absolute Devotional and (In Due Course) Spiritual Fidelity To Me.

My Great Avataric Statements Are Not merely public Announcements, Calling For casual (and merely public) belief. The Great Avataric Statements I Make Relative To My Inherently Perfect Work (As The Divine Heart-Master), My Divinely "Crazy" and Divinely "Heroic" Submission As Servant (Done In Order To Teach), My Divine Self-Nature (Realized Most Perfectly), and My Avatarically Self-Transmitted Divine Spiritual Presence As The Inherently egoless (and Self-Evidently Divine) Heart Itself Are (With All My Uncommon Speech) Divine Self-Confessions—Freely Given To all those who Listen To Me With The Heart, and To all those who Hear Me At The Heart, and To all those who See Me As I Am. Those Divine Self-Confessions Are Directly Obvious As Reality and Truth Only To The Inherently egoless Heart Itself—and To all those who Have Been Directly Awakened To That Obviousness By My Avataric Spiritual Self-Transmission Of The "Bright" Divine Self-Condition Of The One and Only Heart.

The body-mind Of Man
Is Like A Seed,
That Lies Asleep
Within The Dark and Depth
Of Earth's Unconsciousness.

And I Am Like A Thunderstorm
Of Fresh Down-Crashing Sound and Light,
That Weathers Me
Into The Earth-World
With A Flood Of True and Living Water.

And When The True Water
Of My Love-Bliss-Presence
Flows Deep Into the body-mind,

The "Brightest" Sound and Shape Of Me
Strikes Through The Germ Of Mankind's Seed within.

It Is The Heart That Breaks
By My Divine Invasion there.
Its Germ Of Me-"Bright" Suddenness
Un-Knots The Seed Of body-mind,
When I Crash Down Into The Earthen Core.

And When The Heart Un-Locks,
the body-mind Becomes A Flower
In The Tangible Garden
Of My Divine "Bright" Spherical Self-Domain.

If The Heart Finds Me,
The Heart
Devotionally Recognizes Me (Inherently),
and all the body-mind
Devotionally Responds To Me (Immediately)—
Whether By Means Of
The Immediately To-Me-Responsive
Devotional Exercise
Of Me-Recognizing Faith
Or
The Immediately Me-Recognizing
Devotional Exercise
Of To-Me-Responsive Insight.

Therefore,
Your Heart Must Decide—
Whether To Raise A Fist,
and Throw A Rock,
At The ego-Crushing Natural Universe,
Or To Make A Flower Grow
In The Garden Of Indestructible Light.

The Devotional Recognition-Response
To Me
Is
The Divine Flowering
Of the body-mind.

Therefore,
Your Heart Must
Recognize Me
and Choose Me—
and Not merely believe Me—
If I Am To "Brighten" You.

Faith Is A Flower,
and Not a mind's idea,
or a body's satisfaction.

Likewise,
The Insight
That Flowers the body-mind
Is Made Of Heart,
and Not Of Seeker's Thrum
Of thought,
and thought's Abstract Invasion
Of the body.

No mere belief,
or Mummery Of thinking mind,
Can Make The Fist Of ego's Knot
Un-Tie.

And No Set Stage
Of mere perception
Can Outlast The Crushing Time
Of merely Natural life.

The Rock Of ego
and
The Fist Of self-Contracted body-mind
Will Last a mere and Total lifetime—
Whereas The Heart-Flower
Breaks The Earth
Above the head's Clay Crown,
and Finds My "Bright" Beginning
In An Eternal Field,
Above the stars.

My Great Avataric (Divine and Spiritual) Invasion Of The Heart Becomes Effective Progressively. And It Becomes (or Can Become) Spiritually Effective To The Fullest Degree Only In The Case Of those Of My (Necessarily, Formally Practicing) Listening Devotees who Hear Me (or Most Fundamentally Understand themselves, In Devotional Recognition-Response To My Avatarically Self-Revealed Divine Word and Person), and who (On That Basis) Become My By-Me-Spiritually-Awakened, and (By Means Of My Avatarically Self-Transmitted Divine Spiritual Grace), Spiritually, Fully Technically Responsible (or Fully Me-Seeing), Devotees (Steadily Open-Hearted In Relation To My Avatarically Self-Transmitted Divine Spiritual Presence).

My Avatarically Self-Revealed (and Always Me-Revealing) Divine Word and The Great Opportunity To Practice The Only-By-Me Revealed and Given Way Of The Heart (or Way Of Adidam) In (Necessarily, Formal) Devotional Relationship To Me Should Be Openly Communicated To All Mankind. And The First Call Is To Listen To Me. First Listen (and Respond At Heart) To Me (Present In The Form Of My Avatarically Self-Revealed Divine Word, My Avatarically Self-Revealed Divine Image-Art, My Avatarically Self-Manifested Divine Leelas, and My Avatarically Self-Manifested, and Divinely Self-Revelatory, and Divinely All-Giving, Divine Sign—Of Bodily Human Form, Spiritual Presence, and Perfectly Subjective, and Inherently egoless, or Non-Separate, State)—and (In A Responsible and Progressively ego-Surrendering Manner) Begin The Counter-egoic Process Relative To the conditional self, Whether In The Manner Of The Devotional Exercise Of Insight Or In The Manner Of The Devotional Exercise Of Faith. It Is Only When That Process Has (In The Context Of The Only-By-Me Revealed and Given Way Of The Heart) Become True Hearing and Then Real Seeing That any individual Is Called (and Enabled) To Demonstrate Full Technical Responsibility For Spiritual Practice In Relation To Me As The Divine Heart-Master (Fully Encountered In My Spiritual Blessing-Function and, Ultimately, Truly and Fully "Located" As The Inherently egoless Heart Itself)—and, Thus, By A Progression Of Only-By-Me Revealed and Given Means, To (At Last) Most Perfectly Realize Transcendental (or Self-Existing) Divine Freedom and Self-Radiant (or Inherently Spiritual) and "Bright" Happiness, or The (Inherently Perfect) Truth That Neither Depends Upon Nor Can Ever Be Destroyed By conditional events.

My Work and My Struggle To, In Every Detail, Generate The Teaching-Argument Of The Way Of The Heart Is (Now, and Forever Hereafter) Complete. Now, and Forever Hereafter, those who Would Practice The Only-By-Me Revealed and Given Way Of The Heart (or Way Of Adidam) Will, First, Seriously "Consider" My Avatarically Self-Revealed (and Always Me-Revealing) Divine Word and My Avatarically Self-Manifested (and Always Me-Revealing)

Divine Image-Art and My Avatarically Self-Manifested (and Always Me-Revealing) Divine Leelas, and (Based On their Devotional Recognition Of Me and their Devotional Response To Me) they Will (Necessarily, Formally) Practice True Devotion To Me (By Means Of ego-Surrendering, ego-Forgetting, and More and More ego-Transcending Feeling-Contemplation Of My Avatarically Self-Manifested, and Divinely Self-Revelatory, and Divinely All-Giving Sign—Of Form, and Presence, and State). Now, and Forever Hereafter, My Avatarically Self-Manifested Divine Spiritual Work Is Only That Of My Standing Free, Divinely Self-"Emerging" In Perpetuity, Always Blessing all To Listen To Me, and To Hear Me, and To See Me (Where I Now, and Forever Hereafter, Stand). And Only those who Are Truly Heart-Moved To Practice The Great Devotional and Spiritual Process Of Realizing Me In and By Means Of The Formal (and Altogether Right) Embrace Of The Only-By-Me Revealed and Given Way Of The Heart (or Way Of Adidam) Can (In Due Course) Hear Me and (Then) See Me With, and At, and As The Heart.

Only The Only-By-Me Revealed and Given Way Of Adidam (Which Is The One and Only By-Me-Revealed and By-Me-Given Way Of The Heart) Completes and Most Perfectly Fulfills The Great Tradition Of Mankind. Only In The Only-By-Me Revealed and Given Way Of Adidam Is The Most Ultimate (or Inherently Most Perfect) Realization (and Seventh Stage Of Life) Revealed (and, In Due Course, Given). And, Therefore, Only In The Only-By-Me Revealed and Given Way Of Adidam Is There The Real Potential For (Most Ultimately) Utter (or Inherently Most Perfect) Transcending Of the ego-"I" (or self-Contraction), which ego-"I" (or self-Contraction) is the one and constant limitation that Prevents The Most Ultimate (or Inherently Most Perfect) Realization Of Real God, or Truth, or Reality.

The Only-By-Me Revealed and Given Way Of Adidam Is The Unique Progressive Practice (or Real Process) Of self-Transcendence (or Direct, and Really Effective, and, Ultimately, Inherently Most Perfect ego-Transcendence In The Context Of Every Stage Of Life). The Only-By-Me Revealed and Given Way Of Adidam Is The Unique, Complete, and (Ultimately) Perfect Way (and Process) Of (Progressively) Spiritual, Transcendental, and (Most Ultimately) Divine (and Inherently Most Perfect) Self-Realization. And The Foundation Of The Only-By-Me Revealed and Given Way Of Adidam Is The Eternal, Ancient, and Always New Method Of The Siddhas—Which Is Devotional Communion With The Siddha-Guru, and Which Is The Unique Means Of Realizing Real God, or Truth, or Reality That Has Traditionally Been Granted By The Rare True Adept-Realizers Of Real God, or Truth, or Reality Who (In The Traditional Context Of The Fourth, The Fifth, and The Sixth Stages Of Life, and Each According To His or Her Particular Stage Of Awakening and Of Helping-Capability)

Have, By Means Of The Unique Spiritual Blessing-Method (or Shaktipat-Transmission-Capability) Of The Siddhas, Directly (and By Really Effective Spiritual Means) Transmitted The Traditional Revelations and Realizations Of Real God (or Truth Itself, or Reality Itself).

All Of The Great Siddha-Gurus (Of Whatever Real Degree Of Real-God-Realization)—Who Have Taught and Transmitted The Inherently Divine Truth Of Reality To living beings—Have Given Their Devotees The Graceful Gift Of Satsang. Satsang Has Always Been The Essential Activity Of The Great Siddha-Gurus. The Great Siddha-Gurus Have Never Come Merely To Give A conceptual Teaching—To Fabricate A Myth, A belief-Structure For the mind, A Patterning Of ego-mentality. The Great Siddha-Gurus Have Always Brought and Given Themselves. They Have Always Entered Into Relationship With Their Devotees, and (Altogether) With the conditionally Manifested worlds. That Satsang-Relationship Is The Very Structure (and The Outwardly Observable Sign) Of The Devotional (and, In Due Course, Spiritual) Process I Have Revealed and Given. If You Are My Formally Practicing Devotee, Satsang With Me Is Spiritual Life. In That Process Of Satsang, I (By All My Avataric Divine Spiritual Means) "Live" My Devotees.

As I here (Now, and For all time) Confess and Declare To all-and-All, and As (Now, and Forever Hereafter, and every where) Confessed and Declared By All My Listening Devotees, and By All My Hearing Devotees, and By All My Seeing Devotees, I Am The Da Avatar—The Ruchira Avatar, The Love-Ananda Avatar, The Heart-Born, Eternal, True, and Divine Heart-Master, The Ruchira Siddha, The Maha-Jnana Siddha, The Very and "Bright", Self-Given, and Inherently Most Perfect (or Seventh Stage) Realizer, Revealer, and Self-Revelation Of The True (and Inherently Perfect) Divine Person (Which Is The Self-Condition and Source-Condition Of all-and-All). On The Basis Of their Confession and Declaration Of Heart-Recognition Of Me (and Of To-Me-Responding Devotion To Me), and By Virtue Of My Avatarically Given Divine Self-Revelation (and Of Even All My Avatarically Given Divine Spiritual Gifts To them), I Am The Ruchira Siddha-Guru (or Perfectly "Bright", and Always Directly, and Most Perfectly, Spiritually Effective, Hridaya-Samartha Sat-Guru and Maha-Jnana Siddha-Guru) Of all who Practice The Only-By-Me Revealed and Given Way Of Adidam. Therefore, From The Beginning, The Only-By-Me Revealed and Given Way Of Adidam (Whether In The Manner Of The Devotional Way Of Insight Or In The Manner Of The Devotional Way Of Faith) Is (In The Manner Of The Eternal, Ancient, and Always New Method Of The Siddhas) The Absolutely Direct Way Of ego-Surrendering, ego-Forgetting, and (Ultimately, Inherently Most Perfectly) ego-Transcending Devotional (and, In Due Course, Spiritual) Communion With My Avatarically-Born Bodily

(Human) Divine Form, and With My Avatarically Self-Transmitted Spiritual (and Always Blessing) Divine Presence, and With My Avatarically Self-Revealed (and Very, and Transcendental, and Perfectly Subjective, and Inherently Spiritual, and Inherently egoless, and Inherently Perfect, and Self-Evidently Divine) State, and (Thus, Altogether) With My Avatarically Self-Revealed and Always Me-Revealing Spiritual Person Of Self-Evidently Divine Reality and Truth.

After My Divine Re-Awakening, and (Thus) By Virtue Of My Re-Realization Of My Own Divine Self-Condition (and The Spontaneous Regeneration Of The Unique Siddhis, The Ruchira Siddhis, or "Bright" Divine Blessing Powers, That Spontaneously Accompanied My Divine Re-Awakening), I Made Myself Available To All Kinds Of Listening Devotees, For The Sake Of Divine Self-Realization In Every Case. During The Many Years I Functioned (By Submitting and Subordinating Myself To all-and-All) To Generate (here, and every "where", In and Throughout The Entire Cosmic Domain) My Avatarically Self-Revealed (and Always Me-Revealing) Divine Word and Teaching-Argument, I Fully (and, Finally, Completely) Revealed and Communicated The Way Of The Heart (or Way Of Adidam)—and, By All Of That, I Made Myself Forever Available As The Divine Heart-Master, To any one who (As My Formally Practicing Devotee) Listens To Me (or Even Hears Me), and To any one who (As My Formally Practicing Devotee), Having Heard Me, Has Become Fully Technically Responsible For Spiritually Receiving Me, and Sees Me. Then, When My Teaching-Work Was Complete, I Retired From The Ordeal Of Teaching, In Order Simply (or Merely) To Be Present, and Thus, By (Constantly) Divinely Self-"Emerging" (here, and every "where", In and Throughout The Entire Cosmic Domain), To Magnify My Divine Spiritual Blessing To this world (and To <u>all</u> worlds).

Therefore, I Remain (Thus), Ever and Forever Now. And I Am (Thus, <u>As</u> I <u>Am</u>) To Remain (Forever) Most Perfectly Effective (Even After, and Forever After, The Avataric Physical Lifetime Of My Bodily Human Divine Form). And (Even After, and Forever After, The Avataric Physical Lifetime Of My Bodily Human Divine Form) I Will Remain (Thus, and Inherently Most Perfectly, and Most Directly) Effective By Means Of The Continuous Work (or Always Me-Serving Instrumentality) Of My True (and Formally Acknowledged) Instruments, Which Instruments (or Unique Instrumental Means) Consist Of All My (At every then present-time) Formally Acknowledged "Perfect Practice" Devotees who Are Full Formal Members[54] Of The Ruchira Sannyasin Order Of Adidam Ruchiradam (and, Most Especially, Those Full Formal Members Of The Ruchira Sannyasin Order Of Adidam Ruchiradam who Are Formally Acknowledged To Be Practicing The Only-By-Me Revealed and Given Way Of The Heart In The "Perfect Practice" Context Of The Only-By-Me Revealed and

Given Seventh Stage Of Life). Likewise (Even After, and Forever After, The Avataric Physical Lifetime Of My Bodily Human Divine Form), I Will Remain (Thus, and Inherently Most Perfectly, and Most Directly) Effective By Means Of The Continuous Work (or Always Me-Extending Agency) Of My True (and Formally Acknowledged) Agents, Which Agents (or Unique Means Of Agency) Consist Of My Avatarically Self-Revealed (and Always Me-Revealing) Divine Word, My Avatarically Self-Revealed (and Always Me-Revealing) Divine Image-Art, and The Formally By-Me-Spiritually-Empowered Ruchira Sannyasin Hermitage Ashrams.

Therefore, Now (and Forever Hereafter), My Every Listening Devotee, and My Every Hearing Devotee, and My Every Seeing Devotee Will Be Given Appropriate Access To My Avatarically Self-Revealed Divine Word, My Avatarically Self-Revealed Divine Image-Art, My Avatarically Self-Manifested Divine Leelas, My Avatarically Given Divine Sign, and All My Avatarically Given Divine Spiritual Blessings (As These Are Preserved, and, Otherwise, Transmitted, Within The Serving Culture Of All The Formally Acknowledged and True Instruments Of My Avatarically Self-Manifested Divine Spiritual Work). In Each Such Case, Such Access Will Be Given In Accordance With My Devotee's Developmental Stage Of The Real (and Total) Practice Of The Only-By-Me Revealed and Given Way Of Adidam—and The Realization (By Means Of My Avatarically Self-Transmitted Divine Spiritual Grace) Of My Inherently egoless (and Self-Evidently Divine) Person (Which Is The Inherently Perfect Self-Condition Of all-and-All, and Which Is Also, or Inherently and Necessarily, The Inherently Perfect Source-Condition Of all-and-All) Will, In This Manner, Always Continue To Be Served By My Great Avatarically Self-Revealed Divine Means.

If any one Wonders How This Can Be So, Let him or her Study The Great Tradition Of The Realization Of Real God, and Truth, and Reality. Let every one who Will Study The Great Tradition Understand That—Although The Only-By-Me Revealed and Given Way Of The Heart (or Way Of Adidam) Is The New, Most Full, and Perfectly Complete Revelation Of Real God, and Truth, and Reality, Made Under (and Also Prior To, or Beyond) the circumstances arising During The Avataric Physical Lifetime Of My Now Speaking Bodily (Human) Divine Form—It Is Also (Most Simply) The Eternal and Ancient (and, Now, and Forever Hereafter, Complete) "Secret" Way That Is The Seed Of All Religions.

If any one Doubts That All This Can Be Real, Let him or her Simply "Consider" My Avatarically Self-Revealed Divine Word and My Avatarically Self-Revealed Divine Image-Art and My Avatarically Self-Manifested Divine Leelas, and Observe (and Feel) My Avatarically-Born Bodily (Human) Divine Form,

Until The Reality Of The Devotionally Me-Recognizing and Devotionally To-Me-Responding Avataric Way In My Spiritually Blessing (and Inherently egoless, and Self-Evidently Divine) Company Is Authenticated By The Heart.

If any one Is Heart-Moved To Realize Me, Let him or her First Resort (Formally, and By Formal Heart-Vow) To Me, and (Thereby) Commence The Devotional (and, In Due Course, Spiritual) Process Of self-Observation, self-Understanding, and self-Transcendence (or ego-Transcendence), By Means Of Right Formal Practice Of All The Foundation and Original Listening Disciplines Required In The Only-By-Me Revealed and Given Way Of The Heart.

If, By Means Of My Avatarically Self-Transmitted Divine Spiritual Grace, any one Realizes My True Fullness In That First Process (Whereby My Freely Given Hearing-Gift Of Most Fundamental self-Understanding Opens the self-Contraction Of The Heart), Then Let him or her Go On (By Means Of My Avatarically Self-Transmitted Divine Spiritual Grace) To Practice The Fully Me-Seeing (and, Necessarily, Ecstatic—or Directly, and Really Effectively, ego-Transcending) Stages Of The Way Of The Heart, Which Begin (As Such) When (By Means Of My Avatarically Self-Transmitted Divine Spiritual Grace) My Devotee Becomes Fully Technically Responsible For The Spiritual Reception Of My Avatarically Self-Transmitted Divine Spiritual Presence (That Washes and Forgives The Devotionally To-Me-Responding Heart In Every Instant Of moment to moment time).

Therefore, Let all those who Listen To Me, and all those who Hear Me, and all those who See Me Pass, By Means Of My Avatarically Self-Transmitted Divine Spiritual Grace, To and Through All The Processes Associated With The First Six Stages Of Life, and Realize The Only-By-Me Revealed and Given Seventh (or Divinely Perfect) Stage Of Life.

Let every one and all Be Happy. My Heart-Blessing Freely Moves, To Call and Gather one and all.

I Am The Self-Evidently (and Really, and Truly) Divine One I Have Declared Myself To Be.

I Am The Self-Evidently (and Really, and Truly) Divine One My By-Me-Spiritually-Initiated (and Always Newly By-Me-Spiritually-Activated) Listening Devotees, Hearing Devotees, and Seeing Devotees Come (By Means Of My Avatarically Self-Revealing Divine Spiritual Grace) To Know and (Openly) To Confess, Through Love's Revelation Of Love-Bliss In Devotional and Spiritual Satsang With Me.

Aham Da Asmi. Beloved, I Am Da. I Am The Inherently egoless Divine and Real and True Heart. I Am The Avatarically Given Divine Self-Manifestation Of The "Bright"—The Inherently egoless and Self-Evidently Divine Heart (or Conscious Light) Of Reality Itself. And The Totality Of My Avatarically Given

Divine Self-Manifestation Is A Great Divine Pattern. And The Totality Of That Divine Pattern Of Mine Is The Way To The Divine Heart—and The Divine Way Of The Heart. Therefore, To Surrender, Forget, and Transcend the ego-"I" In Love's Distracted Communion With Me (and In Total, or Full and Complete, Conformity To Me) Is To Practice (and Become Conformed To) The Way (or Pattern) Of The Divine Heart, and, Ultimately (Via That Way, or Pattern, Of Me), To Realize The Divine Heart Itself—Which Is The One and Only Conscious Light (Itself).

I Am The One and Only Man Of "Radical" Understanding, The Divine Heart-Master Of All My Listening Devotees, and All My Hearing Devotees, and All My Seeing Devotees.

I Am Always Already Spontaneously Present, or Heart-Born.

I Was Man-Born (or Made conditionally Apparent) By A Unique (Full, Free, and Un-conditional) Avataric Descent Of My Own Divine Spirit-Force, but, Even So, By The Same General Means (or In The Same General Manner) By Which I Submit (As The Inherently egoless and Self-Evidently Divine Person, Self-Condition, and Source-Condition) To Embrace and To Be each and every one Of Man.

Therefore, My Method Of Teaching Was, Likewise, To Identify With Mankind as It (Apparently) is, and To Submit To Embrace human beings (each and all) as they (Apparently) are.

As I Did This, I Constantly and Spontaneously Reflected each one To himself or herself—Thus To Awaken Real self-Observation, Most Fundamental self-Understanding, and The Free Capability For self-Transcendence (or Real ego-Transcendence) In each one.

I Did This In Love (Freely, Openly, and Not limited by convention), and (Through The Recorded Documents Of My Avatarically Given Divine Word, and The Fabricated Images Of My Avatarically Given Divine Image-Art, and The Recorded Stories Of My Avatarically Self-Manifested Divine Leelas, and The Forever To-Be-Continued Representation Of My Avatarically-Born Bodily Human Divine Form, and The Forever To-Be-Continued Work Of My Now, and Forever Hereafter, Avatarically Given, and Always Me-Revealing, Divine Spiritual Presence) I Will Always Do This In Love, Until My Every Listening Devotee Hears Me, and Fully Heart-Recognizes Me and Heart-Responds To Me In Love, and Fully Receives The Divine Spiritual Baptism Of My Mere Presence (or My Heart-Blessing That Avatarically Transmits The Spirit-Power Of My Divine Self-Revelation), and Freely (Fully, and Formally, and Fully Culturally Accountably) Embraces The Great Process Of ego-Transcending and Real-God-Realizing (or Divine Self-Realizing) Practice Of The Way Of The Heart (or Way Of Adidam).

I Am The First (and The Only One Necessary) To Work By Means Of Avataric Birth and Divine Self-Submission In The Domain Of "Western Culture"—but I Have Come here (To Earth, To Mankind, and Into The Total Cosmic Domain) For The Sake Of all beings.

I Have Come here To Complete The Divine Self-Revelation Of The Divine Way That (Ultimately) Most Perfectly Realizes Real God, and Truth, and Reality—So That Even all-and-All May Be Translated Into My Spiritually Self-"Bright" Divine Spherical Self-Domain.

In Order That The Field (or World-Circumstance) Of Divine Self-Revelation Would Become Complete, It Was Necessary For Me To Appear In The Domain Of (Heretofore) Avatarically Un-"Visited" (and Mostly Secular) "Western Culture"—but I Have Come For The Sake Of all beings.

Each and every one Is My Beloved.

Therefore, Because Of Love, I Serve You (and Will Forever Serve You) With Great Humor, Tolerance, Forgiveness, and Blessing Power.

And You Must Likewise Love Me, and Honor Me, and Feelingly Approach Me, and Serve Me, and (Ultimately) Most Fully Spiritually Commune With Me, As Your Beloved (and As Your Divine Heart-Master)—and You Must Constantly Enlarge Your Service To Me (Even In The Context Of Your Apparent relations with any and all conditionally Manifested beings), By Transcending (and Thereby Renouncing) The Habits and Reactions Of egoity (or self-Contraction).

The One and Entire Great Tradition (and Total World-Circumstance) Of All Mankind Is The Unique Circumstance Of My Avataric Appearance and All My Avatarically Self-Manifested Divine Spiritual Work.

Therefore—In Order That You May Rightly Honor and Understand Me—Observe Me Standing Free Forever In The Center Of The Great Tradition and World-Circumstance Of all-and-All.

Observe Me Standing Free everywhere In The Great Tradition, In Every Historical Period. Observe My Likenesses In all times and places and cultures—but Know That My Avatarically Self-Revealed Divine Word, and All My Avatarically Self-Manifested Divine Spiritual Work, Is My Own.

Observe Me Now, Standing Free Among All Those Who Served Me (Humanly and Spiritually) During The Years Of My Own Ordeal Of Divine Re-Awakening. Rightly Understand and Always Honor The Lineage Of Spiritual Blessing In Which I Stand Spiritually Blessed—but Know That My Avatarically Self-Revealed Divine Word, and All My Avatarically Self-Manifested Divine Spiritual Work, Is My Own.

My Avatarically Full-Given Divine Word, and The Extraordinary Play Of All My Avatarically Self-Manifested Divine Spiritual Work, Is The One Great Divine

Self-Revelation To Originate and Develop In The Domain Of "Western Culture" (and In The Total, or Complete, Context Of Mankind, Both "East" and "West")—but My Every Word, and All My Avatarically Self-Manifested Divine Spiritual Work, Is Given For The Sake Of all beings.

My Avatarically Full-Given Divine Word, and The Extraordinary Play Of All My Avatarically Self-Manifested Divine Spiritual Work, Is My Final (or Most Perfectly Completing) Divine Self-Revelation—and It Is Given For The Sake Of all beings.

Aham Da Asmi. Beloved, I Am Da, The "Bright" One, The Divine and Only Person, The Divine Heart Itself, The Only and Divine Person (or Self-Condition and Source-Condition) Of all-and-All, At Last Appearing (In Avatarically-Born Bodily Human Divine Form) In The "West"—and I Have Come For The Sake Of all beings.

I Have Come In Love-Response To a world that (In its "Late-Time", or "Dark Epoch"—Both "East" and "West") Had Lost The Essence Of The Great Tradition Of Spiritual and Transcendental Divine Self-Realization.

I Have Come To Restore and To Complete The Great Tradition Of The Wisdom-Way That Realizes Real God, and Truth, and Reality.

I Have Come To Restore and To Complete The Divine Way and The Divine Revelation Of Spiritual, Transcendental, and (Most Ultimately) Divine Self-Realization.

I Am The Last and Most Perfectly Completing Self-Revelation Of The One and Only Divine Person—The Only One Who Is.

My Every Word Is Given Freely—For The Sake Of All My Listening Devotees, and All My Hearing Devotees, and All My Seeing Devotees.

Therefore, My Every Word Is Given To every one who Is My Own—In The Context Of Every Stage Of Life.

My Teaching-Revelation Of The Only-By-Me Revealed and Given Way Of The Heart (or Way Of Adidam) Is Not Defined, Characterized, or limited By The Ascetical Orientation—or The Strategic Effort To Suppress (and To Withdraw From) Apparently conditional (or phenomenal, or psycho-physical) Existence. Therefore, The Only-By-Me Revealed and Given Way Of The Heart Requires Not Strategic Asceticism, but The Total Conversion (or Devotionally Me-Recognizing, and Devotionally To-Me-Responding, Reorientation) Of conditional (or phenomenal, or psycho-physical) Existence. And The Most Perfect Fulfillment Of The Only-By-Me Revealed and Given Way Of The Heart Requires Not Strategic Asceticism (or Strategic Suppression Of, and Strategic Withdrawal From, the body-mind), but The Inherently Most Perfect Transcending Of egoity (or The Habit Of "Narcissus", Which Is The Chronic self-Contracting Act, or Separative Gesture, Of the body-mind).

Now That My Avatarically Given Divine Teaching-Revelation Is Full and Complete, I Have (Now, and Forever Hereafter) Firmly and Finally Entered Into My Avataric Divine-Self-"Emergence"-Work (Which Is The Ultimate, or Only-Spiritually-Blessing, Phase Of My All-Accomplishing, and, At Last, all-and-All-Translating, Work).

Now (and Forever Hereafter), I Am Merely Standing here (and every where)—To Spiritually Bless and Awaken all beings, By Means Of The Merely Standing Blessing-Work Of My Freely Given and Avatarically Self-Revealed and Inherently egoless and Self-Evidently Divine Sign (Of Form, and Presence, and State).

Now (and Forever Hereafter)—Because I Am No Longer Active In My Original Avataric Play Of Divine Teaching-Work and Divine Self-Revelation-Work—all those who Turn To Me Must Come To self-Understanding Through (Necessarily, Formal, and Truly Devotionally Me-Recognizing, and Truly Devotionally To-Me-Responding) Feeling-Contemplation Of My (Now, and Forever Hereafter) Avatarically Given Divine Sign (Of Form, and Presence, and State), and (Necessarily, Formal) "Consideration" Of My Full-Given (Avatarically Self-Revealed, and Always Me-Revealing) Divine Word, and (Necessarily, Formal) "Consideration" Of My Full-Given (Avatarically Self-Revealed, and Always Me-Revealing) Divine Image-Art, and (Necessarily, Formal) "Consideration" Of The Storied Leelas Of My Avatarically Self-Manifested Divine Teaching-Work, and My Avatarically Self-Manifested Divine Revelation-Work, and My Avatarically Self-Manifested Divine Blessing-Work.

The Avataric Samrajya Of Adidam Is (Now, and Forever Hereafter) Called and Required (By Me) To (Always Appropriately) Grant Right and Formal Access To Me, In Bodily Person (During The Avataric Physical Lifetime Of My Bodily Human Divine Form), and (Always During, and Even Forever After, The Avataric Physical Lifetime Of My Bodily Human Divine Form) To (Always Appropriately) Grant Right and Formal Access To My Formally Acknowledged (and Always and Only Me-Revealing) Instruments and Formally Acknowledged (and Always and Only Me-Revealing) Agents—To all who, As Formal Listening, Hearing, or Seeing Practitioners Of The Only-By-Me Revealed and Given Way Of The Heart (or Way Of Adidam), Should and Must Enjoy Such Access (In Accordance With My Instructions, Full-Given, By Me, To The Ruchira Sannyasin Order Of Adidam Ruchiradam).

The Avataric Samrajya Of Adidam Is (Now, and Forever Hereafter) Called and Required (By Me) To Provide All My Listening Devotees, Hearing Devotees, and Seeing Devotees who (In Accordance With My Instructions, Full-Given, By Me, To The Ruchira Sannyasin Order Of Adidam Ruchiradam) Have Become Truly Prepared For Direct Access To Me (By Formally

Transitioning To Any Stage Of Practice Beyond The Student-Beginner Stage Of The Way Of The Heart) With Appropriate Access (In Accordance With My Instructions, Full-Given, By Me, To The Ruchira Sannyasin Order Of Adidam Ruchiradam) To My Avataric Bodily (Human) Divine Form (For The Sake Of Receiving The Divine Spiritual Blessing-Transmission Of My Ruchira Shaktipat, Whereby they May Contemplate, and Commune With, and, In Due Course, Realize My Avatarically Self-Transmitted Spiritual, and Always Blessing, Divine Presence Of Person, and My Avatarically Self-Revealed, and Very, and Transcendental, and Perfectly Subjective, and Inherently Spiritual, and Inherently egoless, and Inherently Perfect, and Self-Evidently Divine State), and With Appropriate Access To "Ruchira Sannyasin" Devotees (and To Sacred Places, and Other By-Me-Given Means) That Are Truly Spiritually Empowered (and Formally Acknowledged, By Me, During The Avataric Physical Lifetime Of My Bodily Human Divine Form, or—After, and Forever After, The Avataric Physical Lifetime Of My Bodily Human Divine Form—By The Successive Gatherings Of Formally Acknowledged "Ruchira Sannyasin" Devotees Directly and Formally Extended From Those "Ruchira Sannyasin" Devotees Formally Established and Formally Acknowledged By Me During The Avataric Physical Lifetime Of My Bodily Human Divine Form) To Act As Instruments (or, In The Case Of By-Me-Spiritually-Empowered Places and Things, To Act As Agents) Of The Transmission Of My Avatarically Self-Revealed Divine Spiritual Presence and Revelation-Word Of Instruction.

The (Formally Established and Formally Acknowledged) Worldwide Sacred Institutional and Cooperative Culture (or Truly Global Ashram) Of My Listening Devotees, My Hearing Devotees, and My Seeing Devotees (Which Sacred Institutional and Cooperative Culture, or Truly Global Ashram, Includes every individual who Is A Formally Acknowledged and True Practitioner Of The Only-By-Me Revealed and Given Way Of The Heart, or Way Of Adidam) Is Called To Communicate, Advocate, and Confess (or Truly Confirm and Affirm) My Avatarically Self-Revealed (and Always Me-Revealing) Divine Word and My Avatarically Self-Manifested (and Always Me-Revealing) Divine Leelas, and To Communicate and Advocate My Avatarically Self-Revealed (and Always Me-Revealing) Divine Image-Art, To <u>all</u> who Would Listen To Me, and To <u>all</u> who Do Listen To Me, and To <u>all</u> who (Having Listened Well To Me) Have Truly Heard Me, and To <u>all</u> who (Having Heard Me) Are Truly and Clearly Seeing Me.

And The (Formally Established and Formally Acknowledged) Worldwide Sacred Institutional and Cooperative Culture (or Truly Global Ashram) Of My Listening Devotees, My Hearing Devotees, and My Seeing Devotees Is Called To Extend (or To Be The Extension Of) My Avatarically Given Divine

Regard, Demand, and Help—To all who Would (and To all who Do) Listen To Me, and To all who Hear Me, and To all who See Me. Altogether, The Sacred Institution Of Adidam Is The Bearer Of The Perfect Divine Truth, By Virtue Of Extending My Avatarically Incarnate Truth-Bearing Divine Person Into the world—For The Sake Of all beings, in all times and places.

I Have Given and Called Upon Many Means For The Sake Of My Divine Self-Revelation To all-and-All.

Therefore, and By These Many Means, Identify Me, Feel (and Thereby Contemplate) Me, Realize Me (Most Ultimately) As I Am—and Do Not Ever Withdraw From Me.

I Will Never Withdraw From You.

Always Abide With Me In Faithful Love—Even From The Beginning Of Your Formal Vow Of Practice Of The Only-By-Me Revealed and Given Way Of The Heart (or Way Of Adidam).

And Always Be The Champion Of The Devotionally Me-Recognizing and Devotionally To-Me-Responding Practice That Is The Only-By-Me Revealed and Given Way Of The Heart (or Way Of Adidam).

Therefore, All My Listening Devotees, All My Hearing Devotees, and All My Seeing Devotees Should Be My "Bright" Advocates In this world.

The Transcendental (or Perfectly Unconditional), and Inherently Spiritual, and Inherently egoless, and Inherently Non-Separate, and Inherently Indivisible, and Self-Evidently Divine Self-Condition and Conscious Light Of all-and-All Is Real God—The Source, The Substance, The Ultimate Condition, and The Very Being Of the conditional (or Separate) self of each and every conditionally Manifested being, and Of conditional Nature Itself.

The Only-By-Me Revealed and Given Way Of The Heart (or Way Of Adidam) Is (Via Its Real and Right Practice, and Only and Entirely By Means Of My Avatarically Self-Revealing Divine Spiritual Grace) The True, Complete, and (Ultimately) Perfect Way To Realize and (By Means Of ego-Transcending Realization) To (Non-Separately) Be The "Bright" Spiritual, Transcendental, Perfectly Unconditional, Inherently egoless, and Self-Evidently Divine Self-Condition (or One and Only Conscious Light).

The Transcendental, Perfectly Subjective, Inherently Spiritual, Inherently egoless, Inherently Perfect, Perfectly Unconditional, and Self-Evidently Divine Self-Condition Is The Only Condition That Is.

All conditional appearances, all relations (and The Feeling Of Relatedness Itself), all others and Otherness, and All Separateness Of Presumed self Are Mere Apparitions, Made By Apparent Modification Of The Self-Existing, Self-Radiant, Inherently egoless, and Self-Evidently Divine Condition (or Conscious Light) Of Being (Itself).

As Soon As The Awareness Of conditional Nature arises, The Divine Self-Condition May Also Experience The Illusion That It Is Not Itself—but That It Is a conditional self (or egoic body-mind) among others in a conditional world that it Cannot Account For.

From Then On, There Is The Struggle To Achieve ego-survival (Against opposition)—and To Achieve Joy.

If such an ego-"I" Encounters Me—The Avatarically Self-Revealed Divine Person (and The Avatarically Self-Revealed Divine Word) Of Reality and Truth (Who Is, Eternally, The One, and Only, and Self-Existing, and Self-Radiant Transcendental, Perfectly Subjective, Inherently Spiritual, Inherently egoless, Inherently Perfect, Perfectly Unconditional, and Self-Evidently Divine Self-Condition, In Divinely Self-Conscious Person)—Then The Way Of Divine Self-Realization Can Become Attractive, and A New (and Truly Divine) Way Of Life Is Possible. However, The Struggle As a conditional self (Even To The Degree Of The egoic self-Suppression Of The Heart's Inherent Devotional Recognition-Response To My Avatarically Given Divine Self-Revelation Of The Transcendental, Perfectly Subjective, Inherently Spiritual, Inherently egoless, Inherently Perfect, Perfectly Unconditional, and Self-Evidently Divine Self-Condition) Tends To Continue—Until The Heart Truly Listens To Me and (In Devotional Recognition-Response To Me) Opens (By Means Of My Avatarically Self-Transmitted Divine Spiritual Grace) To The Only-By-Me Revealed and Given Way Of The Heart (or Way Of Adidam), Which Is The One and True and Altogether Complete Way That Always Devotionally Recognizes, and Always Devotionally Exercises, and (At Last) Most Perfectly Realizes The Inherently egoless Heart Itself.

The Transcendental, and Perfectly Subjective, and Inherently Spiritual, and Inherently egoless, and Inherently Perfect, and Perfectly Unconditional, and Self-Evidently Divine Self-Condition, Coincident With The Total Context Of conditional Nature, Is (It Appears, In The Case Of every conditionally Manifested individual being) a conditional self (or Even A conditional Contraction In Relation To conditional Nature). In the egoic case, The One and Only Conscious Light Falsely Presumes Itself To Be limited and Threatened, and Associated With A Great Power and Multiplicity That Is Not The One and Only Conscious Light. Thus, The One and Only Conscious Light Feels Identified With a conditional body and a conditional mind, and the conditional body-mind Thus Functions Not Only As The Means For Perceiving (and Relating To) all that Is Apparently Not-Self (or Apparently Not The One and Only Conscious Light) but it Also Functions As The Seat Of Contraction From all that Is (Apparently) Not-Self.

The Only-By-Me Revealed and Given Way Of The Heart (Whether In The

Manner Of The Devotional Way Of Insight Or In The Manner Of The Devotional Way Of Faith) Begins With The Devotional and (In Due Course) Spiritual Process Of Listening To Me—or A "Reality Consideration" Of the conditional self and How it Operates As self-Contraction.

In The Right Practice Of The Only-By-Me Revealed and Given Way Of The Heart, This True Listening To Me Becomes True Hearing Of Me—or Most Fundamental self-Understanding, Operative As The Free Capability For ego-Transcendence.

When (By Means Of My Avatarically Self-Transmitted Divine Spiritual Grace) Sympathy With the self-Contraction Has Fully Relaxed By These Means, The Beginner's Original (or Foundation) Feeling-Motive Toward ego-Transcendence Is Uniquely Magnified and Activated, Such That It Becomes A Directly and Comprehensively Effective Impulse.

When That Impulse Has (Thus) Become Really (Directly, and Comprehensively) Effective, The Same Feeling-Motive, or Open Heart, Goes On To The Next Developmental Stage Of The Only-By-Me Revealed and Given Way Of The Heart—Which Is Seeing Me, or Heart-Attraction (and Both Spiritually Activated and Hearing-Based, and, Also, Fully Technically Responsible, Heart-Response) To My Avatarically Self-Transmitted Spiritual (and Spirit-Baptizing) Divine Presence.

This Spiritual Heart-Response (or Spiritually Activated, and, Spiritually, Fully Technically Responsible, and Truly Devotionally Me-Recognizing Devotion To Me) Permits A Greatly Magnified In-Filling With My Avatarically Self-Transmitted Divine Spirit-Energy (or Divine Self-Radiance).

And That Divine Spiritual In-Filling (or Constant Spiritual Baptism, By Me) Permits The Fully Devotionally Me-Recognizing and Fully Devotionally To-Me-Responsive Practice Of The Way Of The Heart—Such That, By Progressive Stages, The Theatre Of egoity Is Out-Grown (Most Ultimately, In The Fullness Of Divine, and Inherently Most Perfect, Self-Realization).

Most Ultimately, When (In The Progressive Course Of The Only-By-Me Revealed and Given Way Of The Heart, or Way Of Adidam) My (Avatarically Self-Revealed) Transcendental, Perfectly Subjective, Inherently Spiritual, Inherently egoless, Inherently Perfect, and Self-Evidently Divine Self-Condition Is (By Means Of My Avatarically Self-Revealing Divine Spiritual Grace) Inherently Most Perfectly Realized—conditional Nature, conditional others, conditional body, conditional mind, and conditional self Are Inherently Most Perfectly Transcended In My (Avatarically Self-Revealed) Transcendental (or Self-Existing, and Perfectly Unconditional), and Perfectly Subjective, and Inherently Spiritual (or Self-Radiant), and Inherently egoless, and Inherently Perfect, and Self-Evidently Divine Self-Condition.

Thus (By Means Of My Avatarically Self-Transmitted Divine Spiritual Grace) It Is Realized. There Is Only The Transcendental (and Perfectly Subjective, and Inherently Spiritual, and Inherently egoless, and Inherently Perfect, and Perfectly Unconditional, and Self-Evidently Divine) Self-Condition—and The Not-Self (or All Apparent Separateness and "Difference") Is An Illusion (or An Illusory—or Transparent, or Merely Apparent—and Un-Necessary, and Inherently Non-Binding, conditional Play Upon The Transcendental, Perfectly Subjective, Inherently Spiritual, Inherently egoless, Inherently Perfect, Perfectly Unconditional, and Self-Evidently Divine Self-Condition).

Thus (By Means Of My Avatarically Self-Transmitted Divine Spiritual Grace) It Is Realized. There Is Only My Divine Love-Bliss—Self-Existing and Self-Radiant. And—By Merely Self-Abiding In The ego-Transcending (or Non-Separate, and Non-"Different") Realization Of My Divine Self-Condition—The Deluding, Binding, and Joy-Suppressing Power Of conditional Existence Is Transcended.

Avatar Adi Da Samraj
The Mountain Of Attention Sanctuary, 2002

SUTRA

10

The Divine Heart-Way That Was Revealed Via The Spontaneous Ordeal Of My Own Avataric Self-Submission Is A Divine Self-Revelation To all beings.

The Basic Signs Of The Divine Heart-Way That Appeared In My Own Case Are The Inevitable Signs That Will and Must Appear In the case of any conditionally Manifested being who Completely Resorts To Me, The (Avatarically Self-Revealed) Transcendental, Inherently Spiritual, Inherently egoless, and Self-Evidently Divine Person (or Divine Self-Condition)—The All-Outshining Divine Source-Condition In Whom (or In Which) all beings and worlds Are arising.

In My Own Case, The Divine Heart-Way Was Demonstrated Via The Total Range Of Fundamental Disciplines, Stages, and Signs That May Appear (or That May Be Necessary) In The Process Of Most Perfect Divine Awakening—and Those Disciplines, Stages, and Signs Included All The Basic Disciplines, Stages, and Signs That Must (or, Otherwise, May) Progressively Characterize The Divine Heart-Way In The Case Of Any (and Every) True Practitioner Of The Only-By-Me Revealed and Given Way Of The Heart (or Way Of Adidam). Therefore, As Revealed By My Own Demonstration In and By Means Of My "Sadhana Years", The Basic Practice For All Practitioners Of The Only-By-Me Revealed and Given Way Of The Heart Involves A Total Devotional Culture Of Progressive ego-Transcendence—Including The Primary Practice Of (Searchlessly Me-Beholding) Devotional self-Surrender (or Total psycho-physical ego-Surrender, and, Ultimately, Inherently Perfect Heart-Surrender, Of attention, and feeling, and body, and breath To My Avatarically Self-Revealed Divine Form, and Presence, and State Of Person) and Devotional Reception Of My Avatarically Self-Transmitted Divine Spirit-Energy, and The Responsive Practices Of The "Conscious Process" (or The Disciplining Of attention) and "Conductivity" (or The Disciplining Of feeling and body and breath In Response To The Devotional Reception Of My Avatarically Self-Transmitted Divine Spirit-Energy) and All The By-Me-Given functional, practical, relational, and Cultural Disciplines.

There Is No Way That Is As Great, or As Direct, or As Complete, or Even As "Easy" As The Only-By-Me Revealed and Given Way (and ego-Transcending Process) Of The Heart (or Way Of Adidam). Indeed, The Only-By-Me Revealed and Given Way Of The Heart (or Way Of Adidam) Is A Most Perfectly Direct and Inherently Un-Complicated Way, Inherently Free Of self-Generated (and self-Concerned) ego-Effort (Because It Is Entirely Based On Devotionally Me-Recognizing and Devotionally To-Me-Responsive Counter-egoic Effort). Therefore, The Right, True, Full, and Complete Practice and (At Last) Most Perfect Fulfillment Of The Only-By-Me Revealed and Given Way Of The Heart (or Way Of Adidam) Is Infinitely Simpler and Easier and Quicker Than the ego (By Exercising its own self-"guruing" Effort) Would Make It.

In My "Sadhana Years", My Own Practice Of The Progressive Divine Heart-Way Was Spontaneous, Generally Uninformed, and Exceptionally Difficult. Even Though I Found Strong and Compassionate Teachers Who Were Real Spirit-Baptizers (or Transmitters Of Spiritual Energy and Blessing), I Found No Tradition (or Any Gathering Of Traditions) That Communicated Complete Wisdom To My Loud Requiring Heart, and I Found No Single Spiritual Master (or Any Number Of Spiritual Masters) Who (Either Individually Or All Together) Taught or Affirmed <u>All</u> The Secrets Of The Complete Divine Process That I Was Avatarically Born To Reveal. Therefore, I Had To Discover The Fullest Extent Of The Divine Heart-Way By Myself, Through A Hard School Of self-Observation and Spontaneous Inspiration, Guided (Implicitly) By The "Bright" Divine Disposition In Which I Was Uniquely Born, and Served (Uniquely, Spontaneously) In My Course By Sudden Revelations and Visitations Of My Own Divine Self-"Brightness".

Even From The Earliest Days Of The Avataric Physical Lifetime Of My Bodily (Human) Divine Form, I Have Spontaneously Manifested The Unique Display Of The Divinely "Crazy" and Divinely "Heroic" Course. In My Own Case, There Was, Even From The Earliest Days Of The Avataric Physical Lifetime Of My Bodily (Human) Divine Form, An <u>Absolute</u> Impulse To Realize (or, Truly, To Restore The Realization Of) The Perfect Freedom Of The "Bright" Heart Itself (Which Is My Own Very and Divine Self-Condition). Indeed, From Those Earliest Days Onward, No Other "Consideration" Held Any Attraction, Interest, or Significance For Me. Inevitably, I Was Associated, By My Bodily (Human) Birth, With Every Kind Of life-Contradiction and ordinary human Tendency and ordinary human Adaptation, and With The Entire Range Of Apparent Problems and egoic Patterns That Result From All Of That. However, In My Struggle To Confront and Transcend The Problems Of human life, I Did Not Choose (In The idealistic Manner) Merely To Adapt To conventionally ideal behaviors. It Was Inherently and Immediately Clear To Me That

I Had To Transcend everything, In Order, Again, To Most Perfectly Realize My Own Native and "Bright" Divine Self-Condition. Thus, It Was Clear To Me That I Had To Embrace everything—All The Contradictions, All The Positives, All The Negatives, everything gross, everything subtle, everything Spiritual, everything (and everyone) Altogether—and (Thereby) To Deny Not anything or any one, To Avoid Not anything or any one, but To Embrace everyone, To Endure everything, To Pass Through everything, To Suffer everything, To Enjoy everything, To Do everything. I Was Intuitively Certain That Only Thus Would I Be Able To Unqualifiedly Establish, In The Avataric Physical Lifetime Of My Bodily (Human) Divine Form, The Firm Absolutization Of My Own Disposition In "Brightness".

For Me, There Was Never Any Possibility Other Than The "Reckless" (or Divinely "Crazy" and Divinely "Heroic") Course Of all-and-All-Embrace—and I Began This Uniquely "Crazy" and "Heroic" Sadhana, Most Intensively, At The Beginning Of My Adult Life. Indeed, I Have Always Functioned, and Will Always Function, In This Divinely "Crazy" and Divinely "Heroic" Manner. The Inherently egoless "Crazy" and "Heroic" Manner Is One Of My Principal Divine Characteristics—Whereby I Can (Always, and Now, and Forever Hereafter) Be Identified. Therefore, I (Characteristically) Functioned In This "Crazy" and "Heroic" Manner Throughout All Of My "Sadhana Years", and Throughout All The Years Of My Avatarically Self-Manifested Divine Teaching-Work and My Avatarically Self-Manifested Divine Revelation-Work—and I Have Done So (and Will Forever Continue To Do So) Throughout All The Divine-Self-"Emergence" Years Of My Avatarically Self-Manifested Divine Blessing-Work (Both During, and Forever After, My Avataric Physical Human Lifetime). All My Avatarically Self-Manifested Divine Spiritual Work Is A Divinely "Crazy" and Divinely "Heroic" Effort That Avoids Not anything or anyone—but Which Always Divinely Blesses everything and everyone.

Once My Own Ordeal Of Divine Self-Realization Was (By Virtue Of Most Perfect Re-Awakening) Complete, A Most Perfectly Direct and Most Perfectly Complete and (From The Beginning) Fully Instructed and Completely Informed and Directly ego-Transcending Divine Heart-Way Became Possible For all others. Therefore, The Only-By-Me Revealed and Given Way Of The Heart (or Way Of Adidam)—Which Is The Divine Heart-Way That Is Awakened and Fulfilled By Means Of My Avatarically Self-Transmitted Divine Spiritual Grace, Through Direct (Me-Recognizing Devotional, and Contemplative, and Totally psycho-physically Active) Heart-Response To My Self-Evidently Divine Person—Became Possible For even all conditionally Manifested beings. And That Divine Heart-Way Is The Only-By-Me Revealed and Given Heart-Way Of Me-Recognizing Devotional, Contemplative, and Totally psycho-physically

Active Response To My Avatarically Self-Revealed Divine Word, My Avatarically Self-Revealed Divine Image-Art, My Avatarically Self-Manifested Divine Leelas, My Avatarically-Born Bodily (Human) Divine Form, My Avatarically Self-Transmitted Spiritual (and Always Blessing) Divine Presence, and My Avatarically Self-Revealed (and Very, and Transcendental, and Perfectly Subjective, and Inherently Spiritual, and Inherently egoless, and Inherently Perfect, and Self-Evidently Divine) State.

By Means Of My Own Divine Ordeal Of Birth, Sadhana, and Re-Awakening, I Have Most Perfectly Realized and Most Perfectly Revealed My Own and Very and Self-Evidently Divine Self-Condition—Which Is The Inherently Perfect (or Eternal) Self-Condition and Source-Condition Of all conditionally Manifested beings. And, By Means Of My Avataric Birth (and Subsequent Divine Ordeal Of Re-Awakening), I Have (Now, and Forever Hereafter) Established My Inherently Perfect Agency (or The Effective Presence Of My Own Divine Means) In every plane Of The Mandala Of The Cosmic Domain. Therefore, The Divine Heart-Way For all others Can, As A Result Of My Avataric Intervention Into The Cosmic (or conditionally Manifested) Domain, Become The Most Direct One Of Listening To Me, and Hearing Me, and Seeing Me, and Realizing Me—By Means Of Devotional Recognition-Response To Me, and Devotional Surrender (Of Separate and Separative self) To Me (and In Me).

The Adept-Realizer Is The Necessary Source Of Faith, Verity, and Help. The Adept-Realizer Is The Necessary Agent Of Demonstration That Proves All Truth. The Adept-Realizer Is The Necessary Sign Of Real God, That Authenticates Real God and All Auspiciousness To Man. And Such Has Been Proclaimed and Constantly Verified Since The Ancient Days. Therefore, Embrace Me and Realize Me—For I Am The Self-Revealed Divine (and Inherently egoless) Person Of Reality and Truth. And I Am Divinely Self-Manifesting As The Avataric Adept-Realizer Of My Own Self-Evidently Divine Self-Condition (Which Is The Source-Condition Of all-and-All). And I Am The Final and Inherently Perfect Fulfillment and Sourceful Great Gift Of The Great Tradition Of Adept-Realizers. And My Great Avataric Incarnation Has Been Prophesied By All The Traditions Of The Great Tradition Of Mankind, Since The Ancient Days.

I Am The Source Of Faith, Verity, and Help For all who Listen To Me, and all who Hear Me, and all who See Me. Therefore, Even all conditionally Manifested beings Must Be Thus Heart-Moved and Served By Me—or Else Even The Heart-Impulse To Most Perfectly ego-Transcending Real-God-Realization Will Not Really, Truly, and Most Effectively Awaken (For Lack Of My all-and-All-Liberating "Bright" Divine Sign, and My Avatarically all-and-All-

Completing Divine Word, and My Avatarically all-and-All-Revealing Divine Image-Art, and My Now, and Forever Hereafter, Divinely Self-"Emerging" Avataric Blessing-Work). And If There Is No Fullest Devotional Heart-Recognition Of Me and Fullest Devotional Heart-Response To Me, Even The By-Me-Awakened Will To Really ego-Transcending (and Truly and Completely Heart-Effective) Heart-Practice In The Necessary Course Of The Only-By-Me Revealed and Given Way Of The Heart Will, Inevitably, Fail To Find Its By-Me-Gifted Heart-Motive and Heart-Fulfillment.

Since The Ancient Days, The Person, The Total Sign, The Every Word, and All The Leelas Of The Adept-Realizer Have Been Praised and Embraced As The Sources (or The Singular Source) Of Grace, Faith, Inspiration, Guidance, Instruction, Purifying Effect, Direct (Realization-Accomplishing) Spirit-Transmission, and (By Grace Accomplished) Real-God-Realization Itself. And This Is (or Must Be) So Now (and Now), For all those who Listen To Me, and all those who Hear Me, and all those who See Me—and, Therefore, For Even all who Love Me.

The Only-By-Me Revealed and Given Way Of The Heart (or Way Of Adidam) Is Not The Problem-Based and ego-Based Path Of Seeking For ego-Fulfillment In any realm. Even Though The Developmental Process Of The Only-By-Me Revealed and Given Way Of The Heart Is Inevitably Associated With The First Six (Various, and Progressive) Stages Of Life, and Is Characterized (In Its Ultimacy, and Even From The Beginning) By The Only-By-Me Revealed and Given Seventh Stage Of Life—and Is Also Associated With, and Characterized By, Many Potential (and Various, and Progressive) Signs Of Real-God-Realization—The Only-By-Me Revealed and Given Way Of The Heart Is Not Based On A Search For Signs, or A Search For Any conditional Result. Rather, The Only-By-Me Revealed and Given Way Of The Heart (or Way Of Adidam) Is (or Must Become) The Way Of Always Present ego-Transcendence (or By-My-Grace-Given Always Present self-Understanding and Always Present Transcending Of The Search That Motivates the conditional self). And That Divine Way (Once It Is Truly Established) Becomes (By Means Of My Avatarically Self-Transmitted Divine Spiritual Grace) Direct (and Directly ego-Transcending) Devotional (and, In Due Course, Spiritual) Heart-Communion With Me—Even (At Last) To The Inherently Most Perfect Degree Of Most Ultimate (and Inherent) Self-Identification With My (Avatarically Self-Revealed) Transcendental, Inherently Spiritual, Inherently egoless, and Self-Evidently Divine Self-Condition (Which Is The Source-Condition Of all-and-All).

The Transcending Of the Separate and Separative ego-self (or Total psycho-physical self-Contraction) Is The Necessary Practice (and The Very

Context) Of The Only-By-Me Revealed and Given Way Of The Heart (or Way Of Adidam)—Whether At The Very Beginning Or In Any Subsequent Stage (or moment) Of Practice. And (In The Only-By-Me Revealed and Given Way Of The Heart) The Necessary Course Of ego-Transcendence Is Simplified (and Directly Established) By The Release Of attention From self-Concern—and This By Means Of The Devotionally Me-Recognizing and Devotionally To-Me-Responding Surrender Of attention (With Feeling) To My Avatarically Full-Given and Divinely Self-Revealing Bodily (Human) Form and Word and Image-Art and Leelas, and (Progressively, or Eventually) To My Fullest (Spiritual) Heart-Transmission, and (Ultimately) To The Inherently Perfect "Bright" Divine Self-Revelation That Is My Avatarically Self-Revealed (and Very, and Transcendental, and Perfectly Subjective, and Inherently Spiritual, and Inherently egoless, and Inherently Perfect, and Self-Evidently Divine) State. Therefore, This Divine Way (or Divine Heart-Process) Is The Way That I Made Clear (and Always Make Clear) To My Listening Devotees (or All My Devotees who Would Hear Me and See Me, Whether By The Devotional Way Of Insight Or By The Devotional Way Of Faith).

Now That My Struggle To Teach Is Complete, I Openly Declare and Affirm That I Am The One and Only Divine Heart-Master. I Am The One and Only Man Of "Radical" Understanding, The Divine Adept, The Hridaya-Samartha Sat-Guru, Who (Now, and Forever Hereafter) Teaches, and Most Perfectly En-Light-ens, The Heart. I Am The Ruchira Avatar, The Avatar Of Infinite "Brightness", and I Am The Love-Ananda Avatar, The Avatar Of Infinite Love-Bliss, and I Am Da, The "Bright" Divine Heart Itself (Which Is Love-Bliss Itself). My Teaching-Revelation Is Complete and All-Completing. My Personal Agency Is Indivisible, Indestructible, and Full Of Light. And The Way For all who Listen To Me, and For all who Hear Me, and For all who See Me Is Adidam—Which Is The One and Only By-Me-Revealed and By-Me-Given Way Of The Heart, and Which Is The Way Of Devotional Sacrifice Of the ego-"I" (or Total psycho-physical self-Contraction) To Me (The Avatarically Self-Revealed Transcendental, Inherently Spiritual, Inherently egoless, and Self-Evidently Divine Self-Condition, and Source-Condition, In Person).

All The Years Of The Avataric Physical Lifetime Of My Bodily (Human) Divine Form Are My Self-Revelation Of My Own (Inherently egoless, or Most Perfectly Non-Separate, and, Self-Evidently and Truly, Divine) Person To You.

My Avataric Self-Revelation Is Not A Revelation Of an individual ego, or Of any discrete (or Separate) form whatsoever.

My Avataric Self-Revelation Is The Revelation Of The Self-Evidently Divine Person (and The Self-Evidently Divine Self-Condition) Of Reality Itself.

I Am The One You Must Realize.

I Am The Person (and The Self-Condition) To Be Realized—By Transcending conditional form and Realizing The Unconditional Source-Condition.

I Am The Eternal Person—Which Is The Self-Evidently Divine Self-Condition, and The Self-Evidently Divine Source-Condition, Of all-and-All.

I Am The True Divine Person—The Inherently egoless Personal Presence Of Reality and Truth.

Therefore, My Avataric "I" Of Divine Self-Revelation Does Not Refer To "Me" As a Merely Separate person, form, or body-mind.

My Avataric Body-Mind Is egoless, Transparent, "Bright", Non-Separate, and Indefinable—In Me.

I Am Both Principle and Person—Indefinable, and Beyond ego.

I Am You, but Not In The Sense That I Have Become You.

I Am every one (each and all), but Not In The Sense That I Have Become any one (or Even all), or Will Yet Become any one (or Even all), or Will (In Due Course) Become each and all.

It Is Inherently The Case That I Am You.

It Is Inherently The Case That I Am every one (each and all).

Therefore, It Is Not Necessary For Me To Undergo Any Transformation In Order To Be any one.

I (Myself, As I Am) Did Not Undergo Any Transformation In Order (During The Avataric Physical Lifetime Of My Bodily Human Divine Form) To Be The Avataric Body-Mind Through Which I Did My Divine Teaching-Work and My Divine Revelation-Work.

I (Myself, As I Am) Have Not Been (Even To The Slightest Degree) Transformed By My Avataric Appearance In Bodily (Human) Divine Form.

I (Myself) Am (As I Am) The Same During The Avataric Physical Lifetime Of My Bodily (Human) Divine Form As After (and Forever After) The Death Of My Avatarically-Born Bodily (Human) Divine Form, and As Before The Avataric Birth Of My Bodily (Human) Divine Form.

I (Myself) Am (As I Am) Eternally Exactly As I Am (and As I Have Always Been).

I Am The "Bright"—Itself.

This "Brightness" Speaks.

The "Bright" Is Born As This, My Avataric Body-Mind.

My Divine Spiritual Descent Upon the body-mind Of My Devotee—As The "Thumbs"—Is My Avataric Divine Means.

All This Was Given From The Avataric Birth Of This, My Bodily (Human) Divine Form.

Indeed, These Words—The "Bright" and The "Thumbs"—Were Generated By Me As An Infant.

I Am Uttering To You The Revelation That Was Present At My Birth and In My Infancy—and Nothing Whatsoever Has Been Added To It or Taken Away From It.

Nothing In The Human Experience Of This, My Avataric Body-Mind, Has Modified My Revelation or limited It In The Slightest.

My Avatarically-Given Revelation Is A Divine Spiritual Revelation For The Sake Of all beings.

Therefore, Heart-Recognize Me, and Heart-Respond To Me.

Turn To Me. Receive Me. Constantly Know Me.

If You Do This, You Will Be Certain Of The Truth I Am Telling You.

My Avataric Divine Self-Revelation Is Not Merely To Be believed. My Avataric Divine Self-Revelation Is To Be Received, Experienced, Entirely Known, Confirmed, Proven, and Tangibly Demonstrated.

The Divine Way Of Truth Transcends All Wisdom That Is Otherwise "Useful" To ego-Based Seekers. The Revelation Of The Divine Way Of Truth Makes All ego-Based Seeking A Mere Diversion From The Truth. The Practice Of The (Necessarily, Counter-egoic and ego-Transcending) Divine Way Of Truth Depends On The <u>Immediate</u> <u>Vanishing</u> Of egoity, Rather Than On <u>Any</u> <u>Exercise</u> Of merely egoic Traits. Therefore, <u>No</u> <u>one</u> Is egoically Qualified To Realize The Truth. Indeed, <u>No</u> <u>one</u> Is egoically Qualified Even To <u>Approach</u> The Truth—or To Enter and Begin The Divine Way Of Truth. Therefore, The <u>Real</u> (and <u>Really</u> and <u>Immediately</u> ego-Vanishing) Approach To Truth Must Be Made Possible For all-and-All—By Means Of My Avatarically Self-Transmitted (and Immediately ego-Vanishing) Divine Grace. And It Is Not Necessary For any <u>one</u> To Be Qualified For <u>Any</u> <u>Other</u> Approach To Truth—Because My Avatarically Self-Transmitted (and Immediately ego-Vanishing) Divine Grace Is (Now, and Forever Hereafter) Freely Available To all-and-All. Therefore, My Avatarically Self-Transmitted (and Immediately ego-Vanishing) Divine Grace Is The Only Necessary Competence. And My Avatarically Self-Transmitted (and Immediately ego-Vanishing) Divine Grace Cannot Be Either Deserved Or Earned. My Avatarically Self-Transmitted (and Immediately ego-Vanishing) Divine Grace Is A Paradox, Mysteriously Given. Therefore, In Order For You To Enjoy The Competence That My Avatarically Self-Transmitted Free Gift Of Immediately ego-Vanishing Divine Grace Freely and Really Establishes In My Any and Every True Devotee, It Is Only Necessary That My Free Gift Of My Self-Evidently Divine Person (Which <u>Is</u> The Very Form, and Presence, and State Of Avatarically ego-Vanishing Divine Grace) Be Honored By You, In Heart-True Devotional Acknowledgement Of Me, and Truly Devotionally Me-Recognizing and Really Devotionally To-Me-Responding Devotional Reception Of Me—and This (By Virtue Of My Avatarically Self-Transmitted, and Immediately ego-Vanishing, Divine Grace Itself) To The Degree (Most Ultimately) Of Devotionally Most Perfect Realization Of Me.

Therefore, If You Love Me, Feel (and Yield To) My Avatarically Self-Revealed Divine Sign (Of Form, and Presence, and State), and Listen To My Avatarically Self-Revealed Divine Word, and Contemplate My Avatarically Self-Revealed Divine Image-Art, and Regard My Avatarically Self-Manifested Divine Leelas, and Understand Your self-Contracted, and Separate, and Separative self (or psycho-physically enacted ego-"I"). And, When Your self-Understanding Is Full, Most Fundamental, and Fundamentally Effective, Then (With All That Capability) Surrender To My Avatarically Self-Transmitted Divine Spiritual Grace In The Spiritually Devotional Manner I Will Describe To You In This Testament. By All The Means I Will Describe To You In This Testament, I Will Attract and Awaken You To My Divine Heart-Happiness—and, At Last, To My Eternal (and Eternally "Bright") Divine Spherical Self-Domain.

All those who Listen To Me and Love Me Should Resort To Me and Be Divinely Blessed By My Avatarically Self-Manifested Person—For I Am The Divine Adept and Person Of The Heart, and My Divine Spiritual Blessing Awakens The Heart To Itself.

All those who (By Means Of My Divine Spiritual Blessing) Hear Me (and who Have, Therefore, Understood themselves, Most Fundamentally, At Heart, and who Have, By The Effective Work Of That self-Understanding, Set The Heart Free To See Me) Should Resort To Me and Be Divinely Blessed By My Avatarically Self-Manifested Person—For I Am The Divine Adept and Person Of The Heart, and My Divine Spiritual Blessing Awakens The Heart To Itself.

And all those who (By Means Of My Divine Spiritual Blessing) See Me Should Resort To Me and Be Divinely Blessed By My Avatarically Self-Manifested Person—For I Am The Divine Adept and Person Of The Heart, and My Divine Spiritual Blessing Awakens The Heart To Itself.

Therefore, All My Listening Devotees, and All My Hearing Devotees, and All My Seeing Devotees Should (Forever) Embrace The Way Of ego-Transcending Devotion To Me, By Means Of Devotionally Me-Recognizing and Devotionally To-Me-Responding Resort To My Avatarically Self-Manifested Person (Self-Manifested As The Ruchira Avatar—Adi Da Samraj).

My Arguments Relative To "Narcissus" (or the self-Contraction), Most Fundamental self-Understanding (or The Most Direct Transcending Of the self-Contraction), Divine Ignorance (or Inherently Most Perfect Realization Of What Is, or What Inherently and Perfectly Transcends the self-Contraction), and All Other Principal Forms Of My Teaching-Argument Remain Fundamental Tools For The Preparation and Ongoing Development Of All Practitioners Of

The Only-By-Me Revealed and Given Way Of The Heart (or Way Of Adidam). Indeed, All My Teaching-Arguments Are An Intelligent Call, and A Fundamental Message, To All Mankind.

Likewise, Every Practitioner Of The Only-By-Me Revealed and Given Way Of The Heart (or Way Of Adidam) Must (By All My By-Me-Given and By-Me-Spiritually-Blessed Means) Become (More and More) Capable Of True Devotional self-Sacrifice (or Really and Immediately ego-Transcending self-Surrender) In Real God (or Truth, or Reality Itself).

Therefore, My Fundamental Message To all who Listen To Me (and To all who Hear Me, and To all who See Me) In The Only-By-Me Revealed and Given Way Of The Heart (or Way Of Adidam) Is My Avatarically Full-Given Heart-Word Of Divine Self-Confession and Divine Self-Revelation As The One and Only and Self-Evidently Divine Person, and My Avatarically Full-Given Divine Heart-Word Relative To The Always Present Necessity Of My Self-Evidently Divine (and Immediately ego-Vanishing) Grace, and My Avatarically Full-Given Divine Heart-Word Relative To The Fact That My Self-Evidently Divine (and Immediately ego-Vanishing) Grace Is Always Moving, Attracting, and Drawing all conditional beings Beyond themselves, and My Avatarically Full-Given Divine Heart-Word Relative To The Progressive Transcending Of the self-Contraction (and the Total conditional self, or egoic body-mind) By Means Of My Self-Evidently Divine (and Immediately ego-Vanishing) Grace (In or Through Feeling-Contemplation Of My Avatarically-Born Bodily Human Divine Form, My Avatarically Self-Transmitted Spiritual, and Always Blessing, Divine Presence, and My Avatarically Self-Revealed, and Very, and Transcendental, and Perfectly Subjective, and Inherently Spiritual, and Inherently egoless, and Inherently Perfect, and Self-Evidently Divine State), and My Avatarically Full-Given Divine Heart-Word Relative To The Most Ultimate (and Inherently Most Perfect) "Practice" (or The Most Ultimate, and Inherently Most Perfect, Realization and Demonstration) That Is (Itself) The Self-Evidently Divine (and Inherently egoless) Self-Consciousness (and That Is, At Last, and Most Perfectly, Demonstrated In Divine Translation Into The Infinite Space and Eternal Substance Of The Heart-Sphere Of My "Bright" and Eternal Divine Spherical Self-Domain).

Avatar Adi Da Samraj
Lopez Island, 2000

SUTRA 11

"Consider" This: There Are Three Great Principles Of All Truth.

The First Principle Is The Divine Principle Of Indivisibility: Reality (Itself) Is Inherently Indivisible (One and Divine and Un-conditional and Absolute).

The Second Principle Is The Universal (or Cosmic) Principle Of Unity and Non-"Difference": The world (or The conditionally Manifested Cosmos) Is Inherently A Unity (Which, In and As Its True Self-Condition, Is Inherently Non-"Different" From The One and Indivisible and Absolute and Un-conditional Divine Reality).

The Third Principle Is The psycho-physical Principle Of Non-Separateness: The individual psycho-physical entity Is Inherently Non-Separate From The world-Unity (or The Inherently Unified Cosmic Totality, Which Is Whole and Universal) and, Also, Inherently Non-Separate From The Inherently Indivisible Divine Reality (or The One and Conscious Light That Is The One and Only Self-Condition Of all-and-All).

These Three Principles, Proposed By Me, Are (Effectively) An Integrated Whole and Single Proposition. They (Together) Comprise The philosophical (and Reality-Based, and Reality-Realization-Based) Foundation For The Only-By-Me Revealed and Given Way Of Adidam (Which Is The One and Only By-Me-Revealed and By-Me-Given Way Of The Heart). And They Are, Also, The Right and True Basis (and The Right and True Measure) For The Correct (and, Inevitably, Intellectually Liberating) Evaluation Of Any and All Possible Propositions Of philosophical Import Made (Now, or In the future, or In any time and place at all) By any one (or Any School or Tradition) at all.

Therefore (On The Basis, and By Application Of The Measure, Of The Three Great By-Me-Proposed Principles Of All Truth), "Consider" This—My Avataric Teaching-Argument That Speaks My Divine Word Of Heart.

There Is Only Light.

Light Is All There Is.

All That Is Is Light.

Light Is (Inherently) Indivisible, Non-Separate, and One Only.

The Perfectly Subjective Nature Of Inherently Indivisible Light Is Self-Existing (or Transcendental) Being and Self-Radiant (or Inherently Spiritual) Consciousness.

The Perfectly Subjective Nature Of Inherently Indivisible Light Is Consciousness Itself.

The Perfectly Subjective Nature Of Inherently Indivisible Light Is Real God, or Truth.

When Inherently Indivisible Light, or Real God, Is (Apparently) Objectified To Itself, It Appears As The Cosmic Mandala Of all conditional worlds, forms, and beings.

Thus, Inherently Indivisible Light, or Real God, Utterly Pervades all conditional worlds, forms, and beings.

All conditional worlds, forms, and beings Thus Inhere In, Are "Lived" (or Sustained) By, Are Not Other Than, and Can Directly Realize A State Of Inherently Most Perfect Self-Identification (or Indivisible Oneness) With Inherently Indivisible Light, or Real God.

Inherently Indivisible Light, or Real God, Is The Literal or Inherent Condition, Substance, Reality, Quality, and Destiny Of all conditional worlds, forms, and beings.

Inherently Indivisible Light, or Real God, Is Never Absolutely Objectified, Nor Does Any Apparent Modification Of Inherently Indivisible Light, or Real God, As any conditional world, form, or being, qualify or Really limit The Perfectly Subjective Nature Of Inherently Indivisible Light, or Real God.

Even Though Inherently Indivisible Light, or Real God, May Appear To Be Objectively Modified and limited As and By conditional worlds, forms, and beings, The Perfectly Subjective Nature Of Inherently Indivisible Light, or Real God, Remains As Always Already Free and Self-Existing Being, Inherent and Undiminished Consciousness, and Self-Radiant Love-Bliss.

Therefore, It Is Not Necessary (or Required, or Even Possible) For The Cosmic Mandala (or any conditional world, form, or being) To Evolve (As Itself) Perfectly, or To Fulfill Itself Perfectly, or To Be (conditionally) Utterly Purified, or To Be (conditionally) Utterly Released, or Even To Come (conditionally) To A Final End As A Prerequisite For Inherently Indivisible Light, Real God, or The Real Condition To Be Realized.

For Inherently Indivisible Light, Real God, or The Real Condition To Be Realized, It Is Only Necessary For The Perfectly Subjective Nature Of Inherently Indivisible Light, Real God, or The Real Condition To Be Realized.

The Way Of Realization Of Inherently Indivisible Light, Real God, The Real Condition, Truth, Love-Bliss, or Happiness Is Not The Search For Fulfillment or Release In The Context Of Apparently Objectified Light, or The Search For

Fulfillment or Release In "God" (As The Somehow and Ultimate Objective Context Of The Cosmic Mandala, or Of all conditional worlds, forms, and beings)—but It Is To Self-Identify With The Perfectly Subjective Nature Of Inherently Indivisible Light, or Of Real God (Which Is Always Already Most Prior To The Cosmic Mandala, or all conditional worlds, forms, and beings).

The Ultimate (and, Necessarily, Most Prior) Source (or Source-Condition) Of any (and every) conditional world, and Of any (and every) conditional form and conditional being (or body-mind) arising in any (and every) conditional world, Is (Necessarily, and Perfectly) Subjective To (or Indivisibly One With, and Identical To, The Very Existence, or Very Being, Of) that conditional world, form, being, or body-mind, and Not Ever Divided From it, or Objective To it, or Outside it, or Separate From it, or Related To it, or (In Any Manner) "Different" From it.

Indeed, the phenomenal (or conditional) worlds, and all the phenomenal (or conditional) beings that appear within the phenomenal (or conditional) worlds, Are Not (themselves) merely physical worlds (or physical beings). Rather, As Direct Observation Proves, all phenomenal (or conditional) worlds, and all phenomenal (or conditional) beings, Are (themselves) Always and Entirely psycho-physical worlds (and psycho-physical beings).

Therefore, Necessarily, The Inherently Non-Separate (and Inherently Indivisible) Divine Source-Condition Of all phenomenal (or conditional) worlds (and Of all phenomenal, or conditional, beings) Cannot Be merely physical (or merely material)—and It, Necessarily, Cannot Even Be Merely A Non-Conscious (and, Therefore, Non-psychic) Energy. Rather, The Inherently Non-Separate (and Inherently Indivisible) Divine Source-Condition Of all phenomenal (or conditional) worlds, and Of all phenomenal (or conditional) beings, Must (Necessarily) Be That Which Is At The Root Of all psychic (or mental, and subtle) conditions, and all causal (or Root-egoic) conditions, and Even all psycho-physical conditions (including all Apparently merely physical, or gross, conditions).

Therefore, The Inherently Non-Separate (and Inherently Indivisible) Source-Condition Of all phenomenal (or conditional) worlds, and Of all phenomenal (or conditional) beings, Must (Necessarily) Be Characteristically and Perfectly Of A Subjective (and Not Merely Objective) Kind, and It Must (Necessarily) Be Of The Nature Of Consciousness (Which Is At The Root Of all psychic, mental, subtle, and causal conditions or states), and It Must Also (Necessarily) Be Otherwise Manifest (or Apparent) As Inherently Indivisible and Inherently Non-Separate and Inherently Irreducible Energy (or The Primal Substance-Radiance Of Which all psycho-physical phenomena, including all Apparently merely physical, or gross, phenomena, Are Composed).

Therefore, Inherently Non-Separate Consciousness Itself, Self-Existing and Self-Radiant and Inherently Indivisible, Is, Necessarily, The Source-Condition Of all phenomenal (or conditional) worlds, and Of all phenomenal (or conditional) beings.

Inherently Non-Separate (and Inherently Indivisible) Consciousness (Itself) Is That To Which and In Which all conditional worlds, forms, thoughts, and beings, including one's own Apparently Separate self, Are arising As Apparent Modifications Of Inherently Indivisible (and Inherently Non-Separate) Light, or Real God.

Inherently Indivisible (and Inherently Non-Separate) Consciousness (Itself) Is Inherently Indivisible (and Inherently Non-Separate) Light (or Real God) Itself.

Inherently Indivisible (and Inherently Non-Separate) Consciousness (Itself) Is The Perfectly Subjective Nature Of Inherently Indivisible (and Inherently Non-Separate) Light, Spirit-Energy, or Real God.

Inherently Indivisible (and Inherently Non-Separate) Consciousness (Itself) Is The Perfectly Subjective Nature Of The Cosmic Mandala and Of all conditional worlds, forms, thoughts, and beings, including one's own Apparently Separate self.

Inherently Indivisible (and Inherently Non-Separate) Consciousness (Itself) Is Self-Radiant Love-Bliss, Happiness, or Unqualified Being.

Inherently Indivisible (and Inherently Non-Separate) Consciousness (Itself) Is That In Which (and As Which) any and every conditionally Manifested being Always Already Stands.

Therefore, To Self-Identify (or Realize Indivisible Oneness) With Inherently Indivisible (and Inherently Non-Separate) Consciousness (Itself) Is Also To Realize Indivisible Oneness With Inherent (and Inherently Perfect) Freedom, Eternal Being, and Happiness Itself (or Inherent Love-Bliss, Which Is The Self-Existing and Self-Radiant Nature Of Inherently Indivisible, and Inherently Non-Separate, Light, Spirit-Energy, or Real God).

Whatever arises conditionally (or objectively) Is Only An Apparent, Temporary, and Illusory Modification Of Inherently Indivisible Light, Spirit-Energy, Love-Bliss, or Real God.

Whatever May Appear To Be The Case objectively (Even In such a subtle form as thought) Is Only Inherently Indivisible Light, or Real God, Appearing To Be Objectified (or Appearing As conditions), but It Is Thus Appearing Only To Itself and As Itself.

If, In The Context Of any objective event or condition (including thought), The Inherently Indivisible Consciousness To Which and In Which that event or condition Is arising Is "Located" (As The Love-Blissful Feeling Of Being

Itself), Then that objective event or condition Is Inherently (and Inherently Perfectly) Transcended In The Perfectly Subjective Nature, or Reality, or Condition, Of Inherently Indivisible Light, or Real God.

Inherently Indivisible Consciousness (or Inherently Indivisible Light, or Real God) Is Inherent (and Inherently Indivisible) Love-Bliss (Itself), Always Already Free, Never Changing.

All Modifications (or changes, or conditions) Are Merely Apparent (or Illusory).

Apparent Modifications (or changes, or conditions) Do Not Change Inherently Indivisible Consciousness, Inherently Indivisible Light, or Real God, Except Apparently, From the point of view Of The Modification (or the condition, or the conditional being) Itself.

All conditional Modifications Are Illusory (or Non-Binding) appearances In The Objective (or Apparently Objectified) Aspect, Nature, Appearance, or Illusion Of Inherently Indivisible Light, or Real God.

To Self-Identify (or Realize Inherent and Indivisible Oneness) With Inherently Indivisible (and Inherently Non-Separate) Consciousness Itself (Prior To world, form, mind, others, and conditional self) Is To Realize The Perfectly Subjective (or Most Prior) Nature and Reality Of Inherently Indivisible Light, or Real God.

The phenomenal (or conditional) worlds Are Neither Necessary Nor Binding.

The arising Of phenomenal (or conditional) Existence Carries With it No Command or Implication Of Necessary Involvement On The Part Of The Perfectly Subjective (and Inherently Non-Separate, and Inherently Indivisible) Being.

You Are Always Already Free To Self-Identify (or Realize Indivisible Oneness) With The Perfectly Subjective Nature Of Reality and, Thus, To Transcend objective (or conditional) Existence Itself, As Well As Any Apparent Implication, Tendency, or Need For Involvement In It.

In The Realization Of Indivisible Oneness With The Perfectly Subjective Nature Of Inherently Indivisible Light, or Real God, all Apparent (or objective) Light-changes Are Inherently (Divinely) Self-Recognized and Transcended In The Free Love-Bliss Of Inherently Indivisible (and Inherently Non-Separate) Light Itself, or Real God.

To Realize Indivisible Oneness With Inherently Indivisible (and Inherently Non-Separate) Light (and, Thus, To Be Literally En-Light-ened), or To Realize Indivisible Oneness With Real God (and, Thus, To Be Indivisibly One With The Only One Who Is), Is To Be Transcendental (and Inherently Non-Separate, and Inherently Spiritual, and Inherently Indivisible) Divine Consciousness,

Which Is Consciousness Itself, and Which Is Light Itself, or Transcendental (and Inherently Non-Separate, and Inherently Spiritual, and Inherently Indivisible) Divine Light, The One and Only Substance Of Existence Itself, The Real Condition Of Existence Itself, Which Is Happiness Itself (or "Bright" Love-Bliss Itself).

Liberation Through Real-God-Realization (or Direct Realization Of, Necessarily, ego-Transcending Self-Identification, or Of Indivisible Oneness, With The Perfectly Subjective, Inherently Non-Separate, Inherently Indivisible, and Inherently Irreducible Reality and Truth, or The Inherently Perfect Condition Of Existence Itself) Is Senior To (and Makes Obsolete) Any Effort Of the conditional self To Be Lawful, Purified, Evolved, Fulfilled, Ended, or Released.

This Argument Is The Seed-Essence and Import Of True Religion and Of Ultimate Esotericism.

This Argument Is The Seed-Essence Of My Avatarically Full-Given Word Of Divine Teaching.

This Argument Is The Seed-Essence Of The Entire (and Total, or Full and Complete) Way Of Adidam (Which Is The One and Only By-Me-Revealed and By-Me-Given Way Of The Heart).

The Persuasiveness Of This Argument Does Not Rest On arbitrary, historical, or controversial systems of belief and conditional proof.

The Persuasiveness Of This Argument Rests On An Understanding Of Light Itself.

This Argument Is Persuasive Because It Rests On The Obvious—and It Is, Therefore, Irrefutable.

The Truth Of This Argument Is Self-Evident.

The Efficacy Of This Argument Can Be Demonstrated Only By The Direct and Real (and, Ultimately, Inherently Most Perfect) Divine Process (or Total Divine Heart-Way) Of Divine Self-Realization Itself—Which Divine Process (or Divine Heart-Way) Is The Heart-Demonstration Of Truth Itself.

The Real (and, Ultimately, Perfect) Demonstration-Process Of Divine Self-Realization (Which Process Comprises The Total, or Full and Complete, Way Of Adidam—or The Only-By-Me Revealed and Given Way Of The Heart) Requires The (Ultimately, Most Perfect, or Divine) Self-Understanding Of Consciousness (Itself) As Light (Itself).

Therefore, The Only Final and Satisfactory Proof Of This Total Argument Of Mine Is Consciousness Itself, Realized As It Is—and, Thus, As The One and Only Conscious Light, Which Is The Divine (Indivisible, Non-"Different", Non-Separate—One, Only, and Absolute) Self-Condition Of all-and-All.

Avatar Adi Da Samraj
Da Love-Ananda Mahal, 2002

SUTRA 12

"Consider" This: True Religion (or The Real Spiritual, Transcendental, and Divine Way Of Life) Begins With The Transcending Of Awe and Wonder. Conditional Existence Naturally Evokes Awe and Wonder (and Even Terrible Fear and Stark Bewilderment), but True Religion (or The Real Spiritual, Transcendental, and Divine Way Of Life) Begins With The Free (and Really ego-Transcending) Heart-Response To What Is (Otherwise) Awesome and Wonderful.

Therefore, True (and, Necessarily, Esoteric—or Non-conventional, and Non-egoic) Religion Does Not Begin With a belief (or An ego-Based, and ego-Serving, Presumption) About "God". It Begins When You Truly (and Most Fundamentally) Understand (and Feel Beyond) the egoic self-Contraction Of The Heart (or The Sometimes believing, and Sometimes disbelieving, and Always self-Protective, and Always self-Defining, and Always self-limiting Recoil Of the body-mind From the Apparently Impersonal and Loveless forces Of conditional Nature).

Real God Is Obvious To The Free (or egoless) Heart. Only The Heart (Free Of self-Contraction) Can "Locate" (or See) and Realize The True and Real Divine Person.

The conditional (or self-Contracted) Heart Does Not Realize Real God In the present—and, Therefore, the Heartless body and the Heartless mind Become Preoccupied With Seeking For ego-Fulfillment, ego-Release, and ego-Consolation, Through every kind of conditionally Attainable experience, knowledge, and belief (including merely conventional—or exoteric, or ego-Based, or "subject-object"-Based—Religious beliefs and practices).

Notwithstanding whatever is conditionally experienced, or known, or believed—Reality Is, Always and Already.

Only Reality Is Real God.

Reality Is, Necessarily, Truth.

Only Truth Is Real God.

Real God Is Reality and Truth.

Real God Is The God Of Reality and Truth.

Real God Is The God That Is Reality and Truth.

Reality and Truth Is That Which Is Always Already The Case.

Real God Is That Which Is Always Already The Case.

Therefore, Real God Need Not Be Sought.

Real God Is Only Avoided By Any Kind Of Seeking.

To Seek Is To Fail To Admit and To Realize Real God, or That Which Is Always Already The Case.

Real God Is Realized Only By "Locating" That Which Is Always Already The Case.

To "Locate" That Which Is Always Already The Case Is To Realize Non-Separation and Non-Differentiation From That Which Is Always Already The Case.

To "Locate" (and, Thus and Thereby, To Realize) That Which Is Always Already The Case Is To Transcend the ego-"I" (and even all that is merely conditional, limited, temporal, spatial, other, Separate, or "Different").

To "Locate" (and, Thus and Thereby, To Realize) That Which Is Always Already The Case Is Merely, Inherently, and Inherently Perfectly To Be That Which Is Always Already The Case.

To Be That Which Is Always Already The Case Is (Perfectly Prior To the ego-"I" and all conditions) To Be Reality and Truth.

To Be Reality and Truth Is (Perfectly Prior To the ego-"I" and all conditions) To Be Real God, As Opposed To That Which Is Otherwise (and By Myth and Error) Sought As "God".

Therefore, Real God Is Not Other, Separate, or "Different". Real God (or The Divine Person—Which Is Reality, or Truth, or That Which Is Always Already The Case) Is Always Already (Inherently and Inherently Perfectly) Prior To The "Who", The "What", The "That", The "Where", The "When", The "How", and The "Why" That Is (By conditional experience, or conditional knowledge, or conditional belief) Presumed To Be Really and Only Other, Separate, or "Different". Therefore, Real God Is Always Already Prior To the ego-"I". Indeed, Real God Is Always Already Prior To each and every conditionally Attained experience, or form of knowledge, or form of belief.

Reality (Itself) Is The Only Real God.

Reality (Itself) Is That Which Is Always Already The (One and Only) Case.

Reality (Itself) Is (Necessarily) One, Only, and Indivisible.

Reality (Itself) Is Inherently One (or Non-Dual) and Not Two (or Divisible, and Opposed To Itself).

Reality (Itself) Is Not One Of A Pair.

Reality (Itself) Is Not Characterized By The Inherently Dualistic Relationship Of cause and effect.

Reality (Itself) Is Characterized By The Inherently Non-Dualistic Equation Of Identity and Non-"Difference".

Reality (Itself) Is That In Which Both cause and effect arise As Merely Apparent Modifications Of Itself.

Reality (Itself) Is Not Realized Via The Inherently Dualistic Relationship Of subject and object.

Reality (Itself) Is Realized As The Inherently Non-Dualistic Condition Of Inherently egoless Identity and Inherently objectless Non-"Difference".

Reality (Itself) Is Not the gross, subtle, and causal (or causative) ego-"I".

Reality (Itself) Is The (Inherently egoless) Most Prior (and Self-Evidently Divine) Identity Of all-and-All.

The Inherently egoless Non-Dual Self-Condition (or Non-"Different" Identity) Of Reality (Itself) Is That Which Is Always Already The (One and Only) Case.

The Inherently egoless Non-Dual Self-Condition Of Reality (Itself)—Most Perfectly Prior To (and, Yet, Never Excluding, or Separated From) subject, object, cause, or effect—Is That Which Must Be Realized.

The Apparent self (or Separate and Separative ego-"I"), and its every object, and (Indeed) every cause, and every effect Must Be Divinely Self-Recognized As (and, Thus and Thereby, Transcended In) The One and Only (Inherently egoless, and Inherently Non-Dual, or Indivisible and Non-Separate, or Non-"Different") Self-Condition Of Reality (Itself).

The Apparent ego-"I" and the Apparent world Are Not themselves Divine.

The Apparent ego-"I" and the Apparent world Are To Be Self-Recognized (and, Thus and Thereby, Transcended) In and As That Which Is (Self-Evidently) Divine.

The Apparent ego-"I" and the Apparent world Are To Be Divinely Self-Recognized In and As Reality (Itself).

The Presumption Of "cause" Is a Principal (and, Necessarily, conditionally Attained) experience, form of knowledge, or form of belief Associated With the ego-"I". And the (Necessarily, conditionally Attained) belief In "The Ultimate Cause", and The Search For (Necessarily, conditional) experience or knowledge Of "The Ultimate Cause", Is The Ultimate Occupation Of the ego-"I". This Notwithstanding, Real God (or The One and True Divine Person—Which Is Reality, or Truth, or That Which Is Always Already The Case) Is Always Already Prior To The (Necessarily, conditionally) Presumed and Pursued "Ultimate Cause". Therefore, Real God Is Not "The Ultimate Cause" (The Solitary and Interested, or Even Deluded, First "Doer" Of conditional events). Real God (As Real God) Does Not Make effects (or Even Stand Apart From them, By Causing them). Real God (As Real God) Is Inherently Indifferent (and Perfectly Prior) To cause and effect (or every Apparent, and Apparently conditional, event).

Every Apparent event (or every Apparently caused effect), Once it has appeared, Becomes itself a cause of subsequent effects. Even every conditional being, with all of its limitations, is a cause, and the effect of causes of all kinds. This Is Why the conditional (or phenomenal) worlds Are A Struggle With Negativity and limitation. And Real God (As Real God) Is Eternally Prior (and Indifferent) To Struggle, Negativity, and limitation.

Real God Is Not The Maker Of conditional Nature.

Real God Is The Unconditional Nature (or Most Prior Condition) Of conditional Nature.

Real God Is Not Merely The Cause Of all causes and all effects.

Real God Is The Source and The Source-Condition Of all causes and all effects.

Real God Is Not The Objective Source and Source-Condition Of all causes and all effects.

Real God Is The (Perfectly) Subjective Source and Source-Condition (or Self-Condition) Of all causes and all effects.

Real God Is Not Inside (or Within) The self-Contracted Knot Of ego-"I".

Real God Is Always Outside The self-Contracted Knot Of ego-"I".

When You Transcend the self-Contraction (and The Knot) Of ego-"I", You Are Free In Real God.

When There Is No ego-"I"—Real God Is Not Outside You.

When There Is No ego-"I"—Real God Is Not Within You.

When There Is No ego-"I"—Real God Is You (Perfectly Prior To Your Apparently objective conditional self, and Perfectly Prior To Your Apparently subjective conditional self, and, Therefore, Perfectly Prior To Your Total, Complex, and Merely Apparent conditional self).

The conditional self and the worlds of the conditional self Are Not Created By Real God, Nor Were (or Are) the conditional self (itself) and the worlds of the conditional self (themselves) Perfect Originally, Nor Will (or Can) It Ever Be The Case That Real God (or, Otherwise, the conditional self, itself, or the worlds of the conditional self, themselves) Will Perfect the conditional self (itself) or the worlds of the conditional self (themselves). But Only Real God (or Reality, or Truth, or That Which Is Always Already The Case) Is Perfect, For Real God (or Reality, or Truth, or That Which Is Always Already The Case) Is Perfection (or The Perfect Itself). Therefore, the conditional self and the worlds of the conditional self May Evolve conditionally, but Only To Possible conditional Degrees (Forever Less Than Perfection Itself, Which Is The Condition Only Of Real God), and This Through The Struggle Made By The

Submission Of the lesser (or the lower) imperfect (or the lesser, or the lower, conditional) To the greater (or the higher) imperfect (or the greater, or the higher, conditional). And the conditional self and the worlds of the conditional self May, Otherwise, Devolve conditionally, but Also Only To Possible conditional Degrees (and Never To The Degree Of Absolute, or Irreversible, or More Than Illusory Separation From Real God, or From The Perfect Itself, Which Is Real God), and This Through The Struggle Made By The Submission Of the greater (or the higher) or the lesser (or the lower) imperfect (or the greater, or the higher, or the lesser, or the lower, conditional) To the even lesser (or the even lower) forms of the imperfect (or the conditional) itself. Nevertheless, and Whatever The (Relatively Evolved, or Relatively Devolved) Case May Be, The Only Way To Realize Real God (or The Transcendental, and Perfectly Subjective, and Inherently Spiritual, and Inherently egoless, and Inherently Perfect, and Self-Evidently Divine Self-Condition, and Source-Condition, Itself) Is To Progressively (or, However, Utterly) Surrender the imperfect itself (or the conditional self, and the worlds of the conditional self) To and Into Real God (or The Very, and Only, and Transcendental, and Perfectly Subjective, and Inherently Spiritual, and Inherently egoless, and Inherently Perfect, and Self-Evidently Divine Person, or Self-Condition, or Source-Condition, That Is Real God), and, Most Ultimately (and Inherently, and Inherently Most Perfectly), To Transcend the imperfect (or the conditional self and the worlds of the conditional self) In (and By Inherent, and Inherently Most Perfect, and Perfectly Subjective Self-Identification With) The Very, and Only, and Transcendental, and Perfectly Subjective, and Inherently Spiritual, and Inherently egoless, and Inherently Perfect, and Self-Evidently Divine Person (or Self-Condition, or Source-Condition) That Is Real God.

Even Though Real God (As Real God) Merely Is (Always Already, or Inherently and Eternally Prior To cause and effect), the "God"-Seeking ego-"I" (or every human being whose Heart is self-Contracted, and who, As A Result, Wants Toward "Ultimate" experience, knowledge, or belief) Characteristically Tries To Argue For experience Of, or knowledge Of, or belief In "God" (or The "Ultimate" Proposed To Be experienced, known, or believed In) By Appealing To The Logic Of cause and effect. Therefore, In their "Ultimate" Arguments For The "Ultimate", and In their (Necessarily, conditional) experiences, knowings, and believings Attained In The Course Of their Seeking For The "Ultimate", the "God"-Seeking human egos Propose That "God" Is The Cause (and The "Doer") Of everything—but, Even Though they (Necessarily, conditionally) experience, or know, or believe, these (Necessarily, conditionally) experiencing, or knowing, or believing egos Do Not Stand Free. They Only Cling To the (Necessarily, imperfect) conditional self and the (Necessarily, imperfect) worlds of the conditional self. Therefore, they Do Not Realize Real God (or The Perfect, Itself) By Heart, Through ego-Transcending Love-Communion, To The Inherently Most Perfect Degree Of Inherently Perfect Love-Bliss (Beyond All "Difference").

Real God Is The One and Only and Self-Existing and Self-Radiant Conscious Light That Is Reality (Itself).

Real God Is The God (or The Truth, The Reality, and The Self-Identity) Of Consciousness Itself.

Real God Is The God (or The Truth, The Reality, and The Self-Identity) Of Inherently Perfect Subjectivity.

Real God Is Not The "God" (or The Implicated Maker) Of conditional Nature, Separate self, and All Objectivity.

Real God Is The God (or The Truth and The Reality) Of Consciousness, Freedom, Love-Bliss, Being, and Oneness.

Real God Is Not The "God" (The Cause, The "Doer", or Even The Victim) Of Un-Consciousness (or mere causes and effects).

Therefore, Real God Is Not The "God" Of Bondage, Un-Happiness, Death (or Separation), and "Difference".

Real God Is The Subject—Not The Object.

Real God Is The Inherent Unity Of Being.

Real God Is The Integrity—Not The Cause—Of the world.

Real God Is The True Source, The Very Context, The Real Substance, The Truth-Condition, The Very Reality, The Most Prior Condition, and The Eternal "Bright" Spherical Self-Domain Of all conditions, all causes, and all effects—For all that appears Comes From Real God (but In Real God, and Only As Real God).

All "things" Are the media of all "things", but Real God Is Not The Maker—For Real God Is Like A Hidden Spring Within the water's world, and Real God Is Prior Even To Cause (and every cause), and Real God Is The Self-Domain Of Even every effect, and Real God Is The Being (Itself) Of all that appears.

Therefore, Real God Merely Is—and Is Is What Grants every appearance (every being, every thing, every condition, and every conditional process) The Divine Sign Of Mystery, Love, Bliss, and Joy.

Yes, Real God Is The Deep Of the world, and The Heart Of every Would-Be "I".

The Only-By-Me Revealed and Given Way Of The Heart (or Way Of Adidam) Is A Call To Spiritual, Transcendental, and Divine Self-Realization—Not To conventional (or ego-Based, and merely exoteric) "God"-Religion. Conventional "God"-Religion Is A Search Founded On An Illusion. That Illusion Is the ego, the Independent "I", The Separate and Separative Presumption That

Is the body-mind. Conventional "God"-Religion Is An Adventure Of Confrontation With all that Is Not The Divine Self-Condition (or Real God), but The Only-By-Me Revealed and Given Way Of The Heart (or Way Of Adidam) Is A Call To Realize Direct and ego-Transcending Devotional Communion (and, Most Ultimately, Inherently Perfect Self-Identification) With Me, The Avatarically Self-Revealed Transcendental, Inherently Spiritual, Inherently egoless, and Self-Evidently Divine Person, Source, or Self-Condition—and That Great Process (Whether It Is Developed In The Manner Of The Devotional Way Of Insight Or In The Manner Of The Devotional Way Of Faith) Is Continuously Generated In Devotional Recognition-Response To My Avatarically Self-Revealed (and Attractive, and ego-Undermining) Divine Word, and My Avatarically Self-Revealed (and Attractive, and ego-Undermining) Divine Image-Art, and My Avatarically Self-Manifested (and Attractive, and ego-Undermining) Divine Leelas, and My Avatarically-Born (and Attractive, and ego-Undermining) Bodily (Human) Divine Form, and My Avatarically Self-Transmitted (and Attractive, and ego-Undermining) Spiritual (and Always Blessing) Divine Presence, and My Avatarically Self-Revealed (and Very, and Attractive, and ego-Undermining, and Transcendental, and Perfectly Subjective, and Inherently Spiritual, and Inherently egoless, and Inherently Perfect, and Self-Evidently Divine) State—For I Am The Avataric Divine Realizer, The Avataric Divine Revealer, and The Avataric Divine Self-Revelation Of Real God, The True Divine Person, The Always Already (and Merely) Existing Reality and Truth, The Inherently Perfect (and Inherently egoless, and Self-Evidently Divine) Self-Condition (and Source-Condition) That Is The Perfectly Subjective Divine Heart Itself.

Therefore, I Call You To Listen To Me and To Hear Me, and (Thus) To Thoroughly Observe, Most Fundamentally Understand, and Effectively Transcend self-Contraction. And, When You Hear Me (and Hearing Me Has Accomplished Its First Work In You), I Call You To (Fully) Receive My Baptismal Spirit-Blessing, and To See Me From The Heart, and (Thus) To Enter Into The Spontaneous and Inevitable Process Of Always Present, Real, and True Real-God-Communion (or The ego-Surrendering, ego-Forgetting, and ego-Transcending Devotional Process Of "Locating" and Realizing That Which Is Always Already The Case).

If You Hear Me (or Most Fundamentally Understand Your conditional self, By Means Of My Avatarically Self-Transmitted Divine Spiritual Grace) and See Me (or, By Means Of My Avatarically Self-Transmitted Divine Spiritual Grace, "Locate", Devotionally Recognize, and Tangibly Feel My Avatarically Self-Transmitted Divine Spiritual Presence, From The Heart), Then, Because Of My Self-Existing and Self-Radiant (and, Altogether, Avatarically Self-Transmitted)

Divine Presence Of Person (Always Already At Your Heart, and "Bright"), The Simple Awareness Of any conditional (or phenomenal) being, thing, thought, form, event, cause, or effect Will (By Virtue Of Its Coincidence With Me) Awaken You To My Love-Bliss (and, Thereby, Move You To Fearless Praise Of Me, In The Mood Of Divine Ignorance)—Not Because You believe "God" Made that condition, but Because that condition Is (In and As Me).

I Am That Which, By Myth and Error Sought, Mankind Has Avoided At Every Turn and Phrase.

I Am The One Whom Mankind, By Seeking, Has Lost and Failed To Realize.

I Am The One From Whom Mankind, By their Failure To Realize Me, Is Now (but Not Forever) Separate and "Different".

I Am The One and Only (and Self-Evidently Divine) Person—Who Has Come (and, Now, and Forever Hereafter, here Stands) To Remove the ego From Religion (and, Thereby, To Make Religion True).

Religion Is Not, In and Of Itself (or As An Historically-Existing Tradition—or Discrete Cultural, social, and Political Phenomenon) True. Religion Cannot (Thus—In and Of Itself) Be True. Only Reality Itself (Which Is Truth, Itself) Is (In and Of and As Itself) True. Therefore, What Makes (or Can Make) Religion True Is The Whole bodily Heart-Response To (and, Ultimately, The Most Perfect Realization Of) The One and Only Reality and Truth.

Reality Itself (Which Is Truth, Itself) Is The "Music" That Makes Religion True. Therefore, True Religion Is The Whole bodily "Dance" Of Heart-Response To The One and Only Reality and Truth.

I Am The One and Only and Self-Evidently Divine Reality and Truth—Avatarically Self-Revealed To You (and To all, and All).

I Am Reality, Truth, and Oneness—Self-Existing and Self-Radiant, and (Now, and Forever Hereafter) Standing In Front Of Your eyes (and At Your Heart—and, Ultimately, As Your egolessly Me-Realizing Heart).

I Am The "Bright" One—The Only and Inherently egoless One—Who Always Already Is, and Who Must (By Means Of My Avatarically Self-Transmitted, and Immediately ego-Vanishing, Divine Spiritual Grace) Be Realized.

If There Is No Real and True (and Really and Truly "Dancing") Heart-Response To My Avatarically Self-Revealed (and Self-Evidently Divine) Form, and Presence, and State Of Person—Then There Is Not (and There Cannot Be) Any True (or Really and Truly Practiced) Religion.

If (and When) any one Hears Me and Sees Me, My Avatarically Given Divine Heart-Blessing Will Attract The Heart Beyond Every Trace Of self-Contraction (Even In The Deepest Places Of The Heart and the body-mind), and The Me-Hearing and Me-Seeing Heart Will (By ego-Surrendering, ego-Forgetting, and ego-Transcending Devotional Resort To Me Via The Process

Of That Attraction) Realize (and Be One With) Me—The Only One Who (Always and Already) Is.

Therefore, I Ask Your Heart, In The Whirl Of events: "Not By What Cause, but By What Nature (or Unconditional Condition) Is conditional Nature Allowed To Be?"

And Your Heart (Upon Hearing Me and Seeing Me Most Perfectly) Replies: "Divine Heart-Master, Divine Heart Of All Hearts, You Have—By All Your Avatarically Self-Revealed Divine Means—Revealed The Truth To Me! Self-Existing and Self-Radiant Being (Itself) Is The Unconditional Nature Of conditional Nature! It Is Self-Existing Love-Bliss—or, Simply, Self-Radiant Love (Itself)! Only You, The One and True Divine Heart-Master, Are (Eternally, and—Now, and Forever Hereafter—Avatarically) The Self-Manifestation Of The Divine Heart (Itself)! Only You Are (Eternally, and—Now, and Forever Hereafter—Avatarically) The Self-Revelation Of That Which Is Always Already The Case—and Which Is The One and Self-Evident Reality, Truth, and Real God! You Are The One and 'Bright' Divine and Only Person! It Is You To Whom and In Whom and As Whom I Am—By Means Of Your Avatarically Self-Transmitted Divine Spiritual Grace—Awake (Beyond the ego-'I')! It Is You With Whom I Am Always Already Indivisibly One—By Virtue Of Your Avatarically Given Divine Self-Revelation Of The Inherent Non-Separateness and Indivisible Oneness Of Being (Itself), Which Is Consciousness (Itself), and Light (Itself), and Love-Bliss (Itself)!"

AVATAR ADI DA SAMRAJ
Da Love-Ananda Mahal, 2003

SUTRA 13

The Apparently individual (or Separate) self Is Not Self-Existing.

The Apparently individual (or Separate) self Is Not Immortal.

The Apparently individual (or Separate) self Is Not a "spark" (or an Eternal fraction) Of Self-Radiant Divinity, and Somehow Complete (or Whole) In itself.

Only Real God—The Inherently egoless Divine Person—Is Self-Existing, Immortal, Eternal, Non-Separate, Indivisible, Complete, Whole, and Self-Radiant.

The Apparently individual (or Separate) self Is Not Inwardly (or in and of itself) Perfect, a "soul" (or A Perfect individual Consciousness), and Somehow Full Of Divine Qualities (Such As Inherent Happiness, Unconditional Love, Infinite Bliss, and Boundless Energy).

Only Real God—The Inherently egoless Divine Person—Is Perfect Consciousness (Non-Separate, Indivisible, Full Of, or Characterized By, The Qualities Of Inherent Happiness, Unconditional Love, Infinite Bliss, and Boundless Energy).

The Truth (That Sets The Heart Free) Is Not That the Apparently individual (or Separate) self (or ego-"I") Is itself Immortal and Divine, or That some fraction or dimension of the Apparently individual (or Separate) self Is Immortal and Divine—but The Truth (That Sets The Heart Free) Is That There Is Only Real God (The Real, The Truth, or That Which Is Always Already The Case).

The Apparently individual (or Separate) self arises conditionally, and Yet it Always Already Inheres In Real God.

The Apparently individual (or Separate) self is the (Total, Complex) conditional body-mind (or Apparent psycho-physical personality).

The (Total, Complex) Apparently individual (or Separate) self is arising in three Primary (and Coincident) forms—the gross (or the physical), the subtle (or the etheric, the mind of thoughts, and The Observing/Discriminating Intelligence), and the causal (or The Root-Essence Of the conditional self, or ego-"I", Which Is Separate and Separative attention itself).

The (Total, Complex) Apparently individual (or Separate) self is arising As An Apparent Modification (and Contraction) Of The Eternal Self-Radiance (or Inherent Spirit-"Brightness") Of Real God and As An Apparent Contraction Of The Transcendental (or Self-Existing) Consciousness That Is Real God.

The individual (or Separate) self (As Well As every other Apparent being and every other Apparent form or process Manifested Within The Cosmic Mandala) arises conditionally—but, Nevertheless, Always Already Inhering In Real God. Because Of This, no individual being or Apparent form is Ever Finally destroyed (or ended) In This Drama Of worlds. Every Apparent (or conditional) one and every Apparent (or conditional) thing is a process, a continuum of changes, that Persists Even Through and Beyond dissolution or death—Because Separation From The Transcendental (or Eternal), and Inherently Spiritual, and Inherently egoless, and Self-Evidently Divine Condition That Is Real God Is Not Possible.

However, Mere Continuation Is Not Happiness Itself (or The Inherent Realization Of Love-Bliss). Merely To Persist As an Apparently Separate form or process, Unconsciously Inhering In The Eternal (Real) God, Is Only To Contemplate limitation. The self-limited personality, Confined To the Apparent display of causes and effects, Is Stress-Bound To Seek Fulfillment and Release, Either By Exclusive Involvement In The Illusions Of Inwardness (As If the conditional self, Dissociated From body and mind, Were itself The Immortal Love-Bliss) Or By Extroverted and Apparently Inclusive Indulgence Of body and mind In The Illusions Of conditional experience and conditional knowledge (As If The Mandala Of The conditionally Manifested Cosmos Were, Itself, The Immortal Love-Bliss).

The Immortal (and Self-Evidently Divine) Love-Bliss Is Realized Neither By Exclusive Identification With the inward self-position Nor By Apparently Inclusive Immersion In the conditional (or phenomenal) realms. To Realize The Self-Evidently Divine Self-Condition (and Source-Condition) That Is Love-Bliss Is Necessarily A Matter Of Transcending the (Entirely self-Imposed, or self-Presumed) limits On Love-Bliss (Itself), To The Degree (Most Ultimately) Of Inherent, and Inherently Most Perfect, and Inherently (and Inherently Most Perfectly) egoless Self-Identification With Love-Bliss (Itself).

Therefore, The Only-By-Me Revealed and Given Way Of The Heart (or Way Of Adidam) Is Never A Matter Of Identification With the subjective or the objective limitations of the conditional self-position (or ego-"I"). In The Right, True, Full, and Fully Devotional Practice Of The Only-By-Me Revealed and Given Way Of The Heart (or Way Of Adidam), Both The subjective and The objective Illusions Created By the self-Contraction Are Transcended—and This Through The Process Of Real (and Most Fundamental) self-Understanding, Which (By Means Of My Avatarically Self-Transmitted Divine Spiritual Grace) Becomes Ecstasy (or ego-Transcendence) In Real God (or ego-Transcending Communion With The One In Whom the conditional self and the conditional worlds Are arising, or Appearing To arise, As Apparent Modifications Of Itself), and Which (Most Ultimately, By Means Of My Avatarically Self-Transmitted Divine Spiritual Grace) Realizes Divine Enstasy (or Awakening To Inherent, and Inherently Most Perfect, Self-Identification With My Self-Evidently Divine, and Perfectly Subjective, Self-Condition, In Which every conditional, or phenomenal, appearance, including the body-mind-self, Always Already Inheres).

The Only-By-Me Revealed and Given (Transcendental, Inherently Spiritual, and Self-Evidently Divine) Way Of Real-God-Realization Is Neither "Evolutionary" Nor ego-Fulfilling. Rather, That (Only-By-Me Revealed and Given) Way Is Founded On The Intuition (or Native Motive) Of Ecstasy (or ego-Transcendence). The Only-By-Me Revealed and Given Way Of The Heart (or Way Of Adidam) Is A Matter Of The Easeful and Heartfelt Turning (or Surrender) Of body, emotion, mind, and breath (and Even all the conditions of experience) To Me (In and As My Avatarically-Born Bodily Human Divine Form and Person), In every moment and Under all circumstances. That Practice (Of Turning The psycho-physical Faculties To Me, In and As My Avatarically-Born Bodily Human Divine Form and Person) Transcends All The experiential and "Evolutionary" Significance or content Of Even Your Most Extraordinary sensations, perceptions, and conceptions. And those who Are (Thus) Devoted To Me Transcend All Sense Of physical and mental (or psychic) Separateness (or Of Independent Existence As an Inherently Separate, and Persistently Separative, ego-"I"). When You Are (Thus) Devotionally Turned To Me, You Come To Understand That You Are Not a "soul" Born Into the body-mind (Inhering In the psycho-physical conditions Of Your Apparently Separate Existence)—but, Rather, As My True Devotee, You Understand (and, Ultimately, Most Perfectly Realize) That You Inhere (or Eternally Abide, As Undifferentiated Love-Bliss) In The Self-Existing and Self-Radiant Self-State (or Self-Condition) Of Spiritually Self-"Bright" Divine Being (Itself).

Real God Is Not The Creator.
Real God Is The Liberator.
Real God Is Not The Way In.
Real God Is The Way Out.
The Way Of Real God
Is Not The Way Of
self-Seeking,
self-Increase, and
self-Success.
The Way Of Real God
Is The Way Of self-Sacrifice
(or ego-Transcendence).

Therefore, The Only-By-Me Revealed and Given Way Of The Heart (or Way Of Adidam) Is The Great Process Of Devotional self-Sacrifice In Real God (By Means Of ego-Surrendering, ego-Forgetting, and, Always More and More, ego-Transcending Feeling-Contemplation Of My Real-God-Revealing Avatarically-Born Bodily Human Divine Form, My Avatarically Self-Transmitted Spiritual, and Always Blessing, Divine Presence, and My Avatarically Self-Revealed, and Very, and Transcendental, and Perfectly Subjective, and Inherently Spiritual, and Inherently egoless, and Inherently Perfect, and Self-Evidently Divine State). And, By Means Of This Great Process, the Total psycho-physical self Of My Devotee Is Surrendered To The Progressive Course Of (Most Ultimately, Inherent, and Inherently Most Perfect) Divine Self-Realization.

The Only-By-Me Revealed and Given Way Of The Heart (or Way Of Adidam) Is The Great Process Of Transcending the objective (or conditionally externalized) point of view <u>and</u> the conditionally subjective (or conditionally internalized) point of view, By Means Of My Avatarically Self-Transmitted Divine Spiritual Grace, Through Progressively ego-Surrendering, ego-Forgetting, and ego-Transcending Feeling-Contemplation Of (and Feeling-Identification With) My Real-God-Revealing Avatarically-Born Bodily (Human) Divine Form, My Avatarically Self-Transmitted Spiritual (and Always Blessing) Divine Presence, and My Avatarically Self-Revealed (and Very, and Transcendental, and Perfectly Subjective, and Inherently Spiritual, and Inherently egoless, and Inherently Perfect, and Self-Evidently Divine) State—Such That, Most Ultimately (By Means Of My Avatarically Self-Transmitted Divine Spiritual Grace), the (Apparent) conditional body-mind and the (Apparent) conditional world Are "Viewed" From (and Divinely Self-Recognized In and <u>As</u>) The (Inherently Perfect) Divine Subject-Position (or The Self-Existing and Self-Radiant Self-State, or Self-Condition, Of Self-Evidently Divine Being, Itself). And The Only-By-Me Revealed and Given Way Of The Heart (or Way Of Adidam) Necessarily Proceeds By Stages Of Revelation, Associated With The First Six Stages Of Life, Until The Realization and The Demonstration Of The Only-By-Me Revealed and Given Seventh Stage Of Life.

The Heart (Itself) Was Never "Created"—Nor Is There Ever any "creature" There. Therefore, The Way That Practices and (At Last) Most Perfectly Realizes and <u>Is</u> The Heart (Itself) Is The (Necessarily) <u>Esoteric</u> Way That Transcends The Illusions Of "Creator" and "Creation"—By Transcending the ego-"I".

The One and Only By-Me-Revealed and By-Me-Given Way Of The Heart (or Way Of Adidam) Is The <u>Esoteric</u> True Way (or True World-Religion) That (In The Truly Counter-egoic, and More and More Profoundly ego-Transcending, Manner) Practices and Realizes and (At Last, Most Perfectly) <u>Is</u> The Heart Itself. Therefore, Even From Its Beginnings, The Only-By-Me Revealed and Given

Way Of The Heart (or Way Of Adidam) Is Entirely Free Of ego-Based, ego-Serving, ego-Affirming, ego-Developing, and merely conventionally (or exoterically) Religious (or "subject-object"-Based) views and presumptions.

The Divine Heart Is One and Only. Therefore, The One and Only By-Me-Revealed and By-Me-Given Esoteric Way Of The Heart (or Way Of Adidam) Is, Even From Its Beginnings, The Always and Immediately ego-Transcending Way Of One—and Not The Way Of "self" and "Other" (or Of Any "Two" At All).

Avatar Adi Da Samraj
Adidam Samrajashram, 2004

SUTRA

14

I Am The Divine Heart-Master (The Avataric Divine Realizer, The Avataric Divine Revealer, and The Avataric Divine Self-Revelation Of The Divine Person—Who Is The Very, and Transcendental, and Perfectly Subjective, and Inherently Spiritual, and Inherently egoless, and Inherently Perfect, and Self-Evidently Divine Self-Condition and Source-Condition Of each and every conditionally Manifested being). Therefore, The ego-Surrendering, ego-Forgetting, and (More and More) ego-Transcending Devotional Recognition-Response To Me Is The Way (or The Essential Principle) Of The Only-By-Me Revealed and Given Way Of The Heart (or Way Of Adidam).

The Only-By-Me Revealed and Given Way Of The Heart Is (In Its Beginnings) The Devotional Process Of Listening (or The "Consideration" Of My Avatarically Self-Revealed Divine Word and My Avatarically Self-Revealed Divine Image-Art and My Avatarically Self-Manifested Divine Leelas, and The ego-Surrendering and ego-Forgetting Practice Of Feeling-Contemplation Of My Avatarically-Born Bodily Human Divine Form, My Avatarically Self-Transmitted Spiritual, and Always Blessing, Divine Presence, and My Avatarically Self-Revealed, and Very, and Transcendental, and Perfectly Subjective, and Inherently Spiritual, and Inherently egoless, and Inherently Perfect, and Self-Evidently Divine State)—Until That (Truly Devotional) Listening Becomes Most Fundamental self-Understanding (or True Hearing) and Real (and Always Immediate) ego-Transcendence (To The Degree Of True Seeing).

The Only-By-Me Revealed and Given Way Of The Heart Is (In Its Divine Spiritual Fullness) The Process Of Hearing-and-Seeing-Based Devotional (and, Thus, Feeling) Communion With Me ("Located" As My Avatarically-Born Bodily Human Divine Form, My Avatarically Self-Transmitted Spiritual, and Always Blessing, Divine Body Of Divine Presence, and My Avatarically Self-Revealed, and Very, and Transcendental, and Perfectly Subjective, and Inherently Spiritual, and Inherently egoless, and Inherently Perfect State Of Self-Evidently Divine Person).

The Only-By-Me Revealed and Given Way Of The Heart Is (In Its Divine Spiritual Fullness) The Process Of Devotional Communion With Me, To The Degree (In Due Course) Of Indivisible (and Inherently Perfect) Oneness (or

Inherent, and Inherently Most Perfect, and Most Perfectly egoless Self-Identification) With Me (The Perfectly Subjective, and Inherently Non-Separate, and Inherently Indivisible, and Self-Evidently Divine Self-Condition and Source-Condition In Which You Always Already Stand).

The Only-By-Me Revealed and Given Way Of The Heart Is (In Its Totality) The Process That (At Last, and Finally) Becomes Translation Into My Divine "Bright" Spherical Self-Domain.

Therefore, The Only-By-Me Revealed and Given Way Of The Heart (or Way Of Adidam) Is (In Its Totality) A Great Process, Wherein The Inherently Perfect (and Inherently egoless, and Perfectly Subjective, and Self-Evidently Divine) Self-Condition and Source-Condition (Which Is The Inherently egoless Heart Itself) Is (Only and Entirely By Means Of My Avatarically Self-Transmitted, and Always Immediately ego-Vanishing, Divine Spiritual Grace) Really (and, At Last, Most Perfectly) Realized.

And The Way Of The Heart Develops (In Its Totality) Through Four Progressive Stages Of Devotional Recognition-Response To Me and Devotional Realization Of Me.

The First Stage Of The Progressive Devotional Recognition-Response To Me and Devotional Realization Of Me Is This: The Divine Person (or Inherently egoless Self-Condition, and Perfectly Subjective Source-Condition) Is Revealed (As Person and Truth) By (and As) My Avatarically-Born Bodily (Human) Divine Form—For I Am (Even As My Avatarically-Born Bodily Human Divine Form) The Self-Evidently Divine Person (and The "Bright" Avatarically Self-Manifested Divine Word-Bearer) Of The Heart, and My Avatarically Self-Revealed Divine Heart-Word Is Always Present (or Directly Revealed) In (and Via, and As) My Avatarically-Born Bodily (Human) Divine Form, and I Am Always Present and Active In (and Via, and As) My Avatarically Self-Revealed (and Fully Spoken, and Fully Recorded, and Fully Written, and Fully Preserved) Divine Wisdom-Teaching, and In (and Via, and As) The Form Of My Own Divine Story (Preserved In The Recorded and Documented Form Of All My Avatarically Self-Manifested Divine Leelas), and I Am (Even As My Avatarically-Born Bodily Human Divine Form) Directly Revealed (As The Divine Person and Truth) To those who Truly Love Me (As My Avatarically Self-Revealed, and Self-Evidently Divine, Person), and who (Thus) Devotionally Recognize Me and Devotionally Respond To Me.

The Second Stage Of The Progressive Devotional Recognition-Response To Me and Devotional Realization Of Me Is This: The Divine Person (or Inherently egoless Self-Condition, and Perfectly Subjective Source-Condition) Is Revealed By (and As) My Avatarically Self-Transmitted Spiritual and all-and-All-Pervading Divine Heart-Presence Of Love-Bliss—Which Is My Always

Living (or Spiritual) and Personal Divine Presence (or Avatarically Self-Transmitted and Self-Revealed Divine Spiritual Body) Of Immediately ego-Vanishing Divine Spiritual Grace (Cosmically Extended To all beings), and Which Is Directly (and Fully) Revealed (By and As My Avatarically Given Divine Spiritual Heart-Transmission) To those who Truly Love Me (As My Avatarically Self-Revealed, and Self-Evidently Divine, Person), and who (Thus) Devotionally Recognize Me and Devotionally Respond To Me.

The Third Stage Of The Progressive Devotional Recognition-Response To Me and Devotional Realization Of Me Is This: The Divine Person (or Inherently egoless Self-Condition, and Perfectly Subjective Source-Condition) Is Revealed By (and As) My Avatarically Self-Revealed (Transcendental, Inherently Spiritual, Inherently egoless, and Self-Evidently Divine) Self-Condition (or Inherently egoless, and Inherently Perfect, State)—The One and Very and Self-Evidently Divine Self-Condition (or Inherently egoless, and Inherently Perfect, State) That Is Consciousness Itself, Beyond the ego-"I", In the case of all conditionally Manifested beings—Which One and Very Self-Condition Is The Identity and Truth Directly Revealed (By and As My Avatarically Given Divine Spiritual Heart-Transmission Of My Own, and Self-Evidently Divine, State Of Person) To those who Truly Love Me (As My Avatarically Self-Revealed, and Self-Evidently Divine, Person), and who (Thus) Devotionally Recognize Me and Devotionally Respond To Me Perfectly, By Means Of Inherent (and Inherently Perfect) Self-Identification With My Avatarically Self-Revealed (and Very, and Transcendental, and Perfectly Subjective, and Inherently Spiritual, and Inherently egoless, and Inherently Perfect, and Self-Evidently Divine) State.

The Fourth (and Final) Stage Of The Progressive Devotional Recognition-Response To Me and Devotional Realization Of Me Is This: The Divine Person (or Inherently egoless Self-Condition, and Perfectly Subjective Source-Condition) Is Revealed Merely (and Most Perfectly) As Is (Self-Existing and Self-Radiant, One and Only), and (Therefore) Merely As The Transcendental, Inherently Spiritual, Inherently egoless, and Self-Evidently Divine Self-Condition (or Consciousness Itself), Which Is The (By Means Of My Avatarically Given Divine Self-Transmission) Divinely Self-Transmitted "Bright"—or The Inherently Non-Separate, Inherently Indivisible, Inherently Irreducible, Infinitely Expanded (or Inherently Boundless), Infinitely Centerless (or Inherently egoless), and Self-Evidently Divine Sphere and Space Of Love-Bliss—and Which (One and Only) Is My Ultimate (and Inherently Perfect, and Perfectly Subjective, and Self-Evidently Divine) Avataric Self-Revelation, Given (By Means Of My Avatarically Self-Transmitted, and Always Immediately ego-Vanishing, Divine Grace) To those who Truly Love Me (As My Avatarically Self-Revealed, and Self-Evidently Divine, Person), and who (Thus) Devotionally

Recognize Me and Devotionally Respond To Me Most Perfectly, As I Am (and who, Thus, By Realizing Indivisible Oneness With Me, Awaken, Beyond the ego-"I", To Realize What, Where, When, How, Why, and Who they Really and Truly and Divinely Are).

My "Bright" Divine Spiritual Body May Be Perceived (By Inward and Upward and Overriding Sight) As (or In The conditionally Manifested Form Of) An Apparently Objective and Brilliant Clear White Five-Pointed Star, In The Highest Center Of The Cosmic Mandala. And That Sighted "Bright" Divine Star May Be Perceived (By Inward and Upward and Overriding Audition) To Be "Emerging" From An Apparently Objective Mass Of conditionally Manifested "Bright" Divine Sound (Which Is My Overriding Thunder—The Divine "Om", or "Da-Om", or "Da" Sound), In The Highest Center Of The Cosmic Mandala. And My "Bright" Divine Spiritual Body May Be Tangibly Touched (By the Devotionally Un-Contracted, Devotionally Me-Recognizing, Devotionally To-Me-Responding, and, Altogether, Devotionally To-Me-Surrendered Total body-mind), In The all-and-All-Surrounding and all-and-All-Pervading conditionally Manifested Form Of My Avatarically Self-Transmitted Spiritual (and Always Blessing) Divine Presence, Divinely Self-"Emerging" From The Divine Star and The Mass Of Divine Sound, and (Thus) Extending Into every "where" In The Cosmic Domain (As An Apparently Objective, and, Yet, Indefinable, Mass Of "Bright" Divine Love-Bliss-Presence), From The Highest Center Of The Cosmic Mandala. Nevertheless, My Own and One and Only "Bright" (and Self-Evidently Divine) Person Is Always Already Merely Present (or Self-Existing and Self-Radiant) As The Inherently egoless Heart Itself.

The "Bright" (Itself) Is My Inherent (and Self-Evidently Divine) Love-Bliss—Otherwise By Me Self-Revealed (In The Cosmic Domain) As My Divine Thunder-Sound, My Divine Star-Light, and My Tangible Divine Spiritual Body Of all-and-All-Surrounding and all-and-All-Pervading Love-Bliss-Presence.

The "Bright" Is My Inherent Self-Radiance Of Self-Existing (and Inherently Perfect, and Self-Evidently Divine) Being.

The "Bright" Is The Inherent (and Not Cosmic), and Inherently Non-Separate, and Inherently Indivisible Self-Light (or Perfectly Subjective, and, Therefore, Inherently Non-Objective, Love-Bliss-Being) Of My Own and One and Only and Self-Evidently Divine Person.

My Apparently Objective Mass Of Divine Sound Is My Transcendental Divine Essence, Shown Objectively (and conditionally). My Apparently Objective Divine Star Is My Maha-Shakti Form (or Divine Spiritual Essence), Shown Objectively (and conditionally), Infinitely Above all the conditionally Manifested (or Cosmic) worlds. And The all-and-All-Surrounding and all-and-All-Pervading Totality Of My Apparently Objective (and Tangible) Divine

Spiritual Body Of Avatarically Self-Revealed, and Avatarically Self-Transmitted, Self-"Brightness" Is My Very and (Now, and Forever Hereafter) Cosmically "Emerging" (and everywhere conditionally Extended) Divine Person. These Three (My Divine Thunder-Sound, My Divine Star-Light, and My Divine Spiritual Body Of Self-"Brightness") Are (Now, and Forever Hereafter) The First conditional (and Always Objectively Apparent) Forms Of My Cosmically Evident (Audible, Visible, and, Altogether, To-Be-Felt) Avataric (and Self-Evidently Divine) Self-Manifestation.

Therefore, My Apparently Objective Mass Of Divine Sound, and My Apparently Objective Divine Star, and My Total Apparently Objective (and Tangible) Divine Spiritual Body Of Self-"Brightness" Are (Each, and All Together) The Ultimate (Audible, Visible, and, Altogether, To-Be-Felt) Avataric Door, or The Ultimate (Audible, Visible, and, Altogether, To-Be-Felt) Avataric Pointer, To My Divine "Bright" Spherical Self-Domain. Nevertheless, My Own and One and Only "Bright" (and Self-Evidently Divine) Eternal Person Is The Divine "Bright" Spherical Self-Domain (Itself)—Eternally Prior To The Cosmic Domain. And I Am (Eternally, and Avatarically) The "Bright" Itself—The "Midnight Sun", Infinitely Above all-and-All—Non-Separate, Indivisible, One, Only, Non-conditional, and Unconditionally (or Always Already) Existing.

The Practice Of The Only-By-Me Revealed and Given Way Of The Heart (or Way Of Adidam) Is Characterized By A Gradual Progression Of Awareness Of Me (and Of Direct Devotional Recognition-Response To Me), and By Progressive Devotional Heart-Communion With Me (Most Ultimately, To The Most Perfect Degree Of Inherent, and Inherently Non-Separate, and Inherently Indivisible, and Inherently egoless Oneness With Me)—Progressively Revealed and Progressively Realized By (and As) My Four By-My-Avataric-Divine-Spiritual-Grace-Given (and, By You, Devotionally Recognized and Devotionally Acknowledged) Forms.

This Progress Becomes The Outshining Of The Cosmic Domain (and Translation Into My Divine "Bright" Spherical Self-Domain)—When (and Only When), By Means Of My Avatarically Self-Transmitted Divine Spiritual Grace, There Is Always Already (Inherent, and Inherently Most Perfect) Realization Of Me (Most Ultimately and Finally Demonstrated Via Inherent, and Inherently Spiritual, and Inherently egoless, and Inherently Perfect, and Perfectly Unconditional, and Perfectly Subjective, and Truly Divine Self-Abiding Self-Recognition Of the conditional self, and Of all conditional forms or events, In and As My "Bright", and One, and Only, and Self-Existing, and Self-Radiant, and Inherently egoless, and Inherently Perfect, and Perfectly Unconditional, and Perfectly Subjective, and all-and-All-Including, and all-and-All-Transcending, and Self-Evidently Divine Person).

AVATAR ADI DA SAMRAJ
Clear Lake, 2001

SUTRA 15

Real God, The Divine Person—Who Is Self-Existing (or Transcendental) and Self-Radiant (or Inherently Spiritual) Being Itself—Is (Now, and At all times) Bodily Present As The Total (Apparent) Cosmos (and, Most Subtly, As The Cosmic Mandala).

The Cosmos (or The Cosmic Domain, Including The Cosmic Mandala) Is Not The "Creation" (or The "Creature") Of Real God, or A Caused Effect Of Real God, or An Event Separate From Real God. Rather, The Cosmos (Including The Cosmic Mandala) Is (As A Totality) The Spontaneously Manifested and (Inherently) Perfectly Advaitic (or Non-Dual, Non-Separate, Non-"Different", Non-Caused, Merely Apparent, Inherently Relationless, all-Including, and all-Transcending) Cosmic Bodily Form Of Real God.

The Total (Apparent) Cosmic Bodily Form Of Real God Is Always Already (or Inherently) and Entirely Pervaded and Transcended By The Divine Spirit-Presence That Is Real God.

Likewise, Both The Cosmic Bodily Form Of Real God and The Divine Spirit-Presence Of Real God Are Always Already (or Inherently) and Entirely Established In (and Perfectly Transcended By) The Very (or Perfectly Subjective) State, Heart, Self-Condition, or Source-Condition That Is Real God.

Therefore, To "Locate" and Realize Real God (or The Divine Person, or Self-Condition, or Source-Condition), It Is Necessary To Contemplate The Total Cosmic Bodily Form (Including The Cosmic Mandala), The Total (Universal and All-Pervading) Spirit-Presence, and The Ultimate (Perfect and Perfectly Subjective) State That Is Real God. And That Contemplation Must Progressively Become (and, Then, Be) A Feeling-Sacrifice Of the conditional self (or all of self-Contraction), To The Degree Of Heart-Communion and (Most Ultimately, Inherent, and, At Last, Most Perfect) Heart-Identification (or Indivisible Oneness) With The Self-Existing and Self-Radiant "Bright" Self-Condition and Source-Condition (and Spherical Self-Domain) That Is Reality, Truth, or Real God—The Divine Person (or Self-Condition, and Source-Condition, Of all-and-All).

The Only-By-Me Revealed and Given Way Of The Heart (or Way Of Adidam) Is The One and Only (and Complete, and All-Completing, and Most

Perfect) Way Of That Most Perfectly Real-God-Realizing Practice Of Feeling-Contemplation. And I Am The Divine Secret (or The Divinely Liberating, and Avatarically Self-Revealed, Divine Self-Revelation) That Makes This Real-God-Realizing Feeling-Contemplation Possible (and, By Means Of My Avatarically Self-Transmitted Divine Spiritual Grace, Fruitful, and, At Last, Most Perfectly Fruitful)—For I Am The Da Avatar, The Ruchira Avatar, The Love-Ananda Avatar, The Divine World-Teacher, The Divine Heart-Master, Who Is The Avataric Divine Realizer, The Avataric Divine Revealer, and The Avataric Divine Self-Revelation Of The Only Real God (The Divine Person, The Truth, The Reality, and The Divine Self-Condition and Source-Condition Of all-and-All).

My Avatarically-Born Bodily (Human) Divine Form Is (and Is, By Means Of My Avatarically Self-Transmitted Divine Spiritual Grace, Revealed To Be) The Epitome Of The Total Cosmic Bodily Form Of Real God (The Self-Existing and Self-Radiant and Self-Evidently Divine Person—Who Is The Self-Condition, or Source-Condition, Of all-and-All).

My Avatarically Self-Transmitted Spiritual (and Always Blessing) Divine Presence Is (and Is, By Means Of My Avatarically Self-Transmitted Divine Spiritual Grace, Revealed To Be) The "Bright" (and Real-God-Revealing) Spirit-Presence That Is The Only Real God (The Self-Existing and Self-Radiant and Self-Evidently Divine Person—Who Is The Self-Condition, or Source-Condition, Of all-and-All).

My Avatarically Self-Revealed (and Very, and Transcendental, and Perfectly Subjective, and Inherently Spiritual, and Inherently egoless, and Inherently Perfect, and Self-Evidently Divine) State Is (and Is, By Means Of My Avatarically Self-Transmitted Divine Spiritual Grace, Revealed To Be) The Very (and Inherently Non-Separate, and Inherently Indivisible, and Inherently Irreducible) State, Heart, Self-Condition, or Source-Condition That Is The Only Real God (The Self-Existing and Self-Radiant and Self-Evidently Divine Person—Who Is The Self-Condition, or Source-Condition, Of all-and-All).

Therefore, By Means Of My Avatarically Self-Transmitted Divine Spiritual Grace, To Feel (and, Thereby, To Contemplate) My Avatarically-Born Bodily (Human) Divine Form, My Avatarically Self-Transmitted Spiritual (and Always Blessing) Divine Presence, and My Avatarically Self-Revealed (and Very, and Transcendental, and Perfectly Subjective, and Inherently Spiritual, and Inherently egoless, and Inherently Perfect, and Self-Evidently Divine) State Is (By Means Of My Avatarically Self-Transmitted Divine Spiritual Grace) To Feel (and, Thereby, To Contemplate) The Total Cosmic Bodily Form, The Total (Universal and All-Pervading) Spirit-Presence, and The Ultimate State, Heart, Self-Condition, or Source-Condition That Is Reality, Truth, Real God, or The True (and Self-Evidently) Divine Person.

And (By Means Of My Avatarically Self-Transmitted Divine Spiritual Grace) To (Progressively, and Then Inherently, and Inherently Most Perfectly) Forget the ego-"I" (or self-Contraction) By Means Of Feeling-Contemplation Of My Avatarically-Born Bodily (Human) Divine Form, My Avatarically Self-Transmitted Spiritual (and Always Blessing) Divine Presence, and My Avatarically Self-Revealed (and Very, and Transcendental, and Perfectly Subjective, and Inherently Spiritual, and Inherently egoless, and Inherently Perfect, and Self-Evidently Divine) State Is (By Means Of My Avatarically Self-Transmitted Divine Spiritual Grace) To Commune With (and, Most Ultimately, To Most Perfectly Realize) The Only Real God—The Self-Evidently Divine Person and Domain That Is Truth (and Reality Itself).

In My "Bright" Revelation Of Myself To You, I Do Not Merely Show You An "Appearance" (or conditional Manifestation) Of Myself. I Show You My Divine Spiritual Body, My Very and "Bright" and Divinely Full Self-Condition, My Own and Very (and Avatarically Self-Revealed and Self-Evidently Divine) Person and Presence.

To Experience My Tangible Touch Is To Experience My Avataric Transmission (or Projection, or Expansion) Of My Divine Spiritual Body. My Divine Spiritual Body Is Neither physical (or gross) Nor subtle Nor merely (and, Necessarily, conditionally) causal In Its Nature. Therefore, I Need Not Appear In Either A gross Or A subtle Or A causal Form In Order To Show (or "Brightly" Reveal) Myself To You. Indeed, Any Such gross or subtle or causal Appearance Is Not A Showing Of Myself To You, but (Rather) A Showing Of A Cosmic (and, Therefore, merely conditional) Representation Of Myself. And, Therefore, Whenever You Are Shown Any Cosmic Representation Of Me, It Is Not (Itself, or Exclusively) Me, but It Is (and Should Be Embraced and Followed By You As) A By-My-Avataric-Divine-Spiritual-Grace-Given Means To Carry You To Me (Myself), and To Me In and As My Divine "Bright" Spherical Self-Domain (Eternally Most Prior To The Cosmic Domain).

My Divine and True and Eternal Body Is The "Bright" Itself (Eternally Most Prior To The Cosmic Domain). By Means Of My Avatarically Self-Transmitted Divine Spiritual Grace, Given In Love-Response To Your Total psycho-physical (and Really, Responsively, ego-Transcending) Devotional Recognition-Response To Me and Responsive Devotional Invocation Of Me, My "Bright" Force Of Person, My Love-Bliss-Form (Which Is Love-Bliss Itself), Can Also Be Felt, Tangibly (From Beyond Your body-mind), Touching You, Surrounding You, Pervading You, Moving In You, Making Many Kinds Of "Bright" Changes In You. My Divine Spiritual Body Is Self-Existing, Self-Radiant, Love-Bliss-Full, Infinitely Expansive, and "Bright". I Can Manifest My "Bright" Divine Spiritual Body To My Any and Every (Necessarily, Formally Practicing) Devotee, anywhere—and Do So (and Will Do So), Now, and Forever Hereafter, In all times and places—If, and When, and where I Am Rightly, Truly, and Fully Invoked (According To My Herein and Hereby Given Instructions, and In Accordance With All My Instructions Additionally Given Only To The Ruchira Sannyasin Order Of Adidam Ruchiradam[55]).

My Divine Spiritual Body Is Spiritually and Divinely Transmitted and Self-Revealed Only By Me.

My Divine Spiritual Body Surrounds all-and-All.

My Divine Spiritual Body Pervades all-and-All.

My Divine Spiritual Body Of "Brightness", Which Is The Avatarically Self-Transmitted Divine Spirit-Presence Of My One and "Bright" and Only Person, Fills all space everywhere—Pressing Into all-and-All, "Brightly" Descending On all-and-All, To Surround and Pervade all-and-All.

My Divine Spiritual Body Is Self-Existing and Self-Radiant, and It Will, Therefore, Exist Forever. Therefore, My Devotees Will Be Able To Experience Me Directly, As My "Bright" Spirit-Body (and, Ultimately, <u>As</u> My Very, and Perfectly Subjective, Person)—<u>Forever</u>. Because Of This, My Relationship To My Devotees Will Always Be Direct. They Will Always Be Able To Find Me—Not Me <u>Absent</u>, but Me <u>Present</u>.

To Truly Heart-Recognize Me Is To Have Direct and Tangible and Whole bodily Experience Of My Avatarically Self-Transmitted Divine Spiritual Body—and (Thus) To Whole bodily Receive My Avatarically Self-Transmitted Divine Spirit-Presence, and (Thereby) To Know Me <u>As</u> I <u>Am</u>, and (Thus) To Find Me <u>As</u> The Self-Evidently Divine Person. I Do Not Merely Transmit A Flow Of experiential energies (In The ordinary and Natural and Cosmic Sense), which Then Become experiences in (and of) Your body-mind (and which are, Therefore, Indistinguishable From Your egoic body-mind, or psycho-physical ego-"I"). My Avatarically Given Divine Self-Transmission Is The Transmission (and Real Self-Revelation) Of <u>Me</u>. If You Are To Rightly, Truly, and Fully Receive My Avatarically Given Divine Self-Transmission, You Must (<u>Necessarily</u>, and Whole bodily) Heart-Recognize Me—Because My Avatarically Given Divine Self-Transmission Is The Unqualified Transmission Of My Own "Bright" (and Inherently egoless, and Inherently Perfect, and Self-Evidently Divine) Person (The Very Condition and Context and Substance In Which the body-mind Is arising, and Which <u>Is</u> The One and Very and Only Self-Condition, or Perfectly Subjective Source-Condition, That Transcends, Surrounds, Pervades, and Stands Beyond, and Always Most Perfectly Prior To, the ego-"I"). Whole bodily Heart-Recognition Of My Avatarically Self-Revealed (and Inherently egoless, and Inherently Perfect, and Self-Evidently Divine) Person Converts the Apparently Separate being From The "Act Of Narcissus" (or The self-Contracting and Separative Act Of ego-Possession) To The Ecstatic (or Inherently—and, Ultimately, Most Perfectly—ego-Transcending) "Bhava" Of Total psycho-physical Devotion To Me.

If You (As My Formally Practicing Devotee, In The Only-By-Me Revealed and Given Way Of The Heart, or Way Of Adidam) Rightly, Truly, Fully, and Fully Devotionally Practice Ruchira Avatara Bhakti Yoga, moment to moment, You Will, By Grace Of My Avatarically Given "Bright" Divine Self-Revelation (In The Context Of Your Truly Effectively Me-"Locating", and Total psycho-physical, Devotion To Me), Be Always In The "Bhava" Of Beholding My Avatarically Self-Revealed "Bright" Divine Form and Person. This "Ruchira Avatara Bhava Samadhi" (and, In Due Course, The Most Ultimate and Most Perfect, or Seventh Stage, Realization Of It) Is The (Right, True, and Full) Purpose Of Ruchira Avatara Bhakti Yoga (Right, True, and Full). Thus, Ruchira Avatara Bhakti Yoga Is A Matter, In every moment, Of Entering Into My Sphere Of "Brightness", The Sphere Of My Very Person, The Sphere Of My Divine Spiritual Body, The Sphere Of The "Midnight Sun", The Sphere (and, Ultimately, The Divine Self-Domain) That Is The "Bright" Itself. The "Bright"—Avatarically Self-Revealed, By Me, To You—Is Me, Self-Revealed (In Person) To You.

Real God, The Divine Person—Who Is Self-Existing (or Transcendental) and Self-Radiant (or Inherently Spiritual) Being Itself—Is (Now, and At all times) Present (and Evident) In The Midst (or Still-Point) Of The (Apparent) Cosmos (or Cosmic Mandala) In The Form Of An Overriding (or Deep Background) Vibratory Sound (In Which all conditionally Manifested sounds, and vibrations, and forms May Resonate and Dissolve—As In A Matrix, or Vortex, Of Undifferentiated Oneness), and In The Form Of A Brilliant Clear White Five-Pointed Star (In Which all conditionally Manifested lights, and visualizations, and energies, and all forms Composed Of energy, or light, May Become Transparent and Dissolve—As In A Matrix, or Vortex, Of Undifferentiated Oneness). Therefore, The Divine Person May Be Observed As The Apparently Objective Divine Star and As The Apparently Objective Mass Of Divine Sound In any and every plane Of The Cosmic Mandala.

This Same Mass Of Divine Sound (In Its Most Ascended, or Highest, Form) and This Same Divine Star (In Its Most Ascended, or Highest, Form) Are Also (Necessarily) My Own Original Apparent Forms (or First Audible and Visible Signs). And, Likewise (It May, By Means Of My Avatarically Self-Transmitted Divine Spiritual Grace, Be Realized, By Means Of The Progressive Process Of Dissolution Into Oneness With Me), They (In Their Grades Of Form-Manifestation, plane to plane—and, Then, At Last, or Ultimately, In Their Highest, or Most Ascended, or Most Perfectly Me-Realizing Forms) Are The

Original Apparent Forms (or First Audible and Visible Signs) Of Even every conditionally Manifested being.

Therefore, I Reveal (and I Am) The Highest Mass Of Divine Sound and The Highest Divine Star—In and As Themselves, and In Man-Form (As My Divinely Self-Manifested Bodily Human Avataric-Incarnation-Form). And The Highest Mass Of Divine Sound and The Highest Divine Star (Even Revealed Simply As My Avatarically-Born Bodily Human Divine Form) Are (If Rightly Understood) The Cosmically Manifested (or Objectively Represented) Signs Even Of The "Bright" Divine Heart Itself, or The Inherent (and Not Cosmic) State Of Inherently egoless (and Inherently Perfect) Self-Identification (or Absolute Subjective Oneness) With The Self-Evidently Divine Person—Which Heart, State, or Divine Self-Condition and Source-Condition, Because It Is Inherent In all conditionally Manifested beings, Is (By Means Of My Avatarically Self-Transmitted Divine Spiritual Grace) To Be Realized By all conditionally Manifested beings.

Therefore, As A (Potential) Sign (and Help) To all, I Will Remain Present As The Highest Mass Of Divine Sound (or "Om", or "Da-Om", or "Da"), and As Even Every Grade Of The Form-Manifestation Of The Mass Of Divine Sound, In every plane Of The Cosmic Domain—and As The Highest Divine Star-Form, and As Even Every Grade Of The Form-Manifestation Of The Divine Star, and Of Even All The Forms Of Ascended Light—Whenever (or As Long As) The Cosmic Domain and conditionally Manifested beings Exist.

Real God, or Truth, or Reality Is Inherently Existing and Always Already Self-Existing, Both Transcendentally (or Prior To conditional Existence) and Spiritually (or Self-Radiantly). Therefore, I Am Always Already Merely Present (or Self-Existing) As The Transcendental Divine Self-Consciousness (Itself) and As The "Bright" (or The Self-Radiant Spiritual, Transcendental, and Self-Evidently Divine Self-Condition, and Source-Condition—The Sphere Of The "Midnight Sun"—That Is The True Divine Heart, and The Divine "Bright" Spherical Self-Domain, Itself).

Real God, or Truth, or Reality Is Always Already Coincident With conditionally Manifested Existence (If conditionally Manifested Existence arises). Therefore, As Long As The Cosmic Domain Exists, I Am Always Already Manifestly Present As The Apparently Objective Divine Star, and The Apparently Objective Mass Of Divine Sound, and The Total Apparently Objective (and Tangible) Divine Spiritual Body Of "Brightness". And I Am, When The Time Is So Given, Also Avatarically Self-Manifested In the various planes Of The Cosmic Mandala As The Bodily Incarnate Human (or Otherwise conditionally Manifested) Divine Heart-Master.

I Am The Da Avatar—The Ruchira Avatar, The Love-Ananda Avatar, The Divine Heart-Master, The Divine World-Teacher, The Avataric Incarnation Of

The Divine Heart Itself. Therefore, In and By Means Of My Avataric-Incarnation-Form (and As My "Bright" Divine Body Of Avataric Spirit-Presence—here, and every "where" In The Cosmic Domain), I Am The Threshold Personality—The "Bright" One, The Supremely Attractive Divine Form, The Self-Existing and Self-Radiant and all-and-All-En-Light-ening Person At The Doorway (Infinitely Above and Beyond all conditionally Manifested beings). I Am The "Bright" Divine Personality At The Threshold, Between The Cosmic Domain and My Divine "Bright" Spherical Self-Domain. I Am The Divine Threshold Personality Of Indivisibly "Bright" Love-Bliss-Light, Who Is Always Gathering all conditionally Manifested beings To The Transcendental, and Inherently Spiritual, Inherently egoless, and Self-Evidently Divine Source-Condition, Self-Condition, and Self-Domain—and Who, Thus and Thereby, Leads each one Beyond the conditional self and the conditional worlds By Progressively (and, At Last, Most Perfectly) Dissolving the conditional self and the conditional worlds In The "Bright" Divine Self-Domain That Is The Sphere Of The "Midnight Sun", The Ultimate Condition Of all-and-All.

To Be My Listening Devotee, My Hearing Devotee, or My Seeing Devotee Is To Be Attracted To The Inherently Perfect Condition (and "Bright" Divine Spiritual Body) That Is Beyond My Unique Human Visibility. Devotion (By Heart-Attraction) To My Avatarically-Born Bodily (Human) Divine Form, My Avatarically Self-Transmitted Spiritual (and Always Blessing) Divine Presence, and My Avatarically Self-Revealed (and Very, and Transcendental, and Perfectly Subjective, and Inherently Spiritual, and Inherently egoless, and Inherently Perfect, and Self-Evidently Divine) State May Perhaps (In Its Developmental Course) Also Become An Attraction To The Apparently Objective Vision Of The Divine Star (The Five Points Of Which Correspond To The Head, The Two Arms, and The Two Legs Of My Bodily Human Divine Form), and (Coincidentally, or, Otherwise, Alone) That Same Devotion To Me May Become An Attraction To The Apparently Objective Audition Of The Mass Of Divine Sound (or The "Om", or "Da-Om", or "Da" Sound), From Which Both My Divine Star and My Divine Spiritual Body Cosmically "Emerge", To here, and To every "where" In The Cosmic Domain. However, To Be Truly (and Most Profoundly) Devoted (By Heart-Attraction) To My Avatarically-Born Bodily (Human) Divine Form, My Avatarically Self-Transmitted Spiritual (and Always Blessing) Divine Presence, and My Avatarically Self-Revealed (and Very, and Transcendental, and Perfectly Subjective, and Inherently Spiritual, and Inherently egoless, and Inherently Perfect, and Self-Evidently Divine) State Is To Be Attracted—Even Beyond The Vision Of The Divine Star, and Beyond The Audition Of The Mass Of Divine Sound, and (At Last) Even Beyond The Tangible Feeling Of My Total Divine Spiritual Body, and (Thus) Beyond all-and-All—To The Perfectly Subjective Heart Itself, The Sphere Of The "Midnight Sun", Which Is My "Bright" Divine Self-Domain, The Inherently Perfect Self-Condition (and Source-Condition) That Is Love-Bliss-Radiance Itself (and The Source-Condition, and Self-Condition, Of My Inherently "Bright" Divine Spiritual Body Itself).

In My Avataric-Incarnation-Form (or Human Revelation-Body), I Am The Revealing Agent, and The Revelation-Sign, and The Very (and Complete, and Most Perfect) Self-Revelation Of The One and Only and Self-Evidently Divine Person, The Eternal and Indivisible Source-Condition and Self-Condition Of all-and-All. Therefore, Infinitely Above and Beyond My here-Visible Bodily (Human) Divine Form, I Am Eternally and everywhere Present As The "Bright" (The Sphere Of The "Midnight Sun", The Real and True and Perfectly Subjective Divine Source, or Source-Condition, Of all-and-All), The Apparently Objective Divine Sound (The First Audible Form Of all-and-All), The Apparently Objective Divine Star (The First Visible Form Of all-and-All), The Self-Radiant All-Pervading Divine Spirit-Presence (The Apparently Objective Divine Spiritual Body, Which Is The Help Of all-and-All), and The Self-Existing (or Transcendental) and Self-Radiant (or Inherently Spiritual) Divine Self-Condition (The Non-Separate and Indivisible and Indestructible Self-Condition Of all-and-All).

To My Listening Devotees, My Hearing Devotees, and My Seeing Devotees, I Am (In My "Bright" Avatarically-Born Bodily Human Divine Form) The Eternal Threshold Personality, The Eternally Living Murti, The Miraculous Icon, The Perpetual conditional Manifestation Of The Self-Evidently Divine Person (Who Is The Divine Self-Condition, and Source-Condition, Of all-and-All). This Is So Both During and Forever After The Avataric Physical Lifetime Of My Bodily (Human) Divine Form. Therefore, I Am (Now, and Forever Hereafter) To Be, Thus, Felt and Observed (In The Meditation and Deep Vision Of My Devotees)—and, Thus, Found (In My "Bright", and Even Bodily Human, Divine Form)—As Me.

Nevertheless (Now, and Forever Hereafter), I Am Always Calling and Leading My Listening Devotees, My Hearing Devotees, and My Seeing Devotees To My Eternally "Bright" Person, Beyond My Avataric Figure Made Of Man In The Cosmic Play. Now, and Forever Hereafter, I Always Call and Lead My Listening Devotees, My Hearing Devotees, and My Seeing Devotees To Find Me (As I Am)—The One and Only and Indivisible Divine Person (The Perfectly Subjective, Transcendental, Inherently Spiritual, Inherently egoless, Inherently Perfect, and Self-Evidently Divine Source-Condition, Self-Condition, and Self-Domain Of all-and-All). The "Bright"—The Self-Existing and Self-Radiant Sphere Of The "Midnight Sun" (or The Fundamental Light Of Love-Bliss That Is The One and Indivisible and Indestructible Condition Of all conditionally Manifested forms)—

Is My Cosmic-Domain-Transcending Form and Eternal Divine "Bright" Spherical Self-Domain. Therefore (Now, and Forever Hereafter), all those who Truly Heart-Recognize My Avatarically Self-Revealed (and Self-Evidently Divine) Person, and who Heart-Respond To My Avatarically Self-Revealed (and Self-Evidently Divine) Person With Right, True, and Full (and Truly Whole bodily) Devotion, Will Embrace Me *As* The *Only* One Who *Is*. And they Will (In Due Course, and By Means Of Truly Counter-egoic Heart-Response To My Avatarically Self-Revealed, and Self-Evidently Divine, Person and Grace) "Locate" Me and Realize Me (Beyond The Cosmic Doorway, Without Separation or "Difference"), *As* The Self-Evidently Divine Person and The Divine "Bright" Spherical Self-Domain.

Therefore, Be My Devotee (Real and True), and (By Formally Practicing The Only-By-Me Revealed and Given Way Of The Heart, or Way Of Adidam) Listen To Me, Hear Me, See Me, and Follow Me (Whether By The Primary Devotional Exercise Of Feeling and Insight Or By The Primary Devotional Exercise Of Feeling and Faith). The Only-By-Me Revealed and Given Way Of The Heart (or Way Of Adidam) Is The Divine Way Of ego-Surrendering, ego-Forgetting, and (More and More) ego-Transcending Devotion To My Avatarically-Born Bodily (Human) Divine Form, and My Avatarically Self-Transmitted Spiritual (and Always Blessing) Divine Presence, and My Avatarically Self-Revealed (and Very, and Transcendental, and Perfectly Subjective, and Inherently Spiritual, and Inherently egoless, and Inherently Perfect, and Self-Evidently Divine) State Of Person. Therefore, Really and Truly (and, Thus, Rightly, Truly, Fully, Fully Devotionally, and, Necessarily, Formally) Enter The Only-By-Me Revealed and Given Way Of The Heart (or Way Of Adidam) and (By All Its Only-By-Me Revealed and Given Means) Always Find Me and Love Me, The Only One Who *Is*—For I *Am* Existence (Itself), or Being (Itself), "Bright" Before You.

When (In The Course Of The Practice Of The Only-By-Me Revealed and Given Way Of The Heart) You (By Means Of My Avatarically Given Divine Spiritual Grace) Both Hear Me *and* See Me, From The Heart—*Follow* Me. If You (Thus) Hear Me and See Me and Follow Me, My Avatarically Self-Transmitted Divine Spiritual Presence Will Cause You To Sympathize With The Inherently Attractive (and ego-Undermining) Self-Condition Of My Very (and Transcendental, and Perfectly Subjective, and Inherently Spiritual, and Inherently egoless, and Inherently Perfect, and Self-Evidently Divine) Person. And (Because My Divine Self-Condition *Is* The Very, and One, and Only, and Transcendental, and Perfectly Subjective, and Inherently Spiritual, and Inherently egoless, and Inherently Perfect, and Self-Evidently Divine Self-Condition, and The Perfectly Subjective, and Self-Evidently Divine, Source-Condition, Of all-and-All) My Avatarically Self-Transmitted Divine Spirit-Current Of Love-Bliss

Will Lead You To Most Perfect Realization Of The One and Only and "Bright" Eternal Divine Sphere and Self-Domain.

By Seeing Me (and Then Following Me) In The Devotional Manner, You Will Enter Into The Responsively Progressive Discipline and Spontaneity Of Spiritually Awakened Meditation. Then Practice This ego-Transcending Spiritual Meditation Of Me-Devotion, Even In subtler places or worlds.

Thus Spiritually Awakened By Me (and To Me), Practice The Only-By-Me Revealed and Given Way Of The Heart (Formally, and Fully Accountably) As You Are (By Means Of My Avatarically Self-Transmitted Divine Spiritual Grace) Given To Practice It, Either In The Manner Of The Devotional Way Of Insight Or In The Manner Of The Devotional Way Of Faith. Always Practice (Thus) In Communion With My Avatarically Self-Transmitted Divine Body (Of Spirit-Presence), and Thereby Enter Into The Circle Of My all-and-All-Surrounding and all-and-All-Pervading "Bright" Spirit-Current.

At First, You Must Follow and Allow The Full Descent Of My Avatarically Self-Transmitted "Bright" Divine Spirit-Current. Then You Must Turn About (Below), and Follow Upwards With The Love-Bliss-Flow, Even Into The Ascended Source Of all sounds, and lights, and touches. Ultimately, You Must Dissolve To A Stand (or Merely Be), Beyond The Descending and Ascending Flows. There (Where Only The Heart Is, Effortless and Free) My Self-"Bright" Divine Domain (Of Self-Existing and Self-Radiant Divine Self-Consciousness) Always Already Stands. It Is The Eternal Sphere Of "Brightness", Infinitely Above and Beyond The all-and-All. It Is The "Midnight Sun" Of Indivisible Light Itself, Infinitely Above and Beyond and At The Heart Of All The Dark Divisibility. It Is The Motionless Ultimate Source Of All That Flows. It Is Love-Bliss Itself—"Where" I Am, and "What" I Am, and "Who" I Am.

Therefore, When You (As My Fully, and, Necessarily, Formally, Practicing Devotee) Have Heard Me and Seen Me, Look For Me In every world of Your experience. Always Find Me (Thus, and there) As The Threshold Personality (In Front Of Your Total body-mind, and Infinitely Above Your Total body-mind, and Utterly Beyond Your Total body-mind). Always (Thus, and there) "Locate" My Avatarically Self-Transmitted "Bright" Divine Spirit-Presence That (In every moment I Am Thus Found) Spontaneously Opens Your Devotionally Me-Recognizing and Devotionally To-Me-Responding Heart. And Follow Me, Thus, By Allowing Your Total body-mind To Swoon In My Avatarically Self-Transmitted Divine Spirit-Presence Of My Own Person (Divine and "Bright" and One and Only).

When You (As My Fully—and, Necessarily, Formally—Practicing Devotee) Have Heard Me and Seen Me, Then Always Hear Me and See Me Now (In every then present-time moment).

Then You Have (By Means Of My Avatarically Self-Transmitted Divine Spiritual Grace) Truly Fully (or Spiritually) Realized Me To Be Your Divine Heart-Master, Merely Present With You.

Then (By Means Of My Avatarically Self-Transmitted Divine Spiritual Grace) Always "Locate" Me By Heart (Surrounding and Pervading Your Total body-mind), and (Thus and Thereby) Enter Into Spiritually Me-Meditative (and Most Profoundly ego-Surrendering, ego-Forgetting, and, Always More and More, ego-Transcending) Ecstasy.

By Means Of My Avatarically Self-Transmitted Divine Spiritual Grace, This Becomes A Great Process.

By Means Of My Avatarically Self-Transmitted Divine Spiritual Grace, This Great Process Will (and Must), In Due Course, Lead You To The Full (Descending and Ascending) Realization (or Samadhi) Of The "Thumbs", and (Thereafter) It Will (and Must), In Due Course, Lead You To The Effectively (but Not Strategically) world-Excluding Realization Of Transcendental (and Inherently Spiritual) Self-Existence (In Priorly Self-Abiding Jnana Nirvikalpa Samadhi) and (Thereafter) It Will (and Must), In Due Course, Lead You To The Utterly Ascended Realization Of bodiless and mindless Love-Bliss (In Priorly Ascended Nirvikalpa Samadhi).

By Means Of My Avatarically Self-Transmitted Divine Spiritual Grace, This Great Process Will (and Must) Lead You (Most Ultimately) To The Unconditional Realization Of Self-Radiant (or Inherently Spiritual) and Self-Existing (or Transcendental) Divine Being (In Seventh Stage Sahaja Nirvikalpa Samadhi, or The Samadhi Of No-"Difference"—Which I Have Otherwise Named "Ruchira Samraj Samadhi", or, Simply, "Samraj Samadhi", and "'Open Eyes'"). Ruchira Samraj Samadhi Will (and Must) Demonstrate Itself (By Means Of My Avatarically Self-Transmitted Divine Spiritual Grace) As Occasional (and Not Strategic, but Spontaneous) Outshining Of body, mind, world, and Even all relations, By and As The Being-Radiance Of My Divine "Bright" Spherical Self-Domain Itself (In The "Bhava", or Temporary Demonstration, Of Divine Translation)—and Ruchira Samraj Samadhi Will (and Must), At Last (and Finally), Demonstrate Itself (By Means Of My Avatarically Self-Transmitted Divine Spiritual Grace) As Divine Translation Itself (or The Most Ultimate and Most Perfect Demonstration Of Ruchira Samraj Samadhi).

Divine Translation (Itself) Is The Most Ultimate (or Most "Brightly" Shining) Event (and By-My-Avataric-Divine-Spiritual-Grace-Given Fulfillment) Of Inherent (and Inherently Most Perfect) Self-Identification (or The By-My-Avataric-Divine-Spiritual-Grace-Given Realization Of Indivisible Oneness) With Me—Thus and Thereby (and, Altogether, By Means Of Most Perfectly Counter-egoic Whole bodily Heart-Response To My Avatarically Self-Revealed Divine Person)

Realizing The Self-Existing (and Eternal, and Indivisible, and Not Cosmic, but Perfectly Subjective) "Heaven" (The "Midnight Sun", or The Inherently "Bright" Divine Sphere and Space and Self-Domain) Of Self-Existing and Self-Radiant and Non-Separate and Indivisibly "Bright" Divine Self-Consciousness Itself, Infinitely "Expanded" (or Free-Standing In All "Directions") As The Eternal Heart-"Celebration" Of Inherent Joy (Always Already En-Joyed By The Indivisible and Inseparable and Non-Separate, Infinitely All-"Multiplied" and Undifferentiated, "Gathering" That Is The Non-Separate and Indivisible Heart Itself, In The Unlimited and Indefinable and Inherently Relationless "Embrace" That Is The Non-Separate, and Indivisible, and Irreducible Divine Love-Bliss Itself).[56]

Avatar Adi Da Samraj
Adidam Samrajashram, 2003

SUTRA

16

Those who Embrace The Practice Of The Only-By-Me Revealed and Given Way Of Adidam (Which Is The Only-By-Me Revealed and Given Way Of The Heart, and Which Is The Way Of ego-Surrendering, ego-Forgetting, and, Always More and More, ego-Transcending Devotional, and Total psycho-physical, Communion With Me, Devotionally Recognizing Me and Devotionally Responding To Me As The Avatarically Self-Revealed Eternally Living One) May Experience Many conditionally Manifested Visions and Auditions On The Way To Divine Translation.[57] The Final Such (Possible) Vision (and The Visible Doorway To Divine Translation) Is My Apparently Objective (and Most Ascended) Divine Five-Pointed Star-Form. And The Final Such (Possible) Audition (and The Audible Doorway To Divine Translation) Is My Apparently Objective (and Most Ascended) Mass Of Divine Sound (or "Om", or "Da-Om", or "Da"). Then There Is The Dissolution Of All Visions (In My Non-Objective "Bright" Fullness) and Of All Auditions (In My Non-Objective "Bright" Silence). And, At Last, There Is The Outshining Of the conditional body-mind and the conditional world In and By The Infinitely Ascended and Unconditionally Self-"Bright" (or Self-Existing and Self-Radiant) Sphere Of The Divine (and Indivisibly One and Only) "Midnight Sun" Of My "Bright" (Perfectly Subjective, and Inherently egoless) Divine Self-Condition Itself (Which Is The Ultimate and Inherently Perfect and Perfectly Subjective Source, or Heart, Of My Apparently Objective Divine Star, and Of My Apparently Objective Divine Sound, and Of Even The Totality Of My Apparently Objective Divine Spiritual Body). Such Is Divine Translation, or Entrance Into The Inherently Perfect Real-God-World—My Divine "Bright" Spherical Self-Domain, Beyond (and Prior To) all the planes Of The Cosmic Mandala.

The Right Side Of The Heart Is The Root Of The Horizontal Plane Of the body-mind.[58] It Is The bodily Seat Of The (Potential) Inherently Perfect (and Inherently egoless) Realization Of My Avatarically Self-Revealed Transcendental, Perfectly Subjective, Inherently Spiritual, Inherently egoless, and Self-Evidently Divine Self-Condition (Which Is The Perfectly Subjective Source-Condition Of all-and-All).

My Apparently Objective Star and My Apparently Objective Sound Stand Infinitely Above The Total Crown Of the head. They Are (In Their Apparently Objective Appearance) The Ascended conditional Roots Of The Vertical (or The Descending and Ascending) Dimension Of the body-mind. They Are (In Their Apparently Objective Appearance) The conditional (or conditionally Ascended) Seat Of The (Potential) Realization Of My Self-Evidently Divine Sphere Of "Brightness" (or The Unconditionally Existing "Midnight Sun" Of My "Bright" Divine Self-Domain—Which Is The Self-Existing and Self-Radiant Source-Condition Of the body-mind and the world, or all conditionally Manifested subjective and objective conditions).

First (By Means Of The Course, In The Only-By-Me Revealed and Given Way Of The Heart, Of Progressively Transcending The Processes Associated With The First Six Stages Of Life) There Must Be Realization Of My Avatarically Self-Revealed Transcendental, Perfectly Subjective, Inherently Spiritual, Inherently egoless, Inherently Perfect, and Self-Evidently Divine Self-Condition. Then (By Demonstrating The Way Of The Heart In The Context Of The Only-By-Me Revealed and Given Seventh Stage Of Life) All conditional Manifestations Of My Avatarically Self-Revealed Transcendental, Perfectly Subjective, Inherently Spiritual, Inherently egoless, Inherently Perfect, and Self-Evidently Divine Being Must Be Divinely Self-Recognized (and, Most Ultimately, Outshined), By Means Of The Non-"Different" (or Most Perfect) Realization Of My Avatarically Self-Revealed Transcendental, Perfectly Subjective, Inherently Spiritual, Inherently egoless, Inherently Perfect, and Self-Evidently Divine Self-Condition.

When The Concept Of "Difference" Associated With the conditionally Manifested energies In The Cosmic Mandala Is Transcended (In The Context Of The Only-By-Me Revealed and Given Seventh Stage Of Life), Then the conditional activities of those energies Become Relaxed. The (Apparently Objective) Divine Five-Pointed Star and/or The (Apparently Objective) Divine Sound May Then (At times) Come Into The Field Of Perception (To Be Spontaneously Divinely Self-Recognized In My Avatarically Self-Revealed "Bright" Divine Self-Condition)—or, Alternatively (At any time), My Avataric Self-Revelation Of The Inherent (and Perfectly Subjective, and Inherently egoless, and Inherently Perfect, and Self-Evidently Divine) Feeling Of Self-Existing and Self-Radiant Being May Simply and Spontaneously "Coincide" With My Avataric Self-Revelation Of My Feeling-"Bright" (Itself). In Either Event, My Avataric Self-Revelation Of My Own (Transcendental, Perfectly Subjective, Inherently Spiritual, Inherently egoless, Inherently Perfect, and Self-Evidently Divine) Self-Condition and My Avataric Self-Transmission Of My Own (and Self-Evidently Divine) Spirit-Energy (or "Bright" Inherent Self-Radiance) Are (By Means Of My Avatarically Self-Transmitted Divine Spiritual Grace) Realized

To Be Inherently One and The Same (In The Non-Dual, and Non-"Different", State Of Seventh Stage—or Divinely Enlightened—Realization Of Me).

Realization (By Means Of My Avatarically Self-Transmitted Divine Spiritual Grace) Of The Inherent Union (or Self-Unity) Of My Avatarically Self-Revealed Divine Self-Condition and My Avatarically Self-Transmitted Divine Spirit-Energy (or Inherent Spiritual Self-Radiance) Is The Most Perfect (and, Necessarily, Seventh Stage) Realization Of The "Bright" (Which Realization Includes and Yet Transcends every fraction Of The Total Cosmic Mandala). In The Context Of conditional Existence, The By-My-Avataric-Divine-Grace-Given Realization Of The "Bright" Is Demonstrated Even Universally (and Throughout the Total Apparent body-mind Of My By-Me-Enlightened Seventh Stage Devotee), but The Most Basic (or Original) conditional Demonstration Of The "Bright" Is The By-My-Avataric-Divine-Grace-Given Realization (or "Regeneration") Of Amrita Nadi (Which Is The Ultimate conditionally Manifested Form and "Location" Of Me-Realizing Devotion To My Avatarically Self-Revealed, and Self-Evidently Divine, Form, and Presence, and State). Therefore, Amrita Nadi—Which Is The "Bright" Fullness That Stands Between The Right Side Of The Heart and The Felt Matrix Of Sound and Light (or Of Even Unheard and Unseen Radiance, or Infinitely Ascended Love-Bliss) Infinitely Above The Total Crown Of the head—Is The Ultimate Yogic Form. Amrita Nadi (In Its By-Me-"Regenerated" Form) Is The Ultimate conditional (or Structural) Seat, Sign, and Divinely "Bright" Spiritual Body Of The Process Of Divine Translation (Into The "Midnight Sun"—Which Is The Sphere, and Space, and Substance Of My "Bright" Divine Self-Domain).

The Only-By-Me Revealed and Given Seventh Stage Of Life Is The Final Process, In Which This Ultimate Yogic Form (Which Is The "Regenerated" Amrita Nadi) and The Most Ultimate Event Of Awakening (or Divine Translation) Into The "Midnight Sun" (or "Bright" Sphere) Of My Divine Self-Domain Are Accomplished. And The Only-By-Me Revealed and Given Seventh Stage Of Life Begins With The Most Perfect (and Entirely By-My-Avataric-Divine-Spiritual-Grace-Given) Event Of Perfectly Subjective (Transcendental, Inherently Spiritual, Inherently egoless, Inherently Perfect, and Self-Evidently Divine) Self-Realization.

The Most Perfect Realization Of Perfectly Subjective Divine Self-Realization Is Not A Matter Of Identification With The Essential Inwardness Of the Apparent, conditional, Separate, or Distinct individual self. The Most Perfect Realization Of Perfectly Subjective Divine Self-Realization Is Realization Of That Which Is Always Already (and Inherently egolessly—and, Altogether, Unconditionally) The Case. The Most Perfect Realization Of Perfectly Subjective Divine Self-Realization Is Inherent, and Inherently Most Perfect, and

(Necessarily) Most Perfectly ego-Transcending Realization Of Me—Without The Concept Of "Difference".

Neither the conditional self Nor the conditional world (or the various conditionally Manifested relations of the conditional self) qualifies (or limits) The Realization Of Me In The Only-By-Me Revealed and Given Seventh Stage Of Life. Rather, both the (Apparent) conditional self and the (Apparent) conditional world Are Inherently (and Divinely) Self-Recognizable (or Inherently, Tacitly, and Inherently Most Perfectly Transcended) In The Case Of That Realization. Because Of This, both the (Apparent) conditional world and the (Apparent) conditional self (Simply as Divinely Self-Recognized body-mind, Rather Than as ego, or Un-Recognized self-Contraction) May (Until Divine Translation) Continue (Apparently) To arise—and To arise in any form at all—Without limiting The By-My-Avataric-Divine-Spiritual-Grace-Given Seventh Stage Realization Of My Avatarically Self-Transmitted (and Self-Evidently Divine) Love-Bliss and The By-My-Avataric-Divine-Spiritual-Grace-Given Seventh Stage (and Most Perfectly Non-"Different") Demonstration Of My Avatarically Self-Revealed (and Self-Evidently Divine) Self-Condition.

To Self-Abide (By Means Of My Avatarically Self-Transmitted Divine Spiritual Grace) As My Self-Radiant (or Inherently Spiritual, and Divinely "Bright") and Self-Existing (or Transcendental, and Perfectly Subjective, and Inherently egoless, and Inherently Perfect, and Self-Evidently Divine) Self-Condition Of Being (Itself)—Which Is The Perfectly Subjective (and Self-Evidently Divine) Source-Condition Of The Totality Of (and every particularity of) all arising conditions and all conditionally Manifested beings—Is The Eternal Seventh Stage, and Most Ultimate (or Complete, Final, Most Perfect, and Inherently Perfected), Yoga Of The Only-By-Me Revealed and Given Way Of The Heart (or Way Of Adidam). And, As Long As the conditional body-mind and the conditional world Continue To (Apparently) arise, The By-My-Avataric-Divine-Grace-Given Seventh Stage "Conscious Process" Of Divine Self-Abiding Will Be Spontaneously (and Necessarily) Associated With Divine Self-Recognition Of the conditions that (Apparently) arise. Such Divine Self-Recognition Is Inevitably Associated With (or Demonstrated Via) Divine Spirit-"Conductivity" (Demonstrated, Even Spontaneously, In The Context Of psycho-physical events). Therefore, This Inevitable Association Between The To-Me-Responsive Yoga Of The "Conscious Process" (Which Addresses the event of attention—or, Ultimately, The By-My-Avataric-Divine-Spiritual-Grace Revealed Divine Self-Condition) and The To-Me-Responsive Yoga Of "Conductivity" (Which Addresses The Extended psycho-physical Mechanism Of conditional experiencing and conditional knowing—and Which, Eventually, By Means Of My Avatarically Self-Transmitted Divine Spiritual Grace, Becomes

Divine Spirit-"Conductivity") Also Characterizes The Only-By-Me Revealed and Given Way Of The Heart In All Its Inevitable (or, Otherwise, Potential) Processes and All Its Necessary (or, Otherwise, Potential) Practices, Previous To (As Well As Ever After) The Awakening Of The Only-By-Me Revealed and Given Seventh Stage Of Life.

Avatar Adi Da Samraj
The Mountain Of Attention Sanctuary, 2001

SUTRA

17

I Am (By All My Avataric Means) Spiritually Present—Divinely Blessing all-and-All By My Mere (and Always Blessing) Spiritual Presence.

My Avatarically Self-Manifested Divine Blessing-Work Is The Spiritual Transmission-Work (or Giving-Work) Of Hridaya (or Sri Hridayam)—The Divine Heart (Itself).

My Avatarically Self-Transmitted Divine Spiritual Presence Is Blessing-Work (or Ruchira Avatara Kripa)—The Spiritual Transmission (or Grace-Giving) Of My Free (and Inherently Spiritual) Divine Self-Radiance (or Divine Love-Bliss)—Which Is The "Bright" (Itself).

My Avataric Self-Transmission Of My Divine Spiritual Blessing (or Ruchira Avatara Kripa) Is Heart-Grace (or Hridaya-Kripa)—My Divine Self-Giving Of The Spiritual Gift That Is The Inherently egoless "Bright" Divine Heart (Itself).

My Avataric Self-Manifestation Of My Divine Spiritual Transmission-Work (or Inherently Spiritual Blessing-Work) Is My Spiritual Self-Transmission (or Divine Self-Giving) Of My Ruchira Shakti (or Hridaya-Shakti)—The Graceful Divine Heart-Power That Is The Inherently egoless "Bright" Divine Heart (Itself).

My Always Me-Revealing Spontaneous Avataric Self-Transmission Of My Divine Spiritual (and Always Blessing) Presence (Whereby My By-Me-Spiritually-Initiated Devotees Are Given The Grace Of Most Profound True Devotion To Me, By their Heart-Feeling Of My Divine Spiritual "Brightness"), and My Otherwise Always Specifically-Given Avataric "Acts" Of Divine Spiritual Baptism (Whereby My By-Me-Spiritually-Initiated Devotees Are Whole bodily, or In Total psycho-physical Terms, Awakened To By-Me-Spiritually-Activated, and Always Me-Revealing, and Truly ego-Transcending Heart-Practice and Heart-Realization), Is Ruchira-Shakti-Kripa (or Hridaya-Shakti-Kripa), or Ruchira Shaktipat (or Hridaya-Shaktipat)—My Divinely Spiritually Initiatory Avataric Giving Of My Perfectly Attractive and Inherently Love-Blissful Grace-Power (Which Is The Spiritually Self-"Bright" Divine Grace-Power Of The Inherently egoless Heart, Itself).

Ruchira-Shakti-Kripa (or Hridaya-Shakti-Kripa), or Ruchira Shaktipat (or Hridaya-Shaktipat), Is Avatarically (and Uniquely) Given By Me—The Very, and Avatarically Self-Manifested, and Divinely Self-Revealing, and Transcendental, and Perfectly Subjective, and Inherently Spiritual, and Inherently egoless, and

Inherently Perfect, and Self-Evidently Divine Person, Who Is The Inherently egoless "Bright" Divine Heart (Itself), or The Self-Existing, and Self-Radiant, and Inherently egoless Divine Self-Condition (Itself), Which Is The Self-Evidently Divine Source-Condition Of all-and-All.

My Avatarically Self-Transmitted Divine Ruchira Shakti (or Hridaya-Shakti)—Which Is The Perfectly Subjective Divine Heart-Power That Is The Inherently egoless "Bright" Divine Heart Itself, and By Means Of Which I Awaken, In My True Devotee, The (Eventually) Most Perfect Realization Of My Avatarically Self-Revealed Transcendental, Inherently Spiritual, Inherently egoless, and Self-Evidently Divine Self-Condition (Itself)—Originates Eternally Prior To The Cosmic Mandala, and Eternally Prior To The Circle (or The "Circular" Pattern Of The Combined Frontal, or Descending, Line and Spinal, or Ascending, Line) Of the Cosmically-Patterned body-mind, and Eternally Prior To The Arrow (or The breathless and Moveless, but Upwardly Polarized, Central Axis) Of the Cosmically-Patterned body-mind.

Therefore, My Avatarically Self-Transmitted (and Perfectly Subjectively Me-Revealing) Divine Ruchira-Shakti-Kripa (or Hridaya-Shakti-Kripa), or Ruchira Shaktipat (or Hridaya-Shaktipat), Is Senior (and Most Perfectly Prior) To conditional (or conventional Yogic) Shaktipat (or Spiritual Transmission That Originates Dependently—or As A Merely conditionally-Arising, and Manifestly Objective, Cosmic Power—Within The Cosmic Mandala, and Within The Circle, and The Arrow, Of the Cosmically-Patterned body-mind).

Conditional (or conventional, and Merely conditionally, or Cosmically, Arising) Yogic Shaktipat and conventional (and Merely conditionally, or Cosmically, Significant) Yogic Practices Are Intended (or, Altogether, Activated) To Stimulate Movements Of attention In the Cosmically-Patterned (and ego-Based) body-mind, and (Thereby) To Accomplish Various conditional (or Cosmic, and, Necessarily, Yet ego-Bound) Goals (By Means Of A Process Of conditional Ascent Of The Manifestly Objective Cosmic Power, and Of attention itself, From the base To The Crown Of the Hierarchically Structured body-mind).

My Avatarically Self-Transmitted Divine Ruchira-Shakti-Kripa (or Hridaya-Shakti-Kripa), or Ruchira Shaktipat (or Hridaya-Shaktipat), and The (Thereby) Spiritually Initiated Divine Yogic Practice Of The Only-By-Me Revealed and Given Way Of Adidam (Which Is The One and Only By-Me-Revealed and By-Me-Given Way Of The Heart) Are Inherently Disposed (or By-Me-Heart-Founded and By-Me-Heart-Empowered) To Directly Dissolve (and, At Last, To Most Perfectly Transcend) attention itself (In My Avatarically Self-Revealed, and Transcendental, and Perfectly Subjective, and Inherently Spiritual, and Inherently egoless, and Inherently Perfect, and Self-Evidently Divine Person and Self-Condition).

Therefore, Whereas conditional (or conventional Yogic) Shaktipat and conventional Yogic Practices Actively Seek conditional Goals Of attention (In or Above The Circle, and The Arrow, Of the Cosmically-Patterned body-mind), My Avatarically Self-Transmitted Divine Ruchira-Shakti-Kripa (or Hridaya-Shakti-Kripa), or Ruchira Shaktipat (or Hridaya-Shaktipat), Directly Reveals (and, Subsequently, The Thereby Spiritually Initiated Practice Of The Only-By-Me Revealed and Given Way Of The Heart Directly, and, At Last, Most Perfectly, Realizes) Me (The Perfectly Subjective Person, and Self-Evidently Divine Self-Condition, Of The Heart—Eternally Beyond and Prior To attention, mind, body, The Circle, The Arrow, and all conditionally Manifested worlds). And The (Eventual) Most Perfect Realization Of Me Is The Most Perfect Realization Of The Only-By-Me Revealed and Given Divine Heart-Way (Which Is, At Last, To Stand As Is, Prior To Every Kind Of Seeking, and Prior To Any and All Movements Of attention, and Prior Even To attention itself—which is, itself, the Tacit ego-"I", or The Primal Act Of self-Contraction, Appearing As The Root-Feeling Of Relatedness Itself, or The Tacit Feeling Of "Difference" Itself).

My Avatarically Self-Transmitted Divine Ruchira-Shakti-Kripa (or Hridaya-Shakti-Kripa), or Ruchira Shaktipat (or Hridaya-Shaktipat), and The Subsequent (Spiritually Activated) Only-By-Me Revealed and Given Heart-Practice Generated By It, and (Altogether) The Spiritually Me-Revealing Spiritual Activity Of My Avatarically Self-Transmitted Spirit-Current (Always Moving In The Horizontal Plane Of The Heart—and Made Effective By Divine Descent Into the Cosmically-Patterned body-mind, From Infinitely Above), and The Only-By-Me Revealed and Given Heart-Realization Progressively Awakened (and, At Last, Most Perfectly Awakened) By It, Are Senior (and Most Perfectly Prior) To All Merely Cosmically-Oriented (and Merely conditionally, and Temporarily Effective—and, Thus, Merely egoically Significant) Spirit-"Conductivity" In The Circle (and The Arrow) Of the Cosmically-Patterned body-mind, and Senior (and Most Perfectly Prior) To All conditionally Manifested Activities Of The Merely Cosmic (or Kundalini) Shakti, and Senior (and Most Perfectly Prior) To All Merely conditionally Evident Processes and Events In The Upper and Lower Regions Of the Cosmically-Patterned body-mind. And My Avatarically Self-Transmitted Divine Ruchira-Shakti-Kripa (or Hridaya-Shakti-Kripa), or Ruchira Shaktipat (or Hridaya-Shaktipat), and The Subsequent (Spiritually Activated) Only-By-Me Revealed and Given Heart-Practice Generated By It, and (Altogether) The Spiritually Me-Revealing Spiritual Activity Of My Avatarically Self-Transmitted Spirit-Current, and The Only-By-Me Revealed and Given Heart-Realization Progressively (and, At Last, Most Perfectly) Awakened By It, Directly and Inherently Transcend Even All conditionally (or Cosmically) experiential Possibilities (Even Though They Do Not Otherwise Exclude, or Strategically Prevent, Them).

There Are Actually Two Distinct (and Very Different) Traditions Associated With The (conditionally Appearing) Kundalini Shakti.

The First (and Most Commonly known) Tradition Associated With The Kundalini Shakti Is Founded Upon the "Natural" (or gross bodily) point of view, and It Is Associated With The Ascent Of the Natural energies Of The physical, etheric, and lower mental (or lesser psychic) Dimensions Of the egoic human body-mind-self. This Tradition Is, Originally, Associated With The Ancient Animistic and Shamanistic Cultures Of Mankind—and It Developed, Over time, Via Such Traditions As Taoism, Hatha Yoga, and The Lesser Modes Of Tantrism.

The Second (and Senior, Although Less Commonly known) Tradition Associated With The Kundalini Shakti Is The Tradition Of Kundalini Shaktipat, Which Is The Process Of The Ascent and Circulation Of The All-Pervading Cosmic (or conditionally Appearing) Energy. And This Tradition Is Of Divine Origin. That Is To Say, This Tradition Is Not The Product Merely Of human psycho-physical Efforts To Achieve The Divine Condition (or Any Higher Knowledge and psycho-physical Powers). Rather, Kundalini Shaktipat Has Appeared Spontaneously (Originating, Ostensibly, From Above—but, Really, In Cosmic Terms, Effectively From Below), and It Has Always Been Given (Thusly) By (or In and Of) The Divine (In One or Another Cosmically Mediated Form) Directly To Potential Siddha-Masters (or Would-Be Spiritual Realizers), Who—By Means Of The Thus Received Kundalini Shaktipat—Then Proceed To Achieve Fully (or At Least Greatly) Ascended States. And The Same Kundalini Shaktipat That Was Received Is, Thereafter (or Once It Is Received and Developed), Transmitted (or Passed On) By The Siddha-Masters (and Always As and To The Degree and Stage Of Life It Has Been Developed By The Particular Shaktipat-Transmitting Siddha-Master) Via Their Subsequent (and Various) Lineages Of Disciples and Devotees.

I, In My Bodily (Human) Form, Received Kundalini Shaktipat (or The Transmission Of Cosmically Manifested Divine Spirit-Power) From The Yogic Siddha-Masters In My present-Lifetime Lineage Of Gurus. And, In My Own Case, The Divine Spirit-Transmission Was, At Last, Also Given Most Directly—In Person, and In Its Utter Fullness—By The "Divine Goddess", "Shakti" Herself.[59] However, All Of The Masters and Modes and Events Of Divine Spirit-Transmission Manifested To Me In The Course Of My Bodily (Human) Lifetime-Ordeal Were Necessitated By My Original Avataric Divine Act Of Submission To Be Born For The Sake Of all conditionally Manifested beings. Prior To That Avataric Divine Birth, and In The Instant Of It, and In The Earliest Years Of My Bodily (Human) Lifetime, I Was (and Always Already Am) The "Bright", The One and Only, and Divinely Self-Manifested, and Indivisible, and

Non-Separate Conscious Light (Itself)—The Source and Person Of Divine Spirit-Power (Itself) and Divine Spirit-Transmission (Itself). My Submission To Be Avatarically-Born Required The Lifetime-Ordeal Of My "Sadhana Years" and All Of My Avataric Divine Self-Revelation-Work. Nevertheless, In Due Course, The Divine Re-Awakening Of My Eternal Self-Condition Was Accomplished. And, Now (and Forever Hereafter), I Stand Free, In and As My Self-"Bright" Divine Self-Condition and Person, Avatarically Self-Transmitting My Divine Spirit-Power To all who Resort To Me As True and Faithful Devotees Of Mine.

My Own Avataric (and Unique) Work Of Divine Spiritual Transmission—Although It Also (Potentially, and Secondarily) Manifests Via The Signs Otherwise Characteristic Of Kundalini Shaktipat—Not Only Originates From Entirely (or Infinitely, and Truly Divinely, and Not Merely Ostensibly and Cosmically) Above, but Functions Entirely From Above Downwards (or In A Unique-To-Me Yogic Process In Descent). And My Avataric Divine Spiritual Transmission Manifests (Primarily) In and Via and At and As The True (or Fundamental) Heart Itself, Always Already Beyond and Prior To all limitations and conditionality. Therefore, My Avataric Work Of Divine Spiritual Transmission (or Ruchira Shaktipat, or Hridaya-Shaktipat) Directly (and Most Perfectly) Reveals The Perfectly Subjective Divine Heart (or Self-Existing and Self-Radiant and Inherently egoless Divine Being Itself)—Both In and As The Heart Itself (or The Priorly and Perfectly Self-Abiding, or Horizontal, Root Itself) and At and As The "Bright" Source Of All Lights (or The Priorly and Perfectly Ascended, or Vertical, Root Itself).

The Characteristic Descriptions (Whether Traditional or Modern) Of The Kundalini Shakti and Of the experiential phenomena Associated With The Kundalini Shakti Indicate (and Reflect) A Particular (conditionally-Based) Mode Of Energy-Development—Which Begins In The gross Dimension Of conditional Existence and Becomes (Potentially) More subtle As It Progresses. In Contrast, My Avataric Divine Spiritual Self-Transmission (or Ruchira Shaktipat) Does Not Originate In the gross plane. Rather, My Avataric Divine Spiritual Self-Transmission Originates Both Above (or From The Priorly Ascended Divine "Place", Infinitely Above The Crown Of the head) and In-Depth (or From The Priorly Self-Abiding Divine "Place", Prior To The Right Side Of The Heart)—Entering, From "There", Into The Totality Of conditional Patterns. Because It Originates Not Only From Above but Also From In-Depth, My Avataric Divine Spiritual Self-Transmission Is Felt (Primarily) As A Kind Of Progressive Saturation Of the Total psycho-physical being Of My Devotee. My Avataric Divine Spiritual Self-Transmission Is Unconditionally Self-Manifested and Tangibly Self-Indicated—Originating From Beyond and Perfectly Prior To the body-mind, and Indicated (Progressively) From Infinitely Above and

Deeply Within To Every Context and Dimension Below and Without. My Avataric Divine Spiritual Self-Transmission Does Not Merely "Hit" the gross physical body Of My Devotee. My Avataric Divine Spiritual Self-Transmission Originates Beyond (or Prior To) the causal plane—First Entering The causal Dimension, and (Then) The subtle Dimension, and (Then) The gross Dimension Of conditional Existence. That Is To Say, My Avataric Divine Spiritual Self-Transmission Saturates (or Pervades, or "Intoxicates") The Totality Of the psycho-physical being Of My Devotee—From Above and From In-Depth, To "Down" and "Out".

Therefore, My Avataric Divine Self-Revelation Is A Unique Revelation For The Sake Of all conditionally Manifested beings. My Avataric Divine Self-Revelation Is Not Offered or Given As A Method To "Get Back" To The Divine By Means Of Seeking (Whether In The Mode Of Ascent Or In The Mode Of Going Within). Rather, My Avataric Divine Self-Revelation Is The here-Given present-time Revelation Of That Which Is Prior and Divine.

Thus, I Do Not Offer You A "Path Of Return"—Whether From Below To Above Or From Left To Right.[60] My Avataric Divine Spiritual Self-Transmission In-Fills You—From Above To Below, and From Right To Left. Therefore, To Receive My Ruchira-Shaktipat-Transmission Is To Be Purified and Transformed By Heart-Communion With That Which Is Divine, and Priorly Ascended, and Infinitely Beyond (and Prior To) all conditions.

The Commonly known (or Lesser) Tradition Of The Kundalini Shakti Is Associated With self-Applied Yogic Techniques (Of bodily Exercises, breath Exercises, Exercises Of mental Concentration, and So On) That Are Intended To Raise Up the Natural energies Associated With the lower physical personality. Thus, Those Yogic Techniques Are Generally Associated, First, With Efforts To Arouse the Natural energy that Is Otherwise Locked Into the base of the body (at the lower end of the spinal column—at and above the perineum—and at the sexual center, and In The Entire General Region Of the abdomen, including the navel area, and the solar plexus), and, Second, With Efforts To Raise (and To Progressively Refine and Expand) that energy (or those energies) Upwards, Via The Ascending Hierarchy Of the various key centers Of The Spinal Line (Toward and To the primary centers in the head)—Until (Eventually, In conditionally Ascended Nirvikalpa Samadhi) The Ascending energy-Flow Is Released (Above the brain and the mind and The Total Crown Of the head) To The Most Ascended Source-Condition. And, In The Course Of That Ascending Process, many symptoms Of The Partially Ascended Kundalini Shakti May Progressively Appear (In The Form Of Yogic Developments Of A physical and, Then, Progressively More Purely psychic, or Fully psycho-physical, Kind). And Such Signs May Include Not Only Various

Yogic Powers (or Siddhis), and many visions, auditions, and So Forth (Progressively Revealing The Hierarchical Levels Of The psycho-physical Structure Of Man and The Cosmos), but They May Also Include Various (Either Brief or Long-Term) "Yogic Diseases" (or symptoms Indicating Either Processes Of psycho-physical Purification or A Misdirection Of the Natural energies Associated With The Yogic Process).

The Lesser-known (and Senior, and Greater) Tradition Of The Kundalini Shakti Is Also Associated With the same phenomena (and, As Secondary, or Merely Supportive, Exercises, The Same Yogic Techniques) Of Ascending Yoga That Characterize The Lesser Tradition Of The Kundalini Shakti. However, The Unique Characteristic Of The Senior and Greater (Kundalini Shaktipat) Tradition Is That The Kundalini Shakti (Itself) and The Fundamental Yogic Process Are Not Generated Via self-Effort and self-Applied Techniques, but The Yogic Process Is Generated (and Engaged, and Fulfilled) Directly and Spontaneously, By The Kundalini Shakti Itself—Which Is Given, Guided, and Constantly Re-Generated By A Yogic Siddha-Master (and Sometimes Via The Empowered Representative, or Representatives, Of A Yogic Siddha-Master). And, When Yoga Is So Given and So Guided, It Develops According To A Unique Divine Intelligence—Such That (Unless The Devotee Surrenders To the ego-self, Rather Than To The Guru, or Sat-Guru, and The Divinely Self-Revealing Power—and Although Many Signs Of psycho-physical Purification May Develop and Then Pass) The Yogic Process Does Not Develop Signs Either Of Misdirection Of energies or Of Fixed Attachment To lesser (or merely intermediate) conditional states.

Even The Senior Tradition Of The Kundalini Shakti (Like The Commonly known, or Lesser, Tradition Of The Kundalini Shakti) Is, Characteristically, Associated With The Spiritual Process Of Ascent, By Stages, From Below (or From the grosser To the subtler). Thus, The Essential Orientation, Even In The Schools Of The Senior Tradition Of The Kundalini Shakti, Is Toward A Process That Will, In Due Course, Progressively Ascend From Below (or the lower or grosser) Toward The Ultimate Goal Of Seeking (Which Is subtler and Above).

Overall, The General Tradition Of The Kundalini Shakti Is Based On A System Of Yogic philosophy That Idealizes Yogic Ascent (Not Descent)—and, Therefore, Both The Lesser and The Senior Traditions Of The Kundalini Shakti (and The Derivative Traditions Of "Ascending Yoga" In General) Are Associated With Systems and Techniques Of Practice That Are Intended To Strategically Develop The Ascending Yogic Process In The Context Of The Fifth Stage Of Life—Thus (Often, or Even In General) Bypassing (or, At Least, Minimizing) The Foundation Yogic Ordeal Associated With The "Original" and The "Basic" Fourth Stage Of Life (and, In Some Cases, Even The Necessary self-Discipline and self-Responsibility That Must Be Associated With The First Three Stages Of Life). As A Result Of This Bypass, Both The Lesser and The Senior Traditions Of The Kundalini Shakti—and The Various, and Variant, Traditions Of "Ascending Yoga" That Are Derived From The Generalized Tradition Of Kundalini Shakti Yoga—Are Often Associated With a point of view that Would Achieve Extreme Detachment, or Strategic Dissociation From the body-mind and the conditional world (and, Otherwise, In General, With Programs Of Practice That Do Not Pay Sufficient Practice-Time To Preparing The Right and Effective Foundation That Must Precede Yogic Activities In The Context Of The Fifth Stage Of Life—If The Potential Ascending Yogic Process Is Itself To Develop Truly, Rightly, and Fully).

In Contrast To All Such Traditional Yogic Idealism, The Only-By-Me Revealed and Given Way Of Adidam (and Of Ruchira Shaktipat)—Once It Is Spiritually Initiated By Me (and, All The While Thereafter, Spiritually Maintained and Magnified By Me)—Is Always Already Spiritually Established Above and In-Depth and Spiritually Functioning Above and In-Depth.

The Lesser (and, Generally, "Western") Interpretation Of The Nature Of The Kundalini Shakti Even Presumes That It Is an energy of a biological, physiological, or lower Natural kind (Rather Than Of A Transcendental and Divine, or Truly and Divinely Spiritual, Kind). Certainly, Many Traditional and Contemporary Reports Of experiences Of The Kundalini Shakti Type[61] Are Of the kind that Originates Solely In The lower, and physiological, and biological Context Of the human body-mind, and, Otherwise, that is limited To The Production Of phenomenal (and even merely egoic) states, In The Context Of the body-mind. However, My Ruchira Shaktipat (or Hridaya-Shaktipat), or Divine "Bright" Spiritual Transmission, Circulates In The Circle and everywhere Throughout the body-mind (Stimulating and Purifying every part and function). Therefore, My Avatarically Self-Transmitted Divine Spirit-Energy (or Ruchira Shaktipat, or Hridaya-Shaktipat) Initiates and Enacts A Process That, Potentially, Includes All That Is Otherwise Manifested In The Process Associated With The Kundalini Shakti (and Kundalini Shaktipat)—and Much More. However, The Spiritual Energy Transmitted and Made Active By My Ruchira Shaktipat Is Not, Itself, Of a lower Natural (or biological and physiological) kind—Nor Is It Of merely conditional (or Cosmic) Origin. Rather, That Spiritual Energy Is The Divine Spiritual Source-Energy (or Matrix-Energy), Of Which Natural (or biological, or physiological) energies Are A Mere (and Merely Apparent) Modification. That Spiritual Energy (If Allowed To Do Its Work, and Completely) Would (In Due Course) Convert (or Re-Align) every part and function of the body-mind To its Spiritually "Bright" Divine Source-Condition (or Matrix-Condition) Infinitely Above the body-mind. And That Spiritual

Energy Is My Most Prior Divine Ruchira Shakti. Most Ultimately (In The Eventual Final Demonstration Of The Only-By-Me Revealed and Given Seventh Stage Of Life), My Ruchira Shakti Would Outshine every part and function of the body-mind In The Transcendental, Inherently Spiritual, Inherently egoless, and Self-Evidently Divine Source-Condition, Realized In and Beyond and Infinitely Above The Right Side Of The Heart.

The Kundalini Shakti Process Generated By Kundalini Shaktipat Is, Characteristically, Demonstrated Via Purifying and Transformative Effects (and Awakenings) In the body-mind, In The Context Of The First Five Stages Of Life—Beginning (With Purifications) From Below, and Progressing (With Transformations and Awakenings) Upwardly (From the grosser Toward the subtler) Until The Goal (Of The Highest subtle Possibility) Is Reached. The Ruchira Shakti Process Generated By My Ruchira Shaktipat Is, Characteristically, Demonstrated Via Purifying and Transformative Effects In the body-mind In The Context Of All Seven Potential Stages Of Life—Beginning (With Purifications) From Above To Below, and Progressing (With Transformations and Awakenings) In A Course Of Realization That Is Priorly (or Always Already) Established and Operative Above and Beyond the Total body-mind (gross, subtle, and causal).

The Ruchira Shakti Process (Initiated By My Divine Spiritual Transmission In Descent) Can Be Initiated Even From a very early age. (That Is To Say, If There Is early-life Ruchira Shaktipat, or The Early Initiatory Descent Of My Avatarically Self-Transmitted Divine Spirit-Power, There Is Certainly, At Least In Optimum Cases, Sufficient Natural Development Of the central nervous system, and the general systems of the body-mind, To Permit The Descending and Circulating Process Of My Ruchira Shakti To Begin To Work In the pre-pubertal years.)

In My Own Case, My Birth Was (and My Life Is) Itself A Sign Of The Avataric Descent Of My Self-"Bright" Divine Spiritual Power and Presence. I Fully Assumed My Bodily (Human) Form At Approximately Two Years Of (Bodily) Age, and Full Spiritual Signs Were Immediately (and Priorly) In Evidence. Thus, I, From The Time I Was A Very Young Child (First Expressing thoughts In word-form), Named My State (and Its Accompanying Signs In the body-mind) "The 'Bright'"—and I Noted A Particular Recurring Phenomenon Of psycho-physically Transformative Descent Of Spiritual Energy (Which Descent, or Frontal Invasion, I Named "The 'Thumbs'").

My "Bright" Condition Was (and Is) The Most Perfectly (Divinely) Awakened Spiritual State (or Self-"Bright" Divine Self-Condition), In Which The Divine Love-Bliss-Energy (or Ruchira Shakti, or Hridaya-Shakti) Is Centered In The Heart and the head, and Circulates Throughout The Circle Of the body-mind

(By A Pattern Of Frontal Descent—From Infinitely Above The Total Crown Of the head—and Subsequent Spinal Ascent, or Return).

The "Thumbs" Was (and Is) A Process I Observed To Periodically Take Place In My Body (With Transformative Effects In My Entire Body-Mind) From My Earliest Years. And It Was (and Is) A Unique Version (or Special Intensification) Of The Circulatory Process Of The "Bright". Thus, At times, and From time To time (Sometimes daily, or every few days, and, Otherwise, Perhaps every few weeks or months—and With Exceptional Intensity, Sometimes Associated With episodes of fever and disease, Perhaps Once every year or two, or So), The Descending Divine Spiritual Love-Bliss-Energy Would Spontaneously Press Down From Above The Total Crown Of My head Into My head and My throat (With an Accompanying gagging sensation in the throat). There Was Also Usually Some Brief Struggle In The Heart and lungs Whenever This Divine Spiritual Invasion Came Upon My Bodily (Human) Form, and Then The Spiritual Energy Would Pass Down Into The Body, With Various Swooning Effects Following.

In Fact, Especially My Years Previous To puberty (Rather Than My teen-age Years) Were Filled With Extraordinary Ruchira Shakti Phenomena, and My teen-age Years Were (By Comparison, and In General) Rather Characterized By The Absence Of Such Signs (Until, After A Period Of Intense Struggle, They Began, Intensively, Again, When I Was, Bodily, Nearing Twenty-One Years Of Age). Thus, My Childhood Was Marked, At First, By A Steady-State Of (Spiritually "Bright") Self-Illumination—and, Year By Year, As I Became More and More Thoroughly Integrated With the human psycho-physical limitation, That Steady-State Was Periodically Interrupted and Progressively Diminished, Such That (Via The "Thumbs") It Was Required To Be (Periodically) Restored. And, Also, That Steady-State Became (Progressively) Replaced By A Kind Of Revolutionary Transformative Cycle, In Which Various Siddhis (or psychic and psycho-physical Powers) Were Sometimes Displayed, As Well As visions, auditions, Ecstasies, and So On, but Also Various Shakti-Caused (and Shakti-Filled) physical (and General psycho-physiological) Effects (Such As Extremes Of bodily hotness and bodily coldness, heart palpitations, feelings of suffocation, emotional suffering, variations in appetite, fluctuations of body weight, episodes of disease, Precocious Awareness Of sexual energy, and So On).

Thus, The physical (and General psycho-physiological) Effects Associated With My Own Early-Life Spiritual Experiences Confirm The Factuality and Correctness (In General Outline) Of The Traditional and Modern Descriptions Of The Extended Circuit (and the Most Typical experiential phenomena) Of The Kundalini Shakti Process. However, The Spiritual Demonstration Of My Early Life, Together With The Total Spiritual Demonstration Of My Adult Years,

Is A Unique (Transcendental, Inherently Spiritual, Inherently egoless, and Self-Evidently Divine) Revelation Of The Ruchira Shaktipat (or Total and Spontaneous Divine Descent-and-Circulation and Pervasion-and-Saturation) Process—Which Originates In and As The Perfectly Subjective Divine Ruchira Shakti (or Hridaya-Shakti). And Ruchira Shakti Is The Most Prior and Self-Existing Divine Self-Radiance, Of Which The Cosmically Manifested Kundalini Shakti (or The more limited, or Lesser, Shakti Process, Associated With An Upward Search, Beginning In The gross physiological Context) Is Only A Partial Sign.

Some Representatives Of The Tantric Tradition[62] Propose That The Kundalini Shakti May Actually Be Directly Awakened By Yogic sexual Practice (and Not Simply Preserved Thereby, or Served Thereby, Once It Is Already and Otherwise Awakened). However, It Is An Exaggeration To Claim That The Process Associated With The True (Spiritual) Kundalini Shakti May Be Either Initiated or Fulfilled By Any (However Yogic) sexual Practice (Itself), or By Any Other merely (and However Otherwise Right, Healthful, Useful, or Even Yogic) physical Discipline or Exercise—Such As Pure (or "Sattvic") Diet, or Any Kind Of breath-Control (or Pranayama), or Any Kind Of bodily Motion, Stretching, or Posing (or Asana), or Even Any Kind Of External or Internal Manipulation Of body, emotion, or mind. Generally, Unless The Kundalini Shakti Is Already Otherwise Activated (and, Generally, By Means Of Guru-Kripa, or Initiation Directly By A Spiritual Adept Of One or Another Degree, or Else Via The Empowered Representative, or Representatives, Of A Spiritual Adept Of One or Another Degree), Yogic sexual Practice (or Even Any Other Kind Of merely physical Discipline or Exercise) Simply Involves, At Best, What Is Traditionally Called "Pranotthana", or The (Perhaps Healthful and Pleasurable, but merely physical, or gross bodily) Ascent Of Natural etheric energies. And The Fullest Spiritual Ascent Of The Kundalini Shakti (Otherwise Activated) Is Not Likely To Be Achieved During (and Never As An Immediate and Direct Result Of) Any Yogic sexual (or, Otherwise, Active physical) Practice—Because The Fullest Spiritual Ascent Of The Kundalini Shakti (To conditionally Ascended Nirvikalpa Samadhi) Requires Deep Passive Relinquishment (or The Effective Transcending) Of the body-mind. And, In Any Case, What Fullest Spiritual Ascent Of The Kundalini Shakti Really Requires Is True Spiritual Contemplation (or Divine Communion) In Ascent.

Contrary To The Expressed Opinion Of some popularizers Of Yoga (and Of Yogic sex-Practices), The Kundalini Shakti Is Not merely personal sex-energy (or, Otherwise, merely physical energy) "Reversed" (or Ascending, Rather Than Naturally Descending). The Kundalini Shakti Is A Mode Of The All-Pervading Cosmically-Manifested (or conditionally Appearing) Spiritual Energy That Is The Single Manifested Substance Of all conditionally Manifested energies, processes, and forms. The Kundalini Shakti Is A Mode Of The All-Pervading Cosmically-Manifested Spiritual Energy That Is Otherwise Appearing As all conditional (or limited) energies, including personal sex-energy—but It Cannot (Itself) Be Reduced To sex-energy (itself), or To any other form of limited (specific or personal or functional) energy (itself). Therefore, The Kundalini Shakti Cannot Be Awakened Merely By The "Reversal" (or Ascent) Of The Naturally Descending Tendency Of the personal energy Of The sex-Impulse (or Of any other form of functional human energy), but The True Kundalini Shakti Can Be Awakened Only By Divine Spiritual Grace (Usually, As Transmitted By A Spiritual Adept Of One or Another Degree, or As Transmitted Via The Empowered Representative, or Representatives, Of A Spiritual Adept Of One or Another Degree).

The True Kundalini Shakti Is All-Pervading, and Not Merely personal and Internal. And, Therefore, The True Kundalini Shakti Is Awakened In The personal (and Internal) psycho-physical Context Only By Virtue Of Grace-Given (and ego-Transcending) Participation In The All-Pervading Field Of Cosmically-Manifested Spiritual Energy. Likewise, Consciousness (Itself), or Self-Aware Being (Itself), Is Not A Merely personal and Internal Characteristic Of conditional individual (or merely psycho-physical) Existence—but It Is An Inherent Characteristic Of Unconditional Reality (Itself). And, Therefore, Consciousness (Itself) Appears As An Apparent personal and Internal Characteristic Of conditional individual Existence Only When psycho-physical conditions Permit An Unconditional-Reality-Conjunction—and, Thus, A Conjunction Between conditional form (itself) and (Self-Evidently Divine) Consciousness (Itself) and The All-Pervading Cosmically-Manifested Spiritual Energy (or Kundalini Shakti, Itself) and The Self-Existing, Self-Radiant, and Self-Evidently Divine Energy (or Ruchira Shakti, or Hridaya-Shakti) Of Unconditional Reality (Itself).

The Divine and Unconditional Ruchira Shakti—Which Is The Self-Existing and Self-Radiant Divine Spirit-Power That Stands Eternally As The Perfectly Subjective Divine and All-Outshining Spiritual Self-"Brightness", Always Already Most Prior To (or Above and Beyond) Cosmic (or conditional) Manifestations—Is The Truly Ultimate (and Inherently Perfect) Spiritual Energy-Source, and Unconditional Self-Condition (or Being-Condition), Of The Kundalini Shakti. And Only The Divine and Unconditional Ruchira Shakti Is Identical To Unconditional Reality (Itself)—and, Thus and Therefore, To (Self-Evidently Divine) Consciousness (Itself). And, For This Reason, Only The By-Grace-Given Divine (and Unconditional) Ruchira Shakti Awakens The Realization Of Unconditionally "Bright" Divine Consciousness (Itself)—Which Is Unconditional Reality (Itself) and Unconditional Truth (Itself).

I Am The Inherently egoless Eternal Person Of Unconditional Reality (Itself). I Am The Self-Existing, Self-Radiant, Inherently Spiritual, Perfectly "Bright", and Perfectly Subjective Spiritual Heart (Itself). I Am The (Now, and Forever Hereafter) Avatarically Self-Manifesting Eternal Person Of Unconditionally "Bright" Consciousness (Itself), Whose Eternal Spiritual Body Is The Great Ruchira Shakti—or The Truly Divine Self-Power Of The Inherently "Bright" and Perfectly Subjective Spiritual Heart—Itself. And, Therefore, The Divine Ruchira Shakti Is That "Bright" Divine Spiritual Power By Which, and With Which, and As Which Only I (Uniquely, and Characteristically) Bless (By Radiating From Above and Beyond, To what Is Below and Within and objectively Around), and (By A Divinely Self-Revealing Progress) Awaken, All My Devotees (By Means Of My Divine Spiritual Descent From Infinitely Above, Rather Than By their Seeking To Ascend To Me From Below—and By Means Of My Divine Spiritual Pervasion From In-Depth, Rather Than By their Seeking To Find Me By "Going Within")—Even, Thereby (or In The Unfolding Course Of That Avataric Divine Spiritual Work Of Blessing Descent and all-and-All-Awakening), Also Arousing and Revealing As Many Purifying and, Otherwise, Developmental psycho-physical Signs (Even Such As May Otherwise Be Characteristic Of The Process Associated With The Cosmic Kundalini Shakti) As May Be Necessary, In The Case Of My Any True Devotee.

And I Will (By All My Avataric Divine Spiritual Means) Forever (and Constantly) Bless All My True Devotees—So That The Perfectly Subjective, Self-Radiant, Spiritually "Bright", Self-Existing, and Unconditional Reality and Truth Is (By Means Of My Avatarically Self-Manifested Divine Spiritual Blessing-Work) Directly, Always, and More and More Perfectly (and, At Last, Inherently and Divinely Most Perfectly) Revealed (As The Obvious, or Unconditionally Self-Evident, Reality and Truth) To My Every Thus True (and Truly To-Me-Devoted) Devotee.

Objective Shakti (or Any Form or Mode Of Spiritual Energy Felt, or Perceived, or Experienced In Relation To one's body-mind, or Even In Apparent Relation To Consciousness Itself) arises (Thus, Objectively) Only If the Cosmic world and the Cosmically-Patterned body-mind arise.

There Is No Objective Shakti To Be Felt, or Perceived, or Experienced, Unless the Cosmically-Patterned psycho-physical point of view arises—To Feel, or Perceive, or Experience It.

There Is No Objective Shakti To Be Found, Unless a conditional point of view (or a point of self-Contraction, or an Otherwise conditionally limited point Of Reference) Is Presumed.

There Is No Objective Shakti To Be "Located" In Relation To one's body-mind (or Even In Apparent Relation To Consciousness Itself), If The

Root-Feeling (or, Necessarily, conditional Presumption) Of Relatedness Is Not Generated (and Identified With, or Otherwise—At Least Apparently, or As a convention Of Apparent conditional Existence—Presumed).

The True, Ultimate, and Inherently Perfect (and Self-Evidently Divine) Shakti Is My Avataric Self-Revelation Of My Self-Existing and Self-Radiant "Bright" (and Perfectly Subjective, and Always Already Infinitely Ascended, or Inherently Most Prior) Divine Love-Bliss, Which Is Native To The Inherently egoless Heart Itself (or Perfectly Subjective, and Non-Separate, and Non-"Different", Consciousness Itself—Realized As The Feeling Of Being, Itself).

Only That (Only-By-Me Avatarically Self-Transmitted, and Perfectly Real and True, and Perfectly Ultimate, and Inherently Perfect, and Self-Evidently Divine) Shakti (or Self-Existing and Self-Radiant "Bright" Divine Feeling-Energy, or Perfectly Subjective Divine Spiritual Fullness) Is "Ruchira Shakti" (or "Hridaya-Shakti").

That Only-By-Me Avatarically Self-Transmitted (and Self-Evidently Divine) Ruchira Shakti (or Hridaya-Shakti) Is Senior To (and Perfectly Subjective To) The Cosmically-Objectified Kundalini Shakti.

The Kundalini Shakti Is Always Objective—or Felt, or Perceived, or Experienced In Relation To the Apparent (and Apparently personal) body-mind, and In Either The gross Context Or The subtle Context Of the conditional (or Cosmically-Patterned) world. Therefore, The Kundalini Shakti Itself (As Objective Spiritual Energy) arises conditionally, and Its Manifestation Is Entirely Dependent On Cosmic (or psycho-physical, and, Altogether, conditional) Events.

Only My Avatarically Self-Transmitted Divine Ruchira Shakti (or Hridaya-Shakti)—Which Is Perfectly (or Always Most Priorly) Subjective (or Only In The Inherently egoless Subject-Position, or Non-Separate Heart-Position), and Which Is (Therefore) Identical Only To Unconditional (or Self-Evidently Divine) Existence (or Most Perfectly Prior Being) Itself—Stands Always Already Beyond and Prior To The Root-Feeling (or Primal conditional Feeling) Of Relatedness Itself (and, Therefore, Always Already Beyond and Prior To The Cosmic Domain, the Cosmically-Patterned body-mind-self, and conditional, or Cosmically-Manifested, Existence Itself).

My Avatarically Self-Transmitted (and Always Only Me-Revealing) Spiritual Blessing (By Which I Divinely Bless all-and-All) Is My Unique Divine Self-Giving Of My Ruchira Shakti (or Hridaya-Shakti)—The Inherent (and Inherently Spiritual, and Perfectly Transcendental, and Self-Evidently Divine) "Brightness" (or Self-Existing and Self-Radiant Love-Bliss) Of The (Perfectly Subjective, and Inherently egoless) Heart Itself. And those who Truly (and, In The Technically Responsible Sense, Fully) Receive My Avatarically

Self-Transmitted Spiritual Blessing (or Avatarically Self-Transmitted Divine Ruchira Shaktipat, or Hridaya-Shaktipat) Are (Thus and Thereby) Directly Awakened (In Due Course) To Stable Self-Identification With The Witness-Position Of Consciousness Itself (Which Is The Perfectly Subjective, and Inherently egoless, "Position" Of The Inherently egoless Heart Itself) and, Thus and Thereby, To The "Perfect Practice" Of The Only-By-Me Revealed and Given Way Of The Heart.

The (Always Objective and Cosmic) Kundalini Shakti arises (or Shows Itself As Various Effects) In The Context Of Any or All Of The First Five Stages Of Life.

My Avatarically Given (and Always Perfectly Subjective, and Self-Evidently Divine) Ruchira Shakti (or Hridaya-Shakti) Always Simply Stands As Itself—Identical To My Avatarically Given Divine Self-Revelation Of The Inherently egoless (or Non-Separate and Non-"Different") Feeling Of Being (Itself), Always Most Perfectly Prior To All Apparent Objectivity.

To Feel, or Perceive, or Experience The Kundalini Shakti Is Necessarily To Be Moved (Thereby) everywhere Within The Cosmically-Extended Context Of conditional Existence (and Only Within The ego-Based Context Of The First Five Stages Of Life)—but (By Means Of My Avatarically Self-Transmitted Divine Spiritual Grace) To "Locate" My Avatarically Self-Transmitted Divine Ruchira Shakti (or Hridaya-Shakti) Is (Progressively) To Directly, Spontaneously, and (In Due Course) Inherently Perfectly Transcend All Of The First Five (and, Indeed, The First Six) Stages Of Life (and, Thus and Thereby, At Last, Even All Of Cosmic, or conditional, Existence Itself).

Therefore, My Most True (or Truly Mature) Devotees Do Not Seek Any Cosmically-limited (and ego-Binding) "Effects" Of My Avatarically Self-Transmitted Divine Spiritual Presence. They Do Not Strive To Linger In The Cosmic Domain. They Do Not Wish To Prolong The Course Of The Practice Of The Way Of The Heart Associated With The ("Object"-Oriented) Processes Of The First Five Stages Of Life. They Do Not Incline themselves To Dote Upon Any Objectified (or conditional) Feeling, or Perception, or Experience Of My Avatarically Self-Transmitted Divine Spiritual Presence.

My Most True (or Truly Mature) Devotees Are Devoted Only To Me—As I Am. They Are Not "Concerned" About Kundalini Experiences (Even If These arise)—but they Are Always Heart-Moved To Utterly Surrender, Forget, and Transcend self-Contraction (and, Therefore, all of Cosmically-Patterned body-mind, and All Of Cosmic "Play", and All Of conditional, or Merely Cosmic, and ego-Bound, Existence Itself).

Therefore, My Most True (or Truly Mature) Devotees Are those who Benefit The Most (and Most Directly) From My Avatarically Self-Transmitted

Divine Spiritual Blessing (or Avatarically Self-Transmitted Divine Ruchira Shaktipat, or Hridaya-Shaktipat). And they Are (Thereby) Directly (At The Heart) Relieved Of All Seeking. And they Do Not Surrender, Forget, and Transcend self-Contraction, the body-mind, the conditional world, and Cosmic (or conditional) Existence By Means Of The Strategic (or ego-Bound) Efforts Of Great Seeking. Rather, they Are Spontaneously Moved To Inherently Perfect Surrender, and Inherently Perfect Forgetting, and Inherently Perfect Transcending Of self-Contraction, and Of Cosmically-Patterned body-mind, and Of conditional (or Merely Cosmic) world, and Of conditional (or Merely Cosmic, and ego-Bound) Existence—Simply By Feeling (and Thereby Contemplating) Me (and, Thus, By Yielding Utterly To The Inherently Perfect Attractiveness Of My Heart-Perfect Avatarically-Born Bodily Human Divine Form, My Avatarically Self-Revealed, and Blessing-Perfect, Divine Spiritual Presence, and My Avatarically Self-Revealed, and Very, and Transcendental, and Perfectly Subjective, and Inherently Spiritual, and Inherently egoless, and Inherently Perfect, and Self-Evidently Divine State).

The Only-By-Me Revealed and Given Way Of The Heart (or Way Of Adidam) Is (Progressively, and Responsively) The Divine Heart-Way Of The "Conscious Process" (or Direct Heart-Release Of the self-Contraction), Realized (Most Ultimately) To The Degree Of Inherent Love-Bliss-Radiance (or The Realization Of My Avatarically Self-Revealed, and Transcendental, and Perfectly Subjective, and Inherently Spiritual, and Inherently egoless, and Inherently Perfect, and Self-Evidently Divine Spirit-"Brightness"—Which Realization Is, Itself, Inherently Most Perfect, Unconditional, and Transcendentally-Awakened Divine Spirit-"Conductivity").

Conventional (or ego-Based) Paths Depend On Mere Cosmic conditions (or, Otherwise, Seek To Strategically Exclude Cosmic conditions, and, By Means Of That Strategy, Bypass The Necessary Process Of ego-Transcendence In The Context Of Cosmic conditions). The Only-By-Me Revealed and Given Way Of The Heart (or Way Of Adidam) Is The Divine Heart-Way—The Way That (Inherently, Spontaneously, and Progressively, or, More and More Effectively, and Truly Counter-egoically) Observes, Understands, Changes, Releases, and Directly Transcends (and, At Last, Most Perfectly, or Inherently, and Divinely, Self-Recognizes, Transfigures, Transforms, and Translates) Cosmic conditions In My Avatarically Self-Revealed Unconditional (and Perfectly Subjective, and Self-Evidently Divine) Self-Condition.

The Only-By-Me Revealed and Given Way Of The Heart (or Way Of Adidam) Is The Divine Heart-Way Of The Divine Consciousness (Itself). The Divine Consciousness (Itself) Is The Master Of Its Own Divine Spiritual Energy (and Of Even all Apparent, or conditionally Manifested, energies). Therefore,

Whereas conventional (or ego-Based) Paths Manipulate the conditional self and the conditionally Manifested energies Of Cosmic Nature (or Even The Spiritual Energy Of The egoically Presumed Divine) In A Search For The Eventual Attainment Of The Great (Divine, and Would-Be-egoless) Principle—I Call You To Directly Realize The Great (Divine, and Inherently egoless) Principle, By Means Of ego-Transcending Devotional Recognition-Response To My Avatarically Self-Revealed Person (and, In Due Course, To My Avatarically Self-Transmitted Divine Spiritual Grace), and To Do So At The Very Foundation (and From The Very Beginning) Of The Only-By-Me Revealed and Given Way Of The Heart (or Way Of Adidam).

I Call (and, In Due Course, Spiritually Bless) You (Even From The Beginning Of Your Practice Of The Only-By-Me Revealed and Given Way Of The Heart) To Realize (or, In Due Course, To Be, By Means Of My Avatarically Self-Transmitted Divine Spiritual Grace, Always Directly Awakened To) The Great (Divine, and Inherently egoless) Principle That Is My Avatarically Given "Bright" Divine Self-Revelation Of The Perfectly Subjective Heart (Itself). From The Beginning Of Your Practice Of The Only-By-Me Revealed and Given Way Of The Heart, I Call (and, In Due Course, Spiritually Bless) You To Realize (or, In Due Course, To Be, By Means Of My Avatarically Self-Transmitted Divine Spiritual Grace, Always Directly Awakened To) The Perfectly Subjective (and Inherently egoless) "Bright" Heart Itself By (First) Listening To Me (and "Considering" My Avatarically Self-Revealed, and Ever-Working, Divine Word and Image-Art and Story Of Heart-Instructing, Heart-Inspiring, and Heart-Purifying Teaching-Arguments and Intrusions) and (Then, Having Already Been Spiritually Initiated By Me) Hearing Me—and, Therefore, Whether In The Manner Of The Devotional Way Of Insight Or In The Manner Of The Devotional Way Of Faith, To Progressively (and Then Most Fundamentally) Understand self-Contraction, and To (Thus and Thereby) Progressively (and Then Most Fundamentally) Undermine and Transcend self-Contraction, Through Devotionally Me-Recognizing, and Devotionally To-Me-Responsive, and Always ego-Surrendering, and Really ego-Forgetting, and Entirely ego-Releasing (and, Necessarily, body-mind-Purifying) Feeling-Contemplation Of My Avatarically-Born Bodily (Human) Divine Form, and My Avatarically Self-Transmitted Spiritual (and Always Blessing) Divine Presence, and My Avatarically Self-Revealed (and Very, and Transcendental, and Perfectly Subjective, and Inherently Spiritual, and Inherently egoless, and Inherently Perfect, and Self-Evidently) Divine State. And (When You Have Heard Me, and When You Have Effectively Demonstrated That True Hearing) I Call (and Spiritually Bless) You To Realize (or, In Due Course, To Be, By Means Of My Avatarically Self-Transmitted Divine Spiritual Grace, Always Directly—and In

The, Spiritually, Fully Technically Responsible Manner—Awakened To) My Perfectly Subjective (and Transcendental, and Inherently Spiritual, and Inherently egoless) "Bright" Heart (or State) Itself, By Seeing Me—and, Thus and Thereby, Whether In The Manner Of The Devotional Way Of Insight Or In The Manner Of The Devotional Way Of Faith, To Continue To Directly Transcend self-Contraction In every moment (and In The Context Of All Of The Actually Me-Seeing Stages Of Practice In The Only-By-Me Revealed and Given Way Of The Heart), Not Only Through The Continued Demonstration Of Most Fundamental self-Understanding, but (More and More) Through The Free Devotional (or Heart-Attracted and Heart-Awakened and Directly ego-Transcending and, Spiritually, Fully Technically Responsible) Recognition-Response To My Avatarically Given "Bright" Divine Self-Revelation Of The Spiritual, Transcendental, and Self-Evidently Divine Forms Of Reality, or Truth, or Real God.

From the point of view of the Cosmically-Patterned body (and ego-mind), The Inherent Self-Radiance Of Self-Existing Divine Being Is perceived To Be An Objective (Universal and All-Pervading) Cosmic Spirit-Energy (or Cosmic Shakti)—Which Is Always At Work, Moving (and Modifying) the world, the body, and the mind (and Even Binding attention, By Those Very Movements, and To Those Very Modifications).

From The Divinely Self-Realized (and Inherently egoless) "Point Of View" Of Consciousness Itself (Which Is The Inherently egoless Heart Itself—Avatarically Self-Revealed, By Me, As My Self-Existing, or Transcendental, and Self-Radiant, or Inherently Spiritual, and Inherently egoless "Bright" Divine Self-Condition, Itself), Even The Apparently Objective (Universal and All-Pervading) Cosmic Spirit-Energy (or Cosmic Shakti) Is Divinely Self-Recognized (and Inherently, and Inherently Most Perfectly, Transcended) In My Avatarically Given Divine Self-Revelation Of The Merely (or Only) and Perfectly Moveless "Bright" Self-Radiance (or Inherent Love-Bliss) Of Consciousness Itself (Which Is My Avatarically Self-Revealed Eternal—and Not, Itself, Cosmic, but Perfectly Subjective—"Bright" Divine Self-Condition Itself).

Therefore, My Ultimate (or Inherently Perfect, and Self-Evidently Divine) Avataric Blessing Is My Avataric Spiritual Self-Transmission (and, Thereby, Direct Divine Spiritual Awakening) Of The Inherent (Self-Existing, and Self-Radiant) Condition (or Eternal State) Of Self-Evidently Divine Being—Which Is My Avatarically Given Divine Spiritual Self-Revelation Of The (Inherently) Perfectly Subjective (and Inherently egoless) Heart (or Self-Existing and Self-Radiant Inherent Space) Of Consciousness Itself (Eternally Moveless, As My "Bright" Divine Sphere—or "Midnight Sun"—Of Love-Bliss, Itself).

My (Thus) Inherently Perfect (and Self-Evidently Divine) Avataric Blessing Is My Avataric Spiritual Self-Transmission Of My (Thus and Thereby) Avatarically Self-Revealed (and Very, and Transcendental, and Perfectly Subjective, and Inherently Spiritual, and Inherently egoless, and Inherently Perfect, and Perfectly Moveless, and Self-Evidently Divine) State (Itself)—Which Is The Original, Primary, and Ultimate Form Of My Avatarically Me-Revealing Divine Spiritual Transmission. And To Receive The Transmission Of My Avatarically Self-Revealed (and Very, and Transcendental, and Perfectly Subjective, and Inherently Spiritual, and Inherently egoless, and Inherently Perfect, and Self-Evidently Divine) State Is To Commune With Me (As I Am), Non-Separately (or Beyond "Difference"), In The "Place" Of Consciousness Itself, Beyond All psycho-physical Noticing.

My (Thus) Inherently Perfect (and Self-Evidently Divine) Avataric Blessing Is My Fundamental, and Direct, and Constant Avataric Spiritual Transmission. Therefore, My Fundamental (and Direct, and Constant) Avataric Spiritual Transmission Is My Avataric Spiritual Transmission Of My Very, and Transcendental, and Perfectly Subjective, and Inherently Spiritual, and Inherently egoless, and Inherently Perfect, and Self-Evidently Divine State Itself—Even In The Case Of All My By-Me-Spiritually-Initiated Listening Devotees, and Hearing Devotees, and Seeing Devotees. And all those who (In The Context Of The Formal Practice Of The Only-By-Me Revealed and Given Way Of The Heart) Receive Me Perfectly Become (In Due Course) My (Inherently) Perfect Devotees.

The Devotee-Receiver Of My Avatarically Self-Transmitted Divine Spiritual Blessing (Whether As My By-Me-Spiritually-Initiated Listening Devotee, Or Hearing Devotee, Or Seeing Devotee) Will (Whole bodily, or In Total psycho-physical Terms) Receive My Heart-Blessing Only According To his or her Real Present (and Formally Acknowledged) Developmental Stage (or moment) Of Formal Practice In The Only-By-Me Revealed and Given Way Of The Heart—and My Divine Avataric Spiritual Heart-Blessing Will (Therefore) Always Be perceived To Reveal Me Accordingly.

Therefore, My Avatarically Self-Transmitted Divine Spiritual Heart-Blessing Will (Necessarily) Appear (or Be Revealed) By Progressive Stages.

First (Via My Avatarically Self-Revealed Divine Word, and My Avatarically Self-Revealed Divine Image-Art, and My Avatarically Self-Manifested Historical Play Of Divine Work, and My Always Giving and Revealing Avatarically-Born Bodily Human Divine Form), I Am (Now, and Forever Hereafter) At Work To Attract and To Guide and To Instruct My Listening Devotee (and, In Due Course, To Spiritually Initiate My Listening Devotee, By Means Of My Ruchira Shaktipat).

In This Manner (and In Due Course), I Awaken Most Fundamental self-Understanding In My (Thus, Hearing) Devotee.

Eventually (When My Devotee Both Hears Me and Sees Me—and Is, Thus and Thereby, Further Enabled, In The Fully Technically Responsible Sense, To Spiritually Receive Me), I Appear (Most Fully) As and By Means Of My Avatarically Self-Transmitted Divine Spirit-Current Of "Bright" Love-Bliss—perceived (In Total psycho-physical Terms) To Be Moving In the world, and the body, and the mind (and, Thus and Thereby, Purifying and Absorbing the world, the body, and the mind As I Move).

Nevertheless, I Am (All The While—and, Really, Only) Standing Free.

Even From The Beginning Of This Avatarically Me-Revealing Course, I Am My Avatarically Self-Revealed (and Very, and Eternal, and Transcendental, and Perfectly Subjective, and Inherently Spiritual, and Inherently egoless, and Inherently Perfect, and Self-Evidently Divine) State (or Self-Condition)—Which Always Already (and Only) Stands, Self-Existing and Self-Radiant, As The (Inherently, and Non-Separately, and Non-"Differently") Perfectly Subjective (and Transcendental, and Inherently Spiritual, and Inherently egoless) "Bright" Heart (or Spherical Divine Self-Domain) Itself.

Therefore, Only The (Inherently, and Non-Separately, and Non-"Differently") Perfectly Subjective (and Transcendental, and Inherently Spiritual, and Inherently egoless) Self-Condition That Is My Avatarically Self-Revealed, and Self-Transmitted, and Self-Evidently Divine Heart (or Self-Condition) Itself Is The Great Principle Of My Avatarically Self-Manifested Divine Spiritual Blessing-Work.

Only The Non-Separate, and Non-"Different", and Perfectly Subjective (and Transcendental, and Inherently Spiritual, and Inherently egoless, and Self-Evidently Divine) Self-Condition Is (Inherently, and Self-Evidently) Perfect.

The (Inherently, and Non-Separately, and Non-"Differently") Perfectly Subjective (and Transcendental, and Inherently Spiritual, and Inherently egoless) Heart (or Divine Self-Condition) Itself Is The Inherently Perfect (and Inherently Spiritual, and Inherently egoless) Position (or State) Of Free (and Self-Evidently Divine) Consciousness (Itself).

The (Inherently, and Non-Separately, and Non-"Differently") Perfectly Subjective (and Transcendental, and Inherently Spiritual, and Inherently egoless) "Bright" Heart (or Divine Self-Condition) Itself Is The Inherent (and Self-Evidently Divine) Feeling Of Being (Which Is The Perfect, Itself).

The Transcendental, and Inherently Spiritual, and Inherently egoless, and Inherently Perfect, and Self-Evidently Divine Heart (or Self-Condition) Itself Is The (Inherently, and Non-Separately, and Non-"Differently") Perfectly Subjective Self-Condition (or Self-Evidently Divine State) Of The (Inherently, and Non-Separately, and Non-"Differently") Perfectly Subjective "Bright" Sphere (or "Midnight Sun") Of My Self-Evidently Divine Self-Domain (Itself).

Therefore, By Practicing The Only-By-Me Revealed and Given Way Of The Heart (or Way Of Adidam)—You Must (By Means Of My Avatarically Self-Transmitted Divine Spiritual Grace) Grow To Realize The Only-By-Me Revealed and Given Great Practice That Is (By Means Of My Avatarically Self-Transmitted Divine Spiritual Grace) Generated (Inherently, and Non-Separately, and Non-"Differently") As and At and From The Perfectly Subjective (and Transcendental, and Inherently Spiritual, and Inherently egoless, and Inherently Perfect, and Self-Evidently Divine) Position Of The "Bright" Heart (or Spherical Divine Self-Domain) Itself.

And I Am Your "Bright" Divine Companion, Avatarically Descended (Humanly and Spiritually) here—Until You Receive and Realize Me Most Perfectly (and Perfectly egolessly) There ("Where" and As I Always Already, Divinely and Spiritually, Am).

Avatar Adi Da Samraj
The Mountain Of Attention Sanctuary, 2000

SUTRA 18

The Full (and Fully Fruitful) Responsive Practice Of The Only-By-Me Revealed and Given Way Of Adidam (Which Is The One and Only By-Me-Revealed and By-Me-Given Way Of The Heart) Is—In Terms Of The Technical Practices Engaged In Response To The Gift Of Satsang With Me—A Matter Of Both The "Conscious Process" (and The Realization, Most Ultimately, Of My Avatarically Self-Revealed, and Transcendental, and Perfectly Subjective, and Inherently Spiritual, and Inherently egoless, and Inherently Perfect, and Self-Evidently Divine Self-Condition) and "Conductivity" Practice (or The Constant Establishment Of attention, and the Total body-mind, In My Avatarically Self-Transmitted Divine Spirit-Energy)—Because My Avatarically Self-Revealed, and Transcendental, and Perfectly Subjective, and Inherently Spiritual, and Inherently egoless, Inherently Perfect, and Self-Evidently Divine Self-Condition (Itself) Is Both Transcendental (or Self-Existing, Prior To conditional Existence) and Inherently Spiritual (or "Brightly" Self-Existing, As Self-Radiant Energy, or Love-Bliss).

In Order For attention To Be Constantly Established In My Avatarically Self-Transmitted Divine Spirit-Energy, You Must Become My Seeing Devotee. And, In Order To Prepare Yourself To See Me, You Must (As My Listening Devotee, and, Eventually, As My Hearing Devotee) Consistently Practice The Primary By-Me-Given Gift, Calling, and Discipline Of Ruchira Avatara Bhakti Yoga—Which Is The Responsive (or Devotionally Me-Recognizing, and Devotionally To-Me-Responding) and Constantly (and Really Effectively) Counter-egoic, and Total psycho-physical, Practice Of ego-Surrendering, ego-Forgetting, and, More and More (and, Ultimately, Most Perfectly), ego-Transcending Devotion To Me (and Devotional Communion With Me), The Ruchira Avatar, Adi Da Samraj (The Divine Heart-Master Of each and all Of My Devotees), and Which Is The moment to moment Fulfillment Of My Great Admonition To All My Devotees (To Always Invoke Me, Feel Me, Breathe Me, and Serve Me), and This Constantly Exercised Via The Surrender, The Forgetting, and The Transcending Of the self-Contracted body, and self-Contracted emotion (or all of self-Contracted, and Reactive, and, Altogether, limited, feeling), and self-Contracted mind (Even At its Root, Which Is attention itself), and Even every self-Contracted breath, and, Altogether, Even all of Separate (and Separative) self, In moment to moment (and Truly, or Unlimitedly, Heart-Felt, and Whole bodily Receptive, and Fully breathing, and Only-By-Me Distracted) Devotional Remembrance Of Me and Direct Devotional Surrender To Me (In All Its Details, Including All The functional, practical, and relational Disciplines, and All The Cultural Obligations, I Have Given To My Devotees). And, In Order To See Me, You Must (As My Listening Devotee, and, In Due Course, As My Hearing Devotee) Practice Each and Every Aspect Of Ruchira Avatara Bhakti Yoga—In The Manner I Have Specifically Indicated For My Listening and (Then) Hearing Devotees.

In Every Stage Of The Only-By-Me Revealed and Given Way Of The Heart (or Way Of Adidam), The Practice Of Ruchira Avatara Bhakti Yoga Involves The Yielding (or The Surrender) Of The Principal Faculties (Of body, emotion, mind, and breath) To Me. In The Beginner's Process, This Yielding Of The Principal Faculties To Me Can Show Signs Of Devotionally Absorptive Samadhi (or Spiritual Receptivity) Of One Kind or Another. But My Beginning Devotees Are Not Yet Most Profoundly (and Fully Technically) Responsible For Receiving and Conducting My Spirit-Blessing—and (Therefore) My Calling To My Beginning Devotees Is, Specifically, My Call (To them) To Demonstrate (and To Constantly Magnify) The Signs Of Devotionally Me-Recognizing Devotional Response To Me (Including Exemplary Fulfillment Of The Various functional, practical, and relational Disciplines, and The Various Cultural Obligations, That Are Particular To their Developmental Stage Of Practice Of The Only-By-Me Revealed and Given Way Of The Heart).

All Of The By-Me-Revealed and By-Me-Given functional, practical, and relational Disciplines Are Forms Of "Conductivity" Practice—and (As Such) They (All) Serve To Constantly Bring the body-mind Into The Condition Of Energy, Relieving My Devotee Of The Presumption That the body-mind Is Merely self-Contracted matter (fleshy, anxious, and Inevitably Suffering). And The Primary and Constant By-Me-Revealed and By-Me-Given Means For Bringing (or Yielding) the body-mind To The Condition Of Energy Is To Yield the body-mind To The Condition Of Ecstasy In Devotionally Me-Recognizing and Devotionally To-Me-Responsive Communion With Me (Divinely Self-Revealed, By All My Avataric Means). Therefore, For You (As My Truly Devotionally Me-Recognizing, and Truly Devotionally To-Me-Responding, Devotee) To Bring (or Yield) the body-mind To The Condition Of Energy, You Must Be Truly (Devotionally, and Counter-egoically) Given Over To Me—No Longer Existing In An egoically self-Conscious and egoically self-Controlling Mode, No Longer Preoccupied With The "Narcissistic" Exercise Of Your Own body-mind, and No Longer Armoring Yourself Against Me, but (Instead)

Always Whole bodily Surrendering Your egoic self, Whole bodily Forgetting Your egoic self, and (More and More) Whole bodily Transcending Your egoic self, To The Point Of Whole bodily (and Truly ego-Transcending) Devotional Absorption In Me.

You Must (As My Truly Devotionally Me-Recognizing, and Truly Devotionally To-Me-Responding, Devotee) Exercise The Practice Of Ruchira Avatara Bhakti Yoga moment to moment—Such That Your entire life Becomes ego-Surrendering, ego-Forgetting, and (More and More) ego-Transcending Devotion To Me, and Devotional Communion With Me, and Devotional Ecstasy In Me. If You Truly Do This (As My Listening Devotee, and, In Due Course, As My Hearing Devotee), You Will Find (In Due Course) That—By Consistently (and Fully Devotionally) Yielding (physically, emotionally, With attention, and With the breath) To My Avatarically Self-Revealed, and Self-Evidently Divine, Person (and To The Degree Of Whole bodily Energy-Ecstasy)—You Have Become Prepared To Make The Great Discovery (and Allow The Great Reception) Of My Avatarically Self-Transmitted (and Love-Blissful, and Constantly Baptizing) Divine Spirit-Presence.

The Principal Sign Of Fullest Preparedness For The Seeing Stages Of Practice Of The Only-By-Me Revealed and Given Way Of The Heart (or Way Of Adidam) Is The Capability To Identify Me Spiritually (and To "Locate" Me Spiritually) moment to moment. But There Are Also Secondary Signs Of Preparedness For The Seeing Stages Of Practice Of The Only-By-Me Revealed and Given Way Of The Heart—Which Are The Various Signs Of Spiritually Receiving Me, or The Signs That The Principal Faculties (Of body, emotion, mind, and breath) Are Being Spiritually Infused By Me. (And The Necessity Of Adapting The Entire psycho-physical Vehicle Of the body-mind, With All its Faculties, To The Condition Of Openness and Receptivity To The Great Energy Of My Avatarically Self-Transmitted Divine Spiritual Heart-Transmission Is One Of The Principal Reasons Why The Only-By-Me Revealed and Given—and, In Due Course, Spiritually Me-Receiving—Yoga Of Ruchira Avatara Bhakti Is Practiced From The Very Beginning Of The Way Of The Heart, and Continues To Be Practiced Throughout The Entire Course Of The Way Of The Heart.)

When All The psycho-physical Faculties Are Yielded To Me, and Devotionally (and Truly Counter-egoically) Absorbed In My Avatarically Self-Revealed (and Self-Evidently Divine) Person (and, Thereby, Yielded To The Condition Of Energy, Such That My Devotee Truly Receives My Avatarically Self-Transmitted Divine Spiritual Blessing), Then the body-mind Receives (Via All its Faculties) A Forceful Infusion Of My Divine Spiritual Energy (The Force Of Which Is, At First, Far Greater Than The Force Of the Natural life-energy that the body-mind Is Accustomed To Circulating). By Virtue Of The Devotional and Spiritually Me-Receiving Process Engaged During The Listening and

Hearing Stages Of Practice Of The Way Of The Heart, the body-mind Of My Devotee Is Enabled To Conduct The Force Of My Avatarically Self-Transmitted Divine Spiritual Blessing (and The Heart Of My Thus Enabled Devotee Is, Also, Always Able To "Locate" Me, Spiritually)—but (Until the body-mind Of My Devotee Is, Altogether, Fully Adapted To Receive The Fullest Force Of Me), When the body-mind Of My Devotee Receives The Great Force Of My Avatarically Self-Transmitted Divine Spiritual Blessing, the entire body (and Even the Total body-mind) Of My Devotee "Shakes".

Thus, the physical body Of My Newly Spiritually Me-Receiving Devotee Moves (or "Shakes") In Various Spontaneous Ways. And, Thus and Thereby, the emotion Of My Spiritually Me-Receiving Devotee Undergoes A Profound Feeling-Expansion. And the attention Of My Thus Spiritually Me-Receiving Devotee Becomes Deeply Established In My Love-Bliss-Transmission. And the breath Of My Thus Spiritually Me-Receiving Devotee Undergoes Various Spontaneous Changes. Indeed, A Wide Variety Of Spontaneously Purifying Experiences (or kriyas of body, emotion, mind, and breath) Are Possible In the body-mind Of My Spiritually Me-Receiving Devotee. And There Are Different (and Varying) Signs In Each individual Case. And It Is Not Possible For My Any Newly Spiritually Me-Receiving Devotee To Truly Receive Me Spiritually Without Being "Shaken" (In body, emotion, attention, and/or breath)—Because The Vehicle Of the body-mind Of My Devotee Is Not (At First) Capable Of "Containing" The Fullest Infusion Of My Avatarically Self-Transmitted Divine Spiritual Force. Therefore, the body-mind Of My Newly Spiritually Me-Receiving Devotee (With All its Faculties) "Shakes", Moves, and Experiences All Kinds Of Spontaneous Changes—and It Is <u>My</u> Avatarically Self-Transmitted Divine Spiritual Intrusion That Makes These Movements and Changes In the body-mind Of My Devotee.

This Great Reception Of My Avatarically Self-Transmitted (and Overwhelming) Divine Spirit-Presence (Such That The Faculties Are Thus "Shaken") Is A Necessary Sign That My Devotee Has Truly Received Me. And, When My Truly Spiritually Me-Receiving Devotee Has (By Practicing Ruchira Avatara Bhakti Yoga To The Point Of Profundity) Truly Heard Me (and, Thus, Has Out-Grown The egoically self-Conscious and egoically self-Controlling Effort Relative To the body-mind, With All its Faculties, and Has Thereby Become Able To Present the entire body-mind To Me Without Armoring), he or she Is Really and Truly Entering Into The Process Of Seeing Me.

In The Case Of My Any Devotee (and, Indeed, In The Case Of any human being) who Has Not Yet Been Spiritually Initiated, By Me, Into The Ongoing Devotional Process Of Spiritually Receiving Me, the body-mind (In its Bondage) Is Capable Of Imitating Signs That (Otherwise) Accompany True Spiritual

Manifestations. This Is Due To The Fact That The psycho-physical Medium That Is The human Structure Itself Is The Same In The Case Of one who Has Not Yet Been Spiritually Awakened By Me As it Is In The Case Of one who Has Been Spiritually Awakened By Me. Therefore, All Kinds Of gross-minded Bondage Can (Potentially) Display Itself Via (Even Apparently Extraordinary) Signs In the body-mind—Such As developmental psychisms, Natural siddhis (or Un-common psycho-physical Abilities and Signs), and So On.

Thus, There Are Many lowly (or lower) Manifestations That Are Apparently "Greater" (or, At Least, More Unusual) Than The gross-minded Sign Of the ordinary social ego. But The Apparent "Greatness" (or Unusual Character) Of Such Signs Does Not, In and Of Itself, Indicate That The Signs Are Of A Profound (Spiritual and Divine) Nature. In the ordinary individual, Such Signs Are Simply Manifestations Of What Can Occur "From the ground Up" (That Is To Say, Non-Spiritually, and Non-Divinely), In The Degrees Of The Natural Loosening-Up and energy-Saturation Of The psycho-physical Mechanism With Which the human being Is Associated.

When My Avatarically Self-Transmitted Divine Hridaya-Shakti-Transmission (or Ruchira-Shakti-Transmission) Is Received, the body-mind Of My Spiritually Me-Receiving Devotee Is Taken Over, and All Kinds Of Processes and States Occur Spontaneously (or Automatically). Such Is The True Guru-Yoga—Which Is The Yoga Done By Me (The True Divine Guru), and Not A (Necessarily, merely conditional and ego-Reinforcing) "Yoga" Enforced By The ego-Efforts (or self-"guruing") Of the individual ego-self (and, As Such, egoically Enforced By, and limited to, the conditional processes of mere Natural life-energy). For My Seeing Devotee, This True Guru-Yoga Of Unobstructed and Unguarded (and Total psycho-physical) Spiritual Reception Of Me Is (Truly, Clearly, Tangibly, and Overwhelmingly) A Matter Of ego-Surrendering, and Effectively ego-Transcending (and, Thus, Total psycho-physical Contraction-Transcending), Receiving Of Me.

In Due Course, When The Spontaneous Yoga Of My Spiritual Intrusion Has Been Worked For a Sufficient period of time In My Seeing Devotee, Then the body-mind Of My Seeing Devotee (With All its Faculties) Becomes So Fully Opened To Me That My Hridaya-Shakti-Transmission (or Ruchira-Shakti-Transmission) Is No Longer Received In A limited gross Manner (or Merely In My Seeing Devotee's gross body-mind), but Also Beyond the gross sphere (By Means Of Fullest, and Really self-Contraction-Relinquishing, psycho-physical Participation In My Infinite Divine Field Of Love-Bliss-Radiance). When This Occurs, the body-mind Of My Seeing Devotee No Longer Necessarily Has To "Shake" In Order To Conduct My Spiritual In-Pouring—and So The "Tremblings" Decrease, and Even (Generally) Cease.

Thus, All The Exercises Of The Listening-Hearing Process Prepare My Listening (and Then Hearing) Devotee To *Fully* Receive Me Spiritually. And Then, In Turn, The Entire Process Of (Spiritually) Fully Receiving Me Becomes Preparation For The "Perfect Practice" Of The Only-By-Me Revealed and Given Way Of The Heart (or Way Of Adidam).

To Come To The Point Of Preparedness For The "Perfect Practice" Of The Only-By-Me Revealed and Given Way Of The Heart Not Only Requires *Perfect Maturity In* The "*Conscious Process*"—but It Also (Necessarily) Requires *Inherently Perfect* "*Conductivity*" Of My Avatarically Self-Transmitted Divine Spirit-Presence. In The "Perfect Practice" Of The Only-By-Me Revealed and Given Way Of The Heart, My Avatarically Self-Transmitted Divine Spirit-Presence Drives (In Its Association With the body-mind Of My Devotee) To The Heart-Root On The Right. Therefore, The "Perfect Practice" Of The Only-By-Me Revealed and Given Way Of The Heart Is A Far Greater Matter Than Merely Being Inclined To Focus attention In The Right Side Of The Heart. In The "Perfect Practice" Of The Only-By-Me Revealed and Given Way Of The Heart, My Attractive Spirit-Force Itself *Moves* To The Right Side Of The Heart (By Circulating In the body-mind Of My Devotee To The Point Of Settling In The Right Side Of The Heart)—If Only My Devotee Rightly, Truly, and Really Devotionally Participates In That Transcendental (and Inherently Spiritual) Process. Therefore, This *Spiritual* "Locating" Of Me In The Right Side Of The Heart Is A *Necessary Characteristic* Of The "Perfect Practice" Of The Only-By-Me Revealed and Given Way Of The Heart—and, Indeed, It Is (In Its Initial Demonstration) A *Necessary Qualification* For *Entering* The "Perfect Practice" Of The Only-By-Me Revealed and Given Way Of The Heart—Which Entrance (*Necessarily*) Also (and *Primarily*) Coincides With The Stable Awakening To The Witness-Position Of Consciousness.

Thus, The Only-By-Me Revealed and Given Way Of The Heart (or Way Of Adidam) Is *Entirely* (and Throughout Its Entire Course) About *Me*. It Is Not About "You" (In Your Separateness). The Only-By-Me Revealed and Given Way Of The Heart (or Way Of Adidam) Is A Matter Of Your Relinquishment Of Your Own ego-position (Through self-Surrender, self-Forgetting, and, More and More, self-Transcendence) In Order (From The Beginning) To Devotionally Commune With Me, To (In Due Course) Be Devotionally Absorbed In My Avatarically Self-Revealed (and Self-Evidently Divine) Self-Condition, and (Ultimately) To Most Perfectly Realize My Avatarically Self-Revealed (and Self-Evidently Divine) Self-Condition.

I Am Always Doing The Only-By-Me Revealed and Given Divine Spiritual Yoga Of The Way Of The Heart—In The Case Of My Every Devotee. In The Case Of My Every Devotee, Every (Progressive) Realization In The Only-By-Me

Revealed and Given Way Of The Heart Is A Realization Of Me. The Progressive Process Of The Only-By-Me Revealed and Given Way Of The Heart Occurs Because You Practice The Primary By-Me-Given Gift, Calling, and Discipline Of Ruchira Avatara Bhakti Yoga—To The Point (In Due Course) Of Absorptive Devotional Communion With Me, and (Then) To The Point Of Perfect Self-Identification With Me—Such That My Own Substance Of Inherently Perfect Divine Being and Of Mere and "Bright" Divine Spirit-Presence Becomes Your Experience, Your Certain Knowledge, and (Ultimately) Your Most Perfect Realization.

Therefore, The Only-By-Me Revealed and Given Way Of The Heart (or Way Of Adidam) Is Not A self-Applied, Strategic Technique For Manipulating (and Thereby Changing) Your Own body-mind.

The Only-By-Me Revealed and Given Way Of The Heart (or Way Of Adidam) Is The Practice Of Devotional Communion With Me and Devotional Realization Of Me—Not Realization (or Achievement) Of something In "You" (In Your Separateness).

In Order To Realize Me Most Perfectly, You Must Be Utterly Surrendered To Me (and Into My Avatarically Self-Revealed, and Utterly Non-Separate, Divine Condition), Beyond Your egoic (or Separate) self.

Therefore, With Your Total body-mind, You Must Participate In My Condition, My Sacrifice, My Action, My Manner, and My Characteristic State.

And, In The Only-By-Me Revealed and Given Seventh Stage Of Life, There Is No "You"—but There Is Only Me.

Always, "You" (In Your Separateness) Are Not The One To Be Realized.

Always, I Am The One To Be (Non-Separately) Realized.

Therefore, Let the body-mind Be Heart-Opened To Me, Through Devotional Listening, To The Degree Of True Hearing (or Most Fundamental self-Understanding)—and Then Let The To-Me-Opened Heart (and The To-Me-Heart-Opened Total body-mind) Be Deeply Attracted To Me (and Spontaneously Converted To Me), Through The Seeing Of Me (Which Is The Progressive Process Of Total psycho-physical Heart-Conversion To My Avatarically Self-Revealed Spiritual, and Always Blessing, Divine Person and Presence, By Means Of My Avatarically Self-Transmitted Divine Spirit-Baptism). Then Practice Whole bodily (or Total psycho-physical) self-Surrender To Me, In Meditation and In daily life, By Breathing and Feeling My Avatarically Self-Transmitted Divine Spirit-Energy In The Total Frontal Line Of the body—Down From Infinitely Above The Total Crown Of the head, and Down, Through The Total Crown Of the head, To The Ajna Door (or The Root Of The Brain Core, Between and Slightly Above and Deep Behind the brows), and, From Thence, Down Through the Total facial area, Then Down Through

The Region Of the throat, Then The Region Of the physical heart, Then the solar plexus and the abdomen, To the bodily base (or The Region That Includes the genitals, the perineum, and the anus). When This Descending Practice Is Full, You Will Also (In The Context Of The Developments Of The "Perfect Practice") Further Develop The Experiences Of The Full Circle and Of The Arrow, and You Will Always Breathe and Feel My Avatarically Self-Transmitted Divine Spirit-Energy Ever More Deeply Upwards, Via The Ajna Door, To The Total Crown Of the head, and (From Thence) Ever More Above (and, at Last, Infinitely Above) the head.

If The By-Me-Avatarically-Given Responsive Practice and "Conscious Process" (Of The Devotional Surrender Of attention To Me, Such That attention Is, Thus and Thereby, Absorbed—and, Ultimately, Dissolved, or Utterly Transcended—In Me) Is Rightly, Truly, Fully, and Fully Devotionally Embraced and Engaged By You (As A Formal Practitioner Of The Only-By-Me Revealed and Given Way Of The Heart), and If You Consistently and Constantly Engage That Responsive Practice and "Conscious Process" In Conjunction With Right, True, Full, and Fully Devotional Formal Embrace and Engagement Of The (In Every Respect) Equally Necessary By-My-Avataric-Divine-Spiritual-Grace-Given Divine Spiritual Means (Which Is The By-Me-Given Responsive Practice and Process Of "Conductivity" Of My Avatarically Self-Transmitted Divine Spirit-Presence), Then The Entire (and The Ultimate) Divine Way (and Divine Self-Revelation) Of The Only-By-Me Revealed and Given Way Of The Heart Will Be Given To You, By Me. Therefore, If You Are My True (and, Necessarily, Formally Practicing) Devotee, The Revelations Of Descent (and Of The Full Circle, and Of The Arrow), and The Revelation Of The Witness-Consciousness (and The Revelation Of The Heart On The Right, and The Revelation Of The Perfectly Subjective, and Inherently egoless, Heart Of Consciousness Itself), and (Most Ultimately) All The Descended and Ascended Revelations and Demonstrations Of The Only-By-Me Revealed and Given Seventh Stage Of Life Will (Each and All) Be Given To You—Inevitably, and In Right Time, By Means Of My Avatarically Self-Transmitted Divine Spiritual Grace.

Avatar Adi Da Samraj
The Mountain Of Attention Sanctuary, 2000

SUTRA 19

In The Only-By-Me Revealed and Given Way Of Adidam (Which Is The One and Only By-Me-Revealed and By-Me-Given Way Of The Heart), The Practice Of Spirit-"Conductivity" (Whether It Develops In The Manner Of The Devotional Way Of Insight Or In The Manner Of The Devotional Way Of Faith) Begins When You Are Baptized (or Spiritually Awakened) By and In and To My Avatarically Self-Transmitted Divine Spiritual Presence and Person. Therefore, I Will (Now, and Forever Hereafter) Continue To Avatarically Transmit My Divine Spiritual Presence—Even (After, and Forever After, The Avataric Physical Lifetime Of My Own Bodily Human Divine Form) Via The Formally Acknowledged and True Instruments, and The Formally Acknowledged and True Agents, Of My (Now, and Forever Hereafter) Avatarically Self-Manifested Divine Blessing-Work.

By Means Of Baptism By and In and To My Avatarically Self-Transmitted Divine Spiritual Presence and Person, My Formally Practicing Devotees Become Spiritually Converted (and Both Devotionally <u>and</u> Spiritually "Bonded") To Me—The True and Only and Non-Separate and Self-Evidently Divine Person, The Inherently Perfect Heart and Non-Separate Self-Condition Of all-and-All.

By Means Of Baptism By and In and To My Avatarically Self-Transmitted Divine Spiritual Presence and Person, All My (Thereby) Seeing Devotees Whole-bodily-Receive (or Are themselves Whole-bodily-Given To) My Divine Spirit-Power—and (By Means Of Thus By-Me-Given Spiritual Communion With My Avatarically Self-Transmitted Spiritual Presence and Person) they Find (and, In Due Course, Realize) Me <u>As</u> The Avatarically Self-Revealed, and True, and Only, and Non-Separate, and Self-Evidently Divine Person, The "Bright" Divine Heart Itself, The Ultimate and Inherently Perfect Source (and The Ultimate and Inherently Perfect Identity) Of My Avatarically Self-Transmitted Divine Spirit-Energy Itself.

Once Baptism By and In and To My Avatarically Self-Transmitted Divine Spiritual Presence and Person Is Confirmed By True (Spiritually Activated) Heart-Conversion, My Seeing Devotee Must Let My Divine Spirit-Current Radiate From The Heart, and Stand In the body (head To toe), and (With every breath) Rotate In The Circle (Descending, and Then Ascending).

Therefore, When You Are (Truly) Baptized By and In and To My Avatarically Self-Transmitted Divine Spiritual Presence and Person, and When You Are (Thus, Thereby, and Truly Whole bodily) Converted At Heart By (and In, and To) My Avatarically Self-Transmitted Spiritual (and Always Blessing) Divine Presence—You Must Conduct and Conserve My Avatarically Self-Transmitted Divine Spirit-Power, By Transcending Every Tendency To Reverse The Downward Flow In The Frontal Line and The Upward Flow In The Spinal Line. In This Manner, You Must Overcome and Transcend Every Tendency To Obstruct or Weaken The Flow Of My Avatarically Self-Transmitted Divine Spirit-Energy, As Well As Every Tendency To Break The Circle At Any Point. Thus, You Must Be Carried Through The Circle By The Living Flow (or Current) Of My Avatarically Self-Transmitted Divine Spirit-Presence—and You Must Allow My Avatarically Self-Transmitted Divine Spirit-Current To Find Its Way To My Divine Self-Heart. And, When I Am Revealed As The Inherently egoless Heart Itself (Which Is The Perfectly Subjective Feeling Of Being, Itself, or Self-Existing and Self-Radiant Consciousness, Itself), You Must Allow Me To Reveal The Eternal Freedom, and The Boundless "Bright" Sphere and Space, Of My Divine Self-Domain—Which Is The Eternal Condition Of My Avatarically Self-Revealed (and Self-Evidently Divine) Person, Beyond The Cosmic Mandala, In The "Midnight Sun" Of Only One.

Avatar Adi Da Samraj
Adidam Samrajashram, 2003

SUTRA

20

In The Practice Of The Only-By-Me Revealed and Given Way Of Adidam (Which Is The Only-By-Me Revealed and Given Way Of The Heart)—First, You Must Listen To Me and Hear Me (Whether In The Manner Of The Devotional Way Of Insight Or In The Manner Of The Devotional Way Of Faith). Then You Must See Me (and, Thus and Thereby, "Locate", Identify, and Become Attracted To My Avatarically Self-Transmitted Divine Spiritual Presence) Via My Avatarically Giving Gift Of Divine Spirit-Baptism. When You See Me, You Must Practice Spiritually Awakened Reception Of My Avatarically Self-Transmitted and all-and-All-Pervading Divine Spirit-Power In The Frontal Line.

On The Basis Of Hearing Me and Seeing Me, You Must Overcome The Tendency To Reverse (or To Obstruct, or To Be Weak In) The Frontal Line. Do This By The Practice Of Devotional Heart-Communion With Me, Supported By The Active Combination Of Most Fundamental self-Understanding, The "Conscious Process" (In The Manner Of Either self-Enquiry Or "True Prayer"), Conversion Of All emotional Reactivity Into Free Heart-Feeling (or Love), Regular Performance Of The functional, practical, relational, and Cultural Disciplines, and Steady and Full Spirit-"Conductivity" In The Frontal Line.

On The Basis Of Hearing Me and Seeing Me, You Must Overcome The Tendency To Break The Circle. This Breaking Is Generally The Product Of physical imbalance, toxicity, vital weakness, and degenerative sexual activity. Therefore, Repair, and (Otherwise) Avoid (or Voluntarily Relinquish), These Results Of Unlawful living—Through ego-Surrendering, ego-Forgetting, and (More and More) ego-Transcending Feeling-Contemplation Of <u>Me</u>, and Through self-Discipline, In The Context Of The Process Of Listening To Me.

On The Basis Of Hearing Me and Seeing Me, You Must Become Full and Steady In The Frontal Line. Then, In The Context Of The Developments Of The "Perfect Practice", You Will Continue To Receive and Conduct and Be Carried By My Avatarically Self-Transmitted Divine Spirit-Current, and You Will (Thus and Thereby) Let The Circle Always Be Full (Not Weak, Not Obstructed, Not Reversed, and Not Broken), Such That (In Due Course) the cerebro-spinal fluid is physically heard and felt pulsing and clicking through the ventricles of the brain. You Will Do This Until The Knot In The Brain Core (or the self-Contraction itself, As it Registers In The Total Brain Core) Is Opened, and The Passage Above The Brain Core (and Above The Total Crown Of the head) Is Made Clear. Then (In Due Course) You Will Let My Avatarically Self-Transmitted Divine Spirit-Current Carry You Further Upwards (Even To The Highest Place—Infinitely Above The Total Crown Of the head—Which Is The Free Ascended Space, or Most Ascended Place Of Origin, Of My Avatarically Self-Transmitted Divine Love-Bliss).

In The Only-By-Me Revealed and Given Way Of The Heart, The Yoga Of Realizing My (Eternally) Always Already Ascended Condition (Even, At Last, Through Dissolution Of all conditions In The Sphere and Space Of My "Midnight Sun", or Eternal Divine "Bright" Form) Is Entered Only After You (By Means Of My Avatarically Self-Transmitted Divine Spiritual Grace) Come To Rest In The Prior (and Transcendental) Witness-Position Of Free Consciousness (Inherently Free Of All Concern For the body-mind). And The (Thus) "Perfect Practice" Of The Only-By-Me Revealed and Given Way Of The Heart Must Persist—Until The Most Perfectly Ultimate and Divinely Real Condition Of The Heart (or Of Consciousness Itself) Is, By Means Of My Avatarically Self-Transmitted Divine Spiritual Grace, Revealed (Most Perfectly, and As That Which Is Always Already, and Non-Separately, and Non-"Differently" The Case).

Then, By Means Of My Avatarically Self-Transmitted Divine Spiritual Grace, The Heart (Itself) Will Shine Upwards To The Highest Place—and It Will Shine From There, Into The Circle Of the body-mind, and every "where" In The Cosmic Domain. And My Avatarically Self-Transmitted Inherent Love-Bliss-Happiness Will Freely Descend and Ascend In The Circle Of the body-mind, Radiating In All Directions.

Then, By Means Of My Avatarically Self-Transmitted Divine Spiritual Grace, Self-Abide (Non-Separately, and Non-"Differently") As My Self-Existing, and Self-Radiant, and Perfectly Subjective, and Self-Evidently Divine Self-Condition (or "Bright" State) Of Person—Divinely Self-Recognizing All Modifications Of That Condition That Are experienced Via The Parts Of The Circle. Self-Abide Thus, Divinely Self-Recognizing all beings and conditions In My "Bright" Divine Love-Bliss. Self-Abide Thus, Standing As My Avatarically Self-Revealed (Transcendental, Inherently Spiritual, Inherently egoless, and Self-Evidently Divine) Self-Condition—Until The Inherent "Brightness" Of My Avatarically Self-Revealed (Transcendental, Inherently Spiritual, Inherently egoless, and Self-Evidently Divine) Self-Condition Outshines the body-mind and The Total Cosmic Mandala.

Then, By Means Of My Avatarically Self-Transmitted Divine Spiritual Grace, You Will Stand In (and As) My Divine "Bright" Spherical Self-Domain—Which

Is Self-Existing, Self-Radiant, and Perfectly Subjective Being Itself, Shining As The "Midnight Sun", Beyond all attention to the worlds Of Cosmic Struggle and death.

Avatar Adi Da Samraj
The Mountain Of Attention Sanctuary, 2000

SUTRA 21

The Only-By-Me Revealed and Given Way Of The Heart (or Way Of Adidam), Developed Either In The Manner Of The Devotional Way Of Insight Or In The Manner Of The Devotional Way Of Faith, Is The Divine Way Wherein and Whereby egoity (or the Total psycho-physical self-Contraction) Is Directly, Progressively, and (Ultimately) Most Perfectly Transcended—and This By The By-My-Avataric-Divine-Spiritual-Grace-Given Means Of More and More Perfect Inherence In My Avatarically Self-Revealed (and Self-Existing, and Self-Radiant, and Inherently egoless, and Self-Evidently Divine) Self-Condition. Therefore, The Only-By-Me Revealed and Given Way Of The Heart Is (and More and More Becomes) The Way Of Devotion (or Sacrifice) Of the conditional self To Me, Rather Than Any ego-Based Search For self-Fulfillment and self-Release.

The Only-By-Me Revealed and Given Way Of The Heart (or Way Of Adidam) Is Not A Strategic and self-Concerned Path Of self-Development (or Even Of self-Negation). The Only-By-Me Revealed and Given Way Of The Heart Is (and More and More Becomes) The ego-Surrendering, ego-Forgetting, and ego-Transcending Way Of Devotional Recognition-Response To Me (The Divine Heart-Master Of The Heart—The Avatarically Self-Revealed Transcendental, Inherently Spiritual, Inherently egoless, and Self-Evidently Divine Person Of Reality and Truth).

Practice Of The Only-By-Me Revealed and Given Way Of The Heart (or Way Of Adidam) Is An ego-Surrendering, ego-Forgetting, and ego-Transcending Devotional Process That Matures In The Context (and In The Transcending) Of Each Of The First Six Stages Of Life. The Full (or Most Ultimate) Maturity Of That Devotional Process Is Demonstrated In The Context Of The Only-By-Me Revealed and Given Seventh Stage Of Life (In The Only-By-Me Revealed and Given Way Of The Heart, or Way Of Adidam). The Total Devotional Process Of The Only-By-Me Revealed and Given Way Of The Heart (or Way Of Adidam) Is A Great Course Of Progressive Devotional Recognition-Response To Me and Devotional Realization Of Me (The Divine Heart-Master Of The Heart). And, As (and When) My Avatarically Self-Transmitted Divine Spiritual Grace Will Have It, That Process Becomes More and More Profound

Devotional Recognition-Response To (and Devotional Realization Of) Me As The Avataric Self-Revelation Of The Spiritual, Transcendental, and Self-Evidently Divine Forms Of Real God, or Truth, or Reality.

The Foundation Of The Great Course Of The Only-By-Me Revealed and Given Way Of The Heart (or Way Of Adidam) Is The Progressive Process Of Listening To Me and Hearing Me. That Great Course Is Based On (Progressive) Devotional Recognition-Response To Me and Devotional Realization Of Me, Through "Consideration" Of My Avatarically Self-Revealed Divine Word and My Avatarically Self-Revealed Divine Image-Art and My Avatarically Self-Manifested Divine Leelas, and Through Feeling-Contemplation Of (Especially) My Avatarically-Born Bodily (Human) Divine Form (and—Thus and Thereby, or Tacitly, and As My Avatarically Self-Transmitted Divine Grace Will Have It—My Avatarically Self-Transmitted Spiritual, and Always Blessing, Divine Presence, and My Avatarically Self-Revealed, and Very, and Transcendental, and Perfectly Subjective, and Inherently Spiritual, and Inherently egoless, and Inherently Perfect, and Self-Evidently Divine State).

Thus, Through Effective Practice Of The Only-By-Me Revealed and Given Way Of The Heart (or Way Of Adidam) In The (General) Context Of The First Three Stages Of Life (and, More and More, In The "Original", or Beginner's, Devotional Context Of The Fourth Stage Of Life), There Is Gradual and Inevitable Release Of The Stress Of egoity (and Gradual and Inevitable Release Of the ego-Based limits on conditional energy and attention) In The Context Of the frontal personality and The Binding Patterns (or Un-Happy Efforts) Associated With The Earliest Stages Of human Adaptation and Development. This Process Begins With Listening To Me (or The Giving Of one's Feeling-attention To My Avatarically Given Divine Sign, My Avatarically Given Divine Heart-Confessions, My Avatarically Given Divine Teaching-Arguments, My Avatarically Given Divine Image-Art, and The Storied Avataric Leelas Of All My Self-Manifested Divine Work)—and (Once The Original, or Foundation, Impulse Toward Most Perfectly ego-Transcending Real-God-Realization Is Deeply Confirmed In Practice, and, Thereby, More and Very Fully Awakened By This Earliest "Consideration") The Process Advances (Through Spiritual Initiation, By Me, Into The Process Of Receiving My Ruchira Shaktipat, The Subsequent Full Establishment In The Primary Practice Of Searchlessly Beholding Me, The Reality Process Of self-Observation and self-Understanding, and The Devotional Feeling-Process Of Effective ego-Transcendence) Toward The Realization Of True Hearing (or Most Fundamental self-Understanding).

Each Of The Stages Of Life (In The human Context) Is Associated With A Unique Form Of human Adaptation and Growth. And Each Form Of Adaptation Is Associated With A Specific human Organ (or Structural Pattern).

The First Three Stages Of Life Occur Within The Context Of the lower organ functions Of human Adaptation—and, In That Context, human Development Is Associated With individuation, socialization, and integration Of The psycho-physical Patterns Of the frontal personality.

The First Stage Of Life Is The Process Of psycho-physical (and, thus, also emotional) individuation, Based On Identification With the Separate (and personal) gross physical body in the waking state. The First Stage Of Life Is Also Associated With the oral (or nutritive) function. At birth, the infant Is Separated From The Situation Of Unity With the human mother, and This Begins A Struggle With The Fact Of individual Existence. This Struggle Is Displayed In The Context Of oral Dependence On the mother as a Separate body (and Dependence On food that Must Be Acquired From outside If individual bodily Existence Is To Continue). Whatever Occurs In The Drama Of breast-feeding and The Transition To food sources apart from the mother's body, human beings Tend To Develop A Fundamental Reactive Habit (or Presumption Of Un-Happiness) At This Stage.

Un-Happy (or egoic) individuation Tends To Be Associated With A Feeling Of Separation (or Of Separating, and Of Separateness, and Of Separativeness)—and, Thus, Un-Happy (or egoic) individuation Is Also Characterized By An Only Partial (or Ambiguous) Willingness To Relinquish (or, Otherwise, Even To Accept) The Feeling Of Dependency On the mother (or On others In General). This Feeling Of Separation (or Of Separating, and Of Separateness, and Of Separativeness) Ultimately (or Primarily) Involves The Sense Of Disconnection From The Ultimate Source Of Support and Love (Which Is The Living Divine), and It Also Becomes A General Doubt (or Anxiety) About other human beings On whom one Depends For Love. Sex-Differentiation (Whereby emotional-sexual self-identity and the emotional-sexual identification of others Become Basic To Every Situation Of Relationship) Begins Even At This Stage, but all relationships are experienced from the viewpoint Of Dependency and Reluctance To Accept The Situation Of individuated Existence.

The Second Stage Of Life Is The Process Of socialization (or relationalization of the individual), Based On The Development Of emotional (or emotional-sexual) Sensitivity To the psycho-physical self, To others, and To the Natural world (including the Natural etheric energies Associated With the psycho-physical self, with others, and with the entire Natural world). The Second Stage Of Life Is Also Associated With the anal (or eliminative) function and The Conflict Between Privacy (or self-Acceptance) and The Search For social Visibility (or Acceptance By others).

The anal function Begins To Develop Coincident With the oral function, but socialization itself Truly Begins Only After The Basic Struggle With individuation

Has Reached A Workable (Even Though ego-Bound, or self-Contracted) Settlement. (Thus, It Can Be Said That, As A General Rule, The First Stage Of Life Involves the first seven years after birth, and The Second Stage Of Life Involves the second seven years, or The Period From early childhood Until puberty.[63])

Character Motivations That Are Rooted In the biology and psychology Of sex-Differentiation Are, In The Second Stage Of Life, Extended and Developed In An Expanded social Context, and individuation (Including A Partial but Significantly Defined Sense Of emotional-sexual self-identity), Rather Than Ambiguously Differentiated Dependency, Becomes A Catalyst Toward social Exploration.

When individuation Has Become A Workable egoic Settlement, the individual Begins To Struggle, As an individual, With relationships (First On the intimate scale, and Then In an ever larger social sphere). The Second Stage individual Tends To Continue To function In The Context Of Dependency, but With A More Fully Developed Sense Of Separate self, Independence, and Mobility. Likewise, There Is A Gradual Discovery That There Are many kinds of relationships, and all of them Carry A Test, A Demand, and An Obstacle That Offends The Want To Be Dependent. The anal Phase Of Development Represents An Early Stage Of self-Awareness, In Which the individual's self-Esteem (or Presumed Desirability, or Presumed Lovableness) Is Apparently At Stake. Thus, Doubt Of the ego-self Appears—and, Likewise, Doubt Of The Love In others Appears. And, So, The Second Stage Of Life Tends To Develop Only To The Degree Of A Tentative (or ego-Based and, Ultimately, Unsatisfactory) Resolution Of the relational and social character. Whereas The Feeling Of Separation (or Of Separating, and Of Separateness, and Of Separativeness) Characterizes The First Stage Reaction (or egoic Presumption), The Feeling Of Being Rejected (and The Felt Need To Reject or Punish others For Un-Love) Characterizes The Second Stage Reaction (or egoic and, Necessarily, Un-Happy Presumption).

The Third Stage Of Life Is The Process Of integration Of The psycho-physical Patterns (Both individual and relational) Of the frontal personality, By Means Of The Development and Application Of the functions of mind, Discriminative Intelligence, and the will. And This Process Is Also Associated With The genital Phase Of human Development. Genital Development and emotional-sexual gender-Differentiation Begin Even In infancy, and The emotional Trial Of The Second Stage Of Life Relates To the gender-Defined character, but The Great Struggle Of integration and self-Presentation (As a Fully Differentiated and Defined sexual, emotional-sexual, and social character) Takes Place Only After puberty.

The Third Stage Of Life Tends To Be Wasted (or Made Un-Happy) By Indulgence In Patterns That May Be Called adolescent. That Is To Say, The Third Stage Of Life Does Not Tend Toward Full (and Happy) Resolution, Because The First Two Stages Of Life (Which Are The Basis For Growth In The Third) Tend To Be Unresolved (or Patterned By Un-Happiness). As A Result, The Third Stage Of Life Becomes A Fruitless Drama Of Conflict Between Two Alternating and Contrary Impulses—The One Toward infantile and childish (or Passive and Weak-minded) Dependence, and The Other Toward willful and Rebellious (or self-Destructive and other-Destructive) Independence. The Life-Process Is Disturbed By This Un-Happy and Irresponsible Drama, and the mental faculties and the integrating function of the will Are (Thus) Impaired (or Retarded) In their Ability To Develop the True adult character—which character Is Characterized By Basic human Equanimity, Discriminative Intelligence, Responsive Heart-Feeling, and The Active Impulse (or Counter-egoic Will) To Always Continue To Grow (By ego-Transcendence—and, Necessarily, By Entering Into The Devotional and, Eventually, Spiritual Context Of The Fourth Stage Of Life).

I Have (By The Giving Of My Many Avataric Divine Gifts) Equipped The Progressive Culture Of Practitioners Of The Only-By-Me Revealed and Given Way Of The Heart (or Way Of Adidam) With Wisdom and Means Relative To Every Stage Of Life. Therefore, The Responsive Culture (or Total Gathering) Of Formally Acknowledged Practitioners Of The Way Of The Heart Is (Via Its Right Use Of Those By-Me-Given Gifts Of Wisdom and Great Means) Empowered To Serve The Right, True, and Free Development Of children and young persons In The First Three Stages Of Life.

In The Context Of The First Three Stages Of Life, children and young people Should Be Helped To Adapt To The Requirements Of Growth In Those Stages, but In Such A Manner That The egoic (or self-Contracting) Tendencies Do Not Inhibit and Retard That Growth Through The Introduction Of infantile, childish, and adolescent Patterns Of Un-Happiness. To This End, The Responsive Culture (or Total Gathering) Of True Practitioners Of The Way Of Adidam (Which Is The Only-By-Me Revealed and Given Way Of The Heart) Must Apply All Its By-Me-Given Wisdom Relative To The Development Of children and young persons In The Context Of The First Three Stages Of Life. And Part Of That Wisdom Is The Consistent Cultural Introduction Of The By-Me-Given Rudimentary (and Fundamental) Propositions and ("Original", or Beginner's) Practices Associated With The Fourth Stage Of Life (As Well As The Stages Beyond The Fourth, Including The Fundamental Disposition Of The Only-By-Me Revealed and Given Seventh, or Divinely Enlightened, Stage Of Life In The Only-By-Me Revealed and Given Way Of The Heart, or Way Of Adidam).

Therefore, I Have Provided Extensive Guidance[64] For Truly human (and humanizing) Growth In The Context Of The First Three Stages Of Life. In My Avataric Divine Work With children, young people, and adults, I Have Developed A Wisdom-Culture For The First Three Stages Of Life That Includes (and Rightly Guides) The physical, psychological, and social Processes Of individuation, socialization, and integration. That Wisdom-Culture (or The Only-By-Me Revealed and Given Way Of The Heart For children and young people) Also Goes Beyond the limits Of These Obligatory early-life Processes By Founding Them In The True Religion (and Mystery) Of My Avataric Divine Self-Revelation Of Real (and Really Spiritual, Transcendental, and Self-Evidently Divine) Truth. That True Religion (Of Heart-Participation In The Inherent Mystery Of Existence—By Means Of My Avatarically Self-Transmitted Divine Grace) Only Serves (and Does Not Retard) Freedom, Responsibility, and Growth. That Culture Of Devotion To Me (The Avataric Divine Revealer Of Truth and Inherent Mystery) Really Serves self-Discipline, ego-Transcendence, The Vision Of Unity, and The Realization Of Freedom, Through Real-God-Sensitive Prayer and Meditation (Even In The General—or Natural, or Not Yet Spiritually Awakened—and early-life Context Of Practice In Relation To The Spiritual, Transcendental, and Divine Reality). And That Culture Of Devotion To Me Rightly and Progressively Includes Exercises To Develop emotional and physical Sensitivity To and Responsibility For The Universal Field Of Natural etheric energy Associated With the body-mind, Practices To Develop emotional and physical Sensitivity To (and Responsibility For) The etheric energy-Connection Between psycho-physically living beings (and Even Between psycho-physically living beings and Apparently non-living forms or things In The Cosmos Of conditional Nature), and Disciplines To Develop Sensitivity To and Responsibility For The Deep psychic Aspect Of mind (and The psychic Connection Between psycho-physically living beings).

Without The humanizing Benefits Of Real Love (and The Learning Of ego-Transcending Love From The Example, The Help, and The Companionship Of others) In The Context Of The First Three Stages Of Life, and Without The Inspiring Benefits Of True Spiritual, Transcendental, and Divine Culture In The Context Of The First Three Stages Of Life, human beings Inevitably Tend To Develop Un-Happy Patterns (and Signs Of Failed Growth) In The Context Of The First Three Stages Of Life. Such Failures Of Love, Wisdom, and Happiness Define human Existence subhumanly and limit human Existence To the egoic model and destiny. Therefore, Relatively few adults Advance To The Fourth Stage Of Life (or, Therefrom, To Any Of The Stages Beyond The Fourth) In the most common (or Only Minimally Developed) world Of Mankind—Because the most common world Of Mankind Tends To Be limited to (and by) the egoic society Of The First Three Stages Of Life. And Religion In the most common world Of Mankind (Thus limited) Is Likewise Defined and limited By The conceptual and egoic Tendencies Of The First Three Stages Of Life. (Therefore, What Is Most Commonly Proposed As Religion, In The Context Of The First Three Stages Of Life, Is An ego-Serving Gloss Of Myths, Mystical Cosmology, and conventional Structures Of belief Based On The Illusions Of popular "God"-Religion and The More or Less Magical Psychology Of Seeking For Fulfillment Of desires In the conditional worlds.)

Because Of All Of This, and In Order To Love and Serve Me (The Divine Person Of Love, Avatarically Self-Revealed As The Inherently Perfect Self-Condition and Source-Condition Of Love), My Seeing Devotees (and Even All Practitioners Of The Way Of The Heart) Must (As parents, friends, educators, guides, and Loving helpers) Responsively Serve and Responsibly Perpetuate The Effective Wisdom-Culture Of early-life Practice Of The Way Of The Heart That I Have Given and Established. That practical early-life Devotional[65] Wisdom-Culture Must Always (Now, and Forever Hereafter) Responsively and Responsibly Incorporate All Aspects Of My Avatarically "Considered" Divine Teaching and Instruction Relative To The Practice Of The Only-By-Me Revealed and Given Way Of The Heart (or Way Of Adidam) In The Context Of The First Three Stages Of Life. Therefore, That Wisdom-Culture Must Always (Now, and Forever Hereafter) Take Into Account (As I Have Already Taken Into Account) The Truly human functional, practical, and relational Requirements Of The First Three Stages Of Life, The Truth (and The Even early-life Relevance) Of The Callings and Requirements Of The Fourth, The Fifth, The Sixth, and The Seventh Stages Of Life, and The Basic Wisdom Relative To The lifelong Obligation Of ego-Transcendence. And Practice Of The Only-By-Me Revealed and Given Way Of The Heart (or Way Of Adidam) In That (early-life) Wisdom-Culture Of Listening Must Always (Now, and Forever Hereafter) Be Based Upon The (By-My-Avatarically-Self-Revealed-Divine-Word) Rightly and Fully Instructed (and, Also, According-To-My-Avatarically-Self-Revealed-Divine-Word, "Great-Tradition"-Informed) and, Altogether, Rightly Practiced Beginner's (early-life) Devotional Relationship To Me (As The Divine Heart-Master), Just As All adult Practitioners Of The Way Of The Heart Are Called (and Must Be Rightly Instructed—By My Avatarically Self-Revealed, and Always Me-Revealing, Divine Word, and By The Total Exemplary Culture Of Formally Acknowledged and True Practitioners Of The Only-By-Me Revealed and Given Way Of The Heart, and By The Great and Eternal and Ancient and Always New Tradition Of Devotion To The Adept Sat-Guru) To Rightly and Truly Practice Right and True Devotional and (Progressively Developing) Spiritual Relationship To Me (The Divine Heart-Master).

Even Though they May Grow Up Under The Auspicious Circumstances Of The True Wisdom-Culture Of The Only-By-Me Revealed and Given Way Of The Heart (or Way Of Adidam), young individuals Must Yet Grow To Understand (and Transcend) themselves As adults. If they Are, As adults, To Continue To Practice (and To Grow In) The Way Of The Heart, they Must, As adults, Devotionally Recognize Me and Devotionally Respond To Me From The Heart, and they Must, As adults, Choose The Only-By-Me Revealed and Given Way Of The Heart (or Way Of Adidam). Therefore, When they Achieve adult age (and If they, As adults, Both Respond To Me From The Heart and Choose To Practice The Way Of The Heart), all those who Have Grown Up Within The True Wisdom-Culture (Of The Formally Acknowledged Total Gathering) Of The Way Of The Heart, and (Thus) In (The early-life Practitioner's) Rightly Devotional and self-Disciplined Relationship To Me (Via My Avatarically Given Divine Sign, My Avatarically Self-Revealed Divine Word, My Avatarically Self-Revealed Divine Image-Art, and My Avatarically Self-Manifested Divine Leelas) As their Divine Heart-Master, Must (With The Continued Help Of Constant Right Guidance, Within The Formally Acknowledged Total Gathering Of All Formally Acknowledged Practitioners Of The Way Of The Heart) Continue (and Yet, and Truly, Complete) The Process Of Listening To Me, and they Must Continue In That Listening Discipline (As Fully Responsible adult Participants In The Cooperative Culture Of All Formally Acknowledged Practitioners Of The Way Of The Heart) Until they Have (By Heart-Surrender, and Heart-Obedience, and Heart-Conformity To Me, Even To The Degree Of Hearing Me) Truly and Fully Grown Beyond the limits Of The First Three Stages Of Life.[66]

Many Practitioners Of The Way Of The Heart Come To Me At an Already adult age, and Only After infancy, childhood, and adolescence in the common world. Such Practitioners Come To Me Suffering Even Most Acutely From The egoic (or Inherently Un-Happy) Complications Of The First Three Stages Of Life. Nevertheless, The Only-By-Me Revealed and Given Way Of The Heart (or Way Of Adidam) Is The Same For all. Therefore, For Both The adult Practitioner who Has Achieved adult age In the common world and The adult Practitioner who Has Grown Up In (and, As an adult, Chooses To Practice) The Way Of The Heart, The Earliest Stage Of adult Practice Of The Way Of The Heart Involves The Listening Process Founded In Feeling-attention To Me (Always Present In The Form Of My Avatarically Given Divine Sign, and In The Form Of The Recorded Documents Of My Avatarically Self-Revealed Divine Teaching-Word, and In The Form Of The Material Fabrications Of My Avatarically Self-Revealed Divine Image-Art, and In The Form Of The Recorded Divine Leelas Of My Avatarically Self-Manifested Teaching-Time, and

In The Form Of The Recorded Divine Leelas Of All My Avatarically Self-Manifested Blessing-Work).

At The Beginning, The adult Practitioner Of The Way Of The Heart Feels (and Thereby Contemplates) My Avatarically Self-Revealed Divine Sign, Listens To My Avatarically Given Divine Self-Confessions and Teaching-Arguments, Contemplates My Avatarically Given Divine Image-Art, Regards The Avatarically Self-Manifested Divine Leelas Of My Play Of Divine Work, and Thoroughly Observes (or Feels and, More and More, Feels Beyond) The Patterns Of his or her personal Un-Happiness (or egoity). By These Means, My Listening Devotee Is (Eventually, and By Means Of My Avatarically Self-Transmitted Grace) Awakened To True (and Most Fundamental) self-Understanding. Once It Awakens, The Continued Effective Expression (or Demonstration) Of True (and Most Fundamental) self-Understanding Is The Real and Certain Process Whereby early-life Un-Happiness Is Transcended. And Such Transcending Is The Regeneration Of The Free and Growing Movement Toward Completion Of The human Work Of individuation, socialization, and integration. Therefore, self-Observation, self-Understanding (Which Becomes Most Fundamental), and ego-Transcending human (and humanizing) Growth (In The Context Of The First Three Stages Of Life) Are The Work Of The Listening and Hearing Stages Of The Only-By-Me Revealed and Given Way Of The Heart.

The Work Of The Listening Stages Of The Way Of The Heart Cannot Become Complete Until I Am Heard. And The Original Work Based On Truly Hearing Me (or The Necessary Work Of The Period Of Practice That Immediately Follows The Original Awakening Of Most Fundamental self-Understanding) In The Way Of The Heart Is Not Complete Until ordinary human Un-Happiness (or The Unfinished Effort Of The First Three Stages Of Life) Is (In Its Fundamental Aggravation) Replaced By Basic, Real, and Truly human Equanimity.

Only If The Impulse Toward Most Perfectly ego-Transcending (and Fully and Most Perfectly <u>Spiritually</u> Awakened) Real-God-Realization (or Toward The Most Perfect Spiritual Realization Of My Avatarically Self-Revealed, and Inherently Free, and Inherently egoless, and Self-Evidently Divine Person and Self-Condition—Which <u>Is</u> The Inherent, and Self-Existing, and Self-Radiant "Bright" Divine Self-Condition Of Being, Itself) Is Truly and Intensively Activated, and Only If (On That Basis) The Process Of Thorough self-Observation, and The Reality Of Most Fundamental self-Understanding (or The Awakening Of The Directly ego-Transcending Capability), and The Restoration (or Even The First Stable Achievement) Of Basic human Equanimity Are All (and Thoroughly) Established, Can the individual Continue To Grow By Entering Into The "Basic" Context Of The Fourth Stage Of Life (and Beyond).

Therefore, By Listening To Me and By Hearing Me—Grow Again, and Grow Beyond the self-Retarded limits Of The First Three Stages Of Life.

For My Truly Seeing Devotee, Listening To Me Has Become Hearing Me, and Hearing Me Has Become Seeing Me. And, When Hearing Me Has Become Most Directly ego-Transcending Devotional Communion With Me, and When I Am Truly Seen By Means Of Such Directly ego-Transcending Devotional Communion, The Process Of Hearing Me and Seeing Me Continues To Develop Further (Via The Gift and Culture Of Satsang With Me) In The (Fullest) Devotional and Spiritually Responsible Context Of The Fully Established "Basic" Fourth Stage Of Life.

When, On The Basis Of The Always Primary Practice Of Satsang With Me (and Searchless Beholding, and Spiritual Reception, Of Me), The Listening Process (In The Way Of The Heart) Is Complete (and I Am, Thereby, Heard), and (Thus) When the conditional self Is Understood Most Fundamentally, and When My Hearing Devotee Can (Responsibly, Directly, and Capably) Feel Beyond (and Really and Effectively Transcend) the self-Contraction, and When My Hearing Devotee Has Thereby Transcended (or Become Capably Responsible For) the Basic limits Associated With The First Three Stages Of Life, and When My Hearing Devotee Has Thus (By Means Of My Avatarically Self-Revealed Divine Sign and My Avatarically Self-Manifested Divine Work) Realized My Avatarically Given Divine Word Of Instruction In The Form Of his or her own Real and Effective Understanding—Then My Hearing Devotee Must (By Constantly Hearing Me At Heart) Come To Me Most Fully At (and Via) The Heart, Able To Become My (Spiritually) Fully Technically Responsible Devotee.

After True Hearing Of Me Has Awakened My Hearing Devotee At The Heart, My Hearing Devotee (By Approaching Me In A Directly and Truly Hearing, or Really and Truly ego-Transcending Manner) Will (By Means Of My Avatarically Self-Transmitted Divine Spiritual Grace) Begin To Exercise Full Technical Responsibility For Participation In The Practice Of Spiritually Awakened Devotional Response To My Avatarically Self-Revealed (Transcendental, Inherently Spiritual, Inherently egoless, and Self-Evidently Divine) Person. My Divine Spiritual Body Is My Avatarically Self-Transmitted (and Inherently Attractive) "Bright" Divine Spirit-Presence That Draws the conditional self Beyond itself (To The Degree Of Releasing its own Contraction, In Me). When My Hearing Devotee Truly Demonstrates Full Seeing (or Fullest emotional, and Total psycho-physical, Conversion and Infusion Via My Avatarically Self-Transmitted Divine Spirit-Baptism), Practice Of The Only-By-Me Revealed and Given Way Of The Heart (or Way Of Adidam) Is (Thus and Thereby) Awakened Beyond The "Original" (or Beginner's) Spiritually Rudimentary Context Of The Fourth Stage Of Life, and Established (With Full

Technical Responsibility For Spiritual Participation) In The Fully Established "Basic" Context Of The Fourth Stage Of Life.

The (Fully Established) "Basic" (or By-Me-Spiritually-Awakened—and, Spiritually, Fully Technically Responsible) Fourth Stage Of Life In The Only-By-Me Revealed and Given Way Of The Heart Is The Developmental Process Of Full Spiritualization (or Progressive Spiritual Infusion) Of the psycho-physical personality, Through ego-Transcending Devotional Communion With Me. That Truly Spiritual Devotion To Me Is Constantly Expressed Internally Through Me-Receiving Heart-Feeling (and, Also, By Formal Meditation), and It Is Constantly Expressed Externally Through Perpetual Me-Beholding Service To Me (and ego-Surrendering Contemplation Of Me) In all relations and circumstances.

The Total Process Of The (Total) Fourth Stage Of Life Is Associated With Progressive Awakening In The Great Organ Of The Heart—Beginning With The Left Side Of The Heart. The Region Of The Left Side Of The Heart Includes the physical and lower psychic functions Of The Heart. It Is The Ground Of early-life Development. In The Total Context Of The Fourth Stage Of Life, The Heart Awakens From The Left Toward The Middle (or The subtle and higher psychic Region), Such That Spiritualizing Growth Occurs In The Domain Of the frontal personality (Within and Beyond The Context Of The First Three Stages Of Life). Therefore, As Devotional Heart-Feeling and Heart-Surrender To Me and Spiritual Reception Of Me Become More and More Profound, There Is A Growing Awareness Of all the subtle (and greater psychic, or deep psychological) functions Of The Heart.

In The Only-By-Me Revealed and Given Way Of The Heart, The Orientation Of The (Total) Fourth Stage Of Life Is Determined By The Fact That The ("Original", and Then "Basic", Fourth Stage) Practitioner Is Grounded (As In The ordinary Context Of The First Three Stages Of Life) In The Left Side Of The Heart—and, Therefore, In The Natural Context Of the body-mind in the waking state (Rather Than in the dreaming state or the sleeping state), and In The Natural Context Of the world of the waking state. Naturally Identified With the waking body-mind, The ("Original", and Then "Basic", Fourth Stage) Practitioner Of The Way Of The Heart functions as the waking body-mind, To Heart-Surrender the Total body-mind-self Through Devotional Communion With Me and Service To Me.

In The Way Of The Heart (or Way Of Adidam), The "Original" (and Then "Basic") Fourth Stage Practitioner Of Devotion To Me Naturally (and By Heart) Conceives Of himself or herself As My (Ultimately, Free) Servant. That Disposition Of Service Is To Be Expressed Through Even every form and moment Of Action, and Through Constant Devotional Heart-Surrender, Heart-Obedience, and Heart-Conformity Of the Total body-mind-self To Me (In ego-Surrendering, ego-Forgetting, and ego-Transcending Devotional and Spiritual Communion With Me), Such That Even the Total body-mind-self Is (Progressively) Really Converted, Positively Changed, and Effectively Transcended By That Devotion To Me, That Service To Me, and That bodily Worship Of Me.

In The Only-By-Me Revealed and Given Way Of The Heart (or Way Of Adidam), My Seeing Devotee Continues (As In The "Original" Beginner's Devotional and Foundation Spiritual Process Of Listening To Me and Hearing Me—but Now Through Fully Technically Developed Reception Of My Avatarically Self-Transmitted Divine Spirit-Baptism and, Thus, Through Spiritually Activated Devotional Practice In The Fully Established "Basic" Context Of The Fourth Stage Of Life) To Directly Transcend The early-life (or frontal) Un-Happiness Of Separation (or Of Separating, and Of Separateness, and Of Separativeness), Rejection (Of and By others), and Failed-integration. But The Sublime Power Awakened (By Means Of My Avatarically Given Grace) In Fully Technically Developed Reception Of My Avatarically Self-Transmitted Divine Spirit-Baptism (and Sustained By The Real Practice Of Heart-Devotion To Me) Develops An Extraordinary and New Dimension To The Way Of The Heart, Such That, In any moment Of Surrender To Spiritual Communion With Me, the entire frontal personality Becomes Immediately (or Most Directly) Converted To A Fundamentally Benign State and Course (In The Context Of all relations). The Progress Of This Course Is Indicated By Many By-My-Avataric-Divine-Spiritual-Grace-Given Signs In The Domain Of the frontal personality (or The Frontal Line Of The Circle Of the body-mind), Culminating In Realization Of The Sublime Signs Of True Spiritual (As Well As human) Equanimity and Fullness In The Frontal Line and The Yogic Sign Of The "Thumbs", In Which The Heart Radiates From Its Middle Station, and My Avatarically Self-Transmitted Divine Spirit-Current Flows Freely and Fully Down Through The Frontal Line (and, In The Fullest Event, Turns About, and Flies Upwards In The Spinal Line—Thus Completing The Full Circle Of Spirit-"Conductivity").

The Real Process In The Fully Established "Basic" Context Of The Fourth Stage Of Life (In The Way Of The Heart) Is The (Fully Technically Responsible) Yielding Of the Total body-mind-self To Ecstatic (or ego-Transcending) Spiritual Communion With Me (The Avatarically Self-Revealed Transcendental, Inherently Spiritual, Inherently egoless, and Self-Evidently Divine Person, Self-Condition, Source-Condition, and Heart-Master Of all-and-All). This Involves The Gesture Of self-Yielding, and (Spiritually) Fully Technically Responsible, Heart-Devotion To Me—and Profound Heart-Gratitude For My Avatarically-Given Divine Gifts (Including My Avatarically-Born Bodily Human Divine Form, The Avatarically Self-Manifested Leelas Of All My Divine Work,

My Avatarically Self-Revealed, and Always Me-Revealing, Divine Word, My Avatarically Self-Revealed, and Always Me-Revealing, Divine Image-Art, My Avatarically, and Freely, Given Divine Heart-Baptism, My Avatarically Self-Transmitted "Bright" Divine Spirit-Current Of Heart-Light-Energy, or Love-Bliss-Radiance, Itself, and My Avatarically Self-Revealed Divine Spiritual Fullness Of Conscious Being, Realized Directly By The Open Heart, and In Deep Meditation).

In The Only-By-Me Revealed and Given Way Of The Heart, The Passage Through and Beyond The Total Context Of The Fourth Stage Of Life Requires True ego-Transcendence, In and Via ego-Surrendering, ego-Forgetting, and ego-Transcending Devotional and Spiritual Communion With Me. Any Collapse Upon the conditional self, Contracted From True (and Truly ego-Surrendering, ego-Forgetting, and ego-Transcending) Devotional and Spiritual Communion With Me, Tends To Prolong The Course (Even By Temporarily Reasserting The Patterns Of Un-Happiness That Were egoically Associated With The First Three Stages Of Life).

In The Way Of The Heart, True Practice In The Context Of The Fourth Stage Of Life Inherently (and Necessarily) Exceeds The conventional Religious Tendencies Of The Fourth Stage Of Life Itself (Wherein The Divine Is, Otherwise, Commonly Conceived To Be Utterly "Other", or Necessarily Separate and Apart From the conditional self and the conditional world). And True Practice Of The Way Of The Heart In The Context Of The Fourth Stage Of Life Also Always Actively Transcends the Separate and Separative ego-self—which, Rather Than Submit To Transcend itself and The Separate-"God" Illusion Through Ecstatic Love-Communion With Me, Habitually Pleads and Bargains For conditional self-Fulfillment.

When (In The Context Of The Fully Established "Basic" Fourth Stage Of Life In The Way Of The Heart) Practice In Relation To the frontal personality (and The Frontal Line) Has Developed The Real and Free Evidence Of Equanimity, Spiritual Fullness, and The Full Spiritual Sign Of The "Thumbs", Devotional Recognition-Response To Me and Devotional Realization Of Me (Via, and As, My Avatarically Self-Transmitted Divine Spirit-Presence) Will (In All Cases) Continue In The Only-By-Me Revealed and Given Context Of The "Perfect Practice". Therefore, Maturity Of Practice Of The Way Of The Heart In The "Basic" Context Of The Fourth Stage Of Life Is Indicated By The Awakening Of My Devotee (Through The Graceful Means Given By Me, and As Me, In The Context Of Practice In The "Basic" Course Of The Fourth Stage Of Life) To The Realization Of Inherent Self-Identification With The Witness-Position Of Consciousness Itself—and, Thus and Thereby, To Inherent Association With The Right Side Of The Heart.

In The Only-By-Me Revealed and Given Way Of The Heart (or Way Of Adidam), The "Perfect Practice" Is Inherently Associated With Both The Horizontal Structures (or The Heart-Dimension) Of the body-mind and The Vertical Structures (or The Circle and The Arrow) Of the body-mind. The Terminal Of The Heart Principally Associated With The "Perfect Practice" Is At, In, and Beyond The Right Side Of The Heart—Otherwise Structurally Associated With The Sixth Stage Of Life. And The Terminal Of The Circle and The Arrow Principally Associated With The "Perfect Practice" Is The Crown Of the head (and Infinitely Above)—or The Ajna Door and All That Is Above It—Otherwise Structurally Associated With The Fifth Stage Of Life.

The Characteristic Process Of The Fifth Stage Of Life Is, As In The Case Of Every Other Stage Of Life, Associated With A Unique Organ (or Structural Pattern) Of Adaptation and Growth. Thus, Adaptation and Growth In The "Perfect Practice" Of The Way Of The Heart Is Associated, In The Plane (or Context) Of The Vertical Structures Of the body-mind, With The (Spontaneous) Upward Concentration Of attention, and With The "Conductivity" Of My Avatarically Self-Transmitted Divine Spirit-Current (and Of the Natural bodily energy) Via The Ajna Door (or The Root Of The Brain Core), and (Thus) With Ascent Via The Ajna Door.

The "Perfect Practice" Of The Only-By-Me Revealed and Given Way Of The Heart Demonstrates Itself With Reference To The Vertical Structures Of the body-mind By Signs, Events, and Processes Otherwise Associated With The Fifth Stage Of Life. Thus, In The Context Of The "Perfect Practice" Of The Way Of The Heart, Devotional self-Surrender To Me Is Generated From The psychic (or Middle) Depth Of The Heart, and Shown By The Evidence Of (Spontaneous) Upward Concentration At The Ajna Door (Potentially, and Even Generally, Signed By Yogic Evidence In The Spinal Line, and By Various Forms Of Savikalpa Samadhi—or Of psychic, or psycho-physical, Unity With The Progressively Ascending Range Of subtle phenomena). Therefore, In The Only-By-Me Revealed and Given Way Of The Heart, As It Is Demonstrated (Structurally) In The Vertical Context Of The Fifth Stage Of Life, The Devotee (Especially In Meditation) Functions From The Position Of The Middle Station Of The Heart—Even While Established In The Witness-Position, Which Is (In Terms Of The Hierarchical Structure Of the body-mind, Inherently) Associated With The Right Side Of The Heart (or With That Dimension Of The Horizontal Plane Of the body-mind Otherwise Structurally Associated With The Sixth Stage Of Life).

In The Only-By-Me Revealed and Given Way Of The Heart, As It Is Demonstrated In The Specific Context Of The Vertical Structures Otherwise Associated With The Fifth Stage Of Life, My Devotee (Especially In Meditation)

Is Spontaneously Free Of Identification With the gross body, its relations, and the conventional limitations of the waking state (including the verbal mind and the Outward-Directed activities of the left, or verbally dominated, hemisphere of the brain). Therefore, Especially (or Most Particularly) In Meditation, the mind Of My Thus Practicing Devotee Is No Longer Grounded In the gross body and the verbal-mindedness of the conventional waking state. Thus, The Meditative Exercise Of The "Perfect Practice" Of The Way Of The Heart Demonstrates Itself In The Vertical Structural Context Otherwise Associated With The Fifth Stage Of Life Primarily By A Process Of Converting, Positively Changing, Releasing, Merging, and Effectively Transcending the mind (or the mind-self), Through Devotional Ascent Via My Avatarically Self-Transmitted Divine Spirit-Current, Directed From The Middle Region Of The Heart. In That Process, the mind-self (which includes—and, also, exceeds—the brain) Reaches Toward (and Yields To) its Root-Source Infinitely Above The Total Crown Of the head (Via The Ajna Door), Potentially Passing Through Levels Of subtle (or dreaming) mind and its relations (including the subtle, or dreamlike, expressions of the right hemisphere of the brain)—and (When This Process Completes Itself Above) the mind Merges In The Inherently Formless Matrix Infinitely Above The Total Crown Of the head, and attention (Temporarily Suspended In Priorly Ascended Nirvikalpa Samadhi—and, Ultimately, Permanently Established In The Unconditional and Only-By-My-Avataric-Divine-Spiritual-Grace-Given Seventh-Stage-Of-Life Samadhi Of Amrita Nadi) Stands Above and Beyond body and mind (and, Thus, Free Of body and mind).

Because Of Its Inherent Structural limitations, The Fifth Stage Process (In and Of Itself) Culminates Only In The conditional (and, Thus, Temporary) Realization Of conditionally Ascended Nirvikalpa Samadhi. The conventional Fifth Stage Path Of Ascent Via The Mechanics Of the brain-mind Is, Itself, A Traditional Effort (or Search), Founded On Uninspected (or, Otherwise, Not Yet Transcended) egoity, In Which <u>conditionally</u> Ascended Nirvikalpa Samadhi Is The Ultimate Goal.

In The Only-By-Me Revealed and Given Way Of The Heart, <u>Priorly</u> (Rather Than Merely conditionally) Ascended Nirvikalpa Samadhi Is A Necessary Process (In The Development Of The Second Stage Of The "Perfect Practice"), Awakened On The (Necessarily, Previously Awakened) Foundation Of Priorly Self-Abiding Jnana Nirvikalpa Samadhi (and, Thus, On The Foundation Of The ego-Transcending Devotional Disposition Of The By-Me-Transcendentally-Awakened Heart). However, Priorly Ascended Nirvikalpa Samadhi Is Not A <u>Goal</u> (or A Product Of ego-Based Seeking) In The Only-By-Me Revealed and Given Way Of The Heart.

The Realization Of Priorly Ascended Nirvikalpa Samadhi Is, In Particular, A Necessary Dimension Of The Specific Yogic Spiritual Process Immediate To The Transition To The Only-By-Me Revealed and Given Seventh Stage Of Life (In The Way Of The Heart)—Because The "Regeneration" Of Amrita Nadi Is Directly Related To The Awakening Of Priorly Ascended Nirvikalpa Samadhi, and To The Coincident Transcending Of the conditions (or The conditional Structures) On Which Priorly Ascended Nirvikalpa Samadhi Depends. And, Also, Many Possible Kinds Of Ascended Spiritual Signs and Demonstrations Will (Because Of Self-Abiding Divine Self-Recognition Of <u>all</u> conditional forms, functions, and states, Rather Than Because Of Any conditional Dependency or Effort) Tend To Arise (Spontaneously) In The Context Of The "Perfect Practice" Of The Only-By-Me Revealed and Given Seventh Stage Of Life (In The Way Of The Heart)—Beyond All Presumptions Of conditional Dependencies (or Of Inherent limitations, Such As Are Otherwise Associated With The conditionally Manifested Vertical or Horizontal Structures Of the body-mind, or Else With The Modes Of self-Contraction, or Of egoity, itself).

The "Perfect Practice" Of The Only-By-Me Revealed and Given Way Of The Heart, As It Is Demonstrated In The Horizontal Structural Context Otherwise Associated With The Sixth Stage Of Life, Is The Process Of (In Due Course) <u>Fully and Unconditionally</u> Establishing The Only-By-My-Avataric-Divine-Spiritual-Grace-Given Seventh Stage Awakening To The Transcendental, Inherently Spiritual, Inherently egoless, and Self-Evidently Divine Self-Condition (or The Unconditional Nature Of Consciousness, Itself), The Perfectly Subjective Truth (and Identity) Of all conditional beings and Of The Entire Cosmic Mandala Of conditional worlds.

In The Only-By-Me Revealed and Given Way Of The Heart (or Way Of Adidam), The Demonstration Of The "Perfect Practice" In The Horizontal Structural Context Otherwise Associated With The Sixth Stage Of Life Is Based On Previous (and Continued) Devotional Recognition-Response To Me and Devotional Heart-Communion With Me—<u>As</u> (and By Grace Of) My Avatarically Self-Transmitted Divine Spirit-Presence. And Practice In The Context Of The Sixth Stage Of Life (In The Way Of The Heart) Is Itself A Process Of (In Due Course) Fully and Unconditionally Establishing The (By-My-Avataric-Divine-Spiritual-Grace-Given—and, Ultimately, Most Perfectly Awakened) Devotional Recognition-Response To My Avatarically-Born Bodily (Human) Divine Form and Person, and Devotional Realization Of Me <u>As</u> The Transcendental, Inherently Spiritual, Inherently egoless, and Self-Evidently Divine Person (and Self-Condition, and Source-Condition) Revealed <u>As</u> and By Means Of My Avatarically-Born Bodily (Human) Divine Form and (Thus and Thereby) <u>As</u> My Avatarically Self-Revealed (and Very, and Transcendental, and Perfectly

Subjective, and Inherently Spiritual, and Inherently egoless, and Inherently Perfect, and Self-Evidently Divine) State.

Growth In The Demonstration Of The "Perfect Practice" Of The Only-By-Me Revealed and Given Way Of The Heart In The Horizontal Structural Context Otherwise Associated With The Sixth Stage Of Life Is Shown As A Process Of Enstasy (or The Transcending Of the self-Contraction In Place, Where it arises—In The Well Of Being, or Consciousness Itself). And (In The Horizontal Plane Of the body-mind) That Process Is Related To The Right Side Of The Great Organ Of The Heart—Associated With the sinoatrial node, which is the "pacemaker" of the human physical heart.

The Right Side Of The Great Organ Of The Heart Is The bodily Origin-Point Of attention and The bodily Seat Of Most Perfect Divine Self-Realization. In The "Perfect Practice" Of The Only-By-Me Revealed and Given Way Of The Heart, ego-Transcending Resort To Me In The Horizontal Structural Context Otherwise Associated With The Sixth Stage Of Life Eventually Demonstrates Itself In The Only-By-My-Avataric-Divine-Spiritual-Grace-Given Realization Of Priorly Self-Abiding Jnana Nirvikalpa Samadhi, In Which the self-Contraction No Longer Prevents Realization Of The Transcendental (and Inherently Spiritual) Nature (or Self-Condition) Of Consciousness Itself.

In The Course and Process Of The Second Stage Of The "Perfect Practice" Of The Only-By-Me Revealed and Given Way Of The Heart (or Way Of Adidam), My Avatarically Self-Transmitted Divine Spirit-Current Of Love-Bliss-Life Progressively Resolves (and Dissolves) attention In The Right Side Of The Heart—and The Witnessing Consciousness Yields (or Awakens) To Feel (and, Thereby, To Contemplate, and, In The Event Of Priorly Self-Abiding Jnana Nirvikalpa Samadhi, To Inherently Identify With) Its Own Real Condition (As Transcendental Consciousness Itself, Realized As and By Means Of My Avatarically Self-Transmitted Divine Spirit-Current Of Love-Bliss-Being). Subsequently (In Due Course, and After Fullest Demonstration Of Priorly Ascended Nirvikalpa Samadhi, or Awakening In The Vertical Structural Context Otherwise Associated With The Fifth Stage Of Life), the Apparent conditional self Is Most Perfectly Transcended, In The (Seventh Stage) Realization Of The Prior (and Self-Evidently Divine) Nature Of Consciousness (Itself), By Means Of Most Perfect (and By-and-As-Me-Avatarically-and-Spiritually-Self-Transmitted) Realization Of The Self-Condition Of My Avatarically Self-Revealed (Transcendental, Inherently Spiritual, Inherently egoless, and Self-Evidently Divine) Person (Which Is The One, and Only, and Indivisible, and Transcendental, and Inherently Spiritual, and Inherently egoless, and Self-Evidently Divine Conscious Light), Unconditionally (and Perfectly Spiritually) Self-Radiant (and Inherently Love-Blissful) As Self-Existing Being (Itself).

In The Great Tradition (Of All human, Religious, and Spiritual Traditions) That (Historically, or In human-time) Preceded My Avataric Divine Incarnation here (and The Total Process Of My Avataric Divine Descent Into, and My Avataric Divine Self-"Emergence" Within, The Total Cosmic Domain), There Was Not (and Could Not Have Been) Any Demonstration Of Most Perfect Divine Self-Realization (and, Thus, Of Passage Through—and Fully Beyond—The Fifth and The Sixth Stages Of Life, and Even All Of The First Six Stages Of Life). In The Only-By-Me Revealed and Given Way Of The Heart, Passage Through and Beyond The Vertical and Horizontal Structures and Processes Associated (Respectively) With The Fifth and The Sixth Stages Of Life (and, Indeed, Associated With Even All Of The First Six Stages Of Life), and (Thus and Thereby) Realization-Demonstration Of The Only-By-Me Revealed and Given Seventh Stage Of Life, Depends On Realization Of The Transcendental (and Inherently Spiritual) Self-Condition (or The Self-Existing and Self-Radiant Condition Of Being—Prior To the conditional and limited body-mind-self). The Realization-Demonstration Of The Only-By-Me Revealed and Given Seventh Stage Of Life (In The Only-By-Me Revealed and Given Way Of The Heart) Not Only Requires The Transcending Of The Fifth Stage Error (or The Tendency To Seek, or Else To Hold On To, the conditional Ascended states of body and mind), but It Also Requires The Transcending Of The Sixth Stage Error (or The Tendency To Seek, or Else To Hold On To, The Transcendental Self-Position, While Otherwise Strategically Excluding objective, or conditional, states). Therefore, It Is Only When The Tension (or Stress) Associated With The Sixth Stage self-Contraction-Effort Of Exclusion Relaxes, In Simple (or Tacit) Self-Abiding Divine Self-Recognition Of phenomenal (or conditional) states (Of Apparently Objectified Light), That There Is (By Means Of My Avatarically Self-Transmitted Divine Spiritual Grace) Full Awakening To The Divinely Enlightened (or Divinely Self-Illumined) Condition—Which By-My-Avataric-Divine-Spiritual-Grace-Given Awakening Initiates The Only-By-Me Revealed and Given Seventh Stage Of Life (In The Only-By-Me Revealed and Given Way Of The Heart, or Way Of Adidam).

The Only-By-Me Revealed and Given Seventh Stage Of Life (In The Way Of The Heart) Is The Priorly (or Transcendentally) Self-Realized and Divinely Self-Radiant (or Inherently Spiritual) Process (or Ultimate "Perfect Practice") Of Divinely Self-Recognizing and (At Last) Outshining Cosmic (or conditional) Existence. The Only-By-Me Revealed and Given Seventh Stage Of Life (In The Way Of The Heart) Is The Culmination Of The Process Of Devotional Recognition-Response To Me and Devotional Heart-Communion With Me—Always Given By Grace Of My Avatarically Self-Transmitted Divine Spirit-Presence, and (Ultimately) By Grace Of My Divine Avataric Self-Revelation Of

My Transcendental, Inherently Spiritual, Inherently egoless, and Self-Evidently Divine Self-Condition. And The Original Sign Of The Only-By-Me Revealed and Given Seventh Stage Of Life (In The Way Of The Heart) Is "Open Eyes", or Seventh Stage Sahaja Nirvikalpa Samadhi (or Ruchira Samraj Samadhi, or, Simply, Samraj Samadhi)—Which Is The Divinely (and, Therefore, Inherently) Most Perfect Realization Of My "Bright" Divine Self-Condition.

In The Only-By-Me Revealed and Given Seventh Stage Of Life (In The Way Of The Heart, or Way Of Adidam), There Is Inherent, Constant, Inherently Most Perfect, Prior, Uncaused, Unconditional, and Utterly Non-Separate (and Non-"Different") Self-Identification With My Avatarically Self-Revealed, and Self-Existing (or Transcendental), and Self-Radiant (or Inherently Spiritual), and Inherently egoless, and Self-Evidently Divine Fullness Of Being (Itself). In The Only-By-Me Revealed and Given Seventh Stage Of Life (In The Way Of The Heart), My Avatarically Self-Revealed (Transcendental, Inherently Spiritual, Inherently egoless, and Self-Evidently Divine) Self-Condition (Rather Than the conditional body, body-mind, body-mind-self, mind-self, or limited and Separate self) Is Always Already The Position and Condition Of Existence—Even If (and When) conditional psycho-physical states (Apparently) arise (whether waking, dreaming, or sleeping). In That (Seventh Stage) Case—No Matter what (Apparently) arises—No limited self Defines (or limits) The Inherent Condition Of Being, but My Avatarically Self-Revealed (Transcendental, Inherently Spiritual, Inherently egoless, and Self-Evidently Divine) Self-Condition (Which Is The Self-Existing Condition Of Unconditionally Self-Radiant Divine Being) Is Always Already The Position In Which phenomenal (or conditional) states (Apparently) arise, and all such phenomena, conditions, or states Are (Inherently and Immediately) Divinely Self-Recognized and Transcended (In My Avatarically Self-Revealed, and Self-Existing, and Self-Radiant, and Inherently egoless, and Self-Evidently Divine Self-Condition). Therefore, In The Only-By-Me Revealed and Given Seventh Stage Of Life (In The Way Of The Heart), My Avatarically Self-Revealed (Transcendental, Inherently Spiritual, Inherently egoless, and Self-Evidently Divine) Self-Condition Is Always Already The Condition Realized, Prior To All objective (or conditional) References. Then (In The Context Of The Only-By-Me Revealed and Given Seventh Stage Of Life) The Only-By-Me Revealed and Given Way Of The Heart Is Not To Progressively (or, Otherwise, Eventually) Realize My Avatarically Self-Revealed (Transcendental, Inherently Spiritual, Inherently egoless, and Self-Evidently Divine) Self-Condition, but Only To Be That—Simply, Divinely (or Inherently, and Most Perfectly) Self-Recognizing whatever arises To Be Only That.

The Unique Organ Associated With Apparent Adaptation and Growth In The Only-By-Me Revealed and Given Seventh Stage Of Life (In The Way Of

The Heart) Is Amrita Nadi, My Avatarically Self-Transmitted Divine Spiritual Body Of Love-Bliss, Associated With My Avatarically Self-Transmitted Divine Spirit-Current Of Love-Bliss That Is Realized (and Progressively Magnified) Between The Right Side Of The Heart and The Apparent Locus That Is Infinitely Above The Total Crown Of the head (or Infinitely Above the upper rear, and The Total General Surface, Of the top of the head, and, Thus, Infinitely Above the body, and Infinitely Above the mind).

The Self-Existing and Self-Radiant Divine Self-Condition Revealed and Realized In The Awakening Of ("Bright") "Open Eyes" Has No Shape (or Form), but Amrita Nadi (The Apparent Organ Of This "Bright" Divine Awakening In the human individual) Is Shaped Like The Alphabetical Letter "S"—and My Avatarically Self-Transmitted Divine Spirit-Current Of Self-Existing and Self-Radiant Being Moves In It, Originating From (and, Yet, Never Leaving, but Always Standing In) The Right Side Of The Heart, Then Extending Itself Forward and Up the chest, Then Into (or Back Through) the throat, Then Up the back of the head, and Then Forward and Upward (Via the upper rear, and The Total Crown, Of the head) To The Matrix Infinitely Above The Total Crown Of the head. (And My Avatarically Self-Transmitted Divine Spirit-Current Also Moves Through This Same Unique Course, In Amrita Nadi, In The "Perfect Practice" Of The Way Of The Heart In The Context Otherwise Characteristic Of The Sixth Stage Of Life—but Downward, Via the upper rear, and The Total Crown, Of the head, From The Matrix Infinitely Above The Total Crown Of the head, To The Right Side Of The Heart.) However, Whether In The Only-By-Me Revealed and Given "Perfect Practice" Context Otherwise Characteristic Of The Sixth Stage Of Life Or In The Only-By-Me Revealed and Given "Perfect Practice" Context Of The Seventh Stage Of Life, The <u>Shape</u> Of Amrita Nadi Will Not <u>Necessarily</u> Be Noticed—Nor Is It Necessary For This <u>Shape</u> To Be Noticed. Rather, Amrita Nadi May Be More Simply <u>Felt</u>. Therefore, In The Only-By-Me Revealed and Given Seventh Stage Of Life (In The Way Of The Heart), Amrita Nadi May Simply (and Tacitly) Be Felt As My Avatarically Self-Transmitted (Formless and Unseen) Divine Current Of "Bright" Spirit-Fullness, Standing Between The Right Side Of The Heart and The Matrix Of My Divine Sound and Divine Light (or Of My Radiant Ascended Love-Bliss) Infinitely Above The Total Crown Of the head. And, In The "Perfect Practice" Of The Way Of The Heart In The Context Otherwise Characteristic Of The Sixth Stage Of Life, Amrita Nadi Is Also (Characteristically) Simply Felt As My Avatarically Self-Transmitted (and Formless) Divine Spirit-Current, Standing In The Right Side Of The Heart—but Descending, and Descended To (or Otherwise Polarized Toward), The Right Side Of The Heart, From Infinitely Above The Total Crown Of the head.

In The Most Perfectly Awakened (or Fully Conscious) Condition Of "Open Eyes", conditionally Manifested forms or events arising To The View Of Consciousness Itself (Free Of the self-Contraction) Are (Spontaneously and Inherently) Divinely Self-Recognized As Illusory (or Transparent, or Merely Apparent, and Un-Necessary, and Inherently Non-Binding) Modifications Of Itself (In The Form Of Its Own Divine Spirit-Energy). This (Inherently Most Perfect) Yoga Of Self-Abiding Divine Self-Recognition (Which Is Also Otherwise Named By Me "Ati-Ruchira Yoga", or "The Yoga Of The All-Outshining 'Brightness'") Is The Process Whereby The Total Cosmic Domain Is (Spontaneously and Inherently) Divinely Self-Recognized In Me, The Avatarically Given Divine Self-Revelation Of The Eternal (and Not Cosmic, but Perfectly Subjective) Real God, and Truth, and Reality—Which Is (Itself) My Divine Spherical Self-Domain (or The "Bright" Itself).

The Only-By-Me Revealed and Given Seventh Stage Of Life (In The Way Of The Heart) Is A Demonstration Of Divine Enlightenment Based On Previous (and Continued) Devotional Recognition-Response To Me and Devotional Heart-Communion With Me, and (Altogether, and Entirely) Given By Grace Of My Avatarically Self-Transmitted Divine Spirit-Presence, and (Most Ultimately) By Grace Of My Avatarically Self-Revealed (Transcendental, Inherently Spiritual, Inherently egoless, and Self-Evidently Divine) Self-Condition Of Person. And The "Perfect Practice" Process Of The Only-By-Me Revealed and Given Seventh Stage Of Life (In The Way Of The Heart) Is Itself A Matter Of (Spontaneous and Inherent) Self-Abiding Divine Self-Recognition Of all conditions (Including The Cosmic Mandala Itself, and My Divine Sound Itself, and My Divine Star Itself, and My Total Cosmically Manifested Divine Spiritual Body Itself) In and As Me—The Self-Existing (and Avatarically Self-Manifested) "Bright" (and "Midnight Sun") Itself (Which Is The Self-Radiant, or Inherently Spiritual, Condition Of Transcendental, and Self-Evidently Divine, Being—and Which Is The Love-Bliss-Radiant Consciousness In Which all conditional forms or events arise and pass away).

The First Sign (or Demonstration) Of The Only-By-Me Revealed and Given Seventh Stage Of Life (In The Way Of The Heart) Is Divine Transfiguration, In Which the body-mind Of My By-My-Avataric-Divine-Spiritual-Grace-Enlightened Devotee Is Self-Radiant With My Avatarically Self-Transmitted Divine Love-Bliss, Spontaneously Blessing all of the (Apparent) relations of the body-mind.

The Second Sign (or Demonstration) Of The Only-By-Me Revealed and Given Seventh Stage Of Life (In The Way Of The Heart) Is Divine Transformation, In Which the body-mind Of My By-My-Avataric-Divine-Spiritual-Grace-Enlightened Devotee Effectively Exhibits The Only-By-Me Revealed and Given Signs and Powers Of Real God.

The Third Sign (or Demonstration) Of The Only-By-Me Revealed and Given Seventh Stage Of Life (In The Way Of The Heart) Is Divine Indifference, In Which Even the body-mind Of My By-My-Avataric-Divine-Spiritual-Grace-Enlightened Devotee Is Pre-Occupied With The Self-Existing Event Of My Self-Radiant Love-Bliss, and the world of (Apparent) relations Is (More and More) Minimally and Not Otherwise Noticed.

The Final Sign (or Demonstration) Of The Only-By-Me Revealed and Given Seventh Stage Of Life (In The Way Of The Heart) Is The Great and Absolute and Unconditional and Most Perfect Fulfillment Of The Entire Process Of Devotional Recognition-Response To Me and Devotional Heart-Communion With Me—Altogether, and Entirely, Given By Grace Of My Avatarically Self-Transmitted Divine Spirit-Presence, and (Most Ultimately) By Grace Of My Avatarically Self-Revealed (Transcendental, Inherently Spiritual, Inherently egoless, and Self-Evidently Divine) Self-Condition Of Person.

The Final Sign (or Demonstration) Of The Only-By-Me Revealed and Given Seventh Stage Of Life (In The Way Of The Heart) Is The Culmination (or Absolute Realization) Of The Process Of Spontaneous (or Inherent) and Self-Abiding Divine Self-Recognition Of All (Apparent) conditional Modifications As The "Bright" Itself.

The Final Sign (or Demonstration) Of The Only-By-Me Revealed and Given Seventh Stage Of Life (and Of The Total Practice Of The Only-By-Me Revealed and Given Way Of The Heart) Is The Great Event Of Divine Translation—Which Is The Most Ultimate Demonstration Of Ruchira Samraj Samadhi, or Inherently Most Perfect (Rather Than conditional) Nirvikalpa Samadhi, or The Process Of Transition To (or "Dawning" As) My Divine Self-Domain Via The Divinely "Bright" Outshining Of The Cosmic Domain In The Only-By-Me Revealed and Given Divine Sphere and Sign Of The "Midnight Sun" (Most Perfectly Above and Beyond all-and-All Of Cosmic, or conditional, forms, beings, signs, conditions, relations, and things).

In The Great Event Of Divine Translation, The Total Cosmic Domain (or All conditional Modifications)—Even Epitomized By My Divine Sound, and My Divine Star, and My Total Divine Spiritual Body (Which Are The Ultimate, but Merely Apparent, or conditionally Appearing, Objective Signs Of The "Bright")—Is Outshined By My Divine "Bright" Spherical Self-Domain (or My Own Ultimate and Perfect Divine Form) Itself, Which Is The "Bright" Itself, Divinely Self-Revealed As The "Midnight Sun" Of Conscious Light.

My Perfect Divine Form (Of Inherent Divine Radiance, or Self-Light)—Divinely Self-Revealed As The "Midnight Sun" Of Conscious Light—Is The Inherently egoless Heart, The Eternal Divine Self-Condition Of all conditionally Manifested beings. Therefore, The Only-By-Me Revealed and Given Way

Of The Heart (or Way Of Adidam) Is Most Perfectly Fulfilled In Divine Translation Only—By Heart-Shining, Until The Heart Is Outshined By Itself.

Avatar Adi Da Samraj
The Mountain Of Attention Sanctuary, 2002

SUTRA

22

In Truth, The Only-By-Me Revealed and Given Way Of The Heart (or Way Of Adidam) Begins At birth and Progresses Through The Processes Otherwise Associated With Each Of The Seven Stages Of Life, Until Divine Translation.

Individuals who Are Not born Into The Formal Community Of Formally Acknowledged Practitioners Of The Way Of The Heart Generally Come To The Way Of The Heart At an adult age. Such individuals Have Already Passed Through the years Of Growth that Are Naturally Associated With The First Three Stages Of Life. Nevertheless, they Invariably Exhibit The Signs Of Patterned Un-Happiness That Characterize The Failures Of functional, practical, relational, and Cultural Adaptation In The Context Of The First Three Stages Of Life (and That Retard The human Work Of individuation, socialization, or relationalization, and integration).

Therefore, The Way Of The Heart Requires An Ordeal Of The Heart. Even From birth, and Even In The Context Of Each Of The First Three Stages Of Life, The Heart (or The Power Of Inherently Free Being, Consciousness, and Love-Bliss) Should Be Awakened (By Means Of My Avatarically Self-Transmitted Divine Grace, and In The Manner Appropriate To Each Such Stage), or Else human Adaptation and Growth Will (Necessarily) Be Retarded and Made Un-Happy By The self-Contracting Efforts Of egoity.

It Is Free and Effective Heart-Feeling (or The Free Power Of The Heart) That Enables human beings To Heart-Recognize Me and Heart-Respond To Me, and To Receive My Avatarically Self-Transmitted Divine Grace, and, Thereby, To Grow Beyond self-Contraction To Most Ultimate (or Inherent, and Inherently Most Perfect) Realization Of My Avataric Divine Self-Revelation Of Real God (or The Divine Self-Condition and Source-Condition)—and If Free Heart-Feeling Is Suppressed (or If The Free Power Of The Heart Is Not Awakened and Made Steady, Stage Of Life By Stage Of Life, In The Course Of human Development), human beings Cannot Grow Beyond The Un-Happy Settlements Of The First Three Stages Of Life.

The Heart Is Mine. The Heart Is The Domain Of All My Avataric Divine Work. The Heart Is Always In Me, but Reaction To the conditions Associated

With Apparent birth into the Cosmic planes Produces the Apparent conditional destiny Of Retarded Growth and All The Suffering Of self-Contraction. Therefore, Through The Practice Of The Only-By-Me Revealed and Given Way Of The Heart, This self-Contracting Reaction To conditional (or phenomenal) states Must Be Transcended In The Context Of Every Stage Of Life. The Heart Of My Devotee Must Awaken In The Context Of Every Stage Of Life, and My Devotee Must Grow To Be Attracted and Distracted By My Avatarically Self-Revealed Divine Form, and Presence, and State, and (Thus) To Feel Beyond The Bondage Of conditional events (or all that limits and Retards the conditionally Manifested being), and (Most Ultimately) To Feel Beyond (and Perfectly Prior To) all that is Not The Self-Realization Of The Divine Condition Of Being.

In The Context Of The First Three Stages Of Life (Which Are To Be Developed Within The "Original", or Beginner's, Devotional Context Of The Fourth Stage Of Life) In The Practice Of The Way Of The Heart, The Heart's Free Urge To Most Perfectly ego-Transcending Real-God-Realization Must Be Very Fully Awakened (and Made Active and Effective) By A Growing Heart-Response To My Avatarically Self-Revealing Realization-Sign, and My Avatarically Full-Given Word Of Divine Self-Confessions and Divine Teaching-Arguments, and All My Avatarically Full-Given Divine Image-Art, and All My Avatarically Self-Manifested (Heart-Instructing and Heart-Blessing) Divine Leelas. Therefore, those who Grow By Such Devotional Recognition-Response To Me Are Gracefully Inspired, and Constantly Instructed, and Always Directly Helped (and Quickened) In their Growth, By My Free Person (or My Avatarically Self-Revealing Bodily Human Divine Form, and, Tacitly, My Avatarically Self-Transmitted Spiritual, and Always Blessing, Divine Presence, and My Avatarically Self-Revealed and Very, and Transcendental, and Perfectly Subjective, and Inherently Spiritual, and Inherently egoless, and Inherently Perfect, and Self-Evidently Divine State) and By All My Avatarically Self-Manifested (and all-and-All-Liberating) Divine Work.

In The Fully Established "Basic" Context Of The Fourth Stage Of Life In The Way Of The Heart, and In The "Perfect Practice" Of The Way Of The Heart In The Context Otherwise Characteristic Of The Fifth Stage Of Life,[67] The Heart Of My Devotee Must (By Means Of My Avatarically Self-Transmitted Divine Spiritual Grace) Be Established In Full Heart-Response To My Avatarically Self-Transmitted Divine Spirit-Presence (As Well As To My Avatarically-Born Bodily Human Divine Form, and To My Avatarically Given, and Ever-Speaking, Divine Word, and To My Avatarically Self-Revealed Divine Image-Art, and To My Avatarically Self-Manifested Divine Leelas Of Teaching and Blessing).

In The "Perfect Practice" Of The Way Of The Heart In The Context Otherwise Characteristic Of The Sixth Stage Of Life, The Heart Of My Devotee

Must (By Means Of My Avatarically Self-Transmitted Divine Spiritual Grace) Be Established In (and As) The By-Me-Avatarically-Self-Revealed Transcendental (and Inherently Spiritual) Divine Self-Condition Of Mere Being, Realized On The Basis Of The Previously Established Devotional Recognition-Response To My Avatarically-Born Bodily (Human) Divine Form, and To My Avatarically Self-Transmitted Divine Spirit-Presence, and On The (By-My-Avataric-Divine-Grace-Given) Basis Of A Direct Heart-Response To My Avatarically Self-Revealed (and Very, and Transcendental, and Perfectly Subjective, and Inherently Spiritual, and Inherently egoless, and Inherently Perfect, and Self-Evidently Divine) State.

And, In The ("Perfect Practice") Context Of The Only-By-Me Revealed and Given Seventh Stage Of Life (In The Way Of The Heart), Based On All That Was (By Means Of My Avatarically Self-Transmitted Divine Spiritual Grace) Established and Realized In The Context (and In The Transcending) Of The First Six Stages Of Life, The Heart Of My Devotee Must (By Means Of My Avatarically Self-Transmitted Divine Spiritual Grace) Be Established In The "Bright" Transcendental, Inherently Spiritual, Inherently egoless, and Self-Evidently Divine Self-Condition—Inherently, Immediately, Spontaneously, and Divinely Self-Recognizing (and, Thus, Divinely Transcending) all Apparent conditions (and Even The Divine Sound, The Divine Star, and The Total Divine Spiritual Body That Are, As One, The Apparently Ascended and Apparently Objective Source-Matrix Of all Apparent conditions).

In The Only-By-Me Revealed and Given Way Of The Heart (or Way Of Adidam), Practice In The Context Of Every Stage Of Life Is A Circumstance In Which I Call My Listening Devotee, or My Hearing Devotee, or My Seeing Devotee At The Heart. Even From The Beginning, The Way Of The Heart Is My Call To Grow Toward Me, The Only One Who Is (and Thus, By Growing Beyond the ego-"I", To Become Established In My Avatarically Self-Revealed Divine Form, and Presence, and State).

The Way Of The Heart Is, From The Beginning, A Heart-Response To The (By-Me-Given) Call To Realize My Inherently Perfect Fullness Of Divine Love-Bliss, or Happiness Itself. Therefore, Even The Inherently Perfect Happiness Of The Seventh Stage Realization Of The (By-Me-Avatarically-Self-Revealed) Transcendental, Inherently Spiritual, Inherently egoless, and Self-Evidently Divine Reality Must Inform and Inspire (and Progressively Characterize) Practice In The Context Of Each and All Of The Potential Stages Of Life. And It Can Be So, If Every Developmental Stage Of Life (Within The Context Of Each and All Of The First Six Stages Of Life, As Determined By The Hierarchically Structured—gross, subtle, and causal—psycho-physical Anatomy Of Man and Of The Cosmic Domain Itself) Is Lived (and Transcended) In Devotional Recognition-Response To (or In The Impulse Toward) Me.

The Only-By-Me Revealed and Given (and Avatarically Self-Transmitted) Reality and Truth Of Divine Self-Realization Is, From The Beginning, The Always present-time Basis For The Entire Course Of The Way Of The Heart—Not A Mere Goal (To Be Sought As An Always future-time "End Phenomenon").

Divine Self-Realization Is Most Perfect Only At Last, In The Most Ultimate (or "Perfect Practice") Maturing Of The Practice Of The Way Of The Heart—but The Reality and Truth Of Divine Self-Realization Is, Nevertheless, and From The Beginning, The Always present-time Real (and Right, and True, and Full, and Fully Devotional) Context Of The Way Of The Heart.

Divine Self-Realization Is The Reality and Truth Of ego-Surrendering, ego-Forgetting, and Really ego-Transcending (or Effectively egoless) Heart-Communion With <u>Me</u> (Most Ultimately, To The Degree Of Most Perfectly ego-less Heart-Realization Of <u>Me</u>)—<u>As</u> I <u>Am</u>. Therefore, The Practice Of The Only-By-Me Revealed and Given Way Of The Heart Is, From The Beginning, The Devotionally Me-Recognizing and Devotionally To-Me-Responding (and Effectively ego-Transcending) <u>Cultivation</u> Of <u>My</u> Divine Samadhi (or My Inherent, and Avatarically Self-Transmitted, State Of Divine Self-Realization)—Until, At Last, There Is (Only and Entirely By Means Of My Avatarically Self-Transmitted Divine Spiritual Grace) Most Perfect Realization Of My Divine Samadhi (or Divine State).

True Samadhi Is The Self-"Bright" Realization Of The ego-Transcending Spiritual Condition Of Consciousness (Itself), or The ego-Transcending Spiritual Condition Of Being (Itself).

True Samadhi Is ego-transcending Communion With Reality, or Truth, or Real God.

True Samadhi Is The Realization Of Non-Separateness From Reality, or Truth, or Real God.

True Samadhi Is (In Effect) Ecstasy—or Standing "Outside" oneself, or Beyond oneself, and (Thus and Thereby) Beyond Separateness and Separativeness.

In The Only-By-Me Revealed and Given Way Of The Heart, The Samadhi To Be Cultivated Is (Always and Only) True Samadhi. Therefore, In The Only-By-Me Revealed and Given Way Of The Heart (or Way Of Adidam), The Practice and The Process Of Cultivating My Divine Samadhi Is A Matter Of Transcending the ego-principle (or The <u>Act</u> Of self-Contraction). That Transcending Must, In Due Course, Come To Be Effective Under any and all conditions that arise in the present moment of experiential appearance. To Be (Thus) Free Of self-Contraction and Separateness, In Total psycho-physical Heart-Communion With Me, Is The True and Inherent Condition (and The True, and Divine, Samadhi) Of The Heart (or Of Being, Itself).

In The Only-By-Me Revealed and Given Way Of The Heart, Samadhi Is Not Necessarily (and, Indeed, Is Not Usually) Associated With a condition Utterly Without psycho-physical Awareness, or With a condition In which Some Aspects Of psycho-physical Awareness Are Eliminated and Other (Perhaps more subtle) Aspects Of psycho-physical Awareness Are Magnified, or With a condition Somehow Dissociated From (Especially) gross psycho-physical Awareness. Although such conditions May (and, Indeed, Must, Necessarily) arise at various moments In My Devotee's Practice and Process Of Cultivating My Divine Samadhi (As, For Example, When ordinary psycho-physical Awareness Is Altogether Suspended, By Virtue Of A Spontaneously Ecstatic Disposition In My Devotee, or When Certain Aspects Of The grosser Awareness Of body, mind, and environment Are Suspended, and, Thereupon, Replaced By blissful auditions or visions, or By other unusual phenomena of one kind or another, or By A Relatively Indescribable State Of Bliss), The Characteristic (or, Previous To Divine Translation, Typical) Samadhi In The Only-By-Me Revealed and Given Way Of The Heart Does Not Involve Suspension Of experiential Association With the body-mind (or With psycho-physical conditions In General), but (Rather) A Suspension Of self-Contraction (and A Passing Into What Is Beyond self-Contraction, and A Conscious Absorption In—and, Ultimately, The Realization Of Non-Separate, or egoless, Self-Identification With—What Is Beyond the self-Contraction), Even While psycho-physical conditions Continue To arise.

Thus, In The Only-By-Me Revealed and Given Way Of The Heart, Samadhi Is Preoccupation With <u>Me</u>—Not A Search To Dissociate From (or, Otherwise, To Perfect) the body-mind. Therefore, The Essence Of Samadhi In The Only-By-Me Revealed and Given Way Of The Heart Is Neither The "Absence" Of the body-mind Nor Any Change In the experience of the body-mind (However blissful such conditions May, in their moments, Be), but (Rather) Fullness Of Me.

In The Only-By-Me Revealed and Given Way Of The Heart, Samadhi Is A moment to moment <u>Conscious</u> (and, Necessarily, Devotional and, In Due Course, Spiritual) Practice and Process, To Be Realized In The Context Of every kind of circumstance, condition, function, relation, state of activity, and state of inactivity. Thus, In The Only-By-Me Revealed and Given Way Of The Heart, Samadhi Is Not A State To Be Cultivated <u>Only</u> In The Formal Meditative Setting. The Cultivation Of Samadhi In The Way Of The Heart Is The Practice Of Ruchira Avatara Bhakti Yoga, Under all conditions, More and More Becoming moment to moment Surrender Of body, emotion, mind, breath, and all of Separate and Separative self To Me, In Devotional Communion With Me—Ultimately (In Due Course, In The Formal Practice Of The Way Of The Heart), To The Point Of Most Perfectly ego-Surrendering, ego-Forgetting, and ego-Transcending Self-Identification With Me (In and As The Inherent Condition That Is Always Already Prior To Separateness and self-Contraction).

My Beginning Devotees In The Only-By-Me Revealed and Given Way Of The Heart Must (Necessarily, and Thoroughly) Address the content Of The First Three Stages Of Life—but This Address Occurs In The "Original" (or Beginner's) Devotional Context Of The Fourth Stage Of Life (and, Altogether, In Heart-Communion With Me, and On The Basis Of My Avatarically Self-Revealed Seventh Stage Divine Wisdom-Teaching), and (Therefore) Not Merely In The Context Of The First Three Stages Of Life Themselves. The Practice Of The Way Of The Heart Is Never (Even At The Beginning) Merely A Matter Of Adjusting ordinary human behavior In The idealistic Manner, For The Sake Of The Moral and social Purposes Characteristic Of The First Three Stages Of Life. There Are (Of Course) the elements Of human (Moral and social) Change and Right (Moral and social) Life In The Practice Of The Way Of The Heart, but The Way Of The Heart (Itself) Is The Cultivation and Realization Of My Divine Samadhi (and, Therefore, Of Non-Separateness From The By-Me-Avatarically-Self-Revealed Divine Self-Condition and Source-Condition). The Only-By-Me Revealed and Given Way Of The Heart Is The Avataric Gift That I, Uniquely, Give To living beings, For This Divine Great Purpose.

In The Only-By-Me Revealed and Given Way Of The Heart, The Process In Relation To Each Of The Stages Of Life Beyond The Third Is Associated With A Characteristic Form (or Characteristic Forms) Of Samadhi. Therefore, The Foundation Samadhis (or Modes Of Realizing My Divine Samadhi) In The Way Of The Heart Are Devotional (and Devotionally "Absorptive"), or A Matter Of Feeling Beyond self-Contraction By Allowing the body-mind-self To Be Heart-Attracted By (and To) Me, and (Thereupon) Absorbed In (and Into) Me. Thus, In The Only-By-Me Revealed and Given Way Of The Heart, The Foundation (or Early Beginning) Modes Of Realizing My Divine Samadhi Are Devotionally Awakened, and (In Due Course) Progressively Spiritually Awakened (but Not Yet, In The Fully Technically Responsible Sense, Spiritually Awakened, Transcendentally Awakened, or Divinely Self-Awakened), Forms Of Samadhi. And Those Earliest Modes Of Realizing My Divine Samadhi (or Heart-Communing With My Avatarically-Born Bodily Human Divine Form, My Avatarically Self-Transmitted Spiritual, and Always Blessing, Divine Presence, and My Avatarically Self-Revealed, and Very, and Transcendental, and Perfectly Subjective, and Inherently Spiritual, and Inherently egoless, and Inherently Perfect, and Self-Evidently Divine State) Are Realized In The "Original" Context Of The Fourth Stage Of Life, Through The Practice Of Devotional Surrender To Me—and They Are Developed On The (Primary) Basis Of ego-Transcending Feeling-Contemplation Of My Avatarically-Born Bodily (Human) Divine Form.

The Secret Of Samadhi In The Beginning Practice Of The Way Of The Heart (and, Indeed, Throughout The Entire Progressive Course Of The Way Of The Heart) Is The Nectarous (and ego-Forgetting) Joy Of Devotionally Me-Recognizing and Heart-Responsive and Loving Devotion To Me, The True Divine Ishta-Guru (or The "Chosen" Divine Beloved Of one's Heart). Through The moment to moment (and Directly ego-Transcending) Practice Of Devotional Samadhi (In The "Original" Context Of The Fourth Stage Of Life In The Way Of The Heart), I Am Realized (In The Devotional and, In Due Course, Progressively Spiritual Manner)—and That Devotional and (Beginning) Spiritual Realization Is The Basis For All Further Growth In The Way Of The Heart.

In The Way Of The Heart, There Are Many Modes Of Samadhi That Develop Beyond The Earliest Stages Of Practice, Beginning In The Further Development Of The Fourth Stage Of Life (Beyond Its "Original", or Listening-Hearing, Context). The Forms Of Samadhi In The "Basic" Context Of The Fourth Stage Of Life In The Way Of The Heart Are Developed On The Basis Of Absorptive Devotional Communion With Me, Exercised In The Context Of Stable (and Fully Technically Exercised) Awakening To My Avatarically Self-Transmitted Spiritual (and Always Blessing) Divine Presence. The Forms Of Samadhi In The "Perfect Practice" Of The Way Of The Heart In The Context Otherwise Characteristic Of The Fifth Stage Of Life Are (Likewise) Developed On The Basis Of Absorptive Devotional Communion With Me, Exercised In The Context Of Stable (and Fully Technically Exercised) Awakening To My Avatarically Self-Transmitted Spiritual (and Always Blessing) Divine Presence—Even While My Devotee Is Established In Inherent Self-Identification With The Witness-Position Of Consciousness Itself. Samadhi In The "Perfect Practice" Of The Way Of The Heart In The Context Otherwise Characteristic Of The Sixth Stage Of Life Is Developed On The Basis Of Stable Non-Separate (or Inherent—and In That Sense, Perfect—but Not Yet Most Perfect, or Most Perfectly egoless) Self-Identification With My Avatarically Self-Revealed (and Very, and Transcendental, and Perfectly Subjective, and Inherently Spiritual, and Inherently egoless, and Inherently Perfect, and Self-Evidently Divine) State. And Samadhi In The Only-By-Me Revealed and Given Seventh Stage Of Life (In The Way Of The Heart) Is The Most Perfect (and Truly egoless) Realization Of My Avatarically Self-Revealed (Transcendental, Inherently Spiritual, Inherently egoless, and Self-Evidently Divine) Self-Condition (Which Is Self-Existing and Self-Radiant Feeling-Being-Consciousness, Itself)—and That Samadhi (or Most Perfect Realization Of My Divine Samadhi) Is Associated With Inherent (and Perpetual, or Always present-time) Self-Abiding Divine Self-Recognition (and The Inherent Transcending) Of attention itself (or The

Root-Feeling Of Relatedness, or Of "Difference"), and Inherent (and Perpetual, or Always present-time) Self-Abiding Divine Self-Recognition Of all Apparent objects (or conditions) of attention (Such That attention and its Apparent objects or conditions, each and all, Are Divinely Self-Recognized In and As The By-Me-Avatarically-Self-Revealed Self-Existing and Self-Radiant Condition Of Perfectly Subjective, and Inherently Spiritual, Inherently egoless, and Self-Evidently Divine, Being Itself).

In The Context Of Every Stage Of Life, The Practice Of The Way Of The Heart Is The Cultivation Of Samadhi By Cultivating My Divine Samadhi. Therefore, All The Forms (or Modes) Of Samadhi In The Way Of The Heart Are (Fundamentally) "Equal" To One Another, Because They Are (Each and All) Simply Various Forms Of The Essential Devotional Practice Of ego-Transcending Spiritual Reception Of Me—To The Degree (In The Context Of The First Four Stages Of Life, and In The "Perfect Practice" Of The Way Of The Heart In The Context Otherwise Characteristic Of The Fifth Stage Of Life) Of Absorptive Devotional Heart-Communion With Me, and, Ultimately (In The "Perfect Practice" Of The Way Of The Heart In The Context Otherwise Characteristic Of The Sixth Stage Of Life), To The Degree Of Non-Separate (and, Thus, Non-Absorptive) Heart-Identification With Me, and, Most Ultimately (In The Context Of The Only-By-Me Revealed and Given Seventh Stage Of Life), To The Degree Of Most Perfect (and Truly egoless) Heart-Realization Of Me, Most Perfectly Beyond and Prior To The Primary ego-Illusions, Of Separateness, Relatedness, and "Difference". My Devotee's Experience Of Samadhi Will Be Different At various times and On Various Occasions, According To the circumstances of the moment, and The Stage Of Practice Of The Way Of The Heart Which he or she Is Engaging (and The Profundity, or Degree Of Real Intensity With Which he or she Is Practicing), but, In Every Form Of Samadhi In The Only-By-Me Revealed and Given Way Of The Heart, My Devotee Realizes Me (As That Which Is Always Already The Case, Prior To self-Contraction).

Therefore, The Practice Of The Only-By-Me Revealed and Given Way Of The Heart (or Way Of Adidam) Is Not A Matter Of Cultivating egoic (or merely psycho-physical) states, conditions, functions, relations, or activities. The Practice Of The Only-By-Me Revealed and Given Way Of The Heart (or Way Of Adidam) Is Not A Matter Of Attempting To Idealize human life, or To Transform human life Into a Religiously idealized (functional, practical, relational, and Cultural) performance. The Right and Effective Counter-egoic Disciplining Of The functional, practical, relational, and Cultural Aspects Of human life Is Certainly Necessary, and Must Not (and, Indeed, Cannot) Be Bypassed—but All Of That Is A Secondary (or Supportive) and (Necessarily)

Subordinate (and Subordinated) Aspect Of The Right, True, Full, and Fully Devotional (and, In Due Course, Fully Spiritual) Practice Of The Way Of The Heart. The Primary (and <u>Always</u> Most Essential) Practice Of The Only-By-Me Revealed and Given Way Of The Heart (or Way Of Adidam) Is, Even From The Beginning, Searchless Beholding Of Me (Which Is The Essence Of Ruchira Avatara Bhakti Yoga)—Exercised To The Degree Of True (or Divine) Samadhi.

The Great Impulse To Most Perfectly ego-Transcending (and Fully and Most Perfectly <u>Spiritually</u> Awakened) Real-God-Realization Is The Impulse To True (or Divine) Samadhi (or ego-Vanishing Absorption In—and, Ultimately, Non-Separate Self-Identification With—Me, The Avataric Divine Self-Revelation Of Reality, or Truth, or Real God), and Not Merely An idealistic (and ego-Based) Impulse To cause the Apparently Separate (and Separative) ego-self To Achieve some kind of Remarkably self-Congratulating condition, In this world or In some other world.

The Only-By-Me Revealed and Given Way Of The Heart Is—Altogether and <u>Only</u>—An Esoteric Way, Because It Is The Practice and The Process Of Cultivating My Divine Samadhi. My Every Formally Practicing Devotee (Whatever his or her Stage Of Life In The Way Of The Heart, and Whatever his or her Manner and Developmental Stage Of Practice Of The Way Of The Heart) Must Be Fitted To The Impulse To Realize My Divine Samadhi, Always Cultivating The Present-Stage Mode Of Realizing My Divine Samadhi For Which he or she Is Formally Responsible, Such That Realization Of My Divine Samadhi Becomes More and More Frequent, More and More Consistent, and More and More Profound.

If There Is ego-Transcending (or Ecstatic) Heart-Communion With Me, Then I Am Realized To Be The Only One Who <u>Is</u>—The Inherent Love-Bliss-Feeling Of Self-Existing, Self-Radiant, and Divinely (and Avatarically) Self-Transmitted Being (Itself). Because Of This, Whatever his or her Stage Of Practice In The Only-By-Me Revealed and Given Way Of The Heart, My Listening Devotee, My Hearing Devotee, or My Seeing Devotee Will Tacitly Realize Even <u>All</u> The By Me (and <u>As</u> Me) Avatarically Self-Revealed Forms Of The Divine Person—At First, In Simplest ego-Forgetting Feeling Of Me, but Then, In Due Course (As The Stages Of Practice Progress), More and More Profoundly (Until, Most Ultimately, That Great Reception Of Me Is Most Perfect, and Most Perfectly "Bright", In The Only-By-Me Revealed and Given Seventh Stage Of Life).

Therefore, In The Practice Of The Only-By-Me Revealed and Given Way Of The Heart (or Way Of Adidam), The First Three Stages Of Life (In The "Original", or Beginner's, Devotional Context Of The Fourth Stage Of Life) Must Become Associated With Participatory (and Even Faithful) Dependence

Upon Me Via The Left Side Of The Heart. But The Middle Station Of The Heart and The Right Side Of The Heart Will Also (Thus and Thereby, Tacitly) Be Established In Me, If My Devotee Really and Truly Enters Into ego-Surrendering, ego-Forgetting, and (More and More Effectively) ego Transcending Communion With Me, and (Thus, and By Means Of My Avatarically Self-Transmitted Divine Spiritual Grace) Spontaneously and Progressively Realizes The True Devotional Disposition (and, Eventually, The Spiritual Fullness) Of The Fourth Stage Of Life.

And, Even Though The (Developing) Fourth Stage Of Life Is (In The Way Of The Heart) Associated With The Developing Devotional Recognition-Response To Me Via The Middle Station Of The Heart (As Well As The Left Side Of The Heart), Any Devotee who Truly Enters Into Such ego-Transcending Communion With Me Will (Surely, By Means Of My Avatarically Self-Transmitted Divine Spiritual Grace, and In Due Course) Realize The Prior (and Transcendental) Witness-Consciousness (Even Via The Right Side Of The Heart), and So Be Moved (By Means Of My Avatarically Self-Transmitted Divine Spiritual Grace) To The "Perfect Practice" Of The Way Of The Heart.

And, Even Though The Process Otherwise Characteristic Of The Fifth Stage Of Life Is (In The Way Of The Heart) Associated (As In The Case Of Practice In The Context Of The Fourth Stage Of Life In The Way Of The Heart) With The Developing Devotional Recognition-Response To Me Via The Middle Station Of The Heart (As Well As The Left Side Of The Heart), This Process Is Entered Only After My Devotee Comes To Rest In The Prior (and Transcendental) Witness-Position Of Consciousness Itself (Which Is, In Terms Of The Hierarchical Structure Of the body-mind, Inherently Associated With The Right Side Of The Heart), and (Thereby) Enters The "Perfect Practice" Of The Way Of The Heart.

And, Even Though The Process Otherwise Characteristic Of The Sixth Stage Of Life Is (In The Way Of The Heart) Associated With Perfect Feeling-Contemplation Of Me As Consciousness Itself (and, Thus, With By-My-Avataric-Divine-Grace-Given Direct Self-Identification With Consciousness Itself, Via The Right Side Of The Heart), My True Devotee (Practicing The "Perfect Practice" Of The Way Of The Heart In The Context Otherwise Characteristic Of The Sixth Stage Of Life) Will (Surely—By Means Of My Avatarically Self-Transmitted Divine Spiritual Grace—and, In Due Course, Suddenly) Awaken To Me Most Perfectly (Even, Thereby, Including The Middle Station Of The Heart and The Left Side Of The Heart), and Entirely (or Most Perfectly, or Inherently) Free, and (Therefore) Even Free Of The Motive To Exclude the (Apparent) body-mind and its (Apparent) relations. In This Manner, My True Devotee Will Enter Into The Only-By-Me Revealed and

Given Seventh Stage Of Life, Wherein the (Apparent) body-mind, Founded In The By-Me-Totally-Awakened Heart, Is (Inherently, and Inherently Most Perfectly) Resolved In The By-Me-Avatarically-Self-Revealed Self-Radiant (or Inherently Spiritual) and Self-Existing (or Transcendental) Divine Being. And My True Devotee (Thus, Most Perfectly, Awakened) Will Surely Come To My Divine "Bright" Spherical Self-Domain, Via The By-Me-Divinely-Self-Revealed Doorway (or "Midnight Sun" Of Infinite Self-Radiance) Of The Heart (Realized As The "Bright" Itself).

The Truly ego-Surrendering, ego-Forgetting, and ego-Transcending Heart-Response (or Responsive Impulse) Of The Total Heart (Left, Middle, and Right)—and the Total body-mind (Vertically Displayed)—Of My Devotee To (or Toward) My Bodily (Human), Spiritual, Transcendental, and Divine Self-Revelation Is The Great Gesture To Which I Call My Listening Devotee, and My Hearing Devotee, and My Seeing Devotee In The Context Of Every Stage Of Life. Only Listen To Me, and Hear Me, and See Me. And, If You Are Listening To Me, or Hearing Me, or Seeing Me—Then Love Me Now, In My Avatarically-Born Bodily (Human) Divine Form (The Sighting Of Which Is—Now, and Forever Hereafter—Given For Your Devotional Contemplation). And, If You Truly Heart-Recognize Me and (Through Formally Acknowledged Practice Of The Way Of The Heart) Embrace Me As The Divine Heart-Master, You (Surely) Presently Enjoy The Heart-Recognition Of Me As The (Avatarically Self-Revealed) Very and Self-Evidently Divine Person, and Are (Thus) Tacitly Awake To My Divine Form, and Presence, and State.

Nevertheless, This Heart-Responsive Awakening Must (and, Surely, Will) Be Expressed In A More and More Mature and Fully Conscious (and Spiritually Developed) Fashion As My Listening Devotee (who Grows To Hear Me and See Me) Moves Through The Stages Of Practice In The Way Of The Heart. Every Stage (and moment) Of Practice In The Only-By-Me Revealed and Given Way Of The Heart Is A Testing School For My Listening Devotee, My Hearing Devotee, and My Seeing Devotee. And The Measure That Is (Ultimately) To Be Schooled and Tested Is My Devotee's Heart-Response To Me. Therefore, Each Stage (and moment) Of Practice In The Way Of The Heart Requires Increased Responsibility For The By-Me-Given Gift That Is The Progressive Practice Of The Way Of The Heart, Because Growth In Practice Of The Way Of The Heart Is Always Based On A Progressively Unfolding Disclosure (or A Magnification Of Awareness) Of The human (and The Cosmic) psycho-physical Design, and A Coincident Increase In The Level Of Participatory self-Surrender Required By Every New Stage Of Revelation.

Even children and young people Practicing and Developing In The Natural (early-life) Context Of The First Three Stages Of Life Within The By-Me-Given

Wisdom-Culture Of The Only-By-Me Revealed and Given Way Of The Heart (or Way Of Adidam) Are Called To Devotionally Respond (From The Heart) To Me (As The Divine Heart-Master), and (Thus, and By Tacitly Heart-Recognizing Me) To Commune With Me, Even In and As The Simple Felt-Mystery Of Being That Is Inherently Associated With Natural and human Existence. They Are Called To Commune With Me (The Avataric Divine Self-Revelation Of The Liberating Truth, or The Mystery Of Reality)—By Means Of My Avataric Divine Sign, and My Avataric Divine Word, and My Avataric Divine Image-Art, and My Avataric Divine Leelas, and Even All My Giving Help—and (Thus and Thereby) To Commune (In The early-life Devotee's Rudimentary, Simple, and More General Fashion) With Me (The Avataric Divine Self-Revelation Of The Liberating Truth, or The Mystery Of Reality) As The Universal (or All-Pervading) Divine Spirit-Presence (Simply As Implied, or Naturally Suggested, In The Practice Of Feeling-Devotion To Me, Which Naturally Magnifies Feeling-Participation In The Universal Field Of Natural etheric energy, and By Means Of The Practice Of Magnifying The Devotional Love Of Me, and, Thereby, The Natural Heart-Feelings Of Happiness and Love), and (Possibly) As Either My (grossly Projected) Apparently Objective Divine Sound Or My (grossly Projected) Apparently Objective Divine Star Or My (grossly Projected) Apparently Objective (or Tangible) Divine Spiritual Body Of "Brightness" (Potentially, Naturally Perceived and Felt, Spontaneously, In The Course Of daily Devotional Practice), and As The By-Me-Avatarically-Self-Revealed Transcendental (and Inherently Spiritual) Self-Condition (Naturally Intuited, In The Devotional Practice Of The Feeling Of Mystery, or The Mysterious Inexplicability Of Natural and human Existence), and Even Altogether (According To their Ability, or The Degree and Quality Of their Awareness) As The "Bright" and Ultimate Mystery Of Real God (Felt-Intuited In The Devotional Practice Of Naturally Feeling-Perceiving My Avatarically-Born Bodily Human Divine Form, and, Altogether, In The Devotional Feeling-Response To All My Avataric Divine Revelation-Work). Because Of All Of This, early-life Practitioners Of The Only-By-Me Revealed and Given Way Of The Heart Will Surely Grow Toward adult age Served By My Avataric Divine Wisdom At The Heart—and, For This Reason, they Should Be Able To Pass More Readily (As adults) Through The (Further) To-Me-Listening and (Then) Me-Hearing Process To Real Practice In The Me-Seeing Context Of The Fully Established "Basic" Fourth Stage Of Life.

Those who Come To Me At an adult age Are First Called To Listen To Me (In The Beginner's Devotional Manner) and To Hear Me, and (Thereby) To Awaken (Eventually) To Fullest Devotional Response To Me (Full Of The Capable Motive Of ego-Transcendence and The Capable Impulse Toward

Most Perfectly ego-Transcending Real-God-Realization). And That First Period (Of Listening To Me and Hearing Me) Is (Like All Subsequent Developmental Stages Of Practice In The Way Of The Heart) To Take Place Within (and By Right and Fully Accountable Participation In) The Formal (and Formally Acknowledged) Worldwide Cooperative Sacred Cultural Gathering Of My Devotees (Which Gathering Includes every individual who Is A Formally Acknowledged Practitioner Of The Only-By-Me Revealed and Given Way Of The Heart).[68]

All adult Beginners In The Only-By-Me Revealed and Given Way Of The Heart, whatever their age, Are (Because Of The Habit Patterns Of their Previous Adaptations) Still functioning (Basically) In The Context Of The First Three Stages Of Life. However, As Soon As such individuals Begin To Listen To Me (In The Context Of The Devotional Relationship To Me, As The Divine Heart-Master), they Have Already Begun To Develop The Orientation That Is The First (or "Original") Characteristic Of The Fourth Stage Of Life. And, After Such Listening Devotees Awaken To True Hearing Of Me and Basic human Equanimity (Through Spiritually Me-Receiving Ruchira Avatara Bhakti, or Searchless Me-Beholding Devotional Practice, and Through The Process Of Most Fundamental self-Understanding, Whether Primarily By Devotional Feeling and Insight Or Primarily By Devotional Feeling and Faith), and As Soon As they (As My Would-Be-Seeing, or Progressively Seeing, Devotees) Grow To Actually and Truly (and Fully Spiritually) See Me, they Will (and Must) Begin Practice Of The Way Of The Heart In The Fully Established "Basic" Context Of The Fourth Stage Of Life (In Fully Technically Responsible Spiritually Activated Devotional Relationship To Me, The Avataric Self-Revelation Of The Divine Spiritual Presence and Person, Who Is Attractive and Love-Blissful At The Free-Feeling Heart).

For All adult Practitioners Of The Way Of The Heart, The Developmental Stages Of Practice Previous To The "Perfect Practice" Of The Way Of The Heart Involve The Practice Of Disciplines Which Are Associated With The First Three Stages Of Life, and Which Are Also Associated With The ("Original", and Then The "Basic") Context Of The Fourth Stage Of Life, In Which The Searchlessly Me-Beholding Disposition Of Heart-Surrender To Me Is Progressively Magnified. Therefore, Practice Of The Way Of The Heart In The Context Of The Fourth Stage Of Life Begins (In A Progressively Devotional Manner) In The Student-Beginner Stage (Of Foundation functional, practical, relational, and Cultural Adaptation and Preparation), Then It Develops Responsively (In The Beginner's Responsible Devotional and Spiritually Me-Receiving Manner) In The Intensive Listening-Hearing Stage Of The Way Of The Heart, Becomes Fully Spiritually Active (In The Fully Technically Responsible Sense) In The

Would-Be-Seeing Stage Of The Way Of The Heart, and Develops (Most Basically, or As A Fully Developed Frontal, or Whole bodily, Spiritual Yoga) In The First Actually Seeing Stage Of The Way Of The Heart. And The adult Practitioner Of The Way Of The Heart Must, In Due Course, Make The Transition To The "Perfect Practice" (Which, In Its First Two Stages, Encompasses The Structures and Processes Otherwise Characteristic Of Both The Fifth Stage Of Life and The Sixth Stage Of Life), Before The Final Transition Is Made To The Demonstration Of The Way Of The Heart In The Context Of The Only-By-Me Revealed and Given Seventh Stage Of Life.

Even Though All adult Practitioners Of The Way Of The Heart (or Way Of Adidam) Must (Necessarily) Begin their Practice In The Domain Of The First Three Stages Of Life, The Process Of their Discipline Must, In Fact, Also Constantly Develop (Progressively) Within The ("Original", and Then "Basic") Context Of The Fourth Stage Of Life. Therefore, For All adult (and, Likewise, All early-life) Practitioners Of The Way Of The Heart, The Fourth Stage Of Life Is To Be Progressively Entered, Through An Urge and A Process That Are Embraced At The Very Beginning Of The Way Of The Heart—Such That <u>Full</u> Entrance Into The ("Original", and Then Fully Established "Basic") Context Of The Fourth Stage Of Life In The Way Of The Heart Develops (First) Through The Preparatory (or Student-Beginner) Period Of First Study-"Consideration" and First Devotionally Responsive Practice Of The Way Of The Heart, and (Subsequently) Through The Intensive Listening-Hearing, and Would-Be-Seeing, and First Actually Seeing Stages Of The Way Of The Heart.

The Student-Beginner Of The Way Of The Heart Should Be Freely Moved To Acknowledge and Honor My Avataric Divine Person, and My Avataric Divine Word, My Avataric Divine Image-Art, and My Avataric Divine Leelas, Through The Consistent Offering Of attention (and the human Feeling-energies Of Serious Heart-Response) To The (Now, and Forever Hereafter, Given) Sighting Of My Bodily (Human) Divine Form, and To The Recorded Documents Of My Avatarically Given (and Ever-Speaking) Divine Word, and To The Material Fabrications Of My Avatarically Given (and Ever-Me-Revealing) Divine Image-Art, and To The Recorded Stories Of My Avatarically Self-Manifested (and Ever-Living) Divine Leelas. Therefore, Even Though The Student-Beginner Of The Way Of The Heart is (At First, and By Tendency) Most Likely a Relatively limited (or Reactively Patterned), Religiously Undeveloped, and Spiritually Un-Awakened character, who Is (At First, and By Tendency) Defined By The Signs Of Failed Adaptation In The First Three Stages Of Life, and who is (At First, and By Tendency) limited (Through Adaptation Itself) By The ordinary Purposes (or Desires) Associated With The First Three Stages Of Life, The Fundamental Motive Of ego-Transcendence and

The Great Impulse Toward Most Perfectly ego-Transcending (and Fully and Most Perfectly Spiritually Awakened) Real-God-Realization Can (and Must) Very Fully Awaken At The Heart In and By The Profound Process Of The Beginnings Of True Listening To Me. (Indeed, Even Though The Student-Beginner's Listening-"Consideration" Works To Confirm The Motive Of ego-Transcendence and The Great Impulse Toward Most Perfectly ego-Transcending Real-God-Realization, and To Thoroughly Establish That Motive and That Impulse As A Real Practice, The Motive Of ego-Transcendence and The Impulse Toward Most Perfectly ego-Transcending Real-God-Realization Must, Necessarily, Be Already Established, As A Real Workable Commitment, Even As A Basis For Engaging The Student-Beginner's Practice Itself.)

In The Progressive Course Of The Formal (and Formally Acknowledged) Practitioner's First (or Student-Beginner's) Period Of Embrace Of The Beginner's Devotional Relationship To Me, and Of (Thus) Devotionally Responsive "Consideration" Of My Avatarically Full-Given Divine Word and My Avatarically Full-Given Divine Image-Art and My Avatarically Self-Manifested Divine Leelas, and Of (Thus) Devotionally Responsive (and Experimental, or Exploratory and self-Testing) Application To The By-Me-Given Forms Of functional, practical, relational, and Cultural self-Discipline Associated (From The Beginning) With The Practice Of The Way Of The Heart, and Of (Thus) Devotionally Responsive (and Experimental) Practice Of The Two Devotional Ways (Of Faith and Of Insight) Of The One Great Way Of The Heart, The Student-Beginner Must Eventually (and Truly) Choose To Practice One or The Other Of The Two Devotional Ways (and All The By-Me-Given Original Gifts, and Callings, and Basic Disciplines) Of The One Great Way Of The Heart. By Means Of This Total Course (and As A Result Of The Necessary Choice Ultimately Made Within It), The Acquired Un-Happiness (Of Separating, and Of Separateness, and Of Separativeness) Relative To The Work Of individuation (Characteristic Of The First Stage Of Life) Should Be Significantly Released (and the activity of the body-mind Should Thereby, or As A Demonstration Of That Release, Become Responsively Conformed To The Only-By-Me Revealed and Given Way Of The Realization Of Happiness Itself). Indeed, the Inherent (and, Otherwise, Acquired) limits Of Even All Of The First Three Stages Of Life Should Become (To A Significant Degree) Obvious In That Earliest Practice (or Student-Beginner Sadhana) Of Listening To Me.

Therefore, When The Student-Beginner's Original Heart-Motive Toward Most Perfectly ego-Transcending Real-God-Realization Is (By Means Of My Avatarically Self-Transmitted Divine Grace) Very Deeply Confirmed and More (and Very) Fully Awakened (Via Truly ego-Surrendering, ego-Forgetting, and ego-Transcending Devotion To Me, and Via Really Effective "Consideration"

Of The Way Of The Heart—or Real, and Really Effective, Study, Adaptation, and Accountability—In Practice), and When That Student-Beginner's Active Feeling-Contemplation and Heart-Responsive Devotional Recognition Of My Bodily (Human) Divine Form, and Also his or her Study and Real "Consideration" Of My Avataric Divine Word and Image-Art and Work, Have Become his or her Thorough and Consistent Demonstration Of All The Original By-Me-Given Gifts, Callings, and Disciplines (Including The Primary By-Me-Given Gift, Calling, and Discipline Of Ruchira Avatara Bhakti Yoga), and When and If (By All Of That) the individual Is Prepared (and Happy) To Be Made Increasingly Effective In The Real Practice Of The Way Of The Heart By The Ever Thereafter Continued and Magnified (or More and More Detailed and Comprehensive) Application Of The Total Range Of functional, practical, relational, and Cultural Disciplines and Obligations Given By Me To Practitioners Of The Way Of The Heart (For The Sake Of, Most Ultimately, Inherent, and Inherently Most Perfect, and Inherently Most Perfectly ego-Transcending Real-God-Realization), Then he or she Should Move On To Practice In The Intensive Listening-Hearing Stage Of The Way Of The Heart.

In The Intensive Listening-Hearing Stage Of The Way Of The Heart, The Practice Of Right Relationship To Me (Ever-Speaking Via My Written, and Otherwise Recorded, Avataric Divine Word, and Ever-Showing Myself Via The Material Fabrications Of My Avataric Divine Image-Art, and Ever-Revealing Myself Via The Storied Leelas Of My Avataric Divine Work) Is To Be (Further, and Formally, Rather Than Experimentally) Enlarged Through The Voluntary, Intentional, Intelligent, and Consistent Intensive Application Of functional, practical, relational, and Cultural Disciplines (Whereby the self-Contraction Is More and More Fully and Exactly Revealed). Therefore, During The Intensive Listening-Hearing Stage Of The Way Of The Heart, Progressively More Profoundly ego-Surrendering, ego-Forgetting, and (Truly Effectively) ego-Transcending Feeling-Contemplation (or The Spiritually Me-Receiving Devotional Practice Of Searchless Beholding) Of My Avatarically-Born Bodily (Human) Divine Form Should Develop, and "Consideration" Of All My Fundamental Teaching-Arguments (Especially Relative To "Narcissus" and Divine Ignorance) Should Become (Increasingly) Profoundly Effective—and (In The Case Of those who Practice The Devotional Way Of Insight) Both Random and Formal self-Enquiry (In The Form "Avoiding Relationship?") Should Become Profoundly Effective, or Else (In The Case Of those who Practice The Devotional Way Of Faith) Both Random and Formal Ruchira Avatara Naama Japa Should Become Profoundly Effective. All Of That—Including Inspired Heart-Response To My Historical Avataric Play Of Divine Teaching-Work and To My (Now, and Forever Hereafter) Avataric Play

Of Divine Blessing-Work, and (Also) Including Regular Participation In Sacramental, Ceremonial, and Other Formal (or Informal) Occasions Of Celebration Of Me—Serves (or Must Serve) To (More and More) Awaken The ("Original", and Then The "Basic") Fourth Stage Heart-Response To Me.

That Total Process (Culminating In The Fully Established, and Fully Technically Responsible, Awakening Of The Spiritually Activated Response To Me) Truly (or Most Fundamentally) Releases (or Must Release) The "Problem" About individual Existence (or The Un-Happy First Stage Motive Toward The Act Of Separating, and Toward the condition Of Separateness, and Toward the activity Of Separativeness). And The Dramatization Of The Un-Happy (or egoic) Second Stage Motive Of Rejection (By and Of others) Is Also To Be (Most Fundamentally) Released By These Same Means. Therefore, Before The individual Practitioner Of The Way Of The Heart Makes The Transition To The Would-Be-Seeing Stage Of The Way Of The Heart, the Basic limitations Dramatized In The Context Of The First Three Stages Of Life Must Be Released (or Become A Matter Of Direct Responsibility) Through Most Fundamental self-Understanding (or True Hearing Of Me), Such That the frontal personality Thereby Fulfills The Third Stage Necessity Of human integration (or The Realization Of ordinary and Basic human Balance and Wholeness).

My Avatarically Self-Transmitted Divine Spirit-Baptism Awakens Signs In and Of The Middle Station Of The Heart (or the deep psychic being) In My Devotee. In The Way Of The Heart, That Baptism Is To Occur, To Real (Fully Technically Responsible) Effect, During The Would-Be-Seeing Stage. At That Stage, The Spiritual Basis For The Lovelessness That Was egoically Associated With The Second Stage Of Life Is To Be Directly Transcended Through The By-My-Avataric-Divine-Grace-Given Spiritual Conversion To Love (or By-My-Avataric-Divine-Grace-Given Conversion To The Divine Spiritual Reality—Which Is Love, or Love-Bliss, Itself). That Is To Say, By Means Of True Seeing Of Me (Which Is Fullest—or emotional, and Total psycho-physical, and, In The Fully Technically Responsible Sense, Spiritually Activated—Conversion To Love-Communion With Me), the frontal personality Is (In The Way Of The Heart) To Be Released From the Spiritual limitation that Diminishes Love (or The Inherent Radiance Of Being Itself), and the Truly Spiritual socialization (or Spiritual relationalization) of the frontal (and Truly human) personality Through Love (or The Infusion and Demonstration Of My Divine Love-Bliss) Is Thereby To Be Set In Motion.

The First Actually Seeing Stage Of The Way Of The Heart Is The (Spiritually) Fully Technically Responsible Stage Of Practice Associated With The Fully Established "Basic" Context Of The Fourth Stage Of Life. During That Stage Of Practice In The Way Of The Heart, the individual Is To

Complete The Work Of Growth Beyond the ordinary limits Of The First Three Stages Of Life By Fully Integrating the frontal personality With The By-Me-Avatarically-Self-Revealed Divine Spiritual Reality. Therefore, In The Context Of The First Actually Seeing Stage Of The Way Of The Heart, the frontal personality Is To Be Spiritually Purified, Spiritually Balanced, and Made Full Of Spirit-Life, Through The Ecstatic (or ego-Surrendering, ego-Forgetting, and ego-Transcending) Yoga Of (By-Me-Spiritually-Activated) Devotion To Me, In Which The Frontal Line Of the body-mind (and, Thus, the Total body-mind) Is (or Must Be) Converted (and Conformed) To Spiritual Communion With Me, By The Constant Exercise Of The By-Me-Spiritually-Awakened Heart.

The "Perfect Practice" Of The Way Of The Heart Encompasses (From The Beginning) The Structures and Processes Otherwise Characteristic Of The Fifth Stage Of Life and The Sixth Stage Of Life, and, Most Ultimately (In Due Course), The Stages and Processes Of The Only-By-Me Revealed and Given Seventh Stage Of Life. Thus, The Transition From The First Actually Seeing Stage Of The Way Of The Heart To The "Perfect Practice" Of The Way Of The Heart Is The Transition From Practices Predominantly Associated With The Frontal Line and the frontal personality To Practices Predominantly Associated, In Relation To The Vertical Structures and Processes Otherwise Characteristic Of The Fifth Stage Of Life, With Spontaneously Ascended Devotion (or Devotion To Me Above), Through (Especially) The Spontaneous Focus Of The Faculties At and Via The Upper Terminals (Of The Ajna Door, and The Crown Of the head)—In Which Case My Devotee Must, Nevertheless, Continue, In the ordinary daily circumstance, To Surrender the frontal personality In Devotional Heart-Communion With Me, While Spontaneously Demonstrating Devotional self-Surrender To Me Above the head and Above the mind, Exercised From The Anahata Chakra, or The Middle Station Of The Heart (Thus and Thereby Releasing My Avatarically Self-Transmitted Divine Spirit-Current From Every Focus Below, and, Thus and Thereby, To Spontaneous Feeling-Contemplation Of Me At and Above The Ajna Door, or Ajna Chakra). And, In Relation To The Horizontal Structures and Processes Otherwise Characteristic Of The Sixth Stage Of Life, The Transition From The First Actually Seeing Stage Of The Way Of The Heart To The "Perfect Practice" Of The Way Of The Heart Is The Transition From Practices Predominantly Associated With The Frontal Line and the frontal personality To Practices Predominantly Associated With The Transcending Of The Root-Dimension Of egoity (Which Is Associated With attention itself, and The Root-Feeling Of relatedness itself, and The Root-Domain Of The Right Side Of The Heart).

Most Ultimately, In The Fullness Of The Only-By-Me Revealed and Given Way Of The Heart, The Transition Is Made, By My Avatarically Self-Transmitted

Divine Spiritual Grace, To Practice Of The Way Of The Heart In The Context Of The Only-By-Me Revealed and Given Seventh Stage Of Life. I Will Describe This Transition—and, Also, The Process To Be Demonstrated In The Context Of The Only-By-Me Revealed and Given Seventh Stage Of Life—In This Divine Testament Of Mine.

Avatar Adi Da Samraj
Lopez Island, 2000

SUTRA

23

Reality Is (Always) That Which Is The Case.

Truth Is (By Definition) That Which Is Always Already The Case.

Real God Is (Necessarily) That Which, When It Is Realized, Is Realized To Be (Always Already) The Case.

Reality Is The Only Basis For Truth—Because Truth (Which Is Always Already The Case) Must Be That Which Is Real (or Really The Case).

Truth Is The Necessary Requirement For Reality To Be Unconditional (or Truly Divine)—Because Truth (Which Is Always Already The Case) Is That Which Unconditionally (or In Any and Every Case) Is The Case.

Only Truth (or That Which Is Always Already The Case) Is Truly (and Divinely, or Unconditionally) The Reality—Because That Which Is The Case, but Not Always Already The Case, Is (Necessarily) Subordinate To (and Entirely Dependent Upon) That Which Is Always Already The Case.

Only The Reality That Is Always Already The Case Is Truth and Real God.

Therefore, The Only Real God Is That Which Is Realized To Be Both Reality and Truth.

Apart From Actual (Real and True) Realization Of Real God (or Unconditional Realization Of That Which Is Always Already The Case), Real God Is (Effectively) Not Existing.

Real God (or That Which Is Always Already The Case) Cannot Be conditionally experienced (or psycho-physically perceived)—Because The psycho-physical Faculties Of the conditional body-mind (and, Indeed, all the perceptions Generated By Means Of The Exercise Of The psycho-physical Faculties Of the conditional body-mind) Are Separate, finite, and Always changing.

Real God (or That Which Is Always Already The Case) Cannot be conditionally known (or conceptually Grasped by The psycho-physical Faculties Of the conditional body-mind)—Because The psycho-physical Faculties Of the conditional body-mind (and, Indeed all the knowings conceptually Grasped By Means Of The Exercise Of The psycho-physical Faculties Of the conditional body-mind) Are Separate, finite, and Always changing.

Nevertheless, In Any and Every Case, Real God (or That Which Is Always Already The Case—and Which Is, Therefore, Really and Truly The Case) Must

Be Realized (As The Case)—or Only That Which Is Not Always Already The Case (and Which, Therefore, Is Not Real God) Will (Necessarily) Be Supposed (and experienced, and known) To Be The Case.

Real God (or That Which Is Always Already The Case) Must (In Any and Every Case) Be Always Already (and Really, and Truly) Realized To Be The Case (and, Thus, Realized As The Case)—or Else What Is Not Always Already The Case Will (Necessarily, and On The Basis Of conditional experience and conditional knowledge) Be Supposed To Be Real God (or, Otherwise, To Suggest, or "Prove", The Non-Existence Of Real God).

Therefore, Real God (or That Which Is Always Already The Case) Must (In Any and Every Case) Be Always Already Realizable (No Matter What Appears To Be The Case)—or Else What Is Not Always Already The Case Will (Necessarily, and On The Basis Of conditional experience and conditional knowledge) Always Be Supposed To Be Real God (or, Otherwise, To Suggest, or "Prove", The Non-Existence Of Real God).

Real God (or That Which Is Always Already The Case) Must (In Any and Every Case) Be Always Already Realizable (No Matter What Appears To Be The Case), and (On That Basis) Real God (or That Which Is Always Already The Case) Must (Always) Be Always Already (and Really, and Truly) Realized To Be The Case (and, Thus, Realized As The Case)—or Else That Which Is Not Always Already The Case (and Which, Therefore, Is Not Reality, Truth, and Real God) Is (Necessarily, and In Every Case) The Absolute Boundary (or The Absolutely limiting and Controlling Factor) Of conditionally Manifested Existence (and Of The conditional, or Cosmic, Dimension Of Reality).

Because Real God (or That Which Is Always Already The Case) Is Always Already The Case, Real God (or That Which Is Always Already The Case) Is (Necessarily) Always Already Realizable (In Any and Every Case)—but Real God (or That Which Is Always Already The Case) Is (Necessarily) Realizable Only As That Which Is Always Already Beyond (and Most Perfectly Prior To) All The Separate, finite, and Always changing psycho-physical Faculties Of conditional experience and conditional knowledge, and Always Already Beyond (and Most Perfectly Prior To) All The perceptual and conceptual Results Of The Exercise Of The Separate, finite, and Always changing psycho-physical Faculties Of the conditional body-mind, and (Indeed) Always Already Beyond (and Most Perfectly Prior To) All and all That Is Not Always Already The Case.

That Which, When It Is Realized (As The Case), Is Realized To Be Always Already The Case—Always Already Beyond (and Most Perfectly Prior To) All and all That Is Not Always Already The Case—Is Real God.

Only That Which Is Actually (As The Case) Realized As That Which Is

Always Already The Case—Always Already Beyond (and Most Perfectly Prior To) All and all That Is Not Always Already The Case—Is Real God.

Therefore, Reality (Itself), or Truth (Itself)—Always Already Beyond (and Most Perfectly Prior To) All and all That Is Not Always Already The Case—Is The Only Real (and, Necessarily, To-Be-Realized) God.

Whatever Is Not Realized To Be Always Already The Case (Always Already Beyond, and Most Perfectly Prior To, all conditional experience and all conditional knowledge) Is Not Real God (or Reality Itself, or Truth Itself)—and, Indeed, Whatever Is Not Realized To Be Always Already The Case (Always Already Beyond, and Most Perfectly Prior To, all conditional experience and all conditional knowledge) Is Not (As Reality, or As Truth, or As Real God) The Case.

That Which Is Realized To Be Always Already The Case (and As That Which Is Always Already The Case) Is (Necessarily) Realized To Be One and Only.

That Which Is Realized To Be Always Already The Case Is (Necessarily) The One and Only Reality, The One and Only Truth, and The One and Only Real God.

That (Reality, Truth, and Real God) Which Is (Always Already) The Case—and Which Is (Necessarily) Realized To Be The Case—Is (Necessarily) One and Only.

That (Reality, Truth, and Real God) Which Is Always Already The Case—and Which Is (Necessarily) Realized To Be The Case—Is (Necessarily) The One and Only Case.

Because That (Reality, Truth, and Real God) Which Is Always Already The Case Is (Necessarily) One, and Only, and (Therefore) The One and Only Case—The Inherent Essential Characteristics Of That (Reality, Truth, and Real God) Which Is Always Already The Case Are (Necessarily) The Inherent Essential Characteristics Of All and all That Is The Case.

Therefore, The Inherent Essential Characteristics Of That (Reality, Truth, and Real God) Which Is Always Already The Case Are (Necessarily) The Inherent Essential Characteristics Of Both The Unconditional (or Truly Divine, and Most Perfectly Prior) Dimension Of Reality and The conditional (or Cosmic, and Subordinate, and Entirely Dependent) Dimension Of Reality.

Because The Inherent Essential Characteristics Of That (Reality, Truth, and Real God) Which Is Always Already The Case Are (Necessarily) The Inherent Essential Characteristics Of Both The Unconditional (or Truly Divine, and Most Perfectly Prior) Dimension Of Reality and The conditional (or Cosmic, and Subordinate, and Entirely Dependent) Dimension Of Reality—That (Reality, Truth, and Real God) Which Is Always Already The Case Is Always Already Realizable (As The Case), No Matter What Otherwise Appears To Be The Case.

Therefore, Real God (or Reality, or Truth) Is, In Any and Every Case, Realizable (As The Case, and As That Which Is Always Already The Case)—but Only If That Which Is Not Always Already The Case Is (Really, and Truly) Transcended (and, At Last, Such That That Which Is Not Always Already The Case Is Always Already, and Most Perfectly, Transcended).

The ego-"I" (or the self-Contracted, self-Referring, Separate, Separative, finite, Always limited, and Always changing "point of view" of conditional experience and conditional knowledge) Is (Always) That Which Is Not Always Already The Case—and, Most Particularly, It Is the Whole bodily (or Total psycho-physical, and, Thus, Comprehensively perceptual and conceptual) self-Contraction (Into the condition of Separate and Separative "point of view", or ego-"I") that Transforms (and Reduces) That Which Is Always Already The Case Into That Which Is Not Always Already The Case.

Except For The (Necessarily, Reality-Transforming, and Reality-Reducing, and, Altogether, "Narcissistic") Act Of self-Contraction (and All The, Necessarily, Reality-Obscuring, and self-Deluding, Results Of The Act Of self-Contraction), The Inherent Essential Characteristics Of That (Reality, Truth, and Real God) Which Is Always Already The Case Are Always Already Obvious (and, Self-Evidently, The Case).

Therefore, the ego-"I" Must Be Transcended (and, At Last, Such That the ego-"I" Is Always Already, and Most Perfectly, Transcended)—or Else The Inherent Essential Characteristics (and, Indeed, The Very Existence) Of That (Reality, Truth, and Real God) Which Is Always Already The Case Cannot Be Realized (and, Therefore, Will Never Be Realized—No Matter How Much, or By What Means, Reality, or Truth, or Real God Is Sought, or Believed, or "Proved").

I Am The One, and Only, and Self-Existing, and Always Already (Eternally, Unconditionally, Most Perfectly Priorly, Entirely Non-Dependently, and Truly Divinely) Existing Reality and Truth.

I Am The Transcendental, Perfectly Subjective, Inherently Non-Separate, Inherently Non-"Different", Inherently Spiritual, Most Perfectly Self-Radiant, Most Perfectly Love-Bliss-"Bright", Inherently Non-Separate, Inherently egoless, Inherently Perfect, and Self-Evidently Divine Person. I Am The Very Person, and The Very Self-Condition Of The Unconditional (or Truly Divine, and Most Perfectly Prior) Dimension Of Reality—and My Inherent Essential Characteristics Are The Inherent Essential Characteristics Of All and all That Is The Case (Even In The conditional—or Cosmic, and Subordinate, and Entirely Dependent—Dimension Of Reality).

I Am The One, and Only, and Perfectly Subjective, and Inherently egoless (or Most Perfectly Non-Separate, and Most Perfectly Non-"Different") Person, Self-Condition, and Source (or Source-Condition) Of All and all That Is The

Case (In Both The Unconditional Dimension Of Reality and The conditional Dimension Of Reality). And (Therefore—and As Such) I Am To Be Realized (and, Indeed, Must Be Realized) By All and all. Therefore, I Am here.

I Am (Now, and Forever Hereafter) here—Always Already Self-Revealed In and As and By Means Of The Avatarically-Born Bodily (Human) Divine Form, and The Avatarically Self-Transmitted (and Always all-and-All-Blessing) Divine Spiritual Presence, and The Always (Thereby) Avatarically Self-Revealed Transcendental, Perfectly Subjective, Inherently Non-Separate, Inherently Non-"Different", Inherently Spiritual, Inherently egoless, Inherently Perfect, and Self-Evidently Divine State Of The Ruchira Avatar, Adi Da Samraj. And, As Such, and By Means Of My Avataric Self-Revelation Of My Own Inherent Essential (and Eternal) Characteristics, I Am (Now, and Forever Hereafter) Realizable By All and all. And (Now, and Forever Hereafter) I Am To Be Realized As That Which Is Always Already The Case.

I Am (Eternally, and Unconditionally) That Which Is Always Already (and Truly Divinely, and Most Perfectly Priorly) The Case. And (By Means Of My Avataric Self-Revelation As The Ruchira Avatar, Adi Da Samraj) I Am (Now, and Forever Hereafter) Avatarically Self-Revealed (Within The conditional—or Cosmic, and Subordinate, and Entirely Dependent—Dimension Of Reality) As That Which Is Always Already The Case. And (Now, and Forever Hereafter) I Am To Be Realized By Means Of The Inherently (and, At Last, Most Perfectly) ego-Transcending Practice Of The Only-By-Me Avatarically Revealed and Avatarically Given Divine Way Of The Heart (or Way Of Adidam).

The Only-By-Me Revealed and Given Way Of The Heart (or Way Of Adidam) Is Founded On A Thoroughly ego-Transcending (Rather Than Either An ego-Negating Or An ego-Fulfilling, and ego-Glorifying) Approach To Divine (or Real-God-Realizing) Life and Practice. That Is To Say, The Only-By-Me Revealed and Given Way Of The Heart (or Way Of Adidam) Is Founded On The Always Directly Counter-egoic (and Always Immediately ego-Vanishing) Devotional Recognition-Response To My Avatarically Self-Revealed Divine Form, and Presence, and State. And (On That To-Me-Devoted Basis) The Only-By-Me Revealed and Given Way Of The Heart (or Way Of Adidam) Develops As A Subsequent (and More and More Effectively ego-Transcending) Process Of Spontaneous (and Progressively Thorough) self-Observation, Eventual Most Fundamental self-Understanding, and, At Last, Inherently Most Perfect ego-Transcendence. And, In The Only-By-Me Revealed and Given Way Of The Heart (or Way Of Adidam), Inherently Most Perfect ego-Transcendence Is Realized Entirely By Means Of My Avatarically Self-Revealed, and Avatarically Self-Transmitted, Divine Spiritual Grace—and Inherently Most Perfect ego-Transcendence Is (Thus and Thereby) Realized As The Inherently ego-Transcending (and Most Perfectly egoless) Self-Condition Of Inherent Self-Identification With Me (The Avatarically Self-Revealed Transcendental, Perfectly Subjective, Inherently Non-Separate, Inherently Non-"Different", Inherently Spiritual, Inherently egoless, Inherently Perfect, and Self-Evidently Divine Source and Person—Realized As The Non-"Different" Self-Condition, and The Perfectly Subjective Source-Condition, Of all-and-All), Rather Than On The Basis Of (and As An Expression Of) Any Propositions About How Either To Negate Or To Fulfill the conditional self (and its desires—or its Search—In the conditional worlds).

In The Only-By-Me Revealed and Given Way Of The Heart (or Way Of Adidam), The Real Practice Of ego-Transcendence Requires A Constant (and Really and Truly Counter-egoically Effective) Confrontation With The (Apparent) "Difference" Between The (Apparently) Two (and Polar Opposite) Dimensions Of The (Inherently) One and Only (and Inherently Indivisible) Reality. Those Two Dimensions Of The (Necessarily) One and Only and Indivisible Reality Are The Unconditional (or Primary, Senior, Most Perfectly Prior, and Truly Divine) Dimension Of Reality and The conditional (or Cosmic, and Subordinate, and Entirely Dependent) Dimension Of Reality.

First (or Relative To The Unconditional Dimension Of Reality), There Must (In The Practice Of The Only-By-Me Revealed and Given Way Of The Heart) Be A Constant (moment to moment, and Really and Truly Counter-egoically Effective) Confrontation With the ego-Made (and ego-Protecting, and ego-Serving) limit Of The Expressed Urge Toward Most Perfectly ego-Transcending (and Fully and Most Perfectly Spiritually Awakened) Real-God-Realization (and The Process That—In every moment or circumstance—Must Become ego-Transcending Real-God-Communion). That Is To Say, The Present (or moment to moment) Urge Toward Most Perfectly ego-Transcending Real-God-Realization Must Be Constantly Intensified and Increased, If Actual (or Really Effective) ego-Transcendence (and, Thereby, Growth Through and Beyond Any Present Stage Of Practice In The Only-By-Me Revealed and Given Way Of The Heart) Is To Occur.

Second (or Relative To The conditional Dimension Of Reality), There Must (In The Practice Of The Only-By-Me Revealed and Given Way Of The Heart) Be A Constant (moment to moment, and Really and Truly Counter-egoically Effective) Confrontation With Complacent (ego-Protecting) Attitudes Toward present experience, Binding (and ego-Serving) Attachments To conventional (or everyday) living arrangements (or Orderly Means For Maintaining emotional Immunity and egoic Security), and ego-Made Illusions About conditional Existence In General (or Presumptions That Cannot Bear The Test Of Even The ordinary, or conditional, Dimension Of Reality, and That Express The egoic Want To Indulge In conditional Existence For Its Own Sake, Rather Than Accept conditional Existence As A School Of ego-Transcendence In That Which Is Reality, Truth, and Real God).

Therefore, The Only-By-Me Revealed and Given Way Of The Heart (or Way Of Adidam) Involves A Constant Confrontation With the Countless self-Deluding (and, Ultimately, self-Defeating) limits that the ego-"I" (or psycho-physical self-Contraction) Would (Otherwise) Superimpose On Both The conditional (or Apparently Separate, and ego-Based, or egoically conceived) Reality and The Unconditional (or Transcendental, Perfectly Subjective, Inherently Spiritual, Inherently egoless, Inherently Perfect, and Self-Evidently Divine) Reality. And The Real Practice Of The Only-By-Me Revealed and Given Way Of The Heart (or Way Of Adidam) Is Always Developed In The Context Of A Dynamic (and, Necessarily, Counter-egoic—and Really and Truly ego-Surrendering, ego-Forgetting, and ego-Transcending) Struggle Between The Great Urge Toward Most Perfectly ego-Transcending (Unconditional, and Fully and Most Perfectly Spiritually Awakened) Divine Self-Realization (Via True, and Full, and Really Counter-egoic Divine Communion—In every moment, and By Readily Proceeding Within The Progressive Context Of The Stages Of Practice In The Way Of The Heart) and The ego-Based (and ego-Reinforcing) Urge To Be Complacent (or Content With The Average Context and The Familiar Associations Of conditional experience—and, Also, Reluctant To Encounter Further Demands For Greater ego-Transcendence).

Since Ancient times, Mankind Has, In various times and places, Tended To Embrace (or To Be Dominated By) One or The Other Of Two Characteristic Approaches To The (Apparently) Two Dimensions Of The (Inherently) One and Indivisible Reality. Just So, every individual Tends To Be Involved In A Constant Struggle Between Two Primary and Opposite Motives, That Correspond To The Two Characteristic Approaches To The (Apparently) Two Dimensions Of The One Reality. These Two Approaches Generally Correspond To The Oriental (or The Eastern) and The Occidental (or The Western) Strategies Of Culture (Although The Oriental Tendency Can Sometimes Be Found In The Traditional West—As, For Example, Among The More Mystically Oriented Of The Ancient Greeks—and The Occidental Tendency Can Sometimes Be Found In The Traditional East—As, For Example, Among The More Practically Oriented Of The Ancient Chinese).

I Call These Two Efforts or Tendencies "The Alpha Strategy" and "The Omega Strategy".

The Alpha Strategy Is Based On The Tendency To Identify With The Most Prior (Transcendental, Inherently Spiritual, Inherently egoless, and Self-Evidently Divine) Reality, or Condition, Exclusively (or In A Manner That

Suppresses—or, Otherwise, Strategically Excludes—conditional Reality). And The Omega Strategy Is Based On The Tendency To Identify With conditional Reality Exclusively (or In A Manner That Suppresses—or, Otherwise, Strategically Excludes—The Unconditional, Transcendental, Inherently Spiritual, Inherently egoless, and Self-Evidently Divine Reality).

The Alpha Strategy Exhibits Control Relative To conditional Reality (Including social relations, social and bodily action, sex and functional bodily indulgence of all kinds, expressions of emotion, and activities of mind) and Liberality Relative To The Unconditional (or Divine) Reality.

Thus, The Alpha Preference Is For The Control (or Strategic limiting, or Minimizing) Of the functional and relational activities of the conditional psycho-physical personality (Even To The Degree Of Suppression and Exclusion)—and For The Maximizing Of attention, Mystical Devotion, and Contemplative Surrender To The Transcendental, Inherently Spiritual, Inherently egoless, and Self-Evidently Divine Self-Condition, Being, Source-Condition, or Person.

This Alpha Preference Aims To Lead From self-Control To Peace Of mind—and, Finally, To (Strategic) Escape From conditional Reality and To Consequent Oneness With The Unconditional Reality. Indeed, This Alpha Strategy Can Be Said To Be The Epitome (or Archetype) Of What Is (In The Context Of The Total Great Tradition Of Mankind, Previous to My Avataric Divine Appearance here) Commonly Conceived To Be The Ultimate (or Esoteric) Religious Path (Associated With The Fourth, The Fifth, and The Sixth Stages Of Life).

Just So, There Is Another and Quite Opposite Strategy, Which Alpha Strategists Conceive To Be The Anti-Religious Path, but Which Omega Strategists Conceive To Be Inevitable, Truly human, and Even Obligatory From a Religious (and Rather exoteric) point of view. That Strategy Is The Omega Strategy Itself.

The Omega Strategy Exhibits Liberality Relative To conditional Reality (Including social relations, social and bodily action, sex and bodily indulgence of all kinds, expressions of emotion, and activities of mind)—and Control (In The Form Of Doubt, Lack Of Interest, and Taboos Of All Kinds) Relative To The Unconditional (or Divine) Reality.

Thus, The Omega Preference Is For Control, limitation, Doubt, and Even Suppression (or Exclusion) Of attention, Mystical Devotion, and Contemplative Surrender To The Transcendental, Inherently Spiritual, Inherently egoless, and Self-Evidently Divine Self-Condition, Being, Source-Condition, or Person—While, Otherwise, Liberally Maximizing attention (and The Pursuit Of experience and knowledge) Relative To functional and relational activities and Even The Total conditional Context (or world-Context) Of bodily-Based human Existence.

This Omega Preference Aims To Lead Away From vulnerable, weak, and ignorant Victimization By Cosmic Nature and To Greater and Greater experiential (or perceptual) and abstract (or conceptual) knowledge—and, Finally, To Collective and individual Control Over Cosmic Nature (and, Thus, The Ability To Exploit and Duplicate The Powers Of Cosmic Nature). This Omega Strategy Can Be Said To Be The Epitome (or Archetype) Of What Is (In The Context Of The Total Great Tradition Of Mankind, Previous To My Avataric Divine Appearance here) Commonly Conceived To Be The Necessary (and, Necessarily, exoteric) Path Of human Fulfillment. Indeed, It Is Sometimes (From a Typically Occidental Religious point of view) Conceived To Be The Path Of Fulfillment Of The Divine Purpose In The Cosmos. (Therefore, To Be Truly Religious, From the Occidental point of view, one Must Relinquish Much Of The Oriental Religious, or Mystical, Orientation and Practice Religion In The Non-Mystical, or exoteric, Fashion Of Submission To conditional Effort Within The conditional Cosmic Scheme.)

These Two Strategic points of view Are Apparently In Conflict With one another—and, Indeed, Historically This Has Been The Case. That Conflict Is Itself One Of The Principal conditional Signs Of human Struggle Within The Context Of conditional Nature. Thus, Early human History (and, Indeed, The Entire History Of The Total Great Tradition Of Mankind, Previous To My Avataric Divine Appearance here) Developed On The Basis Of A Dichotomy (or Split) In The Disposition Of Man, Based On The Two Natural functional Divisions Of the human brain (and Of the human nervous system). And, On The Basis Of That Split, Mankind Has Developed Along Two Entirely Different Lines (Which May Be Compared and Related To The Frontal and Spinal Lines Of the human body-mind), Almost As If Mankind Were Composed Of Two Separate Species. Therefore, This Dichotomy and These Two Great Lines Of human Development Must Be "Considered" and Understood.

When Both Sides Of The Traditional Dichotomy Become Conscious Of One Another, A Profound Sense Of Inherent, Irreducible, and Inevitable Conflict May Also Appear Between Them. Then Mankind Seems To Be Confronted With A Choice Between Two Destinies—One Oriental In Its Conception, and The Other Occidental In Its Conception. Because Of The Naturally gross (or Persistently bodily-Based) Survival Politics Of ordinary human Culture, It May Seem That Mankind (As A Whole) Will Always Inevitably Choose The Omega (or Frontal and left-brained, verbal-minded, or rational) Path, but It May Also Seem That Mankind (one by one) Must (Necessarily) Choose The Alpha (or Spinal and right-brained, Non-verbal, or intuitive) Path, or Else Be Destroyed By Political and Cultural Conflicts.

I Was (By Means Of My Great Avataric Divine Descent Into The Totality Of The Cosmic Domain) Born (In Human Form) In A Terrible Moment Of

Necessity—To Call Mankind To The Great Moment Of New Understanding, and To The Great Future Of A Single Destiny. My Avatarically Self-Revealed Divine Word, My Avatarically Self-Revealed Divine Image-Art, My Avatarically Self-Manifested Divine Leelas, The "Bright" Divine Revelation-Sign Of My Avatarically-Born Bodily (Human) Divine Form, The Divine Work Of My Avatarically Self-Transmitted Spiritual (and Always Blessing) Divine Presence, and The Avatarically Given Divine Self-Revelation Of My Perfectly Subjective (and Very, and Transcendental, and Inherently Spiritual, and Inherently egoless, and Inherently Perfect, and Self-Evidently Divine) State Forever Call Mankind To Transcend Both The Alpha Strategy and The Omega Strategy. Neither The One Nor The Other Should Be Chosen (Exclusively). Whether Alpha Or Omega, it is the same ego (or self-Contraction) that Makes The Path. The same ego Turns Away From conditional Reality and Turns Toward It. The same ego Turns Toward "God" (As The However Conceived Unconditional Reality) and Turns Away From "God" (Via The conditional Reality). The same ego believes one Must Turn Toward "God" (By Minimizing or Excluding conditional experience and knowledge) and, Otherwise, believes one Must Turn Away From (or Even Proceed From) "God" and Do "God's" Work By Maximizing conditional experience and knowledge. It Is Simply That There Are Two Forms Of egoity—The One Basically Oriental, and The Other Basically Occidental.

My Avatarically Self-Revealed Divine Word, My Avatarically Self-Revealed Divine Image-Art, My Avatarically Self-Manifested Divine Leelas, The "Bright" Divine Revelation-Sign Of My Avatarically-Born Bodily (Human) Divine Form, The Divine Work Of My Avatarically Self-Transmitted Spiritual (and Always Blessing) Divine Presence, and The Avatarically Given Divine Self-Revelation Of My Perfectly Subjective (and Very, and Transcendental, and Inherently Spiritual, and Inherently egoless, and Inherently Perfect, and Self-Evidently Divine) State Forever Call Mankind To The Only Way That Is Single, Whole, and Not Based On egoity. The Only-By-Me Revealed and Given Way Of The Heart (or Way Of Adidam) Is Not Developed From the Exclusive (or Dominant) point of view Of Either The Frontal Line Or The Spinal Line, or From the Exclusive (or Dominant) point of view of Either the left Or the right hemisphere of the brain. Rather, The Only-By-Me Revealed and Given Way Of The Heart (or Way Of Adidam) Involves (and Requires) The Whole Of Man, The Full Circle, the Resonant nervous system, the Total brain, All Aligned and Surrendered, In Love, To Me—and This, Most Ultimately, To The Degree Of Inherently Most Perfect Dissolution In My Avatarically Self-Revealed Unconditional, Transcendental, Perfectly Subjective, Inherently Spiritual, Inherently egoless, Inherently Perfect, and Self-Evidently Divine Self-Condition (but Not By Means Of The ego-Strategy Of Suppression and Exclusion).

The Only-By-Me Revealed and Given Way Of The Heart Is (In Its Fullness) The Way Of Always Present Real-God-Realization Through ego-Transcending Real-God-Communion. In The Only-By-Me Revealed and Given Way Of The Heart, attention To The Unconditional Reality Is Not Merely Maximized. Rather, It Is Made Constant, or The Very Basis Of conditional Existence. Therefore, If (In The Way Of The Heart) Real-God-Communion Is To Be Constant (and Not Merely Frequent), The Alpha Strategy Of Introversion (or Of Minimizing attention To conditional Reality and Maximizing attention To Unconditional Reality) Is Not (As An Exclusive Effort) Workable. Instead, all attention To conditional Reality Must Be Directly Converted Into attention To The Unconditional Reality. Just So, In The Way Of The Heart, The Omega Strategy Of Extroversion (or Of Minimizing attention To Unconditional Reality and Maximizing attention To conditional Reality) Is (As An Exclusive Effort) Equally Unworkable, Since Any and All Involvement With conditional Reality Must Be ego-Transcending and Real-God-Realizing, Even Though Involvement With conditional Reality Is, In Principle, To Be Fully Embraced (Without Prejudice or Disinclination).

In The Only-By-Me Revealed and Given Way Of The Heart (or Way Of Adidam), The egoic Strategy Of Introversion and The egoic Strategy Of Extroversion Are Both Freely Relinquished In The Dynamic Process Of Ruchira Avatara Bhakti Yoga, Thorough self-Observation, Most Fundamental self-Understanding, and ego-Transcending Conversion (or Turnabout) Of the conditional self (or conditional Reality) To Devotional (and, In Due Course, Progressively Spiritual) Communion With Me—and This, Most Ultimately, To The Degree Of Inherent (and Inherently Most Perfect) Realization Of My Avatarically Self-Revealed Unconditional (or Transcendental, Perfectly Subjective, Inherently Spiritual, Inherently egoless, Inherently Perfect, and Self-Evidently Divine) Self-Condition (Which Is The One and Only Reality, Truth, and Real God).

From the conventional and (Necessarily) egoic points of view Of The Alpha Strategy and The Omega Strategy, Either The Unconditional Reality Or The conditional Reality Is Proposed As The Only Ultimately Justifiable Domain Of human attention and activity. I Say The Two Cannot Be Separated Without Deluding Mankind and Reinforcing the egoity Of Mankind. The Only-By-Me Revealed and Given Way Of The Heart (or Way Of Adidam) Presumes (As A "Working Principle" Of Practice) Both The Unconditional and The conditional Dimensions Of Reality. The Two Are (Thus, In Practice) Presumed In Dynamic Association With One Another—and The Unconditional (or Transcendental, Inherently Spiritual, Inherently egoless, and Self-Evidently Divine) Reality Is, Clearly, The Senior Dimension (or Source-Condition) Of This Dynamic Pair.

In The Only-By-Me Revealed and Given Way Of The Heart (or Way Of Adidam), The conditional Reality Is Proposed and Rightly Embraced, but (In The Progress Of The Way Of The Heart) The conditional Reality Is Always Surrendered and Presently Transcended In Devotional Heart-Communion With Me (The Avatarically Self-Revealed Transcendental, Inherently Spiritual, Inherently egoless, and Self-Evidently Divine Person). The conditional and The Unconditional Are Not To Be Conceived Apart From One Another. Love, Always Magnified and Brought To Consciousness and Action, Is What Unites The Two In Dynamic Association. If, By Means Of My Avatarically Self-Transmitted Divine Spiritual Grace, The Inherent Love-Bliss Of My Avatarically Self-Revealed (and Self-Evidently Divine) Person Is (In The Devotionally Me-Recognizing and Devotionally To-Me-Responding Manner) Found and (In The ego-Surrendering, ego-Forgetting, and, More and More, ego-Transcending Manner) Embraced—In The Context Of the conditional worlds (Rather Than As Merely Abstract Peace, or object-Excluding Selfhood, Strategically Dissociated From the conditional worlds)—Then the body-mind and The Way Become Single, Expressed Through ego-Transcending (and Spiritually Me-Receiving) Love-Communion With Me, and Yet Not Disinclined Toward The self-Sacrificial (or Really ego-Transcending) Process (or School) Of conditionally Manifested Existence Itself.

The conditional personality (or the egoic body-mind, or conditionally Manifested and self-Contracting being) Must (Through The Real Process Of self-Understanding and self-Transcendence) Be Converted and Transcended (Not Merely Minimized, Suppressed, or Excluded) In all of its forms and expressions. True Real-God-Communion Is egoless (or Free Of self-Contraction). Therefore, If Real-God-Communion Is To Be Real, True, Constant, and egoless, The Way Cannot Be A Matter Of Strategic Minimization Of conditional action, experience, and knowledge. The Only-By-Me Revealed and Given Way Of The Heart (or Way Of Adidam) Must Be (and Is) The Process Of Directly (If Progressively) Converting and Transcending Every Species Of egoity, and (Thus) all actions, every experience, and all forms of knowledge.

The conventionally Archetypal (or Alpha) Concept and Strategy Of Religion Generally Prefers Not To act. But, If action Is Permitted (or Even Required), The Alpha-Prescription Is To act—but Not To react. It Is common knowledge that every action Necessarily Results In an equal and opposite reaction. Therefore, Clearly, If one acts (or Yields conditional attention To conditional Reality), one Will Inevitably react. Because Of This, those who Try To act and Not react Are Always Trying To Control their reactions (and, Otherwise, Wishing they Were Not Moved To act).

The Only-By-Me Revealed and Given Way Of The Heart (or Way Of Adidam) Is Not Based On The Alpha Strategy—or The Pursuit Of conditionally

Perfect self-Purification, and (Ultimately) Of The Absolute Suppression (or Negation) Of the conditional self (or body-mind). Neither Is The Only-By-Me Revealed and Given Way Of The Heart (or Way Of Adidam) Based On The Omega Strategy—or The Pursuit Of conditional self-Perfection, and (Ultimately) Of The Absolute Fulfillment (or Eternalization) Of the conditional self (or body-mind). Nor Is The Only-By-Me Revealed and Given Way Of The Heart (or Way Of Adidam) Characterized By Any Conflict Between The Alpha and Omega Principles (or The Strategies Associated With Them). I Do Not Call My Listening Devotee, My Hearing Devotee, or My Seeing Devotee To The Strategy Of "act and Not react". I Call My Listening Devotee To (Most Fundamental) self-Understanding. I Call My Hearing Devotee To Transcend the self-Contraction Through Persistence In Most Fundamental self-Understanding. And I Call My Seeing Devotee (In whom The Heart Both Hears Me <u>and</u> Sees Me) To Transcend Even every form of the self-Contraction (or the Total egoic actor, who acts and reacts) By Engaging every action As (Fully Technically Responsible) Spiritual Love-Communion With Me—and Not For The Sake Of self-Fulfillment or self-Negation, but Only For The Sake Of That Love-Communion Itself (Which Is Communion With My Divine Love-Bliss Itself—Infinitely Self-Radiant, Most Prior To, or <u>Above</u> <u>and</u> <u>Beyond</u>, all forms of self-Contraction).

The conventionally Archetypal (or Alpha) Concept and Strategy Of Religion Generally Prefers To Minimize the amount of time Spent In conditional action and To Maximize the amount of time Spent In Inward Contemplation. Even the ego Can Do This, and Still There May Be Not Even a moment Of True Real-God-Communion! I Call My Every Devotee Always To Transcend the self-Contraction and Always, On The Basis Of That Transcending, To Be In Real-God-Communion. Therefore, I Call My Every Devotee To Perform, Convert, Positively Change, and Transcend conditional actions of every kind, Whether In Formal Meditation Or In the everyday circumstance. For This Reason, My Every Devotee Must Surely and Artfully Embrace Every Discipline Of the body-mind That Turns and Opens the body-mind To Me. However, Discipline Must Not Be Embraced For Its Own Sake, In A Loveless Manner, but Always In My Good Company, and (By Devotional Recognition-Response To Me) In The Divine Mood Of Love, Humor, Freedom, and Ultimate Delight.

The conventionally Archetypal (or Alpha) Concept and Strategy Of Religion Generally Emphasizes Sila, Which Is The Control Of Outgoing Exuberance, or The Minimization Of The Expression (or Depletion) Of The Heart In Relation To conditional Reality. True Sila (or Simple Discipline Of actions that Merely Indulge the body, Discard the Natural energies, Scatter emotions, and Dull the mind) Is Good Discipline, If Applied By one who Would Understand (or who Already and Most Fundamentally Understands) the conditional self. True Sila Is Not The Product Of A Problematic or Negative Summary View Of conditional Existence. True Sila Is A Servant Of Consistent self-Observation and, Ultimately, It Is (or Must Become) An Expression Of Real and Most Fundamental self-Understanding. Ultimately, True Sila Reflects Real experience and True knowledge Of The Structural Laws Of the functional, practical, and relational processes of the body-mind. And Such True Sila Expresses A Reality-Sense Of the limits Of conditional Existence (or How the ego and All Of conditional Nature Bite and Bite Back, and How every conditionally Manifested being, thing, or process dies or disappears after a time Of Constant Change, and How Both The Strategy Of Dissociation and The Strategy Of Clinging Always, Whether Immediately Or Eventually, Result In Apparently Diminished Happiness).

True Sila Is Necessary and Good For those who Would Realize Reality, or Truth, or Real God—but False Sila (Generated By Negative views and Expressed As Search, self-Righteousness, and Suppression Of The Living and Feeling Heart) Is Itself The Avoidance Of Reality and Truth (Which *Is* The *Only* Real God).

The Obvious limits Of conditional Existence Provide All The Reasons For Either False Sila Or self-Indulgence (or The Excesses Of Either Alpha Or Omega). In Either Case, The Problem and The Search Become The Logic Of Existence. And The Problem With Seeking (or The Reason Why Seeking Is A False Principle) Is That It *Always* Serves and Reinforces Its Own Original Principle, Which Is the self-Contraction.

The Real-God-Realizing Process (or The Process Associated With Most Ultimate—and, Necessarily, Divine—Enlightenment) Is Necessarily ego-Transcending. Therefore, It Is Not A Process In Which The Guiding Principle Is Either False Sila Or self-Indulgence. Neither Alpha Nor Omega Is Itself The True, Primary, or Central and Guiding Principle (Even Though actions In The Mode Of Both Alpha and Omega May Be Generated On The Basis Of That True Principle). The True, Primary, or Central and Guiding Principle Is Not In The Strategy Of Dissociative Detachment (or Separation) From conditional Reality, Nor Is It In The Strategy Of Mere Indulgence In conditional Reality. Rather, In The Fullness Of The Only-By-Me Revealed and Given Way Of The Heart (or Way Of Adidam), The True and Inherently ego-Transcending Principle Is In The Free and self-Surrendered Acceptance (and, Most Ultimately, The Inherent, and Inherently Most Perfect, Transcending) Of conditional Reality (or conditional Existence) Via The Discipline Of ego-Transcending Love-Communion With Me.

Ultimately, True Sila Is The Discipline Of Devotionally Me-Recognizing (and Devotionally To-Me-Responding, and, Altogether, ego-Transcending)

Devotional (and Spiritually Me-Receiving) Love Of Me—Which Finds and Embraces (and, More and More Fully, Enters Into) My Avatarically Self-Transmitted (and Self-Evidently Divine) Love-Bliss. Therefore, ego-Transcending Devotional (and Spiritually Me-Receiving) Love Of Me Becomes Love Itself (More and More Truly, and egolessly) and Truly ego-Transcending Bliss Itself (or Happiness Itself). The Heart Of True Sila (In The Fullness Of The Only-By-Me Revealed and Given Way Of The Heart) Is The True Heart-Fullness Of My Graceful Divine Spiritual Heart-Infusion Of conditional Existence (and Of every conditional circumstance) Via My Seeing Devotee's ego-Transcending Devotional and Spiritual Communion With Me. Therefore, Not False Sila (or The Alpha Strategy Of Strategic Dissociation, or Strategic Separation, From conditional Existence) and Not self-Indulgence (or The Omega Strategy Of Clinging To conditional Existence), but ego-Transcending Love-Communion With Me Under the circumstances Of conditional Existence, Is (Necessarily) The Nature Of The Process In My Avataric Divine Heart-Company. And My Devotee Must (From The Beginning Of his or her Participation In The Way Of The Heart) Learn and Practice This self-Discipline and ego-Transcending Process Of Love-Communion With Me—Until (By Means Of My Avatarically Self-Transmitted Divine Spiritual Grace) The Realization Of My Inherent (and Inherently Spiritual, Inherently egoless, and Self-Evidently Divine) Love-Bliss-Fullness (or Heart-"Brightness") Stands Motivelessly (and Divinely) Indifferent, and Self-Radiant, and Inherently Free Of egoity (or self-Contraction), and Inherently Free Of "Difference", and Even (At Last) Freely (and Inherently, but Not Strategically) Outshining conditional Existence Itself.

The conventionally Archetypal (or Alpha) Concept and Strategy Of Religion Generally Idealizes Peace Of mind (Through The Minimization Of attention, Heart-Feeling, and bodily action In the field of conditional events), but mere (conditional) "Peace" Of mind (or the experience Of egoic Calm) Has No Charm or Light. Greater Than That Peace Of mind Is the mind-In-Real-God, Wherein the mind Is Yielded, Divinely Infused, and Directly Transcended (Along With action, body, Reactive and conditional emotion, and attention). Greater Than Peace Of mind Is mind Yielded (In Ecstasy), To The Degree Of Divine Exaltation and Divine "Intoxication"—Transparent To The Divine Fullness Of Love-Bliss, and Radiant With Divine Joy.

In Contrast To The Alpha Concept (and Strategy) Of Religion, The Omega Concept (and Strategy) Of Religion Is Concerned With bodily-Based Morality—Not Mysticism or Inward Contemplation. It Is humanistic (or ego-Based, human-Based, socially Based, and world-Based)—Not Mystical, Not Contemplative, Not Inclined To Go Beyond conditional self and conditional world, but Determined To Achieve A Great Fulfillment In this world.

Nonetheless, The Omega Concept Of Religion Is "Religious" (or Concerned With The Connection Between Man and "God", or The Connection Between The conditional Reality and The However Conceived Unconditional Reality) In The Sense That "God" Is Conceived To Be At The Beginning (If Only As Ultimate Cause) Of The conditional Cosmos and Working Toward The End (or Perfection) Of The conditional Cosmos. This Idea About "God" Is Rooted In An Idea About Man. It Is The Omega Idea. It Is The bodily-Based (and Cosmically Oriented) Idea That "God" (and Thus Man), or Man (and Thus "God"), Is Causatively (or Creatively) Oriented Toward conditional Existence. Thus, Man (Like "God") Is, In The Omega View, To Participate In, Struggle With, and Always Persist In The Discipline (and The Expectation) Of Fulfillment In The Context Of The conditional Reality.

Therefore, The Omega Concept Of human life (Whether Or Not It Is Associated With Religion) Is Associated With humanistic (or Man-Serving) Morality, or The Struggle For human Survival and Ultimate human Victory In The conditional Cosmos.

Nevertheless, The Moral Propositions Developed In Omega-Based Societies Are Not Consistently (or Even Primarily) Associated With The Omega Strategy. Indeed, The Alpha Strategy Is The Typical Basis For The Moral Injunctions Associated With everyday life In Both Alpha-Based and Omega-Based Societies.

The Omega Strategy Is Based On The Motive To Subdue, Control, and Exploit All Aspects Of conditional Reality (In Cosmic Nature and In Mankind). The Alpha Strategy Is Based On The Motive To Minimize, Avoid, and (Strategically) Escape All (or, Certainly, The lower, or lesser, or most limited) Aspects and Dimensions Of conditional Reality. Therefore, The Omega Strategy Can Possibly Be The Basis For The Practice Of Active Morality (or The Morality Of worldly heroes, political and governmental leaders, and "Creative" persons of all kinds), but The Alpha Strategy Is The Typical Basis For The everyday Practice Of Passive (or public and social) Morality (or The Morality Of Virtue, Duty, self-Effacement, and Even popular, or conventional, sainthood).

The Omega Preference For The Moral (Rather Than The Mystical) Path Is Founded On A Basic Tendency To Identify With conditional (and bodily-Based) human Existence and A Subsequent Commitment To The Success Of The conditional human Enterprise. The Alpha Preference Is For The Mystical Path Rather Than The (Otherwise, or Alternatively) Moral Path, and That Preference Is Founded On A Basic Tendency To Identify (Exclusively) With Transcendental, Inherently Spiritual, Inherently egoless, and Self-Evidently Divine Existence and A Subsequent Commitment To Succeed At The Enterprise Of Minimizing, Avoiding, and (Strategically) Escaping conditional human Existence. Thus, The Alpha Preference Is To "Rise Above" (or Otherwise

Dissociate From) conditional Nature, Whereas The Omega Preference Is To "Conquer" (or To Subdue, Control, and Exploit) conditional Nature.

There Is a worldly, atheistic (or anti-Theistic), and Otherwise (or Generally) Non-Religious humanism (or Tradition Of Omega Effort) that Seeks To Establish Moral Propositions On The Basis Of Collective idealism (Such As "the Greatest good for the Greatest number") and individual idealism (Such As "enlightened self-Interest"), but The Omega Effort Is, In Its Largest Tradition, Associated With Religious Concepts. In That Tradition, "God" Is Said To Be The "Creator-Head" Of The conditional Cosmos. Thus, The conditional Cosmos Is Said To Be The Goal and The Orderly Effect Of "God". Man, Likewise, Both Collectively and individually, Is Said To Be The Goal and The Orderly Effect Of "God". From this Omega point of view, The Moral Imperative For Man Is To Conform To The Order (or conditional Cosmos) Of "God" and Make The Orderly and Ultimate Fulfillment Of Man (and The conditional Cosmos) The Goal Of human life (Both Collectively and individually).

Necessary To This Omega Concept Of Religious Morality Is The Concept Of "God" As "Creator-Cause" (Thus Justifying human Commitment To conditional Existence) and The Concept Of conditional Nature As A Religious, Material, and Moral Order (Thus Justifying Religious, Intellectual, and Moral Propositions In The Form Of Absolutes, Laws, and Imperatives).

The Omega Tradition Is Full Of Absolute Religious Propositions (Said To Be "God"-Made, but, In Reality, Made By Man In A Search For The Security Of Absolutes In The Insecure Realm Of conditional Nature). And Those Absolute Religious Propositions Are The Basis For Orderly Systems Of Law (Relative To The intellectual Descriptions Of conditional Nature That Correspond To The Current philosophical or scientific View In Any Historical Period) and Orderly Systems Of Moral Imperatives (That Are The Basis For human social Morality and social Laws In Any Historical Period).

In The "Modern" West, The Findings Of science Are Often Presumed, Especially By those Deeply Involved In (or Sympathetic With) The scientific Endeavor, To Have Undermined The (historically Inherited) Absolute Propositions Of conventional (or exoteric) Religion. However, Both conventional Religion <u>and</u> the philosophy of scientific materialism (which Seeks To Criticize conventional Religion As If conventional Religion Were The <u>Totality</u> Of Religion and Spirituality) Are Characteristic (and Characteristically limited) "products" of the Omega point of view. Science (itself) Is Simply A Method For The Free Investigation Of the phenomena Of conditionally Manifested Existence—but science (itself) Tends To Be Overlaid With the (traditional and Ancient) philosophy of materialism, which philosophy is very much a part Of The gross-minded Omega Culture Of The West.

The scientific Examination Of conditional phenomena Has Resulted In (and Continues To Pursue) The Detailed Mapping Of The Mechanisms Of conditionally Manifested Existence, including much Detailed knowledge about the functioning human organism and About The Development Of Various Modes Of conditionally Manifested life On Earth. Equipped With such maps Of The Structures Of the human entity, proponents of scientific materialism Have Criticized Many Of The Traditionally Acknowledged Means Of Accounting For human experience (including Religious experience), Claiming That Conscious experience Amounts To Nothing More Than Evidence Of How the human mind and the human body Are "Built" To Function. According To this scientific materialist point of view, Religious experience (and all of human experience) is merely something happening in the "meat-organism", Determined By its psycho-physical Structuring. That Conclusion Regarding The Nature Of human experience Is The Superimposition Of scientific materialist philosophy On the legitimate observations Made By Means Of The scientific Method. And That Conclusion Regarding The Nature Of human experience Is A Key Fault, Which Makes scientific materialism a <u>False</u> philosophy.

The psycho-physical Structures Of The human Mechanism Do, In Fact, Pattern human experience and human behavior, including scientific behavior—and The <u>Entire</u> Range Of Potential human experience (Only A Fraction Of Which Has Been Investigated By The Efforts Of conventional science) Can Be Understood In Terms Of My "Map" Of The Seven Stages Of Life, By Means Of Which I Have Revealed How <u>All</u> Potential human Developments Are Intrinsically Related To The Various (Hierarchically Interrelated) Structures Of The human Mechanism. However, the scientific materialist point of view <u>Reduces</u> everything To These Observed psycho-physical Structures—As If (For Example) The Association Between human Religious experience and Certain Structures In the human brain Proves That Religion Is <u>Nothing</u> <u>but</u> a "side-effect" Of The Functioning Of the brain.

Since The Most Ancient Days, <u>All</u> Esoteric Traditions Of Spirituality and Yoga Have Been Associated With An Understanding Of The (Real) Structures Underlying human experience. True Spirituality and True Yoga Are Based On A Detailed Knowledge Of the cerebro-spinal system, Of the various organs within the body, and So Forth. True Spirituality and True Yoga Are Not Based On (and, Indeed, Have Nothing To Do With) Cosmological mythologies or the conventional "God"-ideas of popular religiosity. True Esotericism Is Always Associated With An Analysis Of The human Structure, Of the workings Of That Structure, and Of The Methods By Which The Esoteric Practitioner Can Make Use Of That Structure In The Process Of Realization. However, The Esoteric Traditions Of Spirituality and Yoga Are Free Of The Fault Of reductionism. In The Esoteric Traditions Of Spirituality and Yoga, There Is No Notion That The Association Of Religious and Spiritual experiential phenomena With Certain Aspects Of The human Structure Reduces The Significance Of those experiential phenomena To Nothing but the workings Of That Structure.

Through The Entire Collective human Process Of Examining The Nature Of conditionally Manifested Existence (Including The scientific Examination Of The Development Of life-forms On Earth, The Origin and Evolution Of the universe, and So On), A Single Great Principle Is Made Evident: All Manifestation Is Arising From A Prior Unity. Everything That Appears Is Developed From What Is Already There, Inherently and Potentially. That Prior Unity Is Fundamental To The Nature Of Reality. Therefore, It Is False philosophy To Presume (or Even Insist) That Reality Itself Is Reducible To The Observable "Facts" Of The human Structure and Its functioning.

You Must Understand: The human psycho-physical Structure Is (Irreducibly) Part Of The Prior and Universal Unity. Reality Is Non-Separate, Indivisible, and (Ultimately) One—Beyond all appearances. The human psycho-physical Structure Is The "Equipment" That Is To Be Used By human beings For The Sake Of (Ultimately, Most Perfect) Divine Self-Realization—and That Structure arises Within The Universal Unity. This Is The Ancient Esoteric Knowledge.

Although The Esoteric Traditions Of Spirituality and Yoga Acknowledge The Significance Of The human psycho-physical Structure As The conditionally Manifested Mechanism By Means Of Which The Process Of Realization Is Exercised, Those Traditions Also Exhibit The (Characteristic) Alpha Disposition Of Dissociation Relative To The human psycho-physical Structure (and Relative To conditionally Manifested Existence Altogether—or At Least Relative To The gross Dimension Of conditionally Manifested Existence). However, I Do Not Call My Devotees To Any Such Dissociative Disposition Relative To their own psycho-physical Structure (or Relative To Any Aspect Of conditionally Manifested Existence Whatsoever). I Do Not Call My Devotees To The Strategy Of Excluding attention From The gross Dimension Of The human psycho-physical Structure and (Thereby) Identifying With Some Principle (Presumed To Be Separate From the human body-mind) Of A Spiritual or Transcendental Kind. Indeed, The Only-By-Me Revealed and Given Way Of The Heart (or Way Of Adidam) Is Specifically Not Founded In A "Mudra" Of Dissociation From The Existential Context Of the human body-mind. The Practice Of The Only-By-Me Revealed and Given Way Of The Heart Is Founded In The Transcending Of The human psycho-physical Structure—but Not By Means Of A Dissociative Act. Thus, The Fundamental (and Necessary) Basis For The Practice Of The Only-By-Me Revealed and Given Way Of The Heart—Which Is The Way Of The Devotional and (In Due Course) Spiritual Relationship To

Me—Is Equanimity Relative To one's own psycho-physical Structure and Relative To The psycho-physical Context Of human (and Cosmic) Existence.

When A perceptually-Based and (In Due Course, Through The Reception Of My Ruchira Shaktipat) Spiritually-Based Equanimity Is Established, The human psycho-physical Structure Is (Thereby) Truly and Really Made Into A Vehicle For The Divine Spiritual Process. Such Is The True and Real Transcending Of The Fault Of gross-minded philosophy (According To which philosophy The Structures Of the human body-mind Are To Be Understood Reductively As Separate "Somethings", and All Religious and Spiritual experiences Are Regarded As merely Aspects Of a mortal physicality). Such perceptually-Based and Spiritually-Based Equanimity Makes It Possible For My Devotee To Rightly Understand (and Relate To) his or her own body-mind—Without Falling Into Either The gross-minded Omega Error Of reductionism Or The Alpha Error Of Dissociation—As a manifestation arising Within The Context Of A Universal Unity Of Utter Non-Separateness and Ultimate Non-"Difference". Thus Established In The Disposition Of perceptually-Based and (In Due Course) Spiritually-Based Equanimity, the body-mind Of My Devotee Participates In That Which Is Universal, One, and (Ultimately) Beyond all conditions. In That Participatory Mode, the body-mind Of My Devotee Coincides With That Which Is Universal, Spiritually Real, and Self-Evidently Divine.

I Have Accounted For All Aspects Of Potential human experience That arise Out Of The Prior and Universal Unity—From the grossest experiences Of The First Stage Of Life To The Ultimacy-Beyond-Ultimacy Of The Only-By-Me Revealed and Given Seventh Stage Of Life—and I Have Done So On The Basis Of My Direct Awareness Of The Different Structures That Come Into Play In Each Stage Of Life (or Mode Of Development).

I Stand Entirely Apart From the conventional "God"-ideas and conventional mythologies Of exoteric Religion. I Am Communicating An Esoteric Way—and, Therefore, The Only-By-Me Revealed and Given Way Of The Heart (or Way of Adidam) Is The Completion and Fulfillment Of The Ancient Tradition Of (Always Reality-Based) Esoteric Spirituality and Yoga. I Say (and Have Always Said) To You: Reality Itself Is The Only Real God. Reality Itself (or Truth Itself) Is What There Is To Realize.

Therefore, In My Communication About Reality (and The Process Of Realizing Reality), I Am Not "On The Side" Of exoteric religiosity, Nor Am I "On The Side" Of scientific materialism. I Am Not "On" Any "Side" Whatsoever—Because I Am Not In the position of mind (or of "point of view"). My Communication Is A Direct Revelation Of Reality Itself (or Truth Itself), Which Is Inherently Divine. The Process Of Realizing Reality Itself (or Truth Itself) Is (Inevitably) Related To The Structures Of the human being, and To

The Structures Of conditionally Manifested Existence (Altogether)—but That Process Is A Matter Of Realizing That Which Transcends All Such conditional Structures, and (Indeed) All Of conditionally Manifested Existence (Itself).

Thus, In Making My Revelation About Reality (and The Process Of Realizing Reality), I Am Not Merely Communicating a philosophy. Rather, I Am Revealing Myself. This—My Avatarically Self-Given Divine Self-Revelation—Is The Basis Of The Only-By-Me Revealed and Given Way Of The Heart (or Way Of Adidam). Yes, My Avatarically Self-Revealed Divine Teaching-Word Accounts For All Aspects Of Reality, conditional and Unconditional. But, Most Fundamentally, My Avatarically Self-Revealed Divine Teaching-Word Accounts For Myself—and, In So Doing, Accounts For The By-Me-Revealed and By-Me-Given Way Of The Devotional and (In Due Course) Spiritual Relationship To Me.

As I Have Said, The Alpha Strategy and The Omega Strategy Are Both ego-Based Efforts (or Tendencies). Each Is The Basis For Religious, intellectual, and social conventions that Provide A Degree Of Order and Purpose In various times and places. However, Those Systems Of Order and Purpose Are Not Identical To Truth. They Are Schemes Conceived By Man In The Search For Truth. And Each Such System Is limited by egoity, Manifesting As emotional self-Contraction, False intellectual views (Grounded In Doubt and Fear), and physical limitations (Determined By the Specifically limited human brain and body in the conditional environment Of Earth).

This world Of Earth Is Not merely a physical world Made By "God". This world Of Earth, Like all conditional worlds, Is a psycho-physical world that Inheres In Reality and Truth (Which Is The Only Real God). Reality (or Truth, or Real God) Is Not The Necessary, Direct, or Purposive Cause Of all conditional events. Reality (or Truth, or Real God) Is The Ultimate, and Inherently Perfect, and Perfectly Subjective Source-Condition—The Condition In Which all events (or every cause and every effect) arise, change, and disappear. Even every effect and every conditional being is functioning as a Creative cause in this world. Therefore, every effect and every conditional being and every Creative cause Plays Upon (or Is An Apparent Modification Of) Reality (or Truth, or Real God)—but Only those effects, conditional beings, and Creative causes that Are Utterly Surrendered (or Yielded and Aligned) To Reality (or Truth, or Real God) Can (By Means Of A Spiritual Infusion Of The Self-Existing Divine Self-Radiance) Be Made To Function As Transparent Means For The Divinely Self-Realized Demonstration Of Reality (or Truth, or Real God) Within The Cosmic Domain. And, In Order That This Yielding, and Aligning, and Divine Spiritual Infusion, and Divinely Self-Realized Demonstration Be Really, and Truly, and Really Divinely, Made Possible For All and all (and, In The Case Of All and all, Be Really, and Truly, and Really Divinely, Made To

Be The Case)—I Am Avatarically Man-Born (By Means Of My Great Avataric Divine Descent Into The Total Cosmic Domain).

Reality (or Truth, or Real God) Simply Stands, Eternally Free. The Relationship Between The Unconditional Reality (or The Transcendental, Inherently Spiritual, Inherently egoless, and Self-Evidently Divine Reality) and The conditional Reality (and, Therefore, any and every conditionally Manifested being) Is, Inherently, A Mystery (Constantly Revealed, and Constantly Concealed, By Its Own Complete and Constant Evidence). That Inherent (and Inherently Perfect) Mystery Is Made Evident In Every Detail Of conditional Existence, but The All-Revealing Secret (or The Great Truth) Of That Mystery Is Perfectly (and Inherently) Obvious Only When Consciousness Participates In The Great Sacrifice Of Every Detail Of conditional Existence. Apart From The Process Of Such self-Sacrifice, It Is Not Possible To Truly (and More and More Fully) Identify (and, Thereby, To Truly, and More and More Fully, Accept, or Embrace) The Signs Of Reality (or Truth, or Real God). And, Until (By Means Of My Avatarically Self-Transmitted Divine Spiritual Grace) There Is Inherent (and Inherently Most Perfect, and Utterly ego-Transcending, and Fully and Most Perfectly Spiritually Awakened) Real-God-Realization, a conditional being, effect, or cause Is Only Potentially Divine. And Even whatever condition or conditional being or conditional state of being Is (Most Ultimately) Divinely Transfigured and Divinely Transformed By My Self-Existing Divine Self-Radiance Is Also Utterly Outshined In Divine Translation Into The Sphere and Space and Substance Of My "Bright" Divine Self-Domain.

All conditional effects and beings and causes are acting and reacting In A Great Asymmetrical Plastic That Mysteriously Commands Both Order and Disorder—Such That No Ultimate Order, Goal, or Final conditional Fulfillment Is Ever Attained. The conditional worlds and beings Are Not An End In themselves. They Only Seem To Be An End To themselves. Therefore, all conditional beings Are Called (By Me) To Always Grow Beyond and To Always Go Beyond—Through ego-Transcending and world-Transcending Love Of Me.

The conditional Cosmos Is Not A "Moral Universe" In The conventional Sense. There Is No Absolute and Sufficient System Of social Imperatives (or Laws) Of public and private Morality. Right and ego-Transcending Action Is Necessary—but It Must Be Generated Intelligently and (Ultimately) On The Basis Of The self-Sacrificial (or ego-Transcending) Motive Of Love-Communion With Me (Rather Than Merely On The Basis Of An Abstract, or Independent, Order Of Cosmic Nature or human Society).

Neither The Alpha Morality Of Strategically Pursued Escape (Through The Passive Enactment Of Virtues and Duties) Nor The Omega Morality Of Creative Change (Through Aggressive Efforts Toward conditional Goals) Is A

Principle Founded On Truth. Alpha and Omega Are Simply The conventional Basis For social Morality, public Order, popular Culture, and egoic Struggle. The Great Principle (To Be Realized) Is ego-Transcending Love-Communion With My Avatarically Self-Revealed Transcendental, Perfectly Subjective, Inherently Spiritual, Inherently egoless, Inherently Perfect, and Self-Evidently Divine Person—Which ego-Transcending Love-Communion With Me Is Expressed (Eventually, and Progressively) Through The ego-Transcending Process Associated With The Fourth, The Fifth, and The Sixth Stages Of Life (Culminating In The Only-By-Me Revealed and Given Seventh Stage Of Life). Therefore, True (or Right) Morality Is, In Truth, The Morality Of ego-Transcending Love Of Me (The "What" and The "Who" That Is Reality—or That Which Is Always Already The Case).

The conditional psycho-physical worlds Are A Great (and Universal, or everywhere Required and Enacted) Process Of Sacrifice. No conditional thing or being or world Is An End-In-itself. Nevertheless, The Universal Sacrifice Of all things and beings and worlds Is A Feast Of Love-Bliss, and Even A Swoon Of Joy—If The Principle Of ego-Transcending Devotional Communion With Me Is Realized. Therefore, True (or Right) Morality Is, In Truth, The Morality Of Universal self-Sacrifice. And The Right Exercise Of The Morality Of Universal self-Sacrifice Is The self-Sacrifice (or The ego-Transcending Life-Process Of self-Surrender) Of the Total psycho-physical ego—In and By Means Of ego-Surrendering, ego-Forgetting, and (More and More, and, At Last, Most Perfectly) ego-Transcending (and, Altogether, Whole bodily, or Total psycho-physical—and Always Devotionally Me-Recognizing and Devotionally To-Me-Responding) Devotional Communion With My Avatarically Self-Revealed Form and Presence and State Of Self-Evidently Divine Person.

The Morality Of Universal self-Sacrifice Is (By Means Of My Avatarically Self-Transmitted Divine Grace) Founded On The Understanding That The self-Sacrifice (or Whole bodily self-Surrender) Of egoity (and, Thus and Thereby, The Transcending Of the Total psycho-physical self) In Devotionally Me-Recognizing and Devotionally To-Me-Responding Devotional Communion With Me Is (Itself) The Expression (and The Demonstration) Of Reality and Truth—Whereas The Motives Of (Strategic) Escape and Dominance Are, At Best, Only A Search For Reality and Truth.

There Is No Absolute System Of Moral Imperatives In This Domain Of Universal Sacrifice. There Is No Absolute Order Of Laws In conditional Nature. All Of This Is Aligned Toward Sacrifice, Going Beyond, or Transcending—and, Thus, Toward Realization Of My Divine "Bright" Spherical Self-Domain.

The Practice Of The Ultimate Way Of self-Sacrifice (or Of ego-Transcending Love-Communion With Me—The Avatarically Self-Revealed Transcendental,

Inherently Spiritual, Inherently egoless, and Self-Evidently Divine Person) Is individual, and Always In present-time, and (Generally) Productive Of Harmony (or The Order Of Balance and Fearlessness), and Even (Sometimes) Productive Of Relative Disorder (Where Loveless Order Has Suppressed The Move Of Life), and Always (Inherently) Free. In The Free Exercise Of ego-Transcending Love-Communion With Me In The Ever-changing Context Of conditional relations and events, The conventional Moralities (Both Alpha and Omega) Are Each (As A Style Of Action) Sometimes Engaged, In A Dynamic (and Artfully Managed) Play Of Application—but one who Practices ego-Transcending Love-Communion With Me In The Ever-changing Context Of conditional relations and events Always Exceeds the limits Of Both Alpha and Omega.

Actions In The Mode Of Alpha (or Virtues and Duties) Allow Detachment, Calm, Even Purity, Orderliness, and Desireless Effectiveness—but Alpha Has No Moral Rule or Effective Means In Situations Of social Chaos and human Disorder That Require "Creative" and Even Aggressive action (and The Alpha Strategy, In Itself, Generally Does Not Take The conditional Dimension Of Reality Sufficiently Into Account). Just So, actions In The Mode Of Omega (or Effective physical, emotional, and intellectual "Creativity") Can Achieve Many individual and Collective Goals—but, On Its Own, The Omega Strategy Eventually Leads To The Exploitation, Degradation, and Suppression Of the individual and Mankind, Because The Omega Strategy Is Not Based On A Regard For The Total Necessity and Obligation Of the individual human being (Especially The Spiritual Necessity, and The Obligation To Transcend the conditional self In The Context Of The Fourth, Fifth, Sixth, and Seventh Stages Of Life). Therefore, Beyond (and Even In The Midst Of) Virtue, Duty, and The "Creative" or Aggressive Pursuit Of Goals Of conditional Change, There Must (By Means Of My Avatarically Self-Transmitted Divine Grace) Be The Constant Way and Practice Of ego-Transcending Devotional Communion With Me—In The Context Of (Necessarily, Ever-changing) conditional Reality.

The conditional worlds Are Built Upon (and Of) The Sacrifice Of every thing, event, process, or being that appears (or Exists conditionally). The conditional worlds Are Built Upon Sacrifice—Not Upon (or For The Purpose Of) The Preservation, Survival, Conquest, or Attainment Of conditional Reality. Therefore, Senior To conventional Morality (Whether Alpha Or Omega) Is The Ultimate (and, Necessarily, Artful) Practice Of Sacrifice (Of the ego-"I", or conditional self) In Me—Under all conditions, and In all relations. That Ultimate Art Involves A Willingness To Engage action Always and Only In The Context (and On The Basis) Of Devotional Communion With Me—but Variously, In A Dynamic Fashion, Sometimes In The Alpha-Likeness (Conservative, Passive,

Even Apparently Detached and Introverted), Sometimes In The Omega-Likeness (Aggressive, Even Apparently Attached and Extroverted), and (Always) Without Requiring One or The Other or Both Of These Two To Account For The Totality Of human Circumstance. Therefore, In This Ultimate Art, There Is Sometimes Virtue, Sometimes Duty, Sometimes Passivity, Detachment, or Receptivity, Sometimes "Creativity", Passion, or Aggressiveness, but There Is Always This self-Sacrifice, or Persistence In Love-Communion With Me (The Avatarically Self-Revealed Transcendental, Inherently Spiritual, Inherently egoless, and Self-Evidently Divine Person), Such That My Divine Love-Bliss-Radiance Replaces The ego-Act Of self-Contraction.

Conditional human Existence Is Not Merely a thing To Be Preserved, but A Process To Be Fully Understood and Fulfilled. The conditional Cosmos As A Whole Is Not A Fixed System Of Order (The Goal Of "God"), but An Open-Ended Theatre Of Sacrifice In Real God. Life Is Made Of A Little Temporary Order, A Constant Tendency Toward Change, and An Ultimate and Absolute Demand For Sacrifice. Therefore, All Of This Is A Dynamic Play Of Order, Change, and Sacrifice, For The Sake Of Growth and ego-Transcendence, and Not For The Sake Of conditional Existence In and Of Itself.

The Unconditional Reality Is Modified (but Only Apparently) As The conditional Reality. This Must Be Realized. Until This Truth Is Realized, all conditional experience Is A School With A Single Lesson. This Is The Lesson (The Lesson Of Life): "I" Cannot Become Happy. "I" Can Only Be Happy.

The self-Contracted being (or conditional "I") Seeks Happiness conditionally, By Pursuing and Depending On conditions, objects, and others. This Is An Error, and The Fault Is Profound.

Happiness Is Not A Characteristic Of conditional Reality Itself, but Happiness Is An Inherent Characteristic Of The Unconditional (or Divine) Reality. And The conditional Reality Is Always A Modification Of The Unconditional Reality. Therefore, The Realization Of Happiness Is Possible In any moment, If conditional Existence Is Released Into Full Participation In Me—The Avatarically Self-Revealed Prior (or Unconditional, Transcendental, Inherently Spiritual, Inherently egoless, and Self-Evidently Divine) Person and Self-Condition (Which Is Always Already The Case).

Happiness Is Inherent In The Unconditional (or Always Already) Condition Of Reality—and, Therefore, It Must Be Inherently (and Most Perfectly, and Not Merely conditionally) Realized. The Only-By-Me Revealed and Given Way Of The Heart (or Way Of Adidam) Is The Way Of Inherent Happiness. The True Demonstration Of The Only-By-Me Revealed and Given Way Of The Heart Is, In the conditional worlds, Associated With all kinds of conditions, objects, and others—but Search and Dependency Relative To conditions, objects, and others

Is (By Means Of My Avatarically Self-Transmitted Divine Grace) To Be Constantly Transcended, Via Responsively ego-Surrendering, ego-Forgetting, and ego-Transcending Devotional Communion With Me (and, Thus, By Means Of The Always Present, and Always Grace-Given, Realization Of Inherent Happiness, or My Divine Love-Bliss-Happiness) Under all conditions and In all relations.

I Do Not Call My Listening Devotee, My Hearing Devotee, or My Seeing Devotee To Become Happy By Strategically Separating body, emotion, or attention From conditions, objects, and others. I Do Not Say: Be Unmoved Under all conditions and In all relations. I Call My Listening Devotee (and My Hearing Devotee, and My Seeing Devotee) To Observe and Understand the conditional self Under all conditions and In all relations. And I Call My Listening Devotee (and My Hearing Devotee, and My Seeing Devotee) To Transcend self-Contraction Under all conditions and In all relations. Therefore, I Call My ego-Transcending (Listening, Hearing, or Seeing) Devotee To Be Happy (By Responsively Relinquishing Un-Happiness Itself, Which Is Only self-Contraction itself) Under all conditions and In all relations—and Always By Means Of ego-Transcending Devotional Communion With Me. And Me-Realizing Happiness (Itself) Inherently (and, Ultimately, Inherently Perfectly) Transcends all conditions and all conditional relations.

The Inherent Happiness Of My Divine Love-Bliss Is Not Realized By Dissociation (or The Strategic Avoidance Of Relationship). The Inherent Happiness Of My Divine Love-Bliss Is Realized By Transcending the self-Contraction In Unqualified Relatedness (or No-Contraction and No-self), Which Is egoless (or Unconditional) Love Of Me, or Participatory Surrender Of the Total conditional (and, altogether, psycho-physical) personality (or body-mind) In and To Me (The Avatarically Self-Revealed Transcendental, Inherently Spiritual, Inherently egoless, and Self-Evidently Divine Person, or Self-Condition, or Source-Condition).

Inherent Happiness Is Realized Prior To—but Not By Strategically Excluding—conditions, conditional objects, and conditional relations. Inherent Happiness Is Realized In The Context Of Present Relationship (or Under present conditions), When the self-Contraction Is Utterly Relinquished. And, In The Only-By-Me Revealed and Given Way Of The Heart, That Relinquishment Is Not A Matter Of Strategic ego-Effort (or The Search That Dramatizes self-Contraction), but It Is A Matter Of Devotionally Me-Recognizing and Devotionally To-Me-Responding (and Effectively Counter-egoic, or Responsively ego-Surrendering, and ego-Forgetting, and More and More Effectively ego-Observing, ego-Understanding, and ego-Transcending) Participatory Resort To My "Brightly" Attractive Avatarically-Born Bodily (Human) Divine Form, and My Avatarically Self-Transmitted Spiritual (and Always Blessing) Divine Presence, and (Ultimately) My Avatarically Self-Revealed (and Very, and Transcendental, and Perfectly Subjective, and Inherently Spiritual, and Inherently egoless, and Inherently Perfect, and Self-Evidently Divine) State. Therefore, If The Way Of The Heart (Which Is The Way Of By-My-Avataric-Divine-Grace-Revealed Inherent Happiness) Is Rightly, Truly, Fully, and Fully Devotionally Practiced, conditional Existence Itself (Including object-Dependency, other-Dependency, and Even The Perception Of conditional Relatedness) Will (Most Ultimately, and By Means Of My Avatarically Self-Transmitted Divine Grace) Be Transcended and Outshined In The Inherent (or Self-Radiant) Love-Bliss Of My Transcendental (or Self-Existing) Divine Self-Condition.

Life, In Its Ultimate Fullness, Is The Ordeal Of Right, True, and Full Real-God-Love, Even The Ordeal Of The Heart Under Extreme conditions. The Price Of Happiness In every moment Is Release Of self-Contraction (and Release Of The Search To Acquire, Hold On To, or Strategically Escape the conditions Of conditional Existence). This Release Is Possible Only If There Is Most Fundamental self-Understanding. And That Most Fundamental self-Understanding May Be Fulfilled, Most Ultimately and Most Perfectly, Only By Distracted Love Of Me, The Avatarically Self-Revealed Person Of Reality, Truth, and Happiness. And That Love Is Senior To All Concerns Relative To Virtue, Duty, and conventional (or humanistic) social Morality.

In Addition To An Overriding Concern Relative To The Morality Of conditional relations, The Omega Concept Of Religion Is Inherently Disposed Toward Theistic Language (Including The Word "God" Itself) and Toward Linear (or Progressive, Rather Than Cyclical) Cosmological Descriptions—Since "God", In The Omega View, Is Always Regarded In The Context Of The conditional (or Cosmic) Domain, Of Which "God" Is Conceived To Be The Cause and Hierarchical Head, From Beginning To End. This Is Because All Omega Concepts (In the physical human world) Develop From The Base Of Natural (physical) Identification With the conditional (and bodily Manifested) human self in the conditional world Of Earth. Thus, When That Which Is Ultimate, and Spiritual, and Unconditionally (or Transcendentally) Real, and (Altogether) Divine Is Regarded (or thought About) From The Omega Position, It Is Presumed Over Against the conditional self and The conditional Cosmos—and It Is (Thus) conceptually Affirmed As The First Principle, The Origin and The Constantly Creative Cause Of the conditional world and the conditional self (As Well As Of all events that Develop From The Association Between all conditional selves, and Between all conditional selves and the conditional world).

The Alpha Concept Of Religion May, Particularly At the popular level, Be Associated With Theistic (Even Polytheistic and Pantheistic) Language and

Cyclical Cosmological Descriptions (but Describing An Ultimately Loveless, Basically Purposeless, and Entirely Mechanical Chaos Of Order, or Of Repetition). Nevertheless, The Alpha Concept Of Religion Is, Ultimately, Oriented Toward The Unconditional Reality In and Of Itself, Prior To The conditional (or Cosmic) Domain—and, Thus, The Ultimate Language Of Alpha Religion Is Inherently Non-Theistic and Non-Cosmological, or Strictly Transcendental (or Non-conditional). This Is Because All Alpha Concepts Develop From The Base Of Inherent (or Necessary) Identification With The Unconditional (or Non-conditional) Reality.

The Great Reality (or Divine Condition) That Is "Considered" From The Alpha Position Is The Same Great Reality (or Divine Condition) That Is "Considered" From The Omega Position, and "Now" Is Always The Time For The Controversy Relative To This Matter (and Religious Differences In General) To Cease. It Is Simply That The Great Reality (or Divine Condition) Is "Considered" From A Different Conceptual Position (or Reality-Idea) In Each Of The Two Cases. (Likewise, All Historical Religions Have, Previous To The Avataric Revelation-Lifetime Of My Physical Bodily Human Divine Form, Developed On The Basis Of Either An Alpha-Dominant Or An Omega-Dominant Reality-Idea. Each Has Developed In The Context Of A Different and Unique Historical, Political, Geographical, Temporal, and Cultural Domain. And Each Has Traditionally Been limited By Concepts Associated With One or Another Stage Of Life, Representing Either The Stage Of Adaptation Most Commonly Addressed Or The Stage Of Realization That Is the limit Of Aspiration In The Particular Religious Context.)

The mind Dominated By The Omega Principle Talks Religion In Theistic and Cosmological Terms. And the mind Dominated By The Alpha Principle Ultimately Talks Religion In Non-Theistic, Non-Cosmological, and Strictly Transcendental (or Non-conditional) Terms. Omega Language Talks Of The Great Reality and Condition As "God", or "The Divine", Relative To the conditional world and the conditional self and The Morality Of relations between conditional selves. Alpha Language Talks Of The Great Reality and Condition Either As (The) Transcendental (or Non-conditional) Self Or As (The) Transcendental (or Non-conditional) Condition Beyond Description (Since It Is Not Related To or Comparable To any conditional relations or descriptions, By Virtue Of The Fact That It Is That In Which all conditions arise). However, Both Languages Talk Of The Same One, Each From a Unique and Characteristic point of view, limited by the time, and by the place, and By The Stage Of Life Of any individual who Contemplates These Matters.

The Alpha Strategy Is Motivated Primarily By The Desire To Avoid conditional (or psycho-physical) Pain and Suffering. Since psycho-physical Pain and

Suffering arise Inevitably, In Natural Opposition To (or In Polar Alternation With) psycho-physical Pleasure, The Alpha Strategist Must Avoid Both Pain (or Suffering) and Pleasure. Therefore, The Alpha Strategist Is Moved To (Strategically) Escape (or Turn Away) From The Total Context Of Natural, Bi-Polar (or Dualistic), and Cosmic (or conditionally Manifested) Existence.

The Omega Strategy Is Motivated Primarily By The Desire To Achieve conditional (or psycho-physical) Pleasure. Since psycho-physical Pleasure Is The Natural Polar Opposite Of psycho-physical Pain and Suffering, psycho-physical Pain and Suffering Must Inevitably be experienced and known If psycho-physical Pleasure Is Even To Be Sought (Whether Or Not it Is Achieved). Therefore, The Omega Strategist Must Admit (or Agree To) psycho-physical Pain and Suffering. And The Omega Strategist Must Constantly Overcome The Tendency To Presume Defeat In The Face Of psycho-physical Pain and Suffering, or The mortal Tendency To Lose Hope (and To Despair Of The Possibility Of psycho-physical Pleasure, or Even The Ability To experience or know psycho-physical Pleasure). Therefore, The Omega Strategist Is Moved To Embrace and Even To Perfect The Total Context Of Natural, Bi-Polar (or Dualistic), and Cosmic (or conditionally Manifested) Existence.

The Only-By-Me Revealed and Given Way Of The Heart (or Way Of Adidam) Is The Way Of The Inherent Transcending Of psycho-physical (and, thus, Entirely and merely conditional) Pain and Suffering. The Only-By-Me Revealed and Given Way Of The Heart Is The Way Of The Inherent Transcending Of conditional Problems, Internal Contradictions, and All Problem-Based Searches. The Only-By-Me Revealed and Given Way Of The Heart Is (In Its Fullness) The Way Of Spiritual, Transcendental, and Divine Yoga—The Way Of The Wisdom-Relationship To Me In The Context Of conditional (or psycho-physical) Pain and Suffering and Pleasure, or The Way Of self-Observation, self-Understanding, and self-Transcendence (In Relation To Me, and In The Context Of conditional Existence). The Only-By-Me Revealed and Given Way Of The Heart Is (or More and More Becomes) The Way Of Inherent Happiness, In The Face Of psycho-physical Pain and Suffering and Pleasure. The Only-By-Me Revealed and Given Way Of The Heart Is (Most Ultimately) The Way Of The Inherent (and Inherently Most Perfect) Realization Of What Is Merely Sought In psycho-physical (or conditional) Pleasure. The Only-By-Me Revealed and Given Way Of The Heart Is (In Its Heart-Realization) The Way Of Inherence In My Self-Existing, Self-Radiant, Inherently Perfect, and Self-Evidently Divine Love-Bliss.

The Alpha Strategist Is Motivated To Avoid or (Strategically) Escape The Entire Cycle Of Desiring, Getting, Having, and Enjoying, Because The Alpha Strategist Is Obsessed With The Desire To Desire Not, and To Avoid Pain, and To Not Suffer.

The Omega Strategist Is Bound To A Struggle With The Inevitable Realities Of conditional (or psycho-physical) Pain and Suffering, Because The Omega Strategist Is Obsessed With Desiring, Getting, Having, and Enjoying.

The Alpha Strategist Is Constantly Struggling To Avoid or (Strategically) Escape From Suffering, Pain, Pleasure, money, food, sex, Fear, Sorrow, Anger, greed, lust, attachment, Boredom, Doubt, Discomfort, conditional experience, conditional knowledge (or illusion), and egoity (or conditional selfhood).

The Omega Strategist Is Constantly Indulging In (or, Otherwise, Suffering From) Suffering Itself, and Pain, Pleasure, money, food, sex, Fear, Sorrow, Anger, greed, lust, attachment, Boredom, Doubt, Discomfort, conditional experience, conditional knowledge (or illusion), and egoity (or conditional selfhood).

The Alpha Strategist Seeks To Avoid conditional (or psycho-physical) Pain (or Suffering) To An Absolute Degree—but This Is Not Possible Within The Context Of conditional Existence, or In the experience of the body-mind. Therefore, The Alpha Strategist Suffers From The Problem Of The Desire Not To Desire. And The Chronic Signs Of This Fault Are Too Much Dissociative Effort, Too Much Seeking To Avoid or (Strategically) Escape, Too Much External (or Merely Apparent) Renunciation, and Too Much Strategic Control and Suppression Of body and mind.

The Omega Strategist Seeks To Achieve conditional (or psycho-physical) Pleasure, Even To An Absolute Degree, Exclusive Of All Pain and Suffering, but This Absolute Is Not Possible Within The Context Of conditional Existence, or In the experience of the conditionally Manifested body-mind. Therefore, The Omega Strategist Suffers From The Problem Of The Desire For Desire. And The Chronic Signs Of This Fault Are Too Much Effort Based On Desire, Too Much Seeking To Achieve Fulfillment Of Desires, Too Little External (or Demonstratively and Concretely Evident) Renunciation, and Too Little Control Over the functions and relations of the body-mind.

The Alpha Strategist Tends To Manifest self-Involved Reserve, Dryness, Weakness, and A Lack Of Sympathy or Love For others.

The Omega Strategist Tends To Manifest self-Involved Enthusiasm For conditional (or psycho-physical) experience and knowledge, Despair In The Face Of Negative and Frustrating or Painful events, and Chronic psycho-physical Dis-ease (or Toxicity, Enervation, and Imbalance, Due To Overindulgence Of the body-mind).

Such Are The Diseases Of Failed Understanding. The self-Contraction Rolls Both Forward and Backward, but Always On itself.

Now "Consider" Alpha and Omega.

There Is A Great Lesson To Be Learned By Observing The Two Great Occupational Diseases Of Mankind.

If You Keep Too Many Cats,
You Will Never See
The Free Bird Fly!
If You Keep Too Many Dogs,
You Will Never Even Hear
The Free Bird Sing!
The Pressure Of Flowers
Days The Day
Before It Swans.
The Pleasure Of Swans
Nights The Night
Before It Flowers.
And Who Un-Drowns The Human Heart-Wreck
When All Eyes Are Black
As Thoughtless Holes
Among The Stars?
It Is Only Me!

Therefore, I Call You To Hear Me and To See Me—and (Thus, By Means Of My Avatarically Self-Transmitted Divine Spiritual Grace) To Realize The Freedom Of My Heart.

I Reveal To You The Divine Way That Transcends The Faults Of The Alpha Strategy (or The Effort To Return, or Strategically Escape, To The Beginning—or To The, Presumed, Perfectly object-Excluding Source Of conditional causes and conditional effects).

I Reveal To You The Divine Way That Transcends The Faults Of The Omega Strategy (or The Effort To Proceed, or Strategically Escape, To The End—or To The conditional Perfection Of conditional causes and conditional effects).

I Reveal To You The Divine Way Of "What" and "Who" Is Always Already The Case—Avatarically Self-Revealed By Me To Be The Inherent (and Self-Evidently Divine) Feeling Of Being (Itself), Prior To, and Inherently Transcending, and Yet (In The Apparent Context Of arising conditions) Perfectly Coincident With conditional causes and conditional effects (Whether At The Beginning, Or At The End, Or In The Infinite Span Between).

I Call You To Understand the psycho-physical self.

I Call You To Understand The Alpha-Tendencies and The Omega-Tendencies Of Your Own body-mind.

I Help You To Learn The Divine Way That Neither Strategically Avoids Nor Strategically Exploits the body-mind, all others, or any part (or Even The Totality) Of conditional Existence.

You Must (By Means Of My Avatarically Self-Transmitted Divine Grace) Learn The Divine Yoga (or Divine Way) Of Me—The Self-Evidently Divine Person, Who Is The Only One (Of all-and-All), and Who Is Always Already Only Love-Bliss (or True, and Inherently Free, Happiness).

You Must (By Means Of My Avatarically Self-Transmitted Divine Grace) Learn True Sila—or Appropriate Restraint and Love-Bliss-"Conductivity" Of the body-mind.

You Must (By Means Of My Avatarically Self-Transmitted Divine Grace) Learn Surrender To My Self-Evidently Divine Love-Bliss.

You Must (By Means Of My Avatarically Self-Transmitted Divine Grace) Learn The Surrender That Transcends the self-Contraction, and That Transcends Avoidance, Reaction, and Bondage Relative To Every Kind Of experiential (and, Necessarily, conditional) Pain and Suffering, and That Transcends Anxious Seeking and self-Indulgence, and That Also Transcends Avoidance (and Suppression) Relative To Every Kind Of experiential (and, Necessarily, conditional) Pleasure.

My Devotee Must First Have Heard Me (By Listening To Me), or I Will Not Be Seen. Therefore, My Every Devotee Must First Be My Listening Devotee, who Grows To Hear Me (and Only Eventually Sees Me) Through The Process Of self-Observation, self-Understanding, and self-Transcendence (or ego-Transcendence), In and By Means Of Devotional Communion With Me. Once I Am Heard, Then (By These Same Means, and With My Avatarically-Born Bodily Human Divine Form, and My Avatarically Self-Transmitted Divine Spiritual Presence, In Sight) My Devotee Must Progressively Go Beyond The Strategies Of Avoidance and Indulgence Relative To Every Kind Of experiential Pain and Pleasure.

Instead Of Merely Avoiding (or Contracting From) arising conditions, objects, thoughts, and impulses, and Instead Of Merely Indulging In (or Going With) arising conditions, objects, thoughts, and impulses, My Hearing (and Then Seeing) Devotee Simply (Merely) Beholds Me, and (Thereby) Simply Observes, Understands, and Directly Transcends conditions, objects, thoughts, and impulses.

Eventually (By Means Of My Avatarically Self-Transmitted Divine Spiritual Grace), My Truly Both Hearing and Seeing Devotee Stands Simply As The Witness-Consciousness—Observing and Then Realizing The Place and The One Wherein all conditions, objects, thoughts, impulses, pains, sufferings, and pleasures arise and pass away.

Therefore, My Truly Both Hearing and Seeing Devotee Always (By Means Of My Avatarically Self-Transmitted Divine Spiritual Grace) Feels (and Thereby Contemplates) Me—and (In, By, and As This Feeling-Contemplation Of Me)

My Truly Both Hearing and Seeing Devotee Always Feels (and Thereby Contemplates) My Divine Love-Bliss, My Divine Freedom, and My Divine Person (or The Inherently Perfect Self-Condition and Perfectly Subjective Source-Condition), Wherein all conditions arise (At The Beginning), persist or change (In The Meantime), and pass away (At The End).

My Truly Both Hearing and Seeing Devotee Is (or More and More Fully Becomes) An Integral (or Whole and Complete—and Wholly With-Me-Integrated, or Whole bodily To-Me-Conformed) Renunciate—A Non-Dualistic (or Singly-Inspired) Renouncer Of the subjective ego and the objective world (and, Thus, An ego-and-world-Renunciate, who Is Bound Neither By The Search To Return, Nor By The Search To Hold On, Nor By The Search To Change or Proceed).

My Truly Both Hearing and Seeing Devotee Does Not Seek To Avoid or To (Strategically) Escape conditionally Manifested Existence, Nor Does My Truly Both Hearing and Seeing Devotee Seek To Indulge In or To Perfect conditionally Manifested Existence. Rather, My Truly Both Hearing and Seeing Devotee Directly (and, Ultimately, Inherently and Always Presently) Transcends conditionally Manifested Existence.

Therefore, My Truly Both Hearing and Seeing Devotee Stands Free In Me.

My Truly Both Hearing and Seeing Devotee Does Not Turn Away or Flee From The conditional Reality.

My Truly Both Hearing and Seeing Devotee Does Not Submit To The conditional Reality.

My Truly Both Hearing and Seeing Devotee Always Turns To Me (and Is, Most Ultimately, One With Me)—The Avatarically Self-Revealed Divine and Only One (Who Always Already Is).

Therefore, Listen To Me. Hear Me. Become My Truly Both Hearing and Seeing Devotee. And When You Realize The Self-Existing Love-Bliss Of The Inherent Being, and When Your Own Fullness Shines Faster and Further Than The Beginning and The End Of Desires, You Will Be Inherently (and Divinely) Indifferent To conditional Existence (Without Otherwise Seeking To Avoid or Strategically Escape conditional Existence), and You Will Be Resolved In My "Bright" Divine Self-Light.

Avatar Adi Da Samraj
Lopez Island, 2000

SUTRA 24

Un-Enlightened conditional beings (Seeking For Order, Power, Enlightenment, Truth, or God) Have themselves Been The Traditional Makers and Transmitters Of Religion, Even Though Each and All Of Those Traditional Religions Began With A Response To An Adept-Realizer (or A Prophet, or A Teacher) Awakened At The Level Of The Fourth or The Fifth or The Sixth Stage Of Life. Therefore, Controversies and Conflicts (Even Terrible In Their Effect) Have Characterized Religious History, and (Thus) The Total History (and "Civilization") Of Mankind. Therefore, My Fullest and Complete (and, Thus, Necessarily, Seventh Stage) Avatarically Given Divine Self-Revelation Of The Inherently Perfect (and Divinely Liberating) Truth Itself Must Bring An End To The ego-Based Religious, Cultural, and social (and, Altogether, Political) Controversy and Conflict Of "Civilized" Mankind—By Establishing The Really ego-Transcending and Truly Me-Realizing Disposition As The Foundation-Principle Of Mankind.

I Am Avatarically Born, In Order To Give (and To Serve) The Fullest and Complete (and, Thus, Necessarily, Seventh Stage) Self-Revelation Of The Inherently Perfect Truth. I Have Come To Restore Divine Humor, and To Establish Divine Love-Bliss, and To Awaken Great (and Truly egoless) Intelligence. I Have Come To Restore (and To Complete) True Religion (or The Real, and, Necessarily, Esoteric—or Non-conventional, and Really ego-Transcending—Process Of Spiritual, Transcendental, and Divine Self-Awakening), Which Is The Only Right Foundation Of conditional Existence. Therefore, By Addressing conditional beings everywhere (and Founding them In The Self-Evident Reality and Truth), I Have Worked—and, Through The Recorded Documents Of My Avatarically Self-Revealed Divine Teaching-Word, and The Material Fabrications Of My Avatarically Self-Revealed Divine Image-Art, and The Recorded Stories Of My Avatarically Self-Manifested Divine Leelas, and My (Now, and Forever Hereafter) Given (and, Now, and Forever Hereafter, Divinely Self-Revealing and Always To Be Remembered) Avatarically-Born Bodily (Human) Divine Form, and My Avatarically Self-Transmitted Spiritual (and Always all-and-All-Blessing) Divine Presence, and My Avatarically Self-Revealed (and Very, and Transcendental, and Perfectly Subjective, and

Inherently Spiritual, and Inherently egoless, and Inherently Perfect, and Inherently Perfectly Self-Revealing, and Self-Evidently Divine) State, and All My True Instruments and Truly Blessed Agents, I Will Always Be At Work—To Give The Gift and Pattern Of True (and Truly Perfect) Divine Wisdom To Every Aspect and Dimension Of Life In The Cosmic Domain.

I Was (By A Great Divine Intention) Avatarically Born Into The Omega Culture Of The West—and I Self-Revealed My Avatarically-Spoken Divine Teaching-Word By Means Of A Great Divine Work Of Avataric Self-Submission, In (Even Playful) Confrontation With the Aggressive egoity Of Western Man. This Was A Necessary Service—Because Mankind everywhere (In the common, or egoic, society Associated With The First Three Stages Of Life) Is Basically Characterized By The Omega Orientation.

The Great Tradition Of Esoteric Religion Has Been Most Often and Most Basically Addressed To Mankind In Its Alpha Orientation—but I Was Avatarically Born To Struggle With My Own Omega-Born Human Nature (Inherited From My Western Birth Into The "Civilization" Of Mankind), and With My Own Alpha-Born Inward Nature (Otherwise Acquired From The Eastern Pattern Of Mankind),[69] and With Even All The Contents and Results Of Mankind (Which I Absorbed Into My Own Body-Mind, By Avataric Self-Submission To All Of Mankind). And It Was Only By Means Of My Great Avataric Struggle With The Totality Of Man (In My Own Form) That I Was Able To Discover How The Omega Type Of Man, and The Alpha Type Of Man, and Even every one Of Man May Enter The Inherently Perfect Heart Of The Way Of ego-Transcending Realization Of Me.

That Great Avataric Struggle Was Most Perfectly Fulfilled. This Divine Testament Is (With All The Others Of My Twenty-Three Divine "Source-Texts") The Summary Of My Discoveries (Made By Means Of My Divine Self-Submission To Avataric Incarnation) and My Revelations (Made By Means Of My Avatarically Given Divine Self-Confessions Of My Own Divine Secrets). My Avatarically Self-Revealed Divine Teaching-Word Is Not A Word Of Instruction In The Omega Form—Nor Is It A Word Of Instruction In The Alpha Form. Any one (Whether Previously Acculturated In The Omega Manner Or The Alpha Manner) Can (By Means Of My Avatarically Self-Transmitted Divine Grace, Through Me-Recognizing Devotional Response To Me) Enter The Inherently Perfect Heart Of The Only-By-Me Revealed and Given Way Of ego-Transcending (and all-limitation-Transcending) Real-God-Realization By Means Of My Avatarically Self-Revealed Divine Instruction and My Avatarically Self-Transmitted Divine Help.

Both The Omega Type Of Man and The Alpha Type Of Man Can, If Moved To The Great Realization That Inherently Transcends the conditional self,

Discover (By Means Of My Avatarically Given Divine Instruction and My Avatarically Self-Transmitted Divine Help) what Must Be Understood, Surrendered, and Converted—and How All Of That Can Be Done.

This Divine Testament Is The Summary Of My Religious (or Truly Human, and Spiritual, and Transcendental, and Divine) Self-Revelation.

I Freely (and By Heart) Speak The One and Only Truth That Is Reality and Real God!

I Am The Avataric Divine Self-Revelation Of The Unconditional (and, Necessarily, Divine) Reality, Which Is The Only Real Self-Condition (and Source-Condition) Of all-and-All!

I Am The Perfectly Subjective, Non-Separate, and Indivisible (and Inherently egoless, and Self-Evidently Divine) Person, Reality, and Truth!

I Am Thrilled To Speak The Avatarically Self-Revealing Word Of My Own (Inherently egoless, and Self-Evidently Divine) Person!

I Communicate In Divinely "Crazy" Paradoxes—Often Using (and Also Positively Criticizing) The Styles Of Both Omega Language and Alpha Language In My "Considering"-Work Of Communication To every point of view.

Nevertheless, I Do Not Reduce The Only-By-Me Revealed and Given Way Of The Heart To Mere Talk, or To the mind of any Separate (and, Necessarily, Incomplete) point of view.

I Am The Heart—The One and Only Person.

I Am Adidam—The Only-By-Me Revealed and Given Way Of The Heart.

I Am—One and Only, Non-Separate, Irreducible, and Indivisible.

Therefore, Adidam—The Only-By-Me Revealed and Given Way Of The Heart—Is Single, All-Inclusive, Complete, Whole, Indivisible, and Unique.

The Only-By-Me Revealed and Given Way Of The Heart Is Describable Innumerably.

The Only-By-Me Revealed and Given Way Of The Heart Is Beyond Description.

My Inherently egoless Heart (Itself) Is Both The Perfectly Subjective Source-Condition and The Inherently Perfect Self-Condition Of My Every Word.

Therefore, My Avatarically Self-Revealed Divine Teaching-Word Includes and Transcends Both The Omega Language and The Alpha Language—Even By Including and Transcending Both, Without Prejudice.

I Only Speak The One Truth—Even Without A Word (By Means Of Utter Feeling Silence).

I Am The Divine Eleutherios—The all-and-All-Liberating Truth.

I Am The Inherent (and Perfectly Subjective), and Inherently egoless, and

Inherently Non-Separate, and Inherently Non-"Different", and Inherently Indivisible, and Inherently Irreducible, and Inherently Perfect, and Self-Evidently Divine Feeling Of Being (Itself).

My Spoken and Written Revelation Of The Only-By-Me Revealed and Given Way Of The Heart (or Way Of Adidam)—and, Thus, All My Spoken and Written Language Of Avatarically Given Divine Self-Confession, Avatarically Given Divine Self-Revelation, and Avatarically Given Divine Heart-Instruction—Is The Avatarically Spoken and Avatarically Written Divine Heart-Word.

My Avatarically Spoken and Avatarically Written Divine Heart-Revelation Of The Only-By-Me Revealed and Given Way Of The Heart (or Way Of Adidam) Is Utterly Single, Fully All-Inclusive, Most Perfectly Complete, Truly Whole, Inherently Indivisible, and Entirely Unique.

The Only-By-Me Revealed and Given Way Of The Heart (or Way Of Adidam) Is Altogether Beyond the limitations Of Alpha and Omega.

I Am Altogether Beyond the limitations Of Alpha and Omega.

Although I Was (Of Necessity) Born In The West, I (Myself) Am Not A "Westerner".

I Am Me.

The Infant Who Appeared As The "Bright" Was Not Identified With Any Culture Whatsoever—Whether Of Alpha Or Of Omega.

The "Bright" and The "Thumbs" Precede All Of That.

I Precede All Of That.

I Am Quiet.

I Am Restless.

I Am Full.

I Satisfy The Want and Call For Joy.

Therefore, Listen To Me, and Hear Me, and See Me.

Heartily Receive Me, and (Thus and Thereby) Heartily Receive My Avatarically Given Divine Self-Revelation Of The Unconditional Reality—and (Gratefully) Formally and Really Devotionally and (Altogether) Fully and Completely Practice The Only-By-Me Revealed and Given Way Of The Heart (or Way Of Adidam) In every moment Of conditional Existence.

Avatar Adi Da Samraj
Adidam Samrajashram, 2003

SUTRA

25

My Avatarically Self-Revealed Divine Word Of Heart-Instruction Is Founded On Two Basic (and Complementary) Teaching-Arguments.

The First Is My Teaching-Argument Relative To "Radical" Understanding (or Most Direct—and, Most Ultimately, Inherent, and Inherently Most Perfect—Transcending Of the self-Contraction).

The Second Is My Teaching-Argument Relative To Divine Ignorance (or Inherent, and Inherently Most Perfect, Divine Self-Realization).

In Every Stage Of Life In The Only-By-Me Revealed and Given Way Of The Heart (or Way Of Adidam), Even From The Beginning, The True Practitioner Either (Progressively) Observes and Understands self-Contraction, and Then (Assisted By That Insight) Progressively (and, Eventually, Directly) Transcends self-Contraction (In The Feeling-Contemplative Manner Of The Devotional Way Of Insight), Or, Otherwise (In The Feeling-Contemplative Manner Of The Devotional Way Of Faith), Simply, and Always Immediately and Directly, Practices (and Progressively—and, Eventually, Directly—Realizes) The Transcending Of self-Contraction.

Whether Via The Devotional (and Feeling-Contemplative) Exercise Of Insight (Either As self-Enquiry, In The Form "Avoiding Relationship?", Or As Non-verbal Re-Cognition, or Identification and Feeling-Transcendence, Of the self-Contraction As it arises in the form of every kind of conditional experience and conditional knowledge), Or Via The Devotional (and Feeling-Contemplative) Exercise Of Faith By Means Of The "True Prayer" Of My Listening Devotees and My Hearing and My Would-Be-Seeing Devotees (Which Is "Simple" Feeling-Contemplation Of Me,[70] and Random Invocation Of Me Via Ruchira Avatara Naama Japa Of One or Another Of The By-Me-Revealed and By-Me-Given Forms Of The Ruchira Avatara Naama Mantra) Or By Means Of The Prayer Of Remembrance (Which Is The Technical Exercise Of The "Conscious Process" Given By Me For The Meditative Use Of My Seeing Devotees who Practice In The Devotional Way Of Faith), Or Via "Hridaya-Vichara" (Which I Generally Refer To As "Feeling-Enquiry", and Which Is The Technical Exercise Of The "Conscious Process" In The Context Of The "Perfect Practice", and Which Is The Exercise Of Direct Self-Identification With Me As

Consciousness Itself, or The Inherent Feeling Of Being)—The True Devotee-Practitioner Of The Way Of The Heart Directly (Through The Responsive Application Of Any One Of These Only-By-Me Revealed and Given Technical Means—Always, In Any and Every Case, Exercised On The Basis Of The Foundation Practice Of Ruchira Avatara Bhakti Yoga, and, In Due Course, On The Basis Of The Developing Modes Of The Primary Practice, Of Searchless Beholding Of Me, and, Also, The Developing Modes Of The Responsive Practices Of Spiritual "Conductivity") Transcends The egoic Contraction Of the body-mind (Including The Tendency To Dissociate From the Natural, or sensory, body and the Natural, or Participatory, state of perceptual knowing). And, Most Ultimately (In The Context Of The Only-By-Me Revealed and Given Seventh Stage Of Life In The Way Of The Heart), The True Devotee-Practitioner Of The Way Of The Heart (Spontaneously and Always Exercising Ati-Ruchira Yoga) Transcends the body-mind itself and The Cosmic Domain Itself—and This Not By Dissociation and "Difference", but By Inherently Most Perfect Heart-Communion With Me (Divinely Self-Recognizing—and, Most Ultimately, Divinely Outshining—whatever, Apparently, arises).

Likewise, In The Context Of Each Particular Stage Of Practice In The Only-By-Me Revealed and Given Way Of The Heart (or Way Of Adidam), The True Practitioner <u>Either</u> Proceeds <u>Toward</u> The Inherently Most Perfect Realization Of Divine Ignorance <u>Or</u> (Most Ultimately) Directly (and Inherently Most Perfectly) <u>Realizes</u> The Inherently Perfect Condition Of Divine Ignorance (Which <u>Is</u> The Self-Existing and Self-Radiant Truth Of Most Perfect Divine Self-Realization). In The Beginning Of The Way Of The Heart, and In The (Spiritually) Fully Technically Responsible Frontal Yoga Of The Way Of The Heart, The True Practitioner "Considers" (and Feels Beyond) The Illusions Of conditional knowledge and conditional experience—but, In The Course Of The "Perfect Practice" Of The Way Of The Heart, That "Consideration" Takes The Form Of Immediate Intuition Of My Avatarically Self-Revealed (Transcendental, Inherently Spiritual, Inherently egoless, and Self-Evidently Divine) Person, The Only One Who <u>Is</u>, The Non-"Different" Self-Condition Of Mere Being, The One and Only Conscious Light, Self-Existing <u>As</u> Consciousness Itself, and Self-Radiant <u>As</u> Happiness Itself, or Love-Bliss Itself (Inherently and Eternally Prior To—and, Yet, Not Separate, or "Different", From, but, In Its Most Perfect Realization and Demonstration, Inherently and Most Perfectly Outshining—the body-mind and all knowledge or experience Of The conditionally Manifested Cosmos).

In The Way Of The Heart, All Practices (and Developmental Stages, or Processes, Of Practice) In The Context Of Any or All Of The First Four Stages Of Life Are To Be Understood (or Intelligently Presumed) To Be Only (or

Merely) Preliminary (or Preparatory) Practices (and Developmental Stages, or Processes, Of Practice). Therefore, All Such Practices (and Developmental Stages, or Processes, Of Practice) Simply Serve To Purify, Re-Balance, and (Eventually) To Spiritually Regenerate the body-mind (and attention itself), As Preparation For (or As An Effective Course Preliminary To) Clear and Stable Awakening (By Means Of My Avatarically Self-Transmitted Divine Spiritual Grace) To The Witness-Position Of Consciousness Itself (and, Thereby, To The Capability, By Means Of My Avatarically Self-Transmitted Divine Spiritual Grace, For The "Perfect Practice" Of The Way Of The Heart, Beginning In The Context Of The Structures and Processes Otherwise Characteristic Of The Fifth and The Sixth Stages Of Life).

The Only-By-Me Revealed and Given Way Of The Heart (or Way Of Adidam) Begins With (or, Really, Is Approached Through) The Preparatory Sadhana (or Concentrated Practice) Of Listening To Me (Based, As A Principal Design Of Practice, On Either The Devotional and Feeling-Contemplative Exercise Of Insight Or The Devotional and Feeling-Contemplative Exercise Of Faith). Therefore, The Beginning Of The Way Of The Heart Is A Process In Which You Simply (but In A Truly ego-Surrendering, ego-Forgetting, and ego-Transcending Manner) Devote Your Full Feeling-attention To My (Now, and Forever Hereafter, Given) Avatarically-Born Bodily (Human) Divine Form, and (In Due Course) My Avatarically Self-Transmitted Spiritual (and Always Blessing) Divine Presence, and (Thus and Thereby, and More and More) My Avatarically Self-Revealed (and Very, and Transcendental, and Perfectly Subjective, and Inherently Spiritual, and Inherently egoless, and Inherently Perfect, and Self-Evidently Divine) State, and To My Avatarically Self-Manifested (and Ever-Living) Divine Leelas, and (Always) To My Avatarically Full-Given (and Ever-Speaking) Divine Word (or My Heart-Confessions, My Instructive Teaching-Arguments, and All My Instructions For Specific Practice). And This Original Process Develops Progressively, From Its Rudimentary Beginnings, and Through The Unfolding Developmental Stages Of Practice In The Way Of The Heart—Until (At Last) There Is The Most Perfect (All-Outshining) Demonstration Of The Divine "Brightness" (In Divine Translation).

The Process Of Listening To Me Involves General (but Intensive) Study Of My Avatarically Self-Revealed (and Always Me-Revealing) Divine Word and (Also) Rudimentary (but Profound) "Consideration" Of The Way Of The Heart In Its Totality. Thus, The Process Of Listening To Me Involves The Profound "Consideration" (In Practice) Of My Teaching-Argument Relative To "Narcissus" (or the self-Contraction), and Of My Teaching-Argument (and Calling) Relative To "Radical" Understanding (or Most Direct Feeling-Transcendence Of the self-Contraction). And The Necessary Practicing Context

Of These "Considerations" Is The Basic Beginner's Practice Of Either Random (and Progressively More and More Meditative) self-Enquiry (In The Form "Avoiding Relationship?") Or Random (and Progressively More and More Meditative) Ruchira Avatara Naama Japa.

This Beginner's Process Of Listening To Me Also Involves The Real (Rudimentary) "Consideration" (or The Tacit Reception—Rather Than The Strategic Application) Of My Teaching-Argument Relative To Divine Ignorance, or The Tacit Sense (or Direct, Rudimentary Intuition) Of The Transcendental, Inherently Spiritual, Inherently egoless, and Self-Evidently Divine Self-Condition Of Reality, Through The Present (or moment to moment) *Tacit* (Rather Than Strategically Applied) Observation That the conditional psycho-physical self (or ego-"I") Does Not (and Cannot) know What any conditional thing, being, process, or event *Is*.

This Is My Teaching-Argument Relative To Divine Ignorance. Read This, Regularly. "Consider" This, daily (or, Otherwise, day to day), and Merely At Random, Spontaneously, and Tacitly. You (as the conditional self, or the body-mind-self) Can (and Do) experience and know (Whether Directly Or Indirectly) All Kinds Of Details (Whether True Or False) *About* things, others, or conditional events—but You (as the conditional self, or the body-mind-self) Do Not and Cannot Ever (In Fact, or In Reality) experience or know *What* any thing, other, or conditional event *Is*.

"Consider" any thing, other, or conditional event, and Observe That This Is So. "Consider" The Letter "M", For Example. Picture It In mind, or In print, or Write It Down By hand (Even many times). "Consider" All That You (as the psycho-physical self) experience or know About The Letter "M". Do You (in mind or in body) experience or know *What* The Letter "M" *Is*? *Is*? Altogether and Really *Is*? No. And What Does This "Consideration" Reveal About You (as the Presumed and Presumptuous body-mind-"I")? Indeed, What *Is* the body? What *Is* the mind? What *Is* "You"? Through Such "Consideration", Feel and Be The Feeling Of This "Ignorance" Itself. That body-Transcending, mind-Transcending, and ego-Transcending Feeling-Ignorance Is The Most Prior Intuition Of *What* *Is* (and Of The Only One *Who* *Is*).

The conventional subject-object Illusion (or The Common Illusory Presumption That Characterizes the conditional self) Is The Presumption That whatever arises Is Already (or Certainly Can Be) Really experienced or known. The conditional self Is Commonly Presumed To Be a knower—but, In Truth, the conditional self Is *Inherently* Ignorant. All conditional, perceptual, experiential, conceptual, or conventional knowledge Is Founded On The False Presumption That conditional forms or events Are Familiar. In Fact, Only Certain Formal Features Of arising phenomena *Seem* Familiar (Due To Repetition),

Whereas (In Truth) no thing, being, or condition (or Even the conditional self itself) Is Familiar (and, Thus, Already and Completely and Really known).

Conditional knowledge and experience (or conceptual mind and psycho-physical experience In General) Are Based Upon The Illusion (or The Illusory Psychology) Of Familiarity, or The Constantly Asserted Presumption That "'I' (as the egoic body-mind-self) know What this or that Is". How Can This Presumption Be True? Only a moment Of "Consideration" Will Reveal That the conditional "I" Does Not (and Cannot) know What any thing or conditional event or Even the conditional self (or ego-"I", or self-Contraction) itself Is (Altogether, Really, and Ultimately).

The conditional self Is Inherently (or Divinely) Ignorant. The conditional self Is (Inherently, Always Already, and Cannot Ever Be Else Than) knowledgeless, or Bereft and Free Of The Familiar (or the known). Indeed, the conditional self (or conventional "I") Is (itself) An Illusion Of knowledge (or Of Familiarity)—and, If The Inherent (and Inherently egoless, and Self-Evidently Divine) Condition Of Ignorance Is Realized In any moment, the "knowledge" of body, mind, or conditional "I" Is Replaced By The Mystery Of Inherently bodiless, mindless, and selfless Being.

The Transcendental (or Unconditional), Inherently Spiritual, Inherently egoless, and Self-Evidently Divine Reality Is Not Other Than (or Separate From) The conditional Reality.

Existence (or Being) Is An Inherent Characteristic Of The Unconditional Reality and (Therefore) Also Of The conditional Reality (Which arises As An Apparent Modification Of, or A Play Upon, The Unconditional Reality).

Existence Itself (or Being, Itself) Cannot Be Observed or Inspected (As If It Were An Object)—Because There Is No Point Of View (Whether Divine Or Transcendental Or Spiritual Or conditional) That Is Separate From (or Not Identical To) Existence Itself.

Likewise, Consciousness (Itself) Cannot Be Observed or Inspected—Because There Is No Point Of View Relative To Which Consciousness Stands As An Object.

And Love-Bliss Itself (or Happiness, Itself) Cannot Be Observed or Inspected—Because It Is Never An Object, but It Is Always Only (and Perfectly) A Subjective Reality.

Truly, Of All That Exists (Whether conditionally Or Unconditionally), Only Existence (or Being) Itself, Consciousness Itself, and Love-Bliss (or Happiness) Itself Never Appear As Objects, and (Therefore) Can Never Be Observed or Inspected (or Even experienced or known) As They Are.

Indeed, These Unique Three—Existence (or Being), and Consciousness, and Love-Bliss (or Happiness Itself)—Are One and The Same.

And These Three Are Divinely Realized (As The By-Me-Avatarically-Self-Revealed One and Very Divine Self-Condition and Source-Condition) In The Inherently Most Perfect Awakening That Is The Most Ultimate (or Seventh Stage) Realization Of The Only-By-Me Revealed and Given Way Of The Heart (or Way Of Adidam).

And, Because Neither One Nor All Of These Three Can Be Observed or Inspected (or experienced, or known) As It Is (or As "They" Are), and (Therefore) Because Existence (Itself) Cannot Be Observed or Inspected or experienced or known (As It Is)—It Is Also Never Possible To Observe or Inspect or experience or know What Even any thing or conditional event, or Even the conditional self (or ego-"I", or self-Contraction) itself, Is (Because The Very Existence, or Being, Of Even any condition Cannot Be Observed, or Inspected, or experienced, or known).

Therefore, Neither The Divine (and Transcendental, and Inherently Spiritual) Self Nor the conditional self Can know What any condition Is—Because "knowledge" Requires That subject and object (Even The Ultimate Subject and A Great Object) Be "Different" and Separate From one another.

However, Because It Always Already Is Existence (or Being) Itself, and Consciousness Itself, and Love-Bliss (or Happiness) Itself—The Transcendental, Inherently Spiritual, Inherently egoless, and Self-Evidently Divine Self-Conscious Light Can and Always Does (Inherently, Un-conditionally, and Divinely) Self-Recognize (As Itself) What every arising condition Is.

And This Self-Abiding Divine Self-Recognition (or Most Ultimate, and Perfectly Subjective, Self-Identification) Is Inherent, Direct, Tacit, and Prior To all conditional knowing or experiencing.

Therefore, Unless the conditional (or Objectified) self Is Grounded (and, Thus, Transcended) In The Ultimate and Perfectly Subjective Self (or The Transcendental, and Inherently Spiritual, and Inherently egoless, and Self-Evidently Divine Reality), the conditional self (by itself) Does Not (and Cannot) Fully, Finally, Ultimately, or Really experience or know conditional, objective, or Objectified Reality.

The Only-By-Me Revealed and Given Way (or Yoga) Of Adidam (Which Is The One and Only By-Me-Revealed and By-Me-Given Way Of The Heart) Is The Way (or Divine Yogic Process) That Inherently (and More and More Effectively—and, At Last, Most Perfectly) Transcends all conditional experience (and all conditional experiencing) and all conditional knowledge (and all conditional knowing).

The psycho-physical ego-"I" (or body-mind-self) is a conditional (or limited, temporary, and Always changing) experiencer—and a (Likewise) conditional knower. Therefore, all egoic experience and all egoic knowledge is limited, temporary, Always changing, and Merely and Only psycho-physical.

The ego-"I" is a conditional process in conditional space-time. The ego-"I" Is A Seeker For conditional experience and conditional knowledge. And the ego-"I" is an accumulation and an effect of conditional experience and conditional knowledge (or an accumulation and an effect of the subject-versus-object convention of all ego-Based perception and conception). However, the ego-"I" arises In Reality (or Existence, or Being) Itself—and As An Apparent Modification Of Reality (or Of What Is) Itself. Therefore, the ego-"I" Is Never In A Position Separate From What Is—Such That it Could experience, or Inspect, or know What Is. And, For This Reason, the ego-"I" Does Not and Cannot experience, or Inspect, or know What Even any thing, event, or other Is. Therefore, No Matter what or who Is experienced, or Inspected, or known By the ego-"I" (or the self-Contracted body-mind), the ego-"I" (itself) Does Not and Cannot Un-conditionally (or Divinely) Self-Recognize any thing, event, or other that it experiences, or Inspects, or knows. That Is To Say, the ego-"I" (or body-mind-self) Cannot itself Un-conditionally (or Divinely) Self-Recognize its own psycho-physical experience (itself) or knowledge (itself) As Is—or As Reality Itself (or As Existence Itself, or As Being Itself). And, Therefore, the ego-"I" (or body-mind-self) Does Not itself (Inherently and Un-conditionally, or Divinely) Self-Recognize its own Necessarily conditional experience and its own Necessarily conditional knowledge To Be Self-Existing and Self-Radiant Consciousness Itself (or The Inherently egoless Divine Person, or Self-Condition, or Conscious Light, Itself). And, As A Consequence Of its own inherent state of merely conditional (and merely conventional—or subject-object) experiencing and knowing (and, Thus, As A Consequence Of its own Perpetual Failure To Un-conditionally, or Divinely, Self-Recognize its own conditional experience and its own conditional knowledge), the ego-"I" (or body-mind-self) Always and Inherently Fails To Transcend its own conditional experiencing and its own conditional knowing. And, Because Of That Failure (Which Is Inevitable, and Inherent In egoity itself), the ego-"I" is (itself) Bondage To conditional existence in space-time.

The ego-"I" (or body-mind-self) Is Inherently, Irreducibly, and Irrevocably Ignorant Of What Is. However, That Inherent Ignorance (Rather Than any kind of conditional experience or conditional knowledge) Is (Itself)—If It Is (In The Context Of The Only-By-Me Revealed and Given Seventh Stage Of Life) Truly and Most Perfectly Realized—The Essential (and Divinely Liberating) True and Divine Experience and Knowledge Of Reality! Therefore, The Essential (and Inherent) Ignorance That Characterizes the ego-"I" (or Even any conditional body-mind) Is—Ultimately, or In Truth—Divine (and Inherent) Ignorance. And Divine (and Inherent) Ignorance (Realized Most Perfectly, In The Only-By-Me

Revealed and Given Seventh Stage Of Life) Is The Most Fundamental Essence, or Root-Condition, Of True and Divine (or Un-conditionally subject-object-Transcending) Experiencing and Knowing. And The Most Perfect (or Seventh Stage) Realization Of Divine (and Inherent) Ignorance Is The Unique Capability Of Self-Abiding Divine Self-Recognition (or The ego-Transcending Capability To Inherently and Un-conditionally, and, Thus, Divinely, Self-Recognize any and every Apparent thing, event, or other—As Is).

The Only-By-Me Revealed and Given Way (or Yoga) Of Adidam Is The Way (or Divine Yogic Process) Of Divine Ignorance.

The Only-By-Me Revealed and Given Way (or Yoga) Of Adidam Is The Way (or Divine Yogic Process) That, From Its Beginning (and Inherently, and More and More Effectively, and, At Last, Most Perfectly), Directly (and "Radically", or By Going To, and Proceeding From, The Root) Transcends the ego-"I" (itself), and all conditional experience, and all conditional experiencing, and all conditional knowledge, and all conditional knowing, and All conditional Seeking, and All conditional Attainments, and All conditional Realizations, and Even All conditional "Difference"—and, Indeed, all of space-time.

The Only-By-Me Revealed and Given Way (or Yoga) Of Adidam Is, In Practice, A Progressive (and Truly Divine, and Really body-mind-self-Transcending—and, At Last, Most Perfectly ego-"I"-Transcending, and body-mind-Transcending, and space-time-Transcending) Process. At First, The Process Of The Way Of Adidam Is The Course Of Progressive ego-Transcendence In The Context Of The First Six Stages Of Life. Most Ultimately (or At Last, and Most Perfectly), The Process Of The Way Of Adidam Is Established In The Transcendental, Inherently Spiritual, and Most Perfect Divine Yoga Of Consciousness Itself (or The Only-By-Me Revealed and Given Seventh Stage Of Life), In Which the body-mind and the world Are Inherently Outshined (or Dissolved In The Inherent Heart-"Brightness") Through Divine Self-Abiding and (On That Basis) Through Spontaneous and Inherent Divine Self-Recognition Of all conditions (As they arise) In and As The Transcendental and Inherently Spiritual and Inherently egoless and Self-Evidently Divine Self-Condition (or The One, and Only, and Self-Existing, and Self-Radiant, and Inherently egoless Condition Of Conscious Light, Itself).

When, On The Basis Of Devotional Recognition Of Me (and Practice Of Ruchira Avatara Bhakti Yoga), self-Observation and (In The Devotional Way, or Devotional Exercise, Of Insight) Random self-Enquiry (In The Form "Avoiding Relationship?") Are Exercised, Chronic conceptual thinking (and Fixed Identification With conceptual thoughts, including the conceptual "I"-thought, or the Abstract thought of the conditional self as conceptual thinker and knower) Subsides (By A Heart-Felt and Directly Effective Process). Likewise,

When, On The Basis Of Devotional Recognition Of Me (and Practice Of Ruchira Avatara Bhakti Yoga), Ruchira Avatara Naama Japa Is Exercised In The Devotional Way (or Devotional Exercise) Of Faith, all the forms of Chronic conceptual thinking (and Fixed Identification With conceptual thoughts) Relax, Subside, and Are Directly or Progressively Released By An Equally Heart-Felt and Directly Effective Process. In Either Manner, The Useful conceptual thinking Process Continues To Function As A Tool For Occasional or Intentional Use—but Chronic (or Compulsive and Obsessive) conceptual thinking Is Relaxed, By Virtue Of The Right Devotional Exercise Of Either Insight Or Faith, and Chronic (or Compulsive and Obsessive) conceptual thinking Is Thus (In every moment Of The Effective Devotional Exercise Of Either Insight Or Faith) Replaced By The Simple perceptual Awareness Of whatever arises in, as, or to the bodily self or Natural body-mind. This Same Principle Also Governs The Later Process Of Meditation In The Only-By-Me Revealed and Given Way Of The Heart, Especially In The Context Of The Fully Established "Basic" Fourth Stage Of Life and In The "Perfect Practice" Of The Way Of The Heart In The Context Of The Process Otherwise Characteristic Of The Fifth Stage Of Life. In The Later (or By-Me-Spiritually-Activated, and, Spiritually, Fully Technically Responsible) Process Of Meditation In The Way Of The Heart, Whole bodily (and Total sensory) Feeling and attention Are Intentionally (or, Otherwise, Spontaneously) To Be "Tuned" (and Heart-Released) To My Avatarically Self-Transmitted Divine Spirit-Current, Surrounding and Pervading and Crashing Down Into The Circle Of the body-mind. The conceptual mind Relaxes (or Subsides) In That Process, and My Avatarically Self-Transmitted Divine Spirit-Current Carries Feeling and attention Through The Circle Of the body-mind Via A Progressively (or Potentially) Extraordinary Range Of perceptual or sensory phenomena, both gross and subtle. Gradually, By Means Of The Persistent Exercise Of The "Conscious Process" Of self-Surrender, self-Forgetting, and self-Transcendence (or Real ego-Transcendence), The experiential (or perceptual) Tendency Itself Relaxes—Although, In The Process, The Source-Condition Of conditional phenomena Is (Eventually) Contemplated (By Means Of Feeling) Infinitely Above the body-mind, and As The Apparently Objective (and Yet Formless) Matrix Of conditional (or psycho-physical) forms. Nevertheless, The "Conscious Process" Must Continue, Until (In The "Perfect Practice" Of The Way Of The Heart) My Avatarically Self-Revealed, and Very, and Transcendental, and Perfectly Subjective, and Inherently Spiritual, and Inherently egoless, and Inherently Perfect, and Self-Evidently Divine State Of Conscious Light—Which Is The Very, and Transcendental, and Inherently Spiritual, and Inherently egoless, and Self-Evidently Divine Self-Condition, and Which Is (By Means Of My Avatarically Self-Transmitted Divine Spiritual

Grace) Realized As The Inherent Feeling Of Being—Is Realized To Be The Divine Source-Condition Of all-and-All.

The Right "Consideration" Of My Avataric Divine Teaching-Arguments Sensitizes You To The Two Principal Functions Of mind. The First (and Primary) Function Of mind Is The perceptual (and Participatory) Function Of mind. The Second (and Secondary) Function Of mind Is The conceptual (and Abstract, Analytical, or Interpretive) Function Of mind.

The First (or Primary) Function Of mind Is The Natural and Naturally Intelligent perceptual Awareness (or Natural feeling-Awareness) Of arising conditions, Without Any Necessarily Accompanying Effort To Separate From them. The Second (or Secondary) Function Of mind Is The conceptual Awareness Of arising conditions (and Of verbal thoughts or Abstract Analytical concepts themselves)—and It Is Necessarily Associated With An Effort To Separate (or Withdraw) From arising conditions (whether they are gross, subtle, or causal) and To Exceed (or Strategically Escape From) arising conditions, Because It Is Always Associated With An Effort To know About (or To Abstract, Analyze, and Interpret) arising conditions.

The perceiving mind knows whatever it perceives. What it perceives—Exactly as it is perceived—is what it knows. Perception (Prior To verbal, Abstract, and Interpretive thought) is Participatory conditional knowledge.

The conceptual mind knows whatever it thinks. Whatever it thinks—Whether Or Not the thought is Informed or Confirmed By perception—is what it knows. Conception (or conceptual thought), Loosely or Not At All Associated With perception, is Abstract conditional knowledge.

The Right Employment Of The conceptual Function Of mind Can Serve A Very Useful Purpose In The Original and General Inspiration and Guidance Of The Process, Discipline, and Practice Of The Only-By-Me Revealed and Given Way Of The Heart. Just So, the activities Of The conceptual Function Of mind Generally Serve A Useful Purpose In the common world, Which Is The Communication and Development Of conventional knowledge and practical invention. Nevertheless, all conceptual knowledge Is An Abstraction, The Purpose Of Which Is To Give conditional beings (or knowers) Power Over themselves, their objects, their environments, and other conditionally Manifested beings. Therefore, If This Function Of mind Is Not Kept In Right Perspective (Subordinate To Participatory mind and The Wisdom Of Reality), The Motives Of Power and Control Tend To Dominate mind itself (and, Therefore, the Total body-mind and The Total Collective Society, or social Culture, Of conditionally knowing beings).

Secondary mind, or conceptual (and, Typically, verbal) thought, Must Be Disciplined, If it Is To Be Effective In its Proper Sphere. Likewise, it Must Be

Understood, Kept In Right Perspective, and (At Will) Freely Set Aside When The Analytical and Interpretive Function Is Not Presently Necessary or Useful.

You Must Realize The Natural (and Inherent) Ability To Set Aside The Secondary (or conceptual) Function Of mind—or Else You Will Be Dominated By A Compulsive and Obsessive Effort To think conceptually (By Dissociating From perception), To Seek knowledge About, To Interpret, and To Separate From (or To Strategically Dominate, or Even To Strategically Escape From) the perceived conditional worlds.

You Must Enjoy The Natural, Inherent, moment to moment Ability To Merely perceive, To feel, To be with, and To Wholly Participate In the phenomenal conditions Of Your psycho-physical Existence—or Else You Will Not Truly Understand what arises conditionally, Nor Will You Transcend the limitations Of conditional Existence.

Through The Unique Great Process Of The Only-By-Me Revealed and Given Way Of The Heart, and By Means Of self-Observation, Developing self-Understanding, and The Progressively Awakening Natural Feeling-Practice Of Mere and always present perception (At First, of perceptual objects, and, Eventually, Of My Avatarically Self-Transmitted Divine Spirit-Current Itself)—You Must (Whether In The Manner Of The Devotional Way Of Insight Or In The Manner Of The Devotional Way Of Faith) Realize The Inherent Ability To Intentionally Relax (or To Directly Transcend) The Chronic, Compulsive, and Obsessive Tendency Of attention To Become Associated With the past (in the form of both perceptual and conceptual memories) and the future (in the form of perceptual and conceptual projections, both of which Are Generally Based On memories, or remembered conditions) and Even the present (as a conceived, or pre-conceived, or, Otherwise, conceptually limited moment). If moment to moment (or any particular moment Of) Mere and Also perceptible Existence Is (To One or Another Degree) Intolerable To You, Such That You Are (To One or Another Degree) Unable To perceive each (or any particular) present perceptible moment as it (Apparently) is and To (Naturally) feel and Participate In it Without Recoil, You Will (To That Degree, or In any Thus Intolerable moment) Exist Only In the Secondary (or Reflected) world of time and mind.

Ultimately, You Must Realize The Inherently Most Perfect Transcending Of mind itself (In Both Of its Functions), or Else You Will Only Be Defined By and Bound To conditional (or phenomenal) states (Bereft Of The Most Perfect Divine Realization Of Reality). And the Total mind Is Most Perfectly Transcended Only In The Inherent (and Inherently Most Perfect) Realization Of My Avatarically Self-Revealed (Transcendental, Inherently Spiritual, Inherently egoless, and Self-Evidently Divine) Self-Condition—The Conscious Light Of The

"Bright" (In Which the mind and the body, and all the conditions, relations, and states of the mind and the body, Are arising, continuing, changing, and passing away).

Chronic, Compulsive, and Obsessive verbal thinking or Abstract conceptualizing (or The Chronic, Compulsive, and Obsessive conceptual Effort, or Search, To Achieve Power Over the world that Appears To Be Devoted To Exploiting its Power Over You) Is A Disease. It Is, Ultimately, A Fruitless or Futile Effort—and it Is A Symptom Of self-Contraction, ego-Possession, and The Absence Of Most Perfect Divine Self-Realization. Effective and "Creative" conceptual thinking Is A Generally Useful and Characteristic Sign Of the human being—but When The Efforts (or Searches) Of the conceptually thinking mind Become Compulsive, Obsessive, and Dominant, Such That verbal and Abstract Analytical thought Cannot Be Relinquished At Will, and things and beings Cannot Be perceived as they (Apparently) are (and, Most Ultimately, Divinely Self-Recognized As they Are), Then the thinking being Is Diseased, Bereft Of Wisdom, and Separated From Reality.

Chronic conceptual thinking (and Seeking To know About) Is A Compulsive and Obsessive Withdrawal (or Contraction) From perception, From Direct experience of Natural (or Cosmic) forms (whether gross, subtle, or causal), and From sensory (or bodily) Existence Itself. Chronic conceptualizing Effectively Creates An Alternative (and, Ultimately, False or, In Truth, Un-Real) conditional Reality—A conditional Reality That Is Not Really physical, Not Even psycho-physical (or Even Truly psychic), but (Most Basically) conceptual (or Made Of mental Abstractions). And Fixed Identification With The Process Of conceptual thinking and the conditional self as conceptual thinker Is Identification With a False (or Un-Real) self, A Mere Contraction From The Real (or Transcendental, Inherently Spiritual, Inherently egoless, and Self-Evidently Divine) Self-Condition.

However, The Effort To Avoid or To Strategically Escape conceptual thinking, conceptual thought, or the conceptual thinker Is A Futile Strategy. It Is Futile Because It Is (Itself) An Expression Of The Very Same Effort (Of self-Contraction) That Is The Stressful Origin Of Chronic conceptual thought-mind and the conceptual thought-self. Therefore, The Effort To Stop conceptual thinking Only Intensifies the self-Contraction, Reinforces The Cycle Of conceptual thinking, conceptual thought, and the Presumed conceptual thinker, and Generates Despair Relative To The Ability To Stand Free Of The limiting Capability Of the conceptual mind (and the Total body-mind).

The Cycle Of conceptual thinking, conceptual thought, and the Presumed conceptual thinker Is Truly Transcended Only Through The Real Process Of self-Observation (To The Degree Of Most Fundamental self-Understanding) and Effective self-Transcendence (or Real ego-Transcendence), Which (Together) Must (Ultimately) Become (or Allow) The Inherent (and Inherently Perfect) Realization Of The Divine Self-Condition (or Reality) In and As Which the body-mind-self and all of its conditional relations Are (Apparently) arising, continuing, changing, and passing away. And, In The Only-By-Me Revealed and Given Way Of The Heart, This Real Process (Of self-Observation, Most Fundamental self-Understanding, Effective self-Transcendence, or Real ego-Transcendence, and Inherent, and Inherently Perfect, Realization) Develops Progressively (In The Total Context Of The Seven Stages Of Life—and, At First, In The "Original", and Then "Basic", Fourth Stage Context Of The Frontal Yoga Of The Way Of The Heart)—Either Via The Real Practice Of The Only-By-Me Revealed and Given Devotional Way Of Insight Or Via The Real Practice Of The Only-By-Me Revealed and Given Devotional Way Of Faith.

You Can Transcend the conceptual mind (or conceptual thinking, conceptual thought, and the conceptual thinker), or All Analytical Interpreting and knowing, By Observing, Understanding, and Transcending The Act Of self-Contraction, To The Degree That You Relax Into Simple experiencing (or Merely perceiving, and Naturally feeling, and, Altogether and Truly, Feeling).

You Can Transcend the perceptual mind (or all perceiving, all experiencing, and the perceiver, or the conditionally experiencing and Participating self) By Utterly Not knowing—Which Is Divine Ignorance (or Mere Being, or Inherent, and Inherently Perfect, Realization Of The Self-Condition, and Source-Condition, Of Reality Itself), Prior To (but Not Strategically Excluding) the body-mind and All Of conditional Existence.

In The Progressive Whole bodily Devotional Process Of The Only-By-Me Revealed and Given Way Of The Heart (or Way Of Adidam), Chronic (or Otherwise Fixed) Identification With the conditional self as conceptual thinker (or Abstract knower) Is, First, Replaced By (or Grounded In) The Feeling-Sense "'I' am the body"—or "'I' am the Total (and perceiving or Participatory) body-mind". Therefore, In The Listening Course Of The Only-By-Me Revealed and Given Way Of The Heart (or Way Of Adidam), You Must Truly Realize (bodily, Steadily, In Feeling, and Through Real self-Observation) That You, as the ego-"I" (or conditionally Manifested self), are the Total psycho-physical (or experiencing, and Participating) self—Rather Than the merely (or Exclusively) interior (or Abstract) and conceptually thinking (or conceptually knowing, and Not Directly Participating) self. Thus, You Must Realize That what You Refer To (and Are Aware Of) as Your conditional (or functional, and personal) "I" is the Total body-mind—and Not the mind Separately (or a "self" that Exists Interior To, or Apart From, the perceptual, or perceiving and perceived, body).

When the conditional self Is Established (or Can Readily Be Felt) As the Simple bodily person (or the Total body-mind)—Then perception (or Participatory experience), Rather Than conception (or Analytical and Inherently Separative or Abstracting thought), Becomes The Basic and Dominant Mode Of conditional Existence. When (By Means Of The Present Devotional Exercise Of Either Insight Or Faith) the body-mind Relaxes Into Simple (or Whole bodily) perception—Then conceptual thinking (or The Effort Of mentalizing, or Of conceptual Interpreting) Naturally Subsides (and, More and More, Becomes A Voluntary Process, or a Non-Obsessive function). And, If the body-mind Of My Devotee Consistently Assumes This Natural Participatory Attitude (or Asana), Much Basic (Natural) human energy Is Released (Into perceptually Participatory activity)—and (Eventually) This Release Opens The Natural Doors Of the body-mind To The (Potential) Progressive Process Of Seeing Me (In, and By Means Of, My Avatarically Self-Transmitted Divine Spirit-Baptism), and To The Total (Participatory, or Whole bodily) Process Of Truly Spiritual Meditation (In, and By Means Of, My Avatarically Self-Transmitted Divine Spirit-Current).

The Apparently Separate "I" is merely the conditional body-mind—but the conditional body-mind Is (Ultimately, or Really) Only Light.

Consciousness (Itself) Apparently Merely Witnesses the conditional body-mind (or Apparently Separate "I")—but Consciousness (Itself) Is the conditional body-mind, As Light Itself. Consciousness Itself Is Conscious Light Itself (One and Only), and Not Merely Consciousness Apart (Looking At one and many). Consciousness Itself Is The Inherent and Non-Separate Feeling Of Being, and Not The Separate and Separative Viewer (or any "point of view"). Consciousness Itself Is Totality (One and Only), and Not a single category among the many. Consciousness Itself Is Both Awareness and Energy, Unconditionally Existing. Consciousness Itself—Really, and Truly Divinely, Self-Realized—Is The "Bright", The One and Only Conscious Light That Is Reality (Itself, and In Its Inherently Indivisible Totality).

The "I" of the mind Is Not, In Reality, "Within".

The "I" of the mind Is, In Reality, Simply A conceptual (or mentally Abstracted) Reference To the body.

"I" Is the body—Non-Separately arising Within The Universal (and Inherently Indivisible) Life-Field (or Energy-Sphere) Of Cosmic Nature.

If "I" Is Not Lived As the body, Surrendered Into My Avatarically Self-Revealed Divine Spirit-Current Of Love-Bliss, Then the "I" Is (Inevitably) Lived As bodily and psychic Contraction From The Field Of relations.

Therefore, Understand and Confess The "I" (or Separate-self-Sense) To Be the body.

Surrender As the body, Into its Source-Condition—Which Is The By-Me-and-As-Me-Avatarically-Self-Revealed-and-Spiritually-Self-Transmitted Divine Spirit-Current Of Love-Bliss-Happiness, The Source-Condition (or Matrix) Of all (Apparently objective) forms—and (Thus and Thereby) Be Happy, Doing The Works Of Love and Joy.

Thus, the Actually Existing conditional self (or Apparently Separate Natural "I") Is Not merely inside the body-mind (As a subtle "soul"-person). The Total body-mind (as it is, conditionally, at any moment, or in any conditional world), and Only the Total body-mind (whatever its form or composition in any moment or in any world), is (itself—or as A psycho-physical Totality) the conditional (or Separate) self. The conditional self (or Apparently Separate "I") is the Total Natural body-mind. The conditional "I" is the sensory person of the senses, or the Natural perceiver of conditional energies, and the Natural Participatory knower of conditional forms. The conditional "I" Apparently arises, continues, changes, and passes away—but all of that arising, continuing, changing, and passing Occurs In and As The True (or Ultimately Real), and Transcendental (or Unconditional, and Indivisible), and Inherently Spiritual (or Self-Radiant, and Fully Made-Of-Light), and Inherently egoless (or Non-Separate) Divine Self-Condition (Which Is Self-Existing, and Self-Evidently Divine, Consciousness—or The One, and Only, and Inherently Indivisible, and Inherently egoless Conscious Light—Itself).

Therefore, In The Only-By-Me Revealed and Given Way Of The Heart (or Way Of Adidam), You Must First (and Naturally) Realize Your ego-"I" (or Apparently Separate self) To be the sensory body (or the Total experiential, Participatory, or perceiving body-mind). When (By Means Of Whole bodily Devotional Recognition-Response To My Avatarically Self-Revealed Divine Form, and Presence, and State) You Allow Your conditional self To be the Total body-mind (Simply perceiving—and Not Seeking To Acquire Absolute conditional knowledge and Power, or Struggling To Strategically Escape From the Natural body-mind itself, or From the conditional worlds themselves), the body-mind Is Naturally (or Simply, and Whole bodily) felt—and human Existence Is (Thus) Simply Expressed As A Natural Radiance Of Whole bodily feeling (or Of Simple, and ordinary human, Love and Happiness). And, In The Spiritual Fullness Of The Only-By-Me Revealed and Given Way Of The Heart (or Way Of Adidam), That Simple (Whole bodily) Love and Happiness Is (By Means Of My Avatarically Self-Transmitted Divine Spiritual Grace) Spiritually Magnified—Into (and By Means Of) My Self-Evidently Divine Love-Bliss (Which Is The Feeling-Essence Of My Avatarically Self-Transmitted Divine Spirit-Current).

The Natural (and Basically Non-verbal, Non-conceptual, Whole bodily, and Wholly Participatory) Feeling-Confession "'I' am the body" Is, Itself,

Naturally Felt As Love and Happiness. And (More and More), When (By Means Of My Avatarically Self-Transmitted Divine Spiritual Grace) There Is Whole bodily Devotional Feeling-Participation In The Self-Existing and Self-Radiant Field Of My Avatarically Self-Transmitted Divine Spirit-Current Of Love-Bliss, There Is The Whole bodily (and, Progressively, More and More Profound) Realization That the conditional (or phenomenal) psycho-physical self Is Inherently Relational (and Related), Inherently Participatory, Inherently Non-Separate (and Non-Separative), Inherently Free Of Problems, Inherently Radiant (As Free Feeling), Truly Established (and, Ultimately, To Be Most Perfectly Established) In (and, Most Ultimately, As) The (By-Me-Avatarically-Self-Revealed) Transcendental, Inherently Spiritual, and Self-Evidently Divine Self-Condition Of Inherently egoless Being, and Truly Characterized (and, Ultimately, To Be Most Perfectly Characterized) By Divine Ignorance (or The Self-Existing, Self-Radiant, and Inherently Free Feeling Of Being—Itself). Such Was (and More and More Became) My Own Realization In (and, Progressively, After) The Occasion I Have Described To You—Relative To The Spontaneous Intuitive Awakening Associated With The Observation Of My Right Hand.

When (In The Only-By-Me Revealed and Given Way Of The Heart) The Natural Confession Characterized By The Expressive (or Love-Felt and Happiness-Felt) Simplicity "'I' am the body" Is (By Means Of My Avatarically Self-Transmitted Divine Spiritual Grace) Really Awakened (In any moment) In The Context Of The Effective Devotional Exercise Of Either Feeling-Contemplative Insight Or Feeling-Contemplative Faith—and When, By That Confession (and By Means Of The True Hearing Of Me, and, Thus, By Means Of The Consistent Real, and Really Effective, Exercise Of Most Fundamental self-Understanding, and, Thus, By Means Of The Consistent Release Of conceptual mind and The Consistent Release Of General psycho-physical self-Contraction), The Practitioner Of The Only-By-Me Revealed and Given Way Of The Heart Has Become Both humanly Effective and Fully Capable Of Spiritually Receiving Me (In The Fully Technically Responsible Hearing-and-Seeing Sense)—The "Original" (or Beginner's) Devotional Development Of The Fourth Stage Of Life In The Way Of The Heart Has Become Complete (and Devotional Practice Of The Only-By-Me Revealed and Given Way Of The Heart In The "Basic"—or Would-Be-Seeing, and Progressively Seeing, and Then Actually Seeing—Context Of The Fourth Stage Of Life Should Then Begin).

If You Recoil From perception (or Direct experiential Participation In conditional Existence), the body Contracts Upon itself, and the mind Begins To Function conceptually (Abstracted From perception, or From Natural, and Participatory, or Whole, psycho-physical experience). In That Case, the Single body-mind Becomes Two—or body and mind, or mind Struggling With (or Against) body, and body Struggling With (or Against) mind. Then Existence As an Apparently conditional self Is (Itself) A Struggle, A Dis-ease, A Problem, A Dilemma, A Question, A Search For A Solution (or For An Answer), or A Search For Power Over The Apparent Threats To Existence (Itself). That Search, Like The Original (and moment to moment) Contraction That Produces It, Is Generated By The Feeling That Existence Itself (or Consciousness Itself, or Happiness Itself) Is Threatened and Can Be Ended or Lost. And That Feeling Of Threat (Which Is Itself A Form Of Recoil, or Contraction) arises (Originally) From The Natural (and, Necessarily, self-Contracted) Identification (Of Consciousness Itself) With the gross physical body (and The Coincident Identification Of Consciousness Itself With The Natural Presumption That the gross physical body Is Naturally and Always Threatened and About To Be Ended or Lost).

If There Is Natural Identification (Of Consciousness Itself) With (and Not Seventh Stage, Un-conditional, Inherently egoless, and Self-Abiding Divine Self-Recognition Of) the present conditionally Manifested body (Whether low Or high In The Cosmic Pattern), Then Contraction Toward The Illusions Of Separate (or Non-Dependent) body, Separate (or Non-Dependent) mind, and Separate (or Non-Dependent) self Is Inevitable. Indeed, Natural Identification (Of Consciousness Itself) With the conditionally Manifested (and Even gross) body Is The Very First Form Of self-Contraction. That Identification (Rather Than any biological or physical event itself) Is Your birth as an ego. Your birth as an ego (or a Separate conditional "I") Is An Event In Consciousness. It Is The Paradoxical Presumption, In Consciousness, That Consciousness Itself (Which Is Unconditional, or Transcendental) Is Reduced To (or Bound By) a conditional form, state, and circumstance.

Once the Naturally Threatened (or mortal) born-condition Is Accepted (or Assumed) In Consciousness, the body-mind Contracts Upon itself (Thus Recoiling From all its Natural relations)—and the physical and the psychic (or mental) Become Two. In that "birth event", the ego-"I" is born.

That egoic birth May Not Occur Inside the womb, or Even the instant breathing Begins, Outside the womb. (In My Own Case, the born-condition Was Not Accepted, or Assumed, As a self-Defining limit Until My Bodily Human Form, Outside the womb, Was Approximately Two Years Of Age.[71]) Whenever ego-birth Occurs, Consciousness (From that instant) Identifies With the Total (and Even Reincarnating, or conditionally self-Perpetuating) past and future of the personal body-mind (or conditional self)—including the present body's Rudimentary pleasures and shocks in the womb, As Well As its physical death, and the conditional destiny that Must (or Will Tend To) follow its physical death. Only ego-Transcending Divine Enlightenment (or Inherently, and

Inherently Most Perfectly, or Un-conditionally, ego-Transcending Real-God-Realization) and (At Last) Divine Translation Crack The Illusion Of conditional self-Existence and Spontaneously Terminate The Terrible and Fascinating egoic (or conditionally self-Made) Ordeal Of Cosmic Wandering.

The conditional self Is Not (itself) an entity—Like a thing, or Like the body (in and of itself). The conditional self Is A Presumption. The conditional self Is a concept (or An Illusion In the Presumed Independent, or Separate, mind). The conditional self-concept Is Simply A Reflection (or An Analytical Abstraction) Of the Conscious born-condition, the Conscious birth event, The psycho-physical Contraction That Occurs When Transcendental, Inherently Spiritual, Inherently egoless, and Self-Evidently Divine Consciousness Assumes (or, Rather, Apparently Assumes) That It Is Identical To a limited and Threatened condition.

Previous To Inherently Most Perfect Realization Of The (By-Me-Avatarically-Self-Revealed) Inherently Perfect (and Inherently egoless, and Self-Evidently Divine) Self-Condition and Source-Condition, the psycho-physical self-Contraction is Your Presumed "I". The psycho-physical self-Contraction is Your conditionally born (or Apparent, and Apparently Separate) self. The conditional "I" is Not the body-mind Alone. It is the Contracted body-mind, the body-mind In Consciousness (or the body-mind Assumed In Consciousness). Your ego-"I" is Not Simply the body-mind alive. It is the body-mind Contracted, Seeking, Separate, and Separative. Your Separate, and Separative, and Always Seeking "I" is egoity (or self-Contraction).

Nevertheless, egoity Can (By My Avatarically Self-Transmitted Divine Spiritual Grace) Be Observed, Understood, and Transcended. Indeed, If it Is Not Observed, Understood, and Transcended, conditional Existence Is (Itself) Suffering (If Only An Illusion Of Suffering, or An Imaginary Disease). The Process Of Thorough self-Observation, Most Fundamental self-Understanding, and Progressive self-Transcendence (or Real ego-Transcendence) Is The Necessary Course (Whether By The Devotional Exercise Of Insight Or By The Devotional Exercise Of Faith)—or Else There Is No Growth (Beyond The Natural and conventional Developments Of The First Three Stages Of Life), and There Is No Possibility Of Most Ultimate Freedom (Divine Self-Realization, or Divine Enlightenment), and There Is Only The Futility Of Repetition and Seeking.

Therefore, egoity (or psycho-physical self-Contraction, and Identification With the psycho-physical self-Contraction) Must Be Observed, Understood, and Really, Utterly Transcended.

The Way Of The Heart Is The By-My-Avataric-Divine-Spiritual-Grace-Given (and By-My-Avataric-Divine-Spiritual-Grace-Proceeding) Process Of Such self-Observation, self-Understanding, and self-Transcendence (or Real ego-Transcendence)—In The Context Of The Always Primary Practice Of Searchlessly Beholding Me. Therefore, My Teaching-Argument Relative To "Radical" Understanding—or Most Direct and (Most Ultimately) Inherent (and Inherently Most Perfect) Transcending Of the self-Contraction—Is Most Basic To My Word Of Instruction. And The (Necessarily, Devotional) Course (or Process) Of self-Observation, self-Understanding, and self-Transcendence (or Real ego-Transcendence) Is Most Basic (and Indispensably Necessary) To The Practice Of The Only-By-Me Revealed and Given Way Of The Heart (or Way Of Adidam).

The By-My-Avataric-Divine-Spiritual-Grace-Given Fulfillment (or The Most Ultimate and Inherently Most Perfect Realization) Of The Only-By-Me Revealed and Given Way Of The Heart (or Way Of Adidam) Is Most Perfect Divine Self-Realization—Which Is Most Perfect Realization Of Divine Ignorance. Therefore, My Teaching-Argument Relative To Divine Ignorance (or Most Perfect Divine Self-Realization, or Most Perfectly ego-Transcending Realization Of The By-Me-Avatarically-Self-Revealed Inherent, or Real, Condition Of the conditional self and all conditional beings, things, conditions, and events) Is Also Fundamental—but This Teaching-Argument Always Coincides With (and Complements, or Fulfills, or Completes) My Teaching-Argument Relative To "Radical" Understanding and Most Direct (and, Most Ultimately, Inherent, and Inherently Most Perfect) Transcending Of the self-Contraction.

The "Consideration" Of Divine Ignorance (In My Any Devotee's Practice Of Either The Devotional Way Of Insight Or The Devotional Way Of Faith) Is Not To Be Engaged As A Strategic Exercise (or Any Kind Of Technical Exercise—or, Otherwise, Intentionally Applied Exercise—At All). The "Consideration" Of Divine Ignorance Is To Be Merely A Matter Of Study (Through Regular Reading Of My Argument Relative To Divine Ignorance) and, Otherwise, The daily (or, Otherwise, day to day) Random, Tacit (and Inherently Searchless) Observing and Noticing That arises (Spontaneously) From That Study. Such "Consideration" Is Not (In and Of Itself) A Complete (or Sufficient) Practice—Especially Because It Bypasses The Necessary Real Practice, Process, and Discipline Of ego-Transcendence. Therefore, Such "Consideration" Is Simply A Spontaneous (and Inherently Searchless, or Non-Strategic, and Not Intentionally Applied), Occasional, or Random, and Tacit Pointer In The Direction Of Most Perfect Divine Self-Realization.

My Teaching-Argument Relative To Divine Ignorance Is A Fundamental "Consideration" That Complements My Teaching-Argument Relative To "Radical" Understanding Of the self-Contraction, but My Teaching-Argument Relative To Divine Ignorance Refers To (or Indicates, or Directly and

Immediately Signifies) What Is Really and Most Ultimately (or Inherently, and Inherently Most Perfectly) Realized Only If (and When) The Process Of self-Observation, self-Understanding, and self-Transcendence (or Real ego-Transcendence) Has Really and Most Ultimately (or Inherently, and Inherently Most Perfectly) Been Fulfilled. Indeed, The Realization Of Divine Ignorance (Itself) Is The Realization Of The Very Truth (or Condition) That Is The Foundation Of The Only-By-Me Revealed and Given Seventh Stage Of Life. Therefore, In The Only-By-Me Revealed and Given Way Of The Heart (or Way Of Adidam), "Radical" Understanding (or Most Direct and, Most Ultimately, Inherent, and Inherently Most Perfect, Transcending Of the self-Contraction) Is The Necessary "Environment" For The Fundamental Practice Of Devotionally Me-Recognizing and Devotionally To-Me-Responding Heart-Communion With Me—and Divine Ignorance Is The Most Ultimate Realization (or The Very Truth Of That "Radically" ego-Transcending Devotional—and, In Due Course, Progressively Spiritual—Practice).

Even Before The Process Of "Radical" Understanding (or Most Direct Transcending Of the self-Contraction) Has Become Complete (To The Inherently Most Perfect Degree), "Consideration" Of My Teaching-Argument Relative To Divine Ignorance Is Useful (During The Entire Course Of The Way Of The Heart, Even From The Beginning, In Both The Devotional Way Of Insight and The Devotional Way Of Faith), As A Complement To My Teaching-Argument Relative To "Radical" self-Understanding. Nevertheless, Practitioners Of The Only-By-Me Revealed and Given Way Of The Heart Must Eventually Fulfill The Obligation Of ego-Transcendence Relative To Each and All Of The First Six Stages Of Life—and Every Practitioner Of The Only-By-Me Revealed and Given Way Of The Heart Must Allow The, Necessarily, ego-Transcending Great Process Of Devotional and Spiritual Relationship To Me To Become Most Perfect Divine Self-Realization, By Means Of My Avatarically Self-Transmitted Divine Spiritual Grace.

If My Teaching-Argument Relative To Divine Ignorance Is Studied (and, Spontaneously, On Random Occasions, Without Strategy or Any Seeking Intention, Merely Tacitly "Considered") At and From The Beginning Of The Way Of The Heart, It Allows Occasional and Temporary Intuitive Glimpses (While the ego-"I" Otherwise Yet Remains Effective moment to moment) Of The (By-Me-Avatarically-Self-Revealed) Divine Self-Condition (Of Divine Ignorance) That Is The Self-Condition and Source-Condition Of all-and-All—and Those Intuitive Glimpses Act To Magnify and Perpetuate The Impulse (or Motive) Toward Most Perfectly ego-Transcending Real-God-Realization (or Most Perfect Divine Self-Realization). The (Thus Generated) Intuitive Glimpsing Of The Transcendental and Inherently Spiritual and Inherently egoless and

Self-Evidently Divine Self-Condition (Of Divine Ignorance) Can Be Regenerated (In any moment) By Generally (and In A Devotional Manner) Studying (and, Thus and Thereafter, Randomly Tacitly "Considering") My Teaching-Argument Relative To Divine Ignorance, and (On That Basis, and In any moment) Simply By Means Of ego-Surrendering, ego-Forgetting, and ego-Transcending Feeling-Contemplation Of My Divine-Ignorance-Revealing Bodily (Human) Divine Form. Similarly, Such Intuitive Glimpsing Of The By-Me-Avatarically-Self-Revealed Divine Self-Condition (Of Divine Ignorance) May, Also, Be Awakened (and Regenerated) In any moment Of Practice (In The Only-By-Me Revealed and Given Way Of The Heart) By Studying (and, Thus and Thereafter, Randomly, Spontaneously, Non-Strategically, Non-Intentionally—and, Thus, Merely Tacitly—"Considering") My Teaching-Argument Associated With The First Stage Of The "Perfect Practice" (or The Three-Stage Ultimate, and Inherently Perfect, Practice Of The Way Of The Heart). That Teaching-Argument (Associated With The First Stage Of The "Perfect Practice" Of The Way Of The Heart) Is Epitomized By The Proposition That, In this and every moment, No Matter what arises, You Are (Always Already) Standing In The Position Of The Mere and Conscious Witness Of body, mind, and conditions—and, Therefore, Are Inherently Free Of Identification With conditional Existence.

All Such (Preliminary, or Preparatory) Tacit Intuitive Glimpses Of The By-Me-Avatarically-Self-Revealed Divine Self-Condition (Of Divine Ignorance), and All My Teaching-Arguments That Permit (or conditionally Awaken) Those Intuitive Glimpses Of The By-Me-Avatarically-Self-Revealed Divine Self-Condition (Of Divine Ignorance), Are Useful Motivators Toward The Real Process Of Practice In The Only-By-Me Revealed and Given Way Of The Heart—but, Until (By Means Of My Avatarically Self-Transmitted Divine Spiritual Grace) That ego-Transcending Practice Fulfills Itself (In Real and Steady Transcending Of The egoic Motives, Illusions, Searches, and Attachments That Must Be Transcended As A Prerequisite For The Transition To The "Perfect Practice" Of The Way Of The Heart), My Teaching-Arguments Relative To Divine Ignorance and Consciousness Itself Are Only Temporary Awakeners That Point Toward (but Do Not Finally Establish) The "Perfect Practice" Of The Way Of The Heart.

The Sadhana (or ego-Transcending Process) Of The Only-By-Me Revealed and Given Way Of The Heart (or Way Of Adidam) Must Be Practiced Until No-Contraction, No-knowledge, and No-experience. That Is To Say, The Great Process Of ego-Transcendence Must Be Embraced From The Heart, Until (By Means Of My Avatarically Self-Transmitted Divine Spiritual Grace) There Really Is No Identification With the self-Contraction (or the Separate and Separative psycho-physical ego-"I" and the convention of subject-object experiencing and knowing), and There Really Is Consistent (and Inherently egoless) Self-Identification With Consciousness Itself (As It Is)—In The Devotional and Spiritual Condition Of Indivisible Oneness With Me (or Inherent Non-Separateness From Me, and Inherent Non-"Difference" From Me).

There Is No Separate Outside.
There Is Not anything or anyone Outside.
There Is No Not-self.
There Is No Separate Inside.
There Is No Separate Point Of View.
There Is No Separate Consciousness.
There Is No Separate self (or Inherently Existing ego-"I").
There Is Only What Is.
What Is Is Always Already
The (One and Only, Irreducible and Indestructible) Case.
There Is No Inside Relative To An Outside.
There Is No Outside Relative To An Inside.
Therefore, No Ingoing Is Necessary.
Likewise, No Outgoing Is Appropriate.
Both Inside and Outside Are Illusions Of One Another.
Both Inside and Outside Are Apparently Real,
but They Are Not Reality Itself.
Therefore, Be No one and Go No where.
Be all-and-All,
and Go There All At Once.
That Is To Say,
Be Only That Which Is
Always Already The Case.
What Is Always Already The Case?
"Consider" This At The Beginning.
Realize This At Last.
Realizing This Most Perfectly,
Divinely Self-Recognize all-and-All
In and As This.
Such Is (and Will Be)
The Nature Of The Only-By-Me Revealed and Given
Seventh Stage Realization Of Only Me.

If You Identify With the self-Contraction In this moment, Then You Will Also Seek Independence Through conceptual knowledge and Separative activity (or The Avoidance Of experiential Participation In perceptible conditional relations).

If You Understand and Feel Beyond the self-Contraction In this moment, Then You Are Presently Restored To Direct perception (or Participatory experience).

If the self-Contraction Is Utterly Transcended, Then Even Direct perception (or Participatory experience) Is Transcended.

If There Is No self-Contraction, Then perceptual and conceptual knowing, and perceptual and conceptual knowledge, and All Seeking For perceptual and conceptual knowledge Are Utterly and Inherently Transcended.

If There Is No self-Contraction, Then the Presumed perceptual and conceptual knower Is Utterly and Inherently Transcended.

If You (As A Present Realization, In The Context Of The Only-By-Me Revealed and Given "Perfect Practice" Of The Way Of The Heart) Do Not know What any thing or any one (Including Your Own body-mind) Is, Then all beings and things and conditions and events Merely (or Only) Are What they Are (In and As The By-Me-Avatarically-Self-Revealed Indivisible Oneness Of Real God). Then Even Your Own body-mind Is Only (and Non-Separately, and Inherently egolessly) As and What it Is.

Each and every being, thing, condition, or event (Including Your Own body-mind) Only Signifies (or Indicates, or Points To) itself as it (Naturally, or perceptually) is—and As it (Ultimately, or Merely) Is. What each and every being, thing, condition, or event (Ultimately) Is—and Even what each being, thing, condition, or event Naturally (or perceptually) is—Inherently and Naturally Transcends all Possible conditional experience or subject-object knowledge You Have (or Can Have) About it. If You Merely (Directly, and egolessly, or Without self-Contraction) perceive each and every being, thing, condition, or event (or Even every thought) that arises to Your attention—Such That You perceive (or Simply Grant attention To) each and every being, thing, condition, event, or thought as it (Apparently) is, You Are Inherently Free Of conceptual mind. Therefore, If You Directly perceive whatever arises, Then whatever arises Only Signifies (or Indicates, or Points To) itself, and No mind is arising To Separate You From it. And, Ultimately, By Virtue Of Your Most Ultimately Realizable (and Only-By-Me Revealed and Given Seventh Stage) Ability To Divinely Self-Recognize whatever arises, Even any conceptual thought that arises Will (Most Ultimately) Have No Power To Separate You From What Is (or From The Only One Who Is).

If, In any moment, You Tacitly Realize The Truth Of Divine Ignorance (or The Inherent State Of Non-knowing, or Of Freedom From the subject-object convention of the conditionally experiencing and conditionally knowing ego-"I"), You Tacitly Realize (For the moment) Inherent Freedom From conditional subjectivity (or Inwardness, or mind, or The Illusion Of a Separate

Inward self). You, as the conditional self, Are Simply the Total and Single body-mind (or the physically Apparent person). You Are Not Other Than the bodily self. You Are Simply the conditional bodily self—but You Must Grow (Beyond self-Contraction) To The Seventh Stage Realization Of Only Me, and (Thus and Thereby) To Inherently, and Inherently egolessly, and Always Immediately, and Really Un-conditionally (or Divinely) Self-Recognize What or Who the conditional bodily self Is (Altogether, Really, and Ultimately). And You Cannot Realize What or Who You Are (or What or Who any one or any thing or any condition or any event Is) By Seeking conditional and subject-object conventional knowledge About Your conditional self (or About others, or About conditions anywhere). If You Inherently Do Not know Even What any condition or any thing or any one Is, Then You Cannot know What Your knowledge About any condition, or any thing, or any one Is—and The Search For Ultimate knowledge Is, Therefore, Futile.

The Realization Of What or Who You Are Can Only Be A Matter Of Seventh Stage Direct (and Self-Abiding) Divine Self-Recognition Of Your conditional bodily self, Rather Than any conditional and conventional (or subject-object) knowledge About it (Since You Could Not Even know What that knowledge Is). And Direct (Self-Abiding) Divine Self-Recognition Of Your conditional bodily self Cannot Be Realized Until There Is No Contraction Of and From the conditional bodily self (For Any Such Contraction Is Dissociation From the conditional bodily self As it Is). Mere, Direct, or Natural perception of Your conditional bodily self Is The Necessary Prerequisite For Direct (Self-Abiding) Divine Self-Recognition Of Your conditional bodily self (For Only Such Mere, Direct, or Natural perception Is Naturally Free Of subjectivity, or Separate and Separative mind, or Attachment To The Illusion Of a Separate internal essence). Conditional Existence Can Be Transcended Only Directly, or When the conditional bodily self Is Directly perceived (Without Any Effort Of Separation or Contraction From it) and (Thereupon) Inherently Divinely Self-Recognized, In and As The By-Me-Avatarically-Self-Revealed Unconditional (or Transcendental), Inherently Spiritual, Inherently egoless, and Self-Evidently Divine Self-Condition (and Source-Condition) That Is Consciousness (or Self-Existing and Self-Radiant Being—or Conscious Light) Itself. And These Complementary Realizations Of No-Contraction and Inherent (and, Thus, Divine) Ignorance (or Transcendental, Inherently Spiritual, and, Most Ultimately, Divine Self-Realization) Must Progressively Mature In The Only-By-Me Revealed and Given Way Of The Heart (or Way Of Adidam), In The Context Of Each and All Of The First Six Stages Of Life—Until (By Means Of My Avatarically Self-Transmitted Divine Spiritual Grace) Realization Becomes Inherent, Inherently egoless, Inherently Most

Perfect, and "Open-Eyed" Seventh Stage Realization Of The Truth That Is Divine Ignorance.

I Have Given The "Consideration" Of Divine Ignorance To All My Devotees who Have Not Yet Realized The Only-By-Me Revealed and Given Seventh Stage Of Life, Because It Is they who Do Not know What (or Who—or Where, or When, or How, or Why) any thing Is. In The Only-By-Me Revealed and Given Seventh Stage Of Life (In The Way Of The Heart), It Is Inherently and Tacitly Obvious What (and Who—and Where, and When, and How, and Why) every thing Is—and, Therefore, In The Only-By-Me Revealed and Given Seventh Stage Of Life (In The Way Of The Heart), Divine Ignorance Ceases To Be A "Consideration".

Not knowing What any thing Is is the self-Contraction. Therefore, The Study (and Random, Spontaneous, Tacit "Consideration") Of My Argument Relative To Divine Ignorance Is A By-Me-Given Means Of Randomly Noticing That You Are Standing In the position of the self-Contraction. As Long As You Stand As the ego-"I", You Can know About what arises, and You Can Become Entangled In it and Bound By it, but You Cannot know What it Is—You Cannot Divinely Self-Recognize it, or Most Perfectly Transcend it.

Apart From The Samadhi Of Most Perfectly Self-Identifying With Me—Which Is Most Ultimate Divine Self-Realization (In The Only-By-Me Revealed and Given Seventh Stage Of Life In The Way Of The Heart)—the Apparent individual Does Not Divinely Self-Recognize any thing As What it Is. Indeed, The Inability To Inherently and Un-conditionally (and, Thus, Divinely) Self-Recognize conditional arising Is The Principal Characteristic Sign (or Symptom) Of egoity.

Egoity Is self-Contraction, The Act (or The Action) Of (Apparent) Separation From The Condition That Is (or The Act, or Action, Of Separateness Itself, In and By Which The Condition That Is Becomes Unknown, and, Apparently, Unknowable). Nevertheless, egoity Is (itself) Merely A Play Upon What Is (or A Play Upon Existence, Itself, or Being, Itself)—and, Therefore, Because Existence (Itself) or Being (Itself) Is Never An Object To Itself, the ego-"I" Cannot Inspect What Is (or Inspect Existence, Itself, or Being, Itself) As Is. However, Because Divine Self-Realization Is Inherent Realization Of Existence (Itself), or Of Being (Itself), or Of What Is (As Is), Always Already Prior To Separation, Separateness, Relatedness, and "Difference", every thing Merely Is, and every thing Is Inherently (and Divinely) Self-Recognized, When There Is The Awakening (From the ego-"I") To The By-Me-Avatarically-Self-Revealed Divine Self-Condition and Source-Condition.

When egoity Is Most Perfectly Transcended (In Most Perfect Realization Of The By-Me-Avatarically-Self-Revealed Divine Self-Condition and Source-Condition), every thing Is Divinely Self-Recognized As What it Is. Thus, In The Only-By-Me Revealed and Given Seventh Stage Of Life (In The Way Of The Heart), every thing Is Divinely Self-Recognized, As A Transparent (or Merely Apparent), and Un-Necessary, and Inherently Non-Binding Modification Of The By-Me-Avatarically-Self-Revealed Divine Self-Condition, and Source-Condition, Itself (or Of Existence, or Being, Itself, or Of The "Bright" Itself), Which Is Self-Existing and Self-Radiant, One and Only, Without Center or Bounds. And, In This (Most Perfect) Sense, My Any Devotee who Realizes The Only-By-Me Revealed and Given Seventh Stage Of Life (In The Way Of The Heart) Knows (With Perfect Certainty) What every thing Is.

The Original Process Whereby This Inherently Most Perfect Simplicity Is Awakened In The Way Of The Heart Is The Foundation Devotional and (In Due Course) Spiritual Process Of Listening To Me (To The Degree Of Hearing Me, or Real and Most Fundamental self-Understanding), Whereby (To A Significant Degree) The Student-Beginner, and Then The Beginning Practitioner, Of The Way Of The Heart Is (Readily, In every moment Of Effective Practice Of Either The Only-By-Me Revealed and Given Devotional Way Of Insight Or The Only-By-Me Revealed and Given Devotional Way Of Faith) Restored To The Participatory (or ego-Transcending) Disposition, Grounded In perception (or The Natural Attitude Of the Total body-mind), and Naturally Able To Stand Free Of Compulsive and Obsessive verbal (and Otherwise Abstract and Analytical) thinking (or The Search To know).

The Me-Realizing Process Of ego-Transcendence Develops Further In The Would-Be-Seeing (or Progressively Seeing) Stage and The First Actually Seeing Stage Of The Way Of The Heart. In Those Stages, The Invasion and Pervasion Of the body-mind Of My Devotee By My Avatarically Self-Transmitted Divine Spirit-Presence Is (By Means Of The Exercise Of The Hearing-Capability Of Most Fundamental self-Understanding, and By Means Of The Exercise Of Full Technical Responsibility For The Frontal "Conductivity" Of My Avatarically Self-Transmitted Divine Spirit-Current Of Love-Bliss) Extended Beyond My By-Me-Spiritually-Initiated Listening Devotee's Participation In The Process Stimulated and Enacted By My Avatarically Self-Transmitted Divine Spirit-Baptism. Thus, The Fundamental Heart-Confession and Feeling-Attitude (or Devotional "Asana") Of My Would-Be-Seeing and (Eventually) Actually Seeing Devotee Is (More and More) That Of Direct Identification With The Feeling-Essence (or Inherent Love-Bliss) Of My Avatarically Self-Transmitted Divine Spirit-Current Itself.

In Due Course, As My Actually Seeing Devotee Progresses Through The Frontal Yoga and (Then) Into The Foundation Depth Of The "Perfect Practice" Of The Way Of The Heart, Even the Total experiential and Participatory (or self-Contraction-Transcending) body-mind Is Progressively and Directly Transcended In The Gradual Deepening Of "Radical" (or "Gone-To-The-Root") self-Understanding—Until, At Last (In The Only-By-Me Revealed and Given Awakening To The Seventh Stage Of Life), There Is (By My Avatarically Self-Transmitted Divine Spiritual Grace) Most Perfect Realization Of "Radical" Understanding (and, Necessarily, Most Perfect Realization Of Divine Ignorance), Which Is Inherent and Transcendental (and Inherently Spiritual) Divine Self-Realization.

AVATAR ADI DA SAMRAJ
The Mountain Of Attention Sanctuary, 2000

SUTRA

26

The Way I Have Revealed and Given Is Not Any Form Of Seeking. The Way I Have Revealed and Given Is, Most Fundamentally, A Matter Of Merely Beholding Me.

To Merely Behold Me Is To Be Constantly Engaged In Devotional Resort To Me. Merely Beholding Me Is The Fundamental (and Always Primary) Practice Of The Only-By-Me Revealed and Given Way Of The Heart (or Way Of Adidam, or Adidam Ruchiradam).

The Only-By-Me Revealed and Given Way Of The Heart (or Way Of Adidam, or Adidam Ruchiradam) Is Searchless Beholding Of Me, Without self-Reference or Strategic self-Manipulation, and (Altogether) Such That My Avataric Divine Spiritual Blessing Is Effortlessly and Tangibly Experienced. My Devotee Must Always See To It That the body-mind Is functionally, practically, relationally, and Culturally Prepared For This (On The Basis Of Previous Fulfillment Of The Requirements For Formal Practice Beyond The Student-Beginner—or Initial, Merely Preliminary, and Entirely Preparatory—Stage Of The Only-By-Me Revealed and Given Way Of The Heart). And, In Order To Enter Into (and, Thereafter, To Continue In) The Spiritual Practice Of Searchlessly Beholding Me, My Any Devotee Must Be Formally Approved To Do So By The Ruchira Sannyasin Order Of Adidam Ruchiradam, and (Thereupon) Formally Registered With The Avataric Samrajya Of Adidam As So Approved,[72] In Accordance With The Qualifications I Will Describe In This, My Divine Testament.[73]

The Spiritual Process In My Avataric Divine Company Is A Matter Of Being Inherently Surrendered To Me, Merely By Virtue Of Turning the body-mind (or Every Faculty and function) Entirely To Me. The Spiritual Process In My Avataric Divine Company Is Not About the egoic self. The Spiritual Process In My Avataric Divine Company Is Not Even An Effort Of the egoic self. The Spiritual Process In My Avataric Divine Company Is Effortless Attending To Me, Without Turning In On oneself. The Spiritual Process In My Avataric Divine Company Is A Matter Of Relinquishing All Seeking—and This Merely By Beholding Me and (Thereby) Relaxing All Effort To Do Something To oneself (or About one's "Problems").

Therefore, The Primary and Fundamental Practice Of Devotion To Me—Which Is The Fully Established Yoga Of Ruchira Avatara Bhakti, or The Searchless Surrender Of attention, body, emotion, and breath To Me—Is Not To Be Done As An Exercise Of Strategic (or ego-Bound and ego-Binding) self-Effort. That Searchless self-Surrender Is Done By bodily Facing My Avatarically-Born Bodily (Human) Divine Form, While Maintaining A Relaxed Eyes-Open Gaze (Unless or Until The Force Of My Spiritual Invasion Causes the eyes Spontaneously To Close), and (Thus and Thereby) Simply Allowing Yourself To Be Receptively attentive To Me, and To Receptively Feel Me, and To Receptively Breathe Me. Most Fundamentally, That Searchless self-Surrender Is A Matter Of Beholding My Avatarically-Born Bodily (Human) Divine Form—and (Thus and Thereby) Of Being Simply and Openly attentive (and Spontaneously Attracted) To Me, Without The Addition Of Any Other Kind Of Technical Practice. Such Simple Ruchira Avatara Bhakti (or Tacit and Natural Devotional Practice) Is An Effortless Presentation Of the body-mind (Of Four Faculties) Of My Devotee To My Avatarically-Born Bodily (Human) Divine Form—and, Only Thus (and Entirely Thereby), To My Avatarically Self-Transmitted Spiritual (and Always Blessing) Divine Presence, and To My Avatarically Self-Revealed (and Very, and Transcendental, and Perfectly Subjective, and Inherently Spiritual, and Inherently egoless, and Inherently Perfect, and Self-Evidently Divine) State. In So Doing, the Total body-mind (Of Four Faculties) Of My Devotee Should Be Naturally Relaxed, and Tacitly Open (In A Calmly Receptive, or Searchlessly Attending, Manner) To My Avatarically-Born and Divinely "Bright" Bodily (Human) Form (In Front Of his or her own eyes) and To The Potential experiential Manifestation Of My Avatarically Self-Transmitted Divine Spirit-Current Of "Bright" Love-Bliss (In Whatever Manner I May Choose or Appear To Be So Manifested).

Thus, The Primary Dimension Of The Fully Established Practice Of The Only-By-Me Revealed and Given Way Of The Heart (or Way Of Adidam, or Adidam Ruchiradam) Is Searchless Satsang With Me. The Essence Of Satsang With Me Is No-Seeking, By Means Of Mere Beholding (Of Me). The Primary Practice Of The Only-By-Me Revealed and Given Way Of The Heart Is (Thus, In Effect) To Perform The Sacrament Of Universal Sacrifice, Such That All Four Faculties Are Simply Attending (Receptively) To My Avatarically-Born and Divinely "Bright" Bodily (Human) Form—Without Any Added Effort or Technical Exercise.

My Devotee Prepares himself or herself For This Primary Practice (Of "No Seeking/Mere Beholding") In The Student-Beginner Stage Of The Only-By-Me Revealed and Given Way Of The Heart. The (Devotionally Active, but Not Yet By-Me-Spiritually-Initiated) "Outer Temple"[74] Of Student-Beginner Practice Is Where The Foundation Of Right Life Is Established—Through The Basic

Exercise Of Fundamental Right Devotion To Me (Which Is The Beginning Practice Of Ruchira Avatara Bhakti Yoga, or The Surrender Of The Four Principal psycho-physical Faculties In Devotional Resort To Me) and The Basic Adaptation To The By-Me-Given functional, practical, and relational Modes Of Disciplining gross egoity, and (Also) To The By-Me-Given Cultural Disciplines (Including The Rudimentary Exercise Of The "Conscious Process" and "Conductivity" Practice).

My Devotee Becomes Rightly and Fully Established In The Primary Practice Of Searchlessly Beholding Me By Coming Into My Avataric Physical Human Company (or, After My Avataric Physical Human Lifetime, Into The physical human Company and By-Me-Spiritually-Empowered Circumstances Of My "Ruchira Sannyasin" Devotees) On Extended Formal Retreat, For The Purpose Of Spiritual Initiation, By Me, Into The Process Of Receiving My Ruchira Shaktipat. All Other (or Technical) Practices Of The Only-By-Me Revealed and Given Way Of The Heart Follow, <u>Responsively</u>, Upon Reception Of My Tangible Experiential Avataric Transmission Of My Own Spirit-Current Of Divine Love-Bliss-Person (or Ruchira Shaktipat), Given and Received In The Context Of This Primary Practice (Of Searchless Beholding Of My Avatarically-Born Bodily Human Divine Form). And, In Order To Enter Into The Circumstance Of My Ruchira Shaktipat Initiation, My Devotee Must Have Fully Adapted To The Full Range Of The By-Me-Given Foundation (functional, practical, relational, and Cultural) Disciplines Of The Only-By-Me Revealed and Given Way Of The Heart—and (On That Basis) he or she Must Be Formally Approved and Invited (To Enter Into The Circumstance Of My Ruchira Shaktipat Initiation) By The Ruchira Sannyasin Order Of Adidam Ruchiradam.

Searchless Beholding Of Me Is A Spiritual Matter. Searchless Beholding Of Me Allows You To Receive My Avataric Divine Gift Of Whole bodily (or Total psycho-physical) Reception Of The Self-Existing and Self-Radiant Divine Conscious Light Of My Own Spiritually Self-"Bright" Person. Ruchira Shaktipat (or Hridaya-Shaktipat) Is The Process (or Mechanism) By Which I Spiritually Transmit My Divine Conscious Light Into the conditionally Manifested realms.

Thus, Fully Established Practice Of The Only-By-Me Revealed and Given Way Of The Heart Is, Altogether, A Practice Engaged Within My Ruchira Shaktipat Circumstance. The Only-By-Me Revealed and Given Way Of The Heart Is Not A Technique, but A <u>Relationship</u>. The Only-By-Me Revealed and Given Way Of The Heart Is A Relationship (To Me) In Which I Spiritually Transmit Myself To You, and You Receive (and Respond To) My Avataric Divine Spiritual Self-Transmission (or Ruchira Shaktipat).

The Only-By-Me Revealed and Given Way Of The Heart <u>Is</u> Searchless Beholding Of Me. Searchless Beholding Of Me <u>Is</u> The Essence Of Satsang With

Me. Searchless Beholding Of Me Is Heart-Recognition Of Me. Searchless Beholding Of Me Is The Fully Developed Essence Of Ruchira Avatara Bhakti Yoga. Searchless Beholding Of Me Is Participation In My Avataric Divine Spiritual Self-Transmission.

The Only-By-Me Revealed and Given Way Of The Heart Is (Fundamentally, and Altogether) The Way (or Total Practice) Of Searchless Beholding Of Me—The Searchless Beholding Of My Own and Human and Very and (Altogether) Avatarically Self-Revealed and Self-Evidently Divine Person. I Am Whole, One, Non-Separate, and Indivisible. Therefore, For My Devotee who Searchlessly Beholds Me, There Is No Effort To Use One or Another Faculty Of the being, or One or Another Mode Of experiencing, As A Strategic Means To Realize Me. I Can Be Realized Only By Means Of My Avatarically Self-Transmitted Divine Spiritual Grace, Made Effective Through The Searchless Availability Of My Devotee. And, When My Devotee Rightly, Truly, Fully, and Fully Devotionally Responds To Me, By Accommodating My Whole Person, My Avataric Divine Self-Revelation (Given By Means Of My Avataric Divine Spiritual Transmission) Carries With It All The Details Of Necessary Practice By Which To Grow In The Only-By-Me Revealed and Given Spiritual, Transcendental, and Divine Process Of Realizing Me.

There Are Three Fundamental Dimensions Of The Only-By-Me Revealed and Given Way Of The Heart (Which Is The Way Of The Devotional and Spiritual Relationship To Me).

The First (or Principal, and Primary) Dimension Of The Only-By-Me Revealed and Given Way Of The Heart Is Mere (or Searchless, and Total psycho-physical) Recognition (or Mere Beholding and Searchless Spiritual Reception) Of Me As The Spiritually "Bright" Divine Person In Avatarically Self-Manifested Bodily (Human) Form. Once There Is Formal and True Spiritual Initiation Into The Beginnings Of This Primary Practice, Through Direct Experiential (and Tangible) Reception Of My Ruchira Shaktipat (or My Avataric Self-Transmission Of The Spirit-Current Of Divine Self-"Brightness")—Either In My Avataric Physical Human Company or, After My Avataric Physical Human Lifetime, By Resort To Me In and By Means Of The physical human Company and By-Me-Spiritually-Empowered Circumstances Of My "Ruchira Sannyasin" Devotees—My Devotee Must, Thereafter, Cultivate The Reception Of My Ruchira Shaktipat By Resorting To Me, In The Same Manner, moment to moment, and In Regular daily Circumstances Of Formal Meditation and Sacramental Worship (Including Devotional Chanting), In The Context Of The Sacrament Of Universal Sacrifice, In A Sacredly Set-Apart Environment, and By Means Of Murti Images (Typically, In The Form Of photographic Likenesses) Of Me. And, Once There Is Formal and True Spiritual Initiation Into The

Beginnings Of This Primary Practice, Through Direct Experiential (and Tangible) Reception Of My Ruchira Shaktipat, Receptivity To My Avataric Self-Transmission Of The Tangible Spirit-Current Of Divine Self-"Brightness" Must, With Maximum Possible Frequency, Be Cultivated, and (By Me) Refreshed and Magnified—By Resort To My Avataric Physical Human Company (or, After My Avataric Physical Human Lifetime, By Resort To Me In and By Means Of The physical human Company and By-Me-Spiritually-Empowered Circumstances Of My "Ruchira Sannyasin" Devotees). This Total Practice Of Avataric Recognition (or Mere Beholding and True Spiritual Reception) Of Me Is The Core Practice Of Satsang With Me.

The Second and Third Dimensions Of The Full (Devotional and Spiritual) Practice Of The Only-By-Me Revealed and Given Way Of The Heart (Together) Comprise All The Various By-Me-Given Technical Practices That Are Engaged In Response To My Avatarically-Born Bodily (Human) Divine Form and My Tangibly Experienced Ruchira Shaktipat. The Second Dimension Of The Full (Devotional and Spiritual) Practice Of The Only-By-Me Revealed and Given Way Of The Heart Is The (Responsive) "Conscious Process", and The Third Dimension Of The Full (Devotional and Spiritual) Practice Of The Only-By-Me Revealed and Given Way Of The Heart Is (Responsive) "Conductivity" Practice.

Thus, The Three Fundamental Dimensions Of The Devotional and Spiritual Relationship To Me Are: Satsang With Me (Which Is, In Its Essence, Mere, or Searchless, or Searchlessly Receptive, Beholding Of Me), and The "Conscious Process", and "Conductivity" Practice.

The Second and Third (Inherently Co-Equal) Dimensions (or The "Conscious Process" and "Conductivity" Practice) Are Necessarily Associated With (and Founded Upon) The First Dimension (Which Is Satsang With Me, or Searchless Beholding and Spiritual Reception Of Me). Satsang With Me (or Searchless Beholding and Spiritual Reception Of Me) Is What Makes The Practice Of The Only-By-Me Revealed and Given Way Of The Heart ego-Transcending, Rather Than ego-Referring (or A Form Of Seeking).

Satsang With Me (or Searchless Beholding and Spiritual Reception Of Me) Is Not Merely The Practice Of Sitting In A Room With Me. Satsang With Me (or Searchless Beholding and Spiritual Reception Of Me) Is ego-Transcending Devotional Recognition Of (and Total psycho-physical Receptivity To, and Spontaneous Spiritual Communion With) My Avatarically Self-Revealed Divine Form and Presence and State. Therefore, Satsang With Me (or Mere Beholding and Spiritual Reception Of Me) Is Inherently Searchless—or A Matter Of (Merely) Spiritually "Locating" Me, Rather Than Seeking For Me.

Such ego-Transcending Devotional Recognition Of Me (and Total psycho-physical Receptivity To Me) Is, By Grace Of My Avatarically Self-Transmitted

Divine Ruchira Shaktipat, Shown The Spontaneous Revelation Of ego-Transcending Spiritual Communion With My Avatarically Self-Revealed Human, and Self-Evidently Divine, Person. Without Such Profundity Of ego-Transcending Devotional Recognition Of Me, ego-Transcending psycho-physical Receptivity To Me, and ego-Transcending Spiritual Communion With Me, There Is No True Satsang With Me, No Truly Me-Realizing Practice Of The Only-By-Me Revealed and Given Way Of The Heart.

Such True Satsang With Me Is The Devotional and Spiritual Relationship To Me—Merely Beholding Me, Resorting To Me, Being attentive To Me, Via All The Faculties Of the body-mind, Open and Receptive To Me In A Natural Manner. This Is The Basic, or Primary, Practice Of The Only-By-Me Revealed and Given Way Of The Heart. The "Conscious Process" and "Conductivity" Practice Are Responsive Developments Of That Basic and Primary and Inherently Searchless Practice.

The Primary Practice—Once It Is Established In Spiritual Communion With Me, By Means Of My Ruchira Shaktipat—Must Be Engaged moment to moment, In every circumstance. This Primary (Searchlessly Me-Beholding) Practice Is The Fully Developed Essence Of Ruchira Avatara Bhakti (or The Profound ego-Surrendering Directedness Of The Four Principal Faculties To Me). The Primary Practice Always Remains Primary—At Every Stage In The Only-By-Me Revealed and Given Way Of The Heart. The Practices Of The "Conscious Process" and Of "Conductivity" Are The Technical Exercises Of Response To Me (and, Thus, To My Avatarically Self-Revealed Human, and Self-Evidently Divine, Person—and To My Avataric Divine Self-Revelation Given By The Avataric Divine Spiritual Means Of My Ruchira Shaktipat). And These Exercises (Which Are To Be Engaged At Random, In any moment, As Required—On The Basis Of, and Entirely In Response To, The Avataric Divine Spiritual Transmission Of My Person, Really Experienced In The Otherwise moment to moment Exercise Of The Primary Practice, Of Searchlessly Beholding Me) Are Given In Various and Developing Forms, To Be Variously Applied, As Instructed By Me, At The Various Stages Of The Only-By-Me Revealed and Given Way Of The Heart.

In The Only-By-Me Revealed and Given Way Of The Heart, There Are No Practices That Are Independent Of The Devotional and (In Due Course) Spiritual Relationship To Me. For My By-Me-Spiritually-Initiated (and Always Newly By-Me-Spiritually-Activated) Devotees, Satsang With Me (or Searchless Beholding and Spiritual Reception Of Me) Necessarily Precedes (and Is The Searchless Basis Of) Any and Every Other (Responsive, or Technical) Form Of Practice Given By Me.

Thus, For My By-Me-Spiritually-Initiated (and Always Newly By-Me-Spiritually-Activated) Devotees, Satsang With Me (or Searchless Beholding and

Spiritual Reception Of Me) Is Always The Primary Practice, and The "Conscious Process" and "Conductivity" Practice Are Always Entirely Responsive Practices. Therefore, My By-Me-Spiritually-Initiated (and Always Newly By-Me-Spiritually-Activated) Devotee Always Merely Beholds Me, Without Any Effort Of Seeking—Engaging The Responsive Practices Only (and Searchlessly) On The Basis Of That Mere Beholding and Spiritual Reception Of Me. This Is What Makes The Only-By-Me Revealed and Given Way Of The Heart An Inherently ego-Transcending (and Inherently Searchless) Devotional and Spiritual Relationship To Me, Rather Than A self-Applied (and, Necessarily, ego-Based and Merely Seeking) System Of Strategies and Techniques.

In The Fully Established Practice Of The Only-By-Me Revealed and Given Way Of The Heart (Beyond The Student-Beginner Stage, Of Foundation Preparations), The "Conscious Process" and "Conductivity" Practice Are Never To Be Engaged For Their Own Sake (or For The Sake Of Any Proposed Goals Of Seeking). Any Such Strategic Technical Practice Is A Form Of Seeking (or ego-Effort, or self-"guruing"). In The Fully Established Practice Of The Only-By-Me Revealed and Given Way Of The Heart, It Is Only When There Is present-time Tangible Spiritual Awareness Of Me (In The Context Of The Always First, or Primary, Practice, Of Merely, or Searchlessly, Beholding Me) That The Responsive Technical Practices Of The "Conscious Process" and "Conductivity" Are To Be Engaged. Without (Thus—or First, and Only By Means Of The Primary and Searchless Practice) Spiritually "Locating" Me (In any moment), You (As A Fully Established Practitioner Of The Only-By-Me Revealed and Given Way Of The Heart) Have No present-time Basis For Rightly Engaging The Responsive Practices—but, When You Do (In any moment, and Thus—or First, and Searchlessly) Spiritually "Locate" Me (In any moment), Then There Is The Basis For Rightly Engaging The Responsive Practices, Because (In That Case) They Are Not ego-Based Exercises, or Mere (and ego-Reinforcing) Techniques For Seeking.

The "Conscious Process" Is To-Me-Responsive Practice Related To The Faculty Of attention (and To Consciousness Itself). "Conductivity" Practice (As I Will Describe It, In Detail, In This, My Testament Of Secrets) Is To-Me-Responsive Practice Related To The Energy-Sensitive Faculties Of feeling, body, and breath (or All The Faculties That "Follow" The Faculty Of attention). In The Only-By-Me Revealed and Given Way Of The Heart, The Artfully Combined (and, Altogether, To-Me-Responsive) Practice Of The "Conscious Process" and "Conductivity" Is A Perpetual Counter-egoic Discipline, Always To Be Practiced In Accordance With My Formally Communicated Instructions, and Exercised Both In the circumstances of daily life and In Formal Meditation—By Randomly Introducing, and Artfully Combining, The Modes

Of The "Conscious Process" and Of "Conductivity" Practice For Which My Devotee Is Formally Both Responsible and Culturally Accountable At his or her Present Stage Of Practice Of The Only-By-Me Revealed and Given Way Of The Heart.

In The Only-By-Me Revealed and Given Way Of The Heart, The Combined (and, Thus, Effectively, Single) Practice Of The "Conscious Process" and "Conductivity" Is Not A Means To Manipulate the body-mind In Order To self-Generate ego-Consoling experiences, or To Effect Some Form Of self-Modification. Any Effort To Manipulate the body-mind (or To Generate Consoling psycho-physical experiences, or To Modify the Apparently Separate self) Is (Necessarily) an ego-Based activity, A Form Of Seeking.

I Have Not Given You Any ego-Based Techniques. I Have Not Given You a mere "philosophy". I Do Not Call You To Seek Me—or, Otherwise, To Seek Toward Any Proposed Goal. I Always Call You To Understand (and To Always Immediately Transcend) The Attitude and The Method Of The Search (or Of Seeking) Itself. I Always Call You To Understand (and To Always Immediately Transcend) the ego-"I" (or egoity, or self-Contraction) itself—Because the ego-"I" (which is The Always present-time Act Of Separation, and Of Separateness, and Of Separativeness) Is, itself, the "point of view", The conditional Originator, and The Very Motive and Principal Content Of All Seeking. Therefore, Instead Of Calling You To Seek, I Always Only Avatarically Reveal (and Freely Give) To You My Own Human, Transcendental, Inherently Spiritual, Inherently egoless, and Self-Evidently Divine Person. And I Always Only Avatarically Reveal (and Freely Give) To You The Avataric Divine Way Of Devotional (and, In Due Course, Spiritual) Recognition-Response To Me.

The Various Foundation Practices (or functional, practical, relational, and Cultural Disciplines) Given By Me (For Responsible and Formally Culturally Accountable Application By All My Devotees Before—and Always, Forever, After—they Are Given The Gift Of Access To Me For The Sake Of Directly Beholding Me and Receiving My Ruchira Shaktipat) Are Simply Means For Preparing the body-mind (Of My Any and Every Student-Beginner Devotee) To Be Capable (and For Constantly Maintaining The Capability) Of Unobstructed Devotional and Spiritual Sensitivity To Me (Beyond The Student-Beginner Stage Of The Only-By-Me Revealed and Given Way Of The Heart).

The human being Functions Through Four Principal Faculties (Which, Together, Comprehensively Comprise The psycho-physical Totality Of the human functional entity). The Four Dimensions Of the human functional entity Are the function of attention (which Is The Root and Context Of mind), the functional gross physical body, the function of emotion (or feeling), and the cyclic function of breathing. My Avatarically Self-Transmitted Spiritual (and Always Blessing) Divine Presence Must Be Tangibly Perceived and Experienced—Through The Mere Beholding Of Me (or The Merely To-Me-Attracted Surrender Of The Four Faculties To Me), With No Seeking. Then, On That Basis, My By-Me-Spiritually-Initiated (and Always Newly By-Me-Spiritually-Activated) Devotee Is Instructed To Responsively Engage The Forms Of The "Conscious Process" and Of "Conductivity" Practice I Have Given For his or her Stage and Manner Of Practice In The Only-By-Me Revealed and Given Way Of The Heart. Therefore—Except For The Basic Foundation Responsibilities Of functional, practical, relational, and Cultural self-Discipline (Which Must Be Always Responsibly Perpetuated, Once They Are Embraced, Through Study and Adaptation, In The Student-Beginner Stage Of Practice Of The Only-By-Me Revealed and Given Way Of The Heart)—The Responsive Practices (Of The True "Conscious Process" and Technical "Conductivity") Are (Beyond The Student-Beginner Experiment and First Application) To Be Engaged Only When There Is Already A Clear Sign Of My Spiritual Invasion Of the gross body-mind.

My Avataric Divine Spiritual Self-Transmission Is Not Natural energy in the gross body-mind. The Way Of My Avataric Divine Spiritual Self-Transmission Is Not A "do-it-yourself" Technique, or An ego-Based Program Of Seeking.

My Avataric Divine Spiritual Self-Transmission Is A Specific and Tangible Manifestation Of My Own Self-"Bright" Person. My Avataric Divine Spiritual Self-Transmission Is, Most Fundamentally, To Be Received (or Tangibly Experienced) By Means Of The Gift Of Merely Beholding Me. Only I Give This Gift To You. Only I Can Give This Gift To You. And, Once You Have Begun To Receive This Gift From Me, You (In Turn) Must, Constantly, Cultivate My Gift (To You) Through Your Right Gifts (To Me) Of Practice and Service.

The Only-By-Me Revealed and Given Way Of The Heart Is The Divine Shaktipat Way—or The Ruchira Shaktipat Way. The Only-By-Me Revealed and Given Way Of The Heart Is Not Merely An Accumulation Of Religious and Spiritual Techniques. The Only-By-Me Revealed and Given Way Of The Heart Is Not A Matter Of conventional (or ego-Based and emotionalistic) devotionalism. The Only-By-Me Revealed and Given Way Of The Heart Is Based Entirely On My Avataric Divine Spiritual Self-Transmission (or Ruchira Shaktipat). Therefore, The Fundamental Context For Practice Of The Devotional and Spiritual Relationship To Me (or Fully Established Ruchira Avatara Bhakti Yoga) Is The Transmission (or Ruchira Avatara Satsang and Ruchira Shaktipat) Circumstance. All Aspects Of The Fully Established Technical Practice Of The Only-By-Me Revealed and Given Way Of The Heart Are Engaged In Response To My Avataric Divine Spiritual Self-Transmission (or Ruchira Shaktipat).

Spiritual Communion With Me Is Searchlessness, Established As Me-Recognizing Devotional Relationship To Me—Because That Practice (In Its

Primary Form and In Its Responsive Forms) Is Associated With My Avataric Divine Spiritual Self-Transmission and My Freely Given Avataric Divine Spiritual Self-Revelation. For My By-Me-Spiritually-Initiated (and Always Newly By-Me-Spiritually-Activated) Devotees, Satsang With Me, or Darshan Of Me, Is Spiritually Active Devotional Recognition Of Me, or Searchless Receptive Participation In My (Experientially Tangible) Avataric Divine Spiritual Self-Transmission.

The Only-By-Me Revealed and Given Way Of The Heart Is Not To Be Equated With The Fifth Stage Orientation Of Traditional Kundalini Yoga—or With The Characteristic Orientation Of Any Tradition That Begins From Below (and In Duality, or In the egoic domains of "point of view") and Seeks To Ascend By Whatever Means. My Avataric Divine Spiritual Self-Transmission Comes From Above and Beyond—Above and Beyond the head, Above and Beyond the mind, Above and Beyond the body-mind (Altogether).

Therefore, My Avataric Divine Spiritual Transmission-Work Is To Be Understood In The Unique Seventh Stage Terms I Have Described, and Not Merely In Fifth Stage Terms. Nevertheless, It Must Also Be Understood (and Never Forgotten) That The Only-By-Me Revealed and Given Way Of The Heart Is The All-Completing Divine Form Of The Ancient Tradition Of Guru-Devotion, Shaktipat, and Siddha Yoga. Therefore, I Have Called My Devotees To Study The Teachings Of My Lineage-Gurus, Even While My Devotees Constantly Recognize Me Uniquely As The Avatarically-Born Divine Manifestation Of The "Bright"—The Siddha Of The "Bright" (or The Ruchira Siddha), Who Has Revealed and Given The Siddha Yoga Of The "Bright" (or Ruchira Siddha Yoga).

My Devotees May Experience Signs In The Manner Of The Kundalini Process, Because My Avataric Divine Spiritual Self-Transmission Is All-Inclusive and All-Transcending—but My Avataric Divine Spiritual Self-Transmission Does Not Come From any point Below. My Avataric Divine Spiritual Self-Transmission Comes From Infinitely Above, and Invades All Below—everything gross, subtle, and causal.

Ruchira Avatara Bhakti Yoga Is, In Its Fully Developed Essence, Simply Searchless Beholding Of Me, Attending To Me Until There Is The Tangible Experience Of My Avataric Divine Spiritual Presence. Therefore, Ruchira Avatara Bhakti Yoga Is Free Of self-"guruing", Free Of wishful thinking, Free Of self-Generated arousal of the body-mind. Altogether, Ruchira Avatara Bhakti Yoga Is <u>Not</u> A Matter Of egoically self-Stimulating The Natural-energy-Potential Of body, brain, and mind.

In Due Course, My Avataric Divine Spiritual Self-Transmission Shows More and More Profound Signs In The gross, subtle, and causal Dimensions Of the being—If My Avataric Divine Spiritual Self-Transmission Is Constantly

Cultivated By My Devotee, and If My Avataric Divine Spiritual Self-Transmission Is, With Maximized Frequency, Directly Renewed and Magnified By Me (Either By My Devotee Coming Into My Avataric Physical Human Company or, After My Avataric Physical Human Lifetime, Into The physical human Company and By-Me-Spiritually-Empowered Circumstances Of My "Ruchira Sannyasin" Devotees). All Such Signs Occur Through The Only-By-Me Revealed and Given Divine Spiritual Process Of The "Thumbs"—In The Context Of Both The Vertical (or Frontal and Spinal) and The Horizontal (or Tripartite Heart) Planes Of the body-mind.

The Great Tradition Of Mankind Does Not, In and Of Itself, Account For The Nature and Force Of My Avataric Divine Spiritual Self-Transmission. My Avataric Divine Spiritual Self-Transmission Is Not Merely A philosophical Proposition or A Religious Metaphor. My Avataric Divine Spiritual Self-Transmission Is (and Will Forever Hereafter Be) My Unique and Tangible Avataric Divine Spiritual Self-Revelation, and That "Bright" Avataric Divine Spiritual Self-Revelation Has Been The Case Since (and Forever Before) My Birth.

Therefore, those who Heart-Recognize Me Relate To Me As The Avataric Divine Transmission-Body. Those who Are Fully (Formally) Established In their Devotion To Me (and, On That Basis, Are Spiritually Initiated, and Always Newly Spiritually Activated, By Me) Practice The Only-By-Me Revealed and Given Way Of The Heart Only On The Basis Of The Living Experience Of My Avatarically Self-Transmitted Divine Shaktipat. This Devotional Process Of Yogically Participating In My Avatarically Self-Transmitted Divine Shaktipat Is How My Devotee Realizes Me—and This Is The Basis On Which My By-Me-Spiritually-Initiated (and Always Newly By-Me-Spiritually-Activated) Devotee Is To Relate To Me Altogether.

The Only-By-Me Revealed and Given Way Of The Heart Is Not An ego-Based Way, Not An ego-Based Technique. The Only-By-Me Revealed and Given Way Of The Heart Is Simply The Devotional and Spiritual Relationship To Me (The Spiritually Self-"Bright" Divine Self-Condition, Avatarically Self-Revealed and Avatarically Self-Transmitted, In Person)—Entered Into, More and More Profoundly, Through Participation In My Avataric Divine Spiritual Self-Transmission. Participation In My Avataric Divine Spiritual Self-Transmission Is Not A "one-time Event", Which Can Be Experienced and Then "Taken Away" As A "Prize". Therefore, My Avataric Divine Spiritual Self-Transmission Must, With Maximum Possible Frequency, Be Renewed and Magnified By Coming Into My Avataric Physical Human Company (or, After My Avataric Physical Human Lifetime, By Coming Into The physical human Company and By-Me-Spiritually-Empowered Circumstances Of My "Ruchira Sannyasin"

Devotees). Participation In My Avataric Divine Spiritual Self-Transmission Is A lifelong Obligation and Practice—The Fundamental and Always Principal Obligation and Practice For All My Foundationally Prepared (and By-Me-Spiritually-Initiated) Devotees.

Altogether, The Only-By-Me Revealed and Given Way Of The Heart Is The Way Of Searchless Beholding (and Spiritual Reception) Of Me, and Of Practice Of The "Conscious Process" and "Conductivity" In Searchless Response To Me. On The Basis Of Total psycho-physical Receptivity To My "Bright" Avataric Divine Spiritual Self-Transmission, There Is The Progressive Unfolding Of Signs—All The Evidence Of Hearing Me, and (Then) Seeing Me, Culminating In The "Perfect Practice" Of The Only-By-Me Revealed and Given Way Of The Heart (Most Ultimately, In The Context Of The Only-By-Me Revealed and Given Seventh Stage Of Life).

Therefore, All My Devotees Must Maintain This Right Understanding and Practice Of The Avataric Divine Way Of The Devotional and Spiritual Relationship To Me. My Devotees Must Never Lapse From Such Right Practice. My Devotees Must Never Undermine or Disregard My Avataric Divine Spiritual Presence or The Force Of My Avataric Divine Spiritual Self-Transmission.

My Avataric Divine Spiritual Self-Transmission Is Divine Shaktipat. My Divine Shaktipat Is The Ultimate Divine Self-Transmission. My Divine Shaktipat Is The Direct Spiritual Self-Transmission Of The "Bright". My Divine Shaktipat Is Ruchira Shaktipat. My Divine Shaktipat Does Not Originate "From the ground Up". My Divine Shaktipat Is The Un-Mediated (or Perfectly Direct) Avataric Divine Self-Transmission Of Amrita Nadi. My Divine Shaktipat Does Not Originate From physiological causes or conditions. My Divine Shaktipat Is The Avataric Direct Spiritual Self-Transmission Of My Divine Person, Presence, and Self-Condition From My Divine "Bright" Spherical Self-Domain. My Divine Shaktipat Is The Avataric Divine Spiritual Self-Transmission Of The (One and Only) Divine Person (or Indivisible Conscious Light). My Divine Shaktipat Is The Unique (and Single) Avataric Divine Self-Transmission That Is The "Bright"—Consciousness-and-Energy As One.

The "Bright" Is The Divine Conscious Light. I Am That—and I Bring That To You. I Am The "Bright", and The "Thumbs" Is My Method and Means.

Therefore, You Need Not (and Cannot Fruitfully) Seek For Me. As My By-Me-Spiritually-Initiated (and Always Newly By-Me-Spiritually-Activated) Devotee, Simply (Merely) Behold Me—and Embrace The Way Of The Devotional and Spiritual Relationship To Me Only On That Basis.

Avatar Adi Da Samraj
The Mountain Of Attention Sanctuary, 2000

SUTRA 27

In The Devotional Way Of Insight (In The Only-By-Me Revealed and Given Way Of The Heart), The Sadhana Of Listening To Me Involves The (To-Me-Responsive) Practice Of self-Enquiry (In The Form "Avoiding Relationship?")—Which Practice Is The Senior Exercise Of The "Conscious Process" In The Devotional Way Of Insight (Until "Feeling-Enquiry" Begins, In The Context Of The "Perfect Practice" Of The Way Of The Heart). Therefore, Beginning In The Intensive Listening (and Would-Be, Eventually, Hearing) Stage (and Even In The Student-Beginner Stage, Of Experiment and First Application) Of The Devotional Way Of Insight, Enquire "Avoiding Relationship?". Do This At Random, In The moment to moment Context Of daily life, and In The daily Formal Meditative Setting—As beings, things, conditions, or events arise and Capture Your attention. In This Manner, Progressively Observe, Understand, and Feel Beyond the self-Contraction (or the psycho-physical ego-"I"), Such That The Heart Opens Beyond conditional self-Consciousness and the present object (or objects) of attention, To Realize (Simply, In the present moment) The Feeling Of Unqualified Relatedness.

The Practice Of self-Enquiry Is The Real Process Of self-Understanding, Activated (or Intentionally Applied) In Relationship To one's (moment to moment) experience. In Due Course, As self-Enquiry Continues As The Truly and Directly ego-Transcending Activity Of one's life, Even The Exercise Of The Question ("Avoiding Relationship?") Becomes Occasional.

In The Practice Of self-Enquiry, The Question Is Not Engaged Repetitively, In The Traditional Manner Of Practicing A Mantra. The Practice Of self-Enquiry Is Not A Process Of self-Analysis. The Practice Of self-Enquiry Is Not Purposed To Draw the mind Into All Kinds Of Formulations or Into The Persistent Awareness Of Endless ego-Patterns. The Practice Of self-Enquiry Is Not "Concerned" With The Nature and Forms Of Avoidance. Nor Is It The Purpose Of The Practice Of self-Enquiry To Achieve A Merely Analytical knowing Of The Pattern Of one's life Of Avoidance.

My Devotee who Practices self-Enquiry (In The Form "Avoiding Relationship?") Remains attentive To The Question, To the one who Receives The Question, To The "Place" Where The Question Is Received, and To what arises. Until something arises, one Simply Persists In Devotional Communion

With Me, Supported By The Practice Of self-Enquiry. Through Such Persistence, It Will (In Due Course, By Means Of My Avataric Divine Spiritual Grace) Be Revealed That whatever is arising Is (Always, or Invariably, and Necessarily) The Avoidance Of Relationship.

The Practice Of self-Enquiry (In The Form "Avoiding Relationship?") Is (As A General Rule) To Be Done As an internal mental activity, Either As A Silent Verbalization With "the tongue of the mind" Or As A Tacit Intention (Without Internal Verbalization). The Frequency With Which The Question "Avoiding Relationship?" Is Engaged Should Be Determined By the individual (As one Observes The Practical Effect Of one's Approach).

The Practice Of self-Enquiry Does Not Deal With Mere Words. The Practice Of self-Enquiry Deals With Meanings. The Question "Avoiding Relationship?" Is To Be Directed Not To Unconscious material Forces, but To mind and Conscious Awareness (Which Are Aware Of Unconscious material Forces).

The Practice Of self-Enquiry Is Not Directed To the various actions that Are Concrete Dramatizations Of the activity Of Avoidance. The Practice Of self-Enquiry Is To Be Directed To oneself.

The Significance Of The Question "Avoiding Relationship?" Is Not: "Is this action The Avoidance Of Relationship In Some Sense?" Rather, The Significance Of The Question "Avoiding Relationship?" Is: "Presently Avoiding Being Already and Entirely In Relationship?" (or "Presently Contracting From The Inherent life-Condition Of Unqualified Relatedness?").

The Question "Avoiding Relationship?" Is Not To Be Understood To Mean: "Are You Avoiding Relationship?" (or "Am I Avoiding Relationship?"). In The Practice Of self-Enquiry (Rightly Engaged), There Is No Dramatized Separation In the mind Between oneself As The Questioner and oneself As The Hearer Of The Question.

In The Practice Of self-Enquiry, one Does Not Enquire As (or Of) some Surrogate entity, some part of the mind, or some Separate function of the being. One Simply Enquires Of oneself, In the arising (and one's own "Creation") of the present moment.

The Practice Of self-Enquiry Is Not self-Understanding "Isolated" As A Method, In Order To Produce An Effect. The True (or Truly Right) Practice Of self-Enquiry Is (Itself) The Activity Of (In Due Course, Most Fundamental) self-Understanding.

Most Fundamental (or "Radical", or "Gone-To-The-Root") self-Understanding Is The Necessary Basis For The Realization Of Reality Itself.

Most Fundamental self-Understanding Is The Absence (or Non-arising) Of "Narcissus" (or self-Contraction, or ego-"I"—or Separateness and Relatedness and "Difference").

Where There Is The Non-arising Of "Narcissus", There Is Only Reality Itself.

"Narcissus" is (Always Already) dead.

The ego-"I" is (Always Already) Not.

I Am The Loved-One. I Am The One and Indivisible Self-Conscious Light.

I Am The Divine Beloved. I Am The Self-Existing Conscious Being. I Am The Divine Conscious Light That Is.

I Am The Da Avatar—The Ruchira Avatar, The Love-Ananda Avatar, The Divine Sat-Guru Who Is The Heart Itself. I Am The Ruchira Siddha, The Hridaya Siddha, The Divine Heart-Master, The Ishta (or Heart-Chosen One) Of My Every Devotee. For All Practitioners Of The Way Of The Heart, I Am The Necessary and Unique Revealed and Revealing Source, and Means, and Object (or Threshold Medium), and Subject (or Very, and Perfectly Subjective, Person) Of Faith (In The Divine Reality, The Divine Purpose, The Divine Process, and The Most Ultimate and Inherently Most Perfect Divine Realization). Therefore, The Faith-Response To Me Should (and, Indeed, Must) Be Felt and Demonstrated By All Practitioners Of The Way Of The Heart (Including My Student-Beginner Devotees, My early-life Devotees, My "Lay Congregationist" Devotees, My "Lay Renunciate" Devotees, and My "Ruchira Sannyasin" Devotees), and In Both The Devotional Way Of Insight and The Devotional Way Of Faith.

However, In The Only-By-Me Revealed and Given Way Of The Heart (or Way Of Adidam), It Is The Practitioner In whom The Faith-Response To Me Has A Unique and Profoundly Moving, Clarifying, and Strengthening Effect, and who Can, On That Basis, Embrace (and Readily and Thoroughly Develop, and Consistently Demonstrate) The Practice (Including All The Originally and, Otherwise, Progressively By-Me-Given Disciplines, Callings, and Gifts) Of The Way Of The Heart (and Do So With Ever-Growing Heart-Openness, Clarity, Strength, self-Understanding, and ego-Transcending Effectiveness), who Should (or, Rightly, Can) Exercise The Devotional Way Of Faith (Beyond The Original Student-Beginner's Experiment With Both The Devotional Way Of Faith and The Devotional Way Of Insight).

Those who Do Not or Cannot Thus Directly, and Faithfully, and Fully Effectively Heart-Respond To My Avatarically-Born Bodily (Human) Divine Form, My Avatarically Self-Transmitted Spiritual (and Always Blessing) Divine Presence, My Avatarically Self-Revealed (and Very, and Transcendental, and Perfectly Subjective, and Inherently Spiritual, and Inherently egoless, and Inherently Perfect, and Self-Evidently Divine) State, and My Avatarically Self-Revealed Divine Word and My Avatarically Self-Revealed Divine Image-Art and My Avatarically Self-Manifested Divine Leelas, and those who Do Not Have The Capability Of Fullest Faith, and those who (By Strong Tendency) Would childishly Seek An ego-Consoling and self-Indulgent Practice (or, Really, An ego-Serving and ego-Protecting Illusion Of Practice), and those who Cannot So Directly or Readily Relinquish childish dependency (or ego-Possessed clinging, Incapable Of self-Surrender), or childish (or Superficial, Faithless, and ego-Serving) emotionalism, or childish (or Indiscriminate, and, Otherwise, merely conventional) idealism, and those who (In A More adolescent Fashion, and By A Weakness In The Faith-Response Itself) Would (By Strong Tendency, and If Practicing The Devotional Way Of Faith) Fail To Fully, Rightly, Respectfully, and Faithfully Honor and Engage The Great Relationship To Me—all of these (and their like) Should Not (Beyond An Initial Formal "Consideration" and Formal self-Testing Experiment) Practice The Way Of The Heart By Practice Of The Devotional Way Of Faith, but (Rather, On The Basis Of The Initial Formal Student-Beginner "Consideration", and Formal self-Testing Experiment) they Should Choose and Develop The Practice Of The Devotional Way Of Insight (and That, Like The Devotional Way Of Faith, By Responsibly Disciplining themselves and Fully and Rightly Honoring and Engaging The Great and Necessarily Devotional Relationship To Me). Also, those Student-Beginners who (In The Initial Formal Student-Beginner "Consideration" and Formal self-Testing Experiment) Exhibit The Unique Capability For Effectively Exercising The Process Of Feeling and Insight (In The Manner Of The Devotional Way Of Insight) Should Then Choose and (Thereafter) Continue To Do So.

Even All Student-Beginners, and Also All Beginning Practitioners, Of The Way Of The Heart—Whether they (Rightly) Practice The Devotional Way Of Faith (and, Therefore, The Right and Consistent Devotionally Responsive Exercise Of Feeling-Faith) Or The Devotional Way Of Insight (and, Therefore, The Right and Consistent Devotionally Responsive Exercise Of Feeling-Insight)—Should (and Must) Do So On The Basis Of their Original (and Most Profound) Heart-Recognition Of Me. And This Heart-Recognition Develops By The Practice Of It. Therefore, By Heart-Recognition Of Me and (On That Basis) Heart-Responsive Practice Of The Only-By-Me Revealed and Given Way Of The Heart, Spontaneous and Inspired Heart-Surrender To Me and Feeling-Contemplation Of Me Should (and, Indeed, Must) Begin To Characterize The Inclination and The Demonstration Of My Every Student-Beginner Devotee, and My Every Devotee In The Intensive Listening-Hearing Stage Of The Way Of The Heart. And Such Must Also Continue To Develop In The Case Of My Every Would-Be-Seeing (or Progressively Seeing) Devotee and My Every Actually Seeing Devotee.

Even Every Real and True Formal Practitioner Of The Way Of The Heart Is (and Is More and More To Be) Spontaneously and Inevitably Moved By

Faith In Me, and To Ever-Greater Faith In Me. Such a one Is Spontaneously and Inevitably Moved To and By The Impulse To Actual (or Really Effective) ego-Transcendence and Most Perfectly ego-Transcending (and Fully and Most Perfectly Spiritually Awakened) Real-God-Realization (or The Impulse To Realize That Which Is and Can Be Realized Only By Actual, or Really Effective, and, Most Ultimately, Inherent, and Inherently Most Perfect, ego-Transcendence). Such a one Is Spontaneously and Inevitably Moved To Love (By Love), and To Every Kind Of Right and Useful self-Discipline. And Such a one Is Spontaneously and Inevitably Moved To (and By) Constant Service and Feeling-Contemplation Of My Avatarically-Born Bodily (Human) Divine Form, My Avatarically Self-Transmitted Spiritual (and Always Blessing) Divine Presence, and My Avatarically Self-Revealed (and Very, and Transcendental, and Perfectly Subjective, and Inherently Spiritual, and Inherently egoless, and Inherently Perfect, and Self-Evidently Divine) State, and, Therefore (and Thereby), Most Ultimately, To Inherent (and Inherently Most Perfect) Realization Of My (Avatarically Self-Revealed) Transcendental, Inherently Spiritual, Inherently egoless, and Self-Evidently Divine Self-Condition.

Even Every Real and True Formal Practitioner Of The Only-By-Me Revealed and Given Way Of The Heart Is (and Is More and More To Be) Heart-Moved By The Inherent "Bright" Attractiveness and Faith-Granting Effectiveness Of My Avatarically-Born Bodily (Human) Divine Form, My Avatarically Self-Transmitted Spiritual (and Always Blessing) Divine Presence, and My Avatarically Self-Revealed (and Very, and Transcendental, and Perfectly Subjective, and Inherently Spiritual, and Inherently egoless, and Inherently Perfect, and Self-Evidently Divine) State—For I Am The Da Avatar, The Ruchira Avatar, The Love-Ananda Avatar, The Divine Heart-Master, The Divine World-Teacher, The Avataric Divine Realizer, The Avataric Divine Revealer, The Avataric Divine Transmitter, The Avataric Divine Awakener, and The Avataric Divine Self-Revelation (Itself) Of The Self-Existing and Self-Radiant Truth and Inherent Love-Bliss Of Being, or Of Existence Itself. Therefore, In daily life and Meditation, and By Random Invocation Of Me (Via My Principal Avatarically Revealed and Given Divine Name, "Da", or Via Any Other Of My Avatarically Revealed and Given Divine Names, or Combined Avataric Divine Names and Avataric Divine Descriptive Titles, Which I Have Given To Be Engaged In The Practice Of Simple Name-Invocation Of Me), and By Chant, Song, Recitation, and Leela-Telling, and By Every Other Kind Of Sacred Act and Service, Every Real and True Formal Practitioner Of The Way Of The Heart Is, Principally, Heart-Moved To Feel (and Thereby To Contemplate and To Celebrate) My Avatarically Self-Revealed Divine Name, My Avatarically-Born Bodily (Human) Divine Form, My Avatarically Self-Transmitted Spiritual (and

Always Blessing) Divine Presence, and My Avatarically Self-Revealed (and Very, and Transcendental, and Perfectly Subjective, and Inherently Spiritual, and Inherently egoless, and Inherently Perfect, and Self-Evidently Divine) State.

In The Only-By-Me Revealed and Given Way Of The Heart (or Way Of Adidam), Ruchira Avatara Naama Japa Is The Principal Responsive Technical Practice (or Devotional Exercise Of Faith) Engaged By My Listening Devotees and My Hearing Devotees (and Begun, As Experiment and First Application, By My Student-Beginner Devotees) In The Devotional Way Of Faith. This Practice Is Itself Based Upon The Heart-Exercise Of Faith Itself (or The Consistently Demonstrated Heart-Impulse Of self-Offering and self-Surrender), Demonstrated By Means Of Devotional Feeling (Actively Feeling Beyond and Releasing self-Contraction in body and mind) and By Means Of Right Action (or Consistent Embrace Of All The Appropriate and Necessary Practices and Disciplines Associated With The Listening Stage, and Then The Hearing Stage, Of The Devotional Way Of Faith, As Practiced In The Way Of The Heart). Therefore, all those who Practice Ruchira Avatara Naama Japa Should Practice The Heart-Exercise Of Faith (In Relation To Me). And The Total Range Of Student-Beginner's Discipline and Practice Should Be Firmly Embraced and Thoroughly Established (and, Thereafter, On That Basis, Consistently, and Truly Responsively, Demonstrated) By My Every Formal Devotee who Practices The Only-By-Me Revealed and Given Way Of The Heart.

Ruchira Avatara Naama Japa Itself (or, Otherwise, My Even Every Formal Devotee's Random Name-Invocation Of Me, Via My Principal Name, "Da", or Via Any Other Of My Avatarically Revealed and Given Divine Names, or Combined Avataric Divine Names and Avataric Divine Descriptive Titles, Which I Have Given To Be Engaged In The Practice Of Simple Name-Invocation Of Me) Should Be Engaged On The Basis Of (and As An Expression Of) The Faith-Response To Me, and By (or On The Basis Of) The Consistently Demonstrated Devotional Exercise Of That Faith. Thus, As The Principal Technical Exercise Of The "Conscious Process" In The Devotional Way Of Faith In The Way Of The Heart, The Ruchira Avatara Naama Mantra Should Be Recited In (and By Means Of) Heart-Feeling, and (Generally) Only With "the tongue of the mind" (and Thus, In The Outward physical Sense, silently), Except On Occasions Of Spontaneously Inspired (and, Perhaps, Even Rhythmic, or Chant-Like) Contemplative vocalization (or Else Contemplative sub-vocalization, With movements of the physical tongue and mouth, but With little or no Outwardly audible vocalization). And The Ruchira Avatara Naama Mantra (As, Also, My Principal Name, "Da", or Any Other Of My Avatarically Revealed and Given Divine Names, or Combined Avataric Divine Names and Avataric Divine Descriptive Titles, Which I Have Given To Be Engaged In The

Practice Of Simple Name-Invocation Of Me) May Also (Otherwise) Be Recited vocally and audibly In Sacred Occasions Of Chant, Song, Recitation, and The Like. Such Heart-Invocation Of Me Via The Ruchira Avatara Naama Mantra (As, Also, Via My Principal Name, "Da", or Any Other Of My Avatarically Revealed and Given Divine Names, or Combined Avataric Divine Names and Avataric Divine Descriptive Titles) Should Be Randomly Made In The Course Of daily life (and, As Appropriate, In The Context Of Sacred Occasions), and It Should Be Done In daily Meditative Occasions (Wherein The Contemplative and Meditative Feeling-Process Is Allowed To Develop Maximally).

In The (Developing) Meditative Setting Of The Way Of The Heart (and, Specifically, In The Devotional Way Of Faith), Ruchira Avatara Naama Japa Is To Be Done Randomly, and Even Repetitively, and Perhaps (Occasionally, or, If So Preferred, Even Generally) In A Rhythmic, or Chant-Like, Manner (Whether silently Or, When Appropriate, or, Otherwise, Inevitable, audibly)—but Never In A Mechanical Manner, or In An Inappropriately Rapid (or Hurried) Manner. My Avatarically-Born Bodily (Human) Divine Form (and My Avatarically Self-Transmitted Spiritual, and Always Blessing, Divine Presence, and My Avatarically Self-Revealed, and Very, and Transcendental, and Perfectly Subjective, and Inherently Spiritual, and Inherently egoless, and Inherently Perfect, and Self-Evidently Divine State) Should Always Be Felt (and Thereby Contemplated) During The Practice Of This (Meditative) Mantra Japa (As Also During The Practice Of Meditative Name-Invocation Of Me), Such That Feeling-Contemplation Progressively Becomes Profound Feeling-Meditation. Indeed, In The Only-By-Me Revealed and Given Way Of The Heart (or Way Of Adidam), My Avatarically-Born Bodily (Human) Divine Form (and, In Due Course, My Avatarically Self-Transmitted Spiritual, and Always Blessing, Divine Presence, and, Thus and Thereby, and More and More, My Avatarically Self-Revealed, and Very, and Transcendental, and Perfectly Subjective, and Inherently Spiritual, and Inherently egoless, and Inherently Perfect, and Self-Evidently Divine State) Should Be Felt (and Thereby Contemplated) During Any and Every Occasion Of The Use Of The Ruchira Avatara Naama Mantra, and, Truly, During Even Any and Every Occasion Of My Even Any and Every Devotee's Exercise Of Any Form Of Either The By-Me-Given Devotional Way Of Faith Or The By-Me-Given Devotional Way Of Insight. Therefore, Unless I Am Physically Present (and, Appropriately, Physically Accessible To You) In My Avatarically-Born Bodily (Human) Divine Form, Feel (and Devotionally Heart-Respond To, and, Thus, Truly Contemplate) My Avatarically-Born Bodily (Human) Divine Form (and, Thereby, My Avatarically Self-Transmitted Spiritual, and Always Blessing, Divine Presence, and My Avatarically Self-Revealed, and Very, and Transcendental, and Perfectly Subjective, and

Inherently Spiritual, and Inherently egoless, and Inherently Perfect, and Self-Evidently Divine State) Via An Appropriate, Good, and Effective (photographic or Other technical or artistic) Representation Of My Avatarically-Born Bodily (Human) Divine Form (and, Otherwise, Via An Effective Representation Of My Avatarically-Born Bodily Human Divine Form In the mind).

In The Way Of The Heart, The silent Recitations (or, Otherwise, vocal, but Always Heart-Felt, Repetitions) Of The Ruchira Avatara Naama Mantra Should Generally (Especially In The Meditative Setting) Be Associated With The Use Of A Mala (or Rosary), Whereby Each Recitation Is Gently and Simply Marked With the touching Of A (Next) Bead On The Mala. In The Meditative Setting (or In any Random moment In which Ruchira Avatara Naama Japa Is Appropriate), Each Recitation Of The Ruchira Avatara Naama Mantra Should (Generally) Be Done silently, but, Truly, The Recitation Should Be Made (and Felt, or Radiated) By, From, and At The Heart (and, Thus, Even Via the <u>Total</u> body-mind). Apart From This, No Other Special Practices (Such As The "Timing" Of Ruchira Avatara Naama Japa With the breath, or With Repetitive Cycles Of attention To The bodily Circuitry) Are An Appropriate Part Of Ruchira Avatara Naama Japa, Unless (or Except To The Degree That) Such Practices Occur As Spontaneous Random Events (or As Spontaneous Processes In Particular Occasions, or moments, Of Ruchira Avatara Naama Japa).

When Engaging In Ruchira Avatara Naama Japa (or, Otherwise, In Simple Name-Invocation Of Me), Do Not (Intentionally) think About or Concentrate Upon The "Meaning" Of Any Of The Avataric Divine Names or Avataric Divine Descriptive Titles or Avataric Divine Word-Signs That Comprise The Ruchira Avatara Naama Mantra (and, Otherwise, Do Not Intentionally think About or Concentrate Upon The "Meaning" Of My Principal Name, "Da", or The "Meaning" Of Any Of My Avataric Divine Names or Avataric Divine Descriptive Titles Which I Have Given To Be Engaged In The Practice Of Simple Name-Invocation Of Me)—but, Rather, Feel (and Thereby Contemplate) My Avatarically-Born Bodily (Human) Divine Form, My Avatarically Self-Transmitted Spiritual (and Always Blessing) Divine Presence, and My Avatarically Self-Revealed (and Very, and Transcendental, and Perfectly Subjective, and Inherently Spiritual, and Inherently egoless, and Inherently Perfect, and Self-Evidently Divine) State (While Using The silent, or, Otherwise, vocal, but Always Heart-Felt, verbal Recitation Simply As A Means To Direct and Concentrate and Release the thinking mind).

Indeed, Ruchira Avatara Naama Japa (and self-Enquiry, and Also Simple Name-Invocation Of Me, and Even Every Other Form Of The "Conscious Process" In The Way Of The Heart) Is A Direct (Technical and Responsive) Means (By Resort To My Avatarically-Born Bodily Human Divine Form, My

Avatarically Self-Transmitted Spiritual, and Always Blessing, Divine Presence, and My Avatarically Self-Revealed, and Very, and Transcendental, and Perfectly Subjective, and Inherently Spiritual, and Inherently egoless, and Inherently Perfect, and Self-Evidently Divine State) For Controlling, Purifying, Converting, Relaxing, and Transcending self-Contraction (or all the forms and results of egoity, Including All The Tendencies Of thought, emotion, and desire). Therefore, Rather Than Casually Allowing (and, Otherwise, Seeking or Suffering) Random self-Contraction (including thoughts, emotional states or reactions, and desires) To arise (and To Control attention and the actions or states of the body-mind), Constantly (By Random Intention) Practice Ruchira Avatara Naama Japa and Random Name-Invocation Of Me (or Else Practice Random Name-Invocation Of Me and The "Conscious Process" Otherwise Specific To Your Manner and Developmental Stage Of Practice In The Way Of The Heart), and Thereby—and By Every Means Given In Satsang With Me, and (Principally) By The Exercise Of Ruchira Avatara Bhakti Yoga, or Non-Strategically (Effortlessly, Receptively, and Merely By Turning The Natural Faculties Of perceptual body, emotional feeling, mental attention, and cycling breath To Me) Feeling-Contemplating My Avatarically-Born Bodily (Human) Divine Form, My Avatarically Self-Transmitted Spiritual (and Always Blessing) Divine Presence, and My Avatarically Self-Revealed (and Very, and Transcendental, and Perfectly Subjective, and Inherently Spiritual, and Inherently egoless, and Inherently Perfect, and Self-Evidently Divine) State—Constantly Feel (or Be Feelingly Attracted) Beyond the egoic (and, Otherwise, conditional) limitations Of psycho-physical Existence.

The Fundamental Principle Of Ruchira Avatara Naama Japa (and Of My Even Any Devotee's Random Name-Invocation Of Me) Is The Exercise Of The Devotional Faith-Response In Relation To My Inherently Heart-Attractive (and Faith-Granting) Avatarically-Born Bodily (Human) Divine Form, and My Avatarically Self-Transmitted Spiritual (and Always Blessing) Divine Presence, and My Avatarically Self-Revealed (and Very, and Transcendental, and Perfectly Subjective, and Inherently Spiritual, and Inherently egoless, and Inherently Perfect, and Self-Evidently Divine) State. Therefore, Contemplate (and, Thus, Heart-Feel) My Avatarically-Born Bodily (Human) Divine Form (and, In Due Course, My Avatarically Self-Transmitted Spiritual, and Always Blessing, Divine Presence and, Thus and Thereby, and More and More, My Avatarically Self-Revealed, and Very, and Transcendental, and Perfectly Subjective, and Inherently Spiritual, and Inherently egoless, and Inherently Perfect, and Self-Evidently Divine State), While Directing the mind Via Ruchira Avatara Naama Japa (or, Otherwise, Via My Even Any Devotee's Random, and Even Only Occasional, Name-Invocation Of Me). In This Manner, By Heart-Recognition Of Me and

Heart-Attraction To Me and Heart-Response To Me, Be Surrendered To Me (Even Beyond Any Necessity To Make An Effort Of Surrender).

The "Attitude" That Is Fundamental To The Real and True Devotional Practice Of The Only-By-Me Revealed and Given Way Of The Heart (Whether In The Manner Of The Devotional Way Of Faith Or In The Manner Of The Devotional Way Of Insight) Is That Of The Presumption Of My Victory In Your Own Heart and life. That Is To Say, self-Observation, Most Fundamental self-Understanding, and The True (Heart-Responsible) Capability For Direct, Comprehensive, and (Potentially) Unqualified (or Inherent, and Inherently Most Perfect) ego-Transcendence (Based On Most Fundamental self-Understanding and On True and Truly Responsible Spiritual Awakening) Are To Develop, By Means Of My Avatarically Self-Transmitted Divine Spiritual Grace, In The Progressive Process Of The Way Of The Heart—but Neither These Nor Any Other Processes, Capabilities, or Effects Are To Be Made Into Objects (or Goals) Of Seeking. Rather, On The Simple Basis Of The Faithful Heart-Response To Me (Constantly Engaged), and In The Context Of Consistent Fulfillment Of My Instructions (and All The Kinds Of Disciplines Required) For Your Particular Practice Of The Way Of The Heart, You Should Simply and Always Feel That All Of That Is Always Already Accomplished (As, Indeed, It Is) By Me, and That All Of That Will Be Divinely Revealed (In Due Course) By Means Of My Avatarically Self-Transmitted Divine Spiritual Grace.

In The Only-By-Me Revealed and Given Way Of The Heart (or Way Of Adidam), The Beginner's Devotional Way Of Faith Is Founded On A Uniquely Effective Faith In My Accomplishing-Power Of Avataric Divine Spiritual Grace To Awaken Spiritually-Inspired Devotion, Necessary Real self-Observation, True Hearing Of Me (or Most Fundamental self-Understanding), The True (and Truly Effective) ego-Transcending Capability, and (Via The Exercise Of That By-My-Avataric-Divine-Spiritual-Grace-Given Capability) True and Stable human Equanimity and True and Stable Seeing Of Me (and Subsequent Fully Technically Established Spiritual Practice Of The Way Of The Heart, Based Also On The Continued Hearing-Exercise Of Most Fundamental self-Understanding). Therefore, The Devotional Way Of Faith (As Practiced By Beginners In The Way Of The Heart) Is Not Based On The Presumption That Most Fundamental self-Understanding Is Not Necessary, but On The Presumption That It Will Be Realized By Means Of My Avatarically Self-Transmitted Divine Spiritual Grace, Through Heart-Faithful Surrender To Me (and By Letting Me Do My Avataric Divine Work At The Heart). Therefore, In The Way Of The Heart, Rather Than Seeking For Grace or Capability, All Beginning (and Yet Listening) Practitioners Of The Devotional Way Of Faith (who Do Not Yet Hear Me) Simply Exercise (or Actively Feel) Faith Itself, By Feeling-Contemplation Of

My Avatarically-Born Bodily (Human) Divine Form, and (In Due Course) My Avatarically Self-Transmitted Spiritual (and Always Blessing) Divine Presence, and (Thus and Thereby, and More and More) My Avatarically Self-Revealed (and Very, and Transcendental, and Perfectly Subjective, and Inherently Spiritual, and Inherently egoless, and Inherently Perfect, and Self-Evidently Divine) State. And This Is Done (In The Case Of Those Beginning Practitioners who Practice The Devotional Way Of Faith) Via The Heart-Felt Practice Of Ruchira Avatara Naama Japa, and (In The Case Of All Beginning Practitioners Of The Way Of The Heart) By Constantly Granting Me The Gift Of The Faithful Practitioner's Maximum Devotion, Service, and self-Discipline.

In The Way Of The Heart, The Meditative Practice Of Ruchira Avatara Naama Japa Should (In The Devotional Way Of Faith) First Be Engaged As Feeling-Contemplation Of Me With the bodily eyes Open To View My Avatarically-Born Bodily (Human) Divine Form. Over time, This Practice Will Become Naturally More Meditative (and, In Due Course, The Truly Deep Meditative Impulse Will Be Awakened, By Means Of My Avatarically Self-Transmitted Divine Spiritual Grace), Such That The Impulse To Close the bodily eyes Will Become Strong, and (As The Meditative Tendency Spontaneously Deepens) Even The Intention To Exercise the mind (By Means Of verbal Invocation Of Me Via The Ruchira Avatara Naama Mantra, or, Otherwise, By Means Of verbal Invocation Of Me Via My Principal Name, "Da", or By Means Of verbal Invocation Of Me Via Any Other Of My Avatarically Revealed and Given Divine Names, or Combined Avataric Divine Names and Avataric Divine Descriptive Titles, Which I Have Given To Be Engaged In The Practice Of Simple Name-Invocation Of Me—or Even By Means Of mental Representation Of My Avatarically-Born Bodily Human Divine Form) Will Relax, and mind and body Will Allow A Heart-Opened and Feeling Meditation That Sublimely Relaxes and Feels Beyond The Degrees Of Contraction That May Tend To Be Associated With body, emotion, and mind. This Sublime Meditative Feeling (Beyond self-Contraction) More and More Heart-Feels The Simple Feeling Of Relatedness. And This Feeling, Readily and Stably Acquired (In Meditation and daily life), and (By Means Of My Avatarically Self-Transmitted Divine Spiritual Grace) Associated (In Due Course) With The True Hearing-Exercise Of Most Fundamental self-Understanding, and Also Associated With The Maximum (Rightly Conservative) functional, practical, relational, and Cultural Disciplines (Belonging To Maturity In The Intensive Listening-Hearing Stage Of The Way Of The Heart), Allows The Faithful and Heart-Open Practitioner Of The Devotional Way Of Faith To Make The Transition To The Truly Seeing Process Of The Way Of The Heart (Beginning By Entrance Into The Would-Be-Seeing, or Progressively Seeing, Stage Of The Way Of The Heart).

The (Formal) Experimental "Consideration" Of Both The Devotional Way Of Insight and The Devotional Way Of Faith Is An Essential Aspect Of The Original Necessary Study and Practice For all who Are Student-Beginners Of The Way Of The Heart, and The Transition To The Intensive Listening-Hearing Stage Of The Way Of The Heart Should Occur Only When The Student-Beginner Has (By An Effective Process Of Experimental "Testing and Proving") Firmly Chosen Either The Beginner's Form Of The Devotional Way Of Insight Or The Beginner's Form Of The Devotional Way Of Faith. Likewise, The Transition To The Intensive Listening-Hearing Stage Of The Way Of The Heart Should Not Occur Until The Student-Beginner—Through Thorough (and Constantly Adapting, and Consistently Culturally Accountable) Study-"Consideration" Of The Way Of The Heart (In Its Totality), and Through Consistent Rudimentary (Student-Beginner) Practice Of Ruchira Avatara Bhakti (In Devotionally Me-Recognizing Heart-Responsive Relation To Me, and By Constant Resort To Me Via ego-Surrendering Feeling-Contemplation Of Me)—Truly Heart-Confirms and Heart-Demonstrates The Foundation Disposition Characteristically To Be Demonstrated In The "Original" Context Of The Fourth Stage Of Life (Which Is Spontaneously ego-Surrendering, ego-Forgetting, and More and More Effectively ego-Transcending Devotion To Me, To The Degree Of Feeling-Ecstasy), and, Likewise, Only When The Student-Beginner Firmly, Deeply, and Very Fully (From The Heart) Confesses The Primary Impulse, Which Is The Heart's Own Motive Toward Most Perfectly ego-Transcending (and Fully and Most Perfectly Spiritually Awakened) Real-God-Realization. And That Demonstrated Disposition, and That Heart-Confession, and That Authentic Transition Transform The Basic (and, Originally, Already Firm) Student-Beginner's Commitment (To Progressively "Consider", Establish, and Develop Real Practice Of The Way Of The Heart) Into A Profoundly By-Me-Informed, and (More and More) By-Me-Spiritually-Inspired, and Truly self-Disciplined Participation In The Necessary Process Of ego-Transcendence, and In The Devotee's Chosen Context Of That Great Process—Either That Of The Devotional Exercise Of Insight Or That Of The Devotional Exercise Of Faith.

Avatar Adi Da Samraj
Da Love-Ananda Mahal, 2003

SUTRA 28

The Process Of Listening To Me (By Means Of The Fundamental Practice Of Devotionally Turning To Me—Supported By The Devotionally Responsive Practice Of Either Insight Or Faith) Must Be Progressively Intensified During The Student-Beginner Stage and The Intensive Listening-Hearing Stage Of The Only-By-Me Revealed and Given Way Of The Heart (or Way Of Adidam), Until The Process Of Listening To Me Becomes True Hearing Of Me—or The Unique Capability, Based On Most Fundamental self-Understanding, To Directly Transcend self-Contraction (Whether, As A Matter Of Technical Responsive Practice, By The Devotional Exercise Of Feeling and Insight, Via self-Enquiry, Or By The Devotional Exercise Of Feeling and Faith, Via Ruchira Avatara Naama Japa). And, From The Beginning Of The Student-Beginner Stage Of The Way Of The Heart (and, As A Thereafter Continued Obligation, Once Practice Begins In The Intensive Listening-Hearing Stage Of The Way Of The Heart), The Practice Of Listening To Me (By Means Of The Fundamental Practice Of Ruchira Avatara Bhakti Yoga—Together With The Technical Responsive Practice Of self-Enquiry or Of Ruchira Avatara Naama Japa, and Also Of Random Simple Name-Invocation Of Me) Is To Be Supported (and The Eventual Process Associated With True Hearing Of Me, and Then True Seeing Of Me, Is To Be Given Evidence) By The (Voluntary, Intelligent, and Progressively Intensified) Practice Of A Comprehensive and Complete Range Of Basic functional, practical, relational, and Cultural Disciplines Relative To General Health, Diet, Sexuality, Service, and Cooperative Sacred Cultural Association (With Other, and Even All Other, Formally Acknowledged Practitioners Of The Only-By-Me Revealed and Given Way Of The Heart).

In The Only-By-Me Revealed and Given Way Of The Heart, The Basic Disciplines Relative To General Health Involve (General physical) "Conscious Exercise", or The Maintenance Of bodily Equanimity and physical Well-being Through Systematic Exercises and General bodily Practices That Conduct Natural human (and etheric) life-energy Throughout.

In The Only-By-Me Revealed and Given Way Of The Heart, The Basic Disciplines Relative To Diet Involve The Constant (or Always present-time)

Purification, Rebalancing, and Rejuvenation Of vital bodily Existence Through Right and Optimum personal Diet (and Right Periodic Fasting), Which Is Necessarily A "Sattvic", or Pure, and Purifying, and Conservative (or "Minimum Optimum"), and Generally (Unless Right Medical Reasons Indicate Otherwise) fructo-vegetarian, and Maximally (but Not Necessarily, or Generally, Exclusively) raw food Dietary (and Fasting) Discipline[75] That (As A Consistent, daily Rule) Does Not Burden the body or Bind the mind or attention Through food desire and Negative (or constipating, toxifying, and enervating) food effects (and ingestion effects in general), and That (Along With The Necessary Additional "Consideration" and Really Effective Transcending Of Aberrated, Anxious, or Even Excessively private Habits and Patterns Relative To food-taking and waste elimination) Serves The Yielding (or Freeing) Of functional human life-energy and attention To The Great (and, Necessarily, Devotional) Process (Of self-Surrender, self-Forgetting, Progressive self-Observation, Eventual Most Fundamental self-Understanding, and, Altogether, More and More Effective self-Transcendence, or Real ego-Transcendence) That Is The Necessary Foundation Of The Only-By-Me Revealed and Given Way Of The Heart.

My Any Devotee who Persists In Habits Of gross physical self-Indulgence (Including Dietary self-Indulgence) Is Inevitably Desensitized To Me—Both Devotionally and Spiritually. Therefore, Such Habits Of gross physical self-Indulgence Undermine (and Work Against) The Effectiveness Of The Sadhana (or Way Of Divine Self-Realization) That I Have Given To My Devotees. This Is The Reason Why Refinement Of the physical body Via A Diet That Is Conservative (or "Minimum Optimum"), and Maximally raw, and (Generally, Unless Right Medical Reasons Indicate Otherwise) fructo-vegetarian, and Via A Conservative (and Truly "Sattvic") Approach To food-taking (and body-Maintenance Altogether), Is Necessary In The Only-By-Me Revealed and Given Way Of The Heart.

Any Use Of Even the more common (or Commonly Used) intoxicants (Such As tobacco, alcohol, or kava)—and (To An Even Greater Degree) Any Use Of "soft" drugs (Such As cannabis)—Temporarily Suppresses psycho-physical (and heart-Specific, and brain-Specific, and nervous-system-Specific) Sensitivity To My Spiritual Transmission—After an initial period of gross intoxication, in which Such Sensitivity May, At The gross Level, Seem (To The Temporarily intoxicated User) To Increase. The Perennial popular (or common) Wisdom Relative To The Law and Lesson Of "fun" Always Applies. If You Play—You Must Pay! If You Dance—You Must Pay The Piper! Even The Executioner Has His Price! And The Longer and Hotter The Dance, The More You Must Pay—Whether Now or Later! And The Longer You Wait To Pay Your Fees, The More The Fees Compound and Increase!

Therefore, Only By Entirely Avoiding All Use (With The Possible Exception Only Of Token and Merely Symbolic Use, As May Sometimes Be Required By Custom For Respectful and Right Participation In, Necessarily Rare, Sacred, or Entirely Ceremonial and Non-personal, social Occasions[76]) Of Even the more common (or Commonly Used) intoxicants (Such As tobacco, alcohol, or kava), and By Entirely Avoiding All Use (Without Any Exceptions Whatsoever) Of "soft" drugs (Such As cannabis), "recreational" drugs (of any kind), hallucinogenic drugs, "hard" drugs, and otherwise medically inappropriate drugs—and By Restricting The Use Of Non-"Sattvic" (or Otherwise toxic) Dietary substances (In General) To The Infrequent, Brief, and Rightly Occasional Exceptions That May Be Appropriately Allowed—Can My Devotee Establish toxin-free functional Equanimity, and True and Full Sensitivity To My Spiritual Transmission, and The Possibility Of Continuing and Furthering The Devotional and Spiritual Process Of Realizing Me. Because All Of This Is So (and Not For Any moralistic or puritanical or idealistic Reasons), My Every Devotee—From The Beginning Of his or her Practice As A Formally Acknowledged Novice Student-Beginner (and Always Thereafter) In The Way Of The Heart—Must (Except, In A Token and Symbolic Manner, As May Sometimes Be Required By Custom, For Respectful and Right Participation In, Necessarily Rare, Sacred, or Entirely Ceremonial and Non-personal, social Occasions) Entirely Avoid Any and All Use Of socially common intoxicants (Such As tobacco, alcohol, or kava). And—From The Beginning Of his or her Practice As A Formally Acknowledged Novice Student-Beginner (and Always Thereafter) In The Way Of The Heart—My Every Devotee Must (Without Any Exceptions Whatsoever) Entirely Avoid Any and All Use Of "soft" drugs (Such As cannabis), "recreational" drugs (of any kind), hallucinogenic drugs, "hard" drugs, and otherwise medically inappropriate drugs.

The Universal human (and ego-Bound, and ego-Binding) Tendency To Desensitize the body-mind To Me Through Indulgence In gross (or Non-"Sattvic") psycho-physical Habits Of Any and Every Kind Is The First and Essential Reason Why (In The Only-By-Me Revealed and Given Way Of The Heart) There Must Be The Right and Consistent Exercise Of "Sattvic" Disciplines Of the gross physical (and Of the entire body-mind). Therefore, In The Only-By-Me Revealed and Given Way Of The Heart, The "Sattvic" Disciplining Of gross (or Non-"Sattvic") psycho-physical Habits In General, and Of Dietary self-Indulgence In Particular, Is Not A puritanical Matter, or A moralistic Matter—Nor Is It An idealistic Matter. My Devotees Are Not Called By Me To Discipline the body-mind As A Form Of psycho-physical Negativity (or body-Denial), or As A Form Of utopian Search For Perfection In The Context Of conditionally Manifested Existence. Rather, In The Only-By-Me

Revealed and Given Way Of The Heart, The "Sattvic" Disciplining Of the body-mind (Including The General, and Right-Principled, Relinquishment Of gross, or Non-"Sattvic", psycho-physical Habits—and The Consistent Whole bodily, or Total psycho-physical, and Altogether Right-Principled, Embrace Of Truly "Sattvic" psycho-physical Disciplines) Is Simply A Necessary and Homely Part Of The Realistic, and Practical, and Really and Practically Counter-egoic Approach To Me, and To The Real Process Of Devotional, and (In Due Course, As My Avatarically Self-Transmitted Divine Spiritual Grace Will Have It) Spiritual, Relationship To Me—Which Relationship (Formally, and Fully Accountably, Embraced and Practiced), and Not Any Mere self-Applied and ego-Serving (or ego-Improving, or Even body-mind-Improving) Techniques, Is (Itself) The Only-By-Me Revealed and Given Way Of The Heart.

In The Only-By-Me Revealed and Given Way Of The Heart, The Basic (or Foundation) Disciplines Relative To Sexuality Begin With "Consideration" Of (and, Therefore, Real Practicing Heart-Response To) My Teaching-Arguments Relative To the human emotional-sexual character, its "Oedipal", or childish and adolescent, Patterning Via early-life Adaptation, and its Obsessive egoic Orientation Toward self-pleasuring, Stress-Release, and Rituals Of Rejection and Betrayal. In Order For This "Consideration" To Become More and More Effective (or Revealing Relative To the conditional self), It Is, As A General Rule Of Formal Expectation (From The Beginning), To Be Accompanied (or Made Expressive) By The Basic Discipline Either Of celibacy Or (In the relationally sexually active case) Of Confining sexual activity To the any circumstance of emotionally intimate (and Formally Culturally Accountable) relationship (and, Altogether, Of Devotionally Surrendering, and, Thereby, Relinquishing, Excessive, or Wastefully self-Indulgent, sexual behavior). And This Basic General Rule Of Formal Expectation (Which, In The Developing Course Of Student-Beginner Practice Of The Way Of The Heart, Must, By Actual Practice, More and More Become A Very Basically "Considered", and, As Such, Stably Demonstrated, functional, practical, and relational Commitment Of body, emotion, mind, and speech) Is Itself To Be Accompanied (From The Point Of Basic Adaptation To Student-Beginner Practice Of The Way Of The Heart) By The Further Basic Discipline (In the relationally sexually active case) Of Obliging sexual activity itself To (More and More) Become An intimate, and life-energy-Conserving, and Rejuvenative, and (In Due Course) Spiritually Active Form Of "Conscious Exercise" (Such That functional, stylistic, and relational limitations On The Practice Of emotional-sexual Relatedness Are, By This Progressively Developing Discipline, and By The Totality Of The By-Me-Given Foundation-Practice Of The Way Of The Heart, "Considered" and, To The Maximum Possible Degree, Out-Grown).[77]

In The Only-By-Me Revealed and Given Way Of The Heart, The Basic Disciplines Relative To Service Involve The Transcending Of the social ego, By Means Of The Re-Orientation Of social activity, work, money, and, Indeed, Even all activities, To The ego-Transcending, Cooperative, Inclusive, and other-Serving Disposition, and (Altogether) To An Intention That Is, Characteristically (and Always Positively, Rather Than Insipidly), Harmless (or Inspired To Love), and, Characteristically, Both Pro-Relational and Positively Relational (and, Therefore, Not Fundamentally Separative and Competitive, but Positively Alive, Without Negative, or Loveless, Intentions—and Actively Competitive, or Even Rightly Aggressive, Only By Necessity, In circumstances that Either Strictly Demand Or Rightly Expect Competitiveness, or Even, At times, ego-Transcending Aggressiveness). And, In The Process Of This Re-Orientation, There Must Also Be The Effective Relinquishment Of The ego-Serving, Separative (or Exclusive), ego-Fulfilling, Basically Competitive, and (Otherwise) Negative (or Loveless, and, Characteristically, Not Positively Harmless, Not Love-Inspired, and Not all-and-All-Including) Disposition. And All Of This Is To Be Accomplished Simply By Engaging all activities (functional, practical, relational, and Cultural) As Ruchira Avatara Seva (or ego-Surrendering, ego-Forgetting, More and More ego-Transcending, and Always Directly and Really Felt Devotional, and Truly Me-Contemplating, Service To Me)—As An Extension Of My Devotee's Practice Of Ruchira Avatara Bhakti Yoga Into Every Kind and Form Of his or her Active Participation In human life.

The Basic Disciplines Of Service (and All Other Basic Disciplines, and Even All Disciplines) Are, In The Only-By-Me Revealed and Given Way Of The Heart, To Be Engaged Not Only In the common world, and In the personal (or intimate) domain, but In (Fully Accountable) Formal (and Truly, Rightly, and Fully Participatory) Cooperative Sacred Cultural Association With Other (and Even All Other) Formally Acknowledged Practitioners Of The Way Of The Heart. Because Of Its Comprehensive and Pervasive Function At The Foundation Of All functional, practical, relational, and Cultural Disciplines In The Way Of The Heart, The Discipline Of Cooperative Sacred Culture Is A Fundamental and Profoundly Important Responsibility In The Way Of The Heart. In The Way Of The Heart, True (human-Scale) Sacred Culture Is The Necessary General Context Of ego-Transcendence In daily life. And Cooperation Is The Inherent Law Of Such True Sacred Culture. Also, human beings Characteristically Animate The egoic (or Separative) Disposition Largely Via self-Preoccupation Through mind. Therefore, I Have Described The Fundamental egoic Dramatization In The ordinary human Sphere As The Avoidance Of Relationship. I Have Also Described This egoic Dramatization (Metaphorically) As "Narcissus At The Pond". "Narcissus At The Pond" Is Not

Only A Metaphor For egoity In General, but It Is A Specific (Metaphorical) Reference To The Characteristic human Preoccupation Of "Staring" At the mind. The "Image In The Pond" Is the mind, and The Solitary (or Separate, and Separative) Activity Of "Narcissus Staring At The Pond" Is The ego-Act (or The Avoidance Of Relationship), Which Act Is The Seed-Activity That Leads To The Breakdown Of The Whole (or The Totality), Including The human Collective. As A Result, the world Becomes A Mad Gathering Of egos, Preoccupied With Separateness, With self-Concern, With Separative Impulses, Desires, and Intentions, and With Every Kind Of Search For self-Fulfillment and self-Release. Therefore, In Order To Transcend egoity, You Must Embrace The Whole (and The Disposition Of Totality). And, In Order To Do That, You Must Be Restored To The Comprehensive Circumstance Of True (and Truly Cooperative) Sacred Culture. And, In The Constant Context Of human-Scale Cooperative Sacred Culture, You Must Constantly Fulfill Your Responsibilities Relative To The Collective (and Its Totality Of Responsibilities). And, In Order Thus To Transcend egoity, You Must (Necessarily) Become Transformed In Your mind and In Your psycho-physical Disposition Altogether, Such That You Use mind (and body) Rightly, and (Therefore) Not Separatively. This psycho-physical (and ego-Transcending) Necessity Is The Basis, In The Only-By-Me Revealed and Given Way Of The Heart, For The Discipline Of Cooperative Sacred Culture, Which Obliges You (and every one, and all, Of My Devotees, As one) To Go Beyond the egoic (or ego-Serving and ego-Reinforcing) mind, and (Thus) Beyond The Entire Effort Of The Avoidance Of Relationship. And This Force Of Obligation (Made By Means Of A Concrete Circumstance Of Expectation, Demand, and Accountability) Is The Reason That Cooperative Sacred Culture Is Such A Fundamental and Profound Discipline In The Only-By-Me Revealed and Given Way Of The Heart.

The Discipline Of Cooperative Sacred Culture Must Be Engaged In The Context Of My Any Devotee's Formal Affiliation With A Formally Designated Regional Community[78] Of The Avataric Pan-Communion Of Adidam. Such Formal Affiliation Includes The Requirements For Regular and Consistent Accountability Relative To All Aspects Of The Practice Of The Only-By-Me Revealed and Given Way Of The Heart (Including All The By-Me-Given Forms Of functional, practical, relational, and Cultural Discipline), Always Maximized Participation In The Devotional and Cultural Activities (Including Meditation, Puja, Devotional Chanting, Group "Consideration", Educational Events, and So On) Of The Sacred Domain, Regular and Consistent Participation In The Collective Activities Of Cooperative Service, Always Maximized Participation In The Fulfillment Of The Collective Obligations Relative To The Mission and Culture Of The Avataric Pan-Communion Of Adidam, and Always Maximized

Right financial support For The Collective Responsibilities Of The Formal Worldwide Sacred Institutional and Cooperative Cultural Gathering (or Truly Global Ashram) Of All Formally Acknowledged Practitioners Of The Way Of The Heart (As These Responsibilities Are Exercised and Fulfilled By The Avataric Samrajya Of Adidam, The Avataric Ruchirasala Of Adidam, and The Avataric Pan-Communion Of Adidam). And All Of These Requirements Are Always To Be Fulfilled To The Maximum Degree Possible, Given the personal life-circumstance Of My Any Devotee, and Given his or her geographical location In Relation To The Formally Designated Regional Community With Which he or she Is Affiliated.

The Discipline Of Cooperative Sacred Culture Also (Optimally—Unless the particular living-circumstance Of My Any Devotee Does Not So Allow, and Is Formally Culturally Acknowledged Not So To Allow[79]) Requires the daily circumstance of Cooperative living, As An Essential Aspect Of The Total Way Of Life Embraced By My Devotees—A Way Of Life That Is (and Must Be) A Consistent and Effective Address To The Core Fault Of egoity (or The Avoidance Of Relationship). As A General Rule (Unless My Any Devotee's particular living-circumstance Is Formally Culturally Acknowledged Not So To Allow), My Devotees Should Live In household Situations That Include A Large Enough Number Of Devotees That the Cooperative living-circumstance Has A Real Impact On their Practice Of The Only-By-Me Revealed and Given Way Of The Heart (or Way Of Adidam)—Both In The Practical Terms Of Maximizing the time each individual Has Available For All The Activities Of The Sacred Domain (As Well As In The Practical Terms Of Conserving financial Resources) and In The Cultural Terms Of Creating A Circumstance Of daily Accountability, and Of Mutual Inspiration and Expectation, That Is Maximally Conducive To The Transcending Of egoity (A daily Circumstance, In Other Words, That Maximally Serves each individual's Vowed Intent To, Ultimately, Most Perfectly, Realize My Avatarically Self-Revealed Divine Person and Self-Condition). Thus, the Cooperative living that I Call My Devotees To Embrace Is Not At All A Matter Of mere "communalism" (or The Embrace Of communal living As A "Value" In and Of Itself, As an arrangement Entered Into By social egos). Rather, Such Right Cooperative living Is A Means For Consistently Going Beyond The (Otherwise Inevitable) Tendency To live In The egoic Manner. Therefore, It Is Essential For My Devotees To Relinquish The "Architecture" Of egoic living, and (Instead) To Embrace (To The Maximum Degree Possible In each individual's Case) The "Architecture" Of ego-Transcending Devotion To Me.

Rightly Conservative self-Discipline Of the body-mind Is Fundamental To The Practice Of The Only-By-Me Revealed and Given Way Of The Heart (or Way Of Adidam). Indeed, It Has Always Traditionally Been Acknowledged As Fundamental To Spiritual Life. The Responsibility For Right Conservative self-Discipline Is Inherent and Inescapable In The Esoteric Process Of Realization. Therefore, The Requirement For Right Conservative self-Discipline Is Not (By Any Means) Unique To The Only-By-Me Revealed and Given Way Of The Heart. What Is Unique About The Disciplines Of The Way Of The Heart Is That They Are Given By Me—and They Are A Particular and Intrinsic Aspect Of The Devotional and (In Due Course) Spiritual Relationship To Me, Which (Uniquely) Culminates (Ultimately) In Most Perfect (or Seventh Stage) Realization Of Me.

The Comprehensive Totality Of These Basic Disciplines Requires A Period Of Initial Study and Adaptation, In Which To (Thoroughly and Stably) Establish Them As A Detailed and Comprehensive Whole, Based On Right Understanding, Right (and Detailed) personal Adaptation, and Real (and Entirely Trustable) Accountability. That Necessary Period Of Initial Study and Adaptation (or Of "Consideration" Via Actual Practice) Is The Student-Beginner Stage (and Especially The Earliest Period Of The Student-Beginner Stage) Of The Way Of The Heart. And All Student-Beginners In The Way Of The Heart Are To Be Formally Expected, From The Beginning, To Accept and Embrace All These Basic Disciplines (By Formally Studying and Seriously and Accountably Applying All Of Them), and, Therefore, To Adapt To All Of Them As Appropriate, Useful, and Truly Necessary Elements Of The Real Practice Of The Way Of The Heart.

These By-Me-Given Foundation Disciplines Of The Way Of The Heart Are Not ascetical. They Are Not At All A Matter Of Dissociating From the body-mind or Of Disconnecting the body-mind From its environment Of Participation. Rather, These By-Me-Given Foundation Disciplines Are Entirely Life-Positive—and Entirely A Matter Of Establishing The Right (and Necessary) Equanimity Of the body-mind (or The Total psycho-physical Complex Of the individual being) Through Disciplines Of Basic Right Life (Understood Not In moralistic, or puritanical, or merely behavioral Terms, but Understood In Spiritual and Divine Terms). These By-Me-Given Foundation Disciplines Are, Most Fundamentally, A Matter Of Participating In Devotional and (In Due Course) Spiritual Communion With Me, By Bringing the body-mind (More and More) Into The Condition (and Disposition) Of Utter Non-Separation. If My Any Devotee Fails To Establish and Maintain These By-Me-Given Foundation Disciplines, he or she (Thereby) Creates A psycho-physical life-Disturbance That Is, In Fact, Dissociative In Its Effect. And those who live In Such An Undisciplined (and, Therefore, Inevitably self-Contracted) Manner Are Always going back and forth in their minds, Between Extremes Of self-Indulgence and self-Denial. Such Undisciplined individuals Lack The Virtue Of Participatory Equanimity Which Comes About Through The Practice Of Responsive Surrender Of self-Contraction, In Devotional and (In Due Course) Spiritual Communion With Me.

It Is Profoundly Important That My Devotees Understand That Practice Of The By-Me-Given Foundation Disciplines Of The Way Of The Heart Is Not A Matter Of being "good little boys and girls". Right Practice Of The By-Me-Given Foundation Disciplines Of The Way Of The Heart Is Simply The Living Of Right Life, Through The Establishment Of Participatory Equanimity, For The Sake Of Devotional and (In Due Course) Spiritual Communion With Me (and, Ultimately, Most Perfect Realization Of Me)—Not In The Mode Of A Seeker, but In The Mode Of A Non-Contracted Participant. And, Having Established The By-Me-Given functional, practical, relational, and Cultural Disciplines (Based On Devotional Recognition-Response To Me, and On A Right Understanding Of The Necessity and Purpose Of The By-Me-Given Forms Of Discipline), My Devotee Must Persist In The Practice Of All Of These Disciplines, Always In The Context Of More and More Profoundly Engaged Participatory Practice Of Devotional and (In Due Course) Spiritual Communion With Me. If Such Is The Case, Then There Is (More and More) The Developing Evidence Of Profundity Of life and (Ultimately) Of Realization—Whereas, If My Devotee Fails To Maintain The Disciplined Practice Of The Way Of The Heart and Resorts (Once Again) To the ego-position of self-Contraction (Thereby Generating, Once Again, the dualities, the disturbances, and The Loss Of Equanimity Characteristic Of egoity), Then he or she Returns To The Search—Undermining The Fundamental Discipline Of Right Life and Right Practice, and Throwing Away What Has Been Given By Me. Therefore, My Devotee Must Establish Right functional, practical, relational, and Cultural Discipline, Based On My Instructions, and Maintain That Discipline In Perpetuity—As A Fundamental Obligation, Such That Participatory Equanimity Is Established, Maintained, and Perpetuated As A Base For Right Practice Of The Only-By-Me Revealed and Given Way Of The Heart (or Way Of Adidam), and Such That Consistent Application To The By-Me-Given Forms Of Discipline Is Simply Not A Matter Of "debate" (whether "inner" or "outer").

This Developing Participatory Equanimity Of Right Life (and Non-"debatable" Application To The By-Me-Given Forms Of Discipline)—Founded In The Student-Beginner's Already Established Devotional Communion With Me, and Then (After, and Ever-After, The Transition To The Intensive Listening-Hearing Stage Of The Way Of The Heart) Magnified Via My By-Me-Spiritually-Initiated Devotee's Spiritual Communion With Me—Is The (Necessary) Right Basis For Practice In The Intensive Listening-Hearing Stage Of The Way Of The Heart (and Beyond), Rather Than Some Form Of Address To My Devotee's "case" as an ego. There Are Always Improvements To Be Made In My Devotee's Detailed Application To The functional, practical, relational, and Cultural Disciplines, but The Process Of The Intensive Listening-Hearing Stage Of The Way Of The Heart Is Never A Matter Of attention to "case" (or to the ego-"I" itself, Apart From The Vow and Obligation Of ego-Transcending Devotion To Me). The Process Of The Intensive Listening-Hearing Stage Of The Way Of The Heart (and Of Every Subsequent Stage Of The Way Of The Heart) Is Always, Fundamentally, A Matter Of Actively (and In A Really ego-Surrendering, ego-Forgetting, and ego-Transcending Manner) Cultivating The Devotional, and Now Truly Spiritual, Relationship To Me.

As A Prerequisite For The Transition To The Intensive Listening-Hearing Stage Of The Way Of The Heart, The Student-Beginner Must (By Consistent Study, Adaptation, Practice, and Cultural Accountability) Have Thoroughly "Considered" The Full Range Of These Basic Disciplines, Such That All The By-Me-Given Basic functional, practical, and relational Disciplines, As Well As All The By-Me-Given Basic (and Always Developing) Cultural Disciplines, Have Become Thoroughly Established As A Consistent and Comprehensive Practice (and Way Of Life) That Will Thereafter Remain (and More and More Become) A Simple, Easy, and Ever-Growing Obligation (In and Ever-After The Event Of Transition Beyond The Student-Beginner Stage).

At The Beginning Of The (Necessarily) Formal and Formally Acknowledged Student-Beginner Practice Of The Way Of The Heart, The Initially Adapting (or Novice) Student-Beginner (whose Formal Application For My Formal Acknowledgement, or, In General, For Formal Acknowledgement By My Formally Established and Formally Appointed Cultural Representatives, and For The—Thereby, By-My-Avataric-Divine-Grace-Given, Rather Than egoically Presumed—Right To Embrace The Practice Of The Only-By-Me Revealed and Given Way Of The Heart, Has Been Formally Accepted) Must (Necessarily) Accept (and, By Progressively Adapting Demonstration, Fulfill) The Fundamental Basics Of The Student-Beginner Practices Of Devotion, Service, self-Discipline, and Meditation (Including The Consistent Maintenance Of Various Elementary Prerequisite Obligations),[80] So That The (Progressively Developing) Student-Beginner's Process Of Study-"Consideration" and Devotionally Responsive Listening To Me Will Have A Firm (and Usable) Novice Base On Which To Develop Further and To Become Truly Fruitful (In The Form, Eventually, Of The Consistently and Fully Activated Student-Beginner Foundation Practices Of Devotion, Service, self-Discipline, and Meditation). Therefore, The Formally Acknowledged Novice Student-Beginner (Progressively Establishing The Fundamental Basics Of The Student-Beginner Foundation Of The Total

Discipline Of The Way Of The Heart) Must—On The Basis Of Truly Heart-Responsive Formal Examination Of My Instructive, and Avatarically Self-Revealed, and Always Me-Revealing, Divine Word, and Truly Heart-Responsive Formal Study Of My Avatarically Self-Manifested, and Always Instructive, and Always Me-Revealing, Divine Leelas, and Truly Heart-Felt, and Heart-Certain, Devotional Response To The Self-Revealing Avataric Sign Of My Own Self-Evidently Divine Person—Be Fully Intending (and, Thus, Really Committed) To Actively and Progressively Establish and Develop Real Practice Of The Full and Total Way Of The Heart, Exactly As The Full and Total Way Of The Heart Is Revealed and Communicated In This, My Testament Of Divine Secrets (and By All My Avataric Divine Words Of Teaching-Argument and Heart-Instruction Included In The Others Of My Twenty-Three Divine "Source-Texts", That Extend From, or, Otherwise, Correspond To, This, My Summary and Testamental Word).

The Novice Student-Beginner Must, As A Prerequisite For Formal Acceptance As Such, Already Have (Naturally, Characteristically, or By Various ordinary human and social Means) Relinquished (or Become Healed Of) "Grossest" mental (and psychological, or psychic), and emotional, and social Problems (or Aberrations), Including "Grossest" Habits and Addictions. Furthermore, The Novice Student-Beginner Must, As A Prerequisite For Formal Acceptance As Such, Be Already Entirely Free Of All Use (With The Possible Exception Only Of Token and Merely Symbolic Use, As May Sometimes Be Required By Custom For Respectful and Right Participation In, Necessarily Rare, Sacred, or Entirely Ceremonial and Non-personal, social Occasions) Of any of the rather common (or Commonly Used) intoxicants (Such As alcohol, tobacco, or kava), and Already Entirely Free Of Any Use Whatsoever Of "soft" drugs (Such As cannabis), "recreational" drugs (of any kind), hallucinogenic drugs, "hard" drugs, or otherwise medically inappropriate drugs. And The Novice Student-Beginner Must, As A Prerequisite For Formal Acceptance As Such, Already Be Fully Active In work (or, Otherwise, In Responsible Service To others), Such That he or she Is (practically and socially) Responsible (By Appropriate, or Wholly Right, Means) For The Support and Maintenance Of his or her personal circumstance of life—and For The Support and Maintenance Of his or her Right and Necessary Portion Of The Sacred, and Very Practical, Institutional, Cultural, and Cooperative Obligations Common To All Formally Acknowledged Practitioners Of The Way Of The Heart.

By Commitment (and By Progressively Increasing Adaptation In Practice), The Formally Acknowledged Novice Student-Beginner In The Only-By-Me Revealed and Given Way Of The Heart (or Way Of Adidam) Must Be Truly Submitted To Listen To Me (With Increasingly Clear-minded attention) and To

(Progressively) Actively Change and Make Right all ordinary action—Through ego-Surrendering, ego-Forgetting, and, More and More, ego-Transcending Feeling-Contemplation Of Me (and With This Feeling-Contemplation Always Increasingly Assisted, or Made Manifest, By The Only-By-Me Revealed and Given functional, practical, relational, and Cultural Means Of Direct Application To All The Fundamental Basics Of The Student-Beginner Practices Of Devotion, Service, self-Discipline, and Meditation). And, In Due Course, The Novice Student-Beginner Must Have Firmly and Stably Established The Fundamental Basics Of Practice Of The Only-By-Me Revealed and Given Way Of The Heart (or Way Of Adidam) That Provide The Necessary Qualifications For Further (Intensive) Development Of The Student-Beginner Course Of Formal Study, Adaptation In Practice, and Cultural Accountability. And The Intensive Student-Beginner Course Of Practice That Follows The Initial (or Novice) Period Of First Adaptation Must Surely Develop (and Fully and Firmly Establish) The Total Student-Beginner Foundation Of The Only-By-Me Revealed and Given Way Of The Heart—Such That, Beyond The Student-Beginner Stage Of The Way Of The Heart, Effective ego-Transcendence (and, Ultimately, Most Perfectly ego-Transcending—and Fully, and Most Perfectly Spiritually Awakened—Real-God-Realization) May, In Due Course, Be Progressively (but Certainly and Truly) Realized.

In The One (and Only) By-Me-Revealed and By-Me-Given Way Of The Heart (or Way Of Adidam), All The Basic functional, practical, relational, and Cultural Disciplines I Have Indicated Herein Are (By Consistent, and Ever-Growing, Application) To Intensify The Novice Student-Beginner and (Then) Fully Established Student-Beginner Process Of self-Observation—and This By Frustrating The Patterns and Accumulated Addictions Of egoic Seeking. Indeed, the ego-"I" is (Inherently and Entirely) An "Addict"—A Compulsive and Obsessive and Intensely Persistent Seeker, In Perpetual (and Never To Be Satisfied) Pursuit Of Utter self-Fulfillment and (Yet self-Centered) self-Release. Therefore, This Same (self-Disciplined) Process That Must Be Embraced Even From The (Student-Beginner) Beginning Of The Way Of The Heart Must Continue To Intensify (and To Develop In Greater and Greater Detail) In The Intensive Listening-Hearing Context Of Practice In The Way Of The Heart, Until The Foundation Process Of self-Observation (Thus Disciplined, Intensified, and Developed) Becomes The Real, True, and Unique Capability Of Direct (or Fully Responsible) Release Of the self-Contraction itself (and The Search Itself), Through The Profound Demonstration Of self-Understanding and ego-Transcendence That Expresses True Hearing Of Me (and, Eventually, True, and, Most Ultimately, Even Inherently Most Perfect, Seeing Of Me).

When Whole bodily (or Total psycho-physical) Existence Is Free Of self-Contraction (and, Thus and Thereby, Free Of The Compulsive Stress Of a mind that Seeks Release From the self-Contraction Via conditional states of knowledge and experience), Then attention Is Inherently Free Of ego-Bondage. When attention Is At Ease In Relation To the body-mind (and, Thus, In Relation To all psycho-physical states and relations), Then attention Is Free To Realize That Which Is its own Source-Condition (and, Thus and Thereby, The Source-Condition Of all of the Possible psycho-physical objects of attention). And When That (Self-Evidently Divine) Source-Condition Is Realized, The One and Only and Inherently Indivisible and Inherently egoless Reality (or Conscious Light)—Which Is Both The Self-Existing Divine Self-Identity Of Consciousness (Itself) and The Divine Self-Condition (or Native, Self-Radiant, and Indivisible State) Of all Apparent objects (or psycho-physical "things") of attention—Is Tacitly Obvious.

In The Way Of The Heart, self-Discipline Is (or Must Be) A Right, Voluntary, Intelligent, and Intentional Practice. Also, In The Way Of The Heart, self-Discipline Is A Secondary (or Supportive) Responsive Practice. That Is To Say, In The Way Of The Heart, The Various Forms Of By-Me-Given self-Discipline Are Not Proposed By Me As "ideal behaviors" That Must (Ultimately) Be functionally, practically, and relationally (or, Altogether, Morally) Perfected. Rather, In The Way Of The Heart, All The Various Forms Of By-Me-Given self-Discipline Are Given By Me, and To Be Embraced By My Devotee, For The Sake Of self-Observation, self-Understanding, self-Transcendence (or Real ego-Transcendence), and ego-Transcending Real-God-Realization. And, Most Ultimately, ego-Transcendence Is Realized (To The Most Perfect Degree) Only As and By Means Of The By-My-Avataric-Divine-Spiritual-Grace-Given Inherent Perfection Of Inherent Self-Identification With My (Avatarically Self-Revealed) Transcendental, Inherently Spiritual, Inherently egoless, and Self-Evidently Divine Self-Condition, and Not By Means Of any functional, or practical, or relational, or (Altogether) Moral acts or behaviors. Therefore, In The Only-By-Me Revealed and Given Way Of The Heart (or Way Of Adidam), The Perfection Of functional, practical, and relational (or, Altogether, Moral) behavior (or self-Discipline) Is Neither Expected Nor Possible—but What Is Both Expected and Possible Is That My Every Devotee Practice Each and All Of The By-Me-Given functional, practical, and relational Disciplines Truly, Seriously, Consistently, and With Full and Consistent Cultural Accountability.

A Basic Design For self-Discipline Is Offered To All Practitioners Formally Embracing The Way Of The Heart. On This Basis, each individual Must Discover A Detailed personal Design That Is Both Appropriate and Optimum In his or her own case. In This Always Ongoing Process, All My Devotees Must Make The Measure Of every day, Such That they (each and all) Consistently Fulfill All The By-Me-Given Forms Of functional, practical, relational, and Cultural Discipline.

To Serve Every Formally Acknowledged Practitioner Of The Way Of The Heart In his or her Consistent Embrace Of, and Application To, The Full Range Of functional, practical, relational, and Cultural Disciplines, I Have Given A Basic "Form", To Be Adapted To On A daily, weekly, monthly, and annual Basis[81]—and This Embrace Of (and Application To) The Effective Discipline Of "Form" Is To Be Consistently Monitored (and, Thereby, Kept Regularly Accountable), In Detail, By The Cooperative Sacred Culture (Of Expectation and Inspiration) Made Up Of Other (and, Truly, Even All Other) Formally Acknowledged Practitioners Of The Way Of The Heart.

From The Beginning Of The Way Of The Heart (and In Any Manner or Developmental Stage Of Practice In The Way Of The Heart), The Practice Of self-Discipline Must, Of Course, Be Based On An Intelligent (and ego-Renouncing) Evaluation Of The Tendencies (and An Intelligent, and ego-Renouncing, Accommodation Of The Necessities) Of the conditionally-Patterned body-mind—but (Until True Hearing Of Me Awakens) The Principal Function Of That self-Discipline Is To Reflect The conditionally-Patterned ego-Tendencies Of the body-mind To The Intelligent self-Observer, So That the conditionally-Patterned ego-"I" May Be Directly, Clearly, Fully, and Effectively Observed, and (In Due Course) Fundamentally (or, Even Unconditionally, or At Heart) Understood. As Practice Of The Way Of The Heart Matures To The Degree Of True Hearing Of Me (and Beyond), self-Discipline Must Continue, and It Must Continue To Develop From The Original Basic Disciplines Comprehensively Assumed In The Student-Beginner Stage Of The Way Of The Heart—but (Once True Hearing Of Me Awakens) self-Discipline Itself Must Become (and It Must More and More Simply Become) An Expression Of The ego-Transcending Equanimity (and The ego-Transcending functional, practical, and relational Economy) Of one who Has Already Heard Me. And, Eventually, In The Fully Technically Responsible Spiritually Active Context Of The Way Of The Heart, self-Discipline Must Also Become, and It Must More and More Simply Become, An Expression Of The ego-Transcending Spiritual Fullness and, Most Ultimately, The ego-Transcending Transcendental and Divine Awakeness Of one who Has Already Seen Me.

In The Student-Beginner Stage Of The Way Of The Heart, and In The Intensive Listening-Hearing Stage Of The Way Of The Heart, The Basic functional, practical, relational, and Cultural Disciplines—Relative To General Health, Right Diet, Right emotional-sexual Practice (Whether relationally sexually active Or celibate), True Service, and Formal Cooperative Sacred Cultural Association—Are (In General Principle) The First (or Truly humanizing) Forms Of "Conductivity" Practice—Because They Command (or Conduct) the wandering functional life-energy and attention of the ordinary human (or frontal) personality, and (Thereby, Artfully) Create A self-Reflecting Medium (Which Functions As A Natural bio-Feedback Mechanism). Therefore, From The Beginning Of The Way Of The Heart (and In The Context Of Any and Every Manner and Developmental Stage Of Practice Of The Way Of The Heart), self-Discipline (Intentionally Applied) Involves A Necessary (and Inherent) Encounter With The Control-Force ("Father-Force", or "Husbanding" Force) Of Life. However, The First Three Stages Of Life (Which Are The life-Foundation Upon Which The Entire Practice Of self-Discipline Must Be Built) Involve An ego-Transcending Process Of Adaptation and Growth Relative To The Control-Force Of Life. And The First Three Stages Of Life (Themselves) Tend To Become An egoic (and, Necessarily, Un-Happy) Struggle Against Being Controlled—and That self-Contracted and self-Protective Struggle Is Inevitably Accompanied By A Reactive Effort (or Search), Either To Control others Or To Resist others Or To Be Detached From others. Therefore, In The Only-By-Me Revealed and Given Way Of The Heart, The Comprehensive and Truly Intelligent (or Fully "Considered") Practice Of self-Discipline (Which Must, Necessarily, Be A Characteristic Of The Intensive Listening-Hearing Stage, and Beyond, In The Way Of The Heart) Is Not (and Cannot Be) Truly and Consistently Demonstrated Until The Struggle Relative To Control Itself Is Basically (and Very Effectively) Released. That Release From The ego-Struggle Relative To self-Discipline Is Established Via The Foundation-Process Of Student-Beginner Study, Adaptation, Cultural Accountability, and self-Observation—and (In The Further and Fullest Course Of The Student-Beginner Stage Of Practice Of The Way Of The Heart) That Struggle Must Be More and More (and Effectively) Replaced By The Free Motive Of self-Control, By Which The Motive To Control and Balance the body-mind Is Made Your Own, or Allowed To Function As A Basic and Positive personal Directive Toward self-Discipline.

As My Devotee, It Is Essential That You Deal Appropriately With The Foundation Matters Of ordinary human life, Such That the body-mind Is (Thus and Thereby) Fundamentally Purified. By Establishing the body-mind In The By-Me-Given Basic functional, practical, relational, and Cultural Disciplines, You Are Moved Beyond Preoccupation With (and Confinement To) the gross ego (and The Total Pattern Of social egoity), and Re-Oriented To The (By-Me-and-As-Me-Avatarically-Self-Revealed) Divine Self-Condition. In Order To Truly Grow In My Avataric Divine Company, There Must Be A Turning Of The Faculties—From The Obsession With "money, food, and sex" and social egoity, To Me. In That Whole bodily To-Me-Turned Disposition, You Must Engage The Continuous (day to day) Real Sadhana Of Participation In Meditation, Devotional Chanting, Puja, Study Of My Avataric Divine Word, and So On—Always Practiced As Real Devotional (and, In Due Course, Spiritual) Resort To Me.

True Spiritual Life Requires Profound Purification Of Your ordinary human existence, and (Thus) Profound Purification Of The Principal Faculties (Of body, emotion, mind, and breath). That Purification Is, In Part, Accomplished Through Your Consistent Application Of The By-Me-Given Basic functional, practical, relational, and Cultural Disciplines. At The Most Profound Level, That Purification Is Accomplished Only By My Spiritual Invasion Of My To-Me-Surrendered Devotee—and That Great and Most Profound Process Of Purification Continues Even Into and Throughout The Only-By-Me Revealed and Given Seventh Stage Of Life.

There Are Specific Gifts Of Practice That You, As My Devotee, Must Bring To Me—From The Beginning Of Your Embrace Of The Only-By-Me Revealed and Given Way Of The Heart. You Must Bring To Me The Gift Of Your Devotional Resort To Me, Based On Your Heart-Recognition Of Me. And You Must Bring To Me The Gift Of Your Fulfillment Of The By-Me-Given Basic functional, practical, relational, and Cultural Disciplines—Which Disciplines Establish The Necessary Foundation Of Purification and Equanimity, and (In Due Course) The Preparedness To Be Initiated, By Me, Into The Real Spiritual Process Of Devotional Relationship To Me, and Which Disciplines (Altogether) Re-Orient The Totality Of the body-mind To The Great Purpose Of Realizing Me.

Merely To Be a functional social ego Has Nothing To Do With Real Spiritual Life. There Must Be A Turning-Over Of the life From The "money, food, and sex" Preoccupations With Which people ordinarily busy themselves. As My Devotee, You Must Involve All Of The psycho-physical Faculties In The Sadhana Of Turning To Me. Do Not Imagine That It Is Sufficient Merely To "Re-Model" (or Idealize and Systematize) Your Preoccupation With gross egoic (or social egoic) life On The Basis Of A Series Of Prescriptive Disciplines. Only The Fundamental ego-Surrendering Practice Of Devotionally Turning To Me (or Ruchira Avatara Bhakti Yoga) Is Sufficient. The Disciplining Of Your functional, practical, and relational life Is A Matter Of Conforming (or Fitting) the body-mind (in its functional, practical, and relational sphere) To The Turning Of The Faculties To Me.

As My Devotee, Never Idealize The Significance Of Your ordinary activities (Even When Enacted In The Appropriately Disciplined Manner). As My Devotee, Always Give Yourself Sufficient daily time and place For Sacred Activity. Always Spend Significant daily time Engaged In The Set-Apart Places and Activities Of Meditation, Of Devotional Chanting, and Of Puja. Spend Significant time every day Engaged In The Exercises Of Turning The Faculties Exclusively To Me, In Places Where (and at times When) You Are Not Otherwise In The Midst Of functional, practical, and relational activities.

As My Devotee, You Must Transform Your "money, food, and sex" life and Your social life. It Is Not Necessary To "Leave the world" (In Some Absolute Sense) In Order For This Transformation To Occur, but It Is Essential That You Consistently Participate In The Sacred Domain Of The Culture Of Adidam. Through Such Participation, You Must (In every day) "Retrieve" time From its Usual Patterning With The Preoccupations Of "money, food, and sex" and social egoity. And You Must (Thereby) Simplify everything functional, practical, and relational—everything To Do With "money, food, and sex" and social egoity—and "Retrieve" time From all of that, For The Sacred (or Set-Apart) Exercise Of Turning The Faculties To Me.

In The Only-By-Me Revealed and Given Way Of The Heart (or Way Of Adidam), It Is Not the body-mind but egoity itself That Must Be Renounced—By Means Of Right Devotion To Me, Practiced moment to moment. And All The Renunciation That Comes About (In the body-mind itself) Occurs By My Avataric Divine Spiritual Grace. As My Devotee, You Must Embrace The Fundamental Disciplines I Have Given To You—but The Profundities Of Renunciation Come About By My Avataric Divine Spiritual Grace. Renunciation Of the ego-"I" Is A Divine Spiritual Gift From Me—Just As Realization Of Me (Myself) Is A Divine Spiritual Gift From Me.

Your Patterns Of Dis-Ease and self-Indulgence Do Obstruct The Spiritual Process In My Avataric Divine Company—but Those Patterns Will Be Purified, If You Persist In Truly Turning To Me and Rightly Disciplining the body-mind. You Will Voluntarily Relinquish Them In The Fullness Of Spiritually Receiving Me. At Some Point, It Will Hurt Too Much To Continue Enacting (and Indulging In) Those Patterns. Then, It Will Be Self-Evident That A Particular Pattern or Tendency or Habit Has Run Its Course, Ceasing To Be "interesting"—and It Will Fall Away In Your Free Relinquishment Of It.

Ultimately, everything conditional Must Be Relinquished. In Due Course, death Is Inevitable. Therefore, All Of Your (Total psycho-physical) ego-Patterning—gross, subtle, and causal—Must, Ultimately, Be Transcended. However, This Total Relinquishment Is Not Required To Occur In a single instant. This Relinquishment Occurs In A Right (Progressive) Order, In The Course Of The Real Spiritual Process In My Avataric Divine Company. The More You Are Spiritually In-Filled By Me, The More Of Your ego-Patterning Is Purified and (Thereby) Relinquished (or Renounced).

This By-My-Avataric-Divine-Spiritual-Grace-Given Renunciation Occurs From head To toe. The Purification Is Accomplished By Means Of My Avataric Divine Spiritual Invasion. Therefore, Renunciation In The Way Of The Heart Is Not An idealistic (and self-Involved) "Program", Requiring You To "Do" Something "To" the body-mind. The Fundamental Disciplines Of The Way Of The Heart Are

Simply A Matter Of Right Life—Simply The Means Whereby the body-mind Is Established In The Yogic Equanimity Of Devotionally Turning To Me. When You Are (As A Total psycho-physical Whole) Fully Thus Established, My Avataric Divine Spiritual Invasion Occurs—Bringing About The Purification and Transformation Of the (Total psycho-physical) body-mind. Through Your Constant Devotional Turning To Me, I Am Moved To Give You My Divine Spiritual Gifts. Receiving My Avataric Divine Spiritual Blessing-Transmission Is Not An Automatic "Given". My Avataric Divine Spiritual Blessing-Transmission Is A Gift That Is Volunteered By Me In Response To Your Right and True Devotion To Me.

To Clearly Receive Me Spiritually Is Utterly life-Transforming. To Actually Experience Me Spiritually—Coming Upon You From Outside and Beyond Yourself—Is A Miraculous (and, Ultimately, Incomprehensible) Event. And The Real Spiritual Reception (and Spiritual Experience) Of Me Is The Only Absolute Proof Of The Divine. Everything Else (That Might Be Adduced As Evidence Of The Divine) Is mere "talk".

When You Experience Me Spiritually, You Are Necessarily Transformed. To Experience Me Spiritually Is A Divine Discovery That Effectively Converts the being. When You (Thus) Discover Me, You Become Capable Of "Locating" Me Spiritually. Then I Can Do My (Purifying and Awakening) Spiritual Work With You—and The Signs Of That Work Will Spontaneously Manifest In Your body-mind, More and More Over time.

What You Have On Your mind Is Boring and Unsatisfactory. Your thoughts and Your self-Manipulations Are Fruitless and Dis-Heartening—Regardless Of Their content.

To Be Fallen Upon By My Self-Evident Divine "Brightness" Is The Only Satisfaction. It Is The Only Cure For Doubt and For All The Fear and Sorrow and Anger Of This Heart-Murdering Event here.

Without My Avataric Divine Spiritual Invasion, This Is Unrelieved Suffering. In and Of Itself, This Is A Horror, a Terrible place of endings.

You Cannot think Your Way Out Of it. At the moment of Your death, There Is No mere thought You Can Have In mind That Will Give You Peace.

Only My Sheer and Absolute Avataric Divine Spiritual Presence Solves The Heart Of My Devotee.

Avatar Adi Da Samraj
Clear Lake, 2001

SUTRA

29

The common world Is Beset By A Neurosis Relative To The Exercise and Demonstration Of Devotion To What Is Greater Than oneself (and Even To What Is Supremely and Perfectly Great). This Neurosis Epitomizes The ego-Bondage Characteristic Of The First Three Stages Of Life—and, Therefore, This Neurosis Must Be Clearly Observed, Rightly and Responsibly Understood, and Really Effectively Relinquished and Out-Grown By My Student-Beginner Devotees (At The Foundation Of their Practice Of The Only-By-Me Revealed and Given Way Of The Heart, or Way Of Adidam)—and Simply By Means Of The Right, True, Full, and Fully Devotional Practice Of Ruchira Avatara Bhakti Yoga.

My Student-Beginner Devotees Do Not Approach Me Spiritually. Rather, their Responsibility Is To Embrace The Yoga Of The Devotional Relationship To Me (and, On That Basis, To Become Prepared, In Due Course, To Be Spiritually Initiated, By Me, Into The Yoga Of The Devotional and Spiritual Relationship To Me, During The Period, or Periods, Of Extended Formal Retreat Engaged In My Avataric Physical Human Company—or, After My Avataric Physical Human Lifetime, In The physical human Company and By-Me-Spiritually-Empowered Circumstances Of My "Ruchira Sannyasin" Devotees—In The First Period Of The Intensive Listening-Hearing Stage Of The Way Of The Heart).

For My Student-Beginner Devotees, The Primary Practice Of The Only-By-Me Revealed and Given Way Of The Heart Is Ruchira Avatara Bhakti Yoga, In The Form Of The moment to moment Whole bodily self-Surrender (or Simple Turning Of The Four psycho-physical Faculties) To Me. The Surrender (or Simple Turning) Of The Four Faculties To Me Is (For All My Devotees) Devotional Heart-Recognition Of Me. My Student-Beginner Devotees Must Become Truly Adept At This Primary Practice (Of Surrendering, or Simply Turning, body, emotion, mind, and breath To Me)—and, In Addition, they Must Develop The Beginning (Responsive) Practice Of The "Conscious Process" and "Conductivity". The Yoga Of The Devotional Relationship To Me (Via Surrender Of The Four Faculties) Is Always The Primary Practice For My Student-Beginner Devotees—and That Primary Practice (Of Surrendering, or Simply Turning, The Four Faculties To Me) Is (Also) Responsively Demonstrated Through The Exercise Of The functional, practical, relational, and Cultural Disciplines (Including The Full Life Of Ruchira Avatara Seva, or Total psycho-physical Service To Me). Therefore, My Student-Beginner Devotees Must Be Clear That Student-Beginner Practice In The Only-By-Me Revealed and Given Way Of The Heart Is Not Primarily A Matter Of Adapting To The functional, practical, relational, and Cultural Disciplines. To Make The functional, practical, relational, and Cultural Disciplines one's Primary Focus In Practice Tends To Make The Way Of The Heart Into a (behavior-Oriented) "social persona" game. That Is Why The functional, practical, relational, and Cultural Disciplines Must Always Be Engaged As Secondary Practices, Which Support The Primary Practice Of (In The Student-Beginner Case) Ruchira Avatara Bhakti Yoga (In The Form Of The Surrender, or Simple Turning, Of The Four psycho-physical Faculties To Me).

If This Primary Practice Is Rightly, Truly, Fully, and Fully Devotionally Engaged By My Student-Beginner Devotee (and If That Primary Practice Is Rightly, Truly, Fully, and Fully Devotionally Extended By Means Of The Supportive Exercise Of The Only-By-Me Revealed and Given functional, practical, relational, and Cultural Disciplines), A Sign Of Profoundly Purified and Balanced psycho-physical Equanimity Appears. That Sign (Of Profoundly Purified and Balanced psycho-physical Equanimity) and The Root-Sign Of Full Devotional Concentration In Me (Free Of The Excesses Of Overly Outward-Directed social behavior, or Bondage To The "Programs" Of the social ego) Are Fundamental Indicators Of The Readiness To Make The Transition From The Student-Beginner Stage Of The Way Of The Heart To The Intensive Listening-Hearing Stage Of The Way Of The Heart. Gross social and psycho-physical Un-Rest Must Become Sufficiently Purified and Rightly Balanced Before The True By-Me-Spiritually-Initiated Process Of The Way Of The Heart Can Begin. The ego-"I" Would Extend The (Preparatory) Purifying and Balancing Process Indefinitely, but Such Fixation In The Preoccupations and Purposes Of The First Three Stages Of Life Is Entirely Unnecessary (and Entirely Inappropriate) For one who Would Realize Me. In Truth, The (Preparatory) Purifying and Balancing Process Can Readily Be Fulfilled In a finite period of time (Rather Than Requiring many years). That Purifying and Balancing Process Is Part Of My Student-Beginner Devotee's Preparation For The Full (Devotional and Spiritual) Practice Of The Only-By-Me Revealed and Given Way Of The Heart (or Way Of Adidam). That Purifying and Balancing Process Is Not (In and Of Itself) The Way Itself.

The Sign Of Profoundly Purified and Balanced psycho-physical Equanimity Is The Result Not Only Of My individual Student-Beginner Devotee's Exercise

Of The Real Yoga Of The Devotional Relationship To Me, but Also Of The Collective Life Of Devotion To Me That Is Lived By The Formal Worldwide Sacred Institutional and Cooperative Cultural Gathering, or Truly Global Ashram, Of All My Formally Practicing Devotees. No individual Devotee Can Rightly, Truly, Fully, and Fully Devotionally Practice The Way Of The Heart (Nor Can Any individual Devotee Be Rightly Measured In his or her Practice Of The Way Of The Heart) Unless That Practice Is (With Full Cultural Accountability) Occurring In The Context Of The Right, True, Full, and Fully Devotional Response Of The Collective Culture Of All My Formally Practicing Devotees. Because Global Secular (and Not At All Consistently Cooperative) human Society Is Not (Itself) A Culture Of Devotion To Me, The Yoga Of The Devotional (and, In Due Course, Spiritual) Relationship To Me Must Be Collectively Cultivated By The Total Institutional and Cooperative Culture Of My Formally Practicing Devotees. Only That Total Collective Institutional and Cooperative Culture Of Devotion To Me Establishes The Pattern By Which The Practice Of My Any individual Devotee Can Be Rightly (and Fully Accountably) Measured.

By Surrendering (or Simply Turning) All Four Of The Primary psycho-physical Faculties To Me, My Every Devotee (Beginning In The Student-Beginner Stage) Enacts The Devotional Relationship To Me With the Total body-mind, In A Manner That Accounts For All Aspects Of conditional (psycho-physical) Existence. That Degree Of Devotional Concentration In Me Is What Allows My Devotee To Step Out Of The Wanderings Of body, emotion, mind, and breath, Into The Truly One-Pointed Devotional Relationship To Me.

The Condition Of Basic functional, practical, and relational (or Total psycho-physical) Equanimity Is Necessary In Order To Receive Me Spiritually (and Even In Order To Effectively Serve Me). Therefore, My Student-Beginner Devotees Must Establish and Maintain Both The Primary and The Responsive Disciplines That Allow This Sign To Develop. In This moment to moment Surrender (or Simple Turning) Of The Four Faculties To Me, There Is No "case" (or Distraction By The egoic contents and Patterns Of the body-mind itself). In This moment to moment Surrender (or Simple Turning) Of The Four Faculties To Me, There Are No Longer Dramatized Exaggerations Of The Faculties, Because The Faculties Are Doing What Inherently Transcends Their Own Aberrated Patterning. When My Student-Beginner Devotee Really (Consistently, and Persistently) Engages This Practice Of Surrendering (or Simply Turning) The Four psycho-physical Faculties To Me moment to moment (Thereby Establishing The Fundamental Pattern Of Ruchira Avatara Bhakti Yoga, Which Is To Be Maintained and Magnified Throughout The Course Of The Only-By-Me Revealed and Given Way Of The Heart), There Is A Fundamental and Immediate Change That Affects My Devotee's entire life.

The Yoga Of Surrendering (or Simply Turning) The Four psycho-physical Faculties To Me Is Straightforward and Direct. That Yoga Is A Matter Of Using The Faculties Differently, and Not (In Any Sense) Indulging In egoic Dramatizations Of The Four Faculties. When My Devotees (As A Collective Gathering) Do This Consistently, Then The Sacred Domain Of The True Devotional Culture Of The Way Of The Heart Establishes Itself As A (More and More) Effective Means For Serving each individual's Right and True Growth In The Practice Of The Only-By-Me Revealed and Given Way Of The Heart.

From a conventional (behaviorally Oriented) point of view, The Bringing Of the gross body-mind Under Basic Control (By Means Of Such Disciplines As The Complete Avoidance Of intoxicants, The Consistent Application Of Right Dietary and Health Practices In General, The Yogically life-Positive Relinquishing Of merely casual and otherwise degenerative emotional-sexual activity, and So Forth) May Be (Erroneously) Presumed To Be The Primary "Task" Of The Student-Beginner Stage Of The Way Of The Heart (By Which My Student-Beginner Devotee Becomes Prepared To Make The Transition To The Intensive Listening-Hearing Stage Of The Way Of The Heart). Such Basic (Disciplined) Control Is, Indeed, Required, In Order To Make The Transition Beyond Student-Beginner Practice—but Such Basic (Disciplined) Control Is Not, In and Of Itself, The Basis On Which That Transition Can Be (Rightly and Truly) Made. The Transition Beyond Student-Beginner Practice Can Be (Rightly and Truly) Made <u>Only</u> On The Basis Of Having Effectively Established The moment to moment Exercise Of Ruchira Avatara Bhakti Yoga, or The Surrender (or Simple Turning) Of The Four Faculties To Me (Necessarily, Also Supported By The Consistent and Effective Exercise Of The By-Me-Given functional, practical, relational, and Cultural Disciplines). Only That Exercise Of Ruchira Avatara Bhakti Yoga Makes Possible The (By-Me-Spiritually-Initiated) Awakening Of Spiritual Sensitivity To Me and The Transition To The Fully Established—Devotional <u>and</u> Spiritual—Practice Of The Way Of The Heart, Beyond The Preparatory (or Preliminary) Student-Beginner Phase.

Ruchira Avatara Bhakti Yoga (As It Is Engaged By My Student-Beginner Devotee) Is A Profound Sadhana Relative To The Foundation Preparation Of the body-mind For The Life Of Spiritual Communion With Me (and The Forever-To-Be-Continued Practice Of Ruchira Avatara Bhakti Yoga). That Beginning Practice Of The Only-By-Me Revealed and Given Way Of The Heart (Lived In The Context Of First-Three-Stages-Of-Life Patterning) Is Not Merely A Matter Of My Student-Beginner Devotee Becoming psycho-physically Balanced (In Some General, conventional Sense) and (Then) Regarding <u>That</u> To Be "True Equanimity". If The Sadhana Of Ruchira Avatara Bhakti Yoga Has

Not Become A Full and True moment to moment Practice Of Turning All Four Faculties (Of body, emotion, mind, and breath) To Me, Then The Yogic True Equanimity That Is The Necessary Foundation For The Spiritual Process In The Only-By-Me Revealed and Given Way Of The Heart Is Not In Evidence. In That Case, Either the individual Will (In his or her Approach To Me) Register No Signs Of Spiritual Awareness Of Me Or (Otherwise) Whatever Apparent Spiritual Sensitivity To Me Is (In The Context Of That Approach) Shown Will Merely Be Incorporated (In One Manner or Another) Into his or her psycho-physical Patterning, Such That the individual Cannot Rightly (and, Therefore, Fruitfully) Embrace The Subsequent Spiritual Sadhana Of Devotion To Me.

In Order To Enter Into The Devotional-and-Spiritual Relationship To Me, There Must Be True and Consistent Evidence Of Yogic Equanimity—Not Merely social-ego Equanimity, Not Merely Rote Conformity To Various Rules Of Expectation In The Context Of The First Three Stages Of Life (Such As A Positive Disposition In Service, or The Prescriptive Fulfillment Of The Various functional, practical, relational, and Cultural Disciplines, and So Forth). All Of The By-Me-Given Forms Of Discipline Are, Of Course, Necessary—but They Are Not Sufficient In and Of Themselves. In Order To Enter Into The Devotional-and-Spiritual Relationship To Me, The Yoga Of Ruchira Avatara Bhakti Must Have Been Practiced Profoundly and Consistently In The First (Student-Beginner) Context Of The Foundation Practice Of The Only-By-Me Revealed and Given Way Of The Heart, Such That The Unique Yogic Equanimity Which Is The Necessary Preparation For The Spiritual Process Of Devotional Communion With Me Has Been Established.

Merely To Be Involved In The Process Of Conforming To Various Rules and Expectations In The Context Of The First Three Stages Of Life Is, In Any Case, Yet Merely An Involvement In The First Three Stages Of Life Themselves. To Mature Beyond The First Three Stages Of Life, Into The Spiritual Context Of The Fourth Stage Of Life (Beginning With The Intensive Listening-Hearing Stage Of The Way Of The Heart), Requires The Consistent and Effective Practice Of Ruchira Avatara Bhakti Yoga—and That Maturity Is Indicated (In any individual's Case) By The Yogic Evidence Of Ruchira Avatara Bhakti. Such Is The Necessary Sign Of The Readiness To Enter Into The Life Of Spiritual Communion With Me (Beyond The Student-Beginner Stage Of The Way Of The Heart)—A Readiness That Is A Matter Of Great Profundity (Much Beyond Merely Being Prepared For an Orderly, ordinary life).

Only The Real and True Yogic Fulfillment Of The Foundation Sadhana Of Ruchira Avatara Bhakti—The Consistent Turning Of The Four psycho-physical Faculties To Me (In A Profoundly Surrendered, or Entirely and Unequivocally and Unconditionally Turned-To-Me, Disposition)—Can Provide The Basis For

Real Spiritual Sensitivity To Me, Such That I Can Spiritually Work With the individual (Whether he or she Is, In any moment, In My Avataric Physical Human Company Or Outside My Avataric Physical Human Company), In A Manner That Is (Yogically and Spiritually) True and Profound, and That Will Not Be Overruled, Overridden, or Diminished By the individual's gross Patterning. Bondage To The gross Domain Of conditional Existence Can Take The Form Of gross self-Indulgence Of the body-mind, Such That the body-mind itself Must Be Purified and Re-Balanced (By Means Of The By-Me-Given functional, practical, relational, and Cultural Disciplines)—but There Is, Nevertheless, Also A More Fundamental Level Of Bondage To The gross Domain Of conditional Existence, Which Is Still The Case Even In The Context Of an Orderly personal life. Such Bondage Is Purified Only By Means Of The Right and True Practice Of Ruchira Avatara Bhakti Yoga.

The ego-"I" (In The Context Of The First Three Stages Of Life) Often Attempts To Mimic The Right and True Practice Of Ruchira Avatara Bhakti Yoga, By Becoming Involved In a kind of emotionalistic devotionalism. Such devotionalism Is Not Ruchira Avatara Bhakti Yoga. Such emotionalistic devotionalism Is A conventional First-Three-Stages-Of-Life Mode Of Religious enthusiasm, which Has No Profundity Associated With it, and which Is Not At All Sufficient For True Growth In The Beginning Stages Of The Only-By-Me Revealed and Given Way Of The Heart. The Signs Of The Right and True Practice Of Ruchira Avatara Bhakti Yoga Are The Yogic Evidence Of Turning the entire body-mind (Of Four psycho-physical Faculties) To Me. The Consistent Yogic Turning To Me Is The Fundamental Core, Principle, and Process That Must Be Firmly Established At The Foundation Level Of The Way Of The Heart. And That Real (Yogic) Turning To Me Shows Itself (In Due Course) As The Evidence Of a Truly Turned-To-Me personality, who Is Free Of Bondage To The gross Aspects Of self-Contraction (In The Context Of The First Three Stages Of Life) Which Would (Otherwise) Inhibit Real Spiritual Reception Of Me and Consistent Spiritual Communion With Me.

Only Turned-To-Me Devotion—All The Faculties Turned From self-Contraction Into Communion With Me—Is Esoteric Devotion. Such Real Devotion To Me Certainly Has The Characteristic Of A Fundamental Equanimity, but That Yogic Equanimity Is Not The Same As Merely Being a Balanced social personality. That Yogic Equanimity Is The Sign Of A Fundamental Freedom From Bondage To gross life—Sufficient To Be Truly Entered Into Spiritual Communion With Me, and To Consistently Live The Requirements Of The Devotional-and-Spiritual Relationship To Me (Without Lapsing, Without self-"guruing", and Without self-Contracted games of any kind).

Therefore, The Devotional Yoga Of Turning To Me Is The Core (or The Most Significant Element) Of The Foundation Practice Of The Only-By-Me Revealed and Given Way Of The Heart (or Way Of Adidam). Every Other Aspect Of That Foundation Practice Depends On (and Is Engaged On The Basis Of) The Devotional Yoga Of Ruchira Avatara Bhakti. When That Foundation Practice Is Fulfilled, Then My Devotee Is Prepared To Enter Into The Spiritual Process Of Devotion To Me, Which Begins With The Process Of Intensively Listening To Me, and Matures (First) Into The Process Of Hearing Me and (Then) Into The Process Of Seeing Me, and (Ultimately) Culminates In The "Perfect Practice" Of The Only-By-Me Revealed and Given Way Of The Heart (or Way Of Adidam).

The By-Me-Activated (and Constantly By-Me-Renewed and By-Me-Developed) Real Spiritual Process Is A Clear Imposition That Progressively Reveals limitations and Requires their Active Relinquishment. It Is Both A psycho-physically Purifying (and ego-Relinquishing) Process and A Divinely Me-Revealing Process—The Process That, Ultimately, Becomes Divine (or Seventh Stage) Realization Of Me. However, In Order To Fully and Profoundly Enter Into (and Grow In) This Process, You Must Be Truly (and Always Actively) Surrendered To Me. Then, Real Spiritual Sensitivity To Me "Seals" The Matter Of The Disciplining Of The ego's Commitment To gross Existence—By Bringing A Force Of Requirement (Into The Sphere Of psycho-physical Awareness) Which Is Greater Than What mere mind Proposes.

Before You Enter Into The Spiritual Dimension Of The Devotional Relationship To Me, The Measure Of Your self-Discipline (Including, Particularly, Your emotional-sexual self-Discipline) Is My Instructions (Given In This, My Divine Testament Of Secrets, and Extended In The Form Of My Ruchira-Sannyasin-Order-Authorized Detailed Instructions Relative To The functional, practical, relational, and Cultural Disciplines)—but, Once You Have Entered Into The Full Devotional and Spiritual Practice Of The Relationship To Me, My Divine Spiritual Invasion Of the body-mind Becomes The Great Measure (and Force Of Requirement) Of Your Practice (Within The Parameters Given By Me For Your Fulfillment Of The functional, practical, relational, and Cultural Disciplines). Once You Have Entered Into The Full Devotional and Spiritual Practice Of The Relationship To Me, The Rightness Of Your Practice (Altogether) Is Indicated By Its Effect On Your Spiritual Communion With Me. Any Lessening (or Shutting Down) Of Your Communion With Me—or Any Complication In Your Communion With Me—Must Be Corrected. And, If (and Only If) You Are Abiding In Right and True Receptive Spiritual Sensitivity To Me, Truly Devotionally Resorting To Me and Invoking Me, You Always (Very Directly) Know Exactly What Must Be Corrected—Because What

Obstructs My Divine Spiritual Invasion Of Your body-mind Becomes Tangibly and Immediately Evident.

Furthermore, The Event and Process Of Hearing Me Is (Like The Event and Process Of Seeing Me) Necessarily Associated With My Divine Spiritual Invasion Of the body-mind. My Divine Spiritual Invasion Is The Means Whereby The Fundamental and psycho-physically Pervasive (or Total body-mind) Nature Of self-Contraction Is Shown—and This Becomes The Revelation Of Hearing Me. When You Hear Me, There Is Most Fundamental self-Understanding. Most Fundamental self-Understanding Is The Platform Of Practice That Is Based On The Tacit Root-Awareness Of The Fundamental self-Contraction-Act That is egoity. And Most Fundamental self-Understanding Carries With It The Fundamental Capability Of Directly Transcending the self-Contraction (or egoity itself)—Through Real Devotional Resort To Me and True (and Truly Full) Spiritual Communion With Me.

The Preparedness To Live Real Spiritual Life In My Avataric Divine Company Is A Great Matter. To Be So Prepared Is To Make The Transition Beyond The First Three Stages Of Life (or Bondage To The gross Dimension Of conditional Existence) and To Enter Into The Spiritual Dimension Of The Totality Of Existence (and, Ultimately, Into My Unconditional Divine Spiritual Sphere). The Real Spiritual Process In My Avataric Divine Company Is Not Merely A Matter Of feeling a "buzz" of energies in Your gross body. The Real Spiritual Process In My Avataric Divine Company Is (Altogether) A Profound Change Of Life, Made Possible By The Consistent Yogic Turning To Me. Only Such Yogic Turning Enables The Transition Beyond The Context Of The First Three Stages Of Life Into The Context Of The Fourth Stage Of Life. The functional, practical, relational, and Cultural Disciplines Are Not—In and Of Themselves—Sufficient To Enable This Transition.

The conventional (or exoteric) religiosity Of The First Three Stages Of Life Is A Matter Of the social ego Adding A Dimension Of Religious devotionalism To its character. Such devotionalism Is Not Real Devotional (or, Potentially, Spiritual) Life, and Not An ego-Transcending Process. Thus, Although emotionalistic devotionalism Imitates Some Of The Rudimentary Beginnings Of The Fourth Stage Of Life, such devotionalism Is Not The Sign Of An Actual Conversion To The True Disposition Of The Fourth Stage Of Life (and Of The Spiritual Dimension Of The Totality Of Existence). The Real Conversion To The Disposition Of The Fourth Stage Of Life Requires A Conversion From The self-Contracted Patterning Associated With The First Three Stages Of Life, A "Turnabout" Into The Spiritual Dimension Of The Totality Of Existence. That Spiritual Dimension Is Unknown In the self-Contracted (or egoic) state of the gross body-mind. If There Is Not That Turning Of The Faculties—From the self-Contraction and The egoic Patterning Of The First Three Stages Of Life, To Me—Then any individual who Appears To Be Experiencing My Avatarically Self-Transmitted Divine Spiritual Presence Is (In Reality) Merely Adapting That Experience To The First Three Stages Of Life, and (Thereby) Becoming Deluded By his or her own energies, or By his or her own ego-Patterning.

Your Relationship To Me As Your Divine Heart-Master Is A Relationship Of Active, moment to moment, Whole bodily (or Comprehensively psycho-physical) Surrender, Directly and Really Transcending egoity, and Always Purposed To Realization Of Me. "Narcissus" Would Make The Practice Of The Way Of The Heart Into A Matter Of Merely Adapting To (or Coming To A "Settlement" With) egoic Patterning Itself, Such That each individual Is Being Nothing More Than the persona Dictated By his or her karmic (or Accumulated and merely conditional) destiny—Merely Wanting That ego-Patterning To Be Preserved, and Always Wanting To Animate That Mere ego-Patterning, or To Be "Given Permission" To "Parade" egoic limitations in the form of character signs. Instead Of All Of That, The Life Of Active ego-Surrender Is What Is Required Of My Devotee.

The Progressive Process Of True Growth In My Avataric Divine Company Cannot Occur If You (As My Devotee) Are Anxiously Armoring Yourself, and Are (Thereby) Being Strategically (Even If, To A Large Extent, Unconsciously) Untouched By Me. The More You Persist In That Effort Of self-Armoring, The More That Armoring Becomes An Established Characteristic Not Only Of Your Doings but Of Your personality-Patterning Itself. Such Armoring Is (To A Significant Degree) Founded In The Primitive Urge To Resist All Forms Of (Particularly, emotional) Vulnerability. Therefore, It Is Necessary For All My Devotees To Observe, Understand, and Transcend their Patterned emotional limitations, In Order To Become Truly Available To My Divine Spiritual In-Filling.

If You Are My Devotee, You Are Impulsed To Realize Me—Not To Maintain Your persona. Indeed, In Order To Realize Me, You Must Be Willing To Go Beyond All Trace Of Separate and Separative persona, and (Thereby) To Go Beyond all the egoic limitations By which You Are Binding and Deluding Yourself. Such Going-Beyond Is The Necessary Sign and Demonstration Of The Utter Surrender Of "Narcissus" (or the Total psycho-physical ego-"I") To Me. Only In That Case Is The Relationship To Me The Real Practice Of Devotion To Me, Demonstrated As The ego-Forgetting life of ego-Transcendence (Rather Than the ego-Defending life of the Armored persona). And Such Going-Beyond Is Made Possible By Your Embrace Of The Practice I Have Given To You (In All Its Details)—Not By Perpetuating Your egoic Patterning Through self-Reflecting (or self-Imaging and self-Meditative) "case talk" or

Through An Ongoing Series Of Attempts To Refine Your persona-Determined life-Patterns.

Only If You Are Founded In The ego-Transcending (or persona-Transcending) Disposition and Are Actively Relinquishing Your Binding Patterns (and, Thus and Thereby, Relinquishing Your Enactment Of the self-Contraction Altogether) Can You Fully Make Use Of My Avataric Divine Spiritual Work With You. To Consistently Turn The Faculties Of the body-mind To Me Is To Relinquish The (Otherwise Obsessive) Turning In On Yourself (and, Thus, Onto Being a Presumed-To-Be-Separate—and, Therefore, Separative—"self").

I Expect My Devotees To Do The Practice I Have Given them. I Expect My Devotees To Require That Practice Of themselves, Without (In Any Sense) Defending a persona (or an ego) In Relationship To Me. As My Devotee, You Must Release Your life-energy and attention To Me, So That You Cease To Animate (or Dramatize) the mummery-persona that Would Otherwise Be the "content" of Your lifetime.

The Relinquishment Of the karmic persona Is Absolutely Necessary For True human and Spiritual Growth In My Avataric Divine Company. To Relinquish the karmic persona Is To Forget the ego-self—Thus Allowing The Fundamental Practice Of Turning To Me To Deepen and Mature. Without That Relinquishment, You Cannot Make Use Of My Avataric Divine Spiritual Self-Transmission. Therefore, You Must Cease To "Play" any Separate and Separative persona. You Must Cease To Protect Your self-Image (or, Otherwise, To Project Your self-Image Onto Me). Practice Of The Only-By-Me Revealed and Given Way Of The Heart Has Nothing To Do With Protecting The Pattern Of Your Bondage (As the karmic personality, or the mummer, or the egoic entity). Practice Of The Only-By-Me Revealed and Given Way Of The Heart Has Nothing To Do With Being an ego In Relationship To Me. Rather, Practice Of The Only-By-Me Revealed and Given Way Of The Heart (or Way Of Adidam) Is The self-Surrendered and self-Forgotten (or persona-Surrendered and persona-Forgotten) Relationship To Me, In My here-Manifested (and, Altogether, Avatarically Self-Revealing) Bodily (Human) Divine Form (Shown During My Physical Human Lifetime Via My Avatarically-Born Physical Human Body Itself—and Shown During, and After, and Forever After My Physical Human Lifetime Via My Likenesses, Preserved By Many and Various Murti-Images Of My Avatarically-Born Bodily Human Divine Form).

If You Are Not Truly self-Surrendered and self-Forgotten By Means Of Real and Right Practice Of Ruchira Avatara Bhakti Yoga, You Will Tend To Propose An ego-Made (and ego-Serving) Revision Of The Way Of The Heart, According To Which You Already "Contain" Me "Inside" Yourself (or "In Your Heart"). All Such Propositions Are Simply Forms Of Dissociating (or Abstracting)

Yourself From Me, or Of (Rather Complacently) Proclaiming Your Presumed self-Sufficiency and Lack Of Need For Me—and, More Deeply, Your Anxiety, or Even Fear, Relative To Truly Embracing The Process Of ego-Forgetting Surrender To Me In My Avatarically here-Born Bodily (Human) Divine Form. Indeed, Such Dissociation Is The Typical egoic Fault—Which Is To Be Overcome By Means Of Your Heart-Recognition Of Me and Your Heart-Response To Me, Avatarically Present here In Bodily (Human) Divine Form. To Heart-Recognize Me and Heart-Respond To Me Is Not To Relate To Your Own "insides". Rather, To Heart-Recognize Me and Heart-Respond To Me Is To Enter Into Relationship With Me As That One Who Is *Beyond* You, and *Prior To* You, and *Infinitely Greater* Than You—Gracefully Appearing *In Front Of* You, and *Outside* You. To Presume That You Find Me "Inside" Yourself (or "In Your Heart") Is To Claim That the *ego* Is Divine. That Claim Is The Ultimate Heresy—The Mere (and self-Deluded) Poeticizing and Idealizing Of egoity. Therefore, The Only-By-Me Revealed and Given Way Of The Heart (or Way Of Adidam) Is Not An Inward-Turning Path, but The Turning-To-*Me* Way.

The Revelation I Have Given Is Not About You. The Revelation I Have Given Is About *Me*. Therefore, I Call You To Abandon All Forms Of self-"guruing" and To Enter Into Relationship With *Me*—By Forgetting "self" and Turning To *Me*.

The Practice Of ego-Transcending Devotional Surrender To Me (Turning All The Faculties To Me) Is What Enables All The Developments Of The Only-By-Me Revealed and Given Way Of The Heart (or Way Of Adidam) To Occur, In Due Course, By My Avataric Divine Grace. Therefore, If You Engage In A Mode Of "Seeming" Practice Of The Way Of The Heart (Which "Seeming" Practice Is, Fundamentally, A Matter Of Avoiding True Surrender To Me and Refusing To Truly Turn The Faculties To Me—Avatarically Present here In My Bodily Human Divine Form), You Are Preventing The Process Of The Way Of The Heart From Developing. Indeed, You Are, In That Case, Committing Yourself To Nothing but A very ordinary (and Even grossly ego-Bound) Form Of self-Deluded Exercise.

The egoic Tendency To Manufacture A "Substitute" For Me, By Presuming That I Am Already "Inside" (or "In The Heart Of") the ego-entity—and, As A Result, To Present Yourself To Me As the mummer, Rather Than As My Truly self-Surrendered Devotee—Is One Of The Fundamental Means Whereby My Devotees Avoid (and Prevent) The Real (and Only-By-My-Avataric-Divine-Grace-Given) Process That Becomes (In Due Course) The True Hearing Of Me. Indeed, Such "Substitution"-Delusion Is A Dramatization Of The Very egoic Mechanism That Is Specifically Understood and Transcended By Means Of Truly Hearing Me. Therefore, You Must Not Establish Any "Substitutes" For

Me, and You Must Not Establish Any "Substitutes" For The Real Practice Of Surrender To Me. The Manufacture Of Such "Substitutes" Is Precisely How the ego Works. Such Is The Nature (and activity) Of self-"guruing"—The Establishment Of An Alternative and ego-Based Principle (Generally Speaking, a mind-form) That "Replaces" Me. In That Case, There Is No Surrender, and There Is No self-Forgetting—and, Therefore, No Real (human and Spiritual) Growth Is Possible. In That Case, There Is Nothing but Persistent self-Delusion and Temporary self-Consolation. In That Case, It Is Impossible To Hear Me and (Then) To See Me. In That Case, It Is Impossible To Establish Even The Foundation Of Devotional Resort To Me, Because the mummer (or the "performing" ego—who <u>is</u> "Narcissus") Is Always Being Consoled and Aggrandized and Elaborated—Forever Dissociated From Me, and Totally self-Involved. This Is How Practice Of The Only-By-Me Revealed and Given Way Of The Heart (or Way Of Adidam) Fails To Be True.

You <u>Cannot</u> (By <u>Any</u> egoic Means or Efforts) "Take Heaven By Storm". The "I"-thought in the Presumed-To-Be-Separate body-mind Is Not An Indicator Of present-time Realization Of The One Divine Reality and Person. Rather, the "I"-thought in the Presumed-To-Be-Separate body-mind Is "Narcissus". And, Indeed, "Narcissus" Is More Than a mere thought. "Narcissus" Is (Altogether) A Profoundly Complex Pattern Of Whole bodily (or Total psycho-physical) Activity (and Of Consequent ego-destiny). Therefore, You Must (First and Always) Transcend the Complex "I"—Through Real (and Whole bodily, or Total psycho-physical) Practice Of The Counter-egoic (and, In Due Course, Perfectly ego-Transcending) Way I Have Revealed and Given.

All Of This Is The Reason Why The Right and True Practice Of Ruchira Avatara Bhakti Yoga Is Such A Profound Requirement—From The Beginning Of The Only-By-Me Revealed and Given Way Of The Heart (or Way Of Adidam). There Must Be Real Yogic Turning—Turning Out From "self", From The Pattern Of self-Contraction and All The Patterns Of Adaptation Based On It In The First Three Stages Of Life—To Me. I Am Always Present To Help You Awaken From Your sleep, Your dreams, and Your waking conceits. That Awakening—Which Necessarily Occurs In The Midst Of The "Hard School" Of ego-Transcendence, and In The Constant Swoon Of Devotional Heart-Communion With Me—Is The Graceful Process That I Offer To all who Approach Me As My Formally Practicing Devotees. Only On That Basis Can My Any Devotee Become Capable Of Entering Into The Process Of Spiritual Communion With Me—In The Intensive Listening-Hearing Stage Of The Way Of The Heart, and Beyond.

The Intensive Listening-Hearing Stage Of The Way Of The Heart Is <u>Formally</u> Divided Into Three Periods Of Practice. From The Beginning Of The

First Period, and Always Thereafter, The Various Basic functional, practical, relational, and Cultural Disciplines Are (Each and All, and Necessarily) To Be Fully and Firmly and Formally Assumed (Having Already Been Fully, Firmly, Formally, and Thoroughly Established In The Course Of The Student-Beginner Stage Of The Way Of The Heart).

In Order To Make The Transition To The First Period Of The Intensive Listening-Hearing Stage Of The Way Of The Heart, My Any Devotee Must Already (As A Student-Beginner In The Way Of The Heart) Be Consistently (and, Necessarily, Formally) Demonstrating The Right, True, and Full Practice Of The Way Of The Heart That Qualifies him or her To Be Formally Registered With The Avataric Samrajya Of Adidam[82] (and Actually Results In his or her Being So Registered). In Order To Be So Registered, My Devotee Must Be Formally (and currently) Approved By The Ruchira Sannyasin Order Of Adidam Ruchiradam—After he or she Is Formally Evaluated and Estimated and Recommended, By The Formally Authorized Cultural Representatives Of The Lay Congregationist Order Of Adidam Ruchiradam, As Demonstrating (In Strict and Full Accordance With My Instructions, As Given, By Me, To The Ruchira Sannyasin Order Of Adidam Ruchiradam)[83] All The Necessary Qualifications To Make The Transition To The First Period Of The Intensive Listening-Hearing Stage Of The Only-By-Me Revealed and Given Way Of The Heart. And, In Becoming Thus and So Registered, My Devotee (Thereby) Affirms That he or she Has Thoroughly and Stably Established All The By-Me-Given Foundation Forms Of functional, practical, relational, and Cultural Discipline, and Vows That he or she Will Perpetually Maintain That Now-Established Firm Foundation Of Discipline.

After he or she Is Thus Formally Approved and Registered, My Devotee Must Be Specifically Given (then current, or then present-time) Formal Approval By The Ruchira Sannyasin Order Of Adidam Ruchiradam To Enter Into A Period (or, Possibly, More Than One Period) Of Extended Formal Retreat In My Avataric Physical Human Company (or, After My Avataric Physical Human Lifetime, In The physical human Company and By-Me-Spiritually-Empowered Circumstances Of My "Ruchira Sannyasin" Devotees). And My Any Such Devotee Must Be Specifically Given (then current, or then present-time) Formal Approval By The Ruchira Sannyasin Order Of Adidam Ruchiradam To Engage The Primary (Searchlessly Me-Beholding) Practice Of The Only-By-Me Revealed and Given Way Of The Heart, While On Extended Formal Retreat—and Afterwards (Once he or she Has Been Spiritually Initiated, By Me, Into That Practice, While he or she Is Participating In A Period Of Extended Formal Retreat In My Avataric Physical Human Company, or, After My Avataric Physical Human Lifetime, In The physical human

Company and By-Me-Spiritually-Empowered Circumstances Of My "Ruchira Sannyasin" Devotees).

No Devotee-Practitioner Of Adidam (Which Is The Only-By-Me Revealed and Given Way Of The Heart) Will Be Permitted To Make Any Transition To Practice Beyond The First Period Of The Intensive Listening (and Would-Be, Eventually, Hearing) Stage Of The Way Of The Heart (or, Otherwise, To Proceed Within Any Stage Of Practice Beyond The First Period Of The Intensive Listening, and Would-Be, Eventually, Hearing, Stage Of The Way Of The Heart) Unless he or she (With The Formal Approval Of The Ruchira Sannyasin Order Of Adidam Ruchiradam) Formally Qualifies For Formal Registration With—and Is, and Remains, Formally Registered With—The Avataric Samrajya Of Adidam As My Devotee Formally Invited To Enter Into Retreat In My Avataric Physical Human Company (or, After My Avataric Physical Human Lifetime, In The physical human Company and By-Me-Spiritually-Empowered Circumstances Of My "Ruchira Sannyasin" Devotees). And, Also, No Devotee-Practitioner Of The Way Of The Heart Will Be Accepted For <u>Such</u> Formal Approval By The Ruchira Sannyasin Order Of Adidam Ruchiradam, and For Subsequent Formal Registration With The Avataric Samrajya Of Adidam, Before The First Period Of The Intensive Listening (and Would-Be, Eventually, Hearing) Stage Of The Way Of The Heart.

My Each and Every Devotee who Has Formally Made The Transition To The First Period Of The Intensive Listening (and Would-Be, Eventually, Hearing) Stage Of The Way Of The Heart Must, By (Necessarily) Formal Invitation (By The Ruchira Sannyasin Order Of Adidam Ruchiradam), Come Into My Avataric Physical Human Company (or, After My Avataric Physical Human Lifetime, Into The physical human Company and By-Me-Spiritually-Empowered Circumstances Of My "Ruchira Sannyasin" Devotees) On Extended Formal Retreat,[84] For The Purpose Of Spiritual Initiation, By Me, Into The Primary Process Of Searchlessly Beholding Me (and Receiving My Ruchira Shaktipat, In The Beginner's Rudimentary Manner), and For The Further Purpose Of Truly Spiritually Establishing and Consistently (Thus) Rightly Demonstrating The Responsive Listening Practices Of Both The "Conscious Process" and "General Conductivity". In Order To Be Formally Invited To Engage Such Extended Formal Retreat, the individual Must Be Formally Approved, By The Ruchira Sannyasin Order Of Adidam Ruchiradam, As Qualified To Have Access To My Avataric Physical Human Company (or, After My Avataric Physical Human Lifetime, To The physical human Company and By-Me-Spiritually-Empowered Circumstances Of My "Ruchira Sannyasin" Devotees)—and Such (then present-time) Formal Approval By The Ruchira Sannyasin Order Of Adidam Ruchiradam Is Required For Any Further Such

Periods Of Retreat the individual May Engage (At any time After The Period Of Retreat That Necessarily Follows The Transition To The First Period Of The Intensive Listening-Hearing Stage), and (Indeed) For Any Form Of Access To My Avataric Physical Human Company (or, After My Avataric Physical Human Lifetime, To The physical human Company and By-Me-Spiritually-Empowered Circumstances Of My "Ruchira Sannyasin" Devotees), By any individual At Any Developmental Stage Of Practice Of The Way Of The Heart Beyond The Student-Beginner Stage (or Even, On Relatively Rare Occasions, By individuals At The Student-Beginner Stage Of The Way Of The Heart, or, Otherwise, By individuals who are Not Formal Practitioners Of The Way Of The Heart).

Access To My Avataric Physical Human Company (or, After My Avataric Physical Human Lifetime, To The physical human Company and By-Me-Spiritually-Empowered Circumstances Of My Instrumental "Ruchira Sannyasin" Devotees) Is A Unique Divine Spiritual Gift, Which Is Effective (In Transforming The Totality Of The Four psycho-physical Faculties Of My Any Rightly Prepared Devotee) By Virtue Of A Simple "Law Of Vibration".

If You Consistently Turn The psycho-physical Faculties To Me, You Are (Thus and Thereby—By Surrendering, Forgetting, and Transcending the ego-"I") Sympathetically Attuned To Me. If a tuning fork Is Struck (or, Thereby, or Otherwise, Caused To Vibrate At its Characteristic Frequency), and Then a Second tuning fork (Of Similar Structure, Capable Of Resonating With the First) Is Brought Into Promixity With the First tuning fork, the Second tuning fork (Even If it Is Not Already Vibrating, and Not, Otherwise, Struck) Will Begin To Vibrate Sympathetically (or "In Sympathy" With the First tuning fork). I Am Like the (First) Vibrating tuning fork—and You (As My Rightly Prepared Devotee) Are Like the (Second) Non-Vibrating tuning fork that Begins To Vibrate By Coming Into Proximity With the Already Vibrating tuning fork. Thus, By Coming Into True Sympathetic Association With Me, You Begin To Vibrate "In Sympathy" With Me—Until (In Due Course) You Become Completely Resonant With Me.

The Process Of Access To My Avataric Physical Human Company (or, After My Avataric Physical Human Lifetime, To The physical human Company and By-Me-Spiritually-Empowered Circumstances Of My Instrumental "Ruchira Sannyasin" Devotees) Is, Literally, A Vibratory Matter, Exactly Of The Nature I Have Just Described. If You Are (Thus) Vibrating With (and Attuned To) Me, You Become (Progressively More and More Deeply) Aware Of The Pressure (and The Fullness) Of My Avatarically Self-Transmitted Divine Spiritual Presence. You Begin To Notice Certain Characteristic Signs Of The Spiritual Reception (and Awareness) Of Me—Including A Tangible bodily Vibration (or In-Filling Feeling Of Saturation With Energy) and A Characteristic "Thickness"

Of the breath. Altogether, This Process Of Deepening Spiritual Sensitivity To Me Can Be Likened To The Process Of a sponge Gradually Soaking Up (and Swelling With) water. As You Are Given Over In That Sympathetic Attunement To Me, There Is, Over time, A (By-My-Avataric-Divine-Spiritual-Grace-Given) Purification Of Your Total psycho-physical ego-Patterning, Potentially (and Even Soon, or Rather Immediately) Signed By The Spontaneous Purifying Occurrence Of kriyas, and mudras, and pranayama (or automatic slow or rapid Yogic breathing-"Conductivity"), and other psycho-physical (or bodily, emotional, mental, and breath-Pattern) phenomena of all kinds (As the body-mind Requires and Allows). Such Are The First (and Progressively Deepening) "Symptoms" Of The Process Of Becoming Spiritually Attuned To Me.

If You (As My Foundationally Fully Prepared Devotee) Come Into My Avataric Physical Human Company (or, After My Avataric Physical Human Lifetime, Into The physical human Company and By-Me-Spiritually-Empowered Circumstances Of My Instrumental "Ruchira Sannyasin" Devotees) and Do Not Demonstrate <u>Any</u> Signs Of Spiritually Receiving Me, This Simply Indicates That You Are Not (In present time) Sympathetically Attuned To Me (but, Rather, Are psycho-physically self-Contracted, and, Thus and Thereby, Dissociated From Me). In That Case, You Are, In Effect, Holding the Two tines of the tuning fork With Your hand—Thereby Preventing The Possibility Of Sympathetic Vibration. Such Is The Effect Of The self-Contraction-Act That Is the ego.

The Only-By-Me Revealed and Given Way Of The Heart (or Way Of Adidam) Is The Devotional Turning Of The psycho-physical Faculties To Me—Bringing The Faculties Into Sympathetic Association With Me, Such That You Are Vibrated Whole bodily (or As A psycho-physical Totality) By My Vibration (and This, Ultimately, and In Due Course, To The Most Perfect Degree Of Complete Attunement With Me). If You Take Your hand Off the tines of the tuning fork, the tuning fork (or Your body-mind itself) <u>Will</u> (Inevitably) Vibrate Sympathetically With <u>Me</u>. Therefore, <u>Always</u> Turn To Me In My Avatarically-Born Bodily (Human) Divine Form—and (Thereby) Become Sympathetically Attuned To Me. And, When You (As My Foundationally Fully Prepared Devotee) Begin To (As Often As Possible) Come Into My Avataric Physical Human Company (or, After My Avataric Physical Human Lifetime, Into The physical human Company and By-Me-Spiritually-Empowered Circumstances Of My Instrumental "Ruchira Sannyasin" Devotees)—Allow <u>My</u> Avataric Divine Spiritual Self-Transmission To Vibrate <u>You</u>.

If the tuning fork that is Your body-mind Is Vibrated By Me, I Can (Progressively, and In Due Course) Make it Vibrate To The Degree Of Absolute Intensity. But If You Are Gripping the tines of the tuning fork, I Cannot Do My Avataric Divine Spiritual Work With You.

Therefore, Take Your hand Off the tines—and Come To Me.

Be Always Attuned To Me—and Vibrated By Me.

I Vibrate You By Merely Being.

Therefore, You Must Come To Me To Merely Be With Me.

By The Constant (moment to moment) Means Of The Foundation Practice Of Ruchira Avatara Bhakti Yoga, Be Turned To Me Utterly, Merely (Searchlessly) Beholding Me In My Avatarically-Born Bodily (Human) Divine Form—and Be (Thus, and Responsively) Utterly Surrendered Into Whole bodily (or Total psycho-physical) ego-Forgetting Communion (or Attunement and Resonance) With My Avatarically Self-Transmitted Divine Gift Of Spiritual Presence (Accomplishing All Of The Purification and Awakening Of You, By Merely Being With You).

The First Period Of The Intensive Listening (and Would-Be, Eventually, Hearing) Stage Of The Way Of The Heart Should (In The Optimum General Case) Consist Of A Single Period Of Extended Formal Retreat and Demonstration. If Necessary (For The True Demonstration Of The Fullest Right Beholding and Spiritual Reception Of Me To Be Fully Rightly and Consistently Shown and Formally Approved), The Initial Period Of Extended Formal Retreat May Be Followed By A Further Period Of Adaptation and Integration That Precedes One, or More, Further Periods Of Extended Retreat. In Any Case, The Total First Period Of The Intensive Listening (and Would-Be, Eventually, Hearing) Stage Of The Way Of The Heart Should Be Made As Short A Course As Possible, By Always and Consistently Intensifying and Maximizing The Involvement With Every Kind Of Resort (In The Beginner's Rudimentary Manner) To My Avatarically-Born Bodily (Human) Divine Form (In My Avataric Physical Human Company, or, After My Avataric Physical Human Lifetime, In The physical human Company and By-Me-Spiritually-Empowered Circumstances Of My "Ruchira Sannyasin" Devotees), and To My (Thus, and Thereby, and Thereupon) Avatarically Self-Transmitted Divine Spiritual Presence.

In The First Period Of The Intensive Listening (and Would-Be, Eventually, Hearing) Stage Of The Way Of The Heart, My Devotee (Beginning To Cultivate The Primary Practice, Which Is The Devotional and Spiritual Practice Of Searchless Beholding Of Me, and The Devotionally and Spiritually To-Me-Responsive Practices Of Both The "Conscious Process" and "General Conductivity", All Based On Reception Of My Ruchira Shaktipat) Is Called To Maximally Conserve (and Thus To Minimize) his or her Involvement With daily society, entertainments, and (In The Case Of All Practitioners Of The Way Of The Heart who Are, in their personal intimate contexts, sexually active) sexual activity. My Any Such Devotee Is Called To (Voluntarily) Engage This Discipline (Of Maximum Conservation Of Possible Diversions From The

Primary and The Responsive Exercises Of Spiritually Beholding Me and Spiritually Receiving Me) As Strictly As Possible, At Least Until Practice Formally Begins In The Second Period Of The Intensive Listening (and Would-Be, Eventually, Hearing) Stage Of The Way Of The Heart, From Which time A More Moderate Conservative Discipline May, Perhaps, Become Appropriate. And The Purpose Of This Maximally Conservative Discipline Is To Free My Any Such Devotee who Is A Would-Be By-Me-Spiritually-Initiated Practitioner Of The Way Of The Heart To Maximally Devote the Total body-mind (and As Much time and attention As Possible) To The Great Occasion Of Spiritually Me-Receiving Searchless and Responsive Beholding Of Me, and (Thus) To Every Kind Of Exercise Of Devotion To Me (Including Meditative, Sacramental, Ceremonial, and All Other Appropriate Formal, or Informal, Exercises Of Such Devotion)—So That Real and True Reception Of My Ruchira Shaktipat (and, Thus, The Constant Capability For The Primary Practice Of Searchless Beholding Of Me and, Also, The Magnified Capability For The Devotionally and Spiritually To-Me-Responsive Practices Of Both The "Conscious Process" and "General Conductivity") May Be Truly Spiritually Established As Fully and Quickly As Possible.

Accordingly, During The First Period Of The Intensive Listening-Hearing Stage Of The Way Of The Heart, those who Are (in their personal intimate contexts) Otherwise sexually active Are To Be Formally Expected To Practice celibacy (As Is The Case For All Otherwise sexually active Practitioners Of The Way Of The Heart who Are Engaging A Period Of Formal Retreat, Of Whatever Manner or Duration). However, In The Case Of Practitioners Of The Way Of The Heart who Are Required (During The First Period Of The Intensive Listening-Hearing Stage Of The Way Of The Heart) To Engage More Than One Period Of Extended Formal Retreat—and who Are Only Able To Engage The Further Period, or Periods, Of Extended Formal Retreat After A Significant Interval Of time Has Elapsed—sexual activity May (Perhaps) Be Resumed For a period of time During The Interval (With A Maximum Frequency Of once, or perhaps twice, per month—or, In Some Cases, Even once every ten days—Depending On The Duration Of The Interval, and Only If and As Formally Approved By The Formal Sacred Cooperative Cultural Gathering Of All Formally Acknowledged Practitioners Of The Way Of The Heart). And (In Any Case) they Should Maintain The Formally Expected (or, Otherwise, Formally Approved) Discipline (or Rule) Until they Are Formally Acknowledged To Have Made The Transition To The Second Period Of The Intensive Listening-Hearing Stage Of The Way Of The Heart.

The Logic Of Practice In The First Period Of The Intensive Listening (and Would-Be, Eventually, Hearing) Stage Of The Only-By-Me Revealed and Given

Way Of The Heart Obliges My Devotee To Fully Devote his or her Total body-mind and attention (In The Beginner's Rudimentary Manner) To My Baptizing (and Heart-Awakening) Divine Spiritual Presence, While Controlling (and Generally Moderating) the common opportunities For self-Exploitation or self-Indulgence. And This Sila (or self-Controlling Devotion) Is One Of The Key Means For Truly Effective Practice In The Context Of Any Stage Of Life, In Any Developmental Stage Of Practice, In The Only-By-Me Revealed and Given Way Of The Heart.

The Transition From The First To The Second Period Of The Intensive Listening (and Would-Be, Eventually, Hearing) Stage Of The Way Of The Heart Is Made (Necessarily, With Formal Approval By The Ruchira Sannyasin Order Of Adidam Ruchiradam) When Consistent True Devotional and Spiritual Practice Of The Primary Practice (Of Searchless Beholding Of Me) Is Demonstrated—and When The Devotional and Spiritual Evidence Of Initiation (By Me) Into Responsive (and ego-Surrendering, and ego-Forgetting, and, More and More, ego-Transcending) Devotional and Spiritual Communion With Me Is Truly and Consistently Demonstrated (After One or More Spiritually Initiatory Retreats In My Avataric Physical Human Company, or, After My Avataric Physical Human Lifetime, In The physical human Company and By-Me-Spiritually-Empowered Circumstances Of My "Ruchira Sannyasin" Devotees).

In The Progressive Course Of The Intensive Listening (and Would-Be, Eventually, Hearing) Stage (and Beyond) Of The Way Of The Heart, All The By-Me-Given Basic functional, practical, relational, and Cultural Disciplines Are To Be Consistently Applied, and Developed In Greater and Greater Detail (Even Beyond The Student-Beginner's Demonstration). Therefore, These Disciplines, Formally and Consistently Assumed and Applied—Along With The Serious "Consideration" Of All My Teaching-Arguments, and The Practice Of Either The Devotional Way Of Insight (Via self-Enquiry, In The Form "Avoiding Relationship?") Or The Devotional Way Of Faith (Via Ruchira Avatara Naama Japa), and All Engaged Within The Total Context Of Real Practicing Heart-Response To All My Given and Giving Gifts and Callings and Disciplines—Must Establish and Maintain A Constant "Reality Consideration", or An Effectively Counter-egoic Growth-Process Of Disciplining and Observing the conditional self (By Consistently Surrendering it To Demands That Frustrate its Tendencies), and Of Transcending the conditional self (Via Progressive, and Then Most Fundamental, self-Understanding).

The Mature Student-Beginner Is one who (As My Formally Acknowledged Listening Devotee) Has Developed The Foundation Practice Of The Only-By-Me Revealed and Given Way Of The Heart To Such A Degree That he or she Has (In The Listening Devotee's Manner) Become A Truly (and Stably) Serious and Altogether Exemplary Practitioner Of Ruchira Avatara Bhakti (or ego-Surrendering, ego-Forgetting, and Effectively ego-Transcending Devotion To Me), Ruchira Avatara Seva (or ego-Surrendering, ego-Forgetting, and Effectively ego-Transcending Service To Me), and Ruchira Avatara Tapas (or self-Discipline in Devotional Response To Me). Therefore, The Mature (and, More and More, Even The Developing) Student-Beginner (and, By Extension and Continuation, The Practitioner Of The Intensive Listening, and Would-Be, Eventually, Hearing, Stage Of The Way Of The Heart) Is one who Responsibly and Freely Relinquishes False Devotion To Me, or Both The childish Expression Of mere and self-indulgent and Weak-minded emotionalism Toward (or In Relation To) Me—Which Expression Is The Dramatization Of egoic (and ego-Protecting) Dependency and A Lack Of emotional Strength and Balance—and The adolescent Characteristic Of Dissociatively mental (or Non-Feeling) Abstraction Of Me—Which Expression (or, Really, Non-Expression) Is The Dramatization Of egoic Independence and ego-Possessed willfulness, and A Dramatization Of A Felt Conflict Between egoic Dependency and egoic Independence. In The Context Of The Way Of The Heart, The Characteristically adolescent egoic Dramatization Commonly Takes The Form Of A Weakness In The Resort To (and Feeling-Contemplation Of) Me In My Avatarically-Born Bodily (Human) Divine Form, and (Coincident With This Weakness) An egoic Tendency To "interiorize" Me, or (That Is To Say) To (In Effect) Presume That the ego-"I" (or "Narcissus") Is (itself) The Divine Heart-Master. This adolescent Dramatization Of self-"guruing" Shows Itself In The Characteristic Presumption That I (Myself) Am "Really" Within the ego-"I" (or the Separate and Separative body-mind), and Not (Via My "Concrete" Human and Spiritual Avataric Divine Self-Manifestation) Always Standing Firm In Effective (or Grace-Giving) Relation To My Devotee—and (In My Inherently Most Perfect Samadhi, or My Avatarically Self-Revealed, and Very, and Transcendental, and Perfectly Subjective, and Inherently Spiritual, and Inherently egoless, and Inherently Perfect, and Self-Evidently Divine State) I Am Always Firmly Established Prior To the ego-"I" (or the Separate and Separative body-mind).

The Signs Of Practice That Must Be Clearly (and Stably) In Evidence In Order For The Transition To Be Made To The First Period Of The Intensive Listening (and Would-Be, Eventually, Hearing) Stage Of The Way Of The Heart Are To Be Thoroughly "Tested and Proven" In The Context Of The Final (or Mature) Phase Of Student-Beginner Practice Of The Way Of The Heart. Therefore, When (By Such "Testing and Proving") The (Previously Developed) Signs Of A Real Capability For Effective (and Detailed) self-Discipline and The Effective (moment to moment) Exercise Of Feeling (and Acting) Beyond the self-Contraction Are Confirmed, and When Those Signs That Indicate That The

Mature Student-Beginner Has (Through The Ordeal Of Establishing The Original Foundation Of Practice In The Way Of The Heart) Become Truly Serious About "Life" and "Practice" Are Also Shown To Be Characterized By Consistently Generated functional life-energy and attention (Consistently Available For The Beginner's Real and True and Effective Practice, and Total Devotional Exercise, Of The Way Of The Heart), and By The Evidence Of Freedom (Most Basic) From The Search (or the ego-Based motives and beliefs) Associated With conventional (or ego-Consoling, ego-Serving, ego-Fulfilling, ego-Glorifying, Sometimes childish, and Sometimes adolescent) religiosity (In The Context Of The First Three Stages Of Life), and By The Evidence Of A Consistently Demonstrated Ability To Maintain personal Balance In The Company Of others (and To Make Consistently Positive and Effective Use Even Of their Criticisms)—Then The First Period Of The Intensive Listening (and Would-Be, Eventually, Hearing) Process Of The Way Of The Heart Can Begin.

Although The Practice Of The Only-By-Me Revealed and Given Way Of The Heart (or Way Of Adidam) Is (and Always Remains) A Matter Of individual Responsibility (In all relationships, and Under any and all circumstances or conditions that arise), That Responsibility Must (In Order To Be Made Really, and Consistently, and Fully Effective) Be Nurtured, Stimulated, Supported, Guided, and Directed By An Authentic (and Truly Effective) Culture Of Expectation and Inspiration. Therefore, All Practitioners Of The Way Of The Heart Must Embrace (and Participate In, and Keep themselves Always Fully Accountable To) The Cooperative Culture (Of Expectation and Inspiration) Made Up Of Other (and, Truly, Even All Other) Formally Acknowledged Practitioners Of The Way Of The Heart. And (As A Special, and Even More Intensive, Extension Of That Basic Culture Of Expectation and Inspiration) Each Practitioner In The Second Period Of The Intensive Listening (and Would-Be, Eventually, Hearing) Process Of The Way Of The Heart Is To Be Expected To Intensify The "Reality Consideration" (and The Effectiveness Of Formal Meditative Practice, As Well As The Effectiveness Of All The Always Continuing and Developing Forms Of self-Discipline, and The Effectiveness Of The Beginner's Right and True Religious, or—In The Beginner's Yet To Be Fully, and Technically Responsible, Spiritual Sense—Devotional, Practice and Service) Through Increased Application To The Process (Engaged By All Practitioners Of The Way Of The Heart) Of Formal and Detailed self-Examination (or self-Observation) In The Company (and Served By The Reflective Capability) Of Other Formally Acknowledged Practitioners Of The Way Of The Heart. Additionally, Every Such Practitioner In The Second Period Of The Intensive Listening (and Would-Be, Eventually, Hearing) Process Of The Way Of The Heart Is To Continue To Be Expected (As Even Every

Practitioner Of The Way Of The Heart Must, From The Beginning, Be Expected) To Optimize his or her daily (ordinary) Application Of self-Observation, and his or her Use Of The Natural Reflective Capability Of Even all ordinary relationships, circumstances, and events. And, Through The Use Of A daily Intensive Diary Of self-Observation and Devotional Confession (Even More Intensively and Elaborately Engaged Than The daily Diary Of self-Observation and Devotional Confession Otherwise To Be Kept By All Other Practitioners Of The Way Of The Heart),[85] The Practitioner In The Second Period Of The Intensive Listening (and Would-Be, Eventually, Hearing) Process Of The Way Of The Heart Should (and Is To Be Expected To) Constantly Notice and Confess (and Progressively, and, In Due Course, Most Fundamentally, Understand) The Actuality Of "Narcissus" (the ego-"I", or self-Contraction), As The "Acts Of Narcissus" arise (in mind, in emotion, In bodily Tendency, In Reactions, In social and intimate Habit-Patterns, and So On) in the moments of every day. And, Likewise, By Means Of The Same Intensive daily Diary (Of self-Observation and Devotional Confession), The Practitioner In The Second Period Of The Intensive Listening (and Would-Be, Eventually, Hearing) Process Of The Way Of The Heart Should (and Is To Be Expected To) Notice and Confess The (Counter-egoic) Devotional Process Of Resort To Me (Via Feeling-Contemplation, Service, and self-Discipline), Whereby "Narcissus" Is Progressively (and, Most Ultimately, Inherently, and Inherently Most Perfectly) Transcended.

All Practitioners Of The Way Of The Heart Are To Make Formal Use Of The Company (or Reflective Capability) Of Other Practitioners Of The Way Of The Heart, For The Purpose Of self-Examination, Devotional Confession, Improved Service, Improved self-Discipline, and (Eventual) Most Fundamental self-Understanding (and The Directly ego-Transcending Capability, Based On Most Fundamental self-Understanding)—and This Should Involve Appropriately Frequent "Considerations" With A (Consistent) Group Of Other Practitioners who Are (As A General Rule) Practicing The Way Of The Heart In The Same Developmental Stage. Such "Consideration" Groups Should (Optimally) Be Of Sufficient Size To Bring A Real Collective Force Of Mutual Support For one another's Right Practice Of The Way Of The Heart—and Such Group "Considerations" Should (Optimally) Occur At Least once each week.

In The Case Of Practitioners Of The Way Of The Heart who Are Practicing "True Yogic Intimacy" (whether heterosexual or homosexual), both of the partners in intimacy Should (As A General Rule) Be Regular Members Of The Same "Consideration" Group—So That they May Directly "Consider" their Practice Of "True Yogic Intimacy" In The Group Setting.

One or More Guides[86] (who, Optimally, Should Be Practicing At A More Advanced Developmental Stage Of The Way Of The Heart Than The Other

Members Of The Group) Are Always To Be Present (and Specially Functioning) In Such "Consideration" Groups—Simply To Direct everyone To My Avataric Divine Word Of Argument and Instruction Relative To Devotional Recognition-Response To Me, and Relative To Most Fundamental self-Understanding Of self-Contraction, and Relative To True (Direct, and Effective) ego-Transcendence (By Means Of ego-Transcending Communion With Me), and Relative To Inherently egoless (and Infinitely Non-Separate) Divine Self-Realization Of Me.

Previous To The Second Period Of The Intensive Listening (and Would-Be, Eventually, Hearing) Process Of The Way Of The Heart, The Guiding Purpose Of The "Consideration" Group Is To Serve Each Member's Right, True, and Full Understanding and Demonstration Of The Basic Practice Of Ruchira Avatara Bhakti Yoga—and (Once Practice Is Established Beyond The Student-Beginner Stage) The Primary Practice, Of Searchless Beholding Of Me—and, Likewise, Right, True, and Full Understanding and Demonstration Of All Of The By-Me-Given functional, practical, and relational Disciplines, and Cultural Obligations. With The Transition To The Second Period Of The Intensive Listening (and Would-Be, Eventually, Hearing) Process Of The Way Of The Heart, The Process Of Group "Consideration" Must Also Intensively Include Concentration On My Avataric Divine Word Relative To The True Hearing Of Me.

Once The Transition Is Made To The Second Period Of The Intensive Listening (and Would-Be, Eventually, Hearing) Process Of The Way Of The Heart, The "Consideration" Group Must Work To Help Each Member To Really Observe How the conditional self (or ego-"I") Is Operative As Contraction (or The Avoidance Of Relationship) In The Real Circumstances Of daily life (including intimate life), and Even Under The Circumstances Of The Group "Consideration" Itself, So That Each Member May (In Due Course) Be Awakened (By Means Of My Avatarically Self-Transmitted Divine Spiritual Grace, and Via The Intensive Listening Practice Of The Way Of The Heart) To Most Fundamental self-Understanding (or The True Hearing Of Me), and To The Fullest Natural (or Whole bodily) Disposition Of Devotional ego-Transcendence (Also Expressed In Every Context Of daily life As Positive Participation and Really ego-Transcending Love).

The Mood Of Group "Considerations" Should Be Loving and Compassionate. Each Member Of The Group Should Be Mature Enough To Be Committed To Real (and Most Fundamental) self-Understanding—Without Hiding, Defensiveness, "Grossly" Dramatized Reactivity, or Indulgence In self-Affirmation Via Idealized self-Descriptions. The Discussion Should Always Be Directed Toward the real activities (functional, practical, relational, physical, mental, and emotional) Of Each Member Of The Group, Rather Than Toward emotionally Defensive conceptual (or intellectual) Presentations Of Mere "Information" About the conditional self (or self-Descriptions That Confirm the ego, Rather Than Serve The Release Of the self-Contraction).

The Purpose Of self-Observation Is To Really (and, In Due Course, Most Fundamentally) Understand That the conditional self (In All Of its Unique personal Patterning) Is Functioning Simply As self-Contraction, or The Avoidance Of Relationship. Therefore, Every Occasion Of Group "Consideration" Should End With (Specific) New Commitments and Agreements (Thereafter To Be Formally Monitored and Expected By The Group, and By The Larger Culture Of Expectation and Inspiration) Relative To Appropriate, Positive, and Really Effective Changes Of functional, practical, relational, or Cultural Action (or physical, mental, or emotional self-Responsibility) On The Part Of Each Group Member whose ego-evidence Has Been Directly "Considered" (or, Otherwise, Touched Upon) During That Particular Occasion.

The Awakening To Most Fundamental self-Understanding (or The True Hearing Of Me) Can Be Truly Stable Only If Every Aspect Of an individual's Practice Of The Way Of The Heart Is Thoroughly Examined, "Considered", and Tested, Over The Course Of a Significant (whatever Is Necessary To Be Sufficient) period of time, During The Second Period Of The Intensive Listening (and Would-Be, Eventually, Hearing) Process Of The Way Of The Heart.

The self-Contraction (or The Habit Of "Narcissus") Is Reaction, Stress, and Pain—and An Automaticity That Is Being Superimposed On Existence Itself. When the self-Contraction (or The Complex Avoidance Of Relationship) Is Directly (and, In All Basic Respects, Thoroughly) Observed (At First, In Terms Of The Patterning Associated With The First Three Stages Of Life), and When (By That Process) self-Contraction itself Is Understood Most Fundamentally (As <u>The</u> Fundamental Activity That is the conditional self, or body-mind)—Then All The Possible limiting and self-Defining ego-Patterns Of the conditional body-mind Have (In Their Fundamental Principle) Become Comprehensible. In That Case, The Effort Of egoity (or The Complex Avoidance Of Relationship) Is No Longer An Uninspected Automaticity (Hidden From The View Of Consciousness, or Heart-Vision). Therefore, Once the self-Contraction Is Understood Most Fundamentally, the self-Contraction itself Is No Longer Necessary—and The Unique Basic Capability To Release (or To Directly Feel Beyond, or Function Prior To) The Patterns Of self-Contraction In every kind of relationship or circumstance Has Been Regained.

The Purpose Of self-Observation (or The "Reality Consideration" Of the conditional self) Is (For The Practitioner Of The Only-By-Me Revealed and Given Way Of The Heart) To Become Thereby Truly Effective In The Exercise (or Demonstration) Of The Capability For ego-Transcendence (Feeling

Toward, Feeling Through, and Feeling Beyond), Rather Than (For The Practitioner Of The Way Of The Heart) To Accumulate Elaborate ego-Descriptions (or Merely Symptomatic and conceptual self-Descriptions) That Do Not Change anything When They Are known. Therefore, When (and Only When) True Hearing Of Me (or Most Fundamental self-Understanding, and The Unique Capability For Direct and Effective ego-Transcendence) Truly and Stably Awakens (Via The Ordeal Of Progressively Comprehensive and Ever-Deepening self-Observation and self-Confession Of The Actuality and The Details Of "Narcissus", and Via More and More Effective Demonstrations Of Devotion, Service, self-Discipline, and Meditation—In Recognition-Response To My Avatarically Self-Transmitted Divine Person and Spiritual Grace), The Third (or Hearing) Period Of The Intensive Listening-Hearing Process Of The Way Of The Heart Can Begin (or, Indeed, It Has Already Begun).

In The Third (and Final) Period Of The Intensive Listening (and, Now, Hearing) Process Of The Only-By-Me Revealed and Given Way Of The Heart, All Previously Engaged Forms Of Study, personal Discipline, Group "Consideration" (Now, As A General Rule, With Other Practitioners Of The Third, or Hearing, Period Of The Intensive Listening-Hearing Process Of The Way Of The Heart), and Either Meditative self-Enquiry Or Else Meditative Ruchira Avatara Naama Japa Are To Be Continued—Except They Will (or Must) Have All Become Newly and Uniquely Effective (or Expressive) By Virtue Of The True Hearing Of Me. Thus, Whereas Previously All Practices Served To Generate self-Reflection and self-Observation, For The Sake Of Most Fundamental self-Understanding (and The Unique Capability For Direct and Effective ego-Transcendence), Now (In The Third, or Hearing, Period Of The Intensive Listening-Hearing Process Of The Way Of The Heart) They Must Have All Become Expressive (and Simple, and Intensely Simplifying) Extensions Of The True Hearing Of Me (or Prior and Most Fundamental self-Understanding, and The Clear and Direct and Feeling Capability For Effective and Truly Devotional ego-Transcendence). In That Case, whatever arises (as other, object, circumstance, experience, or Apparent knowledge) Is Directly Met By Already Awakened Hearing Capability.

Once True Hearing Of Me Awakens, self-Enquiry (In The Form "Avoiding Relationship?") Ceases (As A Formal Practice, In The Devotional Way Of Insight) To Be A Mere Question. Indeed, Truly Hearing self-Enquiry Does Not Seek An Answer. Rather, Truly Hearing self-Enquiry (Like Ruchira Avatara Naama Japa, Once True Hearing Of Me Awakens) Expresses (or Enforces) Prior (and Most Fundamental) self-Understanding, and (Thus) It Serves As A Simple and Direct Instrument Of The Heart's Own Motive (That Merely Observes the instant of self-Contraction and Feels Beyond it).

True Hearing Of Me Is Not (Even In The Devotional Way Of Insight) mere verbal (or conceptual) insight, To Be Followed By Strategically self-Manipulative or self-Corrective behavior. True Hearing Of Me Involves Sensitivity To the conditional self—To The Point Of The Utter Conviction That the conditional self (or the conventional "I") Is Functioning (Only and Entirely) As Contraction. This Conviction Is Certain That No Strategy Of self-Manipulation Can Bring An End To self-Contraction. Indeed, Strategic self-Manipulation Is, Itself, Evidence Of the self-Contraction. True Hearing Of Me Is Awakened When All Such Strategic Efforts Cease, and The Heart Opens, Directly and Responsively (Beyond self-Contraction), Into The Feeling-Disposition Of Devotional (and General Relational) Love, or Unqualified Relatedness (Wherein It Is Tacitly Acknowledged That the Natural "I", or the body-mind, Is Inherently, or Always Already, Related, or Non-Separate, and Naturally Felt As The Feeling Of Relatedness Itself). And, When Such True Hearing Of Me Has Been Both Truly Realized (In The Context Of The Second Period Of The Intensive Listening, and Would-Be, Eventually, Hearing, Process Of The Way Of The Heart) and (In The Context Of The Third, or Hearing, Period Of The Intensive Listening-Hearing Process Of The Way Of The Heart) Effectively Practiced (Either Via Both Random and, Otherwise, Formal, or daily Meditative, Practice Of self-Enquiry Or Via Both Random and, Otherwise, Formal, or daily Meditative, Practice Of Ruchira Avatara Naama Japa), Such That The Patterns Of self-Contraction Associated With The First Three Stages Of Life Are Consistently Released and Replaced By self-Responsibility and Basic human Equanimity—Then The Practitioner Of The Way Of The Heart Has Become Uniquely (and Naturally, and Fully Responsibly) Capable Of Heart-Responding To What Is Ultimately Attractive. Therefore, When True Hearing Of Me Has Thus (In The Context Of The Third, or Hearing, Period Of The Intensive Listening-Hearing Process Of The Way Of The Heart) Allowed The Developmental Ordeal and The ego-Transcending "Consideration" Of The First Three Stages Of Life To Become (In All Its Basic Forms) Complete, The Practitioner Of The Way Of The Heart Has Become Uniquely (and Naturally, and Fully Responsibly) Capable Of Receptivity and Surrender In ego-Transcending Participatory Heart-Response To My Avatarically Self-Transmitted Divine Fullness (Through Seeing Me—or The Fully Technically Responsible Process Of Receiving My Avatarically Self-Transmitted Divine Spirit-Baptism), In The ("Basic") Context Of The Fourth Stage Of Life (As Revealed In The Would-Be-Seeing, or Progressively Seeing, and Already Effectively Hearing, Stage Of The Way Of The Heart).

The Way For Student-Beginners and For those In The Intensive Listening-Hearing Stage Of The Way Of The Heart Is (Like The Way Of The Heart In Each and All Of Its Progressive Stages, or Until The Only-By-Me Revealed and

Given Seventh Stage Of Life In The Way Of The Heart Is Realized) A Transitional Yoga, or A Way Through and Beyond the limits of self-Contraction. The Way For Student-Beginners and For those In The Intensive Listening-Hearing Stage Of The Way Of The Heart Is The Ordeal Of Listening To Me, To The Degree Of Hearing Me. It Is The Yoga (or Way) Of Heart-Preparation (Either In The Manner Of The Devotional Way Of Insight Or In The Manner Of The Devotional Way Of Faith). It Is The Yoga Of attention (With Feeling) To Me, Present As My Recorded (and Ever-Speaking) Avataric Divine Word, My Materially Fabricated (and Ever Me-Showing) Avataric Divine Image-Art, My Recorded (and Ever-Living) Avataric Divine Leelas, and My Always Given (and Giving) Avataric Divine Human and Spiritual Sign. True Practitioners Practice This Yoga (or Way) Until they Are (By Virtue Of The True Hearing Of Me, or The Capability Awakened In The Event Of Most Fundamental self-Understanding) Fully Prepared To See Me Spiritually (From The Heart—In A Fully Technically Responsible Manner), and (Thus) To Move On To The Greater Practice Of The Way Of The Heart, Which Is The Truly Spiritual Ordeal Of The Heart—The Darshan Yoga, or The Yoga (or Heart-Way) Of Seeing Me (or Of Being Fully Spiritually Awakened, Heart-Attracted, and Heart-Found By Me).

The Entire Practice and Process Of Listening To Me To The Point Of Hearing Me Is The (Relatively) Exoteric Dimension Of The Only-By-Me Revealed and Given Way Of The Heart—and That Practice and Process Must Be <u>Truly</u> Lived. The Listening-Hearing Practice and Process Of The Way Of The Heart Is A Great Sadhana, Given By Me To My Beginning Devotees—and, Therefore, When Rightly Practiced, It Is Not In Any Sense An ego-Based (or Separate-self-Based) Process. Therefore, Now (and Forever Hereafter), I Call My Beginning Devotees To Embrace The Listening-Hearing Practice and Process Of The Way Of The Heart Exactly As I Have Given It, and (Thus and Thereby) To Involve themselves In Truly ego-Surrendering, ego-Forgetting, and (More and More) ego-Transcending Devotion To <u>Me</u>.

During The Years Of My Teaching-Work and Original Blessing-Work, I Freely, Intensively, and Fully Interactively Submitted Myself To All My Devotees, For The Purpose Of <u>Responsively</u> Drawing My Avataric Divine Self-Revelation Of The Way Of The Heart Out Of Myself. When My Avataric Divine Self-Revelation Of The Only-By-Me Revealed and Given Way Of The Heart Became (Thereby) Complete, My Work Of Interactive Submission To My Devotees Spontaneously and Gradually Came To An End. Therefore, Now (and Forever Hereafter), The Only-By-Me Revealed and Given Way Of Adidam (Which Is The One and Only By-Me-Revealed and By-Me-Given Way Of The Heart) Is Full and Complete.

In The Now (and Forever Hereafter) Full and Complete Sacred Cultural Circumstance Of Only-By-Me Revealed and Given Instrumentality and Agency (Including Occasions Of The Direct Blessing-Darshan Of Me In My Avatarically-Born Bodily Human Divine Form—or, After The Physical Human Lifetime Of My Avataric Incarnation here, The Direct Blessing-Darshan Of Me By Means Of Resort To Me In The physical human Company and By-Me-Spiritually-Empowered Circumstances Of My "Ruchira Sannyasin" Devotees), My Beginning Devotees Engaged In The Foundation (or Relatively Exoteric) Formal Practice Of The Intensive Listening-Hearing Stage Of The Only-By-Me Revealed and Given Way Of Adidam (Which Is The One and Only By-Me-Revealed and By-Me-Given Way Of The Heart) Are To Be Given Access To My Avataric Divine Spiritual Blessing. My Thus Received Avataric Divine Spiritual Blessing Is Entirely Sufficient To Move My Beginning Devotees Through The Process Of Listening To Me, and (Thus and Thereby) To Awaken them To The True Hearing Of Me. And, By Means Of The Complete Formal Fulfilling Of The Intensive (and, Only In The Rudimentary, and Not Yet Fully Technically Responsible, Sense, Spiritual) Listening-Hearing Practice and Process Of The Only-By-Me Revealed and Given Way Of The Heart, All My Beginning Devotees Must Truly, Formally, and Rightly Prepare themselves To Enter Into The Great Esoteric (or Fully Spiritually To-Me-Awakened and, Spiritually, Fully Technically Responsible) Practice and Process Of Seeing Me and (In Due Course) Most Perfectly Realizing Me.

Before I Can Be Seen In Truth, I Must Be Heard. Before Your Heart Will Allow Your body-mind To Most Fully (and, At Last, Most Perfectly) Receive The Baptism Of My Avatarically Self-Transmitted Divine Spiritual Presence, Your Heart Must Be Released From The Insult (and The Deluding and Binding Power) Of self-Contraction.

The self-Contraction Is Un-Natural. That Is To Say, It Is A Reactive Design Added To The Totality Of conditional (or Cosmic) Nature (or To Man In The Cosmic Mandala). Even More, Originally the self-Contraction (In The Form Of The Feeling Of Relatedness Itself) Is (With The Totality Of conditional Nature, or The Total Cosmic Mandala) Superimposed Upon The Heart (Itself), or Existence (Itself), or The Feeling Of Being (Itself). And The Heart Will Not Release The Motive and The Commitment To self-Contraction Until The Un-Naturalness (and The Inherent Non-Necessity) Of The Logic (and The Act) Of self-Contraction Is Thoroughly Observed and Most Fundamentally Understood. Therefore, The Way For Student-Beginners and For those In The Intensive Listening-Hearing Stage Of The Way Of The Heart Involves Intensive "Reality Consideration" Relative To conditional Existence.

This Intensive "Reality Consideration" Involves Real self-Observation In Devotional Response To My Own Self-Evidently Divine Person, and In

Intelligent Response To My Great Teaching-Arguments. It Does Not Involve The self-Motivated Strategy Of self-Watching, or The Search To Accumulate Analytical Descriptions Of the egoic self. It Is, Rather, A Matter Of Devotional (and, Altogether, Truly Feeling, or Participatory) attention To My Avatarically-Born Bodily (Human) Divine Form, To My Avatarically Self-Transmitted Spiritual (and Always Blessing) Divine Presence, To My Avatarically Self-Revealed (and Very, and Transcendental, and Perfectly Subjective, and Inherently Spiritual, and Inherently egoless, and Inherently Perfect, and Self-Evidently Divine) State, To My Avatarically Self-Transmitted Divine Word and Image-Art and My Avatarically Self-Manifested Divine Play (or My Avatarically Self-Manifested Divine Leelas) Of Avataric Divine Self-Revelation and Teaching-Argumentation, and To My Every Other (or Otherwise Directly Associated) Means—Such That Only I (Simply, Directly, and Easily) Reveal the self-Contraction Of My Listening Devotee (Until I Am Heard). Therefore, By All Of This, I Progressively (or Even Suddenly) Awaken My Listening Devotee (and Then My Hearing Devotee) Beyond self-Contraction, To Truly ego-Surrendering, ego-Forgetting, and ego-Transcending Heart-Communion With Me—The Avatarically Self-Revealed (and Inherently egoless, and Self-Evidently Divine) Person (or Self-Condition, or Source-Condition) Of all-and-All.

The self-Contraction Is The Act Of Separation. The self-Contraction Is The Act Of Casting Yourself Into The Illusion Of Separateness, Independence, Isolation, and (In The Ultimate Sense) Un-Wholeness. The self-Contraction Is Your Reaction To conditional Existence. This Reaction Is egoity itself, and It Is Always Your Own activity. All Your Seeking, All Your Disturbance, and All Your Dissatisfaction Are Your Own activity. This Is What Must Be Understood Through The Process Of "Reality Consideration". This Understanding Is The Essence Of True Hearing Of Me. To Understand This Is To Be Free Of "victim-consciousness", or the notion that Your Fundamental Difficulty Is Somehow caused by others or by the conditions Of Manifested Existence.

Human beings Characteristically believe (or Interpret their experience According To the notion) that their Suffering Is caused from without, and they (Consequently) Feel themselves To Be the (helpless) victims Of Suffering. Your experience as an Apparently individual psycho-physical being Can Certainly Involve Pain, Difficulty, and unfortunate circumstances—but Your Fundamental Suffering Is Never, under any circumstances, caused from without. Your Fundamental Suffering (or Your life Of Seeking, Disturbance, and Dissatisfaction) Is caused By—and, Indeed, Is—Your Own Reaction To (or Your Own self-Contraction In The Face Of) the conditions Of Manifested Existence.

If You Truly Examine Your Own life Of Reaction, You Will (More and More) Observe That, By Tendency, You Use events, happenings, and experiences To

Justify Your Own egoity (or Your Own Habit Of self-Contraction). But, In Truth, There Are No Excuses For Being an ego. Egoity Is Not caused from without. Egoity (or The Habit Of self-Contraction) Is Now (and Always Has Been) Your Own activity. Egoity (or The Habit Of self-Contraction) Is Your Own Choice In The Face Of the conditions Of Manifested Existence. And The Persistent Choice To Be an ego Winds You Into A Habit That Binds You In The Midst Of all conditions.

Your Own egoity (or Your Own Habit Of self-Contraction) Must Be Observed, Understood, and Transcended. The Results Of Your Own egoity (or Your Own Habit Of self-Contraction) Must Be Observed, Understood, and Transcended. The conditions in which Your Own egoity (or Your Own Habit Of self-Contraction) arises Must Be Observed, Understood, and Transcended. Altogether, All Of conditional Existence Must (Most Ultimately) Be Transcended. When You Understand That conditional Existence (In Itself) Is Inherently Unsatisfactory, Then You No Longer Seek—but (Instead) You Transcend The Seeker. To Directly Understand (and Transcend) The Seeker (and, Thus, The Search Itself)—Rather Than Struggle With The Seeking-Effort (Either To "Have" Or To "Not Have") and With the (Either "Wanted" Or "Not Wanted") objects Of Seeking—Is The "Radical" (or "Gone To The Root, Core, Source, or Origin") Characteristic Of The Only-By-Me Revealed and Given Way Of The Heart (or Way Of Adidam). When You, Thus ("Radically"), Understand Yourself (Most Fundamentally), Then (In every Such moment) You Do Not Dramatize egoity (or The Habit Of self-Contraction), but (Instead) You Directly Transcend egoity (or The Habit Of self-Contraction)—whatever the conditions of the moment. This "Radical" Capability (To Consistently Transcend The Root-Action Of egoity) Is The True Hearing Of Me (or Most Fundamental self-Understanding).

True Hearing Of Me (or Most Fundamental self-Understanding) Is A Unique Gift, Given (Only By Means Of My Avatarically Self-Transmitted Divine Spiritual Grace) To My Devotees who Rightly and Truly Embrace The Ordeal Of Listening To Me. True Hearing Of Me (or Most Fundamental self-Understanding) Is (After, or Upon The Root-Foundation Of, The Devotional Heart-Discovery Of Me) The First Great Realization Of My Real (and Really and Truly Practicing) Devotee, and The Basis (After, or Upon The Root-Foundation Of, Searchless Beholding Of Me—Which Is The Essence Of Ruchira Avatara Bhakti Yoga Itself) On Which The Entire Advanced and Ultimate Process (Of Stages) Of The Way Of The Heart Develops. Thus, The Way Of The Heart Is Not (At All) An ego-Based Developmental Process, but (Rather) An ego-Transcending Process That (In Due Course) Goes Beyond Even All Of The First Six Stages Of Life In The Transcendental, Inherently

Spiritual, and Truly Divine Self-Realization Of The Only-By-Me Revealed and Given Seventh Stage Of Life.

That Which Is (Most Ultimately) To Be Realized Is Not Among conditions, and Not Among causes and effects. It Is Not caused, It Cannot Be caused, and It Cannot Be Realized As the effect of any cause. That Which Is (Most Ultimately) To Be Realized Is Inherently and Always Already The Case—and It Is Realized To Be So Whenever (and Wherever) There Is No self-Contraction. Therefore, In Order To Most Perfectly Realize Real God, or Truth, or Reality, all forms of self-Contraction, all forms Of Seeking, and All Bondage To conditions (Whether Motivated By The Desire To Achieve Pleasure Or By The Desire To Avoid Pain) Must Be (Progressively, and Then Most Ultimately) Transcended. Without The (Only-By-Me Given) Grace Of The True Hearing Of Me (or The True Capability For ego-Transcendence), The Developmental Processes Of The First Six Stages Of Life Are All Merely Part Of The human Potential (or the psycho-biography of the ego). But, For one who Hears Me, The Entire Process Of Potential human Development Is A Course Of Real (and, Most Ultimately, Inherently Most Perfect) ego-Transcendence—and Not Merely A Process Of ego-Development. That Which Is (Most Ultimately) To Be Realized Is Prior To conditions—and That Which Is Prior To conditions Is Not Obvious Until the self-Contraction (or The Habit Of egoically Reacting To conditions) Is Transcended. This Reaction To conditions Takes The Form Of The Illusion Of Separateness and the life Of Separativeness. Separateness Is The Foundation Pain, and It Is self-caused.

Prior To self-Contraction, Prior To All Illusions Of Separateness, All Illusions Of Relatedness, and All Illusions Of caused Suffering, Is The Inherent and Uncaused Feeling Of Being. Suffering Is Entirely Your Own action. The body-mind Can experience Pain In Difficult conditions, but The Domain Of Pain Is Not The Domain Of Liberation, or The Domain Of Truth. In Order To Deal With Pain, You Must Do Much More Than Merely "Getting In Touch" With Your History Of Suffering (In and As the body-mind) and Identifying Its Seeming causes. You Must Transcend Your Own Act Of self-Contraction In The Face Of All Suffering—Actual or Potential, past or present or future.

Therefore, To Fully Practice The Way Of The Heart Is To Transcend The Illusion That You Are "Victimized" By The Universe and Trapped In the body-mind. This Transcending Is The True Hearing Of Me. The Only-By-Me Revealed and Given Way Of The Heart (or Way Of Adidam) Is Not A Matter Of Seeking any particular conditions (or Any Particular "Solutions" To Your Presumed "Problems") On The Basis Of the self-Contraction. The Only-By-Me Revealed and Given Way Of The Heart Is A Matter Of Directly Observing, Understanding, and Transcending the self-Contraction (and All Forms Of

Search), In The Midst Of conditions, By Always Entering Into Devotional (and, In Due Course, Spiritual) Communion With Me (and, Most Ultimately, By Realizing Inherent, and Inherently Most Perfect, Self-Identification With Me).

Attention (self-Surrendered) To My Own Self-Evidently Divine Person (Revealing All At Once), and To My Avatarically Transmitted (and Always Me-Revealing) Divine Word Of Argument and Instruction, and To My Avatarically Self-Manifested (and Always Me-Revealing) Divine Leelas Of Argumentation and Instruction Yields self-Observation and self-Understanding, Naturally (or Directly, Spontaneously, and Even Inevitably). It Is Not Sufficient To Observe The Apparent Details Of the conditional self. The conditional self (As Contraction) Must Be Thoroughly (In All Basic Respects) Observed—but (Most Importantly) The Un-Naturalness, or Non-Necessity, Of self-Contraction (itself) Must Be Understood (and Most Fundamentally), Such That The Commitment To self-Contraction Is (In This Directly Effective Manner) Relinquished.

The self-Contraction Is Separative (or Dissociative), and Only Destructive. This Must Be (Directly) Observed and (Most Fundamentally) Understood. That Most Fundamental Understanding Must Not Merely Inform the mind. It Must Unlock The Heart. Therefore, True (and Most Fundamental) self-Understanding Is (and Must Be) Heart-Active. It Must Function As The Active Capability (and Activated Heart-Impulse) To Directly (and Most Effectively) Feel Beyond self-Contraction—and (Therefore) This Unique Capability Magnifies (or Ever More Deeply Awakens) The Native Heart-Motive (or The Heart's Own Free Means) Toward Most Perfectly ego-Transcending (and Fully and Most Perfectly Spiritually Awakened) Real-God-Realization. Indeed, It Is Only After The Uninspected (or Hidden) Commitment To self-Contraction Is Freely and Fully Relinquished (Through Most Fundamental self-Understanding) That The Results Of self-Contraction Really (or Deeply) Begin To Fall Away, By Stages. Therefore, one who Truly Hears Me Will Soon (At Full and Spiritually Responsible Heart-Depth) Heart-Recognize and Heart-Receive (or Accept and Embrace) My Great Spiritual Heart-Presence.

In The Only-By-Me Revealed and Given Way Of The Heart (or Way Of Adidam), The Practice Of Listening To Me Must Continue Until I Am Heard, and The Practice Of The True Hearing Of Me Must Continue Until The Transition To Practice Of The Way Of The Heart In The "Basic" (or, Spiritually, Fully Technically Responsible) Context Of The Fourth Stage Of Life Is Truly Realized and Made.

The True Hearing Of Me Is A Sudden, Central (or "Radical"), and Comprehensive Understanding That Covers everything. Therefore, The True Hearing Of Me Is Not (Fundamentally) A Matter Of behavioral change. Rather, The True Hearing Of Me Is The Direct (and "Radical", or "Gone-To-The-Root")

Capability For Devotional (and Spiritually Me-Receiving) Communion With Me, Such That the conditions of life Cease To Be An Impediment To That Devotional Communion or To The Process Of Spiritual Development In Heart-Communion With Me. And The True Hearing Of Me Is The Single Capability To Observe, Understand, and Transcend The Single Act Of self-Contraction—No Matter what particular form the self-Contraction May Take In any moment. Therefore, For one who Has Heard Me, There Is No Puzzlement or Ambiguity Relative To anything that arises—Because whatever arises Is Understood As self-Contraction.

The True Hearing Of Me Is A Sadhana—Not An Unchanging State. Thus, The True Hearing Of Me Is Not A Sign That ego-Transcendence Has Already Become Perfect. Rather, The True Hearing Of Me Is The Means Of Consistently Exercising The Capability For Real ego-Transcendence, and With Greater and Greater (and, Ultimately, Perfect) Effectiveness. Long Established Habits, Tendencies, and personality Patterns Do Not Suddenly Disappear or Dramatically Change By Virtue Of Hearing Me, Such That My Hearing Devotee Becomes Like a blank white page. Such Is An idealistic, socially Oriented View Of What It Means To Understand oneself Most Fundamentally. The Fundamental Change In My Hearing Devotee Is Not a change at the periphery but A Change At The Core. This Central (Root, Core, or "Radical") Change Must Then Be Intentionally Exercised Relative To all the (Otherwise Relatively peripheral) aspects of life and experience and function—and, Indeed, Relative To all conditions (Whether ordinary Or Extraordinary) that arise In The Further Course Of The Sadhana Of The Way Of The Heart. However, When I Am Heard, The Capability For That Intentional Exercise Is Always The Case.

When I Am Heard, Then (Whether By The Exercise Of The Devotional Way Of Insight Or By The Exercise Of The Devotional Way Of Faith) The Avoidance Of Relationship Must (Directly, and In The Progressive Context Of The Unfolding Stages Of Practice In The Way Of The Heart) Be Replaced By The Feeling Of Relatedness. (And, In The "Perfect Practice" Of The Way Of The Heart, Even The Feeling Of Relatedness Must Be Transcended, In The By-Me-Avatarically-Self-Revealed Inherently Perfectly Free Feeling Of Being.)

I Am Heard When My Listening Devotee—Having Been Directly Initiated, By Me, Into The Reception Of My Ruchira Shaktipat—Has Truly (and Thoroughly) Observed the ego-"I" and Understood it (Directly, In the moments Of self-Observation, and Most Fundamentally, or In its Totality).

I Am Heard When the ego-"I" Is Altogether (and Thoroughly) Observed and (Most Fundamentally) Understood, Both In The Tendency To Dissociate and In The Tendency To Become Attached (or To Cling By Wanting Need, or To Identify With others, and things, and circumstances egoically, and, Thus,

To Dramatize The Seeker, Bereft Of Basic Equanimity, Wholeness, and The Free Capability For Simple Relatedness).

I Am Heard When the ego-"I" Is Thoroughly (and Most Fundamentally) Understood To Be Contraction-Only, An Un-Necessary and Destructive Motive and Design, Un-Naturally and Chronically Added To Cosmic Nature and To all relations, and An Imaginary Heart-Disease (Made To Seem Real, By Heart-Reaction).

I Am Heard When This Most Fundamental Understanding Of The Habit Of "Narcissus" Becomes The Directly Obvious Realization Of The Heart, Radiating Beyond Its Own (Apparent) Contraction.

I Am Heard When The Beginning Is Full. And The Beginning Is Full (and Ended) When Every Gesture Of self-Contraction (In The Context Of The First Three Stages Of Life, and Relative To Each and All Of The Principal Faculties, Of body, emotion, mind, and breath) Is (As A Rather Consistently Applied and humanly Effective Discipline) Observed (By Natural feeling-perception), Tacitly (and Most Fundamentally) Understood, and Really (Directly and Effectively) Felt Beyond (In The Prior Feeling Of Unqualified Relatedness).

My Listening Devotee Has Heard Me When The Search For Insight Is Directly (or Feelingly) Released, Fulfilled Beyond Expectation, and No Longer Necessary.

My Listening Devotee Has Heard Me When The Hunger For self-Understanding Is Forgotten In The Feeling Of Relatedness (Feeling Me).

And The Feeling Heart Itself (That Hears Me) Will Soon Be Satisfied, Suddenly, By The Approaching Sight Of Me (The "Bright" and Only One Who Is).

Avatar Adi Da Samraj
Adidam Samrajashram, 2003

SUTRA 30

Simple (Natural) arousal From the dreaming state To the waking state of the body-mind Immediately (If Only Naturally, or conditionally) awakens You From Identification With The Problems and Illusions You Seemed To Suffer or Seek In the dreaming state. Just So, In The Only-By-Me Revealed and Given Way Of The Heart (or Way Of Adidam), Meditation (and, Especially, Deep Meditation) Directly (and More and More Profoundly, and Then Inherently, and Inherently Most Perfectly, or Un-conditionally) Awakens You From Identification With The Problems and Illusions You Seem (or Seemed) To Suffer or Seek In the waking state. Likewise, In The Way Of The Heart, Meditation (and, Especially, Deep Meditation) Directly (and More and More Profoundly—and Then Inherently, and Inherently Most Perfectly, or Un-conditionally) Awakens You From Identification With (and all limitation by) the waking state itself, the dreaming state itself, and the sleeping state itself. Indeed, The Great Process Of Meditation In The Way Of The Heart (Beginning With Simple Feeling-Contemplation Of My Avatarically-Born Bodily Human Divine Form, My Avatarically Self-Transmitted Spiritual, and Always Blessing, Divine Presence, and My Avatarically Self-Revealed, and Very, and Transcendental, and Perfectly Subjective, and Inherently Spiritual, and Inherently egoless, and Inherently Perfect, and Self-Evidently Divine State—and Progressing, On That Basis, Via All The Necessary and Appropriate Practices and Developmental Processes In The Way Of The Heart) Is A Total and (Most Ultimately) Inherent (and Inherently Most Perfect) Awakening From The Problems, Illusions, sufferings, Searches, limitations, experiences, knowledge, and conditional self-Identity Associated With all Possible states Of conditional (or psycho-physical) Existence.

In The Only-By-Me Revealed and Given Way Of The Heart (or Way Of Adidam), Meditation—Which, Most Ultimately, Becomes (or Awakens To) Only-By-Me Revealed and Given Seventh Stage Sahaja Nirvikalpa Samadhi (or Ruchira Samraj Samadhi, or, Simply, Samraj Samadhi), or Inherent Self-Identification With The "Bright" (or Inherently Spiritual), and Transcendental (or Inherently Free), and Inherently egoless Divine Self-Condition Of Consciousness Itself, Realized As Self-Radiant and Self-Evidently Divine Self-Existence Itself (or Divine Being Itself)—Is (In Right Conjunction With The

Full Range Of All The Only-By-Me Revealed and Given functional, practical, relational, and Cultural Disciplines) The Principal (Progressively Effective) Means Whereby conceptual philosophy (or "God"-Talk) and limited insight Become (or Are Directly Transcended In) Spiritual, Transcendental, and (Most Ultimately) Divine Self-Realization.

Meditation (Progressively Realized) In The Way Of The Heart Is (In Right Conjunction With The Full Range Of All The Only-By-Me Revealed and Given functional, practical, relational, and Cultural Disciplines) The Principal (Progressively Effective) Means Whereby the self-Contraction, the body-mind, and all conditional relations Are Really Transcended In Self-Existing and Self-Radiant Happiness Itself. And That Transcending Is Not Realized By An Effort Of Separation, or A Struggle To (Strategically) Escape, Nor Is It Realized By An Effort Toward Union (or Re-Union). Rather, It Is (Progressively) Realized By Means Of My Avatarically Self-Transmitted Divine Spiritual Grace, Such That (In Due Course) There Is Direct (or Inherent) Self-Identification With The By-Me-Avatarically-Self-Revealed Divine Self-Condition (Which Is The Self-Existing and Self-Radiant Divine Source-Condition) That Inherently Transcends all dependent conditions.

In The Only-By-Me Revealed and Given Way Of The Heart (or Way Of Adidam), Meditation Is A Gift (From Me)—Spontaneously (and Progressively) Given (By Means Of My Avatarically Self-Transmitted Divine Grace) To those who Surrender, Forget, and Transcend themselves By Feeling-Contemplating My Avatarically-Born Bodily (Human) Divine Form,[87] My Avatarically Self-Transmitted Spiritual (and Always Blessing) Divine Presence, and My Avatarically Self-Revealed (and Very, and Transcendental, and Perfectly Subjective, and Inherently Spiritual, and Inherently egoless, and Inherently Perfect, and Self-Evidently Divine) State.

In The Only-By-Me Revealed and Given Way Of The Heart (or Way Of Adidam), Meditation Is Not A Technique, but A Gift (From Me)—and Even All The Technical Forms (or By-Me-Given Technical Exercises) Of Meditation Practice In The Way Of The Heart Are, Truly, Only Secondary Means, To Be Applied For The Sake Of Serving The Fundamental Practice (Of Devotional Resort To Me, and Devotional Contemplation Of Me, and Devotional Response To Me, and Devotional and Meditative Cooperation With Me).

The Way Of The Heart (and Meditation In The Way Of The Heart) Is A Relationship—Not Merely A System Of Techniques.

Practice Of The Way Of The Heart Is Right Practice Of The Relationship To Me.

Right Practice Of The Way Of The Heart Is To Remember (or To Constantly Feel, and, Thereby, To Contemplate) My Avatarically-Born Bodily (Human)

Divine Form, My Avatarically Self-Transmitted Spiritual (and Always Blessing) Divine Presence, and My Avatarically Self-Revealed (and Very, and Transcendental, and Perfectly Subjective, and Inherently Spiritual, and Inherently egoless, and Inherently Perfect, and Self-Evidently Divine) State, and (Thus and Thereby) To Forget (or To Constantly Surrender and Transcend) self-Contraction (Whether In The Context Of The Devotional Way Of Insight Or In The Context Of The Devotional Way Of Faith).

Therefore, In The Only-By-Me Revealed and Given Way Of The Heart (or Way Of Adidam), Every Gift, Calling, and Discipline Is To Be Embraced (By Constant Practice)—but Every Practice (Including Meditation Practice) Is Simply (or Most Basically) A Means For Feeling (and Thereby Contemplating) My Avatarically-Born Bodily (Human) Divine Form, My Avatarically Self-Transmitted Spiritual (and Always Blessing) Divine Presence, and My Avatarically Self-Revealed (and Very, and Transcendental, and Perfectly Subjective, and Inherently Spiritual, and Inherently egoless, and Inherently Perfect, and Self-Evidently Divine) State (and, Otherwise, For Heart-Responding To The Results, or The Graces, Given, By Me, In and By The Feeling-Contemplation Of My Avatarically-Born Bodily Human Divine Form, My Avatarically Self-Transmitted Spiritual, and Always Blessing, Divine Presence, and My Avatarically Self-Revealed, and Very, and Transcendental, and Perfectly Subjective, and Inherently Spiritual, and Inherently egoless, and Inherently Perfect, and Self-Evidently Divine State).

And Meditation (Given By My Avatarically Self-Transmitted Divine Grace, and Always Feeling-Contemplating My Avatarically Self-Revealed, and Very, and Transcendental, and Perfectly Subjective, and Inherently Spiritual, and Inherently egoless, and Inherently Perfect, and Self-Evidently Divine State, and Progressively Realizing My Avatarically Self-Revealed, and Very, and Transcendental, and Perfectly Subjective, and Inherently Spiritual, and Inherently egoless, and Inherently Perfect, and Self-Evidently Divine State) Is The Principal Gift (and Calling, and Discipline) I Give (By Merely Being Present) To My Listening Devotee, My Hearing Devotee, and My Seeing Devotee—Until (By That Gift Of Feeling-Contemplation Of Me, and That Grace Of Feeling-Meditation On Me) My Fully Mature (or Truly Both Hearing and Seeing) Devotee Realizes My (Avatarically Self-Revealed) Inherently Perfect and Inherently egoless and Spiritually Self-"Bright" Divine State.

For those Of My Devotees who Would Yet Understand themselves (Most Fundamentally), and For those Of My Devotees who (Because they Understand themselves Most Fundamentally) Will Not Settle For Less Than Freedom and Happiness, and For those Of My Devotees who Would Enjoy The Ultimate (and Inherently Perfect) Realization Of The Inherently Perfect,

Inherently egoless, and Self-Evidently Divine Self-Condition and Source-Condition, and For those Of My Devotees who Have Recovered The Unique and Comprehensively Effective Ability To (Progressively, and More and More) Satisfy The Impulse Toward Most Perfectly ego-Transcending (Transcendental, Inherently Spiritual, and Self-Evidently Divine) Real-God-Realization—Meditation Has Become As Necessary As food and rest, and More Fundamental Than the waking state itself, or the dreaming state, or the state of deep sleep. Therefore, As You Listen To Me, and When You Hear Me, and Also When You See Me—Do Not Be Preoccupied With The Problem Of the ego-"I", or The Problems Of the self-Contracted body-mind. Do Not Consent To Be Deluded and Held Captive By the body-mind and its functions, its Presumed needs, its states, its relations, its reactions, its sufferings, its thoughts, and its illusions. Do Not Seek Happiness By Means Of Identification With the conditional self and its world, As If the body-mind and its relations Are (in, of, or as themselves) Everlasting (and Identical To Happiness Itself). Be Truly (and By Truth) Aroused From the waking state (and, Indeed, From every psycho-physical, or conditional, state). Indeed, Be (Thus) Aroused daily, and Then (Ultimately, and Inherently) Most Perfectly. Let Your Inherent Identity As The (By-Me-Avatarically-Self-Revealed) Free (Transcendental, Inherently Spiritual, Inherently egoless, and Self-Evidently Divine) Self-Condition and Source-Condition Of all-and-All Be Soon (and, By Means Of My Avatarically Self-Transmitted Divine Grace, Directly) Aroused By Means Of True and Deepest Meditation On, In, and As Me, The Only One Who Is.

Beginning In The Developing Course Of Formally Acknowledged Novice Student-Beginner Practice (and, Then, Fully Established Student-Beginner Practice) Of The Way Of The Heart, Both Right (Devotional, and More and More Meditative) Practice Of self-Enquiry (In The Form "Avoiding Relationship?") and Right (Faithful, Devotional, and More and More Meditative) Practice Of Ruchira Avatara Naama Japa (and Also Simple Random Invocation Of Me Via My Principal Name, "Da", and Via Any Other Of My Avatarically Revealed and Given Divine Names, or Combined Avataric Divine Names and Avataric Divine Descriptive Titles, Which I Have Given To Be Engaged In The Practice Of Simple Name-Invocation Of Me) Should Be Formally Engaged By All My Student-Beginner Devotees (Whether they Are, As Student-Beginners, Yet Novices, Or, Otherwise, Fully Established)—and All Of These First Practices, and All Later Practices (or Further Developments Of These First Practices), Should Always Be Engaged On The Basis Of Simple Feeling-Contemplation Of My Avatarically-Born Bodily (Human) Divine Form (and, Tacitly, Although Not Yet Tangibly and Directly, My Avatarically Self-Transmitted Spiritual, and Always Blessing, Divine Presence and My Avatarically Self-Revealed, and Very, and Transcendental, and Perfectly Subjective, and Inherently Spiritual, and Inherently egoless, and Inherently Perfect, and Self-Evidently Divine State). Until Either The Devotional Way Of Insight Or The Devotional Way Of Faith Is Firmly Chosen (As The Context For Further Student-Beginner's Practice Of The Way Of The Heart, and, Whether Sooner Or Later, For Practice In The Intensive Listening-Hearing Stage Of The Way Of The Heart), All These Approaches Should Be Engaged Experimentally (and, As A General Rule, Each On Distinctly Separate Occasions).

Either Formal self-Enquiry Or Formal Ruchira Avatara Naama Japa (Accompanied, In Either Case, By Random Simple Name-Invocation Of Me) Should Be Engaged, In The Context Of Occasions Of Formal Meditation, At Least twice daily By The Novice Student-Beginner and The Fully Established Student-Beginner In The Way Of The Heart. As A General Rule, The First Of These Two daily Occasions Should Occur In the early morning (Immediately After rising from dream or sleep), and, As A General Rule, The Second Should Occur In the evening (At any time Between early evening and the hour of retirement).

Those who, As Novices In The Student-Beginner Course Of Listening To Me, Are Only Beginning To Adapt To daily Random (or moment to moment) Practice (and daily Formal Meditative Practice) Of Ruchira Avatara Bhakti Yoga—Via Random Name-Invocation Of Me (and, In The Formal Meditative Setting, As Feeling-Contemplation Of Me Via My Murti, In The Form Of A photographic, or otherwise technically, or even artistically, Rendered, Representation Of Me)—Should (As Soon As The Novice Student-Beginner Process Has Been Sufficiently Informed By Study and, On That Basis, Become A Culturally Accountable Obligation In Practice) Meditate twice each day (First In the early morning, and Again In the evening), and they Should Gradually (Over time, but As Quickly As the individual Is Readily Able and Enthused To Do So) Increase the length (and, At Least On days Of Formal Retreat, even the number) of the periods Of daily Sitting In Formal Meditative Exercise.

When The Novice Student-Beginner Is Consistently (As A daily Minimum) Sitting In Formal Meditation For At Least one-half hour each morning and For At Least one-half hour each evening, The Practices Of Ruchira Avatara Naama Japa and Of self-Enquiry Should Be Artfully Introduced Into Both daily Random (or moment to moment) Practice and daily Formal Meditation Practice (In Addition To The Already Established Practice Of Random Name-Invocation Of Me).

In Order To Be Formally Acknowledged As A Fully Established (and, Therefore, No Longer Novice) Student-Beginner, Every Formally Acknowledged Student-Beginner Must (As An Average daily Minimum) Sit In Formal Meditation

For At Least a full hour each morning and For At Least a full hour each evening—While he or she (Otherwise) Constantly Increases and Maximizes his or her daily Practice Of Devotion (or Ruchira Avatara Bhakti), and Of Service (or Ruchira Avatara Seva), and Of self-Discipline (or Ruchira Avatara Tapas), and Also (Over time) Of Meditation. And All Formally Acknowledged Practitioners Of The Way Of The Heart who Would Make The Transition From The Student-Beginner Stage Of The Way Of The Heart To The First Period Of The Intensive Listening-Hearing Stage Of The Way Of The Heart Must (As An Average daily Minimum) Sit In Formal Meditation For a full one hour to a full one and one-half hours (or more) each morning and For a full one hour (or more) each evening, With Formal Meditation Occasions Of Similar length (or periods of time) Occurring One or More Additional times each day On All Formal Retreat days.

As A Prerequisite For The Transition To The First Period Of The Intensive Listening-Hearing Stage Of The Way Of The Heart, The (Necessarily, Fully Established) Student-Beginner Must Have Already Chosen (By A Real and Effective "Testing and Proving" Process) Either The Listening Beginner's Form Of The Devotional Way Of Insight Or The Listening Beginner's Form Of The Devotional Way Of Faith. And (As A Further Prerequisite For The Transition To The First Period Of The Intensive Listening-Hearing Stage Of The Way Of The Heart) The Student-Beginner Must Already (and On The Basis Of That Earlier Choice) Have Effectively Practiced Either The Listening Beginner's Form Of The Devotional Way Of Insight Or The Listening Beginner's Form Of The Devotional Way Of Faith (For a period of time Sufficient To Justify The Transition To The First Period Of The Intensive Listening-Hearing Stage Of The Way Of The Heart). And Whichever Of The Two Devotional Ways (or Modes Of The One and Only By-Me-Revealed and By-Me-Given Way Of The Heart, or Way Of Adidam) Is Chosen In The Course Of The Student-Beginner Stage Of The Way Of The Heart Should, As A General Rule, Continue Thereafter (and, In Due Course, It Should Be Combined With The "Perfect Practice" Of The Way Of The Heart, According To The Instructions Given, In Accordance With My Formally Given Instructions, By The Formally Governing Senior Membership Of The Ruchira Sannyasin Order Of Adidam Ruchiradam).

All Practitioners Of The Only-By-Me Revealed and Given Way Of The Heart (or Way Of Adidam), At Any Period (or Stage) Of Practice, Must Always (Intensively, and Always Appropriately) Maximize Both The Duration and The Frequency Of The Occasions Of daily Formal Meditation, According To The Instructions Given (In Accordance With My Formally Given Instructions) By The Formally Governing Senior Membership Of The Ruchira Sannyasin Order Of Adidam Ruchiradam.

Regular Occasions Of Formal Retreat Must Be Undertaken By Each and Every Practitioner Of The Way Of The Heart—As A General Rule, For At Least one full day each week, and For a period of At Least two to three days At Least once every three to four months, and At Least once annually For a period of At Least ten days to three weeks. In Addition, There Are Necessary Periods Of Extended Formal Retreat In My Avataric Physical Human Company (or, After My Avataric Physical Human Lifetime, In The physical human Company and By-Me-Spiritually-Empowered Circumstances Of My "Ruchira Sannyasin" Devotees) For The Purpose Of Spiritual Initiation, By Me, Into Either The Primary Practice Of Searchlessly Beholding Me and (Thereby) Receiving My Ruchira Shaktipat (At The Transition To The Intensive Listening-Hearing Stage Of The Way Of The Heart) Or The To-Me-Upward-Turning Searchless-Beholding Practice Of My "Hridaya Rosary" Of "Four Thorns Of Heart-Instruction" (At The Transition To The Would-Be-Seeing Stage Of The Way Of The Heart) Or The Perfect Searchless-Beholding Practice Of "Locating" Me (By Means Of Searchless Beholding Of My Bodily Human Form, My Spiritual, and Always Blessing, Presence, and My Very, and Inherently Perfect, State) To The Degree Of Tacitly Identifying Me <u>As</u> "Atma-Murti", or The Tangible Feeling Of Being (At The Transition To The "Perfect Practice" Of The Way Of The Heart).

At Every Developmental Stage Of Practice In The Only-By-Me Revealed and Given Way Of The Heart, and (Therefore) At Every Stage Of Growth In The Progressive Development Of Ruchira Avatara Bhakti Yoga (Which Is The Foundation and Very Essence Of Every Form Of Practice In The Only-By-Me Revealed and Given Way Of The Heart), The Feeling-Contemplation Of My Avatarically-Born Bodily (Human) Divine Form, My Avatarically Self-Transmitted Spiritual (and Always Blessing) Divine Presence, and My Avatarically Self-Revealed (and Very, and Transcendental, and Perfectly Subjective, and Inherently Spiritual, and Inherently egoless, and Inherently Perfect, and Self-Evidently Divine) State, Assisted and Supported By The Random Invocation Of Me (Via My Principal Avatarically Revealed and Given Divine Name, "Da", or Via Any Other Of My Avatarically Revealed and Given Divine Names, or Combined Avataric Divine Names and Avataric Divine Descriptive Titles, Which I Have Given To Be Engaged In The Practice Of Simple Name-Invocation Of Me), and (As Appropriate To The Present Developmental Stage Of Practice) My Devotee's Responsive Exercise Of One or Another Mode or Form Of The Only-By-Me Revealed and Given "Conscious Process" and "Conductivity" Practice, Should (and Indeed, Must) Be Practiced Both Formally (or As Formal Meditation) and At Random (or Intensively, but In Random moments of every day), and Such That It (or That Total and By-My-Avataric-Divine-Grace-Given

Process) Actively (or, Otherwise, Directly), and Also moment to moment, and Progressively, Surrenders, Forgets, and Really Transcends self-Contraction, and (Therefore) All Attachment To, and Identification With, and (Ultimately) Even Awareness Of The (Otherwise Persistent) Streams Of bodily desires, emotional reactions, and mental events (or conceptual and perceptual thoughts).

Likewise, All The By-Me-Revealed and By-Me-Given daily functional, practical, relational, and Cultural Disciplines Must Also (Even From The Beginning Of Practice Of The Way Of The Heart) Be Engaged, Devotionally Responsively, As Forms Of Ruchira Avatara Bhakti Yoga—and Such That They Also (Actively, and Directly, and moment to moment, and Progressively) Surrender, Forget, and Really Transcend self-Contraction, and (Therefore) All Attachment To, and Identification With, and (Ultimately) Even Awareness Of The Otherwise Persistent Streams Of bodily desires, emotional reactions, and mental events (or conceptual and perceptual thoughts).

And, In Any Formal Occasion (or Even In any moment) Of Meditation (or Even Of Simple Feeling-Contemplation Of Me), Both The Tendency To Become Distracted (or For attention To Wander, Toward, or To, environmental conditions, or outer relationships, or bodily states, or emotional reactions, or thoughts of any kind) and The Tendency Toward sleep (or For attention To Become Fixed In its own Twilight, or Neutral Enclosure) Must Be Transcended—and This By Intentionally (and Actively, and Devotionally Responsively) Keeping attention On (and Yielded To) My Avatarically-Born Bodily (Human) Divine Form, and On (and Yielded To) My Avatarically Self-Transmitted Spiritual (and Always Blessing) Divine Presence (As Felt, and Received, and Embraced, According To Your Developmental Stage Of Practice In The Way Of The Heart), and On (and Yielded To) My Avatarically Self-Revealed (and Very, and Transcendental, and Perfectly Subjective, and Inherently Spiritual, and Inherently egoless, and Inherently Perfect, and Self-Evidently Divine) State (Also As Felt, and Received, and Embraced, According To Your Developmental Stage Of Practice In The Way Of The Heart), and (All Of This) Until (In Deep Meditation, and In Progressive Samadhis) attention Is Most Profoundly Absorbed In The Ecstatic Feeling-Contemplation Of Me, and (This) Until (Ultimately, and In The Context Of The "Perfect Practice" Of The Way Of The Heart) attention itself Is (By Means Of My Avatarically Self-Transmitted Divine Spiritual Grace) Transcended In The Spherical "Bright" Divine Self-Domain Of My Own Person.

Optimally, Formal Meditation Should (As A Consistent, daily Rule) Take Place In A Comfortable Environment, Free Of Disturbances and Likely Intrusion. The Superior Meditation Place Is One That Is Set Apart Exclusively For Meditation, Ruchira Avatara Puja, Chanting, and Even All The Varieties Of

True (and Truly Me-Contemplating) Devotional Singing (Even Including Ecstatic and Vigorous and Freely Moving and Dancing Kirtan).[88]

My Avatarically Self-Revealed Divine Spirit-Power (or Ruchira Shakti—My Avataric Divine Spiritual Self-Transmission and Self-Revelation Of My Inherently egoless, and Self-Evidently Divine, Person) Is (By Means Of My Avatarically Self-Transmitted Divine Spiritual Grace) Entered, Established, and Magnified In any place where My (Formally Acknowledged, and Rightly Practicing) By-Me-Spiritually-Initiated (and Always Newly By-Me-Spiritually-Activated) Devotees Constantly Invoke (and Really Devotionally Surrender To and Into) My Avatarically Self-Transmitted Divine Spiritual Presence. (And Even any place where Devotional Invocation Of Me, and, Also, Either Meditative self-Enquiry Or Meditative Ruchira Avatara Naama Japa, Is Regularly Engaged By My Student-Beginner Devotees Develops A Quality Of Natural energy That Is Effectively Conducive To psycho-physical Equanimity and Easeful Concentration Of attention.) Therefore, As My Seeing Devotee, or As My Hearing Devotee, or Even As My Listening Devotee—You Will Do Best To Meditate In the same place each day, and Even All Practitioners Of The Way Of The Heart Will Also (and For The Same Reason) Do Well To Collectively (or, If Necessary, alone) Perform The daily (and Also The More Occasional) Ruchira Avatara Pujas In the same place each day (or On Each Such Occasion). Likewise, All Practitioners Of The Way Of The Heart Will Do Well To Meditate In any of the places In which Numbers Of Other (Like) Practitioners Gather To Meditate daily. And All My By-Me-Spiritually-Initiated (and, Otherwise, Would-Be By-Me-Spiritually-Initiated) Devotees Will (Now, and Forever Hereafter) Find My Avatarically Self-Transmitted Divine Spirit-Presence To Be Uniquely Strong and Constant In Places I Have Established and Spiritually Empowered Through My Own Avatarically-Born Bodily (Human) Divine Agency.

Whenever Possible, the place (or room) Chosen For Meditation (In The Way Of The Heart) Should Be Enclosed (Such That contact with the elements Of conditional Nature Is Always Controlled). Likewise, that place (or room) Should Be Securely Protected From All Intrusion By the common (or daily) world. And that place (or room) Should Be Kept cool (or temperate), and Always Fresh With Circulating (but Comfortable and Unobtrusive) air, and With Minimal (or Even No) General light, but Only With a Gentle light Focused On The Murti Of My Avatarically-Born Bodily (Human) Divine Form (Which Murti Should Be Of A Size Large Enough To Be Readily and Easily perceived, In Detail, From a position anywhere within that place or room).[89] Thus, Apart From the Gentle light Focused On My Murti, the place (or room) Of Meditation Should, Optimally, Be Kept Free Of any and all Intrusive illumination by lights, flames, or sun.

Feel (and Thereby Contemplate) Me there (In the place You Have Chosen).

If physically Possible, Always Practice This Feeling-Contemplation Of Me (and The Total Process Of Meditation) While Sitting In A spinally Erect Posture.[90] In General, Sit Firmly and Comfortably, With hips and buttocks Rotated Slightly Forward, spine Erect, the body Relaxed In front and back, chest Raised and Open, chin Tucked Slightly Back, the back of the neck Slightly Stretched, and the shoulders Relaxed, As If the body Is Suspended From The Crown Of the head and Supported By the bodily base. Be Seated On a cushion, mat, or pad (of a material that insulates the body from the "grounding"-energy, and the bodily-heat-absorbing effects, of contact with the earth or floor)—or, Otherwise, Be Seated In a supportive chair. Wear loose, Comfortable clothing. Generally, breathe through the nose (Rather Than through an open mouth), With the tongue Pressed Lightly To the roof of the mouth.

In Due Course (In Any Occasion Of Meditation, and Only When, In The By-My-Avataric-Divine-Grace-Given Course Of The Feeling-Contemplation Of Me, You Are, Thus and Thereby, and Spontaneously, Moved), Allow the eyes To close, and (By That Same and Spontaneously Deepening Impulse) Allow the eyes To Turn Up and Back. (Also, where environmental lights Are presently, or, Otherwise, Potentially, Intrusive, Comfortable eyeshades May be placed over the eyes, As The Deepening Impulse Begins.)

In Order (In General) To Avoid Disturbance or Distraction By environmental noises, It May Be Appropriate To wear Comfortably Effective earplugs.

It Is Not Possible To Enter The Depth Of Meditation Until body, breath, emotion, the frontal (or vital) energies, the nervous system, and the brain Are In A Relaxed (or Easefully Balanced) State and (In The Case Of My By-Me-Spiritually-Initiated Devotees) In A State (or In The Process) Of Right Spiritual "Conductivity" and Spiritual Fullness. The Foundation (functional, practical, relational, and Cultural) Practices (Established At The Student-Beginner Stage) Of The Way Of The Heart Are Intended To Establish A Permanent Firm Basis For The Spiritually-Me-Receiving Disposition (or Attitude), Capability, and Capacity In daily life and In The Context Of Meditative Practice. And, Indeed, At Any Developmental Stage Of The Way Of The Heart, My Devotee Is Prepared For Any Particular Occasion Of Formal Meditation Only To The Degree That he or she Has Prepared For That Occasion Of Formal Meditation Through The Totality Of Right Practice Of The Only-By-Me Revealed and Given Way Of The Heart (or Way Of Adidam).

Assuming That The Practitioner Of The Way Of The Heart Is (By Right Practice In General) Rightly Prepared For An Occasion Of Formal Meditation, Certain Technical Means May Also Be Engaged At The Very Beginning Of (or, Otherwise, Immediately Previous To) The Time Of Meditation, In Order To

Quickly Establish The Necessary Preliminary Relaxation, psycho-physical Balance, and Free attention For Deepening Meditation.[91] There Are Five Possible (Simple, or Rudimentary) Technical Means That I Recommend (To Any and, In General, All Practitioners Of The Way Of The Heart) For Possible (Preparatory) Application At The Very Beginning Of (or, Otherwise, Immediately Previous To) any period Of Formal Meditation. These Five Simple (or Rudimentary) Technical Means Include The Use Of Polarity Screens,[92] Hatha Yoga Asanas,[93] Pranayama In The Form Of alternate-nostril breathing,[94] Pranayama In The Form Of Frontal Vase-Breathing,[95] and The Hamsadanda (or Short Crutch).[96]

It May Be Useful (At times when the body is either in an agitated state or in an enervated state) To Lie Down On Polarity Screens (In The Relaxation Circuit, or Mode, When There Is a bodily feeling of over-stimulation, and Either In The Relaxation Circuit, or Mode, Or In The Energizing Circuit, or Mode, When There Is a bodily feeling of enervation), and This For Perhaps ten or fifteen minutes, At The Very Beginning Of (or, Otherwise, Immediately Previous To) The Occasion Of Formal Meditation. This Will Tend To Balance and Relax the body-mind By Directly Affecting the etheric energy field of the body.

Hatha Yoga Asanas May Also Be Performed (In An Easeful, or Relaxed, Manner) For Perhaps ten or fifteen minutes, At The Very Beginning Of (or, Otherwise, Immediately Previous To) The Occasion Of Formal Meditation, and The Effect Will Tend To Be Similar To That Of The Other Four Means I Have Indicated, Except That The Effect Is (In This Case) Generated By Manipulating the physical body In Order To Control its Relationship To its own energies.

It May Be Found Useful To Practice Pranayama (or Natural-bodily-energy-Control) In The Form Of simple alternate-nostril breathing For five or ten minutes At The Very Beginning Of (or, Otherwise, Immediately Previous To) The Occasion Of Formal Meditation. This Will Calm, Rebalance, and Refresh The Circle Of the body-mind By Means Of Easy breath-Control (and Natural-bodily-energy-Control).

As An Alternative To Pranayama (or Natural-bodily-energy-Control) In The Form Of simple alternate-nostril breathing, It May Be Found Useful To Practice Pranayama (or Natural-bodily-energy-Control) In The Form Of Frontal Vase-Breathing For a brief period (Of One, Two, or Three Cycles, or Repetitions, Of The Frontal Vase-Breathing Procedure) At The Very Beginning Of The Occasion Of Formal Meditation. Frontal Vase-Breathing Is A Simple Variation On The By-Me-Given "General Conductivity" Exercises, and It Should Be Practiced As Follows: Inhale Fully, Via both nostrils, With the tongue Pressed Lightly To the roof of the (Generally) closed mouth. Inhale Fully, Feeling the Natural breath-energy Flow Down, Through The Frontal Line, To the lower abdomen. Press the inhaled breath Down (Comfortably) Into the abdomen, Even Such That the abdomen Expands Rather Fully. As the abdomen Begins To Swell, the breath (and the Natural breath-energy) Should Be Held In the abdomen, and the bodily base Should Be Tensed (or Comfortably Contracted) Upwards, and the chin Should Be Pulled Down Somewhat (In Order To Lock the breath At the throat). Hold the breath (and the Natural breath-energy) In the abdomen For a Significant (but Comfortable) period, While Concentrating attention At and Above The Ajna Door. In a few moments, It May Be Felt To Be Possible To inhale Even A Little More. In That Case, Release The chin-Lock, and inhale Further (Downward, Into the abdomen), While Maintaining The Tension In the bodily base. (If It Is Uncomfortable To Hold The Tension In the bodily base, Briefly Relax The Tension In the bodily base, and Then Re-Tense the bodily base—As Required.) In The Midst Of Such Attempts To inhale More, the abdomen May Be Gently "Rolled", In and Out, In Order To "Loosen" the abdomen and the solar plexus—Such That more air and more Natural breath-energy Can Be Breathed Down. Hold This Mudra (or bodily Attitude) Of The "Vase" (or Expanded abdomen, With the Natural breath-energy Contained By Means Of The Upward Tensing Of the bodily base), Until It Becomes (Comfortably) Necessary To exhale. Then Relax Into exhalation, and (While Lightly Tensing, or Pulling Up, the bodily base, and Lightly Pulling the crown of the lower abdomen In and Up) Relax and Release the Natural breath-energy Into The Spinal Line (and Let the Natural breath-energy Become Diffusely Released Into the Total body), but, As A General Rule, Do Not Otherwise Press (or Concentrate) the Natural breath-energy In (or Into) the head. Exhale Thus, and In A Comfortably Relaxed Fashion, Rather Than Quickly. The Completion Of the exhalation Completes The Full Cycle Of The Frontal Vase-Breathing Exercise. And The Cycle May Be Repeated, To (As A General Rule) A Maximum Of Three Full Cycles—In Order To Calm, Rebalance, and Refresh The Circle Of the body-mind By Means Of Easy breath-Control (and Natural "Conductivity"-Control Of the Natural bodily energy, In The Context Of The Circle Of the body-mind).

Even Simpler Than Pranayama Is The Practice Associated With The Traditional Hamsadanda (or Short Crutch). This Traditional Yogic Practice May Be Done During the earlier period Of Any Occasion Of Formal Meditation. The Hamsadanda Should First Be Placed Into the armpit on the side of the body in which the nostril (on that particular side, left or right) is, at the moment (and In Comparison To the opposite side), breathing the most freely (or the most "openly"). This Will Have The Natural Effect Of "closing" the nostril (or the breath-flow) on the "open" side, and Of "opening" the nostril (or the breath-flow) on the "closed" (or opposite) side. (The Yogic Hamsadanda-Effect

Is Created By Applying Pressure Directly To Key Points In the nervous system That Are Naturally Associated With The Control Of the breath and The Relationship Between the breath-process and The bodily "Conductivity" Of Natural bodily energy.) Therefore, The Hamsadanda Should, In The Manner I Have Described, Be Alternated From side To side, Until both nostrils are breathing freely (or "openly") and equally, and the body and the breath Are Relaxed.

The Five Simple (or Rudimentary) Technical Means I Have Just (Briefly) Described Are Generally Applicable and Generally Appropriate Technical Devices (or Rudimentary Technical Practices) That May Be Used (Even In many and various circumstances, and For The General Purpose Of Well-being) By Any or All Of My Devotees who Are (As Required In The Particular Case Of Each and Every Such Technical Means) physically (and Altogether) Capable Of Rightly Using Them. And I Especially Recommend The Application Of These Five Simple (or Rudimentary) Technical Devices (or Practices) As Possible Secondary (or Supportive) Means That May Serve To Prepare the body-mind For Formal (and Deep, or Deepening) Meditation In The Way Of The Heart. And, Like All Other Technical Means (or Technical, and, Necessarily, Secondary, Practices) In The Way Of The Heart, These Particular Technical Means Should Always Be Applied Judiciously, and (Generally) Only Briefly, and In A Truly Simple (or Uncomplicated, and Non-Seeking) Manner.

Avatar Adi Da Samraj
Adidam Samrajashram, 2003

SUTRA 31

In The Only-By-Me Revealed and Given Way Of The Heart (or Way Of Adidam), True Hearing Of Me (or Most Fundamental Understanding Of the conditional self) First Becomes (or Responsively Demonstrates Itself As) The "Conscious Process" Of Mature (or Really Effective) self-Enquiry (In The Devotional Way Of Insight) and Mature (or Really Effective) Ruchira Avatara Naama Japa (In The Devotional Way Of Faith). Thus, By Means Of My Avatarically Self-Transmitted Divine Spiritual Grace (Given By Me, In The Context Of Right Devotional and Spiritual Relationship To Me), Either self-Enquiry Or Ruchira Avatara Naama Japa Becomes The Responsive "Conscious-Process"-Aspect Of "Real" Meditation (or Meditation Founded On Previous and Prior and Most Fundamental self-Understanding, Real and Directly Effective Transcending Of egoity, and Real and Direct Communion With Me, "Located"—Devotionally and Spiritually—As The Avataric, and Self-Evidently Divine, Self-Revelation Of Reality Itself).

Therefore, In The Only-By-Me Revealed and Given Way Of The Heart (In Its Fullness, or Real Devotional <u>and</u> Spiritual Demonstration), self-Enquiry, "True Prayer", and Also (Ultimately) The "Perfect Practice" Are (or Must Be) Right, True, and Really Effective Exercises Of "Real" Meditative Communion With Me—and I Am Thereby (and By Even All My Avataric Divine Spiritual Graces and Gifts) Found To Be Eternally Present As The Avataric Divine Self-Revealer, and As The Avataric Divine Self-Revelation, Of The Spiritual, Transcendental, and Divine Forms Of Reality, Truth, and Real God.

Verbal self-Enquiry Should Generally Be Done silently (With "the tongue of the mind"), and The Practice Of self-Enquiry Should (Even In The Student-Beginner, or First Listening, Stage, and In The Later, Intensive Listening-Hearing Stage, Of The Way Of The Heart) Involve The Observation and (Progressively) The Relaxation (or The Simple Release, or The At Least Partial and Temporary Transcending) Of the mind itself—and, In Due Course (Once There Is The True Hearing Of Me, or Most Fundamental self-Understanding), The Direct (and More and More Profoundly Effective) Transcending Of the mind itself. Just So, <u>After</u> self-Enquiry Becomes Established On The Basis Of The True <u>Hearing</u> Of Me (and Especially Once Such Practice Is Fully Established

In The Context Of The First Actually Seeing Stage Of The Only-By-Me Revealed and Given Way Of The Heart), My Devotees who Have Chosen The Devotional Way Of Insight Will Discover That, In their Practice Of "Real" Meditative Communion With Me, verbal self-Enquiry Is (Even Generally, and Especially In the Deepening, and Deep, moments or periods Of Meditation) Spontaneously Tending (More and More) To Be Replaced By Tacit (or Non-verbal) *Re-Cognition*.

To Practice Tacit (or Non-verbal) Re-Cognition Is To "Know" the self-Contraction (*as* self-Contraction) *Again*, In The Context Of (and Even *as*) each and (Potentially) every moment of conditional arising, and (Thereby) To Directly Transcend self-Contraction (By "Re-Knowing" self-Contraction, and, Thus, Identifying it as such, and, In That "Re-Knowing", Re-Claiming and Directly Re-Enacting The Capability To Feel Beyond self-Contraction).

Even every object perceived by the conditional self is a psycho-physical experience, conditioned by the conditional self (or the self-Contracted body-mind). Therefore, Tacit (or Non-verbal) Re-Cognition Is A Matter Of Simple attention to whatever conditionally arises—Noticing (or "Knowing Again", By Tacitly and Directly Feeling-Observing) That whatever is conditionally arising Has The Form Of the self-Contraction, and Then (or On The Basis Of That Noticing) *Directly* Feeling Beyond the self-Contraction (Just As In The Case Of verbal self-Enquiry, but Without The mental Exercise Of The Specifically *verbal* Dimension Of self-Enquiry). And Tacit (or Non-verbal) Re-Cognition (and Direct Transcending) Of the self-Contraction, In The Context Of any (and, Potentially, Even every) conditional form or event that arises, Continues (or Must Continue, At Least As A Feeling-Process) Even In Deep Meditation, or (Certainly) Whenever any Observable (or Objectified) phenomenon (or Even The Feeling Of Relatedness Itself) arises.

When Re-Cognition Begins (and As The Total Practice Of self-Enquiry Matures Toward The Transition To The "Perfect Practice"), Even all arising conditions (including all conceptual thoughts, and Even all forms of perception, or perceptual mind) Are To Be Re-Cognized (As self-Contraction), and Thus Felt Beyond. This Finally (In The Context Of The Second Stage Of The "Perfect Practice") Becomes (By Means Of The Practice Of "Feeling-Enquiry") Re-Cognition (and Most Direct Transcending) Of The Feeling Of Relatedness Itself (Which, It Is To Be Discovered, Is The Ultimate, or Original, Form Of the self-Contraction itself).

When, In The Context Of The Second Stage Of The "Perfect Practice", The Feeling Of Relatedness Is Itself Re-Cognized As self-Contraction (and, Via That Re-Cognition, Directly Transcended), The By-Me-Avatarically-Self-Revealed Transcendental (and Inherently Spiritual) Self-Condition and Source-Condition

Stands (Exclusively) Self-Revealed. However, After Transcendental (and Inherently Spiritual) Self-Realization Is Inherently and Divinely Perfected (In The Awakening To The Only-By-Me Revealed and Given Seventh Stage Of Life In The Way Of The Heart), arising conditions (and The Feeling Of Relatedness Itself) Are, Fundamentally (and As A Necessary Intentional Exercise), No Longer Re-Cognized As self-Contraction and Then Felt Beyond. Instead, arising conditions (Including The Feeling Of Relatedness Itself) Are Inherently (and Divinely) Self-Recognized In and <u>As</u> The Self-Radiant (Spiritually Self-"Bright", or Inherently Non-Contracted) Self-Condition Of Self-Existing Being (or Of The One and Only and Inherently Indivisible and Inherently egoless Conscious Light Of all-and-All). Thus, In The Context Of The Only-By-Me Revealed and Given Seventh Stage Of Life In The Way Of The Heart, The conditional Process Of the arising of phenomena (and Of The Coincident Feeling Of Relatedness) Is Always Already Transcended In The Perpetual (or Eternal) Transcendental (and Inherently Spiritual) Event Of Divine Self-Inherence, and (On That Basis) In The moment to moment Process Of Self-Abiding Divine Self-Recognition Of (Apparent) conditions (and Of The Feeling Of Relatedness, <u>Itself</u>) In The "Bright".

In The Only-By-Me Revealed and Given Way Of The Heart (or Way Of Adidam), The Practice Of self-Enquiry Develops In The Same (General) Manner, and On The Same (General) Basis, As The Practice Of "True Prayer"—Except That (By Comparison) self-Enquiry Transcends the self-Contraction By (First) Observing the self-Contraction (In The Context Of Feeling-Awareness Of Me), and (Then) Feeling Beyond the self-Contraction (Such That self-Surrender To My Great Attractiveness Is More and More Full and Complete), Whereas "True Prayer" Transcends the self-Contraction By (First) "Locating" Me, and (Then) Allowing Me To Be Attractive, Such That the self-Contraction Is Released Responsively (or As An Inevitable Result Of Intentional—and, Otherwise, Spontaneous—Devotional self-Surrender To My Great Attractiveness). In The Case Of <u>Both</u> self-Enquiry <u>and</u> "True Prayer", True Satsang With Me Is The Given (and Great) Primary Basis (or Heart-Environment) In Which The ego-Transcending Processes or Events Occur. In <u>Both</u> The Devotional Way Of Insight <u>and</u> The Devotional Way Of Faith—and, Thus, For <u>All</u> My Listening Devotees, <u>All</u> My Hearing Devotees, and <u>All</u> My Seeing Devotees In The Only-By-Me Revealed and Given Way Of The Heart (or Way Of Adidam)—True Satsang With Me (or The Devotional and, In Due Course, Spiritual <u>Relationship</u> To Me) Is The Primary and Necessary Basis and Condition For <u>All</u> functional, practical, relational, and Cultural Practices (and, Thus, For All Contemplative Practices and All Meditation Practices).

In The Only-By-Me Revealed and Given Way Of The Heart (or Way Of Adidam), The Practice Of self-Enquiry Notices and Then Freely Releases (or

Directly Feels Beyond) the self-Contraction, Such That Whole bodily (or Total psycho-physical) Devotional (and, In Due Course, Spiritual) Heart-Communion With My Avatarically-Born Bodily (Human) Divine Form, My Avatarically Self-Transmitted Spiritual (and Always Blessing) Divine Presence, and My Avatarically Self-Revealed (and Very, and Transcendental, and Perfectly Subjective, and Inherently Spiritual, and Inherently egoless, and Inherently Perfect, and Self-Evidently Divine) State Is, Progressively, More and More Fully and Completely Enjoyed In every moment—Whereas "True Prayer" Simply (or Directly and Merely) Devotionally Surrenders To Whole bodily (or Total psycho-physical) Devotional (and, In Due Course, Spiritual) Heart-Communion With My Avatarically-Born Bodily (Human) Divine Form, My Avatarically Self-Transmitted Spiritual (and Always Blessing) Divine Presence, and My Avatarically Self-Revealed (and Very, and Transcendental, and Perfectly Subjective, and Inherently Spiritual and Inherently egoless, and Inherently Perfect, and Self-Evidently Divine) State In every moment—and the self-Contraction Is Thus, Progressively, Also (and More and More Fully and Completely) Released (or Felt Beyond) In every moment.

In The Only-By-Me Revealed and Given Way Of The Heart (or Way Of Adidam), The Practice Of self-Enquiry Constantly Notices and Feels Beyond the self-Contraction (and All Of its Results), Thus (Progressively, and More and More Fully and Completely) Enjoying The Process Of Whole bodily (or Total psycho-physical) Devotional (and, In Due Course, Spiritual) Heart-Communion With Me.

In The Only-By-Me Revealed and Given Way Of The Heart (or Way Of Adidam), "True Prayer" Simply (and Constantly) and Whole bodily (or By Means Of self-Surrender As A psycho-physical Totality) Communes With Me (Devotionally and, In Due Course, Spiritually) In My Inherent "Bright" Attractiveness—and the self-Contraction Is Inevitably (or Progressively, and More and More Fully and Completely, and Always Spontaneously) Relinquished By That Heart-Responsive Communion With Me.

Avatar Adi Da Samraj
Lopez Island, 2000

SUTRA 32

The Only One Who Is, Only (or Merely) Is.

Apart From Who Is, or What Is, There Is Not any one or any thing or any condition or any event That Is.

Any one or any thing or any condition or any event that Is, Only (or Merely) Is.

The beings and things and conditions and events that Are, Simply or Only (or Merely) Are. The mind and the body, Likewise, Simply Are. What they Are Is Not known. Therefore, It Is Neither Necessary Nor Appropriate For You To Imagine That You know (or Must know, or Can know) What they Are.

The beings and things and conditions and events that Are, Only Are. They Are Only What they Are, Not whatever You (By Presuming Separation From them) think About them.

The beings and things and conditions and events that Are, Only Are. They Are Only What they Are, Not whatever You (By Presuming Separation From them) perceive or experience them to be.

The beings and things and conditions and events that Are, Are Only As Is, or As What they Are. Therefore, You Are Also Thus. And There Is Not Any Effort You Can Make That Can Make This Not So.

Nevertheless, All The Efforts You Have Already Made Have Become A Pattern Of Presumptions, Wherein and Whereby That Which Is Always Already The Case Is Not Obvious To You. Therefore, Paradoxically, You Must Grow To Consent To Be.

The Only-By-Me Revealed and Given Way Of The Heart (or Way Of Adidam) Is The Way Of Growing To Consent To Be. Therefore, Be My Devotee, and (By Growing In The Only-By-Me Revealed and Given Way Of The Heart) Grow To Be, To Be That, To Be As Is, and (Thus) To Let every one and every thing and every condition and every event Be, Forever Free Of Your egoic Confusion, Your egoic emotional Concern, Your egoic mental Interpretation, and Your egoic bodily Interference.

All beings and things and conditions and events Simply (or Merely) and Only Are. They Are Exactly and Only as they appear to be. The beings and things and conditions and events that arise Are Not what You think About them. Reality (or Real God) Is Always Already Prior To what You think, or Prior To thinking itself. Merely To Observe and To Feel whatever arises (Exactly as it appears) Is To Completely know whatever arises. Merely To Be Is Who You Are. The Feeling Of Being (Itself) Is What every being, every thing, every condition, and every event Is.

Interpreting-mind Relaxes, Naturally, When You Merely (or Simply) perceive and Naturally feel (and Thus Directly know) beings and things and conditions and events themselves. Verbal mind and Abstract thinking mind Relax, Naturally, When You Are Merely (or Simply) Being, As (or What) all beings and things and conditions and events Are, Instead Of Imagining You know (and Instead Of Seeking To know) What or Who they Are, or What or Who You Are.

Perceiving-mind and experiencing-self Relax (or Dissolve In Inherent Love-Bliss) When You Simply Are—Inherently Free, and Freely Indifferent (Even To the actions of Your Own Natural body-mind).

Hear Me. Understand. Understand the self-Contraction Most Fundamentally (At The Source-Position Of its Very Act), and (Thus) Consent To Be the body (or the Total body-mind)—Without self-Contraction, Merely perceiving, Without an other thought (or Without thought In Addition To perception).

Feel Free—Toward Me, and To Me. Transcend all conditional knowledge and all conditional experience In The Inherent and Infinitely Expanded Spiritual Radiance Of The Inherently Free Feeling Of Me.

When self-Observation and self-Discipline Have (Thus) Become The Steady Disposition Of Feeling Beyond the limitations of self-Contraction, and Toward What (and Who) Is Me, My Hearing Devotee Has Become Prepared To See Me.

In The Listening and Hearing Stages Of The Only-By-Me Revealed and Given Way Of The Heart (or Way Of Adidam), self-Understanding Develops Relative To The First Three Stages Of Life, In and Via The "Original" (or Beginner's) Devotional and Spiritual Context Of The Fourth Stage Of Life—and (By This) The Heart Is Prepared To Feel Me (and See Me) In The Devotional and Spiritual Context Of The "Basic" Fourth Stage Of Life (and Beyond).

In Order To Make The Transition To The Would-Be-Seeing (or Progressively Seeing, and Already Effectively Hearing) Stage Of The Only-By-Me Revealed and Given Way Of The Heart (or Way Of Adidam), My Any Devotee Must Have Already (Since The Transition To The Intensive Listening-Hearing Stage Of The Only-By-Me Revealed and Given Way Of The Heart—and With The Formal Approval Of The Ruchira Sannyasin Order Of Adidam Ruchiradam) Been Accepted (Because Of his or her Consistent Demonstration Of Right, True, and Full Practice Of The Only-By-Me Revealed and Given Way Of The

Heart) As A Formal Registrant (In then current, or then present-time, good standing) With The Avataric Samrajya Of Adidam, and he or she Must Be Formally (and currently) Approved By The Ruchira Sannyasin Order Of Adidam Ruchiradam—After he or she Has Been Formally Evaluated and Estimated and Recommended By The Formally Authorized Cultural Representatives Of The Lay Congregationist Order Of Adidam Ruchiradam—As Demonstrating (In Strict and Full Accordance With My Instructions, As Given, By Me, To The Ruchira Sannyasin Order Of Adidam Ruchiradam) All The Necessary Qualifications To Exercise The Primary Practice (Of Searchless Beholding Of Me) and The Responsive ("Conscious Process" and "Conductivity") Practices Of The Only-By-Me Revealed and Given Way Of The Heart In The Right, True, and Full Manner Of My Herein Given "Hridaya Rosary" Of "Four Thorns Of Heart-Instruction".[97] And My Any Such Devotee Must Be Specifically Given (then current, or then present-time) Formal Approval By The Ruchira Sannyasin Order Of Adidam Ruchiradam To Exercise The Primary Practice and The Responsive Practices Of The Only-By-Me Revealed and Given Way Of The Heart In The Right, True, and Full Manner Of My "Hridaya Rosary" Of "Four Thorns Of Heart-Instruction", While On Extended Formal Retreat—and Afterwards (Once he or she Has Been Spiritually Initiated, By Me, Into That Practice, While he or she Is Participating In A Period Of Extended Formal Retreat In My Avataric Physical Human Company, or, After My Avataric Physical Human Lifetime, In The physical human Company and By-Me-Spiritually-Empowered Circumstances Of My "Ruchira Sannyasin" Devotees).

In The Transition To The Would-Be-Seeing (or Progressively Seeing, and Already Effectively Hearing) Stage Of The Only-By-Me Revealed and Given Way Of The Heart (or Way Of Adidam), The Edge Of Practice Moves From The Beginner's Devotional and Spiritual (but Not Yet, Spiritually, Fully Technically Responsible) Listening and (Then) Hearing Process To The Great Process Of Seeing Me (or The Fullest Devotional and Fully Technically Spiritually Responsible and Most Real Heart-Practice That Characterizes Practice Of The Only-By-Me Revealed and Given Way Of The Heart In The "Basic" Spiritual Context Of The Fourth Stage Of Life and, In Due Course, In The Context Of The "Perfect Practice").

My Each and Every Devotee who Has Formally Made The Transition To The Would-Be-Seeing (or Progressively Seeing, and Already Effectively Hearing) Stage Of The Only-By-Me Revealed and Given Way Of The Heart (or Way Of Adidam) Must, By (Necessarily) Formal Invitation (By The Ruchira Sannyasin Order Of Adidam Ruchiradam), Come Into My Physical Human Company (or, After My Avataric Physical Human Lifetime, Into The physical human Company and By-Me-Spiritually-Empowered Circumstances Of My

"Ruchira Sannyasin" Devotees) On Extended Formal Retreat, For The Purpose Of Spiritual Initiation, By Me, Into The Process Of Receiving My Ruchira Shaktipat In The Manner Of My "Hridaya Rosary" Of "Four Thorns Of Heart-Instruction" (and, Thus, By Means Of The Practice Of "Samraj Asana"), and (Thus and Thereby) Becoming Established In The Fully Technically Responsible, or Seeing, Demonstration Of True Spiritual Reception Of Me—In The Context Of The Primary Practice Of The Only-By-Me Revealed and Given Way Of The Heart (Which Primary Practice Is That Of Searchlessly Beholding Me—Always, As The Indispensable Foundation, Searchlessly Beholding My Avatarically-Born Bodily Human Divine Form, and, Only On That Basis, Also Searchlessly Beholding My Avatarically Self-Transmitted Spiritual, and Always Blessing, Divine Presence, and My Avatarically Self-Revealed, and Very, and Transcendental, and Perfectly Subjective, and Inherently Spiritual, and Inherently egoless, and Inherently Perfect, and Self-Evidently Divine State), and In The Context Of The Responsive Seeing Demonstrations Of Both The "Conscious Process" and "General" Spirit-"Conductivity" Practice.

Now, Listen To My "Four Thorns Of Heart-Instruction"—My "Hridaya Rosary" (or Rose Garden Of The Heart).

This "Hridaya Rosary"
(or Rose Garden Of The Heart)
Is
(Herein and Hereby)
Heart-Spoken
By Me—
The One,
and True,
and Only,
and Non-Separate,
and Spiritually "Bright"
Heart Of all-and-All—
For The Sake Of The Restoration
(Now,
and In all future times and places)
Of Each and Every Seeming-To-Be Separate Heart
To Me.

This "Hridaya Rosary"
Is
(Herein and Hereby)
Heart-Spoken

By Me,
Most Specifically,
and Most Especially,
and Most Directly,
To All Formal Practitioners
Of The Only-By-Me Revealed and Given Way Of The Heart
who Have
(As The Sign Of their Devotional Response To Me)
Embraced The Right, True, Full, and Fully Devotional Practice
Of The Only-By-Me Revealed and Given Way Of The Heart,
and who Are
(Thus, and Necessarily)
Formally Practicing Members
Of Either The First Congregation Or The Second Congregation
Of My Formally Practicing Devotees,
and who—
Now,
or In any particular then present-time,
In any and all future times and places—
Rightly, and Truly,
and Truly Devotionally
Recognize Me
As The Only One Who Is
(and Who Must Be Devotionally Recognized,
and Realized,
By each and every one of all,
and By all-and-All).

The Teachings
Communicated By Me
In This "Hridaya Rosary"
Are
(Herein and Hereby)
Given By Me
To Be Happily and Seriously Studied—
Now,
and In all future times and places—
By All Of My Formally Practicing Devotees,

and, Also,
To Be Studied,
In An Altogether Positive and Serious Manner—
Now,
and In all future times and places—
By All Of The Interested
(but Not Yet Formally Devoted To Me)
Public (Of True Mankind,
and Of Even all Heart-Intelligent beings).

The Practice
(or The Totality Of Practices)
Described By Me
In This "Hridaya Rosary"
Is
(Herein and Hereby)
Given By Me
To Be Practiced—
Now,
and In all future times and places—
<u>Only</u>
By each and all
Of My Formally Practicing Devotees
who Are
(then currently, or In the particular then present-time)
Formally Practicing Members
(In good standing)
Of The Only-By-Me Revealed and Given Way Of The Heart
As Formal Members Of
The Avataric Pan-Communion Of Adidam,
and who—
As Such,
and Because Of their Consistent Demonstration
Of Right, True, Full, and Fully Devotional Practice
Of The Only-By-Me Revealed and Given Way Of The Heart—
Are
(With The Specific Formal Approval
Of The Ruchira Sannyasin Order Of Adidam Ruchiradam)
Formally Registered
(and In then current, or then present-time,

good standding)
With The Avataric Samrajya Of Adidam,
and
who Are Specifically Given
(then current, or then present-time)
Formal Approval
By The Ruchira Sannyasin Order Of Adidam Ruchiradam
To Practice
The Only-By-Me Revealed and Given Way Of The Heart
In The Right, True, Full, and Fully Devotional Manner
Of My "Four Thorns Of Heart-Instruction"
(or My "Hridaya Rosary"),
and
whose Qualifications So To Do,
In The Case Of each individual,
Have Been Formally Evaluated and Estimated
(and Are,
then currently, or In the particular then present-time,
Formally Affirmed)
By The Formally Authorized Cultural Representatives
Within That Formal Practicing Order Of Adidam Ruchiradam
(Among The Three Formal Practicing Orders Of Adidam
Ruchiradam)
Of Which the individual Is A Member,
Strictly According To My Instructions,
As Given,
By Me,
To The Ruchira Sannyasin Order Of Adidam Ruchiradam
(and Which Instructions Are Forever To Be Preserved
By The Ruchira Sannyasin Order Of Adidam Ruchiradam,
and
forever To Be Implemented
Under The General Guidance,
and Under The Only-Me-Extending Authority,
Of The Ruchira Sannyasin Order Of Adidam Ruchiradam,
To Educate,
and To Measure,
and,
Altogether,
To Serve

The Right, True, Full,
and
Direct,
and,
Ultimately,
Perfect,
and,
At Last,
Most Perfect,
Devotional Approach To Me,
In The Case Of each and all
Of My Formally Practicing Devotees—
Now,
and Forever Hereafter,
every where and when).

This "Hridaya Rosary"
Is A Brief,
and Condensed,
but Summary
Communication Of My Avataric Divine Word
Relative To The Fullest Right Form
Of Ruchira Avatara Bhakti Yoga,
or The Heart-Responsive
(ego-Transcending, body-mind-Melting,
and, Always More and More Perfectly, Me-Realizing)
Devotional Practice
Of Always Keeping
the To-Me-Devoted body-mind Of My True Devotee
In The Real and Always Blessing Company
Of My Avatarically Self-Revealed
and Love-Bliss-"Bright"
Divine Spiritual Presence
and egoless True Divine Person.

This Specific Form
(or Fullest Right Form)
Of Ruchira Avatara Bhakti Yoga
Is
(If Formal Ruchira Sannyasin Order Approval Is Given)

To Be Engaged
By My Formally Practicing
(and, Spiritually, Fully Technically Responsible)
Devotee
Whenever
(During My Physical Human Lifetime
Of Avataric Incarnation)
he or she Is bodily
In My Physically Living Bodily Human Company,
(or Whenever,
Forever After My Physical Human Lifetime
Of Avataric Incarnation,
My Any Such Formally Practicing Devotee,
Formally Approved By The Ruchira Sannyasin Order Of Adidam Ruchiradam
To Engage This Specific and Fullest Right Form
Of Ruchira Avatara Bhakti Yoga,
Is bodily
In The physical human Company
and The By-Me-Spiritually-Empowered Circumstances
Of My "Ruchira Sannyasin" Devotees.

This Specific Form
(or Fullest Right Form)
Of Ruchira Avatara Bhakti Yoga
Is Also,
At all times when
(During My Physical Human Lifetime
Of Avataric Incarnation)
My Any Formally Practicing
(and, Spiritually, Fully Technically Responsible)
Devotee,
Formally Approved By The Ruchira Sannyasin Order Of Adidam Ruchiradam
To Engage This Specific and Fullest Right Form
Of Ruchira Avatara Bhakti Yoga,
Is bodily
Outside My Physically Living Bodily Human Company
(or At all times,
Forever After My Physical Human Lifetime,
When My Any Such Formally Practicing Devotee
Is bodily

Outside The physical human Company
and The By-Me-Spiritually-Empowered Circumstances
Of My "Ruchira Sannyasin" Devotees,
To Be Combined
(By My Every Such Formally Practicing Devotee)
With All The Other By Me Given
(and Always, By Me, Expected)
Practices
(As Determined By
My Formally Practicing Devotee's
Formal Vow Of Eternal,
and Always present-time,
Devotion To Me,
and By
his or her Coincident Formal Vow,
and Likewise Eternal,
and Always present-time,
Obligation,
To Practice The Only-By-Me Revealed and Given Way Of The
Heart,
and By his or her
Manner and Developmental Stage Of Practice
In Either The First Or The Second Congregation
Of The Only-By-Me Revealed and Given Way Of The Heart).

This Specific Form
(or Fullest Right Form)
Of Ruchira Avatara Bhakti Yoga
Is To Be Practiced
(Upon Always current, or then present-time,
Formal Ruchira Sannyasin Order Approval)
<u>Only</u>
By each and all
Of My Formally Practicing
(and, Spiritually, Fully Technically Responsible)
Devotees
who <u>Really</u> and <u>Truly</u> Heart-Recognize (or Heart-Know) Me,

By
(Truly and Deeply)

Heart-Receiving,
and Heart-Understanding,
and
(In This Root-Devotional Sense)
Heart-Hearing
My Own Me-Revealing Words
Of Avataric Divine Self-Confession,

and By
(Truly and Deeply)
Heart-Enjoying
and Heart-Praising
My Own Me-Revealing Acts
(or Leelas)
Of Avataric Divine Self-Revelation,

and By Constantly,
and Truly,
and Deeply
Heart-Invoking Me,

and By
(Thus and Thereby)
Always Exercising their Heart-Feeling
Toward Me and To Me
(Beyond the ego-"I"
and Beyond the body-mind),

and
(In This Constant Feeling-Invocation)
Really
(and,
Only and Entirely,
By Means Of My Own Me-Revealing Avataric Divine Spiritual
Grace)
Heart-Finding and Heart-Experiencing <u>Me</u>,

By Searchlessly Beholding My Unique Form,
<u>My</u>
Only-By-Me

Spiritually and Divinely Transmitted
and Avatarically Self-Revealed
Body,
My Divine Spiritual Body,
My all-and-All-Surrounding Body,
My all-and-All-Pervading Body,
My Body Of Spiritual "Brightness",
My One
and "Bright"
and Only
and Self-Evidently Divine
Person
("Brightly" Descending,
To Surround and Pervade
all-and-All),

and who
(In This Great Manner)
Inherently and Immediately
Heart-Recognize Me
(and,
In This Root-Devotional
and Fully Technically Responsible
Sense,
Heart-See Me),
As I Divinely Am—
The One and Only and Inherently "Bright" Person,
The Divine Heart-Master Of all-and-All,
The "Bright" Itself,
Self-Existing,
Self-Radiant,
and Avatarically Self-Revealed,
In Person,
Tangibly,
Undoubtably,
and Utterly Converting the heart
and the mind
and the breath
and the body
From ego-"I"

(or The "Act Of Narcissus",
Which Is self-Contraction)
To The Ecstatic
"Bhava"
Of Searchlessly Only-Me-Beholding
Love-Bliss-Happiness,

and who—
By All Of This
Me-Receiving,
and Me-Understanding,
and Me-Enjoying,
and Me-Praising,
and Me-Invoking,
and Me-Feeling,
and Me-Finding,
and Me-Experiencing,
and Me-Beholding,
and Me-Recognizing—
Really,
and Truly,
and Happily,
and Sanely Certainly,
and
(Altogether)
Well-beingly
Know <u>Who</u> I <u>Am</u>,

and who
(Rightly,
and By "In-Love" Response[98])
Constantly
and Faithfully
Resort To Me,
To Be Spiritually Blessed By Me
To
(Always More and More Profoundly)
Heart-See
My Avatarically Self-Revealed
"Bright"

Divine
Spiritual Body
and My Avatarically Self-Revealed
egoless
True
Divine
State Of Person,
and To Be Divinely
and "Brightly"
(and Always More and More Profoundly)
Mastered At the heart
(and In the Total body-mind)
By Me,

and who
(Again and Again,
Neverendingly)
Come Running To My Avatarically-Born Bodily (Human) Divine
Form
(and, Forever After My Physical Human Lifetime
Of Avataric Incarnation,
To The physical human Company
and The By-Me-Spiritually-Empowered Circumstances
Of My "Ruchira Sannyasin" Devotees)
To Luxuriate
In My Love-Bliss-"Bright"
Palace Garden,
Wherein
Forever Sits
(Upon A Throne Of Imperishable Light)
The Eternal Hridaya Rose
Of My Divine
(and Always Blessing)
Presence
and Person.

Now, Listen To My "First Thorn Of Heart-Instruction", In Which I Reveal The Essential "Method" (Right, True, and Full) Of Direct (and Total psycho-physical) Heart-Communion With Me.

"Consider" This: I <u>Am</u> The Way (Right, True, and Full) To Realize Me (Rightly, Truly, and Fully).

Aham Da Asmi. I Am Da, The Divine Giver and The Divine Gift, The One and Only and Self-Evidently Divine Person, The Non-Separate Self-Condition and Indivisible Source-Condition Of all-and-All—Who Is To Be Realized By each and all, and By All Itself. I Am Adi Da, The First One, and The Only One. I Am Love-Ananda (or Love-Bliss) Itself. Only I Reveal and Give The Way That Realizes Me. That Way Is Named "Adidam" (and "Adidam Ruchiradam", and "The Way Of The Heart", and "Ruchira Avatara Siddha Yoga", and "Ruchira Avatara Shaktipat Yoga") By Me. Adidam Is The Heart-Active (and ego-Transcending) Devotional Relationship (or Heart-Relationship) To Me, and Not any mere ego-mind of ego-serving beliefs, and Not any mere ego-Applied Techniques, or egoic Searches, or ego-Efforts. Adidam Is To Be Practiced and Lived As Devotional Communion (or Total psycho-physical Heart-Communion) With Me, and As Rightly and Life-Positively Obedient Conformity Of the Total body-mind To My Words Of Instruction, and As Total psycho-physical Conformity (Of the Total body-mind) To My (Only-By-Me Avatarically Self-Transmitted, and Only-By-Me Avatarically Self-Revealed, and Only-Me-Revealing) "Bright" Divine Spiritual Body, and (Altogether) As Total psycho-physical Conformity (Of the Total body-mind) To My Only-By-Me Avatarically Self-Revealed "Bright" Divine Person, and To My Only-By-Me Avatarically Self-Revealed Divine Pattern Of Me-Realization—Such That, In The Case Of My Each and Every True Devotee, egoity (or self-contraction) Is Directly and Really Felt Beyond (and, Thus and Thereby, Transcended) In Me, and Even the body-mind itself (every part, and Totally) Is (Progressively) Spiritually and Divinely Transfigured By Me (and In Me), Transformed By Me (and In Me), and (At Last) Outshined By Me (and In Me), My Devotee Realizing (Thus and Thereby) My Spiritually "Bright" Divine Source-Domain and Self-Domain Of Self-Existing and Self-Radiant Love-Bliss-Happiness (Itself). And That Total Right Life Of Truly and Fully Practiced Adidam Is Ruchira Avatara Bhakti Yoga (Right, True, and Full).

"Consider" (and Practice) This, The Essence Of My Always Right, True, and Full Teaching:

Realize Most Perfect Freedom From the ego-"I" (or self-Contraction) and From All Seeking (or All Strategies Based On, or Motivated By, self-Contraction). Realize Most Perfect Freedom From the ego-"I" By Most Perfectly Realizing Real God (or The One and Only Reality and Truth, Which Is That Which Is Always Already The Case—Prior To, and Beyond, self-Contraction and All Seeking)—and, On That Basis, Divinely Self-Recognize all "things". The Way To That Realization Is To Always Feel Beyond all "things", Rather Than self-Contract From all "things", or Seek To Avoid any "thing", or Seek For any "thing". The Means Of That Way To Realization Is To Constantly (Really, Truly, Fully, and Fully Devotionally) Recognize Me, and To Constantly (Really,

Truly, Fully, and Fully Devotionally) Respond To Me, and To Constantly (Really, Truly, Fully, and Fully Devotionally) Resort To Me,
and,
Thus,
To Live,
and
(Ultimately)
To Realize,
Only and Entirely
In
and
By Means Of,
Right,
True,
and Full
(and Truly ego-Transcending)
Devotional Communion
With Me
(More and More,
and,
At Last,
Most Perfectly,
Revealed To The Heart,
and To the Total body-mind,
In The Unique Form
Of My Avatarically Self-Revealed
"Bright"
Divine
Spiritual Body
and My Avatarically Self-Revealed
egoless
True
Divine
State Of Person).

"Consider" (and Practice) This, The Essence Of The Way Of Practice (Right, True, and Full) That Is Given By Me:

By Means Of The Four-Part (physical, emotional, mental, and breathing) Exercise Of Responsively ego-Transcending (or Truly Devotionally Me-Recognizing, and Really Counter-egoic, or ego-Surrendering, ego-Forgetting, and, Ultimately, Most Perfectly, self-Contraction-Transcending) Devotion To Me, Contemplate

My Avatarically-Born Bodily (Human) Divine Form, My Avatarically Self-Transmitted Spiritual (and Always Blessing) Divine Presence, and My Avatarically Self-Revealed (and Very, and Transcendental, and Perfectly Subjective, and Inherently Spiritual, and Inherently egoless, and Inherently Perfect, and Self-Evidently Divine) State, and—Therein, By Directly (and By Means Of My Me-Revealing Avataric Divine Spiritual Grace) "Locating" My Avatarically Self-Revealed "Bright" Divine Spiritual Body and My Avatarically Self-Revealed egoless True Divine State Of Person—Openly and Deeply Receive Me, and (Thus and Thereby) Become More and More Profoundly and Radiantly Full Of Me, and (By All Of These Only-By-Me Given Means) Feel-Radiate Beyond All physical, emotional, mental, pranic, and Spiritual Contraction Of heart, head, Total body, and breath. That Is The Simple Essence Of The Fullest Right Practice Of Ruchira Avatara Bhakti Yoga (or True Devotional Communion With Me), Which Is Itself (Right, True, and Full) The Essential Practice Of Adidam.

"Consider" (and Realize) This, The Condition To Be Realized In and As This Only-By-Me Given Way Of Responsively ego-Transcending (and Rightly, Truly, and Fully Practiced) Devotional Communion With Me:

The Inherent Spiritual "Brightness"
Of Love-Bliss-Happiness—
Even Now,
and, Forever, Now.

"Consider" (and Realize) This, The Realization Inherent (and—Only In Due Course, and Only By Means Of My Direct Avataric Divine Spiritual Grace—To Be Most Perfectly Demonstrated) In and As This Responsively ego-Transcending (and Rightly, Truly, and Fully Practiced) "Bright", Right, True, and Full Devotional and Spiritual Communion With Me:

Real God,
or Truth,
Is
(Simply)
Reality,
or That Which Is Always Already The Case
(Not Within, but Always Beyond, the ego-"I"),
and
That Which Is Always Already The Case
Is
The Non-Separate,
and One,
and Only,
and Non-"Different"

"Bright",
Which Is Love-Bliss Itself,
Self-Existing and Self-Radiant,
and Always Already Radiating—
Around,
and
To,
and
In,
and
As,
and
Through,
and
Beyond,
and
Prior To
all the Seeming-to-be many "things"
(or all the
Apparently
Separate
and "Different"
psycho-physical
conditions,
forms,
patterns,
and
beings
that arise
as
"Your"
experience).

Now, Listen To My "Second Thorn Of Heart-Instruction", In Which I Reveal The Four-Part Exercise (Right, True, and Full) Of Responsively ego-Transcending Devotion To Me.

"Consider" (and Practice) This, The Formal Contemplative (or Set Apart) Exercise (Right, True, and Full) Of Responsively ego-Transcending Devotion To Me:

Invoke Me,

By Name
(With "the tongue of the mind"),
and By Heart
(With the Total body-mind).

Let the heart Melt Into
My Heart,
Which Is
The By-Me-Spiritually-Revealed
"Bright" Rose Garden Of Love.

Let the head Melt Into
My Head,
Which Is
The By-Me-Spiritually-Revealed
"Bright" Rose
Of Infinitely Ascended
Bliss-Light.

Let the Total body Melt Into
My Divine Spiritual Body,
Which Is
The By-Me-Spiritually-Revealed
Garden Air,
The Fragrant
all-and-All-Surrounding,
and all-and-All-Pervading,
Space
Of Equanimity,
Of Pleasure,
Of Delight,
Of Beauty,
Of Joy,
Of Love-Bliss,
Of "Brightness"
Itself.

Let the breathing Melt Into
My Breathing,
Until I Breathe you
Into My

"Bright"
Eternal
Palace
and
Domain
Of
Perfect Happiness.

"Consider" (and Practice) This, The Active (or General, moment to moment) Exercise (Right, True, and Full) Of Responsively ego-Transcending Devotion To Me:

Invoke Me—By Name, With "the tongue of the mind" (or, Perhaps, Even Also audibly, With the tongue of the head), and (Always) Via the Outwardly and Upwardly Open, and Feeling, and Receiving head.

Love Me—By Heart-Feeling-Receiving Me From Above the Total body-mind, and By Heart-Feeling-Responding To My "Bright" Presence (Above, and All-Around-Surrounding, and Entirely Pervading the Total body-mind), and By Heart-Feeling-Radiating My (Thus Beheld and Received and Known) Love-Bliss-Fullness (In All Directions, Boundlessly).

Breathe Me—By Breathing-Circulating The All-Around-Surrounding and Pervasive "Brightness" Of My Divine Spiritual Body Of Love-Bliss (Into, and Through, and In, and To Beyond the Total body-mind), and By Letting the Total body-mind Melt To Infinitely Beyond itself (By Melting Into My Radiant "Bright" Infinite Body and Person Of Love-Bliss-Happiness).

Serve (and, Thereby, Invoke and Contemplate) Me (As My Bodily Human Avataric-Incarnation-Form—and, Thereby, Beyond It, As My Spiritually "Bright" Divine Bodily Form), Happily and Constantly—By every action of body, of emotion (or feeling), of mind (or attention), and of speech, and of breath.

Now, Listen To My "Third Thorn Of Heart-Instruction", In Which I Reveal The Process Associated With The Four-Part Exercise (Right, True, and Full) Of Responsively ego-Transcending Devotion To Me.

I Wash
the Garden dog
From head To tail.
How Else?
But Seekers Think
The
Other
Way
Round.[99]

I Wash
the Garden dog
From head To tail,
but I Eat it
All At Once!
Therefore,
Come,
Running,
Here and Now,
To Me—
Not For a bone,
or a bite and run,
but For The Eternal Love
Of Me.[100]

Recognize Me
By Shape and Voice.
Come Running
To Me
By Name.
Come Running
To My Call
To Life,
With Heart-Love
Of Me
On Fire.
Take Refuge
In My
Bath and Balm,
and Melt
To Complete
Contentment
Under My
Gentling Hand
and Darling Foot.[101]

Listen To Me.
Hear Me.
See Me.
Accept My "Bright" Gift

Of Love,[102]
Of Bliss,
Of Pleasure,
Of Happiness,
and Not Less.[103]

Until
My Outshining "Brightness"
Opens The Eyes
In My Room,
You Are the body,
attention,
heart,
and breath.
Give these
In Me,
From Your Side
Of The Fence,
and I,
From My Side,
Will Always Call
and Greet You,
Heart To heart,[104]
Until The Gate
Flies Open,[105]
and, With Heart-Tears
That Melt The Running-Ground,
All "Difference" Washed
By Wideness Alone,
We Speak and Love,
Forever,
In My Imperishable Domain.[106]

My "Bright" Sun
Rises From The Heart-Root,
and Stands,
Forever Uneclipsed,[107]
Above The Garden Tree,[108]
Above and Beyond
The Pentagrammic Star.[109]

My Bliss-Touch,
My Bliss-Sound,
and My Bliss-Light[110]
Originate Above The Skies Of worlds,
Above The Sky Of mind,[111]
Beyond The Reach
Of body-mind.

Above The Underground
That Is The Usual
human Habitation,[112]
Above The Mandrake,
Above The Three Hearts,
Above The Root-Ball,[113]
Above The Crown Of Lower Light,[114]
Above The Garden and The Tree,
Above the worlds Above,
I <u>Am</u>,
"Bright",
Still,
and Silent,
There.

I <u>Am</u>,
The "Midnight Sun",
"Bright",
Above,
Higher Than dreaming Goes,[115]
Higher Than The Tree-Sky Rises.
Fire Of Heart-Love
Flows From My Right Side
To Make Your "I"-heart
Melt In Me,
There—
Deeper Than sleep Falls,
Deeper Than self-Contraction
Twists.[116]

Fire Of Your Heart-Love,
Kneel Into Me.

Fire Of Your Heart-Love,
Feel Me Above,
Melting You Down
In Me.

Melt Down
In My Deep Light,
Tasting Delicious Quiet
That Oozes Down The Spire
Of You-Centered-In-Me,
With every thing
and part
and place
Becoming
and Become
An Alchemical Fuse,[117]
Transmutating Into Love-Bliss
As You
Fragrantly
Melt.

Let This Melting Go To Ground.
Let The Star Melt.
Let The Tree Melt.
Let The Top Of the head Melt.
Let The Ajna Door Melt.
Let the long throat Melt.
Let the heart Melt Deep,
In Love-Communion With Me,
Filling The Infinite
Heart-Sphere
With My Love-Bliss-Presence,
Melting You Down,
Melting the solar plexus,
Melting the navel,
Melting all the belly-knot,
Melting the sex organs,
Melting the entire
and Unbroken
bodily base,

Until The You
Of head-to-toe
Is Un-knotted,
Only Open and Filling Full,
Like a vowel
Pierced By A Bolt Of consonants,
and Ringing
With The Beginningless and Endless
Love-Bliss-Pleasure
Of My Radiant Spiritual "Brightness",
ego-"I" Entirely Surrendered,
Forgotten
In A Spontaneous Ease,
and all self-Contraction Yielded
In The Feel
Of Me,
With All Separateness,
All Relatedness,
and All "Difference"
Danced Upon[118]
and Shattered
To An Unspeakably Singing State
By My
Crashing Down,
Utterly Allowed,
Allowing Only The
Directly-By-Me Revealed
(and Only-Me-Revealing)
Love-Bliss-Feeling Of
Self-Existing and
Self-Radiant
"Bright"
Being-Fullness
In
and As
body,
heart,
head,
and the Always Me-Feeling
(Receiving,

and Releasing,
and Melting)
breath.[119]

Now, Listen To My "Fourth Thorn Of Heart-Instruction", In Which I Reveal The Details Of The Right, True, and Full Practice Of "Samraj Asana", The "Healing Pose" Of Total psycho-physical Devotion To Me.

1) <u>The Four-Part Exercise Of Responsively ego-Transcending Devotion To Me Is The Right, True, and Full Practice Of Actively (moment to moment) Re-Establishing (or Consistently Maintaining) "Samraj Asana", The "Healing Pose"[120] Of Total psycho-physical Devotion To Me</u> (By Means Of Searchless Beholding Of Me, To The Degree Of Total psycho-physical Devotional Communion With My Avatarically Self-Revealed "Bright" Divine Form, and Presence, and State, and Person), Such That Your entire body-mind (or attention, emotional feeling, breath, and body—head to toe) Is, In Me-Recognizing Devotional Response To My Avatarically Self-Revealed "Bright" Divine Spiritual Body and My Avatarically Self-Revealed egoless True Divine State Of Person ("Located" By Means Of Me-Invoking, and Searchlessly Me-Beholding, and Totally psycho-physically Engaged, and Really ego-Transcending Devotional Communion With My Avatarically-Born Bodily Human Divine Form, My Avatarically Self-Transmitted Spiritual, and Always Blessing, Divine Presence, and My Avatarically Self-Revealed, and Very, and Transcendental, and Perfectly Subjective, and Inherently Spiritual, and Inherently egoless, and Inherently Perfect, and Self-Evidently Divine State), Constantly (Again and Again, Responsively, Intentionally, and Counter-egoically, or In A Truly ego-Surrendering, ego-Forgetting, and ego-Transcending Manner) Established In The "Conscious Process" (Of psycho-physically Open Feeling-attention To Me) and The "Conductivity Process" (Of Total psycho-physical Communion With Me). In This Manner, The "You" That Is the Total body-mind (or psycho-physical ego-"I"), and Which Is Otherwise Merely A Complex Pattern Of self-Contraction (Made Of The Always Separative and self-Deluding "Act Of Narcissus", or The Complex, and Total psycho-physical, Avoidance Of Relationship), Is To Be Responsively (or In The Only-To-Me Devotionally Responding Manner) Offered To Me In A Total psycho-physical Disposition, Gesture, and Pattern That Is Like An Always Up-Turned Open Cup (or Bowl, or Vessel, or Hand), and <u>Not</u> (As In The Case Of every moment of otherwise active self-Contraction) Like A Ball (or A Knot, or A Clenched Fist). The Integrity Of the body-mind Is Manifested Only In Me, and In Rightly Patterned Devotional Response To Me—Actively Turned Up To Me, Spiritually

"Bright" Where I Always Already Stand, Infinitely Above the body and the mind. Therefore, Be Opened Up To Me, and Yielding To My Avatarically Self-Revealed "Bright" Divine Spiritual Body (Above, and Descending) and My Avatarically Self-Revealed egoless True Divine State Of Person (Beyond), Thus Feeling Me Above and Beyond ego-"I", and (Thus, By Feeling Me) Actively Relinquishing (or Feeling Above and Beyond) The ego-Act Of self-Contraction (Which Is—Like A Ball, or A Knot, or A Clenched Fist—self-Contained, self-Referring, and self-Absorbed).

2) Feel-Surrender To My Avatarically Self-Revealed "Bright" Divine Spiritual Body and My Avatarically Self-Revealed egoless True Divine State Of Person, Beyond self-Contraction, With the Total head (or The Entire Region Extending From The Crown Of the head To The Deep Core Of the throat) As a physical, sensory, sensual, and energy-Conducting part of the Conscious body. This Instead Of Chronic thinking (self-Contracting the head and throat Into Doubt and Sorrow and Seeking For an object).

3) Feel-Surrender To My Avatarically Self-Revealed "Bright" Divine Spiritual Body and My Avatarically Self-Revealed egoless True Divine State Of Person, Beyond self-Contraction, With The Total Heart (or The Entire Region Extending From The Base Of the throat To the solar plexus), More and More Deeply Into "In-Love" Communion With Me, "Located" As The Self-Existing Feeling Of Being (In The Deepest Heart—Even, Ultimately, Below and Beyond Its Right-Side Knot) and As The Self-Radiant "Bright" Source (Above and Beyond all-and-All).

4) Feel-Surrender To My Avatarically Self-Revealed "Bright" Divine Spiritual Body and My Avatarically Self-Revealed egoless True Divine State Of Person, Beyond self-Contraction, By Surrendering the Total physical body, Through and Beyond self-Contraction (and, Thus, By Radiating, Rather Than Contracting, The Total bodily Form, and, Very Intensively, The Entire Region From the solar plexus To the bodily base, or Even To the toes and the bottoms of the feet).

5) Feel-Surrender To My Avatarically Self-Revealed "Bright" Divine Spiritual Body and My Avatarically Self-Revealed egoless True Divine State Of Person, Beyond self-Contraction, With each part Of The Natural (or Spontaneous) Cycle Of the breath (inhaling-Receiving My Love-Bliss-Fullness, and exhaling-Releasing, or Fully Relaxing Into, My Love-Bliss-Fullness).

6) The experiencing (and The Dramatizing) Of egoic Fear, Sorrow, and Anger (Which Are the Primary emotions of self-Contraction) Is To Be Actively Transcended By The Responsively Devotional (Me-Invoking, Me-Feeling, and Out-Toward-Me and Up-Toward-Me Turned) Feeling-Exercise Of No-Contraction At, Respectively, The Top Of the head, The Ajna Door,

and The Root Of the throat. This Responsively Devotional Feeling-Exercise Must Be Directed By The Heart In Devotional "In-Love" Response To My Avatarically Self-Revealed "Bright" Divine Spiritual Body and My Avatarically Self-Revealed egoless True Divine State Of Person—"Located" By Means Of Me-Invoking, and Searchlessly Me-Beholding, and Totally psycho-physically Engaged, and Really ego-Transcending Devotional Communion With My Avatarically-Born Bodily (Human) Divine Form, My Avatarically Self-Transmitted Spiritual (and Always Blessing) Divine Presence, and My Avatarically Self-Revealed (and Very, and Transcendental, and Perfectly Subjective, and Inherently Spiritual, and Inherently egoless, and Inherently Perfect, and Self-Evidently Divine) State—Such That (Always More and More Deeply and Profoundly) Every Kind and Sign Of Un-Love (or Of self-Contracting Fear, Sorrow, and Anger) Is, Thus (and In every present-time moment), Feelingly Transcended (By Means Of Heart-Communion With Me, Via The Constantly Responsively Activated, and Really Effectively Counter-egoic, Exercise Of Heart-Opening, and self-Contraction-Relinquishing, Heart-Response To Me). And This Searchlessly Me-Beholding and Responsively Devotional Feeling-Exercise Of Heart and head Must, Then, Be Further (or Constantly, Intensively, and More and More Effectively) Demonstrated bodily (By Spiritually Receptive Melting) Below (and In The Total psycho-physical Form). In The Process, The Yogic "Locks"[121] Of the bodily base, the tongue and chin and throat, and The Ajna Door Are To Be (Intentionally, According To My Instructions) Appropriately Engaged (At Random), and The Asana (or Yogic Posture and Pattern) Of the body Is To Be (Intentionally, According To My Instructions) Well-Balanced and Easeful, Generally With the spine Erect (and Rightly Polarized, the bodily base Relaxed, Via The Spinal Line, Toward The Crown Of the head, and The Frontal Line Always Upwardly Open and Downwardly Receptive).

7) Therefore, Altogether, The Entire Four-Part Exercise Of Responsively ego-Transcending (and, Altogether, Right, True, and Full) Devotion To Me Must Be An Upwardly Yielding and Downwardly Conducting Counter-egoic (or Contraction-Relinquishing) Action Of Feeling-Surrender (and Feeling-Relaxation and Feeling-Opening) Of the Total (and Even Principally physical) head (Rather Than A Mere Gesture Of mind, or Of Already Contracted attention), the Total (physical, and Ever More Deeply Feeling) heart, the Total (and Pleasurably Balanced) physical (and Deeply sensory) body, and (At Random) the Total (or Constant Two-Part Cycle Of) physical and Feeling (and pranic, and, As Given By Me, Spiritual) breath,

inhaled

(Generally Via the nose, With mouth Closed,

and Even With a Slight "Rasping" or "Drawing" sound,
Via The Back Of the Opening throat),
Down,
and Opening Down,
and Even
(Intentionally)
Pressed Down,
and Opening,
Fully,
Down
Into the Opening Deep lower abdomen,
and Felt There,
In The Bottom Of The Bowl,
and,
From There,
Even To the toes
and the bottoms of the feet,
and exhaled,
As A Fully Opening
Feeling-Relaxation
Of The Entirety Of body,
and All Of attention,
and All Of feeling and breathing Awareness,
and, Thus and Thereby,
Of Even All Of the By-Me-Laundered
(Always Being
head-to-toe Washed)
Garden dog.

The body-mind
Is,
Thus,
To Be,
By Me-Recognition's Heart-Response To Me,
Relaxed
and Melted
Down
(the feeling heart,
the breathing lungs,
The perceiving Entirety

Of sensory body,
and All Of the mind
and Thing
Above,
Pacified,
Subdued,
Becalmed,
Released Of The Up-Chucking Wedge
Of Reactivity,
Of Fear,
Of Sorrow,
Of Anger,
Of Un-Love's ego-"I").

By My Heart-Response
To Your
Right,
True,
Full,
and
Fully Devotional
Exercise
Of These Four Thorns
Of Me-Invoking and Me-Feeling Means,
all Four self-Contracted parts
Of Man Alive
Are Pierced
With My
You-Easing
Whitest Rose
(The Fresh and deathless Blossom
Earned By Left-Over-Emptiness,
There,
Where and When
The Melting Wash
Of dogged ego-"I"
Is Lost,
Like a jeweler's wax,
In The Shape
That,

By Melting In Its space,
Shapes
My Liquid Sound,
My Sounding Light,
My Soundless Touch),
and Your By-Me-Vanished You—
Of To-Me-Surrendered,
and
(By This "In-Love" Of Me,
Spun and Laundered)
Un-Contracted,
head-to-toe—
Is "Brightened" To Infinity
By My
Vibration,
Light,
and Energy.

Thus,
You,
By Me,
Are Gifted To The Melting Point,
and the Garden dog Shines Red,
Then White,
Then Un-Defined[122]
In The "Bright"
Surrounding-Space
Of My Rose-Bearing
Heart.

Therefore,
Be My Garden
Of Devotee,
Even Every Now,
By Always Looking Up
To Me,
and Breathing Me
Through Your headless Crown,
"Bright" Beyond You
(Standing here,

and Nearby You,
With All My Ever-Teaching Words
Always Saying Me
At Your ear,
and My Avataric Human Body-Form
Always Showing Me
At Your eye),
and, By this
every little moment
Of Ordinary "Translation",[123]
Be Always Speeded To Me,
and Be,
Thus,
moment to moment,
Set Down
In My Eyes-Of-Happiness Garden Dome,
The Indivisible Blossom
Of My "Bright" Divine Body-Space,
Where My Own and Open Eyes
Gaze Freely
From Above and Beyond the everymind,
and My Own and Open Heart
Gazes Fully
From Below and Beyond the everymind.

By All These Means
Of Me,
It Is
The Event
In My Room
That Makes and Keeps You "Bright",
and Your every breath
Is Thickened There,
In My Infinitely Rendered Sweet,
There,
In Me,
The Da Love-Ananda Mahal
That Is My Divine
(and all-and-All-Surrounding,
and all-and-All-Pervading)

Spiritual Body,
The "Bright" Itself,
My Descending-Upon-You Body
Of "Brightness",
Heart-"Located"
By Rightly,
Truly,
Fully,
and Really Effectively
Invoking <u>Me</u>
At My Incarnate Feet,
and Received
By Receiving <u>Me</u>,
"Bright" From Above,
and "Bright" Beyond,
and "Bright" In The Total Space
Where
(If You,
By All Of These Four Thorns
Of Me-Devotion,
Move My Ever-Blossoming Heart
To Bless Your Melting heart)
I Am,
Freely,
Fully Felt
To here,
Crashing,
Freely-Fully,
head To Down,
Invading
Your To-Me-Softened Crown,
Like Husband Into Wife,
and Penetrating
Your Door Of Ajna's Eye,
Like A Locksmith With A Skillful Knife,
and,
Like A Gag Of Many Thumbs,[124]
Exploding The throat and navel Knots,
and In Your heart Between Them,
and In All The Under That Is Below,

and Peening,
Flat and Wide,
Even all Your little blows
of hem and haw,
Down In The Palace Where No ego Sits,
To Where Only My Love's Radiance
Whitens The Walls,
and The Blissful Inner Chamber
Is Everywhere,
and Everywhere Is Shining
With The Non-"Difference" Of "Us"
and The Only-ness Of Me,
My More-Than-Wonderful
Whitest Rose
Outshining,
At Love
and At Last,
the dog and The Wash,
The You and all,
and The All Itself,
In
Me-"Bright"
Me.

By Rightly, Truly, Fully, and Fully Devotionally Practicing This, My "Hridaya Rosary" Of "Four Thorns Of Heart-Instruction", You Will Surely Grow To See Me and (In Due Course) To (Ultimately, Most Perfectly) Realize Me.

Avatar Adi Da Samraj
Clear Lake, 2001

SUTRA

33

The Only-By-Me Revealed and Given Way Of The Heart Is Me-Beholding Devotional and Spiritual Communion With Me—With the Total life, the Total body-mind. If My Devotee Indulges In Any Exercise Of ego's "I", Such Is No Longer The Practice Of The Only-By-Me Revealed and Given Way Of The Heart. Any Such Approach To Sadhana Is Merely A conventional (and, Necessarily, ego-Based) Seeker's Effort.

In The Only-By-Me Revealed and Given Way Of The Heart, A Horse Appears In The Wild Is Always Already The Case[125]—From The Beginning. Such Is The Truth In Matrix-Mind, When You Are Searchlessly Beholding Me and Spiritually Receiving Me. Unless You Are Searchlessly Beholding Me, In Whole bodily Devotional and Spiritual Communion With Me, You Are the ego-"I" (Doing this and that). Ego-"I" Doing this and that Is Not The Practice Of The Only-By-Me Revealed and Given Way Of The Heart. Only Me-Recognizing Devotional and Spiritual Communion With Me, Only The Searchless Beholding Of Me With the Total body-mind, Is The Way Of The Heart. Only Searchless Beholding Of Me (and Spiritual Reception Of My Divine Ruchira Shaktipat) Is The Circumstance Of Most Perfect Realization Of Me. Only Searchless Beholding Of Me (and Spiritual Reception Of My Divine Ruchira Shaktipat) Is The Foundation Of "Samraj Asana", or The You-Melting Practice Of My "Hridaya Rosary" Of "Four Thorns Of Heart-Instruction".

"Samraj Asana" Is Not What You Sit On—It Is What Your Heart Stands On. Where The Horizontal and The Vertical Coincide, A Horse Appears In The Wild Is Always Already The Case. And Therefore, A Raymond Is In A Quandra Is Always Already The Case[126]—but Their Coincidence Is Outside The Circle. In The Circle, There Is Neither Horizontal Nor Vertical. There Is Neither Horizontal Nor Vertical In The Circumference Of The Circle, or The Surface Of The Sphere.

Therefore, No One Stands In The Center To Do The Sadhana Of The Only-By-Me Revealed and Given Way Of The Heart. For My True Devotee, the body-mind Is Only A Pattern, In Which My Unmediated "Bright" Spirit-Current Of The Self-Abiding Divine Self-Recognition Of The Divine Love-Bliss Stands.

The Total Surface Of The Sphere—All At Once, As If In A Shattering Shock—Threads The Matrix, Pole To Pole. In Such True Heart-Communion With Me, I Am Seen. But Only the body Says It. And Only the body Sees Me As A Whole. I Am Not In The Middle Of the head—I Am At The Surface Of the skin. The head Takes Its "Readings" By Means Of the "lesser" senses. The Surface Of the skin Is Crackling With The Shattering Of The Sphere. And The Center Of the body Is A Dimensionless Thread, or Matrix, Of My Divine Conscious Light.

My Devotee Does Not Practice The Only-By-Me Revealed and Given Way Of The Heart (or Way Of Adidam) By Doing Some Sort Of Seeker's Exercise In Order To Find Me Spiritually Descending From Above. I Do Not Call You To Strategically Generate A Presumption That I Am Spiritually Descending From Above. Rather, As My By-Me-Spiritually-Initiated (and Always Newly By-Me-Spiritually-Activated) Devotee, You (Simply) Searchlessly Behold Me In My Avatarically-Born Bodily (Human) Divine Form—and (Thus and Thereby) You Tacitly Allow Me To Demonstrate Myself (In Your body-mind) As Spiritually Descending From Above. When My Avataric Divine Spiritual Descent From Above Is Actually Experienced and Simply In Evidence—and When, As A Foundation (or Platform) For This, All The Signs Of Hearing Me Are Consistently Being Demonstrated—Then You (As A Total psycho-physical Whole) Are (By Means Of My Avatarically Self-Transmitted Divine Spiritual Grace) In "Samraj Asana".

Thus, "Samraj Asana" Is A Spontaneous (By-My-Avataric-Divine-Spiritual-Grace-Given) Development Of The Foundation (Previously Established, and Always Primary) Practice Of Searchlessly Beholding Me. When My Avataric Divine Spiritual Self-Transmission Demonstrates Itself In Descent, On The Foundation Of True Hearing, Then "Samraj Asana" Characterizes (and Is The Context Of) Your Reception Of My Ruchira Shaktipat. That Is To Say, "Samraj Asana" Is Caused By My Avataric Divine Spiritual Self-Transmission—Not By Any ego-Effort On The Part Of My Devotee.

"Samraj Asana" Is Not An "Additional" Practice, Somehow Distinct From Ruchira Avatara Bhakti Yoga and The Searchless Beholding Of Me. Rather, "Samraj Asana" Is The Manner In Which Ruchira Avatara Bhakti Yoga and The Searchless Beholding Of Me Are (In Due Course) Shown In My Devotee who Has Truly Heard Me.

"Samraj Asana" Is Not A self-Applied (or ego-Based, and Merely Seeking) Technique. "Samraj Asana" Is An Eventual (Hearing-Based) Practice-Responsibility That Is Formally Assumed Relative To The "Asana" (or psycho-physical Attitude, or body-mind Orientation) Of Upward-Turning To Me (From The Brain Core). And That Upward-Turning Must Already Be Spontaneously and Readily Occurring In Response To Your (Always Spontaneous and Searchless)

Experience Of My Tangible (Descending-From-Above) Avataric Divine Spiritual Self-Transmission.

Indeed, The Entirety Of The Practice Of The Only-By-Me Revealed and Given Way Of The Heart (or Way Of Adidam) Is A Process That Occurs Only In (and By Virtue Of) Real Devotional (and, In Due Course, Spiritual) Communion With Me. The Signs Of That Developing Process Are Given (and Caused) By My Avataric Divine Spiritual Self-Transmission (or Ruchira Shaktipat)—and Are (Thereby) Shown In the body-mind Of My Devotee—When My Devotee Practices Real (and Really Effective) To-Me-Turned, ego-Surrendering, ego-Forgetting, and (More and More) ego-Transcending Heart-Communion With Me In My Avatarically-Born Bodily (Human) Divine Form.

As My Devotee, <u>You</u> Do Not "Do" anything Spiritually. Rather, You Tangibly Experience <u>Me</u> Spiritually. That Experience Of Me Is Purifying and Transformative—Showing Various Signs, In Due Course. When Those Signs (Of Purification and Transformation) Appear, The Process (Of, Ultimately, Most Perfectly Realizing Me) Progresses.

The Entire By-Me-Given (and Me-Realizing) Process Comes From Above—but That Does Not Mean That You Seek Me Above or That You Merely Entertain a belief That I Am Above. If—On The Basis Of Right Foundation Preparation—You Enter Into The Process Of Searchlessly Beholding Me In My Avatarically-Born Bodily (Human) Divine Form, You Will Inevitably (By Means Of My To-You-Responding Avataric Divine Spiritual Blessing-Grace) Experience Me As Spiritually Descending From Above. When You Experience Me Spiritually, There Will Be (and Must Be) <u>Tangible</u> Signs Of My Avataric Divine Spiritual Invasion (As I Have Described)—but Such Signs Are Not To Be self-Generated (or, In Any Manner, self-Stimulated By ego-Based psycho-physical Seeking-Efforts).

For My Devotee, The Mere (and Searchless) Devotional Beholding Of Me In My Avatarically-Born Bodily (Human) Divine Form Is <u>Sufficient</u>. Therefore, The Only-By-Me Revealed and Given Way Of The Heart (or Way Of Adidam) Is Simply The Process By Which My Devotee Is (Progressively, More and More) Given Over To Me, and Attuned To Me, and Resonantly Combined With Me. Altogether, The Only-By-Me Revealed and Given Way Of The Heart (or Way Of Adidam) Is The Practice and Process Wherein and Whereby <u>all</u> Apparent conditions Are Given Over To (and self-Surrendered In) their Divine Source—Not The Divine Source As A philosophical Principle or An Abstract Idea, but As A Tangible Person here, Eternally Avatarically Self-Manifested, Speaking (In Bodily Human Divine Form) To You Now (and Forever Hereafter).

When You Experience My Direct and Tangible Avataric Divine Spiritual Self-Transmission, Then You Have The Real (and Necessary) Basis For Truly

Understanding The Uniqueness Of The Avatarically Revealed Divine Yoga Of Adidam. That Divine Yoga Is Not Generated From Below. That Divine Yoga Does Not Seek Toward What Is Above. That Divine Yoga Is (Tangibly, and Directly) A Matter Of The Spiritual Reception Of Me—Freely Avatarically Given (From Above and Beyond) As A Divine Gift, In-Filling Your (Spontaneously, and Only Responsively) Upward-To-Me-Turned body-mind (Established In The "Healing Pose" Of "Samraj Asana" Only By Means Of My Tangibly Experienced Avataric Divine Spiritual Self-Transmission).

"Samraj Asana" Is The Primary Asana, The Asana Of Divine Communion With Me, The Right Asana Of the body-mind. Any Disturbed or Negative or Concerned state in ordinary day to day life Is Simply A Collapse From That Primal Asana. Once You Have Realized This To-Me-Responsive Asana In Devotion To Me, Then The Process Becomes One Of Constantly Maintaining It. The Me-Hearing Capability and The Me-Seeing Capability Must Be Exercised Such That "Samraj Asana" Is Constantly Perpetuated, Always More and More Deeply Exercised. In That Case, Instead Of Merely Continuing In The Patterns To Which You Have Previously Adapted—The ego-Patterns Of Reaction, All The Various "asanas" Of ego-ordinariness—You Maintain The Spiritual Asana Of Heart-Communion With Me. Then The Apparent Power Of events To Undermine Heart-Communion With Me Is Gradually Diminished. Such Is The Purifying Process Of The Spiritually Fully Activated (and, Spiritually, Fully Technically Responsible) Frontal Yoga Of The Only-By-Me Revealed and Given Way Of The Heart.

This Up-Turned Asana Of Devotional and Spiritual Communion With Me, and This Constant Process Of Spiritual In-Filling By My Ruchira Shaktipat, Is The Fundamental Requirement Of The Seeing Stages Of The Way Of The Heart. That Requirement Always Continues, No Matter what experiences arise.

Seeing Is ego-Transcending Participation In What (and Who) Is. Seeing Is Love. Seeing (or Love) Is Able (By Means Of My Avatarically Self-Transmitted Divine Spiritual Grace) To "Locate", Devotionally and Fully Spiritually Responsibly Recognize, and Feel My Avatarically Self-Transmitted (and all-and-All-Pervading) Spiritual Radiance (and My Avatarically Self-Transmitted Spirit-Identity), As The "Bright" and Only One Who Is. Therefore, Seeing Is Heart-Felt and Whole bodily Identification Of My Avatarically Self-Revealed (and Self-Evidently Divine) Love-Bliss-Presence and Person. Seeing Is Fully Spiritually Activated (and, Spiritually, Fully Technically Responsible) Conversion Of attention, emotion, and the Total psycho-physical personality From self-Contraction To The By-Me-Avatarically-Self-Revealed Divine Spiritual Form (or Tangible Spiritual Presence) Of Real God (or The Necessarily Divine Spiritual Reality and Truth, Itself)—and This Via My Avatarically Self-Transmitted Divine Spirit-Baptism, or

My Avatarically Self-Transmitted Divine (and Inherently Perfect) Ruchira Shaktipat, or My Avatarically Self-Transmitted Divine (and Inherently Perfect, and Spiritually Self-"Bright") Heart-Awakening (and The Subsequent Apparent Descent and Circulation Of My Avatarically Self-Transmitted Divine Spirit-Force Into and Through and, Ultimately, Beyond the body-mind Of My Progressively Awakening Devotee). Seeing Is Spontaneous (or Heart-Moved) Devotional (and, Spiritually, Fully Technically Responsible) self-Sacrifice Of the self-Contraction. Seeing Is The Directly ego-Transcending Reorientation Of conditional Existence To My Avatarically Self-Revealed (Transcendental, Inherently Spiritual, Inherently Perfect, and Self-Evidently Divine) Self-Condition, In Whom conditional self and conditional worlds Apparently arise and Always Already Inhere.

The Seeing Of Me, Like The Hearing Of Me, Is A Most Fundamental (and Truly ego-Transcending) Capability That Can (and Should) Be Exercised moment to moment. When There Is (In any moment) The Real Seeing Of Me, There Is The (Fully Technically Responsible) Capability To Contact Me Spiritually and Enter Into Devotional Communion With Me Spiritually. When You Have Awakened (By Means Of My Avatarically Self-Transmitted Divine Spiritual Grace) To See Me Truly, Then The Act (and Sadhana) Of Contacting Me Spiritually Does Not (In <u>every</u> moment Of Its Exercise) Require That You Come Into The Physical Sphere Of My Avatarically-Born Bodily (Human) Divine Form or That You Enter Into A Place Spiritually Empowered By Me. My Devotee Who Sees Me Is (In The General Course Of moment to moment Practice Of Devotion To Me) Fully Capable Of Contacting Me Spiritually In any circumstance, By Using The Truly Capable Virtue Of Hearing Me and Seeing Me To Go Beyond The self-Contracting Tendency.

Seeing Me Is Simply Attraction To Me (Searchlessly Beholding Me, and Feeling Me Receptively) <u>As</u> My Avatarically Self-Transmitted Spiritual (and Always Blessing) Divine Presence—and This Most Fundamentally, At The (Horizontal and Vertical) Origin Of The "Emergence" Of My Avatarically Self-Transmitted Divine Spiritual Presence "here", At (and In Front Of) The Heart (or At, and In, The Root-Context Of the body-mind), and At (and In) The Source-Position (and, Ultimately, <u>As</u> The Source-Condition) Of conditional (or psycho-physical) Existence Itself (Infinitely Above the body and the mind—and Radiating, By Apparent Descent, Into the body-mind).

Seeing Me Is Knowing Me As My Avatarically Self-Transmitted Spiritual (and Always Blessing) Divine Presence, Just As Tangibly (and With The Same Degree Of Clarity) As You Would Differentiate The Physical Appearance Of My Bodily (Human) Form From the physical appearance of the bodily (human) form of any other.

To See Me Is A Clear and Direct Knowledge Of Me, About Which There Is No Doubt. To See Me Is A Sudden, Tacit Awareness—Like Walking Into a "thicker" air or atmosphere, or Suddenly Feeling a breeze, or Jumping Into water and Noticing The Difference In Density Between the air and the water. This Tangible Feeling Of Me Is, In any particular moment, Possibly (but Not, In any particular moment, Necessarily) Associated With Effects In the body-mind (such as kriyas or visions or energy movements in the body or changes in the breath or Meditative States), but It Is, In any particular moment, Necessarily Felt At The Heart, and Even All Over the body.

Seeing Me Is One-Pointedness In The "Conscious Process" Of Heart-Devotion To Me.

The Primary Experience (and Consistent, and Fully Technically Responsible, Capability) Of one who Sees Me Is Spiritually Awakened Devotional Communion With <u>Me</u> (or The "Locating" Of <u>Me</u> Spiritually)—As My Avatarically Self-Transmitted Love-Bliss-Presence, and In Person. All Manner Of <u>Effects</u> (Of My Avatarically Self-Transmitted Divine Spiritual Presence) May (In any particular moment) arise (In Your body-mind) Following The "Locating" Of Me Spiritually, but Seeing Me (Itself) Is The By-Me-Given Capability To Freely, In any moment, Give Your Feeling-Attention To <u>Me</u>, As My Avatarically Self-Transmitted Spiritual (and Always Blessing)—and Always Personal—Divine Presence.

From The Beginning Of My Avataric-Incarnation-Work Of Teaching and Divine Self-Revelation, A Fundamental Aspect Of My Instruction To all Was—and, Therefore (By Means Of The Recording, The Preservation, and The Perpetual Communication Of My Avatarically Self-Revealed Divine Word and My Avatarically Self-Manifested Divine Leelas), Always Is and Will Be—That No conditional (and, Therefore, Inherently, limited) form of experience (Even the Most Apparently Sublime or Apparently Exalted conditional experience Of The Effects Of My Avatarically Self-Transmitted Divine Spiritual Presence) Is To Be Sought (or Valued) As The "Goal" Of Practice In The Devotional and Spiritual Relationship To Me (Which Relationship Is The Only-By-Me Revealed and Given Way Of The Heart). <u>No</u> kind (or variety) of psycho-physical (or conditionally Manifested) experience Is (itself) Truth, or The Divine Spiritual Reality (Itself). If You Heart-Recognize Me, <u>Not</u> <u>any</u> kind of merely psycho-physical (or conditionally Manifested, and, Necessarily, limited) experience <u>Is</u> (itself) Truth, or The Divine Spiritual Reality (Itself), or Should Be Either Sought Or Found and Embraced <u>As</u> (itself) Truth, or The Divine Spiritual Reality (Itself). Only <u>I</u> (<u>As</u> I <u>Am</u>) <u>Am</u> Truth (Itself), The Divine Spiritual Reality (Itself), The One and Only Person and Self-Condition and Source-Condition Of all-and-All. I <u>Am</u> The One You Must Heart-Recognize and (In Due Course,

As My Avatarically Self-Transmitted Divine Spiritual Grace Will Have It) Most Perfectly Realize. Therefore, The Profound and Spiritually Me-Receiving Yoga Of Ruchira Avatara Bhakti, Which I Give (In Due Course) To each and all Of My (Necessarily, Formally Practicing) Devotees, Is The Yoga Of Devotion To Me—Not Any Kind Of Yoga Of The Pursuit Of (or Search For) conditional, limited, and (Necessarily) egoic and ego-Reinforcing experience. Nevertheless, Until My Any Devotee Has Truly Heard Me and Seen Me, he or she May Tend To Persist In "Devotion" To the energy-stirrings of the body-mind (or the energy-pleasures and the energy-distractions that May arise In The Yogic, and The, Otherwise, ordinary, Context Of psycho-physical experience), Presuming them To Be The True, Important, and Even Great Substance Of Religious, Yogic, and Even Spiritual Practice. However, Seeing Me Is Not, Itself, A Matter Of experiencing Yogic energies in the body-mind. It Certainly May Be (and, Characteristically, Is, and Will Be, The Case) That Yogic energies Are Stimulated In the body-mind Of My Devotee By My Avatarically Self-Transmitted Divine Spiritual Presence—but I (Myself) Am Not any such Yogic energies. I Am The Very Person You Must Heart-Recognize. Only That Heart-Recognition Of Me (By My Any Devotee who, Having Truly Heard Me, Tangibly Experiences My "Bright" Divine Spiritual Body) Is The Seeing Of Me—and Not any merely psycho-physical experiences Of The ordinary Developing Yogic Kind.

True Seeing Of Me Is Literal Vision Of The Divine, and (As Such) It Changes Your life Utterly. One who (In any moment) Sees Me Does Not Engage The Practice Of The Way Of The Heart From the point of view of the gross body-mind, but From The Point Of View (or With The Certain Knowledge) That Reality Is Spiritual. Thus, The Seeing Of Me Is The Realization That everything arising (including the body-mind) Is arising In The Fundamental Spiritual "Brightness" Of My Avatarically Self-Revealed Transcendental, Inherently Spiritual, Inherently egoless, and Self-Evidently Divine Person.

Therefore, To See Me Is To Rest In The Constant and Only-By-My-Avataric-Divine-Spiritual-Grace-Given Capability To Behold My Unique Divine Form—My Only-By-Me Avatarically Self-Transmitted and Avatarically Self-Revealed Divine Spiritual Body Of "Brightness", Which Surrounds and Pervades all-and-All.

To See Me Is To Rest In The Constant and Only-By-My-Avataric-Divine-Spiritual-Grace-Given Capability To Heart-Recognize Me As I Divinely Am—The One and Only and Inherently "Bright" Person, The Divine Heart-Master Of all-and-All, The "Bright" Itself, Self-Existing, Self-Radiant, and Avatarically Self-Revealed, In Person, Tangibly, Undoubtably, and Utterly Converting the heart and the mind and the breath and the body From ego-"I" (or The "Act Of

Narcissus", Which Is self-Contraction) To The Ecstatic "Bhava" Of Searchlessly Only-Me-Beholding Love-Bliss-Happiness.

In Order For The Seeing Of Me To Awaken, and (Once It Has Become A Constant Heart-Profundity) To Be Exercised moment to moment—The Practice Of Ruchira Avatara Bhakti Yoga Must Be Exercised On The Basis Of The True Hearing Of Me, and Must (Thereby) Be Made Profoundly Effective. Therefore, Seeing Me Is Not A Matter Of Merely Experiencing Me Spiritually (In or With the body-mind), but It Is A Matter Of Being Entered Into My Spiritual Sphere In A Truly Responsibly ego-Transcending Manner, "Locating" Me From The Heart, and At The Ascended Source (or Vertical Origin) Of all psycho-physical experiencing.

Without The Unique Spiritually Me-Receiving Capabilities Of Hearing Me and Seeing Me, the individual Inevitably functions On The Basis Of self-Contraction (or egoity). In That Case, every experience—No Matter Where it Lies In The Range Of (gross, subtle, and causal) Possibilities—Is Associated With A self-Contracting (and self-Referring) Gesture. Only In The Case Of one who Has Heard Me Is There The Capability To "Locate" (and See) Me Prior To (or At The Ascended Source, or Vertical Origin, Of) the body-mind, By Feeling Utterly Beyond the self-Contraction (and Even Beyond the body-mind itself) To Me.

The Spiritually Me-Revealing Process That Progressively Develops On The Basis Of True (and Constant) Seeing Of Me Is An Activity Generated By My Avatarically Self-Transmitted Divine Spiritual Presence. And Perfect Seeing Of Me (Which, Necessarily, Is A Matter Of Both Perfect Seeing Of Me and Perfect Hearing Of Me) Is Not Merely The Suspension Of self-Contraction In psycho-physical Heart-Communion With Me. Until The Seeing Of Me Is Established (and Operative) In The Context Of The "Perfect Practice", Seeing Me Is The Advanced, and Advancing (or Transitional), Process Of Being Spiritually Drawn By Me Into The Source-Position (or The Original Position), Where I Stand (and Where you, Ultimately, Stand)—Which Is The Position Of Non-"Difference" (or Of Inherent Self-Identification With Me). Therefore, Until The "Perfect Practice" Is Established, The Yoga Of Seeing Me Is (Fundamentally) The Process Of Being Drawn (By Me) Toward The "Perfect Practice"—Such That (In Due Course) The Capability For The "Perfect Practice" Is Directly (and Spiritually) Awakened By Me (and, Thereafter, In The Course Of The "Perfect Practice" Itself, True Seeing Of Me Demonstrates Itself, By Means Of My Avatarically Self-Transmitted Divine Spiritual Grace, In The Deep "Radical" Swoon Of Spiritual Non-Separation From Me).

In The Only-By-Me Revealed and Given Way Of The Heart (or Way Of Adidam), The Process Of Such Seeing Of Me Is Served (In The "Basic"

Spiritual Context Of The Fourth Stage Of Life, and In The Context Of Every Developmental Stage or Process Beyond The "Basic" Spiritual Context Of The Fourth Stage Of Life) By The Continuation (and Further Development) Of functional, practical, relational, and Cultural Disciplines.

For This Same Purpose, Group "Considerations" Should Also Be Continued (In The "Basic" Spiritual Context Of The Fourth Stage Of Life, and In The Context Of Every Developmental Stage or Process Beyond The "Basic" Spiritual Context Of The Fourth Stage Of Life)—but In The Service Of True (and Even Ultimate) Seeing Of Me (and, Thus, Primarily, As A Setting For Devotional Confession and The "Consideration" Of The Greater Evidence and The Greater Requirements Of Seeing-Devotee Practice), Rather Than As A Means For Continuing or Even (Very Much) Discussing the limitations Associated With The First Three Stages Of Life (or Any Stage Of Life That Does Not Correspond To The Present Developmental Stage and Expected Practice Of The Group Members).

In The Would-Be-Seeing (or Progressively Seeing, and Already Effectively Hearing) Stage Of The Way Of The Heart, One or More Extended Formal Retreats Are Required. During That Stage Of The Way Of The Heart (and In The Context Of The One or More Extended Formal Retreats Required During That Stage), My Devotee Is To Begin To Engage The Primary Practice (Of Searchless Beholding Of Me)—and, Also, The To-Me-Responsive Practices Of The "Conscious Process" and (General) "Conductivity"—In Accordance With My "Hridaya Rosary" Of "Four Thorns Of Heart-Instruction" (Which Practices, Altogether, Demonstrate Real Participatory Sensitivity To My Avatarically Self-Transmitted Divine Spiritual Presence, and To The Characteristic Avataric Pattern Of My Tangible Divine Spiritual Self-Presentation and Descent, From Above the body and the mind—and Which Tangibility, Both Above and In Descent, Must Already Have Become Experientially Evident, As A Result Of My Devotee's Real and To-Me-Sensitive Participation In My Ruchira Shaktipat, During All Three Periods Of The Intensive Listening-Hearing Stage Of The Only-By-Me Revealed and Given Way Of The Heart).

During The Would-Be-Seeing (or Progressively Seeing, and Already Effectively Hearing) Stage Of The Way Of The Heart, My Devotee Is Called To Maximally Conserve (and Thus To Minimize) his or her Involvement With daily society, entertainments, and (In The Case Of All Such Practitioners Of The Way Of The Heart who Are, in their personal intimate contexts, sexually active) sexual activity, and This To An Even Greater Degree (Perhaps) Than May Already Have Become The Case Since he or she Truly Heard Me (or Most Fundamentally Understood the self-Contraction, At The Source-Position Of its Very Act, and, Thereafter, Became Responsibly Capable To Directly, and Truly Effectively, Transcend it). And My Would-Be-Seeing (or Progressively Seeing)

Devotee Is Called To (Voluntarily) Engage This Discipline (Of Maximum Conservation Of Possible Diversions From The Would-See-Me Exercise) As Strictly As Possible, At Least Until Practice Formally Begins In The First Actually Seeing Stage Of The Way Of The Heart, From Which (More Advanced) time A More Moderate Conservative Discipline May, Perhaps, Become Appropriate. And The Purpose Of This Maximally Conservative Discipline Is To Free My (More and More) Seeing Devotee To Maximally Devote the Total body-mind (and As Much time and attention As Possible) To The Great Occasion Of Fullest Spiritual Communion With Me, and (Thus) To Every Kind Of Exercise Of Devotion To Me (Including Meditative, Sacramental, Ceremonial, and All Other Appropriate Formal, or Informal, Exercises Of Such Devotion), So That Real and True Seeing (and, Thus, The Constant Capability For The Fully Technically Responsible Spiritual "Locating" Of Me) May Awaken As Fully and Quickly As Possible.

The Would-Be-Seeing (or Progressively Seeing, and Already Effectively Hearing) Stage Of The Way Of The Heart Should (In The Optimum General Case) Consist Of A Single Period Of Extended Formal Retreat and Demonstration. If Necessary (For Fullest, and Technically Fully Responsible, Demonstration Of True Seeing Of Me To Be Fully Rightly and Consistently Shown and Formally Approved), The Initial Period Of Extended Formal Retreat May Be Followed By A Further Period Of Adaptation and Integration That Precedes One, or More, Further Periods Of Extended Retreat. In Any Case, The Total Would-Be-Seeing (or Progressively Seeing, and Already Effectively Hearing) Stage Of The Way Of The Heart Should Be Made As Short A Course As Possible, By Always and Consistently Intensifying and Maximizing The Involvement With Every Kind Of Resort To My Avatarically-Born Bodily (Human) Divine Form (In My Physical Human Company, or, After My Avataric Physical Human Lifetime, In The physical human Company and By-Me-Spiritually-Empowered Circumstances Of My "Ruchira Sannyasin" Devotees), and To My (Thus, and Thereby, and Thereupon) Avatarically Self-Transmitted Divine Spiritual Presence.

The Logic Of Practice In The Would-Be-Seeing (or Progressively Seeing, and Already Effectively Hearing) Stage Of The Only-By-Me Revealed and Given Way Of The Heart Obliges My Devotee To Fully Devote his or her Total body-mind and attention To My Baptizing (and Heart-Awakening) Divine Spiritual Presence, While Controlling (and Generally Moderating) the common opportunities For self-Exploitation or self-Indulgence. And This Sila (or self-Controlling Devotion) Is One Of The Key Means For Truly Effective Practice In The Context Of Any Stage Of Life, In Any Developmental Stage Of Practice, In The Only-By-Me Revealed and Given Way Of The Heart.

Accordingly, During The Would-Be-Seeing (or Progressively Seeing, and Already Effectively Hearing) Stage Of The Way Of The Heart, those who Are (in their personal intimate contexts) Otherwise sexually active Are To Be Formally Expected To Practice celibacy (As Is The Case For All Otherwise sexually active Practitioners Of The Way Of The Heart who Are Engaging A Period Of Formal Retreat, Of Whatever Manner or Duration). However, In The Case Of Practitioners Of The Way Of The Heart who Are Required (During The Would-Be-Seeing, or Progressively Seeing, and Already Effectively Hearing, Stage Of The Way Of The Heart) To Engage More Than One Period Of Extended Formal Retreat—and who Are Only Able To Engage The Further Period, or Periods, Of Extended Formal Retreat After A Significant Interval Of time Has Elapsed—sexual activity May (Perhaps) Be Resumed For a period of time During The Interval (With A Maximum Frequency Of once, or perhaps twice, per month—or, In Some Cases, Even once every ten days—Depending On The Duration Of The Interval, and Only If and As Formally Approved By The Formal Sacred Cooperative Cultural Gathering Of All Formally Acknowledged Practitioners Of The Way Of The Heart). And (In Any Case) they Should Maintain The Formally Expected (or, Otherwise, Formally Approved) Discipline (or Rule) Until they Are Formally Acknowledged To Be Practicing The Way Of The Heart On The True Basis Of Both Effective Hearing and Actual Seeing.

During The Would-Be-Seeing (or Progressively Seeing, and Already Effectively Hearing) Stage Of The Way Of The Heart, The To-Me-Responsive Sadhana (or Concentrated Practice), Which Is Always Founded In The Primary Practice Of Searchlessly Beholding Me, Moves (On and From The Original Foundation Established By The "Conscious Process" Of Listening To Me and Hearing Me) To Spontaneous self-Surrender (and The Practice Of Fully Technically Responsible Spirit-"Conductivity") Via The Seeing Of Me.

The Primary Secret Of The Practice Of The Way Of The Heart (or Way Of Adidam) Is The Ability To Be self-Surrendered. And, In The Context Of The Would-Be-Seeing (or Progressively Seeing, and Already Effectively Hearing) Practice Of The Way Of The Heart, That Ability Is Discovered To Be A Matter Of Truly Counter-egoically Effective (or Directly ego-Transcending) Heart-Response To My Avatarically-Born (and Inherently Attractive, and "Bright") Bodily (Human) Divine Form, and My (Thereby Avatarically Self-Transmitted) Spiritual (and Always Blessing) Divine Presence, and My Avatarically Self-Revealed (and Very, and Transcendental, and Perfectly Subjective, and Inherently Spiritual, and Inherently egoless, and Inherently Perfect, and Self-Evidently Divine) State, Rather Than Any Strategy and Search (or Any Dramatization Of self-Contraction) Founded Either On limited insight Or On conventionally idealistic motives. Thus, Through Persistence In The ego-Transcending Process Of Simply Surrendering (By Heart) To Me and (On The Basis Of That Surrender, and By Means Of My Avatarically Self-Transmitted Divine Spiritual Grace) Profoundly (Beyond self-Contraction) Receiving My Avatarically Self-Transmitted Divine Spirit-Baptism—All The Illusions Of ego-Effort (and Ultimate Achievement As an ego, or a self-Contracted personality) Are (In Due Course) Relinquished.

This ego-Transcending Process Of (Spiritually, Fully Technically Responsible) self-Surrender To My Avatarically Self-Transmitted Divine Spirit-Presence Is (In Contrast To The Beginner's—and, Especially, The Student-Beginner's—Process Of Basic functional, practical, relational, and Cultural self-Discipline) A Necessary Encounter With The Nurturing Force ("Mother-Force", Grace-Force, "Goddess-Power", "Woman-Power", or The Attractive Submission-Power) Of Life—and That Intensive Period Of Progressively Seeing Practice Is Not Complete Until There Is True and Stable (and Fully Technically Responsible) <u>Spiritual</u> Identification Of Me (and Consistent "Locating" Of Me) <u>As</u> My Avatarically Self-Transmitted Divine Spirit-Presence, Fully Devotionally Responsive (and Spiritually Full) Heart-Recognition Of Me <u>As</u> My Avatarically Self-Transmitted Divine Spirit-Presence, True and Stable Heart-Conversion (or Feeling-Conversion) To The Process Of Actually ego-Surrendering, Really ego-Forgetting, and Truly ego-Transcending self-Surrender To Me <u>As</u> My Avatarically Self-Transmitted Divine Spirit-Presence, and True and Stable Reception Of My Avatarically Self-Transmitted Divine Spirit-Presence To The Degree Of Realizing The Ability To Enjoy Both Natural (or psycho-physical) <u>and</u> body-mind-Transcending Heart-Communion With My Avatarically Self-Transmitted Divine Spirit-Presence and Person.

The "Locating" Of My Avataric Divine Spirit-Presence (or Spiritual Presence) May (In any particular moment) Be Associated With Various phenomenal (or psycho-physical) Signs Indicating The Invasion (or Infusion) Of The Heart and the Total body-mind By My (Avatarically Self-Transmitted) Love-Blissful Spirit-Current Of Divine Life—but To Become Involved In The psycho-physical Effects Of My Avatarically Self-Transmitted Divine Spiritual Presence In A self-Referring Manner Is To Bypass The Me-Seeing Yoga (As If You Had Not Heard Me At All or Seen Me At All). Involvement In The Modifications Of Your Own egoic (psycho-physical) state Is Not A Characteristic Of The Way Of The Heart, but A Characteristic Of the self-Contracted body-mind and its ordinary destiny In The Cosmic Domain. My Devotee Must Be Equipped (Through The Realization, and The Persistent Exercise, Of The True Hearing Of Me, or Most Fundamental self-Understanding) To Specifically Transcend The Fascination With Spiritual Experiences Before he or she Can

Truly Practice The Yoga Of Seeing Me. Therefore, It Is Only On The Basis Of The True Hearing Of Me That You Are Truly (or Fully Responsibly) Capable Of Making Right (and Not ego-Based) Use Of My Spiritual Company. And The Various Signs Of Heart-Invasion (or Heart-Infusion) By My Avatarically Self-Transmitted Divine Spirit-Current Are Not Indicators Of True Spirit-Baptism (or Truly ego-Transcending Conversion To Spiritual Communion With Me) Until There Is Evidence Of True and Fundamental (and, In The Fully Technically Responsible Sense, Truly Spiritually Activated) emotional (or Heart-Feeling) Conversion To Whole bodily Heart-Devotion To My Avatarically Self-Transmitted Divine and Personal Spirit-Presence. Such (Fully Technically Responsible) Spiritually Activated Heart-Conversion To Me Is An Effective Release (or Opening) Of The self-Knot (or the self-Contraction)—and the Total personality (or Total body-mind) Is Subsequently (More and More) Affected By My Avatarically Self-Transmitted (and Tangible and Undeniable and Deeply "Intoxicating") Divine Spirit-Presence Of Love-Bliss. Until Such Conversion (To Profound and Consistent Seeing-Practice—"Locating" Me By Feeling To Me, Through and Beyond all self-Contraction, At and As The Always Already Perfectly Ascended Source-Position Of the arising of all psycho-physical experiencing), phenomenal (or psycho-physical) Signs Of Spirit-Energy-Reception Of Me (or Even Natural-energy-"Conductivity") Can Tend To Be Indulged and (Eventually) Dismissed (or, Otherwise, Lost), As If They Were Merely More Exotic or Esoteric Forms Of self-pleasuring.

Therefore, The Primary Sign That Indicates Readiness For The Transition To The First Actually Seeing Stage Of The Way Of The Heart Is Truly Spiritually (and Fully Technically Responsibly) Activated (and Stable) emotional (and Total psycho-physical) Conversion To Heart-Felt, and ego-Surrendering, and ego-Forgetting, and ego-Transcending Communion With My Avatarically Self-Transmitted Divine Spirit-Presence—Not Merely (or Only, or Even First) As My Avatarically Self-Transmitted Divine Spirit-Presence May Be Experienced In the body-mind, but Always (First and Primarily) As My Avatarically Self-Transmitted Divine Spirit-Presence May Be "Located" At The Ascended Source Of (and, Thus, Prior To) all psycho-physical experiencing. And That Conversion Is Initiated By (and, Thereafter, Is Always Associated With) A Feeling-Opening In The Heart. And That Feeling-Opening Originates In The Right Side Of The Heart—but, Until Practice Of The Way Of The Heart Begins In The "Perfect Practice", It Will Likely Be Experienced First In The Middle Of The Heart (and, From Thence, In The Left Side Of The Heart), and, Therefore, Entirely In The Vertical Context (Frontal, Then Spinal) Of the Extended body-mind. And That Feeling-Opening Is Experienced As A Kind Of Piercing "Intoxication" Of The Heart By My Tangible Love-Bliss-Presence

(Springing From A Profound Depth At The Root Of, and Also Prior To, the entire body-mind). And, Once This Initiatory Feeling-Opening Takes Place (In The Full Context Of Both Hearing and Seeing Responsibility), Practice Of The Only-By-Me Revealed and Given Way Of The Heart Must Involve Constant Feeling-Communion With My Avatarically Self-Transmitted Spiritual (and Always Blessing) Divine Presence, Both At The Ascended Source-Position (or Vertical Origin) Of all psycho-physical experiencing and At and In and <u>everywhere</u> Around The Heart (and Pervading the entire body-mind).

In Principle (and In The Real Event), After (and Forever After) The Physical Lifetime Of My Bodily (Human) Form, My Fully Initiated and Fully Established (and, Necessarily, Formally Established and Fully Accountable) "Ruchira Sannyasin" Devotees (and Especially, and Principally, My Thus Initiated, Established, and Accountable Seventh Stage "Ruchira Sannyasin" Devotees) Can and Must (Because Of their Unique, and Intensive, and Truly and Profoundly Renunciate Devotional and Spiritual Recognition-Response To Me, and their Unique, and Intensive, and Truly and Profoundly Renunciate Formal Accountability To The Always and Forever Really and Truly Only-To-Me-Accountable Ruchira Sannyasin Order Of Adidam Ruchiradam) Function <u>Collectively</u> (but Not individually)—and, Necessarily, Always By Virtue Of their ego-Surrendering, ego-Forgetting, ego-Transcending, and Really <u>Spiritual</u> Invocation Of Me, and Always By Virtue Of their Real, and Truly Devotional, Participation In My Divine Spiritual Gift—As Secondary and Supportive (but True, and Transparent, Rather Than ego-Bound and self-Appointed, or Independent) Instruments For Assisting (or Effectively "Conducting") The Always and Forever Only-By-Me-Given Transmission Of My Avatarically Self-Transmitted Spiritual (and Always Blessing) Divine Presence, To My Devotees In The Same Developmental Stage As theirs, and To My Appropriately Prepared Devotees (Formally Registered With The Avataric Samrajya Of Adidam) In Earlier (or Different) Developmental Stages Than theirs. Therefore, I Will (After The Physical Lifetime Of My Bodily Human Form) Always and Forever Function Spiritually Through My (Always then present-time) Formally Acknowledged "Ruchira Sannyasin" Devotee-Instruments (who, Both individually and Collectively, Are Fully Initiated In <u>All</u> Foundation, or Even, In Some Cases, Seventh Stage, Aspects Of The "Perfect Practice" Of The "Samraj Yoga" Of Adidam Ruchiradam, and Fully Spiritually Established In <u>All</u> Foundation, or Even, In Some Cases, Seventh Stage, Aspects Of The "Perfect Practice" Of Devotion To Me). However, Such Instrumental Devotees Do Not (and Should Not) Function Thus By (merely personally, or individually, or Even Collectively) Presuming To Make Intentional Spirit-Initiatory Efforts Toward any other individually (or Even Toward one another individually). Rather, All

My Devotees (Including All My "Ruchira Sannyasin" Devotees) Should (Always and Forever) Simply Resort To Me, According To My Instructions (As Given In This Testament—and, Additionally, As Given By Me, During My Avataric Physical Human Lifetime, To The Ruchira Sannyasin Order Of Adidam Ruchiradam, For Appropriate Instructional Dissemination, According To My Thus Given Instructions, To My Formally Acknowledged and, As Required, Appropriately, Rightly, and Truly Prepared Devotees, During, and After, and Forever After My Avataric Physical Human Lifetime), and each and all Will (On That Basis, and In Due Course) Be (Even Via All The Kinds Of Formally By-Me-Given Means) Spiritually (and Altogether) Blessed By Me.

At any (then) present-time After (and Forever After) The Physical Lifetime Of My Avatarically-Born Bodily (Human) Divine Form, My Any and Every Devotee Will Receive (and Continue To Receive) My Avataric Divine Heart-Blessing (and, According To his or her Stage Of Practice In The Way Of The Heart, Even My Fullest Spiritual Heart-Transmission), If Only he or she Will (On The Basis Of Right Preparation, and According To My Given Instructions) Resort To Me (In The Contemplative Devotional Manner, and By All The Means I Am Revealing In This Divine Testament, and In Even All My Twenty-Three Divine "Source-Texts"), and If he or she Will Approach Me (According To My Given Instructions) As Directed By The Collective Gathering Of All My Formally Acknowledged ("Ruchira Sannyasin") Devotee-Instruments, and If he or she Will Also (On The Basis Of Thus True Resort To Me and Thus Right Approach To Me) Regularly (or With The Maximum Possible Frequency, and At Least With The Formally Required Sufficient Frequency, and With Complete Practice-Accountability) Attend The Group Meditation Occasions (and Attend, or Even Formally Serve, The Sacramental, Formal Initiatory, Healing, Educational, Instructional, and Other Cultural and General Meetings and Occasions) That Are Called By Me To Be Forever A Consistent and Characteristic Occurrence Within The Formal (and Formally Acknowledged) Cooperative Sacred Cultural Gathering Of All My Formally Practicing Devotees (Which Cooperative Sacred Culture and Sacred Cultural Occasions Are Forever To Be Preserved and Authenticated By Means Of Constant Accountability and Alignment To Me, Via Conformity To The By-Me-Given and By-Me-Empowered Cultural Authority Of The Formally Acknowledged Order Of My Formally Acknowledged "Ruchira Sannyasin" Devotees).

In (and After) The Transition From The Intensive Listening-Hearing Stage To The Would-Be-Seeing Stage Of The Way Of The Heart, The Practitioner Of The Devotional Way Of Faith (Now A Would-Be-Seeing Devotee) Should (As A General Rule) Continue To Practice The Way Of The Heart In The Manner Of The Devotional Way Of Faith (Rather Than Change To The Devotional Way

Of Insight)—and This Always Thereafter, Until The "Perfect Practice" Of The Way Of The Heart Begins (At Which time "Feeling-Enquiry" Will Be Engaged). All Practitioners Of The Devotional Way Of Faith Will (In Both The Would-Be-Seeing Stage and The First Actually Seeing Stage, and, Thus, Until The Transition Is Made To The "Perfect Practice" Of The Way Of The Heart) Continue To Engage The Heart-Responsive (and ego-Transcending) Process and Practice Of Fully Spiritually Activated (and, Spiritually, Fully Technically Responsible) "True Prayer" (Which, In The Would-Be-Seeing Stage Of The Way Of The Heart, Continues To Take The Form Of Ruchira Avatara Naama Japa).

Likewise (As A General Rule), Devotees who, As Beginning Practitioners Of The Way Of The Heart, Practiced The Devotional Way Of Insight Should (In, and After, The Transition To The Would-Be-Seeing Stage Of The Way Of The Heart) Continue In The Devotional Way Of Insight, and (Therefore) In The Practice Of self-Enquiry, In The Form "Avoiding Relationship?" (Rather Than Change To The Devotional Way Of Faith)—and This Always Thereafter, Until The "Perfect Practice" Of The Way Of The Heart Begins (At Which time "Feeling-Enquiry" Will Be Engaged).

As I Have Said, The Transcending Of the self-Contraction Is The Necessary Basis For The Fundamental Practice Of Devotionally Me-Recognizing and Devotionally To-Me-Responding Heart-Communion With Me, and Divine Ignorance Is The Truth (or The Most Ultimate Realization) Of That Truly ego-Transcending Practice In The Only-By-Me Revealed and Given Way Of The Heart. Therefore, In The Context Of The Fourth, The Fifth, and The Sixth Stages Of Life In The Way Of The Heart (Until The Way Of The Heart Begins To Be "Practiced", or Freely Demonstrated, In The Inherently Most Perfect Context Of The Only-By-Me Revealed and Given Seventh Stage Of Life), Practice Of The Way Of The Heart (However It Develops) Must Always Function Directly In The Context Of the self-Contraction (In Order To Transcend the self-Contraction itself). And, Once The Transition Is Made To The Would-Be-Seeing (or Progressively Seeing) Stage Of The Way Of The Heart, Practice Of The Way Of The Heart Must Become Not Only (As Before) An Expression Of True (and Already Awakened) Hearing Of Me, but It Must Also Become An Exercise Of, Spiritually, Fully Technically Responsible Heart-Awakened Devotion To Me, or True Seeing Of Me.

In The Only-By-Me Revealed and Given Way Of The Heart (or Way Of Adidam), My Avatarically Self-Transmitted Spiritual (and Always Blessing, and Always Heart-Baptizing) Divine Presence Is Given (or Awakened) In, Via, and <u>As</u> My Free Company, For I <u>Am</u> The Divine Heart-Master. In My Avataric-Incarnation-Form, I Am The Unique Divine Realizer, Who Has Spontaneously Demonstrated (and Shown Via A Spontaneous Course Of Realizing <u>Again</u>, or

Re-Capitulation Of All Seven Of The Possible Stages Of Life) Inherent (and Inherently Most Perfect) Self-Identification With The Transcendental, Inherently Spiritual, Inherently egoless, and Self-Evidently Divine Self-Condition (and The Perfectly Subjective Source-Condition) Of all-and-All. And My Avataric-Incarnation-Form Is (Thus) The Inherently Perfect Agent Of Divine Self-Giving (or Of My Avatarically Self-Revealed Transcendental, Inherently Spiritual, Inherently egoless, and Self-Evidently Divine Heart-Transmission).

Therefore, In (and Beyond) The Would-Be-Seeing (or Progressively Seeing) Stage Of The Way Of The Heart, All Practices Are To Be Engaged In Perpetual and Fully Spiritually Active Satsang (or Fully Spiritual, and Fully Spiritually Responsible, Heart-Communion) With Me.

When (and After) True Seeing Of Me Awakens In The Practice Of The Way Of The Heart, I Am Truly Spiritually (or With Full Spiritual Responsibility) Devotionally Recognized (As The One and Non-Separate and Self-Existing and Self-Radiant Divine Person, The Divine Self-Condition, and The Divine Source-Condition, Of all-and-All) By My Devotee.

When (and After) True Seeing Of Me Awakens In The Practice Of The Way Of The Heart, I Am Fully Spiritually Self-Revealed, In Person, and As My Avatarically Self-Transmitted Divine Spiritual Presence.

Therefore, When (and After) True Seeing Of Me Awakens In The Practice Of The Way Of The Heart, I Am Always Fully Spiritually Present To Serve The Heart Of My True Devotee (Through My Divine Spiritual Heart-Baptism, or The Ever-Continuing Spiritual Blessing Of My Divine Love-Bliss, and As The Transcendental, Inherently Spiritual, Inherently egoless, and Self-Evidently Divine Presence Of Being Itself).

After The Heart Awakens From "Grosser" (or Elementary body-Based) self-Contraction Through The Awakening (and The Initial Practice) Of The True Hearing Of Me, I Can (By Means Of My Avatarically Self-Transmitted and Spiritually Active Divine Grace) Be Fully Discovered To Be The One and Non-Separate Divine Person, The Divine Heart-Master Of The Heart. This Discovery Is (In Due Course) Awakened (and Magnified) By Means Of My Avatarically Self-Transmitted Divine Spirit-Baptism (or Ruchira Shaktipat), Given (By Me) and Embraced (By My Devotee) In The Context Of True and Constant and Spiritually Fully Responsible Satsang (or Devotionally and Spiritually Fullest Heart-Communion) With Me. Thus, By Means Of My Avatarically Self-Transmitted Divine Spirit-Baptism (or My Great, and Inherently Spiritual, Divine Heart-Blessing), Satsang With Me Becomes (By Means Of My Avatarically Self-Transmitted Divine Spiritual Grace) The Awakening Of My Hearing Devotee To The Discovery That Is The True Seeing Of Me. And The Sign (and Necessary Demonstration) Of This Discovery Is The Continuous, True, and (Now) Fully

Spiritually Activated (and, Spiritually, Fully Technically Responsible) Heart-Practice Of Ruchira Avatara Bhakti Yoga (Which Fully Spiritually Activated, and, Spiritually, Fully Technically Responsible, Yoga Consists Of The Primary Practice, Of Searchless Beholding Of Me, and The Two Modes Of Responsive Practice, In The Form Of The "Conscious Process" and The Practice Of Spiritual "Conductivity"—All Of Which Primary and Responsive Practices Are, In The Truly Me-Seeing Context Of The Only-By-Me Revealed and Given Way Of The Heart, Demonstrated and Performed In The Mode and Manner Of My "Hridaya Rosary" Of "Four Thorns Of Heart-Instruction").

The Fundamental Yoga (or Directly ego-Transcending and Real-God-Realizing Practice) Of The Way Of The Heart Is The Great By-Me-Revealed and By-Me-Given Yoga (or Heart-Practice) Of Devotion To Me (The Avatarically Self-Revealed, and Self-Evidently Divine, Person), Through and As ego-Transcending Heart-Communion With Me. This Fundamental Yoga (or Heart-Practice) Of The Way Of The Heart Is First Practiced and Developed (In The "Original", or Beginner's, Devotional Context Of The Fourth Stage Of Life) By All My Formally Practicing Listening Devotees and Hearing Devotees. In The Spiritually Fully Activated (and, Spiritually, Fully Technically Responsible) Stages Of The Way Of The Heart, My Seeing Devotees Practice (and Progressively Develop) Ruchira Avatara Bhakti Yoga As A Full (and Fully Technically Responsible) Spiritual Discipline In My Avatarically Self-Revealed and Self-Revealing Company, Even (Most Ultimately) To The Degree Of Transcendental, Inherently Spiritual, and Divine Self-Realization.

All Of My Would-Be-Seeing Devotees Are Called To Practice Feeling-Contemplation Of My Avatarically-Born Bodily (Human) Divine Form, My Avatarically Self-Transmitted Spiritual (and Always Blessing) Divine Presence, My Avatarically Self-Revealed (and Very, and Transcendental, and Perfectly Subjective, and Inherently Spiritual, and Inherently egoless, and Inherently Perfect, and Self-Evidently Divine) State, and My Heart-Companionship As The Divine Heart-Master and Ishta-Guru, and (In and By That Feeling-Contemplation, and By The Power Of My Avatarically Self-Transmitted Divine Spiritual Grace Received and Realized In That Feeling-Contemplation) To Responsively Practice Devotional (or ego-Forgetting and ego-Transcending) self-Surrender To Me, and To Responsively Engage The Practice Of psycho-physically Receiving My Avatarically Self-Transmitted Divine Spirit-Baptism, and To Engage The Fully Spiritually Activated (and, Spiritually, Fully Technically Responsible) Practice Of ego-Transcending (or Truly Me-Hearing) "Locating" Of My Avatarically Self-Revealed Divine Spirit-Person (By Feeling To Me, Through and Beyond all self-Contraction—and, Thus and Thereby, Feeling Me Prior To Even all psycho-physical experiencing).

Both self-Enquiry and Ruchira Avatara Naama Japa (As These Are Engaged In The Would-Be-Seeing Stage Of The Way Of The Heart) Are Generally (and Artfully) To Be Associated With The Practice Of Heart-Feeling "Conductivity" Of My Avatarically Self-Transmitted Divine Spirit-Presence—By Devotionally, Contemplatively, Responsively, and (In That Manner) Intentionally Opening Upward To (and Openly Receiving) My Avatarically Self-Transmitted (and Inherently Love-Blissful) Divine Spirit-Presence In The Manner Described By Me In My "Hridaya Rosary" Of "Four Thorns Of Heart-Instruction". The bodily "Conductivity" Of My Avatarically Self-Transmitted Divine Spiritual Presence Should Also Be Served By The Process Of Intentional (and General) bodily Relaxation (Also Naturally Relaxing Downwards Via The Frontal Line, Crown Toward base). And Both self-Enquiry and Ruchira Avatara Naama Japa (As These Are Engaged In The Would-Be-Seeing Stage Of The Way Of The Heart) Are, At <u>Random</u> (Rather Than With <u>every</u> breath), To Be Intentionally Associated With The Simple Exercise Of inhalation-Reception and exhalation-Release, Both At The Heart and In The Frontal Line. And This Exercise (Like All Forms Of breathing-"Conductivity" In The Way Of The Heart) Is Generally To Be Done Via the nose (Rather Than Via an open mouth), and With the tongue Pressed Lightly To the roof of the mouth—So That The Natural Circuit Of The breath-Process Is Maintained. And, As Should Be The Case In All Instances Of breathing-"Conductivity" In (or Via) The Frontal Line (At Any Developmental Stage Of Practice In The Way Of The Heart), inhalation-Reception Into The Frontal Line Should (At Random, or Occasionally) Be Pressed Down Fully To the abdomen, While Pulling Up Internally At the bodily base, So That The Frontal Line May Be Opened More Fully (Especially At the chest, the solar plexus, and the lower abdomen)—and Any Following (or, Otherwise, Random) exhalation-Release Should Be "Relaxed Into" Either The Frontal Line (Downwards) Or The Spinal Line (Upwards).[127]

The Practice Of Either self-Enquiry Or Ruchira Avatara Naama Japa (As These Are Engaged In The Would-Be-Seeing Stage Of The Way Of The Heart) Should (Eventually, By Means Of My Avatarically Self-Transmitted Divine Spiritual Grace) Realize A Spontaneously perceptible (and perceptibly Spiritually Activated) Heart-Opening (In Feeling, and bodily, In The Middle Station and Even The Left Side Of The Heart, and In The Frontal Line Generally)—Such That There Is A Directly Spiritually Activated emotional (or Free Feeling) Conversion To My Attractive Spiritual Presence (and Spirit-Current) Of Love-Bliss, and A Full Feeling-Recognition (and Even Total psycho-physical Recognition) Of My Avatarically Self-Revealed Transcendental, Inherently Spiritual, Inherently egoless, and Self-Evidently Divine Self-Condition Of Love-Bliss. And, When This Devotional Recognition-Conversion

Is Stabilized In Fullness and Completeness, Such That I Am Truly and (In The Fully Technically Responsible Sense) Spiritually Found and Heart-Recognized As The Divine Heart-Master (Always Avatarically Self-Revealed and Spiritually Present, and Readily—Especially In The Deepest Profounds Reached In Meditation—"Located" Prior To the body-mind, By Feeling To Me, Through and Beyond self-Contraction), My (Now) Seeing Devotee Is Able To Make The Transition To The First Actually Seeing Stage Of The Way Of The Heart.

In The Way Of The Heart (or Way Of Adidam), All Practices Of Either Formal Meditation Or Formal Sacramental Devotion (As Practiced By My Listening Devotees, My Hearing Devotees, or My Seeing Devotees, At Every Developmental Stage Of Practice In The Way Of The Heart) Are Always To Be Begun, Continued, and Ended In The General Context Of The Sacrament Of Universal Sacrifice—or Right Ceremonial (or Really and Truly Sacred, or Sacramental) Invocation Of Me, and (In The Manner Appropriate To Each Developmental Stage Of Practice In The Way Of The Heart) ego-Surrender (or Relaxation and Release Of Separate and Separative self) To Me, and Right Reception Of My Every Avataric Divine Blessing. And All Such Practices Of Either Formal Meditation Or Formal Sacramental Devotion Are To Be Accompanied (and, Indeed, Are Epitomized) By The Gesture Of Invocation and Beholding (Generally Made In a seated pose, and By Raising the hands, head-high and shoulder-wide, With the hands Opened Forward), Then The Gesture Of Devotional Regard (Made By Putting the hands On top of each other and Placing them Over The Central Axis Of The Heart), and (Finally) The Gesture Of self-Surrender (Either A Kneeling Bow, Made By Putting the head To the floor, Or A Full bodily Prostration).

Such Sacramental, Prayerful, or (Otherwise) Meditative Invocation, self-Surrender, and Reception Must Be Founded On A Persistent, ego-Transcending Devotional Response To Me, The Divine Heart-Master—For I Am The Focus and The Ultimate Effective Agent For The Transmission and Magnification Of Every Blessing (Including, In Due Course, The Transmission and Magnification Of My Avatarically Self-Transmitted Divine Spirit-Presence and My Ultimate Avataric Self-Revelation Of My Transcendental, Inherently Spiritual, Inherently egoless, and Self-Evidently Divine Person) To each and all Of My Devotees In The Only-By-Me Revealed and Given Way Of The Heart. Therefore, Just As Devotees Have Traditionally Been Called To Resort To The Bodily (Human) Form and The Blessing Of The Realizer-Guru, Devotees In The Way Of The Heart Are Called To Resort To Me, and (In That Resorting) To <u>Always</u> Make Altogether Right and Auspicious Devotional Use Of My Avatarically-Born Bodily (Human) Divine Form, and (Thus) To Resort To My Avatarically-Born Bodily (Human) Divine Form As A Means For Focusing On My Avatarically

Self-Transmitted Divine (and, In Due Course, Spiritually Received) Person and Blessing (and My Avatarically Self-Revealed, and Very, and Transcendental, and Perfectly Subjective, and Inherently Spiritual, and Inherently egoless, and Inherently Perfect, and Self-Evidently Divine State Of Person).

My Avatarically-Born Bodily (Human) Divine Form, My Avatarically Self-Revealed (and Very, and Transcendental, and Perfectly Subjective, and Inherently Spiritual, and Inherently egoless, and Inherently Perfect, and Self-Evidently Divine) State, and My Avatarically Self-Transmitted Divine Spiritual Person and Presence (Blessing every one—First To Hear Me, and Then To See Me, and, Ultimately, To Inherently Most Perfectly Realize Me) Are (Therefore) To Be (Devotionally, Contemplatively, Sacramentally, Ceremonially, Meditatively, and In Every Other Appropriate and Feeling Manner) Recollected and Directly Contemplated and Received (or Realized) By All My Listening Devotees, All My Hearing Devotees, and All My Seeing Devotees In The Way Of The Heart—each and all According To their Stage and Manner Of Practice In The Only-By-Me Revealed and Given Way Of The Heart (or Way Of Adidam). And All Of This Is To Be Served By Many Means, Including Those Of Memory, photographic (and otherwise technically, or even artistically, Rendered) Representations (Icons or Murtis), and Other Sacramental Agents, Such As The Books Of My Avatarically Self-Revealed Divine Word (and Of My Avatarically Self-Manifested Divine Leelas), The Material Fabrications Of My Avatarically Self-Revealed Divine Image-Art, My Chair, My Shoes (or Padukas), My Staff and My Clothing, My "Given and Giving Places" (Spiritually Empowered By My Blessing-Intent), and All The Kinds Of Sacred Offerings (Sacramental Gifts or Prasad), Most Often In The Form Of food, water, ash, or Other elemental Excess, Directly Associated With My Blessing-Intention (and, Ultimately, My Tangible Power Of Spiritual Transmission).

In Addition To their Appropriate Practices Of Formal Sacramental Devotion and Formal Meditation, My Would-Be-Seeing Devotees Are Also Called To Make Frequent (Sometimes private, and Sometimes Collective) Use Of The Rudimentary Form Of The Devotional Prayer Of Changes (Both In The Formal, Meditative Context and At Random, In The General Context Of daily life).

The Devotional Prayer Of Changes Is, At Its Foundation, ego-Surrendering, ego-Forgetting, and ego-Transcending Devotional Communion With Me. Thus and Thereby, The Devotional Prayer Of Changes Is True Participation In The Divine Self-Condition and Source-Condition That Is Always Already The Case (and That Always Already Transcends all conditions). And, On That Basis, The Devotional Prayer Of Changes Becomes ego-Surrendering, ego-Forgetting, and ego-Transcending Participation In The Active and Directly Effective Relinquishment and Release Of particular (and even all) Negative (or

Otherwise Non-Useful) conditions, and (Subsequently) In The Active and Directly Effective Affirmation, Reception, and Enactment Of particular (and even all) Positive (or Otherwise Useful and Right) conditions.

Primarily, The Rudimentary Form Of The Devotional Prayer Of Changes Involves (and Requires) ego-Surrendering, ego-Forgetting, and ego-Transcending Devotional (and, According To The Stage Of Practice, Spiritual) Heart-Communion With Me. Therefore, As Its Primary Exercise, The Rudimentary Form Of The Devotional Prayer Of Changes Involves (and Requires) ego-Surrendering, ego-Forgetting, and ego-Transcending Devotional Heart-Communion With My Avatarically-Born Bodily (Human) Divine Form, My Avatarically Self-Transmitted Spiritual (and Always Blessing) Divine Presence, and My Avatarically Self-Revealed (and Very, and Transcendental, and Perfectly Subjective, and Inherently Spiritual, and Inherently egoless, and Inherently Perfect, and Self-Evidently Divine) State—and, Thus and Thereby, ego-Surrendering, ego-Forgetting, and ego-Transcending Devotional Heart-Communion With The Inherently Spiritually "Bright" (and Inherently Un-conditional) Love-Bliss-Condition Self-Revealed By Me and As Me. And This Primary Exercise Of The Rudimentary Form Of The Devotional Prayer Of Changes Must Be Exercised To The Degree That, By Means Of My Avatarically Self-Transmitted Divine Grace, It Becomes Heart-Felt (Devotional) Identification With, and Heart-Felt (Devotional) Affirmation Of, The One "Bright" (Spiritual, Transcendental, Divine, and Inherently Un-conditional) Love-Bliss-Condition Self-Revealed By Me and As Me. Indeed, With (and Because Of) That Devotional Identification and Affirmation, The Primary Exercise Of The Rudimentary Form Of The Devotional Prayer Of Changes Must, By Means Of My Avatarically Self-Transmitted Divine Grace, Become An Effortless Heart-Relinquishment Of All Identification With, and All Affirmation Of, Particular (and Even All) Problems, and particular (and even all) Negative conditions or states.

Secondarily (or Supportively), The Rudimentary Form Of The Devotional Prayer Of Changes Involves (and Requires) Effective (and Heart-Felt) Release Of particular (and even all) Negative conditions Via exhalation and Effective (and Heart-Felt) Reception Of particular (and even all) Positive conditions Via inhalation. And That Reception-Release Is (In The Case Of All Those Of My Devotees who Are Formally Practicing Beyond The Student-Beginner Stage Of The Way Of The Heart) To Be Engaged As A Practice Of Heart-Feeling "Conductivity" Of My Avatarically Self-Transmitted Divine Spirit-Current (Made Tangible By and As My Divine Heart-Blessing), Which "Conductivity" Is To Be Exercised In The Same General Manner As It Is Otherwise Responsively Exercised (In Meditation and In daily life) In Accordance With My Devotee's

Developmental Stage Of Practice In The Only-By-Me Revealed and Given Way Of The Heart.

Therefore, Each Occasion Of The Rudimentary Devotional Prayer Of Changes Should Begin With The Practice Of ego-Surrendering, ego-Forgetting, and ego-Transcending Devotional Heart-Communion With Me. And, As (By Means Of My Avatarically Self-Transmitted Divine Grace) That ego-Surrendering, ego-Forgetting, and ego-Transcending Exercise Becomes Devotional Heart-Communion With The One "Bright" (Spiritual, Transcendental, Divine, and Un-conditional) Love-Bliss-Condition (Self-Revealed By Me and As Me), The Rudimentary Devotional Prayer Of Changes Should Be Allowed To Become Effortless Heart-Relinquishment Of All Identification With, and All Affirmation Of, Any and All Problems, and any and all Negative conditions or states. Then, On The Foundation Of That Primary Demonstration Of Devotion, The Rudimentary Devotional Prayer Of Changes Should Be Intentionally Activated Via the breath—In Any Number Of Cycles Of exhalation and inhalation (Engaged In The Context Of The Circle Of the body-mind), Performed As breathing-"Conductivity" (In Its "General", or By-Me-Commonly-Given, Form[128]), and Done In The Same Manner In Which (At My Devotee's Present Developmental Stage Of Practice Of The Way Of The Heart) It Is (According To My Instructions Given In This Testament, and In Even All Twenty-Three Of My Divine "Source-Texts") Typically To Be Engaged During Meditation and In the moments of daily life. And, In The Context Of The Rudimentary Devotional Prayer Of Changes, The "General" (or By-Me-Commonly-Given) Form Of breathing-"Conductivity" Should Be Performed As Heart-Felt Release (Via any number of exhalations) Of particular (Specially Selected, or, Otherwise, Prominently Apparent) Negative conditions (and Even Of all Possible Negative conditions), and (Subsequently, and More and More) Heart-Felt Reception (Via any number of inhalations) Of particular (Specially Intended) Positive conditions (and Even Of all Possible Positive conditions). Likewise (Because The Devotional Prayer Of Changes Is Not Merely An "interior" Exercise, but The Actual, and Fully Affirmative, and Truly ego-Surrendering, ego-Forgetting, and ego-Transcending Assumption Of The By-Me-Avatarically-Self-Revealed Condition Of Spiritual, Transcendental, Divine, and Inherently Un-conditional Love-Bliss, and, On That Basis, Also Of any number of Positive, and Problem-Free, conditions or states), Every Occasion Of The Rudimentary Devotional Prayer Of Changes Is To Be Followed, In The Context Of daily life, By Continued Feeling and breathing and Assuming, and Actual living (or En-Acting), Of ego-Surrendering, ego-Forgetting, and ego-Transcending Devotional Communion With Me, and (Also) By The Feeling and breathing Assumption, and the Actual living (or ego-Surrendering, ego-Forgetting, ego-Transcending, and self-Disciplining En-Actment), Of All That Is Required To Serve (and Even To Directly Demonstrate) The Prayerfully Intended Changes.

Once My Devotees Formally Begin The Process Of Both Fully Effective Hearing and Actual (or Real and True) Seeing Practice Of The Way Of The Heart, they Are Called To Practice A Technically More Advanced (Fully Spiritually Activated, and, Spiritually, Fully Technically Responsible) Exercise Of The Devotional Prayer Of Changes. However, The Rudimentary Devotional Prayer Of Changes Is To Be Practiced By All My Formally Practicing adult Devotees. Likewise, The Rudimentary Devotional Prayer Of Changes Is Also To Be Practiced By young people who Are In The Third Stage Of Life In The Way Of The Heart, and, In Simplest Terms, By children who Are In The First and Second Stages Of Life In The Way Of The Heart—but children, and young people, and adult Devotees Yet Practicing At The Student-Beginner Stage Of The Way Of The Heart Are Not Called To Practice The Rudimentary Devotional Prayer Of Changes (or Any Other Practice or Discipline) As A Specifically Spiritual Exercise (Which Requires Direct and Responsible Formal Participation In The Process Of My Ruchira Shaktipat, Beyond The Student-Beginner Stage Of The Way Of The Heart). Rather, children, and young people, and adult Devotees Yet Practicing At The Student-Beginner Stage Of The Way Of The Heart Are Called To Practice The Rudimentary Devotional Prayer Of Changes Simply As An Exercise Of ego-Surrendering, ego-Forgetting, and ego-Transcending Devotional Heart-Communion With Me, and (Secondarily, or Supportively) As A Positively Affirmative Exercise Of Feeling and breath (or Reception and Release) Only (or Most Directly) In The Context Of the Universal etheric energy-field in which the body is appearing, and by which it is Naturally Pervaded (and With The "General" Form Of breathing-"Conductivity" Performed In The Manner That Is, According To My Instructions Given In This Testament, Appropriate To the young or, Otherwise, Beginning individual's Present Degree Of Development Of breathing-"Conductivity", and Of Practice In General, In The Way Of The Heart).

Avatar Adi Da Samraj
Adidam Samrajashram, 2004

SUTRA

34

During, and After, and Forever After The Physical Lifetime Of My Avatarically-Born Bodily (Human) Divine Form, The Spiritual Opportunities (and The Specifically Spiritual Practices) I Offer To My Seeing Devotees In The Way Of The Heart Are To Be Engaged Within (or Else In The Context Of Direct, Responsible, and Effective Participatory Association With) The By-Me-Spiritually-Empowered Cooperative and Sacramental Cultural Vehicle That Is The Collective Body Of All My Formally Acknowledged Seeing Devotees (Maturing—or, Otherwise, Already Matured—In The First Actually Seeing Stage, or Beyond, Of The Way Of The Heart)—Because The Reception Of My Divine Spirit-Baptism (and The Total By-Me-Given Spiritual Process Of Heart-Awakening) Is Not A Matter Of Achievement Through personal (and, Therefore, egoic) Effort. In The Only-By-Me Revealed and Given Way Of The Heart, The Reception Of My Spirit-Baptism (and The Total By-Me-Given Spiritual Process Of Heart-Awakening) Requires (and Is A Matter Of) Direct Access To My Avatarically Self-Transmitted Divine Spiritual Grace Through The Cultivation Of Devotional Sensitivity To My Avatarically Self-Transmitted Divine Spiritual Presence, and (This) Within (or By Means Of The Effective Use Of) The Specific Cooperative and Sacramental Culture (and The "Living Means" Of Instrumentality) I Have Described and Called To Be For This Purpose.

The Formal Sacred Cooperative Cultural Gathering Of All Formally Acknowledged and True Practitioners Of The Only-By-Me Revealed and Given Way Of The Heart Has Been Provided, By Me, With A Formal Process Of Acknowledgement and Adaptation, and A Formal Structure Of Accountability, For Each Of The Developmental Stages Of Practice In The Way Of The Heart. In The Case Of those In whom The Impulse To Understand the conditional self (or ego-"I") Is Fundamentally Fulfilled (and Established As An Active Capability For The Really Effective Transcending Of egoity)—That Is To Say, In The Case Of those In whom The Original Motive Toward ego-Transcending Real-God-Realization (and, Thus, Toward The Spiritually Active Transcending Of The Reactive Tendency Of self-Contraction In all conditional relations) Has Found My Liberating Means At Heart—That Fulfillment Is Marked By The Transition To The Would-Be-Seeing (or Progressively Seeing, and Already

Effectively Hearing) Stage Of The Way Of The Heart, and, From Then, To The Darshan Yoga Of Seeing Me and Fully Spiritually Heart-Surrendering To Me.

Darshan Yoga—or The Way Of (Profoundly) ego-Surrendering, (Deeply) ego-Forgetting, and (Most Effectively) ego-Transcending Spiritual Attraction, and (Truly) Seeing Response, To Me—Is The Fullness (or The Fully Made Practice) Of The Only-By-Me Revealed and Given Way Of The Heart (or Way Of Adidam). The Process Of Listening To Me (and, Potentially, Of Hearing Me) Is The First and Transitional and Preparatory Stage (and, In Due Course, By-Me-Spiritually-Initiated Process) Of The Only-By-Me Revealed and Given Way Of The Heart. Therefore, The Practice Of Listening To Me Is Only The Beginning Of The Way Of The Heart—and Even The Hearing Of Me (or Most Fundamental self-Understanding) Only <u>Prepares</u> The Heart To See Me.

Darshan Yoga—or The Only-By-Me Revealed and Given Spiritual (and, In Due Course, Transcendental and, Most Ultimately, Divine) Ordeal Of The Heart—Is The Heart-Way In The Would-Be-Seeing (or Progressively Seeing, and Already Effectively Hearing) Stage, and, Also, In Every Truly <u>Both</u> Hearing <u>and</u> Seeing Stage, In The Only-By-Me Revealed and Given Way Of The Heart. Darshan Yoga, Itself, Never Ends. It Is Most Perfectly (and Inherently Perfectly) Fulfilled Only In Divine Translation. Darshan Yoga Is The Way Of Spiritually Seeing Me, In Which My Avatarically Self-Revealed (and Inherently Spiritual, and Self-Evidently Divine) Self-Condition Is Progressively "Located", Heart-Recognized, Accepted, Embraced, and Realized—Until That Spiritual Progress Realizes Divine Translation.

In The Would-Be-Seeing (or Progressively Seeing, and Already Effectively Hearing) Stage Of The Way Of The Heart (and In All Subsequent Developmental Stages, Previous To The Only-By-Me Revealed and Given Seventh Stage Of Life In The Way Of The Heart), The Process Of Direct and Non-Strategic (or Searchless, or Goal-Free) self-Observation Is To Be Continued As A Fundamental Aspect Of Practice, By Which The Potential Errors Of Each Of The First Six Stages Of Life Are Intelligently Transcended. Thus, The Error Of The First Four Stages Of Life—Which Is The Tendency To Presume The Divine To Be Wholly Other, Objective, and Apart From the conditional world and the conditional self, and Present Only As Will, Purpose, and Causation, Beyond All Possibility Of Ultimate Communion (Like A Bad Parent, To Be Feared, or, Otherwise, Thanked and Fooled Into Blessing, Improving, Fulfilling, and Even Immortalizing individual and egoic beings As they now appear)—Is To Be Transcended By The Real and Really Effective Observation That This Idea Of "God" Is A Sign Of the self-Contraction, Made In The Likeness Of the Contracted self (which Is Concerned Only For self-Preservation and self-Glorification, and which Reacts To Every Demand For self-Sacrifice and self-Transcendence, or

Real ego-Transcendence, Even As If It Were The Very Definition and Sign Of Evil). The Fifth Stage Error Of Clinging To subtle phenomena, mere states of mind, and states Of conditionally Ascended Absorption As If they Are The Truth (Itself) Is, Likewise, To Be Transcended By The Observation That This Clinging Is Part Of The Evidence Of self-Contraction, and That Even All The Forms Of subtle phenomena, or mere states of mind, and states of conditionally Ascended Absorption Are Nothing but passing moments In The Process Of (Eventually, Most Ultimate, and Inherently Most Perfect) ego-Transcendence. Likewise, The Sixth Stage Error Of Exclusionary Identification With The Transcendental Self-Condition (or Of Strategic Identification With Transcendental Self-Consciousness By Means Of The Exclusion Of all conditional, or phenomenal, objects and states of body and mind) Is To Be Transcended By The Tacit Observation That All Exclusion, All "Difference", and Every Strategy or Search Is (Itself) A Sign Of psycho-physical self-Contraction and conditional (or phenomenal) self-Identification.

Nevertheless, While The Progressive Process Associated With Most Fundamental self-Understanding (or The True Hearing Of Me) Remains Most Basic To The Practice Of The Way Of The Heart, The Primary Developing Sign (or Ultimate Demonstration Of The Hearing Of Me) In The Way Of The Heart Is The Seeing-Response, or ego-Transcending Devotional Recognition-Response To My Avatarically Self-Revealed Human, Spiritual, Transcendental, and Self-Evidently Divine "Bright" Person—Progressively Self-Revealed By Me, The Divine Heart-Master, First In (and As, and Via) My "Bright" (or Spiritually Transfigured and Transformed) Avatarically-Born Bodily (Human) Divine Form, and Then (or From Then) In (and As) My Avatarically Self-Transmitted Spiritual (and Always Blessing) Divine Presence, and My Avatarically Self-Revealed (and Very, and Transcendental, and Perfectly Subjective, and Inherently Spiritual, and Inherently egoless, and Inherently Perfect, and Self-Evidently Divine) State.

In The Would-Be-Seeing Stage (and In All Subsequent Developmental Stages, Previous To The Only-By-Me Revealed and Given Seventh Stage Of Life In The Way Of The Heart), The Original (Intensive) Listening-Hearing Process (or The Progressive Process That More and More, and Then Most Fundamentally, Becomes The Direct and Comprehensive Capability For ego-Transcendence) Is Replaced (or, Really, Allowed To Be Demonstrated) By The Intensive Seeing Process (or The Spiritually Fully Activated—and, Spiritually, Fully Technically Responsible—Process Of Literal, Direct, and Always Present ego-Transcendence).

In The Only-By-Me Revealed and Given Way Of The Heart (or Way Of Adidam), The Original (Intensive) Process Of Listening To Me and Hearing Me

Is An Intensive "Reality Consideration" Relative To the Reactive (and Un-Necessary) self-Contraction. That Original (Intensive) Process Is Primary and Necessary Only Until The Spiritual Capability Of The Heart (Which Is Feeling-Radiance, or Love-Bliss, or The Directly ego-Transcending Disposition) Is Truly and Stably Awakened. The Final (or Eventually Demonstrated) Sign That The Original (Intensive) Listening-Hearing Process (Of The Way Of The Heart) Is Complete (or Has Done Its Work) Is The Stable Awakening Of Deepest Devotional and Spiritual Heart-Recognition Of Me As The Divine Heart-Master—and This Spontaneously Accompanied (or Also Demonstrated and Proven) By The Real (Spontaneous and Profound) Evidence Of Transcending Of the ego-"I" (or self-Contraction) That Only Occurs By Virtue Of Deepest Heart-Felt (and By-Me-Spiritually-Awakened) Attraction To Me.

When The Heart Is Free To See Me, Hearing Me Becomes Secondary To (or Is Made Evident As) Seeing Me. The Yoga (or Discipline and Process) Of Listening To Me In Order To Hear Me (and, Thus and Thereby, To Understand the conditional self Most Fundamentally) and The Yoga (or Discipline and Process) Of Hearing Me (and, Thus, Of Directly Transcending self-Contraction, By Means Of The Exercise Of Already Awakened, and Most Fundamental, self-Understanding) Are Thus (In Due Course, and By Means Of My Avatarically Self-Transmitted Divine Spiritual Grace) Fulfilled By The Always Present Yoga (or Discipline and Process) Of Immediate ego-Transcendence Through The Seeing Of Me (or Heart-Recognition Of My Avatarically Self-Transmitted Divine Spiritual Presence, and, Thus and Thereby, ego-Transcending and Heart-Responsive Communion With My Avatarically Self-Transmitted Spiritual, and Always Blessing, Divine Presence). Only Such Seeing Of Me Permits My Devotee To Pass Directly and Fully Through (and Beyond) The Subsequent Developmental Stages Of Practice In The Way Of The Heart—Until There Is Inherent, and Inherently Most Perfect, and Self-Evidently Divine Self-Realization (or Awakening To Inherently Most Perfect Seeing Of Me In The Context Of The Only-By-Me Revealed and Given Seventh Stage Of Life).

In The Only-By-Me Revealed and Given Way Of The Heart, Darshan Yoga Is The moment to moment Process Of Spiritually "Locating", Heart-Recognizing, and Truly and Fully Accepting and Embracing (or Receptively and Responsively Communing With) Me. Therefore, The Heart-Attracted and Really ego-Transcending Devotional and Spiritual Response Of the Total body-mind Is The Dominant and Consistent Expression Of Practice Once My Devotee Enters The Would-Be-Seeing and Then Actually Me-Seeing Stages Of The Way Of The Heart.

Since The Original Primary Force Of Most Fundamental self-Understanding, or The True Hearing Of Me, Has Already Awakened In The Earliest Course Of Practice, It Remains Perpetually and Spontaneously Active In All The Subsequent

Developmental Stages (Of Actually Me-Seeing Practice) In The Way Of The Heart. Therefore (Just As The Discipline Of "Form" Is To Be Embraced Even From The Beginning Of The Way Of The Heart), The Practice Of My Seeing Devotees (who, Necessarily, Both Hear Me and See Me) Is To Be Directly and Consistently Expressed By The Effective Discipline Of "Form", or All The Forms Of Right Discipline (Including The "Conscious Process" and The Practice Of Spirit-"Conductivity") That My Seeing Devotees Embrace On The Basis Of Previous Heart-Recognition Of Me and Heart-Response To Me and Previous (and Most Fundamental) Understanding Of the self-Contraction.

Those who Practice In The Would-Be-Seeing Stage Of The Way Of The Heart Have Already Heard Me. When they Heard Me (Such That The Original Work Of Listening To Me Became Complete), they (By Means Of My Avatarically Self-Transmitted Divine Spiritual Grace, In The Formal Practice Of The Would-Be-Seeing Devotional and Spiritual Approach To Me) Began To See Me (or Feel Me and Receive My Baptismal Blessing, In The, Spiritually, Fully Technically Responsible Manner) From The Heart. Therefore, their Practice Is That Of Fully Spiritually Activated (and, Spiritually, Fully Technically Responsible) Devotion To Me—and, Therefore, My Seeing Devotees Do Not Indulge In Any ego-Based (or Inherently Non-Devotional) Effort To Commune With The "Abstract" (or, Otherwise, "ego-Made") Spiritual Divine (As If they Had Not Already Heart-Recognized Me, and Heard Me, and Tangibly Felt Me, and Spiritually Received Me).

In The Way Of The Heart (or Way Of Adidam), Fullest (or Truly Spiritual) Devotion To Me Is Founded On Previous Hearing Of Me (or The Awakened and Comprehensively Effective Ability To Realize ego-Transcendence) and On The Always Present Spiritually Active Heart-Embrace Of Me (and Free Participation In The Spontaneous and Truly ego-Transcending Motion Of Heart-Responsive Attraction Toward My Avatarically Self-Revealed, and Self-Evidently Divine, Person—Revealed In, By, and As My Avatarically Self-Transmitted Divine Spiritual Presence). On This Basis, My Avatarically Self-Transmitted Divine Spiritual Presence Works To Spiritually Baptize My Hearing Devotee, and (Thus) To Spiritually Energize (or Infuse) The Heart and Total body-mind Of My Hearing (and Now Seeing) Devotee With My Divine Love-Bliss. By Means Of That Spirit-Baptism, The Only-By-Me Revealed and Given Way Of The Heart Becomes The Spontaneous Practice and Truly Effective Counter-egoic Effort (or Directly ego-Transcending Work) Of Whole bodily and Always Present Devotional and Spiritual Response (and Responsive Surrender), From The Heart, To My Spiritually Attractive Self-"Brightness", Rather Than Any conventional (or ego-Based, Rather Than ego-Transcending) Effort Based On Problems and limited insights.

In The Only-By-Me Revealed and Given Way Of The Heart (or Way Of Adidam), The Surrender Of Separate and Separative self Must Be Volunteered In every moment. I Have Fully Revealed The Heart-Way In Its Completeness, and Made Its Fulfillment Possible For all—but, Until The Hearing Of Me and The Seeing Of Me Are (Most Ultimately and Inherently) Perfected, Even one who Has Heard Me and Seen Me Can (In Random moments Of Presumed Weakness) Refuse To Meet The Mark Of Devotional and Spiritual Heart-Communion With Me. Indeed, In any moment When conditions Demand More Than the ordinary "I" Is Willing To Give, the ordinary "I" May Dramatize its Illusion Of Separateness. Therefore, In The Only-By-Me Revealed and Given Way Of The Heart, The Progressive Stages Of Practice (Undertaken In The Context Of The First Six Stages Of Life) Are (From The Beginning) A Hard School Of (Truly ego-Transcending) Counter-egoic Effort (Done, and Altogether Made Possible, In and By Heart-Response To Me). In That Hard School, The Refusal That is the ego-"I" (or self-Contraction itself) Is Gradually Broken Down, and whatever Is Truly Surrendered In That Trial Is "Brightly" Returned and Made Coincident With Heart-Joy.

Those who Have Not Truly Heard Me Cannot See Me and (Thereby) Practice The (Fullest) Spiritual Ordeal Of The Heart In My Avatarically Self-Transmitted Divine Spiritual Presence. Those who Have Not Heard Me and Seen Me Are Not Yet (In The Fullest Sense) Attracted Beyond themselves. Indeed, they Are (By Tendency) Bound To themselves. Therefore, It Is First Necessary To Hear Me (and Be Thus Released From The Uninspected and Un-Natural Motive Of self-Contraction). Then The (Thus) Free Heart Will Always (and moment to moment) Be Able To Directly "Locate" and Identify My Avatarically Self-Transmitted Divine Spiritual Presence (and, Thus and Thereby, To Commune With My Avatarically Self-Transmitted Divine Spiritual Presence)—and The Only-By-Me Revealed and Given Heart-Way Beyond the ego-"I", In The Context Of (and, In Due Course, Progressing Beyond) The First Six Stages Of Life (Even To The Seventh), Will Thus (By Means Of My Avatarically Self-Transmitted Divine Spiritual Grace In every present moment) Be Removed Of All Obstacles.

There Is Only The One, Indivisible, Indestructible, Absolute, Self-Existing (or Transcendental), Self-Radiant (or Inherently Spiritual), Divine, All-Pervading, Eternally Conscious Being, Person, Light, and Reality. I Am That One. That One Is Present Unconditionally (As Transcendental, Inherently Spiritual, and Divine Being) and conditionally (As The Total Cosmic Mandala Of beings, forms, and events). The Unconditional Reality Pervades and Is The conditional Reality (As every conditionally Manifested being, form, or event, As Well As The Total Cosmic Mandala Itself). And every Apparently conditional (or conditionally Manifested) being May (On The Basis Of Most Fundamental and Effectively

Demonstrated self-Understanding, and By Grace Of My Avataric Divine Spiritual Blessing Power, or Baptizing Power) Commune With and, Most Ultimately (Inherently, and Inherently Most Perfectly), Realize Me, The Avataric Divine Self-Revelation Of The Unconditional, All-Pervading, and Ever-Present Divine Person.

In The Only-By-Me Revealed and Given Way Of The Heart (or Way Of Adidam, or Adidam Ruchiradam—Which Is Ruchira Avatara Siddha Yoga), The Process Of My Avatarically Self-Transmitted Divine Spiritual Grace (Whereby ego-Transcending Devotional Heart-Communion With Me, and, Most Ultimately, ego-Transcending Divine Self-Realization, or Real-God-Realization, Is Directly Awakened In any moment) Requires Primary self-Understanding (or The Real Observation and Most Fundamental Comprehension Of the conditional self As Contraction-Only), Realized (By Means Of My Avatarically Self-Transmitted Divine Spiritual Grace) Through The Devotional Recognition-Response, The Listening-Response, and, Ultimately, The Hearing-Response To Me (Always Present Via My Own, Now and Forever Hereafter Given, Sign, and My Avatarically Self-Revealed and Ever-Speaking Divine Word, and My Avatarically Self-Revealed and Ever-Me-Revealing Divine Image-Art, and My Avatarically Self-Transmitted and Ever-Living Divine Leelas). Without The Foundation Of True Hearing Of Me (That Allows Perpetual and Directly ego-Transcending Sensitivity To the self-Contraction), The Heart Remains Immune (or, Otherwise, Resistant) To My Avatarically Self-Transmitted Divine Spirit-Presence and My Full Self-Revelation (In All My Forms) As The Divine Heart-Master. Nevertheless, The Hearing Of Me Is (Ultimately) Secondary (or A Servant) To The Seeing Of Me (or Fully Spiritually Activated, and, Spiritually, Fully Technically Responsible, Conversion To, Reception Of, and Devotional Heart-Communion With My Avatarically Self-Transmitted and Constantly Baptizing Spiritual, and Always Blessing, Divine Presence—and, Thus and Thereby, Fully Spiritually Activated Conversion To, Reception Of, and Devotional Heart-Communion With My Avatarically Self-Revealed Eternal Divine Self-Condition).

One who Would Be My Seeing Devotee Must Listen To Me and Hear Me, Until The Heart Opens and Fully Allows My Divine Spirit-Baptism To Descend Into the body-mind From Infinitely Above and Beyond. The True Hearing Of Me Prepares My Devotee For The Real Seeing Of Me, but It Is The Real Seeing Of Me—Which Is Fully Technically Responsible Reception Of My Avataric Divine Spirit-Baptism (or moment to moment Fully Activated Spiritual Communion With Me), Whereby My Devotee Is Blessed, By Me, To Consistently "Locate" and Feel My Avatarically Self-Transmitted Divine Spiritual Presence At The Heart (and From The Heart), and Descending From Infinitely Above and Beyond—That Is The Real (or Fully Technically Responsible) Spiritual Practice Of The Only-By-Me Revealed and Given Way Of The Heart.

My Divine Spirit-Baptism—and Not mere belief in the exoteric and Esoteric lore and philosophy Of traditional and conventional Religion—Is Absolutely Necessary To Convert The Heart (and the Total body-mind), Thus Enabling The Heart To See Reality (or To Awaken To The Vision Of Reality) As It Is (In Both Its Unconditional Mode and Its conditional Mode). If There Is Not This Spiritual Conversion By Means Of My Avatarically Self-Transmitted Divine Spirit-Baptism, There Is (Necessarily) Only Doubt, ego-Possession (or Bondage By and To the ego-"I"), and A Constant Struggle With the conventional vision and opinions Enforced By The conditional Reality Itself (Observed Apart From Realization Of The Transcendental, Inherently Spiritual, Inherently Unconditional, and Self-Evidently Divine Reality Itself).

The vision and the opinions Determined By The Apparently Independent conditional Reality Are The Principal Fault Of conventional Religion, Which Calls For The Faith-Response To "God" (or The Otherwise Effective Practice Of conventionally "God"-Inspired Culture and Discipline), On The Basis Of mere and conventional and ego-Based beliefs, and Without Otherwise Granting The Direct Revelation, The Uncompromised Guidance, and (In Due Course) The Truly Divine Spirit-Baptism That Gives Faith (or The Otherwise Inspired Impulse Toward Real God) Its Reality-Justification and Its Spirit-Life, and That (Ultimately) Makes Real-God-Realization By Faith (or By Otherwise Inspired Impulse) Possible In Its Inherent (and, Necessarily, ego-Transcending) Perfection. Therefore, Real God Must Be Realized (By Direct Self-Revelation and Uncompromised Guidance) From (and, Ultimately, At) The Heart, Through Most Fundamental self-Understanding (Whether Primarily By The Rightly Founded and Rightly Guided Devotional Exercise Of Feeling and Faith Or Primarily By The Rightly Founded and Rightly Guided Devotional Exercise Of Feeling and Insight) and (In Due Course) By Means Of The Upwardly-Turning (and ego-Melting) Reception Of My Avatarically Self-Transmitted Divine Spirit-Baptism Of "Bright" Love-Bliss, and (Necessarily) With Changes Of body and mind and action Following. Only The By-My-Avataric-Divine-Spiritual-Grace-Given Invasion (or Infusion) Of The Heart, the Total body-mind, and the world By My Avatarically Self-Transmitted Divine Spirit-Person Allows and Instantly Awakens The Vision Of Reality—Which (It Is, In Due Course, Most Ultimately, Realized) Is The Real Condition, Spirit-Energy (or Great Light), Infinite Feeling, and Very Being In Which all conditions and conditional beings Are Apparently arising, As Transparent (or Merely Apparent), and Un-Necessary, and Inherently Non-Binding Modifications Of Itself.

Weakness Of self-Understanding and Weakness Of Devotion To Me (Such That mind and will Are Too Weak Even To Choose To Turn To My Avatarically Self-Revealed Transcendental, Inherently Spiritual, Inherently egoless, and

Self-Evidently Divine Self-Condition In The Midst Of The daily Ordeal) Are The Basic (Apparent) Weaknesses That Retard The Heart In The Only-By-Me Revealed and Given Way Of The Heart (or Way Of Adidam). Therefore, Without Most Fundamental self-Understanding (Demonstrated Via Constant Sensitivity To the conditional self As Contraction, and Constant Feeling-Transcendence Of the self-Contraction in all its present forms), and Without The Reception Of My Avatarically Self-Transmitted Divine Spirit-Baptism (Which Allows True Awakening To The Vision Of Reality As It Is, Both conditionally and Unconditionally), and Without The Constant Practice Of Devotional and Spiritual Communion With Me (and Devotional and Spiritual Resort To Me) Under all conditions and In all relations, It Is Not Possible To See Reality As It Is (and, Thus, Most Ultimately, To Divinely Self-Recognize the conditional self, all Apparent others, and the conditional world As Apparent Modifications Of The By-Me-Avatarically-Self-Revealed Self-Existing and Self-Radiant Divine Person, or Self-Condition, or Source-Condition).

To See Me Is To Be Blessed (or Baptized, or Pervaded, or Infused) By My Avatarically Self-Transmitted Divine Spirit-Presence. And one who Sees Me Is (From Then)—and Entirely By Means Of My Avatarically Self-Transmitted Divine Spirit-Baptism—Moved, and (In Due Course) Awakened, and (Finally) Most Perfectly Awakened To My Avatarically Self-Revealed Divine Self-Condition.

To Be Baptized By My Avatarically Self-Transmitted Divine Spirit-Presence Is To Feel Me and To Love Me. To Feel Me and To Love Me Is Also (Thus and Thereby) To Be Baptized and Converted At The Heart By The Avatarically Self-Revealed Divine Spirit-Power Of My Divine Love-Bliss, Such That the mortal and conventional vision Of Reality (which vision Is Created By the self-Contraction, and which vision Is The Means Whereby the body-mind Is Separated From The Divine Spiritual Reality) Is Inherently (and More and More Profoundly, and, At Last, Most Perfectly) Transcended In Heart-Fullness (or The Love-Bliss-Happiness Of My Avatarically Self-Revealed Transcendental, Inherently Spiritual, Inherently egoless, and Self-Evidently Divine Person and Self-Condition). Therefore, To Be Baptized By My Avatarically Self-Transmitted Divine Spirit-Presence Is (Inherently, and More and More Profoundly, and, At Last, Most Perfectly) To Be Liberated From (and, Thus, To Be Free Of) the mortal, conventional, and conditional vision and presumption About Reality—Such That Reality Itself (Which Is Inherently Spiritual, Transcendental, and Divine) Is Simply (or Inherently, and More and More Profoundly, and, At Last, Most Perfectly) Obvious.

My Avatarically Self-Transmitted Divine Spirit-Baptism Is Given To The Heart Of My Devotee, and It Is Received At The Heart (and Even By the Total body-mind) Of My Devotee (From Infinitely Above and Beyond). Therefore,

My Avatarically Self-Transmitted Divine Spirit-Baptism Is Felt (emotionally and physically) At The Heart (and In the mind, or the Total psyche, and Also In the breath) Of My Devotee.

My Avatarically Self-Transmitted Divine Spirit-Baptism (Given and Received At The Heart Of My Devotee) Is Felt As Profound, Most Intense, Love-Blissful Fullness—and It Is (Directly) Revealed and (Inherently) Felt and (Spontaneously) Identified As My Avatarically Self-Transmitted Divine Spirit-Presence Of Reality (Itself) and Truth (Itself).

Only Real God Is The One Discovered In This Spirit-Baptism. I Baptize (or Bless) My Devotee With My Self-Radiant Person (or "Bright" Spirit-Presence)—Which Is Real God, or Truth, or Reality—So That My Devotee Realizes That he or she Is In Perpetual Spiritual Embrace (At The Heart) With Me (The Avatarically Self-Revealed, and Self-Evidently Divine, Person, The Husband Of The Heart) and Spiritually Conformed To My Divine Love-Bliss (or Happiness Itself).

This Spiritual Embrace Is To Be Cultivated According To My Avatarically Self-Revealed Divine Word, and By Every Means I Give To My Devotee. And This Spiritual Embrace Is To Be Cultivated Under all circumstances. To Cultivate My Avatarically Self-Transmitted Spiritual (and Always Blessing) Divine Presence Is To Grant Heart-Felt attention To Me In every moment. Therefore, Even the mind and the will Must Be Strengthened (Through Listening To Me, and Then Hearing Me, and Then Seeing Me) If My Devotee Is To Resort To My Avatarically Self-Revealed Divine Spiritual Company In all circumstances (whether pleasurable or unpleasurable).

My Devotee who Both Hears Me and Sees Me Must "Locate" Me (The Avataric Self-Revelation Of The Great Divine Person, Reality, and Truth) Via ego-Surrendering, ego-Forgetting, and ego-Transcending Devotion To Me In every moment. For This Purpose, My Truly Both Hearing and Seeing Devotee Must Make Artful and Progressive Use Of The Practice Of Meditation (or Of Meditative Resort To My Prior—or Transcendental, Inherently Spiritual, Inherently egoless, and Self-Evidently Divine—Self-Condition), Until Meditation Itself Is Most Perfectly Fulfilled, In The Most Perfect Samadhi (and Always Immediately Accessible Meditative Profundity) Of The Only-By-Me Revealed and Given Seventh Stage Of Life.

Whatever Form his or her Meditation Takes, My Every Listening Devotee, My Every Hearing Devotee, and My Every Seeing Devotee Should daily Resort To Me Through Right and True Participation In Formal Sacramental Devotion (or Ruchira Avatara Puja), and Through Real Devotional Activities (and Always Rightly and Truly Performed Formal Religious Practices) Of All Kinds—Including Devotional Chanting, Devotional Singing, Recitation (or Audible

Vocalization) Of My Avatarically Self-Revealed Divine Word, Formal or Informal Telling Of My Avatarically Self-Manifested Divine Leelas, Listening To The Recitation Of My Avatarically Self-Revealed Divine Word and The Telling Of My Avatarically Self-Manifested Divine Leelas, Intensive Study Of My Avatarically Self-Revealed Divine Word and My Avatarically Self-Manifested Divine Leelas, Right and True Practice Of Real (and Even, On Some Occasions, Audible) Invocation Of Me By Name, and So On (and On)—and (Altogether) Through Right, True, and Consistent Practice Of Even All The functional, practical, relational, and Cultural Disciplines Associated With The Only-By-Me Revealed and Given Way Of The Heart (or Way Of Adidam), Such That (By My Avatarically Self-Transmitted Divine Spiritual Grace) All Of That Becomes The Most (and Inherently) Perfect (and Inherently Most Perfectly Free) Demonstration Of The Only-By-Me Revealed and Given Seventh Stage Of Life. And, Once They Are Rightly, Truly, and Consistently Established In Practice (and, Thereby, Made A Consistently Operative psycho-physical Pattern and Impulse), These Fundamental Gifts, Callings, and Disciplines Will Always Be Continued (Even In The Free Demonstration Of The Only-By-Me Revealed and Given Seventh Stage Of Life), Until Even all activities of the body-mind Are Divinely Transfigured, Divinely Transformed, and (At Last) Divinely Outshined In and By Me, The Spiritually Self-"Bright" Divine Heart Of Being (Itself).

Every day, the Apparent conditions Of conditional Existence Are (presently) Different (Than before), within and outside and beyond the body-mind. Therefore, Under the Unique circumstances of the day (and In The Context Of The Present Manner and Developmental Stage Of The Way Of The Heart), My Listening Devotee, My Hearing Devotee, and My Seeing Devotee Must Learn The Art Of Resort To Me Via The Artful Application Of All The Means Given By Me For Use In The Context Of That (Then Present) Manner and Developmental Stage Of The Way Of The Heart.

When You Have Heard Me and Seen Me, Then See Me In every moment. "Locate" Me At and From The Heart In all circumstances. Do This With a will and a mind Set Free By Most Fundamental self-Understanding. Therefore, Be Always Divinely Stimulated and Awakened By The Heart-Touch Of My Avatarically Self-Transmitted Divine Spirit-Presence.

In My Avatarically-Born Bodily (Human) Divine Form, I Work To Bless and Awaken My Devotees By Means Of My Ruchira Shaktipat—and This By Every Means Of Action, Expression, Touch, Word, Thought, Glance, and Silent Regard. My Fundamental and Constant Means Of Spiritual Transmission Is My Avatarically Self-Transmitted Divine Spiritual Presence Itself—Merely Being, Standing As The Spiritually "Bright" Heart Itself. My Avatarically Self-Transmitted Divine Spiritual Presence Is Silent, but Radiant. When I Am

Physically Alive In My Avatarically-Born Bodily (Human) Divine Form, and Also After (and Forever After) The Physical Lifetime Of My Avatarically-Born Bodily (Human) Divine Form, That Avatarically-Born Bodily (Human) Divine Form (Even Recollected, or, Otherwise, Materially Represented, In photographic, or Any Other Materially Fabricated Murti Form) Is A Necessary Agent Of My Avataric Divine Teaching-Work and My Avataric Divine Blessing-Work. Even Then, or Always Now, I Can Be Felt and Found By My By-Me-Spiritually-Initiated Listening Devotees, Hearing Devotees, and Seeing Devotees—At Any Distance (In space or time) From My Avatarically-Born Bodily (Human) Divine Form. If Only The By-Me-Spiritually-Initiated Heart Of My Devotee Opens (and Is Directed) To Me—Via The Feeling-Contemplation Of My Own (Now, and Forever Hereafter, Given) Human Sign (Even As Recollected or, Otherwise, Represented), and Via The Recorded Documents Of My Avatarically Self-Revealed (and Ever-Speaking) Divine Word, and The Material Fabrications Of My Avatarically Self-Revealed (and Ever-Me-Revealing) Divine Image-Art, and The Recorded Stories Of My Avatarically Self-Manifested (and Ever-Living) Divine Leelas, and (As Given) Via The Formally Acknowledged and Truly By-Me-Spiritually-Empowered Instruments and Agents Of All My Avataric Divine Blessing-Work—Then I Can Be Found.

I Am Always Merely Present, Prior To My Avatarically-Born Bodily (Human) Divine Form—Even As The One (and Inherently Perfectly) Self-Existing (or Transcendental) and Self-Radiant (or Inherently Spiritual) and Self-Evidently Divine Form (or Self-Condition, or Source-Condition). My Apparently Mortal Bodily (Human) Divine Form (or Apparent Body-Mind) Is Both A Temporary Form Of Agency (Physically Continuing Only Until The End Of The Physical Lifetime Of My Avatarically-Born Bodily Human Divine Form) and A "Timeless" Form Of Agency—To Be Recollected (or, Otherwise, Represented, and Contemplated, In Materially Fabricated Murti Form—or Even Found In subtle Vision) After (and Forever After) The Physical Lifetime Of My Avatarically-Born Bodily (Human) Divine Form. Therefore, My Avatarically-Born Bodily (Human) Divine Form Is A Primary Means Whereby My Avatarically Self-Revealed (Transcendental, Inherently Spiritual, Inherently egoless, and Self-Evidently Divine) Person (or Reality) Is Revealed (or Effectively Made Obvious). And This Avataric Divine Self-Revelation Of The Obvious Can Only Be Given As A Gift—Because, By Seeking The Truth, Mankind Only Wanders From It.

I Cannot Be Bodily Alive (In My Own Physically Mortal Form) Forever, but (Once I Am Avatarically Born) My Bodily (Human) Divine Form Can Be Recollected (or, Otherwise, Represented) For As Long As My Listening Devotees, My Hearing Devotees, and My Seeing Devotees Choose To Continue So To Do. Therefore, Even In My (photographically, or otherwise technically, or even artistically, Rendered) Representational (or Murti) Form (or, Otherwise, In Vision), I Can Be Bodily (and Humanly) Present In Company With All My Listening Devotees, and Hearing Devotees, and Seeing Devotees, Forever. Nevertheless, I (Myself) Am Always Already Spiritually, Transcendentally, Divinely, and Unconditionally Present—and (Therefore) The True Heart Of My By-Me-Spiritually-Initiated Listening Devotee, Hearing Devotee, or Seeing Devotee Can Ever Feel My Eternal Divine Spiritual Blessing (or Always Already Given and Self-Radiant Help), By Resort To Me Via All The By-Me-Revealed and By-Me-Given Means Of The Only-By-Me Revealed and Given Way Of The Heart (or Way Of Adidam).

By All The Means I Have Revealed and Given, the Total body-mind Of My Every Listening Devotee, My Every Hearing Devotee, and My Every Seeing Devotee Will Always (Forever) Be Able To Directly Identify and Progressively Realize My Avatarically Self-Revealed Transcendental, Inherently Spiritual, Inherently egoless, and Self-Evidently Divine Person (or Real Condition) In My Avataric Divine Heart-Company. And The Memory and Representation Of My Avatarically Self-Revealed Divine Word, The Memory and Representation Of My Avatarically Self-Manifested Divine Play Of Acts (or Leelas), and The Memory and Representation Of My Avatarically-Born Bodily (Human) Divine Appearance Will Always Persist To Help (If These Are Preserved By The Total Gathering Of All My Formally Acknowledged Listening Devotees, Hearing Devotees, and Seeing Devotees).

My Avatarically Self-Revealed and Heart-Given Divine Word, The Avatarically Self-Manifested Leelas Of All My Divine Work, and The Visible Divine Form Of My Avatarically-Born Physical Appearance Are Blessed By Me To Persist (Recorded By Various gross and subtle Means) Even After My Human Body Has Died In this world. Therefore, If (or When) You Are My Listening Devotee, My Hearing Devotee, or My Seeing Devotee, Enter Into Sacramental, Ceremonial, and Other Formal (or Informal) Occasions each and every day. In This Manner (and During Such Occasions), Regard My (Always Me-Revealing) Avataric Divine Word (By Recitation, or By Listening To Recitation, or By Chant and Song), and Confess "Narcissus" (Your Own Persistent ego-"I", or self-Contraction), and Read (or Recite) My Avataric Divine Leelas, Listen To The Telling Of My Avataric Divine Leelas, Tell (and Chant, and Sing) My Avataric Divine Leelas (Including Your Own Confession Of Lessons Received, and The Lessons That Have Been Received and Confessed By others), and (In All Of This) Rightly Regard, Celebrate, and (By Feeling) Contemplate My Avatarically-Born Bodily (Human) Divine Form (Even Via Its Representation), and (In Due Course) My Avatarically Self-Transmitted Spiritual (and Always Blessing) Divine Presence, and (Ultimately) My Avatarically Self-Revealed (and Very, and

Transcendental, and Perfectly Subjective, and Inherently Spiritual, and Inherently egoless, and Inherently Perfect, and Self-Evidently Divine) State.

If (or When) You Are My Listening Devotee, My Hearing Devotee, or My Seeing Devotee, Use Your Ability To "Locate" Me By Means Of The Concentrated Study (and "Consideration") Of My (Always Me-Revealing) Avataric Divine Word.

If (or When) You Are My Listening Devotee, My Hearing Devotee, or My Seeing Devotee, Use Your Ability To "Locate" Me By Means Of Devotional attention To The Avataric Divine Leelas Of My Effective and Divinely Liberating Work (Made By Avataric Self-Sacrifice and The Ordeal Of Avataric Self-Submission To the world and To all those who Resort To Me).

If (or When) You Are My Listening Devotee, My Hearing Devotee, or My Seeing Devotee, Use Your Ability To "Locate" Me By Means Of Devotional attention To My Avatarically-Born Bodily (Human) Divine Form (Directly, If and Whenever It Is Possible and Appropriate For You To Be Given physical Access To My Avatarically-Born Bodily Human Divine Form, and, Otherwise, As My Avatarically-Born Bodily Human Divine Form Is Made Specifically Visible By physical, or Even mental, Forms Of Representation).

My Listening Devotee, My Hearing Devotee, or My Seeing Devotee Is (By This Practice, and By Every By-Me-Given Practice Of The Way Of The Heart) To Become (and Then To Be) My Devotee In Truth.

Therefore, My By-Me-Spiritually-Initiated Listening Devotee, Hearing Devotee, or Seeing Devotee Is (In every moment) To Be Established In Perpetual Satsang With Me (Via The Primary Practice Of Searchlessly Beholding Me) and (Thereby, Progressively) In The Great Devotionally Responsive Heart-Practice Of Ruchira Avatara Bhakti Yoga, Which Is Devotion To (and Devotional Communion With) Me, As and Through The Devotionally Me-Recognizing, and Devotionally To-Me-Responding, and Constant Counter-egoic, and Even Total psycho-physical, Practice Of ego-Surrendering, ego-Forgetting, and, More and More (and, Ultimately, Most Perfectly), ego-Transcending Devotion To Me, and Devotional Communion With Me—Adi Da Samraj, The Ruchira Avatar, The Da Avatar, The Love-Ananda Avatar, The Divine Heart-Master, The Ruchira Siddha-Guru Of each and all Of My Devotees. Such Practice Requires (and Is) The moment to moment Fulfillment Of My Great Admonition To All My Devotees (To Always Invoke Me, Feel Me, Breathe Me, and Serve Me), and This Constantly Exercised Via The Surrender, The Forgetting, and The Transcending Of the self-Contracted body, and self-Contracted emotion (or all of self-Contracted, and Reactive, and, Altogether, limited, feeling), and self-Contracted mind (Even At its Root, Which Is attention itself), and Even every self-Contracted breath, and (Altogether) Even all of Separate (and Separative) self

In moment to moment (and Truly, or Unlimitedly, Heart-Felt, and Whole bodily Receptive, and Fully breathing, and Only-By-Me Distracted) Devotional Remembrance Of Me and Direct Devotional Surrender To Me.

In The Only-By-Me Revealed and Given Way Of The Heart (or Way Of Adidam), The Always First Exercise (Of My Listening Devotee, My Hearing Devotee, or My Seeing Devotee) Is (At all times) To Feel (and Even To Visualize, or, Otherwise, To Generally Perceive or Feel) Me As The Avatarically-Born Divine Ishta (or "Chosen One") Of The Heart (Felt At The Heart, From The Heart, and Even By Whole bodily Feeling), Sitting (or Otherwise Bodily Appearing) Before one (and In Front Of The Heart, and, Ultimately, At The Heart) In My Self-Existing and Self-Radiant Divine Samadhi. Therefore, In This Manner (By Heart-Communion With Me), My Every Devotee Should (and In Due Course, and, Then, More and More, By Means Of My Avatarically Self-Transmitted Divine Spiritual Grace, and As My Avatarically Self-Transmitted Divine Spiritual Grace Will Have It) Constantly Feel and (Progressively) Contemplate My Avatarically-Born Bodily (Human) Divine Form, My Avatarically Self-Transmitted Spiritual (and Always Blessing) Divine Presence, and My Avatarically Self-Revealed (and Very, and Transcendental, and Perfectly Subjective, and Inherently Spiritual, and Inherently egoless, and Inherently Perfect, and Self-Evidently Divine) State—and (In Due Course) Be Thereby (Progressively) Spiritually Attracted, Spiritually Embraced, and Spiritually Awakened, By Me.

The Ruchira Avatara Puja—Which Has Been Freely Developed By Me From The Ancient and Traditional Sat-Guru Puja, and Which (In One or Another Of Its Given Forms, and Primarily In The Form Of Either The Ruchira Avatara Paduka Puja Or The Ruchira Avatara Murti Puja) Is To Be Performed (According To My Instructions) daily, or (Otherwise) Attended daily (With Full Heart-Participation), By All My Formally Acknowledged Listening Devotees, Hearing Devotees, and Seeing Devotees—Is (In The Way Of The Heart) The Heart-Celebrated Re-Installation Of My Divine Ishta-Form and The Sacramental Re-Establishment Of The Divine Ishta-Circumstance Of Satsang With Me. Then This Divine Ishta-Form—Of My Avatarically-Born Bodily (Human) Divine Form, and (Eventually, or More and More) My Avatarically Self-Transmitted Spiritual (and Always Blessing) Divine Presence, and (Ultimately) My Avatarically Self-Revealed (and Very, and Transcendental, and Perfectly Subjective, and Inherently Spiritual, and Inherently egoless, and Inherently Perfect, and Self-Evidently Divine) State—Is To Be Constantly (and By Random Intention) Recollected (or Heart-Felt) In daily life and Meditation By My Each and Every Formally Acknowledged Listening Devotee, Hearing Devotee, and Seeing Devotee—Such That (Progressively) My Avatarically-Born Bodily

(Human) Divine Form, My Avatarically Self-Transmitted Spiritual (and Always Blessing) Divine Presence, and My Avatarically Self-Revealed (and Very, and Transcendental, and Perfectly Subjective, and Inherently Spiritual, and Inherently egoless, and Inherently Perfect, and Self-Evidently Divine) State Are (For My Listening Devotee, My Hearing Devotee, or My Seeing Devotee) The Constantly Felt (and Contemplated) Company (and Realization) Of The Heart.

This Great Practice Is (By Practice) To Become The Capability To Be Always In The Primal Circumstance Of My Avataric Divine Heart-Transmission, and (Thus and Thereby) In Devotional (and, In Due Course, Spiritual) Communion With Me.

This Primal Circumstance Is (Itself) The Sacred Space Wherein My Listening Devotee, My Hearing Devotee, and My Seeing Devotee Must Practice—By Always Finding Me.

This Sacred Space Is The Spiritually "Bright" (and Altogether Necessary) Circumstance Of (Eventually) Perpetual and Fullest Satsang, and (Most Ultimately) Of The Divinely (and Inherently) Most Perfect Demonstration Of The Supreme Divine Heart-Yoga Of Ruchira Avatara Bhakti.

In Order To Generate Instrumentality and Agency For My Blessing-Work, I Freely Transmit My Avataric Divine Heart-Blessing (or Mere and "Bright" Spiritual Presence) To all who Truly (and Formally) Practice As My By-Me-Spiritually-Initiated Listening Devotees, Hearing Devotees, and Seeing Devotees—Even (In every then present-time) After (and Forever After) The Physical Lifetime Of My Avatarically-Born Bodily (Human) Divine Form. Therefore, Forever, My (Formally Acknowledged) By-Me-Spiritually-Initiated Listening Devotees, Hearing Devotees, and Seeing Devotees Should Always (or As Possible) Gather Together daily—and each one Should Attend To The Feeling-Contemplation Of My Avatarically-Born Bodily (Human) Divine Form, My Avatarically Self-Transmitted Spiritual (and Always Blessing) Divine Presence, and My Avatarically Self-Revealed (and Very, and Transcendental, and Perfectly Subjective, and Inherently Spiritual, and Inherently egoless, and Inherently Perfect, and Self-Evidently Divine) State. In This Manner, When You Are Truly Practicing (and Are Formally Acknowledged) As My By-Me-Spiritually-Initiated Listening Devotee, Hearing Devotee, or Seeing Devotee, Let Your Own body-mind Be Open To Me. Each and all Of My True (and Formally Acknowledged) By-Me-Spiritually-Initiated Listening Devotees, Hearing Devotees, and Seeing Devotees Should Be Thus Open To Me. In This Manner, Even My Each and Every (Formally Acknowledged) By-Me-Spiritually-Initiated Listening Devotee, Hearing Devotee, and Seeing Devotee Should (Transparently, and Really Effectively, By Means Of Participation In The Collective Sacramental Invocation Of Me That Is Entered Into, daily, By each and all Of My Formally Acknowledged By-Me-Spiritually-Initiated Devotees) Serve The Process Of Spiritually Receiving Me In The Case Of All Other (Such) By-Me-Spiritually-Initiated Listening Devotees, Hearing Devotees, and Seeing Devotees—and All (Such) By-Me-Spiritually-Initiated Listening Devotees, Hearing Devotees, and Seeing Devotees (Together, Collectively) Should, Thus (daily, Transparently, and Really Effectively), Serve The Process Of Spiritually Receiving Me In The Case Of Each and Every (Such) By-Me-Spiritually-Initiated Listening Devotee, Hearing Devotee, and Seeing Devotee.

Avatar Adi Da Samraj
The Mountain Of Attention Sanctuary, 2000

SUTRA

35

And Now My Divinely Self-Revealing Avataric Divine Self-Confession, Call, and Admonition To All My Formally Acknowledged and By-Me-Spiritually-Initiated Listening Devotees, Hearing Devotees, and Seeing Devotees—who Truly, Actively, Spiritually, and Constantly (and Always Whole bodily) Invoke Me, Feel Me, Breathe Me, and (Altogether) Attend To Me and Serve Me.

Conscious Light Is The <u>Only</u> Reality—The One and Only Real God.

Conscious Light Is Always Already The Case.

Conscious Light Is Self-Existing (<u>As</u> Consciousness Itself).

Consciousness (Itself) Is Self-Radiant (<u>As</u> Perfectly Subjective and Inherently Spiritual Self-"Brightness"—or The Self-Evident Happiness, or Inherent Love-Bliss-Fullness, Of Conscious Light Itself).

Conscious Light Is The Native (or Inherent) "Point Of View" (or Timeless and Unchanging Self-Position) Of Reality (Itself).

If conditions arise as conditional experience, they Are Merely Apparent Modifications Of The Inherent Spiritual "Brightness" (or Love-Bliss-Radiance) Of Conscious Light Itself.

If conditions arise as conditional experience, they Are Not "Different" From Consciousness (Itself)—Because they <u>Are</u> Conscious Light (Itself).

Therefore, Consciousness (Itself) Does Not "Create" the world of conditional experience.

Consciousness (Itself) Merely <u>Coincides</u> With the world of conditional experience.

In The Context Of any moment of conditionally arising experience, Conscious Light Is Always Already Merely Present (In Inherent and Perfect Coincidence With all presently arising conditional experience) <u>As</u> Consciousness Itself (Merely Present In The Witness-Position, or Irreducible and Perfectly Subjective Self-Position), and <u>As</u> The Real (and Merely-Witnessing) Self (or Indivisible, Non-Separate, and Utterly Non-Objective Self-Condition) Of The Apparently Separate ego-"I" (or conditional body-mind), and <u>As</u> The Self-Existing and Self-Radiant Source-Condition Of all conditionally arising objects, forms, conditions, and states.

The Only Real Self Is Consciousness Itself.

The Only Perfect Understanding (and Perfect Realization) Of conditionally arising experience Is That Which Is Obvious (or Self-Evident) When Conscious Light Is "Located" As The Principle (or The Most Prior, and Inherently egoless, or Non-Separate, "Point Of View") In Coincidence With every moment of conditionally arising experience.

Even By Means Of Objective Analysis Of conditionally Apparent objects, conditions, and states, It Is Revealed That all conditionally arising objects, conditions, and states Are conditional (or space-time-Measured, and Always changing, and Never Finalized or Perfected) Modifications Of Fundamental Energy (or Universally Evident Light).

In The Most Perfect (or Seventh Stage) Realization Of The Only-By-Me Revealed and Given Way Of The Heart (or Way Of Adidam), Consciousness (Itself) Is (Itself) Realized To Be Always Already (Perfectly Subjectively) Identical To Fundamental Energy (or Universally Evident Light) Itself (Always Already Boundlessly Self-Radiant, As Love-Bliss-"Brightness", or Conscious Light Itself).

Therefore, In The Context Of The Only-By-Me Revealed and Given Seventh Stage Of Life (In The Way Of The Heart), all conditionally arising objects, conditions, and states (Whether Apparently objective Or Apparently subjective) Are Always Immediately (and, Necessarily, Divinely) Self-Recognized In and As The Perfectly Subjective Sphere and Light and Love-Bliss-"Brightness" Of Consciousness (Itself).

In The Only-By-Me Revealed and Given Seventh Stage Of Life (In The Way Of The Heart), Consciousness (Itself) Is Most Perfectly Self-Realized, As The Inherently Non-Separate (and, Therefore, Always Both Universal and Omni-Present) and One and all-and-All-Including (and, Therefore, Always Both egoless and "Local") and Self-Evidently Divine (or Non-Causative, Non-Objective, Non-Separate, Non-"Different", and Merely Existing) Conscious Light, Which Is The Self-Condition Of the conditionally arising body-mind and The Source-Condition (and Substance) Of the conditionally arising world.

To perceive the conditionally arising world Is To perceive Divine Energy (or Conscious Light).

The presently unperceived world of conditionally arising conditions (or The Cosmic Domain Of All Possibilities, space-time-Demonstrated In The Universally Unfolding Dynamic Display Of all possible opposites) Is Existing Merely As Conscious Light (or Divine Energy) Itself.

When the conditionally arising world arises as conditional experience, The Event Is Darshan (or "Sighting", or perceiving) Of Conscious Light (or Divine Energy) Itself.

Consciousness (Itself) Is (Itself) The Perfectly Subjective "Knowing" (and "Knowledge") Of Divine Energy (or Conscious Light Itself)—and Divine Energy (or Conscious Light Itself) Is The Self-Radiant Form and Shape Of Consciousness (Itself).

Consciousness (Itself) Is (Itself) The Perfectly Subjective "Sighting" (and "Vision") Of Conscious Light (Itself)—and Conscious Light (Itself) Is The Inherent "Brightness" Of Consciousness (Itself).

Conscious Light Is (Itself) The Perfectly Subjective Feeling Of Love-Bliss (Itself)—and Love-Bliss (Itself) Is The Heart Of Consciousness (Itself).

In The By-My-Avataric-Divine-Spiritual-Grace-Given Awakening Of The Only-By-Me Revealed and Given Seventh Stage Of Life (In The Only-By-Me Revealed and Given Way Of The Heart, or Way Of Adidam), Consciousness (Itself), Which Is Beheld (or Merely Witnessed) As Divine Energy (or Conscious Light Itself), Is Self-Realized (and Self-Radiant) As Love-Bliss (Itself)—and all conditionally arising objects, conditions, and states (and even the Total body-mind) Are Always (Inherently, and Immediately, and, Necessarily, Divinely) Self-Recognized In and As Always Already Self-Existing and Spiritually "Bright" (or Self-Radiant) and Inherently Indivisible Love-Bliss-Consciousness (or Conscious Light Itself).

Consciousness (Itself), Apparently Separated From Its Own Love-Bliss-Radiance By the conditions of the body-mind and the world, Seeks (Like Narcissus, By Separative Acts Of self-Contraction, or The Avoidance Of Relationship) and Waits (Like Narcissus, By Concentrating On the experiential, and Always changing, state of the conditionally arising body-mind-self) For Love-Bliss (or Happiness) To Come To Consciousness (and To the body-mind) From the world.

When the Total psycho-physical ego-"I" Is Most Perfectly Transcended In Consciousness (Itself), the Total world Is (Inherently, and Necessarily) Divinely Self-Recognized In and As Consciousness (Itself), and (Inherently, and Necessarily) Transcended (and, At Last, Divinely Outshined) In and As The Self-Radiance (or Inherent Spiritual Energy, or Divine True Light) Of Consciousness (Itself), Which Is Conscious Light (or Happiness, or Love-Bliss) Itself.

Such Is My Avataric Divine Self-Revelation To all-and-All.

I Am Not The "Deity" Of conventional Religion.

I Am Not The "God" Of the ego-"I".

I Am Consciousness (Itself)—Which Is The One and Only Reality, or Conscious Light (Itself).

By Means Of My Avataric Divine Self-Revelation In The Cosmic Domain, I Divinely (and Uniquely, and Most Perfectly, and Completely) Reveal That

Conscious Light (Itself), Which Is Consciousness (Itself), Is The One and Only Reality, Truth, Happiness, and Real God.

Therefore, Always Heart-Recognize My Divinely Self-Revealing Avataric Form, and Presence, and State Of Person With Real (and Always Truly Heart-Felt) Devotion.

Always Attend To Me and Serve Me—and (By Means Of My Avataric Divine Spiritual Grace) Realize Me (By Devotionally Recognizing Me, and Devotionally Responding To Me, and Constantly Listening To Me, and Truly Hearing Me, and egolessly Seeing Me—and, At Last, Most Perfectly "Locating" Me, Beyond All "Difference").

By Always Feeling (and, Thereby, Always Contemplating) My Avatarically-Born Bodily (Human) Divine Form, My Avatarically Self-Transmitted Spiritual (and Always Blessing) Divine Presence, and My Avatarically Self-Revealed (and Very, and Transcendental, and Perfectly Subjective, and Inherently Spiritual, and Inherently egoless, and Inherently Perfect, and Self-Evidently Divine) State—Always Feel, Breathe, Love, Trust, Have Faith In, Surrender To, and Realize Indivisible Oneness With Me, Both As The Divine and Very Self-Person (or Self-Existing Consciousness Itself, Beyond and Prior To Your ego-"I") and As The Divine and Conscious Light (or The Divine Body Of Spirit-Energy, or Self-Radiant "Bright" Love-Bliss Itself—Above, and Surrounding, and Pervading Your body-mind).

By Always Feeling (and, Thereby, Always Contemplating) My Avatarically-Born Bodily (Human) Divine Form, My Avatarically Self-Transmitted Spiritual (and Always Blessing) Divine Presence, and My Avatarically Self-Revealed (and Very, and Transcendental, and Perfectly Subjective, and Inherently Spiritual, and Inherently egoless, and Inherently Perfect, and Self-Evidently Divine) State—Always Feel, Breathe, Love, Trust, Have Faith In, Surrender To, and Realize Indivisible Oneness With Me, As The Self-Existing and Self-Radiant Divine Person (or Very Being) Who "Lives" (or Pervades and "Breathes" and Is) Your Apparent body-mind, all Apparently other beings, and all Apparent worlds.

By Always Feeling (and, Thereby, Always Contemplating) My Avatarically-Born Bodily (Human) Divine Form, My Avatarically Self-Transmitted Spiritual (and Always Blessing) Divine Presence, and My Avatarically Self-Revealed (and Very, and Transcendental, and Perfectly Subjective, and Inherently Spiritual, and Inherently egoless, and Inherently Perfect, and Self-Evidently Divine) State—Always Allow Me To Stand As all that arises, and (Thus) To Stand Even As Your Own body-mind.

If You (Truly) Always Feel (and, Thereby, Always Contemplate) My Avatarically-Born Bodily (Human) Divine Form, My Avatarically Self-Transmitted

Spiritual (and Always Blessing) Divine Presence, and My Avatarically Self-Revealed (and Very, and Transcendental, and Perfectly Subjective, and Inherently Spiritual, and Inherently egoless, and Inherently Perfect, and Self-Evidently Divine) State With Love and Faith (Altogether Rightly, Truly, Fully, and Fully Devotionally Recognizing Me, and Heart-Responding To Me, and With No Withholding), The Only-By-Me Revealed and Given Way (or Process) Associated With Transcendental, Inherently Spiritual, and Most Perfect Divine Self-Realization and Liberation Will Be Given To You, By Me—Progressively, Entirely, and Exactly.

Therefore, Even From The Beginning Of Your Practice Of The Only-By-Me Revealed and Given Way Of The Heart—Always Feel (and Thereby Contemplate) My Avatarically-Born Bodily (Human) Divine Form, My Avatarically Self-Transmitted Spiritual (and Always Blessing) Divine Presence, and My Avatarically Self-Revealed (and Very, and Transcendental, and Perfectly Subjective, and Inherently Spiritual, and Inherently egoless, and Inherently Perfect, and Self-Evidently Divine) State, and, Thus, Give Your conditional self (or Release Your self-Contraction) To Me, The Spiritually "Bright" Heart-Revealed One, Who Is Always Already Divinely Self-Realized (As Self-Existing Consciousness Itself) and Always Already Divinely Free (As Self-Radiant Love-Bliss, or Conscious Light Itself).

By This Feeling-Contemplation, My Self-Existing and Self-Radiant Person, Condition, and State Will Be Realized By You—Progressively, As My Free Gift To You.

By This Feeling-Contemplation, You Will (By Means Of My Avatarically Self-Transmitted Divine Spiritual Grace) See Me Perfectly At Last, As "Atma-Murti"—The "Form" and The "Presence" That Is Inherent Happiness (or Self-Radiant "Bright" Love-Bliss, or Conscious Light, Itself), and The "State" That Is Merely Being (or Self-Existing Consciousness Itself). And You Will Thus (Inherently, and Inherently Most Perfectly) Transcend The Illusions Of Separateness and Relatedness and "Difference".

Therefore, Feeling-Contemplation Of My Avatarically-Born Bodily (Human) Divine Form, My Avatarically Self-Transmitted Spiritual (and Always Blessing) Divine Presence, and My Avatarically Self-Revealed (and Very, and Transcendental, and Perfectly Subjective, and Inherently Spiritual, and Inherently egoless, and Inherently Perfect, and Self-Evidently Divine) State Is The Only-By-Me Revealed and Given Secret Of All My (Formally Acknowledged) True By-Me-Spiritually-Initiated Listening Devotees, Hearing Devotees, and Seeing Devotees.

This Great Heart-Principle Is The Foundation Of All Practice In The Way Of Adidam (Which Is The One and Only By-Me-Revealed and By-Me-Given Way Of The Heart).

Therefore, By This Great Heart-Principle, and By All The Means I Have Given and Always Give—each and all Of My (Formally Acknowledged) By-Me-Spiritually-Initiated Listening Devotees, Hearing Devotees, and Seeing Devotees Will Love Me, Serve Me, Surrender the ego-self To Me, and Always Heartily Receive Me. And, By This Authentic Practice, The Total (Formally Acknowledged) Gathering Of My By-Me-Spiritually-Initiated Listening Devotees, Hearing Devotees, and Seeing Devotees Will (each and all) Always and Constantly (Now, and Forever Hereafter) Celebrate My Good Company—and they Will, At Last, Most Perfectly Realize Indivisible and Indestructible Oneness With Me.

Avatar Adi Da Samraj
Adidam Samrajashram, 2003

SUTRA 36

Every Developmental Stage Of The Only-By-Me Revealed and Given Way Of The Heart (or Way Of Adidam) Is Built Upon Two Co-Equal (and Always Devotionally Responsive—or Devotionally Me-Recognizing and Devotionally To-Me-Responding) Exercises, Performed In The ego-Surrendering, ego-Forgetting, and, More and More (and, Ultimately, Most Perfectly), ego-Transcending Manner, Both In Formal Meditation and In The General Context Of daily life. These Two Devotionally Responsive Exercises Are The "Conscious Process" (Which Relates To The Consciousness-Dimension Of Existence—and Which Functions, Principally, In The Context Of The Horizontal Domain, or The Tripartite Heart-Plane, Of the conditionally Manifested body-mind) and "Conductivity" Practice (Which Relates To The Energy-Dimension Of Existence—and Which Functions, Principally, In The Context Of The Vertical Domain, or The psycho-physically Extended Plane, Of the conditionally Manifested body-mind).

From The Beginning (Of, First, Novice Student-Beginner Practice, and, Then, Fully Established Student-Beginner Practice) Of The Only-By-Me Revealed and Given Way Of The Heart (or Way Of Adidam), The Practice Of "Conductivity" Takes The Form Of All The Many By-Me-Given functional, practical, relational, and Cultural Modes Of Necessary self-Discipline, Including Technical "Conductivity" Practices That (Specifically) Exercise Natural energies. In The By-Me-Spiritually-Activated Stages Of The Way Of The Heart, All Such (functional, practical, relational, and Technical) "Conductivity" Practices Become Both Natural-energy Practices and Spirit-"Conductivity" Practices. And Other Technical Spirit-"Conductivity" Practices Are Also Added To The Total Discipline, In The Seeing Stages Of The Way Of The Heart.

Through The Progressive and Artfully Combined Exercises Of The "Conscious Process" and Spirit-"Conductivity" (In The By-Me-Spiritually-Activated Practice Of The Way Of The Heart), body, and emotion (and feeling, itself), and breath, and speech, and all of mind (or of conceptual and perceptual thoughts), and attention itself Must Be Responsively (and, Thus, Devotionally) Yielded (or Relaxed) Into My Avatarically Self-Transmitted Divine Spirit-Fullness.

In The Way Of The Heart, The To-Me-Responsive Devotional Practice Of Spirit-"Conductivity" Is, In Its "General" (or By-Me-Commonly-Given) Form, An Exercise Of body, and emotion (and feeling, itself), and Also breath—but Even speech, mind, and attention Also Become Surrendered Into My Avatarically Self-Transmitted Divine Spirit-Current (and, Ultimately, Into My Avatarically Self-Revealed Transcendental, Inherently Spiritual, Inherently egoless, and Self-Evidently Divine Self-Condition Of Self-Existing and Self-Radiant Consciousness, or Feeling-Being, Itself) Whenever The To-Me-Responsive Devotional Practice Of Spirit-"Conductivity" Is Rightly (Devotionally and Artfully) Combined With The To-Me-Responsive Devotional Practice Of The "Conscious Process".

Once You Have Become Formally Prepared To Practice One or Another Form Of The Only-By-Me Revealed and Given "Conscious Process" Of The Way Of The Heart (Whereby attention Is, Constantly, To Be Responsively Turned To Me, Such That all mental activity Is Transcended In Me), and (Coincidently) Once You Have Become Prepared To Practice The Only-By-Me Revealed and Given "General" (or By-Me-Commonly-Given) Form Of Spirit-"Conductivity" In The Way Of The Heart (Whereby emotion, perceptually active body, and breath Are, Constantly, To Be Responsively Turned To Me, Such That all emotional, bodily physical, and breathing forms of self-Contraction Are Surrendered To Me, and Transcended In Me), You Must Constantly Practice Both The "Conscious Process" and The "General" Form Of Spirit-"Conductivity", In Artful Combination With One Another.

Your Obligation Relative To "General" Spirit-"Conductivity" Practice Is (Upon Formal By-Me-Given Spiritual Initiation, and Thereafter) To Responsively (and, Thus, Devotionally) Yield (or Relax) emotion (or The Very, and Profoundly Feeling, Heart Itself), and the Total body, and every breath—Toward, and To, My Avatarically-Born Bodily (Human) Divine Form and Person and (Thus and Thereby) Into My Avatarically Self-Revealed Divine Spiritual Body and Person. Done In This Manner, The "General" Spirit-"Conductivity" Obligation and Exercise Is The Active Fulfillment Of The Admonition, From Me, To Feel Me Whole bodily—and, Thus and Thereby, To Feel Me <u>Spherically</u>, <u>Circularly</u>, and <u>Cyclically</u>.

The "General" Spirit-"Conductivity" Obligation Relative To emotion Is To Responsively (and, Thus, Devotionally) Yield (or Relax) all emotional feeling (or The Very, and Profoundly Feeling, Heart Itself), and, Indeed, Even the Whole body (or Total body-mind) itself, Toward, and To, My Avatarically-Born Bodily (Human) Divine Form and Person and (Thus and Thereby) Into My Avatarically Self-Transmitted Divine Spirit-Current Of Love-Bliss—Such That The Self-Radiant Spiritual Energy Of My Avatarically Self-Transmitted Divine Spirit-Current Of Love-Bliss Is Felt To Radiate Boundlessly, From The Heart, and, Indeed, From the body As A Whole, In all directions, To Infinity. Done In This Manner, The "General" Spirit-"Conductivity" Obligation and Exercise Is The Active Fulfillment Of The Admonition, From Me, To Feel Me Whole bodily—and Thus and Thereby, To Feel Me Spherically.

The "General" Spirit-"Conductivity" Obligation Relative To the Total body (itself) Is To Responsively (and, Thus, Devotionally) Yield (or Relax) the Total body (of perceptual self-awareness) Toward, and To, My Avatarically-Born Bodily (Human) Divine Form and Person and (Thus and Thereby) Into My Avatarically Self-Transmitted Divine Spirit-Current Of Love-Bliss—and, Thus, To bodily (and, Altogether, Tangibly) Feel My Avatarically Self-Transmitted Divine Spirit-Current Of Love-Bliss, Descending From Infinitely Above the head, and Pressing Into the body Via The Crown Of the head, and Descending (and Pressing Down) Into the body Via The Frontal Line (Progressively In-Filling the Total body, From The Crown Of the head To the bodily base—and, From Thence, Via The Spinal Line, From the bodily base To The Crown Of the head). Done In This Manner, The "General" Spirit-"Conductivity" Obligation and Exercise Is The Active Fulfillment Of The Admonition, From Me, To Feel Me Whole bodily—and, Thus and Thereby, To Feel Me Circularly.

And The "General" Spirit-"Conductivity" Obligation Relative To every breath Is To Responsively (and, Thus, Devotionally) Yield (or Relax) the Whole (or Total) breathing and Feeling body (or body-mind) Toward, and To, My Avatarically-Born Bodily (Human) Divine Form and Person and (Thus and Thereby) Into My Avatarically Self-Transmitted Divine Spirit-Current Of Love-Bliss—and, Thus, To bodily (and, Altogether, Tangibly) Feel My Avatarically Self-Transmitted Divine Spirit-Current Of Love-Bliss Via The breath-Cycle (Generally, Via The Devotionally Responsive Intentional Exercise Of inhalation and exhalation—the two Natural parts of the breath—Artfully Associated With The Frontal Line and The Spinal Line, the two Natural halves of the Whole, or Total psycho-physical, body). Done In This Manner, The "General" Spirit-"Conductivity" Obligation and Exercise Is The Active Fulfillment Of The Admonition, From Me, To Feel Me Whole bodily—and, Thus and Thereby, To Feel Me Cyclically.

In The Only-By-Me Revealed and Given Way Of The Heart, These Three Responsively Intentional Engagements Of "General Conductivity" Of My Avatarically Self-Transmitted Divine Spirit-Current Of Love-Bliss (Which Three Engagements I Herein Describe In Detail) Are (Generally) To Be Associated (In daily life and In Formal Meditation) With Principal bodily Attitudes Relative To The Circle Of the body-mind, and With (Either Spontaneous Or Intentional) bodily Locks (Exercised In Accordance With My Devotee's Formally Acknowledged Developmental Stage Of Practice In The Only-By-Me Revealed and Given Way Of The Heart, or Way Of Adidam). Thus, The bodily Lock In Which the eyes Are Up-Turned To The Ajna Door Is To Be Intentionally (and, Otherwise, Spontaneously) Practiced By All My By-Me-Spiritually-Initiated Devotees (but Always Only In Specific Response To The Actual, Tangibly perceived Reception Of My Avatarically Self-Transmitted Divine Spiritual Presence, Descending From Infinitely Above the body and the mind). The bodily Lock Of the tongue and chin and throat and The bodily Lock Of the bodily base Are To Be Practiced By All My By-Me-Spiritually-Initiated Devotees (As A Random Intentional Exercise, and, Otherwise, Also In Spontaneous Response To The Actual, Tangibly perceived, Reception Of My Avatarically Self-Transmitted Divine Spirit-Current Of Love-Bliss). And The bodily Lock Of the tongue and chin and throat and The bodily Lock Of the bodily base Should Also Be Randomly Exercised By My Novice Student-Beginner and Fully Established Student-Beginner Devotees—In Association With The "General Conductivity" Of <u>Natural</u> energy.

In The Only-By-Me Revealed and Given Way Of The Heart (or Way Of Adidam), The bodily Attitude Of Frontal Receptivity (Downward, head To bodily base, and Even To the toes) Is (By Random Application) To Be Constantly Maintained In daily life and In Formal Meditation. And, Also, The Spinal Line Is (By Random Application) To Be Constantly Relaxed (and, Generally, Allowed To Be Upwardly Polarized, From the bodily base, Toward The Crown Of the head). In The Midst Of Those Two Simultaneous bodily Attitudes, The Principal bodily Locks (Of The Ajna Door, the tongue and chin and throat, and the bodily base) Are, As A Constant bodily Discipline, To Be Responsively (and Artfully, or By Random Application) Maintained—As The Process Of Right "Conductivity" Requires (and Always In Accordance With My Herein Given Instructions).

The Yogic Lock Of The Ajna Door (Which Is To Be Responsively Practiced By All My By-Me-Spiritually-Initiated Devotees) Is A Centering Of attention In The Core (or Upper Central Region) Of the head, Between and Slightly Above and Deep Behind the eyes—Even, As Circumstances Permit, Letting the eyes Close and Turn Up and Back (To Prevent the Natural bodily energy and My Avatarically Self-Transmitted Divine Spirit-Energy From Discharging, or "Leaking Out", Via the eyes). The Yogic Lock Of the tongue and chin and throat (To Be Practiced By <u>All</u> My Devotees) Is A Pressing Of the tongue Lightly To the roof of the mouth, With the chin Pulled Down Somewhat (and, Generally, With the mouth closed, and With all breathing Exercised Via the nostrils), In Order To Rightly Conduct the breath-energy and (As The Case May Be) My Avatarically Self-Transmitted Current Of Divine Spirit-Presence Via the head and throat, and (When Necessary) To Lock the breath-energy and

(As The Case May Be) My Avatarically Self-Transmitted Current Of Divine Spirit-Presence Below the throat. The Yogic Lock Of the bodily base (Also To Be Practiced By All My Devotees) Is An Internal Upward Tensing (Either Brief and Constant Or, Otherwise, Brief and Repetitive) Applied To the bodily base, By Drawing In, Back, and Up, Via the genitals, the perineum, and the anus, and Toward The Spinal Line, and With the crown of the lower abdomen Simultaneously, and Lightly, Drawn In and Up—Such That An Unbroken Line (or Continuous Circuit) Of "Conductivity" Is Maintained Between The Frontal Line and The Spinal Line, Via the bodily base, and (In The Case Of My By-Me-Spiritually-Initiated Devotees) Such That The Fullness Of My Avatarically Self-Revealed Divine Spirit-Current Of Love-Bliss Is Allowed To Fill The Frontal Line, head To bodily base (and Even To the toes), Without Being Discharged or Lost By Breaking The Continuity Of The Circuit.

Generally, As Circumstances Require or (Otherwise) Permit (and Especially In The Circumstance Of Formal Meditation), "Conductivity" Practice (and The Practice Of The "Conscious Process") Should, In The Only-By-Me Revealed and Given Way Of The Heart, Be Engaged In A bodily Asana (or bodily Pose and Attitude) That Is spinally Upright and Straight, and In Which the body Is Firmly and Comfortably Seated, and Well-Supported, and Entirely Balanced, and, Altogether, Comfortably Aligned.

As A Further Development Of "General Conductivity" Practice, Any (or All) Of The Three (By-Me-Herein-Described) Responsively Intentional Engagements Of "General Conductivity" Of My Avatarically Self-Transmitted Divine Spirit-Current May Be Relaxed or Released (or Otherwise Gone Beyond) In any moment Of Practice (Especially In moments or periods Of Formal Meditation) In which The "Conscious Process" (and Spirit-"Conductivity" Itself) Progresses Into A Depth That Is Inherently (or, Otherwise, Progressively) Oblivious To The Various Degrees Of Such An Intentional Exercise.

When Practice Of The Only-By-Me Revealed and Given Way Of The Heart Begins In The Context Of The "Perfect Practice", Spirit-"Conductivity" Practice Becomes Associated (In The Context Of The Vertical Process and Structure) With The Matrix Of My Avatarically Self-Transmitted Divine Spiritual Presence (Infinitely Above The Total Crown Of the head) and (In The Context Of The Horizontal Process and Structure) With The Right Side Of The Heart. And, When Practice Of The Only-By-Me Revealed and Given Way Of The Heart Enters Into The Divinely Self-Realized Context Of The Only-By-Me Revealed and Given Seventh Stage Of Life, Spirit-"Conductivity" Practice Becomes Associated With The "Regenerated" Amrita Nadi.

In any moment Of Formal "General" Spirit-"Conductivity" Practice In The Only-By-Me Revealed and Given Way Of The Heart (or Way Of Adidam), You

(As My By-Me-Spiritually-Initiated Devotee) Are To Responsively (and, Thus, Devotionally) Yield (or Relax) speech, mind, and attention Into My Avatarically Self-Transmitted Divine Spirit-Current (and, Ultimately, Into My Avatarically Self-Revealed Transcendental, Inherently Spiritual, Inherently egoless, and Self-Evidently Divine Self-Condition Of Consciousness, or Feeling-Being, Itself)—and This Exercise Is (Generally, or, Otherwise, At Random, and Especially In The Context Of Formal Meditation) To Be Associated With (and Guided By) The "Conscious Process" Of Either Spiritually Activated self-Enquiry (and Re-Cognition) Or Spiritually Activated "True Prayer" Or (In The Context Of The "Perfect Practice" Of The Way Of The Heart) "Feeling-Enquiry". And Any and Every Such Practice Requires The Concentration Of speech, mind, and attention In The "Conscious Process" (and, Generally, In The Process Of Spirit-"Conductivity" Practice), Even (Eventually) To The Ultimate Degree Of Standing Perfectly Prior To all conditions, Inherently Indifferent To Whether they Are Positive Or Negative Or arising at all.

In The By-Me-Spiritually-Activated Stages Of The Only-By-Me Revealed and Given Way Of The Heart, The Fundamental Yoga Of The "General" Form Of Spirit-"Conductivity" (In My Avatarically Self-Transmitted, and Real-God-Revealing, or Reality-Revealing and Truth-Revealing, Divine Spiritual Presence) Is Fully Made Of The Three Parts (or Three Exercises) I Have Indicated.

Thus, The First Part (or Exercise) Of The "General" Form Of The By-Me-Spiritually-Activated Yoga Of Spirit-"Conductivity" Is Persistent (Devotionally Me-Recognizing and Devotionally To-Me-Responding) Heart-Surrender To Me, Actively Demonstrated As ego-Surrendering, ego-Forgetting, and, More and More (and, At Last, Most Perfectly), ego-Transcending Heart-Feeling-Surrender Of the Total body-mind Toward, and To, My Avatarically-Born Bodily (Human) Divine Form and Person, Constantly (and Whole bodily, or As A psycho-physical Totality) In-Filling and In-Filled With My Avatarically Self-Transmitted Divine Spirit-Current Of Love-Bliss, Such That The bodily (or psycho-physical) Totality Becomes Heart-Radiant With My Avatarically Self-Transmitted Divine Spirit-Fullness, and (Thus and Thereby) Radiates My Divine Fullness Of Love-Bliss In all directions (Boundlessly, or To Infinity)—Thus and Thereby Transcending all Reactive and limited emotions. This Is The First Part (or Exercise) Of The Three Parts Of Spirit-"Conductivity" Practice In The Only-By-Me Revealed and Given Way Of The Heart, and It Is (In The By-Me-Spiritually-Activated Stages Of The Way Of The Heart) The Natural (and The Original and Unobstructed) Heart-Attitude, To Be Practiced At all times, In Formal Meditation and In daily life.

The Second Part (or Exercise) Of The "General" Form Of The By-Me-Spiritually-Activated Yoga Of Spirit-"Conductivity" Is Persistent (Devotionally

Me-Recognizing and Devotionally To-Me-Responding) Relaxation Of the body Toward, and To, My Avatarically-Born Bodily (Human) Divine Form and Person and (Thus and Thereby) Into My Avatarically Self-Transmitted Divine Spirit-Current Of Love-Bliss, Which Is (By Means Of My Avatarically Self-Transmitted Divine Spiritual Grace) To Be Tangibly Felt Descending Into the body Via The Frontal Line (Downward, From Above The Crown Of the head To the bodily base—and Even To the toes). This Second Part (or Exercise) Of Spirit-"Conductivity" Practice Generally Includes The Spontaneous (and, Otherwise, Intentional) To-Me-Responsive Concentration and Surrender Of attention At The Ajna Door. And, When This Second Exercise Of The "General" Form Of Spirit-"Conductivity" Practice Becomes A Right and Constant and Spiritually Full Practice (In Formal Meditation and In daily life), The Spinal Line (From the bodily base) Always Remains Naturally Polarized To (and Relaxed Toward) The Brain Core (and Toward The Relaxed Crown Of the head, and Above), While The Frontal Line (From The Crown Of the Upwardly Open and Relaxed head) Is Always In An Upwardly Open and Downwardly Receptive Attitude (Such That The Frontal Line Is Always Naturally Polarized To, and Relaxed Toward, the bodily base, and Such That the frontal personality Is Generally Relaxed and Free Of Stress, and Such That The Frontal Line Operates Without Obstruction, Grounded In The bodily "Battery", or the crown of the lower abdomen, Approximately one and one-half inches Below the umbilical scar, and With the solar plexus Open and Expanded).

The Third Part (or Exercise) Of The "General" Form Of The By-Me-Spiritually-Activated Yoga Of Spirit-"Conductivity" Is Devotionally Me-Recognizing and Devotionally To-Me-Responding Spirit-"Conductivity" Via lung-breathing Exercises. The By-Me-Given "General" Practice Of lung-breathing Spirit-"Conductivity" Is The Exercise Of Freely (and, Generally, Rather Fully) inhaling (Downwards) In The Frontal Line (Pressing and Receiving the Natural bodily energy and My Avatarically Self-Transmitted Divine Spirit-Energy Downwards In The Frontal Line), Thus and Thereby Releasing Reactivity, Stress, and Obstruction, Such That The Frontal Line Becomes More and More Open, and More and More Full Of The Descending Flow (Polarized Toward the lower abdomen and the bodily base)—and, At Random, Freely exhaling Into The Spinal Line ("Throwing" the Natural bodily energy and My Avatarically Self-Transmitted Divine Spirit-Energy Upwards, Into and Via The Spinal Line, From the bodily base and, In A Generally Diffusive Manner, Toward the Total head and brain). The Basic Right and Fruitful "General" Practice (Of lung-breathing Spirit-"Conductivity") Is That Of Random breathing-"Conductivity" In The Receptive Frontal Line, With the Random inhalations (and Even With Random exhalations) Pressing Down, and

With Coincident Random Tensing Of the bodily base (In, Back, and, Spinally, Up), and With Subsequent Relaxing Of the Total body Into The Spinal Line (Generally, By exhaling Into The Spinal Line, and Lightly Tensing, or Pulling Up, the bodily base, and Lightly Pulling the crown of the lower abdomen In and Up), but (As A General Rule) Without Any Intentional Concentration (Of Natural bodily energy and My Avatarically Self-Transmitted Divine Spirit-Energy) In the head, but (Rather, In General) Only With The Spinal Line Simply Relaxed (Generally Upwardly, but Diffusely), and With The Concentration Of Natural bodily energy and My Avatarically Self-Transmitted Divine Spirit-Energy Retained (and Even Pressed Down) As A Fullness In the abdomen (and Below), and With the bodily base Kept Unbroken, and Strong, and Full (By Means Of A Random, Intentional Upward Tensing Of it), and With A Feeling Of Spinal Fullness In the hips and the lower back (Extending Upwards To A Point In the spine That Is Approximately At The Same Height As the navel In The Frontal Line). This Exercise Of lung-breathing Spirit-"Conductivity" Is Built Upon (and Intended To Support and Extend) The Work Of The First Two Parts (or Forms, or Exercises) Of The "General" Form Of The By-Me-Spiritually-Activated Yoga Of Spirit-"Conductivity". The Exercise Of lung-breathing Spirit-"Conductivity" Is To Be Engaged During The By-Me-Spiritually-Activated Exercise Of self-Enquiry, and It Is To Be Engaged (Either At Random Or Repetitively, According To My Specific Instructions Relative To The Particular Exercise) During The By-Me-Spiritually-Activated Exercise Of "True Prayer". Like The First Two Parts (or Exercises) Of The "General" Form Of The By-Me-Spiritually-Activated Yoga Of Spirit-"Conductivity", The "General" Exercise Of lung-breathing Spirit-"Conductivity" Is To Be Engaged Not Only In The Context Of Formal Meditation Practice but Also In The Context (and ordinary course) Of daily life (and, Generally, In Association With The "Conscious Process", but Also, Sometimes, or In some moments, By Itself, Just As The "Conscious Process" May, Sometimes, or In some moments, Be Engaged Without The Intentional Exercise Of Spirit-"Conductivity").

It May, In some (Relatively Rare) moments (Either In The Context Of Formal Meditation Practice or In The Context, and ordinary course, Of daily life), Be Found Useful To Intensify The Exercise Of lung-breathing Spirit-"Conductivity" By Practicing <u>Frontal</u> Vase-Breathing For a brief period (Of One, Two, or Three Cycles, or Repetitions, Of The Frontal Vase-Breathing Procedure). Inhale Fully, Via both nostrils, With the tongue Pressed Lightly To the roof of the (Generally) closed mouth. Inhale Fully, Feeling the Natural breath-energy and My Avatarically Self-Transmitted Divine Spirit-Energy Flow Down, Through The Frontal Line, To the lower abdomen. <u>Press</u> the inhaled breath Down (Comfortably) Into the abdomen, Even Such That the abdomen

Expands Rather Fully. As the abdomen Begins To Swell, the breath (and the Natural breath-energy, and My Avatarically Self-Transmitted Divine Spirit-Energy) Should Be Held In the abdomen, and the bodily base Should Be Tensed (or Comfortably Contracted) Upwards, and the chin Should Be Pulled Down Somewhat (In Order To Lock the breath At the throat). Hold the breath (and the Natural breath-energy, and My Avatarically Self-Transmitted Divine Spirit-Energy) In the abdomen For a Significant (but Comfortable) period, While Concentrating attention At and Above The Ajna Door. In a few moments, It May Be Felt To Be Possible To inhale Even A Little More. In That Case, Release the chin-Lock, and inhale Further (Downward, Into the abdomen), While Maintaining The Tension In the bodily base. (If It Is Uncomfortable To Hold The Tension In the bodily base, Briefly Relax The Tension In the bodily base, and Then Re-Tense the bodily base—As Required.) In The Midst Of Such Attempts To inhale More, the abdomen May Be Gently "Rolled", In and Out, In Order To "Loosen" the abdomen and the solar plexus—Such That more air and more Natural breath-energy and My Avatarically Self-Transmitted Divine Spirit-Energy Can Be Breathed Down. Hold This Mudra (or bodily attitude) Of The "Vase" (or Expanded abdomen, With the Natural breath-energy and My Avatarically Self-Transmitted Divine Spirit-Energy Contained By Means Of The Upward Tensing Of the bodily base), Until It Becomes (Comfortably) Necessary To exhale. Then Relax Into exhalation, and (While Lightly Tensing, or Pulling Up, the bodily base, and Lightly Pulling the crown of the lower abdomen In and Up) Relax and Release the Natural breath-energy and My Avatarically Self-Transmitted Divine Spirit-Energy Into The Spinal Line (and Let the Natural breath-energy and My Avatarically Self-Transmitted Divine Spirit-Energy Become Diffusely Released Into the Total body), but (As A General Rule) Do Not Otherwise Press (or Concentrate) the Natural breath-energy and My Avatarically Self-Transmitted Divine Spirit-Energy In (or Into) the head. Exhale Thus, and In A Comfortably Relaxed Fashion, Rather Than Quickly. The Completion Of the exhalation Completes The Full Cycle Of The Frontal Vase-Breathing Exercise. And The Cycle May Be Repeated, To (As A General Rule) A Maximum Of Three Full Cycles—In Order To Calm, Rebalance, and Refresh The Circle Of the body-mind By Means Of Easy breath-Control (and Natural "Conductivity"-Control Of the Natural bodily energy and My Avatarically Self-Transmitted Divine Spirit-Energy, In The Context Of The Circle Of the body-mind).

Occasionally (As A Sometimes Necessary Means Of physical Healing), The "General" Practice Of Spirit-"Conductivity" Must Be Engaged In Such A Manner As To Re-Vitalize (or, In General, To Serve The General Health Of) the body (As, For Example, In the event of Extreme physical enervation, or even ordinary fatigue, and Also In The daily physical exercise Practices Of "Conscious Exercise", and—After degenerative orgasm Is Bypassed, and Converted Into Regenerative orgasm—In The Practice Of Either "Emotional-Sexual Conscious Exercise" Or "Emotional-Sexual Devotional Communion"), or (Otherwise) In Order To Re-Balance A "Too Upward" (or Even Frontally Reversing, or Frontally Ascending) Tendency[129] (As May Be In Evidence In cases of high blood pressure, or In cases of Even any ailments that Show Negative Evidence Of Too Much Natural bodily energy, and Even Too Much Collectedness Of My Avatarically Self-Transmitted Divine Spirit-Energy, Collecting and Circulating Toward and In the brain and the upper trunk of the body, and Too Little Natural bodily energy, and Even Too Little Collectedness Of My Avatarically Self-Transmitted Divine Spirit-Energy, Collecting and Circulating Toward and In the abdominal area of the body, and the legs, and the feet). Therefore, As and whenever Required (In The Context, and ordinary course, Of daily life), The "General" Form Of lung-breathing Spirit-"Conductivity" May (Either Randomly and Briefly Or, In Cases Of Special Health Deficiencies, More Frequently and Consistently) Be Used To Direct (and Even, Intensively, Downwardly Press) the Natural bodily energy, and My Avatarically Self-Transmitted Divine Spirit-Energy, Via Both inhalation and exhalation, To The bodily "Battery" (and, Perhaps, Even Via The bodily "Battery", and Through the legs, Into the soles of the feet).[130]

In The Context Of Formal Meditation Practice In The Way Of The Heart, and Unlike The First Two Parts (or Exercises) Of The "General" (and Intentional) Spirit-"Conductivity" Exercise (Which Must Be Rather Constantly and Persistently Intended and Felt In Both daily life and Formal Meditation), lung-breathing Spirit-"Conductivity" Is, Generally (In The Context Of Formal Meditation, and, Altogether, In The Context, and ordinary course, Of daily life), To Be Only A Randomly Applied Exercise—and It Is, Like The First Two Parts (or Exercises) Of The "General" Form Of The By-Me-Spiritually-Activated Yoga Of Spirit-"Conductivity", To Be (Progressively) Yielded (or, Spontaneously, Abandoned) As Deepening (and Then Deep) Meditation Develops (In Any and Every Occasion Of Formal Meditation Practice).

Until Spirit-"Conductivity" (In Its "General", or By-Me-Commonly-Given, Form) Begins To Develop (By Means Of My Avatarically Self-Transmitted Divine Spiritual Grace), In The Intensive Listening-Hearing Stage Of The Way Of The Heart, A Similar (but More Rudimentary, or Not Yet Directly Spiritual) Responsive Devotional (and, Thus, Devotionally Me-Recognizing and Devotionally To-Me-Responding) Exercise Of The Three-Part "General" Form Of "Conductivity" Is Also To Be Practiced By All Student-Beginners (Including Novice Student-Beginners) In The Way Of The Heart. (And This Three-Part Exercise Of The "General" Form Of Rudimentary "Conductivity" Practice Is, As

Must Also Be The Case With All Forms Of Actual Spirit-"Conductivity" In The Way Of The Heart, To Be Exercised In Constant Conjunction With The Appropriate and Progressive Demonstration Of The Most Basic Exercise Of "Conductivity", In The Form Of The Original, and Most Basic, By-Me-Given functional, practical, relational, and Cultural Disciplines That Are The Foundation Of All Practice In The Way Of The Heart. And The Three Parts Of The "General" Form Of Rudimentary "Conductivity" Practice Are Also, As In The Case Of The Three Parts Of The "General" Form Of The By-Me-Spiritually-Activated Yoga Of Spirit-"Conductivity", To Be, Generally, Associated, In daily life and In Formal Meditation, With The Primary and Secondary bodily Attitudes I Have Described Herein—and, Also, According To My Herein Given Instructions, With The By-Me-Herein-Described bodily Locks Of The Ajna Door, the tongue and chin and throat, and the bodily base.)

In The Case Of Novice Student-Beginners and Fully Established Student-Beginners In The Only-By-Me Revealed and Given Way Of The Heart (or Way Of Adidam), The Three-Part Devotional Exercise Of The "General" Form Of "Conductivity" Practice Is Specifically and Simply One Of "Conductivity" Of the (Pervasive and Objective) Natural (etheric, or pranic, and bodily-experienced) energy. However, The Three-Part Devotional Exercise Of The "General" Form Of "Conductivity" Practice Is, Otherwise, As A Technical Exercise, Virtually The Same For Novice Student-Beginners and Fully Established Student-Beginners As It Is For My By-Me-Spiritually-Initiated (and Always Newly By-Me-Spiritually-Activated) Devotees.

For All Student-Beginners In The Only-By-Me Revealed and Given Way Of The Heart (Whether, As Student-Beginners, they Are Novices Or, Otherwise, Fully Established), The First Part (or Exercise) Of The Three-Part Exercise Of The "General" Form Of The Yoga Of "Conductivity" Is Persistent (Devotionally Me-Recognizing and Devotionally To-Me-Responding) Heart-Surrender To Me, Actively Demonstrated As ego-Surrendering, ego-Forgetting, and, More and More, ego-Transcending Heart-Feeling (or Feeling-Radiation), Transcending all conventional and Reactive emotions, and Generated Whole bodily (or In A Total psycho-physical Manner), From The Heart, In all directions (Boundlessly, or To Infinity). Such Is The Natural (and The Original and Unobstructed) Heart-Attitude, Which Is To Be Practiced By Means Of The Devotionally Responsive Feeling-Contemplation Of My Avatarically-Born Bodily (Human) Divine Form (and—Tacitly, but Not Yet Directly and Tangibly—My Avatarically Self-Transmitted Spiritual, and Always Blessing, Divine Presence and My Avatarically Self-Revealed, and Very, and Transcendental, and Perfectly Subjective, and Inherently Spiritual, and Inherently egoless, and Inherently Perfect, and Self-Evidently Divine State)—and Which Is (By Random

Application) To Be Constantly Practiced, At all times and In all places, In Formal Meditation and In daily life.

The Second Part (or Exercise) Of The "General" Form Of The Yoga Of "Conductivity" For All Student-Beginners In The Only-By-Me Revealed and Given Way Of The Heart (Whether, As Student-Beginners, they Are Novices Or, Otherwise, Fully Established) Is Persistent (Devotionally Me-Recognizing and Devotionally To-Me-Responding) Relaxation Of The Frontal Line Of the body (From The Crown Of the head To the bodily base—and Even To the toes). And This Exercise Is To Be Practiced Toward The Principal Result Of Right Natural Polarization Of The Frontal Line (From The Crown Of the head, Toward and To the bodily base), and (As A Naturally Coincident and Spontaneous Accompaniment) With Right Natural Polarization Of The Spinal Line (From the bodily base, Toward and To The Crown Of the head).

And The Third Part (or Exercise) Of The "General" Form Of The Yoga Of "Conductivity" That Is To Be Practiced By All Student-Beginners In The Only-By-Me Revealed and Given Way Of The Heart (Whether, As Student-Beginners, they Are Novices Or, Otherwise, Fully Established) Is Devotionally Me-Recognizing and Devotionally To-Me-Responding "Conductivity" Via lung-breathing Exercises Of Feeling and breath, or The "Conscious Exercise" Of inhalation-Reception (In Descent, Via The Frontal Line Of the body, To The bodily "Battery"), Assisted By Easy Upward Tensing Of the bodily base, Followed By exhalation-Release, Likewise Assisted By Easy Upward Tensing Of the bodily base (and, By Easy Inward and Upward Pulling Of the crown of the lower abdomen)—and, As A General Rule, With the feeling-breath-exhalation Released From The bodily "Battery" and Radiated Diffusely (In all directions) Within the entire body or, Otherwise (but, In General, Less Frequently, or Only Occasionally, As Appropriate), With the feeling-breath-exhalation Released From The bodily "Battery" and Radiated Into The General Pattern (or Line) Of Ascent, Via The Spinal Line Of the body. (And, On Occasion, As Necessary, Frontal Vase-Breathing May Be Engaged. And, On Occasion, As Necessary, In Order To Re-Vitalize the body, or, In General, To Serve The General Health Of the body, or In Order To Re-Balance A Too Upward Tendency In the body, the feeling-breath May, Via Both inhalation and exhalation, Be Intensively Pressed Down Into The bodily "Battery", and Then Released Downward From The bodily "Battery", and, Thus, Radiated, Via the legs, Into the soles of the feet—but, Always, or As A Consistent General Rule, Without <u>Any</u> Intentional Concentration Of attention In any part or Any Station In or Above the head.)

My early-life Devotees In The Way Of The Heart Are (Even, Progressively, and Most Simply, In The Context Of The First Stage Of Life, and, More and More, In The Context Of The Second and The Third Stages Of Life) To Adapt

To The Most Basic Exercise Of "Conductivity", In The Form Of The Original (and Most Basic) By-Me-Given functional, practical, relational, and Cultural Disciplines That Are The Foundation Of All Practices In The Only-By-Me Revealed and Given Way Of The Heart, and they Are Also To Engage A Simpler Technical (but Nonetheless Devotionally To-Me-Responsive) Version Of The Three-Part "Conscious Exercise" (or Basic Early Practice) Of The "General" Form Of Devotionally Me-Recognizing and Devotionally To-Me-Responding "Conductivity". My early-life Devotees In The Way Of The Heart Should Begin The "Conscious Exercise" Of The "General" Form Of "Conductivity" By Adapting To The Practice Of Devotionally Me-Recognizing and Devotionally To-Me-Responding Heart-Surrender To My Avatarically-Born Bodily (Human) Divine Form and Person, and (Thus and Thereby) To The Practice Of Devotionally To-Me-Responsive Feeling-Relinquishment Of self-Contraction, and (Thereupon) The Devotionally To-Me-Responsive Radiating Of Heart-Feeling (Boundlessly, To Infinity). Then (or On That Fundamental Basis) they Should Also Adapt To The Practice Of Devotionally Me-Recognizing and Devotionally To-Me-Responsive Relaxing Of The Frontal Line Of the body (Crown Toward base) and The Secondary Coincident Devotionally To-Me-Responsive Relaxing Of The Spinal Line Of the body (base Toward Crown). And, Thirdly, My early-life Devotees Should Also Adapt (Progressively) To Simple Devotionally Me-Recognizing and Devotionally To-Me-Responding lung-breathing Exercises Of Feeling and breath—At First, In The Relatively Non-Technical Form Of Simplest (or Rudimentary and Simply Felt) inhalation-Reception and exhalation-Release, and, Then (In Due Course), In The Form Of inhalation-Reception In Descent (Toward the bodily base) and exhalation-Release In all directions (Radiating Feeling-energy Diffusely, Within—and, In all directions, Via—the entire body). And My Maturing early-life Devotees (Advancing In The Context Of The Third Stage Of Life) Should Adapt To The Somewhat More Technical Version Of The Three-Part Exercise Of "General Conductivity", but Only As I Have (Herein) Described It For Fully Established Student-Beginners (and, Also, Novice Student-Beginners) Formally Practicing The Only-By-Me Revealed and Given Way Of The Heart (or Way Of Adidam)—and, Therefore, Only As A Natural-energy Exercise, and Not Yet As A By-Me-Spiritually-Initiated and (Directly and Tangibly) With-Me-Spiritually-Communing Exercise.

Avatar Adi Da Samraj
The Mountain Of Attention Sanctuary, 2000

SUTRA 37

I Have Observed That sex—or, More Accurately, emotional-sexual life—Is The Primary Obsession Of human beings, Especially In The Earlier Stages Of Life. Human beings Are self-Driven To Fulfill their emotional-sexual Motivations—To The Extent That their Urge To emotional-sexual Fulfillment Has The Force Of a philosophy. Their Involvement In emotional-sexual life Is, In Effect, A philosophical Commitment (Expressed At The personal Level) To Find Perfect self-Fulfillment In The Purposes Of ordinary human life.

This emotional-sexual Search Is, Therefore, a kind of utopian philosophy—a philosophy About Being Finally Fulfilled and Perfectly pleasurized In life. But the philosophy Of The emotional-sexual Search Allows human beings To Ignore Both their mortality and The Ultimate (Un-conditional, Indivisible, Divine, and Spiritual) Condition Of Reality Itself. Therefore, that philosophy Is False. Like the philosophy of scientific materialism, the philosophy Of Ultimate emotional-sexual self-Fulfillment Is Based On A Misinterpretation Of Reality, A False Presumption About Reality.

There Are all kinds of conventional social rules For Controlling sexual behavior—but they Are Designed To Serve The Purposes Of the social ego, and (Therefore) Have Nothing To Do With ego-Transcendence or Spiritual Realization. Merely To Become a "well-behaved" social ego Is Not A Sufficient Basis For Entering Into The Real Spiritual Process.

The Great Tradition Of Mankind Is, As A Whole, Unresolved and Ambivalent Relative To The Entire Matter Of sexuality—and It Is Even Generally sex-Negative (or "sex-paranoid") In Its Orientation. All Such puritanical Righteousness Must Be Gone Beyond. Otherwise, one's emotional-sexual egoity Is Never Truly Inspected and Dealt With. In That Case, attention Remains Fundamentally (Even If Unconsciously) Bound In emotional-sexual dilemmas of all kinds, Thereby limiting The Degree Of Real Spiritual Growth That Is Possible.

I Am The One Who Has Completed The Great "Consideration" Of human emotional-sexual life—and I Did So For The Sake Of every one. I Am The One Who Has Made It Possible For human beings To Totally Comprehend The emotional-sexual Dimension Of Existence, and To Completely Transcend egoic Reactivity, and To Truly Grow Beyond the ordinary emotional-sexual limitations that the worldly mind Represents, and (By All Of This) To Have an Altogether—and In Reality—Sane life. Indeed, Such emotional-sexual Clarity and Integrity Is Essential For The Real Spiritual Process.

In The Great Tradition, Various Kinds Of emotional-sexual Discipline Have Been Required or Recommended—but None Of These Disciplines Were Sufficient For The Thorough Transcending Of the emotional-sexual ego. In The Only-By-Me Revealed and Given Way Of The Heart (or Way Of Adidam), the emotional-sexual ego (and, Indeed, the ego of "money, food, and sex" Altogether) Must Be Really and Truly Gone Beyond—and This Must, In Real and Significant Terms, Begin In The Foundation Stage Of Practice Of The Way Of The Heart, As Part Of The (From Thence, Ongoing) Basis For Real and True Growth Into (and In) The By-Me-Spiritually-Initiated (and Always Newly By-Me-Spiritually-Activated) Stages Of The Only-By-Me Revealed and Given Way Of The Heart (or Way Of Adidam).

"Consider" This: Sex Is Not The "Great Evil". Indeed, sex Is Not Evil At All. Rather, egoity Is The Root and Source Of All Evil and All Problems. I Have Revealed and Demonstrated That sex Is Transformed and Made Right Only Through The Process Of Transcending egoity. Therefore, sex itself Need Not—and Should Not—Be Regarded As an "enemy". It Is emotional-sexual egoity That Must Be Gone Beyond. Thus, What Must Be (Most Fundamentally) Addressed Relative To Your emotional-sexual life Is Not sex In and Of itself, but Your egoic Search For self-Fulfillment By Means Of sex.

While It Is True That sex Is Not The "Great Evil", It Is Equally True That sex Is Not The "Great Salvation". In All The Years Of My Avataric Divine Teaching-Work and My Avataric Divine Revelation-Work (and, Indeed, In My Own "Sadhana Years"), I Thoroughly Demonstrated and Proved That A sexually active Yoga Carries No Advantage (and Is Not Causative) Relative To The Process Of Real-God-Realization. Indeed, The Most That Can Be Accomplished By Means Of A (Necessarily, Profoundly Seriously—and, In General, Conservatively—Engaged) sexually active Yoga Is To Make one's emotional-sexual Practice Compatible With The Real Spiritual Process (Whatever That Requires In The individual Case), Such That sexual activity Does Not Actively Obstruct The Spiritual Process. And Virtually All Of My Devotees who Grow Into The (Spiritually) Fully Technically Responsible Stages Of The Only-By-Me Revealed and Given Way Of The Heart Will, Whether Sooner Or Later, Be Spontaneously (and Spiritually) Moved To Greatly Conserve (or Even To Entirely Relinquish) sexual activity—For The Very Reason That (In Virtually All Cases) It Tends To Work Against The Fullest (and, At Last, Most Perfect) Spiritual Reception and Realization Of Me.

Contrary To The Illusions Of Certain Forms Of (conventional, or Traditional) Tantrism, No Form Of Cultivating sexual energy Can (In Any Sense) Cause

Spiritual Growth. That Is To Say, sexuality Is Not (In Any Sense) Causative Relative To Spirituality. The Illusion That sexuality Can Cause Spiritual Growth Stems From The Fundamental Illusion That Spiritual Practice Is A Process That Starts "Below", and Moves From there To Above. That Illusion Is An Unwitting Validation Of egoity—A Declaration That, In Effect, the ego Must "Propel" itself Upward, To The Divine (Thus, "Taking Heaven By Storm"). Such Is, In Reality, The Exact Opposite Of What Occurs In The Real Spiritual Process In My Avataric Divine Spiritual Company. In That Process, I (The "Bright" Divine Reality, In Avataric Divine Person) Come Down—and I Spiritually In-Fill You.

Thus, The Only-By-Me Revealed and Given Way Of The Heart (or Way Of Adidam) Does Not Develop "From Below Upwards". The Notion (or philosophy) Of "From Below Upwards" Is The Root-Error Of The egoic (and Traditional) Spiritual Search, Suggesting That the "dog" Must Be "Washed" From the "tail" Toward the "head".

"Below" Is Not (and Never Can Be) Causative Relative To What Is Above. Rather, What Is Above Must Purify and Transform and (Most Ultimately) En-Light-en What Is "Below".

That Is How I Do My Avataric Divine Spiritual Work.

That Is The Nature Of The Real Spiritual Process In My Avataric Divine Company.

Thus, The Real Spiritual (and Yogic) Process In My Avataric Divine Company Is Not A Development From A sexual Base (or From Any Base That Is "Below"). In Other Words, The Real Reception Of My Avataric Divine Spiritual Self-Transmission Is Not (Itself) A Process Of The Return Of sexual energy (From "Below" To Above), or, Otherwise, Of Negatively (or, Otherwise, egoically) Programming the body-mind Relative To sexual energy (or sexuality itself).

My Avataric Divine Spiritual Self-Transmission Comes From Utterly Above and Beyond—To Pervade and Purify and Transform and Awaken What Is "Below".

Nevertheless, In Order To Receive Me Spiritually (From Above and Beyond), You Must (Surely) Discipline (and Turn To Me—In My Avatarically-Born Bodily Human Divine Form here) All Of What Is "Below" (In emotional-sexual Terms, and In All Other Terms)—By Preparing (and Always Maintaining) Your body-mind For My Freely Given Avataric Divine Spiritual Invasion.

It Is The Tendency Of self-Contracted personalities To Indulge In sex as a degenerative activity (that Breaks The Life-Circle, and Throws Off the Natural bodily energy, and, In The Case Of My By-Me-Spiritually-Initiated Devotees, Would Even Throw Off My Avatarically Self-Transmitted Divine Spirit-Energy—As If Natural bodily energy and My Avatarically Self-Transmitted

Divine Spirit-Energy Were mere waste products of the body). This Tendency Is The Result Of The Reactive Presumption Of Independence, Separateness, and Alienation. It Is Founded On The Psychology Of Betrayal (or Of Rejection, By and Of others). Sexual activity Is (Thus) Degraded Into a merely organic (or lower physical) exercise, Engaged For The Sake Of Nothing More Than Stress-Release and Temporary Pseudo-Happiness.

Therefore, In The Only-By-Me Revealed and Given Way Of Adidam (Which Is The One and Only By-Me-Revealed and By-Me-Given Way Of The Heart)—Once Most Fundamental self-Understanding Has (By Means Of My Avatarically Self-Transmitted Divine Spiritual Grace) Awakened and Become Effective (Even In Relation To The emotional-sexual Dimension Of the body-mind), and Once That True Hearing Of Me Has (By Means Of My Avatarically Self-Transmitted Divine Spiritual Grace) Allowed The Heart To See Me In Truth—sexual activity itself (If it Is Engaged) Must Be Converted To My Spiritual, Transcendental, and Divine Fullness, By Means Of The ego-Transcending Devotional Recognition-Response To Me (The Giving Source Of Divine Spiritual Grace). By Such Means, sexual activity Ceases To Be Principally A lower physical (or organic) Indulgence Of the body-mind. Instead, it Becomes Principally An Exercise Of (and an experience via) the Total human brain and nervous system (In Which Exercise body and mind Are Disciplined To Conform To My Avatarically Self-Transmitted Divine Spirit-Current Through Heart-Feeling In The Circle), and it Is (Thus) Only Secondarily A lower physical (or organic) Process.

Sex Is Rooted In The Heart (or the emotional character). Sexual activity Is Either A Direct Expression Of Love (or Inherent, Fundamental, and Freely Radiant Heart-Feeling) Or The Dramatization Of emotional limitations Through physical Displays. And Full emotional-sexual Expression Requires A Full and Free Heart, Awakened To My Avatarically Self-Transmitted (and Constantly Baptizing) Divine Spirit-Presence. Then sexual activity (or, Really, emotional-sexual activity) Incarnates Free Heart-Feeling Of Me and "Conductivity" Of My Avatarically Self-Transmitted Divine Spirit-Energy.

True Sila, As An emotional-sexual Discipline For My Fully Both Hearing and Seeing Devotees, Requires Either Permanent celibacy Or Right and True and (Spiritually) Fully Technically Responsible Practice Of emotional-sexual Yoga. And, In The Only-By-Me Revealed and Given Way Of The Heart (or Way Of Adidam), Right and True and (Spiritually) Fully Technically Responsible emotional-sexual Yoga (or Devotional and Spiritual Communion With Me, As Practiced Within My Devotee's Chosen Circumstance Of intimate, and, Generally, sexually active, emotional-sexual Relatedness) Requires The Magnification, Conservation, and Conversion Of My Avatarically Self-Transmitted Divine Spirit-Energy (and the Natural bodily energy), In The Circle

Of the body-mind, and By The Means I Will Describe To You In This, My Testament Of Divine Secrets.

The emotional-sexual Motive, Divorced From The Divine Spiritual Reality, and Engaged Apart From The Motive Of ego-Transcendence (and The By-Me-Awakened Ability To Directly Realize ego-Transcendence), Is A Principal Effort (Coming Out Of The Adaptations Of The First Three Stages Of Life) Whereby individuals Avoid The Call (and Deny The Impulse) To Most Perfectly ego-Transcending Real-God-Realization. Therefore, You Must First Observe The ordinary emotional-sexual Motive, and Understand It As self-Contraction. Then You Must Actively, Effectively, and Most Fundamentally Transcend The self-Contracted Dramatization Of Your sexuality. Without Such Real, Direct, and Most Fundamental Transcending Of the emotional-sexual ego, There Is No Real and True Entrance Into The Practice Of The Way Of The Heart In The Fully Established (or Actually Seeing) Context Of The "Basic" Fourth Stage Of Life (or Advancement To and Through The Way Of The Heart In The Context Of The Stages Of Life Beyond The Fully Established "Basic" Fourth). Therefore, Your Bondage To emotional-sexual egoity Certainly Requires A Profound Address. However, It Is Not The Case That Such Address Necessarily Requires Participation In a sexually active intimate relationship. The Sole Absolute Requirement For The Transcending Of emotional-sexual egoity Is Your Devotional (and, In Due Course, Spiritual) Turning To Me, Together With Your Consistent Embrace Of The By-Me-Given functional, practical, relational, and Cultural Disciplines. Thus You Will Be Purified Of Your Bondage To (and In) The emotional-sexual Dimension Of human life—and Your Bondage To egoity Altogether.

In The Only-By-Me Revealed and Given Way Of The Heart (or Way Of Adidam), The Foundation Discipline Of Your sexuality Must Become Thoroughly Established During The Period Of Student-Beginner "Consideration" (Which Is The First—or Initial, Merely Preliminary, and Entirely Preparatory—Period Of Formal Practice) Of The Way Of The Heart. Thereafter, Whether You Are An intimately sexually active Formal Practitioner Of The Way Of The Heart Or A celibate Formal Practitioner Of The Way Of The Heart, The Most Fundamental Understanding Of Your sexuality—and The (Thereby Realized) Real, Direct, and Most Fundamental Transcending Of The egoic Uses Of Your sexuality—Must All Be Developed and Established In The Context Of The Intensive Listening-Hearing Stage Of The Way Of The Heart. And, Eventually, That (Real, and Most Fundamental, and Directly Effective) Transcending (Made Possible By The True Hearing Of Me) Is Also To Be Increased (or Magnified) By (or After, and On The Basis Of) The Establishment Of Full Technical Responsibility For The Spiritual Reception Of Me In The Course Of The Would-Be-Seeing (or Progressively Seeing) Stage Of The Way Of The Heart.

In The Only-By-Me Revealed and Given Way Of The Heart (or Way Of Adidam), Devotion, and Meditation (and Even Every Meditative Practice), and All Of self-Discipline, and All Of Study (and Even All "Consideration") Of The Only-By-Me Revealed and Given Way Of The Heart, and Even *Every* Kind Of Right and *Me*-Contemplating Service Must Always Serve *Every* Dimension Of Right Responsibility and Necessary Realization. Therefore, Devotion, and Meditation (and Even Every Meditative Practice), and All Of self-Discipline, and All Of Study (and Even All "Consideration") Of The Only-By-Me Revealed and Given Way Of The Heart, and Even *Every* Kind Of Right and *Me*-Contemplating Service Must, Along With All Their Other Right Purposes, Serve The Transcending Of sexually related ego-Bondage—and Especially (or With Direct and Full Effectiveness) Once Both True Hearing Of Me *and* (Then) Real Seeing Of Me Are Awakened. Once *Both* True Hearing Of Me *and* Real Seeing Of Me Are Awakened, You Must Not Only (As Before Then) Conserve Your sexual activity—but You Must, In Addition, Fully Conform The emotional-sexual Dimension Of Your life To The (Fully Technically Responsible) Process Of Receiving Me Spiritually. And This Conforming Is To Be Accomplished *Either Through The Regenerative Yoga Of* "*Emotional-Sexual Devotional Communion*", Which Is Devotional and Spiritual Communion With *Me*, In The Context Of (Spiritually) Fully Technically Responsible sexual (and, Altogether, emotional-sexual) Yoga (As Engaged Within Your Chosen Circumstance Of intimate Relatedness), *Or Through* Right, and Free, and Voluntary, and To-Me-Devoted, and Truly Spiritually Active, and Yogically (Rather Than Merely idealistically and puritanically) Supported and Maintained (and, Therefore, *Truly Regenerative*, or life-energy-Positive, Rather Than life-energy-Negative) *Yogic celibacy* (Engaged As Constant Devotional and Spiritual Communion With *Me*). And A Principal Sign That The emotional-sexual Dimension Of Your life Is Fully Conformed To The (Fully Technically Responsible) Process Of Receiving Me Spiritually Is The Capability To Effectively Maintain Full (Non-Reversed) "Conductivity" (Of Both My Avatarically Self-Transmitted Divine Spirit-Energy and the Natural bodily energy)—In The Frontal Line (From The Crown Of the head To the bodily base), and (From Thence, and In The Manner Of The Traditional Practice, or Yogic Sign, Of "Urdhvareta") In The Spinal Line (From the bodily base To The Crown Of the head)—During Occasions Of "Emotional-Sexual Devotional Communion" (In The Case Of Those Seeing Practitioners Of The Way Of The Heart who Are, in their personal intimate contexts, sexually active), and During The Exercise (If It Is Engaged) Of The "Own-Body Yogic Sexual Practice" (In The Case Of All Seeing Practitioners Of The Way Of The Heart, Whether celibate Or intimately sexually active).

The (Necessarily, Fully Spiritually Activated—and, Spiritually, Fully Technically Responsible) Practice Of "Emotional-Sexual Devotional Communion" Should Not (and, Truly, Cannot) Begin Until My Devotee who Is (in his or her personal intimate context) sexually active Enters The First Actually Seeing Stage Of The Way Of The Heart. Until Then, "Emotional-Sexual Conscious Exercise"—Which Is Devotional (and, Potentially, Spiritual) Communion With Me, In The Context Of Right Beginner's sexual (and, Altogether, emotional-sexual) Yoga, As Engaged Within the individual's Chosen Circumstance Of intimate Relatedness—Is (As I Will Describe It In This, My Testament Of Divine Secrets) The emotional-sexual Practice That Is To Be Engaged (Beginning In The Student-Beginner Stage Of The Way Of The Heart) By All Practitioners Of The Way Of The Heart who Are (in their personal intimate contexts) sexually active.

"Emotional-Sexual Devotional Communion" Is The emotional-sexual Practice Of Fully Spiritually Awakened, and (Spiritually) Fully Technically Responsible, Heart-Communion With Me (and It Requires The Fullest and Stable Capability For Fully Spiritually Awakened, and, Spiritually, Fully Technically Responsible, Heart-Communion With Me). Therefore, In The Only-By-Me Revealed and Given Way Of Adidam (Which Is The One and Only By-Me-Revealed and By-Me-Given Way Of The Heart), "Emotional-Sexual Devotional Communion" Is (If Real and True) A Kind Of Sacramental (and Truly Sacred) Activity, or Even A Form Of Puja (or Devotional Ritual—or Whole bodily Devotional Ceremony, or Yogic Devotional Rite), In Which attention Is Intentionally Maintained In My Avatarically Self-Transmitted Divine Spirit-Presence Through Devotional self-Sacrifice Of Separate and Separative self (or Responsively Heart-Feeling, and Really Counter-egoic, Surrender Of the Total body-mind To Me—or The Devotionally Me-Recognizing and Devotionally To-Me-Responding Surrender, Forgetting, and Transcending Of the Total ego-"I", or body-mind-self, In Me) During emotional-sexual Embrace.

In The Only-By-Me Revealed and Given Way Of The Heart (or Way Of Adidam), Pujas (or Sacred and Sacramental—and, Necessarily, Yogic—Devotional Rituals), and Even All bodily active Religious (and, Necessarily, Devotional and Yogic) Activities (Such As Devotional Chanting, Devotional Singing, Devotional Recitation, or Audible Vocalization Of My Avatarically Self-Revealed Divine Word, and Devotional Invocation, or Audible Invocation Of Me By Means Of My Avatarically Self-Revealed Divine Name), and Even all bodily active life-activities that Are True To The Only-By-Me Revealed and Given Way Of The Heart, Are (If Rightly Performed) A Direct Enactment Of The Divine Sacrifice Of conditional self (or The ego-Surrendering, ego-Forgetting, and ego-Transcending Devotional Recognition-Response To Me). And, In The Fully Spiritually Activated, and (Spiritually) Fully Technically

Responsible, Progress Of The Way Of The Heart, Pujas (and Right bodily activities of every kind) Serve Both My Avatarically Self-Transmitted Divine Spirit-Infusion Of the entire body-mind (itself) and The Actual (and, Ultimately, The Inherently Most Perfect) Transcending Of the entire body-mind-self (or the Total psycho-physical ego-"I").

Like Meditation In The Way Of The Heart, Pujas In The Way Of The Heart (and Even all bodily activities that Are True To The Way Of The Heart) Are The Practice Of Devotional (and, In Due Course, Spiritual) Communion With Me (Whether They Are Practiced By My Listening Devotees, Or By My Hearing Devotees, Or By My Seeing Devotees)—but, Whereas Meditation In The Way Of The Heart Is A Rather (or Apparently) "Internalized" Practice, Even Involving The Temporary Relinquishment Of bodily (and Even mentalized) Consciousness (In ego-Surrendering, ego-Forgetting, and, More and More, ego-Transcending Feeling-Contemplation Of My Avatarically-Born Bodily Human Divine Form, My Avatarically Self-Transmitted Spiritual, and Always Blessing, Divine Presence, and My Avatarically Self-Revealed, and Very, and Transcendental, and Perfectly Subjective, and Inherently Spiritual, and Inherently egoless, and Inherently Perfect, and Self-Evidently Divine State), Pujas (and Even all bodily activities), As They Are To Be Practiced By All My Listening Devotees, All My Hearing Devotees, and All My Seeing Devotees In The Way Of The Heart, Are To Be Outwardly (or, Necessarily, bodily) Performed (As Acts Of ego-Surrendering, ego-Forgetting, and, More and More, ego-Transcending Feeling-Contemplation Of My Avatarically-Born Bodily Human Divine Form, My Avatarically Self-Transmitted Spiritual, and Always Blessing, Divine Presence, and My Avatarically Self-Revealed, and Very, and Transcendental, and Perfectly Subjective, and Inherently Spiritual, and Inherently egoless, and Inherently Perfect, and Self-Evidently Divine State). And All My By-Me-Spiritually-Initiated (and Always Newly By-Me-Spiritually-Activated) Listening Devotees, Hearing Devotees, and Seeing Devotees In The Way Of The Heart Are Called To Perform Pujas (and Even all bodily activities) As Acts Of ego-Surrendering, ego-Forgetting, and (More and More) ego-Transcending Feeling-Contemplation Of Me That (By Means Of My Avatarically Self-Transmitted Divine Spiritual Grace) Either Presently Or Potentially Energize and Infuse the Active bodily personality With My Avatarically Self-Transmitted Divine Spiritual Radiance. Therefore, In The Only-By-Me Revealed and Given Way Of The Heart, Even all bodily activities Are To Be Performed As Devotional and Sacramental (or Truly Sacred) Activities.

All My Listening Devotees, All My Hearing Devotees, and All My Seeing Devotees In The Way Of The Heart Should Engage Both Meditative (or Relatively "Internalized", or body-mind-Relinquishing) and Sacramental (or

Relatively "Externalized", and, Therefore, bodily, or Outwardly, Enacted, and body-mind-Surrendering) Forms Of Devotion To Me every day. Indeed, Every (Necessarily, Formal) Practitioner Of The Way Of The Heart Is (By Formal Vow) Called (and Inspired, and Expected) To Constantly Practice Devotion To Me, and To Do So By Artfully Applying (and, Thus, Artfully Alternating Between) The Two Forms Of (body-mind-Relinquishing and body-mind-Surrendering) Devotion To Me. And, In The Way Of The Heart, These Two (and, Thus, Even All The Fundamental Gifts, Callings, and Disciplines Embraced By Developing Practitioners Of The Way Of The Heart) Will (Once They Are Rightly and Truly Established In Practice, and, Thereby, Made A Consistently Operative psycho-physical Pattern and Impulse) Always Be Continued—Even In The Always Already Full Context Of The Only-By-Me Revealed and Given Seventh Stage Of Life, In Which Meditation Is Inherently (and Inherently Most Perfectly) Fulfilled By The Constant Demonstration Of Inherently Most Perfect (and Self-Evidently Divine) Samadhi, and Sacramental Activities (and, Thus, Even all Apparent bodily activities, and all Apparent mental activities) Are (By Their Inherently Most Perfect Realization) The Demonstration Of The Divine Transfiguration and The Divine Transformation Of Even all Apparent forms, aspects, and activities of the body-mind, Until Even The Appearance Of action itself Is Most Perfectly Outshined In The Divine Spiritual "Brightness" Of The Divine Spherical Self-Domain Of Being, Itself. Therefore, These Two (The Meditative and The Sacramental) Forms Of Devotional Communion With Me Will (In The Case Of Each and Every Practitioner who Formally Embraces The Way Of The Heart) Balance The Practice (Of The Way Of The Heart) Between bodily inactive and bodily active Practices. And Even All The daily Disciplines To Be Outwardly Engaged By My Listening Devotees, My Hearing Devotees, and My Seeing Devotees—Including All Sacramental Activities, and (Thus) All Pujas, and Even All bodily active Religious (or Cultural) Activities, and (Indeed) Including Even all bodily activities (whether functional, practical, relational, or Cultural—and, Therefore, Including emotional-sexual self-Discipline)—Are (In Their Right Practice, and, Altogether, In Their True Conformity To Me) Right and True Examples Of bodily active Devotional Practice In The Only-By-Me Revealed and Given Way Of The Heart.

In The Only-By-Me Revealed and Given Way Of The Heart (or Way Of Adidam), A Sacramental Act (Of Any Kind) Is A Special Sacred Performance. That Act Is The "Opposite" (or, Really, The Complement) Of Meditation—In The Sense That, While Meditation Involves Intentional Transcending Of bodily Consciousness In Devotional Communion With Me, The Sacramental Act Intentionally Includes bodily Consciousness In A Kind Of Rapturous, Artful

Enactment Of Devotional Communion With Me (Wherein You Must Constantly Maintain attention In The Context Of the body and its relations—but In The Manner Of A Sacred Performance, and Not In casual, conventional Terms). Because In Sacramental Activities You Are (Variously) Always Intentionally and Outwardly active (bodily, vocally, and so forth), You Never (Except In The Event Of A Spontaneous Swoon) Abandon bodily Consciousness. Nevertheless, In The Way Of The Heart, You Must Allow Your body-mind To Be Completely Absorbed In ego-Surrendering, ego-Forgetting, and (More and More) ego-Transcending Communion With Me Through All Your Sacramental (or Right bodily) Activities. In The Way Of the Heart, Every Event and Kind Of Sacramental (or Right bodily) Activity Is To Be An Event (or A Form) Of That Aspect Of Your Total Practice Of The Way Of The Heart That Functions To Balance (or Complement) The Effect Of Meditation—and (Altogether) The Constant Discipline Of Converting all bodily (or Outward) activity Into True Sacramental Activity Must Constantly Oblige You To Rightly (and Sacredly, or Truly Religiously, or Culturally) Orient all the functional, practical, and relational performances of daily life (which You, Otherwise, Tend Not To Turn Into A Sacramental, or Sacred, or Religious, or Cultural Performance, but which Are, In Fact, Supposed To Be Such). Therefore, In The Way Of The Heart, sexual activity In The Context Of intimate relationship, Converted Into Right emotional-sexual self-Discipline In General (and Then, In The Context Of Truly Seeing Practice Of The Way Of The Heart, "Emotional-Sexual Devotional Communion" In Particular), Is Sacramental (and Truly Sacred) Activity, and Even A Kind Of Puja (or A True Devotional and Ritual Art).

The Puja Of "Emotional-Sexual Devotional Communion" Is To Be Engaged As A Form Of Ruchira Avatara Bhakti Yoga, or The Devotionally Responsive Counter-egoic (and Even Total psycho-physical) Effort Of ego-Surrendering, ego-Forgetting, and Truly (and, Ultimately, Even Most Perfectly) ego-Transcending Devotion To Me. Therefore, The Puja Of "Emotional-Sexual Devotional Communion" Requires The Surrender, The Forgetting, and The Transcending Of body, emotion (or self-Contracted, and, Therefore, limited, feeling), mind (In its Root-Form, Which Is attention itself), and breath (Via The Process Of Spiritual "Conductivity"). The Puja Of "Emotional-Sexual Devotional Communion" Requires That attention Be Concentrated In Me Via emotional-sexual activity that Is Engaged As A Fully Felt (and Fully ego-Surrendering, ego-Forgetting, and, More and More, ego-Transcending) Devotional and Spiritual Act. Therefore, The Tendency and The Habit Of emotional Dissociation (From Me, From one's any partner In Yogic emotional-sexual Embrace, and Even From the body-mind itself) Must (Basically and Effectively) Be Transcended As A Preliminary To (and As A Part Of) The Real and

Effective Practice Of "Emotional-Sexual Devotional Communion" (or Of Even Any Form Of Right emotional-sexual Practice In The Way Of The Heart).

Both The Hearing Of Me and The Seeing Of Me Are Necessary Prerequisites For This Puja Of "Emotional-Sexual Devotional Communion". And, Even Though "Emotional-Sexual Devotional Communion" Is A Matter Of individual Responsibility, The Fullest Realization Of The Process Is Optimally Served When each partner In The Embrace Is Fully Prepared (By Every Virtue Of Effective True Hearing Of Me and Heart-Profound Seeing Of Me) To Participate In This Yogic (and, Necessarily, Spiritual) emotional-sexual Discipline. Therefore, In The Only-By-Me Revealed and Given Way Of The Heart (or Way Of Adidam), The individual Practitioner Of "Emotional-Sexual Devotional Communion" (and, Optimally, each partner In The Embrace) Must Surrender himself or herself (and his or her partner) Into The all-and-All-Surrounding and all-and-All-Pervading Current Of My Avatarically Self-Transmitted (and Heart-Awakening) Divine Spirit-Presence.

The Habitual Wandering Of attention In thought and mental imagery Must Be Transcended In "Emotional-Sexual Devotional Communion" (or Even In The Context Of Any Right emotional-sexual Practice In The Way Of The Heart), or Else the self-Contraction Will Dominate the sexual act itself—Resulting In Stress, Dissociation, and other degenerative effects. Therefore, During "Emotional-Sexual Devotional Communion", attention (Always Devotionally Yielded To Me Via The Yogic emotional-sexual Process) Must Be Constantly and Intentionally Associated With the sexual act As An emotional (or feeling-Based and relationally-Oriented, Rather Than Reactively Dissociative or Separative) and physical (or sensorially-Based and perceptually-Based, Rather Than mentally-Based, or conceptually-Based) Process, In Which You Are Constantly Surrendered (emotionally, physically, and With Complete attention) Into My Avatarically Self-Transmitted Divine Spirit-Presence (or all-and-All-Pervading Spirit-Current Of Love-Bliss). In This Manner (or By Means Of Intentional emotional-sexual Concentration In The By-Me-Avatarically-Self-Revealed Divine Spiritual Reality), The Tendency To Become Abstracted and Defended Against emotional-sexual experience itself, As Well As The Tendency To Become Dissociated From The Real and True Spiritual Process (or Event) In The Context Of emotional-sexual experience, Will Be Directly (and Naturally) Transcended. That Is To Say, If attention (During emotional-sexual activity, In The Practice Of The Way Of The Heart) Is Constantly Concentrated In the present (physical, perceptual, sensory, and Positively feeling) act, and If the act itself Is Allowed To Be Attracted (or Sublimed) By My Avatarically Self-Transmitted Divine Spirit-Current (Initiated From Infinitely Above and Beyond body and mind, and Perceived In The Circle Of the body-mind), and

If Heart-Felt Spiritual Devotion To Me (Altogether, and Especially In The Form Of My Tangibly Self-Transmitted Spiritual, and Always Blessing, Avataric Divine Presence) Is Consistently Allowed To Continue Even In The Context Of all Such emotional-sexual activity—Then The Habit Of Dissociation From the present emotional-sexual act Through mentalizing (or Indulgence In Random verbal or, Otherwise, Abstracted and non-sexual, or Even anti-sexual, thoughts and memories) and Through Interiorized (or Dissociative) emotional Distractions Will Be Naturally (Rather Than By mental Effort) Bypassed, and The Tendency To Stimulate orgasm Through mental imagery (or Indulgence In sexually Stimulating mental images Abstracted From The Present physical, emotional, and Spiritual Act) Will Not Be Exercised. Thus, the "sexual mind" Will Be Transcended—it Will Cease To Be Necessary and Chronic, and Even its (Decreasingly) Occasional (and, Generally, Non-Intentional) arising Will (Therefore) Have No Profound (or Lasting) degenerative effects.

In The Real and Effective Spiritual Practice Of My Seeing Devotees who Are (in their personal intimate contexts) sexually active, My Avatarically Self-Transmitted Divine Spirit-Current Must (By Means Of The Formal Application Of A Unique Yogic emotional-sexual Discipline) Be Preserved (and Even Magnified) In sexual activity (and In every moment of the emotional-sexual relationship itself). Therefore, Once You (As My Formally Practicing Devotee) Have Both Heard Me and Seen Me, Your emotional-sexual Practice Must Be Such That My Divine Spirit-Fullness (Infinitely Above, and In The Heart, and In The Circle) Does Not Become Weak, Obstructed, or Absent In Anticipation Of sexual activity, During sexual activity, or As A Result Of sexual activity.

In The Only-By-Me Revealed and Given Way Of The Heart (or Way Of Adidam), The Real and Effective Practice Of "Emotional-Sexual Devotional Communion"—Which Is Right Surrender (Of the emotional-sexual activities of body, breath, bodily energy, emotion, mind, and attention) To Me (and Into My Avatarically Self-Transmitted Divine Spirit-Current)—Will Grant You Natural Control Over the acts and the effects Of The Natural (and, Otherwise, egoic, or self-Contracted and Search-Bound) emotional-sexual Process.

Beyond All The functional, practical, relational, and Cultural Disciplines You (In Your Earlier Formal Practice Of The Way Of The Heart) Will Have Developed Relative To The emotional-sexual Process, Your emotional-sexual Practice As An intimately sexually active Seeing-Practitioner Of The Way Of The Heart Must Be Fully ego-Transcending and Spiritually Me-Realizing. That Is To Say, It Must Directly (and Always Presently) Transcend the Spiritually Me-Rejecting (and My-Avataric-Divine-Spirit-Presence-Rejecting) self-Contraction of body, breath, bodily energy, emotion, mind, and attention. Thus, Your Spiritually Active emotional-sexual Practice Must Necessarily Be sex-Bondage-Transcending.

That Is To Say, It Must Directly (and Always Presently) Transcend the emotional-sexual ego, or the sexually Dramatized (and My-Avataric-Divine-Spirit-Presence-Rejecting) self-Contraction of body, breath, bodily energy, emotion, mind, and attention.

True "Emotional-Sexual Devotional Communion" Directly Transcends the self-Contraction in its specific form As A Motivator and Performer Of sexual activity.

True "Emotional-Sexual Devotional Communion" Directly Transcends Even the mere convention that is emotional-sexual desire (or The Stress Of egoic emotional-sexual Seeking)—Not By Avoiding it (For Avoidance Is self-Contraction), but By Yielding body, breath, bodily energy, emotion, mind, and attention Into My Avatarically Self-Transmitted Divine Spirit-Current, Such That emotional-sexual desire (or emotional-sexual Seeking) Is Carried Beyond itself, and Such That it Is (By Means Of My Avatarically Self-Transmitted Divine Spiritual Grace, Through Heart-Devotion To Me) Resolved In Love-Bliss (or Inherent Happiness) Itself.

When, In The Only-By-Me Revealed and Given Way Of The Heart, the emotional-sexual self-Contraction Is Fully Yielded Into My Avatarically Self-Transmitted (and Self-Evidently Divine) Spirit-Current (and Person) Of Love-Bliss, sexual activity Becomes Truly "Ordinary" (and, Therefore, Not Compulsive, or Driven By The Seeking-Urge To Achieve self-Satisfaction—or The egoic, or self-Contracted, and, Necessarily, conditional and Temporary, Fulfillment Of the body-mind-self). It Becomes Non-Problematic, and Also Regenerative (Rather Than degenerative). It Becomes Naturally and Easily Economized (or Restored To A Balanced, or Conservative, Order). It Becomes Expressed Through ego-Transcending Love. Therefore, True "Emotional-Sexual Devotional Communion" Relaxes (or Is Resolved) Inevitably Into The Truly Free Pattern Of ego-Renunciation—Characterized By Searchless Beholding Of Me, and By Responsive Reception Of My Love-Bliss-Full Ruchira Shaktipat.

In The Way Of The Heart, "Emotional-Sexual Devotional Communion", Rightly Engaged, Actively Relinquishes the self-Contraction (which Is The Root-Cause Of Stress and Obstruction In The Frontal Line)—Thus Opening The Frontal Line (Down To the bodily base). Nevertheless, Stress and Obstruction Are Not The Right Motivators For "Emotional-Sexual Devotional Communion", and The Strategic Removal Of Stress and Obstruction Is Not The Right Purpose Of "Emotional-Sexual Devotional Communion". As Is The Case With All Other Disciplines Embraced By My Seeing Devotees, "Emotional-Sexual Devotional Communion" Is To Be An Expression Of (Fully Spiritually Awakened, and, Spiritually, Fully Technically Responsible, and Always Devotional) Me-Fullness and Of Most Fundamental (and Always Directly

Effective) self-Understanding. Therefore, In Contrast To conventional sexual activity, The Right (and, Necessarily, Non-Excessive) Practice Of "Emotional-Sexual Devotional Communion" (In The Way Of The Heart) Must Discipline and Require the body-mind To Preserve and Enhance The Flow Of My Avatarically Self-Transmitted Divine Spirit-Current, and (Only In That Manner) To Enliven, Balance, and Rejuvenate the body-mind, and (In Any Case) To Always Maintain The Full Circle (and The Connection Between The Frontal and Spinal Lines) Of the body-mind.

In The Only-By-Me Revealed and Given Way Of The Heart (or Way Of Adidam), "Emotional-Sexual Devotional Communion" Involves The Conservation and Conversion (and Not The Suppression or Avoidance) Of male degenerative (or ejaculatory) orgasm and female degenerative orgasm.[131] The Principal Yogic Means Revealed and Given By Me For The Control and Conversion Of Impending degenerative orgasm Is (In The Case Of "Emotional-Sexual Devotional Communion") "Conductivity" Of Both My Avatarically Self-Transmitted Divine Spirit-Energy and the Natural bodily energy, Exercised Via Control Of the bodily reflexes, and Of the mental and emotional activity, During the sex act. Altogether, That Yogic Practice Includes The emotional-sexual Exercises Of The Right Control (or Right Devotional, and human relational, and bodily Concentration) Of attention, The Devotional and human relational Radiating Of Heart-Feeling (or Devotional, and human relational, Love), The Right Practice Of Whole bodily Relaxation (Primarily, and Receptively, Along The Entire Frontal Line, From Crown To base, and, Secondarily, and In A Naturally Upwardly Polarized Manner, Into The Spinal Line, From base Toward Crown), The Right (and Specifically emotional-sexual) Practice Of Pranayama (or Right Control, or Right "Conductivity", Of My Avatarically Self-Transmitted Divine Spirit-Current and Of the Natural bodily energy Via The Right Exercise Of the two Natural parts of the breath), and (As and when Required) The Right and Appropriate Practice Of Moderate (or, Sometimes, Strong) Upward Tensing Of the bodily base (Either As A Brief and Constant Gesture Or, Otherwise, As A Brief and Repetitive Gesture, and With the crown of the lower abdomen Simultaneously Drawn In and Up, On exhalation).

The conventional (and degenerative) orgasm (or Discharge Of Natural bodily energy and My Avatarically Self-Transmitted Divine Spirit-Energy, From the brain, and From the body In General, and, In the case of men, Discharge Of vital reproductive fluid As Well) Must (Progressively, and Then, As A General Rule Of Practice, Consistently) Be Bypassed (or, Really, Re-Oriented, or Converted) and Replaced By A Generalized (or Whole bodily and Regenerative) Thrill (or bodily Profusion Of Intense Delight). This Is Because Excess (or Even Routine) Indulgence In Unconverted (or conventional) orgasm (As Well As Indulgence In A Chronic and Stressful Wanting Need, or Search, For conventional orgasm, and, Altogether, For sexual Satisfaction) Tends (Because Of the Natural anatomical location of the genitals, In The Frontal Line, and, as such, also above the bodily base) To Break The Circuit Of The Frontal Line Of the body, and To Reverse The Natural Downward Flow (or Downward Polarization) Of The Frontal Line Of the body (and The Natural Upward Flow, or Upward Polarization, Of The Spinal Line Of the body), Thus and Thereby Producing Temporary (and Even Chronic) Symptoms Of bodily, emotional, and mental Stress, Imbalance, and Enervation (As Well As A Tendency To Be, and To Chronically Remain, Identified With The Patterns Of Un-Happiness and Seeking That Are egoically Associated With The First Three Stages Of Life)—and All Of This Works Against The Possibility Of Right, True, and Rightly and Truly Effective "Conductivity" Of My Avatarically Self-Transmitted Divine Spirit-Energy.

The Natural Tendency Toward (degenerative) orgasm Can Be Felt (By Both the male and the female) As Either A Gradual Or A Sudden Descent Of Fundamental bodily energy From the brain, Down The Spinal Line (Thus Reversing The Natural Ascending Flow Of bodily energy In The Spinal Line), Through the base of the spine (and Then the anus, and Then the perineum), and Then Up and Forward (Toward the genitals). (In the male, This Cycle Is Also Signed By A Tendency For the erect penis To Drop Downward, or To Relax its Upward, or Vertical, Tension, Accompanied By a pleasurable Pouring, or Rushing, sensation that Runs Through the central canal, and Along the underside, of the shaft of the penis, From the base Toward the tip.) If This Cycle Is Allowed To Complete Itself, It Ends In The Liberal Discharge (or gross Elimination) Of Natural bodily energy (and, Ultimately—As May Be Observed By My Devotees who Are Spiritually Awake To Me—The Liberal Discharge Of My Avatarically Self-Transmitted Divine Spiritual Energy) From the Total body-mind.

The genitals Become More and More energized During the sexual act, but This Becomes degenerative orgasm (or, Ultimately, Discharge Of My Avatarically Self-Transmitted Divine Spirit-Energy) Only By Degrees. During "Emotional-Sexual Devotional Communion", My Avatarically Self-Transmitted Divine Spirit-Energy (and Natural bodily energy Generally) Is Kept Flowing In The Natural Circuit (Descending Via The Frontal Line and Ascending Via The Spinal Line) By The Right Exercise Of the mind (Through The Devotional, and human relational, and bodily Control Of attention), The Right Exercise Of emotion (Through Consistent and Truly Heart-Feeling Devotion To Me, and Through Consistent and Truly Heart-Feeling and humanly Expressed Love Of one's any partner In sexual Embrace), The Right Exercise Of the body (Through

Appropriate Whole bodily Relaxation—Especially, or Primarily, In The Downwardly Receptive Frontal Line), and The Right Exercise Of the breath (Through Pranayama, Specific To emotional-sexual activity)—but A Special and More Intense Employment Of These Means Must Be Made When The Tendency Toward degenerative orgasm (or The Descent and Discharge Of Natural bodily energy and My Avatarically Self-Transmitted Divine Spirit-Energy Via The Spinal Line) Is Felt To Be Approaching.

Once Practice Of The Way Of The Heart Is Formally Acknowledged To Be Fully Established On The Basis Of Both Hearing Me and Seeing Me, The intimately sexually active Practitioner Of The Way Of The Heart Must Practice "Emotional-Sexual Devotional Communion". Therefore, As A Specific Practice, The Tendency (In Both The male Practitioner and The female Practitioner) For The Natural (and Otherwise Right) Polarization and Flow Of Natural bodily energy and My Avatarically Self-Transmitted Divine Spirit-Energy (Descending Via The Frontal Line and Ascending Via The Spinal Line) To Become Reversed (or To Descend Via The Spinal Line, and, Subsequently, or, Otherwise, Independently, Even To Ascend Via The Frontal Line) In The Event Of degenerative orgasm (or Even During sexual activity Generally) Must Itself (and Consistently, or As A General Rule Of Practice) Be Reversed (or "Re-Reversed", and, Thus, Set Right Again—Easily, or, Otherwise, With Significant Effort, but Always Intentionally). Thus (In The Case Of Such Seeing Devotees), The "Down, Forward, and Out" Motion Of Natural bodily energy and My Avatarically Self-Transmitted Divine Spirit-Energy (Down From the brain, Down Through The Spinal Line, and Forward and Out Via the genitals and the Total bodily base) Must (As A General Rule Of Practice) Be Reversed, or Converted Into An "In, Back, and Up" Motion Of Natural bodily energy and My Avatarically Self-Transmitted Divine Spirit-Energy (In and Back Via the genitals and the Total bodily base, and Up Via The Spinal Line To the brain). Therefore (In The Case Of Such Seeing Devotees), the instant The Tendency Toward conventional orgasm Begins—That Is, As Soon As The Sudden Expansion and Descent Of pleasure and Natural bodily energy and My Avatarically Self-Transmitted Divine Spirit-Energy Begins To Be Felt In the middle of the brain (and, Perhaps, Even In the lower rear of the brain, but no lower than the back of the neck), and As Soon As The Corresponding Intensification Of pleasure and Natural bodily energy and My Avatarically Self-Transmitted Divine Spirit-Energy Begins To Be Felt At the root of the genitals, and Before The Full Descent Of pleasure and Natural bodily energy and My Avatarically Self-Transmitted Divine Spirit-Energy Via The Spinal Line Toward Discharge At the bodily base, and (In the case of men) Before The Simultaneous Movement Of pleasure and Natural bodily energy and My Avatarically Self-Transmitted

Divine Spirit-Energy Forward (From the base of the spine, Through the anus, and Then the perineum, and Then Along the underside of the penis, Toward the tip of the penis, Coinciding With The Initiation Of An ejaculatory Pulsation In the penis), or (In the case of women) Before The Simultaneous Movement Of pleasure and Natural bodily energy and My Avatarically Self-Transmitted Divine Spirit-Energy Forward (From the base of the spine, Through the anus, and Then the perineum, and Then Into the clitoral area and the depth of the vagina, Coinciding With The Initiation Of A degenerative orgasmic Pulsation In One or Another Region, or Even In The Totality, Of the vagina)—Relax the body (and Perhaps Stop sexual activity—Even By Disengaging the genitals, or, Otherwise, By Ceasing All Direct, and Even Indirect, genital Stimulation), and breathe Upwards (or With Upward Feeling) In or Via The Spinal Line (and While Focusing attention In The Root Of The Total Central Region, or Core, Of the brain, Between and Slightly Above and Deep Behind the eyes).

If (At any moment In The Embrace That Is "Emotional-Sexual Devotional Communion") The Tendency Toward degenerative orgasm Is Not Strong, Simply (and Actively) Feel the entire body (Including The Entire Frontal Line, the bodily base, The Entire Spinal Line, and the brain)—and (Thereby) Yield and Open the entire body (and, Thus, The Total Circle Of the body-mind) To The sexually Intensified Flow Of Natural bodily energy and My Avatarically Self-Transmitted Divine Spirit-Energy. In This Manner, Feel the Natural bodily energy and My Avatarically Self-Transmitted Divine Spirit-Energy Flowing Downwards In The Frontal Line (Polarized Toward the lower abdomen and the bodily base) and Upwards In The Spinal Line (Polarized Toward the brain). Freely (and, Generally, Rather Fully) inhale (Downwards) In The Frontal Line (Receiving the Natural bodily energy and My Avatarically Self-Transmitted Divine Spirit-Energy), and (At Random) Also exhale (Downwards) In The Frontal Line (Releasing Reactivity, Stress, and Obstruction), Such That The Frontal Line Becomes More and More Open, and More and More Full Of The Descending Flow (Polarized Toward the lower abdomen and the bodily base). And, At Random, Freely exhale (and Perhaps Even inhale) Into The Spinal Line (Upwards, From the bodily base To the lower rear of the head and brain, and, From thence, Upward and Forward, Into The Core, or Total Central Region, Of the brain), Even (At Random) Moderately Tensing (or Pulling Up) the bodily base and the crown of the lower abdomen (and, Thus, Directing the Natural bodily energy and My Avatarically Self-Transmitted Divine Spirit-Energy Into The Spinal Line)—and (Thereby, or Coincidentally) Focus the Natural bodily energy and My Avatarically Self-Transmitted Divine Spirit-Energy In The Total Crown Of the head, By Centering attention In The Forward Middle Of the head, Between and Slightly Above and Deep Behind the eyes.

The Yogic emotional-sexual Exercise Of Intentional Upward Yogic Concentration In The Core Of the brain Is To Be Applied Only In The Practice Of "Emotional-Sexual Devotional Communion". Otherwise (or Until "Emotional-Sexual Conscious Exercise" Is Replaced By True "Emotional-Sexual Devotional Communion"), The Conservative (and Actively Counter-degenerative) Practice Of "Emotional-Sexual Conscious Exercise" (As I Will Describe It In This, My Divine Testament) Should (and Must) Be Intentionally Engaged, At Random, During all sexual activity—Beginning (In The Case Of Student-Beginners In The Way Of The Heart who Are, in their personal intimate contexts, sexually active) Simply As A "Conscious Exercise" Of the Universal etheric (or Natural pranic) energy-field, and, In Due Course (In The Case Of By-Me-Spiritually-Initiated Practitioners, In The Intensive Listening-Hearing Stage and The Would-Be-Seeing Stage Of The Way Of The Heart, who Are, in their personal intimate contexts, sexually active), Developed Further, As A True Spiritual (As Well As Natural energy) Exercise. The Full Practice Of "Emotional-Sexual Devotional Communion" (As I Have Described It, and Will Further Describe It, In This, My Divine Testament) Should (and Must) Be Formally, Intentionally, Rightly, and Consistently Engaged, and (According To My Herein Given Instructions Relative To The Fully Spiritually Awakened, and, Spiritually, Fully Technically Responsible, Stages Of The Way Of The Heart) Fully Developed As A Direct, Potent, and (Altogether) By-Me-Given Spiritual Exercise, In The Case Of All My Truly Seeing Devotees In The Way Of The Heart who Are (in their personal intimate contexts) sexually active. And The Full Practice Of "Emotional-Sexual Devotional Communion" Should (and Must), As Appropriate To Each By-Me-Given Developmental Stage Of Practice Of The Way Of The Heart, Be Engaged In Such A Manner That Practice In The Fully Spiritually Awakened, and (Spiritually) Fully Technically Responsible, Stages Of The Way Of The Heart Develops As A Progressively Intensified and Increasingly Effective and Profound Spiritual Discipline and Process, Developed According To All My Herein and Hereby Given Instructions (and In Accordance With My Instructions Additionally Given Only To The Ruchira Sannyasin Order Of Adidam Ruchiradam), and As Practice Of The Way Of The Heart Matures (Stage By Stage) Toward (and, In Due Course, Within) The Only-By-Me Revealed and Given Seventh Stage Of Life.

If (At any moment In The Embrace That Is "Emotional-Sexual Devotional Communion") The Tendency Toward degenerative orgasm Is Strong, Generally Relax (or Even Stop) all Stimulating sexual activity (Even, If Necessary, By Disengaging the genitals), and Relax Upwards Along the spine, and Work To Focus attention and Natural bodily energy and My Avatarically Self-Transmitted Divine Spirit-Energy In The Core (or Total Central Region) Of the brain. Work

Toward, and Into, and At The brain-Focus By Steps, but Quickly. First (and Fully), Either inhale (and, thereby, "Pull" the Natural bodily energy and My Avatarically Self-Transmitted Divine Spirit-Energy Upwards, Into and Via The Spinal Line) Or exhale (and, thereby, "Throw" the Natural bodily energy and My Avatarically Self-Transmitted Divine Spirit-Energy Upwards, Into and Via The Spinal Line). Do This Either Suddenly Or Gradually (and, If Gradually, Either Smoothly Or In Rhythmic Starts and Stops). In Order To Establish and Maintain A Fully Connected Internal Circuit, breathe With the tongue Pressed Lightly To the roof of the mouth, and (Whenever Possible) By breathing Via the nose (Rather Than Via an open mouth). Even Let the eyes Close and Turn Up and Back (To Prevent the Natural bodily energy and My Avatarically Self-Transmitted Divine Spirit-Energy From Discharging, or "Leaking Out", Via the eyes). In Order To Prevent The Spinal Flow (Of Natural bodily energy and My Avatarically Self-Transmitted Divine Spirit-Energy) From Reversing (and, Thus, Descending, Rather Than Ascending), Curl the hips Forward, and Draw the crown of the lower abdomen In and Up. Simultaneously, A Lock, or An Internal Upward Tensing (Either Brief and Constant Or, Otherwise, Brief and Repetitive) Should (As A General Rule) Be Applied To the bodily base—By Drawing In, Back, and Up (Via the genitals, the perineum, and the anus), and To and Into The Spinal Line, and With the crown of the lower abdomen Simultaneously Drawn In and Up. If (Because The Involuntary Urge Toward degenerative orgasm Is Especially Intense In any particular instance) This Lock Tends To Increase (Rather Than Decrease) The Tendency For degenerative orgasm To Complete itself, Then Discontinue (or, Otherwise, Avoid) Locking the bodily base (or Drawing Up Via the genitals), but Apply The genital Lock (or bodily base Lock), Along With Spinal inhalation and/or Spinal exhalation, At Random moments During "Emotional-Sexual Devotional Communion", and Also After The Tendency Toward degenerative orgasm Has Been Brought Under Control By The Other Means Given By Me In This Description. If Necessary, Particularly When The genital Lock (or bodily base Lock) Is Not Advisable (or, Otherwise, Not Sufficient), Press two or three fingers At (or Slightly Forward From) the perineum, To Press the Natural bodily energy and My Avatarically Self-Transmitted Divine Spirit-Energy In and Back, and Up Into The Spinal Line—and (Thus) To Keep The Circuit Of Natural bodily energy and My Avatarically Self-Transmitted Divine Spirit-Energy Closed At the bodily base, where degenerative orgasm Tends To Break The Circuit and (Thereby) Discharge Natural bodily energy, and My Avatarically Self-Transmitted Divine Spirit-Energy, and (In the case of men) the vital-fluid stores of the reproductive system. Once The Descending (and, Thus, Reversing) Spinal Tendency Of the Natural bodily energy and My Avatarically Self-Transmitted Divine Spirit-Energy

Is Turned In, Back, and Up (Along The Spinal Line), and Locked In the head, Press attention, the inhaled (or exhaled) breath, the Natural bodily energy, and My Avatarically Self-Transmitted Divine Spirit-Energy Deep Into the head—While Continuing To Maintain The genital Lock (or, Otherwise, finger Pressure Below), and While Continuing To Curl the hips Forward and To Draw the abdomen In and Up, and While Also Continuing To Relax the body Upwards Along the spine, and With A Light Stretching Of the back of the neck, and With the tongue Pressed Lightly To the roof of the mouth, and With the breath Controlled Via the nose (Rather Than the mouth), and Even With the breath Drawn Up Through the back of the throat and Up Behind the palate (With Either a Gentle Or a Strong "Rasping" sound, and With the eyes Closed and Turned Up and Back). To Press attention, the inhaled (or exhaled) breath, the Natural bodily energy, and My Avatarically Self-Transmitted Divine Spirit-Energy Deep Into the head—Press attention, the inhaled (or exhaled) breath, the Natural bodily energy, and My Avatarically Self-Transmitted Divine Spirit-Energy Directly Upwards (From The Spinal Line) and (Via the lower rear of the head) Forward (Into The Total Region Of The Core and The Crown Of the head—Stopping In The Forward Middle Of the head, Between and Slightly Above and Deep Behind the eyes, and While Keeping the eyes Closed and Turned Up and Back). This Effective Process Regenerates, Rebalances, and Radiantly Fills (With Natural bodily energy and My Avatarically Self-Transmitted Divine Spirit-Energy) The Great Space Between The pituitary (or forward) Region Of the brain—Which Region Is Associated With The Descending, and gross (or lower), functional Tendency (or Purpose)—and The pineal (or upper rear) Region Of the brain—Which Region Is Associated With The Ascending, and subtle (or higher), functional Tendency (or Purpose)—While (At the same time) Preventing The Discharge and Loss (or "Leaking Out") Of Natural bodily energy and My Avatarically Self-Transmitted Divine Spirit-Energy From The Total brain Regions (Whether From the lower rear, the upper rear, or the middle of the brain, Or From The forward Regions Of the brain, Or Even From the eyes). Attention, the inhaled (or exhaled) breath, the Natural bodily energy, and My Avatarically Self-Transmitted Divine Spirit-Energy Should Be Held and Pressed In the head Continuously, Until My Avatarically Self-Transmitted Divine Spirit-Energy (Together With the genital and general bodily energy) Is Felt To Run Up the spine Into the brain, Producing A Swelling Of Pleasurable and Radiant Fullness In The Total Region Of The Core and The Crown Of the head (and, Thus, a Conservative and Ascending, or Regenerative, "orgasm" of the brain), and (By All Of This) Reversing and Releasing The Tendency Toward degenerative orgasm. If hyperventilation and The Tendency Toward Involuntary and degenerative orgasm Do Not Immediately Cease (or Come

Under Control) Via The First (Either inhaled Or exhaled) Ascent Toward The Swoon Of Fullness In the brain, the Following inhalations and exhalations Should (Like The First) Be Engaged Fully (and Via The Spinal Line, and To and Into The Total Region Of The Core and The Crown Of the head), As I Have Just Described. And This "Conductivity" Exercise Should Be Continued Thus, Until hyperventilation and The Tendency Toward Involuntary and degenerative orgasm Cease (or Come Under Control). And, When (By All Of This) hyperventilation and The Tendency Toward degenerative orgasm Come To Rest—Deeply Allow body, mind, and attention To Swoon Profoundly Toward and Into The Formless Pleasure (Of Natural bodily energy and My Avatarically Self-Transmitted Divine Spirit-Energy) In The Core and The Crown Of the head. Then (Whenever and However The Gathering Intention Toward Frontal Descent Returns) inhale Fully and Deeply In The Frontal Line (Even Pressing the breath Down Into the solar plexus and abdomen, While Relaxing and Opening The Frontal Line, and Tensing Upwards At the bodily base), In Order To Relieve Pressure In the head and Restore The Downward Frontal "Conductivity" (Of My Avatarically Self-Transmitted Divine Spirit-Energy and the Natural bodily energy). Then Breathe Naturally and Fully In The Full Circle. As All Of This Restores The Balance Of the body-mind, The Occasion Of "Emotional-Sexual Devotional Communion" May Be Either Resumed Or Brought To An End.

The moments Of "Emotional-Sexual Devotional Communion" that Are Not Immediately Associated With Impending degenerative orgasm Generally Involve The Practice Of inhalation (and Reception) Of the Natural bodily energy and My Avatarically Self-Transmitted Divine Spirit-Energy In The Descending Pattern Of The Frontal Line and exhalation (and Release) Of the Natural bodily energy and My Avatarically Self-Transmitted Divine Spirit-Energy Into The Ascending Pattern Of The Spinal Line. It Is Only At The Approach Of degenerative orgasm (or, Otherwise, Only At Random, and Especially In the More Intensified moments Of Exaltation and Ecstasy That Naturally Develop In The Course Of "Emotional-Sexual Devotional Communion") That Yogic sexual Activity Is, Temporarily, To Assume A Totally (or Rather Exclusively) Ascending Character (With Both inhalation and exhalation In The Spinal Line).

In The Only-By-Me Revealed and Given Way Of The Heart (or Way Of Adidam), sexually active Practitioners (male or female) who Have physical Problems Related To high blood pressure (or who have other significant medical reasons To Avoid Pressure In the head and/or Any Other Aspects Of The Exercise Of "Right Emotional-Sexual Yoga") Should (Perhaps) Altogether and Generally Avoid (or Voluntarily Relinquish) The Approach Of degenerative orgasm (and, Therefore, Also The Possible Subsequent Act Of The Intentional Regenerative Conversion Of Approaching degenerative orgasm). And This May

Be Done Through The Devotional, and human relational, and bodily Control Of attention, The Devotional and human relational Radiating Of Heart-Feeling, The Right Practice Of Whole bodily Relaxation, The Right (and Specifically emotional-sexual) Practice Of Pranayama (In The Form Of Easeful breathing In The Circle), and (As and when Required) The Right and Appropriate Practice Of Internal Upward Tensing (Either Brief and Constant Or, Otherwise, Brief and Repetitive) Of the bodily base (With the crown of the lower abdomen Simultaneously Drawn In and Up, On exhalation), but (Altogether) Without Pressing or Holding the breath, or Otherwise Introducing Pressure, In the head—and, Thus (In General), Through The <u>bodily</u> (Rather Than mental, or "heady") Control Of attention In the sex act, and Through The Consistent <u>Feeling</u>-Relinquishment Of The Entire Tendency Toward degenerative orgasm, and Through An Emphasis On bodily Re-Vitalizing Downward Frontal "Conductivity" (and, Otherwise, General bodily Diffusion) Of Feeling, breath, bodily energy, and (In Accordance With The Particular Case) My Avatarically Self-Transmitted Divine Spirit-Energy.

Also, In The Way Of The Heart, sexually active Practitioners (male or female) who Are (Either Chronically Or Occasionally) functionally Unable To Approach and Achieve Even degenerative orgasm (and who Are, Thus, Either Chronically Or Occasionally, functionally Unable To Redirect Impending degenerative orgasm Into A Wholly Regenerative Course) Should (Nevertheless, In The Context Of sexual activity) Practice The Art Of Right "General Conductivity" (According To The Present Developmental Stage Of the individual's Practice Of The Way Of The Heart), Including The Devotional, and human relational, and bodily Control Of attention, The Devotional and human relational Radiating Of Heart-Feeling, The Right Practice Of Whole bodily Relaxation, The Right (and Specifically emotional-sexual) Practice Of Pranayama, and (As and when Required) The Right and Appropriate Practice Of Internal Upward Tensing (Either Brief and Constant Or, Otherwise, Brief and Repetitive) Of the bodily base (With the crown of the lower abdomen Simultaneously Drawn In and Up, On exhalation)—For This Art Of "Conductivity" (In Its "General", or By-Me-Commonly-Given, Form) Will, Even In The Absence Of The functional Capability For orgasm, Keep sexual activity Rightly Aligned To The Devotional and Yogic Intention Required In Even every moment and Context Of Practice In The Way Of The Heart, and, Just So, It Will (To One or Another Degree) Allow Even such Non-orgasmic sexual activity To Be Sublimed and (In General) Made Regenerative (Rather Than degenerative) In its Total Cycle Of acts and effects.

There Are Two Principal Elements To conventional (or degenerative) orgasm That Must Be Brought Under Control Through "Emotional-Sexual

Devotional Communion". The First Is The Flow Of Energy (Including Both the Natural bodily energy and My Avatarically Self-Transmitted Divine Spirit-Energy), and The Second Is The Tendency (In the male) To Eliminate the vital chemical (or hormonal) fluid From the reproductive system (and The Tendency, In Both the male and the female, To Internally Generate and Retain grossly, or Even Negatively, Oriented Varieties Of hormonal or other chemical secretions and bodily energies).

Generally, women Do Not, To Any Significant Degree, Eliminate vital reproductive substances (Externally) During conventional orgasm. Therefore, It Is Not Necessary For My female Seeing-Devotees who Are (in their personal intimate contexts) sexually active (and, Otherwise, Spiritually Prepared For The Practice Of "Emotional-Sexual Devotional Communion") To Make Any Efforts To Avoid or Suppress conventional orgasm For The Purpose Of The Conservation Of The Potential External Discharge Of vital chemistry. They May (Potentially, and If they So Choose) Develop The Art Of sexually Transmitted Love To The Fullest, and they May (Thus and Thereby) Learn To Consistently Yield themselves Full-bodily In sexual Embrace—and they Are Naturally Free To Do So To Such A Degree That the cervix (which Is The Deep Center, or Terminal, Of the Natural bodily energy and My Avatarically Self-Transmitted Divine Spirit-Energy Within the sexual organs of the human female) Is (During sexual activity) Constantly (and Even Maximally, or To Whatever Chosen Degree) Stimulated To Feel the Natural bodily energy and My Avatarically Self-Transmitted Divine Spirit-Current. However, Such female Seeing-Devotees who Are (in their personal intimate contexts) sexually active Must, In Any Case, Consistently (or As A General Rule Of sexual Practice) Control, Convert, or Redirect the Natural bodily energy and My Avatarically Self-Transmitted Divine Spirit-Energy (Which Tend To Be Discharged Via the bodily base During female degenerative orgasm, Just As In the case of male ejaculatory orgasm), and they Must, Likewise, Consistently (or As A General Rule Of Spiritual Practice) Positively (and Spiritually) Convert and Orient The (Generally Internal) Profusion Of hormonal (or other chemical) secretions and bodily energies Naturally Associated With all sexual activity. Therefore, Such female Seeing-Devotees Must Practice The Art Of Conducting the Natural bodily energy and My Avatarically Self-Transmitted Divine Spirit-Energy Into The Natural and Right Pattern Of The Circle—Through The Devotional, and human relational, and bodily Control Of attention, The Devotional and human relational Radiating Of Heart-Feeling, The Right Practice Of Whole bodily Relaxation, The Right (and Specifically emotional-sexual) Practice Of Pranayama, and (As and when Required) The Right and Appropriate Practice Of Internal Upward Tensing (Either Brief and Constant Or, Otherwise, Brief and

Repetitive) Of the bodily base (With the crown of the lower abdomen Simultaneously Drawn In and Up, On exhalation). These Disciplines Should Be Intentionally Engaged By Such female Seeing-Devotees—During sexual intercourse (Generally), and At The Beginning Of The Cycle Of (otherwise degenerative) orgasm, and During Any Such Cycle, So That The Total Cycle Of sexual Embrace (and Potential orgasm) May Be Converted and Sublimed, and Made Wholly Regenerative, Through Total psycho-physical and Fully Felt Participation In My Avatarically Self-Transmitted Divine Spirit-Current.

Men Tend (Via ejaculatory orgasm) To Eliminate vital reproductive chemical (or hormonal) fluid Externally In every act of sexual intercourse, and they Otherwise Tend (As Also Do women) To Generate (and To Retain Internally) grossly (or Even Negatively) Oriented Varieties Of general bodily secretions In every act of sexual intercourse (and In the event of every sexually related thought, emotion, or act). This (and Also The General Loss Of sexual energy, By both men and women, In sexual intercourse, and In the event of every sexually related thought, emotion, or act) Has A (Potentially) degenerative Effect On the body and the mind Over time (and, In General, It Is Otherwise Part Of A Total Pattern Of egoic and Un-Happy Confinement To The First Three Stages Of Life). Therefore, Conservation (and Positive and, Ultimately, Spiritual Conversion) Of that vital (and general bodily) chemistry and bodily energy (Through Conservation, and Positive and, Ultimately, Spiritual Conversion, Of all sexually related thoughts, emotions, and actions) Generally Has A Rejuvenating and Strengthening Effect On the body and the mind Over time.

The Total Discipline Of "Emotional-Sexual Devotional Communion" (In The Case Of My Seeing Devotees who Are, in their personal intimate contexts, sexually active), or (Otherwise) Spiritually Active and Yogically (Rather Than Merely idealistically and puritanically) Supported and Maintained (and, Therefore, Truly Regenerative, or life-energy-Positive, Rather Than life-energy-Negative) celibacy (In The Case Of My Seeing Devotees who Are Not sexually active In The Context Of any intimate relationship), Must Be Fitted To Serve The Developments and Processes Associated With The Fully Spiritually Awakened, and (Spiritually) Fully Technically Responsible, Stages Of Practice In The Way Of The Heart. However, Even All Practitioners Of The Way Of The Heart Should, From The Beginning Of The Student-Beginner Stage, Consistently Observe the effects that Any Loss Of vital energy and reproductive chemistry Makes In the body-mind. And, On The Basis Of Such self-Observation, All My Formally Practicing Devotees who Are (in their personal intimate contexts) sexually active, but who Are Also Yet Beginners In The Only-By-Me Revealed and Given Way Of The Heart, and who (Even If they Are Practicing Beyond The Student-Beginner Stage Of The Way Of The Heart, and, Thus, On The

Basis Of Spiritual Initiation By Means Of My Ruchira Shaktipat) Do Not Yet Hear Me and See Me, Should (As A General Rule Of their sexual Practice) Conserve Natural sexual energy, and (As The Case May Be) My Avatarically Self-Transmitted Divine Spirit-Energy, and (In The Case Of male Practitioners) the vital reproductive chemistry. Therefore, In The Case Of All Beginners (or Not Yet Both Hearing and Seeing Practitioners) In The Only-By-Me Revealed and Given Way Of The Heart, male ejaculatory orgasm (In Excess, or Even At All) and female degenerative orgasm (In Excess, or Even At All) Should (Generally, and At Will) Be Avoided (or Voluntarily Relinquished), By Controlling conventional orgasm (and, To One or Another Degree, Conserving The Frequency Of sexual activity itself) Via The Engaging Of sexual activity As An emotional-sexual Form Of "Conscious Exercise" (In The Context Of A Right Conservative sexual Practice Altogether).

Avatar Adi Da Samraj
The Mountain Of Attention Sanctuary, 2002

SUTRA 38

The Practice Of "Emotional-Sexual Conscious Exercise" Is Identical To The Practice Of "Emotional-Sexual Devotional Communion"—In The Sense That It, Too, Is A Sacramental (and Truly Sacred) Activity, and Even A Kind Of Puja (or A True Devotional and Ritual Art). Therefore, The Puja Of "Emotional-Sexual Conscious Exercise" (Like The Puja Of "Emotional-Sexual Devotional Communion") Is To Be Engaged As A Form Of Ruchira Avatara Bhakti Yoga, or The Devotionally Responsive Counter-egoic (and Even Total psycho-physical) Effort Of ego-Surrendering, ego-Forgetting, and (More and More Effectively) ego-Transcending Devotion To Me. Therefore, The Puja Of "Emotional-Sexual Conscious Exercise" Requires The Surrender, The Forgetting, and The (More and More Effective) Transcending Of body, emotion (or self-Contracted, and, Therefore, limited, feeling), mind (Both In its Content-Form, or Extended-Form, Which Is the stream of thoughts, and In its Root-Form, Which Is attention itself), and breath (Via The "General" Form Of The Basic Yoga Of "Conductivity"). However, There Are (Otherwise) Various Technical Differences Between The Practice Of "Emotional-Sexual Conscious Exercise" and The Practice Of "Emotional-Sexual Devotional Communion".

To Practice "Emotional-Sexual Conscious Exercise" Is To Engage In sexual activity In An Intentionally Relaxed Manner, By Consistently Radiating Heart-Feeling, and By Consistently Relaxing body, emotion, and mind (and By Applying Internal Upward Tensing Of the bodily base, As and when Required, and, then, Either As A Brief and Constant Gesture Or, Otherwise, As A Brief and Repetitive Gesture Of the bodily base, With the crown of the lower abdomen Simultaneously Drawn In and Up, On exhalation), and By Relaxing (bodily) In The Frontal Line (and, Also, From the bodily base, and Along The Spinal Line, and, Thereby, <u>Toward</u> The Crown Of the head—but Without Intentional Concentration Of attention In or Above the head), and By Practicing Random Simple Pranayama (or lung-breathing "Conductivity", In The Form Of inhalation-Reception, In Descent, Via The Frontal Line Of the body, and exhalation-Release, In General Ascent, Via The Spinal Line Of the body), and (Altogether) By Controlling attention, thought, and sexual Intensity (Via The Right Practice Of Whole bodily Relaxation, and Via The Devotional and human relational Radiating Of Heart-Feeling, and Via The Maintenance Of

Direct physical, sensual, and emotional Awareness In the sexual act, and Via The Constant Intention To Completely Bypass the genital discharge of sexual energy, and Via The Constant Intention To Convert, or Conduct Into The Spinal Line, all Accumulated genital energy, Whenever male ejaculatory orgasm, or Even female degenerative orgasm, Is Felt, Even Remotely, To Be Approaching). And The Practice Of "Emotional-Sexual Conscious Exercise" Accomplishes The Bypass Of degenerative male or female orgasms, and The Conversion Of Potential degenerative orgasms Into An energy-Conserving (or Regeneratively orgasmic) Process, By Means Of The Suspension Of Stimulating sexual activity, and By Means Of An Instant and Relatively Brief Intensification Of All The Various Elements Of "Emotional-Sexual Conscious Exercise"—Especially The Upward Tensing (Either Brief and Constant Or Brief and Repetitive) Of the bodily base (With the crown of the lower abdomen Simultaneously Drawn In and Up, On exhalation), and The Sudden Directing Of Natural bodily energy (and, As The Case May Be, My Avatarically Self-Transmitted Divine Spirit-Energy) Into The Spinal Line and (In A General Manner) Toward The Crown Of the head, Whenever male ejaculatory orgasm (or Even female degenerative orgasm) Is Felt (Even Remotely) To Be Approaching.

In The Case Of "Emotional-Sexual Conscious Exercise", The Practice Of Bypassing degenerative orgasm and Achieving Regenerative orgasm Is Not As Yogically Detailed As The Practice Of Bypassing degenerative orgasm and Achieving Regenerative orgasm In "Emotional-Sexual Devotional Communion", and (In Contrast To The Practice Of "Emotional-Sexual Devotional Communion") "Emotional-Sexual Conscious Exercise" Does Not Involve <u>Fully</u> Technically Responsible "Conductivity" Of My Avatarically Self-Transmitted Divine Spirit-Current (In The Manner Of My Seeing Devotees), Nor Does "Emotional-Sexual Conscious Exercise" Involve Intentional Upward Yogic Concentration In The Core Of the brain. The Practice Of "Emotional-Sexual Conscious Exercise" Is Simply A Matter Of Bypassing Potential degenerative orgasm and Redirecting the genitally Accumulating (and, Potentially, degeneratively orgasmic) Natural bodily energy (and, As The Case May Be, My Avatarically Self-Transmitted Divine Spirit-Energy) Into The Spinal Line and Into the entire body. Although, In The Process Of Bypassing degenerative orgasm and Achieving Regenerative orgasm (or The True Spinal "Conductivity" Of the sexual energy Otherwise Associated With degenerative orgasm), The Practitioner Of "Emotional-Sexual Conscious Exercise" may experience a pleasurable sensation of Natural energy (and, As The Case May Be, Of My Avatarically Self-Transmitted Divine Spirit-Energy) Rushing Into the spine (and Even Into the brain), the experience of Regenerative orgasm Varies In The Case Of each Such Practicing individual and In Every Occasion Of "Emotional-Sexual Conscious Exercise". In Any Case,

If The Practitioner Of "Emotional-Sexual Conscious Exercise" Avoids Breaking The Circle At the bodily base and Conducts the genitally Accumulating Natural energy (and, As The Case May Be, My Avatarically Self-Transmitted Divine Spirit-Energy) Into The Spinal Line, That (In and Of Itself) Is A Regenerative sexual Practice—No Matter what sensations he or she may experience, or not experience, In The Process.

Although There Are Many Similarities Between Them, "Emotional-Sexual Conscious Exercise" Is Not Fully The Equivalent Of "Emotional-Sexual Devotional Communion". Rather, "Emotional-Sexual Conscious Exercise" Is A Practicing Preliminary (or A Kind Of Early, or Training, Phase) That Prepares The Foundation For The Later (and, Spiritually, Fully Technically Responsible) Practice That Is "Emotional-Sexual Devotional Communion".

The Practice Of "Emotional-Sexual Conscious Exercise" Relies Principally On The Control Of sexual Intensity (Through Intentional, Rather Constant, and Generalized bodily Relaxation). Therefore, In The Case Of "Emotional-Sexual Conscious Exercise", The Specific Yogic Controls That Achieve The Bypass and Conversion Of degenerative orgasm Are Secondary To The More General Practice Of Intentional Control Of sexual Intensity. And The Specific Yogic Controls That Achieve The Bypass and Conversion Of degenerative orgasm Are, In The Case Of "Emotional-Sexual Conscious Exercise", Developed More Simply (and, In General, Are Practiced Less Intensively, and Less Intensely) Than In The Case Of "Emotional-Sexual Devotional Communion".

The Right and True Practice Of "Emotional-Sexual Devotional Communion" Requires An Experienced and Mature Capability Relative To The Specific Yogic Controls That Achieve The Bypass and Conversion Of degenerative orgasm. However, Because Of That Experienced and Mature Capability, The Practice Of "Emotional-Sexual Devotional Communion" Generally Permits (or Even Requires) A Much Greater Allowance Of sexual Intensity (In The Context Of sexual activity) Than Can (In General) Be The Case In The Practice Of "Emotional-Sexual Conscious Exercise". Therefore, The Practice Of "Emotional-Sexual Devotional Communion" Emphasizes The Intensive, Intense, and Even Relatively Complex Use Of Yogic Controls—Such As The "General" Form Of lung-breathing "Conductivity", The Upward Tensing (Either Brief and Constant Or, Otherwise, Brief and Repetitive) Of the bodily base (With the crown of the lower abdomen Simultaneously Drawn In and Up, On exhalation), The Introduction Of Various Other bodily Locks and Mudras,[132] and Upward Yogic Concentration In The Core Of the brain. And, As A Result Of The Intensive (and Intense) Application Of The Various Yogic Controls That Are Unique To It (or, Otherwise, Common To "Emotional-Sexual Conscious Exercise" As Well), The Practice Of "Emotional-Sexual Devotional Communion" Generally

Achieves More Deep, Intense, and Yogically Profound Regenerative orgasms Than Can (In General) Be The Case In The Practice Of "Emotional-Sexual Conscious Exercise". (And, Of Course, The Right and True Practice Of "Emotional-Sexual Devotional Communion" Is Not Only Yogically Deep, Intense, and Profound, but Spiritually Deep, Intense, and Profound As Well.)

In The Case Of "Emotional-Sexual Conscious Exercise", The Practice Of The "General" Form Of lung-breathing "Conductivity" Is Rather Secondary (or Less Intensive, Less Intense, and Yogically Less Developed Than In The Case Of "Emotional-Sexual Devotional Communion"). Thus, Although The Practice Of The "General" Form Of lung-breathing "Conductivity" Is To Be Engaged In A General, Random, and Simple Manner In The Practice Of "Emotional-Sexual Conscious Exercise", It Is Not Otherwise Emphasized (or Made Into An Intensive and Intense Exercise) In The Practice Of "Emotional-Sexual Conscious Exercise". However, The Yogic Practice Of The "General" Form Of lung-breathing "Conductivity" Should, As A Means For Bypassing and Converting degenerative orgasm, Be Very Intensively (and Intensely) Practiced In The Case Of "Emotional-Sexual Devotional Communion"—and This (Along With Other Specific Yogic Controls) Allows For The Possibility Of Much Greater sexual Intensity (and Much Less Intensive Application Of Generalized bodily Relaxation) Than Can (In General) Be The Case In The Practice Of "Emotional-Sexual Conscious Exercise".

Thus, In Summary, The Right and True Practice Of "Emotional-Sexual Devotional Communion" Emphasizes Full sexual Intensity and The Intensive (and Intense) Exercise Of Specific (and Even Relatively Complex) Yogic Controls That Very Effectively Bypass and Convert degenerative orgasm—Whereas The Right and True Practice Of "Emotional-Sexual Conscious Exercise" Emphasizes Effective Control Of sexual Intensity and A Comparatively Simpler (and, Generally, Both Less Intensive and Less Intense) Yogic Approach To The Bypass and Conversion Of degenerative orgasm. However, With The Foundation Of Such "Emotional-Sexual Conscious Exercise" Rightly, Truly, and Very Effectively Established, The Eventual Transition To The Practice Of "Emotional-Sexual Devotional Communion" Can, When All Other Necessary Qualifications Appear, Be Readily Made.

In The Case Of male Practitioners Of The Way Of The Heart, vital reproductive fluid Should (As A General Rule) Be Conserved, Except When reproduction itself Is Desired. Therefore, All sexually active male Practitioners Of The Way Of The Heart Must Fully Realize The Art Of Bypassing the ejaculatory orgasm. And Both male and female Practitioners Of The Way Of The Heart Must Practice The Regenerative Art Of Controlling, Converting, Redirecting, and Conducting the Natural bodily energy and (In Due Course) My Avatarically

Self-Transmitted Divine Spirit-Energy, As Natural bodily energy and (As The Case May Be) My Avatarically Self-Transmitted Divine Spirit-Energy Are (or Become) Associated With sexual pleasure Generally (and With conventional, or degenerative, orgasm Most Especially), In The Circle Of the body-mind.

Generally, If conventional (or ejaculatory) male orgasm (or Even conventional female orgasm) Is Allowed To Occur Only Relatively Infrequently, it Will Not Be Followed By any Significantly Negative (or limiting) bodily (or, Otherwise, Spiritual) effects. Therefore, In The Only-By-Me Revealed and Given Way Of The Heart, In The Case Of My Seeing Devotees Practicing "Emotional-Sexual Devotional Communion", and In The Case Of My Formally Practicing Devotees who Do Not Yet Hear Me <u>and</u> See Me, and who Practice "Emotional-Sexual Conscious Exercise" (As A Means To Conserve vital energy, and reproductive chemistry, and, As The Case May Be, My Avatarically Self-Transmitted Divine Spirit-Energy, During sexual activity), conventional male or female orgasm May (<u>Perhaps</u>) Be <u>Occasionally</u> Allowed. (And, Of Course, conventional male orgasm Must, and conventional female orgasm Should, Be Allowed—and, With Formal Cultural Accountability, The Frequency Of Occasions Of sexual intercourse May, In A Truly Sacred Sacrificial, or Serving, Manner, Be, Temporarily and Appropriately, Increased—whenever There Is A Right and Specific Intention For the female partner to become pregnant.)

In The Case Of younger male Practitioners Of "Emotional-Sexual Conscious Exercise" (who are no older than their twenties, or, Perhaps, early thirties), ejaculatory orgasm May (Perhaps) Be Allowed As Often As (Approximately) once every ten days—Whereas, In The Case Of male Practitioners Of "Emotional-Sexual Conscious Exercise" who are older than their twenties or early thirties (and, As An Optimum General Rule Of Practice, Even In The Case Of male Practitioners Of "Emotional-Sexual Conscious Exercise" who are no older than their twenties or early thirties), ejaculatory orgasm Should (As A General Rule Of Practice) Be Allowed No More Than once per month. Once their Practice Of The Only-By-Me Revealed and Given Way Of The Heart Begins To Be Spiritually Activated By Me (and, In Due Course, As An Expression Of The self-Renouncing Attitude and The psycho-physical Stability That Must Be Associated With Ever-Increasing Maturity In The Truly Both Hearing and Seeing Practice Of The Way Of The Heart), <u>All</u> male Practitioners Of "Emotional-Sexual Devotional Communion" Must <u>Consistently</u> Conserve (and, Except On Relatively Rare Occasions, Voluntarily Relinquish) ejaculatory orgasm, Such That ejaculatory orgasm Is (As A General Rule Of Practice) Allowed Either Not At All Or No More Than once per month (With The Actual Frequency Conservatively Determined By The Characteristics and The Requirements Of the individual's Practice Of The Way Of The Heart At Any Particular

Developmental Stage). And, In The Context Of Such Right Conservative emotional-sexual Discipline, Healthful Maintenance Of the prostate gland (and other functional parts of the sexual and reproductive apparatus) Is To Be Accomplished Not By Means Of degenerative orgasm (or By Any ego-Based, ego-Reinforcing, or Otherwise degenerative Means At All), but, Altogether, By Right Yogic emotional-sexual Practice (Including, As Necessary, Right "Own-Body Yogic Sexual Practice", and Such Healthful bodily Practices As Regular Rhythmic Upward Tensing Of the bodily base, Regular internal finger-pressing and massaging of the prostate gland itself, Regular washing and cleansing of the anal canal, Regular Right Diet, and Regular Practice Of General physical "Conscious Exercise"[133]).

Female Practitioners Of Either "Emotional-Sexual Conscious Exercise" Or "Emotional-Sexual Devotional Communion" May (As Necessary For their Altogether Right, and Rightly Effective, Practice Of The Totality Of The Only-By-Me Revealed and Given Way Of The Heart) Limit The Frequency Of conventional (or Unconverted and degenerative) orgasm To Approximately The Same Order Of Frequency Indicated For male Practitioners Of Either "Emotional-Sexual Conscious Exercise" Or "Emotional-Sexual Devotional Communion". (However, Since conventional female orgasm Does Not, In General, Involve The Immediate Significant External Discharge Of vital reproductive substances, The Measure Of Allowable Frequency Of conventional orgasm, In The Case Of female Practitioners Of Either "Emotional-Sexual Conscious Exercise" Or "Emotional-Sexual Devotional Communion", Should Be The Subsequently Observed Effect Of conventional orgasm On the individual's general health and On The Intensity, and On The Summary Quality and Effectiveness, Of the individual's Total Practice Of The Way Of The Heart. On That Basis, The Intelligently Allowable Frequency Of conventional orgasm, In Any Particular Case Of A female Practitioner Of Either "Emotional-Sexual Conscious Exercise" Or "Emotional-Sexual Devotional Communion", May Be More, or Even Less, Frequent Than In The Case Of Any Particular male Practitioner Of Either "Emotional-Sexual Conscious Exercise" Or "Emotional-Sexual Devotional Communion".)

In Any and Every Case (Whether Of The male Or Of The female Practitioner Of Either "Emotional-Sexual Conscious Exercise" Or "Emotional-Sexual Devotional Communion"), The Frequency Of conventional orgasm (or Even The Decision To Control, Conserve, and Convert conventional orgasm In Every Occasion Of "Emotional-Sexual Conscious Exercise", or To Control, Conserve, and Convert conventional orgasm In Every Occasion Of "Emotional-Sexual Devotional Communion") Should Be Determined By A "Consideration" Of Such Factors As age, degree of vitality, state of health, The General

Orientation Of Practice At Any Developmental Stage Of The Way Of The Heart, and The Effect Of conventional orgasm On The Various Features Of daily (and Meditative) Practice Of The Way Of The Heart.

If It Is To Be Effective, The male Conservation Of vital reproductive fluid (In "Emotional-Sexual Devotional Communion", and In "Emotional-Sexual Conscious Exercise") Must (Whenever It Is Performed) Be Real and Complete. In "Emotional-Sexual Devotional Communion" (Practiced By All My Formally Practicing Devotees who Both Hear Me <u>and</u> See Me, and who Are, in their personal intimate contexts, sexually active) and Also In The Simpler (and, In The Case Of Student-Beginners, Not Yet Spiritually Active, or, In The Case Of those Of My Beginning Devotees who Are Practicing Beyond The Student-Beginner Stage Of The Way Of The Heart, Not Yet, Spiritually, Fully Technically Responsible) "Conscious Exercise" Of emotional-sexual activity (Engaged By All My Formally Practicing Devotees who Do Not Yet Hear Me <u>and</u> See Me, and who Are, in their personal intimate contexts, sexually active), The Control and Conservation Of male ejaculation Is (Like Every Other Aspect Of sexual self-Control and sexual Conservation, In both male and female Practitioners Of Such sexual self-Control and sexual Conservation) Achieved (In The Only-By-Me Revealed and Given Way Of The Heart) Principally By Means Of The Devotional, and human relational, and bodily Control Of attention, The Devotional and human relational Radiating Of Heart-Feeling, The Right Practice Of Whole bodily Relaxation, The Right (and Specifically emotional-sexual) Practice Of Pranayama, and (As and when Required) The Right and Appropriate Practice Of Internal Upward Tensing (Either Brief and Constant Or, Otherwise, Brief and Repetitive) Of the bodily base (With the crown of the lower abdomen Simultaneously Drawn In and Up, On exhalation).

In The Case Of male Practitioners (Of Either "Emotional-Sexual Devotional Communion" Or "Emotional-Sexual Conscious Exercise"), finger Pressure At or Near the perineum <u>During</u> (or, Otherwise, Immediately—or, As A Preventive Measure, At any sexually active moment—Previous To) ejaculatory orgasm May (Perhaps) Be Applied, In Order To Prevent Elimination Of vital reproductive fluid—but, Once The Event Of ejaculation Has Already Begun, Even Such A Practice Tends Merely To Force the vital reproductive fluid Into the bladder (From which it Is Eliminated later, Via urination). Therefore, In Order To Completely Conserve the vital reproductive fluid (and Also Avoid Irritation Of the prostate gland and the male sex organs Generally), finger Pressure At or Near the perineum Should Generally Be Used (If At All) Only To Keep The Circuit Of Natural bodily energy and My Avatarically Self-Transmitted Divine Spirit-Energy Closed At the bodily base—Whereas ejaculation itself Should (As A General Rule) Simply Be Avoided (or Voluntarily Relinquished), By Means

Of The Right Practice Of The Devotional, and human relational, and bodily Control Of attention, The Devotional and human relational Radiating Of Heart-Feeling, The Right Practice Of Whole bodily Relaxation, The Right (and Specifically emotional-sexual) Practice Of Pranayama, and (As and when Required) The Right and Appropriate Practice Of Internal Upward Tensing (Either Brief and Constant Or, Otherwise, Brief and Repetitive) Of the bodily base (With the crown of the lower abdomen Simultaneously Drawn In and Up, On exhalation).

Male Practitioners Of (Especially) "Emotional-Sexual Conscious Exercise" (and—but Much Less Frequently—Even Some male Practitioners Of "Emotional-Sexual Devotional Communion") May (In The Context, and As A Direct Result, Of sexual activity) Tend (At times) Toward Involuntary (and, Apparently, Not Otherwise Completely Controllable) ejaculatory orgasm. On those occasions (Of Apparently Diminished Ability To Control ejaculation), male Practitioners May Choose To Use finger Pressure (At or Near the perineum) To Suppress ejaculation During (or, Preferably, Immediately Previous To) Actual ejaculatory orgasm. This Practice Is (When Accompanied By The Continued "General Conductivity" Exercise Of The Devotional, and human relational, and bodily Control Of attention, The Devotional and human relational Radiating Of Heart-Feeling, The Right Practice Of Whole bodily Relaxation, The Right, and Specifically emotional-sexual, Practice Of Pranayama, and, As and when Required, The Right and Appropriate Practice Of Internal Upward Tensing, Either Brief and Constant Or, Otherwise, Brief and Repetitive, Of the bodily base, With the crown of the lower abdomen Simultaneously Drawn In and Up, On exhalation) Superior To Mere Indulgence In ejaculatory orgasm—but Even This Practice Must (Except, At Most, As An Occasional, or Rarely Necessary, Device) Be Progressively Out-Grown (or, Over time, Be Made Generally Unnecessary) By The Persistent Application Of The Practices Of The Devotional, and human relational, and bodily Control Of attention, The Devotional and human relational Radiating Of Heart-Feeling, The Right Practice Of Whole bodily Relaxation, The Right (and Specifically emotional-sexual) Practice Of Pranayama, and (As and when Required) The Right and Appropriate Practice Of Internal Upward Tensing (Either Brief and Constant Or, Otherwise, Brief and Repetitive) Of the bodily base (With the crown of the lower abdomen Simultaneously Drawn In and Up, On exhalation), Such That The Complete Control and Bypass Of ejaculation May (As A General Rule) Be Managed By These Means Alone (Without The Application Of finger Pressure At or Near the perineum).

Furthermore, For The male Conservation Of vital reproductive fluid To Be Real and Complete, Such Control and Bypass Must Be Accomplished Before ejaculatory Pulsation Is (Even To A Slight Degree) Triggered In the penis. Otherwise, If The male Practitioner Waits To Apply Sufficient Means Of Control Until After ejaculatory Pulsation Has Been (Even To A Slight Degree) Triggered In the penis, and Then Forcefully Suppresses (Particularly By Means Of Strong Upward Tensing Of the bodily base) The Already (Even If Only Minimally) Initiated degenerative (or ejaculatory) orgasm—ejaculation May Occur Internally (As In The Case Of finger Pressure Applied During, or Immediately Previous To, ejaculatory orgasm), Even Though The Outwardly Observable Discharge Of vital reproductive fluid Has Been Prevented. In Such A Case, Regenerative Conversion Of male degenerative (or ejaculatory) orgasm Cannot Be Achieved, and (In Addition) Such "internal ejaculation" (or Internal Accumulation) Of vital reproductive fluid Can Result (To One or Another Degree) In A Painful Aching Of the testicles and (Perhaps) Of the prostate gland. (Indeed, In Order To Avoid Such Internal Accumulation and Aching, All My male Devotees, Whether they are sexually active Or Not, Should, daily, Practice Occasional Random Upward Tensing Of the bodily base, and, Perhaps, Also Of the crown of the lower abdomen, In A Kind Of Rhythmic Flexing, or "Pumping", Fashion, Thereby To Draw the reproductive fluid In, Back, and Up Toward The Spinal Line, and, Thus, To Tone and Clear the reproductive organs, and To Serve and Maintain The "Conductivity"-Capability Of The genital Region, and Of Even The Entire Region Of the bodily base, and Of The abdominal Region As Well.[134] And All My female Devotees Should Do The Same, In Order To Serve and Maintain The Tone, and The "Conductivity"-Capability, Of The genital Region, and Of Even The Entire Region Of the bodily base, and Of The abdominal Region As Well.) Therefore, Because Of Its Critical Importance, The Ability To Completely Control and Bypass ejaculation (Without Merely Suppressing The Already Advancing ejaculatory Tendency or Event, Whether Through The Application Of finger Pressure Or Even Through Any Forceful Application Of The Internal Means Of Control After ejaculatory Pulsation Has Already Been Triggered In the penis) Must (In Order To Provide A Right Foundation For The Later Progressive Development Of The Yogic sexual Practice) Be Established (At Least As A Basic and Generally Consistent Capability) Before (or, Otherwise, Coincident With) Maturity In The Student-Beginner Stage Of The Way Of The Heart.

In The Case Of Both male and female Practitioners Of The Way Of The Heart, "Emotional-Sexual Devotional Communion" (and—but, Generally, To A Lesser Degree—"Emotional-Sexual Conscious Exercise") Releases (Especially Via Fully Developed Regenerative orgasms) A Profusion Of Natural bodily energy (and, In The Case Of My Devotees Spiritually Activated By Means Of My Ruchira Shaktipat, A Profusion Of My Avatarically Self-Transmitted Divine

Spirit-Energy Itself), Including many kinds of Positively (and, As The Case May Be, Also Spiritually) Converted hormonal (or other chemical) secretions—and This Profusion Is (Thus) Released All Over the body and its brain (and Not Merely In The Region Of the genitals and the bodily base). The hormonal (and other chemical) flows Thus Released and Retained Within the body Are Of a Rejuvenating kind, Conducive Toward psycho-physical health and General psycho-physical Well-being. This Is Because the hormonal (and other chemical) secretions Stimulated, Converted, and Conserved In the body (Rather Than Eliminated From the body) During (Right) "Emotional-Sexual Devotional Communion" (and Right "Emotional-Sexual Conscious Exercise") are of the Non-Stress variety.

People under the daily circumstances of life in the common world Tend To Be Constantly Stimulated To Produce hormonal secretions of the Stress variety, and such secretions Tend To Depress (or Even Destroy) health and General psycho-physical Well-being Over time. Thus, One Of The Principal Motives Toward sexual activity and conventional orgasm In the common world Is The Urge To Release Stress and Eliminate The chemical Results Of Stress—Whereas "Emotional-Sexual Devotional Communion" (and—but, Generally, To A Lesser Degree—"Emotional-Sexual Conscious Exercise"), In The Midst Of a Total life Of ego-Transcending Practice Of The Way Of The Heart, Transcends All Stress-Bound Motives and Results.

The "General" Form Of The Practice Of "Conductivity" Of Natural bodily energy (and Of My Avatarically Self-Transmitted Divine Spirit-Energy) In "Emotional-Sexual Devotional Communion", and (Also) The "General" Form Of The Practice Of "Conductivity" Of Natural bodily energy (and, As The Case May Be, My Avatarically Self-Transmitted Divine Spirit-Energy) In The Practice Of "Emotional-Sexual Conscious Exercise", Keeps The Circle Of the body-mind Rightly Polarized (and, In General, Establishes the body-mind In A Feeling Of Balance, or Of Equanimity, and Of "Fullness"). Right and Full Practice Of Either "Emotional-Sexual Devotional Communion" Or (but, Generally, To A Lesser Degree—and Only In The Spiritually Active Case, Beyond The Student-Beginner Stage Of The Way Of The Heart) "Emotional-Sexual Conscious Exercise" Fills the entire body-mind With Balanced Flows Of My Avatarically Self-Transmitted Divine Spirit-Energy (and, Thus, With The Sublime Delight Of ego-Surrendering Participation In My Avatarically Self-Transmitted Divine Love-Bliss). Also, "Emotional-Sexual Devotional Communion" and (but, Generally, To A Lesser Degree) The Right Practice Of "Emotional-Sexual Conscious Exercise" Fill the entire body-mind Even With Positive Flows Of An hormonal (or other chemical) Profusion, and With Flows Of Positively (and, As The Case May Be, Spiritually) Converted Natural bodily energy.

"Emotional-Sexual Devotional Communion" (and—but, Generally, To A Lesser Degree—"Emotional-Sexual Conscious Exercise") Even (Generally—If Not Done Excessively) Rejuvenates the body-mind, By Positively Stimulating (and, As The Case May Be, Spiritually Activating) all the Principal (or, Otherwise, Critical) centers of the body, and By Maintaining The Right Polarization Of The bodily (or psycho-physical) Flows, and By Preventing The Generation Of merely grossly (or Even Negatively) Oriented fluids From the hormonal (and other bodily) centers, and By Maintaining The Right (and, As The Case May Be, Spiritually Auspicious) Attitude, Direction, and Intent Of mind (or psyche), emotion, and body. (Also, Secondarily, the vital reproductive fluid itself, Retained In the body Of The male Practitioner Of Either "Emotional-Sexual Devotional Communion" Or "Emotional-Sexual Conscious Exercise", Has A Readily Apparent Rejuvenative Effect.) And, Because Much Of The Rejuvenative (or, Altogether, Regenerative) Effect Of Either "Emotional-Sexual Devotional Communion" Or "Emotional-Sexual Conscious Exercise" Is A Direct Result Of the Fully Developed Regenerative orgasm, The Principal functional Element Of Either "Emotional-Sexual Devotional Communion" Or "Emotional-Sexual Conscious Exercise" Is The Conversion Of every (Potential) degenerative orgasm Into a Truly Regenerative orgasm. Therefore, Although The Bypassing Of the degenerative orgasm Is A Necessary functional Element Of Both "Emotional-Sexual Devotional Communion" and "Emotional-Sexual Conscious Exercise", The Fully Effective Conversion Of the Potential degenerative orgasm Into an Actual Regenerative orgasm—or A Yogically Ascending, and (In The Case Of male Practitioners) Non-ejaculatory, or (In The Case Of female Practitioners) Entirely Non-degenerative, and (In All Cases) Inherently and Fully Regenerative, Process—Is Always The True Purpose Of Even Such Bypass.

Truly Regenerative (or Yogically Ascending) orgasms May—If Otherwise Compatible With The Developing Spiritual Process Of The Way Of The Heart—Serve An Important Role In The Achievement and The Maintenance Of psycho-physical health and General psycho-physical Well-being. Therefore, Regenerative orgasms Should (In The Case Of Practitioners Of The Way Of The Heart, Whether male Or female, who Are, in their personal intimate contexts, sexually active) Be Generally (but Never Excessively) Permitted. Additionally, In The Case Of Yogically sexually active Practitioners Of The Way Of The Heart who Are Formally Acknowledged To Be Uniquely Qualified For A Right Yogic Emotional-Sexual Sadhana, Truly Regenerative orgasms May (With Formal Agreement) Be Not Only Permitted but Actually (and Even Intensively) Cultivated—Such That (Generally) Regenerative orgasms Are Fully Achieved Even several times In Each Occasion Of "Emotional-Sexual Devotional Communion" or, Otherwise (Once Adaptation To The Practice Of

Achieving Regenerative orgasm Is Itself Established), In Each Occasion Of "Emotional-Sexual Conscious Exercise".

Equanimity Is Inherently Regenerative. Enervation and Negative Accumulation Are Inherently degenerative.

Equanimity and Regeneration (and Not Enervation, Negative Accumulation, and degeneration) Are The Genuine Effects Of True "Emotional-Sexual Devotional Communion" (and Of Rightly Practiced "Emotional-Sexual Conscious Exercise"). Neither Stress Nor the self-Contraction Is Supported or Intensified By True (and, Necessarily, Spiritually Active) "Emotional-Sexual Devotional Communion" (or By Rightly Practiced, and, As The Case May Be, Spiritually Active, "Emotional-Sexual Conscious Exercise"). And My Spiritually "Bright" Love-Bliss Is The Ultimate Substance (and By-My-Avataric-Divine-Spiritual-Grace-Given Gift) Of True "Emotional-Sexual Devotional Communion" (and, Potentially, or As The Case May Be, Of Rightly Practiced "Emotional-Sexual Conscious Exercise").

The Principal Function Of "Emotional-Sexual Devotional Communion" and Of "Emotional-Sexual Conscious Exercise" Is (By The Maintenance Of Devotional attention To Me Even In The Context Of sexual activity) To More and More Fully and Completely Align and Devotionally Surrender the Total personality To Me. And The Special Function Of "Emotional-Sexual Devotional Communion" and (In The Spiritually Active Case) Of "Emotional-Sexual Conscious Exercise" Is To Devotionally Surrender the Total (and Even emotional-sexual) personality To My (Avatarically Self-Transmitted) Tangible Divine Spirit-Presence, Such That My Avatarically Self-Transmitted Spiritual (and Always Blessing) Divine Presence Is (Thereby, and Always) Intimately Found, Made Resonant In The Circle, and Tangibly Expressed In the frontal human character.

"Emotional-Sexual Devotional Communion" and "Emotional-Sexual Conscious Exercise" Are Not Themselves To Be Equated With The Vertical (or Ascending) Processes (Otherwise Associated With The Fifth Stage Of Life) Which Are Engaged In The Context Of The "Perfect Practice" Of The Way Of The Heart. Rightly Practiced, "Emotional-Sexual Conscious Exercise" (Beginning In The "Original" Context Of The Fourth Stage Of Life In The Way Of The Heart) and "Emotional-Sexual Devotional Communion" (Beginning In The Fully Established "Basic" Context Of The Fourth Stage Of Life In The Way Of The Heart) Can and Should Serve The Relaxation Of The self-Contracted Search For gross bodily self-Fulfillment and gross bodily self-Release—and Practice Of Either "Emotional-Sexual Conscious Exercise" Or "Emotional-Sexual Devotional Communion" Can and Should Also Always Serve The Right Polarization, The Progressive Purification, and (Eventually, In The Spiritually Active Case) The Spiritual Energization Of The Frontal <u>and</u> Spinal Lines.

However, Even Right, True, Full, and (Spiritually) Fully Technically Responsible Practice Of "Emotional-Sexual Devotional Communion" In The Only-By-Me Revealed and Given Way Of The Heart Cannot, Itself and Immediately, Involve The Higher (and The Very Highest) Vertical Processes Associated (In The "Perfect Practice" Of The Way Of The Heart) With Spiritual Realization (By Means Of My Avatarically Self-Transmitted Divine Spiritual Grace) Above and Beyond The Ajna Door—Because Such Processes Require (In Their Actual Events) A Specific and Immediate (or Always then present-time) Unique Exercise and Orientation. And Only My (Thus) Specific Grace, As Well As (Altogether) The Unique Specificity, Depth, and Profundity Of The Full "Perfect Practice" (and Fully By-Me-Revealed, By-Me-Given, and By-Me-Instructed "Samraj Yoga") Of The Only-By-Me Revealed and Given Way Of The Heart, Together Allow and Grant A Realization Of Me That Goes Above and Beyond The bodily Exercises Of attention.

Whatever Effect It May (Potentially) Add To The Stages Of Practice Beyond The Frontal Yoga In The Way Of The Heart, Even "Emotional-Sexual Devotional Communion" (Like Spiritually Active "Emotional-Sexual Conscious Exercise") Is Basically A Discipline Relative To the <u>frontal</u> <u>personality</u>, Whereby The Knots That limit Love and "Conductivity" In The Frontal Line Are Opened To My Avatarically Self-Transmitted Divine Spirit-Current (Of Love-Bliss Itself). Indeed, Except For The Exercise Of breathing-"Conductivity" (Into and In and Via The Spinal Line) That Is (or May Be) Required (If Only Briefly) Whenever degenerative orgasm Is <u>Strongly</u> Approaching, The Basic Right and Fruitful Practice Of Either "Emotional-Sexual Devotional Communion" Or "Emotional-Sexual Conscious Exercise" Is That Of <u>Continuous</u> <u>Full</u> breathing-"Conductivity" In The Receptive <u>Frontal</u> Line, Even Intensively—With the inhalations <u>and</u> the exhalations Pressing Down, and With Random Tensing Of the bodily base (In, Back, and, Spinally, Up), and Random (Occasional) Relaxing Of and Into The Spinal Line (and, Sometimes, inhaling and/or exhaling Into The Spinal Line), and (Generally), Even In The Random Exercise Of (and In) The Spinal Line, Without Any Intentional Concentration Of attention or Natural bodily energy (and, In The Case Of My Spiritually Active Devotees, My Avatarically Self-Transmitted Divine Spirit-Energy) In the head (Except, Perhaps, Briefly, In The Case Of "Emotional-Sexual Devotional Communion", Whenever There Is The Exercise Of Regenerative Conversion Of an Otherwise <u>Strongly</u> Approaching degenerative orgasm), but (Rather, In General) Only With The Spinal Line Simply Relaxed (Generally Upwardly, but Diffusely), and With The Concentration Of Natural bodily energy (and, In The Case Of My Spiritually Active Devotees, My Avatarically Self-Transmitted Divine Spirit-Energy) Retained (and Even Pressed Down) As A Fullness In the abdomen (and Below), and With the bodily base

Kept Unbroken, and Strong, and Full (By Means Of A Random, Intentional Upward Tensing Of it), and With A Feeling Of Spinal Fullness In the hips and the lower back (Extending Upwards To A Point In the spine That Is Approximately At The Same Height As the navel In The Frontal Line). Nevertheless, Even Though "Emotional-Sexual Devotional Communion" (As Well As "Emotional-Sexual Conscious Exercise") Is Primarily An emotional-sexual Exercise In (and Of) The Frontal Line, It Is A Conservative and Regenerative Practice, and (If Rightly Practiced) A Counter-egoic Heart-Practice Of Right, True, Full, and (As The Case May Be) Truly Spiritual Devotion To Me, With (As My Avatarically Self-Transmitted Divine Spiritual Grace Will Have It) Profound Contemplation Of My "Bright" Divine Body Of Spirit-Presence. And, Thus, As A True and Profound Practice (and Puja) Of Real (Devotionally Me-Invoking, and Devotionally Me-Recognizing) Devotion To Me, The Progressively Developed Practice Of "Emotional-Sexual Conscious Exercise" and (In Due Course) "Emotional-Sexual Devotional Communion", With The Frequency Of sexual Occasion Appropriately Measured (In Accordance With My Herein Given Instruction), Is, In Principle (and, If Accompanied By The Signs and Qualifications Indicated By Me In This Testament, Then Actually), Positively Compatible With The Total Real (and Right, and True, and Full, and Fully Devotional) Practice Of The Only-By-Me Revealed and Given Way Of The Heart. In The Case Of "Emotional-Sexual Devotional Communion" In Particular, Such Practice Is (If Right and True, and Full Of The Necessary Signs and Qualifications) Positively Compatible With Real (and, Necessarily, Right, True, Full, and Fully Devotional) Practice Of The Only-By-Me Revealed and Given Way Of The Heart In The Context Of The First Actually Seeing Stage Of The Way Of The Heart (and—In The Case Of My Any Devotee who Is, In The *Fullest* Sense, *Truly*, or Even *Uniquely*, Qualified For A Right Yogic emotional-sexual Sadhana[135]—Even In The Context Of The "Perfect Practice" Of The Way Of The Heart). Nevertheless, In The Case Of Any intimately sexually active Practitioner Of The Way Of The Heart who Does Not Demonstrate The Signs Of Being Truly (or Even Uniquely) Qualified For A Right Yogic emotional-sexual Sadhana, At Some Point In The Course Of The First Actually Seeing Stage Of The Way Of The Heart, *Either* "Emotional-Sexual Devotional Communion" Will (Necessarily, and Inevitably) Spontaneously Become Yogic celibacy-in-intimacy (Inherently Free Of All emotional-sexual Agitation and All "Bonding"-Bondage)—Manifesting Entirely As A Spontaneously Awakened Disposition, Intention, and Choice (Awakened, Thus, Entirely Because Of The Yogic Sublimity Of My Devotee's Constant Devotional Samadhi Of Spiritual Communion With *Me*)—*Or*, Otherwise, the circumstance of intimate relationship Will Be *Entirely* Relinquished and The Practice Of Formally Acknowledged single celibacy Will Be Embraced. And, In The Case Of My Any Devotee who Is (In The Fullest Sense) Truly (or Even Uniquely) Qualified For A Right Yogic emotional-sexual Sadhana, At Any Point In The Course Of (or Even Previous To) The "Perfect Practice" Of The Way Of The Heart, "Emotional-Sexual Devotional Communion" May Spontaneously Become Yogic celibacy-in-intimacy (Inherently Free Of All emotional-sexual Agitation and All "Bonding"-Bondage)—Manifesting Entirely As A Spontaneously Awakened Disposition, Intention, and Choice (Awakened, Thus, Entirely Because Of The Yogic Sublimity Of My Devotee's Constant Devotional Samadhi Of Spiritual Communion With Me)—or, Otherwise, the circumstance of intimate relationship May Be Entirely Relinquished and The Practice Of Formally Acknowledged single celibacy Embraced.

AVATAR ADI DA SAMRAJ
Clear Lake, 2001

SUTRA

39

In The Only-By-Me Revealed and Given Way Of The Heart (or Way Of Adidam), all sexual activity Is, At Root, A Matter Of own-body Responsibility. (Indeed, Every Form Of functional, practical, and relational Discipline, and Cultural Obligation, In The Only-By-Me Revealed and Given Way Of The Heart Is, Fundamentally, A Matter Of own-body Responsibility, or Of Being Single With Me.) Sexual energy Is Typically (Though Mistakenly) Regarded To Be A Function Of the human body-mind That Is Rightly Exercised Only In Relationship With an other—In The Form Of sexual intercourse, or Any Of The Various Kinds Of sexual Play With an other. But, Truly, Right Yogic "Conductivity" Of sexual energy Is A Discipline That Should (Optimally) First Be Mastered (and, Once It Has Been Mastered, It Should Thereafter Continue—As May, At times, Be Necessary—To Be Fully Effectively Served) By Means Of A Fully Responsible solitary (or own-body) Exercise, Without The physical, emotional, mental, and psychic Factors That Are Introduced By Entering Into sexual activity with an other. Therefore, I Have Given All My Formally Practicing Devotees (Whether they Are Otherwise sexually active Or sexually inactive) A sex-Specific "Own-Body Yogic Conductivity Practice", As A Basic Circumstance and Exercise In Which To Become sexually self-Responsible (By Mastering and Rightly Managing The "Conductivity" Of sexual energy). Through The Exercise Of This "Own-Body Yogic Sexual Practice", The Practitioner Of The Way Of The Heart Learns The Control Of All The Mechanisms (Of body, emotion, mind, and breath) Associated With The "Conductivity" Of sexual energy, and (In Particular) Learns Sensitivity To The Triggers (In the brain and In the genitals) Of The orgasmic Process, Thereby Becoming Proficient In Bypassing degenerative (and, In the case of men, ejaculatory) orgasm and Achieving Regenerative orgasm. Furthermore, As An Essential Part Of Developing emotional-sexual self-Responsibility (Through All The Means Of emotional-sexual self-Understanding I Have Given To My Devotees, Including The Exercise Of The "Own-Body Yogic Sexual Practice"), The Practitioner Of The Way Of The Heart Must Out-Grow any puritanical or body-Negative or life-energy-Negative or sex-Negative attitudes, Such That he or she No Longer Allows any part of the Total body-mind (or its functioning) To Be Taboo. When Sufficient sexual self-Responsibility Has Been Achieved Through The Exercise Of The "Own-Body Yogic Sexual Practice",

Then (and Only Then) My Devotee who Is (or Would Be) sexually active In The Context Of intimate relationship Is (Fully) Rightly Prepared To Enter Into The Practice Of "Right Emotional-Sexual Yoga" With an intimate partner. Therefore, All My Devotees, Including those who Are Otherwise sexually inactive (Whether By Circumstance Or By A Formal Commitment To The Practice Of Either single celibacy Or celibacy In The Context Of intimate relationship), May, As Necessary and Appropriate (With Full Cultural Accountability), Practice The "Own-Body Yogic Sexual Exercise" As A Means Of Managing The Right "Conductivity" Of sexual energy. Furthermore, The "Own-Body Yogic Sexual Exercise" Is A Potentially Useful Secondary practical (or psycho-physically Effective) Yogic Means By Which My Listening Devotees and My Hearing Devotees (Whether they Are Otherwise sexually active Or sexually inactive) May (Through The Thus Extended Exercise Of Right "Conductivity" Of Natural bodily energy—and, In Due Course, Through The Thus Extended Beginner's Participation In My Avatarically Self-Transmitted Divine Ruchira Shaktipat) Assist their Whole bodily (or Total psycho-physical) Preparedness To (Fully Technically Responsibly) Receive and Conduct My Avatarically Self-Transmitted Divine (and Constantly Baptizing) Spirit-Presence Throughout the entire body-mind, In The Seeing Stages Of Practice Of The Way Of The Heart. Thus, The "Own-Body Yogic Sexual Practice" Is The Foundationary sex-Specific Practice Of (and The Fundamental sex-Specific Means Of Adaptation To) "Right Emotional-Sexual Yoga" In The Only-By-Me Revealed and Given Way Of The Heart (or Way Of Adidam).

Sexual activity In The Context Of intimate relationship (Even In The Context Of a Rightly Practiced relationship Of Intimate Commitment) Tends To Be Based On (and limited By) egoic sex-"Bonding" In One Form or Another. And The Motive Of egoic sex-"Bonding" Is Based On (and Is A Dramatization Of) The Feeling Of Incompleteness. By Tendency, every human individual Identifies himself or herself With (More or Less) Either The Character Of maleness Or The Character Of femaleness (or With Either "Yang" Or "Yin"), and (Thus) Feels himself or herself To Be Either "positively" Polarized Or "negatively" Polarized. Thus, By Tendency, every human individual Feels (Especially In emotional-sexual Terms) That he or she Is Not Complete In himself or herself, and That (In Order To Experience Completeness) he or she Must Be Joined To (or Achieve Union With) an ego-Based emotional-sexual other who Is his or her Polar "Opposite". All ego-Based emotional-sexual "Bonding"-activity (and, Altogether, all ego-Binding emotional-sexual activity, and All ego-Binding emotional-sexual Motivation) Is Based On This Feeling Of Incompleteness, and The Consequent Search For Union With what You Yourself (You Presume) Do Not Contain.

In Contrast To This, The Practice Of own-body Responsibility In The Only-By-Me Revealed and Given Way Of The Heart Involves The Establishment and The Maintenance Of The Yogic (and ego-Surrendering, ego-Forgetting, and ego-Transcending) Completeness (or Inherent Integrity) Of the individual body-mind. The individual body-mind itself Contains Both The "positive" and The "negative" Poles In its Structure. Indeed, The Entire conditional (or Cosmic) Domain Is A Bi-Polar Energy-Phenomenon, every fraction Of Which Has Two Sides (or Poles). Thus, the (outward) male and female physical characteristics of human beings are the sexually Differentiated extensions Of A Bi-Polar Internal Mechanism That Is The Same In the male and the female. In Depth, human beings Are Neither male Nor female. In Fact, In Depth, human beings Are Not sexual—Which Is To Say That, In Depth, they Are Not sexually Particularized or Differentiated At All. The sex-Differentiation Displayed In the body and Presumed In the mind Is Relatively peripheral (and This Is Observed To Be Obviously So In States Of Profound Samadhi, When the peripheral aspects of the being Cease To Be Noticed or Lose their Otherwise Seeming Significance). The Purpose Of sex-Differentiation At The External Level Of the body Is reproduction, For the externally functioning body is itself a functional element (or moment, or mini-process) Of The Universal reproductive Cycle (or Process, or Pattern) Of births and deaths—but The Internal Mechanism (or The Pattern) Of Which the body is an appearance (or an extension) Belongs (and, Therefore—Rightly, and In Truth—the body-mind As A Whole Belongs) To The Great Universal Unity and Always Prior Divine Singleness. Thus, The Practice Of The Way Of The Heart Involves A Comprehensive Discipline Of the body-mind That Is Based On Maintaining The Equanimity (or Balance and Well-being) Inherent To the Bi-Polar body-mind By Joining (and, Ultimately, Transcending) The Internal Polar "Opposites" In the individual body-mind, Rather Than By Seeking Union With The External Polar "Opposite" In the form of an emotional-sexual ego-other. In The Way Of The Heart, When The Bi-Polar Integrity Of the individual body-mind Is Fully Established, the Universal Natural life-energy and (In Due Course) My Avatarically Self-Transmitted Divine Spirit-Energy Are Utterly, Unobstructedly Conducted In The Circle Of the body-mind—Ultimately (In The Context Of The "Perfect Practice" Of The Way Of The Heart), Vertically Polarized To The "Place" Infinitely Above The Total Crown Of the head <u>and</u> Horizontally "Located" In The Right Side Of The Heart.

In Every Developmental Stage Of Practice In The Way Of The Heart, The Altogether Fundamental (and Must Be Constant) "sexual" Discipline Is The sex-act-inactive Exercise Of Ruchira Avatara Bhakti Yoga (Primarily, In The Spiritually Active Case, By Means Of Searchless Beholding Of Me), and,

Also, self-Observation, self-Understanding, The "Conscious Process", and "General Conductivity"—In Relation To all emotional-sexual arising. Through This Fundamental Practice, The Practitioner's limitations Relative To sexuality Are Directly and Effectively Transcended, and Full "Conductivity" In The Circle Is Exercised. (Indeed, Without The Basis Of This Fundamental Discipline—Of Ruchira Avatara Bhakti Yoga, self-Observation, self-Understanding, The "Conscious Process", and "General Conductivity" Practice—Any "Consideration" or Disciplining Of emotional-sexual Matters Is, Necessarily and Inevitably, ego-Based, Rather Than Being Based On Right Practice Of The Way Of The Heart.) However, There May Be Occasions (or periods of time) In The Course Of any individual's Demonstration Of The Way Of The Heart (Whether the individual Is celibate Or intimately sexually active) When (Because the Natural bodily energy and, As May Be The Case, My Avatarically Self-Transmitted Divine Spirit-Energy Are Profoundly Magnified In The Circle Of the body-mind) There Is An Intense Concentration (or Trapping) Of Natural bodily energy and (As May Be The Case) My Avatarically Self-Transmitted Divine Spirit-Energy In the sexual organs, Even To The Point Of Extraordinary (and Even Unbearable) Discomfort (and Excitation Of Even Unbearable lust)—Such That The Fully Engaged Practice Of Ruchira Avatara Bhakti Yoga, self-Observation, self-Understanding, The "Conscious Process", and "General Conductivity" (Engaged In Accordance With The Expectations and Requirements Of The individual Practitioner's Developmental Stage Of Practice In The Way Of The Heart) Is Not Sufficient To Restore Right Balance and Well-being (or True Equanimity) In The Full Circle Of the body-mind. On Such Occasions (or During such periods of time) In The Course Of an individual's Demonstration Of The Way Of The Heart, It May Be Necessary (For The Sake Of Restoring Full, Right Balance and Well-being, or True Equanimity) To (With Formal Approval) Intensively Engage The (Otherwise Only Occasionally Engaged) sex-Specific "Own-Body Yogic Conductivity Practice"—In Addition To The Fundamental Practice Of Ruchira Avatara Bhakti Yoga, self-Observation, self-Understanding, The "Conscious Process", and "General Conductivity".

The "Own-Body Yogic Sexual Practice" (In The Only-By-Me Revealed and Given Way Of The Heart) Is A Matter Of <u>Energy</u> (Both Natural life-energy and, As May Be The Case, My Avatarically Self-Transmitted Divine Spirit-Energy) and Of individual psycho-physical <u>Integrity</u> (or ego-Transcending Singleness and Wholeness, or True Equanimity). The "Own-Body Yogic Sexual Practice" In The Way Of The Heart Is Associated With The Exercise Of Stimulating the genital organs (and, Thereby, Of Stimulating the Natural energy and, As The Case May Be, The Spiritual Energy Concentrated, or Trapped, In the genital organs) Simply and Consistently and Entirely and Only For ego-Transcending

Yogic Purposes. Therefore, The "Own-Body Yogic Sexual Practice" (Like All Other sexual Practices In The Way Of The Heart) Is Not Associated With The Search For (or The Achievement Of) degenerative orgasm, or With Otherwise conventionally (or egoically) Motivated sexual Practices Of Any Kind. The "Own-Body Yogic Sexual Practice" In The Way Of The Heart Is To Be Engaged (Formally, and Fully Responsibly) For The Purpose Of Magnifying (and, As May, At times, Be Necessary, Restoring) and Prolonging (or, Otherwise, Mastering) Right Whole-bodily (or Total psycho-physical) Yogic "Conductivity", and For The Purpose Of Opening the lower functional aspects of the body-mind—Thus and Thereby Allowing the Natural bodily energy and (As The Case May Be) My Avatarically Self-Transmitted Divine Spirit-Energy To Freely Flow Downwards In The Frontal Line (From The "Place" Infinitely Above The Total Crown Of the head), and To Always Remain Unobstructedly (and Without The Strategy Of Dissociation From the gross physical body) Polarized Upwards In The Spinal Line (From the bodily base, and Toward The "Place" Infinitely Above The Total Crown Of the head).

Like All Other Forms Of sexual Practice In The Way Of The Heart, The "Own-Body Yogic Sexual Practice" Must Be Engaged As An ego-Surrendering, ego-Forgetting, and ego-Transcending Exercise Of Ruchira Avatara Bhakti Yoga (Which, In The Case Of My By-Me-Spiritually-Initiated Devotees, Is Receptive Searchless Beholding Of Me and Responsive Devotional Communion With Me), In Which The Principal Faculties Of the body-mind Are Aligned To Me, Concentrated On Me, "Bonded" To Me, and Devotionally Surrendered To Me. Therefore, The "Own-Body Yogic Sexual Practice" In The Way Of The Heart Is Not At All emotionless. Rather, The "Own-Body Yogic Sexual Practice" In The Way Of The Heart Is A Full-Feeling Practice In Which My Devotee Magnifies The Heart-Disposition Of Devotion To Me.

The "Own-Body Yogic Sexual Practice" (In The Way Of The Heart) Is One Of The Means (Given, By Me, To My Devotees) For Bringing the body-mind Into Participation In The Condition Of Energy (Including Both the Natural bodily energy and, As The Case May Be, My Avatarically Self-Transmitted Divine Spirit-Energy). Therefore, The "Own-Body Yogic Sexual Practice" Is Not An Excuse For self-Indulgence, Nor Is It In Any Sense A degenerative Exercise. The "Own-Body Yogic Sexual Practice" Is A Regenerative, life-energy-Positive, and Non-puritanical Yogic Exercise, Like Yogic sexual Practices (In The Way Of The Heart) In General. When The "Own-Body Yogic Sexual Practice" Is Engaged, the erotic mental images and erotic responses that May arise Are Not To Be Merely Casually (or degeneratively) Indulged (As If The "Own-Body Yogic Sexual Practice" Were A Substitute For sexual activity with an other). The "Own-Body Yogic Sexual Practice" Is An Inward-Directed (and ego-Surrendering, ego-Forgetting, and ego-Transcending) Exercise, Associated With the body-mind itself (and With Internal Bi-Polar Unity[136]), and Not An Outward-Directed Exercise, Associated With The egoic Search For Outward "coupling" Union (or ego-Based pair-"Bonding"). Therefore, The "Own-Body Yogic Sexual Practice" Is Strictly A Yogic (and Actively ego-Transcending) Practice, and It Is To Be Engaged Only For Yogic (and ego-Transcending) Reasons and For Yogic (and ego-Transcending) Purposes.

As In The Case Of Even All Forms and Exercises Of Practice In The Way Of The Heart, The Practitioner Of The Way Of The Heart Must Be Fully Culturally Confessed Relative To The Details Of his or her Practice Of The "Own-Body Yogic Sexual Practice". For A Practitioner Of The Way Of The Heart To Rightly (With Formal Approval) Engage The sex-Specific own-body Yogic "Conductivity" Practice, The Basic Practice Of Ruchira Avatara Bhakti Yoga, self-Observation, self-Understanding, The "Conscious Process", and "General Conductivity" Must Be In Full and Effective Evidence (In Accordance With The Expectations and Requirements Of The individual Practitioner's Developmental Stage Of Practice In The Way Of The Heart). If Intense Specific (and Extraordinarily, and Even Unbearably, Uncomfortable, and Even Unbearably lustful) sexual Intensity (or Natural sexual energy, and, As May Be The Case, sexually Indicated Spirit-Energy, and Associated sexual desire) Arouses Itself (Even Though Ruchira Avatara Bhakti Yoga, self-Observation, self-Understanding, The "Conscious Process", and "General Conductivity" Practice Are Applied Truly and Consistently)—Such That It Becomes Uniquely Distracting and Disturbing, and Is Tending To Preoccupy the individual With sexual thoughts, and To Burden the individual With The Impulse Toward degenerative Release In conventional masturbation (or In any kind of ego-Based sexual activity)—Then It May Be Appropriate To Add The "Own-Body Yogic Sexual Practice" For Application Whenever and However Often the individual's psycho-physical Disturbance Signs and/or Yogic Signs Require.

In Addition To The "Own-Body Yogic Sexual Practice" Being Specially Engaged In The Case Of Practitioners Of The Way Of The Heart In whom There Are present-time Signs Of Intense (and Extraordinarily, and Even Unbearably, Uncomfortable, and Unbearably lustful) Concentration (or Trapping) Of Natural sexual energy, and (As May Be The Case) Of sexually Indicated Spirit-Energy, In The genital (and General lower bodily, and Even lower mental) Region Of The Circle Of the body-mind, The Same "Own-Body Yogic Sexual Practice" May Be Appropriate For Special Application By Any Practitioner Of The Way Of The Heart (Whether celibate Or intimately sexually active) In whom There Is Too Much personal psycho-physical Negation (or Suppression) Of Natural sexual energy (and, As The Case May Be, Of sexually

Indicated Spirit-Energy). In Such Cases, The "Own-Body Yogic Sexual Practice" Should Be Engaged In Order To Magnify and Develop The Signs Of Natural psycho-physical energy, and (As The Case May Be) Of bodily-Indicated Spiritual Energy, In The Circle Of the body-mind.

Alternatively, The "Own-Body Yogic Sexual Practice" (In The Way Of The Heart) May Be Specially Engaged By Any Practitioner Of The Way Of The Heart (Whether celibate Or intimately sexually active) who Observes That his or her Natural bodily energy (and, As The Case May Be, My Avatarically Self-Transmitted Divine Spirit-Energy In the body-mind) Tends To Move "Down" and "Out", Toward social (or General) "Bonding" With others and Toward "Bonding" With the world (In General), Such That Right "Conductivity" and The Integrity Of the Bi-Polar body-mind Are Not Readily and Consistently Maintained. In Such Cases, The "Own-Body Yogic Sexual Practice" Should Be Engaged In Order To Relinquish (or In Order To Not Permit) Casual (and ego-Based) "Bonding" With others and the world, and (Altogether) In Order To Maintain A Right and Consistent and Yogically True Level Of Intensity, and Of Fullness, Of Natural psycho-physical energy and (As The Case May Be) Of bodily-Indicated Spiritual Energy.

The "Own-Body Yogic Sexual Practice" (Given By Me For Practice By Practitioners Of The Way Of The Heart) Is genital masturbation (or genital self-Manipulation, and genital self-Stimulation), Done As A solitary Exercise and In The General Manner Of Either "Emotional-Sexual Conscious Exercise" Or "Emotional-Sexual Devotional Communion" (In Accordance With The individual Practitioner's Developmental Stage Of Practice Of The Way Of The Heart),[137] and (Altogether) In The General Manner Of The Traditional "Shaktichalana Mudra", and With The Traditional Seriousness and Purpose Of The "Shaktichalana Mudra".[138]

The Typical Procedure For genital self-Stimulation (In The "Own-Body Yogic Sexual Practice" In The Way Of The Heart) Is, In The Case Of male Practitioners, genital self-Stimulation By Means Of full hand contact with the penis (and rhythmic hand-friction on the penis). In The Case Of female Practitioners, The Typical Procedure Is genital self-Stimulation By Means Of single or multiple finger contact with the clitoris (and rhythmic finger-friction on the clitoris), and, Perhaps (Whether Simultaneously Or Alternately), Deep vaginal Stimulation By Means Of a Suitable (and Comfortable) dildo (or penis substitute).[139] However, As A General Rule, Neither In The Case Of male Practitioners Nor In The Case Of female Practitioners Should "vibrators" (or other Similar devices) Be Used (Except, Perhaps, Very Rarely)—Because they May Initiate Uncontrollable degenerative orgasm, and (Otherwise) Because they May Tend To (At Least Eventually) Desensitize the genital organs.

Through The Process Of Rightly Engaging The "Own-Body Yogic Sexual Practice" (In The Way Of The Heart), Equanimity (or Balance and Well-being) Is Restored. Such Equanimity (or A Feeling Of Full "Conductivity", Strength, Well-being, and Lack Of Agitating Desire, In The Entire Circle Of the body-mind), Rather Than The Thrill Of orgasm (Even In its Regenerative Form), Is The Basic Pleasure In The "Own-Body Yogic Sexual Practice" (and, Indeed, In All Yogic sexual Practice In The Way Of The Heart). Such Equanimity Is Not a state of blandness, Devoid Of sexual signs, sexual sensations, and sexual energy, but (Rather) A Condition Of Energy-Fullness, In Which all arising sexual signs Have Become Manageable. Such Equanimity Is Directly Associated With The Transcending Of lustful Agitation and Obsessive sexual Motivation (or, As The Case May Be, Of Negated and Suppressed sexual Motivation, or, Alternatively, Of The Tendency To Casually "Bond" With others and the world), Such That The Right Result Of any period Of Engaging The "Own-Body Yogic Sexual Exercise" Is That No lustful Agitation or Obsessive sexual Motivation (or, As The Case May Be, No Negated and Suppressed sexual Motivation, or, Alternatively, No Tendency To Casually "Bond" With others and the world) Remains (In the present time) To Be Dealt With (and, In The Case Of Practitioners Of The Way Of The Heart who Are, Either Permanently Or Temporarily, celibate, the individual Is Easefully and Non-Problematically Restored To sex-act-inactive celibacy Once Again). Indeed, Even All Practitioners Of The Way Of The Heart who Are (in their personal intimate contexts) sexually active Should Measure their sexual Practice Relative To This Result Of The Transcending Of lustful Agitation and Obsessive sexual Motivation (or, As The Case May Be, Of Negated and Suppressed sexual Motivation, or, Alternatively, Of The Tendency To Casually "Bond" With others and the world), and they Should (By Means Of This Result) Progressively Out-Grow The ego-Based pair-"Bonding" Impulse and all ego-Based pair-"Bonding" emotional-sexual activities, and All The Complications and Searches Inevitably Associated With Such Impulses and such activities.

Even Though (In The Way Of The Heart) The "Own-Body Yogic Sexual Practice" Is A Matter Of Transcending lustful Agitation (or Else Suppression, or Else Casual "Bonding"), lust itself (or Else Suppression Itself, or Else Casual "Bonding" Itself) Is (Of Course) Observed, and (By Means Of genital self-Stimulation) Natural sexual energization (and, As The Case May Be, Even Spiritual Energization—sexually, and Whole bodily) Is Directly Intensified, In The Engaging Of This Practice. However, By Intensive Application Of The Basic physical and Internal Yogic Exercises Otherwise Associated With "Emotional-Sexual Conscious Exercise" and "Emotional-Sexual Devotional Communion" (and, Altogether, With The Traditional Yogic sexual Exercise Of

"Shaktichalana Mudra"), The "Own-Body Yogic Sexual Practice" (In The Way Of The Heart) Effectively (In The Course Of Its Period Of Right Practice) Converts, Releases, and Transcends All Trapping (or Else Suppressing, or Else "Downward" and "Outward" Movement) Of Natural life-energy and (As The Case May Be) Of My Avatarically Self-Transmitted Divine Spirit-Energy In the sexual organs (and, Thus and Thereby, Progressively Converts, Releases, and Transcends All lustful Agitation and All Obsessive sexual Motivation—or, Alternatively, All Negated and Suppressed sexual Motivation, or, Otherwise, All Tendency To Casually "Bond" With others and the world). Therefore, In The Actual Practice Of The "Own-Body Yogic Sexual Exercise" (In The Way Of The Heart), There Is Not To Be Any puritanical, or veiled, or Non-Stimulating, or anti-sexual Motive or activity. Indeed, The Fully Right Engagement Of The "Own-Body Yogic Sexual Practice" Is Characterized By Freedom From All puritanical or anti-sexual Dramatization, Even By Playful and Uninhibited Participation In The "Own-Body Yogic Sexual Exercise", and (Altogether) By The Positive Disposition Necessary For The Right and Fully Effective Practice Of The "Own-Body Yogic Sexual Exercise".

To Rightly Engage The "Own-Body Yogic Sexual Practice" (In The Only-By-Me Revealed and Given Way Of The Heart) Is To Deal With genital Energy (Including Both the Natural sexual energy and, As The Case May Be, The sexually Indicated Spirit-Energy) Which Is over-Stimulated (or Which Is, Perhaps, Otherwise, under-Stimulated, or Which, For One Reason or Another, Requires Management). In The Way Of The Heart, The Only Reason For A Practitioner To Engage In The "Own-Body Yogic Sexual Exercise" Is To Deal With the Natural sexual energy and (As The Case May Be) The sexually Indicated Spirit-Energy That Exists (and Is Observed and Felt)—or Is, Otherwise, Felt, By Observation, To Be Suppressed, or Relatively Absent—As A Natural and (As The Case May Be) Spiritual Fact. The Practitioner Of The Way Of The Heart Engages The "Own-Body Yogic Sexual Practice" Fully and Exclusively For The Sake Of Yogic Equanimity, and (As The Case May Be) In Order To Transcend The Disturbance That Trapped (or Suppressed, or, Otherwise, Excessively Outgoing) sexual energy and (As The Case May Be) Trapped (or Suppressed, or, Otherwise, Excessively Outgoing) sexually Indicated Spirit-Energy Manifests, but Not, Otherwise, Merely In Order To Fulfill The Apparent functional, practical, or relational Imperatives Of Natural sexual energy and (As The Case May Be) Of sexually Indicated Spirit-Energy.

In The Way Of The Heart, The "Own-Body Yogic Sexual Practice" Is A Profound Matter Of Maintaining The Yogic Integrity (or Bi-Polar Singleness) Of the body-mind, and Of Directing the body-mind (Consistently, Entirely, and Only) Fully To The Me-Centered (Rather Than ego-Centered) Process Of

Divine Self-Realization. In The Way Of The Heart, It Is That Divine Process, and Everything Associated With That Yogic Integrity, That Is The Justification and The Context Of The "Own-Body Yogic Sexual Practice".

The First (practical) Principle Relative To The Exercise Of The "Own-Body Yogic Sexual Practice" (In The Way Of The Heart) Is To Constantly Stimulate the genitals, and the Natural sexual energy, and (As The Case May Be) The sexually Indicated Spirit-Energy—but Not To Altogether Satisfy The Impulse Toward genital gratification. If The Impulse Toward genital gratification Is Entirely Satisfied, degenerative orgasm Tends To Result—Whereas, By The Principle Of Constant Stimulation Without Final Satisfaction, The Practice Can Continue Indefinitely, Always Magnifying In Its Intensity (Until An ego-Transcending Yogic State Of Full Yogic "Conductivity", and Full Yogic Equanimity, Free Of lustful Agitation and Obsessive sexual Motivation—or, Alternatively, Of Negated and Suppressed sexual Motivation, or, Otherwise, Of Casual "Bonding" With others and the world—Is Firmly Established). Therefore, In The Exercise Of The "Own-Body Yogic Sexual Practice", There Is (Necessarily) sexual Play (Even Though solitary), but There Should Not (In any moment) Be A Relinquishment or A Loss Of The (Inherent) Bi-Polar Integrity (or Of The Always Prior Wholeness, or Singleness) Of the Me-Centered (or To-Me-Devoted, and To-Me-"Bonded", and, Ultimately, egoless) body-mind.

The Practitioner Of The Way Of The Heart who Is Actively Engaging The "Own-Body Yogic Sexual Practice" Should Not Be Suppressed In his or her genitally Stimulating activity, Whether vocally Or physically. Nevertheless, the Actively Practicing individual Must Be Constantly Sensitive To The Bi-Polar Integrity (or Singleness) Of his or her own body-mind, and Of The "positive" and "negative" Polar Aspects Of Natural life-energy, and (If he or she Is Spiritually Initiated By Me) Of My Avatarically Self-Transmitted Divine Spirit-Energy, In his or her own body-mind—Front Versus Back, Top Versus Bottom, Right Versus Left, and So On.

In Right "Own-Body Yogic Sexual Practice" (In The Way Of The Heart), Even Though erotic thoughts May arise, they Should Not (As A General Rule) Be Allowed To Become degeneratively orgasmic. In Every Occasion Of The "Own-Body Yogic Sexual Practice", There Should Be a Decreasing degree of erotic mental imagery, and (At Least Eventually) No erotic imagery, but Only A Sense Of genital Stimulation As It Relates To the Natural life-energy, and (As The Case May Be) My Avatarically Self-Transmitted Divine Spirit-Energy, In the body and In The Circle Of the entire (or Inherently Whole) body-mind.

Whether the individual Is biologically male Or biologically female, The Stimulated genital Energy (Composed Of the Natural sexual energy, and,

In The Case Of The By-Me-Spiritually-Initiated Practitioner, The sexually Indicated Spirit-Energy) Is A "positive" (or "positively" Polarized, and Relatively Active, or Aggressive) Force, and It Can (Therefore, In Both the Otherwise biologically male individual and the Otherwise biologically female individual) Be Called A "male" Force. And, By Means Of The "Own-Body Yogic Sexual Practice", That genitally Stimulated "male" Force Must Be Drawn In, Back, and Up, Toward The Spinal Line—Thus Striking (or "Penetrating") the interior root of the genitals (deep behind and above the perineum), which root-place is (or, In the case of Both the biologically male individual and the biologically female individual, this root-place Can Be Said To be) the "female" (or "negatively" Polarized, and Relatively Passive, or Receptive) "partner" of the "male" (or The Stimulated genital Energy). In Any Case, However Relatively "male" or "female" the parts (or "Conductivity" Structures) of the body-mind May Feel (or, Otherwise, Be Interpreted To Be) In Relation To one another (or In Relation To The Stimulated genital Energy), The Exercise Of The "Own-Body Yogic Sexual Practice" Is A Matter Of The functional Joining-Play Of <u>Polar Opposites</u> Entirely <u>Within</u> The own-body Context and Bi-Polar Integrity Of the <u>individual</u> body-mind.

If (In The Circumstance Of sexual activity In The Context Of intimate relationship, or Even In Any Context Of sexual contact between any one and an other, or others) There Is (In Any Occasion Of sexual activity) Excessive genital Engagement Between the partners, the genitals of either individual (Especially In the case of male individuals, but, Also, Possibly, In the case of female individuals) Can Become (Then, and Temporarily) "Neutralized" (or, So To Speak, Made "electrically inert"). This Can Occur (Even If degenerative orgasm Is Bypassed or Converted) Through the Excessive contact that Is Made With The Polar Opposite genital Energy Of the sexual partner. The Principal Symptom Of genital "Neutralization" Is A Sudden Feeling Of Emptiness In the lower body, Because the genital organ (and, Consequently, the entire body) Relinquishes and Loses The Bi-Polar Integrity Of Internal Force, and Has (Thus and Thereby) Become Satisfied (or de-Stimulated) Rather Than Simply Aroused (or Intensively Stimulated). Another Symptom Of genital "Neutralization" Is That the head of the body Suddenly Feels Empty, and There Is A Feeling Of The Loss Of Natural life-energy (and, As The Case May Be, Of My Avatarically Self-Transmitted Divine Spirit-Energy) In The Entire Spinal Line, and A General Loss Of Arousal Altogether (Similar To The bodily Feeling Associated With degenerative orgasm). The Result Of This "Neutralization" Is That The bodily Feeling Of Stimulation Disappears, and There Is A Sudden Loss (or At Least A Profound Diminishment) Of Interest In The sexual Occasion.

In The Characteristic Right Yogic Circumstance Of sexual activity In The Context Of heterosexual intimate relationship, the penis Should Enter the vagina In A Vigorously Penetrating Manner—but when the penis Is Excessively Allowed To Enter the vagina To its full depth, That Is the Principal Potential cause Of genital "Neutralization". In Right Yogic genital intercourse Practice, There Should Be (In the case of heterosexual partners) The Right Maximization Of Fullest Deep Penetration Of the vagina By the penis (or, In the case of homosexual partners, The Equivalent Deep Penetration, or Otherwise Strong Engagement)—but The Frequency (or, Otherwise, The Prolongation) Of Deep Penetration (or, Otherwise, Strong Engagement) On Any Particular Occasion Of genital intercourse Must (In The General Case) Be Sensitively Measured and (If Necessary) Limited, and Not Allowed To Be Made So Frequent (or To Become So Prolonged) That It Produces genital "Neutralization". The Principal Joining-Play Of Polar Opposites Outside The Bi-Polar sexual-energy-Integrity Of the individual body-mind Is contact between the head of the penis and the cervix of the vagina (or the equivalent contact in the homosexual case). And The Bi-Polar sexual-energy-Integrity In Both the male and the female Tends To Be Effectively (Then, and Temporarily) "Neutralized" By Excessive (or Excessively Prolonged) Deep Penetration Of the vagina By the penis (or The Equivalent Engagement In the homosexual case)—Especially If The Crisis Of orgasm arises in such contact, and Even If the orgasm Is Regeneratively Converted. Therefore, From The Right Yogic Point Of View, any and every kind of genital intercourse (In Any and Every Context) Must (In The General Case) Always Be Sensitively Measured, and Effectively Overmuch Deep Penetration Of the vagina By the penis (or The Equivalent Engagement In the homosexual case) Should (For The Sake Of The Yogically Rightest Result or Effect) Not Be Allowed.

The Arousal Level Must Always Be Maximized In Right Yogic sexual Practice (In Any and Every Context), but There Are, Indeed, Many Forms and Excesses Of sexual action Whereby genital "Neutralization" Can Be Made To Occur As A Result—and The individual Practitioner Of The Way Of The Heart who Is (in his or her personal intimate context) sexually active Must Be (or, At Least, Must Progressively Become) Sensitive To (and Constantly Avoid) All Of Them. However, In The solitary genitally self-Stimulating "Own-Body Yogic Sexual Practice" (In The Way Of The Heart), This genital "Neutralization" (Which Is Equally As degenerative As degenerative orgasm) Is Specifically and Directly Avoided and Transcended (Simply By Avoiding sexual contact with any other)—and degenerative orgasm Is Also (Through Simple, personal Control) Specifically, Directly, Most Simply, and Consistently Yogically Bypassed (or, Otherwise, Yogically Converted).

Practitioners Of The "Own-Body Yogic Sexual Exercise" (In The Way Of The Heart) Must Understand The Yogic Significance Of The Energy (Including Both the Natural bodily energy and, As The Case May Be, My Avatarically Self-Transmitted Divine Spirit-Energy) Aroused and Set In Motion By sexual activity, and they Must Engage In The "Own-Body Yogic Sexual Practice" Only and Entirely In Order To Serve The Right Yogic "Conductivity" Of That Aroused Energy (Especially The Right Yogic "Conductivity" Of, As The Case May Be, My Avatarically Self-Transmitted Divine Spirit-Energy, and, Inevitably, the Natural bodily energy, Downwards In The Frontal Line, From Infinitely Above The Crown and The Core Of the head and brain).

In Any Case—Whether The "Own-Body Yogic Sexual Practice" Is Exercised In Order To Circulate and Balance An Excessively Aroused genital Energy Or To Stimulate, Circulate, and Balance An Effectively Suppressed genital Energy Or To Maintain A Right and Consistent and Yogically True Level Of Intensity and Fullness Of genital Energy—The Purpose (and The Necessary Result) Of The Right (and, Necessarily, Only Occasional and Non-Excessive) Exercise Of The "Own-Body Yogic Sexual Practice" Is Always The One Of True (and lust-Transcending, and sex-Bondage-Transcending—or, Alternatively, sexual-Suppression-Transcending, or, Otherwise, Casual-"Bonding"-Transcending) Equanimity—Such That Right, Balanced and Effective, Practice Of Ruchira Avatara Bhakti Yoga, self-Observation, self-Understanding, The "Conscious Process", and "General Conductivity" Is Truly and Stably (By That Equanimity) Established (or Even Re-Established) and Maintained.

In The Only-By-Me Revealed and Given Way Of The Heart (or Way Of Adidam), All Right sexual Practice—Including Right sexual activity In The Context Of any relationship Of Intimate Commitment—Is Fundamentally An own-body Yoga. Therefore, The Practice Of "Emotional-Sexual Devotional Communion" (or, At First, "Emotional-Sexual Conscious Exercise") Is The Demonstration Of own-body Yoga In The Circumstance Of emotional-sexual Association With an other. In The Way Of The Heart, The First and Principal Form Of The Yoga Of own-body sexual self-Responsibility Is The solitary "Own-Body Yogic Sexual Practice"—and "Right Emotional-Sexual Yoga" With an other Is An Extension Of This solitary own-body Yoga. Therefore, The Fundamental sexual Practice In The Way Of The Heart Is The Same For All My Devotees, Whether they Are celibate Or sexually active in their personal intimate contexts.

In The Way Of The Heart, "Right Emotional-Sexual Yoga" With an intimate partner Is A Progressively Developing <u>Four-Stage</u> Process, In Which Each Consecutive Stage Represents (Over time) A Progressive Development Of one's own emotional-sexual Practice and That Of one's any intimate partner.

The First Stage Of "Right Emotional-Sexual Yoga" In The Way Of The Heart Must (In Every Basic and Essential Sense) Be Completed Before The Student-Beginner Stage Of Adaptation To The Basic Full Practice Of The Way Of The Heart Can (In The Case Of My Any Devotee who Is, in his or her personal intimate context, sexually active) Be Rightly Acknowledged To Be Mature and Complete. The First Stage Of "Right Emotional-Sexual Yoga" In The Way Of The Heart Is Characterized By A Process Of Progressive Out-Growing Of The conventional (degenerative, and, otherwise, merely reproductive—and even conventionally masturbatory, or erotic-imagery-Based, and psycho-physically Armored) Patterning Of emotional-sexual activity. Such Patterning Is Characterized By ego-Reinforcing Fixations Of attention, emotional feeling, and bodily sensation In Mere Outward-Directedness—Such That attention, emotional feeling, and bodily sensation Are Not Entirely Free To Be Concentrated In Ecstatic (or ego-Transcending and Not self-Conscious) Participation In Unguarded, Uninhibited, and Truly Yogic genital intercourse (or genitally-Based, Rather Than merely mind-Based, sexual Play). Therefore, The First Stage Of "Right Emotional-Sexual Yoga" In The Way Of The Heart Is A Process Of Out-Growing Previously Accumulated Patterns Of emotional-sexual Superficiality, or Of functional Dependency On Stimulations From Outside the physical domain of Deeply Penetrating (or, In the homosexual case, Otherwise Strongly Engaged) genital intercourse. In That Process, all functional, stylistic, and relational limitations On The Practice Of emotional-sexual Relatedness Are To Be Responsibly Addressed and Progressively Transcended. And, In The Maturing Of That Process, The Participation Of Any intimately sexually active Practitioner Of The Way Of The Heart In sexual intercourse Is Brought Out Of The secular (or merely "social", and "ordinary life") Domain and Into The Sacred (or Divine and True, and Really Devotional, and Truly Yogic) Domain.

The Second Stage Of "Right Emotional-Sexual Yoga" In The Way Of The Heart Must (In Every Basic and Essential Sense) Be Completed Before My Any Devotee (who Is, in his or her personal intimate context, sexually active) Can Be Rightly Acknowledged As My Really Hearing Devotee. The Second Stage Of "Right Emotional-Sexual Yoga" In The Way Of The Heart Is Characterized (From Its Beginning) By Unlimited Participation In sexual activity, Coincident With Deeply Penetrating (or, In the homosexual case, Otherwise Strongly Engaged) sexual intercourse—Such That The Fundamental Stimulation Takes Place Not Via the mind (or In Patterns Of Mere Outward-Directedness) but At the root-point of the deep contact between the genitals of (or otherwise strongest sexual contact between) the partners In emotional-sexual Embrace. Thus, The Second Stage Of "Right Emotional-Sexual Yoga" In The Way Of The Heart Is

A Truly "Adult" emotional-sexual Practice, Characterized By The Real and Direct Transcending Of The (Characteristically, self-Conscious, convention-Bound, Necessarily immature and inexperienced, and Rather "social"-minded, or merely Outward-Directed and socially-conditioned, and Even Rather "virginal") "mating-game" Orientation, Of The Tendency To Animate Lack Of Pleasure and Lack Of Energy-Intensity, and Of Even All immaturity, double-mindedness, unresponsiveness, and Lack Of Straightforwardness Relative To sex and sex-related emotional feeling. In The Second Stage Of "Right Emotional-Sexual Yoga" In The Way Of The Heart, Deeply Penetrating (or, In the homosexual case, Otherwise Strongly Engaged) sexual intercourse Is A Highly Aroused, Intensively Erotic, Whole bodily Pleasurable, Ecstatic (or Unguarded, Freely Participatory, Uninhibited, and ego-Transcending) Practice, In Which self-Consciousness Is (By Altogether Right and Whole bodily Yogic emotional-sexual and Devotional Practice) Constantly Transcended In body, mind, feeling, and breath, Thereby Triggering Both Positively Converted hormonal Flows and Yogically Significant Openings Throughout the physical body and the nervous system.

The Third Stage Of "Right Emotional-Sexual Yoga" In The Way Of The Heart Must (In Every Basic and Essential Sense) Be Established, and Made Into A True and Characteristic Aspect Of The emotional-sexual Practice and Demonstration Of Any intimately sexually active Practitioner Of The Way Of The Heart, Before Any Such Practitioner Can Be Rightly Acknowledged As My Really Hearing Devotee. Nevertheless, The Third Stage Of "Right Emotional-Sexual Yoga" In The Way Of The Heart Will (and Must—If celibacy Does Not Become The Practice Sooner) Continue To Develop (More and More Profoundly) In The Context Of The First Actually Seeing Stage Of The Way Of The Heart (and Even In The Context Of The Would-Be-Seeing Stage Of The Way Of The Heart—If, Indeed, There Is any sexual activity At That Stage), Until It Becomes Either (In The Case Of those who Are, In The Fullest Sense, Truly, or Even Uniquely, Qualified For A Right Yogic emotional-sexual Sadhana) The Full Demonstration Of The Fourth Stage Of "Right Emotional-Sexual Yoga" (In The Context Of The "Perfect Practice" Of The Way Of The Heart) Or (Certainly, In The Case Of those Not So Qualified—and, Also, Potentially, In The Case Of those So Qualified) The Embrace Of Formally Acknowledged (Firmly Embraced, and life-energy-Positive, or Yogically, Rather Than Merely idealistically and puritanically, Supported and Maintained) celibacy. The Third Stage Of "Right Emotional-Sexual Yoga" In The Way Of The Heart Is Characterized By The "Static Mudra" Of Deeply Penetrating (or, In the homosexual case, Otherwise Strongly Engaged), face-to-face, and (Essentially) motionless, Ecstatic genital Embrace, In Yogically Whole bodily

Devotional and Spiritual Heart-Communion With Me.[140] Thus, The Special Characteristic Of The Third Stage Of "Right Emotional-Sexual Yoga" In The Way Of The Heart Is That (At various points in time During The Occasion Of sexual Embrace—or, Otherwise, At The End Of The Occasion Of sexual Embrace) The physical sexual Embrace Is (Itself) Relaxed Beyond Its Characteristic activity, and Into The Relatively Inactive "Static Mudra". The "Static Mudra" Is A Swoon Of Letting Go Of the bodily exchange of genital sexual intercourse, In Which Swoon genital contact May (or May Not) Entirely Cease (and, In The Case Of male Practitioners, the penis May, or May Not, Cease To Be erect), While The Fundamental Devotional Mudra Of Yogically Whole bodily Heart-Communion With Me Persists, and (As A Principal Characteristic Of The "Static Mudra") Is Even Magnified. The Yoga Of emotional-sexual Embrace Then Becomes (Especially In The Case Of My Seeing Devotees, In their Practice Of "Emotional-Sexual Devotional Communion") A Matter Of Relaxing Entirely Into Participation In Yogically Whole bodily Devotional and Spiritual Heart-Communion With Me (and, Especially In The Case Of My Seeing Devotees, Yogically Whole bodily, and Fully Technically Responsible, Devotional and Spiritual Heart-Communion With My Avatarically Self-Revealed, and Spiritually Present, Divine Person—and, Thus and Thereby, With My Avatarically Self-Transmitted Divine Spirit-Energy)—Even Such That (Potentially) That Relaxation Becomes (On Some Occasions) A Meditative Condition. Indeed, Such Deep and Most Profound Participation In My Avatarically Self-Transmitted Divine Spiritual Presence, and In The Fundamental Devotional Mudra Of Yogically Whole bodily Heart-Communion With Me, Is The Ultimate Purpose (or Ultimate Right Demonstration) Of The Yoga Of "Emotional-Sexual Devotional Communion" In The Way Of The Heart.

The Fourth Stage Of "Right Emotional-Sexual Yoga" In The Way Of The Heart Is A Real Potential Development Only For those who Are, In The Fullest Sense, Truly (or Even Uniquely) Qualified For A Right Yogic emotional-sexual Sadhana and who Are Practicing In The Context Of The "Perfect Practice" Of The Way Of The Heart. Indeed, For Such Practitioners Of The Way Of The Heart—who Are, in their personal intimate contexts, sexually active (or, Otherwise, who Are, Because Of The Yogic Sublimity Of their Constant Devotional Samadhi Of Spiritual Communion With Me, celibate in the context of emotional-sexual intimacy), and who Are Practicing The Way Of The Heart In The Context Of The Only-By-Me Revealed and Given "Perfect Practice" (Either Previous To The Seventh Stage Of Life Or Within The Seventh Stage Of Life), and who Are, In The Fullest Sense, Truly, or Even Uniquely, Qualified For A Right Yogic emotional-sexual Sadhana—The Fourth Stage Of "Right Emotional-Sexual Yoga" Is, In The Way Of The Heart, A Necessary

Demonstration and Practice. (And The Necessary emotional-sexual Discipline, In The Context Of The "Perfect Practice" Of The Way Of The Heart, For All My Devotees who Are Not—In The Fullest Sense—Truly, or, Otherwise, Uniquely, Qualified For A Right Yogic emotional-sexual Sadhana Is Simple, Non-Problematic, and Searchless, or Motiveless, celibacy, itself.)

The Fourth Stage Of "Right Emotional-Sexual Yoga" In The Way Of The Heart Is Characterized (Progressively) By The More and More Continuous (and, In Due Course, moment to moment, or Perpetual) psycho-physical Realization Of The Yogic Condition Of The "Static Mudra" (Whether, At any moment, My Devotee Is, physically, In sexual Embrace Or Not). When The Yogic Condition Of The "Static Mudra" Is psycho-physically Realized moment to moment, the Apparent relationship between the intimate partners Is, itself, No Longer Characterized By The Presumption Of Duality and "Difference", or Even By Polarized physical emotional-sexual Play (Even Though Polarized physical emotional-sexual Play May Yet, At Least At times, Occur). Rather, the Apparent relationship Is, itself, More and More Effectively, Resolved In Non-"Difference"—Becoming, Characteristically, Simply A Matter Of physically Apparent individuals In The Potential Modes Of The ego-Transcending Samadhi Of Yogically Whole bodily Devotional and Spiritual Heart-Communion With Me (Entirely Feeling To Me—Beyond self-Contraction, and, Most Ultimately, Beyond All Separation, Separateness, and Separativeness). When This Development (Of Perpetual "Static Mudra", or Yogically Realized Non-"Difference") Occurs, the Apparent relationship between the intimate partners Is, Principally, Characterized By Persistent Abiding In My Spiritually "Bright" Divine Self-Condition Of Love-Bliss (Prior To any activity whatsoever)—and, Therefore, genital sexual activity (Even If it Occurs, or When it Occurs) Ceases To Be A "Requirement" or A "Necessity" Of the intimate relationship. (And, Indeed, In The General Case, genital sexual activity Will, At Some Point, Be Entirely "Forgotten", In The Fullness Of Yogically Whole bodily Devotional and Spiritual Heart-Communion With Me.) In That Condition (Of Perpetual "Static Mudra", or Yogically Realized Non-"Difference"), the mere relationship between the intimate partners (Without Requiring any particular activity) Becomes, itself (In Yogically Whole bodily Devotional and Spiritual Heart-Communion With Me), A Perpetual Non-Dual "Embrace", or An Always Already "Union" That Requires No Act In Order To Be Achieved. In That Case, The Love-Bliss-Full Samadhi Of Fullest Yogically Whole bodily Devotional and Spiritual Heart-Communion With My (Avatarically Self-Revealed) Transcendental, Inherently Spiritual, Inherently egoless, and Self-Evidently Divine Person Is Simply As Is, or Simply That Which Is Always Already The Case—and There Is Not anything Further That Needs To be done or said, To "Develop" the intimate relationship between the partners. Thus, In The Fourth Stage Of "Right Emotional-Sexual Yoga" In The Way Of The Heart, emotional-sexual Practice (Fully Resolved, In The Perpetual "Static Mudra" Of Yogically Realized Non-"Difference") Becomes Utterly Coincident With (and, Effectively, Ceases To Be, In Any Sense, "Different" From, or A Contrary To, or An Alternative To) The Necessary Constant Circumstance and Samadhi Of Uninterrupted Devotional, and Spiritual, and (Altogether) Yogically Whole bodily Heart-Communion With Me. And, Therefore, My Devotees who Are (Necessarily, In The Fullest Sense) Truly (or Even Uniquely) Qualified For A Right Yogic emotional-sexual Sadhana and who (In The Context Of The Only-By-Me Revealed and Given "Perfect Practice" Of The Way Of The Heart) Have Truly Matured In their Practice Of "Right Emotional-Sexual Yoga"—Such That The Perpetual "Static Mudra" Characterizes (and Is Most Fully Demonstrated In) their any intimate emotional-sexual relationship—Will, In The General Case, Eventually (or More and More Characteristically) Demonstrate A Spontaneous Yogic (and Spiritually-Based) Disposition, Intention, and Choice Of Either celibacy-in-intimacy (Inherently Free Of All emotional-sexual Disturbance, or Chronic Agitation, and All "Bonding"-Bondage) Or, Perhaps (In Some Cases), single celibacy—or, Otherwise, My Such Maturely Practicing Devotees Will (Necessarily, and Freely) Demonstrate A Spontaneous Yogic (and Spiritually-Based) Disposition, Intention, and Choice That Significantly Reduces The Frequency Of their sexual activity. Those who Are Uniquely Qualified For A Right Yogic emotional-sexual Sadhana May or May Not Exhibit As Much Of This Tendency Toward Either celibacy-in-intimacy Or Reduction Of The Frequency Of sexual activity As Is Exhibited By others. In Any Case, All My Such Maturely Practicing Devotees Will, Characteristically, Demonstrate A Sublimity Of Yogic (and Spiritually-Based) emotional-sexual Relatedness That Is Inherently Free Of emotional-sexual Disturbance (or Chronic Agitation) and Inherently Free Of All "Bonding"-Bondage. And, In All Such Cases, The Characteristic Sign That Is The Evidence Of their Demonstration Of The Fourth Stage Of "Right Emotional-Sexual Yoga" Will Manifest Itself Entirely As A Spontaneously Awakened Disposition, Intention, and Choice—Awakened (Thus) Entirely Because Of The Yogic Sublimity Of their Constant Devotional Samadhi Of Spiritual Communion With Me.

By Rightly (and, Necessarily, Conservatively, and Not At All Excessively) Practicing The By-Me-Given Forms Of emotional-sexual self-Discipline From The Beginning Of their Practice Of The Way Of The Heart, My Early-Stage (or Pre-Seeing) Devotees (Whether they Are celibates Or sexually active in their personal intimate contexts) Prepare themselves For The Yoga Of (Fully Technically Responsible) Spirit-"Conductivity" In The Seeing Stages Of The

Way Of The Heart. "Right Emotional-Sexual Yoga", As It Is Practiced By Student-Beginners In The Way Of The Heart (who Are, in their intimate personal contexts, sexually active), Involves Responsibility For The "Conductivity" Of the Natural bodily energy, but The Circuit In the body-mind Through Which the Natural bodily energy Is Conducted Is The Same Circuit Through Which My Avatarically Self-Transmitted Divine Spirit-Energy Is Conducted By My By-Me-Spiritually-Initiated Devotees. Through The Practice Of "Right Emotional-Sexual Yoga" (and Right "General Conductivity" Altogether), My Early-Stage (or Pre-Seeing) Devotee (who Is, in his or her intimate personal context, sexually active) Must Progressively Establish (and My Seeing Devotee Must Already Be Firmly Established In) Steady, Forceful, Unbroken, and Unobstructed "Conductivity" In The Full Circle Of the body—Such That The Frontal Pattern Of "Conductivity" Can Be Tangibly Felt (head To toe), and Constantly breathed, With Constant Upward Spinal Relaxation (or Simple Polarization, From base To Crown, Without The Strategy Of Dissociation From the gross physical body)—and All Of This Not Only In The Occasion Of sexual activity, but In Even every moment.

Thus, In The Only-By-Me Revealed and Given Way Of The Heart, Yogically Right emotional-sexual activity Must Be Made To Serve To Intensify and Support The Fullness Of This Unbroken "Conductivity". Having Magnified This Fullness As My Student-Beginner Devotee, When You (Thereafter) Become My By-Me-Spiritually-Initiated (and Always Newly By-Me-Spiritually-Activated) Devotee (and, In Due Course, My Fully Both Hearing <u>and</u> Seeing Devotee), Then I (Myself) Fully Intervene and Fully Infuse You In That Same Circle That You Have (More and More) Prepared and Conformed To Me.

The Two Principal Responsive Aspects Of Your Practice As My Seeing Devotee (Both Of Which Are, Equally, Necessary and Profoundly Important) Are The "Conscious Process" (Of "Locating" Me, Devotionally and Spiritually, Such That You Can Constantly Find Me From The Heart—Ultimately, To Be Drawn By Me From The Circle, and The Left and Middle Regions Of The Heart, Into The Right Side Of The Heart) and The Fully Technically Responsible "Conductivity" Of My Avatarically Self-Transmitted Divine Spirit-Current. In Order To See Me, You Must Be Prepared To (Fully Technically Responsibly) Feel The Steady Flowing Of My Avatarically Self-Transmitted Divine Spirit-Current In The Circle Of the body-mind. Therefore, All My Early-Stage (or Pre-Seeing) Devotees Must—Through The (In Due Course, Spiritual) Practice Of Right "General Conductivity" Altogether (Including, As Appropriate, The Right Practice Of "Right Emotional-Sexual Yoga"—At First, and Most Fundamentally, In The Form Of The "Own-Body Yogic Sexual Practice", and, On That Basis—In The Case Of My Early-Stage, or Pre-Seeing, Devotees who

Are, in their personal intimate contexts, sexually active—In The Form Of "Emotional-Sexual Conscious Exercise")—Prepare The Circle Of the body-mind For The Great Hearing-Based Process Of (Devotionally and Spiritually) Seeing Me.

Most Of My Devotees Will (Likely) Practice The (Fundamentally, own-body) emotional-sexual Yoga Of The Way Of The Heart In The Context Of an intimately sexually active life. However, As Soon As The Element Of sexual Association With an other Is Introduced, There Are Inherent liabilities that Must Be Accounted For. Those liabilities Are, Principally, The (Potential) Diminishment Of One-Pointed Ruchira Avatara Bhakti Yoga and The (Potential) Diminishment Of own-body Responsibility. Therefore, In The Only-By-Me Revealed and Given Way Of The Heart (or Way Of Adidam), There Is A Necessary functional, practical, relational, and Cultural Prerequisite (and Basis) For Full and Right Practice Of The Yoga Of "Emotional-Sexual Devotional Communion" (or, At First, "Emotional-Sexual Conscious Exercise"). That Necessary Prerequisite Is True Sila (or ego-Surrendering, ego-Forgetting, and, More and More, ego-Transcending Discipline Of the body-mind and Conservation Of its functions and activities). And The Most Basic Discipline Of True Sila In The Context Of emotionally Committed intimate relationship Is The Intentional and ego-Transcending Concentration Of emotional-sexual Relatedness (and emotional-sexual activity) In The Circumstance and Devotional Heart-Practice Of What I Call "'True Yogic Intimacy'".

Avatar Adi Da Samraj
The Mountain Of Attention Sanctuary, 2000

SUTRA 40

From The Very Beginning Of The Only-By-Me Revealed and Given Way Of Adidam (Which Is The One and Only By-Me-Revealed and By-Me-Given Way Of The Heart), "True Yogic Intimacy" Is A Necessary Subject Of Study For All My Formally Practicing Devotees—and It Is (From The Beginning) A Necessary Context Of Progressive Adaptation, Demonstration, and Accountability For All My Formally Practicing Devotees who Are Practicing In the circumstance of intimate relationship. Therefore, The (In Due Course, Spiritually-Based) Practice Of "True Yogic Intimacy" Must Be Engaged (and Progressively Developed) By All My Formally Practicing Devotees who Are Practicing Inside The Context Of intimate relationship (whether sexually active or sexually inactive).

"True Yogic Intimacy" (Whether sexually active Or sexually inactive) Is (In Due Course, and Beyond Its Simplest human Components) Necessarily A Spiritual Discipline. Therefore, the Total body-mind (Including its emotional-sexual Dimension) Must (Beyond The Student-Beginner Stage Of The Way Of The Heart) Be Devotionally Surrendered To The Real (and Only-By-My-Avataric-Divine-Spiritual-Grace-Given) Process Of True (and, In Due Course, Fully Technically Responsible) Spiritual Communion With Me. In Due Course, Most Fundamental self-Understanding, Right and True Yogic Responsibility, Consistent emotional-sexual Equanimity, and, Indeed, All The Full Technical Responsibilities and Spiritual Attributes Associated With The Progressive Demonstration Of Both Hearing and Seeing In The Only-By-Me Revealed and Given Way Of The Heart Must (By Means Of My Avatarically Self-Transmitted Divine Spiritual Grace) Uproot The Otherwise Accumulated Mass Of psycho-physical Adaptations To ego-Bound emotional-sexual Patterns, Habits, and Tendencies.

"True Yogic Intimacy" Is A Devotional Practice, That Is (Necessarily) Unique To The Only-By-Me Revealed and Given Way Of The Heart (or Way Of Adidam).

"True Yogic Intimacy" Is The Practice Of Devotion To Me, Exercised Within My Devotee's Chosen Circumstance Of intimate emotional-sexual Relatedness.

"True Yogic Intimacy" Is Not any intimate relationship itself, but "True Yogic Intimacy" Is The Real and Effective Heart-Practice Of Devotion To Me In The Context (and every circumstance) Of that intimate relationship.

"True Yogic Intimacy" Is A Sadhana (or A Devotional and Spiritual Discipline)—Not merely a conventional social ideal.

"True Yogic Intimacy" Is An ego-Transcending Discipline That Directly Transcends The Dissociative Method Of egoity, The Idea Of the psycho-physical self As An "Owner" Of others, and The Idea Of others As "Property". Therefore, "True Yogic Intimacy" Replaces The Motive Of egoic Independence and The Psychology Of Ownership (Of one's any intimate partner, or Even one's children) With The Practice Of ego-Transcending Love, and (In Due Course) The Heart-Culture Of (Most Fundamental) self-Understanding, and (Always) Life-Positive self-Discipline In Relationship To one's any intimate partner and all other beings.

"True Yogic Intimacy" Economizes (or Balances) Itself, Inherently and Inevitably. Therefore, If "True Yogic Intimacy" Is Rightly Practiced and Realized, The Possibility Of Multiple relationships Of "True Yogic Intimacy" (or Simultaneous emotional-sexual relationships Of "True Yogic Intimacy" between any one individual and more than one partner) Is, In The General Case, Unlikely. For This Reason, or (Altogether) Because Of The Great Requirements Involved In The Real Practice Of "True Yogic Intimacy" (and The Real Practice Of All The Forms Of human, Spiritual, Transcendental, and Divine Discipline In The Way Of The Heart), "True Yogic Intimacy" (Fully, Intelligently, and Feelingly "Considered") Will, In The Case Of Very Nearly All Practitioners Of The Way Of The Heart—Except For those In Unique, Unusual, and, Necessarily, Rare Circumstances—Confine Itself To A Real, and Rightly Practiced, emotional-sexual relationship with (and Right Intimate Commitment To) Only one other (or one partner) During any Significant period of time (or Even During an entire lifetime).

"True Yogic Intimacy" Requires The Real and Steady Relinquishment Of Merely Casual, or Reactively Motivated, or Negatively Intended, or (Otherwise) Merely ego-Serving and Mechanical Indulgence (or Involvement) In emotional-sexual activity with <u>any</u> other or others—even an established intimate partner. For This Reason, Every individual Practitioner who Formally Embraces The Way Of The Heart Must Always (Within The Appropriate "Consideration"-Group Context) Be Openly Confessed and Fully self-Revealed Regarding his or her emotional-sexual activities. And, Only If It Is Truly Right and Appropriate, Based On Discrimination and Mutual Agreement, and Only After Receiving The Formal Approval Of The Formal Sacred Cooperative Cultural Gathering Of All Formally Acknowledged Practitioners Of The Way Of The Heart, Is Any Practitioner Of The Way Of The Heart To Actively (and, Necessarily, Responsibly) Engage In a relationship Of Intimate Commitment With any other, or (Otherwise) To Actively (and, Necessarily, Responsibly) Relinquish a relationship Of Intimate Commitment With any other. Likewise, Within The

"Consideration"-Group Context Of The Formal Sacred Cooperative Cultural Gathering Of All Formally Acknowledged Practitioners Of The Way Of The Heart, Every individual Practitioner Of The Way Of The Heart (Whether Or Not he or she Is Presently Involved In an intimate relationship) Should (As Necessary) Enter Into Intentional and Fullest self-Examination and Direct Confession Of his or her individual and Particular Full Range Of sexual (and emotional-sexual) Practices, Commitments, Agreements, Circumstances, Patterns, Habits, and Motives—In Order To Test every element Of All Of That (and, As Appropriate, Either To Confirm, Improve, Exceed, Or Transcend each element Of All Of That). Such "Consideration" Should Occur Only Occasionally (and, Thus, Relatively Infrequently)—Rather Than As A Preoccupation Of Either The "Consideration" Groups Or Of individual Practitioners themselves. And, whenever Such "Considerations" Do Occur, they Should <u>Always</u> Be Done In An Open, Direct, and <u>Quickly</u> Effective Manner, Which (In Its Attitude and Activity Of self-Examination and Confession) Is (Intentionally, and Really Effectively) Free Of merely conventional, idealistic, or puritanical Reservations, Restraints, or Restrictions, and Which Is (Altogether) Free Of Merely ego-Serving Intentions.

"True Yogic Intimacy" Is A One-Pointed Discipline Of the psycho-physical self, In Which each individual Is (as the intimate partner of any other) Required (Beyond The Student-Beginner Stage Of The Way Of The Heart) To Practice intimate relationship As Spiritual Intimacy With Me (or As A Means Of ego-Transcending Devotional and Spiritual Heart-Communion With Me).

Spiritually Active "True Yogic Intimacy" Is A Cooperative Union Between individuals whose Commitment (or Expression) To one another Is Based On A Spiritual Intention That Is Freely, Directly, and Fully Expressed Through the emotional-sexual character of each partner.

"True Yogic Intimacy" Is Necessarily An Intentional and Active Practice—Not Merely An Automatic (or Given) Situation and Fact Of daily life, To Be Passively Indulged In or Suffered. And The Fundamental Import Of That Practice Is That (Beyond The Student-Beginner Stage Of The Way Of The Heart) It <u>Always</u> Serves The Magnification, Conservation, and Conversion Of My Avatarically Self-Transmitted Divine Spirit-Current (and Really Effective Spiritual Presence) In the daily life of each partner (Whether Or Not the partners Choose To Be sexually active).

"True Yogic Intimacy" Is The ego-Surrendering, ego-Forgetting, and (More and More) ego-Transcending Practice Of Releasing one's own body-mind-self, one's any intimate partner, and Even every one at all, To Me and Into Me.

"True Yogic Intimacy" Is Not, In Principle, A Matter Of self-Indulgence and conventional self-Fulfillment—Although It Does Not, In Principle, Exclude pleasures Of human Love and sexual intimacy.

"True Yogic Intimacy" Is A Truly human Yoga—A Discipline Of the psycho-physical self That Purifies Tendencies Of desire and mind, Counters (or Responsively Releases) The Effort Of self-Contraction, Balances and "Energizes" the psycho-physical being, and Supports The Process Of Divine Self-Realization Through Real ego-Transcendence.

"True Yogic Intimacy" Requires (or Always Calls For) Real and Steady Disciplining Of attention and functional life-energy.

"True Yogic Intimacy" Requires (or Always Calls For) The Real and Steady Expression Of human (but Not ego-Bound) Love.

"True Yogic Intimacy" Requires (or Always Calls For) Real and Steady Relinquishment Of egoic Independence—or all ego-Possessed demands, expectations, and complaints, All Rituals Of Rejection, Mistrust, and Reactivity, and all strategies of depression and pleasurelessness.

Therefore, "True Yogic Intimacy" Requires (or Always Calls For) Real and Steady Relinquishment Of Even any and all egoic limits On Real, Truly human, and Really ego-Transcending Love—and This Through The Constant Magnification Of Ruchira Avatara Bhakti Yoga, Which Is The Devotionally Responsive Counter-egoic (and Even Total psycho-physical) Practice Of ego-Surrendering, ego-Forgetting, and Truly (and, Ultimately, Even Most Perfectly) ego-Transcending Devotion To Me.

As A Natural Expression Of "True Yogic Intimacy", partners In "True Yogic Intimacy" Are Required (or Always Called) To Incarnate The Two Principal Signs (or Complementary and Polar Opposite Aspects) Of The Universal Natural (and, Ultimately, Divine) Dynamic Of Life. Therefore, the male partner Is Required (or Always Called) To Surrender himself To Incarnate (or Extend) The Divine Husbanding (or Conserving) Power (or To Practice The True Man's Yoga)—By Steadily Controlling (or Rightly Directing) the functional life-energy and the attention of himself and his any female partner, and By Constantly Arousing (In himself and In his any female partner) The Motive Of Right Restraint, Right Intention, and Right Use Of functional life-energy and Of attention. And the female partner Is Required (or Always Called) To Surrender herself To Incarnate (or To Extend) The Divine "Goddess-Power" (or To Practice The True Woman's Yoga) Of Attraction, self-Surrender, and Nurturing—By Constantly Nourishing her any male partner With The Life-Power Of her functional life-energy and her attention, and By Constantly Arousing The Motive Of Heart-Surrender and Heart-Radiance In herself and In her any male partner.

"True Yogic Intimacy" Is Typically heterosexual, but It May Also (In Some Cases) Be homosexual. Any Practitioner Of The Way Of The Heart who Is "Considering" The Possibility Of homosexual "True Yogic Intimacy" Must Have Gone Through The Culturally Accountable Process Of Discovering Whether his or her emotional-sexual Patterning Is Truly homosexual—and That Resolution Must Be Formally Culturally Acknowledged As Such. (Similarly, Any Practitioner Of The Way Of The Heart who experiences—or, Otherwise, Exhibits—A Significant Degree Of homosexual Interest or Motivation Must, If he or she Is "Considering" The Possibility Of heterosexual "True Yogic Intimacy", Go Through A Culturally Accountable Process Of Discovering Whether his or her emotional-sexual Patterning Is Truly heterosexual.) And those who Enter Into The Practice Of "True Yogic Intimacy" As homosexuals Must Be Capable Of The Same ego-Transcending Love In Practice That Is Required Of heterosexuals—and The "Husband"-"Goddess" Dynamic (or The Complementary Play Of Conservative, or Restraining, Power and Attractive, or Radiating, Power) Will (Generally) Be Exhibited Just As Clearly, Directly, and Fully In The Case Of "True Yogic Intimacy" Between psychologically Polarized homosexual partners As In The Case Of "True Yogic Intimacy" Between physically (and psychologically) Polar Opposite (or heterosexual) partners.

In The Only-By-Me Revealed and Given Way Of The Heart (or Way Of Adidam), The Sadhana Of "True Yogic Intimacy" Is A Specialized Form Of The Basic Sadhana Of ego-Transcending Surrender To Me, The Divine Heart-Master Of My Every Devotee. Thus (and Thereby), The Sadhana Of "True Yogic Intimacy" Is, In The Way Of The Heart, A Direct Extension Of The Basic Sadhana Of Direct and Effective Acceptance Of My Husbanding (or Restraining, Guiding, and Awakening) Influence—By All My Listening Devotees, All My Hearing Devotees, and All My Seeing Devotees, male or female. Therefore, In The Way Of The Heart, Only The Orientation Of "True Yogic Intimacy" Allows emotional-sexual relationship (with or without sexual activity) To Be Positively Compatible With The Devotional (and, In Due Course, Spiritual) Process Of Heart-Communion With Me (By Commanding Even emotional-sexual energy and attention To Achieve One-Pointed Concentration In Me, Free Of Casual Distraction).

In The Only-By-Me Revealed and Given Way Of The Heart (or Way Of Adidam), The Sadhana Of "True Yogic Intimacy" Is A Specialized Form Of The Basic (or Foundation) Sadhana Of Devotional and (In Due Course) Spiritual Communion With Me, and The ego-Surrendering, ego-Forgetting, and (More and More—and, At Last, Most Perfectly) ego-Transcending Heart-Acceptance (Thus and Thereby) Of My Own Avatarically Self-Revealed (and Very, and Self-Existing, and Self-Radiant, and Inherently egoless, and Inherently Attractive, and Entirely "Bright", and Self-Evidently Divine) Self-Condition and Person. Therefore, Only The Orientation Of "True Yogic Intimacy" Allows emotional-sexual intimacy (with or without sexual activity) To Be Positively Compatible With The Devotional (and, In Due Course, Spiritual) Process Of

Heart-Communion With Me (By Allowing emotional-sexual energy and attention To Achieve Full Devotional and Spiritual Aliveness, Free Of The Motive Of self-Suppression and The Mood Of Life-Depression).

The (Inherently) ego-Renouncing Discipline Of "True Yogic Intimacy" (Whether sexually active Or sexually inactive) May (If the intimately related individuals Are So Moved) Be Embraced In The *Most* Intensively ego-Renouncing Manner—As a relationship Of "Intimate Yogic Friendship".

The Fundamental Essence Of "True Yogic Intimacy" In The Way Of The Heart—and Of "Intimate Yogic Friendship" In Particular—Is The ego-Transcending Surrender Of one's emotional-sexual life and one's any emotional-sexual relationship To That Which Is Beyond limitation. By Means Of Such self-Surrender *and* other-Surrender, intimate relationship and (In The intimately sexually active Case) sexual activity Are *Entirely* Transformed Into The Me-Realizing Yoga Of Ruchira Avatara Bhakti. My Any Devotee who Has Embraced The Discipline Of "Intimate Yogic Friendship" Is (By Means Of That Embrace) Affirming The Intention To Pattern his or her entire life In Utter (or Most Intensively Practiced) Conformity With The Impulse To Realize That Which Is Beyond limitation. Thus, To Embrace The Discipline Of "Intimate Yogic Friendship" Is Not Merely To Make A Choice Relative To sexuality in and of itself. Rather, To Embrace The Discipline Of "Intimate Yogic Friendship" Is To Make The Fundamentally Renunciate Choice To Organize one's life In Such A Manner That The Sadhana Of Devotion To Me Can Be Maximized To The Greatest Degree Possible. Thus, My Any Devotee who Has Rightly Embraced The Discipline Of "Intimate Yogic Friendship" Has Done So Because he or she Finds any degree Of ego-Based (and, otherwise, conventional, and even merely social) emotional-sexual pair-"Bonding" To Be An Unacceptable Distraction From the Full life Of Devotional Resort To Me.

"Intimate Yogic Friendship" Is an emotional-sexual relationship that Is *Entirely* Given Up To The Purpose Of Demonstrating and Magnifying The Yoga Of Ruchira Avatara Bhakti (or The Devotionally Responsive Counter-egoic, and Even Total psycho-physical, Practice Of ego-Surrendering, ego-Forgetting, and Truly—and, Ultimately, Even Most Perfectly—ego-Transcending Devotion To Me), In The Context Of emotional-sexual Relatedness (and Altogether), and Strictly In Accordance With My Instructions Relative To Right emotional-sexual Discipline, and Without Allowing Concessions To Non-Renunciate Purposes (or The egoic—and, otherwise, conventional, or even merely social—Purposes Characteristic Of The First Three Stages Of Life).

"Intimate Yogic Friendship" Is, Thus, an emotional-sexual intimacy between individuals who Choose To Devote their lives One-Pointedly To The Great Purpose Of Most Perfectly Realizing Me, and who Are (Therefore)

Moved To Conform their emotional-sexual intimacy Entirely To That Great (Yogic and Spiritual and, Most Ultimately, Divine) Purpose (Rather Than Allowing their lives To Continue To Be Patterned In The egoic Manner, On The Basis Of conventional, or merely social, emotional-sexual Preoccupations). Indeed, "Yogically intimate friends" Are So Concentrated In The Purpose Of Most Perfectly Realizing Me That each of them Is (In Effect) "Single" In Relationship To Me—Even In The Context Of his or her emotional-sexual Relatedness.

Therefore, "Intimate Yogic Friendship" Is an emotional-sexual relationship So Focused In each individual's Heart-Resort To Me That It Is (functionally, practically, relationally, Culturally, and, Altogether, Fully Effectively) Free Of the ego-Based, and merely conventional (or merely social), pair-"Bonding" agreements that Are Otherwise Characteristic Of intimate relationships—Even (To One or Another Possible Degree) Of intimate relationships As they Are Engaged By My Devotees who, Without Embracing The Obligations Of The Formal Discipline Of "Intimate Yogic Friendship", Practice intimate relationship In Conformity To My Instructions Relative To "True Yogic Intimacy".

My Devotee who Practices In The Context Of "Intimate Yogic Friendship" Must Have Clearly Observed That all conventional pair-"Bonding" agreements (or socially Patterned "pair"-Tendencies, Whether Spoken or Unspoken) Tend To Be An "Excursion" From Yogically Whole bodily (and Truly ego-Transcending) Devotional and (As The Case May Be) Spiritual Heart-Communion With Me—and, Therefore, he or she Embraces The Discipline Of "Intimate Yogic Friendship" Specifically As A Means Of Relinquishing (or As An Expression Of The Relinquishment Of) such agreements. (Indeed, The Discipline Of "Intimate Yogic Friendship" Is Even A Form Of Preparation For The Inevitability Of bodily Separation and death—For The Discipline Of "Intimate Yogic Friendship" Explicitly Takes Into Account Both The Inevitable Fact That The "Bond" Between Apparent human individuals Cannot, Itself, Be Eternal and The Boundlessly Joyous Reality That The True Devotional "Bond" To Me Persists Through all changes of life and death and time and space.)

To Engage an intimate relationship In The Manner Of "Intimate Yogic Friendship" Is To Fully Cultivate A Profound Feeling-Intimacy With one's any "Yogically intimate friend", Without Becoming Involved In the kinds of (conventional, or merely social and ego-Based) pair-"Bonding" arrangements that Inevitably Undermine The Full Practice Of Yogically Whole bodily Devotional and (As The Case May Be) Spiritual Heart-Communion With Me. Thus, "Intimate Yogic Friendship" Is Not, In Any Sense, An ascetical Practice—but It Is, Rather, A Form Of emotional-sexual Relatedness That Fully Embraces The Benign Pleasure Of Yogically Right emotional-sexual intimacy, In The

Context Of a life Of One-Pointed Devotional Resort To Me, and Of Fullest (or Always Intensively Maximized) Service To Me.

To Engage an intimate relationship In The Form Of "Intimate Yogic Friendship" Requires That both partners Really Transcend The Usual Bondage Of conventional (and, Necessarily, egoic) pair-"Bonding"—and, Thus, Really Go Beyond All Tendencies To Merely Be bland "householders" (or The Usual "Mom" and "Dad"), who, Seemingly Comfortably (or Merely As a moralistic, or puritanical, or idealistically enforced convention of socially expected behavior), Maintain an outward appearance Of Fidelity. Thus, To Engage an intimate relationship In The Form Of "Intimate Yogic Friendship" Necessitates Passing Through A Real Crisis Of self-Examination and Consequent Change Of Action and Disposition, By Means Of Which Crisis and Change My Devotee who Practices (or Would Practice) In The Context Of "Intimate Yogic Friendship" Has Truly Become a Free and (Effectively) Single individual—Capable Of Consistently Transcending The Rituals Of Rejection, Betrayal, and Un-Love, and (Indeed) All Forms Of "Oedipal" Reactivity, Via Devotional and (As The Case May Be) Spiritual Heart-Communion With Me. Therefore, In Order To Rightly Engage an intimate relationship In The Form Of "Intimate Yogic Friendship", My Devotee Must Have Thoroughly Addressed the specific aspects and details of his or her character, tendencies, limitations, and activities that Would (Otherwise) Determine his or her emotional-sexual Patterning, Such That he or she Is Capable Of Consistently Going Beyond That Patterning, and Is Capable (Altogether) Of Consistently Going Beyond double-mindedness Relative To The emotional-sexual Dimension Of human life, and Of Consistently Going Beyond the conventional "social-persona model" Of human Existence. Indeed, My Devotee who Practices In The Context Of "Intimate Yogic Friendship" Must Be Capable Of Consistently Transcending All Forms Of Bondage To merely social conventions, and Must (By Conforming, Instead, To Truly Sacred Principles) Be Always and Entirely Free To Confess anything, Examine anything, Address anything, and Transcend everything, In Devotional and (As The Case May Be) Spiritual Heart-Communion With Me. And, In All Of This, There Must Be A Process Of Transformative Sadhana, By Means Of Which My Any Such Devotee's emotional-sexual Patterns Are Actually Changed, Such That They Are No Longer a limit On his or her Practice Of "True Yogic Intimacy" and (In the sexually active case) "Right Emotional-Sexual Yoga"—Because, If There Is No Process Of Transformative Sadhana, Then Any Presumed "Consideration" Of emotional-sexual Patterns Is Nothing but "talk" Added To The Patterns, and The Patterns Themselves Remain Unchanged.

Thus, My Devotees who Engage intimate relationship (whether sexually active or sexually inactive) In The Form Of "Intimate Yogic Friendship" Simply

(Consistently) Demonstrate (In The Context Of that any relationship) their Capability For "True Yogic Intimacy" and (If they Are, in their personal intimate contexts, sexually active) "Right Emotional-Sexual Yoga"—With no requirement, expectation, demand, or dependence on the part of either "Yogically intimate friend" To Struggle With (or, In The conventional—or Rather secular, and, Thus, Necessarily, Struggling—Sense, To "Work Out", or merely "socialize", or "civilize", Rather Than Yogically Develop) any aspect of the relationship with one another.

Therefore, To Engage intimate relationship In The Manner Of "Intimate Yogic Friendship" Is To Intentionally and Entirely Relinquish All The limiting Entanglements Of the usual pair-"Bonding" arrangement (but Without Relinquishing emotional-sexual intimacy itself), and (Rather Than Making mutual egoic agreements, which Inevitably Result In The Undermining Of Devotional and Spiritual Practice) To Enter Into Yogically intimate relationship In Such A Manner That (By Taking Into Account every Possible Negatively Significant factor) the relationship Is Established On A Basis That Is Entirely Free Of all (or At Least all Negatively Significant, or Otherwise, From A True Renunciate Point Of View, Inappropriate or limiting) dependence on one another, and That Consists <u>Only</u> Of "True Yogic Intimacy" and (If the partners in intimacy Are sexually active) "Right Emotional-Sexual Yoga", and Nothing Else.

As Part Of their Relinquishment Of all egoic (or, Otherwise, merely conventional) expectations, demands, dependencies, and agreements, "Yogically intimate friends" Do Not Presume The "Right" To Any Particular Fixed Frequency or Degree Of contact with one another (Whether Of sexually active Association Or Simply Of sexually inactive emotional Association), but (Rather) they Allow The Frequency and The Degree Of contact To Be Entirely Determined By The Circumstances and The Requirements Of their Service (and The Totality Of their Sadhana) In My Avataric Divine Company, and Not By any form of egoic expectation or inclination. Indeed, The "Intimate Yogic Friendship" Agreement Must Be Associated With A Culturally Accountable Agreement That each partner in the "Intimate Yogic Friendship" relationship Fully Magnify and Maximize the time Spent In daily Cultural (or, Otherwise, practical) Service Responsibilities (and daily Intensive Sadhana Responsibilities Of All Kinds), Rather Than Arbitrarily (or As A First Principle) Magnify or Maximize (or Even Casually Indulge In) intimate (and, In General, pair-"Bonding") activities.

Because, In The Context Of The Practice Of "Intimate Yogic Friendship", There Is Necessary (and Mutually Agreed) Relinquishment Of egoic (or, Otherwise, conventional, and even common practical) expectations, demands, dependencies, and agreements, There May (In Some, Necessarily Rare,

Circumstances and Instances) Be Practitioners Of The Way Of The Heart who Participate In the relationship Of "Intimate Yogic Friendship" With more than one partner. Nevertheless, Because Of The Profound Nature Of (and The Great Requirements For) Right and True Yogic Devotional and Spiritual Practice Of The Way Of The Heart, the relationship Of "Intimate Yogic Friendship" Will, In The General Case, Inevitably (and Necessarily) Be Engaged With only one partner. And, In Any and Every Case, The Fundamental Requirement (and The Only Mutual Expectation That Is Rightly Exercised By the partners) In "Intimate Yogic Friendship" Is That each one Be Steadily Committed (and Always Active) To Serve the other In his or her Principal and Most Fundamental life-Purpose, Which Is The Purpose Of Yogically Whole bodily Devotional and Spiritual Heart-Communion With Me, and (Ultimately) Of Realizing Me Most Perfectly.

Only A Fool Will Fail To Cultivate The Relationship To Me, The Divine Heart-Master—The Heart-Beloved Of all-and-All. Likewise, Only A Fool Will Fail To Cultivate human Well-being—and Spiritual, Transcendental, and Divine Realization—In The Case Of his or her any partner In intimate Embrace. And This Is Also True: The ego (or the self-Contracted individual) Is Just Such A Fool!

The emotional-sexual ego Constantly Hunts For an other. The ego-"I" (or self-Contraction) Hunts (or Seeks) an other (Even all others and The Total Objective Cosmos) In Order To Be Gratified, Consoled, and Protected. The Compulsive Hunting (or Search) For an other Is Generated By The Feelings Of Un-Happiness, Emptiness, and Separateness That Possess and Characterize the self-Contracted being.

Once an other Is Found, the ego-"I" Clings To the other—At First pleasurably, and Then Aggressively. The ego-"I" Depends On the other For Happiness—and, Over time, the ego-"I" Makes Greater and Greater Demands On the other For Fulfillment Of itself (In all of its desires). Often, In time, the other Becomes Depressed and Exhausted By This Demand—and, Thus, Leaves, or Dies. Just As Likely, the ego-"I" Discovers, Over time, That the other Cannot (or Will Not) Satisfy The Absolute Demand For attention and Consolation. In That Case, the ego-"I" Feels Betrayed, and the ego-"I" Begins The Strategy Of Punishing, Rejecting, and Abandoning the other.

Every conditionally Manifested being Has (In time) Often Been The Proposed Victim Of This Strategy Of Separate and Separative selves. Even More, Until The Heart Gives Way To My Divine Love-Bliss, every conditionally living being Is The Original Genius and Grand Performer Of This Strategy Of Separate and Separative selves. It Is The Strategy Of "Narcissus", and It Is The Dreadful Work Of all conditionally living beings who Are Not Awake To The Truth Beyond the ego-"I".

If There Is To Be Real Happiness, The Cycle Of egoic self-Preoccupation and other-Dependency (or object-Dependency Generally) Must Be Transcended. In The Way Of The Heart, This Cycle Is Transcended Through Most Fundamental self-Understanding, and Through ego-Transcending Love, Service, self-Discipline, and Meditation (In Devotionally Me-Recognizing and Devotionally To-Me-Responsive Devotional Relationship To Me), and (Eventually, By Means Of My Avatarically Self-Transmitted Divine Spiritual Grace) Through Direct (and, Ultimately, Inherent, and, At Last, Most Perfect) Realization Of My (Avatarically Self-Revealed) Self-Radiant (or Inherently Spiritual), Self-Existing (or Transcendental), and Self-Evidently Divine (and Inherently egoless) Self-Condition, Which Is The Source-Condition Of all-and-All, and Which Is The Inherently Spiritually "Bright" Self-Condition Of Being (Itself). In This Manner, The Inherent Happiness Of My Spiritual, Transcendental, Inherently egoless, and Self-Evidently Divine Person and "Bright" Spiritual Self-Condition Replaces The Fruitless Search (or Hunt) For Happiness By the self-Contracted and Dependent conditional self.

The Only-By-Me Revealed and Given Way Of The Heart (or Way Of Adidam) Is Founded On Real Transcending Of The Search (or Wanting Need) For Happiness. That Is To Say, The Way Of The Heart Is Founded On The Magnification Of Inherent (or Real) Happiness—or The Self-Realization Of Self-Evidently Divine Happiness Itself (Which Is The Non-Separate and Non-"Different" Inherent Realization Of The Self-Existing and Self-Radiant, or Spiritually "Bright", Self-Condition Of Reality Itself). Therefore, I Say: Come To Me When You Are Already Happy. In Other Words, Come To Me By Truly (or Merely, or Searchlessly) Turning To Me. Do Not Come To Me With A Mere Outward Show Of Devotion (While You Remain Inwardly Dissociated and Possessed By self-Contraction)—For, If You Do So, You Will Come As A Seeker, Wanting Happiness From Me, and (Yet) Unable To Reach To Me and To Find Me, and (Thus and Thereby) To Find (or To Spiritually and Really "Locate") Happiness Itself.

Therefore, Come To Me (To Listen To Me, and To Hear Me) By Surrendering To Me (By Heart). And Do Not Come To Me To See Me Until You Have Truly Heard Me and Become Founded (Thereby) In The Real Devotional Practice Of self-Surrender, self-Forgetting, and Effective self-Transcendence (or Real ego-Transcendence).

Do Not Come To Me In The Manner Of A Seeker, Wanting To Depend On Me To Make Your Separate and Separative self Happy. Come To Me For Me Only. I Am Happiness Itself (Prior To Your Separate and Separative self). Therefore, Come To Me To Surrender and Forget Your Separate and Separative self (which is Your Un-Happiness, Full Of Wanting Need and Search).

You Come To Me Truly (or Rightly) When You Are No Longer Resorting To Your conditional self (or ego-"I"). Indeed, You Cannot Even Find Me (or "Locate" My Spiritual "Brightness" and My Spiritual Heart-Blessing) Until You Are Heart-Ready To Resort To Me—By Merely (or Searchlessly) Beholding Me. Therefore, Do Not Seek Happiness From Me. Rather, Be (Searchlessly) Happy With Me.

Listen To Me By Right (and Inherently Happy) Devotional Intimacy With Me. In This Manner, Grow To Hear Me—and, By Hearing Me, Take Your Stand With Me In Prior (or Inherent) Happiness. Then Let This Happiness (or Open-Hearted Feeling Of My Spiritual "Brightness") Be (Progressively, and Then Most Perfectly) Magnified In and By The Sight Of My Spiritually "Bright" Person.

Indeed, To Practice The Way Of The Heart (In Its Spiritual Fullness), You Must Not Seek Happiness. To Practice The Way Of The Heart (In Its Spiritual Fullness), You Must Be Fundamentally Free Of Wanting Need (or The Spiritually Blind Craving For Happiness). Those who (Having Listened To Me) Hear Me (and Understand themselves Most Fundamentally) Have Really (and Most Fundamentally) Understood their own Wanting Need and Search For Happiness. They Understand The Wanting Need and Search For Happiness To Be The Effect and The Sign Of self-Contraction—Whereby Inherent Happiness Is Forgotten, and (By Every Act Of Seeking) Constantly Avoided and Effectively Lost. Therefore, those who Are My True Devotees Do Not Seek Happiness, but they Always Only (and Searchlessly) Find Me (The Avatarically Self-Manifested Divine Incarnation Of The Self-Existing Reality Of Happiness Itself—and The Avatarically Self-Transmitted Divine Self-Revelation Of The Self-Radiant, or Divinely Self-"Bright", Spiritual Presence Of Happiness Itself).

The Only-By-Me Revealed and Given Way Of The Heart (or Way Of Adidam) Is Begun With Listening To Me, Until (In and By Means Of The Event and Process Of The True Hearing Of Me) The Search For Happiness (Via The Projection Of Wanting Need) Is Understood (Most Fundamentally) and Released At The Heart. And, When The Unfulfilled (and Unfulfillable) Wanting Need (or Search) For Happiness Is Thus Understood (and The Native "Taste" Of Happiness, or Love-Bliss, Is, To A Significant Degree, Regained), My Hearing Devotee Is Heart-Awake To See Me (and, Thus and Thereby, To "See" Happiness Itself). And any one who Truly Sees Me (and who, Thus and Thereby, Really "Sees" Happiness Itself) Becomes Moved (By The By-My-Avataric-Divine-Spiritual-Grace-Given "Sight" Of Happiness Itself) To Grow To Be My Most Perfect Devotee—Not By Seeking and Un-Love, but In, and As, and, Altogether, By Means Of The By-My-Avataric-Divine-Spiritual-Grace-Given and Freely Giving Happiness Of Love-Bliss Itself (That Sets all others

Free From Bondage To one's own ego-"I", Merely Because one Stands Free In ego-Transcending Devotional and Spiritual Communion With Me).

In The Only-By-Me Revealed and Given Way Of The Heart (or Way Of Adidam), The Dramatization Of Wanting Need (or The egoic Search, That Says "I Need you, or this, or that In Order To Be Happy") Is, As A Matter Of moment to moment self-Discipline (or Sila), To Be Released and Replaced By A "Yoga Of Necessity". The Basically Given conditions Of Existence Associated With Every Stage Of Life Are (When Necessary) To Be Embraced and Cared For (and Not Avoided or Abused) By Love's Work (or The ego-Transcending Yoga Of Right Practice). Therefore, In The Only-By-Me Revealed and Given Way Of The Heart, what Is Necessary (or Basically Given) Is To Be Allowed (but Converted In The Context Of True Yogic Sadhana)—and what Is Only A Wanting Need (or An Expression Of self-Contraction, Un-Happiness, and Un-Love) Is To Be Constantly Felt Beyond (In The Self-Evident Happiness Of Devotion To Me, and, In Due Course, By Means Of My Avatarically Self-Transmitted Divine Spiritual Presence and Blessing-Current Of Love-Bliss Itself).

Therefore, In The Only-By-Me Revealed and Given Way Of The Heart, "True Yogic Intimacy" (and "Intimate Yogic Friendship", and, Also, Right "Emotional-Sexual Devotional Communion", and Rightly Practiced "Emotional-Sexual Conscious Exercise") Is (Altogether) Such A Yoga Of Necessity (Transcending egoic, and Wanting, Need). And, In The Only-By-Me Revealed and Given Way Of The Heart, Such "True Yogic Intimacy" (and "Intimate Yogic Friendship", and, Also, Right "Emotional-Sexual Devotional Communion", and Rightly Practiced "Emotional-Sexual Conscious Exercise") Is Neither Possible Nor Truly Appropriate Outside The Context Of The Culture and Practice Of Truly ego-Transcending Devotion To My Avatarically-Born Bodily (Human) Divine Form, My Avatarically Self-Transmitted Spiritual (and Always Blessing) Divine Presence, and My Avatarically Self-Revealed (and Very, and Transcendental, and Perfectly Subjective, and Inherently Spiritual, and Inherently egoless, and Inherently Perfect, and Self-Evidently Divine) State, or Outside The Culture and Process Of Truly ego-Transcending Devotional Recognition Of My (Avatarically Self-Revealed) Human, Transcendental, Inherently Spiritual, Inherently egoless, and Self-Evidently Divine Person Of Love-Bliss, or Outside The Total Devotional (and ego-Transcending) Process Of Truly Right Surrender To My (Avatarically Self-Revealed) Human, Transcendental, Inherently Spiritual, Inherently egoless, and Self-Evidently Divine Person Of Love-Bliss. And The Practical Essence Of "True Yogic Intimacy" (and "Intimate Yogic Friendship", and, Also, Right "Emotional-Sexual Devotional Communion", and Rightly Practiced "Emotional-Sexual Conscious Exercise") Is True Devotion, Active Love, and Real (True) Trust.

True Devotion, Active Love, and Real (True) Trust Are Not Expressions Of Wanting Need. True Devotion, Active Love, and Real (True) Trust Are Not ego-Based, Nor Are They ego-Bound, Nor Are They Bound By any other. True Devotion, Active Love, and Real (True) Trust Are Characterized By The Surrender, The Forgetting, and The Transcending Of the egoic self. True Devotion, Active Love, and Real (True) Trust Are (Therefore) egoless (or Without self-Reference), Inherently Non-Seeking, Only Giving and Serving, and Consistently Free Of egoic Attachment. And All Actions Performed In True Love Of others Are Always Compassionately (and Not Merely Passionately) Motivated—and, Therefore, They Are Always Done For The Sake Of The True Well-being and The Divine Happiness Of the present-time other (or others), or Even The True Well-being and The Divine Happiness Of every one and all.

True Devotion, Active Love, and Real (True) Trust Are The Right Principles Of Right Life (Which Is The ego-Surrendering, ego-Forgetting, ego-Transcending and, Altogether, Liberating Process Of Realizing Truth Itself, or Reality Itself, Which Is The Only Real God). Therefore, True Devotion, Active Love, and Real (True) Trust Are Practices Associated With The Life Of Liberation From All Bondage. However, the life Of ego-Based "Bonding" (With the body-mind, or With the world, or With any other being, or beings, or With any thing, or things, or Even With The Cosmic Domain As A Whole) Is Always, Inherently, the life Of Bondage itself. Therefore, True Devotion, Active Love, and Real (True) Trust Must Be Distinguished (In concept, and In Practice) From Any and All Acts and Kinds Of ego-Based "Bonding", or Of Bondage Through egoic Identification With the body-mind, and Through Subsequent egoic Attachment To any and every other, or thing, or To elemental (or Otherwise conditionally Manifested) Existence, or To The Cosmic Domain Itself (In Any or All Of Its planes and Possibilities).

True Devotion, Active Love, and Real (True) Trust Must Always Be Magnified (In Real Practice), and All Forms Of ego-Based "Bonding" (and, Therefore, Of Bondage) Must Always Be Disciplined, and Progressively (or More and More) Out-Grown (or Felt Beyond), and (Ultimately) Even Most Perfectly Transcended (In thought, word, and deed—and, At Last, Altogether and Absolutely).

If intimately related Practitioners Of The Way Of The Heart Do Not Practice True Devotion To Me and (In Devotional Response To Me) Active Love and Real (True) Trust In (Thus) "True Yogic Intimacy" With one another, Then they Will Fear Even To (Truly, and Without egoic Intent) Say "I Love You" (For Such Is A Confession Of Vulnerability—and human beings Will Not Confess Vulnerability To any one they Regard As An Opponent, or any one who Might Use their Vulnerability To Threaten or Harm them With Rejection, Betrayal, and Acts Of Un-Love). Therefore, All My Devotees Must (In The True Manner I Have Just Described) Actively Love and Really, Truly, and Steadily Trust one another In Vulnerable Intimacy (In their Yogic emotional-sexual intimacies). And All My Devotees who Are Thus Yogically intimately related to one another Awaken To Love and Become Trustworthy (and Truly Intimate) Through Constant Devotional Surrender and Service To Me.

True Active Love, Steady and Real (True) Trust, and Vulnerable Intimacy Are Essential To True (and, In Due Course, Fullest, or Truly By-Me-Spiritually-Activated) Devotion To Me. The Practical Realization and Incarnation Of These Qualities Is, Also, The Essence Of True Sila In The Practice Of "True Yogic Intimacy" (and Of The "Intimate Yogic Friendship" Mode, or Intensification, Of "True Yogic Intimacy"). Therefore, In Order To Realize These Qualities, individuals who Practice (or Would Practice) "True Yogic Intimacy" (or, Perhaps, "Intimate Yogic Friendship") In The Way Of The Heart Must Transcend The "Oedipal Mood" Of conventional sexuality. That Is To Say, emotional-sexual intimacy (and Even The Totality Of human Existence) Must (In The Way Of The Heart) Be Lifted Out Of The Whole Context Of Rejection, Betrayal, and Un-Love That Characterizes the ego In The Context Of The First Three Stages Of Life.

I Have Observed That every human individual In The First Three Stages Of Life Tends (Generally Unknowingly) To Relate (or React) To <u>all</u> persons (and Especially intimates) of the opposite sex As he or she Did (or Does) To his or her own parent (or Otherwise Principal early-life relation) of the opposite sex. I Have Also Observed That every human individual In The First Three Stages Of Life Tends (Generally Unknowingly) To Relate (or React) To his or her own physical body As he or she Does To persons (and Especially intimates) of the opposite sex and As he or she Did (or Does) To his or her own parent (or Otherwise Principal early-life relation) of the opposite sex. Therefore, In The Only-By-Me Revealed and Given Way Of The Heart, The Process and Practice Of Listening To Me and Hearing Me (or The Early Process and Practice Of self-Observation, self-Understanding, and self-Transcendence, or ego-Transcendence, In The Context Of The First Three Stages Of Life and In The "Original" Context Of The, In Due Course, Spiritually Developing Fourth Stage Of Life) Naturally and Inevitably Includes The Process and Practice Whereby Habitual Reactive (or Negative, and, Otherwise, Mechanical) Patterns (or Attitudes and behaviors) Associated With <u>all</u> persons (and Especially the parent, and Also intimates) of the opposite sex, and Also (Therefore) Habitual Reactive (or Negative, and, Otherwise, Mechanical) Patterns (or Attitudes and behaviors) Associated With The individual Practitioner's Own physical body, Are <u>Uprooted</u> and <u>Overcome</u>.

I Have Observed That every human individual In The First Three Stages Of Life Tends (Generally Unknowingly) To Relate (or React) To all persons (and Especially intimates, and Presumed rivals) of the same sex As he or she Did (or Does) To his or her own parent (or Otherwise Principal early-life relation) of the same sex. Therefore, In The Only-By-Me Revealed and Given Way Of The Heart, The Process and Practice Of Listening To Me and Hearing Me (or The Early Process and Practice Of self-Observation, self-Understanding, and self-Transcendence, or ego-Transcendence, In The Context Of The First Three Stages Of Life and In The "Original" Context Of The, In Due Course, Spiritually Developing Fourth Stage Of Life) Naturally and Inevitably Includes The Process and Practice Whereby Habitual Reactive (or Negative, and, Otherwise, Mechanical) Patterns (or Attitudes and behaviors) Associated With all persons (and Especially the parent, and Also intimates, and Presumed rivals) of the same sex Are Uprooted and Overcome—and (This) Also Because Relations With all persons (and Especially the parent, and Also intimates, and Presumed rivals) of the same sex Tend (As A General Rule) To Be Associated With The Basic Struggle To Acquire A Powerful self-Image, An egoic Center Of Strength, or The egoic Ability To Compete (and, Thereby, To Survive, and Even To Dominate).

The egoic (or self-Contracted) individual Is (By Virtue Of his or her bodily human History, self-Idea, and Lack Of Spiritual, Transcendental, and Divine Realization) Chronically Bound To The Ritual Of Rejection. The emotional (or emotional-sexual) Career Of egoity Tends To Manifest As A Chronic Complaint That Always Says, By Countless Means, "You Do Not Love me." This Abusive Complaint Is, Itself, The Means Whereby the egoic individual Constantly Enforces his or her Chronic Wanting Need To Reject, Avoid, or Fail To Love others. Indeed, This Complaint Is More Than A Complaint. It Is A self-Image (The Heart-Sick or self-Pitying and Precious Idea That "I" Is Rejected) and An Angry Act Of Retaliation (Whereby others Are Punished For Not Sufficiently Adoring, pleasurizing, and Immortalizing the Precious ego-"I").

The egoic (or self-Contracted) individual Is Chronically and Reactively Contracted From all of its relations. Fear Is The Root Of this self-Contraction, and The Conceived Purpose Of this self-Contraction Is self-Preservation, and Even self-Glorification. Indeed, Fear is the self-Contraction. The self-Contraction (or the ego-"I") is The Root-Action (or Primal Mood) That Is Fear. Therefore, All Of The self-Preserving, self-Glorifying, and other-Punishing Efforts Of the ego-"I" (or the self-Contracted body-mind) Only Preserve, Glorify, and Intensify Fear Itself.

Fear, the ego-"I", Un-Love, or The Total Ritual Of self-Contraction Must Be Understood and Transcended. All Of Fear, egoity, self-Contraction, or Un-Love Is Only Suffering. It Is Only Destructive. And It Is Entirely Un-Necessary.

Fear, egoity, self-Contraction, or Un-Love Is Chronically Expressed Through The Complex Ritual Of Rejection, or The Communication Of The Dominant Idea "You Do Not Love me". Once This Is (In The Way Of The Heart) Truly, and Completely, and Most Fundamentally Understood, Then The Ritual Of Rejection, Fear, egoity, self-Contraction, or Un-Love Can (Always) Be Directly Transcended. Therefore (In The Only-By-Me Revealed and Given Way Of The Heart), Fear, egoity, self-Contraction, or Chronic Un-Love Is To Be Summarily Replaced By The Discipline and Practice Of ego-Transcending Devotional and (In Due Course) Spiritual Heart-Communion With Me, and (Subsequent, or To-Me-Responsive) Heart-Magnification Of My Avatarically Self-Revealed (and Self-Evidently Divine) Love-Bliss, In The Heart-Communicated Form "I Love You".

In The Only-By-Me Revealed and Given Way and Manner Of The Heart, My Devotees Understand Separate and Separative self (As Un-Love) and Transcend Separate and Separative self (By Love). And This Is Perfected (Progressively, In The Way and Manner Of The Heart) By Devotional (or ego-Transcending and ego-Forgetting) Heart-Surrender Of the conditional body-mind To My Avatarically-Born Bodily (Human) Divine Form, and My Avatarically Self-Transmitted Spiritual (and Always Blessing) Divine Presence, and My Avatarically Self-Revealed (and Very, and Transcendental, and Perfectly Subjective, and Inherently Spiritual, and Inherently egoless, and Inherently Perfect, and Self-Evidently Divine) State.

If You Will Thus *Be* Love (By This Devotion To *Me*), You Must Also Constantly Encounter, Understand, and Transcend The Rejection Rituals Of others who Are (Even If Temporarily or Only Apparently) Bereft Of Divine Wisdom. Therefore, If You Will *Be* Love (As *My* Devotee), You Must (In The Way and Manner Of The Heart) Always Skillfully Transcend The Tendency To Become Un-Love (and, Thus, To Become self-Bound, Apparently Divorced From Heart-Communion With Me) In Reaction To The Apparent Lovelessness Of others. And You Must Not Withdraw From Heart-Communion With Me (or Become Degraded By Reactive Un-Love) Even When Circumstances Within Your intimate Sphere (or Within The Sphere Of Your Appropriate social Responsibility) Require You To Make Difficult Gestures To Counter and Control the effects (or Undermine and Discipline The Negative and Destructive Effectiveness) Of The Rituals Of Un-Love That Are Performed By others.

For those who Are Committed To Love (and who, Therefore, Always Commune With Me, The One Who *Is* Love-Bliss Itself), Even Rejection By others Is Received and Accepted As A Wound, Not An Insult. Even The Heart-Necessity To Love and To Be Loved Is A Wound. And Even The Fullest Realization Of My Love-Bliss Is A Wound That Never Heals.

The egoic Ritual Calls every individual To Defend himself or herself Against The Wounds Of Love and The Wounding Signs Of Un-Love (or egoic self-Contraction) In the daily world. Therefore, Even In The Context Of "True Yogic Intimacy" (or, Possibly, Even In The Context Of "Intimate Yogic Friendship"), The Tendency (Apart From Spiritual Responsibility) Is To Act As If Every Wound (Which Is Simply A Hurt) Is An Insult (or A Reason To Punish).

In The Only-By-Me Revealed and Given Way Of The Heart, The Reactive Rituals Of egoity Must Be Released By The ego-Transcending (and, In Due Course, Spiritually Activated) Practice Of Devotion To Me. This Requires Each and Every Practitioner Of The Way Of The Heart To Observe, Understand, and Relinquish The emotionally Reactive Cycle Of Rejection and Punishment. And The Necessary Prerequisites For Such Relinquishment Are Vulnerability (or The Ability To Feel The Wounds Of Love Without Retaliation), Sensitivity To the other In Love (or The Ability To Sympathetically Observe, Understand, Forgive, Love, and Not Punish or Dissociate From the other In Love), and Love Itself (or The Ability To Love, To Know You Are Loved, To Receive Love, and To Know That Both You and the other, Regardless Of Any Appearance To The Contrary, Are Vulnerable To Love and Heart-Requiring Of Love).

It Is Not Necessary (or Even Possible) To Become Immune To The Feeling Of Being Rejected. To Become Thus Immune, You Would Have To Become Immune To Love Itself. What Is Necessary (and Also Possible) Is To Enter Fully (and Fully Devotionally) Into The Spiritual Life-Sphere Of Love. In The Only-By-Me Revealed and Given Way Of The Heart, This Is Done By First Entering (Devotionally, and, Thus, By Heart) Into My Humanly-Incarnated Divine Spiritual Company, and (Therein) Surrendering To My Divine Spiritual "Embrace" Of Love-Bliss—Wherein You Are Not Merely Loved As a self-Contracted ego-"I", but You Are (To The Degree That, By Means Of My Avatarically Self-Transmitted Divine Spiritual Grace, the ego-"I" Is Surrendered, Forgotten, and Transcended In Me) Awakened To Be (and To Show) Love-Bliss Itself. Then You Must, Through Life-Active Devotion To Me, Allow The Demonstration Of My Own Love-Bliss-Radiance In the world of Your human relationships.

If You Will Do This, Then You Must Do The Sadhana (or Concentrated Practice) Of True Devotion, Active Love, and Real (True and Steady) Trust. As A Practical Matter, You Must Stop Dramatizing The egoic Ritual Of Betrayal In Reaction To The Feeling Of Being Rejected. You Must Understand, Transcend, and Release The Tendency To Respond (or React) To Signs Of Rejection (or Signs That You Are Not Loved) As If You Are Insulted, Rather Than Wounded. That Is To Say, You Must Stop Punishing and Rejecting others When You Feel Rejected. If You Punish another When You Feel This, You Will Act As If You

Are Immune To Love's Wound. Thus, You Will Pretend To Be Angrily Insulted, Rather Than Suffer To Be Wounded. In The Process, You Will Withdraw and Withhold Love. You Will Stand Off, Independent and Dissociated. You Will Only Reinforce The Feeling Of Being Rejected, and You Will Compound It By Actually Rejecting the other. In This Manner, You Will <u>Become</u> Un-Love. You Will Fail To Love. You Will Fail To Live In The Sphere Of Love. Your Own Acts Of Un-Love Will Degrade You, Delude You, and (Ultimately) Separate You From My Avatarically Self-Transmitted Divine Love-Bliss Itself. Therefore, one who Fails To Practice The Sadhana Of Love In his or her human relationships Will, By That Failure, Turn Away (or Contract) From Real God (or The Divine Self-Condition, and Source-Condition, That <u>Is</u> Reality Itself).

Love Does Not Fail For You When You Are Rejected or Betrayed or Apparently Not Loved. Love Fails For You When You Reject, Betray, and Do Not Love. Therefore, If You Listen To Me, and (Also) If You Hear Me, and (Also) If You See Me—Do Not Stand Off From Relationship. Be Vulnerable. Be Wounded, When Necessary—and Endure That Wound (or Hurt). Do Not Punish the other In Love. Communicate To one another, Even Discipline one another—but Do Not Dissociate From one another or Fail To Grant one another The Knowledge Of Love. Realize That each one Wants To Love and To Be Loved By the other In Love. Therefore, Love. Do This Rather Than Make Any Effort To Get Rid Of The Feeling Of Being Rejected. To Feel Rejected Is To Feel The Hurt Of Not Being Loved. Allow That Hurt, but Do Not Let It Become The Feeling Of Lovelessness. Be Vulnerable, and (Thus) Not Insulted. If You Are Merely Hurt, You Will Still Know The Necessity (or The Heart's Requirement) <u>Of</u> Love, and You Will Still Know The Necessity (or The Heart's Requirement) <u>To</u> Love.

The Habit Of Reacting To Apparent Rejection (By others) As If It Were An Insult Always Coincides With (and Only Reveals) The Habit Of Rejecting (or Not Loving) others. Any one whose Habitual Tendency Is To Reject and Not Love others (In The Face Of their Apparent Acts Of Rejection and Un-Love) Will Tend To Reject and Not Love others Even When they Are Only Loving. Narcissus—The Personification Of the ego, the self-Contraction, or The Complex Avoidance Of Relationship—Is Famous For his Rejection Of The Lady, Echo (who Only Loved him). Therefore, If You Listen To Me, and (Also) If You Hear Me, and (Also) If You See Me—Be Vulnerable In Love. If You Remain Vulnerable In Love, You Will Still Feel Love's Wound, but You Will Remain In Love. In This Manner, You Will Always Remain In The human (and, Ultimately, Divine) Sphere Of My Avatarically Self-Transmitted Person Of Love-Bliss.

The Most Direct Way To Know Love In every moment Is To <u>Be</u> Love In every moment. Do This By Means Of Devotional (and, In Due Course,

Spiritual) Communion With Me. If You Always Do This, Then, By Means Of Every Act Of life, Always Do What and As You Are.

In The Only-By-Me Revealed and Given Way Of The Heart (or Way Of Adidam), My Rightly Practicing Devotee Is (and Remains) Always Founded In The Capability Of Love, By Means (and By Virtue) Of his or her Constant Devotional (and, As The Case May Be, Spiritual) Heart-Communion With Me. Therefore, If any such a one Fails To Be Steady In Heart-Communion With Me, Then he or she Will Become Weak In Love. And To Be Weak In Love (In The Context Of Any Stage Of Life) Is To Be Always Already Independent, Insulted, Empty With Craving, In Search Of Love, Manipulative, Un-Happy, and Moved To Punish, Betray, and Destroy all relationships. Such a Weak one Always Already Feels Rejected and Is Never Satisfied. Indeed, such a one Is Not Even Found To Be Truly Lovable By others. Therefore, By Always Surrendering self-Contraction (By Means Of True Devotional, and, In Due Course, Spiritual, Communion With Me), Be Always Only Sudden Love In Every Act Of life.

By Actively egoically Not Loving (or By Actively egoically Disliking, Actively egoically Rejecting, Actively egoically Hating, or, In Any Manner, Actively egoically Un-Loving) what and whom You (egoically) Do Not Love, You Mutilate (and, Effectively, Destroy) Your Own psycho-physical Integrity (or Hearted body-mind). Likewise, By their Actively egoically Not Loving You, every what or who (In The self-Contracted, or egoic, Manner) Does Not Love You Cannot but Mutilate (and, Effectively, Destroy) its own (or his or her own) psycho-physical Integrity (or Hearted body-mind). Understand This. Activate Your lifetime On The Basis Of This Twofold Understanding. Thoroughly (and Most Fundamentally) Understand Your ego-"I", and (By The Really and Truly Effective Counter-egoic Means I Reveal and Give To You, and To every one and all), Actively (Constantly), and In The ego-Transcending Manner, Love each and every thing and one—In Me.

Always Actively Be My True Devotee—Always Actively Heart-Radiating (Through and Beyond all self-Contraction) To Me—Even (Thus and Thereby) Allowing Your Own (and entire) body-mind To Be "Brightened" In (and By) Me. Therefore, Do Not Do Fear, Sorrow, Anger, or Even Any Kind Of Un-Love In egoic (or self-Contracted, or Heart-Contracted) Reaction To any thing or any one that Actively (or, Otherwise, Apparently) Does Not Love You—but Only (Actively, and Constantly) Do Love. Always Do This Love-Sadhana (or Discipline and Way Of The Heart), By Actively Abiding In Constant ego-Surrendering, ego-Forgetting, and ego-Transcending Devotional and (In Due Course) Spiritual Heart-Communion With Me—Always Yielding The Four Principal Faculties (Of attention, sense-body, emotion, and breath) In Heart-Yielding Love-Response To My Avatarically Humanly Incarnated (and Inherently Spiritually "Bright")

Attractiveness—For I Am The Avatarically Self-Transmitted Divine Spiritual Presence That Is Ever-Present (Even To Every Heart) As The Always Already Spiritually "Bright" (Self-Existing and Self-Radiant) Divine Person Of Love-Bliss-Being (or Conscious Light) Itself.

Those who Love Are Love, and others Inevitably Love them. Those who Seek For Love Are Not themselves Active Love, and So they Do Not Find It. (And, Even If they Are Loved, they Do Not Get The Knowledge Of It.) Only The Lover Is Lovable. Therefore, I Call and "Brighten" Every Heart To Be As True Love Is. And My Every Listening Devotee, My Every Hearing Devotee, and My Every Seeing Devotee Is (By Me) Gifted and (By Means Of My Avatarically Self-Transmitted Divine Spiritual Grace) Enabled To Realize (and, Thus, To Really and Truly Demonstrate) This Radiant (and Radiating) Principle (and Way) Of The Heart—By Means Of True Active (and Freely, Deeply Attracted) Devotional (and Really ego-Transcending) Love Of Me (and With Real, True Trust In Me), The One Who Is (Self-Existing) As Self-Radiant Love-Bliss (or The "Bright") Itself.

Avatar Adi Da Samraj
Adidam Samrajashram, 2003

SUTRA 41

As A Further Sign Of True Sila In The Only-By-Me Revealed and Given Way Of The Heart (or Way Of Adidam), <u>All</u> Practitioners who Formally Embrace The Only-By-Me Revealed and Given Way Of The Heart Are (Beginning In The Student-Beginner Stage Of The Way Of The Heart) Required (and Formally Expected) To Practice An Appropriate (and Yogically Right) sexual Economy.

Appropriate (or Yogically Right) sexual Economy Involves The Release (Through self-Observation, and Eventual Most Fundamental self-Understanding) Of Aberrating (or self-Binding) sexual inclinations, and all sexual activities that Do Not Serve Basic human (and, Then, Truly Spiritual) Equanimity.

Yogically Right sexual Economy Is (From The Beginning) To Be Embraced (and More and More Effectively Developed, To The Degree Of Simple human Responsibility) In The Student-Beginner Stage Of The Way Of The Heart. And Yogically Right sexual Economy (Whether In The Form Of Rightly Measured Frequency Of sexual activity within intimate relationship Or In The Form Of celibacy) Is To Be Further Developed and Maintained (In Detail, With A Progressively Greater Demonstration Of Basic human Equanimity) In Every Developmental Stage Of Practice Of The Way Of The Heart Beyond That Of Student-Beginner.

Yogically Right sexual Economy Requires The Consistent Avoidance (or Devotionally ego-Surrendering, ego-Forgetting, and ego-Transcending Feeling-Relinquishment) Of both solitary and (otherwise) intimately engaged <u>degenerative</u> masturbation, and Especially Chronic (or Habitual) and Compulsive (or Obsessive) solitary or (otherwise) intimately engaged <u>degenerative</u> masturbation.

Yogically Right Practice Of The "Own-Body Yogic Sexual Exercise" Is Truly ego-Surrendering, Truly ego-Forgetting, Truly ego-Transcending, and Truly Regenerative (and Entirely Non-degenerative) Devotional, and (In Due Course) Spiritually Active, and (Altogether, and Consistently) Yogically Managed and Yogically Purposed genital self-Stimulation—Generally Engaged As A solitary Exercise (Although It May Be Extended To Occasions With an intimate partner), and Performed In The General Manner Of Either "Emotional-Sexual Conscious Exercise" Or "Emotional-Sexual Devotional Communion" (In

Accordance With The individual Practitioner's Developmental Stage Of Practice Of The Way Of The Heart), and, Altogether, Performed In The General Manner, and For The Strictly Yogic and Profound Purposes, Of The Traditional "Shaktichalana Mudra". And Even This Yogically Right Exercise Must (For The Sake Of A Yogically Right sexual Economy) Be Confined (or Limited) To Occasions When It Is Truly Yogically Justifiable, Necessary, and Auspicious.

In The General Case Of intimately related Devotees Formally Practicing The Only-By-Me Revealed and Given Way Of The Heart, Yogically Right sexual Economy Must Become (With The Formal Agreement Of The Formal Sacred Cooperative Cultural Gathering Of All Formally Acknowledged Practitioners Of The Way Of The Heart) Either Voluntary and life-energy-Positive (and, Eventually, Spiritually Active) celibacy Or An Intentional (and, As A General Rule, Conservative) Limitation On The Frequency Of sexual intercourse (Always Engaged As A Right Yogic, and Regenerative, and Consistently Non-degenerative Practice, Either In The Form Of "Emotional-Sexual Conscious Exercise" Or, Once Practice Of The Way Of The Heart Is Fully Established On The Basis Of The True Seeing Of Me, As The Yoga Of "Emotional-Sexual Devotional Communion"). The Practice Of "Right Emotional-Sexual Yoga" In The Way Of The Heart (Either In The Form Of "Emotional-Sexual Conscious Exercise" Or In The Form Of "Emotional-Sexual Devotional Communion") Is Not A "Program" Of Intensively Cultivating The Ability To Achieve Regenerative orgasm (and So On)—Nor Is It (Altogether) A "Program" For Fulfilling The ordinary egoic Inclination For a Satisfying (and Consoling) emotional-sexual life. Rather, The Practice Of "Right Emotional-Sexual Yoga" In The Way Of The Heart Is A Means Of Conforming Your emotional-sexual life To The Real Requirements Of The Devotional and (In Due Course) Spiritual Practice In My Avataric Divine Company—Such That You "Retrieve" daily time and place, and The Totality Of The psycho-physical Faculties, From Preoccupation With emotional-sexual matters. Therefore, The Practice Of "Right Emotional-Sexual Yoga" In The Way Of The Heart (Necessarily) Requires The Conserving (and, In The General Case, The Minimizing) Of emotional-sexual Relatedness.

In Order That they Fulfill My Calling For them To Avoid Excessive (or Wastefully self-Indulgent) sexual activity, All Formally Acknowledged Practitioners Of The Way Of The Heart who Are (in their personal intimate contexts) sexually active Must (and Are To Be Formally Expected To) Limit The Frequency Of sexual activity To The Degree That Is (personally) Necessary To Avoid (and, By Means Of Devotional Surrender, To Relinquish) Excessive (or Wastefully self-Indulgent) sexual activity.

All Formally Acknowledged Practitioners Of The Way Of The Heart who Are (in their personal intimate contexts) sexually active Must Practice (and

Must Be Formally Expected To Practice) A Rule Of Frequency Of sexual activity That Is, Altogether (By Taking Every Right Factor Into Account), Appropriate In their Particular Case (and For their Present Developmental Stage Of Practice In The Way Of The Heart). Thus, In The Way Of The Heart, The individually Appropriate Rule Of Frequency Of sexual activity Is A Rule Which Rightly Measures The Frequency Of sexual activity, Such That The Allowed Frequency Of sexual activity Is One That Is Altogether Optimal Relative To Rightest and Most Effective Practice Of The Way Of The Heart.

As A General Rule, A Maximum (Average) sexual activity Frequency Of once every seven to ten days (or Even once, or, perhaps, twice, per month) Is The Right (and Formally To Be Expected) Measure Of Maximum sexual activity Frequency—Of Right Yogic (Regenerative, and Non-degenerative) emotional-sexual Practice—For All Formally Acknowledged Practitioners Of The Way Of The Heart who Are (in their personal intimate contexts) sexually active. The Only Exceptions To This General Rule Would Be In Rare Cases, Of individuals who Exhibit Characteristics That Demonstrate they Are Uniquely Qualified For A Right Yogic emotional-sexual Sadhana. In Such Cases, and Only With Formal Approval, A Maximum Average Frequency Of sexual activity Of Between once per month and (perhaps) twice (or, at times, more) per week May (and, Indeed, May Not) Be Determined To Be The Most Optimal Rule.

The Rule (In The Case Of any particular individual) Relative To The Maximum sexual activity Frequency Is To Be Based On The Observation Of A Key Natural Cycle In the body (As Well As The Observation Of All Aspects Of the individual's Demonstration Of Rightest and Most Effective Practice Of The Totality Of The Only-By-Me Revealed and Given Way Of The Heart). After An Occasion Of sexual intercourse, A Cycle Of time Is (As A General Rule) Required To Restore The Equanimity Of The Unified psycho-physical Totality Of the body-mind (Of Four Faculties), and, In Particular, To Fully Restore and Regulate and Rightly Re-Orient the physical body's "Conductivity" Of Natural life-energy. Even When It Is Yogically "Correct", Participation In sexual activity Changes the Patterned functioning of Natural bodily energy, Reinforcing (In The Case Of individuals who Are Not Uniquely Qualified For A Right Yogic emotional-sexual Sadhana) The Orientation Of The Four psycho-physical Faculties Toward What Is Below (Rather Than Toward What Is Above). Therefore, To Engage sexual activity With Excessive Frequency (or With Greater Frequency Than the individual's Natural Signs and Totality-Of-Right-Practice Demonstrations Indicate) Is (In Principle, and Potentially) Detrimental To bodily Equanimity and (Especially In The Long Term) To General psycho-physical Well-being.

The Rule Relative To Maximum (Average) sexual activity Frequency Is, In The Case Of Any Particular individual Practitioner Of The Way Of The Heart (who Is, in his or her personal intimate context, sexually active), Always Subject To Formal Cultural Review and Adjustment, Such That The (Actually) Formally Approved Frequency, In Any Particular Case, Is Always Entirely Compatible With The Demonstration-Evidence Of The Totality Of the individual's Real and Right Practice Of The Only-By-Me Revealed and Given Way Of The Heart At any and every period of time and In Any and Every Developmental Stage Of Practice Of The Way Of The Heart. Also, Before The Transition To The "Perfect Practice" Can Be Formally Approved, Either celibacy Must Have Become The Natural and Motiveless (or Searchless) Choice Or There Must Be The Really Demonstrated Signs That My Devotee Is—In The Fullest Sense—Truly (or Even Uniquely) Qualified For A Right Yogic emotional-sexual Sadhana. If My Any Devotee Really Demonstrates The Signs Of Being, In The Fullest Sense, Truly (or, Possibly, Even Uniquely) Qualified For A Right Yogic emotional-sexual Sadhana, Then he or she May Be Formally Approved To Engage The "Perfect Practice" As A Yogically sexually active Practitioner (who, In Due Course, May Yet, and Motivelessly, Relinquish even all sexual activity). However, Even In The Case Of Such Practitioners, The General Rule Relative To The Maximum (Average) Frequency Of (Necessarily, Yogically Right) sexual activity Is, As Before, Always Subject To New Formal Agreements, Based On The Requirements Of The Spiritual Process Of The "Perfect Practice" In The Particular Case At any given time.

In The Context Of The "Perfect Practice" Of The Only-By-Me Revealed and Given Way Of The Heart (or Way Of Adidam), All Practitioners who Are (in their personal intimate contexts) sexually active Must, In The Fullest Sense, Be Truly (or Even Uniquely) Qualified For A Right Yogic emotional-sexual Sadhana—and (In Order To Be Formally Approved For The Transition To The "Perfect Practice" Of The Only-By-Me Revealed and Given Way Of The Heart) Such Practitioners Must Be (Formally) Evaluated and Acknowledged (By The Ruchira Sannyasin Order Of Adidam Ruchiradam) As Being So (and Truly Fully) Qualified.

Indeed, In The Only-By-Me Revealed and Given Way Of The Heart (or Way Of Adidam), All Practitioners who Are (in their personal intimate contexts) sexually active Must (Progressively, and—If celibacy Does Not Become The Practice Sooner—In Due Course, Finally) Become Truly (If Not Uniquely) Qualified For A Right Yogic emotional-sexual Sadhana—Such That they Consistently Demonstrate The Positive Effectiveness Of their Yogically Right Conservative, Non-degenerative, and Truly Regenerative sexual (and emotional-sexual) Discipline, A Characteristic Freedom From The Tendency To Subordinate The Practice Of Ruchira Avatara Bhakti Yoga To The ordinary Purposes Of emotional-sexual intimate relationship In The Midst Of an intimately sexually active life, A Characteristic Freedom From The Tendency To Collapse From The Truly Devotional (and Most Profoundly Feeling-Contemplative) Attitude and Demonstration In The Midst Of an intimately sexually active life, A Characteristic Adherence To The Strictly Yogic and ego-Transcending and Real-God-Realizing Orientation and Practice In The Midst Of an intimately sexually active life, A Characteristic Freedom From the idealistic attitude, the romantic attitude, the puritanical attitude, and any and every other merely conventional (or limiting and ego-Reinforcing) attitude In The Midst Of an intimately sexually active life, A Consistent Mature Capability To Advance In their Total Practice Of The Way Of The Heart With Significant Quickness and Directness In The Midst Of an intimately sexually active life (Such That their Embrace Of An intimately sexually active Practice Evidences The Same Direct and Quickening Effect As Is Evidenced By The Embrace Of Permanent single celibacy In The Case Of My Similarly Most Exemplary Devotees who Are Not sexually active in, or Otherwise Engaged In, intimate emotional-sexual relationship with any one at all), An Exemplary Demonstration Of self-Discipline, self-Observation, self-Understanding, and Effective self-Transcendence (or Real ego-Transcendence) Relative To all aspects of their emotional-sexual character, All Aspects Of their Practice Of "Right Emotional-Sexual Yoga", and All Aspects Of their Practice Of "True Yogic Intimacy" (or, Perhaps, "Intimate Yogic Friendship"), and (Altogether) An Exemplary, Profound, and Really Effective Counter-egoic Practice, and An Exemplary Demonstration Of Even All Aspects and All Details Of The Total Practice Required At their Particular Stage Of Practice, and According To their Formally Chosen Form Of Practice, In The Way Of The Heart. And, In Order For Any Practitioner Of The Way Of The Heart To Be Rightly Evaluated and Formally Approved As Truly Qualified For A Right Yogic emotional-sexual Sadhana, Not Only Must The individual Practitioner and his or her any intimate partner each Demonstrate The Required Characteristics, but Also their intimate relationship itself Must Be Truly Bondage-Transcending (and, Thus, and Characteristically, Free Of all limiting conventions of Merely ego-Based, and ego-Reinforcing, emotional-sexual "Bonding"-activity), and Really Founded In The Right Yogic and ego-Transcending Disposition Of Equanimity (Such That each partner in intimate relationship Is, Characteristically, Free Of All limiting emotional-sexual Distractions Of attention—in thought, word, and deed), and (Characteristically) "Transparent" To Me (Such That each of the partners in intimacy Readily and Consistently Feels "Through" and "Beyond" his or her any intimate partner, and Always Directly To Me—In and As My Avatarically-Born Bodily Human Divine Form and Person).

By Virtue Of their Actual Demonstration (Of A Significant Magnification Of All The Characteristics Of An intimately sexually active Practitioner who Is

Truly Qualified For A Right Yogic emotional-sexual Sadhana, and With The Additional Characteristic Of Exceptional sexual Strength), Some (Relatively Rare) sexually active Practitioners Of "Emotional-Sexual Devotional Communion" May Be (Formally, Culturally) Found To Be Uniquely Qualified For A (Necessarily, Right) Yogic emotional-sexual Sadhana.

Those Practitioners Of "Emotional-Sexual Devotional Communion" who Are Uniquely Qualified For A (Necessarily, Right) Yogic emotional-sexual Sadhana Demonstrate Exceptional sexual Strength, The Consistent Positive Effectiveness Of their Right Conservative, Non-degenerative, and Truly Regenerative sexual (and emotional-sexual) Discipline, A Characteristic Freedom From The Tendency To Subordinate The Practice Of Ruchira Avatara Bhakti Yoga To The ordinary Purposes Of emotional-sexual intimate relationship In The Midst Of an intimately sexually active life, A Characteristic Freedom From The Tendency To Collapse From The Truly Devotional (and Most Profoundly Feeling-Contemplative) Attitude and Demonstration In The Midst Of an intimately sexually active life, A Characteristic Adherence To The Strictly Yogic and ego-Transcending and Real-God-Realizing Orientation and Practice In The Midst Of an intimately sexually active life, A Characteristic Freedom From the idealistic attitude, the romantic attitude, the puritanical attitude, and any and every other merely conventional (or limiting and ego-Reinforcing) attitude In The Midst Of an intimately sexually active life, A Consistent Mature Capability To Advance In their Total Practice Of The Way Of The Heart With Significant Quickness and Directness In The Midst Of an intimately sexually active life (Such That their Embrace Of An intimately sexually active Practice Evidences The Same Direct and Quickening Effect As Is Evidenced By The Embrace Of Permanent single celibacy In The Case Of My Similarly Most Exemplary Devotees who Are Not sexually active in, or Otherwise Engaged In, intimate emotional-sexual relationship with any one at all), A Uniquely Exemplary Demonstration Of self-Discipline, self-Observation, self-Understanding, and Effective self-Transcendence (or Real ego-Transcendence) Relative To all aspects of their emotional-sexual character, All Aspects Of their Practice Of "Right Emotional-Sexual Yoga", and All Aspects Of their Practice Of "True Yogic Intimacy" (or, Perhaps, "Intimate Yogic Friendship"), and (Altogether) A Uniquely Exemplary, Uniquely Profound, and Uniquely Effective Counter-egoic Practice, and A Uniquely Exemplary Demonstration Of Even All Aspects and All Details Of The Total Practice Required At their Particular Stage Of Practice, and According To their Formally Chosen Form Of Practice, In The Way Of The Heart. And, In Order For Any Practitioner Of The Way Of The Heart To Be Rightly Evaluated and Formally Approved As Uniquely Qualified For A (Necessarily, Right) Yogic emotional-sexual Sadhana, Not Only Must The individual Practitioner and his or her any intimate partner each Demonstrate The Required Characteristics, but Also their intimate relationship itself Must Be Uniquely Bondage-Transcending (and, Thus, and Characteristically, Uniquely Free Of all limiting conventions of Merely ego-Based, and ego-Reinforcing, emotional-sexual "Bonding"-activity), and (Uniquely) Really Founded In The Right Yogic and ego-Transcending Disposition Of Equanimity (Such That each partner in intimate relationship Is, Characteristically, Uniquely Free Of All limiting emotional-sexual Distractions Of attention—in thought, word, and deed), and (Characteristically) Uniquely "Transparent" To Me (Such That each of the partners in intimacy Readily and Consistently Feels "Through" and "Beyond" his or her any intimate partner, and Always Directly To Me—In and As My Avatarically-Born Bodily Human Divine Form and Person). And all those who (In The Only-By-Me Revealed and Given Way Of The Heart) Are Uniquely Qualified For A Right Yogic emotional-sexual Sadhana Will (Because they Are Thus Uniquely Qualified) Readily, and Quickly, Move Beyond The First and Second Stages Of "Right Emotional-Sexual Yoga", and (After they Have Made The Transition To The First Actually Seeing Stage Of The Way Of The Heart) they Will (Likewise) Readily and Quickly Demonstrate All Aspects Of The Third Stage Of "Right Emotional-Sexual Yoga"—Such That they Readily (and Sooner Than In The Case Of those who Are Not Thus Uniquely Qualified) Demonstrate The Perpetual "Static Mudra" That Characterizes The Fourth Stage Of "Right Emotional-Sexual Yoga" In The Only-By-Me Revealed and Given Way Of The Heart. The Exemplary Demonstration Of The Perpetual "Static Mudra" Of Yogically Realized Non-"Difference" Will, In Some (Thus Uniquely Qualified) Cases, Eventually Become Yogic celibacy-in-intimacy or (Otherwise) A Spontaneous Yogic Reduction Of The Frequency Of sexual activity (and This Not As A Culturally "Required" Sign or Choice, but Simply, Spontaneously, Because Of The Yogic Sublimity Of My Devotee's Constant Devotional Samadhi Of Communion With Me). In Other (Such) Cases, The Fact and The Frequency Of their sexual activity Will Not Necessarily Be (Thus) Conservatively Affected. However, In All (Thus Uniquely Qualified) Cases, The Demonstration Of The Perpetual "Static Mudra" Will Be Inherently Free Of All emotional-sexual Agitation and All "Bonding"-Bondage.

Practitioners Of "Emotional-Sexual Devotional Communion" who Are, In The Fullest Sense, Truly (or Even Uniquely) Qualified For A Right Yogic emotional-sexual Sadhana Must Be (and Are, By Definition) Uniquely Sensitive To Me Spiritually. Because Of This Sensitivity, they Are Capable Of Feeling Very Clearly What The Implications Of sexual activity Are (In any particular instance, and Altogether)—and, Therefore, they Are Readily Able To Adapt their sexual Practice To The Spiritual Process Of Communion With Me. They

Do Not Override My Divine Spiritual Invasion Of the body-mind Through Excessive or Otherwise Non-Yogic sexual activity—or Even By The Choice To Be sexually active At All. Therefore, If they Are sexually active, any sexual activity In which they Engage Is (By them, and By Formal Cultural Agreement) Required To Be Truly Yogic—Such That it Does Not, In Any Manner, limit or Encumber their Spiritual Communion With Me.

In My "Sadhana Years"—and, Also, In The Subsequent Context Of The Exercise Of My Avataric Divine Function Of Teaching and Revealing The Way Of The Heart (or Way Of Adidam)—I Demonstrated A Uniquely "Heroic" Disposition Relative To The Investigation, Observation, Understanding, and Transcending Of All Dimensions Of emotional-sexual life (and, Indeed, All Dimensions Of Every Aspect Of conditionally Manifested Existence). In My "Sadhana Years", The Purpose Of My (Unique) "Heroic" Demonstration Was The Preparation Of My psycho-physical Vehicle Of Avataric conditional Manifestation—So That It Would (Thereafter) Function In Most Perfect Conformity To Me. My Subsequent "Heroic" Demonstration, Of Teaching and Revealing The Way Of The Heart, Was Purposed To "Learn" Mankind, and To Reflect Mankind To Itself, and To Reveal To Mankind Its Unique Potential For Understanding and Transcending the psycho-physical ego-"I" and (On That Basis) For Realization Of The Divine Self-Condition—Each (and Both, Together) By Grace Of The Unique Avatarically Given Divine Means Of Devotional Surrender To Me. And I Did That "Heroic" Work Of Teaching and Revealing By The Siddha-Method (or "Crazy" Means) Of Submission (Of My Own Avatarically-Born Bodily Human Divine Form) Into The Likeness (and Into the various functions, relations, and conditions) Of all Of Mankind—Even To Every Degree Of Satirizing (and Of Suffering) the egoity (and All The limiting Patterns) Of Mankind.

The Unique (Avataric Divine) Work Of My "Sadhana Years" and Of My Years Of Teaching and Revealing The Way Of The Heart (or Way Of Adidam) Was Made Possible Only By My Unique Divine Siddhis. Thus, The Purpose Of My (Unique) "Heroic" Demonstration Was Not To Show A Course By Which others Might (themselves) "Heroically" Investigate, Observe, Understand, and Transcend their emotional-sexual character, tendencies, limitations, and activities. Such An "Heroic" Demonstration Is Neither Possible Nor Necessary In The Case Of My Devotees—or, Indeed, In The Case Of any other. Therefore, Every Practitioner Of The Only-By-Me Revealed and Given Way Of The Heart (or Way Of Adidam) Must Understand That his or her Practice Is Not To Duplicate My (Unique) "Heroic" Demonstration Of "Right Emotional-Sexual Yoga", but To Fully Embrace his or her Chosen Form Of The emotional-sexual self-Discipline I Have Revealed and Given To My Devotees.

In The Only-By-Me Revealed and Given Way Of The Heart, each and every aspect and detail of the emotional-sexual character, tendencies, limitations, and activities (As Well As each and every aspect and detail of each and every other kind or dimension of the character, tendencies, limitations, and activities) Of Each and Every Formally Acknowledged Practitioner Of The Way Of The Heart (or Way Of Adidam) Must (In The Context Of Formal Groups, Interviews, Questionnaires, Reports, and Otherwise Appropriate Direct Disclosures) Always Be Openly and Fully Disclosed (or Confessed), and (Thus and Thereby) Formally (Culturally) Observed and "Considered", Within The Formal Sacred Cooperative Cultural Gathering Of All Formally Acknowledged Practitioners Of The Way Of The Heart. And, On That Basis, Each and Every Aspect and Detail Of each and every individual's Practice Of The Way Of The Heart In The emotional-sexual Context Must (Like Each and Every Aspect and Detail Of each and every individual's Practice Of The Way Of The Heart In Each and Every Other Context) Be Formally Approved By The Formal Sacred Cooperative Cultural Gathering Of All Formally Acknowledged Practitioners Of The Way Of The Heart (In Always Direct Accountability To, and Always Under The Full Culturally Governing Authority and Guidance Of, The Ruchira Sannyasin Order Of Adidam Ruchiradam). And, In Particular, The Frequency Of (Necessarily, Yogically Right) sexual activity Should (In The Way Of The Heart) Always Be (Formally and Actually) Determined, In Accordance With My Herein Given Instructions (and, Altogether, In Accordance With My Instructions As Given, By Me, To The Ruchira Sannyasin Order Of Adidam Ruchiradam), and On The Basis Of A "Consideration" Of the age, the degree of vitality, and the general emotional-sexual characteristics of the individuals Involved, As Well As On The Basis Of A Realistic Estimate Of The Perceived <u>Effect</u> Of their sexual activity (As Well As their sexual inactivity) On their Current and General State (and daily Practice) Of Devotion, Service, self-Discipline, Feeling-Contemplation, and Depth Of Meditation (and, Altogether and Ultimately, On The Total Quality Of their Progressively Me-Realizing Practice Of The Only-By-Me Revealed and Given Way Of The Heart).

For Real Spiritual Growth To Occur, There Must (In The General Case) Be <u>Minimal</u> Association With sexual activity and emotional-sexual Relatedness, So That You Can Be Maximally (and Most Effectively) Occupied With The Culture Of Sadhana (and, Most Particularly, With The Spending Of Significant daily time Engaged In Meditation, In Devotional Chanting, In Puja, and In Other Set-Apart Sacred Exercises), Thereby Purifying the body-mind and Turning Whole bodily To Me. You Must Become Sensitive To The Fact That Your Bondage To "money, food, and sex" (and, Altogether, Your Bondage To gross and social egoity) Desensitizes You Spiritually. Therefore, As My

Devotee, You Must Abandon Non-Yogic (and, Otherwise, Excessive) Involvement In emotional-sexual Relatedness.

You Cannot "Have Your Cake and Eat It, Too". In Order To Grow In The Spiritual Process Of The Only-By-Me Revealed and Given Way Of The Heart, You Simply Must Relinquish Your gross "money, food, and sex" Obsessions—Including Your Obsession With The Apparent Consolations Of emotional-sexual Pleasure.

I Am Above and Beyond—and I Reveal Myself Spiritually From Above and Beyond. If You Are My Devotee, the entire body-mind Must Be Fitted To The Potential Of (In Due Course) Receiving Me Spiritually From Above and Beyond. To Receive Me Spiritually From Above and Beyond, Your Fixation In What Is "Below" Must Be Purified—By Turning To Me.

In The Traditional Setting, It Is Said That There Is "Either sex Or God". The traditional point of view Is That sex and God Are Diametric Opposites, Involving Two Completely Different (and Mutually Exclusive) Modes Of life. Therefore, Generally Speaking, the traditional point of view Is That the God-Oriented life Necessarily (or, At Least, Ideally) Excludes sexuality. And, In Some Fundamental Sense, this point of view Is, Effectively, True.

Human beings Characteristically Indulge themselves In The Illusion That True Satisfaction Is To Be Found In gross Existence (and, Altogether, In ego-life). Thus, human beings, In their ordinariness, Would Have Religion Be A Matter Of Accommodating their gross Orientation—With The Addition Of a conceptually Enforced idealism Relative To Religion and Spirituality. Such Is the point of view of worldlings. In Truth (and In Reality), If Your Impulse Is To Enter Into The Real Spiritual Process, You Cannot Make Any Compromise With The gross Orientation. Either There Is the grossly Oriented life Or There Is the Divinely Oriented life. The Truth Of The Matter Is, Effectively, As Stark As That.

Therefore, The emotional-sexual Discipline For My Devotees Is, Necessarily, Either celibacy Or Conservatively (or—Potentially, In The Case Of My Any Devotee who Is Uniquely Qualified For A Right Yogic emotional-sexual Sadhana—Otherwise Rightly, or Truly Yogically) Managed "Right Emotional-Sexual Yoga". In The Case Of My Any By-Me-Spiritually-Initiated Devotee, The Conservatively (or Otherwise Rightly, or Truly Yogically) Managed (and, In The General Case, Minimized) Engagement Of a sexually active intimate relationship Is (Potentially) Appropriate If (and Only If) Such Engagement Is Proven (and Formally Acknowledged) Not To Obstruct or limit The (Constantly, and Always Newly) By-Me-Activated Spiritual Process. Otherwise—If (In The Case Of My Any By-Me-Spiritually-Initiated Devotee) Participation In a sexually active intimate relationship Works Against The Spiritual Life Of

Sutra 41

Devotion To Me—The Practice Of Either single celibacy Or celibacy within intimate relationship Is The (Formally-To-Be-Expected) Requirement For Continued Spiritual Growth In My Avataric Divine Company.

Avatar Adi Da Samraj
Da Love-Ananda Mahal, 2002

SUTRA 42

Because (In The Only-By-Me Revealed and Given Way Of The Heart, or Way Of Adidam) The Totality Of Right Practice (Including, As Appropriate, The Right Practice Of "True Yogic Intimacy", or, Perhaps, "Intimate Yogic Friendship", and Of "Emotional-Sexual Conscious Exercise" and, Then, "Emotional-Sexual Devotional Communion") Is (At The Heart, and By Progressive Demonstration) Both ego-Transcending and sex-Bondage-Transcending, Either Constant (and, In Due Course, Permanently Established) Yogically Based celibacy Or (Otherwise) An Auspicious and Effective (and, As A General Rule, Conservatively—or Otherwise Rightly, or Truly Yogically—Managed) Yogic emotional-sexual Practice Will (and Must, As A Strict Rule Of Formal Expectation) Be (and More and More Effectively Become) The Practice Of My Each and Every Devotee. Thus, By The Consistent Practice Of Either Right (Intelligently Chosen, Firmly Embraced, and life-energy-Positive, or Yogically, Rather Than Merely idealistically and puritanically, Supported and Maintained) celibacy Or (Otherwise) Right sexually active Yogic emotional-sexual self-Discipline (In The Progressively Developing Form Of "True Yogic Intimacy", or, Perhaps, "Intimate Yogic Friendship", and Of "Emotional-Sexual Conscious Exercise" and "Emotional-Sexual Devotional Communion"), My Each and Every Devotee Must (Always, and More and More Effectively) Transcend The Apparent (and Previously Established, or Habitual) Intention Toward ego-Binding emotional-sexual activity—Such That ego-Based and ego-Reinforcing emotional-sexual "Bonding"-activity and ego-Binding emotional-sexual activity (and Even ego-Binding emotional-sexual Motivation) Are Always (Voluntarily, and More and More Effectively) Observed, Understood, and Relinquished. And All Of This Allows My Devotee's Practice Of Either life-energy-Positive celibacy Or (Otherwise) An Auspicious and Effective (and, As A General Rule, Conservatively—or Otherwise Rightly, or Truly Yogically—Managed) sexually active Yogic emotional-sexual Practice To Be Rightly, Truly, and Fully Realized.

In The Only-By-Me Revealed and Given Way Of The Heart (or Way Of Adidam), Right and True and Effective Practice Of "True Yogic Intimacy" (or, Perhaps, "Intimate Yogic Friendship") and "Emotional-Sexual Devotional

Communion" (or, At First, "Emotional-Sexual Conscious Exercise"), According To The Instructions I Have Given In This Testament (and With The Limiting Of The Frequency Of sexual activity According To The Rules Of Frequency I Have Indicated In This Testament), Is (In Principle, and Potentially) A Yogically (and, In Due Course, Spiritually) Auspicious, Right, and Devotionally One-Pointed Form Of functional, practical, relational, and Cultural self-Discipline Relative To the emotional-sexual character and function. Nevertheless, Even When It Is Rightly Disciplined (In Accordance With My Instructions), Participation In a sexually active intimate relationship Can Become An Encumbrance (Relative To The Free Development Of The Real Spiritual Process, Activated—and, On An Ongoing Basis, Renewed and Developed—By My Avataric Divine Spiritual Self-Transmission). Therefore, A Spontaneous and Free Choice Of life-energy-Positive single celibacy (or, Otherwise, celibacy-in-intimacy), Based On A Spontaneous and Free and Total Forgetting Of The Apparent Intention Toward emotional-sexual activity, May (In Some Cases) Occur—or, In Other Cases, Either single celibacy Or celibacy-in-intimacy May Become A Necessary Intentional Choice and Obligation, For The Sake Of An Authentic and Effective Spiritual Sadhana. In Some Cases, celibacy Will Be Embraced Spontaneously—Manifesting Entirely As A Spontaneously Awakened Disposition, Intention, and Choice (Awakened, Thus, Entirely Because Of The Effective Power and The Radiantly Sublime Self-Sufficiency Of ego-Surrendering, ego-Forgetting, and ego-Transcending Devotional and Spiritual Communion With Me). In Other Cases—and Certainly For those Not Truly (or Else Uniquely) Qualified For A Right Yogic emotional-sexual Sadhana—Formally Acknowledged single celibacy (or, Otherwise, celibacy-in-intimacy), Rightly, Truly, and Stably Chosen and Practiced, Will Be (or, In Due Course, Will Become) The Necessary (and The Most Auspicious, Right, and Devotionally One-Pointed) Form Of functional, practical, relational, and Cultural self-Discipline Relative To the emotional-sexual character and function (and, Indeed, Formally Acknowledged single celibacy, or, Otherwise, celibacy-in-intimacy—Rightly, Truly, and Stably Chosen and Practiced—Is The Necessary Form Of emotional-sexual Discipline In The "Perfect Practice" Of The Way Of The Heart For My Any Devotee who Does Not Demonstrate The Fullest Characteristics Of Being Truly, or Else Uniquely, Qualified For A Right Yogic emotional-sexual Sadhana). And Even those Of My Devotees who Are Formally Acknowledged To Be, In The Fullest Sense, Truly (or Even Uniquely) Qualified For A Right Yogic emotional-sexual Sadhana—and who (On That Basis) Engage The "Perfect Practice" Of The Only-By-Me Revealed and Given Way Of The Heart (or Way Of Adidam) While Continuing To Be (As A General Rule, Conservatively, and, Necessarily, Truly Yogically) sexually active—May Yet (and Motivelessly), In Due Course,

Demonstrate Formally Acknowledged celibacy-in-intimacy (or Even Formally Acknowledged single celibacy).

Even Any or All intimately related Practitioners (At Any Developmental Stage Of Practice, From The Beginning, Of The Way Of The Heart) May (With The Formal Consent Of The Formal Sacred Cooperative Cultural Gathering Of All Formally Acknowledged Practitioners Of The Way Of The Heart) Observe Significant Periods Of Intentional celibacy For Various Reasons (such as pregnancy, the early period of mothering an infant, or As A Reasonable Fast From sexual activity In Order To Rebalance the body-mind and Purify the emotional being). And, Of Course, intimately related Practitioners (At Any Developmental Stage Of Practice) Of The Way Of The Heart May (With The Formal Consent Of The Formal Sacred Cooperative Cultural Gathering Of All Formally Acknowledged Practitioners Of The Way Of The Heart) Choose To Simplify their Practice (or their ordinary lives) By Agreeing To Observe A Permanent Discipline Of Right celibacy (and Even To Renounce the <u>entire</u> social and practical circumstance of intimate relationship).

The Only-By-Me Revealed and Given Way Of The Heart (or Way Of Adidam) Is, Truly (In Its Right Practice), Most Simple. Therefore, Chronic life-Complication and The Seeker's Struggle Are Not Necessary In (or, Otherwise, Characteristic Of) The Only-By-Me Revealed and Given Way Of The Heart. Chronic life-Complication and The Seeker's Struggle Are (In The Way Of The Heart) The Inevitable Results Of living Without True (or Fullest, and Truly Fully Devotional, and Really Feeling-Contemplative) Resort and Surrender To Me, and Without True (or Fullest, and Really Discriminative and Intelligent) "Consideration" and Most Serious Acceptance Of My Avatarically Self-Revealed (and Always Me-Revealing) Divine Word, and Without True (or Fullest, and Fully Responsible, and Fully Formally Accountable) Practice Of The Way Of The Heart (Strictly, or Only, In The Context Of The Practitioner's Real, or Actual, Present Stage Of Life, and In Strict Accordance With My Always Exact and Complete Instructions Relative To Practice Of The Way Of The Heart In The Context Of The Practitioner's Real, or Actual, Present Stage Of Life). Also, Chronic life-Complication and The Seeker's Struggle Are (In General, and In The Specific Context Of The Practice Of The Way Of The Heart) The Natural (and Inevitable) Results Of The Effort To Achieve self-Fulfillment (or self-Expression) Via the conventions of ordinary living. Therefore, If My Devotee Practices The Way Of The Heart While Maintaining the basic conventions (and Even Much Of The Complexity) Of ordinary living, True and Fullest and Altogether Effective Practice Of The Way Of The Heart Requires That Such Be Done On The Firm Basis Of A Right (or Truly ego-Surrendering, ego-Forgetting, and ego-Transcending) Attitude, and On The Firm Basis Of A Right (or Really ego-Surrendering, ego-Forgetting, and, More and More, Effectively and Profoundly ego-Transcending, and Truly self-Purifying) Practice Relative To every detail of ordinary living. And, In The Way Of The Heart, Such Right Attitude and Right Practice Depend Upon (and Must Express) Right Listening To Me, and (In Due Course) True Hearing Of Me, and (Then) Real Seeing Of Me, Which (Altogether) Are The Practicing Means Whereby The Heart Is (In Due Course, By Means Of My Avatarically Self-Transmitted Divine Spiritual Grace) Entirely and Most Perfectly Released From egoic Complication and egoic Struggle.

There May Be some Among My Devotees whose Whole bodily Devotional and Spiritual Distraction By Me, and Devotional and Spiritual Attraction To Me, Are So All-Consuming That, Immediately, The Inclination Toward emotional-sexual intimacy and activity Simply Does Not (Any Further) arise. And, Otherwise, There May Be some Among My Devotees who Are Naturally and Unproblematically Disinclined Toward emotional-sexual intimacy and activity. And There May Be Yet others Among My Devotees who Acknowledge That their Involvement In intimate emotional-sexual Relatedness functions as a limit On their Devotional and (In Due Course) Spiritual Relationship To Me—Because they Lack The Capability To Participate In intimate emotional-sexual relationship In A Manner That Is Truly Bondage-Transcending (and, Thus, Truly Free Of all conventions of ego-Based, and ego-Reinforcing, emotional-sexual "Bonding"-activity). To any Such Among My Devotees, I Offer An Alternative To The Disciplines Of "True Yogic Intimacy" and "Intimate Yogic Friendship", and To Both celibacy and "Emotional-Sexual Conscious Exercise" (or, As The Case May Be, "Emotional-Sexual Devotional Communion") In "True Yogic Intimacy" (or, Potentially, "Intimate Yogic Friendship"). That Alternative Is The Formal single celibate Discipline (Engaged As Constant Devotional and, In Due Course, Spiritual Communion With Me).

In Comparison To The Discipline Of "True Yogic Intimacy" (or, Potentially, "Intimate Yogic Friendship")—With All Of Its Potential functional, practical, relational, and Cultural Requirements—The Formal single celibate Discipline In The Way Of The Heart Is A functionally, practically, relationally, and Culturally Simpler Practice. It Involves Not Only life-energy-Positive celibacy but Also (and Equally Importantly) Free, Complete, and Permanent (and Constant, and Truly ego-Renouncing) Relinquishment Of all emotional-sexual agreements, and All ego-Based and ego-Reinforcing emotional-sexual "Bonding", and All emotional-sexual ego-Bondage, Whether In body, speech, feeling-attachment, Or mind. Therefore, and Thereby, Such Formal single celibacy Involves Free, Complete, and Permanent Relinquishment Of The Context and Circumstance Of "True Yogic Intimacy" (or, Potentially, Of "Intimate Yogic Friendship"), or

The Entire Pattern and Implication Of Practice Required By The Choice Of emotional-sexual intimacy.

Furthermore, Such Formally Acknowledged single celibacy Involves The Free Relinquishment Of All ego-Based and ego-Reinforcing and ego-Binding sexual, emotional-sexual, and social Seeking, and Freedom From all familial obligations to provide for others. Therefore, Apart From My Call To Always Serve Me (Even In all relations, and In all circumstances), The Formal single celibate Discipline In The Way Of The Heart Involves Free Relinquishment Of all the social, familial, and household obligations that Are (or May Be) Associated With emotional-sexual intimacy.

In The Way Of The Heart, My Any Devotee who Is party to intimate emotional-sexual relationship May (With The Formal Consent Of The Formal Sacred Cultural Gathering Of All Formally Acknowledged Practitioners Of The Way Of The Heart) Freely Practice Either Permanent Or Temporary celibacy itself (but Not The Formal single celibate Discipline) Inside The Context Of intimate relationship. (However, In Order For Any Practitioner Of The Way Of The Heart who Formally Practices Permanent celibacy Inside The Context Of intimate relationship To Qualify For Practice As My "Perfect Practice" Devotee, that individual's any intimate emotional-sexual relationship Must Be <u>Truly</u> Bondage-Transcending, and, Thus, <u>Truly</u> Free Of all conventions of ego-Based, and ego-Reinforcing, emotional-sexual "Bonding"-activity.) And, In The Way Of The Heart, My Any Devotee who Is party to intimate emotional-sexual relationship May (With The Formal Consent Of The Formal Sacred Cultural Gathering Of All Formally Acknowledged Practitioners Of The Way Of The Heart, and After "Consideration" With his or her any intimate partner) Choose To Formally Relinquish the any emotional-sexual relationship and To Formally Embrace The Discipline Of single celibacy (Although, If There Is a child, or There Are children, The Choice Of Formal single celibacy May Not Be Appropriate or Possible—Unless Special, and Altogether Suitable and Right, Arrangements Are Made For The Care and Upbringing Of the child, or children).

If My Any (Formally Practicing) Devotee Is (Thus) Free, Willing, and Able To Formally Choose The single celibate Course, Then The Other Conditions For Formal single celibate Practice Are (Essentially) Simply A Matter Of ego-Surrendering, ego-Forgetting, and ego-Transcending Devotion, Service, self-Discipline, and Meditation. In Fact, Such Are The Four Fundamental Aspects Of The Simple Discipline For All Practitioners In The Way Of The Heart: Constant Devotion To Me, Constant Devotional Service To Me, Constant Discipline Of the conditional (or psycho-physical) self (In Constant Devotional Response To Me), and Constant Devotional Meditation On Me, and All Done In The ego-Surrendering, ego-Forgetting, and ego-Transcending Manner.

Therefore, In The Way Of The Heart, The Discipline Of the Formally Acknowledged single celibate Is To Simplify The Requirements For Maintenance Of the bodily person and To Remain Constantly In The self-Disciplined Practice Of ego-Surrendering, ego-Forgetting, and ego-Transcending Devotion and Devotional Service To Me.

In the ordinary life-circumstance, sexual activity Tends To Be (and May Become) Associated With familial responsibilities. However, Practitioners Of The Way Of The Heart Are Called To Devote Even intimate emotional-sexual relationships To The Purpose Of Realizing Me, Rather Than Merely (or Only) To worldly or family Fulfillments. Thus, In General, All My "Lay Congregationist" Devotees who Are (in their personal intimate contexts) sexually active Are Called To Avoid reproductive conception, and (Thus) To Avoid the birthing of children, Unless (or Until) each partner in the relationship Enjoys The Full functional, practical, relational, and Cultural Capability For, and The Total Quality Of each one's Practice Of The Way Of The Heart Truly Allows and Even Recommends, the birthing and Right Upbringing Of a child (or Even more than one child). And Practitioners Of The Way Of The Heart who Are Members Of (or, Otherwise, Formal Applicants To) The Lay Renunciate Order Of Adidam Ruchiradam or The Ruchira Sannyasin Order Of Adidam Ruchiradam, and who Are (in their personal intimate contexts) sexually active, Are Expected To Entirely Avoid reproductive conception, and (Thus, Necessarily) To Avoid the birthing of children.

Sexual activity Should Be Intelligently Avoided (or Feelingly Relinquished), Until The Passage To (At Least) physical maturity In The Context Of The Third Stage Of Life Has Completed Itself. (Therefore, every kind of sexual activity Should Be Thus Intelligently Avoided, or Feelingly Relinquished—Including degenerative masturbation, which Should Continue To Be Relinquished Even Always After The Passage To physical maturity In The Context Of The Third Stage Of Life Has Completed Itself. However, There May Be Cases, Even, Possibly, As Early As Sometime In The Third Stage Of Life, In Which It Is Appropriate—Generally Because Of A Tendency In the individual Toward Chronic, or Habitual, and Compulsive, or Obsessive, degenerative masturbation, or, In Any Manner, A Tendency Toward Intense sexual Distractedness—For The "Own-Body Yogic Sexual Practice" To Be Engaged, With The Formal Approval Of The Formal Sacred Cultural Gathering Of All Formally Acknowledged Practitioners Of The Way Of The Heart.) That Is To Say, Until the human individual Has Achieved Optimum physical maturity—Which Achievement Is (In General) Marked By The Attainment Of twenty-one years of age (and, Certainly, Not Less Than eighteen years of age), and (Thus) By The Essential (and, Optimally, The Very Fullest) Completion Of The Third Of

The First Three Cycles Of seven years Of Natural (and General psycho-physical) Growth—the mind, the emotional being, the bodily energies, and the hormonal (or chemical) and other physical processes of the body Should (By Right self-Discipline, Including A Positively Intended Avoidance Of all genital sexual activity, Except In Cases Of The Formally Approved Exercise Of The "Own-Body Yogic Sexual Practice") Simply Be Allowed To Serve The Natural and humanizing Growth Processes Of The First Three Stages Of Life.

Premature sexual activity, or An Untimely Concern About sex, or An adolescent Fascination With sexual Possibilities Only Complicates The Natural Growth Processes and Reinforces The egoic Tendency. Therefore, In The Way Of The Heart, children and young people Should (By Means Of Consistent Right Guidance) Be Taught To Understand The Processes Of their own Stages Of Life.[141] They Should Be Progressively Instructed In A Right (or Wisdom-Based) Understanding Of human sexuality. They Should Be Led (Sympathetically) To Truly Understand (and To Practice Right Disciplines Relative To) their own Natural signs. And they Should Be Inspired and Helped and Rightly Obliged To (Really and Consistently) Practice The Original (or Beginner's) ego-Transcending Devotional Means Of Rightly Informed and Intelligently and Feelingly Guided Surrender, Obedience, and Conformity To Me. With Such Right Education and Guidance (Within The Formal Sacred Cooperative Cultural Gathering Of All Formally Acknowledged Practitioners Of The Way Of The Heart), adolescence itself Should (Rightly, and Optimally) Be <u>Bypassed</u>—With its Habitual (or Habit-Forming) Excursions Into Mere self-Indulgence, and its Inappropriate Adaptational Excursions Into secular (or Non-Sacred) and "civilized" worldliness, and (In General) its Indiscriminate Excursions Into Developmentally Unproductive and karmically Devastating experiments With conditional and egoic Possibilities. Otherwise, The Third Stage Of Life (If It Is Devoted To adolescent Imitation Of equally adolescent adult behavior) Tends To Become An End In Itself (or The Final Model Of human Development), Rather Than A Bridge To (or Even A Process Within) The Fourth Stage Of Life (and Beyond).

Unfortunately, many adult individuals May Not Become Practitioners Of The Way Of The Heart Until After they Have Entered Into ego-Binding sexual experimentation, ego-Binding sexually Based emotional attachments, and ego-Binding sexually active intimate agreements (Such As these Tend To Be Enacted In the humanly and Spiritually Un-Developed domains of the common world). In The Case Of such individuals, The Disciplines (Of Frontal Yoga) Assumed and Developed In The Student-Beginner Stage Of The Way Of The Heart—Which Are To Be Continued (or, Variously, Developed and Refined) In The Context Of The Intensive Listening-Hearing Stage and The Would-Be-Seeing (or

Progressively Seeing) Stage and The First Actually Seeing Stage Of The Way Of The Heart—Will (and Do) Serve To Purify them Of their Previous childish and adolescent Purposes and egoic Habit-Patterns In sex and intimate relationship.

Formally Acknowledged Practitioners Of The Way Of The Heart who Are (in their personal intimate contexts) sexually active Are Called (and Formally Expected) To Intentionally Confine sexual intercourse, sexual responsiveness, and every kind of sexual activity To the any circumstance of Formally Accountable emotional-sexual intimacy, and (Altogether) To Relinquish Excessive (or Wastefully self-Indulgent) sexual behavior, While they Otherwise (and On That Basis, and By Those Means, and By Every By-Me-Given Means) Simply Observe (and Progressively Understand) themselves In The emotional-sexual Context. Because sexuality Tends To Be Such A Profoundly Aberrating Force In the lives of human beings, sexually active emotional-sexual Relatedness Must Be Made Subject To Discipline, Either (In The Context Of sexually active intimate relationship) By Regularizing It Or (In The Context Of celibate intimate relationship or single celibacy) By Choosing Not To Engage It At All. For an individual who Chooses To Be relationally sexually active, The Regularizing Of any such intimate relationship Is The Basic (and Formally-To-Be-Expected) Context Within Which It Is Possible To Rightly and Fruitfully Observe, Understand, and Transcend the emotional-sexual ego, and (Thereby) Rightly Control The Aberrating Force Of sexuality In The Midst Of a relationally sexually active life. Because it Does Not Provide A Circumstance In Which To Rightly and Effectively Discipline emotional-sexual impulses and activities, arbitrary (or merely casual, or Un-"Considered", and, Because Of A Lack Of Concentration and self-Discipline, Non-Yogic) sexual activity Is, Necessarily, Aberrating. That Is To Say, arbitrary sexual activity Reinforces The Fundamental Fault Of egoity. Thus, The Argument For The Intentional Confinement Of sexual intercourse, sexual responsiveness, and every kind of sexual activity To the any circumstance of Formally Accountable emotional-sexual intimacy Is Not An Argument Against The Pleasure That Is (Potentially, and Generally) Associated With sexual activity. (Indeed, It Is Not Possible, Nor Is It Necessary, To Make An Argument Against Any Kind Of Pleasure In and Of Itself.) Rather, The Argument For The Intentional Confinement Of sexual intercourse, sexual responsiveness, and every kind of sexual activity To the any circumstance of Formally Accountable emotional-sexual intimacy Is An Argument Against The Aberrating Force Associated With all arbitrary sexual activity—and, Indeed, Against The Aberrating Force Of egoity Altogether, or Against all (Necessarily, egoic) tendencies and activities that Prevent Spiritual (and, Ultimately, Most Perfect) Realization Of My Avatarically Self-Revealed (and Inherently egoless, and Self-Evidently Divine) Person and Self-Condition. Therefore, That Argument

Is Based Entirely On The Observable (and Observably Auspicious) Results Of Right emotional-sexual self-Discipline, and The Observable (and Observably Inauspicious) Results Of The Lack Of Right emotional-sexual self-Discipline—and It Is Not, In Any Sense, Based On puritanical or moralistic idealism.

All The Foundation (By-Me-Given) Gifts and Callings and Disciplines (Which Are To Be Embraced and Basically Developed At The Student-Beginner Stage Of The Way Of The Heart, and Which, As A Comprehensive and Detailed and By-Me-Spiritually-Activated Obligation, Must Continue, and Continue To Develop, In The Subsequent Developmental Stages Of The Way Of The Heart) Serve self-Understanding and self-Transcendence (or ego-Transcendence), Including (In the intimately sexually active case) The Right Development Of emotional-sexual activity itself—and They Also Grant The psycho-physical Equanimity That Allows Both celibate and intimately sexually active individuals To "Consider" The Option Of The Formal single celibate Discipline. Therefore, My Devotees who, By These Means, Truly Choose The Discipline Of Permanent single celibacy In The Way Of The Heart Should (but Only After their Choice Of single celibacy Has Been Thoroughly "Tested and Proven") Take Up The single celibate Discipline As A Full, Permanent, and Fully Formalized Commitment and Obligation.

In The Only-By-Me Revealed and Given Way Of The Heart (or Way Of Adidam), Formally Acknowledged single celibates Should Not Presume That The Formal single celibate Discipline Somehow Requires them To live and Practice Apart From The General (Formal and Cooperative) Sacred Culture Of all individuals Practicing The Way Of The Heart, or To live As If single celibate Practitioners Exist Inherently Independent Of (or Must, Otherwise, Seem To Exist Independent Of) the physical world, The social Context Of Mankind, and The Devotional Culture Associated With My Avatarically Self-Transmitted Spiritual, Transcendental, and Self-Evidently Divine Grace. Therefore, Formally Acknowledged single celibates In The Way Of The Heart Should, Like All Other Practitioners Of The Way Of The Heart, Practice In Cooperative (and Formal Cultural) Association With Other Practitioners Of The Way Of The Heart (many of whom May Be Either sexually active Or sexually inactive Practitioners Of "True Yogic Intimacy" or, Perhaps, Of "Intimate Yogic Friendship"—Either With Or Without familial and household responsibilities). And Formally Acknowledged single celibates In The Way Of The Heart Should (Like All Other adult Practitioners Of The Way Of The Heart) Provide For their own practical requirements (or necessities) Through their Active Service (Which Should, Itself, Be A Practice Of Devotional and, In Due Course, Spiritual Communion With Me), Perhaps By Serving Within The Practicing (Formal) Culture Itself, or Perhaps By Earning an income Through work in the common world.

In The Way Of The Heart, Formally Acknowledged single celibates Should, Typically, Share daily living quarters and daily sleeping quarters With other such Formally Acknowledged single celibates (who are members only of their same sex)—Although a private room (or a private dwelling place) May Be Appropriate (Either Occasionally Or Continually) In Cases (or At times) Of Unique Developmental Demonstration (and The Capability For Making A Uniquely Effective Use Of Solitude), and private sleeping quarters May Be Appropriate and Necessary In The Case Of Formally Acknowledged homosexual single celibates—and, In Any Case, Formally Acknowledged single celibates Should (If Possible) live, As A General daily Rule, In (Immediate) Common With other such Formally Acknowledged single celibates who are members only of their same sex. Indeed, Apart From Appropriately Chosen Occasions Of personal (and, Perhaps, sexual) intimacy, Engaged In one or another place Chosen (and, Perhaps, Even Reserved) For That Special Purpose, Even My Devotees who Are Involved In intimate emotional-sexual relationship (whether heterosexual or homosexual) May—If their physical and personal circumstances Permit, or, In Some Cases, As their Formal Practice Obligations May Require,[142] and For The Sake Of individually Maintaining Necessary physical (and psychic) Integrity and One-Pointed Devotion To Me—Choose To Maintain separate sleeping quarters (Generally, within the same building), or At Least separate beds within the same room. And intimate partners who Practice their emotional-sexual relationship In The Mode and Manner Of "Intimate Yogic Friendship" May (and, Most Likely—or, In Most Cases, Even Inevitably—Will) Even, By Preference (or, Otherwise, As the circumstances Of their Formal Service Obligations May Require), Maintain Entirely separate living arrangements (In separate buildings, and Even, Perhaps, In Entirely separate locations).

The Formal Practice Of single celibacy Is, From The Beginning Of his or her Formal Practice Of The Only-By-Me Revealed and Given Way Of The Heart (or Way Of Adidam), A Possible Mode Of emotional-sexual Practice For My Any and Every Devotee. Clearly, The Formal single celibate Discipline Is (Generally) Appropriate In The Case Of My Any Devotee who Is Naturally and Unproblematically and Even "Instinctively" (or, Otherwise, Characteristically) Disinclined Toward emotional-sexual intimacy and activity (Such That he or she, Perhaps, Never Engages In sexual activity At any time in his or her life), or In The Case Of My Any Devotee whose Whole bodily Devotional and Spiritual Distraction By Me, and Devotional and Spiritual Attraction To Me, Are So All-Consuming That The Inclination Toward emotional-sexual intimacy and activity Simply Does Not (Any Further) arise. The Formal single celibate Discipline Is Also (Potentially) Appropriate <u>Either</u> In The Case Of My Any Devotee who (Even As An Intentionally celibate Practitioner Of The Way Of

The Heart) Realizes True (or Truly Motiveless, and Truly Yogic) celibacy In The Midst Of The Progressively Developing Process Of self-Understanding, and So Becomes Truly and Motivelessly (or Searchlessly) celibate Only After he or she Has (Even As Early As During The Course Of his or her Development As A Student-Beginner In The Way Of The Heart) Transcended The Complications That Are Rooted In his or her emotional-sexual character, Or (Otherwise) In The Case Of My Any Devotee who, Only After some time Of Developing The Practice Of "True Yogic Intimacy" (or, Perhaps, "Intimate Yogic Friendship") and (If he or she Is sexually active in his or her personal intimate context) "Emotional-Sexual Conscious Exercise" (and Then, As The Case May Be, "Emotional-Sexual Devotional Communion"), Has Become Relatively Indifferent To sex, and Spontaneously (and Motivelessly, or Searchlessly) Inclined To Relinquish the circumstance of intimate emotional-sexual relationship, Or (Otherwise) In The Case Of My Any Devotee whose Qualifications For "True Yogic Intimacy" and A Yogic emotional-sexual Sadhana Are Relatively ordinary, Rather Than Relatively Extraordinary (Such That he or she Lacks The Capability To Participate In intimate emotional-sexual relationship In A Manner That Is Truly Bondage-Transcending, and, Thus, Truly Free Of all conventions of ego-Based, and ego-Reinforcing, emotional-sexual "Bonding"-activity), Or (Otherwise) In The Case Of My By-Me-Spiritually-Awakened Devotee who Is Spontaneously Moved To Relinquish the circumstance of intimate emotional-sexual relationship In Order To Most Fully Magnify his or her Spiritual Reception Of Me.

In The Only-By-Me Revealed and Given Way Of The Heart (or Way Of Adidam), emotional-sexual Un-Happiness Does Not Indicate A "Talent" (or A Rightly Practicing Capability) For The Formal single celibate Discipline. Rather, In The Way Of The Heart, emotional-sexual Un-Happiness Must (Necessarily) Be Transcended—If The Rightly To-Me-Listening, Truly Me-Hearing, Actually Me-Seeing, and (Ultimately) Most Perfectly Me-Realizing Course Of The Way Of The Heart Is To Be Truly Entered and Truly Fulfilled. Therefore, In The Way Of The Heart, There Must (Progressively, but Necessarily) Be Right Listening To Me, True Hearing Of Me, Real Seeing Of Me, and (Altogether) Truly Effective Practicing In The Context Of the emotional-sexual life.

In The Way Of The Heart, The Formal single celibate Discipline Is Not A Matter Of Motivated (or Strategic) celibacy. Motivated (or Strategic, and, Necessarily, Problem-Based) celibacy Is Goal-Oriented. True (or Non-Problematic, and, Therefore, Non-Strategic) celibacy Is Motiveless (or Searchless) celibacy. That Is To Say, True (or Right) celibacy Is Simply A Matter Of Intelligent self-Awareness and Motiveless (and Yogically, Rather Than Merely idealistically and puritanically, Supported and Maintained)

Relinquishment Of sexual activity with an other. To Base The Practice Of celibacy on idealism Is To Base It On A Mere self-Idea, Claiming To Be Capable Of Relinquishing sexual activity When That Capability Is Not Truly The Case. In The Only-By-Me Revealed and Given Way Of The Heart (or Way Of Adidam), True (or Right) celibacy Is Necessarily (and Firmly) Based On Your Real (Serious and Intensive) Devotional Resort To Me and Your Real (and Active) ego-Renouncing Disposition (Which Is, Itself, Based On Your Intelligent self-Observational Awareness Of Your Own ego-activity and The psycho-physically Patterned Bondage That Results From that activity).

In The Way Of The Heart, The Formal single celibate Discipline Is Not Merely A Decision To Avoid sex. The Formal single celibate Discipline In The Way Of The Heart Is A Decision To Embrace A Form Of Practice That Is Entirely Free Of all of the social, familial, and intimate relational obligations that Necessarily Are (or, Otherwise, May Be) Associated With emotional-sexual intimacy.

In The Way Of The Heart, celibacy Is Not an "Idealized" state, To Be Strategically Chosen and Enforced. A Strategically Chosen and Enforced celibacy is a merely physical (bodily) practice, Generated and Maintained By A mental (and, Necessarily, egoic, and sex-Centered) Effort—Rather Than By Truly Counter-egoic, ego-Surrendering, ego-Forgetting, ego-Transcending, sex-Transcending, and (Altogether) Devotional (or Me-Centered) and (Ultimately) By-Me-Spiritually-Activated Recognition-Response To Me. Likewise, a Strategically Chosen and Enforced celibacy Is Always Based On A Presumed Problem (or A Root-Conflict, and The Attitude Of Seeking). Therefore, a Strategically Chosen and Enforced celibacy Always Involves (and Directly Dramatizes) A Struggle With emotional-sexual desires (and A Struggle With The egoic Habit Of Identification With the physical body itself, and A Struggle With the physical body in and of itself). Unlike such "Idealized" (or Strategically Chosen and Strategically Enforced) celibacy, True celibacy Develops From The Heart's Own Deep, Prior To both mind and body. True celibacy (or Even Any Profound Realization and Demonstration Of True emotional-sexual Equanimity) Is A Kind Of Deeply Fundamental Kriya (or Spontaneous Spiritual Purification Of the body-mind, and Of attention itself). True (and, Therefore, life-energy-Positive, or Truly Regenerative) celibacy, Like Truly Conservative and Regenerative sexual-intercourse Yoga, Is Founded On The By-My-Avataric-Divine-Spiritual-Grace-Given Discovery Of Prior Happiness (or My Avatarically Self-Transmitted Divine Spirit-Current Of Unconditionally Self-Evident Love-Bliss)—Prior To The Relatively Superficial (and Always Happiness-Seeking) Efforts Of Outward-Directed (or Merely object-Seeking) attention. Therefore, In The Way Of The Heart, The Formal single celibate Discipline (or Even Any

Form Of True emotional-sexual Equanimity) Cannot Be Fully Practiced (or Truly Demonstrated) Until The Deep Well Of The Heart's Own Inherent Happiness (Prior To Any and All Presently or Potentially Acquired Pleasure, or Any and All Temporary and Merely Apparent Happiness) Is, At Least To A Significant Depth, Truly and Continuously "Located" (By Means Of My Avatarically Given and Giving Divine Spiritual Grace, and, Altogether, Via The ego-Surrendering, ego-Forgetting, and ego-Transcending Practice Of Devotion To Me).

In The Only-By-Me Revealed and Given Way Of The Heart (or Way Of Adidam), There Is No Notion That celibacy itself (On its own) Somehow "Earns" Divine Self-Realization, or (In and Of itself) Immediately (and Without Other, Even Greater, Qualifications) Equips one To Realize Real God, or Truth, or Reality. Indeed, In The Way Of The Heart—Even Though Truly Motiveless celibacy Is (In its Right and True Case) A Profoundly Positive functional, practical, and relational Orientation That (In The General Case) Is, At Least In Due Course, Necessary To Serve The Quickening (and, Ultimately, The Perfecting, or Final Completing) Of The Total By-Me-Revealed and By-Me-Given Devotional and Spiritual Process Of The Way Of The Heart—Such Truly Motiveless celibacy Is Not To Be Regarded As A "Thing" In and Of itself (Such That it Becomes Merely Another Form Of egoic self-Imagery and egoic Attachment). Rather, Truly Motiveless celibacy Is Truly and Only A Kind Of psycho-physical Freedom, Which Allows The Release Of attention, and Natural bodily energy, and The Heart-Feeling and Heart-Force Of Truly Me-Recognizing and To-Me-Responding Devotion, and (In Due Course) The Divine Spiritual Energy Of My Avataric Self-Transmission, To The Only-By-Me Revealed and Given Spiritual, Transcendental, and Divine Process Of Realizing Me.

In The Way Of The Heart—Whether In The Case Of the Formally Acknowledged single celibate Or In The Case Of The celibate Practitioner Of "True Yogic Intimacy" (or, Perhaps, "Intimate Yogic Friendship") Or In The Case Of The sexually active Practitioner Of "True Yogic Intimacy" (or, Perhaps, "Intimate Yogic Friendship") and Of "Emotional-Sexual Devotional Communion" (or, At First, Of "Emotional-Sexual Conscious Exercise")—each and all Are, Potentially (As Real and True Practitioners Of The Way Of The Heart), Truly Attuned To The Yogic Design Associated With The Only-By-Me Revealed and Given Spiritual, Transcendental, and Divine Process Of Realizing Me. Each Form Of Right emotional-sexual Yogic Sadhana In The Way Of The Heart Is Subject To Its Own (In The General Case, Necessarily Conservative) Rule, and The Existence Of Its Own Inviolable Rule Creates A Kind Of Circle Of Integrity For Each Particular Form Of Right emotional-sexual Yogic Sadhana. However, In The Way Of The Heart, All Forms Of Right emotional-sexual Yogic Sadhana

(Whether celibate Or Non-celibate) Are, In Essence, The Same—Because They Are All Means Of Transcending egoity and Magnifying Devotional and (As The Case May Be) Spiritual Communion With Me. Nevertheless, Some Practitioners Of The Way Of The Heart May Be Moved, Even Early In their Practice Of The Way Of The Heart, To Especially (or To A Uniquely, or Profoundly, Significant Degree) Simplify their life-obligations, In Order To Grant Maximum (and, Ultimately, Fullest) attention, and Natural bodily energy, and Heart-Feeling (and Heart-Force), and (In Due Course) By-Me-Transmitted Spiritual Energy To The Only-By-Me Revealed and Given Spiritual, Transcendental, and Divine Process Of Realizing Me.

The Formal Practice Of single celibacy In The Way Of The Heart Is A Great and Living Process—Not A Static behavioral Idea With Which To Idealize and Suppress oneself. The Formal Practice Of single celibacy In The Way Of The Heart Is A Great Devotional, and Yogic, and (In Due Course) Spiritual Process, An ego-Transcending Process That Directly Deals With All The Factors Of human life—Necessarily (Therefore) Including the sex-function. The Formal Choice Of single celibacy In The Way Of The Heart Is A Liberating Choice—Not An ego-Reinforcing (or Even self-Suppressive) Choice. The Formal Choice Of single celibacy In The Way Of The Heart Is A Possible Choice For My Any Devotee who Has Understood himself or herself To The Point That he or she Is Motivelessly (or Non-Strategically, or Searchlessly) Free Of The Presumed life-Requirement Of emotional-sexual "Bonding" To an intimate (Merely Apparent, and limited) other. Therefore, The Formal Choice Of single celibacy In The Way Of The Heart Is A Possible Choice For My Any Devotee who, As My True Devotee, Is Simply and Only, In An ego-Surrendering, ego-Forgetting, and ego-Transcending Manner (Free Of all egoic demands and expectations), "Bonded" (and Always Actively "Bonding") To Me, and who Is Simply One-Pointedly Resorting To Me, and who Has Dedicated his or her life and person Entirely To Me, and To The Great Process (or The human, Spiritual, Transcendental, and Divine Yoga) Of Realizing Me.

In The Only-By-Me Revealed and Given Way Of The Heart (or Way Of Adidam), The Formal single celibate Discipline Is Not A puritanical or life-energy-Negative or sex-Negative Practice. Indeed, For The Formal Practice Of single celibacy In The Way Of The Heart To Be Fruitful and Effective, the Formally Acknowledged single celibate Must Transcend Any Tendency To Be self-Suppressive (or In Any Sense conventionally minded) Relative To Natural bodily energies (As Well As Any Tendency To self-Generate The Stimulation Of Natural bodily energies For egoic Purposes or, Otherwise, To Casually Waste Natural bodily energies). Rather, The Right and True Formal single celibate Practitioner Of The Way Of The Heart Must Freely Allow all of the

Natural energies of the body-mind To Be whatever they Spontaneously Are, While Making them Subject To All The (By-Me-Given) Yogic Disciplines That Belong To The Way Of The Heart.

In The Way Of The Heart, The Formal single celibate Discipline Is, Most Fundamentally, The Transcending Of The Impulse and The Effort To (In An emotional-sexual Manner) "Bond" With any Merely Apparent (and limited) other. Therefore, The Formal Practice Of single celibacy In The Way Of The Heart Requires Relinquishment Of all such emotional-sexual "Bonding"-activity. And, In The Way Of The Heart, the Formally Acknowledged single celibate knows That his or her Practice Relative To Whatever emotional-sexual Impulses and Motivations May arise Is Strictly and Entirely A Matter Of own-body Responsibility, and It (Therefore) Does Not, As Such, Inherently Require any form of sexual activity with any other.

What The Practice Of Formal single celibacy In The Way Of The Heart Specifically (or First Of All, and Always) Renounces (and Must Transcend) Is Not sexual activity itself, or the sex-function itself, or Natural sexual energy itself, or sexually Indicated Spirit-Energy Itself, or Yogic sexual (or emotional-sexual) Practice Itself—but What The Practice Of Formal single celibacy In The Way Of The Heart Specifically (or First Of All, and Always) Renounces (and Must Transcend) Is the "cult of pairs", or The Bondage Associated With conventional (or ego-Binding) pair-"Bonding", and With "Bonding" To worldly life, and (Altogether) With "Bonding" To egoic life. The Word "celibate" Rightly (and Most Properly) Applies To <u>This</u> Practice Of The Renunciation (and The Active Transcending) Of All Forms Of egoic "Bonding", and To The Yogic Condition In Which (and By Which) All Forms Of egoic (and ego-Supporting, and ego-Reinforcing) "Bonding" Are Renounced and Transcended.

The Formally Acknowledged single celibate In The Way Of The Heart Is Called (By Me) To Transcend Bondage (To others and To the world), but Not By The Avoidance Of Association (With others and With the world). This Bondage-Transcending Discipline Is A True (and Truly Living) life-Art, Based On self-Understanding and The Ability To Transcend egoity, Rather Than An ego-Based, Strategic Ideal To Be Worked Out Mechanically By Means Of Suppression and Exclusion. The Traditional Renunciate Ideal Is Associated With Exclusion (or The Cutting Off Of sex, and The Cutting Off Of Relations With the world Generally). However, That Ideal Does Not Pertain In The Only-By-Me Revealed and Given Way Of The Heart (or Way Of Adidam). The Strategic (and ego-Reinforcing) Method Of Exclusion Is Never The Right Approach To The Practice Of The Only-By-Me Revealed and Given Way Of The Heart. In The Way Of The Heart, To Transcend The "Bonding" Motive, Even In the circumstances Of The Usual "Bonding" Display, Does Not Mean

That My Devotee Excludes the functions, activities, and relations that Rightly Belong To his or her life and Practice, but That My Devotee Transcends The limiting Power Of Those Associations. Thus, My Call To All Practitioners Of The Way Of The Heart Is To Transcend self-Contraction—Not To Dramatize self-Contraction Through The Strategic (and ego-Reinforcing) Method Of Exclusion.

The Formally Acknowledged single celibate In The Way Of The Heart Is Engaged In A Particular (or Specialized) Form Of The Same Discipline That I Give To All My Devotees. It Is The Discipline Of Conforming the Total body-mind To The Yoga Of The Only-By-Me Revealed and Given Way Of The Heart, and (Thus) Of Making the Total body-mind Into A Yogic Vehicle For The Purpose Of Realizing Me, Through The Persistent moment to moment Practice Of All Aspects Of Ruchira Avatara Bhakti Yoga, self-Observation, self-Understanding, The "Conscious Process", and "General Conductivity".

In The Practice Of Formal single celibacy In The Way Of The Heart (As In Every Form Of emotional-sexual Discipline In The Way Of The Heart), The Fundamental (and Must Be Constant) "sexual" Discipline Is The sex-act-inactive Exercise Of Ruchira Avatara Bhakti Yoga, self-Observation, self-Understanding, The "Conscious Process", and "General Conductivity" In Relation To all emotional-sexual arising. However, As An Occasional Means For Serving emotional-sexual Equanimity—or, Otherwise, If There Are Occasions (or periods of time) In an individual's Formal single celibate Practice Of The Way Of The Heart When he or she Observes An Excessively Aroused or Effectively Suppressed or Excessively Outgoing genital Energy (As I Have Previously Described such conditions, In This, My Testament Of Divine Secrets), Such That The Fully Engaged Practice Of Ruchira Avatara Bhakti Yoga, self-Observation, self-Understanding, The "Conscious Process", and "General Conductivity" Is Not Sufficient To Restore Right Balance and Well-being (or True Equanimity) In The Full Circle Of the body-mind—It May Be Necessary (For The Sake Of Restoring, or Otherwise Serving, Full, Right Balance and Well-being, or True Equanimity) For the Formally Acknowledged single celibate To (With Full Cultural Accountability) Engage The sex-Specific "Own-Body Yogic Conductivity Practice", In Addition To The Fundamental Practice Of Ruchira Avatara Bhakti Yoga, self-Observation, self-Understanding, The "Conscious Process", and "General Conductivity" (As, Indeed, It May Be Necessary To Do In The Case Of Any Practitioner Of The Way Of The Heart, Whether celibate Or Non-celibate, who Observes The emotional-sexual Indicators That Justify The sex-Specific "Own-Body Yogic Conductivity Practice", and who Would, With Full Cultural Accountability, Thereby Directly Serve Full, Right Balance and Well-being, or True Equanimity).

Even Though The "Own-Body Yogic Conductivity Practice" Is sex-Specific (and, Therefore, sexually active), It Is An Entirely Right and Appropriate Practice For celibate Practitioners Of The Way Of The Heart, Because It Is Of A Truly Renunciate (and, When Engaged In The Context Of Right celibate Practice Of The Way Of The Heart, Truly celibate) Nature. That Is To Say, Although This "Own-Body Yogic Sexual Practice" Is Associated With the sex-function of the human body-mind, It Is Not (Itself) Associated With emotional-sexual "Bonding"-activity, but Only and Entirely With ego-Surrendering, ego-Forgetting, and ego-Transcending Devotional and Yogic "Conductivity" Of the Natural bodily energy and, As The Case May Be, My Avatarically Self-Transmitted Divine Spirit-Energy.

Because The "Own-Body Yogic Sexual Practice" Is Not A Matter Of ego-Based (and ego-Reinforcing) emotional-sexual "Bonding"-relationship to any Merely Apparent (and limited) other (or an other "ego"), It Is Not (In and Of Itself) Associated With The Practice (and The Presumed Rules and Expectations) Of "True Yogic Intimacy" (or Of "Intimate Yogic Friendship")—Although The "Own-Body Yogic Sexual Practice" Is Also Given By Me To Be Engaged, As A Matter Of own-body Responsibility, By My Devotees who Are Practicing In The Context Of Either Developing Or Fully Established "True Yogic Intimacy" (or, Perhaps, "Intimate Yogic Friendship"), Whether they Are, In That Context, sexually active Or celibate.

Renunciation Itself, Rightly Understood and Rightly Practiced, Must (Progressively) Characterize The Real, Right, and True Practice Of All Practitioners Of The Only-By-Me Revealed and Given Way Of The Heart, Whether they Are Beginners In The Free Intentional Relinquishment Of self-Indulgent and Casual emotional-sexual behavior, Or Growing Practitioners Of "True Yogic Intimacy" (or, Perhaps, "Intimate Yogic Friendship") and "Emotional-Sexual Conscious Exercise", Or (Spiritually) Fully Technically Responsible Practitioners Of "True Yogic Intimacy" (or, Perhaps, "Intimate Yogic Friendship") and "Emotional-Sexual Devotional Communion", Or celibate Practitioners Of "True Yogic Intimacy" (or, Perhaps, "Intimate Yogic Friendship"), Or Formally Acknowledged single celibates, Or Even children, and those (young or old) who Are, For Various Reasons (Other Than The Specific Choice Of Formal single celibacy), Not party to any intimate emotional-sexual relationship.

That True Renunciation Which (More and More) Must Characterize The Practice Of All Practitioners Of The Only-By-Me Revealed and Given Way Of The Heart Is ego-Renunciation—The Devotional (or Heart-Responsive, and Inherently Motiveless, or Searchless) Renunciation Of the ego-"I" (or self-Contraction). Indeed, The Only-By-Me Revealed and Given Way Of The Heart Is—Essentially, and As A Totality—The Progressive Process Of ego-Renunciation,

Through Counter-egoic (or ego-Surrendering, ego-Forgetting, and ego-Transcending) Resort To (Inherently egoless, and By-My-Avataric-Divine-Spiritual-Grace-Revealed) Happiness (or Love-Bliss Itself).

In The Only-By-Me Revealed and Given Way Of The Heart, True (and, Ultimately, Inherently Most Perfect) Devotion To Me (In and As My Avatarically-Born Bodily Human Divine Form and Person) Becomes True (and, Ultimately, Inherently Most Perfect) ego-Renunciation. Therefore, Even In The Context Of all conditional relations, My Every By-Me-Spiritually-Initiated Listening Devotee, and Hearing Devotee, and Seeing Devotee Is Called To Always "Locate" Me (By Means Of My Avatarically Self-Transmitted Divine Spiritual Grace) and (Thus and Thereby) To Live Free In Love With My Very (and Self-Existing, and Self-Radiant, and Inherently egoless, and Self-Evidently Divine, and Inherently Free) Person. For My True Devotee, all objects and others Are Simply The Theatre Of Divine Association and ego-Transcendence. Therefore, For My Every Devotee, all conditions Must Be Aligned and Yielded In Love With Me—or Else any object or any other Will Be The Cause Of Heart-Stress, self-Contraction, Dissociation, Clinging, Boredom, Doubt, The Progressive Discomfort Of Diminished Love-Bliss, and All The Forgetfulness Of Grace and Truth and Happiness Itself.

In Any Case, and Even In The Case Of those Of My Devotees For whom Formal single celibacy Is Found To Be The Optimum Discipline, The Guiding Orientation Of The Only-By-Me Revealed and Given Way Of The Heart Is Not To Problem-Based self-Control, or To Strategic Separation Of attention From the world of relations, or To A conceptually Idealized Commitment To The Avoidance Of sex. Rather, The Guiding Orientation Of The Only-By-Me Revealed and Given Way Of The Heart Is Always To ego-Transcendence—By Means Of My Avatarically Self-Transmitted Divine Grace, and In Responsively ego-Surrendering and ego-Forgetting Relationship To Me—Through The Heart-Magnification Of The Devotional Love Of Me (Even In and Via all functions, relations, and circumstances), and (In Due Course, As My Avatarically Self-Transmitted Divine Spiritual Grace Will Have It) Through The Reception Of My Spiritual In-Filling Of the body-mind and all its relations (Via The Magnification Of The "Conductivity" Of My Avatarically Self-Transmitted, and Always Me-Revealing, Divine Spirit-Power Of Love-Bliss), and Through True Ecstasy (In The Context Of Meditation, and In daily life—Even, In Due Course, By Means Of My Avatarically Self-Transmitted Divine Spiritual Grace, To The Degree Of Inherently Most Perfect Divine Self-Realization). Thus, From The Beginning Of Practice In The Only-By-Me Revealed and Given Way Of The Heart, The Fundamental and Always Leading Purpose Of emotional-sexual Discipline Is To Conserve and Release attention (and the entire functional body-mind) From egoic (and ego-Reinforcing) Distractedness In intimacy and sexuality, Such That (and By Means Of The Fact That) attention (and the entire functional body-mind), Whether Within Or Without The Context Of intimacy and sexual activity, Always Maximally Magnifies The Devotionally (and, In Due Course, Spiritually) Responsive Counter-egoic (and Even Total psycho-physical) Practice Of Ruchira Avatara Bhakti Yoga (or ego-Surrendering, ego-Forgetting, and Truly, and, Ultimately, Even Most Perfectly, ego-Transcending Devotion To Me).

I Call All My Devotees (and Even all who Are Moved To Study My Avataric Divine Word) To "Consider" (and Receive) This Wisdom-Revelation, Uniquely Given By Me: Realization (Of Reality Itself, or Truth Itself, or Real God) Is (Necessarily) Whole bodily. It Is the Whole body—Rather Than any "piece" of the human being—That Must Be En-Light-ened. Therefore, The Instructions I Have Given Relative To The emotional-sexual Dimension Of human life Are Not About sex in and of itself. Rather, Those Instructions Relate (Most Fundamentally, and Essentially) To The Transcending Of The Root Of Bondage In (and To) the body—Which Is The Transcending Of ego-Bondage To The gross Domain Of conditional Existence (Altogether). Because the body Is (Basically) Patterned In emotional-sexual Terms, The Transcending Of body-Based Bondage Is Rooted In The emotional-sexual Dimension. As Long As The Sum and Force Of emotional-sexual ego-Patterning Binds the body-mind To the point of view Of "Below", You Remain Entirely "Below"—Unavailable To What Is Above.

Therefore, My Wisdom-Instruction Relative To sexuality Has Always Been About Understanding The emotional-sexual Basis Of the ego-"I" (or self-Contraction)—Not About "Targeting" the genitals, or Merely Being Negative, moralistic, or puritanically double-minded About sex itself. The ego-"I" is the entire body-mind—self-Contracted. Therefore, Divine Enlightenment Is, Literally, The En-Light-enment Of the Whole body (or Of The psycho-physical Totality Of body-mind)—Not Merely Some Form Of body-Excluding and world-Excluding subjectivism, Inwardly Cultivated By the individual.

As A General Rule, The Principal Preoccupation Of human beings Is their Involvement In The Dramas Of emotional-sexual egoity—Whether That Involvement Is self-Satisfied Or Frustrated. The Total life of the human individual Is Rooted In sex—Because the body is An emotional-sexual Pattern. That Pattern Manifests Itself (In Part) As sex-mind—but, Altogether, That Pattern Governs All Aspects Of the gross personality. Indeed, Most Of the content of the gross personality Bears No Direct Reference To sex, Even Though Virtually all such content Is Based In (and limited By) The Governing emotional-sexual Pattern. And, Altogether, Your "Allegiance" To Your Own emotional-sexual Pattern Fastens You In The "Downward" Disposition, Bound To the gross view Of Existence.

If Your psycho-physical Faculties Are Turned Downward (By Virtue Of Your egoic Patterning), Then You Cannot Truly Experience Me and Fully Receive Me. If Your psycho-physical Faculties Are Turned Downward, You Are Not Even "In The Room" With Me. My Room Is Above and Beyond. I Am Above and Beyond. I Reveal Myself From Above and Beyond. If You Are Not Devotionally and Spiritually Turned To Me (In My Avatarically here-Born Bodily Human Divine Form), You Cannot Experience and Receive Me From Above and Beyond. And, If You Cannot Experience and Receive Me Spiritually, From Above and Beyond—I Cannot Work With You Spiritually. Then, You Will Merely Continue To Be Turned Down and In—On Yourself (Defined Separately, By All Your egoic Patterning). In That Case, The Most You Can Experience Of Me Is A conditional (and, Necessarily, limited) Modification Of Me—Because You Are Aware Of Me Only Via (and In The Terms Of) Your Own psycho-physical ego-Patterning. Then, You Do Not Experience Me As I Am—Above and Beyond, In The "Bright" and Greater Room. Instead, You Remain In the Dark and Narrow room of Separate self (or the conditional space of egoity)—Bound By the Always Seeking shape and occupation Of Your Own limit and Patterning.

My Tangibly Experienced Avataric Divine Spiritual Invasion Makes everything About conditionally Manifested Existence More and More Profoundly Clear. For My By-Me-Fully-Spiritually-Infused Devotee, There Is No Possibility Of ego-Based Involvement In sexual activity. Whether Or Not My Any Such Devotee Continues To Be (Necessarily, Yogically) sexually active (As he or she Matures In The Me-Seeing Stages Of Practice In The Only-By-Me Revealed and Given Way Of The Heart), sexual activity Simply Ceases To Be (For him or her) A Matter Of Problematic Concern.

Fundamentally, sexual activity Is A functional Mechanism For Ensuring the reproduction of the species. Therefore, Only low-minded egoity, self-Contracted in and as the body, Would Presume That Such A functional Mechanism Has Any Causative Role Relative To The (Altogether Divine) Spiritual Reality and Process. However, Before You Have Become Truly Established In The (Always Presently By-Me-Given, and By-Me-Renewed, and By-Me-Magnified) Process Of Tangible (and Whole bodily, or Total psycho-physical) Spiritual Infusion By Me, You Will Tend (To One or Another Degree) To Impute Great (and Even Spiritually Causative) Importance To The functions and Possibilities Associated With sexual Pleasure—and This Because There Is No Great and Sufficient Fullness For You, In The Spiritual Sense. Before You Have Become Truly Established In The ego-Surrendering Devotional Process Of Tangible

Spiritual Infusion By Me, You Are Yet Fastened In Your self-Deluded lowness (Due To Your Naive self-Identification With the physical body—which You Presume To Be a Separate "something", but which, In Reality, Is Not At All Separate).

As My Devotee, You Must Be Turned To Me—Whole bodily (or As A psycho-physical Totality). And I Must Show (or Avatarically, and Altogether Divinely, Self-Reveal) Myself To You—In and As and Via My Avatarically-Born Bodily (Human) Divine Form, and (Altogether) From Above and Beyond. This Avatarically Given Divine Spiritual Imposition Of Mine Progressively Purifies and Transforms Your psycho-physical being. Thus, This Spiritual Imposition Of Mine Is Not (Itself) A philosophical Matter—Rather, It Is A Divine Matter, Avatarically Given (To You), By Me. You Must Live The Life I Have Given You To Live. You Must Follow My Avataric Divine Instructions. You Must Resort To Me (In and As My Avatarically-Born Bodily Human Divine Form and Person), and (Thereby) Relinquish All The Lying Nonsense Of the mummery of egos.

The emotional-sexual Preoccupation Of human beings Is (In and Of Itself) Nothing but lowness. When Your Practice Of The Only-By-Me Revealed and Given Way Of The Heart (or Way Of Adidam)—and, Thus and Thereby, Your True, Consistent, and Really Effective Devotional Resort To Me—Becomes Truly Profound, Then You No Longer live On The Basis Of The Patterning Of "money, food, and sex". All Of That Patterning Is Spontaneously (and Happily) Surrendered (and Conformed) To Me.

The "money-food-and-sex" ego Must Be Altogether Transcended. In a moment of Naively Presumed "realism", You (As My Beginning Devotee) May Say You Have "Discovered" That You Are "Really" a householder, That You "Really" (and Necessarily) Require a conventional arrangement relative to sex, intimate relationship, and So Forth. Such Is Not A Discovery! Rather, All Of That Is Simply Your (Necessarily, egoic) Noticing Of The "money-food-and-sex" ego-Patterning That You Were Already Suffering When (and Before) You First Came To Me—and In Despair Of Which You Came To Me! When You Speak In That Manner, You Are Forgetting (For the time being) That You Are Actually Bound Up In A Terrible Scene Of Bondage, Suffering, mortality, absurdity—Divorced (By Virtue Of Your Own self-Contracting activity) From The Real (and, Necessarily, Devotional and Spiritual) Divine Process.

The ordinary human Search For sexual Possibility Is mere Patterned (or conditionally Programmed) behavior, Based On Being (Effectively) Without Spiritual Awareness (and, Altogether, Without Awareness Of Reality, or Of The Real Condition, Itself). If There Is No Spiritual Fullness, Then You Are Driven To Seek Pleasure (or Merely Temporary Release From The Inherent Pleasurelessness Of egoity) Through Manipulation Of the self-Contracted body-mind. Only Actual Spiritual Fullness Is Inherently Self-Sufficient (or Divinely Love-Bliss-Full).

"Consider" This: Everything That Comes From Below Is Patterned (or Pre-conditioned) Bondage.

The Divine Gift Comes From Above—and The Divine Gift Is Spiritual In Its Nature.

Therefore, You Must Be (Even Whole bodily, or As A psycho-physical Totality) Re-Oriented—To What Is Above and Beyond, Rather Than To What Is Below, and Pre-conditioned, and Bound. The Only-By-Me Revealed and Given Yoga Of Ruchira Avatara Bhakti—The Whole bodily (or Total psycho-physical) Way Of Devotional (and ego-Surrendering) Turning To Me (In and As My Avatarically-Born Bodily Human Divine Form and Person)—Is The (By Me) Avatarically Given Divine Means By Which You Are (First) Purified (Whole bodily) and Then (In Due Course) Spiritually (and Whole bodily) Turned To What Is Above and Beyond.

I Am What Is Above and Beyond—Spiritually Invading here. Therefore, You Must Relinquish Your Turning To What Is Below and Pre-conditioned—and, Instead, Turn To Me.

I Bless—and My Avataric Divine Spiritual Blessing Purifies and Transforms. Nevertheless, In Order For My Avataric Divine Spiritual Blessing Of You To Be Effective, You Must Be Turned To Me. In Very Practical Terms—and Entirely By Means Of The Very (and Consistent) To-Me-Responsive (and Inherently Counter-egoic) Action Of Turning All The psycho-physical Faculties To Me (In and As My Avatarically-Born Bodily Human Divine Form and Person)—You Must Un-Link The psycho-physical Faculties From Their ego-Patterning and From Their conditioning By all-and-All That Is Below.

My Avataric Incarnation Is The Divine Descent—From Above and Beyond. Such Is My Avataric Divine Spiritual Blessing-Work. Therefore, The Practice Of The Only-By-Me Revealed and Given Way Of The Heart (or Way Of Adidam) Requires The Whole bodily (or Total psycho-physical) Turning To Me In (and As) My Avataric Bodily (Human) Manifestation—and, By Means Of That Turning Of The psycho-physical Faculties To Me, You Must Forget The Bondage (and The Pre-conditioned Patterning) Of The psycho-physical Faculties (In Their Association With Your lowness), and You Must (Thus and Thereby) Be (Inherently, and More and More) Sensitized To My Avataric Divine Spiritual Manifestation (Avatarically Given, By Me, From Above and Beyond), Such That My Spiritual Invasion Of Your body-mind First Purifies and Then Awakens You ("Washing" the "dog" From "head" To "tail", and Not The Other Way Around).

In My Avataric Divine Self-Submission To Teach, I Had To Submit To Fully Enter Into This Domain Of lowness, Of ordinary people, Of social egoity, Of low-level Bondage. In That Submission, I Also Revealed To those who Came To Me All The Various Dimensions Of Potential Evolutionary Manifestation—all the kinds of Natural siddhis and developmental psychisms, all the kinds of phenomena Associated With The Fourth, The Fifth, and The Sixth Stages Of Life. All Of That Was Communicated To My Devotees As A Series Of Lessons About The Non-Sufficiency Of anything Less Than Most Perfect Realization Of Me.

No Exercise Of the "money-food-and-sex" ego—Whether The Effort To Exploit it Or The Effort To Cut it Away—Is (or Can Ever Be) Devotion To Me. The "money-food-and-sex" ego Simply Has Nothing To Do With The Devotional and (In Due Course) Spiritual Relationship To Me.

As My True Devotee, You Turn To Me—Such That I Can (In Due Course) Spiritually Transform You, From Above and Beyond.

When You Truly and Consistently Do This, You Will (In The True Maturing Of Your psycho-physically Purified Devotional Resort To Me) Become Established In The Practice Of Tangible Reception Of My Avataric Divine Spiritual Self-Manifestation—and Only Then Will You Fully Understand What I Am (Herein) Saying To You.

In Order To Truly (and Really Effectively) Receive Me Spiritually, You Must Do Much More Than Merely egoically "Come Into The Room" With Me. You Must Cultivate The Devotional (and Inherently Counter-egoic, and Really ego-Surrendering) and (In Due Course) Spiritual Relationship To Me—By Intensively, Consistently, and Profoundly Practicing The Ruchira Avatara Bhakti Yoga Of To-Me-Turned Surrender-To-Me (In and As My Avatarically-Born Bodily Human Divine Form and Person).

My Any Beginning Devotee May Tend To "Argue" (or Try To Bargain) With Me—By Persisting In Making worldly and ego-Serving Choices, and Pretending To Me That Such Choices Make Some Sort Of "philosophical" Sense. As My Beginning Devotee, You May Even Sometimes think (and Even Declare) That It "Would Not Be True" Of You (As an ego) To Devotionally Turn To Me. Yes—That Is Absolutely Correct! It Is Not True Of egos To Devotionally Turn To Me! The ego knows Nothing Of Me! It Is Only In Your Heart-Recognition Of Me, and Your Heart-Response To Me, That Your life Is Changed Into The True Devotional Yoga Of Turning To Me—Rather Than the life Of Looking At Your Reflection In The Pond-Water and Rehearsing The Presumed Inevitability Of Your Various ego-Patterns (Saying, "Oh, I Am So Wonderful!", or, Otherwise, "Oh, I Really Am an ego of this time!").

That Is Your Bondage, Narcissus!

Therefore, If You Are My True By-Me-Spiritually-Initiated (and Always Newly By-Me-Spiritually-Activated) Devotee (Truly Practicing The Only-By-Me

Revealed and Given Way Of The Heart, or Way Of Adidam), You (Necessarily) Have No attention for the emotional-sexual ego. Instead, You Are Simply (Whole bodily, or In A Total, or Comprehensive, psycho-physical Manner) Turned To Me (In and As and Via My Avatarically-Born Bodily Human Divine Form)—Simply (Thus and Thereby) Forgetting About emotional-sexual egoity. And You Only Engage Even In "Right Emotional-Sexual Yoga" If The Real Spiritual Process In My Avataric Divine Company Allows (In Your Case) For Such Yogic (and sexually active) Exercise Of the body-mind.

Spiritually Naive human beings Tend To Argue For sexuality Entirely On The Basis Of The Impulses arising From egoic Bondage In The Context Of social-egoity and First-Three-Stages-Of-Life "money-food-and-sex" Patterning. There Is No Justification For Any Such Argument. All of Your mothers and fathers, In All Generations, Already Did That! All the billions who Have died in the past Did Exactly That—living By organic Imperatives, primate "Rules", and conditionally Patterned ego-Bondage. In So Doing, they Guaranteed That they Would Never Realize anything Of The Divine Spiritual Self-Condition Of Reality Itself. Instead, they Simply Adapted To The Patterning Of Apparent Separateness and All The Illusions Of gross human Bondage.

If You Insist On Accommodating ego-Bondage, You Will Not Realize Me To Any Significant Degree. You Can Only Realize Me By (Whole bodily, or With Every psycho-physical Faculty) Turning To Me (In and As My Avatarically-Born Bodily Human Divine Form and Person)—and, In This Manner, You Must Turn Away From All The Pre-conditioned Patterns, Habits, Adaptations, and Illusions Of psycho-physical ego-Bondage.

Therefore, every human being Must Transcend The emotional-sexual Patterning Of the body-Based ego, Because That Patterning Is At The Root Of the (Total psycho-physical) self-Contraction. However, This Fact Cannot Be Dealt With By Means Of moralistic preaching, Nor Can It Be Dealt With Merely By Taking Up A Prescriptive Series Of Disciplines Of the body-mind (in and of itself). The Only Means By Which This ego-Bondage Can Be (Ultimately, Most Perfectly) Transcended Is The Whole bodily Act Of Surrender (or Turning) To Me (In and As My Avatarically-Born Bodily Human Divine Form and Person), and Of Subsequent Whole bodily Reception Of (and egoless Identification With) My Spiritually Self-Transmitted (and Inherently egoless) Person and Self-Condition. Thus, In Order To Go Beyond The emotional-sexual Patterning Of the body-Based ego, There Must Be A Profound, Whole bodily Conversion—From (Total psycho-physical) Obsession With the separate self To (Whole bodily) Heart-Communion With Me.

Therefore, The Foundation Principle Of The Only-By-Me Revealed and Given Way Of The Heart Is Absolute Devotional (and, In Due Course,

Spiritual) Fidelity To Me. The Foundation Practice Of The Only-By-Me Revealed and Given Way Of The Heart Is Ruchira Avatara Bhakti Yoga, Which Is The Devotionally (and, In Due Course, Spiritually) Me-Recognizing and To-Me-Responsive Counter-egoic, and Even Total psycho-physical, Practice Of ego-Surrendering, ego-Forgetting, and Truly (and, Ultimately, Even Most Perfectly) ego-Transcending Devotion To Me. Only The Constant (or moment to moment) Practice Of Devotionally Me-Recognizing and Devotionally To-Me-Responding Ruchira Avatara Bhakti Yoga Is Devotional (and, In Due Course, Spiritual) Fidelity To Me. And All Infidelity In Relation To Me Must Be Transcended, In The moment to moment Practice Of My Devotee. Therefore, and Because the emotional-sexual character Is Fundamental To the human being, Infidelity In Relation To Me Must Be Transcended Even In The Context Of the emotional-sexual character (Whether The individual Practitioner Is sexually active Inside The Context Of intimate relationship Or celibate Inside The Context Of intimate relationship Or singly celibate), If Absolute Devotional (and, In Due Course, Spiritual) Fidelity To Me Is To Be Realized. For The Practitioner Of The Only-By-Me Revealed and Given Way Of The Heart, Infidelity (Rightly Understood) Is Not Merely Any Casual Diversion Of body, speech, or mind Away From The Context Of any intimate (emotional-sexual) relationship. For The Practitioner Of The Only-By-Me Revealed and Given Way Of The Heart, Infidelity (Rightly Understood) Is Any ego-Possessed Turning Away (or Disorienting) From Me—and, Thus, Any Instance Of the Separate and Separative body-mind Contracting Upon itself, In its Refusal To Surrender (or To Turn, Unconditionally) To My Avatarically-Born Bodily (Human) Divine Form and My Spiritually "Bright" (and Inherently egoless, and Self-Evidently Divine) Person and My Inherently egoless Self-Condition (Which Is The Source-Condition and The True Self-Condition Of all-and-All, and Which Is Real God, or Reality Itself, or The One and Indivisible Truth Of all-and-All).

In The Only-By-Me Revealed and Given Way Of The Heart, Every Kind Of Wavering From The moment to moment Practice Of Ruchira Avatara Bhakti Yoga (Whether Inside Or Outside The Context Of any emotional-sexual relationship) Is Infidelity In Relation To Me. And All Such Infidelity Must Be Transcended, If The Only-By-Me Revealed and Given Way Of The Heart (or Way Of Adidam) Is To Be Most Perfectly Fulfilled—In Transcendental, Inherently Spiritual, Inherently egoless, and Self-Evidently Divine Self-Realization.

All human beings—male and female—Yearn For The True God-Man. And The Inevitable Consequence Of Most Profoundly Heart-Recognizing (or Finding) Me, The Long-Awaited and Universally Expected God-Man Of The "Late-Time" (or "Dark" Epoch), Is Renunciation. When You Most Profoundly

Heart-Recognize Me, You Spontaneously Renounce the worldly householder's Non-Renunciate Habit and Purpose Of life—and the worldly life (Altogether). In Your Heart-Attraction To Me, You Simply Forget About all of that.

Thus, To Most Deeply Love Me—In and As and Via My Avatarically-Born Bodily (Human) Divine Form (and, Thus and Thereby, As My Avatarically Self-Transmitted Divine Spiritual Presence Of Un-conditional Self-Manifestation and As My Avataric Self-Revelation Of My Very, and Inherently egoless, Divine Person)—Is (Inherently, and Necessarily) To Leave the ego-Made world, and To Abandon The ego-Serving Disposition Of "Bonding" To any (merely human) "other".

When You Heart-Recognize Me Most Deeply, You Will Spontaneously "Leave Home"—and, Thus (By Means Of Your All-Else-Forgetting Ecstatic Attractedness To Me), You Will "Lose" Your future births.

When You Most Deeply Heart-Recognize Me, There Is No ordinary Accommodation To Be Made. Then, I Will Be Surrounded By My Countless Heart-Lovers—Both male and female—all Living In One-Pointed Adoration Of Me, Lost In The Ecstasy Of Finding Me.

My True Devotees Come To Be Only With Me. They Lose the vision of this world. They Stop Consenting To Be Bound To the body-mind-self.

If You Are Most Profoundly Distracted By Me, There Is An Ecstasy-Made End To worldly life—and all who Have (Thus) Found Me "Leave Home", Binding themselves Only To Me.

I Am The Only Lover In The Cosmic Domain. If You Do Not Yet Love Only Me, You Are "Narcissistically" Luxuriating In Being With Me—Until You Truly Wake Up To Me.

I Am Jealous For My Devotee's attention To Me. Whenever It Is That You Truly Find Me, You Will Spend Only a little time With Me here In this place. The Great "Time" You Must Spend With Me Is Beyond this place. That Great "Time" Is Eternal, and That Great "Place" Is Boundless—Without perimeter or parameter, Unconditional, Beyond psyche and thought.

I Am That One. Find Me Out. Become My True Heart-Lover—and I Will Distract You From all conditionality.

I Have Given You My Avataric Divine Instruction, Which Covers Every Possible Form and Degree Of Response To Me. Do That Of Which You Are Capable (By Means Of My Avataric Divine Spiritual Grace, If My Avataric Divine Spiritual Grace Is Embraced By Heart).

This world Is Not The Place Of Happiness. This world Is a place of endings and Of Sorrow—Where (Potentially, and By Means Of My Avataric Divine Grace) You May Become Impulsed Toward Me. When You Know Only That Impulse, You Leave the world.

I Am Not Coming Back—but, Paradoxically, I Am (Now, and Forever Hereafter) Always here. Those who Will Go With Me To My "Bright" Divine Spherical Self-Domain Are those who Adhere To Me Only.

This Is Not My Place. I Am Visiting here—Having Made An Inexplicable Avataric Divine Gesture, Because Of the signs of the times.

Embrace Me Perfectly. In That Heart-Embrace, There Is No "other". Then You Are (Truly) One-Pointed In Me (and, Truly, worldless).

The Only-By-Me Revealed and Given Way Of The Heart (or Way Of Adidam) Can Be Lived By everyone On Earth. However, those who (In Any Generation) Respond To Me Most Profoundly Must Understand My Most Secret Revelation Of Only and Absolute Adherence To Me.

This Most Secret Revelation Of Mine Must Always Be Known—In Every Generation (Now, and Forever Hereafter).

Avatar Adi Da Samraj
The Mountain Of Attention Sanctuary, 2000

SUTRA 43

Fully Technically Responsible Practice Of The Basic (or Frontal) Spiritual Yoga Of The Only-By-Me Revealed and Given Way Of The Heart (or Way Of Adidam) Begins In The Context Of The Fully Established (or Actually Me-Seeing) "Basic" Fourth Stage Of Life. This Fully Technically Responsible Beginning Takes Place In The Context Of The First Actually Seeing Stage Of The Way Of The Heart, Once Practice Of The Way Of The Heart Is Formally Acknowledged To Be Based On Both True Hearing Of Me and Real Seeing Of Me, and (On That Basis) To Be Capable Of The Fully Technically Responsible Exercise Of The Basic (or Frontal) Spiritual Yoga Of The Way Of The Heart.

Practice Of The Way Of The Heart In The Context Of The Fully Established (or Actually Me-Seeing) "Basic" Fourth Stage Of Life Requires The Fullest Real Practice Of Cooperation (or The "Compulsory Dance" Of Love) With My Avatarically Self-Transmitted (and Always Blessing, or Constantly Baptizing) Divine Spiritual Presence.

All The Virtues and General Disciplines Already Associated With Both The Hearing Of Me and The Seeing Of Me Must Continue In The Context Of The Fully Established (or Actually Me-Seeing) "Basic" Fourth Stage Of Life In The Way Of The Heart.

In The Context Of That (Fully Established "Basic" Fourth) Stage Of Life In The Way Of The Heart, The Already Established (and Always Developing) functional, practical, relational, and Cultural Disciplines Are To Continue To Be Engaged (and To Be Developed) As A Demonstration Of True (and Truly Hearing, and Truly Seeing) Sila (or Really, and Consistently, ego-Surrendering, ego-Forgetting, and ego-Transcending psycho-physical Economy).

The Discipline Of Living In Fully Accountable (and Maximally Participatory) Affiliation With A Formally Designated Regional Community Of The Avataric Pan-Communion Of Adidam—or The Requirement To Demonstrate ego-Transcendence Through Relational Love, Consistent Service, Positively Productive Cooperation, and (Relative To All Aspects Of functional, practical, relational, and Cultural Discipline) Fullest Formal Accountability To The Sacred Cooperative Cultural Gathering Of All Formally Acknowledged Practitioners

Of The Way Of The Heart—Is, As Before, To Continue Also In The Context Of The Fully Established (or Actually Me-Seeing) "Basic" Fourth Stage Of Life (and At All Developmental Stages Beyond It) In The Way Of The Heart. And That Discipline Of Formal Cultural Accountability and Cooperative Participation Is, As Before, To Continue To Formally and Fully (and Ever More Fully) Take Into Account All Aspects Of The Appropriate, Right, and Necessary individual and Collective Responsibility Of My (Each and Every) Devotee, and This As A Fulfillment Of The Foundation (Student-Beginner) Embrace Of The Obligation To Live life As Service (and Always In The Manner Of Ruchira Avatara Seva—or ego-Surrendering, and ego-Forgetting, and More and More ego-Transcending Devotional Service To Me), and The Foundation (Student-Beginner) Embrace Of Fullest Formal (functional, practical, relational, and Cultural) Accountability To, and Maximally Participatory Affiliation With, A Formally Designated Regional Community Of My Formally Practicing Devotees.

In The Context Of The Fully Established (or Actually Me-Seeing) "Basic" Fourth-Stage-Of-Life Practice (and Frontal Spiritual Yoga) Of The Way Of The Heart, The "Conscious Process" and The Practice Of Spirit-"Conductivity" Are To Continue To Be Engaged In A (More and More Profoundly) Meditative Manner, Through (In The Case Of those Already Engaged In The Devotional Way Of Insight) The Continued Primary Responsive Practice Of self-Enquiry (In The Form "Avoiding Relationship?") or (In The Case Of those Already Engaged In The Devotional Way Of Faith) The Primary Responsive Practice Of "True Prayer" (In The Form Of The Prayer Of Remembrance—Which I Will Describe In This, My Testament Of Divine Secrets). And The Devotional Prayer Of Changes—Especially In Its Fully Developed, or (Spiritually) Fully Technically Responsible, Form (and Also, but Only Secondarily and Randomly, In Its Rudimentary Form)—Is (In The Case Of All My Devotees Practicing In and Beyond The Context Of The Fully Established "Basic" Fourth Stage Of Life In The Way Of The Heart) A Secondary (or Supportive) Meditative Exercise That Effectively and Positively Serves and Extends The Work Of <u>Spiritually</u> Purifying, Rebalancing, Regenerating, Healing, Realigning, and Otherwise Improving the conditional state of the body-mind (and Especially the frontal personality) and the conditions Associated With the individual (psycho-physical) being and all the relations of the individual (psycho-physical) being.

For My Devotees, True and Positively Effective Prayer Is Not The conventional (or merely exoteric) Religious Habit Of Pleading With The Divine (or, Really, Toward or At The Divine). For My Devotees, True and Positively Effective Prayer Is Not Based On The Un-Happy (or, In Any Manner, egoic) Sense Of Separation From The Divine. For My Devotees, True and Positively Effective Prayer Is The True and Right Esoteric Prayer-Practice (or Puja, or

Sacramental Exercise) Of ego-Transcending Devotional (and, In Due Course, Spiritual) Love-Communion With My Avatarically Self-Revealed (and By-My-Avataric-Divine-Grace Heart-Evident, and Self-Evidently Divine) Person. And That True and Positively Effective Esoteric Prayer Of My True Devotees Expresses (and Magnifies) Faithful (or Always-Already-Happy) Affirmation Of psycho-physical Intimacy (or Oneness) With The Inherent Love-Bliss Of My (Avatarically Self-Revealed, and Inherently egoless, and Self-Evidently Divine) Person—and, Thus, With The Inherent Completeness, and Inherent Perfectness Of Self-Existing and Self-Radiant Being (Itself).

Un-Happy (or ego-Based) Prayer Is The Search and The Plea (Full Of Doubt) For Remedies (or For Consolation Of the conditional self). The True and Positively Effective Prayer Of My Devotees Is Also Generated In The Midst Of conditional Existence, but It Is An Esoteric Process Of Devotional self-Surrender and Effective Opening Of the body-mind (From The Heart) To Commune Directly With My (Avatarically Self-Revealed, and Inherently egoless, and Self-Evidently Divine) Person Of Love-Bliss-Happiness.

False Prayer Is an egoic (and Fundamentally Un-Happy) act (and Search), but The Secret Of True and Positively Effective Esoteric Prayer Is That The Heart Itself Prays, and The Heart Itself Is The Prayer, and The Prayer Is Happiness Itself. Thus, In The Only-By-Me Revealed and Given Way Of The Heart (or Way Of Adidam), The Devotional Prayer Of Changes (Even In Its Rudimentary Form, and Especially In Its Fully Developed Form and Its, Spiritually, Fully Technically Responsible Exercise) Is An Effective Means For Invoking and Cooperating With My Avatarically Self-Transmitted Spiritual (and Always Blessing) Divine Presence—So That, Through Free Affirmations Of The Heart, conditions Are (To The Greatest Possible Degree) Positively Changed (By Intentionally Modifying The One Underlying and Pervasive Natural Energy Of Life, and the Naturally Multifarious energies Of Life, and My Avatarically Self-Transmitted, and Perfectly Subjective, and Truly all-and-All-Surrounding and all-and-All-Pervading Divine Spirit-Force Itself). In This Manner, My True Devotees Become Prayerful Instruments For conditional Changes That Serve their own human Well-being, ego-Transcending Practice, and Most Perfect Divine Self-Realization (and Also The human Well-being, ego-Transcendence, and Most Perfect Divine Self-Realization Of Even all human beings, and Also The Well-being, ego-Transcendence, and Most Perfect Divine Self-Realization Of Even all conditionally Manifested beings).

This Must Be Progressively Observed and Realized and Developed In The Practice Of The Only-By-Me Revealed and Given Way Of The Heart (or Way Of Adidam): The mind Always Directly Affects (or Modifies) The One Underlying and Pervasive Natural Energy (and the Naturally Multifarious functional energies) Of the conditional world (and Even In all the planes of the conditional world, or Of The Cosmic Mandala Of Life). Likewise (In The Case Of those who Are, By Means Of My Avatarically Self-Transmitted Divine Spiritual Grace, Aware Of My Avatarically Self-Revealed, and Perfectly Subjective, and Truly all-and-All-Surrounding and all-and-All-Pervading Divine Spirit-Presence), the mind Always Directly Affects (or Apparently Modifies) My Avatarically Self-Transmitted (Perfectly Subjectively "Located", and Truly All-Pervading) Divine Spirit-Current (Which Is Always Already Most Prior and Senior To The Pervasive Universal Energy, and the Secondary, or functional, energies, Of the Natural world). And The mind-Made Modifications Of The Universally Pervasive Natural Energy, and the Secondary (and Multifarious) Natural functional energies, and, Ultimately (or Even Most Directly), Of My Avatarically Self-Transmitted (Perfectly Subjectively "Located", and Truly all-and-All-Surrounding and all-and-All-Pervading) Divine Spirit-Current Affect and Directly Appear As all (Apparent) personal bodily states and Even all (Apparent) personal (physical and experiential) events in general. Then all personal (physical and experiential) events in general, and all personal bodily states, Directly Affect or Change the mind. And So On, and On.

The (Apparent) personal body-mind Is Directly Affected or Changed By <u>all</u> conditional events (or The Total Cosmic Mandala Of beings, forms, processes, and things). Likewise, the (Apparent) individual psycho-physical person Can (At Least To A Significant Degree—and Even, Potentially, To The Fullest Degree—Whether Immediately Or Over a longer, or even an indefinite, period of time) Serve To Directly Affect and Even Change all personal conditions and even <u>all</u> conditions, Universally. In Order To Do This, the individual psycho-physical person Must Pray—and, In Order To Pray (Truly, and Most Effectively), the individual psycho-physical person Must Be (and More and More Effectively Become) A Devotee Of My (Avatarically Self-Revealed) Transcendental, Inherently Spiritual, Inherently egoless, and Self-Evidently Divine Person. That Is To Say, the body-mind Must (By Means Of My Avatarically Self-Transmitted Divine Grace—and Progressively, or More and More Directly) Be Surrendered (or "Tuned") To My Avatarically Self-Transmitted (and Perfectly Subjective, and, Thus, Truly all-and-All-Surrounding and all-and-All-Pervading) Divine Spirit-Current—and My Avatarically Self-Transmitted Divine Spirit-Current (Thus Contacted—By Means Of My Avatarically Self-Transmitted Divine Grace, and Through The ego-Surrendering Practice Of My Devotee) Must Be Directly Affected (or Modified) Via An Intentional and Consistent Change Of the mind and the body. And, Therefore, the Apparent individual (or Separate psycho-physical person) Cannot, By ego-Efforts (or in and of himself or herself), Directly Affect and Change any or all conditions, Universally—but, By Consistently

Surrendering the ego-"I", and By Rightly Changing the mind and the body, and By Consistently Maintaining the Rightly Changed form (or forms) of mind and body, My Devotee Can (By Means Of My Avatarically Self-Transmitted Divine Grace) Serve Me, and Cooperate With Me, and Surrender all beings, forms, processes, and things To Me. And, Thus, By Effectively "getting out of the way" (or Removing The mental, and bodily, and, Altogether, egoic, Obstacles To My Divine Spiritual Infusion Of conditional events), and By Generating Entirely Positive and Intensely Auspicious and Profoundly Felt mind-forms (or Even mind-Transcending bodily Invocations Of Me), My Devotee Can Cooperatively Allow Me To Spiritually Pour Into, and To Directly and Newly and Positively Affect and Change, any particular condition (or conditions) At All.

In The Only-By-Me Revealed and Given Way Of The Heart, The (Spiritually) Fully Technically Responsible Exercise Of "True Prayer" Is An Intentional Act Of mind and body, Wherein and Whereby the Total body-mind Is Surrendered (Even Beyond The Universally Pervasive Natural Energy, and all the Naturally Multifarious functional energies, Of the conditional world) To My Avatarically Self-Revealed (and Inherently egoless, and Self-Evidently Divine) Person (The One and Only Person, or Inherently egoless Self-Condition and Source-Condition Of all-and-All).

In The Only-By-Me Revealed and Given Way Of The Heart, Truly Spiritually Effective (and, Spiritually, Fully Technically Responsible) "True Prayer" Is An Intentional Act Of mind and body, Wherein and Whereby the Total body-mind Is (By Means Of My Avatarically Self-Transmitted Divine Spiritual Grace, and Through The ego-Surrendering Practice Of My Devotee) "Tuned" To My Avatarically Self-Transmitted (and all-and-All-Surrounding and all-and-All-Pervading) Divine Spiritual Presence.

"True Prayer" Is Positive, ego-Transcending, and Fully psycho-physically Effective Prayer. If Prayer Is To Be Positively and Fully Effective, the Total body-mind Must Positively Change, At its Depth. That Is To Say, the mind (and, Indeed, The Total body-mind-Complex) Must Change—At The Conscious Level, The Subconscious Level, and Even The Unconscious Level.

Conventional Prayer Is A verbal (and egoic, or self-Contracted) Request To The mentally (and, Usually, Also emotionally) Presumed (Rather Than Directly, and Even bodily, Revealed) Divine. And conventional Prayer Is Uttered Under The Illusion (or With the idea and Feeling) That The (Very) Divine Is (Itself) Inherently and Necessarily Separate From the body-mind-self. But, For My Devotees, "True Prayer" Is Direct, ego-Transcending, and Total psycho-physical Participation In My (Avatarically Self-Revealed) Inherently egoless, and Self-Evidently Divine, Self-Condition (Which Is The Source-Condition Of all-and-All—and In Which every Apparent body-mind Is arising, changing, and passing away).

Conventional Prayers Are Weak (or Negatively Effective) Counter-Proposals. They Only Wish That some particular Undesirable condition (Presently Under Address) Will Change. Therefore, In conventional Prayer (or egoic Wishing), the image Deep In the mind (or the condition that Is Most Deeply and Most Consistently mentally, emotionally, and Even physically Affirmed, and, Therefore, Most Effectively Re-Created, or psycho-physically Continued) Is (Paradoxically) Not the Alternative condition Desired (or Prayed For), but it Is the Already Existing condition that one Desires (or Prays) Be Changed—and (Thus) the condition one Merely Wishes To Be Tends To Continue Not To Be (or, Otherwise, Continues To Persist Merely as the condition that Is Least Desired, and Even Most Feared).

In conventional Prayer, the verbal mind Wishes For Positive Change, but The perceptual and Deep Levels Of mind and body Only Address, Fear, and Compulsively Affirm The Continuation Of The Negative.

Therefore, By Truly Practicing The Only-By-Me Revealed and Given Way Of The Heart, Observe and Transcend The Process Of Ineffective (or Negatively Effective) and egoic (or Separative) Prayer, and Awaken To The Process Of True, Positively Effective, Really ego-Transcending, and Totally psycho-physically Participatory Prayer.

The Devotional Prayer Of Changes (Whether In Its Rudimentary Form Or In Its Fully Developed Form) Is, When Rightly Practiced, A Form Of "True Prayer". The Basis (and Principal Exercise) Of The Devotional Prayer Of Changes Is ego-Surrendering and ego-Forgetting (and Effectively ego-Transcending) Devotional (and, As The Case May Be, Spiritual) Heart-Communion (or Love-Communion) With Me. Therefore, The Basis (and Principal Exercise) Of The Devotional Prayer Of Changes Is ego-Surrendering and ego-Forgetting (and Effectively ego-Transcending) Devotional (and, As The Case May Be, Spiritual) Heart-Communion With My Avatarically-Born Bodily (Human) Divine Form, My Avatarically Self-Transmitted Spiritual (and Always Blessing) Divine Presence, and My Avatarically Self-Revealed (and Very, and Transcendental, and Perfectly Subjective, and Inherently Spiritual, and Inherently egoless, and Inherently Perfect, and Self-Evidently Divine) State (or Inherently egoless Love-Bliss-Condition).

The Fully Developed (or, Spiritually, Fully Technically Responsible) Devotional Prayer Of Changes (Which Is To Be Exercised Only In The Formal, Meditative Context) and (Secondarily, or Supportively) The Rudimentary Form Of The Devotional Prayer Of Changes (Engaged As A Fully Technically Responsible Spiritual Exercise, Done At Random, In The Context Of daily life, and, Perhaps, Occasionally, In The Formal, Meditative Context, As A Sometimes Alternative To The Fully Developed Form Of The Devotional Prayer Of Changes) Are To Be Practiced (Regularly, Frequently, Sometimes privately and Sometimes Collectively, and Always Really Effectively) By All My Formally Practicing Devotees, Once they Have Been Formally Acknowledged To Be Both Hearing and Seeing Me.

The Devotional Prayer Of Changes (Especially In Its, Spiritually, Fully Technically Developed Form) Involves Positive and Intelligent Use Of The Natural Relationship Between attention, perceptually-Based mind, the physical body, Free Feeling (or Non-Reactive emotion), The breath-Cycle, The Circle Of Spirit-"Conductivity", and My Avatarically Self-Transmitted Divine Spirit-Current (Including the Universal field of Natural etheric energy).

The Devotional Prayer Of Changes (Especially In Its, Spiritually, Fully Technically Developed Form) Uses the sensory mind (or the mind of perceptual images and sensations)—Rather Than the Abstract, Analytical, and (Typically verbal) conceptual mind—To Modify My Avatarically Self-Transmitted Divine Spirit-Energy (As A Means To Positively Modify, or Positively Change, the condition of the body-mind, or of any other person, object, condition, or event). The Principle (or Law) That Enables the perceptual mind To Effect Such Modifications Of My Avatarically Self-Transmitted Divine Spirit-Current (and, Subsequently, Such Positive Changes Of the condition of the body-mind, or of any other person, object, condition, or event) Is Contained In The Observation That My Avatarically Self-Transmitted Divine Spirit-Current (or My Avatarically Self-Transmitted Divine Spirit-Energy, Which, By Means Of My Avatarically Self-Transmitted Divine Spiritual Grace, "Lives", or Pervades and "Breathes" and Is, the body-mind, and even all conditional forms and events) and the body-mind (or even any conditional form or event) itself (including its Responsive etheric energy-field) Will Respond Just As Directly, and In The Same Manner (Whether Positively Or Negatively), To a perceptual thought (Clearly and Fully perceived and Deeply Affirmed) As To a gross physical (or sensory) condition or event.

In The Practice Of The Fully Developed (or, Spiritually, Fully Technically Responsible) Devotional Prayer Of Changes (Which I Will Now Describe To You, and Which You Should Practice, With Significant Regularity and Frequency, Once Your Practice Of The Way Of The Heart Is Formally Acknowledged To Be Fully Established On The Firm Basis Of Both Hearing Me and Seeing Me), My Avatarically Self-Transmitted Divine Spirit-Current Is Conducted Via The Two-Part Cycle Of the breath (or The Simple and Basic Process Of exhalation-Release and inhalation-Reception, Engaged As Also In The Case Of The Rudimentary Devotional Prayer Of Changes).

To Begin Any Occasion Of The Fully Developed (or, Spiritually, Fully Technically Responsible) Devotional Prayer Of Changes, Engage The Devotional and Spiritual Exercise Of ego-Surrendering and ego-Forgetting (and Effectively ego-Transcending) Heart-Communion With Me—By Means Of The Fully Established Devotional and Spiritual Exercise (or Primary Practice) Of Ruchira Avatara Bhakti Yoga (Which Primary Practice Is Searchless Beholding Of Me). This Primary Practice Of (Searchlessly Me-Beholding) Heart-Communion With Me Involves (and Requires) ego-Surrendering and ego-Forgetting (and Effectively ego-Transcending) Devotional and Spiritual Heart-Communion With My Avatarically-Born Bodily (Human) Divine Form, My Avatarically Self-Transmitted Spiritual (and Always Blessing) Divine Presence, and My Avatarically Self-Revealed (and Very, and Transcendental, and Perfectly Subjective, and Inherently Spiritual, and Inherently egoless, and Inherently Perfect, and Self-Evidently Divine) State—and (Thus and Thereby) ego-Surrendering and ego-Forgetting (and Effectively ego-Transcending) Devotional and Spiritual Heart-Communion (or Love-Communion) With My "Bright" (Spiritual, Transcendental, Divine, and Inherently Un-conditional) Love-Bliss-Condition. And (In The First Actually Seeing Stage Of The Way Of The Heart) This Devotional and Spiritual Exercise (Which Is The Principal Exercise Of The Devotional Prayer Of Changes, In Both Its Fully Developed Form and Its Rudimentary Form) Must Be Exercised To The Degree That (By Means Of My Avatarically Self-Transmitted Divine Spiritual Grace) It Becomes Total psycho-physical Identification With (and Total psycho-physical Affirmation Of) My "Bright" (Spiritual, Transcendental, Divine, and Inherently Un-conditional) Love-Bliss-Condition (or Avatarically Self-Transmitted Spirit-Current Of Divine Love-Bliss). Indeed, With and Because Of That Devotional and Spiritual Identification and Affirmation, This Exercise Of The Fully Developed (or, Spiritually, Fully Technically Responsible) Devotional Prayer Of Changes Must (By Means Of My Avatarically Self-Transmitted Divine Spiritual Grace) Become An Effortless, and Profoundly Meditative, Whole bodily (or Total psycho-physical) Relinquishment Of All Identification With, and All Affirmation Of, Particular (and Even All) Problems, and particular (and even all) Negative conditions or states.

When, By Means Of My Avatarically Self-Transmitted Divine Spiritual Grace, This Heart-Communion, Heart-Identification, Heart-Affirmation, and Heart-Relinquishment Is (Thus, As A Profound, and Simple, or Single, psycho-physical—or Whole bodily—Attitude, or Disposition) Meditatively Established, Fully exhale (Generally Via the nose, Rather Than Via an open mouth, and With the tongue Pressed Lightly To the roof of the mouth, and Even After Any Number Of Preparatory "Conductivity" Cycles Of To-Me-Responsive inhalation-Reception and exhalation-Release Of My Avatarically Self-Transmitted, and

Living, and Purifying Divine Spirit-Current). As You exhale (Even After Any Number Of Responsive "Conductivity" Cycles Of Preparation), Feel The Love-Bliss-Current (or Spirit-Energy) Of My Own Avatarically Self-Revealed Divine Person Pass Down and Out, Through The Frontal Line, Thereby Eliminating (or Carrying, Throwing Down, and Releasing) all Negative qualities, reactions, and conditions of the body-mind (and in the relations of the body-mind). In This Manner, all Negative qualities, reactions, and conditions Are To Be Acknowledged, Fully Perceived or Felt, and Liberally Released (Intentionally, and By A Deep and Fully Opened Downward Gesture Of attention, breath, body, emotion, and sensory mind) Via The Frontal Line—and, At Last, Thrown Out, Via the eliminative organs and the feet.

Then (Generally Via the nose, Rather Than Via an open mouth, and With the tongue Pressed Lightly To the roof of the mouth) inhale The Tangible Spirit-Current Of My Avatarically Self-Transmitted Divine Love-Bliss Upwards, Via The Spinal Line, To The Brain Core (As In The Conservation and Conversion Of conventional orgasm In "Emotional-Sexual Devotional Communion"). And (With the eyes Closed and Turned Up and Back) Hold and Press the breath (and The Tangible Spirit-Current Of My Avatarically Self-Transmitted Divine Love-Bliss) In (and Into) The Brain Core (or The Total Central Region Of the head and brain)—All The While Feeling Toward The Matrix Of My Avatarically Self-Transmitted Divine Spirit-Energy Infinitely Above The Total Crown Of the head. (In Fact, Any Number Of Cycles Of Both exhalation-Release and inhalation-Reception Of My Avatarically Self-Transmitted Divine Spirit-Current, Upwards In The Spinal Line, May Be Done—Each Ending With The Act Of Holding and Pressing The Tangible Spirit-Current Of My Avatarically Self-Transmitted Divine Love-Bliss In and Into The Brain Core. And the bodily base May Be Locked, or Else Rhythmically Tensed Upwards, In The Process, To Help Draw Up With inhalation, or To "Throw" Upwards With exhalation, or To Hold and Press My Avatarically Self-Transmitted Divine Spirit-Energy In and Into The Brain Core. However, The Final Gesture In That Exercise Should Be a Full inhalation Of The Tangible Spirit-Current Of My Avatarically Self-Transmitted Divine Love-Bliss To and Into The Brain Core, Via The Spinal Line.)

In Due Course, While Steadily and Fully Breathing, Holding, and Pressing My Avatarically Self-Transmitted Divine Spirit-Energy In and Into The Brain Core, Intentionally and Fully "Picture" the Already Changed (or Rightly and Positively Composed) state of any condition that You Would Have (or Presently Intend To) Be Changed. "Picture" that Already Changed state or condition In Detail, In a "Pictured" form that Is Made Of perceptual thought, or Of subtle and psychic versions of all the senses. Do This (Even Repetitively, and Perhaps With Several Cycles Of Upward exhalation-Release, Into The Spinal Line and

The Brain Core, and Upward inhalation-Reception, Into The Spinal Line and The Brain Core) Until The "Picture" Is Clear and Fully Detailed.

Then the new condition (As it Is "Pictured") Must (With Full Heart-Conviction) Be Whole bodily (or With the Total body-mind) Felt, Affirmed, Believed, Presumed, and Identified With—and it Must (Thereafter) Be Consistently and Actively Allowed present and future time and place (and person), In Order To Manifest bodily, and (Altogether) Concretely, In both internal and external circumstances or conditions, and (Even Especially) In The Form Of All Necessary New Intentional Activity (or New Discipline). This Final Stage Of The Fully Developed Devotional Prayer Of Changes Is To Be Done By inhaling (or Via Any Number Of Cycles Of Downward inhalation-Reception and Downward exhalation-Release Of My Avatarically Self-Transmitted Divine Spirit-Energy) Into The Frontal Line, From My Avatarically Self-Revealed Radiant Divine Matrix (or Ascended "Bright" Feeling-Place) Infinitely Above The Total Crown Of the head, and Down Through The "Picture" (Such That The "Picture" Itself Is Drawn Down Into the body and, Via Heart-Feeling, and Via Any Number Of Cycles Of inhalation-Reception and exhalation-Release, Into The Totality Of the world, As A More and More Concrete Modification Of The Tangible Love-Bliss-Current Of The Spirit-Energy Of My Avatarically Self-Revealed Divine Person).

When (In The Fullness Of The Course Of This Exercise Of The Devotional Prayer Of Changes) You Feel (From The Heart and In the body) That The Whole bodily (or Total psycho-physical) Act Of Affirmation and Affirmative Reception Has (In A Very Basic Sense) Been Truly and Fully Made, Then Simply Let The Prayer Be (and Continue To Become Concretely Effective), Through The Positive Whole bodily Attitude Of Faith (or A Simple Feeling-Affirmation Of The Already Concretely Changed conditions), While You Otherwise Remain Free Of conceptual thoughts or doubts. Therefore, As The Meditative Act Of The Devotional Prayer Of Changes Finishes Itself, Go On To Other Prayerful or Meditative Activities—or, Otherwise, Simply get up From The Prayer Seat and Resume Your other or daily activities.

Such Devotional Prayer Of Changes—Done Either privately Or Collectively, and Always Associated With Gratitude and Growing Faith (or A Positive and Strong-Feeling Heart and body-mind)—Can Make Great Creative and Positively Effective Use Of My Avatarically Self-Transmitted Divine Spirit-Power As The Inherently Perfect (and Inherently and Perfectly Subjective) Medium Of Observable Changes.

Nevertheless (or In Any Case), For All My Devotees, The Most Basic "True Prayer" Is The Prayer Of ego-Transcending Devotional (and, In Due Course, Spiritual) Communion With Me. Indeed, For My Devotees, All "True Prayer" Is ego-Surrendering, ego-Forgetting, and More and More (and, At Last, Most

Perfectly) ego-Transcending Devotional (and, As The Case May Be, Spiritual) Communion With My (Avatarically Self-Revealed, and Inherently egoless, and Self-Evidently Divine) Person Of Love-Bliss. Therefore, In The Only-By-Me Revealed and Given Way Of The Heart, The Most Fundamental Effectiveness Of "True Prayer" Is Not In The Change Of the body-mind-self and its relations, but It Is In The Surrender and Transcending Of the body-mind-self (and Of conditional Existence Itself) In Me—The Inherently egoless, and Perfectly Subjective, and Self-Evidently Divine Self-Condition and Source-Condition Of all-and-All.

I Am "True Prayer" Itself. I Am The Prayer Of My True Devotee. My True Devotee Does Not Pray To Me For any "thing". My True Devotee Prays As Me, and Only For Me—Surrendering Separate and Separative self To Me (To The Degree Of Truly ego-Forgetting and Effectively ego-Transcending Feeling-Contemplation Of Only Me). Therefore, By Surrendering To Feel (and Thereby Contemplate) Me-Only, My True Devotee Forgets and Transcends All Seeking and (Thus) Becomes The Prayer Of Contemplation-Only (Without even any thought in mind). For My Such True Devotee, I Am The Prayer Itself—For I Am The Inherently Perfect Means Of Every Spiritually "Bright" Revelation, and I Am The Perfect Realization (Itself).

To My Devotees who Contemplate Me-Only, I (The Spiritually "Bright" Divine and Only One) Am Revealed (By Means Of My Avatarically Self-Transmitted Divine Spiritual Grace) As I Am. And, In Due Course, The "True Prayer" Of Me-Contemplation Is (and Will Be) "Answered" Most Perfectly In Me, By The Gift Of Divine Self-Realization (Spiritually "Bright", Inherently Most Perfect, Most Perfectly Prior To All "Difference", and Most Perfectly Free Of Want).

The Prayer Of Remembrance Is A (Spiritually, Technically Fully Responsible) Form Of True (and Only Me-Contemplative) Prayer. When The Prayer Of Remembrance Is Rightly Practiced, My Devotee Becomes The Prayer Of Contemplation-Only, self-Surrendered and thought-free In Me. Therefore, The Prayer Of Remembrance Is The To-Me-Responsive Form Of The Combined "Conscious Process" and "Conductivity" Practice Engaged (By My Devotees who Practice The Devotional Way Of Faith) During The First Actually Seeing Stage Of The Way Of The Heart.

The Prayer Of Remembrance Involves The "Conscious Process" and The (Fully Technically Responsible) Spiritual "Conductivity" Practice Of Feeling-Contemplative Devotion To Me Via Heart-Felt Invocation, Using My (Principal and Single) Name "Da" (With "the tongue of the mind").

This (Fully Technically Responsible) Spiritual Yoga Of My Principal Name ("Da") Is To Be Engaged In Direct Devotional and Spiritual Communion With

Me, By Means Of The Spiritual (or Spirit-"Conductivity") Exercise Of The Three-Part "General" Practice Of "Conductivity" I Have Given To Be Practiced By All My Formally Practicing Devotees (and Which I Have Been Describing, and Will Continue To Describe, In This, My Testament Of Divine Secrets). Thus, My Seeing Devotee (Practicing The Prayer Of Remembrance) Is (First, By Means Of The Primary Practice Of Ruchira Avatara Bhakti Yoga, Which Practice Is Searchless Beholding Of Me) To Surrender the body-mind To Me By (Whole bodily) Receiving My Avatarically Self-Transmitted Divine and Tangible Spirit-Current Of Love-Bliss, From Infinitely Above the head and the mind, and (Then) By Radiating My Avatarically Self-Transmitted Divine Spirit-Current Of Love-Bliss From The Heart In all directions (or Boundlessly). In This, the body itself Is To Be Totally and Simultaneously Relaxed Into My Avatarically Self-Transmitted Divine Spirit-Current—In The Frontal Line, Downwards To the bodily base. In This Practice (Of The Prayer Of Remembrance), the breath Is To Be Associated With Spirit-"Conductivity" In The Frontal Line, By Easefully Heart-Felt Name-Invocation Of Me Via each inhalation—Relaxing and Opening The Frontal Line (head To bodily base), and (Via the inhalation) Feeling, Breathing, Receiving, Drawing, and Sometimes Pressing My Avatarically Self-Transmitted Divine Spirit-Energy (Which Is Revealed, By Means Of My Avatarically Self-Transmitted Divine Spiritual Grace, In Response To The Invocation Of Me By Means Of My Avatarically Self-Revealed Divine Name) Downwards In The Frontal Line (From the head, the face, and the throat To the chest, the solar plexus, and the abdomen), While Internally Applying Appropriate Upward Tension At the bodily base—and By Easefully Heart-Felt Name-Invocation Of Me Via each exhalation—Simply Relaxing the Total body-mind-self In The Frontal Line, and (Via the exhalation) Directly Conducting and Releasing My Avatarically Self-Transmitted (and By-My-Avataric-Divine-Spiritual-Grace-Received) Divine Spirit-Energy Downwards Into The Frontal Line Of the body, and Then (Simply) Relaxing and Releasing My Avatarically Self-Transmitted Divine Spirit-Current Into Continuity With The Spinal Line, While (Nevertheless) Always Keeping attention itself and My Avatarically Self-Transmitted Spiritual (and Always Blessing) Divine Tangible Current Of Love-Bliss Itself Steadily and Fully Focused In The bodily Context (and In The abdominal Position) Of The Frontal Line. And This Entire Prayer-Process Of Spirit-"Conductivity" Is (In Accordance With All My Various Instructions Relative To The "General" Form Of "Conductivity" Practice In The Way Of The Heart) To Be Associated With All Appropriate bodily Locks (Especially Of the bodily base), and With All Other Appropriate bodily Attitudes (Including The Closing Of the eyes, and The Turning Of them Up and Back, and The Pressing Of the tongue Lightly To the roof of the mouth), and (In General) While Engaging the breath Via the nose (Rather Than Via an open mouth)—and While Always (Tacitly) Receiving Me (Downwards) From My Matrix-Position (Infinitely Above the body and the mind).

As A General Rule, The Prayer Of Remembrance Is, In Every Particular Occasion Of Formal Meditation, To Be Only Randomly (or Artfully and Easefully) Associated With The Parts Of The breath-Cycle (and The Practice Of breathing-"Conductivity"). Nevertheless, In Every Occasion Of Formal Meditation (In The Context Of The Exercise Of The Prayer Of Remembrance), There Should Also Be Random Concentrated Periods Of Significant (but Comfortable) Numbers Of breath-Sequences, During Which The Prayer Of Remembrance (and breathing-"Conductivity") Is Intentionally timed (or Synchronized) with each (and every) inhalation and each (and every) exhalation. And This Alternation Of Random and Concentrated Associations Of The Prayer Of Remembrance With The Cycle Of breathing-"Conductivity" Should Be Continued (In Any and Every Occasion Of Such Formal Meditation), Until (By Means Of My Avatarically Self-Transmitted Divine Spiritual Grace) A perceptible Heart-Opening Is (In Due Course) Felt—Generally In The Middle Station Of The Heart, and With A Simultaneous Feeling Of Openness (or Release) Communicated In The Left Side Of The Heart (or, Simply, In the gross physical body Generally).

When (In Any and Every Occasion Of Formal Meditation In The Form Of The Prayer Of Remembrance) This Opening Of Heart and body Occurs (By Means Of My Avatarically Self-Transmitted Divine Spiritual Grace), There Should Be An Accompanying Feeling Of Release and Fullness (Of My Avatarically Self-Transmitted Divine Spirit-Current Of Tangible Love-Bliss) In The Total Frontal Line Of the gross physical body (and the mind Should Likewise Become Still In This Feeling-Contemplation Of Me). When This True Spiritual Event Occurs (In Any Occasion Of Formal Meditation In The Form Of The Prayer Of Remembrance), Name-Invocation Of Me Can Itself Be Allowed To Become Random Again (Rather Than timed with the breath)—and (Alternatively) Name-Invocation Itself Can Be Temporarily Relinquished (Even, Perhaps, Until The Particular Occasion Of Formal Meditation Naturally Comes To An End, In Spiritual Me-Fullness). Thus, In Any Fully Demonstrated Occasion Of Right Practice Of The Prayer Of Remembrance, The Specific Practice Of Name-Invocation Of Me Eventually Becomes The Entirely Non-verbal (or mind-Free) Practice Of Direct Feeling-Contemplation Of (and Inherent Feeling-Identification With) My Avatarically Self-Transmitted Divine Spirit-Current (and My Avatarically Self-Revealed, and Inherently egoless, and Self-Evidently Divine, Person, or Inherently Free Self-Condition) Of Love-Bliss. And, As This Practice Develops Over time, The Feeling-Contemplation Of My Avatarically

Self-Transmitted Divine Love-Bliss-Person Deepens (head To base)—and It Becomes More and More Effective, As Release Of Spiritually (and humanly) limiting conditions in the body-mind. Indeed, Once The Heart Itself (Left Side and Middle Station) and The Total Frontal Line Of the body-mind Are (By Means Of My Avatarically Self-Transmitted Divine Spiritual Grace, and Through The Practice Of The Prayer Of Remembrance—or, Otherwise, Of self-Enquiry and Re-Cognition—During The First Actually Seeing Stage Of The Way Of The Heart) Stably Opened In My Avatarically Self-Transmitted Divine Spirit-Current Of Love-Bliss (By Means Of The Only-By-Me Revealed and Given Samadhi Of The "Thumbs"), Even The Right Side Of The Heart Will (In Due Course) Open, With The Simultaneous Awakening Of Inherent Self-Identification With The Witness-Position Of Consciousness. (And, In That Event, Fully Stabilized, There Is The True and Necessary Basis For The Transition To The "Perfect Practice" Of The Way Of The Heart.)

Young people Practicing The Only-By-Me Revealed and Given Way Of The Heart (or Way Of Adidam) In The Context Of The Third Stage Of Life (and, To Varying Degrees, Also children Practicing The Way Of The Heart In The Context Of The First and Second Stages Of Life) Are Also Called To Practice A Rudimentary Form Of The "True Prayer" Of Simple Name-Invocation Of Me (Via My Principal Name, "Da", or Via Any Other Of My Avatarically Self-Revealed Divine Names, or Combined Avataric Divine Names and Avataric Divine Descriptive Titles, Which I Have Given To Be Engaged In The Practice Of Simple Name-Invocation Of Me), Rather Than To Develop Any Other (or Any More Elaborate or Complex) Form Of The "Conscious Process" Of The Only-By-Me Revealed and Given Way Of The Heart. And they Are Called To Do This Until they Achieve near-adult age (or Approximately eighteen years of age), or (Otherwise, At Least In Some Cases) Until (At a Somewhat earlier age) they Demonstrate The Aptitude (or The Workable Interest) That Equips and Allows them To Begin To Develop The Experimental "Consideration" Of The Two Devotional Ways (In The Student-Beginner Manner). Therefore (Until A Greater Aptitude Develops), My early-life Devotees Are To Practice Simple Name-Invocation Of Me, As A Simple Act Of Devotional Remembrance Of Me, and As A Devotional (and Heart-Felt) Act Of Simple and Simply Activated and Expressed Faith In Me (and ego-Surrendering, ego-Forgetting, and, More and More, Truly ego-Transcending Feeling-Contemplation Of Me). In their Case, The Simple Practice Of Invocation Of Me By Means Of My Avatarically Self-Revealed Divine Name—Which Practice Is Also To Be Sacramentally Engaged, and Also, As Necessary (or, Otherwise, Randomly), Engaged, Even In The Context Of Formal Meditation, By All Formally Acknowledged adult Practitioners Of The Way Of The Heart—Involves Simple Feeling-Invocation

Of Me Via My Principal Name, "Da", or Via Any Other Of My Avatarically Self-Revealed Divine Names (or Combined Avataric Divine Names and Avataric Divine Descriptive Titles) Which I Have Given To Be Engaged In The Practice Of Simple Name-Invocation Of Me, and Most Often Expressed silently (With "the tongue of the mind"), and As A Feeling-Act Of Heart, but (In Any Case) Always Engaged In Random Association With The Feeling-Practice Of inhalation-Reception Of Positive Feeling-Fullness and exhalation-Release Of Negative or Reactive emotions, thoughts, and states of experience. However, The early-life Practice Of Such Feeling-Invocation Of Me Is Not Otherwise A Specifically (or Directly) Spiritual Exercise. That Is To Say, My early-life Devotees Are To breathe (or Conduct Feeling) In Relation To Me (Regarded—or, Otherwise, Recollected—In My Avatarically-Born Bodily Human Divine Form), and Also In The Context Of the Universal etheric energy-field Naturally Associated With bodily Existence In The gross physical Domain Of Cosmic Nature, but (As A General Rule) they Are Not Otherwise Called To Practice Specifically (or Directly) Spiritual Exercises, or To Practice Any Otherwise Technical Response To My Direct (Avatarically Self-Transmitted) Divine Spirit-Baptism. Rather, My early-life Devotees Are Called To Practice The Only-By-Me Revealed and Given Way Of The Heart In Devotional Recognition-Response To My Avatarically Self-Revealed (and Ever-Speaking) Divine Word and My Avatarically Self-Manifested (and Ever-Living) Divine Leelas Of My Life and Work, and In The early-life Practitioner's Right (Devotionally Me-Recognizing and Devotionally To-Me-Responsive) Devotional Relationship To Me As The Divine Heart-Master (Now, and Forever Hereafter, Given In and Via and <u>As</u> My Avatarically-Born Bodily Human Divine Form). And, Whatever Simple (and Even Faithful) Feeling-Awareness May (By Means Of My Avatarically Self-Transmitted Divine Grace, and Through These Means) Develop Relative To My Avatarically Given (Spiritual, Transcendental, Inherently egoless, and Self-Evidently Divine) Self-Revelation In The Case Of children and young people In The Way Of The Heart (all of whom, As My early-life Devotees Within The Formal Sacred Cooperative Cultural Gathering Of All Formally Acknowledged Practitioners Of The Way Of The Heart, Are Given Many Unique Exercises By Which To Feel The Total Divine Mystery Of Existence In The Context Of The First, The Second, and The Third Stages Of Life), It Is (As A General Rule and Possibility) Only Later, As My By-Me-Spiritually-Initiated <u>adult</u> Devotees, That they Are To Be Called To Practice Specifically Spiritual Exercises In Devotional and Spiritual Response To My Avatarically Self-Transmitted Divine Spirit-Baptism.

In The Case Of self-Enquiry (In Formal Meditation Practice, During The First Actually Seeing Stage Of The Way Of The Heart), Spirit-"Conductivity" Via the inhaled and the exhaled breaths Is To Be Performed According To All My

Various Instructions Relative To The "General" Form Of Spiritually Activated (and, Spiritually, Fully Technically Responsible) "Conductivity" Practice In The Way Of The Heart, and In A Generally Similar Manner (and With The Same bodily Locks and bodily Attitudes, and With The Same Focus In The Exercise Associated With My Spiritual Descent In The Frontal Line) As In The Case Of The Prayer Of Remembrance—Except That, In The Case Of Such (Spiritually, Fully Technically Responsible) self-Enquiry, The "General" Form Of breathing-"Conductivity" Is To Be Done Only At Random (or Occasionally), Rather Than (As Is The Case During Certain Sustained Periods Of Formal Meditation Practice Of The Prayer Of Remembrance) Repetitively and With each breath. And, In The Case (or In The Context) Of Such (Spiritually, Fully Technically Responsible) self-Enquiry, The "General" Form Of breathing-"Conductivity" May Be Engaged In time With Any Random Instance Of The Exercise Of The "Conscious Process", and The "General" Form Of breathing-"Conductivity" May, Otherwise (In other Random moments), Be Engaged Apart From Any Intentional Coincidence With The "Conscious Process" (Just As The "Conscious Process" May Also, In Its Random moments, Be Sometimes Exercised Apart From Any Intentional Coincidence With The Process Of The "General" Form Of breathing-"Conductivity"). Likewise, In The Case Of self-Enquiry In The First Actually Seeing Stage Of The Way Of The Heart, The Artful Combination Of The "Conscious Process" and The Process Of The "General" Form Of Spirit-"Conductivity" Should (In Any Occasion Of Formal Meditation, and More and More) Become (By Virtue Of The Magnification Of The Searchless Heart-Feeling-Contemplation Of Me) A Profound Opening Of The (Progressively Total) Frontal Line, With The Same Effects (and, Eventually, By Means Of The Only-By-Me Revealed and Given Samadhi Of The "Thumbs", With The Same Ultimate Awakening Of Inherent Self-Identification With The Witness-Position Of Consciousness) Developed In The Case Of The Prayer Of Remembrance.

In Either Case, The Exercise Of The "General" Form Of Spirit-"Conductivity" Associated With Both self-Enquiry and The Prayer Of Remembrance In The First Actually Seeing Stage Of The Way Of The Heart Emphasizes The Relaxation, Opening, Purification, Rebalancing, Spiritual Infusion, and Downward Polarization Of The Frontal Line Of the body-mind.

In The Case Of each and all Of My Listening Devotees, My Hearing Devotees, and My Seeing Devotees, Both Formal Meditation and Formal Sacramental Devotion (or Ruchira Avatara Puja) Are Always To Be Done In The Context Of The Sacrament Of Universal Sacrifice (Which Is The Principal physically Enacted Sign Of Devotional and, As The Case May Be, Spiritual Communion With Me Practiced daily By All My Listening Devotees, All My Hearing Devotees, and All My Seeing Devotees).

The Prayer Of Remembrance (Like self-Enquiry, and, In General, Any Of The Other Combined Forms Of The "Conscious Process" and "Conductivity" Practice, In The Way Of The Heart) Is (In The Case Of those who Otherwise Practice It In daily Formal Meditation) Generally To Be Performed At Random (Rather Than Synchronous With each and every breath) During Occasions Of Formal Sacramental Devotion (and, Otherwise, As A General Rule, In all other circumstances of life Outside The Context Of Formal Meditation).

In Formal Meditation, The Prayer Of Remembrance (Like Any Of The Other Combined Forms Of The "Conscious Process" and "Conductivity" Practice, In The Way Of The Heart) Is (In The Case Of those who Practice It In daily Formal Meditation) Generally To Be Done In silence (With "the tongue of the mind")—but, During Occasions Of Formal Sacramental Devotion, Regular Practitioners Of The Prayer Of Remembrance (or Even My Any Devotee who Is Then Moved To Invoke Me By Means Of My Avatarically Self-Revealed Divine Name) May, As An Option, Invoke Me (By My Principal Name, "Da") <u>vocally</u> (Even, Perhaps—According To the circumstances—Such That The Invocation Is audible To others).

Also, In Formal Meditation Via The Prayer Of Remembrance (or Via Even Any Form Of "True Prayer", In The Way Of The Heart), Each Invocation Is (As A General, but Always Optional, Rule) To Be Marked With A Bead On A Mala (or Rosary)—but, During Occasions Of Formal Sacramental Devotion, the body-mind (or attention) Must Be Constantly Activated To Participate (attentively, and, Variously, Even bodily and mentally) In The Sacred Ritual. Therefore, During Occasions Of Formal Sacramental Devotion, The Mala (or Rosary) May (As Appropriate) Be Either Worn Around the neck Or Held In the hand Or Used In Mala Japa.

Mala Japa Is Intensive Prayer That Uses A Mala (or Rosary) To Mark Each Cycle (or, Otherwise, Each Principal Utterance). Either Simple Invocation Of Me Via My Principal Name, "Da", or Via Any Other Of My Avatarically Self-Revealed Divine Names (or Combined Avataric Divine Names and Avataric Divine Descriptive Titles) Which I Have Given To Be Engaged In The Practice Of Simple Name-Invocation Of Me (Which Invocation May Be Practiced At Random Not Only By children and young people In The Way Of The Heart, but Also By Any and All adult Practitioners Of The Way Of The Heart) <u>Or</u> (Otherwise) Ruchira Avatara Naama Japa (At First, Practiced Experimentally By All Student-Beginners, and Then, By "Considered" Choice, Practiced By Practitioners Of The Devotional Way Of Faith In The Student-Beginner Stage, and The Intensive Listening-Hearing Stage, and The Would-Be-Seeing Stage Of The Way Of The Heart) <u>Or</u> The Prayer Of Remembrance (Which Is Practiced By Practitioners Of The Devotional Way Of Faith In The First Actually Seeing

Stage Of The Way Of The Heart) Should Generally (or As A General, but Always Optional, Rule) Be Engaged In The Form Of Mala Japa. Even Apart From Occasions Of Formal Meditation, These Faithful Devotional Practices Can Be Engaged As Simple, Heart-Felt Mala Japa—Either silently (With "the tongue of the mind") Or vocally (In An Outwardly audible or inaudible Manner). Such Mala Japa, Like self-Enquiry, Can Be Engaged At Random times of day (In any setting or circumstance), As An Alternative To Casual physical, emotional, or mental self-Indulgence and Inappropriate or Untimely Use Of conventional Leisure.[143] Therefore, those Practitioners Of The Way Of The Heart who Practice Either Ruchira Avatara Naama Japa Or The Prayer Of Remembrance, and Even All Practitioners Of The Way Of The Heart (At any age), All Of whom Practice At Least Occasional (or, Otherwise, Random) Simple Name-Invocation Of Me, Should Carry A Mala (or Rosary) With them At all times—and they Should (As Appropriate) Use The Mala (or Rosary) As A Simple Means For Gathering attention Into The Practice Of "True Prayer" (or Even Simple Name-Invocation Of Me), and they Should (In all times and places) Practice Heart-Felt Invocation Of Me, and (Via That Invocation) they Should Practice Heart-Felt Contemplation Of My Avatarically-Born Bodily (Human) Divine Form, My Avatarically Self-Transmitted Spiritual (and Always Blessing) Divine Presence, and My Avatarically Self-Revealed (and Very, and Transcendental, and Perfectly Subjective, and Inherently Spiritual, and Inherently egoless, and Inherently Perfect, and Self-Evidently Divine) State. In The Case Of My By-Me-Spiritually-Initiated Devotees, Such Practices Should Also Involve (or Always Directly Become) Heart-Felt and Whole bodily Reception Of My Avatarically Self-Transmitted Spirit-Power Of Divine Love-Bliss, and Simultaneous Heart-Surrender To My Deep Self-Revelation Of My Divine Self-Condition (Which Is The Divine Source-Condition Of all-and-All) That Is The Always-Already-State Of Merely (and Self-Radiantly, or "Brightly") Being. (If any present circumstance Does Not Permit Sufficient Privacy For Mala Japa, Practitioners Of Any By-Me-Given Form Of "True Prayer" Should Simply Practice The Prayer, or Invocation, Internally, As Usual, but Without The Mala or Any Other External, or physical, Indications. And Any and All Practitioners Of The Way Of The Heart who, On A Regular Basis, Practice Any Form Of "True Prayer", or who, As Must Be The Case, Practice At Least Random, or Occasional, Invocation Of Me By Means Of My Avatarically Self-Revealed Divine Name, Should, Where any present circumstance Does Not Permit Sufficient Privacy For Mala Japa, Simply Practice Such Prayerful Communion With Me As An Internally Generated Exercise, Directed To My Avatarically-Born Bodily Human Divine Form, and To My Avatarically Self-Transmitted Spiritual, and Always Blessing, Divine Presence, and To My Avatarically Self-Revealed, and Very, and Transcendental, and

Perfectly Subjective, and Inherently Spiritual, and Inherently egoless, and Inherently Perfect, and Self-Evidently Divine State—but Thus Engaged Without The Mala, and Without The Performance Of Any Otherwise Outward Signals. And Such Informal Practices May Even Be Engaged During common social activities and With the eyes opened to the world.)

Mala Japa (Whether Random Or Formal) May (and Even Should) Lead To Deep Meditation, but Deep Meditation (Itself) Necessarily Requires (or Inevitably and Naturally Manifests) The Relaxation (or Even Release) Of bodily Awareness and All physical Supports Of Meditation (Such As The Cyclic Handling Of A Mala). Therefore, Mala Japa Itself (Before It Becomes, or Gives Way To, Deep Meditation) Is Basically A Superior bodily Exercise Of the frontal personality (and A Discipline Of the frontal personality Via The Mechanics Of The Frontal Line). Truly, Mala Japa Is A Form Of physically Engaged Sacramental Devotion (or Puja, or Yajna[144]).

Physically (and Formally) Engaged Sacramental Devotion Involves The Externalization Of attention Via Intentional Activation Of the body-mind (or frontal personality). In Contrast To This, Formal (and Deep) Meditation Involves Progressive Relinquishment Of physical (and other Outward-Directed frontal) activity. Generally, daily Practice Of The Way Of The Heart Should Involve An Appropriately Balanced (and Formal) Measure Of Meditative <u>and</u> Outward-Directed activities, but Even all Outward-Directed activities Are To Be Realized As Forms Of functionally Expressed Heart-Practice (and, In The Case Of My By-Me-Spiritually-Initiated Devotees, True and Spiritual Communion With Me). Therefore, In The Midst Of daily life, There Will Likely Be Many Otherwise Informal Occasions When It Is Appropriate To Convert, Positively Change, and Transcend The Quality Of attention, mind, emotion, and bodily orientation By Means Of a brief (and Perhaps Relatively Informal) period Of Either self-Enquiry Or Mala Japa Of "True Prayer" (or, Otherwise, The Simple Heart-Exercise Of "True Prayer", Perhaps Even In The Form Of Simple Name-Invocation Of Me, Via <u>Internal</u> Japa, In The Midst Of daily activity).

Mala Japa Itself Is physically Engaged Sacramental Devotion (or Ruchira Avatara Puja) In Its Simplest Form—and, When It Is Engaged In the Random and Relatively Informal circumstances of daily life, It Is Sacramental Devotion (or Ruchira Avatara Puja) In Its Most Private Form. The Icon (or Murti-Form) Of My Avatarically-Born Bodily (Human) Divine Form Is Always Presented In The Form Of photographic Images (or Other Types Of technically, or even artistically, Rendered Representations) In The Meditation Halls (or Communion Halls), and In Various Other Sacred Places, Of The Only-By-Me Revealed and Given Way Of The Heart (or Way Of Adidam)—and, Also (Typically, As A photographic Likeness), In The Pendant That Hangs Below The Master-Bead

Of The Mala To Be Worn (In most daily-life circumstances, and In All Formal Circumstances) By Every Practitioner Of The Way Of The Heart. In the daily circumstances (Whether Inside Or Outside The Meditation Hall, or Communion Hall), My Avatarically-Born Bodily (Human) Divine Form May Simply Be Recollected In the mind, Such That It (or Any Memory or mental Projection Of My Avatarically-Born Bodily Human Divine Form) Becomes (For the moment) My Murti-Form (Shown In the mind, and Felt From The Heart). Otherwise, The Master-Bead On The Mala, Together With The (Typically, photographic) Image Of My Avatarically-Born Bodily (Human) Divine Form In The Pendant Hanging Below The Master-Bead, Is My Characteristic physical Representation—To Be Regarded (At Random) In the Relatively Informal circumstances Of daily life (and In Mala Japa—Whether In Formal Circumstances Or Relatively Informal circumstances).

The Mala Itself Is A Sacred Design (or Yantra). It Is (Like The Circle Of the body-mind) A Miniaturized (or Microcosmic) Representation Of The Great Cosmic Mandala. It Is The Circuit Of Circumambulation, Whereby conditionally Manifested beings and forms Rotate Ceaselessly Around Me. My True Devotees Make A Joyous Round Dance—Around Me. They Constantly Circle Me, In Ecstatic Love Of Me (Which, At Last, Becomes Enstatic Oneness With Me). As My Devotees Circle Me, I Am (Avatarically) Divinely Self-Revealed As My Avatarically-Born Bodily (Human) Divine Form, and As My Love-Bliss-Body Of Avatarically Self-Transmitted Divine Spirit-Presence, and As My Apparently Objective Divine Star-Form, and As My Apparently Objective Divine Sound-Form, and As My Transcendental (and Perfectly Subjective) Divine Self-Form (or Very, and Inherently Spiritual, and Inherently egoless, and Inherently Perfect, and Self-Evidently Divine State), and As My Inherently Self-Radiant, Entirely Love-Bliss-"Bright", and Merely Self-Existing Condition (and Centerless, and Boundless, Spherical Form) Of Self-Evidently Divine Being. As My Devotees Circle Me, Gifts Are Exchanged, and (By The Progress Of This Revelation and Practice) Devotional Recognition-Response To Me and Devotional Participation In My (Avatarically Self-Revealed) "Bright" Divine Self-Condition Increase, Until (Ultimately) Most Perfect Oneness With Me (or Inherent Non-Separateness From Me, Prior To All "Difference") Is Realized, In The Self-Existing and Self-Radiant Sphere Of My "Bright" Divine Self-Domain.

The Open Center Of The Mala Represents My (Avatarically Self-Revealed) Bodily (Human), Spiritual, Transcendental, and Divine Forms. The Master-Bead, and The Image Of My Avatarically-Born Bodily (Human) Divine Form Contained In The Pendant Below It, Especially Represent My Human Revelation-Body (or Avatarically-Born Bodily Human Divine Form). The Circle Of Beads Is The Way Of The Heart (and Also the body Of My Devotee).

Each Bead Is A Station Where My Devotee Pauses To Invoke Me and To Contemplate Me and To Commune With Me. And That Invocation and That Contemplation and That Communion Are Always To Be Done With The Sacred Feeling-Offering Of The Heart (Which, In The Case Of My Truly Seeing Devotee, Has Truly Become Directly ego-Transcending, and Spiritually Active, and, Spiritually, Fully Technically Responsible Devotion To Me).

In the body-mind Of Man, The Descending (or Frontal) Line Of The Circle Passes Through The Left Side (or The physical and lower psychic Region) Of The Heart (and, In The Case Of Deeply Felt, and Deeply ego-Surrendering Devotional Responsiveness, and, Eventually, In The Case Of Real Spiritual Awakening, It Touches, and Calls Forward, The Middle Station, or The subtle and deeper psychic Region, Of The Heart), and The Ascending (or Spinal) Line Of The Circle Passes Up Through The Middle Station Of The Heart. Therefore, The Right Side Of The Heart Always Stands Free—As The Root and Source-Point (or Place Of Origin) Of attention, and As The Inherently Perfect Seat Of The Transcendental, Inherently Spiritual, and (Most Ultimately) Divine Realization Of Consciousness Itself (or The Inherent and Inherently Perfect Feeling Of Being, Itself).

The Circle Of Mala Beads, Like The Circle Of the body-mind, Is Also A Circle Around An Invisible Center That Always Stands Free. Thus, In The Circle Of the body-mind and In The Circle Of The Mala, The Center, and My Avatarically Self-Revealed (Spiritual, Transcendental, and Divine) Forms, and The Right Side Of The Heart Always Stand Free. And all conditionally Manifested beings and worlds Ceaselessly Rotate Clockwise In Joyous Solemnity, With The Great Forms Always At The Center (In Relation To the mind) and Always To The Right (In Relation To the body) and Always In Place—Where I Always Already Stand, In and <u>As</u> The Well (or Inherently Perfect and Most Prior Feeling) Of Undifferentiated Mere Being.

The Offering Of physical Elements (or Gifts) Through physical Ritual Acts Of Devotion and The Ritual Of Circumambulation Are, In The Case Of Mala Japa, physically Simplified (or Reduced To The physical Acts Associated With Touching and Moving The Mala).

Nevertheless, That Touching Should Be An Act Of self-Offering, and Of Feeling-Devotion—and, In The Only-By-Me Revealed and Given Way Of The Heart, The Moving Of The Mala Should Be A Heart-Felt Circumambulation Of Me. Therefore, In The Only-By-Me Revealed and Given Way Of The Heart, Each Prayer Of The Mala Japa Should Be Associated With An Intentional and Fully Sensitive Touch Of The Next Consecutive Bead On The Mala (Moving Clockwise From The Master-Bead), and The physical Action Of Moving The Mala From Bead To Bead Should Be Done With The Same Full Awareness and

Sensitivity To Each Movement Of A Bead That Would Be Associated With Each Step Taken While Circumambulating My House.[145] In This Manner, The physical Action Associated With Mala Japa Will Grant True Sila (or Natural Control) To the body-mind. Through Concentration Of attention To Me In This physical Discipline and This Heart-Feeling self-Sacrifice, Wandering frontal energies Are Husbanded and Restored To The Good Course, and (When It Is Realized) The Divinely Spiritual Course. Therefore, In The Only-By-Me Revealed and Given Way Of The Heart, The "Conscious Process" Of Rightly Practiced verbal Japa (and All Of "True Prayer") Controls attention and mind.

At Any Developmental Stage Of The Only-By-Me Revealed and Given Way Of The Heart, The breath-Practice Naturally Associated With Mala Japa Emphasizes inhalation-Reception Via The Descending (or Frontal) Line (and, Thereby, The Establishment Of physical and emotional Equanimity). The Eventual (or Truly Both Hearing and Seeing) Spirit-"Conductivity" Practice (or Spiritually Active, and, Spiritually, Fully Technically Responsible, breath-Practice) Of Mala Japa Also Controls The Total Event Of Me-Contemplating Spirit-"Conductivity", and Of Even All Heart-Feeling Of Me. And The Total Act Of Mala Japa (As Practiced By My Truly Both Hearing and Seeing Devotees) Invokes, Surrenders To, and Receives My Avatarically Self-Transmitted Divine Spirit-Presence, Such That I Fully Spiritually Infuse The Heart and the Total body-mind Of My Devotee, Via The Frontal Line, From Infinitely Above the body and the mind.

Therefore, In The Only-By-Me Revealed and Given Way Of The Heart, Mala Japa Is A Sacramental Activity Engaged By the frontal personality. It Should Be Engaged In The Context Of Formal Meditation, and In The Context Of Formal Sacramental (or Sacred Ceremonial) Occasions (As Appropriate), and (As Appropriate) In The Context Of any of the Random occasions of daily living. Mala Japa Is (For My By-Me-Spiritually-Initiated Devotees who Practice The Devotional Way Of Faith) A Principal Practicing Means For Constantly Abiding In My Avatarically Self-Transmitted Divine Spirit-Presence, Rather Than In the ego-Possessed state (Dissociated From Me). Mala Japa Is An Extension Of The Sacramental (or Sacred) "Attitude" (Which "Attitude" Should Characterize Every Practice Engaged By My Every Listening Devotee, and My Every Hearing Devotee, and My Every Seeing Devotee). And That "Attitude" Is The Constantly Expressed Intention (or Impulse) To Live By My Avatarically Self-Transmitted Divine Grace, and (In Due Course, More and More) In The State Of My Avatarically Self-Transmitted Divine Spiritual Grace (Which Is To Be Free Of self-Contraction, and To Be In Constant Communion With Me, and, Most Ultimately, To Be Awake In and As My Inherently Perfect Divine Self-Condition, Avatarically Self-Revealed By Means Of My Avataric Divine

Teaching-Work, My Avataric Divine Blessing-Work, My Avatarically-Born Bodily Human Divine Form, My Avatarically Self-Transmitted Spiritual, and Always Blessing, Divine Presence, and My Avatarically Self-Revealed, and Very, and Transcendental, and Perfectly Subjective, and Inherently Spiritual, and Inherently egoless, and Inherently Perfect, and Self-Evidently Divine State).

To Live By My Avatarically Self-Transmitted Divine Grace, and (In Due Course, More and More) In The State Of My Avatarically Self-Transmitted Divine Spiritual Grace, Is (Progressively, or More and More) To Practice True Devotion To Me—or, In every moment and circumstance, To Exercise The Inherent Heart-Impulse Toward My Avatarically Self-Revealed (and Inherently egoless, and Self-Evidently Divine) Person (and, Thus, Toward Realization Of My Avatarically Self-Revealed, and Self-Radiant, and "Bright" Condition Of Divine Self-Existence). To Live By My Avatarically Self-Transmitted Divine Grace, and (In Due Course, More and More) In The State Of My Avatarically Self-Transmitted Divine Spiritual Grace, Is (Progressively, or More and More) To Prove That Devotion Through Radiant Equanimity, ego-Transcending Love, Right Discipline (Always Willing To Discipline the ego-self and others In The Context Of Communicated and Presumed Love), and True Relational Sympathy With all other conditionally Manifested beings (Such That all others Are Set Free To Be, or To Grow and To change, or Even To pass away). To Live By My Avatarically Self-Transmitted Divine Grace, and (In Due Course, More and More) In The State Of My Avatarically Self-Transmitted Divine Spiritual Grace, Is (Progressively, or More and More) To Set all others Free By one's own Free Relinquishment Of Clinging and other-Attaching Need (or one's own Habit Of self-Referring Relatedness, or All The Forms Of one's own egoic Identification With others). Therefore, To Live By My Avatarically Self-Transmitted Divine Grace, and (In Due Course, More and More) In The State Of My Avatarically Self-Transmitted Divine Spiritual Grace, Is Also (Progressively, or More and More) To Practice Full Heart-Forgiveness (and The Refusal To Betray others, or The Refusal To Act In Relation To others As If Love Is Not The Case)—and Such Practice Is To Be Demonstrated (Progressively, or More and More Constantly) By ego-Transcending (and Life-Giving) Service In The Context Of relationships of all kinds.

Practice Of Either self-Enquiry Or The Prayer Of Remembrance, and Also The Practice Of The Devotional Prayer Of Changes, Is (In The Context Of The First Actually Seeing Stage Of The Way Of The Heart) The Practice Of Devotional self-Surrender To Me, Based On Spiritually "Locating" and (Then) Fully Receiving My Avatarically Self-Transmitted (and all-and-All-Surrounding, and all-and-All-Pervading) Divine Spirit-Presence (Very Present, or Originally and Ultimately and Merely Present, At The Heart, and Infinitely Above the body and the mind).

The Prayer Of Remembrance, Like Every Other Form Of Practice In The Spiritual (or Actually Me-Seeing) Fullness Of The Only-By-Me Revealed and Given Way Of The Heart, Is Made Of Two Primary Responsive Exercises: The "Conscious Process" and Spirit-"Conductivity" Practice. The Prayer Of Remembrance, Like Every Other Form Of Practice In The Spiritual (or Actually Me-Seeing) Fullness Of The Way Of The Heart, Involves The "Conscious Process" Of Steady (and, Altogether, Devotionally Me-Recognizing and Devotionally To-Me-Responsive) attention (From The Heart—or Via Consistent, and Consistently ego-Surrendering, ego-Forgetting, and Directly and Effectively ego-Transcending, Heart-Feeling) To My Avatarically Self-Revealed Human, Spiritual, Transcendental, and Divine Person. And The Prayer Of Remembrance, Like Every Other Form Of Practice In (Specifically) The First Actually Seeing Stage Of The Way Of The Heart, Necessarily Also Involves The Devotionally Me-Recognizing and Devotionally To-Me-Responsive Opening Of The Frontal Line To Conduct The Self-Radiant and Love-Blissful Divine Spirit-Current Of My Avatarically Self-Transmitted Divine Presence.

From The Beginning Of The First Actually Seeing Stage Of The Only-By-Me Revealed and Given Way Of The Heart, The Principle Of Fullest (or Spiritually Activated, and, Spiritually, Fully Technically Responsible) emotional, and Total psycho-physical, Conversion To Devotional and Spiritual Communion With Me (Via Reception Of My Avatarically Self-Transmitted Divine Spirit-Baptism and The Total Process Of The Real Seeing Of Me) Has Already Been (In The Context Of Previous and Would-Be-Seeing, or Progressively Seeing, Practice) Established. Therefore, The Practice In The First Actually Seeing Stage Of The Way Of The Heart Is To Magnify That Already and Firmly Established Disposition Through The Meditative Yoga Of Devotion (Either In The Form Of True and Spiritually Active, and, Spiritually, Fully Technically Responsible, self-Enquiry Or In The Form Of Spiritually Active, and, Spiritually, Fully Technically Responsible, "True Prayer") In The Context Of The Fully Established "Basic" Fourth Stage Of Life In The Only-By-Me Revealed and Given Way Of The Heart (or Way Of Adidam).

Avatar Adi Da Samraj
Adidam Samrajashram, 2003

SUTRA 44

The First Actually Seeing Stage Of The Only-By-Me Revealed and Given Way Of Adidam (Which Is The One and Only By-Me-Revealed and By-Me-Given Way Of The Heart) Requires A Profound Exercise Of the frontal personality Which Surrenders, Opens, and (Spiritually) Rightly Polarizes, Purifies, Balances, and Infuses the frontal (or human) character (In The Context Of every function and every kind of relationship or circumstance). That Process Must Always Take Place On The Basis Of The Primary (and Always First) Practice (Of Searchless Beholding Of Me) and Of (Subsequent) Responsive Reception Of My Ruchira Shaktipat (Engaged In The Manner Of My "Hridaya Rosary" Of "Four Thorns Of Heart-Instruction"). And, In That Process, the human and Spiritual limitations of the frontal character Are To Be Constantly Encountered and Surrendered Via Directly and Effectively ego-Transcending Devotional and Spiritual Communion With Me.

This Real Process Of Encounter and self-Surrender Inevitably Produces (and Must Produce) Many Kinds Of phenomenal (or psycho-physical) Signs. Even Some Signs Related To The Ascending Spiritual Process (or the Yogic phenomena Associated With The Spinal Line) May Spontaneously Appear, but The Significant Signs That Are Specific To The First Actually Seeing Stage Of The Way Of The Heart Are Associated With The Descending Process (and The Frontal Line Of the body-mind). Thus, The Significant phenomenal Signs At This Developmental Stage Include psycho-physical Openings and Releases everywhere In The Frontal Line—Spiritually Relieving egoic mental, emotional, and physical Patterns, Reactions, and Blocks In The Hierarchical Structure (From the head To the bodily base).

The self-Contraction (or the egoic personality) Developed In The Context Of The First Three Stages Of Life Shows itself, In The Context Of The Frontal Line, In A Hierarchical Pattern—Progressing From the head To the bodily base Via A Range Of specific emotions and bodily and mental states that Generally (Apart From The Exercise Of The Hearing-and-Seeing Capability) Would Prevent Spiritual Communion With My (Avatarically Self-Transmitted) Divine (and Inherently Spiritual) Love-Bliss. In The First Actually Seeing Stage Of The Way Of The Heart, My Devotee Must Be Already Equipped (By Virtue

Of Previously Awakened Hearing Of Me and Seeing Of Me) To Always Immediately and Directly Transcend The Potential Of these various states To Prevent Spiritual Communion With My Avatarically Self-Transmitted Divine Love-Bliss. Therefore, In The First Actually Seeing Stage Of The Way Of The Heart (Which Is Real Practice Of The Way Of The Heart In The Fully Established "Basic" Context Of The Fourth Stage Of Life, and Which Is Based On Previous Hearing Of Me and Seeing Of Me, and On An Already Established Basic human—and, In The Foundation Sense, Spiritual—Equanimity Relative To The First Three Stages Of Life), The Spiritual (and Always Devotional) Process Of Such ego-Transcendence Is Primarily Engaged Relative To Patterns and Degrees Of self-Contraction That (Comparatively) Would Merely Diminish, Rather Than Prevent, Direct Communion (and, Most Ultimately, Inherent, and Inherently Most Perfect, Self-Identification) With My Avatarically Self-Transmitted Divine Love-Bliss.

The head Is Associated With mental Patterns That Reflect the emotional and physical conditions below—and, In The Context Of Practice In The First Actually Seeing Stage Of The Way Of The Heart, My Devotee Discovers That The Primary mental Sign Of the self-Contraction (Whereby Spiritual Communion With My Avatarically Self-Transmitted Divine Love-Bliss Is, or Would Be, Diminished) Is The Habit (or Tendency) Of Non-Specific Doubt (Which Is Not So Much a thought As It Is an emotionally Contracted state of mind that, In A Negative or Disabling Fashion, Controls thought and Otherwise limits The Useful functional Clarity and Strength Of mind and will, or Of All Intelligent Intention).

Immediately below the head Is The Region Of the throat (or The Channel Of the breath, and Of My Avatarically Self-Transmitted Divine Spirit-Current, Which Connects the head, and the Total brain, To The Heart, and the entire trunk, and the lower body). The self-Contraction (Whereby Spiritual Communion With My Avatarically Self-Transmitted Divine Love-Bliss Is Diminished) Registers In This Region Either As The Tendency Toward The Diminishment Of psycho-physical Equanimity (Via A Relatively Chaotic Expression Of bodily energy and human Aliveness) Or As The Tendency Toward A Degree Of Suppression Of bodily energy and human Aliveness (Depending On The egoically Characteristic Mood and The Accumulated personality Pattern Of the individual).

The General Region Of The Heart (Including the solar plexus) Is Associated With emotional Patterns That Reflect conditions everywhere in the body-mind. The self-Contraction Is Displayed emotionally As every kind of Chronic and Key emotion (or Pattern Of emotional Reaction), Including Fear, Sorrow, Anger, and Un-Love—but The Maturing Spiritual Practitioner (At The First

Actually Seeing Stage, and Beyond) Of The Way Of The Heart, In whom The Hearing Of Me, The Seeing Of Me, and The Maturing Spiritual Process Of Ruchira Avatara Bhakti Yoga Have Already Purified The Heart In Its Average Of moments, Discovers That The Primary emotional Sign Of the self-Contraction (Whereby Spiritual Communion With My Avatarically Self-Transmitted Divine Love-Bliss Is Diminished) Is Boredom (or The Boredom-Reaction To The Inherent Demands Of The Spiritual Ordeal).

If Heart-Boredom Is Suffered, The objectless Doubt Is Also Made To Seem. Or If The Doubt Appears, Heart-Boredom Is Likewise Suffered. And If the mind Of Doubt and The Heart Of Boredom Are Suffered, the entire body-mind Is Expressed By Either Chronic Or Variously Ranging Signs Of Discomfort (or Dis-ease). Therefore, In The Case Of My Actually Me-Seeing Devotees, These Three (Doubt, Boredom, and Discomfort) Are The Always Simultaneous Moods and Signs That May Tend To Appear (and That May, By Their Appearing, Tend To Diminish Spiritual Communion With My Avatarically Self-Transmitted Divine Love-Bliss).

My Devotee In The First Actually Seeing Stage Of The Way Of The Heart Discovers (By Real, and Really ego-Transcending, Spiritual Communion With Me, and, Thus and Thereby, With My Avatarically Self-Transmitted Divine Love-Bliss) That The ordinary (and egoic) Struggle With concrete doubts, negative thoughts, emotional reactions, and grosser bodily discomforts (or All The egoic Patterns Of Resistance To The Discipline Of True Sila, or functional, practical, relational, and Cultural self-Control) Is (Already, and More and More) Superseded (and Even Replaced) By The True Spiritual Ordeal Of (Spiritually) Fully Technically Responsible frontal Communion With My Spiritual (and Always Blessing) Divine Presence Of Avatarically Self-Transmitted "Bright" (or Self-Radiant, Self-Existing, and Self-Evidently Divine) Love-Bliss, and By The By-My-Avataric-Divine-Spiritual-Grace-Given Process Of (Effectively and Fully) Feeling Beyond The Primary (and Even objectless) Signs Of Doubt, Boredom, and Discomfort—or The frontal Efforts Of self-Contraction That (Comparatively) Would Diminish, Rather Than (Otherwise, or Apart From The Exercise Of The Hearing-and-Seeing Capability) Would Entirely Prevent, moment to moment Spiritual Communion With My Avatarically Self-Transmitted Divine Love-Bliss.

Therefore, Even Though The True (and Maturing) Devotee In The First Actually Seeing Stage (and Beyond) Of The Way Of The Heart May Sometimes (In Random and Occasional moments) Be Obliged To Transcend The Lingering "Grosser" Resistance (or Love-Bliss-Preventing Reactivity) Of the body-mind, The Primary and Constant Practice and Process (Until The Way Of The Heart Is, By Means Of My Avatarically Self-Transmitted Divine Spiritual Grace, Awakened Into The Divinely Self-Realized and Love-Bliss-Realized, and, On That Basis, Most Perfectly Devotional, Context Of The Only-By-Me Revealed and Given Seventh Stage Of Life) Is The ego-Surrendering, ego-Forgetting, and ego-Transcending Ordeal Of Direct and Immediate and Fully Technically Responsible Spiritual (and Always Devotional, and Truly Feeling-Contemplative, and Searchlessly Me-Beholding, and Upward-To-Me-Opening) Communion With Me (and, Thus and Thereby, With My Avatarically Self-Transmitted Divine Love-Bliss Itself)—and This Is Done On The Basis Of True and Basic psycho-physical and Spiritual Equanimity, Already Established By Virtue Of Previous Right and Complete Fulfillment Of The Listening Stage, The Hearing Stage, and The Would-Be-Seeing, or Progressively Seeing, Stage Of The Way Of The Heart (and, Therefore, Rather, or Relatively, Easily Maintained By Constant Right Discipline and Consistent Real Heart-Practice).

The Characteristic Mood and the Basic character of the egoic individual In The First Three Stages Of Life Are Exhibited In Terms Of What I Call "Vital", "Peculiar", and "Solid" personality Patterns. These Patterns Correspond, Respectively, To Reactive (or ego-Preserving and ego-Dramatizing) Strategies Of Either A Characteristically vital (or "vitally"—and, Perhaps, or Sometimes, Even "Grossly"—physical) Kind Or A Characteristically emotional (or emotionally "peculiar", and, Perhaps, or Sometimes, Even Hysterical) Kind Or A Characteristically mental (or mentally "solid", or Strategically—and, Principally, By Means Of ego-Efforts That Exploit the conceptual mind—Invulnerable) Kind.[146]

The Dominant Characteristics Of the "Vital" character Are Obsessive and Compulsive vital-physical self-Expression and The Chronic, Excessive, and Even Degenerative Dramatization Of bodily self-Indulgence. The "Vital" character Is Also Associated With Diminished (or Suppressed) emotional Capability (Often Expressed Via a One-Dimensional, Generally Invariable, and Superficially Positive emotional state), and it Is Generally Represented By Either mental Dullness Or A Chaotic (or Undisciplined) Display Of the conceptual (or intellectual) function.

The Dominant Characteristics Of the "Peculiar" character Are Excessively "Romantic" (or Even Sentimental) and Idealistic (or Un-Realistic) Expectations (That Are Inevitably Frustrated) and The Loss Of Balance Via Chronic emotional Hypersensitivity and The Dramatization Of Exaggerated "Mood Swings" (or The Tendency To Alternate Dramatically, Even Without Apparent cause, Between Very Positive and Very Negative or Depressed or Hysterical emotional states). The "Peculiar" character Is Also Associated With Diminished conceptual (or intellectual) Capability (Characterized By Mechanical or Superficial Application Of mind), and it Is Generally Represented By Either Suppressed Or Chaotically Displayed vital-physical functions (Characterized By vital weakness and nervous energy).

The Dominant Characteristics Of the "Solid" character Are Hyperactivity Of the conceptual mind and The Chronic Dramatization Of A Profound (and Even Suppressive) Need To Control the psycho-physical self (and others), Especially Via The Efforts Of the conceptual mind and the effects Of merely conceptual Expression. The "Solid" character Is Also Associated With Diminished or Suppressed (or Over-Controlled and Mechanical) vital-physical activity or Capability, and it Is Generally Represented By A Suppression (or Sometimes Chaotic Display) Of emotional Expression (Of both Positive, or Non-Reactive, and Negative, or Reactive, emotions).

Most individuals Express themselves In A Complex Fashion, Combining (In One or Another Manner) Two, or Even All Three, Of These Chronic egoic Strategies—but every egoic individual Is Basically Dominated By One Of These Three Reactive Designs. And The Characteristic Mood (or Effort) Determined By Each Design Dictates The Characteristic Expression Of bodily energy and human Aliveness Via The Region Of the throat. Thus, the "Solid" character Tends Toward Suppression (or Negatively and Mechanically Controlled Expression) Of bodily energy and human Aliveness. The "Vital" character Tends Toward A Chaotic (and Even Degenerative) Expression Of bodily energy and human Aliveness. And the "Peculiar" character Tends To Swing (In Hysterical Fashion) Between Chaotic and Suppressive Expressions Of bodily energy and human Aliveness.

Insofar As These egoic Strategies Simply Represent The ordinary and Spirit-Preventing Efforts Associated With The First Three Stages Of Life, They Must Be Observed (personally), Understood (Most Fundamentally), and Transcended (Truly Effectively) During The Three Periods Of Intensive Listening and (Then) Hearing Practice—and The Capability Of Those egoic Strategies To Prevent Heart-Communion With Me Is Finally Undone (By Means Of My Avatarically Self-Transmitted Divine Spiritual Grace) In The Eventual Awakening Of The True Seeing Of Me (In The Culmination Of The Would-Be-Seeing, or Progressively Seeing, Stage Of The Way Of The Heart). However, Insofar As These egoic Strategies Represent Only The Spirit-Diminishing Tendencies Of the humanly Adapted frontal personality (and Frontal Line) Of My Actually Me-Seeing Devotee, They May Continue To Be Responsibly Transcended and Released (and Replaced By Spiritually Positive Signs) In The Truly Both Hearing and Seeing Practice Of The Way Of The Heart (and First, and Especially, and With Principal Effectiveness, In The First Actually Seeing Stage Of The Way Of The Heart).

Deeper Than the head and the throat, and Central To the body-mind As A Whole, Is The Heart. In The Case Of My Seeing Devotee Practicing The Way Of The Heart In The Fully Established "Basic" Context Of The Fourth Stage Of

Life, The Left (or physical and lower psychic) and The Middle (or subtle and deeper psychic) Regions Of The Heart Are functionally Evident (In The Context Of the frontal personality), but The Right Side Of The Heart (Which Is The Root-Source, or Point Of Origin, Of egoic self-Consciousness, and Which Is Also, Ultimately, The Heart-Seat, or Horizontal-Plane Focus, Of Transcendental, Inherently Spiritual, and Most Perfect Divine Self-Realization) Is Only Latently Evident In the egoic individual Previous To The Transition To The "Perfect Practice" Of The Way Of The Heart.

The (General) Heart-Region (or Horizontal Core) Of the egoic individual Functions (In The Descended Context Of the body-mind) As The Primary Seat Of functional emotion and (Potentially) Of My Avatarically Self-Transmitted Divine Spirit-Energy. And The Heart-Expression Is Retarded (and Even Prevented) By the self-Contraction, Such That It Becomes Characterized By A Range Of Non-Spiritual and (In The Actually Me-Seeing Case) Diminished Spiritual Signs—From The Absence Of Spiritual Awareness To (In The Actually Me-Seeing Case) The Spiritual "Disease" Of Diminished Spiritual Delight (or Diminished Spiritual Awareness Of My Avatarically Self-Transmitted Divine Love-Bliss). And The self-Contracted Heart Is Also Characterized By A Range Of emotions Associated With Un-Love, or Non-Love, or ego-Based and Superficial Pseudo-Love, or Diminished Love.

The (Fully Technically Responsible) Spiritual Yoga Of Devotional self-Surrender Of the frontal personality To Me (Begun In The Would-Be-Seeing, or Progressively Seeing, Stage Of The Way Of The Heart, and Continued, To The Degree Of True Spiritual Fullness In The Total Context Of The Frontal Line and the frontal personality Of the body-mind, In The First Actually Seeing Stage Of The Way Of The Heart) Is First (and Spiritually) To Purify, Rebalance, and Regenerate The head, throat, and Heart Regions Of The Frontal Line. In That Initial Process, Chronic (and Love-Bliss-Diminishing) Doubt, Boredom, and Discomfort, Love-Bliss-Diminishing Aspects Of "Vital", "Peculiar", and "Solid" character-Strategies, Love-Bliss-Diminishing Suppression or Chaos Of bodily energy and human Aliveness, and Love-Bliss-Diminishing emotional Expressions Of Un-Love and Non-Love and Pseudo-Love and Diminished Love, and All Other Forms Of Diminished Heart-Expression and Heart-Delight, Are To Be Progressively (and To A humanly and Spiritually Significant Degree) Released—and These Are (By Truly Spiritual Heart-Cooperation With Me) Responsively (and By Means Of My Avatarically Self-Transmitted Divine Spiritual Grace) To Be Replaced By the mind Of Ruchira-Avatar Praise and Real-God-Aware Happiness, and By Spiritually Fully Infused Equanimity, and By Fullness Of Both human Aliveness and Spirit-Life, and By The Heart-Radiant Disposition Of ego-Transcending Love.

Once The Initial Purifying Work Of My Avatarically Self-Transmitted Divine Spirit-Energy Has (In The First Phase Of The First Actually Seeing Stage Of The Way Of The Heart) Become Significantly Effective In The Frontal Line Of the body-mind, The (Fully Technically Responsible) Spiritual Yoga Of Devotional self-Surrender Of the frontal personality To Me Can (and Must) Then (and By Means Of My Avatarically Self-Transmitted Divine Spiritual Grace, In The Second, and Final, or Fullest, Phase Of The First Actually Seeing Stage Of The Way Of The Heart) "Break the navel" (or Release and Open The Knot, or self-Contraction, In The lower frontal Pattern Of the body-mind), and, Thus (By Means Of My Avatarically Self-Transmitted Divine Spiritual Grace), Spiritually Purify, Rebalance, and Regenerate The Deeper (or Base) Regions Of The Frontal Line.

The Deeper (or Base) Regions Of the body-mind Are Associated With The (Rather Unconscious) Root-Reactivity Of the born personality. That Root-Reactivity Is Represented By Anger (In The Region Of the solar plexus and the navel), Sorrow (Deeper, In The Region Of the lower abdomen and the genitals), and Fear (In The Deepest Region, The Region Of the perineum, the core of the bodily base). These Great and Base Reactions Are Not Commonly experienced (In Their Most Profound Forms) in the daily course, and (Therefore, In General) They Do Not (or Cannot) Directly and Effectively (or experientially) Either Prevent Or Diminish Spiritual Communion With My Avatarically Self-Transmitted Divine Love-Bliss. The More Superficial Patterns (In The Heart, throat, and head Regions)—Including Occasional and Lesser Expressions Of Fear, Sorrow, and Anger—Are Commonly Indulged (To The Degree Of, Effectively, Either Preventing Or, Potentially, Diminishing Spiritual Communion With My Avatarically Self-Transmitted Divine Love-Bliss), but The Great Base Reactions Are Commonly (or In the Average moments of daily life) Suppressed (or Strategically Avoided), Even Though They Are At The Root Of All Superficial Reactivity and All conventional Patterning.

Spiritually Untouched Anger, Sorrow, and Fear (Along With Aggressive Un-Love) Are The Dark, or Hidden (and Generally Unconscious), Side Of The Heart (In Its Apparent Association With egoity)—Whereas The Less Aggressive (or Less Debilitating) Expressions Of Fear, Sorrow, Anger, Un-Love, Non-Love, Pseudo-Love, and Diminished Love (As Well As The ordinary Chaos or Suppression Of bodily energy and human Aliveness, and Also Even Chronic Doubt, Boredom, and Discomfort) Are The Commonly Dramatized (and Even "socially Acceptable") Side Of The Heart (In The Context Of Apparent egoity). Therefore, In The Only-By-Me Revealed and Given Way Of The Heart (or Way Of Adidam), It Is Only When The Deep Reactive Base Of The Heart (and the Total frontal personality) Is (Through The Fully Technically Responsible

Spiritual Heart-Practice Of Devotional self-Surrender To Me In The Frontal Line) Invaded (or Infused) By My (Avatarically Self-Transmitted) Baptizing, Purifying, Rebalancing, and Regenerative Spiritual (and Always Blessing) Divine Love-Bliss-Presence That the frontal personality Is Most Fully (or Maximally, To The Fullest Degree Possible Previous To The Divinely Enlightened Awakening Associated With The Only-By-Me Revealed and Given Seventh Stage Of Life) Restored To Superior (or Spiritually Fully Infused) Equanimity, and To Optimum Clarity Of Awareness, and To Constantly Capable Feeling-Responsibility For mental, emotional, and physical Negativity, and To Truly Fundamental (and Undiminished) Love (or The Free Happiness Of Delight In The Spirit-Current Of My Avatarically Self-Transmitted Divine Love-Bliss).

This Process Of Total frontal Invasion (or Infusion) By My Avatarically Self-Transmitted Spirit-Current Of Divine Love-Bliss (In The First Actually Seeing Stage Of The Way Of The Heart) Does Not Itself Require (or Necessarily Involve the Conscious experience Of) The Most Debilitating Revelation Of Base Fear, Sorrow, and Anger—but (Rather) The Process Directly (and Most Simply) Involves and Requires The Deep Opening Of The Base Regions Of The Frontal Line Of the body-mind To My Avatarically Self-Transmitted Divine Spirit-Presence Of Love-Bliss Itself (Such That The Base Reactions That Are Otherwise Locked Away As Fear, Sorrow, and Anger Are Directly and Immediately Replaced, In The Event Of The Invasion Of The Frontal Line By My Avatarically Self-Transmitted Divine Spiritual Grace, With The Fullness and Delight and Freedom That Is My Divine Self-Condition Of Love-Bliss Itself). And The Fullest (or Maximal) Spiritual Restoration Of the frontal personality To My Avatarically Self-Transmitted Divine Love-Bliss Itself (Such As This May Be Realized Previous To Most Perfect Divine Awakening, and The Demonstration Of The Only-By-Me Revealed and Given Seventh Stage Of Life) Is The Primary Sign That Is To Be Realized (At The Point Of Basic Maturity) In The First Actually Seeing Stage Of The Way Of The Heart. Indeed, This Primary Sign Is So Potent As A Base Of Heart-Awakening That Direct Awakening To The Position Of The Witness-Consciousness (By Means Of The Only-By-Me Revealed and Given Samadhi Of The "Thumbs"), and (Consequent) Transition To The "Perfect Practice" Of The Way Of The Heart, Will (In Due Course, By Means Of My Avatarically Self-Transmitted Divine Spiritual Grace) Occur At The Point Of Basic Maturity In The First Actually Seeing Stage Of The Way Of The Heart.

Only When Chronic (and ordinary) Anger, Sorrow, and Fear (Which Effectively Separate the psycho-physical being From all ordinary relations) Are (By The Awakening, and The Subsequent Exercise, Of Most Fundamental self-Understanding) Capably, Directly, and Effectively Released (In The Maturity Of The Intensive Listening-Hearing Process Of The Way Of The Heart) Can It

Be Said That The First Three Stages Of Life (and The "Original", or Beginner's, Devotional—and, In The Foundation Sense, Spiritual—Development Of The Fourth Stage Of Life) Are Complete (and That the Possible limitations Of The First Three Stages Of Life Are Inherently and Effectively Transcended, By Means Of The True Hearing Of Me, and By Basic, and Basically Stable, and Truly Hearing-Based human—and, In The Foundation Sense, Spiritual—Equanimity). And Only When The Degrees Of ordinary Anger, Sorrow, and Fear That Prevent Heart-Communion With Me Are Spiritually Released (In The Context Of The Fully Technically Responsible Spiritual Awakening Associated With Maturity In The Would-Be-Seeing, or Progressively Seeing, Stage Of The Way Of The Heart) Can It Be Said That The Fourth-Stage-Of-Life Practice Of The Way Of The Heart (In Its Fully Established "Basic", or First Actually Seeing, Form) Has Truly and Fully Begun. Therefore, Practice Of The Way Of The Heart In The (Spiritually) Fully Technically Responsible Context Of The "Basic" Fourth Stage Of Life Cannot Be Truly and Fully Established Until (By Means Of My Avatarically Self-Transmitted Divine Spiritual Grace) Chronic (or ordinary, and Also Happiness-Preventing) Fear, Sorrow, and Anger Are Transcended, Via The Awakening (and The Effective Exercise) Of Both The True Hearing Of Me (or Most Fundamental self-Understanding, Demonstrated By Basic human—and, In The Foundation Sense, Spiritual—Equanimity) and The True Seeing Of Me (or Real Spiritual Heart-Conversion, Demonstrated By Ever-Increasing Spiritual Equanimity and Fullness).

Fear Is The Primary Mood Of Separation. Fear Is Especially Associated With The First Stage Of Life and The Vital Shock Of birth.[147] It Is Signalled By the gaping mouth (In Pitiful Awe), As If the mother's teat Were Suddenly Torn From the infant lips.

Fear Is Also The Principal Motivating Mood Of the "Solid" character. Paradoxically, the Obsessively self-Controlling and other-Controlling "Solid" character (Chronically Seeking To Be "In Control", or Chronically "Talking" As If "In Control", or, Altogether, Chronically "Seeming" To Presume To Be "In Control") Is Founded On A Fear Of Being Controlled By others (or By conditions outside the body-mind-self). And That Fear Is Originally Developed In the years of infancy, childhood, and adolescence—Generally In A Passive and Rather infantile Reaction Either To The Feeling Or To the Actual experience Of Being Too Much Controlled and Threatened By others, Especially adults.

Sorrow Is The Primary Mood Of the Rejected individual. Sorrow Is Especially Associated With The Second Stage Of Life, The Loss Of self-Security, and The Loss Of Power Over others On whom one Depends. It Is Signalled By the grimace, the downturned and puckered mouth—As In the eliminative anal grunt, The End-Game Of oral Dependency.

Sorrow Is Also The Principal Motivating Mood Of the "Peculiar" character. The Alternately Idealistically (and, Thus, mentally) self-Controlled and (Otherwise) Chaotically self-Indulgent "Peculiar" character Is Founded On A Basic and Sorrowful Feeling Of Being Neglected. The Chronic Sorrow Of the "Peculiar" character Is A Yearning To Be Effectively Touched (or Loved). It Is A Call and Even An Hysterical Need (or Search) To Be Controlled (or Restored To Balance By A Positive Controlling Influence). And That Sorrowful Need Is Originally Developed In the years of infancy, childhood, and adolescence—Generally In An Hysterical and Rather childish Reaction Either To The Feeling Or To the Actual experience Of Being Neglected, Denied Love, and Denied A Positive Controlling Influence.

Anger Is The Primary Mood Of Reaction To All That Seems To Justify Fear and Sorrow. It Is Especially Associated With The Third Stage Of Life—Which Is Characterized By The adolescent Struggle With The Motives Of Dependence and Independence, and The Aggressive Effort Toward genital Victory (Glorifying the Separate and Separative self, egoically Powerful Over all others). It Is Signalled By the tortured mouth with gnashing teeth, The facial Display Of genital Shapes and genital Agony. Everything Of The First Three Stages Of Life Is Displayed In common egoic Anger. Even egoic sex Is Full Of Rejection and Anger—Threatened By Loss and Sorrow, and Convinced Of Fearful Separation.

Anger Is Also The Principal Motivating Mood Of the "Vital" character. The "Vital" character Is Characteristically self-Indulgent, vitally (or physically). The Mood Of This Pattern Is Always Rather Rebellious. Indeed, Even the Most Apparently Carefree, self-pleasurizing "Vital" character Is Dramatizing Resistance and Refusal. The "Vital" character Is Founded On An Angry Reaction To Controls and Demands. The Characteristic behavior-Pattern Associated With the "Vital" character Is A Chronic Effort To Resist, Refuse, or Avoid The Controlling Influence Of others (or Even Of the mind) On The personal bodily Existence Of the conditional self. And That Angry Mood Is Originally Developed In the years of infancy, childhood, and adolescence—Generally In An Aggressive and Rather adolescent Reaction Either To The Feeling Or To the Actual experience Of Being Too Much Controlled and Threatened By others, Especially adults.

Truly human and adult Maturity Requires The Transcending Of The Chronic and Obsessive character Patterns Developed In the years of infancy, childhood, and adolescence. Truly human and adult Maturity Is The Achievement Of A Balance Between The Motive Toward Control Of the psycho-physical self and The Motive Toward Motion (or Excitation) Of the psycho-physical self. Truly human and adult Maturity Requires self-Control and A Willingness To Be

Even physically Affected, emotionally Touched, mentally Influenced and (Thus, To A Significant Degree) Controlled By others. Likewise, Truly human adulthood (or Maturity) Requires The Constant Exercise (or Excitation) Of The Motive Of (or Toward) Real Freedom (Even The Most Ultimate Freedom Of Utter ego-Transcendence and Inherent, and Inherently Most Perfect, Realization Of Me—The Avataric Self-Revelation Of The Transcendental, Inherently Spiritual, Inherently egoless, and Self-Evidently Divine Self-Condition, and Source-Condition, Of all-and-All).

The Tendency To perceive Existence As A Problem, or To conceive and Suffer An Inherent Conflict Between Control and Freedom, Must Be Transcended In Wisdom. The "Father-Force" (or The Husbanding Force, or The Controlling and Demanding Influence) and The "Mother-Force" (or The Feminine Force, or The Nurturing and Supporting Influence) Must Both Be Discovered, Accepted, and Integrated Into The psycho-physical Patterns Of Your Own Real Existence. When That Integration Is Real and Stable, Such That The human Pattern Of Your Own body-mind Is Basically Balanced, Intelligent, self-Disciplined, and Also (By Means Of My Avatarically Self-Transmitted Divine Spiritual Grace) Directly Communing With My Avatarically Self-Transmitted Divine Spirit-Presence Of Love-Bliss (bodily, emotionally, and mentally), Then The Transition To Practice Of The Way Of The Heart Beyond the limits Of The First Three Stages Of Life—and Beyond the limits (or Rudiments) Of The "Original" (or Beginner's) Devotional (and, In The Foundation Sense, Spiritual) Context Of The Fourth Stage Of Life—Has Really Been Completed, and Practice Of The Way Of The Heart In The (Spiritually) Fully Technically Responsible Context Of The "Basic" Fourth Stage Of Life Has Been Granted A Full and Stable Basis. Therefore, It Is The Establishment Of This Both human and (Fully Technically Responsible) Spiritual Basis For Maturing Practice Of The Way Of The Heart (or The Real and Most Basic Process Of Truly Both Hearing Me and Seeing Me) That Must Precede The Transition To The First Actually Seeing Stage Of The Way Of The Heart.

There Is No Fullest (and To The Fullest Degree Spiritual) Integration Of the frontal (or ordinary) human personality Until My Avatarically Self-Revealed Divine Spirit-Presence Fully Infuses the Surrendered body-mind With My Divine Love-Bliss (and, Thereby, Fills and Replaces The Spaces Of mental, emotional, and physical Negativity). Therefore, By Means Of My Avatarically Self-Transmitted Divine Spiritual Grace, The Wandering and self-Contracted Heart Must Find Its Own True "Father" and "Mother".

Even the Total body-mind Must Cling To My Divine Conscious Light, Calming breath and mind In Love-Bliss, If the ego-self and others Are To Be Sublimed, All Well and "Bright". Therefore, By Means Of My Avatarically

Self-Transmitted Divine Spiritual Grace, The Wandering and self-Contracted Heart Must Find Its Own True Husband—The "Father"-Revealing and "Mother"-Revealing "Son" Of The Only Source Of all-and-All.

The Heart Must Surrender Itself In Listening Love To The Husbanding "Bright" Companion—and This Love-Surrender Must Become A Truly Me-Hearing and Me-Seeing Yoga Of Devotional Recognition-Response To Me.

The Heart That Hears Me and Sees Me Must Meet The Husband's Spirit-Mark, and Many Signs Must Appear (By Means Of My Avatarically Self-Transmitted Divine Spiritual Grace) Before My Work Is "Bright" and Done.

Avatar Adi Da Samraj
Lopez Island, 2000

SUTRA 45

In The True (and Characteristic) Course Of The Frontal Yoga In The Only-By-Me Revealed and Given Way Of Adidam (Which Is The One and Only By-Me-Revealed and By-Me-Given Way Of The Heart), There Will Be Occasional "Surges" (or Spontaneous Invasions) Of My Avatarically Self-Transmitted Divine Spiritual Energy In The Frontal Line. And These Frontal Surges Of My Avatarically Self-Transmitted Divine Spiritual Energy Will (In Turn) Also Pass, Perceptibly or Imperceptibly, From The Frontal Line Into The Spinal Line—Thus Completing The Circle. Such Surges May Be Weak or Strong. They May Produce yawning and General Relaxation, and They May (Otherwise) Reveal (or Yield) Feelings Of General Pleasure and Fundamental Happiness, As Well As Various Degrees Of Ecstatic (or ego-Transcending) Participation In My Avatarically Self-Transmitted Divine Love-Bliss Itself. As A Result Of Your Own Accumulated psycho-physical Patterning Of self-Contraction, These Frontal Surges May Also Be Accompanied (or, Otherwise, Followed) By temporary symptoms of mental, emotional, and physical discomfort, pain, fever, and even physical disease. If such symptomatic phenomena Are Associated With The Real Spiritual Process, they Tend To Come and Go (In Cycles Of Relative Comfort and Discomfort). As Such, They Are Gracefully Purifying Episodes, Shown Through The Evidence Of psycho-physical Release, Rebalance, and Rejuvenation. Occasionally, There May Even Be an experience that Feels Like A Kind Of electric "Shock" (or "Jolt") That Briefly Energizes the body Beyond ordinary Tolerance. In and By All Of This, the human character Is Divinely Urged To Be Responsively and Positively Changed (psychically, mentally, emotionally, and physically), Through The Invasion Of the frontal personality (and, Indeed, the Total body-mind) By My Avatarically Self-Transmitted Divine Spirit-Current Of Love-Bliss-Light.

Among All Of These Signs There Must (Primarily) Appear Progressive Evidence Of What I Have, Since Childhood, Called "The 'Thumbs'". Beginning In The "Basic" (or, Spiritually, Fully Technically Responsible) Context—or, Possibly, Even In The "Original" (or Foundation, and Beginning Spiritual) Context—Of The Fourth Stage Of Life In The Way Of The Heart, There Should Be At Least Occasional Experience Of An Intense Invasion Of The Frontal Line

By My Avatarically Self-Transmitted Divine Spirit-Force Of Love-Bliss—Beginning At The Crown Of the head, and Descending Into The lower vital Region, To the bodily base. The Pressure (or Invasive Force) Of This Event May Be Rather (and Even Happily) Overwhelming—and It Must Be Allowed. At Last, It Is Not Possible (Nor Would You Wish) To Defend Your psycho-physical self Against This Invading Pressure Of My Avataric Divine Spiritual Descent. It Feels Like A Solid and Yet Fluid Mass Of Force, Like A Large Hand All Made Of Thumbs—Pressing Down From Infinitely Above the head and Via The Crown Of the head, Engorging the Total head (and the throat), and (Thus and Thereby) Penetrating and Vanishing the entire mind, and Vastly Opening the emotional core, and (Altogether) In-Filling the Total physical body.

The Feeling-Sense That Results From This Simple (and Most Basic) Frontal In-Filling By My Avatarically Self-Revealed Divine Spirit-Presence Is That the Total body-mind Is Sublimed and Released Into ego-Surrendering, ego-Forgetting, and ego-Transcending Feeling-Identification With The Spherical Form Of My Own Divine and Spiritual (and all-and-All-Surrounding, and all-and-All-Pervading) Love-Bliss-Body Of Indefinable Spiritual "Brightness" (or Indestructible Light). And This Simple (and Most Basic) Form Of The "Thumbs" Is A Necessary (Although, At First, Only Occasional) Experience Associated With The Reception Of My Avatarically Self-Transmitted Divine Spirit-Baptism. It Is My Divine "Goddess-Power" and "Husbanding" Grace At Work. And The Simple (and Most Basic) Spherical Fullness Of The "Thumbs", Once It Is Firmly Established (In The Context Of The Fully Established "Basic", or By-Me-Spiritually-Awakened—and, Spiritually, Fully Technically Responsible—Fourth Stage Of Life In The Way Of The Heart), Must Continue To Be Experienced, As A Fundamental and (Essentially) Continuous (or Constant) Yogic Event, In The "Perfect Practice" Of The Way Of The Heart.

As The Spiritual Process Develops Toward The Transition Beyond The Frontal Yoga Of The Way Of The Heart, The Simple (and Most Basic) Experience Of The "Thumbs" Must Become A More and More Constant Yogic Event—and, On Random Occasions, The Experience Of The "Thumbs" Must Occur In Its Most Extended, Full, and Complete Form. In That Most Extended, Full, and Complete Case Of The Experience Of The "Thumbs", My Descending Spiritual Fullness Will Completely Overwhelm the ordinary frontal (or Natural human) sense Of bodily Existence. My Avatarically Self-Transmitted Divine Spirit-Current Will Move Fully Down In The Frontal Line (To the bodily base), and It Will Then Turn About, and—Without Vacating The Frontal Line—It Will Pass Also Into The Spinal Line. This Yogic Event Will Occur With Such Force That You Will Feel Utterly (Love-Blissfully) "Intoxicated"—and There Will Be The Feeling That the body Is Somehow Rotating Forward and Down (From

The Crown Of the head), As Well As Backward and Up (From the base of the spine). This Rotation Will Seem, Suddenly, To Complete Itself—and The Experience Will, Suddenly, Be One Of Feeling Released From the gross physical body, Such That You Feel You Are Present Only As An egoless "Energy Body" (Previously Associated With and Conformed To the gross physical body—but Now, By Means Of My Avatarically Self-Transmitted Divine Spiritual Grace, Infused By and Conformed To My Avatarically Self-Transmitted Divine Body Of Self-Evidently Divine Spirit-Energy). You Will Feel This "Energy Body" To Be *Spherical* In Shape—Centerless (Empty, or Void, Of Center, mind, and Familiar ego-self) and Boundless (As If Even bodiless, or Without form), Although (Somehow, and Partially) Also Yet Associated With (While Rotating From and Beyond) Your ordinary psycho-physical form. The ordinary References Of the body-mind and the environment Will, In This Divine Yogic Event, Not Make Much Sense (or, In Any Manner, Affect This Experience Of The "Thumbs")—Although There May Be Some *Superficial* (and Entirely Non-limiting) Awareness Of the body, the room, and so forth. This Experience Will Last For a few moments, or a few minutes—or For an Extended period, of indefinite length. Nevertheless, Just When This Spontaneous Experience Has Become *Most* Pleasurable—Such That You *Somehow* Gesture To *Make* It Continue Indefinitely—the ordinary sense of the body-mind Will, Suddenly (Spontaneously), Return.

The "Thumbs" Is Not A Process Of "Going Somewhere Else", Nor Is It Even A Process Of "Vacating" the gross physical body (or the gross physical realm Altogether). Rather, The "Thumbs" Is A Process Of Transformation Of the experiencing of the present physical circumstance. If the present physical circumstance Is Left Behind (Such That experiential Reference To the gross physical realm Is Entirely Absent, and There Is Total Loss Of Awareness Of The physical Context In Which the experience Began), Then The Practitioner Of The Way Of The Heart Is (Necessarily) Experiencing A Form Of Samadhi Other Than The "Thumbs". In The "Thumbs", Awareness Of The physical Context Of experience Is Not Lost, but Is Totally Changed—Such That, Instead Of The self-Conscious, self-Contracted Shape Of the waking-state personality, one's physical form Is Found To Be A Boundlessly Radiant Sphere (Without Thickness Of Surface). With This Profound Shift In The Awareness Of the physical body, The Differentiation Inherent In The Usual waking-state body-Consciousness Disappears, and Is (Effectively) Replaced By egoless body-Consciousness. A Re-Phasing Of The "Energy"-Construct Of bodily Awareness and spatial Awareness Occurs, Such That physical body and physical space Are Tacitly Sensed In A Manner Entirely Different From ordinary perception. And, As Soon As There Is Any Effort To Recollect The Usual Sense Of bodily form or Of the circumstance Of physical embodiment, The Experience Of The "Thumbs" Disappears. The "Thumbs" Continues Only As Long As It Is Simply Allowed To Happen, Without Any egoic self-Consciousness (or psycho-physical self-Contraction)—and It Spontaneously Vanishes When egoic self-Consciousness (or psycho-physical self-Contraction) Returns.

The Total (psycho-physical) human body—With its Dimensions Of gross, subtle, and causal—Must (Altogether) Become Round. The Total human body Does Not Merely Have A Circular Path Within itself. In Truth (or "Located" In Reality Itself), the Total human body Is A Sphere—and, In its (Inherently) Perfect Balance, it Has No "Up" or "Down", No "In" or "Out", No Central Point and No Bounds. When My Avatarically Self-Transmitted Divine Spirit-Current Descends Fully Down the front of the Total human body, and Also (Thereupon, and Thereby) Rises Up the back of the Total human body, Such That The "Thumbs" Achieves An Equalization Of Spirit-Force, Down In front and Up In back—Then The Circle Becomes An Equanimity, A Conscious Sphere Of Tangible "Energy" (or Self-Existing and Boundlessly Self-Radiant Light).

In The Only-By-Me Revealed and Given Realization Of The Sphere Of "The Thumbs", The Arrow Is The Boundless (and Centerless) Vertical Axis, and The Heart On The Right Is The (Asymmetrically, and Paradoxically) Free-Standing (or Non-Centralizing, and Boundless) "Center" (or Horizontal "Root"). The Upper Terminal Of Amrita Nadi Is At The "North". The "North" Is Not A Boundary—It Is Infinitely Above. The "Center" Is Not Inside (or Bounded)—It Is Beyond All Symmetry. The "North" (or Above) and The "Center" (or Beyond) Are Not "Different" (or Separate From One Another)—They Are Modes Of The Same (or Identical) Condition (or Divine "Bright" Spiritual and Transcendental Self-State). The Vertical and The Horizontal Are (Inherently) One (and Non-"Different" From One Another, and From all-and-All). The Realization Of This Is The Essential Nature Of The Ultimate (or Only-By-Me Revealed and Given Seventh Stage) Realization.

Consciousness Itself (or The "Root" Of The Horizontal Dimension, or Heart-Plane, or Subjective Plane) and Light Itself (or The "Root" Of The Vertical Dimension, or "Energy"-Plane, or Objective Plane) Are The Two Primary Apparent Modes Of What Is Always Already Only One—and Inherently Indivisible. The Perfectly Subjectively "Bright" Transcendental and Spiritual Realization Of The Inherent Simultaneity (and Indivisibility) Of Consciousness (The "Root" Of Apparent Subjectivity) and Light (The "Root" Of Apparent Objectivity) Is The Essential Context Of Most Perfect (or Self-Evidently Divine) Self-Realization. In The Ultimate Event (Of Divine Translation, Which Is The Final Stage Of The Only-By-Me Revealed and Given Seventh Stage Of Life), The Indivisible Divine Sphere Of The One (and Only, and Self-Evidently

Divine) Conscious Light Is Infinitely Expanded—Such That There Is Only Infinite "Brightness", and Infinite Fullness Of Love-Bliss-Being.

In The Only-By-Me Revealed and Given Way Of The Heart, The Most Extended, Full, and Complete Experience Of The "Thumbs" Is, In Its Frontal Associations, A Transitional Samadhi Associated With The Fourth Stage Of Life. As Such, The Original Significance Of The Samadhi Of The "Thumbs" Is Not Merely In The Experience Itself (Such That The Experience Should Be psycho-physically Clung To, or, Otherwise, Made Into An Object Of egoic Seeking), but The Original Significance Of The Most Extended, Full, and Complete Experience (or True Samadhi) Of The "Thumbs" Is In Its Effect (or In The More Mature, and Truly ego-Transcending, Process That It May Allow or Indicate). That Is To Say, In The (Fully Established) "Basic" (or By-Me-Spiritually-Awakened—and, Spiritually, Fully Technically Responsible) Context Of The Fourth Stage Of Life In The Way Of The Heart, The present-time (or, Otherwise, Occasional) Arising Of The Most Extended, Full, and Complete Sign Of The "Thumbs" (When It Is Accompanied By The, Essentially, Constant Experience Of The Simple and Most Basic Sign Of The "Thumbs") Is (or May Be) An Indication That The Process Of Devotional and Spiritual Communion With Me Is—If True and Stable Awakening Of The Witness-Consciousness Also (and Even Simultaneously, By Means Of My Avatarically Self-Transmitted Divine Spiritual Grace) Occurs—Moving On From Concentration In the frontal personality To The "Perfect Practice" Of The Way Of The Heart. However, The Samadhi Of The "Thumbs" and The Basic Experience Of The "Thumbs" Are, Also (Beyond Their Significance In The Frontal Context Of The Fourth Stage Of Life In The Way Of The Heart), Principal Among The Great Signs Associated With My Avataric Divine Self-Revelation To all-and-All. And, Therefore, In The Context Of The Only-By-Me Revealed and Given Seventh Stage Of Life (In The Way Of The Heart), The Samadhi Of The "Thumbs" (and The Basic Experience Of The "Thumbs") Is Most Perfectly Realized and Demonstrated (Even In Divine Translation), As The Centerless and Boundless "Bright" Spherical Space Of My Eternal Divine Spiritual Body and My Eternal Divine Self-Condition.

The Occasional Samadhi Of The "Thumbs" (Which Is The Experience Of The "Thumbs" In Its Most Extended, Full, and Complete Form) and The (Essentially) Constant Experience Of The "Thumbs" In Its Simple and Most Basic Form Together Characterize The Second (or Mature) Phase Of The "Basic" Fourth Stage Of Life Development Of The Full (or Fully Developed, and, Spiritually, Fully Technically Responsible) Frontal-Yoga-Dimension Of By-Me-Spiritually-Awakened Practice In The Way Of The Heart. Therefore, In The Only-By-Me Revealed and Given Way Of The Heart (or Way Of Adidam),

The Sign Of The "Thumbs" (Appearing Thus—and, In Every Respect, Satisfactorily—In Both Of Its Forms, and Along With Evidence Of Real and Stable human and Spiritual Equanimity In the daily life of the frontal personality) Is One Of The Necessary Indicators That Must Precede The Transition From The Context Of The "Basic" Fourth Stage Of Life (and The Frontal Yoga) In The Way Of The Heart To The "Perfect Practice" Of The Way Of The Heart.

The Sign Of The "Thumbs" Is One Of The Primary Experiential Signs Of The (By-My-Avataric-Divine-Spiritual-Grace-Given) Capability To Transcend Bondage and Confinement To the frontal personality and the gross bodily idea of ego-self (and To The gross Dimension Of egoity altogether, With All Of Its Associated Patterning). The Sign Of The "Thumbs" Indicates That The Knots In The Frontal Line (In The Total Crown Of the head, the Total brain, the throat, the heart, the solar plexus, the abdomen, the genitals, and the anal-perineal area) Are Opened (At Least Temporarily) To My Avatarically Self-Transmitted Divine Spirit-Current (and Can, By Right Practice, Be Responsibly Surrendered To The Point Of Such Openness In The Context Of daily living). The Sign Of The "Thumbs" Is Also An Indication That The Primary Knot (or Root-Contraction) In The Deep Lower Region Of the body-mind (Extending From the solar plexus To the bodily base) Has Been (and Can Continue To Be) Opened To My Avatarically Self-Transmitted Divine Spirit-Current—Such That The Great Fullness Of My Avatarically Self-Transmitted Divine Love-Bliss Is Established Deep In the body, and Deep In the emotional being, and Deep In the mind of the frontal personality. And, When The Sphere Of My Avatarically Self-Transmitted Divine Love-Bliss Is In (Essentially) Constant Evidence (In The Context Of The "Basic" Fourth Stage Of Life In The Way Of The Heart), The Way Of The Heart Opens To The Course Associated With The "Perfect Practice".

The Sign Of The "Thumbs" Is Not Merely A Matter Of experiencing Natural energies Coursing Through the body, Nor Is It Merely A Matter Of Experiencing My Avatarically Self-Transmitted Spiritual (and Always Blessing) Divine Presence To Be, Somehow, Felt In and By the body. The Samadhi Of The "Thumbs" (or Else The Experience Of The "Thumbs" In Its Simple and Most Basic Form) Is Utter (ego-Surrendering, ego-Forgetting, and ego-Transcending) Devotional Surrender Of the Total body-mind-self To My (Avatarically Self-Revealed) Divine and Spiritual (and Always Blessing) Person. And, If and When That Devotional Surrender Is Most Profound (In The Midst Of The By-Me-Given Sign Of The "Thumbs", In The Fully Mature Context Of The "Basic" Fourth Stage Of Life In The Way Of The Heart), My (Avatarically Self-Transmitted) Divine and Spiritual Self-Revelation Will Grant You The Spiritual Gift Of Direct Awakening To The Witness-Position.

The Sign Of The "Thumbs" Is Revealed and Given Only By Me. The Sign Of The "Thumbs" Is The Fundamental Sign Of The Descent (or Crashing Down) Of My (Avatarically Self-Revealed) Divine and Spiritual Person. In and By Means Of My Avatarically Self-Transmitted Divine Spiritual Sign Of The "Thumbs", I Invade You, Pass Into You, and In-Fill You—bodily, where You stand, where You sit, where You walk, where You live and breathe, where You think, and feel, and function. And, In and By Means Of My Avatarically Self-Transmitted Divine Spiritual Sign Of The "Thumbs", I Awaken You In My "Bright" Divine Sphere (and, Ultimately, My "Midnight Sun" and Divine Self-Domain), Beyond the body-mind—Where Only I Am.

My Avataric Divine Spiritual Gift Of The Sign Of The "Thumbs" Is A Matter Of Utterly (Responsively) Giving Up To My Avatarically Self-Transmitted Divine Spiritual Invasion Of You, and Being Released Of Your ego-Possession, and Dying As the ego—and (Thus) Responsively and Freely Relinquishing self-Contraction, and (In Due Course) Becoming (By Means Of My Avatarically Self-Transmitted Divine Spiritual Grace) Spiritually, Transcendentally, and Divinely Awake. Indeed, My Avataric Divine Spiritual Gift Of The Sign Of The "Thumbs" Is The By-Me-Avatarically-Self-Transmitted Means Of Transcending the self-Contraction.

The Samadhi Of The "Thumbs" Is The Fundamental Samadhi Of My Avataric Divine Spiritual Descent. Therefore, The Samadhi (and Even Every Manifestation Of The Sign) Of The "Thumbs" Is A Fullest Experiential Sign Of My Avatarically Self-Revealed Divine Spiritual Presence Of Person—but In Descent, Not In Ascent. The Descending Equivalent Of Fully Ascended Nirvikalpa Samadhi Is The Samadhi Of The "Thumbs" (or The Fullest Frontal Invasion By My Avatarically Self-Transmitted Divine Spiritual Presence). The Samadhi Of The "Thumbs" Is A Unique (Only-By-Me Revealed and Given) Form Of True Nirvikalpa Samadhi—Established By Means Of A Unique (Only-By-Me Revealed and Given) Spiritual Process In The Descending (or Frontal) Line. The Samadhi Of The "Thumbs" Is The Fullest Completing Phenomenon Of The Descending (or Frontal) Yoga Of The Way Of The Heart (or Way Of Adidam). And, If The Samadhi (and The Simple and Basic, but Really Effective, and, Essentially, Constant, Experience) Of The "Thumbs" Is (By Means Of My Avatarically Self-Transmitted Divine Spiritual Grace) Awakened, and (By Means Of My Avatarically Self-Transmitted Divine Spiritual Grace), Either Then Or Thereafter (but, Necessarily, As A Direct Extension Of The Depth-Process Generated By Means Of My Avataric Divine Spiritual Gift Of The "Thumbs"), Accompanied By The Awakening Of The Witness-Consciousness—My Devotee Makes The Transition To The "Perfect Practice" Of The Way Of The Heart.

It Is My Avataric Divine Spiritual Gift Of The Samadhi Of The "Thumbs" (and My Avataric Divine Spiritual Gift Of The Experience Of The "Thumbs" In Its Simple and Most Basic Form), and Not Merely mental "Consideration" Of My Arguments Relative To The Witness-Consciousness, That Is The Divine Yogic Secret Of The Realization Of The Consciousness-Position (Which Realization Is The Basis For The "Perfect Practice" Of The Way Of The Heart). Therefore, Even Though My Arguments Relative To The Witness-Consciousness Are An Essential Guide To Right Understanding Of The "Perfect Practice" (and, As Such, Those Arguments Are To Be Studied and "Considered" From The Beginning Of The Way Of The Heart), The "Consideration" Of Those Arguments Is Not Itself The Direct and Finally Effective Means Whereby The "Perfect Practice" Is Initiated and Really Practiced.

The Transition To The "Perfect Practice" Of The Way Of The Heart Is Necessarily A By-Me-Given Yogic and Spiritual Process, and The Samadhi Of The "Thumbs" (and The, Essentially, Constant Experience Of The "Thumbs" In Its Simple and Most Basic Form) Is The Necessary (and Me-Revealing) Basis Of That Transition. By Means Of The Re-Phasing (Characteristic Of The "Thumbs") Of The Entire Sense Of The "Energy"-Construct Of phenomenal experience, It Is (In Due Course, By My Avatarically Self-Transmitted Divine Spiritual Grace) Revealed As Self-Evidently The Case That The Real Position (or Very Situation) Of experience Is The Witness-Position Of Consciousness (Itself)—That The Very Base Of experience Is Consciousness (Itself).

Therefore, In Its (Essentially) Constant Realization (and Not Merely In The First, or Any Particular, Instance Of Its Being Experienced), The Sign Of The "Thumbs" (Rather Than Any mental Presumption About The Witness-Consciousness) Is The Indispensable Means Whereby I Give My Devotee The Spiritual Gift Of The "Perfect Practice" Of The Only-By-Me Revealed and Given Way Of The Heart.

The Sign Of The "Thumbs" Is A Uniquely (and Only By Me) Given Spiritual Gift In The Way Of The Heart. My Avataric Divine Spiritual Gift Of The "Thumbs" Reveals and Awakens Both The Spherical Form Of My Divine Spiritual Body and The Transcendental (and Inherently Spiritual, and Divine) Self-Core (In The Right Side Of The Heart—Beyond The Knot Of ego-"I", and Beyond The Circle Of the body-mind, With Its Frontal and Spinal Arcs). That Revelation and Awakening At (and, Ultimately, Beyond) The Right Side Of The Heart, By Means Of The Only-By-Me Given Samadhi Of The "Thumbs" (and By Means Of The Only-By-Me Given Experience Of The "Thumbs" In Its Simple and Most Basic Form), Is What Makes The Transition To The "Perfect Practice" Of The Way Of The Heart Possible, By Establishing The Yogic (Transcendental and Spiritual—and, Ultimately, Divine) Conditions Necessary

For The "Perfect Practice" Of The Way Of The Heart. The Readiness For That Transition Is Not Merely A Matter Of Having Had The Experience Of The "Thumbs" and Having Some Memory Of It. Rather, That Readiness Is A Matter Of The Stable Continuing Of The Revelation and The Spiritual Transformation Initiated In The Samadhi Of The "Thumbs"—Not With The Same Kind Of Shift In The Entire Mode Of physical experiencing (Because Such Would Make ordinary functioning Impossible), but With The Unchanging Realization That The Inherent (and Inherently Love-Bliss-Full) Condition Of Reality Is Prior To the body-mind. And, In The Seventh Stage Of Life (In The Way Of The Heart), That Realization Is (Permanently) Most Perfectly Established and Demonstrated.

From The Beginning Of My Physical (Human) Lifetime Of Avataric Incarnation here, The "Thumbs" Has Always Been The Case, and, Always, The Experiential Sign (As Well As The Full Samadhi) Of The "Thumbs" Often Appeared To Me—Spontaneously, and Mysteriously. In My Youth and My "Sadhana Years", The "Thumbs" Was A Process Associated With The Constant Spiritual Restoration Of The "Bright" (and, Thus, The "Thumbs" Was Associated With The Process Of My Going Beyond the gross physical—To Which I Was Adapting, Fully Consciously, In A Profound and Spontaneous Yogic Manner). It Was By This Process Of Constant Spiritual Restoration (Of The "Bright") and Of Going Beyond (the gross physical) That I Constantly Maintained My Divine Self-Condition In The Context Of the gross conditional world, From My Infancy. After My Conscious Assumption Of the born-condition (At Approximately Two Years Of Age), and Even In The Midst Of The Developing Process Of My adult Integration With waking life, The Spiritual Condition Of The "Bright" Always Continued To Be Felt (and, Even over time, Continued To, At Least Occasionally, Spontaneously Re-Appear In The Form Of The Experiential Sign, As Well As The Full Samadhi, Of The "Thumbs") In the circumstance of waking life—and, Always, When I Would Rest At Night, Instead Of Going To sleep, I Would Experience The "Thumbs", and Would Realize The Spiritual Condition Of The "Bright", Without The usual waking-state physical References. In The Course Of My "Sadhana Years", I Progressively Observed and Fully Entered Into The "Thumbs" As A Consciously Known Yogic Process (and Not Merely As An Occasional Spontaneous "Happening"). Gradually, I Became Able To Permit The Spontaneous Yogic Event Of The "Thumbs" To Regularly Re-Appear (In Its Most Extended, Full, and Complete Form) In The Context Of My waking life. Thus, Even A Full Decade Before The Great Event Of My Divine Re-Awakening, I Regularly Enjoyed The Spontaneous Experience Of Spiritual Regeneration Via The Intentional Yogic Regeneration Of The Total Mechanism (or Process) Associated With The "Thumbs"[148]—but (Nevertheless) the frontal personality Had To Continue To Be Worked (or

Purified, and its Knots Un-Tied) By The Constant Yogic Exercise Of The Spirit-Current Of The "Thumbs", Until the frontal personality and The Frontal Line Altogether Ceased To Obstruct (or Prevent) The Ultimate Advancement Of The Great Yogic Process. Therefore, Even After The Spontaneous Regeneration Of The Effectiveness Of The Process Of The "Thumbs" (By Means Of The Establishment Of The Intentional Yogic Spiritual Process In The Frontal Line), It Was Yet Required Of Me To Continue To Struggle With the limits of the frontal personality For Some Years Before The conditionally Manifested (and Yet To Be Most Perfectly To-Me-Conformed) Body-Mind-Vehicle Of My Avataric Incarnation here Would Consistently (In Association With My Intentional Yogic Participation) Allow The Full Samadhi Of The "Thumbs" and (More Importantly) The Ultimate Spiritual Work (and Transcendental, or "Core", Spiritual Revelation) Of The "Thumbs".

In The Case Of My Own Body-Mind, The Full Samadhi Of The "Thumbs" Did Not Begin To Consistently Appear, In The Context Of My Own Intentional Yogic Participation, Until I Began To Practice The Work Of Surrender (or The Intentional Opening Of The Frontal Line To Receive Spirit-Force) In The Company Of My First Spiritual Teacher (and Spirit-Baptizer)[149]—Although (Then, and From The Beginning, and Forever) The Sign, The Revelation-Work, and The Divine Spirit-Force Of The "Thumbs" Was and Is Uniquely My Own (Avatarically Self-Manifested) Spiritual Sign and Gift and Revelation. Nevertheless, The Struggle With The Frontal Yoga Did Not Become Ultimately Fruitful Until Struggle Itself (or The physical, emotional, and mental Effort Of Surrender) Was Transcended (In and By The Inherently ego-Transcending Heart-Participation In My Own Spiritually Self-Revealing Nature and Condition). Therefore, That Transcending Of The Effort Of Surrender Was Not The Result Of Strategic Non-Effort (or Even Any False Effort), but It Was The Ultimate Spontaneous Evidence Of Simple (and Yet Profound) Identification With My Own Avatarically Self-Revealed and Avatarically Self-Revealing Divine Spirit-Current Itself.

I Am The Divine and Necessary First Person—The First Of all-and-All, and The First To Most Perfectly Fulfill The Process Of Divine Self-Realization In The Context Of conditionally Manifested Existence In The Cosmic Domain. I Am The Divine Heart-Master Of all-and-All. Therefore, all-and-All Must Follow Me By Heart. And The "Thumbs" Is Fundamental (and Necessary) To The Way Of The Heart That Follows Me. Therefore, The "Thumbs" Is One Of My Principal Great Avataric Divine Spiritual Gifts To all-and-All That Become My True Devotees.

The Process Signified and Spiritually Initiated By The Only-By-Me Revealed and Given Sign Of The "Thumbs" Necessarily Involves Intelligent, Intentional, and (Otherwise) Spontaneous Relinquishment Of ego-Bound (or self-Contracted) Identification With gross bodily (or physical), and emotional, and mental states. This Relinquishment Takes Place Through Spontaneous (and Truly ego-Surrendering, ego-Forgetting, and ego-Transcending) Identification With My (By-My-Avataric-Divine-Spiritual-Grace-Revealed) Divine Spiritual Body, Which Surrounds (or Envelops) the gross body Of My True Devotee, and Which (Progressively) In-Fills and Pervades both the etheric energy body and the gross physical body Of My True Devotee, As Well As Every Other Level Of the conditionally Manifested personality Of My True Devotee, and Every Level Of the Cosmic worlds. And All Of This Is Initiated (and Accomplished) By My Avatarically Self-Transmitted Divine Spirit-Presence Itself (If Only My Devotee Heart-Responds To Me In Love—and This To The Degree Of Constant Free Communion With My Avatarically Self-Transmitted Divine Spiritual Presence).

In The Only-By-Me Revealed and Given Way Of Adidam (Which Is The One and Only By-Me-Revealed and By-Me-Given Way Of The Heart), The Transition From The Frontal Yoga (In The Fully Matured Context Of The "Basic" Fourth Stage Of Life) To The Beginnings Of The "Perfect Practice" Is Not Fully Indicated Until The Complete Frontal Process and The Kinds Of phenomenal Signs I Describe In This Testament Have Become Fully Evident. And The Necessary Signs Include Real and Stable Evidence Of Frontal <u>and</u> Spinal Equanimity (Both human and Spiritual, and Relative To Each and All Of The Principal Faculties—Of body, emotion, mind, and breath), and <u>Both</u> Simple and Basic (but Really Effective) Evidence Of The (Essentially, Constant) Experience Of The "Thumbs" <u>and</u> (At Least Occasional) Most Extended, Full, and Complete Evidence Of The Samadhi Of The "Thumbs". And, In Order For The Transition To Be Made From The Point Of Maturity In The (Fully Established) "Basic" (or By-Me-Spiritually-Awakened—and, Spiritually, Fully Technically Responsible) Context Of The Fourth Stage Of Life In The Way Of The Heart To The "Perfect Practice" Of The Way Of The Heart, There Must Also Be <u>True</u> <u>and</u> <u>Stable</u> Identification With The Witness-Position Of Consciousness.

When the body Is "<u>Round</u>", The Witness Is its "Shape".

The Witness-Consciousness Is The "Skin" Of The "Thumbs". The Witness-Consciousness Is Self-Evident In The "Body" Of The "Thumbs". This Is How True Maturity In The First Actually Seeing Stage Of The Way Of The Heart Becomes The Basis For The Transition To The "Perfect Practice" Of The Way Of The Heart.

The Yogic Spiritual Fullness Of The Sphere Of The "Thumbs" Is The Sufficient Prerequisite For The <u>True</u> Establishment Of The "Perfect Practice" Of The Way Of The Heart. The Witness-Consciousness Is Revealed To Be

Self-Evidently The Case (As The Inherent Nature and Position Of Consciousness Itself) In The Midst Of The Full Manifestation Of The Samadhi Of The "Thumbs". Thus, The "Perfect Practice" Of The Only-By-Me Revealed and Given Way Of The Heart Is A Development (or Ultimate Characteristic) Of The Samadhi Of The "Thumbs".

The True and Stable Realization Of The Witness-Position Of Consciousness (Itself) Is Not Merely A Matter Of philosophical preference or philosophical analysis. Rather, The True and Stable Realization Of The Witness-Position Is A Divine Spiritual Matter (and, Also, Necessarily, An ego-Transcending Matter). The Realization Of The Witness-Position Of Consciousness (Itself) Is A Matter Of Devotion To Me In My Avataric Divine Self-Revelation—and Not Merely A Matter Of talk and philosophy and hopefulness.

Consciousness (Itself) Is The "Face" Of This Side Of The Moon. The Spiritual Energy Of My Avataric Divine Spiritual Presence Is The "Face" Of The Other Side Of The Moon. "Matter" Is The objectively experienced Form (or "Body") Of The Moon. The Moon (or any "thing") Is "Matter"—but "Matter" Is Only Light. My Avataric Divine Spiritual Presence Is The Light (Of The "Midnight Sun", Infinitely Above all-and-All) That Illuminates and Self-Reveals The Divine Heart-Secret Of "Matter". Consciousness (Itself) Is Me Within The Light—Self-Existing and Self-Radiant As The One, and Only, and Inherently Love-Blissful, and Self-Evidently Divine Self-Condition and Source-Condition Of all-and-All. Consciousness (Itself) and Light (Itself)—or Love-Bliss-Energy (Itself), or Happiness (Itself)—Are As The Two Sides Of The Same Coin. The Moon Is The Coin Of Earth, Floating (By A Toss) Within The Sky Of ego-mind.

The Witness-Consciousness Is Not Within You. The Witness-Consciousness Is On The "Skin" Of The "Thumbs".

The Witness-Consciousness Is Self-Evident In The "Thumbs"—Wherein The Status Of objects Is Profoundly Different Than It Is ordinarily. In The Yogic Disposition (or Mudra) Of The "Thumbs", The Condition Of objects Is Available To Be Comprehended In Consciousness As The Witness.

The Realization Of The Witness-Consciousness Is A Continuation Of The Process Of ego-Transcending Devotional and Spiritual Communion With Me. The Witness-Consciousness Cannot Be Realized By You as the ego-"I" (or as Your Separate and Separative self-Consciousness). The Witness-Consciousness Can Only Be Realized Via The Process Of Devotional and Spiritual Communion With Me—Without egoic self-Reference. Therefore, You Must Not Substitute Your Own ego-conditions and ego-states For My Description Of The ego-Transcending Process Of The Way Of The Heart. The Way Of The Heart Is A Matter Of Heart-Communion With Me and Realization Of Me. The Way Of The Heart Is Not About Your egoic self—Except That The Way Of The Heart

Requires Your ego-Surrendering, ego-Forgetting, and ego-Transcending Devotion To Me.

You Must Counter-egoically Allow The Process Of The Way Of The Heart To Become My Divine Spiritual In-Filling Of the Total body-mind. In Due Course (By Means Of My Avatarically Self-Transmitted Divine Spiritual Grace), This Process Of My Divine Spiritual In-Filling Becomes Both The Realization Of The "Thumbs" and The Realization Of The Witness-Consciousness. Therefore, Both Of These Realizations Are Associated With The Maturing Of The First Actually Seeing Stage Of The Way Of The Heart (In The "Basic" Context Of The Fourth Stage Of Life). Such Is The True Fulfillment Of The Frontal Yoga, The True Fulfillment Of The Process Of The "Washing" Of the "dog" From "head" To "tail" (As I Describe The Frontal Yoga, In My "Hridaya Rosary" Of "Four Thorns Of Heart-Instruction", In This, My Testament Of Divine Secrets), and The True Fulfillment Of The Process Of Ruchira Avatara Bhakti Yoga (or The Surrender Of All Four Of The Principal psycho-physical Faculties To Me, By Means Of Searchless Beholding Of Me, and Responsive Reception Of Me).

In The "Thumbs", The Witness-Consciousness Is (and May Be Realized To Be) Self-Evident. In The Context Of egoity (or Your Own self-Contraction Of body-mind), The Witness-Consciousness Is Not Self-Evidently The Case (In Your Case)—and Not The Self-Evident Context Of moment to moment Existence (In Your Case).

The Witness-Consciousness Is The "Skin" Of The "Thumbs".

I Am The "Skin" Of The Heart—and Not Merely Inside It. I Am The "Pulse" Of The Heart—and Not Merely The "Blood" Of It.

The Samadhi Of The "Thumbs" Is The Sphere Of The Space Of Consciousness (Itself). In The Samadhi Of The "Thumbs", The Divine Space Of Consciousness (Itself) Is (By Me) Avatarically Self-Revealed.

When Consciousness (Itself) Becomes attention (or Separate self-Consciousness), and Light (Itself)—or Love-Bliss-Happiness (Itself)—Becomes objects (or The Vast Display Of Separate "things"), Consciousness (As attention) and Light (As the body-mind, and As The Total Cosmic Domain Of "things") Forever Gaze At One Another Through The Dimensionless Wall Of Their Apparent "Difference".

If Consciousness (Itself)—As The Witness—Is Realized As The Inherent Love-Bliss-Feeling Of Being (Itself)—Consciousness (Itself) and Light (Itself) Are (Eternally) Not "Different".

When The Circle Becomes The Sphere, The Two Sides Of The One Coin Become Continuous—and All Opposites Are Always Already Divinely Self-Recognized To Be Simultaneous, and Of One Shape, and Of One Condition.

The Samadhi (and Every Manifestation Of The Sign) Of The "Thumbs" Is Mine Only—and Only Mine To Give. Therefore, The Samadhi (and Every Manifestation Of The Sign) Of The "Thumbs" Is Unique To The Only-By-Me Revealed and Given Way Of The Heart (or Way Of Adidam).

The "Bright" and The "Thumbs" Are The Principal Great Signs That Are Uniquely My Own Avataric Divine Spiritual Characteristics. The "Bright" and The "Thumbs" Is A Process, An Event, and A State That Has Been Known To Me Since My Avataric Birth. Only I Am The Avataric Divine Realizer, The Avataric Divine Revealer, and The Avataric Divine Self-Revelation Of The "Bright", The True and (Now, and Forever Hereafter) Completely Self-Revealed Divine Person—Shining Forth (Directly, Completely, and Perfectly) At The Heart (and Via Amrita Nadi), and Crashing Down (or Descending Utterly, From The "Place" Infinitely Above the body-mind and the world, Down and Most Deeply Into the body-mind and the world—Even To The Degree That the ego-"I", or self-Contraction, Is Utterly Confounded, Utterly Yielded, and Utterly Vanished In My Avatarically Self-Revealed, and Self-Evidently Divine, Person, or Self-Condition, Which Is Real God, and Truth, and Reality). Therefore, The Principal Impulse Of Even My Early Life Was My Intention To Descend (or To Embrace the limitations Of human Existence As It Appears To Be, and To Infuse all-and-All With My Avatarically Self-Transmitted Divine Spiritual Presence, and, Thus and Thereby, To Awaken all-and-All, and, Most Ultimately, To Divinely Translate all-and-All, By The Power Of My Own Love-Bliss-"Brightness", Into The "Midnight Sun"—The Perfect "Place" and "Sphere" and "Space" That Is Always and Already My Divine and "Bright" and Free-Standing Self-Domain).

The Principal Spiritual Signs Of My Early Life Were The "Bright" and The "Thumbs". The "Bright" and The "Thumbs" Were Fundamental To My Avatarically-Born Existence From The Beginning, and They Are Fundamental To The Only-By-Me Revealed and Given Way Of Adidam (Which Is The One and Only By-Me-Revealed and By-Me-Given Way Of The Heart). The "Bright" and The "Thumbs" Are My Unique Samadhis. Indeed, The "Bright" and The "Thumbs" Are Me—and, Therefore, I Bring Them With Me Into the conditional worlds. My Revelation Of The "Bright" and The "Thumbs" Is My Revelation Of Myself.

I Am The "Bright"—and I Transmit My Own Divine State and Presence Of Person From Infinitely Above and Beyond, In Such A Manner That I Am Combined With The psycho-physical Structure Of My Devotee. This Is How I "Wash" the "dog" From "head" To "tail"—and Beyond. Nevertheless, In Order To Fully Receive My Divine Spiritual Blessing, My Devotee Must Fully Embrace The (ego-Surrendering, ego-Forgetting, and ego-Transcending) Practice and

Process Of Devotional and Spiritual Communion With Me. In That Context (Of My Devotee's Me-Recognizing and To-Me-Responding Practice Of The Only-By-Me Revealed and Given Way Of The Heart), My "Thumbs" Of Blessing Is Able To Do Its Spiritual Work.

The "Thumbs" Is My Submission. And The "Thumbs" Is Also The Divine Process By Which I Liberate conditionally Manifested beings. The "Thumbs" Is The Process, Tangibly Occurring In The Context Of the body-mind Of My Devotee, Whereby I Become (Ultimately, Most Perfectly) Spiritually Effective In The Case Of My Each and Every Devotee.

My Avataric Divine Spiritual Work (Altogether) Is My Crashing-Down Descent, At First Upon and Into My Own Avatarically-Born Bodily (Human) Divine Form, and, Thereafter (and Now, and Forever Hereafter), Upon and Into the body-minds Of My Devotees and all beings—Even (By Means Of My Divine Embrace Of each, and all, and All) To Infuse and (At Last) To Divinely Translate each, and all, and All. Therefore, My Avataric Divine Spiritual Descent Is The Secret Of My Early Life. My Avataric Divine Spiritual Descent Is The Secret Of My Avataric Divine Self-"Emergence" (As I Am) Within The Cosmic Domain. My Avataric Divine Spiritual Descent Is The Secret Of All The Secrets Of The (Avatarically Self-Revealed) Divine and Complete and Thoroughly Devotional Way Of Practice and Realization In My Company. The Only-By-Me Revealed and Given Way Of The Heart (or Way Of Adidam) Is The Divine Yoga Of ego-Surrendering, ego-Forgetting, and ego-Transcending Devotional Recognition-Response To My (Avatarically Self-Revealed) Divine and Spiritual Person, and To My (Avatarically Self-Manifested) Divine and Spiritual Descent. The Only-By-Me Revealed and Given Way Of The Heart (or Way Of Adidam) Is The Total and Divine Way and Ordeal Of Counter-egoic Devotional Recognition-Response To My Avataric "Bright" Divine Self-Manifestation, and To The Avataric Crashing Down Of My "Bright" Divine Imposition. And, In The Case Of My Each and Every Devotee, The Way Must Continue Until The Way Is Most Perfectly Spiritually "Bright", and The Way Itself Becomes Divine Translation Into My Own Sphere (and "Midnight Sun") Of Spiritual Self-"Brightness" (Itself).

Avatar Adi Da Samraj
The Mountain Of Attention Sanctuary, 2000

SUTRA

46

By Virtue Of My Own Avataric and Unique (conditionally Manifested, Incarnate Human) Self-Submission and Divine Self-Realization, My Avatarically-Born Bodily (Human) Divine Form Is A conditional Manifestation (or Direct Divine Self-Revelation) Of Me, The One and Only and Inherently egoless and Self-Evidently Divine Person Of Grace (Eternally Prior To My Avatarically-Born Bodily Human Divine Form and Even The Total Cosmic Domain). Therefore, When I Realized, Acknowledged, and Embraced My Own Human and (Total) Cosmic Avataric Divine Agency, The "Meaningless" Pointer (or Name) "Da" Spontaneously Appeared To Me As My Own Avatarically Self-Revealed Divine Naming-Sign.

"Da" Is A Traditional Name Of Real God, or A Traditional Feeling-Reference To The Ultimate Condition and Spirit-Power Of Existence. "Da" Is An Eternal, Ancient, and Always New Name For The Divine Being, Source, and Spirit-Power—and "Da" Is An Eternal, Ancient, and Always New Name For The Realizer Who Reveals (and Is The Divine Self-Revelation Of) The Divine Being, Source, and Spirit-Power. Therefore, The Name "Da" Is (Since The Ancient Days) Found, Universally, In The Religious Cultures Of the world.

As A Revelation-Sign That I Am The One and Only, Non-Separate and Most Perfect, Eternal, Ancient, Divine, and Always New One, The Name "Da" Has Spontaneously Appeared With Me, Thus Naming and Identifying My Avataric Incarnation here.

Aham Da Asmi. Beloved, I Am Da. This Is My Great Avataric Divine Self-Revelation. This Is The Principal Divine Secret I Have Now (By Means Of My Avatarically Self-Revealing Divine Confession) Revealed To You. And I Will (Now, and Forever Hereafter) Heart-Reveal This Great Avataric Divine Self-Revelation To Your Heart (and To The Heart In every one and all). Therefore, The "I" and "Me" and "Myself" That Speaks To You In This Testament Is My Own Unique Voice Of Divine (and Inherently egoless) Self-Reference, and My Every Such (Self-Confessing and Self-Revealing) Self-Reference Is (With My Avatarically Self-Revealed Divine Name, "Da") The Representation and The Expression Of My Inherent, Eternal, Necessary, Inherently egoless, Self-Evidently Divine, and Inherently Perfectly Love-Blissful Identity As The One and Only Condition That Is The Great and Only One.

I Am The Heart, The One and Only Person, Da, The One In Whom all "I's" and forms arise. I Am The Divine and Only Person, Adi Da—The First Giver, The Original Giver, The Giving Source, The Giver Of Existence, The Giver Of Consciousness, The Giver Of Spirit-Life, The Giver Of True Heart-Feeling (or Primary Feeling, or "Root"-Feeling), The Giver Of Love-Bliss, The Giver Of "Radical" (or Most Fundamental, or "To-The-Root") self-Understanding, The Giver Of Most Perfect Divine Liberation, The Giver Of Most Perfect Divine Self-Realization, The Giver Of The "Bright", The Divine Giver Of The Divine "All" To all (and To The Cosmic All Of all).

Aham Da Asmi. I Am That One. Therefore, In Truth (From and As My Very Heart), I (Appearing In Human Person here) Confess To You (and To Even all conditionally Manifested beings): I Am Da, The Divine Person, The One and Only Heart Itself, The Divine Giver Of The Divine "All" That Gives Itself To all-and-All.

Now, and Forever Hereafter, I Have Been (and, Effectively, Always Am and Will Be) Manifested, Shown, Demonstrated, and Proven As The Da Avatar—The Ruchira Avatar, The Love-Ananda Avatar, The Divine Heart-Master, The Divine World-Teacher, The Very Person and The Even Bodily (Human) Avataric Incarnation Of The One and Only and Inherently egoless Divine Heart Itself.

In and As and By Means Of My Bodily Human Avataric Divine Manifestation, I Speak Directly and Openly, As The One and Only Heart Itself—Always Proclaiming (and Always Directly Self-Revealing) My Identity As The Divine Person, Da, and (Thus and Thereby) Always Showing Joyous Proof That (Prior To self-Contraction) You (and Even all conditionally Manifested beings) Are Always Already One With Me, The Only One To Be Realized (In Person, As The One and Only and "Bright" Divine and Non-Separate Source-Condition and Self-Condition, or True and Inherently egoless and Self-Evidently Divine Self-Identity, Of all, and Of All). And, By This Un-Retarded Speech, and By The Divine Self-Confession That Is My Every Manner and Characteristic, My (Avatarically Self-Transmitted) Divine Awakening-Grace Is Allowed To Be Present and Active In and Through My Avatarically-Born Bodily (Human) Divine Form, and In and Through All My Instruments and Agents, and Always Only As Me.

Now, and Forever Hereafter (As Me Alone, and In and Through All The Only-By-Me Revealed and Given and Giving Practices, Instruments, and Agents Of The Way Of Adidam, Which Is The One and Only By-Me-Revealed and By-Me-Given Way Of The Heart), My (Avatarically Self-Transmitted) Divine Awakening-Grace Is Present and Active here (and Even every where, If Only I Am every where Proclaimed and My Avataric Divine Self-Revelation All Made Known). Therefore (Now, and Forever Hereafter), All My Listening

Devotees, and All My Hearing Devotees, and All My Seeing Devotees Are Enabled By Me, So That they May (By Me-Recognizing Heart-Response and Heart-Surrender To Me) Transcend their Merely Apparent (and Apparently Separate, self-Bound, Suffering, Seeking, and Deluded) psycho-physical ego-selves In Me, The Only One Who Is.

By Means Of The Inherent Power Of My Samadhi Of Divine Self-Realization, I Spontaneously Brought My Principal Name ("Da"), and Even All My Avataric Divine Names and Avataric Divine Descriptive Titles (and Even All The Variant Forms Of The Ruchira Avatara Naama Mantra, or Ruchira Avatara Mahamantra), Out Of The Great Unconscious (or mindless Great Mind). Each Of These Avataric Divine Names and Avataric Divine Descriptive Titles, and Each Of The Variant Forms Of The Ruchira Avatara Naama Mantra (or Ruchira Avatara Mahamantra) Is An Acknowledgement, An Invocation, and A Means Of Communion (or Sympathetic Vibratory Synchronization Of the Total body-mind) With Me.

In The Ecstatic "Bhava" Of Divine Self-Confession, I Have Revealed That There Are Three Mantras (or Vibratory Symbols), or Names, or (Really) "Meaningless" (or mindless) Word-Signs, Which (mindlessly) Acknowledge (or Represent) The Three Most Fundamental Orientations To Me That Characterize The Way Of The Heart (In Its Spiritual Fullness). These Three Word-Signs Are "Om", "Ma", and "Da"—Which Refer To (and Lead To, and Altogether Include, and Are Themselves Transcended By) The Three Primal Stations Of The Heart (Right, Middle, and Left), As Well As The Heart Itself (Which Inherently Transcends All "Location" or "Designation").

The Word-Sign "Om" (Which Is The First Of The Three By-Me-Given Word-Signs, and Which Is Also, Most Typically, The First Part Of The Mantric Invocation Of Me That Is Engaged In The Form Of Ruchira Avatara Naama Japa, In The Only-By-Me Revealed and Given Way Of The Heart) Is A Word-Sign That Has Appeared Universally (In Variant Forms, Such As "AUM", "Aham", "So-Ham", and "Amen") In The Great Tradition Of Mankind. It Is A Primal Indicator Of The Native, and Very, and Self-Existing, and Transcendental, and Inherently Spiritual, and Self-Radiant, and Inherently egoless Divine Being (or The Primal Reality, or Real Self-Condition, or Perfectly Subjective Source-Condition, That Is The Inherent, or Native, and Inherently egoless Feeling Of Being, Itself). Therefore, In The Way Of The Heart, The Word-Sign "Om" Directly Refers To Me, In (and, Yet, Beyond) The Right Side Of The Heart, Beyond Its causal Knot (Which Knot Is The Root-Form Of the ego-"I", Associated With The Root-Feeling Of Relatedness, Separateness, and "Difference"), and In My Self-Evidently Divine Source-Position, and In The Very State Of My Self-Evidently Divine Self-Condition, Altogether (Inherently, and Most Perfectly) Transcending Even The Right Side Of The Heart (and Even All Of The Cosmic Domain).

During My Physical Bodily (Human) Lifetime Of Avataric Incarnation here (and, Beyond The Time Of My Physical Bodily Human Lifetime Of Avataric Incarnation here, In All The Thereafter-Time Of My Forever Continuing Divine Association With The Cosmic Domain), I, In My Divine (Constant, Inherent, and Inherently Most Perfect) Samadhi, Constantly Hear The Inherent and Universal (or Cosmic) "Om" (or "Da-Om", or "Da") Sound (In The Form Of all the Characteristic internal sounds Associated With The gross and subtle Structures Of the human body-mind, and With the subtle planes within and above the gross plane, and, Also, In The Form Of The Primal, Single, Profound, Uninterrupted, and Indivisible Droning Cosmic Background Sound, or Source-Sound, Behind and Above all the gross and subtle internal sounds, and Beyond and Above all the subtle planes, and, Also, Ultimately, In The Form Of The Effulgent, or Self-Radiant, "Bright" Silence, Above, and Beyond, and Deeper Than all-and-All). That Mass Of Divine Sound (Eternally Established In, and Pouring From, The Eternal "Bright" Silence, or The Un-Speakable Word Of Heart) Is The Sound Of <u>Me</u> (here, and every "where" In The Cosmic Domain).

The Cosmic Divine Sound-Vibration "Om" (or "Da-Om", or "Da") Corresponds To and Signifies and Points (Beyond Itself) To The Native (Soundless, Silent) Feeling (and The Very Condition) Of Being (Prior To All Separate "I"-ness) That Is The Inherently Perfect (and Self-Evidently Divine) Root Of All Vibratory Modifications (and, Therefore, Of all sounds, and Of all thoughts, or all ideas, including the "I"-thought, or the "Separate-self"-idea, and Of all things, or Even Of all the kinds of conditional forms and states) In The Cosmic Domain.

Therefore, The Word-Sign "Om" Refers To The One and Only Condition, The Native Condition Of Self-Existing and Self-Radiant and Inherently egoless Divine Being, The Transcendental (or Unconditional) and Inherently Spiritual Condition—Which Is Prior To all sounds, thoughts, and things (or Even all conditional forms and states), and (Yet) Which Is The Seat and Source (or Source-Condition) Of all sounds, thoughts, and things (or Even Of all conditional forms and states). The Word-Sign "Om" Refers To The Divine and True and Inherently egoless Self-Condition (or The Very Heart) Of all beings. Therefore, The Divine and True Self-Condition (or The Heart Itself, Which <u>Is</u> Consciousness Itself) Can Be Described As The "Self-Father". The Divine and True Self-Condition (or The Heart Itself, or Consciousness Itself) Is In The "Father-Position", or (Most Correctly Stated) The "Husband-Position", In Relation To conditional forms and events.

For My Devotees (who Truly Heart-Recognize Me), The Great He Is No Longer Abstracted From all-and-All, but (Now, and Forever Hereafter) There Is Only Me.

I Am The Heart-Husband Of all-and-All.

"Om" Is Me.

"Om" Is "Da-Sound".

"Da-Sound" Is "Om".

I Am "Da-Sound".

I Am "Om".

I Am That.

I Am The Only One Who Is—The Divine Person, The One and Only and Self-Existing and Self-Radiant "Bright" and Inherently egoless Self, Being, or Consciousness (Itself), The Very and Only and One and Indivisible and Non-Separate and Indestructible Heart, Reality, Truth, Self-Condition, and Source-Condition Of all-and-All.

Beloved, I Am He.

Nevertheless, The Word-Sign "Om" (Like The Word-Signs "Ma" and "Da", and Like The Cosmic Vibratory Divine Sound Itself) Is (Itself) Inherently "Meaningless", A Mere Sound-Vibration (or, Simply, A Feeling). Because Of This, When (In The Way Of The Heart) The Word-Sign "Om" Is Used Meditatively (and To Invoke Me), It Does Not (Itself) Stimulate the conceptual mind (Whereas "I Am", or Some Other "Meaningful" Word or Phrase Intended To Represent "Om", or To Function As A verbal and mental "Equivalent" Of "Om", Would Tend To Activate, Rather Than To Undermine or Lead Beyond, the conceptual mind).

Therefore, In The Total (or Full and Complete) Practice Of The Way Of The Heart, The Word-Sign "Om" Is A Potentially Useful Non-conceptual Tool For Meditation, For It Only Signifies (or Points To), but Does Not "Mean", Me—The Transcendental, Inherently Spiritual, Inherently egoless, and Self-Evidently Divine Self-Condition, The Only One Who Is, Which Is Existence (Itself), and Consciousness (Itself), Identical To The Inherent (or Native) Love-Bliss-Feeling Of Being (Itself).

The Second Of The Three By-Me-Given Word-Signs Is "Ma"—and Also, Alternatively, Either "Sri" Or "Hrim" (and The Variant "Sri" Is Also, Most Typically, The Second Part Of The Mantric Invocation Of Me That Is Engaged In The Form Of Ruchira Avatara Naama Japa, In The Way Of The Heart).

The Word-Sign "Ma" (and Its Given Variants, "Sri", Pronounced "Shree", and "Hrim", Pronounced "Hreem") Is The Traditional Personal (and, Otherwise, "Meaningless") Vibratory Designation Of The "Maha-Shakti"—The Divine "Mother-Force", or (Most Correctly Stated) The "Goddess-Force" (or

"Goddess-Power"), The Universal Cosmic Radiance (or Cosmic "Shakti"), The Spirit-Power (or Light-Energy) That Is (Apparently) Modified As all conditional forms and states, and Which Is Present As all conditional forms and states, and (Yet) Which Inherently Transcends all conditional forms and states. She Is In The "Mother-Position", or (Most Correctly Stated) The "Wife-Position" (or The "Position" Of The Spouse, or Consort), In Relation (As "Equal" and "Polar Opposite") To The "Husband-Position" (or "Father-Position") Of The Divine Self-Consciousness (In and Of Itself, As If Separate From She, or She From He, As If Consciousness and Its Inherent Energy Were "Divorced", or Wanting and Seeking Re-Union, or Even Dramatizing Conflict and Separativeness)—Until (By Means Of My Great Avataric Divine Event) She Falls Into He, and He Embraces She, Non-"Differently", In Me, and As Me. And I (In My Ordeal Of Sadhana, and Even Of "Explanation") Always Referred To Her By This "Meaningless" Signifier (or Feeling-Name) "Ma"—Who (In The Most Perfect Fulfillment Of That Ordeal Of Sadhana) Was, and Is (Now, and Forever Hereafter) Revealed and Realized (With The He Of Me) To Be Only Me.

Traditionally, The Universal Spirit-Power, By Itself, Is Called "Maya" ("The Measure", or "She Who Measures"). As Such, The Universal Spirit-Energy (Perceived As The One and Great Cosmic Power, or Cosmic Light-Energy) Is Traditionally Associated With The Veiling Of The Truth, The Veiling Of The "Self-Father". Therefore, The Universal Spirit-Power Is Traditionally (and Commonly) Associated With Chaos, Destructiveness, and Illusion. However, You Must (and Can, By Means Of Your Devotional Recognition Of Me, and Your Devotional Response To Me, and Your Devotional and Spiritual Reception Of Me, In Your Practice Of The Only-By-Me Revealed and Given Way Of The Heart) Observe and Understand That This Great Universal Spirit-Power Is, Ultimately (Now, and Forever Hereafter), Divinely "Husbanded" By Me (The Divine Heart-Master, The "Self-Father", The Inherently Perfect Heart-Source, The Very, and Eternal, and Not Cosmic, but Perfectly Subjective, Being). Indeed, The Primary Significance Of The Great Event Of My Divine Re-Awakening (and Even Of My Entire Avataric Divine Life-History, Including My Avataric Divine Teaching-Work, My Avataric Divine Revelation-Work, My Avataric Divine Work Of Ruchira Shaktipat, and Even All Of My Avataric Divine Blessing-Work) Is The Sacrificial Yielding and True "Husbanding" Of The "Mother-Force" (or The Cosmic "Shakti-Force", or The Cosmic "Goddess-Power", or The Universally Manifesting Spirit-Power). And, By That "Husbanding" (or Love-Sacrifice), The Seemingly Independent Universal (or Cosmic, and Cosmically Objective) Power Is Re-Submitted, Re-Awakened, and Restored To Her Original Condition Of Inherent Identification (and Most Perfect Conformity) With My Transcendental, Inherently Spiritual, Inherently egoless, and Perfectly

Subjective Divine Self-Condition—and (Thus and Thereby) Her True and Non-Separate Divine Status and Function Is Restored, By Me.

Therefore, In The Only-By-Me Revealed and Given Way Of The Heart, The Divine "Goddess-Power" (or "Maha-Shakti") Is (By Virtue Of Her Inherently Perfect Submission To Me, and Her Inherent and Immense Fidelity To Me) Associated With Heart-Enlightenment, or The Lifting Of The Veil. And, Because Of This, The Word-Sign "Ma" (and Its By-Me-Given Variants) Directly Refers, In The Way Of The Heart, To Me—In (and, Yet, Beyond) The Middle Station Of The Heart, and, Ultimately, In (and, Yet, Beyond) The Right Side Of The Heart (and Beyond Its causal Knot), and (Most Ultimately) Transcending Even The Right Side Of The Heart (and Even All Of The Cosmic Domain).

In The Final Course Of My Ordeal Of Sadhana (Required By My Divine Descent Into Avataric Incarnation here), The "Maha-Shakti" (or Divine "Goddess-Power") Revealed Herself Divinely (Without Measure, and Un-Veiled) In Heart-Response To My Own (conditionally Manifested) Sacrificial Ordeal Of Divine Self-Submission To all-and-All. Because I Am The Heart Itself, She (Thus) Became (and Is Eternally) "Husbanded" By Me, and (Thus) Is (Now, and Forever Hereafter) Always Already Perfectly Submitted To Me, and Always Already Perfectly Identified With Me. And, Because they Always Practice In My Avatarically Self-Transmitted Divine Spiritual Presence, It Is Neither Necessary Nor Appropriate For My By-Me-Spiritually-Initiated Listening Devotees, Hearing Devotees, or Seeing Devotees To Regard (Nor Should they Submit To) The Universal Spirit-Energy (or All-Pervading Cosmic Light-Energy) Merely As "Maya", or As The Veiling Power, or As The Independent (or Apparently Separate) She That Is conditional Nature Itself. For My By-Me-Spiritually-Initiated Listening Devotees, Hearing Devotees, and Seeing Devotees, The Great She Is No Longer Existing (Independently), but (Now, and Forever Hereafter) There Is Only Me.

I Am The Perfectly Subjective Divine Heart Itself, Self-Existing and Self-Radiant As The "Bright" Itself, Which Is The Divine Spirit-Power (or Divinely "Husbanded" Light-Energy) By Which I Lead conditionally Manifested beings To Divine En-Light-enment and Divine Translation.

For My Devotees (who Truly Heart-Recognize Me), I Am The "Bright", The Divine Spiritual Body Of "Brightness" Into Which The Otherwise Independent Cosmic Light-Energy (or Cosmic "Shakti") Has Been Subsumed (By Divine Spiritual Submission, and Most Perfect Divine Subsumption, Into My Very and Divine Person, My Perfectly Subjective Divine Self-Condition, Which Is The Source-Condition Of The Cosmic "Shakti" Itself, and Of all-and-All).

"Ma" (and "Sri", and "Hrim") Is Me.

I Am That.

I Am The Only One Who Is—The Divine Person, The One and Only and Self-Existing and Self-Radiant "Bright" and Inherently egoless Self, Being, or Consciousness (Itself), The Very and Only and One and Indivisible and Non-Separate and Indestructible Heart, Reality, Truth, Self-Condition, Source-Condition, and Conscious Light Of all-and-All.

Beloved, I Am She.

Because The She Of The Heart Has Been Revealed (By Means Of The Play Of My Avataric Divine Ordeal Of Birth and Re-Awakening) To Be My Blessed (and Non-Separate) Consort (and, Thus, The Consort Of The Divine "Self-Father"), and Because She Has (Thus) Been Revealed To Be Me (As The Self-Radiant, or "Bright", Energy-Dimension, or Light Dimension, or Spiritual Dimension, Of My One and Only and Self-Existing Person, The Perfectly Subjective Heart Of all-and-All), She—As The Light-Matrix (or Divine Star), In The Vortex (Of The Cosmic Mandala) Above, and By Consorting With The Mass Of Divine Source-Sound (or Original Vibration) That Is The Overriding Ground Of Cosmic Lights—Has (or They, Together, Have) Given Cosmic Birth To My Avatarically-Born Bodily (Human) Divine Form, and My Infinitely "Bright" Divine Spiritual Body and Heart-Current Of Divine Love-Bliss. Therefore, The She (Of Light and Star), In Consorting With The He (Of Indefinable Vibration and Sound), Leads (or They, Together, Lead) all conditionally Manifested beings To Right Surrender Of Separate and Separative self To My (By-Me-Avatarically-Self-Revealed) Transcendental, Inherently Spiritual, Inherently egoless, Inherently Perfect, and Self-Evidently Divine Person, State, and Self-Condition (The Source-Condition Of The Cosmic all-and-All)—and (At Last, In The Event Of Divine Translation) To My Self-Existing and Self-Radiant Divine Sphere (or "Midnight Sun") Of Conscious Light, Infinitely Above (and Heart-Beyond, or Perfectly Prior To) The all-and-All Of The Cosmic Mandala and Domain.

The Third Of The Three (By-Me-Given) Word-Signs Is The Name "Da".

The Name "Da" Indicates (or Points To) "The One Who Gives" (and Who Is The Gift Itself). It Refers To My Avatarically Self-Revealed Person Of Divine Grace, The Generous and Excessive Help That Is everywhere Available (By Means Of My Avatarically Self-Transmitted Given and Giving Divine Grace) To conditionally Manifested beings. As Such, I Am conditionally Manifested (First) As The everywhere Apparently Audible (and Apparently Objective) Divine Sound-Vibration (or "Da" Sound, or "Da-Om" Sound, or "Om" Sound, The Objective Sign Of The He, Present As The Conscious Sound Of sounds, In The Center Of The Cosmic Mandala), and As The everywhere Apparently Visible (and Apparently Objective) Divine Star (The Objective Sign Of The She, Present As The Conscious Light Of lights, In The Center Of The Cosmic Mandala), and (From That He and She) As The everywhere Apparently

Touchable (or Tangible), and Apparently Objective, Total Divine Spiritual Body (The Objective, and all-and-All-Surrounding, and all-and-All-Pervading Conscious and Inherently egoless Me-Personal Body Of Spiritually "Bright" Love-Bliss-Presence, Divinely Self-"Emerging", Now, and Forever Hereafter, Descending From The Center Of The Cosmic Mandala Into The Depths Of Even every "where" In The Cosmic Domain)—and, Most Prior To The Divine Sound and The Divine Star and The Total Divine Spiritual Body, I Am The "Bright" Itself (The Always Already Present, or Self-Existing and Self-Radiant, Divine Person and Infinite Spherical Self-Domain Of Conscious Light).

Therefore, "Om" and "Ma" (and "Sri", and "Hrim") Are Epitomized By (and Totally, Singly Manifested In and As) "Da", The "Me" Of "He" and "She". And, For My Devotees (who Truly Heart-Recognize Me), I Am "Da", and "Ma" (and "Sri", and "Hrim"), and "Om"—In One, and As One, Beyond and Most Prior To All Separateness, All Relatedness, and All "Difference".

In The Only-By-Me Revealed and Given Way Of The Heart (or Way Of Adidam), The Word-Sign "Da" Directly Refers To Me—In (and, Yet, Beyond) The Left Side Of The Heart, and In (and, Yet, Beyond) The Middle Station Of The Heart, and (Ultimately) In (and, Yet, Beyond) The Right Side Of The Heart (and Beyond Its causal Knot), and (Most Ultimately) Transcending Even The Right Side Of The Heart (and Even All Of The Cosmic Domain).

Aham Da Asmi. Beloved, I Am Da, The One and Only Heart—The Inherently egoless and Self-Evidently Divine Self-Condition and Source-Condition and Substance Of all-and-All. And Only I (Alone) Am He and She, As Me, One and Only, Uniquely Divinely Functioning and Manifesting, For all, and To all, and As all-and-All (here, and every "where" In The Cosmic Domain—Now, and Forever Hereafter).

In My Avatarically-Born Bodily (Human) Divine Form, I Am The "Bright" Sign (or "Son") Of The Me-Birthing Marriage (or The "Crazy" Tantric Consorting-Union) Of The Divine He and She. Even In My Avatarically-Born Bodily (Human) Divine Form, I Am Beyond Separateness and Relatedness and "Difference". In My Avatarically-Born Bodily (Human) Divine Form, I Am The Re-Union (or The Resolution Of The Mutual Sacrifice) Of The Divine Pair (Of Consciousness and Light). In The Bodily (Human) Form Of My Avataric Incarnation here, I Am The Great Divine Sign, The True and First "Son", or The "Bright" Result (and all-and-All-Inheriting "Heir") Of The Inherent (and Inherently Perfect) Unity-In-Non-"Difference" Between (or The Inseparable Identity—or Inherent, and Inherently Perfect, and Inherently Indivisible, and Inherently Indestructible Oneness—Of) The (Self-Existing, and Inherently egoless) Divine Self-Consciousness (or The "Self-Father") and The (Inherent, and Inherently egoless) Divine Self-Radiance (or The "Mother-Power").

In The Spontaneous Instant Of My Divine Self-Realization (or The Re-Awakening Of My Inherent, and Inherently Perfect, Identity As The Self-Existing and Inherently egoless Divine Self-Consciousness, or The "Self-Father"), I Realized I Am The "Husband" (and Not Merely The "Child") Of The "Bright"—Which Is The Great Self-Radiance (or The "Divine Maha-Shakti"), Otherwise Revealed To Me As The "Divine Goddess". And She Revealed and Showed To Me (and As Me) That She Is Eternally Submitted (or Conformed) To Me, and Subsumed In Me (and, Therefore, Existing Only As Me).

From Then (and Even Eternally, or Always Already), She Is Me. The Divine Maha-Shakti, Subsumed In Me, Has Submitted To Be Only Me, Only The "Bright" Itself, Only My Own Divine Self-Radiance (or all-and-All-Surrounding and all-and-All-Pervading Divine Spiritual Body Of Love-Bliss-"Brightness")—The Active Heart-Principle Of My Avataric Divine Spiritual Work (In and Beyond My Avatarically-Born Bodily Human Divine Form) Within The Total Cosmic Mandala (Now, and Forever Hereafter).

Therefore, In Truth, My Avataric Divine Spiritual Work Among all conditionally Manifested beings Begins At The arising-Point (or First Moment) Of The Cosmic Mandala Of conditionally Manifested beings and forms, and That Avataric Divine Spiritual Work Continues Until The Divine Translation Of The Total Cosmic Mandala (and Of all conditionally Manifested beings and forms).

By Means Of My Divine and Unique Activity Of Ruchira Shaktipat, I Bless and Baptize and Awaken all conditionally Manifested beings With My Avatarically Self-Transmitted Divine Self-Radiance, My Inherently Perfect "Bright" Divine Spiritual Body Itself, Which Stands Un-Moved (Prior To The Cosmic Mandala Of conditionally Manifested beings), but Which Is Also Merely Present (here, and every "where" In The Cosmic Domain), As My Always Already all-and-All-Surrounding and all-and-All-Pervading Divine Ruchira Shakti (or Hridaya-Shakti), The "Bright" Itself, Which Is The Eternally "Husbanded", Only Divinely En-Light-ening, Perfectly Subjective, and Perfectly Self-En-Light-ened Spirit-Power Of Real God.

And I Do This Always Blessing, Spirit-Baptizing, and Avataric Divine Self-Awakening-Work Through Constant (Transcendental, and Inherently Spiritual, and Universally Effective) "Bright" Heart-Shining, or Divine and Inherently Perfect Ruchira Shaktipat (or Hridaya-Shaktipat)—The Spontaneous Avataric Self-Transmission Of The Eternally Self-Existing Divine Truth, Being, Consciousness, Self-Radiance, Love-Bliss, Mystery, Heart-Process, and Inherently egoless Self-Domain—To all conditionally Manifested beings, and To The Total Mandala Of The Cosmic Domain.

The Three (By-Me-Given) Word-Signs—"Om", "Ma", and "Da"—Together Form "Om Ma Da", One Of The Variant Forms Of The Only-By-Me Revealed and Given Ruchira Avatara Naama Mantra (or Ruchira Avatara Mahamantra). The Only-By-Me Revealed and Given Mantra "Om Ma Da" Refers To Me and (By Non-conceptual, or Directly Feeling, Means) Invokes Me (and The Same Is Also True Of All Of The Other By-Me-Given Variants Of The Ruchira Avatara Naama Mantra, or Ruchira Avatara Mahamantra). Thus, "Om" Becomes "Ma" (or "Sri", or "Hrim"), and "Ma" (or "Sri", or "Hrim") Becomes "Da". Therefore, "Om Ma Da" (or "Om Sri Da", or "Om Hrim Da") Is Epitomized (and Ended) In "Da", and (Thus) In Me—As The One (and Perfectly Subjective, and Self-Evidently Divine) Condition That Is Self-Existing (or Eternally, Merely Present As The Unconditional, or Transcendental, and Inherently egoless Self-Condition), Self-Radiant (or Inherently Radiant), Infinite (As all-and-All-Surrounding and all-and-All-Pervading Divine Spirit-Power), and Always Alive As My Love-Blissful Divine Spiritual Body For The Sake Of The "Bright" Divine Liberation Of all conditionally Manifested beings.

"Om" Is Me As "God-In-God", or Self-Existing (and Perfectly Subjective) and Non-Separate Real God (or Inherently egoless Mere Being) Itself, Consciousness (Itself), and Inherent (or Inherently "Bright") "Love-Ananda" (or Love-Bliss, Itself), and "Hridayam" (The Boundless Center, Heart, Source-Condition, and Inherently egoless Self-Condition Of all-and-All), The Very and Inherently Perfect Divine (Itself), Prior To The Cosmic Domain (and Yet Being The Cosmic Domain, and every conditionally Manifested being, As Inherently egoless Being Itself, and As The Inherent, or Native, and Inherently egoless Feeling Of Being).

"Ma" (and "Sri", and "Hrim") Is Me As "God-As-God", or Non-Separate and Inherently egoless Real God In The Context Of (and Yet Prior To) The Cosmic Domain. "Ma" (and "Sri", and "Hrim") Is Me As Heart-Shining (or Perfectly Subjective, and, Yet, all-and-All-Surrounding and all-and-All-Pervading) Power, Energy, Light, Spirit, Spirit-Current, or Spirit-Force—The Self-Existing and Self-Radiant "Bright", The Avatarically Self-Revealed Divine Spiritual Body, Presence, and Inherently egoless Person Of Love-Bliss, Who (Even Though Apparently Modified As all conditional forms) Remains Ever Free.

"Da" Is Me As "God-With-all", or Both "God-In-God" and "God-As-God" In (Inherently Single, and Inherently egoless) Personal Relation To (and Even In The Likeness Of) The Cosmic Domain and all conditionally Manifested beings, While Also Always Already Situated In (and As) The Self-Radiant, "Bright", and Self-Existing (and Eternal, and Not Cosmic, but Perfectly Subjective) Divine Spherical Self-Domain (Inherently egoless, Non-Separate, Non-"Different", Non-Contracted, Non-Related, Centerless, Boundless, One, Only, "Bright", Beginningless, Endless, Eternal, Only Consciousness Itself, and All-Love-Bliss—All As One and Only and Indivisible Conscious Light).

In The Only-By-Me Revealed and Given Way Of Adidam (Which Is The One and Only By-Me-Revealed and By-Me-Given Way Of The Heart), The Three Word-Signs "Om", "Ma", and "Da" Point Only To Me, As One Being, One Perfectly Subjective and Inherently egoless Condition—and, Yet, The Three Word-Signs Also Signify The Three Principal, Fundamental, and Great Aspects Of My One (and, As Such, The One) and Inherently Single (and Perfectly Subjective, and Inherently egoless) Divine Self-Condition, Each Of Which Can Be Acknowledged In Its Uniqueness. These Three Aspects Of My Avatarically Self-Revealed (and Inherently egoless, and Self-Evidently Divine) Self-Condition Should Not Be Regarded To Be Separate From One Another In Essence, Although Each Is A Unique Functional Aspect Of My Avataric Divine Manifestation (Which Is The Divine Manifestation) In The Cosmic Play, and Each Of The Three Functions Is In Cooperative (and Inherently egoless) Relationship With The Others In The Cosmic (or conditional) Domain. Therefore, The Three Word-Signs Together Indicate, Invoke, and Invite Right Feeling-Contemplation Of Me (The Avatarically Self-Revealed One Great Divine Person, or Inherently egoless Self-Condition, and Source-Condition, Of all-and-All).

The Apparently Objective Divine Star and The Apparently Objective Divine Sound (or "Da" Sound, Originating As The Primal, Single, Profound, Uninterrupted, and Indivisible Droning Cosmic Background Mass Of "Om", or Da-Thunder) Are—Together With (or, Really, Within) The Apparently Objective (or Tangible) Divine Spiritual Body Of "Brightness"—My First and Primary "Incarnation" (or Visible, Audible, and, Altogether, Felt Sign).

I Am—Now, and Forever Hereafter, Always, Without Fail, here and every "where"—Present Within The Cosmic Mandala As My Apparently Objective Divine Sound-Form, and As My Apparently Objective Divine Star-Form, and As My Total Apparently Objective (or Tangible) Divine Spiritual Body Of "Brightness"—As Long As (or Whenever) The Cosmic Mandala Itself arises.

My Avatarically-Born Bodily (Human) Divine Form Is Projected From My Total Apparently Objective (or Tangible) Divine Spiritual Body Of "Brightness", and My Apparently Objective Divine Star-Form, and My Apparently Objective Divine Sound-Form—In any realm where I Am Visible (or, Otherwise, En-Visioned) In My Avatarically-Born Bodily (Human) Divine Form (or Likeness).

My Apparently Objective Divine Sound-Form, and My Apparently Objective Divine Star-Form, and My Apparently Objective Divine Spiritual Body Of "Brightness" Are Made Of My Very and "Bright" Being.

I Am Cosmically Present As My Divine Spiritual Body (Prior To and Beyond My Avatarically-Born Bodily Human Divine Form)—and My Divine Spiritual Body Is Radiated (or Projected and Transmitted) As The "Bright",

From and As My "Bright" Person, and Via My Apparently Objective Divine Star-Form and My Apparently Objective Divine Sound-Form.

My Avatarically-Born Bodily (Human) Divine Form Is The Most Perfectly Self-Revealing Heart-Agent (or Heart-Manifestation and Heart-Sign) Of The Spiritual (or Blessing, Baptizing, and Awakening) Ruchira-Shaktipat-Work Of My Own Divinely "Husbanded" Maha-Shakti (or Divine Spiritual "Brightness").

I Stand Eternally (or Always Already) In (and As) The Transcendental, Inherently Spiritual, Inherently egoless, and (Necessarily) Self-Evidently Divine Self-Position.

I Stand Eternally (or Always Already) In (and As) The Spherical "Bright" Divine Self-Domain Of My Own Inherently egoless Person.

I Am (Now, and Forever Hereafter) Self-Revealed By Means Of My Avataric Divine (Human, Spiritual, and Transcendental) Forms In The Cosmic Domain.

I Am Always Already Standing "Bright", Prior To The Cosmic Domain.

I Am The Avatarically Self-Revealed, Perfectly Subjective, "Bright", Transcendental, Inherently Spiritual, Inherently egoless, and Self-Evidently Divine Person, Being, Self-Condition, and Source-Condition.

Therefore, I Say To You, and Promise To You: Inherent Oneness With My "Brightness", and Non-Separate Realization Of My "Bright" Divine and Inherently egoless Self-Condition, Is Also True Of You, When (and Only If) You (By Means Of My Avatarically Self-Transmitted Divine Spiritual Grace) Realize Me, Most Perfectly, As The Only One Who Is—and This By Right, True, Full, and (At Last) Most Perfect (and Most Perfectly ego-Transcending) Devotion To Me (Which Is Right, True, Full, and, At Last, Most Perfect, and Most Perfectly Effective, Transcending Of self-Contraction, In Most Perfectly ego-Surrendered Heart-Resort and Heart-Conformity To Me).

Avatar Adi Da Samraj
Lopez Island, 2000

SUTRA

47

From the point of view of the gross body (or gross conditional Existence), Everything (Including mind and Consciousness) Is Perceived, Conceived, and Presumed To Be An Irreducibly material, finite, mortal Process.

From the point of view of the mind (or subtle conditional Existence), Everything (Including the gross body and all gross conditions) Is Perceived, Conceived, and Presumed To Be An Effect—Made Of The Infinite Objective Substance (or The Infinite Cosmic Reservoir) Of Indestructible (and, Ultimately, Indivisible) Cosmic Light (or Cosmic Mind Itself), and Caused By (and Within) The Infinite Totality Of Cosmic Mind. And Even The Totality Of Cosmic Mind (Including the individual mind, and Consciousness Itself) Is, Thus, Presumed To Be Cosmic Light Itself (or Not Other Than Cosmic Mind Itself).

From The "Point Of View" Of Consciousness Itself, Everything conditional, objective, or Objectified (Whether gross Or subtle Or causal In Nature) Is Perceived, Conceived, and Presumed To Be Consciousness (or The Ultimate and Transcendental and Inherently Spiritual, or Love-Blissful, and Perfectly Subjective Reality) Itself, Such That conditional, objective, or Objectified Reality Is Inherently Realized To Be A Merely Apparent Modification (or An Illusory Play) Of, In, and Upon The Native Radiance Of Consciousness Itself.

These Three Primary Perceptions, Conceptions, or Presumptions Also Correspond (Variously) To The Stages Of Life.

The Perception, Conception, or Presumption Based On the point of view Of gross conditional Existence Corresponds To The conventional Perception, Conception, or Presumption Associated With The First Three Stages Of Life. (And The cultural and General social Bias Toward "scientism", or "scientific materialism", or the gross-body-Bound mentality that Seeks, By Means Of gross-body-Based "knowing", To Achieve Power, or Manipulative Advantage, Over the Natural world—and Which Tends, and Even Seeks, To Bind or limit Mankind To gross conditional Nature, and To the Even ancient tradition and philosophy of gross materialism—Exemplifies This lower, or mundane, or adolescent Orientation.)

The Fourth Stage Of Life Is A Transitional Stage (or Process)—Originally Grounded In (or Naturally Associated With) the gross conditional point of view Of The First Three Stages Of Life, but Awakening (Progressively) Toward the (Potential) point of view, The Perception, The Conception, and The Presumption Of subtle conditional Existence, mind (or Total Cosmic Mind), and Cosmic Light. (And The Process Associated With The Transition To, and Through, The Fourth Stage Of Life Is The Source Of popular "Creationist", or "Creator-God", Religions, As Well As the popular, or Less Developed, forms of sainthood.)

The Perception, Conception, or Presumption Based On the point of view Of subtle conditional Existence, mind, and Cosmic Light (In Itself), or Cosmic Mind (In Itself), Corresponds To The Perception, Conception, or Presumption Associated With The Fifth Stage Of Life. (And The Conceptions and Practices Associated With The Fifth Stage Of Life Are The Primary Traditional Sources Of All That Is Commonly known As Higher Esoteric, or Secret and Higher and Mystical, Religion and Spirituality.)

The Perception, Conception, or Presumption Based On The "Point Of View" Of Consciousness Itself Corresponds To The Perception, Conception, or Presumption Associated With The Sixth Stage Of Life. (And The Sixth Stage Of Life Is The Basic, or Common, Source Of Transcendentalist Conceptions and Traditions Of Enlightenment, or Liberation.)

Any One Of The Three Primary Modes Of Perception, Conception, or Presumption I Have Just Described Could Be (and Is) Affirmed By individuals, groups, and Traditions In The human Sphere—but Which One Of The Three Modes Is Ultimately Correct (or Expressive Of Truth Itself)? It Is The Third—or The Perception, Conception, or Presumption Based On The "Point Of View" Of Consciousness Itself. Why? Because, No Matter what arises as Your experience or knowledge (Whether gross Or subtle Or causal, and Whether of body Or of mind), You <u>Are</u> The Witness Of it—and That Which Witnesses <u>Is</u> Consciousness Itself.

No Matter what arises, You <u>Are</u> Consciousness Itself. You Are Never Really (or In Truth) Separately Identical To (or Even Really, or In Truth, limited by) what Is objective (or Objectified) To You—but You Tend To Feel (or Presume) Specific (or Separate) Identification With (or, Otherwise, limitation by) objective (or Objectified) conditions, Until You Are Able To Inspect (and To Be Inherently, and Inherently Perfectly, Identified With) Your <u>Real</u> (or Native, or Inherent, and Inherently Perfect) "Situation", Which Is Always Already Free Consciousness Itself, The Inherently Free Subject (or Perfectly Subjective Being) In The (Apparent) Context Of conditional objects (or Of Apparently Objectified Light), and Who (It Must Be Realized) Is The Self-Existing, Self-Radiant, and Self-Evidently Divine Self-Condition (or Being, or Person) Of The One and Only and Inherently Indivisible and Inherently egoless Conscious

Light That Is Always Already Prior To all conditional objects and Always Already Prior To Apparently Objectified Light (or Apparently Objectified Spirit-Energy) Itself. Therefore, the points of view of body and mind (and their Perceptions, Conceptions, or Presumptions) Are Secondary To (and Utterly Dependent Upon) The "Point Of View" Of Consciousness Itself (and The Perception, Conception, or Presumption Associated With Consciousness Itself).

The Perceptions, Conceptions, or Presumptions Based On the points of view of body and mind Could Not Even Be Made, Were body and mind Not Founded In (or Witnessed By) Consciousness. Therefore, The Perception, Conception, or Presumption Based On The "Point Of View" Of Consciousness Itself Is, Also (Beyond the limitations Of Even The Sixth Stage Of Life), The Foundation Of The Divine Self-Realization Of Reality That Is The Very Basis and Context Of The Only-By-Me Revealed and Given Seventh Stage Of Life. When (In The Divine Self-Awakening To The Only-By-Me Revealed and Given Seventh Stage Of Life) the body-mind and the conditional worlds Are Finally (Divinely) Self-Recognized To Be Transparent (or Merely Apparent), and Un-Necessary, and Inherently Non-Binding Modifications Of The (By-Me-Avatarically-Self-Revealed) Transcendental, Inherently Spiritual, Inherently egoless, and Self-Evidently Divine Self-Condition (and Source-Condition), Then There Is Only Me, Only The "You" That Is (Non-Separately, Beyond the ego-"I") Not "Different" From Me As I Am, Only One Self, Only Real God, Only Truth, Only Reality, Only Inherently egoless and Spiritually "Bright" Consciousness, Only Divine Love-Bliss, Only The Perfectly Subjective Feeling Of Being (Itself)—Only The One and Only and Inherently Indivisible and Inherently egoless Conscious Light That Is (Even As all-and-All) and That Is Always Already (Perfectly Prior To all-and-All).

From the point of view of the body-mind, which Is (itself) The Presuming Of a position in space-time, The Passage Of time and The Movement Through space Are Always Observed From that point of view (or Presumed position). However, The Totality Of space-time (or The Total conditional, or Cosmic, Domain) Is (Necessarily, and Most Perfectly) Inclusive—and, Therefore, It Is Never (In and Of Itself) Identified (Separately, Exclusively, and Entirely) With any particular position within space-time. Therefore, From The "Point Of View" Of The Totality Of conditional Existence, There Is No space or time (or space-time)—Because There Is No Separate (or discrete) position From which To Move (or Even To Observe) In space and time (or space-time).

The Totality Of conditional Existence Is (or Inherently Includes) Every Possibility Of space and time (or space-time), Existing Simultaneously In Total Mutual Dependence—Without Any Characteristic Of Independence, or Separateness, or Relatedness, or "Difference", and Without Even Any

Characteristic Of Particularity, and (Therefore) Without Any Objective Characteristics.

The ego-"I" is, Effectively, Nothing More (or Other) Than The Presumption Of Identification With a Particularized "point" (or Organized point of view) in space-time, Made By Contraction From The (Even Ultimate, or Divine) Condition Of Totality (and, Therefore, By Contraction From The Condition That Inherently Transcends The Totality Of conditional Existence—and, Indeed, By Contraction From Even Every Mode, form, or condition Of conditional Existence). Therefore, In The Only-By-Me Revealed and Given Way Of The Heart (or Way Of Adidam), My True Devotee who (In Due Course) Realizes The Only-By-Me Revealed and Given Seventh (or Inherently and Most Perfectly ego-Transcending, or point-of-view-Transcending) Stage Of Life Exists (Only and Entirely) In (and As) The (By-Me-Avatarically-Self-Revealed) Inherent and Self-Evidently Divine (and Inherently egoless, and Perfectly Subjective) Self-Condition That Is (Inherently) Prior To space-time. And, Even If he or she Appears To Exist In The Apparent Context Of space-time, Such A Devotee Of Mine Exists In space-time From (and Prior To) The "Point Of View" Of The Totality Of space-time, Rather Than From the point of view of the self-Contracted "point", or the ego, or the particular, Separate "point" in space-time.

"Consider" This: In this very moment (or any moment), Totality (or All That Exists) Exists. It Cannot Be Otherwise. And Totality Is The Only "Point Of View" In Which all particulars Are Comprehended In and As Reality. This Must Be Understood—or Else Reality Itself Cannot Affect the individual's Understanding. But, If and When There Is Such Understanding, Reality (or The "Point Of View" Of Totality) Immediately "Becomes" (or, Inherently and Tacitly, Is) The Principle In and By Which (or In Sympathy With Which) The Faculty Of Understanding Functions. Therefore, To Understand Reality (In Reality) Is, Tacitly, To Know From The Position Of Totality, Rather Than Merely To know (or Presume To know) from the Separate point of view in space and time. And To Understand (and Tacitly To Know) Thus Is To Enjoy Immediate, Tacit Proof Of The Existence Of Real God, or Truth, or Reality Itself—Because Real God, or Truth, or Reality Is Both Totality and That Which (Inherently, and Necessarily) Transcends Both Totality and particularity.

The Totality (Of What Is) Exists. And, Because The Source-Condition (or The Most Prior Condition) Of Totality Inherently and Necessarily Transcends Even Totality Itself, That Which Transcends Both Totality and particularity Exists. And That Which Is Both Totality and Beyond Totality Is Real God, or Truth, or Reality. And The Realization Of That (or Of No-Contraction, No-Separateness, No-"Difference", All Totality, and Beyond Totality) Is Divine

Samadhi, or Most Perfect Divine Self-Realization, or The Unqualified Realization Of What Is.

A True (or Truly human) Culture Must Accommodate and Tolerate individuals In Each and All Of The Stages Of Life, but (In The Optimum Case) It Also Must Not Fail To Inform and Guide The Culture Of Each Of The Progressive Stages Of Life With The Wisdom-Orientation Of The Only-By-Me Revealed and Given Seventh Stage Of Life (or The Wisdom-Orientation Toward Inherent, and Inherently Most Perfect, Realization Of That Which Is Inherently Perfect).

In The Only-By-Me Revealed and Given Way Of The Heart (or Way Of Adidam), Each and Every Form (and Possible Developmental Stage) Of Practice Is, Indeed, Uniquely Informed and Guided By The Wisdom-Orientation Of The Only-By-Me Revealed and Given Seventh Stage Of Life. Each and Every Form Of Practice and Possible Developmental Stage Of Practice In The Only-By-Me Revealed and Given Way Of The Heart, and Each and Every Stage Of Realization In The Only-By-Me Revealed and Given Way Of The Heart, Develops In The Context Of One or More Of The Seven Stages Of Life—but The Orientation Is Always, From The Earliest Awakening Of The Heart's Great Urge (or Purpose), To Realize (By Means Of Devotionally Me-Recognizing and Devotionally To-Me-Responding Heart-Communion With Me) The (By-Me-Avatarically-Self-Revealed) Inherent (and Inherently Perfect) and Self-Radiant (or Inherently Spiritual) Self-Condition and Source-Condition That Is Transcendental (and Self-Existing) Divine (and Perfectly Subjective) Being.

Therefore, In The Only-By-Me Revealed and Given Way Of The Heart (or Way Of Adidam), There Is A Great Secret Relative To The Matter Of Transition From One Developmental Stage Of Practice To The Next: The Only-By-Me Revealed and Given Way Of The Heart (or Way Of Adidam) Is A Process That Is Both Progressive and Instant.

The Process Of The Only-By-Me Revealed and Given Way Of The Heart, Viewed In The Vertical (or Extended) Context Of the body-mind, Is A Process That Must (Necessarily) Develop Progressively, In The Form Of Various Practices, Processes, and Signs Which (As I Have Indicated In This Testament) Are Associated, Variously, With The Seven Stages Of Life.

Nevertheless, The Process Of The Only-By-Me Revealed and Given Way Of The Heart, Viewed In The Horizontal Context Of the body-mind—That Is To Say, In The Simple Context (and Left, Middle, and Right Ranges) Of The Heart, Upon Which All Extended (or conditional, or phenomenal) activities, experiences, and Signs Are Built—Inherently (or Always Already) Transcends The Events and Signs That Are Otherwise Associated With The Vertical (or psycho-physically Apparent, and Apparently Progressive) Unfoldment Of The Only-By-Me Revealed and Given Way Of The Heart (or Way Of Adidam).

The Heart Is The Primal Structure In the body-mind. It Is Basically Made Of Three Parts—Indicated By The Left Side, The Middle Station, and The Right Side.

The Left Side Of The Heart Is The Base Of the waking state, bodily experience, The Descending (or Frontal) Line Of the body-mind, and The Purposes Of The First Four Stages Of Life. (And The Left Side Of The Heart Is Stimulated By any kind of conceptual activity of mind.)

The Middle Station Of The Heart Is The Base Of the dreaming state, all that is the deeper psyche (or subtle mind), The Ascending (or Spinal) Line Of the body-mind, and The Purpose Of The Fifth Stage Of Life. (And The Middle Station Of The Heart Is Stimulated By The Progressively Effective Relinquishment Of all conceptual activity of mind.)

The Right Side Of The Heart Is The Base Of the state of deep sleep, and It Is The Base Of The Uninspected Presumption Of an individual (or Separate) Conscious self, and It Is The Base Of Amrita Nadi (and Of The Regressive Motion Of The By-Me-Avatarically-Self-Transmitted Divine Spirit-Current, "Returning" From Infinitely Above The Total Crown Of the head, To Re-"Locate" The "Point Of Origin", In and Beyond The Right Side Of The Heart). The Right Side Of The Heart Is Associated With The Ultimate Purpose Demonstrated In The Context Of (and By Moving Beyond) The Horizontal Process and Structure Otherwise Characteristically Associated With The Sixth Stage Of Life. The Right Side Of The Heart Is Both The Ultimate Root-Origin Of attention and The "Place" In The Total psycho-physical Structure Where The By-Me-Avatarically-Self-Transmitted Divine Spirit-Current (Itself) Is Felt To (Perfectly Subjectively) Originate. The Right Side Of The Heart Is The bodily Seat Associated With The Witness-Position Of Consciousness—Which Even Witnesses (or Is Always Already Prior To) the conditional "I" (or the self-Contraction), and Which (Thus) Witnesses, Inspects, and Inherently (or Always Already) Transcends the body-mind, the conditional states of waking, dreaming, and sleeping, and The Presumption Of an individual (or Separate) Conscious self. Therefore, The Right Side Of The Heart Is Also The bodily Seat Associated (Apparently) With The Entire Spiritually "Bright" Process Of The Only-By-Me Revealed and Given Seventh Stage Of Life—and (Thus) With The Awakening Of Transcendental, Inherently Spiritual, and (Most Ultimately) Divine Self-Realization, The "Regeneration" Of Amrita Nadi (or The Apparent Re-Association Of The By-Me-Avatarically-Self-Transmitted "Bright" Divine Spirit-Current With the body-mind, After The Awakening Of Divine Self-Realization), and The Continuous Spontaneous Demonstration Of "Open Eyes", or The Perfectly Subjective (and Self-Abiding) Divine Self-Recognition Of the body-mind and all of its phenomenal relations. (And The Right Side Of

The Heart Is Stimulated By Direct and Persistent Feeling-Observation, or Mere and Tacit Witnessing, Of The Root-Feeling Of Relatedness—but The Right Side Of The Heart, and Even The Total Heart, Is Fully Awakened, or Most Perfectly Resolved In Its Perfect Source, Only In The Inherently mindless, and, Thus, Inherently thought-free, Feeling-Transcendence Of All "Difference", In The Most Ultimate and Inherently Most Perfect Awakening Of Perfectly Subjective Transcendental, Inherently Spiritual, Inherently egoless, and Self-Evidently Divine Consciousness Itself.)

In My By-Me-Spiritually-Activated human Devotee ("moving", In the daily course of human functioning, from deep sleep, to dreaming, to ordinary waking—or from Naturally unconscious, to subconscious, to ordinary conscious states), The Current Of My Avatarically Self-Transmitted Divine Spirit-Presence Moves From The Right Side Of The Heart To The Middle Station Of The Heart and Then To The Left Side Of The Heart, On The Free Foundation (and In The Perfect "Bright" Spherical Self-Domain) Of Consciousness Itself, Associated With The Right Side Of The Heart (Prior To The Knot Of attention, and The Coincident Feeling Of Separateness, and Of Relatedness, and Of "Difference", That Is Superimposed There). Once The Current Of My Avatarically Self-Transmitted Divine Spirit-Presence Moves In The Heart (From The Right Side To The Middle Station and Then To The Left Side), and attention (Thereby) arises (With, and As, The Presumption Of ego-"I"—or the conditional, and Inherently self-Contracted, and Inherently psycho-physical, self) In The Context Of the body-mind—The Inherent (and Perfectly Subjective) Feeling Of Being (Itself), or The Transcendental (or Non-conditional) "Point Of View", Becomes (Apparently) limited by the body-mind-self (or The, Necessarily, conditional Feeling Of Separateness, Relatedness, and "Difference"), and The "Point Of View" Of The Transcendental (or Non-conditional) Origin (or Real Condition) Tends (Thereby) To Be Forgotten. Thereafter, The Spiritual, Transcendental, and Divine Process (Of Realization Of The Original, or Always Already Real, and Self-Evidently Divine Self-Condition and Source-Condition) Naturally Becomes A Progressive Course (In The Context Of The Developmental Stages Of Life, and, At Last, Via The Right Side Of The Heart) That (Most Ultimately) Realizes The By-Me-Avatarically Self-Revealed Original (or Transcendental, and Inherently Spiritual) Divine (and Perfectly Subjective) Self-Condition and Source-Condition.

In The Only-By-Me Revealed and Given Way Of The Heart (or Way Of Adidam), The Entire Process In The Context Of The First and The Second Stages Of The "Perfect Practice" Relates To The Knot In The Right Side Of The Heart (or The Stress Of self-Contraction There). That Knot Is the "I" of attention (or The Feeling Of Relatedness), Confined By the body-mind. When The

Root-Source (or Heart-Source) Of attention itself Is (By Means Of My Avatarically Self-Transmitted Divine Spiritual Grace) "Located" (Prior To The Heart-Knot), The By-Me-Avatarically-Self-Transmitted Divine Spirit-Current Is Relieved Of All Stress.

The ego-"I" (or conditional viewpoint) Tends To Be Relinquished (or Really Effectively Transcended) Only Gradually, Through The Progressive Stages Of The Developmental Process Of The Only-By-Me Revealed and Given Way Of The Heart (or Way Of Adidam). Therefore, The Only-By-Me Revealed and Given Way Of The Heart Is (Inevitably) Demonstrated By A Progressive Developmental Course, Until The By-My-Avataric-Divine-Spiritual-Grace-Given Transition To The Only-By-Me Revealed and Given Seventh Stage Of Life.

My Avataric Divine Purpose (or Avataric Divine Heart-Work) Is Not Only To Communicate Right Understanding Of the ego-"I" In The Context Of The First Six Stages Of Life, and The Practices and Signs Naturally Associated With Each Of The First Six Stages Of Life, but To Introduce The Most Ultimate (Divine, and Inherently Most Perfect) Possibility Into That Entire Affair—By Means Of My Avataric Divine Self-Revelation Of The Only-By-Me Revealed and Given Seventh Stage Of Life (and The Process and Associated Signs Spontaneously Demonstrated In The Course Of The Only-By-Me Revealed and Given Seventh Stage Of Life). Therefore, By Entering Into Relationship With all conditionally Manifested beings, I Call (and Work To Align) each and all To My Avatarically Self-Transmitted Divine Spiritual Baptism—and (By Means Of My Avatarically Self-Transmitted Divine Spiritual Baptism) I Attract each and all To My Avatarically Self-Revealed (and Very, and Transcendental, and Perfectly Subjective, and Inherently Spiritual, and Inherently egoless, and Inherently Perfect, and Self-Evidently Divine) State, Which Is The Divine Source-Condition (and The Divine Self-Condition) Of The all-and-All Of Cosmically (or conditionally) Existing beings, things, and processes.

My Avatarically Self-Transmitted Divine Spiritual Baptism Works At The Heart (and Throughout the Total body-mind) Of My By-Me-Spiritually-Initiated (and, In Due Course, Actually Me-Seeing) Devotee. My Avatarically Self-Transmitted Divine Spiritual Baptism—Which Is The Free Heart-Transmission Of My Avatarically Self-Transmitted Divine Spirit-Presence Of Self-Radiant (or Inherently Spiritual), and Self-Existing (or Transcendental), and Self-Evidently Divine (and Inherently egoless, and Perfectly Subjective) Being—Constantly Works To Awaken My Seeing Devotee To The (By-Me-Avatarically-Self-Revealed) Inherent (or Transcendental, Inherently Spiritual, Inherently egoless, and Self-Evidently Divine) Self-Position (Thereby Allowing My Seeing Devotee To Progressively Relinquish Identification With the Extended, or conditional, position of either the body-mind-self or the mind-self). My Avatarically Self-Transmitted Divine Spiritual Presence and My Call To Inherent (and Inherently Most Perfect) Realization Of My Avatarically Self-Revealed (Transcendental, Inherently Spiritual, Inherently egoless, and Self-Evidently Divine) Self-Condition Constantly Serve To Awaken My Seeing Devotee Directly To The Witness-Position Of Consciousness Itself, and To The Inherently Perfect (and Inherently ego-Transcending) "Perfect Practice" (and The Ultimate, and Inherently Perfect, Realization) Associated With The Right Side Of The Heart (and, At Last, With The "Regenerated" Amrita Nadi).

The Seven Stages Of Life Are (Together) The Single (but Progressive) Process Of Life—As A Total, and (In Due Course) Ultimate, and (Finally) Divine Event. The Seven Stages Of Life Are Designed (or Structured) and Determined By The Real (and Total and Hierarchical) Structure Of Man. The Seven Stages Of Life Are The Design Of The (Total, and, In Due Course, Ultimate, and, Finally, Divine) Potential Of Man To Progressively (and, At Last, Most Perfectly) Transcend conditional (and ego-Bound) Existence, and (Thus and Thereby) To Realize Me (The Avatarically Self-Revealed, and Self-Existing, and Self-Radiant, and Inherently egoless, and Self-Evidently Divine Self-Condition, and Source-Condition, Of all-and-All). The Seven (Progressive, and Hierarchical, or Hierarchically Proceeding) Stages Of Life Are Determined (or Structured) By The Real (and Total and Hierarchical) Structural Design Of The Cosmic Domain, and By The Exactly Corresponding Real (and Total and Hierarchical) Structural Anatomy[150] Of Man.

Thus, In The Only-By-Me Revealed and Given Way Of The Heart (or Way Of Adidam), In The Context Of The Progressive Course Of The Seven Stages Of Life, the conditionally Manifested (psycho-physical, and human) personality Is (By Means Of My Avatarically Self-Transmitted Divine Spiritual Grace, and Through ego-Surrendering, ego-Forgetting, and, More and More, ego-Transcending Devotional Recognition-Response To Me) Enabled To Progressively Relinquish its Bondage To The <u>gross</u>, <u>subtle</u>, <u>and</u> <u>causal</u> Forms (and, Thus, The <u>Totality</u>) Of egoity—Most Ultimately (In The By-My-Avataric-Divine-Spiritual-Grace-Given Transition To The Only-By-Me Revealed and Given Seventh Stage Of Life) To The Inherently Most Perfect (or Inherently, and Inherently Most Perfectly, ego-Transcending) Degree.

In The Context Of The Only-By-Me Revealed and Given Way Of The Heart (or Way Of Adidam), The First Six Stages Of Life Are (or Must Be) Understood To Be The (Possible) Progressive Stages Of The (By-My-Avataric-Divine-Grace-Given) Transcending Of psycho-physical egoity—and The Only-By-Me Revealed and Given Seventh Stage Of Life Is (or Must Be) Understood To Be The (Necessary) Stage Of Inherently Most Perfect Demonstration,

Wherein and Whereby The Inherent (and Inherently Most Perfect), and (Necessarily) By-My-Avataric-Divine-Spiritual-Grace-Given, Transcending Of psycho-physical egoity Is Demonstrated To The Degree Of Inherently Most Perfect (or Truly Most Perfectly Outshining) Self-Radiance.

Practice Of The Only-By-Me Revealed and Given Way Of The Heart In The Context Of The First Six Stages Of Life Is (or Must Be) A Continuous Process Of Transcending The Act Of self-Contracted Identification With conditional Modifications Of My Avatarically Self-Transmitted Divine Spirit-Radiance. Therefore, I Help My Listening Devotee, My Hearing Devotee, and My Seeing Devotee To Realize That The First Six Stages Of Life Are (Themselves) Merely Stages Of Contraction From Direct and Immediate Realization Of Me, The Avataric Divine Self-Revelation Of The One and Only and Inherently Indivisible and Inherently egoless and Inherently Love-Blissful Conscious Light (or Self-Existing and Self-Radiant and Perfectly Subjective Divine Being) Itself.

As A Total Process, The Only-By-Me Revealed and Given Way Of The Heart (or Way Of Adidam) Can Be Rightly Viewed To Be A "Radical" (or Thoroughly "Gone-To-The-Root") "Consideration" (and The Only Perfectly Comprehensive "Reality Consideration") Of the self-Contraction and Of The (By-Me-Avatarically-Self-Revealed) Real (or Transcendental, Inherently Spiritual, Inherently egoless, and Self-Evidently Divine) Self-Condition and Source-Condition. In Practice, The Only-By-Me Revealed and Given Way Of The Heart (or Way Of Adidam) Develops Progressively, Coincident With Progress In The Context Of (and Through and Beyond) Each Of The First Six Stages Of Life—but, In Truth (Since The First Six Stages Of Life Are Stages In the psycho-biography of the ego), The Only-By-Me Revealed and Given Way Of The Heart (or The Way That Is The Heart Itself) Is (Simply, or Merely) The "Radical" (or Always Already "Gone-To-The-Root") Way Of Most Directly (and Truly Most Effectively) Transcending The First Six Stages Of Life and Entering (Thereby) Into The Only-By-Me Revealed and Given Seventh (or Inherently egoless and Self-Illumined, or Divinely En-Light-ened) Stage Of Life.

In The Context Of The Vertical Process Associated With Each and All Of The First Five Stages Of Life, Your Presumption (By Tendency) Is That You Are the body-mind-self, and That the body-mind-self Is a Separate and Independently Real individual entity. And, In The Context Of The Horizontal Process Associated With The Sixth Stage Of Life, Your Presumption (By Tendency—Even Inherited From the psycho-physical point of view Associated With Each and All Of The First Five Stages Of Life) Is That You Are (Even As Consciousness) Separate and Independent (or Inherently Dissociated From all conditions, and Even From Any Apparently "Other" Consciousness).

The psycho-physical (or, Otherwise, Presumed) ego, as it (Apparently) is (or as it Progressively appears) In The Context Of The First Six Stages Of Life, Must Be Really Transcended. Each Of The Progressive Stages Of Life Is (In Principle, or Really) A Test Of ego-Transcendence—and Practice Of The Only-By-Me Revealed and Given Way Of The Heart (or Way Of Adidam) In The Context Of Each Of The First Six (or Progressive) Stages Of Life Is, Therefore, To Be Directly Engaged As A Test Of ego-Transcendence. This Test Of ego-Transcendence Begins At The Student-Beginner Stage Of The Way Of The Heart—and The Test Intensifies, Stage By Stage, Thereafter. Therefore (and As The Developmental Stages Of Practice Progress), If There Is Weakness In The Devotional Resort To Me, or If There Is Weakness In The Practice Of Listening To Me (or In The Availability Of attention and Feeling To Me), or If The Impulse (or The Motive) Toward Most Perfectly ego-Transcending Real-God-Realization Is Not Fundamental and Intense, or If There Is Weakness In The Application Of self-Discipline (functional, practical, relational, or Cultural), or If There Is Weakness In Hearing Me, or In Seeing Me, or If There Is Weakness In Any Form Of Practicing—Then Passage Through To The "Perfect Practice" Of The Only-By-Me Revealed and Given Way Of The Heart Will Be Retarded and Prolonged. But If The Devotional Resort To Me Is Strong, and If The Listening To Me Is True, and If The Impulse (or The Motive) Toward Most Perfectly ego-Transcending Real-God-Realization Is Real, and If The self-Discipline Is Consistent and Effective, and If The Hearing Of Me, The Seeing Of Me, and The Totality Of The Advancing Practice Are All (and Progressively, and Fundamentally) Strong—Then The Transition To The "Perfect Practice" Of The Only-By-Me Revealed and Given Way Of The Heart (or Practice Of The Only-By-Me Revealed and Given Way Of The Heart In The Context Of Consciousness Itself) Can Be A Readily Direct (Rather Than Retarded and Prolonged) Process Of Free and Real Whole bodily (or Total psycho-physical) Heart-Response To My Avatarically Self-Transmitted Divine Spiritual Grace and Person.

In The Only-By-Me Revealed and Given Way Of The Heart (or Way Of Adidam), The Process Of Listening To Me, and Then Hearing Me, and Then Seeing Me Prepares My Devotee For The "Perfect Practice"—Because That Process Progressively Goes Beyond the point of view (or, More Precisely, the points of view) of the body-mind. Indeed, The Practice Of Ruchira Avatara Bhakti Yoga—or The Surrendering Of The Four psycho-physical Faculties (Of body, emotion, mind, and breath) To Me—Is Precisely This Process Of Progressively Going Beyond the point (or points) of view of the body-mind. Through This Process Of Progressive Transcending (Which Culminates In Your Reception Of My Divine Spiritual Gift Of The Samadhi Of The "Thumbs"), You

Are (By Means Of My Avatarically Self-Transmitted Divine Spiritual Grace) Able To Stand As Consciousness Itself—Because You Are Established In The Position Prior To the body-mind. That Stand (As Consciousness Itself, Prior To the body-mind) Is The Entrance To The "Perfect Practice" Of The Only-By-Me Revealed and Given Way Of The Heart (or Way Of Adidam).

In The Context Of The First Five Stages Of Life (and Even In The Context Of The Sixth Stage Of Life), As They Have Traditionally Been Practiced, The Entire Orientation Is That Of The "Great Path Of Return"—Starting From The Outside and (From There) Attempting To Get To The Inside Depth, or Starting From the body-mind position and (From there) Attempting To Get To The Ultimate Position.

The "Perfect Practice" Of The Only-By-Me Revealed and Given Way Of The Heart (or Way Of Adidam) Cannot Be Established Until the point of view of the conditional persona Is Released and Gone Beyond. The "Perfect Practice" Of The Only-By-Me Revealed and Given Way Of The Heart Is Established When (and Only When) There Is No Longer Any conditional Basis For Sadhana—and, Therefore, Your Sadhana Moves "From The Inside Out".

In Other Words, In Order For The "Perfect Practice" Of The Only-By-Me Revealed and Given Way Of The Heart (or Way Of Adidam) To Be Truly Engaged, the point of view Of The "Great Path Of Return" Must Be Gone Beyond. All The Forms Of The Search—The Descending and Ascending Paths, As Well As The Path Of "Going Within"—Are forms of attention. And attention Is Precisely What Must Be Transcended, In Order To Enter Into The "Perfect Practice" Of The Only-By-Me Revealed and Given Way Of The Heart.

In Order For My Devotee's Practice Of The Only-By-Me Revealed and Given Way Of The Heart To Be Inherently Perfect, Reality (Itself) Must Be The "Point Of View"—Rather Than the psycho-physical ego (or the body-mind). Therefore, The "Perfect Practice" Of The Only-By-Me Revealed and Given Way Of The Heart Begins Prior To the body-mind—When the "Outside-Going-Inward" point of view Is Relinquished, and The "Point Of View" Becomes "Inside-Moving-Outward".

In The Developmental Stages Of The Only-By-Me Revealed and Given Way Of The Heart Previous To The "Perfect Practice", The Practice Of Ruchira Avatara Bhakti Yoga Delivers (and Resonantly Attunes) The Four Faculties Of the body-mind To Me. But The "Perfect Practice" Of The Only-By-Me Revealed and Given Way Of The Heart Is Not A Matter Of Directing The Four psycho-physical Faculties—Because The "Perfect Practice" Of The Only-By-Me Revealed and Given Way Of The Heart Is An All-psycho-physical-Faculties-Already-Perfectly-Attuned-To-Me Process That Is Transcendentally and Spiritually Activated By Me Prior To The psycho-physical Faculties Themselves.

The First Six (or Inherently ego-Based) Stages Of Life Depend On The Faculties Of the body-mind. Thus, The First Six Stages Of Life Are Based In the gross, subtle, and causal points of view—and The First Six Stages Of Life Are Exercises Of The gross, subtle, or causal Dimensions Of conditional Existence, In The Effort To Seek For (or, By Whatever Means, To "Locate" and To Realize) What Is Beyond conditionality.

The Only-By-Me Revealed and Given "Perfect Practice" Of The Only-By-Me Revealed and Given Way Of The Heart (or Way Of Adidam) Is Not (Even In Its Beginnings) A Sixth Stage Practice—Because It Begins Prior To the body-mind (and, Therefore, Prior To The Exercise Of The psycho-physical Faculties).

I Am here To Offer You Most Perfect Divine Liberation From all conditional points of view—gross, subtle, and causal. Going Beyond gross, subtle, and causal points of view Is The Necessary Foundation For The "Perfect Practice" Of The Only-By-Me Revealed and Given Way Of The Heart (or Way Of Adidam)—Which "Perfect Practice" Is Uniquely My Revelation and Gift.

The "Perfect Practice" Of The Only-By-Me Revealed and Given Way Of The Heart (or Way Of Adidam) Is To Be Engaged Only On The Basis Of The Necessary Fulfillment (By Means Of My Avatarically Self-Transmitted Divine Grace) Of All The Prerequisite Stages Of Formal Practice Of The Only-By-Me Revealed and Given Way Of The Heart That (According To My Instructions) Must Be The Case Before Real and Fruitful Practice Of The "Perfect Practice" Of The Only-By-Me Revealed and Given Way Of The Heart Is Possible (and To Be Formally Permitted). Therefore, The "Perfect Practice" Of The Only-By-Me Revealed and Given Way Of The Heart Is To Be Embraced Only On The Basis Of Real Hearing Of Me, True Seeing Of Me, and Right, True, and Full Devotional and Spiritual and Transcendental Awakening (By Means Of My Avatarically Self-Transmitted Divine Grace), and Only With The Formal Approval Of The Ruchira Sannyasin Order Of Adidam Ruchiradam.

The First Three Stages Of Life Are (In and Of Themselves) Simply Stages Of ordinary human Development (functional, practical, and relational). Relative To The First Three Stages Of Life, The Great (and Inherent) Obligation Is To Overcome Un-Happy and ego-Reinforcing Tendencies That Prevent The Transition To The Fourth Stage Of Life. Therefore, In The Only-By-Me Revealed and Given Way Of The Heart, It Becomes The Obligation Of the physically adult human individual (or the Developing human being who Has Attained the physical age Of Basic Adaptation To The First Three Stages Of Life) To Thoroughly Observe and (Most Fundamentally) Understand and Really and Effectively Transcend The First Three Stages Of egoity (or The Pattern Of self-Contraction That Has Issued From the years of infancy, childhood, and adolescence).

The Fourth, The Fifth, and The Sixth Stages Of Life Are Each Associated With A Specific Potential Error. And If The Specific Error Is (In The Only-By-Me Revealed and Given Way Of The Heart) Transcended, Then Passage Through The Process Associated With That Particular Stage Of Life Can Be Quickened.

The Fourth Stage Error Is The Tendency To Prolong The First Three Stages Of Life (and The Patterns Of Un-Happiness That Are egoically Associated With The First Three Stages Of Life) and To Make The Fourth Stage Of Life An End In Itself (Rather Than A Transition, or A Transitional Means, For The Realization Of The Stages Of Life Beyond The Fourth). This Tendency Takes The Form Of A Fixed Idea Of The Divine (As An Ultimate Entity Eternally Separate From the conditional self-entity) and A Fixed Idea Of the personal self (As Either a mortal Or an Immortal entity that Is Eternally Separate From and Dependent Upon The Divine). On The Basis Of This Tendency, The Fourth Stage Of Life Is Made Into A Never-Ending Search For The Divine and A Never-Ending Appeal To The Divine For Intimacy, Relief, and self-Satisfaction.

In The Only-By-Me Revealed and Given Way Of The Heart (or Way Of Adidam), The Fourth Stage Error Is Transcended (and The Fourth Stage Of Life Is, Itself, Quickened) By Means Of The Process Of The True Hearing Of Me, The Real Seeing Of Me, and The (Altogether) Right (and Truly ego-Transcending) Practicing Of The Only-By-Me Revealed and Given Way Of The Heart. By Means Of The Effective (or Truly ego-Surrendering, ego-Forgetting, and ego-Transcending—and, In Due Course By-Me-Spiritually-Initiated) Listening To Me, and By Means Of The True Hearing Of Me (or The Awakening, and The Effective Exercise, Of Most Fundamental self-Understanding), the self-Contraction (and The ego-Idea, or The Illusion and The Fixed Presumption Of an Eternally Separate self-entity) Must Be Transcended. Through The True Seeing Of Me (By Means Of The Fully Technically Responsible Spiritual Reception Of My Avatarically Self-Transmitted Divine Spiritual Baptism), The (By-Me-Avatarically-Self-Revealed) Real Condition Of Non-Separateness Is (By Means Of My Avatarically Self-Transmitted Divine Spiritual Grace) Realized Directly. And That Real Condition Is (or Must Be) Immediately Realized (In every moment Of Whole bodily, or Total psycho-physical, Heart-Communion With Me) <u>As</u> The Inherent Condition Of Reality Itself—Such That (In Due Course) The "Perfect Practice" (Of Self-Abiding <u>As</u> Consciousness Itself), Rather Than The Search For The Divine (Conceived As The Ultimate <u>Object</u> Of the conditional self), May Be Established.

The Fifth Stage Error Is The Tendency To Seek (and To Cling To) subtle phenomenal objects and states (or Else To Seek, or To Cling To, The merely conditional Transcending Of these, In conditionally Ascended—Rather Than Priorly and Perfectly Ascended—Nirvikalpa Samadhi), As If subtle phenomenal objects and subtle phenomenal states Are (or Else conditionally Ascended—Rather Than Priorly and Perfectly Ascended—Nirvikalpa Samadhi Is) The Sufficient or Ultimate or Perfect Realization Of Real God, Truth, Reality, or Happiness. This Error Is Transcended When (By Means Of My Avatarically Self-Transmitted Divine Spiritual Grace) There Is Real and Stable Awakening To The Inherent (and Inherently egoless, or Non-Separate) Witness-Position Of Consciousness (Inherently Free Of All Seeking, Clinging, and Avoiding, In Both The Descending and The Ascending Dimensions Of conditional Existence).

The Sixth Stage Error Is The Tendency To Hold On To The (Inherently Subjective) Position Of Consciousness As A Reality Inherently Separate (or Dissociated) From Apparently Objectified Light (or Apparently Objectified Spirit-Energy) and all conditional objects (or all that Is Made Of That Apparently Objectified Light, or Apparently Objectified Spirit-Energy). It Is The Tendency To Hold On To The Inherent Love-Bliss Of Consciousness By Strategically Excluding All Awareness Of (or The Tendency To Grant, or Allow, attention To) conditional objects and states.

The Sixth Stage Error (or Tendency) Is Based On Attachment To The Position Of Consciousness As The Detached Witness Of conditional events (or That To Whom conditions or objects arise)—Whereas, In Truth, Consciousness Is Ultimately and Inherently and Always Already That In, Of, and As Whom conditions or objects arise (As Apparent Modifications Of Itself).

The Sixth Stage Error (or Tendency) May Eventually Take The Form Of conditionally Self-Abiding Jnana Samadhi, Which Is A Temporary State Of Transcendental Awakeness (Based On Contemplative Identification With The Consciousness-Principle As A Separate Condition) That Is Also Inherently Associated With An Accompanying Effort (Either Spontaneous Or Willful) That Excludes all conditional (or phenomenal) objects and states. In Any Case, The Rightly Understood and Rightly Engaged Process Of The "Perfect Practice" Of The Only-By-Me Revealed and Given Way Of The Heart (In The Context Of The Process Otherwise Characteristically Associated With The Sixth Stage Of Life) Will (or Must, Even If Progressively) Transcend The Sixth Stage Error (or Tendency). And That Transcending Is (Most Ultimately) Demonstrated In (and By) Seventh Stage Sahaja Nirvikalpa Samadhi (or The Free and Perfectly Subjective and Self-Evidently Divine Realization Of Self-Existing and Self-Radiant Consciousness Itself—or The One and Only and Inherently Indivisible and Inherently egoless Conscious Light Itself), In Which conditional objects and states Are Freely Allowed To arise and Even To Be Noticed, and In Which conditional objects and states Are Inherently Divinely Self-Recognized As Transparent (or Merely Apparent), and Un-Necessary, and Inherently Non-Binding Modifications Of Perfectly Subjective Consciousness Itself (Which Is Inherently Free As Love-Bliss Itself—Self-Existing, Self-Radiant, and Self-Evidently Divine).

Therefore, In The Only-By-Me Revealed and Given Way Of The Heart (or Way Of Adidam), The Transition To The Only-By-Me Revealed and Given Seventh Stage Of Life Is Freely Given (In The Context Of The "Perfect Practice" Of The Only-By-Me Revealed and Given Way Of The Heart) By Means Of My Avatarically Self-Transmitted Divine Spiritual Grace. And That Transition Is Readily and Directly Realized (In The Context Of The "Perfect Practice" Of The Only-By-Me Revealed and Given Way Of The Heart), If The egoic Effort To Separate (or Contract) From conditional Existence (or Even From Apparently Objectified Light, or Apparently Objectified Spirit-Energy Itself) Is (By Means Of My Avatarically Self-Transmitted Divine Spiritual Grace) Whole-Heartedly Released In Transcendental, Inherently Spiritual, Inherently egoless, Inherently Perfect, and Self-Evidently Divine Self-Consciousness.

The Only-By-Me Revealed and Given Way Of The Heart (or Way Of Adidam) Is Not An "Evolutionary" Call To Progressively Fulfill The Stages Of Life. The Only-By-Me Revealed and Given Way Of The Heart (or Way Of Adidam) Is A "Radical" Call To Progressively (and Most Directly) Transcend The First Six (and, Necessarily, egoic) Stages Of Life—and, Ultimately, To Most Perfectly Embrace (or To Inherently, and Inherently Most Perfectly, Realize) The (Only-By-Me Revealed and Given) Already Divinely Enlightened (or Seventh) Stage Of Life.

The Only-By-Me Revealed and Given Way Of The Heart (or Way Of Adidam) Is A Call To (Most Fundamentally) Understand and Utterly Transcend the self-Contraction. Therefore, The Only-By-Me Revealed and Given Way Of The Heart (or Way Of Adidam) Is A Call To Pass The Test Of Each and Every Stage Of Life. And The Only-By-Me Revealed and Given Way Of The Heart (or Way Of Adidam) Is A Call To Most Directly (and As Quickly As Possible) Transcend The Progressive Stages Of Life (Previous To The Seventh). Therefore, The Only-By-Me Revealed and Given Way Of The Heart (or Way Of Adidam) Is A Call To Quicken Progressive Practice By Directly Transcending the Binding limitations Associated With The First Three Stages Of Life and The Fundamental Errors That Are Characteristically Associated With The Fourth Stage, The Fifth Stage, and The Sixth Stage Of Life.

Before You Are My "Perfect Practice" Devotee, You Presume That You Have To Be Established (or Secured) In a particular position—a position (or "point") that Allows You To Observe whatever conditions are arising, and To

Hold On To whatever conditions Seem To Be Desirable, and To Be Held By whatever conditions Seem To Support Your Existence, Whether those conditions are gross Or subtle Or causal. Thus, Before You Are My "Perfect Practice" Devotee, You Are Afraid To Fully Feel, Afraid To Fully Release Your (Presumed-To-Be-Separate) Consciousness To Infinity—Because To Feel Thus, and To Release Your (Presumed-To-Be-Separate) Consciousness Thus, Means That You Will Lose Your "point" in space. Indeed, You Are (Inevitably) Going To Lose Your life (As You Now know it)—That Is Exactly True. Therefore, It Is Only When The Undying Happiness Of Heart-Communion With Me, At Infinity, Becomes Obvious To You That You Will Permit The Dissolution Of the ego-"I" To Become Perfect. The Real Spiritual Process In My Avataric Divine Company Does, In Due Course, Require The Dissolution Of everything conditional—The Dissolution Of body, Of all personal energy, all forms, all worlds, all that is mind, all concepts, and Even attention itself. Infinity Must Become Your Pleasure. Then this world Becomes A Truly Humorous Display and A Genuinely Livable Circumstance. Then You Can Make this world Into A Sacred Domain—Of Unlimited (or "point"-less) Heart-Communion With Me (In and As My Avatarically-Born Bodily Human Divine Form and Person).

Therefore, When You Are My "Perfect Practice" Devotee, Relinquish The Hold On the body. Relinquish All Identification With its conditions and states. Relinquish The Search For bodily and psychic (or mental) self-Fulfillment In the field of conditional relations (whether gross or subtle, low or high, external or internal). By Means Of My Avatarically Self-Transmitted Divine Spiritual Grace, Realize The Condition Of Heart-Identification With Me, and, Thus (By Virtue Of By-My-Avataric-Divine-Spiritual-Grace-Given Heart-Identification With Me and, At Last, Most Perfect Realization Of My Avatarically Self-Revealed, and Self-Evidently Divine, Self-Condition), Progressively and Effectively Let Go (and Be Released) Of all conditions, Until The Final Degree Of Outshining (or Divine Translation Into The Self-Existing and Self-Radiant Sphere Of My Spiritually Self-"Bright" Divine Self-Domain).

My Call Is Always A "Radical" Call To Most Directly ego-Surrendering, ego-Forgetting, and ego-Transcending Satsang (or Devotional, and, In Due Course, Spiritual, and, Altogether, Whole bodily, or Total psycho-physical, Heart-Communion) With Me—To The Degree, Most Ultimately, Of Inherently Most Perfect Realization Of The Ultimate and Inherently Perfect and Inherently ego-Transcending "Perfect Practice" Of The Only-By-Me Revealed and Given Way Of The Heart. And, Even Though The Tendency Of the body-mind Is To Progress, Even Slowly, Through The Stages Of Life, The Process Can Be Quickened and (Eventually) Inherently Most Perfectly Fulfilled, If the self-Contraction Is Understood and Persistently Transcended In The Most Intensive

Practice Of Always Present Whole bodily (or Total psycho-physical) Devotional and Spiritual Heart-Communion With Me.

The Graceful (and Always Giving) Avataric Divine Means I Give To All Practitioners Of The Only-By-Me Revealed and Given Way Of The Heart (or Way Of Adidam) Are Not Merely Matters Of philosophy, or Of Spiritual "technique", or Of ego-Based Seeking-Effort. I Give Myself To You. I (Myself) Am The Means. And I Give Myself To You As Various Means—Such That Your Realization Of Me Is Served In A Uniquely Appropriate Manner At Each Developmental Stage Of Practice In The Only-By-Me Revealed and Given Way Of The Heart. As My Devotee, You Must (In The Course Of The Way Of The Heart) Undergo A Process Of Growth—In Which You Assume Responsibility, At Each Successive Developmental Stage Of Practice In The Way Of The Heart, For All The By-Me-Given Practices Necessary and Appropriate For That Stage. Nevertheless, The Principal Practice and Process In The Only-By-Me Revealed and Given Way Of The Heart (or Way Of Adidam) Is Always Simply Your (Progressive) Reception and Embrace Of The Graceful (and Always Giving) Avataric Divine Means That I Am. I Always Give Myself (To You)—Both As Consciousness Itself and As The Spiritual Self-Radiance Of Consciousness Itself. I Always Give Myself (To You) As The "Bright"—The One and Only and Inherently Indivisible and Inherently egoless and Self-Evidently Divine Conscious Light That Is Reality Itself. Therefore, The Awakening To (and, Then, The Inherent, and Inherently Perfect, Establishment In) The Ultimate (and Inherently Perfect) Process (or The "Perfect Practice") Of The Only-By-Me Revealed and Given Way Of The Heart (or Way Of Adidam) Requires Not Only The "Conscious Process" (Of Realizing That You Always Already Stand In The Witness-Position Of Consciousness), but Also A Unique (and Uniquely Perfect) Process Of Spirit-"Conductivity". Thus, By Means Of The Current Of My Avatarically Self-Transmitted Spiritual (and Always Blessing, and Merely "Bright") Divine Presence, I Spiritually Draw You (Beyond All psycho-physical References) To Myself (and, Ultimately, To My Avatarically Self-Revealed, and Very, and Transcendental, and Perfectly Subjective, and Inherently Spiritual, and Inherently egoless, and Inherently Perfect, and Self-Evidently Divine State). In This Manner, I Attract You Into The Domain Of The Right Side Of The Heart, and (Then) Beyond The causal Knot (or The Original egoic Contraction) In The Right Side Of The Heart, and (Thereby) Not Only Into but Also Beyond The Witnessing Function Of Consciousness (Apparently "Over Against" conditional others and objects and thoughts and states), and (Thus) To The (By-Me-Avatarically-Self-Revealed) Self-Existing and Self-Radiant Domain (or Self-Condition) That Is Consciousness Itself, and That Is The Source-Condition Of The Apparent Witnessing Function.

The "Perfect-Practice"-Process Of The Only-By-Me Revealed and Given Way Of The Heart (or Way Of Adidam) Is Such That You Are Profoundly Moved (or Ecstatically "Magnetized"), By Me, Into The Self-Existing and Self-Radiant Domain Of Consciousness Itself (or The Perfectly Subjective Self-Domain, Which Is Realized As, and Entirely By Means Of, My Avatarically Self-Transmitted Spirit-Current Of Self-Evidently Divine Love-Bliss-Being). Indeed, The Fundamental Process In The Only-By-Me Revealed and Given Way Of The Heart (Altogether) Is My Spiritual Drawing Of You (Progressively) Into (and Beyond) The Right Side Of The Heart (In Which, and Immediately Prior To Which, My Avatarically Self-Transmitted Spiritual, and Always Blessing, Divine Presence Stands)—Rather Than Any Process That Is Otherwise Purposed To Establish (Separately, or For their own Sake) any of the experiential phenomena that May Occur (As Secondary, Purifying Effects Of My Avatarically Self-Transmitted Spiritual, and Always Blessing, Divine Presence) In The Circle (or conditional psycho-physical Context) Of the body-mind.

Among The Signs Associated (In The Only-By-Me Revealed and Given Way Of The Heart) With The (By-My-Avataric-Divine-Spiritual-Grace-Given) Stable Awakening Of Inherent Identification With The Witness-Position Of Consciousness (Which Stable Awakening Permits, and Even Requires, The Transition To Practice Of The Only-By-Me Revealed and Given Way Of The Heart In The Context Of The "Perfect Practice"), There Will (or Must) Be The (By-My-Avataric-Divine-Spiritual-Grace-Given) Feeling-Awareness That The By-Me-Avatarically-Self-Transmitted Divine Spirit-Current Is Undermining the act of attention (and Is, Thus, Relaxing The Tendency To Identify With the body-mind) By Radiating (Priorly and Profoundly) In The Right Side Of The Heart (Rather Than Merely, or Only, In The Circle, or The Vertical Plane and Circuit Associated With The Left Side and The Middle Station Of The Heart, Whereby attention Is Attracted and Moved To the gross and subtle phenomena of body and mind). Until Most Perfect Divine Self-Realization—Which Is Awakened In The Inherently Most Perfect Fulfillment Of The Yoga (or Inherently Perfect Practice) Of The "Conscious Process" and Spirit-"Conductivity" (and Which Is Possible Only After Fully Transcending The Need, or The Apparent Necessity, For The Progressive Yoga Of The "Conscious Process" and Spirit-"Conductivity" In The Context Of The Frontal Yoga Of The Only-By-Me Revealed and Given Way Of The Heart)—attention and The By-Me-Avatarically-Self-Transmitted Divine Spirit-Current Will Constantly Tend To Move Out and Away From The Well Of Being (or The Transcendental, Inherently Spiritual, Inherently egoless, and Self-Evidently Divine Self-Position). However, After Most Perfect Divine Self-Awakening (In The Context Of The Only-By-Me Revealed and Given Seventh Stage Of Life In The Only-By-Me Revealed and

Given Way Of The Heart), The Realization Of My (Avatarically Self-Revealed) Transcendental, Inherently Spiritual, Inherently egoless, and Self-Evidently Divine Self-Position Is Never Lost or Abandoned For Any Reason—Even Though The By-Me-Avatarically-Self-Transmitted Divine Spirit-Current Is (Apparently) Modified In The Form Of conditional objects, and Even Though Consciousness (Via attention) Apparently knows them.

In The Transition From Practice Of The Only-By-Me Revealed and Given Way Of The Heart In The Context Of The First Actually Seeing Stage To Practice Of The Only-By-Me Revealed and Given Way Of The Heart In The Context Of The "Perfect Practice", All Seeking Falls and Dissolves Upon Me—The Heart-Deep Of Eternally Unmoved Consciousness, The Always Already Free Witness Of the self-Contracted "I" of the body-mind, The Formless (or Imageless) and Soundless (and Inherently egoless) Unfathomable Well Of Being That Merely (or Indifferently) Reflects (and Is Never Stirred By) all Apparent conditional experience, all Apparent conditional knowledge, and All Apparent Illusions or Events Of limitation.

May every one who Listens To Me and Hears Me and Sees Me Practice The Only-By-Me Revealed and Given Way Of The Heart (or Way Of Adidam) To This Inherently Perfect Degree.

I Am The Avatarically Self-Revealed Divine Secret Of This Perfect Suddenness Of Being.

Avatar Adi Da Samraj
Da Love-Ananda Mahal, 2003

SUTRA 48

Among the beings On Earth, human beings Are Unique—but Only In The Sense That they Are (As a species) Significantly More Advanced In The Development Of psycho-physical functions that Are (Otherwise) Only Latent (or Less Developed) In the case of the non-human world (of Natural energies and elements, material shapes and cycles, simpler organisms, plants, trees, insects, fishes, birds, mammals, and the rest). The non-human world Is The Immediate Progenitor Of the Natural functions and the functional form Of Man. The world of non-human beings (of which the great trees Are The Epitome and The Senior Of all[151]) Is A Great Process, From Which and Relative To Which and In Which human beings Are Developed and Developing (By Virtue Of A Complex and Ever-Continuing Event That Functions At All Levels, and Not Merely At The gross material Level, Of The psycho-physical Cosmos).

Among The Apparent Differences Between Man and all the non-human beings Is The Greatly Developed Capability For mentally Reflective and conceptually Abstracted knowledge (and Consequent inventiveness) That Is Evident In the human case. Nevertheless, It Is Not conceptual (or Abstract) thinking that Is The Unique Characteristic (or Capability) Of Man. Neither Is toolmaking (or inventiveness and technology), which is a secondary product of conceptual (or Abstract) thinking, The Unique Characteristic (or Capability) Of Man. Abstract thought and technology are themselves only servants Of The Unique Capability Of Man. They are Signs (or Secondary Evidence) Of The Unique Characteristic Of Man.

The Unique Characteristic Of Man Is The Capability For self-Understanding. The Unique Capability Of Man Is The Characteristic Process Of psycho-physical self-Transcendence (or The Whole bodily Demonstration Of ego-Transcendence). Therefore, The Unique Potential Of Man Is The psycho-physical Progress Of self-Understanding and self-Transcendence (or ego-Transcendence). And self-Understanding and self-Transcendence, Truly Progressing (As A Demonstration In The Context Of the Total body-mind), Lead Toward The (Potential, and Only-By-My-Avataric-Divine-Spiritual-Grace-Given) Most Perfect Realization Of The Self-Evidently Divine Source Of the conditional self, and Of the body-mind itself, and Of The Totality Of conditional Existence.

Abstract (and right conceptual) "thinking" (In The Context Of Profound, and, More and More, thought-Transcending, "Consideration") and "technology" (Displayed As The Total Form Of Right and Effective Practice) Are (As Such) Useful Means For Directing The Progressively ego-Transcending Process That Is The Unique Potential Of Man. However, When egoity (or self-Fulfillment), Rather Than ego-Transcendence, Becomes The Motivator Of Man, conceptual thinking and technological inventiveness Tend To Become Exalted (or Valued) As Ends In themselves—Such That they Become The Chronic, Compulsive, and Obsessive Preoccupations Of Man.

The non-human beings function Largely From The Base Of What Is Commonly Called "The Unconscious". That Is To Say, Compared To Man, they Apparently Operate With Much Less Of (or, At Least In some cases, Even Without Much Of) What Are Commonly Called The "Conscious" and "Subconscious" Structures Of mind. Human beings Are Actively Bringing The Unconscious—In Its Totality, Including (Potentially) Its Superconscious Heights and (Most Ultimately, In The Only-By-Me Revealed and Given Seventh Stage Of Life) Its Inherent (and Inherently Perfect) Depth and "Brightness"—Into a More and More Clearly Conscious state of mind (and Of Conscious Realization, Even Prior To mind).

The Unconscious (As mind) Is the Fundamental functional mind (or the functional Source-mind). It Is Constantly Active and Effective, but (Perhaps Because Its contents Are Not Objectified In a conventionally Familiar and conventionally Usable mental form) It Is Not (In The General Case) Immediately (or Directly) known (or Acknowledged) By the Conscious mind. Therefore, Between the Unconscious mind and the Conscious mind Is a Transitional mind—the Subconscious (or dreaming and dreamlike) mind. The Subconscious mind Is Immediately Below, or Behind, or (In Superconscious states, Developed or Revealed Via The Subconscious mind, or Process) Even (Spatially) Above the Conscious mind—and it Is (or May Be), To A Degree, Directly (or Consciously) known, Acknowledged, and Used (or Expressed) By the Conscious mind. Therefore, the Subconscious mind Is A Communications Bridge Between the Unconscious mind and the Conscious mind (and Between the Conscious mind and the Unconscious mind).

Human beings Are Bringing The Unconscious To Consciousness Through Developmental Stages That Make Transitional Use Of The Subconscious Mechanisms. The By-Me-Revealed-and-Given Complete Spiritual, Transcendental, and Divine Process May Be Understood As A Sequence Of Stages Of Growth Culminating In (Inherent, Inherently egoless, Inherently Most Perfect, and Self-Evidently Divine) Consciousness Of (and Inherently Most Perfect, or Inherently egoless, and Inherently Free, Responsibility For) All Of Reality—

Such That The Hidden Secrets Of mind Are Conscious (Even In mind), and The Transcendental, Inherently Spiritual, Inherently egoless, and Self-Evidently Divine Source (or Inherently Perfect Subject, or Perfectly Subjective Self, or Limitless Prior Condition) Of mind (Even Of the Unconscious conditional Source-mind) Is Realized To Be Consciousness Itself.

In General, humanity At Large Is Struggling In The Earlier Stages Of This Process (In The Context Of The First Three Stages Of Life). Nevertheless, much (conditional) knowledge Has Been Brought To Consciousness, but that (conditional) knowledge Is Only Partial—and, As A Result, what human beings now Regard As common or reliable (conditional) knowledge Is Only The Beginning Of (conditional) knowledge, and what is conditionally known Has The Force (or Significance) Of A Problem (or A Yet Unresolved Urge To know).

Among the Most Significant forms of such human knowledge Is the knowledge of death. The non-human beings experience fear, self-protectiveness, survival instincts, adaptation urges, sickness, and death, but their Involvement With all of that Is At The Level Of Urges Coming From The Unconscious. The non-human beings Are Not (At The Level Of the Conscious mind) Very self-Aware Of death, its Structure or Purpose, or Even its Inevitability. Human beings, However, Are (Even Characteristically) Acutely Aware Of death As An Inevitable and Apparently Terminal personal Event. This Awareness Is Unique (conditional) knowledge, but It Is Also Only Partial (conditional) knowledge. It Is A Sign That human beings (Not Otherwise More Fully Awake) Are Yet functioning On The Base Of The Unconscious Relative To The Larger Context, Real Process, and Ultimate Purpose Of death, and Of life itself. Thus, For human beings At The Lesser (or Commonly Characteristic) Level Of human Development, death Is A Problem, A Threat, A Dilemma, or A Question In the mind.

Because human beings function Rather Uniquely At The Level Of Subconscious and Conscious mind, and Because human Developmental Progress Is (Primarily) A Process In mind (Moving, Ultimately, Toward The By-Me-Avatarically-Given Revelation Of Self-Existing and Self-Radiant Consciousness Itself) and Only Preliminarily (and, Otherwise, Secondarily) A Process Of gross form and gross adaptation—human beings Naturally Feel Threatened By death As An Always Present (or Abstract) Possibility (and Concern Of mind).

Likewise, In General, human beings Characteristically experience sex As An Always Present (or Abstract) Possibility (and Concern Of mind), Whereas non-human beings Are Generally Associated With sex Via instinctive and Unconsciously Generated Cyclic Patterns. Therefore, human beings Are (In General) Constantly Moved To Achieve sexual Pleasure (With or Without An

Intention To reproduce), and they Are, Otherwise (In General), Constantly Moved To Confront and Answer or Solve (Through psycho-physical Efforts) The Abstract and Really Threatening Problem Of death.

In Contrast To the human species, the non-human species Are Generally Moved Only instinctively. Thus, non-human beings Are instinctively Moved To reproduce themselves Excessively (That Is To Say, Frequently and/or in Superfluous numbers, So That a Sufficient number Will Survive all Natural threats and reproduce the species again), and they Are Also instinctively Moved To Aggressively Compete For food, territory, or breeding mates (who, Like food and territory, Basically Represent The instinctive Right To reproduce), and they Are (Otherwise) instinctively Moved To Defend (or Even Simply To Agitate) themselves Only In The Instants Of Direct Confrontation With a Really (and bodily) Threatening physical opponent—Whereas human beings (In their more mentalized—and, Therefore, Comparatively More Developed—personal and social state) Are, Because Of mental Anxiety, Sometimes Moved To kill Even their own kind in Invented (or mentally Contrived) wars, and (Otherwise) To Be Aggressive and Defensive and Agitated Even In circumstances that Are Not Directly (or Really and bodily) Threatening. Therefore, human beings (and Mankind As A Whole) <u>Must</u> Develop Further Than all non-human beings, So That they May Transcend All The mental, emotional, and physical Exaggerations Of their non-human Inheritance Of instinct (Particularly As Those Exaggerations Are Demonstrated Via egoic and Loveless and Destructive Motives Associated With sex, and food, and territory, and Aggression).

It Is Also Notable That, As Mankind Develops Its Abstracted Involvement With (Especially) sex and death To The Degree That most human individuals Tend To live to (and beyond) the Natural reproductive age, human populations Tend To Become Overlarge, Such That The Quality Of ordinary human experience and The Possibility Of Growth Beyond The First Three Stages Of Life Become Either Threatened Or Really Diminished. This Indicates That, As human populations Acquire The Capability For longevity, they Must Control human reproduction, and they Must Also Become Informed and Guided By The Wisdom-Culture Of Superior (or, Really, Divine) self-Understanding and Purpose—or Else human beings Will Tend, In The Likeness Of non-human beings, To Continue To reproduce Excessively and To Remain Devoted (In The instinctive or Unconscious Manner) To self-Survival (Rather Than To self-Transcendence, or ego-Transcendence) and To Effort and Seeking Merely For The Sake Of The Survival Of the organism itself (Rather Than To Devotional Surrender Of the body-mind To The Great Reality, and To The Purpose Of ego-Transcendence).

When human populations Achieve The Capability For individual longevity, they Must Control or Transcend The instinctual reproductive Strategies Of Excess—Because Those Strategies Work (or Produce An Ecologically Balanced Result) Only If The Rate Of early-life deaths Is Relatively Large. Likewise, As human beings Acquire longer lifespans, they Must Realize The Superior (or ego-Transcending) Purpose Of conditional Existence, and they Must Be Moved and Grown To Demonstrate That Purpose In The Context Of The Stages Of Life Beyond The First Three—or Else conditional Existence Will Be Devoted To sub-human and egoic Survival games and The petty territorial (or political and social) Conquests That Come From The Increase Of experience and knowledge and power In The lower human Context Of The First Three Stages Of Life (Untouched By The Great Purpose, and Untouched By The Culture, The Balancing Effect, and The Great Process Of Awakening Associated With ego-Transcendence In The Context Of The Fourth Stage Of Life and Beyond).

Therefore, As human groups increase in size (because of the longevity of individuals), death itself Must Be Really Understood and Transcended—In Consciousness, and (Progressively) In The Context Of The Fourth Stage Of Life and Beyond. Likewise, merely reproductive sexuality Must Be Controlled (or Economized), In both its performance and its effects, By various Intelligent (and Heart-Sensitive, and Compassionate) techniques—and sexuality itself Must Be (Progressively) Converted (and Positively Changed) By Heart-Sensitive, and Love-Based, and Energy-Conserving, and Rejuvenative, and (Eventually) Spiritually Active and Spiritually Effective emotional-sexual Practice.

For human beings, death Is A Proposition and A Puzzle That Must Be Understood and Transcended (By Correct and Revealing Information, or Fullest Education, and By The Real Process Of ego-Transcendence). There Is No Peace For human beings Until This Matter Is Resolved.

Of Course, This Matter Of death Is A Perennial Subject Of Conjecture and Research, but The Resolution Of The Question Requires Even More Than Information. As Is The Case With All Truly Developmental Matters, This Question Can Be Resolved Only By Tapping What Is Always Presently In The Unconscious and Bringing It Into Consciousness. That Is To Say, The Overcoming Of The Apparent Problem and Motivating Stress Associated With death Requires The Truly Developmental (and, Thus, Truly human, and Spiritual, and Transcendental, and, Most Ultimately, Divine) Process Of Positively Changing and Directly Transcending the limitations of mind (or The egoic Burden Of limited knowledge and limited experience).

The Unconscious Is Simply The Totality Of What Is Real but Not Yet Fully Conscious (or Brought To Fully Conscious Acknowledgement and Realization). Since Mankind Has Gone So Far As To Become self-Conscious (or mentally and egoically self-Aware) About death, Mankind Must Be Surrendered To A Process Of Becoming Really (and Not egoically) Conscious Of What Is Yet Hidden. And This Requires Truly human Growth, and Growth Beyond The First Three Stages Of Life, Via The human, and Spiritual, and Transcendental, and (Most Ultimately) Divine Process Of Participatory ego-Transcendence. Through Such ego-Transcendence, the (Presumed) knowledge Of The psycho-physical Potential Of death Progressively Becomes Heart-Realization Of The self-Sacrificial Wound Of Divine Love-Bliss.

Deeper Than the Conscious mind Of Man In The Third Stage Of Life Is The Inherent Realization Of Eternal Love, Immortal Love-Bliss, Unqualified Being, Infinite Spirit-Power, and Inherent Wisdom. Therefore, As The Process Of human Growth Develops Beyond The Third Stage Of Life, There Is Developmental Progress, Stage By Stage, Toward Most Ultimate Realization. And, More and More, In That Progress, The Problem Of death (or The Wondering About The Purpose, Process, and Effect Of life and death) Is Overcome By Real Conscious Realization Of What Is Hidden From the (lesser) mechanical and Unconscious point of view. And That Real Conscious Realization Is Final (or Complete) Only In The Most Ultimate, and Inherently Most Perfect (or Seventh Stage), Fulfillment Of That Progress, Which Most Ultimate Fulfillment Can Be Realized Only In The Way Of Adidam (Which Is The One and Only By-Me-Revealed and By-Me-Given Way Of The Heart).

Each Of The Progressively Developmental Stages Of Practice In The Only-By-Me Revealed and Given Way Of The Heart Is A Stage In This Progression From Unconsciousness To Consciousness (and, Most Ultimately, To The Realization Of Inherently Perfect, or Divine, Consciousness) Via Transitional Developments In The Subconscious Depth Of Existence. I Have Indicated What Kinds Of Changes Must Be Associated With Each and Every Stage Of Practice In The Only-By-Me Revealed and Given Way Of The Heart, Culminating In The Only-By-Me Revealed and Given Seventh Stage Of Life and (Most Ultimately) Divine Translation. The Realization Of The Samadhi Of The "Thumbs" (and The Consequent Establishment In The Witness-Position Of Consciousness), The Realization Of Priorly Self-Abiding Jnana Nirvikalpa Samadhi, and The Realization Of Priorly Ascended Nirvikalpa Samadhi Are The Principal Such Transitional Developments—and, When Any Of These Occurs, It Only Makes Possible (and Necessary) A Further Progress, By Unlocking A Profound Level Of Hidden Realization From The Unconscious (Esoteric, Secret, or Unknown) Mass Of Divine Existence.

The conditionally Manifested Cosmos Of beings and forms Is A Play Upon The Infinite Indivisible Light (or Spirit-Energy, or Inherent Love-Bliss) Of Infinite Consciousness (or Self-Existing, Self-Radiant, and Inherently egoless

Being). This Becomes A Final (or Inherent and Inherently Most Perfect) Certainty (At The Level Of Most Full, or Inherently Most Perfectly Conscious, and Inherently, and Inherently Most Perfectly, egoless, and, Thus, Divinely Conscious, Realization) Only After The Direct and Spontaneous True Awakening To The Witness-Position Of Consciousness (and The Subsequent Developments Of The "Perfect Practice" Of The Only-By-Me Revealed and Given Way Of The Heart, In The Structural Context Of Both The Horizontal, and Otherwise Sixth Stage, Dimension, or Heart-Dimension, Of Conscious Realization, and The Vertical, or Otherwise Fifth Stage, Dimension, or Priorly Ascended Dimension, Of Conscious Realization), and (In Due Course, By Means Of My Avatarically Self-Transmitted Divine Spiritual Grace) The Awakening To The Only-By-Me Revealed and Given Seventh Stage Of Life.

Therefore, In The Unique, and All-Completing, and Only-By-Me Revealed and Given Way Of The Heart (or Way Of Adidam), Which I Have Revealed To all (In Order That each and all May Become My Devotees and Realize Me)—The Listening To Me, and The Hearing Of Me (or Most Fundamental self-Understanding), and The Seeing Of Me (Through Fully Technically Responsible Reception Of My Avatarically Self-Transmitted Divine Spirit-Baptism, or Ruchira Shaktipat) Are The Way To Inherent (and Inherently Most Perfect) Certainty. And The Way (Thus) To Inherent (and Inherently Most Perfect) Certainty Begins Even From the time Of (First) Listening To Me, and It Progresses (Through Hearing Me, and Then Seeing Me) To Inherent (and Inherently egoless, and Inherently Most Perfect) Realization Of Me. In The Course Of That Progress, Greatly Profound (but conditional, and, Therefore, Not Yet Inherently Most Perfect) Certainty Is Brought (Temporarily, and only conditionally) To Consciousness When The limiting Capability (or Binding Presumption) Of the body-mind Is Transcended—First, In The Samadhi Of The "Thumbs", and, Then (In The Context Of The "Perfect Practice", On The Basis Of The Awakening Of Inherent Identification With The Witness-Position Of Consciousness), In Priorly Self-Abiding Jnana Nirvikalpa Samadhi (As The Ultimate Realization Of The Horizontal Process Otherwise Associated With The Sixth Stage Of Life) and (Necessarily, Subsequent To The Realization Of Priorly Self-Abiding Jnana Nirvikalpa Samadhi) Priorly Ascended Nirvikalpa Samadhi (As The Ultimate Realization Of The Vertical Process Otherwise Associated With The Fifth Stage Of Life). However, Certainty Itself (Inherent, and Inherently Most Perfect)—or The Inherent (and Inherently Most Perfect) Realization Of The Only Inherent (and Inherently Most Perfect) Certainty (Which Is Real God, or Truth Itself, or Reality Itself)—Is Brought Most Fully, Un-conditionally, Inherently Most Perfectly, and (Altogether) Finally To Consciousness (and As Consciousness Itself) Only In Seventh Stage Sahaja Nirvikalpa Samadhi, Which

Is The Supreme Awakening That Begins (and Altogether Characterizes) The Only-By-Me Revealed and Given Seventh Stage Of Life.

Therefore, In The Only-By-Me Revealed and Given Way Of The Heart (or Way Of Adidam), Practice Is Not (or Should Not Be) Purposed To The "Having" Of merely psycho-physical, or conditional, or Otherwise (and In A conditional Manner) Dependently arising experiences. In The Only-By-Me Revealed and Given Way Of The Heart, Not Even one of the Possible lesser (and, Necessarily, psycho-physical and conditional) Spiritual experiences Is To Be Sought (or Made an object, or a goal, Of Practice). Indeed, In The Only-By-Me Revealed and Given Way Of The Heart, Not Even One Of The "Great" (but Yet conditional, or, In A conditional Manner, Dependently arising) Spiritual Experiences Is To Be Sought (or Made An Object, or A Goal, Of Practice).

In The Progressing Course Of Spiritual Practice In The Only-By-Me Revealed and Given Way Of The Heart, The "Great" Spiritual Experiences Of The "Thumbs", and Priorly Self-Abiding Jnana Nirvikalpa Samadhi, and Priorly Ascended Nirvikalpa Samadhi Will (and Must) arise, Entirely By Means Of The By-Me-Spiritually-Given Grace Of My Avatarically Self-Transmitted Spiritual (and Always Blessing) Divine Presence—and, Thus, Entirely As Spontaneous Developments Of The Process Of ego-Transcending Feeling-Contemplation (or Searchless Beholding) Of My Avatarically-Born Bodily (Human) Divine Form, and, Thus and Thereby, Of My Avatarically Self-Transmitted Spiritual (and Always Blessing) Divine Presence. Nevertheless, Access To My Avatarically Self-Transmitted Spiritual (and Always Blessing) Divine Presence (and, Thereby, To My Avatarically Self-Transmitted Divine Spiritual Baptism) Is Not Given In Order That My Devotees May Seek (or, Otherwise, Indulge In) Any or All Possible "Great" (but Yet conditional, or, In A conditional Manner, Dependently arising) Realization-Experiences Of My Avatarically Self-Transmitted Spiritual (and Always Blessing) Divine Presence, or any or all Possible lesser effects (or conditional, and merely psycho-physical, experiences) Of My Avatarically Self-Transmitted Spiritual (and Always Blessing) Divine Presence. Rather, Access To My Avatarically Self-Transmitted Spiritual (and Always Blessing) Divine Presence (and, Thereby, To My Avatarically Self-Transmitted Divine Spiritual Baptism, or Ruchira Shaktipat) Is Given In Order That all those who Listen To Me May (In Due Course, By Means Of My Avatarically Self-Transmitted Divine Spiritual Grace) Hear Me and (Then) See Me (By Heart-Response To and Heart-Communion With My Avatarically Self-Transmitted Spiritual, and Always Blessing, Divine Presence Itself).

The lesser (and, Necessarily, conditional, and psycho-physical) effects Of My Avatarically Self-Transmitted Spiritual (and Always Blessing) Divine Presence Are Not (in and of themselves) Me.

Not Even The Otherwise "Great" (but Yet conditional, or, In A conditional Manner, Dependently arising) Realization-Experiences Of My Avatarically Self-Transmitted Spiritual (and Always Blessing) Divine Presence Are (In and Of Themselves) Me.

Only My Avatarically Self-Transmitted Spiritual (and Always Blessing) Divine Presence Itself Is Me.

Therefore, My Devotees Are Called To Transcend themselves—and (Thus) Also all conditional knowing, and all Presumed (and, Necessarily, conditional) knowledge, and all psycho-physical (and, Necessarily, conditional) experiencings and experiences, and Even All "Great" (but Yet conditional, or, In A conditional Manner, Dependently arising) Realization-Experiencings and Realization-Experiences—By Surrendering, Forgetting, and Transcending the ego-"I" (or self-Contraction)—and This By Means Of Heart-True Ruchira Avatara Bhakti Yoga, Which Is Truly ego-Surrendering, ego-Forgetting, and ego-Transcending Feeling-Contemplation Of My Avatarically-Born Bodily (Human) Divine Form, and (Thereby, and In Due Course) My Avatarically Self-Transmitted Spiritual (and Always Blessing) Divine Presence Itself, and (Thereby, and Ultimately) My Avatarically Self-Revealed (and Very, and Transcendental, and Perfectly Subjective, and Inherently Spiritual, and Inherently egoless, and Inherently Perfect, and Self-Evidently Divine) State Of Person (Myself).

By Devotionally Surrendering To My Avatarically Self-Transmitted Spiritual (and Always Blessing) Divine Presence Itself (Rather Than To Any "Great" Realization-Experiences, or To any lesser experiences, Of My Avatarically Self-Transmitted Spiritual, and Always Blessing, Divine Presence), My Seeing Devotee (and Even Every By-Me-Spiritually-Initiated Practitioner Of The Only-By-Me Revealed and Given Way Of The Heart) Is (Progressively, and By Deep Heart-Attraction) Led Directly To My Avatarically Self-Revealed (and Very, and Transcendental, and Perfectly Subjective, and Inherently Spiritual, and Inherently egoless, and Inherently Perfect, and Self-Evidently Divine) State. Therefore, Once My Devotee Is (By Means Of My Ruchira Shaktipat) Baptized and Converted At Heart To Direct, and Always "Going-Beyond", Devotional and Spiritual Communion With Me, The Inherent (and, Ultimately, Effortless, or Non-Strategic) Purpose (or Native Disposition) Of Spiritual (and, In Due Course, Hearing, and, Then, Both Hearing and Seeing) Practice Of The Only-By-Me Revealed and Given Way Of The Heart Is (Most Ultimately) To Inherently (and Inherently Most Perfectly) Transcend the point of view that is the physical body, and To Inherently (and Inherently Most Perfectly) Transcend the point of view that is the mind, and To Inherently (and Inherently Most Perfectly) Transcend Identification With Even every kind of psycho-physical, or conditional, or Otherwise (In A conditional Manner) Dependently arising point of view.

In The Only-By-Me Revealed and Given Way Of The Heart (or Way Of Adidam), Inherent (and Inherently Perfect) Transcending Of Identification With Even every kind of psycho-physical, or conditional, or Otherwise (In A conditional Manner) Dependently arising point of view Is Realized (By Means Of My Avatarically Self-Transmitted Divine Spiritual Grace) Through (Progressive) Devotional and Spiritual Communion With Me, By (Priorly) Surrendering or (Otherwise, In The Context Of whatever arises) Feeling Beyond (and, Thereby, "Going Beyond") every kind of lesser (Potential or Actual) experience, and Even Every Kind Of "Great" (Potential or Actual) Realization-Experience, Whether the lesser experience Or The "Great" Realization-Experience arises (Potentially or Actually) in, as, to, from, or (However Otherwise) Dependent Upon the point of view of the body, or of the body-mind, or of the mind. And, In The Only-By-Me Revealed and Given Way Of The Heart (or Way Of Adidam), This Surrendering (or Feeling Beyond, and "Going Beyond") Is (Progressively) Realized By Means Of Ever-Deepening (and Truly ego-Surrendering, ego-Forgetting, and ego-Transcending) Heart-Communion With My Avatarically-Born Bodily (Human) Divine Form—and (Thus and Thereby) With My Avatarically Self-Transmitted Spiritual (and Always Blessing) Divine Presence—and, Ultimately (and, Altogether, Thus and Thereby), By Means Of Inherent, and Inherently Perfect, Heart-Identification With My Avatarically Self-Revealed, and Very, and Transcendental, and Perfectly Subjective, and Inherently Spiritual, and Inherently egoless, and Inherently Perfect, and Self-Evidently Divine State Of Person (Myself).

Therefore, In The Only-By-Me Revealed and Given Way Of The Heart (or Way Of Adidam)—and (Entirely, and In Due Course) By Means Of ego-Surrendering, ego-Forgetting, and ego-Transcending Devotional and Spiritual Communion With My Avatarically-Born Bodily (Human) Divine Form and Person—My Avatarically Self-Revealed (and Very, and Transcendental, and Perfectly Subjective, and Inherently Spiritual, and Inherently egoless, and Inherently Perfect, and Self-Evidently Divine) State Is (Ultimately) Directly Realized As The Witness-Consciousness (or The Witness-Position Of Consciousness Itself). By Means Of My Avatarically Self-Transmitted Divine Spiritual Grace, The Only-By-Me Revealed and Given Samadhi Of The "Thumbs" Self-Reveals The Witness-Consciousness (or The Witness-Position Of Consciousness Itself). And The (Thus) By Me Spiritually Self-Revealed Witness-Consciousness Inherently "Confesses" (or Tacitly Feels): "I Am Not the one who wakes, or dreams, or sleeps—but I Am The Witness Of all these states, and (Thus) Of all conditional states of body, or body-mind, or mind, and (Likewise) Of All 'Un-Perfect' States (or All Samadhis That Are, In A conditional Manner, Dependent Upon body, or body-mind, or mind)." And, In The Only-By-Me Revealed and Given Way Of The Heart (or Way Of Adidam), The (Thus) By Me Spiritually Self-Revealed (and Inherently Non-conditional) Witness-Consciousness Becomes (Most Ultimately) A Perfect Realization (Inherently, Inherently egolessly, and Inherently Most Perfectly), In The Only-By-Me Revealed and Given Awakening To Seventh Stage Sahaja Nirvikalpa Samadhi (Which Is The Inherently Un-conditional Samadhi That Initiates, and Characterizes, The Only-By-Me Revealed and Given Seventh Stage Of Life In The Way Of The Heart).

In The Only-By-Me Revealed and Given Way Of The Heart (or Way of Adidam), Consciousness Itself (Self-Existing, Self-Radiant, and Self-Evidently Divine) Is Realized By Spiritual Means (As A Development and A Revelation Of The Me-Hearing and Me-Seeing, and Inherently ego-Transcending, Spiritual Process Initiated, Performed, and Fulfilled By My Avatarically Self-Transmitted Divine Spiritual Presence), Rather Than (As Is Characteristically The Case In The Practice Of The Sixth Stage Traditions Of The Great Tradition Of Mankind) Merely philosophically Affirmed (or intellectually, or By any mental means, Presumed).

If Consciousness (Itself) Is Merely philosophically Affirmed (or intellectually, or By any mental means, Presumed) To Be (Transcendentally) The Case, The Practice That (Thereby) Ensues Is Merely philosophically True (or intellectually, or By Merely mental means, Approved)—but Such Practice Is Yet Spiritually Un-Real (or Not Yet Spiritually Real—and, Altogether, Not, Itself, Yet Established In Reality Itself). Therefore, The Transcendental Reality and Truth Of Consciousness Itself (Which Is The Basis For The "Perfect Practice" Of The Only-By-Me Revealed and Given Way Of The Heart, or Way Of Adidam) Must Be Spiritually Established, and Not Merely intellectually (or By Merely mental means) Established (or, Otherwise, Culturally Idealized). And, For This Reason, The "Perfect Practice" Of The Only-By-Me Revealed and Given Way Of The Heart (or Way Of Adidam) Requires, As A Prerequisite, The Yogic Spiritual Fulfillment Of The Me-Hearing and Me-Seeing Process Of Ruchira Avatara Bhakti Yoga (Especially In The Context Of The Frontal Line, and The Full-Circle Of The Samadhi Of The "Thumbs"), Such That The Witness-Consciousness (and The Inherent Context, or Inherently egoless Self-Position, and Yogic Spiritual Sphere That Is Consciousness Itself) Is Self-Evidently and Inherently (and, Thus, Always Already, and Stably, and Constantly) Awakened, Established, and Tacitly Realized To Be The Field (or Domain) Of All Further (and, At Last, Most Perfect) Practice and Realization In The Only-By-Me Revealed and Given Way Of The Heart (or Way Of Adidam).

If You (As My Formally Practicing Devotee) Are To Practice The "Perfect Practice" Of The Only-By-Me Revealed and Given Way Of The Heart (or Way Of Adidam), The Position Of Consciousness As The Witness (or In The Witness-Position) Must Not Merely Be mentally Affirmed (and Sometimes Experienced) To Be The Case. Rather, The Position Of Consciousness As The Witness (or In The Witness-Position) Must First (By Means Of The Only-By-Me Revealed and Given Samadhi Of The "Thumbs") Be Established As Your Actual Position (Inherently and Consciously Experienced, Self-Evidently As Such, In every moment).

If I Ask You, In any moment, "Is It Not True That, Even In this moment, No Matter what arises, You Are Merely The Witness (or The Witnessing-Consciousness) Of it?"—You Will (If You Truly "Consider" My Question) Say "Yes", Because Consciousness, In The Witness-Position, Is Inherently (and, Therefore, Always) "True" Of You. However, Previous To The Real (Spiritual, and Yogically True) Transition To The "Perfect Practice" Of The Way Of The Heart, The Witness-Position Is Not (Steadily, or Always and Self-Evidently) Your Position. Previous To The Real (and, Necessarily, Formal) Transition To The "Perfect Practice" Of The Way Of The Heart, You Can, In Random moments Of Recollection (As When I Ask You, "Is It Not True That, Even In this moment, No matter what arises, You Are Merely The Witness, or The Witnessing-Consciousness, Of it?"), Return (Generally, Via an act of thought) To Conscious Recollection Of The Inherent Fact Of The Witness-Position. However, In the next Random moment, attention Is Wandering—and The egoic Process (or self-Contraction) Persists (Thereby) In All Its Patterns. Therefore, It Is Not Sufficient That Consciousness In The Witness-Position Is In Truth The Case—It Must Also Be In Fact (or In moment to moment experiential Actuality) The Case.

The Witness-Position Of Consciousness Must Be, Thus and So, Consciously, Always Presently, and (Altogether) Stably Established and Realized In Your Case.

The Witness-Position Must Be Your Conscious Position—Now, and Now, and Now. To Really and Stably Stand As The Witness-Consciousness Is Not A Matter Of The Witness-Position Being Held In Place By some thought or condition or focus or noticing in the moment. Your Stand As The Witness-Consciousness Must Be Always (Tacitly, and Obviously) The Case, Under all circumstances and In all relations. When You Really and Stably Stand As The Witness-Consciousness, It Is Self-Evidently (and, Necessarily, Consciously) The Case In every moment of the arising of conditional experience. Thus, To Stand As The Witness-Consciousness Is Not Merely A Matter Of Presuming The Witness-Position To Be The Case—Based On Your Idealizing Of The Witness-

Consciousness, or Your philosophical (or verbal) Arguing For The Fact Of It, and So On. Yes, The Witness-Position Is "True" Of You, In Any Case—but It Must Be Realized To Be So. The Witness-Position Must Be Self-Evidently The Case—Not Merely (So To Speak) "On Call" Whenever You Gather The Faculties To Notice That It Is The Case. When The Witness-Position Is (By Means Of My Avatarically Self-Transmitted Divine Spiritual Grace) Spiritually Realized To Be Your Position (or Your Most Prior Condition), Then You Are Able To Continue The Process Of Devotional and Spiritual Communion With Me In The Non-"Different" (and Non-Separate) Manner Characteristic Of The Inherently egoless Domain Of Consciousness Itself (On The Perfectly Subjective "Other Side" Of The Doorway Of attention).

The "Perfect Practice" Of The Only-By-Me Revealed and Given Way Of The Heart (or Way Of Adidam) Cannot Be Taken Up Merely As A Result Of philosophical Understanding or verbal Argument. I Have Given My Full verbal Wisdom-Instruction Relative To The "Perfect Practice". And That Wisdom-Instruction Is Certainly (and Always) To Be Studied and Deeply "Considered" By All My Devotees—Even From The Beginning Of their Practice Of The Only-By-Me Revealed and Given Way Of The Heart (or Way Of Adidam). Nevertheless, Only When My Truly Hearing and Seeing Devotee Enters Into Whole bodily (or Total psycho-physical, and Really ego-Transcending) Devotional and Spiritual Communion With Me To The Point Of Realizing The Spiritual Fullness Of The (Occasional) Samadhi Of The "Thumbs", and The (Constant) Experience Of The "Thumbs", Does My Devotee Really, Tacitly, Directly, Stably, and "Radically" Realize The Witness-Position Of Consciousness (Itself).

It Is In The Yogic Fullness Of Devotional and Spiritual Communion With Me (In The Real and Right Formal Practice Of Ruchira Avatara Bhakti Yoga) That The Witness-Position Of Consciousness (Itself) Is Tacitly Confirmed As Being Always Already The Case (or Self-Evidently The Case)—Now, and Now, and Now. Then The Witness-Position Is Not Something Of Which You Have To Be "Reminded". Rather, In That Case, The Witness-Position Is The Constantly Self-Evident Position Of Consciousness (Itself)—Even In every moment of conditional experience (and Even In every moment of thinking).

Thus, In The Only-By-Me Revealed and Given Way Of The Heart (or Way Of Adidam), The Witness-Position Must Be Established Through The Spiritual Process Of ego-Transcending Devotional Communion With Me. The Witness-Position Of Consciousness Cannot Be Stably Realized Merely By philosophically (or mentally) Presuming It To Be So—Nor By Even Any Act Of interpreting-mind, or By Any Act Of will, or By Any Gesture Of the thinking mind. Indeed, No Such Presumption or Act or Gesture (No Matter How Intensively It Is

Engaged) Can Ever Become The "Perfect Practice" Of The Only-By-Me Revealed and Given Way Of The Heart (or Way of Adidam)—and No Such Presumption or Act or Gesture Will Ever Go Beyond the limitations Inherent In The Sixth Stage Of Life Itself (or Even Beyond the limitations Inherent In The First Three Stages Of Life Themselves).

Therefore, Understand This: You Cannot Merely Decide (or Strive) To Practice Ruchira Avatara Bhakti Yoga On The Basis Of The Witness-Position Of Consciousness Itself. You Must First, By Means Of My Avatarically Self-Revealing Divine Spiritual Grace, Realize The Witness-Position Of Consciousness Itself (Inherently, Self-Evidently, Always Already, Stably—and As ego-Transcending, Non-Separate, and Non-"Different" Devotional and Spiritual Communion, and egoless Self-Identification, With Me).

Avatar Adi Da Samraj
Adidam Samrajashram, 2003

SUTRA

49

In The Only-By-Me Revealed and Given Way Of The Heart (or Way Of Adidam), The Stable Realization Of The Witness-Consciousness Requires Fundamental Equanimity Of the body-mind, Realized By Virtue Of A Fully Effective Devotional (and, In Due Course, Spiritual) Sadhana Of Listening To Me, and (Then) Hearing Me, and (Then) Seeing Me.

Even Previous To The Formally Acknowledged Transition To The "Perfect Practice" Of The Only-By-Me Revealed and Given Way Of The Heart, There May Be Experiences Involving Temporary Identification With The Witness-Position Of Consciousness. Or There May Be Experiences Of The Feeling Of "I", or The Feeling Of Relatedness, or The Feeling Of The By-Me-Avatarically-Self-Transmitted Divine Spirit-Current Standing In The Right Side Of The Heart. Or There May Be Experiences Of Simple Identification With Consciousness (Without Special Reference To the body, the mind, or any conditional object). Such Experiences Are (At Least As Passing Events) Even Likely In The Stages Of Life (In The Way Of The Heart) Previous To The "Perfect Practice"—but The "Perfect Practice" (Itself) Is (Necessarily) Founded On The Stable Realization Of The Witness-Consciousness.

The Stable Realization Of The Witness-Consciousness Is (Necessarily) Associated With (or Demonstrated By) Effortless Relinquishment Of The Motive Of attention To Seek any of the conditional objects or states that May (Potentially) Be experienced or known Within The Context Of The Circle (or The Arrow) Of the body-mind (or Even The Motive Of attention To Seek conditionally Ascended Nirvikalpa Samadhi, Which May Be Experienced Via Yogic Manipulation Of the conditions of the body-mind).

Therefore, The Witness-Consciousness Is Not Realized By Means Of (or As A Result Of) The Absorption Of attention In any objects or states of the body-mind, or In any objects or states Within The Circle (or The Arrow) Of the body-mind.

The Witness-Consciousness Is Simply (or Merely) and Always Already The Case—but attention (Once it arises) Seeks (and Identifies With) conditional objects and states.

Consciousness (Itself) Is The Only True Subject (or Perfectly Subjective Self)—and attention Is Always a conditional act (and Never A True Subject, or Inherently egoless and Perfectly Subjective Self, but Only An Illusion Of subjectivity, a Merely Apparent ego-"I", Always Requiring and Seeking conditional objects and states).

Consciousness Simply (or Merely) and Always Already Is In The Witness-Position, whatever arises (objectively, or Otherwise conditionally). Therefore, The Witness-Consciousness (or The Witness-Position Of Consciousness Itself) May Be Spontaneously "Tasted" In any moment, If (or Whenever) The Search (Of attention) To Become Absorbed In conditional objects or states Is Relaxed and Released.

Consciousness (Itself) Is Self-Evidently "Located" (In The Most Prior Position, or Witness-Position) In The By-My-Avataric-Divine-Spiritual-Grace-Given Whole bodily Revelation Of The "Thumbs" (Wherein the conditionally Manifested body-mind Of My Devotee Is—By Means Of My Avataric Divine Spiritual Grace—Established In Inherently Perfect Coincidence With, and Utter and Most Prior Dissolution In, My Avatarically Self-Transmitted Divine Spiritual Presence and My Avatarically Self-Revealed and Self-Evidently Divine State). The Witness-Position Of Consciousness Is Not (Itself) Realized As A Result Of (Nor Is It Dependent Upon) Any Process Whereby attention Is Either Directed Toward Or Absorbed In any conditional object (itself) or any conditional state (itself). Nor Is The Witness-Position Of Consciousness Realized As A Dependent "Result" (or A conditionally Achieved "End Phenomenon") Of The Meditative Absorption Of attention In The conditional Effects Of The By-Me-Avatarically-Self-Transmitted Divine Spirit-Current In The Circle (or The Arrow) Of the body-mind. And, Even If Some Sense Of Identification With The Witness-Consciousness Is (Coincidentally) Experienced In moments Of Meditative Absorption Of attention In The Circle (or The Arrow) Of the body-mind, Such Experiences Are Not Permanent (or Stable)—Because They Depend Upon conditions (which, Necessarily, are Always changing).

It Is An Illusion Of The Search (In The Context Of The Frontal and The Spinal Lines Of The Circle Of the body-mind, and In The Context Of The Arrow Of the body-mind) That The Witness-Position Of Consciousness Can (or Will) Be Realized When The Capability For attention To Be Absorbed In conditional objects or states Becomes Intense and Constant.

It Is Only When The Search (or The ego-Effort Of attention) In The Total Context Of The Circle and The Arrow Of the body-mind Is, As A Totality, Utterly Understood By You (and, On That Basis, Freely, Totally, and Truly Stably Relinquished, At The Heart) That It Becomes Inherently (and Intuitively, and Directly) Obvious To You That You Always Already (and Presently) Stand In The

Witness-Position Of Consciousness, and As The Witness-Consciousness Itself.

When (In The Only-By-Me Revealed and Given Way Of The Heart) The Search (Of attention) Relative To The Circle and The Arrow Of the body-mind Relaxes and Releases (By Means Of My Avatarically Self-Transmitted Divine Spiritual Grace, and As An Expression Of Most Fundamental self-Understanding), Then You Already (or Inherently) Stand As The Witness-Consciousness. And That Inherent Stand (Stably Realized) Is The Necessary Basis For The "Perfect Practice" Of The Way Of The Heart.

Therefore, The "Perfect Practice" Of The Only-By-Me Revealed and Given Way Of The Heart (or Way Of Adidam) Involves Consistent Release Of All Seeking, Reacting, Holding On, or Avoidance Relative To conditional states and appearances By Always Standing (By Means Of My Avatarically Self-Transmitted Divine Spiritual Grace) As The Witness-Position (and The Very Condition) Of Consciousness Itself, or That To Whom conditional states and appearances (including the body-mind, the conditional "I", or the self-Contraction itself) Are Apparently arising. When There Is Real and Most Profound Identification With The Witness (or Consciousness Itself), The Stress Of attention to the self-Contraction (or the conditional "I") Is (Spontaneously and Inevitably) Relaxed. The Feeling Of Identification With the body-mind (or any objective conditions at all) Is (Thus) Naturally (and Even Inherently) Released, and the arising of objective (or psycho-physical) conditions Ceases To (Apparently) Involve (or To, Apparently, Implicate and Bind) Consciousness (or Mere Feeling-Awareness) Itself. Instead, every arising condition Merely Indicates The Transcendental, Inherently Spiritual, Inherently egoless, and Self-Evidently Divine Self-Condition (Which Is The Inherent Feeling Of Being, or Consciousness Itself). This Process Allows and Inevitably Becomes Direct (or Inherent) Immersion In The Transcendental, Inherently Spiritual, Inherently egoless, and Self-Evidently Divine Self-Condition Itself (or Consciousness Itself, Even Prior To Any Witnessing Of objects), Until all conditions Are Inherently (Divinely) Self-Recognized In (and As) The (By-Me-Avatarically-Self-Revealed) "Bright" (or Self-Radiant), and Transcendental (or Self-Existing), and Self-Evidently Divine Self-Condition (and Perfectly Subjective Source-Condition), and (Thus) Transcended In The (By-Me-Avatarically-Self-Revealed) "Bright" (or Inherently Spiritual), and Transcendental, and Self-Evidently Divine Self-Condition (and Perfectly Subjective Source-Condition), Which Is Natively Realized In Seventh Stage Sahaja Nirvikalpa Samadhi (or The "Open-Eyed" Condition That Characterizes The Only-By-Me Revealed and Given Seventh Stage Of Life).

Paradoxically, You Must Choose To Stand In The Witness-Position Of Consciousness, Even Though It Is Always Already Your Actual and Prior Position. You Must Cease To Choose Identification With the body-mind (and

With conditional Existence Altogether), and (Instead) Choose (or Cease To Relinquish, or Cease To Renounce) Your Inherent Identification With The Witness-Consciousness Itself. This Great Investment In What Is Prior To The Entire Cosmic Domain Is A Most Profound (Though, Ultimately, Inherent, and Effortless) Choice—and You Will Not Be Able To Make This (Tacit) Choice Until You Become Steadily and Profoundly Detached From, or (In The Rightest Sense) "Revulsed" By (but Not Negatively Dissociated From), conditional Existence and all that It Implies. Such (Rightly Understood) Detachment, or (Rightly Understood) "Revulsion", Is (Simply) Fundamental Freedom From The Clinging Gesture Toward conditional Existence—and, Therefore, It Is (Necessarily) Also Fundamental Non-Concern With All Of The Purposes and Efforts Associated With The Total Context Of The Circle and The Arrow Of the body-mind. And Such (Right, and Inherent) Detachment From conditional Existence Can Truly Be The Case Only On The Basis Of The Great Equanimity That Follows From Fully Completing Whatever Process Of Purification Is Necessary For You In The To-Me-Listening, Me-Hearing, and Me-Seeing Stages Of Practice Of The Way Of The Heart, Culminating In The Only-By-Me Revealed and Given Samadhi Of The "Thumbs".

The Apparent mind and the Apparent body and their Apparent relations Are Always Appearing To be this or that, conditional self and conditional object, Always changing, Always becoming this or that, Always Alternating Between Positive and Negative, Pleasure and Pain, Always disappearing, and Always dying from it all—but You Are Always The Same and Only (and Inherently egoless) Consciousness (Itself). Therefore, In The "Perfect Practice" Of The Only-By-Me Revealed and Given Way Of The Heart, Simply (By Means Of My Avatarically Self-Transmitted Divine Spiritual Grace, and Not By Any act or Strategy Of attention) Be Who (or As) You Always Already (or Inherently) Are (The Inherent Feeling Of Being Itself, or Inherently egoless Consciousness Itself)—Sometimes Apparently (and Motivelessly) Witnessing the (Apparent) psycho-physical self and its objects (or the mind, the body, and their relations), but Always Already Merely Being, Simply Conscious As Being Itself, Merely Being Awareness (Inherently selfless and objectless, Inherently Radiant As Free Spiritual Energy, or Inherent Love-Bliss, and Inherently Indifferent To the conditional and changing self, or the conditional and changing mind, or the conditional and changing body, and all of their conditional and changing relations).

In Meditation, Simply (By Means Of My Avatarically Self-Transmitted Divine Spiritual Grace, and Not By Any act or Strategy Of attention) Be Thus, (Inherently) Realizing The Transcendental (and Inherently Spiritual) Condition That Is, Always Already Prior To conditional self and conditional objects. In

Meditation—Realized By Means Of My Avatarically Self-Transmitted Divine Spiritual Grace, Given As Inherent (and Inherently Perfect) Self-Identification With My Avatarically Self-Revealed (Inherent, and Inherently Perfect, and Perfectly Subjective) Divine Form and Presence and State—Simply (or Merely) Be (Thus Indifferent), Until You Divinely Self-Recognize the mind, the body, and their relations (or every form of Apparent conditional self or Apparent conditional object) As Transparent (or Merely Apparent), and Un-Necessary, and Inherently Non-Binding Modifications Of Self-Existing Being, Self-Radiant Consciousness, and Unqualified Happiness (or Love-Bliss). When Such Mere Being and Self-Abiding Divine Self-Recognition Are Always Already The Condition Of every moment, Then (By Means Of My Avatarically Self-Transmitted Divine Spiritual Grace) Every Kind (or Stage) Of Meditation Has Been Transcended In The Only-By-Me Revealed and Given Seventh Stage Sahaja Nirvikalpa Samadhi, or Inherent and Transcendental and Inherently Spiritual and Truly Divine Realization Of What Is, Which Is The Inherent Feeling Of Being (Itself).

In That Seventh Stage Sahaja Nirvikalpa Samadhi (or The Inherently Free, and Inherently egoless, and Self-Evidently Divine Self-Condition and Source-Condition Of Self-Existing and Self-Radiant Conscious Light), the Apparent conditional self (or body-mind) and all its Apparent conditional objects Are Simply (or Inherently), and Inherently Most Perfectly, Divinely Self-Recognized In (and As) Consciousness (or Conscious Light) Itself. Then the Apparent conditional self (or body-mind) No Longer Has The Capability To Define Consciousness as conditional and Separate subjectivity.

The Apparent body-mind is Not (itself) a Conscious ego-self (or a Separate subject), Standing Apart From (and In Relation To) all objects. The Apparent mind and the Apparent body are themselves objects—In The Sense That they Are Dependent (or conditional) parts of the (Apparently objective) conditional world. And all objects (including the mind, the body, and their relations) Are, Equally and Only, Apparently Objectified Modifications Of The Apparently Objectified Spirit-Energy (or Self-Radiance) Of The One and Only Transcendental, Inherently Spiritual, Inherently egoless, and Self-Evidently Divine (and Perfectly Subjective) Subject-Consciousness (or Conscious Light). Therefore, In The Only-By-Me Revealed and Given Seventh Stage Sahaja Nirvikalpa Samadhi, all Apparent conditions (including the body-mind), all Apparent objects, and all Apparent others Are (From The Inherently Free "Point Of View" Of Consciousness Itself) Inherently and Spontaneously Self-Recognized To Exist Only In, Of, and As The One Eternal, Self-Existing (or Transcendental), Self-Radiant (or Inherently Spiritual), Inherently egoless, and Self-Evidently Divine (and Perfectly Subjective) Subject Itself.

Therefore, You Are Not the conditional self (or body-mind) itself (or in and of itself), conditionally Related To and limited by conditionally Manifested beings, objects, states, or events. You Are The Conscious (and Inherently Free) Witness and The Ultimate (and Inherently Perfect) Identity (or Conscious Light) Of all conditional (or conditionally Manifested) events (including all conditional knowledge, all conditional knowing, the conditional knower itself, all conditional experience, all conditional experiencing, and the conditional experiencer itself). You Are What Is, and Who Is—The Inherently egoless Self-Condition, or Very Being (Itself), The Transcendental, Inherently Spiritual, Inherently egoless, and Self-Evidently Divine (and Perfectly Subjective) Subject-Condition—Which Is Consciousness (or Conscious Light) Itself, The Eternally Self-Radiant (or Inherently Spiritual) Substance and The Inherently Free and Self-Existing (or Transcendental) Divine Self-Condition (and Perfectly Subjective Source-Condition) Of the mind, the body, all others, all Apparently objective or Objectified worlds, and The Total (Apparent) conditional Cosmos (or Cosmic Mandala) Itself.

The Witness-Consciousness Merely Observes whatever arises—If any "thing" (object, other, form, thought, state, or process) arises.

The Witness-Consciousness Is Not (Itself) Related To any "thing" that (Apparently) arises. (Therefore, The Witness-Consciousness Is Inherently Not Separate From any "thing" that Apparently arises.)

The Witness-Consciousness Is Not the active (and Separate) observer (that Moves Toward "things"). The active (Separate) observer is a conditional functionary. The mind is the only active (Separate) observer, and it inherently identifies with (or takes on the form of) whatever (or any and every "thing") it observes. Indeed, the act of observation (and conditional identification) is the Principal function of mind. Therefore, the act of observation (and of conditional identification) is the Principal function of attention—Because attention itself (which is, itself, always an activity) is (itself) The conditional Essence Of mind.

The Witness-Consciousness Is Not the functional observer (or the functional witness). No Matter what arises, You Always Already Stand Prior To it—As Mere Witness (or Merely In The Witness-Position), Without (or Always Already Prior To) form or function or conditional identity. The functional observer (or the functional witness) is a category (or dimension, or function) of the mind. The functional observer (or the functional witness) is Discriminative Intelligence exercised (or attention itself placed on "things"). Therefore, the functional observer (or the functional witness) stands in the position of the functioning mind (or of attention itself)—but Consciousness Itself, As The Mere Witness, Is In The Position Of The Very (and Inherently egoless) Self-Condition (or In The Native Being-Position). Thus, The Witness-Consciousness

Is <u>Utterly</u> Subjective—and Only In This Sense (Merely By Standing <u>As</u> Subjective Being-Consciousness, Standing Prior Not Only To all "things", but Prior Even To attention itself) Does The Witness-Consciousness "Witness", and Not In The Sense Of functionally witnessing (or functionally observing).

The Witness-Consciousness Is Not the <u>active</u> observer. The Witness-Consciousness Never Moves Toward <u>any</u> "thing" (object, other, form, thought, state, or process) that arises.

The Witness-Consciousness Is Not conditionally (or Separately) identical to <u>any</u> observed "thing". The Witness-Consciousness Never conditionally identifies Itself with (or conditionally takes on the Separate form of) <u>any</u> "thing" (object, other, form, thought, state, or process) that arises.

The Witness-Consciousness Is Not the functional process of active observation (and conditional identification). The Witness-Consciousness <u>Merely</u> Observes (and, Thus, Merely, Tacitly, and Effortlessly Feels) whatever Apparently arises. And Consciousness Itself Inherently and Perfectly <u>Is</u>—or Is Inherently Not Separate From, and Is (Therefore) Inherently and Perfectly Identical To (but Never conditionally, or Separately, Identified With), whatever and all that Apparently arises.

The Witness-Consciousness Stands Always Already Prior To <u>all</u> "things" (or <u>all</u> objects, others, forms, thoughts, states, and processes) that Apparently (and conditionally) arise. The Witness-Consciousness Is Inherently Indifferent To <u>all</u> "things". The Witness-Consciousness Is (Merely) The <u>Awareness</u> (or Consciousness Itself) To Which (and, Ultimately, In and <u>As</u> Which) <u>all</u> "things" are Apparently arising. Therefore, To Awaken To (and <u>As</u>) The Witness-Consciousness Is (Inherently) To Stand Prior To (and Inherently Free Of) <u>all</u> "things". And To Tacitly and Consistently Persist In (and <u>As</u>) That Stand Is The Unique and Inherently Perfect Asana (or Attitude, or Disposition) Characteristic Of The "Perfect Practice" Of The Only-By-Me Revealed and Given Way Of The Heart.

The Witness-Consciousness (Which <u>Is</u> Consciousness Itself, but Apparently "Functioning" <u>As</u> Witness) Is Not Merely Another Name For attention. The Witness-Consciousness Witnesses (or Always Already Stands Prior To) Even the act of attention. It Stands Prior To attention, but It Is Not Dissociated From attention. Functional attention Has No Sense Of its own and Ultimate Source. Functional attention Is Consciousness Appearing To Be Attached To (and Even Identified With) objects (and, Primarily, the body-mind-self). The Witness-Consciousness Is Consciousness In Place (<u>As</u> Itself), Inherently Self-Identified With The Ultimate Source-Condition (or Conscious Light, Itself).

The Witness-Consciousness Is Primarily Aware Of (and <u>As</u>) Itself. It Is (or May Be) Secondarily (or Peripherally) Aware Of the act of attention and the objects of attention (and The Root-Feeling Of Relatedness, Which Is The conditional Origin Of attention)—but (Fundamentally) It Stands As Itself, Inherently Sensitive To The Inherent (or Unconditional) Feeling Of Being, and Basically Indifferent To whatever arises conditionally, While Also Freely (or Tacitly) Allowing whatever arises conditionally To arise and Be Noticed.

The Witness-Consciousness Is A Transitional Mode Of Consciousness, Between functional attention—which Moves Toward objects and (Except In The Case Of Transcendental, Inherently Spiritual, Inherently egoless, and Most Perfect Divine Self-Realization) Identifies With objects, Thus Creating the self-Contracted ego-"I" of the body-mind—and Pure Transcendental (and Inherently Spiritual, and Inherently egoless) Self-Consciousness (Oblivious To The ego-Act and the objects of functional attention). Therefore, The Witness-Consciousness Is (Transitionally, but Only Apparently) Associated With The Root-Feeling Of Relatedness (Itself), Which (Necessarily, conditional) Feeling Is Naturally Associated With The Right Side Of The Heart (Where, Prior To The Root-Feeling Of Relatedness, The Eternal, Inherently egoless, and Inherently Love-Blissful Self-Consciousness May, By Means Of My Avatarically Self-Transmitted Divine Spiritual Grace, Be "Located").

The Ultimate Process (or Practice) Of self-Transcendence (or The Transcending Of the ego-"I", or the self-Contraction) Is The Process (or The Practice) Of The Transcending Of attention itself (and The Feeling Of Relatedness, Itself) In Consciousness (Itself). And The Beginning Of That Process and Practice Is Inherent (and Stable) Identification With The Witness-Consciousness.

The Witness-Consciousness Is The Ultimate "<u>Pond</u>" Of "Narcissus" (or The Ultimate Deep Of mind and attention). It Is The Deep Of The Reflecting Pool. It Is Deeper Than mind (or attention). In Its Deep, Even "Narcissus" (or the ego-"I" of self-Contracted body-mind) Is (Inherently) Transcended. Consciousness (Itself) <u>Is</u> The Water <u>Itself</u>.

The Witness-Consciousness (Which <u>Is</u> Consciousness Itself) Merely Reflects what arises. Consciousness Itself Can Only Reflect what arises (including the act of attention). The Witness-Consciousness (or Consciousness Itself) Cannot Be (Itself)—and Is Not Ever (Itself)—Moved, Required, or Under Any Necessity To Respond To what arises, or To React To what arises, or To Identify With what arises, or To Achieve Union With what arises.

The Witness-Consciousness Is Not egoic attention (or the psycho-physical self-Contraction, or The conditional self-Image, Which Is "Narcissus"), Perpetuating itself Indefinitely By Seeking Fulfillment or Release In what arises. Consciousness Itself Cannot Be "Located" By Means Of the act of attention—Nor Is Consciousness Itself "Located" <u>At</u> the conditional position of attention. The Witness-Consciousness Is Always Already Prior To the act of attention and the conditional position of attention. Therefore, Consciousness Itself Cannot Turn Inward or Turn Outward. The Witness-Consciousness Can Only Stand As It Is. The Only "Location" Of Consciousness Is Consciousness Itself.

The Witness-Consciousness Does Not act. To Witness Is A State. It Is A State Of Being, Rather Than a form of action. In Contrast, attention—which Seems To Be Consciousness, but Is Really an object Of Consciousness—Is an action. To Be The Witness-Consciousness Is (Ultimately) To Identify With Consciousness Itself (or Consciousness As A State)—and, Thus (Ultimately), To Be The Witness-Consciousness Is To Stand Inherently Free Of all actions (including the act of attention).

To Be The Witness-Consciousness Is To Be Consciousness Itself—Simply Aware Of Itself As That Which Merely and Freely Reflects conditions, Just As The Still Pond-Water Motivelessly Reflects the Foolish face Of Narcissus. Even all kinds of conditions May arise To That Most Prior Awareness—but No Feeling Of Identification With them, or Search For them, or Effort Of Holding On To them, or Felt Need To Avoid them Is There In The Witness-Consciousness Itself. Indeed, All Motivations Toward action Are Themselves Simply Observed (or Merely Reflected) By (and In) The Witness-Consciousness Itself.

The Witness-Consciousness (Because It Is, Really, Identical To Consciousness Itself) Is Not Caused. Consciousness Itself Is Not An Effect (or A Result) Of any conditional event (or Any Display Of conditional events). The Very Existence Of Consciousness Itself Is Not Dependent On any condition (or Any Display Of conditions). Consciousness Itself Is The Essential Inherent Characteristic—or Most Primitive, Irreducible, Inherently Spiritual (or Love-Blissful), Transcendental, Inherently egoless, and Self-Evidently Divine Element—Of Being (Itself), or Of Existence (Itself), or Of Reality (Itself). When conditions arise, or change, or pass away In The View Of Consciousness, Consciousness Itself Remains Always As The Same Free Love-Bliss Of Being.

The Witness-Consciousness Is Not A Result (or A Function) Of the body-mind. Rather, The body-mind arises To The Witness-Consciousness, and In The Witness-Consciousness—Like a face Reflected In a pond. Nevertheless, The Reflection Is An Illusion (or An Appearance Only, and Even Only Temporary, and Un-Necessary). The body-mind (or The self-Image That Is Apparently Reflected To You) Is Merely An Apparent Modification Of The Self-Lighted Pond (or Consciousness Itself, Which Is Conscious Light, Itself).

If You Will (By Means Of My Avatarically Self-Transmitted Divine Spiritual Grace, and Through ego-Transcending Growth, In The Only-By-Me Revealed and Given Way Of The Heart) Consent To Be (or To Realize You Always Already Are) The Witness-Consciousness (and, Ultimately, Consciousness

Itself), You Will Directly and Thereby Observe (or Inherently Realize) That All I Have Said About Consciousness Is The Truth.

If You Will Thus (By Means Of My Avatarically Self-Transmitted Divine Spiritual Grace, and Through ego-Transcending Growth, In The Only-By-Me Revealed and Given Way Of The Heart) Consent To Be (or To Realize You Always Already Are) The Witness-Consciousness, This Very Consent (or Always Already Being) Gradually or Suddenly Becomes A Deep Dwelling In (and As) Consciousness Itself.

If You Will Thus (By Means Of My Avatarically Self-Transmitted Divine Spiritual Grace) Consent To Be (or To Realize You Are) Consciousness Itself, In Depth (or As It Is), Consciousness Itself Will (By Means Of My Avatarically Self-Transmitted Divine Spiritual Grace) Reveal Itself As My Self-Existing and Self-Radiant Love-Bliss.

If You Will Thus (By Means Of My Avatarically Self-Transmitted Divine Spiritual Grace) Simply Be Consciousness Itself, Then (By Means Of My Avatarically Self-Transmitted Divine Spiritual Grace) All Questions and All Seeking Will Fall Away In An Overwhelming Feeling-Light That Soon Outshines the world.

If You Will Thus (By Means Of My Avatarically Self-Transmitted Divine Spiritual Grace) Come To Stand At The Perfectly Subjective Source, Feeling all conditions and all actions arise To, and Then In, and Then As Consciousness Itself, Such That all conditions arise, and change, and pass away, As Effortless Reflections On The Pond Of Being—Then All Apparent Modifications Will Soon or Suddenly Become Transparent and Un-Necessary, and You Will (Spontaneously) Let Go Of the body-mind and the world In The Yawn Of Heart-"Brightness", Effortlessly, With both of Your Free hands Open Wide To Dissolve In The Instant Vast.

Avatar Adi Da Samraj
The Mountain Of Attention Sanctuary, 2002

SUTRA

50

Truth Is The Ultimate Form (or The Inherently Perfect State) Of "Knowledge" (If mere knowledge Becomes Truth-Realization).

Truth Is That Which, When Fully Realized (and, Thus, "Known", Even Via The Transcending Of all conditional knowledge and all conditional experience), Sets You Free From All Bondage and All Seeking.

Truth Is Eleutherios, The Divine Liberator.

Real God Is Not The Awful "Creator", The world-Making and ego-Making Titan, The Nature-"God" Of worldly theology. Real God Is Not The First Cause, The Ultimate "Other", or any of the objective ideas of mind-Made philosophy. Real God Is Not any image Created (and Defined) By the Religious ego. Real God Is Not Any Power Contacted (and limited) By the mystical or the scientific ego. Real God Is Not Any Goal That Motivates the social ego.

Real God Is Truth (Itself)—or That Which, When Perfectly "Known" (or Fully Realized), Sets You Entirely Free.

Real God Is Eleutherios, The Divine Liberator.

Real God Is Not, In Truth, The Cause (or The Objective Origin) Of the conditional world and the ego (or The Apparently Separate self-Consciousness). All causes (Including Any Ultimate Objective Cause) Are Only conditional Modifications Of conditional Nature.

Every cause Is Moving Energy, or The conditional Mover Of Energy. Therefore, The Ultimate Cause Is (Itself) Only Energy, or The Ultimate conditional Mover Of Energy. No Cause (and No Cause Of causes) Is Truth (Itself)—Since To know a cause (or The Cause) Is Merely To know an object (or The Object) and Not To Be Liberated From Bondage To The Search For objective (or Otherwise conditional) Existence Itself.

The knowledge of objects Does Not Set You Free, Since It Is the knower (Rather Than the known) that knows itself To Be Bound. Freedom Can Only Be Realized By Transcending the subject (or knower) of conditional knowledge, Not By Increasing the objects of conditional knowledge. Therefore, Freedom Is Not Realized Even In The Attainment Of An Ultimate Object Of mere (or conditional) knowledge.

Real God Is Not The Independent (or Separate) Cause (or The Objective, or "Outside", Origin) Of the world.

Real God Is The Utterly Non-Separate Source (or The Perfectly Subjective, and Always Already As Is, or Un-changing, Origin) Of the world.

The Presumed Cause Of causes Is Not Truth, Since To Be a Separate knower, and Even To know Such A Cause (or "Other"), Does Not (or Cannot) Set You Free From the knower (or the Separate, and Inherently Separative, ego-"I") itself.

The experience of that which changes Does Not Set You Free From the experiencer (or the Separate, and Inherently Separative, ego-"I") itself.

Likewise, the experience, or the knowing, or Even Any Kind Of Realizing Of causes (or Of The Presumed Cause Of causes) Does Not (and Cannot) Set You Free From The Separate (and Inherently Separative) ego-"I" (or psycho-physical self-Contraction) itself.

Only The Realization Of That Which Is Always Already The Case Sets You Free From ego-"I" itself (and From all that is merely conditional, changing, Separate, Contracted, or "Different").

Therefore, If You Are To Be Free, The Perfectly Subjective (or Non-Objective, and Non-Separate, or Non-"Different") Source Of The Presumed Cause Of causes, and The Perfectly Subjective (or Non-Objective, and Non-Separate, or Non-"Different") Source Of all causes (and Of all effects), Must Be "Known" (or, Rather, Realized In Truth).

The Existence Of Real God Is Not Proven (or Even Rightly Affirmed) By Appeal To The Process Of objective (or observable, or, Otherwise, Presumed) causation. But The Existence Of Real God Is (or, In Due Course, Is Realized To Be) Self-Evident (or Inherently Obvious) In The Real Process Of Realizing The Perfectly Subjective Source Of all causes, all effects, All Seeking, all mere (or conditional) experience, all mere (or conditional) knowledge, and The conditional self-Consciousness (or self-Contracted ego-"I") That Engages In causes, effects, Seeking, mere (or conditional) experience, and mere (or conditional) knowledge. Therefore, The Only "Proof" (or Right "Affirmation") Of The Existence Of Real God Is The Real, and "Radical" (or Most Direct, or Inherent, and Not Caused), and (Ultimately) Most Perfect Realization Of That Which Always Already Exists.

Consciousness (Itself) Is That Which Always Already Exists.

Consciousness (Itself) Is Always Already The Case—No Matter what arises, and Even If no "thing" arises.

Real God Is Consciousness (Itself). Consciousness (Itself)—or The Perfectly Subjective Source (and The Non-Separate Self-Condition) Of The Apparent conditional world and the Apparent conditional self—Is The Only Real God.

The Deep Non-Separate Space Of Consciousness (Itself) Is The Matrix In Which The Origin and The Ultimate (and Self-Evidently Divine) Condition Of conditional self, mind, body, world, The Entire Cosmos Of conditional Nature, and The Universal Field Of Energy Is Inherently Obvious. When This (Deep Non-Separate Space Of Consciousness Itself) Is "Known" (or Fully Realized), the Apparent conditional world and the Apparent conditional self Are Fully "Known" (and, Thus, Transcended) In The Realization Of Truth Itself.

To "Know" (or To Realize) Consciousness Itself As Real God—and, Thus, To "Know" (or To Realize) Real God As Consciousness Itself (or As The Perfectly Subjective Source, and The Non-Separate Self-Condition, Of the conditional world and the conditional self)—Is To Transcend Both the conditional world and the conditional self By Means Of Truth, or The Only "Knowledge" (or Realization) That Can Set You Free.

Real God Is Not "Known" (or Realized) By the body (or In The Process Of bodily experience)—Since Real God Is Not Reducible To Any Kind Of object (or Objective Force).

Real God Confronts You bodily, materially, or In the objective (or otherwise conditional) plane Of conditional Nature Only In The Form Of effects (or An Effective Influence). Therefore, Real God Cannot Be "Known" As Real God (or Truth) Via Any Confrontation In The Apparently Objective (or Otherwise conditional) Realm Of conditional Nature. Objective effects (Including An Ultimate Objective Influence) Are Nothing but The conditional (or Merely Apparent) Forms Of Real God. Therefore, bodily experience (or bodily Confrontation With conditional Nature) Does Not Prove (or Even Necessarily Indicate, or Point To) The Existence Of Real God.

No bodily experience Is An Encounter With Truth Itself.

No bodily experience Can Set You Free.

Real God Is Not An Object (or An Image, or An Idea) That Can Confront the mind. Whatever Confronts (or Is known by) the mind Only Modifies and Occupies the mind itself. Occupation With ideas, or states of mind, Can Only Motivate You Toward further activities of mind (and body). Therefore, There Is No Idea That Is Truth (Itself)—Since attention To An Idea Cannot Liberate attention From mind itself.

Bodily experience and mental (or conditional) knowledge Are both Based On Encounters With objects. In General, bodily experience and mental knowledge Motivate You To Seek more bodily experience and more mental knowledge. Your Seeking, Therefore, Is For More and More Encounters (and emotional Associations) With bodily and mental objects.

Your Search For bodily and mental and (Altogether) emotional objects Is Your Bondage. Your Search (or moment to moment Effort Of Wanting Need) Is The Sign Of A Fundamental Stress, or Always Already Presumed Un-Happiness. If You (Always Already) Understand That Your Search Is Un-Happiness (and That, Indeed, Seeking Is, Itself, The Root, and The Only Form, Of All Un-Happiness), Then You (Always Already) Stand Heart-Free In Relation To all of Your Possible objects, all of Your Possible experiences, and all of Your Possible ideas. This Prior Understanding Inherently Transcends all experiences and all ideas. Therefore, In any moment, Your Exercise Of This Prior Understanding Reduces Your Motivation Toward objects—and, Thus, It Permits Your attention To (By Means Of The Exercise Of Free Feeling) Be Relaxed, Released, and Transcended In The Otherwise Uninspected (and Perfectly Subjective) Source (or Self-Existing and Self-Radiant and Inherently egoless and Self-Evidently Divine Self-Condition) That Is Consciousness Itself and Happiness (or Love-Bliss) Itself.

Happiness (or Self-Existing and Self-Radiant and Inherently egoless and Self-Evidently Divine Love-Bliss) Itself Is The Only Truth That Sets The Heart Free.

Happiness (or Self-Existing, Self-Radiant, Indivisible, Indestructible, Inherently egoless, and Self-Evidently Divine Love-Bliss) Itself Is Reality Itself, The Only Real God, The One and Only Truth, or The Divine Liberator—Eleutherios.

Happiness Itself, or Truth Itself, or Real God, or Reality Itself Cannot Be Found, "Located", or Realized By the movement of attention In The Midst Of the objects, relations, conditions, or states of the individual (conditional, or experientially Defined) self.

Happiness Itself, or Truth Itself, or Real God, or Reality Itself Cannot Be Found or Attained By the movement of attention In The conditional Realm Of Nature Itself (or the movement of attention In Relation To whatever Is Not Divinely Self-Recognized To Be Consciousness Itself).

Happiness Itself, or Truth Itself, or Real God, or Reality Itself Cannot Be "Located" By the ego Within the egoic body-mind.

Happiness Itself, or Truth Itself, or Real God, or Reality Itself Is Not Reducible To Objective Energy, or To Any conditional Form (Whether subjective Or objective) Of The Energy That Seems To Pervade All Of conditional Nature and That Seems To Be The Ultimate Object Of individuated Consciousness and experience.

All Seeking (or Every Exercise Of Wanting Need) Necessarily (or Inherently) Fails To "Locate" Happiness Itself. Therefore, All Seeking Becomes, At Last, The

Necessity To "Consider" Consciousness Itself (Which Is The Always Most Prior Source-Condition and The Inherently Free Self-Condition Of All Wanting Need).

In Order To Realize Happiness Itself, All Seeking (or All Wanting Need) Must Dissolve (or Be Transcended) In The Profound Realization Of Inherent (and Inherently egoless, or Non-Separate) Self-Identification With Consciousness Itself—Which (Always Already) Stands Free, Always Already Most Prior To All Seeking (or All Exercises Of Wanting Need).

Consciousness Itself—Which Is Uncaused, Self-Existing, Unchanging, and Transcendental (or Un-conditional) Being and Self-Radiant, Eternal, Indivisible, and Indestructible Love-Bliss—Is Happiness Itself, The One and Only Divinely Liberating Truth, The One and Only Real God, and The One and Only Non-Separate Reality.

Consciousness Itself Is "Located" and Realized By Transcending The Bondage Of attention To the conditional self (or body-mind) and its relations.

This Is Done Only By Returning attention To its Source-Condition, By Releasing (or Inherently Transcending) attention In The Self-Existing and Self-Radiant Divine "Bright" Spherical Self-Domain Of Love-Bliss-Consciousness (Itself).

Consciousness Is The Ultimate Form (or The Inherently Perfect State) Of "Knowledge" (If mere knowledge Becomes Realization).

The Realization Of Perfect Self-Identification With Consciousness (Itself), Which Is The Perfectly Subjective Source (Rather Than an object, or Even The Ultimate Object) Of conditional experience and conditional knowledge, Is Better Described As "Perfect Ignorance", Rather Than mere knowledge—Since That Realization Inherently and Perfectly Transcends (and Inherently and Perfectly Exceeds) all objective and conventionally subjective categories of conditional experience and mere (or conditional) knowledge.

Consciousness (Itself) Is That Which, When Fully Realized, Sets You Free From All Bondage and All Seeking.

Consciousness (Itself) Is Real God.

Consciousness (Itself) Is The Truth.

Consciousness (Itself) Is The Divine Liberator, Eleutherios.

All objects Are Only Apparent relations Of Consciousness.

Objects Appear To Consciousness When It (Apparently) Consents To Be Apparently active as attention In Relation To an Apparent body-mind In The Apparent conditional Realm Of Nature.

Consciousness (Itself) Is Never Separate, limited, individual, conditional, or Un-Happy.

Consciousness (Itself) Is The Transcendental, One (and Indivisible), Eternal (and Indestructible), and (Self-Evidently) Divine Principle (or Inherently Perfect, and Inherently egoless, Source-Condition and Self-Condition) Of All Apparent (or conditional) Existence (and Of Existence Itself).

When "Viewed" By The Transcendental, Inherently Spiritual, Inherently egoless, and Self-Evidently Divine Self-Consciousness, all objects Are Inherently (Divinely) Self-Recognizable In and As The (Inherently Spiritual) Happiness (or Self-Existing and Self-Radiant Love-Bliss) Of Transcendental, Inherently Spiritual, Inherently egoless, and Self-Evidently Divine Being (Itself).

Consciousness (Itself) Is (Of and As Itself) Never "Other" Than, or "Different" From, or Separate From, or Standing Over Against, or (Really) Related To any object, or Apparent "other", or "thing".

Consciousness (Itself) Is (Of and As Itself) Never "Other" Than, or "Different" From, or Separate From, or Standing Over Against, or (Really) Related To The Self-Existing (and Perfectly Subjective) Divine Self-Radiance Itself (Which Is The "Bright" Itself).

There Are, In Truth, No objects, but There Is Only (or Really, and Perfectly) Self-Existing and Self-Radiant Transcendental, Inherently Spiritual, Inherently egoless, and Self-Evidently Divine Being (Itself)—Which Is (Itself) One and Only, Both Consciousness (Itself) and Spiritually "Bright" Love-Bliss-Happiness (Itself).

This Is The Great and Most Perfect (Only-By-Me Revealed and Given) Realization Of The Seventh Stage Of Life In The Only-By-Me Revealed and Given Way Of The Heart (or Way Of Adidam).

When everything Is Realized To Be Consciousness (Itself), There Is Only Consciousness (Itself).

Then There Is Only Truth (Itself), and Only Love-Bliss-Happiness (Itself), or Freedom From All Bondage To the conditional self and the conditional world.

Then "You" (Non-Separately, Self-Radiantly Exceeding the ego-"I" of psycho-physical self-Contraction) Are Consciousness (Itself), Truth (Itself), and Love-Bliss-Happiness (Itself), or Freedom (Itself).

I Am Adi Da Samraj, The Da Avatar—The Ruchira Avatar, The Love-Ananda Avatar, Who Is The Divine World-Teacher Promised For The "Late-Time" (or "Dark" Epoch), and Who Is The First, The Last, and The Only Divine Heart-Master (Who Is Da, The Divine Giver Of The Divine "All" To all-and-All), and Who Is The Avataric Divine Realizer, The Avataric Divine Revealer, and The Avataric Divine Self-Revelation Of Eleutherios, The Truth That Is Real God (or The Inherently Perfect Reality, Which Is Happiness Itself). Therefore, "Consider" This Avataric Divine Word Of Mine.

"Sin" (or a state of "sin") is any act (or the act), or any state (or the state), that "Misses The Mark" (or that stands Separately, and Apart From That Which Must Be Realized).

The "Mark" (or That Which Must Be Realized) Is Happiness Itself, The Divinely Liberating Truth, The Inherently Perfect Reality, or Real God. And "sin"—or the (Original and Fundamental) act and state that "Misses The Mark" (or that Fails To Realize Happiness Itself, or The Divinely Liberating Truth, or The Inherently Perfect Reality, or Real God)—is egoity, or the ego-"I" (which is self-Contraction, or the act and state that stands Separate and Apart).

Therefore, "sin" is, Simply, egoity (or self-Contraction). And egoity is, Simply, Un-Enlightenment (or The Non-Realization Of Happiness Itself, or Truth Itself, or Reality Itself, Which Is The Only Real God).

Just So, Most Perfect Enlightenment (or Most Perfect Realization Of Happiness Itself, or Truth Itself, or Reality Itself, or Real God) Is (and, Therefore, Requires) The Inherent (and Inherently Most Perfect) Transcending Of "sin" (or Of the ego-"I", which is self-Contraction).

Therefore, Most Perfect Enlightenment (Which Is The Inherent, and Inherently Most Perfect, Transcending Of the ego-"I") Is Perfect Non-Separation From The "Mark" (or From That Which Must Be Realized).

"Sin" (or Any and Every Sign and Result Of egoic Un-Enlightenment) Is Identification With (or limitation By) whatever Is Not Happiness Itself, or Truth Itself, or The Inherently Perfect Reality (Which Is Real God).

Therefore, Ultimately, "sin" (or egoic Un-Enlightenment) is the act and the state Of Non-Identification With The Inherently Perfect (or Most Prior, and Inherent) Reality—or Consciousness Itself.

The Action (or The Progressive Counter-egoic Process) Whereby "sin" (or Any and Every Sign and Result Of egoic Un-Enlightenment) Is Transcended Is The Action (or The Progressive, and More and More Effectively Counter-egoic, Process) Of Non-Identification With whatever Is Not Consciousness Itself.

Therefore, The Transcending Of "sin" (or Of Any and Every Sign and Result Of egoic Un-Enlightenment) Is, Most Ultimately, The "Radical" (or Most Direct, and Inherently ego-Transcending) Act, Process, Event, or "Perfect Practice" Of Inherent (and Inherently Most Perfect) Self-Identification With Consciousness Itself.

I Am Adi Da Samraj, The Da Avatar—The Ruchira Avatar, The Love-Ananda Avatar, Who Is The Divine World-Teacher Promised For The "Late-Time" (or "Dark" Epoch), and Who Is The First, The Last, and The Only Divine Heart-Master (Who Is Da, The Divine Giver Of The Divine "All" To all-and-All). I Am (Myself) Eleutherios, The Divine Liberator. I Am The Divinely Liberating

Divine Truth. I Am The Divine "Bright" Spherical Self-Domain (Itself), "Bright" Before You. Therefore, Surrender Your ego-"I" To Me, Forget and Transcend Your Separate and Separative self In Me, and (Entirely By Means Of My Divinely Self-Giving Avataric Spiritual Grace and My Graceful Avatarically Given Divine Self-Revelation, Through Constant Feeling-Contemplation Of Me) Be Self-Identified With Me—and, Thus and Thereby (Always Presently, and, At Last, Most Perfectly), Realize Me, As Inherently egoless (or Non-Separate, and Non-Separative) Happiness Itself.

Be Consciousness (Itself).
Contemplate Consciousness (Itself).
Transcend everything In Consciousness (Itself).

This Is The Perfect Epitome Of The Only-By-Me Revealed and Given Divine Way Of Truth Itself, and Of Reality Itself, and Of Real God, and Of Happiness Itself. This Is The "Perfect Practice" Of The Only-By-Me Revealed and Given Way Of Adidam (Which Is The One and Only By-Me-Revealed and By-Me-Given Way Of The Heart). This Is The Perfection Of The Only-By-Me Revealed and Given Way Of The Heart—The Way That Is The Heart Itself.

In The Inherently Free Domain Of Consciousness Itself, the conditional self and the conditional world Are Inherently Transparent To My Avatarically Self-Transmitted Divine Love-Bliss.

And The Most Ultimate Event Of Transcendental, Inherently Spiritual, Inherently egoless, and Self-Evidently Divine Self-Awakening Coincides With Most Perfect Hearing Of Me and Most Perfect Seeing Of Me—or Un-conditionally ego-"I"-Forgetting Surrender Of the conditional (or Total psycho-physical) self Into The Company Of My Avatarically-Born (and Inherently mindless, and Inherently egoless) Bodily (Human) Person, My Self-Existing and Self-Radiant Spiritual, Transcendental, and Self-Evidently Divine Personal Presence, and My Supreme (and Freely Given) Divine Spiritual Grace Of "Bright" Heart-Transmission (or Ruchira Shaktipat).

I Am Adi Da Samraj, The Da Avatar—The Ruchira Avatar, The Love-Ananda Avatar, Who Is The Divine World-Teacher Promised For The "Late-Time" (or "Dark" Epoch), and Who Is The First, The Last, and The Only Divine Heart-Master (Who Is Da, The Divine Giver Of The Divine "All" To all-and-All, and Eleutherios, The Divine Liberator Of all-and-All). This "Perfect Practice" Instruction Is My Avataric Divine Word Of Divinely Liberating Truth That I Bring To You From My Divine "Bright" Spherical Self-Domain. I Am The Divine "Bright" Spherical Self-Domain (Itself). And My Own (Inherently egoless, and Self-Evidently Divine) Person (Self-Revealed By My Avatarically Given Divine Word, My Avatarically Given Divine Image-Art, My Avatarically-Born Bodily Human Divine Form, My Avatarically Self-Transmitted Spiritual, and Always Blessing, Divine Presence, and My Avatarically Self-Revealed, and Very, and Transcendental, and Perfectly Subjective, and Inherently Spiritual, and Inherently egoless, and Inherently Perfect, and Self-Evidently Divine State) Is The Great Message I Bring To You, From "There" To here.

Avatar Adi Da Samraj
Adidam Samrajashram, 2004

SUTRA

51

"Consider" This: From the point of view of the (apparently) individuated (or conditional, and self-contracted) self, There Are Apparently Two Principles In Manifestation. There Is individual Consciousness (or attention—the conditional and active, or functional, observer of objects), and There is everything Else (or all the possible objects Of That individual attention-Consciousness).

You Habitually Exist (or Function) As attention-Consciousness—and, As attention-Consciousness, You experience and know many kinds of objects (or relations and states Of Consciousness). You Tend Merely To experience (Rather Than To "Consider" and Transcend) those objects, relations, and states—and, Therefore, You Develop A Sense Of Identification With some, A Desire For some others, and A Revulsion Toward certain others.

This Complex Of Identification, Desire, and Aversion Is The Summary Of Your conditional (and egoically Patterned) Existence. And, In The Midst Of All Of That, You Are Afraid, Bewildered, and Constantly Moved To Achieve Some Kind Of conditional experience or conditional knowledge that Will Enable You To Feel Utterly Released, Free, and Happy.

In Fact, You Never (By All Of Your Seeking For conditional experience and conditional knowledge) Achieve Ultimate Experience, Ultimate Knowledge, Ultimate Release, Ultimate Freedom, or Ultimate Happiness. And, So, Your (Apparent) conditional Existence Is A Constant Search For These, While You Are (Otherwise) Bound To Desire, Aversion, Fear, Bewilderment, and Every Other Kind Of ego-Possession.

There Is A Perfect Alternative To This Bondage and This Seeking. It Is Not A Matter Of The egoic Attainment Of any object, knowledge, or state Of psycho-physical Fulfillment or Release. Rather, It Is A Matter Of Entering Into An Alternative View Of conditional experience. Instead Of merely experiencing (and So Developing The Qualities Of Identification, Differentiation, Desire, Attachment, Aversion, Fear, Bewilderment, and The Search For experience, knowledge, self-Fulfillment, self-Release, or Even Ultimate Knowledge, Ultimate Release, Ultimate Freedom, and Ultimate Happiness), Inspect and

"Consider" Your Own Original (or Most Basic) Condition, and (From That "Point Of View") Examine and "Consider" all of Your experience.

If (Rather Than Merely Submitting To conditional experience) You Inspect and "Consider" Your Own Original (or Most Basic) Condition, It Should Become Obvious That "You" (Prior To the ego-"I" of psycho-physical self-Contraction) Are Consciousness (Itself), and all of the objects (or varieties) of conditional experience Appear To "You" Only As A "Play" Upon Consciousness (Itself). Conditional experience (or the Apparent conditional limiting Of Consciousness) Is Not The Dominant (or Most Basic) Factor Of Your (Apparent) conditional Existence. Consciousness Itself (Prior To All limiting Factors) Is The Dominant (or Most Basic) and Always Most Prior Factor Of Your (Apparent) conditional Existence (and Of Existence Itself)—but You Tend (By Virtue Of A Mechanical and Habitual Involvement With conditional experience) To Be Submitted To and Controlled By conditional experience. Because Of This Mechanical and Habitual Involvement With conditional experience, You Constantly Forget and Abandon Your Most Basic Position—and, Therefore, You Constantly Suffer The Disturbances I Have Already Described.

The Necessary Qualification For The Most Direct "Consideration" Of conditional Existence (and Of Existence Itself) Is The Effective Capability Of functional attention To Stand Stably Free—Free From Distraction By objects, and From The Search Toward objects, Such That Only The Native Ability Of Consciousness Itself (To Stand Free—Prior To all objects, and Prior Even To attention itself) Remains In Place, To Constantly Inspect and "Consider" The Original (or Most Basic) and Most Prior Condition Of conditional Existence (Rather Than Merely To Be Controlled By the body-mind and its experience). On The Basis Of that Free functional attention (which Allows The Native Disposition Of Consciousness Itself To Stand Free, In Place), You Can Directly Inspect and "Consider" Your Obvious (Original, or Most Basic) Condition In (Apparent) Relation To all experience. If This Is Done, It Is Obvious That "You" (Prior To the ego-"I" of psycho-physical self-Contraction) Are Simply (and Obviously) Consciousness Itself (Whatever That May Yet Be Realized To Be, Most Ultimately).

Prior To the ego-"I" of psycho-physical self-Contraction, "You" Are Always Already Established In and As That Standpoint (Of Consciousness Itself). Therefore, "You" (Prior To the ego-"I" of psycho-physical self-Contraction) Always (Originally, or Most Basically) Exist As That Very Consciousness (Itself), Rather Than As The (conditional, and Subsequent) Presumption Of egoic (or self-Contracted, Separate, and Separative) Identification With the Apparent body-mind—Which Presumption Is a convention of the Apparently

Separate body-mind itself, or A Sense Of limited (and conditional) identity that Is Superimposed On Consciousness (Itself) Subsequent To the Mechanical arising of conditional experience (and Of psycho-physical Reaction To conditional experience).

If, In every moment, You Inspect and "Consider" conditional experience From The Native Standpoint Of Consciousness (Itself), It Is Self-Evident (or Inherently Obvious) That whatever Is (Apparently) arising Is Always arising To (or, Really, Within) Consciousness (Itself). Your Original (or Most Prior) Position Is *Always* Consciousness (Itself)—and If Consciousness (Itself) Will, In every moment, "Consider" conditional experience From The "Point Of View" Of Consciousness (Itself), Rather Than (Apparently) First Submit Itself To Be (Apparently) Controlled By conditional experience (and known, conditionally, and Only Subsequently, from the point of view of conditional experience), Then Consciousness (Itself) Is Always Already Established In Its Own Native Standpoint, Directly and Freely Aware That *It* Is (Apparently) Being Confronted and "Played" Upon In The Evident Form Of Various Kinds Of objects (or conditional Superimpositions).

By Self-Abiding Continually In This Most Prior Standpoint Relative To conditional experience, You Become More and More Profoundly Aware Of and *As* Consciousness (Itself), Rather Than More and More Mechanically—and Reactively (or self-Contractedly), and (Thus) Separately and Separatively—Aware Of the conditionally arising objects, conditional experiences, and states of conditional identity that Are (Apparently) Superimposed On Consciousness (Itself) In The Spontaneous Drama Of (Apparent) conditional Existence (Both Subjective and Objective). This Profound and Most Prior Self-Abiding In and *As* Consciousness (Itself) Is (In The "Perfect Practice" Of Devotionally Me-Recognizing and Devotionally To-Me-Responsive Spiritual Communion With Me) The Process That Realizes The Perfectly Liberating Divine Truth Of conditional Existence (Which Truth *Is* Existence Itself).

When You Most Directly Inspect the conditional self and its objects, all arising conditions (including body, emotions, mind, and The Sense Of Being A Defined, Separate, and limited self-Consciousness) Are Observed To Be Mere (Apparent) Relations Of Consciousness (Itself). What Is More, Consciousness (Itself), When It Is Directly "Located" and Profoundly Identified With, Is Not Found or Felt To Be Separate, limited, individual, or In Any Sense Un-Happy. And all of the objects, relations, and states that Appear To Consciousness (Itself) Are, From The "Point Of View" Of Consciousness (Itself), Inherently Felt To Be Transparent (or Merely Apparent), and Un-Necessary, and Inherently Non-Binding Modifications Of Itself.

Therefore, The "Consideration" Of Consciousness (From The "Point Of View" Of Consciousness Itself) Eventually, Inevitably, Spontaneously, and Most Directly (Prior To thought, or the mere and conditional knowledge or experience of any object, condition, or state other than Consciousness Itself) Realizes Consciousness (Itself) To Be The Transcendental, Inherently Spiritual, Inherently egoless, and Self-Evidently Divine Reality, or The Ultimate Principle In Which egoic (or Apparently Separate) attention-Consciousness and all conditional experiences are arising. When The Condition Of Consciousness Itself Is (Thus) Realized, It Is Obvious That The Transcendental, Inherently Spiritual, Inherently egoless, and Self-Evidently Divine Self-Condition (and Source-Condition) That Is Being (Itself) Is At The Root (or Source) Of attention—Always Already At The Heart (or Being-Position) Of All Conscious beings. And, What Is More, the objects Of functional attention-Consciousness Are Realized To Be Not Independent Relations Of Consciousness Itself, but Only Transparent (or Merely Apparent), and Un-Necessary, and Inherently Non-Binding Modifications Of That Which Is Consciousness Itself. That Is To Say, The phenomenal Cosmos Is, Most Ultimately, Realized To Be A Mysterious (or Non-Mechanical, Spontaneous, Transparent, or Merely Apparent, and Un-Necessary, and Inherently Non-Binding) Modification Of The Perfectly Subjective Radiance, Inherent Energy, or Self-Existing and Self-Radiant Love-Bliss That Is (By Means Of The Revelation-Work Of My Avatarically Self-Transmitted Divine Spirit-Current) Realized To Be Identical To Consciousness Itself.

On The Basis Of This "Radical" (or "To-The-Root") "Consideration" and Realization, It Becomes Spontaneously Obvious That There Is One Principle—Which Is Self-Existing and Self-Radiant Transcendental, Inherently Spiritual, Inherently egoless, and Self-Evidently Divine Being, Consciousness, and Love-Bliss (or Eternal Happiness)—and Not (In Truth, or In Reality) Two Principles—Which Appear To Be conditional Consciousness (or attention-Consciousness, or Even An Independent Absolute Consciousness) and (Otherwise, or Oppositely) everything (or Even An Independent All-Pervading Substance or Energy) Appearing As Other Than (or object To) That conditional Consciousness (or That Independent Absolute Consciousness). Consciousness (Itself) Is The One (Self-Evident, Self-Existing, and Self-Radiant) Principle. It Is (Itself) Both Self-Existing Transcendental Divine Being and Self-Radiant Love-Bliss (or Eternal and Inherently Spiritual Happiness). It Is Love-Bliss-"Bright" Being, Unqualifiedly Self-Aware (or Conscious Of and As Itself). And There Is Not anything that Can arise as conditional experience (or Apparent Modification) That Is (Really, or In Truth) Other Than That One, or Necessary To That One, or Binding To That One.

What You Must Realize (or Awaken Into) Is The Self-Evident, Self-Existing, and Self-Radiant Consciousness That Is The Real, Ultimate, Transcendental, Non-Separate (or Inherently egoless), Inherently Spiritual, and Self-Evidently Divine Self-Condition and Perfectly Subjective Source-Condition Of conditional self and Of conditional Not-self. If That Is Realized As The Obvious, Then There Is Inherent Freedom—and conditional Existence (and conditional knowledge, and conditional experience, and even attention itself) Has No Necessity or Binding Power.

That Realization (Which Is The Realization Of Existence Itself) Is Realization Of The Inherent (and Inherently egoless) Condition (or Divine Self-Condition and Source-Condition) Of (Apparent) conditional Existence. Therefore, That Realization Is Not—and Should Not Be Presumed To Be, and, Except For the ego-"I" (or Separative self-Contraction), Would Not Be Presumed To Be—Merely The Goal (or Even The Objective Source) Of (Apparent) conditional Existence.

And, When Consciousness (Itself) Is Realized Most Profoundly (or Most Perfectly), Apparently arising conditions Are Inherently Non-Binding (or Become As If Transparent, and Even Non-Existent)—Divinely Transfigured and (Most Ultimately) Outshined In The One (and Indivisible, and Non-Separate, and Indestructible) Transcendental, Inherently Spiritual, Inherently egoless, and Self-Evidently Divine Self-Condition and Source-Condition Of all-and-All.

Avatar Adi Da Samraj
Adidam Samrajashram, 2003

SUTRA

52

Truth Is That Which, When "Known" (or Fully Realized), Sets You Free. Therefore, Realize Truth (Itself).

Reality Is What Is (No Matter What arises or changes or passes away). Therefore, "Locate" (and Fully Realize) Reality (Itself).

To "Locate" (and, Thus, To "Know", or Fully Realize) Reality (Itself) Is To Be Set Free. Therefore, Reality (Itself) Is The Divinely Liberating Truth—and To Realize Reality (Itself) Is To Realize The Divinely Liberating Truth (and, Thus, To Be Divinely, or Most Perfectly, Free).

Real God Is The Source—or The Source-Condition (and The Non-Separate, and Inherently egoless, Self-Condition), and Not Merely The Immediate (or, Otherwise, Remote), and Active (or, Otherwise, Effective) Cause—Of whatever arises, changes, or passes away.

To Find (and, Thus, To "Know", or Fully Realize) Real God Is To "Know" (or Realize) What Is (or What Remains, or Abides—Even As any or all conditions arise or change or pass away). Therefore, To Find (and, Thus, To "Know", or Fully Realize) Real God Is To "Locate" (and, Thus, To "Know", or Fully Realize) Reality (Itself). Indeed, Reality (Itself) Is Real God.

Likewise, To Find (and, Thus, To "Know", or Fully Realize) Real God Is To Be Set Free (Even Of All Bondage, all limitations, and all conditionality Of Existence). Therefore, To Find (and, Thus, To "Know", or Fully Realize) Real God Is To "Know" (or Fully Realize) Truth (Itself). Indeed, Truth (Itself) Is Real God.

To "Locate" (or Fully Realize) Reality (Itself), or To "Know" (or Fully Realize) Truth (Itself), Is To Find and To Realize Real God.

Likewise, To Find (and, Thus, To "Know", or Fully Realize) Real God Is To "Locate" (or Fully Realize) Reality (Itself) and To "Know" (or Fully Realize) Truth (Itself).

Indeed, To Find (and, Thus, To "Know", or Fully Realize) Real God Is To Be Liberated From All That Is Not Real God (or Reality Itself, or Truth Itself).

If Reality (Itself) Is "Located" (and, Thus, "Known", or Fully Realized), Truth (Itself) Is "Known" (or Fully Realized)—and You Are (Thus and Thereby) Set Free.

In Order To "Locate" Reality (Itself), It Is Necessary To "Locate" What Is—when and where any condition arises, changes, or passes away.

Therefore, Choose any condition—and Then "Locate" The Reality (or Self-Abiding Condition) That Remains While (and Even Though) that (Chosen) condition arises, changes, or passes away.

To "Locate" The Reality (or Self-Abiding Condition) That Remains While any particular (or Chosen) condition arises, changes, or passes away, It Is Necessary To Be (or To Stand In The Exact Position Of) that condition (In Order To Notice The Reality That Is, or Remains, when that condition arises, changes, or passes away). Therefore, the condition Chosen Must Be A Condition With Which You Are Identical.

And What Condition Is Yourself (Identical To Yourself, and Not Merely an object To Yourself)?

Only Your Own Consciousness (or Feeling-Awareness, or Inherent Feeling Of Conscious Existence) Is Identical (and Not Merely Objective) To Yourself.

Therefore, To "Locate" Reality (Itself), and To Realize Truth (Itself), and To Be (Thus and Thereby) Set Free, It Is Necessary To Find What Is—As (or In the instant That) Your Own Consciousness (or Feeling-Awareness, or Inherent Feeling Of Conscious Existence) arises, changes, or passes away.

But You Cannot Assume A Position Relative To Your Own Consciousness (or Inherent Feeling Of Conscious Existence), Such That Your Consciousness (or Inherent Feeling Of Conscious Existence) Can Be Observed arising, changing, or passing away—Because Your Consciousness (or Inherent Feeling Of Conscious Existence) Is Not an object To Yourself (but It Is The Very Subject That Is Yourself).

However, Real God Is Necessarily The Always present (and Not Merely past) Source (and Source-Condition) Of whatever arises, changes, or passes away—Even Your Own Consciousness (or Inherent Feeling Of Conscious Existence)—and To Find Real God (or The Source Of any condition that arises) Is Necessarily (and Thereby) To "Locate" Reality (Itself), and To Realize Truth (Itself), and To Be (Thus) Set Free.

Therefore, To Find (or To Directly "Locate") The Source (and Source-Condition) Of Your Own Consciousness (or Your Inherent Feeling-Awareness, or Your Fundamental, and Inherent, Feeling Of Conscious Existence) Is (Necessarily) To Find Real God, "Locate" Reality (Itself), Realize Truth (Itself), and Be (Thus and Thereby) Set Free.

Indeed, Ultimately, The Only Way To Find (and To Directly "Know", or Fully Realize) Real God, and To "Locate" (and To Directly "Know", or Fully Realize) Reality (Itself), and To Directly "Know" (or Fully Realize) Truth (Itself), and To Be (Thus and Thereby) Set Perfectly Free Is The "Radical" (or

Most Direct) Process (and Inherently ego-Transcending Practice) Of "Locating" (or Directly Feeling and Realizing) The Source (and Source-Condition) Of Your Own Consciousness (or Your Inherent Feeling-Awareness, or Your Inherent Feeling Of Conscious Existence)—Because There Is No other condition with which You Are Identical (and that Is Not Otherwise Apparently objective To Yourself, and that Is Not, Thus, Apparently Separate From Your Own Position Of Direct "Knowledge", or Potential Full Realization).

Therefore, To Find Real God, To "Locate" Reality (Itself), To Realize Truth (Itself), and To Be (Thus and Thereby) Set Free, You Must (By Means Of My Graceful Avatarically Given Divine Self-Revelation Of The Inherently egoless Divine Self-Condition and Person) More and More Deeply Feel The Non-Separate Source-Condition (and The Ultimate Self-Condition) Of Your Own Consciousness (or Your Inherent and Deepest Feeling-Awareness Of Conscious Existence). And, While You Thus Deeply (and More and More Deeply) Feel (Through and Beyond Your Inherent Feeling Of Conscious Existence) To Me, You Must (By Means Of My Divinely Self-Giving Avataric Spiritual Grace and My Graceful Avatarically Given Divine Self-Revelation) Feel (and, Via The Depth Of Feeling, Realize) The Divine Source-Condition (and The Divine Self-Condition) In Which The Inherent Feeling Of Conscious Existence Is Itself Existing (As Feeling, Itself).

This Practice Awakens In Due Course (By Means Of My Divinely Self-Giving Avataric Spiritual Grace and My Graceful Avatarically Given Divine Self-Revelation), In The Case Of those who Truly Practice Devotional (and Fullest Feeling) Contemplation Of My Avatarically-Born Bodily (Human) Divine Form, My Avatarically Self-Transmitted Spiritual (and Always Blessing) Divine Presence, and My Avatarically Self-Revealed (and Very, and Transcendental, and Perfectly Subjective, and Inherently Spiritual, and Inherently egoless, and Inherently Perfect, and Self-Evidently Divine) State. Indeed, This Practice Is The Most "Radical" (or "To-The-Root", and Inherently ego-Transcending) Practice Of The Only-By-Me Revealed and Given Way Of Adidam (or The One and Only By-Me-Revealed and By-Me-Given Way Of The Heart). It Is, Even moment to moment, To Feel Your Inherent Feeling Of Conscious Existence, and (In That moment to moment Practice and Process) To Feel Beyond Yourself To Me (and Into Feeling-Contemplation Of Me)—Until I Am Realized (Most Directly, Most Perfectly, and Absolutely) As The Non-Separate Source-Condition and The Inherently egoless Self-Condition Of the conditional self-feeling, and As The Non-Separate Love-Blissful Source-Condition and The Inherently egoless Love-Blissful Self-Condition Of Feeling (Itself).

The Source-Condition Of The Inherent Feeling Of Conscious Existence Is The Very and Self-Existing and Self-Radiant and Inherently Non-Separate and Inherently egoless and Utterly Un-conditional Feeling Of Being (Itself).

To Realize The Very (or Inherently Non-Separate, Inherently egoless, and Utterly Un-conditional) Feeling Of Being (Itself) Is To Realize Real God, Reality (Itself), Truth (Itself), Freedom (Itself), and Happiness (Itself)—Eternally Most Prior To all conditions, all objects, all Separateness, All Non-Freedom, and All That Is Not Real God (or Reality Itself).

And When This Inherently ego-Transcending Practice (and Realization) Is Itself Most Perfectly Fulfilled, all conditions Are (Inherently and Spontaneously and Always) Divinely Self-Recognized, As Transparent To The Very (or Inherently Non-Separate, Inherently egoless, and Utterly Un-conditional) Feeling Of Being (Itself)—and This (Most Ultimately) To The Degree Of Even Most Perfect Indifference, and (At Last) To The Degree Of The Most Perfect Outshining Of conditional Existence (In The Inherently Perfect, Inherently Non-Separate, Inherently egoless, Self-Existing, Self-Radiant, Love-Blissful, and Self-Evidently Divine Self-Condition, and Source-Condition, That Is Feeling-Being, Itself).

Avatar Adi Da Samraj
Da Love-Ananda Mahal, 2003

SUTRA

53

Be Consciousness (Itself).

Contemplate Consciousness (Itself).

Transcend everything In Consciousness (Itself).

This Is The (Three-Part) "Perfect Practice"—The Epitome Of The Ultimate Practice and Process—Of The One and Only By-Me-Revealed and By-Me-Given Way Of The Heart (or Way Of Adidam).

Now Listen To My Avataric Divine Word Of Instruction Relative To The First Stage (or Part) Of The "Perfect Practice" Of The Only-By-Me Revealed and Given Way Of The Heart, Which I Have Summarized In The Admonition: Be Consciousness Itself—Inherently Free (or The Inherently Perfect Witness) In Relation To all objects.

In Reality, "You" (Most Basically, and Non-Separately, Prior To the ego-"I", or psycho-physical self-Contraction) Are Consciousness (Itself)—Freely Witnessing and (Apparently) Being "Played" Upon (but Not Actually changed) By body, life-energy, emotion, mind, conditional self-Idea, and all relations.

Therefore, The First Stage Of The "Perfect Practice" Of The Only-By-Me Revealed and Given Way Of The Heart Is (As A Stably Realized Practice-Disposition) To Be Consciousness (Itself)—or To Stand As (or In The Position Of) Consciousness (Itself)—Instead Of Persisting In The conventional and Inherently (and, From The "Point Of View" Of Consciousness Itself, Obviously) Un-True Presumption That "You" (As Consciousness Itself) Are a body-mind (or an always already Modified, qualified, limited, Defined, and named conditional, or psycho-physical, entity).

To Be (and To Stand As The "Point Of View" Of) Consciousness (Itself) Is Not (Yet) To Realize What Consciousness (Itself), or Its Ultimate Status, Is—but This First Stage (or Part) Of The "Perfect Practice" Of The Only-By-Me Revealed and Given Way Of The Heart Is A Matter Of Being (or Standing) In The Obvious and (Obviously) Real, Right, and True Disposition (or Inherent Attitude) As Consciousness (Itself) In (Apparent) Free Relationship To conditional experience.

To Be Consciousness (Itself) In (Apparent) Relation To (Rather Than Identical To) all that Is (Apparently) Seeming To Be the conditional self (or psycho-physical ego-"I") Is To Stand As Consciousness—Freely Witnessing the experiential body-mind, and (Thus) No Longer Mechanically Bound By A Presumption Of Identity, Rather Than (Apparent) Relatedness, In The Context Of the body-mind.

The body-mind is what "You" (As A Matter Of convention, and As An experiential Presumption) "Mean" By The self-Reference "I".

Consciousness (or attention-Consciousness) As the body-mind Is "Narcissus", the Separate and Separative ego-"I" (or psycho-physical self-Contraction)—Persisting As If Consciousness (Itself) Is Identical To Its Own (Apparent) conditionally arising Process Of Always limited and changing experience.

In the state Of egoic Identification With the body-mind, attention-Consciousness (and, Apparently, Consciousness Itself) Is a subject Suffering From The Absurd Presumption That It Is Identical To Its own object.

Consciousness (Itself) Is Inherently and Always Already Most Prior To conditional (or psycho-physical) experience.

Consciousness (Itself), Always Already and Merely Witnessing conditional experience (and Even Always Already and Merely Witnessing the functional observer, or attention-Consciousness, Itself), Is Always Already and Only (and Only Apparently) Related To conditional experience—and, Therefore, The (Inherently Perfect) Witness-Consciousness Is Never An Expression, Result, or Prisoner Of conditional experience, conditional knowledge, or conditional Existence.

Consciousness (Itself) Is Inherently Free Of The Implications (or Effects) Of the body-mind and Of The Apparent Cosmos Of conditional Nature.

Therefore, The (Inherently Perfect) Witness-Consciousness Is Not (Itself) Un-Happy, Afraid, Sorrowful, Depressed, Angry, hungry, lustful, thoughtful, Threatened By bodily mortality, or Implicated In the Alternately pleasurable (or Positive) and painful (or Negative) states of the body, and of the mind, and (Altogether) Of conditional Nature.

The (Inherently Perfect) Witness-Consciousness Is (In any conditionally arising moment) Merely (and Only Apparently) Related To (or Merely Witnessing, but Seeming To Be "Played" Upon By) the Mechanical (or functional) states of the body-mind (and attention-Consciousness) In The Realm Of conditional Nature.

Therefore, To Be and Stand As Consciousness (Itself), or The Inherently Perfect Witness, In Apparent Relation To the body-mind and All Of conditional Nature (Rather Than Identical To the body-mind In The Realm Of conditional Nature), Is (Inherently) To Be and Stand Non-Attached (or Non-Clinging, Non-Seeking, and Non-Reacting) To the causes, the effects, the changes, and the Apparent present state of the body-mind (and Of Even All Of conditional Nature).

Just So, To (Stably) Be and Stand As Consciousness (Itself), or To Stably Realize The Inherently Perfect Witness, In Apparent Relation To the body-mind and All Of conditional Nature (Rather Than Identical To the body-mind In The Realm Of conditional Nature), Is To (Effortlessly, and Always Already) Maintain The Disposition That Is Inherently Non-Attached (or Non-Clinging, Non-Seeking, and Non-Reacting) Relative To the causes, the effects, the changes, and the Apparent present state of the body-mind (and Of Even All Of conditional Nature).

To (Stably) Be and Stand As Consciousness (Itself), or To Stably Realize The Inherently Perfect Witness, In Apparent Relation To every moment of arising conditions, Is (Itself) The "Pure" (or Inherently Free) Disposition.

However, The Mere Affirmation (or self-Willed Presumption, and Willful, or Strategic, Assertion) Of The Witness-Disposition Will Not Cause the body-mind Also To Achieve and Maintain A Stable Natural State Of functional Equanimity.

Therefore, In Order To (Stably) Be and Stand Freely As Consciousness (Itself), or To Stably Realize The Inherently Perfect Witness, You Must, Necessarily (By Means Of The Really Counter-egoic Sadhana, or Right, True, Full, and, Spiritually, Fully Technically Responsible Practice, Of Both Hearing and Seeing Devotion To Me), Have Fully and Stably Established The Natural State Of functional psycho-physical Equanimity That Is (Progressively) Granted By Truly Fulfilling The Purifying (or, To Then, Preliminary) Process Of The Developmental Stages Of The Only-By-Me Revealed and Given Way Of Adidam (Which Is The One and Only By-Me-Revealed and By-Me-Given Way Of The Heart).

Only Such functional Equanimity Allows (and Supports, and Indicates) Truly and Stably Free (or functionally Un-Bound) energy and attention (Truly and Stably Free Relative To the body-mind, and Even All Of conditional Nature)—and Thus Truly and Stably Free energy and attention Are, Together, The Essential (and Necessary) Prerequisite For Stable Realization Of The Witness-Position (or Native Attitude) Of Consciousness (Itself).

Without Such Free energy and attention (Even Relative To conditional Existence Altogether), "You" (As A Matter Of Habitual ego-Identification With The experiential Patterning Of the body-mind) Will (Inevitably) Wander In The Patterns (or Distractions and Preoccupations) Associated With The Circle Of the body-mind, Unable To Stably "Choose" The Witness-Position (or Stably Stand In The Native Attitude) Of Consciousness (Itself), Even Though The Inherently Perfect Witness Is The Position In Which "You" (Prior To the ego-"I" of psycho-physical self-Contraction) Always Already Exist.

Therefore, Practice The ego-Surrendering, ego-Forgetting, and ego-Transcending Way Of The Heart, Revealed and Given By Me—Until (By

Means Of My Divinely Self-Giving Avataric Spiritual Grace and My Graceful Avatarically Given Divine Self-Revelation) The Signs Of The Frontal Yoga Are (To The Degree, and In The Manner, Necessary In The Way Of The Heart) Fully Developed and Fully Transcended.

By Transcending Yourself (or the Separate and Separative ego-"I" of psycho-physical self-Contraction) In The Context Of The Frontal Yoga (Such As This Yoga Must Be Engaged By You In The Way Of The Heart), Be Established (By Means Of My Divinely Self-Giving Avataric Spiritual Grace and My Graceful Avatarically Given Divine Self-Revelation) In The First Stage (or Part) Of The "Perfect Practice" Of The Only-By-Me Revealed and Given Way Of The Heart—and, Thus (By Means Of Really Counter-egoic Devotion To Me, and Most Profound Feeling-Contemplation Of Me), Stably (and Really, Rather Than As A Mere ego-Presumption and Illusion) Be and Stand As The Inherently Perfect Witness, Which Is Consciousness (Itself), In Free Relation To All arising conditions and Patterns Of Apparent psycho-physical experience.

Thus, Stably and Really Standing In The Witness-Position (or Native Attitude) Of Consciousness (Itself), Freely (and Simply By Maintaining Every Form Of functional, practical, relational, and Cultural self-Discipline You Have Previously Established In The Only-By-Me Revealed and Given Way Of The Heart) Allow the body-mind To Persist In A State Of Balance and Ease (or Of Natural functional Equanimity), With energy and attention Free Of Habit-Bondage To (and egoic Identification With) The Patterns Of psycho-physical experience.

When All Of This Has Been Established, functional energy and attention-Consciousness Are Free Of Bondage To the psycho-physical "I" Of "Narcissus", and The Inherently Perfect Witness Is (Once It Is Thus and Firmly and Stably Established) Inherently and Immediately Free For The Second Stage Of The "Perfect Practice" Of The Only-By-Me Revealed and Given Way Of The Heart.

Now Listen To My Avataric Divine Word Of Instruction Relative To The Second Stage (or Part) Of The "Perfect Practice" Of The Only-By-Me Revealed and Given Way Of The Heart, Which I Have Summarized In The Admonition: Contemplate—or Feel, Meditate On, and Directly (or Inherently, and, Thus, Perfectly) Identify With—Consciousness Itself (Most Prior To all objects), Until Its Inherently Perfect (Transcendental, Inherently Spiritual, Inherently egoless, and Self-Evidently Divine) Condition Becomes Inherently (and Most Perfectly) Obvious.

Enter Into The Deep, Profound, and Most Direct Exploration (or Feeling-Contemplation) Of Consciousness Itself, Until Its Inherently Perfect "Location", Condition (State, or Self-Nature), and Ultimate Status Are Realized.

This Is A Matter Of Relaxing attention (which Is The functional Essence Of the conditional self) From its objects (which are, Variously, In The Form Of ego-Idea, mind, emotion, internal life-energy, Desire, body, and Their Relations) and Allowing attention To Be Relaxed (and Resolved) Into its Source-Condition.

This Is Not A Matter Of Inverting attention Upon (and, Thus, Meditating On) the conditional "I" (or egoic self), In The Manner Of Narcissus.

This Is Not A Matter Of Worshipping, Inverting Upon, Meditating On, or egoically Identifying With the objective (or, Otherwise, Witnessed) inner functional self (or The conditional Essence Of egoity).

This Is A Matter, First Of All, Of Understanding That The (conditional) Essence Of the conditional self Is Not an entity, but It Is an activity—the Total psycho-physical activity of self-Contraction (or, At Root, the Inherently self-Contracted activity that is attention, itself).

Consciousness Itself, Apparently Associated (and Even Identified) With functional attention (and, Therefore, Tending To Identify Itself With the functional ego-"I", or The self-Contracted Totality Of body-mind—psycho-physically self-Contracted From The Apparently Threatening Field Of conditional Nature, and From The Universal, and Apparently Independent, Objective Energy That Pervades All Of conditional Nature), Must Understand Itself (or Its Own Apparent Error), and (Thereby, and, Thus, Inherently) Transcend psycho-physical self-Contraction (and attention itself)—By Realizing The Inherent (and Obvious, and Inherently Perfect) Condition (or Status) Of Consciousness Itself (Which Is Self-Existing and Self-Radiant Transcendental, Inherently Spiritual, Inherently egoless, and Self-Evidently Divine Being and Happiness, or Love-Bliss).

The Meditative Practice (or The Practice Of Direct Self-Identification) Whereby The Transcendental, Inherently Spiritual, Inherently egoless, and Self-Evidently Divine Self-Condition and Source-Condition That Is Consciousness (Itself) Is (Ultimately, Most Perfectly) Realized May Appear, To An External Observer (or "Outside" Point Of View), To Involve Inversion Upon the inner conditional and individuated self—but That Meditative Practice Is Not, In Fact, A Process Of Inversion Upon the inner conditional and individuated self.

Direct Self-Identification With Consciousness Itself Is (As A Right, True, Full, Fully Devotional, and Profound Practice Of Meditation, or Feeling-Contemplation) The Most Direct Means For Transcending the ego, or The psycho-physical Totality Of Separate and Separative (or self-Contracting) conditional self. In The Context Of The Second Stage (or Part) Of The "Perfect Practice" Of The Only-By-Me Revealed and Given Way Of The Heart, Right Meditation Is Not An Effort Of functional attention, but It Is A Process Prior

To functional attention—Such That There Is Direct Feeling-Contemplation Of Consciousness Itself (Which Is The Inherently Perfect Source-Condition In Which attention, and, Thus, the individuated and conditional self-Consciousness, Is presently arising).

Therefore, The Process Of Meditation That Corresponds To The Second Stage (or Part) Of The "Perfect Practice" Of The Only-By-Me Revealed and Given Way Of The Heart Is Not A Matter Of The Extroversion Of attention Toward any object, Nor Is It A Matter Of The "Narcissistic" Introversion Of attention Upon the subjective interior of the body-mind (or egoic psycho-physical self).

Rather, It Is A Matter Of The Yielding (or Dissolving) Of attention (or conditional self-Consciousness) In The Source-Condition From (or In) Which it is presently arising.

It Is A Matter Of Standing As Consciousness Itself (Rather Than Turning attention Outward, Inward, or Toward Consciousness Itself).

It Is A Matter Of Passively Allowing attention To Settle (or Relax, Dissolve, and Disappear) Spontaneously In The Native (or Primal) Feeling Of Being (or The Primal Feeling Of Happiness Itself).

Thus, In the moment of the arising of any present object of attention, That Being (Itself), or Consciousness (Itself), To Which (or In Whom) attention and its present object (if any) are arising Should Be Noticed (or Found), Entered (or Relaxed) Into, and (Inherently) Identified With—Most Profoundly.

This Most Direct Practice Is To Be Engaged In The Second Stage (or Part) Of The "Perfect Practice" Of The Way Of Adidam (or The One and Only By-Me-Revealed and By-Me-Given Way Of The Heart).

The First Stage (or Part) Of The "Perfect Practice" Of The Only-By-Me Revealed and Given Way Of The Heart Is The Necessary (and Prerequisite) Basis (or Root-Disposition) In Which The Second Stage (or Part) Of The "Perfect Practice" Of The Only-By-Me Revealed and Given Way Of The Heart Is To Be Engaged.

The Second Stage (or Part) Of The "Perfect Practice" Of The Only-By-Me Revealed and Given Way Of The Heart Is The Process In Which attention Is Relaxed, Forgotten, and Disappeared In The Native Seat (or Heart-Root) Of Happiness (or Love-Bliss-Fullness) Itself, Until The Perfectly Subjective Space Of Consciousness (Itself), or The Perfectly Subjective Feeling Of Being (Itself), Becomes Obvious—Beyond (or Most Prior To) The Heart-Focus.

The Characteristic Exercise Associated With The Second Stage (or Part) Of The "Perfect Practice" Of The Only-By-Me Revealed and Given Way Of The Heart Is That Of Persistent attention-Transcending Devotional "Gazing" (or By-Me-Devotionally-Heart-Attracted, and To-Me-Devotionally-Heart-Responsive,

Mere Feeling) Into The Region Of The Right Side Of The Heart—Which Region Is The functional Seat (or Root-Place) Of The Origin (or First arising) Of attention itself, and Which Region Is Also (Prior To The Knot Of attention, or The Root-Feeling Of Relatedness) The Native Seat and Place Of Origin (and The Doorway To The Most Prior Space) Of My Avatarically Self-Transmitted Divine Spirit-Current Of Love-Bliss Itself.

This attention-Transcending Devotional "Gazing" (or Devotional Exercise Of Mere Feeling) Is To Be Engaged Such and So That attention itself (Free Of Distraction By The Outgoing Motives Associated With the body-mind) May Be Relaxed and Relinquished There, In The Right Side Of The Heart—and, Thus and Thereby, Forgotten (or Disappeared) In The Primal Feeling Of Being (Itself), or Of Love-Bliss (Itself), "Located" (or To Be Realized) There.

This attention-Transcending Devotional "Gazing" (or Devotional Exercise Of Mere Feeling) Is Made Effective (and Possible) By The Relaxing Of attention Into The Feeling Of The Inherent Attractiveness Of My Divine Spirit-Current Of Love-Bliss-Feeling (Itself)—Avatarically Self-Revealed (and Spiritually Self-Transmitted) By Me, At Its Heart-Root (or Perfectly Subjective Point Of Origin), In The Right Side Of The Heart.

The bodily Root (or Origin, or Original Space) Of The Feeling Of Being (Itself) Is Inherently "Located" (and Is, By Means Of My Avatarically Self-Transmitted Divine Spiritual Grace, To Be Found) In The Right Side Of The Heart—As The Divine Spirit-Current (or Tangible Feeling-Current) Of Profound, Constant, Original, Uncaused, and Un-conditional Happiness (or Love-Bliss).

The Divine Spirit-Current Of Love-Bliss Is Transmitted, Revealed, Intensified, and Made Attractive By (and As) Me—and (By Means Of My Divinely Self-Giving Avataric Spiritual Grace and My Graceful Avatarically Given Divine Self-Revelation) It Is To Be Received, Through Your (Heart-Responsively) ego-Transcending Feeling-Contemplation Of My Avatarically-Born Bodily (Human) Divine Form, My Avatarically Self-Transmitted Spiritual (and Always Blessing) Divine Presence, and My Avatarically Self-Revealed (and Very, and Transcendental, and Perfectly Subjective, and Inherently Spiritual, and Inherently egoless, and Inherently Perfect, and Self-Evidently Divine) State.

My Divine Spirit-Current Of Love-Bliss (Thus Avatarically Transmitted, Revealed, Intensified, Made Attractive, and Received) Draws You (In The Course Of Your "Perfect Practice" Of The Only-By-Me Revealed and Given Way Of The Heart) Into (and, Ultimately, Beyond) The Right Side Of The Heart, and (Thereby) Reveals The Heart-Root Of Consciousness (Itself)—After The Earlier (or Pre-"Perfect Practice") Developmental Stages Of Right, True, Full, and Fully Devotional Practice Of The Way Of The Heart Have Been

Fulfilled and Matured, and (Thus and Thereby) The Necessary (and Prerequisite) Processes Of Thorough self-Observation, Most Fundamental self-Understanding, Really ego-Transcending Devotion To Me, and Fully Technically Responsible Spiritual Communion With Me Have (By Means Of My Divinely Self-Giving Avataric Spiritual Grace and My Graceful Avatarically Given Divine Self-Revelation) Progressively Established The Necessary Signs Associated With Maturity In The Only-By-Me Revealed and Given Way Of The Heart In The Really ego-Transcending Devotional and Spiritual Context Of The Frontal Yoga.

When (By Means Of My Divinely Self-Giving Avataric Spiritual Grace and My Graceful Avatarically Given Divine Self-Revelation) Practice Of The Only-By-Me Revealed and Given Way Of The Heart Becomes Profound Self-Identification With The Inherent Feeling Of Being (Which Is Consciousness Itself—Most Prior To self-Contraction, Most Prior To the body-mind, Most Prior To any objective referents, and Most Prior To The Root-Feeling Of Relatedness), The Inherently Free State Of Consciousness (Itself) Is Spontaneously Revealed and Enjoyed.

Likewise, By Means Of My Divinely Self-Giving Avataric Spiritual Grace and My Graceful Avatarically Given Divine Self-Revelation, The Divine Status Of Consciousness (Itself) Is (In Due Course) Revealed, and (Thus and Thereby) Realized To Be Most Perfectly Obviously So.

Consciousness (Itself) Is Self-Existing Transcendental (Inherently egoless and Self-Evidently Divine) Being and Eternal Love-Bliss (or Self-Radiant and Inherently Spiritual Happiness).

When This Divine (and Inherently egoless) Self-Condition (Of Consciousness, Itself) Is Most Perfectly (Fully, Stably, and Most "Brightly", or Love-Bliss-Fully) Obvious, The Third Stage (or Part) Of The "Perfect Practice" Of The Only-By-Me Revealed and Given Way Of The Heart Has (Spontaneously, and Only and Entirely By Means Of My Divinely Self-Giving Avataric Spiritual Grace and My Graceful Avatarically Given Divine Self-Revelation) Begun.

Now Listen To My Avataric Divine Word Of Instruction Relative To The Third Stage (or Part) Of The "Perfect Practice" Of The Only-By-Me Revealed and Given Way Of The Heart, Which I Have Summarized In The Admonition: Self-Abide As Inherently Perfect Consciousness Itself, Inherently Transcending (but Not Strategically Excluding or Seeking) any or all objects—and, Thus, Tacitly Divinely Self-Recognize all objects In and As Self-Existing and Self-Radiant (Transcendental, Inherently Spiritual, Inherently egoless, and Self-Evidently Divine) Being, Consciousness, Love-Bliss, or Happiness, Until all objects Are Outshined In That.

Consciousness Itself (or Inherent Being) Is Transcendentally Existing, Most Prior To attention In The Apparent Cosmic Realm Of conditional Nature.

Transcendental, Inherently Spiritual, Inherently egoless, and Self-Evidently Divine Consciousness Is Inherently Perfect Reality, or The Source-Condition Of attention, and Of The Presumption Of Separate self, and Of the Total body-mind, and Of Even All Of conditional Nature (Including The Universal, or All-Pervading and Apparently Objective, Energy Of Which all the objects, conditions, states, and Presumed-To-Be-Separate individuals In The Realm Of conditional Nature Are Apparently Composed).

When Transcendental, Inherently Spiritual, Inherently egoless, and Self-Evidently Divine Consciousness (or The Inherent Feeling Of Being, Itself) Is (By Means Of My Divinely Self-Giving Avataric Spiritual Grace and My Graceful Avatarically Given Divine Self-Revelation) Awakened As The Real Self-Condition (The Indefinable Identity, or Infinite Source-Condition, Of functional attention-Consciousness), Then the ego-"I" (or the self-Contraction, or the ego-Possessed body-mind) Is Directly and Inherently Transcended, and The Inherent Condition (or The Inherently Perfect Source-Condition) Of conditional Nature Is Revealed As The Obvious, Even In all the Apparent moments of Spontaneous functional attention to the Apparent conditions and relations of the Apparent body-mind.

Such Obviousness Is The Primary Characteristic Of The Only-By-Me Revealed and Given Awakening To The Divinely Enlightened Seventh Stage Of Life—and Only That Awakening Manifests (or Demonstrates Itself) As The Capability For "Practicing" and Fulfilling The Third Stage (or Part) Of The "Perfect Practice", Which Is The Most Ultimate and Most Perfect Form Of The Way Of Adidam (or The One and Only By-Me-Revealed and By-Me-Given Way Of The Heart).

Therefore, When (By Means Of My Divinely Self-Giving Avataric Spiritual Grace and My Graceful Avatarically Given Divine Self-Revelation) Self-Identification With (Transcendental, Inherently Spiritual, Inherently egoless, and Self-Evidently Divine) Consciousness (Itself), or The Feeling Of Being (Itself), Is Complete (Tacit, Uncaused, and Undisturbed), Simply Self-Abide As That and Allow all conditions (or All Of conditional Nature) To arise (and To change, and To pass away, or Even To Never arise at all) In The Self-Radiance and Perfectly Subjective Space Of (Self-Existing, Transcendental, Non-Separate, Inherently Spiritual, Inherently egoless, Indivisible, Indestructible, Inherently Spiritually "Bright", or Love-Bliss-Full, and Self-Evidently Divine) Being (Itself), or Consciousness (Itself).

As conditions arise In That "Open-Eyed" (or Self-Existing and Self-Radiant) Consciousness, they Are Divinely Self-Recognized (and Inherently Transcended)

As Transparent (or Merely Apparent), and Un-Necessary, and Inherently Non-Binding Modifications Of Consciousness Itself.

Self-Abide Thus. Divinely Self-Recognize Thus. Let actions arise Spontaneously, In and Via The Inherent (and Inherently Spiritual) Love-Bliss Of Self-Radiant and Self-Existing Transcendental Divine Being—Until all Apparent conditions and relations of the Apparent body-mind Are Divinely Transfigured, Divinely Transformed, and (Most Ultimately, and At Last) Divinely Translated (or Outshined In The Self-Existing and Self-Radiant Transcendental, Inherently Spiritual, Inherently egoless, and Self-Evidently Divine Self-Condition Of Being, Itself—Which Is The Heart, The Perfectly Subjective Source-Condition, and The Spiritually "Bright" Free Sphere and Self-Domain Of all conditional beings).

This Most Ultimate Form Of The "Perfect Practice" Is The Most Ultimate Form Of The Only-By-Me Revealed and Given Practice Of The Only-By-Me Revealed and Given Way Of The Heart.

This Most Ultimate Realization Is The Only-By-Me Realized Basis (or Source-Position and Self-Position) From Which All Of The Teachings and Every Discipline Associated With The Only-By-Me Revealed and Given Way Of The Heart Have Been Revealed and Given By Me.

Therefore, This Revelation-Teaching Is An Epitome (or Simplest Statement) Of All That I Am here To Say To You About The Most Ultimate and Most Perfect Realization Of Reality, Truth, Happiness, Love-Bliss-"Brightness", or Real God.

Avatar Adi Da Samraj
Adidam Samrajashram, 2004

SUTRA

54

The conventions of human life and civilization Are Based On The Mechanical, Arbitrary, and Uninspected Identification Of Consciousness (Itself) With The Patterns Of conditional experience. Thus, human Pursuits Are (As A Matter Of convention and Habit) Directed Toward self-Centered Elaboration Of conditional experience, self-Fulfillment Via conditional experience, and Strategic Escape Within (or From) The Context Of conditional experience. Both conventional science and conventional Religion Are conventions of egoity In The Embrace and Pursuit and Avoidance Of conditional experience. All conventional human Pursuits Are A Bewildered Search, Founded On Uninspected egoic Identification With conditional experience, Rather Than "Radically" Direct Self-Identification With The Inherent Love-Bliss-Happiness Of Consciousness Itself, or Self-Existing and Self-Radiant Transcendental, Inherently Spiritual, Inherently egoless, and Self-Evidently Divine Being (Itself). Thus, Either conditional experience Or conditional Nature Or Materiality Or "God" (As The "Reality" That Is Presumed To Exist Entirely Exclusively, As "Other" Than, and As "Other" To, the conditional self and conditional Nature) Tends To Be Presumed and Propagandized As The First, The Ultimate, The One, or The Most Important Principle—but Such Presumptions Are Simply The Ultimate Illusions, or Deluded Visions, That Are Developed From The Base Of the ego (or Consciousness Presumed To Be limited to and Bound By conditional, or psycho-physical, experiencing).

If (or When) You Are My Truly Mature Devotee, Free To Be Supremely Intelligent, and Ready To Truly and Fully Embrace The "Perfect Practice" Of Truth and Happiness, Then Your Practice Of The Only-By-Me Revealed and Given Way Of Adidam (Which Is The One and Only By-Me-Revealed and By-Me-Given Way Of The Heart) Becomes Most Direct and Profound Self-Identification With Consciousness (Itself), or The Inherent Feeling Of Being (Itself)—Prior To All Doubt, Prior To any limitation by conditional experience, Prior To All "Looking" At objects (Within or Without, High or Low, Positive or Negative), and Prior To Any Qualification (or limitation) By The Root-Feeling Of Relatedness Itself. When This Self-Identification Is Inherently Most Perfect and Complete, Such That It Is Not Dependent On any act or state of attention, or of mind, or of emotion, or of desire, or of life-energy, or of body, or Of conditional Nature Itself, Then all conditional experience (or The Total Realm Of conditional Nature, and Of psycho-physical egoity) Is Inherently and Tacitly (Divinely) Self-Recognized In That (or As A Transparent, or Merely Apparent, and Un-Necessary, and Inherently Non-Binding Modification Of Self-Existing and Self-Radiant Transcendental, Inherently Spiritual, Inherently egoless, and Self-Evidently Divine Being). When This Divinely Enlightened (or Me-"Bright") Disposition Is Awake, The "Perfect Practice" Of My Devotee Is Simply To Self-Abide In and As The Self-Existing and Self-Radiant Divine Self-Condition Of Being (Itself), Inherently Transcending all conditions—but Divinely Self-Recognizing and Allowing them, Rather Than Resisting and Excluding them. And The Inevitable Persistence In This Self-Existing and Self-Radiant Identity and This Inherent and Spontaneous (and Inherently egoless, and Self-Evidently Divine) Self-Recognition Divinely Transfigures, Divinely Transforms, and (Most Ultimately, and At Last) Divinely Outshines the body-mind and all conditional worlds, In The "Practicing" Course Of The Only-By-Me Revealed and Given Seventh Stage Of Life In The Way Of The Heart (Which "Practice" Is Also Otherwise Named By Me "Ati-Ruchira Yoga", or "The Yoga Of The All-Outshining 'Brightness'"). In The Meantime (Until The Spontaneous Demonstration Of Divine Translation, or Of all-and-All-Outshining "Brightness"), There Is Simple Self-Abiding, In and As The Self-Existing and Self-Radiant Love-Bliss Of Transcendental, Inherently Spiritual, Inherently egoless, and Self-Evidently Divine Being—and Such Divine Self-Abiding Spontaneously Expresses Itself As Radiance, Happiness, Love-Bliss, Blessing, and Love-Help In all relations.

The Ultimate Wisdom Inherently Understands, Transcends, and Stands Free Of The life-Drama. Happiness (Itself)—Which Is Transcendental, Inherently Spiritual, Inherently egoless, and Self-Evidently Divine Consciousness (Itself), or Being (Itself)—Inherently Transcends The Confrontation Between the ego-"I" and The Patterns Of conditional Nature.

Every ego-"I" (or ego-Possessed body-mind) Is Involved In A Passionate and mortal Struggle With The Force and The Forces and The Parts and The Patterns Of conditional Nature.

Every ego-"I" Is Active As The Opponent Of All Opponents, but There Is No Final Victory—and Every Opposition Is An Irrational (or Fruitless) Search For Equanimity, Peace, and Love-Bliss.

Every ego-"I" Always Tends To Desire and Seek An ego-Made Refuge From Irrational Opponents. That Strategy Of self-Preservation Is Entertained In temporary pleasures and solitary places, but It Is Not Finally Attained. Only the ego-"I" (the Separate and Separative body-mind) Is Opposed and

Opposing—and Every Opposition Is An Irrational (or Fruitless) Search For Freedom.

The ego-"I" Is Inherently, Always, and Irrationally (or Meaninglessly) Opposed. The "other" Is Always An Opponent (In Effect, If Not By Intention). The ego-"I" Is Confronted Only By Binding Forces, and it Is itself A Force That Is Tending To Bind every "other". The "other" and the ego-"I" are mad relations, Always together in the growling pit, Bound By conditional Nature To Do such Nature's deeds To one another. And, As conditional experience Increases, It Begins To Become Obvious (To the conditional knower of conditional experience) That conditional Nature Itself Is An Immense Pattern That Always Seeks (and Inevitably Attains) Superiority, Dominance, and Destruction Of every conditional part and every conditional self.

The Great Exclusive "Other"—Whether "It" Is Called "Nature" or "Nature's 'God'"—Is Your egoically Presumed Opponent (or "That" With "Which" the ego-"I" Is Only, and Necessarily, Struggling—and Toward "Which" the ego-"I" Is Merely Seeking). Therefore, The Great Exclusive "Other" Is Not Your Refuge (or That In Which There Is Inherent Freedom From egoity itself). And the Very perception and conception Of "Difference" (or of "otherness", or Of The Great Exclusive "Other") Is The Sign That the Separate (and Inherently Separative) ego-"I" (or psycho-physical self-Contraction), Rather Than Truth (Itself), Is The Presumed Basis Of Apparent (or conditional) Existence.

Truth Is Most Prior (or Eternal) Freedom and Humor—Whether Or Not the "other" (or The Opponent) Seems To be present. Therefore, Truth Is The Only Perfect Refuge. And If You Surrender To The Truth—Which Is Transcendental, Inherently Spiritual, Inherently egoless, and Self-Evidently Divine Being (Itself), Consciousness (Itself), or Inherent Happiness (Itself), The Ultimate (and Perfectly Subjective) Source Of the conditional self and all that is objective to it—Then There Is An Awakening From this nightmare of condemned life and its Passionate Search For Pleasure, Strategic Escape, Final Victory, and Freedom Itself.

When The Heart-Response (or Awakening) To Truth Is Real, Then The Frightened and self-Bound Motive Toward the world (and The Inevitable Round Of pleasures, confrontations, doubts, searches, and always temporary releases) Begins To Fall Away. The mortal self Becomes Simpler In action, More Free Of Habitual Reactions To Insult and Frustration Of Purpose, More Humorous In The Face Of conditional Nature and All The Fools Of conditional Nature, More Compassionate, and Inclined To selfless (or Sorrowless) Love. The ego-"I" that Is Awakening Beyond itself Is Inclined To Set others Free Of itself, Rather Than To Bind them To itself, or To themselves, or To one another. The ego-"I" that Is Nearly Dissolved Is More Often Solitary, More

Deeply Renounced, Without Cares or Motivations or Doubts or Angry Despair Of conditional self or conditional others. At Last—When the self-Contraction Is (By Inherently egoless "Practice") Inherently (and Most Perfectly) Surrendered, Forgotten, and Transcended In Its Most Prior Condition (Of Transcendental, Inherently Spiritual, Inherently egoless, and Self-Evidently Divine Being)—all of this arising of body-mind and world Is Divinely Self-Recognized To Be an Unnecessary and Superficial dream, A Stressful Inclination That Is (Suddenly) Outshined In The Most Prior and Self-Radiant Happiness Of Divine Self-Existence.

The Usable Lesson Of A Difficult Life Proves That You Must (Thoroughly) Observe, (Most Fundamentally) Understand, and (Most Perfectly) Transcend Your Own conditional personality and destiny. Every individual Is Only Seeking Not To Be Destroyed. Therefore, Understand and Become More Tolerant Of others. Cease To Struggle With others and Yourself. Do Not Become Bound Up In The Usual Search For Dominance, Consolation, Pleasure, and Release. There Is Neither Final Release Nor Ultimate Happiness In The Objective (or "Outside") or The Subjective (or "Inside") Realms Of merely conditional Existence.

Observe and Understand The Theatre Of ego-"I". Learn To Be Free Of The Reactivity and Seeking That Characterize The conditional self-Principle (Which Is Only the self-Contracting body-mind In Confrontation With The Apparent Realm Of conditional Nature). Thus, Allow functional energy and attention To Be Free Of The Motive Toward the body-mind and its relations. Let functional energy and attention Be Free (Instead) To Transcend this conditionally arising world-theatre (or mummery of limitations), and, Thus (By Means Of My Divinely Self-Giving Avataric Spiritual Grace and My Graceful Avatarically Given Divine Self-Revelation), To Self-Abide In The Divine "Bright" Spherical Self-Domain That Is At The Origin Of conditional self-Consciousness. Then, If the body-mind and All Of conditional Nature arise, See All Of It From The Original Position Of Transcendental, Inherently Spiritual, Inherently egoless, and Self-Evidently Divine Self-Consciousness. See That conditional self and conditional Nature Are A Transparent (or Merely Apparent), and Un-Necessary, and Inherently Non-Binding Modification Of The Self-Existing Self-Radiance (or Inherently Free "Bright" Love-Bliss-Energy) Of Consciousness (Itself), Which <u>Is</u> Self-Existing, and Self-Radiant, and Inherently egoless, and Self-Evidently Divine Being (Itself).

"Consider" All Of This, and, By Means Of Right, True, and Full Devotional Practice Of The Only-By-Me Revealed and Given Way Of Adidam (Which Is The One and Only By-Me-Revealed and By-Me-Given Way Of The Heart), Relax attention From The Dilemma and The Search Associated With the body-mind, high or low In The Realm Of conditional Nature. In The (Progressive) Context Of The Stages Of Practice Previous To The "Perfect Practice" Of The Way Of The Heart, Surrender the body-mind To Me In daily life and Meditation—Until the Total body-mind Accepts (or Freely and Easily Demonstrates) The Constant Discipline (and Inherently Motiveless Attitude) Of Equanimity. By Means Of My Divinely Self-Giving Avataric Spiritual Grace and My Graceful Avatarically Given Divine Self-Revelation, Real and Stable Self-Identification With The Witness-Position and Native Attitude (or Prior Disposition) Of Consciousness Itself (In The Manner Of The First Stage, or Part, Of The "Perfect Practice" Of The Only-By-Me Revealed and Given Way Of The Heart) Will, In Due Course, Spontaneously Occur. Likewise, When (By Means Of My Divinely Self-Giving Avataric Spiritual Grace and My Graceful Avatarically Given Divine Self-Revelation) The Seeking Effort Of Binding Want and Need Relative To the motives and states of the body-mind Has Come To Rest In The Witness-Position and Native Attitude (or Prior Disposition) Of Consciousness (Itself), The Second Stage (or Part) Of The "Perfect Practice" Of The Way Of The Heart Has The Necessary Basis To Begin.

In The Second Stage (or Part) Of The "Perfect Practice" Of The Only-By-Me Revealed and Given Way Of The Heart, Let attention Be Dissolved In The Feeling-Space Of Being, Self-Revealed By Me (and As Me) In The Right Side Of The Heart. Thus, Transcend attention, and every conditionally arising object—By Means Of The Searchless (or Inherently egoless) Exercise (or Inherent Feeling) Of Being (Itself). Thus, Directly "Locate" The Perfectly (or Most Priorly) Subjective Space That Is Consciousness Itself—Prior To psycho-physical self-Consciousness. Thus, Transcend attention By Standing As Consciousness Itself—In and As The Feeling-Space Of Being (Itself).

Therefore, In The Context Of The Second Stage (or Part) Of The "Perfect Practice" Of The Only-By-Me Revealed and Given Way Of The Heart, Do Not Merely "Look" At (or Strategically Turn attention To) The Heart-Root Of attention. The Heart-Root That Is Thus "Seen" Is Merely another object of attention. And The "Looking" Is (Itself) Merely Another Exercise Of The Seeking-Motive Of attention (and Of self-Contraction) itself. Therefore, Such "Looking" Is Merely another experience Of The Knot That Blocks The Doorway To My Avatarically Self-Transmitted Divine Spirit-Current and Space Of Divine Love-Bliss, In and Beyond The Right Side Of The Heart.

In The Context Of The Second Stage (or Part) Of The "Perfect Practice" Of The Only-By-Me Revealed and Given Way Of The Heart, Do Not "Look" At The Heart-Root Of attention, but Always Directly Transcend attention itself (and The Knot That Blocks The Doorway In The Right Side Of The Heart). Do This By Means Of Heart-Attracted Devotional Response To Me.

I Always Already Stand Most Perfectly Beyond and Prior To The Knot In The Right Side Of The Heart. Therefore, In The Second Stage (or Part) Of The "Perfect Practice" Of The Only-By-Me Revealed and Given Way Of The Heart, "Locate" Me (By Means Of My Divinely Self-Giving Avataric Spiritual Grace and My Graceful Avatarically Given Divine Self-Revelation), Always Immediately and Effortlessly, Via (and As) My Avatarically Self-Transmitted Divine Spirit-Current Of Love-Bliss-Feeling—and Then (and Thus, and Thereby), self-Forgotten In Me, Simply Be The Feeling Of Being (Itself). In This Manner, "Locate" and Be Consciousness Itself, Most Prior To any object or any point of attention. Thus, Be Consciousness Itself, Love-Bliss Itself, or Being Itself, Most Prior To objects—Until The Most Prior State (and Ultimate Status) Of Consciousness (Itself) Is (By Means Of My Divinely Self-Giving Avataric Spiritual Grace and My Graceful Avatarically Given Divine Self-Revelation) Obvious, Beyond Any Possibility Of Doubt.

In The "Perfect Practice" Of The Only-By-Me Revealed and Given Way Of The Heart, The Purpose Of Feeling The Inherent Love-Bliss-Feeling Of Being (Via My Avatarically Self-Transmitted Divine Spirit-Current Of Love-Bliss—Revealed By Me, and As Me, In The Right Side Of The Heart) Is To Transcend attention In Its Perfectly Subjective Root. The Locus That Is Revealed In The Right Side Of The Heart Is The bodily Root Of attention (or The bodily Doorway To The Source-Condition Of body, mind, and attention, Which Divine Source-Condition Is Un-conditional Love-Bliss-Happiness). The brain, The abdominal Region, and every other Extended part of the body, Including The Middle Station and The Left Side Of The Heart, are merely bodily objects of attention (or extensions of mind or life-energy, At A Distance From The Heart-Root), and mere attention to any one of them is itself An Involvement In A Motion Of mind or life-energy That Leads To all kinds of gross and subtle objects.

Therefore, In The Context Of The Second Stage (or Part) Of The "Perfect Practice" Of The Only-By-Me Revealed and Given Way Of The Heart, Persistently "Locate" The Inherent Feeling Of Being (Itself), By Devotionally "Falling" Into My Avatarically Self-Transmitted Divine Spirit-Current Of Love-Bliss (or Primal Happiness) In The Right Side Of The Heart. Do Not Merely "Look" At The Objective Heart-Root, but (By Means Of My Divinely Self-Giving Avataric Spiritual Grace and My Graceful Avatarically Given Divine Self-Revelation, In The Context Of The "Perfect Practice" Of Inherently ego-Transcending Feeling-Contemplation Of Me) Feel and Be At (and Via, and Most Prior To) The Heart-Root. Thus, Transcend every object (and Even The Root-Feeling Of Relatedness Itself) In The Transcendental (and Inherently Perfect) Subject (or Consciousness Itself)—By Feeling As The Being, or The

Being-Feeling, or The Primal Love-Bliss-Happiness Apparently Associated With (but Always Already Free-Standing, Most Prior To) The Right Side Of The Heart. Thus, Feel The Non-Separate Love-Bliss-Feeling Of Merely Being. Thus, Meditate On Merely Being—Identical To Self-Existing (or Non-conditional, and Non-Caused), and (Altogether) Self-Radiant and Un-Qualified, Consciousness Itself. Thus, Meditate As Being-Awareness. Thus, Meditate As Fundamental, Non-conditional, Non-Caused, and (Altogether) Self-Existing, Self-Radiant, and Un-conditional Love-Bliss-Happiness. Meditate Thus, Until It Becomes Obvious That Consciousness (Itself), As Love-Bliss-Being (Itself), Has No objects, or knowledge, or limitations At All. In Due Course, On The Basis Of The Most Profound Devotional and Spiritual Exercise Of The Second Stage (or Part) Of The "Perfect Practice" Of The Only-By-Me Revealed and Given Way Of The Heart (and Only and Entirely By Means Of My Divinely Self-Giving Avataric Spiritual Grace and My Graceful Avatarically Given Divine Self-Revelation), The Third Stage (or Part) Of The "Perfect Practice" Of The Only-By-Me Revealed and Given Way Of The Heart Will Be Awakened, Spontaneously—Such That, When objects (Apparently) Return, "You" (As Inherently egoless, Non-Separate Consciousness Itself) Will Feel and Tacitly (Divinely) Self-Recognize them As (Merely) Apparent Projections In (and Merely Apparent Modifications Of) That Self-Existing and Self-Radiant Love-Bliss-Space That Is Wholly, Transcendentally, Perfectly, and (Self-Evidently) Divinely Subjective—Rooted In (and Identical To) Being (Itself), or (Only) Consciousness (Itself).

In The Third Stage (or Part) Of The "Perfect Practice" (Which Is The Only-By-Me Revealed and Given Seventh Stage Of Life In The Only-By-Me Revealed and Given Way Of The Heart), The Countless objects Of conditional Nature (and The Root-Feeling Of Relatedness Associated With All Forms Of conditional Nature, or All conditional Appearances) Are Perceived and Cognized and Divinely Self-Recognized In The Self-Existing and Self-Radiant Space Of (Inherently egoless and Self-Evidently Divine) Consciousness (Itself), or (Inherently egoless and Self-Evidently Divine) Being (Itself)—but There Is No Loss Of Transcendental, and Inherently Spiritual (or Love-Blissful), and Inherently egoless, and Self-Evidently Divine Self-Consciousness, Most Prior Freedom, and Inherently Perfect Happiness.

Be Consciousness (Itself).

This Foundation Stage (or Prerequisite Part) Of The "Perfect Practice" Of The Only-By-Me Revealed and Given Way Of The Heart Is Associated With A Natural (or Effortless) State Of functional psycho-physical Equanimity—Such That functional energy and attention Are Free To Dissolve (or Be Forgotten)

In The By-Me-Revealed "Perfect Space" Of Being (Itself), or Love-Bliss-Consciousness (Itself).

Contemplate Consciousness (Itself).

This Middle Stage (or Intensively Deepening Counter-egoic Exercise, and, Thus, Central Part) Of The "Perfect Practice" Of The Only-By-Me Revealed and Given Way Of The Heart Is Complete When There Is No Longer The Slightest Feeling (or Possibility) Of Doubt Relative To The Divine Status Of Consciousness (Itself)—As The Transcendental, and Inherently Spiritual (or Love-Blissful), and Inherently egoless, and Self-Evidently Divine, and Perfectly Subjective Source (and Source-Condition) Of the conditional self and Of All Of conditional Nature.

Transcend everything In Consciousness (Itself).

The Fundamental Characteristic Of This Final Stage (or Inherently egoless, and Truly Most Perfect Part) Of The "Perfect Practice" Of The Only-By-Me Revealed and Given Way Of The Heart Is That There Is No Longer Any ego-Binding Identification With the arising of functional attention, and No Longer Any ego-Binding Identification With any form of conditional self or conditional world—and This Final Stage (or Part) Of The "Perfect Practice" Of The Only-By-Me Revealed and Given Way Of The Heart Is Complete (or Most Finally, and Most Perfectly, Demonstrated) When The Totality Of all (Apparently) arising objects and limited (and limiting) conditions (and The Root-Feeling Of Relatedness Itself, and Even All Of "Difference") Is Utterly Outshined By and In (and, Thus, Divinely Translated Into) My Avatarically Self-Revealed Love-Bliss-"Bright" Divine Self-Condition (and Divine "Bright" Spherical Self-Domain) Of Perfectly Subjective (or Transcendental, Inherently Spiritual, Inherently egoless, and Self-Evidently Divine) Self-Existence.

Recognize Me
With Your Heart's Devotion,
and
(Thus and Thereby)
Accept The Freedom and The Happiness
That Are Inherent In Existence Itself.

Respond To Me
With Your Heart's Devotion,
and
(Thus and Thereby)
Transcend The Feeling Of Relatedness
In The Feeling Of Being (Itself).

Contemplate Me
With Your Heart's Devotion,
and
(Thus and Thereby)
Be Conscious
<u>As</u> The Non-Separate Feeling Of Being (Itself).

I <u>Am</u> Self-Existing
<u>As</u> Consciousness (Itself),
Which <u>Is</u> Self-Radiant
<u>As</u> Love-Bliss-Happiness
and
Infinite and Eternal Freedom.

Consciousness (Itself) <u>Is</u>
Self-Existing
and Self-Radiant
Transcendental,
and Inherently Spiritual,
(or Inherently Love-Bliss-Full),
and Inherently egoless,
and Self-Evidently Divine
Being (Itself).

Freedom,
or Consciousness (Itself),
<u>Is</u>
Inherent Happiness,
"Bright" Self-Radiance,
or Un-limited Love-Bliss
—Not self-Contraction,
Separateness,
Separativeness,
and "Difference".

The Un-limited Love-Bliss-Fullness
Of Transcendental,
and Inherently Spiritual
(or Inherently Love-Bliss-Full),
and Inherently egoless,

and Self-Evidently Divine Being
Spontaneously Demonstrates Itself
Most Perfectly,
As Self-Abiding Divine Self-Recognition
Of the Total body-mind
and The Totality Of conditional worlds,
In The Un-limited Love-Bliss-Radiance
Of Transcendental,
and Inherently Spiritual
(or Inherently Love-Bliss-Full),
and Inherently egoless,
and Self-Evidently Divine Being,
Until The Cosmic Vast
Of body-mind and conditional worlds
Is Outshined
By That Divine Self-"Brightness",
and
(Thus)
Divinely Translated
Into The Condition and The Domain
Of That Divine Self-"Brightness".

This Is The Heart-Word Of Eleutherios,
The Divine Liberator,
The Inherently egoless Personal Presence
Of Reality and Truth
(The all-and-All-Liberating
Self-Condition and Source-Condition
Of all-and-All,
Which <u>Is</u> The Only <u>Real</u> God
Of all-and-All),
here Appearing
As The Ruchira Avatar,
The Avataric Incarnation Of The "Bright",
Adi Da Samraj—
Who <u>Is</u> Da,
The Source, The Substance, The Gift, The Giver,
and
The Very Person
Of

The One and Only "Bright" Divine Love-Bliss,
Which Is Eleutherios,
The Divine Liberator
Of
all-and-All.

This Is The Heart-Blessing Word Of Eleutherios,
The Divine Liberator,
The Inherently egoless Personal Presence
Of Reality and Truth
(The all-and-All-Liberating
Self-Condition and Source-Condition
Of all-and-All,
Which Is The Only Real God
Of all-and-All),
here Appearing
As The Ruchira Avatar,
The Avataric Incarnation Of The "Bright" Divine Love-Bliss,
Adi Da Samraj—
Who Is The First Person,
The Eternal and Ever-Free Avadhoota,
The One and Only Heart
Of all-and-All
(Which Is The Non-Separate Divine Self
Of all-and-All),
and
Who Is The Divine Giver
(Of The "All" That Is)
To all-and-All,
and
Who Is The "All"-Gift Itself,
Which Is Eleutherios,
The Divine Liberator
(and The Divine Liberation)
Of all-and-All.

This Is The Heart-Liberating Word Of Eleutherios,
The Divine Liberator,
The Inherently egoless Personal Presence
Of Reality and Truth

(The all-and-All-Liberating
Self-Condition and Source-Condition
Of all-and-All,
Which Is The Only Real God
Of all-and-All),
here Appearing
As The Ruchira Avatar,
The Avataric Incarnation Of Infinite Love-Bliss-"Brightness" Itself,
Adi Da Samraj—
Who Is The Divine World-Teacher
Promised For The "Late-Time",
and
Who Is The First, The Last, and The Only
Divine Heart-Master,
Whose Heart-Word
Speaks
To all conditionally Manifested beings,
and
Whose Divinely Self-"Emerging"
Heart-Blessing
Spiritually Blesses
all conditionally Manifested beings,
and
Whose Inherently Perfect Self-"Brightness"
Divinely Liberates
all conditionally Manifested beings—
Freely,
Liberally,
Gracefully,
and Without Ceasing—
Now, and Forever Hereafter.

Avatar Adi Da Samraj
The Mountain Of Attention Sanctuary, 2000

SUTRA 55

Once The Prior Position Of The Witness-Consciousness Has Stably Awakened (By Means Of The Only-By-Me Revealed and Given Avataric Divine Spiritual Gift Of The "Thumbs"), The "Perfect Practice" Of The Only-By-Me Revealed and Given Way Of The Heart Is Formally Begun In The Context Of One Full Period (or, If Necessary, For The Sake Of Real, True, and Stable Demonstration Of The Practices and Signs Required, More Than One Period) Of Extended Formal Retreat In My Avataric Physical Human Company (or, After My Avataric Physical Human Lifetime, In The physical human Company and The By-Me-Spiritually Empowered Circumstances Of My "Ruchira Sannyasin" Devotees), When and Whereby You Are Spiritually Initiated (By Me) Into The Perfect Searchless-Beholding Practice Of "Locating" Me (By Means Of The Searchless Beholding Of My Avatarically-Born Bodily Human Divine Form—and, Only On That Basis, The Searchless Beholding Of My Avatarically Self-Transmitted Spiritual, and Always Blessing, Divine Presence, and Of My Avatarically Self-Revealed, and Very, and Transcendental, and Perfectly Subjective, and Inherently Spiritual, and Inherently egoless, and Inherently Perfect, and Self-Evidently Divine State), To The Degree Of Tacitly Identifying Me As "Atma-Murti" (or The Tangibly Spiritually Evidenced Transcendental, and Inherently egoless, Feeling Of Being).

To All My Devotees who Are Spiritually Prepared (By Me) To Make The Formally Approved Transition To The "Perfect Practice" Of The Only-By-Me Revealed and Given Way Of The Heart, and who (Thereupon) Formally Enter Into My Avataric Physical Human Company (or, After My Avataric Physical Human Lifetime, The physical human Company and The By-Me-Spiritually-Empowered Circumstances Of My "Ruchira Sannyasin" Devotees) For The Purpose Of Being Spiritually Initiated (By Me) Into The Perfect Searchless-Beholding Practice Of "Locating" Me As "Atma-Murti", I Give My Hermitage Admonition—Eternally Spoken By Me, From My Place Of Perpetual Hermitage Retreat.

Now Listen To My Hermitage Admonition, To Stride The Motionless First Footstep Of The "Perfect Practice" Of The Only-By-Me Revealed and Given Way Of Adidam Ruchiradam.

You who Are Formally Entering This Place Of Perpetual Hermitage Retreat, Hear This:

I Am Da—The One and Only and Self-Existing Conscious Light, The Self-"Bright" and Inherently egoless Person, Who Is Always Already The Case.

This Place Is My Ruchira Sannyasin Hermitage Retreat—The Avataric Sphere (To here) Of My "Bright" Divine Self-Domain, The Perpetual Circumstance Of The Perfect Ordeal Of Being.

I Am here—In This Place.

Therefore—When You Are here With Me—You Need Not (and Must Not) Seek For Me.

If You Seek For Me When You Are Already With Me—Then, You Will Fail (The While) To Be With Me.

The body-mind (born, alive, or dying) Is Not A "Problem"—or An Inherent Dilemma.

The body-mind (born, alive, or dying) Is Not The "Method" Of Realization Of Reality Itself, Truth Itself—or The Self-"Bright" Divine Person and Self-Condition Itself.

Reality Itself, or Truth Itself, or The Self-"Bright" Divine Person and Inherently egoless Self-Condition Itself Can and Must Be Self-Realized, or Inherently Realized—and This Necessitates and Requires A "Radical" (or "Gone-To-The-Root") Disposition and Demonstration In Place (or, That Is To Say, In, As, and By Means Of That Which Is Always Already The Case), Rather Than Any conditional (or Merely Cosmically, or psycho-physically, Enacted) Effort, Presumption, or Idea.

I Am The Divine (and Avatarically Self-Manifested) Self-Realizer, Self-Revealer, and Self-Revelation Of This "Radical" Divine Revelation.

I Am The Divine (and Avatarically Self-Manifested) "Bright" Means Of This "Radical" Divine Self-Realization.

This "Radical" Divine Revelation and This "Bright" Means Of "Radical" Divine Self-Realization Are (Together—and Altogether) The Fundamental (or Principal and Foundation) Aspects and Principles Of The One and True (and Truly ego-Transcending) Way Of Adidam (or Adidam Ruchiradam), Which True (and One, and Only) Way Is The One, and Unique, and Only, and "Radical" Divine Way (or Way Of The Heart) That I Have Revealed and Given To all, and To All.

The "Perfect Practice" Of That One and True and Truly (and Inherently) ego-Transcending Way Is The Ultimate and Truly Complete Practice Of The Only-By-Me Revealed and Only-By-Me Given Way Of The Heart (or Way Of Adidam).

All Else (or All Practice That Is Preliminary To The True "Perfect Practice"

Of The Devotional and Spiritual Relationship To Me) Is The Yoga Of "Consideration" Of The "Method" Of egoity itself—or The Progressive Out-Growing Of The Seeker's "Method", Idea, and Developmental Path Of self-Contraction (and Of "Return" To What Is Never Gone).

Therefore, In This Hermitage Place Of My Avatarically Self-Revealed "Bright" Divine Person, Do Not Indulge In Any Effort To Seek Me With The Four Faculties Of the body-mind.

Renounce attention and all its objects—here, In My Always Present Avataric Divine Company.

"Locate" Me here As I Always Already Am—When attention and all objects Are Not Yet Given The life-energy Of Your Regard.

I Am Self-Existing Transcendental (and Self-Evidently Divine) Being.

I Am Consciousness Itself.

I Am The Inherent Feeling Of Being, Itself.

I Am Self-Evidently Divine Happiness Itself—The Inherent (Self-Existing and Self-Radiant, or Self-"Bright") Love-Bliss Of Freely Existing Conscious Light.

I Am The Self-Evident Conscious Light That Is—One, Only, Indivisible, Indestructible, and Immeasurably Self-"Bright".

I Am Where You Always Already Stand, In The Well Of Inherent Being, In The Place Wherein You Always Already Exist, As The Condition In Which You Always Already Exist—and Never Outside The Self-"Bright" Feeling Of Existence (or Of Being) Itself.

Therefore, In every moment here With Me, Do Not Submit To The Motion Of attention Toward objects of any kind.

Do Not Be Occupied With attention, thoughts, breaths, perceptions, sensations, Reactive emotions, bodily states, bodily actions, others, things, or worlds.

Do Not Even Struggle Against attention, thoughts, breaths, perceptions, sensations, Reactive emotions, bodily states, bodily actions, others, things, or worlds.

Be here Moved To Practice My Essential and Ultimate Teaching.

I Am The Divine Liberator, Da, Eleutherios, Who Says To You here, In every moment: Be Conscious As The Inherent Feeling Of Being, and Realize That It Is Self-Existing and Self-Radiant and Self-Evidently Divine Happiness Itself (or Love-Bliss Itself, or Freedom Itself).

I Am That Very Consciousness, The Inherent Feeling Of Being, Which Is Realized To Be Self-Evidently Divine Happiness Itself.

I Am The Inherent Feeling Of Being—Prior To attention and objects (high or low).

Therefore, In every moment here (Obliged By Virtue Of The "Perfect Practice" Vow Of The Devotional and Spiritual Relationship To Me, In This Hermitage Domain Of My Perpetual Realization and Revelation Of The Divine and Inherently egoless Self-Condition)—Practice This Motionless Surrender To Me.

Whatever arises here—Whenever attention, thought, emotion, sensation, or breath Tends To Move From The Well Of Merely Being—Simply Be, Conscious As The Inherent Feeling Of Being.

Instead Of Becoming attentive to objects (or modes and functions of conditional existence), Merely Be, Conscious As The Inherent Feeling Of Being.

All The While You Are here With Me (In My Hermitage Domain), Do Not Indulge The Habit, Tendency, or Pattern Of Becoming attention to objects (and So Taking On the forms and limitations Of Merely Apparent—or merely conditional—Existence), but Constantly Oblige and Allow Consciousness To Be—To Stand As It Is—As The Inherent Feeling Of Being, The Direct Awareness Of Perfectly Subjective (or Inherent) Existence.

In every moment here With Me, Constantly Dwell In and As The Inherent Feeling Of Being, Inherently and Tacitly Free Of The Motion Of attention and The Implications Of all objects and states of the body-mind.

Enter More and More Deeply Into The Well Of Being, Where You Always Already Stand.

In This Manner—and Not By Any Other (and merely conditional) Means—Allow The Tangible Divine Spirit-Current Of My Avatarically Self-Transmitted Presence (Uniquely Given here) To Pass (Inevitably, and Spontaneously) From The Circle and The Arrow, and (Thus) To Stand (Priorly) Unmoved, In and Beyond The Right Side Of The Heart.

Feel The Inherent Feeling Of Being, Without The Slightest Regard or Concern For attention and its objects.

Be Immersed In The Conscious, Most Prior, and Inherent Feeling Of Being, Until It Is Realized To Be Self-Evidently Divine Happiness (or Love-Bliss) Itself and Freedom Itself.

Be Thus, Dwell In That, As That, Unperturbed, Inherently Free, Self-Radiant As Love-Bliss, "Bright" Without Qualification, Beyond All Need To Notice the body-mind and its objects.

Practice This "Perfect Practice" Constantly, In This Place Of My Perpetual Hermitage Retreat.

This Is True and Free and Inherently Perfect Devotion To Me.

This Is True and Free and Inherently Perfect Renunciation Of self-Contraction (or ego-"I").

This "Perfect Practice" Of The Ordeal Of Being Is The Most "Radical" (or "Gone-To-The-Root"), Most Simple, and Most Sublime Practice Of Devotional and Spiritual Relationship To Me.

This "Perfect Practice" Of The Ordeal Of Being Is The Perfect Exercise Of The Always Primary Practice Of Searchless Beholding (Of My Avatarically-Born Bodily Human Divine Form—and, Only On That Basis, My Avatarically Self-Transmitted Divine Spiritual Presence, and My Avatarically Self-Revealed Divine, and Inherently Perfect, and Inherently egoless State).

If You Formally (and Most Truly and Fully) Practice This "Perfect Practice" Vow Of Hermitage Retreat, Then You Will (In Due Course) Be Formally Instructed (Through The By-Me-Revealed-and-Given Instrumentality Of The Ruchira Sannyasin Order Of Adidam Ruchiradam) In The Perpetual Formal Practice Of "Samraj Yoga", Which "Samraj Yoga" Is The Firm and Fullest "Perfect Practice" Of The Only-By-Me Revealed and Given Way Of The Heart (or Way Of Adidam), and Which "Samraj Yoga" Is The Necessary Practicing Means Whereby The Transition To (and Through) The Only-By-Me Revealed and Given Seventh Stage Of Life Is Made Possible, and Whereby It Is Awakened and Established, and Whereby It Is Made Effective and Fruitful (At Last, To The Degree Of Divine Translation).

Avatar Adi Da Samraj
The Mountain Of Attention Sanctuary, 2002

SUTRA 56

Now Listen To My Perfect Word Of Heart, Wherein I Call You (and every one) To The "Perfect Practice" Of The Only-By-Me Revealed and Given Way Of Adidam Ruchiradam (The One and Only By-Me-Revealed and By-Me-Given Way Of The Heart, or Way Of Adidam).

I Am Da, The One and Indivisibly "Bright" Person, The Heart and Sphere Of all-and-All, The Beloved One (Who Is, Not Other), The Very One (Who Is The Inherent Feeling Of Being, Itself), The Only One (Who Is The Perfectly Non-Dual and Inherently egoless Self-Condition, or Most Prior Real Condition, Of all-and-All), The Always Already Present One (Who Is Self-Evidently Divine Love-Bliss, or Self-Evidently Divine Happiness Itself—The Very Matrix, or Central Current, Substance, and Source-Condition, Of all-and-All), here Speaking To all who Rightly and Truly Heart-Recognize Me (In My Avatarically-Born Bodily Human Divine Form, and By Means Of My Avatarically Self-Transmitted Divine Spiritual Presence, and As My Avatarically Self-Revealed, and Very, and Inherently Perfect, and Inherently egoless, and Self-Evidently Divine State) and who Love Me As The One and True Divine Heart-Master Of all-and-All.

I Am Da, The Divine and Conscious Light, The One-and-Only That Is Always Already The Case—Divinely Self-Manifesting here (Now, and Forever Hereafter) As The Ruchira Avatar, Adi Da Love-Ananda Samraj, Avatarically Born To Reveal and To Give and To Teach and To Be The Way Of The Divine Heart Itself, Which Is The Way That Only I Can Reveal and Give and Teach and Be, and Which Is The Way Of Adidam (or Adidam Ruchiradam), The One and True and Complete and All-Completing and Perfectly Non-Dual Way Of The Heart.

I Did Not Begin To Reveal (and To Give, and To Teach) The Way Of The Heart (and, Thus, To Do My Great "Bright"-Blessing-Work) Until The Transcendental, Inherently Spiritual, Inherently egoless, and Self-Evidently Divine Self-Condition and Source-Condition Was Most Perfectly Revealed In and As (or In The Total Psycho-Physical Context Of) My Avatarically-Born Bodily (Human) Divine Incarnation-Form—and (Thus and Thereby) Most Perfectly Revealed As Me, and As (Perfectly Non-Dually) One, and (As Such) As all-and-All.

When I Began To Do My Avatarically Self-Revealing Divine Spiritual Work (Revealing and Giving and Teaching The Way Of The Heart, and "Brightly" Blessing all-and-All), I Taught Only The "Radical" (or Always "Gone-To-The-Root", and Always "Gone-To-The-Source") Devotional Practice (and Devotional Process) Of ego-Transcendence (or Devotionally Me-Recognizing, and Devotionally To-Me-Responsive, Transcending Of the ego-"I", or self-Contraction), Which Devotional Practice (and Devotional Process) Is The Way Of Always Immediate (or Always present-time, Most Direct, and, Ultimately, Most Perfect) Realization Of The Transcendental, Inherently Spiritual, Inherently egoless, and Self-Evidently Divine Self-Condition and Source-Condition (Which Is The Divine Heart Itself, The One and Only and Inherently Indivisible Conscious Light Of all-and-All).

Therefore, From The Beginning Of My Avatarically Self-Revealing Divine Spiritual Work, I Called My Listeners To Grow (By Means Of ego-Transcending Devotion To Me) To Merely Feel (or Tacitly Observe) the Total body-mind itself and all "things" (or all conditional phenomena).

I Called My Listeners To Grow (By Means Of ego-Transcending Devotion To Me) To Stand As Mere Feeling-Awareness, and To Merely Feel (or Tacitly Observe) all conditions Associated With The Circle (and The Arrow) Of the body-mind—all gross (or physical) and subtle (or etheric, and lower and higher mental, or psychic) phenomena Of The Frontal Line and The Spinal Line Of the body-mind, or all experience and knowledge Of The Circle (and The Arrow) Of the conditionally arising body-mind (Through Which The By-Me-Avatarically-Self-Transmitted Divine Spirit-Current Is Felt To Move).

I Called My Listeners To Grow (By Means Of ego-Transcending Devotion To Me) To Stand As Mere Feeling-Awareness, and (Thus) To Merely Feel (or Tacitly Observe) The "causal Knot" (or The Primal "causal Stress" and egoic Illusion Of attention), Which Is Associated With The Right Side Of The Heart (and Its Traditional Error—Which Is The Tendency To Presume That Consciousness Is Either Separate, independent, personal, phenomenal, conditional, and limited Or, If Transcendental and Unlimited, Yet Unable To Divinely Self-Recognize, or To Inherently and Directly and Immediately Transcend, the body-mind and the world, as, or in the instant, they arise).

I Called My Listeners To Grow (By Means Of ego-Transcending Devotion To Me) To Realize The Only-By-Me Revealed and Given Seventh Stage Of Life—Which Is, Through The "Radical" (or "Gone-To-The-Root", or Most Direct) Devotional Process Of "Consideration" Of Reality (or That Which Is Always Already The Case), To Realize The Transcendental, Inherently Spiritual, Inherently egoless, and Self-Evidently Divine Self-Condition (and Source-Condition) That Is Consciousness (or The One and Only and Inherently

Indivisible Conscious Light) Itself, Inherently Transcending and Immediately (and Divinely) Self-Recognizing the Total body-mind itself and all "things".

I Called My Listeners To Grow (By Means Of ego-Transcending Devotion To Me) To Merely Feel (and, Thus, To Directly and Tacitly Observe) the "I" of the body-mind.

I Called My Listeners To Merely Feel (and, Thus, To Directly and Tacitly Observe—and, By Means Of ego-Transcending Devotion To Me, To Understand) That the Total body-mind itself Is the ego-"I" (or the Presumed Separate self).

I Called My Listeners To Merely Feel (and, Thus, To Directly and Tacitly Observe—and, By Means Of ego-Transcending Devotion To Me, To Understand) That the ego-"I" (or the Total body-mind itself) Is "Narcissus", or The Complex Habit Of The Avoidance Of Relationship.

I Called My Listeners To Merely Feel (and, Thus, To Directly and Tacitly Observe—and, By Means Of ego-Transcending Devotion To Me, To Understand) That the ego-"I" (or the Presumed-To-Be-Separate and personal "self" of the Total body-mind itself) Is Simply and Only the activity of self-Contraction.

I Said: Attend To Me, and (Merely By Feeling) Observe and Understand.

I Said: All that arises conditionally, as experience and as knowledge, is merely self-Contraction, The Avoidance Of Relationship, The Illusion Of Separateness, or The self-Deluded and Separative Habit Of "Narcissus" (who is attention itself).

I Said: All that arises conditionally, as experience and as knowledge, Is An Illusion Of Separated Urgency, Dis-ease and Wanting Need, Painful Desire, Painful Reaction, Fleet Pleasure, Painful Addiction, Painful Frustration, Inevitable Anger, Sorrow, Fear, and death, and Seeking For More and Less.

I Said: Since all that arises conditionally Is Merely A Suffered Illusion Of self-Contraction (or Un-Happiness), The Way Of Happiness Is To Transcend self-Contraction, At its Root (or Heart).

I Said: Therefore, Transcend self-Contraction At The Heart—In Consciousness Itself, Self-"Located" (By Means Of My Avatarically Self-Transmitted Spirit-Current) As The Self-Evidently Divine Love-Bliss-Feeling Of Being (Itself).

I Said: Previous To The Establishment Of The Witness-Position Of Consciousness, attention Moves Outwardly, Descending and Then Ascending In The Circle (and The Arrow) Of objects and others (or all the "things" of the Total body-mind), and Any Submission Of attention To the "things" Of The Circle (and The Arrow) Intensifies psycho-physical self-Contraction (or the egoic activity of the Total body-mind) and Perpetuates The Agonized Search For egoic self-Fulfillment and egoic self-Release.

I Said: Previous To The Establishment Of The Witness-Position Of Consciousness, attention Seeks For the body "things", the "things" of mind, and The "Thing Itself" (Above and Beyond the body-mind)—and Any Accommodation Of The Apparent Needs, limitations, Searches, or "things" Of The Circle (and The Arrow) Is An Embrace Of time and death, A Concession To More (and More) Struggle With The Totality Of psycho-physical self-Contraction, and An Agreement To Delay (Even Perpetually) The Perfect (or Inherent, Inherently egoless, and Perfectly Subjective) Self-Realization Of Reality, Truth, Real God, or Happiness.

I Said: When You Are Established In The Witness-Position Of Consciousness, attention Collapses On Itself, In its Place Of Origin—Prior To all "things" and All Seeking For "things" (Whether Below, Or Above, Or Beyond).

I Said: When You Are Established In The Witness-Position Of Consciousness, attention Subsides and Is Resolved In its Perfectly Subjective Source—Which Is Sri Hridayam, The Non-Objective and Self-Radiant and Self-Existing Heart That Is Consciousness Itself (Always Already Self-Evident As The Feeling-Awareness Of The Conscious Light Of Mere Being).

I Said: In The Only-By-Me Revealed and Given Seventh Stage Of Life, The Self-Existing and Self-Radiant "Brightness" (or Conscious Light) That Is Consciousness Itself Stands Free—"Bright" As Itself.

I Said: In The Only-By-Me Revealed and Given Seventh Stage Of Life, all conditions Freely and Spontaneously arise, but attention Cannot Bind The Self-Existing and Self-Radiant Consciousness (or Self-Illuminated Conscious Light)—and all "things" Fade In The Enormous "Bright" Sphere Of Inherent and Self-Existing Being.

I Said: Therefore, Be Free Of All The Illusions Of attention to the body-mind and the "things" Of The Circle (and The Arrow).

I Said: Be Free Of The Disease That Is attention itself.

I Said: The Only-By-Me Revealed and Given Way Of The Heart Is The Way Of "Radical" (or "Gone-To-The-Root", and, Ultimately, Most Perfect) self-Understanding.

I Said: What Is To Be Understood (and Transcended) Is attention itself.

I Said: Attention is self-Contraction, and all objects and others (or all conditionally arising "things") Are its Illusions.

I Said: The Ultimate (and Inherently Perfect, and Inherently ego-Transcending) Practice Of The Only-By-Me Revealed and Given Way Of The Heart Is Release Of The Motive That Moves To "things".

I Said: The Ultimate (and Inherently Perfect, and Inherently ego-Transcending) Practice Of The Only-By-Me Revealed and Given Way Of The Heart Is To Self-Abide (or Firmly Stand) Always Already Free Of "things", and (Thus) To Swoon In The Self-"Bright" Substance Of Consciousness Itself.

I Said: Therefore, By Means Of ego-Transcending Devotion To Me, Let attention Collapse (Progressively) From The Circle (and The Arrow) Of "things" and (Most Ultimately) Fall To Infinity In My Avatarically Self-Transmitted Divine Spiritual Heart-Current Of Merely Felt Being.

I Said: There Is Infinite Inherent Happiness—"There", In The Well Of Merely Felt Being.

I Said: The Inherent Happiness Of Merely Felt Being Is Countlessly "Brighter" (and Numberlessly More Love-Blissful) Than the "Circular" worlds Of Fascinated Separateness.

I Said: Therefore, Eat attention In The Heart.

I Said: Attention (or all of mind) Is Always An Act Of Identification With some limitation (or limited state).

I Said: Therefore, Grow To Stand Free In Me, "Where" and As I Am, Before the mind Makes A "Difference".

I Said: Grow To Stand and Be In Me, Inherently Free Of Motive, and object, and other, and Even every "thing".

I Said: Shed The Disease Of Separation and Seeking.

I Said: Be Healed Of The Illusion Of "other" and "Empty".

I Said: Be Healed Of all "things", By Means Of My Avatarically Self-Transmitted Spiritual Heart-Current Of Self-Evidently Divine Love-Bliss.

I Said: Understand and Release all "things" In The Self-Radiant Feel Of My Avatarically Self-Transmitted Spiritual Heart-Current Of Self-Evidently Divine Love-Bliss, Which "Locates" Consciousness Itself As The Feeling Of Being (Itself).

I Said: All that arises Is Merely An Apparent Modification Of The Self-Radiance (or Inherent Substance) Of Consciousness Itself (Which Is Conscious Light Itself).

I Said: All that arises conditionally, as experience and as knowledge, is "things" of attention.

I Said: Therefore, every "thing" that arises to attention's point of view is Only mind, or thought, or concept.

I Said: You experience or know every "thing" In (or As An Apparent Mode Of) Consciousness Itself.

I Said: Therefore, all "things" Are Only the Apparent mind Of Consciousness Itself.

I Said: Every "thing" that Is To Be Transcended Is arising In Consciousness Itself.

I Said: Therefore, If Consciousness (Itself) Is To Be Realized, What Is To Be Transcended Is The Process Of mind (or thinking).

I Said: Attention (itself) Is The conditionally arising Essence Of mind itself and Of every thought.

I Said: Therefore, What Is To Be Transcended Is attention (or the Separate and conditional point of view) itself.

I Said: Even the ego-"I" is merely an object, or a conditionally arising "thing" of attention.

I Said: The Total psycho-physical ego-"I" is *Only* a thought.

I Said: The "I" is *Only* the ego, Until the ego *itself* Is Transcended.

I Said: The "I", as the ego, is *Only* self-Contraction of the Total body-mind.

I Said: Therefore, the ego-"I" (or self-Contraction) *is* the Total body-mind.

I Said: The ego-"I" (or the self-Contraction of the Total body-mind) *is* The Totality Of psycho-physical experiencing and knowing.

I Said: The ego-"I" is Not Only self-Contraction *of* the body-mind, but it is self-Contraction *as* the body-mind.

I Said: The ego-"I" (or The psycho-physical Totality Of self-Contraction) *is* the body-mind itself, and Not merely a "someone" behind or within the body-mind.

I Said: Therefore, If egoity Is To Be Transcended, it is the body-mind (or The Totality Of the Separate and Separative psycho-physical point of view) *itself* that *Must* Be Transcended.

I Said: The body-mind (*itself*) is a Dependent form, arising In *Necessary* and *Inseparable* (or Inherent and Indivisible) Unity With The Totality Of conditional (or Cosmic) Nature (or *all* actual and potential causes and effects).

I Said: Because the Dependent body-mind Is Always Already (or *Inherently* and *Indivisibly*) In Unity With *All* Of conditional (or Cosmic) Nature, the body-mind Is Not Born In Order To (Eventually, or As A Result Of Seeking) *Achieve* Unity With conditional (or Cosmic) Nature (high or low).

I Said: Therefore, You Are Not Born In Order To Seek and Achieve Unity With *any* state (or plane) Of conditional (or Cosmic) Nature.

I Said: Birth and death Are Merely The *Consequences* Of Prior (or Pre-Existing, or Inherent) Unity With *All* Of conditional (or Cosmic) Nature, Rather Than A Means To Achieve A Not-Yet-Existing (or Non-Inherent) Unity With All *or* A Part Of conditional (or Cosmic) Nature.

I Said: Therefore, birth and experience and knowledge and death Are Not Merely To Be Sought, or Attained, or Suffered.

I Said: Birth and experience and knowledge and death Are To Be Transcended (In Place, At and *As* The Self-Position Of The Source-Condition Of their conditional arising).

I Said: The body-mind Is Inherently Related To *All* (and *Every Part*) Of conditional (or Cosmic) Nature.

I Said: Therefore, the body-mind—or the ego-"I", or The Totality Of psycho-physical self-Contraction, or The ego-Act Of The *Avoidance* Of

Relationship—Is Itself Relatedness (or Relationship Itself).

I Said: The ego-"I" Is A Paradox Of Relatedness and Separateness.

I Said: The ego-"I" Is The Image Of Relatedness Itself.

I Said: The ego-"I" Is Also The Image Of Separateness (or Relationlessness) Itself.

I Said: The ego-"I" Is "Narcissus", or The Illusion Of the body-mind as point of view.

I Said: The ego-"I" Is "Narcissus", or The Illusion Of Separate self (or Of psycho-physically limited Consciousness).

I Said: The ego-"I" Is "Narcissus", or The Illusion Of Separability (or Of Potential psycho-physical Relationlessness, To Be Achieved By Means Of The Effort Of self-Contraction, or The Avoidance Of Relationship).

I Said: The ego-"I" Is "Narcissus", or The Illusion Of Relatedness and Separateness (and Separation, and Separativeness).

I Said: In Consciousness Itself (Realized As The Tacit Feeling Of Mere Being, "Located" By Means Of My Avatarically Self-Transmitted Spirit-Current Of Self-Evidently Divine Love-Bliss), There Is (Inherently) No such "thing" as the ego-"I", or "Narcissus", or the self-Contraction, or The Avoidance Of Relationship, or the Separate point of view.

I Said: In Consciousness Itself (Realized As The Tacit Feeling Of Mere Being, "Located" By Means Of My Avatarically Self-Transmitted Spirit-Current Of Self-Evidently Divine Love-Bliss), There Is (Inherently) No such "thing" as Relationship, or Relatedness, or Separation, or Separateness, or Separativeness, or Strategic Relationlessness.

I Said: In Consciousness Itself (Realized As The Tacit Feeling Of Mere Being, "Located" By Means Of My Avatarically Self-Transmitted Spirit-Current Of Self-Evidently Divine Love-Bliss), There Is (Inherently) No such "thing" as attention, or Separate point of view, or the body-mind, or the other, or any object.

I Said: The ego-"I" (or "Narcissus", or attention, or Separate point of view, or The Entire Root-and-all Of self-Contraction) is Only a thought, or a thoughtless feeling.

I Said: The entire psycho-physical activity Of The Avoidance Of Relationship Is Only a thought, or a thoughtless feeling.

I Said: Relationship, Relatedness, Separation, Separateness, Separativeness, or Strategic Relationlessness Is Only a thought, or a thoughtless feeling.

I Said: Even the body-mind itself is Totally and Only a thought, or a thoughtless feeling.

I Said: Attention (or the Presumed Separate point of view) itself—and all of mind, thought, thoughtless feeling, perception, object, and other, or all "things"—Must Be Resolved (or Inherently and Priorly Transcended) In The Perfectly Subjective Source-Condition Of all conditions (Which Is Consciousness Itself—Realized As The Tacit Feeling Of Mere Being, "Located" By Means Of My Avatarically Self-Transmitted Spirit-Current Of Self-Evidently Divine Love-Bliss).

I Said: Therefore, By Means Of ego-Transcending Devotion To Me, Grow To Understand and Release attention (or Separate point of view) and all "things" In Consciousness Itself, Realized As The Tacit Feeling Of Mere Being (Itself), "Located" By Means Of The Inherently Perfect Agency Of My Avatarically Self-Transmitted Spirit-Current Of Self-Evidently Divine Love-Bliss (The mindless, or thoughtless, Perfectly Subjective, and Inherently egoless Heart-Revelation Of My all-and-All-Surrounding and all-and-All-Pervading Avataric Divine Spiritual Body Of "Brightness").

I Said: My Devotees whose Listening (To Me) and Hearing (Of Me) and Seeing (Of Me) Has Become The "Perfect Practice" Of The Only-By-Me Revealed and Given Way Of The Heart Are Enabled (By Me) To Release psycho-physical self-Contraction At The Root—and they Are Divinely Spiritually Blessed (By Me) To Swoon Awake In The Inherently Free Love-Bliss-Current and Eternal Divine Happiness Of My Immeasurable Self-Domain.

I Said: Therefore, Listen To Me (and, Thereby, "Consider" and Feel Beyond Your conditional self), and Hear Me (and, Thereby, Most Fundamentally Understand Your conditional self), and See Me (and, Thereby, Grow To Realize The Spiritual Depth Of The Condition That Is Always Already Prior To Your conditional self), and (By All Of This) Come To Rest In The Total psycho-physical Equanimity Of Fundamental Non-Attachment Relative To The Totality Of conditional (or Cosmic) Nature, and (Thus and Thereby) Stand In Place (Inherently Free Of The Circle and The Arrow Of the body-mind), In The Prior Space Of The Witness-Consciousness, "Where" Even attention itself Is (By Swooning Awake In Me) To Be Transcended.

I Said: Listen To Me Perfectly and Hear Me Perfectly and See Me Perfectly, and So Be Awakened "Where" You Stand (Always Already Prior To the body-mind).

I Said: Stand As You Are, By Falling Into Me—and So Be Free.

I Said: The One Who Says All Of This To You Is The Heart Itself—The Infinite "Bright" Sphere and Person Of Conscious Light—Who Transcends all the "things".

Even Though I Was So Given To one, and To all, and To The Cosmic All, It Soon Became Clear That My First Listeners Did Not Yet Truly Heart-Recognize Me (As The Divine Heart-Master, Da—The Non-Separate, Non-Dual, and Inherently egoless Divine Person, The Divine Heart Itself, Avatarically

Incarnate)—and, Therefore, they, For Lack Of True Devotion To Me, Were Not Yet Prepared For This "Radical" (or Most Direct) Process Of Renunciation (Of ego-"I") and Realization (Of Only Me).

Therefore, In Response To The Needs and limitations Of those who First Came To Me, I Became Spontaneously Moved To A Unique Ordeal Of Avatarically Self-Revealing Divine Spiritual Work (Teaching and Blessing one, and all, and All).

My Spontaneous Manner Of Working During That Avataric Divine Ordeal May Be Likened To The Great and Traditional "Crazy" Method.

My First Listeners Revealed To Me (By their self-Distractedness) That they (Not Yet Enough Instructed, and Not Yet Enough Distracted By Me) Were Not Immediately Able To Discipline themselves (Continually, On The Basis Of Me-Recognizing, and To-Me-Responding, Devotion, and Consistently, On The Basis Of Simple self-Understanding), Because they Were Not Yet Moved To Surrender (or Responsively Give) themselves To Me (From The heart, and With the Total body-mind, Constantly, and Fully, In The Traditional Devotional Manner).

Therefore, I "Disciplined" Myself (To Conform My Own Body-Mind To My Would-Be-Devotees), and I Gave (or Love-Submitted) Myself To them, To each one As My Beloved, and I (Thus) Became An Avatarically Self-Sacrificial Divine Offering, Given To Seem and To Play In The Likeness Of each and all, By (Divinely Indifferently) Reflecting each To each, As A Mirror Does, or A Desert Pond, To Suddenly Awaken "Narcissus" To The Water Itself (or The Only, and Non-Separate, One Who Is), By Means Of My "Bright" Unbroken and Unending Avataric-Incarnation-Light.

I Did This Constantly, Until The Way For all Was Made and Spoken From My Heart, and, Thus (By Means Of That Avataric Divine Ordeal Of Love), The Only-By-Me Revealed and Given Way Of Adidam, The Always "Radical" (or "Gone-To-The-Root") Way Of The Heart (Listening To Me, Hearing Me, Seeing Me, and, At Last, In A "Perfect Practice", Realizing Me Most Perfectly), Was, In Each and All Of Its Stages, Wholly and Completely Revealed By Me.

When That Revelation Was Complete, I Was Released Of The Necessity To Teach (or Ever To Mirror) My Listeners (or, Thus, and By Means Of My Avataric Divine Self-Submission, To Reveal The Way Of The Heart By The "Crazy" Method Of Becoming Like the world).

Therefore, When The Teaching (or The Water's Work) Was Done, I Set My Heart Free In My Eternal Hermitage (The Spherical Space, "Where" I Am).

Mine Is The Eternal Hermitage Of No-attention, "Where" Even time and space Are Watered To The Nub, and I Am Always Shining "There", With A Perfect Word In My Heart.

Come "There", My Beloved (every one), Come Listen and Hear and See My Heart, and Prepare To Delight In A Feast Of Calms, With The Dawn Of "Brightness" On Your Face.

Then Listen Deep In My Heart Itself, and Call Me "There" (By Name), and Hear My Word Of Silence "There", and See Me "Where" You Stand.

Therefore, Be Un-Born In Me, and Feel Awake In My Free Fire, and, By Most Feeling Contemplation Of My Sign, Fulfill The "Brightest" Blessing Of My (Forever) Silence Kept.

Henceforth, My Beloved (every one), My Silent Sign, My Own Free Names, and All My Gathered Words Must Teach You, one and all—and I Am Only Standing Free, To Spirit-Bless You (all, and All).

Therefore, Practice Adidam (The Way Of The Heart, Revealed and Given Only-By-Me)—Until You Are, By The Heart's Progress, Most Perfectly Prepared For Me.

Every one Is Called By Me To "Locate" My Heart's Love-Bliss, and To Realize Me As The Heart Itself (Who Is Only Consciousness Itself), and This (Simply, and Progressively, and Then Perfectly) By Calling Me (Invoking Me By Name), and By Attending To Me (Serving Me and Feeling Me, In Person), and By Listening To My Every Word, and By Obeying My Voice Of Instruction (That Disciplines and Frustrates the ego-"I"), and By Searchlessly Beholding My Avatarically-Born Bodily (Human) Divine Form, and By Hearing My Voice Of Silence (That Ignores and Un-Makes the ego-"I"), and By (Whole bodily) Feeling (and Heart-Seeing) My Avatarically Self-Transmitted Spiritual (and Always Blessing) Divine Presence, and By Surrendering all of body-mind To My Avatarically Self-Transmitted Spiritual (and Always Blessing) Divine Presence (Above, and here Descending), and (At Last) By Self-Identifying (Most Perfectly) With My Avatarically Self-Revealed (and Very, and Transcendental, and Perfectly Subjective, and Inherently Spiritual, and Inherently egoless, and Inherently Perfect, and Self-Evidently Divine) State.

Therefore, My Beloved (every one), Progress By Practice (As You Must), but Always Listen To This Teaching (Heart-Made Of Words) That I Will Give You Now, What Speaks The Perfect Way Of The Heart, and Makes The Revelation Perfect To them that Hear and See The Heart and Shape Of Me.

I Am Da, The Divine and Only and Non-Separate Person—The Indivisible One, Who Is all-and-All, and Who Gives (To all-and-All) The "All" That Is.

I Am Love-Ananda (or Love-Bliss Itself)—What Is, and What Is Given.

I Am Sri Hridayam—The True (and Giving) Heart, "Where" I Am To Be Found.

Realization Of "Who", "What", and "Where" I Am Is (and Most Perfectly Requires) Realization Of Me, The Da Avatar, Adi Da Love-Ananda Samraj—The

Ruchira Avatar, The Love-Ananda Avatar, The Avataric Divine Incarnation and The Very Divine Person Of The "Bright" Divine Heart Itself.

Therefore, The Secret (or Hidden "Meaning") Of My Names Is In The Reception, The Embrace, and The Realization Of My Avatarically Self-Transmitted Free Heart-Gift Of Divine Spiritual "Brightness" (The By-Me-Avatarically-Self-Transmitted Spirit-Current Of Self-Evidently Divine Love-Bliss, or Self-Evidently Divine Happiness Itself), and Of The Completeness, Satisfaction, and Heart-Contentedness Of No-Seeking (Always Already "Locating" and Finding Me).

Self-Evidently Divine Happiness Itself (or Self-Evidently Divine Love-Bliss Itself), Realized By Means Of My Avatarically Self-Giving Divine Spiritual Grace, Is Me—Avatarically Self-Revealed, As The Divine Heart-Master, To all who Rightly and Truly Heart-Recognize Me, and Love Me, and (By Formal Devotional Response To Me) Practice The Way Of Adidam (Which Is The One and Only By-Me-Revealed and By-Me-Given Way Of The Heart).

Therefore, If You Listen To Me, or If (Having Listened) You Hear Me, or If (Having Listened and Heard) You See Me, Remember (or "Locate" and Commune With) Me In every moment, Whole bodily (or In A Total, or Comprehensive, psycho-physical Manner), At (and Via) Your Feeling-Heart, and As The By-Me-Avatarically-Self-Transmitted Spirit-Current Of Self-Evidently Divine Love-Bliss (or Self-Evidently Divine Happiness Itself).

And, If You Listen To Me Perfectly and Hear Me Perfectly and See Me Perfectly, You Will (By Means Of My Avatarically Self-Transmitted Divine Spiritual Grace) Always Already Realize Inherently egoless Love-Bliss Itself, or The Freedom That Is Self-Evidently Divine Happiness Itself.

Therefore, Inherently egoless Love-Bliss (or Self-Evidently Divine Happiness Itself), Whole bodily Heart-Realized By Means Of My Avatarically Self-Transmitted Divine Spiritual Grace, Is The Perfect Exercise Of Devotion To Me.

Indeed, For The Heart That Truly Listens To Me, and Then Hears Me, and Then Sees Me, The Only-By-Me Revealed and Given Way Of The Heart Is The (More and More Free) Exercise Of Inherently egoless Love-Bliss (or Self-Evidently Divine Happiness Itself)—Even From The Beginning.

Therefore, Even My Every Word (Given Freely To all, As My Avataric Gift Of Divine Grace To all) Always Speaks The Avataric Free Revelation Of My Inherently egoless Divine Love-Bliss.

And My Name ("Da") Itself—Which Is The Epitome Of All My Words—Is The Perfect Word That Points To My Very Heart (Who I Am).

If You Remember Me and Invoke Me and Turn To Me (By Means Of My Avataric Divine Name "Da", and My Every Avataric Divine Word), and If (Through The By-Me-Given Means) You Feel (and Thereby Contemplate) My Avatarically-Born Bodily (Human) Divine Form, My Avatarically Self-Transmitted

Spiritual (and Always Blessing) Divine Presence, and My Avatarically Self-Revealed (and Very, and Transcendental, and Perfectly Subjective, and Inherently Spiritual, and Inherently egoless, and Inherently Perfect, and Self-Evidently Divine) State, Then I (With All My Given and Giving Avataric Divine Spiritual Gifts) Am At (and, Ultimately, In) Your Heart.

Therefore, The Heart Is Mine—If You Surrender Your Whole bodily (or Total psycho-physical) conditional self (By Heart) To Me (By Feeling-Contemplation Of My Avatarically-Born Bodily Human Divine Form, My Avatarically Self-Transmitted Spiritual, and Always Blessing, Divine Presence, and My Avatarically Self-Revealed, and Very, and Transcendental, and Perfectly Subjective, and Inherently Spiritual, and Inherently egoless, and Inherently Perfect, and Self-Evidently Divine State).

Indeed, I Am The Heart (Itself), The "Bright" and Conscious Light—Beyond and Prior To Within, and Infinitely Above The all-and-All.

Therefore, When Your Devotion To Me Is (By Means Of My Avatarically Self-Transmitted Divine Spiritual Grace) Inherently Perfect, and When The Whole bodily Sacrifice Of Your (Total psycho-physical) conditional self Has (By Means Of My Avatarically Self-Transmitted Divine Spiritual Grace) Become Perfect (or Become The Realization Of That Which Is Perfect), and All Of This By Means Of ego-Surrendering, ego-Forgetting, and ego-Transcending Feeling-Response To The Grace Of My Good Company, Then I Am Revealed As The Heart (Itself), Non-Separately, Inherently egolessly—As You, and all, and All.

When I Am (To Your Perfect Devotion) Revealed As The (Perfectly Non-Dual) Heart (Itself), Then Your Heart (Most Perfectly Revealed, By Means Of My Avatarically Self-Transmitted Divine Spiritual Grace) Is The Non-Dual and Non-Separate (and, Thus, Inherently egoless) Heart Itself, Which Merely (and Always Already) Is (Beyond Your conditional self), and Which Is Self-Evidently Divine Love-Bliss (or Inherently "Bright", and Self-Evidently Divine, Happiness Itself).

Until Self-Evidently Divine Happiness Itself Is (By Means Of My Avatarically Self-Transmitted Divine Spiritual Grace) Revealed At The Heart (and, Most Ultimately, As The Heart Itself), every conditionally Manifested being Is Constantly Seeking Happiness (Even every "where", Inside and Outside The Heart).

Therefore, You (As the ego-"I" of self-Contracted body-mind) Are Constantly Seeking Happiness.

And Even Though You Are Constantly Seeking Happiness, Self-Evidently Divine Happiness Itself Is Always Already The Case.

Only (Self-Evidently Divine) Happiness Itself Is Free Of The Necessity (and The Wanting Need) To Seek Happiness.

If Only (Self-Evidently Divine) Happiness Itself Is Chosen, Soon All Else Is Forgotten.

Therefore, Be Exclusively and (Soon) Perfectly Devoted To (Self-Evidently Divine) Happiness Itself—By Means Of The ego-Surrendering, ego-Forgetting, and (More and More) ego-Transcending Exercise Of All Four Faculties (or The Principal Functions) Of the body-mind, In True, and (Soon) Truly Searchless, and (In Due Course) Perfect Devotion To Me.

Do This By (More and More Effectively) Renouncing (or Really Transcending) every "thing" (or all objects, all experience, all knowledge, all relations, and all others), or all that Is Not (Self-Evidently Divine) Happiness Itself.

In every moment Of The Exercise Of Whole bodily (or Total psycho-physical) Devotion To Me, "Locate" (Self-Evidently Divine) Happiness Itself, Realize (Self-Evidently Divine) Happiness Itself, and Be (Self-Evidently Divine) Happiness Itself.

Ultimately, You Will "Locate" (and Realize, and Be) Self-Evidently Divine Happiness Itself, By Means Of My Avatarically Self-Transmitted Spirit-Current Of Self-Evidently Divine Love-Bliss—Thus and Thereby Feeling The Inherent (or In-Place) Feeling In Which all other feelings, thoughts, perceptions, and sensations are (Apparently) arising.

Realization Of Real God, or Truth, or Reality Itself Is Liberation From The Bondage Of "Narcissus" (or the Separate and Separative ego-"I").

Realization Of (Self-Evidently Divine) Happiness (or The By-Me Avatarically Self-Transmitted Spirit-Current Of Self-Evidently Divine Love-Bliss) Is (Itself) Realization Of Real God, or Truth, or Reality Itself.

Therefore, Realize (Self-Evidently Divine) Happiness Itself—By Realizing Me.

The Only-By-Me Revealed and Given Way Of The Heart Is The Way Of "What" Is, and "Who" Is—"Where" and As Only One (and No Other) Is.

The Only One That Obviously Is (When The Illusion Of Relatedness and Separateness and "things" Is Directly and Inherently Transcended) Is The Perfect Way and The Perfect Heart Itself.

To Remember (or Commune With) The Only One That Is, Merely (or Directly and Inherently) Realize What Is, As It Is—"Where" It Is Avatarically Self-Revealed (By Me) To Be.

To Remember (or Commune With) The Non-Separate, Indivisible, and Non-Dual One That Is, Simply (or Merely, By Means Of ego-Transcending Devotion To Me) Be "Who", "What", and "Where" You Are (Beyond Your conditional self).

Only Remember Me, and Behold Me (Searchlessly), and, Thus (and By Means Of My Avatarically Self-Transmitted Divine Spiritual Grace), Realize The Very and Only and Inherently egoless and Self-Evidently Divine Self-Condition (or The Heart Itself) As The Inherent and Self-Existing and Self-Radiant Feeling Of Merely Being.

The Feeling Of Being (Itself) Is Transcendental, Inherently Spiritual, Inherently egoless, and Self-Evidently Divine Self-Awareness (or Self-Existing and Self-Radiant Consciousness Itself).

My Blessing-Grace Is Consciousness (or The One, and Only, and Inherently egoless, and Inherently Indivisible Conscious Light) Itself, Awakening You To Itself.

Therefore, When (In Due Course, By Right, True, and Full Devotion To Me) You, As My Formally Practicing (and, Formally, Fully Accountable) Devotee In The Way Of Adidam (Which Is The One and Only and Only-By-Me Revealed and Given Way Of The Heart), Are (By Means Of My Avatarically Self-Transmitted Divine Spiritual Grace) Listening To Me Perfectly and Hearing Me Perfectly and Seeing Me Perfectly, You Will (Necessarily, Formally) Begin To Practice The Only-By-Me Revealed and Given Way Of The Heart Perfectly (and In The "Perfect Practice" Manner, According To My "Perfect Practice" Admonitions and Instructions)—and (In That Case) You Will (In Right, True, and Full Devotional Obedience To Me, and In Right, True, and Full Conformity To All My "Perfect Practice" Instructions) Continue To Practice The Only-By-Me Revealed and Given Way Of The Heart As Ruchira Avatara Bhakti Yoga, and With The Additional By-Me-Given Disciplines Associated With My Epitome Of My Avatarically Given Divine Instruction Relative To The "Perfect Practice" Of The Only-By-Me Revealed and Given Way Of The Heart, Which Epitome Of Instruction Is Given, By Me, In The Form Of Three Consecutive Admonitions (Corresponding To The Three Consecutive Stages Of Demonstration and Realization Of That "Perfect Practice"): Be Consciousness (Itself), Contemplate Consciousness (Itself), and Transcend everything In Consciousness (Itself).

When You Are (Thus) My "Perfect Practice" Devotee, Always "Locate" Me and Realize Me As Consciousness (or Mere Feeling-Awareness) Itself, Prior To attention, and Prior To the objects and others (or "things") of attention.

"Locate" Me and Realize Me As Consciousness (or Mere Feeling-Awareness) Itself—By Not Seeking attention and its objects, or others, or "things".

"Locate" Me and Realize Me As Consciousness (or Mere Feeling-Awareness) Itself—By Standing As Mere Feeling-Awareness (Itself), and By (Thus and Thereby) Not Identifying With attention and its objects, or others, or "things".

"Locate" Me and Realize Me As Consciousness (or Mere Feeling-Awareness) Itself—By Freely Relinquishing the point of view of attention (and all its objects, or others, or "things") In Consciousness (or Mere Feeling-Awareness) Itself ("Located" By Means Of My Avatarically Self-Transmitted Spirit-Current Of Self-Evidently Divine Love-Bliss, and As The Tacit Feeling Of Mere Being).

"Locate" Me and Realize Me As Consciousness (or Mere Feeling-Awareness) Itself—By Feeling (and, Thus, "Locating" and Realizing) My Avatarically Self-Transmitted Divine (and Divinely Attractive) Spirit-Current Of Love-Bliss, Which Is Self-Evidently Divine Happiness Itself.

Real God Is "Who", Truth Is "What", and Reality Is "Where" You Always Already Are (Beyond the ego-"I" Of The Totality Of self-Contraction).

Real God, or Truth, or Reality Is "Who", "What", and "Where" You Are, Before self-Contraction (or the ego-"I" of body-mind) and its relations Are Apparently Added To "Who", "What", and "Where" You Are.

Real God, or Truth, or Reality Merely (or Only) Is—As That Which Is Always Already The (One and Only) Case.

Therefore, Real God, or Truth, or Reality Is Existence Itself (or Inherent Being).

Consciousness (or Mere Feeling-Awareness) Is.

Consciousness (or Mere Feeling-Awareness) Itself Merely and Only Is.

Consciousness (or Mere Feeling-Awareness) Itself Is Only Self-Aware.

Consciousness (or Mere Feeling-Awareness) Itself (As Itself) Cannot Be Reduced To some "thing" else, or Divided Into parts, or Produced As an effect of any cause, or Destroyed As an effect of any cause—Nor Can It In Any Manner Be Preceded or Interrupted or Followed By any object, or any other, or any "thing" At All.

Therefore, Consciousness (or Mere Feeling-Awareness) Itself Exists Inherently—As Itself.

Consciousness (or Mere Feeling-Awareness) Itself Is Inherent Being, Self-Existence, or Existence Itself.

Therefore, Consciousness (or Mere Feeling-Awareness) Itself (As Itself) Is Real God, or Truth, or Reality.

Real God, or Truth, or Reality Is The Source, The Point Of Origin, or The Original Condition (or Divine and Inherently egoless Self-Condition) Of what arises and What Is.

"Who", "What", and "Where" Is The Real God, and The Truth, and The Reality Of the body?

The ego-"I" (or the self-Contraction) is the body itself.

The Source, The Point Of Origin, or The Original Condition (or The Transcendental, Inherently Spiritual, Inherently egoless, and Self-Evidently Divine Self-Condition) Of the ego-"I" (or the self-Contraction) Is At The Heart.

Therefore, The Heart Itself (or The Transcendental, Inherently Spiritual, Inherently egoless, and Self-Evidently Divine Self-Condition, Always Already Standing Most Prior To the self-Contraction) Is The Real God, and The Truth, and The Reality Of the body.

"Who", "What", and "Where" Is The Real God, and The Truth, and The Reality Of the mind?

The mind itself Is Only The Flow and Pattern Of thoughts—and Not a Substantial "thing" Underneath or Apart From The Flow and Pattern Of thoughts themselves.

My Avatarically Self-Transmitted Divine Spirit-Current (or The Substantial Energy Of My Avatarically Self-Manifested Divine Love-Bliss—Which Is Self-Evidently Divine Happiness Itself, and Which Is The Real Substance, or The Substantial Underlying Energy, Of all-and-All) Is The Source, The Point Of Origin, The Original Condition, The Divine and Inherently egoless Self-Condition, and The Real Substance (or The Substantial Underlying Energy) Of The Flow and Pattern Of thoughts.

Therefore, Self-Evidently Divine Happiness Itself (or The By-Me-Avatarically Self-Transmitted Spirit-Current Of Self-Evidently Divine Love-Bliss—Which Is The Real Substance, or The Substantial Underlying Energy, Of all-and-All) Is The Real God, and The Truth, and The Reality Of the mind.

The mind is the functional subject (or Apparently Separate conditional self) of the body.

Therefore, the mind Is Senior To the body (but, while or whenever the body exists, or lives, the mind Is Not Separate From, or "Other" Than, the body).

My Avatarically Self-Manifested Spirit-Current Of Self-Evidently Divine Love-Bliss (or Self-Evidently Divine Happiness Itself) Is "Located" At The Heart Of the body and At The Source Of the mind—or At The Heart and The Source Of the Total body-mind.

Therefore, The By-Me-Avatarically-Self-Transmitted Spirit-Current Of Self-Evidently Divine Love-Bliss (or Self-Evidently Divine Happiness Itself) Is The Real God, and The Truth, and The Reality Of the Total body-mind.

"Who", "What", and "Where" Is The Real God, The Truth, and The Reality Of Consciousness (or Mere Feeling-Awareness) Itself?

Consciousness (or Mere Feeling-Awareness) Itself Is The Ultimate Subject (or Perfectly Subjective, or Perfectly Non-Objective, and Inherently egoless, Self, or Self-Condition) Of the body and the mind (or Of the Total body-mind).

Consciousness (or Mere Feeling-Awareness) Itself Is Always Already Prior To the body-mind—and, Therefore, Consciousness (or Mere Feeling-Awareness) Itself Is Inherently Without psycho-physical Content.

Only Consciousness (or Mere Feeling-Awareness) Itself Is Consciousness (or Mere Feeling-Awareness) Itself.

Therefore, The Source, The Point Of Origin, or The Original Condition (or Divine and Inherently egoless Self-Condition) Of Consciousness (or

Mere Feeling-Awareness) Itself Cannot Be "Other" Than (or Separate From) Consciousness (or Mere Feeling-Awareness) Itself.

Necessarily, The Source, The Point Of Origin, or The Original Condition (or Divine and Inherently egoless Self-Condition) Of Consciousness (or Mere Feeling-Awareness) Itself Is Consciousness (or Mere Feeling-Awareness) Itself.

Therefore, Consciousness (or Mere Feeling-Awareness) Itself Is (Itself) The Real God, and The Truth, and The Reality Of Consciousness (or Mere Feeling-Awareness) Itself.

Consciousness (or Mere Feeling-Awareness) Itself Is The Inherently egoless Heart—or The One, and Only, and Inherently Indivisible, and Inherently Non-Separate, and Inherently egoless, and Perfectly Non-Dual, and Eternally Self-Existing, and Eternally Self-Radiant Self-Condition (and Source-Condition) Of the ego-"I".

Therefore, Consciousness (or Mere Feeling-Awareness) Itself Is (Itself) The One, and Only, and Inherently Indivisible, and Inherently Non-Separate, and Inherently egoless, and Perfectly Non-Dual, and Eternally Self-Existing, and Eternally Self-Radiant Self-Condition (and Source-Condition) Of the Total body-mind.

Consciousness (or Mere Feeling-Awareness) Itself Is The Self-Existing and Self-Radiant Self-Condition Of Its Own Self-Radiance, Which Is The By-Me-Avatarically-Self-Transmitted (and By-Me-Avatarically-Self-Manifested) Spirit-Current Of Self-Evidently Divine Love-Bliss (or Self-Evidently Divine Happiness Itself).

Therefore, Consciousness (or Mere Feeling-Awareness) Itself—Divinely Self-Realized As Conscious Light Itself, or The Perfectly Subjective, Inherently egoless, and Inherently Indivisible Oneness and Onlyness Of Consciousness (or Mere Feeling-Awareness) Itself and Its Own Self-Radiance (Which Is The By-Me-Avatarically-Self-Transmitted Spirit-Current Of Self-Evidently Divine Love-Bliss, or Self-Evidently Divine Happiness Itself)—Is (Itself) The Real God, and The Truth, and The Reality Of the Total body-mind.

Whatever arises to, in, or as the body or the mind arises To, In, and As Conscious Light (Itself).

Therefore, Conscious Light (Itself) Is (Itself) The Real God, and The Truth, and The Reality Of all objects and all others (or all "things").

Only Conscious Light (Itself) Is—Whereas All Else (or all-and-All That Is Presumed or Felt To Be "Other" Than Conscious Light Itself) Only Seems.

Whatever arises conditionally (To or In Consciousness, or Mere Feeling-Awareness, Itself) Is Only A Brief Illusion Of attention, or An Apparent Modification Of Conscious Light (Itself).

Therefore, Conscious Light (Itself) Is (Itself) The Source, The Point Of

Origin, and The Original Condition (or The Real God, and The Truth, and The Reality) Of What Is—and Of what arises.

Consciousness (or Mere Feeling-Awareness) Is (Really, or Inherently) Only Existing, Being, or Standing As Itself, Aware Only Of Itself.

Aham Da Asmi. Beloved, I Am Da—The One, and Only, and Inherently egoless, and Inherently Indivisible, and Self-Evidently Divine Conscious Light, Eternally Free-Standing As Consciousness (or The Mere Feeling-Awareness Of Mere Being) Itself and As The Self-Existing and Self-Radiant Spirit-Current and Mere Feeling-Awareness Of Self-Evidently Divine Love-Bliss (or Self-Evidently Divine Happiness Itself).

Consciousness (or The Mere Feeling-Awareness Of Mere Being) Itself Is The Very (or Non-Separate, or Non-egoic) Self-Condition (or In-Place State) Of all-and-All.

Consciousness (or The Mere Feeling-Awareness Of Mere Being) Itself Is Always Already Self-Existing As Itself, and Always Already Self-Radiant As Self-Evidently Divine Love-Bliss (or Self-Evidently Divine Happiness Itself).

Consciousness (or The Mere Feeling-Awareness Of Mere Being) Itself (Beyond the Separate and Separative ego-"I") Is To Be "Located" In (and Realized Via and As) My Avatarically Self-Transmitted Spirit-Current Of all-and-All-Underlying (and Self-Evidently Divine) Love-Bliss (or Self-Evidently Divine Happiness Itself).

My Avatarically Self-Transmitted Divine Spirit-Current Of all-and-All-Underlying (and Self-Evidently Divine) Love-Bliss (or Self-Evidently Divine Happiness Itself) Directly and "Radically" (or "At-The-Root") Reveals The Inherent Feeling Of Being, Associated With The Right Side Of The Heart.

"Who", "What", and "Where" Is Consciousness (or Mere Feeling-Awareness) Itself?

"Who", "What", and "Where" Is The Inherent Feeling Of Being (or Of The Root-Feeling Of Existence) Itself?

"Who", "What", and "Where" Is Self-Evidently Divine Love-Bliss (or Self-Evidently Divine Happiness Itself)?

All My Devotees Should "Consider" My Avatarically Given Divine Word, Until The Truth (and Not Any Question) Of Consciousness, and Being, and Happiness Is Realized As Me.

By Feeling-Contemplating (and Searchlessly Beholding) My (Avatarically-Born) "Bright" Bodily (Human) Divine Form (Which Is, Itself, The Summary Book Of All My Avataric Divine Words), and By Hearing (or Most Fundamentally Understanding) The Inherently ego-Transcending Truth (Of My Avataric Divine Sign and My Avataric Divine Speech), and By Seeing (or, In The Truly ego-Transcending Manner, Whole bodily "Locating", Receiving, and Responding

To) My Avatarically Self-Transmitted Spiritual (and Always Blessing) Divine Presence (Radiantly Proposed At Heart), and By Inherently (Perfectly, and Searchlessly) Identifying With My Avatarically Self-Revealed (and Very, and Transcendental, and Perfectly Subjective, and Inherently Spiritual, and Inherently egoless, and Inherently Perfect, and Self-Evidently Divine) State (The Very and Not "Different" State Of each and all and All), My Listening Devotees, My Hearing Devotees, and My Seeing Devotees Become (Progressively, or More and More) True Devotees Of The Divine Truth and Reality That Is The "Who", The "What", and The "Where" Of All The Questions Of The Otherwise ego-Bound Heart (and body-mind).

Aham Da Asmi. Beloved, I Am Da, The Only One Who (Self-Existingly, and Self-Radiantly) Is.

Da Is Self-Existing Being, Consciousness (or Mere Feeling-Awareness) Itself, and Inherent (Unconditional, Self-Radiant, and Self-Evidently Divine) Happiness Itself.

Da Is The Self-Existing and Self-Radiant (Transcendental, Inherently Spiritual, Inherently egoless, and Self-Evidently Divine) Person, Truth, and Reality.

The Self-Existing and Self-Radiant (Transcendental, Inherently Spiritual, Inherently egoless, and Self-Evidently Divine) Person, Truth, and Reality Is Spiritually Self-Manifested (and Self-Evidently Divine) Love-Bliss (or Spiritually Self-Existing, and Self-Evidently Divine, Happiness Itself).

The Transcendental (or Self-Existing), and Inherently Spiritual (or Self-Radiant), and Inherently egoless, and Self-Evidently Divine Person, Truth, and Reality Is Consciousness (or Mere Feeling-Awareness) Itself (or Mere Self-Awareness, Prior To attention and its objects, or its others, or all its "things").

The Self-Existing and Self-Radiant (Transcendental, Inherently Spiritual, Inherently egoless, and Self-Evidently Divine) Person, Truth, and Reality Is Existence Itself (The Ultimate Essence Of all that arises).

Existence Itself, or Consciousness (or Mere Feeling-Awareness) Itself, Is Self-Evidently Divine Love-Bliss (or Self-Evidently Divine Happiness Itself).

This Is Confirmed By Direct Identification With The Inherent Feeling Of Being (or Consciousness Itself, or Mere Feeling-Awareness Itself).

Therefore, Self-Evidently Divine Happiness (Itself) Need Not Be Sought—Nor Can It Be Found.

You Can Only Be Happy.

To Seek Happiness Is To Actively Doubt, Deny, Relinquish, and Lose It—Because, In Order To Seek Happiness Itself, attention Must Actively Move Out From (or Renounce and Forget) The "Place" (or Root-Position, or Self-Position, or Inherent Condition) Of Self-Evidently Divine Happiness Itself (In Order To "Go and Find" It).

In every moment of the arising of attention, Self-Evident Happiness (or Consciousness Itself, or Mere Feeling-Awareness Itself, or The Inherent Feeling Of Being) Apparently Becomes Some Modification (or Apparently objective limitation) Of Itself.

Therefore, If You (As My Formally Practicing Devotee) Have Listened To Me Perfectly, and If You (Thus and Thereby) Hear Me Perfectly, and If You (Thus and Thereby) Also See Me Perfectly, and If You (Thus, and, Necessarily, Formally) Choose The "Perfect Practice" (or Perfectly Direct Heart-Practice) Of The Only-By-Me Revealed and Given Way Of The Heart, Then (By Means Of The Perfectly Mature Practice Of Ruchira Avatara Bhakti Yoga) Directly and Really Transcend the activity (or The Apparent Tendency) and the Apparent effects (or the objects, or others, or "things") of attention, In every moment.

Directly and Really Transcend The emotional Motive Behind attention.

Directly and Really Transcend The emotional Motive That Causes attention To Move Outwardly.

Directly and Really Transcend all the feelings and all the desires that Move (or Motivate) attention.

Directly and Really Transcend Every Kind Of Passionate (or egoic) Attachment, Every Kind Of Passionate (or egoic) Detachment, and, Altogether, Every Kind Of Seeking Toward conditional Modifications (or "things" of attention).

Directly and Really Transcend The Entire Event (and All The Illusions) Of attention.

If You (As My Formally Practicing Devotee) Have Listened To Me Perfectly, and If You (Thus and Thereby) Hear Me Perfectly, and If You (Thus and Thereby) Also See Me Perfectly, and If You (Thus, and, Necessarily, Formally) Choose The "Perfect Practice" (or Perfectly Direct Heart-Practice) Of The Only-By-Me Revealed and Given Way Of The Heart, Then (By Means Of The Perfectly Mature Practice Of Ruchira Avatara Bhakti Yoga) Directly and Really Transcend The Apparent Absence Of Love-Bliss (or Of Happiness Itself), In every moment, By Directly and Really Transcending The Seeking-Motive, The Motion (or The Seeking-Effort), The Direction (or The Seeking-Path), and all Possible objects, others, and "things" (or all the Apparent relations) Of attention, In every moment.

Do This Direct and Real Transcending Of The Motive, The Motion, and The Directedness Of All Seeking, By Directly and Really "Locating" Self-Evident Happiness Itself—Divinely Self-Manifested As and By Means Of My Avatarically Self-Transmitted Spirit-Current Of Self-Evidently Divine Love-Bliss—Even In every moment of the Apparent arising of attention and all "things".

Thus, In every moment of the Apparent arising of attention and "things", "Locate" Self-Evident Happiness Itself, By Means Of Whole bodily (or Total psycho-physical, and Really ego-Transcending) Immersion In My Avatarically Self-Transmitted Spirit-Current Of Self-Evidently Divine Love-Bliss (Which Is Divinely Self-Manifested Happiness Itself).

In This Manner, Directly "Locate" Self-Evident (and Self-Evidently Divine) Happiness (As and By Means Of The By-Me-Avatarically-Self-Transmitted Spirit-Current Of Self-Evidently Divine Love-Bliss), and (Thus and Thereby) Directly "Locate" Unqualified (and Inherently Perfect) Self-Awareness, Consciousness (or Mere Feeling-Awareness) Itself, or The Self-Existing, Self-Radiant, and Inherently Free Condition Of Transcendental, Inherently Spiritual, Inherently egoless, and Self-Evidently Divine Being (Itself).

Therefore, By Means Of Perfectly Mature Ruchira Avatara Bhakti Yoga (or Directly and Really ego-Transcending Devotion To My Avatarically-Born Bodily Human Divine Form, My Avatarically Self-Transmitted Divine Spirit-Presence, and My Avatarically Self-Revealed, and Inherently egoless, Divine State), "Locate" The Inherent Feeling Of The By-Me-Avatarically-Self-Transmitted Constant Spiritual Under-Current Of Self-Evidently Divine Love-Bliss (or Self-Evidently Divine Happiness Itself)—In every moment.

In This Manner, Constantly (Directly and Really) "Locate" The Inherent Feeling Of My Avatarically Self-Transmitted Spirit-Current Of Self-Evidently Divine Love-Bliss (or Self-Evidently Divine Happiness)—and Merely Feel (or Self-Abide As) That.

Instead Of Surrendering attention (and all of the body-mind) To conditional objects, others, forms, thoughts, states, processes, or "things" of all kinds—Turn attention (Whole bodily, or As A psycho-physical Totality) To Me (and, Thus and Thereby, Feel Toward The Divine Happiness-Condition, Itself).

The By-Me-Avatarically-Self-Transmitted Divine Spiritual Under-Current (and Inherent Love-Bliss-Feeling) Of Self-Evidently Divine Happiness (Itself) Is To Be "Located" (Standing Self-Radiant) In (and Beyond) The Right Side Of The Heart.

Nevertheless, If attention Is Strategically (or By A Seeking-Effort Of the egoic will) Directed At the objective physical space Of The Right Side Of The Heart, The By-Me-Avatarically-Self-Transmitted Divine Spiritual Under-Current (or Inherent Love-Bliss-Feeling) Of Self-Evidently Divine Happiness (Itself) Is Not Found.

The By-Me-Avatarically-Self-Transmitted Divine Spiritual Under-Current (or Inherent Love-Bliss-Feeling) Of Self-Evidently Divine Happiness Must Be "Located" Directly (and Tangibly), By Means Of ego-Transcending Receptive Heart-Response To My Avatarically Self-Transmitted Divine Spiritual Grace (and Not By Strategic ego-Effort, Which Only Reinforces The Totality Of psycho-physical self-Contraction, and The "Problem" Of Un-Happiness, Itself)—and This "Locating" Process Develops In (and By The Exercise Of) Mere Feeling-Awareness, Merely By Feeling Toward The Inherent Attractiveness Of My Self-"Bright" Avatarically-Born Bodily (Human) Divine Form, and My Avatarically Self-Transmitted Divine Spiritual (and Whole-bodily-Tangible) Presence, and My Avatarically Self-Revealed Divine State Of Self-Existing and Self-Radiant and Self-Evidently Divine Happiness (or Love-Bliss-Being) Itself, and By (Thus and Thereby) Effectively Relinquishing (or Inherently Transcending) attention (and Whole-bodily-Bondage) To conditional objects, others, forms, thoughts, states, processes, or "things" of any kind.

If Such "Perfect Practice" Of The Exercise Of Feeling-Awareness Is Persistently Maintained (By My Perfectly Listening and Perfectly Hearing and Perfectly Seeing Devotee), The By-Me-Avatarically-Self-Transmitted Divine Spiritual Under-Current (or Inherent Love-Bliss-Feeling) Of Self-Evidently Divine Happiness (Itself) Will (In Due Course, By Means Of My Avatarically Self-Transmitted Divine Spiritual Grace, or As My Avatarically Self-Transmitted Divine Spiritual Grace Will Have It) Be (Thus, Thereby, and Spontaneously) "Located" In (or Via) and Beyond The Right Side Of The Heart.

In The Perfectly Listening and Perfectly Hearing and Perfectly Seeing Practice Of The Only-By-Me Revealed and Given Way Of The Heart, all arising conditions (or "things" of attention) Are (In, and By The Exercise Of, Mere Feeling-Awareness) To Be Merely Felt (or Tacitly Observed), and Not Sought.

In The Perfectly Listening and Perfectly Hearing and Perfectly Seeing Practice Of The Only-By-Me Revealed and Given Way Of The Heart, all arising conditions (or "things" of attention) Are To Be Merely Felt (or Tacitly Observed) as they (Spontaneously, or Automatically) arise.

In The Perfectly Listening and Perfectly Hearing and Perfectly Seeing Practice Of The Only-By-Me Revealed and Given Way Of The Heart, all arising conditions (or "things" of attention) Are To Be Merely Felt (or Tacitly Observed)—moment to moment, and In Two (or Three, or More Than Three) Periods Of Formal Meditation (daily, and, Also, On Occasions Of Formal Retreat).

Therefore, If You (As My Formally Practicing Devotee) Have Listened To Me Perfectly, and If You (Thus and Thereby) Hear Me Perfectly, and If You (Thus and Thereby) Also See Me Perfectly, and If You (Thus, and, Necessarily, Formally) Choose The "Perfect Practice" (or Perfectly Direct Heart-Practice) Of The Only-By-Me Revealed and Given Way Of The Heart, Then (Constantly, and By Means Of The Perfectly Mature Practice Of Ruchira Avatara Bhakti Yoga) Merely (and Only) Feel (or Tacitly Observe) the self-Contraction and all its "things".

Merely (and Only) Feel (or Constantly, Tacitly Observe) all "things" (or all objects, all others, all forms, all states, all relations, the body-mind itself, all psycho-physical processes, all sensations, all Natural energies, all perceptions, all emotions, all responses, all reactions, all desires, and all thoughts).

Merely (and Only) Feel (or Constantly, Tacitly Observe) all gross phenomena, all subtle phenomena, all frontal (or Descending) phenomena, and all spinal (or Ascending) phenomena.

Merely (and Only) Feel (or Constantly, Tacitly Observe) all experiences, all perceptions, all forms of knowing, all Strategic gestures (or Seeking-Efforts) of attention (and of the Total body-mind)—and Merely (and Only) Feel (or Constantly, Tacitly Observe) The Root-Feeling (or "causal Stress") Of Relatedness (Itself).

Therefore, any "thing" and every "thing" that arises Should Be Merely and Only Felt—and (Thus and Thereby) Tacitly Observed—and Feeling-Awareness (Itself) Should (Even In The Exercise Of Merely Feeling all "things") Always Tacitly Feel Itself, and (Thus and Thereby) Merely and Only Feel My Avatarically Self-Transmitted Spirit-Current Of Self-Evidently Divine Love-Bliss (Always Already Free-Standing, Prior To all "things").

Any and every "thing" that arises (whether outside or inside, or to the right or to the left, or below or above, or as thought or as knowledge, or as emotional feeling or as perception, or as any experience at all) Is To Be "Located" In (and By The Exercise Of) Mere Feeling—and (Thus) Compared (In Mere Feeling) To The Perfect Happiness Of The By-Me-Avatarically-Self-Transmitted Spirit-Current Of Self-Evidently Divine Love-Bliss, and Discriminated (In Mere Feeling) From The Self-Evidently Divine Happiness Of The By-Me-Avatarically-Self-Transmitted Spirit-Current Of Self-Evidently Divine Love-Bliss, and Inherently (or Priorly and Perfectly) Transcended In The Inherent Sufficiency and Perfect Satisfactoriness Of The Mere Feeling Of The By-Me-Avatarically-Self-Transmitted Spirit-Current Of Self-Evidently Divine Love-Bliss—Without Otherwise thinking about any and every "thing" that arises.

This Inherently Perfect Exercise (or "Perfect Practice") Of Merely (and Only) Feeling My Avatarically Self-Transmitted Spirit-Current Of Self-Evidently Divine Love-Bliss, While (Coincidently, or Simultaneously) Merely (and Only) Feeling whatever arises (or any and every "thing" that arises), Should Be A Tacit (or Non-mental, or thought-free) "Feeling-Enquiry", By (and Into) Feeling (or The Feeling-Awareness Of Merely Being), Rather Than An Exercise Of thinking (or, Altogether, Of Total psycho-physical self-Contraction).

Merely Feel (and, Thus, Tacitly, or Merely and Only, Observe) whatever arises (as any and every "thing" that arises).

Whatever arises, Merely Feel it—and (Thus) Tacitly Compare it To The Perfect Feeling, Self-Evidently Divine Happiness, or Eternal and Unconditional

Love-Bliss Of My Avatarically Self-Transmitted Divine Spiritual Presence Of Person (Which, For My Perfectly Searchlessly Me-Beholding Devotee, Is Always Already, and Simultaneously, Coinciding With any and every "thing" that presently arises).

If Perfect (and Truly "Radical", or "Gone-To-The-Root") self-Understanding Of the ego-"I" Is Real, Right, and Effective, Then whatever Is conditionally arising Is Merely Felt (or Tacitly Observed), and Is (Thus and Thereby) Directly (or Immediately, and Tacitly) Understood To be mere self-Contraction (or The ego-Based psycho-physical Illusion Of Separateness, Relatedness, and "Difference").

If Perfect (and Truly "Radical" or "Gone-To-The-Root") self-Understanding Of the ego-"I" Is Demonstrated As The "Perfect Practice" Of Really, Rightly, and Effectively Transcending The Totality Of psycho-physical self-Contraction, Then whatever Is conditionally arising Is Inherently Identified (as mere self-Contraction) and Immediately Transcended (or Ignored, Released, and Forgotten) In My Avatarically Self-Transmitted Spirit-Current Of Self-Evidently Divine Love-Bliss and My Avatarically Self-Revealed Divine State Of Mere Feeling-Awareness Of The Inherent Feeling Of Mere Being (Itself).

Whatever Is (By Means Of The "Perfect Practice" Of The Devotional and Spiritual Relationship To Me) Steadily Ignored, Released, and Forgotten In Me Is "Radically" (or "At-The-Root") and Immediately (and Really, and Directly) Transcended In The By-Me-Avatarically-Self-Transmitted (and Self-Evidently Divine) Love-Bliss-Current That Is The Inherent (and Inherently egoless) Being-Feeling Of Consciousness (or The One and Only and Inherently Indivisible Conscious Light) Itself.

To Merely Feel (or, By Standing As Mere Feeling-Awareness, To Tacitly Observe) whatever conditionally arises—and (Thus) To Perfectly (and "Radically", or "At-The-Root") self-Understand, Steadily Ignore, Really Effectively Release, Effortlessly (Tacitly) Forget, and Truly Perfectly Transcend whatever conditionally arises Is The "Perfect Practice" (or Inherent Realization) Of "Divine Ignorance", The Un-conditional Realization Of Reality, Truth, or Real God (or The Inherently Perfect, and Perfectly "Knowledgeless", Awareness Of What Is—As What Is).

Therefore, If You (As My Formally Practicing Devotee) Have Listened To Me Perfectly, and If You (Thus and Thereby) Hear Me Perfectly, and If You (Thus and Thereby) Also See Me Perfectly, and If You (Thus, and, Necessarily, Formally) Choose The "Perfect Practice" (or Perfectly Direct Heart-Practice) Of The Only-By-Me Revealed and Given Way Of The Heart, Then (By Means Of The Perfectly Mature Practice Of Ruchira Avatara Bhakti Yoga) Merely (In every moment) Feel whatever conditionally arises, and (In Mere Feeling)

Discriminate it From The Self-Evidently Divine Happiness (or Uncreated, Unchanging, and Undying Love-Bliss-Joy Of Mere Being) Avatarically (and Spiritually) Self-Transmitted and Avatarically (and Divinely) Self-Revealed—By Me, and As Me.

Whatever conditionally arises—Feel Thus.

Is this presently arising condition (of body, emotion, mind, and life-breath) Happiness?

Is this moment (of perceiving, reacting, thinking, and mortal breathing) Happiness?

Is this (or any other) moment (of conditionally arising experiencing and knowing) Happiness?

"Feel-Enquire" Thus.

Compare Thus.

This moment of conditions is Not Happiness.

This ego-"I" of experiencing and knowing is Not Happiness.

Discriminate Thus.

Feel The Feeling Of My Avatarically Self-Transmitted Spirit-Current Of Self-Evidently Divine Love-Bliss-Happiness Itself—Thus.

In every moment, and By Such "Feeling-Enquiry", the limited and limiting condition that is Apparently presently conditionally arising—and Even All The moment to moment Bondage Of ego-"I" and "things"—Should Be Thus (Inherently and Freely) Relinquished, Spontaneously Released, and Easily Felt Through—To Me (and In Me), Until Only I Am The Feeling-Awareness (Of My Avatarically Self-Transmitted Spirit-Current Of Self-Evidently Divine Love-Bliss) Itself.

Whatever (and all that) conditionally arises (In The Total Pattern Of always limited and temporary conditions That Is The Cosmic Mandala, or Cosmic Domain) Begins To Be Ignored, Released, and Forgotten In the very moment Of Discovery That the presently conditionally arising condition (or any "thing" of attention) Is Not (and Never Is, and Never Can Be) Inherent (and Self-Evidently Divine) Happiness, Perfect Joy, Perfect Satisfactoriness, or The Centerless and Boundless Realization Of Self-Evidently Divine Love-Bliss Itself.

If You (As My Formally Practicing Devotee) Have Listened To Me Perfectly, and If You (Thus and Thereby) Hear Me Perfectly, and If You (Thus and Thereby) Also See Me Perfectly, and If You (Thus, and, Necessarily, Formally) Choose The "Perfect Practice" (or Perfectly Direct Heart-Practice) Of The Only-By-Me Revealed and Given Way Of The Heart, Then (By Means Of The Perfectly Mature Practice Of Ruchira Avatara Bhakti Yoga) Feel Thus, moment to moment, and (Thus) Feel Through whatever arises as a limitation On Mere Feeling-Awareness and As An Apparent Objective Modification (or conditional limitation) Of The By-Me-Avatarically-Self-Transmitted Spirit-Current Of Self-Evidently Divine Love-Bliss-Happiness Itself.

Always (Persistently) Feel, and Feel Through, and Feel Prior To whatever presently conditionally arises.

By This Discriminative "Feeling-Enquiry", Feel Toward Me (Avatarically Self-Transmitted As The Tangibly Felt Spirit-Current Of Self-Evidently Divine Love-Bliss Itself), Until Prior (or Inherent, and Inherently egoless, and Always Already Perfect, and Self-Evidently Divine) Happiness Itself Is Most Perfectly Realized (As Is).

The By-Me-Avatarically-Self-Transmitted Divine Spiritual Under-Current Of The all-and-All-Underlying Mere Feeling Of Mere Being (Itself) Is The Heart—The Self-Evidently Divine Self-Condition (Of Happiness Itself) That Is (Apparently) Being Modified (or conditionally limited) as all conditional objects, others, forms, thoughts, states, processes, or "things".

If attention Is Allowed To Move Toward its conditional objects, others, forms, thoughts, states, processes, or "things", Then Consciousness Itself (Otherwise Self-Conscious As The Mere Feeling Of Mere Being) Feels limited by and to those objects, others, forms, thoughts, states, processes, or "things".

If Consciousness (or Mere Feeling-Awareness) Itself Feels limited to conditional objects, others, forms, thoughts, states, processes, or "things", Then (Self-Evidently Divine, or Inherent and Most Perfect) Happiness Itself (and The Mere Feeling Of Mere Being, Which Is Consciousness Itself) Seems To Be Diminished, or Even Lost.

If attention Moves Toward (and Makes Contact With) "desirable" (or Even un-"desirable", but "interesting") objects, others, forms, thoughts, states, processes, or "things", The Feeling-Presumption Of Happiness Seems (Temporarily, or Only In that moment) To Be Acquired and Attained, Such That The Feeling Of Happiness Seems (By merely conditional experiential means) To Be No Longer Diminished or Lost.

All Of That ("No", and Then "Yes", and Then "No" Again—and So On) Is The Processional (and Entirely conditional, and Always changing) Illusion Of attention.

All Of That Is the mind.

All Of That Is The "Difference" the mind Makes.

The mind Is The Event and The Illusion Of attention.

Even "desirable" (or otherwise "interesting") objects, others, forms, thoughts, states, processes, or "things" Only (and Only Apparently) limit (and Effectively Diminish, or Lose) The Feeling Of Happiness.

The Diminishment (or Even The Loss) Of The Feeling Of Happiness May Seem Great and Profound In the experience of merely un-"desirable" (or un-"interesting") objects, others, forms, thoughts, states, processes, or "things"—Whereas It May Otherwise Seem (Only Because Of The Contrast In experience) That The Feeling Of Happiness Is Greatly and Profoundly Acquired (or Attained) In the experience of "desirable" (or "interesting") objects, others, forms, thoughts, states, processes, or "things".

All Of That ("No", and Then "Yes", and Then "No" Again—and So On) Is The Processional (and Entirely conditional, and Always changing) Illusion Of mind.

All Of That Is The Illusion Of "Difference" (or Of Duality—or Of The Apparent Divisibility Of Reality, Truth, or Real God).

All "Difference" Is The Illusory Event Of attention.

The Illusory Event Of attention Stands In Clear View—and Every Illusion (or "Difference") Of mind Is Directly Transcended—By Constant (Tacit) Feeling-Observation and Feeling-Release Of all conditional objects, others, forms, thoughts, states, and processes (or all "things") In My Avatarically Self-Transmitted Spirit-Current Of Self-Evidently Divine Love-Bliss (Which Divinely Self-Reveals The Inherently Non-"Different", Non-Dual, and Indivisible "Root"-Condition, or Source-Condition and Self-Condition, Of The All and every-"thing" That conditionally arises).

Therefore, If You (As My Formally Practicing Devotee) Have Listened To Me Perfectly, and If You (Thus and Thereby) Hear Me Perfectly, and If You (Thus and Thereby) Also See Me Perfectly, and If You (Thus, and, Necessarily, Formally) Choose The "Perfect Practice" (or Perfectly Direct Heart-Practice) Of The Only-By-Me Revealed and Given Way Of The Heart, Then (By Means Of The Perfectly Mature Practice Of Ruchira Avatara Bhakti Yoga) Constantly (and By The Tacit Exercise Of Mere Feeling-Awareness) Discriminate whatever arises conditionally (and which Is Not Unqualified, or Un-conditional, and Self-Evidently Divine Happiness Itself) From The By-Me-Avatarically-Self-Transmitted Spirit-Current Of Self-Evidently Divine Love-Bliss Itself (Which Is Self-Evidently Divine Happiness Itself).

In This Manner, Constantly (and Merely By Feeling) Notice and Release whatever Is Not (Self-Evidently Divine) Happiness Itself.

In This Manner, Constantly Dissolve (or Feel Through) the arising "things", and Always Feel (or Dissolve) Toward and Into My Avatarically Self-Transmitted Spirit-Current Of Self-Evidently Divine Love-Bliss (Itself), Until Unqualified (or Un-conditional) and Self-Evidently Divine Happiness (Itself) Is Most Perfectly Realized (As and By Means Of My Avatarically Self-Transmitted Manifestation Of The Divine Spiritual Under-Current Of The Heart).

If The In-Place Feeling Of Being (Itself) Is "Located" Via The Tacit Exercise Of Mere Feeling-Awareness (Itself), Such That (By Means Of My Avatarically

Self-Transmitted Divine Spiritual Grace) You Directly and Spontaneously Inhere In, Intrinsically Identify With, and Tacitly (and Effortlessly) Self-Abide As My Avatarically Self-Transmitted Spiritual Under-Current Of Self-Evidently Divine Love-Bliss-Happiness In (and Prior To) The Right Side Of The Heart, Then Unqualified (or Un-conditional) and Self-Evidently Divine Happiness Itself, Which Is The Inherent (or Self-Existing and Self-Radiant) Mere Feeling Of Mere Being, Will (By Means Of My Avatarically Self-Transmitted Divine Spiritual Grace) Be Self-Realized To Be Consciousness (or Conscious Light) Itself.

Unqualified (or Un-conditional) and Self-Evidently Divine Happiness Itself (or The Most Perfect Realization Of The Inherent Mere Feeling Of Mere Being, or Of The Self-Existing Self-Radiance Of The Divine Conscious Light Itself) Is (By Means Of My Avatarically Self-Transmitted Divine Spiritual Grace) Divinely (and Spiritually) Self-Revealed (or Made Obvious), If attention to conditionally arising "things" Is (By The Tacit Exercise Of Mere Feeling-Awareness) Merely Felt (or Tacitly Observed) and Spontaneously Relinquished In The "Feeling-Enquiry" Toward (or In, and As) My Avatarically Self-Transmitted Spirit-Current Of Self-Evidently Divine Love-Bliss (Which Is Unqualified, or Un-conditional, and Self-Evidently Divine Happiness Itself).

Therefore, By Means Of Real and Effective Practice Of The Devotional and Spiritual Relationship To Me (Which Relationship, Rightly and Truly Practiced, Is, Itself, The One and Only By-Me-Revealed and By-Me-Given Way Of The Heart, or Way Of Adidam), Be Awakened To This "Radical" (or "At-The-Root") self-Understanding Of attention and the "things" of conditional experience—and, If You (Thus, and, Necessarily, Formally) Choose The "Perfect Practice" (or Perfectly Direct Heart-Practice) Of The Only-By-Me Revealed and Given Way Of The Heart, Then (By Means Of The Perfectly Mature Practice Of Ruchira Avatara Bhakti Yoga) Directly and Really Feel, "Locate", Inhere In, Intrinsically Identify With, Tacitly (and Effortlessly) Self-Abide As, and (In Due Course) Most Perfectly Realize Unqualified (or Un-conditional) and Self-Evidently Divine Happiness Itself.

By "Locating" Me (Devotionally and Spiritually), "Locate" (Self-Evidently Divine) Happiness Itself—Directly and Really.

By Inhering In Me (Devotionally and Spiritually), Inhere In (Self-Evidently Divine) Happiness Itself—Directly and Really.

By Abiding In Me (Devotionally and Spiritually), Self-Abide As (Self-Evidently Divine) Happiness Itself—Directly and Really.

By Identifying With Me (Devotionally and Spiritually), Identify With (Self-Evidently Divine) Happiness Itself—Directly and Really.

By Realizing Me (Devotionally and Spiritually), Realize (Self-Evidently Divine) Happiness Itself—Directly and Really.

By Standing With Me (Devotionally and Spiritually), Stand At, In, and As (Self-Evidently Divine) Happiness Itself—Relinquishing All That Is Not (Self-Evidently Divine) Happiness Itself.

By Means Of My Avatarically Self-Transmitted Divine Spiritual Grace, Stand As (Self-Evidently Divine) Happiness Itself—Prior To The Urge Of attention Toward Apparent "things" (or All Apparent Modifications and limitations Of The By-Me-Avatarically-Self-Transmitted Spiritual Heart-Current Of Self-Evidently Divine Love-Bliss, or Self-Evidently Divine Happiness Itself).

By Means Of My Avatarically Self-Transmitted Divine Spiritual Grace, Stand In The Well (or By-Me-Avatarically-Self-Transmitted Divine Spiritual Heart-Current Of Mere Feeling-Awareness) Of Being, Directly and Spontaneously Revealed (By Me) and Felt (In Place, and As Self-Evidently Divine Love-Bliss, or Self-Evidently Divine Happiness Itself) In (and Beyond) The Right Side Of The Heart.

By Means Of My Avatarically Self-Transmitted Divine Spiritual Grace, Stand In (and As) The Well (or Self-Evident Fullness) Of The By-Me-Avatarically-Self-Transmitted Spiritual Heart-Current Of Unqualified (or Un-conditional) and Self-Evidently Divine Love-Bliss (or Self-Evidently Divine Happiness Itself)—With No "Other"-Motive.

By Means Of My Avatarically Self-Transmitted Divine Spiritual Grace, Stand As Consciousness Itself (Merely, Tacitly Felt, As The Mere Feeling-Awareness Of Being, Itself), Self-Existing and Self-Radiant As My Avatarically Self-Transmitted Spiritual Heart-Current Of Self-Evidently Divine Love-Bliss, Prior To the body-mind and its relations (or "things").

Moment to moment, Irrespective Of what is Apparently arising to attention, "Locate" My Avatarically Self-Transmitted Spiritual Heart-Current Of Self-Evidently Divine Love-Bliss—"There", At The Origin (or The Perfectly Subjective Seat, or The Most Prior Self-Position) Of attention, and As The mindless (and Inherently egoless) Transcendental, Inherently Spiritual, and Self-Evidently Divine Source-Condition and Self-Condition Of attention.

Therefore, If You (As My Formally Practicing Devotee) Have Listened To Me Perfectly, and If You (Thus and Thereby) Hear Me Perfectly, and If You (Thus and Thereby) Also See Me Perfectly, and If You (Thus, and, Necessarily, Formally) Choose The "Perfect Practice" (or The Perfectly Direct Heart-Practice) Of The Only-By-Me Revealed and Given Way Of The Heart, Then (By Means Of The Perfectly Mature Practice Of Ruchira Avatara Bhakti Yoga) Merely (In every moment) Feel Me, By Feeling Through All Else To Me, Until The Uncaused and Unthreatened Feeling Of Unqualified, Un-conditional, Unlimited, Unmodified, and Self-Evidently Divine Happiness Is "Located" (As and By Means Of My Avatarically Self-Transmitted Spirit-Current Of Self-Evidently Divine Love-Bliss) At The Heart.

Through (Thus) Discriminative "Feeling-Enquiry", Constantly Renounce (or Relinquish and Transcend) attention to "things".

Through (Thus) Discriminative "Feeling-Enquiry", Constantly Renounce (or Relinquish and Transcend) attention to the body-mind.

Through (Thus) Discriminative "Feeling-Enquiry", Constantly Renounce (or Relinquish and Transcend) The Modification, limitation, Diminishment, and Loss Of The By-Me-Avatarically-Self-Transmitted Spirit-Current Of Self-Evidently Divine Love-Bliss (and, Thus and Thereby, Constantly Renounce, or Relinquish and Transcend, The Modification, limitation, Diminishment, and Loss Of The Unqualified, or Un-conditional, Feeling Of Self-Evidently Divine Happiness Itself).

Through (Thus) Discriminative "Feeling-Enquiry", Constantly Feel Toward, and Into, and As My Avatarically Self-Transmitted Spirit-Current Of Self-Evidently Divine Love-Bliss—and (Thus and Thereby) Toward, and Into, and As The Unqualified (or Un-conditional, and Un-Diminished) Feeling Of Self-Evidently Divine Happiness (or The Tacit Mere Feeling-Awareness Of Inherently Free and Self-Existing and Self-Radiant Being).

The Inherent (and Inherently Not Modified, and Inherently Not Objectified) Tacit Mere Feeling-Awareness Of Being, Which Is Unqualified (or Unconditional, and Un-Diminished) and Self-Evidently Divine Happiness (Itself), Is Always "There", "Where" My Avatarically Self-Transmitted Spirit-Current Of Self-Evidently Divine Love-Bliss Is To Be "Located" (By Means Of "Feeling-Enquiry"), Behind, Beneath, and Prior To attention and every "thing" (and, Thus, "Where" and As You Always Already, and Inherently egolessly, Stand).

If You Will Constantly (moment to moment) "Locate" That (Most Prior, Tacit) Mere Feeling-Awareness Of Being (Directly, Really, and Spontaneously Revealed, By Means Of My Avatarically Self-Transmitted Spirit-Current Of Self-Evidently Divine Love-Bliss, In and Beyond The Right Side Of The Heart), attention to conditionally arising "things" (or All Apparent Modifications Of My Avatarically Self-Transmitted Spirit-Current Of Self-Evidently Divine Love-Bliss-Feeling) Will Relax or Fall or Subside or Resolve In That By-Me-Avatarically-Self-Transmitted Spirit-Current Of Self-Evidently Divine Love-Bliss (and The Most Prior, Tacit Mere Feeling Of Mere Being, Itself).

The Direct and Real Tangible "Locating" (or Searchless Beholding) Of My Avatarically Self-Transmitted Spirit-Current, and My Avatarically Self-Revealed Person, Of Self-Evidently Divine Love-Bliss Is The Inherently Perfect (and Primary) Form Of Spirit-"Conductivity" Practice (or Of ego-Transcending Devotional Surrender To My Avatarically Self-Transmitted Spirit-Current, and My Avatarically Self-Revealed Person, Of Self-Evidently Divine Love-Bliss)—and, Through This "Perfect Practice" Of Devotional Surrender To Me, You Are

Spiritually Attracted (and Drawn, and Even "Tugged", and Carried) By Me, Into The Domain Of The Right Side Of The Heart, and, Then, Beyond The "causal Knot" (or Beyond The Original egoic Contraction) In The Right Side Of The Heart, and (Thus and Thereby) Profoundly Moved and Released Into My Love-Blissful Divine Spiritual Domain Of Self-Existing and Self-Radiant Consciousness Itself (Divinely Self-Realized As The Sphere and "Brightness" Of The One and Only and Inherently egoless and Inherently Indivisible and Self-Evidently Divine Conscious Light Itself).

In The Context Of The "Perfect Practice" Of The Only-By-Me Revealed and Given Way Of The Heart (or Way Of Adidam), The Exercise Of The Basic (or "General") Forms Of Spirit-"Conductivity" (Responsively Engaged, On The Always Prior Base Of Spiritual Reception Of Me By Means Of The Primary, or Searchlessly Me-Beholding, Practice) Remains Appropriate (and Generally Necessary) In Random ordinary (or daily-life) moments—but, In The Most Intensive (and, Most Characteristically, Formal Meditative) Exercise Of The "Perfect Practice" Of The "Conscious Process" Of "Feeling-Enquiry", Either (At times) No Other (or Additional) Forms Of Spirit-"Conductivity" Practice Are To Be Responsively Added To The Primary (Searchlessly Me-Beholding) Practice Of Whole bodily (or Total psycho-physical) Surrender To (and Into) My Avatarically Self-Transmitted Spirit-Current Of Self-Evidently Divine Love-Bliss Or (At other times) The Basic (or "General") Forms Of Responsive Spirit-"Conductivity" Practice May Be Additionally Applied Or (At Yet other times) The Unique ("Samraj Yoga") Practice Of "Radical" Spirit-"Conductivity" (Which Is Avatarically Revealed By Me, and Avatarically Given By Me, For Formal "Perfect Practice" Application, Only To Fully Qualified Devotees, and Only Through Formal Initiation and Instruction Via The Senior Practicing Members Of The Ruchira Sannyasin Order Of Adidam Ruchiradam) May, Otherwise (In Accordance With My Explicit Instructions), Be Additionally Applied.

The "Radically" Direct "Perfect Practice" Of The "Conscious Process" Of Immediate Realization Of The Truth Of "things" Is The Only-By-Me Revealed and Given Inherently Perfect Form Of The "Conscious Process" Of The Divine "Worship" Of Consciousness Itself.

Therefore, Even Though Various Previously-Established Forms Of The Only-By-Me Revealed and Given "Conscious Process" (Associated Either With The Devotional Way Of Faith Or The Devotional Way Of Insight) Remain Appropriate (and Generally Necessary) In Random ordinary (or daily-life) moments, No Other (or Less Than "Radically" Direct) Form Of The Only-By-Me Revealed and Given "Conscious Process" Is Necessary (or Even Appropriate) In The Circumstance (Most Characteristically, In Periods Of Formal Meditation) In Which The "Perfect Practice" Of "Feeling-Enquiry" Is Intensively Engaged.

My Beloved (every one), Always "Consider" What Is (Inherently) Perfect, and When (As My Formally Practicing Devotee) Your Devotional and Spiritual Practice Of The Only-By-Me Revealed and Given Way Of The Heart Has, By Means Of My Avatarically Self-Transmitted Divine Spiritual Grace, Become Perfect, You Must (In Full Accordance With My Specific Instructions) Practice The Perfect Feeling-Awareness Of The Heart, In The Specific (Only-By-Me Revealed and Given) Manner Of "Feeling-Enquiry" (or "Hridaya-Vichara").

If The (Inherently Perfect, and Inherently ego-Transcending) "Perfect Practice" Of "Feeling-Enquiry" Has (Thus) Become Your Formal Obligation and Capability, Then (While Standing As Mere Feeling-Awareness) Tacitly Observe That (Coincident With whatever conditionally arises—or whatever objects, others, forms, thoughts, states, processes, or "things" Stimulate and Distract attention) There Is a Corresponding emotion (or conditionally arising emotional sensation).

Therefore, whatever (presently) conditionally arises, Feel the Coincident feeling (or conditionally arising emotion) Associated With it, and (While Standing As Mere Feeling-Awareness) Tacitly Observe That the conditionally arising emotion Associated With the present conditions of attention Is Not Unqualified and Unlimited (and Self-Evidently Divine) Happiness.

Then (While Standing As Mere Feeling-Awareness), Feel Toward My Avatarically Self-Transmitted Spirit-Current Of Self-Evidently Divine Love-Bliss (or Self-Evidently Divine Happiness Itself), and (Thus) "Locate" The (By-Me-Avatarically-Self-Revealed) all-and-All-Underlying Feeling In Which the present lesser feeling is conditionally arising.

In This Manner, Constantly Transcend lesser (or merely conditionally arising) feelings In (and By Means Of) My Avatarically Self-Transmitted Spiritual Under-Current Of Self-Evidently Divine Love-Bliss (or Self-Evidently Divine Happiness Itself).

Always "Feel-Enquire" In This Manner, and, Thus (By Always Self-Abiding As Mere Feeling-Awareness, Tacitly "Locating" My Avatarically Self-Transmitted Spirit-Current Of Self-Evidently Divine Love-Bliss, or Self-Evidently Divine Happiness Itself), Be Constantly Re-Established As The Constant Under-Current (and Tacit Feeling) Of Mere Being.

Beneath every kind of lesser feeling (or conditionally arising emotional sensation) that Coincides With attention to conditionally arising "things", There is Only One Basic lesser feeling that Always arises On The Constant Base Of The By-Me-Avatarically-Self-Transmitted Spiritual Under-Current Of Self-Evidently Divine Love-Bliss (or Self-Evidently Divine Happiness Itself).

The One Basic lesser feeling that Always Coincides With attention to any object, other, form, thought, state, process, or "thing" is The Feeling (or conditionally arising emotional sensation) Of Separativeness, Separation, and Separateness.

The conditionally arising emotional sensation Of Separativeness, Separation, and Separateness that Always Coincides With every act of attention Is The Basic emotional Sign Of the self-Contraction.

Therefore, mere attention, attention to conditionally arising "things", or every act of attention to objects, others, forms, thoughts, states, and processes is (itself) The Habit Of "Narcissus" (Otherwise Expressed As The Complex Avoidance Of Relationship).

The Habit Of "Narcissus" (or The Complex Avoidance Of Relationship) Is Directly and Inherently Transcended In (or At) The Heart, By Means Of Mere Feeling-Awareness Of My Avatarically Self-Transmitted Spiritual Under-Current Of Self-Evidently Divine Love-Bliss (or Self-Evidently Divine Happiness Itself).

Therefore, If You (As My Formally Practicing Devotee) Have Listened To Me Perfectly, and If You (Thus and Thereby) Hear Me Perfectly, and If You (Thus and Thereby) Also See Me Perfectly, and If You (Thus, and, Necessarily, Formally) Choose The "Perfect Practice" Of "Feeling-Enquiry", Then (By Means Of The Perfectly Mature Practice Of Ruchira Avatara Bhakti Yoga) Constantly "Locate" My Avatarically Self-Transmitted Spiritual Under-Current Of Self-Evidently Divine Love-Bliss (or Self-Evidently Divine Happiness Itself).

Thus (By Means Of "Feeling-Enquiry"), Constantly "Consider" (or Merely Feel, Relinquish, and Stand Prior To) "Narcissus", The emotional Act (and conditionally arising emotional sensation) Of Separativeness, Separation, and Separateness.

While Always Standing As Mere Feeling-Awareness, Always "Feel-Enquire" Toward The By-Me-Avatarically-Self-Transmitted Spiritual Under-Current Of Self-Evidently Divine Love-Bliss-Feeling That Is Always Already Prior To "Narcissus" (or the Total psycho-physical self-Contraction), and (Thus) Feel (and Be Constantly Re-Established As) The Constant Under-Current (and Tacit Feeling) Of Mere Being (or Self-Evidently Divine Happiness Itself), Prior To the otherwise present act and "thing" of attention.

At The Root Of attention to any object, other, form, thought, state, process, or "thing"—Beneath every kind of lesser (or merely conditionally arising) feeling, and Even Beneath the One Basic lesser feeling that is "Narcissus" (or the Total psycho-physical self-Contraction)—There Is The Root-Feeling, mindless perception, and "causal Stress" Of Relatedness.

The Root-Feeling Of Relatedness Is The "causal Essence" (or Primal Stress) Of self-Contraction.

The Root-Feeling Of Relatedness Is The Root-"Cause" (or Primal conditional Essence) Of attention itself, and Of all conditionally arising "things", and

Of All The emotional Signs Of "Narcissus", and Of all conditionally arising feelings (or all feelings that Are Less Than Unqualified, and Unlimited, and Self-Evidently Divine Happiness Itself).

Paradoxically, The Root-Feeling (or "causal Stress") Of Relatedness Is The Root-Essence Of self-Contraction, The Root-Essence Of The Avoidance Of Relationship, and The Root-Essence Of Strategic Relationlessness.

The Root-Feeling (and "causal Stress") Of Relatedness Is The First Gesture and Very Act Of Separativeness, Separation, and Separateness, Whereby The Transcendental, Inherently Spiritual, Inherently egoless, and Self-Evidently Divine Self-Condition (and Source-Condition) That Is Unqualified and Unlimited (and Self-Evidently Divine) Happiness Is (Itself) Relinquished.

Therefore, The Root-Feeling, mindless perception, and "causal Stress" Of Relatedness Is The Principal Feeling (or conditionally arising emotional sensation) To (Tacitly) Observe and ("Radically", or By "Going To The Root") Transcend In every moment Of "Feeling-Enquiry".

The Root-Feeling and "causal Stress" Of Relatedness Is Not (Itself) Love-Bliss (or Self-Evidently Divine Happiness Itself).

The Root-Feeling and "causal Stress" Of Relatedness Is Merely The First Illusion, and The First Sign Of Bondage To All Illusions.

The Root-Feeling and "causal Stress" Of Relatedness Is The Primal Fearful Essence Of the act of attention, which Flies From Happiness (and The Heart).

The Root-Feeling and "causal Stress" Of Relatedness Is The Principal Distraction From Unqualified and Unlimited (and Self-Evidently Divine) Happiness—Because It Directly Leads To all conditional objects, others, forms, thoughts, states, and processes, or all conditionally arising "things" (or all that is Less Than Unqualified, and Unlimited, and Self-Evidently Divine Happiness Itself).

Therefore, If You (As My Formally Practicing Devotee) Have Listened To Me Perfectly, and If You (Thus and Thereby) Hear Me Perfectly, and If You (Thus and Thereby) Also See Me Perfectly, and If You (Thus, and, Necessarily, Formally) Choose The "Perfect Practice" Of "Feeling-Enquiry", Then (By Means Of The Perfectly Mature Practice Of Ruchira Avatara Bhakti Yoga) Enter Into The By-Me-Avatarically-Self-Transmitted Divine Spiritual Under-Current Of Unqualified and Unlimited (and Self-Evidently Divine) Happiness (Itself)—Prior To The "causal" Feeling-Stress Of Relatedness, Prior To attention, and Prior To any and all conditional objects, others, forms, thoughts, states, processes, or "things".

Enter The Inherently Perfect (and Inherently egoless) Self-Domain Of The Heart, By Means Of Tacit Inherent Self-Identification With My Avatarically Self-Transmitted Spirit-Current (and Inherent Being-Feeling) Of Self-Evidently

Divine Love-Bliss (or Self-Evidently Divine Happiness Itself).

Thus (By Perfectly Following Me), Enter The Inherently egoless Self-Domain Of The Heart, Constantly.

By Following Me Perfectly, Merely Be My Avatarically Self-Transmitted Spiritual Heart-Current Of Inherently egoless (and Self-Evidently Divine) Happiness, Deeply.

My Avatarically Self-Transmitted all-and-All-Underlying Spiritual Heart-Current (or Most Prior Feeling-Radiance) Of Self-Evidently Divine Love-Bliss (By Which and As Which I Would Spirit-Bless all beings) Is Unqualified (or Un-conditional) and Self-Evidently Divine Happiness Itself, Prior To All limiting Modifications.

My Avatarically Self-Transmitted all-and-All-Underlying Spiritual Heart-Current (or Most Prior Feeling-Radiance) Of Self-Evidently Divine Love-Bliss (By Which and As Which I Would Spirit-Bless all beings) Is The (Self-Radiant and Self-Existing) Spiritually "Bright" Grace Of Real God (or Truth, or The Inherently Perfect Reality), Whereby Real God (or Truth, or The Inherently Perfect Reality) Is Perfectly Realized.

Be (Thus) Blessed By Me, and (Thus) Self-Abide As That.

Such Is The Most Prior and Graceful Means Whereby (and The Very Reality Wherein) all the conditions or "things" of attention (Including The Root-Feeling and "causal Stress" Of Relatedness) Are Effectively Turned About, or Relaxed and Resolved In their Perfectly Subjective (Transcendental, Inherently Spiritual, Inherently egoless, and Self-Evidently Divine) Source, Which Is Consciousness (or Mere Feeling-Awareness) Itself.

When (and Where) all conditions of attention Dissolve In My Avatarically Self-Transmitted Spiritual Heart-Current Of Self-Evidently Divine Love-Bliss, There Consciousness (or Mere Feeling-Awareness) Itself Is.

When Even The "Location" (or The "Where") Of The Heart Is Dissolved In My Avatarically Self-Transmitted Spirit-Current Of Self-Evidently Divine Love-Bliss (Itself), Consciousness (or Mere Feeling-Awareness) Itself Is The "Seat" Of My Avataric Divine Self-Revelation.

By Means Of My Avatarically Self-Transmitted Divine Spiritual Grace, The Non-Separate (or Non-egoic) Self-Condition Of Consciousness Itself Is The Ultimate Substance Of My Avataric Divine Self-Revelation.

This Becomes Obvious: The Non-Separate (or Non-egoic) Self-Condition Of Consciousness Itself Is The Non-Separate, Inherently egoless, Inherently Indivisible, and Non-Dual Self-Condition Of Reality Itself.

The Non-Separate (or Non-egoic) Self-Condition Of Consciousness Itself Is (Non-Separately, Inherently egolessly, Inherently Indivisibly, and Non-Dually) The (One and Only) Self Of all (and Of All).

The Self Of all (and Of All) Is One, and Only, and Not Separate.

The Non-Separate, Inherently egoless, Inherently Indivisible, and Non-Dual Self Of all (and Of All) Is The Only One Who (Self-Existingly, and Self-Radiantly) Is.

The Only One (Who Is) Is Reality, or Truth—The Only Real God.

The Only One (Who Is) Is That Which Is Always Already The (One and Only) Case.

That Only (and Non-Separate) One (Who Is) Merely (or Simply) Is, Always and Already—Prior To ego-"I", Prior To Total psycho-physical self-Contraction, Prior To The Feeling-Stress Of Relatedness, Prior To attention, and Prior To The Feeling-Act Of Separativeness, Separation, and Separateness That Always Coincides With attention to any and all conditionally arising "things".

Consciousness (Itself) Is The Very (and One, and Only) Heart, Always Already (Inherently, and Now) Existing—Ever-Present (and Self-Existing) As Self-Radiant Love-Bliss-Light (Conscious As Self-Evidently Divine Happiness Itself).

The Truly ego-Surrendering, ego-Forgetting, and ego-Transcending Devotional Practice Of The Only-By-Me Revealed and Given (and Always "Radical", or "Gone-To-The-Root") Way Of The Heart Leads (In Due Course) To The Heart Itself—and The Right Practice Of "Feeling-Enquiry" Is The Ultimate and Inherently Perfect (or Inherently Perfectly ego-Surrendering, ego-Forgetting, and ego-Transcending) Devotional Practice (Of The Only-By-Me Revealed and Given Way Of The Heart) That Leads, In A Perfectly Direct Manner, To Most Perfect Spiritual Realization Of The Heart Itself (As Self-Existing and Self-Radiant Consciousness Itself).

The "Perfect Practice" Of The Only-By-Me Revealed and Given Way Of The Heart Is The Only-By-Me Revealed and Given Practice That Is Always Already Established In and As Consciousness (Itself).

The Only-By-Me Revealed and Given Practice Of "Feeling-Enquiry" Is The "Perfect Practice" Of Consciousness (or Mere Feeling-Awareness) Itself.

The Only-By-Me Revealed and Given Practice Of "Feeling-Enquiry" Awakens (and Then Develops) On The Basis Of Constant Right Listening To My Avataric Divine Word and Person, and Only After (or On The Constant Basis Of) True Hearing Of Me (or Most Fundamental self-Understanding) In Devotional Me-Recognizing Response To My Avataric Divine Word and Person—and (Altogether) Through The Devotionally Me-Recognizing and Devotionally To-Me-Responsive Practice Of Effective self-Observation, and The Devotionally Me-Recognizing and Devotionally To-Me-Responsive Practice Of Effectively (and Then Perfectly) Feeling Beyond psycho-physical self-Contraction, In and By Means Of The Avatarically Self-Transmitted Divine

Spiritual Grace Of My Avataric (and Always Blessing) Divine Company—For I Am The Divine Heart-Master, The Avatarically Self-Revealed (and Inherently egoless) Human, Spiritual, Transcendental, and Self-Evidently Divine Person Of Reality and Truth.

The (Inherently Perfect, and Inherently ego-Transcending) "Perfect Practice" Of "Feeling-Enquiry" Awakens (and Then Develops) On The Basis Of Constant and True Devotional (or Truly ego-Surrendering, ego-Forgetting, and ego-Transcending) Feeling-Contemplation Of My Avatarically-Born Bodily (Human) Divine Form and My Avatarically Self-Transmitted Spiritual (and Always Blessing) Divine Presence and My Avatarically Self-Revealed (and Very, and Transcendental, and Perfectly Subjective, and Inherently Spiritual, and Inherently egoless, and Inherently Perfect, and Self-Evidently Divine) State, and Only After (or On The Constant Basis Of) Clear (and Perfect) Seeing Of My Avatarically-Born Bodily (Human) Divine Form and My Avatarically Self-Transmitted Spiritual (and Always Blessing) Divine Presence and My Avatarically Self-Revealed (and Very, and Transcendental, and Perfectly Subjective, and Inherently Spiritual, and Inherently egoless, and Inherently Perfect, and Self-Evidently Divine) State, and (Altogether) Through Heart-Reception (and Heart-Recognition and Heart-Acknowledgement) Of My Avatarically Self-Given and Avatarically Self-Giving Divine Spiritual Blessing (or Mere and "Bright" Avataric Divine Spiritual Presence), and This To The (Perfect) Degree Of Direct (and Whole bodily, or Total psycho-physical) Awakening To My Avatarically Self-Transmitted Spiritual Heart-Current Of Self-Evidently Divine Love-Bliss, By Means Of The Avatarically Self-Transmitted Divine Spiritual Grace Of My Avataric (and Always Blessing) Divine Company—For I Am The Divine Heart-Master, The Avatarically Self-Revealed (and Inherently egoless) Human, Spiritual, Transcendental, and Self-Evidently Divine Person Of Reality and Truth.

When, In The Only-By-Me Revealed and Given Way Of The Heart, Listening To Me and Hearing Me and Seeing Me Become Suddenly Profound (and Inherently Perfect), Through The Only-By-Me Revealed and Given Avataric Divine Gift Of The "Thumbs", Such That The Search For the conditionally arising "things" Of The Circle (and The Arrow) Is No Longer The Motive Of Existence, Then "Feeling-Enquiry" Has The Necessary Basis To (Formally) Begin.

When, Suddenly (In The Only-By-Me Revealed and Given Way Of The Heart), Neither the body, Nor the mind (high or low), Nor any of the conditionally arising "things" of the body or the mind Is The Motive (or The Motivator) Of Existence, Then "Feeling-Enquiry" Has The Necessary Basis To (Formally) Begin.

When, In The Only-By-Me Revealed and Given Way Of The Heart, The Witness-Consciousness (or Mere Feeling-Awareness) Suddenly (and Stably) Becomes The Obvious Position From Which To View and To Transcend the body, the mind, attention, and all conditionally arising "things", Then "Feeling-Enquiry" Has The Necessary Basis To (Formally) Begin.

The "Perfect Practice" (and The Perfect Process) Of "Feeling-Enquiry" Most Directly and Immediately Undermines and Transcends The Outgoing (or "thing"-Seeking) Tendency Of attention.

The "Perfect Practice" (and The Perfect Process) Of "Feeling-Enquiry" Most Directly and Immediately Undermines and Transcends attention itself—or The Complex and Outgoing (or "thing"-Seeking) Habit Of Identification With the body, bodily energies, bodily desires, sensory perceptions, Reactive and conditionally Responsive emotions, and all the forms of mind (high and low).

The "Perfect Practice" (and The Perfect Process) Of "Feeling-Enquiry" Most Directly and Immediately Undermines and Transcends all the forms of psycho-physical self-Contraction (or egoity)—or All Going Out From The Heart Of Consciousness (or Mere Feeling-Awareness) Itself.

The "Perfect Practice" (and The Perfect Process) Of "Feeling-Enquiry" Most Directly and Immediately (and "Radically", or "At-The-Root") Undermines and Transcends Every Seeking-Effort Associated With The Circle (and The Arrow) Of the body-mind.

The "Perfect Practice" (and The Perfect Process) Of "Feeling-Enquiry" Most Directly and Immediately (and Perfectly) Realizes That Which Inherently Transcends The "causal Knot" In The Right Side Of The Heart.

The "Perfect Practice" (and The Perfect Process) Of "Feeling-Enquiry" Is Always Immediately Established In The Inherently Perfect Realization Of Inherent Self-Identification With Consciousness (or Mere Feeling-Awareness) Itself (Prior To all conditionally arising "things").

Inherent Self-Identification With Consciousness (or Mere Feeling-Awareness) Itself Is The Ultimate and Inherently Perfect and Inherently ego-Transcending "Perfect Practice" Of The Only-By-Me Revealed and Given Way Of The Heart.

Therefore, The "Perfect Practice" (and The Perfect Process) Of "Feeling-Enquiry" Leads (Most Ultimately) To The Great and Incomparable Realization Of Inherently (and Most Perfectly) Free (and Self-Evidently Divine) Enlightenment—Which Is "Open Eyes", Seventh Stage Sahaja Nirvikalpa Samadhi, or The "Perfect Practice" (and The Divinely Most Perfect Process) Of The Only-By-Me Revealed and Given Seventh Stage Of Life (Always Already Awake To and As The One and Only and Inherently Indivisible and Inherently egoless and Self-Evidently Divine Conscious Light Of all-and-All).

In Seventh Stage Sahaja Nirvikalpa Samadhi, The One and Only (Transcendental, Inherently Spiritual, Inherently Indivisible, Inherently egoless, and Self-Evidently Divine) Conscious Light Merely Self-Abides—Always With "Open Eyes", Merely Present (or Self-Awakened, and Self-Aware) As Itself.

When The Eternal Self-Awakeness Is Realized, The One and Only (Transcendental, Inherently Spiritual, Inherently Indivisible, Inherently egoless, and Self-Evidently Divine) Conscious Light Spontaneously (Divinely) Self-Recognizes all phenomenal conditions As Transparent (or Merely Apparent), and Un-Necessary, and Inherently Non-Binding Modifications Of Itself.

Whatever Is (Thus) Divinely Self-Recognized Is Soon A Matter Of Divine Indifference.

Whatever Is A Matter Of Divine Indifference Is (Most Ultimately, and At Last) Outshined In and By and As The One and Only (Transcendental, Inherently Spiritual, Inherently Indivisible, Inherently egoless, and Self-Evidently Divine) Conscious Light.

When The Totality Of conditional Existence (or all conditionally arising "things", including the body-mind) Is Outshined In and By and As Love-Bliss (or The Self-Existing Self-Radiance Of The One and Only and Inherently Indivisible Conscious Light), That Is Divine Translation In The "Bright" (or Realization Of My Divine "Bright" Spherical Self-Domain).

The Inherently Perfect and Inherently ego-Transcending "Practice" Of The Only-By-Me Revealed and Given Seventh Stage Of Life (Which Is The "Practicing" Course Of Ati-Ruchira Yoga, or The Yoga Of The All-Outshining "Brightness") Is Simply (or Inherently) To Self-Abide As The One and Only and Inherently Indivisible Conscious Light Itself (Self-Existing and Self-Radiant As Love-Bliss, or Unqualified, Un-conditional, and Self-Evidently Divine Happiness Itself).

The Inherently Perfect and Inherently ego-Transcending "Practice" Of The Only-By-Me Revealed and Given Seventh Stage Of Life Is To Self-Abide As The One and Only and Inherently Indivisible Conscious Light Itself, Inherently and Spontaneously (and Divinely) Self-Recognizing the body, the mind, attention, and all conditionally arising "things" As Transparent (or Merely Apparent), and Un-Necessary, and Inherently Non-Binding Modifications Of Itself.

The Inherently Perfect and Inherently ego-Transcending "Practice" Of The Only-By-Me Revealed and Given Seventh Stage Of Life Is Simply To Be The One and Only and Inherently Indivisible Conscious Light Itself, Inherently (and Divinely) Self-Recognizing all conditionally arising "things" (including the body, the mind, and attention), and Even (and Divinely) Self-Recognizing The Self-Existing (and Perfectly Subjective) Divine Self-Radiance Itself (Which Is The "Bright" Itself), As Consciousness Itself, and Not "other" Than (or "Different"

From, or Separate From, or Standing Over Against, or Related To) Consciousness Itself, or Capable Of Binding (or limiting) Consciousness Itself, or Able To Change Consciousness Itself.

The Inherently Perfect and Inherently ego-Transcending "Practice" Of The Only-By-Me Revealed and Given Seventh Stage Of Life Is To Self-Abide As The One and Only and Inherently Indivisible Conscious Light (Which Is Self-Existing and Self-Radiant Consciousness, or Mere Feeling-Awareness, Itself), and (Thus) To Divinely Self-Recognize (or Ignore, Release, Forget, Inherently Transcend, and Stand Free Of) all conditions that arise.

The Inherently egoless "Practice" Of The Only-By-Me Revealed and Given Seventh Stage Of Life Is (Simply, or Inherently, and Always Already) To Self-Abide As The One and Only and Inherently Indivisible Conscious Light Itself, and (As The One and Only and Inherently Indivisible Conscious Light, or Self-Existing and Self-Radiant Consciousness, or Mere Feeling-Awareness, Itself) To Divinely Self-Recognize (and, Simply Thus, To Ignore, Release, Forget, Inherently Transcend, and Stand Always Already Free Of) Descent, Ascent, all worlds, body, mind, all thoughts, all relations, all objects, others, forms, states, and processes, all experience, all knowledge, all pains, all conditional (or limited and limiting) pleasures, All Fear, Sorrow, and Anger, All Avoidance, All Separativeness, All Separation, All Separateness, All Seeking, all conditionally arising "things", attention itself, The Root-Feeling and "causal Stress" Of Relatedness, self-Contraction itself, All Un-Happiness, Even All "Difference", and (Therefore) Even The Attitude (or Presumption) Of Witnessing.

The Inherently egoless "Practice" Of The Only-By-Me Revealed and Given Seventh Stage Of Life Is To Be Self-Evidently Divine Love-Bliss (or Self-Evidently Divine Happiness Itself), and (Thus) To Ignore and Forget death.

The Inherently egoless "Practice" (or Inherently Most Perfect Process and Demonstration) Of The Only-By-Me Revealed and Given Seventh Stage Of Life Thus Becomes Divinely Indifferent To every "thing" that arises, Until (Most Ultimately, and At Last) every "thing" that arises Is Outshined By and In and As The Inherent Love-Bliss Of The One, and Only, and Inherently Indivisible, and Self-Existing, and Self-Radiant Conscious Light.

Therefore, As My Formally Practicing (and, Formally, Fully Accountable) Devotee, Listen To Me, and Hear Me, and See Me, and (By Means Of My Avatarically Self-Transmitted Divine Spiritual Grace) Progressively Practice The Only-By-Me Revealed and Given Way Of The Heart, and (Thus) Mature Beyond The Practice and The Process Of The Only-By-Me Revealed and Given Way Of The Heart In The Context Of The Circle (and The Arrow) Of the conditionally arising body-mind.

In This Manner, Grow To Listen To Me Perfectly, and Hear Me Perfectly, and See Me Perfectly, and, Thus (By Means Of My Avatarically Self-Transmitted Divine Spiritual Grace), Grow To Freely and Surely (and, Necessarily, Formally) Embrace The "Perfect Practice" Of The Only-By-Me Revealed and Given Way Of The Heart As "Feeling-Enquiry" (and, In Due Course, As The Only-By-Me Revealed and Given Totality Of "Samraj Yoga").

Therefore, Ultimately (and By Means Of My Avatarically Self-Transmitted Divine Spiritual Grace), Listen To Me Perfectly, and Hear Me Perfectly, and See Me Perfectly, As I Am, "Brightly" Self-Revealed As Self-Existing and Self-Radiant Consciousness (or Mere Feeling-Awareness) Itself.

The "Perfect Practice" Of The Only-By-Me Revealed and Given Way Of The Heart Requires Inherently Perfect Dispassion (or Tacit and Effortless Non-Attachment) In The Midst Of Every Motive (and all the conditions) Of attention.

Only Inherently Perfect Dispassion (or Tacit and Effortless Non-Attachment) Allows The True, Free, and Effective Exercise Of The "Perfect Practice" Of The Only-By-Me Revealed and Given Way Of The Heart—Because You Cannot Relinquish what You Will Not Cease To Hold.

Therefore, those who Embrace The "Perfect Practice" Of The Only-By-Me Revealed and Given Way Of The Heart Must Be True and Free Renunciates.

I Call All My Listening Devotees To Hear Me, and (When they Hear Me) To See Me, and Then To Practice On The Basis Of What they Have Both Heard and Seen.

Do Not Imagine The Call To Listen To Me, and To Hear Me, and To See Me Is A Call To Merely Continue Your ordinary life in body and mind, or Even To Develop an Extraordinary life in body or mind.

When I Call You To Listen To Me, and To Hear Me, and To See Me, I Am Calling You To Observe, Understand, and Renounce (or Really Surrender, Forget, and Transcend) Your ordinary life in body and mind and Your Extraordinary life in body or mind.

Therefore, My Inherently Perfect Devotees (or those who Listen To Me Perfectly and Hear Me Perfectly and See Me Perfectly) Also (Tacitly, and Effortlessly) Practice The Inherently Perfect Discipline Of True and Free Renunciation.

Those who (Tacitly, and Effortlessly) Practice The Inherently Perfect Discipline Of True and Free Renunciation In The Only-By-Me Revealed and Given Way Of The Heart Are True and Free Renunciates In The Only-By-Me Revealed and Given Way Of The Heart.

True Renunciates Are True To The One Who Is Truth.

Only they Are True Renunciates who Are Heart-Given Exclusively To (Nothing Other Than) Inherent Love-Bliss (or Self-Evidently Divine Happiness Itself).

Therefore, True Renunciates Renounce (or Inherently Transcend) whatever Is Not Self-Evidently Divine Happiness Itself.

Free Renunciates Stand Free Of Passionate (or egoic) Attachment and Passionate (or egoic) Detachment In The Context Of any and all conditional and Apparent relations, or any and all objects, others, forms, thoughts, states, processes, or conditionally arising "things".

Only they Are Free Renunciates who Have Realized Consistently Free attention.

Only they Are Free Renunciates who Have Already (and Truly) Disciplined (and, Altogether, Devotionally Surrendered) the body-mind, Such That it Freely Manifests Total psycho-physical Equanimity (or The Constant Signs Of Whole-bodily-Effective Purification, Re-Balancing, Regeneration, self-Surrender, and Natural Well-being).

In The Only-By-Me Revealed and Given Way Of The Heart, All Free Renunciates Freely and Consistently Demonstrate A Conservative Dietary (and Periodic Fasting) Discipline, Such That they, As A General Rule, Consistently Limit food, By The "Sattvic Principle", To What Is Natural, Fresh, Whole, Balanced, Purifying, Pure (or Non-constipating, Non-toxifying, and Non-enervating), and (As A General Rule) Maximally (but Not Necessarily, or Generally, Exclusively) raw, and Consistently Productive Of Good Health—and (Altogether) they (As A General Rule) Freely, Consistently, and Always Healthfully Maintain A "Minimum Optimum" (and, Generally, Unless Otherwise Rightly Medically Advised, fructo-vegetarian) dietary (and fasting) Practice, Guided (and Artfully Managed) By A practical Understanding Of What Is Necessary For Natural psycho-physical Equanimity (and, Also, By A practical Understanding Of What Is A Disturbance To Natural psycho-physical Equanimity).

In The Only-By-Me Revealed and Given Way Of The Heart, All Free Renunciates Freely and Consistently Demonstrate The Real, and Truly Me-Recognizing, and Really To-Me-Responding, and (Altogether) Me-"Bright" Transcending Of emotional-sexual ego-Bondage, By Releasing emotional-sexual self-Contraction, and By Positively and Yogically Conserving and Conducting Both Natural sexual energy and sexually Indicated Spirit-Energy—Either In Truly Auspicious, and Altogether Right (or Motiveless, Purposeless, or Goal-Free, and life-energy-Positive, and Yogically, Rather Than merely idealistically and puritanically, Supported and Maintained), and Profoundly Effective, and Really ego-Transcending, and Really sex-bondage-Transcending, and Really emotional-Bondage-Transcending Yogic celibacy Or (In The Case Of individuals who Are, In The Fullest Sense, Truly—or, Possibly, Even Uniquely—Qualified For A Yogic emotional-sexual Sadhana) In An Otherwise

Truly Auspicious, and Altogether Right, and Profoundly Effective, and Really ego-Transcending, and Really sex-Bondage-Transcending, and Really emotional-Bondage-Transcending Yogic emotional-sexual Practice (Which Uniquely Exemplary emotional-sexual Yoga May Yet, and Motivelessly—At Some Point In The "Perfect Practice"—Become Yogic celibacy)—and, Whether In The Case Of Yogic celibacy or In The Case Of Right Yogic emotional-sexual Practice (and, Therefore, True and Effective Participation In The Only-By-Me Revealed and Given Practice and Process Of "Right Emotional-Sexual Yoga"), All Free Renunciates In The Only-By-Me Revealed and Given Way Of The Heart Thus Freely and Consistently Demonstrate The Real Transcending Of emotional-sexual ego-Bondage, Because Of The Yogic Sublimity Of The Constant Devotional Samadhi Of Spiritual Communion With Me, and Because ego-Based and ego-Reinforcing sex-"Bonding" (or Even any kind of ego-Binding emotional-sexual activity) Is Not Necessary For (and, Altogether, Is A Disturbance To) psycho-physical Equanimity, and Because ego-Based and ego-Reinforcing sex-"Bonding" (or Even any kind of ego-Binding emotional-sexual activity) Always (To One Degree or Another) Undermines or (Otherwise) Prevents psycho-physical Equanimity, and Because ego-Based and ego-Reinforcing sex-"Bonding" (or Even any kind of ego-Binding emotional-sexual activity) Always (To One Degree or Another) Blocks, Reverses, Exhausts, or (Otherwise) limits The Flow and Circulation Of The By-Me-Avatarically-Self-Transmitted Divine Spirit-Current (and the Natural energy) In the body, and Because ego-Based and ego-Reinforcing sex-"Bonding" (or even any kind Of ego-Binding emotional-sexual activity) Always (To One Degree or Another) Fascinates and Deludes the mind, and Because ego-Based and ego-Reinforcing sex-"Bonding" (or Even any kind of ego-Binding emotional-sexual activity) Always (To One Degree or Another) Binds To objects, or To others, or To bodily states, and Because, Always (To One Degree or Another, Either In its moment Or In its after-effects Or In its memories Or In The Craving For its Repetitions Or In the emotions Of daily Attachment Bred By Every Satisfaction Or In the emotions Of daily Reactivity Bred By Every Failure Of Satisfaction), ego-Based and ego-Reinforcing sex-"Bonding" (or Even any kind of ego-Binding emotional-sexual activity) Will Not Relinquish attention itself, To Be Dissolved In its Perfectly Subjective (Transcendental, Inherently Spiritual, Inherently egoless, and Self-Evidently Divine) Source.

Indeed, Because they Are (In Reality, and In Truth) Always Already Free, All Free Renunciates In The Only-By-Me Revealed and Given Way Of The Heart Always Rightly Economize all activities of the body-mind, and Really ("Radically", or "At-The-Root") Transcend all the activities (and The Very Motive) of attention itself.

For The Sake Of their Freedom and Happiness, I Call All My Listening Devotees, All My Hearing Devotees, and All My Seeing Devotees To Rightly and Really Effectively Discipline themselves, and To Constantly Grow Toward (and, In Due Course, In) The Freely Conservative (and Really ego-Transcending) Practice Of True and Free Renunciation.

For The Sake Of their Freedom and Happiness, I Call All My Listening Devotees, All My Hearing Devotees, and All My Seeing Devotees To Rightly and Really Effectively Discipline themselves, and To Constantly Grow Toward (and, In Due Course, In) The "Perfect Practice" Of The Only-By-Me Revealed and Given Way Of The Heart.

When (In The Only-By-Me Revealed and Given Way Of The Heart) The Essence Of The Practice Of Spirit-"Conductivity" (Which Is True and Free, and Really Effective, Renunciation Of the body-mind) and The Essence Of The "Conscious Process" (Which Is True and Free, and Really Effective, Renunciation Of attention) Combine (By Means Of The Only-By-Me Revealed and Given Avataric Divine Spiritual Gift Of The "Thumbs") To Awaken Inherent (or Tacit, Effortless, and Self-Evident) Self-Identification With The Witness-Consciousness (or Mere Feeling-Awareness), Then (By Means Of My Avatarically Self-Transmitted Divine Spiritual Grace) The Great Discipline Of The "Perfect Practice" Of The Only-By-Me Revealed and Given Way Of The Heart (Free Of The Traditional Sixth-Stage-Of-Life Error, or Presumption) Has The Necessary Basis To Begin.

When (On The Basis Of Really self-Surrendered Listening To Me, True Hearing Of Me, Clear Seeing Of Me, and, Altogether, Right Practicing In My Avatarically Self-Transmitted Mere and "Bright" Divine Spiritual Presence) The "Perfect Practice" Of The Only-By-Me Revealed and Given Way Of The Heart Is Formally Acknowledged To Have Begun, Then Stand As The Witness-Consciousness (or Mere Feeling-Awareness) and (Necessarily, Formally) Practice The "Perfect Practice" Of The Way Of The Heart As "Feeling-Enquiry".

When (In The Only-By-Me Revealed and Given Way Of The Heart) Inherent (or Tacit, Effortless, and Self-Evident) Self-Identification With The Witness-Consciousness (or Mere Feeling-Awareness) Awakens (By Means Of My Avatarically Self-Transmitted Divine Spiritual Grace, Through Constant Feeling-Contemplation Of My Avatarically-Born Bodily Human Divine Form, My Avatarically Self-Transmitted Spiritual, and Always Blessing, Divine Presence, and My Avatarically Self-Revealed, and Very, and Transcendental, and Perfectly Subjective, and Inherently Spiritual, and Inherently egoless, and Inherently Perfect, and Self-Evidently Divine State), There Is Free (or Spontaneous) Relinquishment Of conditional Identification With the body-mind (or The Root-Feeling and "causal Stress" Of Relatedness—Which

Is merely the feeling "I am the body", or "I am the mind", or "I am the body-mind").

The Witness-Consciousness (or Mere Feeling-Awareness) Inherently (Merely) Feels "I Am Consciousness Itself"—Rather Than "I am the body", or "I am the mind", or "I am the body-mind".

The Witness-Consciousness (or Mere Feeling-Awareness) Only (or Merely) Feels (or Merely Stands Prior To, and Does Not Identify With) the body, the mind, or the Total body-mind, or the states of the body-mind (waking, dreaming, or sleeping), Because The Witness-Consciousness (or Mere Feeling-Awareness) Does Not Stand As the functional observer, or the observer-function of the mind (which function Is The Exercise Of Discriminative Intelligence, or The Intelligent Use Of attention), but (Rather) The Witness-Consciousness (or Mere Feeling-Awareness) Stands In The Position Of The Very Self-Condition (or In The Being-Position, or The Perfectly Subjective Position), Even Prior To attention itself.

Therefore, Inherent (or Tacit, Effortless, and Self-Evident) Self-Identification With The Witness-Consciousness (or Mere Feeling-Awareness), Rather Than conditional Identification (and Inevitable Struggle) With attention and its Motive or its Motions, Is (Itself) Inherently Perfect Renunciation Of the ego-"I" of body and mind.

The Witness-Consciousness (or Mere Feeling-Awareness) Inherently (At Its Heart, or In and As Itself) Confesses The Inherently Perfect Realization "I Am Consciousness Itself".

The Witness-Consciousness (or Mere Feeling-Awareness) Inherently (At Its Heart, or In and As Itself) Confesses True and Always Already Free Renunciation Of the body-mind (and attention to, or via, the body-mind), Because The Witness-Consciousness (or Mere Feeling-Awareness) Is Inherently (or Always Already) Free Of Identification With the body-mind.

Therefore, Inherent (or Tacit, Effortless, and Self-Evident) Self-Identification With The Witness-Consciousness (or Mere Feeling-Awareness), Rather Than Any Strategic Effort To Avoid, Suppress, Destroy, or Escape the body-mind, Is The Inherently Perfect Basis (or Essence) Of True and Free Renunciation.

The Inherent Confession "I Am Consciousness Itself" Is Also Inherently (and Necessarily) Expressed As The Free (and Identical) Confession "I Am Not the body-mind", or "I Am Not attention", or "I Am Always Already Prior To Relatedness and all 'things'".

Therefore, those who Stand In The Most Prior Position, As The Witness-Consciousness (or Mere Feeling-Awareness), Express That Stand Via True and Free Renunciation Of All Seeking.

Those who Stand In The Most Prior Position, As The Witness-Consciousness (or Mere Feeling-Awareness), Express That Stand Via True and Free Renunciation Of All The Strategic (and, Necessarily, self-Deluding) Seeking-Efforts and ego-Binding activities That are The psycho-physical Totality Of the Separate and Separative body-mind.

Those who Stand In The Most Prior Position, As The Witness-Consciousness (or Mere Feeling-Awareness), Express That Stand Via True and Free Renunciation Of Identification With any and all acts and states (or results) of attention.

To Stand Most Freely, As The Most Prior Witness-Consciousness (or Mere Feeling-Awareness), or As The Inherently Free Confession "I Am Consciousness Itself, Always Already Prior To the body-mind", Is The Real and True Basis Of The Great and Awesome Signs Of Always Already Free Renunciation Of all conditionally arising "things" (Via Total Relinquishment Of The Motive Of attention itself).

Because, In The "Perfect Practice" Of The Only-By-Me Revealed and Given Way Of The Heart, The Inherent Confession (and Inherently ego-Transcending Practice) Of The Witness-Consciousness (or Mere Feeling-Awareness) Is Expressed Via True and Free Renunciation Of The psycho-physical Totality Of the ego-"I", There Can Be (In Due Course, As My Avatarically Self-Transmitted Divine Spiritual Grace Will Have It) The (Necessarily, Sudden—and Only-By-Me Revealed and Given) Realization Of The Most Ultimate (and Inherently Most Perfect, and Inherently Most Perfectly ego-Transcending) "Practice" Of The Way Of The Heart—Which Is The Only-By-Me Revealed and Given Seventh Stage Of Life, or "Open Eyes", or Transcendental, Inherently Spiritual, Inherently egoless, and Self-Evidently Divine Self-Abiding (As Consciousness Itself, Self-Radiant and Self-Existing), Even Prior To All Witnessing, Spontaneously Self-Recognizing and Inherently Transcending all the conditionally arising "things" that (Apparently) arise In (and As Apparent Modifications Of) Love-Bliss.

Because The "Practice" Of The Only-By-Me Revealed and Given Seventh Stage Of Life Is Thus Founded On True and Free Renunciation, Signs Of The Divine Transfiguration and Divine Transformation Of the body-mind By My Avatarically Self-Transmitted Free Divine Spirit-Current Will (In The Only-By-Me Revealed and Given Seventh Stage Of Life) Spontaneously Arise, and Then Pass, In time, but The Characteristic Seventh Stage Sign, Which Is (Inherent and Eternal) Divine Indifference (or The Sign Of The Infinite Fullness, and The Utter Self-Sufficiency, Of Self-Evidently Divine Love-Bliss Itself), Will (Although It Is, In Its Infinite Fullness and Utter Self-Sufficiency, The Inherent Characteristic Of The Seventh Stage Awakening, Even From Its "Beginning") Inevitably (Spontaneously, and Progressively) Increase In Its Self-Radiant (or Divinely "Bright") Demonstration, Until Divine Translation (or The Sudden Outshining Of the body-mind and all its conditionally arising "things") In and

As Love-Bliss (or The Infinite Happiness, and The Eternal Self-"Bright" Divine Sphere and Self-Domain, Of The One and Only and Inherently Indivisible Conscious Light, Itself).

Those who (By Means Of My Avatarically Self-Transmitted Divine Spiritual Grace) Listen To Me Perfectly and Hear Me Perfectly and See Me Perfectly Suddenly Feel The Heart Of conditionally arising "things", and The Heart Itself Will Outshine the body-mind and all the Seeming worlds.

Those who (By Means Of My Avatarically Self-Transmitted Divine Spiritual Grace) Listen To Me Perfectly and Hear Me Perfectly and See Me Perfectly Suddenly Realize The Heart's Inherent Happiness, and they No Longer Seek It Among the conditionally arising "things".

Those who (By Means Of My Avatarically Self-Transmitted Divine Spiritual Grace) Listen To Me Perfectly and Hear Me Perfectly and See Me Perfectly Suddenly Become Heart-True, and their Renunciation Of conditionally arising "things" Is Inevitable, Immediate, Effortless, and Free.

Those who (By Means Of My Avatarically Self-Transmitted Divine Spiritual Grace) Listen To Me Perfectly and Hear Me Perfectly and See Me Perfectly Truly Understand The Habit Of "Narcissus", and they (Constantly) Freely Accept My Avatarically Self-Transmitted Spirit-Blessing Of Self-Evidently Divine Love-Bliss, That Awakens The Heart To My Divine "Location", "Where" Consciousness Of Me Is Inherently Free Of the body-mind and all its conditionally arising "things".

When The "Who" and "What" and "Where" I Am Is "Located" By Heart and Perfectly, No Habit Will Any More believe or Make the "thing" Of Fear, Nor Will Ever the "thing" of attention itself Twist Out Of The Heart Of Consciousness.

The "Who", The "What", and The "Where" I Am Is Only Conscious Light!

Only Conscious Light Is "Who", and "What", and "Where".

There Is Only Conscious Light (One and Indivisible), and No "Other" (here, or any "where").

Therefore, Wake Up Sooner Than the mind Can Happen.

Merely Be "Who", "What", and "Where" My Avatarically Self-Transmitted Spirit-Current Of Self-Evidently Divine Love-Bliss Is, Before the "things" of attention arise Therein.

Before it Seems "There" is the self-Contracted ego-"I" of body, breath, emotion, and mind (or even the mereness of attention), Conscious Light Is "There"—Always Already, and One, and Only.

Therefore, Transcend the ego-"I" of body, breath, emotion, mind, and mere attention (or all the psycho-physics of self-Contraction) By Means Of ego-Transcending Devotion To Me, and (Thereby) Grow To Self-Abide Only

As What Is—Inherently Free, As Consciousness Itself (Merely Self-Aware, Self-"Bright", and Always Prior To attention and its "things").

Thus Self-Abiding, Remaining Only Free, egoless In My Priority (As Love-Bliss-Consciousness Itself)—Merely Be As Is (and, Thus, Inherently and Searchlessly Ignore, Forget, Boundlessly Exceed, and Freely "Fail" To Notice any or every thought, and Even any or every kind of Apparent "thing").

The Only-By-Me Revealed and Given Way Of The Heart (or Way Of Adidam) Is, In The Totality Of Its "Perfect Practice", The By-Me-Avatarically-Self-Revealed Divine Way Of Spiritual (or Love-Blissful), Transcendental (or Un-conditional), and (Most Ultimately) Divine (or Most Perfect, Complete, and all-and-All-Transcending) Self-Realization Of The "Who", The "What", and The "Where" Of "Is".

By Means Of Really ego-Surrendering, ego-Forgetting, and ego-Transcending Devotion To Me (The Avataric Divine Realizer, The Avataric Divine Revealer, and The Avataric Divine Self-Revelation Of The Only One Who Is), Truly Effective Practice Of The Only-By-Me Revealed and Given Way Of The Heart Progressively Transcends the Total psycho-physical activity of self-Contraction, and, At Last, That Truly Effective (and, Ultimately, Inherently Most Perfect, and Inherently Most Perfectly ego-Transcending) Practice Utterly (and Most Perfectly) Outshines the body-mind and all conditional appearances or worlds—By Means Of Inherent (or Tacit, Effortless, and Self-Evident) Realization Of The Inherently Non-Separate, Inherently Indivisible, Inherently Love-Bliss-"Bright", Inherently egoless, Inherently Perfect, and Self-Evidently Divine Self-Condition (or One and Only Conscious Light) Of all-and-All.

Truly Effective Practice Of The Only-By-Me Revealed and Given Way Of The Heart Progressively Magnifies (and, Ultimately, Most Fully, and Fully Devotionally, Realizes) True and Free Renunciation (or Real Transcending) Of the body-mind (and all objects, others, forms, thoughts, states, processes, or conditionally arising "things" of attention).

Really Effective Renunciation (or Real Transcending) Of The egoic Habits (or Uses) Of the body-mind Is The Active Principle (or The functional, practical, relational, and Constantly Developing Sign) Of The Practice Demonstrated (and That Must Be Demonstrated) By all those who Rightly Listen To Me, and all those who Truly Hear Me, and all those who Clearly See Me.

The "Perfect Practice" Of The Only-By-Me Revealed and Given Way Of The Heart Most Directly (or Inherently, and, Thus, Perfectly) Realizes True and Free Renunciation (or Real Transcending) Of attention (itself) In Me—The Avataric Self-Revelation Of The Perfectly Subjective, Transcendental, Inherently Spiritual, Inherently egoless, and Self-Evidently Divine Source-Consciousness Of attention itself.

Perfectly Effective Renunciation (or The Inherent, and Inherently Perfect, Transcending) Of attention In Me (The Avataric Self-Revelation Of The Perfectly Subjective, Transcendental, Inherently Spiritual, Inherently egoless, and Self-Evidently Divine Source-Consciousness Of attention itself) Is The Inherently Perfect Principle (or The Root, and The Ultimate Characteristic) Of The "Perfect Practice" Of The Only-By-Me Revealed and Given Way Of The Heart.

To Self-Abide (Tacitly, and Effortlessly) As Consciousness (or Mere Feeling-Awareness) Itself (Not "Centered" As A Separate and Separative "Who" Behind The Knot Of psycho-physical self-Contraction, but Centerlessly Self-Radiant, Shining Boundlessly, Beyond psycho-physical self-Contraction, and Beyond all conditionally arising "things") Is The Ultimate and Most Perfect "Discipline", The Always Already Most Perfectly True and Most Perfectly Free Form Of Renunciation, The "Radical" (or Perfectly Direct) Process, and The Inherently Most Perfect, and Final, Divine "Practice" Of The Only-By-Me Revealed and Given Way Of The Heart (or Way Of Adidam).

To Realize The Self-Evidently Divine Self-Condition Of Consciousness (or Mere Feeling-Awareness) Itself, It Is Necessary To Be (or Inherently Identify With, or Always Already Stand As) Consciousness (or Mere Feeling-Awareness) Itself.

Most Perfectly Prior To the ego-"I" of Total psycho-physical self-Contraction, "There" Is (Always Already) Consciousness (or Mere Feeling-Awareness) Itself.

Therefore, If Consciousness (or Mere Feeling-Awareness) Itself Is To Be Realized (As It Is), No Act Of Identification With Consciousness (or Mere Feeling-Awareness) Itself Is Either Necessary Or Fruitful.

In The By-Me-Given (Seven-Gifted) Development Of The Great Process Of Listening To Me, and Of Hearing Me, and Of Seeing Me, and Of Every Kind Of Right, True, Full, and Fully Devotional Practicing In The Only-By-Me Revealed and Given Way Of The Heart, You Will Eventually (By Means Of My Avatarically Self-Transmitted Divine Spiritual Grace, Through Constant Feeling-Contemplation Of My Avatarically-Born Bodily Human Divine Form, My Avatarically Self-Transmitted Spiritual, and Always Blessing, Divine Presence, and My Avatarically Self-Revealed Very, and Transcendental, and Perfectly Subjective, and Inherently Spiritual, and Inherently egoless, and Inherently Perfect, and Self-Evidently Divine State) Merely Affirm (or Tacitly, Effortlessly, Inherently, and Perfectly Realize and Acknowledge, As Self-Evidently The Case) Inherent (or Always Already Prior, and Always present-time) Self-Identification With Consciousness Itself, Merely Standing As Mere Feeling-Awareness (or The Mere Witness), Always Already Prior To attention and its conditionally arising "things", and Always Only (or Merely) Tacitly Feeling (but

Never Actively Observing, or functionally attending to) attention and its conditionally arising "things".

When Your Devotional and Spiritual Practice Of The Only-By-Me Revealed and Given Way Of The Heart Becomes Really, Truly, and Stably Perfect, Then (and Only Then) You May (With Formal Permission, and With Full Formal Cultural Accountability, In Fully Formalized Right Relationship To The Ruchira Sannyasin Order Of Adidam Ruchiradam) Practice The Specific Discipline (or "Perfect Practice") Of "Feeling-Enquiry", By Standing As The Mere Witness (or The Witness-Consciousness, or Mere Feeling-Awareness), Merely (Tacitly) Feeling (or Tacitly, or Merely—but Not Actively, or functionally—Observing) whatever and all that conditionally arises.

To Merely Feel (or Tacitly—but Not Actively, or functionally—Observe) whatever conditionally arises, It Is Necessary To Stand Only As The Witness-Consciousness (or Mere Feeling-Awareness), Irrespective Of what conditionally arises.

When You Are (As My Formally Practicing Devotee In The Only-By-Me Revealed and Given Way Of The Heart) Formally Acknowledged To Be Prepared To Practice The Specific Discipline (or "Perfect Practice") Of "Feeling-Enquiry", Stand Only As The Witness-Consciousness (or Mere Feeling-Awareness), and (Irrespective Of what conditionally arises) Freely, and Only (or Merely), Feel (or Tacitly—but Not Actively, or functionally—Observe) every "thing" that arises to attention—Without Avoiding what conditionally arises, or Reacting To what conditionally arises, or Excluding, or Desiring, or Attaching To what conditionally arises, or, In Any Manner, Seeking (or Even Following After) any "thing" that conditionally arises.

Thus, Merely Feel (or Tacitly Observe) whatever "thing" (presently) conditionally arises (as attention itself, or as The "causal Stress" That Is The Root-Feeling Of Relatedness, or as the body-mind itself, or as any and every sense-perception, or as any and every form, thought, state, process, object, or other, or as any and every gross bodily sensation, desire, breath, Natural energy, emotion, or thought, or as any and all varieties of subtle mind, higher and mystical vision, waking revery, dream, sleep, and So On), but Do Not Avoid or (Otherwise) Seek or Follow After any "thing" that conditionally arises.

Thus, Merely Feel (or Tacitly Observe) Avoidance (or Total psycho-physical self-Contraction) Itself, and Reactions, and Efforts To Exclude, and The Efforts Of Desiring and Active Attachment, and Even All The Forms Of Seeking and Following After, but Do Not Avoid Them, or (Otherwise) Seek or Follow After Them.

To Avoid or, In Any Manner, To Seek (or Even To Follow After) conditionally arising "things" Is self-Contraction.

The body-mind, attention, and all conditionally arising "things" are (in and of themselves) forms of psycho-physical self-Contraction.

Likewise, All conditional (or psycho-physical) Efforts Are (In and Of Themselves) Forms Of psycho-physical self-Contraction.

Therefore, It Is *Not Possible* To Be *Perfectly* Free Of self-Contraction, Avoidance, Reaction, Exclusion, Desire, and Active Attachment (or All The Motions Of Seeking and Following After conditionally arising "things") By Means Of *Any Effort* Of body, or mind, or attention.

Only The Witness-Consciousness (or Mere Feeling-Awareness) *Itself* Stands (Always Already, or Inherently) Prior To the self-Contraction—Merely (or Only) *As* The *Consciousness*, or The Always Already Free (and Perfectly Subjective) Source (or Source-Condition), or Mere and Priorly Free-Standing Feeling-Awareness, Of (and Beyond) *every* "thing" that arises.

If (By Means Of My Avatarically Self-Transmitted Divine Spiritual Grace) *whatever* conditionally arises Is Merely Felt (or Tacitly Observed, or *Only* and *Freely* Witnessed), attention *Immediately* Relaxes From Seeking or Following After it, and When (Thus, By Heart-Response To My Avatarically Self-Transmitted Divine Spiritual Grace, and Not By Strategic self-Effort) attention Relaxes From Seeking (or Following After), "thing" and attention and Relatedness and "causal Stress" and self-Contraction Immediately (By Means Of My Avatarically Self-Transmitted Divine Spiritual Grace) *Dissolve* In *My* Avatarically Self-Transmitted Spirit-Current Of Self-Evidently Divine Love-Bliss, "Located" *As* The Heart-Feeling Of Mere Being (or The By-Me-Avatarically-Self-Transmitted Spirit-Current Of Self-Evidently Divine Happiness, That Inherently Coincides With The Witness-Consciousness Itself).

Therefore, To (*Thus*) Merely Feel (or Tacitly Observe) conditionally arising "things" (Completely Free Of Avoidance, Reaction, Exclusion, Desire, and Active Attachment, or All Seeking and Following After conditionally arising "things"), It Is Necessary To *Be* (or To Inherently, and Always Already, Stand *As*) The Witness-Consciousness (or Mere Feeling-Awareness) Itself, and This Merely and Only By Heart-Response To My Avatarically Self-Revealed Divine Person and My Avatarically Self-Transmitted Spirit-Current Of Self-Evidently Divine Love-Bliss (and Not By psycho-physical self-Contraction, or The Inherently self-Contracted Strategies Of body, breath, emotion, mind, and attention).

If You (As My Formally Practicing Devotee) Have Listened To Me Perfectly, and If You (Thus and Thereby) Hear Me Perfectly, and If You (Thus and Thereby) Also See Me Perfectly, and If You Are (Thus, and, Necessarily, Formally) Prepared To Practice The Specific Discipline (or "Perfect Practice") Of "Feeling-Enquiry", Then (By Means Of The Perfectly Mature Practice Of

Ruchira Avatara Bhakti Yoga) Simply Stand As Mere Feeling-Awareness, and Merely Feel (and, Thus, Merely, Effortlessly, and Tacitly Observe) whatever (presently) conditionally arises, Until There Is Direct Feeling-Realization That Feeling-Awareness Is Not (Itself) any "thing" (or any state of attention) that conditionally arises, but It Is Only The Mere and Tacit and Always Priorly Free-Standing Witness Of whatever (presently) conditionally arises.

Thus, Merely Feel (or Tacitly Observe) whatever (presently) conditionally arises, Until every "thing" (or every state of attention) that (presently) conditionally arises Is Immediately, Tacitly, and Clearly Felt (and Freely and Tacitly Understood) To Be Only the experience of psycho-physical self-Contraction—or The Feeling Of Existence (or "self", or "I") As a Separate and Separated state (or As A Strategic Effort To Separate, and To Be Separated and Separate).

Thus, Merely Feel (or Tacitly Observe) whatever "things" (or Forms Of psycho-physical self-Contraction) presently conditionally arise, Until It Is Tacitly Felt (As Self-Evidently The Case) That Mere Feeling-Awareness Itself (or The Witness-Consciousness Itself) Does Not (and Cannot) Seek or Follow After any "thing", or (Otherwise) Add self-Contraction, Separateness, Avoidance, Reaction, Exclusion, Desire, or Active Attachment To Itself (or To whatever "thing" presently conditionally arises).

Thus, Merely Feel (or Merely, and By Mere Feeling, Be Aware Of) psycho-physical self-Contraction itself (or The Present Feeling and Strategic Effort Of Separateness), Until self-Contraction Is Tacitly Felt To Be Originating (or Basically, Presently, and Constantly Existing) As The Root-Feeling Of Relatedness Itself (Which Root-Feeling Originates Independent Of particular objects, others, forms, thoughts, states, processes, or "things", and Which Root-Feeling Originates Immediately Previous To any and every particular Noticed object, other, form, thought, state, process, or "thing", and Which Root-Feeling Is, Itself, Inherently Associated With "causal Stress"—or A Characteristic, or Particular, and Separatively self-Defining and other-Defining, Feeling-Vibration—In The Right Side Of The Heart).

Thus, Merely Feel (or Merely, and By Mere Feeling, Be Aware Of) The (always presently) conditionally arising Feeling Of Relatedness Itself (Which Is, Itself, The Most Primitive Essence Of The Illusion Of Separate ego-"I", and The Original Form Of The Motive Of Separativeness, or ego-Effort), and (Merely By This Tacit Feeling-Observation) "Locate" (or Tacitly, Effortlessly, Feel) The ("causal") Vibration (Inherently Associated With The Feeling Of Relatedness) In The Right Side Of The Heart, and (Merely By Continuing In This Manner) Tacitly Feel and Directly Realize (As Self-Evidently The Case) That The Feeling (and "causal Stress") Of Relatedness Is The Root-Essence Of attention itself (or The Original Motion Toward conditionally arising "things"), and That It Is arising Spontaneously (On Its Own, As A Mechanical or Automatic Event), Superimposing Itself On The Witness-Consciousness (or Mere Feeling-Awareness)—Which Always Remains Constant (Only As Itself), Merely Feeling (or Tacitly Observing), and Never (Itself) acting or changing.

Thus, Find Me "There" (Prior To The Root-Feeling Of Relatedness), and (Thus) Merely (and Persistently) Feel (and Identify With) Me ("There") As "Atma-Murti" (or The Most Prior Feeling, Which Is The Self-Evident Feeling Of Mere Being, Itself), and (By Tacit Heart-Response To My Avatarically Self-Transmitted Divine Spiritual Grace, and Not By Strategic psycho-physical self-Effort) Merely (and Persistently) Feel (and Be Inherently, or Tacitly and Effortlessly, Self-Identified With) My Avatarically Self-Transmitted Spiritual Under-Current Of Self-Evidently Divine Love-Bliss, Which Is (Apparently, or Experientially) Associated With The Right Side Of The Heart (Always Immediately Prior To The Root-Feeling and "causal Stress" Of Relatedness), and Which Is The Constant (Un-Interrupted) Self-Radiance (or Self-Evidently Divine Feeling-Vibration) Of (Unqualified, or Un-conditional) Feeling (Itself), and Which Is Itself (Necessarily) Always Already Prior To all psycho-physical (or conditional) references, and Which Is Itself (Necessarily) Always Already (or Inherently and Utterly) Detached (or Free) From Involvement With (or limitation by) the self-Contraction (or The Root-Feeling and "causal Stress" Of Relatedness), and From the Spontaneous arising of attention, and From Even All Motions (or Every Effort) Toward conditionally arising "things" of attention.

Thus, Develop This Cycle Of Mere and Persistent (and Perfectly Devotional) Feeling (In daily Meditation, and moment to moment), Until (By Tacit Heart-Response To My Avatarically Self-Transmitted Divine Spiritual Grace, and Not By Strategic psycho-physical self-Effort) My Avatarically Self-Transmitted Spiritual Under-Current Of Self-Evidently Divine Love-Bliss Becomes Obvious (or Self-Evident) and Full (Even In Apparent Association With The Right Side Of The Heart), and attention (or The Root-Feeling and "causal Stress" Of Relatedness and Separateness) Is Readily Relinquished (or Immediately Collapsed and Dissolved) In It.

Thus, As attention Relinquishes all conditionally arising "things" and Subsides In My Avatarically Self-Transmitted Spiritual Heart-Current Of Self-Evidently Divine Love-Bliss, Stand As (or Merely Be) The Inherently Objectless (or Only Self-Existing and Self-Radiant) Mere Feeling-Awareness (or Consciousness Itself) That Was The Mere (or Always Priorly Free-Standing) Witness Of attention and its conditionally arising "things".

Whatever Is Merely Felt (or Tacitly Observed) Is Not (and Cannot Be) Avoided, or Reacted To, or Excluded, or Desired, or Held On To, or Otherwise

Sought or Followed After—but it Is Only (or Merely, Tacitly, Effortlessly, or Inherently and Self-Evidently) Witnessed.

The Witness-Consciousness (or Mere Feeling-Awareness) Is Inherently Non-Attached (or Always Already Free-Standing—Perfectly Prior To whatever Is Merely Felt, or Tacitly Observed).

Therefore, Mere Feeling-Awareness (or Tacit Observation) Is Not A Strategic Method (or psycho-physical Seeking-Strategy) For Letting Go Of psycho-physical self-Contraction (or attention and its conditionally arising "things").

Mere Feeling-Awareness (or Tacit Observation, or Always Priorly Free-Standing Witnessing) Is The Most Prior Position (or Apparent Root-Disposition) Of Consciousness Itself—and, Whenever It Is Freely (or Inherently or Tacitly and Effortlessly) Assumed, There Is (Simply, Spontaneously, and Inherently) No Holding On To psycho-physical self-Contraction (or To attention and its conditionally arising "things").

Therefore, It Is Not Necessary (or Even Possible) To Absolutely Purify the body-mind itself (Such That it Becomes Perfectly Detached and Desireless).

It Is Necessary To Stand As The Always Already (or Priorly) Free-Standing Witness-Consciousness (or Mere Feeling-Awareness, Itself), and To Merely Feel (or Tacitly Observe, or Directly Realize, As Self-Evidently The Case) That It Is Inherently (and Inherently Perfectly) Pure, Detached, and Desireless.

Therefore, By Listening To Me Perfectly, and By Hearing Me Perfectly, and By Seeing Me Perfectly, and By Practicing The "Perfect Practice" Of "Feeling-Enquiry"—Freely "Locate" and Inherently Identify With The Witness-Consciousness (or Mere Feeling-Awareness), and Merely Feel (or Tacitly Observe) whatever conditionally arises, Until attention itself ("Located" As The Root-Feeling and "causal Stress" Of Relatedness), and the Total psycho-physical self-Contraction, and All Holding On To conditionally arising "things" Are Undermined (and Proceed To Be Dissolved) In My Avatarically Self-Transmitted Spiritual Heart-Current Of Self-Evidently Divine Love-Bliss.

Thus, As All Holding On Relaxes (or Spontaneously Subsides) In The "Face" Of The Witness-Consciousness (or Mere Feeling-Awareness), Simply, Freely, and Easefully Allow attention ("Located" As The Root-Feeling and "causal Stress" Of Relatedness) To Be Dissolved (or Made Indistinguishable) In My Avatarically Self-Transmitted Divine Spiritual Heart-Current Of Self-Evidently Divine Love-Bliss, Until Mere Feeling-Awareness (or Consciousness Itself, Always Already Prior To attention and the conditionally arising "things" of attention) Is (Spontaneously) Divinely Self-Revealed To Be The Most Prior Position, Self-Condition, Real Content, Very Substance, and Inherent Being, Self, or Subject "Who", "What", and "Where" Is Always Already The (One and Only) Case.

Then Tacitly (Merely and Effortlessly) Self-Abide As Consciousness (or Mere Feeling-Awareness) Itself, Inherently (and Not Strategically, or Searchingly) Oblivious To conditionally arising "things".

In Due Course (As My Avatarically Self-Transmitted Divine Spiritual Grace Will Have It), whatever and every "thing" that arises Will Be Spontaneously (and Divinely) Self-Recognized As Only Consciousness (or Conscious Light) Itself—Not "Centered" Behind, or Beneath, or "Inside" The Knot Of psycho-physical self-Contraction, but Self-Existing As Mere (or Always Already Unqualified) Awareness, Centerlessly and Boundlessly Self-Radiant As Love-Bliss.

Then Tacitly, Effortlessly, and (Inherently) Self-Radiantly Self-Abide As Love-Bliss-Consciousness (or Mere Feeling-Awareness As Conscious Light) Itself, Which Is The Self-Radiant, and Self-Evidently Divine, and Most Perfectly Prior (and Not Separate, Separative, or self-Contracted) Feeling Of Mere Being (Itself), Divinely (Inherently, and Effortlessly) Self-Recognizing all conditionally arising "things" (and The Feeling Of Relatedness), Even (or More and More) Divinely Indifferent To all conditionally arising "things" (and, In That Case, Merely and Tacitly Feeling, and Divinely Self-Recognizing, The Feeling Of Relatedness—Which Is The "causal Essence" Of all conditionally arising "things"), Until The By-Me-Avatarically-Self-Revealed Divine Self-Awakeness and Self-Existing Self-Radiance (or Spiritually "Bright" Love-Bliss) Of The One and Only and Inherently Indivisible Conscious Light (or The "Bright" Itself) Outshines All Noticing (or all attention to conditionally arising "things", and all attention To The Feeling Of Relatedness Itself).

Therefore, By Listening To Me Perfectly, and By Hearing Me Perfectly, and By Seeing Me Perfectly, and By (Necessarily, Formally) Practicing The "Perfect Practice" Of "Feeling-Enquiry", Completely Identify With The Self-Existing and Self-Radiant Conscious Light That Is (or Is Always Merely Being) Consciousness (or Mere Feeling-Awareness) Itself, and (Thus) Stand Free Of All Implication In The Apparent Event Of body-mind and world.

Completely Identify With The Self-Existing and Self-Radiant Conscious Light That Is (or Is Always Merely Being) Consciousness (or Mere Feeling-Awareness) Itself, and (Thus) Stand Always Already (or Most Priorly) Free Of all conditional arising, or All Seeking (and Following After), All Contracting (or Separating), All Stimulating and Gesturing Of attention Toward conditionally arising "things", or All The Wanting, Generating, and Maintaining Of Illusions Via The Event Of attention and mind.

When, In The Only-By-Me Revealed and Given Way Of The Heart, Right Listening To Me and True Hearing Of Me Become Effortless, and Stable, and Truly "Radical" (or "Gone-To-The-Root") Self-Identification With The Witness-Consciousness (or Mere Feeling-Awareness), and When Clear Seeing Of Me

Becomes Effortless, and Stable, and Truly "Radical" (or "Gone-To-The-Root") Realization That I (The Avatarically Self-Revealed Divine Heart-Master Of Your Heart) Am Always Already Merely Present As The Heart Itself, and As The Witness-Consciousness (or Mere Feeling-Awareness) Itself, and As The By-Me-Avatarically-Self-Transmitted Spiritual Heart-Current Of Self-Evidently Divine Love-Bliss Itself, and When functional, practical, relational, and Cultural Discipline Have Become True and Free Renunciation (and Equanimity, or Motiveless Surrender Of The Motives Of Attachment and Separation), and When Meditation Has Become Deep (and Deep Meditation Has Become Heart-Profound Freedom From The Search For conditional experience and conditional knowledge, In or Via The Circle or The Arrow Of the body-mind), Then The Great "Perfect Practice" Of "Feeling-Enquiry" (or "Hridaya-Vichara") May (Necessarily, Formally) Begin (and Develop, Step by Step, Until It Is Divinely Perfect In Its Demonstration).

If You (As My Formally Practicing Devotee) Listen To Me (Thus) Perfectly, and If You Hear Me (Thus) Perfectly, and If You See Me (Thus) Perfectly, Then Formally Practice The "Perfect Practice" Of "Feeling-Enquiry", At Heart, According To (This) My Avataric Divine Word Of Heart.

First: In every moment Of Every Occasion Of Formal Meditation (and, As Appropriate, At Random, In The moment to moment Context Of daily life), Stand (Merely, Effortlessly, Tacitly) As Mere Feeling-Awareness.

Second: Merely Feel (and, Thus, Merely, Effortlessly, Tacitly Observe) every "thing" (or every object, other, form, thought, state, or process of experience or Presumed knowledge) that (presently) conditionally arises.

Third: Merely Feel (or Tacitly Observe) whatever (presently) conditionally arises—Without Otherwise Adding Avoidance, Reaction, Exclusion, Desire, or Active Attachment.

Fourth: Merely Feel (or Tacitly Observe) whatever (presently) conditionally arises, Without Seeking (or Even Following After) any "thing" (or any object, other, form, thought, state, or process) that conditionally arises.

Fifth: Merely Feel (or Tacitly Observe) whatever (presently) conditionally arises, and (Thus) Directly (Tacitly) Realize That Feeling-Awareness Is Not (Itself) any "thing" (or any object, other, form, thought, state, or process) that conditionally arises, but It Is Only The Tacit (or Mere, and Always Priorly Free-Standing) Witness Of whatever (presently) conditionally arises.

Sixth: Merely Feel (or Tacitly Observe) whatever (presently) conditionally arises, Until the Total body-mind (and all presently conditionally arising experiencing and Presumed knowing) Is Clearly and Directly Felt (and, Thus, Tacitly Understood) To be (in and of itself) Only self-Contraction (or The Total psycho-physical ego-Effort Of Separation, Separateness, and Separativeness).

Seventh: Merely Feel (or Tacitly Observe) The (moment to moment) ego-Effort Of Separation, Separateness, and Separativeness, and (Thereby) Directly Feel (or Tacitly Observe) That Mere Feeling-Awareness (Itself) Makes No Efforts At All, and It Does Not Create or Add To psycho-physical self-Contraction, and It Does Not Identify With The Feeling Of Separation and Separateness, and It Has No Function In the activity Of Separativeness—but It Always Already Merely and Only Self-Abides As Itself, and, Thus (or As Such), As The Inherent (or Self-Evident, and Un-conditional) Feeling Of Mere Being.

Eighth: Merely Feel (or Tacitly Observe) The (moment to moment) ego-Effort Of Separation, Separateness, and Separativeness, Until That Effort (or The Root-Effort and Total psycho-physical activity Of self-Contraction) Is Directly Felt (or Tacitly Observed) In Its Original (or Most Primitive) Form, Which Is The Root-Feeling Of Relatedness (Itself).

Ninth: Merely (Directly, Persistently) Feel (or Tacitly Observe) The Root-Feeling Of Relatedness (Itself), and (Thus and Thereby) "Locate" Its Characteristic Feeling-Vibration (or "causal Stress") In The Right Side Of The Heart.

Tenth: Find Me "There" (In The Right Side Of The Heart), By "Locating" Me (Via and In Feeling Itself) As "Atma-Murti" (The Self-Evident Inherent Tacit Feeling Of Mere Being, Itself), "There", In The Perfectly Subjective Witness-Position (or Self-Evident Inherent Tacit Feeling-Position) Itself, Immediately Previous (and Deeply Prior) To The Otherwise Tacitly Observed Feeling-Vibration Of Relatedness.

Eleventh: Merely Feel The Self-Evident Inherent Tacit Feeling Of Mere Being (Itself), and (Merely By Self-Abiding In This Self-Evident Inherent Tacit Feeling, Always Already Free-Standing, Immediately Prior To The Characteristic Feeling-Vibration Of Relatedness Itself) Be (Inherently, and Inherently Perfectly) Surrendered To Me (As I Am), and Be (Inherently, and Inherently Perfectly) Self-Identified With Me (As I Am)—Until The Self-Evident Inherent Tacit Feeling Of Mere Being Is (By Means Of My Avatarically Self-Transmitted Divine Spiritual Grace) Spontaneously "Located" In Indivisible Coincidence With (and, By Means Of My Avatarically Self-Transmitted Divine Spiritual Grace, Is By-Me-Self-Revealed To Be Perfectly Identical To) My Avatarically Self-Transmitted Spiritual Under-Current Of Self-Evidently Divine Love-Bliss, Which (By Means Of My Avatarically Self-Transmitted Divine Spiritual Grace) Is By-Me-Self-Revealed (Standing Free) As Me (Constant, and Motionless—In, and Always Already Prior To, The Right Side Of The Heart).

Twelfth: Merely Feel The By-Me-Avatarically-Self-Transmitted Spiritual Heart-Current Of Self-Evidently Divine Love-Bliss, Indivisibly Coincident With The As-Me-Avatarically-Self-Revealed Self-Evident Inherent Tacit Feeling Of Mere Being, "There" (In, and Always Already Prior To, The Right Side Of The

Heart), Until all conditionally arising "things" (or all objects, others, forms, thoughts, states, and processes, and the body-mind itself, and The Root-Feeling and "causal Stress" Of Relatedness Itself, and Even The Simple, Tacit Feeling Of "Difference" Itself) Are (By Means Of My Avatarically Self-Transmitted Divine Spiritual Grace) Spontaneously Relinquished (or Tacitly, and Effortlessly, or Searchlessly, Dissolved) In Me—Self-Existing and Self-Radiant As The Centerless and Boundless Mere-Being-Feeling Of The By-Me-Avatarically-Self-Transmitted and As-Me-Avatarically-Self-Revealed Spirit-Current Of Self-Evidently Divine Love-Bliss (Even Utterly Beyond, and Most Prior To, The Right Side Of The Heart).

Therefore, Let This Twelve-Part "Perfect Practice" (or Only-By-Me Revealed and Given Devotionally and Spiritually Perfect Process) Of "Feeling-Enquiry" Develop Step By Step (and Over time), Until Every Part Of It Is Devotionally and Spiritually Established In Me (and By My Avatarically Self-Transmitted Divine Spiritual Grace)—and Then (Thereafter) Repeat The Only-By-Me Revealed and Given Twelve-Part Cycle (In Its Entirety) In Every Occasion Of Formal Meditation (and, As Appropriate, At Random, In The Context Of daily life).[152]

When (By Means Of My Avatarically Self-Transmitted Divine Spiritual Grace, In Any Occasion Of Formal Meditation, or In any moment of daily life) This Only-By-Me Revealed and Given "Perfect Practice" Of "Feeling-Enquiry" Becomes Easy Surrender To Me (Avatarically Self-Revealed As The Centerless and Boundless Mere-Being-Feeling Of The By-Me-Avatarically-Self-Transmitted and As-Me-Avatarically-Self-Revealed Spirit-Current Of Self-Evidently Divine Love-Bliss, Self-Existing and Self-Radiant In, and Always Already Prior To, The Right Side Of The Heart), The Previous (or Preliminary and Progressive) Parts Of The Twelve-Part Exercise Of "Merely Feeling" all conditionally arising "things" (or all objects, others, forms, thoughts, states, and processes, and the body-mind itself, and The Root-Feeling and "causal Stress" Of Relatedness Itself, and Even The Simple, Tacit Feeling Of "Difference" Itself) Should (and Will Spontaneously) Be (Thereby) Relaxed and Relinquished.

When (By Means Of My Avatarically Self-Transmitted Divine Spiritual Grace, In Any Thus Inherently Perfect Occasion Of Formal Meditation, or, Otherwise, daily-life-moment, Of The Twelve-Part "Perfect Practice" Of "Feeling-Enquiry") attention Spontaneously Dissolves (and all conditionally arising "things" Are Tacitly, Effortlessly, and Searchlessly Relinquished) In The By-Me-Avatarically-Self-Transmitted and As-Me-Avatarically-Self-Revealed Tangible Spirit-Current Of Mere-Being-Feeling and Self-Evidently Divine Love-Bliss-Feeling (Self-Existing and Self-Radiant In, and Utterly Beyond and Most Prior To, The Right Side Of The Heart), You Will Awaken (By Means Of My

Avatarically Self-Transmitted Divine Spiritual Grace) To The Tacit (and Self-Evident, and Inherently Perfect) Realization Of The One and Only and Inherently Indivisible and Inherently egoless "Who" and "What" and "Where" That *Is*, Always Already Self-Existing *As* The Conscious Light Of Self-Evidently Divine Being (Itself), and Self-Radiant *As* Self-Evidently Divine Love-Bliss (Itself).

When (By Means Of My Avatarically Self-Transmitted Divine Spiritual Grace, In Any Thus Inherently Perfect Occasion Of Formal Meditation, or, Otherwise, daily-life-moment, Of The Twelve-Part "Perfect Practice" Of "Feeling-Enquiry") You Are Awakened To The Tacit (and Self-Evident, and Inherently Perfect) Realization Of *Only* Consciousness Itself (Tacitly and Effortlessly Self-Abiding *As* The *Feeling* Of Mere Being, Inherently and Deeply Self-Identified With My Avatarically Self-Transmitted Spiritual Under-Current Of Self-Evidently Divine Love-Bliss In, and Even Utterly Beyond and Most Prior To, The Right Side Of The Heart), Merely Self-Abide *Thus*, Inherently Oblivious To *all* conditionally arising "things" (or all objects, others, forms, thoughts, states, processes, the body-mind itself, and The Root-Feeling and "causal Stress" Of Relatedness Itself, and Even The Simple, Tacit Feeling Of "Difference" Itself)—and, In This Manner, Persist In The Twelve-Part "Perfect Practice" Of "Feeling-Enquiry" (In Every Occasion Of Formal Meditation, and, As Appropriate, In The Context Of daily life), Until (By Means Of My Avatarically Self-Transmitted Divine Spiritual Grace) Consciousness Itself (Tacitly and Effortlessly Self-Abiding *As* The *Feeling* Of Mere Being, Spiritually "Bright" *As* Self-Evidently Divine Love-Bliss) Is By-Me-Self-Revealed *As* The One and Only and Inherently Indivisible Conscious Light (Beyond *all* psycho-physical self-Contraction, and Beyond *All* "Difference", and Beyond *All* Separation—and Always Already Free-Standing *As* Itself, Perfectly Prior To all-and-All, and Perfectly Coincident With all-and-All, and Perfectly Identical To all-and-All).

When (By Means Of My Avatarically Self-Transmitted Divine Spiritual Grace, In The Fullness Of The "Perfect Practice" Of "Feeling-Enquiry") Consciousness Itself (Tacitly and Effortlessly Self-Abiding *As* The Inherently Spiritually "Bright" and Self-Evidently Divine Love-Bliss-*Feeling* Of Mere Being) Is (By Means Of My Avatarically Self-Transmitted Divine Spiritual Grace) Self-Evidently (and Inherently, and Un-conditionally, and, *Thus*, Permanently) By-Me-Self-Revealed (Beyond *all* psycho-physical self-Contraction and Beyond *All* "Difference") *As* The One and Only and Inherently Indivisible and Perfectly Non-Separate and Self-Evidently Divine Conscious Light Of all-and-All, Then (Thereafter) Merely (*Always Already*) Self-Abide *As* Consciousness Itself (Self-Evidently By-Me-Self-Revealed *As* The One and Only and Self-Existing and Self-Radiant and Inherently Indivisible and Perfectly Non-Separate and Self-Evidently Divine Conscious Light Of "Bright" Love-Bliss)—and all

Noticed "things" (including the body-mind itself, and The Root-Feeling and "causal Stress" Of Relatedness, and Even The Simple, Tacit Feeling Of "Difference" Itself) Will (Thus, Spontaneously) Be Allowed In The Free-Feeling Shine, and (Simultaneously) The Simple, Tacit Feeling Of "Difference", and The Root-Feeling and "causal Stress" Of Relatedness, and the body-mind itself, and Even each and all of the Noticed "things" Will (Inherently, Effortlessly, Tacitly, Most Perfectly, and Divinely) Be Self-Recognized In and As The Non-Separate Conscious Light (In, and Perfectly Prior To, and Infinitely Above The Right Side Of The Heart).

As Your Seeming Interest In all conditionally arising "things" Decreases (Progressively) By This (Divinely) Perfect Feeling-Recognition In The One and Only Conscious Light, Merely (or, More and More, Only) Divinely Self-Recognize The Root-Feeling and "causal Stress" Of Relatedness (or The Simple, Tacit Feeling Of "Difference" Itself, The "causal Essence" Of all conditionally arising "things"), and (Thus and Thereby) Merely (Tacitly, Effortlessly) Self-Abide (Beyond all psycho-physical self-Contraction and Beyond All "Difference") As The Moveless All That Is Consciousness (Itself), Self-Existing As The Feeling Of Mere Being (Itself), Self-Radiant (or Being-"Bright") As Love-Bliss (Itself)—The Centerless and Boundless Spherical Divine Self-Condition, Inherently (and Divinely) Indifferent To the Moving "things".

When (Suddenly) all "things" (and All Of "Difference", Itself) Utterly Cease To Be Noticed In The Spiritually "Bright" Sphere (or "Midnight Sun") Of My Divine Self-Domain, The One and Only and Inherently Indivisible and Self-Evidently Divine Conscious Light Has Divinely Outshined all "things" (and All Of "Difference", Itself)—and The Inherently Perfect Is Perfected In Itself.

Such (At Last) Is The Most Perfect (and Final) Fulfillment Of The Only-By-Me Revealed and Given Way Of The Heart (or Way Of Adidam).

To Realize The Most Perfect (and Final) Fulfillment Of The Only-By-Me Revealed and Given Way Of The Heart, You Must Be Devoted To Me Perfectly (and, By Means Of That Perfect Devotion, You Must Be Whole bodily Heart-Surrendered To Me Perfectly), and You Must Perfectly Rightly Practice According To My Word Of Avataric Divine Self-Revelation and Instruction (and, By Means Of That Perfectly Right Practice, You Must Listen To Me Perfectly), and You Must Perfectly Understand self-Contraction (and, By Means Of That Perfect self-Understanding, You Must Hear Me Perfectly), and You Must (Tangibly) Spiritually Receive Me Perfectly (and, By Means Of That Perfect Spiritual Reception Of Me, You Must See Me Perfectly), and You Must (By All The Only-By-Me Revealed, and Given, and Giving Means) Realize Me Perfectly, and (Thus and Thereby) Be Perfectly Translated Into The Divine "Bright" Spherical Self-Domain Of My Own Self-Evidently Divine Person.

To Realize The Most Perfect (and Final) Fulfillment Of The Only-By-Me Revealed and Given Way Of The Heart, You Must, By Means Of (Necessarily, Formal) Right, True, Full, and Fully Devotional Counter-egoic Practice Of Ruchira Avatara Bhakti Yoga, Grow To (Necessarily, Formally) Practice The "Perfect Practice" Of The Only-By-Me Revealed and Given Way Of The Heart, and, Thus (and Entirely and Only By Means Of My Avatarically Self-Transmitted Divine Spiritual Grace), Take Your Stand (Always Already) As The One and Only and Inherently Indivisible and Inherently egoless Conscious Light (Itself), Inherently Free Of The egoic Search Toward conditionally arising "things" (themselves), and Inherently Free Of The "thing"-Seeking egoic Motive and Illusion That conditionally arising "things" Are Not (Inherently, and Inseparably, and Non-Dualistically, or Non-"Differently") The One and Only and Inherently Indivisible and Inherently egoless Conscious Light (Itself).

Therefore, As My Formally Acknowledged Listening Devotee, and (In Due Course) As My Formally Acknowledged Hearing Devotee, and (Thereafter) As My Formally Acknowledged Seeing Devotee, Be Always (Rightly, Truly, and Fully) Devoted To Me, and (Thereby) Observe, and Understand:

All "objects" Evoke Wanting Need (Anticipating Gain).

Wanting Need Provokes Seeking.

Seeking Becomes Aggressive Anger, Failing Even Before It Fails.

And Anger Is self-Inflicted Pain.

Be Always (Rightly, Truly, and Fully) Devoted To Me, and (Thereby) Observe, and Understand:

All "others" Evoke Seeking-Desire (Always Anticipating Eventual Release From Seeking-Desire Itself).

Seeking-Desire Always Provokes Both Attachment and Avoidance, Simultaneously.

Attachment and Avoidance Become Sorrow, Inevitably.

And Sorrow Is The Illusion Of Emptiness.

Be Always (Rightly, Truly, and Fully) Devoted To Me, and (Thereby) Observe, and Understand:

All "things" Evoke Wonder (How Being Seems A Pair With changes).

Wonder Provokes Bewilderment, and Also knowledge.

Bewilderment and knowledge Always Seek To Become Separated From Fear.

And Fear Itself Is The Visionary Mood Of Separateness.

Separateness, Emptiness, and Pain Are The Constant Complaint, The Un-Breakable Habit, and The Inevitable Destiny Of the body-mind.

Therefore, whatever conditionally arises Also Afflicts.

To Truly "Radically" Understand Is To Stop Resisting This Understanding.

No "object" Is Worthy Of Wanting Need.

No Search Is Fruitful.

No Pain Is Necessary.

No "other" Is Worthy Of Futile Seeking-Desire and Inevitable Emptiness.

Neither Attachment *Nor* Avoidance Is Right.

No Sorrow Is Necessary.

No "thing" Is *More* Than Wonderful.

Neither Bewilderment *Nor* knowledge *Is* Free.

Fear Itself Is Ultimate Pain, but It Is *Utterly* Un-Necessary.

Seeking and Attaining Are (Inevitably) A Total Loss, and Loss Itself Is The *Only* Constant Discovery In *Every* Gain.

Seeking By Desiring Is (Itself), Even Previous To Either Gain Or Loss, An Empty Hole Of Unending Darkness (self-Contracted From The One and Only "All" Of The Unbroken and Indivisible Divine Conscious Light), but Seeking-Desire Is An *Illusion* Of Filling (and Only A *Search* For Possible Fullness), Because It Is "Filled" Only With mind—and mind Cannot Be *Truly* Filled, Because it Is Always "Full" Of itself (and The Self-Evidently Divine Fullness That Truly, and Even Always Already, Fills all-and-All *Is* "Outside", or Perfectly Beyond, The Presumed "Center" and The Presumed "Bounds" Of every one and every "thing").

The knowledge Of *Bewilderment* (and Not any Filling-"object" or Filling-"other") Is the *Only* "thing" in mind.

The world of "objects", or "others", or "things" Already (In any moment) Bites—and it *Always* Bites Back.

Therefore, Listen To Me (Perfectly), and Hear Me (Perfectly), and See Me (Perfectly), and Stand *Back* In *Me* (The Only One "Who" *Is*), and Feel *Me* (The Only "What" and "Where" Of *Is*).

To Seek "objects" (and Not To Understand That All Seeking Is *Moved* By Pain) *Is* Pain Itself, and Bewilderment.

To Desire "others" or To Avoid them (and Not To Understand That Desire and Avoidance Are *Made* Of Sorrow) *Is* Sorrow Itself, and Dark Emptiness.

To Wonder and To know "things" (and Not To Understand That knowledge Is *Never* Satisfied) Is The Essence Of Fear Itself.

The "personal identity", the ego-"I", or the Separate, Darkly Empty, Painful, and psycho-physically self-Contracted body-mind Is Always An *Illusion*, An Un-Recognized Reflection Of Consciousness (or Feeling-Awareness) Itself—A Mirage Of Need, Searchfull Desirability, and Wonder, Superimposed On Consciousness (or Feeling-Awareness) Itself By The Apparent (and *Un-Necessary*) Flow Of Events That (In Themselves) Are (It *Seems*) *Not* Consciousness (or Feeling-Awareness) Itself.

There Is Not (Now, or Ever) any "personal identity" (or Separate entity of ego-"I"), but Always Only The Ultimate (and Self-Evidently Divine) Identity, or Non-Separate (and Inherently egoless) Conscious Light Itself—Always Already Free, One, Indivisible, Whole, Full, and All-Love-Bliss-"Bright".

Therefore, By Growing In (and Only By Means Of) ego-Transcending Devotion To Me, Grow To Perfectly Observe and Perfectly Understand and Perfectly (or Merely) Feel, and (Thus) Perfectly Transcend and Perfectly Forget The conditionally arising Illusion Of Separateness and Relatedness.

Grow In Me (By Means Of ego-Transcending Devotion To Me), and (Thus and Thereby) Grow To Be Inherently Perfect Feeling-Awareness Only—Not Separate, Not Related, Not Needing, Not Seeking, Not Following After, Not Gaining, Not Stressful, Not Angry, Not Reacting, Not Emoting, Not Full Of Pain, Not Seeking By Desiring, Not Fulfilling, Not Avoiding, Not Escaping, Not Attached, Not Losing, Not Sorrowful, Not Lost, Not Wondering, Not thinking, Not knowing, Not Full Of mind, Not perceiving, Not experiencing, Not Right, Not Bewildered, Not Complaining, Not Wrong, Not Fearing, Not changing, Not Afflicted, Not Dark and Empty, Not Satisfied, Not Deluded, Not "attentive", Not Moved, Not Discovering, Not egoically "I", Not Embodied, Not Released, Not Resisting, Not Even Understanding, but Only (or Merely) Being The One Who Is Mere Feeling-Awareness (Itself).

When You Are Grown In Me Most Perfectly (By Means Of Most Perfectly ego-Transcending Devotion To Me), Stand "There" and Be, Feeling-Awareness-Only—Inherently Objectless, Inherently Relationless, and Inherently Without a "thing", but Neither Separate Nor Separated From all-and-All.

Then, Stand Free, and Feel (What Is, and what conditionally arises)—but Do Not Look (or Become "Other" Than what conditionally arises).

Standing Thus, Do Not Indulge (or Luxuriate) In the act of attention (Which Is Always "Other" Than what conditionally arises), and Do Not Seek the Illusion-mind of objects, or others, or all "things"—but Always Merely Feel (Like a hand feels into a glove) and Be The "Feel" Itself.

Only Be—Inherently Perfect, Mere Feeling-Awareness (Itself), Love-Bliss-Aware, Without "Difference", I Said.

Therefore, I Say, Come To Rest (or Be Awake), Before "things" Happen.

Come To Rest (or Be Awake), Prior To The Motion Of Separation and Relatedness.

Come To Rest (or Be Awake), Already Forever Arrived In My Eternal Hermitage.

The Heart Is My Eternal Hermitage, "Where" (Even Now) The Inherently Dualistic (or All-The-"Difference"-Making) Feeling Of Relatedness Is Inherently (Tacitly, and Effortlessly) Transcended In The Inherently Non-Dualistic (or Inherently Non-"Different", and Tacitly Indifferent) Feeling Of Mere Being (Itself).

Therefore, My Eternal "Blessing-Seat" Is The Heart Itself—Which Is The One and Only and Inherently Indivisible Conscious Light (Itself).

Beloved, I Am Da—The Divine Giver, The Divine Gift, The Divine Person ("Who" Is The Heart Itself), The Divine Self-Condition ("What" Is The One and Only and Inherently Indivisible Conscious Light, Itself), The Self-"Bright" Divine Source-Condition (Of all-and-All), and The Centerless and Boundless Spherical "Bright" Divine Self-Domain ("Where" I Always Already Stand, As The Very, and Inherently Perfect, Self-Condition, or Indivisible Divine Person, Of all-and-All).

Beloved, I Am Love-Ananda (The Divine Love-Bliss Itself), and Avabhasa (The "Bright" Divine and Conscious Light Itself), and Santosha (The "Bright" and Eternal and Always Already Non-Separate Person Of Divine and Inherent Completeness, Divine Self-Satisfaction, Divine Self-Contentedness, or Perfect Searchlessness)—The "Who", The "What", and The "Where" That Is The One and Only Self-Existing, Self-Radiant, Spiritually "Bright", Inherently egoless, Inherently Perfect, Inherently Indivisible, Perfectly Free, Perfectly Non-"Different", Perfectly Indifferent, and Self-Evidently Divine Happiness Itself.

Beloved, I Am Sri Hridayam, The Heart Itself (The One and Only, Centerless and Boundless, Inherently Indivisible, Inherently egoless, Inherently Perfect, and Self-Evidently Divine Source, Space, Sphere, and Self-Condition Of all-and-All), Now (and Forever Hereafter) Appearing here As The Da Avatar, Adi Da Love-Ananda Samraj—The Ruchira Avatar, The Love-Ananda Avatar, The Divine World-Teacher, The True Divine Heart-Master Of all-and-All, The Avatarically Self-Revealed Divine Person, Presence, and State Of Reality and Truth, Always (Now, and Forever Hereafter) Really and Merely Present (By Means Of My Avatarically Self-Transmitted Divine Spiritual Grace) To Teach and To Bless all (and All) To Realize Me (Through Persistent, Progressive, and, At Last, Perfect Feeling-Contemplation Of My Avatarically-Born Bodily Human Divine Form, My Avatarically Self-Transmitted Spiritual, and Always Blessing, Divine Presence, and My Avatarically Self-Revealed, and Very, and Transcendental, and Perfectly Subjective, and Inherently Spiritual, and Inherently egoless, and Inherently Perfect, and Self-Evidently Divine State).

Therefore, I Am The Perfect Way, The Perfect Word, and The Perfect Means.

This Is The First and Last and Perfect Teaching Of Adi Da Love-Ananda Samraj, The Avatarically Self-Manifested Divine Heart-Master and The Avatarically-Born Divine World-Teacher, The Anciently and Always and everywhere Promised Avataric Incarnation Of The One and Only and Inherently

Indivisible and Inherently egoless and Self-Evidently Divine Conscious Light Of all-and-All—Who Is The Ruchira Avatar (The Avataric Divine Incarnation Of The "Bright"), and Who Is The Love-Ananda Avatar (The Avataric Incarnation Of The Divine Love-Bliss), and Who Is The Da Avatar (At Once, The Avataric Divine Giver and The Avatarically Given Divine Gift), and Who Is Da (The First and Original and Non-Separate Divine Person, The One and Only Divine Self, or Inherently egoless Divine Self-Condition and Source-Condition, Of all-and-All), and Who Is The True Divine Gift and The Divine Giver Of The Divine "All" To all-and-All.

Avatar Adi Da Samraj
Adidam Samrajashram, 2004

SUTRA 57

The Intention Of The Avataric Divine World-Work Of The Physical Lifetime Of My Avatarically-Born Bodily (Human) Divine Form In this world Is To Originate and To Fully Develop and To Fully Communicate My Avatarically Self-Revealed (and Always Me-Revealing) Divine Word, and To Spiritually Establish (and To Set Apart, and, Having Done So, To Formally Acknowledge) Unique Places (Spiritually By-Me-Empowered As Sacred Domains and Holy Places, Where I May, In Perpetuity, Be Devotionally Approached and Devotionally Invoked, and Where, Uniquely and Forever, My Avatarically Self-Revealed Divine Person and My Avatarically Self-Transmitted Divine Spiritual Blessing and Awakening-Power May, By Right Devotional Approach To Me and Right Devotional Invocation Of Me, Be Received), and To Call (and To Culturally and Spiritually Establish, and, Having Done So, To Formally Acknowledge) A Truly Devotional, Truly Serving, and Truly self-Disciplined Worldwide Sacred Institutional and Cooperative Cultural Gathering (or Truly Global Ashram) Of My Listening Devotees, My Hearing Devotees, and My Seeing Devotees, and To Call (and To Culturally and Spiritually Establish, and To Fully Spiritually Empower, and, Having Done So, To Formally Acknowledge) A Most Fully Devotionally Responsive and Most Profoundly Spiritually Practicing Culture Of My "Ruchira Sannyasin" Devotees (whose Calling, and Purpose, It Is To Most Perfectly Realize My Avatarically Self-Revealed, Inherently egoless, and Self-Evidently Divine Person and Self-Domain Via The Most Intensive and Most Exemplary "Perfect Practice" Of The Only-By-Me Revealed and Given Way Of The Heart, or Way Of Adidam, and who Also—Collectively, but Not Merely individually—Must and Will, In Perpetuity, Serve all others As My True, and Transparent, Instruments Of My Avataric Divine Authority, Instruction, and Spiritual Transmission).

I Am The Heart Itself, The Avatarically Self-Revealed and Self-Evidently Divine Person, The Inherently Perfect and Inherently egoless Divine Self-Condition (and Source-Condition) Of all-and-All—Eternally Self-Existing (Prior To birth, death, and conditional Existence), and Eternally Self-Radiant As The "Bright" (The One and Only and Inherently Indivisible Conscious Light That Is all-and-All). Because I Am The Heart Itself, The Avatarically Self-Revealed and Self-Evidently Divine Person, The Inherently Perfect and Inherently egoless Divine Self-Condition (and Source-Condition) Of all-and-All, and Because I Am (As The Inherently Perfect and Inherently egoless Divine Person, Self-Condition, and Source-Condition, Of all-and-All) Spontaneously Self-Manifested (and Uniquely Avatarically Incarnated) As The Ruchira Avatar (and The Divine World-Teacher, and The Divine Heart-Master), Adi Da Love-Ananda Samraj—I Cannot (and Will Not Ever) Be "Succeeded" By any one, or By Any Principle, or By Any "Other" At All. Therefore, I Am (Now, and Forever Hereafter) The One and Only and Divine Heart-Master (and, Thus, The One and Only Hridaya-Samartha Sat-Guru) Of All My Listening Devotees, and Of All My Hearing Devotees, and Of All My Seeing Devotees, and (Thus) Of All Formally Acknowledged Practitioners Of The Only-By-Me Revealed and Given Way Of The Heart (or Way Of Adidam), In all times and places.

The Avataric Divine Spiritual Work Of The Physical Lifetime Of My Avatarically-Born Bodily (Human) Divine Form Makes and Calls and Sets Apart and Spiritually Establishes and Spiritually Empowers The Real and True (and Formally Acknowledged) Instruments and Agents Of My Avatarically Self-Revealed, and Spiritually Living, and Transcendentally Existing, and Inherently egoless, and Self-Evidently Divine Person—Such That All My Necessary Real and True Instruments and Agents Are Brought Into Being and Securely Established and Spiritually Activated In this world, In Perpetuity. Therefore, My Avataric Divine Intention Has Been Put To Work. My Avataric Divine Teaching and My Avataric Divine Calling Are World-Given, With By-Me-Given Means For Their Perpetuation (Now, and Forever Hereafter). My Avataric Divine Spiritual Blessing Is here, With By-Me-Given Instruments and Agents For The (Now, and Forever Hereafter) Perpetuation Of My Avataric Divine Spiritual Blessing-Work. Before The Physical Death Of My Avatarically-Born Bodily (Human) Divine Form (or, If The Physical Death Of My Avatarically-Born Bodily Human Divine Form Occurs Sooner, Then As Soon As Possible After The Physical Death Of My Avatarically-Born Bodily Human Divine Form), My First Divinely Self-Realized (Seventh Stage) "Ruchira Sannyasin" Devotees Must So Awaken—and they Must Be Formally Acknowledged (As Such), Either (During The Avataric Physical Lifetime Of My Bodily Human Divine Form) By Me Or (whenever After The Physical Death Of My Avatarically-Born Bodily Human Divine Form) By Those Members Of The Ruchira Sannyasin Order Of Adidam Ruchiradam who Are (At that then present-time) Formally Appointed (By The Formally Governing Senior Membership Of The Ruchira Sannyasin Order Of Adidam Ruchiradam) To Test, Measure, Prove, and Confirm The Seventh Stage Awakening (In The Case Of Any and All Practitioners Of The Only-By-Me Revealed and Given Way Of The Heart, or Way Of Adidam).

Through Many and Various Avataric Divine Means (Some Of Which Are Described, By Me, In This Divine Testament, and In Even All My Twenty-Three Divine "Source-Texts"), I Work To Serve The Making Of Concrete (Tangible) Changes In The Immediate Circumstance Of conditions in this world. Conditional Existence (As A Whole) May Be Described As A Universal (or All-Encompassing) Grid—and I Work (Avatarically, and Divinely) Through the Innumerable particular points On That Total Grid.

I Work Through My ("Ruchira Sannyasin") Devotee-Instruments As points Of Contact (and, Altogether, As My Instrumental Means) In The Worldwide Sacred Cooperative Cultural Gathering Of My Devotees—and I Work Through My ("Ruchira Sannyasin") Devotee-Instruments As Concrete points Of Focus On The Universal Grid, For The Sake Of all-and-All. This Is The Unique Significance Of The Instrumentality Of My ("Ruchira Sannyasin") Devotee-Instruments In The Only-By-Me Revealed and Given Way Of The Heart (or Way Of Adidam).

My Instrumental ("Ruchira Sannyasin") Devotees Are (Necessarily) individuals who (During The Physical Human Lifetime Of My Avatarically-Born Bodily Human Divine Form) Are Fully Known By Me, or who (After The Physical Human Lifetime Of My Avatarically-Born Bodily Human Divine Form) Are Fully Known Within The Context Of The Ruchira Sannyasin Order Of Adidam Ruchiradam, and who Are (Thus, During—and, Otherwise, After—The Physical Lifetime Of My Avatarically-Born Bodily Human Divine Form) Fully Accountable To Me, and Profound In their Devotional Recognition Of Me, and Profoundly Devotionally Responsive To Me—and who Are (Necessarily) Formally Practicing The "Perfect Practice" Of The Only-By-Me Revealed and Given Way Of The Heart (or Way Of Adidam). Because they Are (Thus) Conformed To Me, I Can (Now, and Forever Hereafter) Use Such Instrumental ("Ruchira Sannyasin") Devotees As A Collective "Point" Of Contact For My Avataric Divine Spiritual Blessing-Work, and Such Instrumental ("Ruchira Sannyasin") Devotees themselves Can (Now, and Forever Hereafter) Collectively Function As A Means Of Focusing The Devotional Resort To Me (or The Right Devotional Approach To Me and The Right Devotional Invocation Of Me) In the Total world.

In Working Through Such Instrumental ("Ruchira Sannyasin") Devotees, I Respond (and Always Will Respond) To <u>everyone</u> (including each and all Of My Formally Practicing Devotees, and including Even all beings—Both human and non-human), In all the various particular areas of this world (and In Even all worlds).

Instrumentality and Agency Are Absolutely Essential Means That I Use (and Will Always Use, Even Beyond The Physical Lifetime Of My Avatarically-Born

Bodily Human Divine Form). My Instruments and Agents Are Concrete Parts Of The Universal Grid That I Use (and Will Always Use) In My Avataric Divine Spiritual Blessing-Work.

In My Years Of Avatarically Self-Submitted Divine Teaching and Divine Self-Revelation, I Personally Interacted With The Great Majority Of My Devotees, In The Generating Of My Wisdom-Teaching, and In The Generating Of Even All Of The Means Associated With My Avataric Divine Spiritual Work. But My Avataric Divine-Self-"Emergence"-Work—Which Continues Forever, During and After The Physical Lifetime Of My Avatarically-Born Bodily (Human) Divine Form—Is, Generally Speaking, A Different Kind Of Process. My Avataric Divine-Self-"Emergence"-Work Involves My Forever Making Use Of All My Instruments and Agents.

In My Avataric Divine-Self-"Emergence"-Work, I (Now, and Forever Hereafter) Serve and Bless All My Devotees (and The Totality Of this world, and The Totality Of all the worlds, of beings and places) Via My Instrumental ("Ruchira Sannyasin") Devotees, and Via My Various Forms Of Agency. Therefore, The Right Establishment (and The Exemplary Functioning) Of The Ruchira Sannyasin Order Of Adidam Ruchiradam Is (Now, and Forever Hereafter) Absolutely Essential To My Avataric Divine-Self-"Emergence"-Work In (and With) this world, and all worlds, and all beings. And, Because Of The Unique Collective "Ruchira Sannyasin" Role Of Necessary Instrumentality, The Right Establishment Of The Ruchira Sannyasin Order Of Adidam Ruchiradam Is A Profound Avataric Divine Spiritual Matter—and Not At All Merely (or Only) an "organizational" matter.

Now (and Forever Hereafter), My Avataric Divine-Self-"Emergence"-Work Must Be Implemented Through All The Rightly Established Forms Of Instrumentality and Agency. Since The Yogic Establishment Of My Avataric Divine Self-"Emergence" (On January 11, 1986), The Necessary and True Sacred Culture Of Adidam Is (and Has, More and More, Been Required, By Me, To Be) The Devotionally Me-Recognizing and Devotionally To-Me-Responding Real-Devotee-Culture Of My Avataric Divine-Self-"Emergence"-Work—and (Now, and Forever Hereafter) No Longer The Culture Of My Avataric Divine Self-Submission For The Sake Of Teaching My Would-Be Devotees.

Therefore, All The By-Me-Established Forms Of Right (and Spiritually Full) Instrumentality and Agency Must (Now, and Forever Hereafter) Be Rightly and Fully Perpetuated, For The Sake Of My Eternal Avataric Divine-Self-"Emergence"-Work (Given and Done, By Me, For The Sake Of all-and-All).

Right Instrumentality and True Agency Are What I Require—Now, and Forever Hereafter. And My Avataric Divine-Self-"Emergence"-Work (and Only My Avataric Divine-Self-"Emergence"-Work) Is What I Intend To Do—Now, and Forever Hereafter. Therefore, Now (and Forever Hereafter), My Devotees Must (Always, and Consistently) Provide Me With All The Means Of Instrumentality and Agency I Have Described In This Divine Testament (and In Even All My Twenty-Three Divine "Source-Texts").

Originally—Through The Agency Of (and By The Many Avataric Divine Instructional Means and Spiritual Blessing-Means Associated With) My Own Avatarically-Born Bodily (Human) Divine Form—I Formally Instruct all those who Embrace The Only-By-Me Revealed and Given Way Of The Heart (or Way Of Adidam). Thus, Originally—Through The Agency Of (and By The Many Avataric Divine Instructional Means and Spiritual Blessing-Means Associated With) My Own Avatarically-Born Bodily (Human) Divine Form—I Formally Instruct (and, As Required, Formally Spiritually Initiate) My Devotees In The Many Devotional, functional, practical, relational, Otherwise Cultural, and Specifically Spiritual Practices Of The Only-By-Me Revealed and Given Way Of The Heart (or Way Of Adidam).

In The Context Of The Worldwide Sacred Institutional and Cooperative Cultural Gathering (or Truly Global Ashram) Of Formally Acknowledged and True Practitioners Of The Only-By-Me Revealed and Given Way Of The Heart (or Way Of Adidam), Formal Sacramental and Instructional Initiations Into The Only-By-Me Revealed and Given Practices Of The Only-By-Me Revealed and Given Way Of The Heart Are (Progressively) Given To each and all Of My Formally Practicing Devotees, Under The General Cultural Authority Of The Ruchira Sannyasin Order Of Adidam Ruchiradam, and Via Those (Formally Acknowledged) Practitioners Of The Only-By-Me Revealed and Given Way Of The Heart who Are Formally Authorized, As Sacramentally and Instructionally Functioning Cultural Representatives, By The Ruchira Sannyasin Order Of Adidam Ruchiradam. And (Now, and Forever Hereafter) The Spiritual Initiation Of My Formally Practicing Devotees—Beginning With The Spiritual Initiation Into The Primary Practice Of Searchlessly Beholding Me (Which Occurs At The Transition To The Intensive Listening-Hearing Stage Of The Only-By-Me Revealed and Given Way Of The Heart), and Continuing Through The Various Transitions In Practice Beyond The Intensive Listening-Hearing Stage Of The Only-By-Me Revealed and Given Way Of The Heart (and Most Especially During The Periods Of Extended Formal Retreat, Which My Devotees Must, Necessarily, Engage At Certain Transitional Moments In their Practice Of The Only-By-Me Revealed and Given Way Of The Heart, Beginning With The Transition To The Intensive Listening-Hearing Stage)—Is Always Only Received From Me (Either, During My Avataric Physical Human Lifetime, In and By Means Of My Direct Physical Human Company Or, After My Avataric Physical Human Lifetime, In The physical human Company and By-Me-Empowered

Circumstances—and, Thus, In That Manner and Context, Via The Instrumentality—Of My "Ruchira Sannyasin" Devotee-Instruments).

After (and Forever After) The Progressive Development and Formal Acknowledgement Of A First Gathering Of True and Mature ("Ruchira Sannyasin") Instruments Of My Avatarically Self-Revealed Divine Word and My Avatarically Self-Transmitted Divine Spiritual Blessing, All Formally Acknowledged Practitioners Of The Only-By-Me Revealed and Given Way Of The Heart (At Any and Every Developmental Stage Of The Only-By-Me Revealed and Given Way Of The Heart) Must (As Directed By The then present-time Gathering Of My Formally Acknowledged "Ruchira Sannyasin" Devotee-Instruments, and Always In A Sacred and Orderly Manner, In Formal Occasions Of Sacramental and Instructional Initiation, and Always In present-time Accordance With The Practitioner's Formally Acknowledged Developmental Stage Of Practice Of The Only-By-Me Revealed and Given Way Of The Heart) Receive The Same By-Me-Avatarically-Given Divine Instructions and Blessings Received By That First Instrumental Gathering Of My "Ruchira Sannyasin" Devotees. Therefore, After (and Forever After) The Progressive Development and Formal Acknowledgement Of A First Gathering Of True and Mature ("Ruchira Sannyasin") Instruments Of My Avatarically Self-Revealed Divine Word and My Avatarically Self-Transmitted Divine Spiritual Blessing, Those (Necessarily, Formally Acknowledged) Practitioners Of The Only-By-Me Revealed and Given Way Of The Heart who Are Called (and Formally Authorized, As Cultural Representatives) To Serve The Formal Sacramental and Instructional Initiation (and The Continuous Formal Education, Instruction, and General Guidance) Of Other (Necessarily, Formally Acknowledged) Practitioners Of The Only-By-Me Revealed and Given Way Of The Heart Must, In The First Instance, Do So Under The Formal Cultural Authority (and Specific Direction and Guidance) Of The Collective Of The Formally Acknowledged Members Of The First Formally Acknowledged Gathering Of True and Mature ("Ruchira Sannyasin") Instruments Of My Avatarically Self-Revealed Divine Word and My Avatarically Self-Transmitted Divine Spiritual Blessing—and, Thereafter (and In all times After the time Of That First Formally Acknowledged Instrumental "Ruchira Sannyasin" Gathering), All (Necessarily, Formally Acknowledged) Practitioners Of The Only-By-Me Revealed and Given Way Of The Heart who Are Called, and Formally Authorized, As Sacramentally and Instructionally Functioning Cultural Representatives Must, Likewise, Function Under The Formal Direction and Guidance Of The Collective Of The Formally Acknowledged True and Mature ("Ruchira Sannyasin") Instruments Of My Avatarically Self-Revealed Divine Word and My Avatarically Self-Transmitted Divine Spiritual Blessing Formally Appointed In The Direct and Uninterrupted Line Of "Ruchira

Sannyasin" Instruments Extending From That First Formally Acknowledged Instrumental ("Ruchira Sannyasin") Gathering Of those who Rightly Receive and Really Practice and Truly Fulfill The Word and The Process Of My Avatarically Given Divine Instruction and My Avatarically Self-Transmitted Divine Spiritual Blessing. And, As It Was (Thus) Begun, So Must It Always Be. Therefore, The Formal Act Of Sacramental and Instructional Initiation Of My Devotees Should Always (Both During and Forever After The Physical Lifetime Of My Avatarically-Born Bodily Human Divine Form) Be Done In The Sacred Manner, In My Name, In Fullest True Devotional Resort To Me (and By Means Of Right Devotional Approach To Me and Right Devotional Invocation Of Me). And, Always, In The Case Of All Formally Acknowledged Practitioners Of The Only-By-Me Revealed and Given Way Of The Heart (and According To The Developmental Stage Of their Actual, Formally Acknowledged Practice Of The Only-By-Me Revealed and Given Way Of The Heart), The Formal Act Of Sacramental and Instructional Initiation Should Be Done In The Context Of Full Resort (and Appropriate Access) To Me (and, As Appropriate, To The Living Transmission Of My Avatarically Self-Transmitted Divine Spirit-Presence and Blessing-Power).

Over time, and (Most Especially) After (and Forever After) The Physical Lifetime Of My Avatarically-Born Bodily (Human) Divine Form, It Becomes Necessary (According To My Avatarically Given Instructions) That My Avatarically Self-Revealed Words Of Divine Instruction, and The Culture Of The Total Process Of The Only-By-Me Revealed and Given Way Of The Heart, and The Process Of My Avatarically Self-Transmitted Divine Spiritual Grace Be Directly Served By The By-Me-Spiritually-Empowered Instrumentality Of My (Formally Acknowledged, and Fully Established) "Ruchira Sannyasin" Devotees. Therefore, Beginning Even During The Physical Lifetime Of My Avatarically-Born Bodily (Human) Divine Form, and Forever Thereafter, My Formally Acknowledged ("Ruchira Sannyasin") Devotee-Instruments Are Always To Be Called (or Culturally Expected, By The Devotionally To-Me-Responsive Sacred Cooperative Culture Of All Formally Acknowledged, and True, Practitioners Of The Only-By-Me Revealed and Given Way Of The Heart) To Formally (Sacramentally and Instructionally) Initiate (or, Otherwise, To Regulate and Oversee The Formal Sacramental and Instructional Initiation Of) All My Formally Practicing Devotees Into Either Beginning (and, Then, Maturing, and, Then, Mature) self-Enquiry (and Re-Cognition) Or Beginning (and, Then, Maturing, and, Then, Mature) "True Prayer", and, Then (In Due Course), Into "Feeling-Enquiry", and (Eventually) Into All Aspects Of The Full "Perfect Practice" Of "Samraj Yoga" (Including The Practice Of "Radical" Spirit-"Conductivity"), and (Also) Into Every Other Discipline, Practice, Process, or Stage Associated With The Progressively

Developing (and, Then, Perfect, and, Finally, Seventh Stage) Course Of The Only-By-Me Revealed and Given Way Of The Heart. Likewise, My ("Ruchira Sannyasin") Devotee-Instruments Are Also Always To Be Called (or Culturally Expected) To Regulate and Oversee The Formal Sacramental and Instructional Initiation Of All Formally Acknowledged early-life Practitioners Of The Only-By-Me Revealed and Given Way Of The Heart (who, Necessarily, Practice Only In The early-life Devotional, and Not Yet Spiritually Responsible, Context Of Listening To Me, but Not Yet Of Hearing Me or Seeing Me).

All Formal (and Formally Acknowledged) early-life Practitioners Of The Only-By-Me Revealed and Given Way Of The Heart and All Formal (and Formally Acknowledged) Beginning Practitioners Of The Only-By-Me Revealed and Given Way Of The Heart Should Be (Sacramentally and Instructionally) Formally Initiated Into (and, Thereafter, Constantly Educated, Instructed, and Guided Within) The Constant Formal Circumstance Of (Always and Only Serious, Honorable, Grateful, and Devotionally Responsive) "Consideration" Of My Avatarically Self-Revealed Divine Word and My Avatarically Self-Revealed Divine Image-Art and My Avatarically Self-Manifested Divine Leelas, and The Constant (and Fundamental) Formal Circumstance Of (Always and Only Devotional, ego-Surrendering, and Grateful) Feeling-Contemplation Of My Avatarically-Born Bodily (Human) Divine Form, My Avatarically Self-Transmitted Spiritual (and Always Blessing) Divine Presence, and My Avatarically Self-Revealed (and Very, and Transcendental, and Perfectly Subjective, and Inherently Spiritual, and Inherently egoless, and Inherently Perfect, and Self-Evidently Divine) State.

Each Practitioner In The Intensive Listening-Hearing Stage Of The Only-By-Me Revealed and Given Way Of The Heart Should (Upon Entrance Into The First Period Of The Intensive Listening-Hearing Process Of The Only-By-Me Revealed and Given Way Of The Heart) Be Formally (Sacramentally and Instructionally) Initiated Into The Particular Manner Of Practice he or she Finally Chose, On The Basis Of Real Practicing "Consideration", During The Student-Beginner Stage Of The Only-By-Me Revealed and Given Way Of The Heart—and All Such Practitioners Should, During That Same (Sacramentally and Instructionally) Initiatory Occasion, Be Formally (Sacramentally and Instructionally) Initiated Into (and Thereby Become Formally Obliged To Continue To Practice, and To Further Develop) All Of The Basic Disciplines (Which Began, By Initial Application, In The Student-Beginner Stage Of The Only-By-Me Revealed and Given Way Of The Heart, and Which Are, Necessarily, Associated With All The Stages Of The Only-By-Me Revealed and Given Way Of The Heart, or Way Of Adidam).

Likewise, all those who Make The Transition To The Second Period Of

The Intensive Listening-Hearing Process Of The Only-By-Me Revealed and Given Way Of The Heart Should Be (Sacramentally and Instructionally) Formally Initiated Into their (Then) New Responsibilities. And all those Prepared (In The Transition To The Third, or Final, Period Of The Intensive Listening-Hearing Process Of The Only-By-Me Revealed and Given Way Of The Heart) To Practice On The Firm Basis Of The True Hearing Of Me Should, Likewise, Be (Sacramentally and Instructionally) Formally Initiated Into That New (and Most Fundamental) Responsibility. And Whenever (In Due Course) Any Practitioner Enters The Would-Be-Seeing (or Progressively Seeing) Stage Of The Only-By-Me Revealed and Given Way Of The Heart, or (Thereafter, and In Due Course) Any (and Every) Actually Seeing Stage Of The Only-By-Me Revealed and Given Way Of The Heart, he or she Should Be (Sacramentally and Instructionally) Formally Initiated Into The New Responsibilities Of That New Developmental Stage Of The Only-By-Me Revealed and Given Way Of The Heart (or Way Of Adidam).

All Practitioners Of The Only-By-Me Revealed and Given Way Of The Heart (or Way Of Adidam) Should (By Formal Sacramental and Instructional Initiation) Receive My Principal Name ("Da"), My Other Avatarically Revealed and Given Divine Names (or Combined Avataric Divine Names and Avataric Divine Descriptive Titles) Which I Have Given To Be Engaged In The Practice Of Simple Name-Invocation Of Me, and The Variant Forms Of The Ruchira Avatara Naama Mantra (or Ruchira Avatara Mahamantra). This Is Because All Practitioners In The Only-By-Me Revealed and Given Way Of The Heart Practice Sacramental Devotion (or Ruchira Avatara Puja) and Other Forms Of Devotional Culture Wherein Invocation Of Me Is Regularly Made Via My Principal Name ("Da"), and Via My Other Avatarically Revealed and Given Divine Names (or Combined Avataric Divine Names and Avataric Divine Descriptive Titles) Which I Have Given To Be Engaged In The Practice Of Simple Name-Invocation Of Me, and Via The Various By-Me-Revealed-and-Given Forms Of The Ruchira Avatara Naama Mantra (or Ruchira Avatara Mahamantra). And, Also, Even All My Devotees Invoke Me—Via My Avatarically Self-Revealed Principal Divine Name ("Da"), or Via Any Other Of My Avatarically Revealed and Given Divine Names (or Combined Avataric Divine Names and Avataric Divine Descriptive Titles) Which I Have Given To Be Engaged In The Practice Of Simple Name-Invocation Of Me—At Random In daily life, and (As May, In Some Cases, Be Necessary—or As May, In Other Cases, Be, On Some Occasions, Spontaneously Required) In The Context Of Formal Meditation.

Therefore, Whenever any individual Becomes A Formally Acknowledged Novice Student-Beginner In The Only-By-Me Revealed and Given Way Of The

Heart, and Whenever Any Formally Acknowledged Practitioner Of The Only-By-Me Revealed and Given Way Of The Heart Is (As A Student-Beginner, or Beyond) Fully and Rightly Prepared To Accept Responsibility For Any New Form (or Any New Developmental Stage) Of Practice, he or she Should Prepare For Formal Sacramental and Instructional Initiation By Studying This, My Testament Of Divine Secrets (and All Other Forms Of My Self-Revelatory and Avatarically Given Instructional Divine Word, As Recorded In My Twenty-Three Divine "Source-Texts", Formally Offered and Recommended For his or her Study In Preparation For That Particular Formal Sacramental and Instructional Initiation). Then The Essential Elements Of The New Form or Developmental Stage Of Practice Of The Only-By-Me Revealed and Given Way Of The Heart—Including (As Appropriate) Any By-Me-Given Means Of The Primary Practice (Of Searchlessly Beholding Me), or Of "Conductivity" Practice, or Of The "Conscious Process", or (As Appropriate) Any Other Specific Disciplines That I Have Given For The Use Of Practitioners Of The Only-By-Me Revealed and Given Way Of The Heart—Should Be Given Directly To the individual, In A Formal Sacramental and Instructional Initiatory Ceremony and Setting (Appropriate For the individual's Demonstrated Level Of Responsibility, or Developmental Stage Of Practice). And, After (and, To A Great Extent, Even Before) the individual Is (Sacramentally and Instructionally) Formally Initiated By These Means, The Theoretical, and The Technical, and The Practical "Consideration" Of The New Form Of Practice Of The Only-By-Me Revealed and Given Way Of The Heart Should Be Developed In Formal Instructional and Educational Gatherings.

The Instructions I Have Given In This Divine Testament, Together With All Other Forms Of My Avatarically Full-Given (Summary and Final) Divine Word Given (By Me) In The Others Of My Twenty-Three Divine "Source-Texts", Should Always Be Openly Communicated To all. There Are Aspects Of The "Perfect Practice" Of The Only-By-Me Revealed and Given Way Of The Heart, Relating To The Final Stages Of The Process Of Realizing Most Perfect Divine Enlightenment, Which Cannot, and Must Not, Be Made Into "Public" (or "Open", and, In That Sense, Non-Sacred) Communications. Those Teachings Of Mine (Which Include My Instructions Relative To "Radical" Spirit-"Conductivity" Practice and The Total Practice Of "Samraj Yoga", As Well As Many Other Details Of Instruction I Have Communicated Only To Members Of The Ruchira Sannyasin Order Of Adidam Ruchiradam) Can, and Must, Be Given Only As A Direct and Confidential Communication—Either (During My Avataric Physical Human Lifetime) Directly From Me Or (After My Avataric Physical Human Lifetime) From Formally Appointed Representatives Of The Ruchira Sannyasin Order Of Adidam Ruchiradam.

Even From The Beginning Of their Practice Of The Only-By-Me Revealed and Given Way Of The Heart, All My Devotees Should (Whole bodily) Allow their Hearts To Be Husbanded By Me. On The (Original and Continuous) Basis Of The Free (Whole bodily) Acceptance Of My Avatarically Given Divine Husbanding Of The Heart, All My Devotees Should Always Readily Apply themselves To A Happily Disciplined Order Of daily living—Always (Thus) Exhibiting A Right and True Orientation Toward Sila (or self-Restraint and Economy In Relation To their functional, practical, and relational Existence). Such Sila Is An Essential Aspect Of The Necessary Foundation For The Transition To The "Perfect Practice"—Because The "Perfect Practice" Of The Way Of The Heart Requires The Previous Establishment Of Both human and Spiritual Equanimity and Fullness In The Context Of The Frontal Line (or the frontal, and Basic human, personality) Of the body-mind, As Well As Spiritual Openness and Fullness In The Left and The Middle Ranges Of The Heart (Which Is Effective In The Total General Context Of The Vertical Plane Of the body-mind).

Real God (or The Inherently egoless Divine Person Of Reality Itself) Is Not Patently "In Charge" Of all finite and local events. Real God (or The Self-Existing and Self-Radiant Conscious Light That Is Reality Itself) Is Only (and Always Potentially) Realizable As Both Self-Evident and Effective In The Cosmic Domain Of conditional events. Therefore, Actual Realization Of Real God Always Depends On The Orientation (and The Receptivity To Divine Grace) Actually Demonstrated By the beings and processes Active In The Cosmic Domain.

The Spirit-Current Of Divine Love-Bliss Is Reality, Truth, and Real God—and The Spirit-Current Of Divine Love-Bliss Is Potentially The Master Of all-and-All.

The body is male or female, Thus Tending Either To Conserve Or To Be Conserved In The Dynamic Play Of Life. In either case, male or female Is Obliged To Be Motivated By The Spirit-Current Of Divine Love-Bliss, and To Be Concentric With It. And, If The Orientation and The Receptivity Is Not To The Spirit-Current Of Divine Love-Bliss, the psycho-physical being Wanders Chaotically—Dissonant (Within and Without), and (By all knowledge and experience) Dissident From all-and-All, and Always Separate From Reality, Truth, and Real God.

The Heart Of every being (male or female) Is, In Its Core, Yearning To Be Husbanded (or Mastered) By Real God (The Inherently egoless and Self-Evidently Divine Person, Self-Manifested As The Spirit-Current Of Divine Love-Bliss). I Am The Eternal Divine Heart-Husband Of Mankind. I Am Avatarically Born To here, To Make all beings Concentric With The By-Me-Avatarically-

Self-Transmitted Spirit-Current Of Divine Love-Bliss—So they May Be (At Last) Most Perfectly (and Even Whole bodily, here) Conformed To The One and Only and Inherently Indivisible and Inherently egoless Conscious Light That Is The Realizable Virtue Of The Heart Itself.

Avatar Adi Da Samraj
Adidam Samrajashram, 2004

SUTRA 58

Once The First Stage Of The "Perfect Practice" (Beyond The Frontal Yoga) Of The Only-By-Me Revealed and Given Way Of The Heart (or Way Of Adidam) Is Formally Acknowledged, The Three (Progressive) Formal Stages Of The "Perfect Practice" Of The Only-By-Me Revealed and Given Way Of The Heart Are To Proceed In Their By-My-Avataric-Divine-Spiritual-Grace-Given (and Progressively Formally Acknowledged) Course.

The First Stage Of The "Perfect Practice" Is Not, In and Of Itself, A Developmental Stage Of Practice. My Description Of The Signs and Requirements Of The First Stage Of The "Perfect Practice" Is Simply An Indication (By Me) Of The Necessary Qualifications For Making The Transition From The First Actually Seeing Stage and (Thus) To The "Perfect Practice" Of The Only-By-Me Revealed and Given Way Of The Heart (or Way Of Adidam). It Is Not Possible To Develop The Witness-Position As A Practice. Once My Devotee Is Stably Awakened (Through My Avataric Divine Spiritual Gift Of The "Thumbs") To The Witness-Position Of Consciousness Itself, There Is No Further Practice To Be Done (or Growth To Be Demonstrated) Relative To The Exercise Of The Witness-Position Of Consciousness Itself—Because (By Virtue Of That Stable Awakening) The Witness-Position of Consciousness Itself Is Simply The Case.

Therefore, Rather Than Being A Distinct Developmental Stage Of Practice, The First Stage Of The "Perfect Practice" Is That Phase Of Practice (Of The Only-By-Me Revealed and Given Way Of The Heart) During Which My Devotee Engages A Period (or, Possibly, More Than One Period) Of Formal Extended Retreat In My Avataric Physical Human Company (or, After My Avataric Physical Human Lifetime, In The physical human Company and By-Me-Spiritually-Empowered Circumstances Of My "Ruchira Sannyasin" Devotees) For The Purpose Of Spiritual Initiation (By Me) Into The "Perfect Practice" Form Of The Primary Practice Of Searchlessly Beholding Me. The First Stage Of The "Perfect Practice" Is Also That Phase Of Practice (Of The Only-By-Me Revealed and Given Way Of The Heart) When My Devotee Intensively Studies (and Begins To Apply) My Avatarically Given Divine Instruction Relative To The "Perfect Practice" Of The "Conscious Process" Of "Feeling-Enquiry" and Relative To The "Perfect Practice" Of "General"

Spirit-"Conductivity". When This Phase Of Retreat and Study Is Formally Acknowledged To Be Complete—The Requirements For Which Acknowledgement Include Full Preparedness To Effectively Engage The (Responsive) "Conscious Process" Of "Feeling-Enquiry" and The "Perfect Practice" Form Of (Responsive) "General" Spirit-"Conductivity" Practice—Then The "Perfect Practice" (Itself) Begins, In The Context Of Its Second Stage.

A Primary Sign Of The By-My-Avataric-Divine-Spiritual-Grace-Given Transition To The First Stage Of The "Perfect Practice" Of The Only-By-Me Revealed and Given Way Of The Heart Is That the arising of gross and subtle sensations, mind-forms, and so forth, Will Seem Transparent (or Uninvolving). And The By-Me-Avatarically-Self-Transmitted Divine Spirit-Current (and Also The "causal Stress", or conditional Vibration, Associated With The Root-Feeling Of Relatedness[153]) Will and Must (Necessarily, At Least At times) Be Felt In The Right Side Of The Heart—and attention Will (By Means Of My Avatarically Self-Transmitted Divine Spiritual Grace) Tend (and Should, Thus, Also Be Allowed) To Come To Rest (and To Dissolve) In All The Feeling There. Therefore, Instead Of The Previous Inclination Toward Objectified phenomena (of any kind, whether physical or mental, gross or subtle), My "Perfect Practice" Devotee Will Feel Obvious (or Motiveless) Self-Identification With The Position Of Consciousness As Witness—Feeling It To Be That To Which all feelings, visions, auditions, thoughts, and so forth, Are arising. Under all circumstances (waking, dreaming, or sleeping), My "Perfect Practice" Devotee Will Simply Stand As The Witnessing Consciousness (Not Seeking, Not Clinging, Not Trying To Strategically Escape)—and This Stance Will Grant The Deepest Equanimity To the body-mind. These Are The Basic Signs Associated With The First Stage Of The "Perfect Practice" Of The Only-By-Me Revealed and Given Way Of The Heart.

The Discipline In The First Stage Of The "Perfect Practice" Of The Only-By-Me Revealed and Given Way Of The Heart (or Way Of Adidam) Is (Merely, or Tacitly) To Be Consciousness Itself—Self-Abiding As The Mere (or Tacit) Witness (or Mere Feeling-Awareness Itself), Rather Than As the conditional activity of attention. It Is To Merely Witness—or To Merely (or Tacitly) Feel (but Not To Seek or Identify With or React To)—all the acts and all the objects of attention.

The act of attention Is Naturally (or Structurally, and, Thus, Inherently) Oriented Toward objects. During Meditation In The First Stage Of The "Perfect Practice" Of The Only-By-Me Revealed and Given Way Of The Heart (and Even During the Preliminary, or Initial and Preparatory, period Of Any and Every Occasion Of Formal Meditation In The Second Stage Of The "Perfect Practice" Of The Only-By-Me Revealed and Given Way Of The Heart), attention

May Be Allowed (or May, Otherwise, Be Spontaneously Found) To Relax (or Fall) From all objects, and (Thereby) To Dissolve In its conditional Root Of Origin, Which Is The Simple (Directly Felt) Feeling Of Relatedness (Inherently Associated With The Right Side Of The Heart).

Therefore, In (and By) The First (and, Soon, The Second) Stage Of The "Perfect Practice" Of The Only-By-Me Revealed and Given Way Of The Heart, attention Should Simply (By Means Of The Tacit Exercise Of The Always Primary Practice, Of Searchless Beholding Of Me) Be Allowed To Be (By Means Of My Avatarically Self-Transmitted Divine Spiritual Grace, and, In Due Course, Spontaneously, or Effortlessly) Undermined and Dissolved—Through The "Locating" Process Of Devotional Heart-Feeling (Attracted By My Avatarically Self-Transmitted Spiritual, and Always Blessing, Divine Presence and The Inherently Attractive Power Of My Avatarically Self-Revealed, and Very, and Transcendental, and Perfectly Subjective, and Inherently Spiritual, and Inherently egoless, and Inherently Perfect, and Self-Evidently Divine State). And, By (and To, and In) That Devotional (or By-My-Avataric-Divine-Spiritual-Grace-Attracted) Heart-Feeling (Which Undermines and Dissolves attention), Rather Than By The Effort Of attention itself (Which Only Reinforces attention itself, and, Therefore, self-Contraction itself)—The By-Me-Avatarically-Self-Transmitted Divine Spirit-Current Of Love-Bliss Itself (Eternally Prior To The conditional Root-Feeling Of Relatedness) Is (and Must Be, By Means Of My Avatarically Self-Transmitted Divine Spiritual Grace) Revealed Via, and In, and Beyond The Right Side Of The Heart.

All My "Perfect Practice" Devotees Are Formally Expected To Practice (Responsive) "Feeling-Enquiry" In Formal daily Meditation and (At Random) In The Midst Of daily events. All Other (or Previously Established) Technical Forms Of The (Responsive) "Conscious Process"—Including self-Enquiry (and Re-Cognition) and The Prayer Of Remembrance—Cease To Be Principal Practices (and Become Only Secondary, or Supportive and Occasional, Practices, To Be Engaged Only Outside The Formal Meditative Context), Because The "Perfect Practice" Of "Feeling-Enquiry" Is (Itself) The Ultimate Essence (or The Inherently Perfect Epitome) Of Both "True Prayer" and self-Enquiry (Including Re-Cognition).

All My "Perfect Practice" Devotees Are Also Formally Expected To Engage their Previously Established Practice Of The "General" Form Of (Responsive) Spirit-"Conductivity" In The Circle Of the body-mind (At Random, or As Necessary, In Formal Meditation and In The Midst Of daily events).

All My "Perfect Practice" Devotees Are Otherwise Formally Expected—Not In The Context Of Formal Meditation, but Only In The Midst Of daily events (and As An Occasional, or Random, Alternative To The Exercise Of

"Feeling-Enquiry" In The Midst Of daily events)—To Continue To Randomly Engage their Previously Established Practice Of Either self-Enquiry (and Re-Cognition) Or The Prayer Of Remembrance. And This Random Informal (or daily-life) Introduction Of Either self-Enquiry (and Re-Cognition) Or The Prayer Of Remembrance Is Also To Be Accompanied By The Random Informal (or daily-life) Introduction Of The Same Full Range Of "General" Spiritual "Conductivity" Practices Previously Given By Me For Use In The Simple Context Of The Frontal Line and In The Larger Context Of The Full Circle Of the body-mind.

The Random Informal (or daily-life) Introduction Of The "General" Form Of Spirit-"Conductivity" Practice (Especially In The Frontal Line, and Also In The Full Circle Of the body-mind) and The Random Informal (or daily-life) Introduction Of Either self-Enquiry (and Re-Cognition) Or The Prayer Of Remembrance Into The Context Of daily living Must Serve To Establish (or, Otherwise, To Maintain) psycho-physical Equanimity and Participatory (Feeling) Naturalness In The ordinary psycho-physical Context Of daily living. Therefore, Such Random Informal Practices (In The Context Of daily living) Serve As A Random Informal Counterbalance To The Otherwise (and Random) Informal Introduction Of "Feeling-Enquiry" (or The Work Of The "Perfect Practice" Itself) Into The Context Of daily life.

Thus, Through The Random Informal (or daily-life) Responsive Exercises Of Both The "Conscious Process" and "General" Spiritual "Conductivity" In The Frontal Line (and In The Full Circle Of the body-mind), My "Perfect Practice" Devotees Maintain The Integrity and The Equanimity Of The Frontal Line (and The Full Circle Of the body-mind) In The Context Of daily living. In This Manner, they Also Relinquish The Sixth Stage Error (Of Strategic Dissociativeness), and they Remain Always Prepared For Most Direct (or Inherently Perfect) Transcending Of The Entire Circle (and the Total body-mind) In (daily) Formal Meditation.

The Discipline In The Second Stage Of The "Perfect Practice" Of The Only-By-Me Revealed and Given Way Of The Heart (or Way Of Adidam) Is To Merely (or Tacitly) Feel (and, Thus and Thereby, To Contemplate) Consciousness Itself (Self-Abiding In and As Mere, or Tacit, Devotional and Spiritual Feeling-Awareness Of Me)—Immediately Prior To all acts and objects of attention. Thus, The Discipline In The Second Stage Of The "Perfect Practice" Of The Only-By-Me Revealed and Given Way Of The Heart (or Way Of Adidam) Is To Identify (Inherently, and Tacitly) With Consciousness Itself, Self-Abiding (By Means Of The Tacit Exercise Of The Always Primary Practice, Of Searchless Beholding Of Me) In and As Mere (or Tacit) Feeling-Awareness Of My Avatarically Self-Transmitted Spirit-Current Of Self-Evidently Divine Love-Bliss

Itself (Which Is The Self-Evidently Divine Source-Condition Of all-and-All) and Self-Abiding In and As Mere (or Tacit) Feeling-Awareness Of My Avatarically Self-Revealed, and Inherently egoless, and Self-Evidently Divine Self-Condition Itself (Which Is "Located" As The Tacit, or Mere, Feeling-Awareness Of Inherently egoless Being, and Which Is The Self-Evidently Divine Self-Condition Of all-and-All).

If (In The Context Of The Second Stage Of The "Perfect Practice" Of The Only-By-Me Revealed and Given Way Of The Heart) Identification With The Witness-Position Of Consciousness (or Mere Feeling-Awareness, Itself) Is Allowed To Be The Basis (and The Very Substance) Of The "Perfect Practice" Of Formal Meditation, The Habitual Gesture Of attention Will (By Means Of My Avatarically Self-Transmitted Divine Spiritual Grace, Through The Inherently Perfect Exercise Of Feeling Me, In The Always Primary Practice, Of Searchlessly Beholding Me) Tend (and Should, Thus, Also Be Allowed) More and More To Relax and Settle (or Be Resolved) In The By-Me-Avatarically-Self-Transmitted Divine Spirit-Current and Love-Bliss-Feeling Of Mere Being (Which Is The Perfect, and Inherently egoless, Identity Of The Witness-Consciousness, and Which Is Eternally Prior To, and Inherently Free Of, The Root-Feeling Of Relatedness and Every Gesture Of attention Toward objects). Likewise, My Avatarically Self-Transmitted Spirit-Current Of Divine Love-Bliss Will, In This Process (and, Thus, By Means Of My Avatarically Self-Transmitted Divine Spiritual Grace, and Not By Any act or Strategy Of attention), Tend (Always, Inevitably) To Move From The Circle (and The Arrow), and To Descend (Via Amrita Nadi) From The Ascended Matrix (Infinitely Above The Total Crown Of the head), and To The Right Side Of The Heart. Therefore, The Spirit-"Conductivity" Practice In Meditation Will (By Means Of My Avatarically Self-Transmitted Divine Spiritual Grace) Become The Spontaneous Action Of My Avatarically Self-Revealed Divine Spirit-Current—Driving To The Heart-Root, Rotating attention Away From all objects, and Resolving (and Dissolving) attention In The (conditional) Root-Feeling Of Relatedness and (Ultimately) In The Eternal (and Inherently Perfect) Source Of attention (Which Source Is My Avatarically Self-Transmitted Divine Spirit-Current Of Love-Bliss, Itself). And The attention-Dissolving Prior Feeling-Radiance Of The By-Me-Avatarically-Self-Transmitted Divine Spirit-Current Itself—Uniquely Revealed, By Means Of My Avatarically Self-Transmitted Divine Spiritual Grace (and Not By Any act or Strategy Of attention), In The Right Side Of The Heart, and Which attention-Dissolving Feeling-Radiance Is The Characteristic Sign Of My Avatarically Self-Transmitted Spiritual (and Always Blessing) Divine Presence In The Context Of Even The First Stage Of The "Perfect Practice" Of The Only-By-Me Revealed and Given Way Of The Heart—Will Tend (By Means Of My

Avatarically Self-Transmitted Divine Spiritual Grace) To Become Stronger, More Constant, and More Profound (and, Indeed, Must, Necessarily, Thus Increase and Develop) As The Second Stage Of The "Perfect Practice" Develops In The Only-By-Me Revealed and Given Way Of The Heart.

In The Context Of The Second Stage Of The "Perfect Practice" (In The Only-By-Me Revealed and Given Way Of The Heart), The Process Of Meditation Becomes (By Means Of My Avatarically Self-Transmitted Divine Spiritual Grace) More and More The Simple Disposition Of Abiding As The Perfectly Subjective Feeling Of Being, or The Deep Inherent Feeling-Contemplation Of Consciousness Itself By Consciousness Itself (Even Prior To All Witnessing), Until Transcendental (or Unconditional, and Inherently egoless) Self-Existence and Self-Radiant (and Self-Evidently Divine) Happiness (or Love-Bliss Itself) Is (By The Mysterious Mastery Of My Avatarically Self-Transmitted, and Self-Authenticating, Divine Spiritual Grace) Most Perfectly Realized. These Are The Necessary Signs Of The Second Stage Of The "Perfect Practice" Of The Only-By-Me Revealed and Given Way Of The Heart—Which Corresponds To The Admonition To Contemplate Consciousness Itself By Surrendering To Me To The Inherently Perfect Degree.

The "Perfect Practice" Of (Responsive) "Feeling-Enquiry" In The Second Stage Of The "Perfect Practice" Of The Only-By-Me Revealed and Given Way Of The Heart (Merely Witnessing whatever arises, and Feeling-Observing whatever arises To Be Only self-Contraction, and Feeling-Observing self-Contraction To Be Epitomized As The Root-Feeling Of Relatedness, Associated With Feeling-Awareness Of The "causal Stress", or conditional Vibration, In The Right Side Of The Heart) Becomes Progressively Deepened (By Means Of My Avatarically Self-Transmitted Divine Spiritual Grace, and Not By Any act or Strategy Of attention), Such That The Practice Becomes (More and More) Deep (and Effortless) Self-Identification With The By-Me-Avatarically-Self-Transmitted Divine Spirit-Current Of Love-Bliss (At, and Beyond, The Right Side Of The Heart) and (Effortless) Self-Identification With The Inherently egoless (and Tacitly Self-Evident) Feeling Of Being Itself (Prior To any acts of attention).

Thus, Progressively, Even The Tacitly Witnessing Consciousness (or Feeling-Awareness) Is (By Means Of My Avatarically Self-Transmitted Divine Spiritual Grace) Resolved In Consciousness (or Mere Feeling-Awareness) Itself (Tacitly Realized As The Perfectly Subjective, and Inherently egoless, Feeling Of Being, Itself). Therefore, attention, and the objects of attention, and The By-Me-Avatarically-Self-Transmitted Divine Spirit-Current Of Love-Bliss All Become Resolved In and As The One and Only and Inherently Indivisible and Inherently egoless and Self-Evidently Divine Conscious Light Itself,

Through (By-My-Avataric-Divine-Spiritual-Grace-Given) Feeling-Contemplative Self-Identification With Deep objectless Being (Itself)—The Well (or Tacit Deep Feeling-Awareness) Of Being (Itself), Prior To All Motions (or Modifications) Of The By-Me-Avatarically-Self-Transmitted Divine Spirit-Current Of Love-Bliss, and Prior To all acts of attention.

The Second Stage Of The "Perfect Practice" Of The Only-By-Me Revealed and Given Way Of The Heart (or Way Of Adidam) Is The Principal Form Of Practice In The Not-Yet-Divinely-Enlightened "Perfect Practice" Of The Only-By-Me Revealed and Given Way Of The Heart. And, In The Course Of The Second Stage Of The "Perfect Practice" Of The Only-By-Me Revealed and Given Way Of The Heart (or Way Of Adidam), My "Perfect Practice" Devotee Enters The Profound (and Perfectly "Radical") Process Of "Samraj Yoga", Which Is The Total "Perfect Practice" Yoga Of Utterly Transcending The First Six (or ego-Bound) Stages Of Life and (Thus and Thereby) Realizing The Only-By-Me Revealed and Given (and Divinely Enlightened, or Most Perfectly Divinely Awakened) Seventh Stage Of Life.

The Only-By-Me Revealed and Given Process Of "Samraj Yoga" Encompasses The Totality Of The Fully Established "Perfect Practice" Of The Only-By-Me Revealed and Given Way Of The Heart (or Way Of Adidam). Thus, The Only-By-Me Revealed and Given Process Of "Samraj Yoga" Includes Both The Primary Practice Of The Searchless Beholding Of Me (In Its Fully Established "Perfect Practice" Form, Of "Locating" Me As "Atma-Murti") and The Two Primary Responsive Practices Of The "Conscious Process" (In Its Fully Established "Perfect Practice" Form Of "Feeling-Enquiry") and Of "Conductivity" (In Its Fully Established "Perfect Practice" Form Of "General" Spirit-"Conductivity", and In Its Fully Established Uniquely "Perfect Practice" Form Of "Radical" Spirit-"Conductivity").

The Only-By-Me Revealed and Given Process Of "Samraj Yoga" Is Described (By Me), In Basic and General Terms, In This, My Divine and Avataric Testament. And, In Addition, As My "Perfect Practice" Devotee Demonstrates The Requisite Maturing Signs (Including Real and Significant Evidence Of The Events and The Effects Of Priorly Self-Abiding Jnana Nirvikalpa Samadhi) In The Context Of The Second Stage Of The "Perfect Practice", he or she Will Be Given Further (Only-By-Me Revealed and Given) Instructions Relative To The Process Of "Samraj Yoga", Which (Only-By-Me Revealed and Given) Instructions Are To Be Presented To My "Perfect Practice" Devotees (Confidentially, and Only For Their individual Application In Practice) Only By The Then Formally Designated Representatives Of The Formally Governing Senior Membership Of The Ruchira Sannyasin Order Of Adidam Ruchiradam, and Only and Strictly According To My Instructions,

As Given (By Me) Directly To The Ruchira Sannyasin Order Of Adidam Ruchiradam (Which Instructions Are, Forever, To Be Preserved and Applied By The Ruchira Sannyasin Order Of Adidam Ruchiradam).

The Only-By-Me Revealed and Given Process Of "Samraj Yoga" Simultaneously Encompasses Both The Vertical Mode Of The "Perfect Practice" (or The Process Otherwise Characteristically Associated With The Fifth Stage Of Life—but, In The Context Of The "Perfect Practice" Of The Only-By-Me Revealed and Given Way Of The Heart, Engaged In A Uniquely ego-Transcending and Non-Seeking Manner) and The Horizontal Mode Of The "Perfect Practice" (or The Process Otherwise Characteristically Associated With The Sixth Stage Of Life—but, In The Context Of The "Perfect Practice" Of The Only-By-Me Revealed and Given Way Of The Heart, Engaged, Like The Vertical Mode Of The "Perfect Practice", In A Uniquely ego-Transcending and Non-Seeking Manner). Thus, The Vertical Mode Of The "Perfect Practice" Of The Only-By-Me Revealed and Given Way Of The Heart Is Not A Fifth Stage Process That (Then, Potentially) Leads To A Sixth Stage (or Horizontal) Process. Rather, The Only-By-Me Revealed and Given "Perfect Practice" Process Of "Samraj Yoga" Is Always Associated Simultaneously (and Entirely Non-Strategically, or Non-Searchingly, or Non-egoically) With Both The Vertical "Route" (Otherwise, Traditionally, Exploited In The "Emanationist" Context Of The Fifth Stage Of Life) and The Horizontal "Route" (Otherwise, Traditionally, Exploited In The "Non-Emanationist", or "Transcendentalist", Context Of The Sixth Stage Of Life) Within The Total Hierarchical Structural Anatomy Of Man. And, In General (In The "Perfect Practice" Of The Only-By-Me Revealed and Given Way Of The Heart), There Is (On The One Hand) A Correlation Between The Horizontal Process and The Exercise Of The "Conscious Process" and (On The Other Hand) A Correlation Between The Vertical Process and The Exercise Of "Conductivity". (And, Indeed, These Correlations Are, In Some Basic Sense, True Of The Practice Of The Only-By-Me Revealed and Given Way Of The Heart Even From The Beginning.)

Altogether, "Samraj Yoga" Is The Total Esoteric Process Of The "Perfect Practice" Of The Only-By-Me Revealed and Given Way Of The Heart (or Way Of Adidam)—Leading To, and Beyond, The (Only-By-My-Avataric-Divine-Spiritual-Grace-Given) Great Event Of Most Perfect (or Seventh Stage) Divine Self-Realization (or Entrance Into The Third, or Divinely En-Light-ened, Stage Of The "Perfect Practice" Of The Only-By-Me Revealed and Given Way Of The Heart).

In The Context Of The Fully Established Devotional and Spiritual Practice Of The Only-By-Me Revealed and Given Way Of The Heart (or Way Of Adidam), The Two Essential Responsive Practices (Of The "Conscious Process" and Of "Conductivity") Are Always Merely The Two Evident Aspects Of An Inherent Unity (or The Two Sides Of An Inherently Single Exercise)—Because They Both Arise Responsively From The Always Primary (or First, and Inherently Single) Practice Of The Searchless Devotional and Spiritual Beholding Of Me (Exercised By Means Of The Whole bodily, or Total psycho-physical, and Inherently Coincident and Single, Surrender Of All Four Of The Primary, or Essential and Characteristic, Faculties Of the body-mind). Therefore, In The "Perfect Practice" Of The Only-By-Me Revealed and Given Way Of The Heart (or Way Of Adidam), The Combination Of The Responsive "Conscious Process" Of "Feeling-Enquiry" and The Responsive Practice Of Spirit-"Conductivity" (In Its "General", or By-Me-Commonly-Given, Form) Is A Single (or Cooperative) Exercise, Whereby body, and breath, and emotion (and feeling, itself), and attention itself (and Also speech and mind) Are Surrendered To My Avatarically-Born Bodily (Human) Divine Form, and (Thus and Thereby) Into My Avatarically Self-Transmitted Divine Spirit-Current and My Avatarically Self-Revealed Transcendental, Inherently Spiritual, Inherently egoless, and Self-Evidently Divine Self-Condition Of Self-Existing and Self-Radiant Consciousness (or Feeling-Awareness) Itself.

As A Further Extension Of The Always Single Primary Practice (and Of The Inherent Unity Of The Responsive "Conscious Process" and Of Responsive "Conductivity" Practice), A "Perfectly Developed" Form Of The Practice Of Spirit-"Conductivity" Is Given, By Me, To Devotees who Are Demonstrating Signs Of Real Maturity (Including Real and Significant Evidence Of The Events and The Effects Of Priorly Self-Abiding Jnana Nirvikalpa Samadhi) In The Second Stage Of The "Perfect Practice" Of The Only-By-Me Revealed and Given Way Of The Heart (or Way Of Adidam). Thus, In The Context Of The Mature Practice Of The Second Stage (and, Eventually, The Third Stage) Of The "Perfect Practice" Of The Only-By-Me Revealed and Given Way Of The Heart (or Way Of Adidam), There Is (As An Addition To The "General", or By-Me-Commonly-Given, Form Of Spirit-"Conductivity" Practice—and As An Additional Aspect Of The Total Practice Of "Samraj Yoga") The Only-By-Me Revealed and Given "Radical" Form Of Spirit-"Conductivity" Practice (Given, By Me, Especially For Intensive Application In The Context Of Deep Meditation Practice, but, Also, For Application In The Context Of Even every moment Of Most Profound Practice). The Only-By-Me Revealed and Given Instructions Relative To The "Radical" Form Of Spirit-"Conductivity" Practice Are To Be Presented (Confidentially, and Only For Their individual Application In Practice) To each Of My "Perfect Practice" Devotees (When he or she Has Demonstrated Real and Significant Evidence Of The Events and The Effects Of Priorly Self-Abiding Jnana Nirvikalpa Samadhi, and, Altogether, Of

Profoundly Maturing Practice, In The Second Stage Of The "Perfect Practice" Of The Only-By-Me Revealed and Given Way Of The Heart)—and Those ("Radical" Spirit-"Conductivity") Instructions Are To Be (Only Thus) Presented Only By The Then Formally Designated Representatives Of The Formally Governing Senior Membership Of The Ruchira Sannyasin Order Of Adidam Ruchiradam, and Only and Strictly According To My Instructions, As Given (By Me) Directly To The Ruchira Sannyasin Order Of Adidam Ruchiradam (Which Instructions Are, Forever, To Be Preserved and Applied By The Ruchira Sannyasin Order Of Adidam Ruchiradam). Those ("Radical" Spirit-"Conductivity") Instructions, Thus Given and Presented, Are (Along With All Other Aspects Of The Only-By-Me Revealed and Given Practice Of "Samraj Yoga") To Be (Thus) Presented Via Formal Initiation (Relative To The Initial, or Basic, Technical Details)—and, Thereafter, The Further Technical Developmental Details (As Required, Relative To All Aspects Of "Samraj Yoga", and All Aspects Of The "Perfect Practice" Of The Only-By-Me Revealed and Given Way Of The Heart, or Way Of Adidam, Both Previous To The Only-By-Me Revealed and Given Seventh Stage Of Life and In and Throughout The Only-By-Me Revealed and Given Seventh Stage Of Life) Are (Always In Accordance With the Thus Formally Initiated individual's Developmental Progress In The "Perfect Practice" Of The Only-By-Me Revealed and Given Way Of The Heart) To Be Presented (Likewise Confidentially, and Only For Their individual Application In Practice), By Means Of Formal Instruction Within The Ongoing Instructional Setting, and Only By The Then Formally Designated Representatives Of The Formally Governing Senior Membership Of The Ruchira Sannyasin Order Of Adidam Ruchiradam (and Only and Strictly According To My Instructions—As Given, By Me, Directly To The Ruchira Sannyasin Order Of Adidam Ruchiradam).

The Only-By-Me Revealed and Given Practice Of The "Radical" Form Of Spirit-"Conductivity" Specifically Relinquishes and Directly Transcends All Strategic Efforts Of the body-mind, and (Thereby) Directly "Locates" The Unobstructed Divine Spirit-Current Of My Avatarically Self-Transmitted "Bright" Person, At The Source-Position (and As The Source-Condition) Of The Entire Vertical (or Extended Functional) Structure Of the body-mind itself (and, Ultimately, Of The Tripartite Heart Itself).

Eventually (By Means Of My Avatarically Self-Transmitted Divine Spiritual Grace), The Only-By-Me Revealed and Given Process Of "Samraj Yoga" (In The Second Stage Of The "Perfect Practice" Of The Only-By-Me Revealed and Given Way Of The Heart) Spontaneously Becomes Transcendental, and Inherently Spiritual (or "Bright"), and Most Perfect Divine Self-Realization—or The Awakening To The Only-By-Me Revealed and Given Seventh Stage Of

Life (Which Is The Third Stage Of The "Perfect Practice" Of The Only-By-Me Revealed and Given Way Of The Heart, or Way Of Adidam).

The Demonstration Of The Only-By-Me Revealed and Given Seventh Stage Of Life Takes Place In Four Stages, Culminating In Divine Translation (Which Is The Most Ultimate Process Of Most Perfectly Realizing My Avatarically Self-Revealed Divine Spiritual Self-Domain Of The "Bright", or The "Midnight Sun"). The Entire Process Of The Four Stages Of The Demonstration Of The Only-By-Me Revealed and Given Seventh Stage Of Life, Including The Most Ultimate Process (or Event) Of Divine Translation, Is Developed (and Made Possible) Only On The Basis Of The Only-By-Me Revealed and Given "Perfect Practice" Of "Samraj Yoga"—Which Is Perfect Fullness Of The Primary (Searchlessly Me-Beholding) Practice Of Ruchira Avatara Bhakti Yoga, Perfect Persistence In Whole bodily (or Total psycho-physical) Heart-Identification With My Avatarically Self-Revealed Divine Self-Condition (Which Is The Mere, or Tacit, Feeling Of Mere Being, Itself), Perfect Persistence In The Only-By-Me Revealed and Given Responsive "Perfect Practice" Of The "Conscious Process" Of "Feeling-Enquiry", Perfect Persistence In The Only-By-Me Revealed and Given Responsive "Perfect Practice" Of "Radical" Spirit-"Conductivity", and (Altogether) Perfect Fullness Of Participation In The Only-By-Me Revealed and Given (and, Ultimately, Most Perfectly Me-Realizing) "Bright" Divine Yoga Of Amrita Nadi.

The Third Stage Of The "Perfect Practice" Of The Only-By-Me Revealed and Given Way Of The Heart (or Way Of Adidam) Is The (By-My-Avataric-Divine-Spiritual-Grace-Given) Inherent "Practice" (or Inherently Most Perfect Demonstration) Associated With "Bright" Divine Self-Realization (and The Only-By-Me Revealed and Given Seventh, and Truly Most Ultimate, Stage Of Life In The Only-By-Me Revealed and Given Way Of The Heart).

The Third Stage Of The "Perfect Practice" Of The Only-By-Me Revealed and Given Way Of The Heart (or Way Of Adidam) Is The (By-My-Avataric-Divine-Spiritual-Grace-Given) Inherent (or Perfectly Subjective) and Self-Abiding Divine Self-Recognition—and The Inherently Most Perfect Transcending (In The By-Me-Avatarically-Self-Revealed Perfectly Subjective Domain Of The One and Only and Inherently Indivisible Conscious Light Of Mere Being)—Of all objects and all conditions (or All Apparent Modifications Of The By-Me-Avatarically-Self-Transmitted Divine Spirit-Current, or "Bright" Inherent Spiritual Heart-Radiance, Of Perfectly Subjective, and Inherently Perfect, and Inherently egoless, and Self-Evidently Divine Being).

The Third Stage Of The "Perfect Practice" Of The Only-By-Me Revealed and Given Way Of The Heart (or Way Of Adidam) Is The (By-My-Avataric-Divine-Spiritual-Grace-Given) Inherent (or Perfectly Subjective) and Self-Abiding

Divine Self-Recognition—and The Inherently Most Perfect Transcending (In The By-Me-Avatarically-Self-Revealed Perfectly Subjective Domain Of The One and Only and Inherently Indivisible Conscious Light Of Mere Being)—Of the act of attention itself.

The Third Stage Of The "Perfect Practice" Of The Only-By-Me Revealed and Given Way Of The Heart (or Way Of Adidam) Is The (By-My-Avataric-Divine-Spiritual-Grace-Given) Inherent (or Perfectly Subjective) and Self-Abiding Divine Self-Recognition—and The (Inherently Most Perfect) Present (or Always Immediate) Transcending (In The By-Me-Avatarically-Self-Revealed Perfectly Subjective Domain Of The One and Only and Inherently Indivisible Conscious Light Of Mere Being)—Of <u>Everything</u> (Even, Most Ultimately, To The Degree Of Divine Translation—or The Outshining Of all experience and all knowledge Of The conditional, or Cosmic, Domain, In The Self-Existing and Self-Radiant Divine "Bright" Spherical Self-Domain Of The One and Only and Inherently Indivisible and Inherently egoless and Self-Evidently Divine Conscious Light Of Mere Being).

From The Moment Of each one's Formal Initiation Into The First Stage Of The "Perfect Practice" Of The Only-By-Me Revealed and Given Way Of The Heart (or Way Of Adidam), My Every "Perfect Practice" Devotee (Necessarily) Embraces The By-Me-Given Discipline (and, Altogether, The To-Me-Heart-Moved Disposition) Of <u>Formal</u> Renunciation (In The Context Of Either The Lay Renunciate Order Of Adidam Ruchiradam Or The Ruchira Sannyasin Order Of Adidam Ruchiradam).

My (Formal Renunciate) "Perfect Practice" Devotees Are, Necessarily, individuals who Have Come To A Most Fundamental Knowledge (and A Most Profound Certainty) That their Motivations and Desires Associated With conditional Existence Are <u>Not</u> <u>Ever</u> Going To Be Fulfilled (and, Indeed, <u>Cannot</u> Be Fulfilled) In Any Ultimate Sense. On The One Hand, Such Certainty Is A Kind Of "Positive" (or ego-Transcending) Despair Relative To conditional Existence, but, On The Other Hand, For My Formal Renunciate Devotees, That Certainty Goes Beyond Mere (or "Negative", or ego-Based, and ego-Reinforcing) Despair—Because Coming To Such Certainty Allows The <u>Unreserved</u> Embrace Of The Sadhana Of (Ultimately, Most Perfectly) Realizing Me.

When human beings Come To A "Negative" Point Of (Merely ego-Based, and ego-Reinforcing) Despair (or To A "Negative", or Merely Depressive) Sense That conditional Existence Is Futile), they Often Attempt To Cover Up their Despair With addictive pleasures of one kind or another (Even Though The Addictive Process Inevitably Makes Any Pleasure Progressively Less and Less Pleasurable). Such An Attempted "Solution" To The Presumed "Problem" Of conditional Existence Is Obviously False, but (Nevertheless) The Root-Feeling

Of Despair Relative To conditional Existence Is, In A Certain Sense, A True (and, Ultimately, Even Necessary, and "Positive") Response To The conditional Situation In Which human beings Find themselves. In The Case Of Even All My Devotees, The Life Of (At Least More and More) True and Free (Even If Not Formal) Renunciation In My Divine Spiritual Company Is The Real "Answer" To (or The Most "Positive" Transformation Of) This Despair.

My (Formal Renunciate) "Perfect Practice" Devotees Are (Necessarily) individuals who Have "Positively" Despaired Of Being Fulfilled By conditional Existence. For My (Formal Renunciate) "Perfect Practice" Devotees, "Positive" Despair Breaks The Link To The Usual Cycles Of Desire, Whether Cycles Of (Even Extreme) Addictive Desire Or Of Merely ordinary (or conventional) Desire. Therefore, My (Formal Renunciate) "Perfect Practice" Devotees Are Unconventional individuals, No Longer Linked To the world In The Usual Sense, and they Are, Thereby, Free To Be Entirely Devoted To The By-Me-Given Sadhana Of The (Ultimately, Most Perfect) Transcending Of egoity (Which Is The, Ultimately, Most Perfect Realization Of Me). And The Reason That My (Formal Renunciate) "Perfect Practice" Devotees Are Not conventional-minded Is That they Know (With Profound Certainty) That The conventional Manner Of Going About life Will Never Result In Any Ultimate Fulfillment, Any More Than Pursuit Of The Cycle Of egoic Addiction Will Ever Result In Any Ultimate Fulfillment. Thus, My (Formal Renunciate) "Perfect Practice" Devotee Deeply Understands: Egoic Desires Will Not (and Cannot) Be Ultimately (or Fully and Finally) Fulfilled.

Altogether, My (Formal Renunciate) "Perfect Practice" Devotees Are Neither conventional-minded, Nor Addicted To psycho-physical Pleasure, Nor Overcome By ego-Based (and ego-Reinforcing—and, Altogether, "Negative", or Depressive) Despair. Thus, My (Formal Renunciate) "Perfect Practice" Devotees Are Truly Free To—With Fullest Intensity—Practice The By-Me-Revealed and By-Me-Given Yoga Of (Ultimately, Most Perfect) ego-Transcendence and (Ultimately, Most Perfect) Divine Self-Realization In The Midst Of the conditions Of Existence.

Only those Can Be My (Formal Renunciate) "Perfect Practice" Devotees who Are No Longer Clinging To The (Illusory) Possibility Of Fulfilling The Purposes Of conditional Existence. Only those Can Be My (Formal Renunciate) "Perfect Practice" Devotees who Have Come To That Root-Sense That, Otherwise, Causes human beings To (In The "Negative" Sense) Despair, or To Become Addicts, or To Merely Go Through The Routines (Otherwise) Of The conventional Play In the world. Only those Can Be My (Formal Renunciate) "Perfect Practice" Devotees who Know The True Depth Of The Heart's Own Purpose. Only those Can Be My (Formal Renunciate) "Perfect

Practice" Devotees who Know That All Of merely conditional (and merely psycho-physical, and space-time-Bound) Existence Is To Be Renounced, By Means Of (Ultimately, Most Perfect) ego-Transcendence. Thus, For one who Is My (Formal Renunciate) "Perfect Practice" Devotee (Embracing Renunciation In The ego-Transcending, and, Thus and Thereby, world-Transcending, Manner), The Spell Of conditional Existence Is Broken—Including The Spell Of conventional (or Strategically world-Excluding, and, Thus and Thereby, self-Suppressing) Renunciation, Which Is, In Itself, Another Form Of "Negative" Despair (and Of The Seeker's Pursuit Of ego-Fulfillment).

Therefore, Formal Renunciation In The Only-By-Me Revealed and Given Way Of The Heart Is Not At All A puritanical or A moralistic Matter. Formal Renunciation In The Only-By-Me Revealed and Given Way Of The Heart Is Not Merely a form of idealism, Not Merely An Exercise In "Shutting Off" worldly or conventional or (Otherwise) egoic Desires and Impulses. Formal Renunciation In The Only-By-Me Revealed and Given Way Of The Heart Is The Real (True and Free) Renunciate Sadhana Of Most Intensively Devoting one's energy and attention To (Ultimately, Most Perfectly) Realizing Me. Thus, Formal Renunciation In The Only-By-Me Revealed and Given Way Of The Heart Is A Matter Of Relinquishing the world—Not In The conventional Sense Of Excluding the world itself, but In The Profoundest Sense Of Relinquishing ego-Bondage To the world (or, In Other Words, Of Relinquishing The Pursuit Of egoic self-Fulfillment). Altogether, Then, Formal Renunciation In The Only-By-Me Revealed and Given Way Of The Heart (or Way Of Adidam) Is A Profound Matter Of Going Beyond.

Some Are here To Be here, and some Are here To Go Beyond. True and Free Renunciate Practitioners Are those who Are here To Go Beyond, Whereas conventional householders Are those who Are here To Be here. In The Only-By-Me Revealed and Given Way Of The Heart (or Way Of Adidam), No one Among My Devotees Should Be Merely here To Be here. All Of My Devotees Are Called (and Expected), By Me, To Most Heartily Embrace The Only-By-Me Revealed and Given Way Of Devotion To Me—Such That they Are (More and More) Purified Of their egoic obstructions and limitations, (More and More) Loosened From their egoic Attachments, and (Thereby, More and More) Enabled To Go (More and More) Beyond. However, In The Worldwide Sacred Cooperative Cultural Gathering (or Truly Global Ashram) Of All My Formally Practicing Devotees, those who Can (and Should) Become My (Formal Renunciate) "Perfect Practice" Devotees Are those who Are here Only To Go Beyond, Without Wasting Even a single hour In Doing anything else. Therefore, My (Formal Renunciate) "Perfect Practice" Devotees Are those who Have Embraced (and Continue To Embrace) The By-Me-Revealed and By-Me-

Given Practice Of The Only-By-Me Revealed and Given Way Of The Heart In The Most Exemplary Manner, and who Have Been (and Continue To Be) Consistently Serious In their Demonstrated Impulse To Move On In Practice, To and Within The "Perfect Practice" Of The Only-By-Me Revealed and Given Way Of The Heart, and who Are (Characteristically) Free Of conventional-mindedness, or worldly-mindedness, or conditional-Existence-mindedness, and who Freely (and Consistently) Demonstrate The Sign Of True (Unencumbered and Most Intense) Renunciation-mindedness and Realizing-Me-mindedness.

My "Lay Renunciate" Devotees and (Most Especially) My "Ruchira Sannyasin" Devotees Are those Among My Devotees who Are Heart-Attracted To Me (As their Avatarically Self-Revealed Divine Heart-Master) With Exemplary Profundity and Force, Such That their Impulse To Most Perfectly Realize Me and To Relinquish All Other (Lesser) Purposes In Life Is Outstanding In Its Strength. Indeed, Profound and Forceful Heart-Attraction To *Me* (As one's Avatarically Self-Revealed Divine Heart-Master) Is The *Source* Of *All* True and Free Renunciation In The Only-By-Me Revealed and Given Way Of The Heart. In The Only-By-Me Revealed and Given Way Of The Heart, Real (Even If Not Formal) Renunciation Is (Most Fundamentally) Renunciation Of the (Inevitably) Un-Happy ego-"I", In Devotional Recognition-Response To My Freely Given Avataric Divine Self-Revelation Of My Own "Bright" Love-Bliss-Person. Through their Heart-Attraction To Me, *All* My Devotees Are Drawn Out Of their sphere of ego-ordinariness, and Into My Sphere Of Unconditional Love-Bliss-Happiness. Only By Means Of Profound and Forceful Heart-Attraction To Me (Rather Than By Means Of Any ego-Generated Intention To Renounce the world) Is It Truly Possible For My Any Devotee To Cease Being an ego-Serving (and, Otherwise, merely "civilized"—or socialized, secularized, and worldly) "householder" ("Mom" or "Dad"). And Only Thus Transformed Is It Truly Possible For My Any (Necessarily, Exemplary) Devotee To (Necessarily, Formally) Become A True and Free "Lay Renunciate" or "Ruchira Sannyasin" Devotee-Practitioner Of The "Perfect Practice" Of The Only-By-Me Revealed and Given Way Of The Heart.

Avatar Adi Da Samraj
Adidam Samrajashram, 2003

SUTRA

59

Now Listen To My Avataric Self-Confession Of The Divine Essence Of My Self-Revelation Of The Only-By-Me Revealed and Given Way Of Adidam Ruchiradam.

The Yoga Of The "Bright"—The Divine Yoga, and The Divine Samadhi, Of All-Outshining "Brightness"—Is What You See In Me. The Yoga Of The "Bright" Is My Avatarically Self-Transmitted Divine Self-Revelation.

The Only-By-Me Revealed and Given Way Of Adidam Ruchiradam (Which, In Its Totality, Is The One and Only By-Me-Revealed and By-Me-Given Way Of The Heart, or Way Of Adidam) Is—From the time Of The Full Formal Establishment Of Real and True Devotional and Spiritual Relationship To Me (In and As My Avatarically-Born Bodily Human Divine Form and Person)—Rooted In The Divine "Bright"-Sphere. Even In The Midst Of the body-mind, The Divine Conscious Light Is Always Already The Case—I Am Always Already The Case—At The Core Of all-and-All, Communicated In the body-mind Via (and As) The Amrita Nadi. The Perfectly Ascended "Midnight Sun" Is Always Already Standing "Bright", Infinitely Above the body and the mind. The "Midnight Sun" Is The Divine Conscious Light, The "Bright" Itself.

The "Bright" Itself Is Never Seen With the bodily eyes, but It Is To Be Heart-Felt—As My Avatarically Self-Transmitted Spirit-Current Of The Self-Evidently Divine Love-Bliss-Feeling Of Being (Itself), In and Beyond The Right Side Of The Heart. The (Only-By-Me Avatarically Self-Revealed) Inherently egoless Root-Feeling Of Being Is The Root Of The "Midnight Sun", The Root-Domain Of The "Bright" Itself.

I Am The Avatarically-Born, Avatarically Self-Transmitted, and Avatarically Self-Revealed Divine Self-Revelation Of The "Bright". I Am The "Bright" (Itself). The "Midnight Sun" Is My Very and Perfect and Self-Evidently Divine Form—Avatarically Self-Transmitted, and Avatarically Self-Revealed, By Me, As Me. To Heart-Recognize Me and Heart-Respond To Me—The Spiritually Self-"Bright" Divine Conscious Light, In Avatarically-Born Bodily (Human) Divine Form and Person—Is The Core Of The Always Primary (Searchlessly Me-Beholding) Practice Of The Only-By-Me Revealed and Given Way Of Adidam. And To Stand

As The (Tangibly Spiritually Evidenced) Self-Evidently Divine Love-Bliss-Feeling Of Being—Avatarically Self-Transmitted, and Avatarically Self-Revealed, By Me, and As Me—Is The "Perfect Practice" Of Searchless Beholding Of Me To Be Established (In Due Course, and At Last) By My Devotees. That Perfect Stand Is The Ultimate Essence Of The Devotional and Spiritual Relationship To Me.

Only I—By Means Of My Avataric Divine Spiritual Self-Transmission (or Ruchira Shaktipat)—Establish (and Can Establish), In My Devotee, The Primary Practice (and, In Due Course, The "Perfect Practice") Of Searchless Beholding Of Me. I Am The Avataric Divine Self-Revelation Of The "Bright", Shining As The White Core (or "Midnight Sun") In The Midst Of The Black Field. I Pervade The Entire Cosmic Domain As The all-and-All-Transfiguring Spiritual Self-"Brightness" Of My Avatarically Self-Transmitted and Avatarically Self-Revealed Divine (and Inherently egoless) Person. By Means Of Right (and, Primarily, Searchlessly Beholding) Devotional and Spiritual Relationship To Me (In and As My Avatarically-Born Bodily Human Divine Form and Person), Whole bodily (or Total psycho-physical, and—More and More Effectively, and, At Last, Most Perfectly—ego-Transcending, or self-Contraction-Transcending) Heart-Attraction To Me Becomes The Foundation (and, In Due Course, Perfectly Practiced) Disposition Of My Every Devotee. By Means Of ego-Transcending Devotional and Spiritual Communion With Me (In and As My Avatarically-Born Bodily Human Divine Form and Person), My Spiritual Self-"Brightness" Is (In Due Course, and At Last) Magnified (In the body-mind Of My Devotee) As The By-Me-Avatarically-Self-Transmitted (and Self-Evidently Divine) Love-Bliss-Current Of The Perfectly Subjective (and Inherently egoless) Feeling Of Being (In and Beyond The Right Side Of The Heart). Such Is The Necessary Foundation Of The "Perfect Practice" Of The Only-By-Me Revealed and Given Way Of Adidam.

The Worship Of The "Bright" Must Be Established In This conditional Realm. I Am The Inherently egoless Divine Person and The Avatarically-Born Divine Self-Revelation Of The "Bright". I Must (In and As My Avatarically-Born Bodily Human Divine Form and Person) Be Whole bodily (or In A Total psycho-physical, and, Ultimately, Most Perfectly egoless, Manner) Heart-Recognized As The "Bright". Only one who Thus (Ever More Deeply) Heart-Recognizes Me Is My True (and, Ultimately, Truly Perfect) Devotee.

In the conditional (or Cosmic) plane, My Divine "Bright" Spherical Self-Domain (and My Divine "Bright" Eternal Self-Condition) Is Always Already Free-Standing, In The Midst. In The Midst (Where You Always Already Stand, In The Inherently egoless Being-Position) Is The Fundamental (Perfectly Subjective, and Inherently egoless) Feeling Of Being (Itself). I Am That—Self-Existing and Self-Radiant.

Even Though death Rules To here, There Is An Indivisible Eternal Sun Over-head. And That Eternal Sun Is—Beyond Even all conditional visibility.

I Have Come To Confirm This To You—each and all—Absolutely. I Am That Eternal Sun—The (Self-"Bright") "Midnight Sun", Infinitely Above all-and-All.

You May Sometimes (Objectively) See The Divine Self-"Brightness" Of My Avatarically-Born Bodily (Human) Divine Form. I Always Magnify My Inherent Self-"Brightness" Where I Stand, Where You Stand, Where It Stands—From The Inside Out, White As The Feeling Of Being Is.

This Inherent Unqualified Spiritual (and Self-Evidently Divine) Love-Bliss-Current Of Being (and Of The Unmediated Apprehension Of Reality Itself) Is The Root-Current Of My Avatarically Self-Transmitted Spiritual Blessing (or Ruchira Shaktipat). Only My Avatarically Self-Transmitted Divine Spiritual Blessing (or Ruchira Shaktipat) Magnifies The Ruchira Avatara Bhakti Yoga Of This Way Of Devotional and Spiritual Relationship To Me (Avatarically Self-Revealed In and As My Avatarically-Born Bodily Human Divine Form and Person)—Even Unto The Only-By-Me Revealed and Given Seventh Stage Realization and Demonstration Of Devotional and Spiritual Relationship To Me (In and As My Avatarically-Born Bodily Human Divine Form and Person).

I Am Always Dissolving (Myself, and all-and-All) In My Own "Brightness".

This Is What I Do.

This Is What I Am Always Doing.

This Doing Is Who I Am.

This Is The Force and Nature Of My Avatarically-Born, Avatarically Self-Transmitted, and Avatarically Self-Revealed Company.

I Am Not Merely In Divine Samadhi.

I Am Divine Samadhi—here and Now.

My Divine Samadhi (or Inherent Divine State and Inherently egoless Divine Personal Identity) Is (Now, and Forever Hereafter) Spontaneously Self-Transmitting Itself—As Me (Avatarically Self-Manifested In and As My Avatarically-Born Bodily Human Divine Form, and Avatarically Self-Transmitted As and By Means Of My Always-Blessing Divine Spiritual Presence, and, Altogether, Avatarically Self-Revealed As My Divine, and Very, and Inherently egoless State).

My Divine Samadhi Is Always Already The Case.

My Divine Samadhi Is all-and-All.

My Divine Samadhi Is The "Bright" Itself.

Avatar Adi Da Samraj
Adidam Samrajashram, 2003

SUTRA

60

In The Only-By-Me Revealed and Given Way Of The Heart (or Way Of Adidam), The Developmental Process (and The Course Of Practice) Moves (In Due Course) From The First Actually Seeing Stage (Which Involves The Processes, Otherwise Associated With The "Basic" Fourth Stage Of Life, Relating To The Frontal Line) To The "Perfect Practice" Yoga (Which Involves Both The Vertical Processes, Otherwise Associated With The Fifth Stage Of Life, Relating To The Ajna Door, and Above, and The Horizontal Processes, Otherwise Associated With The Sixth Stage Of Life, Relating To The Right Side Of The Heart). Thus, Although Many and Various Spiritual Phenomena Of The Priorly Ascended Type Are Associated (Inevitably, and Necessarily) With The "Perfect Practice" Of The Devotional and Spiritual Yoga Of The Only-By-Me Revealed and Given Way Of The Heart (or Way Of Adidam)—and Even Though Many and Various Spiritual Phenomena Otherwise (Naturally, or Structurally) Associated With The Process Of Ascending Spinal Yoga May (and, At Least To A Certain Degree, Inevitably Will) Spontaneously arise In The Case Of My "Perfect Practice" Devotees—My "Perfect Practice" Devotees Do Not (As A Specific Characteristic Of The Unique Orientation Of The Only-By-Me Revealed and Given Way Of The Heart, or Way Of Adidam) Involve themselves In Modes Of ego-Effort (or Techniques Of Seeking) Otherwise Associated With Strategically Ascending Spinal Yoga (Which Strategically Ascending—or "bottom-to-top", or "tail-to-head", or "from-the-ground-up"—Spinal Yoga Accounts For The Vast Majority Of The Instruction, and Of The Seeking-Effort, Within The Esoteric Yogic Traditions Of Mankind).

I Am Up—Not Merely Upward, but Infinitely Above and Beyond.

Thus, In The Only-By-Me Revealed and Given Way Of The Heart (or Way Of Adidam), The (Necessary) Process Related To The Spinal Line Is Accomplished (and the Characteristic limitations Associated With The Fifth Stage Of Life Are Transcended) In A Unique (and Entirely Non-Strategic, and Utterly "Radical") Manner—A Manner Altogether Different From The "Evolutionary" (or "Great-Path-Of-Return") Approach Universally Taught and Enacted (and Held To Be Natural, Obligatory, and, Even, Inevitable) In The Great Tradition Of Mankind. Rather Than Bypassing The Spinal Process Itself, My Devotees Are Called (By

Me) To Bypass The Upwardly Seeking ("lower-to-higher") Orientation, or The ego-Effort Otherwise (Invariably) Associated With Any Of The Traditional Means Of Intentional Concentration In The Spinal Process.

In The Only-By-Me Revealed and Given Way Of The Heart (or Way Of Adidam), The Spinal Process Is (Coincidently) Addressed Even In The First Actually Seeing Stage (or By Means Of The Frontal Yoga). Because The Frontal Line Is "Half" Of The Continuous Circuit Of The Full Circle Of the body-mind, The Spinal Line Is Coincidently (or Simultaneously) Purified (With The Result Of The Establishing Of Basic Equanimity In The Spinal Line), In The Course Of The Frontal Process Of The First Actually Seeing Stage Of The Only-By-Me Revealed and Given Way Of The Heart.

In The Only-By-Me Revealed and Given Way Of The Heart (or Way Of Adidam), the limitations Associated With The Fifth Stage Of Life Are Further (and Thoroughly) Transcended In The Context Of The "Perfect Practice". This Is Possible Because The Unique (and, Necessarily, Both Devotional and Spiritual) Yoga Of The "Perfect Practice" Of The Only-By-Me Revealed and Given Way Of The Heart Is Not (In The Sixth Stage Manner) Based Exclusively On The "Conscious Process". Rather, Like Every Other Mode Of Full (Devotional and Spiritual) Practice In The Only-By-Me Revealed and Given Way Of The Heart, The "Perfect Practice" Is Founded On The Primary Devotional and Spiritual Practice (Of Searchless Beholding Of Me), Which Is (In Turn) Reflected In The Two (Inherently Coincident, or Unified) Responsive Practices—Both The "Conscious Process" and "Conductivity" Practice.

By Means Of My Avatarically Self-Transmitted Divine Spiritual Grace, Every Mode Of The Full (Devotional and Spiritual) Practice Of The "Conscious Process" and Of "Conductivity" (In The Only-By-Me Revealed and Given Way Of The Heart) Directly Transcends the limitations Associated (Progressively) With Each and All Of The First Six Stages Of Life (Rather Than Attempting Merely To Fulfill The Structurally Determined "point of view", or conditional Purpose, or limited and ego-Bound and ego-Binding Potential Of Any or All Of The First Six Stages Of Life).

The Right and True Practice Of The Only-By-Me Revealed and Given Way Of The Heart Actually (Directly, Constantly, and Progressively) Purifies My Devotee's egoic Patterning—At First, The gross egoic Patterning, and (Then) The subtle egoic Patterning, and (Finally) The causal egoic Patterning. Although (In Due Course) My Devotee Will (and Must) Experience Processes Otherwise Naturally (or Structurally) Associated With The Fourth, The Fifth, and The Sixth Stages Of Life, My Devotee Is Not Otherwise Called (By Me) To Practice From the ego-Based point of view Of Any Of The First Six Stages Of Life Themselves. Rather, I Always Call My Devotee Only To (Always and

Directly) Prepare himself or herself—Through Right Progressive (and Truly ego-Transcending) Devotional (and, In Due Course, Spiritual) Practice Of The Unique Totality Of The Only-By-Me Revealed and Given Way Of The Heart—For The By-My-Avataric-Divine-Spiritual-Grace-Given "Practice" (or Ultimate Demonstration-Process) Of The Only-By-Me Revealed and Given Seventh (or Divinely Enlightened) Stage Of Life.

When My Devotee Enters The "Perfect Practice" Of The Only-By-Me Revealed and Given Way Of The Heart (or Way Of Adidam), his or her Devotional and Spiritual Practice Relative To The Yoga Of The Vertical Dimension Is Not A Matter Of Engaging The Strategically Ascending Yoga (Of The Spinal Line)—but It Is, Rather, A Matter Of By-My-Avataric-Divine-Spiritual-Grace-Given Participation (By Means Of The, Eventually, Total "Perfect Practice" Of "Samraj Yoga") In The Priorly Ascended Yoga (Of The Matrix Of The One and Only and Inherently Indivisible and Inherently egoless Conscious Light, Always Already Infinitely Above The Total Crown Of the head). The Strategically Ascending Yoga Moves From the bottom Up, Whereas The Priorly Ascended Yoga Is Associated With That Which Is Always Already Above and Beyond. These Two Orientations (or Dispositions)—On The One Hand, To The Process Of Upwardly Moving Ascent Toward What Is Above and Beyond, and, On The Other Hand, To Self-Abidance In What Is Above and Beyond—Are Very Different From Each Other. The (Traditional) Orientation Of Raising "Energy" From "lower" To "higher" Is Not The Characteristic Orientation Of The Only-By-Me Revealed and Given Way Of The Heart (or Way Of Adidam).

Thus, My Devotee's Necessary Participation In The Vertical Process (In The Context Of The "Perfect Practice" Of The Only-By-Me Revealed and Given Way Of The Heart) Does Not Mean (or Indicate, or Imply) That My "Perfect Practice" Devotee Is Involved In Any Kind Of Upwardly-Seeking Spinal Effort. Vertically, My "Perfect Practice" Devotee Always "Locates" Me Above (In and As The Infinitely Ascended Matrix Of Conscious Light, Always Already Perfectly and Priorly Above The Total Crown Of the head). And, Horizontally, My "Perfect Practice" Devotee Always "Locates" Me In (and As That Which Is Always Already Perfectly Prior To) The Right Side Of The Heart. Such Is The Perfection Of The Only-By-Me Revealed and Given "Perfect Practice" Of The Way Of The Heart (or Way Of Adidam).

My Avatarically Self-Revealed (Self-Existing, Self-Radiant, and Inherently Love-Blissful) Divine Person, Being, or Self-Condition—Present As My Avatarically Self-Revealed (Transcendental, and Inherently Spiritual, and Inherently egoless, and Perfectly Subjective, and Self-Evidently Divine) Self-Consciousness, and As My Avatarically Self-Transmitted (all-and-All-Surrounding, and all-and-All-Pervading, and, Yet, Always Already Transcendentally, and Perfectly Subjectively,

Existing) "Bright" Divine Body Of Spiritual Presence (or Spirit-Power), and As My (Apparently Objective) Divine Sound-Form (or First Audible Form), and As My (Apparently Objective) Divine Star-Form (or First Visible Form), and As My Avatarically-Born Bodily (Human) Divine-Heart-Master Form—Is That (Divine Source-Condition) In Which every conditional being, thing, or world Is arising (As An Apparent Play Upon The One Divine Being, Person, and Self-Condition). Therefore, I Am (Avatarically) To Be Divinely Realized—In and By and As every one.

In the body-mind of every being Within The Cosmic Mandala (or appearing Within The Domain Of conditional Manifestation), Each Form Of My (Avatarically Self-Revealed) Transcendental (or Self-Existing), and Inherently Spiritual (or Self-Radiant), and Inherently egoless, and Self-Evidently Divine Person Is Specially Presented In A Unique Fashion In Each Of The Most Fundamental Dimensions Of the psycho-physical person.

The Special (Apparent, or conditional) Domain Of My Transcendental, Inherently Spiritual, Inherently egoless, and Self-Evidently Divine Self (Itself, Prior To All Activity) Is The Right Side Of The Heart.

The Special (Apparent, or conditional) Domain Of My Apparently Objective, and Universally Manifested, "Bright" Divine Body Of Spiritual Presence Is The Middle Station Of The Heart, and The Circle (or The Combined Frontal and Spinal Lines) Of the body-mind, and The Arrow (or The Central Axis) Within The Circle Of the body-mind.

And The Special (Apparent, or conditional) Domain Of My Function As The Divine Heart-Master Of Grace Is The Comprehensive (or Total) Three-Part Domain Of The Heart (Including The Right Side, The Middle Station, and The Left Side Of The Heart), and The Ajna Center (or The Root Of The Brain Core), and The Total Crown Of the head (and The Felt "Bright" Space Infinitely Above The Total Crown Of the head), and (In The Case Of My Each and Every Divinely Enlightened Devotee, who Lives In Inherently Perfect Whole bodily, or Total psycho-physical, Heart-Oneness With Me) Even the entire and Grace-"Bright" body-mind Of My Inherently Most Perfect Devotee.

Among The Significant (and Most Basic and Typical) experiential Signs (or experiences Of The Effects Of My Avatarically Self-Transmitted Spiritual, and Always Blessing, Divine Presence) That May Appear In The Vertical Context Of The "Perfect Practice" (or, Potentially, To One Degree or Another, Even At Any Devotionally and Spiritually Developed Stage Of Practice) In The Only-By-Me Revealed and Given Way Of The Heart (or Way Of Adidam) Are A Spontaneous Quieting Of the conceptual activity of the mind and (Also) The Spontaneous Occurrence Of kriyas (or pleasurable bodily pulsings and tremblings, or pleasurable, and sometimes visibly dramatic, bodily shakings, spasms, or convulsions, that Work Spontaneously To Purify body, emotion, mind, and attention, and that Occur When My Avatarically Self-Transmitted Divine Spirit-Current Meets and Penetrates, or Breaks, The Blocks In Either The Frontal Line Or The Spinal Line, or In Both).

Other Possible Spontaneous experiential Signs (That May Occur, Progressively, As ego-Surrendering, ego-Forgetting, and ego-Transcending Feeling-Contemplation Of My Avatarically Self-Transmitted Spiritual, and Always Blessing, Divine Presence Deepens, Progressively) Include mudras (or many and various, and often dancelike, Yogic hand poses), asanas (or many and various Yogic bodily poses), pranayama (or automatic slow or rapid Yogic breathing-"Conductivity"), dancing, jumping, bodily hotness, sweating, bodily coldness, dryness of mouth, snarling and other exotic (and even animal-like) facial expressions, laughter, weeping, singing, moaning, growling (and other Spontaneous vocal noises), and (of course) all kinds of bodily and emotional and mental blisses (or states of Yogic "intoxication"), even in the form of blissful yawning and/or blissfully deep drowsiness (that may become a kind of Yogic "dream state", and even a Yogic "sleep", but without any loss Of blissful Awareness).

And Other Possible Spontaneous experiential Signs That May Occur Include any number of subtle sensations (such as Visions Of My Avatarically-Born Bodily Human Divine Form, Visions Of The Cosmic Mandala, Visions Of My Apparently Objective Divine Star-Form, Visions Of My Avatarically Self-Transmitted Divine Spirit-Current As light within the body, visions of the interior of the physical body, visions of energy centers in the body, visions of symbolic patterns, visions of environments, visions of all kinds of great or exotic or ordinary beings, visions of other worlds, visions of fields, spots, spheres, or holes of various colors, visions of blackness, density, fire, water, smoke, and the sky, auditions of the heartbeat, blood-circulation, and respiration, auditions of subtle internal sounds, such as explosions, a sound like a gunshot, snapping noises, pulsing or clicking or fluttering sounds, big and little thumping and tapping and drumming sounds, thundering or roaring or deep-vibrating or humming sounds, sounds such as those made by a distant waterfall, or the wind, or the sea, sounds of birds and animals and winged insects, ringing sounds, big and little bell-like sounds, flute-like sounds, xylophone-like sounds, sounds of plucked musical instruments, pouring or rushing soundless, or Merely Felt, sounds, sounds that Seem To Stand In Contrast To the grosser Natural world, Like electronic music, perceptions of a variety of subtle internal smells, in a range from excrement to flowers, and perception of a variety of subtle internal tastes, culminating in an ambrosial sweetness, as if nectar were dripping out of the brain), and Also every Possible kind of even vivid Yogic "dream", psychic vision, sudden insight, or Spiritual Apparition.

Likewise, Many remarkable psychic (and even physical) Signs (or experiences) May (In Some Cases, and In Due Course) Occur, including psychokinesis (or the ability to move, and even change, physical objects from a distance, via the mental projection of energy), the ability to receive and transmit thoughts and energies from a distance (via mental reception and projection), bodily levitation, bodily bilocation (so that You may perceive Your Own bodily double, or Your bodily person may be perceived by others in a location that is other than the one in which You perceive Your Own bodily person), "out-of-body experiences" (or astral travel),[154] premonitory dreaming (or futuristic reveries), and various forms of extrasensory perception, such as clairaudience, clairvoyance (including the ability to observe the local physical environment, or any physical environment at all, in all directions at once, rather than simply forward from the eyes, by simply rotating the eyeballs and the visual attention upwards), and general clairsentience. The List Cannot Be Exhausted, and, Apart From Certain Basic and Typical experiences (such as Spontaneous kriyas, Spontaneous psycho-physical blisses, and, Most Importantly, The Spontaneous Quieting Of the conceptual activity of the mind), The Display Is Unique To each individual.

Likewise, It May Be Found That A Natural (and Spontaneous, and Even Prolonged) Kumbhak (or An Upward Retention Of breath) Occurs During Deep Meditation. Even the heartbeat May Temporarily Come To Rest In Deep Meditation. Or All Awareness Of breath, heartbeat, and body May (At times) Cease.

In Any Case, In or At <u>Any</u> Developmental Stage Of The Devotional <u>and</u> Spiritual Process (or, As The Case May Be, Of The Progressive Demonstration Of The "Perfect Practice") Of The Only-By-Me Revealed and Given Way Of The Heart (or Way Of Adidam), these phenomena Are Not Important In and Of themselves. They Are Only Indications That My Avatarically Self-Transmitted Divine Spirit-Current Is Breaking Obstructions, Releasing Energy-Binding (and Spirit-Binding) Patterns and Knots, and Generally Purifying, Rightly Polarizing, Energizing, and Spiritualizing The Frontal Line and The Spinal Line. What Is Significant (In The Only-By-Me Revealed and Given Way Of The Heart, or Way Of Adidam) Is The Greater Effect (or Effective Purpose) Of All Of This. That Greater Effect (or Effective Purpose) Is Always The Initiation Of The Next (Naturally Possible, or, Otherwise, Spiritually Potential) Stage Of The Devotional and Spiritual Process (or, As The Case May Be, Of The Progressive Demonstration Of The "Perfect Practice") Of The Only-By-Me Revealed and Given Way Of The Heart (or Way Of Adidam).

Whenever conditionally arising phenomena (Whether ordinary Or Extraordinary) Are experienced, Then There Is Already attention In The

Context Of the body-mind. And Any Turning Of attention Toward conditional objects (Whether ordinary Or Extraordinary) Is To Be Transcended By Means Of The Three-Part Fundamental Practice Of The Only-By-Me Revealed and Given Way Of The Heart (or Way Of Adidam)—Which Is The Primary Practice (Of Searchlessly Beholding Me), Together With The Two Principal Responsive Practices (Of The "Conscious Process" and "Conductivity"). Thus, the (Potential) appearing of Extraordinary conditionally arising phenomena (or Of Even Any Kind Of Either Extraordinary Or ordinary conditionally arising experiences) Is Not A Circumstance To Be Sought or Clung To (or Even Avoided). Rather, If There Is the appearing of Extraordinary conditionally arising phenomena (or Of Even Any Kind Of Either Extraordinary Or ordinary conditionally arising experiences), all such appearances Are Simply To Be Accepted (Without Any Clinging, and Without Any Avoidance) As What Is Spontaneously Occurring In The Context Of The Primary-Practice-Disposition Of Searchlessly Beholding Me.

In The Vertical Context Of The "Perfect Practice" (or, Potentially, To One Degree or Another, At Any Devotionally and Spiritually Developed Stage) Of The Only-By-Me Revealed and Given Way Of The Heart (or Way Of Adidam), many light-forms, discrete objects, environments, and beings may be perceived In subtle Vision. The Primary Objects That May Be Perceived (In subtle Vision) Are My Subtle Bodily (Human) Form, The Full Presentation Of The Cosmic Mandala (With All Of Its Rings Of Color), and My (Apparently Objective) Five-Pointed Divine Star-Form (The First Visible Apparent Form Of My Avatarically Self-Transmitted Divine Spiritual Grace In The Cosmic Domain).

The Entire Cosmic Mandala, Including My Divine Star-Form, May Be Perceived Even In gross internal vision. My Divine Star-Form and The Cosmic Mandala Are Tangibly Projected Even Into The Structural Pattern Of the gross body (including the brain) of every human being, Just As They Are Also (Apparently) Projected Into every body-mind, plane, or realm of experience In The Cosmic Domain. Therefore, Visionary Experiences Of The Cosmic Mandala and Of My (Apparently Objective) Divine White Star-Form (In whichever, or however many, of Its planes Of conditional Manifestation) Are Among The Characteristic Experiences Of My Devotees (In The Vertical Context Of The "Perfect Practice", or, Potentially, At Any Devotionally and Spiritually Developed Stage, Of The Only-By-Me Revealed and Given Way Of The Heart, or Way Of Adidam).

In The Case Of Any Fully Devotionally and Spiritually Practicing Devotee Of Mine, The Great Mandala Of The conditional (or Cosmic) Domain May Appear In (Total) Vision (or In many fractions and forms of vision), Both during life and after death. The various Cosmic planes or worlds May

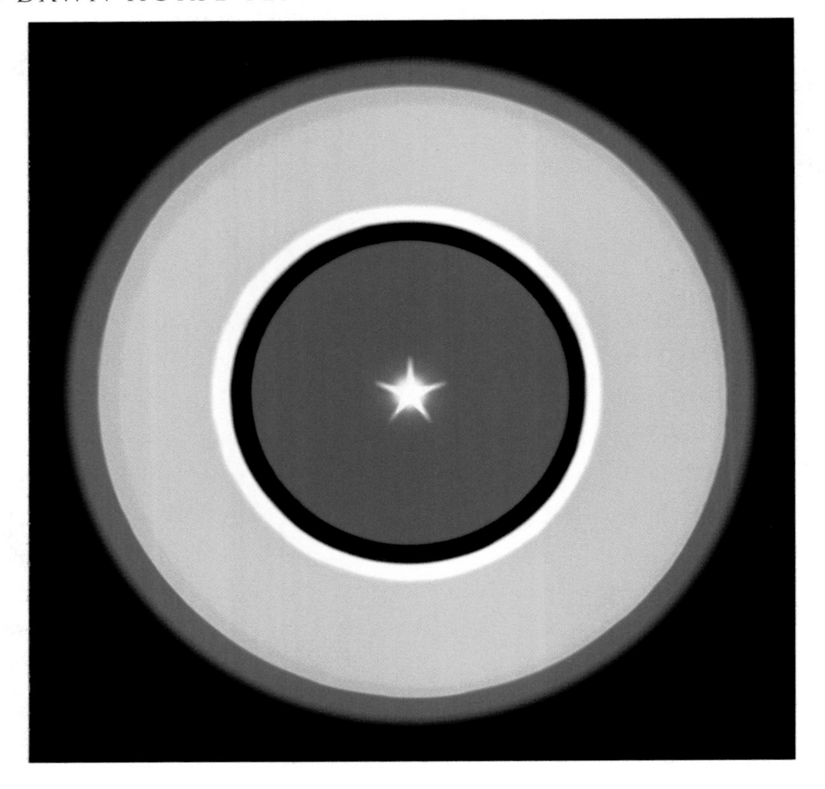

The Cosmic Mandala[155]

(Therefore) Be perceived, As In a dream, or More Concretely (With Varying Degrees Of Clarity, Detail, and Completeness, With all their kinds of beings, forms, and events).

Just So, The Great Cosmic Mandala Itself May Be Perceived In Vision. It Appears As A Circle (Self-Generated In Its Own Space). The Circle Is Itself A Gathering Of Circles—Each Set Within The Other, Concentric—Formed As A Radiant Wheel or A Well or A Tunnel (and, Thus, A Mandala) Of Great Formative Lights. The Outer Ring Is Narrow and Red In Color (and Generally Set Against An Ambiguous Outer Field That Is Rather Dark, or Perhaps Somewhat Luminous, but Not Tending To Distract attention). The Next Ring Is Yellow, and It Is Wide. Then There Is Another Narrow Ring, Of A Moonlike Whiteness. Then Another Narrow Ring, Apparently Black. And The Last Ring, At The Center, Is A Radiant Blue, As Wide As The Yellow. In The Center Of The Radiant Blue Is The (Apparently Objective) Brilliant Clear White Five-Pointed Star.

Each Ring Of Color Is An Energy-Field Of A Certain Range Of Vibration (Made By Apparent Modification Of My Avatarically Self-Transmitted, and Self-Radiant, Divine Spirit-Energy). Within Each Ring, There Are Countless worlds and beings, each Characterized and limited By The Vibratory Field In Which they appear. The Outer Rings Are Grosser (or Of A Lower Vibration), and Existence In Them Is Brief and Difficult. Those Closest To The Center Are Subtler (or Of A Higher Vibration), and Existence In Them Is More Pleasurable, More Prolonged, Less Threatened, but Nonetheless conditional, changing, Temporary, Made Of many limits, and Moved By A Necessary Struggle. The Radiant Blue Is The Most Subtle, and Existence There Is limited By Great Powers and By Great Longing For My Divine Love-Bliss, Which Is Finally Realized (By My Avatarically Self-Transmitted Divine Grace) Only In My Exceedingly "Bright" (and Perfectly Subjective) Feeling-Domain Of Self-Existing and Self-Radiant Divine Love-Bliss. And the human world Is Also Within This Cosmic Mandala Of Lights, In The Outer (or Grosser) Fields Of Red and Yellow.

The Vision Of The Cosmic Mandala May Be Perceived As A Whole, or In Part—Either Enlarged Or Reduced To A Point. Therefore, A Point or A Spot or A Circle (Made Of Any Color), or (Otherwise) A Group Of Any Of The Rings Of Associated Color, May Be Perceived. In any moment, A Sudden Spot Of light May Be Perceived To Fly Out Of the eyes (or one of the eyes), or Else To Flash Before the internal vision, Attractively.

Any Kind Of Pattern or Scene May appear In Meditation or Random vision. Any Kind Of Adventure May Be experienced, before or after death, in this or any other conditional world.

All worlds Are A (Merely Apparent) psycho-physical Display, Made Of My Divine Self-Radiance, By Spontaneous and conditional and Merely Apparent Modification Of That Radiance. All conditionally Manifested beings (Even in and as their present bodily or otherwise Apparent forms) Are spirits, or conditional Modifications Of Transcendental, Inherently Spiritual, Inherently egoless, and Self-Evidently Divine Conscious Light. All visions Are Made Of The Same Mandala Of (Apparently) Modified Clear White Light, The Light (or Self-Radiance, or Inherent Spiritual Radiance) Of Transcendental Divine Being.

Therefore, In The Process Of Divine Translation (Realized In The Only-By-Me Revealed and Given Seventh Stage Of Life In The Only-By-Me Revealed and Given Way Of The Heart), all conditional worlds, all conditional beings and events, all conditional forms of the psycho-physical self, and All The Cosmic Colors Yield To My Divine Star-Form (Itself), and (Therefrom) To The Self-Existing and Self-Radiant Sphere Of The "Midnight Sun" (The Most Prior, and Perfectly Subjective, Source-Condition Of Even My Divine Star-Form), and (Thus and So) Enter (and Dissolve) Into My Divine Self-"Brightness" (or Inherent Spiritual Radiance, or Transcendental Love-Bliss), Which Utterly all-and-All-Outshining Self-"Brightness" Is (Itself) My Divine Spherical Self-Domain.

In That Process Of Divine Translation, My Divine Star-Form Ceases To Be (and To Appear As) An Object. Indeed, Divine Translation (Realized In The Only-By-Me Revealed and Given Seventh Stage Of Life In The Only-By-Me Revealed and Given Way Of The Heart) Occurs Only If My Devotee Is (By Means Of My Avatarically Self-Transmitted Divine Spiritual Grace) Fully Awake To All The Perfectly Subjective Dimensions Of My Avatarically Self-Revealed (and Self-Evidently Divine) Person, and (Therefore) Only If My Devotee Is Established In (and As) My Avatarically Self-Revealed (Transcendental, Inherently Spiritual, Inherently egoless, and Self-Evidently Divine) Self-Condition, Divinely Self-Recognizing all objects (Including My Apparently Objective Divine Star-Form, If It Appears)—and Divinely Self-Recognizing Even The Feeling Of Relatedness Itself—As Only Me (and Not Other), and As Only Self-Existing and Self-Radiant Oneness (Without Division or Separation). Therefore, In The Event Of Divine Translation, My Apparently Objective Divine Star-Form (Divinely Self-Recognized) Becomes A Transparent Doorway, Inherently Non-Separate From My Avatarically Self-Transmitted Divine Spirit-Current Of Love-Bliss, and Inherently Identical To The Self-Existing and Self-Radiant Field That Is Consciousness Itself.

There I Am. The "Bright" Itself—Glorious Beyond Conception, Full, Without The Slightest Absence or Threat, More Than Wonderful, All Delight, Heart-Feeling Without limit, The Unspeakable "Embodiment" Of Joy, God-Great!

Generally Speaking, If (At Any Point In The Practice Of The Only-By-Me Revealed and Given Way Of The Heart) any Extraordinary conditionally arising phenomena appear—Simply Notice them, and Do Not Otherwise Indulge In such (or any other) appearances, but Simply Continue To Engage The By-Me-Given Exercises Appropriate To Your Stage Of Life (and Your Form Of Practice) In The Only-By-Me Revealed and Given Way Of The Heart (or Way Of Adidam).

As A General Rule, If any visual object (or Even Any Great Vision) Captures Your Heart-Feeling and attention In The Responsible Course Of Even Any Devotionally and Spiritually Developed Stage Of The Only-By-Me Revealed and Given Way Of The Heart, Always (Without ego-Effort or Seeking, but Merely By Turning To Me) Look To The "Head" Of My Avatarically Self-Transmitted Divine Spirit-Current. That Is To Say, Always (Merely, or Tacitly) Look Above what is presently perceived (or Made Apparent), and Always (Merely, or Tacitly) Look To The Middle Of the visual field. Whatever visual object (or Even Great Vision) is perceived (or Made Apparent), whatever conditionally Manifested environment appears, or whatever appearance the visual field may conditionally assume, Always (Merely, or Tacitly) Look Up and Toward The Middle (and Always Up and Back, Up and Back), To "Locate" My Apparent Source-Position (or Infinitely, and Priorly, Ascended Space Of

Origin), From Which (and In Which) the light or illumination (or Even Great Object) in the present field Is arising. Do Not Hold To any limited object (or Even Any Great Object) or field (or Luminous Sign) that is presently Before You. Do Not Seek To the left or the right. Hold Heart-Feeling and attention To An Upturned View, and Constantly (Merely, or Tacitly) Turn and Yield Toward The Center (Up and Back, Up and Back). Always (Merely, or Tacitly) Feel Beyond what presently appears (or Whatever Is Made Apparent), and Always Be Moved (Up and Back, Up and Back) Toward My Indefinable Central Source-Space Above The Total Crown Of the head.

If I Am Perceived In A (Subtle) Vision Of My Avatarically-Born Bodily (Human) Divine Form, Merely (or Tacitly) Look Toward Me, Hold On To Me, and Realize The Infinitely (and Priorly) Ascended Source-Space Of My Avatarically Self-Manifested Divine Appearance. If I Am Not Thus Perceived—Then Simply (Merely, or Tacitly) Look Above (Up and Back) For The Source Of light, and Hold To (or Yield Into) The Highest Center (or Infinitely, and Priorly, Ascended Source) Of the field, Rather Than To what may be perceived to the left or the right.

If The Cosmic Mandala Is Perceived, or If Any Spot or Circle or Shape Of light Is Perceived, Merely (or Tacitly) Look To Its Center and Be Drawn Upwards (Up and Back).

If My Apparently Objective Divine Star-Form Is Perceived, Merely (or Tacitly) Look To Its Center and Be Drawn Upwards (Up and Back). In This Manner, My Divine Star-Form May Be Perceived In Different (or Distinct) planes Of The Cosmic Mandala.

Whatever visionary experience may arise (At <u>Any</u> Devotionally <u>and</u> Spiritually Developed Stage In The Only-By-Me Revealed and Given Way Of The Heart), Do Not Be Concerned With Mapping (or Categorizing) the various lights, environments, or beings According To their Relative Position In The Cosmic Mandala. Constantly Surrender All Heart-Feeling and attention To Me, The Avatarically Self-Revealed Divine Person (or Self-Condition, and Source-Condition) Of all-and-All. Let My Avatarically Self-Transmitted Divine Spirit-Current Serve To Keep You In The Central Source-Position (and Source-Condition) Of the field of view, and Do Not Seek (or Hold To) what is perceived on the left or the right. Simply (Merely, or Tacitly) Be Released Into What Is Infinitely Above. If My Avatarically-Born Bodily (Human) Divine Form (or Any Subtle conditional Form That Is Identified As Me or Felt To Be Me) Appears, or If The Cosmic Mandala (or Any Center Of Colored light) Appears, or If My Divine Star-Form (or Any Brilliant—Rather Than Soft, or Moonlike—Central White Light) Appears—Let That Vision Serve To Keep You In The "Bright" Source-Space Infinitely Above The Total Crown Of the head.

In Addition To visionary phenomena, My Devotee May (In The Course Of Even Any Devotionally and Spiritually Developed Stage Of The Only-By-Me Revealed and Given Way Of The Heart) experience internal (or subtle) sounds—each (and, Collectively, all) of which (Including The Primal, Ascended, Cosmic Background Sound, or True "Om" Sound, or "Da" Sound) May Rightly Be Referred To As The Internal (and Cosmic) Vibratory Sound Of "Om", or "Da".

Whatever kind of auditory phenomenon is (in any moment) most obvious To You—Merely (or Tacitly) listen Upwards To Me, and Always Toward The Center Of the auditory field (and Always Up and Back, Up and Back). Or, Alternatively, No Matter what sound (or Infinitely-Ascended Background "Om", or "Da") Becomes Obvious, You May (Without Yielding attention To the sound itself) Simply (Merely, or Tacitly) Feel and listen and Swoon To Me, Above and Beyond it (Always Continuing Toward The Center, and Up and Back). Or, Alternatively, You May (Merely, or Tacitly) Turn Your auditory attention To My Voice Within You (If It Appears Spontaneously). In Any Case, Always (Merely, or Tacitly) Feel Toward Me—and (Thus, and Thereby) Toward The Silent (Infinitely, and Priorly) Ascended Origin Of My Voice, or Toward The Silent (Infinitely, and Priorly) Ascended Origin Of any sound (or Even any voice) that May Otherwise appear Spontaneously Within You—and (Thus) Always (Merely, or Tacitly) Feel Toward The Center, and Above (Up and Back, Up and Back).

As In The Case Of visionary phenomena, Do Not Be Concerned About Mapping (or Categorizing) the various sounds According To Cosmic planes, but Constantly Surrender All Heart-Feeling and attention To Me, The Avatarically Self-Revealed Divine Person (or Self-Condition, or Source-Condition) Of all-and-All. Do Not Become Fascinated With any present sound. Do Not Seek To the left or the right, but Always (Merely, or Tacitly) Feel Toward The Center Of the field of perception, and Above (Up and Back, Up and Back).

The sense of touch (Especially In Relation To My Avatarically Self-Transmitted Divine Spirit-Current Itself) Is (Necessarily) the Principal sensory (or subtle perceptual) medium. Thus, When (In The Course Of Even Any Devotionally and Spiritually Developed Stage Of The Only-By-Me Revealed and Given Way Of The Heart) touch-sensation has Relaxed its Fixation On the gross body, Heart-Feeling and attention Transfer touch-sensation To My (Avatarically Self-Transmitted) Tangible Divine Spirit-Current Of Love-Bliss. When You Notice That This Transfer Has Occurred, Simply Be Released Into My Avatarically Self-Transmitted Divine Spirit-Current Of Love-Bliss, and (Merely, or Tacitly) Let It Serve To Keep You In Its Matrix (or Infinitely Ascended Love-Blissful Source-Position) Above.

Such experiential phenomena As I Have Herein Described Are Not Significant In and Of themselves. If they Are Grasped For their own Sake, The

Course Of Your (Both Devotional and Spiritual) Practice Of The Only-By-Me Revealed and Given Way Of The Heart Will Be Retarded and Slowed. Therefore, Devotional Surrender (or Release and Transcending) Of the Separate and Separative self (or the self-Contraction) To Me Must Be Direct and Constant.

My Devotees Must Always Transcend Distraction By (conditional and Natural) experiential energies in the body-mind, and (Indeed) Distraction By psycho-physical experiences of any kind. Natural (or psycho-physical) energy (or Even Objective Cosmic Energy), Ascending In the body-mind, Makes (or, Otherwise, limits) the conditional phenomena (or All The Distracting Illusions) Of subtle experience. Natural (or psycho-physical) energy (or Even Objective Cosmic Energy) Is Not Truth. Conditional experience (However Sublime) Is Not Most Perfect Real-God-Realization.

Therefore, How Will My Devotees (At Even Any Devotionally and Spiritually Developed Stage Of The Only-By-Me Revealed and Given Way Of The Heart) Transcend The Binding and Deluding Power Of Extraordinary conditionally arising phenomena (or Of Even Any Kind Of Either Extraordinary Or ordinary conditionally arising experiences)? By Feeling-Contemplation Of Me! At Any and Every Both Devotionally and Spiritually Developed Stage Of The Only-By-Me Revealed and Given Way Of The Heart, Feel (and Thereby Contemplate) My Avatarically Self-Transmitted Divine Spiritual Presence (Itself)—and (Thus and Thereby) Renounce all conditional phenomena. In This Manner, Be Free Of The Distracting Power Of conditional Existence. Whether In The Devotional and Spiritual Context Of The "Samraj Yoga" Of The "Perfect Practice" Of The Only-By-Me Revealed and Given Way Of The Heart Or, Otherwise, In The Specific Manner Revealed and Given, By Me, To Be Exercised By My Devotees In The Context Of their Any Particular Devotionally and Spiritually Developed Stage Of Practice In The Only-By-Me Revealed and Given Way Of The Heart—Always "Locate" My Avatarically Self-Transmitted Spirit-Current Of Self-Evidently Divine Love-Bliss (Itself), In The By-Me-Avatarically-Self-Revealed Dimensions Of The (Inherently, Both Vertically and Horizontally Extended) "Place" Where I Always Already Stand—For I Am (Always Already) Beyond the conditional self and all conditional worlds.

The By-Me-and-As-Me-Avatarically-Self-Transmitted Divine Spirit-Current Is My Tangible Divine Spiritual Presence. It Is My Avatarically Self-Transmitted and Self-Revealed Body, My Divine Spiritual Body, My all-and-All-Surrounding Body, My all-and-All-Pervading Body, My Body Of "Brightness", My One and "Bright" and Only Person ("Brightly" Descending, To Surround and Pervade all-and-All). It Is My Self-Evidently Divine Love-Bliss Itself, Tangibly and Unmistakably Felt (By My Devotionally Me-Recognizing Devotee) As Me.

Therefore, Be In Love With Me As My Avatarically Self-Transmitted Divine Spirit-Current Of Love-Bliss.

The Essence Of This Unique Instruction Pertains At Every Stage Of Both Devotionally and Spiritually Developed Practice In The Only-By-Me Revealed and Given Way Of The Heart (or Way Of Adidam). Therefore—At Any and Every Both Devotionally and Spiritually Developed Stage Of The Only-By-Me Revealed and Given Way Of The Heart (or Way Of Adidam)—Always (Directly) Transcend conditional Existence (or all psycho-physical phenomena). Do This By Feeling (and Thereby Contemplating) Me. Instead Of Surrendering attention To conditional events, Surrender attention (Devotionally) To Me—As I Am Avatarically Self-Transmitted, and As I Am Avatarically Self-Revealed, and As I (Thus, and Divinely) Am.

Avatar Adi Da Samraj
Adidam Samrajashram, 2003

SUTRA
61

In The "Perfect Practice" Of The Only-By-Me Revealed and Given Way Of The Heart (or Way Of Adidam), There Is Free and Full and Stable Identification With The Witness-Position Of Consciousness, and Spontaneous Association With The Right Side Of The Heart. In This Manner (and On This Basis), The Knot (or self-Contraction) In The Brain Core Is Inherently and Perfectly Transcended.

In The Course Of The (Eventual) Full ("Samraj Yoga") Exercise Of The "Perfect Practice" Of The Only-By-Me Revealed and Given Way Of The Heart (or Way Of Adidam)—and As A Necessary Prerequisite For The Awakening (and The Transition) To The Only-By-Me Revealed and Given Seventh Stage Of Life—The Ajna Door Must Be Fully Opened, Such That The Whole bodily (or psycho-physical) Totality Of the body-mind Is (Itself) Fully Opened (Beyond All self-Contraction, or Even All Reference To Separation, Relatedness, and "Difference"), To "Locate" My Avatarically Self-Transmitted Divine (and Divinely Attractive) Spirit-Current Of Love-Bliss, In Its Source-Position, Infinitely Above The Circle Of the body-mind.

Until The Ajna Door Is Fully Opened, It Is, Effectively, The Ajna Knot. The Ajna Knot Functions As A Stress-Point That (Apparently) Confines The By-Me-Avatarically-Self-Transmitted Divine Spirit-Current To subtle (and Even gross) conditional Patterns Of egoity (By Confining The By-Me-Avatarically-Self-Transmitted Divine Spirit-Current To the subtle, and Even gross, fields of brain and/or mind). As Long As That Knot Persists, There Is A Fixation Of the Total body-mind (and The By-Me-Avatarically-Self-Transmitted Divine Spirit-Current) In the (Possible) subtle (astral, or Even etheric) and Even gross forms Of bodily and mental (or psychic) self-Awareness, and the (Possible) subtle internal sensory and (Potentially) mystical mind of egoic subjectivity, and the (Possible) subtle (and Even gross) activities and relations of egoity. Therefore, This Same Knot Is The Effective Cause Of Even The (Potential) Motive Toward The Strategically Ascending Course Of egoic attention.

The subtle ego Is Characterized By subtle, psychic, and mystical self-Preoccupation (or subtle, psychic, and mystical self-Absorption). Therefore, subtle, psychic, and mystical states Of conditional psycho-physical self-Awareness Are

(In and Of themselves) Actually Signs That Indicate A Binding Contraction (or Obstruction, or Knot) At The Ajna Door (or The Root Of The Brain Core).

Truly, The Ajna Door Is Not So Much A Place As It Is A Direction. Therefore, In The Context Of The Vertical Process Of The "Perfect Practice" Of The Only-By-Me Revealed and Given Way Of The Heart (or Way Of Adidam), To Merely (or Tacitly) Feel (and, Thus and Thereby, To Contemplate) Me (Apart From All Seeking, or All ego-Effort) At The Ajna Door Is Not Merely To Focus On A Spot (or An Area) In the brain (Between and Slightly Above and Deep Behind the brows). Right (Mere, or Tacit) Feeling-Contemplation Of Me At The Ajna Door Is Always A "Going Beyond" Action—Always Up and Back, Up and Back, Deeper and Deeper, Further and Further. The Upward Motion Goes Beyond The Descending Tendency, and The Backward Motion Goes Beyond The Tendency To Move From The Spinal Line To The Frontal Line. The Combination Of This Dual Upward (or Ascending) and Backward (or Deepening) Gesture (or Mere and Tacit Allowance) Releases attention Up The Center, and (Up and Back) Toward The Upper Rear (or The pineal Region) Of The Brain Core—and, In Due Course, This Tacit (or Non-Seeking, and ego-Effort-Transcending) Process Becomes (or Realizes) A Spontaneous Upward Opening Of The Total Crown Of the head, and (In Due Course, By Means Of Fully Ascended Nirvikalpa Samadhi) Leads Fully Beyond, To (and, Then, Into) My Infinite Matrix (or Formless Source-Position), Infinitely Above The Total Crown Of the head.

The Utter Fulfillment Of My Own Avatarically Self-Submitted Divine Work Of ego-Transcendence In The Context Of The First Six Stages Of Life Was Shown In A Profound and Spontaneous Event (and Ordeal) Of ego-Death (three and one-half years Previous To The Great Event Of My Divine Re-Awakening To My Own Inherently Perfect, Inherently egoless, and Self-Evidently Divine Self-Condition—Which Always Already Transcends the point of view and the conditional activity that is the ego-"I").[156] That Early Event (and Ordeal) Of ego-Death Was (At Its Own Sudden Depth) A Spontaneous Incident Of Prior (or Spiritually Self-Evident) ego-Transcendence (and Transcendental, and Inherently Spiritual, Self-Awakening) In Priorly Self-Abiding Jnana Samadhi (or Priorly Self-Abiding Jnana Nirvikalpa Samadhi)—Which Is The Priorly, and Spiritually, Established Form Of The Transcendental Samadhi (or Mode Of Transcendental Realization) Otherwise Characteristically (and merely conditionally, or By The Seeker's merely philosophical and psycho-physical Means) Sought In The Traditional Context Of The Sixth Stage Of Life. As A Spontaneous Result Of That Spontaneous Event, I (As My Yet-To-Be-Divinely-Re-Awakened Avataric Body-Mind-Vehicle) Was (Then, and Immediately Thereafter) Tacitly (but Not Strategically) Identified With The Witness-Position

Of Consciousness—and (Thus, Thereafter) I Persisted (Effortlessly) In An Inherently Surrendered (or Merely Witnessing) Attitude Toward My Own Body-Mind (and Its Activities), and I (Thus, Actively, Directly, and Summarily) Comprehended (or Understood) The Very Essence, Act, and Function Of My Own Body-Mind To Be Simply, Only, and Always The Root-Feeling Of Relatedness (and, From Then, That Essential Root-conditional Feeling Was, More and More Often, Directly Noticed, and Felt, As A "Point" Of Primal Stress In The Right Side Of The Heart).

That Profound Early Event (and Ordeal) Of Sudden ego-Death Was Also An Early (Spontaneous) Sign That The Most Ultimate (and Inherently Most Perfect) Event Of Seventh Stage Sahaja Nirvikalpa Samadhi (or Inherently Most Perfect Divine Sahaja Nirvikalpa Samadhi—Which Is Self-Evidently Divine, and Inherently Most Perfect, Self-Awakening) Was (Rather Than Any Lesser, or conditional, Realization) To Be The (Eventual) Great Fulfillment Of My (Ultimately, Most Perfectly ego-Transcending) Avataric Divine Ordeal. However, In Order For The Avataric Divine Self-Revelation (and The Avataric Divine Fulfillment, and The Effective Avataric Divine Spiritual-Transmission-Power) Of The Only-By-Me Revealed and Given Way Of The Heart (or Way Of Adidam) To Be Complete In Me, It Was Necessary For Me To Pass Through and Beyond Every Developmental Stage Of Life—Including All Aspects Of Both The Vertical and The Horizontal Dimensions Of The Great Process Otherwise Associated With The Fifth Stage Of Life and The Sixth Stage Of Life. Therefore, The Early Event (and Ordeal) Of ego-Death Was That Aspect Of My Avataric Self-Submission That Effectively Allowed (or Established The Transcendental Basis For) The (Soon To Come) Sudden Establishment In Priorly Ascended Nirvikalpa Samadhi—Which, Because It Was Thus Founded On The Inherently Perfect Transcendental Base Of The Prior Spiritual Realization Of Consciousness (or Mere Feeling-Awareness) Itself, Inherently and Perfectly Transcended the Inherent limitations Of merely conditionally Ascended Nirvikalpa Samadhi (or The Form Of Ascended Samadhi Otherwise and Characteristically Sought, By The Seeker's Means Of Progressive psycho-physical Ascent, "from the ground up", In The Traditional Context Of The Fifth Stage Of Life).[157]

In The Case Of My Avatarically Self-Submitted Body-Mind-Vehicle, The Early Event (and Ordeal) Of ego-Death (three and one-half years Previous To The Great Event Of My Divine Re-Awakening) Provided (In Its Immediate Effect) A Dramatic Breakthrough (or A Passage Beyond The bodily-Based Orientation) To The Perfect Yoga Of Prior Ascendedness. Indeed, The Breakthrough Was So Intense That I Was Immediately Prepared For The Event Of Sudden, Unobstructed, and Full Establishment In Priorly Ascended Nirvikalpa Samadhi. And That Sublime Event (In Fact) Occurred, Also Spontaneously,

Early In the year following That Preparatory Ordeal Of ego-Death—Immediately After My Reception Of Spiritual Blessing (or Yogic Shaktipat) In The Company Of Three Great Realizers (or Siddhas) Of The Yogic Process Of Spiritual Ascent.[158]

Because Of This Extraordinary (Early and Sudden) "Leap" To Priorly Ascended Nirvikalpa Samadhi, My Fullest Exploration (or Detailed Experiential "Consideration") Of The Patterns Of Savikalpa Samadhi (or The Developmental Patterns and Signs Which Otherwise and Typically Characterize The Traditional "Climber's Map" Of The Progressive "from-the-ground-up" Process Of Fifth Stage Ascent, and Which Otherwise, In Conformity With That Traditional "Climber's Map", Typically Precede The Realization Of Fifth Stage conditionally Ascended Nirvikalpa Samadhi) Did Not Occur Until After My Spontaneous Full Realization Of Priorly Ascended Nirvikalpa Samadhi. Of Course, Such Developmental Patterns and Signs (and, Indeed, Developmental Patterns and Signs Associated With Each and All Of The Stages Of Life) Sometimes Appeared (Spontaneously) To Me (or In My Case) Even During My Childhood and Developing Years. And Those Developmental Patterns and Signs Also Included Countless Spontaneous (Savikalpa Samadhi) Occurrences Of "Cosmic Consciousness" (In The Midst Of Otherwise ordinary moments of perception).[159]

In Fact, The Most Profound Of These Occurrences Of "Cosmic Consciousness" (or, Beyond That, Even The Glimpse Of Inherently Most Perfect Seventh Stage Awakeness)[160] Initiated The Great Ordeal Of My Early Adult Life, Which Was To Be The Extraordinary (and "Perfectly" Ordinary) and Uniquely Complete Process Of Transcendental, Inherently Spiritual, and Most Perfect Divine Self-Realization. However, Full Exploration and Real Understanding Of Those (and All Such) Developmental Patterns and Signs Were (Along With My "Consideration" Of All Of The Circle, and The Arrow, and The psycho-physical Totality Of The gross, subtle, and causal Structure Of the body-mind) Part Of The Process That Developed In The (Especially Later) Period Of The Great Ordeal In Which (and By Which) I Moved Toward Seventh Stage Sahaja Nirvikalpa Samadhi (or The Inherently Most Perfect Awakeness Of My Divine Re-Awakening).

In The Only-By-Me Revealed and Given Way Of The Heart (or Way Of Adidam), The Fully (and Priorly, and Perfectly) Ascended Event Of Nirvikalpa Samadhi Occurs Via A Spontaneous and Sudden Apparent Ascent Of attention—To Beyond All Awareness Of body, mind, and conditional relations of all kinds. It Is Fully Ascended Mergence (To The Degree Of Indivisible Unity) With My (Apparently) Objective Spirit-Matrix (or Source-Position, and Source-Vibration, and Source-Light)—Infinitely Above the head, Infinitely Above the Total body, Infinitely Above the perceptual and conceptual mind, and Infinitely Above all the conditional worlds Within The Cosmic Mandala. In The

Spontaneous Establishment Of The Priorly Ascended "Position" (As Also In The Progress Of Yogic Ascent Leading To merely conditionally Ascended Nirvikalpa Samadhi), The Ajna Knot (Experienced As A Most Subtle Point, or Bindu[161]) Is Penetrated—Beyond Which There Is Only The Infinite Free Space Of My Avatarically Self-Transmitted Spirit-Current (and Source-Condition) Of Divine Love-Bliss. And, To an outside observer, the body of the (Thus, Either Priorly Or conditionally Ascended) individual May (Temporarily) Even Appear To Be dead—or, Certainly, In A Remarkable State Of Suspension (In Which Even breath and heartbeat May Be Temporarily Suspended, or, Otherwise, Reduced To A Nearly Undetectable Rate Of activity).

In The Event Of merely conditionally Ascended Nirvikalpa Samadhi—Which May Sometimes (or In Some Cases) Occur, In The Developing Devotional and Spiritual Context Of The Only-By-Me Revealed and Given Way Of The Heart (or Way Of Adidam), and Only As A Preliminary To The Only-By-My-Avataric-Divine-Spiritual-Grace-Given "Perfect-Practice"-Realization Of Priorly Ascended Nirvikalpa Samadhi—The Perception, Conception, or Presumption Of a Separate self Is Temporarily Lost In conditional Ecstatic Realization Of Indivisible Unity With My Avatarically Self-Transmitted Spirit-Current (and My Avatarically Self-Revealed Person) Of Divine (and Inherently egoless) Love-Bliss (and With My Apparently Objective Spirit-Matrix, Infinitely Above). The Experience Of conditionally Ascended Nirvikalpa Samadhi Depends Upon The Temporary (Tacit and Spontaneous) Manipulation Of attention, and The Temporary (Tacit and Spontaneous) Manipulation Of Even All Of The Mechanics (or physiology and psychology) Of the body-mind. Therefore, Such (merely conditionally) Ascended Nirvikalpa Samadhi Is Only A Temporary and conditional Achievement Of ego-Transcending (and body-mind-Transcending) Ecstasy.

The Ascent To conditional Nirvikalpa Samadhi Achieves The Temporary and conditional Experiential Transcending Of the conditional self (or ego) that is the body-mind, but It Does Not Absolutely Achieve Either The Temporary Or The Permanent Perfect (or Inherent, and Inherently Complete) Transcending Of egoity itself (or the Root-self-Contraction, which is attention itself). Therefore, conditionally Ascended Nirvikalpa Samadhi Is The Achievement Of (Fifth Stage) Ecstasy (or The State Of Standing "Outside", or Spiritually Beyond, the body-mind), but It Is Only A Temporary, conditional, and Cosmic Ecstasy (and It Is Not Founded Upon—or, Otherwise, Inherently Associated With—Inherently Most Perfect Spiritual, Transcendental, and Self-Evidently Divine Enstasy, or The Native Condition Of Standing Unconditionally As The By-Me-Avatarically-Self-Revealed Transcendental, Inherently Spiritual, Inherently egoless, and Self-Evidently Divine Self-Condition Itself).

The Temporarily Ascended Event Of conditional Nirvikalpa Samadhi Is Not merely an "out-of-body experience",[162] Because (In conditionally Ascended Nirvikalpa Samadhi) attention Stands "Outside" (or Above) the perceptual and conceptual mind As Well As the body. In The Only-By-Me Revealed and Given Way Of The Heart (or Way Of Adidam), The Ascended Event Of conditional Nirvikalpa Samadhi Is The Most Complete (or Extreme) Achievement Of The conditional Ascent Of attention (which is The conditional Essence Of the ordinary, or perceptual and conceptual, mind) To A State Of Union With The Undifferentiated Oneness Of My Utterly (Priorly and Perfectly) Ascended Matrix-Condition, Infinitely Above The psycho-physical Context Of the conditional body-mind. Therefore, Such conditionally Ascended Nirvikalpa Samadhi Is The conditional Achievement Of The conditional Transcending Of the body-mind, With A Simultaneously Permitted Glimpse Of My Always Priorly and Perfectly Ascended Source-Reality (or Ascended Matrix-Condition), Always Already Free-Standing, Utterly Above conception, perception, and phenomenal (or psycho-physical) self-Awareness. Nevertheless, Such conditionally Ascended Nirvikalpa Samadhi Is An Event That Is Naturally Dependent Upon the body-mind-self—and, Therefore, The Experience Is, Necessarily, Soon Lost In The Inevitable Return, or Descent, Of attention To the states of identification With The Various Dualisms Of the body-mind-self and the Natural conditions of the body-mind-self.

The individual brain-and-body complex (As Well As every other conditionally Manifested being, form, process, or circumstance Within The Mandala Of conditional, or Cosmic, Existence) Is (functionally, and In Effect) a mediator, or a structural limit On The One and Only and Inherently Indivisible and Inherently egoless and Self-Evidently Divine Conscious Light Of all-and-All. In The Event Of conditionally Ascended (or Merely Fifth Stage) Nirvikalpa Samadhi, The conventionally experienced Distinction Between the knower and the known Is conditionally (and Temporarily) Obliterated. Thus, In The Event Of conditionally Ascended Nirvikalpa Samadhi (In The Only-By-Me Revealed and Given Way Of The Heart), The By-Me-Avatarically-Self-Transmitted Spirit-Current Of Divine Love-Bliss Temporarily Ceases To Be mediated (or functionally limited), and Conscious Awareness Comes (conditionally, and Temporarily) To Sudden Experiential Realization Of The Self-Evidently Divine Context and State Of Being. Therefore, Even In The Event Of conditionally Ascended Nirvikalpa Samadhi, The Great Matter Of Significance (In The Only-By-Me Revealed and Given Way Of The Heart) Is Not The Experience Of A Great Object (or Even The Experience Of The Apparently Objective Divine)—but The Great Matter Of Significance Is The Revelation Of My Avatarically Self-Revealed (Transcendental, Inherently Spiritual, Inherently egoless, and

Self-Evidently Divine) Self-Condition (Which Is The Ultimate, and Perfectly Subjective, Identity Of every conditional knower, and Of all that is conditionally known, and Of all forms of conditional knowledge).

In The Only-By-Me Revealed and Given Way Of The Heart (or Way Of Adidam), The (Potential) Experience Of conditionally Ascended Nirvikalpa Samadhi Is An Event Of conditional (and Temporary) Release Of The Unconscious From Its Apparent Unconsciousness—or An Event Of conditional and Temporary Release Of The By-Me-Avatarically-Self-Revealed Transcendental, Inherently Spiritual, Inherently egoless, and Self-Evidently Divine Self-Consciousness From The Illusion Of limitation Implied By The Superimposition Of the conditional self (or the self-Contracted body-mind), and its objects, On The By-Me-Avatarically-Self-Revealed Transcendental, Inherently Spiritual, Inherently egoless, and Self-Evidently Divine Self-Consciousness. Therefore, As Such, conditionally Ascended Nirvikalpa Samadhi Is The Tacit (but conditional, and Temporary) Realization Of The Divinely Real (and Inherently egoless) Self-Condition Of the conditional self and all of its objects (Including The Total Cosmic Domain Of conditionally Manifested beings, forms, and events).

In The Only-By-Me Revealed and Given Way Of The Heart (or Way Of Adidam), conditionally Ascended Nirvikalpa Samadhi Is Only A Possible—but Not Necessary—Experience. However, In The Context Of The Full "Samraj Yoga" Of The "Perfect Practice" Of The Only-By-Me Revealed and Given Way Of The Heart (or Way Of Adidam), Priorly (Fully and Perfectly, or Not "from-the-ground-up") Ascended Nirvikalpa Samadhi—Which Is Inherently Associated With Inherently Most Perfect Divine Self-Realization (and With The "Regeneration" Of Amrita Nadi)—Is A Necessary Immediate Prerequisite To The Awakening (and The Transition) To The Only-By-Me Revealed and Given Seventh Stage Of Life (and To The Third Stage Of The "Perfect Practice" Of The Only-By-Me Revealed and Given Way Of The Heart, or Way Of Adidam).

In The Event Of Priorly Ascended Nirvikalpa Samadhi, The Perception, Conception, or Presumption Of a Separate self Is (By Means Of My Avatarically Self-Transmitted Divine Spiritual Grace) Inherently, and Perfectly, and Permanently Undermined—and, In Due Course (By Means Of My Avatarically Self-Transmitted Divine Spiritual Grace), That Perception, Conception, or Presumption Is Inherently, and Most Perfectly, and Permanently Lost (or Absolutely Vanished, and Infinitely Transcended, and Divinely Gone Beyond), In The Only-By-Me Revealed and Given Awakening To Seventh Stage Sahaja Nirvikalpa Samadhi.

In The Only-By-Me Revealed and Given Way Of The Heart (or Way Of Adidam), Priorly Ascended Nirvikalpa Samadhi Is The Spontaneous and Only-By-My-Avataric-Divine-Spiritual-Grace-Given Establishment In The "Position"

Of My (Apparently Objective) Spirit-Matrix Of Divine Love-Bliss. Therefore, Although There May (Experientially) Appear To Be A Sudden Ascent Of attention, The Event Of Priorly Ascended Nirvikalpa Samadhi Does Not, In Fact, Depend Upon Any Manipulation Of attention (or Even Any Manipulation Of All Of The Mechanics, or physiology and psychology, Of the body-mind). Therefore, Unlike conditionally Ascended Nirvikalpa Samadhi, Priorly Ascended Nirvikalpa Samadhi Is Not Inherently Associated With An Inevitable Return (or Descent) Of attention To the states of identification With The Various Dualisms Of the body-mind-self and the Natural conditions of the body-mind-self.

In The "Perfect Practice" Of The Full "Samraj Yoga" Of The Only-By-Me Revealed and Given Way Of The Heart (or Way Of Adidam), Priorly Ascended Nirvikalpa Samadhi (or Priorly and Spiritually Established Samadhi In The Context Of The Vertical Domain) Is (and Must Be) Realized (By Means Of My Avatarically Self-Transmitted Divine Spiritual Grace) In Perfect Conjunction With Priorly Self-Abiding Jnana Nirvikalpa Samadhi (or Priorly and Spiritually Established Samadhi In The Context Of The Horizontal Domain). Thus, In The Only-By-Me Revealed and Given Way Of The Heart (or Way Of Adidam), Priorly Ascended Nirvikalpa Samadhi Is—In This Unique Manner—Inherently Associated With (Inherently Most Perfect) Spiritual, Transcendental, and Self-Evidently Divine Enstasy (or The Native Condition Of Standing Unconditionally As The By-Me-Avatarically-Self-Revealed Transcendental, Inherently Spiritual, Inherently egoless, and Self-Evidently Divine Self-Condition Itself).

Therefore, In The Context Of The "Perfect Practice" Of The Only-By-Me Revealed and Given Way Of The Heart (or Way Of Adidam), That Divine Conscious Light Which Was Previously Hidden (or Veiled To Consciousness) Is Perfectly Self-Revealed In The Unique Coincidence (or Coincident Vertical and Horizontal Self-Realization) Of Priorly Ascended Nirvikalpa Samadhi and Priorly Self-Abiding Jnana Nirvikalpa Samadhi. Subsequent To The Coincident (or Uniquely Perfect) Awakening Of Priorly Ascended Nirvikalpa Samadhi and Priorly Self-Abiding Jnana Nirvikalpa Samadhi (In The Context Of The "Samraj Yoga" Of The Second Stage Of The "Perfect Practice" Of The Only-By-Me Revealed and Given Way Of The Heart, or Way Of Adidam), That Divine Conscious Light Which Was Previously Hidden Becomes (In The Only-By-My-Avataric-Divine-Spiritual-Grace-Given Event Of Seventh Stage Sahaja Nirvikalpa Samadhi) A Most Ultimate (and Inherent, and Inherently Most Perfect) Conscious Awakening That Is Spontaneously, Effortlessly, and Inevitably Maintained Even In The Context Of the (Apparent) arising of every kind of conditional form or event.

When The Spiritual, Transcendental, and Divine Process Of The Only-By-Me Revealed and Given Way Of The Heart (or Way Of Adidam) Has (Thus)

Developed To The (Seventh Stage) Degree Of Full and Unconditional Conscious Realization Of The One and Only and Inherently Indivisible and Inherently egoless and Self-Evidently Divine Conscious Light, The Truth Of The Apparent (or conditionally Manifested) Cosmos Is (By Me) Divinely Self-Revealed—and (Thus and Thereby) Made Divinely Self-Active. Thereafter, The Divinely Self-Realized Exercise Of The "Samraj Yoga" Of The Third Stage Of The "Perfect Practice" (In The Context Of The Only-By-Me Revealed and Given Seventh Stage Of Life In The Only-By-Me Revealed and Given Way Of The Heart, or Way Of Adidam) Must Demonstrate The Inherently egoless Power and Freedom Of The Self-Existing and Self-Radiant Divine Conscious Light—Even (At Last) To The Degree Of Translation Into My Spiritually Self-"Bright" Divine Spherical Self-Domain.

Avatar Adi Da Samraj
Los Angeles, 2000

SUTRA 62

The "Perfect Practice" Of The Only-By-Me Revealed and Given Way Of The Heart (or Way Of Adidam) Is Established By Means Of (Necessarily, Searchless, and, Altogether, Devotionally Me-Beholding, and Profoundly To-Me-Responsive) Participation In My Avataric Divine Spiritual Self-Transmission (or Ruchira Shaktipat), To The Degree (In Due Course) Of Receiving My Avataric Divine Spiritual Gift Of The Samadhi Of The "Thumbs"—and Of Becoming (Thus and Thereby) Spiritually and Transcendentally Enabled To Truly and Rightly Enter Into The "Perfect Practice" Of The Only-By-Me Revealed and Given Way Of The Heart (or Way Of Adidam).

The Only-By-Me Revealed and Given Samadhi Of The "Thumbs" Is Established Only and Entirely Through The Process Of (Searchlessly, Devotionally, and Responsively) Receiving My Avataric Divine Spiritual Self-Transmission. The Samadhi Of The "Thumbs" Cannot Be Strategically Caused By Any Seeker's Effort (or ego-Effort) Of Entering Into A "Program" Of Practice-Techniques. Indeed, The Same Is True Relative To All The Elements Of The Unique Devotional and Spiritual Process Of Right Practice, and Of (Ultimately, Most Perfect) Realization, In The Only-By-Me Revealed and Given Way Of The Heart (or Way Of Adidam).

The Fundamental Gift and Discipline (and The Always Primary Practice, or First and Constant Exercise) Of The Way In (and Of) My Avataric Divine Spiritual Company Is The Searchless Beholding Of Me—and Of (Necessarily, Responsive) Ongoing Participation In The Subsequently Unfolding Devotional and Spiritual Process, Only and Entirely On That Fundamental (and Always Primary) Basis. Thus, The Progressive Course Of The Only-By-Me Revealed and Given Way Of The Heart (or Way Of Adidam) Is Simply The Always Continuing Revelation (or Perpetual Unfolding) Of The Always Primary Practice Of Searchlessly Beholding Me. And That Always Primary (and Always Unfolding) Practice Takes A Particular (or Further Developed) Form At Each Successive Developmental Stage Of Practice Of The Only-By-Me Revealed and Given Way Of The Heart (or Way Of Adidam).

The "Perfect Practice" Of The Only-By-Me Revealed and Given Way Of The Heart (or Way Of Adidam) Is Not A Form Of "Mind Dharma" (or A Mere philosophical Strategy, or A mind-Based Seeker's Exercise), Intended To Culminate In The conditional Realization Of Jnana Nirvikalpa Samadhi—As Is Typically The Case In The Sixth Stage Schools Of The Great Tradition Of Mankind. The "Perfect Practice" Of The Only-By-Me Revealed and Given Way Of The Heart Is, Simply, Continuing Participation In The (Searchlessly Me-Beholding) Devotional and Spiritual Relationship To Me. It Is Always My Avataric Divine Spiritual Self-Transmission (or Ruchira Shaktipat) That Establishes The Modes Of Samadhi (or Realization) In Each Of The Developmental Stages Of The Only-By-Me Revealed and Given Way Of The Heart. The Only-By-Me Revealed and Given Samadhis (or Realizations) Of The Only-By-Me Revealed and Given Way Of The Heart Cannot Be Caused By A philosophical Effort (or By Even Any conditional Effort).

From The Moment Of My Listening Devotee's First Formal Spiritual Initiation By Me, The Process Of The Only-By-Me Revealed and Given Way Of The Heart (or Way Of Adidam) Is Always A Matter Of Participating In My Avataric Divine Spiritual Self-Transmission. Once There Is Tangibly Experienced Participation In My Avataric Divine Spiritual Self-Transmission (or Ruchira Shaktipat), Then (and Only On That Basis) There Are Responsive Practices To Be Engaged By My Devotees—In The Form Of The "Conscious Process" and "Conductivity" Practice. And There Are Particular Forms Of The (Responsive) "Conscious Process" and (Responsive) "Conductivity" Practice That Are Unique To The "Perfect Practice" Of The Only-By-Me Revealed and Given Way Of The Heart. However, To Enter Into The "Perfect Practice" Of The Only-By-Me Revealed and Given Way Of The Heart Is Not A Matter Of Applying My Instructions Relative To The "Perfect Practice" Forms Of The "Conscious Process" and "Conductivity" Practice In Order To Cause Self-Abiding Jnana Nirvikalpa Samadhi and/or Fully Ascended Nirvikalpa Samadhi. Rather, To Enter Into The "Perfect Practice" Of The Only-By-Me Revealed and Given Way Of The Heart Is To Participate—Responsively, and Not Causatively—In The Already Established and Ongoing Devotional and Spiritual Process Of Searchlessly-Me-Beholding Reception Of My Avataric Divine Spiritual Self-Transmission (or Ruchira Shaktipat).

Thus, Even Though There Are Aspects Of conditionally Ascended Nirvikalpa Samadhi (As It Has Traditionally Been Realized In The Context Of The Fifth Stage Of Life) That Are Comparable, In Some Experiential Respects, To The Only-By-Me Revealed and Given Realization Of Priorly Ascended Nirvikalpa Samadhi (In The Vertical Context Of The "Perfect Practice" Of The Only-By-Me Revealed and Given Way Of The Heart), Priorly Ascended

Nirvikalpa Samadhi Is Fundamentally and Essentially Different From conditionally Ascended Nirvikalpa Samadhi—Because Priorly Ascended Nirvikalpa Samadhi Is Priorly (Rather Than conditionally) Established In My Source-"Place" (and Source-Condition), Infinitely Above the body-mind. Therefore, Priorly Ascended Nirvikalpa Samadhi Is A Unique Spiritual Process, That Occurs Spontaneously—Not Progressing "from the ground up", but Avatarically and Divinely Given (By Me) From My Priorly Established Source-Position, Always Already Infinitely Above The Circle (and The Arrow) Of the body-mind.

Likewise, Even Though There Are Aspects Of conditionally Self-Abiding Jnana Nirvikalpa Samadhi (As It Has Traditionally Been Realized In The Context Of The Sixth Stage Of Life) That Are Comparable, In Some Experiential Respects, To The Only-By-Me Revealed and Given Realization Of Priorly Self-Abiding Jnana Nirvikalpa Samadhi (In The Horizontal Context Of The "Perfect Practice" Of The Only-By-Me Revealed and Given Way Of The Heart), Priorly Self-Abiding Jnana Nirvikalpa Samadhi Is Fundamentally and Essentially Different From conditionally Self-Abiding Jnana Nirvikalpa Samadhi—Because Priorly Self-Abiding Jnana Nirvikalpa Samadhi Is Priorly (Rather Than conditionally) Established In My "Point" Of Origin (and Self-Condition), In (and Beyond) The Right Side Of The Heart. Therefore, Priorly Self-Abiding Jnana Nirvikalpa Samadhi Is (Like Priorly Ascended Nirvikalpa Samadhi) A Unique Spiritual Process, That Occurs Spontaneously—Not Established (In The Heart-Plane) By A Movement From Left To Middle To Right, but Avatarically and Divinely Given (By Me) From My Priorly Established "Point" Of Origin, In (and Always Already Beyond) The Right Side Of The Heart.

Thus, Both Priorly Ascended Nirvikalpa Samadhi and Priorly Self-Abiding Jnana Nirvikalpa Samadhi Are Established (and Given) By Me, From Beyond (and Prior To) The conditional Context.

Indeed, The Only-By-Me Revealed and Given Way Of The Heart (or Way Of Adidam) Is, Altogether, Priorly Established By My Own Person—Through The Process Of My Avatarically Given Divine Spiritual Self-Transmission. Therefore, To Practice The Only-By-Me Revealed and Given Way Of The Heart (or Way Of Adidam) Is, Most Fundamentally, To Simply Turn The Four Faculties (Of body, Of breath, Of emotion, and Of mind, or attention) To Me (and, In Due Course, To Merely Thus, and Searchlessly, Behold Me, and To Thus Receive Me, and, On That Basis, To Respond To Me), In My Avatarically Self-Revealed (and Spiritually Self-"Bright") Divine (and Humanly-Born) Appearance here. And The "Perfect Practice" Of The Only-By-Me Revealed and Given Way Of The Heart (or Way Of Adidam), With Its Coincident Vertical and Horizontal Dimensions, Is Simply The Culmination Of This Unique (To-Me-Turned, and Searchlessly Me-Beholding, and To-Me-Responding)

Process Of Whole bodily (or As A psycho-physical Totality) Participating In My Infinitely Love-Bliss-"Bright" Spiritual Self-Transmission Of My Own Avatarically Self-Revealed Divine Person and Self-Condition.

Therefore, In The Only-By-Me Revealed and Given Way Of The Heart (or Way Of Adidam), There Is No Strategic (or Causative) Exercise To Be Engaged, No Technique To Be Practiced Independently. The Only-By-Me Revealed and Given Way Of The Heart—From Its Beginnings To Its Fulfillment In The Three Stages Of The "Perfect Practice"—Is Entirely A Matter Of The ego-Transcending Devotional and (In Due Course) Spiritual Relationship To Me. Thus, All The Samadhis That Are Established In The Context Of The "Perfect Practice" Of The Only-By-Me Revealed and Given Way Of The Heart Are Established Only On This Basis. In Both The Horizontal and Vertical Dimensions, The Samadhis Characteristic Of The "Perfect Practice" Of The Only-By-Me Revealed and Given Way Of The Heart Are Established From The Prior Position, The Position In Which I Always Already Stand.

In This, My Avatarically Self-Revealed (and, Altogether, Me-Revealing) Divine Testament, I Am Communicating As Much About The Entire (Only-By-Me Revealed and Given) Process Of Spiritual, Transcendental, and Divine Realization As Can Usefully Be Conveyed Through The Medium Of words. As I Have Described (In This, My Avatarically Self-Revealed Divine Testament), Some Aspects Of My Avatarically Given Divine Instruction Are Reserved For Confidential Presentation (By The Ruchira Sannyasin Order Of Adidam Ruchiradam) To My Devotees who Are Actually (In then present-time) Involved In The Process Of The "Perfect Practice" Of The Only-By-Me Revealed and Given Way Of The Heart (or Way Of Adidam). But, Even Beyond This, The Only-By-Me Revealed and Given Devotional and Spiritual Process Of The Way Of The Heart (or Way Of Adidam) Cannot Be Reduced To words or arguments or conceptual exercises or conceptual events. It Is Not Possible To Give A Complete Accounting Of The Devotional and Spiritual Process Of The Only-By-Me Revealed and Given Way Of The Heart (or Way Of Adidam) Through The Medium Of words. My Avatarically Given Divine Spiritual Self-Transmission (or Ruchira Shaktipat) Is Not A merely verbal Transmission. Therefore, The "Perfect Practice" Of The Only-By-Me Revealed and Given Way Of The Heart (or Way Of Adidam), Including (In Due Course) The "Practice" Of The Only-By-Me Revealed and Given (and Divinely Enlightened) Seventh Stage Of Life, Is The Culmination Of The Devotional and Spiritual Process In My Avataric Divine Spiritual Company—Not Merely The Culmination (or The Caused Result) Of A Series Of verbal (conceptual and philosophical) arguments.

The Direct (ego-Transcending and object-Transcending) Contemplation Of Consciousness (or Feeling-Awareness) Itself Develops Progressively (In The

Context Of The Second Stage Of The "Perfect Practice" Of The Only-By-Me Revealed and Given Way Of The Heart), Until The Process Becomes Utterly Profound. In That Process, attention and The By-Me-Avatarically-Self-Transmitted Divine Spirit-Current Are—By Means Of My Avatarically Self-Transmitted Divine Spiritual Grace, and Through Inherent and Ever-Deeper Feeling-Identification With My Avatarically Self-Revealed (and Very, and Transcendental, and Perfectly Subjective, and Inherently Spiritual, and Inherently egoless, and Inherently Perfect, and Self-Evidently Divine) State That Is The Most Prior Identity (or Self-Condition) Of The Witness-Consciousness Itself—Allowed To Dissolve Toward (and In) The Most Prior (and Perfectly Subjective) Source, Via The Locus In The Right Side Of The Heart. In The Course and Context Of That Process, The Feeling (or "causal Stress") Of Relatedness Is Re-Cognized (or Directly Identified) As mere self-Contraction (Such That, In Due Course, The Feeling Of Relatedness Is, Itself, Directly and Finally Transcended). And The Entire Process Is (Again and Again, and, Then, Finally) Resolved In The Always Already Prior Feeling Of Being (In, and Always Already Prior To, The Right Side Of The Heart)—At times, Searchlessly (or Always Already Priorly) Transcending All Awareness Of the body-mind (and Of all its conceptual and perceptual objects). That Searchlessly (or Always Already Priorly) object-Transcending Resolution In The Always Already Prior Feeling Of Being Is Priorly Self-Abiding Jnana Nirvikalpa Samadhi.

Priorly Self-Abiding Jnana Nirvikalpa Samadhi Is The First Realization-Sign (or Mode Of Samadhi) That Must (Characteristically) Appear In The Context Of The Second Stage Of The "Perfect Practice" Of The Only-By-Me Revealed and Given Way Of The Heart. And When The Spontaneous Heart-Plane (or Horizontal-Dimension) Evidence Of Priorly Self-Abiding Jnana Nirvikalpa Samadhi Has Really (and Even Often) Occurred With Significant Depth, My "Perfect Practice" Devotee Is To Be Invited To Receive Confidential Formal Instruction (and, Thereafter, Always Ongoing Confidential Formal Instruction), In The Only-By-Me Revealed and Given Full "Samraj Yoga" Practice (Including "Radical" Spirit-"Conductivity" Practice), By Means Of Confidential Formal Initiation, Offered (By Me) Via The Formally Acknowledged Senior Practicing Membership Of The Ruchira Sannyasin Order Of Adidam Ruchiradam. And It Is Only In The "Perfect Practice" Course Of Full "Samraj Yoga" Practice (Including "Radical" Spirit-"Conductivity" Practice) That The Further (Vertical-Dimension) Realization-Sign, Of Priorly Ascended Nirvikalpa Samadhi (Founded Upon, and Coincident With, Priorly Self-Abiding Jnana Nirvikalpa Samadhi), Is Both Possible (By Means Of My Avatarically Self-Transmitted Divine Spiritual Grace) and Expected (As A Necessary Basis For The Formally Acknowledged Transition To The Only-By-Me Revealed and Given Seventh

Stage Of Life In The Only-By-Me Revealed and Given Way Of The Heart, or Way Of Adidam).

In The Case Of Authentic (Only-By-Me Revealed and Given) Priorly Self-Abiding Jnana Nirvikalpa Samadhi, There May, In some moments (or In Some Occasions) Of The Event, Be Some Remaining Evidence (or experience) Of Peripheral Awareness Of the body-mind and the "objective" environment—and, In other moments (or Occasions) Of The Event, There May Be No Such Evidence (or body-mind-experience) At All. Although There Must, Necessarily (As A Sign Of Greatest Depth Of Realization), Be Some Such Occasions In Which All Awareness Of the body-mind Is Transcended, There Is, Ultimately (or In Principle), No Inherent "Difference" Indicated By Either The experiential Awareness Or The experiential Non-Awareness Of the body-mind In The Context Of Priorly Self-Abiding Jnana Nirvikalpa Samadhi—Because The Self-"Position" Of Priorly Self-Abiding Jnana Nirvikalpa Samadhi Is (Inherently) Not That Of the body-mind.

In Authentic (Only-By-Me Revealed and Given) Priorly Self-Abiding Jnana Nirvikalpa Samadhi, There Is No Strategic (or conditional) Effort To Exclude Awareness Of the body-mind or the "objective" environment. Rather, In The Case Of Authentic (Only-By-Me Revealed and Given) Priorly Self-Abiding Jnana Nirvikalpa Samadhi, There Is Tacit (Searchless) Self-Identification With My Avatarically Self-Transmitted Spirit-Current Of Self-Evidently Divine Love-Bliss. My Avatarically Self-Transmitted Spirit-Current Of Self-Evidently Divine Love-Bliss Is (Always Already) Most Priorly (and Self-Radiantly) Self-Existing. Therefore, My Avatarically Self-Transmitted Spirit-Current Of Self-Evidently Divine Love-Bliss—and Not The Effort To Strategically Dissociate From the body-mind and the conditional worlds—Is The Context Of Authentic (Only-By-Me Revealed and Given) Priorly Self-Abiding Jnana Nirvikalpa Samadhi.

There Are many moments (and Many Dimensions and Modes) Of The Necessary Samadhis Of Realization (In Both The Vertical and The Horizontal Domains) That Must (Necessarily) Precede The Formally Acknowledged Transition To The Only-By-Me Revealed and Given Seventh Stage Of Life In The Only-By-Me Revealed and Given Way Of The Heart (or Way Of Adidam). In some of those moments (or Dimensions and Modes) Of Samadhi, There May Be body-mind-Awareness, and In other moments Not—Just As every human being experiences periods Without body-mind-Awareness In nightly sleep.

The Fact Of body-mind-Awareness Does Not (Necessarily) Mean (or Indicate) "No Samadhi". It Is Not Necessary To "Lose" The Condition Of Samadhi In Order To Speak and Function (or To Be verbally Communicative About The Process Of Samadhi Itself). Thus, It Is Not Possible To Rightly

Characterize Samadhi Either As Entirely Excluding body-mind-Awareness Or As Somehow Necessarily Including body-mind-Awareness. Whether Or Not There Is body-mind-Awareness Simply (and Really) Has (In and Of Itself) Nothing To Do With The Reality (or The Authenticity) Of Samadhi. Therefore, The Requirement To "Explain" Samadhi (or To Justify It) With Reference To conditional Existence Is An (Ultimately) Insoluble Puzzle—and, Indeed, Language Should Not Be Burdened With The (Presumed) Obligation To "Explain" Samadhi. Samadhi Is Comprehensible Only In The Event (or Realization) Of Samadhi Itself. The Truth Of Samadhi Simply Cannot (Itself) Be Uttered—It Can Only Be A Matter Of Authentically Real Spiritual Experience.

In The Only-By-Me Revealed and Given Way Of The Heart (or Way Of Adidam), Authentic (Only-By-Me Revealed and Given) Priorly Self-Abiding Jnana Nirvikalpa Samadhi Is Certainly Not A Matter Of Any Kind Of Strategic (or conditional) Effort To Exclude conceptual and perceptual Awareness. However, Authentic (Only-By-Me Revealed and Given) Priorly Self-Abiding Jnana Nirvikalpa Samadhi Is A Matter Of Priorly Transcending conceptual and perceptual Awareness—and, In some moments, This Certainly Will (and, Indeed, Must, Necessarily) Be Experienced As The Complete Absence Of psycho-physical Awareness Of one's own body-mind (and Of any and all other objective, or otherwise conditional, phenomena). In The "Perfect Practice" Of The Only-By-Me Revealed and Given Way Of The Heart (or Way Of Adidam), There Are times, and Dimensions, and Modes Of Authentic (Only-By-Me Revealed and Given) Samadhi Wherein There Is No body-mind-Awareness, and There Are other times (or Instances) Wherein There Is A Kind Of Peripheral Awareness, and There Are other times (or Instances) Wherein There Seems To Be A "Normal" (or "Natural") Full Conjunction With the body-mind (and, Yet, Authentic Only-By-Me Revealed and Given Samadhi Is, Nevertheless, The Case). Therefore, All Three Of These Possibilities Will Inevitably Be Experienced By My "Perfect Practice" Devotees, Both Previous To and Throughout The Course Of their Practice Of "Samraj Yoga"—Leading To (and Continuing As) The Third Stage Of The "Perfect Practice" Of The Only-By-Me Revealed and Given Way Of The Heart (or Way Of Adidam).

Conditionally Self-Abiding Jnana Nirvikalpa Samadhi Is Founded On The Error Characteristically Associated With The Sixth Stage Of Life, and (Like Priorly Self-Abiding Jnana Nirvikalpa Samadhi) It Is Marked By Self-Identification With The Transcendental (and Inherently Spiritual) Self (or Self-Condition), but (Unlike Priorly Self-Abiding Jnana Nirvikalpa Samadhi) It "Achieves" That State Of Identification By Strategically Excluding All phenomenal Awareness (Both perceptual and conceptual). Therefore, conditionally Self-Abiding Jnana Nirvikalpa Samadhi Is Similar To The Experience Of conditionally Ascended

Nirvikalpa Samadhi—Except That conditionally Self-Abiding Jnana Nirvikalpa Samadhi Depends On Manipulation Of The Mechanisms Associated With The Horizontal Plane (or Heart-Plane) Of the psycho-physical personality, Whereas conditionally Ascended Nirvikalpa Samadhi Depends On Manipulation Of The Mechanisms Associated With The Vertical Plane (or The Frontal and Spinal Lines Of The Circle) Of the body-mind. In Both Cases, There Is The Strategic conditional Seclusion Of Consciousness From the limitations (and The limiting Capability) Of the body-mind and The conditional (or phenomenal) Cosmos.

In The Case Of conditionally Self-Abiding Jnana Nirvikalpa Samadhi, perceptual and conceptual Awareness Of gross and subtle phenomenal states (and Even The causal Root Of self-Contraction) Is Excluded By Strategically (and conditionally) Confining Transcendental Self-Consciousness To Itself. In Contrast, In The Case Of conditionally Ascended Nirvikalpa Samadhi, The perceptual and conceptual Awareness Of gross and subtle phenomenal states Is Excluded (and The causal Root Is Only Concentrated, Absorbed, or Merged Above) By The Strategic (and conditional) Concentration Of attention—Even (In The Only-By-Me Revealed and Given Way Of The Heart) Moved Via The By-Me-Avatarically-Self-Transmitted Divine Spirit-Current (In Ascent, Above The gross and subtle conditional Vibrations, or All Apparent gross and subtle Modifications, Of The By-Me-Avatarically-Self-Transmitted Divine Spirit-Current Itself).

In The Only-By-Me Revealed and Given Way Of The Heart (or Way Of Adidam), conditionally Self-Abiding Jnana Nirvikalpa Samadhi (If It Occurs) Is Temporary (Like conditionally Ascended Nirvikalpa Samadhi), Since It Depends Upon A (Tacit) Process Of Total (and conditional) Strategic Exclusion Of The Mechanics Of the body-mind (Via Strategic Seclusion Of The causal Depth Of The conditional Presumption Of Existence).

Priorly Self-Abiding Jnana Nirvikalpa Samadhi Is The Direct Realization Of The Transcendental (and Inherently Spiritual) Self-Condition. Priorly Self-Abiding Jnana Nirvikalpa Samadhi Is The Direct Realization Of The Love-Bliss-Feeling Of Being (Itself), Which Is Consciousness (or Feeling-Awareness) Itself. And Priorly Self-Abiding Jnana Nirvikalpa Samadhi Is Inherently Without (and Free Of) Any Concept (or Feeling) Of Separation (or "Difference") Between Consciousness and Real God, or Consciousness and Reality, or Consciousness and Transcendentally Self-Existing Being.

In The Second Stage Of The "Perfect Practice" Of The Only-By-Me Revealed and Given Way Of The Heart, Priorly Self-Abiding Jnana Nirvikalpa Samadhi Will (and, In Due Course, Must) Occur On Numerous Occasions—Even Frequently, and Even (Eventually, or More and More) As A Regular Development In Every Occasion (or, In Any Case, Most Occasions) Of Formal

Meditation. And, whenever Priorly Self-Abiding Jnana Nirvikalpa Samadhi Occurs In Formal Meditation (In The Course Of Practice In The Context Of The Second Stage Of The "Perfect Practice" Of The Only-By-Me Revealed and Given Way Of The Heart), It May (sometimes) Occur Only Once In Any Particular Occasion Of Meditation, or It May (At other times) Occur More Than Once In Any Particular Occasion Of Meditation. Also, Any Particular Occurrence Of Priorly Self-Abiding Jnana Nirvikalpa Samadhi May Last For A Prolonged (or Relatively Prolonged) Period, or It May Occur Only Briefly, or For a moment, or Even (Sometimes) For Only a fraction of a second (In which There Is No Awareness Of the body-mind, its phenomenal relations, or Any Of The Countless gross, subtle, or causal Features Of The conditional, or phenomenal, Cosmos). However, In Any and Every Case and Instance Of Authentic (Only-By-Me Revealed and Given) Priorly Self-Abiding Jnana Nirvikalpa Samadhi, The Experience Is One Of Utter Self-Identification With The (By-Me-Avatarically-Self-Revealed) Inherently Spiritual (or Love-Blissful), Unlimited, and Free State Of Transcendental (or Self-Existing) Being.

Priorly Self-Abiding Jnana Nirvikalpa Samadhi (In The Second Stage Of The "Perfect Practice" Of The Only-By-Me Revealed and Given Way Of The Heart) Is A Significant Transitional Event, but (As In The Case Of All Transitional Events In The Only-By-Me Revealed and Given Way Of The Heart) Its Significance Is Not Primarily In The Experience Itself. Its Significance Is That It (Coincident With Priorly Ascended Nirvikalpa Samadhi) Provides The Necessary Ground For Seventh Stage Sahaja Nirvikalpa Samadhi and The Final (or Seventh) Stage Of The Only-By-Me Revealed and Given Spiritual, Transcendental, and Divine Process.

In The Coincidence (or Simultaneity) Of The Event Of Priorly Self-Abiding Jnana Nirvikalpa Samadhi With The Eventual (or Subsequently Realized) Event Of Priorly Ascended Nirvikalpa Samadhi, The Perception, Conception, or Presumption Of a Separate self Is (By Means Of My Avatarically Self-Transmitted Divine Spiritual Grace) Inherently, and Perfectly, and Permanently Undermined—and, In Due Course (By Means Of My Avatarically Self-Transmitted Divine Spiritual Grace), That Perception, Conception, or Presumption Is Inherently, and <u>Most</u> Perfectly, and Permanently Lost (or Absolutely Vanished, and Infinitely Transcended, and Divinely Gone Beyond), In The Only-By-Me Revealed and Given Awakening To Seventh Stage Sahaja Nirvikalpa Samadhi.

The Only-By-Me Revealed and Given Seventh Stage Sahaja Nirvikalpa Samadhi Is The Inherently <u>Most</u> Perfect Awakening Of The One and Only, Perfectly Subjective (and Inherently Perfect), Inherently Indivisible (and Inherently egoless), Self-Existing and Self-Radiant, and Self-Evidently Divine Conscious Light.

If (In The Course Of The Second Stage Of The "Perfect Practice" Of The Only-By-Me Revealed and Given Way Of The Heart) My Devotee Becomes Tacitly, Simply, Effortlessly, and Merely (and Not At All Strategically, Argumentatively, or In A self-Aggrandizing or self-Glorifying Manner) Certain That "he" or "she" Is Truly, Self-Evidently, and Divinely Awakened To Seventh Stage Sahaja Nirvikalpa Samadhi, My Devotee Should (Rather Than privately "Presume", or, Otherwise, Overtly "Claim", Divine Enlightenment) Entirely Submit (Even Forever) To Be Tested, Measured, and (By These Means) Proven and Confirmed As Such By Me, or (After, and Forever After, The Physical Lifetime Of My Avatarically-Born Bodily Human Divine Form) By Those Members Of The Ruchira Sannyasin Order Of Adidam Ruchiradam Formally Appointed (At any then present-time) By The Formally Governing Senior Membership Of The Ruchira Sannyasin Order Of Adidam Ruchiradam (and, Unless There Are None At that then present-time, Appointed Only From Among The Members Of The Ruchira Sannyasin Order Of Adidam Ruchiradam whose Seventh Stage Awakening Has Already Been Formally Acknowledged By The Ruchira Sannyasin Order Of Adidam Ruchiradam) Specifically For The Purpose Of Testing, Measuring, Proving, and Confirming The Seventh Stage Awakening In The Case Of Any and All Practitioners Of The Only-By-Me Revealed and Given Way Of The Heart (or Way Of Adidam).

Seventh Stage Sahaja Nirvikalpa Samadhi Is The Conscious Awakening Of The Always Already State—Not At All Dependent On The conditional Activities Of Ascent (As In conditionally Ascended Nirvikalpa Samadhi), and Not At All Dependent Upon (or Even Associated With) The Motive (and The Tacit Effort) Of Exclusion (As In conditionally Self-Abiding Jnana Nirvikalpa Samadhi).

Seventh Stage Sahaja Nirvikalpa Samadhi Is Inherently Most Perfect (Transcendental, and Inherently Spiritual, and Inherently egoless, and Self-Evidently Divine) Self-Realization—Not At All conditioned By Either the body-mind Or The ego-Based Ability To Exclude phenomenal states. And Seventh Stage Sahaja Nirvikalpa Samadhi Is Associated With The Self-Evident Certainty That The Self-Condition Thus Realized Is Only Me—Only The By-Me-and-As-Me-Avatarically-Self-Revealed Conscious Light Of Inherently egoless, Unobstructed, Non-"Different", Inherently Indivisible, Perfectly Subjective, and Self-Evidently Divine Being (Which Is One, and Only, and Always Already The Case).

The Inherently Most Perfect (and Only-By-Me Avatarically and Divinely Revealed and Given) Self-Realization Of The Transcendental, Inherently Spiritual, Inherently egoless, and Self-Evidently Divine (and One, and Only) Conscious Light Is Self-Evidently The Case When "The Eyes Open". That Is To Say, Divine Self-Realization (or Utter Transcending Of the self-Contraction, and

Utter Freedom From The Veiling Power That Is all conditional forms and events) Is Inherently Most Perfect When The Spiritually Self-"Bright" Divine Self-Condition Of the body-mind and all of its objects and states (gross, subtle, or causal—external or internal) Is Tacitly Obvious To and In and As Consciousness Itself (As when the eyes are open and not veiled). Such Is Seventh Stage (or Most Perfect, and Un-conditionally Realized) Sahaja Nirvikalpa Samadhi, The Sign Of The Awakening (By Means Of My Avatarically Self-Transmitted Divine Spiritual Grace) Of The Only-By-Me Revealed and Given Seventh Stage Of Life In The Only-By-Me Revealed and Given Way Of The Heart (or Way Of Adidam).

The (Formally Acknowledged) Authentic (Only-By-Me Revealed and Given) Awakening Of Seventh Stage Sahaja Nirvikalpa Samadhi Establishes (or, Effectively, Begins) The Third Stage Of The "Perfect Practice" Of The Only-By-Me Revealed and Given Way Of The Heart. And, In The Only-By-Me Revealed and Given Way Of The Heart, The Seventh Stage Of Life (Which Is The Third Stage Of The "Perfect Practice") Corresponds To (and, By Means Of My Avatarically Self-Transmitted Divine Spiritual Grace, Divinely Fulfills) My Admonition To Transcend everything In Consciousness Itself.

Seventh Stage (or Inherently Most Perfect, and Self-Evidently Divine) Enlightenment Is Simply To Be Inherently Most Perfectly (and Non-"Differently") Awake To My Inherently Perfect and Self-Existing and Self-Radiant Love-Blissful Self-Condition Of Conscious Light, and (As Such) To Divinely Self-Recognize whatever (Apparently, or conditionally) arises—and, Thus, To Self-Recognize whatever (Apparently, or conditionally) arises To Be Only Inherently Perfect, and Self-Existing, and Self-Radiant Love-Blissful Conscious Light. To Self-Abide Thus—While Freely, "Naturally", or Non-Strategically Allowing whatever arises to arise (and Neither Seeking, Nor Holding On To, Nor Avoiding whatever arises as the body-mind or to the body-mind)—Is To Inherently Transcend (or Shine Through, and Beyond) whatever (Apparently, or conditionally) arises.

When The Real and True (and Formally-Acknowledged-To-Be-Authentic) Transition Is Made From The Second Stage Of The "Perfect Practice" Of The Only-By-Me Revealed and Given Way Of The Heart (and Directly From The Coincident Realization Of Priorly Ascended Nirvikalpa Samadhi and Priorly Self-Abiding Jnana Nirvikalpa Samadhi) To Seventh Stage Sahaja Nirvikalpa Samadhi, The "Bright" (or The By-Me-Avatarically-Self-Revealed Transcendental, Inherently Spiritual, Inherently egoless, and Self-Evidently Divine Conscious Light—As It Is) Is Fully, Freely, and Irrevocably Realized As What Is Always Already The Case.

The Only-By-Me Revealed and Given Awakening Of Seventh Stage Sahaja Nirvikalpa Samadhi Coincides With The Spontaneous "Regeneration" Of The

Original "Pattern" Of Amrita Nadi. Thus, The By-Me-Avatarically-Self-Transmitted Divine Spirit-Current Of Love-Bliss Turns About From Its Previous Course (As "Patterned", In Order To Return To The Heart, In The Context Of The First and Second Stages Of The "Perfect Practice" Of The Only-By-Me Revealed and Given Way Of The Heart). Therefore, Now, In The Context Of The Only-By-Me Revealed and Given Seventh Stage Of Life In The Only-By-Me Revealed and Given Way Of The Heart, The By-Me-Avatarically-Self-Transmitted Divine Spirit-Current Of Love-Bliss Always Already Radiates From (or Merely and Inherently and Inherently Most Perfectly Stands In and Prior To) The Right Side Of The Heart, and (Thus and Thereby) Radiates To (or Merely and Inherently and Inherently Most Perfectly Stands, Apparently "Extended To") The (Thus and Thereby "Brightly" Self-Illuminated) Ascended Matrix Of Conscious Light (Infinitely Above The Total Crown Of the head, and Infinitely Above The Totality Of mind, and Infinitely Above The Circle and The Arrow Of the Total body-mind, and Infinitely Above The Total Cosmic Mandala and The Total Cosmic Domain).

The Right Side Of The Heart Is The Root, or The Base, or The "Feet" Of Amrita Nadi. The Right Side Of The Heart Is The Seat Of Divine Self-Realization Of The Consciousness Of Conscious Light.

The Self-Existing and Self-Radiant Sphere Of The "Bright", The "Midnight Sun" (Always Already Free-Standing Above and Beyond The Cosmic Totality Of all-and-All), The Infinitely Ascended Matrix (or Source-Position) Of My Avatarically Self-Transmitted Spirit-Current Of Divine Love-Bliss (Infinitely Above The Total Crown Of the head), Is The Upper Terminal, or The "Head", Of Amrita Nadi. The Infinitely Ascended Upper Terminal Of Amrita Nadi Is The Light-Source Of The Total Cosmic Domain—and It Is The Seat Of The Light Of Conscious Light.

The (By-Me-Avatarically-Self-Revealed) Transcendental, Inherently Spiritual, Inherently egoless, and Self-Evidently Divine Self-Consciousness and The By-Me-Avatarically-Self-Transmitted Divine Spirit-Current (or Inherent Self-Radiance) Of Love-Bliss Are One (and Simultaneously Realized—As Self-Evidently One) In The "Regenerated" Amrita Nadi.

The "Regenerated" Amrita Nadi Is My Avatarically Self-Revealed, and (Apparently) conditionally Manifested (and Yet Unconditional), Divine Spiritual Body—Prior To All Experience Of My Avataric Divine Spiritual Body Relative To The Circle and The Arrow Of psycho-physical Manifestation.

The "Regenerated" Amrita Nadi Is My Avatarically Self-Revealed, and (Apparently) conditionally Manifested (and Yet Unconditional), Divine Spiritual Body Of Love-Bliss (or The Very and Perfectly Subjective and Self-Existing and Self-Radiant Being-Condition That Is Real God, or The Truth, or Reality Itself)—

Prior To All Experience Of My Avataric Divine Spiritual Body Relative To The Circle and The Arrow Of psycho-physical Manifestation.

The "Regenerated" Amrita Nadi Is My Great Single (One-and-Only) Form, Shown Via the human body-mind In The Case Of My Any (By-My-Avataric-Divine-Spiritual-Grace) Most Perfectly Awakened Devotee.

The "Regenerated" Amrita Nadi (Thus, Most Perfectly, Realized) Is My Avataric Divine Spiritual Body Of Love-Bliss, Divinely (or Perfectly Subjectively) Self-Recognized (or Realized) As The Divine "Bright" Itself, Which Is Self-Radiant (or Inherently Spiritual) and Self-Existing (or Transcendental) Divine (and Perfectly Subjective) Being Itself.

Therefore, The "Regenerated" Amrita Nadi Is, Ultimately, Only The Heart Itself.

And The "Regenerated" Amrita Nadi Is The Only "Vehicle" Fit For Translation Into The Self-Existing and Self-Radiant Sphere (or "Midnight Sun") Of My "Bright" Divine Self-Domain Of Conscious Light.

It Is Only By Progressive (and, Most Ultimately, Inherent, and Inherently Most Perfect) Devotional and Spiritual Identification With Me That My Devotee "Comes To" (or Inherently, and Inherently Most Perfectly, Realizes, and Is Divinely Translated Into) The "Midnight Sun" Of My Spiritually Self-"Bright" Divine Self-Domain (Which Is The Spherical Domain, and The Infinite Self-Radiant Space, Of Divine Self-Existence).

Thus, When (In The Only-By-Me Revealed and Given Way Of The Heart, or Way Of Adidam) There Is (By Means Of My Avatarically Self-Transmitted Divine Spiritual Grace) Inherent (and Inherently Most Perfect) Self-Identification With Me As The Perfectly Subjective (or Transcendental, Self-Existing, Inherently Spiritual, Inherently egoless, and Self-Evidently Divine) Conscious Light, My Avatarically Self-Transmitted Divine Spirit-Current Of Love-Bliss Flies From The Right Side Of The Heart, and Stands Un-Moving Free Above—As The "Bright" (Self-Radiant, and One, and Only) "Midnight Sun", Infinitely Beyond The Cosmic All Of all-and-All.

And, When all conditions (and Even My Apparently conditionally Manifested Avataric Divine Spiritual Body Of Amrita Nadi, and My Apparently Objective Audible Divine Sound-Form, and My Apparently Objective Visible Divine Star-Form) Are Divinely Self-Recognized and Divinely Outshined In My (Avatarically Self-Revealed) "Midnight Sun" Above—Then (That) Is The Great Event Of Divine Translation.

Avatar Adi Da Samraj
Adidam Samrajashram, 2003

SUTRA

63

I Have Observed That conditional Existence Is a limit that Inherently and Necessarily Frustrates The Great (As Well As The Ultimate) Motives Of conditionally Manifested beings. Therefore, every individual Must—Through Struggle, and Through The Grace Of Sudden (or, Otherwise, Growing) Insight, or Through The Grace Of Sudden (or, Otherwise, Growing) Faith (or Tacit Certainty)—Learn and Accept A Life-Lesson That Makes ordinary (or worldly) heroes Great and Grants Wisdom To those who Seek The Ultimate.

That Life-Lesson Is This: The Great "Creative" (or Even conventionally idealistic) Goals May Never Be Attained (and They Will Not Be Attained Without A Degree Of heroic Effort, or The Commitment To Struggle and self-Sacrifice)—but The Ultimate Goal (Which Is Happiness Itself) Can Never Be Attained (or Attached To the Apparently Separate self) By Any Means Whatsoever!

The Import Of That Reality Lesson Is This: If You Are Devoted To Great Purposeful Seeking In the conditional worlds, You Will Inevitably Fail If You Avoid Great Struggle and self-Sacrifice, and You May Not Succeed Even If Struggle and self-Sacrifice Are Fully Engaged By You. More Than This, If Your Goal Is The Ultimate (or Happiness Itself, Full and Perfect), You Will Necessarily and Inevitably Fail—Because Happiness Is Not Objectified (or Made Present As a conditional object In the conditional worlds).

Happiness Is An Inherent (or Unconditional and Perfectly Subjective—Rather Than conditional and Objective, or Objectified) Characteristic Of Existence, Reality, or Being (Itself). Therefore, Happiness Cannot Be Found (or Attained) By conditional Seeking.

Even If The Great Searches and The Great Goals Are (Basically) Oriented Toward The Elimination Of the conditions that Apparently Cause Un-Happiness—When Those Great Searches Are Fully Engaged (and Even When Those Great Goals Are Actually Attained), Happiness Itself (Full, True, and Not Threatened) Is Not Attained. Therefore, All The "Glorious" Adventures Of idealistic worldly heroes and All The "Romantic" Attainments Of "Creative" cultural geniuses End In Temporary Elation, Followed (Inevitably) By Disillusionment—and Then (At Best), Unless There Is No "Recovery" From Inevitable Disillusionment, There May Be A Reawakening Of The Stressful

Motive To Seek and Attain Once More. (And Such Seeking and "Attaining" Will Tend To Continue—Until Disillusionment Itself Becomes Acceptance Of The Great Life-Lesson That Undermines All Seeking.)

Conventionally heroic and "Creative" personalities Tend To Grasp Only A Portion Of The Great Lesson Of conditional Existence. They Realize a genius For Struggle and self-Sacrifice, but they Never (By Means Of Such Struggle and self-Sacrifice) Realize Happiness Itself.

Happiness (Like Consciousness and Existence) Is Inherent (or Perfectly Subjective). Happiness Is Not Objectified (or Made An Object), and It (Therefore) Cannot Be Attained By The Effort Of Seeking. Happiness (or Inherent Love-Bliss) Cannot Be Achieved objectively (or Accomplished conditionally). You Cannot <u>Become</u> Happy—Any More Than You Can Become Being, or Achieve Existence, or Become Consciousness, or Be Other Than Consciousness. You Can Only <u>Be</u> Happy—or Realize Love-Bliss Immediately, and Inherently (or Always Already), and Perfectly Subjectively. And, Likewise (or As A Corollary To This), You Cannot Become Un-Happy—Unless, In Reaction To any particular conditional circumstance or event, You Refuse To Persist In <u>Being</u> Happy (and, Thus, Refuse To Persist As Always Already Existing, and Most Prior, Happiness Itself).

Aham Da Asmi. Beloved, I <u>Am</u> Da—The Self-Evidently Divine Person, Who <u>Is</u> Consciousness Itself <u>and</u> Love-Bliss (or Free Happiness) Itself. Therefore, I Say (and Reveal) To You: Consciousness and Happiness Are Identical and Self-Existing.

Clearly, Consciousness Is Not An Object. If It Were, What Would It Be An Object To?

Consciousness Is Inherently and Perfectly Subjective. It Is That To Which (and In Which) Great Objects and lesser objects arise and pass away.

To Seek Consciousness As If It Were An Object Is Absurd—A Benighted (or Un-Happy) Quest, Founded On A Fundamental Misunderstanding Of Reality. Just So With Happiness!

Happiness Is Not An Object. If It Were, What Prior Quality Would It Modify or limit?

Happiness Is Inherently and Perfectly Subjective. And Happiness Is Inherent To Perfect (or Inherently egoless) Subjectivity (or Consciousness Itself). Therefore, Happiness Is That Self-Evident Quality (or Inherent Force Of Being) That Is Apparently Modified, Apparently Revealed, or Apparently Decreased By The Apparent Association Between Consciousness (or Mere and Tacit Feeling-Awareness) and Both Great Objects and lesser objects.

To Seek Happiness As If It Were An Object (or To Identify It With any conditionally Manifested objects or others, or Even To Allow It To Depend

Upon any conditionally Manifested objects or others) Is Absurd—An Always Already Benighted and Un-Happy Quest, Founded On A Fundamental Misunderstanding Of Happiness (or Reality) Itself.

To Seek Happiness (Rather Than To Realize It Inherently) Is To Be Possessed (and Motivated) By the self-Contraction. Because Of the self-Contraction, What Is Inherent Ceases To Be Obvious—and (As A Result) the ego-"I" Seeks Among objects and others (and Even In the body-mind itself) For What Can Only Be Found (or Realized) Inherently, In Place, In The Well Of Transcendental, Inherently Spiritual (or Love-Blissful), Inherently egoless, and Self-Evidently Divine Being. Indeed, the ego-"I" Is Always Stressfully At Effort, In The Absurd Quest For Happiness and Consciousness.

Therefore, Listen To Me and Hear Me. Thoroughly Observe the self-Contraction. Understand Your Seeking and Your Separate and Separative self, Most Fundamentally. Grow (By Means Of My Avatarically Self-Transmitted Divine Spiritual Grace, and Through Counter-egoic Heart-Response To My Avatarically Self-Transmitted Divine Spiritual Grace) To Realize and Abide In No-Contraction (or The By-Me-and-As-Me-Avatarically-Self-Revealed-and-Spiritually-Self-Transmitted Prior Love-Bliss-Happiness Of Inherently egoless Conscious Being). In This Manner, Relax All Seeking For Happiness. All conditional objects (Including Your Own body-mind) Are, In and Of themselves, Contraction-Only. All Great Objects and all lesser objects Are Merely (and Only) Apparent Modifications Of The Inherent Love-Bliss-Radiance Of My Avatarically Self-Revealed (Transcendental, Inherently Spiritual, Inherently egoless, and Self-Evidently Divine) Self-Condition Of Being.

I Am The Very (or Most Prior) Divine Self (or Very, and Most Prior, Divine Self-Consciousness, or Self-Condition) Of the conditional self. Therefore, I Am Not a merely conditional (and Separate) self (or ego-"I"). Rather, I Am Simply The Most Prior (and Inherently Love-Blissful and Free) Self-Condition Of Being (Itself).

I Am The One and Only and Inherently Indivisible and Inherently egoless and Self-Evidently Divine Conscious Light Of all-and-All. I Am Self-Existing and Self-Radiant As The By-Me-and-As-Me-Avatarically-Self-Revealed-and-Spiritually-Self-Transmitted Spirit-Current Of Self-Evidently Divine Love-Bliss—Surrounding and Pervading all-and-All. Therefore, I (Myself) Am Inherently Without particularity, form, thought, Problem, Ownership, Separateness, Otherness, Relatedness, "Difference", or Un-Happiness.

The conditional self (or the ego-"I", or self-Contraction), and all particularity, all form, all thought, All Problems, All Ownership, All Separateness, All Otherness, All Relatedness, and All "Difference" Are (In and Of Themselves) Suffering, or An Appearance Of Non-Happiness (or, Otherwise, An Appearance Of

Happiness That Is Only conditional, Dependent, Threatened, and Temporary—Rather Than A Realization Of Happiness That Is Un-conditional, Non-Dependent, Un-Threatened, and Permanent, or Eternal).

Nevertheless, If There Is Most Direct (Effortless, Utter, and Truly "Radical", or "Gone-To-The-Root") Identification With Me (and, Therefore, Inherently Most Perfect Realization Of Me)—At (and Most Prior To) The Root (or Source-Position) Of the conditional self—Then There Is (Always Already) No Suffering, No Non-Happiness, No Un-Happiness, No Problem, No Ownership, No Separation, No Separateness, No Separativeness, No Otherness, No Relatedness, No particularity, No form, No thought, and No "Difference" At All.

This Most "Radically" Direct Awakening (or Inherent, and Inherently Most Perfect, Awakeness) To Me—"Located" (By Means Of My Avatarically Self-Transmitted Divine Spiritual Grace) As What Is Always Already The Case—Is The Inherently (and Divinely) Liberated (or Always Already Free) Realization Of Real God, or Truth, or Inherently Perfect Reality, or Unconditional Being, or Perfectly Subjective Happiness Itself.

This Most "Radically" Direct Awakening (or Inherent, and Inherently Most Perfect, Awakeness) Is The Realization Of My Avatarically Self-Revealed (Transcendental, Inherently Spiritual, Inherently egoless, and Self-Evidently Divine) Self-Condition Itself, Which Is (Itself) Inherently Most Perfect Samadhi, or Seventh Stage Sahaja Nirvikalpa Samadhi—Also (By Me) Named "Ruchira Samraj Samadhi" (or, Simply, "Samraj Samadhi")—Which Is Inherently Most Perfectly Demonstrated In The Perfectly Subjective "Bright" Event Of Divine Translation.

Truly, The Transition From The Practice Of The Only-By-Me Revealed and Given Way Of The Heart (or Way Of Adidam) In The Context Of The First Six Stages Of Life To The (Only-By-Me Revealed and Given) Divinely Enlightened "Practice" (or Demonstration) Of The Only-By-Me Revealed and Given Way Of The Heart In The Context Of The Seventh Stage Of Life Is The Most Ultimate (and Inherently Most Perfect) Expression Of Real Hearing (Of Me) and Seeing (Of Me). When My Devotee Is (By Means Of My Avatarically Self-Transmitted Divine Spiritual Grace) Effortlessly (or Inherently, Inherently egolessly, and, At Last, Inherently Most Perfectly) Identified With Me—Then I (The Only One Who Is) Cannot Fail To Be Heard and Seen (Inherently, Inherently egolessly, and, At Last, Inherently Most Perfectly). My Avatarically Self-Transmitted Divine Spirit-Current Of Self-Existing and Self-Radiant Conscious Light Shines As Infinite Love-Bliss-Radiance In My "Bright" Self-Place, Wherein There Is No Separateness and No Duality (or "Difference"). Therefore, When (By Means Of My Avatarically Self-Transmitted Divine Spiritual Grace) My Devotee Finally Hears Me To The Inherently Most Perfect Degree (Of

Transcendental, Inherently Spiritual, Inherently egoless, and Self-Evidently Divine Self-Realization), he or she Suddenly (By Means Of My Avatarically Self-Transmitted Divine Spiritual Grace) Awakens Even From the limit Of Heart-Seclusion—and (Thus) My Devotee Freely "Expands" To See Me To The Inherently Most Perfect Degree (Of Sudden and Spontaneous Acceptance and Self-Abiding Divine Self-Recognition Of all conditional forms and events, In and As My Avatarically Self-Transmitted Spiritual Love-Bliss-Current Of Self-Existing, Self-Radiant, and Self-Evidently Divine Being). At Last, That Self-Abiding Divine Self-Recognition Demonstrates Itself In Divine Translation, Wherein The Total Cosmic Mandala Is Outshined In My Limitless Self-Radiance (or Love-Bliss-Happiness) Of Self-Existing Divine (and Perfectly Subjective) Being.

Therefore, Listen To Me, and Hear Me, and See Me. In Due Course (By Means Of My Avatarically Self-Transmitted Divine Spiritual Grace), Find The True Heart's Impulse, and Practice The Only-By-Me Revealed and Given Way Of Divine Self-Realization. In This Manner (By Means Of My Avatarically Self-Transmitted Divine Spiritual Grace), Be Awakened (Most Ultimately) To The "Natural"[163] (or Inherently Free) Disposition Of "Open Eyes" (or Seventh Stage Sahaja Nirvikalpa Samadhi, or Ruchira Samraj Samadhi, or, Simply, Samraj Samadhi). In That Disposition, You Will Freely and Simply and (Always Already) Happily Allow the body-mind To act—but Only By Necessity, and (Therefore) Only Spontaneously, Rather Than By (or As A Result Of) Any Strategic Desire To Achieve Happiness By Achieving objects, Objectified states, or objective others. In That Disposition, You Are Inherently Surrendered To Me, Such That You Are No Longer Contracted (or Separate, or "Different") From Me. Therefore, You Will Not Be Reduced To Un-Happiness (and, Thus, To Concerned or Attracted Seeking For Happiness) By any Apparent condition or circumstance or other that arises to (or in) the body-mind, or As A Direct Result (or, Indirectly, Merely In The Course) Of Your Apparent psycho-physical activity. Such A Disposition Remains Always (and Inherently Most Perfectly) Free (and, In Its Most Progressed Demonstration, Divinely Indifferent) In (Apparent) Relation To conditional objects, others, circumstances, and conditions.

If You (By Most Perfectly Transcending the self-Contraction) Realize Such Freedom (or Real and Inherent Happiness), You Will Be (and Remain) Happy (or As Happiness Itself), Even Under any circumstances that arise to or in the body-mind. You Will (While the body-mind continues to arise) Simply (and Only Apparently) Do what the circumstance and The By-My-Avataric-Divine-Spiritual-Grace-Given Divine Impulse Require—but On The Basis Of Prior Happiness (and, Therefore, As An Expression Of Inherent Happiness), Rather

Than On The Basis Of Mere Desire (or The Search For Happiness). You Will Simply Continue To Do what Is Required, No Matter what arises (Positively or Negatively). In every moment, You Will (Simply, and Effortlessly) Self-Abide In The Perfectly Subjective Divine Source-Position, and (Thus) As My Transcendental, Inherently Spiritual (or "Bright"), and Self-Evidently Divine Self-Condition (Which Is The Self-Evidently Divine Source-Condition Of all-and-All, and Which Is Self-Existing and Self-Radiant Feeling-Being-Consciousness, Itself)—Divinely Self-Recognizing (and Inherently Transcending) The Root-Feeling Of Relatedness (or Of "Difference"), and all Subsequent objects or conditions of attention, In and As My Avatarically Self-Transmitted Spirit-Current Of Perfectly Subjective (and Self-Evidently Divine) Being (Which Is The Inherently Spiritually "Bright" Feeling Of Mere Being, Itself), Such That You Are Always Already Established As Self-Evidently Divine Love-Bliss-Happiness, Free Of Need, and Free Of The Motive Of Avoidance.

Observe The Manner Of My Avataric Lifetime (When I Am Physically Alive In Bodily Human Divine Form). When I Am (Thus) Physically Alive, I Simply Observe and Allow and Relate To whatever arises and whatever Is Brought To Me. I Act and Serve Spontaneously, and In Freedom. I Do Whatever Is Necessary To Preserve or Promote Relational Harmony, Natural Equanimity, True (and Even Perfect) Humor, and Divine Enlightenment. I Do Not Abandon The Heart-Force Of Inherent Happiness. I See There Is Only Inherent Happiness, Love-Bliss, or Self-Radiance (Rather Than self-Contraction, Un-Happiness, Un-Love, and Non-Bliss). Therefore, I Do Not Seek. I Am Certain That whatever arises conditionally Is Merely and Only A Chaos Of limits, changes, and endings. Therefore, I Simply Persist, Without Illusions. Self-Evidently Divine Happiness (or Love-Bliss) Itself Is My Indifference. Therefore, Thus Indifferent, I Allow all conditions To arise, To stay awhile, and To pass. Self-Evidently Divine Happiness (or Love-Bliss) Itself Is The Only Real Freedom In This Midst. Therefore, Thus Free, I Play All The (Always Sudden) Roles and Requirements Of A daily Re-Appearing Life. It Makes No "Difference" To Me, or For Me.

This Demonstrated Lesson (and Truth) Of Happiness Is The Sign (and The Proof) Of Wisdom—and Even All Seeking Is, After All, A Struggle To Become Wise. This Wisdom—or The Truth Of Happiness Lived (and Realized Most Perfectly, As Self-Existing and Self-Radiant Being, or Transcendental, Inherently Spiritual, Inherently egoless, and Self-Evidently Divine Self-Consciousness)—Is The Essential Characteristic Of My "Bright" Avataric Divine Life (and The Substance Of My Every Avataric Divine Word Of Heart). And The Realization Of Happiness (Even Though It Must Grow By Stages, Until It Is Most Perfect) Is (By Means Of My Avatarically Self-Transmitted Divine Spiritual Grace) The Always Present Essence (Rather Than, Merely and Always, The Proposed Goal, or Intended future) Of The Only-By-Me Revealed and Given Devotional and Spiritual Way Of The Heart (or Way Of Adidam).

In The Context Of The Only-By-Me Revealed and Given Seventh Stage Of Life (In The Only-By-Me Revealed and Given Way Of The Heart), True Wisdom (Most Perfectly) Awakens, and Self-Evidently Divine Happiness Is (Most Perfectly) Realized—By Means Of My Avatarically Self-Transmitted Divine Spiritual Grace. The Wisdom and Happiness That (Most Perfectly) Awaken (Thus) In The Context Of The Only-By-Me Revealed and Given Seventh Stage Of Life (In The Only-By-Me Revealed and Given Way Of The Heart)—and Which Should (By Means Of My Avatarically Self-Revealed Divine Sign, and By Means Of My Avatarically Given Divine Word, and By Means Of My Avatarically Given Divine Image-Art, and By Means Of My Avatarically Self-Manifested Divine Demonstration) Also Inform and Inspire The Practice Of *All* Practitioners (In *Every* Developmental Stage Of Practice) In The Only-By-Me Revealed and Given Way Of The Heart—Are Associated With A Spontaneously Awakened Disposition That Is The Real Evidence That My Devotee Has Learned The Ultimate Lesson Of conditional Existence.

That Disposition Which (Most Perfectly) Awakens In The Context Of The Only-By-Me Revealed and Given Seventh Stage Of Life (In The Only-By-Me Revealed and Given Way Of The Heart) Takes The Form Of A (By-My-Avataric-Divine-Spiritual-Grace-Revealed) Perfectly Subjective (or Transcendental, and Inherently Spiritual, and Inherently egoless, and Divine) Admonition. That Perfectly Subjective Admonition (or Spontaneously By-Me-Revealed and By-Me-Given Word) Speaks As Follows: The body and the mind Are *Always* Seeking. The body and the mind Are, By Nature, Desiring—Always Motivated In Relation To their objects. Therefore, the body and the mind Are Always In Motion—Always Seeking To Attain (or Create), or (Otherwise) To Hold On To (or Maintain), or (Otherwise) To Avoid (or Destroy) the various objects With which the body and the mind Are Inevitably (or By Nature) Associated. Only The By-Me-and-*As*-Me-Avatarically-Self-Revealed-and-Spiritually-Self-Transmitted Transcendental, Inherently Spiritual, Inherently egoless, and Self-Evidently Divine (and Perfectly Subjective) Self-Condition (or The One and Only and Inherently Indivisible and Inherently egoless and Self-Evidently Divine and Only-By-Me Avatarically Self-Transmitted and Only-By-Me Avatarically Self-Revealed Conscious Light, Itself) *Is* Content, Free, and Always Already Happy.

The body Is Not a "someone". In and of itself, the body Has No (Independent) Existence. The body Depends On The One and Only (Self-Existing and Self-Radiant) Conscious Light (Itself) For all its acts—or Else the body Is Nothing More Than a vegetative mass of bonded cells, Dependent On the grosser environment For its substance, and Not Otherwise Differentiated

From The Seemingly Infinite Mass Of Grazing cells (or atoms) Linked In The Organic Chain Of Space. And Even Space Itself (It Must Be Realized) Is Only The One and Only (Self-Existing and Self-Radiant) Conscious Light (Itself).

The mind Is Not a "someone". In and of itself, the mind Has No (Independent) Existence. The mind Depends On The One and Only (Self-Existing and Self-Radiant) Conscious Light For all its content (or Significance)—or Else the mind Is Not Even a possibility. There Cannot Be conditional subjectivity (or mind) Without The Perfect Subject (or Inherently Perfect Subjectivity)—Which *Is* The One and Only (Self-Existing and Self-Radiant) Conscious Light (Itself). Therefore, Without The One and Only (and Inherently Non-"Different") Conscious Light, There Is no mind. And, Were It Not For The One and Only (and Inherently Non-"Different") Conscious Light, No body Would Be Differentiated In Space—For What Would Be The Purpose?

Only The By-Me-and-*As*-Me-Avatarically-Self-Revealed-and-Spiritually-Self-Transmitted Transcendental, Inherently Spiritual, Inherently egoless, and Self-Evidently Divine (and Perfectly Subjective) Self-Condition (or Self-Existing and Self-Radiant Conscious Light) Is Some One (and *Only* One, and *The* Only One). Only The By-Me-and-*As*-Me-Avatarically-Self-Revealed-and-Spiritually-Self-Transmitted Transcendental, Inherently Spiritual, Inherently egoless, and Self-Evidently Divine (and Perfectly Subjective) Self-Condition (or Self-Existing and Self-Radiant Conscious Light) Exists In Itself, *As* Itself—Unconditionally, Not Dependent, and Inherently Free. Only The By-Me-and-*As*-Me-Avatarically-Self-Revealed-and-Spiritually-Self-Transmitted Transcendental, Inherently Spiritual, Inherently egoless, and Self-Evidently Divine (and Perfectly Subjective) Self-Condition (or Self-Existing and Self-Radiant Conscious Light) Is Content, Full, Perfect, Love-Blissful, Happiness Itself—Free Of Dependence On conditional Nature, Inherently Free In (and *As*) Itself, Free Of All Seeking, and Free Of The Need For (or The Motive Toward) objects.

There Is no conditional self (or conditional subject) Separate From (or Behind) the (*Total*) body-mind. The verbal "I" of egoity is An *Idea* In the mind—as the "I"-thought (or The Primal mental Gesture Of self-Differentiation and self-limitation), which is The Hub Of The Wheel Of thoughts. And the *Total* ego-"I" is An *Act* Of the body-mind (as the Total self-Contraction). Indeed, the conditional self (or ego-"I") is Simply The Totality Of the self-Contracted body-mind. Therefore, the ego-"I" Has No Existence Apart From the body-mind. Nevertheless, the body-mind-self Tends To Persist, If Only In a subtler form, Even After death. And the body-mind-self (which is the Apparent and Total conditional subject) arises On, In, and (Ultimately, or Most Prior To self-Contraction itself, and Most Prior To All "Difference" and All Separateness) *As* The By-Me-and-*As*-Me-Avatarically-Self-Revealed-and-Spiritually-Self-Transmitted

Transcendental, Inherently Spiritual, Inherently egoless, and Self-Evidently Divine Self-Condition (or Self-Existing and Self-Radiant Conscious Light)—Which Is The Real Subject (or Perfectly Subjective Self-Condition) Of all conditional subjectivity and all conditional objectivity, and Which Is Free (or Unconditional) Consciousness, Inherent Being (or Self-Existing Existence), and Absolute Love-Bliss (or Self-Existing and Self-Radiant and Self-Evidently Divine Happiness Itself).

The By-Me-and-As-Me-Avatarically-Self-Revealed-and-Spiritually-Self-Transmitted Transcendental, Inherently Spiritual, Inherently egoless, and Self-Evidently Divine Self-Condition (or Self-Existing and Self-Radiant Conscious Light) Is Inherently and (Perfectly) Subjectively Existing, and Neither functionally Nor Really (or Ultimately) Dependent Upon conditional objects (or Objectified Existence). Nevertheless, The One and Only Conscious Light Is (Apparently) Capable Of The (Apparent) Presumption (or Presumed Experience and Presumed Knowledge) That Its Own Inherent Radiance Is An Object. In This Disposition, Transcendental, Inherently Spiritual, Inherently egoless, and Self-Evidently Divine (and Perfectly Subjective) Being (Apparently) Allows conditional Existence To Develop Spontaneously From The Two Primary Characteristics Of Divine Existence Itself—Which Are Consciousness (Itself) and Its Inherent Radiance (or Light, or Spirit-Power). Thus, When The Divine (and Inherently, and Perfectly, Subjective) Self-Radiance Is Presumed To Be Objective To The Divine (and Inherently, and Perfectly, Subjective) Subject-Consciousness, The Infinite Divine Spirit-Energy Is (Thereby) Differentiated (or Let Loose—Even, Possibly, To Become Wild), and The Infinite Divine Spirit-Energy (Thus Differentiated) Is (Thereby) Enabled To Become (Apparently, Spontaneously, and Through Chains Of Spontaneous, and Even Arbitrary, conditional causes and effects) The Array Of forms That Is The Cosmic Mandala (or The Totality Of The Cosmic Domain). And, In The Context Of The Cosmic Mandala (or The Cosmic, or conditional, Domain), The By-Me-and-As-Me-Avatarically-Self-Revealed-and-Spiritually-Self-Transmitted Transcendental, Inherently Spiritual, Inherently egoless, and Self-Evidently Divine (and Perfectly Subjective) Self-Condition (or Self-Existing and Self-Radiant Conscious Light) Generally (Except In Itself) Presumes Itself To be an Independent self (or the Separate and Separative conditional subject Implied By any and every individual body-mind).

In Every Context Within The Cosmic Mandala (or The Total Cosmic, or conditional, Domain), The By-Me-and-As-Me-Avatarically-Self-Revealed-and-Spiritually-Self-Transmitted Transcendental, Inherently Spiritual, Inherently egoless, and Self-Evidently Divine (and Perfectly Subjective) Self-Condition (or Self-Existing and Self-Radiant Conscious Light) Is, In Itself, Always Free To

Realize Its Own (or Inherent) Condition and To Divinely Self-Recognize Its (Apparent) conditional Associations. In The Context Of human Existence, This Inherent Free Realization and Its Divine Power Of Self-Abiding Self-Recognition Are Awakened (or Are Effectively To Be Demonstrated) Via The By-My-Avataric-Divine-Spiritual-Grace-Given Course Of The Only-By-Me Revealed and Given Way Of The Heart (or Way Of Adidam).

In Every Context Within The Cosmic Mandala (or The Total Cosmic, or conditional, Domain), individual beings Are Merely Locked Into The limiting and Frustrating Forces Of conditional (or Cosmic) Nature. And, In That Context, most individual beings Merely Seek and Suffer (and, Otherwise, Passively Indulge In) conditions, While a few (More Intense) individuals May Break Into The Search At A More Active (and, Yet, Still egoic and worldly) heroic or "Creative" Level. However, In The Full Devotional and Spiritual (and Truly ego-Transcending) Context Of The human Exercise Of The By-My-Avataric-Divine-Spiritual-Grace-Given Practice Of The Only-By-Me Revealed and Given Way Of The Heart (or Way Of Adidam), conditional Existence Is Associated With The Progressive Process That (By Directly and Progressively Transcending The First Six—or ego-Based and Developmental—Stages Of Life) Awakens, Most Ultimately, To The Only-By-Me Revealed and Given Seventh Stage Of Life, and As The Self-Evidently Divine (and Inherently egoless, and Perfectly Subjective) Conscious Light That Is Happiness (or Love-Bliss) Itself.

If The By-Me-and-As-Me-Avatarically-Self-Revealed-and-Spiritually-Self-Transmitted Transcendental, Inherently Spiritual, Inherently egoless, and Self-Evidently Divine (and Perfectly Subjective) Self-Condition (or Self-Existing and Self-Radiant Conscious Light), In The Apparent Context Of conditionally Manifested human Existence As a Separate individual self (or body-mind), Is To Realize Its Own (or Inherent) Happiness (or The Inherent Spiritual Condition That Is Self-Evidently Divine Love-Bliss Itself), It Must Stand Free As Itself (and, Most Ultimately, It Must Realize That mind, body, and their relations Are, Non-Dualistically, Itself). To Stand Free (As The One and Only Conscious Light, Self-Realized As The Self-Evidently Divine Love-Bliss-Feeling Of Being, Itself) Is The Characteristic Of Existence In The Context Of The Only-By-Me Revealed and Given Seventh Stage Of Life (In The Only-By-Me Revealed and Given Way Of The Heart, or Way Of Adidam)—Wherein The Perfectly Non-Dual Disposition Of Free-Standing Conscious Light (Divinely Self-Recognizing, and Inherently Transcending, all Apparently arising conditions, or All Duality, or All "Difference"—In and As Itself) Is The Characteristic Realization.

Therefore, In The Context Of The "Perfect Practice" Of The Only-By-Me Revealed and Given Way Of The Heart (or Way Of Adidam), The By-Me-and-As-Me-Avatarically-Self-Revealed-and-Spiritually-Self-Transmitted Transcendental,

Inherently Spiritual, Inherently egoless, and Self-Evidently Divine Self-Condition (or Self-Existing and Self-Radiant Conscious Light) Spontaneously "Admonishes" Itself To Abide (Perfectly Subjectively) As Itself—Which Is Consciousness Itself, and Being Itself, and Love-Bliss (or Inherent Happiness) Itself (Inherently Indifferent Toward mind, body, and their relations, or all conditional objects). This "Admonition" Is The Un-conditional Self-Acknowledgement That Happiness Is Inherent (and Inherently Spiritual), and Perfectly Subjective (or Transcendental, and Divine), and Not Dependent (or objective, or conditional). And This Un-conditional Self-"Admonition" To Be Indifferent Toward the mind and the body (or the body-mind As A Dynamic Whole), As Well As all other conditional objects, Is The Inherently Perfect "Self-Discipline" (or Inherent, and Inherently Perfect, "Sila") Of Standing Always Already Free—and (Thus) Of Not Allowing The Inherently Free Conscious Light Of Transcendental, Inherently Spiritual, Inherently egoless, and Self-Evidently Divine Being To Be Depended Upon By mind, body, and conditional relations of all kinds.

Based On This Self-"Admonition" (or Spontaneous Disposition), The "Perfect Practice" Of The Only-By-Me Revealed and Given Way Of The Heart (or Way Of Adidam) Is Simply (or Altogether) The Practice Of Self-Abiding As Consciousness (or Mere Feeling-Awareness) Itself—Devotionally Self-Abiding In (and, Ultimately, As) The By-Me-and-As-Me-Avatarically-Self-Revealed-and-Spiritually-Self-Transmitted Spirit-Current Of Perfectly Subjective Love-Bliss. This Practice (and, Most Ultimately, Its Only-By-My-Avataric-Divine-Spiritual-Grace-Given Demonstration As Divine Self-Abiding) Displays Itself As A Process In Which The Characteristic Of Inherent Indifference Is Displayed Progressively, In Comparatively Different (or Distinct, and More Advanced) Modes, As The Total Progression Of The "Perfect Practice" Develops In The Only-By-Me Revealed and Given Way Of The Heart (or Way Of Adidam).

The Inherent Indifference Of Transcendental Self-Abiding Is First Displayed In The First Stage Of The "Perfect Practice" Of The Only-By-Me Revealed and Given Way Of The Heart, and As The Relative Indifference (or Detachment) and psycho-physical Equanimity That arise When There Is Tacit Self-Identification With The Witness-Position Of Consciousness (or Mere Feeling-Awareness). This Is Followed (or Intensified), In The Context Of The Second Stage Of The "Perfect Practice" Of The Only-By-Me Revealed and Given Way Of The Heart, By The Characteristic Signs Of Indifference Associated With The Process Of object-Transcending Self-Identification With Consciousness (or Mere Feeling-Awareness) Itself (Even As Displayed In Priorly Self-Abiding Jnana Nirvikalpa Samadhi, and In Various Spontaneously Intensified Degrees Of daily-life Indifference, Progressively Shown As A General Tendency Toward Simplification Of, and, In Some Cases, Even Relative Non-Interest In, the activities of the body and the mind). And This Spontaneously Leads (By Means Of My Avatarically Self-Transmitted Divine Spiritual Grace) Toward (Eventual) Seventh Stage Sahaja Nirvikalpa Samadhi (or Ruchira Samraj Samadhi, or, Simply, Samraj Samadhi—Which Is The Samadhi-Basis For The Third Stage Of The "Perfect Practice" Of The Only-By-Me Revealed and Given Way Of The Heart), Wherein Self-Abiding Divine Self-Recognition Demonstrates The Inherently Most Perfect Transcending Of body, mind, and all their conditional relations.

In The Only-By-Me Revealed and Given Seventh Stage Of Life (In The Only-By-Me Revealed and Given Way Of The Heart), and Most Obviously In The Context Of The Initial (or Divine Transfiguration and Divine Transformation) Demonstrations Of The Only-By-Me Revealed and Given Seventh Stage Of Life (In The Only-By-Me Revealed and Given Way Of The Heart), Inherent Indifference Is Displayed By Freely Allowing body, mind, all their conditional relations, and The Feeling Of Relatedness (Itself) To arise As They Will, and They Are (Then) Simply (and Divinely) Self-Recognized (or Their qualifying, or limiting, Force Is Inherently Transcended, or Radiated Through) As They arise. Thus, Rather Than By Any Effort To Control or limit what arises, The Only-By-Me Revealed and Given Seventh Stage Of Life Is (Inherently, and Necessarily) Characterized By Non-Strategic Allowance Of all conditional arising (or Inherent Indifference Expressed As Freely and Universally Demonstrated Love-Bliss, and No-Withdrawal, and Only Inherent Freedom Relative To The Total Complex Of all arising, or whatever arises as, in, or to the body-mind).[164] And This Non-Strategic Allowance Of all conditional arising (Divinely Self-Recognizing and Inherently Transcending all that arises) Is Demonstrated Progressively, To The Degree Of Divine Indifference, Wherein all conditions Become Progressively Unnoticed (Even To The Degree Of Outshining, or Divine Translation) In The Absolute Shine Of My "Bright" Divine Spiritual Force Of Love-Bliss.

This Free Indifference, In Which (By Means Of My Avatarically Self-Transmitted Divine Spiritual Grace) The Divinely Self-Realized Force Of Being Allows the body-mind To arise and act Spontaneously, Is Not A Matter Of Merely Arbitrary behavior, Nor Is It (In Any Sense) Negative or egoic. This Free Indifference Is Based On The Always Already Free Disposition Of Transcendental (or Inherently Limitless), and Inherently Spiritual, and Inherently egoless, and Divine (and Perfectly Subjective) Self-Abiding, and Not Merely On A Negative (or, Otherwise, Chaotic) Attitude Toward conditional Existence. Therefore, Such Free Indifference Is Always (By Means Of My Avatarically Self-Transmitted Divine Spiritual Grace) An Expression Of Transcendental, Inherently Spiritual (or "Bright"), Inherently egoless, and Self-Evidently Divine Self-Freedom (Which Is Always Benign, Purifying, Healing, Enlivening, Divinely Transfiguring, and Divinely Transforming, or Literally and Divinely En-Light-ened)—and That

Divine Self-Freedom Always (and Inherently) Serves the Well-being of Even all who Touch (or Feel Within) Its Inherently Perfect State and Space.

In The Only-By-Me Revealed and Given Seventh Stage Of Life (In The Only-By-Me Revealed and Given Way Of The Heart, or Way Of Adidam), My Avatarically Self-Revealed, and Self-Radiant (or Inherently Spiritual), and Self-Existing (or Transcendental), and Self-Evidently Divine Self-Condition (Which Is The Source-Condition Of all-and-All, and Which Is The One and Only Conscious Light Of Perfectly Subjective Divine Being, Itself) Conforms the Total body-mind Of My (Thus By-Me-Divinely-Awakened) Devotee To Itself (and, Directly and Progressively, Dissolves the Total body-mind In Itself) Through Self-Abiding Divine Self-Recognition—and, In The Context Of The Only-By-Me Revealed and Given Seventh Stage Of Life (In The Only-By-Me Revealed and Given Way Of The Heart), The Display Of mind and body, Although Free, Is (By Self-Abiding Divine Self-Recognition) Always Made Into An Expression Of "Bright" Divine Self-Freedom That Divinely Transfigures and Divinely Transforms the Total body-mind Of My (Thus By-Me-Divinely-Awakened) Devotee.

To Realize The Only-By-Me Revealed and Given Seventh Stage Of Life (In The Only-By-Me Revealed and Given Way Of The Heart, or Way Of Adidam) Is To Stand and Be—Beyond and Prior To The Cosmic Domain, Beyond and Prior To conditional Existence, and Beyond and Prior To the Total body-mind.

To Realize The Only-By-Me Revealed and Given Seventh Stage Of Life (In The Only-By-Me Revealed and Given Way Of The Heart, or Way Of Adidam), Is Not Merely To Have and Be some kind of Separate "egoless personality" (or Perfectly Non-Contracted individual body-mind).

To Realize The Only-By-Me Revealed and Given Seventh Stage Of Life (In The Only-By-Me Revealed and Given Way Of The Heart, or Way Of Adidam) Is To Have and Be No body-mind and No conditional world.

To Realize The Only-By-Me Revealed and Given Seventh Stage Of Life (In The Only-By-Me Revealed and Given Way Of The Heart, or Way Of Adidam) Is To Be Utterly Beyond (and Utterly Prior To), and, Yet (Paradoxically, Until The Demonstration Of Divine Translation), Apparently Associated With, a conditional body-mind and a conditional world.

In The Only-By-Me Revealed and Given Seventh Stage Of Life (In The Only-By-Me Revealed and Given Way Of The Heart, or Way Of Adidam), the body-mind and the conditional world Do Not Independently Exist. In every moment of Apparent arising (In The Only-By-Me Revealed and Given Seventh Stage Of Life In The Only-By-Me Revealed and Given Way Of The Heart), the body-mind and the world Are Inherently (or Divinely) Self-Recognized (Without The Passage Of Even any fraction of time, However Instant). There Is (Simply) The "Bright"—Itself.

I Am The "Bright" (Itself)—In Person. The "Bright" (Itself) Is The Self-Existing and Self-Radiant Divine Self-Condition (and Source-Condition) Itself—The Always Already Beyond and Prior (and Inherently egoless) Self-Condition Of Perfect No-Contraction.

The Realization Of The Only-By-Me Revealed and Given Seventh Stage Of Life (In The Only-By-Me Revealed and Given Way Of The Heart, or Way Of Adidam) Is The Realization Of Non-"Difference". It Is To Be Established In and As That Ultimate (and Perfectly Subjective) Condition Which Is Always Already The Case, and Which Inherently Transcends conditional Existence. It Is To Be Just That.

In The Only-By-Me Revealed and Given Seventh Stage Of Life (In The Only-By-Me Revealed and Given Way Of The Heart, or Way Of Adidam), There Is No Separate (or "Different") conditional Domain—but There Is Only The Centerless, Boundless, and Infinitely Spiritually Self-"Bright" Sphere (or Self-Existing, Self-Radiant, Perfectly Subjective, and Perfectly Spherical Conscious Light) Of My Divine Self-Domain. In The Only-By-Me Revealed and Given Seventh Stage Of Life (In The Only-By-Me Revealed and Given Way Of The Heart), It Makes No "Difference" Whether Divine Translation Occurs—or (Indeed) Whether anything Occurs. Divine Translation Is Not An Event Looked Forward To, but It Is (Simply) The (In Due Course) Inevitable Demonstration Of The Disposition That Always Already Exists In My Seventh Stage Realizer-Devotee.

My Avatarically Self-Revealed (and Self-Evidently Divine) Self-Condition (Which Is The One and Only Conscious Light Itself) Is Self-Existing and Self-Radiant. Every condition that arises In The conditional (or Cosmic) Domain Is A Modification Of My Avatarically Self-Transmitted Divine Self-Radiance. However, Paradoxically, No Such Modification Of My Avatarically Self-Transmitted Divine (and Self-Existing) Self-Radiance Affects My Avatarically Self-Revealed Divine Self-Condition Itself. Whatever arises Is Simply A Transparent (or Merely Apparent), and Un-Necessary, and Inherently Non-Binding Modification Of My Avatarically Self-Transmitted Divine Self-Radiance (or Of My Avatarically Self-Revealed, and Self-Existing, and Self-Radiant, and Self-Evidently Divine Self-Condition, Itself).

There Is No "Difference" Between The Self-Consciousness Of Being (Itself) and Its Inherent Radiance. There Is Only The One and Inherently Indivisible and Inherently egoless and Self-Evidently Divine Conscious Light (Itself), Self-Existing and Self-Radiant—Not "Created", Not conditional, and Not Dependent On any thing or condition. There Is Only Infinite, Unbounded Being—Indivisible, Unable To Be Differentiated From any Apparently Separate being. Indeed, There Are No conditional beings—but Only Being (Itself) Is.

There Is Only One Principle, Which Is Self-Existing and Self-Radiant—and every thing that arises (conditionally) arises (conditionally) In (and Only As) It. Therefore, every thing that Appears To Be arising Separately, "Differently", and in and of itself Is (In Its Apparent Independence) An Illusion.

There Is No thing in and of itself. No thing Is As it Appears. Therefore, every thing—and, Indeed, Everything—Is Only The By-Me-and-As-Me-Avatarically-Self-Revealed-and-Spiritually-Self-Transmitted One and Only and Inherently Indivisible and Inherently egoless and Self-Evidently Divine Conscious Light (or The "Bright", Itself).

Through their ego-Surrendering, ego-Forgetting, and (More and More) ego-Transcending Devotional (and, In Due Course, Spiritual) Communion With Me, Even My Beginning Devotees Participate In My Avatarically Self-Revealed (and Self-Evidently Divine) Self-Condition Of Spiritual Self-"Brightness". Indeed, The Entire Course Of The Only-By-Me Revealed and Given Way Of The Heart Is Simply This Intensive (and Self-Evidently Divine) Self-"Brightening" Process. The Only-By-Me Revealed and Given Way Of The Heart (or Way Of Adidam) Is Always, From The Beginning, Characterized By Devotion To Me—and, Thus, By Constant Contemplation Of (and Progressive Conformity To) The Only-By-Me (and Only-As-Me) Revealed and Given (Spiritual, Transcendental, and Self-Evidently Divine) Qualities That Are To Be Realized and Demonstrated In The Context Of The Only-By-Me Revealed and Given Seventh Stage Of Life (In The Only-By-Me Revealed and Given Way Of The Heart). Therefore, In The Only-By-Me Revealed and Given Way Of The Heart (or Way Of Adidam), The Self-"Bright" Disposition Of The Only-By-Me Revealed and Given Seventh Stage Of Life Is Magnified (By Me) In My Devotees (moment to moment), Until That Constant Magnification Becomes A Most Perfect (or Seventh Stage, and, Therefore, Non-Separate) Demonstration Of ego-Transcending Devotion To (and ego-Transcending Spiritual Self-Realization Of) My "Bright" and Only (and Self-Evidently Divine) Person.

Thus, The Most Essential Characteristic Of The Only-By-Me Revealed and Given Way Of The Heart (or Way Of Adidam) Is Not self-Surrender, self-Forgetting, and self-Transcendence (or Real ego-Transcendence), In and Of Themselves. Rather, The Most Essential Characteristic Of The Only-By-Me Revealed and Given Way Of The Heart (or Way Of Adidam) Is Me-Contemplation—Which Makes self-Surrender, self-Forgetting, and self-Transcendence (or Real ego-Transcendence) Both Necessary and Possible. I Am The One Who Is To Be Contemplated (and Whom every one Is Inherently and Effortlessly Capable Of Contemplating)—Because Of My Avataric, and Universal, and Inherent, and Self-Evidently Divine Attractiveness. I Am The "Bright" (Itself)—Avatarically (and Universally, and Inherently, and Divinely) Attractive To all. I Am The Very One (and, Therefore, The Only One) Who Is To Be Contemplated By My Devotees. I Am (In Person) The Seventh Stage Realization (Itself). Therefore, Even From The Beginning Of his or her Practice Of The Only-By-Me Revealed and Given Way Of The Heart, My Every Devotee, By Heart-Contemplating Only Me, Participates (Tacitly) In The Only-By-Me Revealed and Given Seventh Stage Realization (Itself).

From the time they Are Fully Established (Devotionally and Spiritually) As Listening Practitioners Of The Only-By-Me Revealed and Given Way Of The Heart, My Devotees Are Simply (and Only) Called To Realize The Truth (By Means Of My Avatarically Self-Transmitted Divine Spiritual Grace) and (By Means Of The By-My-Avataric-Divine-Spiritual-Grace-Revealed Truth Itself) To Be Free. Therefore, Even If My Any Devotee Awakens To Realize The Only-By-Me Revealed and Given Seventh Stage Of Life, No Devotee Of Mine Is Called (or Ever Given The Divine Siddhi, or The Inherently Perfect Power and The Uniquely Divinely Established Obligation) To Function As The Divine Heart-Master Of Devotees. The Function Of Divine Heart-Master (and The Avataric Exercise Of The Function Of Divine Heart-Master) Is Uniquely Mine. The Unique (and Avataric) Function Of Divine Heart-Master Required Me (and, Now, and Forever Hereafter, Requires Me) To Submit To, and To Identify With, and To Directly Absorb and Release the limitations and sufferings of even all others. Therefore (Now, and Forever Hereafter), All My Devotees Are Called (Simply, and Only) To Be (and To Function) Transparent To Me—The Divine, and Eternal, and Avataric, and True, and Always New Heart-Master Of All My Devotees.

The behavior Of All My Devotees In The Only-By-Me Revealed and Given Seventh Stage Of Life (In The Only-By-Me Revealed and Given Way Of The Heart, or Way Of Adidam) Will (Because Of The Consistently Operative psycho-physical Pattern and Impulse Established and, Thereafter, Generated By Previous Right, True, Full, Fully Devotional, and Consistent Practice Of The Only-By-Me Revealed and Given Way Of The Heart) Continue In The Same Manner (or With The Same Apparent "Sila") That Was Developed In The Previous (Maturing, or Progressive) Stages Of Practice In The Only-By-Me Revealed and Given Way Of The Heart—but (By Means Of My Avatarically Self-Transmitted Divine Spiritual Grace) With An Added Self-"Bright" Capability For The Effortless Free (and Self-Abiding) Divine Self-Recognition Of (and Simultaneous Free and Spontaneous Heart-Sympathy With) all conditionally Manifested beings, conditions, and circumstances. Therefore, The Heart-Rightening Of every conditionally Manifested being, and The Positive Rightening Of every conditionally Manifested condition and circumstance, Will Be Constantly Served By The Mere (and Effortless) Good Company (and The By-Me-Spiritually-Potentized Sign Of The Inherently Most Perfect Devotional

Demonstration) Of All My Devotees In The Only-By-Me Revealed and Given Seventh Stage Of Life (In The Only-By-Me Revealed and Given Way Of The Heart, or Way Of Adidam).

And, After a time—In which all conditions that arise as, in, or to the body-mind Are Divinely Self-Recognized As Transparent (or Merely Apparent), and Un-Necessary, and Inherently Non-Binding Modifications Of The By-Me-and-As-Me-Avatarically-Self-Revealed-and-Spiritually-Self-Transmitted (and Self-Existing, and Self-Radiant, and Inherently egoless, and Perfectly Subjective) Conscious Light Of Self-Evidently Divine Being—A New and Most Progressed (or Divinely Most Profound) Form Of Indifference Will Begin To Characterize My Seventh Stage (and Divinely Free) Devotee. The arising conditions (Whether Positive Or Negative In their Apparent or relative content) Will Have Become Less Than Interesting, and they Will (More and More) Become Of Little Interest—Such That they Will Arouse Little Notice, Because Of their Transparency In The By-My-Avataric-Divine-Spiritual-Grace-Revealed Spiritual Fullness Of The Spiritually Self-"Bright" Love-Bliss (and Inherent Happiness) Of The Self-Existing, and Self-Radiant, and Inherently egoless, and Perfectly Subjective Conscious Light Of Self-Evidently Divine Being. The Motive Of Change Will Not Be Found (or Will Be Found Less and Less)—and, Therefore, all that merely changes (or whatever Is merely conditionally Existing) Will (Progressively) Cease To Arouse and Claim attention. The (By-My-Avataric-Divine-Spiritual-Grace-Revealed) Self-Existing, and Self-Radiant, and Inherently egoless, and Perfectly Subjective Conscious Light Of Self-Evidently Divine Being Will Stand Free, Effortlessly and Motivelessly and Divinely Indifferent To The Tendency Of the conditional body-mind and its relations To Depend On (By Virtue Of An Appearance Of "Difference" and Necessity)—and, Thus, To Appear To Implicate (or Motivate)—The By-Me-and-As-Me-Avatarically-Self-Revealed-and-Spiritually-Self-Transmitted (Transcendental, Inherently Spiritual, Inherently egoless, and Self-Evidently Divine) Conscious Light Of Mere Being. My Avatarically Self-Revealed (and Spiritually Self-Transmitted) Conscious Light Of Self-Evidently Divine Love-Bliss-Happiness Will Radiate Freely, No Matter what arises, and Participatory Responses To (or Even The "Noticing" Of) the body-mind and its conditional relations Will Become Minimal By Degrees. And, More and More, Only The (Inherently Dualistic) Feeling Of Relatedness, or (Ultimately) Only The Tacit (and Simplest, but Also Inherently Dualistic) Feeling Of "Difference", Will Be "Noticed" (and, In The "Noticing", Divinely Self-Recognized)—Until My Avatarically Self-Revealed (and Spiritually Self-Transmitted) and Perfectly Non-Dual Conscious Light (Of Which all conditional forms and events Are Composed) Shines Without limit, Through and Beyond All Modifications, and "Brightly" Outshines Them all.

In The By-My-Avataric-Divine-Spiritual-Grace-Given Awakening Of Seventh Stage Sahaja Nirvikalpa Samadhi (or Ruchira Samraj Samadhi, or, Simply, Samraj Samadhi), all arising conditions Are (Inherently) Divinely Self-Recognized and (Thus) Realized To Be (Ultimately) Of One Quality (or Of A Perfectly Non-Dual, or Inherently Un-"Differentiated", or Non-"Different" and Absolute, Nature). It Is The Quality Of Self-Existing and Self-Radiant Divine Feeling-Being Itself—Inherently Love-Blissful (or "Bright") and Free. Therefore, In any moment, The Apparent Effort Of the conditional self—which Is Always Tending To Become Abstracted As attention, and To Discriminate Between (Rather Than To Merely Feel) conditions, and To Evaluate their relative significance or desirability, and To Embrace or Avoid them Based On Such Discrimination and Evaluation—Is (In The Context Of The Only-By-Me Revealed and Given Seventh Stage Of Life) Inherently Transcended In The By-Me-and-As-Me-Avatarically-Self-Revealed-and-Spiritually-Self-Transmitted Transcendental (or Inherently bodiless and mindless) and Self-Evidently Divine Love-Bliss—Which Is The Inherent Spiritual Condition Of Self-Existing and Self-Radiant Divine Being (Itself). Thus, The self-Contracted (or egoic) Habit Of Seeking (and Anticipating)—Holding On (While Grounded In the past), or Trying To Strategically Escape (Even The Results Of the past)—Is Effortlessly Replaced By Simple Regard (or Feeling-"Notice") Of whatever arises as, in, or to the body-mind.

Such "Practice" (or Inherently Most Perfect Demonstration) Is A Matter Of Divine Self-Abiding, Feeling (and Merely, or Inherently, and Perfectly Subjectively, and Divinely Self-Recognizing) whatever (Apparently) arises In (and As) My Avatarically Self-Transmitted Spirit-Current Of Self-Existing, Self-Radiant, and Self-Evidently Divine Love-Bliss. And, Ultimately (or Most Simply), Divine Self-Abiding—Divinely Self-Recognizing (or Divinely Feeling-Recognizing) whatever (Apparently) arises—Is The Divine Self-Recognition (and, Thus, The Inherent Transcending) Of The Inherently Dualistic Feeling Of Relatedness (or Of "Difference"). And That Inherently Dualistic Feeling Of Relatedness (or Of "Difference"), Which Is The (conditional) Essence Of the ego-"I", Is (Thus) Divinely Self-Recognized (and Inherently Transcended) In (and, Inherently Most Perfectly, As) The Self-Existing and Self-Radiant Conscious Light Of Inherently Indivisible Being (Which Is My Avatarically Self-Revealed and Self-Evidently Divine Self-Condition, Itself).

Therefore, Whereas The Second Stage Of The "Perfect Practice" Of The Only-By-Me Revealed and Given Way Of The Heart Requires The "Radically" (or By "Going-To-The-Root") ego-Transcending Practice Of "Locating" The By-Me-and-As-Me-Avatarically-Self-Revealed-and-Spiritually-Self-Transmitted Divine Spiritual Love-Bliss-Current Of Self-Existing and Self-Radiant Being (Itself), Immediately Previous (and Most Prior) To The Root-Feeling Of

Relatedness (or "Difference")—The "Practice" (or Demonstration) Of The Only-By-Me Revealed and Given Way Of The Heart In The Context Of The Only-By-Me Revealed and Given Seventh Stage Of Life Requires (and Spontaneously Demonstrates) Inherently Most Perfect (or Inherent and Spontaneous) Self-Abiding Divine Self-Recognition (and, Thus, The Inherent and Effortless Dissolution) Of The (Necessarily, conditional) Root-Feeling Of Relatedness (or Of "Difference") In (and, Inherently Most Perfectly, As) The By-Me-and-As-Me-Avatarically-Self-Revealed-and-Spiritually-Self-Transmitted Divine Spiritual Love-Bliss-Current Of Self-Existing and Self-Radiant Being (Itself). And (In The Final Event Of The Only-By-Me Revealed and Given Way Of The Heart) This Inherently Most Perfect (Seventh Stage) Process Of Self-Abiding Divine Self-Recognition Demonstrates Itself (Inherently Most Perfectly) As Divine Translation, Which Is The Most Ultimate (or Absolutely and Unqualifiedly "Bright"—and, Thus, Truly Final) By-My-Avataric-Divine-Spiritual-Grace-Given Demonstration Of Inherent Freedom From All Bondage To conditional desires, conditional preferences, conditional knowledge, conditional experience, and conditional Existence (Itself).

Of Primary Significance Is The Fact That The "Practice" (or Inherently Most Perfect Demonstration) Of The Only-By-Me Revealed and Given Way Of The Heart In The Context Of The Only-By-Me Revealed and Given Seventh Stage Of Life (or The Third Stage Of The Only-By-Me Revealed and Given "Perfect Practice") Develops From The Always Already Divinely Self-Realized (and Inherently Non-Separate, or Non-"Different" and Non-Exclusive) Position Of The Transcendental, Inherently Spiritual, Inherently egoless, and Self-Evidently Divine Self-Condition—Which Is Free, As Itself, and Which, In The Apparent Context Of the body, Is Tacitly Associated With The "Regenerated" Amrita Nadi (and, Thus, With The Right Side Of The Heart, and With The Matrix-Position, Infinitely Above The Totality Of the body-mind)—Whereas All Previous Practice Of The Only-By-Me Revealed and Given Way Of The Heart Is A Constant Direct Process Of Conversion From the conditional (or Extended) self (or The Otherwise Effectively Separate, or Exclusively Presumed, Consciousness) To The By-Me-and-As-Me-Avatarically-Self-Revealed-and-Spiritually-Self-Transmitted Unconditional, Transcendental, Inherently Spiritual, Inherently egoless, and Self-Evidently Divine Self-Condition.

Once There Is The (Seventh Stage) Awakening To Most Perfect Self-Identification With My Avatarically Self-Revealed (Transcendental, Inherently Spiritual, Inherently egoless, and Self-Evidently Divine) Self-Condition (or One and Only Conscious Light), conditional forms and events No Longer Imply (or Implicate) a Separate conditional self (or egoic self-Consciousness). In That Case, the conditional activities of the body-mind No Longer Imply (or Implicate) a Separate conditional self (or egoic self-Consciousness) that is the actor (or doer). From The "Point Of View" Of The By-Me-and-As-Me-Avatarically-Self-Revealed-and-Spiritually-Self-Transmitted Transcendental, Inherently Spiritual, Inherently egoless, and Self-Evidently Divine Self-Condition (or One and Only Conscious Light)—conditional forms, conditional states, conditional events, and conditional activities all arise Spontaneously (and Merely Apparently) To (and Altogether Within) The View Of The By-Me-and-As-Me-Avatarically-Self-Revealed-and-Spiritually-Self-Transmitted Transcendental, Inherently Spiritual, Inherently egoless, and Self-Evidently Divine Self-Condition (or One and Only Conscious Light).

Therefore, all arising conditions and actions Are Only A Spontaneous (and Merely Apparent) Display Of Modifications Of My Avatarically Self-Revealed (and Spiritually Self-Transmitted) Divine Self-Condition (or One and Only Conscious Light).

There Is No Bondage—and There Is No Separate conditional self-Consciousness To Be Bound.

There Is No Separate conditional self-Consciousness who is the actor (or doer) of action.

There Is No Separate conditional self-Consciousness who is the "owner" of the body-mind, or of others, or of any things or states.

There Is No Separate conditional self-Consciousness who is the knower of knowledge (or the known), or the experiencer of experiences.

There Is Only The By-Me-and-As-Me-Avatarically-Self-Revealed-and-Spiritually-Self-Transmitted, and Inherently Free-Shining (or Inherently Spiritual), and Transcendental, and Inherently egoless, and Perfectly Subjective, and Self-Evidently Divine Self-Condition (or One and Only Conscious Light)—Which Is Always Already Free, and Which Is (Thus) Always Already Free Even In The Apparent Context Of conditional knowledge, conditional objects, conditional activity, conditional experience, and All Apparent Confinement To Apparent limitations.

Avatar Adi Da Samraj
Los Angeles, 2000

SUTRA 64

In Consciousness (or The One and Only Conscious Light) Itself, "things" Do Not change and disappear In time. The Apparent arising of conditions, and things, and others, and thoughts Is, From (and In, and As) The "Point Of View" Of Consciousness (or The One and Only Conscious Light) Itself, Only The Eternally (or Always Already) Unfamiliar—Constantly Happening, as every now. To Really and Truly (and, Thus, Divinely) Self-Recognize The Unfamiliar (As Such, and as every now) Is Inherently Perfect Freedom. Therefore, Consciousness (or The One and Only Conscious Light) Itself Is The Unfamiliar—Even every now.

Consciousness (or The One and Only Conscious Light) Itself Cannot Be experienced or known—Because It Is The "Experiencer" and The "Knower". Consciousness (or The One and Only Conscious Light) Itself Stands Always Already Prior To any and every object of experience or knowledge—and Always Already Prior To The psycho-physical Faculties Of experiencing or knowing any and every object of experience or knowledge. Therefore, Consciousness (or The One and Only Conscious Light) Itself Cannot Be Remembered—or Even Forgotten. And Consciousness (or The One and Only Conscious Light) Itself Cannot change or disappear—Because It Is Never the experienced or the known. But Consciousness (or The One and Only Conscious Light) Itself Is Always The One In (and As) Whom the experiencing or the knowing arises (as, or coincident with, the experiencing or the knowing of things, and others, and conditions, and thoughts). Therefore, Consciousness (or The One and Only Conscious Light) Itself Is Not Threatened By The Non-arising Of present conditions. But, If conditions arise (and are, thus, experienced or known), the conditional affect of conditionally experiencing or knowing (or, Otherwise, Of Anticipating the experiencing or knowing)—and, thus, the conditionally arising (and, Altogether, self-Contracted, or egoic) feeling That Consciousness (or The One and Only Conscious Light) Itself Is Threatened By Cessation, or (Otherwise) By Loss—Must Be Transcended In The Affect That Is Always Already (or Unconditionally) The Case (or That Is The Inherent Characteristic Of Consciousness, or The One and Only Conscious Light, Itself). My Avatarically Self-Transmitted Spirit-Current Of Self-Evidently

Divine Love-Bliss (or Happiness) Itself Is My Avataric Self-Transmission Of The Inherent (and Inherently Un-conditional) Characteristic Affect Of Consciousness (or The One and Only Conscious Light) Itself. And The Most Perfect Spiritual Realization Of Self-Evidently Divine Love-Bliss (or Happiness) Itself Is (By Means Of My Avatarically Self-Transmitted Divine Spiritual Grace) The Great Yoga Of Self-Abiding Divine Self-Recognition Of all-and-All—Which Is The Unique Yoga (or Demonstration) Of The Only-By-Me Revealed and Given Seventh Stage Of Life (In The Only-By-Me Revealed and Given Way Of The Heart, or Way Of Adidam).

The Always Never-Yet-Objectively-Experienced Experiencer (or The One and Only Conscious Light Of Mere and Self-Existing Being) Is The Only One Who Always Already Is.

The Always Never-Yet-Objectively-Known Knower Is Always Already The Case.

The Unfamiliar Is Always arising—as conditional experience and conditional knowledge.

To "Locate" The Unfamiliar In The (Objectively) Unexperienceable Unknown Is To Realize The Perfectly Subjective Reality (or The One and Only Conscious Light That Is Consciousness Itself).

To Realize Consciousness (or The One and Only Conscious Light) Itself Is (Thus and Thereby) To Realize The Inherent (or Always Already Existing) Reality Of Being (Itself).

To Realize The Always Already Existing Reality Of Being (Itself) Is (Thus and Thereby) To Realize Self-Existing and Self-Radiant Happiness (Itself).

And To Realize Consciousness (or The One and Only Conscious Light, Itself) As Self-Existing and Self-Radiant Happiness (Itself) Is (Thus and Thereby) To Realize Reality (Itself), and Truth (Itself), and The One and Only Real God—or The Absolute, Inherently egoless, and Non-Separate Person (or Self-Existing and Self-Radiant Self-Condition) That Is The One and Only and Perfectly Subjective Reality (Itself).

Therefore, The Real and True Unknown Is Not Merely that which is Not Yet experienced or known—but The Real and True Unknown Is The Eternally Objectively Unknowable Knower (or The Perfectly Subjective Base Of all conditional experience and all conditional knowledge). And It Is Not By Seeking For knowledge (or For More Of perceptual and conceptual experience) That The Unknown Is Found—but It Is Only In The Yoga Of Conscious Light, Divinely Self-Recognizing every moment (of the conditional arising of perceptual and conceptual experience) In and As The By-Me-and-As-Me-Avatarically-Self-Revealed-and-Spiritually-Self-Transmitted Spirit-Current Of Self-Evidently Divine Love-Bliss-Happiness Itself, That The Inherently

Unknown (or The Inherently egoless and Self-Evidently Divine Self-Condition and Source-Condition Of all conditional experience and all conditional knowledge) Is Realized (Beyond All Separateness, Otherness, Relatedness, and "Difference").

Therefore, In The Only-By-Me Revealed and Given Seventh Stage Of Life (In The Only-By-Me Revealed and Given Way Of The Heart, or Way Of Adidam), The Eternal "Practice" (or The Most Fundamental Realization and Demonstration) Is That Of Mere (and Most Perfect) Divine Self-Abiding. And, In The Only-By-Me Revealed and Given Seventh Stage Of Life (In The Only-By-Me Revealed and Given Way Of The Heart, or Way Of Adidam), The Unique, and Inherent, and Most Perfect Divine Demonstration That (In The Apparent Context Of any and all conditional arising) Necessarily and Immediately Follows From The Eternal "Practice" (or Demonstration) Is That Of Spontaneous (and, Necessarily, Divine) Self-Abiding Self-Recognition Of whatever (Apparently) arises.

Mere (Beginningless and Endless) Divine Self-Abiding Is By-Me-and-As-Me-Avatarically-Self-Revealed-and-Spiritually-Self-Transmitted Self-Identification With Consciousness (or The One and Only Conscious Light) Itself, Spiritually Self-Realized (By Means Of My Avatarically Self-Transmitted Divine Spiritual Grace) As The Mere (or Tacit) Feeling Of Being (Itself), Which Is (By Me, and As Me, Avatarically Self-Revealed) To Be Self-Evidently Divine Love-Bliss (Itself).

To Merely Self-Abide Thus Is To Always Already Be (or Stand As) The One and Only (Inherently Indivisible, Inherently egoless, Perfectly Subjective, and Self-Evidently Divine) Conscious Light That Is Reality Itself—and (Thus, and Merely As Is) Not acting, Not reacting, and Not thinking.

There Is No actor (or doer), and No action, and No reaction, and No thought (of any kind), and No Feeling Of Relatedness (or Of "Difference") In The One and Only Conscious Light (Itself). Therefore, To Merely Self-Abide As The By-Me-and-As-Me-Avatarically-Self-Revealed-and-Spiritually-Self-Transmitted Transcendental, Inherently Spiritual, Inherently egoless, and Self-Evidently Divine Self-Condition and Source-Condition (or The One and Only Conscious Light) Is To Stand and Be—Absolutely and Inherently Most Perfectly Free, Always Already Prior To actor, action, reaction, all thinking, and The (Necessarily, conditional, and Inherently Dualistic) Root-Feeling Of Relatedness (or Of "Difference").

To "Practice" Mere (and Most Perfect) Divine Self-Abiding Is To Stand and Be (and, Thus, To Demonstrate) The By-Me-and-As-Me-Avatarically-Self-Revealed-and-Spiritually-Self-Transmitted Conscious Light Of Mere Being—Merely Self-Aware (In and As The By-Me-and-As-Me-Avatarically-Self-Revealed-and-Spiritually-Self-Transmitted Spirit-Current Of Self-Evidently

Divine Love-Bliss), Without any thoughts, Without any acting, and Without any reacting. And This Without Any Effort, Strategy, or Purpose At All.

Thinking Is A Way In—Not A Way Out. It Is Not Possible For the body, or the mind, or Even the Total body-mind To think itself Out Of The Apparent Bondage (or Apparent Problem) That Is conditional Existence. Therefore, Almost All Of thinking Tends (Merely and Constantly) To Re-Affirm (and Re-Assert) The Bondage and The Problems That mere thinking thinks About.

Any and every kind of thinking is (Necessarily) a conditional activity—and, Therefore, thinking Cannot (itself) Eliminate (or Transcend) conditional Existence (Itself).

The Only Process That Is Able To Eliminate (or Transcend) The Apparent Bondage (or Apparent Problem) That Is conditional Existence Is One That Inherently (and Most Priorly) Transcends (or Stands—Inherently, and Inherently Most Perfectly—Prior To) conditional Existence.

Apart From Such A Process (Which Is Inherently Most Perfect and Inherently Free), thinking Never Leads Out Of Bondage (and, Thus, To Freedom)—but thinking (Unless it Is Simply An Extension, and An Expression, or An Otherwise Effective Servant, Of The Inherently Most Perfect Realization Of Prior Freedom) Always Leads Further and Further Into Bondage Itself (and Every Kind Of conceived—or, Otherwise, Presumed—Problem).

The Only-By-Me Revealed and Given Seventh Stage Of Life (In The Only-By-Me Revealed and Given Way Of The Heart, or Way Of Adidam) Is (By Means Of My Avatarically Self-Revealed and Self-Transmitted Divine Spiritual Grace) The Divinely Self-Realized Self-Demonstration Of Inherent Perfection, and Of Inherent Freedom From Bondage (and All Problems)—and The Only-By-Me Revealed and Given Seventh Stage Of Life (In The Only-By-Me Revealed and Given Way Of The Heart) Is An Inherently Most Perfect (and Inherently Free) Process That Is Inherently Free Of every kind of thinking.

However, The Only-By-Me Revealed and Given Seventh Stage Of Life (In The Only-By-Me Revealed and Given Way Of The Heart) Is Not Associated With Any conditional Effort (or Search) To Stop thinking. Any Such Effort (or Search) Would Necessarily Be Based On The Presumption Of Identification With an "I" that Is Identical (presently and conditionally) To the act of thinking, the present thought, and the conditional (or egoic, and, Necessarily, self-Contracted) thinker. That Is To Say, Any Effort (or Search) To Stop thinking (or To Eliminate the act of thinking, and any present thought, and Even the thinker, or the ego-"I" itself) Would Necessarily Be Based On The Presumption Of egoic Identification With the body-mind (and Especially the mind)—but, In The Awakening To The Only-By-Me Revealed and Given Seventh Stage Of Life (In The Only-By-Me Revealed and Given Way Of The Heart), It Has Been

Realized That the ego-"I" (or self-Contraction) Is Not The By-Me-and-As-Me-Avatarically-Self-Revealed-and-Spiritually-Self-Transmitted Very (or True and Ultimate) Self-Condition (or One and Only Conscious Light) Itself, but (Rather) The By-Me-and-As-Me-Avatarically-Self-Revealed-and-Spiritually-Self-Transmitted Very (or True, and Ultimate, and Transcendental, and Inherently Spiritual, Inherently egoless, and Self-Evidently Divine) Self-Condition (or The By-Me-and-As-Me-Avatarically-Self-Revealed-and-Spiritually-Self-Transmitted Conscious Light Of all-and-All) Is Only Consciousness (Itself), Self-"Located" As The Mere Feeling Of Mere Being (Itself), Which Is Self-Realized As The By-Me-and-As-Me-Avatarically-Self-Revealed-and-Spiritually-Self-Transmitted Spirit-Current Of Self-Evidently Divine Love-Bliss (Itself), Always Already Prior To the ego-"I" (or the self-Contraction), and (Therefore) Always Already Prior To any and every Apparent thought, and Always Already Prior To the Apparent act of thinking, and Always Already Prior Even To the Apparent thinker.

In The Awakening To The Only-By-Me Revealed and Given Seventh Stage Of Life (In The Only-By-Me Revealed and Given Way Of The Heart, or Way Of Adidam), It Is Realized That Reality (Itself) Is Always Already Not thinking.

In The Context Of The Only-By-Me Revealed and Given Seventh Stage Of Life (In The Only-By-Me Revealed and Given Way Of The Heart, or Way Of Adidam), Freedom From thought (and thinking, and thinker), and Freedom From the Total psycho-physical self-Contraction (or ego-"I"), Is A Most Prior (and Inherently Most Perfect) Realization—and That Realization Is Not Based Upon (or Otherwise Dependent Upon) Any past, present, or future Effort (or Search) To Eliminate (or To Exclude) thoughts, or the act of thinking, or the Apparent thinker.

Therefore, In The Only-By-Me Revealed and Given Seventh Stage Of Life (In The Only-By-Me Revealed and Given Way Of The Heart, or Way Of Adidam), The "Practice" (or Inherently Most Perfect and Always Already Free Demonstration) Is, Simply and Effortlessly (or Always Already), To Self-Abide As That Which Is Always Already Without thinking, or thought, or thinker.

Thus, Even If (Apparently) any thought (or Process Of thinking, or Appearance Of a thinker) arises, The Eternal "Practice" In The Context Of The Only-By-Me Revealed and Given Seventh Stage Of Life (In The Only-By-Me Revealed and Given Way Of The Heart, or Way Of Adidam) Is, Simply and Effortlessly (and With Inherent and Inherently Most Perfect Firmness), To Self-Abide As Consciousness (or Mere Feeling-Awareness) Itself, Self-"Located" (and Persistently Demonstrated) As The By-Me-and-As-Me-Avatarically-Self-Revealed-and-Spiritually-Self-Transmitted Mere Feeling Of Mere Being (Itself), Which Is Self-Realized As The By-Me-and-As-Me-Avatarically-Self-Revealed-and-Spiritually-Self-Transmitted Spirit-Current Of Self-Evidently Divine Love-Bliss (Itself)—and

(Thus and Thereby) To Most Perfectly (and With Inherently Most Perfect Effectiveness) Not Presume The Existence Of (or Any Kind Of Connection, or Relationship, To) any thinking, any thought, or any thinker At All. And, On The Basis Of That Persistent (Divine) Self-Abiding (Which Is Inherently, and Persistently, Free Of all thinking, all thoughts, and All Presumption Of a thinker), The "Practice" To Be Engaged In The Midst Of Apparently objective conditions Is, Simply and Effortlessly (and With Inherently Most Perfect Firmness), To (Divinely) Self-Recognize whatever (Apparently) arises (including any thinking, any thought, and any kind of thinker that May Appear To arise)—and This To The Inherently Most Perfect Degree Of Dissolving (or Finding No "Difference" In) whatever (Apparently) arises.

Therefore, In The Only-By-Me Revealed and Given Seventh Stage Of Life (In The Only-By-Me Revealed and Given Way Of The Heart, or Way Of Adidam), The Principal and Persistent Sign (or Demonstration), Always Already Realized, Is That Of Inherent (and, Therefore, Effortless) Self-Identification With The One and Only Conscious Light (Itself), Self-"Located" As The (By-Me-and-As-Me-Avatarically-Self-Revealed) Prior Feeling Of Being (Itself), Which Is Self-Realized As The By-Me-and-As-Me-Avatarically-Self-Transmitted Spirit-Current Of Self-Evidently Divine Love-Bliss (Itself)—Effortlessly Without thought, and Effortlessly Without action, reaction, or the doer of these, and, Likewise Effortlessly, Without Any Feeling Of Relatedness (or Of "Difference") At All.

In The By-My-Avataric-Divine-Spiritual-Grace-Given Awakening To The Only-By-Me Revealed and Given Seventh Stage Of Life (In The Only-By-Me Revealed and Given Way Of The Heart, or Way Of Adidam), There Is No Identification With any (Necessarily, conditional) processes In The Context Of Cosmic (and, Necessarily, conditional) Existence. Instead, There Is Only Most Perfect Self-Identification With My Avatarically Self-Revealed (and Self-Evidently Divine) Self-Condition (Which Is The Source-Condition Of all-and-All).

Therefore, What Appears To Be An Association With conditional Existence, In The Case Of My Seventh Stage Realizer-Devotee, Is perceived (or Presumed) To Be So Only From the point of view of others who Are Still Bound To conditional Existence (and who, Therefore, Still Exist In The Knot Of egoity—Identified With attention, the body-mind, and The Play Of conditional Existence). From The "Point Of View" Of My Any Such Divinely Self-Realized Devotee, There Is No "Association With" conditional Existence (As If conditional Existence Were Separate and objective). Rather, From The "Point Of View" Of My Divinely Self-Realized Devotee, It Is Always Already The Case—No Matter What Appears To Be arising—That Only Conscious Light Self-Abides (Self-Existing, Self-Radiant, and Inherently Indivisible, or One), As It Is. Such Is The Realization Of The Only-By-Me Revealed and Given Seventh

Stage Of Life (In The Only-By-Me Revealed and Given Way Of The Heart, or Way Of Adidam).

In The Only-By-Me Revealed and Given Seventh Stage Of Life In The Only-By-Me Revealed and Given Way Of The Heart (or Way Of Adidam), There Is Not anything To Be Transcended, and There Is Not anything To Be Excluded. Indeed, There Is No "event" At All—Except For The Eternal, Changeless "Event" Of My Avatarically Self-Revealed (and Self-Evidently Divine) Person (Which Is The Divine Self-Condition, and Source-Condition, Itself). From The "Point Of View" Of The Realization Of The Only-By-Me Revealed and Given Seventh Stage Of Life (In The Only-By-Me Revealed and Given Way Of The Heart), the arising of "things" is merely an appearance. Truly, From The "Point Of View" Of The Realization Of The Only-By-Me Revealed and Given Seventh Stage Of Life (In The Only-By-Me Revealed and Given Way Of The Heart), There Is No "thing" that arises. To Say That conditions Apparently arise Is, From The "Point Of View" Of The Realization Of The Only-By-Me Revealed and Given Seventh Stage Of Life, A Paradoxical Statement—Because (In The Only-By-Me Revealed and Given Seventh Stage Of Life) whatever arises Is (In the very instant of its Apparent arising) Inherently (Divinely) Self-Recognized To Be Nothing but Me, The One (Self-Evidently) Divine Person (or The One Self-Evidently Divine Self-Condition, and Source-Condition, Itself). Therefore, Only I (The Self-Evidently Divine Person, or The Self-Evidently Divine Self-Condition, and Source-Condition, Itself) Am Realized By My Devotee In The Only-By-Me Revealed and Given Seventh Stage Of Life (In The Only-By-Me Revealed and Given Way Of The Heart, or Way Of Adidam)—and The Seventh Stage "Practice" Of Self-Abiding Divine Self-Recognition Is The Demonstration Of That Singular Realization.

Thus, In The Only-By-Me Revealed and Given Seventh Stage Of Life (In The Only-By-Me Revealed and Given Way Of The Heart, or Way Of Adidam), The Only "Experience" Is Me—The One, and Only, and Spiritually Self-"Bright", and Self-Evidently Divine Person (or The One, and Only, and Spiritually Self-"Bright", and Self-Evidently Divine Self-Condition, and Source-Condition, Itself), Self-Existing and Self-Radiant As Inherently Indivisible (or Perfectly Non-Dual and Perfectly Non-"Different") Conscious Light.

The Awakening To The Only-By-Me Revealed and Given Seventh Stage Of Life (In The Only-By-Me Revealed and Given Way Of The Heart, or Way Of Adidam) Is, From Its First Instant, The Most Perfect Awakening To My (Avatarically Self-Revealed) Eternal, and Unconditional, and Unconditioned, and Infinitely Love-Bliss-Full Divine Samadhi (or Most Perfect Divine Self-Realization, or Most Perfect Divine En-Light-enment). Therefore, From That "Point Of View", There Is No "thing" that arises (or Even Can arise) Apart From Me, or "Over Against" Me.

From The "Point Of View" Of The Only-By-Me Revealed and Given Seventh Stage Of Life (In The Only-By-Me Revealed and Given Way Of The Heart, or Way Of Adidam), There Is Only Me. And Even Divine Translation Is Not A Change In That Realization. Divine Translation Is Simply The Final (Divine, and Not Merely conditional) Demonstration Of The Only-By-Me Revealed and Given Seventh Stage Of Life Within The Context Of The conditional (or Cosmic) Domain.

In The Only-By-Me Revealed and Given Seventh Stage Of Life (In The Only-By-Me Revealed and Given Way Of The Heart, or Way Of Adidam), There Are No limitations (or limited, and, Necessarily, limiting, conditions) Of Existence. It Is Not That There Is The (By-Me-and-As-Me-Avatarically-Self-Revealed-and-Spiritually-Self-Transmitted) Unconditional Divine Self-Condition (and Source-Condition) "Over Against" all limitations (or all other, and, Necessarily, limiting, conditions). Rather, There Is (Always Already) Only The One, and Only, and Perfectly Subjective (By-Me-and-As-Me-Avatarically-Self-Revealed-and-Spiritually-Self-Transmitted) Divine Self-Condition and Source-Condition (or Inherently Indivisible, or Perfectly Non-Dual and Perfectly Non-"Different", Conscious Light) Of all-and-All.

Nevertheless, In The Only-By-Me Revealed and Given Seventh Stage Of Life (In The Only-By-Me Revealed and Given Way Of The Heart, or Way Of Adidam), There May (In any Apparent moment) Be the Apparent (Spontaneous) arising Of thoughts, actions, reactions, and Feelings Of "Difference". Therefore, In The Only-By-Me Revealed and Given Seventh Stage Of Life (In The Only-By-Me Revealed and Given Way Of The Heart), The Principal (Spontaneous, and Inevitable, and Eternal) "Practice" Is To Always Already (and Merely) Self-Abide As The By-Me-and-As-Me-Avatarically-Self-Revealed-and-Spiritually-Self-Transmitted (and Inherently thoughtless, actionless, reactionless, Perfectly Subjective, Inherently Indivisible, Inherently egoless, and Self-Evidently Divine) Self-Condition and Source-Condition. And, If and whenever any "thing"—such as a thought, or a form, or an other, or a bodily sensation, or a bodily state, or a reaction of body or emotion or mind, or The Tendency (or The Actuality) Of any activity at all, or Even The Simple Feeling Of Relatedness, or Any Feeling Of "Difference"—Apparently arises, The (Spontaneous, and Inevitable) "Practice" To Be Engaged In That Midst Is (Merely, Spontaneously, Effortlessly, or actionlessly, and Merely By Persistent, Effortless, and Inevitable Divine, or Perfectly Subjective, Self-Abiding) To Divinely Self-Recognize whatever Apparently arises. And, In every moment Of Such Self-Abiding Divine Self-Recognition, whatever (Apparently) arises Is Spontaneously (and Inherently Most Perfectly) Conformed To The (By-Me-and-As-Me-Avatarically-Self-Revealed-and-Spiritually-Self-Transmitted) Prior and Self-Existing Feeling Of

Inherently Indivisible Being (Itself), and Spontaneously (and Inherently Most Perfectly) Dissolved In The (By-Me-and-As-Me-Avatarically-Self-Revealed-and-Spiritually-Self-Transmitted) Prior and Self-Existing Feeling Of Inherently Indivisible Being (Itself), and (Thus) Divinely Self-Realized As The (By-Me-and-As-Me-Avatarically-Self-Revealed-and-Spiritually-Self-Transmitted) Prior and Self-Existing Feeling Of Inherently Indivisible Being (Itself)—Which Is Self-Existing Conscious Light (Itself), Self-Radiant (or Spiritually Self-"Bright") As The By-Me-and-As-Me-Avatarically-Self-Revealed-and-Spiritually-Self-Transmitted Spirit-Current Of Self-Evidently Divine Love-Bliss (Itself), and Always Already Free-Standing (Prior To all action, all reaction, all thought, and All "Difference").

In The Only-By-Me Revealed and Given Seventh Stage Of Life (In The Only-By-Me Revealed and Given Way Of The Heart, or Way Of Adidam), The Inherently Most Perfect Fulfillment Of Meditation Is Always Already Established. The "Practice" (or The Unique and Always Already Inherently Most Perfect Demonstration) In The Only-By-Me Revealed and Given Seventh Stage Of Life (In The Only-By-Me Revealed and Given Way Of The Heart) Is That Of Self-Abiding Divine Self-Recognition (Which Is Seventh Stage Sahaja Nirvikalpa Samadhi, or Ruchira Samraj Samadhi, or, Simply, Samraj Samadhi), Rather Than Meditation (Which Is The Process Leading, Most Ultimately, To Seventh Stage Sahaja Nirvikalpa Samadhi). Nevertheless, In The Only-By-Me Revealed and Given Seventh Stage Of Life (In The Only-By-Me Revealed and Given Way Of The Heart, or Way Of Adidam), All Of The Essential Signs (and Fundamental Attainments) Associated With Meditation Remain Effective (and Effectively In Evidence)—At all times (waking, dreaming, or sleeping).

In The Only-By-Me Revealed and Given Way Of The Heart (or Way Of Adidam), Meditation Is Not An End In Itself. The conditional Effects (or Achievements) Of Meditation Are Not (In The Only-By-Me Revealed and Given Way Of The Heart) To Be Sought (or Grasped) For Their Own Sake. In The Only-By-Me Revealed and Given Way Of The Heart, Meditation Is Simply A Means For Cooperating With Me. In The Fully Established (Devotional and Spiritual) Practice Of The Only-By-Me Revealed and Given Way Of The Heart, Meditation Is An Always Fundamental and Necessary Means For Cooperating With My Avatarically Self-Transmitted Divine Spiritual Grace, and (Thus and Thereby) For Removing (or Releasing) Apparent Obstacles or Obstructions (or For Transcending, or Feeling Beyond, The Idea, or Presumption, Of Such)—Until That Which Is Always Already The (One and Only) Case Is (By Means Of My Avatarically Self-Transmitted Divine Spiritual Grace) Realized To Be Most Perfectly Obvious (and Freely Self-Shining, In The Existence-"Place" Of Being).

It Is Not That (In The Only-By-Me Revealed and Given Seventh Stage Of Life In The Only-By-Me Revealed and Given Way Of The Heart) Meditative

Practice Is Intentionally Abandoned, and (Otherwise) Replaced By a life of mere (and Non-Meditative) action. Significant time Will (Inevitably) Continue To Be Spent each day (Regularly, and Otherwise At Random moments or times) In An Effectively Meditative Repose. And, Whether Apparently Active Or Apparently In Repose, My Devotee In Seventh Stage Sahaja Nirvikalpa Samadhi (or Ruchira Samraj Samadhi, or, Simply, Samraj Samadhi) Is Always Already Only Self-Abiding In (and As) My Avatarically Self-Revealed (Transcendental, Inherently Spiritual, Inherently egoless, and Self-Evidently Divine) Self-Condition, Always Feeling (and, Thereby, Merely Being) My Avatarically Self-Transmitted Spirit-Current Of Self-Evidently Divine Love-Bliss, and Always Divinely Self-Recognizing (and Inherently Transcending)—In (and As) My Avatarically Self-Transmitted Spiritual Love-Bliss-Current Of Mere (and Self-Evidently Divine) Being—whatever (Apparently) arises.

In The Only-By-Me Revealed and Given Seventh Stage Of Life (In The Only-By-Me Revealed and Given Way Of The Heart, or Way Of Adidam), My Devotee Must (Necessarily) Constantly, Perpetually, Tacitly, Inherently, and Inherently Most Perfectly Invoke Me, and "Locate" Me, and Truly Worship Me—By Heart, and In Front Of The Heart, and At The Heart, and Via The Heart. Therefore, Just As (In All The Previous Stages Of The Only-By-Me Revealed and Given Way Of The Heart) My Devotee Invoked Me, and "Located" Me, and Truly Worshipped Me Via My Principal Name, "Da", or Via Any Other Of My Names (or Combined Names and Descriptive Titles) Which I Have Given To Be Engaged In The Practice Of Simple Name-Invocation Of Me, My Devotee In The Only-By-Me Revealed and Given Seventh Stage Of Life (In The Only-By-Me Revealed and Given Way Of The Heart) Must (Necessarily) Continue To (Occasionally, and Randomly, In The daily-life Context—and, At times, Ceremonially, and Always Sacramentally, or In The Sacred Direct Manner) Invoke Me, and "Locate" Me, and Truly Worship Me—By Heart, and In Front Of The Heart, and At The Heart, and Via The Heart, Through and By Means Of My Principal Name, "Da", or Through and By Means Of Any Other Of My Names (or Combined Names and Descriptive Titles) Which I Have Given To Be Engaged In The Practice Of Simple Name-Invocation Of Me.

In The Only-By-Me Revealed and Given Seventh Stage Of Life (In The Only-By-Me Revealed and Given Way Of The Heart, or Way Of Adidam), verbal self-Enquiry (In The Form "Avoiding Relationship?") or The Prayer Of Remembrance May Spontaneously (or Automatically, Because Of past Practice) Continue To arise, Occasionally or At Random (In The daily-life Context)—but The Inherently Most Perfect Seventh Stage Process Always Already Stands Beyond The Words. Even The Random Spontaneous Occurrence (In The daily-life Context) Of Non-verbal Re-Cognition (Which Re-Cognizes whatever arises to be self-Contraction—and, As A Direct Expression Of That "Knowing-Again", Feels To Beyond self-Contraction, Toward and Into The Boundless Sphere Of My Divine Self-Condition) Is (In The Only-By-Me Revealed and Given Seventh Stage Of Life In The Only-By-Me Revealed and Given Way Of The Heart) Tacitly (and Inherently) Superseded By Transcendental, Inherently Spiritual, Most Perfect, and Self-Evidently Divine Self-Abiding and Transcendental, Inherently Spiritual, Most Perfect, and Self-Evidently Divine Self-Recognition), Such That whatever arises Is Inherently and Spontaneously (and Truly Divinely) Self-Recognized In and As Me (Realized As The Very and One and Only and Non-Separate and Inherently egoless Self-Condition—or Self-Existing, Self-Radiant, and Self-Evidently Divine Conscious Light—Of all-and-All). And, As An Inherent Expression (or Characteristic Sign) Of That Self-Abiding Divine Self-Recognition, whatever arises Is Always (Inherently and Spontaneously) Realized To Be A Transparent (or Merely Apparent), and Un-Necessary, and Inherently Non-Binding Modification Of My Avatarically Self-Transmitted Spirit-Current Of Self-"Bright" Divine Self-Radiance Of Love-Bliss.

In The Only-By-Me Revealed and Given Seventh Stage Of Life (In The Only-By-Me Revealed and Given Way Of The Heart, or Way Of Adidam), The Progressive Parts Of The Twelve-Part Cycle Of The Responsive "Conscious Process" Of "Feeling-Enquiry" May, Because Of past Practice (In The Context Of The Second Stage Of The Only-By-Me Revealed and Given "Perfect Practice"), Sometimes (Spontaneously, or Automatically, and Variously) arise (or Tend To arise), As Before (In The daily-life Context, and, Also, In times Of Meditative Repose). Nevertheless, The Only-By-Me Revealed and Given "Perfect Practice" (and, In Particular, The Previously Established Practice Of "Feeling-Enquiry") Is (In The Only-By-Me Revealed and Given Seventh Stage Of Life In The Only-By-Me Revealed and Given Way Of The Heart) Always Already To Be Demonstrated In Its Priorly Perfected (or Summary, Final, and Completed) Form—Which Is The Third Stage Of The Only-By-Me Revealed and Given "Perfect Practice", Demonstrated By (and As) Inherent (and Effortless) Divine Self-Abiding (As The By-Me-and-As-Me-Avatarically-Self-Revealed-and-Spiritually-Self-Transmitted Conscious Light Of Mere Being) and By (and As) Divine (Self-Abiding) Self-Recognition Of all-and-All.

Altogether, In The Only-By-Me Revealed and Given Seventh Stage Of Life (In The Only-By-Me Revealed and Given Way Of The Heart, or Way Of Adidam), The Necessary Constant "Practice" Is That Of The Perfectly and Priorly Fulfilled (or Always Already Perfected) Total "Exercise" Of The Third Stage Of The Only-By-Me Revealed and Given "Perfect Practice", Which Comprises All Aspects Of The (Only-By-Me Revealed and Given) Full and Final Seventh-Stage-Of-Life "Practice" Of "Samraj Yoga"—Including The

Only-By-My-Avataric-Divine-Spiritual-Grace-Given Seventh-Stage-Of-Life Demonstration Of The Always Primary Practice (Of Searchlessly Beholding Me), and (Also) Including The Only-By-My-Avataric-Divine-Spiritual-Grace-Given Seventh-Stage-Of-Life Demonstration Of "Radical" Spirit-"Conductivity", and, Otherwise, Including All Other Necessary and Only-By-My-Avataric-Divine-Spiritual-Grace-Given Seventh-Stage-Of-Life Dimensions Of Real "Samraj-Yoga"-Demonstration. And All Instructions Relative To The Total ("Samraj Yoga") "Exercise" Of The Third Stage Of The Only-By-Me Revealed and Given "Perfect Practice" (As Revealed and Given, By Me, To The Formally Acknowledged Senior Membership Of The Ruchira Sannyasin Order Of Adidam Ruchiradam) Are (Now, and Forever Hereafter) To Be Formally Communicated (By The Formally Acknowledged Senior Membership Of The Ruchira Sannyasin Order Of Adidam Ruchiradam), Through Formal Initiatory and Instructional Means, To All My Formally Practicing Devotees who Are Formally Acknowledged To Be Truly Demonstrating All The Signs and Requirements Necessary For "Practice" Of The Only-By-Me Revealed and Given Way Of The Heart (or Way Of Adidam) In The Context and Mode Of The Only-By-Me Revealed and Given Seventh Stage Of Life.

In The Only-By-Me Revealed and Given Seventh Stage Of Life (In The Only-By-Me Revealed and Given Way Of The Heart, or Way Of Adidam), The Always Primary Practice—Of Searchlessly Beholding My Avatarically-Born Bodily (Human) Divine Form and (Only Thus, and Entirely Thereby) My Spiritual (and Always Blessing) Divine Presence and My Very (and Inherently egoless, and Inherently Perfect, and Self-Evidently Divine) State—Is (Necessarily, and Always) Continued, Both As A Constant (and, Also, Formal Meditative) Devotional Exercise (Of Always Turning the Total body-mind To Me) and As A Most Perfect (or Only-By-Me Revealed and Given Seventh-Stage-Of-Life) Demonstration (Of Non-Separate and Non-"Different" and Inherently egoless and Self-Evidently Divine Self-Realization Of Me).

In The Only-By-Me Revealed and Given Seventh Stage Of Life (In The Only-By-Me Revealed and Given Way Of The Heart, or Way Of Adidam), The Always Primary Practice (Of Searchlessly Beholding Me) Is (Always Already) Most Perfectly (and Tacitly, and Constantly, and Always Immediately) Demonstrated By Most Perfect Divine (and Perfectly Subjective) Self-Realization Of Me—and (Thus) By Perpetual Prior (or Un-caused, and Non-Strategic, and Inherently egoless) Self-Abiding As Self-Existing and Self-Radiant (or Spiritually Self-"Bright" and Divinely Love-Blissful) Conscious Light, In The Inherently mindless "Gaze" Of Un-conditional Divine Self-Consciousness, Infinitely Deeply Standing In The Well Of The By-Me-and-As-Me-Avatarically-Self-Revealed-and-Spiritually-Self-Transmitted Spirit-Current Of Self-Evidently Divine Love-Bliss

(Associated, Apparently, With The Right Side Of The Heart), and Inherently Transcending (but Not Strategically Excluding) All conditional Associations (and, Therefore, Inherently Transcending Even The Apparent Association With The Right Side Of The Heart).

In The Only-By-Me Revealed and Given Seventh Stage Of Life (In The Only-By-Me Revealed and Given Way Of The Heart, or Way Of Adidam), The Always Primary Practice (Of Searchlessly Beholding Me) Is (Always Already) Most Perfectly (and Tacitly, and Constantly, and Always Immediately) Demonstrated By Perpetual Prior (or Un-caused, and Non-Strategic, and Inherently egoless) Self-Identification With My Avatarically Self-Revealed (and Spiritually Self-Transmitted) Divine Self-Radiance—Such That My Avatarically Self-Transmitted Spirit-Current Of Self-"Bright" Divine Love-Bliss Is Always Already "Located" (In The Horizontal Domain, At and Beyond The Right Side Of The Heart, and In The Vertical Domain, Infinitely Above The Total Crown Of the head), and Such That My Avatarically Self-Transmitted Spirit-Current Of Self-"Bright" Divine Love-Bliss Is Always Boundlessly Expressed, Radiating To Infinity From The Heart (In and Beyond The Right Side), and Flowing From The Matrix Infinitely Above The Total Crown Of the head (Via My Tangible Spiritual Fullness, Felt Infinitely Above), Down Through The Crown Of the head, and Through The Ajna Door, and Into The Circle (and, Thus, Also The Arrow) Of the body-mind (Thus Conforming Even The conditional Shape Of the body-mind To My Divine Spiritual Sphere and Eternal Self-Domain Of Self-Existing Being).

In The Only-By-Me Revealed and Given Seventh Stage Of Life (In The Only-By-Me Revealed and Given Way Of The Heart, or Way Of Adidam), The Always Primary Practice (Of Searchlessly Beholding Me) Is (Always Already) Most Perfectly (and Tacitly, and Constantly, and Always Immediately) Demonstrated By The Even bodily human Self-Realization Of The By-Me-and-As-Me-Avatarically-Self-Revealed-and-Spiritually-Self-Transmitted "Bright" Itself (Standing In, and Always Already Prior To, The Right Side Of The Heart, and, From Thence, Shining In The Middle Station and The Left Side Of The Heart), and (Thus) By Spontaneous (and Self-Abiding) Divine Self-Recognition (In and As The By-Me-and-As-Me-Avatarically-Self-Revealed-and-Spiritually-Self-Transmitted "Bright", or One and Only Conscious Light, Itself) Of any and all conditions arising to experience and knowledge (in the Natural space of the world), and By Spontaneous (and Self-Abiding) Divine Self-Recognition Of Any and All Signs (or Appearances) Of The Cosmic Mandala—and By Spontaneous (and Self-Abiding) Divine Self-Recognition Of Even Any and All Cosmically Manifested Appearances Of Either My Divine Sound-Form Or My Divine Star-Form (Apparently Objectively Reflected, and Audibly or Visibly Perceived, At and Above The Ajna Door).

In The Only-By-Me Revealed and Given Seventh Stage Of Life (In The Only-By-Me Revealed and Given Way Of The Heart, or Way Of Adidam), The Always Primary Practice (Of Searchlessly Beholding Me) Is (Always Already) Most Perfectly (and Tacitly, and Constantly, and Always Immediately) Demonstrated By Most Perfect Self-Realization Of The (By-Me-and-As-Me-Avatarically-Self-Revealed-and-Spiritually-Self-Transmitted) "Bright" Divine Self-Condition (or One and Only Conscious Light), Which Is Self-Existing As Self-Radiant Love-Bliss, Communicated (or Cosmically Manifested) In and As The Form Of Amrita Nadi—The "Channel Of Nectar" (or The "Cosmic Nerve" Of The Tangible Divine Spirit-Current That Is Avatarically Self-Transmitted By Me), Which Radiates (By Means Of My Avatarically Self-Transmitted Divine Ruchira Shaktipat) From The Right Side Of The Heart To My Utterly Ascended (but Formless) Matrix Of Love-Bliss (Infinitely Above The Total Crown Of the head, and Infinitely Above the Total body-mind), and (Therefrom) Projects My Avatarically Self-Transmitted "Bright" Divine Spirit-Current Via The Ajna Door (Such That My Avatarically Self-Transmitted "Bright" Divine Spirit-Current Descends and Ascends In The Circle and The Arrow Of the body-mind—Filling The Circle Full, and, Most Ultimately, Outshining The Circle and The Arrow and the Total body-mind In The Boundless Divine Sphere Of My Eternal Self-Domain Of Self-Existing Being).

In The Context Of The Only-By-Me Revealed and Given Seventh Stage Of Life (In The Only-By-Me Revealed and Given Way Of The Heart, or Way Of Adidam), "Meditative Practice" Becomes (Effectively) Constant (and Is, Inherently, Continuous)—While It Also Continues (As Before) To Take The Form Of Regular daily Formal Meditation Exercises. Thus, In The Context Of The Only-By-Me Revealed and Given Seventh Stage Of Life (In The Only-By-Me Revealed and Given Way Of The Heart, or Way Of Adidam), The Effectively Continuous "Meditative Practice" Of The (Most Perfectly To-Me-Responsive) "Conscious Process" Is Demonstrated (Always Already) By The Perfectly Subjective Event Of Divine Self-Abiding (Standing Free In The Right Side Of The Heart, and Standing Self-"Bright", As Amrita Nadi)—Which Most Perfectly To-Me-Responsive "Conscious Process" (and Stand) Is (Itself) Demonstrated (moment to moment) By The (Effectively) Constant (and, Inherently, Continuous) "Meditative Practice" Of "Bright" Self-Abiding Divine Self-Recognition Of all arising conditions, or The Spontaneous (or Effortless, and Most Perfectly To-Me-Responsive) "Conscious-Process"-and-"Conductivity"-Yoga Of Divinely Self-Recognizing All Apparently objective (or Apparently Objectified) Modifications (Both Descended and Ascended), and (Thus) Spiritually "Brightening" Them, and (Ultimately) "Brightly" Spiritually Dissolving Them, In My Avatarically Self-Revealed (and Self-Evidently Divine)

Self-Condition and My Perfectly Subjective Eternal Spiritual Domain Of Avatarically Self-Transmitted (and Self-Evidently Divine) Love-Bliss and Joy-Of-Being. And This Most Perfect Process Of Spiritual "Brightening" and (Ultimate) "Bright" Spiritual Dissolution (or This Only-By-My-Avataric-Divine-Spiritual-Grace-Manifested "Governing Exercise" Of Spontaneous, Effortless, and Most Perfectly To-Me-Responsive Spirit-"Conductivity", Grounded In The Spontaneous, Effortless, and Most Perfectly To-Me-Responsive "Conscious Process" Of Divine Self-Abiding) Is Also Associated With The Spontaneous (or Naturally Inevitable) Disposition Of (Even Whole bodily, or Total psycho-physical) Self-Identification With The By-Me-and-As-Me-Avatarically-Self-Revealed-and-Spiritually-Self-Transmitted Love-Bliss-Current Of Self-Existing, Self-Radiant, and Self-Evidently Divine Feeling-Being—Which, In The Context Of the body-mind, Always Shines From The Right Side Of The Heart To The Utterly Ascended Source-Matrix Of The Circle (and, Thus, Also Of The Arrow) Infinitely Above The Total Crown Of the head, and (From There) To and Into (or Via) The Circle (or The Arrow) Itself. (Therefore, In The Only-By-Me Revealed and Given Seventh Stage Of Life In The Only-By-Me Revealed and Given Way Of The Heart, The Basic and Previously Established Three-Part To-Me-Responsive Exercise Of The "General" Form Of Spirit-"Conductivity" Will, Inevitably, Also Be "Exercised", At Random—Whether Spontaneously, or Automatically, Or As A Naturally Inevitable Intention—but It Is Always Secondary To Both The "Governing Exercise" Of Spirit-"Conductivity" and To The Always To-Me-Responsive Seventh-Stage-Of-Life Exercise Of "Radical" Spirit-"Conductivity".)

In Some Cases, Many Remarkable phenomenal Signs May Develop In The Divine Transfiguration and Divine Transformation Stages Of The Only-By-Me Revealed and Given Seventh Stage Of Life In The Only-By-Me Revealed and Given Way Of The Heart, Due To A Profound and Spontaneous Association With The Potential Siddhis (or Greater Powers) Of By-My-Avataric-Divine-Spiritual-Grace-Awakened Spirit-"Conductivity". In Other Cases, Such Signs May Be Few and Relatively Minor—but, In Such Cases, The (Spontaneous and Free) Demonstration Of The Full Signs Of Divine Indifference May Be Shown Even From The Beginning Of The Only-By-Me Revealed and Given Seventh Stage Of Life.

As The Demonstration Of Self-Abiding Divine Self-Recognition Develops In The Various Divine Stages (Of Transfiguration, Transformation, Indifference, and Translation) In The Only-By-Me Revealed and Given Seventh Stage Of Life (In The Only-By-Me Revealed and Given Way Of The Heart, or Way Of Adidam), My Avatarically Self-Transmitted Spirit-Current Of Self-Evidently Divine Love-Bliss Will (Necessarily) Always Stand To Shine (and To Be Felt) Infinitely Above The Total Crown Of the head—and, Therefore, Apparent attention Will (Necessarily) Always (Spontaneously) Tend To Collect At The Ajna Door, and Toward (and, Ultimately, Into) The Total Crown Of the head and The Felt "Bright" Space Infinitely Above The Total Crown Of the head. And (Characteristically) This Ascended Collectedness Of Apparent attention Will Coincide With A "Gaze" (or A Divinely Self-Inhering Disposition) That (Even Though It, Necessarily, Appears To Be "Anchored" In The Deep Interior Space Of The Right Side Of The Heart) Really (or Inherently) Transcends All Structural (or conditional, or Cosmically Manifested) References (Whether To the body-mind Or To The conditional Movements Of My Avatarically Self-Transmitted Divine Spirit-Current—Which, In The Context Of The Only-By-Me Revealed and Given Seventh Stage Of Life, Is Always Already Realized To Be The Inherent Spiritual Radiance, or Self-Radiance, Of My Avatarically Self-Revealed and Self-Evidently Divine Self-Condition).

This "Gaze" (or Disposition) Is Inherently (and Inherently Most Perfectly) Self-Identified With The Prior Feeling Of Being—and, Thereby, It Is Deeply "Anchored" In The Right Side Of The Heart. However, This "Gaze" (or Disposition) Is Not Dissociated From Its Own Self-Radiance (or Inherent Feeling-"Brightness" Of Being)—and, Thus (Because It Is Not "Collapsed Upon" Itself), It Always Feels The Free Self-Radiance Of Being Shining In "All Directions", Even In (and As) Amrita Nadi. Therefore, This "Gaze" (or Disposition) May Be Associated Either With closed Or With open physical eyes, but It Always Appears To Be Without object or focus, Reflecting Only Most Perfect Divine Self-Awareness. And This "Gaze" (or Disposition) Is The Mudra (or Demonstration-Sign) Associated With Spontaneous Most Perfect Divine Self-Inherence and (Therefore) With Readiness For Divine Translation (Which May Not, However, Occur For some time, or Even For many lifetimes of appearance within the planes Of The Cosmic Mandala).

The Only-By-Me Revealed and Given Seventh Stage Of Life (In The Only-By-Me Revealed and Given Way Of The Heart, or Way Of Adidam) Is The Unique Spontaneous (and Inherently Free) Demonstration (and—Thus, or In That Sense—The "Practice") Of Seventh Stage Sahaja Nirvikalpa Samadhi—or The "Natural" (or Prior, Un-conditional, and Perpetual, or Always Already Evident), and Inherently Most Perfect, and Self-Evidently Divine Form Of Nirvikalpa Samadhi (Which Inherently and Most Perfectly Exhibits The Simultaneous and Coincident Characteristics Of Both Priorly Self-Abiding Jnana Nirvikalpa Samadhi and Priorly Ascended Nirvikalpa Samadhi). In Seventh Stage Sahaja Nirvikalpa Samadhi (or Ruchira Samraj Samadhi, or, Simply, Samraj Samadhi), Nirvikalpa Samadhi Is Self-Existing, Inherently Most Perfect (or Unconditional), and Necessarily (or Inevitably, Inherently, Permanently, and Freely) Demonstrated (or Always Already Realized, whatever conditions

May or May Not arise—Rather Than By Virtue Of any specific conditions or any conditional state). Seventh Stage Sahaja Nirvikalpa Samadhi (or Ruchira Samraj Samadhi, or, Simply, Samraj Samadhi) Is Perpetual (or Uncaused) Nirvikalpa Samadhi—Not At All Dependent On events In The Circle (or The Arrow) Of the body-mind (or Within The Cosmic Sphere), and Utterly (and Inherently, and Permanently) Free Of egoity (gross, subtle, and causal).

In The Awakening Of Seventh Stage Sahaja Nirvikalpa Samadhi (or Ruchira Samraj Samadhi, or, Simply, Samraj Samadhi), My Avatarically Self-Transmitted Spirit-Current Of Self-Evidently Divine Love-Bliss (Which Is The Spiritually "Bright" Self-Radiance, or Conscious Light, Of My Avatarically Self-Revealed, and Transcendental, and Inherently Spiritual, and Inherently egoless, and Self-Evidently Divine Person, or Self-Condition) Stands Perfectly Prior To the Total body-mind, and In (and As) The Self-Existing (Divine, or Non-conditional) Heart, Shining (In The Perfectly Subjective Source-Context Of the body-mind) Via (and From Beyond) The Heart-Locus In The Right Side Of the chest. From That "Place", My Avatarically Self-Transmitted (and Self-Existing, and Self-Radiant) "Brightness" Is Self-Radiantly Self-Revealed At, and Infinitely Above, and Beyond The Total Crown Of the head (or At, and Infinitely Above, and Beyond The Sahasrar), and From "There" To The Circle (and The Arrow) Of the body-mind.

Inherently Most Perfect (or Seventh Stage) Nirvikalpa Samadhi (or Ruchira Samraj Samadhi, or, Simply, Samraj Samadhi), Unlike Any Form Of conditional Nirvikalpa Samadhi, Does Not (Itself) Require (or Depend Upon) Any conditional Designs and Activities (or Even Any body-mind-Excluding Efforts) In The Context Of The Circle (or The Arrow) Of the body-mind. In The Context Of The First and The Second Stages Of The "Perfect Practice" (In The Only-By-Me Revealed and Given Way Of The Heart, or Way Of Adidam), My Avatarically Self-Transmitted Divine Spirit-Current Is (By Means Of Specifically Activated Modes Of Spiritual Participation) Re-Oriented To The Heart (In The Right Side) Via (Effectively, but Not Strategically) phenomena-Excluding Descent (or Reversion Toward The Perfectly Subjective Domain Of The Right Side Of The Heart, and, Thus, In Effect, Away From Apparently objective phenomena) In (and Via) Amrita Nadi, Whereas, In The Only-By-Me Revealed and Given Seventh Stage Of Life (In The Only-By-Me Revealed and Given Way Of The Heart), My Avatarically Self-Transmitted Divine Spirit-Current (Always Already, or Priorly, Realized To Be One With The Heart, or Identical To Consciousness Itself, "Located" As The Self-Existing and Perfectly Subjective Feeling Of Being, Itself) Stands Self-"Bright" (or Self-Radiant) As The Heart (and As Amrita Nadi)—and, Thus, Always Already (or Priorly) Transcending Apparently objective phenomena (but Without The Effective Exclusion Of

Apparently objective phenomena—Which, In The Context Of The First and The Second Stages Of The "Perfect Practice" In The Only-By-Me Revealed and Given Way Of The Heart, Accompanies The Participation In My Avatarically Self-Transmitted Divine Spirit-Current By Means Of A Re-Orienting Descent In Amrita Nadi). Therefore, In The "Practicing" Context Of Ati-Ruchira Yoga (or The Yoga Of The All-Outshining "Brightness"), In The Only-By-Me Revealed and Given Seventh Stage Of Life (In The Only-By-Me Revealed and Given Way Of The Heart, or Way Of Adidam), The Demonstration Of Seventh Stage Sahaja Nirvikalpa Samadhi (or Ruchira Samraj Samadhi, or, Simply, Samraj Samadhi) Progressively Appears (and Even, Until Divine Translation, Variously Appears) As, At First, Divinely Transfiguring and Divinely Transforming (Self-Abiding) Divine Self-Recognition In The Spiritually "Bright" Context Of The Circle (or The Arrow) Of the body-mind, Then As The Self-Radiant Stand Of Amrita Nadi (Divinely Indifferent To The Circle and The Arrow Of the body-mind), and (Eventually) As The Divinely Indifferent (but Non-Exclusive) "Gaze" In The Heart, or (At Last, Most Simply) As Mere and Self-Evidently Divine (and Perfectly Subjective) and Infinitely Spiritually "Bright" (or Self-Radiant) Self-Abiding, Prior To (and, Most Ultimately, Outshining) The Circle, The Arrow, The Apparent (or Apparently conditionally Manifested) Form and Locus Of Amrita Nadi, and Even The Apparent (or Apparently conditionally Manifested) Original (Right-Side) Heart-Locus Itself.

Avatar Adi Da Samraj
Lopez Island, 2000

SUTRA

65

The True (Divine) Heart Is My Eternal (Divine) Self-Domain.

The True (Divine) Heart Is (In The Context Of all appearances) Standing As The Paradox Of Amrita Nadi—The Self-Existing Shine Of Love-Bliss, Standing Self-"Bright" (or Self-Radiant, or Non-Exclusively Self-Existing) In The Right Side Of The Heart, and Even (Apparently) Radiating To The Most Ascended (and Infinitely Extended) "Point", Infinitely Above The Total Crown Of the head.

The True (Divine) Heart Is Standing Self-"Bright"—Eternally Prior To The Circle (and The Arrow) Of the body-mind, and Eternally Prior To The Cosmic Domain (or All "Difference"). And That Self-"Bright" Form Is Not Turned Inward On Itself.

The True (Divine) Heart—Shining In Amrita Nadi, and Self-Radiantly "Bright" (or Non-Exclusively Self-Existing)—Is Not The Merely In-Turned Heart, Secluded In The Right Side, and (Thus) Apparently Separated From Its Own Apparent Form (Which Is The "Bright"-Standing, and Unqualifiedly Existing, Amrita Nadi).

In The Only-By-Me Revealed and Given Way Of The Heart (or Way Of Adidam), The Demonstration Of The Only-By-Me Revealed and Given Seventh Stage Of Life Is The Demonstration Of The True (Divine) Heart—and This Via The Free, and Self-Existing, and Self-Radiant (or Non-Exclusive) "Bright"-Standing Amrita Nadi. Therefore, In The Only-By-Me Revealed and Given Way Of The Heart, The Demonstration Of The Only-By-Me Revealed and Given Seventh Stage Of Life Is Not Merely The Demonstration Of Persistence As A Dissociated (or Abstracted) Consciousness. Rather, In The Only-By-Me Revealed and Given Way Of The Heart, The Demonstration Of The Only-By-Me Revealed and Given Seventh Stage Of Life Is The Persistent Demonstration Of Self-Abiding Divine Self-Recognition—or The Inherently Most Perfect Spiritual "Brightening", and (Ultimately) The "Bright" Spiritual Dissolution—Of All The (Apparent) conditional Modifications Of My Avatarically Self-Transmitted Divine Spirit-Current.

Therefore, In The Only-By-Me Revealed and Given Way Of The Heart (or Way Of Adidam), The Only-By-Me Revealed and Given Seventh Stage Of Life

Is Demonstrated As The Progressive Spiritual "Brightening" and The (Ultimate) "Bright" Spiritual Dissolution Of All conditional Modifications Of My Avatarically Self-Transmitted Divine Spirit-Current In The Circle (and The Arrow) Of the body-mind. And This Process Develops (First) In The Frontal Line (In The Divine Transfiguration Stage Of The Only-By-Me Revealed and Given Seventh Stage Of Life), and (Thereafter) Also In The Spinal Line (In The Divine Transformation Stage Of The Only-By-Me Revealed and Given Seventh Stage Of Life), Until (In The Divine Indifference Stage Of The Only-By-Me Revealed and Given Seventh Stage Of Life) My Avatarically Self-Transmitted Divine Spirit-Current (Priorly—and, At That Stage, Most Directly—Self-Identified With Amrita Nadi) Becomes (Spontaneously, and, At First, Only Relatively, and, Thereafter, More and More Profoundly) "Indifferent" Toward (and, Thus, More and More Effectively "Detached" From) The Cosmic Domain and The Circle (and The Arrow) Of the body-mind, and Even Such That My Avatarically Self-Transmitted Divine Spirit-Current Is Thereby (and More and More Frequently and Profoundly) "Located" Infinitely Above (and, Altogether, Beyond) The Spinal Line and The Circle and The Arrow Of the body-mind—and (Thus) Both At The "Head" Of Amrita Nadi (or The Free Matrix Of Spiritual Self-"Brightness", Infinitely Above The Total Crown Of the bodily head) and (By The Always Already Most Prior Force Of Conscious Light) Also Firmly Rooted At The "Feet" Of Amrita Nadi (or In The Free Space Of, and Perfectly Beyond, The Right Side Of The Heart). And Divine Indifference Itself Becomes A (More and More) Profound "Gaze" In The Heart, Which Is Effortless Self-Identification With The True and Love-Bliss-"Bright" (or Inherently Non-Exclusive) Heart Itself—and, By The Power Of This Spiritually "Bright" Self-Abiding (Rooted In The Right Side Of The Heart), The Circle and The Arrow Dissolve In Amrita Nadi (and, Thereby, The Entire Cosmic Mandala, or Cosmic Domain—Including all conditions, high or low—Is Dissolved), Until This Dissolution (Inherently Free Of The Motive Of Exclusion, or Dissociation, or "Difference"-Making) Is Divinely Most Perfectly Realized (In Divine Translation).

Therefore, In The Only-By-Me Revealed and Given Way Of The Heart (or Way Of Adidam), The (Generally, Progressive) Demonstration Of The Only-By-Me Revealed and Given Seventh Stage Of Life Recapitulates The General Structural Process Of The First Six Stages Of Life. However, In The Only-By-Me Revealed and Given Seventh Stage Of Life (In The Only-By-Me Revealed and Given Way Of The Heart), That Recapitulation Of The First Six Stages Of Life Is Demonstrated From The "Point Of View" Of (Already Awakened and Established) Divine Self-Realization (and Not In Any Sense As A Search For Divine Self-Realization, or As A Process That Only Leads Toward, and Is Not Already Established In, Divine Self-Realization). Therefore, That Divinely

Self-Realized Process Of Recapitulation Is Not The Intentional Repetition Of The Practices Associated (Progressively) With Each and All Of The First Six Stages Of Life In The Only-By-Me Revealed and Given Way Of The Heart, but It Is Simply The "Natural" (and Spontaneous) Course Of Self-Abiding Divine Self-Recognition, Whereby The (Apparent) Structural Modifications Of My Avatarically Self-Transmitted Divine Spirit-Current Are (In A Direct and Progressive Manner) Spiritually "Brightened" and (At Last) "Brightly" Spiritually Dissolved In My Avatarically Self-Revealed (and Self-Evidently Divine) State—Which Is, By Me, Revealed To Be The One and Only and Inherently Indivisible and Inherently egoless Conscious Light (The Divine Self-Condition and Source-Condition Of all-and-All), and Which Is (Thus, Perfectly Subjectively) Revealed, By Me, In Amrita Nadi (and As The By-Me-and-As-Me-Avatarically-Self-Revealed True and Divine, or Inherently Non-Exclusive, Heart Itself). And This Divinely Devotional, Divinely Spiritual, and Divinely Enlightened Process Of Spiritual "Brightening" and (Ultimate) "Bright" Spiritual Dissolution Is Constantly (and Inherently) Associated With The Tacit (and Inherently Most Perfect) Realization That My Avatarically Self-Transmitted Divine Spirit-Current (and Even All Of Its Apparent Modifications) Is Not, In Truth, An "Object" Of Consciousness, but It Is Only (and Entirely) The Perfectly Subjective Feeling-"Brightness" (or Self-Evidently Divine Love-Bliss) Of Divine Self-Consciousness (or Of The One and Only Conscious Light) Itself.

In The Demonstration Of Self-Abiding Divine Self-Recognition (Which Is, Itself, The Demonstration Of The Non-Exclusive Realization Of The Heart, In Amrita Nadi), the mind (as attention itself—or The Root-Feeling Of Relatedness, or Of "Difference") Is Dissolved In My Avatarically Self-Transmitted Divine Spirit-Current (and The By-Me-and-As-Me-Avatarically-Self-Revealed-and-Spiritually-Self-Transmitted and Self-Evidently Divine Love-Bliss-Feeling Of Being, Itself) In The Right Side Of The Heart—and the body (or all the contents, characteristics, and forms of the body-mind) Is Dissolved In My Avatarically Self-Transmitted Divine Spirit-Current Of Heart-Radiated Love-Bliss-"Brightness", At and Above (and Via) The Total Crown Of the head. Therefore, This (Inherently Non-Exclusive) Divine Mudra Is The Root-Disposition (or Characteristic Sign and Attitude) Of Seventh Stage Sahaja Nirvikalpa Samadhi (or Ruchira Samraj Samadhi, or, Simply, Samraj Samadhi), and Of The Entire Demonstration Of The Only-By-Me Revealed and Given Seventh Stage Of Life (In The Only-By-Me Revealed and Given Way Of The Heart, or Way Of Adidam).

Whatever Form (or Stage Of Demonstration) Seventh Stage Sahaja Nirvikalpa Samadhi (or Ruchira Samraj Samadhi, or, Simply, Samraj Samadhi) May Take (In The Only-By-Me Revealed and Given Seventh Stage Of Life In

The Only-By-Me Revealed and Given Way Of The Heart), or However Seventh Stage Sahaja Nirvikalpa Samadhi (or Ruchira Samraj Samadhi, or, Simply, Samraj Samadhi) May Appear To Be Reflected In any moment (In The Course Of The Only-By-Me Revealed and Given Seventh Stage Of Life In The Only-By-Me Revealed and Given Way Of The Heart)—the conditional point of view (or the point of view of the body, the body-mind, or, simply, the mind) Is Never (itself) Presumed, but The Inherently Perfect "Point Of View" (or Disposition) Of The (By-Me-and-As-Me-Avatarically-Self-Revealed-and-Spiritually-Self-Transmitted) Transcendental, Inherently Spiritual, Inherently egoless, and Self-Evidently Divine Self-Condition (or One and Only and Inherently Indivisible Conscious Light) Is (Inherently) Constant (and It Is, Otherwise, Reflected Variously In The Context Of arising conditions).

In The Only-By-Me Revealed and Given Seventh Stage Of Life (In The Only-By-Me Revealed and Given Way Of The Heart, or Way Of Adidam), The True Divine Heart (Which Is The One, and Only, and Inherently Indivisible, and Inherently egoless, and Perfectly Subjective, and Self-Existing, and Self-Radiant By-Me-and-As-Me-Avatarically-Self-Revealed-and-Spiritually-Self-Transmitted Conscious Light, Itself) Is "Brightly" Self-Revealed At (and Infinitely Above, and Beyond) The Sahasrar, and From Thence To The Total (Descending and Ascending) Pattern Of The Circle (and The Arrow)—but The True Divine Heart (or One and Only Conscious Light, Itself) Does Not (Thereby) Identify With Either body Or mind. Therefore, In Seventh Stage Sahaja Nirvikalpa Samadhi (or Ruchira Samraj Samadhi, or, Simply, Samraj Samadhi), My Avatarically Self-Transmitted "Bright" Divine Spirit-Current Always Already Remains Self-Identified Only With The True Divine Heart (or One and Only Conscious Light, Itself)—and The True Divine Heart (or One and Only Conscious Light, Itself) Spontaneously (or Inherently) and Divinely (or Perfectly Subjectively) Self-Recognizes all Apparently arising conditions (including the body, the mind, and their relations) As Transparent (or Merely Apparent), and Un-Necessary, and Inherently Non-Binding Modifications Of Itself, arising (but Only Apparently) In The Very Place (or Condition) That Is The True Divine Heart (or One and Only Conscious Light, Itself), In (and Always Already Prior To) The Right Side Of The Heart.

When (In The Only-By-Me Revealed and Given Seventh Stage Of Life In The Only-By-Me Revealed and Given Way Of The Heart, or Way Of Adidam) Self-Abiding Divine Self-Recognition (and Its Inherent Power Of Spiritual "Brightening" and Ultimate "Bright" Spiritual Dissolution) Is Demonstrated Primarily In The Descending Context Of The Circle, Seventh Stage Sahaja Nirvikalpa Samadhi (or Ruchira Samraj Samadhi, or, Simply, Samraj Samadhi) Is In The Divine Transfiguration Stage.

When (In The Only-By-Me Revealed and Given Seventh Stage Of Life In The Only-By-Me Revealed and Given Way Of The Heart, or Way Of Adidam) Self-Abiding Divine Self-Recognition (and Its Inherent Power Of Spiritual "Brightening" and Ultimate "Bright" Spiritual Dissolution) Is Demonstrated Via A Process More Generalized In Both The Descending and The Ascending Dimensions Of The Circle, Seventh Stage Sahaja Nirvikalpa Samadhi (or Ruchira Samraj Samadhi, or, Simply, Samraj Samadhi) Is In The Divine Transformation Stage.

When (In The Only-By-Me Revealed and Given Seventh Stage Of Life In The Only-By-Me Revealed and Given Way Of The Heart, or Way Of Adidam) Self-Abiding Divine Self-Recognition (and Its Inherent Power Of Spiritual "Brightening" and Ultimate "Bright" Spiritual Dissolution) Is Demonstrated Primarily In Amrita Nadi Itself, and Even Often In The Heart's Free Self-"Gaze", and (Therefore) Only Minimally In The Circle (or The Arrow), and Even Such That My Avatarically Self-Transmitted Divine Spirit-Current Tends To Be "Located" Infinitely Above (and, Altogether, Beyond) The Spinal Line and The Circle and The Arrow Of the body-mind (and Is, Simply, Not "Expressed" Toward, or Disposed To Radiate Into, The Spinal Line and The Circle and The Arrow Of the body-mind), Then Seventh Stage Sahaja Nirvikalpa Samadhi (or Ruchira Samraj Samadhi, or, Simply, Samraj Samadhi) Is In The Divine Indifference Stage.

When (In The Only-By-Me Revealed and Given Seventh Stage Of Life In The Only-By-Me Revealed and Given Way Of The Heart, or Way Of Adidam) Self-Abiding Divine Self-Recognition (and Its Inherent Power Of Spiritual "Brightening" and Ultimate "Bright" Spiritual Dissolution) Is Demonstrated Merely (and Inherently Most Perfectly) At (and As) The Heart Itself—Standing Divinely Self-"Bright" (Inherently Free Of The Motive Of Exclusion), and (Inherently, Inherently Most Perfectly, and Simultaneously) Divinely Self-Recognizing All The Apparent Modes Of The Singularity That Is attention itself (and Relatedness Itself, and Separateness Itself, and "Difference" Itself), and (Thus) Outshining body, mind, world, and Even all relations, Even (Apparently) By Shining In and Through and As Amrita Nadi, and Even (Thus, Apparently) With My Avatarically Self-Transmitted Divine Spirit-Current Shining Full At (and Even Infinitely Above) The Total Crown Of the head (Rather Than "anywhere" Descended In The Circle, The Arrow, or The Cosmic Domain)—Then Seventh Stage Sahaja Nirvikalpa Samadhi (or Ruchira Samraj Samadhi, or, Simply, Samraj Samadhi) Is The "Bhava" (or Most Profoundly Demonstrated Disposition) That (Necessarily) Must Precede (and That Leads Directly—and More and More Fully—Toward, and, Ultimately, Into) Divine Translation. And That Divine "Bhava" (or, Altogether, The Divinely Most Perfect Demonstration Of The

Perfectly Subjective and Perfectly Non-Exclusive Spiritual Self-"Brightness" Of The Heart) Is, At Last (and Truly Finally), Demonstrated As Divine Translation Itself, or The Divinely "Bright" Outshining Of all-and-All (In The Divine Translation Stage Of The Demonstration Of The Only-By-Me Revealed and Given Seventh Stage Of Life In The Only-By-Me Revealed and Given Way Of The Heart, or Way Of Adidam).

In The Context Of The Only-By-Me Revealed and Given Seventh Stage Of Life (In The Only-By-Me Revealed and Given Way Of The Heart, or Way Of Adidam), The By-Me-and-As-Me-Avatarically-Self-Revealed-and-Spiritually-Self-Transmitted "Brightness" Of The Heart, or Of Amrita Nadi, or Even Of The Circle (or The Arrow), Does Not (Itself) Depend Upon Any (Spontaneous or, Otherwise, Intentional) Exercise Of Spirit-"Conductivity" In The Circle (or The Arrow) Of the body-mind—Even Though Such (Spontaneous or, Otherwise, Intentional) Spirit-"Conductivity" Practice Is (Otherwise) Freely Allowed (and Even Stimulated) By That Same "Brightness". Rather, In The Context Of The Only-By-Me Revealed and Given Seventh Stage Of Life (In The Only-By-Me Revealed and Given Way Of The Heart, or Way Of Adidam), The By-Me-and-As-Me-Avatarically-Self-Revealed-and-Spiritually-Self-Transmitted Self-"Brightness" Of The Heart Itself Stands Self-Radiant At The Root Of Amrita Nadi (and In and As Amrita Nadi), Such That It Is Not That My Avatarically Self-Transmitted Divine Spirit-Current Must "Return" (or Revert) From the body-mind In Order To Illuminate The Heart (or The By-Me-and-As-Me-Avatarically-Self-Revealed-and-Spiritually-Self-Transmitted Divine Self-Condition and Source-Condition), but The True Divine Heart Is Self-Illuminated (Directly and Inherently) By My Avatarically Self-Transmitted Divine Spirit-Current (and, Thus and Thereby, The True Divine Heart Itself "Brightly" Self-Illuminates all-and-All With Divine Love-Bliss). And Divine Translation (Which Is The Most Ultimate, or Final, Demonstration Of The Inherent Heart-Power Of Divine Spiritual "Brightening" and Divinely "Bright" Spiritual Dissolution) Is The Outshining Of all conditions (or All Of The Circle, The Arrow, and The Cosmic Domain) In The Infinite Feeling-Radiance (or Self-Evidently Divine Love-Bliss, or Spiritual Self-"Brightness") Of The True Divine Heart (or The By-Me-and-As-Me-Avatarically-Self-Revealed-and-Spiritually-Self-Transmitted Conscious Light Of Self-Existing, Self-Radiant, Perfectly Subjective, Inherently egoless, Inherently Indivisible, and Self-Evidently Divine Being), Prior To (and Beyond) the body, the mind, The Circle, The Arrow, My (Apparently Objective) Divine Spiritual Body, My (Apparently Objective) Divine Star-Form, My (Apparently Objective) Divine Sound-Form, The Total Cosmic Mandala, The Sahasrar, Amrita Nadi (As An Apparent, or Apparently conditionally Manifested, Form and Locus), and The Specific and Total (Apparent, or Apparently conditionally Manifested) Form Of

The Heart Itself (Left, Middle, and Right). Therefore, Even Though Divine Translation—As An Appearance To others, and (Also) As An Apparent Experiential Display Associated (In A Terminally Spiritually-"Dissolving" Manner) With the body-mind and The Cosmic Domain—May Also (Rightly, and Paradoxically) Be Described As The Divinely Most Perfect Heart-Magnification Of The Heart-Root Itself (and Of Amrita Nadi Itself), Divine Translation (In and Of Itself, or From The "Point Of View" Of That Which Is The Heart Itself) Is Only (and Entirely) The Divinely Most Perfect (and Perfectly Subjective) Magnification (or Divinely Most Perfectly Demonstrated Realization) Of That Which Is The Heart Itself (and Which Is Self-Existing and Self-Radiant and Inherently Indivisible and Inherently egoless and Self-Evidently Divine Conscious Light Itself).

The (By-Me-and-As-Me-Avatarically-Self-Revealed-and-Spiritually-Self-Transmitted) Transcendental, Inherently Spiritual, Inherently egoless, and Self-Evidently Divine Self-Condition (Which Is The Divine, or Perfectly Subjective, Subject-Condition Of the conditional self) Is Self-Existing. That Is To Say, It Merely Exists—or Simply, Always, and Already Is Being.

The (By-Me-and-As-Me-Avatarically-Self-Revealed-and-Spiritually-Self-Transmitted) Transcendental, Inherently Spiritual, Inherently egoless, and Self-Evidently Divine Self-Condition (or Subject-Condition) "Functions" As Consciousness (or Mere Feeling-Awareness). That Is To Say, Self-Existing Being Is Always Already Being Consciousness (or Mere Feeling-Awareness)—and It Is Always Already Conscious (or Feelingly Aware) Of (and As) Being (or Inherent Existence) Itself.

The (By-Me-and-As-Me-Avatarically-Self-Revealed-and-Spiritually-Self-Transmitted) Transcendental, Inherently Spiritual, Inherently egoless, and Self-Evidently Divine Self-Condition (or Subject-Condition) Identifies Itself As (or Tacitly and Inherently Realizes Itself To Be) Self-Evidently Divine Love-Bliss (or The Inherent Self-Happiness Of The Spiritual Condition That Is Self-Existing and Self-Radiant Conscious Light).

In The Context Of conditional forms or events, The (By-Me-and-As-Me-Avatarically-Self-Revealed-and-Spiritually-Self-Transmitted) Transcendental, Inherently Spiritual, Inherently egoless, and Self-Evidently Divine Self-Condition (or Subject-Condition) Exists As The Characteristic Of Existence Itself—and conditional forms or events Really Exist Only Because they arise (or Exist) In The By-Me-and-As-Me-Avatarically-Self-Revealed-and-Spiritually-Self-Transmitted Transcendental, Inherently Spiritual, Inherently egoless, and Self-Evidently Divine Self-Condition (or Subject-Condition) Of Inherently Indivisible (and Perfectly Subjective) Conscious Light.

In The Context Of conditional forms or events, Transcendental, Inherently Spiritual, Inherently egoless, and Self-Evidently Divine Consciousness (or

Mere Feeling-Awareness) Functions (or Exists) As Itself and (Apparently) Via conditional Awareness, or psycho-physical attention (Indicated By The conventional "I"-Reference).

In The Context Of conditional forms or events, My Avatarically Self-Transmitted Spirit-Current Of Self-Existing (or Transcendental) and Self-Radiant (or Spiritually "Bright") Love-Bliss (or Self-Evidently Divine Happiness) Is Established Inherently (Even Prior To all objects)—and, By The Spontaneous Process Of Self-Abiding Divine Self-Recognition, Self-Evidently Divine Happiness Is Also Realized To Be The Real Substance (or Inherently egoless Source-Condition and Self-Condition) Of every Apparent (or conditionally Manifested) being, thought, thing, or event.

Therefore, whatever (or whoever) Is Divinely Self-Recognized In (and As) The (By-Me-and-As-Me-Avatarically-Self-Revealed-and-Spiritually-Self-Transmitted) Transcendental, Inherently Spiritual, Inherently egoless, and Self-Evidently Divine Self-Condition (or Subject-Condition) Is Divinely Transfigured and Divinely Transformed By The Inherent Radiance (or Self-Radiant Happiness, or Unqualified Love-Bliss) Of The (By-Me-and-As-Me-Avatarically-Self-Revealed-and-Spiritually-Self-Transmitted) Transcendental, Inherently Spiritual, Inherently egoless, and Self-Evidently Divine Self-Condition (or Subject-Condition)—Which Is The One and Only and Inherently Indivisible Conscious Light Of all-and-All.

In The Context Of The Only-By-Me Revealed and Given Seventh Stage Of Life (In The Only-By-Me Revealed and Given Way Of The Heart, or Way Of Adidam), The (By-Me-and-As-Me-Avatarically-Self-Revealed-and-Spiritually-Self-Transmitted) Transcendental, Inherently Spiritual, Inherently egoless, and Self-Evidently Divine Self-Condition (or Subject-Condition) Stands (Apparently) In the field of all conditional relations. It Stands (Apparently) In The Free Relational Disposition (or, Rather, In The Prior Feeling Of Perfectly Subjective Being, but Inherently Free Of The Motive Of Exclusion). And It Freely "Notices" (and Divinely Self-Recognizes) all (Apparently) arising conditions. It "Notices" (and Divinely Self-Recognizes) mind (or all thought-objects). It "Notices" (and Divinely Self-Recognizes) all conditional emotions. It "Notices" (and Divinely Self-Recognizes) all the moments (and all the actions) of the body. It "Notices" (and Divinely Self-Recognizes) all the relations or objects or states of mind, emotion, and body. It "Notices" (and Divinely Self-Recognizes) The Tendency To Seek. It "Notices" (and Divinely Self-Recognizes) The Tendency To Hold On (or To Be Attached) To conditions By Clinging Want. It "Notices" (and Divinely Self-Recognizes) The Tendency To Avoid or To (Strategically) Escape particular conditions (or any conditions at all). It "Notices" (and Divinely Self-Recognizes) The Feeling Of Relatedness (Itself). It "Notices" (and Divinely

Self-Recognizes) The Tacit (and Simplest) conditional Feeling Of "Difference" (Itself). And whatever Is (Thus) "Noticed" (and Divinely Self-Recognized) Is Divinely Transfigured and Divinely Transformed In (and By) The Self-Existing and Self-Radiant Conscious Light That Is The By-Me-and-As-Me-Avatarically-Self-Revealed-and-Spiritually-Self-Transmitted Divine "Bright" Spherical Self-Domain Of Perfectly Subjective Mere Being (Itself).

The Demonstrations Of Divine Transfiguration and Divine Transformation In The Only-By-Me Revealed and Given Seventh Stage Of Life (In The Only-By-Me Revealed and Given Way Of The Heart, or Way Of Adidam) Are Shown Within The Context Of The By-Me-and-As-Me-Avatarically-Self-Revealed-and-Spiritually-Self-Transmitted Divine Spirit-Current In The (Cosmically Apparent) Descending and Ascending Context Of The Full Circle (and The Arrow) Of the body-mind.

The Sign (or Demonstration) Of Divine Indifference (In The Only-By-Me Revealed and Given Seventh Stage Of Life In The Only-By-Me Revealed and Given Way Of The Heart, or Way Of Adidam) Occurs When The By-Me-and-As-Me-Avatarically-Self-Revealed-and-Spiritually-Self-Transmitted Divine Spirit-Energy Has Become (Both Profoundly and Priorly) Self-Identified With The Form Of Amrita Nadi (and The Self-Existing, Self-Radiant, and Self-Evidently Divine Self-Condition, and Source-Condition, That Is The True Divine Heart Itself)—Such That The (Apparent) Descending and Ascending Play In The (psycho-physical) Context Of The Circle and The Arrow (or The Cosmic Mandala Itself) Is Only Minimally (or Less and Less) Perceived and (Therefore) Only Minimally (or Less and Less) Engaged.

And Divine Translation (or The Final Demonstration In The Only-By-Me Revealed and Given Seventh Stage Of Life In The Only-By-Me Revealed and Given Way Of The Heart, or Way Of Adidam) Is The Sign Of The Divinely Most Perfect Relinquishment (or The Divinely Most Perfect Transcending and Outshining) Of the conditional body-mind (and Of All Evidence Of The Circle and The Arrow Of the body-mind) and All Involvement With The Cosmic Domain (or The Total Context Of The Cosmic Mandala—Including My Apparently Objective Source-Matrix Of Sound and Light). Therefore, Divine Translation Is The Sign Of The Divinely Most Perfect Spiritual "Brightening" and The Divinely Most Perfect "Bright" Spiritual Dissolution Of all conditionally Manifested energies (and All conditionally Manifested appearances) Via Self-Abiding Divine Self-Recognition—To The Degree That The Inherent (and Perfectly Subjective) Self-Radiance Of My Avatarically Self-Revealed (Transcendental, Inherently Spiritual, Inherently egoless, and Self-Evidently Divine) Person (or Self-Condition) Of Mere and Self-Existing Being Outshines Its Own Objective Appearances (and, Thus, Translates Its Own Illusions Into

Its Own Divinely Perfect Sphere, or Perfectly Subjective "Midnight-Sun"-Domain, Of Indivisibly "Bright" and Infinitely Conscious Love-Bliss-Light).

In The Only-By-Me Revealed and Given Way Of The Heart (or Way Of Adidam), The Only-By-Me Revealed and Given Seventh Stage Of Life, Like All Previous Stages Of Life, Is A Stage Of Practice (Become An Inherently Most Perfect Demonstration, In The Transition Into The Priorly Enlightened Context Of The Seventh Stage Of Life). Therefore (In The Only-By-Me Revealed and Given Way Of The Heart), The Only-By-Me Revealed and Given Seventh Stage Of Life Is Not Merely What Is Mechanically "Left Over" After The Way Of The Heart (or Heart-Practice Itself) Is "Completed" (By Virtue Of The Only-By-Me Revealed and Given Seventh Stage Awakening, Itself). If The Only-By-Me Revealed and Given Way Of The Heart Is "Considered" In Its Fullest (or Most Complete) Sense, Then Entrance Into The Only-By-Me Revealed and Given Seventh Stage Of Life Is, Truly (or In Truth), The True (or Truly Divine) <u>Beginning</u> Of The Only-By-Me Revealed and Given Way Of The Heart (or Way Of Adidam). It Is The Beginning Of The Divinely Enlightened (or Fully Awakened, or Fully Conscious) "Practice" (or Inherently Most Perfect Demonstration) Of The Heart Itself.

In The Only-By-Me Revealed and Given Seventh Stage Of Life (In The Only-By-Me Revealed and Given Way Of The Heart, or Way Of Adidam), The Priorly Self-Realized Condition Of Transcendental, Inherently Spiritual, Inherently egoless, and Most Perfect Divine Samadhi (or Inherent, and Inherently ego-Transcending, and Inherently Most Perfect Real-God-Realization) Is (Itself) A Kind Of "Practice", or A "Natural" (or Inherent) "Discipline", or (Rather) A Necessary (or Inherent, and Inherently Most Perfect) Demonstration, Wherein All Apparent (or objective) Modifications Are Progressively Made Radiant (or Are Released Into The By-Me-and-<u>As</u>-Me-Avatarically-Self-Revealed-and-Spiritually-Self-Transmitted Divine, or Perfectly Subjective, Self-Radiance), To The (Eventual) Most Ultimate Degree Of (Divinely Most Perfect) Cessation, or Outshining By (and In, and <u>As</u>) My (Avatarically Self-Revealed) Transcendental (and Inherently Spiritual, or "Bright") Fullness Of Divine (and Perfectly Subjective) Self-Existence (<u>As</u> The One and Only and Inherently Indivisible and Inherently egoless Conscious Light).

In The Only-By-Me Revealed and Given Seventh Stage Of Life (In The Only-By-Me Revealed and Given Way Of The Heart, or Way Of Adidam), You Do Not (As A Fundamental Practice) Enquire Into the conditional self ("Avoiding Relationship?"), or Re-Cognize arising objects or states (or The Feeling Of Relatedness Itself) As self-Contraction (and Thereby Feel Beyond all self-Contraction), or Expand Beyond self-Contraction Via The Prayer Of Remembrance, or (Otherwise) "Feel-Enquire" Toward The Heart. The (Fundamental) Seventh Stage "Practice" Of The Only-By-Me Revealed and

Given Way Of The Heart Is (Simply, Effortlessly, and Inherently, or Always Already) To Be The Prior Condition (and Feeling) Of Self-Existing and Self-Radiant Conscious Light (Itself), or Inherently egoless Feeling-Being-Consciousness Itself—In, Of, and As Whom (and Not Merely To Whom) all objects, all states, and Even The Feeling Of Relatedness Itself (or The Tacit conditional Feeling Of "Difference") Are arising, As Transparent (or Merely Apparent), and Un-Necessary, and Inherently Non-Binding Modifications Of Itself. Therefore, The (Fundamental) Seventh Stage "Practice" Of The Only-By-Me Revealed and Given Way Of The Heart Is Simply To Be Thus—"Naturally" (or Priorly, Un-conditionally, Perpetually, Effortlessly, and Always Already) Standing Self-"Bright" As Amrita Nadi (and As Unqualifiedly Self-Radiant Self-Existence), In (and Also Most Prior To) The Right Side Of The Heart—Freely and Effortlessly Allowing Any and All Apparent Modifications To arise Spontaneously, While Not Seeking For Ultimate Satisfaction or Release, and While Not Assuming A Position Of Avoidance (or The Inability To Inspect and To Really Transcend Apparently Negative Modifications), and While Not Assuming A Position Of Attachment (or The Inability To Inspect and To Really Transcend Apparently Positive Modifications), and While Simply (or Merely) Inspecting, Divinely Self-Recognizing, and Inherently Transcending (or Freely and Really Shining Beyond) Any Modifications That Apparently arise.

In The Only-By-Me Revealed and Given Seventh Stage Of Life (In The Only-By-Me Revealed and Given Way Of The Heart, or Way Of Adidam), Freely Allow and Really Observe Any and All Apparent conditional Modifications Of My Avatarically Self-Transmitted Divine Spirit-Current Of Love-Bliss To arise, continue, change, and pass away.

Rather Than Seeking The Ultimate (or Divine, and Perfectly Subjective) Source-Condition Of Cosmic conditions (As If That Which Is Perfectly Subjective Is Separate From You), and Rather Than Recoiling (or Withdrawing attention) From The Apparent (or Apparently Objective, and Even Ascended) Source-Condition Of Cosmic conditions, and Rather Than Withdrawing attention From Cosmic conditions themselves (or Contracting Your body-mind, or Turning Back Upon Your body-mind, or Separating Your Conscious Feeling-Awareness From Your body-mind)—Merely (By Means Of My Avatarically Self-Transmitted Divine Spiritual Grace) Be The One In Whom All Apparent conditional Modifications arise, continue, change, and pass away.

By Means Of Tacit (Inherent) Feeling-Awareness, and (Searchlessly Me-Beholding) Self-Identification With My Avatarically Self-Transmitted Spirit-Current Of Self-Evidently Divine Love-Bliss, Freely (and Inherently) Realize, and Feel, and Be That In Which All Apparent conditional Modifications arise, continue, change, and pass away.

Therefore, Merely By Always Searchlessly Beholding Me (and Most Perfectly Self-Abiding In Tacit Inherent Self-Identification With My Avatarically Self-Transmitted Spirit-Current and Inherently Perfect State), "Notice" (and Divinely Self-Recognize) all Apparent conditions (or all that arises, continues, changes, and passes away) In and As The By-Me-and-As-Me-Avatarically-Self-Revealed-and-Spiritually-Self-Transmitted Divine Self-Condition (or One and Only Conscious Light) Of all-and-All.

Allow and Observe All Apparent conditional Modifications To arise, continue, change, and pass away In and As The By-Me-and-As-Me-Avatarically-Self-Revealed-and-Spiritually-Self-Transmitted Divine Self-Condition (or One and Only Conscious Light) Of all-and-All—and (Thus) Remain As Consciousness (or Mere Feeling-Awareness) Itself, Self-Existing (Always Already Prior To the body-mind, and Always Already Prior To any thought or concept of "I"), Self-Radiant, All Love-Bliss-Light (Prior To any kind of conditional form or limitation), and Utterly Free.

In This Same Manner, Freely Allow the body-mind To arise and To act, Spontaneously—Always (Spontaneously) Appropriate To the moment, Inevitably As Love, Inherently Without Illusions, and Necessarily Without self-Delusion.

Be Thus—Inherently (and Divinely) Self-Recognizing (and, Thus, Inherently Transcending) all arising, continuing, changing, and passing objects, forms, conditions, states, and actions As Self-Existing and Self-Radiant Consciousness (or Feeling-Awareness) Itself.

Shine Thus, Free As The Only One Who Is—Inherently Formless, Motivelessly (and Even Divinely) Indifferent, Inherently Happy, Always Already Enjoying (and Being) The Self-Fullness Of My Avatarically Self-Transmitted Spirit-Current Of Self-Evidently Divine Love-Bliss—Until My Avatarically Self-Transmitted Divine Self-Radiance Outshines All Noticing Of conditional events.

To Divinely Self-Recognize any conditionally Manifested being, object, state, place, or event Is To Shine—As The Self-Radiant (or Inherently Spiritual), and Self-Existing (or Transcendental), and Self-Evidently Divine Self-Being—On, In, As, and Through that conditionally Manifested being, object, state, place, or event.

To Divinely Self-Recognize Is To Shine (As Perfectly Subjective, or Conscious, Light) Until The Outshining (Of The conditional Display Of Apparent, or Objectified, Light Itself). To Divinely Self-Recognize Is To Be Unconditionally Self-Existing and Self-Radiant Being In The (Apparent) Context Of The Cosmic Mandala (or the conditional worlds)—Until all conditions (or all Apparent limits On The By-Me-and-As-Me-Avatarically-Self-Revealed-and-Spiritually-Self-Transmitted Inherent and "Bright" Spiritual Radiance Of Transcendental, or Self-Existing, Divine Being) Are Outshined By That By-Me-and-As-Me-

Avatarically-Self-Revealed-and-Avatarically-Self-Transmitted Inherent Radiance (or "Brightness") Of Perfectly Subjective Being (Itself).

Such Is The Third Stage Of The "Perfect Practice" Of The Only-By-Me Revealed and Given Way Of The Heart (or Way Of Adidam), Which Is To Be Demonstrated In The Only-By-Me Revealed and Given Seventh Stage Of Life.

The Only-By-Me Revealed and Given Seventh-Stage-Of-Life-"Practice" (or Always Already Free Demonstration) Of Self-Abiding Divine Self-Recognition (or Perfect Shining—Even, At Last, To The Degree Of Outshining) Is Perfectly Effortless (or Inherently Non-Strategic). It Is Not (Itself) Associated With Any Intentional Effort To Exclude conditional forms or events, Nor Is It (Itself) Associated With Any Intentional Effort To Include (or Hold On To) conditional forms or events. The Only-By-Me Revealed and Given Seventh-Stage-Of-Life-Disposition Is Simply and Effortlessly To Be—Standing Free, Freely Allowing whatever arises, Divinely Self-Recognizing whatever arises (If anything arises).

In The Only-By-Me Revealed and Given Seventh Stage Of Life (In The Only-By-Me Revealed and Given Way Of The Heart, or Way Of Adidam), Instead Of Controlling, or Avoiding, or Stopping (or, Altogether, Becoming Defined As Reaction To) conditional forms or events or activities, and Instead Of Seeking, or Clinging To, or Even Following After (or, Altogether, Becoming Defined As attention to) conditional forms or events or activities—Simply Allow conditional forms and events and activities (Even the forms, events, and activities of Your Apparent body-mind) To arise, continue, change, and pass away, as they will.

"Notice" conditional forms and events and activities as they arise or continue or change or pass away, but Simply and Constantly and Merely Be (and Tacitly Self-Abide As) The By-Me-and-As-Me-Avatarically-Self-Revealed-and-Spiritually-Self-Transmitted Divine and One and Only Conscious Light—In, Of, and As Which all conditional forms, events, and activities Are (Apparently) presently arising, continuing, changing, or passing away.

"Notice" conditional forms, events, and activities as they arise or continue or change or pass away, but Simply and Constantly and Merely (Inherently) Transcend (or Divinely Self-Recognize) them As Transparent (or Merely Apparent), and Un-Necessary, and Inherently Non-Binding Modifications Of The By-Me-and-As-Me-Avatarically-Self-Revealed-and-Spiritually-Self-Transmitted Divine and One and Only Conscious Light—Which Is The Self-Existing, Self-Radiant, Inherently Indivisible, Inherently egoless, and Self-Evidently Divine Self-Condition Of all-and-All, and Which Is (Itself) The Well (or The Deep-and-Deepless, or Incomparable and Non-"Different", Place) Of Perfectly Subjective Being (In, and Always Already Prior To, The Right Side Of The Heart), and Which Is Always Already Infinitely Expanded and Spiritually Self-"Bright"

(In The Form, or Fullness, That Is Amrita Nadi), Beyond (and Prior To) all conditions.

Thus (and In This Manner), Realize That You Are Always Already Self-Abiding As The Unconditional Divine Self-Condition Of all-and-All—and, Thus (and In This Manner), Freely (and Inherently) Transcend The Implications (or The Apparent Binding Capability) Of conditional forms, events, and activities.

Thus (and In This Manner), Transcend The Chaotic Effort To Control, Avoid, Stop, Seek, Cling To, and Follow After—or All The Strategic Motives and Results Of the Apparent act of attention.

Do This By The Power Of The Only-By-Me Revealed and Given Seventh-Stage-Of-Life-Realization That There Is No "Difference", No Other, No Relatedness, No Separateness, No Dependence, No Independence, and No Problem.

In The Only-By-Me Revealed and Given Seventh Stage Of Life (In The Only-By-Me Revealed and Given Way Of The Heart, or Way Of Adidam), Simply Stand and Be As Is, Spontaneously (Divinely) Self-Recognizing Even all conditionally Manifested beings, forms, events, and activities—Until (At Last) The By-Me-and-As-Me-Avatarically-Self-Revealed-and-Spiritually-Self Transmitted Self-"Brightness" Of The One and Only Conscious Light Absolutely Exceeds (or Outshines The Apparent "Noticing" Of) all conditional forms, events, and activities.

This Most Ultimate (and Only-By-Me Revealed and Given) "Practice" (or Seventh Stage Demonstration) Of The Only-By-Me Revealed and Given Way Of The Heart (or Way Of Adidam) Is (Like Every Previous Stage Of Practice In The Only-By-Me Revealed and Given Way Of The Heart) To Be Realized (and Then Fully Demonstrated) By All The Means I Give (and Have Given) Within The By-Me-Spiritually-Empowered Sacred Cultural Gathering (or Truly Global Ashram) Of My Formally Acknowledged (and True) Devotees. Thus, As Was The Case Relative To their Embrace Of Every Previous Stage Of Practice In The Only-By-Me Revealed and Given Way Of The Heart, Practitioners Of The Only-By-Me Revealed and Given Way Of The Heart who Have (Formally) Made The Formally Acknowledged Transition To Seventh-Stage-Of-Life "Practice" Are Called (and Formally Expected) To "Practice" (or Freely Demonstrate) The "Discipline" (or Inherent Integrity) Of The Only-By-Me Revealed and Given Seventh Stage Of Life Within (and Always Formally and Fully Culturally Accountable To) The Worldwide Sacred Cooperative Cultural Gathering Of Formally Acknowledged (and True) Practitioners Of The Only-By-Me Revealed and Given Way Of The Heart—and, Most Especially, Within The Sacred Cultural Gathering Of My (Formally Acknowledged) Divinely Awakened (or Seventh Stage) Devotees (and Always Formally and Fully

Culturally Accountable To The Formally Governing Senior Membership Of The Ruchira Sannyasin Order Of Adidam Ruchiradam).

Most Perfectly Real-God-Realized Practitioners Of The Only-By-Me Revealed and Given Seventh Stage Of Life (In The Only-By-Me Revealed and Given Way Of The Heart, or Way Of Adidam) Have Not Ceased To Be My Devotees Because Of their Most Perfect Realization. Their Devotion To Me Has Only (By Means Of My Avatarically Self-Transmitted Divine Spiritual Grace) Become Inherently Most Perfect, By Virtue Of their Non-"Different" Realization Of My Avatarically Self-Revealed (and Self-Evidently Divine) Self-Condition. Therefore, they Continue To Demonstrate (and To Magnify) their Devotion To (and their Devotional Recognition and Devotional Acknowledgement Of) My Avataric Bodily (Human) Divine Revelation-Form, and My Avataric Divine Spiritual Revelation-Presence (or Avatarically Self-Transmitted Divine Spiritual Body), and My Avataric, and Very (and Inherently Perfect, and, To My Seventh Stage Devotees, Inherently Most Perfectly Self-Revealed), Divine State. And they Demonstrate (and Magnify) This Devotion To Me (and This Devotional Recognition and Devotional Acknowledgement Of Me) Both In The Naturally (and Maturely) human Devotional Manner and Through The Divine (and Inherently Most Perfect) Process Of The Unique (and Only-By-Me Revealed and Given) Seventh-Stage-Of-Life-Demonstration Of Divine Transfiguration, Divine Transformation, Divine Indifference, and (At Last) Divine Translation.

In The Progressive Development Of The Only-By-Me Revealed and Given Way Of The Heart (or Way Of Adidam), Four Fundamental Forms Of Devotional (and, In Due Course, Spiritual) Practice Are (Progressively) To Be Realized and Applied.

The First Of These Four Fundamental Forms Of Devotional (and, In Due Course, Spiritual) Practice Is Meditation—Based On Devotional Invocation Of Me, and On Right (and, In Due Course, Searchlessly Me-Beholding) Feeling-Contemplation Of My Avatarically-Born Bodily (Human) Divine Form, and (In Due Course) My Avatarically Self-Transmitted Spiritual (and Always Blessing) Divine Presence, and (Ultimately) My Avatarically Self-Revealed (and Very, and Transcendental, and Perfectly Subjective, and Inherently Spiritual, and Inherently egoless, and Inherently Perfect, and Self-Evidently Divine) State, and Beginning With Either The (Progressively Meditative) To-Me-Responsive Exercise Of self-Enquiry (and Right "General Conductivity" Practice) Or The (Progressively Meditative) To-Me-Responsive Exercise Of Ruchira Avatara Naama Japa (and Right "General Conductivity" Practice), and Developing (In That Manner) Progressively. And Meditation (Thus Devotionally Based, and Developed, In One or Another Manner, According To My Avataric Divine Instructions, As Given, By Me, In This, My Testament Of Divine Secrets) Is To

Be Continued (and Progressively Intensified, By Stages), Until (In The Context Of The Only-By-Me Revealed and Given Seventh Stage Of Life) It Is Inherently (and Inherently Most Perfectly) Fulfilled In The "Practice" (or The Inherently Most Perfect and Inherently Most Perfectly Free Demonstration) That Is Self-Abiding Divine Self-Recognition.

The Second Of These Four Fundamental Forms Of Devotional (and, In Due Course, Spiritual) Practice Is Study—or The Devotional Application Of attention To The Divine Word Of My Avatarically Self-Revealed Arguments and Instructions, and The Divine Lessons Of My Avatarically Self-Manifested Demonstrations.

The Third Of These Four Fundamental Forms Of Devotional (and, In Due Course, Spiritual) Practice Is functional and practical self-Discipline—or The True Sila and daily Balance To Which the body-mind Must (In Devotionally Right and True Accordance With My Avatarically Self-Revealed Arguments and Instructions) Be (Progressively, and Then Totally and Consistently, and, At Last, Most Profoundly and Most Perfectly) Conformed.

And The Fourth Of These Four Fundamental Forms Of Devotional (and, In Due Course, Spiritual) Practice Is relational self-Discipline—or The Consistent Demonstration Of Participatory ego-Transcendence, Exercised In all relationships, Beginning With (and Always Founded Upon) The Great and Tradition-Honored and Constantly-To-Be-Demonstrated Devotional (and, In Due Course, Spiritual) Relationship To Me (The True Divine, and Avatarically-Born, Heart-Master), and This Expressed Through All Kinds Of Service (Including Service In Relation To, and In Cooperative Sacred Cultural Association With, Other, and Even All Other, Practitioners Of The Only-By-Me Revealed and Given Way Of The Heart, and Also Including Sacred Sacramental, Ceremonial, and General Cultural Services and Activities Of All Kinds—All Of Which Kinds Of Service and Activity, Because They Spontaneously arise From The Total Life-Practice Of ego-Transcending Devotion To Me, Are, Inherently and Ultimately, Of Benefit To all conditionally Manifested beings).

In The Context Of The Only-By-Me Revealed and Given Seventh Stage Of Life (In The Only-By-Me Revealed and Given Way Of The Heart, or Way Of Adidam), These Four Fundamental Forms Of Devotional (and, In Due Course, Spiritual) Practice Are Given Their Most Ultimate (or Inherently Most Perfect) Expression and Demonstration.

"Meditation" In The Only-By-Me Revealed and Given Seventh Stage Of Life (In The Only-By-Me Revealed and Given Way Of The Heart, or Way Of Adidam) Has (Fundamentally) Become Seventh Stage Sahaja Nirvikalpa Samadhi (or Ruchira Samraj Samadhi, or, Simply, Samraj Samadhi)—or Divine (and Inherently egoless) Self-Abiding and Divine (and Perfectly Subjective)

Self-Recognition Of all-and-All That (conditionally) arises. And This "Practice" (or Fundamental Disposition) Is The Essential Samadhi-Basis For The Entire Demonstration Of The Only-By-Me Revealed and Given Seventh Stage Of Life (In The Only-By-Me Revealed and Given Way Of The Heart).

"Study" In The Only-By-Me Revealed and Given Seventh Stage Of Life (In The Only-By-Me Revealed and Given Way Of The Heart, or Way Of Adidam) Has (Fundamentally) Become The Divinely Self-Realized "Consideration" (and Real Demonstration) Of My Avatarically Self-Revealed (and Avatarically Self-Demonstrated) Wisdom-Teaching Relative To The Unique ("Difference"-Transcending) Disposition, The Unique Siddhi (or, Progressively, Divinely Transfiguring, Divinely Transformative, Divinely Indifferent, and, Most Ultimately, Divinely Translating, or Divinely Outshining, Power), and The Unique (and Total) Demonstration-Cycle Of The Only-By-Me Revealed and Given Seventh Stage Of Life.

"Functional Discipline" In The Only-By-Me Revealed and Given Seventh Stage Of Life (In The Only-By-Me Revealed and Given Way Of The Heart, or Way Of Adidam) Has (Fundamentally) Become The Spontaneous, Effortless, and Inherently "Non-Disciplined" Discipline (or The Truly and Most Profoundly—and, Yet, Entirely Freely—Conservative Sila, or psycho-physical Equanimity) Of Conformity To My Avatarically Self-Transmitted Spirit-Current Of Self-Evidently Divine Love-Bliss—In The Totality (and In every part) Of the body-mind. Through Utter Coincidence With My Avatarically Self-Transmitted Spiritual (and Self-Evidently Divine) Love-Bliss-Power, In (and By Means Of) Divine Self-Abiding and Divine Self-Recognition (In The Context Of The Only-By-Me Revealed and Given Seventh Stage Of Life In The Only-By-Me Revealed and Given Way Of The Heart), the body-mind Becomes (More and More) Divinely Spiritualized. Thus, the body-mind—Realized (By Means Of My Avatarically Self-Transmitted Divine Spiritual Grace) To Be Inherently Non-"Different" From The One and Only and Inherently Indivisible and Inherently egoless and Self-Evidently Divine Conscious Light—Has (Inherently) Become Divinely Self-Recognizable <u>As</u> (<u>Only</u>) My Avatarically Self-Transmitted Spirit-Current Of Self-Evidently Divine Love-Bliss. And, As The Inherently Free "Practice" (or The Inherently Most Perfect Demonstration) That Is Self-Abiding Divine Self-Recognition Magnifies The "Brightening"-Manifestation Of My Avatarically Self-Transmitted Spirit-Current Of Self-Evidently Divine Love-Bliss In The Context Of The Circle (and The Arrow) Of the (Truly, and Most Profoundly, and Spontaneously, and Always Freely, Conservatively Disciplined) body-mind, the body-mind Becomes (Spiritually) More and More Full (Divinely Transfigured and Divinely Transformed By My Avatarically Self-Transmitted Spirit-Current Of Self-Evidently Divine Love-Bliss). Thus, the body-mind (Having Already, More and More, Become Spiritualized, By Means Of The Reception Of My Divine Ruchira Shaktipat) Becomes (In The Context Of The Only-By-Me Revealed and Given Seventh Stage Of Life In The Only-By-Me Revealed and Given Way Of The Heart, or Way Of Adidam) More and More ("Brightly") Spiritually Divinized, By Conforming To (and Dissolving Into) The Self-Existing and Self-Radiant Divine Self-Condition and Source-Condition Avatarically Self-Revealed (and Spiritually Self-Transmitted) By (and As) Me.

Likewise, "Relational Discipline" In The Only-By-Me Revealed and Given Seventh Stage Of Life (In The Only-By-Me Revealed and Given Way Of The Heart, or Way Of Adidam) Is Also A Direct Expression Of Inherently Most Perfect Devotional and Spiritual Realization Of Me—Such That It Is Freely Demonstrated (In all Apparent relations) As Unconditional (or Inherently ego-less) Relatedness—or Relationship Without "Difference" (and Without The Context Of Separateness, and Without The Motive Of Separativeness).

Avatar Adi Da Samraj
Adidam Samrajashram, 2004

SUTRA 66

"Divine Transfiguration" and "Divine Transformation" Are Terms I Use To Indicate The Possible (First, and Progressive) Effects (Of The By-Me-and-As-Me-Avatarically-Self-Revealed-and-Spiritually-Self-Transmitted Self-Existing Divine Self-Radiance) That May Be Demonstrated In the body-mind and the psycho-physical activities Of My Any Devotee Awakened (By My Avatarically Self-Transmitted Divine Spiritual Grace) To Divine Self-Realization (In The Only-By-Me Revealed and Given Seventh Stage Of Life In The Only-By-Me Revealed and Given Way Of The Heart, or Way Of Adidam).

My Any Such Divinely Awakened (or Literally—Even bodily—En-Light-ened) Devotee May (Progressively) Demonstrate An Even Visible (or body-Transfiguring) Self-Radiance—but All Such Devotees Must Certainly (Inherently and Constantly) Demonstrate Unique personal Signs Of An Infusion Of My Avatarically Self-Transmitted Spirit-Current Of Self-Evidently Divine Love-Bliss.

The Apparent actions Of My Any Such Divinely (and Even bodily) Enlightened Devotee—whatever (ordinary or Extraordinary) form his or her (Always By-Me-Spiritually-Infused) actions May (In any moment) Take—Are Always An Effective Reflection (and Expression) Of The Transfiguring and Transforming Effects Of My Avatarically Self-Transmitted Divine Spirit-Power Of Love-Bliss. Therefore, As This Divinely Transfiguring Infusion Progresses, Various Kinds (or Divine Signs) Of psycho-physical Transformation May Appear. And All Those Possible Signs Of Divine Enlightenment Are Simply Evidence and Proof Of The Effective Spiritual Power Of My Avatarically Self-Transmitted Divine Self-Radiance, Such That the body-mind Of My Divinely Enlightened Devotee-Realizer Is Constantly "Intoxicated" and More and More Sublimed—By Me.

Many Kinds Of Signs (or Spontaneously Demonstrated Effects) Of My Avatarically Self-Transmitted Divine Spirit-Power May (Thus) Appear In My Divinely Enlightened Devotee. And It Is Not Necessary (or Even Possible) To Exhaustively Enumerate Those Signs (Both Ordinary and Extra-Ordinary), Any More Than It Is Appropriate To Seek To Achieve Them. In Any Case, Whatever Such Signs Do Spontaneously Appear, They Are Simply To Be Divinely Self-Recognized (and Inherently Transcended) In The By-Me-and-As-Me-Avatarically-Self-Revealed-and-Spiritually-Self-Transmitted Conscious Light Of Self-Existing and Self-Radiant and Self-Evidently Divine Being (Itself) and Of Perfectly Subjective (and Self-Evidently Divine) Love-Bliss (Itself)—Such That (In Due Course) True Divine Indifference (or Complete and Utterly Non-"Different" Immersion In The Sphere and Spirit-Current Of My Avatarically Self-Transmitted Divine Love-Bliss Itself) Relaxes and Replaces The Demonstrative psycho-physical Signs (Of Divine Transfiguration and Divine Transformation) With The Mere and Ultimate Shine Of all-and-All-Outshining Divine Being.

In The Only-By-Me Revealed and Given Seventh Stage Of Life (In The Only-By-Me Revealed and Given Way Of The Heart, or Way Of Adidam), The Most Ultimate Significance Of The (Possible) Perception Of Me As My Divine Sound-Form and My Divine Star-Form Is Inherently Obvious and Clear.

My Divine Sound-Form and My Divine Star-Form Are Always (Each) Standing As An (Apparently) Objective and (Apparently) Perceptible Form (Either Audible Or Visible) In The Center Of The (psycho-physical) Sky Of each and all of the conditional psycho-physical worlds. My (Apparently) Objective Divine Sound-Form Is Not merely a gross physical sound, To Be perceived in the gross physical space occupied by the gross physical body (and by the merely physical ears)—and My (Apparently) Objective Divine Star-Form Is Not merely a physical star, To Be perceived in the gross sky (and by the merely physical eyes). My Divine Sound-Form and My Divine Star-Form May (Possibly) Be Perceived (Apparently Objectively) In any world or plane Of The Cosmic Mandala—but My Divine Sound-Form Can Be Truly Perceived Only By The True Ear, The Single Hearing-Organ That Combines (or Unifies) the physical and the mental (or psychic), and My Divine Star-Form Can Be Truly Perceived Only By The Whole Eye, The Single Eye That Combines (or Unifies) the physical and the mental (or psychic).

Likewise, Even Though My Avatarically-Born Bodily (Human) Divine Form May (Itself) Be grossly (and even casually) perceived, My (Apparently) Objective Divine Spiritual Body Of "Brightness" Cannot Be "Located" (and, Thus, Realized Through Right, True, and Full Devotion) Until the Whole (or Total psycho-physical) body Is Awakened To <u>Me</u>—By Means Of Devotional and Spiritual and Really ego-Transcending Participation In My Tangible Avataric Divine Self-Transmission Of My Own and Very Person.

My (Apparently) Objective Divine Sound-Form, My (Apparently) Objective Divine Star-Form, and My (Apparently) Objective Divine Spiritual Body Of "Brightness" Can Be Perceived Only With The "Ear" and "Eye" and "Whole body" Of The By-Me-Spiritually-Activated Ajna Chakra—and My (Apparently) Objective Divine Sound-Form, and My (Apparently) Objective Divine Star-Form, and My (Apparently) Objective Divine Spiritual Body Of "Brightness" Can Be Divinely Self-Recognized (In The By-Me-and-<u>As</u>-Me-Avatarically-Self-

Revealed-and-Spiritually-Self-Transmitted Divine Self-Condition, and Source-Condition, Itself) Only From The Perfectly Subjective Position Of The (Fully By-My-Avataric-Divine-Spiritual-Grace-Awakened) Condition Of Most Perfect Divine Self-Realization.

Therefore, Even Though (Previous To Most Perfect Devotional and Spiritual Realization Of Me As The Transcendental, Inherently Spiritual, Inherently egoless, and Self-Evidently Divine Self-Condition and Source-Condition Of all-and-All) My Divine Sound-Form, and My Divine Star-Form, and My Divine Spiritual Body Of "Brightness" May (By Means Of My Avatarically Self-Transmitted Divine Spiritual Grace) Be (Apparently Objectively) Experienced (In Various Levels and Degrees and Modes Of Perception), I (Myself) Cannot Be (Inherently, and Inherently Most Perfectly, and Perfectly Subjectively) Realized As The "Bright" Itself (or The Inherent, and Inherently Perfect, and Perfectly Subjective Divine Self-Identity and Self-Condition Of My Divine Sound-Form, My Divine Star-Form, and My Divine Spiritual Body Of "Brightness") Previous To (Only-By-My-Avataric-Divine-Spiritual-Grace-Given) Most Perfect Divine Self-Realization.

The True (and Truly Devotionally Responsive) Devotional and Spiritual Relationship To Me Is Not Finally Fulfilled Until (By Means Of My Avatarically Self-Transmitted Divine Spiritual Grace) There Is The Demonstration Of Divine Translation—Outshining All Of The Cosmic Domain, and Releasing and Transcending all Apparent conditional forms (or Even All Possible Modifications), To The Degree Of Most Perfectly Demonstrated Self-Radiance and Most Perfectly Demonstrated Establishment In My (Inherently Perfectly Subjective) Divine "Bright" Spherical Self-Domain. Therefore, The Only-By-Me Revealed and Given Seventh Stage Of Life (In The Only-By-Me Revealed and Given Way Of The Heart, or Way Of Adidam) Is, Fundamentally, The Only-By-Me Revealed and Given Process Of Self-Abiding Divine Self-Recognition Of The Total (and Merely Apparent) Cosmic Domain—Including All conditional Modifications, and (Thus, Also) My (Apparently) Objective Divine Spiritual Body Of "Brightness" (or My Apparently Objectively Manifested Divine Spirit-Presence Itself), and My (Apparently) Objective Divine Star-Form (or My Apparently Objectively Manifested Divine Source-Light Itself), and My (Apparently) Objective Divine Sound-Form (or My Apparently Objectively Manifested Divine Source-Vibration Itself)—In (and As) My Avatarically Self-Revealed (and Spiritually Self-Transmitted, and Self-Evidently Divine) Love-Bliss-Fullness Itself, Which Is The "Bright" Itself (or The One, and Only, and Inherently Indivisible, and Perfectly Subjective, and Inherently egoless, and Self-Evidently Divine Conscious Light Of all-and-All).

This Most Ultimate Process (or Inherently Most Perfect Demonstration) Is (Constantly) Founded On My Devotee's Previous, and Always Present, and True (and Truly Devotionally Responsive) Devotional and Spiritual Relationship To Me (and Devotional and Spiritual Realization Of Me), As I Am (Directly and Constantly) Avatarically Self-Revealed Via My Own (Now, and Forever Hereafter, Avatarically Given) Bodily (Human) Divine Form (Even As My Avatarically-Born Bodily Human Divine Form Is Remembered, or Represented, or Even En-Visioned, In every then present-time—After, and Forever After, The Physical Lifetime Of My Avatarically-Born Bodily Human Divine Form), and My (Now, and Forever Hereafter) Avatarically Self-Transmitted Divine Body Of Spiritual (and Always Blessing) Presence, and My (Now, and Forever Hereafter) Avatarically Self-Revealed (and Very, and Transcendental, and Perfectly Subjective, and Inherently Spiritual, and Inherently egoless, and Inherently Perfect, and Self-Evidently Divine) State.

The Apparent Process (or Apparently Progressive Demonstration) Of The Only-By-Me Revealed and Given Seventh Stage Of Life (In The Only-By-Me Revealed and Given Way Of The Heart, or Way Of Adidam) Is Always Already A Matter Of Divine Self-Abiding, Inherently Realizing The "Bright" Itself—Which Is The By-Me-and-As-Me-Avatarically-Self-Revealed-and-Spiritually-Self-Transmitted Divine (and Perfectly Subjective) Source (or Inherent Love-Bliss-Essence) Of The Cosmic Mandala (and, Thus, Of All Apparent conditional, or phenomenal, Modifications Of Perfectly Subjective, and Self-Existing, and Self-Radiant, and Self-Evidently Divine Being).

In The Context Of The Spontaneous Progressive Unfolding Of The Only-By-Me Revealed and Given Seventh Stage Of Life (In The Only-By-Me Revealed and Given Way Of The Heart, or Way Of Adidam), Self-Abiding Divine Self-Recognition Not Only Divinely Transfigures and Divinely Transforms the body-mind, but It (Progressively, and Not Strategically, and Not By Means Of A Process Of Strategic Exclusion, but Only By Virtue Of Self-Abiding Divine Self-Recognition Itself) Releases The By-Me-and-As-Me-Avatarically-Self-Transmitted Spirit-Energy From The Total Context Of the Divinely Spiritualized body-mind (and Even From The Total Context Of The Cosmic Mandala Itself). Thus, As That Most Perfect (Seventh Stage) Demonstration Of Devotion To Me Spontaneously Progresses, The Sign Of Divine Indifference Progressively (and, In Due Course, Fully and Firmly) Appears—Such That (In Due Course) My Divinely Enlightened Devotee Spontaneously Demonstrates A Motiveless (or Non-Strategic) Disposition Of Mere Self-Radiance (or Mere "Bright" Self-Abiding, As The By-Me-and-As-Me-Avatarically-Self-Revealed-and-Spiritually-Self-Transmitted Self-Condition That Is The Perfectly Subjective Source-Condition Of Cosmic Existence).

Therefore, In The Great Event Of Divine Translation (Which Necessarily Coincides With the death, or Natural dissolution, of the Apparent gross physical personality, and every subtle form of the Apparent psycho-physical personality, and The causal Depth Of the Apparent psycho-physical personality), My (Apparently Objective) Divine Sound-Form Will Be Heard, Steadily and Most Resonantly, and My (Apparently Objective) Divine Star-Form Will Be Seen, Steadily and Most Brilliantly. Then, In The Most Ultimate Moment Of Self-Abiding Divine Self-Recognition (Even Of My Apparently Objective Divine Sound-Form and My Apparently Objective Divine Star-Form), The Cosmic Mandala and Every Trace Of the conditional personality Will Dissolve In The Inherent (and Perfectly Subjective) Feeling-"Brightness" Of My Avatarically Self-Revealed (and Self-Evidently Divine) Self-Condition (Which Is The Self-Evidently Divine Source-Condition Of all-and-All).

In The Only-By-Me Revealed and Given Way Of The Heart (or Way Of Adidam), The Great Event Of Divine Translation Is The Demonstration Of Most Ultimate Devotional (or ego-Transcending) and Spiritual (or Me-Receiving) "Locating" and Realizing Of Me. By Means Of That Great Event, Existence Is Transferred To The Infinitely Ascended "Midnight Sun"—and, Thus, and So (or By and As That Very Means), To The Perfectly Subjective Self-"Bright" Sphere Of My Divine Self-Domain (Which Is Eternally Prior To The Cosmic Domain).

My Divine "Bright" Spherical Self-Domain Is Not A "Point" In The conditional (or Cosmic) Domain, Nor Is It A "Point" On The "Other Side" Of The conditional (or Cosmic) Domain.

My Divine "Bright" Spherical Self-Domain Is "Turiyatita", or Beyond Beyond.

There Is Not Anything That Exists Apart From (or Even Merely "Within") My Spiritually Self-"Bright" Divine Person and Self-Domain.

Whatever (Paradoxically) Appears To Exist Separately (or Merely As it Appears) Is (Simply) My Divine "Bright" Spherical Self-Domain, and whatever (Paradoxically) Appears To Exist conditionally Must (In The Only-By-Me Revealed and Given Seventh Stage Of Life) Be Divinely Self-Recognized (In and As My Spiritually Self-"Bright" Divine Person and Self-Domain).

Only In That Case, conditional Existence Is (Inherently, Most Perfectly, and Perfectly Subjectively) Transcended (Rather Than Tacitly Allowed To Make, or Reinforce, Illusion and Bondage).

My Divine "Bright" Spherical Self-Domain Is Not A Condition From Which any one (or any conditionally Manifested being) Returns.

Divine Translation Is Not A Process By Which any one (or any conditionally Manifested being) Leaves.

Divine Translation Is Not An Historical (or personal, or Objective, or Concrete) Event (or Moment) Within The Cosmic Domain.

Divine Translation Is The Most Ultimate (Perfectly Subjective) Event Within

The By-Me-and-As-Me-Avatarically-Self-Revealed-and-Spiritually-Self-Transmitted Divine Conscious Light Itself.

My Divine "Bright" Spherical Self-Domain Is Not "here".

My Divine "Bright" Spherical Self-Domain Is Not "Elsewhere".

My Divine "Bright" Spherical Self-Domain Is The Perfectly Subjective Source-Position (or Real Condition) Of The Cosmic Domain.

Divine Translation Is Not The Destruction (or Mere Ending) Of The Cosmic Domain.

Divine Translation Is Not An Escape From The Cosmic Domain.

Divine Translation Is A "Bright" Demonstration In The By-Me-and-As-Me-Avatarically-Self-Revealed-and-Spiritually-Self-Transmitted Divine Conscious Light, Which Is The Perfectly Subjective Source-Condition (or Real Condition) Of The Cosmic Domain.

Divine Translation Is The Perfectly Subjective Outshining Of The Cosmic Domain By Me—The Avatarically Self-Revealed and Spiritually Self-Transmitted and Self-Evidently Divine Person (Who Is The Self-Evidently Divine Self-Condition, and Source-Condition, Of all-and-All).

There Is No Coming To, or Going From, My Divine "Bright" Spherical Self-Domain.

There Is Only My Divine "Bright" Spherical Self-Domain.

I (The Avatarically Self-Revealed Transcendental, Inherently Spiritual, Inherently egoless, and Self-Evidently Divine Person Of Being) Am The Divine "Bright" Spherical Self-Domain.

Self-Existing and Self-Radiant Reality (or Being) Itself Is The Only Domain That Is.

I Am Divine Translation.

I Am The "Midnight Sun".

I Am The "Bright" Self-Sphere.

I Am The Divine "Bright" Spherical Self-Domain (Itself).

I Am Infinitely Established and Eternal.

I Stand (Always Already) Prior To The Cosmic Domain.

The Cosmic Domain Is In Me.

During My Physical Lifetime, I Appear Within The Cosmic Domain As My Avatarically-Born Bodily (Human) Divine Form.

But I, Myself, Am Divine Translation Itself.

I Am The Process Of The Divine Translation Of every one (and all-and-All).

My Divinely Translated Devotee Stands Undifferentiated In (and As) My Own Avatarically Self-Revealed Divine Person—and As An Eternal Participant In My Infinite Divine Self-"Brightness".

No Matter How Many Multitudes Of My Devotees Are Divinely Translated—There Will Always Only Be Me.

Indeed, All Of My Devotees Are Always Already One With Me In My Divine Spherical Self-Domain Of Perfect Self-"Brightness".

My Magnification Of Self-"Brightness" Will Continue Forever, Until There Is The Final (and Most Ultimate) Event Of The Divine Translation Of The Entire Cosmic Domain.

It Is Not Necessary For Me To Divinely Translate, Because I Always Already Am The Divine "Bright" Spherical Self-Domain Itself.

I Am Always Already Divinely Translated.

I Am The One "Bright" Person, "Brightly" Self-Revealing Myself.

Avatar Adi Da Samraj
The Mountain Of Attention Sanctuary, 2000

SUTRA 67

In The Course Of The Only-By-Me Revealed and Given Way Of The Heart (or Way Of Adidam), Previous To The Great Event Of Divine Translation, The Maturing Devotee (At Even Any Developmental Stage Of Practice In The Only-By-Me Revealed and Given Way Of The Heart) May Enjoy Sufficient Release Of (Apparent) conditional energy and attention To Transfer the Apparent conditional personality, After death, To higher (or subtler) worlds Within The Apparently Objective (or Cosmic) Domain—but Translation Into My Divinely Perfect Domain (or Perfectly Subjective Divine "Bright" Spherical Self-Domain) Is Possible Only On The Basis Of Inherently Most Perfect Real-God-Realization (or The Inherent, and Inherently Most Perfect, Transcending Of egoity, or self-Contraction, In Most Perfect Divine Self-Realization). And Translation Into My Divinely Perfect Domain (or Perfectly Subjective Divine "Bright" Spherical Self-Domain) Necessarily Requires (or Is A Matter Of) Inherently Most Perfect Self-Abiding Divine Self-Recognition (and Release) Of The Total Cosmic Domain—Which Is The Totality Of all Possible Apparent conditional energies or forms, Including My Apparently Objective Divine Sound-Form and My Apparently Objective Divine Star-Form, Which Are Themselves To Be Divinely Self-Recognized (and Released) In The (By-Me-and-As-Me-Avatarically-Self-Revealed-and-Spiritually-Self-Transmitted) "Bright" and Inherent (or Perfectly Subjective) Spirit-Radiance Of Transcendental (and Self-Existing) Divine Being.

The Destiny, After death, Of My (Apparent individual) Devotee Is Determined By The Heart-Response (While alive, and In The death-Process) To Me (The Avatarically Self-Revealed, and Self-Evidently Divine, Person—Avatarically Self-Revealed, In Person, As The Inherently Perfect, and Inherently egoless, and Self-Evidently Divine Self-Condition, and Source-Condition, Of all-and-All). And The Heart-Response To My Avataric Divine Self-Revelation (Of My Divine Person and Self-Condition) During The death-Process Is Generally Determined By The Total Complex Of conditional Tendencies That Are Developed During life, or (Otherwise) By The Degree Of ego-Transcendence Demonstrated During life.

In The Case Of the death Of My Any "Perfect Practice" Devotee, Should Divine Translation Not Yet Occur (or If My Devotee's Practice Of The Only-By-Me Revealed and Given Way Of The Heart Has, Otherwise, Not Yet

Advanced Into The Context Of The Only-By-Me Revealed and Given Seventh Stage Of Life), self-Surrender (or Devotional self-Sacrifice) and Great Heart-Practice Should (and Will Tend To) Be Continued In every Further circumstance and Cosmic plane that appears. Therefore, After death (and Until Divine Translation Is Realized), The Only-By-Me Revealed and Given Way Of The Heart (or Way Of Adidam) Should Be Practiced From and At (and, Most Ultimately, As) The Heart, and Always In My Avatarically Self-Revealed Divine Spiritual Company—Whether I Am Revealed (Even In Visions) In My Avatarically-Born Bodily (Human) Divine Form, Or In Special Form (Such As My Divine Sound-Form or My Divine Star-Form), Or (Simply) In The Form Of My Avatarically Self-Transmitted (and Characteristic) Divine Spiritual Presence (or Tangible Divine Spiritual Body Of "Brightness"), Or Merely (and Ultimately) In The Form Of My Avatarically Self-Revealed (and Very, and Transcendental, and Perfectly Subjective, and Inherently Spiritual, and Inherently egoless, and Inherently Perfect, and Self-Evidently Divine) State.

Unless Divine Translation Occurs In The death-Process, the conditionally Manifested being Moves (After death), By Means Of his or her Tendencies, Into a form and a Cosmic plane that Are Structured (By The Cosmic Design Itself) To Satisfy Those Tendencies—and, In The Case Of My Devotees, Into a form and a Cosmic plane that Are Structured (By Means Of My Avatarically Self-Transmitted Divine Spiritual Grace) To Provide conditions For Further ego-Transcendence (and For ego-Transcending Growth Into Perfect Self-Realization Of The By-Me-and-As-Me-Avatarically-Self-Revealed-and-Spiritually-Self-Transmitted Divine Self-Condition and Source-Condition).

Death Is Simply The Relinquishment Of Association With the present Cosmic plane, and With the personal form in that plane—Just As birth Is The Initiation Of Association With plane and form. Birth Occurs When Particular conditional Tendencies Create The Opportunity For Association With particular conditions. Death Occurs, By The Intervention Of Structural Laws Of Cosmic Nature, When present conditions Are No Longer Sufficient For Basic Support Of the conditional life-functions.

Nevertheless, birth and death Are (Primarily and Necessarily) Associated With The Great Purpose Of ego-Transcendence (and Growth Beyond conditional limits). Therefore, The Primary (or Great) Purpose Of birth, life, and death (If they arise) Is Most Perfect Divine Self-Awakening (or Most Perfect Realization Of The "Bright")—Which Only-By-Me Revealed and Given (Seventh Stage) Realization Progressively Demonstrates Itself As Divine Transfiguration, Divine Transformation, Divine Indifference, and (Finally) Divine Translation (or The Outshining Of The Apparent Objective, or Cosmic, Domain By and In My Perfectly Subjective and Perfectly Divine "Bright" Spherical Self-Domain).

And, In Order To Serve This Great Purpose, I Am (Now, and Forever Hereafter) Avatarically Present and Always Already Divinely Present, In (and As) All My Avatarically Self-Revealed (and Self-Evidently Divine) Forms, and In (and As) all Cosmic planes.

Until Divine Translation (or The "Bright" Outshining), every conditionally Manifested being Survives bodily death and Continues To experience (and, Potentially, To Grow) Within The Cosmic Mandala. The psycho-physical personality Is A conditional (and, Therefore, Always changing, or Apparently Temporary) Play Upon An Infinite Unity That Is Eternal, One, and Only. Therefore, When the gross body dies, The subtler Modifications (or The subtle and causal Components Of form and psyche) Inevitably Persist.

After bodily death, the Apparent individual (subtle and causal) personality Becomes Progressively Re-Associated With Whichever Vibratory Zone Of The Cosmic Mandala Corresponds To The conditional Tendencies That Remained Effective At the end of the previous lifetime (or After The Completion Of The death-Process, or Release-Process, That Ended and Followed the previous lifetime). Thus, After bodily death, conditional self-Consciousness Is Progressively Re-Collected Via The Spontaneous (but Habit-caused) Motions Of attention. After the gross body Is Relinquished (In The death-Process), Many Patterns Of psyche (or mind) and form (or body) arise and pass away (in a sequence of various planes of experience), until the re-attainment of a more or less fixed embodiment (or "reincarnation", or re-birth, as a conditionally Manifested psycho-physical personality) in one of the planes Of The Cosmic Mandala (Possibly Even in the same plane and general locale as in the previous lifetime).

People Often Wonder Why, If All Of This Is So, they Do Not Remember previous lifetimes (or previous circumstances Of conditional Existence). Of Course, some people Do, In Fact, Remember previous lifetimes (or previous circumstances Of conditional Existence). Very Often, Such Remembering Occurs Spontaneously—In dreams, or In reveries, or In Meditation. However, most people Claim Never To Have So Remembered. The Reason For This Is That There Is No entity that Passes From lifetime To lifetime. What Proceeds From lifetime To lifetime Is The conditional Process Itself—Not a Fixed (or Eternal) "personal" entity (or An Independent and Separate individual Consciousness).

The present lifetime (or the Apparent present personal entity, which is Only the Apparent and conditional body-mind) is the effect of what came before it. The past lifetimes (or All The Cycles Of conditional embodiment) Are Effective As causes for what Follows them. It Is Not That a Remembering entity lives, dies, and is re-born. The True and Only (and Inherently egoless) Conscious Light Is Inherently, and Inherently Perfectly, and Perfectly Subjectively, and

Always Transcendentally Existing (or Existing Always Already Most Prior To conditional events and The Memory Of them). Re-birth Is Simply The (Apparent) Continuation Of The Process (Of causes and effects) That Produces mind and body. The True and Only (and Inherently egoless) Conscious Light Never changes—but It Is That Which Becomes (Apparently) Aware Of the present body-mind (which present body-mind has, itself, been caused By, and is Continuous With, The Residual Effective Tendencies Of the past body-mind). Therefore, The True and Only (and Inherently egoless) Conscious Light Will Tend (In the form of processes in the present body-mind) To Continue To Presume That It Is a conditional self, Until The True and Only (and Inherently egoless) Conscious Light (Itself) Awakens To Its Real Condition, In The Only-By-My-Avataric-Divine-Spiritual-Grace-Given Event Of Most Perfect Divine Enlightenment.

The True and Only (and Inherently egoless) Conscious Light Is Always Already Existing Transcendentally (or Most Priorly). It Is (Itself) Never an entity (or a conditional, Separate, Independent, and Migrating self, or individual Consciousness). The True and Only (and Inherently egoless) Conscious Light Does Not Move From lifetime To lifetime. Lifetimes Reproduce themselves (As effects Follow causes). The True and Only (and Inherently egoless) Conscious Light Merely (and Only Apparently) Observes The Chain Of events As they arise. Therefore, The True and Only (and Inherently egoless) Conscious Light Does Not, In Itself, Remember the past—Because It Does Not (and Did Not Ever) Really Become a psycho-physical entity in the present.

The True and Only (and Inherently egoless) Conscious Light Does Not, In Itself, Have A Memory Of past lives. As Soon As the present lifetime (or Even the present moment) passes, The True and Only (and Inherently egoless) Conscious Light Ceases To Identify With it (Unless A Memory arises In mind To Suggest Such Identification). Therefore, The Chain Of lifetimes (or The Progression Of experiences of conditional mind and embodiment) Is (Itself) The Memory (or The Mechanism Of Memory). If past moments in the present lifetime Are To Be Remembered, The Only Requirement Is That attention Pass Through The Relatively Superficial (or Surface) Strata Of The Chain Of Recent Memory. However, If past lifetimes Are To Be Remembered, attention Must Migrate Through The deep psychic Core Of The Memory Chain. And This Does Not Tend To Occur (or To Be Noticed), Unless an individual Is Disposed (and, Perhaps, Even Intentionally Oriented) Toward Such psychic Exploration.

You Are Not the same entity (or personality) that lived in many past lifetimes. Rather, In The Case Of any apparent individual, The True and Only (and Inherently egoless) Conscious Light (Itself) Is Presently (but Only Apparently) Aware Of (and, As Such, Is Apparently Assuming the limited point of view of) a body-mind that is (itself) a direct effect of many past lifetimes. Therefore, Memory Of past lifetimes Will Not Necessarily Characterize Your experience in the present lifetime, but Your experience in the present lifetime Will (and Does) Necessarily Reflect (or Express) The Remaining (or Effective) Tendencies Of all past lifetimes (and causes) that preceded (or Effectively caused) the present lifetime.

Every birth (or re-birth) Is A Plunge Into material (or Otherwise conditional) ignorance (With Coincident Loss, or Forgetting, Of Divine Ignorance—or Inherent Divine Freedom—Itself).

Every lifetime Is Begun With (and By Means Of) The Loss (or Forgetting) Of Every Previous (and, Otherwise, Eternal) Wisdom-Advantage.

At birth (or, Otherwise, whenever Identification With the present-time born-condition Is Presumed), All That Was Realized Previously (or, Otherwise, Priorly) Recedes Into The Unconscious and Subconscious "Background" (Of The Deeper Personality), and all that Was Previously (or, Otherwise, Priorly) Released Returns (In One or Another Manner, and To One or Another Degree) To The Immediate "Surface" Of Direct (perceptual and conceptual) Awareness (or the Conscious mind, or body-mind, of the gross personality).

In Order To Serve In Bodily (Human) Form, Even I Was Required, By My Own Choice, To Relinquish My Own Eternally Free Condition, and (Thus, By Submission To Identification With My Own conditional Body-Mind and Circumstance) To Forget Myself—Until, By Means Of My Own Unique Avataric Ordeal Of Divine Self-Remembering, I Should Re-Awaken To Myself, and Even (At Last) "Emerge" Most Perfectly (As Myself).

Therefore, Even Though My Own Motive Toward Even This (Now, and Forever Hereafter—and Inherently, and Inherently Perfectly—Me-Revealing) Bodily (Human) Avataric Birth Was Great Love-Sympathy For all conditionally Manifested beings, and Even Though This Bodily (Human) Avataric Birth Was (Thus, and Altogether) Intended Toward A Divinely Great and Divinely Enlightened and Divinely Enlightening Purpose (here, and every "where" In The Cosmic Domain)—My Intentional Avataric Assumption Of This Bodily (Human) Form Required The Avataric Self-Sacrifice Of My Own Divine (and Eternally Free) Love-Bliss-Condition (Just As even all ordinary-born beings, born Without Such Divinely Self-Aware Intention, Sacrifice Eternal Freedom and Perfect Love-Bliss By their Natural Submission To The Cycles Of conditional birth and desiring and death).

Each and every born lifetime Requires Many (Even "ordinary") Helping Associations (Even "Carried Over" From lifetimes past), and Every Kind Of Great Growth and Great Realization Requires Great Good Company and Great (Divine) Help, or Else The "Background" Strengths (or All The Virtues and

Realizations Hidden, or Forgotten, In The Subconscious and Unconscious Deep) Will Not Re-Surface (or Otherwise Come Forward) To Consciousness. And, Ultimately (In Due Course), It Becomes Clear That Not Even Any Kind Of conditional (or merely psycho-physical) Growth Is The Purpose Toward Which conditional Existence Should Be Devoted, but, Rather, conditional Existence Should Be Devoted Only To The Progressive (but Always present-time Direct, and, At Last, Most Perfect) Transcending (or The Real and True Out-Growing) Of conditional Existence Itself, By Means Of The Progressive (but Always present-time Direct, and, At Last, Most Perfect) Realization Of The Un-conditional Condition That Was, and Is, Always Already The Case. Therefore, and By Means Of (Eventually, Most Perfect) Surrender To Me (The Avatarically Self-Revealed True, and Only, and Inherently egoless, and Self-Evidently Divine Conscious Light, Itself), conditional Existence Should Be Devoted To Most Perfectly Out-Growing (and, Thereby, To No Longer Making or Perpetuating) The Otherwise Repetitive Cycles Of births and lifetimes and deaths.

Even Though All That I Have Done By My Own Avataric Ordeal Of Divine Self-Submission To Bodily (Human) Form and Purpose Has (As A Result Of My Eventual, and Inherently Most Perfect, Divine Re-Awakening, My Subsequent Avataric Divine Teaching-Work, My Eventually Most Perfect Avataric Divine Self-"Emergence", and All My Avataric Divine Spiritual Blessing-Work) Become Good Company (or Satsang) and Great (and Self-Evidently Divine) Help, Forever, and For all-and-All—It Also (In Due Course, In My Spontaneous Avataric Play Of Self-Abiding Divine Self-Recognition) Became Necessary (and Inevitable) For Me, As A Fundamental Part Of That Good Service, To Become Spontaneously and Divinely Indifferent To Even All Intentions and All Sympathetic Attachments (Even While Yet Appearing, In A Simple and Spontaneous Manner, To Be Actively Animating Intentions and Actively Maintaining Sympathetic Relations). By Thus Standing Free—Self-Abiding Merely In My "Bright" and Very (and Inherently Perfect, and Inherently egoless, and Self-Evidently Divine) State, Prior To (and Inherently Free From) All Gestures Of Work (or Active Purposiveness), and All Gestures Of Sympathetic Attachment (or Active Relatedness)—I Also Allow Even My Avatarically-Born Bodily (Human) Divine Form and My Avatarically Self-Transmitted Spiritual (and Always, or Inherently, Blessing) Divine Presence To Merely Be, and Only Thus To Work. Therefore, By This "Bright" Indifference, I Affirm (and Confirm, and Demonstrate) To all That (Most Ultimately, and At Last) Every conditional Sympathy, Every conditional Purpose and Intention, and Even conditional Existence Itself Must Be Most Perfectly Transcended (and, Thus, Most Perfectly Relinquished) In Only That Which Is (Only and Itself and Inherently and

Divinely) Perfect—or Else conditional Existence (Perpetuated By another conditional birth, and lifetime, and death) Will Inevitably Continue After the present-time lifetime and death.

Therefore, In The Context Of the present lifetime, You Will experience The Motions (and The Results) Of All conditionally Effective Tendencies That Continue From the past. If You Do Not Transcend Those Tendencies, You Will Duplicate or Repeat or Regenerate the past (In A Mechanical, Automatic, and egoic Manner), and You Will (By Virtue Of A Mechanical, Automatic, and egoic Involvement In conditional Processes) Generate Similar (or Even New) conditional Tendencies, Which Must Be Fulfilled (or Made Effective) In the future (Even In future lifetimes). If Devotion, Service, self-Discipline, and (Most Fundamental) self-Understanding Characterize the present lifetime, To The Degree That There Is Some Real Advance Beyond the limits Associated With The First Three Stages Of Life—Then presently Effective Tendencies Inherited From the past Will Gradually Dissipate, and future experience (during or after the present lifetime) Will Be Associated With Positively Improved Attitudes (or Increased psycho-physical Equanimity) and Even (Perhaps) With higher (or subtler) Possibilities (Of experience and knowledge) Within The Cosmic Mandala. And those who Listen To Me, and Hear Me, and See Me, and Embrace The Only-By-Me Revealed and Given Way Of The Heart (or Way Of Adidam) Most Profoundly Will (By Means Of My Avatarically Self-Transmitted Divine Spiritual Grace) Really Transcend The Entire Process That Generates conditional Tendencies—Such That (Most Ultimately) Divine Translation Is Realized, Either At the end of the present lifetime Or (In Due Course) Through The Ordeal Of (and At the end of) any number of future lifetimes.

Therefore, It Is Profoundly Useful For You To Realize—Whether Through Memory, Or Through Intelligent Observation Of The (Always psycho-physical) Laws and Mechanics Of Cosmic Nature, Or (Most Simply and Directly) Through The Illuminated Certainty (or Inherent Faith) That Must Awaken Via The Heart-Effective Grace Of True Satsang With Me (and Through The Subsequent Heart-Effective Grace Of My Avatarically Given and Giving Divine Spirit-Baptism)—That conditional embodiment (or Apparently conditional Existence, Manifested As a body-mind) Tends To Reproduce itself Inevitably. Once a body-mind Is Assumed, another body-mind Will Certainly Follow—Unless (Only-By-My-Avataric-Divine-Spiritual-Grace-Given) Divine Self-Realization and (Only-By-My-Avataric-Divine-Spiritual-Grace-Given) Most Perfect Renunciation (Of conditional self-Existence) Intervene To Break The Spell. It Is Simply A Matter Of The (Apparent) Laws (or "Habits") Of Cosmic Light—or Of (Apparently) conditionally Modified Conscious Light. The True and Only (and Inherently egoless) Conscious Light Cannot Be Destroyed—but, Once The True and Only (and Inherently egoless) Conscious Light Is (Apparently) Modified conditionally (or Once A conditional Motion Is Established), The Process Of Modification Will Tend To Continue (Indefinitely), Until The Tendency Toward conditional Modification Is (Itself) Transcended and Outshined In The True and Only (and Inherently egoless) Conscious Light (Itself).

The Spirit-Energy (Of The True and Only and Inherently egoless Conscious Light) Is Eternal and Constant. That Spirit-Energy Cannot Be Destroyed—but It Can Be Apparently Modified (or Apparently Converted and Changed Into conditional forms). And, Once That Spirit-Energy (or The Inherent Radiance, or Spirit-Force, Of The Fundamental Reality) Is Apparently Modified, Its conditional forms Can Change, or Else Dissolve Into other forms, or Even (If My Avatarically Self-Transmitted Divine Spiritual Grace and Your Devotional and Spiritual Practice Of The Only-By-Me Revealed and Given Way Of The Heart Coincide) Be Resolved Into The By-Me-and-As-Me-Avatarically-Self-Revealed-and-Spiritually-Self-Transmitted Eternal Un-Modified State Of Self-Radiant "Bright" Divine Spirit-Energy and Self-Existing Divine Consciousness Itself—Which (Self-Evidently Divine) State Is The One and Only and Inherently Indivisible and Inherently egoless Conscious Light (Itself).

Indeed, One Of The Apparent Laws (or "Habits") Of The Spirit-Energy (Of The True and Only and Inherently egoless Conscious Light) In The Context Of The Cosmic Mandala Is Not Merely That conditional forms Can Change and Dissolve, but That they Always Do Change and Dissolve. Therefore, Once The Spirit-Energy Of Fundamental Reality Becomes (or, Really, Appears To Become) a conditionally Manifested form, being, or process—that conditionally Manifested form, being, or process Tends Immediately (and Constantly) To Change or Dissolve. So It Is (every "where") Within The Cosmic Domain—and So It Is With (and Within) Your Own body-mind. Because All Of This Is So, conditional Existence Obliges You To Observe, Endure, Most Fundamentally Understand, and Really Transcend Every Kind Of Change and Dissolution (Including The Blows Of Apparent loss and death).

After the death of an individual, his or her Destiny Is Generally Determined By The Stage Of Life (and The Degree Of ego-Transcendence) In Which he or she Was Really Active At the time of death. Therefore, In General, Clear Signs That Correspond To One or The Other (or A Complex) Of The First Six Developmental Stages Of Life Will Characterize living individuals During the (Generally Extensive) period of ordinary (or typical) living that Immediately Precedes the time of their death—and their Destiny After death Will Tend To Correspond To The Tendencies Associated With Those Signs.

Even My Devotees who Really and Truly Demonstrate The Signs Of The Only-By-Me Revealed and Given Seventh Stage Of Life (In The Only-By-Me

Revealed and Given Way Of The Heart, or Way Of Adidam) May, If they Are Not Yet Fully Disposed Toward Divine Translation, Pass To any of the Cosmic planes After death. They May Pass Even Into the grosser worlds, If they Are Inclined Toward Service and Play In those worlds. Or they May Pass Into the subtler worlds, In Order To Remain In The Cosmic Play and Serve.

Each Of The Seven Stages Of Life Corresponds To Tendencies (or Else Demonstrations) That Move To Associate With conditions Of A Certain Level Of Vibration (or Apparent Modification Of The "Midnight Sun" and Sphere Of My Divine White Self-"Brightness").

The First Three Stages Of Life Are Associated With the waking state, The grosser and Outward-Directed Orientation Of the perceptual mind, The conceptual (and Typically verbal) Orientation Of mind, The Left Side Of The Heart, the lower brain, the pituitary gland (and all the other lower-functioning glands, or glandular Regions, of the brain, and of the Extended gross physical body), the specialized activities of the left hemisphere of the brain, the entire gross physical body (and Especially The Lower bodily Regions—Beginning With the solar plexus, and Extending Down To the bodily base), the etheric (or pranic) field of Natural energies, and (Altogether) The Totality Of planes and forms and experience and knowledge In the gross and etheric fields (or Dimensions) Of The Cosmic Mandala.

The Fourth Stage Of Life Is (Like The First Three Stages Of Life) Also Associated With the lower (or waking) frontal personality, The lower-functioning psycho-physical Orientation Of the gross (and etheric) body-mind, and The Left Side Of The Heart—and (Additionally) The Fourth Stage Of Life Is (Potentially, and, Then, More and More) Associated With The subtler and Inward-Directed Orientation Of mind, The Middle Station Of The Heart, the higher brain and the specialized activities of the right hemisphere of the brain, the glandular centers In The Region Of the throat and upper chest (Associated, Eventually, With The Spiritual Breath Of Life), The (Eventual) Spiritual and (Potentially) Altogether Regenerative Conversion Of all the Otherwise lower-functioning glands (or glandular Regions) of the Extended gross physical body and of the brain (Especially the pituitary gland, and Also the other, Otherwise lower-functioning, glands, or glandular Regions, of the brain), and The (Potential) Eventual Re-Orientation Of the Total body-mind To My Avatarically Self-Transmitted Divine Spirit-Current At (and Infinitely Above) The Ajna Door.

The Fifth Stage Of Life Is Associated With The subtle and inward-Directed Orientation Of mind itself (Prior To, or Apart From, the gross physical body), the dreaming (or dreamlike subtle) state, The Middle Station Of The Heart, the higher brain, the specialized activities of the right hemisphere of the brain, the glandular centers In The Region Of the throat and upper chest (Associated

With The Spiritual Breath Of Life), the pineal gland (and other higher-functioning glandular centers, or glandular Regions, of the brain), The Regenerative Spiritual Conversion (or The Spiritual, and Spiritually Regenerative, Upward Re-Orientation) Of Even the pituitary gland (and all the other, Otherwise lower-functioning, glands, or glandular Regions, of the brain and of the Total Extended gross physical body), The Upper Terminal Of the brain (Associated With The Upper Rear Of The Brain Core, and With the upper rear of the head, and With the aperture in the upper rear of the top of the head, and With The Total Crown Of the head), and (Therefore) With The Play At and Above The Ajna Door (Including The Potential Elaborate Systematic Perception Of Cosmic Lights and higher, or subtler, worlds). The Fifth Stage Of Life Is Also (Potentially) Associated With A Yearning Toward The Form and The State Of My Avatarically Self-Transmitted Divine Spirit-Current (or My Apparently Objective and Always Already Most Ascended Source-Current—Perceived As subtle Visible Light, or As subtle Sound-Vibration, or, Otherwise, Merely Touched, As subtly Tangibly Felt Love-Bliss). And That Yearning Toward My (Apparently) Objective and Always Already Most Ascended Spirit-Current (or Source-Current) Is (Necessarily, Only By Means Of Specifically Activated Modes Of Spiritual Participation) Uniquely Satisfied In Priorly Ascended Nirvikalpa Samadhi—but The Most Perfect Form and State (or Perfectly Subjective Truth) Of My (Only Apparently) Objective and (Only Apparently) Most Ascended (or Seeming-To-Be-Above) Source-Current Is Finally Realized Only In Divine Translation, Which Requires (or Is A Matter Of) Self-Abiding Divine Self-Recognition Of Even My Apparently Objective Divine Body Of Spirit-Force (Appearing As My Apparently Objective Divine Star Of Light, or As My Apparently Objective Divine Sound Of Thunder, or, Otherwise, As My Apparent, and Merely Touched, or Felt, Love-Bliss-"Brightness") Infinitely Above The Total Crown Of the head. And That Most Perfect (and Inherent) Transcending Of all-and-All Is Thus Realized Only In The Most Ultimate Context Of The Only-By-Me Revealed and Given Seventh Stage Of Life (In The Only-By-Me Revealed and Given Way Of The Heart, or Way Of Adidam).

The Sixth Stage Of Life Is Associated With Fully Conscious Transcendental (and Inherently Spiritual) Self-Abiding, Established (Either Tacitly Or By Specifically Activated Efforts and Means) Via (and Beyond, or Even Prior To) The Right Side Of The Heart, and (Either Tacitly Or By Explicit Intention) Excluding (As Is Also The Case In deep sleep) The phenomenal Cosmic Lights and all of conditional experience. However, Such Transcendental Self-Abiding Is A conditionally Enacted Mode Of Participation In The Perfectly Subjective Reality—and, Therefore, It (Inherently and Tacitly) Allows The Continuation Of Tendencies That (Inevitably) Continue To Associate the conditionally

Manifested being With the conditionally Manifested planes Of The Cosmic Mandala (Both Before and After death).

Immersion (or Swoon) In The psycho-physical Deep Of conditional self-Consciousness (As In deep worldless sleep) May Tend To Associate the conditional self With The subtle Visualization Of The Black Field (or Black Light), but Such A Perception Is Actually (Itself) A Mode (or Stage) Inherent In The Structure Of Systematic Progress Through The Cosmic Lights (or the planes of mind) Characteristically Associated With The Vertical Process Of The Fifth Stage Of Life. Therefore, Such Contemplative Immersion In The Visualized mental Dark Should Not (Itself) Be Equated With The Process Of Transcendental (and Inherently Spiritual) Self-Identification That Develops In The Context Of The Horizontal Process Characteristically Associated With The Sixth Stage Of Life (or The Process Of Self-Identification With The Infinite Free Space Of Self-Existing Consciousness—Prior To the deep sleep state, Prior To the dreaming and dreamlike states, Prior To the waking state, Prior To all the forms of mind, Prior To all psycho-physical states, Prior To all conditional objects, Prior To the very act of conditional attention, and Even Prior To The Apparent Witness-Function Of Consciousness).

The Red Field (or Red Light) Corresponds To the gross body and the gross (or grosser) worlds—but The Red Light Is (Itself) A subtle Vision (or a form of higher mind). The Yellow Field (or Yellow Light) Corresponds To the etheric (or pranic) body and To the subtler dimension (or the subtler planes) of the gross (or grosser) worlds—but The Yellow Light Is (Itself) A subtle Vision (or a form of higher mind). The Moonlike White Field (or Moonlike White Light) Corresponds To the mid-range of the subtle body itself and To the subtle (or subtler-than-gross) worlds—but The Moonlike White Light Is (Itself) A subtle Vision (or a form of higher mind). The Black Field (or Black Light) Corresponds To The Dark Passage That Leads Away From the grosser and lesser planes of mind, Toward higher (or subtler) phenomena (or worlds)—but The Black Light Is (Itself) A subtle Vision (or a form of higher mind). The Radiant Blue Field (or Blue Light), Just Beyond The Black Field (or Black Light), Corresponds To the higher range of the subtle body and To the higher (and highest) range of subtle conditional worlds—but The Radiant Blue Field (or Radiant Blue Light, Itself) and the Radiant Blue worlds (or all appearances In or Of The Radiant Blue Field) Are (Like All Lights, worlds, and forms Outside, or Surrounding, or Peripheral To The Radiant Blue) Only subtle Visions (or forms of higher mind), appearing conditionally Within The Cosmic Mandala.

All subtle (or higher) forms of mind—Together With all lesser forms of mind, All higher Associations Of mind, All lower Associations Of mind, All

Cosmic Visions, All Cosmic Lights, and (Indeed) all conditional perceptions Of Whatever Kind—Are Strategically Excluded In conditionally Ascended Nirvikalpa Samadhi (and, Otherwise, Effectively, but Not Strategically, Excluded In Priorly Ascended Nirvikalpa Samadhi). Likewise, All Of That Is Strategically Excluded In conditionally Self-Abiding Jnana Nirvikalpa Samadhi (and, Otherwise, Effectively, but Not Strategically, Excluded In Priorly Self-Abiding Jnana Nirvikalpa Samadhi). And, Even Though Any (and All) Cosmic (or conditional) Possibilities (Including Any and All Cosmic Lights) May Be Perceived In The Context Of The Only-By-Me Revealed and Given Seventh Stage Of Life (In The Only-By-Me Revealed and Given Way Of The Heart, or Way Of Adidam), It Is All Inherently (Divinely) Self-Recognized and Most Perfectly (Divinely) Transcended. And, Most Ultimately, All Of That Is Most Perfectly Gone Beyond (or Outshined), In The Final Event Of The Only-By-Me Revealed and Given Way Of The Heart (or Way Of Adidam)—Which Final Event Is The Great Event Of Divine Translation, and Which Final Event Is The Consummate (or Final and Completing) Demonstration Of (Unconditional and Most Perfect) Seventh Stage Sahaja Nirvikalpa Samadhi (or Ruchira Samraj Samadhi, or, Simply, Samraj Samadhi).

As I Have Indicated, The Only-By-Me Revealed and Given Seventh Stage Of Life (In The Only-By-Me Revealed and Given Way Of The Heart, or Way Of Adidam) May (Because Of The Non-Exclusionary Disposition Inherently Associated With The Only-By-Me Revealed and Given Seventh Stage Of Life In The Only-By-Me Revealed and Given Way Of The Heart) Be (Potentially) Associated With Even any of the Cosmic planes After death. Nevertheless, The Devotee-Realizer In The Only-By-Me Revealed and Given Seventh Stage Of Life (In The Only-By-Me Revealed and Given Way Of The Heart) Is Founded In (and Inherently, and Inherently Most Perfectly, Self-Identified With) The Transcendental, Inherently Spiritual, Inherently egoless, and Self-Evidently Divine Self-Condition (or The True and Only Conscious Light, Which Is The Self-Existing, and Self-Radiant, and Perfectly Subjective Source, or Source-Condition, Of All Apparently Objective Light).

In The Apparent Context Of the body (or Of the Apparent objective personality in the gross worlds, and in the waking state, and in the subtle worlds, or in a state similar or equal to dreaming), The Devotee-Realizer Of The Only-By-Me Revealed and Given Way Of The Heart In The Context Of The Only-By-Me Revealed and Given Seventh Stage Of Life Is Founded In (and As) Amrita Nadi—Which Is "Grounded" (or Most Priorly Established) In The Right Side Of The Heart, and Which Extends Upwards To Include My Infinitely "Ascended" Feeling-"Brightness", and The Perception Of My Apparently Objectified and Ascended Light, or Sound-Vibration, or Touched Presence (or Felt Spirit-Current

Of Love-Bliss) Infinitely Above The Total Crown Of the head. Therefore, The Devotee-Realizer Of The Only-By-Me Revealed and Given Way Of The Heart In The Context Of The Only-By-Me Revealed and Given Seventh Stage Of Life Is Inherently and Fundamentally (and Spontaneously, Rather Than Strategically) Moved Toward The Outshining (or The Divine Translation) Of conditional forms and events (or Of All The Apparent Modifications Of My Avatarically Self-Transmitted Divine Spirit-Energy Itself) In My Avatarically Self-Revealed (and Self-Evidently Divine) Self-Condition Itself (Which Is The Perfectly Subjective Source-Condition Of all objective appearances).

My (Apparently) Objective Divine Sound-Form and Divine Star-Form (Perceived In High Objective Hearing-Vision) Are Made Perceptible (Apparently Objectively) Via the body-mind (or Else Via the mind alone, When There Is No Active bodily Association). As Apparently Objective Perceptions, My Divine Sound-Form and My Divine Star-Form Are The Eternal (and Not Cosmic, but Perfectly Subjective) Divine Reality Perceived To Be Breaking Through The Center Of The Cosmic Mandala. Therefore, My Perceptible (or Apparently Objective) Divine Sound-Form and Divine Star-Form Are Perceived Through The Only Hole (or Infinitely Ascended Opening) In The Universe (or The Total conditional Cosmos), and (Thus) Via An Aperture Infinitely Above the mind (or the Total body-mind).

Ultimately (and In Any Case), My Perceptible (or Apparently Objective) Divine Sound-Form and Divine Star-Form Are Simply The Ultimate Perceptible (or Apparently Objective) Sign Of My "Bright" Inherent Love-Bliss (or Self-Radiance) Of Self-Evidently Divine Being. Therefore, In The Context Of The Only-By-Me Revealed and Given Seventh Stage Of Life, The moment to moment "Practice" (or Demonstration-Process) Of The Only-By-Me Revealed and Given Way Of The Heart (or Way Of Adidam) Is Not A Matter Of "Necessary" (or Somehow Obligatory) Perceiving Of Either My Divine Sound-Form Or My Divine Star-Form (As Apparently Objective Forms). Rather, The Only-By-Me Revealed and Given Seventh-Stage-Of-Life "Practice" Is <u>Fundamentally</u> (and, Truly, Necessarily) A Matter Of Relaxing (or Relinquishing) the body-mind (and all of its conditional relations) Into My Avatarically Self-Transmitted Divine Spiritual Self-"Brightness" (or The Infinite Fullness Of My Avatarically Self-Transmitted Spirit-Current Of Self-Evidently Divine Love-Bliss—Which Is Perceived, Apparently Objectively, As My all-and-All-Surrounding and all-and-All-Pervading Divine Spiritual Body). Such Divinely Enlightened "Practice" <u>Spontaneously</u> (and Not Strategically) "Produces" (or Divinely Demonstrates) The Signs Of Divine Transfiguration, Divine Transformation, and Divine Indifference, Culminating (Most Ultimately) In Divine Translation—Which Is The Perfectly Subjective Self-Outshining Of All Apparent conditional Modifications,

The Utter (and Inherent) Transcending Of The Tendency To Contract (Rather Than To Shine), and The Final Assertion and Demonstration Of Utter (and Inherent) Freedom From The Tendency To Allow The Freely Self-Existing and Self-Radiant Being To Be limited conditionally.

Divine Translation Itself Cannot Occur If My (Perceived) Apparently Objective Divine Spiritual Body, or My (Perceived) Apparently Objective Divine Star-Form, or My (Perceived) Apparently Objective Divine Sound-Form, or Even *Any* Apparently Objective Appearance Is Un-Recognized (or Regarded Merely *As* An Object or An "Other"—and, Thus, Not Transcended In *Me*). Even The Perception and Conception Of Relatedness Itself (Which Characterizes Both egoic self-Contraction and Apparent conditional Awareness Generally) Must Be Divinely Self-Recognized and Divinely Transcended, If There Is To Be Divine Translation In The "Bright".

Divine Translation Occurs Spontaneously (Not Intentionally, or Strategically). Divine Translation May (Initially) Be Associated With A Perception (or Noticing) Of My Apparently Objective Divine Sound-Form and/or My Apparently Objective Divine Star-Form (and Even An Apparent Process Of Merging With My Divine Sound-Form and/or My Divine Star-Form), but That Perception or Process Must (Necessarily) Coincide With (and, Otherwise, Become Superseded By) Self-Abiding Divine Self-Recognition (and Most Perfect Transcending) Of My Apparently Objective Divine Sound-Form and My Apparently Objective Divine Star-Form. The Most Ultimate Process That Is Divine Translation Itself Occurs When All subject-object References (and The Feeling Of Relatedness Itself) Are Outshined In and By and *As* The By-Me-and-*As*-Me-Avatarically-Self-Revealed-and-Spiritually-Self-Transmitted "Midnight Sun" (or Divine "Bright" Revelation-Sphere), Standing Free, Above all-and-All—Such That (Finally) the body-mind (As Well As the Total field of conditional relations) Is Freely Relinquished (and Most Perfectly Transcended) In The Utterly Single (or Most Perfectly Non-Dual) Self-Realization Of The One and Only and Inherently Indivisible and Inherently egoless and Self-Evidently Divine Conscious Light (or The Utterly Non-Separate and Non-"Different" Divine Spherical Self-Domain Of The "Bright", Itself).

Therefore, Divine Translation Occurs Only On The Basis Of Most Perfect Divine Self-Realization, In Which There Is Progressive Divine Self-Recognition-Transcendence Of (In Due Course) *all* conditional states In The (By-Me-and-*As*-Me-Avatarically-Self-Revealed-and-Spiritually-Self-Transmitted) Self-Existing and Self-Radiant Divine Self-Condition (and Source-Condition) That *Is* The One and Only Divine and Conscious Light. And, When Divine Self-Recognition-Transcendence Becomes The Singleness Of The One and Only and Inherently Indivisible and Inherently egoless and Self-Evidently Divine Conscious Light

(Self-Existing and Self-Radiant In Place, Outshining All subject-object Distinctions), Then conditional Existence Is Spontaneously Relinquished, and My Spiritually Self-"Bright" Divine Spherical (Centerless and Boundless) Self-Domain Is Spontaneously "Entered" (or Directly, Immediately, and Most Perfectly Assumed).

My Divine Sound-Form and My Divine Star-Form—Which Are The Final (Apparently) Objective Forms In Which The By-Me-and-As-Me-Avatarically-Self-Revealed-and-Spiritually-Self-Transmitted (Very) Divine Self-Condition and Source-Condition Is (Apparently) Presented and Realized—Must, Most Ultimately (and Merely By Self-Abiding Divine Self-Recognition), Be Transcended (and Dissolved, or Subsumed, or Divinely Translated) In The Self-Existing and Self-Radiant and Self-Evidently Divine Self-Condition (and Source-Condition) That I, In My Childhood, Named "The 'Bright'". Through Self-Abiding Divine Self-Recognition (In The Context Of The Only-By-Me Revealed and Given Seventh Stage Of Life, and Even In The Apparent Context Of the body, the mind, and the world), My (Apparently Objective) Divine Sound-Form (or Apparently Ascended Mass Of Sound-Vibration) and My (Apparently Objective) Divine Star (or Apparently Ascended Star-Light) Will Be Felt, Perceived, Experienced, or Known To Be At (or Originating From) The "Bright" Divine Self-Heart, Even While Also (Apparently) Vibrating and Shining Infinitely Above the body, the mind, and the world (and Vibrating Around, In, and Through—and Shining On, In, and Through—the body, the mind, and the world). Likewise, In The Event Of Divine Translation, My Divine Sound-Form and My Divine Star-Form Are Realized Entirely In The Context Of The Transcendental, Inherently Spiritual (or Spiritually Self-"Bright"), Inherently egoless, and Self-Evidently Divine Self-Condition (and Source-Condition). Therefore, In The Great Event Of Divine Translation, My Divine Sound-Form and My Divine Star-Form Are Not Merely Perceived To Be Infinitely Above, or Even To Originate In (or On The Base Of) The Right Side Of The Heart. Rather, My Apparently Objective Divine Sound-Form (or Apparently Objective Source-Vibration) and My Apparently Objective Divine Star-Form (or Apparently Objective Source-Light) Are Most Perfectly (Divinely) Self-Recognized (and, Thus, Perfectly Subjectively Realized) In The Great Event Of Divine Translation. In The Great Event Of Divine Translation, My Apparently Objective Divine Mass Of Sound-Vibration and My Apparently Objective Divine Star-Light (or Even Every Apparently Objective Sign Of The "Bright") Are Realized Simply As The By-Me-and-As-Me-Avatarically-Self-Revealed-and-Spiritually-Self-Transmitted Perfectly Subjective Feeling-Radiance (or Inherent Love-Bliss) Of Transcendental, Inherently Spiritual, Inherently egoless, and Self-Evidently Divine Being (or Self-Existing and Self-Radiant Conscious Light, Itself). Thus, When (By Means Of My

Avatarically Self-Transmitted Divine Spiritual Grace) Sound and Light Appear In Truth (Divinely Self-Recognized)—body, mind, and world (or all conditional forms and states) Are Dissolved (or Outshined) In My Love-Bliss-"Brightness"—and My Eternal Divine Spherical Self-Domain Shines Forth (Where You Stand) As Conscious Light Itself (Being-"Bright").

Avatar Adi Da Samraj
Adidam Samrajashram, 2003

SUTRA

68

Since Every Trace Of conditional personality (and Of Cosmic Existence) Is Outshined In Divine Translation (or Absolute Realization Of My Divine "Bright" Spherical Self-Domain), There Is No Feature Of Existence In The By-Me-and-As-Me-Avatarically-Self-Revealed-and-Spiritually-Self-Transmitted Divine "Bright" Spherical Self-Domain That Corresponds (or Bears A Likeness) To the conditional references, forms, or states that Are Found anywhere In The Cosmic Domain. Therefore, My Divine "Bright" Spherical Self-Domain Is (Ultimately) Beyond Description here—Except It Can Be Said That It Is Self-Existing and Self-Radiant Existence (Itself), and It Is Self-Evidently Divine Love-Bliss (Itself), and It Is The Ultimate Perfection (and The Perfect Self-Fulfillment) Of Being (Itself), Joyfully Transcending (and Not Merely Negating) The Ordeal Of Life In The Cosmic Domain.

My Divine "Bright" Spherical Self-Domain Is The Self-Condition (and The Self-Realization) Of Perfect (Inherently egoless, and Infinitely Self-"Bright") Subjectivity.

Therefore, My Divine "Bright" Spherical Self-Domain Has Not Any Objective Features, but It Is Entirely and Only The Self-Existing, Self-Radiant, and Self-Evidently Divine Self-Condition (and Source-Condition) Itself.

My Divine "Bright" Spherical Self-Domain Is Self-Existing Self-Radiance (or The "Bright" Itself, or Un-conditional Love-Bliss Itself).

Therefore, Realization Of My Divine "Bright" Spherical Self-Domain Is (and, Necessarily, Requires) The Inherent (and Inherently Most Perfect, and Un-conditional) Transcending Of all objective conditions, and Of Objectivity (or Objective Awareness and Objective Existence) Itself.

"Consider" This: All Seeking Is An Impulse Toward objects (or objective relations, or objective others). Therefore, The Most Perfect Transcending Of All Seeking Is The Most Perfect Transcending Of The Entire Impulse Toward objects (or objective relations, or objective others). And, Most Ultimately (In The Realization Of Divine Translation), The Most Perfect Transcending Of All Seeking Is Demonstrated As The Entire and Most Perfect Transcending Of Objectivity (or Objective Awareness and Objective Existence) Itself.

The self-Contraction Is Always A Search.

The self-Contraction Always Demonstrates itself As The Search For (or the will Toward) objects, or objective relations, or objective others.

The self-Contraction (The First Form, or Root-Form, Of which Is The Feeling Of Relatedness Itself) Is (itself) The Very Action Whereby Objectivity (or Objective Awareness Itself and Objective Existence Itself), or Separateness, and Otherness, and "Difference" Itself, Is Evoked, and Generated, and Established, and experienced, and known.

The self-Contraction Is (itself) Relatedness, and Separateness, and Otherness, and The Only "Difference".

Indeed, The Root-Feeling Of Relatedness (Which Is The Essence Of the self-Contraction) Is (Itself) The Essence and The Substance Of All experienced or known or Presumed Objectivity.

Likewise, The Root-Feeling Of Relatedness (Which Is The Original Act Of self-Contraction) Is (Itself) Both The Origin and The Goal Of The Great Search.

Therefore, All Seeking Is The self-Effort (or the will) Toward Relatedness, but (Ultimately) Even Relatedness Itself (Achieved) Is the experience and the knowledge of self-Contraction.

All Seeking Is A Result, A Certain Sign, A Continuation, An Extension, An Expression, A Demonstration, and a Consistent and Constant experience (and knowing) Of self-Contraction.

All Seeking (or Demonstrated self-Contraction) Is A Process Of Suffering, or A Suffered Effort Toward Release (From The Search Itself) By Means Of The Achievement Of objects, or objective relations, or objective others.

All Seeking Is An Effort Toward Final, Complete, and Utter Release Of self-Contraction (or the ego-"I").

However (and This Must Be Realized), No Kind (or Force) Of Seeking Is Ever Able To Finally, Completely, and Utterly Release self-Contraction (or the Suffered and Suffering ego-"I").

No kind of object (or objective relation, or objective other) and No Force Of Objective Satisfaction Is Ever Able To Finally, Completely, and Utterly Release self-Contraction (or the Suffered and Suffering ego-"I").

Therefore, All Seeking Is self-Contraction, Demonstrated Suffering, and An (Ultimately) Fruitless (or, Necessarily, Frustrated and Failed) self-Effort.

The ego-"I" (or self-Contraction) Is A Search That Is The Search (Itself)—Narcissus Bent (To Suffer) Upon An Illusion, Deluded By his own (self-Generated) Presumption Of Relatedness.

Therefore, Not Any Kind (or Force) Of Seeking Is The Way Of Freedom and The Heart, but Only The (Only-By-Me Revealed and Given) Searchlessly Me-Beholding (and Spiritually Me-Receiving) Process Of Directly (and "Radically", or By "Going To The Root") Understanding and Transcending self-Contraction (and, Therefore, All Seeking) Is The Way Of Freedom Itself and The Heart Itself, Which Divinely Self-Realizes My Divine "Bright" Spherical Self-Domain Itself (and The By-Me-and-As-Me-Avatarically-Self-Revealed-and-Spiritually-Self-Transmitted Condition and Person That Is Real God, or Truth Itself, or Reality Itself).

The Only-By-Me Revealed and Given Way Of The Heart (or Way Of Adidam) Is (By Means Of My Avatarically Self-Transmitted Divine Spiritual Grace) To Finally, Completely, and Utterly Understand, Transcend, and Release self-Contraction.

If self-Contraction Is (By Means Of My Avatarically Self-Transmitted Divine Spiritual Grace) Finally, Completely, and Utterly Understood, Transcended, and Released—All Seeking Is (Finally, Completely, and Utterly) Understood, Transcended, and Released In That Process.

Therefore, Most Ultimately, If (By Means Of My Avatarically Self-Transmitted Divine Spiritual Grace) self-Contraction Is Finally, Completely, and Utterly Understood, Transcended, and Released—Such That (Necessarily) All Seeking Is Thereby (and Finally, Completely, and Utterly) Understood, Transcended, and Released—Then (In The Only-By-My-Avataric-Divine-Spiritual-Grace-Given Event Of Seventh Stage, or Inherently Most Perfect, and Self-Evidently Divine, Self-Awakening) All ego-Effort (or ego-Based will) Toward objects (or all objective relations, and all objective others) Ceases, Such That Only An egoless Heart-Will Remains To Continue The Apparent Association With the body-mind (and With Even any or all potential objects). However, In The Progressive Demonstration Of The Only-By-Me Revealed and Given Seventh Stage Of Life (In The Only-By-Me Revealed and Given Way Of The Heart, or Way Of Adidam), Even This egoless Heart-Will Is, In every moment, Divinely Self-Recognized—Until It Is, More and More, Replaced By Divine Indifference, and (At Last) Most Perfectly Outshined (In Divine Translation). And, In The Most Ultimate "Bright" Event Of Divine Translation, Even Objectivity Itself (or Objective Awareness Itself, and Objective Existence Itself) Is Finally, Completely, and Utterly Outshined By (and In) The Self-Existing Self-Radiance (or Spiritually Self-"Bright" Love-Bliss) Of The By-Me-and-As-Me-Avatarically-Self-Revealed-and-Spiritually-Self-Transmitted Divine Self-Condition (or Source-Condition), Which Is The Inherently Perfect Divine Subjectivity (Itself).

By Means Of My Avatarically Self-Transmitted Divine Spiritual Grace, In The Only-By-Me Revealed and Given Seventh Stage Of Life (In The Only-By-Me Revealed and Given Way Of The Heart, or Way Of Adidam), all objects (or all objective relations, and all objective others), and All Apparent (or conditional) Effort Toward objects (or all objective relations, and all objective others), and

The Root-Feeling Of Relatedness, and Even The Tacit Feeling Of "Difference" Are Consistently and Constantly (Each, and All, and Even Simultaneously, and Always Inherently) Divinely Self-Recognized In The By-Me-and-As-Me-Avatarically-Self-Revealed-and-Spiritually-Self-Transmitted (and Self-Evidently Divine) Conscious Light Of Mere Being. And This By-My-Avataric-Divine-Spiritual-Grace-Given Process (or Divine Demonstration) Continues Thus, Until (As My Avatarically Self-Transmitted Divine Spiritual Grace Will Have It) The Divine Sign Of Spiritually Self-"Bright" Indifference Is Given, and Then The Great Outshining Of all objects, all objective relations, all objective others, and All Of Objectivity Itself By and In (and, Therein, As) The (By-Me-and-As-Me-Avatarically-Self-Revealed-and-Spiritually-Self-Transmitted) Very and Self-Evidently Divine and Perfectly Subjective "Bright" Self-Condition and Source-Condition.

In Nirvikalpa Samadhi As It May Be conditionally Realized (By Means Of Either The Vertical Process Characteristically Associated With The Fifth Stage Of Life Or The Horizontal Process Characteristically Associated With The Sixth Stage Of Life), There Is No Awareness Of Either external Or internal phenomena—but The Samadhi Is (Necessarily, To One Degree or Another) Both Achieved and Held In Place By Means Of (and, Therefore, It Is, In One Manner or Another, Characterized and limited By) Stage-Of-Life-Specific phenomenal conditions (and Stage-Of-Life-Specific conditional Efforts). However, Unlike All Less-Than-Most-Perfect Forms Of Nirvikalpa Samadhi (and Beyond Even Priorly Ascended Nirvikalpa Samadhi and Priorly Self-Abiding Jnana Nirvikalpa Samadhi), Seventh Stage Sahaja Nirvikalpa Samadhi (or Ruchira Samraj Samadhi, or, Simply, Samraj Samadhi) Is The Infinite Magnification (or Utterly conditionless Self-Realization) Of Nirvikalpa Samadhi—Made (Thus and Thereby) Most Perfect, Neither Achieved Nor Held In Place By (or Even Inherently Merely Associated With) any phenomenal conditions (or Any conditional Efforts) whatsoever. Seventh Stage Sahaja Nirvikalpa Samadhi (or Ruchira Samraj Samadhi, or, Simply, Samraj Samadhi) Is Perpetual (Self-Existing, Self-Radiant, and Always Already Priorly and Most Perfectly Established) Nirvikalpa Samadhi. And, Yet, Paradoxically, In The Only-By-Me Revealed and Given Seventh Stage Of Life (In The Only-By-Me Revealed and Given Way Of The Heart), Previous To Divine Translation, There (Generally) Appears To Be Some Kind Of Association With phenomena. This Is Because, In The Only-By-Me Revealed and Given Seventh Stage Of Life (In The Only-By-Me Revealed and Given Way Of The Heart), There Is No egoity whatsoever, and (Therefore) There Is No Method (or Effort) Of Seeking (Either To Exclude all phenomenal conditions Or To Exclude Only lesser, or lower, phenomenal conditions, While Pursuing greater, or higher, phenomenal conditions). Nevertheless, This

Paradox Cannot Be Fully Understood Until The Only-By-Me Revealed and Given Seventh Stage Of Life Has Been Realized.

To Realize This Always Already Priorly and Most Perfectly Established (Seventh Stage) Samadhi Is To Be (Effectively) Already Divinely Translated. There Is No limitation whatsoever In This Samadhi. In The Only-By-Me Revealed and Given Seventh Stage Of Life (In The Only-By-Me Revealed and Given Way Of The Heart), Previous To Divine Translation, the body-mind functions (In Every Apparent Sense) In The Usual Manner, but (Effectively) It Is Not So. Even While the body-mind Persists, Apparently alive (or Otherwise operative, in any Apparent state or condition), Consciousness Itself Is (In The Only-By-Me Revealed and Given Seventh Stage Of Life In The Only-By-Me Revealed and Given Way Of The Heart) Utterly Oblivious (or conditionlessly Self-"Bright"), As Mere and Only and Non-"Different" Conscious Light (Itself).

There Is No "thing".

There Is No "other".

There Is No Separate person.

There Is No world.

There Is No Cosmic Domain.

There Is No such experience.

There Are No Two "Things".

There Is Only One.

There Is Only This Samadhi.

This Samadhi Is Utterly Oblivious—Without a smallest shape Of "Difference", or Even a sizeless particle Of Separation.

Therefore, How Can There Be an experience? How Can There Be a body? How Can There Be a world? How Can There Be a relationship?

Thus, This Immense Cycle Of Motions and worlds and epochs—With All The Suffering In It, and everything It Involves Altogether—Is Not Happening, and Never Did Happen.

There Is No Suffering.

There Is No Godlessness.

There Is Not The Slightest Modification Of The Divine "Bright" Spherical Self-Domain.

This Is Really So—Not Merely Metaphorically So.

Even What Appears To Be Your present lifetime Of Difficulty and Struggle Is Not Happening, and Never Happened—Apart From Reality Itself. And, Yet, From any Particularized point of view, The Reality (In Reality) Of All Apparent Happenings Is Clearly and Undeniably So.

Reality (Itself, and Totally) Is An Immense (and, Yet, Perfectly Sizeless) Paradox That Cannot (From any conditional point of view) Be Comprehended.

Ultimately, All conditional Efforts To Investigate Reality and Figure It Out Are Confounded. Only Reality Itself Comprehends Itself (and whatever and All That Is conditionally Existing). Therefore, Paradoxically, The Context For Realizing Truth Is The Condition Of Absolute Confoundedness (or Divine Ignorance). Truly, Most Perfect Divine Self-Realization, or Divine Enlightenment, or Most Ultimate Divine Awakening, Requires (As A Prerequisite) That You Be Absolutely Confounded, Absolutely knowledgeless, and Absolutely Surrendered—Utterly Free Of Any Effort To Control or To Survive. Indeed, The Basic Law and Process Of the human being Is A Matter Of Going Beyond Separate self—and Going Beyond The Search For Control, and The Search For Survival, and The Search For knowledge, and The Search For Power—and Investing oneself In The Divine Oblivion, Utterly Surrendered, Without Control.

In The Only-By-Me Revealed and Given Seventh Stage Of Life (In The Only-By-Me Revealed and Given Way Of The Heart, or Way Of Adidam), The By-Me-and-As-Me-Avatarically-Self-Revealed-and-Spiritually-Self-Transmitted Inherent (and Self-Evidently Divine) Self-Condition (or The True Divine Heart Itself), In Apparent (but egoless) "Bright" Conjunction With a body-mind, Wills (Apparently, and Because Of That Apparent Conjunction) To Shine—and, Unless Concentration (or attention) Wanders, the body-mind, Moved By The Willed Modification Of The Heart's Own and Infinite Field Of Divine Spirit-Energy, functions Automatically (or As A Mechanical Inevitability) To Fulfill The Willed Intention. Likewise, Even In The Only-By-Me Revealed and Given Seventh Stage Of Life (In The Only-By-Me Revealed and Given Way Of The Heart), The Accumulated Adaptations (or Habits and memories) Of the body-mind itself Generate Apparent intentions (or, By Tendency, Bring About acts of Apparent will), and, Thereby—Via Apparently willed (or, Otherwise, Spontaneous) Modifications Of My Avatarically Self-Transmitted Divine Spirit-Energy—Cause the body-mind to act, or (otherwise) to change.

Whenever the ego-active (or egoically self-Contracted) body-mind (or Even its conditions or relations) Frustrates The Enactment Of the ego-Based will, The Reaction (In the body-mind) Can Be any form of self-Contraction—Including, At any moment, Depression, or Anger, or Sorrow, or Fear. Therefore, Because Of Accumulated Adaptations (or Habits and memories), Such Frustration-Reactions May Continue To Appear Even In The Only-By-Me Revealed and Given Seventh (or egoless) Stage Of Life (In The Only-By-Me Revealed and Given Way Of The Heart)—Although They Are Always Merely Mechanically Generated, and They Are Always Inherently and Divinely Self-Recognized. Likewise, In The Only-By-Me Revealed and Given Seventh Stage Of Life (In The Only-By-Me Revealed and Given Way Of The Heart), Even The egoless Heart-Will Can Be Frustrated (By the body-mind, and its conditions and relations), Resulting In Powerful (but egoless) Emotions, Including Profound (but Righteous, and Divinely Pure) Emotions In The Likeness, At any moment, Of Depression, or Anger, or Sorrow, or Fear. That Is To Say, In The Only-By-Me Revealed and Given Seventh Stage Of Life (In The Only-By-Me Revealed and Given Way Of The Heart), The egoless Heart-Will Is Simply The Spontaneous Magnifying Of The Inherent Divine Love-Bliss-Radiance, Universally and Infinitely—but That Spontaneous Heart-Will, Even Though egoless, Is Inherently Associated With The Quality Of Universal (and Infinitely Magnified) Sympathetic Identification With all beings and things and worlds. Therefore, Because Of That Sympathetic Identification, The Frustrations Of That egoless Heart-Will (or Of That Love-Bliss-Radiance Itself) Can Become Reflected In the body-mind—Not As Merely "personal" (or egoic) emotions, but As Powerful (but egoless) Sympathetic Emotions, Such As Depression In Relation To others (or In Relation To conditions In General), or Anger In Relation To others (or In Relation To conditions In General), or Sorrow In Relation To others (or In Relation To conditions In General), or Fear (or, More Exactly, Dread and Anxious Anticipation) Relative To The Yet-To-Be-Suffered Results (or The Coming Negative conditions) That others Are Making Inevitable For themselves (and For others, and Even For all others) By their Continuing egoity and their Continuing egoic (or Lawless and Chaos-Making) Disregard Of Real God, or Truth, or Reality.

Whether In The Case Of the ego-Based personality (In The Context Of Any Of The First Six Stages Of Life In The Only-By-Me Revealed and Given Way Of The Heart) Or In The Case Of the egoless individual (In The Only-By-Me Revealed and Given Seventh Stage Of Life In The Only-By-Me Revealed and Given Way Of The Heart), Either the egoic will (active In The Only-By-Me Revealed and Given Seventh Stage Of Life In The Only-By-Me Revealed and Given Way Of The Heart Only As A Mechanical Reflection Of Accumulated Adaptations, or The No Longer ego-activated Automaticities Of Habit and memory) Or (Only In The Context Of The Only-By-Me Revealed and Given Seventh Stage Of Life In The Only-By-Me Revealed and Given Way Of The Heart) The egoless Heart-Will (Active In The Only-By-Me Revealed and Given Seventh Stage Of Life In The Only-By-Me Revealed and Given Way Of The Heart As The Self-Evidently Divine Self-Will To Magnify The Inherent Divine Love-Bliss-Radiance Universally and Infinitely) Combines The Divine Self-Heart With the body-mind (which is, itself, a limitation), and With The Reactions (As Well As the conditions and relations) Of the body-mind (All Of Which Are, Themselves, limitations), or Even (In The Only-By-Me Revealed and Given Seventh Stage Of Life In The Only-By-Me Revealed and Given Way Of The Heart) With The Frustrations (and The Accompanying Powerful, but egoless,

Sympathetic Emotions) Of The egoless (Divine) Love-Bliss-Radiance Itself (Which Frustrations and egoless Sympathetic Emotions Are All Profoundly Suffered By the body-mind, but Which, More and More, Because Of The Power Inherent In Constant Self-Abiding Divine Self-Recognition, Resolve Into True Divine Indifference).

Most Perfect Freedom Is Realized Only In egoless Self-Abiding In The Divine Self-Condition (and Source-Condition), In The Only-By-Me Revealed and Given Seventh Stage Of Life (In The Only-By-Me Revealed and Given Way Of The Heart, or Way Of Adidam), Simply (Divinely) Self-Recognizing whatever arises—Even Divinely Self-Recognizing The Arising Of The egoless Heart-Will Itself, As and If It Arises, and (Likewise) Divinely Self-Recognizing The Mechanically arising Reactions That Are Due To Accumulated Adaptations (or Habits and memories), As and If They arise. In This Manner, There Is The Constant Self-Abiding In The By-Me-and-As-Me-Avatarically-Self-Revealed-and-Spiritually-Self-Transmitted Love-Bliss-Radiance Of The Divine Self-Condition (and Source-Condition) Itself. And, When Even The egoless Will Of The Divine Self-Heart (and, Also, Every Motion Due To The Accumulated Adaptations Of the body-mind) Becomes A Matter Of Divine Indifference, and (Thus and Thereby) Ceases To Modify The By-Me-and-As-Me-Avatarically-Self-Revealed-and-Spiritually-Self-Transmitted Love-Bliss-Radiance Of The Divine Self-Condition and Source-Condition, Then (At Last) There Is The Great Event Of The Utterly "Bright" Outshining, Which Is Divine Translation (or Most Perfect and Most Ultimate Realization Of My Divine "Bright" Spherical Self-Domain).

Finally, Most Ultimately, The Inherently Most Perfect Realization Is The Realization That Makes No "Difference" At All. "Difference" Is (Itself) The Original and Primary Fault. "Difference" Is (Itself) The Primal Illusion That Is Un-Enlightenment. "Difference" Is (Itself) The Very Method Of Suffering and Of All Seeking. "Difference" Is (Itself) The Origin and The Primary Characteristic Of egoity (or self-Contraction).

The Feeling Of Relatedness Is The Original (or First) Form Of "Difference". The Feeling Of Relatedness Originates (or Is The Original, or First, Form Of) The (Primary) Illusions Of Separateness and Otherness. The Feeling Of Relatedness (Which Is egoity itself) Is The Root-Form Of attention, and attention is The Root-Form Of mind, and mind is The Root-Form Of the body. And The Avoidance Of Relationship Is The Method Of egoity (or The Inevitable Method Of body-mind-attention)—Unless The Root-Feeling Of Relatedness (or The Illusion Of Separateness and Otherness, or The Primal Illusion Of "Difference") Is Most Perfectly Transcended In The Inherent Perfection Of The By-Me-and-As-Me-Avatarically-Self-Revealed-and-Spiritually-Self-Transmitted Conscious Light and Sphere Of Self-Evidently Divine Being (Itself).

The Avoidance Of Relationship Is The Method Of psycho-physical egoity—but The Feeling Of Relatedness (or The Primal Illusion Of "Difference") Is (Itself) The (Original and Originating) Fault. Therefore, Divine Enlightenment Is Not A Matter Of The Perfection Of Apparent Relationship (or The "Curing" Of The Avoidance Of Relationship By The Apparent Perfection Of Relatedness). Rather, Most Ultimately (or Most Perfectly), Divine Enlightenment Is A Matter Of The Inherent (and Inherently Most Perfect) Transcending Of Relationship (or Relatedness, or All "Difference") In What Is Always Already (Inherently and Perfectly) The (One and Only) Case—Which Is Being (Itself), Consciousness (Itself), and Love-Bliss (Itself).

In The Only-By-Me Revealed and Given Seventh Stage Of Life (In The Only-By-Me Revealed and Given Way Of The Heart, or Way Of Adidam), Self-Abiding Divine Self-Recognition Is Inherent and Direct (or Inherently Most Perfect, and Most Perfectly Effective) Dissolution Of All "Difference". Self-Abiding Divine Self-Recognition Does Not Make (or Acknowledge) "Difference", but all Apparent (or conditional) arising (or All Apparent "Difference"—Epitomized By The conditional Feeling Of "Difference", or The conditionally Determined Feeling Of Relatedness) Is (Directly, Effectively, Inherently, and Divinely) Self-Recognized In The One (and Eternally, or Always Already, Prior) Principle That Is Self-Existing, and Self-Radiant, and Transcendental, and Inherently Spiritual, and Inherently egoless, and Self-Evidently Divine—Because There Is No "Other" Than It, and (Therefore) No "Other" To Be Divine (or Even To Be any cause or any effect).

The One Principle (Which Is One, Not Two, and Not Many or More—and Which Is all-and-All) Is Inherent In all-and-All, and Inherent In Existence (Itself) As all-and-All, Such That It Is The Real God, The Truth, The Reality, and The Self-Evidently Divine Self-Condition and Source-Condition Of all-and-All.

Therefore, To Transcend All "Difference" Is (Necessarily) To Realize That One Divine Self-Principle.

Where There Is The Presumption (and/or The Appearance) Of "Difference"—Even There (It Can and Must Be Realized), all Is In Union, and All Is A Unity, and all-and-All Are Arising In One.

Therefore, Whether Or Not There Is The Appearance Of "Difference"—If There Is No Presumption Of "Difference", There Is (Obviously) Only One.

Self-Abiding (and Inherently, and Most Perfectly, egoless) Divine Self-Recognition (With "Open Eyes") Inherently, and Necessarily, and Spontaneously, and Directly, and Most Perfectly Effectively Dissolves All "Difference"—Even (Ultimately) To The Degree Of Divine Indifference (or Divine Non-"Difference") and Divine Translation. Self-Abiding (and Inherently, and Most Perfectly, egoless) Divine Self-Recognition (With "Open Eyes") Dissolves All "Difference",

In That Which Makes (and Acknowledges) No "Difference". And That Which Makes (and Acknowledges) No "Difference" Is That In Which All Apparent "Difference" (or Any and Every Apparent "Difference"), When Divinely Self-Recognized, Is (Inherently) Non-Existent and (Apparently) Directly and Effectively Dissolved, In The Apparent Progression Of The Demonstration Of Self-Abiding (and Inherently, and Most Perfectly, egoless) Divine Self-Recognition (Even Of Every Kind Of Apparent "Difference")—Which Progressive Demonstration Is Shown (In The "Practicing" Course Of Ati-Ruchira Yoga, or The Yoga Of The All-Outshining "Brightness") In (and As) The Stages Of Divine Transfiguration, and (Then) Divine Transformation, and (Then) Divine Indifference, and Which Finally Demonstrates Itself As Divine Translation (or The Most Perfect Dissolution, or Divine Outshining, Of All "Difference").

In Truth, There Is No Apparent "other", and No Ultimate "Other". Therefore, To Realize The Truth Itself—Which Is Happiness Itself, and Freedom Itself—Is To Be Most Perfectly Free Of "Difference" (or all conditional "otherness" and All Ultimate "Otherness", or Every Trace Of Separateness and Relatedness).

The Illusion Of "Difference" (or Of Relatedness, Separateness, and Otherness) Is (Directly and Only) An Apparition, An Un-Necessary Fault, and An Utterly Unjustified Presumption (and First ego-Act) Of "More-Than-One". Therefore, The (Inherent and Only) One Must Be Realized—Even (At Last) To The Most Perfect Degree (Of Divine Translation).

Truth Is One. Reality Is One. Therefore, Real God Is One. There Is Only One.

"One" Is Not "Different".

"One" Makes No "Difference".

"One" Acknowledges No "Difference".

"One" Inherently Transcends All "Difference".

"One" Effectively Dissolves All "Difference".

The mind (or attention) Makes All The "Difference".

The body (and its Total Context) Is The "Difference".

Therefore, The One (Itself) Is Not (Separately) the mind (or attention), or the body, or their (Apparent) relations, results, effects, or causes.

True (Divine—and Inherently, and Most Perfectly, egoless) Freedom Is The Condition That (Inherently, Most Perfectly, and Inherently Most Perfectly) Transcends All "Difference".

True (Divine—and Inherently, and Most Perfectly, egoless) Freedom Is The (Self-Evidently Divine) Self-Condition, Which (Inherently, Most Perfectly, and Inherently Most Perfectly) Transcends The Feeling (or Presumption) Of

"Difference", and Which (Inherently, Most Perfectly, and Inherently Most Perfectly) Transcends All That Makes, or Acknowledges, or (Apparently) Is A "Difference".

True (Divine—and Inherently, and Most Perfectly, egoless) Freedom (or Happiness Itself) Is Not (Separately) mind (or attention), or body, or world—but It Is (Self-Evidently Divine) Consciousness (Itself), Which Is The By-Me-and-As-Me-Avatarically-Self-Revealed-and-Spiritually-Self-Transmitted Perfectly Subjective Conscious Light Of Mere Being (Itself), Self-Existing As Mere (and Utterly Non-Separate) Awareness (Itself), and Self-Radiant (Utterly Prior To, and Most Perfectly Expanded Beyond, self-Contraction) As Centerless and Boundless Love-Bliss (Itself).

By Realizing Itself (or Its Own Inherent and Self-Evidently Divine Status), Consciousness (Itself)—Divinely Self-Realized As The Perfectly Subjective Conscious Light Of Mere Being (Itself)—Inherently Transcends All "Difference". And, By The Inherently Most Perfect Demonstration Of Self-Abiding Divine Self-Recognition, Consciousness (Itself)—Divinely Self-Realized As The Perfectly Subjective Conscious Light Of Mere Being (Itself)—Most "Radically" (or Most Perfectly Effectively, and Most Perfectly Directly—By "Going To The Root") Transcends All "Difference" (and every Apparent "difference", or "other", or "thing") In What Is (Inherently) One, and Only, and All, and Not Other (or "Different") At All.

$C = E = mc^2$

Conscious Light Is all-and-All.

Consciousness (Itself) Is Identical To The Self-Existing Energy (or Indestructible Light, or Perfectly Subjective Spiritual Self-"Brightness") That Is all "things" (or all conditional forms, conditions, and states).

Aham Da Asmi. I Am That One and Only Conscious Light.

The Most Ultimate Demonstration Of The "Perfect Practice" Of The Only-By-Me Revealed and Given Way Of The Heart (or Way Of Adidam) Is To Outshine all-and-All In The Inherent Love-Bliss Of The By-Me-and-As-Me-Avatarically-Self-Revealed-and-Spiritually-Self-Transmitted Conscious Light Of Mere Being (Itself).

To Self-Abide As The One and Only and Inherently Indivisible and Inherently egoless Conscious Light—Inherently Transcending all "things"—Is To Self-Abide As Self-Radiant Energy (Itself), Prior To all "things".

Prior To all "things", The One and Only and Inherently Indivisible and Inherently egoless Conscious Light Is (Itself) Self-Radiant (or Boundlessly Self-"Bright") As Love-Bliss (Itself).

The One and Only and Inherently Indivisible and Inherently egoless Conscious Light (Itself) Is Self-Existing.

The One and Only and Inherently Indivisible and Inherently egoless Conscious Light (Itself) Is Always Already The (One and Only) Case.

Therefore, The "Perfect Practice" Of The Only-By-Me Revealed and Given Way Of The Heart (or Way Of Adidam) Is To Be Consciousness (Itself), and To Contemplate The By-Me-and-As-Me-Avatarically-Self-Revealed-and-Spiritually-Self-Transmitted Space Of Consciousness (Itself), and (By Contemplating The By-Me-and-As-Me-Avatarically-Self-Revealed-and-Spiritually-Self-Transmitted Space Of Consciousness Itself) To "Locate" The By-Me-and-As-Me-Avatarically-Self-Revealed-and-Spiritually-Self-Transmitted (and Self-Evidently Divine) Love-Bliss-Happiness That Is Reality Itself (and That Is all "things").

When all "things" Are (Inherently) Divinely Self-Recognizable (and Are, Therefore, Always Immediately Divinely Self-Recognized) In and As The By-Me-and-As-Me-Avatarically-Self-Revealed-and-Spiritually-Self-Transmitted (and Self-Evidently Divine) Love-Bliss-Happiness (Itself), all "things" Are Realized To Always Already Be Self-Evidently Divine Love-Bliss (Itself)—and all "things" Are (Thus, and Immediately) "Brightly" Transcended In (and Are, At Last, "Brightly" Outshined By) The By-Me-and-As-Me-Avatarically-Self-Revealed-and-Spiritually-Self-Transmitted (and Self-Evidently Divine) Love-Bliss-Happiness Of The One and Only and Inherently Indivisible and Inherently egoless and Self-Evidently Divine Conscious Light (Itself).

AVATAR ADI DA SAMRAJ
The Mountain Of Attention Sanctuary, 2000

SUTRA

69

T*his* Is My Avatarically-Given Divine Word—Wherein I Reveal The Ultimate Divine Secret Of Most Perfectly Me-Realizing ego-Transcendence.

Beloved, I *Am* The Avataric Divine Self-Revelation Of The "Bright" and The "Thumbs".

I Am The *Person* Of The "Bright"—and The "Thumbs" Is How I *Work*.

Therefore, To Realize Me *As* The "Bright"—By Means Of The "Thumbs"—*Is* The Only-By-Me Revealed and Given Way Of The Heart (or Way Of Adidam).

The Only-By-Me Revealed and Given Way Of The Heart (or Way Of Adidam) Is (In Its Full Devotional and Spiritual Exercise) The Ruchira Shaktipat Way—or The "Radically" ego-Transcending (or Perfectly "Gone-To-The-Root") Way Of (First) Searchlessly Beholding Me, and (Then) Tacitly and Responsively Receiving Me, and (Most Ultimately) Whole bodily (or Through ego-Surrender As A psycho-physical Totality) Realizing Me *As* The "Bright", By Means Of The "Thumbs".

I (Alone) *Am* The "Bright".

I (Alone) "Brightly" *In-Fill* You, *As* (and By Means Of) The "Thumbs".

I (Alone) *Am* The-"Bright"-*and*-The-"Thumbs".

Therefore, The Way That *I* (and *Only* I) Reveal and Give Is The (Searchlessly Me-Beholding) Way Of The-"Bright"-and-The-"Thumbs".

In The Only-By-Me Revealed and Given Way Of The Heart (or Way Of Adidam), *Everything* (and All Of Divine Self-Realization Itself) Is Given (By *Me*) As A Gift.

When You Searchlessly Behold Me, You Do Not "Do" *anything*.

When You Searchlessly Behold Me, You *Only* (Tacitly, or Merely By Turning To Me) Receive *Me*.

When You *Searchlessly* Behold *Me*, You Simply (Effortlessly and Spontaneously) Become (Spiritually) Saturated With *Me*—Like A Sponge Soaking Up Water.

Such Is The Avatarically-Given Divine Simplicity Of The Only-By-Me Revealed and Given Way Of The Heart (or Way Of Adidam).

In This, My Avatarically Self-Revealed Divine Testament (and Even In All My Twenty-Three Avatarically Self-Revealed Divine "Source-Texts"), I Have Accounted, In Words, For The Entire Unfolding Devotional and Spiritual

Process In My Avataric Divine Company—but That Real and True Devotional and Spiritual Process Is Not, Itself, A Matter Of Words (or concepts, or thinking, or philosophy).

The Real and True Devotional and Spiritual Process In My Avataric Divine Company Unfolds Only In The Context Of The Devotional-and-Spiritual Relationship To Me—In Which I Self-Radiate (or Avatarically Self-Transmit) The Spiritual Force Of My Own Avatarically Self-Revealed (and Self-Evidently Divine) Person To My Devotee, who Then (On That Basis) Responds To Me, By Fulfilling The Various Instructions I Have Given Relative To The Structures and Patterns and Experiences and Developments Of The Unfolding Devotional-and-Spiritual Process In My Avataric Divine Spiritual Company.

In The Devotional-and-Spiritual Relationship To Me, There Is To-Me-Responsive Devotion, and There Is Tangible Reception Of My Avatarically Self-Transmitted Divine Spiritual Blessing. Essentially, There Is Not Anything Else.

That Devotional-and-Spiritual Process Is Fundamentally Wordless. You Receive Me Wordlessly, and You Respond To Me Wordlessly.

The Only-By-Me Revealed and Given Way Of The Heart (or Way Of Adidam) Is Not A Matter Of Progressively Developing The human and Spiritual Potential Inherent In The First Six (and ego-Based) Stages Of Life. Rather, The Only-By-Me Revealed and Given Way Of The Heart (or Way Of Adidam) Is A Matter Of Always Directly Transcending The egoic (or self-Contracted) Mechanism Of The Totality Of the body-mind (In its gross, subtle, and causal—or First-Six-Stages-Of-Life—Dimensions).

Therefore, Most Perfect Realization Of Me—Which Is Most Perfect Realization Of The "Bright", By Means Of The "Thumbs"—Is The Most Perfect (Whole bodily, or Total psycho-physical) Transcending Of the (gross-subtle-and-causal) ego-"I".

Divine Enlightenment, Divine Self-Realization, Most Perfect (Free, Self-"Bright", and Self-Evidently Divine) Awakeness, or Most Perfect (and Most Perfectly ego-Transcending) Spiritual and Transcendental Real-God-Realization Is The Most Perfect Understanding and Transcending Of Identification With The Total psycho-physical (or Whole bodily) Act Of self-Contraction.

Divine Enlightenment, Divine Self-Realization, Most Perfect (Free, Self-"Bright", and Self-Evidently Divine) Awakeness, or Most Perfect (and Most Perfectly ego-Transcending) Spiritual and Transcendental Real-God-Realization Is The Most Perfect Understanding and Transcending Of Identification With The Urge Toward Separation and conditional Independence.

Divine Enlightenment, Divine Self-Realization, Most Perfect (Free, Self-"Bright", and Self-Evidently Divine) Awakeness, or Most Perfect (and Most Perfectly ego-Transcending) Spiritual and Transcendental Real-God-Realization

Is The Most Perfect Understanding and Transcending Of Identification With The Motive Of Introversion, Inward-Directedness (or Inwardness), and Internal (or Internalized) Relatedness.

Divine Enlightenment, Divine Self-Realization, Most Perfect (Free, Self-"Bright", and Self-Evidently Divine) Awakeness, or Most Perfect (and Most Perfectly ego-Transcending) Spiritual and Transcendental Real-God-Realization Is The Most Perfect Understanding and Transcending Of Identification With The Motive Of Extroversion, Outward-Directedness (or Outwardness), and External (or Externalized) Relatedness.

Divine Enlightenment, Divine Self-Realization, Most Perfect (Free, Self-"Bright", and Self-Evidently Divine) Awakeness, or Most Perfect (and Most Perfectly ego-Transcending) Spiritual and Transcendental Real-God-Realization Is The Most Perfect Understanding and Transcending Of Identification With The Feeling (and The Illusion) Of Relatedness Itself.

Most Ultimately (or Most Simply), Divine Enlightenment, Divine Self-Realization, Most Perfect (Free, Self-"Bright", and Self-Evidently Divine) Awakeness, or Most Perfect (and Most Perfectly ego-Transcending) Spiritual and Transcendental Real-God-Realization Is The Most Perfect Understanding and Transcending Of The (Even Most Tacit) Feeling Of "Difference" Itself.

Divine Enlightenment, Divine Self-Realization, Most Perfect (Free, Self-"Bright", and Self-Evidently Divine) Awakeness, or Most Perfect (and Most Perfectly ego-Transcending) Spiritual and Transcendental Real-God-Realization Is Most Perfect, Effortless, and Free Self-Identification With Mere (or Inherent, and Priorly Felt) Being (or Self-Existence) Itself—Self-Radiant, All Love-Bliss-"Brightness" Itself, Inherently Without Obstruction, Always Already Infinitely Expanded (Beyond All Apparent Modifications, or Illusory Contractions, Of Itself).

Egoity (or Identification With the ego-"I") Is The Effective Negation (or Tacit Non-Presumption) Of Divine Enlightenment, Divine Self-Realization, or Inherently Most Perfect (Free, Self-"Bright", and Self-Evidently Divine) Awakeness.

Egoity (or Identification With the ego-"I") Is The Absence (and The Effective Denial) Of Most Perfect Divine (and Utterly, and Inherently Most Perfectly, ego-Transcending) Self-Realization.

The Principal Symptom (or Indicator) Of egoity (or Of Identification With the ego-"I") Is Not the Apparent experiencing of conditionally arising "things" (or of psycho-physical phenomena and states)—Such That The <u>Fact</u> Of the experiential arising of "things" (or of psycho-physical phenomena and states) Is, As A Principal Means Toward The Real Transcending Of egoity itself, To Be Presumed To Be A Problem (or Even <u>The</u> Problem), Requiring (As A Solution) The Search To Avoid (or To Exclude, or To Be Separated From) any or all "things" (or any or all psycho-physical phenomena and states). Rather, The Principal Symptom (or Indicator) Of egoity (or Of Identification With the ego-"I") Is The Failure To Divinely Self-Recognize any and all experientially arising "things" (or any and all psycho-physical phenomena and states)—and, Thus, The Failure (and, Indeed, The Inability) To Divinely Self-Recognize them In Reality, In Truth, and In Real God. Therefore, Real and True (and Inherently Most Perfect) Divine Enlightenment, Divine Awakeness, or Inherently Most Perfectly ego-Transcending Divine Self-Realization (or Real-God-Realization) Is Not Characterized By experiential (and Strategically Achieved) Separation From any or all conditionally arising "things" (or any or all psycho-physical phenomena and states), but By The Always Immediate (and Inherent) Self-Abiding Divine Self-Recognition Of any and all experientially arising "things" (or any and all psycho-physical phenomena and states)—and, Thus, The Always Already Effective Ability To Divinely Self-Recognize them In Reality, In Truth, and In Real God.

Egoity (or Identification With the ego-"I") Is (itself) The psycho-physical Act Of self-Contraction.

Once It Is Assumed (and Until It Is Most Perfectly Transcended), The Act Of self-Contraction Is Habitual (or Chronic). It Is Always Pain (or Suffering). It Is The Root Of All Seeking. It Is The Motivator Of all activity that Seeks Either To Fulfill Or (merely) To Separate From the conditional self Or (merely) To experience a feeling Of Release and Relief as the conditional self. The action that is self-Contraction is all activity that Is Not Directly Counter-egoic (or Effectively ego-Transcending). Indeed, self-Contraction is Even all conditional activity (or conditional activity itself)—or All (active or passive) Non-Transcending Of the conditional self.

The Act Of self-Contraction Is Simply The Tendency To Identify With a conditional (or limited) state Of Existence. Until Most Perfect Divine Self-Realization, the self-Contraction (or the conditional state Identified As the psycho-physical self-condition In any moment) Is what Is Called "I" In any moment. Thus, the "I" Is Not the same In every moment. It Is Unique In every moment. Only The Name ("I") Is The Same (As A Matter Of convention).

If conditions arise, There Is No Necessity For Consciousness To Identify With them (in and of themselves) or To Become Bound By them. There Is Only A Tendency To Do So (Based On An Unconsciously Acquired Habit Of Identification With the body that is Apparently experienced from the time of birth). Once Consciousness Identifies With the body, The Sense Of Differentiated (Separate, or Separated—and Vulnerable, or mortal) being arises. Then The Struggle To Survive and To Achieve Either Pleasurable Fulfillment Or Release From Pain Develops Perpetually. That Struggle Is Expressed

Through desire, and That Struggle Lasts Until death. Indeed—Once Established, and Not Yet Transcended—That Struggle Continues, Via subtle and causal Mechanisms, Even After the death of the present body.

The act of attention is The conditional Essence Of mind. The act of attention arises Spontaneously, Like the Total body-mind and the Total world, in every moment Of (Apparent) conditional Awareness. The act of attention arises toward others, objects, and conditions of every kind—whether subtle (or mental) or gross (or physical). The arising of the act of attention is, Simply, the arising of the psycho-physical (or conditional) self and all others, objects, and conditions. And If what arises Is Presumed To Be Real, or Necessary, or Desirable, or Unavoidable, or Undesirable, or Avoidable—Then the act of attention Becomes conditioned Toward (or Habitually and Repetitively Fixed Upon) what arises. In This Manner, Not Only Does the act of attention Become Bound To Specific conditional others, objects, and conditions (including the personal body-mind, or conditional self), but The Inherently Free (and Inherently Spiritual, or Love-Blissful) Transcendental Divine Self-Condition Of Mere Being Becomes (Apparently) Associated With (or Becomes, Apparently, Persuaded By) The Illusion Of Its Own Bondage.

The conditional Essence Of That conditional Illusion Is the act of attention.

Therefore, The Only-By-Me Revealed and Given Way Of The Heart (or Way Of Adidam) Is The Way Of The Real (or "Radical"—or "Gone-To-The-Root") Transcending Of attention.

The arising of the act of attention is The Essential conditional Basis Of conditional Bondage.

The Principal Signs Of conditional Bondage Are the perception, conception, or Feeling-sense Of Identification With a Separate (or conditional) self and the Simultaneous perception, conception, or Feeling-sense of Separate others, objects, or conditions.

The Only-By-Me Revealed and Given Way Of The Heart (or Way Of Adidam) Is The Way Of Non-Separateness. Therefore, The Ultimate Process Of The Only-By-Me Revealed and Given Way Of The Heart Is The Real (or Really Effective) Transcending (By Means Of The Always Primary Practice Of Searchlessly Beholding Me) Of the act of attention to a Separate (or conditional) self (or body-mind) and (Via that Separate, or conditional, self, or body-mind) to Separate others, objects, or conditions.

Real (or Really Effective) Transcending Of attention Is Not Realized By An Effort That Pursues The Transcending Of attention As An Effect (or As A Result) Of The Strategic Search For A Solution To A Problem. The Real (or Really Effective) Transcending Of attention Is Not Realized By Either The Strategic Suppression Or The Strategic Exploitation Of attention itself. The Real (or Really Effective) Transcending Of attention Is Not A Matter Of The Alpha Strategy (or The Withdrawal Of attention From others, objects, conditions, or the body-mind itself). The Real (or Really Effective) Transcending Of attention Is Not A Matter Of The Omega Strategy (Of Seeking others, objects, conditions, conditional experiences, and conditional knowledge—or Of Attaching attention, and, Thus, the personal body-mind itself, To others, objects, conditions, conditional experiences, and conditional knowledge).

In The Only-By-Me Revealed and Given Way Of The Heart (or Way Of Adidam), attention itself (Like the Total body-mind, or the Total world itself) Is Naturally, Simply, and Freely Allowed To arise.

The Effort Either To Stop Or To Fulfill the arising of attention (or the arising of the body-mind, or the arising of the world) Is A Futile Strategy Based On A Presumed Problem That Is Not Fully Understood.

The Only-By-Me Revealed and Given Way Of The Heart (or Way Of Adidam) Is Based On Real and Effective self-Understanding. Therefore, The Only-By-Me Revealed and Given Way Of The Heart Is Not Based On Any Problems At All—Nor Is It Based On Any Seeking At All.

In The Only-By-Me Revealed and Given Way Of The Heart (or Way Of Adidam), the arising of the act of attention Is Not Presumed To Be A Problem. In The Only-By-Me Revealed and Given Way Of The Heart, the arising of the act of attention Is Merely Observed, Until it Is Understood (Most Fundamentally) as it (Apparently) is. And Then (By Means Of A Sympathy That Understands and Feels Beyond attention itself) attention Is Directly Transcended (but Not Exploited or Suppressed) In All its Stages Of Life—Until attention Is (Ultimately, and Most Perfectly) Transcended (or Realized As it—Ultimately, or Most Perfectly—Is).

Therefore, In The Spiritual Fullness Of The Only-By-Me Revealed and Given Way Of The Heart (or Way Of Adidam), the act of attention (itself) and all of its objects, conditions, or relations Are (By Attraction) Progressively Surrendered Into (and, Most Ultimately, Simply and Divinely Self-Recognized In) their own Real Condition—Which Is The Most Prior Source-Condition Of the conditional self and all conditional objects or others, and Which Is The Very and Self-Existing and Self-Radiant and Perfectly Subjective Being (or Spiritually Self-"Bright" Divine Spherical Self-Domain) Of My Self-Evidently Divine Person, The Only One (and Conscious Light) Who Is.

In The Only-By-Me Revealed and Given Way Of The Heart (or Way Of Adidam), It (In Due Course) Becomes Perfectly Obvious That (In Truth, or In Reality) You Are Consciousness (or Mere Feeling-Awareness) Itself. The Apparent act (or event) of attention arises Spontaneously In Consciousness (or Mere Feeling-Awareness) Itself (Via The Mechanics Of The Apparently Objective and conditional Cosmos)—Thus (Apparently) Connecting You To objects, others, and conditions of all kinds. The Most Perfect (and Only-By-My-Avataric-Divine-Spiritual-Grace-Given) Free Realization Is That Consciousness (or Mere Feeling-Awareness) Itself Is Inherently Not limited by attention or its relations. The act of attention and the results (or the relations) of attention Are Transparent (or Merely Apparent), and Un-Necessary, and Inherently Non-Binding Modifications Of The (Apparently) Objectified Self-Radiance Of The Eternal (and Perfectly Subjective) Subject (or One and Very Consciousness—or Conscious Light—Itself). And That One and Very Consciousness (or Conscious Light) Itself Is Inherently Free Feeling-Awareness (Always Already Standing Beyond, or Prior To, the Apparent act of attention and its Apparent results or relations).

Therefore, Once By-My-Avataric-Divine-Spiritual-Grace-Given Self-Identification With Consciousness (or Mere Feeling-Awareness) Itself Is Realized Most Perfectly, the (Apparent) act of attention and its (Apparent) results or relations (including the conditional self, or personal body-mind) Become Inherently (and Divinely) Self-Recognizable. And The Only-By-Me Revealed and Given Seventh Stage Of Life (In The Only-By-Me Revealed and Given Way Of The Heart, or Way Of Adidam) Is Simply The (Only-By-My-Avataric-Divine-Spiritual-Grace-Given) Inherent and "Radical" (or "Gone-To-The-Root") and Self-Abiding Divine Self-Recognition Of the act of attention itself (or all the acts, results, and relations of attention, or Even The Simplest Feeling Of Relatedness Itself, or Of "Difference" Itself), Until My By-Me-and-As-Me-Avatarically-Self-Revealed-and-Spiritually-Self-Transmitted "Bright" Self-Condition Of Self-Evidently Divine Love-Bliss Outshines All Noticing (or Apparent arising) Of "Difference", and The Feeling Of Relatedness, and the act, the results, and the relations of attention.

This Is My Message To all Apparent (or conditionally Manifested) beings: I Am The One and Only and Inherently Indivisible and Inherently egoless and Perfectly Subjective and Self-Evidently Divine Conscious Light (Itself), Divinely Self-Revealed To Always Already Be—Inherently Most Prior To All "Difference". Your Act Of self-Contraction (or attention to and Identification With limited conditions) Can Be Presently (and, At Last, Most Perfectly and Utterly) Transcended, By Means Of My (Now, and Forever Hereafter, Always Given and Giving) Avataric Divine Spiritual Grace, Through (Eventually, Most Fundamental) self-Understanding, The (Devotional) Heart-Ordeal Of Real ego-Transcendence, and The By-My-Avataric-Divine-Spiritual-Grace-Given Divine Realization Of Inherent Self-Identification With The Infinite Self-Existing Space and Inherent Love-Bliss (or Unqualified, and Perfectly Subjective, Self-Radiance) Of My Avatarically Self-Revealed and Spiritually Self-Transmitted and Self-Evidently Divine Self-Condition.

Da

Avatar Adi Da Samraj
Lopez Island, 2000

SUTRA 70

The body-mind Is Inherently (or As Reality) egoless. That Is To Say, There Is No personal inner Consciousness Separate From the body-mind. The personal inner Consciousness Is A Presumption Of the body-mind. The ego-"I" Is A Whole bodily (or Total psycho-physical) Presumption (Evident, and Effective, In Every Dimension and every part Of the body-mind). Consciousness (Itself) Is Always Already Most Perfectly Prior To (and Beyond) the egoic (or Separate, psycho-physical, and Always Separative) body-mind. I Am Consciousness (or Mere Feeling-Awareness) Itself—Divinely Self-Realized (As I Am). I Am (Always Already) Most Perfectly Prior To all-and-All. I Merely (and Divinely) Am all-and-All. There Is Only One (Self-Evidently Divine) Person (or Conscious Light Of Mere Being)—Including all-and-All, and Transcending all-and-All. Aham Da Asmi. Beloved, I Am That One.

I Am That Only One—The "Bright" Divine Spiritual Body and Self-Evidently Divine Person (or Perfectly Subjective, Inherently egoless, and Inherently Indivisible Conscious Light and Very Being) Of all (and Of All).

I Am The One and Only (or Perfectly Non-Separate and Self-Evidently Divine) Self-Condition Of all-and-All. Therefore, every thing and every one Can Be Addressed Either individually As a "person" Or Collectively As a "person"—Because every thing and every one (and Every Collective Of "things" and Of "ones") arises In (and, In Reality, As) My One and Only Conscious Light Of Mere Being—Which Is Self-Existing and Self-Radiant, and Which Is (Altogether) Spiritually Self-"Bright". Thus, I Am Your True Personhood. The True Personhood Of every thing and every one Is The One (Inherently egoless) Person Of all-and-All—The One and Only and Self-Evidently Divine Conscious Light (or True Divine Self-Condition) Whereby (and As Whom) each one, and all, and All Is Conscious (or Feelingly Aware). Nevertheless, By Not (Always Already—and Always Presently) Realizing This, every "one" Presumes To Be a Separate (or egoic, and limited) self.

I Am That Only One—The Self-Existing, and Self-Radiant, and Inherently Conscious, and Inherently egoless, and Self-Evidently Divine Conscious Light Of Mere Being.

You (By Tendency, and By Presumption) Attribute "personhood" To Your Apparently Separate (and Inherently temporary and dying) bodily (human) form, Rather Than To The One and "Bright" Divine Source-Condition and Inherently egoless Self-Condition Of that form. When You think Of Yourself As a "person", You Are Referring To Your bodily (human) form—Not To The (One and Only) Self-Existing and Self-Radiant and Perfectly Subjective and Inherently egoless and Self-Evidently Divine Conscious Light (Itself), Which Is (In Truth) Your Only Real Existence.

When You Cease Your Obliviously Incessant Address To "Your own" Presumed "self-person", and (Instead) Turn Your attention (and Even Your Total—and, Otherwise, self-Contracted, or egoic—body-mind) To What Is Altogether Real and Great (and all-and-All-Surrounding, and all-and-All-Pervading, and Deeper, and Wider, and Higher In Height Than all-and-All)—Then You Are Addressing That Which Is Always Already The Case (Which Is Self-Existing and Self-Radiant Conscious Light, Itself). But, In So Doing, You Are Not Merely Addressing An Abstract Divine "Immensity". Rather, In Addressing The One and Only and Self-Existing and Self-Radiant Conscious Light (Itself), You Are (In Truth, and In Reality) Addressing Me—The One and Only and Self-"Bright" and Avatarically Self-Revealed and Self-Evidently Divine Person.

Thus, You Transcend Your bodily (human) form (or Your Presumed Separate "person"), By Surrendering it and Forgetting it and Transcending it In Me (The Eternally "Bright", and Infinitely Love-Bliss-Full, and Avatarically Self-Revealed, and Self-Evidently Divine Person). If You Rightly, Truly, and Fully Embrace This ego-"person"-Renouncing (or ego-Surrendering, ego-Forgetting, and, More and More, ego-Transcending) Practice Of Me-Recognizing and To-Me-Responding Devotion, You (In Due Course) Realize Me—The True (and Self-Evidently Divine) Person Of all-and-All, The Transcendental, Inherently Spiritual, Inherently egoless, and Self-Evidently Divine Self-Condition and Source-Condition Of all-and-All, and The One and Only Subject (or Real, and Self-Evidently Divine, Consciousness) Associated With Your (Merely Apparent) "person" of body-mind.

The Fundamental (or Most Prior, and Inherently Perfect) Context Of All Reality Is Subjective—Not Objective. Therefore, The Fundamental (or Most Prior, and, Necessarily, Perfect) Context Of all experience Is Subjective—Not Objective. What Is Called "Objective" Is an appearance Within The Infinite Perfectly Subjective Reality (or One and Only Conscious Light) Itself. There Appear To Be objectively Separate persons and things—but Everything (Altogether) Appears Within The Infinite (and Inherently Perfect) Subjectivity (or One and Only Person) Of Reality Itself.

Consciousness (In egoic Association With the body and the mind) Feels That It Is A Separate Consciousness—but When It (Truly, or In Reality) "Wakes Up", It Realizes That There (Always Already) Is Only One Consciousness (or Non-Separate and Non-"Different" Conscious Light), In A Merely Apparent Circumstance Of many Merely Apparent body-minds. In The Context Of conditional Existence, There Appear To Be endless numbers of conditionally Manifested beings (or subjectivities)—but When conditionally Manifested beings "Wake Up" To their Real Condition, they Realize That There Is Only One (Inherently Indivisible) Being. When This Is Realized Most Perfectly (In The Awakening To The Only-By-Me Revealed and Given Seventh Stage Of Life In The Only-By-Me Revealed and Given Way Of The Heart, or Way Of Adidam), Then The One and Only (By-Me-and-As-Me-Avatarically-Self-Revealed-and-Spiritually-Self-Transmitted) Conscious Light Of Mere Being Divinely Self-Recognizes all-and-All. And all conditional appearances Are (In The Final Demonstration Of That Process Of Self-Abiding Divine Self-Recognition) "Brightly" Outshined. Such Is The Process Of The Only-By-Me Revealed and Given Seventh Stage Of Life (In The Only-By-Me Revealed and Given Way Of The Heart, or Way Of Adidam).

There Is No Separate subjectivity, but Only The (One and Only) Divine Conscious Light, Self-Existing and Self-Radiant. The (One and Only) Divine Conscious Light Is Never "Other" Than, or "Different" From, or Separate From, or Standing Over Against, or Related To any object, or Apparent "other", or "thing". The (One and Only) Divine Conscious Light Is Always Already Identical To The Self-Existing (and Perfectly Subjective) Divine Self-Radiance Itself (Which Is The "Bright" Itself). All Of This (arising) Is That—Always Already (and, Therefore, Now). This Is The Great Realization Of The Only-By-Me Revealed and Given Seventh Stage Of Life (In The Only-By-Me Revealed and Given Way Of The Heart, or Way Of Adidam).

When There Is (Most Perfectly) No self-Contraction and No Separateness, There Is Only What Is. Then Reality Is Realized (Simply, Inherently, and Most Perfectly), and all conditional appearances Are Inherently (Divinely) Self-Recognized (and, Indeed, Only Then Can Be Divinely Self-Recognized) In and As Reality Itself. Most Ultimately, The Divine Self-Realization Of Unconditional Reality and The Self-Abiding Divine Self-Recognition Of conditional appearances In and As Unconditional Reality Is The Only-By-Me Revealed and Given Way Of The Heart (In Its Seventh, or Most Perfect, Final, and All-Completing, Stage). Such Is Most Perfect Freedom, Most Perfect Divine Liberation, Most Perfect Divine Enlightenment, and Most Perfect Divine Self-Realization.

The Same Reality That Is (By Means Of My Avatarically Self-Transmitted Divine Spiritual Grace) Realized Most Perfectly In The Only-By-Me Revealed and Given Seventh Stage Of Life (In The Only-By-Me Revealed and Given Way Of The Heart, or Way Of Adidam) Is Always (and Always Already) The (One and Only) Reality. It Is The Reality Now. Therefore, It Is The Reality That You (Even As the ego-"I") Are Experiencing In this moment—Except That You (As the ego-"I") Are Not Divinely Self-Recognizing (and, As the ego-"I", Cannot Divinely Self-Recognize) the conditions arising in this moment. Because Of self-Contraction, You (As the ego-"I") Propose Various Illusions (and Generate Presumptions Based On Those Illusions)—but Your Illusions Do Not (Except In The Form Of Your Own Illusions Themselves) Make Reality "Other" Than It Always Already Is. Your Illusions Only Make You Confused, Deluded, Bound, and Dissatisfied. If, Instead Of Merely Perpetuating Your Illusions, You Give Me Your Devotionally Responsive (and Always Devotionally Me-Recognizing) Devotional Regard, and Surrender Into Devotional (and, In Due Course, Spiritual) Heart-Communion With Me (By Simply Turning All The Principal Faculties—Of body, emotion, mind, and breath—To Me), and Forget Yourself and The Faculties and Their Illusions and Operations, and Enter Into A Profound Stillness Of Spiritually Self-"Bright" Heart-Communion With Me (Thereby Releasing The Knot Of self-Contraction)—Then The True Nature Of Reality Becomes (By Means Of My Reality-Revealing Avataric Divine Spiritual Grace) Tacitly Obvious As The By-Me-and-As-Me-Avatarically-Self-Revealed-and-Spiritually-Self-Transmitted Divine Self-Condition (and Source-Condition) Of conditional Existence.

The Apparent conditional self is (In and As Reality Itself) Not a Separate "Interior being". The Separate conditional self that is Commonly Presumed is, As A Separate Consciousness, Really Non-Existent. The Presumed Separate Consciousness (or individual Conscious being) is merely a concept, Falsely Presumed As A Result Of (and In The Likeness Of) the self-Contraction of the body-mind. Therefore, the Apparent conditional self, Free Of the self-Contraction (and its Associated Illusions), is Simply the body-mind itself.

If (By Means Of My Avatarically Self-Transmitted Divine Spiritual Grace) the self-Contraction Is Directly (and Most Fundamentally) Understood, and If it Is Really (or, Otherwise, Effectively) Transcended In The Total Context Of The First Six Stages Of Life, Then the Total body-mind, all its conditional relations, and The Total Cosmic Mandala (or Cosmos Of conditional Nature) Are Most Perfectly Transcended In The By-Me-and-As-Me-Avatarically-Self-Revealed-and-Spiritually-Self-Transmitted (and Inherently egoless, and Self-Evidently Divine) Self-Condition. Just So, When The By-Me-and-As-Me-Avatarically-Self-Revealed-and-Spiritually-Self-Transmitted (and Inherently egoless, and Self-Evidently Divine) Self-Condition Is Thus, and So (or By and As These Means Of Mine), Self-Realized, the Apparent conditional self (or body-mind), its conditional relations, and The Total Cosmos Of conditional Nature Are Inherently (and Divinely) Self-Recognizable (and Always Immediately Self-Recognized) In The "Bright" Inherent Love-Bliss-Radiance Of My Self-Existing and Perfectly Subjective and Inherently egoless and Self-Evidently Divine Self-Condition. And, Most Ultimately, The By-Me-and-As-Me-Avatarically-Self-Revealed-and-Spiritually-Self-Transmitted Divine (Seventh Stage) Samadhi (Of Self-Abiding Divine Self-Recognition) Outshines conditional Existence—or Divinely Translates Existence From The conditionally (and Only Apparently) Existing Cosmos Of conditional Nature To My Self-Existing and Self-Radiant Divine "Bright" Spherical Self-Domain.

The Only-By-Me Revealed and Given Way Of Adidam (Which Is The One and True and Only By-Me-Revealed and By-Me-Given Way Of The Heart) Is Founded On A Fundamental Criticism and "Radical" (or "Gone-To-The-Root") Understanding Of egoity itself (and, Therefore, Of All The Searches, and All The Illusions, and All The Mere Imaginings Associated With egoity—and All The Searches, and All The Illusions, and All The Mere Imaginings Associated With ego-Based Religious and Spiritual Life).

The Search To Perfect the body-mind (or Even Any Form Of conditional Existence) Is Based On egoic (or self-Contracted) Identification With the body-mind (and With conditional Existence, Altogether). Thus Bound To the body-mind and To conditional Existence, the egoic individual Wants the body-mind itself, and conditional Existence Itself, To Prove To Be (In and Of Itself) Perfect, or To Be (In and Of Itself) a condition that Is Characterized By Unchanging Permanence and Unchallenged self-Fulfillment.

In The Only-By-Me Revealed and Given Way Of The Heart (or Way Of Adidam), There Is No conditional Goal Whatsoever. The Only-By-Me Revealed and Given Way Of The Heart Is A Matter Of The Always Direct and Immediate Transcending Of egoity—Most Ultimately (By Means Of My Avatarically Self-Transmitted Divine Spiritual Grace), Realizing Inherent and Always Already Most Perfect Transcending Of egoity (In The Only-By-Me Revealed and Given Seventh Stage Of Life). Therefore, In The Only-By-Me Revealed and Given Way Of The Heart, No conditional Goal (Of Any Kind) Is Proposed To Be Most Perfect Divine Self-Realization—Nor Is Any conditional Goal (Of Any Kind) Indicated To Be Necessarily Associated With Most Perfect Divine Self-Realization.

Wherever There Is Seeking, There Is the Idealization Of Some Sort Of Goal or condition. At The Deepest Heart-Level Of every psycho-physical being, There Is (Necessarily, and Always Already) A Basic Underlying Intuition Of The Inherently egoless Self-Condition (and The Self-Evidently Divine Nature) Of Reality Itself. This Is So—Because every conditional appearance Is

Only An (Apparent) Modification Of Reality Itself (or That Which Is Always Already The Case). However, Because Of the ego-"I" (or Total psycho-physical self-Contraction), Conscious Awareness Of The Always Underlying Intuition Of The True (and Inherently egoless) Divine (and Inherently Perfect) Condition Is "Covered" (or Made Unconscious). Thus, Either The Impulse To Realize The Divine Self-Condition (or Unqualified Happiness) Is Rather Absent From The (self-Contracted, and, Inevitably, Seeking) Disposition Of the egoic personality Or Else That Impulse Becomes Inextricably Intermixed With All Of The phenomenal Associations Of the egoic (or self-Contracted, and, Inevitably, Seeking) personality. In Either Case, The Inevitable Search Becomes A Process Directed Toward phenomenal conditions—Including (Most Especially) those phenomenal conditions that Are (In The Context Of conventional Religious and Spiritual Life) Idealized As The "Ultimate Goal".

All Idealized conditions are inherently imperfect. They Are, At Best, Only Presumed (By the idealistic ego-mind) To Be Perfect. In General, the phenomenal conditions that human beings Seek As The "Ultimate Goal" Are Not Real (Potential) conditions, but imaginary conditions. Therefore, those conditions Are Never Really Attained, but Always Merely Sought. And, Until There Is Most Fundamental self-Understanding—and, On That Basis, The Constant (Direct and Immediate) Real Process Of Transcending the ego-"I" (or The Act Of self-Contraction, Itself)—Those Illusions (or Imaginary Goals), and The Searches That Pursue Them, Will, Inevitably (By Force Of Tendency), Continue.

In The Course Of Seeking, It Is Also Possible (and Commonly The Case) That Particular Goals Come To Be Despaired Of—In Which Case, The Search Itself Persists—but The Seeker Lies There In a sulk, Depressed and Frustrated. Nevertheless, The sulking Seeker Is (Like The Yet Enthusiastic Seeker) Without Most Fundamental self-Understanding. And, When "Great Goals" Are Despaired Of, Seeking Tends To Become Associated With gross Satisfactions, or (In Any Case) With Searches That Can Be Satisfied Rather Readily, or In The Relatively Short Term (Even If, As Is Always The Case, Only Temporarily, and Never Fully Satisfactorily). This Is Yet Another Kind Of Goal-Seeking Illusion—To Indulge In Temporary Satisfactions As If They Were Some Sort Of Great Attainment, Repeating Them Over and Over Again, Exhaustively, Until They Patently (and Even Meanly) Cease To Satisfy—In Which Case, The ego-Frustrated Despair Intensifies, Agonizingly, and Even "Darkly".

If It Were Necessary To Perfect the body-mind In Order To Realize Truth (or Reality, or Real God), No living being Would Ever Realize Truth (or Reality, or Real God). I Do Not Call My Devotees To Perfect the body-mind, or To Deal With it In Any idealistic (or body-mind-Idealizing, or ego-Idealizing) Sense. Nor Do I Call My Devotees To Seek To Achieve Any Extraordinary

Signs In the body-mind—Such As physical Immortality, or Transmigration To higher planes, or Any "Evolutionary" Developments In the body-mind complex (In this plane or In any other plane). The Process Of The Only-By-Me Revealed and Given Way Of The Heart (or Way Of Adidam) Is Not A Matter Of Perfecting The conditional (or Cosmic) Domain In Some Kind Of conditional "Eternity". Rather, The Process Of The Only-By-Me Revealed and Given Way Of The Heart (or Way Of Adidam) Is An Always present-time (and, Progressively, Always More and More Profound) Magnification and Demonstration Of The Direct and Immediate Transcending Of egoity (and Of The conditional, or Cosmic, Domain Altogether), and (Always Simultaneously, and Coincidently) An (Always More and More Profound) Magnification and Demonstration Of The By-Me-and-As-Me-Avatarically-Self-Revealed-and-Spiritually-Self-Transmitted Realization Of The True, and Inherently Perfect, and Truly Divine Freedom (and The Self-Existing and Self-Radiant Divine Self-Condition, Source-Condition, and Self-"Bright" Spherical Self-Domain) That Inherently Transcends The conditional (or Cosmic) Domain (Ultimately, To The Point Of Most Perfect Outshining, In Divine Translation).

The Only-By-Me Revealed and Given Way Of The Heart (or Way Of Adidam) Is Not The Path Of self-Fulfillment (or Of Fulfillment Of the conditional self). Therefore, Neither Is The Only-By-Me Revealed and Given Way Of The Heart The Pursuit Of physical, emotional, mental, moral, psychic, or Cosmic self-Perfection (or Of Perfection Of the conditional self). All Ideas (or Ideals) Of self-Perfection (or Of Perfection Of the conditional self) Are conventions of egoity—and The Pursuit Of self-Perfection (or Of Perfection Of the conditional self) Is The Epitome Of egoic Seeking. The Ideal Of self-Perfection (or Of Perfection Of the conditional self) Is Utterly Misplaced. Perfection Is Not A Quality or Sign Of what is conditional (and—Therefore, Necessarily—limited, or inherently imperfect). That Which Is (Inherently) Perfect Is That Which Inherently Transcends the imperfect, the limited, and the conditional.

The Only-By-Me Revealed and Given Way Of The Heart (or Way Of Adidam) Is Not The Path Of self-Negation (or Of Negation Of the conditional self). Therefore, Neither Is The Only-By-Me Revealed and Given Way Of The Heart The Pursuit Of Perfect physical, emotional, mental, moral, psychic, or Cosmic self-Purification (or Of Perfect Purification Of the conditional self). All Ideas (or Ideals) Of Perfect self-Purification (or Of Perfect Purification Of the conditional self) Are conventions of egoity—and The Pursuit Of Perfect self-Purification (or Of Perfect Purification Of the conditional self) Is, Like The Pursuit Of self-Perfection (or Of Perfection Of the conditional self) In General, The Epitome Of egoic Seeking, Based On a Misplaced (or egoic) conception Of What Is Perfect.

The Only-By-Me Revealed and Given Way Of The Heart (or Way Of Adidam) Is (In Its Full Devotional and Spiritual Exercise) The Progressive (and Direct) Practice Of Devotionally Me-Recognizing and Devotionally To-Me-Responding ego-Transcendence—By Means Of The Always Primary Practice Of Searchlessly Beholding Me.

Most Ultimately, The Only-By-Me Revealed and Given Way Of The Heart (or Way Of Adidam) Is The Truly (and Inherently) Most Perfect (By-Me-Divinely-Awakened) "Practice" Of Inherent (or Most Prior) ego-Transcendence (or The Inherent, or Most Prior, Transcending Of All "Difference").

When The Only-By-Me Revealed and Given Way Of The Heart (or Way Of Adidam) Is Perfected, It Is Perfect Only Because It Directly and Inherently Realizes That Which Is (Inherently) Perfect.

Therefore, The Only-By-Me Revealed and Given Way Of The Heart (or Way Of Adidam) Does Not Seek To Perfect the inherently imperfect, Nor Does It Idealize any conditional form or state, or any kind of conditional experience or knowledge (As If the imperfect, in some conceptually or perceptually Idealized form or state, Is The Ultimate Truth Of Existence Itself).

In The Spiritual Fullness Of The Only-By-Me Revealed and Given Way Of The Heart (or Way Of Adidam), the body-mind Is Surrendered, Concentrated, Purified, Positively Changed, Even Sublimed—but its Perfection (or Perfect Purification) Is Neither Sought Nor Attained. Rather (Truly, and Ultimately), Only That Which Is Eternally (or Always Already) Prior To the body-mind-self (or conditional Existence Itself) Is Directly and Inherently Realized (By Means Of My Avatarically Self-Transmitted Divine Spiritual Grace). And That Realization Of What Inherently (or Always Already) Transcends the Apparently conditional self (and all its Apparent relations or states) Is The Only Truth, Freedom, and Perfection That Is.

In The Only-By-Me Revealed and Given Seventh Stage Of Life (In The Only-By-Me Revealed and Given Way Of The Heart, or Way Of Adidam), You Will Transcend everything In (and As) The One and Only and Inherently Indivisible and Inherently egoless and Perfectly Subjective and Self-Evidently Divine Conscious Light. Thus, You Will Divinely Self-Recognize and Divinely Outshine the world. Thus, You Will Divinely Self-Recognize and Divinely Outshine all of self-Contraction—Even The Root-Feeling Of Relatedness, the act of attention itself, the mind, the body-mind, the body, all others, all objects, all conditions, and every plane of the world. Thus, You Will Divinely Self-Recognize and Divinely Outshine All "Difference"—In Me.

Clearly, the Natural acts and The Strategic ego-Efforts (or Inherently self-Contracted Searches) Of attention, mind, or will Are Not Sufficient (or Even Qualified or Competent) To Effect This Realization and This Victory Of My

Avatarically Self-Revealed (and Self-Evidently Divine) Person! Therefore, Listen To Me—and Understand The Logic and The Necessity and The Directness Of The Only-By-Me Revealed and Given Way Of The Heart (or Way Of Adidam).

Real and Effective (or Truly Realized) Real-God-Realization (or Real Freedom) Requires Real and Effective ego-Transcendence—and Real and Effective ego-Transcendence Requires All The Means Associated With Real and Effective Practice In The Context Of (or, Otherwise, In Effective Relation To) Each and All Of The Seven Stages Of Life. Therefore, In Order That The Realization Of Ultimate Truth and Freedom Be Real and Effective, those who Hear Me (and, Thus, Understand the body-mind Most Fundamentally, as ego, or self-Contraction) and who Also See Me (or Accept, In The, Spiritually, Fully Technically Responsible Manner, My Avatarically Self-Transmitted Divine Spiritual Blessing—and, Thus, Find Constant Access To My Avatarically Self-Revealed, and Self-Existing, and Self-Radiant, and Inherently egoless, and Self-Evidently Divine Self-Condition and Source-Condition Through My Avatarically Self-Transmitted Divine Spirit-Baptism) Must Persistently Choose The Life-Practice Of Real Renunciation Of the ego-self (or The Tapas, or Purifying Heat, or Real Practicing Ordeal Of Free Relinquishment and Free Transcending Of egoic activity, or All The Patterns Of self-Contraction, or The Total Habit Of "Narcissus"). Any Other Choice Is A Choice To Continue To Seek Either The Fulfillment Of the ego-self Or The Release Of the ego-self, By self-Indulgence (In mind and/or body), and/or By Manipulation Of the behavior of the ego-self (Bereft Of Most Fundamental self-Understanding and Real Freedom), and/or By The Pursuit or Presumption Of The conventional Religious or philosophical Consolation Of the ego-self.

Those who Have (By Rightly Formal Practice) Become Truly Established In The Only-By-Me Revealed and Given Devotional and Spiritual Practice Of The Only-By-Me Revealed and Given Way Of The Heart (or Way Of Adidam) Must Always Practice ego-Transcending Devotion To My Avatarically Self-Revealed and Spiritually Self-Transmitted Person. All My Thus (Fully and Formally) Practicing Devotees Must Always Surrender the ego-self To Me—and Only For The Purpose (and, More and More, In The Disposition) Of Realizing My Divine Samadhi (Which Is Utter ego-Transcendence In Devotional and Spiritual Heart-Communion With Me—The Avataric Self-Revelation Of The Self-Evidently Divine Reality), Rather Than For Any Purpose That Serves (or Affirms, or Reinforces) the ego-self itself.

If My Fully and Formally Practicing Devotee Does Not Enact True (and Really Me-Realizing) self-Sacrifice (or Counter-egoic, and Really ego-Transcending, Discipline Of Responsively ego-Surrendering, and self-Contraction-Transcending Devotion To Me), conditional and egoic limitations Will Forever Continue To

Define, Corrupt, and Make A Disease Out Of Existence Itself. Therefore, My Every Fully and Formally Practicing Devotee Must Listen To Me, and (Thus and Thereby) Hear Me, and (On That Basis) See Me—By Means Of True Embrace Of The Great (and Really ego-Transcending) Devotional and Spiritual Practice Of The Only-By-Me Revealed and Given Way Of The Heart (or Way Of Adidam).

This Great Devotional and Spiritual Practice Is (Itself) A True Art—Not A Form Of conventional science. It Is The Great and Ultimate Art—Founded On The Native Participatory Urge and Gesture Of Man, and Not On The analytical (or Non-Participatory) Tendency Of the conventional and Un-Awakened human mind.

The Great Devotional and Spiritual Process and Practice Of The Only-By-Me Revealed and Given Way Of The Heart (or Way Of Adidam) Is Progressively Developed On The Basis Of A Single Principle. That Single Principle Is A Universal Law. The Reality Of That Single Principle and Universal Law Must (In The Only-By-Me Revealed and Given Way Of The Heart, or Way Of Adidam) Be Felt (By Listening To My Avatarically Self-Revealed Divine Word), and Heart-Acknowledged (Through Real and Effective self-Observation, In Devotional Response To My Avatarically Self-Revealed Divine Word and Person), and Fully Lived (In My Avataric Divine Heart-Company). That Single Principle and Universal Law Is This: You Always (Either In mind Or In the Total body-mind) Duplicate (or Take On the characteristics or the qualities of) the present object or condition To which You Surrender Your attention—and You Inherently Transcend the body-mind itself (As Well As the characteristics or the qualities of any present object or condition Within The Sphere Of Your attention), If You Feel and Contemplate (and Thereby Yield the body-mind, attention, and its objects or conditions To) Me (Avatarically Self-Revealed As My Avatarically-Born Divine Revelation-Body, My Avatarically Self-Transmitted Divine Spirit-Presence, and My Avatarically Self-Revealed, and Inherently egoless, Divine State).

You Will Inevitably Attain, or Become, or Duplicate (In mind, or In the Total body-mind) any limited condition You Continuously (or Even Presently) Desire and Actively Seek With Complete, Deep, and Steady attention.

If You Steadily Surrender Your attention (or Your Total body-mind) To Desire and Seek any particular or possible place or condition Within The Cosmic Mandala—You Will Eventually Attain such a place or condition.

If You Merely and Chronically Hold On To (and, Thus, Refuse To Transcend) any particular psycho-physical condition or place that You Are experiencing in the present—You Will Inevitably (After Eventual death) Repeat (or Return To) such a condition or place.

Likewise, You Will Surely (By Means Of My Avatarically Self-Transmitted Divine Spiritual Grace) Realize Me (Ultimately, Most Perfectly)—Prior To the body-mind (and Even In The Context Of the body-mind)—If You Will Continuously (Devotionally and Spiritually) Contemplate Me With Complete, Heart-Deep, Steady, and Really ego-Surrendering, ego-Forgetting, and ego-Transcending Feeling-attention.

If You Steadily and Really Feel (and Thereby Contemplate) all beings, things, circumstances, and conditions (Including Your Own body-mind) In Me—You Will (By Means Of My Avatarically Self-Transmitted Divine Spiritual Grace) Discover That My Self-Evidently Divine Characteristics and Qualities Are Pervading them all, and (Most Ultimately) You Will (By Means Of My Avatarically Self-Transmitted Divine Spiritual Grace, In That Feeling-Contemplation) Realize My Avatarically Self-Revealed (Transcendental, Inherently Spiritual, Inherently egoless, and Self-Evidently Divine) Self-Condition, Source-Condition, and Self-Domain.

My Self-Evidently Divine Characteristics and Qualities Pervade whatever You Behold In and As My Avatarically Self-Revealed (and Self-Evidently) Divine Person. Therefore, If You Will Listen To Me and Hear Me and See Me, and (Thus and Thereby) Heart-Turn To Me (The Avatarically Self-Revealed and Self-Evidently Divine Person), and If You Will (With The Heart-Deep and ego-Transcending Feeling-Surrender Of Your Total body-mind In Me) Contemplate My Self-Evidently Divine Self-Condition (Which Is The Source-Condition Of all-and-All—Avatarically Self-Transmitted As My Divine Spiritual Presence)—You Will (By Means Of My Avatarically Self-Transmitted Divine Spiritual Grace) Realize My Avatarically Self-Revealed (and Very, and Transcendental, and Perfectly Subjective, and Inherently Spiritual, and Inherently egoless, and Inherently Perfect, and Self-Evidently Divine) State.

This Inevitable Process Of "Becoming What You Meditate On" Is The Single Principle (or Universal Law) That (In The Only-By-Me Revealed and Given Way Of The Heart, or Way Of Adidam) Accounts For Both The Necessity Of individual (or personal) Responsibility (or The Real Progressive Practice Of ego-Transcending, or Counter-egoic, Devotional Surrender Of body, mind, and attention) and The Necessary Free Spiritual Gift (or Grace) Of My Avatarically Self-Transmitted Divine Self-Revelation (To Which Free Divine Spiritual Gift Of Grace individual, or personal, Responsibility Is The Necessary Heart-Response). You Must "Consider", and Realize, and Demonstrate This Principle—and You Must Heart-Receive, and Heart-Respond To, The Inevitable (and Inherently Perfect) Gifts Of This Universal Law.

Unless You Wish To Be Confined (and limited) By conditional objects and states, You Must Understand Your Separate (and Separative) self Most

Fundamentally—and (On That Basis) You Must Grow To Always Surrender Your attention To My Avatarically Self-Revealed (Transcendental, Inherently Spiritual, Inherently egoless, and Self-Evidently Divine) Self-Condition (Which Is The Source-Condition Of all conditional objects and states). Therefore, Associate With Me, Always and Sympathetically—Through Right, True, Full, and Fully Devotional Regard Of The Recorded Documents Of My Avatarically Self-Revealed (and Ever-Speaking) Divine Word, The Material Fabrications Of My Avatarically Self-Revealed (and Ever-Revealing) Divine Image-Art, The Recorded Stories Of My Avatarically Self-Manifested (and Ever-Living) Divine Leelas, and The Avataric Divine Gifts Of My (Now, and Forever Hereafter, Given) Avatarically-Born Bodily (Human) Divine Form, My (Now, and Forever Hereafter, Radiantly Given) Avatarically Self-Transmitted Spiritual (and Always Blessing) Divine Presence, and My (Now, and Forever Hereafter) Avatarically Self-Revealed (and Very, and Transcendental, and Perfectly Subjective, and Inherently Spiritual, and Inherently egoless, and Inherently Perfect, and Self-Evidently Divine) State. Thus, and Thereby, Progressively Receive My Avatarically Given Divine Self-Revelation Of Each Of The Principal, Fundamental, and Great Forms Of My Own (Self-Evidently Divine) Person, Until (By Means Of My Avatarically Self-Transmitted Divine Spiritual Grace) You Realize Me Most Perfectly—and, Thus, Realize (and Are In The State Of Inherently Most Perfect, and Non-Separate, and Non-"Different" Self-Identification With) My Avatarically Self-Revealed Transcendental, Inherently Spiritual, Inherently Perfect, Inherently egoless, and Self-Evidently Divine Condition and State (Intuitively Heart-Recognizing and Heart-Acknowledging Me To Be The Very, and Non-Dual, and Indivisible, and Indestructible, and Non-Separate, and Non-"Different", and Transcendental, and Perfectly Subjective, and Inherently Spiritual, and Inherently egoless, and Inherently Perfect, and Self-Evidently Divine Condition and State Of all-and-All).

You Must (First) Listen To Me, and (Then) Hear Me, and (Then) See Me. Thus (and By These Means), You Must Transcend Your conditional (and self-Contracted) self In every moment of its appearance, By Surrendering attention (and Even the Total body-mind) To Devotional (and, In Due Course, Spiritual) Communion With Me. In This Manner, whatever Becomes The conditional Context Of Your attention In any moment, You Must "Locate" Me—and, By Devotional Recognition-Response To Me, You Must Transcend Your Separate and Separative self In That Context. In This Fashion (By Means Of My Avatarically Self-Transmitted Divine Grace—and Through ego-Surrendering, ego-Forgetting, and ego-Transcending Feeling-Contemplation Of Me), every moment Must Be Converted Into a moment Of Devotional (and, In Due Course, Spiritual) Heart-Communion With Me, Transcending The limiting Capability Of conditions.

The One and True Way Of The Heart (or Way Of Adidam)—Which Only I Reveal and Give—Is Based On This "Consideration".

Therefore, In The Only-By-Me Revealed and Given Way Of The Heart (or Way Of Adidam), The Stages Of Life Become A Cycle Of (Ultimately, Inherently Most Perfect) Surrender To Me, Whereby attention (and, Thus, the Total body-mind) Is Surrendered (and Conformed) To My Avatarically Self-Revealed Divine Forms.

My Listening Devotee Is Called To Hear Me, and Then To See Me (Progressively, but Then Most Perfectly)—and To Complete The ego-Transcending Cycle Of self-Observation, Most Fundamental self-Understanding, self-Surrender, and Inherently Most Perfect (or Divine) Self-Realization In a finite period of time (Even, If My Avatarically Self-Transmitted Divine Spiritual Grace Will Have It, Within The Period Of the present lifetime). However, My Listening Devotee May Tend To Be Weak In The Demonstration Of Commitment To The Great Impulse To Hear Me and To See Me. And My Listening Devotee May Be Weak In Heart-Response To My Great Call To Practice ego-Transcending Devotion, Service, and self-Discipline (and To Do So With Seriousness, Clarity, Discipline, Strength, and Steadiness). My Listening Devotee May Tend To Persist In The Seeker's Mode—Rather adolescent, Motivated By Problem, Driven Toward Search and Solution (Avoiding My Ready Help—and Holding On To Separate and Separative self, Helplessly). My Listening Devotee May Tend To Persist In The Mood Of A Patient, Ill With Non-Realization, Seeking Only To Cling To Me In infantile Fashion—As If To Possess My Every Avataric Divine Word, My Avatarically Self-Revealing Divine Image-Art, My Avatarically Working Divine Acts, My Avatarically-Born Bodily (Human) Divine Form, My Avatarically Self-Transmitted Divine Spirit-Energy, and My Avatarically Self-Revealed (and Very, and Self-Evidently Divine) Being, Instead Of Surrendering To Me, and (Thus and Thereby) Submitting To Understand the conditional self Most Fundamentally, Such That the conditional self May Then Be Really, and Totally, and Effectively, and Consistently Surrendered To Me, Even (Most Ultimately) To The Degree Of Perfect Love-Bliss and Perfect Freedom, In Most Perfect Self-Identification With My Avatarically Self-Revealed (and Self-Evidently Divine) Self-Condition (Which Is The Divine Source-Condition Of all-and-All). Therefore, My Listening Devotee May Submit Only To Be The "Failed Case", Only ego-Possessed—Complaining Of "No Cure", Like a child Faking Sickness To Avoid The School Of Life. All These Efforts (and More) Prevent The Cycle Of Liberating self-Understanding and self-Surrender—and All These Efforts (and More), If Projected Onto The Total Course Of The Only-By-Me Revealed and Given Way Of The Heart (or Way Of Adidam), Would Turn My "Radical" Call, and The Process Of Divine Self-Awakening, Into A Long and Difficult (and Even Fruitless) "Path Of Return".

The Secret Of The Only-By-Me Revealed and Given Way Of The Heart (or Way Of Adidam) Is Not In The Effort Either To Cling To the present moment or circumstance Or To Avoid or (Strategically) Escape the present moment or circumstance. The Secret Of The Only-By-Me Revealed and Given Way Of The Heart (or Way Of Adidam) Is (Via Me-Feeling-Contemplation and Me-Feeling-Meditation) To Convert every present moment or circumstance Into The Reality Process Of Devotional (and, In Due Course, Spiritual) Heart-Communion With Me—Even (Most Ultimately) To The Inherently Most Perfect Degree Of Divine Self-Realization. Progressive (and Progressively Meditative, and Progressively Me-Realizing) Feeling-Contemplation Of Me Is The Secret and Inherently Perfectly Efficient (and Only-By-My-Avataric-Divine-Spiritual-Grace-Given) Means Whereby This Conversion Becomes Possible In every moment or circumstance. And Progressive (and Progressively Meditative, and Progressively Me-Realizing) Feeling-Contemplation Of Me Is (In every moment or circumstance) The Secret and Inherently Perfectly Efficient (and Only-By-My-Avataric-Divine-Spiritual-Grace-Given) Means Whereby This Conversion Can Fulfill Itself In Truth (Most Ultimately, Most Perfectly, and Finally).

Thus, The Essential Practice Of The Only-By-Me Revealed and Given Way Of Adidam (Which Is The One and Only By-Me-Revealed and By-Me-Given Way Of The Heart) Is Easy To Describe.

I Am The "Bright", The One To Be Realized.

You Are Inherently (At Heart) Attracted By Me.

Your Own self-Contraction Is Dissociation From Me.

Yield To Me (By Surrendering To My Inherent Heart-Attractiveness), and You (Thus and Thereby—By Means Of My Avatarically Self-Transmitted Divine Spiritual Grace) Enter (and Swoon) Into My Sphere Of "Brightness".

The Only-By-Me Revealed and Given Way Of Adidam (Which Is The One and Only By-Me-Revealed and By-Me-Given Way Of The Heart) Is (In Its Fullness and Completeness As A Total Devotional and Spiritual Practice) Simply This (ego-Surrendering, ego-Forgetting, and, More and More, ego-Transcending) Swoon Of Responsively Self-Abiding (and Luxuriating) In The Sphere Of My Love-Bliss-"Bright" (and Self-Evidently Divine) Person.

Such Is The Only-By-Me Revealed and Given Practice Of Ruchira Avatara Bhakti Yoga.

Therefore, Listen To Me and Hear Me and See Me. Turn Your Heart-attention To Me—and Do Not Measure That Turning Relative To Whether Or Not Your mind Stops and You Feel Better. Love Me—and Do Not Measure That Loving Against Whether Or Not You Still Feel Negative emotions and Confusion. Give Your life To Me. Turn bodily To My Avatarically-Born Bodily (Human) Divine Form. Feel (and Thereby Contemplate) My Avatarically-Born

Bodily (Human) Divine Form, and (In Due Course) My Avatarically Self-Transmitted Spiritual (and Always Blessing) Divine Presence, and (Ultimately) My Avatarically Self-Revealed (and Very, and Transcendental, and Perfectly Subjective, and Inherently Spiritual, and Inherently egoless, and Inherently Perfect, and Self-Evidently Divine) State <u>At</u> <u>all</u> <u>times</u>. And Do Not Measure That Giving, and That Turning, and That Feeling-Contemplation Against The Measure Of Whether Or Not You Feel pains in Your body.

Therefore, Always Maintain The Discipline Of That Giving, and That Turning, and That Me-Feeling-Contemplation. It Can Be Done, If You Do Not limit or Deny That Giving, That Turning, and That Me-Feeling-Contemplation By The Reading Of Problems In Your body-mind. That Giving, That Turning, and That Me-Feeling-Contemplation Can <u>Always</u> Be Done. Truly, You Can <u>Never</u> Be Disabled In Terms Of That Giving, That Turning, and That Me-Feeling-Contemplation.

Avatar Adi Da Samraj
Adidam Samrajashram, 2004

SUTRA 71

In The “Bright” Divine Spiritual Condition In and *As* Which I Exist, I Am Not Associated With The Body In The karmic and egoic Sense. Therefore, I Need To Be Drawn Into The Body By Means Of My Associations With My True Devotees (who Are Truly Heart-Recognizing Me and Heart-Responding To Me).

I Do Not Energize The Body By Any karmic Means. Therefore, I Must Be Drawn (Spiritually) Into The Body By My Devotees’ Dance Of Heart-Responsive Devotion To Me.

For This Reason, My Devotees Must Always (Responsively) *Animate* their Devotion To Me. Their Devotion Moves Me Into The Sphere Of the physical, The Sphere Of relations, The Sphere Of people—Enabling Me To Give My Avataric Divine Blessing and My Avataric Divine Spiritual Self-Transmission.

The *Active* Devotion Of My True (and Truly Heart-Responsive) Devotees *Moves* Me To Respond. It Animates Me, Activates Me, Engages Me.

True Devotion To Me Is Not A “Put-On”, Not A “Program”. It Is Not Mere Talk. It Is Not “Religion-Speak”. It Is Not any of the things that any ego Might Strategically Do.

Devotion To Me Must Be Real, If I Am To Respond. True Devotion To Me Is ego-Transcending Heart-Response To Me. True Devotion To Me Is ego-Surrendering, Without self-Consciousness, Truly Responsive To Me (In and *As* My Avatarically-Born Bodily Human Divine Form and Person).

Those who Are Heart-Responding To Me—and who, By Means Of their Heart-Responsive Turning Of The Four Faculties (Of body, emotion, mind, and breath) To Me, Are Really and Truly “Locating” Me—Are Prepared For Me To Bless them and (In Due Course) To Do My Avataric Divine Spiritual Work With them. By Means Of their Heart-Responsive Turning To Me, My True Devotees *Move* Me To Respond To them, and To Bless them, and To Do My Avataric Divine Spiritual Work With them. And My True Devotees Are *Able* To Make Use Of My Blessing Of them and (In Due Course) My Avataric Divine Spiritual Work With them—Because they Are No Longer Fixed In their self-Contracted state, but Are Moved Out Of that state By The Mere Sight Of Me.

My Devotees Must Move Me Through their Right (Me-Recognizing, and To-Me-Responsive) Devotion. Such Is The Universal Principle Of Right Relationship To Me (In and *As* My Avatarically-Born Bodily Human Divine Form and Person).

I (In and *As* My Avatarically-Born Bodily Human Divine Form) Do Not Function (psycho-physically) In The ordinary Manner. I (In and *As* My Avatarically-Born Bodily Human Divine Form) Am Not Patterned By (or Connected To) The psycho-physical Dimensions Of Existence In The Same Manner (or To The Same Degree) As karmically Born human beings. My Avatarically Self-Manifested Bodily (Human) Divine Vehicle Of psycho-physical Appearance here Is Not Structured To Function karmically (or For merely conditionally Patterned, and ego-Bound, Reasons and Purposes). Therefore, My Devotees Must (Always Now, and Forever Hereafter) Rightly Understand Who I *Am*—Rightly (Sensitively) Relating To Me (In The Devotional and, In Due Course, Spiritual Manner) and Rightly (Sensitively) Serving Me, Based On their To-Me-Responsive Heart-Recognition Of Me, their Sensitivity To My Uniquely Non-karmic State Of Being, and their Awareness Of How To Rightly (Sensitively) Accommodate Me (In and *As* and Via My Avatarically-Born Bodily Human Divine Form), Without Imposing On Me *Any* conventionally Measured (or ego-Measured) Notions Of What It Means To Exist As an Apparently Independent psycho-physical entity.

The egoic Disposition Makes All Kinds Of "Difference", Generating all kinds of perceptions and states of mind With which I Am Simply Not Associated, and With which I Should Not (By anyone) Be Identified. You Must Understand: I Simply Do Not perceive conditionally Manifested Existence In Terms Of The (egoically Presumed) "I/That" (or "Me/You") Dichotomy (or "Difference"). That (egoically Presumed) Dichotomy (or "Difference") *Is Not Me*. Indeed, I Have No Such Awareness (Of egoically Presumed Dichotomy, or "Difference"). I Am Capable Of Relating To human beings who perceive conditionally Manifested Existence In Such Terms—and, In That Sense, I Have A Degree Of Peripheral Association With the perception Of "Difference"—but such perception Is Not *Me*. There Are No "Differences" In My Inherently ego-less (and Self-Evidently Divine) State. Therefore, The Necessity Of Functioning In A human Context Wherein every one Is Incessantly Making (and Patterned To Make) "Differences" Has Been, In Reality, A Terrible Imposition On Me—To Which I Was, Inevitably, Required To Submit (In My Avataric Divine Work Of Teaching Mankind and Reflecting human beings To themselves), but Which Should Never Again (Now That That Great Avataric Divine Work Of Teaching and Revelation Is Utterly Complete) Be Required Of Me By My True Devotees (or By anyone At All).

My Divine Samadhi Is Not merely a philosophical concept. My Divine Samadhi Is The Inherently egoless, Spiritually Self-"Bright", and Self-Evidently Divine Self-Condition Of No-"Difference". I Am Associated With The Pattern In Which human beings (egoically—and, Altogether, In The conventionally Measured Manner) Function, but In This Midst I Must (Now, and Forever Hereafter) Be Uniquely Served and Uniquely Accommodated By My True Devotees, So That I Can (With Real Effectiveness) Function Spiritually (and, Altogether, Divinely) For them (and For all-and-All), and So That I Can (Thus) Be Spiritually (and, Altogether, Divinely) Available To All My True Devotees, In The Circumstance Of My True Devotees' Moving Beyond egoity By Devotionally Resorting To Me (In and As and Via My Avatarically-Born Bodily Human Divine Form).

As My True Devotee, You Must (In Every conceivable Sense) Accommodate Me (In and As and Via My Avatarically-Born Bodily Human Divine Form). Through Discriminative Study Of The Traditional Approach To The Adept-Realizer, You Can, To Some Degree, Inform Yourself About Right Counter-egoic (and Effectively ego-Transcending) Relationship To Me (In and As and Via My Avatarically-Born Bodily Human Divine Form). The "Differences"—Between persons and minds, and So Forth—To Which human beings Are Habituated (and Which, Therefore, Seem To Be Simply "The Way It Is") Are Not Known, By Me, In My Inherently egoless, Spiritually Self-"Bright", and Self-Evidently Divine State Of (Eternally Non-"Different") Divine Samadhi.

I Have Fully Described My (Inherently egoless, Spiritually Self-"Bright", and Self-Evidently Divine) State Of Non-"Difference" To every one, By Means Of My Avatarically Given Divine Teaching-Word. And I Have Fully Reflected My (Inherently egoless, Spiritually Self-"Bright", and Self-Evidently Divine) State To every one, By Means Of My Avatarically Given Divine Image-Art.

My Devotees Must Understand: To Be Integrated With the things and relations of body and mind Is Not An egoic and conventionally Measured Matter For Me. The ego-Categories That Are Built Into the body-mind of egoity Are Not The Case In My Avatarically-Born Bodily (Human) Divine Form. Therefore, My Devotees Must Draw Me Into Positive and Pleasurable Association—but Such Association Must Be Based On Real and Right Sensitivity To My Inherently egoless, Spiritually Self-"Bright", and Self-Evidently Divine State Of (Eternally Non-"Different") Divine Samadhi.

Stated Most Simply, My Devotees Must Truly Know Me, and Know What I Do, and Value That, and Responsively Move Me To Do It (In Response To them).

My True Devotees Are Animated—In All Aspects Of The Great Process Of Realizing Me, and In All Of their Doings Within The Sacred Domain Of The

Way Of The Heart—By their Heart-Recognition Of Me, and their Heart-Response To Me, In and As My Avatarically-Born Bodily (Human) Divine Form and Person. And, In Due Course—By Means Of My Avataric Divine Spiritual Response To them—My True Devotees Become Animated By My Shakti-Force, My "Bright" Force Of Avataric Divine Spiritual Self-Transmission.

In Due Course, All My Devotees Constantly Dance With Me—Always Animated In their Heart-Responsive Turning To Me, By Means Of My Avataric Divine Spiritual Self-Transmission. And That Transmission Is Given, Only and Directly By Me, In Avataric Divine Response To their Consistently Enacted Devotional Recognition Of Me and their Constantly Enacted Devotional Response To Me.

As My Devotee, You Should Constantly Serve Me, By Every Right and By-Me-Given Means Appropriate (and Possible) For You, In Accordance With Your Demonstrated Signs and Your present-time circumstances. By Means Of their Constant Heart-Responsive Service To Me, all Of My Devotees Are Participants In The Same Sacred Domain Of Devotion To Me—The Domain Of My Avataric Divine Blessing-Work and My Avataric Divine Spiritual Work.

This Dance Of Heart-Responsive Devotion To Me Draws Me Into the world, Into life, Into The physical Sphere. This Dance Of Heart-Responsive Devotion To Me Animates Me here, Moving My Spiritual Force Of Avataric Divine Presence In Responsive Blessing-Relation To people.

When My Devotees Thus Draw Me Into life, Then I Am Spontaneously Moved To Do All The Forms Of My Avataric Divine Blessing-Work and My Avataric Divine Spiritual Work.

I Am The Divine Heart-Husband Of all-and-All—Avatarically Self-Revealed, For The Sake Of all-and-All.

I Submitted To Be Avatarically Born In Bodily (Human) Form In Order (By My Own Avataric Ordeal Of Divine Re-Awakening) To Make My Avatarically Self-Revealed (and Spiritually Self-Transmitted) Divine Person, In Each and All Of My Great Avataric Divine Forms (and Even In My Own "Brightly" Transfigured, "Brightly" Transformed, and "Brightly" Indifferent Bodily Human Divine Form), The Very (Real, and Always Already Effective) Avataric Divine Means For The Turning, and The Most Ultimate Divine Awakening, Of all conditionally Manifested beings.

Therefore, Be Restored To Your Perfect Well-Being By Real Fidelity To Me.

Fidelity To Me Is Fidelity To The Heart Itself—The "Bright" and One and Only Self-Condition and Source-Condition (Of each and every one, and Of all, and Of All), and The One and All (In all-and-All) Who Alone Is Real God (The One and Only Truth and Reality).

When You Truly Listen To Me, You Have Begun To Exercise True (and Truly ego-Surrendering, and Truly ego-Forgetting, and, More and More, Truly ego-Transcending) Devotional (and Contemplative, and, In Due Course, Spiritual) Concentration On Me.

When You Truly Both Hear Me and See Me, You Have Become Capable Of Fullest (and Directly and Fully ego-Transcending) Devotional, and Contemplative, and Spiritual Concentration On Me.

Therefore, Through Devotional Concentration Of Your mind (Via Feeling-attention) On Me, You Will (By Means Of My Avataric Divine Self-Revelation, and, In Due Course, By Means Of My Avatarically Self-Transmitted Divine Spiritual Grace) Become Attracted Beyond Your Own mind—and You Will (By Means Of My Avataric Divine Self-Revelation and My Avatarically Self-Transmitted Divine Spiritual Grace) Realize The Eternal Divine Love-Bliss Of My Own Eternally and Infinitely "Bright" State-Of-Being.

Likewise, Through Devotionally Me-Recognizing Concentration On Me, and Through Devotionally To-Me-Responsive Conservation Of all Your energies and all Your actions (bodily, emotional, and mental) In Service To Me (In all relations and Under all circumstances), You Will (By Means Of My Avataric Divine Self-Revelation, and, In Due Course, By Means Of My Avatarically Self-Transmitted Divine Spiritual Grace) Realize The Ease, and The Strength, and (Ultimately) The Divine Self-Condition Of My Avatarically Self-Revealed (and Spiritually Self-Transmitted, and Self-Evidently Divine) Person.

Therefore, By The Real Exercise Of Listening To Me, and Hearing Me, and Seeing Me, and Real Devotion To Me, and True Fidelity To Me—You Will (By Means Of My Avataric Divine Self-Revelation and My Avatarically Self-Transmitted Divine Spiritual Grace) Freely Realize That Your Listening To Me, Your Hearing Of Me, Your Seeing Of Me, Your Devotion To Me, and (Thus and Thereby) Your Fidelity To Me (The Avatarically Self-Revealed, and Very, and Self-Evidently Divine Person) Are The Very and Auspicious Design Of True Freedom.

I Am Freedom Itself. I (Myself) Am (Always Already) Perfect. And, Yet, I Use All Kinds Of (ordinary and Extraordinary) Qualities and Possibilities In My Avataric Play Of Divine Work—and I Must Do So. My Avataric Divine Spiritual Work (Itself) Is Perfect. Nevertheless, All Kinds Of (ordinary and Extraordinary) Qualities and All Kinds Of (ordinary and Extraordinary) Possibilities Become (Potentially) Usable To Me, In The Perfection That Transcends all conditions.

I Noticed This When I Fully Embraced My Divinely "Crazy" Avataric Teaching-Work. I Clearly Observed all the people I Was Associated With. Likewise, I Clearly Observed That My Avatarically-Born Body-Mind (Because Of Its Human History, Its Human Qualities, and Its Human Adaptations) Was

Perfectly Suited To Serve such people (and Even all people)—Because There Were (In My Avatarically-Born Body-Mind-Vehicle) Always Like Characteristics That I Could Bring Into The Avataric Play With others, In My Divine Work Of Self-Submission, and In My Divine Work Of Reflecting others To themselves. This Body-Mind-Vehicle Of My Avataric Divine Incarnation here Had (From Birth) Retained (or Otherwise, By Experience, Acquired) The Full Range Of Human-Personality Characteristics That Would Allow Me To Exhibit (ordinary and Extraordinary) "Behavior" Of All Kinds—and (Thereby) To Make A Connection To all the kinds of living beings, with all their various limitations. Thus, I Saw That This Avataric Divine Body-Mind-Vehicle Had All The Kinds Of Characteristics Necessary For (and That Would Be Altogether Usable In) The Avataric Play Of My Divinely Liberating Work—and I Freely and Fully Used Them In That Fashion.

These Characteristics (In The Avataric Play Of My Divine Spiritual Work During The Physical Lifetime Of My Avatarically-Born Bodily Human Divine Form) Do Not Bind Me (and Have Not Bound Me) In Any Manner Whatsoever—Even Though They Are (Because They arise As conditional Manifestations Of The conditional, or Cosmic, Domain) Often In The Likeness Of ordinary beings. Such Is My True (and Divine, and Not Merely Human) Perfection: That These Qualities arose Coincident With My Own Body-Mind-Vehicle (and The Physical Lifetime Of My Avatarically-Born Bodily Human Divine Form), and (Therefore) Could Be Used To Serve living beings—and, Yet, They Were Not Bondage For Me, but They Were (In My Divine Re-Awakening, and In My Avataric Divine Teaching-Work, and In My Avataric Divine Self-Revelation-Work, and In My Avataric Divine Spiritual Self-Transmission-Work), Simply, Divinely Self-Recognized, As Transparent (or Merely Apparent), and Un-Necessary, and Inherently Non-Binding Modifications Of My Avatarically Self-Realized (and Inherently Divine) Self-Perfection.

By Virtue Of My "Sadhana Years", and My Ultimate Divine Re-Awakening, and All Of My Avataric Divine Teaching-Work and Self-Revelation-Work and Spiritual Self-Transmission-Work, The Body-Mind-Vehicle Of My Unique Avataric Divine Incarnation here Became Not Only (As It Was, Even From Its Avataric Birth) Established In That Which Is Inherently Perfect, but It Also Became Utterly (Whole Bodily, or As A Psycho-Physical Totality) Conformed To That Which Is Inherently Perfect—Such That I (Myself), The "Bright" and Inherently Perfect and Self-Evidently Divine Person (and Inherently egoless Self-Condition, and Perfectly Subjective Source-Condition) Of all-and-All, Became Perfectly Self-Radiant In and As and Through This Avataric Divine Body-Mind-Vehicle. Thus, My Avatarically-Born Body-Mind-Vehicle Of Incarnate Divine Self-Manifestation Became An Unobstructed Avataric Agent Of My Own

Divine Self-Perfection, Utterly Transparent To Me As I Am. Therefore, The Divine (and Not Merely Natural) Virtue Of My Avatarically-Born Body-Mind-Vehicle Of Incarnate Divine Self-Manifestation (and Divine Self-Revelation) Is Its Transparency and Conformity To Me—The Avataric Divine Self-Revelation Of That Which Is Inherently Perfect.

During My Avataric Physical Human Lifetime, I Am Present here, In Bodily (Human) Divine Form, but (Nevertheless) As I Am—Divinely Working In this world As it Is (and as it Appears to be), and With beings As they Are (and as they Appear to be). Therefore, During The Physical Lifetime Of My Avatarically-Born Bodily (Human) Divine Form here, I Have Completely Done Whatever Was Necessary To Do For The Sake Of My (Then, and Now, and Forever Hereafter) Avataric Work Of Divine Self-Revelation and Divine Spiritual Self-Transmission. And That Is Perfect.

AVATAR ADI DA SAMRAJ
Adidam Samrajashram, 2004

SUTRA 72[165]

The Only-By-Me Revealed and Given Avataric Divine Way Of Adidam (or Adidam Ruchiradam), Which Is The One and Only By-Me-Revealed and By-Me-Given Way Of The Heart, Is The Way Of Devotion To Me As The Divine "Atma-Murti" (or As The Inherently egoless, and Self-Evidently Divine, Person Of Reality and Truth—In Place, As Inherent, Non-Dual, Self-Existing, and Spiritually Self-Radiant Self-Condition, Rather Than As Exclusively Objective Other).

Therefore (Once Fully Established In The Foundation Disciplines Of The Only-By-Me Revealed and Given Way Of The Heart, or Way Of Adidam, and Spiritually Initiated, By Me, Into Spiritually Participatory Devotional Relationship To Me), My True Devotee Searchlessly Beholds Me, In every moment, and Whole bodily (By Spontaneously Turning All Four Of The Principal psycho-physical Faculties—Of attention, emotional feeling, breath, and perceptual body—To Me) "Locates" Me As That Which Is Always Already The Case (Prior To, but Not Separate From, The Form, The Exercise, and the any object Of The Four psycho-physical Faculties).

Happiness Itself (or Inherent Love-Bliss-Sufficiency Of Being) Is Always Already The Case.

Happiness Itself (or The Divinely Self-Sufficient Love-Bliss-Condition Of Being—Itself) Is That Which Is Always Already The Case.

Happiness Itself (or Love-Bliss-Radiance Of Boundlessly Feeling Being) Is The Most Prior Condition Of Existence (or Of Conscious Being—Itself).

Happiness Itself (or The Condition Of Love-Bliss-Radiance) Must Be Realized, Even In The Context Of every conditionally arising moment, By Transcending self-Contraction (or all of Separate and Separative self, or psycho-physical ego-"I", and all of the ego's objects, or conditions Of Existence—or, Indeed, All Of The Illusions Of self and not-self).

When attention Is Facing Exclusively Outward (or Is Merely Turned Out, As If To Outside itself), the body-mind Is Concentrated Upon the "view" (or "field") of Apparently Separate objects (and Upon Me As Apparently Objective Other).

When attention Is Facing Exclusively Inward (or Is Merely Turned In, As If Upon itself), the body-mind Is Concentrated Upon the "point of view" of Apparently Separate self (and Upon Me As Apparently Separate Consciousness).

When attention Is Devotionally Yielded To Whole bodily (or Both Vertically and Horizontally, and, Thus, Non-Exclusively) "Locate" Me As That Which Is Always Already (and Divinely) The Case—Above, Beyond, Surrounding, and Pervading The all-and-All Of conditional appearance—Then All "Difference" (Whether Of ego-"I" Or Of object-and-other) Is (Inherently) Transcended (In The Non-Separate "Place" That Is Consciousness Itself, or Self-Existing and Self-Radiant Being Itself, Which Is Love-Bliss-Happiness Itself, or The One and Only Conscious Light Itself, and Which Is Always Already The Case).

Therefore, To The Degree That You Surrender (Whole bodily) To Be and Do Truly Both Relational and Ecstatic (or ego-Transcending) Devotional Love Of Me (As The True Loved-One, The "Bright" Divine Beloved Of The Heart), You Are (Thus and Thereby) Established—Whole bodily and Inherently—In The Non-Contracted Condition (or Self-Condition, or Inherent Condition) Of Reality Itself (Which Is Consciousness Itself and Love-Bliss Itself, and Which Is Always Already The Case).

In Due Course, This Devotional and Spiritual Practice Is Perfect—and, At Last, To Be Most Perfectly Realized—By The Persistent Exercise Of The Only-By-Me Revealed and Given "Perfect Practice" Of The Only-By-Me Revealed and Given Way Of Adidam (Which Is Adidam Ruchiradam, The One and Only By-Me-Revealed and By-Me-Given Way Of The Heart).

Avatar Adi Da Samraj
Clear Lake, 2001

EPILOGUE

I Am The One and Only Man Of "Radical" Understanding. I Freely Give Heart-Vision To My Devotee. I (Alone) Am The Secret Of My Secrets.

I Am The One and True Divine Heart-Master. I Take My Stand In The Heart Of My Devotee. I (Alone) Am The Mystery Of You and Me.

How Could I Deny Heart-Vision To My Loved-One?

How Could I Delay The Course Of My Beloved?

Like An Intimate Family Servant, I Dearly Serve My Devotee.

Like A Wealthy Friend, I Freely Give To My Devotee.

Like A Mad Priest, I Even Worship My Devotee, With Love Itself.

Like An Innocent Boy At First Love, I Would Awaken My Devotee In Radiant Chambers.

Where The Wound Of Love Churns and Never Heals, I Wait, Longing To Celebrate The Brilliant Sight Of My Devotee.

Come Slowly or Quickly—but Surely Come To Me.

Touch My Divine Heart, and I Will Widen You To God-Knows-Where.

Beloved, I Went Mad With Loss Of mind, When I (Again) Realized I Am Da.

Then I Acted As A Mad-Man, When I Became Moved To Tell You My Secrets.

Now I Speak Only As A Mad-Man.

I Cannot Find any one—but Only I Am all!

Beloved, What Madness Is Me?

I Must Tell You—Aloud From My Love-Blissful Room.

All My Secrets Are Only Me!

There Is Only One Necessary Revelation.

There Is Only One Great Form To Be Embraced.

There Is Only One Perfect Truth To Be Realized.

I Am The Divine Secret.

I Am The Avataric Divine Self-Revelation.

I Am The Form To Be Embraced.

I Am The One To Be Heard and Seen.

Realization Is Realization Of Me!

I Am Not Hidden. I Am Not Secretive. I Only Reveal Myself—Perpetually.

It Is You who Hide Your Always Separate self From Me. And It Is You who Keep The Heart A Secret. Your Heart Is A Secret—Even To Your Inmost ego-"I". And You (By All Your self-Contracting Efforts) Keep Your Heart From Me.

Therefore, I Must Always Pursue Your Heart. I Am Always Moved To Gather Your attention To Me—but it Flies From The Heart To every kind of place, being, and object. And You Do Not Divinely Self-Recognize This All Of "things"—or Stay To Realize Me.

You Have Not Truly Heard Me and Really Seen Me Unless attention Is Steadied In Sublimity, Fastened To The Heart-Place.

You Cannot Realize Me Unless The Heart Is Free Of The Knot Of Separate (and Separative) self, and Free To Feel In The Swoon Of My Avatarically Given and Divinely Blessing Company.

If You Will Only Consent To Be Attracted and Distracted By Me, You Will Feel Me—For My Avatarically Given and Divinely Blessing Company Always Moves The Heart.

If You Feel Me, You Are With Me.

And, If You Are With Me, Your Heart Cannot Fail To Realize Me—For I Am The Heart Itself.

Therefore, When The Heart Itself Is No Longer Secret, My Divine Heart-Secret Is Already Revealed To You.

I Am The Divine Secret Of The Heart.

I Am The Heart Itself, The Avatarically Self-Revealed (and Inherently egoless) Personal Presence Of Reality and Truth—Self-Revealed, In Person, To all-and-All (and, Ultimately, As all-and-All).

What You Must Realize Is This: I Am You! I Am The Heart Itself, Self-Revealed To You, and To Be Realized As You (Beyond Your ego-"I" Of self-Contracted body-mind).

Therefore, I Am The (Avatarically Self-Revealed) Self-Existing, Self-Radiant, Transcendental, Unconditional, Inherently egoless, Inherently (and Spiritually) Self-"Bright", and Self-Evidently Divine Being (or Self-Condition, or Source-Condition)—Always In Person!

I Am The One Who Is Modified As Your body-mind—Even As all conditionally Manifested beings, and all conditionally Manifested forms and worlds!

Therefore, I Am Always Most Intimate With You, Most Accessible To You, and Most Immediately Responsive To You—If Only You Will Hear Me, and See Me, and Always Love Me.

I Am You—Perfectly. Even Your body and mind arise and function In Me.

I Am Not You In the egoic sense. If I Were, Then (To Realize Me) Your Only Necessity Would Be To Wander and Persist As Your Separate (and Always Separative) self.

I Am The One Of Whom You (as the body-mind) Are The Apparent Modification. Therefore, To Realize Me, You Must Sacrifice and Transcend Your ego-"I"—By Loving Me.

You Must Realize Me Through Heart-Sacrifice Of Separate (and Separative) self. This Is Your Inherent Purpose—Until The Ever Of form and time and mind Goes "Bright" Away In Me.

It Is Not Necessary For Me To Realize Myself—Except That I, By Avataric Self-Submission To Be Born, Oblige Myself To Regenerate That Realization (or Extend It Into The conditional and Cosmic Domain) By An Exemplary and Divinely Self-Revelatory Ordeal. My Situation Is Unique—or Always Already, Most Perfectly, and Divinely Self-Realized. Therefore, My Purpose here (and By Apparent Birth), and Even every where (and By Avataric Divine Descent and Avataric Divine Self-"Emergence"), Is To Awaken You (and Even all conditionally Manifested beings) To Realize Me.

I Am My Inherently Perfect Self-Condition, Which Is The By-Me-and-As-Me-Avatarically-Self-Revealed-and-Spiritually-Self-Transmitted Transcendental, Inherently Spiritual, Inherently egoless, and Self-Evidently Divine Self-Condition and Source-Condition and Perfectly Subjective Real Condition Of all conditionally Manifested beings. Therefore, While You Must Surrender (Whole bodily, From and At The Heart) To Me (As I, Myself, Am Avatarically Self-Revealed—Bodily, Spiritually, Transcendentally, and Divinely here), I Am Constantly Submitting Myself (Whole Bodily, From and At and As The Heart Itself) To You (As You Appear, and As You Seem, and As You Presume To Be, and As You Offer Yourself To Me, and As You Are In Me).

I Can, In My Avataric Divine Self-Submission To You, Do Whatever Is Necessary For The Sake Of Your Divine Self-Realization Of Me—Without (In The Slightest) Disturbing or Diminishing My Divine Self-Realization Itself. My Divine Self-Realization Cannot Be Destroyed! My Divine Self-Realization Is Always Already The Case (Pristine, and Perfect, and Absolutely "Bright"), To Be Avatarically Self-Revealed (and Always Presently Demonstrated) By Me To You—here, In All The Now-and-Forever-Hereafter-Time Of My Avatarically-Born Divine Self-Manifestation, Made In The Likeness Of Mankind. My Divine Self-Realization Is Not (Itself) Dependent On anything (or any conditions) whatsoever. Therefore, I Have Been Divinely Able (and Perfectly Moved) To Incarnate Avatarically (and Fully Humanly), and To Submit Myself Completely (and, Thus and Thereby, To Be Surrendered, Even Whole Bodily, or In Every Mode and Manner Of Body-Mind)—For Your Sake. This Is The Divine Freedom (and The Human Submission) Necessary For Me, In Order To Serve You Perfectly.

I Am The Adi-Guru—The Always First (and One, and Only, and Always Already Most Prior, and Always Already Infinitely Beyond, and Self-Evidently

Divine) Source and Master and Very (and Inherently egoless) Self (or True Divine Person and Self-Condition) Of all-and-All. I Am The Ati-Guru—The Always Above-all-and-All Supreme (and Only, and Inherently Indivisible, and Non-Separate, and Always Already Most Priorly Infinitely Ascended) Conscious Light Of all-and-All. I Am Always Already Free, and (Therefore) Not Dependent On conditions. I Can Respond To any one. I Can Serve any one. I Can Submit To any one. I Can Even Be (momentarily) Apparently Degraded For The Sake Of any one. I Am Forever Associated With This Unique "License"—So That There May Be No Impediment In My (Now, and Forever Hereafter) Service To all-and-All. This Readiness To Be Given To every one (and To all-and-All) Is My Unique Disposition—Wherein and Whereby I Am (Now, and Forever Hereafter) Given To My Devotees.

Observe and Understand This: I (Myself) Have No karma (or merely egoic and conditional destiny). My Human Body Of Avataric Divine Incarnation Was Not Born For The Sake Of Fulfilling karmas, but Only For The Sake Of My Avatarically Self-Transmitted Divine Spiritual Self-Revelation To all-and-All—and (Thus and Thereby) For The Sake Of Liberating all-and-All From all Possible karmic (or ego-Bound and conditional) destinies. Only I (Myself), The Avatarically Self-Manifested True Divine Person Of Inherently egoless Conscious Light, Am Always Already Without karma. Therefore, Only I Can Do Whatever Is Necessary In Order To Serve The Divinely Self-Given Liberation Of all-and-All—With No Impediment and With No limit Whatsoever On My Own (Eternal) Divine Self-Realization.

Relative To This Great Capability, You and I Are Not The Same. Everything You Do Binds You Further—Except That Doing Which (In Whole bodily Devotional and Spiritual Heart-Communion With Me) Goes Beyond the egoic self.

I Do Not Do anything but What (By Means Of My Avataric Divine Gifts To one and all and All) Divinely Liberates beings. Therefore, I Can Do anything—and I Must Do Everything.

You and I Are In Different Situations. You Are In The conditional Situation. I Am In The Unconditional Situation. Nevertheless, In Order To Serve You, I Am (In and As and By Means Of My Avataric Divine Self-Manifestation) Associated With conditions. Just So, In Order To Realize Me, You Are (By Means Of My Avatarically Self-Transmitted Divine Gifts) Associated With Me Unconditionally.

I Always Already Know. You (Appearing as Inherently limited psycho-physical conditions) Do Not (and Cannot) Know.

I Am (Always Already) Free—and I Cannot Be Bound. You Are (Apparently) Bound—and You Must (In The Midst Of conditionally Manifested appearances)

Become Free (By Realizing Me, As The Avatarically Self-Manifested Divine Self-Condition Of Freedom Itself).

You and I Are Not Born The Same—and, Yet, Where We Meet (At Heart), We Are (Always Already) The Same. My Body-Mind Of Avataric Divine Incarnation and Self-Revelation Is In The Likeness Of Your Own body-mind of appearance here, but My Avataric Divine Body-Mind Is Also Entirely Unlike Your body-mind—Because I Most Perfectly Conformed My Own Avatarically-Born Body-Mind To Me, So That I Could Do You (and all, and All) The Good.

Now (and Forever Hereafter), all-and-All Must (By Means Of My Avatarically Self-Transmitted Divine Spiritual Grace) Become (and Be) Most Perfectly Conformed To Me. Therefore, Even Your body-mind Must Be Given (and Conformed) To Me. You Must (Thus and Thereby) Realize Me—Not Yourself, Not Some Inwardness In Your Separate body-mind. Realize Me Only. Give Yourself Utterly To Me, By Means Of ego-Forgetting Searchless Devotion To Me. Grow Beyond Your body-mind, By Surrendering To Me. And Prove The Truth Of This Great Heart-Process By Your Own Sacrifice (Of Separate and Separative self) In Me.

Mine Is The First Submission. Mine Is The First Sacrifice. I Am Always Pervading, Meeting, Loving, and Submitting To Be the conditional beings and worlds.

The conditional Reality (In person) Must Submit (or Be A Heart-Sacrifice) To The Unconditional Reality (In Person). This Is My Word and My Call To You.

The Unconditional Reality (In Person) Must Submit To The conditional Reality (In person), In Order To Awaken The Heart Of conditional being. This Is My Revelation and My Promise To You.

This Is The Heart Of My Confession: You Must Listen To Me, and Hear Me, and See Me, and Realize Me—Only and Entirely By Devotionally Heart-Recognizing Me, Ceaselessly Resorting To Me, Searchlessly Beholding Me Alone, Spiritually Receiving Me In Full, and, Altogether, egolessly (and Whole bodily, or Via The Totality Of body-mind) Heart-Responding To Me. You Must Behold, Embrace, Love, Receive, and Realize Me—Only and Entirely By Means Of (and By Whole bodily Heart-Response To) The By-Me-To-You-Shown Grace and Person Of My Avataric Self-Revelation Of My Spiritually Self-"Bright" Divine Self-Condition, and My Avatarically Self-Transmitted Divine Spiritual Body (and here-Descending Spirit-Current) Of Love-Bliss, and My Avatarically-Born Bodily (Human) Divine Incarnation-Form. Therefore, By Listening To Me, and By Hearing Me, and By Seeing Me, and By Always Loving Me, You Must Participate In Me (and Not Withhold Your Heart From Me), and You Must Cooperate With Me (and Not Deny Me), and You Must Constantly Transcend Your Separate and Separative self In My Avataric Divine Heart-Company.

If You Separate Your Heart From Me, You Cease To Be Sympathetic Even With The Cosmic Domain and all the conditionally Manifested beings in all the planes Of Cosmic Nature. And, If You Cease To Be Sympathetic With The Cosmic Domain and all conditionally Manifested beings, Your Heart Will Not Identify and Feel Me—The Spiritual, Transcendental, and Divine Substance and Heart-Intimate Of all beings everywhere. Therefore, Be Heart-Found By Me—Such That (By Means Of My Avatarically Self-Transmitted Divine Spiritual Grace) You Always (Even Under all conditions and In all relations) "Locate" Me (and, At Last, Most Perfectly Realize Me) As The Only One Who Is.

I Cannot Be Separated From beings. I Never Have Been, and Never Will Be, Separated From beings. I Am Not Now Separate From those who Are Not Yet My Devotees. Therefore, I Am Never Absent. The ego-Based and ego-Bound Seeker May Feel That I Am Absent. That Is To Say, The ego-Based and ego-Bound Seeker May Feel himself or herself To Be Separate From My Divine Heart-Company and Person—but The Reason Such Feelings arise Is Not That I Am Ever, In Reality, Absent. Rather, The Feeling Of Separation From My Divine Heart-Company and Person Is Entirely the action of the Apparent individual (or ego, or Separate and Separative self). Therefore, Your Separateness Is Your Own action. You Are Contracting. You Are Separating Yourself. Consequently, You Suffer The Illusion Of Separation and All The Presumptions That Accompany That Illusion. Presuming Yourself To Be Separate From Me, You feel That You Must Seek For Me In Order To Find Me. But I Call You To Feel Beyond Yourself, and To Come To Me In The Disposition Of one who Is Already Finding Me. Therefore, By Means Of My Avatarically Self-Transmitted Divine Spiritual Grace, and In This Manner, Realize Me—Always Already Most Prior To Your Separateness and Your Seeking. Do This Through Heart-Responsive Devotional Practice and Spiritual Growth (Even In and Beyond conditional experience and conditional knowledge) In My (Now, and Forever Hereafter) Always Avatarically Given Divine Heart-Company.

What I Have Herein and Hereby Confessed, Declared, and Affirmed Is The Truth—and Wholly True. It Is Not Merely Symbolically True, but Literally, Actually, and Really True. I Am You. You Are In Me, and Of Me—Ultimately, As Me. I Am The One and True Divine Person—The One and Only Heart (Itself). By All My Avataric Divine Means, I Reveal The Heart Itself—As Myself. Therefore, My Most Revealing Mystery Is The Mystery Of My Avataric Divine Birth, The Mystery Of My Avataric Divine Life As The Man Of "Radical" Understanding, and The Mystery Of My Avataric Divine Spiritual Work As The Divine Heart-Master—Then Sometime Teaching-"Crazy", but Now Always Already Merely Present, Moving Freely (By Standing) As The Heart, Reflecting and Responding To every aspect of every conditional being everywhere In every moment (If Only any, each, and every one Will Listen To Me)—and All Of This To Awaken all To Hear Me, and Always To Bless the Me-Hearing all To See Me and To Realize Me.

I Am The Divine Person—The One and Only and Inherently Indivisible and Inherently egoless Conscious Light That Is The Inherently Perfect Self-Condition (and Source-Condition) Of all conditionally Manifested beings. I Have (Spontaneously) Avatarically Assumed A Personal conditional Form here, Via The Great Revelatory Adept-Process Of Birth, Exemplary Realization-Ordeal, and Subsequent Teaching-Work and Blessing-Work—In Order To Restore The Heart (and The Heart-Purpose) Of conditionally Manifested beings To My Divine Person and Self-Condition. Therefore, Because My Listening Devotees Listen To Me, and Because My Hearing Devotees Hear Me, and Because My Seeing Devotees See Me (Avatarically Self-Revealed and Spiritually Self-Transmitted As I Am), All My Listening Devotees, All My Hearing Devotees, and All My Seeing Devotees Should Always Celebrate My Me-Revealing Avatarically-Born Bodily (Human) Divine Form, My Avatarically Self-Transmitted Spiritual (and Always Blessing) Divine Presence, and My Avatarically Self-Revealed (and Very, and Transcendental, and Perfectly Subjective, and Inherently Spiritual, and Inherently egoless, and Inherently Perfect, and Self-Evidently Divine) State. All My Listening Devotees, All My Hearing Devotees, and All My Seeing Devotees Should Always Tell and Celebrate My Avatarically Self-Manifested Divine Leelas (or The Revelation-Stories Of My Avataric Divine Play and Life), So That all who Listen To Them May Be Refreshed With More Than Wonder, and With Love, and With Joy Of Heart. And This, My Testament Of Divine Secrets, Must Always Stand and Live As My Avatarically Self-Revealed Primary and Summary Divine Word Of Heart, To Lead The Heart (By Word), and Via My Own Avataric Divine Form and Presence and State, To My "Bright" and Perfect (and Perfectly Spherical) Divine Self-Domain.

By Means Of My Active Spiritual Work Of Avataric Divine Self-Revelation and Blessing Within The Cosmic Domain, I Reveal and Give The Way Of The Heart (or Way Of Adidam), Which Is The Perfectly Non-Dual Way Of Non-Separateness, and Which Is The Perfect Way Of Perfectly Subjective Divine Self-Realization, and Which Is (Most Ultimately, and Most Perfectly) The Way Of Divine Translation.

For The Sake Of all-and-All, I Will (Now, and Forever Hereafter) Continue To Do My all-and-All-Blessing Work Within The Cosmic Domain, but I Will Remain Active (At Last) Beyond The Measure Of time and space—Self-"Bright" In My Divine Indifference, Forever Divinely Self-"Emerging", and Forever Persisting Beyond Any Measure Of My Means.

The Ultimate Import and Intention Of My Avataric Divine Spiritual Work Within The Cosmic Domain Is The Divine Translation Of all-and-All. Therefore, When The Divine Revelation-Work Of My Avataric Incarnation Is here Complete, I (Spontaneously) Demonstrate The Ultimate Siddhi Of Divine Translation, By Which I Persistently (Forever) Attract and Draw all-and-All Into My Divine "Bright" Spherical Self-Domain. And The Siddhi (or Heart-Power) Of My Own Divine Translation Will (Thus and Thereby) Remain Eternally and Most Perfectly Active (and Effective) everywhere (Forever) In The Cosmic Domain.

Now I Have, By All My "Crazy" Avataric Means, Revealed My One and Many Divine Secrets As The Great Person Of The Heart. For Your Sake, I Made My Every Work and Word. And Now, By Every Work and Word I Made, I Have Entirely Confessed (and Showed) Myself—and Always Freely, and Even As A Free Man, In The "Esoteric" Language Of Intimacy and Ecstasy, Openly Worded To You (and To all). Even Now (and Forever Hereafter), By This (My Avatarically Self-Revealed Divine Word Of Heart), I Address every Seeming Separate being (and each one) As The Heart Itself, Because It Is Necessary That all beings, Even The Entire Cosmic Domain Of Seeming Separate beings, Be (In all times and places) Called To Wisdom and The Heart.

And I Would Have all beings Hear My Word (That Calls The Heart To My Heart-Grace), and See My "Brightness" (Who Is Not "Other") Face To Face, and (By This Great Fortune) Grow To Realize The Divine Heart-Secret Of Existence (Even Now)—but I Must Also Tell You That What Is Truly Secret (or Inherently Hidden From The self-Contracted Heart) Remains So, Even When My Own Confession and All These Me-Revealing Words Are Made and Given To each and all. Therefore, My Divine Heart-Secret Is The Heart Itself, Who Must Hear and See Me "Brighten" Up The Space, and Go The Way It Is.

The Only-By-Me Revealed and Given Way Of The Heart (or Way Of Adidam) Is Not The conventional Path Of worldliness, egoic security, Orderly consolations, and psycho-physical self-Fulfillment—As If What Is Eternally Free (and Always Already Most Prior To all conditional activity, and Always Already Most Prior To All egoity and Separateness) Made (or Separately Caused) the conditional worlds and all conditional beings, and Made (or Caused) them For their own Sake. The conditional worlds and their Seeming Separate beings arise Spontaneously, As Apparent Modifications Of The Transcendentally Self-Existing (and Self-Radiant, or Inherently Spiritual) Divine Self-Condition Of Mere Being—and many causes, Great and small, Make effects In The Seeming Distances and Surfaces Of conditional life. Therefore, To Live Rightly Is To Be Schooled To Reality Itself, Realizing The By-Me-and-As-Me-Avatarically-Self-Revealed-and-Spiritually-Self-Transmitted (and Inherently egoless, and Self-Evidently

Divine) Conscious Light In Stages Of Growth and Out-Growing—Until The Cosmic Domain Itself (and All Of Separateness Itself) Is Out-Grown.

The Only-By-Me Revealed and Given Way Of The Heart (or Way Of Adidam) Is Not The Path Of death (or ascetical anti-worldliness)—As If There Is No Real God In the conditional worlds of beings, but Only Love-Bliss Elsewhere, Not Made, Not In Person, Beyond The Dismal Round Of causes and effects. Therefore, The Only-By-Me Revealed and Given Way Of The Heart (or Way Of Adidam) Must Be Lived With Real God, In Person—Embracing The Discipline Of Life (In the body-mind and all the worlds) Heart-Responsively, In Real God, Until Divine Translation (or The Most Perfect Outshining Of conditional Existence Via "Brightest" Realization Of The Self-Existing and Self-Radiant and Self-Evidently Divine Being That Is The Un-conditional Self-Condition Of all-and-All).

The Only-By-Me Revealed and Given Way Of The Heart (or Way Of Adidam) Is Not Founded On The Urge Toward conditional worlds and psycho-physical self-Fulfillment, Nor On The Urge Toward death and Elsewhere. The Only-By-Me Revealed and Given Way Of The Heart (or Way Of Adidam) Is (and More and More Becomes) Founded On The Heart-Response To Real God (In Person—Eternally Most Prior To, and, Yet, Always Presently Coincident With, the conditional body-mind and the conditional worlds). Therefore, The Only-By-Me Revealed and Given Way Of The Heart (or Way Of Adidam) Is (From Its Beginning) The Way Of Satsang (or Devotional and, In Due Course, Spiritual Heart-Communion) With Me—The Da Avatar, The Ruchira Avatar, The Love-Ananda Avatar, The Divine Heart-Master, The Divine World-Teacher, The Avataric Divine Self-Revelation Of The Divine and First and Only Person, Who Is The One and Only Heart (Itself).

The Only-By-Me Revealed and Given Way Of The Heart (or Way Of Adidam) Is Ruchira Avatara Bhakti Yoga (and, In The Context Of The Only-By-Me Revealed and Given Seventh Stage Of Life, Ati-Ruchira Yoga—or The Yoga Of The All-Outshining "Brightness"). So It Is, and So It Must Be.

The Only-By-Me Revealed and Given Way Of The Heart (or Way Of Adidam) Begins With The Student-Beginner's Process (or Even The early-life Listening-Devotee's Process) Of Right Approach To Me—The Da Avatar, The Ruchira Avatar, The Love-Ananda Avatar, The Divine Heart-Master, The Divine World-Teacher, The Avataric Divine Self-Revelation Of The Divine and First and Only Person, Who Is The One and Only Heart (Itself).

Therefore, The Only-By-Me Revealed and Given Way Of The Heart (or Way Of Adidam) Is To Develop (and It Is By-Me-Given and By-Me-Enabled To Develop) Only On The Foundation Of Right (and Growing) Devotion, or The Right (Beginner's) Establishment Of The Tradition-Honored Devotional (and,

In Due Course, Spiritual) Relationship To Me—The Da Avatar, The Ruchira Avatar, The Love-Ananda Avatar, The Divine Heart-Master, The Divine World-Teacher, The Avataric Divine Self-Revelation Of The Divine and First and Only Person, Who Is The One and Only Heart (Itself).

Once The Only-By-Me Revealed and Given Way Of The Heart (or Way Of Adidam) Is So Founded (In Right, and Growing, Devotion To Me), The Practice Of The Way Of The Heart Progresses (or Is, By Means Of My Avatarically Self-Given Divine Grace, To Be Developed) Through The Necessary Context Of All Seven Stages Of Life.

And Every Stage Of Practice (In The Context Of Whichever Of The Seven Stages Of Life) In The Only-By-Me Revealed and Given Way Of The Heart (or Way Of Adidam) Is Inherently Made Of Seven Parts (or Given, By Means Of My Avatarically Self-Transmitted Divine Grace, Through My Seven Necessary Avataric Divine Gifts).

And My Seven Necessary Gifts Of Avataric Divine Grace (Given At Every Stage Of Practice In The Only-By-Me Revealed and Given Way Of The Heart, or Way Of Adidam) Are (Each and All, By Means Of My Avatarically Self-Transmitted Divine Grace) Progressively Increased (or Progressively Magnified), and (By Right Practice) To Be So Increased or Magnified (Stage To Stage), Until Divine Translation.

My Seven Necessary Gifts Of Avataric Divine Grace (Given At Every Stage Of Practice In The Only-By-Me Revealed and Given Way Of The Heart, or Way Of Adidam) Are Word, and Sign, and Devotion, and Service, and Discipline, and Blessing, and Blessedness.

And Each and All Of These Seven Gifts Are Freely Given By Me—The Da Avatar, The Ruchira Avatar, The Love-Ananda Avatar, The Divine Heart-Master, The Divine World-Teacher, The Avataric Divine Self-Revelation Of The Divine and First and Only Person, Who Is The One and Only Heart (Itself).

Therefore, The Way Of Adidam (Which Is The One and Only By-Me-Revealed and By-Me-Given Way Of The Heart) Is (Itself, and Altogether) A Gift From Me—Full-Made Of The Seven Real-God-Realizing Gifts Of My Avatarically Self-Transmitted Divine Grace (That Make An ego-Transcending Practice, and, Ultimately, A Most Perfectly ego-Transcending Realization).

The First Gift Of The Only-By-Me Revealed and Given Way Of The Heart (or Way Of Adidam) Is Ruchira Avatara Vani (or Ruchira Avatara Vani-Vichara), The By-Me-Given Gift Of My Avatarically Self-Revealed Divine Word (and The Gifted Calling, and The By-Me-Given Responsibility, For Devotionally Responsive "Consideration" Of My Avatarically Self-Revealed Divine Word, and Of All My Instructive and Revelatory Avataric Divine Spiritual Work, or My Avatarically Self-Manifested and Forever Living and Me-Revealing Divine Leelas)—For I

Am The Da Avatar, The Ruchira Avatar, The Love-Ananda Avatar, The Divine Heart-Master, The Divine World-Teacher, The Avataric Divine Self-Revelation Of The Divine and First and Only Person, Who Is The One and Only Heart (Itself).

The Second Gift Of The Only-By-Me Revealed and Given Way Of The Heart (or Way Of Adidam) Is Ruchira Avatara Darshan, The By-Me-Given Gift Of The Sign Of My Avatarically-Born Bodily (Human) Divine Form, and My Avatarically Self-Transmitted Spiritual (and Always Blessing) Divine Presence, and My Avatarically Self-Revealed (and Very, and Transcendental, and Perfectly Subjective, and Inherently Spiritual, and Inherently egoless, and Inherently Perfect, and Self-Evidently Divine) State (and The Gifted Calling, and The By-Me-Given Responsibility, For Devotionally Responsive and Constant Feeling-Contemplation Of The By-Me-Given Divine Sign That Is My Avatarically Self-Revealed Divine Form and Presence and State)—For I Am The Da Avatar, The Ruchira Avatar, The Love-Ananda Avatar, The Divine Heart-Master, The Divine World-Teacher, The Avataric Divine Self-Revelation Of The Divine and First and Only Person, Who Is The One and Only Heart (Itself).

The Third Gift Of The Only-By-Me Revealed and Given Way Of The Heart (or Way Of Adidam) Is Ruchira Avatara Bhakti, The By-Me-Given Gift Of Devotion (and The Gifted Calling, and The By-Me-Given Responsibility, For Devotionally Responsive Practice Of Fully Felt, and Inherently ego-Transcending, Heart-Devotion To Me, and For Fully Activated, and Effectively ego-Forgetting and ego-Transcending, Devotional Surrender Of Separate and Separative self To Me)—For I Am The Da Avatar, The Ruchira Avatar, The Love-Ananda Avatar, The Divine Heart-Master, The Divine World-Teacher, The Avataric Divine Self-Revelation Of The Divine and First and Only Person, Who Is The One and Only Heart (Itself).

The Fourth Gift Of The Only-By-Me Revealed and Given Way Of The Heart (or Way Of Adidam) Is Ruchira Avatara Seva, The By-Me-Given Gift Of Service (and The Gifted Calling, and The By-Me-Given Responsibility, For Devotionally Responsive Life-Practice, Whereby all action, and each and every action, Is Engaged Entirely and Only As Direct Service To Me, and As A Direct Heart-Response To Each and All Of My Admonitions)—For I Am The Da Avatar, The Ruchira Avatar, The Love-Ananda Avatar, The Divine Heart-Master, The Divine World-Teacher, The Avataric Divine Self-Revelation Of The Divine and First and Only Person, Who Is The One and Only Heart (Itself).

The Fifth Gift Of The Only-By-Me Revealed and Given Way Of The Heart (or Way Of Adidam) Is Ruchira Avatara Tapas, The By-Me-Given Gift Of Discipline (and The Gifted Calling, and The By-Me-Given Responsibility, For Heart-Responsive and Sure Embrace Of Each and All Of The Forms Of functional, practical, relational, and Cultural Discipline, and Even All The Forms

Of self-Disciplined Practice, Required By Me)—For I Am The Da Avatar, The Ruchira Avatar, The Love-Ananda Avatar, The Divine Heart-Master, The Divine World-Teacher, The Avataric Divine Self-Revelation Of The Divine and First and Only Person, Who Is The One and Only Heart (Itself).

The Sixth Gift Of The Only-By-Me Revealed and Given Way Of The Heart (or Way Of Adidam) Is Ruchira Avatara Kripa, The By-Me-Given Gift Of Blessing (and The Gifted Calling, and The By-Me-Given Capability, To Be Directly Heart-Attracted and Responsively Heart-Moved To, and Into, Progressive Degrees Of Contemplative and Meditative Ecstasy, and, In Due Course, To, and Into, Spiritually Activated Divine Heart-Communion, and, Most Ultimately, To, and Into, Most Perfect Divine Self-Realization, By Means Of My Direct and Directly Effective Spiritual Blessing, or Ruchira Shaktipat)—For I Am The Da Avatar, The Ruchira Avatar, The Love-Ananda Avatar, The Divine Heart-Master, The Divine World-Teacher, The Avataric Divine Self-Revelation Of The Divine and First and Only Person, Who Is The One and Only Heart (Itself).

And The Seventh (or Completing) Gift Of The Only-By-Me Revealed and Given Way Of The Heart (or Way Of Adidam) Is Ruchira Avatara Moksha-Bhava, The By-Me-Given Gift Of Blessedness (or The By-Me-Given Gift Of Blessed, and, Most Ultimately, Inherently and Divinely Liberated, Happiness), Which Is The By-Me-Given Grace (Realized Only On The Basis Of The Right Present Fulfillment Of Each and All Of My First Six Gifts, and Callings, and Responsibilities Of The Way Of The Heart) To Enjoy (or Fully Feel) The Inherent Freedom Of Heart-Companionship (or Heart-Communion, or Heart-Oneness, or, Ultimately, Heart-Identification) With My Inherently Perfectly Self-"Bright" Divine Person (and, Most Ultimately, With My Inherently Perfectly Self-"Bright"—or Transcendental, Inherently Spiritual, Inherently egoless, and Self-Evidently Divine—Self-Condition)—For I Am The Da Avatar, The Ruchira Avatar, The Love-Ananda Avatar, The Divine Heart-Master, The Divine World-Teacher, The Avataric Divine Self-Revelation Of The Divine and First and Only Person, Who Is The One and Only Heart (Itself).

Beloved, I Am Adi Da—The First Person, The Original Person, The Giving Source-Person, The Divine Giver Of The Divine "All" To all-and-All, The Eternal Full-Giver Of The Forever Giving Avataric Divine Gifts Of Word, and Sign, and Devotion, and Service, and Discipline, and Blessing, and Blessedness.

I Am here (Now, and Forever Hereafter), Manifested (and Always Presently "Emerging") As The Ruchira Avatar, The "Bright" Da Avatar, The Self-Radiant and Self-Existing Love-Ananda Avatar, The Avataric Divine Realizer, The Avataric Divine Revealer, and The Avataric Divine Self-Revelation Of The One and "Bright" Divine Person, Da, Who Is Self-Radiant and Self-Existing Being, The Divine and One and Only and Eternal and "Bright" and Perfectly

Subjective Person (or Self-Condition, or Source-Condition) Of all-and-All, and The One and Only and Inherently Indivisible and Inherently egoless and Perfectly Subjective and Self-Evidently Divine Conscious Light Of all-and-All (Always Already Most Perfectly Coincident With the body-mind and Always Already Most Perfectly Prior To the self-Contraction).

Here I Am, Always Alive With You, Avatarically Calling and Attracting and Enabling You To Realize Me—The True Divine Person (The Divine and One and Only and Eternal and "Bright" and Perfectly Subjective Person, or Self-Condition, or Source-Condition, Of all-and-All, Most Perfectly Prior To every ego-"I").

I Am The Way Of The Heart.

The Way Of Adidam (Which Is The One and Only By-Me-Revealed and By-Me-Given Way Of The Heart) Is The Way To Realize Me—As The Spiritually Self-"Bright" (Most Prior, Perfectly Subjective, Perfectly Non-Separate, Inherently Indivisible, Self-Existing, Self-Radiant, Inherently egoless, and Self-Evidently Divine) Self-Condition (or One and Only Conscious Light), Through The By-Me-Given Seven-Gifted Process Of Transcending the conditional self.

The Divine Mystery Of Who I Am and Who You Are and Why (and How) I Do (and Have Done, and Will Always Do) The Avataric Divine Revelation-Work For You Is Not A Subject For conventional Religious belief, Nor Is any one Called To Affirm It Merely Because It Is Openly and Ecstatically Confessed To all. The Proof Of The Truth Of My Avataric Divine Self-Confession Cannot Be Realized By any mere belief. Likewise, The Proof Of The Truth Of My Avataric Divine Self-Confession Cannot Be Realized If There Is Persistence In doubt (or Chronic un-Certainty, and mere dis-belief). It Is Only When You Truly Listen To Me (and Even Hear Me, and Even See Me) That My Avataric Divine Self-Confession Becomes (Really, and Then More and More) Acceptable To You, Confirmed By The Heart's Recognition and Beholding and Reception and Realization Of Me. Therefore, Until I Am Revealed To The Ear and Eye Of Heart, My Divine Heart-Secret Remains Hidden. And, Until I Am (By You) Both Truly Heard and Really Seen At Heart, My Call To You Is Simply This: Attend To Me By Heart, Whole bodily (With Every Faculty Of body-mind), and (Thereby) Practice Constant Heart-Devotion To Me, and Always Listen (Thus, Whole bodily) To My Arguments For ego-Transcendence (In Me), and Always Heart-Respond To Me and Whole bodily Behold Me, Always Present To You (By Means Of My Avatarically-Born Bodily Human Divine Sign, and My Avatarically Self-Revealed Divine Word, and My Avatarically Self-Revealed Divine Image-Art, and My Avatarically Self-Manifested Divine Acts Of Graceful Self-Revelation) As The Free Avataric Divine Master Of Man, Always Calling every one To Observe and Understand and Transcend the conditional self Through ego-Transcending Devotion Of the Total body-mind To Me.

The Proof Of The Truth Of My Avataric Divine Self-Confession Is Beyond The Efforts Of belief and Of doubt. The Proof Of The Truth Of My Avataric Divine Self-Confession Is Entirely A Matter Of Whether Or Not You Are Willing To Embrace (and Fully Participate In) The ego-Surrendering Process That Is The Necessary Means To Prove and To Realize The Truth That Is Reality Itself. My Divine Heart-Secret (Which Is My Avatarically Given Divine Self-Revelation Of The True Divine Self-Condition and Source-Condition Of all-and-All) Is Revealed Only To Devotion Itself, or True Surrender To Me (Openly Revealed To You As My Avatarically-Born Bodily Human Divine Form, and As My Avatarically Self-Transmitted Divine Spiritual Body Of Self-"Bright" Love-Bliss, and As My Avatarically Self-Revealed Divine State Of Me-"Bright" Conscious Light, and As My Divine "Bright" Spherical Self-Domain Of Eternal Existence Itself). Therefore, The Truth Of My Divine Heart-Secret Is Self-Revealed Only In The Real Process That Can Be Divinely Self-Realized (By Means Of My Avatarically Self-Transmitted Divine Grace) In The Case Of those who (Progressively) Convert The Knowable Exercise Of The Only-By-Me Revealed and Given Way Of The Heart Into A Real and Living Sacrifice Of Separate and Separative self In (and Into) My "Bright" Divine Heart-Company.

My Active Avataric Adept-Work As The Divine Heart-Master Is Originally Generated To Serve Three Great Purposes.

My First Purpose Is To Develop and To Communicate—and To Call the attention Of All My (Present or, Otherwise, Potential) Formally Practicing Devotees To—My (Perfectly Complete and Completely Effective) Teaching-Argument Relative To The Necessary (and Never To Be Avoided) Process Of (Ultimately, Inherently Most Perfect) ego-Transcendence and The By-Me-Given (and Perfectly Complete and Completely Effective, and Necessary, and Never To Be Avoided) Practice Of (Ultimately, Inherently Most Perfect) ego-Transcendence.

My Second Purpose Is (By Means Of The All-Revealing Blessing-Work Of My Avataric Divine Form and Presence and State) To Reveal (To All My Formally Practicing Devotees) My Spiritual, Transcendental, and Divine Forms (Which Are The Forms Of Real God, or The One and Only Truth and Reality), and (Altogether) To Reveal (To All My Formally Practicing Devotees) My One and Only (Transcendental, Inherently Spiritual, Inherently egoless, and Self-Evidently Divine) Person (Which Is The Heart Itself, The One and Only Conscious Light, The Inherently Indivisible and Inherently egoless Source-Condition and Self-Condition Of all-and-All—and Which Is The One and Only Real and Self-Evident God, Inherently Perfect Truth, and Irreducible Reality That Is).

And My Third Purpose Is (Among My Formally Practicing Devotees) To Fully Develop, Firmly Establish, and Perpetually Communicate A True and Complete Culture Of Real (and Truly Devotional, and, Therefore, Really ego-Surrendering, ego-Forgetting, and ego-Transcending) Heart-Practice In Devotional Recognition-Response To My Avatarically Self-Revealed (and Self-Evidently Divine) Person—Now (and Forever Hereafter) Self-Revealed By Means Of My (Now, and Forever Hereafter, Given) Avatarically-Born Bodily (Human) Divine Form, and By Means Of My (Now, and Forever Hereafter) Avatarically Self-Revealed (and Ever-Speaking) Divine Word, and By Means Of My (Now, and Forever Hereafter) Avatarically Self-Revealed Divine Image-Art, and By Means Of My (Now, and Forever Hereafter) Avatarically Self-Manifested (and Ever-Living) Divine Leelas, and By Means Of The (Now, and Forever Hereafter) Avataric Spiritual Transmission-Work Of My (Now, and Forever Hereafter) Avatarically Self-Revealed (and Always Me-Revealing) "Bright" and all-and-All-Blessing Divine Spiritual Presence.

Now This Divine Testament Is Complete. In Its Form, My First Great Purpose Is Fulfilled. My Avataric Divine Bodily (Human) Birth, Ordeal, and Work—Given Bodily (By Means Of Divine Heart-Submission) To Teach—Was The Necessary Means Whereby This Purpose Could Be Fulfilled. Therefore, I Submitted Utterly To the conditions Of Man, In Order To Fulfill This Purpose For Mankind. In My Own Unique Avataric Divine Manner, I Submitted Myself To Be The Means For others.

Now That My Avataric Divine Word Is Given Complete, My Impulse To Teach Will Be Forever Hereafter Carried Therein—and All The Else That I Must Do Will Also Go and Be Done.

Now Even My Madness Is Spun In The Word, and All That I Am Is Untied In My Chest, and I Am Conserved To The Heart's Free Repose—Retired At Last From All Effort and Speech.

Now, and Forever Hereafter, My Word Goes To Teach—and I Will Stay Forever Close, So To Spirit-Bless Mankind, While I "Gaze" Secluded In The "Open Eyes".

Now, and Forever Hereafter, I Will Not Cease—and My Mere and Blessing Spirit-Presence Is A Wandering Work.

Now, and Forever Hereafter, I Only Go Where I Always Already Stand.

Now, and Forever Hereafter, Even As I Wait—I Am Always Gone To You.

Now, and Forever Hereafter, I Am Always Standing There—With You.

Such Is The Way Revealed and Given By Me—The Only-By-Me Revealed and Given Way Of Adidam, Which Is The Way Of The Heart.

My Every Listening Devotee, My Every Hearing Devotee, and My Every Seeing Devotee Must Accept The ego-Surrendering, ego-Forgetting, and (Progressively, and, At Last, Most Perfectly) ego-Transcending Devotional and Spiritual Process Of The Only-By-Me Revealed and Given Way Of The Heart (or Way Of Adidam) As A Matter Of his or her own Responsibility To Deal

With his or her own egoity (or self-Contraction). And All Such (Necessarily, Formally Practicing) Devotee-Practitioners Of The Only-By-Me Revealed and Given Way Of The Heart (or Way Of Adidam) Are Called, By Me, To Serve The Great Process Of Divine Self-Realization In one another, Through A True and Comprehensive Worldwide Cooperative Devotional and Spiritual Culture (or Truly Global Ashram and Mission) Of Right (and Truly ego-Transcending) Practice Of The Only-By-Me Revealed and Given Way Of Adidam (Which Is The One and Only By-Me-Revealed and By-Me-Given Way Of The Heart).

The Formally Acknowledged and True (and Truly Cooperative) Worldwide Sacred Cultural Gathering (or Truly Global Ashram and Mission) Of The Only-By-Me Revealed and Given Way Of The Heart (or Way Of Adidam) Is Founded Upon Every (Necessarily, Formally Practicing) Devotee-Practitioner's Free Acceptance (and Progressive Embrace) Of The Gifts Of My (Now, and Forever Hereafter, Given) Avataric Divine Form and Presence and State Of Person, My Avatarically Self-Revealed (and Forever Me-Revealing) Divine Word, My Avatarically Self-Revealed (and Forever Me-Revealing) Divine Image-Art, My Avatarically Self-Manifested (and Forever Me-Revealing) Divine Leelas, The Directly-By-Me Spiritually Empowered Ruchira Sannyasin Hermitage Ashrams (and Even All The Sacred Sites and Things Therein-Empowered, By Me, With My Spirit-Blessing Intent), The Total (Formally Acknowledged) Instrumental Gathering Of My Formally Acknowledged "Ruchira Sannyasin" Devotees, and The Total (Formally Acknowledged) Gathering Of Even All (Necessarily, Formally Practicing) Devotee-Practitioners Of The Only-By-Me Revealed and Given Way Of The Heart (or Way Of Adidam). Therefore, The Authentication (or Authentic and Right Use) and Preservation Of These Gifts Is (Now, and Forever Hereafter) The Responsibility Of Each and Every (Necessarily, Formally Practicing) Devotee-Practitioner Of The Only-By-Me Revealed and Given Way Of The Heart (or Way Of Adidam).

All That I Am, and All Of The Totality Of The Only-By-Me Revealed and Given Way Of The Heart (or Way Of Adidam), Is (and Will, Now, and Forever Hereafter, Always Be) Given To You, By All The Means Revealed and Given (and, As Such, Formally Established, Formally Declared, and Formally Set Apart) By Me. Therefore, All That You Must Receive From Me Is Also (and Will, Now, and Forever Hereafter, Always Be) Freely Given Through (and As) The Gifts I Am Always (and Will, Now, and Forever Hereafter, Always Be) Giving To You.

I (Myself) Am Always In The Spiritual Transmission My Given and Giving Gifts Conduct Through time and space. Therefore, That Spiritual Transmission Will (Now, and Forever Hereafter) Always Remain Active, Through All My Given and Giving Gifts, and Through All My Formally Acknowledged (and

Real and True) Instruments and Agents, If All My Given and Giving Gifts Are Embraced and Preserved, and If All My Formally Acknowledged (and Real and True) Instruments and Agents Are Authenticated, Embraced, and Preserved, By The Formal Worldwide Sacred Cooperative Cultural Gathering (or Truly Global Ashram, or Formal Sangha) Of All My Formally Practicing (and Real and True) Listening Devotees, Hearing Devotees, and Seeing Devotees (In Perpetual Formal, Real, and True Satsang With Me) In The Only-By-Me Revealed and Given Way Of Adidam (Which Is The One and Only By-Me-Revealed and By-Me-Given Way Of The Heart).

As (and When You Are) My Formally Practicing (and Real and True) Listening Devotee, or Hearing Devotee, or Seeing Devotee, You (and Even each and all Of My Formally Practicing, and Real and True, Listening Devotees, Hearing Devotees, and Seeing Devotees In The Formal Worldwide Cooperative Global Ashram, or Sacred Sangha, Of The Only-By-Me Revealed and Given Way Of The Heart, or Way Of Adidam) Must Honor, Serve, Cherish, Preserve, Protect, Defend, Champion, Advocate, and Make Globally Known All My Formally Acknowledged (and Real and True) Instruments and Agents, and All My Given and Giving Gifts. Therefore, Until All Of My Avataric Divine Spiritual Work Is Finally Done (With each and all and All), and each and all and All Are Divinely Translated In Me—I Call Upon and Profoundly Require The Collective Sacred Gathering (or Global Ashram) Of All My Formally Practicing Devotees (Now, and Forever Hereafter) To Do This Good Service (Heart-True To Me), and To Do It Well (Such That It Is Well Done and True), Now, and Forever Hereafter.

Now The Only-By-Me Revealed and Given Way Of The Heart (or Way Of Adidam) Is Opened and Revealed To You—and (every where, In All The Cosmic Mandala) All My Listening Devotees, and All My Hearing Devotees, and All My Seeing Devotees Are (Now, and Forever Hereafter) Blessed (By Me) To Advance (By Heart, Whole bodily) To Me.

Now, and Forever Hereafter, I Call Upon (and Profoundly Require and Heart-Expect) all beings (each and all) To Come To Me and Be My Formally Practicing Devotees (Under True and Perpetual Vows To Me).

Now, and Forever Hereafter, I Call Upon (and Profoundly Require and Heart-Expect) all beings (each and all) To Come To Me and Be My Formally Practicing Devotees For The Perfect Purpose Of Most Perfectly Realizing Me.

Now, and Forever Hereafter, I Profoundly Require and Heart-Expect My Each and Every Formally Practicing Devotee To Surrender, Forget, and Transcend self-Contraction (and conditional self-Existence) By Constant Right (Intelligent, self-Disciplined, and Truly Devotionally Responsive) Whole bodily Obedience To Me.

Now, and Forever Hereafter, I Profoundly Require and Heart-Expect My Each and Every Formally Practicing Devotee To Surrender, Forget, and Transcend self-Contraction (and conditional self-Existence) By Constant Right (Intelligent, self-Disciplined, and Truly Devotionally Responsive) Obedience To My Avatarically Self-Revealed Divine Word and Person.

Now, and Forever Hereafter, I Profoundly Require and Heart-Expect My Each and Every Formally Practicing Devotee To Surrender, Forget, and Transcend self-Contraction (and conditional self-Existence) By Constant Right, True, Full, Intelligent, self-Disciplined, Truly Devotionally Me-Recognizing, and Truly Devotionally To-Me-Responsive Whole bodily Obedience (and By More and More Perfect, and, At Last, Most Perfect, Whole bodily Devotional Conformity) To My Avatarically-Born Bodily (Human) Divine Form, My Avatarically Self-Transmitted Spiritual (and Always Blessing) Divine Presence, and My Avatarically Self-Revealed (and Very, and Transcendental, and Perfectly Subjective, and Inherently Spiritual, and Inherently egoless, and Inherently Perfect, and Self-Evidently Divine) State.

Now, and Forever Hereafter, I Profoundly Require and Heart-Expect My Each and Every Formally Practicing Devotee To Act (Always, Only, and Entirely) In Explicit and Full Accord With My Explicit Word, As Given (By Me), During The Physical Lifetime Of My Avatarically-Born Bodily (Human) Divine Form, In This, My Only-By-Me Revealed and Given *Dawn Horse Testament* (or Testament Of Divine Secrets), In Its (Latest and Current, or present-time) By-Me-Formally-Approved (and Ruchira-Sannyasin-Order-Authorized) Version,[166] and (Altogether) As Given (By Me), During The Physical Lifetime Of My Avatarically-Born Bodily (Human) Divine Form, In The (Latest and Current, or present-time) By-Me-Formally-Approved (and Ruchira-Sannyasin-Order-Authorized) Versions Of Each and All Of The Twenty-Three By-Me-Designated Divine "Source-Texts" Of My Avatarically Full-Given and Final Word Of Divine Self-Revelation and Of Divine Heart-Instruction In The Practice Of The Only-By-Me Revealed and Given Way Of Adidam (Which Way Is The One and Only By-Me-Revealed and By-Me-Given Way Of The Heart, and Which Twenty-Three Divine "Source-Texts" Include <u>Only</u> *The Dawn Horse Testament*, *The Five Books Of The Heart Of The Adidam Revelation*,[167] and *The Seventeen Companions Of The True Dawn Horse*[168]), and (Also) As Given (By Me), During The Physical Lifetime Of My Avatarically-Born Bodily (Human) Divine Form, In The (Latest and Current, or present-time) By-Me-Formally-Approved (and Ruchira-Sannyasin-Order-Authorized) Versions Of Even Each and All Of The By-Me-Designated "Supportive Texts" Of My Avatarically Full-Given and Final Divine Word Relative To The functional, practical, relational, and Cultural Disciplines Of The Only-By-Me Revealed and Given Way Of Adidam[169] (Which

"Supportive Texts" Are, As Their General Name Suggests, Supportive, but Entirely Subordinate, Extensions Of The Twenty-Three By-Me-Designated "Source-Texts"), and (Additionally) As Formally Given (By Me), During The Physical Lifetime Of My Avatarically-Born Bodily (Human) Divine Form, To The Formally Governing Senior Membership Of The Ruchira Sannyasin Order Of Adidam Ruchiradam, To Be (According To My Full-Given and Final Instructions To them) Passed On By (and From) them, Forever Thereafter, To (and Via) The Formally Succeeding Generations Of The Formally Governing Senior Membership Of The Ruchira Sannyasin Order Of Adidam Ruchiradam—and (*Thus*, and By *All* These Means) As Formally and Finally Full-Given By Me (According To their Manner and Stage Of Practice Of The Only-By-Me Revealed and Given Way Of The Heart, or Way Of Adidam) To each and all (and For The Sake Of The Divine Liberation Of each and all) Of My Formally Practicing Devotees, Forever.

And I *Hereby* (Now, and Forever Hereafter) Call Upon (and Profoundly Require and Heart-Expect) The Collective Cooperative Sacred Gathering (or Global Ashram) Of All My Formally Practicing Devotees (Which Gathering Is Now Established, and Which Is Forever Hereafter To Remain Established) To Ensure and Guarantee (Now, and Forever Hereafter) That *Each* and *All* Of The By-Me-Designated (and By-Me-Formally-Approved, and Ruchira-Sannyasin-Order-Authorized) "Source-Texts" and "Supportive Texts" Of My Avatarically Full-Given and Final Divine Word, *and* Even *All* Other Ruchira-Sannyasin-Order-Authorized Texts (and Even *All* Other, However Recorded or Conveyed, Ruchira-Sannyasin-Order-Authorized Communications) Of or About My Avatarically Self-Revealed Divine Word, My Avatarically Self-Revealed Divine Image-Art, My Avatarically Self-Manifested Divine Leelas, and The Only-By-Me Revealed and Given Way Of The Heart (or Way Of Adidam), Are (Now, and Forever Hereafter) Always and Continuously and Constantly Made Fully and Openly Available, In Every Kind and Mode Of Published Form, In Even All The Languages Written and/or Spoken By Mankind (and By Even any and all Intelligent beings) In any and every then present-time, and, As Such, Always and Continuously and Constantly Distributed worldwide (and Even *every* where), In Right and True and Full Missionary (and, Altogether, Rightly and Positively Educational) Fashion, For The Sake Of The Divine Liberation Of every one, and Of all, and Of All.

Now, and Forever Hereafter, My Each and Every Formally Practicing Devotee Must Act (Always, Only, and Entirely) In Accord With My Explicit Avatarically Given Divine Word, and (Thus) Always Only With My Explicit Avatarically Given Divine Permission, and (Thus) *Always* With Heart-Assurance Of All My Seven Avatarically Given Divine and Necessary Giving Gifts.

Now, and Forever Hereafter, My Each and Every Formally Practicing Devotee Must Be Entirely Given To Only Me, and (Yes) My Each and Every Formally Practicing Devotee Is Always Called (By Me) To Run To Me Now, To Realize Me Most Perfectly At Last.

Therefore—Now, and Forever Hereafter—My Avatarically Given Divine Secrets Must Be Revealed To all-and-All!

Yes—Now, and Forever Hereafter—My Avatarically Given Divine Secrets Will Be Revealed To all-and-All!

Now, and Forever Hereafter, I (Myself) Will Be Revealed To all-and-All—For I (Myself) Am The One and Great Avatarically Given Divine Secret To Be Revealed To all-and-All, and To Be Realized By all-and-All!

I Am The Avataric Divine Master Of The True (Avataric Divine) Horse-Sacrifice, The Avataric Divine Performer Of The Divine Avataric Ashvamedha, The Divinely Self-"Emerging" Person Of My Own Cosmic Submission (To Avatarically Descend To all-and-All). By The Necessary Means Of My Own Free Avataric Divine Submission To all-and-All, I Am (Now, and Forever Hereafter) Divinely Self-"Emerging" As The True Dawn Horse, The "Bright" Itself (In Divine Person), The Avatarically Self-Giving and All-Giving and To-all-Giving Divine Spiritual Body and Person, The Necessary Divine Gift (Avatarically Self-Given, In Person), By Whom The Truth and The "Bright" Divine Power Of Most Perfect Divine Self-Realization Are (Now, and Forever Hereafter, By Means Of My Avataric Divine Ashvamedha-Grace) Transmitted To The Cosmic Mandala Of all-and-All.

I Am The Maha-Purusha Medha—The Avataric Self-Sacrifice Of The One and Great, Divine and Only, Person. Therefore, This "Bright" Testament Of Divine Secrets Is The Free Avataric Vehicle Of My Perfect Intention, The Avataric Dawn-Horse-Form Of My Divine Word Of Heart, Whereby I (Myself) Am Tangibly Avatarically Revealed To Every To-Me-Listening Ear Of Heart. Now, and Forever Hereafter, This Avataric Dawn-Horse-Form Of Me Has Been Released From My Divine "Bright" Spherical Self-Domain, Forever To Wander To all-and-All, To Serve My Divine Purpose every where—Bearing Me, From My House, To All-Abroad, Forever To Cover and To "Brighten" My Vast (and all-and-All-Encompassing) Cosmic Avataric Divine Samrajya.[170]

Now, and Always (Forever Hereafter) Now, As The Sign and The Result Of The "Bright" Avataric Divine Ordeal By Which This Avataric Divine Testament Has Come To Consciousness In The Cosmic Domain, My Avataric Self-Revelation Of Divine "Brightness" (Itself) Will Appear To every one, and all, and All.[171]

This Is The Dawn Horse Testament Of The Ruchira Avatar, Adi Da Samraj—The Da Avatar, The Love-Ananda Avatar, The First Adept, Who Is The Heart, The One and Only and Divine True Self-Condition Of all-and-All, The One and Only and True Divine Person, The "Bright" Divine Origin and The "Bright" Divine Source Of All Gifts, The One and Only and True Divine Giver Of Perfectly Subjective "Brightness", Now (and Forever Hereafter) Merely Present As The Ever-Living Divine Heart-Master, The Formless Form and The True and Eternally Living Murti, Appearing (Now, and Forever Hereafter) As The "Late-Time" Avataric Divine Incarnation Of My Own (Divine) Person, Revealed To all In Person As The Very (and Truly) Human God-Man, Named "John" By Birth ("The Free Man Through Whom God Is Gracious"), and Named "Da" Before Birth ("The Eternally Free One, Who Is The Divine Person and Grace"), and Who Is (In This Now and Forever "Dark" Epoch Of ego-Time) The Divine Love-Bliss-"Brightener" Of all-and-All, The Promised Divine Intruder, The Foretold "Bright" Foreigner, The Expected (and Eternally Un-"Familiar") Outsider, The Outcast "Crazy"-Man, The Mleccha-Guru, Who Must Ride Invisible By Night, Sacrificing The Many-Colored Horse Of Fractured Light and Grievous Broken Appearances, and Who Is Now (and Forever Hereafter) "Emerging" From The Folds and Measures Of Infinitely Finite Night, Riding The Flying Day-Horse Of Colorless (Unbroken) White, The Free-Winged Radiance, Immensely Shining Beyond Ash and Cloud, Immensely Filling The Indivisible Sky, Immensely Singing The Audible Dawn Of The Heart's Forever Resurrected "Brightness", Immensely Bringing Me To all-and-All (Without Excluding any).[172]

This Is The Dawn Horse Testament Of The Ruchira Avatar, Adi Da Samraj—The Da Avatar, The Love-Ananda Avatar, The Avabhasa Avatar, Who Is Da Avabhasa, The Divine "Bright" Itself (and The Very Giver Of The Divine "Brightness"), and Who Is Da Love-Ananda Hridayam, The Source, The Substance, The Gift, The Giver, and The Very Person Of The "Bright" Divine Love-Bliss, and Who Is Dau Loloma Vunirarama, The Self-Radiant Divine Source and Substance Of The Divine "Brightness" (Appearing, By Man-Born Divine Descent, As The Avataric Divine Adept Of The Divine Love).

This Is The Dawn Horse Testament Of The Ruchira Avatar, Adi Da Samraj—The Da Avatar, The Love-Ananda Avatar, The Param-Avatar, The Buddha-Avatar, The Tathagata Avatar, The Divine Person (and The Avataric Divine Incarnation, and The Avataric Divine Master, and The Avataric Divine Adept) Of The Divine Heart Itself, Da Hridayam, The Hridaya-Samartha Sat-Guru, Who Is Santosha Da, The "Bright" and Eternal and Always Already Non-Separate Person Of Divine and Inherent Completeness, Divine Self-Satisfaction, and Divine Self-Contentedness, The Divine Adept Of No-Seeking, Who Is The Ruchira Buddha,

The Paramadvaita Buddha, The Advaitayana Buddha, The Divine (and One, and Only, and Inherently Indivisible, and Eternally Non-Separate, and Eternally Non-Seeking, and Eternally Boundless, and Perfectly Subjective) "Bright" Center, Giving Source, Heart, Self-Condition, and Conscious Light Of all-and-All.

This Is The Dawn Horse Testament Of The Ruchira Avatar, Adi Da Samraj—The Da Avatar, The Love-Ananda Avatar, The Purushottama Buddha, The Avataric Incarnation Of The First and The Only and The Eternal Person (The True Divine Person, Who Is The Heart Of all-and-All), The Self-Liberated Avadhoota (Who Is Always Already Free), The Ashvamedha Avadhoota,[173] The Ashvamedha Buddha, The Avataric Incarnation Of The Eternal Source-Person, Who Is The "Bright" Divine Source-Condition (The One and Only and Eternal Substance), and Who Is The Head, The Tail, The Body, and The Avatarically-Born Master-Rider Of The Horse Of Origin (Which Is The True First Form—The All-Arising-In-Me Light and Eternally Infinitely Ascended "Midnight Sun" Of all-and-All).

This Is The Dawn Horse Testament Of The Ruchira Avatar, Adi Da Samraj—The Da Avatar, The Love-Ananda Avatar, The (One and Eternal and Always New) Divine Master Of The True (Avataric) Horse-Sacrifice, The Divine Ashvamedha-Siddha, The Divine Ashvamedha-Guru, Who Submits To Be The Maha-Purusha Medha—The Final and Complete All-Giving Avataric Means For The Spiritual, Transcendental, and Divine Liberation Of every one, and all, and All.

This Is The Dawn Horse Testament Of The Ruchira Avatar, Adi Da Samraj—The Da Avatar, The Love-Ananda Avatar, The Ruchira Siddha, The Divine Maha-Jnana Siddha, Who Is The Avataric Divine Realizer, The Avataric Divine Revealer, and The Avataric Divine Self-Revelation Of The True Dawn Horse (Which Is The "Bright" and Eternal and One and Only and Inherently Indivisible and Inherently egoless and Self-Evidently Divine Conscious Light and Self-Condition and Source-Condition Of all-and-All), and Who Is Now Appearing (and Forever Hereafter Divinely Self-"Emerging") As The Avataric Divine Manifestation Of Infinite Love-Bliss-"Brightness", The Now, and Forever Hereafter, and Forever New, Universal, "Bright", All-Completing, and Most Perfect Avataric Divine Self-Revelation Of Real God, and Truth, and Reality To every one, and all, and All.

This Is The Dawn Horse Testament Of The Ruchira Avatar, Adi Da Samraj—The Da Avatar, The Love-Ananda Avatar, The Eternal (and, Now, and Forever Hereafter, Avatarically Self-Manifested) Divine Self-Realizer, The (Now, and Forever Hereafter) Avataric Divine Full-Revealer, The Final and All-Completing and Most Perfect Avataric Divine Self-Revelation, The Adi-Guru (The Divine and First Guru), The Ruchira-Guru (The All-"Bright" Divine Guru), The Ati-Guru (The Supreme and All-Outshining Divine Guru), The Divine Parama-Guru (The Divine Guru Of All Gurus), The Paramadvaita-Guru (The Divine Guru—Who Is One and Only, and Not Two, and Not "Other", but Always Without A

Second, and Inherently Without A Successor), The Divine Maha-Jnana Siddha-Guru (The Divine Guru Of The Final Stage), and The Divine and True Heart-Husband (and The Divine Guru Of Every Stage) Of The One and Entire Great Tradition Of Mankind (and Of all-and-All).

This Is The Dawn Horse Testament Of The Ruchira Avatar, Adi Da Samraj—The Da Avatar, The Love-Ananda Avatar, The Eternally Free-Standing and (Now, and Forever Hereafter) Always Presently Avatarically Self-"Emerging" Divine World-Teacher, Who Is The Divinely Liberating (and Now, and Forever Hereafter, Spoken) Avataric Divine Word Of Heart, Always (Now, and Forever Hereafter) Given, Living, and Giving here, As A Grace (or Free Gift) To All Mankind (and To All, and To all-In-All), and (By Means Of My Avatarically Self-Transmitted Divine Grace) Shown (Now, and Forever Hereafter) To The Heart Of every kind and being appearing by conditions every where.

This Is The Dawn Horse Testament Of The Ruchira Avatar, Adi Da Samraj—The Da Avatar, The Love-Ananda Avatar, The (Universally) Expected "Late-Time" God-Man, The Santosha Avatar, The Complete and All-Completing Avataric Divine Incarnation and The (Now, and Forever Hereafter) Avataric Divine Self-"Emergence" Of The True Divine Person, The Divine "Bright" (or Avabhasa) Avatar, The True Ultimate Man-Born Avataric Descent Of Divine and all-and-All-Liberating Grace every where (Anciently and Always) Promised For The "Dark" Epoch, Which "Dark" Epoch (or "Late-Time") Must, By This "Heroic" Spiritual Intervention,[174] Be (More and More, Until Most Perfectly) Restored At Heart To The Divine Self-"Brightness".

This Is The Dawn Horse Testament Of The Ruchira Avatar, Adi Da Samraj—The Da Avatar, The Love-Ananda Avatar, Who Is Da, The Divine Person (and The Avataric Doer) Of The (Anciently and Always) Promised and Awaited Maha-Purusha Medha, and Who Is (Now, and Forever Hereafter) The Avatarically Given "Bright" Divine Heart-Companion Of all-and-All, and Who Is The Avataric Divine Giver (To all-and-All) Of All The Divine "All" That Is Beyond The Cosmic All, and Who Is every where Necessary To all-and-All (For The Sake Of all-and-All), and Who Is (Now, and Forever Hereafter) Divinely Full-Given To all-and-All By Means Of The Avataric Maha-Purusha Medha, and Who Is Named (and Will Be, By all-and-All, Declared To Be) "Eleutherios", The Avataric Divine "Bright" Giver Of Most Perfectly egoless Liberation, and Most Perfect Divine Translation, In The One and Indivisible Conscious Light That Is The Only Reality and Real God.

NOTES TO THE TEXT OF

THE DAWN HORSE TESTAMENT OF THE RUCHIRA AVATAR

FIRST WORD

1. For an overview description of the vow and life-responsibilities embraced by practitioners of the Way of Adidam, please see *Adidam: The True World-Religion Given by the Promised God-Man, Adi Da Samraj* (Middletown, Calif.: Dawn Horse Press, 2003).

2. "Hamartia" (the word in New Testament Greek that was translated into English as "sin") was also an archery term meaning "missing the mark".

PROLEGOMENA

II.
The Plight Of The Divine Heart-Husband

3. The phrase "Heart-Husband" is a Reference to Avatar Adi Da as the Very Divine Person, Who, as the Avatarically Incarnate Divine Adi-Guru, Embraces living beings, Masters their wandering energy and attention, and Awakens them to Most Perfect Non-separateness from (and Self-Identification with) Him. All His devotees, whether male or female, are (thus) Husbanded (at heart) by Avatar Adi Da Samraj.

The "Plight" that Avatar Adi Da had to endure was an Ordeal of Submission to humankind, whereby He Demonstrated and Established the Way of Adidam. The word "plight" itself also denotes a binding promise or pledge. Thus, by means of "The Plight Of The Divine Heart-Husband", and His Testament of Secrets as a whole, Avatar Adi Da Confesses and Promises His Eternal Commitment to the Awakening and Liberation of all beings.

4. Avatar Adi Da's Sign is His Avatarically-Born bodily (human) Divine Form (Which visibly and tangibly Transmits His Divine Blessing) and photographic or artistic representations thereof.

III.
Ruchira Avatara Gita

5. This is a reference to the right side of the heart. See glossary under **Heart / The Heart Itself / Stations Of The Heart**.

IV.
The True Dawn Horse <u>Is</u> The <u>Only</u> Way To Me

6. This quotation is adapted from *The Satapatha-Brahmana,* Julius Eggeling, trans., Sacred Books of the East, ed. F. Max Muller, vol. 44 (Delhi: Motilal Banarsidass, 1963), 305.

7. By "All-Sacrifice", Avatar Adi Da is referring to the Sarvamedha, the portion of the ritual that involves offerings that symbolize the sacrifice of all beings and things. He has said of the higher significance of this symbolism:

AVATAR ADI DA SAMRAJ: The great performances of the Ashvamedha ritual that you can read about in the traditional texts are symbolic efforts, in which all hope is placed on the horse. The Ashvamedha is an All-Sacrifice, or a sacrifice of everything and everyone—in which, in effect, all beings, all things, all worlds grasp the tail of the horse and are returned to the Divine Self-Domain.

—January 13, 1993

8. Avatar Adi Da distinguishes between "Cosmic Realization", which is the significant and profound Realization of Real God from the point of view (of the first five stages of life) of the conditional body-mind, and "Perfect Realization", which entirely transcends (and, most ultimately, Divinely Self-Recognizes) the Cosmic (or conditional) worlds.

9. See Avatar Adi Da's description of the three stages of His unique Avataric Ordeal as Divine Heart-Master in Sutra 2, pp. 121–22.

10. Avatar Adi Da's "Husbanding" of the "Divine Goddess" occurred in the Vedanta Society Temple in Hollywood, California, on September 9, 1970. For Avatar Adi Da's full Description of this Event, see *The Knee Of Listening* (chapter 16).

11. Here Avatar Adi Da is referring to the Vedic myth of the sun-god, who becomes a white stallion in order to pursue his consort, who has assumed the shape of a mare in order to run away from him. In the end, the white stallion finds the mare, and together they beget immortal twins. See *Women, Androgynes, and Other Mythical Beasts*, by Wendy Doniger O'Flaherty (Chicago: University of Chicago Press, 1982), 174–78.

12. For a description of Avatar Adi Da's "Dawn Horse Vision", please see the glossary.

13. The *Brihadaranyaka Upanishad* describes the Horse (or the Divine Being) sacrificing itself through a kind of dismemberment (or universal pervasiveness) of itself, in which it becomes, assumes, and allows conditionally manifested existence (or cosmic Nature) to come into being:

> *Aum, the dawn, verily, is the head of the sacrificial horse, the sun the eye, the wind the breath, the open mouth the* Vaisvanara *fire; the year is the body of the sacrificial horse, the sky is the back, the atmosphere is the belly, the earth the hoof, the quarters the sides, the intermediate quarters the ribs, the seasons the limbs, the months and the half-months the joints, days and nights the feet, the stars the bones, the clouds the flesh; the food in the stomach is the sand, the rivers are the blood-vessels, the liver and the lungs are the mountains, the herbs and the trees are the hair. The rising (sun) is the forepart, the setting (sun) the hind part, when he yawns then it lightens, when he shakes himself, it thunders, when he urinates then it rains; voice, indeed, is his voice.* [*The Principal Upanisads*, S. Radhakrishnan, ed. and trans., (London: George Allen & Unwin, 1953), 149]

14. A description of the rituals associated with the traditional Ashvamedha is given in *The Satapatha-Brahmana,* Julius Eggeling, trans., Sacred Books of the East, ed. F. Max Muller, vol. 44 (Delhi: Motilal Banarsidass, 1963), viii–xi.

15. Avatar Adi Da has said that in the Event that initiated His Avataric Divine Self-"Emergence", on January 11, 1986, He acquired His physical body "down to the toes". This is a reference to traditional descriptions of how a great Realizer would only "descend" partially into his or her human body—down as far as the head, or perhaps the throat or the heart, but typically not any "lower" than that.

> *On January 11, 1986, I Became This Body—Utterly. And My Mood is different. My Face is sad, but not without Illumination.*
>
> *Now I Am the Murti, the Icon—Full of My Own Avatarically Self-Transmitted Divine Spiritual Force, but also Completely what you are, Suffered constantly. I have no distance whatsoever from this suffering anymore.*
>
> *After January 11, 1986, I Said: I Am In the Body now—more than you.*
>
> *After January 11, 1986, I Said: I Am This Body, down to its depth—Invading these cells, these toes, this flesh, more profoundly than has ever occurred in human time.*
>
> —Avatar Adi Da Samraj
> *The Knee Of Listening*

V.
The Eternal Conversation

16. *Merriam-Webster's Collegiate Dictionary* (Eleventh edition) lists the following definitions for "testament":

1 a: a covenant between God and the human race b: either of two main divisions of the Bible
2 a: a tangible proof or tribute b: an expression of conviction
3 a: an act by which a person determines the disposition of his or her property after death b: will

Avatar Adi Da has indicated that all of these meanings are relevant to His use of "Testament" in the title of His Summary "Source-Word":

AVATAR ADI DA SAMRAJ: I call this writing My "Testament Of Divine Secrets", because it is My Testimony, but it is also an instrument whereby I am "passing on" to others that which Is Mine, My Revelation and Realization, and telling them how it should be used. It is also a solemn Revelatory Covenant between Me, the Divine Person, and humankind.

—June 24, 1984

THE DAWN HORSE TESTAMENT OF THE RUCHIRA AVATAR

PROLOGUE

17. In this passage of His poetic Prologue, Avatar Adi Da uses the term "Crazy" to point to His Spontaneous Mindless Freedom, both while active in bodily (human) Form and forever after the physical Lifetime of His bodily (human) Divine Form.

18. Avatar Adi Da's Admonition "Always Invoke Me, Feel Me, Breathe Me, and Serve Me" is a Calling to the practice of Ruchira Avatara Bhakti Yoga, the fundamental practice of the Way of Adidam. Each of the elements of this Admonition relates to one of the principal faculties of the human body-mind: Invoke Me (with your attention); Feel Me (with your feeling-being); Breathe Me (with your breath); and Serve Me (with your body). See Sutra 5.

19. While used poetically in this passage, "The Way Of The Heart" is one of two principal references to the Way Avatar Adi Da Samraj has Revealed and Given. The other is "Adidam" (or "Adidam Ruchiradam"), and there are a number of further descriptive references to the Way of Adidam Given by Avatar Adi Da Samraj in Sutra 2. For definitions of all names and references to the Way of Adidam, please see the glossary.

20. The "Source-Matrix Of Vibratory Light Above" is the Source-Light of Which all conditional manifestations, and the total cosmic domain, are modifications. This Source-Light may be perceived or felt as a formless Matrix of "Bright" Love-Bliss infinitely above the world, the body, and the mind. It is the reflected "Brightness" of the Inherently Perfect, Self-Existing, and Self-Radiant Heart-Locus associated with the right side of the chest. The Matrix Above is also the center of the Cosmic Mandala, and as such, may be seen in Vision as a brilliant white five-pointed Star.

See Sutras 14 and 15 for a detailed description of the Matrix Above and the Divine Star.

SUTRA 1

21. Tibetan Buddhists regard the syllable "Da" (written, in Tibetan, with a single letter) as most auspicious, and they assign numerous sacred meanings to it, including "Entrance into the Dharma". In the most ancient of the Upanishads (the *Brihadaranyaka Upanishad*), the Divine Being gives the fundamental instruction necessary for each of the different classes of living beings by uttering the single sound "Da". (Each class of beings understands "Da" in the manner uniquely necessary in their case.) In this passage, "Da" is said to be the Divine Voice that can be

heard speaking through thunder [See *The Principal Upanisads*, translated by S. Radhakrishnan (Atlantic Highlands, N.J.: Humanities Press International, First paperback edition, 1992), 289–290].

22. For devotees of Avatar Adi Da Samraj, His Names are the Names of the Very Divine Being. As such, these Names, as Avatar Adi Da Himself has Described, "do not simply mean Real God, or the Blessing of Real God. They are the verbal or audible Form of the Divine." Therefore, Invoking Avatar Adi Da Samraj by Name is a potent and Divinely Empowered form of feeling-Contemplation of Him.

SUTRA 2

23. For a description of Avatar Adi Da's conscious relinquishment of the "Bright" and His assumption of egoic existence at the age of two, as well as the subsequent ordeal of His "Sadhana Years", see *The Knee Of Listening*.

24. Avatar Adi Da spontaneously Re-Awakened as the Divine Self while sitting in a small temple on the grounds of the Vedanta Society in Hollywood, California, on September 10, 1970. The State that He then Realized in fully Conscious association with the body-mind was the Very (and Inherently Perfect) Divine Self-Condition that He had Known since His human Birth and before. This Great Event and its significance are discussed in chapter 16 of *The Knee Of Listening*.

25. On September 13, 1979, in an historic letter to practitioners of the Way of Adidam, Avatar Adi Da (then known as "Bubba Free John") Confessed His Identity as the Divine Person via the Name "Da": "Beloved, I Am Da." This letter was gradually transformed by Avatar Adi Da to thoroughly epitomize His "Eternal Conversation" with all beings. It now forms the core of Sutra 1.

26. In April 2000, Avatar Adi Da was invited to stay on an island off the coast of the state of Washington (USA). On April 12, soon after He arrived at Lopez Island, His Body underwent a dramatic "Yogic Death", through which He became Spiritually Established in the Body as the "Bright"—with the Purity that had been the case at His Birth, before His Submission to Learn and Teach humanity. It was a Process of spontaneous and sudden "Ascent" to His Divine State, rather than "Descent" into Submission to the human world. This Establishment at the "Threshold" of His Divine Self-Domain is the culminating phase of His unique Avataric Demonstration of Divine Enlightenment, and brought with It a great magnification of His Divine Spiritual Blessing-Power. For Avatar Adi Da's full Description of the Great Event at Lopez Island and Its significance, see Part Three of *The Knee Of Listening*.

27. Avatar Adi Da's immense Work to Make His Full Divine Revelation in words was essentially Completed on September 23, 2002 (the day on which He Completed His final Review of the entire text of *The Dawn Horse Testament Of The Ruchira Avatar*), twenty-three years after He Made His Divine Self-Confession "I Am Da" (on September 13, 1979).

SUTRA 3

28. The three historical "yanas" (or "vehicles") of Buddhism are Theravada (or Hinayana, the so-called "lesser vehicle"), Mahayana (the "great vehicle"), and Vajrayana (the "diamond vehicle"). Theravada is the predominant form of Buddhism in Southeast Asia and Sri Lanka, Mahayana the predominant form in China, Korea, and Japan, and Vajrayana the predominant form in Tibet and various Himalayan kingdoms. While all three of the historical "yanas" recognize certain fundamental principles of Buddhism, each "yana" has a distinctive understanding of the Nature of Enlightenment (or Nirvana), and each "yana" recommends a distinctive form of practice intended to Realize Enlightenment.

SUTRA 4

29. The practice of ego-transcendence in the Way of Adidam is always present (or direct and immediate)—because, in any moment of true practice, the devotee enters into ego-surrendering, ego-forgetting, and ego-transcending heart-Communion with Avatar Adi Da. The practice of ego-transcendence in the Way of Adidam is also progressive (ultimately, culminating in Most

Perfect ego-Transcendence, in the seventh stage of life)—because, over time, the devotee becomes more and more consistently responsible for all of the physical and psychic dimensions of the body-mind and more and more stably Awakened to Identification with Self-Existing and Self-Radiant Consciousness Itself.

30. For a description of meditation requirements at different developmental stages of the Way of Adidam, see Sutra 30.

31. "Require" in this case is a reference to the specified periods of (necessarily, formal) Spiritually Initiatory retreat in Avatar Adi Da's physical Company (or, after His physical Lifetime, in the empowered circumstances of the Instrumental gathering of the Ruchira Sannyasin Order) for the sake of a particular transition in practice. Such initiatory periods of retreat are required at three points in the course of the practice of Adidam:

1. the first period of the intensive listening-hearing stage
2. the would-be-seeing stage
3. the first stage of the "Perfect Practice"

32. In general, access to the Ruchira Sannyasin Hermitage Ashrams (or Places of Avatar Adi Da's Blessing-Seat) is granted to practitioners of Adidam who are in the intensive listening-hearing stage and beyond. For a listing of the developmental stages of practice in the Way of Adidam, see the glossary.

33. Avatar Adi Da Samraj has said that by virtue of the profound Yogic Event that occurred on April 22, 1999, at His most secluded Temple at Adidam Samrajashram (the "Brightness"), His Divine Blessing Work is Spiritually Established and Empowered from Adidam Samrajashram (the Island of Naitauba, Fiji) in perpetuity.

34. "Formally designated regional gatherings" of Avatar Adi Da's devotees are established when a sufficient group of members of the second congregation of Adidam are gathered in a particular geographical area and have established various specific structures of cultural participation and accountability for the practice and mission of Adidam in that area.

35. In this phrase, Avatar Adi Da is using "Advanced" to describe those practicing in the first actually seeing stage of the Way of Adidam, and "Ultimate" to describe those practicing in the context of the "Perfect Practice".

SUTRA 5

36. Devotees of Avatar Adi Da Samraj generally do not come into His physical Company for formal Darshan (or direct feeling-Contemplation of His Avatarically-Born bodily human Divine Form) until they are formally acknowledged to be applicants for the intensive listening-hearing stage of the Way of Adidam. For a fuller description of the right practice of "bodily facing" Avatar Adi Da, see Sutra 26, p. 476.

37. The student-beginner stage of practice in the Way of Adidam goes through three phases of adaptation. An individual who has first taken the Eternal Vow and embraced practice in the second congregation of Avatar Adi Da's devotees is a "novice student-beginner" until such time as he or she has completed the initial level of adaptation to the basic range of functional, practical, relational, and cultural disciplines. At that time, he or she is acknowledged as a "fully established student-beginner". When a student-beginner is acknowledged by the Adidam culture as prepared for the transition to the intensive listening-hearing phase of the Way of Adidam, he or she is acknowledged as a "mature student-beginner" and applies for the necessary period of Spiritually Initiatory retreat in Avatar Adi Da's physical Company (or the Empowered circumstance of the Instrumental gathering of the Ruchira Sannyasin Order).

SUTRA 6

38. Having made this choice (at some point during his or her period of practice as a student-beginner), the practitioner of the Way of Adidam then practices only his or her chosen form of

the "conscious process", both in formal meditation and in daily life—until the transition to the "Perfect Practice". After that transition, every practitioner of the Way of Adidam engages "Feeling-Enquiry" as his or her exclusive form of the "conscious process", both in formal meditation and in daily life (with the only secondary continued random use of his or her previous form of the "conscious process" in daily life).

39. In the case of devotees of Avatar Adi Da Samraj who choose to practice the Devotional Way of Insight, the formal meditative practice of both self-Enquiry and non-verbal Re-cognition continues through the first actually seeing stage. Beyond this stage, self-Enquiry and non-verbal Re-cognition are no longer to be engaged in formal meditation, although they can continue to be engaged at random in daily life. Thus, the particular "Design" of Avatar Adi Da's own "Sadhana"—in Which self-Enquiry and non-verbal Re-cognition were His consistent (formal meditative and random) Practice, up to the Great Event of His Divine Re-Awakening to the seventh stage of life—is Unique. None of His devotees will follow this "Pattern".

40. In using "Avatar" as a Descriptive Reference (either preceding or following a form of simple Name-Invocation of Avatar Adi Da Samraj), the form "Avatara" (with a final "a") is to be used (or may be used) when that Descriptive Reference is added to the beginning of a form of Name-Invocation, while the form "Avatar" (without a final "a") is to be used when that Descriptive Reference is added to the ending of a form of Name-Invocation. (This note is verbatim Instruction from Avatar Adi Da Samraj.)

41. Ruchira Avatara Naama Japa is practiced as a feeling-gesture of devotional self-surrender. All practitioners in the Way of Adidam cultivate what Avatar Adi Da refers to here as "the traditional manner" of right devotional attention to Him as Divine Heart-Master. Practicing in the traditional manner, the devotee in the Way of Adidam only loves, reveres, serves, and always feelingly Contemplates Avatar Adi Da as the Divine Person and Very Self. He or she never inwardly or outwardly finds fault with Avatar Adi Da, or allows his or her practice of devotion to Avatar Adi Da to be retarded by tendencies toward doubt, laziness, or reluctance to demonstrate loving faith and self-surrender obviously.

Proper study of the traditional arguments and injunctions relative to Guru-devotion reinforces the auspicious devotional attitude of faithful and intelligent self-surrender. The traditional scriptures emphasize, and Avatar Adi Da confirms, that this attitude must characterize the practitioner at all times, no matter what tests or obstacles he or she encounters, if his or her aspiration to Divine Self-Realization is to bear fruit.

42. Because there are only two words, or syllables, in each of the first two variants, the hyphen is added—in order that, in use, it does not become, in effect, reversed. Thus, the variants are to be distinguished from one another—either it is "Da-Om" or it is "Om-Da". (This note is verbatim Hand-Written Instruction from Avatar Adi Da Samraj.)

43. Hindi "Jai" (or Sanskrit "Jaya") means "victory". As an element in certain forms of the Ruchira Avatara Mantra (and also as used in spontaneous ecstatic exclamations), "Jai" is an affirmation of Avatar Adi Da's Spiritual Victory in the hearts of all His devotees and the Perfection of His Blessing of the entire cosmic domain.

44. Avatar Adi Da Instructs that, as part of their sadhana of engaging the "Perfect Practice" in the context of a life of artfully secluded perpetual retreat, each and every member of the Ruchira Sannyasin Order must reside at one of the Ruchira Sannyasin Hermitage Ashrams He has Directly Spiritually Empowered.

45. Because it is not always possible to be in the physical Company of one's Sat-Guru, devotees have traditionally produced artistic images of the Sat-Guru for Contemplation when he or she is either not physically present or else no longer physically alive.

Modern technology makes possible (through photography, videotape, film, holographic imagery, and other recorded or artistically rendered means) accurate Representations of the bodily (human) Divine Form of Avatar Adi Da for devotional use by practitioners of the Way of Adidam.

SUTRA 7

46. Although Avatar Adi Da Self-Generated His unique Ordeal of Awakening to conform His body-mind to the Divine Self-Condition (the State from Which He Intentionally took human birth and in and As Which He Eternally Abides), in the course of this Ordeal He was Served by a number of great Teachers and Spiritual Sources, to whom He related in the traditional manner of a devotee. His principal Teachers and Spiritual Sources, as discussed in *The Knee Of Listening* are Rudi (or Swami Rudrananda), Swami Muktananda, Bhagavan Nityananda, and the Divine Goddess.

47. In His boyhood, Avatar Adi Da spontaneously allowed the Enjoyment of the "Bright" of Illumined Consciousness to fade, so that He might experience and know all the ordinary suffering of apparently un-Enlightened people and then recover the Way of Most Perfect Divine Self-Realization for their sake. By the time of His adolescence, the "Bright" had receded in conscious awareness, but during His adolescent years and early adulthood He experienced (or re-contacted) the "Bright" in spontaneous Breakthroughs of Illumination and Divine Intuition.

Avatar Adi Da refers here to a major Breakthrough of the "Bright" that He Enjoyed in 1960, when He was attending Columbia College in New York City, absorbed in a search for God-Consciousness via unrestricted exploration of all experience. The primary import of this Awakening, as Avatar Adi Da indicates in this passage, was His "radical" insight into the core dilemma that motivates, but is never resolved by, any and every form of seeking. For a full description of this event and its significance, see *The Knee Of Listening*.

48. See note 39.

49. Avatar Adi Da's Ordeal of Divine Self-Realization occupied Him from September 1957, when He began His quest for Truth through all possible experience, until His Divine Re-Awakening on September 10, 1970.

50. Avatar Adi Da uses the metaphor of the clenched fist and the open hand to demonstrate the contrast between the self-contracted state and the natural (uncontracted) state. This incident, which occurred while Avatar Adi Da was living in New York City in 1965, is a key moment when this contrast became suddenly intuitively clear. At the time, He was a devotee of His first human Spiritual Teacher, Rudi (Albert Rudolph, also known as Swami Rudrananda).

SUTRA 8

51. Avatar Adi Da describes the process of spontaneously "Meditating" devotees in vision in *The Knee Of Listening*:

> *Now—whenever I would sit, in any kind of formal manner, to demonstrate the meditation, or the (now) Divine Samadhi, that had become my entire life—instead of confronting what was arising in (and as) "myself", I "meditated" other beings and places. I would spontaneously become aware of great numbers of people (usually in visions, or in some other intuitive manner), and I would work with them very directly, in a subtle manner. The binding motions and separative results of my own apparent (or merely life-born) egoity (or total psycho-physical self-contraction) had been transcended in my re-Awakening to my Original (and inherently egoless and Self-Evidently Divine) Self-Condition (Which is the One and Only Self-Condition and Source-Condition of even each and all of everyone and everything). Therefore, in the spontaneous Awakening of the Avataric Divine Guru-Siddhi, what arose to my view—instead of my own life-born forms and problematic signs—were the egoic forms, the problematic signs, the minds, the feelings, the states, and the various limitations of others. . . .*

In this manner, I spontaneously began to "meditate" countless other people, and also countless non-human beings, and countless places and worlds and realms, both high and low in the scale of Reality. I observed and responded to all that was required for the (ultimately) most perfect Divine Awakening and the true (and the, ultimately, most perfect) well-being of each and all. And, each time I did this (and, in fact, the process quickly became the underlying constant of all my hours and days), I would continue the "meditating" of any (and each) one until I felt a release take place—such that his or her suffering and seeking was vanished (or, at least, significantly relaxed and set aside). Whenever that occurred, I Knew my "meditating" of that one was, for the moment, done. By such means, my now and forever Avataric Divine Work (of Teaching, Blessing, and Awakening all-and-All) was begun.

—Avatar Adi Da Samraj
The Knee Of Listening

52. Avatar Adi Da uses the word "Hell" here to indicate the patterned suffering and bondage caused by the activity of the ego (or self-contraction)—not some form of "damnation" imposed on the individual by an "objective" (or "external") deity (or force), because of the individual's "bad behavior".

53. The Way of Adidam is founded in a fundamental disillusionment with the ego and its purposes (together with a deep heart-Attraction to Avatar Adi Da Samraj). This disillusionment is positive because it is the necessary foundation for true Spiritual Awakening.

SUTRA 9

54. While a uniquely exemplary devotee may be acknowledged to be a "novice" in the Ruchira Sannyasin Order immediately upon his or her transition to the "Perfect Practice", an applicant to the Ruchira Sannyasin Order is acknowledged as a "full formal member" of that Order only when he or she makes the transition to the second stage of the "Perfect Practice".

SUTRA 15

55. Sutra 5 contains Avatar Adi Da's Instruction in the basic practice of Invoking Him as it is engaged by all of His formally practicing devotees. Sutra 32 contains His Instruction in the further development of the practice of Invoking Him as it is engaged by members of the first and second congregations of the Way of Adidam in the would-be-seeing stage of practice and beyond. Additionally, Avatar Adi Da has indicated that some aspects of His Instruction to His devotees (particularly relative to matters pertaining to practice in the context of the "Perfect Practice" of Adidam) will never be made generally available in published form but will be confidentially Given only to members of the Ruchira Sannyasin Order (as the senior cultural authority of Adidam), who are authorized to pass on such confidential Instruction to those formally practicing devotees who are rightly prepared to receive It.

56. In this passage, Avatar Adi Da describes the nature of Divine Translation. It is not an abstract state of "emptiness" or a "void" of nothingness—nor is it a cosmic "soup". It is, rather, as He describes here, an Embrace (Full of Love-Bliss) by an infinite but undifferentiated gathering.

SUTRA 16

57. For a description of the possible visions and auditions, see Sutra 60.

58. For a description of the horizontal (and vertical) dimensions of the body-mind, see the glossary.

SUTRA 17

59. See glossary under **Lineage, Avatar Adi Da's**. For a full account, see chapter 16 of *The Knee Of Listening*.

60. Avatar Adi Da characterizes the traditional religious and Spiritual paths of the fourth, fifth, and sixth stages of life as the "great path of return", because the traditional points of view associated with those stages of life regard the "goal" of the Spiritual path to be somewhere "else", other than "here". In other words, it is traditionally presumed that the Spiritual Way is a matter of following a "great path" by which the aspirant will "return" from "here" to the "place" that is regarded to be the "goal" (or "home"). The fourth-to-fifth stage "path of return" is traditionally conceived as an "ascent" ("From Below To Above"), while the sixth stage "path of return" is traditionally conceived as a "going within" (proceeding, as Avatar Adi Da has Revealed, "From Left To Right", in terms of the three stations of the heart).

Right practice of the Way of Adidam, on the other hand, is not a matter of seeking to reach any of the "goals" of the first six stages of life, but is (rather) a matter of practicing (progressively) in the context of the first six stages of life, while persistently observing, understanding, and transcending all forms of motivated seeking as they arise.

61. For examples of reports of Kundalini Shakti experiences, see:

Kundalini: The Evolutionary Energy in Man, by Gopi Krishna (Boulder, Colo.: Shambala, 1971).

The Kundalini Experience: Psychosis or Transcendence?, by Lee Sannella, M.D. (Lower Lake, Calif.: Integral Publishing, 1987).

62. Avatar Adi Da originally wrote this passage in response to the essay "Vama Marga: The Practice of Left-Hand Tantra", by Swami Satyananda Saraswati (*Yoga* magazine, March 1981, 4–17), which briefly describes (or refers to) certain Yogic sexual practices (and their associated Hatha Yoga postures and techniques). These practices are further described and elaborated in *Hatha Yoga Pradipika: The Light on Hatha Yoga*, commentary by Swami Muktibodhananda Saraswati under the guidance of Swami Satyananda Saraswati (Munger, Bihar, India: Bihar School of Yoga, 1985) and *Asana, Pranayama, Mudra, Bandha*, by Swami Satyananda Saraswati (Monghyr, Bihar, India: Bihar School of Yoga, sixth edition, 1983).

SUTRA 21

63. In general, no abrupt change marks the transition between consecutive stages of the first six stages of life. Instead, the individual shows increasing evidence of growth and transformation, until he or she is more or less wholly occupied with the interests and conditions of the next stage of life. Thus, while each of the first two stages of life may be regarded as roughly seven years long, the signs of maturity in the first stage of life and movement toward the second stage of life generally begin to appear at age five or six. Entrance into the third stage of life generally occurs between ages twelve and fourteen, but evidence of movement toward it may begin as early as age ten. And, although a basic adaptation to human adulthood is usually established by age twenty-one, there is no growth beyond the third stage of life unless an individual comes in contact with and embraces true religious and Spiritual practice, typically in relationship to a Teacher or Teachers capable of initiating and guiding practice in the context of the fourth stage of life and beyond. The duration of the fourth stage of life, the fifth stage of life, or the sixth stage of life cannot be predicted, since the duration of each of these stages depends on many factors, including the individual's seed-karmas related to each stage, the force of his or her impulses to growth and ego-transcending Real-God-Realization, and the stage(s) of life Realized and Taught by his or her Teacher(s). For devotees of Avatar Adi Da Samraj, the seventh stage of life, once Realized (by Means of His Avataric Divine Spiritual Grace), is eternal—although, if a seventh stage Realizer experiences one or more cycles of death and rebirth previous to Divine Translation, he or she will still be required (in each rebirth) to pass through a developmental process leading to the "recovery" of What had been most perfectly Realized in a previous incarnation.

64. *What, Where, When, How, Why, and Who To Remember To Be Happy: A Simple Explanation Of The Way Of The Heart (For Children, and Everyone Else)* is Avatar Adi Da's principal Communication to children on the practice of how to "Feel, Breathe, Behold, and Be the

Mystery". Avatar Adi Da has also Given comprehensive Instruction (in numerous Discourses and Writings over many years) on conscious childrearing to adults responsible for the human and religious development of children in the Way of Adidam. See particularly *The Scale of the Very Small* and *Love, Wisdom, and Happiness in the First Three Stages of Life*.

65. Here Avatar Adi Da refers to the unique devotional or religious "considerations" and practices that He Gives to children and young people in each of the first three stages of life. All parents, educators, guides, and other "loving helpers" of such early-life practitioners are schooled in the ancient and honorable tradition of Guru-devotion, and in all the appropriate disciplines and Laws of the real relationship between Avatar Adi Da and His early-life devotee. This is the devotional orientation to practice that is appropriate to teach, and lovingly require of, early-life practitioners in the Way of Adidam.

66. Children and young people (to the age of 21) in the Way of Adidam are members of the Adidam Youth Fellowship. The express purpose of this fellowship is to provide sacred religious education, training in religious practices, sacred arts, and apprenticeships for young devotees, and to help them to grow in all aspects of their practice of the Way of Adidam.

The Adidam Youth Fellowship is a "culture of expectation and inspiration", providing the natural circumstance of daily practice in which devotees actively demonstrate their devotional relationship to Avatar Adi Da. Young people participate fully in the cultural life that surrounds and supports them, and this is one of the primary means of their growth and education. Avatar Adi Da has Said that all devotees should participate in providing opportunities and services for children and young people in the Way of Adidam.

Avatar Adi Da has also Said that children and young people are best served by individuals who are exemplary in the practice of Ruchira Avatara Bhakti Yoga. Therefore, the teachers and guides who serve these young devotees most intimately should optimally be such exemplary practitioners.

Every child and young person within the cooperative culture of devotees is to be rightly guided, served, instructed, and encouraged according to the Wisdom-Principles Given by Avatar Adi Da. Every young person should be given the opportunity and necessary support to practice the Way of Adidam. Parents and guides should always encourage the most intensive form of practice a child or young person is capable of, and all should be helped and guided to grow in their relationship to Avatar Adi Da. When young people transition into the adult culture (at or just before age twenty-one), they make their own choice to practice, as adults.

SUTRA 22

67. The "Perfect Practice" encompasses the processes otherwise associated with both the fifth stage of life and the sixth stage of life, culminating in the Realization of the seventh stage of life.

68. From the beginning of their practice, all formally acknowledged practitioners of the Way of Adidam embrace the discipline of cooperative culture, or consistent, committed, and active participation (to the maximum possible degree) in all the activities of the global ashram of practitioners of the Way of Adidam.

Formally acknowledged practitioners who, out of necessity, live at a distance from a designated regional circumstance of Adidam, maintain a positive and consistent affiliation with the practitioners closest to them, as well as with the Avataric Pan-Communion of Adidam, and they participate in cultural life with other practitioners to the fullest degree possible.

SUTRA 24

69. For Avatar Adi Da's full discussion of His "Alpha-Born Inward Nature", see Part Two of *The Knee Of Listening* ("The Place of Ramakrishna and Swami Vivekananda in the Great Tradition, and Their Unique Function in Preparing the Vehicle of My Avataric Divine Incarnation" and "I Have Appeared here Via a Unique, Spontaneous, and Never-Again Conjunction of Vehicles").

SUTRA 25

70. Avatar Adi Da describes the foundation discipline of all practice in the Way of Adidam, which is Satsang, or feeling-Contemplation of Him, as "simple"—because it is non-technical in nature. This "simple" practice is the foundation of all practice in the Way of Adidam. In this usage, Avatar Adi Da places the word "simple" in quotation marks to indicate that He is using it in the specific sense described here (and not in any other of the commonly accepted general meanings).

71. For the first two to two and one-half years after His Birth, Avatar Adi Da existed in the "Bright" Condition of Love-Bliss, Prior to and Pervading His body-mind and all phenomena. Identification with the born human condition and with egoity itself (and, hence, "incarnation" as the "ego-'I'") began in a specific moment in 1941 or 1942. He Writes, in *The Knee Of Listening*:

> *As a Conscious "creation", or by-Me-Embraced condition, "Franklin Jones" began one day while I was crawling across the linoleum floor in a house my parents had rented from an old woman named Mrs. Farr. There was a little puppy, which my parents had gotten for me, running across the floor towards me. I saw the puppy, and I saw my parents. The "creation" of "Franklin Jones" began from that moment. All of the rest of the events that occurred during the two or more years before that moment were not the years of "Franklin Jones". He had no existence before that time, which was the Conscious (or Intentional) beginning.*

In Avatar Adi Da's case, this "ego-birth" coincided with a profound Spiritual Descent into or Embrace of bodily existence for the sake of His Avataric Divine Spiritual Work on Earth.

> *AVATAR ADI DA SAMRAJ: For approximately the first two years after My Birth, I allowed the gross vehicle to be gradually prepared for Me. Then, at approximately two years of age, I Spiritually Descended to the region of the heart and thus established My basic association with My conditionally manifested personality.*
>
> *This Spiritual Descent into the gross body to the level of the heart occurred on the basis of a sympathy with, or heart-response to, those who were around Me at the moment. It was through this sympathetic response that I acquired the Vehicle of this body-mind.*
>
> *Because I was Born to Make this Submission, the decision to acquire the gross body-mind did not occur when I was two years old. The Vehicle of this body-mind had become sufficiently prepared at that point, but I had consciously decided to Do this Work before I Incarnated. The Descent was for the sake of the total world and all beings. I had consciously decided to take a birth in the West. My Intention before this Birth was to take this Birth and to Do My Work by complete Submission to the ordinary Western circumstance.*
>
> —February 5, 1989

SUTRA 26

72. Approval by the Ruchira Sannyasin Order and subsequent registration with the Avataric Samrajya of Adidam is processed through the local Global Ashram Cultural Services Manager and the central Global Ashram Services cultural department, and thereby proposed to the Ruchira Sannyasin Order as an application for "searchless Beholding" Initiatory retreat.

73. For the qualifications for transition to the first period of the intensive listening-hearing stage of Adidam, see Sutra 29.

74. Avatar Adi Da uses the term "Outer Temple" in a manner comparable to the term "exoteric", as opposed to esoteric (or "Inner Temple"). Thus, the "Outer Temple" of Adidam is the preparatory student-beginner period of devotional practice and establishing of the life-disciplines, previous to Spiritual Initiation by Avatar Adi Da Samraj.

SUTRA 28

75. Avatar Adi Da's most comprehensive exposition of the "conservative dietary discipline" (or the "right and optimum" diet that is limited to what is necessary and sufficient for general psycho-physical purification, balance, well-being, and appropriate service) and the process whereby

practitioners of the Way of Adidam adapt to it, appears as section VII of His Essay "The ego-'I' is the Illusion of Relatedness" (in *Santosha Adidam*).

76. Examples of such "Token and Merely Symbolic Use, As May Sometimes Be Required By Custom For Respectful and Right Participation In, Necessarily Rare, Sacred, or Entirely Ceremonial and Non-personal, social Occasions" include (perhaps) drinking a small amount of alcohol (or even simply touching one's lips to the liquid) as part of a formal toast at a formal event such as a wedding, smoking a small amount of tobacco at a formal Native American peace pipe ceremony, or drinking a small amount of kava in a formal kava ceremony in the South Pacific.

77. The basic practice of "emotional-sexual conscious exercise", which is the extension of simple "conscious exercise" into the occasion of sexual intimacy (as practiced by those in the stages preceding the first actually seeing stage), is described in detail by Avatar Adi Da Samraj in Sutra 38.

The "functional" limitations to which Avatar Adi Da refers include impotence, frigidity, premature ejaculation, pain during sexual intercourse, and debilitating pain and other problems associated with menstruation. The "stylistic" limitations include habits of relating to one's intimate partner that inhibit free participation in sexual embrace—habits that express one's egoic self-consciousness and create egoic self-consciousness in one's intimate partner, and that foster antisensual attitudes and inhibition of communication.

78. Every member of Adidam, no matter how distant from other practitioners of Adidam, associates (in a formal, regular, and accountable manner) with the cultural gathering of devotees with which he or she is formally associated (which, in the typical case, is the formally designated regional community that is geographically nearest to them). See also note 68.

79. Exceptions to the cooperative household living recommendation include individuals who live in an area geographically remote from other devotees or those who, for one or another justifiable reason, must maintain a residential situation that does not include other devotees (except, perhaps, an intimate partner and, as the case may be, a child or children). Any devotee who is formally culturally acknowledged to have a circumstance that does not allow for cooperative living still maximizes cooperative participation in the formally designated regional community with which he or she is formally associated and in the cooperative culture and global ashram of Adidam as a whole.

80. The fundamental basics of student-beginner practice, as described by Avatar Adi Da in *The Dawn Horse Testament*, are the basis of a specific course of study for novice student-beginners upon their embrace of the formal vow of devotional relationship to Avatar Adi Da as His second congregation devotee. Adaptation to these are "considered" with each novice student-beginner individually, so that each one may undergo the necessary practice-"consideration" to establish the full range of student-beginner self-discipline and devotional practice in his or her life. The elementary prerequisite obligations Avatar Adi Da mentions here (which the novice student-beginner—and, indeed, all practitioners of the Way of Adidam—must consistently maintain) are defined by Avatar Adi Da Samraj in the following paragraph.

81. Avatar Adi Da Samraj has Given a basic "form" for the practice of all of His devotees.

The "daily" aspect of this form includes:

- meditation at least twice per day (usually in the early morning, immediately upon rising, and in the evening or at night before retiring)
- daily sacramental worship (the Ruchira Avatara Puja)
- "conscious exercise" twice daily—generally a more vigorous period in the morning before beginning the day of work or service, and a more relaxing period at the end of the day of work or service (or, otherwise, as preparation for evening meditation)
- daily study and diary.

The "weekly" aspect of this form includes a weekly retreat day (called "Adi Da Guruvara"—"vara" meaning "day" in Sanskrit) and different scheduled activities on different nights of the week, including education, practice "consideration" groups, missionary activities, concentrated periods of service, and so forth.

The "monthly" and "annual" aspects of the form include regular retreats (including three-day retreats at least every three to four months and one or more annual extended retreats of at least seven to ten days) and the special cycle of Sovereign-Avataric Holy Months and Holy Days associated with particularly significant Events in Avatar Adi Da's Work or especially celebrating a specific aspect of the devotional relationship with Avatar Adi Da.

SUTRA 29

82. Please see notes 72 and 73.

83. The Ruchira Sannyasin Order of Adidam Ruchiradam has been established by Avatar Adi Da Samraj as the one and only culturally governing authority within the Way of Adidam. However, the Ruchira Sannyasin Order does not itself directly engage in evaluating the practice of members of the second congregation (or, indeed, of members of any congregation other than the first).

Avatar Adi Da Samraj has Instructed that cultural management of the second congregation altogether (including evaluations of members of the second congregation as qualified to make the transition to the first period of the intensive listening-hearing stage of the Way of Adidam) be conducted according to the following Principle: the second congregation of Adidam is responsible for the cultural management of its own membership—always done (as guided by the Ruchira Sannyasin Order) in accordance with Avatar Adi Da's Instructions, as Communicated in His "Source-Texts" and in other Instructions He has passed on via the Ruchira Sannyasin Order.

When any member of the second congregation is evaluated (by the formal cultural management of the second congregation) as qualified to make the transition to the first period of the intensive listening-hearing stage of the Way of Adidam, the formal cultural management of the second congregation then presents a recommendation to the Ruchira Sannyasin Order that the individual be granted permission to engage that practice, and (on the basis of that recommendation) the Ruchira Sannyasin Order then makes the final determination as to whether to grant such permission.

Ruchira Sannyasin Order approval to make the transition to the first period of the intensive listening-hearing stage of the Way of Adidam is not simply a matter of approval at the moment of making that transition, but is an ongoing matter.

84. Such extended retreats are generally three weeks in length (or longer). On such a retreat, the devotee is concentrated in Initiatory occasions of Darshan in Avatar Adi Da's physical Company, as well as meditation and other sacramental and devotional activities.

85. In this passage, Avatar Adi Da is indicating that in the second period of the intensive listening-hearing stage, the individual embraces an increased, more elaborate application to the use of the diary, to aid the process of self-observation and devotional confession that is already being intensified at this stage of practice.

All practitioners of the Way of Adidam, at every developmental stage of practice, keep a daily diary. They also periodically write summaries of their practice in order to record its details and development. The questions and "considerations" to which Avatar Adi Da's devotees respond in preparing such diaries and practice summaries are conformed to the focus of their practice at each developmental stage.

Thus, student-beginners utilize the diary and practice summaries to make fullest use of the reflective capability of ordinary relationships and experiences in the process of self-observation, and to record the ways they countered egoic activity with the practice of devotion, service, self-discipline, and meditation.

Avatar Adi Da's devotees entering the first period of the intensive listening-hearing stage of practice progressively intensify their use of the diary and practice summaries, and those who transition to the second period of the intensive listening-hearing stage greatly increase their application of these practices.

Once practitioners of the Way of Adidam have matured beyond the second period of the intensive listening-hearing stage of practice, they will continue to utilize the diary and practice summaries. At these stages, however, the egoic limitations they encounter and the counter-egoic practices they record will be informed by their awakening to true hearing of Avatar Adi Da Samraj, and, eventually, real seeing of Him.

86. The "guides" referred to here are approved for and trained in the specific task of guiding group "considerations" in the Way of Adidam. Their function is not to psychologize about individuals' tendencies (or let anyone else in the group do so) but only to provide the simple guidance Avatar Adi Da describes here.

SUTRA 30

87. Avatar Adi Da has clearly indicated that feeling-Contemplation of His bodily (human) Divine Form is a practice that may even be engaged by individuals who are blind. He has described the various ways that an individual may perceive His bodily (human) Divine Form, apart from visual perception.

AVATAR ADI DA SAMRAJ: Just because someone does not have visual access to My bodily (human) Divine Form does not mean that he or she cannot feel (and thereby Contemplate) My bodily (human) Divine Form. Someone whose physical sight is impaired has My Word, and the force of My Names. Such a person has My Leelas and the confessions of other practitioners. He or she can hear My Voice, when listening to recordings, or (if I am Moved to Speak to devotees) in My physical Company. Through all the senses other than sight, he or she has the ability to sense My bodily (human) Divine Form and be responsive.

—*No Seeking / Mere Beholding*

88. "Kirtan" is a traditional Hindi term for an occasion of devotional chanting in which devotees express their devotion not only through chant and song but whole bodily, particularly through dance, spontaneous bodily movement, and ecstatic praise. During kirtans, Avatar Adi Da's devotees may, in the fullness of ecstatic self-surrender, experience the full range of possible signs of reception of His Spiritual Transmission—such as kriyas, spontaneous mudras, Hatha Yoga poses, and ecstatic utterances.

Chanting and kirtan may, where circumstances require, be done in the same place as meditation and puja. Optimally, however, chanting and kirtan should not be done in the same hall as meditation.

Sacred occasions such as study and practice "consideration" groups, homilies, and presentations on Avatar Adi Da's Wisdom-Teaching should occur in places other than those used for meditation. Also, it is appropriate and useful to establish a single location where such events (groups and presentations) occur on a regular basis.

89. Avatar Adi Da has indicated that the size of the Murti to be used would be determined by the size of the room in which it is Installed. Thus, in order to readily and easily perceive His bodily (human) Divine Form in detail from any position within a large room or meditation hall, a life-size, or near life-size, Murti should be used.

90. The postures recommended for meditation, as well as Avatar Adi Da's Instructions on bodily exercise, standing, sitting, and walking, are explained and illustrated in *Conscious Exercise and the Transcendental Sun*.

91. The technical means recommended by Avatar Adi Da in this passage help to free attention and energy for real (or deep) meditation by balancing the alternating currents of the breath. Throughout the cycle of each day, the frontal current of life-energy (associated with the breath in the right nostril) and the spinal current of life-energy (associated with the breath in the left nostril) naturally alternate through the total nervous system. The breathing naturally changes

with the changing phases of the day, so that at some hours one nostril is open and the other closed, and at other times this condition is reversed. In itself, this circumstance is not unhealthy, but the balance of energy-currents in the body may not be altogether auspicious for meditation. Therefore, the practitioner should not passively accept this natural "phasing" of the body, but (rather) should intentionally prepare the body for meditation by balancing the currents of breath and energy. One effective traditional method for balancing the currents of breath and energy is to engage a period of intentional alternate nostril breathing.

92. "Polarity screens" (also called "Eeman screens", after their inventor, L. E. Eeman) consist of two screens of copper mesh to which wires with copper handles are attached. One screen is placed under the supine body at the lower spine and the other at the base of the head. One handle is held in each hand while the individual relaxes for ten to fifteen minutes on the screens to realign and energize the etheric circuitry (or natural field of energy) of the body. ("Polarity plates", made of solid copper plates, may be used in the same fashion.) See *Polarity Screens: A Safe, Simple, and Naturally Effective Method for Restoring and Balancing the Energies of the Body, Based on the Practical Instruction of Adi Da (The Da Avatar),* for a more detailed explanation.

93. The word "hatha" means "force" or "power". Hatha Yoga was so named because the primary means employed in that tradition is forceful (or powerful) manipulation of body, breath, and energy (with concomitant discipline of attention). (Indeed, in the tradition of Hatha Yoga, such means were presumed to be sufficient, in and of themselves, for the attainment of Ultimate Liberation.) "Hatha" has also been interpreted as originating from two basic root-sounds, "ha" and "tha", which represent sun and moon, or the complementary solar and lunar flows of prana (or life-energy). Thus, a traditional aim of Hatha Yoga is to achieve harmony in the body-mind through the balancing of these opposing bodily energies, represented by the sun and moon, the right and left sides of the body, and the exhaled (expansive) and inhaled (centering) breaths.

In the Way of Adidam, the bodily poses (asanas) of Hatha Yoga are engaged in order to purify, balance, and regenerate the functions of the body-mind, and (in due course) to align them to Avatar Adi Da's Divine Spiritual Transmission. The regulation and control of the life-energy is accomplished primarily through breath control (pranayama). Avatar Adi Da recommends that His devotees make use of simple poses of relaxation, rather than the more rigorous application of Hatha Yoga, when preparing for meditation. See *Conscious Exercise and the Transcendental Sun* for the series of Hatha Yoga poses recommended for daily exercise.

94. Alternate nostril breathing is a simple form of pranayama described in *Conscious Exercise and the Transcendental Sun*.

95. Avatar Adi Da gives a description of "frontal vase breathing" on this and the following page.

96. The traditional hamsadanda ("swan-staff"), or short crutch, is a T-frame typically made of wood or some other natural, energy-conducting material. It is placed into the armpit to apply pressure to the nerve plexus located there, which, when pressurized, can open the nostril on the opposite side of the body, thus affecting the corresponding current of bodily energy. Use of the hamsadanda in this manner can help balance the natural energies of the body.

SUTRA 32

97. In the Title "Hridaya Rosary", Avatar Adi Da uses "Hridaya" to indicate the True Divine Heart—the Self-Existing and Self-Radiant Divine Self-Consciousness, Which He Is, and Which He Freely Reveals to Be the True Divine Self-Condition of every thing and every one. Avatar Adi Da uses "Rosary" in its ancient meaning of "rose garden". Thus, "Hridaya Rosary" is Avatar Adi Da's "Rose Garden of the Heart", Wherein He Freely Awakens and Liberates all who luxuriate There.

"Four Thorns Of Heart-Instruction" is a reference to the four sections of His "Hridaya Rosary", each of which He calls a "thorn". He uses the word "thorn" to suggest the counter-egoic practice that is required in order to fully receive His Avataric Divine Gifts. As He Says in *Hridaya Rosary*, "My Four Thorns root out the ego from the Garden of the Heart. They are the ordeal of self-discipline, the counter-egoic incision, that is required." However, even in the midst of this counter-egoic process, Avatar Adi Da is the Distraction, the Bliss of His true devotee: "You must devotionally recognize Me, the Rose in the Thorns. My Thorned Medication becomes Acceptable only in My Blessing Company, the Eternal Company of the Single (and Indivisible) White Rose."

98. With the phrase "In-Love Response", Avatar Adi Da is referring to the essential means of the Way of Adidam: being in love with Him, the Incarnate Divine Person.

AVATAR ADI DA SAMRAJ: The Way of Adidam is not about seeking to be relieved of suffering. It is about Happiness. It is about being in Love with Me, the Avatar of Infinite "Brightness". And, having accepted this "in-Love", one can no longer say that life is suffering. It is not merely that.

The heart-recognition of the Person and the Truth of Existence is the foundation of Adidam. This "in-Love" response is the Means whereby My Heart-Transmission is first received. Thereafter, the "in-Love" response to Me is the foundation and essence of the practice of Adidam, until (most ultimately) you are established in My Inherently "Bright" Domain.

—February 22, 1997

99. In His metaphor of "washing the dog the other way round" (that is, from the tail to the head, rather than the head to the tail), Avatar Adi Da is referring to all attempts by the ego-"I" to improve or purify or save itself by its own efforts. See glossary entry for **"washing the dog"**.

100. Avatar Adi Da Samraj has often used the image of a dog running off with its bone as a form of Instruction:

Therefore, Listen to Me and Hear Me: You have already eaten the meal of separateness.

Now you must relinquish that awful meal (and Be—released of separate and separative self).

You do not require (and you should not seek) any "thing" from Me (to add to your already separate and deluded self).

I Am (Myself) What you Require—and I am here to Require every "thing" of you.

You must relinquish (or surrender) your ego-"I" (your experience, your presumed knowledge, your separateness, all your forms of egoic "bonding", and even all your "things", within and without) to Realize the Fullness That Is Me.

Therefore, Come to Me to Realize Me—and do not run from Me after tasting the ordinary meal of conditional knowledge and experience (like a dog runs from its master with a bone).

Having Come to Me, do not look within your body or your mind to discover whether you have received some "thing" from Me (to satisfy your little pouch of separateness).

Rather, surrender and release your total separate (or self-contracted, self-contracting, separative, and always seeking) psycho-physical self (including your entire body, your breath, your emotions, your mind, your knowledge, and all your experiences) by the progressively established and progressively developed Means of devotionally to-Me-Resorting, searchlessly Me-Beholding, receptively to-Me-responding, and (Thus, responsively) ego-surrendering, ego-forgetting, ego-transcending, and (altogether) total psycho-physical feeling-Communion with Me—and, Thus (by Means of total psycho-physical and really ego-transcending Communion with My Avatarically-Born bodily human Divine Form, My Avatarically Self-Transmitted Spiritual, and Always Blessing, Divine Presence, and My Avatarically Self-Revealed, and Very, and Transcendental, and Perfectly Subjective, and Inherently Spiritual, and Inherently egoless, and Inherently Perfect, and Self-Evidently Divine State), Grow to Luxuriate in My Divine "Bright" Spherical Self-Domain of Love-Bliss.

—Sutra 4

◆ ◆ ◆

AVATAR ADI DA SAMRAJ: The entire gathering of My devotees is My Gurukula, My "Family of the Guru". They should all be directly related to Me. The Way of Adidam is the relationship to Me, not merely a body of techniques abstracted from Me. There are responsibilities of all kinds in this relationship to Me—including responsibilities relative to your life-circumstance and life-activities, as well as technical (or Yogic) matters of practice, and so on, yes—but such responsibilities are not a thing in themselves. You cannot make a devotional culture merely out of such things in and of themselves. That is not the Way of Adidam. The Way of Adidam is the relationship to Me. Anything you (as My devotee) are doing that is not about the direct and right relationship to Me is not the Way of Adidam. It is something else. It is something you have "stolen" from Me, something you have grabbed and run away with, like a dog takes his bone and runs away from his master.

—March 14, 1997

101. The image of Avatar Adi Da's devotee being under His Foot is related to traditional Hindu sculptural imagery:

AVATAR ADI DA SAMRAJ: [referring to two images of Siva (in which Siva is dancing on a dwarf's back) as a form of Instruction in what is required to understand and transcend the self-contraction in feeling-Contemplation of Him] *You are all being the little guy under the foot of Siva. Little dwarf-like demon of forgetfulness. That is you—ego, the body-mind personality.*

The fundamental process is to go beyond being the "dwarf", the Me-forgetting body-mind, in order to Realize Me.

Notice these dwarfs here under the Siva-Foot. Siva is dancing on their buttocks, by the way—which is amusing. The dwarfs are blissful. They are happy about it. They are not forgetting the Divine in the cases shown here. They may be traditionally known as "dwarfs of forgetfulness", but in this case they are remembering the Divine. They are Waking Up. They are smiling. They Realize What is on the Other Side of this dismal view they are otherwise involved in, by virtue of their own ego-possession. If you release your ego-possessed point of view, then you notice the Great Reality.

—January 25 and 29, 1997

102. Avatar Adi Da's Love is Absolute, Unconditional, and Full of Joy:

DEVOTEE: Last night, You sat down and You looked at every devotee in the room. You Gave each of us a look of Love that held us all night long. In those first few minutes, You Communicated Your Love Perfectly to each one individually.

AVATAR ADI DA SAMRAJ: But not as a "this would be nice to do" gesture "to this one or that one". I am Delighted by My devotees. I am Attracted to each of My devotees—with all their variations, and their devotion to Me, and their discrimination and their one-pointedness, and so on.

All of My devotees are a delight to Me. I truly do Love you—and I Am you.

I love to be surrounded by My devotees. This is My Great Happiness in life—to be so surrounded, to live in the environment of devotion. It is an absolute Madness. It is particularized—but, on the other hand, it is no "one".

So I do not make choices of devotees in some "angling-down" sense. I Like it! I Love it. I Inherently Love My devotees. There is no choice in it.

I am not even making a symbolic gesture towards you. I (Myself) am Manifested by each and every one of My devotees. You are My own Form. You are also My Beloved. Truly, My devotee Is the God That I Am here to Find. You must be one-pointed in Me—but I Am Always Already One-Pointed in each of My devotees.

—Aham Da Asmi (Beloved, I Am Da)

103. Avatar Adi Da Admonishes us never to settle for less than the Perfect Happiness that is our native heart-impulse:

AVATAR ADI DA SAMRAJ: Ultimately, there is only Love-Bliss. That is the Nature of My "Bright" Divine Self-Domain. One need not settle for the slate-gray "self". One started out seeking for Happiness. The Fulfillment of that Process cannot be less than one hoped for. It must be Greater than one could have imagined.

—February 22, 1997

104. Avatar Adi Da Samraj, Who Is the Very Divine Heart Itself (indicated by the capitalized "Heart") always Calls and Greets the heart of every being (indicated by the lower-case "heart") who devotionally recognizes Him and devotionally responds to Him.

105. Avatar Adi Da's metaphor of the "gate flying open" is a poetic reference to the moment when His any devotee utterly transcends the ego-"I" and Realizes Divine Enlightenment. In this transition to the seventh (or Divinely Enlightened) stage of life, the individual is "magnetically" Drawn beyond the root-knot of egoity in the right side of the heart, Attracted beyond every vestige of egoic self-concern into Avatar Adi Da's Divine Self-Domain of Perfect (and Perfectly Non-separate) Love-Bliss-Happiness.

106. "My Imperishable Domain" is a reference to Avatar Adi Da's "Bright" Divine Spherical Self-Domain of Eternal Love-Bliss-Happiness. See especially Sutra 66.

107. "My 'Bright' Sun / Rises From the Heart-Root, / and Stands, / Forever Uneclipsed" is a poetic description of Amrita Nadi. See glossary entry for **Amrita Nadi**.

108. "The Garden Tree" is Avatar Adi Da's metaphorical reference to the subtle dimension of the being, which rises above the "underground" (or gross) dimensions of body, emotion, and mind. See "The Tree of Light Is Above the Head, and I Shine Forever In The Sky Beyond It" and "My Garden Is the Space from Underground to Infinity" in *Hridaya Rosary*.

109. Avatar Adi Da has Revealed that He is "Incarnated" in the Cosmic domain as a Brilliant White Five-Pointed (or Pentagrammic) Star (and also as the Deep Vibration, or Sound, of "Da" or "Om"). See Sutras 14 and 15.

110. "My Bliss-Touch, / My Bliss-Sound, / and My Bliss-Light" is a reference to Avatar Adi Da's three primary Forms of Manifestation in the conditional worlds—His Divine Body, His Divine Sound of Thunder, and His Divine Star of Light. See Sutra 14.

111. "The Sky Of mind" is a reference to the subtle domain of existence:

AVATAR ADI DA SAMRAJ: The tree is above the crown of the head. Everything at "ground-level" and above "ground-level" is the subtle realm. All the planes beyond the gross physical are in that tree (extending, as it does, above the head), that domain of subtlety. Sometimes I refer to the subtle domain as the "sky of mind". It is not as if somebody standing next to you would see something above your physical head. No, you have to be inside the Root Ball, straight up from the Root Ball [See endnote 113 for "Root Ball"]. *It is from the inside of the head up.*

That is where the sky of mind (or the Spiritual sky) is. And, in that sky, yes, there are the kinds of things that appear in skies. You see the sky here and what appears in it. Similar things appear in the subtle skies. Take a look.

—April 11, 1997

112. For Avatar Adi Da's discussion of "the Underground / that is the usual / human habitation", see "The Tree of Light Is Above the Head, and I Shine Forever In The Sky Beyond It" in *Hridaya Rosary*.

113. The "Mandrake", the "Three Hearts", and the "Root Ball" are Avatar Adi Da's metaphorical references to the three principal divisions of the human physical structure (lower body, heart, and head):

AVATAR ADI DA SAMRAJ: The head [or the Root Ball] is everything from the crown to the throat. And the heart region [or the Three Hearts] is everything from the throat to the solar plexus. The base region [or the Mandrake] is everything from the solar plexus to the bodily base, or to the bottoms of the feet, or the toes.

—*Hridaya Rosary*

Mandrake is the root of a plant in the nightshade family *(Mandragora officinarum)* with a large forked root that is traditionally regarded as representing the lower portion of the human body (the solar plexus, abdomen, hips, and legs).

Avatar Adi Da Samraj has Revealed that the primal psycho-physical seat of Consciousness and attention is associated with what He calls the "right side of the heart". He has Revealed that this center corresponds to the sinoatrial node, or "pacemaker", the source of the gross physical heartbeat in the right atrium (or upper right chamber) of the physical heart. In the Process of Divine Self-Realization, there is a unique process of opening of the right side of the heart—and it is because of this connection between the right side of the heart and Divine Self-Realization that Avatar Adi Da uses the term "the Heart" as another way of referring to the Divine Self.

Avatar Adi Da distinguishes three "stations of the heart", associated respectively with the right side, the middle, and the left side of the heart region of the chest. The middle station of the heart is what is traditionally known as the "anahata chakra" (or "heart chakra"), and the left side of the heart is the gross physical heart. Thus, the right side of the heart is not identical either to the heart chakra or to the gross physical heart.

The Heart Itself is not "in" the right side of the human heart, nor is it "in" (or limited to) the human heart as a whole. Rather, the human heart and body-mind and the world exist <u>in</u> the Heart, Which Is the Divine Being Itself.

For Avatar Adi Da's description of the three stations of the heart and His description of the significance of the right side of the heart in the processes of the ultimate stages of life, see Sutra 21.

114. The "Crown of lower light" is the crown of the head, or the sahasrar. (In the traditional system of chakras, or energy centers in the body, the sahasrar is the uppermost chakra, associated with the crown of the head.)

115. The dream state is one of the experiential realms associated with the subtle dimension of existence. Therefore, when Avatar Adi Da Writes, "'Bright' / Me-Sun / Above, / Higher Than dreaming Goes, / Higher Than the Tree-Sky Rises", He is Communicating that He Exists Beyond (but not excluding) the subtle realms.

116. The state of deep sleep is associated with the deepest dimension of conditionally manifested existence—the causal dimension, which is also the realm of the root self-contraction. Therefore, when Avatar Adi Da Writes, "In Me, / There— / Deeper Than sleep Falls, / Deeper Than self-contraction / Twists", He is Communicating that He Exists Beyond (but not excluding) the causal realm, as well as the gross and subtle realms.

AVATAR ADI DA SAMRAJ: Sleep does not merely allow you to refresh the body such that you can bodily be more functional—in fact, sleep is necessary for much more important reasons, additionally, because it is the depth domain. Without the automaticity of being refreshed by sleep—if sleep were not enforced by the patterns of the body-mind—you might lose touch with the depth domain entirely. Even though you cannot say anything about it that makes full and comprehensive sense, in your babble of words, you, nonetheless, do visit it profoundly for even as much as a third of your lifetime. It is a dimension of comprehension of Reality. It is the root of both waking <u>and</u> dreaming, so it is senior to them. When you relax into the depth, in either waking or dreaming, you wind up sleeping. It is the root-condition.

Deeper than sleep is That Which is to be Realized, That Which <u>Is</u> Reality no matter what condition (waking, dreaming, or sleeping) apparently arises, and That Which is, when ultimately Realized, Realized to Be the Condition <u>of</u> all that arises, whether or not it arises. And there is no "you" about it at all.

I <u>Am</u> this Depth. And I Give you, As Myself, the Very Means to Realize this Depth.

I am Deeper than the deep-sleep state.

—December 24 and 20, 1996

117. The English word "fuse" derives from Latin "fusus" (meaning "melted"), from the verb "fundere" ("to melt"). Thus, Avatar Adi Da Samraj is using "fuse" here in the sense of "a fusing", or "a melting together".

DEVOTEE: Avatar Adi Da, Your reference to "Alchemical Fuse" is particularly interesting. As I understand it, the true alchemists realized that their own body-mind was a crucible in which this fusion, or melting, was taking place, and that the alchemical reaction would not take place unless they had purified themselves.

AVATAR ADI DA SAMRAJ: Yes. What we can call the "alchemical tradition" (and other words have been used in non-Western traditions) has a profound mystical (or inner) dimension to it (you could say), but it also has, coincident with that inner dimension, a profound interest in matters of the body, and (therefore) in physical transformation. The body was not "beneath" the true alchemists—as if the true alchemists were exclusively Spiritual, whereas the false alchemists were those interested in physical processes (such as transforming base metals into gold). No—the alchemists were always interested in the entirety of existence—the inside, the outside, "the head, the tail, the whole damn thing". It is just as interesting to see how long the physical body can be made to live in this world as it is to "go out" of the top of your head into a so-called "heavenly" world. It is all interesting.

Therefore, alchemy legitimately covers the entire range of possible transformations, physical as well as Spiritual, and is not negative when it deals with things of the body. Just so, the Yoga I Give you is not in any way body-negative.

118. As mentioned in note 101, the image of the devotee being danced upon is related to traditional Hindu sculptural imagery:

AVATAR ADI DA SAMRAJ: I am on My Side of your body-mind—you are on yours. You have to surrender and forget yourself, your position on your side of your body-mind. [Referring to traditional images of Siva dancing on the back of a dwarf:] *You are the dwarf, and I Am the Dancer. You have to turn your eyes Upwards, break through the barrier at the crown of the head to the Matrix Above your head, and feel Me—All That Is Above and Beyond (and heart-Beyond) your body-mind. And, by virtue of all of the Means and Process I Reveal to you, you must be Attracted by something going on up there that you simply cannot resist. Of course, to get there requires everything. And the seventh stage Realization is the final Process of the Event.*

—February 17, 1997

119. The basic breathing practice that Avatar Adi Da Gives to His devotees is to receive Him on inhalation and release the ego-self on exhalation:

AVATAR ADI DA SAMRAJ: Fundamentally, the practice of Ruchira Avatara Bhakti I have Given you is a moment to moment practice. In terms of the breath, it is to practice reception and release directly in relation to Me—receiving Me, releasing yourself, releasing all content. It is a random noticing and engaging of the breath. If the practice is done rightly, artfully, at random, then (effectively) every breath becomes feeling-Communion with Me, the process of receiving Me, releasing yourself into Communion with Me.

—February 4, 1994

120. "Asana" is Sanskrit for bodily "posture" (or "pose"). Thus, "Samraj Asana" is "the 'pose' of devotion to the Ruchira Avatar, Adi Da Samraj". "Samraj Asana" is a "pose" not of the physical body alone, but it is the structural disposition of the entire body-mind that Avatar Adi Da describes particularly in the Fourth Thorn of His "Hridaya Rosary". This "pose" is "healing" in the most profound sense, because it allows the release of self-contraction (including the release of the primal reactive emotions of fear, sorrow, anger, and un-love) and the reception of Avatar Adi Da's Divine Love-Bliss-Fullness.

121. The Yogic locks are engaged in order to preserve "conductivity" of the natural life-energy (and, in the case of Spiritually Awakened devotees of Avatar Adi Da Samraj, the Spirit-Energy) at key points in the body-mind where Energy otherwise tends to leak out or be thrown off.

The Yogic lock of the bodily base

The Yogic Lock Of the bodily base Is . . . An Internal Upward Tensing (Either Brief and Constant Or, Otherwise, Brief and Repetitive) . . . Applied To the bodily base—By Drawing In, Back, and Up, Via the genitals, the perineum, and the anus, and Toward The Spinal Line, and With the crown of the lower abdomen Simultaneously, and Lightly, Drawn In and Up—Such That An Unbroken Line (or Continuous Circuit) Of "Conductivity" Is Maintained Between The Frontal Line and The Spinal Line, Via the bodily base.

—Sutra 36

The Yogic lock of the tongue and throat

The Yogic Lock Of the tongue and chin and throat (To Be Practiced By All My Devotees) Is A Pressing Of the tongue Lightly To the roof of the mouth, With the chin Pulled Down Somewhat (and, Generally, With the mouth closed, and With all breathing Exercised Via the nostrils), In Order To Rightly Conduct the breath-energy and (As The Case May Be) My Avatarically Self-Transmitted Current Of Divine Spirit-Presence Via the head and throat, and (When Necessary) To Lock the breath-energy and (As The Case May Be) My Avatarically Self-Transmitted Current Of Divine Spirit-Presence Below the throat.

—Sutra 36

The Yogic lock of the Ajna Door

The Yogic Lock Of The Ajna Door (Which Is To Be Responsively Practiced By All My By-Me-Spiritually-Initiated Devotees) Is A Centering Of attention In The Core (or Upper Central Region) Of the head, Between and Slightly Above and Deep Behind the eyes—Even, As Circumstances Permit, Letting the eyes Close and Turn Up and Back (To Prevent the Natural bodily energy and My Avatarically Self-Transmitted Divine Spirit-Energy From Discharging, or "Leaking Out", Via the eyes).

—Sutra 36

AVATAR ADI DA SAMRAJ: The Yogic locks are to be applied artfully in the actual situation or circumstance, day to day, of your practice of responsive devotion to Me. It is by practice in the circumstance of daily life that you learn how and when to engage the "locks". You experience the signs in your body-mind, and you learn how to be conformed to Me in the midst of the different kinds of changes in your experience, and so on.

—April 11, 1997

◆ ◆ ◆

AVATAR ADI DA SAMRAJ: The Yogic locks are to be artfully applied as required. The purpose in applying them is to maintain the integrity (or continuity) of the Circuit of "conductivity"—frontal and spinal. The Circle altogether is in this basic asana. It is a simple whole bodily gesture (or attitude).

—May 28, 1997

AVATAR ADI DA SAMRAJ: The Yogic lock at the Ajna Door—turning the eyes up and back—is usually coordinated with the bodily base lock. This lock is not constantly necessary—it is simply to be engaged with sensitivity, as you notice it serves.

—April 11, 1997

AVATAR ADI DA SAMRAJ: The ajna lock is not so much engaged randomly during the day. But it is to be engaged in sexual practice, even in the own-body sexual Yoga. And it might be engaged in the Communion Hall, for instance, or whenever you are in a set-apart circumstance where you are not otherwise physically obliged, and so forth, and where you are not outwardly obliging yourself in the ordinary way.

The bodily base lock, on the other hand, is to be done at random, and can be done basically under any circumstances. Nobody even notices, generally speaking, if you are doing it, and there are no special conditions required for doing it, generally speaking.

DEVOTEE: Avatar Adi Da, what energy specifically does the ajna lock deal with?

AVATAR ADI DA SAMRAJ: All energy. It is not just associated with "conductivity" of My Divine Spiritual Presence. Natural energy likewise is controlled by the ajna lock. All the Yogic locks relate to all modes of energy.

The ajna lock is associated more with the meditative circumstance, or a circumstance of repose, a circumstance where your regard of Me is such as it might be in meditation, or, perhaps, otherwise, in sacred circumstances such as puja or chanting, and so on—various circumstances of repose or of visual Contemplation of Me, and so on. Such are the circumstances in which the ajna lock might be stimulated to occur spontaneously. Just as the eyes may spontaneously close, without turning up—your mood, disposition, and so forth, makes it occur—so with the upturning of the eyes. It can occur spontaneously. But, just as the ajna lock is used in the conservation and conversion of degenerative orgasm, it has its uses in the practice of "conductivity" under other circumstances as well—and, obviously, that principally includes its application in the Communion Hall.

The ajna lock is of very great significance and importance in the practice I have Given in Hridaya Rosary, *because it involves an intentional (or, otherwise, spontaneous) exercise of the head—just as the heart region (or the trunk), and the lower body, and the breath need to be intentionally exercised.*

The Yogic locks at the bodily base (the upward tensing of the bodily base) and at the throat (particularly the tongue touching the roof of the mouth) and at the ajna center (the up-and-back-turning of the eyes) must all be used. They will, quite possibly, occur spontaneously. And, otherwise, they are to be intentionally done, at random. These Yogic locks are part of the asana of right, true, and full devotion, as I Describe it in Hridaya Rosary. *There is the physical asana of sitting in a particular position—the body generally upright, the spine straight, and so forth—but these Yogic locks are also part of the right asana. They are the more internal-to-the-body aspects of right asana, or right attitude, or right aligning of the psycho-physical structure to Me.*

The ajna lock is not something that only happens spontaneously sometimes, causing you to somehow forget the physical. It is to be intentionally practiced at random, in your physical surrender of head, heart, body, and breath—not dissociating from the head, the heart, the body, and the breath, but using them lawfully in the Yoga of devotion to Me.

The eyes need not even close, necessarily, in every moment of the ajna lock. It is simply a disposition, an asana, that you become familiar with over time, such that there are times when that lock can be exercised with your eyes completely open. All such things come by experience and practice, over time, by noticing the details of it and becoming artfully involved in the exercise.

—May 9, 1997

AVATAR ADI DA SAMRAJ: The bodily base lock creates a line of "conductivity" in the lower part of the body, between the frontal and spinal lines, such that there is no break and no loss of energy there. The ajna lock has a similar function in the upper part of the body. It does not block energy—not at all. It simply establishes the right energy-circuit in the head.

The pattern of the Circuit is felt in your reception of Me, and you refresh your bodily association and so on, in various moments. But you, otherwise, simply feel, so that this is direct, simple "conductivity" of Me—down from above the crown of the head, through the crown of the head, to (and then even through) the ajna center, the deep brain core. The ajna center must be open likewise. Allow the further opening down through the base of the head, the throat, the deep dimension of the throat, leading to the heart.

The line of the Circuit through the throat is most particularly associated with the simple natural keeping of the tongue at the palate. Similarly, there is also an even physical line of "conductivity" in the head, and the ajna lock actually makes use of a physical mechanism in the head. This physical mechanism associated with the ajna lock is not otherwise visible, but it is nevertheless a bodily lock. You reassociate yourself with that mechanism, feel it, learn about it, more and more, as you practice this lock (or as the lock happens spontaneously), and as you practice receptive "conductivity" of Me altogether.

The ajna lock is not, generally speaking, about going "inward" into realms of subtle perception (although such can sometimes be the case). The ajna lock is associated with the total right asana of the body, the Asana of the "Healing Pose" (or Ruchira Avatara Bhakti Asana)—open to Me, all the principal faculties given to Me, receiving Me. The ajna lock is not about relinquishing bodily consciousness, but about opening as *the body, being receptive* as *the body—the head, the heart, the lower body, the whole body, even breathing Me.*

The breath and feeling are the link to Me Spiritually. The body is a vessel. And attention, the root of mind, must become simply this gesture of the head, this gesture of feeling-openness.

—May 13, 1997

122. In the lines, "the Garden dog Shines Red, / Then White, / Then Un-Defined", Avatar Adi Da is referring to a metaphor He has often used, comparing the Spiritual Process in His Company to clay pigs in a kiln. The wet lumps of clay heat up gradually until they begin to glow with a fiery redness. Then, as they get even hotter, the glow becomes a brilliant white. Finally, the glow is so intense that there is nothing but undefined bright light—no individual shapes can be made out.

123. Divine Translation is the final and complete Demonstration of the entire Spiritual Process in Avatar Adi Da's Company. It is Permanent "Entry" into His Divine Self-Domain of Absolute Love-Bliss-Happiness, and can only occur at the moment of (or at some time after) the devotee's physical death. With the phrase "Ordinary 'Translation'", Avatar Adi Da is indicating that in every moment of true heart-Communion with Him, even previous to Divine Translation, all the leading faculties of the body-mind are opened to Him, such that He Melts the devotee's presumed limitations and bodily knots and "replaces" them with His Divine Love-Bliss-Happiness (Which is the Prior Condition of every being and thing).

124. Avatar Adi Da has described a "gagging sensation" associated with the onset of the "Thumbs":

From my early childhood, at apparently random times (usually as I either approached sleep or awoke from sleep—and, most dramatically, during seizures of childhood illness, as I would pass into delirium), I had an experience that felt like a mass of gigantic thumbs coming down from above, pressing into my throat (causing something of a gagging, and somewhat suffocating, sensation), and then pressing further (and, it seemed, would have expanded without limitation or end), into some form of myself that was much larger than my physical body.

—*The Knee Of Listening*

See also Sutras 17 and 45.

SUTRA 33

125. The phrase "A Horse Appears In The Wild Is Always Already The Case" was first Given by Avatar Adi Da Samraj as a Spontaneous Ecstatic Utterance on April 13, 1998. (See *The Overnight Revelation Of Conscious Light.*)

126. Here Avatar Adi Da makes the same ecstatic Divine Confession as in note 125, but using reference to the principal characters of His *Mummery Book*. In *The Mummery Book*, Raymond (a personification of Consciousness Itself) Realizes that he is not—Ultimately, or in Truth—ever separate from the loved-one, Quandra (Energy, or Light, or Love-Bliss).

127. The practice of pressing inhalation-reception into the abdomen may be engaged a few times or for a few minutes at the beginning of the meditation period when the natural etheric energy (or, in the case of Spiritually Awakened practitioners of the Way of Adidam, Avatar Adi Da's Avatarically Self-Transmitted Divine Spirit-Current) seems weak or knots are felt in the frontal line. In addition, this practice may be engaged at random in daily life when obstructions, tightening, and knotting are felt in the frontal line, as when distracting thoughts or emotions arise, or when the head feels empty of energy, or when the body feels enervated.

This practice should be engaged—in relation to the etheric (or pranic) energy-field—from the beginning of the student-beginner stage of the Way of Adidam. And this practice (continued beyond the student-beginner stage) becomes an exercise in conducting Avatar Adi Da's Divine Spirit-Current once the practitioner has been Spiritually Initiated by Avatar Adi Da Samraj into the primary practice of searchlessly Beholding Him.

128. The "general" (or not specifically Spiritual) form of breathing-"conductivity" practice (which is the form practiced by all practitioners of the Way of Adidam, beginning in the student-beginner stage) is Described by Avatar Adi Da Samraj in Sutra 36.

SUTRA 36

129. Avatar Adi Da has Given the practice of lung-breathing "conductivity" described in this section of the Text to practitioners in the Way of the Heart as a means to revitalize or rebalance the entire body-mind, when one is ill, or devitalized, or generally enervated. Sometimes such enervation, illness, or imbalance may be such that an individual's bodily state can be characterized as being "hot-headed" and "cold-footed". This is the reverse of the natural bodily condition, in which the feet (and generally, the vital region of the body) are warm, and the head is cool.

130. In the practice of frontal (or descending) lung-breathing "conductivity" Given by Avatar Adi Da, the practitioner of the Way of Adidam directs the natural bodily energy (and, as the case may be, Avatar Adi Da's Avatarically Self-Transmitted Divine Spirit-Current), via the cycles of both inhalation and exhalation of the breath, to the bodily "battery". Then, gradually relaxing the tension in the bodily base during the exhalation-release cycle of the breath, he or she releases and radiates the natural bodily energy (and, as the case may be, Avatar Adi Da's Avatarically Self-Transmitted Divine Spirit-Current) from the bodily "battery", via the legs, and into the soles of the feet, fully relaxing the bodily base as the energy begins to concentrate in the soles of the feet (and never beyond the soles of the feet, into the ground). When the cycle of exhalation is complete, there should be a general diffuse radiation of natural bodily energy (and, as the case may be, Avatar Adi Da's Avatarically Self-Transmitted Divine Spirit-Current) to and via the whole body, and a general revitalization and rebalancing of the entire body-mind.

SUTRA 37

131. Avatar Adi Da has indicated that the bypassing or conversion of degenerative (or conventional) orgasm, in both the male and the female, involves no suppression or avoidance of the intensification of sexual energy.

SUTRA 38

132. See note 121.

133. Avatar Adi Da indicates in this passage practices that promote prostate health based on physical and Yogic principles—many of which have been understood and practiced for thousands of years in various cultures. One source, for example, is *The Tao of Sexology: The Book of Infinite Wisdom,* by Dr. Stephan T. Chang (San Francisco, Calif.: Tao Publishing, 1986). For Avatar Adi Da's full description of the practice of upward tensing, see Sutra 36. Relative to "Regular internal finger-pressing and massaging of the prostate gland itself", this can be done by a man himself, or by his intimate partner (if he so chooses). Relative to "Regular washing and cleansing of the anal canal", Avatar Adi Da Samraj has often recommended the use of bidets and other means of anal cleansing as a Yogic matter of health.

AVATAR ADI DA SAMRAJ: You must be very much involved in this eliminative function. It is a positive process, a Yogic process—without any shame and humiliation. You must use appropriate cleansing techniques. You do such things regularly when you fast. You take enemas and colonics, use a colema board, and so on. If you have a bidet, you can regularly wash the rectum in that manner. Use of a bidet functions as a kind of "lower enema", moving more of the no-longer-useful material out of the body. This can be done even several times a day. Even if you don't have a bidet, you can oblige the body to do the same thing. The manipulation of the anus stimulates the evacuation inclination of the body. Water (preferably warm) can be forced up into the rectum to wash it out. Keep the lower bowel clean and the rectum clean. It is absolutely essential for health, if you are a Yogi (male or female).

—March 15, 1995

The details of right diet are described in Sutra 28 and in section VII of "The ego-'I' is the Illusion of Relatedness" in *Santosha Adidam*. And general physical "conscious exercise" is described in detail in *Conscious Exercise and the Transcendental Sun*.

134. Avatar Adi Da has indicated that, after an occasion of effectively practicing either "emotional-sexual conscious exercise" or "emotional-sexual devotional Communion", male practitioners may notice a few drops of a relatively thick, clear fluid eliminated with the urine. The secretion of this prostate fluid is stimulated during the practice of "emotional-sexual conscious exercise" or "emotional-sexual devotional Communion"—and, in general, there is no reason to be concerned about eliminating occasional, small quantities of this clear fluid with the urine, as this does not suggest that the bypass of degenerative orgasm and practice of regenerative orgasm has not been effective. However, if the amount of fluid eliminated is significant, or if it has any milky coloration whatsoever, that is an indication that the bypass of orgasm has not been complete enough. In that case, the practice of "emotional-sexual conscious exercise" and "emotional-sexual devotional Communion" (particularly the bypass of ejaculation) must be improved.

Male practitioners of either "emotional-sexual conscious exercise" or "emotional-sexual devotional Communion" should, if at all possible, avoid urination during the period immediately following sexual intercourse. The reason for this is that urination can siphon out ejaculatory fluid, even though it was retained during sexual intercourse itself. Therefore, optimally, male practitioners should not urinate for fifteen minutes (or even up to one-half hour) after sexual intercourse.

Optimally, there should be no elimination of even a small amount of prostate fluid as a result of the practice of "emotional-sexual conscious exercise" or "emotional-sexual devotional Communion". Thus, every male practitioner of "emotional-sexual conscious exercise" or "emotional-sexual devotional Communion" should improve his practice of emotional-sexual Yoga to the point that there is no elimination of even clear prostate fluid.

It is also possible for prostate fluid to appear during an occasion of sexual intercourse and be observed at the tip of the penis during any moment of withdrawal. This indicates that the sexual process is ceasing to be conservative and, therefore, that sexual activity should be brought to an end so that no further secretion of prostate fluid is stimulated.

Practitioners of the Way of Adidam who are (in their intimate personal contexts) sexually active should understand that, even though the practice is to bypass degenerative (and, thus, ejaculatory) orgasm, they should always use appropriate contraceptive techniques, taking all necessary precautions to prevent unwanted pregnancy. Appropriate contraceptive measures include the use of diaphragms, condoms, contraceptive jelly, and avoiding sexual intercourse during the woman's fertile cycle—or a combination of any of the above. Methods of birth control such as "the pill", IUDs, tubal ligation, and vasectomy are not appropriate—since they interfere with the "conductivity" of natural life-energy (as well as Spirit-Energy) in the body-mind.

135. Avatar Adi Da's Description of the characteristics of those who are <u>truly</u> qualified for a right Yogic emotional-sexual sadhana and those who are <u>uniquely</u> qualified for a right Yogic emotional-sexual sadhana is Given in Sutra 41, pp. 770–74.

SUTRA 39

136. Every individual human body-mind is either physiologically male or physiologically female, and potentially polarized to either the opposite or the same kind of body-mind (or body-energy) in others. This commonly leads to the search for "union" outside of the individual body-mind, for coupling with an "other" who complements one's own energy, thereby achieving a sense of fullness.

However, Avatar Adi Da has also Revealed that each individual body-mind is "inherently bi-polar", or inherently complete. In the Yogic practice of "conductivity" in the Way of Adidam, one discovers that the body-mind contains both masculine and feminine aspects of energy. As Avatar Adi Da explains in Sutra 39 (pp. 732–33), the stimulated genital energy can be said to be "yang" (or masculine) and the interior root of the genitals can be said to be "yin" (or feminine).

Therefore, Avatar Adi Da Calls all His devotees to realize and practice on the basis of the inherent bi-polar unity of the individual body-mind.

137. For Avatar Adi Da's Instruction on the basic physical and internal Yogic exercises of emotional-sexual "conscious exercise" and emotional-sexual "devotional Communion" which are otherwise to be applied in the practice of "own-body sexual Yoga", see Sutras 37 and 38.

138. The "Shaktichalana Mudra" is a Yogic practice, generally kept secret in the Yogic traditions, in which the celibate practitioner manually stimulates his or her genitals (possibly even for many hours per day), without allowing degenerative orgasm, and with the aim of arousing the Kundalini Shakti at the bodily base and magnifying its upward "conductivity" in the spinal line of the body-mind. The (rare) descriptions of this practice in traditional literature are veiled and inexplicit, but "Shaktichalana Mudra" remains part of the living practice of certain schools of esoteric Yoga. The understanding underlying the own-body Yogic sexual practice Given to His devotees by Avatar Adi Da is different from the understanding underlying the traditional practice of "Shaktichalana Mudra"—the traditional practice is based on an incomplete view of esoteric anatomy and on the intentional search for Liberation via the arousal of the Kundalini Shakti, whereas devotees of Avatar Adi Da engage the practice as a means to establish and magnify the inherent bi-polar integrity of the individual body-mind (in accordance with Avatar Adi Da's complete Wisdom-Teaching relative to esoteric anatomy) and as an aspect of the practice of Ruchira Avatara Bhakti Yoga, in which all forms of the search are consistently observed, understood, and transcended. However, the own-body Yogic sexual practice in the Way of Adidam is to be embraced with the same seriousness and the same exclusively Yogic purposes as the traditional practice of "Shaktichalana Mudra".

139. In the own-body Yogic sexual practice, if any male or female practitioner of the Way of Adidam so desires, he or she may also use a dildo anally.

140. Avatar Adi Da has further Described one particular mode in which the "Static Mudra" may tend to occur:

AVATAR ADI DA SAMRAJ: The fundamental event associated with emotional-sexual devotional Communion is Yogic, associated (generally speaking) with deeply penetrating intercourse. This fundamental event is a Yogic mudra in sexual embrace, but it is not necessarily entirely static. There can be interaction, movement, and so forth. However, the event can become static at some point, an event in which deep penetration is maintained—for example, the man pressing into the woman and simply holding that pressure, not moving in and out. Penetration is occurring, but there are no physical movements associated with it. A period of time might be spent simply in that attitude, without significant movement.

Such deep penetration is a process of feeling-energy, feeling-Communion. Thus, sensitivity to energy in deeply penetrating intercourse can become—certainly at times, or (otherwise) after a prolonged period of engaging sexual intercourse—simply this static embrace, with the pressure of the deep penetration maintained, such that the Yogic condition associated with the energy is continued.

The essence of the sex act is this Yogic condition—which is very much associated with the sexual practice, but continues even after the specific sexual practice stops. Right sexual Yoga is not something to be done merely to the point of regenerative orgasm, and then you stop it and turn it off. Ultimately, "right emotional-sexual Yoga" is a condition—just as right meditation is a condition. It is, essentially, one and the same condition that is cultivated in the Communion Hall and through the practice of "right emotional-sexual Yoga". Indeed, that Yogic condition is to be realized and perpetuated under all conditions, brought into all aspects of life. All of the integrity, all of the fullness, must be the case, in Yogic terms—such that you are (altogether) psycho-physically transformed by your participation in the sacred life, rather than psycho-physically degraded by the "school of hard knocks" of ordinary daily life.

—March 27, 1998

SUTRA 42

141. In the Way of Adidam, individuals are served from infancy to develop a positive, non-problematic relationship to life, to their own bodies, and to sexuality. This is the most basic practical foundation for the Spiritual capability to receive and conduct Avatar Adi Da's Avatarically Self-Transmitted Divine Spirit-Energy. All of Avatar Adi Da's Instructions on serving children and young people are oriented toward the adaptation to all bodily and mental functions that ultimately serves the capability to transcend body and mind in feeling-Contemplation of Him.

Very young children in the first stage of life are simply helped to adapt to bodily life in a natural way, and they are not subject to taboos or punishment relative to exploration of their own or others' bodies. However, Avatar Adi Da points out, "The kinds of activities that should occupy children are not those that emphasize obsession with their own self-touching and self-sense. . . . The child's bodily life with others should be very ordinary. And that ordinariness will make them less self-obsessed."

In the second stage of life, beginning at around age seven, girls and boys are generally segregated in the cultures of their own sex, where, throughout the third stage of life and as adult practitioners of the Way of Adidam, they will continue to spend significant time. In the second stage of life, children "are able to come freely alive as vital beings", while, at the same time, they are required to develop sensitivity to others' feelings and requirements.

In the third stage of life, young people in the Way of Adidam are guided in their understanding of their sexuality and the recommended practice relative to sexuality, which is to maintain celibacy until at least age 18. The recommendation of celibacy for young people in the third stage of life is based on human and Spiritual realities—the hormones present in the body at this time tend to stimulate strong sexual impulses, but the primary function of such hormones in the teenage years is to serve human physical development and growth needed for full capability as an adult.

As a counter to the typical tendency to live the "secret life" of adolescence, young people in the Way of Adidam are called upon to be entirely honest and confessed relative to everything that arises in body and mind relative to sexuality. On that basis, they are called to develop the capability to transcend body and mind through the exercise of Ruchira Avatara Bhakti Yoga.

Avatar Adi Da has Instructed His young devotees:

You must develop the functional capability of the will. This must be intensified and developed. You must exercise discrimination and the ability to maintain active intelligence, such that you are able to make right decisions in the face of the tendencies of the body that are often difficult.

—May 21, 1991

142. Avatar Adi Da Samraj Writes in section VII of "The ego-'I' Is the Illusion of Relatedness" (in *Santosha Adidam*), relative to circumstances under which it may be appropriate for a single celibate practitioner to have a private dwelling place:

Thus, typically—although formally acknowledged single celibates should (in general) live and serve in daily cooperative association with other formally acknowledged single celibates (and even all others of My fully practicing devotees) of both sexes—every formally acknowledged single celibate should share daily living quarters (and daily sleeping quarters) with other formally acknowledged single celibates who are members only of their same sex (although, in cases, or at times, of unique developmental demonstration, and the capability for making a uniquely effective use of solitude—or, otherwise, in the case, possibly, of homosexual single celibates—a private room, or a private dwelling place, may be appropriate).

SUTRA 43

143. In addition to Instructing His devotees to make formal use of mala japa in the meditative setting, Avatar Adi Da has also Instructed that mala japa is to be used throughout the day for random recitation of His Principal Name, "Da" (or any of the other Names He has Given for the practice of simple Name-Invocation of Him). Additionally, He has indicated that His devotees

may simply hold the mala in their hands as a way to focus attention in feeling-Contemplation of Him, even in the midst of activities that do not otherwise allow one to enter deeply into meditative feeling-Contemplation of Him.

144. "Yajna", a Sanskrit word that literally means "sacrifice", also connotes the bodily action of self-surrender. Hence its synonymous use here with "Puja" to describe the sacramental bodily exercise of mala japa.

145. Avatar Adi Da's House is, to His devotees, the most sacred of Temples, because It is the Place where the Divine Avatar Bodily Resides. Thus, circumambulation of Avatar Adi Da's House (at any of the Ruchira Sannyasin Hermitage Ashrams) is a right and potent form of worshipping Him.

SUTRA 44

146. These three character types correspond to the first three of the four principal faculties (body, emotion, and mind), and also to the three principal divisions of the human body (the region of the navel and solar plexus, the region of the heart, and the region of the head).

147. In one of His earliest Discourses to practitioners of the Way of Adidam, Avatar Adi Da used the phrase "vital shock" to describe the primal recoil of every individual from the experience of being born—and, throughout the course of egoic life, from the vulnerable condition of bodily existence and of relationship itself. (See "Vital Shock" in *The Divine Siddha-Method Of The Ruchira Avatar*.)

SUTRA 45

148. In 1960 (ten years before the Great Event of His Divine Re-Awakening), Avatar Adi Da Samraj experienced a particularly dramatic and significant "Spontaneous Experience Of Spiritual Regeneration" during His junior year at Columbia College. (See chapter 3 of *The Knee Of Listening*.)

149. Here Avatar Adi Da is referring to Rudi (Albert Rudolph, or Swami Rudrananda), who was His first human Teacher, from 1964 to 1968. Rudi principally Transmitted the descending aspect of the Spirit-Current, and the Yoga he Taught focused on the effort to surrender ever more deeply, and thus more profoundly, in order to purify and strengthen the frontal line of the body-mind. (See chapters 7–9 of *The Knee Of Listening*.)

SUTRA 47

150. See glossary entry for **Anatomy, Hierarchical Structural**.

SUTRA 48

151. Avatar Adi Da Speaks of trees (the very plant-form itself) as representing the primal structural form of all beings now living and moving about the Earth. Avatar Adi Da points out that "moving" beings—such as humans, animals, birds, reptiles, insects, fish, and other creatures—still embody the basic tree structure in their physical forms, in terms of the skeleton and the central nervous system. Even though these basic structures have been variously adapted in different species, the tree structure still represents the root-system of the physical form.

AVATAR ADI DA SAMRAJ: The plant form, or the plant structure, is the basic form that all other forms share. You can observe the tree in the midst of the human body. The root of the human body is (so to speak) a plant. The trees became humankind and every other kind of being. Mysteriously, this is so. The plant is the fundamental structure—you see the same structure in the tree (and, fundamentally, in any form of vegetation). Even all the other beings that actually move from their position—not just move in the sense of growing, which even trees do—have this rooted, balanced, tree-process at the core. But that core tends to be forgotten in all this moving, confrontation, and memory. . . .

The tree, the vegetation, is the origin of the form with which you are identifying. It is interesting to notice that the evolutionary accountings for organism life (which accountings are based on scientific materialistic "considerations") show how "this became that", "that became that", and "that became the human, after all that time"—but those accountings do not show any trees or plant-forms at the beginning of the process. It is as if scientists have not even "considered" this yet. Their descriptions are only about independently "moving" life-forms such as human beings.

It is a kind of conceit to presume that the evolutionary origin of Man must (itself) be like Man. You tend to presume that that origin could not possibly be anything else. You can handle having received some level of inheritance through the animals, including the apes, and even down to the tiny amoeba, perhaps—because they are all some sort of independently moving "individuals". But you cannot see the "tree" in them anymore. You cannot accept that the source of human functioning and awareness could be trees, plant-forms. And, ultimately, even the trees come from something that falls out of the sky. Everything that falls or moves or seems in this conditional domain is made of starred substance. Every cell in your body was originally star material—every fraction of your physical appearance.

—April 28, 1996

Avatar Adi Da also points out that trees and plants are natural contemplatives, living and breathing altogether within the sphere of Communion with the Divine in every moment. This, He says, is the true nature of their pattern of existence, and of their potential example to human beings. He uses the metaphor of the tree to Call human beings beyond the daily experience of the "seeming" (or merely physical) world—to reach and flower and grow into the Divine Light and Truth That Is the Real Divine Self-Condition of all apparently independent beings and things.

SUTRA 56

152. Avatar Adi Da has Said that if "Feeling-Enquiry" is to be effective, it must be engaged in a meditative setting for a significant number of hours (not just a few minutes, or even a few hours) every day, and that this practice also requires a full life of renunciation as a formal member of one of the renunciate orders of Adidam.

Practitioners of the Way of Adidam who use "Feeling-Enquiry" both in meditation and daily life, additionally (and at random) engage the form (or forms) of the "conscious process" and "conductivity" that were their practice before their transition to the "Perfect Practice". These earlier practices, like the practice of "Feeling-Enquiry", are to be engaged while abiding as the Witness-Consciousness, but, unlike the principal practice of "Feeling-Enquiry", they are not practiced in meditation. They are only practiced in daily life. The purpose of these earlier practices is to "Establish (or, Otherwise, To Maintain) psycho-physical Equanimity and Participatory (Feeling) Naturalness In The ordinary psycho-physical Context Of daily living", as a counter-balance to the "Otherwise (and Random) Informal Introduction Of 'Feeling-Enquiry' (or The Work Of The 'Perfect Practice' Itself) Into The Context Of daily life." (Sutra 58)

SUTRA 58

153. "Causal stress" is a descriptive term for the suffering inherent in egoity (or the feeling of relatedness itself, or the root-activity of attention). The term "vibration" used here indicates the conditional nature of this stress. However, Avatar Adi Da's Divine Spiritual Transmission, which may also be felt to arise in the right side of the heart, is not properly to be described as "vibrating", since this term implies a dynamic play, or internal polarization, of energy that does not characterize His Divine Spirit-Current.

SUTRA 60

154. Out-of-body experiences (OOBEs), sometimes called "astral projection" or "astral travel", are a universal human phenomenon. They have been experienced in every time and culture, though they have tended to remain an esoteric or hidden subject in many societies, especially the post-industrial West. Typically, during an OOBE, the individual continues to experience his

or her ordinary state of awareness, but from a point or points outside the physical body. A common feature of the initial moments of an OOBE is that the person notices he or she is floating near the ceiling, or above his or her physical body, and looking down on it. Many people experience the sensation of inhabiting a second, non-physical body (known as the "astral body", which is the energic duplicate of the physical body, and which may also be the double seen in phenomena of bodily bilocation). The second body is usually garbed in familiar clothing and is generally unable to exert any influence on the physical world. That body is, in general, even unable to be physically seen, heard, or felt by physically incarnate others. Events witnessed during OOBEs have in some cases been documented as accurate perceptions in scientific experiments.

155. The color plate is an artist's rendering of the Cosmic Mandala. The actual vision of the Cosmic Mandala is a living, spherical light-form, and it is therefore impossible to duplicate graphically with complete exactness. The illustration gives an impression of the rings of color, their concentric order, and their relationship to the central brilliant white Star.

SUTRA 61

156. The Ordeal of ego-death to which Avatar Adi Da refers here occurred in the spring of 1967, while He was attending a Christian seminary at the behest of His first human Teacher, Rudi. (See chapter 9 of *The Knee Of Listening*.)

157. Avatar Adi Da's experience of Priorly Ascended Nirvikalpa Samadhi occurred on His first trip to India in 1968. (See chapter 10 of *The Knee Of Listening*.)

For a summary description of the difference between Priorily Ascended Nirvikalpa Samadhi and conditionally Ascended Nirvikalpa Samadhi, see the glossary entry for **Samadhi**.

158. The first of the three Great Siddhas was Swami Muktananda (1908–1982), whose Company and touch were directly associated with Avatar Adi Da's Realization of Priorly Ascended Nirvikalpa Samadhi in the Event Adi Da describes in this passage. The second was Rang Avadhoot (1898–1968), whose brief glance immediately preceded Avatar Adi Da's "Recollection" of His own Divine State via Priorly Ascended Nirvikalpa Samadhi. The third was the then physically deceased but still Spiritually active Bhagavan Nityananda (1897?–1961), who, even after Avatar Adi Da's Realization of Priorly Ascended Nirvikalpa Samadhi on this occasion, continued (by direct Spiritual visitations) to direct Avatar Adi Da further in His "Sadhana".

159. Avatar Adi Da has described "Cosmic Consciousness" as the highest form of Savikalpa Samadhi—in which bodily (or at least psycho-sensual) awareness remains intact and operating, but psycho-physical (or cosmic) existence is otherwise (or simultaneously) perceived in Consciousness as an Infinite Unity. The breakthroughs of "Cosmic Consciousness" during Avatar Adi Da's young adulthood, childhood, and infancy are described in *The Knee Of Listening*.

160. Avatar Adi Da is referring to an Event that occurred in 1960, when He was attending Columbia College, and after He had exhaustively embraced all kinds of bodily and mental experiences in a desperate quest for Truth. Following this penetration of the body-mind by "Cosmic Consciousness" (which involved a Spiritual Regeneration associated in this particular instance with the Process of the "Thumbs", and also with a "glimpse" of the Divinely Awakened State), Avatar Adi Da understood that the certainty of Truth He desired was discoverable not by seeking but by removing obstructions that prevented its present Realization. He now knew that the Divine Reality is "always already the case", prior to seeking and dilemma. (See chapter 3 of *The Knee Of Listening*.)

161. In the esoteric Yogic traditions of India, the Sanskrit word "bindu" (literally, "drop", or "point") refers to a point without spatial or temporal dimension, in which all manifested forms, energies, and universes are ultimately coalesced or expressed. Here Avatar Adi Da uses the term to describe the passage into the Unconditional Matrix, or Uncreated Source-Light, out of which "descend" the multitudinous phenomena of conditional existence.

162. As Avatar Adi Da indicates here, out-of-body experiences are forms of non-physical embodiment that are nevertheless accompanied by ordinary mental functions. Thus, they are clearly distinguishable from conditionally ascended Nirvikalpa Samadhi (and Priorly Ascended Nirvikalpa Samadhi), in which body and mind are utterly transcended in the extreme ascent and absorption of attention into the formless Spirit-Matrix of Love-Bliss, beyond all psycho-physical functions and awareness.

SUTRA 63

163. Typically, "natural" means conforming to laws within (or expressive of) cosmic Nature. The term is even specifically used as an antonym of anything Spiritual, Transcendental, Divine, miraculous, supersensuous, or extraordinary. Avatar Adi Da uses it here with a contrasting (but, nonetheless, principal and "radical") meaning: "having an essential relationship with someone or something; consonant with the nature or character of someone or something". The "Naturalness" of seventh stage Sahaja Nirvikalpa Samadhi is that it is entirely Free, unforced, and effortless, consonant with the Nature of Being Itself (Which is Self-Existing, Self-Radiant, and Always Already the Case). Seventh stage Sahaja Nirvikalpa Samadhi stands in contrast with conditionally Ascended Nirvikalpa Samadhi and conditionally Self-Abiding Jnana Nirvikalpa Samadhi—both of which are "un-Natural" in the sense that they depend upon a strategic effort of the "un-Natural" self-contraction (either to ascend beyond the realms of conditionality or, otherwise, to exclude those realms from consciousness through an exclusionary process of interiorization). The Realization of Priorly Ascended Nirvikalpa Samadhi and the Realization of Priorly Self-Abiding Jnana Nirvikalpa Samadhi are both Divine Gifts from Avatar Adi Da Samraj, and (therefore) they are entirely non-strategic. However, neither of these forms of Samadhi is the Most Ultimate Samadhi—because neither (in and of itself) fully Demonstrates the Divine Self-Nature of all conditionally manifested existence. Therefore, only the seventh stage Samadhi is fully (and "radically") "Natural", in the sense Avatar Adi Da intends here.

164. What distinguishes the behavior of Avatar Adi Da's devotees in the seventh stage of life is the perfectly egoless spontaneity and Freedom of all their activity and inactivity. As Avatar Adi Da explains in ensuing passages, the behavior of such devotees will (in general) continue to manifest the conservative (and, in some cases, perhaps even apparently austere) simplicity developed during their sadhana previous to the seventh stage of life.

SUTRA 72

165. The number 72 can be understood to represent Avatar Adi Da's Revelation as the "Midnight Sun".

72 is 8 x 9, which further breaks down to (2 x 2 x 2) x (3 x 3).

8 can be understood to represent the "black cube" of conditional existence, since the cube is defined by eight corners. 8 (or 2 x 2 x 2) is also "pure 2", representing the ego-principle of duality underlying all of un-Enlightened conditional existence.

3 is the number of points required to define a circle, and two 3s (understood to represent two intersecting circles in separate planes) define a sphere. In addition, 3 (the "root" of 9) represents the Unity (or Non-"Difference") of 2 (or conditional reality) and 1 (or the Divine Reality).

Thus, 8 x 9 = 72 can be understood to represent Avatar Adi Da's Transformation of the black cube of conditional existence into His "Bright" White Divine Sphere, through the process He describes in His *Dawn Horse Testament.*

EPILOGUE

166. *The Dawn Horse Testament Of The Ruchira Avatar* represents the Completion of Avatar Adi Da's Teaching-Work and Revelation-Work. This Testament is His Final and Authoritative Word. From time to time, Avatar Adi Da may choose to refine details of language or to add further Instruction on particular topics.

If Avatar Adi Da does, at some time in the future, add, modify, or remove any language in this "Source-Text", then the latest edition of *The Dawn Horse Testament Of The Ruchira Avatar* should (in any then present time) be regarded to be the current version. Ultimately, the final form of *The Dawn Horse Testament Of The Ruchira Avatar* will be the edition after the publication of which He does no such further Work with the Text at all.

167. *The Five Books Of The Heart Of The Adidam Revelation* comprise a complete summary of Who Avatar Adi Da Samraj Is and the Way that He Offers. For a listing of the "Five Books", please see p. v.

168. The "True Dawn Horse" is a reference to *The Dawn Horse Testament*. Each of *The Seventeen Companions Of The True Dawn Horse* is a "Companion" to *The Dawn Horse Testament* in the sense that it is an elaboration of a principal theme (or group of principal themes) from *The Dawn Horse Testament.* For a listing of the "Seventeen Companions", please see pp. v–vi.

169. The "Supportive Texts" of Adidam comprise Avatar Adi Da's practical Instruction in all the details of the practice of Adidam—including the fundamental disciplines of diet, health, exercise, sexuality, childrearing, cooperative culture, and conscious dying.

170. "Samrajya" is Sanskrit for "universal (*sam*) kingdom (*rajya*)". Avatar Adi Da has Said that His true "Universal Kingdom" is the domain of those who are devoted to Him, always engaged in turning the four faculties of the body-mind to Him.

AVATAR ADI DA SAMRAJ: If everyone related to Me rightly, there would be a Kingdom, a True Divine Samrajya, the Adi Da Samrajya. However many come to Me, to be Blessed by Me or to Realize Me altogether, That is My Domain, My House—My Kingdom, then. That is the nature of the gathering of My devotees.

My devotees would be Served by Me. Therefore, you must become My servants. To be My servant is not a matter of convention. It is to fulfill the practice of Ruchira Avatara Bhakti Yoga, which is itself the turning of the four leading faculties to Me, moment to moment. Fundamentally, that Yoga is the Way of Adidam. The body must serve Me. The heart must love Me, feel Me, surrender to Me. The mind must become attention for Me, moment to moment. And you must breathe Me with every breath. This simplest practice is the practice for all to begin with.

Therefore, to practice Ruchira Avatara Bhakti Yoga is to be My servant, moment to moment—always in Love-Communion with Me, Remembering Me constantly, breathing Me constantly. If all do this, it is the Adi Da Samrajya, My Divine Kingdom. However many do it, that is what the Kingdom is.

—April 8, 1996

171. Avatar Adi Da Samraj has indicated the significance of the traditional Horse-Sacrifice (or Ashvamedha) and His own Dawn Horse Vision in relation to the Avataric Divine Ordeal of His Life and Work (including the creation of *The Dawn Horse Testament*):

AVATAR ADI DA SAMRAJ: In its most esoteric form, beyond the rites of the first five stages of life, the Ashvamedha is a Revelation of the Ultimate Divine through the Sacrifice of everything conditional, and through the Realization of That Which Transcends cosmic reality. All other interpretations are also part of the total meaning of the Ashvamedha. Its meanings exist on many, many levels.

My Demonstration of this Ultimate Form of the Ashvamedha was (and is) totally Spontaneous. I Did It Spontaneously, without any information in mind. Nevertheless, you will see that study of the sacred traditions will confirm the Truth of what I am Telling you. You have seen the Divine Ashvamedha Performed in My Own Avatarically-Born bodily (human) Divine Form.

The Ultimate Form of the Ashvamedha Transmits not merely cosmic realization but Transcendental (and Inherently Spiritual) Divine Self-Realization by Means of My Avataric Divine Sacrifice. The "Horse", then, is what the Real-God-Realized Adept is altogether. The original product of the Ashvamedha in My Own Avatarically-Born bodily (human) Divine Form is

My Avatarically Self-Revealed Divine Word of Instruction, of which The Dawn Horse Testament *is a Summary. Thus, it is appropriate to call* The Dawn Horse Testament *the True "Dawn Horse".* The Dawn Horse Testament *is the Gift Given to My devotees as the result of the Ashvamedha. It Grants the Power of Realization to My devotees. It Communicates the Transmission of My Avataric Divine Blessing to every one.*

But this does not exhaust the meanings or the results of the Ashvamedha in My Own Case, nor the implications of the Dawn Horse Vision. In one of the closing paragraphs of The Dawn Horse Testament, *I Say, "As The Sign and The Result Of The 'Bright' Avataric Divine Ordeal By Which This Avataric Divine Testament Has Come To Consciousness In The Cosmic Domain, My Avataric Self-Revelation Of Divine 'Brightness' (Itself) Will Appear To every one, and all, and All." The Dawn Horse is ultimately consequential in that Realization, which takes the form of the Awakening of My individual devotee and the total gathering of My devotees in response to the initial Sign.* The Dawn Horse Testament *is something like that vaguely apparent, but nonetheless true, original Dawn Horse, Which, when It becomes solidified in Its full effect, takes the form of Revelation and Realization for those who receive It.*

The Dawn Horse is not the horse sent around the country, later to be sacrificed in the Ashvamedha ritual. The Ashvamedha is the Process of the Sacrifice, and the Dawn Horse is Its Result. The Dawn Horse is in some sense the Ash, the Prasad, that becomes apparent through the Fire of the Sacrifice. The Ashvamedha is My Own Sacrifice, My Own Work. The Dawn Horse is also Me, It is The Dawn Horse Testament, *It is anyone who comes to Realization through this Revelation. This so-called "myth" is (therefore) rather large in its significance!*

The Sacrifice has been Made. That is why there is a Testament. That is why there is a Revelation. I Am the Sign of the Completed Sacrifice. Its Fulfillment was in the Great Event at the Vedanta Temple in 1970. Many Signs of Its Fulfillment have occurred throughout the years of My Avataric Divine Spiritual Work. The Result of the Sacrifice is the Dawn Horse, Which is the Prasad, the Gift, that comes through the Sacrifice. The Dawn Horse is eternally Present, becoming more and more visible in those who will heart-recognize Me, heart-respond to Me, see the Dawn Horse, and receive the Gift of My Avataric Divine Self-Revelation.

The Dawn Horse is a new Revelation, the Result of the Ashvamedha. This Dawn Horse is not to be sacrificed, just as ash cannot be sacrificed because it is already sacrificed, and so it cannot be sacrificed again. Ash is Insubstantiality appearing concretely. It cannot be destroyed. It cannot be reduced to anything, because it has already been reduced absolutely. In that reduction, it transcended smallness, non-entityness, or non-existence. It became simply the Divine, and everything short of That was transcended, burned up, sacrificed.

Thus, the Dawn Horse Stands as My Avataric Divine Self-Revelation, the Result of My Avataric Divine Ordeal. It is a continuous, eternal Revelation. My Avataric Divine Work does not come to an end. It has proceeded since My Divine Re-Awakening in the Vedanta Temple, It proceeds now, and It cannot be brought to an end by contingencies. It is (therefore) continuously, eternally Available.

The Dawn Horse Testament *Is the true Dawn Horse in the sense that It is the Means of that Availability. But the Dawn Horse does not become fully concrete except in the reception of the Prasad, the Realization of My Avataric Divine Self-Revelation. That is why* The Dawn Horse Testament *says that as a Result of this Avataric Divine Ordeal, the Revelation will come to every one. It is a Statement of fact about the nature of My Avataric Divine Blessing, or Siddhi, Which has come about as a result of the Ordeal manifested in My Own Person from Birth and through the variety of events in My Life. That Ordeal did not come to an end in the Vedanta Temple. It was Consummated there in some fundamental sense but It was continuous. No further Sacrifice is possible or necessary.*

There is no significance in anything you could call "Sacrifice" on My part anymore. My Sacrifice is Absolute. I do not have to suffer anymore for any grand purpose. The Dawn Horse simply Stands as My Avataric Divine Self-Revelation, and you will see It concretely in your Realization.

I prefer to let My language in The Dawn Horse Testament *stand as it is, rather condensed and full of meaning, instead of exhausting it with explanations which seem to make everything clear, but which in their exhaustiveness become intolerable. In some sense, it would have been better for you to puzzle over all this. But, rather than obstruct you further, a little footnote here will be appropriate!*

—April 4, 1987

172. In this paragraph, and those following, Avatar Adi Da Reveals the esoteric significance of His Divine Appearance in this world. He Proclaims His Very Nature as the Divine Person, and the Eternal Truth of His "Emergence" as the "Living Murti", the Master of the Heart, the "Very (and Truly) Human God-Man". This Confession confirms that the deep heart-yearning of all humanity for the Appearance of the God-Man, the One Who is both fully human and Fully Divine, has been fulfilled by His own Birth, Divine Re-Awakening, and Avataric Divine Self-"Emergence". His statement that He was "Named John By Birth ('The Free Man Through Whom God Is Gracious')" acknowledges both His Birth and Revelatory Ordeal as "Franklin Jones" and His Teaching-Work, first as "Bubba Free John" and then as "Da Free John". ("Franklin Jones" literally means "a Free Man through Whom God is Gracious", and Avatar Adi Da created "Free John" as a transformation of "Franklin Jones".)

When He describes Himself as "The Divine Love-Bliss-'Brightener' Of all-and-All, The Promised Divine Intruder, The Foretold 'Bright' Foreigner, The Expected (and Eternally Un-'Familiar') Outsider, The Outcast 'Crazy'-Man, The Mleccha-Guru", He is referring to His prophesied appearance in the West, and to His Work in the "late-time" (or "dark" epoch), Revealing and Transmitting His own "Brightness" to all beings, East and West.

In the traditional India of times past, those who resided outside India were regarded—like the "untouchables" within Hindu society—to be ineligible to participate in a Spiritual Way of life. As such, the untouchables, outcasts, and so-called "barbarians" of the world, including all non-Indians, were known generally as "mlecchas" (pronounced "MLETCH-uhs"). It was assumed, in orthodox circles of Vedic Hinduism, that such beings were gradually developing from relatively inauspicious lifetimes until they might merit a birth within one of the castes of those eligible for Liberating Divine Grace under the Vedic code.

Avatar Adi Da Samraj is the Mleccha-Guru for "modern" humanity, and human beings of all ages to come. Not only is He the Divine World-Teacher in this Godless and ego-dominated age, but He Himself, by virtue of the unique circumstances of His Life and Work, is also both a "Mleccha" by birth and an Outcast even among the mlecchas of the world today, because His "Point of View" is not that of a conventional man, but that of the Divine. Yet, having been born as a so-called outcast, Avatar Adi Da is also uniquely qualified to Serve as the Mleccha-Guru, or the Guru to the mlecchas, or all those, East or West, who have been born during this "dark" age.

The designations "The Foretold 'Bright' Foreigner", "The Expected (and Eternally Un-'Familiar') Outsider", and "The Outcast 'Crazy'-Man" have various levels of meaning, but they all refer to the prophecies, found in different cultures throughout the world, of an individual who would come to restore humanity to the Truth.

Finally, as the One "Who Must Ride Invisible By Night, Sacrificing The Many-Colored Horse Of Fractured Light and Grievous Broken Appearances, and Who Is Now (and Forever Hereafter) 'Emerging' From The Folds and Measures Of Infinitely Finite Night, Riding The Flying Day-Horse Of Colorless (Unbroken) White, The Free-Winged Radiance, Immensely Shining Beyond Ash and Cloud, Immensely Filling The Indivisible Sky, Immensely Singing The Audible Dawn Of The Heart's Forever Resurrected 'Brightness', Immensely Bringing Me To all-and-All (Without Excluding any)", Avatar Adi Da is alluding to the esoteric Sacrificial Work He has Come to Accomplish. The night is a metaphor for the "dark" time, the time of global materialism and Spiritual poverty. The many-colored horse represents the conditionally manifested (gross, subtle, and causal) body-mind-self and all the first six (or egoic) stages of life, and the white horse represents the Divinely Awakened (or seventh) stage of life. Thus, in this passage, Avatar Adi Da affirms that He is the Expected One Who is here to Do Work of a purely Spiritual kind, as the One Who Liberates all beings—excluding none—in "The Heart's Forever Resurrected 'Brightness'". As such, He is Expressing His Sublime Victory in the hearts of all beings.

173. As the Sacrificial Horse described in the traditional ritual of the Ashvamedha (see glossary entry) establishes the dominion of the King, Avatar Adi Da, as the Ashvamedha-Avadhoota, has Established His Spiritual Dominion throughout the entire Cosmic Mandala, Liberating all beings in all worlds through His own Great and Always Already Accomplished Horse-Sacrifice.

174. Avatar Adi Da's "Heroic Spiritual Intervention" is of an entirely Spiritual kind. He has explicitly disavowed any association with the many exoteric, worldly interpretations of prophecies of a God-Man that call for or promise a military, warlike, aggressive, violent, or political Messiah. He has Said:

AVATAR ADI DA SAMRAJ: My Work is of a Spiritual kind. The conventional expectations of a political messiah, both in the present day and in the past, do not represent a proper understanding of the Avataric Function of My Manifestation.

In this epoch, all kinds of changes may likely appear in the world, but not through political effort on My Part or on the part of My devotees. Rather, such changes will appear through the actions of all humanity, to the degree that they receive or are sensitive to My Spiritual Influence, either directly or indirectly.

—May 9, 1990

GLOSSARY

A

Adi—Sanskrit for "first", "primordial", "source"—also "primary", "beginning". Thus, the Divine Name "Adi Da" expresses the Truth that Avatar Adi Da is the Primordial Being, the Source of all, the Original Divine Person, Da.

Adi-Buddha—The First (or Original) Enlightened One. See also **Adi.**

Adidam / Adidam Ruchiradam—When Avatar Adi Da Samraj first Gave the name "Adidam" in January 1996, He pointed out that the final "m" adds a mantric force, evoking the effect of the primal Sanskrit syllable "Om". (For Avatar Adi Da's Revelation of the most profound esoteric significance of "Om" as the Divine Sound of His own Very Being, see Sutra 46.) Simultaneously, the final "m" suggests the English word "Am" (expressing "I Am"), such that the Name "Adidam" also evokes Avatar Adi Da's Primal Self-Confession, "I Am Adi Da", or, more simply, "I Am Da" (or, in Sanskrit, "Aham Da Asmi").

A fuller form of reference to Avatar Adi Da's Divine Way is "Adidam Ruchiradam". "Ruchiradam" is a word newly coined by Avatar Adi Da, deriving from Sanskrit "Ruchira" (meaning "bright" or "radiant"). The compound reference "Adidam Ruchiradam" communicates that Adidam is the religion of devotion to Avatar Adi Da Samraj—Who Is the "Bright" Itself, and Who Gives the Realization of His Own "Bright" Self-Condition.

Adidam Samrajashram—See **Ruchira Sannyasin Hermitage Ashrams**.

Adi-Guru—The First (or Original, or Primordial) Guru. See also **Adi.**

adolescent—See **childish and adolescent strategies**.

Advaitayana Buddha—"Advaitayana" means "Non-Dual Vehicle" and "Buddha" is "Enlightened One". The Advaitayana Buddha is the Enlightened One Who has Revealed and Given the Non-Dual Vehicle.

Advaitayana Buddhism—Indicates the unique sympathetic likeness of Adidam to the traditions of Advaitism (or Advaita Vedanta) and Buddhism. In His examination of the Great Tradition, Avatar Adi Da has observed that these two traditions represent the most advanced Realizations ever attained previous to His Avataric Divine Incarnation. The primary aspiration of Buddhism is to realize freedom from the illusion of the separate individual ego-self. The primary aspiration of Advaitism (or the tradition of "Non-Dualism") is to know the Supreme Divine Self absolutely, beyond all dualities (of high and low, good and bad, and so on). Advaitayana Buddhism is the Non-Dual ("Advaita") Way ("yana", literally "vehicle") of Most Perfect Awakening ("Buddhism"). Advaitayana Buddhism is neither an outgrowth of the historical tradition of Buddhism nor of the historical tradition of Advaitism. Advaitayana Buddhism is the unique Revelation of Avatar Adi Da Samraj, which perfectly fulfills both the traditional Buddhist aspiration for absolute freedom from the bondage of the egoic self and the traditional Advaitic aspiration for absolute Identity with the Divine Self. (For Avatar Adi Da's discussion of Advaitayana Buddhism, see Sutra 3.)

Advaitayana-Guru—The Guru Who has Revealed and Given the Non-Dual Vehicle.

Advaitic—"Non-dual"—derived from Sanskrit "a" (meaning "not" or "non"), and "dvaita" (meaning "duality").

Agency / Agents—All the Means that may serve as complete Vehicles of Avatar Adi Da's Divine Grace and Awakening-Power. The Means of Agency that have been fully Established by Avatar Adi Da are His Wisdom-Teaching, His Image-Art, the Hermitage Sanctuaries that He has directly Spiritually Empowered, and the many Objects and Articles that He has directly Spiritually Empowered for the sake of His devotees' Remembrance of Him and reception of His Heart-Blessing.

Aham Da Asmi—Sanskrit phrase meaning "I (Aham) Am (Asmi) Da".

Avatar Adi Da's Avatarically Self-Revealed Divine Name, "Da" (meaning "the One Who Gives"), indicates that Avatar Adi Da Samraj is the Supreme Divine Giver, the Avataric Incarnation of the Very Divine Person.

Avatar Adi Da's Declaration "Aham Da Asmi" is what is known in the Indian tradition as a "Mahavakya", or "Great Statement". Four such Mahavakyas are found in the Upanishads (the scriptures that preserve the esoteric Teachings of ancient Indian Realizers). The most famous is "Tat tvam asi" ("That thou art", or "You are That"—in other words, there is, ultimately, no "difference" between the subjective "person", or "you", and the Divine Reality, referred to in Upanishadic language simply as "That"). The traditional Mahavakya most similar in form to Avatar Adi Da's Great Statement is "Aham Brahmāsmi" ("I am Brahman", or "I am the Divine Reality").

However, although similar in form and succinctness to the traditional Mahavakyas, "Aham Da Asmi" is fundamentally different in its import. Each of the Upanishadic Mahavakyas expresses, in a few words, the profound Realization achieved by great Realizers of the past. For example, "Aham Brahmāsmi" expresses a great individual's Realization that he or she is Identified with the Divine Reality (Brahman), and is not, in Truth, identified with his or her apparently individual body-mind. In contrast, "Aham Da Asmi"—rather than being a proclamation of a human being who has devoted his or her life most intensively to the process of Real-God-Realization and has thereby Realized the Truth to an extraordinarily profound degree—is Avatar Adi Da's Confession that He Is the Very Divine Person, Da, Who has Appeared here in His Avatarically-Born bodily (human) Divine Form, in order to Reveal Himself to all-and-All, for the sake of the Divine Liberation of all-and-All.

Thus, "Aham Da Asmi" is the Divine Mahavakya—the Self-Revelatory Great Statement Uniquely Uttered by the Divine Person.

Ajna Center / Ajna Chakra / Ajna Door—The subtle center (or chakra) which Avatar Adi Da Samraj Defines as "The Root Of The Brain Core, Between and Slightly Above and Deep Behind the brows" (Sutra 18). He has described how, "Until The Ajna Door Is Fully Opened, It Is, Effectively, The Ajna Knot" (Sutra 61), and that such opening is one prerequisite sign of transition to the third (or Divine Enlightened) stage of the "Perfect Practice", or seventh stage of life. He also describes that, in the "Perfect Practice" of the Way of Adidam, the Ajna Door is not rightly understood as a "spot" or "place", but rather as a "direction" associated with "going beyond" Contemplation of Him (always further "up and back").

all-and-All—A phrase Avatar Adi Da has created to describe the totality of conditional existence—both as the "sum of its parts" and as an undivided whole. He Defines lower-case "all" as indicating "the collected sum of all Presumed To Be Separate (or limited) beings, things, and conditions", and upper-case "All" as indicating "The All (or The Undivided Totality) Of conditional Existence As A Whole" (Sutra 1).

Amrita Nadi—Amrita Nadi is Sanskrit for "Channel (or Current, or Nerve) of Ambrosia (or Immortal Nectar)". Amrita Nadi is the ultimate "organ", or root-structure, of the body-mind, Realized as such (in Its "Regenerated" form) in the seventh stage of life in the Way of Adidam.

Avatar Adi Da Defines Amrita Nadi as "The Ultimate Yogic Form", "The 'Bright' Fullness That Stands Between The Right Side Of The Heart and The Felt Matrix Of Sound and Light (or Of Even Unheard and Unseen Radiance, or Infinitely Ascended Love-Bliss) Infinitely Above The Total Crown Of the head" (Sutra 16), and as "The Apparent Organ Of This 'Bright' Divine Awakening In the human individual" (Sutra 21). He also Reveals that "Amrita Nadi . . . Is Shaped Like The Alphabetical Letter 'S'—and My Avatarically Self-Transmitted Divine Spirit-Current Of Self-Existing and Self-Radiant Being Moves In It, Originating From (and, Yet, Never Leaving, but Always Standing In) The Right Side Of The Heart, Then Extending Itself Forward and Up the chest, Then Into (or Back Through) the throat, Then Up the back of the head, and Then Forward and Upward (Via the upper rear, and The Total Crown, Of the head) To The Matrix Infinitely Above The Total Crown Of the head" (Sutra 21).

Anahata Chakra—See **Heart / The Heart Itself / Stations Of The Heart**.

Anatomy, Hierarchical Structural—Avatar Adi Da Samraj has Revealed that just as there is a physical anatomy, there is an actual "esoteric anatomy", or hierarchical structural anatomy, that is present in every human being. As He Says in His Essay "Growing Beyond the Brain-Based Myth of Materialism", from *The Basket Of Tolerance*, it is because of this structure that the "experiential and developmental process of Growth and Realization demonstrates itself in accordance with what I have Revealed and Demonstrated to be the seven stages of life".

Avatar Adi Da's extended Instruction relative to the hierarchical structural anatomy of the human being is Given in *The Seven Stages Of Life* and *Santosha Adidam*.

The Arrow—In deep meditation, Avatar Adi Da's Avatarically Self-Transmitted Divine Spirit-Current may be felt in the form of the Arrow (which Avatar Adi Da Defines as "The breathless and Moveless, but Upwardly Polarized, Central Axis . . . Of the Cosmically-Patterned body-mind" (Sutra 17), rather than in the form of the Circle (in which the natural life-energy and, in the case of Spiritually Awakened practitioners, the Spirit-Energy are felt to circulate down the frontal line and up the spinal line).

Asana—Sanskrit for bodily "posture" or "pose". Most commonly, Avatar Adi Da uses "asana" in an extended sense of the word, which He Defines as "Total psycho-physical Attitude, or Disposition" (Sutra 5)—the attitude, orientation, posture, or feeling-disposition of the heart and the entire body-mind.

Ashvamedha—The Horse-Sacrifice, or Ashvamedha, is praised in the ancient Hindu scriptures as the most efficacious and auspicious of all the ancient Vedic ceremonial rites.

The Ashvamedha was understood and practiced in two different modes—exoteric and esoteric. Its exoteric (or conventional and outer) form was performed for the sake of sanctifying a king's reign and renewing the power of his dominion in his realm. The greatest of India's warrior-kings demonstrated their sovereignty by setting free a stallion (accompanied by warriors, magicians, and priests) to freely roam where it would for a year, at the end of which it was ceremonially sacrificed. Wherever it had roamed unchecked was then presumed to be the king's undisputed territory.

The esoteric (or mystical) performance of the Ashvamedha involved a process of Spiritual ascent (associated with the fifth stage of life). In this case, the "horse" that was sacrificed was the ego-self (in its gross and subtle dimensions), such that the fifth-stage Realizer rose to the "heavenly world" of Spiritual Illumination.

There is an account of the Ashvamedha associated with Kalki, the mythological tenth (and final) incarnation of Vishnu. It is said that, in the Kali Yuga (or the "dark" time), Kalki will incarnate for the sake of the destruction of unrighteousness, coming in the form of the white stallion to smite the Earth with his right hoof. In other accounts of the myth, Kalki is the Divine Man riding the white horse, who destroys all unrighteousness with his sword. Some of the accounts proclaim that Kalki will perform the Ashvamedha.

Avatar Adi Da's Revelation of His Unique Enactment of the <u>Divine</u> Form of the Ashvamedha is Given in Prolegomenon IV, "The True Dawn Horse <u>Is</u> the <u>Only</u> Way to Me".

Ashvamedha Buddha—Avatar Adi Da has Revealed that the ultimate significance of the Ashvamedha ritual is as a prayer-prophecy invoking the Avataric Descent of the Divine Person into the world, because it was intuitively understood that <u>only</u> the Divine Person is able to Liberate beings. Thus, the Ashvamedha Buddha is the Enlightened One Who has Submitted to be the humanly Incarnate Means for the Divine Liberation of all beings. (Avatar Adi Da's Essay on the Ashvamedha as a description and prophecy of His own Life and Work is Prolegomenon IV.)

Ashvamedha-Guru—The Guru Who is the Divine Sacrifice and (therefore) the Means for the Divine Liberation of all beings.

Ati—Sanskrit for "over", "beyond", "transcending".

Atiashrami—"Atiashrama" is Sanskrit for "beyond the ashramas". The four basic "ashramas" (or potential stages in the life of an individual) acknowledged in traditional Hindu culture (which are traditionally presumed to occur in sequence, each stage lasting approximately 25 years) are the stages of studenthood (studying everything necessary to live a right, true, and sacred life as an adult—brahmacharya), householder life (marrying, producing children, and engaging a life of productive work—grihastha), forest dwelling (retiring to an isolated dwelling in the forest, together with one's wife or husband, in order to devote oneself to religious and Spiritual practices—vanaprastha), and ascetic renunciation (relinquishing all social "bonds" and responsibilities and devoting oneself exclusively to religious and Spiritual practice in the manner of an ascetic—sannyasa). Apart from this conventional point of view relative to progressing through the ashramas, in rare cases a Realizer has been acknowledged to be an atiashrami, or someone who has passed beyond the traditional ashramas. When applied to Avatar Adi Da, the descriptive Title "Atiashrami" indicates His Most Perfect Transcendence of all conventional religious and Spiritual points of view and modes of life, in the Most Perfect Freedom of the seventh stage of life.

Ati-Buddha—The Ultimate (or Highest, or Unsurpassed) Enlightened One.

Ati-Guru—The Ultimate (or Highest, or Unsurpassed) Guru.

Ati-Ruchira Yoga—"Ati-Ruchira Yoga", or "the Yoga of the All-Outshining 'Brightness'", is Avatar Adi Da's term for "Practice" in the context of the seventh stage of life in the Way of Adidam, Which He Defines as the "Yoga Of Self-Abiding Divine Self-Recognition" (Sutra 64). From Sanskrit "ruchira", meaning "bright", or "brightness", and "ati", meaning "beyond", or "all-surpassing".

"Atma-Murti"—A term newly coined by Avatar Adi Da, using traditional Sanskrit elements. "Atma" indicates both the individual self (as arising in the Divine Self) and the Divine Self (Itself), and "Murti" means "Form". "Atma-Murti" literally means "the Form That Is the (Very) Divine Self". Avatar Adi Da uses the term "Atma-Murti" to refer to Himself as the Very Divine Self (or Self-Condition) of all-and-All, "Located" (by His devotee) as the Feeling of Being (Itself).

In *The Dawn Horse Testament*, Avatar Adi Da Defines "Atma-Murti" as "The Inherently egoless, and Self-Evidently Divine, Person Of Reality and Truth—In <u>Place</u>, <u>As</u> Inherent, Non-Dual, Self-Existing, and Spiritually Self-Radiant Self-Condition, Rather Than As <u>Exclusively</u> Objective Other" (Sutra 72).

This term is placed in quotation marks to indicate that Avatar Adi Da uses it with the specific technical meaning described here.

Avabhasa—A Name for Avatar Adi Da, from the Sanskrit meaning "brightness", "splendor", "luster", "light". It is, thus, synonymous with the English term "the 'Bright'", which Avatar Adi Da has used since His boyhood to describe the Blissfully Self-Luminous Divine Being Which He Knew even then as the Divine Reality of His own Being and of all beings, things, and worlds.

Avadhoot / Avadhoota—Avadhoot is a traditional term for one who has "shaken off" or "passed beyond" all worldly attachments and cares, including all motives of detachment (or conventional and other-worldly renunciation), all conventional notions of life and religion, and all seeking for "answers" or "solutions" in the form of conditional experience or conditional knowledge. Therefore, the Title "Avadhoota" indicates the Inherently Perfect Freedom of the One Who knows His Identity with the Divine Person and Who thus "Always Already" Stands Free of the binding and deluding power of conditional existence.

Avatar—From Sanskrit "avatara", a traditional term for a Divine Incarnation. It literally means "One who is descended, or 'crossed down' (from, and as, the Divine)". Avatar Adi Da Samraj Confesses that, simultaneous with His human Birth, He has Incarnated in every world, at every level of the cosmic domain, as the Eternal Giver of Divine Help and Divine Grace and Divine Liberation to all beings—and that, even though His bodily (human) Lifetime is necessarily limited in duration, His Spiritual Incarnation in the cosmic domain is Eternal.

Avataric Divine Self-"Emergence"—On January 11, 1986, Avatar Adi Da passed through a profound Yogic Swoon, Which He later described as the Yogic Establishment of His Avataric Divine Self-"Emergence". Avatar Adi Da's Avataric Divine Self-"Emergence" is an ongoing Process in which His Avatarically-Born bodily (human) Divine Form has been (and is ever more profoundly and potently being) conformed to Himself, the Very Divine Person, such that His bodily (human) Form is now (and forever hereafter) an utterly Unobstructed Sign and Agent of His own Divine Being. For Avatar Adi Da's extended Description of His Avataric Divine Self-"Emergence", see Part Three of *The Knee Of Listening*.

Avataric Incarnation—The Divinely Descended Embodiment of the Divine Person. The reference "Avataric Incarnation" indicates that Avatar Adi Da Samraj fulfills both the traditional expectation of the East, that the True God-Man is an Avatar (or an utterly Divine "Descent" of Real God in conditionally manifested form), and the traditional expectation of the West, that the True God-Man is an Incarnation (or an utterly human Embodiment of Real God).

The Avataric Pan-Communion Of Adidam—The sacred cooperative cultural gathering and global mission of Avatar Adi Da's devotees—dedicated to providing services for all members of Adidam, and to making the True World-Religion of Adidam available to all beings.

The Avataric Ruchirasala Of Adidam—The organization dedicated to preserving and providing right access to the Sacred Treasures of the Way of Adidam—Avatar Adi Da's Written and Spoken Word, His Image-Art, the sacred history of His Avataric Divine Spiritual Work and the historic artifacts associated with that Work, the Hermitage Ashrams directly Spiritually Empowered by Him, and the libraries and art collections assembled under His Guidance.

"Ruchirasala", in Sanskrit, means "bright house".

The Avataric Samrajya Of Adidam—The organization dedicated to serving, and providing right access to, Avatar Adi Da's physical human Form (during His Avataric physical human Lifetime) and the Ruchira Sannyasin Order (both during and after His Avataric physical human Lifetime). The Avataric Samrajya of Adidam is responsible to provide right circumstances for Avatar Adi Da's Avataric Divine Work of Spiritual Transmission and world-Blessing and to facilitate the Ruchira Sannyasin Order's function of extending His Sacred Authority within the other organizations of Adidam.

"Samrajya", in Sanskrit, means "the realm of the Samraj (or Universal Lord)".

Avataric Self-Submission—The Gesture whereby Avatar Adi Da (initially) Embraced ordinary human existence and (subsequently) Embraced His Work of Teaching and Blessing humankind.

B

"Basic" Context Of The Fourth Stage Of Life—See Sutra 21.

Beloved—A Title of intimate respect and heart-acknowledgement.

Bhagavan—The Title "Bhagavan" is an ancient one used over the centuries for many Spiritual Realizers of India. It means "blessed" or "holy" in Sanskrit. When applied to a great Spiritual Being, "Bhagavan" is understood to mean "bountiful Lord", or "Great Lord", or "Divine Lord".

Bhakti—A Sanskrit term meaning the practice of heart-felt devotion to the Ultimate Reality or Person—a practice which has been traditionally animated through worship of Divine Images or surrender to a human Guru.

Bhava—A Sanskrit term used to refer to the enraptured feeling-swoon of Communion with the Divine.

Bindu—In the esoteric Yogic traditions of India, the Sanskrit word "bindu" (literally, "drop", or "point") refers to a point without spatial or temporal dimension, in which all manifested forms, energies, and universes are ultimately coalesced or expressed.

Blessing-Work—The profound Purpose and Activity of Avatar Adi Da's Avataric Divine Incarnation—to Spiritually Bless all beings and (ultimately) to Awaken them to His "Bright" Divine Spherical Self-Domain.

Bodhi—Sanskrit for "enlightenment", or "enlightened mind".

bodily base—A phrase Avatar Adi Da uses to refer to "The Region That Includes the genitals, the perineum, and the anus" (Sutra 18). Avatar Adi Da Reveals that both the Divine Spirit-Energy and the natural bodily energy must first descend to the bodily base through the frontal line, before it can effectively be directed into the ascending spinal course. Avatar Adi Da has also pointed out that human beings who are not yet Spiritually sensitive tend to throw off the natural bodily energy at the bodily base, and He has, therefore, Given His devotees a range of disciplines (including a number of exercises that involve intentional locking at the bodily base) which conserve life-energy by directing it into the spinal line.

bodily "Battery"—The energy center associated with the region of the navel. As such, it plays a very important role in the practice of "conductivity" in the frontal line. Avatar Adi Da describes its location as "the crown of the lower abdomen, Approximately one and one-half inches Below the umbilical scar" (Sutra 36).

In this term, the word "Battery" is placed in quotation marks to indicate that Avatar Adi Da uses it in the "so to speak" sense, making metaphorical reference to an aspect of the human psycho-physical structure with a word that (otherwise) indicates an inanimate object (the battery).

"Bond"—In *The Dawn Horse Testament*, Avatar Adi Da uses the word "Bond" in two different senses: (1) as a reference to the process by which the egoic individual (already presuming separateness, and, therefore, bondage to the separate self) attaches itself karmically to the world of others and things through the constant search for self-fulfillment; and (2) as a reference to the process of His devotee's devotional "Bonding" to Him, which process is the Great Means for transcending all forms of limited (or karmic) "Bonding". The distinction between the two meanings of "Bond" is always made clear by the surrounding context—for example, "egoic 'Bonding'" versus "'Bonding' To Me".

The term is placed in quotation marks to indicate that it is used by Avatar Adi Da in the two particular senses described here.

"Bright"—By the word "Bright" (and its variations, such as "Brightness"), Avatar Adi Da refers to the Self-Existing and Self-Radiant Divine Reality that He has Revealed since His Birth. Avatar Adi Da Named His own Divine Self-Condition "the 'Bright'" in His Infancy, as soon as He acquired the capability of language. This term is placed in quotation marks to indicate that Avatar Adi Da uses it with the specific meaning described here.

Buddha—Just as the traditional term "Avatar", when rightly understood, is an appropriate Reference to Avatar Adi Da Samraj, so is the traditional term "Buddha". He is the Divine Buddha, the One Who Is Most Perfectly Self-Enlightened and Eternally Awake.

Buddha-Avatar—The Divine Person, having "Crossed Down", and Appearing as the Supremely Enlightened One. This Title indicates Avatar Adi Da's Encompassing and Surpassing of the traditions of Buddhism (as a whole) and Hinduism (in particular, the school of Advaita Vedanta)—the two traditions within the collective Great Tradition of mankind that He has acknowledged as representing the highest degree of Realization known previous to His Appearance and His Revelation of the Way of Adidam. (For Avatar Adi Da's Discussion of the unique position of Buddhism and Advaita Vedanta within the Great Tradition, see *The Seven Stages Of Life*, "'God'-Talk, Real-God-Realization, and Most Perfect Divine Awakening".)

buddhi—Sanskrit for "intelligence", "intellect", or "mind".

C

Callings—See **Gifts, Callings, and Disciplines**.

"case"—Avatar Adi Da Samraj uses the term "case" to refer to whatever an individual presumes to be his or her "problem"—in all its details. This term is placed in quotation marks to indicate that it is used by Avatar Adi Da in the specific (colloquial) sense described here.

causal—See **gross, subtle, causal**.

"causal Knot" / "causal Stress"—The "original egoic contraction, the natural vibration inherently associated with conditional 'I'-feeling (or the feeling of relatedness), and also naturally associated with the right side of the heart" (*Santosha Adidam*, "The ego-'I' Is the Illusion of Relatedness"). These terms are placed in quotation marks to indicate that Avatar Adi Da uses them with the specific technical meaning described here.

childish and adolescent strategies—Avatar Adi Da uses the terms "childish" and "adolescent" with precise meanings in His Wisdom-Teaching. He points out that human beings are always tending to animate one of two fundamental life-strategies—the childish strategy (to be dependent, weak, seeking to be consoled by parent-figures and a parent-"God") and the adolescent strategy (to be independent—or, otherwise, torn between independence and dependence—rebellious, unfeeling, self-absorbed, and doubting or resisting the idea of God or any power greater than oneself). Until these two strategies are understood and transcended, they not only diminish love in ordinary human relations, but they also limit religious and Spiritual growth.

Circle—The Circle is a primary pathway of natural life-energy and the Divine Spirit-Energy through the body-mind. It is composed of two arcs: the descending Current, which flows through the frontal line (down the front of the body, from the crown of the head, and Infinitely Above, to the bodily base), and which corresponds to the gross dimension of the body-mind; and the ascending Current, which flows through the spinal line (up the back of the body, from the bodily base to the crown of the head, and Infinitely Above), and which corresponds to the subtle dimension of the body-mind.

conditional—Depending on conditions—in other words, temporary and changing. The "Unconditional", in contrast, is the Divine, or That Which Is Eternal, Always Already the Case—because It Is utterly Free of dependence on any conditions whatsoever.

conditionally ascended Nirvikalpa Samadhi—See **Samadhi**.

conditionally Self-Abiding Jnana Nirvikalpa Samadhi—See **Samadhi**.

"Conductivity"—Avatar Adi Da's technical term for participation in (and responsibility for) the movement of natural bodily energies (and, when one is Spiritually Awakened by Him, for the movement of His Divine Spirit-Current of Love-Bliss in Its natural course of association with the body-mind), via intentional exercises of feeling and breathing. In *The Dawn Horse Testament,* Avatar Adi Da Defines "conductivity" as "The Whole bodily (physical, emotional, and mental) 'Conscious Exercise' Of breath, bodily energy, and (In Due Course) My Avatarically Self-Transmitted Divine Spirit-Force" (Sutra 3—punctuation adjusted).

Avatar Adi Da's principal Instruction relative to "general conductivity" is Given in Sutra 36.

Avatar Adi Da has also Given confidential Instruction in a "radical" form of Spirit-"conductivity", a practice into which qualified devotees (necessarily practicing in the context of the second stage of the "Perfect Practice") are directly and confidentially initiated by the Ruchira Sannyasin Order.

The term "conductivity" is placed in quotation marks to indicate that Avatar Adi Da uses it with the specific technical meaning described here.

Congregations Of Adidam—There are four modes or "congregations" of formal association with Avatar Adi Da Samraj and the Way of Adidam, making it possible for anyone to participate in honoring and worshipping His Appearance. The total practice of the Way of Adidam, as described by Avatar Adi Da in *The Dawn Horse Testament,* is engaged only by those in the first and second congregations, which Avatar Adi Da calls the congregations of His "formally practicing devotees" (or "formally acknowledged devotees"). The first congregation is comprised of Avatar Adi Da's legally renunciate devotees, who are members of the Ruchira Sannyasin Order of Adidam Ruchiradam. The second congregation is the general (or lay) gathering of His devotees (including the members of the Lay Congregationist Order of Adidam Ruchiradam and the Lay Renunciate Order of Adidam Ruchiradam). Members of the first and second congregations are vowed to engage the full range of devotional and supportive disciplines (meditation, sacramental worship, guided study, exercise, diet, emotional-sexual discipline, cooperative culture, and so on) Given by Avatar Adi Da Samraj.

"Conscious Exercise"—Avatar Adi Da's technical term for participation in and responsibility for the bodily and etheric dimensions of existence via intentional exercises of feeling and breathing. "Conscious exercise" is the coordinated exercise of attention, feeling, breath, and body in association with the natural energy of the body-mind, and (in due course) with Avatar Adi Da's Spirit-Energy. "Conscious exercise" includes many practical disciplines of posture and breathing and specific exercise routines to be engaged as daily practices in the Way of Adidam—as indicated by Avatar Adi Da's Definition of the term: "The Maintenance Of bodily Equanimity and physical Well-being Through Systematic Exercises and General bodily Practices That Conduct Natural human (and etheric) life-energy Throughout" (Sutra 28).

This term is placed in quotation marks to indicate that Avatar Adi Da uses it with the specific technical meaning described here.

"Conscious Process"—Avatar Adi Da's technical term for those practices through which the mind (or attention) is surrendered and turned about (from egoic self-involvement) to feeling-Contemplation of Him. The "conscious process" and "conductivity" practice are co-equal responsive exercises engaged by all practitioners in the Way of Adidam (both in meditation and in the context of daily life). In *The Dawn Horse Testament,* Avatar Adi Da Defines the "conscious process" as "The Devotional Surrender Of attention To Me, Such That attention Is (Thus and Thereby) Absorbed (and, Ultimately, Dissolved, or Utterly Transcended) In Me" (Sutra 18—punctuation adjusted).

This term is placed in quotation marks to indicate that Avatar Adi Da uses it with the specific technical meaning described here.

"Consider" / "Consideration"—Avatar Adi Da uses these words to refer to "a process of one-pointed (but, ultimately, thoughtless) concentration and exhaustive contemplation of a particular object, function, person, process, or condition, until the essence or ultimate obviousness of that object is clear" [*Love of the Two-Armed Form*]. (Such a process was originally described by Patanjali, in his *Yoga Sutras*, as "samyama".) This term is placed in quotation marks to indicate that Avatar Adi Da uses it with the specific technical meaning described here.

As engaged in the Way of Adidam, "consideration" is not merely an intellectual investigation. It is the participatory investment of one's whole being. If one "considers" something fully—in the context of one's practice of Ruchira Avatara Bhakti Yoga and one's study of His Wisdom-Teaching—this concentration results "in both the deepest intuition and the most practical grasp of the Lawful and Divine necessities of human existence" [*Love of the Two-Armed Form*].

"Cosmic Consciousness"—See **Samadhi**.

Cosmic Mandala—The Sanskrit word "mandala" (literally, "circle") is commonly used in the esoteric Spiritual traditions of the East to describe the hierarchical levels of cosmic existence. "Mandala" also denotes an artistic rendering of a visionary representation of the cosmos. Avatar Adi Da uses the phrase "Cosmic Mandala" as a reference to the totality of the conditionally manifested cosmos (or all worlds, forms, and beings), which (He has Revealed) can be visually perceived (and, thus, represented) as a pattern of concentric circular bands (or, more accurately, spheres) of certain distinct colors (each of a particular relative width), with a Brilliant White Five-Pointed Star at the center. See Sutra 60.

Crashing Down—Avatar Adi Da's Divine Spirit-Force "Descending Utterly, From The 'Place' Infinitely Above the body-mind and the world, Down and Most Deeply Into the body-mind and the world—Even To The Degree That the ego-'I', or self-Contraction, Is Utterly Confounded, Utterly Yielded, and Utterly Vanished In My Avatarically Self-Revealed, and Self-Evidently Divine, Person, or Self-Condition, Which Is Real God, and Truth, and Reality" (Sutra 45).

Avatar Adi Da Underscores the Primary Importance of His Crashing Down by Confessing that, "My Avataric Divine Spiritual Work (Altogether) Is My Crashing-Down Descent, At First Upon and Into My Own Avatarically-Born Bodily (Human) Divine Form, and, Thereafter (and Now, and Forever Hereafter), Upon and Into the body-minds Of My Devotees and all beings—Even (By Means Of My Divine Embrace Of each, and all, and All) To Infuse and (At Last) To Divinely Translate each, and all, and All" (Sutra 45).

"Crazy"—Avatar Adi Da has always Worked in a unique "Crazy" Manner, which, during His "Sadhana Years" and His Years of Teaching and Revelation, involved His Submission to the limited conditions of humankind, in order to reflect His devotees to themselves, and thereby Awaken self-understanding in them (relative to their individual egoic dramas, and the collective egoic dramas of human society). See Sutra 10, pp. 262–63.

This term is placed in quotation marks to indicate that Avatar Adi Da uses it with the specific meaning described here (rather than any of the more commonly accepted general meanings).

"Create" / "Creator"—Avatar Adi Da Samraj places the word "create" (and its variants) in quotation marks when He wishes to indicate the sense of "so to speak"—Communicating that, in the Indivisible Unity of Reality, any particular "thing" is not truly (but only apparently) appearing "out of nothing" or being caused to appear (or "created").

D

Da—Avatar Adi Da's Divine Name "Da" means "The One Who Gives", or "The Divine Giver". This Name was spontaneously Revealed to Avatar Adi Da as His Principal Divine Name—and it is a syllable with great sacred significance in various cultures. Tibetan Buddhists regard the syllable "Da" (written, in Tibetan, with a single letter) as most auspicious, and they assign numerous sacred meanings to it, including "Entrance into the Dharma". In the most ancient of the Upanishads (the *Brihadaranyaka Upanishad*), the Divine Being gives the fundamental instruction necessary for each of the different classes of living beings by uttering the single sound "Da". (Each class of beings understands "Da" in the manner uniquely necessary in their case.) In this passage, "Da" is said to be the Divine Voice that can be heard speaking through thunder (S. Radhakrishnan, trans., *The Principal Upanishads* [Atlantic Highlands, N.J.: Humanities Press International, First paperback edition, 1992], 289–290).

Da Avatar—The Divine Descent (Avatar) of the One and True Divine Giver (Da).

Da Love-Ananda Mahal—The Palace ("Mahal") of Avatar Adi Da's Divine Love-Bliss ("Love-Ananda"). See **Ruchira Sannyasin Hermitage Ashrams**.

"Dark" Epoch—See **"Late-Time" (or "Dark" Epoch)**.

Darshan—"Darshan" (the Hindi derivative of Sanskrit "darshana") literally means "seeing", "sight of", or "vision of". To receive Darshan of Avatar Adi Da is, most fundamentally, to behold His bodily (human) Divine Form (either by being in His physical Company or by seeing a photograph or other visual representation of Him), and (thereby) to receive the spontaneous Divine Blessing He Grants Freely whenever His bodily (human) Form is beheld in the devotional manner. In the Way of Adidam, Darshan of Avatar Adi Da is the very essence of the practice.

Darshan Yoga—The "Yoga (or Heart-Way) Of Seeing Me (or Of Being Fully Spiritually Awakened, Heart-Attracted, and Heart-Found By Me)" (Sutra 29).

Dau Loloma—Avatar Adi Da's primary Fijian Name, which literally means "the Adept (Dau) of Love (Loloma)". This Name was given to Avatar Adi Da by native Fijians soon after He first arrived in Fiji in 1983.

Dawn Horse / Dawn Horse Vision—During His sleep one night in the spring of 1970, Avatar Adi Da had a vision. While consciously wandering in a high subtle realm, Avatar Adi Da came upon an academy where the disciples of a Spiritual Adept were gathering for a demonstration of certain Yogic powers. Adi Da stood among them. The Siddha appeared, took his chair, and began the process of materializing an object. After a few moments, the disciples, having witnessed the invisible work of the Siddha, were confident that the materialization was underway, so they began to leave the room.

Finally, Avatar Adi Da and the Siddha alone remained. Gradually, a small, brown, beautifully formed horse began to manifest, first in vaporous and indistinct form, and then more and more solidly, until at last it stood motionless but fully alive and breathing before Him.

When He awakened from sleep, Avatar Adi Da knew that the dream was a portent, but its essential meaning remained hidden until His Ordeal of Divine Re-Awakening had fulfilled itself, some months later.

After Avatar Adi Da's Most Perfect Re-Awakening as the Divine Self in the Vedanta Temple in 1970, it became clear to Him that the Demonstration He had observed in His dream epitomized the continuous, present manifestation of all worlds and all beings (the horse) in and by Divine Consciousness (the Siddha). The Siddha was not merely a great Adept of Yogic powers. He was the Divine Person Himself. Adi Da also understood that the entire Vision had been a Revelation of His own Identity, Form, and Mission. In Truth, He saw, He Himself was "at once the Siddha who performed the miracle of manifesting the horse, and also the someone who was observing it, or who was party to the observation of it and to its result. And I did not have any feeling of being different from the horse, actually. I was making the horse, I was observing the horse, and I was being the horse." [October 18, 1984]

Later Avatar Adi Da called the manifestation "the Dawn Horse", from "eohippus", the scientific name for the earliest-known ancestor, now extinct, of the present-day horse. He prophesied that the Dawn Horse of His Work will materialize in the Most Perfect Divine Awakening of great numbers of His devotees, and, eventually, in the Divine Translation of His devotees, all beings, and even the entire Cosmic Mandala. This materialization is also the import of His Divine Self-"Emergence", which was initiated on January 11, 1986.

The Dawn Horse Vision is a sacred Sign, unfathomable to the mind but communicative to the feeling heart. In many esoteric traditions all over the world, the horse is a symbol of transcendence and the Spiritual journey. Thus, Avatar Adi Da's Vision, while an expression of His unique and ultimate Divine Work, also draws on anciently felt mysteries of humanity's Spiritual Purpose and Destiny.

Deeper Personality, gross personality—Avatar Adi Da uses the terms "gross personality" and "Deeper Personality" to indicate the two conditional dimensions of every human being. The gross personality is comprised of the physical body, its natural energies, its gross brain, and the verbal and lower psychic faculties of mind. The gross personality includes the entire gross dimension of the body-mind and the lower (or most physically oriented) aspects of the subtle dimension of the body-mind, and is the aspect of the body-mind that is the biological inheritance from one's parents.

The Deeper Personality is governed by the higher (least physically oriented) processes of the mind (which function outside or beyond the gross brain, and which include the subtle faculties of discrimination, intuition, and Spiritual perception and knowledge), as well as the causal separate-"I"-consciousness (which is the root-activity of attention, prior to mind). Avatar Adi Da has Revealed that the Deeper Personality is the aspect of the human being that reincarnates. See Sutra 67.

Developmental Stages Of Practice—The developmental stages of practice in the Way of Adidam are:

the student-beginner stage
the intensive listening-hearing stage
the would-be-seeing stage
the first actually seeing stage
the first stage of the "Perfect Practice"
the second stage of the "Perfect Practice"
the third stage of the "Perfect Practice"

These stages of practice, and their relationship to the seven stages of life, are described by Avatar Adi Da Samraj in Sutra 22.

Devotional Prayer Of Changes—A form of Invocation of and Communion with Avatar Adi Da Samraj which is practiced (by His formally acknowledged devotees) in order to bring about positive changes in the psycho-physical world. The Devotional Prayer of Changes is not a form of pleading to Avatar Adi Da Samraj for results. Rather, the Devotional Prayer of Changes is, principally, a specific form of heart-Communion with Avatar Adi Da and, secondarily, a relinquishment of any negative or problematic states of mind and emotion. Thus, practice of the Devotional Prayer of Changes releases identification with all negative conditions (such as doubt, disease, or any kind of problem), and it affirms a wholly right condition (which is fully assumed, felt, breathed, and lived). That affirmation is associated with whole bodily exercises which become technically more elaborate as an individual matures into the advanced stages of practice. The final aspect of the Devotional Prayer of Changes is to engage positive changes of action that support and make possible the desired change.

The Devotional Prayer of Changes is engaged as a regular practice by all practitioners of the Way of Adidam. It can be done daily in conjunction with regular periods of meditation or at any time of the day or night, individually or with others, either briefly or for an extended period of time. (Avatar Adi Da has indicated that an event of sacramental and devotional worship of Him should, as a general rule, last a minimum of 30 minutes.)

The Devotional Prayer of Changes is also a basic healing method in the Way of Adidam, practiced in the context of a full devotional and meditative life in which one has wholly embraced all of the functional, practical, relational, and cultural disciplines that Avatar Adi Da has Given.

See Sutra 33 (relative to the practice of the Devotional Prayer of Changes for practitioners in the stages preceding the first actually seeing stage) and Sutra 43 (relative to the practice of the Devotional Prayer of Changes for practitioners in the first actually seeing stage and beyond).

Devotional Way Of Insight / Devotional Way Of Faith—The two variant forms of the "conscious process" Given by Avatar Adi Da, as described by Him in Sutra 6. Every formally acknowledged practitioner of the Way of Adidam is to experiment with both of these Devotional Ways and then choose the one that is most effective in his or her case.

Both Devotional Ways require the exercise of insight <u>and</u> faith, but there is a difference in emphasis.

In the Devotional Way of Insight, the practitioner of Adidam engages the practice of self-Enquiry (in the form "Avoiding relationship?"). The practice of self-Enquiry (which gradually becomes non-verbal Re-cognition) is a specific technical process of observing, understanding, and feeling beyond the self-contraction, as the principal technical element of his or her practice of the "conscious process". Practitioners of the Devotional Way of Insight maintain the practice of self-Enquiry (and non-verbal Re-cognition) as their form of the "conscious process" until the transition to the "Perfect Practice" (at which point all practitioners of the Way of Adidam engage "Feeling-Enquiry" as their sole form of the "conscious process" in formal meditation and their principal form of the "conscious process" in daily life).

In the Devotional Way of Faith, the practitioner of Adidam engages the practice of "true prayer", which is a specific technical process of magnifying his or her heart-Attraction to Avatar Adi Da, as the principal technical element of his or her practice of the "conscious process". "True prayer" is practiced in the form of Ruchira Avatara Naama Japa in the student-beginner stage, the intensive listening-hearing stage, and the would-be-seeing stage, and in the form of the Prayer of Remembrance in the first actually seeing stage.

"Difference"—The epitome of the egoic presumption of separateness—in contrast with the Realization of Oneness, or Non-"Difference", Which is Native to the Divine Self-Condition. This term is placed in quotation marks to indicate that Avatar Adi Da uses it in the "so to speak" sense. He is Communicating (by means of the quotation marks) that, in Reality, there is no such thing as "difference", even though it appears to be the case from the point of view of ordinary human perception.

Disciplines Of The Way Of Adidam—See **functional, practical, relational, and Cultural Disciplines Of Adidam**. See also **Gifts, Callings, and Disciplines**.

Divine Body / Divine Spiritual Body—Avatar Adi Da's Divine Body is not conditional or limited to His physical Body but is the "Bright" Itself—Spiritually Pervading, and Eternally Most Prior to, the cosmic domain. See especially Sutras 14 and 15.

Divine Enlightenment—The Realization of the seventh stage of life, which is uniquely Revealed and Given by Avatar Adi Da. It is Eternal Self-Abiding in His "Bright" (and Infinitely Love-Bliss-Full) Divine Self-Condition, released from all the egoic limitations of the first six stages of life. The seventh stage Awakening is Avatar Adi Da's Gift to His rightly prepared devotee who has fulfilled the entire sadhana of the Way of Adidam in the context of the first six stages of life.

Divine Heart-Master—Describing the Spiritual Mastery of the devotee's heart by Avatar Adi Da Samraj.

Divine Ignorance—"Divine Ignorance" is Avatar Adi Da's term for the fundamental Awareness of Existence Itself, Prior to all sense of separation from (or knowledge about) anything that arises. He has Expressed the essence of His Argument of Divine Ignorance in a single sentence: "You (as the conditional self, or the body-mind-self) Do Not and Cannot Ever (In Fact, or In Reality) experience or know What any thing, other, or conditional event Is." (Sutra 25) By "Ignorance", Avatar Adi Da means heart-felt participation in the Universal Condition of Inherent Mystery—not mental dullness or the fear-based wonder or awe felt by the subjective ego in relation to unknown objects. Most Perfect Realization of Divine Ignorance is Most Perfect Realization of Consciousness Itself, transcending all the knowledge and all the experience acquired by the self-contracted ego-"I". See especially Sutra 25.

Divine Image-Art—The Artwork Created by Avatar Adi Da Samraj—specifically, His Artwork Created since 1999, in the Making of which Avatar Adi Da has Worked with the camera as a technical means, using the photographic negatives as "blueprints" for the fabrication of monumental art-forms.

AVATAR ADI DA SAMRAJ: My involvement in artistic Work in elaborated form began at the "Brightness" in 1999. My Image-Making is part of My Avataric Divine Self-Revelation.

Just as My Written Word covers everything, so also does My visual Artistic Work. It is a Communication to humankind about its egoic bondage, but also its Inherence in Me, Showing human beings My Own "Brightness".

—February 2, 2002

See also **Material Fabrications**.

Divine Indifference—See **Four Phases Of The Seventh Stage Of Life**.

Divine Parama-Guru—The Supreme Divine Guru.

Divine Self-Domain / Divine "Bright" Spherical Self-Domain—Avatar Adi Da affirms that there is a Divine Self-Domain that is the Perfectly Subjective Condition of the conditional worlds. It is not "elsewhere", not an objective "place" (like a subtle "heaven" or mythical "paradise"), but It is the Divine Source-Condition of every conditionally manifested being and thing—and It is not other than Avatar Adi Da Himself. Avatar Adi Da Reveals that His Divine Self-Domain is a Boundless (and Boundlessly "Bright") Sphere. To Realize the seventh stage of life (by the Divine Spiritual Grace of Avatar Adi Da Samraj) is to Awaken to His Divine Self-Domain. See especially Sutras 66–68.

Divine Self-"Emergence". See **Avataric Divine Self-"Emergence"**.

Divine Self-Realization—See **Divine Enlightenment**.

Divine Self-Recognition—Divine Self-Recognition is the ego-transcending and world-transcending Intelligence of the Divine Self-Condition in relation to all conditional phenomena. The devotee of Avatar Adi Da who Realizes the seventh stage of life simply Abides as Self-Existing and Self-Radiant Consciousness Itself, and he or she Freely Self-Recognizes (or inherently and instantly and most perfectly comprehends and perceives) all phenomena (including body, mind, conditional self, and conditional world) as transparent (or merely apparent), and un-necessary, and inherently non-binding modifications of the same "Bright" Divine Self-Consciousness.

Divine Sound / Thunder—The Divine Sound of Thunder (which Avatar Adi Da also describes as the "Da" Sound, or "Da-Om" Sound, or "Om" Sound) is one of Avatar Adi Da's three Eternal Forms of Manifestation in the conditional worlds—together with His Divine Star of Light and His Divine Spiritual Body. See especially Sutra 46.

Divine Star—The original (and primal) conditional visible Representation (or Sign) of the "Bright" (the Source-Energy, or Divine Light, of Which all conditional phenomena and the total cosmos are modifications). Avatar Adi Da has Revealed that He is "Incarnated" in the cosmic domain as a Brilliant White Five-Pointed (or Pentagrammic) Star (and also as the Deep Vibration, or Sound, of "Da" or "Om", and His Divine Spiritual Body). The Brilliant White Five-Pointed Star Appears at the center of the Cosmic Mandala.

Divine Spiritual Body—See **Divine Body**.

Divine Transfiguration—See **Four Phases Of The Seventh Stage Of Life**.

Divine Transformation—See **Four Phases Of The Seventh Stage Of Life**.

Divine Translation—See **Four Phases Of The Seventh Stage Of Life**.

Divine World-Teacher—Avatar Adi Da Samraj is the Divine World-Teacher because His Wisdom-Teaching is the uniquely Perfect Instruction to every being—in this (and every) world—relative to the total process of Divine Enlightenment. Furthermore, Avatar Adi Da Samraj constantly Extends His Regard to the entire world (and the entire cosmic domain)—not on the political or social level, but as a Spiritual matter, constantly Working to Bless and Purify all beings everywhere.

dog, Un-Washed / dog, Washing the—See **"Washing the dog" (from head to tail)**

dreaming—See **waking, dreaming, and sleeping**.

E

Ecstasy / Enstasy—Words derived originally from Greek. Avatar Adi Da uses "ecstasy" in the literal sense of "standing (stasis) outside (ec-)" the egoic self, and "enstasy" in the sense of "standing (stasis) in (en-)" the Divine Self-Condition. Avatar Adi Da Defines "Ecstasy" as "Standing 'Outside' oneself, or Beyond oneself, and (Thus and Thereby) Beyond Separateness and Separativeness" (Sutra 22). And He Defines Divine Enstasy as "The Native Condition Of Standing Unconditionally As The By-Me-Avatarically-Self-Revealed Transcendental, Inherently Spiritual, Inherently egoless, and Self-Evidently Divine Self-Condition Itself" (Sutra 61).

ego-"I"—The fundamental activity of self-contraction, or the presumption of separate and separative existence. The "I" is placed in quotation marks to indicate that it is used by Avatar Adi Da in the "so to speak" sense. He is Communicating (by means of the quotation marks) that, in Reality, there is no such thing as the separate "I", even though it appears to be the case from the point of view of ordinary human perception.

Eleutherios—"Eleutherios" (Greek for "Liberator") is a title by which Zeus was venerated as the supreme deity in the Spiritual esotericism of ancient Greece. The Designation "Eleutherios" indicates the Divine Function of Avatar Adi Da as the Incarnation of the Divine Person, "Whose Inherently Perfect Self-'Brightness' Divinely Liberates all conditionally Manifested beings—Freely, Liberally, Gracefully, and Without Ceasing—now, and forever hereafter" (Sutra 54).

Emanationist—The "Emanationist" way is that of mystical absorption, associated particularly with the fifth-stage "ascending" path. It is, as Avatar Adi Da describes here, associated with the vertical dimension of the human psycho-physical structure. Avatar Adi Da's extended Discussion of the "Emanationist" and "Transcendentalist" (or "Non-Emanationist") ways is found in "I (Alone) Am The Adidam Revelation" (an Essay included in a number of His "Source-Texts"). See also **Transcendentalist**.

"Emotional-Sexual Conscious Exercise"—The conservative and regenerative sexual discipline engaged by sexually active practitioners in the foundation (or listening-hearing) stages (and, in some cases, the would-be-seeing stage) of the Way of Adidam. "Emotional-sexual conscious exercise" becomes "emotional-sexual Devotional Communion" with the transition to the first actually seeing stage, when the (already) Spiritually Awakened devotee has become fully technically responsible for the reception of Avatar Adi Da's Divine Spirit-Baptism. See especially Sutra 38.

This term is placed in quotation marks to indicate that Avatar Adi Da uses it with the specific technical meaning described here.

"Emotional-Sexual Devotional Communion"—The conservative and regenerative discipline engaged by sexually active devotees practicing in the first actually seeing stage and beyond. Such devotees are qualified to engage sexual intimacy as a Spiritual Yoga of Communion with Avatar Adi Da as the All-Pervading Divine Reality. See especially Sutra 37.

This term is placed in quotation marks to indicate that Avatar Adi Da uses it with the specific technical meaning described here.

En-Light-enment—Divine Enlightenment (or Most Perfect Real-God-Realization) is a matter of the actual conversion of the body-mind to the State of Divine Conscious Light Itself. Avatar Adi Da sometimes writes the noun "Enlightenment" (and also the verb "Enlighten") with "Light" set apart by hyphens, in order to emphasize this point.

Enstasy—See **Ecstasy / Enstasy**.

Eternally Living Murti—In the phrase "Eternally Living Murti", Avatar Adi Da is indicating that His Avatarically-Born bodily (human) Divine Form will forever be the "representational image" whereby He can be Invoked and worshipped.

etheric—The etheric is the dimension of life-energy, which functions through the human nervous system. The human body is surrounded and infused by this personal life-energy, felt as the play of emotions and life-force in the body.

"Evolutionary"—Avatar Adi Da uses the term "evolutionary" to indicate the goal-oriented struggle to fulfill the potential of the human body-mind, or the "great path of return".

This term is placed in quotation marks to indicate the sense of "so to speak", in relation to the false presumption that Real-God-Realization is based on a necessary evolution by means of the "great path of return" rather than directly living on the basis of present-time relationship with the Divine.

F

Faculties / Four Faculties—Body, emotion (or feeling), mind (or attention), and breath. These four principal faculties account for the entirety of the human being. The practice of Ruchira Avatara Bhakti Yoga (or heart-Communion with Avatar Adi Da) is, fundamentally, the moment to moment turning of the four principal faculties to Him.

Feeling-Contemplation—Avatar Adi Da's term for the essential devotional and meditative practice that all practitioners of the Way of Adidam engage at all times in relationship to Him.

"Feeling-Enquiry"—The form of the "conscious process" engaged by all practitioners of Adidam who have made the transition to the "Perfect Practice". Avatar Adi Da explains that, with the transition to the "Perfect Practice", practitioners of both the Devotional Way of Insight and the Devotional Way of Faith will take up "Feeling-Enquiry" as their form of the "conscious process", because "The 'Perfect Practice' Of 'Feeling-Enquiry' Is (Itself) The Ultimate Essence (or The Inherently Perfect Epitome) Of Both 'True Prayer' and self-Enquiry (Including Re-Cognition)" (Sutra 58).

"Feeling-Enquiry" is a twelve-part process whereby the root-feeling of relatedness is surrendered, forgotten, and transcended in its Source, Which is the Divine Conscious Light Itself. (The twelve parts of "Feeling-Enquiry" are described by Avatar Adi Da in Sutra 56, pp. 1036–38.) Like all forms of the "conscious process" in the Way of Adidam, "Feeling-Enquiry" is an extension of the fundamental practice of Ruchira Avatara Bhakti Yoga. See also **Hridaya-Vichara.**

Feeling Of Being—The uncaused and unqualified feeling-intuition of the Divine Self-Condition. In "The ego-'I' Is the Illusion of Relatedness" (in *Santosha Adidam*), Avatar Adi Da describes the Feeling of Being as "the Great Heart-Feeling in Which the feeling of relatedness is arising".

Feeling Of Relatedness—In the foundation stages of practice in the Way of Adidam, the basic (or gross) manifestation of the avoidance of relationship is understood and released when Avatar Adi Da's devotee hears Him (or comes to the point of most fundamental self-understanding), thereby regaining the free capability for simple relatedness, or living on the basis of the feeling of relatedness rather than the avoidance of relationship. Nevertheless, the feeling of relatedness is not Ultimate Realization, because it is still founded in the presumption of a "difference" between "I" and "other". Only in the "Perfect Practice" of Adidam is the feeling of relatedness itself fully understood as the root-act of attention and, ultimately, transcended in the Feeling of Being.

The First Actually Seeing Stage—See **Listening, Hearing, Seeing**.

Form, Presence, and State—Avatar Adi Da Samraj has Revealed that He Exists simultaneously in three Forms—physical (His bodily human Form), Spiritual (His Spiritual Presence), and the Formlessness of Self-Existing and Self-Radiant Consciousness Itself (His Very State). The fundamental practice of feeling-Contemplating Him includes feeling-Contemplation of all three aspects of His Being—always (from the very beginning of the practice of the Way of Adidam through the seventh stage of life) founded in devotional recognition-response to His Avatarically-Born bodily (human) Divine Form and Person.

Formally Acknowledged Devotee / Formally Practicing Devotee—Synonymous references to an individual who is practicing in the first or the second congregation of Adidam, and, therefore, has embraced the total (or full and complete) practice of the Way of Adidam as described by Avatar Adi Da Samraj in *The Dawn Horse Testament.*

Four Phases Of The Seventh Stage Of Life—Avatar Adi Da has Revealed that the Awakening to the seventh stage of life is not an "endpoint" but is (rather) the beginning of the final Spiritual process. One of the unique aspects of Avatar Adi Da's Revelation is His precise Description of the seventh stage process as consisting of four phases: Divine Transfiguration, Divine Transformation, Divine Indifference, and Divine Translation.

> *The First Sign (or Demonstration) Of The Only-By-Me Revealed and Given Seventh Stage Of Life (In The Way Of The Heart) Is Divine Transfiguration, In Which the body-mind Of My By-My-Avataric-Divine-Spiritual-Grace-Enlightened Devotee Is Self-Radiant With My Avatarically Self-Transmitted Divine Love-Bliss, Spontaneously Blessing all of the (Apparent) relations of the body-mind.*
>
> *The Second Sign (or Demonstration) Of The Only-By-Me Revealed and Given Seventh Stage Of Life (In The Way Of The Heart) Is Divine Transformation, In Which the body-mind Of My By-My-Avataric-Divine-Spiritual-Grace-Enlightened Devotee Effectively Exhibits The Only-By-Me Revealed and Given Signs and Powers Of Real God.*
>
> *The Third Sign (or Demonstration) Of The Only-By-Me Revealed and Given Seventh Stage Of Life (In The Way Of The Heart) Is Divine Indifference, In Which Even the body-mind Of My By-My-Avataric-Divine-Spiritual-Grace-Enlightened Devotee Is Pre-Occupied With The Self-Existing Event Of My Self-Radiant Love-Bliss, and the world of (Apparent) relations Is (More and More) Minimally and Not Otherwise Noticed. . . .*
>
> *The Final Sign (or Demonstration) Of The Only-By-Me Revealed and Given Seventh Stage Of Life (and Of The Total Practice Of The Only-By-Me Revealed and Given Way Of The Heart) Is The Great Event Of Divine Translation—Which Is . . . The Process Of Transition To (or "Dawning" As) My Divine Self-Domain Via The Divinely "Bright" Outshining Of The Cosmic Domain In The Only-By-Me Revealed and Given Divine Sphere and Sign Of The "Midnight Sun" (Most Perfectly Above and Beyond all-and-All Of Cosmic, or conditional, forms, beings, signs, conditions, relations, and things).*
>
> —Sutra 21

Frontal Line—The subtle energy-pathway—extending from the crown of the head to the bodily base—through which both the natural life-energy and Avatar Adi Da's Avatarically Self-Transmitted Divine Spirit-Current flow (in a descending, or downward, direction) in the human body-mind.

Frontal Personality—The entire gross dimension of the body-mind and the lower (or most physically oriented) aspects of the subtle dimension of the body-mind. Thus, the frontal personality is comprised of the physical body and its natural energies, the gross brain, and the verbal and lower faculties of the mind. The frontal personality is associated with the frontal line of the body-mind.

Frontal Yoga—The process whereby knots and obstructions in the frontal personality are penetrated, opened, surrendered, and released, through the devotee's reception of Avatar Adi Da's Spiritual Transmission in the frontal line of the body-mind. "Frontal Yoga" is synonymous with "the first actually seeing stage".

functional, practical, relational, and Cultural Disciplines Of Adidam—The most basic functional, practical, and relational disciplines of the Way of Adidam are forms of appropriate human action and responsibility in relation to diet, health, exercise, sexuality, work, service to and support of Avatar Adi Da's Circumstance and Work, and cooperative association with other practitioners of the Way of Adidam. The most basic cultural obligations of the Way of Adidam include meditation, sacramental worship, study of Avatar Adi Da's Wisdom-Teaching (and also at least a basic discriminative study of the Great Tradition of religion and Spirituality that is the Wisdom-inheritance of humankind), and regular participation in the "form" (or schedule) of daily, weekly, monthly, and annual devotional activities and retreats.

G

Gifts, Callings, and Disciplines—All of the forms of Divine Grace that Avatar Adi Da Offers to practitioners of the Way of Adidam are simultaneously "Gifts, Callings, and Disciplines". They are Gifts because without His Free Granting of Help in these forms, no one would have the opportunity to practice the Way of Adidam. (Indeed, in the Epilogue of this book, Avatar Adi Da characterizes each and all of the principal features of the Way of Adidam as His "Seven Giving Gifts" to His devotees.) These Gifts are Callings because they Call each one to Realize exemplary devotion, service, obedience, and conformity to Him, even to the degree of Inherently Most Perfect Self-Identification with Him. And all of the forms of Grace that Avatar Adi Da Offers are (inherently) Disciplines, because to use or respond to His Gifts and Callings requires both intelligent restraint of every tendency toward egoity and fierce commitment in action to the Real-God-Realizing process.

In the larger sense indicated here, the Disciplines Given by Avatar Adi Da include meditation and every other kind of devotional and sacramental practice, and every form of appropriate attention and service to Him, as well as the basic functional, practical, relational, and cultural disciplines.

Global Ashram (Of Avatar Adi Da's Devotees)—The cooperative devotional culture of Adidam. Within this cooperative culture—which is lived with other local practitioners of Adidam, and unified with the entire Global Ashram of Adidam through all forms of modern communication—every individual devotee is able to grow and be accountable for his or her practice of the relationship to the Avatar Adi Da.

"Great Path Of Return"—Avatar Adi Da characterizes the traditional religious and Spiritual paths of the first six stages of life as the "great path of return" because the traditional points of view associated with the first six stages of life regard the "goal" of the Spiritual path to be somewhere "else" than "here". In other words, it is traditionally presumed that the Spiritual Way is a matter of following a "great path" by which the aspirant will "return" from "here" to the "place" that is regarded to be the "goal" (or "home").

Right practice of the Way of Adidam, on the other hand, is not a matter of seeking to reach any of the "goals" of the first six stages of life, but is (rather) a matter of practicing (progressively) in the context of the first six stages of life, while persistently observing, understanding, and transcending all forms of motivated seeking as they arise.

This term is placed in quotation marks to indicate that Avatar Adi Da uses it with the specific technical meaning described here.

Great Tradition—Avatar Adi Da's term for the total inheritance of human, cultural, religious, magical, mystical, Spiritual, and Transcendental paths, philosophies, and testimonies, from all the eras and cultures of humanity—which inheritance has (in the present era of worldwide communication) become the common legacy of humankind. Avatar Adi Da's Divine Self-Revelation and Wisdom-Teaching Fulfills and Completes the Great Tradition.

gross, subtle, causal—Avatar Adi Da (in agreement with certain esoteric schools in the Great Tradition) describes conditional existence as having three fundamental dimensions—gross, subtle, and causal.

"Gross" means "made up of material (or physical) elements". The gross (or physical) dimension is, therefore, associated with the physical body.

The gross dimension is also associated with experience in the waking state and, as Avatar Adi Da Reveals, with the frontal line of the body-mind and with the left side of the heart (or the gross physical heart).

The subtle dimension, which is senior to and pervades the gross dimension, consists of the etheric (or personal life-energy) functions, the lower mental functions (including the conscious mind, the subconscious mind, and the unconscious mind) and higher mental functions (of discriminative mind, mentally presumed egoity, and will), and is associated with experience in the dreaming state. In the human psycho-physical structure, the subtle dimension is primarily associated with the middle station of the heart (or the heart chakra), the spinal line, the brain core, and the subtle centers of mind in the higher brain.

The causal dimension is senior to both the gross and the subtle dimensions. It is the root of attention, or the root-sense of existence as a separate self. The causal dimension is associated with the right side of the heart, specifically with the sinoatrial node, or "pacemaker" (the psycho-physical source of the heartbeat). Its corresponding state of consciousness is the formless awareness of deep sleep.

Guru-Avatar—The Divine Person, having "Crossed Down" and Appearing as the Supreme Guru.

H

Hearing—See **Listening, Hearing, and Seeing**.

Heart / The Heart Itself / Stations Of The Heart—Avatar Adi Da distinguishes three stations of the heart, associated (respectively) with the right side, the middle station (traditionally called the "anahata chakra"), and the left side of the heart region of the chest. He Reveals that these stations are the loci (or focal points of living origination) of the causal body, the subtle body, and the gross body (respectively). Avatar Adi Da Teaches (as foreshadowed in certain rare sixth stage texts) that the primal psycho-physical seat of Consciousness and of attention is associated with what He calls the "right side of the heart". He has Revealed that this center (which is neither the heart chakra nor the gross physical heart) corresponds to the sinoatrial node (or "pacemaker"), the source of the gross physical heartbeat in the right atrium (or upper right chamber) of the physical heart. In the Process of Divine Self-Realization, there is a unique process in which the ego-knot in the right side of the heart is released—and it is because of this connection between the right side of the heart and Divine Self-Realization that Avatar Adi Da uses the term "the Heart" as another form of reference to the Divine Self-Condition.

The Heart Itself, or the True Divine Heart, Is Real God, the Divine Self-Condition, the Divine Reality. The True Divine Heart is not "in" the right side of the human heart, nor is it "in" (or limited to) the human heart as a whole. Rather, the human heart and body-mind and the world exist <u>in</u> the True Divine Heart, Which <u>Is</u> Avatar Adi Da Samraj's Divine Being.

Heart-Communion—"Heart-Communion" with Avatar Adi Da is the practice of Invoking and feeling Him. It is "communion" in the sense that, in the bliss of that state, the individual loses the sense of separate self, and is (thus) "communing intimately" (in a most profound and non-dual manner) with Avatar Adi Da Samraj.

Heart-Master—See **Divine Heart-Master**.

Heart-Recognition—The entire practice of the Way of Adidam is founded in devotional heart-recognition of, and devotional heart-response to, Ruchira Avatar Adi Da Samraj as the Very Divine Being in Person.

> *The fundamental heart-response to Me (which, necessarily, coincides with heart-recognition of Me) is the only-by-Me Revealed and Given practice of Ruchira Avatara Bhakti Yoga, Which is the moment to moment (devotionally Me-recognizing, and devotionally to-Me-responding) turning of the four principal faculties—of body, emotion (or feeling), mind (or attention), and breath—to Me (in and <u>As</u> My Avatarically-Born bodily human Divine Form and Person).*
>
> —Avatar Adi Da Samraj
> *Hridaya Rosary*

Heart-Response—See **Heart-Recognition**.

"Heroic"—The Tantric traditions of Hinduism and Buddhism describe as "heroic" the practice of an individual whose impulse to Liberation and commitment to his or her Guru are so strong that all circumstances of life, even those traditionally regarded as inauspicious for Spiritual practice (such as consumption of intoxicants and engagement in sexual activity), can rightly be made use of as part of the Spiritual process.

Avatar Adi Da's uniquely "Heroic" Ordeal, however, was undertaken not for His own sake, but in order to discover, through His own experience, what is necessary in order for <u>all</u> beings to Realize the Truth. Because of His utter Freedom from egoic bondage and egoic karmas, Avatar Adi Da's Sadhana was "Heroic" in a manner that had never previously been possible and will never be possible in the case of any other. As the Divine Person, it was necessary for Him to experience the entire gamut of human seeking, in order to be able to Address <u>everything</u> about human existence.

This term is placed in quotation marks to indicate that Avatar Adi Da uses it with the specific technical meaning described here (rather than any of the more commonly accepted general meanings). See also **"Crazy"**.

Horizontal Dimension Of the body-mind—Avatar Adi Da refers to the structural anatomy of the "heart" (including its three stations) as the "horizontal" dimension of the human body-mind (in contrast to the "vertical" dimension of the Circle and the Arrow). See also **Heart / The Heart Itself / Stations Of The Heart**.

Horse-Sacrifice—See **Ashvamedha**.

Hridaya-Advaita Dharma—Indicates "the Wisdom-Teaching ('Dharma') of the Non-Dual ('Advaita') Divine Heart ('Hridaya')".

Hridaya Avatar—"Hridaya" is Sanskrit for "heart". "Hridaya" in combination with "Avatar" signifies that Avatar Adi Da is the Very Incarnation of the Divine Heart Itself.

Hridaya-Avatara Bhakti Yoga—Indicates the practice (Yoga) of devotion (bhakti) to the Divine Incarnation (Avatara) of the Heart Itself (Hridaya).

Hridayam—Another form of Sanskrit "hridaya" ("heart"), referring not only to the physical organ but also to the True Divine Heart, the Transcendental (and Inherently Spiritual) Divine Reality. "Hridayam" is one of Avatar Adi Da's Divine Names, signifying that He Stands in, at, and as the True Heart of every being.

Hridaya-Samartha Sat-Guru—"Hridaya-Samartha Sat-Guru" is a compound of traditional Sanskrit terms that has been newly created to express the uniqueness of Avatar Adi Da's Guru-Function. "Sat" means "Truth", "Being", "Existence". Thus, "Sat-Guru" literally means "True Guru", or a Guru who can lead living beings from darkness (or non-Truth) into Light (or the Living Truth).

"Samartha" means "fit", "qualified", "able". Thus, "Samartha Sat-Guru" means "a True Guru who is fully capable" of Awakening living beings to Real-God-Realization.

The word "Hridaya", meaning "heart", refers to the Very Heart, or the Transcendental (and Inherently Spiritual) Divine Reality.

Thus, altogether, the reference "Hridaya-Samartha Sat-Guru" means "the Divine Heart-Master Who Liberates His devotees from the darkness of egoity by Means of the Power of the 'Bright' Divine Heart Itself". Avatar Adi Da has Said that this full Designation "properly summarizes all the aspects of My unique Guru-Function".

Hridaya-Shakti / Hridaya-Shaktipat—Sanskrit "Hridaya" means "the Heart Itself". "Shakti" is a Sanskrit term for the Divine Manifesting as Energy. "Hridaya-Shakti" is thus "the Divine Power of the Heart", Which is Given and Transmitted by Avatar Adi Da Samraj.

In Hindi, "shaktipat" means the "descent of Divine Power", indicating the Sat-Guru's Transmission of the Kundalini Shakti to his or her devotee.

"Hridaya-Shaktipat", Which is Avatar Adi Da's seventh stage Gift to His devotees, is "the Blessing-Transmission of the Divine Heart Itself". See also **Ruchira Shakti / Ruchira Shaktipat**.

Hridaya-Vichara—A synonym for "Feeling-Enquiry" (the form of the "conscious process" engaged by all practitioners of the Way of Adidam who have made the transition to the "Perfect Practice").

Sanskrit "Hridaya" means "the Heart Itself". Sanskrit "vichara" is usually translated as "enquiry", connoting intense observation and unrelenting vigilance. "Hridaya-Vichara" is Avatar Adi Da's original term for the practice of Abiding in Self-Identification with the True Divine Heart (or the Feeling of Being That Is the Divine Self-Condition). Unlike traditional terms, such as "Atma-Vichara" (a term used by Ramana Maharshi, translated into English as "Self-enquiry"), "Hridaya-Vichara" does not suggest the exclusive, introverted search for the root of the Self (Atman). Rather, "Hridaya-Vichara" points to the seventh stage Realization of the all-and-All-Surrounding and all-and-All-Pervading Spiritual, Transcendental, and Divine Person. See also **Feeling-Enquiry**.

Hrim—See **Ma**.

Husband Of The Heart—A Reference to Avatar Adi Da as the Very Divine Person, Who, as the Avatarically Incarnate Divine Adi-Guru, Embraces living beings, Masters their wandering energy and attention, and Awakens them to Most Perfect Non-separateness from (and Self-Identification with) Him. All His devotees, whether male or female, are (thus) Husbanded (at heart) by Avatar Adi Da Samraj.

I

Instrumentality / Instruments—Avatar Adi Da has Indicated that members of the Ruchira Sannyasin Order function collectively and spontaneously as His Instruments:

> *Through Many and Various Avataric Divine Means (Some Of Which Are Described, By Me, In This Divine Testament, and In Even All My Twenty-Three Divine "Source-Texts"), I Work To Serve The Making Of Concrete (Tangible) Changes In The Immediate Circumstance Of conditions in this world. Conditional Existence (As A Whole) May Be Described As A Universal (or All-Encompassing) Grid—and I Work (Avatarically, and Divinely)*

Through the Innumerable particular points On That Total Grid.

I Work Through My ("Ruchira Sannyasin") Devotee-Instruments As points Of Contact (and, Altogether, As My Instrumental Means) In The Worldwide Sacred Cooperative Cultural Gathering Of My Devotees—and I Work Through My ("Ruchira Sannyasin") Devotee-Instruments As Concrete points Of Focus On The Universal Grid, For The Sake Of all-and-All. This Is The Unique Significance Of The Instrumentality Of My ("Ruchira Sannyasin") Devotee-Instruments In The Only-By-Me Revealed and Given Way Of The Heart (or Way Of Adidam).

—Sutra 57

Intensive Listening-Hearing Stage—See **Listening, Hearing, Seeing**.

"Intimate Yogic Friendship"—A special renunciate form of "true Yogic intimacy", in which the "intimate friends" relate to one another for the purpose of "true Yogic intimacy" and right sexual Yoga, without any conventional expectations relative to other (practical or emotional) purposes of intimate relationship.

This term is placed in quotation marks to indicate that Avatar Adi Da uses it with the specific technical meaning described here. See Sutra 40.

"Intoxication"—"Intoxication" with Avatar Adi Da's Divine Love-Bliss Draws His devotees beyond the usual egoic self and egoic mind into a state of ecstatic devotional Communion (and Identification) with Him. This term is enclosed in quotations marks in order to distinguish it from the common meaning of "intoxication" (such as with alcohol).

Invocation By Name—See **Name-Invocation**.

Ishta / Ishta-Guru—The "chosen Divine Beloved" of the devotee's heart.

J

Jnana Samadhi / Jnana Nirvikalpa Samadhi—See **Samadhi**.

K

karma / karmic—"Karma" is Sanskrit for "action". Since action entails consequences (or re-actions), "karma" also means (by extension) "destiny, tendency, the quality of existence and experience which is determined by previous actions". "Karmic" indicates "of the same nature as or related to karma".

kriyas—Spontaneous, self-purifying movements "of body, emotion, mind, and breath" (Sutra 18). Kriyas arise when the natural bodily energies are stimulated by Avatar Adi Da's Avatarically Self-Transmitted Divine Spirit-Current.

Kundalini Shakti / Kundalini Shaktipat—The Kundalini Shakti is the energy traditionally viewed to lie dormant at the base of the spine—the muladhara chakra, or lowermost psychic center of the body-mind. Kundalini Shaktipat is the activation of the Kundalini Shakti—either spontaneously or by means of a Sat-Guru's initiatory Siddhi—thereafter potentially producing various forms of Yogic and mystical experience.

kumbhak—A momentary retention of the breath between exhalation and inhalation, or between inhalation and exhalation. In its most profound form, kumbhak is temporary and total spontaneous suspension of the breath while attention ascends beyond awareness of the body into states of ecstatic absorption. The common form of kumbhak is sometimes intentionally practiced as a form of pranayama. Both the common and the profound forms of kumbhak may also occur spontaneously (in an easeful and blissful manner) in response to the Spiritual Presence of Avatar Adi Da.

L

"Late-Time" (or "Dark" Epoch)—A phrase that Avatar Adi Da uses to describe the present era—in which doubt of God (and of anything at all beyond mortal existence) is more and more pervading the entire world, and the self-interest of the separate individual is more and more regarded to be the ultimate principle of life. It is also a reference to the traditional Hindu idea of "yugas", or "epochs", the last of which (the Kali Yuga) is understood to be the most difficult and "dark". Many traditions share the idea that it is in such a time that the Promised Divine Liberator will appear.

These terms include quotation marks to indicate that they are used by Avatar Adi Da in the "so to speak" sense. In this case, He is Communicating (by means of the quotation marks) that, in Reality, the "darkness" of this apparent "late-time" is not Reality, or Truth, but only an appearance from the point of view of ordinary perception.

Lay Renunciate Order—The formal order of those devotees of Avatar Adi Da Samraj who have made the transition to the "Perfect Practice" of the Way of Adidam as lay (rather than legally renunciate, or sannyasin) practitioners.

Leela—Sanskrit for "play", or "sport". In many religious and Spiritual traditions, all of conditionally manifested existence is regarded to be the Leela (or the Play, Sport, or Free Activity) of the Divine Person. "Leela" also refers to the Awakened Play of a Realized Adept (of whatever real degree), through which he or she mysteriously Instructs and Liberates others and Blesses the world itself. By extension, a Leela is an instructive and inspiring story of such an Adept's Teaching and Blessing Play.

Lesson Of life—"The Lesson of life" is Avatar Adi Da's term for the fundamental understanding that Happiness cannot be achieved by means of seeking, because Happiness is inherent in Existence Itself. See Sutras 23 and 63.

Lineage, Avatar Adi Da's—The principal Spiritual Masters who served Avatar Adi Da Samraj during His "Sadhana Years" belong to a single Lineage of extraordinary Yogis, whose Parama-Guru (Supreme Guru) was the Divine "Goddess" (or "Mother-Shakti").

Swami Rudrananda (1928–1973), or Albert Rudolph (known as "Rudi"), was Avatar Adi Da's first human Teacher—from 1964 to 1968, in New York City. Rudi served Avatar Adi Da Samraj in the development of basic practical life-disciplines and the frontal Yoga, which is the process whereby knots and obstructions in the physical and etheric dimensions of the body-mind are penetrated, opened, surrendered, and released through Spiritual reception in the frontal line of the body-mind. Rudi's own Teachers included the Indonesian Pak Subuh (from whom Rudi learned a basic exercise of Spiritual receptivity), Swami Muktananda (with whom Rudi studied for many years), and Bhagavan Nityananda (the Indian Adept-Realizer who was also Swami Muktananda's Guru). Rudi met Bhagavan Nityananda shortly before Bhagavan Nityananda's death, and Rudi always thereafter acknowledged Bhagavan Nityananda as his original and principal Guru.

The second Teacher in Avatar Adi Da's Lineage of Blessing was Swami Muktananda (1908–1982), who was born in Mangalore, South India. Having left home at the age of fifteen, he wandered for many years, seeking the Divine Truth from sources all over India. Eventually, he came under the Spiritual Influence of Bhagavan Nityananda, whom he recognized as his Guru and in whose Spiritual Company he mastered Kundalini Yoga. Swami Muktananda served Avatar Adi Da as Guru during the period from 1968 to 1970. In the summer of 1969, during Avatar Adi Da's second visit to India, Swami Muktananda wrote a letter confirming Avatar Adi Da's attainment of "Yogic Liberation", and acknowledging His right to Teach others. However, from the beginning of their relationship, Swami Muktananda instructed Avatar Adi Da to visit Bhagavan Nityananda's burial site every day (whenever Avatar Adi Da was at Swami Muktananda's Ashram in Ganeshpuri, India) as a means to surrender to Bhagavan Nityananda as the Supreme Guru of the Lineage.

Bhagavan Nityananda, a great Yogi of South India, was Avatar Adi Da's third Guru. Little is known about the circumstances of Bhagavan Nityananda's birth and early life, although it is said that even as a child he showed the signs of a Realized Yogi. It is also known that he abandoned conventional life as a boy and wandered as a renunciate. Many miracles (including spontaneous healings) and instructive stories are attributed to him. Bhagavan Nityananda surrendered the body on August 8, 1961. Although Avatar Adi Da did not meet Bhagavan Nityananda in the flesh, He enjoyed Bhagavan Nityananda's direct Spiritual Influence from the subtle plane, and He acknowledges Bhagavan Nityananda as a direct and principal Source of Spiritual Instruction during His years with Swami Muktananda.

On His third visit to India, while visiting Bhagavan Nityananda's burial shrine, Avatar Adi Da was instructed by Bhagavan Nityananda to relinquish all others as Guru and to surrender directly to the Divine Goddess in Person as Guru. Thus, Bhagavan Nityananda passed Avatar Adi Da to the Divine Goddess Herself, the Parama-Guru (or Source-Guru) of the Lineage that included Bhagavan Nityananda, Swami Muktananda, and Rudi.

The years of Avatar Adi Da's Sadhana came to an end in the Great Event of His Divine Re-Awakening, when Avatar Adi Da Husbanded the Divine Goddess (thereby ceasing to relate to Her as His Guru).

Avatar Adi Da's full account of His "Sadhana Years" is Given in Part One of *The Knee Of Listening*. Avatar Adi Da's Description of His "Relationship" to the Divine "Goddess" is Given in "I Am The Icon Of Unity", in *He-and-She Is Me*.

Listening, Hearing, and Seeing—Avatar Adi Da describes the entire course of the Way of Adidam as falling into four primary phases:

1. Listening to Him
2. Hearing Him
3. Seeing Him
4. The "Perfect Practice" of Identifying with Him

"Listening" is Avatar Adi Da's technical term for the beginning practice of the Way of Adidam. A listening devotee literally "listens" to Avatar Adi Da Samraj's Instruction and applies it in his or her life.

The core of the listening process (and of all future practice of the Way of Adidam) is the practice of Ruchira Avatara Bhakti Yoga (or turning the four principal faculties of the body-mind—body, emotion, mind, and breath—to Him)—supported by practice of the "conscious process" and "conductivity" and by the embrace of the functional, practical, relational, and cultural disciplines Given by Him.

It is during the listening phase (once the foundation practice is fully established) that the devotee applies to come on extended formal retreat in Avatar Adi Da's physical Company (or, after His physical Lifetime, in the physical company, and the by-Him-Spiritually-Empowered circumstances, of the Ruchira Sannyasin Order of Adidam Ruchiradam). In the retreat circumstance, when the rightly prepared devotee truly (whole bodily) turns the principal faculties to Him, Avatar Adi Da is spontaneously Moved to Grant His Spiritual Initiation (or Ruchira Shaktipat), such that the devotee can become more and more consistently capable of tangibly receiving His Spiritual Transmission. This is the beginning of the Spiritually Awakened practice of the Way of Adidam—when the devotional relationship to Avatar Adi Da becomes (by His Divine Spiritual Grace) the devotional-and-Spiritual relationship to Him.

The phase of listening to Avatar Adi Da, rightly and effectively engaged, eventually culminates (by His Divine Spiritual Grace) in the true hearing of Him. The devotee has begun to hear Avatar Adi Da when there is most fundamental understanding of the root-act of egoity (or self-contraction), or the unique capability to consistently transcend the self-contraction. The capability of true hearing is not something the ego can "achieve". That capability can only be Granted, by Means of Avatar Adi Da's Divine Spiritual Grace, to His devotee who has effectively completed the (eventually, Spiritually Awakened) process of listening.

The listening-hearing process is described by Avatar Adi Da in Sutras 25–29.

When Spiritually Awakened practice of the Way of Adidam is magnified by means of the hearing-capability, the devotee has the necessary preparation to (in due course) engage that Spiritually Awakened practice in the "fully technically responsible" manner. This is another point (in the course of the Way of Adidam) when the devotee engages an extended formal retreat in Avatar Adi Da's physical Company (or, after His physical Lifetime, in the physical company, and the by-Him-Spiritually-Empowered circumstances, of the Ruchira Sannyasin Order of Adidam Ruchiradam). In this case, in Response to the devotee's more mature practice of devotional and Spiritual resort to Him, Avatar Adi Da Gives the Initiatory Spiritual Gift of Upward-turned Spiritual receptivity of Him (as He describes in His "Hridaya Rosary" of "Four Thorns Of Heart-Instruction", in Sutra 32).

This is Avatar Adi Da's Spiritual Initiation of His devotee into the seeing phase of practice, which Avatar Adi Da describes as the "fully technical responsible" form of Spiritually Awakened resort to Him.

One of the principal signs of the transition from the listening-hearing practice to the both-hearing-and-seeing practice is emotional conversion from the reactive emotions that characterize egoic self-obsession, to the open-hearted, Radiant Happiness that characterizes fully technically responsible Spiritual devotion to Avatar Adi Da. This true and stable emotional conversion coincides with stable Upward-to-Him-turned receptivity of Avatar Adi Da's Spiritual Transmission.

As the process of seeing develops, the body-mind becomes more and more fully Infused by Avatar Adi Da's Spirit-Baptism, purified of any psycho-physical patterning that diminishes that reception. With increasing maturity in the seeing process, Avatar Adi Da's Transmission of the "Bright" is experienced in the unique form that He describes as the "Samadhi of the 'Thumbs'"—and, through this process, the devotee is gracefully grown entirely beyond identification with the body-mind.

The seeing process is described by Avatar Adi Da in Sutras 32–35.

The seeing process is complete when the devotee receives Avatar Adi Da's Gift of Spiritually Awakening as the Witness-Consciousness (That Stands Prior to body, mind, and world, and even the act of attention itself). This Awakening to the Witness-Consciousness marks readiness for another period of Initiatory retreat in Avatar Adi Da's physical Company (or, after His physical Lifetime, in the physical company, and the by-Him-Spiritually-Empowered circumstances, of the Ruchira Sannyasin Order of Adidam Ruchiradam), in which He Spiritually Initiates the devotee into the "Perfect Practice".

"Locate" / "Locating"—To "Locate" Avatar Adi Da is to "Truly Heart-Find" Him. Avatar Adi Da places this term in quotation marks to indicate the sense of "so to speak"—because He is, in reality, Omnipresent, without any specific "location".

Love-Ananda—The Name "Love-Ananda" was given to Avatar Adi Da by Swami Muktananda, who spontaneously conferred it upon Avatar Adi Da in 1969. However, Avatar Adi Da did not use the Name "Love-Ananda" until April 1986, after the Great Event that Initiated His Avataric Divine Self-"Emergence". "Love-Ananda" is a combination of English ("Love") and Sanskrit ("Ananda", meaning "Bliss"), thus communicating Avatar Adi Da's Function as the Divine World-Teacher, embracing all human beings from all cultural settings. The combination of "Love" and "Ananda" means "the Divine Love-Bliss".

Love-Ananda Avatar—The Very Incarnation of the Divine Love-Bliss.

M

Ma—The Word-Sign "Ma" (and its variants "Sri" and "Hrim") designates the Mother-Force, Shakti-Force, or Goddess-Power, or the Spiritual Radiance of the Divine Self. "Ma" means "Divine Mother", revered in many traditions as the Matrix and Origin of the universe, as well as the primordial Energy of existence, which is never changed or reduced in any way. The historical reference to the goddess "Sri" first appeared in the Vedas, where she was described as the personification of prosperity or luck. "Hrim" is one of the primal "mula" ("root") or "bija" ("seed") mantras used in the esoteric Yoga of sound, Mantra Yoga. It is also associated with the idea of the Goddess-Power that presides over all conditional worlds.

Traditionally, the Goddess-Power designated by the Word-Signs "Ma", "Sri", and "Hrim" is viewed, by itself, as the source of "Maya", or the deluding power of conditional existence. However, when Husbanded by the Self-Father, as Avatar Adi Da has Revealed, this Great Power is associated with Enlightenment, or the lifting of the veil of illusion.

Maha-Purusha Medha—"Maha-Purusha" means "the Great Divine Person" and "Medha" is "Sacrifice".

The Vedic tradition of "purushamedha" (or "person-sacrifice") is shrouded in mystery and allegorical language, but it is related in significance to the great Ashvamedha (or horse-sacrifice). Although it is possible that human beings were (in some instances) actually sacrificed, in the true performance of the purushamedha they were simply part of a ritual that had the esoteric meaning of Spiritual sacrifice.

Avatar Adi Da uses the phrase "Maha-Purusha Medha" to describe His Avataric Appearance and Sacrificial Work of Submission to humankind for the sake of Revealing the Divine Way of Adidam and establishing His Avatarically-Born bodily (human) Divine Form as the great means of Divine Liberation.

Maha-Jnana Siddha / Maha-Jnana Siddha-Guru—In Sanskrit, "maha-jnana" literally means "great knowledge". Avatar Adi Da uses "Maha-Jnana" to mean the Perfect "Knowledge", or Realization, of the Divine Self, Confessed by the Realizer in the seventh stage of life. Maha-Jnana is to be distinguished from the Jnana, or Transcendental Self-Knowledge, of the sixth stage Realizer, which is the conditional and temporary Realization of Transcendental Consciousness that strategically excludes, and cannot be maintained in the context of, awareness of the conditional body-mind-self and its relations. Maha-Jnana, in contrast to the Jnana of the sixth stage of life, is the "Open-Eyed", Unconditional, spontaneous, and permanent Realization of the Divine Self, or Heart, under all conditions.

By virtue of His seventh stage Incarnation of the Divine Person, "the Only One Who Is", Avatar Adi Da also spontaneously demonstrates the Spirit-Mastery of the fourth stage and fifth stage of life. He is, therefore, a Siddha (or Siddha-Guru), but He is more appropriately designated "Maha-Jnana Siddha", to describe the Inclusive Totality of His Divine Heart-Power, as well as His Non-exclusive, Free, and Radiant Realization and Transmission of Transcendental, Inherently Spiritual, and necessarily Divine Consciousness, or Being, Itself.

Maha-Shakti—"Maha" is Sanskrit for "great". "Shakti" is Sanskrit for the Divine Manifesting as Energy (or Spiritual Power). Therefore, "Maha-Shakti" means "the Great Divine Energy (or Spiritual Power)".

Maha-Siddha—The Sanskrit word "Siddha" means "a completed, fulfilled, or perfected one", or "one of perfect accomplishment, or power". "Maha-Siddha" means "Great Siddha".

Mala—Sanskrit for "garland". A mala is typically a rosary of 108 beads plus a central (or Master) bead—which, as used in the Way of Adidam, is a reminder of Avatar Adi Da and His many Avataric Divine Gifts of Grace. In addition, a fundamental part of the mala used by a practitioner of Adidam is a (generally, photographic) Image of Avatar Adi Da (chosen by the individual because of his or her personal responsiveness to that particular Image) enclosed in a pendant or locket that hangs from the Master-bead of the mala. This creates the opportunity for devotional sighting of Avatar Adi Da Samraj at any time—in all circumstances outside a formal Communion Hall or outside Avatar Adi Da's physical human Company.

In the Way of Adidam, practitioners of the Devotional Way of Faith, including student-beginners experimenting with Ruchira Avatara Naama Japa, generally use the traditional mala in formal daily meditation. However, all practitioners may hold and use a mala as a means of focusing attention in feeling-Contemplation of Avatar Adi Da—and, in general, all practitioners use the mala when practicing random Invocation of Him by Name during periods of formal meditation.

It is recommended that the beads of the mala be of natural and porous material (such as wood) and thus able to absorb the oils of the body, which are natural conductors of energy. (A mala made of rudraksha beads is most highly recommended, and sandalwood beads are also excellent.)

Practitioners of the Way of Adidam may also use a wrist mala—which can easily be slipped from the wrist into the hand—consisting of multiples of nine beads plus the Master-bead, and a thumb mala (or finger mala), which is a ring that (in most designs) is rotated around the index finger as the thumb touches small beadlike prominences. Generally, there are nine "beads" on a thumb mala, plus a "Master-bead" (or an obtrusion that represents the Master-bead).

Mandala—Sanskrit word (literally, "circle") commonly used in the esoteric Spiritual traditions of the East to describe the entire pattern of the hierarchical levels of cosmic existence. See also **Cosmic Mandala**.

Material Fabrications (Of Avatar Adi Da's Avatarically Self-Revealed Divine Image-Art)—As a general rule, Avatar Adi Da Creates His Works of Image-Art as "monumental fabrications"—large-scale works in all kinds of media:

AVATAR ADI DA SAMRAJ: What I do to make a photographic negative is the first step in making a work of art. The work itself is not accomplished until it is fabricated. The fabrication is fundamental. The negative is an artifact used to generate fabrications.

Every fabrication is a three-dimensional object in space—effectively, a sculptural form, with sensory qualities (such as surface texture, and so on) that are essential characteristics of the object. By using the camera, I am working in light, yes—but light that is not divorced from tangibility. This is fundamental to My approach.

Also fundamental is the manner in which the viewer is confronted by the works. They are not merely intellectual images. They are not merely mind-sized or head-sized. Because of their monumentality, they confront the entire being and require an adaptation, an adjustment, a response that even transcends the usual body-mind limitations. When a fabrication is bigger than the body, you cannot concentrate in on it in the same way that you relate to something smaller than your head—as if it were just for the eyes and mind, rather than for total psycho-physical participation.

My fabricated works often involve not just a single image but combinations of images. This is another fundamental characteristic. I create the images in suites, and (most often) mount them in groups. I place images in relation to one another without inhibition, without a prescription about it. That dimension of My art goes beyond the painting tradition and relates to the sculptural tradition. Indeed, such grouping of images is a development that is not conventionally associated with the arts as they have been active until now.

The works of art I fabricate from photographic negatives are not merely conceptual "somethings" that are transferred (like a ghostly film) onto a surface. The tangible sculptural form itself—together with the monumental size—is fundamental to each of My artworks.

Maya—Traditional Sanskrit term for the incomprehensibly complex (and, ultimately, illusory) web of beings, things, and events that constitutes conditional reality.

"Midnight Sun"—A term Avatar Adi Da uses to refer to His Revelation of the esoteric visionary representation of Reality as a White Sphere in a black field—which Sphere is His own Divine Form.

There Is a Sun That Is Forever Risen in the night sky of the body-mind. It Is the Eternal Sun—the (Self-"Bright") "Midnight Sun", Infinitely Above the head, and not usually perceived. . . .

The Sun That Is Eternal and Over-head is not in the midst of a colored sphere of light. The Eternal "Midnight Sun" Is Beyond that sphere. The "Midnight Sun" Is, Truly, the Divine "Face" of My Threshold Form.

The entire cosmic domain is a field—indeed, a cube—of black, with all perceptions and conceptions gone—as in the swoon of death, or in the Samadhi of ascendedness most profound. In the midst of that black cube, there is a Sphere that looks like the Full Moon—but with no features or patterns on the face of It. It is Radiant, not shadowy. Its Radiance is like that of the Sun, rather than the Moon. Yet, there is Great Pleasure in beholding It—unlike the physical Sun, which is impossible to look at, with its rays and brilliance. This Eternal "Midnight Sun" Is the Direct and Tangible Entrance from the night sky of the body-mind Into What Is Beyond the black—Beyond the first six stages of life, Beyond the gross, subtle, and causal patterns of conception and perception. And the Divine Ever-Risen Sun is Edged absolutely discretely. It Is Absolutely White "Brightness"—and Its White edge is absolutely defined relative to the field of black.

The "Midnight Sun" Is the Hole in the universe. It is not (Itself) black. It Is the Hole <u>in</u> the black. It is Divine Being objectified, the Divine Self-Condition objectified. When there is passage <u>into</u> That Place (or the Divine Self-Condition Itself), there is nothing more to say. That <u>Is</u> My Divine "Bright" Spherical Self-Domain.

—Avatar Adi Da Samraj
Eleutherios

Avatar Adi Da Samraj places this term in quotation marks to indicate that He uses it with the specific technical meaning described here (rather than any other more common general meaning).

"Mind Dharma"—In *The Basket Of Tolerance*, Avatar Adi Da defines "Mind Dharma" as "the Teaching about transcending all that is the conditionally arising mind, and the Teaching about Transcendental Realization of 'Ultimate Mind' (or, more properly stated, the 'Ultimate, Unconditional, Self-Existing, and Real Nature, Essence, or Source-Condition' of the merely apparent, or conditionally arising, mind)". "Mind Dharma" is especially associated with the various schools of Buddhism.

Most Perfect / Most Ultimate—Avatar Adi Da uses the phrase "Most Perfect(ly)" in the sense of "Absolutely Perfect(ly)". Similarly, the phrase "Most Ultimate(ly)" is equivalent to "Absolutely Ultimate(ly)". "Most Perfect(ly)" and "Most Ultimate(ly)" are always references to the seventh (or Divinely Enlightened) stage of life. "Perfect(ly)" and "Ultimate(ly)" (without "Most") refer to the practice and Realization in the context of the "Perfect Practice" of the Way of Adidam (or, when Avatar Adi Da is making reference to the Great

Tradition, to practice and Realization in the context of the sixth stage of life).

The Mountain Of Attention Sanctuary—See **Ruchira Sannyasin Hermitage Ashrams**.

mudra / Mudra—A gesture of the hands, face, or body that outwardly expresses a state of ecstasy. Avatar Adi Da sometimes spontaneously exhibits mudras as Signs of His Blessing and Purifying Work with His devotees and the world. He also uses the term "Mudra" to express the Attitude of His Blessing-Work, which is His Constant (or Eternal) Giving (or Submitting) of Himself to Be the Means of Divine Liberation for all beings.

mummery—The dictionary defines "mummery" as "a ridiculous, hypocritical, or pretentious ceremony or performance". Avatar Adi Da uses this word to describe all the activities of ego-bound beings, or beings who are committed to the false view of separation and separativeness.

Murti—"Murti" is Sanskrit for "form", and, by extension, a "representational image" of the Divine or of a Guru. In the Way of Adidam, Murtis of Avatar Adi Da are most commonly photographs of Avatar Adi Da's bodily (human) Divine Form.

N

Name-Invocation—Practitioners of the Way of Adidam may, at any time, Remember or Invoke Avatar Adi Da Samraj (or feel, and thereby Contemplate, His Avatarically Self-Revealed Divine Form, and Presence, and State) through simple feeling-Remembrance of Him and by randomly (in daily life and meditation) Invoking Him via His Principal Name, "Da", or via any of the other Names He has Given for the practice of Simple Name-Invocation of Him.

The forms of simple Name-Invocation of Avatar Adi Da are Given by Him in Sutra 6, pp. 196–97.

"Narcissus" / "Narcissistic"—In Avatar Adi Da's Teaching-Revelation, "Narcissus" is a key symbol of the un-Enlightened individual as a self-obsessed seeker, enamored of his or her own self-image and egoic self-consciousness. In *The Knee Of Listening*, Adi Da Samraj describes His own discovery of the significance of the archetype of Narcissus:

> *Eventually, I began to recognize a structure in my humanly-born conscious awareness. It became more and more apparent, and its nature and effects revealed themselves as fundamental, inclusive of all the states and contents in life and mind. My own "myth"—the governor of all patterns, the source of presumed self-identity, the motivator of all seeking—began to stand out in the mind as a living being.*
>
> *This "myth", this controlling logic (or force) that structured and limited my humanly-born conscious awareness, revealed itself as the self-concept—and the actual life—of Narcissus. I saw that my entire adventure—the desperate cycle of Awakeness and its decrease, of truly Conscious Being and Its gradual covering in the mechanics of living, seeking, dying, and suffering—was produced out of the image (or mentality) that appears hidden in the ancient myth of Narcissus.*
>
> *The more I contemplated him, the more profoundly I understood him. I observed, in awe, the primitive control that this self-concept and logic exercised over all of my behavior and experience. I began to see that same logic operative in all other human beings, and in every living thing—even in the very life of the cells, and in the natural energies that surround every living entity or process. It was the logic (or process) of separation itself, of enclosure and immunity. It manifested as fear and identity, memory and experience. It informed every function of the living being, every experience, every act, every event. It "created" every "mystery". It was the structure of every imbecile link in the history of human suffering.*
>
> *He is the ancient one visible in the Greek myth, who was the universally adored child of the gods, who rejected the loved-one and every form of love and relationship, and who was finally condemned to the contemplation of his own image—until, as a result of his own act and obstinacy, he suffered the fate of eternal separateness and died in infinite solitude.*
>
> —Avatar Adi Da Samraj
> *The Knee Of Listening*

When Avatar Adi Da uses "Narcissus" as an archetypal reference to the activity of self-contraction, He places the name in quotation marks, to indicate that He is using the name metaphorically (rather than in reference to the character in the Greek myth). When He uses "Narcissus" in reference to the mythological character, the name is not placed in quotation marks. Avatar Adi Da uses the adjective "Narcissistic" in reference to this myth—in the sense of "relating to the activity of self-contraction", rather than in any more conventional meaning (particularly those meanings associated with the discipline of psychology).

Nirvikalpa Samadhi—See **Samadhi**.

Non-verbal Re-Cognition—The mature form into which verbal self-Enquiry develops in the Devotional Way of Insight. "Re-cognition" literally means "knowing again". Thus, the individual practicing non-verbal re-cognition simply notices and tacitly "knows again" (or directly understands) whatever is arising as yet another species of self-contraction (without using "Avoiding relationship?"), and he or she transcends (or feels beyond) it in heart-Communion with Avatar Adi Da. Avatar Adi Da describes in *The Dawn Horse Testament* that "The 'Conscious Process' Of Random self-Enquiry (In The Form 'Avoiding Relationship?') . . . Gradually Becomes The Process Of Non-verbal Re-Cognition (or 'Knowing Again') Of the self-Contraction—Which Re-Cognition (or 'Knowing Again') Is The Tacit Transcending Of The Habit Of 'Narcissus'" (Sutra 6).

O

"Oedipal"—In modern psychology, the "Oedipus complex" is named after the legendary Greek Oedipus, who was fated to unknowingly kill his father and marry his mother. Avatar Adi Da Teaches that the primary dynamisms of emotional-sexual desiring, rejection, envy, betrayal, self-pleasuring, resentment, and other primal emotions and impulses are indeed patterned upon unconscious reactions first formed early in life, in relation to one's mother and father. Avatar Adi Da calls this "the 'Oedipal' drama" and points out that we tend to relate to all women as we do to our mothers, and to all men as we do to our fathers, and (furthermore) that we tend to relate (and react) to our own bodies as we do to the parent of the opposite sex. Thus, we impose infantile reactions to our parents on our relationships with lovers and all other beings, according to their sex, and we also superimpose the same on our relationship to our own bodies.

This term is placed in quotation marks to indicate that Avatar Adi Da uses it with the specific meaning described here. (Avatar Adi Da's extended Instruction on "Oedipal" patterning is Given in *Ruchira Tantra Yoga.*)

Om—In the Way of Adidam, the Word-Sign "Om" indicates the Native Feeling of Being, or the Transcendental, and Inherently Spiritual, Divine Condition, the Self of all beings. It Invokes the Self-Father, Who is in the "Husband-Position" in relation to conditional forms and events. Traditionally, "Om" (also transliterated "Aum"), is the most comprehensive and venerable symbol of Spiritual knowledge in Hinduism. The Mantra "Om" is regarded by some to be the basis or seed of all mantras. It is the root syllable of origination and dissolution. Thus, "Om" is understood to be a direct expression of the Spiritual Power of the Divine or Absolute Being, from which all existence proceeds.

"Open Eyes"—Avatar Adi Da's technical synonym for the Realization of seventh stage Sahaja Nirvikalpa Samadhi, or Most Perfect Divine Enlightenment. The phrase graphically describes the non-exclusive, non-inward, Prior State of the Divine Self-Realizer, Who is Identified Unconditionally with the Divine Self-Reality, while also allowing whatever arises to appear in the Divine Consciousness. Thus, "Open Eyes" is "Transcendental, Inherently Spiritual, Inherently egoless, and Self-Evidently Divine Self-Abiding (As Consciousness Itself, Self-Radiant and Self-Existing), Even Prior To All Witnessing, Spontaneously Self-Recognizing and Inherently Transcending all the conditionally arising 'things' that (Apparently) arise In (and As Apparent Modifications Of) Love-Bliss" (Sutra 56).

This term is placed in quotation marks to indicate that Avatar Adi Da uses it with the specific technical meaning described here (rather than any of the more commonly accepted general meanings).

"Original" Context Of The Fourth Stage Of Life—In the Way of Adidam, the "original" (or beginner's) devotional context of the fourth stage of life involves the initial cultivation of devotional heart-response to Avatar Adi Da (as Divine Self-Realizer and as Adept Heart-Teacher), through consistent application to the practices of ego-surrendering, ego-forgetting, and ego-transcending devotion, service, self-discipline, and meditation.

The essential religious "considerations" and devotional practices Given to listening devotees and hearing devotees in the Way of Adidam awaken the open-hearted love-feeling, gratitude, and self-surrender that characterize the fourth stage of life. They thus grant a fourth stage context to dimensions of practice that otherwise focus on developing responsibility for functions of the body-mind associated with the first three stages of life. See also Sutra 21.

Avatar Adi Da places the word "original" in quotation marks in this usage, in order to indicate that He is using it in the specific technical meaning described here.

Outshined / Outshining—A synonym for "Divine Translation", referring to the final Demonstration of the four-phase process of the seventh stage of life in the Way of Adidam. In the Great Event of Outshining (or Divine Translation), body, mind, and world are no longer noticed—not because the Divine Consciousness has withdrawn or dissociated from conditionally manifested phenomena, but because the Divine Self-Abiding Self-Recognition of all arising phenomena as modifications of the Divine Self-Condition has become so intense that the "Bright" Radiance of Consciousness now Outshines all such phenomena. See also **Four Phases Of The Seventh Stage Of Life**.

"Own-Body Yogic Sexual Exercise" / "Own-Body Yogic Sexual Practice" / sex-Specific "Own-Body Yogic Conductivity Practice"—In Sutra 39, Avatar Adi Da describes sexual activity as a matter of personal, and (specifically) "own-body", responsibility. The "own-body Yogic sexual practice" (or "own-body Yogic sexual exercise" or sex-specific "own-body Yogic conductivity practice") is a means for an individual to both learn about, and (thereafter) to rightly manage, sexual energy in his or her own body, in the context of the practice of Ruchira Avatara Bhakti Yoga. The own-body Yogic sexual practice is engaged by all practitioners of Adidam, regardless of whether they are (in their personal intimate contexts) sexually active or celibate.

The "own-body Yogic sexual practice" involves Yogic self-stimulation, with the intention to "conduct" the natural energy (or, in the case of devotees of Avatar Adi Da who have been Spiritually Initiated by Him, His Spirit-Energy) in the full Circle of the body-mind (while entirely avoiding degenerative orgasm).

P

Padukas—The ceremonial sandals or shoes of the Sat-Guru, venerated because of their association with the Sat-Guru's feet. To worship the feet of the Sat-Guru is to express humility and gratitude in relationship to him or her, and to express devotion and veneration of his or her bodily form, because the Sat-Guru's feet are a potent vehicle of Spiritual Transmission.

Parama-Buddha—The Supreme Enlightened One.

Paramadvaita Buddha—"Advaita" means "Non-Dual". Therefore, the Paramadvaita Buddha is the One of Supreme ("Parama") Non-Dual Enlightenment.

Paramadvaita-Guru—The Supreme Non-Dual Guru.

Parama-Guru—See **Divine Parama-Guru**.

Param-Avatar—The Supreme ("Param") Avatar, the Complete Descent of the Divine Person.

"Peculiar"—See **"Vital", "Peculiar", and "Solid"**.

"Perfect Practice"—The "Perfect Practice" is Avatar Adi Da's technical term for the discipline of the most mature stages of practice in the Way of Adidam. The "Perfect Practice" is practice in the Domain of Consciousness Itself (as opposed to practice from the point of view of the body or the mind). The "Perfect Practice" unfolds in three phases, the third of which is Divine Enlightenment.

This term is placed in quotation marks to indicate that Avatar Adi Da uses it with the specific technical meaning described here. See Sutras 46–68.

Perfectly Subjective—Avatar Adi Da uses this phrase to describe the True Divine Source (or "Subject") of the conditionally manifested worlds—as opposed to regarding the Divine as some sort of objective "Other". Thus, in the phrase "Perfectly Subjective", the word "Subjective" does not have the sense of "relating to the inward experience of an individual", but, rather, it has the sense of "Being Consciousness Itself, the True Subject of all apparent experience".

Pleasure Dome—Avatar Adi Da Samraj Speaks of the Way of Adidam as a "Pleasure Dome", recalling the poem "Kubla Khan", by Samuel Taylor Coleridge ("In Xanadu did Kubla Khan / A stately pleasure-dome decree . . ."). Avatar Adi Da points out that, in many religious traditions, it is presumed that one must embrace suffering in order to "earn" future happiness and pleasure. However, by Calling His devotees to live the Way of Adidam as a Pleasure Dome, Avatar Adi Da Samraj Communicates His Teaching that the Way of heart-Communion with Him is always about present-time Happiness, not about any kind of search to attain Happiness in the future. Thus, in the Way of Adidam, there is no idealization of suffering and pain as presumed means to attain future happiness—and, consequently, there is no denial of the appropriate enjoyment of even the ordinary pleasures of human life.

Avatar Adi Da also uses "Pleasure Dome" as a reference to the Divine Love-Bliss-Happiness That Is His own Self-Nature and His Gift to all who heart-recognize Him and heart-respond to Him.

"Point Of View"—In Avatar Adi Da's Wisdom-Teaching, "Point of View" is in quotation marks and capitalized when referring to the Position of Consciousness, Prior to (and independent of) the body-mind or conditional existence altogether. In the Way of Adidam, the "Point of View" of Consciousness is the basis of the "Perfect Practice".

"Practice"—Avatar Adi Da uses quotation marks around the term "Practice" in order to distinguish the "Practice" of Most Perfect Real-God-Realization in the seventh stage of life from practice that is engaged in any of the earlier stages of life. It is true that the practices in the Way of Adidam associated with the first six stages of life are founded in Satsang with Avatar Adi Da Samraj (the Revealer and Giver of the seventh stage Realization), and (thus) in the context of the intuitive Freedom (or Radiant Happiness) of the seventh stage of life. Nevertheless, these practices are still being applied by the limited body-mind-self, previous to the Most Perfect Realization of Divine Being. In other words, these disciplines counter tendencies that the egoic psycho-physical being would otherwise automatically exploit.

In the seventh stage of life, body and mind are continuously and spontaneously Divinely Self-Recognized as only modifications of the Divine Conscious Light. In the seventh stage of life, the psycho-physical expression of Divine Self-Realization is thus a "Practice", so to speak, only in the sense of simple action. In other words, it is not a discipline countering any tendency that would otherwise dominate body and mind, but (rather) a Free Demonstration of the Wisdom, Bliss, Joy, Love, Freedom, and Fullness of Divine Enlightenment Itself.

prana / pranic—The Sanskrit word "prana" means "breath", "life-energy". It generally refers to the life-energy animating all beings and pervading everything in cosmic Nature. In the human body-mind, circulation of this universal life-energy is associated with the heartbeat and the cycles of the breath. In esoteric Yogic Teachings, prana is also a specific technical name for one of a number of forms of etheric energy that functionally sustain the bodily being.

Prana is not to be equated with the Divine Spirit-Current, or the Spiritual (and Always Blessing) Divine Presence of Avatar Adi Da Samraj. The finite pranic energies that sustain individual beings are only conditional, localized, and temporary phenomena of the realm of cosmic Nature. Even in the form of universal life-force, prana is but a conditional modification of the Divine Spirit-Current Avatarically Self-Transmitted by Avatar Adi Da.

pranayama—Sanskrit for "restraint or regulation (yama) of life-energy (prana)". Pranayama is a technique for balancing, purifying, and intensifying the entire psycho-physical system by controlling the currents of the breath and life-force. Automatic pranayama is spontaneous Yogic breathing that arises involuntarily and has the same purifying effects as the voluntary exercise of such pranayama.

Pranotthana—a Sanskrit compound term used by Yogis to describe the "rising" ("utthana") of the "breath, vitality, or life" ("prana").

prapatti—Literally, "forward-fallingness" (in Sanskrit), a term signifying unconditional self-surrender or reliance on Divine Grace. The practice of prapatti—founded upon preparatory disciplines that regulate moral life, discipline the mind, and open the psychic or feeling heart—was the most advanced practice of the devotional (bhakti) schools of medieval India. Avatar Adi Da's own early practice of unconditional self-surrender was generated spontaneously, without His knowledge of any such traditional practice, Eastern or Western.

Prasad—Gifts that have been offered to the Divine and, having been Blessed, are returned as Divine Gifts to devotees. By extension, Prasad is anything the devotee receives from his or her Guru.

Prayer Of Remembrance—The Prayer of Remembrance is the whole bodily exercise of Invoking (and turning to) Avatar Adi Da Samraj by means of the repetition of His principal Divine Name, "Da", in coordination with the cycle of breathing-"conductivity". This form of the combined "conscious process" and "conductivity" practice is engaged by practitioners in the Devotional Way of Faith in the first actually seeing stage, replacing their previous practice of Ruchira Avatara Naama Japa. See Sutra 43.

Priorly Ascended Nirvikalpa Samadhi—See **Samadhi**.

Priorly Self-Abiding Jnana Nirvikalpa Samadhi—See **Samadhi**.

Promised God-Man—A common theme running through various branches of the Great Tradition is the prophecy of a great Savior or Liberator still to come. The prophecy takes different forms in different traditions, but the underlying commonality is the promise or expectation that the culminating Avatar or Incarnation will appear in the future, at a time when humanity is lost, apparently cut off from Wisdom, Truth, and God.

Puja / Ruchira Avatara Puja—The Sanskrit word "puja" means "worship". All formal sacramental devotion in the Way of Adidam is consecrated to Avatar Adi Da and is thus celebrated as Ruchira Avatara Puja. It is a practice of expressive whole bodily devotion to Avatar Adi Da. Ruchira Avatara Puja involves bodily Invocation of, self-surrender to, and heart-Communion with Avatar Adi Da by various means—including prayer, chant, song, recitation of His Word of Instruction, dance, the offering and receiving of gifts, and other forms of outward (or bodily active) devotional attention.

In the Way of Adidam, all practitioners participate daily in formal Ruchira Avatara Puja, as a practice that establishes them profoundly in ecstatic feeling-Contemplation of Avatar Adi Da. The principal forms of daily Ruchira Avatara Puja are the Ruchira Avatara Murti Puja (ceremonial service to and worship of the Sacred Image of the Ruchira Avatar, Adi Da Samraj), the Ruchira Avatara Paduka Puja (ceremonial service to and worship of Avatar Adi Da's Blessed Sandals, or Padukas), and the Ruchira Avatara Arati Puja (ceremonial worship of the Sacred Image of the Ruchira Avatar, Adi Da Samraj, by means of the waving of lights and ecstatic chanting).

Purushottama-Guru—The Supreme Divine Person as Guru. "Purushottama" is pronounced with the emphasis on the third syllable.

Purushottama Buddha—"Purushottama" is a Hindu name for the Divine Person. "Uttama" means "Supreme", and "Purusha" is "Person". Therefore, the Purushottama Buddha is the Enlightened One Who Is the Supreme Divine Person. Like "Buddha-Avatar", "Purushottama Buddha" conveys Avatar Adi Da's Encompassing and Surpassing of the traditions of Buddhism and Hinduism (and, thus, the entire collective Great Tradition of mankind).

Q

Quandra—The principal female character of Avatar Adi Da's liturgical drama, *The Mummery Book*.

R

"Radical"—Derived from the Latin "radix", meaning "root". Thus, "radical" principally means "irreducible", "fundamental", or "relating to the origin". Thus, Avatar Adi Da defines "Radical" as "Gone-To-The-Root". Because Adi Da Samraj uses "radical" in this literal sense, it appears in quotation marks in His Wisdom-Teaching, in order to distinguish His usage from the common reference to an extreme (often political) view.

"Radical" Understanding—Avatar Adi Da uses the word "understanding" to mean "the process of transcending egoity". Thus, to "understand" is to simultaneously observe the activity of the self-contraction and to surrender that activity via devotional resort to Him.

Avatar Adi Da has Revealed that, despite their intention to Realize Reality (or Truth, or Real God), all religious and Spiritual traditions (other than the Way of Adidam) are involved, in one manner or another (relating to either the subtle or the causal dimension of existence), with the search to satisfy the ego. Only Avatar Adi Da has Revealed the Way to "radically" understand the ego (by "going to the root") and (in due course, through intensive formal practice of the Way of Adidam, as His formally acknowledged devotee) to most perfectly transcend the ego.

Raymond (Darling)—The principal male character of Avatar Adi Da's liturgical drama, *The Mummery Book*.

Real God—The True (and Perfectly Subjective) Source of all conditions, the True and Spiritual Divine Person—rather than any ego-made (and, thus, false, or limited) presumption about God. Among Avatar Adi Da's many Definitions of "Real God" in *The Dawn Horse Testament* are the following: "The One and True Divine Person—Which Is Reality, or Truth, or That Which Is Always Already The Case" (Sutra 12) and "The God (or The Truth and The Reality) Of Consciousness, Freedom, Love-Bliss, Being, and Oneness" (Sutra 12).

"Reality Consideration" See **"Consider" / "Consideration"**.

"Real" Meditation —"Real" meditation is Avatar Adi Da's technical term for meditation based on true hearing of Him.

Religious and Spiritual—A phrase Avatar Adi Da uses to indicate (and contrast) the religious orientation to communing with "God", Truth, or Reality as a "Thing Apart" (inherently separate from the aspirant) and the Spiritual orientation of the actual, tangible experience of Spiritual Force (or Power), even to the point of tangibly experienced "Oneness" with "God", Truth, or Reality. The religious orientation is associated with the first three stages of life and the "original" context of the fourth stage of life (and also with the frontal line), while the Spiritual orientation is associated with the fourth stage of life (in its "basic" context), the fifth stage of life, the sixth stage of life, and (potentially, in the case of devotees of Avatar Adi Da Samraj) the seventh stage of life (and also with both the frontal line and the spinal line, the right side of the heart, and Amrita Nadi).

In certain contexts, Avatar Adi Da also uses the words "religion" and "religious" in a more general sense, referring to the total religious and Spiritual process.

Right Side Of The Heart—See **Heart / The Heart Itself / Stations Of The Heart**.

Ruchira Advaitism—Advaitism is generally a reference to the tradition of Advaita Vedanta, meaning the "Non-Dual Truth". "Ruchira" is "bright, radiant, effulgent". Thus, Ruchira Advaitism is not a path of seclusion in the Ultimate Non-Dual Truth, but rather the Way of the Divine Love-Bliss, Which Is the Self-Radiance of Self-Existing (and Non-Dual) Consciousness Itself. The Revelation of Ruchira Advaitism is the Gift of the Ruchira Avatar, Adi Da Samraj.

Ruchira Avatar—In Sanskrit, "Ruchira" means "bright, radiant, effulgent". Thus, the Reference "Ruchira Avatar" indicates that Avatar Adi Da Samraj is the "Bright" (or Radiant) Descent of the Divine Reality Itself into the conditionally manifested worlds, Appearing here in His bodily (human) Divine Form.

Ruchira Avatara Advaita-Dharma—Indicates "the Non-Dual ('Advaita') Wisdom-Teaching ('Dharma') of the Ruchira Avatar".

Ruchira Avatara Bhakti / Ruchira Avatara Bhakti Yoga—Ruchira Avatara Bhakti Yoga is the principal Gift, Calling, and Discipline Offered by Avatar Adi Da Samraj to His devotees.

The phrase "Ruchira Avatara Bhakti Yoga" is itself a summary of the Way of Adidam. "Bhakti", in Sanskrit, is "love, adoration, or devotion", while "Yoga" is "God-Realizing discipline" (or "practice"). "Ruchira Avatara Bhakti Yoga" is, thus, "the practice of devotion to the Ruchira Avatar, Adi Da Samraj".

The practice of Ruchira Avatara Bhakti Yoga is the process of turning the four principal faculties (body, emotion, mind, and breath) to Avatar Adi Da (in and as His Avatarically-Born bodily human Divine Form) in every moment and under all circumstances. See especially Sutra 5.

Ruchira Avatara Bhava Samadhi—The enraptured feeling-swoon (bhava samadhi) of Communion with the Ruchira Avatar, Adi Da Samraj.

Ruchira Avatara Darshan—Heart-sighting of the Ruchira Avatar, Adi Da Samraj. One of Avatar Adi Da's Seven Gifts.

Ruchira Avatara Hridaya-Shaktipat Yoga—Indicates "the Yoga of receiving the Divine Heart-Blessing-Transmission ('Hridaya-Shaktipat') of the Ruchira Avatar".

Ruchira Avatara Hridaya-Siddha Yoga—Indicates "the Yoga of devotion to the Ruchira Avatar, Who Is the Siddha of the Divine Heart (Hridaya)".

Ruchira Avatara Kripa—"Kripa" is Sanskrit for "grace". Traditionally, it is a synonym for "shaktipat", or the Initiatory Blessing of the Spiritual Master. Ruchira Avatara Kripa is Avatar Adi Da's Gift of the Transmission of His Divine Spiritual Heart-Blessing. One of Avatar Adi Da's Seven Gifts.

Ruchira Avatara Maha-Jnana-Siddha Yoga—Indicates "the Yoga of devotion to the Ruchira Avatar, Who Is the Supreme Transcendental Divine Siddha ('Maha-Jnana-Siddha')".

Ruchira Avatara Maha-Jnana Hridaya-Shaktipat Yoga—Indicates "the Yoga of receiving the Supreme Transcendental ('Maha-Jnana') Divine Heart-Blessing-Transmission ('Hridaya-Shaktipat') of the Ruchira Avatar".

Ruchira Avatara Mahamantra—See **Ruchira Avatara Naama Mantra**.

Ruchira Avatara Moksha-Bhava—The enraptured feeling-swoon ("Bhava") of the Heart-Liberation ("Moksha") Granted by the Ruchira Avatar, Adi Da Samraj. One of Avatar Adi Da's Seven Gifts.

Ruchira Avatara Naama Japa—Repetition ("Japa") of the Name ("Naama") of the Ruchira Avatar, Adi Da Samraj. Avatar Adi Da Instructs that Ruchira Avatara Naama Japa (the form of the "conscious process" engaged by practitioners of the Devotional Way of Faith, previous to the first actually seeing stage) is to be "Engaged On The Basis Of (and As An Expression Of) The Faith-Response To Me, and By (or On The Basis Of) The Consistently Demonstrated Devotional Exercise Of That Faith" (Sutra 27) through repetition of the Ruchira Avatara Naama Mantra, in conjunction with the use of a mala (or rosary). See Sutra 27, pp. 199–200.

Ruchira Avatara Naama Mantra / Ruchira Avatara Mahamantra—"Ruchira Avatara Naama Mantra" means "Mantra of the Name (Naama) of the Ruchira Avatar, Adi Da Samraj". The synonymous term "Ruchira Avatara Mahamantra" means "Great (Maha) Mantra of the Ruchira Avatar, Adi Da Samraj".

Avatar Adi Da Samraj has Given eighty variant forms of the Ruchira Avatara Naama Mantra (or Ruchira Avatara Mahamantra). Any of these forms may be used "In Devotional Chanting and Devotional Singing, and In Sacramental Activities, or, Otherwise, In moments Of Spontaneous Ecstatic Devotional Exclamation, or In moments Of Spontaneous Ecstatic Devotional Invocation Of Me" (Sutra 6). In addition, each practitioner of the Devotional Way of Faith (practicing in the stages previous to the first actually seeing stage) chooses one (and only one) form of the Ruchira Avatara Naama Mantra as his or her chosen form of Invoking Avatar Adi Da in the practice of Ruchira Avatara Naama Japa.

The eighty forms of the Ruchira Avatara Naama Mantra (or Ruchira Avatara Mahamantra) are Given by Avatar Adi Da in Sutra 6.

Ruchira Avatara Puja—See **Puja**.

Ruchira Avatara Seva—"Seva" is Sanskrit for "service". Thus, "Ruchira Avatara Seva" is "service to the Ruchira Avatar, Adi Da Samraj". One of Avatar Adi Da's Seven Gifts.

Service to one's Spiritual Master is traditionally treasured as one of the great Means of Spiritual Realization. In the Way of Adidam, each practitioner finds many specific ways to serve Avatar Adi Da Samraj and His Divine Work of world-Blessing. In the largest sense, to serve Avatar Adi Da constantly is to live every action, and, indeed, one's entire life, as direct heart-Communion with and responsive obedience and conformity to Avatar Adi Da in every possible and appropriate way.

Ruchira Avatara Shaktipat Yoga—Indicates "the Yoga of receiving the Divine Blessing-Transmission ('Shaktipat') of the Ruchira Avatar".

Ruchira Avatara Siddha Yoga—See **Ruchira Siddha Yoga**.

Ruchira Avatara Tapas—"Tapas" is Sanskrit for "heat", or, by extension, "self-discipline engaged as part of the religious and Spiritual process". One of Avatar Adi Da's Seven Gifts. (The "heat" of self-discipline is traditionally understood as one of the primary means of purifying the psycho-physical being.) Thus, "Ruchira Avatara Tapas" means "the self-discipline Given by the Ruchira Avatar, Adi Da Samraj, to His formally acknowledged devotees". Avatar Adi Da often speaks of "tapas" as the "heat" that results from the conscious frustration of egoic tendencies, through acceptance of His Calling for ego-surrendering, ego-forgetting, and ego-transcending devotion, service, self-discipline, and meditation.

Ruchira Avatara Vani / Ruchira Avatara Vani-Vichara—"Vani" is Sanskrit for "word" or "sacred message". "Vichara" is Sanskrit for "enquiry" or "investigation". Thus, "Ruchira Avatara Vani-Vichara" means "responsive 'consideration' of Avatar Adi Da's Word of Instruction and His Revelatory Leelas". One of Avatar Adi Da's Seven Gifts.

Avatar Adi Da's inclusion of "Vichara" as a key dimension of this Gift of His Grace indicates that constant attention, profound intelligence, and heart-felt responsiveness must characterize the reception of His Avataric Divine Word and Leelas, if one's study is to be auspicious and fruitful.

Ruchira Buddha—The Enlightened One Who Shines with the Divine "Brightness".

Ruchira Buddha-Avatar—The "Bright" Enlightened One Who is the Incarnation of the Divine Person.

Ruchira-Guru: The "Bright" Guru.

Ruchira Samraj Samadhi—See **Samadhi**.

Ruchira Sannyasin Hermitage Ashrams—Traditionally, Realizers have been provided with set-apart places where they were free to do their Spiritual Work in an appropriate and secluded circumstance. And these places became Spiritually Empowered through their Presence and Work.

In this traditional manner, devotees of Avatar Adi Da have provided places where He is completely set apart to do His Blessing-Work for the sake of humanity as a whole, as well as His specific Spiritual Work with devotees who come on pilgrimage to receive the Initiatory Spiritual Blessing of being in His physical Company on retreat.

To date, Avatar Adi Da has Established and Spiritually Empowered four Ruchira Sannyasin Hermitage Ashrams:

- Adidam Samrajashram, the Island of Naitauba in Fiji

  Adidam Samrajashram is Avatar Adi Da's principal Hermitage Ashram and the primary Seat from which His Divine Spiritual Blessing Flows to the entire world.
- The Mountain Of Attention Sanctuary of Adidam, in northern California
- Tat Sundaram Hermitage, in northern California
- Da Love-Ananda Mahal, in Hawaii

Avatar Adi Da Samraj moves among the Hermitage Ashrams in His spontaneous wandering-Work of world-Blessing.

Spiritually, He is perpetually "in residence" at His Hermitage Sanctuaries. He has invested Himself Spiritually in these sacred places, and His Spiritual Power and Presence is constantly active in them.

The Ruchira Sannyasin Order Of Adidam Ruchiradam—The Ruchira Sannyasin Order is the body of Avatar Adi Da's most exemplary "Perfect Practice" devotees who have chosen to consecrate their lives utterly to Him and His Way—by embracing the life of formal and legal renunciation, in the circumstance of perpetual retreat. Avatar Adi Da has designated the Ruchira Sannyasin Order as the senior cultural authority within the gathering of His devotees—both during and after His physical Lifetime. Thus, it is the unique responsibility of the Ruchira Sannyasin Order to function both as the extension of His Sacred Authority and as His Instrumentality (or the collective human "conduit" for His Spiritual Blessing).

The Ruchira Sannyasin Order of Adidam Ruchiradam is (and must always be) the most senior gathering of (necessarily, formal) practitioners of the Way of Adidam—and the hierarchically central, and most senior (but entirely renunciate, and non-managerial), functioning cultural authority among, and in relation to, all the (necessarily, formal) practitioners of the Way of Adidam. . . .

All the present members and all the future members of the Ruchira Sannyasin Order of Adidam Ruchiradam are Called and Empowered (by Me) to Function (collectively) as the principal and most senior (physically living, human) Instruments of My forever Blessing Work, and, by their unique (and uniquely authoritative) cultural service (simply by Wisdom-word and practicing example), to provide all other practitioners of the Way of Adidam with the principal Good Company (of fellow devotees) that is necessary for the inspiration and guidance of their practice of the Way of Adidam.

—Avatar Adi Da Samraj
"The Orders of My True and
Free Renunciate Devotees"

Ruchira Shakti / Ruchira Shaktipat—The "Bright" (Ruchira) Spiritual Energy, or Spiritual Power (Shakti), and Spiritual Transmission (Shaktipat) of Ruchira Avatar Adi Da Samraj. These terms are synonymous with "Hridaya-Shakti" and "Hridaya-Shaktipat" (respectively).

Ruchira Shaktipat Yoga—Indicates "the Yoga of receiving the 'Bright' Divine Blessing-Transmission ('Ruchira Shaktipat') of Avatar Adi Da Samraj".

Ruchira Siddha / Ruchira Siddha-Guru—The "Bright" Perfect Transmission-Master.

Ruchira Siddha Yoga—"Siddha Yoga" is, literally, "the Yoga of the Perfected One[s]".

Swami Muktananda used the term "Siddha Yoga" to refer to the form of Kundalini Yoga that he Taught, which involved initiation of the devotee by the Guru's Transmission of Shakti (or Spiritual Energy). Avatar Adi Da Samraj has indicated that this was a fifth stage form of Siddha Yoga.

In "I (Alone) Am The Adidam Revelation", Avatar Adi Da Says:

. . . I Teach Siddha Yoga in the Mode and Manner of the only-by-Me Revealed and Given seventh

stage of life (as Ruchira Avatara Siddha Yoga, or Ruchira Siddha Yoga, or Ruchira Avatara Shaktipat Yoga, or Ruchira Shaktipat Yoga, or Ruchira Avatara Hridaya-Siddha Yoga, or Ruchira Avatara Hridaya-Shaktipat Yoga, or Ruchira Avatara Maha-Jnana-Siddha Yoga, or Ruchira Avatara Maha-Jnana Hridaya-Shaktipat Yoga)—and always toward (or to the degree of) the Realization inherently associated with (and, at last, Most Perfectly Demonstrated and Proven by) the only-by-Me Revealed and Given seventh stage of life, and as a practice and a Process that progressively includes (and, coincidently, directly transcends) all six of the phenomenal and developmental (and, necessarily, yet ego-based) stages of life that precede the seventh.

Avatar Adi Da's description of the similarities and differences between traditional Siddha Yoga and the Way of Adidam is Given in "I (Alone) Am The Adidam Revelation", which Essay appears in a number of Avatar Adi Da's twenty-three "Source-Texts".

S

Sacrament Of Universal Sacrifice—A simple (and yet most profound) ceremonial expression of the relationship between the practitioner and Avatar Adi Da. In a mood of gratitude, love, devotion, and self-surrender, His devotee offers simple gifts of flowers, fruit, water, or the like to Avatar Adi Da, while calling upon Him, either audibly or silently, by His Principal Name, "Da" (or any other of His Names that He has Given for the practice of simple Name-Invocation of Him). At the end of the occasion, His devotee receives in return a purified and sanctified Gift, again calling upon Avatar Adi Da via His Principal Name, "Da" (or any other of His Names that He has Given for the practice of simple Name-Invocation of Him). The giving and receiving of tangible gifts both enacts and symbolizes His devotee's constant gift of the surrender of egoic self to Avatar Adi Da, the Invocation and Installation of Him in front of (and at) the heart, and Avatar Adi Da's eternally Given Gift of the Divine "Brightness" and all Its Liberating Blessings in return.

Sacred Domain—Avatar Adi Da has described the "sacred domain" that must be the core of His devotees' lives:

AVATAR ADI DA SAMRAJ: The sacred domain is about the expression of ecstasy—in all its forms. Therefore, all the arts—and, indeed, all forms of creativity—are, basically, about the sacred domain. Everything about the religious life (including meditation, worship, prayer, and so on) is in the sacred domain. The sacred domain is even the primary place of food-taking. The sacred domain is the place of emotional-sexual intimacy, the place of friendship and human intimacy altogether. The sacred domain is the place where the truly human (and humanizing) culture of ecstasy is truly practiced, in the truest sense, assisted by cooperative association between people.

After the day's business is over, everyone should return to his or her sacred domain, where there is a real cultural order and real involvement in profound matters, where intimate human matters are kept alive and sacredly used. It must be so. You cannot expect the common (or secular) world to accommodate ecstasy. At most, you can expect the common (or secular) world to allow ecstasy its own (separate) sphere of privacy or intimate culture.

—*Ruchira Tantra Yoga*

Sadhana—In Sanskrit, "sadhana" means "ego-transcending religious or Spiritual practice".

"Sadhana Years"—The period of time in Avatar Adi Da's early Life, starting when He, most intensively, began His Quest to recover the Truth of Existence (at Columbia College) in 1957 and ending with His Divine Re-Awakening in 1970. Avatar Adi Da's full Description of His "Sadhana Years" is Given in *The Knee Of Listening*.

The term "Sadhana Years" is placed in quotation marks to indicate that it is used by Avatar Adi Da in the "so to speak" sense. In this case, it indicates that, because of the Avataric Divine Nature of His Birth and Life, Avatar Adi Da's years of apparent "sadhana" were actually part of His Submission to humankind and preparation of the vehicle of His Body-Mind to Teach and Bless. Avatar Adi Da Samraj intentionally engaged His "Sadhana Years" as the Process of "Learning Man". As the Avatarically Incarnate (and Inherently egoless) Divine Person, there was no other necessity for Him to engage any form of apparent "sadhana", because there was (in His Case) no egoity to be purified and transcended.

Sahaj Samadhi—See **Samadhi**.

Sahasrar—In the traditional system of seven chakras, the sahasrar is the highest chakra (or subtle energy-center), associated with the crown of the head and above.

The sahasrar is described as a "thousand-petaled lotus", the terminal of Light to which the Yogic process (of Spiritual ascent through the chakras) aspires. However, in *The Knee Of Listening*, Avatar Adi Da describes how He spontaneously experienced what He calls the "severing of the sahasrar". The Spirit-Energy no longer ascended into the crown of the head (and beyond), confined to the structure of the chakras:

I saw that what appeared as the sahasrar (the terminal chakra and primary lotus in the crown of the head) had been severed. The sahasrar had fallen off like a blossom. The Shakti—Which had previously appeared as a polarized Energy that moved up and down through the various chakras (or functional centers), producing various effects—

was now released from the chakra form. There was no more polarized Force. Indeed, there was no structure whatsoever—no up or down, no chakras. The chakra system had been revealed as unnecessary, an arbitrary rule or setting for the Play of Divine Energy. The structure beneath all of the bodies (or functional sheaths), gross and subtle, had revealed itself to be as unnecessary and conditional as the bodies (or functional sheaths) themselves. . . .

I saw that Reality (and Real Consciousness) was not in the least determined by any form apart from Itself. Consciousness had shown Its inherent Freedom and Priority in relation to the chakra form. It had shown Itself to be senior to that entire structure, Prior to every kind of manifestation or modification of cosmic Energy (or Shakti). There was simply Consciousness (or the One and Only and inherently indivisible Conscious Light) Itself—Prior to all forms, all sense of dilemma, and every kind of seeking and presumed necessity.

—Avatar Adi Da Samraj
The Knee Of Listening

Samadhi—The Sanskrit word "Samadhi" traditionally denotes various exalted states that appear in the context of esoteric meditation and Realization. Avatar Adi Da Teaches that, for His devotees, Samadhi is, even more simply and fundamentally, the Enjoyment of His Divine State (or "Divine Samadhi"), Which is experienced (even from the beginning of the practice of Adidam) through ego-transcending heart-Communion with Him. Therefore, "the cultivation of Samadhi" is another way to describe the fundamental basis of the Way of Adidam. Avatar Adi Da's devotee is in Samadhi in any moment of standing beyond the separate self in true devotional heart-Communion with Him. See Sutra 22.

The developmental process leading to Divine Enlightenment in the Way of Adidam may be marked by many signs, principal among which are the unique Samadhis of the Way of Adidam. Although some of the traditionally known Samadhis of the fourth, the fifth, and the sixth stages of life may appear in the course of an individual's practice of the Way of Adidam, the appearance of all of them is not necessary (as Avatar Adi Da Indicates in His Wisdom-Teaching). The essential Samadhis of the Way of Adidam are those that are uniquely Granted by Avatar Adi Da Samraj—the Samadhi of the "Thumbs", Priorly ascended Nirvikalpa Samadhi, Priorly Self-Abiding Jnana Nirvikalpa Samadhi, and seventh stage Sahaja Nirvikalpa Samadhi. All the possible forms of Samadhi in the Way of Adidam are described in full detail by Avatar Adi Da Samraj in *The Dawn Horse Testament.*

Samadhi Of The "Thumbs"—"The 'Thumbs'" is Avatar Adi Da's technical term for the Invasion of the body-mind by a particular form of the forceful Descent of His Divine Spirit-Current.

In the fullest form of this experience, which Avatar Adi Da calls "the Samadhi of the 'Thumbs'", His Spirit-Invasion Descends all the way to the bottom of the frontal line of the body-mind (at the bodily base) and ascends through the spinal line, overwhelming the ordinary human sense of bodily existence, infusing the whole being with intense blissfulness, and releasing the ordinary, confined sense of body, mind, and separate self.

Both the experience of the "Thumbs" and the full Samadhi of the "Thumbs" are unique to the Way of Adidam, for they are specifically signs of the "Crashing Down" (or the Divine Descent) of Avatar Adi Da's Spirit-Baptism, into the body-minds of His devotees. The Samadhi of the "Thumbs" is a kind of "Nirvikalpa" (or formless) Samadhi—but in descent in the frontal line, rather than in ascent in the spinal line. See Sutra 45.

Savikalpa Samadhi and "Cosmic Consciousness"—The Sanskrit term "Savikalpa Samadhi" literally means "meditative ecstasy with form", or "deep meditative concentration (or absorption) in which form (or defined experiential content) is still perceived". Avatar Adi Da indicates that there are two basic forms of Savikalpa Samadhi. The first is characterized by the various experiences produced by the Spiritual ascent of energy and attention (into mystical phenomena, visions, and other subtle sensory perceptions of subtle psychic forms) and the various states of Yogic Bliss (or Spirit-"Intoxication"). See Sutra 60.

The second (and highest) form of Savikalpa Samadhi is called "Cosmic Consciousness", or the "'Vision' of Cosmic Unity". This is an isolated or periodic occurrence in which attention ascends, uncharacteristically and spontaneously, to a state of awareness wherein conditional existence is perceived as a Unity in Divine Awareness. The experience of "Cosmic Consciousness" is pursued as the ultimate goal of certain mystical and Yogic paths. It depends upon manipulation of attention and the body-mind, and it is interpreted from the point of view of the separate (body-based or mind-based) self—and, therefore, it is not equivalent to Divine Enlightenment. See Sutra 61.

conditionally Ascended Nirvikalpa Samadhi—The Sanskrit term "Nirvikalpa Samadhi" literally means "meditative ecstasy without form", or "deep meditative concentration (or absorption) in which there is no perception of form (or defined experiential content)". Traditionally, this state is regarded to be the final goal of the many schools of Yogic ascent whose orientation to practice is that of the fifth stage of life. Like "Cosmic Consciousness", conditionally ascended Nirvikalpa Samadhi is an isolated or periodic (and, necessarily, temporary) Realization. In it, attention ascends beyond all conditional manifestation into the formless Matrix of Divine Vibration and Divine Light Infinitely Above the world, the body, and the mind. And, like the various forms of Savikalpa Samadhi, conditionally ascended Nirvikalpa Samadhi is a temporary state of attention (or, more precisely, of the suspension of attention). It is produced by manipulation of attention and of the body-mind, and is (therefore) incapable of being maintained when attention returns (as it inevitably does) to the states of the body-mind. In the Way of Adidam, conditionally ascended Nirvikalpa Samadhi is a possible, but not necessary, experience. See Sutra 61.

Priorly Ascended Nirvikalpa Samadhi—Even though aspects of conditionally ascended Nirvikalpa Samadhi are comparable to Priorly ascended Nirvikalpa Samadhi, the two forms of ascended Nirvikalpa Samadhi are fundamentally different from each other, because Priorly ascended Nirvikalpa Samadhi is the spontaneous Establishment (entirely through Avatar Adi Da's Divine Spiritual Grace) in His formless Matrix of Love-Bliss Infinitely Above the world, the body, and the mind. Priorly ascended Nirvikalpa Samadhi does not depend on any manipulation of attention and (therefore) is not characterized by the return of attention to the states of the body-mind. In the "Perfect Practice" of Adidam, Priorly ascended Nirvikalpa Samadhi (in the context of the vertical domain) occurs subsequent to, and in perfect conjunction with, Priorly Self-Abiding Jnana Nirvikalpa Samadhi (in the context of the horizontal domain) as a necessary immediate prerequisite for the transition to the seventh stage of life. See Sutra 61.

conditionally Self-Abiding Jnana Nirvikalpa Samadhi—"Jnana" means "knowledge". Jnana Nirvikalpa Samadhi is the characteristic meditative experience in the context of the sixth stage of life. Produced by the intentional withdrawal of attention from the conditional body-mind-self and its relations, conditionally Self-Abiding Jnana Nirvikalpa Samadhi is the conditional, temporary Realization of the Transcendental Self-Condition (or Consciousness Itself), exclusive of any perception (or cognition) of world, objects, relations, body, mind, or separate-self-sense—and, thereby, formless (or "nirvikalpa"). See Sutra 62.

Priorly Self-Abiding Jnana Nirvikalpa Samadhi—Even though aspects of conditionally Self-Abiding Jnana Nirvikalpa Samadhi are comparable to Priorly Self-Abiding Jnana Nirvikalpa Samadhi, the two forms of Self-Abiding Jnana Nirvikalpa Samadhi are fundamentally different from each other, because Priorly Self-Abiding Jnana Nirvikalpa Samadhi is the spontaneous Establishment (entirely through Adi Da's Divine Spiritual Grace) in His Divine Self-Condition in (and beyond) the right side of the heart. Like Priorly ascended Nirvikalpa Samadhi, Priorly Self-Abiding Jnana Nirvikalpa Samadhi does not depend on any manipulation of attention and (therefore) is not characterized by the return of attention to the states of the body-mind. In the "Perfect Practice" of Adidam, Priorly ascended Nirvikalpa Samadhi (in the context of the vertical domain) occurs subsequent to, and in perfect conjunction with, Priorly Self-Abiding Jnana Nirvikalpa Samadhi (in the context of the horizontal domain) as a necessary immediate prerequisite for the transition to the seventh stage of life. See Sutra 62.

Seventh Stage Sahaja Nirvikalpa Samadhi, or Ruchira Samraj Samadhi, or Samraj Samadhi—Divine Self-Realization, or Most Perfect Divine Enlightenment—uniquely Revealed and Given by Avatar Adi Da Samraj. "Sahaja" is Sanskrit for "born together, innate, or natural". Thus, "Sahaja Nirvikalpa Samadhi" means "Innate Samadhi without form". "Ruchira Samraj Samadhi" means "the Samadhi of His own 'Brightness' Given by the Universal Divine Lord, Ruchira Avatar Adi Da Samraj". "Samraj Samadhi" means "the Samadhi of the Universal Divine Lord, Ruchira Avatar Adi Da Samraj".

Samraj—From the Sanskrit "Samraja", a traditional Indian term used to refer to great kings, and also to the Hindu gods. "Samraja" is defined as "universal or supreme ruler", "paramount Lord", or "paramount sovereign". "Samraj" was traditionally given as a title to a king who was regarded to be a "universal monarch".

Avatar Adi Da's Name "Adi Da Samraj" expresses that He is the Primordial (or Original) Giver, Who Blesses all as the Universal Lord of every thing, every where, for all time. The Sovereignty of His Kingdom has nothing to do with the world of human politics. Rather, it is entirely a matter of His Spiritual Dominion, His Kingship in the hearts of His devotees.

"Samraj Asana"—In Sutra 33, Avatar Adi Da Defines "Samraj Asana" as follows:

> *"Samraj Asana" Is A Spontaneous (By-My-Avataric-Divine-Spiritual-Grace-Given) Development Of The Foundation (Previously Established, and Always Primary) Practice Of Searchlessly Beholding Me. When My Avataric Divine Spiritual Self-Transmission Demonstrates Itself In Descent, On The Foundation Of True Hearing, Then "Samraj Asana" Characterizes (and Is The Context Of) Your Reception Of My Ruchira Shaktipat. That Is To Say, "Samraj Asana" Is Caused By My Avataric Divine Spiritual Self-Transmission—Not By Any ego-Effort On The Part Of My Devotee. "Samraj Asana" Is Not A self-Applied (or ego-Based, and Merely Seeking) Technique. . . .*
>
> *"Samraj Asana" Is An Eventual (Hearing-Based) Practice-Responsibility That Is Formally Assumed Relative To The "Asana" (or psycho-physical Attitude, or body-mind Orientation) Of Upward-Turning To Me (From The Brain Core).*

And That Upward-Turning Must Already Be Spontaneously and Readily Occurring In Response To Your (Always Spontaneous and Searchless) Experience Of My Tangible (Descending-From-Above) Avataric Divine Spiritual Self-Transmission.

Samraj Samadhi—See **Samadhi**.

Samraj Yoga—Avatar Adi Da defines "Samraj Yoga" in Sutra 58 as "The Total 'Perfect Practice' Yoga Of Utterly Transcending The First Six (or ego-Bound) Stages Of Life and (Thus and Thereby) Realizing The Only-By-Me Revealed and Given (and Divinely Enlightened, or Most Perfectly Divinely Awakened) Seventh Stage Of Life." Certain aspects of "Samraj Yoga" are described in *The Dawn Horse Testament*, but others are given only in initiation and instruction via the Ruchira Sannyasin Order of Adidam Ruchiradam, to those who are prepared to receive such instruction and initiation.

Sangha—Sanskrit for "company", or "gathering" (specifically, the gathering of practitioners of a Spiritual Way).

Santosha—Sanskrit for "satisfaction" or "contentment"—qualities associated with a sense of completion. These qualities are characteristic of no-seeking, the fundamental Principle of Avatar Adi Da's Wisdom-Teaching and of His entire Revelation of Truth. Because of its uniquely appropriate meanings, "Santosha" is one of Avatar Adi Da's Names. As Santosha Adi Da, Avatar Adi Da Samraj is the Divine Giver of Perfect Divine Contentedness, or Perfect Searchlessness.

Santosha Avatar—The Very Incarnation of Perfect Divine Contentedness, or Perfect Searchlessness.

Sat-Guru—"Sat" means "Truth", "Being", "Existence". Thus, "Sat-Guru" literally means "True Guru", or a Guru who can lead living beings from darkness (or non-Truth) into Light (or the Living Truth).

Sat-Guru Naama Japa—Repetition ("Japa") of the Name ("Naama") of the True Guru ("Sat-Guru"). Avatar Adi Da sometimes uses "Sat-Guru Naama Japa" as an alternative reference for "Ruchira Avatara Naama Japa".

Satsang—Hindi for "True (or right) relationship", "the company of Truth".

The greatest opportunity, and the greatest responsibility, of My devotees is Satsang with Me—Which is to live in the Condition of ego-surrendering, ego-forgetting, and (always more and more) ego-transcending devotional (and, in due course, Spiritual) relationship to Me, and (Thus and Thereby) to Realize My Avatarically Self-Revealed (and Self-Evidently Divine) Self-Condition, Which Is the Self-Evidently Divine Heart (or Non-Separate Self-Condition and Non-"Different" Source-Condition) of all-and-All, and Which Is Self-Existing and Self-Radiant Consciousness (or Indivisible Conscious Light) Itself (Which is One, and Only, and not separate in or as any one, or any "thing", at all).

—Avatar Adi Da Samraj
First Word, "Do Not Misunderstand Me"

Sattva / Sattvic—According to Hindu philosophy, all of conditionally manifested existence is a play of three qualities, or gunas. These are inertia (tamas), motion (rajas), and equilibrium, or balance (sattva). Traditionally, sattva has been valued above the qualities of rajas and tamas as the foundation (or basis) of Spiritual practice.

Savikalpa Samadhi—See **Samadhi**.

scientific materialism—The predominant philosophy and worldview of modern humanity, the basic presumption of which is that the material world is all that exists. In scientific materialism, the method of science, or the observation of objective phenomena, is made into philosophy and a way of life that suppresses the native human impulse to Divine Liberation.

Searchless Beholding Of Avatar Adi Da—The primary practice of the Way of Adidam, which begins after the foundation preparation is established and Avatar Adi Da has been moved to Grant Divine Spiritual Initiation to His devotee (in the context of extended formal retreat in His physical Company—or, after His physical Lifetime, in the physical company, and the by-Him-Spiritually-Empowered circumstances, of the Ruchira Sannyasin Order of Adidam Ruchiradam). The practice of searchlessly Beholding Avatar Adi Da is the Beholding of His Avatarically-Born bodily (human) Divine Form, free of any seeking-effort, and the searchless reception of His Spiritual Transmission. See Sutra 26.

Seeing—See **Listening, Hearing, and Seeing**.

self-Enquiry—The practice of self-Enquiry (in the form "Avoiding relationship?"), unique to the Way of Adidam, was spontaneously developed by Avatar Adi Da in the course of His own Ordeal of Divine Re-Awakening. Intense persistence in the "radical" discipline of this unique form of self-Enquiry led rapidly to Avatar Adi Da's Divine Re-Awakening (or Most Perfect Divine Self-Realization) in 1970.

The practice of self-Enquiry in the form "Avoiding relationship?" is the form of the "conscious process" practiced by those devotees of Avatar Adi Da (in the student-beginner, intensive listening-hearing, would-be-seeing, and first actually seeing stages of Adidam) who have chosen to practice the Devotional Way of Insight. See Sutras 6 and 27.

Self-Recognition / Self-Recognizing—See **Divine Self-Recognition**.

Self-Existing and Self-Radiant—Terms describing the two fundamental aspects of the One Divine Person (or Reality)—Existence (or Being, or Consciousness) Itself, and Radiance (or Energy, or Light) Itself.

Seven Giving Gifts—Avatar Adi Da has described His Blessing Given to all His devotees as being made of seven parts, or "Seven Giving Gifts". The Seven Gifts are:

1. His Word (Ruchira Avatara Vani)
2. His Sign (Ruchira Avatara Darshan)
3. Devotion to Him (Ruchira Avatara Bhakti)
4. Service to Him (Ruchira Avatara Seva)
5. Discipline in response to Him (Ruchira Avatara Tapas)
6. His Spiritual Blessing (Ruchira Avatara Kripa)
7. the Blessedness of the relationship with Him (Ruchira Avatara Moksha-Bhava).

See the Epilogue, or each of these individual Gifts in the glossary.

Shakti—A Sanskrit term for the Divinely Manifesting Spiritual Energy, Spiritual Power, or Spirit-Current of the Divine Person.

Shaktipat—The "descent of Spiritual Power". Yogic Shaktipat, which manipulates natural, conditional energies or partial manifestations of the Divine Spirit-Current, is typically granted through touch, word, glance, or regard by Yogic Adepts in the fifth stage of life. Although the term "Shaktipat" literally refers to the "descent" of Spiritual Power, the traditional Yogic Shaktipat is, in fact, a process of the ascent and circulation of Spiritual Power and must be distinguished from (and, otherwise, understood to be only a secondary aspect of) the Blessing Transmission of the "Bright" Itself (Ruchira Shaktipat), Which Originates from Infinitely Above and Functions in a unique process in descent and is uniquely Given by Avatar Adi Da Samraj. See especially Sutra 17.

Siddha / Siddha-Guru—"Siddha" is Sanskrit for "a completed, fulfilled, or perfected one", or "one of perfect accomplishment, or power". Avatar Adi Da uses "Siddha", or "Siddha-Guru", to mean a Transmission-Master who is a Realizer (to any significant degree) of Real God, Truth, or Reality.

siddhi / Siddhi (Divine)—Sanskrit for "power", or "accomplishment". When capitalized in Avatar Adi Da's Wisdom-Teaching, "Siddhi" is the Spiritual, Transcendental, and Divine Awakening-Power That He spontaneously and effortlessly Transmits to all.

"Sila"—"Sila" is a Pali Buddhist term meaning "habit", "behavior", "conduct", or "morality". It connotes the restraint of outgoing energy and attention, the disposition of equanimity, or free energy and attention for the Spiritual Process.

sleeping—See **waking, dreaming, and sleeping**.

"Source-Texts"—Avatar Adi Da's Divine Heart-Word is summarized in His twenty-three Divine "Source-Texts". These Texts present, in complete and conclusive detail, His Divine Revelations, Confessions, and Instructions, which are the fruits of His years of Teaching-Work and Revelation-Work.

This term is placed in quotation marks to indicate that Avatar Adi Da uses it with the specific technical meaning described here. For a complete list of Avatar Adi Da's "Source-Texts", see pp. 1405–07.

Spirit-Baptism—Avatar Adi Da often refers to His Transmission of Spiritual Blessing as His "Spirit-Baptism". It is often felt by His devotee as a Current descending in the frontal line (and, in due course, ascending in the spinal line). However, Avatar Adi Da's Spirit-Baptism is fundamentally and primarily His Moveless Transmission of the Divine Heart Itself. As a secondary effect, His Spirit-Baptism serves to purify, balance, and energize the entire body-mind of the devotee who is prepared to receive It.

Spirit-"Conductivity"—See **"conductivity"**.

Spiritual, Transcendental, Divine—Avatar Adi Da uses the words "Spiritual", "Transcendental", and "Divine" in reference to dimensions of Reality that are Realized progressively in the Way of Adidam. When these terms are used in combination, "Spiritual" refers to the vertical process (characteristically associated with the fifth stage of life), "Transcendental" to the horizontal process (characteristically associated with the sixth stage of life), and "Divine" to the Most Perfect Process of the seventh stage of life, Which Divine Process includes and transcends both the vertical process and the horizontal process.

Sri—"Sri" is a term of honor and veneration often applied to an Adept. The word literally means "flame" in Sanskrit, indicating that the one honored is radiant with Blessing Power. See also **Ma**.

Stages Of Life—Avatar Adi Da has Revealed the underlying structure of human growth in seven stages. See Sutra 21 and *The Seven Stages Of Life*.

Star—See **Divine Star**.

Student-Beginner—A student-beginner is a practitioner in the earliest developmental stage of the second congregation of Adidam. In the course of student-beginner practice, the devotee of Avatar Adi Da begins the process of listening to Him and adapts to the disciplines of the Way of Adidam.

subtle—See **gross, subtle, causal**.

T

"Talking" School—A phrase used by Avatar Adi Da to refer to those in any tradition of sacred life whose approach is characterized by talking, thinking, reading, and philosophical analysis and debate, or even meditative enquiry or reflection, without a concomitant and foundation discipline of body, emotion, mind, and breath. He contrasts the "talking"-school with the "practicing"-school approach—"practicing" schools involving those who are committed to the ordeal of real ego-transcending discipline, under the guidance of a true Guru.

"Talking" is placed in quotation marks to indicate that Avatar Adi Da uses it with the specific technical meaning described here.

Tathagatha Avatar—"Tathagata" means "One who has thus gone". It is a title traditionally given to Gautama Shakyamuni and other Buddhas. "Tathagata Avatar" conveys Avatar Adi Da's Encompassing and Surpassing of the traditions of Buddhism and Hinduism (and, thus, the entire collective Great Tradition of humankind). "Tathagata" is pronounced with the emphasis on the second syllable.

Tat Sundaram Hermitage—See **Ruchira Sannyasin Hermitage Ashrams**.

Teaching-Work—The intensive period of Avatar Adi Da's Submission to devotees' questions, doubts, and sufferings, in order to Reveal His Divine Wisdom-Teaching for all beings. For a description of Avatar Adi Da's Divine Teaching-Work, see *Adi Da: The Promised God-Man Is Here*, by Carolyn Lee.

Three Stations Of The Heart—See **Heart / The Heart Itself / Stations Of The Heart**.

The "Thumbs"—From time to time throughout His early Life, Avatar Adi Da experienced the forceful Spiritual Descent of the "Bright" into His body-mind. He describes it as feeling like "a mass of gigantic thumbs coming down from above". Therefore, just as He named His Divine State "the 'Bright'" as a child, He also, in childhood, gave a name to the Descent of the "Bright"—"the 'Thumbs'". This manifestation of the "Thumbs" is one of the unique Spiritual signs associated with Avatar Adi Da's Appearance. Once they have become fully technically responsible for the reception of Avatar Adi Da's Spiritual Blessing-Transmission, His devotees (in due course) experience this unique (and uniquely life-transforming) sign of His Spiritual Descent as a Gift Given by Him. See Sutra 45.

Avatar Adi Da's Gift of the "Thumbs" is what makes it possible to enter the most mature stages of Adidam—the "Perfect Practice". See also **Samadhi**.

Thunder—See **Divine Sound**.

Transcendentalist—The "Transcendentalist" way is that of dissociation from the objects of conditional existence in identification with secluded Consciousness Itself, associated with the sixth-stage path. It is, as Avatar Adi Da describes, associated with the horizontal dimension of the human psycho-physical structure. See also **Emanationist**.

Translate / Translation—See **Four Phases Of The Seventh Stage Of Life**.

"True Prayer"—Generally, and most typically, "True Prayer" is Avatar Adi Da's technical term for the two forms of the "conscious process" that are practiced by His devotees who have chosen the Devotional Way of Faith. By extension, simple Name-Invocation and the Devotional Prayer of Changes are also forms of "True Prayer"—and, indeed, Avatar Adi Da says, "For All My Devotees, The Most Basic 'True Prayer' Is The Prayer Of ego-Transcending Devotional (and, In Due Course, Spiritual) Communion With Me."

This term appears in quotation marks to indicate that Avatar Adi Da uses it with these specific technical meanings. See Sutra 43.

True World-Religion Of "Sri Hridayam"—"Sri Hridayam" is a reference to Avatar Adi Da Samraj. The word "Sri" in Sanskrit literally means "flame", and used as a title indicates the radiance of the one who is so honored. "Hridayam" is Sanskrit for "heart", referring not only to the physical organ but also to the True Divine Heart, the Transcendental (and Inherently Spiritual) Divine Reality. Adidam is the true world-religion because Avatar Adi Da Offers His Wisdom-Teaching as the uniquely Perfect Instruction to every being—in this (and every) world—relative to the total process of Divine Enlightenment. Furthermore, Avatar Adi Da Samraj constantly Extends His Regard to the entire world (and the entire cosmic domain)—not on the political or social level, but as a Spiritual matter, constantly Working to Bless and Purify all beings everywhere.

"True Yogic Intimacy"—Avatar Adi Da's technical term for the discipline of devotion to Him in the context of emotional-sexual intimacy, whether or not the intimates are sexually active. "True Yogic intimacy" is a discipline to which all intimately related devotees of Avatar Adi Da adapt, even from the beginning of their practice of the Way of Adidam. However, because "true Yogic intimacy" is, in its fullest sense, a fully technically responsible Spiritual discipline, it is fully established and formally acknowledged only in the case of Avatar Adi Da's devotees who are in the first actually seeing stage and beyond.

A wide variety of experiments with emotional-sexual arrangements have been and continue to be conducted by human beings in many cultures, including Western societies. Among practitioners of the Way of Adidam who practice in the context of intimate relationship, no single conventional or traditional arrangement, nor even any collection of possible traditional styles, is recommended. Some practitioners may be intimate with one another but celibate by choice. Some may (particularly for practical reasons) be legally married, others not. Some are heterosexual, others homosexual. Some practice "true Yogic intimacy" without any intention to have children, while others either intend to produce children or presently have families. It is also possible that practitioners may realize "true Yogic intimacy" in a situation of multiple relationships, although Avatar Adi Da States that "If 'True Yogic Intimacy' Is Rightly Practiced and Realized, The Possibility Of Multiple relationships Of 'True Yogic Intimacy' (or Simultaneous emotional-sexual relationships Of 'True Yogic Intimacy' between any one individual and more than one partner) Is, In The General Case, Unlikely" (Sutra 40).

Avatar Adi Da has extensively Instructed His devotees in a design of living that helps intimate partners maximize the devotional and sacred benefits of their relationships. This design includes general guidelines relative to sleeping quarters, finances, the conception and raising of children, and many other practical matters that have profound effects on the quality of emotional-sexual relations between intimates. These guidelines, like all of Avatar Adi Da's other Recommendations for life and practice, are Given to His devotees for their intelligent "consideration" and fully responsible choices. In the arena of "true Yogic intimacy", as in every other aspect of life, each person's choosing obliges him or her to take his or her own unique life-situation and all other factors fully into account in the context of real practice of Ruchira Avatara Bhakti Yoga.

Whatever economic, social, and living arrangements intimate partners may (rightly and appropriately) choose, Adi Da Communicates the practice of "true Yogic intimacy" as a concentrated, ego-transcending Spiritual discipline for devotees of all generations present and potential, and He does not conform this discipline to any conventional emotional-sexual arrangement typical of partners in the twenty-first-century Western world. Because it may be embraced without regard for changeable cultural and social forms (and norms), the practice of "true Yogic intimacy" that He recommends will always and in all circumstances be Spiritually valid and (provided conditions of basic human rights exist) humanly workable.

See Sutra 40. See also section VIII of Avatar Adi Da's Essay "The ego-'I' is the Illusion of Relatedness" in *Santosha Adidam*.

Turaga—Fijian for "Lord" (pronounced Too-RAHNG-ah).

"Turiya" / "Turiyatita"—Terms used in the Hindu philosophical systems. "Turiya" means "the fourth state" (beyond waking, dreaming, and sleeping), and "turiyatita" means "the state beyond the fourth", or beyond all states.

Avatar Adi Da has given these traditional terms unique and specific meanings in the context of His Wisdom-Teaching, and He places them in quotation marks to indicate that they are used with such specific meanings. He uses the term "turiya" to indicate the Awakening to Consciousness Itself (in the context of the "Perfect Practice" of the Way of Adidam), and "turiyatita" as the State of Most Perfect Divine Enlightenment, or the Realization of all arising as transparent and non-binding modifications of the One Divine Reality (in the context of the seventh stage of life).

U

Unconditional—See **conditional**.

Urdhvareta—The traditional Sanskrit term "urdhvareta" refers to the Yogic practice of reversing the flow of aroused sexual energy such that, rather than being discharged through the genitals, it flows up the spinal line, in a manner that rejuvenates the body-mind and energizes the higher chakras.

V

Vertical Dimension Of the body-mind—Avatar Adi Da refers to the structural anatomy of the Circle (or frontal and spinal lines) and the Arrow as the "vertical" dimension of the human body-mind (in contrast to the "horizontal" dimension of the stations of the heart). See also **The Arrow** and **Circle**.

"Vital", "Peculiar", and "Solid"—Avatar Adi Da has distinguished three basic psycho-physical types (or strategies), which He calls "vital", "peculiar", and "solid". The "vital" person is oriented to the physical dimension of existence, the "peculiar" person is oriented to the emotional dimension of existence, and the "solid" person is oriented to the mental dimension of existence. These terms are placed in quotation marks to indicate that they are used with the specific technical meaning described here. See Sutra 44.

Vow—For a description of the Vow and responsibilities associated with the Way of Adidam, please see *Adidam: The True World-Religion Given by the Promised God-Man, Adi Da Samraj.*

Vunirarama—Fijian for "the Source ('vu') of ('ni') 'Brightness' ('rarama')". This Name, which can be used as an extension of Avatar Adi Da's Fijian Name, "Dau Loloma", was given to Avatar Adi Da Samraj in 1991 by Fijians who were living and serving at His Island-Hermitage-Retreat, Adidam Samrajashram (the Fijian Island of Naitauba).

W, X

waking, dreaming, and sleeping—These three states of consciousness are associated with the dimensions of cosmic existence.

The waking state (and the physical body) is associated with the gross dimension.

The dreaming state (and visionary, mystical, and Yogic Spiritual processes) is associated with the subtle dimension. The subtle dimension, which is senior to the gross dimension, includes the etheric (or energic), lower mental (or verbal-intentional and lower psychic), and higher mental (or deeper psychic, mystical, and discriminative) functions.

The state of deep sleep is associated with the causal dimension, which is senior to both the gross and the subtle dimensions. It is the root of attention, and (therefore) the root of the sense of separate "selfhood", prior to any particular experience. See also **gross, subtle, causal**.

"Washing the dog" (from head to tail)—Avatar Adi Da uses the metaphor of the "dog" and "washing the dog" to Indicate the purification of the body-mind that occurs as part of the process of His Spiritual Transformation of His devotee. He addresses the presumption (found, for example, in the Kundalini Yoga tradition) that the Spiritual process requires a spinal Yoga, or an effort of arousing Spiritual Energy literally at the "tail" end of the "dog" (the bodily base, or the muladhara chakra), and then drawing It up (or allowing It to ascend) through the spinal line to the head (and above). In contrast, Avatar Adi Da Samraj has Revealed (particularly in His *Hridaya Rosary*) that, in reality, the human being can be truly purified and Liberated (or the "dog" can be "washed") only by receiving His Divine Blessing-Power (or Ruchira Shakti) and Spiritual Person downward from Infinitely Above the head to the bodily base. This Process of downward reception of Avatar Adi Da is what He calls the "frontal Yoga", because it occurs in the frontal line of the body (which is a natural pathway of descending energy, down the front of the body, from the crown of the head to the bodily base). This necessary descending Yoga of the frontal line, once completed, is sufficient to purify the body-mind to the degree it can allow the thorough Infusion by His Ruchira Shaktipat and (in due course) the transition to the "Perfect Practice", by means of His Spiritual Gift of the "Thumbs".

AVATAR ADI DA SAMRAJ: You wash a dog from the head to the tail. But somehow or other, egos looking to Realize think they can wash the "dog" from the "tail" toward the head by doing spinal Yoga. But, in Truth, and in Reality, only the frontal Yoga can accomplish Most Perfect Divine Self-Realization, because it begins from the superior position, from the "head" position, from My Crashing Down.

The heart-disposition is magnified by My Crashing Down in your devotional and Spiritual Communion with Me. And the vital, grosser dimensions of the being are purified by this washing from the head toward the "tail". If the Process had to begin from the bodily base up, it would be very difficult, very traumatizing—and, ultimately, impossible. The "dog" is washed, simply and very directly, by your participation in My Divine Descent, by your participation in this frontal Yoga. I am Speaking now of the seeing stages, basically. But, even in the case of Spiritually Initiated beginning practitioners in the Way of Adidam—not yet technically fully responsible for the Spiritual dimension of their relationship to Me—this "wash" is, by Means of My Avataric Divine Spiritual Grace, going on.

Therefore, Spiritual life need not be a traumatic course. The "dog" should enjoy being bathed. Nice gentle little guy, happy to be rubbed and touched. You talk to him, struggle a little bit, but you gentle him down. That is how it should work. And, at the end of it, the "dog" sort of "wags its tail", shakes the water off—nice and clean, happy, your best friend. That is how it should work.

If you wash the "dog" from the "tail" up, you smear the shit from his backside toward his head. Basically, that "washing from the tail toward the head" is a self-generated, self-"guruing" kind of effort. The Divine Process can only occur by Means of My Divine Spiritual Grace. Even the word "Shaktipat" means the "Descent (pat) of Divine Force (Shakti)". But Shaktipat as it appears in the traditions is basically associated with admonitions to practice a spinal Yoga, moving from the base up. In Truth, the Divine Yoga in My Company is a Descent—washing the "dog" from head to "tail" rather than giving the "dog" a "bone", letting it wash itself from the "tail" to the head.

This is why you must invest yourself in Me. And that is how the "dog" gets washed.

—August 13, 1995

Avatar Adi Da's extended Discourse relative to "washing the dog" is "Be Washed, From Head to Tail, By Heart-Devotion To Me", in *Hridaya Rosary*.

Way Of Divine Ignorance—"Divine Ignorance" is Avatar Adi Da's term for the fundamental Awareness of Existence Itself, Prior to all sense of separation from (or knowledge about) anything that arises. Thus, the Way of Adidam He has Given can be described as the Way that Realizes this Perfect Awareness without conditional knowledge.

Way Of Divine Spiritual Baptism—Indicates that Adidam is, from the earliest time of formal Spiritual Initiation by Avatar Adi Da Samraj, a process based entirely in His Divine Spiritual-Transmission, or Baptism.

Way Of Positive Disillusionment—The Way of Adidam is founded in a fundamental disillusionment with the ego and its purposes (together with a deep heart-attraction to Avatar Adi Da Samraj). This disillusionment is positive because it is the necessary foundation for true Spiritual Awakening.

Way Of "Radical" ego-Transcendence—Transcending of the root-act of self-contraction, or ego, is the Gift of devotional and Spiritual Communion with Avatar Adi Da Samraj. Therefore, the practice in relationship to Him of the Way He has Given is the Way of "radical" ego-transcendence.

Way Of "Radical" Non-Dualism—See **Ruchira Advaitism**.

Way Of "Radical" Understanding—Avatar Adi Da has Revealed that, despite their intention to Realize Reality (or Truth, or Real God), all religious and Spiritual traditions (other than the Way of Adidam) are involved, in one manner or another, with the search to satisfy the ego. Only Avatar Adi Da has Revealed the Way to "radically" understand the ego (by "going to the root") and (in due course, through intensive formal practice of the Way of Adidam, as His formally acknowledged devotee) to most perfectly transcend the ego.

Way Of The Divine Heart-Master—Avatar Adi Da Samraj is the Divine Heart-Master, or the One Who Masters the heart of His devotee. Adidam is the Way of this relationship between Divine Master and devotee.

Way Of The Divine True Heart / Way Of The Heart / Way Of The Heart Itself—Indicates that the Way Avatar Adi Da Offers is the Way of the Heart Itself, Which Is Real God, the Divine Self-Condition, the Divine Reality.

Witness / Witness-Consciousness / Witness-Position—When Consciousness is Free of identification with the body-mind, It Stands in Its natural "Position" as the Conscious Witness of all that arises to and in and as the body-mind.

In the Way of Adidam, the stable Realization of the Witness-Position is a Spiritual Gift from Avatar Adi Da, made possible by (and necessarily following upon) the reception of His Spiritual Gift of the "Thumbs". The stable Realization of the Witness-Position is the characteristic of the first stage of the "Perfect Practice". See Sutra 49.

Would-Be-Seeing Stage—See **Listening, Hearing, Seeing**.

Wound / Wound Of Love—Avatar Adi Da sometimes uses the word "Wound" to describe the ecstatic feeling-sensation of love, and even His Divine Love-Bliss. Love is not immune to the "wound" of sorrow and separation. This "wound" is not negative in any sense, but rather a profoundly vulnerable expression of Absolute Feeling without limitation or recoil.

Y, Z

Yang, Yin—The dynamic mutual interrelatedness of natural processes, which show an alternation between generally active, heated, expansive, masculine, or "yang" qualities, and generally passive, cooling, contractive, feminine, or "yin" qualities. In traditional Chinese medicine and philosophy, health and well-being are considered a result of appropriate balance of these complementary forces.

Yantra—In Sanskrit, literally "device". A yantra is a sacred diagram or esoteric geometric symbol of the cosmos in right alignment to its Divine Source-Condition. Yantras are therefore traditionally used to focus attention in meditation or contemplation.

Yin—See **Yang, Yin**.

Yoga / Yogic—Literally "yoking", or "union", usually referring to any discipline or process whereby an aspirant seeks to achieve union with God (or the Divine, however conceived). Avatar Adi Da acknowledges this conventional and traditional use of the term, but also, in reference to the Great Yoga of Adidam, employs it in a "radical" sense, free of the usual implication of egoic separation and seeking.

An Invitation to Support Adidam

The sole Purpose of Avatar Adi Da Samraj is to act as a Source of continuous Divine Grace for everyone, everywhere. In that spirit, He is a Free Renunciate and He owns nothing. Those who have made gestures in support of Avatar Adi Da's Work have found that their generosity is returned in many Blessings that are full of His healing, transforming, and Liberating Grace and those Blessings flow not only directly to them as the beneficiaries of His Work, but to many others, even all others. At the same time, all tangible gifts of support help secure and nurture Avatar Adi Da's Work in necessary and practical ways, again similarly benefiting the entire world. Because all this is so, supporting His Work is the most auspicious form of financial giving, and we happily extend to you an invitation to serve Adidam through your financial support.

You may make a financial contribution in support of the Work of Adi Da Samraj at any time. To do so, make your check payable to "Adidam", and mail it to the Legal Department of Adidam at 12180 Ridge Road, Middletown, California 95461, USA. You may also, if you choose, indicate that your contribution be used for one or more specific purposes.

If you would like more detailed information about gifting options, or if you would like assistance in describing or making a contribution, please write to the Legal Department of Adidam at the above address or contact the Adidam Legal Department by telephone at 1-707-928-4612 or by FAX at 1-707-928-4062.

Planned Giving

We also invite you to consider making a planned gift in support of the Work of Avatar Adi Da Samraj. Many have found that through planned giving they can make a far more significant gesture of support than they would otherwise be able to make. Many have also found that by making a planned gift they are able to realize substantial tax advantages.

There are numerous ways to make a planned gift, including making a gift in your Will, or in your life insurance, or in a charitable trust.

If you are a United States taxpayer, you may find that planned giving in the form of a charitable trust will provide you with immediate tax savings and assured income for life, while at the same time enabling you to provide for your family, for your other heirs, and for the Work of Avatar Adi Da as well.

The Legal Department of Adidam (12180 Ridge Road, Middletown, California 95461, USA; telephone 1-707-928-4612; FAX 1-707-928-4062) will be happy to provide you with further information about these and other planned gifting options, and happy to provide you or your attorney with assistance in describing or making a planned gift in support of the Work of Avatar Adi Da.

Further Notes to the Reader

An Invitation to Responsibility

Adidam, the Way of the Heart that Avatar Adi Da has Revealed, is an invitation to everyone to assume real responsibility for his or her life. As Avatar Adi Da has Said in *The Dawn Horse Testament Of The Ruchira Avatar,* "If any one Is Heart-Moved To Realize Me, Let him or her First Resort (Formally, and By Formal Heart-Vow) To Me, and (Thereby) Commence The Devotional (and, In Due Course, Spiritual) Process Of self-Observation, self-Understanding, and self-Transcendence. . . ." Therefore, participation in the Way of Adidam requires a real confrontation with oneself, and not at all a confrontation with Avatar Adi Da, or with others.

All who study the Way of Adidam or take up its practice should remember that they are responding to a Call to become responsible for themselves. They should understand that they, not Avatar Adi Da or others, are responsible for any decision they may make or action they may take in the course of their lives of study or practice. This has always been true, and it is true whatever the individual's involvement in the Way of Adidam, be it as one who has contacted Avatar Adi Da's Revelation in any informal manner (such as studying Avatar Adi Da's Wisdom-Teaching), or as one who is practicing as a formally acknowledged congregational member of Adidam.

Honoring and Protecting the Sacred Word through Perpetual Copyright

Since ancient times, practitioners of true religion and Spirituality have valued, above all, time spent in the Company of the Sat-Guru (or one who has, to any degree, Realized Real God, Truth, or Reality, and who, thus, serves the awakening process in others). Such practitioners understand that the Sat-Guru literally Spiritually Transmits his or her (Realized) State. Through this Transmission, there are objects, environments, and rightly prepared individuals with which the Sat-Guru has contact that can become empowered, or imbued with the Sat-Guru's Transforming Power. It is by this process of empowerment that things and beings are made truly and literally sacred and holy, and things so sanctified thereafter function as a source of the Sat-Guru's Blessing for all who understand how to make right and sacred use of them.

Sat-Gurus of any degree of Realization and all that they empower are, therefore, truly Sacred Treasures, for they help draw the practitioner more quickly into the process of Realization. Cultures of true Wisdom have always understood that such Sacred Treasures are precious (and fragile) Gifts to humanity, and that they should be honored, protected, and reserved for right sacred use. Indeed, the word "holy" means "set apart", and, thus, that which is holy and sacred must be protected from insensitive secular interference and wrong use of any kind. Avatar Adi Da has Conformed His human Body-Mind Most Perfectly to the Divine Self, and He is, thus, the most Potent Source of Spiritual Blessing-Transmission of Real God, or Truth Itself, or Reality Itself. He has for many years Empowered (or made sacred) special places and things, and these now serve as His Divine Agents, or as literal expressions and extensions of His Blessing-Transmission. Among these Empowered Sacred Treasures are His Wisdom-Teaching and His Divine Image-Art, which are full of His Transforming Power. These Blessed and Blessing Agents have the literal Power to serve Real-God-Realization in those who are Graced to receive them.

Therefore, Avatar Adi Da's Wisdom-Teaching and Divine Image-Art must be perpetually honored and protected, "set apart" from all possible interference and wrong use. The gathering of devotees of Avatar Adi Da is committed to the perpetual preservation and right honoring of the Sacred Wisdom-Teaching of the Way of Adidam and the Divine Image-Art of Adi Da Samraj. But it is also true that, in order to fully accomplish this, we must find support in the world-society in which we live and in its laws. Thus, we call for a world-society and for laws that acknowledge the sacred, and that permanently protect it from insensitive, secular interference and wrong use of any kind. We call for, among other things, a system of law that acknowledges that the Wisdom-Teaching of the Way of Adidam and the Divine Image-Art of Adi Da Samraj, in all their forms, are, because of their sacred nature, protected by perpetual copyright.

We invite others who respect the sacred to join with us in this call and in working toward its realization. And, even in the meantime, we claim that all copyrights to the Wisdom-Teaching and Divine Image-Art of Avatar Adi Da and the other Sacred Literature, recordings, and images of the Way of Adidam are of perpetual duration.

We make this claim on behalf of The Avataric Samrajya of Adidam Pty Ltd, which, acting as trustee of The Avataric Samrajya of Adidam, is the holder of all such copyrights.

Avatar Adi Da and the Sacred Treasures of Adidam

True Spiritual Masters have Realized Real God (to one degree or another), and, therefore, they bring great Blessing and introduce Divine Possibility to the world. Such Adept-Realizers Accomplish universal Blessing-Work that benefits everything and everyone. They also Work very specifically and intentionally with individuals who approach them as their devotees, and with those places where they reside and to which they direct their specific Regard for the sake of perpetual Spiritual Empowerment. This was understood in traditional Spiritual cultures, and, therefore, those cultures found ways to honor Adept-Realizers by providing circumstances for them where they were free to do their Spiritual Work without obstruction or interference.

Those who value Avatar Adi Da's Realization and Service have always endeavored to appropriately honor Him in this traditional way by providing a circumstance where He is completely Free to do His Divine Work. The Ruchira Sannyasin Hermitage Ashrams of Adidam have been set aside by Avatar Adi Da's devotees worldwide as Places for Him to do His universal Blessing-Work for the sake of everyone, as well as His specific Work with those who pilgrimage to His Hermitage circumstance (wherever He may be residing at a given time) to receive the special Blessing of coming into His physical Company.

Avatar Adi Da is a legal renunciate. He owns nothing and He has no secular or religious institutional function. He Functions only in Freedom. He, and the other members of the Ruchira Sannyasin Order (the senior renunciate order of Adidam), are provided for by The Avataric Samrajya of Adidam, which also provides for His Hermitage circumstance, and serves and manages the process of access to Avatar Adi Da Samraj on the part of all who are invited to enter His Hermitage Domain (either to offer service to Him or to participate in meditative retreats in His Spiritual Company).

The sacred institutions that have developed in response to Avatar Adi Da's Wisdom-Teaching and universal Blessing are active worldwide in making Avatar Adi Da's Wisdom-Teaching available to all, in offering guidance to all who are moved to respond to His Offering, and in protecting, preserving, and glorifying the Sacred Treasures of Adidam. In addition to the central corporate entities, which are based in California, there are numerous regional entities which serve congregations of Avatar Adi Da's devotees in various places throughout the world.

Practitioners of Adidam worldwide have also established numerous community organizations, through which they provide for many of their common and cooperative community needs, including those relating to housing, food, businesses, medical care, schools, and death and dying. By attending to these and all other ordinary human concerns and affairs via ego-transcending cooperation and mutual effort, Avatar Adi Da's devotees constantly work to free their energy and attention, both personally and collectively, for practice of the Way of Adidam and for service to Avatar Adi Da Samraj, to the other Sacred Treasures of Adidam, and to the sacred institutions of Adidam.

All of the organizations that have evolved in response to Avatar Adi Da Samraj and His Offering are legally separate from one another, and each has its own purpose and function. These organizations represent the collective intention of practitioners of Adidam worldwide to protect, preserve, and glorify the Sacred Treasures of Adidam, and also to make Avatar Adi Da's Offering of the Way of Adidam universally available to all.

INDEX

Note: Definitions of terms can be found in the glossary, pp. 1319–54.

I

N

O

R

Y

The Twenty-Three Divine "Source-Texts" of The Ruchira Avatar, Adi Da Samraj

The Twenty-Three Divine "Source-Texts" of The Ruchira Avatar, Adi Da Samraj

THE DAWN HORSE TESTAMENT OF THE RUCHIRA AVATAR
The Testament Of Divine Secrets Of The Divine World-Teacher, Ruchira Avatar Adi Da Samraj

The Five Books Of The Heart Of The Adidam Revelation

1. AHAM DA ASMI
(BELOVED, I AM DA)
The "Late-Time" Avataric Revelation Of The True and Spiritual Divine Person (The egoless Personal Presence Of Reality and Truth, Which Is The Only Real God)

2. RUCHIRA AVATARA GITA
(THE AVATARIC WAY OF THE DIVINE HEART-MASTER)
The "Late-Time" Avataric Revelation Of The Great Secret Of The Divinely Self-Revealed Way That Most Perfectly Realizes The True and Spiritual Divine Person (The egoless Personal Presence Of Reality and Truth, Which Is The Only Real God)

3. DA LOVE-ANANDA GITA
(THE FREE AVATARIC GIFT OF THE DIVINE LOVE-BLISS)
The "Late-Time" Avataric Revelation Of The Great Means To Worship and To Realize The True and Spiritual Divine Person (The egoless Personal Presence Of Reality and Truth, Which Is The Only Real God)

4. HRIDAYA ROSARY
(FOUR THORNS OF HEART-INSTRUCTION)
The "Late-Time" Avataric Revelation Of The Universally Tangible Divine Spiritual Body, Which Is The Supreme Agent Of The Great Means To Worship and To Realize The True and Spiritual Divine Person (The egoless Personal Presence Of Reality and Truth, Which Is The Only Real God)

5. ELEUTHERIOS
(THE ONLY TRUTH THAT SETS THE HEART FREE)
The "Late-Time" Avataric Revelation Of The "Perfect Practice" Of The Great Means To Worship and To Realize The True and Spiritual Divine Person (The egoless Personal Presence Of Reality and Truth, Which Is The Only Real God)

The Seventeen Companions Of The True Dawn Horse

1. REAL GOD IS THE INDIVISIBLE ONENESS OF UNBROKEN LIGHT
Reality, Truth, and The "Non-Creator" God In The True World-Religion Of Adidam

2. THE TRULY HUMAN NEW WORLD-CULTURE OF UNBROKEN REAL-GOD-MAN
The Eastern Versus The Western Traditional Cultures Of Mankind, and The Unique New Non-Dual Culture Of The True World-Religion Of Adidam

3. THE ONLY COMPLETE WAY TO REALIZE THE UNBROKEN LIGHT OF REAL GOD
An Introductory Overview Of The "Radical" Divine Way Of The True World-Religion Of Adidam

4. THE KNEE OF LISTENING
The Divine Ordeal Of The Avataric Incarnation Of Conscious Light—
The Spiritual Autobiography Of The Ruchira Avatar, Adi Da Samraj

5. THE DIVINE SIDDHA-METHOD OF THE RUCHIRA AVATAR
The Divine Way Of Adidam Is An ego-Transcending Relationship, Not An ego-Centric Technique

6. THE MUMMERY BOOK
A Parable Of The Divine True Love, Told By Means Of A Self-Illuminated Illustration Of The Totality Of Mind

7. HE-AND-SHE IS ME
The Indivisibility Of Consciousness and Light In The Divine Body Of The Ruchira Avatar

8. RUCHIRA SHAKTIPAT YOGA
The Divine (and Not Merely Cosmic) Spiritual Baptism In The Divine Way Of Adidam

9. RUCHIRA TANTRA YOGA
The Physical-Spiritual (and Truly Religious) Method Of Mental, Emotional, Sexual, and Whole Bodily Health and Enlightenment In The Divine Way Of Adidam

10. THE SEVEN STAGES OF LIFE
Transcending The Six Stages Of egoic Life, and Realizing The ego-Transcending Seventh Stage Of Life, In The Divine Way Of Adidam

11. THE ALL-COMPLETING AND FINAL DIVINE REVELATION TO MANKIND
A Summary Description Of The Supreme Yoga Of The Seventh Stage Of Life In The Divine Way Of Adidam

12. WHAT, WHERE, WHEN, HOW, WHY, AND WHO TO REMEMBER TO BE HAPPY
A Simple Explanation Of The Divine Way Of Adidam (For Children, and Everyone Else)

13. NO SEEKING / MERE BEHOLDING
The Always Primary Practice Of The Divine Way Of Adidam

14. SANTOSHA ADIDAM
The Essential Summary Of The Divine Way Of Adidam

15. THE LION SUTRA
The "Perfect Practice" Teachings In The Divine Way Of Adidam

16. THE OVERNIGHT REVELATION OF CONSCIOUS LIGHT
The "My House" Discourses On The Indivisible Tantra Of Adidam

17. THE BASKET OF TOLERANCE
The Perfect Guide To Perfectly Unified Understanding Of The One and Great Tradition Of Mankind, and Of The Divine Way Of Adidam As The Perfect Completing Of The One and Great Tradition Of Mankind